The Linux Bible
The GNU Testament

Third Edition

Yggdrasil Computing Inc.
San Jose, CA

Yggdrasil Computing Inc.
4880 Stevens Creek Blvd. Suite 205
San Jose, CA 95129-1034
© 1994-1995 by Yggdrasil Computing Inc.
First edition published 1994. Second Edition 1994
Third edition published 1995
Printed in the United States of America
97 96 95   5 4 3 2 1

Library of Congress Cataloging-in-Publication Data

The Linux bible : the GNU testament. – 3rd ed.
        p.   cm.
    Includes bibliographical references and Index.
    Written by Matt Welsh and others.
    ISBN 1-883601-12-6
    1. Linux. 2. Operating systems (Computers)   I. Welsh, Matt.
    II. Yggdrasil Computing Inc.
    QA76.76.O63R692   1994
    005.4'3–dc20   95-4437
                                                        CIP

ISBN 1-883601-12-6

See the next page for Copyright information for the individual works that make up The Linux Bible.

Individual Copyrights:

As a collection, The Linux Bible, The GNU Testament–3rd Edition is Copyright©1994-1995 Yggdrasil Computing Incorporated. The individual works that make up the Linux Bible are copyright by their respective authors and have their own copying terms and conditions. The individual copyrights are listed below.

Contents

Part I

Linux Installation and Getting Started

Copyright © 1992–1994 Matt Welsh

Version 2.2.2, 11 February 1995.

This book is an installation and new-user guide for the Linux system, meant for UNIX novices and gurus alike. Contained herein is information on how to obtain Linux, installation of the software, a beginning tutorial for new UNIX users, and an introduction to system administration. It is meant to be general enough to be applicable to any distribution of the Linux software.

This book is freely distributable; you may copy and redistribute it under certain conditions. Please see the copyright and distribution statement on page 12.

Contents

Preface

"You are in a maze of twisty little passages, all alike."

Before you looms one of the most complex and utterly intimidating systems ever written. Linux, the free UNIX clone for the personal computer, produced by a mishmash team of UNIX gurus, hackers, and the occasional loon. The system itself reflects this complex heritage, and although the development of Linux may appear to be a disorganized volunteer effort, the system is powerful, fast, and free. It is a true 32-bit operating system solution.

My own experiences with Linux began several years ago, when I sat down to figure out how to install the only "distribution" available at the time—a couple of diskettes made available by H.J. Lu. I downloaded a slew of files and read pages upon pages of loosely-organized installation notes. Somehow, I managed to install this basic system and get everything working together. This was long before you could buy the Linux software on CD-ROM from worldwide distributors; before, in fact, Linux even knew how to access a CD-ROM drive. This was before XFree86, before Emacs, before commercial software support, and before Linux became a true rival to MS-DOS, Microsoft Windows, and OS/2 in the personal computer market.

You hold in your very hands the map and guidebook to the world of Linux. It is my hope that this book will help you to get rolling with what I consider to be the fastest, most powerful operating system for the personal computer. Setting up your own Linux system can be a great deal of fun—so grab a cup of coffee, sit back, and read on.

Grab a cup for me, too, while you're at it. I've been up hacking Linux for days.

Audience

This book is for any personal computer user who wants to install and use Linux on their system. We assume that you have basic knowledge about personal computers and operating systems such as MS-DOS. No previous knowledge about Linux or UNIX is assumed.

Despite this, we strongly suggest that UNIX novices invest in one of the many good UNIX books out there. Several of them are listed in Appendix A.

Organization

This book contains the following chapters.

Chapter 1, *Introduction to Linux*, gives a general introduction to what Linux is, what it can do for you, and what is required to run it on your system. It also provides helpful hints for getting help and reducing overall stress.

Chapter 2, *Obtaining and Installing Linux*, explains how to obtain the Linux software, as well as how to install it—from repartitioning your drive, creating filesystems, and loading the software on the system. It contains instructions meant to be general for any distribution of Linux, and relies on the documentation provided for your particular release to fill in any gaps.

Chapter 3, *Linux Tutorial*, is a complete introduction to using the Linux system for UNIX novices. If you have previous UNIX experience, most of this material should be familiar.

Chapter 4, *System Administration*, introduces many of the important concepts of system administration under Linux. This will also be of interest to UNIX system administrators who want to know about the Linux-specific issues of running a system.

Chapter 5, *Advanced Features*, introduces the reader to a number of advanced features supported by Linux, such as the X Window System and TCP/IP networking. A complete guide to configuring XFree86-3.1 is included.

Appendix A, *Sources of Linux Information*, is a listing of other sources of information about Linux, including newsgroups, mailing lists, online documents, and books.

Appendix B, *Linux Vendor List*, provides a short list of software vendors offering Linux software and services.

Appendix C, *FTP Tutorial and Site List*, is a tutorial for downloading files from the Internet with FTP. This appendix also includes a listing of FTP archive sites which carry Linux software.

Appendix C.8, *Linux BBS List*, is a listing of bulletin board systems worldwide which carry Linux software. Because most Linux users are do not have access to the Internet, it is important that information on BBS systems becomes available.

Appendix D, *The GNU General Public License*, contains a copy of the GNU GPL, the license agreement under which Linux is distributed. It is very important that Linux users understand the GPL; many disagreements over the terms of the GPL have been raised in recent months.

Acknowledgments

This book has been long in the making, and many people are responsible for the outcome. In particular, I would like to thank Larry Greenfield and Karl Fogel for their work on the first version of Chapter 3, and to Lars Wirzenius for his work on Chapter 4. Thanks to Michael K. Johnson for his assistance with the LDP and the LATEX conventions used in this manual, and to Ed Chi, who sent me a printed copy of the book for edition.

Thanks to Melinda A. McBride at SSC, Inc., who did an excellent job completing the index for Chapters 3, 4, and 5. I would also like to thank Andy Oram, Lar Kaufman, and Bill Hahn at O'Reilly and Associates for their assistance with the Linux Documentation Project.

Thanks to Linux Systems Labs, Morse Telecommunications, Yggdrasil Computing, and others for their support of the Linux Documentation Project through sales of this book and other works.

Much thanks to the many activists, including (in no particular order) Linus Torvalds, Donald Becker, Alan Cox, Remy Card, Ted T'so, H.J. Lu, Ross Biro, Drew Eckhardt, Ed Carp, Eric Youngdale, Fred van Kempen, Steven Tweedie, and a score of others, for devoting so much time and energy to this project, and without whom there wouldn't be anything to write a book about.

Special thanks to the myriad of readers who have sent their helpful comments and corrections. There are far too many to list here. Who needs a spell checker, when you have an audience?

Matt Welsh
13 January 1994

Credits and Legalese

The Linux Documentation Project is a loose team of writers, proofreaders, and editors who are working on a set of definitive Linux manuals. The overall coordinator of the project is Matt Welsh, aided by Lars Wirzenius and Michael K. Johnson.

This manual is but one in a set of several being distributed by the Linux Documentation Project, including a Linux User's Guide, System Administrator's Guide, and Kernel Hacker's Guide. These manuals are all available in LaTeX source format and Postscript output for anonymous FTP from sunsite.unc.edu, in the directory /pub/Linux/docs/LDP.

We encourage anyone with a penchant for writing or editing to join us in improving Linux documentation. If you have Internet e-mail access, you can join the DOC channel of the Linux-Activists mailing list by sending mail to

```
linux-activists-request@niksula.hut.fi
```

with the line

```
X-Mn-Admin:  join DOC
```

as the first line of the message body.

Feel free to get in touch with the author and coordinator of this manual if you have questions, postcards, money, or ideas. Matt Welsh can be reached via Internet e-mail at mdw@sunsite.unc.edu, and in real life at

205 Gray Street
Wilson, N.C. 27896
U.S.A.

UNIX is a trademark of X/Open.

Linux is not a trademark, and has no connection to UNIX™ or X/Open.

The X Window System is a trademark of the Massachusetts Institute of Technology.

MS-DOS and Microsoft Windows are trademarks of Microsoft, Inc.

The author encourages distributors of Linux software in any medium to use the book as an installation and new user guide. Given the copyright above, you are free to print and distribute copies of this book with your software. You may either distribute this book free of charge, or for profit. If doing so, you may wish to include a short "installation supplement" for your release.

The author would like to know of any plans to publish and distribute this book commercially. In this way, we can ensure that you are kept up-to-date with new revisions. And, should a new version be right around the corner, you might wish to delay your publication of the book until it is available.

If you are distributing this book commercially, donations, royalties, and/or printed copies are greatly appreciated by the author. Contributing in this way shows your support for free software and the Linux Documentation Project.

All source code in *Linux Installation and Getting Started* is placed under the GNU General Public License. See Appendix D for a copy of the GNU "GPL."

Documentation Conventions

These conventions should be obvious, but we'll include them here for the pedantic.

Bold   Used to mark **new concepts**, **WARNINGS**, and **keywords** in a language.

italics   Used for *emphasis* in text, and occasionally for quotes or introductions at the beginning of a section. Also used to indicate commands for the user to type when showing screen interaction (see below).

⟨**slanted**⟩   Used to mark **meta-variables** in the text, especially in representations of the command line. For example,

ls -l ⟨*foo*⟩

where ⟨*foo*⟩ would "stand for" a filename, such as /bin/cp.

Typewriter   Used to represent screen interaction, as in

```
$ ls –l /bin/cp
-rwxr-xr-x  1 root     wheel    12104 Sep 25 15:53 /bin/cp
```

Also used for code examples, whether it is C code, a shell script, or something else, and to display general files, such as configuration files. When necessary for clarity's sake, these examples or figures will be enclosed in thin boxes.

Key   Represents a key to press. You will often see it in this form:

Press return to continue.

◇   A diamond in the margin, like a black diamond on a ski hill, marks "danger" or "caution." Read paragraphs marked this way carefully.

Chapter 1

Introduction to Linux

Linux is quite possibly the most important achievement of free software since the original *Space War*, or, more recently, Emacs. It has developed into the operating system for businesses, education, and personal productivity. Linux is no longer just for UNIX wizards who sit for hours in front of the glowing console (although we assure you that quite a number of users fall into this category). This book will help you get the most out of it.

Linux (pronounced with a short *i*, as in *LIH-nucks*) is a clone of the UNIX operating system that runs on Intel 80386 and 80486 computers. It supports a wide range of software, from TEX to X Windows to the GNU C/C++ compiler to TCP/IP. It's a versatile, bona fide implementation of UNIX, freely distributed by the terms of the GNU General Public License (see Appendix D).

Linux can turn any 386 or 486 PC into a workstation. It will give you the full power of UNIX at your fingertips. Businesses are installing Linux on entire networks of machines, using the operating system to manage financial and hospital records, a distributed user computing environment, telecommunications, and more. Universities worldwide are using Linux for teaching courses on operating systems programming and design. And, of course, computing enthusiasts everywhere are using Linux at home, for programming, productivity, and all-around hacking.

What makes Linux so different is that it is a *free* implementation of UNIX. It was and still is developed by a group of volunteers, primarily on the Internet, exchanging code, reporting bugs, and fixing problems in an open-ended environment. Anyone is welcome to join in the Linux development effort: all it takes is interest in hacking a free UNIX clone and some kind of programming know-how. The book that you hold in your hands is your tour guide.

1.1 About This Book

This book is an installation and entry-level guide to the Linux system. The purpose is to get new users up and running with the system by consolidating as much important material as possible into one book. Instead of covering many of the volatile technical details, those things which tend to change with rapid development, we give you enough background to find out more on your own.

Linux is not difficult to install and use. However, as with any implementation of UNIX, there is often some black magic involved to get everything working correctly. We hope that this book will get you on the Linux tour bus and show you how groovy this operating system can be.

In this book, we cover the following topics.

- What is Linux? The design and philosophy of this unique operating system, and what it can do for you.

- All of the details of what is needed to run Linux, including suggestions on what kind of hardware configuration is recommended for a complete system.

- How to obtain and install Linux. There are many distributions of the Linux software. We present a general discussion of Linux software distributions, how to obtain them, and generic instructions for installing the software (which should be applicable to any distribution).

  This edition also contains specific instructions for the Slackware distribution of Linux.

- A brief introductory UNIX tutorial, for those users who have never had experience with UNIX before. This tutorial should, hopefully, provide enough material for complete novices to have enough basic know-how to find their way around the system.

- An introduction to systems administration with Linux. This covers the most important tasks that new Linux administrators will need to be familiar with, such as creating users, managing filesystems, and so forth.

- Information on configuring more advanced aspects of Linux, such as the X Window System, networking with TCP/IP and SLIP, and the setup of electronic mail and news systems.

This book is for the personal computer user wishing to get started with Linux. We don't assume previous UNIX experience, but do expect novices to refer to other materials along the way. For those unfamiliar with UNIX, a list of useful sources of information is given in Appendix A. In general, this book is meant to be read along with another book on basic UNIX concepts.

1.2   A Brief History of Linux

UNIX is one of the most popular operating systems worldwide because of its large support base and distribution. It was originally developed as a multitasking system for minicomputers and mainframes in the mid-1970's, but has since grown to become one of the most widely used operating systems anywhere, despite its sometimes confusing interface and lack of central standardization.

The real reason for UNIX's popularity? Many hackers feel that UNIX is the Right Thing—the One True Operating System. Hence, the development of Linux by an expanding group of UNIX hackers who want to get their hands dirty with their own system.

Versions of UNIX exist for many systems—ranging from personal computers to supercomputers such as the Cray Y-MP. Most versions of UNIX for personal computers are quite expensive and cumbersome. At the time of this writing, a one-machine version of AT&T's System V for the 386 runs at about US$1500.

Linux is a freely distributable version of UNIX developed primarily by Linus Torvalds [1] at the University of Helsinki in Finland. Linux was developed with the help of many UNIX programmers and wizards across the Internet, allowing anyone with enough know-how and gumption the ability to develop and change the system. The Linux kernel uses no code from AT&T or any other proprietary source, and much of the software available for Linux is developed by the GNU project at the Free Software Foundation in Cambridge, Massachusetts. However, programmers all over the world have contributed to the growing pool of Linux software.

Linux was originally developed as a hobby project by Linus Torvalds. It was inspired by Minix, a small UNIX system developed by Andy Tanenbaum, and the first discussions about Linux were on the USENET

---

[1]`torvalds@kruuna.helsinki.fi.`

newsgroup `comp.os.minix`. These discussions were concerned mostly with the development of a small, academic UNIX system for Minix users who wanted more.

The very early development of Linux was mostly dealing with the task-switching features of the 80386 protected-mode interface, all written in assembly code. Linus writes,

> "After that it was plain sailing: hairy coding still, but I had some devices, and debugging was easier. I started using C at this stage, and it certainly speeds up development. This is also when I start to get serious about my megalomaniac ideas to make 'a better Minix than Minix'. I was hoping I'd be able to recompile `gcc` under Linux some day...
>
> "Two months for basic setup, but then only slightly longer until I had a disk-driver (seriously buggy, but it happened to work on my machine) and a small filesystem. That was about when I made 0.01 available [around late August of 1991]: it wasn't pretty, it had no floppy driver, and it couldn't do much anything. I don't think anybody ever compiled that version. But by then I was hooked, and didn't want to stop until I could chuck out Minix."

No announcement was ever made for Linux version 0.01. The 0.01 sources weren't even executable: they contained only the bare rudiments of the kernel source, and assumed that you had access to a Minix machine to compile and play with them.

On 5 October 1991, Linus announced the first "official" version of Linux, version 0.02. At this point, Linus was able to run `bash` (the GNU Bourne Again Shell) and `gcc` (the GNU C compiler), but not very much else was working. Again, this was intended as a hacker's system. The primary focus was kernel development—none of the issues of user support, documentation, distribution, and so on had even been addressed. Today, the Linux community still seems to treat these ergonomic issues as secondary to the "real programming"—kernel development.

Linus wrote in `comp.os.minix`,

> "Do you pine for the nice days of Minix-1.1, when men were men and wrote their own device drivers? Are you without a nice project and just dying to cut your teeth on a OS you can try to modify for your needs? Are you finding it frustrating when everything works on Minix? No more all-nighters to get a nifty program working? Then this post might be just for you.
>
> "As I mentioned a month ago, I'm working on a free version of a Minix-lookalike for AT-386 computers. It has finally reached the stage where it's even usable (though may not be depending on what you want), and I am willing to put out the sources for wider distribution. It is just version 0.02...but I've successfully run `bash`, `gcc`, `gnu-make`, `gnu-sed`, `compress`, etc. under it."

After version 0.03, Linus bumped the version number up to 0.10, as more people started to work on the system. After several further revisions, Linus increased the version number to 0.95, to reflect his expectation that the system was ready for an "official" release very soon. (Generally, software is not assigned the version number 1.0 until it is theoretically complete or bug-free.) This was in March of 1992. Almost a year and a half later, in late December of 1993, the Linux kernel was still at version 0.99.pl14—asymptotically approaching 1.0. As of the time of this writing, the current kernel version is 1.1 patchlevel 52, and 1.2 is right around the corner.

Today, Linux is a complete UNIX clone, capable of running X Windows, TCP/IP, Emacs, UUCP, mail and news software, you name it. Almost all of the major free software packages have been ported to Linux, and commercial software is becoming available. Much more hardware is supported than in original versions of the kernel. Many people have executed benchmarks on 80486 Linux systems and found them comparable with mid-range workstations from Sun Microsystems and Digital Equipment Corporation.

Who would have ever guessed that this "little" UNIX clone would have grown up to take on the entire world of personal computing?

1.3 System Features

Linux supports most of the features found in other implementations of UNIX, plus quite a few that aren't found elsewhere. This section is a nickel tour of the Linux kernel features.

Linux is a complete multitasking, multiuser operating system (just like all other versions of UNIX). This means that many users can be logged into the same machine at once, running multiple programs simultaneously.

The Linux system is mostly compatible with a number of UNIX standards (inasmuch as UNIX has standards) on the source level, including IEEE POSIX.1, System V, and BSD features. It was developed with source portability in mind: therefore, you are most likely to find commonly-used features in the Linux system which are shared across multiple implementations. A great deal of free UNIX software available on the Internet and elsewhere compiles on Linux out of the box. In addition, all source code for the Linux system, including the kernel, device drivers, libraries, user programs, and development tools, is freely distributable.

Other specific internal features of Linux include POSIX job control (used by shells such as csh and bash), pseudoterminals (pty devices), and support for national or customized keyboards using dynamically-loadable keyboard drivers. Linux also supports **virtual consoles**, which allow you to switch between multiple login sessions from the system console in text mode. Users of the "screen" program will find the Linux virtual console implementation familiar.

The kernel is able to emulate 387-FPU instructions itself, so that systems without a math coprocessor can run programs that require floating-point math instructions.

Linux supports various filesystem types for storing data. Various filesystems, such as the *ext2fs* filesystem, have been developed specifically for Linux. Other filesystem types, such as the Minix-1 and Xenix filesystems, are also supported. The MS-DOS filesystem has been implemented as well, allowing you to access MS-DOS files on hard drive or floppy directly. The ISO 9660 CD-ROM filesystem type, which reads all standard formats of CD-ROMs, is also supported. We'll talk more about filesystems in Chapters 2 and 4.

Linux provides a complete implementation of TCP/IP networking. This includes device drivers for many popular Ethernet cards, SLIP (Serial Line Internet Protocol, allowing you to access a TCP/IP network via a serial connection), PLIP (Parallel Line Internet Protocol), PPP (Point-to-Point Protocol), NFS (Network File System), and so on. The complete range of TCP/IP clients and services is supported, such as FTP, telnet, NNTP, and SMTP. We'll talk more about networking in Chapter 5.

The Linux kernel is developed to use the special protected-mode features of the Intel 80386 and 80486 processors. In particular, Linux makes use of the protected-mode descriptor-based memory management paradigm and many of the other advanced features of these processors. Anyone familiar with 80386 protected-mode programming knows that this chip was designed for a multitasking system such as UNIX (or, actually, Multics). Linux exploits this functionality.

The Linux kernel supports demand-paged loaded executables. That is, only those segments of a program which are actually used are read into memory from disk. Also, copy-on-write pages are shared among executables, meaning that if several instances of a program are running at once, they will share pages in physical memory, reducing overall memory usage.

In order to increase the amount of available memory, Linux also implements disk paging: that is, up to

256 megabytes of "swap space"[2] can be allocated on disk. When the system requires more physical memory, it will swap out inactive pages to disk, thus allowing you to run larger applications and support more users at once. However, swap is no substitute for physical RAM—it is much slower due to drive access latency times.

The kernel also implements a unified memory pool for user programs and disk cache. In this way, all free memory is used for caching, and the cache is reduced when running large programs.

Executables use dynamically linked shared libraries, meaning that executables share common library code in a single library file found on disk, not unlike the SunOS shared library mechanism. This allows executable files to occupy much less space on disk, especially those that use many library functions. There are also statically-linked libraries for those who wish to use object debugging or maintain "complete" executables without the need for shared libraries to be in place. Linux shared libraries are dynamically linked at run-time, allowing the programmer to replace modules of the libraries with their own routines.

To facilitate debugging, the Linux kernel does core dumps for post-mortem analysis. Using a core dump and an executable linked with debugging support, it is possible to determine what caused a program to crash.

1.4 Software Features

In this section, we'll introduce you to many of the software applications available for Linux, and talk about a number of common computing tasks. After all, the most important part of the system is the wide range of software available for it. The fact that most of this software is freely distributable is even more impressive.

1.4.1 Basic commands and utilities

Virtually every utility that you would expect to find on standard implementations of UNIX has been ported to Linux. This includes basic commands such as `ls`, `awk`, `tr`, `sed`, `bc`, `more`, and so on. You name it, Linux has it. Therefore, you can expect your familiar working environment on other UNIX systems to be duplicated on Linux. All of the standard commands and utilities are there. (Novice Linux users should see Chapter 3 for an introduction to these basic UNIX commands.)

Many text editors are available, including `vi`, `ex`, `pico`, `jove`, as well as GNU Emacs and variants such as Lucid Emacs (which incorporates extensions for use under X Windows) and `joe`. Whatever text editor you're accustomed to using has more than likely been ported to Linux.

The choice of a text editor is an interesting one. Many UNIX users still use "simple" editors such as `vi` (in fact, the author wrote this book using `vi` under Linux). However, `vi` has many limitations, due to its age, and more modern (and complex) editors such as Emacs are gaining popularity. Emacs supports a complete LISP-based macro language and interpreter, a powerful command syntax, and other fun-filled extensions. Emacs macro packages exist to allow you to read electronic mail and news, edit the contents of directories, and even engage in an artificially intelligent psychotherapy session (indispensible for stressed-out Linux hackers).

One interesting note is that most of the basic Linux utilities are GNU software. These GNU utilities support advanced features not found in the standard versions from BSD or AT&T. For example, GNU's version of the `vi` editor, `elvis`, includes a structured macro language which differs from the original AT&T

---

[2]Swap space is inappropriately named: entire processes are not swapped, but rather individual pages. Of course, in many cases entire processes will be swapped out, but this is not necessarily always the case.

implementation. However, the GNU utilities strive to remain compatible with their BSD and System V counterparts. Many people consider the GNU versions of these programs superior to the originals.

The most important utility to many users is the **shell**. The shell is a program which reads and executes commands from the user. In addition, many shells provide features such as **job control** (allowing the user to manage several running processes at once—not as Orwellian as it sounds), input and output redirection, and a command language for writing **shell scripts**. A shell script is a file containing a program in the shell command language, analogous to a "batch file" under MS-DOS.

There are many types of shells available for Linux. The most important difference between shells is the command language. For example, the **C Shell** (csh) uses a command language somewhat like the C programming language. The classic **Bourne Shell** uses a different command language. One's choice of a shell is often based on the command language that it provides. The shell that you use defines, to some extent, your working environment under Linux.

No matter what shell you're accustomed to, some version of it has probably been ported to Linux. The most popular shell is the GNU Bourne Again Shell (bash), a Bourne shell variant which includes many advanced features, such as job control, command history, command and filename completion, an Emacs-like interface for editing the command line, and powerful extensions to the standard Bourne shell language. Another popular shell is tcsh, a version of the C Shell with advanced functionality similar to that found in bash. Other shells include zsh, a small Bourne-like shell; the Korn shell (ksh); BSD's ash; and rc, the Plan 9 shell.

What's so important about these basic utilities? Linux gives you the unique opportunity to tailor a custom system to your needs. For example, if you're the only person who uses your system, and you prefer to exclusively use the vi editor, and bash as your shell, there's no reason to install other editors or shells. The "do it yourself" attitude is prevalent among Linux hackers and users.

1.4.2 Text processing and word processing

Almost every computer user has a need for some kind of document preparation system. (How many computer enthusiasts do you know who still use pen and paper? Not many, we'll wager.) In the PC world, *word processing* is the norm: it involves editing and manipulating text (often in a "What-You-See-Is-What-You-Get" environment) and producing printed copies of the text, complete with figures, tables, and other garnishes.

In the UNIX world, *text processing* is much more common, which is quite different than the classical concept of word processing. With a text processing system, text is entered by the author using a "typesetting language", which describes how the text should be formatted. Instead of entering the text within a special word processing environment, the source may be modified with any text editor such as vi or Emacs. Once the source text (in the typesetting language) is complete, the user formats the text with a separate program, which converts the source to a format suitable for printing. This is somewhat analogous to programming in a language such as C, and "compiling" the document into a printable form.

There are many text processing systems available for Linux. One is groff, the GNU version of the classic nroff text formatter originally developed by Bell Labs and still used on many UNIX systems worldwide. Another modern text processing system is TEX, developed by Donald Knuth of computer science fame. Dialects of TEX, such as LATEX, are also available.

Text processors such as TEX and groff differ mostly in the syntax of their formatting languages. The choice of one formatting system over another is also based upon what utilities are available to satisfy your needs, as well as personal taste.

For example, some people consider the groff formatting language to be a bit obscure, so they use TEX, which is more readable by humans. However, `groff` is capable of producing plain ASCII output, viewable on a terminal, while TEX is intended primarily for output to a printing device. However, various programs exist to produce plain ASCII from TEX-formatted documents, or to convert TEX to `groff`, for example.

Another text processing system is `texinfo`, an extension to TEX used for software documentation by the Free Software Foundation. `texinfo` is capable of producing a printed document, or an online-browsable hypertext "Info" document from a single source file. Info files are the main format of documentation used by GNU software such as Emacs.

Text processors are used widely in the computing community for producing papers, theses, magazine articles, and books (in fact, this book was produced using LATEX). The ability to process the source language as a plain text file opens the door to many extensions to the text processor itself. Because source documents are not stored in an obscure format, readable only by a particular word processor, programmers are able to write parsers and translators for the formatting language, extending the system.

What does such a formatting language look like? In general, the formatting language source consists mostly of the text itself, along with "control codes" to produce a particular effect, such as changing fonts, setting margins, creating lists, and so on.

As an example, take the following text:

Mr. Torvalds:

We are very upset with your current plans to implement *post-hypnotic suggestion* in the **Linux** terminal driver code. We feel this way for three reasons:

1. Planting subliminal messages in the terminal driver is not only immoral, it is a waste of time;

2. It has been proven that "post-hypnotic suggestions" are ineffective when used upon unsuspecting UNIX hackers;

3. We have already implemented high-voltage electric shocks, as a security measure, in the code for `login`.

We hope you will reconsider.

This text would appear in the LATEX formatting language as the following:

```
\begin{quote}
Mr. Torvalds:

We are very upset with your current plans to implement {\em post-hypnotic
suggestion\/} in the {\bf Linux} terminal driver code. We feel this
way for three reasons:
\begin{enumerate}
\item Planting subliminal messages in the kernel driver is not only
      immoral, it is a waste of time;
\item It has been proven that ''post-hypnotic suggestions'' are ineffective
      when used upon unsuspecting UNIX hackers;
\item We have already implemented high-voltage electric shocks, as a
      security measure, in the code for {\tt login}.
\end{enumerate}
We hope you will reconsider.
\end{quote}
```

The author enters the above "source" text using any text editor, and generates the formatted output by processing the source with LaTeX. At first glance, the typesetting language may appear to be obscure, but it's actually quite easy to learn. Using a text processing system enforces typographical standards when writing. For example, all enumerated lists within a document will look the same, unless the author modifies the definition of the enumerated list "environment". The primary goal is to allow the author to concentrate on writing the actual text, instead of worrying about typesetting conventions.

WYSIWYG word processors are attractive for many reasons; they provide a powerful (and sometimes complex) visual interface for editing the document. However, this interface is inherently limited to those aspects of text layout which are accessible to the user. For example, many word processors provide a special "format language" for producing complicated expressions such as mathematical formulae. This is identical text processing, albeit on a much smaller scale.

The subtle benefit of text processing is that the system allows you to specify exactly what you mean. Also, text processing systems allow you to edit the source text with any text editor, and the source is easily converted to other formats. The tradeoff for this flexibility and power is the lack of a WYSIWYG interface.

Many users of word processors are used to seeing the formatted text as they edit it. On the other hand, when writing with a text processor, one generally does not worry about how the text will appear when formatted. The writer learns to expect how the text should look from the formatting commands used in the source.

There are programs which allow you to view the formatted document on a graphics display before printing. For example, the xdvi program displays a "device independent" file generated by the TeX system under the X Windows environment. Other software applications, such as xfig, provide a WYSIWYG graphics interface for drawing figures and diagrams, which are subsequently converted to the text processing language for inclusion in your document.

Admittedly, text processors such as nroff were around long before word processing was available. However, many people still prefer to use text processing, because it is more versatile and independent of a graphics environment. In either case, the idoc word processor is also available for Linux, and before long we expect to see commercial word processors becoming available as well. If you absolutely don't want to give up word processing for text processing, you can always run MS-DOS, or some other operating system, in addition to Linux.

There are many other text-processing-related utilities available. The powerful METAFONT system, used for designing fonts for TeX, is included with the Linux port of TeX. Other programs include ispell, an interactive spell checker and corrector; makeindex, used for generating indexes in LaTeX documents; as well as many groff and TeX-based macro packages for formatting many types of documents and mathematical texts. Conversion programs to translate between TeX or groff source to a myriad of other formats are available.

1.4.3 Programming languages and utilities

Linux provides a complete UNIX programming environment, including all of the standard libraries, programming tools, compilers, and debuggers that you would expect to find on other UNIX systems. Within the UNIX software development world, applications and systems programming is usually done in C or C++. The standard C and C++ compiler for Linux is GNU's gcc, which is an advanced, modern compiler supporting many options. It is also capable of compiling C++ (including AT&T 3.0 features) as well as Objective-C, another object-oriented dialect of C.

Besides C and C++, many other compiled and interpreted programming languages have been ported to Linux, such as Smalltalk, FORTRAN, Pascal, LISP, Scheme, and Ada (if you're masochistic enough to program in Ada—we're not going to stop you). In addition, various assemblers for writing protected-mode 80386 code are available, as are UNIX hacking favorites such as Perl (the script language to end all script languages) and Tcl/Tk (a shell-like command processing system including support for developing simple X Windows applications).

The advanced `gdb` debugger has been ported, which allows you to step through a program to find bugs, or examine the cause for a crash using a core dump. `gprof`, a profiling utility, will give you performance statistics for your program, letting you know where your program is spending most of its time executing. The Emacs text editor provides an interactive editing and compilation environment for various programming languages. Other tools include GNU `make` and `imake`, used to manage compilation of large applications; and RCS, a system for source locking and revision control.

Linux implements dynamically-linked shared libraries, which allow binaries to be much smaller as the subroutine code is linked at run-time. These DLL libraries also allow the applications programmer to override function definitions with their own code. For example, if a programmer wished to write her own version of the `malloc()` library routine, the linker would use the programmer's new routine instead of the one found in the libraries.

Linux is ideal for developing UNIX applications. It provides a modern programming environment with all of the bells and whistles. Various standards such as POSIX.1 are supported, allowing software written for Linux to be easily ported to other systems. Professional UNIX programmers and system administrators can use Linux to develop software at home, and then transfer the software to UNIX systems at work. This not only can save a great deal of time and money, but will also let you work in the comfort of your own home.[3] Computer Science students can use Linux to learn UNIX programming and to explore other aspects of the system, such as kernel architecture.

With Linux, not only do you have access to the complete set of libraries and programming utilities, but you also have the complete kernel and library source code at your fingertips.

1.4.4   The X Window System

The X Window System is the standard graphics interface for UNIX machines. It is a powerful environment supporting many applications. Using X Windows, the user can have multiple terminal windows on the screen at once, each one containing a different login session. A pointing device such as a mouse is often used with the X interface, although it isn't required.

Many X-specific applications have been written, such as games, graphics utilities, programming and documentation tools, and so on. With Linux and X, your system is a bona fide workstation. Coupled with TCP/IP networking, you can even display X applications running on other machines on your Linux display, as is possible with other systems running X.

The X Window System was originally developed at MIT, and is freely distributable. However, may commercial vendors have distributed proprietary enhancements to the original X Windows software. The version of X Windows available for Linux is known as XFree86, a port of X11R5 made freely distributable for 80386-based UNIX systems such as Linux. XFree86 supports a wide range of video hardware, including VGA, Super VGA, and a number of accelerated video adaptors. This is a complete distribution of the X Windows software, containing the X server itself, many applications and utilities, programming libraries, and documentation.

Standard X applications include `xterm` (a terminal emulator used for most text-based applications within an X window); `xdm` (the X Session Manager, which handles logins); `xclock` (a simple clock display);

---

[3]The author uses his Linux system to develop and test X Windows applications at home, which can be directly compiled on workstations elsewhere.

xman (an X-based man page reader), and more. The many X applications available for Linux are too numerous to mention here, but the base XFree86 distribution includes the "standard" applications found in the original MIT release. Many others are available separately, and theoretically any application written for X Windows should compile cleanly under Linux.

The look and feel of the X Windows interface is controlled to a large extent by the **window manager**. This friendly program is in charge of the placement of windows, the user interface for resizing, iconifying, and moving windows, the appearance of window frames, and so on. The standard XFree86 distribution includes twm, the classic MIT window manager, although more advanced window managers such as the Open Look Virtual Window Manager (olvwm) are available as well. One window manager that is popular among Linux users is fvwm. This is a small window manager, requiring less than half of the memory used by twm. It provides a 3-D appearance for windows, as well a virtual desktop—if the user moves the mouse to the edge of the screen, the entire desktop is shifted as if the display were much larger than it actually is. fvwm is greatly customizable, and allows all functions to be accessed from the keyboard as well as the mouse. Many Linux distributions use fvwm as the standard window manager.

The XFree86 distribution contains programming libraries and include files for those wily programmers who wish to develop X applications. Various widget sets, such as Athena, Open Look, and Xaw3D are supported. All of the standard fonts, bitmaps, man pages, and documentation are included. PEX (a programming interface for 3-D graphics) is also supported.

Many X applications programmers use the proprietary Motif widget set for development. Several vendors sell single and multiple-user licenses for a binary version of Motif for Linux. Because Motif itself is relatively expensive, not many Linux users own it. However, binaries statically linked with Motif routines may be freely distributed. Therefore, if you write a program using Motif and wish to distribute it freely, you may provide a binary so that users without Motif can use the program.

The only major caveats with X Windows are the hardware and memory requirements. A 386 with 4 megabytes of RAM is capable of running X, but 8 megabytes or more of physical RAM are needed to use it comfortably. A faster processor is nice to have as well, but having enough physical RAM is much more important. In addition, to achieve really slick video performance, an accelerated video card (such as a local bus S3-chipset card) is strongly recommended. Performance ratings in excess of 140,000 xstones have been achieved with Linux and XFree86. With sufficient hardware, you'll find that running X and Linux is as fast, or faster, than running X on other UNIX workstations.

In Chapter 5 we'll discuss how to install and use X on your system.

1.4.5 Networking

Interested in communicating with the world? Yes? No? Maybe? Linux supports the two primary networking protocols for UNIX systems: **TCP/IP** and **UUCP**. TCP/IP (Transmission Control Protocol/Internet Protocol, for acronym aficionados) is the set of networking paradigms that allow systems all over the world to communicate on a single network known as the Internet. With Linux, TCP/IP, and a connection to the network, you can communicate with users and machines across the Internet via electronic mail, USENET news, file transfers with FTP, and more. There are many Linux systems currently on the Internet.

Most TCP/IP networks use Ethernet as the physical network transport. Linux supports many popular Ethernet cards and interfaces for personal computers, including the D-Link pocket Ethernet adaptor for laptops.

However, because not everyone has an Ethernet drop at home, Linux also supports **SLIP** (Serial Line Internet Protocol), which allows you to connect to the Internet via modem. In order to use SLIP, you'll need to have access to a SLIP server, a machine connected to the network which allows dial-in access.

Many businesses and universities provide such SLIP servers. In fact, if your Linux system has an Ethernet connection as well as a modem, you can configure it as a SLIP server for other hosts.

NFS (Network File System) allows your system to seamlessly share files with other machines on the network. FTP (File Transfer Protocol) allows you to transfer files between other machines. Other applications include `sendmail`, a system for sending and receiving electronic mail using the SMTP protocol; NNTP-based electronic news systems such as C-News and INN; `telnet`, `rlogin`, and `rsh`, which allow you to login and execute commands on other machines on the network; and `finger`, which allows you to get information on other Internet users. There are literally tons of TCP/IP-based applications and protocols out there.

The full range of mail and news readers are available for Linux, such as `elm`, `pine`, `rn`, `nn`, and `tin`. Whatever your preference, you can configure your Linux system to send and receive electronic mail and news from all over the world.

If you have experience with TCP/IP applications on other UNIX systems, Linux will be very familiar to you. The system provides a standard socket programming interface, so virtually any program which uses TCP/IP can be ported to Linux. The Linux X server also supports TCP/IP, allowing you to display applications running on other systems on your Linux display.

In Chapter 5 we'll discuss configuration and setup of TCP/IP, including SLIP, for Linux.

UUCP (UNIX-to-UNIX Copy) is an older mechanism used to transfer files, electronic mail, and electronic news between UNIX machines. Classically, UUCP machines connected to each other over the phone lines via modem, but UUCP is able to transport over a TCP/IP network as well. If you do not have access to a TCP/IP network or a SLIP server, you can configure your system to send and receive files and electronic mail using UUCP. See Chapter 5 for more information.

1.4.6   Telecommunications and BBS software

If you have a modem, you will be able to communicate with other machines using one of the telecommunications packages available for Linux. Many people use telecommunications software to access bulletin board systems (BBSs), as well as commercial online services such as Prodigy, CompuServe, and America On-Line. Other people use their modems to connect to a UNIX system at work or school. You can even use your modem and Linux system to send and receive facsimiles. Telecommunications software under Linux is very similar to that found under MS-DOS or other operating systems. Anyone who has ever used a telecommunications package will find the Linux equivalent familiar.

One of the most popular communications packages for Linux is Seyon, an X application providing a customizable, ergonomic interface, with built-in support for various file transfer protocols such as Kermit, ZModem, and so on. Other telecommunications programs include C-Kermit, `pcomm`, and `minicom`. These are similar to communications programs found on other operating systems, and are quite easy to use.

If you do not have access to a SLIP server (see the previous section), you can use `term` to multiplex your serial line. `term` will allow you to open multiple login sessions over the modem connection to a remote machine. `term` will also allow you to redirect X client connections to your local X server, through the serial line, allowing you to display remote X applications on your Linux system. Another software package, KA9Q, implements a similar SLIP-like interface.

Running a bulletin board system (BBS) is a favorite hobby (and means of income) for many people. Linux supports a wide range of BBS software, most of which is more powerful than what is available for other operating systems. With a phone line, a modem, and Linux, you can turn your system into a BBS, providing dial-in access to your system to users worldwide. BBS software for Linux includes XBBS and the UniBoard BBS packages.

Most BBS software locks the user into a menu-based system where only certain functions and applications are available. An alternative to BBS access is full UNIX access, which would allow users to dial into your system and login as a regular user. While this would require a fair amount of maintenance on the part of the system administrator, it can be done, and providing public UNIX access from your Linux system is not difficult to do. Along with a TCP/IP network, you can provide electronic mail and news access to users on your system.

If you do not have access to a TCP/IP network or UUCP feed, Linux will also allow you to communicate with a number of BBS networks, such as FidoNet, with which you can exchange electronic news and mail via the phone line. More information on telecommunications and BBS software under Linux can be found in Chapter 5.

1.4.7   Interfacing with MS-DOS

Various utilities exist to interface with the world of MS-DOS. The most well-known application is the Linux MS-DOS Emulator, which allows you to run many MS-DOS applications directly from Linux. Although Linux and MS-DOS are completely different operating systems, the 80386 protected-mode environment allows certain tasks to behave as if they were running in 8086-emulation mode, as MS-DOS applications do.

The MS-DOS emulator is still under development, yet many popular applications run under it. Understandably, however, MS-DOS applications which use bizarre or esoteric features of the system may never be supported, because it is only an emulator. For example, you wouldn't expect to be able to run any programs which use 80386 protected-mode features, such as Microsoft Windows (in 386 enhanced mode, that is).

Applications which run successfully under the Linux MS-DOS Emulator include 4DOS (a command interpreter), Foxpro 2.0, Harvard Graphics, MathCad, Stacker 3.1, Turbo Assembler, Turbo C/C++, Turbo Pascal, Microsoft Windows 3.0 (in *real* mode), and WordPerfect 5.1. Standard MS-DOS commands and utilities (such as `PKZIP`, and so on) work with the emulator as well.

The MS-DOS Emulator is meant mostly as an ad hoc solution for those people who need MS-DOS only for a few applications, but use Linux for everything else. It's not meant to be a complete implementation of MS-DOS. Of course, if the Emulator doesn't satisfy your needs, you can always run MS-DOS as well as Linux on the same system. Using the LILO boot loader, you can specify at boot time which operating system to start. Linux can coexist with other operating systems, such as OS/2, as well.

Linux provides a seamless interface for transferring files between Linux and MS-DOS. You can mount an MS-DOS partition or floppy under Linux, and directly access MS-DOS files as you would any other.

Currently under development is a project known as **WINE**—a Microsoft Windows emulator for the X Window System under Linux. Once WINE is complete, users will be able to run MS-Windows applications directly from Linux. This is similar to the proprietary WABI Windows emulator from Sun Microsystems. At the time of this writing, WINE is still in the early stages of development, but the outlook is good.

In Chapter 5 we'll talk about the MS-DOS tools available for Linux.

1.4.8   Other applications

A host of miscellany is available for Linux, as one would expect from such a hodgepodge operating system. Linux's primary focus is currently for personal UNIX computing, but this is rapidly changing. Business and scientific software is expanding, and commercial software vendors are beginning to contribute to the growing pool of applications.

Several relational databases are available for Linux, including Postgres, Ingres, and Mbase. These are full-featured, professional client/server database applications similar to those found on other UNIX platforms. /rdb, a commercial database system, is available as well.

Scientific computing applications include FELT (a finite element analysis tool); gnuplot (a plotting and data analysis application); Octave (a symbolic mathematics package, similar to MATLAB); xspread (a spreadsheet calculator); xfractint, an X-based port of the popular Fractint fractal generator; xlispstat (a statistics package), and more. Other applications include Spice (a circuit design and analysis tool) and Khoros (an image/digital signal processing and visualization system).

Of course, there are many more such applications which have been, and can be, ported to run on Linux. Whatever your field, porting UNIX-based applications to Linux should be quite straightforward. Linux provides a complete UNIX programming interface, sufficient to serve as the base for any scientific application.

As with any operating system, Linux has its share of games. These include classic text-based dungeon games such as Nethack and Moria; MUDs (multi-user dungeons, which allow many users to interact in a text-based adventure) such as DikuMUD and TinyMUD; as well as a slew of X games such as xtetris, netrek, and Xboard (the X11 version of gnuchess). The popular shoot-em-up arcade-style *Doom* has also been ported to Linux.

For audiophiles, Linux has support for various sound cards and related software, such as CDplayer (a program which can control a CD-ROM drive as a conventional CD player, surprisingly enough), MIDI sequencers and editors (allowing you to compose music for playback through a synthesizer or other MIDI-controlled instrument), and sound editors for digitized sounds.

Can't find the application you're looking for? The Linux Software Map, described in Appendix A, contains a list of many software packages which have been written and ported to Linux. While this list is far from complete, it contains a great deal of software. Another way to find Linux applications is to look at the INDEX files found on Linux FTP sites, if you have Internet access. Just by poking around you'll find a great deal of software just waiting to be played with.

If you absolutely can't find what you need, you can always attempt to port the application from another platform to Linux. Most freely distributable UNIX-based software will compile on Linux with few problems. Or, if all else fails, you can write the application yourself. If it's a commercial application you're looking for, there may be a free "clone" available. Or, you can encourage the software company to consider releasing a Linux binary version. Several individuals have contacted software companies, asking them to port their applications to Linux, and have met with various degrees of success.

1.5   About Linux's Copyright

Linux is covered by what is known as the GNU *General Public License*, or *GPL*. The GPL was developed for the GNU project by the Free Software Foundation. It makes a number of provisions for the distribution and modification of "free software". "Free" in this sense refers to freedom, not just cost. The GPL has always been subject to misinterpretation, and we hope that this summary will help you to understand the extent and goals of the GPL and its effect on Linux. A complete copy of the GPL is included in Appendix D.

Originally, Linus Torvalds released Linux under a license more restrictive than the GPL, which allowed the software to be freely distributed and modified, but prevented any money changing hands for its distribution and use. On the other hand, the GPL allows people to sell and make profit from free software, but does not allow them to restrict the right for others to distribute the software in any way.

First, it should be explained that "free software" covered by the GPL is *not* in the public domain. Public domain software is software which is not copyrighted, and is literally owned by the public. Software covered by the GPL, on the other hand, is copyrighted to the author or authors. This means that the software is protected by standard international copyright laws, and that the author of the software is legally defined. Just because the software may be freely distributed does not mean that it is in the public domain.

GPL-licensed software is also not "shareware". Generally, "shareware" software is owned and copyrighted by the author, but the author requires users to send in money for its use after distribution. On the other hand, software covered by the GPL may be distributed and used free of charge.

The GPL also allows people to take and modify free software, and distribute their own versions of the software. However, any derived works from GPL software must also be covered by the GPL. In other words, a company could not take Linux, modify it, and sell it under a restrictive license. If any software is derived from Linux, that software must be covered by the GPL as well.

The GPL allows free software to be distributed and used free of charge. However, it also allows a person or organization to distribute GPL software for a fee, and even to make a profit from its sale and distribution. However, in selling GPL software, the distributor cannot take those rights away from the purchaser; that is, if you purchase GPL software from some source, you may distribute the software for free, or sell it yourself as well.

This might sound like a contradiction at first. Why sell software for profit when the GPL allows anyone to obtain it for free? As an example, let's say that some company decided to bundle a large amount of free software on a CD-ROM and distribute it. That company would need to charge for the overhead of producing and distributing the CD-ROM, and the company may even decide to make profit from the sales of software. This is allowed by the GPL.

Organizations which sell free software must follow certain restrictions set forth in the GPL. First, they cannot restrict the rights of users who purchase the software. This means that if you buy a CD-ROM of GPL software, you can copy and distribute that CD-ROM free of charge, or resell it yourself. Secondly, distributors must make it obvious to users that the software is indeed covered by the GPL. Thirdly, distributors must provide, free of charge, the complete source code for the software being distributed. This will allow anyone who purchases GPL software to make modifications of that software.

Allowing a company to distribute and sell free software is a very good thing. Not everyone has access to the Internet to download software, such as Linux, for free. The GPL allows companies to sell and distribute software to those people who do not have free (cost-wise) access to the software. For example, many organizations sell Linux on diskette, tape, or CD-ROM via mail order, and make profit from these sales. The developers of Linux may never see any of this profit; that is the understanding that is reached between the developer and the distributor when software is licensed by the GPL. In other words, Linus knew that companies may wish to sell Linux, and that he may not see a penny of the profits from those sales.

In the free software world, the important issue is not money. The goal of free software is always to develop and distribute fantastic software and to allow anyone to obtain and use it. In the next section, we'll discuss how this applies to the development of Linux.

1.6   The Design and Philosophy of Linux

When new users encounter Linux, they often have a few misconceptions and false expectations of the system. Linux is a unique operating system, and it is important to understand its philosophy and design in order to use it effectively. Time enough for a soapbox. Even if you are an aged UNIX guru, what follows is probably of interest to you.

In commercial UNIX development houses, the entire system is developed with a rigorous policy of quality assurance, source and revision control systems, documentation, and bug reporting and resolution. Developers are not allowed to add features or to change key sections of code on a whim: they must validate the change as a response to a bug report and consequently "check in" all changes to the source control system, so that the changes can be backed out if necessary. Each developer is assigned one or more parts of the system code, and only that developer may alter those sections of the code while it is "checked out".

Internally, the quality assurance department runs rigorous regression test suites on each new pass of the operating system, and reports any bugs. It is the responsibility of the developers to fix these bugs as reported. A complicated system of statistical analysis is employed to ensure that a certain percentage of bugs are fixed before the next release, and that the operating system as a whole passes certain release criteria.

In all, the process used by commercial UNIX developers to maintain and support their code is very complicated, and quite reasonably so. The company must have quantitative proof that the next revision of the operating system is ready to be shipped; hence, the gathering and analysis of statistics about the operating system's performance. It is a big job to develop a commercial UNIX system, often large enough to employ hundreds (if not thousands) of programmers, testers, documentors, and administrative personnel. Of course, no two commercial UNIX vendors are alike, but you get the general picture.

With Linux, you can throw out the entire concept of organized development, source control systems, structured bug reporting, or statistical analysis. Linux is, and more than likely always will be, a hacker's operating system.[4]

Linux is primarily developed as a group effort by volunteers on the Internet from all over the world. Across the Internet and beyond, anyone with enough know-how has the opportunity to aid in developing and debugging the kernel, porting new software, writing documentation, or helping new users. There is no single organization responsible for developing the system. For the most part, the Linux community communicates via various mailing lists and USENET newsgroups. A number of conventions have sprung up around the development effort: for example, anyone wishing to have their code included in the "official" kernel should mail it to Linus Torvalds, which he will test and include in the kernel (as long as it doesn't break things or go against the overall design of the system, he will more than likely include it).

The system itself is designed with a very open-ended, feature-minded approach. While recently the number of new features and critical changes to the system have diminished, the general rule is that a new version of the kernel will be released about every few months (sometimes even more frequently than this). Of course, this is a very rough figure: it depends on a several factors including the number of bugs to be fixed, the amount of feedback from users testing pre-release versions of the code, and the amount of sleep that Linus has had this week.

Let it suffice to say that not every single bug has been fixed, and not every problem ironed out between releases. As long as the system appears to be free of critical or oft-manifesting bugs, it is considered "stable" and new revisions will be released. The thrust behind Linux development is not an effort to release perfect, bug-free code: it is to develop a free implementation of UNIX. Linux is *for* the developers, more than anyone else.

Anyone who has a new feature or software application to add to the system generally makes it available in an "alpha" stage—that is, a stage for testing by those brave or unwary users who want to bash out problems with the initial code. Because the Linux community is largely based on the Internet, alpha software is usually uploaded to one or more of the various Linux FTP sites (see Appendix C) and a message posted to one of the Linux USENET newsgroups about how to get and test the code. Users who download and test alpha software can then mail results, bug fixes, or questions to the author.

---

[4]What I mean by "hacker" is a feverishly dedicated programmer, a person who enjoys exploiting computers and generally doing interesting things with them. This is in contrast to the common denotation of "hacker" as a computer wrongdoer or outlaw.

After the initial problems in the alpha code have been fixed, the code enters a "beta" stage, in which it is usually considered stable but not complete (that is, it works, but not all of the features may be present). Otherwise, it may go directly to a "final" stage in which the software is considered complete and usable. For kernel code, once it is complete the developer may ask Linus to include it in the standard kernel, or as an optional add-on feature to the kernel.

Keep in mind that these are only conventions—not rules. Some people feel so confident with their software that they don't need to release an alpha or test version. It is always up to the developer to make these decisions.

You might be amazed that such a nonstructured system of volunteers, programming and debugging a complete UNIX system, could get anything done at all. As it turns out, it is one of the most efficient and motivated development efforts ever employed. The entire Linux kernel was written *from scratch*, without employing any code from proprietary sources. A great deal of work was put forth by volunteers to port all of the free software under the sun to the Linux system. Libraries were written and ported, filesystems developed, and hardware drivers written for many popular devices.

The Linux software is generally released as a *distribution*, which is a set of pre-packaged software making up an entire system. It would be quite difficult for most users to build a complete system from the ground up, starting with the kernel, adding utilities, and installing all of the necessary software by hand. Instead, there are a number of software distributions including everything that you need to install and run a complete system. Again, there is no standard distribution—there are many, each with their own advantages and disadvantages. We'll talk more about the various available Linux distributions in Section 2.1.

Despite the completeness of the Linux software, you will still need a bit of UNIX know-how to install and run a complete system. No distribution of Linux is completely bug-free, so you may be required to fix small problems by hand after installation. Running a UNIX system is not an easy task, not even for commercial versions of UNIX. If you're serious about Linux, bear in mind that it will take a considerable amount of effort and attention on your part to keep the system running and take care of things: this is true of *any* UNIX system, and Linux is no exception. Because of the diversity of the Linux community and the many needs which the software is attempting to meet, not eveything can be taken care of for you all of the time.

1.6.1 Hints for UNIX novices

Installing and using your own Linux system does not require a great deal of background in UNIX. In fact, many UNIX novices successfully install Linux on their systems. This is a worthwhile learning experience, but keep in mind that it can be very frustrating to some. If you're lucky, you will be able to install and start using your Linux system without any UNIX background. However, once you are ready to delve into the more complex tasks of running Linux—installing new software, recompiling the kernel, and so forth—having background knowledge in UNIX is going to be a necessity.

Fortunately, by running your own Linux system you will be able to learn the essentials of UNIX necessary for these tasks. This book contains a good deal of information to help you get started—Chapter 3 is a tutorial covering UNIX basics, and Chapter 4 contains information on Linux system administration. You may wish to read these chapters before you attempt to install Linux at all—the information contained therein will prove to be invaluable should you run into problems.

Nobody can expect to go from being a UNIX novice to a UNIX system administrator overnight. No implementation of UNIX is expected to run trouble- and maintenance-free. You must be aptly prepared for the journey which lies ahead. Otherwise, if you're new to UNIX, you may very well become overly frustrated with the system.

1.6.2 Hints for UNIX gurus

Even those people with years of UNIX programming and systems administration experience may need assistance before they are able to pick up and install Linux. There are still aspects of the system that UNIX wizards will need to be familiar with before diving in. For one thing, Linux is not a commercial UNIX system. It does not attempt to uphold the same standards as other UNIX systems you have may have come across. To be more specific, while stability is an important factor in the development of Linux, it is not the *only* factor.

More important, perhaps, is functionality. In many cases, new code will make it into the standard kernel even though it is still buggy and not functionally complete. The assumption is that it is more important to release code which users can test and use than delay a release until it is "complete". As an example, WINE (the Microsoft Windows Emulator for Linux) had an "official" alpha release before it was completely tested. In this way, the Linux community at large had a chance to work with the code, test it, and help develop it, while those who found the alpha code "good enough" for their needs could use it. Commercial UNIX vendors rarely, if ever, release software in this manner.

If you have been a UNIX systems administrator for more than a decade, and have used every commercial UNIX system under the Sun (no pun intended), Linux may take some getting used to. The system is very modern and dynamic. A new kernel release is made approximately every few months. New software is constantly being released. One day your system may be completely up-to-date with the current trend, and the next day the same system is considered to be in the Stone Age.

With all of this dynamic activity, how can you be expected to keep up with the ever-changing Linux world? For the most part, it is best to upgrade incrementally; that is, upgrade only those parts of the system that *need* upgrading, and then only when you think an upgrade is necessary. For example, if you never use Emacs, there is little reason to continuously install every new release of Emacs on your system. Furthermore, even if you are an avid Emacs user, there is usually no reason to upgrade it unless you find that some feature is missing that is in the next release. There is little or no reason to always be on top of the newest version of software.

We hope that Linux will meet or exceed your expectations of a homebrew UNIX system. At the very core of Linux is the spirit of free software, of constant development and growth. The Linux community favors expansion over stability, and that is a difficult concept to swallow for many people, especially those so steeped in the world of commercial UNIX. You cannot expect Linux to be perfect; nothing ever is in the free software world. However, we believe that Linux really is as complete and useful as any other implementation of UNIX.

1.7 Differences Between Linux and Other Operating Systems

It is important to understand the differences between Linux and other operating systems, such as MS-DOS, OS/2, and other implementations of UNIX for the personal computer. First of all, it should be made clear that Linux will coexist happily with other operating systems on the same machine: that is, you can run MS-DOS and OS/2 along with Linux on the same system without problems. There are even ways to interact between the various operating systems, as we'll see.

1.7.1 Why use Linux?

Why use Linux instead of a well-known, well-tested, and well-documented commercial operating system? We could give you a thousand reasons. One of the most important, however, is that Linux is an excellent choice for personal UNIX computing. If you're a UNIX software developer, why use MS-DOS at home? Linux will allow you to develop and test UNIX software on your PC, including database and X Windows applications. If you're a student, chances are that your university computing systems run UNIX. With Linux, you can run your own UNIX system and tailor it to your own needs. Installing and running Linux is also an excellent way to learn UNIX if you don't have access to other UNIX machines.

But let's not lose sight. Linux isn't just for personal UNIX users. It is robust and complete enough to handle large tasks, as well as distributed computing needs. Many businesses—especially small ones—are moving to Linux in lieu of other UNIX-based workstation environments. Universities are finding Linux to be perfect for teaching courses in operating systems design. Larger commercial software vendors are starting to realize the opportunities that a free operating system can provide.

The following sections should point out the most important differences between Linux and other operating systems. We hope that you'll find that Linux can meet your computing needs, or (at least) enhance your current computing environment. Keep in mind that they best way to get a taste for Linux is just to try it out—you needn't even install a complete system to get a feel for it. In Chapter 2, we'll show you how.

1.7.2 Linux vs. MS-DOS

It's not uncommon to run both Linux and MS-DOS on the same system. Many Linux users rely on MS-DOS for applications such as word processing. While Linux provides its own analogues for these applications (for example, TEX), there are various reasons why a particular user would want to run MS-DOS as well as Linux. If your entire dissertation is written using WordPerfect for MS-DOS, you may not be able to easily convert it to TEX or some other format. There are many commercial applications for MS-DOS which aren't available for Linux, and there's no reason why you can't use both.

As you might know, MS-DOS does not fully utilize the functionality of the 80386 and 80486 processors. On the other hand, Linux runs completely in the processor's protected mode, and exploits all of the features of the processor. You can directly access all of your available memory (and beyond, using virtual RAM). Linux provides a complete UNIX interface not available under MS-DOS—developing and porting UNIX applications under Linux is easily done, while under MS-DOS you are limited to a small subset of the UNIX programming functionality. Because Linux is a true UNIX system, you do not have these limitations.

We could debate the pros and cons of MS-DOS and Linux for pages on end. However, let it suffice to say that Linux and MS-DOS are completely different entities. MS-DOS is inexpensive (compared to other commercial operating systems), and has a strong foothold in the PC computing world. No other operating system for the PC has reached the level of popularity of MS-DOS—largely because the cost of these other operating systems is unapproachable to most personal computer users. Very few PC users can imagine spending $1000 or more on the operating system alone. Linux, however, is free, and you finally have the chance to decide.

We will allow you to make your own judgments of Linux and MS-DOS based on your expectations and needs. Linux is not for everybody. If you have always wanted to run a complete UNIX system at home, without the high cost of other UNIX implementations for the PC, Linux may be what you're looking for.

There are tools available to allow you to interact between Linux and MS-DOS. For example, it is easy to access MS-DOS files from Linux. There is also an MS-DOS emulator available, which allows you to run many popular MS-DOS applications. A Microsoft Windows emulator is currently under development.

1.7.3   Linux vs. The Other Guys

A number of other advanced operating systems are on the rise in the PC world. Specifically, IBM's OS/2 and Microsoft's Windows NT are becoming very popular as more users move away from MS-DOS.

Both OS/2 and Windows NT are full multitasking operating systems, much like Linux. Technically, OS/2, Windows NT, and Linux are quite similar: they support roughly the same features in terms of user interface, networking, security, and so forth. However, the real difference between Linux and The Other Guys is the fact that Linux is a version of UNIX, and hence benefits from the contributions of the UNIX community at large.

What makes UNIX so important? Not only is it the most popular operating system for multiuser machines, it is also the foundation for the majority of the free software world. If you have access to the Internet, nearly all of the free software available there is written specifically for UNIX systems. (The Internet itself is largely UNIX-based.)

There are many implementations of UNIX, from many vendors, and no single organization is responsible for distribution. There is a large push in the UNIX community for standardization in the form of open systems, but no single corporation controls this design. Hence, any vendor (or, as it turns out, any hacker) may implement these standards in an implementation of UNIX.

OS/2 and Windows NT, on the other hand, are proprietary systems. The interface and design are controlled by a single corporation, and only that corporation may implement that design. (Don't expect to see a free version of OS/2 anytime in the near future.) In one sense, this kind of organization is beneficial: it sets a strict standard for the programming and user interface unlike that found even in the open systems community. OS/2 is OS/2 wherever you go—the same holds for Windows NT.

However, the UNIX interface is constantly developing and changing. Several organizations are attempting to standardize the programming model, but the task is very difficult. Linux, in particular, is mostly compliant with the POSIX.1 standard for the UNIX programming interface. As time goes on, it is expected that the system will adhere to other such standards, but standardization is not the primary issue in the Linux development community.

1.7.4   Other implementations of UNIX

There are several other implementations of UNIX for the 80386 and 80486. The 80386 architecture lends itself to the UNIX design, and a number of vendors have taken advantage of this.

Feature-wise, other implementations of UNIX for the PC are quite similar to Linux. You will see that almost all commercial versions of UNIX support roughly the same software, programming environment, and networking features. However, there are some strong differences between Linux and commercial versions of UNIX.

First of all, Linux supports a different range of hardware from commercial implementations. In general, Linux supports the most well-known hardware devices, but support is still limited to that hardware which developers actually have access to. However, commercial UNIX vendors generally have a wider support base, and tend to support more hardware, although Linux is not far behind. We'll cover the hardware requirements for Linux in Section 1.8.

Secondly, commercial implementations of UNIX usually come bundled with a complete set of documentation as well as user support from the vendor. In contrast, most of the documentation for Linux is limited to documents available on the Internet—and books such as this one. In Section 1.9 we'll list sources of Linux documentation and other information.

As far as stability and robustness are concerned, many users have reported that Linux is at least as stable as commercial UNIX systems. Linux is still under development, and certain features (such TCP/IP networking) are less stable but improve as time goes by.

The most important factor to consider for many users is price. The Linux software is free, if you have access to the Internet (or another computer network) and can download it. If you do not have access to such a network, you may need to purchase it via mail order on diskette, tape, or CD-ROM (see Appendix B). Of course, you may copy Linux from a friend who may already have the software, or share the cost of purchasing it with someone else. If you are planning to install Linux on a large number of machines, you need only purchase a single copy of the software—Linux is not distributed on a "single machine" license.

The value of commercial UNIX implementations should not be demeaned: along with the price of the software itself, one usually pays for documentation, support, and assurance of quality. These are very important factors for large institutions, but personal computer users may not require these benefits. In any case, many businesses and universities are finding that running Linux on a lab of inexpensive personal computers is preferrable to running a commercial version of UNIX in a lab of workstations. Linux can provide the functionality of a workstation on PC hardware at a fraction of the cost.

As a "real-world" example of Linux's use within the computing community, Linux systems have traveled the high seas of the North Pacific, managing telecommunications and data analysis for an oceanographic research vessel. Linux systems are being used at research stations in Antarctica. As a more mundane example, perhaps, several hospitals are using Linux to maintain patient records. It is proving to be as reliable and useful as other implementations of UNIX.

There are other free or inexpensive implementations of UNIX for the 386 and 486. One of the most well-known is 386BSD, an implementation and port of BSD UNIX for the 386. 386BSD is comparable to Linux in many ways, but which one is "better" depends on your own personal needs and expectations. The only strong distinction that we can make is that Linux is developed openly (where any volunteer can aid in the development process), while 386BSD is developed within a closed team of programmers who maintain the system. Because of this, serious philosophical and design differences exist between the two projects. The goals of the two projects are entirely different: the goal of Linux is to develop a complete UNIX system from scratch (and have a lot of fun in the process), and the goal of 386BSD is in part to modify the existing BSD code for use on the 386.

NetBSD is another port of the BSD NET/2 distribution to a number of machines, including the 386. NetBSD has a slightly more open development structure, and is comparable to 386BSD in many respects.

Another project of note is HURD, an effort by the Free Software Foundation to develop and distribute a free version of UNIX for many platforms. Contact the Free Software Foundation (the address is given in Appendix D) for more information about this project. At the time of this writing, HURD is still in early stages of development.

Other inexpensive versions of UNIX exist as well, such as Coherent (available for about $99) and Minix (an academic but useful UNIX clone upon which early development of Linux was based). Some of these implementations are of mostly academic interest, while others are full-fledged systems for real productivity. Needless to say, however, many personal UNIX users are moving to Linux.

1.8 Hardware Requirements

Now you must be convinced of how wonderful Linux is, and all of the great things that it can do for you. However, before you rush out and install the software, you need to be aware of the hardware requirements and limitations that Linux has.

Keep in mind that Linux was developed by its users. This means, for the most part, that the hardware which is supported by Linux is only the hardware which the users and developers actually have access to. As it turns out, most of the popular hardware and peripherals for 80386/80486 systems are supported (in fact, Linux supports more hardware than some commercial implementations of UNIX). However, some of the more obscure and esoteric devices aren't supported yet. As time goes on, a wider range of hardware is supported, so if your favorite devices aren't listed here, chances are that support for them is forthcoming.

Another drawback for hardware support under Linux is that many companies have decided to keep the hardware interface proprietary. The upshot of this is that volunteer Linux developers simply can't write drivers for those devices (if they could, those drivers would be owned by the company that owned the interface, which would violate the GPL). The companies that maintain proprietary interfaces write their own drivers for operating systems such as MS-DOS and Microsoft Windows; the end user (that's you) never needs to know about the interface. Unfortunately, this does not allow Linux developers to write drivers for those devices.

There is very little that can be done about the situation. In some cases, programmers have attempted to write hackish drivers based on assumptions about the interface. In other cases, developers will work with the company in question and attempt to obtain information about the device interface, with varying degrees of success.

In the following sections, we'll attempt to summarize the hardware requirements for Linux. The Linux *Hardware HOWTO* (see Section 1.9) contains a more complete listing of hardware supported by Linux.

Disclaimer: a good deal of hardware support for Linux is currently in the development stage. Some distributions may or may not support these experimental features. This section primarily lists hardware which has been supported for some time and is known to be stable. When in doubt, consult the documentation for the distribution of Linux you are using (see Section 2.1 for more information on Linux distributions).

1.8.1   Motherboard and CPU requirements

Linux currently supports systems with an Intel 80386, 80486, or Pentium CPU. This includes all variations on this CPU type, such as the 386SX, 486SX, 486DX, and 486DX2. Non-Intel "clones", such as AMD and Cyrix processors, work with Linux as well.

If you have a 80386 or 80486SX, you may also wish to use a math coprocessor, although one isn't required (the Linux kernel can do FPU emulation if you do not have a math coprocessor). All standard FPU couplings are supported, such as IIT, Cyrix FasMath, and Intel coprocessors.

The system motherboard must use ISA or EISA bus architecture. These terms define how the system interfaces with peripherals and other components on the main bus. Most systems sold today are either ISA or EISA bus. IBM's MicroChannel (MCA) bus, found on machines such as the IBM PS/2, is not currently supported.

Systems which use a local bus architecture (for faster video and disk access) are supported as well. It is suggested that you have a standard local bus architecture such as the VESA Local Bus ("VLB").

1.8.2   Memory requirements

Linux requires very little memory to run compared to other advanced operating systems. You should have at the very least 2 megabytes of RAM; however, it is strongly suggested that you have 4 megabytes. The more memory you have, the faster the system will run.

Linux can support the full 32-bit address range of the 386/486; in other words, it will utilize all of your RAM automatically.

Linux will run happily with only 4 megabytes of RAM, including all of the bells and whistles such as X Windows, Emacs, and so on. However, having more memory is almost as important as having a faster processor. 8 megabytes is more than enough for personal use; 16 megabytes or more may be needed if you are expecting a heavy user load on the system.

Most Linux users allocate a portion of their hard drive as swap space, which is used as virtual RAM. Even if you have a great deal of physical RAM in your machine, you may wish to use swap space. While swap space is no replacement for actual physical RAM, it can allow your system to run larger applications by swapping out inactive portions of code to disk. The amount of swap space that you should allocate depends on several factors; we'll come back to this question in Section 2.2.3.

1.8.3 Hard drive controller requirements

You do not need to have a hard drive to run Linux; you can run a minimal system completely from floppy. However, this is slow and very limited, and many users have access to hard drive storage anyway. You must have an AT-standard (16-bit) controller. There is support in the kernel for XT-standard (8 bit) controllers; however, most controllers used today are AT-standard. Linux should support all MFM, RLL, and IDE controllers. Most, but not all, ESDI controllers are supported—only those which do ST506 hardware emulation.

The general rule for non-SCSI hard drive and floppy controllers is that if you can access the drive from MS-DOS or another operating system, you should be able to access it from Linux.

Linux also supports a number of popular SCSI drive controllers, although support for SCSI is more limited because of the wide range of controller interface standards. Supported SCSI controllers include the Adaptec AHA1542B, AHA1542C, AHA1742A (BIOS version 1.34), AHA1522, AHA1740, AHA1740 (SCSI-2 controller, BIOS 1.34 in Enhanced mode); Future Domain 1680, TMC-850, TMC-950; Seagate ST-02; UltraStor SCSI; Western Digital WD7000FASST. Clones which are based on these cards should work as well.

1.8.4 Hard drive space requirements

Of course, to install Linux, you'll need to have some amount of free space on your hard drive. Linux will support multiple hard drives in the same machine; you can allocate space for Linux across multiple drives if necessary.

The *amount* of hard drive space that you will require depends greatly on your needs and the amount of software that you're installing. Linux is relatively small as UNIX implementations go; you could run a complete system in 10 to 20 megabytes of space on your drive. However, if you want to have room for expansion, and for larger packages such as X Windows, you will need more space. If you plan to allow multiple users to use the machine, you will need to allocate storage for their files.

Also, unless you have a large amount of physical RAM (16 megabytes or more), you will more than likely want to allocate swap space, to be used as virtual RAM. We will discuss all of the details of installing and using swap space in Section 2.2.3.

Each distribution of Linux usually comes with some literature that should help you to gauge the precise amount of required storage depending on the amount of software you plan to install. You can run a minimal system with less than 20 megabytes; a complete system with all of the bells and whistles in 80 megabytes or less; and a very large system with room for many users and space for future expansion in the range of

100-150 megabytes. Again, these figures are meant only as a ballpark approximation; you will have to look
at your own needs and goals in order to determine your specific storage requirements.

1.8.5   Monitor and video adaptor requirements

Linux supports all standard Hercules, CGA, EGA, VGA, IBM monochrome, and Super VGA video cards
and monitors for the default text-based interface. In general, if the video card and monitor coupling works
under another operating system such as MS-DOS, it should work fine with Linux. Original IBM CGA cards
suffer from "snow" under Linux, which is not pleasant to use.

Graphical environments such as the X Window System have video hardware requirements of their own.
Instead of listing these requirements here, we relegate the discussion to Section 5.1.1. In short, to run the
X Window System on your Linux machine, you will need one of the video cards listed in that section.

1.8.6   Miscellaneous hardware

The above sections described the hardware which is required to run a Linux system. However, most users
have a number of "optional" devices such as tape and CD-ROM storage, sound boards, and so on, and are
interested in whether or not this hardware is supported by Linux. Read on.

1.8.6.1   Mice and other pointing devices

For the most part, you will only be using a mouse under a graphical environment such as the X Window
System. However, several Linux applications not associated with a graphics environment do make use of
the mouse.

Linux supports all standard serial mice, including Logitech, MM series, Mouseman, Microsoft (2-button)
and Mouse Systems (3-button). Linux also supports Microsoft, Logitech, and ATIXL busmice. The PS/2
mouse interface is supported as well.

All other pointing devices, such as trackballs, which emulate the above mice, should work as well.

1.8.6.2   CD-ROM storage

Almost all CD-ROM drives use the SCSI interface. As long as you have a SCSI adaptor supported by Linux,
then your CD-ROM drive should work. A number of CD-ROM drives have been verified to work under
Linux, including the NEC CDR-74, Sony CDU-541, and Texel DM-3024. The Sony internal CDU-31a and
the Mitsumi CD-ROM drives are supported by Linux as well.

Linux supports the standard ISO-9660 filesystem for CD-ROMs.

1.8.6.3   Tape drives

There are several types of tape drives available on the market. Most of them use the SCSI interface, all
of which should be supported by Linux. Among the verified SCSI tape drives are the Sanyo CP150SE;
Tandberg 3600; Wangtek 5525ES, 5150ES, and 5099EN with the PC36 adaptor. Other QIC-02 drives should
be supported as well.

Drivers are currently under development for various other tape devices, such as Colorado drives which
hang off of the floppy controller.

1.8.6.4 Printers

Linux supports the complete range of parallel printers. If you are able to access your printer via the parallel port from MS-DOS or another operating system, you should be able to access it from Linux as well. The Linux printing software consists of the UNIX standard `lp` and `lpr` software. This software also allows you to print remotely via the network, if you have one available.

1.8.6.5 Modems

As with printer support, Linux supports the full range of serial modems, both internal and external. There is a great deal of telecommunications software available for Linux, including Kermit, `pcomm`, `minicom`, and Seyon. If your modem is accessible from another operating system on the same machine, you should be able to access it from Linux with no difficulty.

1.8.7 Ethernet cards

Many popular Ethernet cards and LAN adaptors are supported by Linux. These include:

- 3com 3c503, 3c503/16

- Novell NE1000, NE2000

- Western Digital WD8003, WD8013

- Hewlett Packard HP27245, HP27247, HP27250

- D-Link DE-600

The following clones are reported to work:

- LANNET LEC-45

- Alta Combo

- Artisoft LANtastic AE-2

- Asante Etherpak 2001/2003,

- D-Link Ethernet II

- LTC E-NET/16 P/N 8300-200-002

- Network Solutions HE-203,

- SVEC 4 Dimension Ethernet

- 4-Dimension FD0490 EtherBoard 16

Clones which are compatible with any of the above cards should work as well.

1.9   Sources of Linux Information

As you have probably guessed, there are many sources of information about Linux available apart from this book. In particular, there are a number of books, not specific to Linux but rather about UNIX in general, that will be of importance, especially to those readers without previous UNIX experience. If you are new to the UNIX world, we seriously suggest that you take the time to peruse one of these books before you attempt to brave the jungles of Linux. Specifically, the book *Learning the UNIX Operating System*, by Grace Todino and John Strang, is a good place to start.

Many of the following sources of information are available online in some electronic form. That is, you must have access to an online network, such as the Internet, USENET, or Fidonet, in order to access the information contained therein. If you do not have online access to any of this material, you might be able to find someone kind enough to give you hardcopies of the documents in question. Read on.

1.9.1   Online documents

If you have access to the Internet, there are many Linux documents available via anonymous FTP from archive sites all over the world. If you do not have direct Internet access, these documents may still be available to you: many Linux distributions on CD-ROM contain all of the documents mentioned here. Also, they are distributed on many other networks, such as Fidonet and CompuServe. If you are able to send mail to Internet sites, you may be able to retrieve these files using one of the `ftpmail` servers which will electronically mail you the documents or files from FTP archive sites. See Appendix C for more information on using `ftpmail`.

There is a great number of FTP archive sites which carry Linux software and related documents. A list of well-known Linux archive sites is given in Appendix C. In order to reduce network traffic, you should always use the FTP site which is geographically (network-wise) closest to you.

Appendix A contains a listing of some of the Linux documents which are available via anonymous FTP. The filenames will differ depending on the archive site in question; most sites keep Linux-related documents in the `docs` subdirectory of their Linux archive space. For example, on the FTP site `sunsite.unc.edu`, Linux files are stored in the directory `/pub/Linux`, with Linux-related documentation being found in `/pub/Linux/docs`.

Examples of available online documents are the *Linux FAQ*, a collection of frequently asked questions about Linux; the Linux *HOWTO* documents, each describing a specific aspect of the system—including the *Installation HOWTO*, the *Printing HOWTO*, and the *Ethernet HOWTO*; and, the Linux META-FAQ, a list of other sources of Linux information on the Internet.

Most of these documents are also regularly posted to one or more Linux-related USENET newsgroups; see Section 1.9.4 below.

1.9.2   Linux on the World Wide Web

The Linux Documentation Home Page is available for World Wide Web users at the URL

```
http://sunsite.unc.edu/mdw/linux.html
```

This page contains many HOWTOs and other documents in HTML format, as well as pointers to other sites of interest to Linux users.

1.9.3 Books and other published works

At this time, there are few published works specifically about Linux. Most noteworthy are the books from the Linux Documentation Project, a project carried out over the Internet to write and distribute a bona fide set of "manuals" for Linux. These manuals are analogues to the documentation sets available with commercial versions of UNIX: they cover everything from installing Linux, to using and running the system, programming, networking, kernel development, and more.

The Linux Documentation Project manuals are available via anonymous FTP from the Internet, as well as via mail order from several sources. Appendix A lists the manuals which are available and covers means of obtaining them in detail.

There are not many books specifically about Linux currently available. However, there are a large number of books about UNIX in general which are certainly applicable to Linux—as far as using and programming the system is concerned, Linux does not differ greatly from other implementations of UNIX. In short, almost everything you want to know about using and programming Linux can be found in sources meant for a general UNIX audience. In fact, this book is meant to be complemented by the large library of UNIX books currently available; here, we present the most important Linux-specific details and hope that you will look to other sources for more in-depth information.

Armed with a number of good books about using UNIX, as well as the book you hold in your hands, you should be able to tackle just about anything. Appendix A includes a list of highly-recommended UNIX books, both for UNIX newcomers and UNIX wizards alike.

There is also a monthly magazine about Linux, called the *Linux Journal*. It is distributed worldwide, and is an excellent way to keep in touch with the many goings-on in the Linux community—especially if you do not have access to USENET news (see below). See Appendix A for information on subscribing to the *Linux Journal*.

1.9.4 USENET newsgroups

USENET is a worldwide electronic news and discussion forum with a heavy contingent of so-called "newsgroups"—discussion areas devoted to a particular topic. Much of the development of Linux has been done over the waves of the Internet and USENET, and not suprisingly there are a number of USENET newsgroups available for discussions about Linux.

The original Linux newsgroup was `alt.os.linux`, and was created to move some of the discussions about Linux out of `comp.os.minix` and the various mailing lists. Soon, the traffic on `alt.os.linux` grew to be large enough that a newsgroup in the `comp` hierarchy was warranted; a vote was taken in February of 1992, and `comp.os.linux` was created.

`comp.os.linux` quickly became one of the most popular (and loudest) USENET groups; more popular than any other `comp.os` group. In December of 1992, a vote was taken to split the newsgroup in order to reduce traffic; only `comp.os.linux.announce` passed this vote. In July of 1993, the group was finally split into the new hierarchy. Almost 2000 people voted in the `comp.os.linux` reorganization, making it one of the largest USENET Call For Votes ever.

If you do not have direct USENET access, but are able to send and receive electronic mail from the Internet, there are mail-to-news gateways available for each of the newsgroups below.

`comp.os.linux.announce`

> `comp.os.linux.announce` is a moderated newsgroup for announcements and important postings about the Linux system (such as bug reports, important patches to software,

and so on). If you read any Linux newsgroups at all, read this one. Often, the important postings in this group are not crossposted to other groups. This group also contains many periodic postings about Linux, including many of the online documents described in the last section and listed in Appendix A.

Postings to this newsgroup must be approved by the moderators, Matt Welsh and Lars Wirzenius. If you wish to submit and article to this group, in most cases you can simply post the article as you normally would (using `Pnews` or whatever posting software that you have available); the news software will automatically forward the article to the moderators for approval. However, if your news system is not set up correctly, you may need to mail the article directly; the submission address is `linux-announce@tc.cornell.edu`.

The rest of the Linux newsgroups listed below are unmoderated.

`comp.os.linux.help`
This is the most popular Linux newsgroup. It is for questions and answers about using, setting up, or otherwise running a Linux system. If you are having problems with Linux, you may post to this newsgroup, and hopefully receive a reply from someone who might be able to help. However, it is strongly suggested that you read all of the available Linux documentation before posting questions to this newsgroup.

`comp.os.linux.admin`
This newsgroup is for questions and discussion about running a Linux system, most commonly in an active, multi-user environment. Any discussion about administrative issues of Linux (such as packaging software, making backups, handling users, and so on) is welcome here.

`comp.os.linux.development`
This is a newsgroup for discussions about development of the Linux system. All issues related to kernel and system software development should be discussed here. For example, if you are writing a kernel driver and need help with certain aspects of the programming, this would be the place to ask. This newsgroup is also for discussions about the direction and goals behind the Linux development effort, as described (somewhat) in Section 1.6.

It should be noted that this newsgroup is not (technically) for discussions about development of software *for* Linux, but rather for discussions of development *of* Linux. That is, issues dealing with applications programming under Linux should be discussed in another Linux newsgroup; `comp.os.linux.development` is about developing the Linux system itself, including the kernel, system libraries, and so on.

`comp.os.linux.misc`
This newsgroup is for all discussion which doesn't quite fit into the other available Linux groups. In particular, advocacy wars (the incessant "Linux versus Windows NT" thread, for example), should be waged here, as opposed to in the technical Linux groups. Any nontechnical or metadiscourse about the Linux system should remain in `comp.os.linux.misc`.

It should be noted that the newsgroup `comp.os.linux`, which was originally the only Linux group, has been superseded by the new hierarchy of groups. If you have access to `comp.os.linux`, but not to the newer Linux groups listed above, encourage your news administrator to create the new groups on your system.

1.9.5   Internet mailing lists

If you have access to Internet electronic mail, you can participate in a number of mailing lists even if you do not have USENET access. Note that if you are not directly on the Internet, you can join one of these mailing lists as long as you are able to exchange electronic mail with the Internet (for example, UUCP, FidoNET, CompuServe, and other networks all have access to Internet mail).

The "Linux Activists" mailing list is primarily for Linux developers and people interested in aiding the development process. This is a "multi-channel" mailing list, in which you join one or more "channels" based on your particular interests. Some of the available channels include: NORMAL, for general Linux-related issues; KERNEL, for kernel development; GCC, for discussions relating to the gcc compiler and library development; NET, for discussions about the TCP/IP networking code; DOC, for issues relating to writing and distributing Linux documentation; and more.

For more information about the Linux Activists mailing list, send mail to

```
linux-activists@niksula.hut.fi
```

You will receive a list of currently available channels, including information on how to subscribe and unsubscribe to particular channels on the list.

Quite a few special-purpose mailing lists about and for Linux exist as well. The best way to find out about these is to watch the Linux USENET newsgroups for announcements, as well as to read the list of publicly-available mailing lists, periodically posted to the USENET group news.answers.

1.10   Getting Help

You will undoubtedly require some degree of assistance during your adventures in the Linux world. Even the most wizardly of UNIX wizards occasionally is stumped by some quirk or feature of Linux, and it's important to know how and where to find help when you need it.

The primary means of getting help in the Linux world are via Internet mailing lists and USENET newsgroups, as discussed in Section 1.9. If you don't have online access to these sources, you might be able to find comparable Linux discussion forums on other online services, such as on local BBS's, CompuServe, and so on.

A number of businesses are providing commercial support for Linux. This will allow you to pay a "subscription fee" which will allow you to call the consultants for help with your Linux problems. Appendix B contains a list of Linux vendors, some of which provide commercial support. However, if you have access to USENET and Internet mail, you may find the free support found there to be just as useful.

Keeping the following suggestions in mind will greatly improve your experiences with Linux and will guarantee you more success in finding help to your problems.

Consult all available documentation. . . first! The first thing you should do when encountering a problem is consult the various sources of information listed in Section 1.9 and Appendix A. These documents were laboriously written for people like you—people who need help with the Linux system. Even books written for UNIX in general are applicable to Linux, and you should take advantage of them. More than likely, you will find the answer to your problems somewhere in this documentation, as impossible as it may seem.

If you have access to USENET news or any of the Linux-related mailing lists, be sure to actually *read* the information there before posting for help with your problem. Many times, solutions to common problems are not easy to find in documentation, and instead are well-covered in the newsgroups and mailing lists devoted to Linux. If you only post to these groups, and don't actually read them, you are asking for trouble.

Learn to appreciate self-maintenance. In most cases, it is preferable to do as much independent research and investigation into the problem as possible before seeking outside help. After all, you asked for it, by running Linux in the first place! Remember that Linux is all about hacking and fixing problems yourself. It is not a commercial operating system, nor does it try to look like one. Hacking won't kill you. In fact, it will teach you a great deal about the system to investigate and solve problems yourself—maybe even enough to one day call yourself a Linux guru. Learn to appreciate the value of hacking the system, and how to fix problems yourself. You can't expect to run a complete, homebrew Linux system without some degree of handiwork.

Remain calm. It is vital to refrain from getting frustrated with the system, at all costs. Nothing is earned by taking an axe—or worse, a powerful electromagnet—to your Linux system in a fit of anger. The authors have found that a large punching bag or similar inanimate object is a wonderful way to relieve the occasional stress attack. As Linux matures and distributions become more reliable, we hope that this problem will go away. However, even commercial UNIX implementations can be tricky at times. When all else fails, sit back, take a few deep breaths, and go after the problem again when you feel relaxed. Your mind and conscience will be clearer.

Refrain from posting spuriously. Many people make the mistake of posting or mailing messages pleading for help prematurely. When encountering a problem, do not—we repeat, do *not*—rush immediately to your nearest terminal and post a message to one of the Linux USENET newsgroups. Often, you will catch your own mistake five minutes later and find yourself in the curious situation of defending your own sanity in a public forum. Before posting anything any of the Linux mailing lists or newsgroups, first attempt to resolve the problem yourself and be absolutely certain what the problem is. Does your system not respond when switched on? Perhaps the machine is unplugged.

If you do post for help, make it worthwhile. If all else fails, you may wish to post a message for help in any of the number of electronic forums dedicated to Linux, such as USENET newsgroups and mailing lists. When posting, remember that the people reading your post are not there to help you. The network is not your personal consulting service. Therefore, it is important to remain as polite, terse, and informative as possible.

How can one accomplish this? First, you should include as much (relevant) information about your system and your problem as possible. Posting the simple request, "I cannot seem to get e-mail to work" will probably get you nowhere unless you include information on your system, what software you are using, what you have attempted to do so far and what the results were. When including technical information, it is usually a good idea to include general information on the version(s) of your software (Linux kernel version, for example), as well as a brief summary of your hardware configuration. However, don't overdo it—including information on the brand and type of monitor that you have probably is irrelevant if you're trying to configure networking software.

Secondly, remember that you need to make some attempt—however feeble—at solving your problem before you go to the Net. If you have never attempted to set up electronic mail, for instance, and first decide to ask folks on the Net how to go about doing it, you are making a big mistake. There are a number of documents available (see the Section 1.9) on how to get started with many common tasks under Linux. The idea is to get as far along as possible on your own and *then* ask for help if and when you get stuck.

Also remember that the people reading your message, however helpful, may occasionally get frustrated by seeing the same problem over and over again. Be sure to actually read the Linux newsgroups and mailing lists before posting your problems. Many times, the solution to your problem has been discussed repeatedly, and all that's required to find it is to browse the current messages.

Lastly, when posting to electronic newsgroups and mailing lists, try to be as polite as possible. It is much more effective and worthwhile to be polite, direct, and informative—more people will be willing to help you if you master a humble tone. To be sure, the flame war is an art form across many forms of electronic communication, but don't allow that to preoccupy your and other people's time. Save the network undue wear and tear by keeping bandwidth as low as possible, and by paying as much attention to other sources of information which are available to you. The network is an excellent way to get help with your Linux problems—but it is important to know how to use the network *effectively*.

Chapter 2

Obtaining and Installing Linux

In this chapter, we'll describe how to obtain the Linux software, in the form of one of the various pre-packaged distributions, and how to install the distribution that you choose.

As we have mentioned, there is no single "official" distribution of the Linux software; there are, in fact, many distributions, each of which serves a particular purpose and set of goals. These distributions are available via anonymous FTP from the Internet, on BBS systems worldwide, and via mail on diskette, tape, and CD-ROM.

Here, we present a general overview of the installation process. Each distribution has its own specific installation instructions, but armed with the concepts presented here you should be able to feel your way through any installation. Appendix A lists sources of information for installation instructions and other help, if you're at a total loss.

This book contains additional sections detailing the Slackware distribution of Linux.

2.1 Distributions of Linux

Because Linux is free software, no single organization or entity is responsible for releasing and distributing the software. Therefore, anyone is free to put together and distribute the Linux software, as long as the restrictions in the GPL are observed. The upshot of this is that there are many distributions of Linux, available via anonymous FTP or via mail order.

You are now faced with the task of deciding upon a particular distribution of Linux which suits your needs. Not all distributions are alike. Many of them come with just about all of the software you'd need to run a complete system—and then some. Other Linux distributions are "small" distributions intended for users without copious amounts of diskspace. Many distributions contain only the core Linux software, and you are expected to install larger software packages, such as the X Window System, yourself. (In Chapter 4 we'll show you how.)

The Linux *Distribution HOWTO* (see Appendix A) contains a list of Linux distributions available via the Internet as well as mail order. Appendix B also lists contact addresses for a number of Linux mail-order vendors. If you purchased this book in printed the form, the publisher should also be able to provide you with a Linux distribution or tell you who can.

How can you decide among all of these distributions? If you have access to USENET news, or another computer conferencing system, you might want to ask there for personal opinions from people who have installed Linux. Even better, if you know someone who has installed Linux, ask them for help and advice.

There are many factors to consider when choosing a distribution, however, everyone's needs and opinions are different. In actuality, most of the popular Linux distributions contain roughly the same set of software, so the distribution that you select is more or less arbitrary.

This book contains information on installing the popular Slackware and Slackware Pro distributions of Linux.

2.1.1 Getting Linux from the Internet

If you have access to the Internet, the easiest way to obtain Linux is via anonymous FTP.[1] Appendix C lists a number of FTP archive sites which carry Linux software. One of these is sunsite.unc.edu, and the various Linux distributions can be found in the directory

```
/pub/Linux/distributions
```

there.

Many distributions are released via anonymous FTP as a set of disk images. That is, the distribution consists of a set of files, and each file contains the binary image of a floppy. In order to copy the contents of the image file onto the floppy, you can use the RAWRITE.EXE program under MS-DOS. This program copies, block-for-block, the contents of a file to a floppy, without regard for disk format.[2]

RAWRITE.EXE is available on the various Linux FTP sites, including sunsite.unc.edu in the directory

```
/pub/Linux/system/Install/rawrite
```

Therefore, in many cases, you simply download the set of diskette images, and use RAWRITE.EXE with each image in turn to create a set of diskettes. You boot from the so-called "boot diskette" and you're ready to roll. The software is usually installed directly from the floppies, although some distributions allow you to install from an MS-DOS partition on your hard drive. Some distributions allow you to install over a TCP/IP network. The documentation for each distribution should describe these installation methods if they are available.

Other Linux distributions are installed from a set of MS-DOS format floppies. For example, the Slackware distribution of Linux requires only the boot and root diskettes to be created using RAWRITE.EXE. The rest of the diskettes are copied to MS-DOS format diskettes using the MS-DOS COPY command. The system installs the software directly from the MS-DOS floppies. This saves you the trouble of having to use RAWRITE.EXE for many image files, although it requires you to have access to an MS-DOS system to create the diskettes.

Each distribution of Linux available via anonymous FTP should include a README file describing how to download and prepare the diskettes for installation. Be sure to read all of the available documentation for the release that you are using.

When downloading the Linux software, be sure to use *binary* mode for all file transfers (with most FTP clients, the command "binary" enables this mode).

See Section 2.1.4, below, for information on obtaining the Slackware distribution from the Internet.

---

[1] If you do not have direct Internet access, you can obtain Linux via the ftpmail service, provided that you have the ability to exchange e-mail with the Internet. See Appendix C for details.

[2] If you have access to a UNIX workstation with a floppy drive, you can also use the dd command to copy the file image directly to the floppy. A command such as "dd of=/dev/rfd0 if=foo bs=18k" will "raw write" the contents of the file foo to the floppy device on a Sun workstation. Consult your local UNIX gurus for more information on your system's floppy devices and the use of dd.

2.1.2   Getting Linux from other online sources

If you have access to another computer network such as CompuServe or Prodigy, there may be a means to download the Linux software from these sources. In addition, many bulletin board (BBS) systems carry Linux software. A list of Linux BBS sites is given in Appendix C.8. Not all Linux distributions are available from these computer networks, however—many of them, especially the various CD-ROM distributions, are only available via mail order.

2.1.3   Getting Linux via mail order

If you don't have Internet or BBS access, many Linux distributions are available via mail order on diskette, tape, or CD-ROM. Appendix B lists a number of these distributors. Many of them accept credit cards as well as international orders, so if you're not in the United States or Canada you still should be able to obtain Linux in this way.

Linux is free software, although distributors are allowed by the GPL to charge a fee for it. Therefore, ordering Linux via mail order might cost you between US$30 and US$150, depending on the distribution. However, if you know someone who has already purchased or downloaded a release of Linux, you are free to borrow or copy their software for your own use. Linux distributors are not allowed to restrict the license or redistribution of the software in any way. If you are thinking about installing an entire lab of machines with Linux, for example, you only need to purchase a single copy of one of the distributions, which can be used to install all of the machines.

2.1.4   Getting Slackware

Slackware is a popular distribution of Linux maintained by Patrick Volkerding.[3] It is easy to install and fairly complete, and may be obtained both from the Internet as well as on CD-ROM from a number of vendors (see Appendix B).

The Slackware distribution consists of a number of "disk sets", each one containing a particular type of software (for example, the d disk set contains development tools such as the gcc compiler, and the x disk set contains the X Window System software). You can elect to install whatever disk sets you like, and can install new ones later.

The version of Slackware described here is 2.0.0, of 25 June 1994. Installation of later versions of Slackware should be very similar to the information given here.

2.1.4.1   Slackware disk sets

Unfortunately, Slackware does not maintain a complete list of diskspace requirements for each disk set. You need at least 7 megabytes to install just the "A" series of disks; a very rough estimate of the required diskspace would be 2 or 2.5 megabytes per disk.

The following disk sets are available:

A   The base system. Enough to get up and running and have elvis and comm programs
                     available. Based around the 1.0.9 Linux kernel, and the new filesystem standard (FSSTND).

---

[3]Patrick Volkerding can be reached on the Internet at volkerdi@mhd1.moorhead.msus.edu.

These disks are known to fit on 1.2M disks, although the rest of Slackware won't. If you have only a 1.2M floppy, you can still install the base system, download other disks you want and install them from your hard drive.

AP   Various applications and add ons, such as the manual pages, `groff`, `ispell` (GNU and international versions), `term`, `joe`, `jove`, `ghostscript`, `sc`, `bc`, and the quota patches.

D   Program development. GCC/G++/Objective C 2.5.8, make (GNU and BSD), `byacc` and GNU `bison`, `flex`, the 4.5.26 C libraries, `gdb`, kernel source for 1.0.9, `SVGAlib`, `ncurses`, `clisp`, `f2c`, `p2c`, `m4`, `perl`, `rcs`.

E   GNU Emacs 19.25.

F   A collection of FAQs and other documentation.

I   Info pages for GNU software. Documentation for various programs readable by `info` or Emacs.

N   Networking. TCP/IP, UUCP, `mailx`, `dip`, `deliver`, `elm`, `pine`, `smail`, `cnews`, `nn`, `tin`, `trn`.

OOP   Object Oriented Programming. GNU Smalltalk 1.1.1, and the Smalltalk Interface to X (STIX).

Q   Alpha kernel source and images (currently contains Linux 1.1.18).

TCL   Tcl, Tk, TclX, blt, itcl.

Y   Games. The BSD games collection, and Tetris for terminals.

X   The base XFree86 2.1.1 system, with `libXpm`, `fvwm` 1.20, and `xlock` added.

XAP   X applications: X11 `ghostscript`, `libgr13`, `seyon`, `workman`, `xfilemanager`, `xv` 3.01, GNU `chess` and `xboard`, `xfm` 1.2, `ghostview`, and various X games.

XD   X11 program development. X11 libraries, server linkkit, PEX support.

XV   XView 3.2 release 5. XView libraries, and the Open Look virtual and non-virtual window managers.

IV   Interviews libraries, include files, and the `doc` and `idraw` apps.

OI   ParcPlace's Object Builder 2.0 and Object Interface Library 4.0, generously made available for Linux developers according to the terms in the "copying" notice found in these directories. Note that these only work with `libc`-4.4.4, but a new version may be released once `gcc` 2.5.9 is available.

T   The TEX and LATEX text formatting systems.

You must get the "A" disk set; the rest are optional. We suggest installing the A, AP, and D sets, as well as the X set if you plan to run the X Window System.

2.1.4.2   Getting Slackware from the Internet

The Slackware release of Linux may be found on any number of FTP sites worldwide. Appendix C lists several of the Linux FTP sites; we suggest that you try to find the software on the FTP site nearest you, to reduce net traffic. However, two of the major Linux FTP archives are `sunsite.unc.edu` and `tsx-11.mit.edu`.

The Slackware release may be found at least on the following sites:

- `sunsite.unc.edu:/pub/Linux/distributions/slackware`

- `tsx-11.mit.edu:/pub/linux/packages/slackware`

- `ftp.cdrom.com:/pub/linux/slackware`

`ftp.cdrom.com` is Slackware's home site.

2.1.4.2.1   Downloading the files   You should download the following files using FTP. Be sure to use binary mode when transferring. Appendix C contains a complete tutorial on using FTP.

- The various `README` files, as well as `SLACKWARE_FAQ`. Be sure to read these files before attempting to install the software, to get any updates or changes to this document.

- A bootdisk image. This is a file that you will write to a floppy to create the Slackware boot disk. If you have a 1.44 megabyte boot floppy (3.5"), look in the directory `bootdsks.144`. If you have a 1.2 megabyte boot floppy (5.25"), look in the directory `bootdsks.12`.

You need one of the following bootdisk files.

  - `bare.gz`. This is a boot floppy that has only IDE hard drive drivers. (No SCSI, CD-ROM, or networking support.) Use this if you only have an IDE hard drive controller and aren't going to be installing over the network or from CD-ROM.

  - `cdu31a.gz`. Contains IDE, SCSI, and the Sony CDU31A/33A driver.

  - `mitsumi.gz`. Contains IDE, SCSI, and the Mitsumi CD-ROM driver.

  - `modern.gz`. An experimental boot disk with a newer kernel, and all drivers except those for network cards and the Sony 535 CD-ROM.

  - `net.gz`. Contains IDE and network drivers.

  - `sbpcd.gz`. Contains IDE, SCSI, and SoundBlaster Pro/Panasonic CD-ROM drivers.

  - `scsi.gz`. Contains IDE, SCSI, and SCSI CD-ROM drivers.

  - `scsinet.gz`. Contains IDE, SCSI, SCSI CD-ROM, and network drivers.

  - `sony535.gz`. Contains IDE, SCSI, and Sony 535/531 CD-ROM drivers.

  - `xt.gz`. Contains IDE and XT hard drive drivers.

You need only *one* of the above bootdisk images, depending on the hardware that you have in your system.

The issue here is that some hardware drivers conflict with each other in strange ways, and instead of attempting to debug hardware problems on your system it's easier to use a boot floppy image with only certain drivers enabled. Most users should try `scsi.gz` or `bare.gz`.

- A rootdisk image. This is a file that you will write to a floppy to create the Slackware installation disk. As with the bootdisk image, look in `rootdsks.144` or `rootdsks.12` depending on the type of boot floppy drive that you have.

  You need one of the following files:

  - `color144.gz`. The menu-based color installation disk for 1.44 megabyte drives. Most users should use this rootdisk.

  - `umsds144.gz`. A version of the `color144` disk for installing with the UMSDOS filesystem, which allows you to install Linux onto a directory of an MS-DOS filesystem. This installation method is not discussed in detail here, but it will prevent you from having to repartition your drive. More on this later.

  - `tty144.gz`. The terminal-based installation disk for 1.44 megabyte drives. If `color144.gz` doesn't work for you, try `tty144.gz` instead.

  - `colrlite.gz`. The menu-based color installation disk for 1.2 megabyte drives.

  - `umsds12.gz`. A version of the `colrlite` disk for installing with the UMSDOS filesystem. See the description of `umsds144.gz`, above.

  - `tty12.gz`. The terminal-based installation disk for 1.2 megabyte drives. Use this rootdisk if you have a 1.2 megabyte boot floppy and `colrlite.gz` doesn't work for you.

  Again, you need only *one* of the above rootdisk images, depending on the type of boot floppy drive that you have.

- `GZIP.EXE`. This is an MS-DOS executable of the `gzip` compression program used to compress the boot and rootdisk files (the `.gz` extension on the filenames indicates this). This can be found in the `install` directory.

- `RAWRITE.EXE`. This is an MS-DOS program that will write the contents of a file (such as the boot and rootdisk images) directly to a floppy, without regard to format. You will use `RAWRITE.EXE` to create the boot and root floppies. This can be found in the `install` directory as well.

  You only need `RAWRITE.EXE` and `GZIP.EXE` if you plan to create the boot and root floppies from an MS-DOS system. If you have access to a UNIX workstation with a floppy drive instead, you can create the floppies from there, using the `dd` command. See the man page for `dd` and ask your local UNIX administrators for assistance.

- The files in the directories `slakware/a1`, `slakware/a2`, and `slakware/a3`. These files make up the "A" disk set of the Slackware distribution. They are required. Later, you will copy these files to MS-DOS floppies for installation (or, you can install from your hard drive). Therefore, when you download these files, keep them in separate directories; don't mix the `a1` files with the `a2` files, and so on.

  Be sure that you get the files without periods in the filenames as well. That is, within FTP, use the command "`mget *`" instead of "`mget *.*`".

- The files in the directories `ap1`, `ap2`, etc., depending on what disk sets you are installing. For example, if you are installing the "X" disk series, get the files in the directories `x1` through `x5`. As with the "A" disk set, above, be sure to keep the files in separate directories when you download them.

2.1.4.3 Getting Slackware on CD-ROM

Slackware is also available on CD-ROM. Most Slackware CD-ROMs simply contain a copy of the files as they appear on the FTP archive sites, as described above. Therefore, if you have a Slackware CD-ROM, you have all of the files that you need.

You will have to create a boot and root floppy from the files on the CD-ROM. See Section 2.1.4.2.1, above, for a discussion on the available boot and root disk images.

First, decide which boot and root disk images you will use. They should all be on the CD-ROM. Below, we will describe how to create these floppies.

2.1.4.4   Installation methods

Slackware provides several different means of installing the software. The most popular is installing from an MS-DOS partition on your hard drive; another is to install from a set of MS-DOS floppies created from the disk sets that you downloaded.

If you have Slackware on a CD-ROM, you can install the files directly from there. The Slackware Pro distribution, from Morse Telecommunications, allows you to install Slackware so that many files are accessed directly on the CD-ROM. This can save a great deal of space on your hard drive, with the tradeoff that running certain applications will be slower.

2.1.4.4.1   Creating the boot and root floppies
You must create floppies from the bootdisk and rootdisk images that you downloaded (or have on CD-ROM), no matter what type of installation you will be doing.

On an MS-DOS system, you must uncompress the bootdisk and rootdisk images using GZIP.EXE. For example, if you're using the bare.gz bootdisk image, issue the MS-DOS command:

```
C:\> GZIP -D BARE.GZ
```

which will uncompress bare.gz and leave you with the file bare. If you are installing from CD-ROM, you can copy the bootdisk image (such as bare.gz) to you hard drive, and run GZIP.EXE from the CD-ROM to uncompress it.

You must similarly uncompress the rootdisk image. For example, if you are using the rootdisk color144.gz, issue the command:

```
C:\> GZIP -D COLOR144.GZ
```

which will uncompress the file and leave you with color144.

Next, you must have two *high-density* MS-DOS formatted floppies. (They must be of the same type; that is, if your boot floppy drive is a 3.5" drive, both floppies must be high-density 3.5" disks.) You will use RAWRITE.EXE to write the boot and rootdisk images to the floppies.

Issue the command:

```
C:\> RAWRITE
```

Answer the prompts for the name of the file to write (such as bare, or color144) and the floppy to write it to (such as A:). RAWRITE will copy the file, block-by-block, directly to the floppy. Also use RAWRITE for the root disk image. When you're done, you'll have two floppies: one containing the boot disk, the other containing the root disk. Note that these two floppies will no longer be readable by MS-DOS (they are "Linux format" floppies, in some sense).

Be sure that you're using brand-new, error-free floppies. The floppies must have no bad blocks on them.

Note that you do not need to be running MS-DOS in order to install Slackware. However, running MS-DOS makes it easier to create the boot and root floppies, and it makes it easier to install the software (as you can install directly from an MS-DOS partition on your system). If you are not running MS-DOS on your system, you can use someone else's MS-DOS system just to create the floppies, and install from there.

It is not necessary to use `GZIP.EXE` and `RAWRITE.EXE` under MS-DOS to create the boot and root floppies, either. You can use the `gzip` and `dd` commands on a UNIX system to do the same job. (For this, you will need a UNIX workstation with a floppy drive, of course.) For example, on a Sun workstation with the floppy drive on device `/dev/rfd0`, you can use the commands:

```
$ gunzip bare.gz
$ dd if=bare of=/dev/rfd0 obs=18k
```

You must provide the appropriate block size argument (the `obs` argument) on some workstations (e.g., Suns) or this will fail. If you have problems the man page for `dd` will be instructive.

2.1.4.4.2 Preparing for installation from hard drive   If you're planning on installing the Slackware software directly from the hard drive (which is often faster and more reliable than a floppy installation), you will need an MS-DOS partition on the system that you're installing Slackware to.

Note: If you plan to install Slackware from an MS-DOS partition, that partition must NOT be compressed with DoubleSpace, Stacker, or any other MS-DOS drive compression utility. Linux currently cannot read DoubleSpace/Stacker MS-DOS partitions directly. (You can access them via the MS-DOS Emulator, but that is not an option when installing the Linux software.)

To prepare for hard drive installation, simply create a directory on the hard drive to store the Slackware files. For example,

```
C:\> MKDIR SLACKWAR
```

will create the directory `C:\SLACKWAR` to hold the Slackware files. Under this directory, you should create subdirectories `A1`, `A2`, and so on, for each disk set that you downloaded, using the `MKDIR` command. All of the files from the `A1` disk should go into the directory `SLACKWAR\A1`, and so forth.

2.1.4.4.3 Preparing for floppy installation   If you wish to install Slackware from floppies instead of the hard drive, you'll need to have one blank, MS-DOS formatted floppy for each Slackware disk that you downloaded. These disks must be high-density format.

The `A` disk set (disks `A1` through `A3`) may be either 3.5" or 5.25" floppies. However, the rest of the disk sets must be 3.5" disks. Therefore, if you only have a 5.25" floppy drive, you'll need to borrow a 3.5" drive from someone in order to install disk sets other than `A`. (Or, you can install from the hard drive, as explained in the previous section.)

To make the disks, simply copy the files from each Slackware directory onto an MS-DOS formatted floppy, using the MS-DOS `COPY` command. As so:

```
C:\> COPY A1\*.* A:
```

will copy the contents of the `A1` disk to the floppy in drive `A:`. You should repeat this for each disk that you downloaded.

You do *not* need to modify or uncompress the files on the disks in any way; you merely need to copy them to MS-DOS floppies. The Slackware installation procedure takes care of uncompressing the files for you.

2.1.4.4.4 Preparing for CD-ROM installation If you have Slackware on a CD-ROM, you are ready to install the software once you have created the boot and root floppies. The software will be installed directly from CD.

2.2 Preparing to Install Linux

After you have obtained a distribution of Linux, you're ready to prepare your system for installation. This takes a certain degree of planning, especially if you're already running other operating systems. In the following sections we'll describe how to plan for the Linux installation.

2.2.1 Installation overview

While each release of Linux is different, in general the method used to install the software is as follows:

1. **Repartition your hard drive(s).** If you have other operating systems already installed, you will need to *repartition* the drives in order to allocate space for Linux. This is discussed in Section 2.2.4, below.

2. **Boot the Linux installation media.** Each distribution of Linux has some kind of installation media— usually a "boot floppy"—which is used to install the software. Booting this media will either present you with some kind of installation program, which will step you through the Linux installation, or allow you to install the software by hand.

3. **Create Linux partitions.** After repartitioning to allocate space for Linux, you create Linux partitions on that empty space. This is accomplished with the Linux fdisk program, covered in Section 2.3.3.

4. **Create filesystems and swap space.** At this point, you will create one or more *filesystems*, used to store files, on the newly-created partitions. In addition, if you plan to use swap space, you will create the swap space on one of your Linux partitions. This is covered in Sections 2.3.4 and 2.3.5.

5. **Install the software on the new filesystems.** Finally, you will install the Linux software on your newly-created filesystems. After this, it's smooth sailing—if all goes well. This is covered in Section 2.3.6. Later, in Section 2.5, we describe what to do if anything goes wrong.

Many distributions of Linux provide an installation program which will step you through the installation process, and automate one or more of the above steps for you. Keep in mind throughout this chapter that any number of the above steps may be automated for you, depending on the distribution.

The Slackware distribution of Linux, covered in this book, only requires you to repartition your drive, using fdisk, and use the setup program to accomplish the other steps.

Important hint: While preparing to install Linux, the best advice that we can give is to *take notes* during the entire procedure. Write down everything that you do, everything that you type, and everything that you see that might be out of the ordinary. The idea here is simple: if (or when!) you run into trouble, you want to be able to retrace your steps and find out what went wrong. Installing Linux isn't difficult, but there are many details to remember. You want to have a record of all of these details so that you can experiment with other methods if something goes wrong. Also, keeping a notebook of your Linux installation experience is useful when you want to ask other people for help, for example, when posting a message to one of the Linux-related USENET groups. Your notebook is also something that you'll want to show to your grandchildren someday.[4]

---

[4] The author shamefully admits that he kept a notebook of all of his tribulations with Linux for the first few months of working with the system. It is now gathering dust on his bookshelf.

2.2.2 Repartitioning concepts

In general, hard drives are divided into *partitions*, where a single partition is devoted to a single operating system. For example, on one hard drive, you may have several separate partitions—one devoted to, say, MS-DOS, another to OS/2, and another to Linux.

If you already have other software installed on your system, you may need to resize those partitions in order to free up space for Linux. You will then create one or more Linux partitions on the resulting free space for storing the Linux software and swap space. We call this process *repartitioning*.

Many MS-DOS systems utilize a single partition inhabiting the entire drive. To MS-DOS, this partition is known as C:. If you have more than one partition, MS-DOS names them D:, E:, and so on. In a way, each partition acts like a separate hard drive.

On the first sector of the disk is a **master boot record** along with a **partition table**. The boot record (as the name implies) is used to boot the system. The partition table contains information about the locations and sizes of your partitions.

There are three kinds of partitions: **primary**, **extended**, and **logical**. Of these, primary partitions are used most often. However, because of a limit in the size of the partition table, you can only have four primary partitions on any given drive.

The way around this four-partition limit is to use an extended partition. An extended partition doesn't hold any data by itself; instead, it acts as a "container" for logical partitions. Therefore, you could create one extended partition, covering the entire drive, and within it create many logical partitions. However, you may have only one extended partition per drive.

2.2.3 Linux partition requirements

Before we explain how to repartition your drives, you need to have an idea of how much space you will be allocating for Linux. We will be discussing how to create these partitions later, in Section 2.3.3.

On UNIX systems, files are stored on a **filesystem**, which is essentially a section of the hard drive (or other medium, such as CD-ROM or diskette) formatted to hold files. Each filesystem is associated with a specific part of the directory tree; for example, on many systems, there is a filesystem for all of the files in the directory /usr, another for /tmp, and so on. The **root filesystem** is the primary filesystem, which corresponds to the topmost directory, /.

Under Linux, each filesystem lives on a separate partition on the hard drive. For instance, if you have a filesystem for / and another for /usr, you will need two partitions to hold the two filesystems.

Before you install Linux, you will need to prepare filesystems for storing the Linux software. You must have at least one filesystem (the root filesystem), and therefore one partition, allocated to Linux. Many Linux users opt to store all of their files on the root filesystem, which is in most cases easier to manage than several filesystems and partitions.

However, you may create multiple filesystems for Linux if you wish—for example, you may want to use separate filesystems for /usr and /home. Those readers with UNIX system administration experience will know how to use multiple filesystems creatively. In Chapter 4 we discuss the use of multiple partitions and filesystems.

Why use more than one filesystem? The most commonly stated reason is safety; if, for some reason, one of your filesystems is damaged, the others will (usually) be unharmed. On the other hand, if you store all of your files on the root filesystem, and for some reason the filesystem is damaged, then you may lose all of your files in one fell swoop. This is, however, rather uncommon; if you backup the system regularly you should be quite safe.[5]

Another reason to use multiple filesystems is to divvy up storage between multiple hard drives. If you have, say, 40 megabytes free on one hard drive, and 50 megabytes free on another, you might want to create a 40-megabyte root filesystem on the first drive and a 50-megabyte /usr filesystem on the other. Currently it is not possible for a single filesystem to span multiple drives; if your free hard drive storage is fragmented between drives you will need to use multiple filesystems to utilize it all.

In summary, Linux requires at least one partition, for the root filesystem. If you wish to create multiple filesystems, you will need a separate partition for each additional filesystem. Some distributions of Linux automatically create partitions and filesystems for you, so you may not need to worry about these issues at all.

Another issue to consider when planning your partitions is swap space. If you wish to use swap space with Linux, you have two options. The first is to use a *swap file* which exists on one of your Linux filesystems. You will create the swap file for use as virtual RAM after you install the software. The second option is to create a *swap partition*, an individual partition to be used only as swap space. Most people use a swap partition instead of a swap file.

A single swap file or partition may be up to 16 megabytes in size. If you wish to use more than 16 megabytes of swap, you can create multiple swap partitions or files—up to eight in all. For example, if you need 32 megabytes of swap, you can create two 16-megabyte swap partitions.

Setting up a swap partition is covered in Section 2.3.4, and setting up a swap file in Chapter 4.

Therefore, in general, you will create at least two partitions for Linux: one for use as the root filesystem, and the other for use as swap space. There are, of course, many variations on the above, but this is the minimal setup. You are not required to use swap space with Linux, but if you have less than 16 megabytes of physical RAM it is strongly suggested that you do.

Of course, you need to be aware of how much *space* these partitions will require. The size of your Linux filesystems (containing the software itself) depends greatly on how much software you're installing and what distribution of Linux you are using. Hopefully, the documentation that came with your distribution will give you an approximation of the space requirements. A small Linux system can use 20 megabytes or less; a larger system anywhere from 80 to 100 megabytes, or more. Keep in mind that in addition to the space required by the software itself, you need to allocate extra space for user directories, room for future expansion, and so forth.

The size of your swap partition (should you elect to use one) depends on how much virtual RAM you require. A rule of thumb is to use a swap partition that is twice the space of your physical RAM; for example, if you have 4 megabytes of physical RAM, an 8-megabyte swap partition should suffice. Of course, this is mere speculation—the actual amount of swap space that you require depends on the software which you will be running. If you have a great deal of physical RAM (say, sixteen megabytes or more), you may not wish to use swap space at all.

Important note: Because of BIOS limitations, it is usually not possible to boot from partitions using cylinders numbered over 1023. Therefore, when setting aside space for Linux, keep in mind that you may not want to use a partition in the >1023-cylinder range for your Linux root filesystem. Linux can still *use* partitions with cylinders numbered over 1023, however, you may not be able to *boot* Linux from such a partition. This advice may seem premature, but it is important to know while planning your drive layout.

If you absolutely must use a partition with cylinders numbered over 1023 for your Linux root filesystem, you can always boot Linux from floppy. This is not so bad, actually—it only takes a few seconds longer to

---

[5]The author uses a single 200-megabyte filesystem for all of his Linux files, and hasn't had any problems (so far).

boot than from the hard drive. At any rate, it's always an option.

2.2.4 Repartitioning your drives

In this section, we'll describe how to resize your current partitions (if any) to make space for Linux. If you are installing Linux on a "clean" hard drive, you can skip this section and proceed to Section 2.3, below.

The usual way to resize an existing partition is to delete it (thus destroying all of the data on that partition) and recreate it. Before repartitioning your drives, *backup your system*. After resizing the partitions, you can reinstall your original software from the backup. However, there are several programs available for MS-DOS which are able to resize partitions nondestructively. One of these is known as "FIPS", and can be found on many Linux FTP sites.

Also, keep in mind that because you'll be shrinking your original partitions, you may not have space to reinstall everything. In this case, you need to delete enough unwanted software to allow the rest to fit on the smaller partitions.

The program used to repartition is known as fdisk. Each operating system has its own analogue of this program; for example, under MS-DOS, it is invoked with the FDISK command. You should consult your documentation for whatever operating systems you are currently running for information on repartitioning. Here, we'll discuss how to resize partitions for MS-DOS using FDISK, but this information should be easily extrapolated to other operating systems.

Please consult the documentation for your current operating systems before repartitioning your drive. This section is meant to be a general overview of the process; there are many subtleties that we do not cover here. You can lose all of the software on your system if you do not repartition the drive correctly.

A warning: Do not modify or create partitions for any other operating systems (including Linux) using FDISK under MS-DOS. You should only modify partitions for a particular operating system with the version of fdisk included with that operating system; for example, you will create Linux partitions using a version of fdisk for Linux. Later, in Section 2.3.3, we describe how to create Linux partitions, but for now we are concerned with resizing your current ones.

Let's say that you have a single hard drive on your system, currently devoted entirely to MS-DOS. Hence, your drive consists of a single MS-DOS partition, commonly known as "C:". Because this repartitioning method will destroy the data on that partition, you need to create a bootable MS-DOS "system disk" which contains everything necessary to run FDISK and restore the software from backup after the repartitioning is complete.

In many cases, you can use the MS-DOS installation disks for this purpose. However, if you need to create your own system disk, format a floppy with the command

```
FORMAT /s A:
```

Copy onto this floppy all of the necessary MS-DOS utilities (usually most of the software in the directory \DOS on your drive), as well as the programs FORMAT.COM and FDISK.EXE. You should now be able to boot this floppy, and run the command

```
FDISK C:
```

to start up FDISK.

Use of FDISK should be self-explanatory, but consult the MS-DOS documentation for details. When you start FDISK, use the menu option to display the partition table, and *write down* the information displayed there. It is important to keep a record of your original setup in case you want to back out of the Linux installation.

To delete an existing partition, choose the FDISK menu option "Delete an MS-DOS Partition or Logical DOS Drive". Specify the type of partition that you wish to delete (primary, extended, or logical) and the number of the partition. Verify all of the warnings. Poof!

To create a new (smaller) partition for MS-DOS, just choose the FDISK option "Create an MS-DOS Partition or Logical DOS Drive". Specify the type of partition (primary, extended, or logical), and the size of the partition to create (specified in megabytes). FDISK should create the partition and you're ready to roll.

After you're done using FDISK, you should exit the program and reformat any new partitions. For example, if you resized the first DOS partition on your drive (C:) you should run the command

```
FORMAT /s C:
```

You may now reinstall your original software from backup.

2.3   Installing the Linux software

After you have resized your existing partitions to make space for Linux, you are ready to install the software. Here is a brief overview of the procedure:

- Boot the Linux installation media;

- Run fdisk under Linux to create Linux partitions;

- Run mke2fs and mkswap to create Linux filesystems and swap space;

- Install the Linux software;

- Finally, either install the LILO boot loader on your hard drive, or create a boot floppy in order to boot your new Linux system.

As we have said, one (or more) of these steps may be automated for you by the installation procedure, depending on the distribution of Linux which you are using. Please consult the documentation for your distribution for specific instructions.

2.3.1   Booting Linux

The first step is to boot the Linux installation media. In most cases, this is a "boot floppy" which contains a small Linux system. Upon booting the floppy, you will be presented with an installation menu of some kind which will lead you through the steps of installing the software. On other distributions, you will be presented with a login prompt when booting this floppy. Here, you usually login as root or install to begin the installation process.

The documentation which came with your particular distribution will explain what is necessary to boot Linux from the installation media.

If you are installing the Slackware distribution of Linux, all that is required is to boot the boot floppy which you created in the previous section.

Most distributions of Linux use a boot floppy which allows you to enter hardware parameters at a boot prompt, to force hardware detection of various devices. For example, if your SCSI controller is not detected when booting the floppy, you will need to reboot and specify the hardware parameters (such as I/O address and IRQ) at the boot prompt.

Likewise, IBM PS/1, ThinkPad, and ValuePoint machines do not store drive geometry in the CMOS, and you must specify it at boot time.

The boot prompt is often displayed automatically when booting the boot floppy. This is the case for the Slackware distribution. Other distributions require you to hold down `shift` or `ctrl` while booting the floppy. If successful, you should see the prompt

```
boot:
```

and possibly other messages.

To try booting without any special parameters, just press `enter` at the boot prompt.

Watch the messages as the system boots. If you have a SCSI controller, you should see a listing of the SCSI hosts detected. If you see the message

```
SCSI: 0 hosts
```

then your SCSI controller was not detected, and you will have to use the following procedure.

Also, the system will display information on the drive partitions and devices detected. If any of this information is incorrect or missing, you will have to force hardware detection.

On the other hand, if all goes well and you hardware seems to be detected, you can skip to the following section, Section 2.3.2.

To force hardware detection, you must enter the appropriate parameters at the boot prompt, using the following syntax:

```
ramdisk ⟨parameters...⟩
```

There are a number of such parameters available; here are some of the most common.

hd=⟨*cylinders*⟩, ⟨*heads*⟩, ⟨*sectors*⟩
> Specify the hard drive geometry. Required for systems such as the IBM PS/1, ValuePoint, and ThinkPad. For example, if your drive has 683 cylinders, 16 heads, and 32 sectors per track, enter
>
> ```
> ramdisk hd=683,16,32
> ```

tmc8xx=⟨*memaddr*⟩, ⟨*irq*⟩
> Specify address and IRQ for BIOS-less Future Domain TMC-8xx SCSI controller. For example,
>
> ```
> ramdisk tmc8xx=0xca000,5
> ```
>
> Note that the `0x` prefix must be used for all values given in hexadecimal. This is true for all of the following options.

st0x=⟨*memaddr*⟩, ⟨*irq*⟩
> Specify address and IRQ for BIOS-less Seagate ST02 controller.

`t128=`⟨*memaddr*⟩`,`⟨*irq*⟩

> Specify address and IRQ for BIOS-less Trantor T128B controller.

> `ncr5380=`⟨*port*⟩`,`⟨*irq*⟩`,`⟨*dma*⟩ Specify port, IRQ, and DMA channel for generic NCR5380 controller.

`aha152x=`⟨*port*⟩`,`⟨*irq*⟩`,`⟨*scsi_id*⟩`,1`

> Specify port, IRQ, and SCSI ID for BIOS-less AIC-6260 controllers. This includes Adaptec 1510, 152x, and Soundblaster-SCSI controllers.

For each of these, you must enter `ramdisk` followed by the parameter that you wish to use.

If you have questions about these boot-time options, please read the Linux *SCSI HOWTO*, which should be available on any Linux FTP archive site (or from wherever you obtained this book), as well as the Linux *CD-ROM HOWTO*. These documents describe hardware compatibility in much more detail.

2.3.2   Drives and partitions under Linux

Many distributions require you to create Linux partitions by hand using the `fdisk` program. Others may automatically create partitions for you. Either way, you should know the following information about Linux partitions and device names.

Drives and partitions under Linux are given different names than their counterparts under other operating systems. Under MS-DOS, floppy drives are referred to as `A:` and `B:`, while hard drive partitions are named `C:`, `D:`, and so on. Under Linux, the naming convention is quite different.

Device drivers, found in the directory `/dev`, are used to communicate with devices on your system (such as hard drives, mice, and so on). For example, if you have a mouse on your system, you access it through the driver `/dev/mouse`. Floppy drives, hard drives, and individual partitions are all given individual device drivers of their own. Don't worry about the device driver interface for now; it is important only to understand how the various devices are named in order to use them.

Table 2.1 lists the names of these various device drivers.

A few notes about this table. Note that `/dev/fd0` corresponds to the first floppy drive (`A:` under MS-DOS) and `/dev/fd1` corresponds to the second floppy (`B:`).

Also, SCSI hard drives are named differently than other drives. IDE, MFM, and RLL drives are accessed through the devices `/dev/hda`, `/dev/hdb`, and so on. The individual partitions on the drive `/dev/hda` are `/dev/hda1`, `/dev/hda2`, and so on. However, SCSI drives are named `/dev/sda`, `/dev/sdb`, etc., with partition names such as `/dev/sda1` and `/dev/sda2`.

Here's an example. Let's say that you have a single IDE hard drive, with 3 primary partitions. The first two are set aside for MS-DOS, and the third is an extended partition which contains two logical partitions, both for use by Linux. The devices referring to these partitions would be:

First MS-DOS partition (`C:`)	`/dev/hda1`
Second MS-DOS partition (`D:`)	`/dev/hda2`
Extended partition	`/dev/hda3`
First Linux logical partition	`/dev/hda5`
Second Linux logical partition	`/dev/hda6`

Note that `/dev/hda4` is skipped; it corresponds to the fourth primary partition, which we don't have in this example. Logical partitions are named consecutively starting with `/dev/hda5`.

Device	Name
First floppy (A:)	/dev/fd0
Second floppy (B:)	/dev/fd1
First hard drive (entire drive)	/dev/hda
First hard drive, primary partition 1	/dev/hda1
First hard drive, primary partition 2	/dev/hda2
First hard drive, primary partition 3	/dev/hda3
First hard drive, primary partition 4	/dev/hda4
First hard drive, logical partition 1	/dev/hda5
First hard drive, logical partition 2	/dev/hda6
⋮	
Second hard drive (entire drive)	/dev/hdb
Second hard drive, primary partition 1	/dev/hdb1
⋮	
First SCSI hard drive (entire drive)	/dev/sda
First SCSI hard drive, primary partition 1	/dev/sda1
⋮	
Second SCSI hard drive (entire drive)	/dev/sdb
Second SCSI hard drive, primary partition 1	/dev/sdb1
⋮	

Table 2.1: Linux partition names

2.3.3 Creating Linux partitions

Now you are ready to create Linux partitions with the fdisk command. As described in Section 2.2.3, in general you will need to create at least one partition for the Linux software itself, and another partition for swap space.

After booting the installation media, run fdisk by typing

    fdisk ⟨drive⟩

where ⟨drive⟩ is the Linux device name of the drive you plan to add partitions to (see Table 2.1). For instance, if you want to run fdisk on the first SCSI disk in your system, use the command fdisk /dev/sda. /dev/hda (the first IDE drive) is the default if you don't specify one.

If you are creating Linux partitions on more than one drive, run fdisk once for each drive.

    # fdisk /dev/hda

    Command (m for help):

Here fdisk is waiting for a command; you can type m to get a list of options.

    Command (m for help): m
    Command action
    a toggle a bootable flag
    d delete a partition
    l list known partition types
    m print this menu

```
n add a new partition
p print the partition table
q quit without saving changes
t change a partition's system id
u change display/entry units
v verify the partition table
w write table to disk and exit
x extra functionality (experts only)

Command (m for help):
```

The n command is used to create a new partition. Most of the other options you won't need to worry about. To quit fdisk without saving any changes, use the q command. To quit fdisk and write the changes to the partition table to disk, use the w command.

The first thing you should do is display your current partition table and write the information down, for later reference. Use the p command.

```
Command (m for help):  p
Disk /dev/hda:  16 heads, 38 sectors, 683 cylinders
Units = cylinders of 608 * 512 bytes

   Device Boot   Begin   Start     End   Blocks   Id  System
/dev/hda1    *       1       1     203   61693    6  DOS 16-bit >=32M


Command (m for help):
```

In this example, we have a single MS-DOS partition on /dev/hda1, which is 61693 blocks (about 60 megs).[6] This partition starts at cylinder number 1, and ends on cylinder 203. We have a total of 683 cylinders in this disk; so there are 480 cylinders left to create Linux partitions on.

To create a new partition, use the n command. In this example, we'll create two primary partitions (/dev/hda2 and /dev/hda3) for Linux.

```
Command (m for help):  n
Command action
e extended
p primary partition (1-4)
p
```

Here, fdisk is asking the type of the partition to create: extended or primary. In our example, we're creating only primary partitions, so we choose p.

```
Partition number (1-4):
```

fdisk will then ask for the number of the partition to create; since partition 1 is already used, our first Linux partition will be number 2.

```
Partition number (1-4):  2
First cylinder (204-683):
```

---

[6]A block, under Linux, is 1024 bytes.

Now enter the starting cylinder number of the partition. Since cylinders 204 through 683 are unused, we'll use the first available one (numbered 204). There's no reason to leave empty space between partitions.

```
First cylinder (204-683):  204
Last cylinder or +size or +sizeM or +sizeK (204-683):
```

fdisk is asking for the size of the partition to create. We can either specify an ending cylinder number, or a size in bytes, kilobytes, or megabytes. Since we want our partition to be 80 megs in size, we specify +80M. When specifying a partition size in this way, fdisk will round the actual partition size to the nearest number of cylinders.

```
Last cylinder or +size or +sizeM or +sizeK (204-683):  +80M

Warning:  Linux cannot currently use 33090 sectors of this partition
```

If you see a warning message such as this, it can be ignored. fdisk prints the warning because it's an older program, and dates before the time that Linux partitions were allowed to be larger than 64 megabytes.

Now we're ready to create our second Linux partition. For sake of demonstration, we'll create it with a size of 10 megabytes.

```
Command (m for help):  n
Command action
e extended
p primary partition (1-4)
p
Partition number (1-4):  3
First cylinder (474-683):  474
Last cylinder or +size or +sizeM or +sizeK (474-683):  +10M
```

At last, we'll display the partition table. Again, write down all of this information—especially the block sizes of your new partitions. You'll need to know the sizes of the partitions when creating filesystems, later. Also, verify that none of your partitions overlap.

```
Command (m for help):  p
Disk /dev/hda:  16 heads, 38 sectors, 683 cylinders
Units = cylinders of 608 * 512 bytes
```

Device	Boot	Begin	Start	End	Blocks	Id	System
/dev/hda1	*	1	1	203	61693	6	DOS 16-bit >=32M
/dev/hda2		204	204	473	82080	81	Linux/MINIX
/dev/hda3		474	474	507	10336	81	Linux/MINIX

As you can see, /dev/hda2 is now a partition of size 82080 blocks (which corresponds to about 80 megabytes), and /dev/hda3 is 10336 blocks (about 10 megs).

Note that many distributions (such as Slackware) require you to use the t command in fdisk to change the type of the swap partition to "Linux swap", which is usually numbered 82. You can use the L command to print a list of known partition type codes, and then use t to set the type of the swap partition to that which corresponds to "Linux swap".

In this way, the installation software will be able to automatically find your swap partitions based on type. If the installation software doesn't seem to recognize your swap partition, you might want to re-run fdisk and use the t command on the partition in question.

In the example above, the remaining cylinders on the disk (numbered 508 to 683) are unused. You may wish to leave unused space on the disk, in case you wish to create additional partitions later.

Finally, we use the w command to write the changes to disk and exit fdisk.

```
Command (m for help):  w

#
```

Keep in mind that none of the changes you make while running fdisk will take effect until you give the w command, so you can toy with different configurations and save them when you're done. Also, if you want to quit fdisk at any time without saving the changes, use the q command. Remember that you shouldn't modify partitions for operating systems other than Linux with the Linux fdisk program.

Remember that you may not be able to boot Linux from a partition using cylinders numbered over 1023. Therefore, you should try to create your Linux root partition within the sub-1024 cylinder range. Again, if this is impossible, you can simply boot Linux from floppy.

Some Linux distributions require you to reboot the system after running fdisk. This is to allow the changes to the partition table to take effect before installing the software. Newer versions of fdisk automatically update the partition information in the kernel, so rebooting isn't necessary. To be on the safe side, after running fdisk you should reboot the installation media, as before, before proceeding.

2.3.4   Creating the swap space

If you are planning to use a swap partition for virtual RAM, you're ready to prepare it for use.[7] In Chapter 4 we will discuss the preparation of a swap file in case you don't want to use an individual partition.

Many distributions require you to create and activate swap space before installing the software. If you have a small amount of physical RAM, the installation procedure may not be successful unless you have some amount of swap space enabled.

The Slackware distribution requires you to create swap space, before installation, if you have 4 megabytes of RAM or less. If this is not the case, the Slackware installation procedure can be used to prepare swap space automatically. If in doubt, go ahead and follow the procedure described here; it can't hurt.

The command used to prepare a swap partition is mkswap, and it takes the form

```
mkswap -c ⟨partition⟩ ⟨size⟩
```

where ⟨partition⟩ is the name of the swap partition, and ⟨size⟩ is the size of the partition, in blocks.[8] For example, if your swap partition is /dev/hda3 and is 10336 blocks in size, use the command

```
# mkswap -c /dev/hda3 10336
```

The -c option tells mkswap to check for bad blocks on the partition when creating the swap space.

If you are using multiple swap partitions, you will need to execute the appropriate mkswap command for each partition.

After formatting the swap space, you need to enable it for use by the system. Usually, the system automatically enables swap space at boot time. However, because you have not yet installed the Linux software, you need to enable it by hand.

The command to enable swap space is swapon, and it takes the form

---

[7]Again, some distributions of Linux will prepare the swap space automatically for you, or via an installation menu option.

[8]This is the size as reported by fdisk, using the p menu option. A block under Linux is 1024 bytes.

```
swapon (partition)
```

In the example above, to enable the swap space on /dev/hda3, we use the command

    # *swapon /dev/hda3*

2.3.5   Creating the filesystems

Before you can use your Linux partitions to store files, you must create **filesystems** on them. Creating a filesystem is analogous to formatting a partition under MS-DOS or other operating systems. We discussed filesystems briefly in Section 2.2.3.

There are several types of filesystems available for Linux. Each filesystem type has its own format and set of characteristics (such as filename length, maximum file size, and so on). Linux also supports several "third-party" filesystem types such as the MS-DOS filesystem.

The most commonly used filesystem type is the **Second Extended Filesystem**, or *ext2fs*. The *ext2fs* is one of the most efficient and flexible filesystems; it allows filenames up to 256 characters and filesystem sizes of up to 4 terabytes. In Chapter 4, we'll discuss the various filesystem types available for Linux. Initially, however, we suggest that you use the *ext2fs* filesystem.

If you are installing the Slackware distribution, filesystems are created automatically for you by the installation procedure described in the next section. If you wish to create your filesystems by hand, however, follow the procedure described here.

To create an *ext2fs* filesystem, use the command

```
mke2fs -c (partition) (size)
```

where ⟨**partition**⟩ is the name of the partition, and ⟨**size**⟩ is the size of the partition in blocks. For example, to create a 82080-block filesystem on /dev/hda2, use the command

    # *mke2fs –c /dev/hda2 82080*

If you're using multiple filesystems for Linux, you'll need to use the appropriate mke2fs command for each filesystem.

If you have encountered any problems at this point, see Section 2.5 at the end of this chapter.

2.3.6   Installing the software

Finally, you are ready to install the software on your system. Every distribution has a different mechanism for doing this. Many distributions have a self-contained program which will step you through the installation. On other distributions, you will have to **mount** your filesystems in a certain subdirectory (such as /mnt) and copy the software to them by hand. On CD-ROM distributions, you may be given the option to install a portion of the software on your hard drives, and leave most of the software on the CD-ROM.

Some distributions offer several different ways to install the software. For example, you may be able to install the software directly from an MS-DOS partition on your hard drive, instead of from floppies. Or, you may be able to install over a TCP/IP network via FTP or NFS. See your distribution's documentation for details.

For example, the Slackware distribution only requires you to create partitions with fdisk, optionally create swap space with mkswap and swapon (if you have 4 megs or less of RAM), and then run the setup program. setup leads you through a very self-explanatory menu system to install the software. Use of setup is described in detail below.

The exact method used to install the Linux software differs greatly with each distribution. We're hoping that installing the Linux software should be self-explanatory, as it is with most distributions.

2.3.6.1   Installing Slackware with setup

If you are installing Slackware, after creating partitions (and possibly swap space), use the command

    # *setup*

This will present you will a menu-based procedure to walk you through the remaining steps of installation.

The procedure described here corresponds to that found on the color144 and colrlite root disks; the other root disks may have slightly different procedures.

The setup menu consists of the following items. Use the arrow keys to move over the items, and press enter or spacebar to select an item.

Help   View the setup help file.

Keymap   This option allows you to specify the keyboard mapping for your system if you do not have a US keyboard. A list of keymaps will be presented; select the appropriate item from the list.

Quick   This allows you to select between "quick" and "verbose" installation modes. "Verbose" is the default, and is recommended for most installations (unless you've installed Slackware a dozen times, in which case you already know this).

Make tags   This allows Slackware installation experts to create customized "tag files" for preselecting packages. This is only necessary for customizing the installation procedure in some way; you shouldn't have to concern yourself with this.

Addswap   This will be the first item that most users will select to install Slackware. A list of available swap partitions will be displayed (those partitions with type "Linux swap" as set in fdisk). You will be able to specify which partitions you wish to use for swap space. You will then be asked if you wish to run mkswap on these partitions.

              If you have already executed mkswap and swapon (as described in Section 2.3.4) on your swap partitions, then you should *not* allow setup to execute mkswap on these partitions.

              Even if you have already executed mkswap and swapon, it is necessary to use the Addswap menu item: This ensures that your swap partitions will be available once you have the system installed.

              Be warned! Creating swap space on a partition will destroy data on that partition. Be sure that you're not wiping out data that you want to keep.

              If you select this menu item, you will be automatically prompted if you wish to proceed with the following items. In general, you should do this.

Target   This item allows you to specify the partitions upon which Linux is to be installed. A list of available partitions (those with type "Linux native", as specified by fdisk) will be

displayed, and you will be asked to enter the name of your Linux root partition, such as
/dev/hda2. You will then be prompted for the type of filesystem that you wish to create;
we suggest using the ext2fs filesystem type as described in Section 2.3.5. This will create
a filesystem on the named partition—somewhat analogous to "formatting" the partition
under MS-DOS.

You will also be prompted for any other partitions that you might wish to use for Linux.
For example, if you created a separate partition for /usr (see Section 2.2.3), you will be
able to specify the name of the partition and the location where it should be mounted (as
in /usr or /usr/bin).

◇ Be warned! Creating a filesystem on a partition will destroy all data on that partition. Be
sure that you're not wiping out data that you want to keep.

Even if you already created your filesystems using mke2fs (see Section 2.3.5), you must
use the Target menu item to specify the partitions where Linux will be installed.

Source   This menu item allows you to specify where you will be installing Slackware from, such as
floppy, hard drive, or CD-ROM.

If you are installing from hard drive, you will be asked what partition the Slackware files
are found on, as well as the type of partition. For example, if you have the Slackware files
on an MS-DOS partition, enter the name of the partition (such as /dev/hda1) and select
MS-DOS FAT as the type. You will then be asked what directory the files may be found
under on this partition. For example, if you have the Slackware files stored under the
directory C:\SLACK on your MS-DOS partition, enter

    /slack

as the location. Note that you should use forward slashes, not backslashes, in the pathname.

If you are installing from CD-ROM, you will be asked the type of CD-ROM device that
you are using, as well as what directory on the CD-ROM the files may be found in. Many
CD-ROMs have the files contained within the directory /slakware, but this depends on
the release.

If you are installing Slackware Professional,[9] two directories are used on the CD-ROM.
slakware is used for the standard system which will install the files directly to your hard
drive. slackpro is used for the CD-ROM-based system where many files are accessed
directly from the CD-ROM. This can save diskspace, but accessing many files is also noticeably slower. Several other Slackware vendors provide the ability to run the software
from the CD-ROM as well. However, if you have the diskspace to spare, we recommend
not running Slackware from the CD-ROM itself. Performance is generally slower.

If you are attempting a hard drive or CD-ROM install, Slackware may report that there is a
mount error at this point. This is usually an indication that there was a problem accessing
the hard drive or CD-ROM. See Section 2.5.3 for more information if you see such an error
message.

Disk sets   This menu option allows you to select the disk sets that you wish to install. You must install
at least the A disk set. Simply use the arrow keys and spacebar to select which disk sets
you wish to install.

Note that selecting a particular disk set does not mean that all packages on the disk set will
be installed; you will be prompted before installing packages on the disk set marked as

---

[9]Slackware Professional is a version of Slackware available from Morse Telecommunications.

"optional" or "recommended."

Install
At long last, this menu item will install the software on your system. You will be prompted for the prompting method; most users should select "normal." For each disk set that you selected, the "required" packages will be installed, and you will be prompted when installing the "optional" and "recommended" packages. If you are installing from floppy you will be asked to insert each floppy in succession.

As each package is installed a short description will be printed. Unless you have background in UNIX or Linux, many of these descriptions will not mean much to you. Take note of which packages are being installed, so you know what's there, but don't worry about trying to jot down everything that's printed on the display.

The most common error encountered here is that a file cannot be found on a floppy, or an I/O error when attempting to read the floppy. The former is an indication that the files on your floppy might be corrupted or incomplete; the latter that the floppy itself is bad. Any floppies which give these errors should be replaced, and you should re-install the disk set containing those floppies. See Section 2.5.3 for suggestions.

You may also have read errors when attempting to access a CD-ROM; be sure that the CD-ROM is clean, has no fingerprints, etc.

Configure
This menu item performs some post-installation configuration of your system. This is covered in the following section.

2.3.7   Creating the boot floppy or installing LILO

Every distribution provides some means of booting your new Linux system after you have installed the software. In many cases, the installation procedure will create a "boot floppy" which contains a Linux kernel configured to use your newly-created root filesystem. In order to boot Linux, you would boot from this floppy, and control would be transferred to your hard drive after booting. On other distributions, this "boot floppy" is the installation floppy itself.

Many distributions give you the option of installing **LILO** on your hard drive. LILO is a program that is installed on your drive's master boot record. It is able to boot a number of operating systems, including MS-DOS and Linux, and allows you to select at startup time which to boot.

For the Slackware distribution, the Configure item in the setup menu will allow you to create a boot floppy as well as install LILO. These options should be fairly self-explanatory. The Configure menu item also allows you to specify your modem, mouse, and timezone information.

In order for LILO to be installed successfully, it needs to know a good deal of information about your drive configuration—for example, which partitions contain which operating systems, how to boot each operating system, and so on. Many distributions, when installing LILO, attempt to "guess" at the appropriate parameters for your configuration. Although it's not often, the automated LILO installation provided by some distributions can fail, and leave your master boot record in shambles (although it's very doubtful that any damage to the actual data on your hard drive will take place). In particular, if you use OS/2's Boot Manager, you should *not* install LILO using the automated procedure—there are special instructions for using LILO with the Boot Manager, which will be covered later.

In many cases, it is best to use a boot floppy, until you have a chance to configure LILO yourself, by hand. If you're feeling exceptionally trustworthy, though, you can go ahead with the automated LILO installation if it is provided with your distribution.

In Chapter 4, we'll cover in detail how to configure and install LILO for your particular setup.

If everything goes well, then congratulations! You have just installed Linux on your system. Go have a Diet Coke or something—you deserve it.

In case you did run into any trouble, the next section will describe the most common sticking points for Linux installations, and how to get around them.

2.3.8 Additional installation procedures

Some distributions of Linux provide a number of additional installation procedures, allowing you to configure various software packages such as TCP/IP networking, the X Window System, and so on. If you are provided with these configuration options during installation, you may wish to read ahead in this book for more information on how to configure this software. Otherwise, you should put off these installation procedures until you have a complete understanding of how to configure the software.

It's up to you; if all else fails, just go with the flow and see what happens. It's very doubtful that anything that you do incorrectly now cannot be undone in the future. (Knock on wood.)

2.4 Postinstallation procedures

After you have completed installing the Linux software, there should be very little left to do before you can begin to use the system. In most cases, you should be able to reboot the system, login as root, and begin exploring the system. (Each distribution has a slightly different method for doing this.)

At this point it's a good idea to explain how to reboot and shutdown the system as you're using it. You should never reboot or shutdown your Linux system by pressing the reset switch or with the old "Vulcan Nerve Pinch"—that is, by pressing $\boxed{\texttt{ctrl-alt-del}}$ in unison.[10] You shouldn't simply switch off the power, either. As with most UNIX systems, Linux caches disk writes in memory. Therefore, if you suddenly reboot the system without shutting down "cleanly", you can corrupt the data on your drives, causing untold damage.

The easiest way to shut down the system is with the shutdown command. As an example, to shutdown and reboot the system immediately, use the following command as root:

    # shutdown –r now

This will cleanly reboot your system. The man page for shutdown describes the other command-line arguments that are available.[11]

Note, however, that many Linux distributions do not provide the shutdown command on the installation media. This means that the first time you reboot your system after installation, you may need to use the $\boxed{\texttt{ctrl-alt-del}}$ combination after all. Thereafter, you should always use the shutdown command.

After you have a chance to explore and use the system, there are several configuration chores that you should undertake. The first is to create a user account for yourself (and, optionally, for any other users that might have access to the system). Creating user accounts is described in Section 4.4. Usually, all that you have to do is login as root, and run the adduser (sometimes useradd) program. This will lead you through several prompts to create a new user account.

---

[10]On most Linux systems, however, $\boxed{\texttt{ctrl-alt-del}}$ will cause the system to shutdown gracefully, as if you had used the shutdown command.

[11]Use the command man shutdown to see the manual page for shutdown.

If you created more than one filesystem for Linux, or if you're using a swap partition, you may need to edit the file /etc/fstab in order for those filesystems to be available automatically after rebooting. (For example, if you're using a separate filesystem for /usr, and none of the files that should be in /usr appear to be present, you may simply need to mount that filesystem.) Section 4.8 describes this procedure. Note that the Slackware distribution of Linux automatically configures your filesystems and swap space at installation time, so this usually isn't necessary.

2.5   Running Into Trouble

Almost everyone runs into some kind of snag or hangup when attempting to install Linux the first time. Most of the time, the problem is caused by a simple misunderstanding. Sometimes, however, it can be something more serious, such as an oversight by one of the developers, or a bug.

This section will describe some of the most common installation problems, and how to solve them. If your installation appears to be successful, but you received unexpected error messages during the installation, these are described here as well.

2.5.1   Problems with booting the installation media

When attempting to boot the installation media for the first time, you may encounter a number of problems. These are listed below. Note that the following problems are *not* related to booting your newly-installed Linux system. See Section 2.5.4 for information on these kinds of pitfalls.

- **Floppy or media error when attempting to boot.**

  The most popular cause for this kind of problem is a corrupt boot floppy. Either the floppy is physically damaged, in which case you should re-create the disk with a *brand new* floppy, or the data on the floppy is bad, in which case you should verify that you downloaded and transferred the data to the floppy correctly. In many cases, simply re-creating the boot floppy will solve your problems. Retrace your steps and try again.

  If you received your boot floppy from a mail order vendor or some other distributor, instead of downloading and creating it yourself, contact the distributor and ask for a new boot floppy—but only after verifying that this is indeed the problem.

- **System "hangs" during boot or after booting.**

  After the installation media boots, you will see a number of messages from the kernel itself, indicating which devices were detected and configured. After this, you will usually be presented with a login prompt, allowing you to proceed with installation (some distributions instead drop you right into an installation program of some kind). The system may appear to "hang" during several of these steps. During all of these steps, be patient; loading software from floppy is very slow. In many cases, the system has not hung at all, but is merely taking a long time. Verify that there is no drive or system activity for at least several minutes before assuming that the system is hung.

  1. After booting from the LILO prompt, the system must load the kernel image from floppy. This may take several seconds; you will know that things are going well if the floppy drive light is still on.

  2. While the kernel boots, SCSI devices must be probed for. If you do not have any SCSI devices installed, the system will "hang" for up to 15 seconds while the SCSI probe continues; this usually occurs after the line

```
lp_init:  lp1 exists (0), using polling driver
```

appears on your screen.

3. After the kernel is finished booting, control is transferred to the system bootup files on the floppy. Finally, you will be presented with a login prompt, or be dropped into an installation program. If you are presented with a login prompt such as

```
Linux login:
```

you should then login (usually as `root` or `install`—this varies with each distribution). After entering the username, the system may pause for 20 seconds or more while the installation program or shell is being loaded from floppy. Again, the floppy drive light should be on. Don't assume that the system is hung.

Any of the above items may be the source of your problem. However, it is possible that the system actually may "hang" while booting, which can be due to several causes. First of all, you may not have enough available RAM to boot the installation media. (See the following item for information on disabling the ramdisk to free up memory.)

The cause of many system hangs is hardware incompatibility. Section 1.8 in the last chapter presented an overview of supported hardware under Linux. Even if your hardware is supported, you may run into problems with incompatible hardware configurations which are causing the system to hang. See Section 2.5.2, below, for a discussion of hardware incompatibilities.

- **System reports out of memory errors while attempting to boot or install the software.**

  This item deals with the amount of RAM that you have available. On systems with 4 megabytes of RAM or less, you may run into trouble booting the installation media or installing the software itself. This is because many distributions use a "ramdisk", which is a filesystem loaded directly into RAM, for operations while using the installation media. The entire image of the installation boot floppy, for example, may be loaded into a ramdisk, which may require more than a megabyte of RAM.

  The solution to this problem is to disable the ramdisk option when booting the install media. Each release has a different procedure for doing this; on the SLS release, for example, you type "`floppy`" at the LILO prompt when booting the `a1` disk. See your distribution's documentation for details.

  You may not see an "out of memory" error when attempting to boot or install the software; instead, the system may unexpectedly hang, or fail to boot. If your system hangs, and none of the explanations in the previous section seem to be the cause, try disabling the ramdisk.

  Keep in mind that Linux itself requires at least 2 megabytes of RAM to run at all; some distributions of Linux require 4 megabytes or more.

- **The system reports an error such as "`permission denied`" or "`file not found`" while booting.**

  This is an indication that your installation bootup media is corrupt. If you attempt to boot from the installation media (and you're sure that you're doing everything correctly), you should not see any errors such as this. Contact the distributor of your Linux software and find out about the problem, and perhaps obtain another copy of the boot media if necessary. If you downloaded the bootup disk yourself, try re-creating the bootup disk, and see if this solves your problem.

- **The system reports the error "`VFS: Unable to mount root`" when booting.**

  This error message means that the root filesystem (found on the boot media itself), could not be found. This means that either your boot media is corrupt in some way, or that you are not booting the system correctly.

  For example, many CD-ROM distributions require that you have the CD-ROM in the drive when booting. Also be sure that the CD-ROM drive is on, and check for any activity. It's also possible that the system is not locating your CD-ROM drive at boot time; see Section 2.5.2 for more information.

If you're sure that you are booting the system correctly, then your bootup media may indeed be corrupt. This is a very uncommon problem, so try other solutions before attempting to use another boot floppy or tape.

2.5.2   Hardware problems

The most common form of problem when attempting to install or use Linux is an incompatibility with hardware. Even if all of your hardware is supported by Linux, a misconfiguration or hardware conflict can sometimes cause strange results—your devices may not be detected at boot time, or the system may hang.

It is important to isolate these hardware problems if you suspect that they may be the source of your trouble. In the following sections we will describe some common hardware problems and how to resolve them.

2.5.2.1   Isolating hardware problems

If you experience a problem that you believe to be hardware-related, the first thing that you should to do is attempt to isolate the problem. This means eliminating all possible variables and (usually) taking the system apart, piece-by-piece, until the offending piece of hardware is isolated.

This is not as frightening as it may sound. Basically, you should remove all nonessential hardware from your system, and then determine which device is actually causing the trouble—possibly by reinserting each device, one at a time. This means that you should remove all hardware other than the floppy and video controllers, and of course the keyboard. Even innocent-looking devices such as mouse controllers can wreak unknown havoc on your peace of mind unless you consider them nonessential.

For example, let's say that the system hangs during the Ethernet board detection sequence at boot time. You might hypothesize that there is a conflict or problem with the Ethernet board in your machine. The quick and easy way to find out is to pull the Ethernet board, and try booting again. If everything goes well, then you know that either (a) the Ethernet board is not supported by Linux (see Section 1.8 for a list of compatible boards), or (b) there is an address or IRQ conflict with the board.

"Address or IRQ conflict?" What on earth does that mean? All devices in your machine use an *IRQ*, or *interrupt request line*, to tell the system that they need something done on their behalf. You can think of the IRQ as a cord that the device tugs when it needs the system to take care of some pending request. If more than one device is tugging on the same cord, the kernel won't be able to detemine which device it needs to service. Instant mayhem.

Therefore, be sure that all of your installed devices are using unique IRQ lines. In general the IRQ for a device can be set by jumpers on the card; see the documentation for the particular device for details. Some devices do not require the use of an IRQ at all, but it is suggested that you configure them to use one if possible (the Seagate ST01 and ST02 SCSI controllers being good examples).

In some cases, the kernel provided on your installation media is configured to use a certain IRQ for certain devices. For example, on some distributions of Linux, the kernel is preconfigured to use IRQ 5 for the TMC-950 SCSI controller, the Mitsumi CD-ROM controller, and the bus mouse driver. If you want to use two or more of these devices, you'll need to first install Linux with only one of these devices enabled, then recompile the kernel in order to change the default IRQ for one of them. (See Chapter 4 for information on recompiling the kernel.)

Another area where hardware conflicts can arise is with DMA (direct memory access) channels, I/O addresses, and shared memory addresses. All of these terms describe mechanisms through which the system interfaces with hardware devices. Some Ethernet boards, for example, use a shared memory address as well as an IRQ to interface with the system. If any of these are in conflict with other devices, then the system may behave unexpectedly. You should be able to change the DMA channel, I/O or shared memory addresses for your various devices with jumper settings. (Unfortunately, some devices don't allow you to change these settings.)

The documentation for your various hardware devices should specify the IRQ, DMA channel, I/O address, or shared memory address that the devices use, and how to configure them. Again, the simple way to get around these problems is just to temporarily disable the conflicting devices until you have time to determine the cause of the problem.

Table 2.2 is a list of IRQ and DMA channels used by various "standard" devices found on most systems. Almost all systems will have some of these devices, so you should avoid setting the IRQ or DMA of other devices in conflict with these values.

Device	I/O address	IRQ	DMA
ttyS0 (COM1)	3f8	4	n/a
ttyS1 (COM2)	2f8	3	n/a
ttyS2 (COM3)	3e8	4	n/a
ttyS3 (COM4)	2e8	3	n/a
lp0 (LPT1)	378 - 37f	7	n/a
lp1 (LPT2)	278 - 27f	5	n/a
fd0, fd1 (floppies 1 and 2)	3f0 - 3f7	6	2
fd2, fd3 (floppies 3 and 4)	370 - 377	10	3

Table 2.2: Common device settings

2.5.2.2 Problems recognizing hard drive or controller

When Linux boots, you should see a series of messages on your screen such as:

```
Console:  colour EGA+ 80x25, 8 virtual consoles
Serial driver version 3.96 with no serial options enabled
tty00 at 0x03f8 (irq = 4) is a 16450
tty03 at 0x02e8 (irq = 3) is a 16550A
lp_init:  lp1 exists (0), using polling driver
...
```

Here, the kernel is detecting the various hardware devices present on your system. At some point, you should see the line

```
Partition check:
```

followed by a list of recognized partitions, for example:

```
Partition check:
hda:  hda1 hda2
hdb:  hdb1 hdb2 hdb3
```

If, for some reason, your drives or partitions are not recognized, then you will not be able to access them in any way.

There are several things that can cause this to happen:

- **Hard drive or controller not supported.** If you are using a hard drive controller (IDE, SCSI, or otherwise) that is not supported by Linux, the kernel will not recognize your partitions at boot time.

- **Drive or controller improperly configured.** Even if your controller is supported by Linux, it may not be configured correctly. (This is particularly a problem for SCSI controllers; most non-SCSI controllers should work fine without any additional configuration).

  Refer to the documentation for your hard drive and/or controller for information on solving these kinds of problems. In particular, many hard drives will need to have a jumper set if they are to be used as a "slave" drive (for example, as the second hard drive). The acid test for this kind of condition is to boot up MS-DOS, or some other operating system, known to work with your drive and controller. If you can access the drive and controller from another operating system, then it is not a problem with your hardware configuration.

  See Section 2.5.2.1, above, for information on resolving possible device conflicts, and Section 2.5.2.3, below, for information on configuring SCSI devices.

- **Controller properly configured, but not detected.** Some BIOS-less SCSI controllers require the user to specify information about the controller at boot time. Section 2.5.2.3, below, describes how to force hardware detection for these controllers.

- **Hard drive geometry not recognized.** Some systems, such as the IBM PS/ValuePoint, do not store hard drive geometry information in the CMOS memory, where Linux expects to find it. Also, certain SCSI controllers need to be told where to find drive geometry in order for Linux to recognize the layout of your drive.

  Most distributions provide a bootup option to specify the drive geometry. In general, when booting the installation media, you can specify the drive geometry at the LILO boot prompt with a command such as:

      boot: *linux hd=⟨cylinders⟩,⟨heads⟩,⟨sectors⟩*

  where ⟨*cylinders*⟩, ⟨*heads*⟩, and ⟨*sectors*⟩ correspond to the number of cylinders, heads, and sectors per track for your hard drive.

  After installing the Linux software, you will be able to install LILO, allowing you to boot from the hard drive. At that time, you can specify the drive geometry to the LILO installation procedure, making it unnecessary to enter the drive geometry each time you boot. See Chapter 4 for more about LILO.

2.5.2.3   Problems with SCSI controllers and devices

Presented here are some of the most common problems with SCSI controllers and devices such as CD-ROMs, hard drives, and tape drives. If you are having problems getting Linux to recognize your drive or controller, read on.

The Linux SCSI HOWTO (see Appendix A) contains much useful information on SCSI devices in addition to that listed here. SCSI can be particularly tricky to configure at times.

- **A SCSI device is detected at all possible ID's.** This is caused by strapping the device to the same address as the controller. You need to change the jumper settings so that the drive uses a different address from the controller itself.

- **Linux reports sense errors, even if the devices are known to be error-free.** This can be caused by bad cables, or by bad termination. If your SCSI bus is not terminated at both ends, you may have errors accessing SCSI devices. When in doubt, always check your cables.

- **SCSI devices report timeout errors.** This is usually caused by a conflict with IRQ, DMA, or device addresses. Also check that interrupts are enabled correctly on your controller.

- **SCSI controllers using BIOS are not detected.** Detection of controllers using BIOS will fail if the BIOS is disabled, or if your controller's "signature" is not recognized by the kernel. See the Linux SCSI HOWTO for more information about this.

- **Controllers using memory mapped I/O do not work.** This is caused when the memory-mapped I/O ports are incorrectly cached. Either mark the board's address space as uncacheable in the XCMOS settings, or disable cache altogether.

- **When partitioning, you get a warning that "cylinders > 1024", or you are unable to boot from a partition using cylinders numbered above 1023.** BIOS limits the number of cylinders to 1024, and any partition using cylinders numbered above this won't be accessible from the BIOS. As far as Linux is concerned, this affects only booting; once the system has booted you should be able to access the partition. Your options are to either boot Linux from a boot floppy, or boot from a partition using cylinders numbered below 1024. See Section 2.3.7 for information on creating a boot diskette or installing LILO.

- **CD-ROM drive or other removeable media devices are not recognized at boot time.** Try booting with a CD-ROM (or disk) in the drive. This is necessary for some devices.

If your SCSI controller is not recognized, you may need to force hardware detection at boot time. This is particularly important for BIOS-less SCSI controllers. Most distributions allow you to specify the controller IRQ and shared memory address when booting the installation media. For example, if you are using a TMC-8xx controller, you may be able to enter

        boot: *linux tmx8xx=⟨interrupt⟩,⟨memory-address⟩*

at the LILO boot prompt, where ⟨*interrupt*⟩ is the IRQ of controller, and ⟨*memory-address*⟩ is the shared memory address. Whether or not you will be able to do this depends on the distribution of Linux you are using; consult your documentation for details.

2.5.3   Problems installing the software

Actually installing the Linux software should be quite trouble-free, if you're lucky. The only problems that you might experience would be related to corrupt installation media or lack of space on your Linux filesystems. Here is a list of these common problems.

- **System reports "`Read error`", "`file not found`", or other errors while attempting to install the software.** This is indicative of a problem with your installation media. If you are installing from floppy, keep in mind that floppies are quite succeptible to media errors of this type. Be sure to use brand-new, newly-formatted floppies. If you have an MS-DOS partition on your drive, many Linux distributions allow you to install the software from the hard drive. This may be faster and more reliable than using floppies.

  If you are using a CD-ROM, be sure to check the disc for scratches, dust, or other problems which might cause media errors.

The cause of the problem may be that the media is in the incorrect format. For example, if using floppies, many Linux distributions require that the floppies be formatted in high-density MS-DOS format. (The boot floppy is the exception; it is not in MS-DOS format in most cases.) If all else fails, either obtain a new set of floppies, or recreate the floppies (using new diskettes) if you downloaded the software yourself.

- **System reports errors such as** "`tar:   read error`" **or** "`gzip:   not in gzip format`". This problem is usually caused by corrupt files on the installation media itself. In other words, your floppy may be error-free, but the data on the floppy is in some way corrupted. For example, if you downloaded the Linux software using text mode, rather than binary mode, then your files will be corrupt, and unreadable by the installation software.

- **System reports errors such as** "`device full`" **while installing.** This is a clear-cut sign that you have run out of space when installing the software. Not all Linux distributions will be able to cleanly pick up the mess; you shouldn't be able to abort the installation and expect the system to work.

  The solution is usually to re-create your filesystems (with the `mke2fs` command) which will delete the partially-installed software. You can then attempt to re-install the software, this time selecting a smaller amount of software to install. In other cases, you may need to start completely from scratch, and rethink your partition and filesystem sizes.

- **System reports errors such as** "`read_intr:   0x10`" **while accessing the hard drive.** This is usually an indication of bad blocks on your drive. However, if you receive these errors while using `mkswap` or `mke2fs`, the system may be having trouble accessing your drive. This can either be a hardware problem (see Section 2.5.2), or it might be a case of poorly specified geometry. If you used the

  > hd=⟨cylinders⟩,⟨heads⟩,⟨sectors⟩

  option at boot time to force detection of your drive geometry, and incorrectly specified the geometry, you could be prone to this problem. This can also happen if your drive geometry is incorrectly specified in the system CMOS.

- **System reports errors such as** "`file not found`" **or** "`permission denied`". This problem can occur if not all of the necessary files are present on the installation media (see the next paragraph) or if there is a permissions problem with the installation software. For example, some distributions of Linux have been known to have bugs in the installation software itself. These are usually fixed very rapidly, and are quite infrequent. If you suspect that the distribution software contains bugs, and you're sure that you have not done anything wrong, contact the maintainer of the distribution to report the bug.

If you have other strange errors when installing Linux (especially if you downloaded the software yourself), be sure that you actually obtained all of the necessary files when downloading. For example, some people use the FTP command

```
mget *.*
```

when downloading the Linux software via FTP. This will download only those files that contain a "`.`" in their filenames; if there are any files without the "`.`", you will miss them. The correct command to use in this case is

```
mget *
```

The best advice is to retrace your steps when something goes wrong. You may think that you have done everything correctly, when in fact you forgot a small but important step somewhere along the way. In many cases, just attempting to re-download or re-install the Linux software can solve the problem. Don't beat your head against the wall any longer than you have to!

Also, if Linux unexpectedly hangs during installation, there may be a hardware problem of some kind. See Section 2.5.2 for hints.

2.5.4 Problems after installing Linux

You've spent an entire afternoon installing Linux. In order to make space for it, you wiped your MS-DOS and OS/2 partitions, and tearfully deleted your copies of SimCity and Wing Commander. You reboot the system, and nothing happens. Or, even worse, *something* happens, but it's not what should happen. What do you do?

In Section 2.5.1, we covered some of the most common problems that can occur when booting the Linux installation media—many of those problems may apply here. In addition, you may be victim to one of the following maladies.

2.5.4.1 Problems booting Linux from floppy

If you are using a floppy to boot Linux, you may need to specify the location of your Linux root partition at boot time. This is especially true if you are using the original installation floppy itself, and not a custom boot floppy created during installation.

While booting the floppy, hold down ⎡shift⎦ or ⎡ctrl⎦. This should present you with a boot menu; press ⎡tab⎦ to see a list of available options. For example, many distributions allow you to type

    boot: *linux hd=⟨partition⟩*

at the boot menu, where ⟨**partition**⟩ is the name of the Linux root partition, such as /dev/hda2. Consult the documentation for your distribution for details.

2.5.4.2 Problems booting Linux from the hard drive

If you opted to install LILO, instead of creating a boot floppy, then you should be able to boot Linux from the hard drive. However, the automated LILO installation procedure used by many distributions is not always perfect. It may make incorrect assumptions about your partition layout, in which case you will need to re-install LILO to get everything right. Installing LILO is covered in Chapter 4.

- **System reports** "Drive not bootable---Please insert system disk." You will get this error message if the hard drive's master boot record is corrupt in some way. In most cases, it's harmless, and everything else on your drive is still intact. There are several ways around this:

  1. While partitioning your drive using fdisk, you may have deleted the partition that was marked as "active". MS-DOS and other operating systems attempt to boot the "active" partition at boot time (Linux pays no attention to whether the partition is "active" or not). You may be able to boot MS-DOS from floppy and run FDISK to set the active flag on your MS-DOS parirition, and all will be well.

     Another command to try (with MS-DOS 5.0 and higher) is

```
FDISK /MBR
```
This command will attempt to rebuild the hard drive master boot record for booting MS-DOS, overwriting LILO. If you no longer have MS-DOS on your hard drive, you'll need to boot Linux from floppy and attempt to install LILO later.

2. If you created an MS-DOS partition using Linux's version of `fdisk`, or vice versa, you may get this error. You should create MS-DOS partitions only using MS-DOS's version `FDISK`. (The same applies to operating systems other than MS-DOS.) The best solution here is either to start from scratch and repartition the drive correctly, or to merely delete and re-create the offending partitions using the correct version of `fdisk`.

3. The LILO installation procedure may have failed. In this case, you should either boot from your Linux boot floppy (if you have one), or from the original installation media. Either of these should provide options for specifying the Linux root partition to use when booting. Hold down `shift` or `ctrl` at boot time, and press `tab` from the boot menu for a list of options.

- **When booting the system from the hard drive, MS-DOS (or another operating system) starts instead of Linux.** First of all, be sure that you actually installed LILO when installing the Linux software. If not, then the system will still boot MS-DOS (or whatever other operating system you may have) when you attempt to boot from the hard drive. In order to boot Linux from the hard drive, you will need to install LILO (see Chapter 4).

  On the other hand, if you *did* install LILO, and another operating system boots instead of Linux, then you have LILO configured to boot that other operating system by default. While the system is booting, hold down `shift` or `ctrl`, and press `tab` at the boot prompt. This should present you with a list of possible operating systems to boot; select the appropriate option (usually just "`linux`") to boot Linux.

  If you wish to select Linux as the default operating system to boot, you will need to re-install LILO. See Chapter 4.

  It also may be possible that you attempted to install LILO, but the installation procedure failed in some way. See the previous item.

2.5.4.3 Problems logging in

After booting Linux, you should be presented with a login prompt, like so:

```
linux login:
```

At this point, either the distribution's documentation or the system itself will tell you what to do. For many distributions, you simply login as `root`, with no password. Other possible usernames to try are `guest` or `test`.

Most newly-installed Linux systems should not require a password for the initial login. However, if you are asked to enter a password, there may be a problem. First, try using a password equivalent to the username; that is, if you are logging in as `root`, use "`root`" as the password.

If you simply can't login, there may be a problem. First, consult your distribution's documentation; the username and password to use may be buried in there somewhere. The username and password may have been given to you during the installation procedure, or they may be printed on the login banner.

One cause of this may be a problem with installing the Linux login and initialization files. If this is the case, you may need to reinstall (at least parts of) the Linux software, or boot your installation media and attempt to fix the problem by hand—see Chapter 4 for hints.

2.5.4.4 Problems using the system

If login is successful, you should be presented with a shell prompt (such as "#" or "$") and can happily roam around your system. However, there are some initial problems with using the system that sometimes creep up.

The most common initial configuration problem is incorrect file or directory permissions. This can cause the error message

```
Shell-init: permission denied
```

to be printed after logging in (in fact, any time you see the message "permission denied" you can be fairly certain that it is a problem with file permissions).

In many cases, it's a simple matter of using the chmod command to fix the permissions of the appropriate files or directories. For example, some distributions of Linux once used the (incorrect) file mode 0644 for the root directory (/). The fix was to issue the command

> # *chmod 755 /*

as root. However, in order to issue this command, you needed to boot from the installation media and mount your Linux root filesystem by hand—a hairy task for most newcomers.

As you use the system, you may run into places where file and directory permissions are incorrect, or software does not work as configured. Welcome to the world of Linux! While most distributions are quite trouble-free, very few of them are perfect. We don't want to cover all of those problems here. Instead, throughout the book we help you to solve many of these configuration problems by teaching you how to find them and fix them yourself. In Chapter 1 we discussed this philosophy in some detail. In Chapter 4, we give hints for fixing many of these common configuration problems.

Chapter 3

Linux Tutorial

3.1 Introduction

New users of UNIX and Linux may be a bit intimidated by the size and apparent complexity of the system before them. There are many good books on using UNIX out there, for all levels of expertise from novice to expert. However, none of these books covers, specifically, an introduction to using Linux. While 95% of using Linux is exactly like using other UNIX systems, the most straightforward way to get going on your new system is with a tutorial tailored for Linux. Herein is such a tutorial.

This chapter does not go into a large amount of detail or cover many advanced topics. Instead, it is intended to get the new Linux user running, on both feet, so that he or she may then read a more general book about UNIX and understand the basic differences between other UNIX systems and Linux.

Very little is assumed here, except perhaps some familiarity with personal computer systems, and MS-DOS. However, even if you're not an MS-DOS user, you should be able to understand everything here. At first glance, UNIX looks a lot like MS-DOS (after all, parts of MS-DOS were modeled on the CP/M operating system, which in turn was modeled on UNIX). However, only the very superficial features of UNIX resemble MS-DOS in any way. Even if you're completely new to the PC world, this tutorial should be of help.

And, before we begin: *Don't be afraid to experiment.* The system won't bite you. You can't destroy anything by working on the system. UNIX has some amount of security built in, to prevent "normal" users (the role which you will now assume) from damaging files which are essential to the system. Even so, the absolute worst thing that can happen is that you'll delete all of your files—and you'll have to go back and re-install the system. So, at this point, you have nothing to lose.

3.2 Basic UNIX Concepts

UNIX is a multitasking, multiuser operating system. This means that there can be many people using one computer at the same time, running many different applications. (This differs from MS-DOS, where only one person can use the system at any one time.) Under UNIX, for users to identify themselves to the system, they must **log in**, which entails two steps: Entering your **login name** (the name which the system identifies you as), and entering your **password**, which is your personal secret key to logging into your account. Because only you know your password, no one else can login to the system under your username.

On traditional UNIX systems, the system administrator will assign you a username and an initial password when you are given an account on the system. However, because you are the system administrator, you must set up your own account before you can login—see Section 3.2.1, below. For the following discussions, we'll use the imaginary username "larry".

In addition, each UNIX system has a **hostname** assigned to it. It is this hostname that gives your machine a name, gives it character and charm. The hostname is used to identify individual machines on a network, but even if your machine isn't networked, it should have a hostname. In Section 4.10.2 we'll cover setting your system's hostname. For our examples, below, the system's hostname is "mousehouse".

3.2.1   Creating an account

Before you can use the system, you must set up a user account for yourself. This is because it's usually not a good idea to use the root account for normal use. The root account should be reserved for running privileged commands and for maintaining the system, as discussed in Section 4.1.

In order to create an account for yourself, you need to login as root and use the useradd or adduser command. See Section 4.4 for information on this procedure.

3.2.2   Logging in

At login time, you'll see a prompt resembling the following on your screen:

```
mousehouse login:
```

Here, enter your username, and press the `Return` key. Our hero, larry, would type the following:

```
mousehouse login:  larry
Password:
```

Now, enter your password. It won't be echoed to the screen when you login, so type carefully. If you mistype your password, you'll see the message

```
Login incorrect
```

and you'll have to try again.

Once you have correctly entered the username and password, you are officially logged into the system, and are free to roam.

3.2.3   Virtual consoles

The system's **console** is the monitor and keyboard connected directly to the system. (Because UNIX is a multiuser operating system, you may have other terminals connected to serial ports on your system, but these would not be the console.) Linux, like some other versions of UNIX, provides access to **virtual consoles** (or VC's), which allow you to have more than one login session from your console at a time.

To demonstrate this, login to your system (as demonstrated above). Now, press `alt-F2`. You should see the login: prompt again. You're looking at the second virtual console—you logged into the first. To switch back to the first VC, press `alt-F1`. *Voila!* You're back to your first login session.

A newly-installed Linux system probably allows you to access the first four VC's, using `alt-F1` through `alt-F4`. However, it is possible to enable up to 12 VC's—one for each function key on your keyboard. As you can see, use of VC's can be very powerful—you can be working on several different VC's at once.

While the use of VC's is somewhat limiting (after all, you can only be looking at one VC at a time), it should give you a feel for UNIX's multiuser capabilities. While you're working on VC #1, you can switch over to VC #2 and start working on something else.

3.2.4   Shells and commands

For most of your explorations in the world of UNIX, you'll be talking to the system through the use of a **shell**. A shell is just a program which takes user input (e.g., commands which you type) and translates them into instructions. This can be compared to the COMMAND.COM program under MS-DOS, which does essentially the same thing. The shell is just one interface to UNIX. There are many possible interfaces—such as the X Window System, which lets you run commands by using the mouse and keyboard in conjunction.

As soon as you login, the system starts the shell, and you can type commands to it. Here's a quick example. Here, Larry logs in, and is left sitting at the shell **prompt**.

```
mousehouse login:   larry
Password:   larry's password
Welcome to Mousehouse!

/home/larry#
```

"/home/larry#" is the shell's prompt, indicating that it's ready to take commands. (More on what the prompt itself means later.) Let's try telling the system to do something interesting:

```
/home/larry# make love
make:   *** No way to make target 'love'.   Stop.
/home/larry#
```

Well, as it turns out make was the name of an actual program on the system, and the shell executed this program when given the command. (Unfortunately, the system was being unfriendly.)

This brings us to one burning question: What are commands? What happens when you type "make love"? The first word on the command line, "make", is the name of the command to be executed. Everything else on the command line is taken as arguments to this command. Examples:

```
/home/larry# cp foo bar
```

Here, the name of the command is "cp", and the arguments are "foo" and "bar".

When you type a command, the shell does several things. First of all, it looks at the command name, and checks to see if it is a command which is internal to the shell. (That is, a command which the shell knows how to execute itself. There are a number of these commands, and we'll go into them later.) The shell also checks to see if the command is an alias, or substitute name, for another command. If neither of these conditions apply, the shell looks for a program, on the disk, with the command's name. If it finds such a program, the shell runs it, giving the program the arguments specified on the command line.

In our example, the shell looks for the program called make, and runs it with the argument love. Make is a program often used to compile large programs, and it takes as arguments the name of a "target" to compile. In the case of "make love", we instructed make to compile the target love. Because make can't find a target by this name, it fails with a humorous error message, and we are returned to the shell prompt.

What happens if we type a command to a shell, and the shell can't find a program with the command name to run? Well, we can try it:

```
/home/larry# eat dirt
eat:  command not found
/home/larry#
```

Quite simply, if the shell can't find a program with the name given on the command line (here, "eat"), it prints an error message which should be self-explanatory. You'll often see this error message if you mistype a command (for example, if you had typed "mkae love" instead of "make love").

3.2.5 Logging out

Before we delve much further, we should tell you how to log out of the system. At the shell prompt, use the command

```
/home/larry# exit
```

to logout. There are other ways of logging out as well, but this is the most foolproof one.

3.2.6 Changing your password

You should also be aware of how to change your password. The command passwd will prompt you for your old password, and your new password. It will ask you to reenter the new password for validation. Be careful not to forget your password—if you do, you will have to ask the system administrator to reset it for you. (If you're the system administrator, see Section 4.4.)

3.2.7 Files and directories

Under most operating systems (UNIX included), there is the concept of a **file**, which is just a bundle of information which is given a name (called a **filename**). Examples of files would be your history term paper, an e-mail message, or an actual program which can be executed. Essentially, anything which is saved on disk is saved in an individual file.

Files are identified by their filenames. For example, the file containing your history paper might be saved with the filename history-paper. These names usually identify the file and its contents in some form which is meaningful to you. There is no standard format for filenames as there is under MS-DOS and other operating systems; in general, filenames may contain any character (except /—see the discussion of pathnames, below), and are limited to 256 characters in length.

With the concept of files comes the concept of directories. A **directory** is just a collection of files. It can be thought of as a "folder" which contains many different files. Directories themselves are given names, with which you can identify them. Furthermore, directories are maintained in a tree-like structure; that is, directories may contain other directories.

A file may be referred to by its **pathname**, which is made up of the filename, preceded by the name of the directory which contains the file. For example, let's say that Larry has a directory called papers, which contains three files: history-final, english-lit, and masters-thesis. (Each of these three files contains information for three of Larry's ongoing projects.) To refer to the file `english-lit`, Larry can specify the file's pathname:

    `papers/english-lit`

As you can see, the directory and file names are separated by a single slash (`/`). For this reason, filenames themselves cannot contain the `/` character. MS-DOS users will find this convention familiar, although in the MS-DOS world, the backslash (`\`) is used instead.

As mentioned, directories can be nested within each other as well. For example, let's say that Larry has another directory, within `papers`, called `notes`. This directory contains the files `math-notes` and `cheat-sheet`. The pathname of the file `cheat-sheet` would be

    `papers/notes/cheat-sheet`

Therefore, the pathname really is a "path" which you take to locate a certain file. The directory above a given subdirectory is known as the **parent directory**. Here, the directory `papers` is the parent of the `notes` directory.

3.2.8   The directory tree

Most UNIX systems have a standard layout for files, so that system resources and programs can be easily located. This layout forms a directory tree, which starts at the "`/`" directory, also known as "the root directory". Directly underneath `/` are some important subdirectories: `/bin`, `/etc`, `/dev`, and `/usr`, among others. These directories in turn contain other directories which contain system configuration files, programs, and so on.

In particular, each user has a **home directory**, which is the directory set aside for that user to store his or her files. In the examples above, all of Larry's files (such as `cheat-sheet` and `history-final`) were contained in Larry's home directory. Usually, user home directories are contained under `/home`, and are named for the user who owns that directory. Therefore, Larry's home directory is `/home/larry`.

In Figure 3.2.8 a sample directory tree is represented. It should give you some idea of how the directory tree on your system is organized.

3.2.9   The current working directory

At any given time, commands that you type to the shell are given in terms of your **current working directory**. You can think of your working directory as the directory in which you are currently "located". When you first login, your working directory is set to your home directory—`/home/larry` in our case. Whenever you reference a file, you may refer to it in relationship to your current working directory, instead of specifying the full pathname of the file.

Here's an example. Larry has the directory `papers`, and `papers` contains the file `history-final`. If Larry wants to look at this file, he can use the command

    `/home/larry#` *more /home/larry/papers/history-final*

The `more` command simply displays a file, one screen at a time. However, because Larry's current working directory is `/home/larry`, he can instead refer to the file *relative* to his current location. The command would be

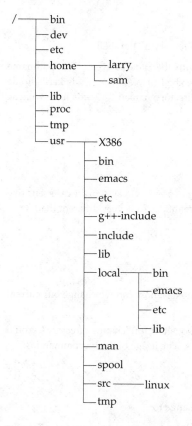

Figure 3.1: A typical (abridged) Unix directory tree.

`/home/larry#` *more papers/history-final*

Therefore, if you begin a filename (such as `papers/final`) with a character other than "/", the system assumes that you're referring to the file in terms relative to your current working directory. This is known as a **relative pathname**.

On the other hand, if you begin a filename with a "/", the system interprets this as a full pathname—that is, a pathname including the entire path to the file, starting from the root directory, `/`. This is known as an **absolute pathname**.

3.2.10   Referring to home directories

Under both `tcsh` and `bash`,[1] your home directory can be referred to using the tilde character ("~"). For example, the command

`/home/larry#` *more ~/papers/history-final*

is equivalent to

---

[1] `tcsh` and `bash` are two *shells* running under Linux. The shell is the program which reads user commands and executes them; most Linux systems enable either `tcsh` or `bash` for new user accounts.

```
/home/larry# more /home/larry/papers/history-final
```

The "~" character is simply replaced with the name of your home directory by the shell.

In addition, you can specify other user's home directories with the tilde as well. The pathname "~karl/letters" translates to "/home/karl/letters" by the shell (if /home/karl is karl's home directory). The use of the tilde is simply a shortcut; there is no directory named "~"—it's just syntactic sugar provided by the shell.

3.3   First Steps into UNIX

Before we begin, it is important to note that all file and command names on a UNIX system are case-sensitive (unlike operating systems such as MS-DOS). For example, the command make is very different than Make or MAKE. The same hold for file and directory names.

3.3.1   Moving around

Now that we can login, and know how to refer to files using pathnames, how can we change our current working directory, to make life easier?

The command for moving around in the directory structure is cd, short for "change directory". You'll notice that many often-used Unix commands are two or three letters. The usage of the cd command is:

   cd ⟨**directory**⟩

where ⟨**directory**⟩ is the name of the directory which you wish to change to.

As we said, when you login, you begin in your home directory. If Larry wanted to move down into the papers subdirectory, he'd use the command

```
/home/larry# cd papers
/home/larry/papers#
```

As you can see, Larry's prompt changes to reflect his current working directory (so he knows where he is). Now that he's in the papers directory, he can look at his history final with the command

```
/home/larry/papers# more history-final
```

Now, Larry is stuck in the papers subdirectory. To move back up to the parent directory, use the command

```
/home/larry/papers# cd ..
/home/larry#
```

(Note the space between the "cd" and the "..".) Every directory has an entry named ".." which refers to the parent directory. Similarly, every directory has an entry named "." which refers to itself. Therefore, the command

```
/home/larry/papers# cd .
```

gets us nowhere.

You can also use absolute pathnames in the cd command. To cd into Karl's home directory, we can use the command

```
/home/larry/papers# cd /home/karl
/home/karl#
```

Also, using cd with no argument will return you to your own home directory.

```
/home/karl# cd
/home/larry#
```

3.3.2 Looking at the contents of directories

Now that you know how to move around directories you probably think, "So what?" The basic skill of moving around directories is fairly useless, so let's introduce a new command, ls. ls prints a listing of files and directories, by default from your current directory. For example:

```
/home/larry# ls
Mail
letters
papers
/home/larry#
```

Here we can see that Larry has three entries in his current directory: Mail, letters, and papers. This doesn't tell us much—are these directories or files? We can use the -F option on the ls command to tell us more.

```
/home/larry# ls -F
Mail/
letters/
papers/
/home/larry#
```

From the / appended to each filename, we know that these three entries are in fact subdirectories.

Using ls -F may also append "*" to the end of a filename. This indicates that the file is an **executable**, or a program which can be run. If nothing is appended to the filename using ls -F, the file is a "plain old file", that is, it's neither a directory, or an executable.

In general, each UNIX command may take a number of options in addition to other arguments. These options usually begin with a "-", as demonstrated above with ls -F. The -F option tells ls to give more information about the type of the files involved—in this case, printing a / after each directory name.

If you give ls a directory name, it will print the contents of that directory.

```
/home/larry# ls -F papers
english-lit
history-final
masters-thesis
notes/
/home/larry#
```

Or, for a more interesting listing, let's see what's in the system's /etc directory.

```
/home/larry#  ls /etc

Images          ftpusers        lpc             rc.new          shells
adm             getty           magic           rc0.d           startcons
bcheckrc        gettydefs       motd            rc1.d           swapoff
brc             group           mount           rc2.d           swapon
brc~            inet            mtab            rc3.d           syslog.conf
csh.cshrc       init            mtools          rc4.d           syslog.pid
csh.login       init.d          pac             rc5.d           syslogd.reload
default         initrunlvl      passwd          rmt             termcap
disktab         inittab         printcap        rpc             umount
fdprm           inittab.old     profile         rpcinfo         update
fstab           issue           psdatabase      securetty       utmp
ftpaccess       lilo            rc              services        wtmp
/home/larry#
```

(For those MS-DOS users out there, notice how the filenames can be longer than 8 characters, and can contain periods in any position. It is even possible to have more than one period in a filename.)

Let's cd up to the top of the directory tree, using "cd ..", and then down to another directory: /usr/bin.

```
/home/larry#  cd ..
/home#  cd ..
/#  cd usr
/usr#  cd bin
/usr/bin#
```

You can also move into directories in multiple steps, as in cd /usr/bin.

Try moving around various directories, using ls and cd. In some cases, you may run into a foreboding "Permission denied" error message. This is simply the concept of UNIX security kicking in: in order to ls or to cd into a directory, you must have permission to do so. We'll talk more about this in Section 3.9.

3.3.3   Creating new directories

It's time to learn how to create directories. This involves the use of the mkdir command. Try the following:

```
/home/larry#  mkdir foo
/home/larry#  ls -F
Mail/
foo/
letters/
papers/
/home/larry#  cd foo
/home/larry/foo#  ls
/home/larry/foo#
```

Congrats! You've just made a new directory and moved into it. Since there aren't any files in this new directory, let's learn how to copy files from one place to another.

3.3.4 Copying files

Copying files is done with the command `cp`:

```
/home/larry/foo# cp /etc/termcap .
/home/larry/foo# cp /etc/shells .
/home/larry/foo# ls –F
shells      termcap
/home/larry/foo# cp shells bells
/home/larry/foo# ls –F
bells      shells      termcap
/home/larry/foo#
```

The `cp` command copies the files listed on the command line to the file or directory given as the last argument. Notice how we use the directory "`.`" to refer to the current directory.

3.3.5 Moving files

A new command named `mv` moves files, instead of copying them. The syntax is very straightforward.

```
/home/larry/foo# mv termcap sells
/home/larry/foo# ls -F
bells      sells      shells
/home/larry/foo#
```

Notice how `termcap` no longer exists, but in its place is the file `sells`. This can be used to rename files, as we have just done, but also to move a file to a completely new directory.

◇ **Note:** `mv` and `cp` will overwrite the destination file (if it already exists) without asking you. Be careful when you move a file into another directory: there may already be a file with the same name in that directory, which you'll overwrite!

3.3.6 Deleting files and directories

You now have an ugly rhyme developing with the use of the `ls` command. To delete a file, use the `rm` command. ("`rm`" stands for "remove").

```
/home/larry/foo# rm bells sells
/home/larry/foo# ls -F
shells
/home/larry/foo#
```

We're left with nothing but shells, but we won't complain. Note that `rm` by default won't prompt you before deleting a file—so be careful.

A related command to `rm` is `rmdir`. This command deletes a directory, but only if the directory is empty. If the directory contains any files or subdirectories, `rmdir` will complain.

3.3.7   Looking at files

The commands `more` and `cat` are used for viewing the contents of files. `more` displays a file, one screenful at a time, while `cat` displays the whole file at once.

To look at the file `shells`, we can use the command

> /home/larry/foo# *more shells*

In case you're interested what `shells` contains, it's a list of valid shell programs on your system. On most systems, this includes `/bin/sh`, `/bin/bash`, and `/bin/csh`. We'll talk about these different types of shells later.

While using `more`, press ⎡Space⎤ to display the next page of text, and ⎡b⎤ to display the previous page. There are other commands available in `more` as well, these are just the basics. Pressing ⎡q⎤ will quit `more`.

Quit `more` and try `cat /etc/termcap`. The text will probably fly by much too quickly for you to read it. The name "cat" actually stands for "concatenate", which is the real use of the program. The `cat` command can be used to concatenate the contents of several files and save the result to another file. This will be discussed later.

3.3.8   Getting online help

Almost every UNIX system, Linux included, provides a facility known as "manual pages", or "man pages" for short. These man pages contain online documentation for all of the various system commands, resources, configuration files, and so on.

The command used to access man pages is `man`. For example, if you're interested in finding out about the other options of the `ls` command, you can type

> /home/larry# *man ls*

and the man page for `ls` will be displayed.

Unfortunately, most of the man pages out there are written for those who already have some idea of what the command or resource does. For this reason, man pages usually only contain the hardcore technical details of the command, without a lot of tutorial. However, man pages can be an invaluable resource for jogging your memory if you forget the syntax of a command. Man pages will also tell you a lot about the commands which we won't tell you in this book.

I suggest that you try `man` for the commands we've already gone over, and whenever I introduce a new command. You'll notice some of these commands won't have man pages. This could be for several reasons. For one, the man pages haven't been written yet (the Linux Documentation Project is responsible for man pages under Linux as well. We are gradually accumulating most of the man pages available for the system). Secondly, the the command might be an internal shell command, or an alias (as discussed in Section 3.2.4), in which case it would not have a man page of its own. One example is `cd`, which is a shell internal command. The shell actually processes the `cd`—there is no separate program which contains this command.

3.4   Summary of Basic Commands

This section introduces some of the most useful basic commands on a UNIX system, including those covered in the last section.

Note that options usually begin with a "-", and in most cases multiple one-letter options may be combined using a single "-". For example, instead of using the command `ls -l -F`, it is adequate to use `ls -lF`.

Instead of listing all of the options available for each of these commands, we'll only talk about those which are useful or important at this time. In fact, most of these commands have a large number of options (most of which you'll never use). You can use `man` to see the manual pages for each command, which list all of the available options.

Also note that many of these commands take a list of files or directories as arguments, denoted by "⟨file1⟩ ... ⟨fileN⟩". For example, the `cp` command takes as arguments a list of files to copy, followed by the destination file or directory. When copying more than one file, the destination must be a directory.

`cd`	Change the current working directory.

`cd`   Change the current working directory.
Syntax: `cd` ⟨**directory**⟩
⟨**directory**⟩ is the directory to change to. ("`.`" refers to the current directory, "`..`" the parent directory.)
Example: `cd ../foo` sets the current directory to `../foo`.

`ls`   Displays information about the named files and directories.
Syntax: `ls` ⟨**file1**⟩ ⟨**file2**⟩ ... ⟨**fileN**⟩
Where ⟨**file1**⟩ through ⟨**fileN**⟩ are the filenames or directories to list. Options: There are more options than you want to think about. The most commonly used are `-F` (used to display some information about the type of the file), and `-l` (gives a "long" listing including file size, owner, permissions, and so on. This will be covered in detail later.)
Example: `ls -lF /home/larry` will display the contents of the directory `/home/larry`.

`cp`   Copies file(s) to another file or directory.
Syntax: `cp` ⟨**file1**⟩ ⟨**file2**⟩ ... ⟨**fileN**⟩ ⟨**destination**⟩
Where ⟨**file1**⟩ through ⟨**fileN**⟩ are the files to copy, and ⟨**destination**⟩ is the destination file or directory.
Example: `cp ../frog joe` copies the file `../frog` to the file or directory `joe`.

`mv`   Moves file(s) to another file or directory. This command does the equivalent of a copy followed by the deletion of the original. This can be used to rename files, as in the MS-DOS command `RENAME`.
Syntax: `mv` ⟨**file1**⟩ ⟨**file2**⟩ ... ⟨**fileN**⟩ ⟨**destination**⟩
Where ⟨**file1**⟩ through ⟨**fileN**⟩ are the files to move, and ⟨**destination**⟩ is the destination file or directory.
Example: `mv ../frog joe` moves the file `../frog` to the file or directory `joe`.

`rm`   Deletes files. Note that when files are deleted under UNIX, they are unrecoverable (unlike MS-DOS, where you can usually "undelete" the file).
Syntax: `rm` ⟨**file1**⟩ ⟨**file2**⟩ ... ⟨**fileN**⟩
Where ⟨**file1**⟩ through ⟨**fileN**⟩ are the filenames to delete.
Options: `-i` will prompt for confirmation before deleting the file.
Example: `rm -i /home/larry/joe /home/larry/frog` deletes the files `joe` and `frog` in `/home/larry`.

`mkdir`   Creates new directories.
Syntax: `mkdir` ⟨**dir1**⟩ ⟨**dir2**⟩ ... ⟨**dirN**⟩
Where ⟨**dir1**⟩ through ⟨**dirN**⟩ are the directories to create.

Example: `mkdir /home/larry/test` creates the directory `test` under `/home/larry`.

`rmdir`   This command deletes empty directories. When using `rmdir`, your current working directory must not be within the directory to be deleted.
Syntax: `rmdir` ⟨**dir1**⟩ ⟨**dir2**⟩ ...⟨**dirN**⟩
Where ⟨**dir1**⟩ through ⟨**dirN**⟩ are the directories to delete.
Example: `rmdir /home/larry/papers` deletes the directory `/home/larry/papers`, if it is empty.

`man`   Displays the manual page for the given command or resource (that is, any system utility which isn't a command, such as a library function.) Syntax: `man` ⟨**command**⟩
Where ⟨**command**⟩ is the name of the command or resource to get help on.
Example: `man ls` gives help on the `ls` command.

`more`   Displays the contents of the named files, one screenful at a time.
Syntax: `more` ⟨**file1**⟩ ⟨**file2**⟩ ...⟨**fileN**⟩
Where ⟨**file1**⟩ through ⟨**fileN**⟩ are the files to display.
Example: `more papers/history-final` displays the file `papers/history-final`.

`cat`   Officially used to concatenate files, `cat` is also used to display the entire contents of a file at once.
Syntax: `cat` ⟨**file1**⟩ ⟨**file2**⟩ ...⟨**fileN**⟩
Where ⟨**file1**⟩ through ⟨**fileN**⟩ are the files to display.
Example: `cat letters/from-mdw` displays the file `letters/from-mdw`.

`echo`   Simply echoes the given arguments.
Syntax: `echo` ⟨**arg1**⟩ ⟨**arg2**⟩ ...⟨**argN**⟩
Where ⟨**arg1**⟩ through ⟨**argN**⟩ are the arguments to echo.
Example: `echo "Hello world"` displays the string "Hello world".

`grep`   Display all of the lines in the named file(s) matching the given pattern.
Syntax: `grep` ⟨**pattern**⟩ ⟨**file1**⟩ ⟨**file2**⟩ ...⟨**fileN**⟩
Where ⟨**pattern**⟩ is a regular expression pattern, and ⟨**file1**⟩ through ⟨**fileN**⟩ are the files to search.
Example: `grep loomer /etc/hosts` will display all lines in the file `/etc/hosts` which contain the pattern "`loomer`".

3.5   Exploring the File System

The **file system** is the collection of files and the hierarchy of directories on your system. I promised before to escort you around the filesystem and the time has come.

You have the skills and the knowledge to make sense out of what I'm saying, and you have a roadmap. (Refer to Figure 3.2.8 on page 83).

First, change to the root directory (`cd /`), and do an `ls -F`. You'll probably see these directories[2]: `bin`, `dev`, `etc`, `home`, `install`, `lib`, `mnt`, `proc`, `root`, `tmp`, `user`, `usr`, and `var`.

Let's take a look at each of these directories.

---

[2]You may see others, and you might not see all of them. Don't worry. Every release of Linux differs in some respects.

/bin   /bin is short for "binaries", or executables. This is where many essential system programs reside. Use the command "ls -F /bin" to list the files here. If you look down the list you may see a few commands that you recognize, such as cp, ls, and mv. These are the actual programs for these commands. When you use the cp command, you're running the program /bin/cp.

Using ls -F, you'll see that most (if not all) of the files in /bin have an asterisk ("*") appended to their filenames. This indicates that the files are executables, as described in Section 3.3.2.

/dev   Next on our stop is /dev. Take a look, again with ls -F.

The "files" in /dev are known as **device drivers**—they are used to access system devices and resources, such as disk drives, modems, memory, and so on. For example, just as you can read data from a file, you can read input from the mouse by accessing /dev/mouse.

The filenames beginning with fd are floppy disk devices. fd0 is the first floppy disk drive, fd1 the second. Now, the astute among you will notice that there are more floppy disk devices then just the two I've listed above: they represent specific types of floppy disks. For example, fd1H1440 will access high-density, 3.5" diskettes in drive 1.

Here is a list of some of the most commonly used device files. Note that even though you may not have some of the devices listed below, the chances are that you'll have entries in /dev for them anyway.

- /dev/console refers to the system's console—that is, the monitor connected directly to your system.

- The various /dev/ttyS and /dev/cua devices are used for accessing serial ports. For example, /dev/ttyS0 refers to "COM1" under MS-DOS. The /dev/cua devices are "callout" devices, which are used in conjunction with a modem.

- The device names beginning with hd access hard drives. /dev/hda refers to the *whole* first hard disk, while hda1 refers to the first *partition* on /dev/hda.

- The device names beginning with sd are SCSI drives. If you have a SCSI hard drive, instead of accessing it through /dev/hda, you would access /dev/sda. SCSI tapes are accessed via st devices, and SCSI CD-ROM via sr devices.

- The device names beginning with lp access parallel ports. /dev/lp0 refers to "LPT1" in the MS-DOS world.

- /dev/null is used as a "black hole"—any data sent to this device is gone forever. Why is this useful? Well, if you wanted to suppress the output of a command appearing on your screen, you could send that output to /dev/null. We'll talk more about this later.

- The device names beginning with /dev/tty refer to the "virtual consoles" on your system (accessed via by pressing alt-F1 , alt-F2 , and so on). /dev/tty1 refers to the first VC, /dev/tty2 refers to the second, and so on.

- The device names beginning with /dev/pty are "pseudo-terminals". They are used to provide a "terminal" to remote login sessions. For example, if your machine is on a network, incoming telnet logins would use one of the /dev/pty devices.

/etc   /etc contains a number of miscellaneous system configuration files. These include /etc/passwd (the user database), /etc/rc (the system initialization script), and so on.

/sbin   sbin is used for storing essential system binaries, to be used by the system administrator.

/home   /home contains user's home directories. For example, /home/larry is the home directory
               for the user "larry". On a newly-installed system, there may not be any users in this
               directory.

/lib   /lib contains **shared library images**. These files contain code which many programs share
               in common. Instead of each program containing its own copy of these shared routines, they
               are all stored in one common place, in /lib. This makes executable files smaller, and saves
               space on your system.

/proc   /proc is a "virtual filesystem", the files in which are stored in memory, not on the drive.
               They refer to the various **processes** running on the system, and allow you to get information
               about what programs and processes are running at any given time. We'll go into more detail
               in Section 3.11.1.

/tmp   Many programs have a need to generate some information and store it in a temporary file.
               The canonical location for these files is in /tmp.

/usr   /usr is a very important directory. It contains a number of subdirectories which in turn
               contain some of the most important and useful programs and configuration files used on
               the system.

               The various directories described above are essential for the system to operate, but most of
               the things found in /usr are optional for the system. However, it is those optional things
               which make the system useful and interesting. Without /usr, you'd more or less have
               a boring system, only with programs like cp and ls. /usr contains most of the larger
               software packages and the configuration files which accompany them.

/usr/X386   /usr/X386 contains The X Window System, if you installed it. The X Window System is a
               large, powerful graphical environment which provides a large number of graphical utilities
               and programs, displayed in "windows" on your screen. If you're at all familiar with the
               Microsoft Windows or Macintosh environments, X Windows will look very familiar. The
               /usr/X386 directory contains all of the X Windows executables, configuration files, and
               support files. This will be covered in more detail in Section 5.1.

/usr/bin   /usr/bin is the real warehouse for software on any UNIX system. It contains most of the
               executables for programs not found in other places, such as /bin.

/usr/etc   Just as /etc contained miscellaneous system programs and configuration files, /usr/etc
               contains even more of these utilities and files. In general, the files found in /usr/etc are
               not essential to the system, unlike those found in /etc, which are.

/usr/include
               /usr/include contains **include files** for the C compiler. These files (most of which end
               in .h, for "header") declare data structure names, subroutines, and constants used when
               writing programs in C. Those files found in /usr/include/sys are generally used when
               programming on the UNIX system level. If you are familiar with the C programming
               language, here you'll find header files such as stdio.h, which declares functions such as
               printf().

/usr/g++-include
               /usr/g++-include contains include files for the C++ compiler (much like

/usr/include).

/usr/lib /usr/lib contains the "stub" and "static" library equivalents to the files found in /lib. When compiling a program, the program is "linked" with the libraries found in /usr/lib, which then directs the program to look in /lib when it needs the actual code in the library. In addition, various other programs store configuration files in /usr/lib.

/usr/local /usr/local is a lot like /usr—it contains various programs and files not essential to the system, but which make the system fun and exciting. In general, those programs found in /usr/local are specialized for your system specifically—that is, /usr/local differs greatly between UNIX systems.

Here, you'll find large software packages such as TEX (a document formatting system) and Emacs (a large and powerful editor), if you installed them.

/usr/man This directory contains the actual man pages. There are two subdirectories for every man page "section" (use the command man man for details). For example, /usr/man/man1 contains the source (that is, the unformatted original) for man pages in section 1, and /usr/man/cat1 contains the formatted man pages for section 1.

/usr/src /usr/src contains the source code (the uncompiled program) for various programs on your system. The most important thing here is /usr/src/linux, which contains the source code for the Linux kernel.

/var /var holds directories that often change in size or tend to grow. Many of those directories used to reside in /usr, but since we are trying to keep it relatively unchangeable, the directories that change often have been moved to /var. Some of those directories are:

/var/adm /var/adm contains various files of interest to the system administrator, specifically system logs, which record any errors or problems with the system. Other files record logins to the system, as well as failed login attempts. This will be covered in Chapter 4.

/var/spool /var/spool contains files which are to be "spooled" to another program. For example, if your machine is connected to a network, incoming mail will be stored in /var/spool/mail, until you read it or delete it. Outgoing or incoming news articles may be found in /var/spool/news, and so on.

3.6 Types of shells

As I have mentioned too many times before, UNIX is a multitasking, multiuser operating system. Multitasking is *very* useful, and once you get used to it, you'll use it all of the time. Before long, you'll be able to run programs in the "background", switch between multiple tasks, and "pipeline" programs together to achieve complicated results with a single command.

Many of the features we'll be covering in this section are features provided by the shell itself. Be careful not to confuse UNIX (the actual operating system) with the shell—the shell is just an interface to the underlying system. The shell provides a great deal of functionality on top of UNIX itself.

The shell is not only an interpreter for your interactive commands, which you type at the prompt. It is also a powerful programming language, which allows you to write **shell scripts**, to "batch" several shell commands together in a file. MS-DOS users will recognize the similarity to "batch files". Use of shell scripts is a very powerful tool, which will allow you to automate and expand your usage of UNIX. See

Section 3.13.1 for more information.

There are several types of shells in the UNIX world. The two major types are the "Bourne shell" and the "C shell". The Bourne shell uses a command syntax like the original shell on early UNIX systems, such as System III. The name of the Bourne shell on most UNIX systems is /bin/sh (where sh stands for "shell"). The C shell (not to be confused with sea shell) uses a different syntax, somewhat like the programming language C, and on most UNIX systems is named /bin/csh.

Under Linux, there are several variations of these shells available. The two most commonly used are the Bourne Again Shell, or "Bash" (/bin/bash), and Tcsh (/bin/tcsh). Bash is a form of the Bourne shell with many of the advanced features found in the C shell. Because Bash supports a superset of the Bourne shell syntax, any shell scripts written in the standard Bourne shell should work with Bash. For those who prefer to use the C shell syntax, Linux supports Tcsh, which is an expanded version of the original C shell.

The type of shell that you decide to use is mostly a religious issue. Some folks prefer the Bourne shell syntax with the advanced features of Bash, and some prefer the more structured C shell syntax. As far as normal commands, such as cp and ls, are concerned, the type of shell you're using doesn't matter—the syntax is the same. Only when you start to write shell scripts or use some of the advanced features of the shell do the differences between shell types begin to matter.

As we're discussing some of the features of the shell, below, we'll note those differences between Bourne and C shells. However, for the purposes of this manual, most of those differences are minimal. (If you're really curious at this point, read the man pages for bash and tcsh).

3.7 Wildcards

A key feature of most Unix shells is the ability to reference more than one filename using special characters. These so-called **wildcards** allow you to refer to, say, all filenames which contain the character "n".

The wildcard "*" refers to any character or string of characters in a filename. For example, when you use the character "*" in a filename, the shell replaces it with all possible substitutions from filenames in the directory which you're referencing.

Here's a quick example. Let's suppose that Larry has the files frog, joe, and stuff in his current directory.

```
/home/larry# ls
frog      joe      stuff
/home/larry#
```

To access all files with the letter "o" in the filename, we can use the command

```
/home/larry# ls *o*
frog      joe
/home/larry#
```

As you can see, the use of the "*" wildcard was replaced with all substitutions which matched the wildcard from filenames in the current directory.

The use of "*" by itself simply matches all filenames, because all characters match the wildcard.

```
/home/larry# ls *
frog      joe      stuff
/home/larry#
```

Here are a few more examples.

```
/home/larry# ls f*
frog
/home/larry# ls *ff
stuff
/home/larry# ls *f*
frog        stuff
/home/larry# ls s*f
stuff
/home/larry#
```

The process of changing a "*" into filenames is called **wildcard expansion** and is done by the shell. This is important: the individual commands, such as ls, *never* see the "*" in their list of parameters. The shell expands the wildcard to include all of the filenames which match. So, the command

```
/home/larry# ls *o*
```

is expanded by the shell to actually be

```
/home/larry# ls frog joe
```

One important note about the "*" wildcard. Using this wildcard will *not* match filenames which begin with a single period ("."). These files are treated as "hidden" files—while they are not really hidden, they don't show up on normal ls listings, and aren't touched by the use of the "*" wildcard.

Here's an example. We already mentioned that each directory has two special entries in it: "." refers to the current directory, and ".." refers to the parent directory. However, when you use ls, these two entries don't show up.

```
/home/larry# ls
frog      joe      stuff
/home/larry#
```

If you use the -a switch with ls, however, you can display filenames which begin with ".". Observe:

```
/home/larry# ls -a
.         ..        .bash_profile    .bashrc     frog      joe      stuff
/home/larry#
```

Now we can see the two special entries, "." and "..", as well as two other "hidden" files—.bash_profile and .bashrc. These two files are startup files used by bash when larry logs in. More on them in Section 3.13.3.

Note that when we use the "*" wildcard, none of the filenames beginning with "." are displayed.

```
/home/larry# ls *
frog      joe      stuff
/home/larry#
```

This is a safety feature: if the "*" wildcard matched filenames beginning with ".", it would also match the directory names "." and "..". This can be dangerous when using certain commands.

Another wildcard is "?". The "?" wildcard will only expand a single character. Thus, "ls ?" will display all one character filenames, and "ls termca?" would display "termcap" but *not* "termcap.backup". Here's another example:

```
/home/larry# ls j?e
joe
/home/larry# ls f??g
frog
/home/larry# ls ????f
stuff
/home/larry#
```

As you can see, wildcards allow you to specify many files at one time. In the simple command summary, in Section 3.4, we said that the cp and mv commands actually can copy or move multiple files at one time. For example,

```
/home/larry# cp /etc/s* /home/larry
```

will copy all filenames in /etc beginning with "s" to the directory /home/larry. Therefore, the format of the cp command is really

cp ⟨file1⟩ ⟨file2⟩ ⟨file3⟩ ... ⟨fileN⟩ ⟨destination⟩

where ⟨file1⟩ through ⟨fileN⟩ is a list of filenames to copy, and ⟨destination⟩ is the destination file or directory to copy them to. mv has an identical syntax.

Note that if you are copying or moving more than one file, the ⟨destination⟩ must be a directory. You can only copy or move a *single* file to another file.

3.8 UNIX Plumbing

3.8.1 Standard input and output

Many UNIX commands get input from what is known as **standard input** and send their output to **standard output** (often abbreviated as "stdin" and "stdout"). Your shell sets things up so that standard input is your keyboard, and standard output is the screen.

Here's an example using the command cat. Normally, cat reads data from all of the filenames given on the command line and sends this data directly to stdout. Therefore, using the command

```
/home/larry/papers# cat history-final masters-thesis
```

will display the contents of the file history-final followed by masters-thesis.

However, if no filenames are given to cat as parameters, it instead reads data from stdin, and sends it back to stdout. Here's an example.

```
/home/larry/papers# cat
Hello there.
Hello there.
Bye.
```

```
Bye.
ctrl-D
/home/larry/papers#
```

As you can see, each line that the user types (displayed in italics) is immediately echoed back by the `cat` command. When reading from standard input, commands know that the input is "finished" when they receive an EOT (end-of-text) signal. In general, this is generated by pressing ctrl-D.

Here's another example. The command `sort` reads in lines of text (again, from stdin, unless files are given on the command line), and sends the sorted output to stdout. Try the following.

```
/home/larry/papers# sort
bananas
carrots
apples
ctrl-D
apples
bananas
carrots
/home/larry/papers#
```

Now we can alphabetize our shopping list... isn't UNIX useful?

3.8.2 Redirecting input and output

Now, let's say that we wanted to send the output of `sort` to a file, to save our shopping list elsewhere. The shell allows us to **redirect** standard output to a filename, using the ">" symbol. Here's how it works.

```
/home/larry/papers# sort > shopping-list
bananas
carrots
apples
ctrl-D
/home/larry/papers#
```

As you can see, the result of the `sort` command isn't displayed, instead it's saved to the file `shopping-list`. Let's look at this file.

```
/home/larry/papers# cat shopping-list
apples
bananas
carrots
/home/larry/papers#
```

Now we can sort our shopping list, and save it, too! But let's suppose that we were storing our unsorted, original shopping list in the file `items`. One way of sorting the information and saving it to a file would be to give `sort` the name of the file to read, in lieu of standard input, and redirect standard output as we did above. As so:

```
/home/larry/papers# sort items > shopping-list
/home/larry/papers# cat shopping-list
```

```
apples
bananas
carrots
/home/larry/papers#
```

However, there's another way of doing this. Not only can we redirect standard output, but we can redirect standard *input* as well, using the "<" symbol.

```
/home/larry/papers# sort < items
apples
bananas
carrots
/home/larry/papers#
```

Technically, `sort < items` is equivalent to `sort items`, but the former allows us to demonstrate the point: `sort < items` behaves as if the data in the file `items` was typed to standard input. The shell handles the redirection. `sort` wasn't given the name of the file (`items`) to read; as far as `sort` is concerned, it was still reading from standard input as if you had typed the data from your keyboard.

This introduces the concept of a **filter**. A filter is a program which reads data from standard input, processes it in some way, and sends the processed data to standard output. Using redirection, standard input and/or standard output can be referenced from files. `sort` is a simple filter: it sorts the incoming data and sends the result to standard output. `cat` is even simpler: it doesn't do anything with the incoming data, it simply outputs whatever was given to it.

3.8.3 Using pipes

We've already demonstrated how to use `sort` as a filter. However, these examples assumed that you had data in a file somewhere, or were willing to type the data to standard input yourself. What if the data you wanted to sort came from the output of another command, such as `ls`? For example, using the `-r` option with `sort` sorts the data in reverse-alphabetical order. If you wanted to list the files in your current directory in reverse order, one way to do it would be:

```
/home/larry/papers# ls
english-list
history-final
masters-thesis
notes
/home/larry/papers# ls > file-list
/home/larry/papers# sort -r file-list
notes
masters-thesis
history-final
english-list
/home/larry/papers#
```

Here, we saved the output of `ls` in a file, and then ran `sort  -r` on that file. But this is unwieldy and causes us to use a temporary file to save the data from `ls`.

The solution is to use **pipelining**. Pipelining is another feature of the shell which allows you to connect a string of commands in a "pipe", where the stdout of the first command is sent directly to the stdin of the second command, and so on. Here, we wish to send the stdout of ls to the stdin of sort. The "|" symbol is used to create a pipe:

```
/home/larry/papers# ls | sort -r
notes
masters-thesis
history-final
english-list
/home/larry/papers#
```

This command is much shorter, and obviously easier to type.

Another useful example—using the command

```
/home/larry/papers# ls /usr/bin
```

is going to display a long list a files, most of which will fly past the screen too quickly for you to read them. Instead, let's use more to display the list of files in /usr/bin.

```
/home/larry/papers# ls /usr/bin | more
```

Now you can page down the list of files at your own leisure.

But the fun doesn't stop here! We can pipe more than two commands together. The command head is a filter which displays the first lines from an input stream (here, input from a pipe). If we wanted to display the last filename in alphabetical order in the current directory, we can use:

```
/home/larry/papers# ls | sort -r | head -1
notes
/home/larry/papers#
```

where head -1 simply displays the first line of input that it receives (in this case, the stream of reverse-sorted data from ls).

3.8.4 Non-destructive redirection

Using ">" to redirect output to a file is destructive: in other words, the command

```
/home/larry/papers# ls > file-list
```

overwrites the contents of the file file-list. If, instead, you redirect with the symbol ">>", the output will be appended to the named file, instead of overwriting it.

```
/home/larry/papers# ls >> file-list
```

will append the output of the ls command to file-list.

Just keep in mind that redirection and using pipes are features provided by the shell—the shell provides this handy syntax using ">" and ">>" and "|". It has nothing to do with the commands themselves, but the shell.

3.9   File Permissions

3.9.1   Concepts of file permissions

Because there are multiple users on a UNIX system, in order to protect individual user's files from tampering by other users, UNIX provides a mechanism known as **file permissions**. This mechanism allows files and directories to be "owned" by a particular user. As an example, because Larry created the files in his home directory, Larry owns those files, and has access to them.

UNIX also allows files to be shared between users and groups of users. If Larry so desired, he could cut off access to his files, such that no other user could access them. However, on most systems the default is to allow other users to read your files, but not modify or delete them in any way.

As explained above, every file is owned by a particular user. However, files are also owned by a particular **group**, which is a system-defined group of users. Every user is placed into at least one group when that user is created. However, the system administrator may also grant the user access to more than one group.

Groups are usually defined by the type of users which access the machine. For example, on a university UNIX system, users may be placed into the groups student, staff, faculty or guest. There are also a few system-defined groups (such as bin and admin) which are used by the system itself to control access to resources—very rarely do actual users belong to these system groups.

Permissions fall into three main divisions: read, write, and execute. These permissions may be granted to three classes of users: the owner of the file, the group to which the file belongs, and to all users, regardless of group.

Read permission allows a user to read the contents of the file, or in the case of directories, to list the contents of the directory (using ls). Write permission allows the user to write to and modify the file. For directories, write permission allows the user to create new files or delete files within that directory. Finally, execute permission allows the user to run the file as a program or shell script (if the file happens to be a program or shell script, that is). For directories, having execute permission allows the user to cd into the directory in question.

3.9.2   Interpreting file permissions

Let's look at an example to demonstrate file permissions. Using the ls command with the -l option will display a "long" listing of the file, including file permissions.

```
/home/larry/foo# ls -l stuff

-rw-r--r--   1 larry     users          505 Mar 13 19:05 stuff

/home/larry/foo#
```

The first field printed in the listing represents the file permissions. The third field is the owner of the file (larry), and the fourth field is the group to which the file belongs (users). Obviously, the last field is the name of the file (stuff), and we'll cover the other fields later.

This file is owned by larry, and belongs to the group users. Let's look at the file permissions. The string -rw-r--r-- lists, in order, the permissions granted to the file's owner, the file's group, and everybody else.

The first character of the permissions string ("-") represents the type of file. A "-" just means that this is a regular file (as opposed to a directory or device driver). The next three letters ("rw-") represent the permissions granted to the file's owner, larry. The "r" stands for "read" and the "w" stands for "write". Thus, larry has read and write permission to the file stuff.

As we mentioned, besides read and write permission, there is also "execute" permission—represented by an "x". However, there is a "-" here in place of the "x", so Larry doesn't have execute permission on this file. This is fine, the file stuff isn't a program of any kind. Of course, because Larry owns the file, he may grant himself execute permission for the file if he so desires. This will be covered shortly.

The next three characters, r--, represent the group's permissions on the file. The group which owns this file is users. Because only an "r" appears here, any user which belongs to the group users may read this file.

The last three characters, also r--, represent the permissions granted to every other user on the system (other than the owner of the file and those in the group users). Again, because only an "r" is present, other users may read the file, but not write to it or execute it.

Here are some other examples of group permissions.

-rwxr-xr-x   The owner of the file may read, write, and execute the file. Users in the file's group, and all other users, may read and execute the file.

-rw-------   The owner of the file may read and write the file. No other user can access the file.

-rwxrwxrwx   All users may read, write, and execute the file.

3.9.3 Dependencies

It is important to note that the permissions granted to a file also depend on the permissions of the directory in which the file is located. For example, even if a file is set to -rwxrwxrwx, other users cannot access the file unless they have read and execute access to the directory in which the file is located. For example, if Larry wanted to restrict access to all of his files, he could simply set the permissions on his home directory /home/larry to -rwx------. In this way, no other user has access to his directory, and all files and directories within it. Larry doesn't need to worry about the individual permissions on each of his files.

In other words, to access a file at all, you must have execute access to all directories along the file's pathname, and read (or execute) access to the file itself.

Usually, users on a UNIX system are very open with their files. The usual set of permissions given to files is -rw-r--r--, which will allow other users to read the file, but not change it in any way. The usual set of permissions given to directories is -rwxr-xr-x, which will allow other users to look through your directories, but not create or delete files within them.

However, many users wish to keep other users out of their files. Setting the permissions of a file to -rw------- will not allow any other user to access the file. Likewise, setting the permissions of a directory to -rwx------ will keep other users out of the directory in question.

3.9.4 Changing permissions

The command chmod is used to set the permissions on a file. Only the owner of a file may change the permissions on that file. The syntax of chmod is:

chmod {a,u,g,o}{+,-}{r,w,x} (*filenames*)

Briefly, you supply one or more of **all**, **user**, **group**, or **other**. Then you specify whether you are adding rights (+) or taking them away (-). Finally, you specify one or more of read, write, and execute. Some examples of legal commands are:

```
chmod a+r stuff
```
> Gives all users read access to the file.

```
chmod +r stuff
```
> Same as above—if none of a, u, g, or o is specified, a is assumed.

```
chmod og-x stuff
```
> Remove execute permission from users other than the owner.

```
chmod u+rwx stuff
```
> Allow the owner of the file to read, write, and execute the file.

```
chmod o-rwx stuff
```
> Remove read, write, and execute permission from users other than the owner and users in the file's group.

3.10   Managing file links

Links allow you to give a single file multiple names. Files are actually identified to the system by their **inode number**, which is just the unique filesystem identifier for the file[3]. A directory is actually a listing of inode numbers with their corresponding filenames. Each filename in a directory is a **link** to a particular inode.

3.10.1   Hard links

The `ln` command is used to create multiple links for one file. For example, let's say that you have the file `foo` in a directory. Using `ls -i`, we can look at the inode number for this file.

```
# ls -i foo
22192 foo
#
```

Here, the file `foo` has an inode number of 22192 in the filesystem. We can create another link to `foo`, named `bar`:

```
# ln foo bar
```

With `ls -i`, we see that the two files have the same inode.

```
# ls -i foo bar
22192 bar    22192 foo
#
```

---

[3]The command `ls -i` will display file inode numbers.

Now, accessing either `foo` or `bar` will access the same file. If you make changes to `foo`, those changes will be made to `bar` as well. For all purposes, `foo` and `bar` are the same file.

These links are known as *hard links* because they directly create a link to an inode. Note that you can only hard-link files on the same filesystem; symbolic links (see below) don't have this restriction.

When you delete a file with `rm`, you are actually only deleting one link to a file. If you use the command

```
# rm foo
```

then only the link named `foo` is deleted; `bar` will still exist. A file is only actually deleted on the system when it has no links to it. Usually, files have only one link, so using the `rm` command deletes the file. However, if a file has multiple links to it, using `rm` will only delete a single link; in order to delete the file, you must delete all links to the file.

The command `ls -l` will display the number of links to a file (among other information).

```
# ls -l foo bar
-rw-r--r--   2 root     root          12 Aug  5 16:51 bar
-rw-r--r--   2 root     root          12 Aug  5 16:50 foo
#
```

The second column in the listing, "2", specifies the number of links to the file.

As it turns out, a directory is actually just a file containing information about link-to-inode translations. Also, every directory has at least two hard links in it: "`.`" (a link pointing to itself), and "`..`" (a link pointing to the parent directory). The root directory (`/`) "`..`" link just points back to `/`.

3.10.2 Symbolic links

Symbolic links are another type of link, which are somewhat different than hard links. A symbolic link allows you to give a file another name, but it doesn't link the file by inode.

The command `ln -s` will create a symbolic link to a file. For example, if we use the command

```
# ln -s foo bar
```

we will create the symbolic link `bar` pointing to the file `foo`. If we use `ls -i`, we will see that the two files have different inodes, indeed.

```
# ls -i foo bar
22195 bar   22192 foo
#
```

However, using `ls -l`, we see that the file `bar` is a symlink pointing to `foo`.

```
# ls -l foo bar
lrwxrwxrwx   1 root     root           3 Aug  5 16:51 bar -> foo
-rw-r--r--   1 root     root          12 Aug  5 16:50 foo
#
```

The permission bits on a symbolic link are not used (they always appear as `rwxrwxrwx`). Instead, the permissions on the symbolic link are determined by the permissions on the target of the symbolic link (in our example, the file `foo`).

Functionally, hard links and symbolic links are similar, but there are some differences. For one thing, you can create a symbolic link to a file which doesn't exist; the same is not true for hard links. Symbolic links are processed by the kernel differently than hard links are, which is just a technical difference but sometimes an important one. Symbolic links are helpful because they identify what file they point to; with hard links, there is no easy way to determine which files are linked to the same inode.

Links are used in many places on the Linux system. Symbolic links are especially important to the shared library images in /lib. See Section 4.7.2 for more information.

3.11 Job Control

3.11.1 Jobs and processes

Job control is a feature provided by many shells (Bash and Tcsh included) which allows you to control multiple running commands, or **jobs**, at once. Before we can delve much further, we need to talk about **processes**.

Every time you run a program, you start what is known as a *process*—which is just a fancy name for a running program. The command ps displays a list of currently running processes. Here's an example:

```
/home/larry# ps

 PID TT STAT  TIME COMMAND
  24  3 S     0:03 (bash)
 161  3 R     0:00 ps

/home/larry#
```

The PID listed in the first column is the **process ID**, a unique number given to every running process. The last column, COMMAND, is the name of the running command. Here, we're only looking at the processes which Larry is currently running[4]. These are bash (Larry's shell), and the ps command itself. As you can see, bash is running concurrently with the ps command. bash executed ps when Larry typed the command. After ps is finished running (after the table of processes is displayed), control is returned to the bash process, which displays the prompt, ready for another command.

A running process is known as a *job* to the shell. The terms *process* and *job* are interchangeable. However, a process is usually referred to as a "job" when used in conjunction with **job control**—a feature of the shell which allows you to switch between several independent jobs.

In most cases users are only running a single job at a time—that being whatever command they last typed to the shell. However, using job control, you can run several jobs at once, switching between them as needed. How might this be useful? Let's say that you're editing a text file and need to suddenly interrupt your editing and do something else. With job control, you can temporarily suspend the editor, and back at the shell prompt start to work on something else. When you're done, you can start the editor back up, and be back where you started, as if you never left the editor. This is just one example. There are many practical uses for job control.

3.11.2 Foreground and background

Jobs can either be in the **foreground** or in the **background**. There can only be one job in the foreground at any one time. The foreground job is the job which you interact with—it receives input from the keyboard

---
[4]There are many other processes running on the system as well—"ps -aux" lists them all.

and sends output to your screen. (Unless, of course, you have redirected input or output, as described in Section 3.8). On the other hand, jobs in the background do not receive input from the terminal—in general, they run along quietly without need for interaction.

Some jobs take a long time to finish, and don't do anything interesting while they are running. Compiling programs is one such job, as is compressing a large file. There's no reason why you should sit around being bored while these jobs complete their tasks; you can just run them in the background. While the jobs are running in the background, you are free to run other programs.

Jobs may also be **suspended**. A suspended job is a job that is not currently running, but is temporarily stopped. After you suspend a job, you can tell the job to continue, in the foreground or the background as needed. Resuming a suspended job will not change the state of the job in any way—the job will continue to run where it left off.

Note that suspending a job is not equal to *interrupting* a job. When you interrupt a running process (by hitting your interrupt key, which is usually `ctrl-C`)[5], it kills the process, for good. Once the job is killed, there's no hope of resuming it; you'll have to re-run the command. Also note that some programs trap the interrupt, so that hitting `ctrl-C` won't immediately kill the job. This is to allow the program to perform any necessary cleanup operations before exiting. In fact, some programs simply don't allow you to kill them with an interrupt at all.

3.11.3   Backgrounding and killing jobs

Let's begin with a simple example. The command `yes` is a seemingly useless command which sends an endless stream of y's to standard output. (This is actually useful. If you piped the output of `yes` to another command which asked a series of yes and no questions, the stream of y's would confirm all of the questions.)

Try it out.

```
/home/larry# yes
y
y
y
y
y
```

The y's will continue *ad infinitum*. You can kill the process by hitting your interrupt key, which is usually `ctrl-C`. So that we don't have to put up with the annoying stream of y's, let's redirect the standard output of `yes` to `/dev/null`. As you may remember, `/dev/null` acts as a "black hole" for data. Any data sent to it will disappear. This is a very effective method of quieting an otherwise verbose program.

```
/home/larry# yes > /dev/null
```

Ah, much better. Nothing is printed, but the shell prompt doesn't come back. This is because `yes` is still running, and is sending those inane y's to `/dev/null`. Again, to kill the job, hit the interrupt key.

Let's suppose that we wanted the `yes` command to continue to run, but wanted to get our shell prompt back to work on other things. We can put `yes` into the background, which will allow it to run, but without need for interaction.

One way to put a process in the background is to append an "`&`" character to the end of the command.

---

[5]The interrupt key can be set using the `stty` command. The default on most systems is `ctrl-C`, but we can't guarantee the same for your system.

```
/home/larry# yes > /dev/null &
[1] 164
/home/larry#
```

As you can see, we have our shell prompt back. But what is this "[1] 164"? And is the yes command really running?

The "[1]" represents the **job number** for the yes process. The shell assigns a job number to every running job. Because yes is the one and only job that we're currently running, it is assigned job number 1. The "164" is the process ID, or PID, number given by the system to the job. Either number may be used to refer to the job, as we'll see later.

You now have the yes process running in the background, continuously sending a stream of y's to /dev/null. To check on the status of this process, use the shell internal command jobs.

```
/home/larry# jobs
[1]+  Running                  yes >/dev/null  &
/home/larry#
```

Sure enough, there it is. You could also use the ps command as demonstrated above to check on the status of the job.

To terminate the job, use the command kill. This command takes either a job number or a process ID number as an argument. This was job number 1, so using the command

```
/home/larry# kill %1
```

will kill the job. When identifying the job with the job number, you must prefix the number with a percent ("%") character.

Now that we've killed the job, we can use jobs again to check on it:

```
/home/larry# jobs

[1]+  Terminated               yes >/dev/null

/home/larry#
```

The job is in fact dead, and if we use the jobs command again nothing should be printed.

You can also kill the job using the process ID (PID) number, which is printed along with the job ID when you start the job. In our example, the process ID is 164, so the command

```
/home/larry# kill 164
```

is equivalent to

```
/home/larry# kill %1
```

You don't need to use the "%" when referring to a job by its process ID.

3.11.4 Stopping and restarting jobs

There is another way to put a job into the background. You can start the job normally (in the foreground), **stop** the job, and then restart it in the background.

First, start the `yes` process in the foreground, as you normally would:

```
/home/larry# yes > /dev/null
```

Again, because `yes` is running in the foreground, you shouldn't get your shell prompt back.

Now, instead of interrupting the job with `ctrl-C`, we'll *suspend* the job. Suspending a job doesn't kill it: it only temporarily stops the job until you restart it. To do this, you hit the suspend key, which is usually `ctrl-Z`.

```
/home/larry# yes > /dev/null
ctrl-Z
[1]+  Stopped                    yes >/dev/null
/home/larry#
```

While the job is suspended, it's simply not running. No CPU time is used for the job. However, you can restart the job, which will cause the job to run again as if nothing ever happened. It will continue to run where it left off.

To restart the job in the foreground, use the command `fg` (for "foreground").

```
/home/larry# fg
yes >/dev/null
```

The shell prints the name of the command again so you're aware of which job you just put into the foreground. Stop the job again, with `ctrl-Z`. This time, use the command `bg` to put the job into the background. This will cause the command to run just as if you started the command with "`&`" as in the last section.

```
/home/larry# bg
[1]+ yes >/dev/null &
/home/larry#
```

And we have our prompt back. `jobs` should report that `yes` is indeed running, and we can kill the job with `kill` as we did before.

How can we stop the job again? Using `ctrl-Z` won't work, because the job is in the background. The answer is to put the job in the foreground, with `fg`, and then stop it. As it turns out you can use `fg` on either stopped jobs or jobs in the background.

There is a big difference between a job in the background and a job which is stopped. A stopped job is not running—it's not using any CPU time, and it's not doing any work (the job still occupies system memory, although it may be swapped out to disk). A job in the background is running, and using memory, as well as completing some task while you do other work. However, a job in the background may try to display text on to your terminal, which can be annoying if you're trying to work on something else. For example, if you used the command

```
/home/larry# yes &
```

without redirecting stdout to /dev/null, a stream of y's would be printed to your screen, without any way of interrupting it (you can't use ctrl-C to interrupt jobs in the background). In order to stop the endless y's, you'd have to use the fg command, to bring the job to the foreground, and then use ctrl-C to kill it.

Another note. The fg and bg commands normally foreground or background the job which was last stopped (indicated by a "+" next to the job number when you use the command jobs). If you are running multiple jobs at once, you can foreground or background a specific job by giving the job ID as an argument to fg or bg, as in

        /home/larry# *fg %2*

(to foreground job number 2), or

        /home/larry# *bg %3*

(to background job number 3). You can't use process ID numbers with fg or bg.

Furthermore, using the job number alone, as in

        /home/larry# *%2*

is equivalent to

        /home/larry# *fg %2*

Just remember that using job control is a feature of the shell. The commands fg, bg and jobs are internal to the shell. If for some reason you use a shell which does not support job control, don't expect to find these commands available.

In addition, there are some aspects of job control which differ between Bash and Tcsh. In fact, some shells don't provide job control at all—however, most shells available for Linux support job control.

3.12   Using the vi Editor

A **text editor** is simply a program used to edit files which contain text, such as a letter, C program, or a system configuration file. While there are many such editors available for Linux, the only editor which you are guaranteed to find on any UNIX system is vi— the "visual editor". vi is not the easiest editor to use, nor is it very self-explanatory. However, because it is so common in the UNIX world, and at times you may be required to use it, it deserves some documentation here.

Your choice of an editor is mostly a question of personal taste and style. Many users prefer the baroque, self-explanatory and powerful **Emacs**—an editor with more features than any other single program in the UNIX world. For example, Emacs has its own built-in dialect of the LISP programming language, and has many extensions (one of which is an "Eliza"-like AI program). However, because Emacs and all of its support files are relatively large, you may not have access to it on many systems. vi, on the other hand, is small and powerful, but more difficult to use. However, once you know your way around vi, it's actually very easy. It's just the learning curve which is sometimes difficult to cross.

This section is a coherent introduction to vi—we won't discuss all of its features, just the ones you need to know to get you started. You can refer to the man page for vi if you're interested in learning about more of this editor's features. Or, you can read the book *Learning the vi Editor* from O'Reilly and Associates. See Appendix A for information.

3.12.1 Concepts

While using `vi`, at any one time you are in one of three modes of operation. These modes are known as *command mode*, *insert mode*, and *last line mode*.

When you start up `vi`, you are in *command mode*. This mode allows you to use certain commands to edit files or to change to other modes. For example, typing "x" while in command mode deletes the character underneath the cursor. The arrow keys move the cursor around the file which you're editing. Generally, the commands used in command mode are one or two characters long.

You actually insert or edit text within *insert mode*. When using `vi`, you'll probably spend most of your time within this mode. You start insert mode by using a command such as "i" (for "insert") from command mode. While in insert mode, you are inserting text into the document from your current cursor location. To end insert mode and return to command mode, press `esc`.

Last line mode is a special mode used to give certain extended commands to `vi`. While typing these commands, they appear on the last line of the screen (hence the name). For example, when you type ":" from command mode, you jump into last line mode, and can use commands such as "wq" (to write the file and quit `vi`), or "q!" (to quit `vi` without saving changes). Last line mode is generally used for `vi` commands which are longer than one character. In last line mode, you enter a single-line command and press `enter` to execute it.

3.12.2 Starting `vi`

The best way to understand these concepts is to actually fire up `vi` and edit a file. In the example "screens" below, we're only going to show a few lines of text, as if the screen was only six lines high (instead of twenty-four).

The syntax for `vi` is

    `vi` ⟨*filename*⟩

where ⟨*filename*⟩ is the name of the file that you wish to edit.

Start up `vi` by typing

    `/home/larry#` *vi test*

which will edit the file `test`. You should see something like

```
~
~
~
~
~
~
"test" [New file]
```

The column of "~" characters indicates that you are the end of the file.

3.12.3 Inserting text

You are now in command mode; in order to insert text into the file, press `i` (which will place you into insert mode), and begin typing.

```
Now is the time for all good men to come to the aid of the party.
~
~
~
~
```

While inserting text, you may type as many lines as you wish (pressing `return` after each, of course), and you may correct mistakes using the backspace key.

To end insert mode, and return to command mode, press `esc`.

While in command mode, you can use the arrow keys to move around the file. Here, because we only have one line of text, trying to use the up- or down-arrow keys will probably cause vi to beep at you.

There are several ways to insert text, other than using the i command. For example, the a command inserts text beginning *after* the current cursor position, instead of on the current cursor position. For example, use the left arrow key to move the cursor between the words "good" and "men".

```
Now is the time for all good_men to come to the aid of the party.
~
~
~
~
```

Press `a`, to start insert mode, type "wo", and then hit `esc` to return to command mode.

```
Now is the time for all good women to come to the aid of the party.
~
~
~
~
```

To begin inserting text at the line below the current one, use the o command. For example, press `o` and type another line or two:

```
Now is the time for all good women to come to the aid of the party.
Afterwards, we'll go out for pizza and beer.
~
~
~
~
```

Just remember that at any time you're either in command mode (where commands such as i, a, or o are valid), or in insert mode (where you're inserting text, followed by `esc` to return to command mode), or last line mode (where you're entering extended commands, as discussed below).

3.12.4 Deleting text

From command mode, the x command deletes the character under the cursor. If you press `x` five times, you'll end up with:

```
Now is the time for all good women to come to the aid of the party.
Afterwards, we'll go out for pizza and_
~
~
~
~
```

Now press `a`, insert some text, followed by `esc`:

```
Now is the time for all good women to come to the aid of the party.
Afterwards, we'll go out for pizza and Diet Coke_.
~
~
~
~
```

You can delete entire lines using the command `dd` (that is, press `d` twice in a row). If your cursor is on the second line, and you type `dd`,

```
Now is the time for all good women to come to the aid of the party.
~
~
~
~
```

To delete the word which the cursor is on, use the `dw` command. Place the cursor on the word "good", and type `dw`.

```
Now is the time for all women to come to the aid of the party.
~
~
~
~
```

3.12.5   Changing text

You can replace sections of text using the `R` command. Place the cursor on the first letter in "party", press `R`, and type the word "hungry".

```
Now is the time for all women to come to the aid of the hungry_.
~
~
~
~
```

Using `R` to edit text is much like the `i` and `a` commands, but `R` overwrites text, instead of inserting it.

The `r` command replaces the single character under the cursor. For example, move the cursor to the beginning of the word "Now", and type `r` followed by `C`, you'll have:

```
Cow is the time for all women to come to the aid of the hungry.
~
~
~
~
~
```

The "~" command changes the case of the letter under the cursor from upper- to lower-case, and vise versa, For example, if you place the cursor on the "o" in "Cow", above, and repeatedly press ⟨ ~ ⟩, you'll end up with:

```
COW IS THE TIME FOR ALL WOMEN TO COME TO THE AID OF THE HUNGRY.
~
~
~
~
~
```

3.12.6   Moving commands

You already know how to use the arrow keys to move around the document. In addition, you can use the h, j, k, and l commands to move the cursor left, down, up, and right, respectively. This comes in handy when (for some reason) your arrow keys aren't working correctly.

The w command moves the cursor to the beginning of the next word; the b moves it to the beginning of the previous word.

The 0 (that's a zero) command moves the cursor to the beginning of the current line, and the $ command moves it to the end of the line.

When editing large files, you'll want to move forwards or backwards through the file a screenful at a time. Pressing ⟨ ctrl-F ⟩ moves the cursor one screenful forward, and ⟨ ctrl-B ⟩ moves it a screenful back.

In order to move the cursor to the end of the file, type G. You can also move to an arbitrary line; for example, typing the command 10G would move the cursor to line 10 in the file. To move to the beginning of the file, use 1G.

You can couple moving commands with other commands, such as deletion. For example, the command d$ will delete everything from the cursor to the end of the line; dG will delete everything from the cursor to the end of the file, and so on.

3.12.7   Saving files and quitting vi

To quit vi without making changes to the file, use the command :q!. When you type the ":", the cursor will move to the last line on the screen; you'll be in last line mode.

```
COW IS THE TIME FOR ALL WOMEN TO COME TO THE AID OF THE HUNGRY.
~
~
~
~
~
:_
```

In last line mode, certain extended commands are available. One of them is q!, which quits vi without saving. The command :wq saves the file and then exits vi. The command ZZ (from command mode, without the ":") is equivalent to :wq. Remember that you must press ⟨enter⟩ after a command entered in last line mode.

To save the file without quitting vi, just use :w.

3.12.8 Editing another file

To edit another file, use the :e command. For example, to stop editing test, and edit the file foo instead, use the command

```
COW IS THE TIME FOR ALL WOMEN TO COME TO THE AID OF THE HUNGRY.
~
~
~
~
~
:e foo_
```

If you use :e without saving the file first, you'll get the error message

```
No write since last change (":edit!" overrides)
```

which simply means that vi doesn't want to edit another file until you save the first one. At this point, you can use :w to save the original file, and then use :e, or you can use the command

```
COW IS THE TIME FOR ALL WOMEN TO COME TO THE AID OF THE HUNGRY.
~
~
~
~
~
:e! foo_
```

The "!" tells vi that you really mean it—edit the new file without saving changes to the first.

3.12.9 Including other files

If you use the :r command, you can include the contents of another file in the current file. For example, the command

```
:r foo.txt
```

would insert the contents of the file foo.txt in the text at the current cursor location.

3.12.10 Running shell commands

You can also run shell commands from within vi. The :r! command works like :r, but instead of reading a file, it inserts the output of the given command into the buffer at the current cursor location. For example, if you use the command

```
:r!  ls -F
```

you'll end up with

```
COW IS THE TIME FOR ALL WOMEN TO COME TO THE AID OF THE HUNGRY.
letters/
misc/
papers/

~

~
```

You can also "shell out" of `vi`, in other words, run a command from within `vi`, and return to the editor when you're done. For example, if you use the command

```
:!  ls -F
```

the `ls -F` command will be executed, and the results displayed on the screen, but not inserted into the file which you're editing. If you use the command

```
:shell
```

`vi` will start an instance of the shell, allowing you to temporarily put vi "on hold" while you execute other commands. Just logout of the shell (using the `exit` command) to return to `vi`.

3.12.11   Getting help

`vi` doesn't provide much in the way of interactive help (most UNIX programs don't), but you can always read the man page for `vi`. `vi` is a visual front-end to the `ex` editor; it is `ex` which handles many of the last-line mode commands in `vi`. So, in addition to reading the man page for `vi`, see `ex` as well.

3.13   Customizing your Environment

The shell provides many mechanisms to customize your work environment. As we've mentioned before, the shell is more than a command interpreter—it is also a powerful programming language. While writing shell scripts is an extensive subject, we'd like to introduce you to some of the ways that you can simplify your work on a UNIX system by using these advanced features of the shell.

As we have mentioned before, different shells use different syntaxes when executing shell scripts. For example, Tcsh uses a C-like syntax, while Bourne shells use another type of syntax. In this section, we won't be running into many of the differences between the two, but we will assume that shell scripts are executed using the Bourne shell syntax.

3.13.1   Shell scripts

Let's say that you use a series of commands often, and would like to shorten the amount of required typing by grouping all of them together into a single "command". For example, the commands

```
/home/larry# cat chapter1 chapter2 chapter3 > book
/home/larry# wc -l book
/home/larry# lp book
```

would concatenate the files `chapter1`, `chapter2`, and `chapter3` and place the result in the file `book`. Then, a count of the number of lines in `book` would be displayed, and finally `book` would be printed with the `lp` command.

Instead of typing all of these commands, you could group them into a **shell script**. We described shell scripts briefly in Section 3.13.1. The shell script used to run all of these commands would look like

```
#!/bin/sh
# A shell script to create and print the book

cat chapter1 chapter2 chapter3 > book
wc -l book
lp book
```

If this script was saved in the file `makebook`, you could simply use the command

/home/larry# *makebook*

to run all of the commands in the script. Shell scripts are just plain text files; you can create them with an editor such as `emacs` or `vi` [6].

Let's look at this shell script. The first line, "`#!/bin/sh`", identifies the file as a shell script, and tells the shell how to execute the script. It instructs the shell to pass the script to `/bin/sh` for execution, where `/bin/sh` is the shell program itself. Why is this important? On most UNIX systems, `/bin/sh` is a Bourne-type shell, such as Bash. By forcing the shell script to run using `/bin/sh`, we are ensuring that the script will run under a Bourne-syntax shell (instead of, say, a C shell). This will cause your script to run using the Bourne syntax even if you use Tcsh (or another C shell) as your login shell.

The second line is a *comment*. Comments begin with the character "`#`" and continue to the end of the line. Comments are ignored by the shell—they are commonly used to identify the shell script to the programmer.

The rest of the lines in the script are just commands, as you would type them to the shell directly. In effect, the shell reads each line of the script and runs that line as if you had typed it at the shell prompt.

Permissions are important for shell scripts. If you create a shell script, you must make sure that you have execute permission on the script in order to run it[7]. The command

/home/larry# *chmod u+x makebook*

can be used to give yourself execute permission on the shell script `makebook`.

3.13.2 Shell variables and the environment

The shell allows you to define **variables**, as most programming languages do. A variable is just a piece of data which is given the name.

◇   Note that Tcsh, as well as other C-type shells, use a different mechanism for setting variables than is described here. This discussion assumes the use of a Bourne shell, such as Bash (which you're probably using). See the Tcsh man page for details.

When you assign a value to a variable (using the "`=`" operator), you can access the variable by prepending a "`$`" to the variable name, as demonstrated below.

---

[6]`vi` is covered in Section 3.12.

[7]When you create text files, the default permissions usually don't include execute permission.

```
/home/larry# foo="hello there"
```

The variable foo is given the value "hello there". You can now refer to this value by the variable name, prefixed with a "$" character. The command

```
/home/larry# echo $foo
hello there
/home/larry#
```

produces the same results as

```
/home/larry# echo "hello there"
hello there
/home/larry#
```

These variables are internal to the shell. This means that only the shell can access these variables. This can be useful in shell scripts; if you need to keep track of a filename, for example, you can store it in a variable, as above. Using the command set will display a list of all defined shell variables.

However, the shell allows you to **export** variables to the **environment**. The environment is the set of variables which all commands that you execute have access to. Once you define a variable inside the shell, exporting it makes that variable part of the environment as well. The export command is used to export a variable to the environment.

◇   Again, here we differ between Bash and Tcsh. If you're using Tcsh, another syntax is used for setting environment variables (the setenv command is used). See the Tcsh man page for more information.

The environment is very important to the UNIX system. It allows you to configure certain commands just by setting variables which the commands know about.

Here's a quick example. The environment variable PAGER is used by the man command. It specifies the command to use to display man pages one screenful at a time. If you set PAGER to be the name of a command, it will use that command to display the man pages, instead of more (which is the default).

Set PAGER to "cat". This will cause output from man to be displayed to the screen all at once, without breaking it up into pages.

```
/home/larry# PAGER="cat"
```

Now, export PAGER to the environment.

```
/home/larry# export PAGER
```

Try the command man ls. The man page should fly past your screen without pausing for you.

Now, if we set PAGER to "more", the more command will be used to display the man page.

```
/home/larry# PAGER="more"
```

Note that we don't have to use the export command after we change the value of PAGER. We only need to export a variable once; any changes made to it thereafter will automatically be propagated to the environment.

The man pages for a particular command will tell you if the command uses any environment variables; for example, the man man page explains that PAGER is used to specify the pager command. Some commands share environment variables; for example, many commands use the EDITOR environment variable to specify the default editor to use when one is needed.

The environment is also used to keep track of important information about your login session. An example is the HOME environment variable, which contains the name of your home directory.

```
/home/larry/papers# echo $HOME
/home/larry
```

Another interesting environment variable is PS1, which defines the main shell prompt. For example,

```
/home/larry# PS1="Your command, please: "
Your command, please:
```

To set the prompt back to our usual (which contains the current working directory followed by a "#" symbol),

```
Your command, please:  PS1="\w# "
/home/larry#
```

The bash man page describes the syntax used for setting the prompt.

3.13.2.1 The PATH environment variable

When you use the ls command, how does the shell find the ls executable itself? In fact, ls is found in /bin/ls on most systems. The shell uses the environment variable PATH to locate executable files for commands which you type.

For example, your PATH variable may be set to:

```
/bin:/usr/bin:/usr/local/bin:.
```

This is a list of directories for the shell to search, each directory separated by a ":". When you use the command ls, the shell first looks for /bin/ls, then /usr/bin/ls, and so on.

Note that the PATH has nothing to do with finding regular files. For example, if you use the command

```
/home/larry# cp foo bar
```

The shell does not use PATH to locate the files foo and bar—those filenames are assumed to be complete. The shell only uses PATH to locate the cp executable.

This saves you a lot of time; it means that you don't have to remember where all of the command executables are stored. On many systems, executables are scattered about in many places, such as /usr/bin, /bin, or /usr/local/bin. Instead of giving the command's full pathname (such as /usr/bin/cp), you can simply set PATH to the list of directories that you want the shell to automatically search.

Notice that PATH contains ".", which is the current working directory. This allows you to create a shell script or program and run it as a command from your current directory, without having to specify it directly (as in ./makebook). If a directory isn't on your PATH, then the shell will not search it for commands to run—this includes the current directory.

3.13.3   Shell initialization scripts

In addition to shell scripts that you create, there are a number of scripts that the shell itself uses for certain purposes. The most important of these are your **initialization scripts**, scripts automatically executed by the shell when you login.

The initialization scripts themselves are simply shell scripts, as described above. However, they are very useful in setting up your environment by executing commands automatically when you login. For example, if you always use the `mail` command to check your mail when you login, you place the command in your initialization script so it will be executed automatically.

Both Bash and Tcsh distinguish between a **login shell** and other invocations of the shell. A login shell is a shell invoked at login time; usually, it's the only shell which you'll use. However, if you "shell out" of another program, such as `vi`, you start another instance of the shell, which isn't your login shell. In addition, whenever you run a shell script, you automatically start another instance of the shell to execute the script.

The initialization files used by Bash are: `/etc/profile` (set up by the system administrator, executed by all Bash users at login time), `$HOME/.bash_profile` (executed by a login Bash session), and `$HOME/.bashrc` (executed by all non-login instances of Bash). If `.bash_profile` is not present, `.profile` is used instead.

Tcsh uses the following initialization scripts: `/etc/csh.login` (executed by all Tcsh users at login time), `$HOME/.tcshrc` (executed a login time and by all new instances of Tcsh), and `$HOME/.login` (executed at login time, following `.tcshrc`). If `.tcshrc` is not present, `.cshrc` is used instead.

To fully understand the function of these files, you'll need to learn more about the shell itself. Shell programming is a complicated subject, far beyond the scope of this book. See the man pages for `bash` and/or `tcsh` to learn more about customizing your shell environment.

3.14   So You Want to Strike Out on Your Own?

Hopefully we have provided enough information to give you a basic idea of how to use the system. Keep in mind that most of the interesting and important aspects of Linux aren't covered here—these are the very basics. With this foundation, before long you'll be up and running complicated applications and fulfilling the potential of your system. If things don't seem exciting at first, don't despair—there is much to be learned.

One indispensable tool for learning about the system is to read the man pages. While many of the man pages may appear confusing at first, if you dig beneath the surface there is a wealth of information contained therein.

We also suggest reading a complete book on using a UNIX system. There is much more to UNIX than meets the eye—unfortunately, most of it is beyond the scope of this book. Some good UNIX books to look at are listed in Appendix A.

Chapter 4

System Administration

This chapter is an overview to Linux system administration, including a number of advanced features which aren't necessarily for system administrators only. Just as every dog has its day, every system has its administrator, and running the system is a very important and sometimes time-consuming job, even if you're the only user on your system.

We have tried to cover here the most important things about system administration you need to know when you use Linux, in sufficient detail to get you comfortably started. In order to keep it short and sweet, we have only covered the very basics, and have skipped many an important detail. You should read the *Linux System Administrator's Guide* if you are serious about running Linux. It will help you understand better how things work, and how they hang together. At least skim through it so that you know what it contains and know what kind of help you can expect from it.

4.1 About Root, Hats, and the Feeling of Power

As you know, UNIX differentiates between different users, so that what they do to each other and to the system can be regulated (one wouldn't want anybody to be able to read one's love letters, for instance). Each user is given an **account**, which includes a username, home directory, and so on. In addition to accounts given to real people, there are special system-defined accounts which have special privileges. The most important of these is the **root account**, for the username `root`.

4.1.1 The `root` account

Ordinary users are generally restricted so that they can't do harm to anybody else on the system, just to themselves. File permissions on the system are arranged such that normal users aren't allowed to delete or modify files in directories shared by all users (such as `/bin` and `/usr/bin`. Most users also protect their own files with the appropriate file permissions so that other users can't access or modify those files.

There are no such restrictions on `root`. The user `root` can read, modify, or delete any file on the system, change permissions and ownerships on any file, and run special programs, such as those which partition the drive or create filesystems. The basic idea is that the person or persons who run and take care of the system logs in as `root` whenever it is necessary to perform tasks that cannot be executed as a normal user. Because `root` can do anything, it is easy to make mistakes that have catastrophic consequences when logged in using this account.

For example, as a normal user, if you inadvertently attempt to delete all of the files in /etc, the system will not permit you to do so. However, when logged in as root, the system won't complain at all. It is very easy to trash your system when using root. The best way to prevent accidents is to:

- Sit on your hands before you press return on a command which may cause damage. For example, if you're about to clean out a directory, before hitting return, re-read the entire command and make sure that it is correct.

- Don't get accustomed to using root. The more comfortable you are in the role of the root user, the more likely you are to confuse your privileges with those of a normal user. For example, you might *think* that you're logged in as larry, when you're really logged in as root.

- Use a different prompt for the root account. You should change root's .bashrc or .login file to set the shell prompt to something other than your regular user prompt. For example, many people use the character "$" in prompts for regular users, and reserve the character "#" for the root user prompt.

- Only login as root when absolutely necessary. And, as soon as you're finished with your work as root, log out. The less you use the root account, the less likely you'll be to do damage on your system.

Of course, there is a breed of UNIX hackers out there who use root for virtually everything. But every one of them has, at some point, made a silly mistake as root and trashed the system. The general rule is, until you're familiar with the lack of restrictions on root, and are comfortable using the system without such restrictions, login as root sparingly.

Of course, everyone makes mistakes. Linus Torvalds himself once accidentally deleted the entire kernel directory tree on his system. Hours of work were lost forever. Fortunately, however, because of his knowledge of the filesystem code, he was able to reboot the system and reconstruct the directory tree by hand on disk.

Put another way, if you picture using the root account as wearing a special magic hat that gives you lots of power, so that you can, by waving your hand, destroy entire cities, it is a good idea to be a bit careful about what you do with your hands. Since it is easy to move your hand in a destructive way by accident, it is not a good idea to wear the magic hat when it is not needed, despite the wonderful feeling.

4.1.2   Abusing the system

Along with the feeling of power comes the tendency to do harm. This is one of the grey areas of UNIX system administration, but everyone goes through it at some point in time. Most users of UNIX systems never have the ability to wield this power—on university and business UNIX systems, only the highly-paid and highly-qualified system administrators ever login as root. In fact, at many such institutions, the root password is a highly guarded secret: it is treated as the Holy Grail of the institution. A large amount of hubbub is made about logging in as root; it is portrayed as a wise and fearsome power, given only to an exclusive cabal.

This kind of attitude towards the root account is, quite simply, the kind of thing which breeds malice and contempt. Because root is so fluffed-up, when some users have their first opportunity to login as root (either on a Linux system or elsewhere), the tendency is to use root's privileges in a harmful manner. I have known so-called "system administrators" who read other user's mail, delete user's files without warning, and generally behave like children when given such a powerful "toy".

Because `root` has such privilege on the system, it takes a certain amount of maturity and self-control to use the account as it was intended—to run the system. There is an unspoken code of honor which exists between the system administrator and the users on the system. How would you feel if your system administrator was reading your e-mail or looking over your files? There is still no strong legal precedent for electronic privacy on time-sharing computer systems. On UNIX systems, the `root` user has the ability to forego all security and privacy mechanisms on the system. It is important that the system administrator develop a trusting relationship with the users on the system. I can't stress that enough.

4.1.3 Dealing with users

UNIX security is rather lax by design. Security on the system was an afterthought—the system was originally developed in an environment where users intruding upon other users was simply unheard of. Because of this, even with security measures, there is still the ability for normal users to do harm.

System administrators can take two stances when dealing with abusive users: they can be either paranoid or trusting. The paranoid system administrator usually causes more harm than he or she prevents. One of my favorite sayings is, "Never attribute to malice anything which can be attributed to stupidity." Put another way, most users don't have the ability or knowledge to do real harm on the system. 90% of the time, when a user is causing trouble on the system (by, for instance, filling up the user partition with large files, or running multiple instances of a large program), the user is simply unaware that what he or she is doing is a problem. I have come down on users who were causing a great deal of trouble, but they were simply acting out of ignorance—not malice.

When you deal with users who are causing potential trouble, don't be accusative. The old rule of "innocent until proven guilty" still holds. It is best to simply talk to the user, and question about the trouble, instead of causing a confrontation. The last thing you want to do is be on the user's bad side. This will raise a lot of suspicion about you—the system administrator—running the system correctly. If a user believes that you distrust or dislike them, they might accuse you of deleting files or breaching privacy on the system. This is certainly not the kind of position that you want to be in.

If you do find that a user has been attempting to "crack" the system, or was intentionally doing harm to the system, don't return the malicious behavior with malice of your own. Instead, simply provide a warning—but be flexible. In many cases, you may catch a user "in the act" of doing harm to the system— give them a warning. Tell them not to let it happen again. However, if you *do* catch them causing harm again, be absolutely sure that it is intentional. I can't even begin to describe the number of cases where it appeared as though a user was causing trouble, when in fact it was either an accident or a fault of my own.

4.1.4 Setting the rules

The best way to run a system is not with an iron fist. That may be how you run the military, but UNIX was not designed for such discipline. It makes sense to lay down a simple and flexible set of guidelines for users—but remember, the fewer rules you have, the less chance there is of breaking them. Even if your rules for using the system are perfectly reasonable and clear, users will always at times break these rules without intending to. This is especially true in the case of new UNIX users, who are just learning the ropes of the system. It's not patently obvious, for example, that you shouldn't download a gigabyte of files and mail them to everyone on the system. Users need help understanding the rules, and why they are there.

If you do specify usage guidelines for your system, make sure that the reason behind a particular guideline is made clear. If you don't, then users will find all sorts of creative ways to get around the rule, and not know that they are in fact breaking it.

4.1.5   What it all means

We can't tell you how to run your system to the last detail. Most of the philosophy depends on how you're using the system. If you have many users, things are much different than if you only have a few users, or if you're the only user on the system. However, it's always a good idea—in any situation—to understand what being the system administrator really means.

Being the system administrator doesn't make you a UNIX wizard. There are many system admins out there who know very little about UNIX. Likewise, there are many "normal" users out there who know more about UNIX than any system administrator could. Also, being the system administrator does not allow you to use malice against your users. Just because the system gives you the privilege to mess with user files does not mean that you have any right to do so.

Lastly, being the system administrator is really not a big deal. It doesn't matter if your system is a little 386 or a Cray supercomputer. Running the system is the same, regardless. Knowing the `root` password isn't going to earn you money or fame. It will allow you to maintain the system, and keep it running. That's it.

4.2   Booting the System

There are several ways to boot the system, either from floppy or from the hard drive.

4.2.1   Using a boot floppy

Many people boot Linux using a "boot floppy" which contains a copy of the Linux kernel. This kernel has the Linux root partition coded into it, so it will know where to look on the hard drive for the root filesystem. (The `rdev` command can be used to set the root partition in the kernel image; see below.) This is the type of floppy created by Slackware during installation, for example.

To create your own boot floppy, first locate the kernel image on your hard disk. It should be in the file `/Image` or `/etc/Image`. Some installations use the file `/vmlinux` for the kernel.

You may instead have a compressed kernel. A compressed kernel uncompresses itself into memory at boot time, and takes up much less space on the hard drive. If you have a compressed kernel, it may be found in the file `/zImage` or `/etc/zImage`.

Once you know where the kernel is, set the root device in the kernel image to the name of your Linux root partition with the `rdev` command. The format of the command is

    `rdev` ⟨*kernel-name*⟩ ⟨*root-device*⟩

where ⟨**kernel-name**⟩ is the name of the kernel image, and ⟨**root-device**⟩ is the name of the Linux root partition. For example, to set the root device in the kernel `/etc/Image` to `/dev/hda2`, use the command

    # *rdev /etc/Image /dev/hda2*

`rdev` can set other options in the kernel as well, such as the default SVGA mode to use at boot time. Just use "`rdev -h`" to get a help message.

After setting the root device, you can simply copy the kernel image to the floppy. Whenever copying data to a floppy, it's a good idea to MS-DOS format the floppy first. This lays down the sector and track information on the floppy, so it can be detected as either high or low density.

For example, to copy the kernel in the file /etc/Image to the floppy in /etc/fd0, use the command

  # *cp /etc/Image /dev/fd0*

This floppy should now boot Linux.

4.2.2 Using LILO

Another method of booting is to use LILO, a program which resides in the boot sector of your hard disk. This program is executed when the system is booted from the hard disk, and can automatically boot up Linux from a kernel image stored on the hard drive itself.

LILO can also be used as a first-stage boot loader for several operating systems, allowing you to select at boot time which operating system (such as Linux or MS-DOS) to boot. When you boot using LILO, the default operating system is booted unless you press ctrl, alt, or shift during the bootup sequence. If you press any of these keys, you will be provided with a boot prompt, at which you type the name of the operating system to boot (such as "linux" or "msdos"). If you press tab at the boot prompt, a listing of available operating systems will be provided.

The easy way to install LILO is to edit the configuration file, /etc/lilo.conf, and then run the command

  # */sbin/lilo*

The LILO configuration file contains a "stanza" for each operating system that you want to boot. The best way to demonstrate this is with an example LILO config file. The below setup is for a system which has a Linux root partition on /dev/hda1, and an MS-DOS partition on /dev/hda2.

```
# Tell LILO to modify the boot record on /dev/hda (the first
# non-SCSI hard drive). If you boot from a drive other than /dev/hda,
# change the following line.
boot = /dev/hda

# Name of the boot loader. No reason to modify this unless you're doing
# some serious hacking on LILO.
install = /boot/boot.b

# Have LILO perform some optimization.
compact

# Stanza for Linux root partition on /dev/hda1.
image = /etc/Image    # Location of kernel
   label = linux      # Name of OS (for the LILO boot menu)
   root = /dev/hda1   # Location of root partition
   vga = ask          # Tell kernel to ask for SVGA modes at boot time

# Stanza for MSDOS partition on /dev/hda2.
other = /dev/hda2     # Location of partition
   table = /dev/hda   # Location of partition table for /dev/hda2
   label = msdos      # Name of OS (for boot menu)
```

The first operating system stanza in the config file will be the default OS for LILO to boot. You can select another OS to boot at the LILO boot prompt, as discussed above.

Remember that every time you update the kernel image on disk, you should rerun /sbin/lilo in order for the changes to be reflected on the boot sector of your drive.

Also note that if you use the "root =" line, above, there's no reason to use rdev to set the root partition in the kernel image. LILO sets it for you at boot time.

The Linux FAQ (see Appendix A) provides more information on LILO, including how to use LILO to boot with OS/2's Boot Manager.

4.3 Shutting Down

Shutting down a Linux system is a bit tricky. Remember that you should never just turn off the power or hit the reset switch while the system is running. The kernel keeps track of disk I/O in memory buffers. If you reboot the system without giving the kernel the chance to write its buffers to disk, you can corrupt your filesystems.

Other precautions are taken at shutdown time as well. All processes are sent a signal, which allows them to die gracefully (writing and closing all files, and so on). Filesystems are unmounted for safety. If you wish, the system can also alert users that the system is going down and give them a change to log off.

The easiest way to shutdown is with the shutdown command. The format of the command is

    shutdown ⟨**time**⟩ ⟨*warning-message*⟩

The ⟨**time**⟩ argument is the time to shutdown the system (in the format *hh:mm:ss*), and ⟨*warning-message*⟩ is a message displayed on all user's terminals before shutdown. Alternately, you can specify the ⟨**time**⟩ as "now", to shutdown immediately. The -r option may be given to shutdown to reboot the system after shutting down.

For example, to shutdown the system at 8:00pm, use the command

    # *shutdown -r 20:00*

The command halt may be used to force an immediate shutdown, without any warning messages or grace period. halt is useful if you're the only one using the system, and want to shut down the system and turn it off.

◇   Don't turn off the power or reboot the system until you see the message:

    The system is halted

It is very important that you shutdown the system "cleanly" using the shutdown or halt commands. On some systems, pressing ctrl-alt-del will be trapped and cause a shutdown; on other systems, however, using the "Vulcan nerve pinch" will reboot the system immediately and may cause disaster.

4.4 Managing Users

Whether or not you have many users on your system, it's important to understand the aspects of user management under Linux. Even if you're the only user, you should presumably have a separate account for yourself (an account other than root to do most of your work).

Each person using the system should have his or her own account. It is seldom a good idea to have several people share the same account. Not only is security an issue, but accounts are used to uniquely identify users to the system. You need to be able to keep track of who is doing what.

4.4.1 User management concepts

The system keeps track of a number of pieces of information about each user. They are summarized below.

username   The username is the unique identifier given to every user on the system. Examples of usernames are `larry`, `karl`, and `mdw`. Letters and digits may be used, as well as the characters "`_`" (underscore) and "`.`" (period). Usernames are usually limited to 8 characters in length.

user ID   The user ID, or UID, is a unique number given to every user on the system. The system usually keeps track of information by UID, not username.

group ID   The group ID, or GID, is the ID of the user's default group. In Section 3.9 we discussed group permissions; each user belongs to one or more groups defined by the system administrator. More about this below.

password   The system also stores the user's encrypted password. The `passwd` command is used to set and change user passwords.

full name   The user's "real name" or "full name" is stored along with the username. For example, the user `schmoj` may have the name "Joe Schmo" in real life.

home directory

The home directory is the directory in which the user is initially placed at login time. Every user should have his or her own home directory, usually found under `/home`.

login shell   The user's login shell is the shell which is started for the user at login time. Examples are `/bin/bash` and `/bin/tcsh`.

The file `/etc/passwd` contains this information about users. Each line in the file contains information about a single user; the format of each line is

```
username:encrypted password:UID:GID:full name:home directory:login shell
```

An example might be:

```
kiwi:Xv8Q981g71oKK:102:100:Laura Poole:/home/kiwi:/bin/bash
```

As we can see, the first field, "`kiwi`", is the username.

The next field, "`Xv8Q981g71oKK`", is the encrypted password. Passwords are not stored on the system in any human-readable format. The password is encrypted using itself as the secret key. In other words, you need to know the password to decrypt it. This form of encryption is fairly secure.

Some systems use "shadow password" in which password information is relegated to the file `/etc/shadow`. Because `/etc/passwd` is world-readable, `/etc/shadow` provides some degree of extra security because it is not. Shadow password provides some other features such as password expiration and so on; we will not go into these features here.

The third field, "102", is the UID. This must be unique for each user. The fourth field, "100", is the GID. This user belongs to the group numbered 100. Group information, like user information, is stored in the file /etc/group. See Section 4.4.5 for more information.

The fifth field is the user's full name, "Laura Poole". The last two fields are the user's home directory (/home/kiwi) and login shell (/bin/bash), respectively. It is not required that the user's home directory be given the same name as the username. It does help identify the directory, however.

4.4.2 Adding users

When adding a user, there are several steps to be taken. First, the user must be given an entry in /etc/passwd, with a unique username and UID. The GID, fullname, and other information must be specified. The user's home directory must be created, and the permissions on the directory set so that the user owns the directory. Shell initialization files must be provided in the new home directory and other system-wide configuration must be done (for example, setting up a spool for incoming e-mail for the new user).

While it is not difficult to add users by hand (I do), when you are running a system with many users it is easy to forget something. The easiest way to add users is to use an interactive program which asks you for the required information and updates all of the system files automatically. The name of this program is useradd or adduser, depending on what software was installed. The man pages for these commands should be fairly self-explanatory.

4.4.3 Deleting users

Similarly, deleting users can be accomplished with the commands userdel or deluser depending on what software was installed on the system.

If you'd like to temporarily "disable" a user from logging into the system (without deleting the user's account), you can simply prepend an asterisk ("*") to the password field in /etc/passwd. For example, changing kiwi's /etc/passwd entry to

```
kiwi:*Xv8Q981g71oKK:102:100:Laura Poole:/home/kiwi:/bin/bash
```

will restrict kiwi from logging in.

4.4.4 Setting user attributes

After you have created a user, you may need to change attributes for that user, such as home directory or password. The easiest way to do this is to change the values directly in /etc/passwd. To set a user's password, use the passwd command. For example,

> # *passwd larry*

will change larry's password. Only root may change other user's password in this manner. Users can change their own passwords with passwd as well.

On some systems, the commands chfn and chsh will be available to allow users to set their own fullname and login shell attributes. If not, they will have to ask the system administrator to change these attributes for them.

4.4.5 Groups

As we have mentioned, each user belongs to one or more groups. The only real importance of group relationships pertains to file permissions, as you'll recall from Section 3.9, each file has a "group ownership" and a set of group permissions which defines how users in that group may access the file.

There are several system-defined groups such as `bin`, `mail`, and `sys`. Users should not belong to any of these groups; they are used for system file permissions. Instead, users should belong to an individual group such as `users`. If you want to be cute, you can maintain several groups of users such as `student`, `staff`, and `faculty`.

The file `/etc/group` contains information about groups. The format of each line is

```
group name:password:GID:other members
```

Some example groups might be:

```
root:*:0:
users:*:100:mdw,larry
guest:*:200:
other:*:250:kiwi
```

The first group, `root`, is a special system group reserved for the `root` account. The next group, `users`, is for regular users. It has a GID of 100. The users `mdw` and `larry` are given access to this group. Remember that in `/etc/passwd` each user was given a default GID. However, users may belong to more than one group, by adding their usernames to other group lines in `/etc/group`. The `groups` command lists what groups you are given access to.

The third group, `guest`, is for guest users, and `other` is for "other" users. The user `kiwi` is given access to this group as well.

As you can see, the "password" field of `/etc/group` is rarely used. It is sometimes used to set a password on group access. This is seldom necessary. To protect users from changing into privileged groups (with the `newgroup` command), set the password field to "`*`".

The commands `addgroup` or `groupadd` may be used to add groups to your system. Usually, it's easier just to add entries in `/etc/group` yourself, as no other configuration needs to be done to add a group. To delete a group, simply delete its entry in `/etc/group`.

4.5 Archiving and Compressing Files

Before we can talk about backups, we need to introduce the tools used to archive files and software on UNIX systems.

4.5.1 Using `tar`

The `tar` command is most often used to archive files.

The format of the `tar` command is

```
tar ⟨options⟩ ⟨file1⟩ ⟨file2⟩ ... ⟨fileN⟩
```

where ⟨**options**⟩ is the list of commands and options for `tar`, and ⟨*file1*⟩ through ⟨*fileN*⟩ is the list of files to add or extract from the archive.

For example, the command

    # *tar cvf backup.tar /etc*

would pack all of the files in `/etc` into the tar archive `backup.tar`. The first argument to `tar`—"`cvf`"— is the `tar` "command". "`c`" tells `tar` to create a new archive file. The "`v`" option forces `tar` into verbose mode—printing each filename as it is archived. The "`f`" option tells `tar` that the next argument— `backup.tar`—is the name of the archive to create. The rest of the arguments to `tar` are the file and directory names to add to the archive.

The command

    # *tar xvf backup.tar*

will extract the tar file `backup.tar` in the current directory. This can sometimes be dangerous—when extracting files from a tar file, old files are overwritten.

Furthermore, before extracting tar files it is important to know where the files should be unpacked. For example, let's say you archived the following files: `/etc/hosts`, `/etc/group`, and `/etc/passwd`. If you use the command

    # *tar cvf backup.tar /etc/hosts /etc/group /etc/passwd*

the directory name `/etc/` is added to the beginning of each filename. In order to extract the files to the correct location, you would need to use the following commands:

    # *cd /*
    # *tar xvf backup.tar*

because files are extracted with the pathname saved in the archive file.

If, however, you archived the files with the command

    # *cd /etc*
    # *tar cvf hosts group passwd*

the directory name is not saved in the archive file. Therefore, you would need to "`cd /etc`" before extracting the files. As you can see, how the tar file is created makes a large difference in where you extract it. The command

    # *tar tvf backup.tar*

may be used to display an "index" of the tar file before unpacking it. In this way you can see what directory the filenames in the archive are stored relative to, and can extract the archive from the correct location.

4.5.2 `gzip` **and** `compress`

Unlike archiving programs for MS-DOS, `tar` does not automatically compress files as it archives them. Therefore, if you are archiving two 1-megabyte files, the resulting tar file will be two megabytes in size. The `gzip` command may be used to compress a file (the file to compress need not be a tar file). The command

> # *gzip -9 backup.tar*

will compress `backup.tar` and leave you with `backup.tar.gz`, the compressed version of the file. The `-9` switch tells `gzip` to use the highest compression factor.

The `gunzip` command may be used to uncompress a gzipped file. Equivalently, you may use "`gzip -d`".

`gzip` is a relatively new tool in the UNIX community. For many years, the `compress` command was used instead. However, because of several factors[1], `compress` is being phased out.

`compressed` files end in the extension `.Z`. For example, `backup.tar.Z` is the compressed version of `backup.tar`, while `backup.tar.gz` is the gzipped version[2]. The `uncompress` command is used to expand a `compressed` file; `gunzip` knows how to handle `compressed` files as well.

4.5.3 Putting them together

Therefore, to archive a group of files and compress the result, you can use the commands:

> # *tar cvf backup.tar /etc*
> # *gzip -9 backup.tar*

The result will be `backup.tar.gz`. To unpack this file, use the reverse set of commands:

> # *gunzip backup.tar.gz*
> # *tar xvf backup.tar*

Of course always make sure that you are in the correct directory before unpacking a tar file.

You can use some UNIX cleverness to do all of this on one command line, as in the following:

> # *tar cvf - /etc | gzip -9c > backup.tar.gz*

Here, we are sending the tar file to "`-`", which stands for `tar`'s standard output. This is piped to `gzip`, which compresses the incoming tar file, and the result is saved in `backup.tar.gz`. The `-c` option to `gzip` tells `gzip` to send its output to stdout, which is redirected to `backup.tar.gz`.

A single command used to unpack this archive would be:

> # *gunzip -c backup.tar.gz | tar xvf -*

Again, `gunzip` uncompresses the contents of `backup.tar.gz` and sends the resulting tar file to stdout. This is piped to `tar`, which reads "`-`", this time referring to `tar`'s standard input.

Happily, the `tar` command also includes the `z` option to automatically compress/uncompress files on the fly, using the `gzip` compression algorithm.

For example, the command

> # *tar cvfz backup.tar.gz /etc*

---

[1] These factors include a software patent dispute against the `compress` algorithm and the fact that `gzip` is much more efficient than `compress`.

[2] To add further confusion, for some time the extension `.z` (lowercase "z") was used for gzipped files. The official `gzip` extension is now `.gz`.

is equivalent to

> # *tar cvf backup.tar /etc*
> # *gzip backup.tar*

Just as the command

> # *tar xvfz backup.tar.Z*

may be used instead of

> # *uncompress backup.tar.Z*
> # *tar xvf backup.tar*

Refer to the man pages for `tar` and `gzip` for more information.

4.6   Using Floppies and Making Backups

Floppies are usually used as backup media. If you don't have a tape drive connected to your system, floppy disks can be used (although they are slower and somewhat less reliable).

You may also use floppies to hold individual filesystems—in this way, you can **mount** the floppy to access the data on it.

4.6.1   Using floppies for backups

The easiest way to make a backup using floppies is with `tar`. The command

> # *tar cvfzM /dev/fd0 /*

will make a complete backup of your system using the floppy drive `/dev/fd0`. The "M" option to `tar` allows the backup to be a multivolume backup; that is, when one floppy is full, `tar` will prompt for the next. The command

> # *tar xvfzM /dev/fd0*

can be used to restore the complete backup. This method can also be used if you have a tape drive (`/dev/rmt0`) connected to your system.

Several other programs exist for making multiple-volume backups; the `backflops` program found on `tsx-11.mit.edu` may come in handy.

Making a complete backup of the system can be time- and resource-consuming. Most system administrators use a incremental backup policy, in which every month a complete backup is taken, and every week only those files which have been modified in the last week are backed up. In this case, if you trash your system in the middle of the month, you can simply restore the last full monthly backup, and then restore the last weekly backups as needed.

The `find` command can be useful in locating files which have changed since a certain date. Several scripts for managing incremental backups can be found on `sunsite.unc.edu`.

4.6.2   Using floppies as filesystems

You can create a filesystem on a floppy just as you would on a hard drive partition. For example,

>   # mke2fs /dev/fd0 1440

creates a filesystem on the floppy in /dev/fd0. The size of the filesystem must correspond to the size of the floppy. High-density 3.5" disks are 1.44 megabytes, or 1440 blocks, in size. High-density 5.25" disks are 1200 blocks.

In order to access the floppy, you must **mount** the filesystem contained on it. The command

>   # mount -t ext2 /dev/fd0 /mnt

will mount the floppy in /dev/fd0 on the directory /mnt. Now, all of the files on the floppy will appear under /mnt on your drive. The "-t ext2" specifies an ext2fs filesystem type. If you created another type of filesystem on the floppy, you'll need to specify its type to the mount command.

The "mount point" (the directory where you're mounting the filesystem) needs to exist when you use the mount command. If it doesn't exist, simply create it with mkdir.

See Section 4.8 for more information on filesystems, mounting, and mount points.

◇   Note that any I/O to the floppy is buffered just as hard disk I/O is. If you change data on the floppy, you may not see the drive light come on until the kernel flushes its I/O buffers. It's important that you not remove a floppy before you unmount it; this can be done with the command

>   # umount /dev/fd0

Do not simply switch floppies as you would on an MS-DOS system; whenever you change floppies, umount the first one and mount the next.

4.7   Upgrading and Installing New Software

Another duty of the system administrator is upgrading and installing new software.

The Linux community is very dynamic. New kernel releases come out every few weeks, and other software is updated almost as often. Because of this, new Linux users often feel the need to upgrade their systems constantly to keep up the the rapidly changing pace. Not only is this unnecessary, it's a waste of time: to keep up with all of the changes in the Linux world, you would be spending all of your time upgrading and none of your time using the system.

So, when should you upgrade? Some people feel that you should upgrade when a new distribution release is made—for example, when Slackware comes out with a new version. Many Linux users completely reinstall their system with the newest Slackware release every time. This, also, is a waste of time. In general, changes to Slackware releases are small. Downloading and reinstalling 30 disks when only 10% of the software has been actually modified is, of course, pointless.

The best way to upgrade your system is to do it by hand: only upgrade those software packages which you know that you should upgrade. This scares a lot of people: they want to know what to upgrade, and how, and what will break if they don't upgrade. In order to be successful with Linux, it's important to overcome your fears of "doing it yourself"— which is what Linux is all about. In fact, once you have your system working and all software correctly configured, reinstalling with the newest release will no doubt wipe all of your configuration and things will be broken again, just as they were when you first installed your system. Setting yourself back in this manner is unnecessary—all that is needed is some know-how about upgrading your system, and how to do it right.

You'll find that when you upgrade one component of your system, other things should not break. For example, most of the software on my system is left over from an ancient 0.96 MCC Interim installation. Yet, I run the newest version of the kernel and libraries with this software with no problem. For the most part, senselessly upgrading to "keep up with the trend" is not important at all. This isn't MS-DOS or Microsoft Windows. There is no important reason to run the newest version of all of the software. If you find that you would like or need features in a new version, then upgrade. If not, then don't. In other words, only upgrade what you have to, and when you have to. Don't just upgrade for the sake of upgrading. That will waste a lot of time and effort trying to keep up.

The most important software to upgrade on your system is the kernel, the libraries, and the `gcc` compiler. These are the three essential parts of your system, and in some cases they all depend on each other for everything to work successfully. Most of the other software on your system does not need to be upgraded periodically.

4.7.1   Upgrading the kernel

Upgrading the kernel is simply a matter of getting the sources and compiling them yourself. You must compile the kernel yourself in order to enable or disable certain features, as well as to ensure that the kernel will be optimized to run on your machine. The process is quite painless.

The kernel sources may be retrieved from any of the Linux FTP sites (see Section C for a list). On `sunsite.unc.edu`, for instance, the kernel sources are found in `/pub/Linux/kernel`. Kernel versions are numbered using a version number and a patchlevel. For example, kernel version 0.99 patchlevel 11 is usually written as `0.99.pl11`, or just `0.99.11`.

The kernel sources are released as a gzipped tar file[3]. For example, the file containing the 0.99.pl11 kernel sources is `linux-0.99.11.tar.gz`.

Unpack this tar file from the directory `/usr/src`; it creates the directory `/usr/src/linux` which contains the kernel sources. You should delete or rename your existing `/usr/src/linux` before unpacking the new version.

Once the sources are unpacked, you need to make sure that two symbolic links in `/usr/include` are correct. To create these links, use the commands

    # ln -sf /usr/src/linux/include/linux /usr/include/linux
    # ln -sf /usr/src/linux/include/asm /usr/include/asm

Once you have created these links once, there is no reason to create them again when you install the next version of the kernel sources. (See Section 3.10 for more about symbolic links.)

Note that in order to compile the kernel, you must have the `gcc` and `g++` C and C++ compilers installed on your system. You may need to have the most recent versions of these compilers: see Section 4.7.3, below, for more information.

To compile the kernel, first `cd` to `/usr/src/linux`. Run the command `make config`. This command will prompt you for a number of configuration options, such as what filesystem types you wish to include in the new kernel.

---

[3]Often, a patch file is also released for the current kernel version which allows you to patch your current kernel sources from the last patchlevel to the current one (using the program `patch`). In most cases, however, it's usually easier to install the entire new version of the kernel sources.

Next, edit `/usr/src/linux/Makefile`. Be sure that the definition for `ROOT_DEV` is correct—it defines the device used as the root filesystem at boot time. The usual definition is

```
ROOT_DEV = CURRENT
```

Unless you are changing your root filesystem device, there is no reason to change this.

Next, run the command `make dep` to fix all of the source dependencies. This is a very important step.

Finally, you're ready to compile the kernel. The command `make Image` will compile the kernel and leave the new kernel image in the file `/usr/src/linux/Image`. Alternately, the command `make zImage` will compile a compressed kernel image, which uncompresses itself at boot time and uses less drive space.

Once you have the kernel compiled, you need to either copy it to a boot floppy (with a command such as "`cp Image /dev/fd0`") or install it using LILO to boot from your hard drive. See Section 4.2.2 for more information.

4.7.2 Upgrading the libraries

As mentioned before, most of the software on the system is compiled to use shared libraries, which contain common subroutines shared among different programs.

If you see the message

```
Incompatible library version
```

when attempting to run a program, then you need to upgrade to the version of the libraries which the program requires. Libraries are back-compatible; that is, a program compiled to use an older version of the libraries should work with the new version of the libraries installed. However, the reverse is not true.

The newest version of the libraries can be found on the Linux FTP sites. On `sunsite.unc.edu`, they are located in `/pub/Linux/GCC`. The "release" files there should explain what files you need to download and how to install them. Briefly, you should get the files `image-`*version*`.tar.gz` and `inc-`*version*`.tar.gz` where *version* is the version of the libraries to install, such as `4.4.1`. These are gzipped tar files; the `image` file contains the library images to install in `/lib` and `/usr/lib`. The `inc` file contains include files to install in `/usr/include`

The `release-`*version*`.tar.gz` should explain the installation procedure in detail (the exact instructions vary for each release). In general you need to install the library `.a` and `.sa` files in `/usr/lib`. These are the libraries used at compilation time.

In addition, the shared library image files, `libc.so.`*version* are installed in `/lib`. These are the shared library images loaded at runtime by programs using the libraries. Each library has a symbolic link using the major version number of the library in `/lib`.

For example, the `libc` library version 4.4.1 has a major version number of 4. The file containing the library is `libc.so.4.4.1`. A symbolic link of the name `libc.so.4` is also in `/lib` pointing to this file. You need to change this symbolic link when upgrading the libraries. For example, when upgrading from `libc.so.4.4` to `libc.so.4.4.1`, you need to change the symbolic link to point to the new version.

◇ It is very important that you change the symbolic link in one step, as given below. If you somehow delete the symbolic link `libc.so.4`, then programs which depend on the link (including basic utilities like `ls` and `cat`) will stop working. Use the following command to update the symbolic link `libc.so.4` to point to the file `libc.so.4.4.1`:

```
#  ln -sf /lib/libc.so.4.4.1 /lib/libc.so.4
```

You also need to change the symbolic link `libm.so.`*version* in the same manner. If you are upgrading to a
different version of the libraries substitute to appropriate filenames above. The library release notice should
explain the details. (See Section 3.10 for more information about symbolic links.)

4.7.3 Upgrading `gcc`

The `gcc` C and C++ compiler is used to compile software on your system, most importantly the kernel. The
newest version of `gcc` is found on the Linux FTP sites. On `sunsite.unc.edu`, it is found in the directory
`/pub/Linux/GCC` (along with the libraries). There should be a `release` file for the `gcc` distribution
detailing what files you need to download and how to install them.

4.7.4 Upgrading other software

Upgrading other software is usually just a matter of downloading the appropriate files and installing them.
Most software for Linux is distributed at gzipped tar files, including either sources or binaries or both. If
binaries are not included in the release, you may need to compile them yourself; usually, this means typing
`make` in the directory where the sources are held.

Reading the USENET newsgroup `comp.os.linux.announce` for announcements of new software
releases is the easiest way to find out about new software. Whenever you are looking for software on an
FTP site, downloading the `ls-lR` index file from the FTP site and using `grep` to find the files in question
is the easiest way to locate software. If you have `archie` available to you, it can be of assistance as well[4].
See Appendix A for more details.

One handy source of Linux software is the Slackware distribution disk images. Each disk contains
a number of `.tgz` files which are simply gzipped tar files. Instead of downloading the disks, you can
download the desired `.tgz` files from the Slackware directories on the FTP site and install them directly.
If you run the Slackware distribution, the `setup` command can be used to automatically load and install a
complete series of disks.

Again, it's usually not a good idea to upgrade by reinstalling with the newest version of Slackware,
or another distribution. If you reinstall in this way, you will no doubt wreck your current installation,
including user directories and all of your customized configuration. The best way to upgrade software is
piecewise; that is, if there is a program that you use often that has a new version, upgrade it. Otherwise,
don't bother. Rule of thumb: If it ain't broke, don't fix it. If your current software works, there's no reason
to upgrade.

4.8 Managing Filesystems

Another task of the system administrator is taking care of filesystems. Most of this job entails periodically
checking the filesystems for damage or corrupted files; many systems automatically check the filesystems
at boot time.

---

[4]If you don't have `archie`, you can telnet to an `archie` server such as `archie.rutgers.edu`, login as "archie" and use the
command "`help`"

4.8.1 Mounting filesystems

First, a few concepts about filesystems. Before a filesystem is accessible to the system, it must be **mounted** on some directory. For example, if you have a filesystem on a floppy, you must mount it under some directory, say /mnt, in order to access the files on it (see Section 4.6.2). After mounting the filesystem, all of the files in the filesystem appear in that directory. After unmounting the filesystem, the directory (in this case, /mnt) will be empty.

The same is true of filesystems on the hard drive. The system automatically mounts filesystems on your hard drive for you at bootup time. The so-called "root filesystem" is mounted on the directory /. If you have a separate filesystem for /usr, for example, it is mounted on /usr. If you only have a root filesystem, all files (including those in /usr) exist on that filesystem.

The command mount is used to mount a filesystem. The command

```
mount -av
```

is executed from the file /etc/rc (which is the system initialization file executed at boot time; see Section 4.10.1). The mount -av command obtains information on filesystems and mount points from the file /etc/fstab. An example fstab file appears below.

```
# device        directory       type      options
/dev/hda2       /               ext2      defaults
/dev/hda3       /usr            ext2      defaults
/dev/hda4       none            swap      sw
/proc           /proc           proc      none
```

The first field is the device—the name of the partition to mount. The second field is the mount point. The third field is the filesystem type—such as ext2 (for ext2fs) or minix (for Minix filesystems). Table 4.1 lists the various filesystem types available for Linux.[5] Not all of these filesystem types may be available on your system; your kernel must have support for them compiled in. See Section 4.7 for information on building the kernel.

Filesystem	Type name	Comment
Second Extended Filesystem	ext2	Most common Linux filesystem.
Extended Filesystem	ext	Superseded by ext2.
Minix Filesystem	minix	Original Minix filesystem; rarely used.
Xia Filesystem	xia	Like ext2, but rarely used.
UMSDOS Filesystem	umsdos	Used to install Linux on an MS-DOS partition.
MS-DOS Filesystem	msdos	Used to access MS-DOS files.
/proc Filesystem	proc	Provides process information for ps, etc.
ISO 9660 Filesystem	iso9660	Format used by most CD-ROMs.
Xenix Filesystem	xenix	Used to access files from Xenix.
System V Filesystem	sysv	Used to access files from System V variants for the x86.
Coherent Filesystem	coherent	Used to access files from Coherent.
HPFS Filesystem	hpfs	Read-only access for HPFS partitions (DoubleSpace).

Table 4.1: Linux Filesystem Types

The last field of the fstab file contains mount options—usually, this is set to "defaults".

---

[5]This table is current as of kernel version 1.1.37.

As you can see, swap partitions are included in /etc/fstab as well. They have a mount directory of none, and type swap. The swapon -a command, executed from /etc/rc as well, is used to enable swapping on all swap devices listed in /etc/fstab.

The fstab file contains one special entry—for the /proc filesystem. As mentioned in Section 3.11.1, the /proc filesystem is used to store information about system processes, available memory, and so on. If /proc is not mounted, commands such as ps will not work.

◊   The mount command may only be used by root. This is to ensure security on the system; you wouldn't want regular users mounting and unmounting filesystems on a whim. There are several software packages available which allow regular users to mount and unmount filesystems (floppies in particular) without compromising system security.

The mount -av command actually mounts all filesystems other than the root filesystem (in the table above, /dev/hda2). The root filesystem is automatically mounted at boot time by the kernel.

Instead of using mount -av, you can mount a filesystem by hand. The command

   # mount -t ext2 /dev/hda3 /usr

is equivalent to mounting the filesystem with the entry /dev/hda3 in the fstab example file above.

In general, you should never have to mount or unmount filesystems by hand. The mount -av command in /etc/rc takes care of mounting the filesystems at boot time. Filesystems are automatically unmounted by the shutdown or halt commands before bringing the system down.

4.8.2   Checking filesystems

It is usually a good idea to check your filesystems for damage or corrupt files every now and then. Some systems automatically check their filesystems at boot time (with the appropriate commands in /etc/rc).

The command used to check a filesystem depends on the type of the filesystem in question. For ext2fs filesystems (the most commonly used type), this command is e2fsck. For example, the command

   # e2fsck -av /dev/hda2

will check the ext2fs filesystem on /dev/hda2 and automatically correct any errors.

It is usually a good idea to unmount a filesystem before checking it. For example, the command

   # umount /dev/hda2

will unmount the filesystem on /dev/hda2, after which you can check it. The one exception is that you cannot unmount the root filesystem. In order to check the root filesystem when it's unmounted, you should use a maintenance boot/root diskette (see Section 4.11.1). You also cannot unmount a filesystem if any of the files in it are "busy"—that is, being used by a running process. For example, you cannot unmount a filesystem if any user's current working directory is on that filesystem. You will receive a "Device busy" error if you attempt to unmount a filesystem which is in use.

Other filesystem types use different forms of the e2fsck command, such as efsck and xfsck. On some systems, you can simply use the command fsck, which will determine the filesystem type and execute the appropriate command.

◊   It is important that you reboot your system immediately after checking a mounted filesystem if any corrections were made to that filesystem. (However, in general, you shouldn't check filesystems while they are mounted.) For example, if e2fsck reports that it corrected any errors with the filesystem, you should immediately shutdown -r in order to reboot the system. This is to allow the system to re-sync its information about the filesystem when e2fsck modifies it.

The /proc filesystem never needs to be checked in this manner. /proc is a memory filesystem, managed directly by the kernel.

4.9   Using a swap file

Instead of reserving an individual partition for swap space, you can use a file. However, to do so you'll need install the Linux software and get everything going *before* you create the swap file.

If you have a Linux system installed, you can use the following commands to create a swap file. Below, we're going to create a swap file of size 8208 blocks (about 8 megs).

> # *dd if=/dev/zero of=/swap bs=1024 count=8208*

This command creates the swap file itself. Replace the "count=" with the size of the swap file in blocks.

> # *mkswap /swap 8208*

This command will initialize the swapfile; again, replace the name and size of the swapfile with the appropriate values.

> # */etc/sync*
> # *swapon /swap*

Now we are swapping on the file /swap which we have created, after syncing, which ensures that the file has been written to disk.

The one major drawback to using a swapfile in this manner is that all access to the swap file is done through the filesystem. This means that the blocks which make up the swap file may not be contiguous. Therefore, performance may not be as great as using a swap partition, for which blocks are always contiguous and I/O requests are done directly to the device.

Another drawback in using a swapfile is the chance to corrupt your filesystem data—when using large swap files, there is the chance that you can corrupt your filesystem if something goes wrong. Keeping your filesystems and swap partitions separate will prevent this from happening.

Using a swap file can be very useful if you have a temporary need for more swap space. For example, if you're compiling a large program and would like to speed things up somewhat, you can temporarily create a swap file and use it in addition to your regular swap space.

To get rid of a swap file, first use swapoff, as in

> # *swapoff /swap*

And you can safely delete the file.

> # *rm /swap*

Remember that each swap file (or partition) may be as large as 16 megabytes, but you may use up to 8 swap files or partitions on your system.

4.10   Miscellaneous Tasks

Believe it or not, there are a number of housekeeping tasks for the system administrator which don't fall into any major category.

4.10.1   System startup files

When the system boots, a number of scripts are executed automatically by the system before any user logs in. Here is a description of what happens.

At bootup time, the kernel spawns the process /etc/init. init is a program which reads its configuration file, /etc/inittab, and spawns other processes based on the contents of this file. One of the important processes started from inittab is the /etc/getty process started on each virtual console. The getty process grabs the VC for use, and starts a login process on the VC. This allows you to login on each VC; if /etc/inittab does not contain a getty process for a certain VC, you will not be able to login on that VC.

Another process executed from /etc/inittab is /etc/rc, the main system initialization file. This file is a simple shell script which executes any initialization commands needed at boot time, such as mounting the filesystems (see Section 4.8) and initializing swap space.

Your system may execute other initialization scripts as well, such as /etc/rc.local. /etc/rc.local usually contains initialization commands specific to your own system, such as setting the hostname (see the next section). rc.local may be started from /etc/rc or from /etc/inittab directly.

4.10.2   Setting the hostname

In a networked environment, the hostname is used to uniquely identify a particular machine, while in a standalone environment the hostname just gives the system personality and charm. It's like naming a pet: you can always address to your dog as "The dog," but it's much more interesting to assign the dog a name such as Spot or Woofie.

Setting the system's hostname is a simple matter of using the hostname command. If you are on a network, your hostname should be the full hostname of your machine, such as goober.norelco.com. If you are not on a network of any kind, you can choose an arbitrary host and domainname, such as loomer.vpizza.com, shoop.nowhere.edu, or floof.org.

When setting the hostname, the hostname must appear in the file /etc/hosts, which assigns an IP address to each host. Even if your machine is not on a network, you should include your own hostname in /etc/hosts.

For example, if you are not on a TCP/IP network, and your hostname is floof.org, simply include the following line in /etc/hosts:

```
127.0.0.1      floof.org localhost
```

This assigns your hostname, floof.org, to the loopback address 127.0.0.1 (used if you're not on a network). The localhost alias is also assigned to this address.

If you are on a TCP/IP network, however, your real IP address and hostname should appear in /etc/hosts. For example, if your hostname is goober.norelco.com, and your IP address is 128.253.154.32, add the following line to /etc/hosts:

```
  128.253.154.32      goober.norelco.com
```

If your hostname does not appear in `/etc/hosts`, you will not be able to set it.

To set your hostname, simply use the `hostname` command. For example, the command

> # *hostname -S goober.norelco.com*

sets the hostname to `goober.norelco.com`. In most cases, the `hostname` command is executed from one of the system startup files, such as `/etc/rc` or `/etc/rc.local`. Edit these two files and change the `hostname` command found there to set your own hostname; upon rebooting the system the hostname will be set to the new value.

4.11 What To Do In An Emergency

On some occasions, the system administrator will be faced with the problem of recovering from a complete disaster, such as forgetting the root password or trashing filesystems. The best advice is, *don't panic*. Everyone makes stupid mistakes—that's the best way to learn about system administration: the hard way.

Linux is not an unstable version of UNIX. In fact, I have had fewer problems with system hangs than with commercial versions of UNIX on many platforms. Linux also benefits from a strong complement of wizards who can help you get out of a bind.

The first step in investigating any problem is to attempt to fix it yourself. Poke around, see how things work. Too much of the time, a system administrator will post a desperate plea for help before looking into the problem at all. Most of the time, you'll find that fixing problems yourself is actually very easy. It is the path to guruhood.

There are very few cases where reinstalling the system from scratch is necessary. Many new users accidentally delete some essential system file, and immediately reach for the installation disks. This is not a good idea. Before taking such drastic measures, investigate the problem and ask others to help fix things up. In almost all cases, you can recover your system from a maintenance diskette.

4.11.1 Recovering using a maintenance diskette

One indispensable tool for the system administrator is the so called "boot/root disk"—a floppy which can be booted for a complete Linux system, independent of your hard drive. Boot/root disks are actually very simple—you create a root filesystem on the floppy, place all of the necessary utilities on it, and install LILO and a bootable kernel on the floppy. Another technique is to use one floppy for the kernel and another for the root filesystem. In any case, the result is the same: you are running a Linux system completely from floppy.

The canonical example of a boot/root disk is the Slackware boot disks[6]. These diskettes contain a bootable kernel and a root filesystem, all on floppy. They are intended to be used to install the Slackware distribution, but come in very handy when doing system maintenance.

The H.J Lu boot/root disk, available from `/pub/Linux/GCC/rootdisk` on `sunsite.unc.edu`, is another example of such a maintenance disk. Or, if you're ambitious, you can create your own. In most cases, however, using a pre-made boot/root disk is much easier and will probably be more complete.

---

[6]See Section 2.1.1 for information on downloading these from the Internet. For this procedure, you don't need to download the entire Slackware release—only the boot and root diskettes.

Using a boot/root disk is very simple. Just boot the disk on your system, and login as `root` (usually no password). In order to access the files on your hard drive, you will need to mount your filesystems by hand. For example, the command

> # *mount -t ext2 /dev/hda2 /mnt*

will mount an ext2fs filesystem on `/dev/hda2` under `/mnt`. Remember that `/` is now on the boot/root disk itself; you need to mount your hard drive filesystems under some directory in order to access the files. Therefore, `/etc/passwd` on your hard drive is now `/mnt/etc/passwd` if you mount your root filesystem on `/mnt`.

4.11.2   Fixing the root password

If you forget your root password, no problem. Just boot the boot/root disk, mount your root filesystem on `/mnt`, and blank out the password field for `root` in `/mnt/etc/passwd`, as so:

```
root::0:0:root:/:/bin/sh
```

Now `root` has no password; when you reboot from the hard drive you should be able to login as `root` and reset the password using `passwd`.

Aren't you glad you learned how to use `vi`? On your boot/root disk, other editors such as Emacs probably aren't available, but `vi` should be.

4.11.3   Fixing trashed filesystems

If you somehow trash your filesystems, you can run `e2fsck` (if you use the ext2fs filesystem type, that is) to correct any damaged data on the filesystems from floppy. Other filesystem types use different forms of the `fsck` command; see Section 4.8 for details.

When checking your filesystems from floppy, it's best for the filesystems to not be mounted.

One common cause of filesystem damage is superblock corruption. The *superblock* is the "header" of the filesystem that contains information on the filesystem status, size, free blocks, and so forth. If you corrupt your superblock (for example, by accidentally writing data directly to the filesystem's partition), the system may not recognize the filesystem at all. Any attempt to mount the filesystem could fail, and `e2fsck` won't be able to fix the problem.

Happily, the *ext2fs* filesystem type saves copies of the superblock at "block group" boundaries on the drive—usually, every 8K blocks. In order to tell `e2fsck` to use a copy of the superblock, you can use a command such as

> # *e2fsck -b 8193 ⟨partition⟩*

where ⟨**partition**⟩ is the partition on which the filesystem resides. The `-b 8193` option tells `e2fsck` to use the copy of the superblock stored at block 8193 in the filesystem.

4.11.4   Recovering lost files

If you accidentally deleted important files on your system, there's no way to "undelete" them. However, you can copy the relevant files from the floppy to your hard drive. For example, if you deleted `/bin/login` on your system (which allows you to login), simply boot the boot/root floppy, mount the root filesystem on `/mnt`, and use the command

># *cp -a /bin/login /mnt/bin/login*

The `-a` option tells `cp` to preserve the permissions on the file(s) being copied.

Of course, if the files you deleted weren't essential system files which have counterparts on the boot/root floppy, you're out of luck. If you made backups, you can always restore from them.

4.11.5 Fixing trashed libraries

If you accidentally trashed your libraries or symbolic links in `/lib`, more than likely commands which depended on those libraries will no longer run (see Section 4.7.2). The easiest solution is to boot your boot/root floppy, mount your root filesystem, and fix the libraries in `/mnt/lib`.

Chapter 5

Advanced Features

This chapter will introduce you to some of the more interesting features of Linux. This assumes that you have at least basic UNIX experience, and understand the information contained in the previous chapters.

The most important aspect of Linux that distinguishes it from other implementations of UNIX is its open design and philosophy. Linux was not developed by a small team of programmers headed by a marketing committee with a single goal in mind. It was developed by an ever-increasing group of hackers, putting what they wanted into a homebrew UNIX system. The types of software and diversity of design in the Linux world is large. Some people dislike this lack of uniformity and conformity—however, some call it one of the strongest qualities of Linux.

5.1 The X Window System

The X Window System is a large and powerful (and somewhat complex) graphics environment for UNIX systems. The original X Window System code was developed at MIT; commercial vendors have since made X the industry standard for UNIX platforms. Virtually every UNIX workstation in the world runs some variant of the X Window system.

A free port of the MIT X Window System version 11, release 6 (X11R6) for 80386/80486/Pentium UNIX systems has been developed by a team of programmers originally headed by David Wexelblat[1]. The release, known as XFree86[2], is available for System V/386, 386BSD, and other x86 UNIX implementations, including Linux. It includes all of the required binaries, support files, libraries, and tools.

Configuring and using the X Window System is far beyond the scope of this book. You are encouraged to read *The X Window System: A User's Guide*—see Appendix A for information on this book. In this section, we'll give a step-by-step description of how to install and configure XFree86 for Linux, but you will have to fill in some of the details yourself by reading the documentation released with XFree86 itself. (This documentation is discussed below.) The Linux *XFree86 HOWTO* is another good source of information.

5.1.1 Hardware requirements

As of XFree86 version 3.1, released in September 1994, the following video chipsets are supported. The documentation included with your video adaptor should specify the chipset used. If you are in the market for a new video card, or are buying a new machine that comes with a video card, have the vendor find

---

[1] David may be reached on the Internet at dwex@XFree86.org.

[2] XFree86 is a trademark of The XFree86 Project, Inc.

out exactly what the make, model, and chipset of the video card is. This may require the vendor to call technical support on your behalf; in general vendors will be happy to do this. Many PC hardware vendors will state that the video card is a "standard SVGA card" which "should work" on your system. Explain that your software (mention Linux and XFree86!) does not support all video chipsets and that you must have detailed information.

You can also determine your videocard chipset by running the `SuperProbe` program included with the XFree86 distribution. This is covered in more detail below.

The following standard SVGA chipsets are supported:

- Tseng ET3000, ET4000AX, ET4000/W32

- Western Digital/Paradise PVGA1

- Western Digital WD90C00, WD90C10, WD90C11, WD90C24, WD90C30, WD90C31, WD90C33

- Genoa GVGA

- Trident TVGA8800CS, TVGA8900B, TVGA8900C, TVGA8900CL, TVGA9000, TVGA9000i, TVGA9100B, TVGA9200CX, TVGA9320, TVGA9400CX, TVGA9420

- ATI 18800, 18800-1, 28800-2, 28800-4, 28800-5, 28800-6, 68800-3, 68800-6, 68800AX, 68800LX, 88800

- NCR 77C22, 77C22E, 77C22E+

- Cirrus Logic CLGD5420, CLGD5422, CLGD5424, CLGD5426, CLGD5428, CLGD5429, CLGD5430, CLGD5434, CLGD6205, CLGD6215, CLGD6225, CLGD6235, CLGD6420

- Compaq AVGA

- OAK OTI067, OTI077

- Avance Logic AL2101

- MX MX68000, MX680010

- Video 7/Headland Technologies HT216-32

The following SVGA chipsets with accelerated features are also supported:

- 8514/A (and true clones)

- ATI Mach8, Mach32

- Cirrus CLGD5420, CLGD5422, CLGD5424, CLGD5426, CLGD5428, CLGD5429, CLGD5430, CLGD5434, CLGD6205, CLGD6215, CLGD6225, CLGD6235

- S3 86C911, 86C924, 86C801, 86C805, 86C805i, 86C928, 86C864, 86C964

- Western Digital WD90C31, WD90C33

- Weitek P9000

- IIT AGX-014, AGX-015, AGX-016

- Tseng ET4000/W32, ET4000/W32i, ET4000/W32p

Video cards using these chipsets are supported on all bus types, including VLB and PCI.

All of the above are supported in both 256 color and monochrome modes, with the exception of the Avance Logic, MX and Video 7 chipsets, which are only supported in 256 color mode. If your video card has enough DRAM installed, many of the above chipsets are supported in 16 and 32 bits-per-pixel mode (specifically, some Mach32, P9000, S3 and Cirrus boards). The usual configuration is 8 bits per pixel (that is, 256 colors).

The monochrome server also supports generic VGA cards, the Hercules monochrome card, the Hyundai HGC1280, Sigma LaserView, and Apollo monochrome cards. On the Compaq AVGA, only 64k of video memory is supported for the monochrome server, and the GVGA has not been tested with more than 64k.

This list will undoubtedly expand as time passes. The release notes for the current version of XFree86 should contain the complete list of supported video chipsets.

One problem faced by the XFree86 developers is that some video card manufacturers use non-standard mechanisms for determining clock frequencies used to drive the card. Some of these manufacturers either don't release specifications describing how to program the card, or they require developers to sign a non-disclosure statement to obtain the information. This would obviously restrict the free distribution of the XFree86 software, something that the XFree86 development team is not willing to do. For a long time, this has been a problem with certain video cards manufactured by Diamond, but as of release 3.1 of XFree86, Diamond has started to work with the development team to release free drivers for these cards.

The suggested setup for XFree86 under Linux is a 486 machine with at least 8 megabytes of RAM, and a video card with a chipset listed above. For optimal performance, we suggest using an accelerated card, such as an S3-chipset card. You should check the documentation for XFree86 and verify that your particular card is supported before taking the plunge and purchasing expensive hardware. Benchmark ratings comparisons for various video cards under XFree86 are posted routinely to the USENET newsgroups `comp.windows.x.i386unix` and `comp.os.linux.misc`.

As a side note, my personal Linux system is a 486DX2-66, 20 megabytes of RAM, and is equipped with a VLB S3-864 chipset card with 2 megabytes of DRAM. I have run X benchmarks on this machine as well as on Sun Sparc IPX workstations. The Linux system is roughly 7 times faster than the Sparc IPX (for the curious, XFree86-3.1 under Linux, with this video card, runs at around 171,000 xstones; the Sparc IPX at around 24,000). In general, XFree86 on a Linux system with an accelerated SVGA card will give you much greater performance than that found on commercial UNIX workstations (which usually employ simple framebuffers for graphics).

Your machine will need at least 4 megabytes of physical RAM, and 16 megabytes of virtual RAM (for example, 8 megs physical and 8 megs swap). Remember that the more physical RAM that you have, the less that the system will swap to and from disk when memory is low. Because swapping is inherently slow (disks are very slow compared to memory), having 8 megabytes of RAM or more is necessary to run XFree86 comfortably. A system with 4 megabytes of physical RAM could run *much* (up to 10 times) more slowly than one with 8 megs or more.

5.1.2   Installing XFree86

The Linux binary distribution of XFree86 can be found on a number of FTP sites. On `sunsite.unc.edu`, it is found in the directory `/pub/Linux/X11`. (As of the time of this writing, the current version is 3.1; newer versions are released periodically).

It's quite likely that you obtained XFree86 as part of a Linux distribution, in which case downloading the software separately is not necessary.

If you are downloading XFree86 directly, This table lists the files in the XFree86-3.1 distribution.

One of the following servers is required:

File	Description
XF86-3.1-8514.tar.gz	Server for 8514-based boards.
XF86-3.1-AGX.tar.gz	Server for AGX-based boards.
XF86-3.1-Mach32.tar.gz	Server for Mach32-based boards.
XF86-3.1-Mach8.tar.gz	Server for Mach8-based boards.
XF86-3.1-Mono.tar.gz	Server for monochrome video modes.
XF86-3.1-P9000.tar.gz	Server for P9000-based boards.
XF86-3.1-S3.tar.gz	Server for S3-based boards.
XF86-3.1-SVGA.tar.gz	Server for Super VGA-based boards.
XF86-3.1-VGA16.tar.gz	Server for VGA/EGA-based boards.
XF86-3.1-W32.tar.gz	Server for ET4000/W32-based boards.

All of the following files are required:

File	Description
XF86-3.1-bin.tar.gz	The rest of the X11R6 binaries.
XF86-3.1-cfg.tar.gz	Config files for xdm, xinit and fs.
XF86-3.1-doc.tar.gz	Documentation and man pages.
XF86-3.1-inc.tar.gz	Include files.
XF86-3.1-lib.tar.gz	Shared X libraries and support files.
XF86-3.1-fnt.tar.gz	Basic fonts.

The following files are optional:

File	Description
XF86-3.1-ctrb.tar.gz	Selected contrib programs.
XF86-3.1-extra.tar.gz	Extra XFree86 servers and binaries.
XF86-3.1-lkit.tar.gz	Server linkkit for customization.
XF86-3.1-fnt75.tar.gz	75-dpi screen fonts.
XF86-3.1-fnt100.tar.gz	100-dpi screen fonts.
XF86-3.1-fntbig.tar.gz	Large Kanji and other fonts.
XF86-3.1-fntscl.tar.gz	Scaled fonts (Speedo, Type1).
XF86-3.1-man.tar.gz	Manual pages.
XF86-3.1-pex.tar.gz	PEX binaries, includes and libraries.
XF86-3.1-slib.tar.gz	Static X libraries and support files.
XF86-3.1-usrbin.tar.gz	Daemons which reside in /usr/bin.
XF86-3.1-xdmshdw.tar.gz	Shadow password version of xdm.

The XFree86 directory should contain README files and installation notes for the current version.

All that is required to install XFree86 is to obtain the above files, create the directory /usr/X11R6 (as root), and unpack the files from /usr/X11R6 with a command such as:

    # *gzip –dc XF86-3.1-bin.tar.gz | tar xfB –*

Remember that these tar files are packed relative to /usr/X11R6, so it's important to unpack the files there.

After unpacking the files, you first need to link the file /usr/X11R6/bin/X to the server that you're using. For example, if you wish to use the SVGA color server, /usr/bin/X11/X should be linked to /usr/X11R6/bin/XF86_SVGA. If you wish to use the monochrome server instead, relink this file to XF86_MONO with the command

ln –sf /usr/X11R6/bin/XF86_MONO /usr/X11R6/bin/X

The same holds true if you are using one of the other servers.

If you aren't sure which server to use, or don't know your video card chipset, you can run the
`SuperProbe` program found in `/usr/X11R6/bin` (included in the `XF86-3.1-bin` listed above). This
program will attempt to determine your video chipset type and other information; write down its output
for later reference.

You need to make sure that `/usr/X11R6/bin` is on your path. This can be done by editing your
system default `/etc/profile` or `/etc/csh.login` (based on the shell that you, or other users on your
system, use). Or you can simply add the directory to your personal path by modifying `/etc/.bashrc` or
`/etc/.cshrc`, based on your shell.

You also need to make sure that `/usr/X11R6/lib` can be located by `ld.so`, the runtime linker. To do
this, add the line

```
/usr/X11R6/lib
```

to the file `/etc/ld.so.conf`, and run `/sbin/ldconfig`, as `root`.

5.1.3   Configuring XFree86

Setting up XFree86 is not difficult in most cases. However, if you happen to be using hardware for which
drivers are under development, or wish to obtain the best performance or resolution from an accelerated
graphics card, configuring XFree86 can be somewhat time-consuming.

In this section we will describe how to create and edit the `XF86Config` file, which configures the
XFree86 server. In many cases it is best to start out with a "basic" XFree86 configuration, one which uses
a low resolution, such as 640x480, which should be supported on all video cards and monitor types. Once
you have XFree86 working at a lower, standard resolution, you can tweak the configuration to exploit the
capabilities of your video hardware. The idea is that you want to know that XFree86 works at all on your
system, and that something isn't wrong with your installation, before attempting the sometimes difficult
task of setting up XFree86 for real use.

In addition to the information listed here, you should read the following documentation:

- The   XFree86   documentation
  in `/usr/X11R6/lib/X11/doc` (contained within the `XFree86-3.1-doc` package). You should
  especially see the file `README.Config`, which is an XFree86 configuration tutorial.

- Several video chipsets have separate `README` files in the above directory (such as `README.Cirrus`
  and `README.S3`). Read one of these if applicable.

- The man page for `XFree86`.

- The man page for `XF86Config`.

- The man page for the particular server that you are using (such as `XF86_SVGA` or `XF86_S3`).

The main XFree86 configuration file is `/usr/X11R6/lib/X11/XF86Config`. This file contains information on your mouse, video card parameters, and so on. The file `XF86Config.eg` is provided with the
XFree86 distribution as an example. Copy this file to `XF86Config` and edit it as a starting point.

The `XF86Config` man page explains the format of this file in detail. Read this man page now, if you have not done so already.

We are going to present a sample `XF86Config` file, piece by piece. This file may not look exactly like the sample file included in the XFree86 distribution, but the structure is the same.

◇   Note that the `XF86Config` file format may change with each version of XFree86; this information is only valid for XFree86 version 3.1.

◇   Also, you should not simply copy the configuration file listed here to your own system and attempt to use it. Attempting to use a configuration file which doesn't correspond to your hardware could drive the monitor at a frequency which is too high for it; there have been reports of monitors (especially fixed-frequency monitors) being damaged or destroyed by using an incorrectly configured `XF86Config` file. The bottom line is this: Make absolutely sure that your `XF86Config` file corresponds to your hardware before you attempt to use it.

Each section of the `XF86Config` file is surrounded by the pair of lines `Section "`⟨*section-name*⟩`"`... `EndSection`. The first part of the `XF86Config` file is `Files`, which looks like this:

```
Section "Files"
    RgbPath      "/usr/X11R6/lib/X11/rgb"
    FontPath     "/usr/X11R6/lib/X11/fonts/misc/"
    FontPath     "/usr/X11R6/lib/X11/fonts/75dpi/"
EndSection
```

The `RgbPath` line sets the path to the X11R6 RGB color database, and each `FontPath` line sets the path to a directory containing X11 fonts. In general you shouldn't have to modify these lines; just be sure that there is a `FontPath` entry for each font type that you have installed (that is, for each directory in `/usr/X11R6/lib/X11/fonts`).

The next section is `ServerFlags`, which specifies several global flags for the server. In general this section is empty.

```
Section "ServerFlags"
# Uncomment this to cause a core dump at the spot where a signal is
# received.  This may leave the console in an unusable state, but may
# provide a better stack trace in the core dump to aid in debugging
#    NoTrapSignals

# Uncomment this to disable the <Crtl><Alt><BS> server abort sequence
#    DontZap
EndSection
```

Here, we have all lines within the section commented out.

The next section is `Keyboard`. This should be fairly intuitive.

```
Section "Keyboard"
    Protocol    "Standard"
    AutoRepeat  500 5
    ServerNumLock
EndSection
```

Other options are available as well—see the `XF86Config` file if you wish to modify the keyboard configuration. The above should work for most systems.

The next section is `Pointer` which specifies parameters for the mouse device.

```
Section "Pointer"

    Protocol     "MouseSystems"
    Device       "/dev/mouse"

# Baudrate and SampleRate are only for some Logitech mice
#     BaudRate   9600
#     SampleRate 150

# Emulate3Buttons is an option for 2-button Microsoft mice
#     Emulate3Buttons

# ChordMiddle is an option for some 3-button Logitech mice
#     ChordMiddle

EndSection
```

The only options that you should concern yourself with now are `Protocol` and `Device`. `Protocol` specifies the mouse *protocol* that your mouse uses (not the make or brand of mouse). Valid types for `Protocol` (under Linux—there are other options available for other operating systems) are:

- BusMouse

- Logitech

- Microsoft

- MMSeries

- Mouseman

- MouseSystems

- PS/2

- MMHitTab

`BusMouse` should be used for the Logitech busmouse. Note that older Logitech mice should use `Logitech`, but newer Logitech mice use either `Microsoft` or `Mouseman` protocols. This is a case in which the protocol doesn't necessarily have anything to do with the make of the mouse.

`Device` specifies the device file where the mouse can be accessed. On most Linux systems, this is `/dev/mouse`. `/dev/mouse` is usually a link to the appropriate serial port (such as `/dev/cua0`) for serial mice, or to the appropriate busmouse device for busmice. At any rate, be sure that the device file listed in `Device` exists.

The next section is `Monitor`, which specifies the characteristics of your monitor. As with other sections in the `XF86Config` file, there may be more than one `Monitor` section. This is useful if you have multiple monitors connected to a system, or use the same `XF86Config` file under multiple hardware configurations. In general, though, you will need a single `Monitor` section.

```
Section "Monitor"

    Identifier  "CTX 5468 NI"

    # These values are for a CTX 5468NI only! Don't attempt to use
```

```
# them with your monitor (unless you have this model)

Bandwidth    60
HorizSync    30-38,47- 50
VertRefresh  50-90

# Modes: Name      dotclock  horiz              vert

ModeLine "640x480"   25     640 664 760 800    480 491 493 525
ModeLine "800x600"   36     800 824 896 1024   600 601 603 625
ModeLine "1024x768"  65     1024 1088 1200 1328 768 783 789 818
```

```
EndSection
```

The `Identifier` line is used to give an arbitrary name to the `Monitor` entry. This can be any string; you will use it to refer to the `Monitor` entry later in the `XF86Config` file.

they are listed below.

`HorizSync` specifies the valid horizontal sync frequencies for your monitor, in kHz. If you have a multisync monitor, this can be a range of values (or several comma-separated ranges), as seen above. If you have a fixed-frequency monitor, this will be a list of discrete values, such as:

```
HorizSync    31.5, 35.2, 37.9, 35.5, 48.95
```

Your monitor manual should list these values in the technical specifications section. If you do not have this information available, you should either contact the manufacturer or vendor of your monitor to obtain it. There are other sources of information, as well;

`VertRefresh` specifies the valid vertical refresh rates (or vertical synchronization frequencies) for your monitor, in Hz. Like `HorizSync` this can be a range or a list of discrete values; your monitor manual should list them.

`HorizSync` and `VertRefresh` are used only to double-check that the monitor resolutions that you specify are in valid ranges. This is to reduce the chance that you will damage your monitor by attempting to drive it at a frequency for which it was not designed.

The `ModeLine` directive is used to specify a single resolution mode for your monitor. The format of `ModeLine` is

```
ModeLine ⟨name⟩ ⟨clock⟩ ⟨horiz-values⟩ ⟨vert-values⟩
```

⟨*name*⟩ is an arbitrary string, which you will use to refer to the resolution mode later in the file. ⟨*dot-clock*⟩ is the driving clock frequency, or "dot clock" associated with the resolution mode. A dot clock is usually specified in MHz, and is the rate at which the video card must send pixels to the monitor at this resolution. ⟨*horiz-values*⟩ and ⟨*vert-values*⟩ are four numbers each which specify when the electron gun of the monitor should fire, and when the horizontal and vertical sync pulses fire during a sweep.

How can you determine the `ModeLine` values for your monitor? The file `VideoModes.doc`, included with the XFree86 distribution, describes in detail how to determine these values for each resolution mode that your monitor supports. First of all, ⟨**clock**⟩ must correspond to one of the dot clock values that your video card can produce. Later in the `XF86Config` file you will specify these clocks; you can only use video modes which have a ⟨**clock**⟩ value supported by your video card.

There are two files included in the XFree86 distribution which may include `ModeLine` data for your monitor. These files are `modeDB.txt` and `Monitors`, both of which are found in `/usr/X11R6/lib/X11/doc`.

You should start with `ModeLine` values for the VESA standard monitor timings, which most monitors support. `modeDB.txt` includes timing values for VESA standard resolutions. In that file, you will see entries such as

```
# 640x480@60Hz Non-Interlaced mode
# Horizontal Sync = 31.5kHz
# Timing: H=(0.95us, 3.81us, 1.59us), V=(0.35ms, 0.064ms, 1.02ms)
#
# name        clock    horizontal timing      vertical timing        flags
  "640x480"   25.175   640  664  760  800     480  491  493  525
```

This is a VESA standard timing for a 640x480 video mode. It uses a dot clock of 25.175, which your video card must support to use this mode (more on this later). To include this entry in the `XF86Config` file, you'd use the line

```
ModeLine "640x480" 25.175  640 664 760 800  480 491 493 525
```

Note that the ⟨*name*⟩ argument to `ModeLine` (in this case `"640x480"`) is an arbitrary string—the convention is to name the mode after the resolution, but ⟨*name*⟩ can technically be anything descriptive which describes the mode to you.

For each `ModeLine` used the server will check that the specifications for the mode fall within the range of values specified with `Bandwidth`, `HorizSync` and `VertRefresh`. If they do not, the server will complain when you attempt to start up X (more on this later). For one thing, the dot clock used by the mode should not be greater than the value used for `Bandwidth`. (However, in many cases it is safe to use modes with a slightly higher bandwidth than your monitor can support.)

If the VESA standard timings do not work for you (you'll know after trying to use them later) then the files `modeDB.txt` and `Monitors` include specific mode values for many monitor types. You can create `ModeLine` entries from the values found in those two files as well. Be sure to only use values for the specific model of monitor that you have. Note that many 14 and 15-inch monitors cannot support higher resolution modes, and often resolutions of 1024x768 at low dot clocks. This means that if you can't find high resolution modes for your monitor in these files, then your monitor probably does not support those resolution modes.

If you are completely at a loss, and can't find working `ModeLine` values for your monitor, you can follow the instructions in the `VideoModes.doc` file included in the XFree86 distribution to generate `ModeLine` values from the specifications listed in your monitor's manual. While your mileage will certainly vary when attempting to generate `ModeLine` values by hand, this is a good place to look if you can't find the values that you need. `VideoModes.doc` also describes the format of the `ModeLine` directive and other aspects of the XFree86 server in gory detail.

Lastly, if you do obtain `ModeLine` values which are almost, but not quite, right, then it may be possible to simply modify the values slightly to obtain the desired result. For example, if while running XFree86 the image on the monitor is shifted slightly, or seems to "roll", you can follow the instructions in the `VideoModes.doc` file to try to fix these values. Also, be sure to check the knobs and controls on the monitor itself! In many cases it is necessary to change the horizontal or vertical size of the display after starting up XFree86 in order for the image to be centered and be of the appropriate size. Having these controls on the front of the monitor can certainly make life easier.

◇   You shouldn't use monitor timing values or `ModeLine` values for monitors other than the model that you own. If you attempt to drive the monitor at a frequency for which it was not designed, you can damage or even destroy it.

The next section of the `XF86Config` file is `Device`, which specifies parameters for your video card. Here is an example.

```
Section "Device"
        Identifier "#9 GXE 64"

        # Nothing yet; we fill in these values later.

    EndSection
```

This section defines properties for a particular video card. Identifier is an arbitrary string describing the card; you will use this string to refer to the card later.

Initially, you don't need to include anything in the Device section, except for Identifier. This is because we will be using the X server itself to probe for the properties of the video card, and entering them into the Device section later. The XFree86 server is capable of probing for the video chipset, clocks, RAMDAC, and amount of video RAM on the board.

Before we do this, however, we need to finish writing the XF86Config file. The next section is Screen, which specifies the monitor/video card combination to use for a particular server.

```
Section "Screen"
        Driver      "Accel"
        Device      "#9 GXE 64"
        Monitor     "CTX 5468 NI"
        Subsection "Display"
            Depth       16
            Modes       "1024x768" "800x600" "640x480"
            ViewPort    0 0
            Virtual     1024 768
        EndSubsection
    EndSection
```

The Driver line specifies the X server that you will be using. The value values for Driver are:

- Accel: For the XF86_S3, XF86_Mach32, XF86_Mach8, XF86_8514, XF86_P9000, XF86_AGX, and XF86_W32 servers;

- SVGA: For the XF86_SVGA server;

- VGA16: For the XF86_VGA16 server;

- VGA2: For the XF86_Mono server;

- Mono: For the non-VGA monochrome drivers in the XF86_Mono and XF86_VGA16 servers.

You should be sure that /usr/X11R6/bin/X is a symbolic link to the server that you are using.

The Device line specifies the Identifier of the Device section corresponding to the video card to use for this server. Above, we created a Device section with the line

```
Identifier "#9 GXE 64"
```

Therefore, we use "#9 GXE 64" on the Device line here.

Similarly, the Monitor line specifies the name of the Monitor section to be used with this server. Here, "CTX 5468 NI" is the Identifier used in the Monitor section described above.

Subsection "Display" defines several properties of the XFree86 server corresponding to your monitor/video card combination. The XF86Config file describes all of these options in detail; most of them are icing on the cake and not necessary to get the system working.

The options that you should know about are:

- Depth. Defines the number of color planes—the number of bits per pixel. Usually, Depth is set to 8. For the VGA16 server, you would use a depth of 4, and for the monochrome server a depth of 1. If you are using an accelerated video card with enough memory to support more bits per pixel, you can set Depth to 16, 24, or 32. If you have problems with depths higher than 8, set it back to 8 and attempt to debug the problem later.

- Modes. This is the list of video mode names which have been defined using the ModeLine directive in the Monitor section. In the above section, we used ModeLines named "1024x768", "800x600", and "640x48"0. Therefore, we use a Modes line of

        Modes   "1024x768" "800x600" "640x480"

The first mode listed on this line will be the default when XFree86 starts up. After XFree86 is running, you can switch between the modes listed here using the keys ctrl alt numeric + and ctrl alt numeric - .

It might be best, when initially configuring XFree86, to use lower resolution video modes, such as 640x480, which tend to work on most systems. Once you have the basic configuration working you can modify XF86Config to support higher resolutions.

- Virtual. Sets the virtual desktop size. XFree86 has the ability to use any additional memory on your video card to extend the size of your desktop. When you move the mouse pointer to the edge of the display, the desktop will scroll, bringing the additional space into view. Therefore, even if you are running at a lower video resolution such as 800x600, you can set Virtual to the total resolution which your video card can support (a 1-megabyte video card can support 1024x768 at a depth of 8 bits per pixel; a 2-megabyte card 1280x1024 at depth 8, or 1024x768 at depth 16). Of course, the entire area will not be visible at once, but it can still be used.

The Virtual feature is a nice way to utilize the memory of your video card, but it is rather limited. If you want to use a true virtual desktop, we suggest using fvwm, or a similar window manager, instead. fvwm allows you to have rather large virtual desktops (implemented by hiding windows, and so forth, instead of actually storing the entire desktop in video memory at once). See the man pages for fvwm for more details about this; most Linux systems use fvwm by default.

- ViewPort. If you are using the Virtual option described above, ViewPort sets the coordinates of the upper-left-hand corner of the virtual desktop when XFree86 starts up. Virtual 0 0 is often used; if this is unspecified then the desktop is centered on the virtual desktop display (which may be undesirable to you).

Many other options for this section exist; see the XF86Config man page for a complete description. In practice these other options are not necessary to get XFree86 initially working.

5.1.4 Filling in video card information

Your XF86Config file is now ready to go, with the exception of complete information on the video card. What we're going to do is use the X server to probe for the rest of this information, and fill it into XF86Config.

Instead of probing for this information with the X server, the XF86Config values for many cards are listed in the files modeDB.txt, AccelCards, and Devices. These files are all found in /usr/X11R6/lib/X11/doc. In addition, there are various README files for certain chipsets. You should look in these files for information on your video card, and use that information (the clock values, chipset type, and any options) in the XF86Config file. If any information is missing, you can probe for it as described here.

In these examples we will demonstrate configuration for a #9 GXE 64 video card, which uses the XF86_S3 chipset. This card happens to be the one which the author uses, but the discussion here applies to any video card.

The first thing to do is to determine the video chipset used on the card. Running SuperProbe (found in /usr/X11R6/bin) will tell you this information, but you need to know the chipset name as it is known to the X server.

To do this, run the command

```
X -showconfig
```

This will give the chipset names known to your X server. (The man pages for each X server list these as well.) For example, with the accelerated XF86_S3 server, we obtain:

```
XFree86 Version 3.1 / X Window System
(protocol Version 11, revision 0, vendor release 6000)
Operating System: Linux
Configured drivers:
  S3: accelerated server for S3 graphics adaptors (Patchlevel 0)
      mmio_928, s3_generic
```

The valid chipset names for this server are mmio_928 and s3_generic. The XF86_S3 man page describes these chipsets and which videocards use them. In the case of the #9 GXE 64 video card, mmio_928 is appropriate.

If you don't know which chipset to use, the X server can probe it for you. To do this, run the command

```
X -probeonly > /tmp/x.out 2>&1
```

if you use bash as your shell. If you use csh, try:

```
X -probeonly &> /tmp/x.out
```

You should run this command while the system is unloaded, that is, while no other activity is occurring on the system. This command will also probe for your video card dot clocks (as seen below), and system load can throw off this calculation.

The output from the above (in /tmp/x.out should contain lines such as the following:

```
XFree86 Version 3.1 / X Window System
(protocol Version 11, revision 0, vendor release 6000)
Operating System: Linux
Configured drivers:
  S3: accelerated server for S3 graphics adaptors (Patchlevel 0)
      mmio_928, s3_generic
```
Several lines deleted...

```
(--) S3: card type: 386/486 localbus
(--) S3: chipset:   864 rev. 0
(--) S3: chipset driver: mmio_928
```

Here, we see that the two valid chipsets for this server (in this case, XF86_S3) are mmio_928 and s3_generic. The server probed for and found a video card using the mmio_928 chipset.

In the Device section of the XF86Config file, add a Chipset line, containing the name of the chipset as determined above. For example,

```
Section "Device"
        # We already had Identifier here...
        Identifier "#9 GXE 64"
        # Add this line:
        Chipset "mmio_928"
EndSection
```

Now we need to determine the driving clock frequencies used by the video card. A driving clock frequency, or dot clock, is simply a rate at which the video card can send pixels to the monitor. As we have seen, each monitor resolution has a dot clock associated with it. Now we need to determine which dot clocks are made available by the video card.

First you should look into the files (modeDB.txt, and so forth) mentioned above and see if your card's clocks are listed there. The dot clocks will usually be a list of 8 or 16 values, all of which are in MHz. For example, when looking at modeDB.txt we see an entry for the Cardinal ET4000 video board, which looks like this:

```
# chip   ram   virtual   clocks                          default-mode  flags
 ET4000  1024  1024 768   25  28  38  36  40  45  32   0  "1024x768"
```

As we can see, the dot clocks for this card are 25, 28, 38, 36, 40, 45, 32, and 0 MHz.

In the Devices section of the XF86Config file, you should add a Clocks line containing the list of dot clocks for your card. For example, for the clocks above, we would add the line

```
        Clocks 25 28 38 36 40 45 32 0
```

to the Devices section of the file, after Chipset. Note that the order of the clocks is important! Don't resort the list of clocks or remove duplicates.

If you cannot find the dot clocks associated with your card, the X server can probe for these as well. Using the X -probeonly command described above, the output should contain lines which look like the following:

```
(--) S3: clocks: 25.18  28.32  38.02  36.15  40.33  45.32  32.00  00.00
```

We could then add a Clocks line containing all of these values, as printed. You can use more than one Clocks line in XF86Config should all of the values (sometimes there are more than 8 clock values printed) not fit onto one line. Again, be sure to keep the list of clocks in order as they are printed.

Be sure that there is no Clocks line (or that it is commented out) in the Devices section of the file when using X -probeonly to probe for the clocks. If there is a Clocks line present, the server will *not* probe for the clocks—it will use the values given in XF86Config.

Note that some accelerated video boards use a programmable clock chip. (See the XF86_Accel man page for details; this generally applies to S3, AGX, and XGA-2 boards.) This chip essentially allows the X server to tell the card which dot clocks to use. If this is the case, then you may not find a list of dot clocks for the card in any of the above files. Or, the list of dot clocks printed when using X -probeonly will only contain one or two discrete clock values, with the rest being duplicates or zero.

For boards which use a programmable clock chip, you would use a ClockChip line, instead of a Clocks line, in your XF86Config file. ClockChip gives the name of the clock chip as used by the video card; the man pages for each server describe what these are. For example, in the file README.S3, we see that several S3-864 video cards use an "ICD2061A" clock chip, and that we should use the line

```
ClockChip "icd2061a"
```

instead of Clocks in the XF86Config file. As with Clocks, this line should go in the Devices section, after Chipset.

Similarly, some accelerated cards require you to specify the RAMDAC chip type in the XF86Config file, using a Ramdac line. The XF86_Accel man page describes this option. Usually, the X server will correctly probe for the RAMDAC.

Some video card types require you to specify several options in the Devices section of XF86Config. These options will be described in the man page for your server, as well as in the various files (such as README.cirrus or README.S3. These options are enabled using the Option line. For example, the #9 GXE 64 card requires two options:

```
Option "number_nine"
Option "dac_8_bit"
```

Usually, the X server will work without these options, but they are necessary to obtain the best performance. There are too many such options to list here, and they each depend on the particular video card being used. If you must use one of these options, fear not—the X server man pages and various files in /usr/X11R6/lib/X11/doc will tell you what they are.

So, when you're finished, you should end up with a Devices section which looks something like this:

```
Section "Device"
        # Device section for the #9 GXE 64 only !
        Identifier "#9 GXE 64"
        Chipset "mmio_928"
        ClockChip "icd2061a"
        Option "number_nine"
        Option "dac_8_bit"
EndSection
```

Most video cards will require a Clocks line, instead of ClockChip, as described above. The above Device entry is only valid for a particular video card, the #9 GXE 64. It is given here only as an example.

There are other options that you can include in the Devices entry. Check the X server man pages for the gritty details, but the above should suffice for most systems.

5.1.5   Running XFree86

With your XF86Config file configured, you're ready to fire up the X server and give it a spin. First, be sure that /usr/X11R6/bin is on your path.

The command to start up XFree86 is

```
startx
```

This is a front-end to xinit (in case you're used to using xinit on other UNIX systems).

This command will start the X server and run the commands found in the file .xinitrc in your home directory. .xinitrc is just a shell script containing X clients to run. If this file does not exist, the system default /usr/X11R6/lib/X11/xinit/xinitrc will be used.

A standard .xinitrc file looks like this:

```
#!/bin/sh

xterm -fn 7x13bold -geometry 80x32+10+50 &
xterm -fn 9x15bold -geometry 80x34+30-10 &
oclock -geometry 70x70-7+7 &
xsetroot -solid midnightblue &

exec twm
```

This script will start up two xterm clients, an oclock, and set the root window (background) color to midnightblue. It will then start up twm, the window manager. Note that twm is executed with the shell's exec statement; this causes the xinit process to be replaced with twm. Once the twm process exits, the X server will shut down. You can cause twm to exit by using the root menus: depress mouse button 1 on the desktop background—this will display a pop up menu which will allow you to Exit Twm.

Be sure that the last command in .xinitrc is started with exec, and that it is not placed into the background (no ampersand on the end of the line). Otherwise the X server will shut down as soon as it has started the clients in the .xinitrc file.

Alternately, you can exit X by pressing `ctrl`-`alt`-`backspace` in combination. This will kill the X server directly, exiting the window system.

The above is a very, very simple desktop configuration. Many wonderful programs and configurations are available with a bit of work on your .xinitrc file. For example, the fvwm window manager will provide a virtual desktop, and you can customize colors, fonts, window sizes and positions, and so forth to your heart's content. Although the X Window System might appear to be simplistic at first, it is extremely powerful once you customize it for yourself.

If you are new to the X Window System environment, we strongly suggest picking up a book such as *The X Window System: A User's Guide*. Using and configuring X is far too in-depth to cover here. See the man pages for xterm, oclock, and twm for clues on getting started.

5.1.6   Running into trouble

Often, something will not be quite right when you initially fire up the X server. This is almost always caused by a problem in your XF86Config file. Usually, the monitor timing values are off, or the video card dot clocks set incorrectly. If your display seems to roll, or the edges are fuzzy, this is a clear indication that the monitor timing values or dot clocks are wrong. Also be sure that you are correctly specifying your video card chipset, as well as other options for the Device section of XF86Config. Be absolutely certain that you are using the right X server and that /usr/X11R6/bin/X is a symbolic link to this server.

If all else fails, try to start X "bare"; that is, use a command such as:

```
X > /tmp/x.out 2>&1
```

You can then kill the X server (using the ctrl - alt - backspace key combination) and examine the contents of /tmp/x.out. The X server will report any warnings or errors—for example, if your video card doesn't have a dot clock corresponding to a mode supported by your monitor.

The file VideoModes.doc included in the XFree86 distribution contains many hints for tweaking the values in your XF86Config file.

Remember that you can use ctrl - alt - numeric + and ctrl - alt - numeric - to switch between the video modes listed on the Modes line of the Screen section of XF86Config. If the highest resolution mode doesn't look right, try switching to lower resolutions. This will let you know, at least, that those parts of your X configuration are working correctly.

Also, check the vertical and horizontal size/hold knobs on your monitor. In many cases it is necessary to adjust these when starting up X. For example, if the display seems to be shifted slightly to one side, you can usually correct this using the monitor controls.

The USENET newsgroup comp.windows.x.i386unix is devoted to discussions about XFree86. It might be a good idea to watch that newsgroup for postings relating to your video configuration—you might run across someone with the same problems as your own.

5.2   Accessing MS-DOS Files

If, for some twisted and bizarre reason, you would have need to access files from MS-DOS, it's quite easily done under Linux.

The usual way to access MS-DOS files is to mount an MS-DOS partition or floppy under Linux, allowing you to access the files directly through the filesystem. For example, if you have an MS-DOS floppy in /dev/fd0, the command

```
# mount -t msdos /dev/fd0 /mnt
```

will mount it under /mnt. See Section 4.6.2 for more information on mounting floppies.

You can also mount an MS-DOS partition of your hard drive for access under Linux. If you have an MS-DOS partition on /dev/hda1, the command

```
# mount -t msdos /dev/hda1 /mnt
```

will mount it. Be sure to umount the partition when you're done using it. You can have your MS-DOS partitions automatically mounted at boot time if you include entries for them in /etc/fstab; see Section 4.8 for details. For example, the following line in /etc/fstab will mount an MS-DOS partition on /dev/hda1 on the directory /dos.

```
/dev/hda1      /dos     msdos      defaults
```

The Mtools software may also be used to access MS-DOS files. For example, the commands mcd, mdir, and mcopy all behave as their MS-DOS counterparts. If you installed Mtools, there should be man pages available for these commands.

Accessing MS-DOS files is one thing; running MS-DOS programs from Linux is another. There is an MS-DOS Emulator under development for Linux; it is widely available, and even distributed with SLS. It can be retrieved from a number of locations, including the various Linux FTP sites (see Appendix C for details). The MS-DOS Emulator is reportedly powerful enough to run a number of applications, including WordPerfect, from Linux. However, Linux and MS-DOS are vastly different operating systems. The power of any MS-DOS emulator under UNIX is somewhat limited.

In addition, work is underway on a Microsoft Windows emulator to run under X Windows. Watch the newsgroups and FTP sites for more information.

5.3   Networking with TCP/IP

Linux supports a full implementation of the TCP/IP (Transport Control Protocol/Internet Protocol) networking protocols. TCP/IP has become the most successful mechanism for networking computers worldwide. With Linux and an Ethernet card, you can network your machine to a local area network, or (with the proper network connections), to the Internet—the worldwide TCP/IP network.

Hooking up a small LAN of UNIX machines is easy. It simply requires an Ethernet controller in each machine and the appropriate Ethernet cables and other hardware. Or, if your business or university provides access to the Internet, you can easily add your Linux machine to this network.

The current implementation of TCP/IP and related protocols for Linux is called "NET-2". This has no relationship to the so-called NET-2 release of BSD UNIX; instead, "NET-2" in this context means the second implementation of TCP/IP for Linux.

Linux NET-2 also supports SLIP—Serial Line Internet Protocol. SLIP allows you to have dialup Internet access using a modem. If your business or university provides SLIP access, you can dial in to the SLIP server and put your machine on the Internet over the phone line. Alternately, if your Linux machine also has Ethernet access to the Internet, you can set up your Linux box as a SLIP server.

For complete information on setting up TCP/IP under Linux, we encourage you to read the Linux NET-2 HOWTO, available via anonymous FTP from sunsite.unc.edu. The NET-2 HOWTO is a complete guide to configuring TCP/IP, including Ethernet and SLIP connections, under Linux. The Linux Ethernet HOWTO is a related document that describes configuration of various Ethernet card drivers for Linux. The *Linux Network Administrator's Guide*, from the Linux Documentation Project, is also available. See Appendix A for more information on these documents.

Also of interest is the book *TCP/IP Network Administration*, by Craig Hunt. It contains complete information on using and configuring TCP/IP on UNIX systems.

5.3.1   Hardware Requirements

You can use Linux TCP/IP without any networking hardware at all—configuring "loopback" mode allows you to talk to yourself. This is necessary for some applications and games which use the "loopback" network device.

However, if you want to use Linux with an Ethernet TCP/IP network, you need one of the following Ethernet cards: 3com 3c503, 3c503/16; Novell NE1000, NE2000; Western Digital WD8003, WD8013; Hewlett Packard HP27245, HP27247, HP27250.

The following clones are reported to work: WD-80x3 clones: LANNET LEC-45; NE2000 clones: Alta Combo, Artisoft LANtastic AE-2, Asante Etherpak 2001/2003, D-Link Ethernet II, LTC E-NET/16 P/N 8300-200-002, Network Solutions HE-203, SVEC 4 Dimension Ethernet, 4-Dimension FD0490 EtherBoard 16, and D-Link DE-600, SMC Elite 16.

See the Linux Ethernet HOWTO for a more complete discussion of Linux Ethernet hardware compatibility.

Linux also supports SLIP, which allows you to use a modem to access the Internet over the phone line. In this case, you'll need a modem compatible with your SLIP server—most servers require a 14.4bps V.32bis modem.

5.3.2 Configuring TCP/IP on your system

In this section we're going to discuss how to configure an Ethernet TCP/IP connection on your system. Note that this method should work for many systems, but certainly not all. This discussion should be enough to get you on the right path to configuring the network parameters of your machine, but there are numerous caveats and fine details not mentioned here. We direct you to the *Linux Network Administrators' Guide* and the NET-2-HOWTO for more information.[3]

First of all, we assume that you have a Linux system that has the TCP/IP software installed. This includes basic clients such as `telnet` and `ftp`, system administration commands such as `ifconfig` and `route` (usually found in `/etc`), and networking configuration files (such as `/etc/hosts`). The other Linux-related networking documents described above explain how to go about installing the Linux networking software if you do not have it already.

We also assume that your kernel has been configured and compiled with TCP/IP support enabled. See Section 4.7 for information on compiling your kernel. To enable networking, you must answer "yes" to the appropriate questions during the `make config` step, and rebuild the kernel.

Once this has been done, you must modify a number of configuration files used by NET-2. For the most part this is a simple procedure. Unfortunately, however, there is wide disagreement between Linux distributions as to where the various TCP/IP configuration files and support programs should go. Much of the time, they can be found in `/etc`, but in other cases may be found in `/usr/etc`, `/usr/etc/inet`, or other bizarre locations. In the worst case you'll have to use the `find` command to locate the files on your system. Also note that not all distributions keep the NET-2 configuration files and software in the same location—they may be spread across several directories.

The following information applies primarily to Ethernet connections. If you're planning to use SLIP, read this section to understand the concepts, and follow the SLIP-specific instructions in the following section.

5.3.2.1 Your network configuration

Before you can configure TCP/IP, you need to determine the following information about your network setup. In most cases, your local network administrator can provide you with this information.

- IP address. This is the unique machine address in dotted-decimal format. An example is 128.253.153.54. Your network admins will provide you with this number.

  If you're only configuring loopback mode (i.e. no SLIP, no ethernet card, just TCP/IP connections to your own machine) then your IP address is 127.0.0.1.

- Your network mask ("netmask"). This is a dotted quad, similar to the IP address, which determines which portion of the IP address specifies the subnetwork number, and which portion specifies the host on that subnet. (If you're shaky on these TCP/IP networking terms, we suggest reading some introductory material on network administration.) The network mask is a pattern of bits, which when

---

[3]Some of this information is adapted from the NET-2-HOWTO by Terry Dawson and Matt Welsh.

overlayed onto an address on your network, will tell you which subnet that address lives on. This is very important for routing, and if you find, for example, that you can happily talk to people outside your network, but not to some people within your network, there is a good chance that you have an incorrect mask specified.

Your network administrators will have chosen the netmask when the network was designed, and therefore they should be able to supply you with the correct mask to use. Most networks are class C subnetworks which use 255.255.255.0 as their netmask. Other Class B networks use 255.255.0.0. The NET-2 code will automatically select a mask that assumes no subnetting as a default if you do not specify one.

This applies as well to the loopback port. Since the loopback port's address is always 127.0.0.1, the netmask for this port is always 255.0.0.0. You can either specify this explicitly or rely on the default mask.

- Your network address. This is your IP address masked bitwise-ANDed the netmask. For example, if your netmask is 255.255.255.0, and your IP address is 128.253.154.32, your network address is 128.253.154.0. With a netmask of 255.255.0.0, this would be 128.253.0.0.

  If you're only using loopback, you don't have a network address.

- Your broadcast address. The broadcast address is used to broadcast packets to every machine on your subnet. Therefore, if the host number of machines on your subnet is given by the last byte of the IP address (netmask 255.255.255.0), your broadcast address will be your network address ORed with 0.0.0.255.

  For example, if your IP address is 128.253.154.32, and your netmask is 255.255.255.0, your broadcast address is 128.253.154.255.

  Note that for historical reasons, some networks are setup to use the network address as the broadcast address, if you have any doubt, check with your network administrators. (In many cases, it will suffice to duplicate the network configuration of other machines on your subnet, substituting your own IP address, of course.)

  If you're only using loopback, you don't have a broadcast address.

- Your gateway address. This is the address of the machine which is your "gateway" to the outside world (i.e. machines not on your subnet). In many cases the gateway machine has an IP address identical to yours but with a ".1" as its host address; e.g., if your IP address is 128.253.154.32, your gateway might be 128.253.154.1. Your network admins will provide you with the IP address of your gateway.

  In fact, you may have multiple gateways. A *gateway* is simply a machine that lives on two different networks (has IP addresses on different subnets), and routes packets between them. Many networks have a single gateway to "the outside world" (the network directly adjacent to your own), but in some cases you will have multiple gateways—one for each adjacent network.

  If you're only using loopback, you don't have a gateway address. The same is true if your network is isolated from all others.

- Your nameserver address. Most machines on the net have a name server which translates hostnames into IP addresses for them. Your network admins will tell you the address of your name server. You can also run a server on your own machine by running named, in which case the nameserver address is 127.0.0.1. Unless you absolutely *must* run your own name server, we suggest using the one provided to you on the network (if any). Configuration of named is another issue altogether; our priority at this point is to get you talking to the network. You can deal with name resolution issues later.

  If you're only using loopback, you don't have a nameserver address.

SLIP users: You may or may not require any of the above information, except for a nameserver address. When using SLIP, your IP address is usually determined in one of two ways: Either (a) you have a "static" IP address, which is the same every time you connect to the network, or (b) you have a "dynamic" IP address, which is allocated from a pool available addresses when you connect to the server. In the following section on SLIP configuration this is covered in more detail.

NET-2 supports full routing, multiple routes, subnetworking (at this stage on byte boundaries only), the whole nine yards. The above describes most basic TCP/IP configurations. Yours may be quite different: when in doubt, consult your local network gurus and check out the man pages for `route` and `ifconfig`. Configuring TCP/IP networks is very much beyond the scope of this book; the above should be enough to get most people started.

5.3.2.2   The networking `rc` files

`rc` files are systemwide configuration scripts executed at boot time by `init`, which start up all of the basic system daemons (such as `sendmail`, `cron`, etc.) and configure things such as the network parameters, system hostname, and so on. `rc` files are usually found in the directory `/etc/rc.d` but on other systems may be in `/etc`.

Here, we're going to describe the `rc` files used to configure TCP/IP. There are two of them: `rc.inet1` and `rc.inet2`. `rc.inet1` is used to configure the basic network parameters (such as IP addresses and routing information) and `rc.inet2` fires up the TCP/IP daemons (`telnetd`, `ftpd`, and so forth).

Many systems combine these two files into one, usually called `rc.inet` or `rc.net`. The names given to your `rc` files doesn't matter, as long as they perform the correct functions and are executed at boot time by `init`. To ensure this, you may need to edit `/etc/inittab` and uncomment lines to execute the appropriate `rc` file(s). In the worst case you will have to create the `rc.inet1` and `rc.inet2` files from scratch and add entries for them to `/etc/inittab`.

As we said, `rc.inet1` configures the basic network interface. This includes your IP and network address, and the routing table information for your network. The routing tables are used to route outgoing (and incoming) network datagrams to other machines. On most simple configurations, you have three routes: One for sending packets to your own machine, another for sending packets to other machines on your network, and another for sending packets to machines outside of your network (through the gateway machine). Two programs are used to configure these parameters: `ifconfig` and `route`. Both of these are usually found in `/etc`.

`ifconfig` is used for configuring the network device interface with the parameters that it requires to function, such as the IP address, network mask, broadcast address and the like. `route` is used to create and modify entries in the routing table.

For most configurations, an `rc.inet1` file that looks like the following should work. You will, of course, have to edit this for your own system. Do *not* use the sample IP and network addresses listed here for your own system; they correspond to an actual machine on the Internet.

```
#!/bin/sh
# This is /etc/rc.d/rc.inet1 -- Configure the TCP/IP interfaces

# First, configure the loopback device

HOSTNAME='hostname'

/etc/ifconfig lo 127.0.0.1      # uses default netmask 255.0.0.0
/etc/route add 127.0.0.1        # a route to point to the loopback device
```

```
# Next, configure the ethernet device. If you're only using loopback or
# SLIP, comment out the rest of these lines.

# Edit for your setup.
IPADDR="128.253.154.32"        # REPLACE with YOUR IP address
NETMASK="255.255.255.0"        # REPLACE with YOUR netmask
NETWORK="128.253.154.0"        # REPLACE with YOUR network address
BROADCAST="128.253.154.255"    # REPLACE with YOUR broadcast address, if you
                               # have one. If not, leave blank and edit below.
GATEWAY="128.253.154.1"        # REPLACE with YOUR gateway address!

/etc/ifconfig eth0 ${IPADDR} netmask ${NETMASK} broadcast ${BROADCAST}

# If you don't have a broadcast address, change the above line to just:
# /etc/ifconfig eth0 ${IPADDR} netmask ${NETMASK}

/etc/route add ${NETWORK}

# The following is only necessary if you have a gateway; that is, your
# network is connected to the outside world.
/etc/route add default gw ${GATEWAY} metric 1

# End of Ethernet Configuration
```

Again, you may have to tweak this file somewhat to get it to work. The above should be sufficient for the majority of simple network configurations, but certainly not all.

rc.inet2 starts up various servers used by the TCP/IP suite. The most important of these is inetd. inetd sits in the background and listens to various network ports. When a machine tries to make a connection to a certain port (for example, the incoming telnet port), inetd forks off a copy of the appropriate daemon for that port (in the case of the telnet port, inetd starts in.telnetd). This is simpler than running many separate, standalone daemons (e.g., individual copies of telnetd, ftpd, and so forth)—inetd starts up the daemons only when they are needed.

syslogd is the system logging daemon—it accumulates log messages from various applications and stores them into log files based on the configuration information in /etc/syslogd.conf. routed is a server used to maintain dynamic routing information. When your system attempts to send packets to another network, it may require additional routing table entries in order to do so. routed takes care of manipulating the routing table without the need for user intervention.

Our example rc.inet2, below, only starts up the bare minimum of servers. There are many other servers as well—many of which have to do with NFS configuration. When attempting to setup TCP/IP on your system, it's usually best to start with a minimal configuration and add more complex pieces (such as NFS) when you have things working.

Note that in the below file, we assume that all of the network daemons are held in /etc. As usual, edit this for your own configuration.

```
#! /bin/sh
# Sample /etc/rc.d/rc.inet2

# Start syslogd
if [ -f /etc/syslogd ]
```

```
then
        /etc/syslogd
fi

# Start inetd
if [ -f /etc/inetd ]
then
        /etc/inetd
fi

# Start routed
if [ -f /etc/routed ]
then
        /etc/routed -q
fi

# Done!
```

Among the various additional servers that you may want to start in `rc.inet2` is `named`. `named` is a name server—it is responsible for translating (local) IP addresses to names, and vice versa. If you don't have a nameserver elsewhere on the network, or want to provide local machine names to other machines in your domain, it may be necessary to run `named`. (For most configurations it is not necessary, however.) `named` configuration is somewhat complex and requires planning; we refer interested readers to a good book on TCP/IP network administration.

5.3.2.3 `/etc/hosts`

`/etc/hosts` contains a list of IP addresses and the hostnames that they correspond to. In general, `/etc/hosts` only contains entries for your local machine, and perhaps other "important" machines (such as your nameserver or gateway). Your local name server will provide address-to-name mappings for other machines on the network, transparently.

For example, if your machine is `loomer.vpizza.com` with the IP address 128.253.154.32, your `/etc/hosts` would look like:

```
127.0.0.1               localhost
128.253.154.32          loomer.vpizza.com loomer
```

If you're only using loopback, the only line in `/etc/hosts` should be for 127.0.0.1, with both `localhost` and your hostname after it.

5.3.2.4 `/etc/networks`

The `/etc/networks` file lists the names and addresses of your own, and other, networks. It is used by the `route` command, and allows you to specify a network by name, should you so desire.

Every network you wish to add a route to using the `route` command (generally called from `rc.inet1`— see above) *must* have an entry in `/etc/networks`.

As an example,

```
default 0.0.0.0 # default route    - mandatory
```

```
loopnet 127.0.0.0 # loopback network - mandatory
mynet 128.253.154.0 # Modify for your own network address
```

5.3.2.5 `/etc/host.conf`

This file is used to specify how your system will resolve hostnames. It should contain the two lines:

```
order hosts,bind
multi on
```

These lines tell the resolve libraries to first check the `/etc/hosts` file for any names to lookup, and then ask the nameserver (if one is present). The `multi` entry allows you to have multiple IP addresses for a given machine name in `/etc/hosts`.

5.3.2.6 `/etc/resolv.conf`

This file configures the name resolver, specifying the address of your name server (if any) and your domain name. Your domain name is your fully-qualified hostname (if you're a registered machine on the Internet, for example), with the hostname chopped off. That is, if your full hostname is `loomer.vpizza.com`, your domain name is just `vpizza.com`.

For example, if your machine is `goober.norelco.com`, and has a nameserver at the address 128.253.154.5, your `/etc/resolv.conf` would look like:

```
domain     norelco.com
nameserver 127.253.154.5
```

You can specify more than one nameserver—each must have a `nameserver` line of its own in `resolv.conf`.

5.3.2.7 Setting your hostname

You should set your system hostname with the `hostname` command. This is usually called from `/etc/rc` or `/etc/rc.local`; simply search your system `rc` files to determine where it is invoked. For example, if your (full) hostname is `loomer.vpizza.com`, edit the appropriate `rc` file to execute the command:

```
/bin/hostname loomer.vpizza.com
```

Note that the `hostname` executable may not be found in `/bin` on your system.

5.3.2.8 Trying it out

Once you have all of these files set up, you should be able to reboot your new kernel and attempt to use the network. There are many places where things can go wrong, so it's a good idea to test individual aspects of the network configuration (e.g., it's probably not a good idea to test your network configuration by firing up Mosaic over a network-based X connection).

You can use the `netstat` command to display your routing tables; this is usually the source of the most trouble. The `netstat` man page describes the exact syntax of this command in detail. In order to test network connectivity, we suggest using a client such as `telnet` to connect to machines both on your local subnetwork and external networks. This will help to narrow down the source of the problem. (For example, if you're unable to connect to local machines, but can connect to machines on other networks, more than likely there is a problem with your netmask and routing table configuration). You can also invoke the route command directly (as root) to play with the entries in your routing table.

You should also test network connectivity by specifying IP addresses directly, instead of hostnames. For example, if you have problems with the command

    $ *telnet shoop.vpizza.com*

the cause may be incorrect nameserver configuration. Try using the actual IP address of the machine in question; if that works, then you know that your basic network setup is (more than likely) correct, and the problem lies in your specification of the name server address.

Debugging network configurations can be a difficult task, and we can't begin to cover it here. If you are unable to get help from a local guru we strongly suggest reading the *Linux Network Administrators' Guide* from the LDP.

5.3.3 SLIP Configuration

SLIP (Serial Line Internet Protocol) allows you to use TCP/IP over a serial line, be that a phone line, with a dialup modem, or a leased asynchronous line of some sort. Of course, to use SLIP you'll need access to a dial-in SLIP server in your area. Many universities and businesses provide SLIP access for a modest fee.

There are two major SLIP-related programs available—dip and slattach. Both of these programs are used to initiate a SLIP connection over a serial device. It is *necessary* to use one of these programs in order to enable SLIP—it will not suffice to dial up the SLIP server (with a communications program such as kermit) and issue ifconfig and route commands. This is because dip and slattach issue a special *ioctl()* system call to seize control of the serial device to be used as a SLIP interface.

dip can be used to dial up a SLIP server, do some handshaking to login to the server (exchanging your username and password, for example) and then initate the SLIP connection over the open serial line. slattach, on the other hand, does very little other than grab the serial device for use by SLIP. It is useful if you have a permanent line to your SLIP server and no modem dialup or handshaking is necessary to initiate the connection. Most dialup SLIP users should use dip, on the other hand.

dip can also be used to configure your Linux system as a SLIP server, where other machines can dial into your own and connect to the network through a secondary Ethernet connection on your machine. See the documentation and man pages for dip for more information on this procedure.

SLIP is quite unlike Ethernet, in that there are only two machines on the "network"—the SLIP host (that's you) and the SLIP server. For this reason, SLIP is often referred to as a "point-to-point" connection. A generalization of this idea, known as PPP (Point to Point Protocol) has also been implemented for Linux.

When you initiate a connection to a SLIP server, the SLIP server will give you an IP address based on (usually) one of two methods. Some SLIP servers allocate "static" IP addresses—in which case your IP address will be the same every time you connect to the server. However, many SLIP servers allocate IP addresses dynamically—in which case you receive a different IP address each time you connect. In general, the SLIP server will print the values of your IP and gateway addresses when you connect. dip is capable of reading these values from the output of the SLIP server login session and using them to configure the SLIP device.

Essentially, configuring a SLIP connection is just like configuring for loopback or ethernet. The main differences are discussed below. Read the previous section on configuring the basic TCP/IP files, and apply the changes described below.

5.3.3.1   Static IP address SLIP connections using `dip`

If you are using a static-allocation SLIP server, you may want to include entries for your IP address and hostname in `/etc/hosts`. Also, configure these files listed in the above section: `rc.inet2`, `host.conf`, and `resolv.conf`.

Also, configure `rc.inet1`, as described above. However, you only want to execute `ifconfig` and `route` commands for the loopback device. If you use `dip` to connect to the SLIP server, it will execute the appropriate `ifconfig` and `route` commands for the SLIP device for you. (If you're using `slattach`, on the other hand, you *will* need to include `ifconfig/route` commands in `rc.inet1` for the SLIP device—see below.)

`dip` *should* configure your routing tables appropriately for the SLIP connection when you connect. In some cases, however, `dip`'s behavior may not be correct for your configuration, and you'll have to run `ifconfig` or `route` commands by hand after connecting to the server with `dip` (this is most easily done from within a shell script that runs `dip` and immediately executes the appropriate configuration commands). Your gateway is, in most cases, the address of the SLIP server. You may know this address before hand, or the gateway address will be printed by the SLIP server when you connect. Your `dip` chat script (described below) can obtain this information from the SLIP server.

`ifconfig` may require use of the `pointopoint` argument, if `dip` doesn't configure the interface correctly. For example, if your SLIP server address is 128.253.154.2, and your IP address is 128.253.154.32, you may need to run the command

```
ifconfig sl0 128.253.154.32 pointopoint 128.253.154.2
```

as `root`, after connecting with `dip`. The man pages for `ifconfig` will come in handy.

Note that SLIP device names used with the `ifconfig` and `route` commands are `sl0`, `sl1` and so on (as opposed to `eth0`, `eth1`, etc. for Ethernet devices).

In Section 5.3.4, below, we explain how to configure `dip` to connect to the SLIP server.

5.3.3.2   Static IP address SLIP connections using `slattach`

If you have a leased line or cable running directly to your SLIP server, then there is no need to use `dip` to initiate a connection. `slattach` can be used to configure the SLIP device instead.

In this case, your `/etc/rc.inet1` file should look something like the following:

```
#!/bin/sh
IPADDR="128.253.154.32"          # Replace with your IP address
REMADDR="128.253.154.2" # Replace with your SLIP server address

# Modify the following for the appropriate serial device for the SLIP
# connection:
slattach -p cslip -s 19200 /dev/ttyS0
/etc/ifconfig sl0 $IPADDR pointopoint $REMADDR up
/etc/route add default gw $REMADDR
```

`slattach` allocates the first unallocated SLIP device (`sl0`, `sl1`, etc.) to the serial line specified.

Note that the first parameter to `slattach` is the SLIP protocol to use. At present the only valid values are `slip` and `cslip`. `slip` is regular SLIP, as you would expect, and `cslip` is SLIP with datagram header compression. In most cases you should use `cslip`; however, if you seem to be having problems with this, try `slip`.

If you have more than one SLIP interface then you will have routing considerations to make. You will have to decide what routes to add, and those decisions can only be made on the basis of the actual layout of your network connections. A book on TCP/IP network configuration, as well as the man pages to `route`, will be of use.

5.3.3.3 Dynamic IP address SLIP connections using `dip`

If your SLIP server allocates an IP address dynamically, then you certainly don't know your address in advance—therefore, you can't include an entry for it in `/etc/hosts`. (You should, however, include an entry for your host with the loopback address, 127.0.0.1.)

Many SLIP servers print your IP address (as well as the server's address) when you connect. For example, one type of SLIP server prints a string such as,

```
Your IP address is 128.253.154.44.
Server address is 128.253.154.2.
```

`dip` can capture these numbers from the output of the server and use them to configure the SLIP device.

See Section 5.3.3.1, above, for information on configuring your various TCP/IP files for use with SLIP. Below, we explain how to configure `dip` to connect to the SLIP server.

5.3.4 Using `dip`

`dip` can simplify the process of connecting to a SLIP server, logging in, and configuring the SLIP device. Unless you have a leased line running to your SLIP server, `dip` is the way to go.

To use `dip`, you'll need to write a "chat script" which contains a list of commands used to communicate with the SLIP server at login time. These commands can automatically send your username/password to the server, as well as get information on your IP address from the server.

Here is an example `dip` chat script, for use with a dynamic IP address server. For static servers, you will need to set the variables `$local` and `$remote` to the values of your local IP address and server IP address, respectively, at the top of the script. See the `dip` man page for details.

```
main:
  # Set Maximum Transfer Unit. This is the maximum size of packets
  # transmitted on the SLIP device. Many SLIP servers use either 1500 or
  # 1006; check with your network admins when in doubt.
  get $mtu 1500

  # Make the SLIP route the default route on your system.
  default

  # Set the desired serial port and speed.
  port cua03
  speed 38400

  # Reset the modem and terminal line. If this causes trouble for you,
  # comment it out.
```

```
reset

# Prepare for dialing. Replace the following with your
# modem initialization string.
send ATT&C1&D2\\N3&Q5%M3%C1N1W1L1S48=7\r
wait OK 2
if $errlvl != 0 goto error
# Dial the SLIP server
dial 2546000
if $errlvl != 0 goto error
wait CONNECT 60
if $errlvl != 0 goto error

# We are connected.  Login to the system.
login:
sleep 3
send \r\n\r\n
# Wait for the login prompt
wait login: 10
if $errlvl != 0 goto error

# Send your username
send USERNAME\n

# Wait for password prompt
wait ord: 5
if $errlvl != 0 goto error

# Send password.
send PASSWORD\n

# Wait for SLIP server ready prompt
wait annex: 30
if $errlvl != 0 goto error

# Send commands to SLIP server to initate connection.
send slip\n
wait Annex 30

# Get the remote IP address from the SLIP server. The 'get...remote'
# command reads text in the form xxx.xxx.xxx.xxx, and assigns it
# to the variable given as the second argument (here, $remote).
get $remote remote
if $errlvl != 0 goto error
wait Your 30

# Get local IP address from SLIP server, assign to variable $local.
get $local remote
if $errlvl != 0 goto error

# Fire up the SLIP connection
done:
print CONNECTED to $remote at $rmtip
print GATEWAY address $rmtip
```

```
    print LOCAL address $local
    mode SLIP
    goto exit
 error:
    print SLIP to $remote failed.

 exit:
```

`dip` automatically executes `ifconfig` and `route` commands based on the values of the variables `$local` and `$remote`. Here, those variables are assigned using the `get...remote` command, which obtains text from the SLIP server and assigns it to the named variable.

If the `ifconfig` and `route` commands that `dip` runs for you don't work, you can either run the correct commands in a shell script after executing `dip`, or modify the source for `dip` itself. Running `dip` with the `-v` option will print debugging information while the connection is being set up, which should help you to determine where things might be going awry.

Now, in order to run `dip` and open the SLIP connection, you can use a command such as:

```
/etc/dip/dip -v /etc/dip/mychat 2>&1
```

Where the various `dip` files, and the chat script (`mychat.dip`), are stored in `/etc/dip`.

The above discussion should be enough to get you well on your way to talking to the network, either via Ethernet or SLIP. Again, we strongly suggest looking into a book on TCP/IP network configuration, especially if your network has any special routing considerations, other than those mentioned here.

5.4 Networking with UUCP

UUCP (UNIX-to-UNIX Copy) is an older mechanism used to transfer information between UNIX systems. Using UUCP, UNIX systems dial each other up (using a modem) and transfer mail messages, news articles, files, and so on. If you don't have TCP/IP or SLIP access, you can use UUCP to communicate with the world. Most of the mail and news software (see Sections 5.5 and 5.6) can be configured to use UUCP to transfer information to other machines. In fact, if there is an Internet site nearby, you can arrange to have Internet mail sent to your Linux machine via UUCP from that site.

The *Linux Network Administrator's Guide* contains complete information on configuring and using UUCP under Linux. Also, the Linux UUCP HOWTO, available via anonymous FTP from `sunsite.unc.edu`, should be of help. Another source of information on UUCP is the book *Managing UUCP and USENET*, by Tim O'Reilly and Grace Todino. See Appendix A for more information.

5.5 Electronic Mail

Like most UNIX systems, Linux provides a number of software packages for using electronic mail. E-mail on your system can either be local (that is, you only mail other users on your system), or networked (that is, you mail, using either TCP/IP or UUCP, users on other machines on a network). E-mail software usually consists of two parts: a *mailer* and a *transport*. The mailer is the user-level software which is used to actually compose and read e-mail messages. Popular mailers include `elm` and `mailx`. The transport is the low-level software which actually takes care of delivering the mail, either locally or remotely. The user never sees the transport software; they only interact with the mailer. However, as the system administrator, it is important to understand the concepts behind the transport software and how to configure it.

The most popular transport software for Linux is `Smail`. This software is easy to configure, and is able to send both local and remote TCP/IP and UUCP e-mail. The more powerful `sendmail` transport is used on most UNIX systems, however, because of its complicated setup mechanism, many Linux systems don't use it.

The Linux Mail HOWTO gives more information on the available mail software for Linux and how to configure it on your system. If you plan to send mail remotely, you'll need to understand either TCP/IP or UUCP, depending on how your machine is networked (see Sections 5.3 and 5.4). The UUCP and TCP/IP documents listed in Appendix A should be of help there.

Most of the Linux mail software can be retrieved via anonymous FTP from `sunsite.unc.edu` in the directory `/pub/Linux/system/Mail`.

5.6   News and USENET

Linux also provides a number of facilities for managing electronic news. You may choose to set up a local news server on your system, which will allow users to post "articles" to various "newsgroups" on the system. . . a lively form of discussion. However, if you have access to a TCP/IP or UUCP network, then you will be able to participate in USENET—a worldwide network news service.

There are two parts to the news software—the *server* and the *client*. The news server is the software which controls the newsgroups and handles delivering articles to other machines (if you are on a network). The news client, or *newsreader*, is the software which connects to the server to allow users to read and post news.

There are several forms of news servers available for Linux. They all follow the same basic protocols and design. The two primary versions are "C News" and "INN". There are many types of newsreaders, as well, such as `rn` and `tin`. The choice of newsreader is more or less a matter of taste; all newsreaders should work equally well with different versions of the server software. That is, the newsreader is independent of the server software, and vice versa.

If you only want to run news locally (that is, not as part of USENET), then you will need to run a server on your system, as well as install a newsreader for the users. The news server will store the articles in a directory such as `/usr/spool/news`, and the newsreader will be compiled to look in this directory for news articles.

However, if you wish to run news over the network, there are several options open to you. TCP/IP network-based news uses a protocol known as NNTP (Network News Transmission Protocol). NNTP allows a newsreader to read news over the network, on a remote machine. NNTP also allows news servers to send articles to each other over the network—this is the software upon which USENET is based. Most businesses and universities have one or more NNTP servers set up to handle all of the USENET news for that site. Every other machine at the site runs an NNTP-based newsreader to read and post news over the network via the NNTP server. This means that only the NNTP server actually stores the news articles on disk.

Here are some possible scenarios for news configuration.

- You run news locally. That is, you have no network connection, or no desire to run news over the network. In this case, you need to run C News or INN on your machine, and install a newsreader to read the news locally.

- You have access to a TCP/IP network and an NNTP server. If your organization has an NNTP news server set up, you can read and post news from your Linux machine by simply installing an NNTP-based newsreader. (Most newsreaders available can be configured to run locally or use NNTP). In this case, you do not need to install a news server or store news articles on your system. The newsreader will take care of reading and posting news over the network. Of course, you will need to have TCP/IP configured and have access to the network (see Section 5.3).

- You have access to a TCP/IP network but have no NNTP server. In this case, you can run an NNTP news server on your Linux system. You can install either a local or an NNTP-based newsreader, and the server will store news articles on your system. In addition, you can configure the server to communicate with other NNTP news servers to transfer news articles.

- You want to transfer news using UUCP. If you have UUCP access (see Section 5.4), you can participate in USENET as well. You will need to install a (local) news server and a news reader. In addition, you will need to configure your UUCP software to periodically transfer news articles to another nearby UUCP machine (known as your "news feed"). UUCP does not use NNTP to transfer news; simply, UUCP provides its own mechanism for transferring news articles.

The one downside of most news server and newsreader software is that it must be compiled by hand. Most of the news software does not use configuration files; instead, configuration options are determined at compile time.

Most of the "standard" news software (available via anonymous FTP from `ftp.uu.net` in the directory `/news`) will compile out-of-the box on Linux. Necessary patches can be found on `sunsite.unc.edu` in `/pub/Linux/system/Mail` (which is, incidentally, also where mail software for Linux is found). Other news binaries for Linux may be found in this directory as well.

For more information, refer to the Linux News HOWTO from `sunsite.unc.edu` in `/pub/Linux/docs/HOWTO`. Also, the LDP's *Linux Network Administrator's Guide* contains complete information on configuring news software for Linux. The book *Managing UUCP and Usenet*, by Tim O'Reilly and Grace Todino, is an excellent guide to setting up UUCP and news software. Also of interest is the USENET document "How to become a USENET site," available from `ftp.uu.net`, in the directory `/usenet/news.announce.newusers`.

Appendix A

Sources of Linux Information

This appendix contains information on various sources of Linux information, such as online documents, books, and more. Many of these documents are available either in printed form, or electronically from the Internet or BBS systems. Many Linux distributions also include much of this documentation in the distribution itself, so after you have installed Linux these files may be present on your system.

A.1 Online Documents

These documents should be available on any of the Linux FTP archive sites (see Appendix C for a list). If you do not have direct access to FTP, you may be able to locate these documents on other online services (such as CompuServe, local BBS's, and so on). If you have access to Internet mail, you can use the `ftpmail` service to receive these docucments. See Appendix C for more information.

In particular, the following documents may be found on `sunsite.unc.edu` in the directory `/pub/Linux/docs`. Many sites mirror this directory; however, if you're unable to locate a mirror site near you, this is a good one to fall back on.

You can also access Linux files and documentation using `gopher`. Just point your `gopher` client to port 70 on `sunsite.unc.edu`, and follow the menus to the Linux archive. This is a good way to browse Linux documentation interactively.

The Linux Frequently Asked Questions List

        The Linux Frequently Asked Questions list, or "FAQ", is a list of common questions (and answers!) about Linux. This document is meant to provide a general source of information about Linux, common problems and solutions, and a list of other sources of information. Every new Linux user should read this document. It is available in a number of formats, including plain ASCII, PostScript, and Lout typesetter format. The Linux FAQ is maintained by Ian Jackson, `ijackson@nyx.cs.du.edu`.

The Linux META-FAQ

        The META-FAQ is a collection of "metaquestions" about Linux; that is, sources of information about the Linux system, and other general topics. It is a good starting place for the Internet user wishing to find more information about the system. It is maintained by Michael K. Johnson, `johnsonm@sunsite.unc.edu`.

The Linux INFO-SHEET

The Linux INFO-SHEET is a technical introduction to the Linux system. It gives an overview of the system's features and available software, and also provides a list of other sources of Linux information. The format and content is similar in nature to the META-FAQ; incidentally, it is also maintained by Michael K. Johnson.

The Linux Software Map

The Linux Software Map is a list of many applications available for Linux, where to get them, who maintains them, and so forth. It is far from complete—to compile a complete list of Linux software would be nearly impossible. However, it does include many of the most popular Linux software packages. If you can't find a particular application to suit your needs, the LSM is a good place to start. It is maintained by Lars Wirzenius, `lars.wirzenius@helsinki.fi`.

The Linux HOWTO Index

The Linux HOWTOs are a collection of "how to" documents, each describing in detail a certain aspect of the Linux system. They are maintained by Matt Welsh, `mdw@sunsite.unc.edu`. The HOWTO Index lists the HOWTO documents which are available (several of which are listed below).

The Linux Installation HOWTO

The Linux Installation HOWTO describes how to obtain and install a distribution of Linux, similar to the information presented in Chapter 2.

The Linux Distribution HOWTO

This document is a list of Linux distributions available via mail order and anonymous FTP. It also includes information on other Linux-related goodies and services. Appendix B contains a list of Linux vendors, many of which are listed in the *Distribution HOWTO*.

The Linux XFree86 HOWTO

This document describes how to install and configure the X Window System software for Linux. See the section "5.1" for more about the X Window System.

The Linux Mail, News, and UUCP HOWTOs

These three HOWTO documents describe configuration and setup of electronic mail, news, and UUCP communications on a Linux system. Because these three subjects are often intertwined, you may wish to read all three of these HOWTOs together.

The Linux Hardware HOWTO

This HOWTO contains an extensive list of hardware supported by Linux. While this list is far from complete, it should give you a general picture of which hardware devices should be supported by the system.

The Linux SCSI HOWTO

The Linux SCSI HOWTO is a complete guide to configuration and usage of SCSI devices under Linux, such as hard drives, tape drives and CD-ROM.

The Linux NET-2-HOWTO

The Linux NET-2-HOWTO describes installation, setup, and configuration of the "NET-2" TCP/IP software under Linux, including SLIP. If you want to use TCP/IP on your Linux system, this document is a must read.

The Linux Ethernet HOWTO

Closely related to the NET-2-HOWTO, the Ethernet HOWTO describes the various Ethernet devices supported by Linux, and explains how to configure each of them for use by the Linux TCP/IP software.

The Linux Printing HOWTO

This document describes how to configure printing software under Linux, such as `lpr`. Configuration of printers and printing software under UNIX can be very confusing at times; this document sheds some light on the subject.

Other online documents

If you browse the `docs` subdirectory of any Linux FTP site, you'll see many other documents which are not listed here: A slew of FAQ's, interesting tidbits, and other important information. This miscellany is difficult to categorize here; if you don't see what you're looking for on the list above, just take a look at one of the Linux archive sites listed in Appendix C.

A.2   Linux Documentation Project Manuals

The Linux Documentation Project is working on developing a set of manuals and other documentation for Linux, including man pages. These manuals are in various stages of development, and any help revising and updating them is greatly appreciated. If you have questions about the LDP, please contact Matt Welsh (`mdw@sunsite.unc.edu`).

These books are available via anonymous FTP from a number of Linux archive sites, including `sunsite.unc.edu` in the directory `/pub/Linux/docs/LDP`. A number of commercial distributors are selling printed copies of these books; in the future, you may be able to find the LDP manuals on the shelves of your local bookstore.

Linux Installation and Getting Started, by Matt Welsh

A new user's guide for Linux, covering everything the new user needs to know to get started. You happen to hold this book in your hands.

The Linux System Administrators' Guide, by Lars Wirzenius

This is a complete guide to running and configuring a Linux system. There are many issues relating to systems administration which are specific to Linux, such as needs for supporting a user community, filesystem maintenance, backups, and more. This guide covers them all.

The Linux Network Administrators' Guide, by Olaf Kirch

An extensive and complete guide to networking under Linux, including TCP/IP, UUCP, SLIP, and more. This book is a very good read; it contains a wealth of information on many subjects, clarifying the many confusing aspects of network configuration.

The Linux Kernel Hackers' Guide, by Michael Johnson

The gritty details of kernel hacking and development under Linux. Linux is unique in that the complete kernel source is available. This book opens the doors to developers who wish to add or modify features within the kernel. This guide also contains comprehensive coverage of kernel concepts and conventions used by Linux.

A.3   Books and Other Published Works

Linux Journal is a monthly magazine for and about the Linux community, written and produced by a number of Linux developers and enthusiasts. It is distributed worldwide, and is an excellent way to keep in touch with the dynamics of the Linux world, especially if you don't have access to USENET news.

At the time of this writing, subscriptions to *Linux Journal* are US$19/year in the United States, US$24 in Canada, and US$29 elsewhere. To subscribe, or for more information, write to Linux Journal, PO Box 85867, Seattle, WA, 98145-1867, USA, or call +1 206 527-3385. Their FAX number is +1 206 527-2806, and e-mail address is `linux@ssc.com`. You can also find a *Linux Journal* FAQ and sample articles via anonymous FTP on `sunsite.unc.edu` in `/pub/Linux/docs/linux-journal`.

As we have said, not many books have been published dealing with Linux specifically. However, if you are new to the world of UNIX, or want more information than is presented here, we suggest that you take a look at the following books which are available.

A.3.1   Using UNIX

Title:	*Learning the UNIX Operating System*
Author:	Grace Todino & John Strang
Publisher:	O'Reilly and Associates, 1987
ISBN:	0-937175-16-1, $9.00

> A good introductory book on learning the UNIX operating system. Most of the information should be applicable to Linux as well. I suggest reading this book if you're new to UNIX and really want to get started with using your new system.

Title:	*Learning the* `vi` *Editor*
Author:	Linda Lamb
Publisher:	O'Reilly and Associates, 1990
ISBN:	0-937175-67-6, $21.95

> This is a book about the `vi` editor, a powerful text editor found on every UNIX system in the world. It's often important to know and be able to use `vi`, because you won't always have access to a "real" editor such as Emacs.

A.3.2   Systems Administration

Title:	*Essential System Administration*
Author:	Æleen Frisch
Publisher:	O'Reilly and Associates, 1991
ISBN:	0-937175-80-3, $29.95

> From the O'Reilly and Associates Catalog, "Like any other multi-user system, UNIX requires some care and feeding. *Essential System Administration* tells you how. This book strips away the myth and confusion surrounding this important topic and provides a compact, manageable

introduction to the tasks faced by anyone responsible for a UNIX system." I couldn't have said it better myself.

Title:	*TCP/IP Network Administration*
Author:	Craig Hunt
Publisher:	O'Reilly and Associates, 1990
ISBN:	0-937175-82-X, $24.95

A complete guide to setting up and running a TCP/IP network. While this book is not Linux-specific, roughly 90% of it is applicable to Linux. Coupled with the Linux NET-2-HOWTO and *Linux Network Administrator's Guide*, this is a great book discussing the concepts and technical details of managing TCP/IP.

Title:	*Managing UUCP and Usenet*
Author:	Tim O'Reilly and Grace Todino
Publisher:	O'Reilly and Associates, 1991
ISBN:	0-937175-93-5, $24.95

This book covers how to install and configure UUCP networking software, including configuration for USENET news. If you're at all interested in using UUCP or accessing USENET news on your system, this book is a must-read.

A.3.3   The X Window System

Title:	*The X Window System: A User's Guide*
Author:	Niall Mansfield
Publisher:	Addison-Wesley
ISBN:	0-201-51341-2, ??

A complete tutorial and reference guide to using the X Window System. If you installed X windows on your Linux system, and want to know how to get the most out of it, you should read this book. Unlike some windowing systems, a lot of the power provided by X is not obvious at first sight.

A.3.4   Programming

Title:	*The C Programming Language*
Author:	Brian Kernighan and Dennis Ritchie
Publisher:	Prentice-Hall, 1988
ISBN:	0-13-110362-8, $25.00

This book is a must-have for anyone wishing to do C programming on a UNIX system. (Or any system, for that matter.) While this book is not obstensibly UNIX-specific, it is quite applicable to programming C under UNIX.

Title:	*The Unix Programming Environment*
Author:	Brian Kernighan and Bob Pike
Publisher:	Prentice-Hall, 1984
ISBN:	0-13-937681-X, ??

An overview to programming under the UNIX system. Covers all of the tools of the trade; a good read to get acquainted with the somewhat amorphous UNIX programming world.

Title:	*Advanced Programming in the UNIX Environment*
Author:	W. Richard Stevens
Publisher:	Addison-Wesley
ISBN:	0-201-56317-7, $50.00

This mighty tome contains everything that you need to know to program UNIX at the system level—file I/O, process control, interprocess communication, signals, terminal I/O, the works. This book focuses on various UNI standards, including POSIX.1, which Linux mostly adheres to.

A.3.5 Kernel Hacking

Title:	*The Design of the UNIX Operating System*
Author:	Maurice J. Bach
Publisher:	Prentice-Hall, 1986
ISBN:	0-13-201799-7, ??

This book covers the algorithms and internals of the UNIX kernel. It is not specific to any particular kernel, although it does lean towards System V-isms. This is the best place to start if you want to understand the inner tickings of the Linux system.

Title:	*The Magic Garden Explained*
Author:	Berny Goodheart and James Cox
Publisher:	Prentice-Hall, 1994
ISBN:	0-13-098138-9, ??

This book describes the System V R4 kernel in detail. Unlike Bach's book, which concentrates heavily on the algorithms which make the kernel tick, this book presents the SVR4 implementation on a more technical level. Although Linux and SVR4 are distant cousins, this book can give you much insight into the workings of an actual UNIX kernel implementation. This is also a very modern book on the UNIX kernel—published in 1994.

Appendix B

Linux Vendor List

This appendix lists contact information for a number of vendors which sell Linux on diskette, tape, and CD-ROM. Many of them provide Linux documentation, support, and other services as well. This is by no means a complete listing; if you purchased this book in printed form, it's very possible that the vendor or publishing company also provides Linux software and services.

The author makes no guarantee as to the accuracy of any of the information listed in this Appendix. This information is included here only as a service to readers, not as an advertisement for any particular organization.

Fintronic Linux Systems
1360 Willow Rd., Suite 205
Menlo Park, CA 94025 USA
Tel: +1 415 325-4474
Fax: +1 415 325-4908
linux@fintronic.com

InfoMagic, Inc.
PO Box 30370
Flagstaff, AZ 86003-0370 USA
Tel: +1 800 800-6613, +1 602 526-9565
Fax: +1 602 526-9573
Orders@InfoMagic.com

Lasermoon Ltd
2a Beaconsfield Road, Fareham,
Hants, England. PO16 0QB.
Tel: +44 (0) 329 826444.
Fax: +44 (0) 329 825936.
info@lasermoon.co.uk

Linux Journal
P.O. Box 85867
Seattle, WA 98145-1867 USA
Tel: +1 206 527-3385
Fax: +1 206 527-2806
linux@ssc.com

Linux Systems Labs
18300 Tara Drive
Clinton Twp, MI 48036 USA
Tel: +1 313 954-2829, +1 800 432-0556
Fax: +1 313 954-2806
`info@lsl.com`

Morse Telecommunication, Inc.
26 East Park Avenue, Suite 240
Long Beach, NY 11561 USA
Tel: +1 800 60-MORSE
Fax: +1 516 889-8665
`Linux@morse.net`

Nascent Technology
Linux from Nascent CDROM
P.O. Box 60669
Sunnyvale CA 94088-0669 USA
Tel: +1 408 737-9500
Fax: +1 408 241-9390
`nascent@netcom.com`

Red Hat Software
P.O. Box 4325
Chapel Hill, NC 27515 USA
Tel: +1 919 309-9560
`redhat@redhat.com`

SW Technology
251 West Renner Suite 229
Richardson, TX 75080 USA
Tel: +1 214 907-0871
`swt@netcom.com`

Takelap Systems Ltd.
The Reddings, Court Robin Lane,
Llangwm, Usk, Gwent, United Kingdom NP5 1ET.
Tel: +44 (0)291 650357
Fax: +44 (0)291 650500
`info@ddrive.demon.co.uk`

Trans-Ameritech Enterprises, Inc.
2342A Walsh Ave
Santa Clara, CA 95051 USA
Tel: +1 408 727-3883
`roman@trans-ameritech.com`

Unifix Software GmbH
Postfach 4918

D-38039 Braunschweig
Germany
Tel: +49 (0)531 515161
Fax: +49 (0)531 515162

Yggdrasil Computing, Incorporated
4880 Stevens Creek Blvd., Suite 205
San Jose, CA 95129-1034 USA
Tel: +1 800 261-6630, +1 408 261-6630
Fax: +1 408 261-6631
info@yggdrasil.com

Appendix C

FTP Tutorial and Site List

FTP ("File Transfer Protocol") is the set of programs that are used for transferring files between systems on the Internet. Most UNIX, VMS, and MS-DOS systems on the Internet have a program called ftp which you use to transfer these files, and if you have Internet access, the best way to download the Linux software is by using ftp. This appendix covers basic ftp usage—of course, there are many more functions and uses of ftp than are given here.

At the end of this appendix there is a listing of FTP sites where Linux software can be found. Also, if you don't have direct Internet access but are able to exchange electronic mail with the Internet, information on using the ftpmail service is included below.

If you're using an MS-DOS, UNIX, or VMS system to download files from the Internet, then ftp is a command-driven program. However, there are other implementations of ftp out there, such as the Macintosh version (called Fetch) with a nice menu-driven interface, which is quite self-explanatory. Even if you're not using the command-driven version of ftp, the information given here should help.

ftp can be used to both upload (send) or download (receive) files from other Internet sites. In most situations, you're going to be downloading software. On the Internet there are a large number of publicly-available **FTP archive sites**, machines which allow anyone to ftp to them and download free software. One such archive site is sunsite.unc.edu, which has a lot of Sun Microsystems software, and acts as one of the main Linux sites. In addition, FTP archive sites **mirror** software to each other—that is, software uploaded to one site will be automatically copied over to a number of other sites. So don't be surprised if you see the exact same files on many different archive sites.

C.1 Starting ftp

Note that in the example "screens" printed below I'm only showing the most important information, and what you see may differ. Also, commands in *italics* represent commands that you type; everything else is screen output.

To start ftp and connect to a site, simply use the command

    ftp ⟨hostname⟩

where ⟨hostname⟩ is the name of the site you are connecting to. For example, to connect to the mythical site shoop.vpizza.com we can use the command

```
ftp shoop.vpizza.com
```

C.2   Logging In

When `ftp` starts up we should see something like

```
Connected to shoop.vpizza.com.
220 Shoop.vpizza.com FTPD ready at 15 Dec 1992 08:20:42 EDT
Name (shoop.vpizza.com:mdw):
```

Here, `ftp` is asking us to give the username that we want to login as on `shoop.vpizza.com`. The default here is `mdw`, which is my username on the system I'm using FTP from. Since I don't have an account on `shoop.vpizza.com` I can't login as myself. Instead, to access publicly-available software on an FTP site you login as `anonymous`, and give your Internet e-mail address (if you have one) as the password. So, we would type

```
Name (shoop.vpizza.com:mdw): anonymous
331-Guest login ok, send e-mail address as password.
Password: mdw@sunsite.unc.edu
230- Welcome to shoop.vpizza.com.
230- Virtual Pizza Delivery[tm]:  Download pizza in 30 cycles or less
230- or you get it FREE!
ftp>
```

Of course, you should give your e-mail address, instead of mine, and it won't echo to the screen as you're typing it (since it's technically a "password"). `ftp` should allow us to login and we'll be ready to download software.

C.3   Poking Around

Okay, we're in. `ftp>` is our prompt, and the `ftp` program is waiting for commands. There are a few basic commands you need to know about. First, the commands

```
ls ⟨file⟩
```

and

```
dir ⟨file⟩
```

both give file listings (where ⟨file⟩ is an optional argument specifying a particular filename to list). The difference is that `ls` usually gives a short listing and `dir` gives a longer listing (that is, with more information on the sizes of the files, dates of modification, and so on).

The command

```
cd ⟨directory⟩
```

will move to the given directory (just like the `cd` command on UNIX or MS-DOS systems). You can use the command

```
cdup
```

to change to the parent directory[1].

The command

```
help ⟨command⟩
```

will give help on the given ftp ⟨command⟩ (such as ls or cd). If no command is specified, ftp will list all of the available commands.

If we type dir at this point we'll see an initial directory listing of where we are.

```
ftp> dir
200 PORT command successful.
150 Opening ASCII mode data connection for /bin/ls.
total 1337


dr-xr-xr-x   2 root       wheel          512 Aug 13 13:55 bin
drwxr-xr-x   2 root       wheel          512 Aug 13 13:58 dev
drwxr-xr-x   2 root       wheel          512 Jan 25 17:35 etc
drwxr-xr-x  19 root       wheel         1024 Jan 27 21:39 pub
drwxrwx-wx   4 root       ftp-admi      1024 Feb  6 22:10 uploads
drwxr-xr-x   3 root       wheel          512 Mar 11  1992 usr


226 Transfer complete.
921 bytes received in 0.24 seconds (3.7 Kbytes/s)
ftp>
```

Each of these entries is a directory, not an individual file which we can download (specified by the d in the first column of the listing). On most FTP archive sites, the publicly available software is under the directory /pub, so let's go there.

```
ftp> cd pub
ftp> dir
200 PORT command successful.
150 ASCII data connection for /bin/ls (128.84.181.1,4525) (0 bytes).
total 846


-rw-r--r--   1 root       staff         1433 Jul 12  1988 README
-r--r--r--   1 3807       staff        15586 May 13  1991 US-DOMAIN.TXT.2
-rw-r--r--   1 539        staff        52664 Feb 20  1991 altenergy.avail
-r--r--r--   1 65534      65534        56456 Dec 17  1990 ataxx.tar.Z
-rw-r--r--   1 root       other      2013041 Jul  3  1991 gesyps.tar.Z
-rw-r--r--   1 432        staff        41831 Jan 30  1989 gnexe.arc
-rw-rw-rw-   1 615        staff        50315 Apr 16  1992 linpack.tar.Z
-r--r--r--   1 root       wheel        12168 Dec 25  1990 localtime.o
-rw-r--r--   1 root       staff         7035 Aug 27  1986 manualslist.tblms
drwxr-xr-x   2 2195       staff          512 Mar 10 00:48 mdw
-rw-r--r--   1 root       staff         5593 Jul 19  1988 t.out.h
```

---

[1]The directory above the current one.

```
226 ASCII Transfer complete.
2443 bytes received in 0.35 seconds (6.8 Kbytes/s)
ftp>
```

Here we can see a number of (interesting?) files, one of which is called README, which we should download (most FTP sites have a README file in the /pub directory).

C.4   Downloading files

Before downloading files, there are a few things that you need to take care of.

- **Turn on hash mark printing.** *Hash marks* are printed to the screen as files are being transferred; they let you know how far along the transfer is, and that your connection hasn't hung up (so you don't sit for 20 minutes, thinking that you're still downloading a file). In general, a hash mark appears as a pound sign (#), and one is printed for every 1024 or 8192 bytes transferred, depending on your system.

  To turn on hash mark printing, give the command hash.

  ```
  ftp> hash
  Hash mark printing on (8192 bytes/hash mark).
  ftp>
  ```

- **Determine the type of file which you are downloading.** As far as FTP is concerned, files come in two flavors: *binary* and *text*. Most of the files which you'll be downloading are binary files: that is, programs, compressed files, archive files, and so on. However, many files (such as READMEs and so on) are text files.

  Why does the file type matter? Only because on some systems (such as MS-DOS systems), certain characters in a text file, such as carriage returns, need to be converted so that the file will be readable. While transferring in binary mode, no conversion is done—the file is simply transferred byte after byte.

  The commands bin and ascii set the transfer mode to binary and text, respectively. *When in doubt, always use binary mode to transfer files.* If you try to transfer a binary file in text mode, you'll corrupt the file and it will be unusable. (This is one of the most common mistakes made when using FTP.) However, you can use text mode for plain text files (whose filenames often end in .txt).

  For our example, we're downloading the file README, which is most likely a text file, so we use the command

  ```
  ftp> ascii
  200 Type set to A.
  ftp>
  ```

- **Set your local directory.** Your *local directory* is the directory on your system where you want the downloaded files to end up. Whereas the cd command changes the remote directory (on the remote machine which you're FTPing to), the lcd command changes the local directory.

  For example, to set the local directory to /home/db/mdw/tmp, use the command

  ```
  ftp> lcd /home/db/mdw/tmp
  Local directory now /home/db/mdw/tmp
  ftp>
  ```

Now you're ready to actually download the file. The command

```
get ⟨remote-name⟩ ⟨local-name⟩
```

is used for this, where ⟨*remote-name*⟩ is the name of the file on the remote machine, and ⟨*local-name*⟩ is the name that you wish to give the file on your local machine. The ⟨*local-name*⟩ argument is optional; by default, the local filename is the same as the remote one. However, if for example you're downloading the file README, and you already have a README in your local directory, you'll want to give a different ⟨*local-filename*⟩ so that the first one isn't overwritten.

For our example, to download the file README, we simply use

```
ftp> get README
200 PORT command successful.
150 ASCII data connection for README (128.84.181.1,4527) (1433 bytes).
#
226 ASCII Transfer complete.
local:  README remote:  README
1493 bytes received in 0.03 seconds (49 Kbytes/s)
ftp>
```

C.5 Quitting FTP

To end your FTP session, simply use the command

```
quit
```

The command

```
close
```

can be used to close the connection with the current remote FTP site; the open command can then be used to start a session with another site (without quitting the FTP program altogether).

```
ftp> close
221 Goodbye.
ftp> quit
```

C.6 Using `ftpmail`

`ftpmail` is a service which allows you to obtain files from FTP archive sites via Internet electronic mail. If you don't have direct Internet access, but are able to send mail to the Internet (from a service such as CompuServe, for example), `ftpmail` is a good way to get files from FTP archive sites. Unfortunately, `ftpmail` can be slow, especially when sending large jobs. Before attempting to download large amounts of software using `ftpmail`, be sure that your mail spool will be able to handle the incoming traffic. Many systems keep quotas on incoming electronic mail, and may delete your account if your mail exceeds this quota. Just use common sense.

`sunsite.unc.edu`, one of the major Linux FTP archive sites, is home to an `ftpmail` server. To use this service, send electronic mail to

```
ftpmail@sunsite.unc.edu
```

with a message body containing only the word:

```
help
```

This will send you back a list of `ftpmail` commands and a brief tutorial on using the system.

For example, to get a listing of Linux files found on `sunsite.unc.edu`, send mail to the above address containing the text

```
open sunsite.unc.edu
cd /pub/Linux
dir
quit
```

You may use the `ftpmail` service to connect to any FTP archive site; you are not limited to `sunsite.unc.edu`. The next section lists a number of Linux FTP archives.

C.7   Linux FTP Site List

Table C.1 is a listing of the most well-known FTP archive sites which carry the Linux software. Keep in mind that many other sites mirror these, and more than likely you'll run into Linux on a number of sites not on this list.

Site name	IP Address	Directory
tsx-11.mit.edu	18.172.1.2	/pub/linux
sunsite.unc.edu	152.2.22.81	/pub/Linux
nic.funet.fi	128.214.6.100	/pub/OS/Linux
ftp.mcc.ac.uk	130.88.200.7	/pub/linux
fgb1.fgb.mw.tu-muenchen.de	129.187.200.1	/pub/linux
ftp.informatik.tu-muenchen.de	131.159.0.110	/pub/Linux
ftp.dfv.rwth-aachen.de	137.226.4.105	/pub/linux
ftp.informatik.rwth-aachen.de	137.226.112.172	/pub/Linux
ftp.ibp.fr	132.227.60.2	/pub/linux
kirk.bu.oz.au	131.244.1.1	/pub/OS/Linux
ftp.uu.net	137.39.1.9	/systems/unix/linux
wuarchive.wustl.edu	128.252.135.4	/systems/linux
ftp.win.tue.nl	131.155.70.100	/pub/linux
ftp.ibr.cs.tu-bs.de	134.169.34.15	/pub/os/linux
ftp.denet.dk	129.142.6.74	/pub/OS/linux

Table C.1: Linux FTP Sites

`tsx-11.mit.edu`, `sunsite.unc.edu`, and `nic.funet.fi` are the "home sites" for the Linux software, where most of the new software is uploaded. Most of the other sites on the list mirror some combination of these three. To reduce network traffic, choose a site that is geographically closest to you.

C.8   Linux BBS List

Printed here is a list of bulletin board systems (BBS) which carry Linux software. Zane Healy (`healyzh@holonet.net`) maintains this list. If you know of or run a BBS which provides Linux software which isn't on this list, you should get in touch with him.

The Linux community is no longer an Internet-only society. In fact, it is now estimated that the majority of Linux users don't have Internet access. Therefore, it is especially important that BBSs continue to provide and support Linux to users worldwide.

C.9   United States

Citrus Grove Public Access, 916-381-5822.   ZyXEL 16.8/14.4 Sacramento, CA. Internet: `citrus.sac.ca.us`

Higher Powered BBS, 408-737-7040. ? CA. RIME ->HIGHER

hip-hop, 408-773-0768. 19.2k Sunnyvale, CA. USENET access

hip-hop, 408-773-0768. 38.4k Sunnyvale, CA.

Unix Online, 707-765-4631. 9600 Petaluma, CA. USENET access

The Outer Rim, 805-252-6342. Santa Clarita, CA.

Programmer's Exchange, 818-444-3507. El Monte, CA. Fidonet

Programmer's Exchange, 818-579-9711. El Monte, CA.

Micro Oasis, 510-895-5985. 14.4k San Leandro, CA.

Test Engineering, 916-928-0504. Sacramento, CA.

Slut Club, 813-975-2603. USR/DS 16.8k HST/14.4K Tampa, FL. Fidonet 1:377/42

Lost City Atlantis, 904-727-9334. 14.4k Jacksonville, FL. FidoNet

Aquired Knowledge, 305-720-3669. 14.4k v.32bis Ft. Lauderdale, FL. Internet, UUCP

The Computer Mechanic, 813-544-9345. 14.4k v.32bis St. Petersburg, FL. Fidonet, Sailnet, MXBBSnet

AVSync, 404-320-6202. Atlanta, GA.

Information Overload, 404-471-1549. 19.2k ZyXEL Atlanta, GA. Fidonet 1:133/308

Atlanta Radio Club, 404-850-0546. 9600 Atlanta, GA.

Rebel BBS, 208-887-3937. 9600 Boise, ID.

Rocky Mountain HUB, 208-232-3405. 38.4k Pocatello, ID. Fionet, SLNet, CinemaNet

EchoMania, 618-233-1659. 14.4k HST Belleville, IL. Fidonet 1:2250/1, f'req LINUX

UNIX USER, 708-879-8633. 14.4k Batavia, IL. USENET, Internet mail

PBS BBS, 309-663-7675. 2400 Bloomington, IL.

Third World, 217-356-9512. 9600 v.32 IL.

Digital Underground, 812-941-9427. 14.4k v.32bis IN. USENET

The OA Southern Star, 504-885-5928. New Orleans, LA. Fidonet 1:396/1

Channel One, 617-354-8873. Boston, MA. RIME ->CHANNEL

VWIS Linux Support BBS, 508-793-1570. 9600 Worcester, MA.

WayStar BBS, 508-481-7147. 14.4k V.32bis USR/HST Marlborough, MA. Fidonet 1:333/14

WayStar BBS, 508-481-7293. 14.4k V.32bis USR/HST Marlborough, MA. Fidonet 1:333/15

WayStar BBS, 508-480-8371. 9600 V.32bis or 14.4k USR/HST Marlborough, MA. Fidonet 1:333/16

Programmer's Center, 301-596-1180. 9600 Columbia, MD. RIME

Brodmann's Place, 301-843-5732. 14.4k Waldorf, MD. RIME ->BRODMANN, Fidonet

Main Frame, 301-654-2554. 9600 Gaithersburg, MD. RIME ->MAINFRAME

1 Zero Cybernet BBS, 301-589-4064. MD.

WaterDeep BBS, 410-614-2190. 9600 v.32 Baltimore, MD.

Harbor Heights BBS, 207-663-0391. 14.4k Boothbay Harbor, ME.

Part-Time BBS, 612-544-5552. 14.4k v.32bis Plymouth, MN.

The Sole Survivor, 314-846-2702. 14.4k v.32bis St. Louis, MO. WWIVnet, WWIVlink, etc

MAC's Place, 919-891-1111. 16.8k, DS modem Dunn, NC. RIME ->MAC

Digital Designs, 919-423-4216. 14.4k, 2400 Hope Mills, NC.

Flite Line, 402-421-2434. Lincoln, NE. RIME ->FLITE, DS modem

Legend, 402-438-2433. Lincoln, NE. DS modem

MegaByte Mansion, 402-551-8681. 14.4 V,32bis Omaha, NE.

Mycroft QNX, 201-858-3429. 14.4k NJ.

Steve Leon's, 201-886-8041. 14.4k Cliffside Park, NJ.

Dwight-Englewood BBS, 201-569-3543. 9600 v.42 Englewood, NJ. USENET

The Mothership Cnection, 908-940-1012. 38.4k Franklin Park, NJ.

The Laboratory, 212-927-4980. 16.8k HST, 14.4k v.32bis NY. FidoNet 1:278/707

Valhalla, 516-321-6819. 14.4k HST v.32 Babylon, NY. Fidonet (1:107/255), UseNet (`die.linet.org`)

Intermittent Connection, 503-344-9838. 14.4k HST v.32bis Eugene, OR. 1:152/35

Horizon Systems, 216-899-1086. USR v.32 Westlake, OH.

Horizon Systems, 216-899-1293. 2400 Westlake, OH.

Centre Programmers Unit, 814-353-0566. 14.4k V.32bis/HST Bellefonte, PA.

Allentown Technical, 215-432-5699. 9600 v.32/v.42bis Allentown, PA. WWIVNet 2578

Tactical-Operations, 814-861-7637.   14.4k V32bis/V42bis State College, PA. Fidonet 1:129/226, `tac_ops.UUCP`

North Shore BBS, 713-251-9757. Houston, TX.

The Annex, 512-575-1188. 9600 HST TX. Fidonet 1:3802/217

The Annex, 512-575-0667. 2400 TX. Fidonet 1:3802/216

Walt Fairs, 713-947-9866. Houston, TX. FidoNet 1:106/18

CyberVille, 817-249-6261. 9600 TX. FidoNet 1:130/78

splat-ooh, 512-578-2720. 14.4k Victoria, TX.

splat-ooh, 512-578-5436. 14.4k Victoria, TX.

alaree, 512-575-5554. 14.4k Victoria, TX.

Ronin BBS, 214-938-2840. 14.4 HST/DS Waxahachie (Dallas), TX. RIME, Intelec, Smartnet, etc.

VTBBS, 703-231-7498. Blacksburg, VA.

MBT, 703-953-0640. Blacksburg, VA.

NOVA, 703-323-3321. 9600 Annandale, VA. Fidonet 1:109/305

Rem-Jem, 703-503-9410. 9600 Fairfax, VA.

Enlightend, 703-370-9528. 14.4k Alexandria, VA. Fidonet 1:109/615

My UnKnown BBS, 703-690-0669. 14.4k V.32bis VA. Fidonet 1:109/370

Georgia Peach BBS, 804-727-0399. 14.4k Newport News, VA.

Top Hat BBS, 206-244-9661. 14.4k WA. Fidonet 1:343/40

victrola.sea.wa.us, 206-838-7456. 19.2k Federal Way, WA. USENET

C.10   Outside of the United States

Galaktische Archive, 0043-2228303804. 16.8 ZYX Wien, Austria. Fidonet 2:310/77 (19:00-7:00)

Linux-Support-Oz, +61-2-418-8750. v.32bis 14.4k Sydney, NSW, Australia. Internet/Usenet, E-Mail/News

500cc Formula 1 BBS, +61-2-550-4317. V.32bis Sydney, NSW, Australia.

Magic BBS, 403-569-2882. 14.4k HST/Telebit/MNP Calgary, AB, Canada. Internet/Usenet

Logical Solutions, 299-9900 through 9911. 2400 AB, Canada.

Logical Solutions, 299-9912, 299-9913. 14.4k Canada.

Logical Solutions, 299-9914 through 9917. 16.8k v.32bis Canada.

V.A.L.I.S., 403-478-1281. 14.4k v.32bis Edmonton, AB, Canada. USENET

The Windsor Download, (519)-973-9330. v32bis 14.4 ON, Canada.

r-node, 416-249-5366. 2400 Toronto, ON, Canada. USENET

Synapse, 819-246-2344. 819-561-5268 Gatineau, QC, Canada. RIME->SYNAPSE

Radio Free Nyongwa, 514-524-0829. v.32bis ZyXEL Montreal, QC, Canada. USENET, Fidonet

DataComm1, +49.531.132-16. 14.4 HST Braunschweig, NDS, Germany. Fido 2:240/550, LinuxNet

DataComm2, +49.531.132-17. 14.4 HST Braunschweig, NDS, Germany. Fido 2:240/551, LinuxNet

Linux Server /Braukmann, +49.441.592-963. 16.8 ZYX Oldenburg, NDS, Germany. Fido 2:241/2012, LinuxNet

MM's Spielebox, +49.5323.3515. 14.4 ZYX Clausthal-Zfd., NDS, Germany. Fido 2:241/3420

MM's Spielebox, +49.5323.3516. 16.8 ZYX Clausthal-Zfd., NDS, Germany. Fido 2:241/3421

MM's Spielebox, +49.5323.3540. 9600 Clausthal-Zfd., NDS, Germany. Fido 2:241/3422

Bit-Company / J. Bartz, +49.5323.2539. 16.8 ZYX MO Clausthal-Zfd., NDS, Germany. Fido 2:241/3430

Fractal Zone BBS /Maass, +49.721.863-066. 16.8 ZYX Karlsruhe, BW, Germany. Fido 2:241/7462

Hipposoft /M. Junius, +49.241.875-090. 14.4 HST Aachen, NRW, Germany. Fido 2:242/6, 4:30-7,8-23:30

UB-HOFF /A. Hoffmann, +49.203.584-155. 19.2 ZYX+ Duisburg, Germany. Fido 2:242/37

FORMEL-Box, +49.4191.2846. 16.8 ZYX Kaltenkirchen, SHL, Germany. Fido 2:242/329, LinuxNet (6:00-20:00)

BOX/2, +49.89.601-96-77. 16.8 ZYX Muenchen, BAY, Germany. Fido 2:246/147, info magic: LINUX (22-24,0:30-2,5-8)

Die Box Passau 2+1, +49.851.555-96. 14.4 V32b Passau, BAY, Germany. Fido 2:246/200 (8:00-3:30)

Die Box Passau Line 1, +49.851.753-789. 16.8 ZYX Passau, BAY, Germany. Fido 2:246/2000 (8:00-3:30)

Die Box Passau Line 3, +49.851.732-73. 14.4 HST Passau, BAY, Germany. Fido 2:246/202 (5:00-3:30)

Die Box Passau ISDN, +49.851.950-464. 38.4/64k V.110/X.75 Passau, BAY, Germany. Fido 2:246/201 (8:00-24:00,1:00-3:30)

Public Domain Kiste, +49.30.686-62-50. 16.8 ZYX BLN, Germany. Fido 2:2403/17

CS-Port / C. Schmidt, +49.30.491-34-18. 19.2 Z19 Berlin, BLN, Germany. Fido 2:2403/13

BigBrother / R. Gmelch, +49.30.335-63-28. 16.8 Z16 Berlin, BLN, Germany. Fido 2:2403/36.4 (16-23:00)

CRYSTAL BBS, +49.7152.240-86. 14.4 HST Leonberg, BW, Germany. Fido 2:2407/3, LinuxNet

Echoblaster BBS #1, +49.7142.213-92. HST/V32b Bietigheim, BW, Germany. Fido 2:2407/4, LinuxNet (7-19,23-01h)

Echoblaster BBS #2, +49.7142.212-35. V32b Bietigheim, BW, Germany. Fido 2:2407/40, LinuxNet (20h-6h)

LinuxServer / P. Berger, +49.711.756-275. 16.8 HST Stuttgart, BW, Germany. Fido 2:2407/34, LinuxNet (8:3-17:5,19-2)

Rising Sun BBS, +49.7147.3845. 16.8 ZYX Sachsenheim, BW, Germany. Fido 2:2407/41, LinuxNet (5:30-2:30)

bakunin.north.de, +49.421.870-532. 14.4 D 2800 Bremen, HB, Germany. kraehe@bakunin.north.de

oytix.north.de, +49.421.396-57-62. ZYX HB, Germany. mike@oytix.north.de, login as gast

Fiffis Inn BBS, +49-89-5701353. 14.4-19.2 Munich, Germany. FidoNet 2:246/69,Internet,USENET,LinuxNet

The Field of Inverse Chaos, +358 0 506 1836. 14.4k v32bis/HST Helsinki, Finland. USENET; ichaos.nullnet.fi

Modula BBS, +33-1 4043 0124. HST 14.4 v.32bis Paris, France.

Modula BBS, +33-1 4530 1248. HST 14.4 V.32bis Paris, France.

STDIN BBS, +33-72375139. v.32bis Lyon, Laurent Cas, France. FidoNet 2:323/8

Le Lien, +33-72089879. HST 14.4/V32bis Lyon, Pascal Valette, France. FidoNet 2:323/5

Basil, +33-1-44670844. v.32bis Paris, Laurent Chemla, France.

Cafard Naum, +33-51701632. v.32bis Nantes, Yann Dupont, France.

DUBBS, +353-1-6789000. 19.2 ZyXEL Dublin, Ireland. Fidonet 2:263/167

Galway Online, +353-91-27454. 14.4k v32b Galway, Ireland. RIME, @iol.ie

Nemesis' Dungeon, +353-1-324755 or 326900. 14.4k v32bis Dublin, Ireland. Fidonet 2:263/150

nonsolosoftware, +39 51 6140772. v.32bis, v.42bis Italy. Fidonet 2:332/407

nonsolosoftware, +39 51 432904. ZyXEL 19.2k Italy. Fidonet 2:332/417

Advanced Systems, +64-9-379-3365. ZyXEL 16.8k Auckland, New Zealand. Singet, INTLnet, Fidonet

Thunderball Cave, 472567018.   Norway. RIME ->CAVE

DownTown BBS Lelystad, +31-3200-48852. 14.4k Lelystad, Netherlands. Fido 2:512/155, UUCP

MUGNET Intl-Cistron BBS, +31-1720-42580. 38.4k Alphen a/d Rijn, Netherlands. UUCP

The Controversy, (65)560-6040. 14.4k V.32bis/HST Singapore. Fidonet 6:600/201

Pats System, +27-12-333-2049. 14.4k v.32bis/HST Pretoria, South Africa. Fidonet 5:71-1/36

Gunship BBS, +46-31-693306. 14.4k HST DS Gothenburg Sweden.

Baboon BBS, +41-62-511726. 19.2k Switzerland. Fido 2:301/580 and /581

The Purple Tentacle, +44-734-590990. HST/V32bis Reading, UK. Fidonet 2:252/305

A6 BBS, +44-582-460273. 14.4k Herts, UK. Fidonet 2:440/111

On the Beach, +444-273-600996. 14.4k/16.8k Brighton, UK. Fidonet 2:441/122

Appendix D

The GNU General Public License

Printed below is the GNU General Public License (the *GPL* or *copyleft*), under which Linux is licensed. It is reproduced here to clear up some of the confusion about Linux's copyright status—Linux is *not* shareware, and it is *not* in the public domain. The bulk of the Linux kernel is copyright ©1993 by Linus Torvalds, and other software and parts of the kernel are copyrighted by their authors. Thus, Linux *is* copyrighted, however, you may redistribute it under the terms of the GPL printed below.

GNU GENERAL PUBLIC LICENSE
Version 2, June 1991

Copyright ©1989, 1991 Free Software Foundation, Inc. 675 Mass Ave, Cambridge, MA 02139, USA
Everyone is permitted to copy and distribute verbatim copies of this license document, but changing it is not allowed.

D.1 Preamble

The licenses for most software are designed to take away your freedom to share and change it. By contrast, the GNU General Public License is intended to guarantee your freedom to share and change free software– to make sure the software is free for all its users. This General Public License applies to most of the Free Software Foundation's software and to any other program whose authors commit to using it. (Some other Free Software Foundation software is covered by the GNU Library General Public License instead.) You can apply it to your programs, too.

When we speak of free software, we are referring to freedom, not price. Our General Public Licenses are designed to make sure that you have the freedom to distribute copies of free software (and charge for this service if you wish), that you receive source code or can get it if you want it, that you can change the software or use pieces of it in new free programs; and that you know you can do these things.

To protect your rights, we need to make restrictions that forbid anyone to deny you these rights or to ask you to surrender the rights. These restrictions translate to certain responsibilities for you if you distribute copies of the software, or if you modify it.

For example, if you distribute copies of such a program, whether gratis or for a fee, you must give the recipients all the rights that you have. You must make sure that they, too, receive or can get the source code. And you must show them these terms so they know their rights.

We protect your rights with two steps: (1) copyright the software, and (2) offer you this license which gives you legal permission to copy, distribute and/or modify the software.

Also, for each author's protection and ours, we want to make certain that everyone understands that there is no warranty for this free software. If the software is modified by someone else and passed on, we want its recipients to know that what they have is not the original, so that any problems introduced by others will not reflect on the original authors' reputations.

Finally, any free program is threatened constantly by software patents. We wish to avoid the danger that redistributors of a free program will individually obtain patent licenses, in effect making the program proprietary. To prevent this, we have made it clear that any patent must be licensed for everyone's free use or not licensed at all.

The precise terms and conditions for copying, distribution and modification follow.

D.2   Terms and Conditions for Copying, Distribution, and Modification

0. This License applies to any program or other work which contains a notice placed by the copyright holder saying it may be distributed under the terms of this General Public License. The "Program", below, refers to any such program or work, and a "work based on the Program" means either the Program or any derivative work under copyright law: that is to say, a work containing the Program or a portion of it, either verbatim or with modifications and/or translated into another language. (Hereinafter, translation is included without limitation in the term "modification".) Each licensee is addressed as "you".

   Activities other than copying, distribution and modification are not covered by this License; they are outside its scope. The act of running the Program is not restricted, and the output from the Program is covered only if its contents constitute a work based on the Program (independent of having been made by running the Program). Whether that is true depends on what the Program does.

1. You may copy and distribute verbatim copies of the Program's source code as you receive it, in any medium, provided that you conspicuously and appropriately publish on each copy an appropriate copyright notice and disclaimer of warranty; keep intact all the notices that refer to this License and to the absence of any warranty; and give any other recipients of the Program a copy of this License along with the Program.

   You may charge a fee for the physical act of transferring a copy, and you may at your option offer warranty protection in exchange for a fee.

2. You may modify your copy or copies of the Program or any portion of it, thus forming a work based on the Program, and copy and distribute such modifications or work under the terms of Section 1 above, provided that you also meet all of these conditions:

   a. You must cause the modified files to carry prominent notices stating that you changed the files and the date of any change.

   b. You must cause any work that you distribute or publish, that in whole or in part contains or is derived from the Program or any part thereof, to be licensed as a whole at no charge to all third parties under the terms of this License.

   c. If the modified program normally reads commands interactively when run, you must cause it, when started running for such interactive use in the most ordinary way, to print or display an announcement including an appropriate copyright notice and a notice that there is no warranty (or else, saying that you provide a warranty) and that users may redistribute the program under these conditions, and telling the user how to view a copy of this License. (Exception: if the Program itself is interactive but does not normally print such an announcement, your work based on the Program is not required to print an announcement.)

These requirements apply to the modified work as a whole. If identifiable sections of that work are not derived from the Program, and can be reasonably considered independent and separate works in themselves, then this License, and its terms, do not apply to those sections when you distribute them as separate works. But when you distribute the same sections as part of a whole which is a work based on the Program, the distribution of the whole must be on the terms of this License, whose permissions for other licensees extend to the entire whole, and thus to each and every part regardless of who wrote it.

Thus, it is not the intent of this section to claim rights or contest your rights to work written entirely by you; rather, the intent is to exercise the right to control the distribution of derivative or collective works based on the Program.

In addition, mere aggregation of another work not based on the Program with the Program (or with a work based on the Program) on a volume of a storage or distribution medium does not bring the other work under the scope of this License.

3. You may copy and distribute the Program (or a work based on it, under Section 2) in object code or executable form under the terms of Sections 1 and 2 above provided that you also do one of the following:

   a. Accompany it with the complete corresponding machine-readable source code, which must be distributed under the terms of Sections 1 and 2 above on a medium customarily used for software interchange; or,

   b. Accompany it with a written offer, valid for at least three years, to give any third party, for a charge no more than your cost of physically performing source distribution, a complete machine-readable copy of the corresponding source code, to be distributed under the terms of Sections 1 and 2 above on a medium customarily used for software interchange; or,

   c. Accompany it with the information you received as to the offer to distribute corresponding source code. (This alternative is allowed only for noncommercial distribution and only if you received the program in object code or executable form with such an offer, in accord with Subsection b above.)

The source code for a work means the preferred form of the work for making modifications to it. For an executable work, complete source code means all the source code for all modules it contains, plus any associated interface definition files, plus the scripts used to control compilation and installation of the executable. However, as a special exception, the source code distributed need not include anything that is normally distributed (in either source or binary form) with the major components (compiler, kernel, and so on) of the operating system on which the executable runs, unless that component itself accompanies the executable.

If distribution of executable or object code is made by offering access to copy from a designated place, then offering equivalent access to copy the source code from the same place counts as distribution of the source code, even though third parties are not compelled to copy the source along with the object code.

4. You may not copy, modify, sublicense, or distribute the Program except as expressly provided under this License. Any attempt otherwise to copy, modify, sublicense or distribute the Program is void, and will automatically terminate your rights under this License. However, parties who have received copies, or rights, from you under this License will not have their licenses terminated so long as such parties remain in full compliance.

5. You are not required to accept this License, since you have not signed it. However, nothing else grants you permission to modify or distribute the Program or its derivative works. These actions

are prohibited by law if you do not accept this License. Therefore, by modifying or distributing the Program (or any work based on the Program), you indicate your acceptance of this License to do so, and all its terms and conditions for copying, distributing or modifying the Program or works based on it.

6. Each time you redistribute the Program (or any work based on the Program), the recipient automatically receives a license from the original licensor to copy, distribute or modify the Program subject to these terms and conditions. You may not impose any further restrictions on the recipients' exercise of the rights granted herein. You are not responsible for enforcing compliance by third parties to this License.

7. If, as a consequence of a court judgment or allegation of patent infringement or for any other reason (not limited to patent issues), conditions are imposed on you (whether by court order, agreement or otherwise) that contradict the conditions of this License, they do not excuse you from the conditions of this License. If you cannot distribute so as to satisfy simultaneously your obligations under this License and any other pertinent obligations, then as a consequence you may not distribute the Program at all. For example, if a patent license would not permit royalty-free redistribution of the Program by all those who receive copies directly or indirectly through you, then the only way you could satisfy both it and this License would be to refrain entirely from distribution of the Program.

   If any portion of this section is held invalid or unenforceable under any particular circumstance, the balance of the section is intended to apply and the section as a whole is intended to apply in other circumstances.

   It is not the purpose of this section to induce you to infringe any patents or other property right claims or to contest validity of any such claims; this section has the sole purpose of protecting the integrity of the free software distribution system, which is implemented by public license practices. Many people have made generous contributions to the wide range of software distributed through that system in reliance on consistent application of that system; it is up to the author/donor to decide if he or she is willing to distribute software through any other system and a licensee cannot impose that choice.

   This section is intended to make thoroughly clear what is believed to be a consequence of the rest of this License.

8. If the distribution and/or use of the Program is restricted in certain countries either by patents or by copyrighted interfaces, the original copyright holder who places the Program under this License may add an explicit geographical distribution limitation excluding those countries, so that distribution is permitted only in or among countries not thus excluded. In such case, this License incorporates the limitation as if written in the body of this License.

9. The Free Software Foundation may publish revised and/or new versions of the General Public License from time to time. Such new versions will be similar in spirit to the present version, but may differ in detail to address new problems or concerns.

   Each version is given a distinguishing version number. If the Program specifies a version number of this License which applies to it and "any later version", you have the option of following the terms and conditions either of that version or of any later version published by the Free Software Foundation. If the Program does not specify a version number of this License, you may choose any version ever published by the Free Software Foundation.

10. If you wish to incorporate parts of the Program into other free programs whose distribution conditions are different, write to the author to ask for permission. For software which is copyrighted by the Free Software Foundation, write to the Free Software Foundation; we sometimes make exceptions for this. Our decision will be guided by the two goals of preserving the free status of all derivatives of our free software and of promoting the sharing and reuse of software generally.

NO WARRANTY

11. BECAUSE THE PROGRAM IS LICENSED FREE OF CHARGE, THERE IS NO WARRANTY FOR THE PROGRAM, TO THE EXTENT PERMITTED BY APPLICABLE LAW. EXCEPT WHEN OTHERWISE STATED IN WRITING THE COPYRIGHT HOLDERS AND/OR OTHER PARTIES PROVIDE THE PROGRAM "AS IS" WITHOUT WARRANTY OF ANY KIND, EITHER EXPRESSED OR IMPLIED, INCLUDING, BUT NOT LIMITED TO, THE IMPLIED WARRANTIES OF MERCHANTABILITY AND FITNESS FOR A PARTICULAR PURPOSE. THE ENTIRE RISK AS TO THE QUALITY AND PERFOR-MANCE OF THE PROGRAM IS WITH YOU. SHOULD THE PROGRAM PROVE DEFECTIVE, YOU ASSUME THE COST OF ALL NECESSARY SERVICING, REPAIR OR CORRECTION.

12. IN NO EVENT UNLESS REQUIRED BY APPLICABLE LAW OR AGREED TO IN WRITING WILL ANY COPYRIGHT HOLDER, OR ANY OTHER PARTY WHO MAY MODIFY AND/OR REDIS-TRIBUTE THE PROGRAM AS PERMITTED ABOVE, BE LIABLE TO YOU FOR DAMAGES, IN-CLUDING ANY GENERAL, SPECIAL, INCIDENTAL OR CONSEQUENTIAL DAMAGES ARISING OUT OF THE USE OR INABILITY TO USE THE PROGRAM (INCLUDING BUT NOT LIMITED TO LOSS OF DATA OR DATA BEING RENDERED INACCURATE OR LOSSES SUSTAINED BY YOU OR THIRD PARTIES OR A FAILURE OF THE PROGRAM TO OPERATE WITH ANY OTHER PRO-GRAMS), EVEN IF SUCH HOLDER OR OTHER PARTY HAS BEEN ADVISED OF THE POSSIBILITY OF SUCH DAMAGES.

END OF TERMS AND CONDITIONS

D.3 Appendix: How to Apply These Terms to Your New Programs

If you develop a new program, and you want it to be of the greatest possible use to the public, the best way to achieve this is to make it free software which everyone can redistribute and change under these terms.

To do so, attach the following notices to the program. It is safest to attach them to the start of each source file to most effectively convey the exclusion of warranty; and each file should have at least the "copyright" line and a pointer to where the full notice is found.

⟨one line to give the program's name and a brief idea of what it does.⟩ Copyright ©19yy ⟨name of author⟩

This program is free software; you can redistribute it and/or modify it under the terms of the GNU General Public License as published by the Free Software Foundation; either version 2 of the License, or (at your option) any later version.

This program is distributed in the hope that it will be useful, but WITHOUT ANY WARRANTY; without even the implied warranty of MERCHANTABILITY or FITNESS FOR A PARTICULAR PURPOSE. See the GNU General Public License for more details.

You should have received a copy of the GNU General Public License along with this program; if not, write to the Free Software Foundation, Inc., 675 Mass Ave, Cambridge, MA 02139, USA.

Also add information on how to contact you by electronic and paper mail.

If the program is interactive, make it output a short notice like this when it starts in an interactive mode:

```
Gnomovision version 69, Copyright (C) 19yy name of author Gnomovision comes
with ABSOLUTELY NO WARRANTY; for details type 'show w'. This is free
software, and you are welcome to redistribute it under certain conditions;
type 'show c' for details.
```

The hypothetical commands 'show w' and 'show c' should show the appropriate parts of the General Public License. Of course, the commands you use may be called something other than 'show w' and 'show c'; they could even be mouse-clicks or menu items–whatever suits your program.

You should also get your employer (if you work as a programmer) or your school, if any, to sign a "copyright disclaimer" for the program, if necessary. Here is a sample; alter the names:

> Yoyodyne, Inc., hereby disclaims all copyright interest in the program 'Gnomovision' (which makes passes at compilers) written by James Hacker.
>
> ⟨signature of Ty Coon⟩, 1 April 1989
> Ty Coon, President of Vice

This General Public License does not permit incorporating your program into proprietary programs. If your program is a subroutine library, you may consider it more useful to permit linking proprietary applications with the library. If this is what you want to do, use the GNU Library General Public License instead of this License.

Part II

The Linux Kernel Hackers' Guide

A hodgepodge collection of information, speculation, and ramblings about the Linux kernel. This is only a draft. Please mail any corrections, amplifications, suggestions, etc. to Michael K. Johnson, johnsonm@nigel.vnet.net, Editor.

Editorial comments look like this: [**This is an editorial comment.**] I invite answers to any questions in these comments. The more help I get on these, the fewer of these ugly comments newer versions of the guide will have. Some of these are merely large notices to myself to finish some task I started. If you would like to help by working on a section that has notes like this, please contact me to see what help I need.

This work is currently rather fragmented, and will remain in that state until most of the sections have been written, so that revision combining those sections can be done intelligently. Substantial revision to occur at that time should address the problems with unnecessarily duplicated information and lack of structure, and make the guide easier to follow and more succinct.

However, the section on device drivers should be helpful to some. Other sections are mostly a little out of date and in need of revision anyway. Please bear with me, or better yet, help.

Introduction

The *The Linux Kernel Hackers' Guide* is inspired by all of us "kernel hacker wannabees" who just did not know enough about Unix systems to hack the Linux kernel when it first came out, and had to learn slowly. This guide is designed to help you get up to speed on the concepts that are not intuitively obvious, and to document the internal structures of Linux so that you don't have to read the whole kernel source to figure out what is happening with one variable, or to discover the purpose of one function call.

Why Linux? Well, Linux is the first free Unix clone for the 386 to be freely available. It is a complete re-write, and has been kept small, so it does not have a lot of the time-honored baggage that other free operating systems (like 386BSD) carry, and so is easier to understand and modify.

Unix has been around for over twenty years, but only in the last few years have microcomputers become powerful enough to run a modern protected, multiuser, multitasking operating system. Furthermore, Unix implementations have not been free. Because of this, very little free documentation has been written, at least for the kernel internals.

Unix, though simple at first, has grown more and more appendages, and has become a very complex system, which only "wizards" understand. With Linux, however, we have a chance to change this, for a few reasons:

- Linux has a simple kernel, with well-structured interfaces.

- One person, Linus Torvalds, has control of what code is added to Linux, and he does this work gratis. This means that random pieces of code are not forced into the kernel by some company's politics, and the kernel interfaces stay relatively clean.

- The source is free, so many people can study it and learn to understand it, becoming "wizards" in their own right, and eventually contribute code to the effort.

It is our hope that this book will help the nascent kernel hacker learn how to hack the Linux kernel, by giving an understanding of how the kernel is structured.

Thanks to...

Linus Torvalds, of course, for starting this whole time sink, and for gently providing explanations whenever necessary. He has done a wonderful job of keeping the kernel source code understandable and neat. I can't imagine having learned so much in the past few years without Linux.

Krishna Balasubramanian and **Douglas Johnson,** for writing much of the section on memory management, and helping with the rest.

Stanley Scalsky, for helping document the system call interface.

Rik Faith, for writing the section on how to write a SCSI device driver.

Robert Baruch, for the review of *Writing UNIX Device Drivers* and for his help with the section on writing device drivers.

Linux Journal, for providing me with a Linux-related job, and for allowing me to do work on the KHG on their time.

Kim Johnson, my wife, for tolerating and encouraging me even when I spend my time on crazy stuff like Linux.

Copyright Acknowledgements:

Linux Memory Management: The original version of this document is copyright © 1993 Krishna Balasubramanian. Some changes copyright © 1993 Michael K. Johnson and Douglas R. Johnson.

How System Calls Work: The original version of this document is copyright © 1993 Stanley Scalsky. Some changes copyright © 1993 Michael K. Johnson

Writing a SCSI Device Driver The original version of this document is copyright © 1993 Rickard E. Faith. Some modifications are copyright © 1993 Michael K. Johnson. The author has approved the inclusion of this material, despite the slightly more restrictive copyright on this whole document. The original copyright restrictions, *which still apply to any work derived solely from this work,* are:

> Copyright © 1993 Rickard E. Faith (faith@cs.unc.edu). All rights reserved. Permission is granted to make and distribute verbatim copies of this paper provided the copyright notice and this permission notice are preserved on all copies.

If you wish to make a derived work, please start from the original document. To do so, please contact Rickard E. Faith, `faith@cs.unc.edu`. The original is available for anonymous ftp as ftp.cs.unc.edu:/pub/faith/papers/scsi.paper.tar.gz.

Contents

Chapter 0

Before You Begin...

0.1 Typographical Conventions

Bold   Used to mark **new concepts**, **WARNINGS**, and **keywords** in a language.

italics   Used for *emphasis* in text, and occasionally for quotes or introductions at the beginning of a section.

slanted   Used to mark **meta-variables** in the text, especially in representations of the command line. For example,

```
ls -l foo
```

where *foo* would "stand for" a filename, such as /bin/cp. Sometimes, this might be difficult to see, and so the text is put in angle brackets, like this: ⟨slanted⟩.

Typewriter   Used to represent screen interaction, as in

```
ls -l /bin/cp
-rwxr-xr-x  1 root     wheel    12104 Sep 25 15:53 /bin/cp
```

Also used for code examples, whether it is "C" code, a shell script, or something else, and to display general files, such as configuration files. When necessary for clarity's sake, these examples or figures will be enclosed in thin boxes.

Key   Represents a key to press. You will often see it in this form:

Press return to continue.

◇   A diamond in the margin, like a black diamond on a ski hill, marks "danger" or "caution." Read paragraphs marked this way carefully.

0.2 Assumptions

To read *The Linux Kernel Hackers' Guide*, you should have a reasonably good understanding of C. That is, you should be able to read C code without having to look up everything. You should be able to write simple C programs, and understand struct's, pointers, macros, and ANSI C prototyping. You do not have to have a thorough knowledge of the standard I/O library, because the standard libraries are not available in the kernel. Some of the more often used standard I/O functions have been rewritten for use within the kernel, but these are explained in this book where necessary.

You should be able to use a good text editor, recompile the Linux kernel, and do basic system administration tasks, such as making new device entries in /dev/.

You should also be able to read, as I do not offer support for this book. . .

> *"Hello, sir, I'm having some problems with this book you wrote."*
> *"Yes?"*
> *"I can't read it."*
> *"Is it plugged in?"*
> *"Yes. I also tried a lamp in that socket, so I know it is getting power. But I really don't think that's the problem."*
> *"Why not?"*
> *"I can't read."*
> *" Oh. Well, let's start here. See this? Repeat after me: The cat sat on the rat. . ."*

0.3 Hacking Wisdom

This is a collection of little things that you need to know before you start hacking. It is rather rambling, and almost resembles a glossary in form, but it is not a reference, but rather a hacker's narrative, a short course in kernel hacking.

Static variables

Always initialize static variables. I cannot overemphasize this. Many seemingly random bugs have been caused by not initializing static variables. Because the kernel is not really a standard executable, the **bss** segment may or may not be zeroed, depending on the method used for booting.

libc **unavailable**

Much of libc is unavailable. That is, all of libc is unavailable, but many of the most common functions are duplicated. See the section **[not here yet]** for simple documentation of these functions. Most of the documentation for these are the section 3 and section 9 man pages.

Linux is not UNIX™

However, it is close. It is not plan 9, nor is it Mach. It is not primarily intended to be a great commercial success. People will not look kindly upon suggestions to change it fundamentally to attain any of these goals. It has been suggested that part of the reason that the quality of the Linux kernel is so high is the unbending devotion of the Linux kernel hackers to having fun playing with their new kernel.

Useful references

You will encounter certain references that you will need to understand. For instance, "Stevens" and "Bach". Read the annotated bibliography (Appendix A) for a list of books that you should at least recognize references to, even if you have not read them.

Read the FAQ

Chapter 1

Device Drivers

1.1 What is a Device Driver?

Making hardware work is tedious. To write to a hard disk, for example, requires that you write magic numbers in magic places, wait for the hard drive to say that it is ready to receive data, and then feed it the data it wants, very carefully. To write to a floppy disk is even harder, and requires that the program supervise the floppy disk drive almost constantly while it is running.

Instead of putting code in each application you write to control each device, you share the code between applications. To make sure that that code is not compromised, you protect it from users and normal programs that use it. If you do it right, you will be able to add and remove devices from your system without changing your applications at all. Furthermore, you need to be able to load your program into memory and run it, which the operating system also does. So, an operating system is essentially a privileged, general, sharable library or low-level hardware and memory and process control functions and routines.

All versions of UN⋆X have an abstract way of reading and writing devices. By making the devices act as much as possible like regular files, the same calls (read(), write(), etc.) can be used for devices and files. Within the kernel, there are a set of functions, registered with the filesystem, which are called to handle requests to do I/O on "device special files," which are those which represent devices.[1]

All devices controlled by the same device driver are given the same **major number,** and of those with the same major number, different devices are distinguished by different **minor numbers.**[2]

This chapter explains how to write any type of Linux device driver that you might need to, including character, block, SCSI, and network drivers. **[Well, it will when it is done**...] It explains what functions you need to write, how to initialize your drivers and obtain memory for them efficiently, and what function are built in to Linux to make your job easier.

Creating device drivers for Linux is easier than you might think. It merely involves writing a few functions and registering them with the Virtual Filesystem Switch (VFS), so that when the proper device special files are accessed, the VFS can call your functions.

However, a word of warning is due here: Writing a device driver **is** writing a part of the Linux kernel. This means that your driver runs with kernel permissions, and can do anything it wants to: write to any memory, reformat your hard drive, damage your monitor or video card, or even break your dishes, if your

---

[1]See mknod(1,2) for an explanation of how to make these files.

[2]This is not strictly true, but is close enough. If you understand where it is not true, you don't need to read this section, and if you don't but want to learn, read the code for the tty devices, which uses up 2 major numbers, and may use a third and possibly fourth by the time you read this.

dishwasher is controlled by your computer. Be careful.

Also, your driver will run in kernel mode, and the Linux kernel, like most UN*X kernels, is not pre-emptible. This means that if you driver takes a long time to work without giving other programs a chance to work, your computer will appear to "freeze" when your driver is running. Normal user-mode preemptive scheduling does not apply to your driver.

If you choose to write a device driver, you must take everything written here as a guide, and no more. I cannot guarantee that this chapter will be free of errors, and I cannot guarantee that you will not damage your computer, even if you follow these instructions exactly. It is highly unlikely that you will damage it, but I cannot guarantee against it. There is only one "infallible" direction I can give you: **Back up!** Back up before you test your new device driver, or you may regret it later.

1.2 User-space device drivers

It is not always necessary to write a device driver for a device, especially in applications where no two applications will compete for the device. The most useful example of this is a memory-mapped device, but you can also do this with devices in I/O space (devices accessed with `inb()` and `outb()`, etc.). If your process is running as superuser (root), you can use the `mmap()` call to map some of your process memory to actual memory locations, by `mmap()`'ing a section of /dev/mem. When you have done this mapping, it is pretty easy to write and read from real memory addresses just as you would read and write any variables.

If your driver needs to respond to interrupts, then you really need to be working in kernel space, and need to write a real device driver, as there is no good way at this time to deliver interrupts to user processes. Although the DOSEMU project has created something called the SIG (Silly Interrupt Generator) which allows interrupts to be posted to user processes (I believe through the use of signals), the SIG is not particularly fast, and should be thought of as a last resort for things like DOSEMU.

An interrupt (for those who don't know) is an asynchronous notification posted by the hardware to alert the device driver of some condition. You have likely dealt with 'IRQ's when setting up your hardware; an IRQ is an "Interrupt ReQuest line," which is triggered when the device wants to talk to the driver. This may be because it has data to give to the drive, or because it is now ready to receive data, or because of some other "exceptional condition" that the driver needs to know about. It is similar to user-level processes receiving a **signal,** so similar that the same `sigaction` structure is used in the kernel to deal with interrupts as is used in user-level programs to deal with signals. Where the user-level has its signals delivered to it by the kernel, the kernel has interrupt delivered to it by hardware.

If your driver must be accessible to multiple processes at once, and/or manage contention for a resource, then you also need to write a real device driver at the kernel level, and a user-space device driver will not be sufficient or even possible.

1.2.1 **Example:** vgalib

A good example of a user-space driver is the `vgalib` library. The standard `read()` and `write()` calls are really inadequate for writing a really fast graphics driver, and so instead there is a library which acts conceptually like a device driver, but runs in user space. Any processes which use it **must** run setuid root, because it uses the `ioperm()` system call. It is possible for a process that is not setuid root to write to /dev/mem if you have a group `mem` or `kmem` which is allowed write permission to /dev/mem and the process is properly setgid, but only a process running as root can execute the `ioperm()` call.

There are several I/O ports associated with VGA graphics. `vgalib` creates symbolic names for this with #define statements, and then issues the ioperm() call like this to make it possible for the process to read and write directly from and to those ports:

```
if (ioperm(CRT_IC, 1, 1)) {
    printf("VGAlib: can't get I/O permissions \n");
    exit (-1);
}
ioperm(CRT_IM,  1, 1);
ioperm(ATT_IW, 1, 1);
```

[...]

It only needs to do error checking once, because the only reason for the ioperm() call to fail is that it is not being called by the superuser, and this status is not going to change.

◇   After making this call, the process is allowed to use inb and outb machine instructions, but only on the specified ports. These instructions can be accessed without writing directly in assembly by including <linux/asm>, but will only work if you compile **with optimization on,** by giving the -O? to gcc. Read <linux/asm> for details.

After arranging for port I/O, vgalib arranges for writing directly to kernel memory with the following code:

```
/* open /dev/mem */
if ((mem_fd = open("/dev/mem", O_RDWR) ) < 0) {
    printf("VGAlib: can't open /dev/mem \n");
    exit (-1);
}

/* mmap graphics memory */
if ((graph_mem = malloc(GRAPH_SIZE + (PAGE_SIZE-1))) == NULL) {
    printf("VGAlib: allocation error \n");
    exit (-1);
}
if ((unsigned long)graph_mem % PAGE_SIZE)
    graph_mem += PAGE_SIZE - ((unsigned long)graph_mem % PAGE_SIZE);
graph_mem = (unsigned char *)mmap(
    (caddr_t)graph_mem,
    GRAPH_SIZE,
    PROT_READ|PROT_WRITE,
    MAP_SHARED|MAP_FIXED,
    mem_fd,
    GRAPH_BASE
);
if ((long)graph_mem < 0) {
    printf("VGAlib: mmap error \n");
    exit (-1);
}
```

It first opens /dev/mem, then allocates memory enough so that the mapping can be done on a page (4 KB) boundary, and then attempts the map. GRAPH_SIZE is the size of VGA memory, and GRAPH_BASE is the first address of VGA memory in /dev/mem. Then by writing to the address that is returned by mmap(), the process is actually writing to screen memory.

1.2.2   Example: mouse conversion

If you want a driver that acts a bit more like a kernel-level driver, but does not live in kernel space, you can also make a FIFO, or named pipe. This usually lives in the /dev/ directory (although it doesn't need to) and acts substantially like a device once set up. However, FIFOs are one-directional only — they have one reader and one writer.

For instance, it used to be that if you had a PS/2-style mouse, and wanted to run XFree86, you had to create a FIFO called /dev/mouse, and run a program called mconv which read PS/2 mouse "droppings" from /dev/psaux, and wrote the equivalent microsoft-style "droppings" to /dev/mouse. Then XFree86 would read the "droppings" from /dev/mouse, and it would be as if there were a microsoft mouse connected to /dev/mouse.[3]

1.3   Device Driver Basics

We will assume that you decide that you do not wish to write a user-space device, and would rather implement your device in the kernel. You will probably be writing writing two files, a .c file and a .h file, and possibly modifying other files as well, as will be described below. We will refer to your files as foo.c and foo.h, and your driver will be the `foo` driver.

[Should I include at the beginning of this section an example of chargen and charsink? Many writers do, but I don't know that it is the best way. I'd like people's opinions on this.]

1.3.1   Namespace

One of the first things you will need to do, before writing any code, is to name your device. This name should be a short (probably two or three character) string. For instance, the parallel device is the "lp" device, the floppies are the "fd" devices, and SCSI disks are the "sd" devices. As you write your driver, you will give your functions names prefixed with your chosen string to avoid any namespace confusion. We will call your prefix `foo`, and give your functions names like `foo_read()`, `foo_write()`, etc.

1.3.2   Allocating memory

Memory allocation in the kernel is a little different from memory allocation in normal user-level programs. Instead of having a `malloc()` capable of delivering almost unlimited amounts of memory, there is a `kmalloc()` function that is a bit different:

- Memory is provided in pieces whose size is a power of 2, except that pieces larger than 128 bytes are allocated in blocks whose size is a power of 2 minus some small amount for overhead. You can request any odd size, but memory will not be used any more efficiently if you request a 31-byte piece than it will if you request a 32 byte piece. Also, there is a limit to the amount of memory that can be allocated, which is currently 131056 bytes.

- `kmalloc()` takes a second argument, the priority. This is used as an argument to the `get_free_page()` function, where it is used to determine when to return. The usual priority is `GFP_KERNEL`. If it may be called from within an interrupt, use `GFP_ATOMIC` and be truly prepared for it to fail (i.e. don't panic). This is because if you specify `GFP_KERNEL`, `kmalloc()` may sleep, which

---

[3]Even though XFree86 is now able to read PS/2 style "droppings", the concepts in this example still stand. If you have a better example, I'd be glad to see it.

cannot be done on an interrupt. The other option is GFP_BUFFER, which is used only when the kernel is allocating buffer space, and never in device drivers.

To free memory allocated with kmalloc(), use one of two functions: kfree() or kfree_s(). These differ from free() in a few ways as well:

- kfree() is a macro which calls kfree_s() and acts like the standard free() outside the kernel.

- If you know what size object you are freeing, you can speed things up by calling kfree_s() directly. It takes two arguments: the first is the pointer that you are freeing, as in the single argument to kfree(), and the second is the size of the object being freed.

See section 1.6 for more information on kmalloc(), kfree(), and other useful functions.

The other way to acquire memory is to allocate it at initialization time. Your initialization function, foo_init(), takes one argument, a pointer to the current end of memory. It can take as much memory as it wants to, save a pointer or pointers to that memory, and return a pointer to the new end of memory. The advantage of this over statically allocating large buffers (char bar[20000]) is that if the foo driver detects that the foo device is not attached to the computer, the memory is not wasted. The init() function is discussed in Section 1.3.6.

Be gentle when you use kmalloc. Use only what you have to. Remember that kernel memory is unswappable, and thus allocating extra memory in the kernel is a far worse thing to do in the kernel than in a user-level program. Take only what you need, and free it when you are done, unless you are going to use it right away again.

[I believe that it is possible to allocate swappable memory with the vmalloc function, but that will be documented in the VMM section when it gets written. In the meantime, enterprising hackers are encouraged to look it up themselves.]

1.3.3   Character vs. block devices

There are two main types of devices under all UN*X systems, character and block devices. Character devices are those for which no buffering is performed, and block devices are those which are accessed through a cache. Block devices must be random access, but character devices are not required to be, though some are. Filesystems can only be mounted if they are on block devices.

Character devices are read from and written to with two function: foo_read() and foo_write(). The read() and write() calls do not return until the operation is complete. By contrast, block devices do not even implement the read() and write() functions, and instead have a function which has historically been called the "strategy routine." Reads and writes are done through the buffer cache mechanism by the generic functions bread(), breada(), and bwrite(). These functions go through the buffer cache, and so may or may not actually call the strategy routine, depending on whether or not the block requested is in the buffer cache (for reads) or on whether or not the buffer cache is full (for writes). A request may be asynchronous: breada() can request the strategy routine to schedule reads that have not been asked for, and to do it asynchronously, in the background, in the hopes that they will be needed later. A more complete explanation of the buffer cache is presented below in Section **?? [When that section is written. . .]**

The sources for character devices are kept in . . . /kernel/chr_drv/, and the sources for block devices are kept in . . . /kernel/blk_drv/. They have similar interfaces, and are very much alike, except for reading and writing. Because of the difference in reading and writing, initialization is different, as block devices have to register a strategy routine, which is registered in a different way than the foo_read() and foo_write() routines of a character device driver. Specifics are dealt with in Section 1.4.1 and Section 1.5.1

1.3.4   Interrupts vs. Polling

Hardware is slow. That is, in the time it takes to get information from your average device, the CPU could be off doing something far more useful than waiting for a busy but slow device. So to keep from having to **busy-wait** all the time, **interrupts** are provided which can interrupt whatever is happening so that the operating system can do some task and return to what it was doing without losing information. In an ideal world, all devices would probably work by using interrupts. However, on a PC or clone, there are only a few interrupts available for use by your peripherals, so some drivers have to poll the hardware: ask the hardware if it is ready to transfer data yet. This unfortunately wastes time, but it sometimes needs to be done.

Also, some hardware (like memory-mapped displays) is as fast as the rest of the machine, and does not generate output asynchronously, so an interrupt-driven driver would be rather silly, even if interrupts were provided.

In Linux, many of the drivers are interrupt-driven, but some are not, and at least one can be either, and can be switched back and forth at runtime. For instance, the `lp` device (the parallel port driver) normally polls the printer to see if the printer is ready to accept output, and if the printer stays in a not ready phase for too long, the driver will sleep for a while, and try again later. This improves system performance. However, if you have a parallel card that supplies an interrupt, the driver will utilize that, which will usually make performance even better.

There are some important programming differences between interrupt-driven drivers and polling drivers. To understand this difference, you have to understand a little bit of how system calls work under UN⋆X. The kernel is not a separate task under UN⋆X. Rather, it is as if each process has a copy of the kernel. When a process executes a system call, it does not transfer control to another process, but rather, the process changes execution modes, and is said to be "in kernel mode." In this mode, it executes kernel code which is trusted to be safe.

In kernel mode, the process can still access the user-space memory that it was previously executing in, which is done through a set of macros: `get_fs_*()` and `memcpy_fromfs()` read user-space memory, and `put_fs_*()` and `memcpy_tofs()` write to user-space memory. Because the process is still running, but in a different mode, there is no question of where in memory to put the data, or where to get it from. However, when an interrupt occurs, any process might currently be running, so these macros cannot be used — if they are, they will either write over random memory space of the running process or cause the kernel to panic.

[Explain how to use `verify_area()`, which is only used on CPUs that don't provide write protection while operating in kernel mode, to check whether the area is safe to write to.]

Instead, when scheduling the interrupt, a driver must also provide temporary space in which to put the information, and then sleep. When the interrupt-driven part of the driver has filled up that temporary space, it wakes up the process, which copies the information from that temporary space into the process' user space and returns. In a block device driver, this temporary space is automatically provided by the buffer cache mechanism, but in a character device driver, the driver is responsible for allocating it itself.

1.3.5   The sleep-wakeup mechanism

[Begin by giving a general description of how sleeping is used and what it does. This should mention things like all processes sleeping on an event are woken at once, and then they contend for the event again, etc...]

Perhaps the best way to try to understand the Linux sleep-wakeup mechanism is to read the source for the `__sleep_on()` function, used to implement both the `sleep_on()` and `interruptible_sleep_on()`

calls.

```
static inline void __sleep_on(struct wait_queue **p, int state)
{
    unsigned long flags;
    struct wait_queue wait = { current, NULL };

    if (!p)
        return;
    if (current == task[0])
        panic("task[0] trying to sleep");
    current->state = state;
    add_wait_queue(p, &wait);
    save_flags(flags);
    sti();
    schedule();
    remove_wait_queue(p, &wait);
    restore_flags(flags);
}
```

A wait_queue is a circular list of pointers to task structures, defined in <linux/wait.h> to be

```
struct wait_queue {
    struct task_struct * task;
    struct wait_queue * next;
};
```

state is either TASK_INTERRUPTIBLE or TASK_UNINTERRUPTIBLE, depending on whether or not the sleep should be interruptible by such things as system calls. In general, the sleep should be interruptible if the device is a slow one; one which can block indefinitely, including terminals and network devices or pseudodevices.

add_wait_queue() turns off interrupts, if they were enabled, and adds the new struct wait_queue declared at the beginning of the function to the list p. It then recovers the original interrupt state (enabled or disabled), and returns.

save_flags() is a macro which saves the process flags in its argument. This is done to preserve the previous state of the interrupt enable flag. This way, the restore_flags() later can restore the interrupt state, whether it was enabled or disabled. sti() then allows interrupts to occur, and schedule() finds a new process to run, and switches to it. Schedule will not choose this process to run again until the state is changed to TASK_RUNNING by wake_up() called on the same wait queue, p, or conceivably by something else.

The process then removes itself from the wait_queue, restores the original interrupt condition with restore_flags(), and returns.

Whenever contention for a resource might occur, there needs to be a pointer to a wait_queue associated with that resource. Then, whenever contention does occur, each process that finds itself locked out of access to the resource sleeps on that resource's wait_queue. When any process is finished using a resource for which there is a wait_queue, it should wake up and processes that might be sleeping on that wait_queue, probably by calling wake_up(), or possibly wake_up_interruptible().

If you don't understand why a process might want to sleep, or want more details on when and how to structure this sleeping, I urge you to buy one of the operating systems textbooks listed in Appendix A and look up **mutual exclusion** and **deadlock**.

[This is a cop-out. I should take the time to explain and give examples, but I am not trying to write an OS text, and I want to keep this under 1000 pages...]

1.3.5.1 More advanced sleeping

If the `sleep_on()`/`wake_up()` mechanism in Linux does not satisfy your device driver needs, you can code your own versions of `sleep_on()` and `wake_up()` that fit your needs. For an example of this, look at the serial device driver (.../kernel/chr_drv/serial.c) in function `block_til_ready()`, where quite a bit has to be done between the `add_wait_queue()` and the `schedule()`.

1.3.6 The VFS

The Virtual Filesystem Switch, or **VFS**, is the mechanism which allows Linux to mount many different filesystems at the same time. In the first versions of Linux, all filesystem access went straight into routines which understood the `minix` filesystem. To make it possible for other filesystems to be written, filesystem calls had to pass through a layer of indirection which would switch the call to the routine for the correct filesystem. This was done by some generic code which can handle generic cases and a structure of pointers to functions which handle specific cases. One structure is of interest to the device driver writer; the `file_operations` structure.

From /usr/include/linux/fs.h:

```
struct file_operations {
    int  (*lseek)   (struct inode *, struct file *, off_t, int);
    int  (*read)    (struct inode *, struct file *, char *, int);
    int  (*write)   (struct inode *, struct file *, char *, int);
    int  (*readdir) (struct inode *, struct file *, struct dirent *,
                     int count);
    int  (*select)  (struct inode *, struct file *, int,
                     select_table *);
    int  (*ioctl)   (struct inode *, struct file *, unsigned int,
                     unsigned int);
    int  (*mmap)    (struct inode *, struct file *, unsigned long,
                     size_t, int, unsigned long);
    int  (*open)    (struct inode *, struct file *);
    void (*release) (struct inode *, struct file *);
};
```

Essentially, this structure constitutes a partial list of the functions that you may have to write to create your driver.

This section details the actions and requirements of the functions in the `file_operations` structure. It documents all the arguments that these functions take. **[It should also detail all the defaults, and cover more carefully the possible return values.**

1.3.6.1 The `lseek()` function

This function is called when the system call `lseek()` is called on the device special file representing your device. An understanding of what the system call `lseek()` does should be sufficient to explain this function, which moves to the desired offset. It takes these four arguments:

```
struct inode * inode
```
> Pointer to the inode structure for this device.

```
struct file * file
```
> Pointer to the file structure for this device.

```
off_t offset
```
> Offset **from origin** to move to.

```
int origin
```     0 = take the offset from absolute offset 0 (the beginning).
         1 = take the offset from the current position.
         2 = take the offset from the end.

`lseek()` returns `-errno` on error, or $\geq 0$ the absolute position after the lseek.

If there is no `lseek()`, the kernel will take the default action, which is to modify the `file->f_pos` element. For an `origin` of 2, the default action is to return `-EINVAL` if `file->f_inode` is NULL, otherwise it sets `file->f_pos` to `file->f_inode->i_size + offset`. Because of this, if `lseek()` should return an error for your device, you must write an `lseek()` function which returns that error.

### 1.3.6.2  The `read()` and `write()` functions

The read and write functions read and write a character string to the device. If there is no `read()` or `write()` function in the `file_operations` structure registered with the kernel, and the device is a character device, `read()` or `write()` system calls, respectively, will return `-EINVAL`. If the device is a block device, these functions should not be implemented, as the VFS will route requests through the buffer cache, which will call your strategy routine. See Section 1.5.2 for details on how the buffer cache does this. The read and write functions take these arguments:

```
struct inode * inode
```
> This is a pointer to the inode of the device special file which was accessed. From this, you can do several things, based on the `struct inode` declaration about 100 lines into /usr/include/linux/fs.h. For instance, you can find the minor number of the file by this construction: `unsigned int minor = MINOR(inode->i_rdev);` The definition of the `MINOR` macro is in `<linux/fs.h>`, as are many other useful definitions. Read fs.h and a few device drivers for more details, and see section 1.6 for a short description. `inode->i_mode` can be used to find the mode of the file, and there are macros available for this, as well.

```
struct file * file
```
> Pointer to file structure for this device.

```
char * buf
```   This is a buffer of characters to read or write. It is located in *user-space* memory, and therefore must be accessed using the `get_fs*()`, `put_fs*()`, and `memcpy*fs()` macros detailed in section 1.6. User-space memory is inaccessible during an interrupt, so if your driver is interrupt driven, you will have to copy the contents of your buffer into a queue.

```
int count
```     This is a count of characters in `buf` to be read or written. It is the size of `buf`, and is how you know that you have reached the end of `buf`, as `buf` is not guaranteed to be null-terminated.

### 1.3.6.3   The `readdir()` function

This function is another artifact of `file_operations` being used for implementing filesystems as well as device drivers. Do not implement it. The kernel will return `-ENOTDIR` if the system call `readdir()` is called on your device special file.

### 1.3.6.4   The `select()` function

The `select()` function is generally most useful with character devices. It is usually used to multiplex reads without polling — the application calls the `select()` system call, giving it a list of file descriptors to watch, and the kernel reports back to the program on which file descriptor has woken it up. It is also used as a timer. However, the `select()` function in your device driver is not directly called by the system call `select()`, and so the `file_operations select()` only needs to do a few things. Its arguments are:

`struct inode * inode`
> Pointer to the inode structure for this device.

`struct file * file`
> Pointer to the file structure for this device.

`int sel_type`
> The select type to perform:
>
> | | |
> |--------|-----------|
> | SEL_IN | read |
> | SEL_OUT | write |
> | SEL_EX | exception |

`select_table * wait`
> If `wait` is not NULL and there is no error condition caused by the select, `select()` should put the process to sleep, and arrange to be woken up when the device becomes ready, usually through an interrupt. If `wait` is NULL, then the driver should quickly see if the device is ready, and return even if it is not. The `select_wait()` function does this already.

If the calling program wants to wait until one of the devices upon which it is selecting becomes available for the operation it is interested in, the process will have to be put to sleep until one of those operations becomes available. This does **not** require use of a `sleep_on*()` function, however. Instead the `select_wait()` function is used. (See section 1.6 for the definition of the `select_wait()` function). The sleep state that `select_wait()` will cause is the same as that of `sleep_on_interruptible()`, and, in fact, `wake_up_interruptible()` is used to wake up the process.

However, `select_wait()` will not make the process go to sleep right away. It returns directly, and the `select()` function you wrote should then return. The process isn't put to sleep until the system call `sys_select()`, which originally called your `select()` function, uses the information given to it by the `select_wait()` function to put the process to sleep. `select_wait()` adds the process to the wait queue, but `do_select()` (called from `sys_select()`) actually puts the process to sleep by changing the process state to `TASK_INTERRUPTIBLE` and calling `schedule()`.

The first argument to `select_wait()` is the same `wait_queue` that should be used for a `sleep_on()`, and the second is the `select_table` that was passed to your `select()` function.

After having explained all this in excruciating detail, here are two rules to follow:

1. Call `select_wait()` if the device is not ready, and return 0.

2. Return 1 if the device is ready.

If you provide a `select()` function, do not provide timeouts by setting `current->timeout`, as the `select()` mechanism uses `current->timeout`, and the two methods cannot co-exist, as there is only one `timeout` for each process. Instead, consider using a timer to provide timeouts. See the description of the `add_timer()` function in section 1.6 for details.

### 1.3.6.5  The `ioctl()` function

The `ioctl()` function processes ioctl calls. The structure of your `ioctl()` function will be: first error checking, then one giant (possibly nested) switch statement to handle all possible ioctls. The ioctl number is passed as `cmd`, and the argument to the ioctl is passed as `arg`. It is good to have an understanding of how `ioctl`s ought to work before making them up. If you are not sure about your ioctls, do not feel ashamed to ask someone knowledgeable about it, for a few reasons: you may not even need an ioctl for your purpose, and if you do need an ioctl, there may be a better way to do it than what you have thought of. Since ioctls are the least regular part of the device interface, it takes perhaps the most work to get this part right. Take the time and energy you need to get it right.

`struct inode * inode`
> Pointer to the inode structure for this device.

`struct file * file`
> Pointer to the file structure for this device.

`unsigned int cmd`
> This is the ioctl command. It is generally used as the switch variable for a case statement.

`unsigned int arg`
> This is the argument to the command. This is user defined. Since this is the same size as a `(void *)`, this can be used as a pointer to user space, accessed through the fs register as usual.

**Returns:**         `-errno` on error
> Every other return is user-defined.

If the `ioctl()` slot in the `file_operations` structure is not filled in, the VFS will return `-EINVAL`. However, in all cases, if `cmd` is one of `FIOCLEX`, `FIONCLEX`, `FIONBIO`, or `FIOASYNC`, default processing will be done:

`FIOCLEX`         0x5451
> Sets the close-on-exec bit.

`FIONCLEX`        0x5450
> Clears the close-on-exec bit.

`FIONBIO`         0x5421
> If `arg` is non-zero, set O_NONBLOCK, otherwise clear O_NONBLOCK.

`FIOASYNC`        0x5452
> If `arg` is non-zero, set O_SYNC, otherwise clear O_SYNC. O_SYNC is not yet implemented, but it is documented here and parsed in the kernel for completeness.

Note that you have to avoid these four numbers when creating your own ioctls, since if they conflict, the VFS ioctl code will interpret them as being one of these four, and act appropriately, causing a very hard to track down bug.

### 1.3.6.6   The `mmap()` function

`struct inode * inode`
> Pointer to inode structure for device.

`struct file * file`
> Pointer to file structure for device.

`unsigned long addr`
> Beginning of address in main memory to `mmap()` into.

`size_t len`   Length of memory to `mmap()`.

`int prot`   One of:

| | |
|---|---|
| `PROT_READ` | region can be read. |
| `PROT_WRITE` | region can be written. |
| `PROT_EXEC` | region can be executed. |
| `PROT_NONE` | region cannot be accessed. |

`unsigned long off`
> Offset in the file to `mmap()` from. This address in the file will be mapped to address `addr`.
>
> **[Here, give a pointer to the documentation for the new vmm (Virtual Memory Management) interface, and show how the functions can be used by a device `mmap()` function. Krishna should have the documentation for the vmm interface in the memory management section.]**

### 1.3.6.7   The `open()` and `release()` functions

`struct inode * inode`
> Pointer to inode structure for device.

`struct file * file`
> Pointer to file structure for device.

`open()` is called when a device special files is opened. It is the policy mechanism responsible for ensuring consistency. If only one process is allowed to open the device at once, `open()` should lock the device, using whatever locking mechanism is appropriate, usually setting a bit in some state variable to mark it as busy. If a process already is using the device (if the busy bit is already set) then `open()` should return `-EBUSY`. If more than one process may open the device, this function is responsible to set up any necessary queues that would not be set up in `write()`. If no such device exists, `open()` should return `-ENODEV` to indicate this. Return 0 on success.

`release()` is called only when the process closes its last open file descriptor on the files. If devices have been marked as busy, `release()` should unset the busy bits if appropriate. If you need to clean up `kmalloc()`'ed queues or reset devices to preserve their sanity, this is the place to do it. If no `release()` function is defined, none is called.

#### 1.3.6.8   The `init()` function

This function is not actually included in the `file_operations` structure, but you are required to implement it, because it is this function that registers the `file_operations` structure with the VFS in the first place — without this function, the VFS could not route any requests to the driver. This function is called when the kernel first boots and is configuring itself. `init()` is passed a variable holding the address of the current end of used memory. The init function then detects all devices, allocates any memory it will want based on how many devices exist (this is often used to hold such things as queues, for interrupt driven devices), and then, saving the addresses it needs, it returns the new end of memory. You will have to call your `init()` function from the correct place: for a character device, this is `chr_dev_init()` in .../kernel/chr_dev/mem.c. In general, you will only pass the `memory_start` variable to your `init()` function.

While the `init()` function runs, it registers your driver by calling the proper registration function. For character devices, this is `register_chrdev()`.[4] `register_chrdev()` takes three arguments: the major device number (an int), the "name" of the device (a string), and the address of the *device*_fops `file_operations` structure.

When this is done, and a character or block special file is accessed, the VFS filesystem switch automagically routes the call, whatever it is, to the proper function, if a function exists. If the function does not exist, the VFS routines take some default action.

The `init()` function usually displays some information about the driver, and usually reports all hardware found. All reporting is done via the `printk()` function.

## 1.4   Character Device Drivers

**[Write appropriate blurb here]**

### 1.4.1   Initialization

Besides functions defined by the `file_operations` structure, there is at least one other function that you will have to write, the `foo_init()` function. You will have to change `chr_dev_init()` in chr_drv/mem.c to call your `foo_init()` function. `foo_init()` will take one argument, `long mem_start`, which will be the address of the current end of allocated memory. If your driver needs to allocate more than 4K of contiguous space at runtime, here is the place. Simply save `mem_start` in an appropriate variable, add however much space you need to `mem_start`, and return the new value. Your driver will now have exclusive access to the memory between the old and new values of `mem_start`.

`foo_init()` should first call `register_chrdev()` to register itself and avoid device number contention. `register_chrdev()` takes three arguments:

`int major`   This is the major number which the driver wishes to allocate.

`char *name`   This is the symbolic name of the driver. It is currently not used for anything, but this may change in the future.

`struct file_operations *f_ops`
This is the address of your `file_operations` structure defined in Section ??

---

[4]See section??

**Returns:**          0 if no other character device has registered with the same major number.

non-0 if the call fails, presumably because another character device has already allocated that major number.

Generally, the `foo_init()` routine will then attempt to detect the hardware that it is supposed to be driving. It should make sure that all necessary data structures are filled out for all present hardware, and have some way of ensuring that non-present hardware does not get accessed. **[detail different ways of doing this.]**

## 1.4.2 Interrupts vs. Polling

In a polling driver, the `foo_read()` and `foo_write()` functions are pretty easy to write. Here is an example of `foo_write()`:

```
static int foo_write(struct inode * inode, struct file * file,
                     char * buf, int count)
{
    unsigned int minor = MINOR(inode->i_rdev);
    char ret;

    while (count > 0) {
        ret = foo_write_byte(minor);
        if (ret < 0) {
            foo_handle_error(WRITE, ret, minor);
            continue;
        }
        buf++ = ret; count--
    }
    return count;
}
```

`foo_write_byte()` and `foo_handle_error()` are either functions defined elsewhere in foo.c or pseudocode. `WRITE` would be a constant or `#define`.

It should be clear from this example how to code the `foo_read()` function as well.

Interrupt-driven drivers are a little more difficult. Here is an example of a `foo_write()` that is interrupt-driven:

```
static int foo_write(struct inode * inode, struct file * file,
                     char * buf, int count)
{
    unsigned int minor = MINOR(inode->i_rdev);
    unsigned long copy_size;
    unsigned long total_bytes_written = 0;
    unsigned long bytes_written;
    struct foo_struct *foo = &foo_table[minor];

    do {
        copy_size = (count <= FOO_BUFFER_SIZE ? count : FOO_BUFFER_SIZE);
        memcpy_fromfs(foo->foo_buffer, buf, copy_size);

        while (copy_size) {
```

```
            /* initiate interrupts */

            if (some_error_has_occurred) {
                /* handle error condition */
            }

            current->timeout = jiffies + FOO_INTERRUPT_TIMEOUT;
                /* set timeout in case an interrupt has been missed */
            interruptible_sleep_on(&foo->foo_wait_queue);
            bytes_written = foo->bytes_xfered;
            foo->bytes_written = 0;
            if (current->signal & ~current->blocked) {
                if (total_bytes_written + bytes_written)
                    return total_bytes_written + bytes_written;
                else
                    return -EINTR; /* nothing was written, system
                                      call was interrupted, try again */
            }
        }

        total_bytes_written += bytes_written;
        buf += bytes_written;
        count -= bytes_written;

    } while (count > 0);

    return total_bytes_written;
}

static void foo_interrupt(int irq)
{
    struct foo_struct *foo = &foo_table[foo_irq[irq]];

    /* Here, do whatever actions ought to be taken on an interrupt.
       Look at a flag in foo_table to know whether you ought to be
       reading or writing. */

    /* Increment foo->bytes_xfered by however many characters were
       read or written */

    if (buffer too full/empty)
        wake_up_interruptible(&foo->foo_wait_queue);
}
```

Again, a foo_read() function is written analogously. foo_table[] is an array of structures, each of which has several members, some of which are foo_wait_queue and bytes_xfered, which can be used for both reading and writing. foo_irq[] is an array of 16 integers, and is used for looking up which entry in foo_table[] is associated with the irq generated and reported to the foo_interrupt() function.

To tell the interrupt-handling code to call foo_interrupt(), you need to use either request_irq() or irqaction(). This is either done when foo_open() is called, or if you want to keep things simple, when foo_init() is called. request_irq() is the simpler of the two, and works rather like an old-style signal handler. It takes two arguments: the first is the number of the irq you are requesting, and the second is a pointer to your interrupt handler, which must take an integer argument (the irq that was generated) and have a return type of void. request_irq() returns -EINVAL if irq > 15 or if the pointer to the interrupt handler is NULL, -EBUSY if that interrupt has already been taken, or 0 on success.

irqaction() works rather like the user-level sigaction(), and in fact reuses the sigaction structure. The sa_restorer() field of the sigaction structure is not used, but everything else is the same. See the entry for irqaction() in Section 1.6, **Supporting Functions**, for further information about irqaction().

1.4.3 TTY drivers

[The reasons that this section has not been written are that I don't know enough about TTY stuff yet. Ted re-wrote the tty devices for the 1.1 series, but I haven't studied them yet.]

1.5 Block Device Drivers

To mount a filesystem on a device, it must be a block device driven by a block device driver. This means that the device must be a random access device, not a stream device. In other words, you must be able to seek to any location on the physical device at any time.

You do not provide read() and write() routines for a block device. Instead, your driver uses block_read() and block_write(), which are generic functions, provided by the VFS, which will call the **strategy** routine, or request() function, which you write in place of read() and write() for your driver. This strategy routine is also called by the **buffer cache** (See section ??), which is called by the VFS routines (See chapter ??) which is how normal files on normal filesystems are read and written.

Requests for I/O are given by the buffer cache to a routine called ll_rw_block(), which constructs lists of requests ordered by an **elevator algorithm,** which sorts the lists to make accesses faster and more efficient. It, in turn, calls your request() function to actually do the I/O.

Note that although SCSI disks and CDROMs are considered block devices, they are handled specially (as are all SCSI devices). Refer to section 1.7, Writing a SCSI Driver, for details.[5]

1.5.1 Initialization

Initialization of block devices is a bit more complex than initialization of character devices, especially as some "initialization" has to be done at compile time. There is also a register_blkdev() call that corresponds to the character device register_chrdev() call, which the driver must call to say that it is present, working, and active.

1.5.1.1 The file blk.h

At the top of your driver code, after all other included header files, you need to write two lines of code:

```
#define MAJOR_NR DEVICE_MAJOR
#include "blk.h"
```

---

[5]Although SCSI disks and CDROMs are block devices, SCSI tapes, like other tapes, are generally used as character devices.

where **DEVICE**_MAJOR is the major number of your device. drivers/block/blk.h requires the use of the MAJOR_NR define to set up many other defines and macros for your driver.

Now you need to edit blk.h. Under `#ifdef MAJOR_NR`, there is a section of defines that are conditionally included for certain major numbers, protected by `#elif (MAJOR_NR == **DEVICE**_MAJOR)`. At the end of this list, you will add another section for your driver. In that section, the following lines are required:

```
#define DEVICE_NAME "device"
#define DEVICE_REQUEST do_dev_request
#define DEVICE_ON(device) /* usually blank, see below */
#define DEVICE_OFF(device) /* usually blank, see below */
#define DEVICE_NR(device) (MINOR(device))
```

DEVICE_NAME is simply the device name. See the other entries in blk.h for examples.

DEVICE_REQUEST is your strategy routine, which will do all the I/O on the device. See section 1.5.3 for more details on the strategy routine.

DEVICE_ON and DEVICE_OFF are for devices that need to be turned on and off, like floppies. In fact, the floppy driver is currently the only device driver which uses these defines.

DEVICE_NR(device) is used to determine the number of the physical device from the minor device number. For instance, in the hd driver, since the second hard drive starts at minor 64, DEVICE_NR(device) is defined to be (MINOR(device)>>6).

If your driver is interrupt-driven, you will also set

```
#define DEVICE_INTR do_dev
```

which will become a variable automatically defined and used by the remainder of blk.h, specifically by the SET_INTR() and CLEAR_INTR macros.

You might also consider setting these defines:

```
#define DEVICE_TIMEOUT DEV_TIMER
#define TIMEOUT_VALUE n
```

where *n* is the number of jiffies (clock ticks; hundredths of a second on Linux/386) to time out after if no interrupt is received. These are used if your device can become "stuck": a condition where the driver waits indefinitely for an interrupt that will never arrive. If you define these, they will automatically be used in SET_INTR to make your driver time out. Of course, your driver will have to be able to handle the possibility of being timed out by a timer. See section ?? for an explanation of how to do this.

1.5.1.2 Recognizing PC standard partitions

[Inspect the routines in genhd.c and include detailed, correct instructions on how to use them to allow your device to use the standard dos partitioning scheme.]

1.5.2 The Buffer Cache

[Here, it should be explained briefly how ll_rw_block() is called, about getblk() and bread() and breada() and bwrite(), etc. A real explanation of the buffer cache is reserved for the VFS reference section, where something on the complexity order of Bach's treatment of the buffer cache should exist.

For now, we assume that the reader understands the concepts behind the buffer cache. If you are a reader and don't, please email me and I'll help you, which will also help me put my thoughts together for that section.]

1.5.3 The Strategy Routine

All reading and writing of blocks is done through the **strategy routine**. This routine takes no arguments and returns nothing, but it knows where to find a list of requests for I/O (CURRENT, defined by default as blk_dev[MAJOR_NR].current_request), and knows how to get data from the device into the blocks. It is called with interrupts **disabled** so as to avoid race conditions, and is responsible for turning on interrupts with a call to sti() before returning.

The strategy routine first calls the INIT_REQUEST macro, which makes sure that requests are really on the request list and does some other sanity checking. add_request() will have already sorted the requests in the proper order according to the elevator algorithm (using an insertion sort, as it is called once for every request), so the strategy routine "merely" has to satisfy the request, call end_request(1), which will take the request off the list, and then if there is still another request on the list, satisfy it and call end_request(1), until there are no more requests on the list, at which time it returns.

If the driver is interrupt-driven, the strategy routine need only schedule the first request to occur, and have the interrupt-handler call end_request(1) and the call the strategy routine again, in order to schedule the next request. If the driver is not interrupt-driven, the strategy routine may not return until all I/O is complete.

If for some reason I/O fails permanently on the current request, end_request(0) must be called to destroy the request.

A request may be for a read or write. The driver determines whether a request is for a read or write by examining CURRENT->cmd. If CURRENT->cmd == READ, the request is for a read, and if CURRENT->cmd == WRITE, the request is for a write. If the device has separate interrupt routines for handling reads and writes, SET_INTR(*n*) must be called to assure that the proper interrupt routine will be called.

[Here I need to include samples of both a polled strategy routine and an interrupt-driven one. The interrupt-driven one should provide separate read and write interrupt routines to show the use of SET_INTR.]

1.5.4 Example Drivers

[I'm not sure this belongs here — we'll see. I'll leave the stub here for now.]

1.6 Supporting Functions

Here is a list of many of the most common supporting functions available to the device driver writer. If you find other supporting functions that are useful, please point them out to me. I know this is not a complete list, but I hope it is a helpful one.

```
add_request()
            static void add_request(struct blk_dev_struct *dev,
                            struct request * req)
```

This is a static function in ll_rw_block.c, and cannot be called by other code. However, an understanding of this function, as well as an understanding of `ll_rw_block()`, may help you understand the strategy routine.

If the device that the request is for has an empty request queue, the request is put on the queue and the strategy routine is called. Otherwise, the proper place in the queue is chosen and the request is inserted in the queue, maintaining proper order by insertion sort.

Proper order (the elevator algorithm) is defined as:

a. Reads come before writes.

b. Lower minor numbers come before higher minor numbers.

c. Lower block numbers come before higher block numbers.

The elevator algorithm is implemented by the macro `IN_ORDER()`, which is defined in drivers/block/blk.h

Defined in: drivers/block/ll_rw_block.c
See also: `make_request()`, `ll_rw_block()`.

add_timer()   void add_timer(struct timer_list * timer)

```
#include <linux/timer.h>
```

Installs the timer structures in the list `timer` in the timer list.

The `timer_list` structure is defined by:

```
struct timer_list {
        struct timer_list *next;
        struct timer_list *prev;
        unsigned long expires;
        unsigned long data;
        void (*function)(unsigned long);
};
```

In order to call `add_timer()`, you need to allocate a `timer_list` structure, and then call `init_timer()`, passing it a pointer to your `timer_list`. It will nullify the `next` and `prev` elements, which is the correct initialization. If necessary, you can allocate multiple `timer_list` structures, and link them into a list. Do make sure that you properly initialize all the unused pointers to `NULL`, or the timer code may get very confused.

For each struct in your list, you set three variables:

expires   The number of jiffies (100ths of a second in Linux/86) after which to time out.

function   Kernel-space function to run after timeout has occurred.

data   Passed as the argument to `function` when `function` is called.

Having created this list, you give a pointer to the first (usually the only) element of the list as the argument to `add_timer()`. Having passed that pointer, keep a copy of the pointer handy, because you will need to use it to modify the elements of the list (to set a new timeout when you need a function called again, to change the function to be called, or to change the data that is passed to the function) and to delete the timer, if necessary.

Note: This is *not* process-specific. Therefore, if you want to wake a certain process at a timeout, you will have to use the sleep and wake primitives. The functions that you install through this mechanism will run in the same context that interrupt handlers run in.

Defined in: kernel/sched.c
See also: `timer_table` in include/linux/timer.h, `init_timer()`, `del_timer()`.

`cli()`   `#define cli() __asm__ __volatile__ ("cli"::)`

`#include <asm/system.h>`

Prevents interrupts from being acknowledged. `cli` stands for "CLear Interrupt enable".

See also: `sti()`

`del_timer`   `void del_timer(struct timer_list * timer)`

`#include <linux/timer.h>`

Deletes the timer structures in the list `timer` in the timer list.

The timer list that you delete must be the address of a timer list you have earlier installed with `add_timer()`. Once you have called `del_timer()` to delete the timer from the kernel timer list, you may deallocate the memory used in the `timer_list` structures, as it is no longer referenced by the kernel timer list.

Defined in: kernel/sched.c
See also: `timer_table` in include/linux/timer.h, `init_timer()`, `add_timer()`.

`end_request()`

`static void end_request(int uptodate)`

`#include "blk.h"`

Called when a request has been satisfied or aborted. Takes one argument:

uptodate   If not equal to 0, means that the request has been satisfied.
            If equal to 0, means that the request has not been satisfied.

If the request was satisfied (`uptodate != 0`), `end_request()` maintains the request list, unlocks the buffer, and may arrange for the scheduler to be run at the next convenient time (`need_resched = 1`; this is implicit in `wake_up()`, and is not explicitly part of `end_request()`), before waking up all processes sleeping on the `wait_for_request` event, which is slept on in `make_request()`, `ll_rw_page()`, and `ll_rw_swap_file()`.

Note: This function is a static function, defined in drivers/block/blk.h for every non-SCSI device that includes blk.h. (SCSI devices do this differently; the high-level SCSI code itself provides this functionality to the low-level device-specific SCSI device drivers.) It includes several defines dependent on static device information, such as the device number. This is marginally faster than a more generic normal C function.

Defined in: kernel/blk_drv/blk.h
See also: `ll_rw_block()`, `add_request()`, `make_request()`.

`free_irq()`   `void free_irq(unsigned int irq)`

`#include <linux/sched.h>`

Frees an irq previously acquired with `request_irq()` or `irqaction()`. Takes one argument:

irq   interrupt level to free.

Defined in: kernel/irq.c
See also: `request_irq()`, `irqaction()`.

get_user*()   `inline unsigned char get_user_byte(const char * addr)`
                `inline unsigned short get_user_word(const short * addr)`
                `inline unsigned long get_user_long(const int *addr)`

                `#include <asm/segment.h>`

Allows a driver to access data in user space, which is in a different segment than the kernel.

Note: these functions may cause implicit I/O, if the memory being accessed has been swapped out, and therefore preemption may occur at this point. Do not include these functions in critical sections of your code even if the critical sections are protected by `cli()`/`sti()` pairs, because that implicit I/O will violate the integrity of your `cli()`/`sti()` pair. If you need to get at user-space memory, copy it to kernel-space memory *before* you enter your critical section.

These functions take one argument:

addr   Address to get data from.

Returns: Data at that offset in user space.

Defined in: include/asm/segment.h
See also: `memcpy_*fs()`, `put_user*()`, `cli()`, `sti()`.

inb(), inb_p()

                `inline unsigned int inb(unsigned short port)`
                `inline unsigned int inb_p(unsigned short port)`

                `#include <asm/io.h>`

Reads a byte from a port. `inb()` goes as fast as it can, while `inb_p()` pauses before returning. Some devices are happier if you don't read from them as fast as possible. Both functions take one argument:

port   Port to read byte from.

Returns: The byte is returned in the low byte of the 32-bit integer, and the 3 high
                     bytes are unused, and may be garbage.

Defined in: include/asm/io.h
See also: `outb()`, `outb_p()`.

init_timer()

                Inline function for initializing `timer_list` structures for use with `add_timer()`.

                Defined in: include/linux/timer.h
                See also: `add_timer()`.

irqaction()

int irqaction(unsigned int irq, struct sigaction *new)

#include <linux/sched.h>

Hardware interrupts are really a lot like signals. Therefore, it makes sense to be able to register an interrupt like a signal. The sa_restorer() field of the struct sigaction is not used, but otherwise it is the same. The int argument to the sa.handler() function may mean different things, depending on whether or not the IRQ is installed with the SA_INTERRUPT flag. If it is not installed with the SA_INTERRUPT flag, then the argument passed to the handler is a pointer to a register structure, and if it is installed with the SA_INTERRUPT flag, then the argument passed is the number of the IRQ. For an example of handler set to use the SA_INTERRUPT flag, look at how rs_interrupt() is installed in . . . /kernel/chr_drv/serial.c

The SA_INTERRUPT flag is used to determine whether or not the interrupt should be a "fast" interrupt. Normally, upon return from the interrupt, need_resched, a global flag, is checked. If it is set (≠ 0), then schedule() is run, which may schedule another process to run. They are also run with all other interrupts still enabled. However, by setting the sigaction structure member sa_flags to SA_INTERRUPT, "fast" interrupts are chosen, which leave out some processing, and very specifically do not call schedule().

irqaction() takes two arguments:

irq   The number of the IRQ the driver wishes to acquire.

new   A pointer to a sigaction struct.

Returns: -EBUSY if the interrupt has already been acquired,
                -EINVAL if sa.handler() is NULL,
                0 on success.

Defined in: kernel/irq.c
See also: request_irq(), free_irq()

IS_*(inode)   IS_RDONLY(inode) ((inode)->i_flags & MS_RDONLY)
               IS_NOSUID(inode) ((inode)->i_flags & MS_NOSUID)
               IS_NODEV(inode)   ((inode)->i_flags & MS_NODEV)
               IS_NOEXEC(inode) ((inode)->i_flags & MS_NOEXEC)
               IS_SYNC(inode)   ((inode)->i_flags & MS_SYNC)

#include <linux/fs.h>

These five test to see if the inode is on a filesystem mounted the corresponding flag.

kfree*()   #define kfree(x) kfree_s((x), 0)
               void kfree_s(void * obj, int size)

#include <linux/malloc.h>

Free memory previously allocated with kmalloc(). There are two possible arguments:

obj   Pointer to kernel memory to free.

size   To speed this up, if you know the size, use kfree_s() and provide the correct size. This way, the kernel memory allocator knows which bucket cache the object belongs to, and doesn't have to search all of the buckets.

(For more details on this terminology, read mm/kmalloc.c.)

Defined in: mm/kmalloc.c, include/linux/malloc.h
See also: `kmalloc()`.

`kmalloc()`   `void * kmalloc(unsigned int len, int priority)`

`#include <linux/kernel.h>`

`kmalloc()` used to be limited to 4096 bytes. It is now limited to 131056 bytes ((32 * 4096) −
16). Buckets, which used to be all exact powers of 2, are now a power of 2 minus some
small number, except for numbers less or equal to 128. For more details, see the
implementation in mm/kmalloc.c.

`kmalloc()` takes two arguments:

len   Length of memory to allocate. If the maximum is exceeded, kmalloc
                will log an error message of "`kmalloc of too large a block (%d
                bytes).`" and return NULL.

priority   GFP_KERNEL or GFP_ATOMIC. If GFP_KERNEL is chosen, `kmalloc()` may
                sleep, allowing preemption to occur. This is the normal way of calling
                `kmalloc()`. However, there are cases where it is better to return immedi-
                ately if no pages are available, without attempting to sleep to find one. One
                of the places in which this is true is in the swapping code, because it could
                cause race conditions, and another in the networking code, where things
                can happen at much faster speed that things could be handled by swapping
                to disk to make space for giving the networking code more memory. The
                most important reason for using GFP_ATOMIC is if it is being called from
                an interrupt, when you cannot sleep, and cannot receive other interrupts.

Returns: NULL on failure.
                Pointer to allocated memory on success.

Defined in: mm/kmalloc.c
See also: `kfree()`

`ll_rw_block()`

        `void ll_rw_block(int rw, int nr, struct buffer_head *bh[])`

        `#include <linux/fs.h>`

No device driver will ever call this code: it is called only through the buffer cache. However,
an understanding of this function may help you understand the function of the strategy
routine.

After sanity checking, if there are no pending requests on the device's request queue,
`ll_rw_block()` "plugs" the queue so that the requests don't go out until all the requests
are in the queue, sorted by the elevator algorithm. `make_request()` is then called for
each request. If the queue had to be plugged, then the strategy routine for that device is
not active, and it is called, **with interrupts disabled. It is the responsibility of the strategy
routine to re-enable interrupts.**

Defined in: devices/block/ll_rw_block.c
See also: `make_request(), add_request().`

MAJOR()
```
#define MAJOR(a)  (((unsigned)(a))>>8)
```
```
#include <linux/fs.h>
```
This takes a 16 bit device number and gives the associated major number by shifting off the minor number.

See also: MINOR().

make_request()
```
static void make_request(int major, int rw, struct buffer_head *bh)
```
This is a static function in ll_rw_block.c, and cannot be called by other code. However, an understanding of this function, as well as an understanding of ll_rw_block(), may help you understand the strategy routine.

make_request() first checks to see if the request is read-ahead or write-ahead and the buffer is locked. If so, it simply ignores the request and returns. Otherwise, it locks the buffer and, except for SCSI devices, checks to make sure that write requests don't fill the queue, as read requests should take precedence.

If no spaces are available in the queue, and the request is neither read-ahead nor write-ahead, make_request() sleeps on the event wait_for_request, and tries again when woken. When a space in the queue is found, the request information is filled in and add_request() is called to actually add the request to the queue.

Defined in: devices/block/ll_rw_block.c
See also: add_request(), ll_rw_block().

MINOR()
```
#define MINOR(a)  ((a)&0xff)
```
```
#include <linux/fs.h>
```
This takes a 16 bit device number and gives the associated minor number by masking off the major number.

See also: MAJOR().

memcpy_*fs()
```
inline void memcpy_tofs(void * to, const void * from,
                        unsigned long n)
inline void memcpy_fromfs(void * to, const void * from,
                          unsigned long n)
```
```
#include <asm/segment.h>
```
Copies memory between user space and kernel space in chunks larger than one byte, word, or long. Be very careful to get the order of the arguments right!

Note: these functions may cause implicit I/O, if the memory being accessed has been swapped out, and therefore preemption may occur at this point. Do not include these functions in critical sections of your code, even if the critical sections are protected by cli()/sti() pairs, because implicit I/O will violate the cli() protection. If you need to get at user-space memory, copy it to kernel-space memory *before* you enter your critical section.

These functions take three arguments:

to   Address to copy data to.

from   Address to copy data from.

n   Number of bytes to copy.

Defined in: include/asm/segment.h
See also: get_user*(), put_user*(), cli(), sti().

outb(), outb_p()

```
inline void outb(char value, unsigned short port)
inline void outb_p(char value, unsigned short port)
#include <asm/io.h>
```

Writes a byte to a port. outb() goes as fast as it can, while outb_p() pauses before
returning. Some devices are happier if you don't write to them as fast as possible. Both
functions take two arguments:

value   The byte to write.

port   Port to write byte to.

Defined in: include/asm/io.h
See also: inb(), inb_p().

printk()   int printk(const char* fmt, ...)

```
#include <linux/kernel.h>
```

printk() is a version of printf() for the kernel, with some restrictions. It cannot handle
floats, and has a few other limitations, which are documented in kernel/vsprintf.c. It takes
a variable number of arguments:

fmt   Format string, printf() style.

...   The rest of the arguments, printf() style.

Returns: Number of bytes written.

Note: printk() may cause implicit I/O, if the memory being accessed
has been swapped out, and therefore preemption may occur at this point.
Also, printk() will set the interrupt enable flag, so **never use it in code
protected by** cli(). Because it causes I/O, it is not safe to use in protected
code anyway, even it if didn't set the interrupt enable flag.

Defined in: kernel/printk.c.

put_user*()   inline void put_user_byte(char val, char *addr)
                inline void put_user_word(short val, short *addr)
                inline void put_user_long(unsigned long val, unsigned long *addr)

```
#include <asm/segment.h>
```

Allows a driver to write data in user space, which is in a different segment than the kernel.
When entering the kernel through a system call, a selector for the current user space segment
is put in the fs segment register, thus the names.

◇

Note: these functions may cause implicit I/O, if the memory being accessed has been swapped out, and therefore preemption may occur at this point. Do not include these functions in critical sections of your code even if the critical sections are protected by `cli()`/`sti()` pairs, because that implicit I/O will violate the integrity of your `cli()`/`sti()` pair. If you need to get at user-space memory, copy it to kernel-space memory *before* you enter your critical section.

These functions take two arguments:

val   Value to write

addr   Address to write data to.

Defined in: asm/segment.h
See also: `memcpy_*fs()`, `get_user*()`, `cli()`, `sti()`.

register_*dev()

```
int register_chrdev(unsigned int major, const char *name,
                    struct file_operations *fops)
int register_blkdev(unsigned int major, const char *name,
                    struct file_operations *fops)

#include <linux/fs.h>
#include <linux/errno.h>
```

Registers a device with the kernel, letting the kernel check to make sure that no other driver has already grabbed the same major number. Takes three arguments:

major   Major number of device being registered.

name   Unique string identifying driver. Used in the output for the /proc/devices file.

fops   Pointer to a `file_operations` structure for that device. This must **not** be NULL, or the kernel will panic later.

Returns: `-EINVAL` if major is ≥ `MAX_CHRDEV` or `MAX_BLKDEV` (defined in `<linux/fs.h>`), for character or block devices, respectively.
`-EBUSY` if major device number has already been allocated.
0 on success.

Defined in: fs/devices.c
See also: `unregister_*dev()`

request_irq()

```
int request_irq(unsigned int irq, void (*handler)(int),
                unsigned long flags, const char *device)

#include <linux/sched.h>
#include <linux/errno.h>
```

Request an IRQ from the kernel, and install an IRQ interrupt handler if successful. Takes four arguments:

`irq`	The IRQ being requested.
`handler`	The handler to be called when the IRQ occurs. The argument to the handler function will be the number of the IRQ that it was invoked to handle.
`flags`	Set to `SA_INTERRUPT` to request a "fast" interrupt or 0 to request a normal, "slow" one.
`device`	A string containing the name of the device driver, *device*.
Returns:	`-EINVAL` if `irq` > 15 or `handler` = `NULL`. `-EBUSY` if `irq` is already allocated. 0 on success.

If you need more functionality in your interrupt handling, use the `irqaction()` function. This uses most of the capabilities of the `sigaction` structure to provide interrupt services similar to to the signal services provided by `sigaction()` to user-level programs.

Defined in: kernel/irq.c
See also: `free_irq()`, `irqaction()`.

`select_wait()`

```
inline void select_wait(struct wait_queue **wait_address,
                        select_table *p)
```
```
#include <linux/sched.h>
```

Add a process to the proper `select_wait` queue. This function takes two arguments:

`wait_address`	
	Address of a `wait_queue` pointer to add to the circular list of waits.
`p`	If `p` is `NULL`, `select_wait` does nothing, otherwise the current process is put to sleep. This should be the `select_table *wait` variable that was passed to your `select()` function.

Defined in: linux/sched.h
See also: `*sleep_on()`, `wake_up*()`

`*sleep_on()`
```
void sleep_on(struct wait_queue ** p)
void interruptible_sleep_on(struct wait_queue ** p)
```
```
#include <linux/sched.h>
```

Sleep on an event, putting a `wait_queue` entry in the list so that the process can be woken on that event. `sleep_on()` goes into an uninterruptible sleep: The only way the process can run is to be woken by `wake_up()`. `interruptible_sleep_on()` goes into an interruptible sleep that can be woken by signals and process timeouts will cause the process to wake up. A call to `wake_up_interruptible()` is necessary to wake up the process and allow it to continue running where it left off. Both take one argument:

`p`	Pointer to a proper `wait_queue` structure that records the information needed to wake the process.

Defined in: kernel/sched.c

See also: `select_wait()`, `wake_up*()`.

`sti()`   `#define sti() __asm__ __volatile__ ("sti"::)`

`#include <asm/system.h>`

Allows interrupts to be acknowledged. `sti` stands for "SeT Interrupt enable".

Defined in: asm/system.h

See also: `cli()`.

`sys_get*()`   `int sys_getpid(void)`
`int sys_getuid(void)`
`int sys_getgid(void)`
`int sys_geteuid(void)`
`int sys_getegid(void)`
`int sys_getppid(void)`
`int sys_getpgrp(void)`

These system calls may be used to get the information described in the table below, or the information can be extracted directly from the process table, like this:

`foo = current->`**`pid`**`;`

`pid`	Process ID
`uid`	User ID
`gid`	Group ID
`euid`	Effective user ID
`egid`	Effective group ID
`ppid`	Process ID of process' parent process
`pgid`	Group ID of process' parent process

The system calls should not be used because they are slower *and* take more space. Because of this, they are no longer exported as symbols throughout the whole kernel.

Defined in: kernel/sched.c

`unregister_*dev()`
`int unregister_chrdev(unsigned int major, const char *name)`
`int unregister_blkdev(unsigned int major, const char *name)`

`#include <linux/fs.h>`
`#include <linux/errno.h>`

Removes the registration for a device device with the kernel, letting the kernel give the major number to some other device. Takes two arguments:

`major`   Major number of device being registered. Must be the same number given to `register_*dev()`.

`name`   Unique string identifying driver. Must be the same number given to `register_*dev()`.

Returns: `-EINVAL` if major is $\geq$ `MAX_CHRDEV` or `MAX_BLKDEV` (defined in `<linux/fs.h>`), for character or block devices, respectively, or if there have not been file operations registered for major device major, or if name is not the same name that the device was registered with.

0 on success.

Defined in: fs/devices.c

See also: register_*dev()

wake_up*()   void wake_up(struct wait_queue ** p)
                void wake_up_interruptible(struct wait_queue ** p)

#include <linux/sched.h>

Wakes up a process that has been put to sleep by the matching *sleep_on() function. wake_up() can be used to wake up tasks in a queue where the tasks may be in a TASK_INTERRUPTIBLE or TASK_UNINTERRUPTIBLE state, while wake_up_interruptible() will only wake up tasks in a TASK_INTERRUPTIBLE state, and will be insignificantly faster than wake_up() on queues that have only interruptible tasks. These take one argument:

p   Pointer to the wait_queue structure of the process to be woken.

Note that wake_up() does not switch tasks, it only makes processes that are woken up runnable, so that the next time schedule() is called, they will be candidates to run.

Defined in: kernel/sched.c

See also: select_wait(), *sleep_on()

1.7 Writing a SCSI Device Driver

This is (with the author's explicit permission) a modified copy of the original document. If you wish to reproduce just this section, you are advised to get the original version by ftp from ftp.cs.unc.edu:/pub/faith/papers/scsi.paper.tar.gz

1.7.1 Why You Want to Write a SCSI Driver

Currently, the Linux kernel contains drivers for the following SCSI host adapters: Adaptec 1542, Adaptec 1740, Future Domain TMC-1660/TMC-1680, Seagate ST-01/ST-02, UltraStor 14F, and Western Digital WD-7000. You may want to write your own driver for an unsupported host adapter. You may also want to re-write or update one of the existing drivers.

1.7.2 What is SCSI?

The foreword to the SCSI-2 standard draft [ANS] gives a succinct definition of the Small Computer System Interface and briefly explains how SCSI-2 is related to SCSI-1 and CCS:

The SCSI protocol is designed to provide an efficient peer-to-peer I/O bus with up to 8 devices, including one or more hosts. Data may be transferred asynchronously at rates that only depend on device implementation and cable length. Synchronous data transfers are supported at rates up to 10 mega-transfers per second. With the 32 bit wide data transfer option, data rates of up to 40 megabytes per second are possible.

SCSI-2 includes command sets for magnetic and optical disks, tapes, printers, processors, CD-ROMs, scanners, medium changers, and communications devices.

In 1985, when the first SCSI standard was being finalized as an American National Standard, several manufacturers approached the X3T9.2 Task Group. They wanted to increase the mandatory requirements of SCSI and to define further features for direct-access devices. Rather than delay the SCSI standard, X3T9.2 formed an ad hoc group to develop a working paper that was eventually called the Common Command Set (CCS). Many disk products were designed using this working paper in conjunction with the SCSI standard.

In parallel with the development of the CCS working paper, X3T9.2 began work on an enhanced SCSI standard which was named SCSI-2. SCSI-2 included the results of the CCS working paper and extended them to all device types. It also added caching commands, performance enhancement features, and other functions that X3T9.2 deemed worthwhile. While SCSI-2 has gone well beyond the original SCSI standard (now referred to as SCSI-1), it retains a high degree of compatibility with SCSI-1 devices.

1.7.2.1 SCSI phases

The "SCSI bus" transfers data and state information between interconnected SCSI devices. A single transaction between an "initiator" and a "target" can involve up to 8 distinct "phases." These phases are almost entirely determined by the target (e.g., the hard disk drive). The current phase can be determined from an examination of five SCSI bus signals, as shown in Table 1.1 [LXT91, p. 57].

-SEL	-BSY	-MSG	-C/D	-I/O	PHASE
HI	HI	?	?	?	BUS FREE
HI	LO	?	?	?	ARBITRATION
I	I&T	?	?	?	SELECTION
T	I&T	?	?	?	RESELECTION
HI	LO	HI	HI	HI	DATA OUT
HI	LO	HI	HI	LO	DATA IN
HI	LO	HI	LO	HI	COMMAND
HI	LO	HI	LO	LO	STATUS
HI	LO	LO	LO	HI	MESSAGE OUT
HI	LO	LO	LO	LO	MESSAGE IN

I = Initiator Asserts, T = Target Asserts, ? = HI or LO

Table 1.1: SCSI Bus Phase Determination

Some controllers (notably the inexpensive Seagate controller) require direct manipulation of the SCSI bus—other controllers automatically handle these low-level details. Each of the eight phases will be described in detail.

BUS FREE Phase

The BUS FREE phase indicates that the SCSI bus is idle and is not currently being used.

ARBITRATION Phase

The ARBITRATION phase is entered when a SCSI device attempts to gain control of the SCSI bus. Arbitration can start only if the bus was previously in the BUS FREE phase. During arbitration, the arbitrating device asserts its SCSI ID on the DATA BUS. For example, if the arbitrating device's SCSI ID is 2, then the device will assert 0x04. If multiple devices attempt simultaneous arbitration, the device with the highest SCSI ID will win. Although ARBITRATION is optional in the SCSI-1 standard, it is a required phase in the SCSI-2 standard.

SELECTION Phase

After ARBITRATION, the arbitrating device (now called the initiator) asserts the SCSI ID of the target on the DATA BUS. The target, if present, will acknowledge the selection by raising the -BSY line. This line remains active as long as the target is connected to the initiator.

RESELECTION Phase

The SCSI protocol allows a device to disconnect from the bus while processing a request. When the device is ready, it reconnects to the host adapter. The RESELECTION phase is identical to the SELECTION phase, with the exception that it is used by the disconnected target to reconnect to the original initiator. Drivers which do not currently support RESE-LECTION do not allow the SCSI target to disconnect. RESELECTION should be supported by all drivers, however, so that multiple SCSI devices can simultaneously process commands. This allows dramatically increased throughput due to interleaved I/O requests.

COMMAND Phase

During this phase, 6, 10, or 12 bytes of command information are transferred from the initiator to the target.

DATA OUT and DATA IN Phases

During these phases, data are transferred between the initiator and the target. For example, the DATA OUT phase transfers data from the host adapter to the disk drive. The DATA IN phase transfers data from the disk drive to the host adapter. If the SCSI command does not require data transfer, then neither phase is entered.

STATUS Phase

This phase is entered after completion of all commands, and allows the target to send a status byte to the initiator. There are nine valid status bytes, as shown in Table 1.2 [ANS, p. 77]. Note that since bits[6] 1–5 are used for the status code (the other bits are reserved), the status byte should be masked with 0x3e before being examined.

The meanings of the three most important status codes are outlined below:

GOOD   The operation completed successfully.

CHECK CONDITION
                An error occurred. The REQUEST SENSE command should be used to find out more information about the error (see section 1.7.3).

BUSY   The device was unable to accept a command. This may occur during a self-test or shortly after power-up.

MESSAGE OUT and MESSAGE IN Phases

---

[6]Bit 0 is the least significant bit.

Value[†]	Status
0x00	GOOD
0x02	CHECK CONDITION
0x04	CONDITION MET
0x08	BUSY
0x10	INTERMEDIATE
0x14	INTERMEDIATE-CONDITION MET
0x18	RESERVATION CONFLICT
0x22	COMMAND TERMINATED
0x28	QUEUE FULL

[†] After masking with 0x3e

Table 1.2: SCSI Status Codes

Additional information is transferred between the target and the initiator. This information may regard the status of an outstanding command, or may be a request for a change of protocol. Multiple MESSAGE IN and MESSAGE OUT phases may occur during a single SCSI transaction. If RESELECTION is supported, the driver must be able to correctly process the SAVE DATA POINTERS, RESTORE POINTERS, and DISCONNECT messages. Although required by the SCSI-2 standard, some devices do not automatically send a SAVE DATA POINTERS message prior to a DISCONNECT message.

1.7.3 SCSI Commands

Each SCSI command is 6, 10, or 12 bytes long. The following commands must be well understood by a SCSI driver developer.

REQUEST SENSE
    Whenever a command returns a CHECK CONDITION status, the high-level Linux SCSI code automatically obtains more information about the error by executing the REQUEST SENSE. This command returns a sense key and a sense code (called the "additional sense code," or ASC, in the SCSI-2 standard [ANS]). Some SCSI devices may also report an "additional sense code qualifier" (ASCQ). The 16 possible sense keys are described in Table 1.3. For information on the ASC and ASCQ, please refer to the SCSI standard [ANS] or to a SCSI device technical manual.

TEST UNIT READY
    This command is used to test the target's status. If the target can accept a medium-access command (e.g., a READ or a WRITE), the command returns with a GOOD status. Otherwise, the command returns with a CHECK CONDITION status and a sense key of NOT READY. This response usually indicates that the target is completing power-on self-tests.

INQUIRY
    This command returns the target's make, model, and device type. The high-level Linux code uses this command to differentiate among magnetic disks, optical disks, and tape drives (the high-level code currently does not support printers, processors, or juke boxes).

Sense Key	Description
0x00	NO SENSE
0x01	RECOVERED ERROR
0x02	NOT READY
0x03	MEDIUM ERROR
0x04	HARDWARE ERROR
0x05	ILLEGAL REQUEST
0x06	UNIT ATTENTION
0x07	DATA PROTECT
0x08	BLANK CHECK
0x09	(Vendor specific error)
0x0a	COPY ABORTED
0x0b	ABORTED COMMAND
0x0c	EQUAL
0x0d	VOLUME OVERFLOW
0x0e	MISCOMPARE
0x0f	RESERVED

Table 1.3: Sense Key Descriptions

READ and WRITE

These commands are used to transfer data from and to the target. You should be sure your driver can support simpler commands, such as TEST UNIT READY and INQUIRY, before attempting to use the READ and WRITE commands.

1.7.4   Getting Started

The author of a low-level device driver will need to have an understanding of how interrupts are handled by the kernel. At minimum, the kernel functions that disable (`cli()`) and enable (`sti()`) interrupts should be understood. The scheduling functions (e.g., `schedule()`, `sleepon()`, and `wakeup()`) may also be needed by some drivers. A detailed explanation of these functions can be found in section 1.6.

1.7.5   Before You Begin: Gathering Tools

Before you begin to write a SCSI driver for Linux, you will need to obtain several resources.

The most important is a bootable Linux system—preferably one which boots from an IDE, RLL, or MFM hard disk. During the development of your new SCSI driver, you will rebuild the kernel and reboot your system many times. Programming errors may result in the destruction of data on your SCSI drive *and* on your non-SCSI drive. *Back up your system before you begin.*

The installed Linux system can be quite minimal: the GCC compiler distribution (including libraries and the binary utilities), an editor, and the kernel source are all you need. Additional tools like `od`, `hexdump`, and `less` will be quite helpful. All of these tools will fit on an inexpensive 20-30 MB hard disk.[7].

Documentation is essential. At minimum, you will need a technical manual for your host adapter. Since Linux is freely distributable, and since you (ideally) want to distribute your source code freely, avoid

---

[7] A used 20 MB MFM hard disk and controller should cost less than US$100.

non-disclosure agreements (NDA). Most NDAs will prohibit you from releasing your source code—you might be allowed to release an object file containing your driver, but this is simply not acceptable in the Linux community at this time.

A manual that explains the SCSI standard will be helpful. Usually the technical manual for your disk drive will be sufficient, but a copy of the SCSI standard will often be helpful.[8]

Before you start, make hard copies of `hosts.h`, `scsi.h`, and one of the existing drivers in the Linux kernel. These will prove to be useful references while you write your driver.

1.7.6   The Linux SCSI Interface

The high-level SCSI interface in the Linux kernel manages all of the interaction between the kernel and the low-level SCSI device driver. Because of this layered design, a low-level SCSI driver need only provide a few basic services to the high-level code. The author of a low-level driver does not need to understand the intricacies of the kernel I/O system and, hence, can write a low-level driver in a relatively short amount of time.

Two main structures (`Scsi_Host` and `Scsi_Cmnd`) are used to communicate between the high-level code and the low-level code. The next two sections provide detailed information about these structures and the requirements of the low-level driver.

1.7.7   The `Scsi_Host` Structure

The `Scsi_Host` structure serves to describe the low-level driver to the high-level code. Usually, this description is placed in the device driver's header file in a C preprocessor definition, as shown in Figure 1.1.

```
#define FDOMAIN_16X0   { "Future Domain TMC-16x0",              \
                         fdomain_16x0_detect,                   \
                         fdomain_16x0_info,                     \
                         fdomain_16x0_command,                  \
                         fdomain_16x0_queue,                    \
                         fdomain_16x0_abort,                    \
                         fdomain_16x0_reset,                    \
                         NULL,                                  \
                         fdomain_16x0_biosparam,                \
                         1, 6, 64, 1 ,0, 0}
  #endif
```

Figure 1.1: Device Driver Header File

The `Scsi_Host` structure is presented in Figure 1.2. Each of the fields will be explained in detail later in this section.

---

[8]The October 17, 1991, draft of the SCSI-2 standard document is available via anonymous ftp from `sunsite.unc.edu` in `/pub/Linux/development/scsi-2.tar.Z`, and is available for purchase from Global Engineering Documents (2805 McGaw, Irvine, CA 92714), (800)-854-7179 or (714)-261-1455. Please refer to document X3.131-199X. In early 1993, the manual cost US$60–70.

```
typedef struct
{
    char                    *name;
    int                     (* detect)(int);
    const char              *(* info)(void);
    int                     (* queuecommand)(Scsi_Cmnd *,
                             void (*done)(Scsi_Cmnd *));
    int                     (* command)(Scsi_Cmnd *);
    int                     (* abort)(Scsi_Cmnd *, int);
    int                     (* reset)(void);
    int                     (* slave_attach)(int, int);
    int                     (* bios_param)(int, int, int []);
    int                     can_queue;
    int                     this_id;
    short unsigned int      sg_tablesize;
    short                   cmd_per_lun;
    unsigned                present:1;
    unsigned                unchecked_isa_dma:1;
} Scsi_Host;
```

Figure 1.2: The Scsi_Host Structure

1.7.7.1 Variables in the Scsi_Host structure

In general, the variables in the Scsi_Host structure are not used until after the detect() function (see section 1.7.7.2.1) is called. Therefore, any variables which cannot be assigned before host adapter detection should be assigned during detection. This situation might occur, for example, if a single driver provided support for several host adapters with very similar characteristics. Some of the parameters in the Scsi_Host structure might then depend on the specific host adapter detected.

1.7.7.1.1 name

name holds a pointer to a short description of the SCSI host adapter.

1.7.7.1.2 can_queue

can_queue holds the number of outstanding commands the host adapter can process. Unless RESELECTION is supported by the driver and the driver is interrupt-driven,[9] this variable should be set to 1.

1.7.7.1.3 this_id

Most host adapters have a specific SCSI ID assigned to them. This SCSI ID, usually 6 or 7, is used for RESELECTION. The this_id variable holds the host adapter's SCSI ID. If the host adapter does not have an assigned SCSI ID, this variable should be set to -1 (in this case, RESELECTION cannot be supported).

---

[9]Some of the early Linux drivers were not interrupt driven and, consequently, had very poor performance.

1.7.7.1.4 `sg_tablesize`

The high-level code supports "scatter-gather," a method of increasing SCSI throughput by combining many small SCSI requests into a few large SCSI requests. Since most SCSI disk drives are formatted with 1:1 interleave,[10] the time required to perform the SCSI ARBITRATION and SELECTION phases is longer than the rotational latency time between sectors.[11] Therefore, only one SCSI request can be processed per disk revolution, resulting in a throughput of about 50 kilobytes per second. When scatter-gather is supported, however, average throughput is usually over 500 kilobytes per second.

The `sg_tablesize` variable holds the maximum allowable number of requests in the scatter-gather list. If the driver does not support scatter-gather, this variable should be set to `SG_NONE`. If the driver can support an unlimited number of grouped requests, this variable should be set to `SG_ALL`. Some drivers will use the host adapter to manage the scatter-gather list and may need to limit `sg_tablesize` to the number that the host adapter hardware supports. For example, some Adaptec host adapters require a limit of 16.

1.7.7.1.5 `cmd_per_lun`

The SCSI standard supports the notion of "linked commands." Linked commands allow several commands to be queued consecutively to a single SCSI device. The `cmd_per_lun` variable specifies the number of linked commands allowed. This variable should be set to 1 if command linking is not supported. At this time, however, the high-level SCSI code will not take advantage of this feature.

Linked commands are fundamentally different from multiple outstanding commands (as described by the `can_queue` variable). Linked commands always go to the same SCSI target and do not necessarily involve a RESELECTION phase. Further, linked commands eliminate the ARBITRATION, SELECTION, and MESSAGE OUT phases on all commands after the first one in the set. In contrast, multiple outstanding commands may be sent to an arbitrary SCSI target, and *require* the ARBITRATION, SELECTION, MESSAGE OUT, and RESELECTION phases.

1.7.7.1.6 `present`

The `present` bit is set (by the high-level code) if the host adapter is detected.

1.7.7.1.7 `unchecked_isa_dma`

Some host adapters use Direct Memory Access (DMA) to read and write blocks of data directly from or to the computer's main memory. Linux is a virtual memory operating system that can use more than 16 MB of physical memory. Unfortunately, on machines using the ISA bus[12], DMA is limited to the low 16 MB of physical memory.

If the `unchecked_isa_dma` bit is set, the high-level code will provide data buffers which are guaranteed to be in the low 16 MB of the physical address space. Drivers written for host adapters that do not use DMA should set this bit to zero. Drivers specific to EISA bus[13] machines should also set this bit to zero, since EISA bus machines allow unrestricted DMA access.

---

[10]"1:1 interleave" means that all of the sectors in a single track appear consecutively on the disk surface.

[11]This may be an over-simplification. On older devices, the actual command processing can be significant. Further, there is a great deal of layered overhead in the kernel: the high-level SCSI code, the buffering code, and the file-system code all contribute to poor SCSI performance.

[12]The so-called "Industry Standard Architecture" bus was introduced with the IBM PC/XT and IBM PC/AT computers.

[13]The "Extended Industry Standard Architecture" bus is a non-proprietary 32-bit bus for 386 and i486 machines.

1.7.7.2 Functions in the `Scsi_Host` Structure

1.7.7.2.1 `detect()`

The `detect()` function's only argument is the "host number," an index into the `scsi_hosts` variable (an array of type `struct Scsi_Host`). The `detect()` function should return a non-zero value if the host adapter is detected, and should return zero otherwise.

Host adapter detection must be done carefully. Usually the process begins by looking in the ROM area for the "BIOS signature" of the host adapter. On PC/AT-compatible computers, the use of the address space between `0xc0000` and `0xfffff` is fairly well defined. For example, the video BIOS on most machines starts at `0xc0000` and the hard disk BIOS, if present, starts at `0xc8000`. When a PC/AT-compatible computer boots, every 2-kilobyte block from `0xc0000` to `0xf8000` is examined for the 2-byte signature (`0x55aa`) which indicates that a valid BIOS extension is present [Nor85].

The BIOS signature usually consists of a series of bytes that uniquely identifies the BIOS. For example, one Future Domain BIOS signature is the string:

```
FUTURE DOMAIN CORP. (C) 1986-1990 1800-V2.07/28/89
```

found exactly five bytes from the start of the BIOS block.

After the BIOS signature is found, it is safe to test for the presence of a functioning host adapter in more specific ways. Since the BIOS signatures are hard-coded in the kernel, the release of a new BIOS can cause the driver to mysteriously fail. Further, people who use the SCSI adapter exclusively for Linux may want to disable the BIOS to speed boot time. For these reasons, if the adapter can be detected safely without examining the BIOS, then that alternative method should be used.

Usually, each host adapter has a series of I/O port addresses which are used for communications. Sometimes these addresses will be hard coded into the driver, forcing all Linux users who have this host adapter to use a specific set of I/O port addresses. Other drivers are more flexible, and find the current I/O port address by scanning all possible port addresses. Usually each host adapter will allow 3 or 4 sets of addresses, which are selectable via hardware jumpers on the host adapter card.

After the I/O port addresses are found, the host adapter can be interrogated to confirm that it is, indeed, the expected host adapter. These tests are host adapter specific, but commonly include methods to determine the BIOS base address (which can then be compared to the BIOS address found during the BIOS signature search) or to verify a unique identification number associated with the board. For MCA bus[14] machines, each type of board is given a unique identification number which no other manufacturer can use—several Future Domain host adapters, for example, also use this number as a unique identifier on ISA bus machines. Other methods of verifying the host adapter existence and function will be available to the programmer.

1.7.7.2.1.1 Requesting the IRQ

After detection, the `detect()` routine must request any needed interrupt or DMA channels from the kernel. There are 16 interrupt channels, labeled IRQ 0 through IRQ 15. The kernel provides two methods for setting up an IRQ handler: `irqaction()` and `request_irq()`.

The `request_irq()` function takes two parameters, the IRQ number and a pointer to the handler routine. It then sets up a default `sigaction` structure and calls `irqaction()`. The code[15] for

---

[14]The "Micro-Channel Architecture" bus is IBM's proprietary 32 bit bus for 386 and i486 machines.

[15]Linux 0.99.7 kernel source code, `linux/kernel/irq.c`

the `request_irq()` function is shown in Figure 1.3. I will limit my discussion to the more general `irqaction()` function.

```
int request_irq( unsigned int irq, void (*handler)( int ) )
{
  struct sigaction sa;

  sa.sa_handler  = handler;
  sa.sa_flags    = 0;
  sa.sa_mask     = 0;
  sa.sa_restorer = NULL;
  return irqaction( irq, &sa );
}
```

Figure 1.3: The `request_irq()` Function

The declaration[16] for the `irqaction()` function is

```
int irqaction( unsigned int irq, struct sigaction *new )
```

where the first parameter, `irq`, is the number of the IRQ that is being requested, and the second parameter, `new`, is a structure with the definition[17] shown in Figure 1.4.

```
struct sigaction
{
  __sighandler_t sa_handler;
  sigset_t       sa_mask;
  int            sa_flags;
  void           (*sa_restorer)(void);
};
```

Figure 1.4: The `sigaction` Structure

In this structure, `sa_handler` should point to your interrupt handler routine, which should have a definition similar to the following:

```
void fdomain_16x0_intr( int irq )
```

where `irq` will be the number of the IRQ which caused the interrupt handler routine to be invoked.

The `sa_mask` variable is used as an internal flag by the `irqaction()` routine. Traditionally, this variable is set to zero prior to calling `irqaction()`.

---

[16]Linux 0.99.5 kernel source code, `linux/kernel/irq.c`
[17]Linux 0.99.5 kernel source code, `linux/include/linux/signal.h`

The `sa_flags` variable can be set to zero or to `SA_INTERRUPT`. If zero is selected, the interrupt handler will run with other interrupts enabled, and will return via the signal-handling return functions. This option is recommended for relatively slow IRQs, such as those associated with the keyboard and timer interrupts. If `SA_INTERRUPT` is selected, the handler will be called with interrupts disabled and return will avoid the signal-handling return functions. `SA_INTERRUPT` selects "fast" IRQ handler invocation routines, and is recommended for interrupt driven hard disk routines. The interrupt handler should turn interrupts on as soon as possible, however, so that other interrupts can be processed.

The `sa_restorer` variable is not currently used, and is traditionally set to `NULL`.

The `request_irq()` and `irqaction()` functions will return zero if the IRQ was successfully assigned to the specified interrupt handler routine. Non-zero result codes may be interpreted as follows:

-EINVAL   Either the IRQ requested was larger than 15, or a `NULL` pointer was passed instead of a valid pointer to the interrupt handler routine.

-EBUSY   The IRQ requested has already been allocated to another interrupt handler. This situation should never occur, and is reasonable cause for a call to `panic()`.

The kernel uses an Intel "interrupt gate" to set up IRQ handler routines requested via the `irqaction()` function. The Intel i486 manual [Int90, p. 9-11] explains the interrupt gate as follows:

> Interrupts using...interrupt gates...cause the TF flag [trap flag] to be cleared after its current value is saved on the stack as part of the saved contents of the EFLAGS register. In so doing, the processor prevents instruction tracing from affecting interrupt response. A subsequent IRET [interrupt return] instruction restores the TF flag to the value in the saved contents of the EFLAGS register on the stack.
>
> ... An interrupt which uses an interrupt gate clears the IF flag [interrupt-enable flag], which prevents other interrupts from interfering with the current interrupt handler. A subsequent IRET instruction restores the IF flag to the value in the saved contents of the EFLAGS register on the stack.

1.7.7.2.2   Requesting the DMA channel

Some SCSI host adapters use DMA to access large blocks of data in memory. Since the CPU does not have to deal with the individual DMA requests, data transfers are faster than CPU-mediated transfers and allow the CPU to do other useful work during a block transfer (assuming interrupts are enabled).

The host adapter will use a specific DMA channel. This DMA channel will be determined by the `detect()` function and requested from the kernel with the `request_dma()` function. This function takes the DMA channel number as its only parameter and returns zero if the DMA channel was successfully allocated. Non-zero results may be interpreted as follows:

-EINVAL   The DMA channel number requested was larger than 7.

-EBUSY   The requested DMA channel has already been allocated. This is a very serious situation, and will probably cause any SCSI requests to fail. It is worthy of a call to `panic()`.

1.7.7.2.3   `info()`

The `info()` function merely returns a pointer to a static area containing a brief description of the low-level driver. This description, which is similar to that pointed to by the `name` variable, will be printed at boot time.

1.7.7.2.4 `queuecommand()`

The `queuecommand()` function sets up the host adapter for processing a SCSI command and then returns. When the command is finished, the `done()` function is called with the `Scsi_Cmnd` structure pointer as a parameter. This allows the SCSI command to be executed in an interrupt-driven fashion. Before returning, the `queuecommand()` function must do several things:

1. Save the pointer to the `Scsi_Cmnd` structure.

2. Save the pointer to the `done()` function in the `scsi_done()` function pointer in the `Scsi_Cmnd` structure. See section 1.7.7.2.5 for more information.

3. Set up the special `Scsi_Cmnd` variables required by the driver. See section 1.7.8 for detailed information on the `Scsi_Cmnd` structure.

4. Start the SCSI command. For an advanced host adapter, this may be as simple as sending the command to a host adapter "mailbox." For less advanced host adapters, the ARBITRATION phase is manually started.

The `queuecommand()` function is called *only* if the `can_queue` variable (see section 1.7.7.1.2) is nonzero. Otherwise the `command()` function is used for all SCSI requests. The `queuecommand()` function should return zero on success (the current high-level SCSI code presently ignores the return value).

1.7.7.2.5 `done()`

The `done()` function is called after the SCSI command completes. The single parameter that this command requires is a pointer to the same `Scsi_Cmnd` structure that was previously passed to the `queuecommand()` function. Before the `done()` function is called, the `result` variable must be set correctly. The `result` variable is a 32 bit integer, each byte of which has specific meaning:

Byte 0 (LSB)   This byte contains the SCSI STATUS code for the command, as described in section 1.7.2.1.

Byte 1   This byte contains the SCSI MESSAGE, as described in section 1.7.2.1.

Byte 2   This byte holds the host adapter's return code. The valid codes for this byte are given in `scsi.h` and are described below:

        DID_OK   No error.

        DID_NO_CONNECT
                SCSI SELECTION failed because there was no device at the address specified.

        DID_BUS_BUSY
                SCSI ARBITRATION failed.

        DID_TIME_OUT

A time-out occurred for some unknown reason, probably during SELEC-
TION or while waiting for RESELECTION.

DID_BAD_TARGET

The SCSI ID of the target was the same as the SCSI ID of the host adapter.

DID_ABORT   The high-level code called the low-level abort() function (see sec-
               tion 1.7.7.2.7).

DID_PARITY   A SCSI PARITY error was detected.

DID_ERROR   An error occurred which lacks a more appropriate error code (for example,
               an internal host adapter error).

DID_RESET   The high-level code called the low-level reset() function (see sec-
               tion 1.7.7.2.8).

DID_BAD_INTR

An unexpected interrupt occurred *and* there is no appropriate way to handle this interrupt.

Note that returning DID_BUS_BUSY will force the command to be retried, whereas returning DID_NO_CONNECT will abort the command.

Byte 3 (MSB)   This byte is for a high-level return code, and should be left as zero by the low-level code.

Current low-level drivers do not uniformly (or correctly) implement error reporting, so it may be better
to consult scsi.c to determine exactly how errors should be reported, rather than exploring existing
drivers.

1.7.7.2.6 command()

The command() function processes a SCSI command and returns when the command is finished. When
the original SCSI code was written, interrupt-driven drivers were not supported. The old drivers are much
less efficient (in terms of response time and latency) than the current interrupt-driven drivers, but are also
much easier to write. For new drivers, this command can be replaced with a call to the queuecommand()
function, as demonstrated in Figure 1.5.[18]

The return value is the same as the result variable in the Scsi_Cmnd structure. Please see sections 1.7.7.2.5 and 1.7.8 for more details.

1.7.7.2.7 abort()

The high-level SCSI code handles all timeouts. This frees the low-level driver from having to do timing,
and permits different timeout periods to be used for different devices (e.g., the timeout for a SCSI tape drive
is nearly infinite, whereas the timeout for a SCSI disk drive is relatively short).

The abort() function is used to request that the currently outstanding SCSI command, indicated by
the Scsi_Cmnd pointer, be aborted. After setting the result variable in the Scsi_Cmnd structure, the

---

[18]Linux 0.99.5 kernel, linux/kernel/blk_drv/scsi/aha1542.c, written by Tommy Thorn.

```
static volatile int internal_done_flag    = 0;
static volatile int internal_done_errcode = 0;
static void         internal_done( Scsi_Cmnd *SCpnt )
{
  internal_done_errcode = SCpnt->result;
  ++internal_done_flag;
}

int aha1542_command( Scsi_Cmnd *SCpnt )
{
  aha1542_queuecommand( SCpnt, internal_done );

  while (!internal_done_flag);
  internal_done_flag = 0;
  return internal_done_errcode;
}
```

Figure 1.5: Example `command()` Function

`abort()` function returns zero. If code, the second parameter to the `abort()` function, is zero, then `result` should be set to `DID_ABORT`. Otherwise, `result` should be set equal to code. If code is not zero, it is usually `DID_TIME_OUT` or `DID_RESET`.

Currently, none of the low-level drivers is able to correctly abort a SCSI command. The initiator should request (by asserting the -ATN line) that the target enter a MESSAGE OUT phase. Then, the initiator should send an ABORT message to the target.

1.7.7.2.8 `reset()`

The `reset()` function is used to reset the SCSI bus. After a SCSI bus reset, any executing command should fail with a `DID_RESET` result code (see section 1.7.7.2.5).

Currently, none of the low-level drivers handles resets correctly. To correctly reset a SCSI command, the initiator should request (by asserting the -ATN line) that the target enter a MESSAGE OUT phase. Then, the initiator should send a BUS DEVICE RESET message to the target. It may also be necessary to initiate a SCSI RESET by asserting the -RST line, which will cause all target devices to be reset. After a reset, it may be necessary to renegotiate a synchronous communications protocol with the targets.

1.7.7.2.9 `slave_attach()`

The `slave_attach()` function is *not* currently implemented. This function would be used to negotiate synchronous communications between the host adapter and the target drive. This negotiation requires an exchange of a pair of SYNCHRONOUS DATA TRANSFER REQUEST messages between the initiator and the target. This exchange should occur under the following conditions [LXT91]:

> A SCSI device that supports synchronous data transfer recognizes it has not communicated with the other SCSI device since receiving the last "hard" RESET.

A SCSI device that supports synchronous data transfer recognizes it has not communicated with the other SCSI device since receiving a BUS DEVICE RESET message.

1.7.7.2.10 `bios_param()`

Linux supports the MS-DOS[19] hard disk partitioning system. Each disk contains a "partition table" which defines how the disk is divided into logical sections. Interpretation of this partition table requires information about the size of the disk in terms of cylinders, heads, and sectors per cylinder. SCSI disks, however, hide their physical geometry and are accessed logically as a contiguous list of sectors. Therefore, in order to be compatible with MS-DOS, the SCSI host adapter will "lie" about its geometry. The physical geometry of the SCSI disk, while available, is seldom used as the "logical geometry." (The reasons for this involve archaic and arbitrary limitations imposed by MS-DOS.)

Linux needs to determine the "logical geometry" so that it can correctly modify and interpret the partition table. Unfortunately, there is no standard method for converting between physical and logical geometry. Hence, the `bios_param()` function was introduced in an attempt to provide access to the host adapter geometry information.

The `size` parameter is the size of the disk in sectors. Some host adapters use a deterministic formula based on this number to calculate the logical geometry of the drive. Other host adapters store geometry information in tables which the driver can access. To facilitate this access, the `dev` parameter contains the drive's device number. Two macros are defined in `linux/fs.h` which will help to interpret this value: `MAJOR(dev)` is the device's major number, and `MINOR(dev)` is the device's minor number. These are the same major and minor device numbers used by the standard Linux `mknod` command to create the device in the `/dev` directory. The `info` parameter points to an array of three integers that the `bios_param()` function will fill in before returning:

`info[0]`   Number of heads

`info[1]`   Number of sectors per cylinder

`info[2]`   Number of cylinders

The information in `info` is *not* the physical geometry of the drive, but only a *logical* geometry that is identical to the *logical* geometry used by MS-DOS to access the drive. The distinction between physical and logical geometry cannot be overstressed.

1.7.8 The `Scsi_Cmnd` Structure

The `Scsi_Cmnd` structure,[20] as shown in Figure 1.6, is used by the high-level code to specify a SCSI command for execution by the low-level code. Many variables in the `Scsi_Cmnd` structure can be ignored by the low-level device driver—other variables, however, are extremely important.

1.7.8.1 Reserved Areas

1.7.8.1.1 Informative Variables

`host` is an index into the `scsi_hosts` array.

---

[19]MS-DOS is a registered trademark of Microsoft Corporation.
[20]Linux 0.99.7 kernel, `linux/kernel/blk_drv/scsi/scsi.h`

```
typedef struct scsi_cmnd
{
    int             host;
    unsigned char   target,
                    lun,
                    index;
    struct scsi_cmnd *next,
                    *prev;

    unsigned char   cmnd[10];
    unsigned        request_bufflen;
    void            *request_buffer;

    unsigned char   data_cmnd[10];
    unsigned short  use_sg;
    unsigned short  sglist_len;
    unsigned        bufflen;
    void            *buffer;

    struct request  request;
    unsigned char   sense_buffer[16];
    int             retries;
    int             allowed;
    int             timeout_per_command,
                    timeout_total,
                    timeout;
    unsigned char   internal_timeout;
    unsigned        flags;

    void (*scsi_done)(struct scsi_cmnd *);
    void (*done)(struct scsi_cmnd *);

    Scsi_Pointer    SCp;
    unsigned char   *host_scribble;
    int             result;

} Scsi_Cmnd;
```

Figure 1.6: The Scsi_Cmnd Structure

target stores the SCSI ID of the target of the SCSI command. This information is important if multiple outstanding commands or multiple commands per target are supported.

cmnd is an array of bytes which hold the actual SCSI command. These bytes should be sent to the SCSI target during the COMMAND phase. cmnd[0] is the SCSI command code. The COMMAND_SIZE macro, defined in scsi.h, can be used to determine the length of the current SCSI command.

result is used to store the result code from the SCSI request. Please see section 1.7.7.2.5 for more information about this variable. This variable *must* be correctly set before the low-level routines return.

1.7.8.1.2   The Scatter-Gather List

use_sg contains a count of the number of pieces in the scatter-gather chain. If use_sg is zero, then request_buffer points to the data buffer for the SCSI command, and request_bufflen is the length of this buffer in bytes. Otherwise, request_buffer points to an array of scatterlist structures, and use_sg will indicate how many such structures are in the array. The use of request_buffer is non-intuitive and confusing.

Each element of the scatterlist array contains an address and a length component. If the unchecked_isa_dma flag in the Scsi_Host structure is set to 1 (see section 1.7.7.1.7 for more information on DMA transfers), the address is guaranteed to be within the first 16 MB of physical memory. Large amounts of data will be processed by a single SCSI command. The length of these data will be equal to the sum of the lengths of all the buffers pointed to by the scatterlist array.

1.7.8.2   Scratch Areas

Depending on the capabilities and requirements of the host adapter, the scatter-gather list can be handled in a variety of ways. To support multiple methods, several scratch areas are provided for the exclusive use of the low-level driver.

1.7.8.2.1   The scsi_done() Pointer

This pointer should be set to the done() function pointer in the queuecommand() function (see section 1.7.7.2.4 for more information). There are no other uses for this pointer.

1.7.8.2.2   The host_scribble Pointer

The high-level code supplies a pair of memory allocation functions, scsi_malloc() and scsi_free(), which are guaranteed to return memory in the first 16 MB of physical memory. This memory is, therefore, suitable for use with DMA. The amount of memory allocated per request *must* be a multiple of 512 bytes, and *must* be less than or equal to 4096 bytes. The total amount of memory available via scsi_malloc() is a complex function of the Scsi_Host structure variables sg_tablesize, cmd_per_lun, and unchecked_isa_dma.

The host_scribble pointer is available to point to a region of memory allocated with scsi_malloc(). The low-level SCSI driver is responsible for managing this pointer and its associated memory, and should free the area when it is no longer needed.

1.7.8.2.3 The `Scsi_Pointer` Structure

The `SCp` variable, a structure of type `Scsi_Pointer`, is described in Figure 1.7. The variables in this struc-

```
typedef struct scsi_pointer
{
  char                *ptr;             /* data pointer */
  int                 this_residual;    /* left in this buffer */
  struct scatterlist  *buffer;          /* which buffer */
  int                 buffers_residual; /* how many buffers left */

  volatile int        Status;
  volatile int        Message;
  volatile int        have_data_in;
  volatile int        sent_command;
  volatile int        phase;
} Scsi_Pointer;
```

Figure 1.7: The `Scsi_Pointer` Structure

ture can be used in *any* way necessary in the low-level driver. Typically, `buffer` points to the current entry in the `scatterlist`, `buffers_residual` counts the number of entries remaining in the `scatterlist`, `ptr` is used as a pointer into the buffer, and `this_residual` counts the characters remaining in the transfer. Some host adapters require support of this detail of interaction—others can completely ignore this structure.

The second set of variables provide convenient locations to store SCSI status information and various pointers and flags.

1.8 Acknowledgements

Thanks to Drew Eckhardt, Michael K. Johnson, Karin Boes, Devesh Bhatnagar, and Doug Hoffman for reading early versions of this paper and for providing many helpful comments. Special thanks to my official COMP-291 (Professional Writing in Computer Science) "readers," Professors Peter Calingaert and Raj Kumar Singh.

1.9 Network Device Drivers

[I have not written this section because I don't know anything about it. I would appreciate help with this.

Note that Donald Becker has written an excellent skeleton device driver which is a very good start towards writing a network device driver.]

Chapter 2

The /proc filesystem

The proc filesystem is an interface to several kernel data structures which behaves remarkably like a filesystem. Instead of having to read /dev/kmem and have some way of knowing where things are,[1] all an application has to do is read files and directories in /proc. This way, all the addresses of the kernel data structures are compiled into the proc filesystem at kernel compile time, and programs which use the /proc interface need not be recompiled or updated when the kernel is recompiled. It is possible to mount the proc filesystem somewhere other than /proc, but that destroys the nice predictability of the proc filesystem, so we will conveniently ignore that option. The information should somewhat resemble Linux 1.0.

2.1 /proc Directories and Files

[This section should be severely cut, and the full version put in the LPG when that is available. In the mean time, better here than nowhere.]

In /proc, there is a subdirectory for every running process, named by the number of the process's pid. These directories will be explained below. There are also several other files and directories. These are:

self   This refers to the process accessing the proc filesystem, and is identical to the directory named by the process id of the process doing the look-up.

kmsg   This file can be used instead of the syslog() system call to log kernel messages. A process must have superuser privileges to read this file, and only one process should read this file. This file should **not** be read if a syslog process is running which uses the syslog() system call facility to log kernel messages.

loadavg   This file gives an output like this:

```
0.13 0.14 0.05
```

These numbers are the numbers normally given by uptime and other commands as the load average—they are the average number of processes trying to run at once in the last minute, in the last five minutes and in the last fifteen minutes, more or less.

meminfo   This file is a condensed version of the output from the free program. Its output looks like this:

---

[1]Usually a file called a namelist file, often /etc/psdatabase.

254

```
              total:    used:     free:    shared:  buffers:
   Mem:     7528448  7344128    184320   2637824  1949696
   Swap:    8024064  1474560   6549504
```

Notice that the numbers are in bytes, not KB. Linus wrote a version of free which reads this file and can return either bytes (-b) or KB (-k, the default). This is included with the procps package at tsx-11.mit.edu and other places. Also notice that there is **not** a separate entry for each swap file. The Swap: line summarizes all the swap space available to the kernel.

uptime   This file contains two things: the time that the system has been up, and the amount of time it has spent in the idle process. Both numbers are given as decimal quantities, in seconds and hundredths of a second. The two decimal digits of precision are not guaranteed on all architectures, but are currently accurate on all working implementations of Linux, due to the convenient 100 Hz clock. This file looks like this:

```
   604.33 205.45
```

In this case, the system has been running for 604.33 seconds, and of that time, 205.45 seconds have been spent in the idle task.

kcore   This is a file which represents the physical memory in the current system, in the same format as a 'core file'. This can be used with a debugger to examine variables in the kernel. The total length of the file is the physical memory plus a 4KB header to make it look like a core file.

stat   The stat file return various statistics about the system in ASCII format. An example of stat file is the following:

```
   cpu  5470 0 3764 193792
   disk 0 0 0 0
   page 11584 937
   swap 255 618
   intr 239978
   ctxt 20932
   btime 767808289
```

The meaning of the lines being

cpu   The four numbers represent the number of jiffies the system spent in user mode, in user mode with low priority (nice), in system mode, and in the idle task. The last value should be 100 times the second entry in the uptime file.

disk   The four dk_drive entries in the kernel_stat structure are currently unused.

page   This is the number of pages the system brought in from the disk and out to the disk.

swap   Is the number of swap pages the system brought in and out.

intr   The number of interrupts received from system boot. **[The format of this line has changed in more recent kernels.]**

ctxt   The number of context switches the system underwent.

btime   The boot time, in seconds since the epoch.

modules   This return the list of kernel modules, in ASCII form. The format is not well defined at this point, as it has changed from version to version. This will stabilize with later versions of Linux as the modules interface stabilizes.

malloc   This file is present only if CONFIG_DEBUG_MALLOC was defined during kernel compilation.

version   This file contains a string identifying the version of Linux that is currently running. An example is:

```
Linux version 1.1.40 (johnsonm@nigel) (gcc version 2.5.8) #3 \
   Sat Aug 6 14:22:05 1994
```

Note that this contains the version of Linux, the username and hostname of the user that compiled it, the version of gcc, the "iteration" of the compilation (each new compile will increase the number), and the output of the 'date' command as of the start of the compilation.

net   This is a directory containing three files, all of which give the status of some part of the Linux networking layer. These files contain binary structures, and are therefore not readable with cat. However, the standard netstat suite uses these files. The binary structures read from these files are defined in <linux/if*.h> The files are:

unix   **[I do not yet have details on the unix interface. These details will be added later.]**

arp   **[I do not yet have details on the arp interface. These details will be added later.]**

route   **[I do not yet have details on the route interface. These details will be added later.]**

dev   **[I do not yet have details on the dev interface. These details will be added later.]**

raw   **[I do not yet have details on the raw interface. These details will be added later.]**

tcp   **[I do not yet have details on the tcp interface. These details will be added later.]**

udp   **[I do not yet have details on the udp interface. These details will be added later.]**

Each of the process subdirectories (those with numerical names and the self directory) have several files and subdirectories, as well. The files are:

cmdline   This holds the complete command line for the process, **unless the whole process has been swapped out,** or unless the process is a zombie. In either of these later cases, there is nothing in this file: i.e. a read on this file will return as having read 0 characters. This file is null-terminated, but **not** newline-terminated.

cwd
: A link to the current working directory of that process. To find out the cwd of process 20, say, you can do this:

```
(cd /proc/20/cwd; pwd)
```

environ
: This file contains the environment for the process. There are no newlines in this file: the entries are separated by null characters, and there is a null character at the end. Thus, to print out the environment of process 10, you would do:

```
cat /proc/10/environ | tr "\000" "\n"
```

This file is also null-terminated and not newline terminated..

exe
: This is a link to the executable. You can type

```
/proc/10/exe
```

to run another copy of whatever process 10 is.

fd
: This is a subdirectory containing one entry for each file which the process has open, named by its file descriptor, and which is a link to the actual file. Programs that will take a filename, but will not take the standard input, and which write to a file, but will not send their output to standard output, can be effectively foiled this way, assuming that -i is the flag designating an input file and -o is the flag designating an output file:

```
... | foobar -i /proc/self/fd/0 -o /proc/self/fd/1 | ...
```

Voilá. Instant filter! Note that this will not work for programs that seek on their files, as the files in the fd directory are not seekable.

maps
: This is a file which contains a listing of all the memory mappings that the process is using. The shared libraries are mapped in this way, so there should be one entry for each shared library in use, and some processes use memory maps for other purposes as well. Here is an example:

```
00000000-00013000 r-xs 00000400 03:03 12164
00013000-00014000 rwxp 00013400 03:03 12164
00014000-0001c000 rwxp 00000000 00:00 0
bffff000-c0000000 rwxp 00000000 00:00 0
```

The first field is a number defining the start of the mapped range.
the second field is a number defining the end of the mapped range.
The third field gives the flags:
r means readable, - means not.
w means writable, - means not.
x means executable, - means not.
s means shared, p means private.
The fourth field is the offset at which it is mapped.
The fifth field indicates the *major:minor* device number of the file being mapped.
The sixth field indicates the inode number of the file being mapped.

mem
: This is **not** the same as the mem (1,1) device, despite the fact that it has the same device numbers. The /dev/mem device is the physical memory before any address translation is done, but the mem file here is the memory of the process that accesses it. This cannot be mmap()ed currently, and will not be until a general mmap() is added to the kernel.

root   This is a pointer to the root directory of the process. This is useful for programs that call
              chroot(), such as ftpd.

stat   This file contains a lot of status information about the process. The fields, in order, with
              their proper scanf() format specifiers, are:

          pid %d   The process id.

          comm (%s)   The filename of the executable, in parentheses. This is visible whether or
                              not the executable is swapped out.

          state %c   One character from the string "RSDZT" where R is running, S is sleeping in
                              an interruptible wait, D is sleeping in an uninterruptible wait or swapping,
                              Z is zombie, and T is traced or stopped (on a signal).

          ppid %d   The pid of the parent.

          pgrp %d   The pgrp of the process.

          session %d   The session id of the process.

          tty %d   The tty the process uses.

          tpgid %d   The pgrp of the process which currently owns the tty that the process is
                              connected to.

          flags %u   The flags of the process. Currently, every flag has the math bit set, because
                              crt0.s checks for math emulation, so this is not included in the output. This
                              is probably a bug, as not *every* process is a compiled c program. The math
                              bit should be a decimal 4, and the traced bit is decimal 10.

          min_flt %u   The number of minor faults the process has made, those which have not
                              required loading a memory page from disk.

          cmin_flt %u   The number of minor faults that the process and its children have made.

          maj_flt %u   The number of major faults the process has made, those which have re-
                              quired loading a memory page from disk.

          cmaj_flt %u   The number of major faults that the process and its children have made.

          utime %d   The number of jiffies that this process has been scheduled in user mode.

          stime %d   The number of jiffies that this process has been scheduled in kernel mode.

          cutime %d   The number of jiffies that this process and its children have been scheduled
                              in user mode.

          cstime %d   The number of jiffies that this process and its children have been scheduled
                              in kernel mode.

          counter %d   The current maximum size in jiffies of the process' next timeslice, of what
                              is currently left of its current timeslice, if it is the currently running process.

          priority %d   The standard UN*X nice value, plus fifteen. The value is never negative in the kernel.

timeout %u	The time in jiffies of the process' next timeout.

it_real_value %u

The time in jiffies before the interval timer mechanism causes a SIGALRM to be sent to the process.

start_time %d	Time the process started in jiffies after system boot.
vsize %u	Virtual memory size

rss %u

Resident Set Size: number of pages the process has in **real** memory, minus 3 for administrative purposes. This is just the pages which count towards text, data, or stack space. This does **not** include pages which have not been demand-loaded in, or which are swapped out.

rlim %u	Current limit on the size of the process, 2GB by default.
start_code %u	The address above which program text can run.
end_code %u	The address below which program text can run.
start_stack %u	The address of the start of the stack.

kstk_esp %u

The current value of esp (32 bit stack pointer), as found in the kernel stack page for the process.

kstk_eip %u

The current value of eip (32 bit instruction pointer), as found in the kernel stack page for the process.

signal %d	The bitmap of pending signals (usually 0).
blocked %d	The bitmap of blocked signals (usually 0, 2 for shells).
sigignore %d	The bitmap of ignored signals.
sigcatch %d	The bitmap of catched signals.

wchan %u

This is the "channel" in which the process is waiting. This is the address of a system call, and can be looked up in a namelist if you need a textual name.

statm

This file contains special status information that takes a bit longer to cook than the information in stat, and is needed rarely enough that it has been relegated to a separate file. For each field in this file, the proc filesystem has to look at each of the 0x300 entries in the page directory, and count what they are doing. Here is a description of these fields:

size %d

The total number of pages that the process has mapped in the virtual memory space, whether they are in physical memory or not.

resident %d

The total number of pages that the process has in physical memory. This should equal the rss field from the stat file, but is calculated rather than read from the process structure.

shared %d   The total number of pages that the process has that are shared with at least one other process.

trs %d   Text Resident Size: the total number of text (code) pages belonging to the process that are present in physical memory. Does **not** include shared library pages.

lrs %d   Library Resident Size: the total number of library pages used by the process that are present in physical memory.

drs %d   Data Resident Size: the total number of data pages belonging to the process that are present in physical memory. Include dirty library pages and stack.

dt %d   The number of library pages which have been accessed (i.e., are dirty).

2.2 Structure of the /proc filesystem

The proc filesystem is rather interesting, because none of the files exist in any real directory structure. Rather, the proper vfs structures are filled in with functions which do gigantic case statements, and in the case of reading a file, get a page, fill it in, and put the result in user memory space.

One of the most interesting parts of the proc filesystem is the way that the individual process directories are implemented. Essentially, every process directory has the inode number of its PID shifted left 16 bits into a 32 bit number greater than 0x0000ffff. Within the process directories, inode numbers are reused, because the upper 16 bits of the inode number have been masked off after choosing the right directory.

Another interesting feature is that unlike in a "real" filesystem, where there is one file_operations structure for the whole filesystem, as file lookup is done, different file_operations structures are assigned to the f_ops member of the file structure passed to those functions, dynamically changing which functions will be called for directory lookup and file reading.

[Expand on this section later — right now it is mostly here to remind me to finish it. . .]

2.3 Programming the /proc filesystem

◇ **Note:** the code fragments in this section won't match the sources for your own kernel exactly, as the /proc filesystem has been expanded since this was originally written, and is being expanding still more. For instance, the root_dir structure has nearly doubled in size from the one quoted here below.

Unlike in most filesystems, not all inode numbers in the proc filesystem are unique. Some files are declared in structures like

```
static struct proc_dir_entry root_dir[] = {
        { 1,1,"." },
        { 1,2,".." },
        { 2,7,"loadavg" },
        { 3,6,"uptime" },
        { 4,7,"meminfo" },
        { 5,4,"kmsg" },
        { 6,7,"version" },
        { 7,4,"self" }  /* will change inode # */
        { 8,4,"net" }
```

```
};
```

and some files are dynamically created as the filesystem is read. All the process directories (those with numerical names and `self`) essentially have inode numbers that are the pid shifted left 16 bits, but the files within those directories reuse low (1–10 or so) inode numbers, which are added at runtime to the pid of the process. This is done in inode.c by careful re-assignment of `inode_operation` structures.

Most of the short read-only files in the root directory and in each process subdirectory one use a simplified interface provided by the `array_inode_operations` structure, within array.c.

Other directories, such as /proc/net/, have their own inode numbers. For instance, the net directory itself has inode number 8. The files within that directory use inode numbers from the range 128–160, and those are uniquely identified in inode.c and the files given the proper permissions when looked up and read.

Adding a file is relatively simple, and is left as an exercise for the reader. Adding a new directory is a little bit harder. Assuming that it is not a dynamically allocated directory like the process directories, here are the steps:[2]

1. Choose a **unique** range of inode numbers, giving yourself a reasonable amount of room for expansion. Then, right before the line

   ```
   if (!pid) { /* not a process directory but in /proc/ */
   ```

   add a section that looks like this:

   ```
   if ((ino >= 128) && (ino <= 160)) { /* files withing /proc/net */
       inode->i_mode = S_IFREG | 0444;
       inode->i_op = &proc_net_inode_operations;
       return;
   }
   ```

   but modify it to to to do what you want. For instance, perhaps you have a range of 200–256, and some files, inodes 200, 201, and 202, and some directories, which are inodes 204 and 205. You also have a file that is readable only by root, inode 206.

   Your example might look like this:

   ```
   if ((ino >= 200) && (ino <= 256)) { /* files withing /proc/foo */
       switch (ino) {
           case 204:
           case 205:
               inode->i_mode = S_IFDIR | 0555;
               inode->i_op = &proc_foo_inode_operations;
               break;
           case 206:
               inode->i_mode = S_IFREG | 0400;
               inode->i_op = &proc_foo_inode_operations;
               break;
           default:
               inode->i_mode = S_IFREG | 0444;
               inode->i_op = &proc_foo_inode_operations;
   ```

---

[2]Unless you are making a subdirectory of the replicating, dynamically allocated process directory, you would have to create a new filesystem type, similar to the proc filesystem in design. Subdirectories of the process directories are supported by the mechanism which dynamically creates the process directories. I suggest going through this explanation of how to add a non-dynamically-allocated directory, understand it, and then read the code for the process subdirectories, if you wish to add subdirectories to the process subdirectories.

```
                    break;
            }
            return;
    }
```

2. Find the definition of the files. If your files will go in a subdirectory of /proc, for instance, you will look in root.c, and find the following:

```
static struct proc_dir_entry root_dir[] = {
    { 1,1,"." },
    { 1,2,".." },
    { 2,7,"loadavg" },
    { 3,6,"uptime" },
    { 4,7,"meminfo" },
    { 5,4,"kmsg" },
    { 6,7,"version" },
    { 7,4,"self" },   /* will change inode # */
    { 8,4,"net" }
};
```

You will then add a new file to this structure, like this, using the next available inode number:

```
[...]
    { 6,7,"version" },
    { 7,4,"self" },   /* will change inode # */
    { 8,4,"net" },
    { 9,3,"foo" }
};
```

You will then have to provide for this new directory in inode.c, so:

```
if (!pid) { /* not a process directory but in /proc/ */
    inode->i_mode = S_IFREG | 0444;
    inode->i_op = &proc_array_inode_operations;
    switch (ino)
      case 5:
            inode->i_op = &proc_kmsg_inode_operations;
            break;
      case 8: /* for the net directory */
            inode->i_mode = S_IFDIR | 0555;
            inode->i_op = &proc_net_inode_operations;
            break;
      default:
            break;
            return;
}
```

becomes

```
if (!pid) { /* not a process directory but in /proc/ */
    inode->i_mode = S_IFREG | 0444;
    inode->i_op = &proc_array_inode_operations;
    switch (ino)
      case 5:
            inode->i_op = &proc_kmsg_inode_operations;
            break;
      case 8: /* for the net directory */
```

```
                              inode->i_mode = S_IFDIR | 0555;
                              inode->i_op = &proc_net_inode_operations;
                              break;
                   case 9: /* for the foo directory */
                              inode->i_mode = S_IFDIR | 0555;
                              inode->i_op = &proc_foo_inode_operations;
                              break;
                   default:
                              break;
                              return;
         }
```

3. You now have to provide for the contents of the files within the foo directory. Make a file called proc/foo.c, following the following model:[3] **[The code in** proc_lookupfoo() **and** proc_readfoo() **should be abstracted, as the functionality is used in more than one place.]**

```
/*
 *   linux/fs/proc/foo.c
 *
 *   Copyright (C) 1993 Linus Torvalds, Michael K. Johnson, and Your N. Here
 *
 *   proc foo directory handling functions
 *
 *   inode numbers 200 - 256 are reserved for this directory
 *   (/proc/foo/ and its subdirectories)
 */

#include <asm/segment.h>
#include <linux/errno.h>
#include <linux/sched.h>
#include <linux/proc_fs.h>
#include <linux/stat.h>

static int proc_readfoo(struct inode *, struct file *, struct dirent *, int);
static int proc_lookupfoo(struct inode *,const char *,int,struct inode **);
static int proc_read(struct inode * inode, struct file * file,
                     char * buf, int count);

static struct file_operations proc_foo_operations = {
         NULL,                    /* lseek - default */
         proc_read,               /* read */
         NULL,                    /* write - bad */
         proc_readfoo,            /* readdir */
         NULL,                    /* select - default */
         NULL,                    /* ioctl - default */
         NULL,                    /* mmap */
         NULL,                    /* no special open code */
         NULL                     /* no special release code */
};

/*
 * proc directories can do almost nothing..
 */
```

---

[3]This file is available as file proc/foo.c in the *The Linux Kernel Hackers' Guide* source mentioned on the copyright page.

```
struct inode_operations proc_foo_inode_operations = {
        &proc_foo_operations,   /* default foo directory file-ops */
        NULL,                   /* create */
        proc_lookupfoo,         /* lookup */
        NULL,                   /* link */
        NULL,                   /* unlink */
        NULL,                   /* symlink */
        NULL,                   /* mkdir */
        NULL,                   /* rmdir */
        NULL,                   /* mknod */
        NULL,                   /* rename */
        NULL,                   /* readlink */
        NULL,                   /* follow_link */
        NULL,                   /* bmap */
        NULL,                   /* truncate */
        NULL                    /* permission */
};

static struct proc_dir_entry foo_dir[] = {
        { 1,2,".." },
        { 9,1,"." },
        { 200,3,"bar" },
        { 201,4,"suds" },
        { 202,5,"xyzzy" },
        { 203,3,"baz" },
        { 204,4,"dir1" },
        { 205,4,"dir2" },
        { 206,8,"rootfile" }
};

#define NR_FOO_DIRENTRY ((sizeof (foo_dir))/(sizeof (foo_dir[0])))

unsigned int get_bar(char * buffer);
unsigned int get_suds(char * buffer);
unsigned int get_xyzzy(char * buffer);
unsigned int get_baz(char * buffer);
unsigned int get_rootfile(char * buffer);


static int proc_read(struct inode * inode, struct file * file,
                     char * buf, int count)
{
        char * page;
        int length;
        int end;
        unsigned int ino;

        if (count < 0)
                return -EINVAL;
        page = (char *) get_free_page(GFP_KERNEL);
        if (!page)
                return -ENOMEM;
        ino = inode->i_ino;
        switch (ino) {
```

```
                    case 200:
                            length = get_bar(page);
                            break;
                    case 201:
                            length = get_suds(page);
                            break;
                    case 202:
                            length = get_xyzzy(page);
                            break;
                    case 203:
                            length = get_baz(page);
                            break;
                    case 206:
                            length = get_rootfile(page);
                            break;
                    default:
                            free_page((unsigned long) page);
                            return -EBADF;
            }
            if (file->f_pos >= length) {
                    free_page((unsigned long) page);
                    return 0;
            }
            if (count + file->f_pos > length)
                    count = length - file->f_pos;
            end = count + file->f_pos;
            memcpy_tofs(buf, page + file->f_pos, count);
            free_page((unsigned long) page);
            file->f_pos = end;
            return count;


    }


    static int proc_lookupfoo(struct inode * dir,const char * name, int len,
            struct inode ** result)
    {

            unsigned int pid, ino;
            int i;

            *result = NULL;
            if (!dir)
                    return -ENOENT;
            if (!S_ISDIR(dir->i_mode)) {
                    iput(dir);
                    return -ENOENT;
            }
            ino = dir->i_ino;
            i = NR_FOO_DIRENTRY;
            while (i-- > 0 && !proc_match(len,name,foo_dir+i))
                    /* nothing */;
            if (i < 0) {
                    iput(dir);
                    return -ENOENT;
            }
```

```
        if (!(*result = iget(dir->i_sb,ino))) {
                iput(dir);
                return -ENOENT;
        }
        iput(dir);
        return 0;
}

static int proc_readfoo(struct inode * inode, struct file * filp,
        struct dirent * dirent, int count)
{
        struct proc_dir_entry * de;
        unsigned int pid, ino;
        int i,j;

        if (!inode || !S_ISDIR(inode->i_mode))
                return -EBADF;
        ino = inode->i_ino;
        if (((unsigned) filp->f_pos) < NR_FOO_DIRENTRY) {
                de = foo_dir + filp->f_pos;
                filp->f_pos++;
                i = de->namelen;
                ino = de->low_ino;
                put_fs_long(ino, &dirent->d_ino);
                put_fs_word(i,&dirent->d_reclen);
                put_fs_byte(0,i+dirent->d_name);
                j = i;
                while (i--)
                        put_fs_byte(de->name[i], i+dirent->d_name);
                return j;
        }
        return 0;
}


unsigned int get_foo(char * buffer)
{

/* code to find everything goes here */

        return sprintf(buffer, "format string", variables);
}


unsigned int get_suds(char * buffer)
{

/* code to find everything goes here */

        return sprintf(buffer, "format string", variables);
}


unsigned int get_xyzzy(char * buffer)
```

```
        {

        /* code to find everything goes here */

                return sprintf(buffer, "format string", variables);
        }


        unsigned int get_baz(char * buffer)
        {

        /* code to find everything goes here */

                return sprintf(buffer, "format string", variables);
        }


        unsigned int get_rootfile(char * buffer)
        {

        /* code to find everything goes here */

                return sprintf(buffer, "format string", variables);
        }
```

4. Filling in the directories dir1 and dir2 is left as an exercise. In most cases, such directories will not be needed. However, if they are, the steps presented here may be applied recursively to add files to a directory at another level. Notice that I saved a range of 200–256 for /proc/foo/ and all its subdirectories, so there are plenty of unused inode numbers in that range for your files in dir1 and dir2. I suggest reserving a range for each directory, in case you need to expand. Also, I suggest keeping all the extra data and functions in foo.c, rather than making yet another file, unless the files in the dir1 and dir2 directories are significantly different in concept than foo.

5. Make the appropriate changes to fs/proc/Makefile. This is also left as an exercise for the reader.

[Please note: I have made changes similar to these (I wrote the /proc/net/ support). However, this has been written from memory, and may be unintentionally incomplete. If you notice any inadequacies, please explain them to me in as complete detail as possible. My email address is johnsonm@sunsite.unc.edu]

Chapter 3

The Linux scheduler

[This is still pretty weak, but I think that I have removed most or all of the inaccuracies that were in previous versions. Jim Wisner appears to have dropped from the face of the Net, so I have not been able to get his help at making this chapter more meaningful. If anyone has a copy of the paper he wrote on the scheduler, please get in touch with me, as he promised me a copy, and I'd at least like to see what he had to say about the scheduler.]

[I'm not going to spend any further time on this until the new scheduler is added to Linux. The current one doesn't handle lots of tasks at once very well, and some day a new one will be put in.]

The scheduler is a function, `schedule()`, which is called at various times to determine whether or not to switch tasks, and if so, which task to switch to. The scheduler works in concert with the function `do_timer()`, which is called 100 times per second (on Linux/x86), on each system timer interrupt, and with the system call handler part `ret_from_sys_call()` which is called on the return from system calls.

When a system call completes, or when a "slow" interrupt completes, `ret_from_sys_call()` is called. It does a bit of work, but all we care about are two lines:

```
cmpl $0,_need_resched
jne reschedule
```

These lines check the `need_resched` flag, and if it is set, `schedule()` is called, choosing a new process, and then after `schedule()` has chosen the new process, a little more magic in `ret_from_sys_call()` restores the environment for the chosen process (which may well be, and usually is, the process which is already running), and returns to user space. Returning to user space causes the new process which has been selected to run to be returned to.

In `sched_init()` in kernel/sched.c, `request_irq()` is used to get the timer interrupt. `request_irq()` sets up housekeeping before and after interrupts are serviced, as seen in <asm/irq.h>. However, interrupts that are serviced often and that must be serviced quickly, such as serial interrupts, do *not* call `ret_from_sys_call()` when done and do as little as possible, to keep the overhead down. In particular, they only save the registers that C would clobber, and assume that if the handler is going to use any others, the handler will deal with that. These "fast" interrupt handlers must be installed with the `irqaction()` function described in section 1.6.

The Linux scheduler is significantly different from the schedulers in other unices, especially in its treatment of 'nice level' priorities. Instead of scheduling processes with higher priority first, Linux does round-robin scheduling, but lets higher priority processes run both sooner and longer. The standard UN*X scheduler instead uses queues of processes. Most implementations use two priority queues; a standard queue and a "real time" queue. Essentially, all processes on the "real time" queue get executed before processes on the standard queue, if they are not blocked, and within each queue, higher nice-level processes run before lower ones. The Linux scheduler gives much better interactive performance at the expense of some "throughput."

3.1   The code

Here is a copy of the relevant code from /usr/src/linux/kernel/sched.c, annotated and abridged.

```
void schedule(void)
{
        int i,next,c;
        struct task_struct ** p;

/* check alarm, wake up any interruptible tasks that have got a signal */

        need_resched = 0;
        for(p = &LAST_TASK ; p > &FIRST_TASK ; --p) {
```

The process table is an array of pointers to `struct task_struct` structures.   See /usr/include/linux/sched.h for the definition of this structure.

```
            if (!*p || ((*p)->state != TASK_INTERRUPTIBLE))
                    continue;
            if ((*p)->timeout && (*p)->timeout < jiffies) {
```

If a process has a timeout and has reached it, then `jiffies` (the number of 100ths of a second since system start) will have passed `timeout`. `timeout` was originally set as `jiffies +` *desired_timeout*.

```
                (*p)->timeout = 0;
                (*p)->state = TASK_RUNNING;
            } else if ((*p)->signal & ~(*p)->blocked)
```

If the process has been sent a signal, and is no longer blocked, then let the process be allowed to run again, when its turn comes.

```
                (*p)->state = TASK_RUNNING;

        }
```

At this point, all runnable processes have been flagged as runnable, and we are ready to choose one to run, by running through the process table. What we are looking for is the process with the largest counter. The counter for each runnable process is incremented each time the scheduler is called by an amount that is weighted by the priority, which is the kernel version of the 'nice' value. (It differs in that the priority is never negative.)

```
/* this is the scheduler proper: */

        while (1) {
                c = -1;
                next = 0;
                i = NR_TASKS;
```

```
                    p = &task[NR_TASKS];
                    while (--i) {
                            if (!*--p)
```

If there is no process in this slot then don't bother...

```
                                    continue;
                            if ((*p)->state == TASK_RUNNING && (*p)->counter > c)
                                    c = (*p)->counter, next = i;
```

If the counter is higher than any previous counter, then make the process the next process, unless, of course, an even higher one is encountered later in the loop.

```
                    }
                    if (c)
                            break;
                    for(p = &LAST_TASK ; p > &FIRST_TASK ; --p)
                            if (*p)
                                    (*p)->counter = ((*p)->counter >> 1) +
                                                    (*p)->priority;
```

Here is where the counter is set. It is first divided by 2, and then the priority is added. Note that this happens only if no process has been found to switch to, because of the break; line.

```
            }
            sti();
            switch_to(next);
    }
```

sti() enables interrupts again, and switch_to() (defined in linux/sched.h) sets things up so that when we return to ret_to_sys_call(), we will return from ret_to_sys_call() into the *new* process.

I have truncated do_timer() extremely, only showing the pieces that relate specifically to schedule(). For information on the rest, see the appropriate section. For instance, for commentary on the itimer mechanism see the section on itimers. **[I suppose I need to *write* that section now...I will need to put a reference here to that section.]** I have specifically left out all the accounting stuff, all the timer stuff, and the floppy timer.

```
    static void do_timer(struct pt_regs * regs)
    {
            unsigned long mask;
            struct timer_struct *tp = timer_table+0;
            struct task_struct ** task_p;

            jiffies++;
```

Here is where jiffies is incremented. This is all-important to the rest of the kernel, because all time calculations (except for timed delay loops) are based on this variable.

```
            if (current == task[0] || (--current->counter)<=0) {
                    current->counter=0;
```

```
                    need_resched = 1;
            }
    }
```

Don't let task 0 run if anything else can run, because task 0 doesn't do anything. If task 0 is running, the machine is idle, but don't let it be idle if anything else is happening, so run schedudule as soon as possible. Set the need_resched flag if necessary so that schedule gets called again as soon as possible.

Chapter 4

How System Calls Work

[This needs to be a little re-worked and expanded upon, but I am waiting to see if the iBCS stuff makes any impact on it as I write other stuff.]

This section covers first the mechanisms provided by the 386 for handling system calls, and then shows how Linux uses those mechanisms. This is not a reference to the individual system calls: There are very many of them, new ones are added occasionally, and they are documented in man pages that should be on your Linux system.

[Ideally, this chapter should be part of another section, I think. Maybe, however, it should just be expanded. I think it belongs somewhere near the chapter on how to write a device driver, because it explains how to write a system call.]

4.1   What Does the 386 Provide?

The 386 recognizes two event classes: exceptions and interrupts. Both cause a forced context switch to new a procedure or task. Interrupts can occur at unexpected times during the execution of a program and are used to respond to signals from hardware. Exceptions are caused by the execution of instructions.

Two sources of interrupts are recognized by the 386: Maskable interrupts and Nonmaskable interrupts. Two sources of exceptions are recognized by the 386: Processor detected exceptions and programmed exceptions.

Each interrupt or exception has a number, which is referred to by the 386 literature as the vector. The NMI interrupt and the processor detected exceptions have been assigned vectors in the range 0 through 31, inclusive. The vectors for maskable interrupts are determined by the hardware. External interrupt controllers put the vector on the bus during the interrupt-acknowledge cycle. Any vector in the range 32 through 255, inclusive, can be used for maskable interrupts or programmed exceptions. See figure 4.1 for a listing of all the possible interrupts and exceptions. [Check all this out to make sure that it is right.]

4.2   How Linux Uses Interrupts and Exceptions

Under Linux the execution of a system call is invoked by a maskable interrupt or **exception** class transfer, caused by the instruction `int 0x80`. We use vector 0x80 to transfer control to the kernel. This interrupt vector is initialized during system startup, along with other important vectors like the system clock vector.

0	divide error
1	debug exception
2	NMI interrupt
3	breakpoint
4	INTO-detected Overflow
5	BOUND range exceeded
6	invalid opcode
7	coprocessor not available
8	double fault
9	coprocessor segment overrun
10	invalid task state segment
11	segment not present
12	stack fault
13	general protection
14	page fault
15	reserved
16	coprocessor error
17–31	reserved
32–255	maskable interrupts

Figure 4.1: Interrupt and Exception Assignments

HIGHEST	Faults except debug faults
	Trap instructions INTO, INT n, INT 3
	Debug traps for this instruction
	Debug traps for next instruction
	NMI interrupt
LOWEST	INTR interrupt

Figure 4.2: Priority of simultaneous interrupts and exceptions

As of version 0.99.2 of Linux, there are 116 system calls. Documentation for these can be found in the man (2) pages. When a user invokes a system call, execution flow is as follows:

- Each call is vectored through a stub in libc. Each call within the libc library is generally a syscall**X**() macro, where **X** is the number of parameters used by the actual routine. Some system calls are more complex then others because of variable length argument lists, but even these complex system calls must use the same entry point: they just have more parameter setup overhead. Examples of a complex system call include open() and ioctl().

- Each syscall macro expands to an assembly routine which sets up the calling stack frame and calls _system_call() through an interrupt, via the instruction int $0x80

For example, the setuid system call is coded as

```
_syscall1(int,setuid,uid_t,uid);
```

Which will expand to:

```
_setuid:
  subl $4,%exp
  pushl %ebx
```

```
        movzwl 12(%esp),%eax
        movl %eax,4(%esp)
        movl $23,%eax
        movl 4(%esp),%ebx
        int $0x80
        movl %eax,%edx
        testl %edx,%edx
        jge L2
        negl %edx
        movl %edx,_errno
        movl $-1,%eax
        popl %ebx
        addl $4,%esp
        ret
    L2:
        movl %edx,%eax
        popl %ebx
        addl $4,%esp
        ret
```

The macro definition for the `syscallX()` macros can be found in /usr/include/linux/unistd.h, and the user-space system call library code can be found in /usr/src/libc/syscall/

- At this point no system code for the call has been executed. Not until the int $0x80 is executed does the call transfer to the kernel entry point `_system_call()`. This entry point is the same for all system calls. It is responsible for saving all registers, checking to make sure a valid system call was invoked and then ultimately transferring control to the actual system call code via the offsets in the `_sys_call_table`. It is also responsible for calling `_ret_from_sys_call()` when the system call has been completed, but before returning to user space.

  Actual code for `system_call` entry point can be found in /usr/src/linux/kernel/sys_call.S Actual code for many of the system calls can be found in /usr/src/linux/kernel/sys.c, and the rest are found elsewhere. `find` is your friend.

- After the system call has executed, `_ret_from_sys_call()` is called. It checks to see if the scheduler should be run, and if so, calls it.

- Upon return from the system call, the `syscallX()` macro code checks for a negative return value, and if there is one, puts a positive copy of the return value in the global variable `_errno`, so that it can be accessed by code like `perror()`.

4.3 How Linux Initializes the system call vectors

The `startup_32()` code found in /usr/src/linux/boot/head.S starts everything off by calling `setup_idt()`. This routine sets up an IDT (Interrupt Descriptor Table) with 256 entries. No interrupt entry points are actually loaded by this routine, as that is done only after paging has been enabled and the kernel has been moved to 0xC0000000. An IDT has 256 entries, each 4 bytes long, for a total of 1024 bytes.

When `start_kernel()` (found in /usr/src/linux/init/main.c) is called it invokes `trap_init()` (found in /usr/src/linux/kernel/traps.c). `trap_init()` sets up the IDT via the macro `set_trap_gate()` (found in /usr/include/asm/system.h). `trap_init()` initializes the interrupt descriptor table as shown in figure 4.3.

0	divide_error
1	debug
2	nmi
3	int3
4	overflow
5	bounds
6	invalid_op
7	device_not_available
8	double_fault
9	coprocessor_segment_overrun
10	invalid_TSS
11	segment_not_present
12	stack_segment
13	general_protection
14	page_fault
15	reserved
16	coprocessor_error
17	alignment_check
18–48	reserved

Figure 4.3: Initialization of interrupts

At this point the interrupt vector for the system calls is not set up. It is initialized by sched_init() (found in /usr/src/linux/kernel/sched.c). A call to set_system_gate (0x80, &system_call) sets interrupt 0x80 to be a vector to the system_call() entry point.

4.4   How to Add Your Own System Calls

1. Create a directory under the /usr/src/linux/ directory to hold your code.

2. Put any include files in /usr/include/sys/ and /usr/include/linux/.

3. Add the relocatable module produced by the link of your new kernel code to the ARCHIVES and the subdirectory to the SUBDIRS lines of the top level Makefile. See fs/Makefile, target fs.o for an example.

4. Add a #define _NR_xx to unistd.h to assign a call number for your system call, where xx, the index, is something descriptive relating to your system call. It will be used to set up the vector through sys_call_table to invoke you code.

5. Add an entry point for your system call to the sys_call_table in sys.h. It should match the index (xx) that you assigned in the previous step. The NR_syscalls variable will be recalculated automatically.

6. Modify any kernel code in kernel/fs/mm/, etc. to take into account the environment needed to support your new code.

7. Run make from the top level to produce the new kernel incorporating your new code.

At this point, you will have to either add a syscall to your libraries, or use the proper _syscalln() macro in your user program for your programs to access the new system call.

The *386DX Microprocessor Programmer's Reference Manual* is a helpful reference, as is James Turley's *Advanced 80386 Programming Techniques.* See the Annotated bibliography in Appendix A.

Chapter 5

Linux Memory Management

[This chapter needs to be made much friendlier. I'd hate to remove detail, but it needs to be less daunting. Many have told me that this is a daunting chapter, and it need not be. I'll re-work it later. In the meantime, please bear with me.]

5.1   Overview

The Linux memory manager implements demand paging with a copy-on-write strategy relying on the 386's paging support. A process acquires its page tables from its parent (during a `fork()`) with the entries marked as read-only or swapped. Then, if the process tries to write to that memory space, and the page is a copy-on-write page, it is copied, and the page is marked read-write. An `exec()` results in the reading in of a page or so from the executable. The process then faults in any other pages it needs.

Each process has a page directory which means it can access 1 KB of page tables pointing to 1 MB of 4 KB pages which is 4 GB of memory. A process' page directory is initialized during a fork by `copy_page_tables()`. The idle process has its page directory initialized during the initialization sequence.

Each user process has a local descriptor table that contains a code segment and data-stack segment. These user segments extend from 0 to 3 GB (0xc0000000). In user space linear addresses[1] and logical addresses[2] are identical.

The kernel code and data segments are privileged segments defined in the global descriptor table and extend from 3 GB to 4 GB. The swapper page directory (`swapper_page_dir` is set up so that logical addresses and physical addresses are identical in kernel space.

The space above 3 GB appears in a process' page directory as pointers to kernel page tables. This space is invisible to the process in user mode but the mapping becomes relevant when privileged mode is entered, for example, to handle a system call.

Supervisor mode is entered within the context of the current process so address translation occurs with respect to the process' page directory but using kernel segments. This is identically the mapping produced by using the `swapper_pg_dir` and kernel segments as both page directories use the same page tables in

---

[1]In the 80386, linear address run from 0GB to 4GB. A linear address points to a particular memory location within this space. A linear address is **not** a physical address — it is a virtual address.

[2]A logical address consists of a selector and an offset. The selector points to a segment and the offset tells how far into that segment the address is located.

this space. Only task[0] (the idle task[3] **[This should be documented earlier in this guide. . .]**) uses the swapper_pg_dir directly.

- The user process' segment_base = 0x00, page_dir private to the process.

- user process makes a system call: segment_base=0xc0000000 page_dir = same user page_dir.

- swapper_pg_dir contains a mapping for all physical pages from 0xc0000000 to 0xc0000000 + end_mem, so the first 768 entries in swapper_pg_dir are 0's, and then there are 4 or more that point to kernel page tables.

- The user page directories have the same entries as tt swapper_pg_dir above 768. The first 768 entries map the user space.

The upshot is that whenever the linear address is above 0xc0000000 everything uses the same kernel page tables.

The user stack sits at the top of the user data segment and grows down. The kernel stack is not a pretty data structure or segment that I can point to with a "yon lies the kernel stack." A kernel_stack_frame (a page) is associated with each newly created process and is used whenever the kernel operates within the context of that process. Bad things would happen if the kernel stack were to grow below its current stack frame. **[Where is the kernel stack put? I know that there is one for every process, but where is it stored when it's not being used?]**

User pages can be stolen or swapped. A user page is one that is mapped below 3 GB in a user page table. This region does not contain page directories or page tables. Only dirty pages are swapped.

Minor alterations are needed in some places (tests for process memory limits comes to mind) to provide support for programmer defined segments.

5.2   Physical memory

Here is a map of physical memory before any user processes are executed. The column on the left gives the **starting** address of the item, numbers in *italics* are approximate. The column in the middle names the item(s). The column on the far right gives the relevant routine or variable name or explains the entry.

0x110000	FREE	memory_end or high_memory
	mem_map	mem_init()
	inode_table	inode_init()
	device data	device_init()†
0x100000	more pg_tables	paging_init()
0x0A0000	RESERVED	
0x060000	FREE	
	low_memory_start	
0x006000	kernel code + data	
	floppy_track_buffer	
	bad_pg_table	used by page_fault_handlers to kill processes
	bad_page	gracefully when out of memory.
0x002000	pg0	the first kernel page table.
0x001000	swapper_pg_dir	the kernel page directory.
0x000000	null page	

---

[3]Sometimes called the swapper task, even though it has nothing to do with swapping in the Linux implementation, for historical reasons

†device-inits that acquire memory are(main.c): `profil_buffer`, `con_init`, `psaux_init`, `rd_init`, `scsi_dev_init`. Note that all memory not marked as FREE is RESERVED (`mem_init`). RESERVED pages belong to the kernel and are **never** freed or swapped.

5.3   A user process' view of memory

0xc0000000	The invisible kernel	reserved
	initial stack	
	room for stack growth	4 pages
0x60000000	shared libraries	
brk	unused	
	malloc memory	
end_data	uninitialized data	
end_code	initialized data	
0x00000000	text	

Both the code segment and data segment extend all the way from 0x00 to 3 GB. Currently the page fault handler `do_wp_page` checks to ensure that a process does not write to its code space. However, by catching the SEGV signal, it is possible to write to code space, causing a copy-on-write to occur. The handler `do_no_page` ensures that any new pages the process acquires belong to either the executable, a shared library, the stack, or lie within the `brk` value.

A user process can reset its `brk` value by calling `sbrk()`. This is what `malloc()` does when it needs to. The text and data portions are allocated on separate pages unless one chooses the `-N` compiler option. Shared library load addresses are currently taken from the shared image itself. The address is between 1.5 GB and 3 GB, except in special cases.

User process Memory Allocation

	swappable	shareable
a few code pages	Y	Y
a few data pages	Y	N?
stack	Y	N
pg_dir	N	N
code/data page_table	N	N
stack page_table	N	N
task_struct	N	N
kernel_stack_frame	N	N
shlib page_table	N	N
a few shlib pages	Y	Y?

[What do the question marks mean? Do they mean that they might go either way, or that you are not sure?] The stack, shlibs and data are too far removed from each other to be spanned by one page table. All kernel `page_tables` are shared by all processes so they are not in the list. Only dirty pages are swapped. Clean pages are stolen so the process can read them back in from the executable if it likes. Mostly only clean pages are shared. A dirty page ends up shared across a fork until the parent or child chooses to write to it again.

5.4   Memory Management data in the process table

Here is a summary of some of the data kept in the process table which is used for memory management:
[These should be much better documented. We need more details.]

- Process memory limits: `ulong start_code, end_code, end_data, brk, start_stack;`

- Page fault counting: `ulong min_flt, maj_flt, cmin_flt, cmaj_flt`

- Local descriptor table: `struct desc_struct ldt[32]` is the local descriptor table for task.

- `rss`: number of resident pages.

- `swappable`: if 0, then process' pages will not be swapped.

- `kernel_stack_page`: pointer to page allocated in fork.

- `saved_kernel_stack`: V86 mode stuff.

- `struct tss`

    - Stack segments

      `esp0` kernel stack pointer (`kernel_stack_page`)

      `ss0` kernel stack segment (0x10)

      `esp1 = ss1 = esp2 = ss2 = 0`
          unused privilege levels.

    - Segment selectors: `ds = es = fs = gs = ss = 0x17, cs = 0x0f`
      All point to segments in the current `ldt[]`.

    - `cr3`: points to the page directory for this process.

    - `ldt`: `_LDT(n)` selector for current task's LDT.

5.5   Memory initialization

In `start_kernel()` (main.c) there are 3 variables related to memory initialization:

`memory_start`	starts out at 1 MB. Updated by device initialization.
`memory_end`	end of physical memory: 8 MB, 16 MB, or whatever.
`low_memory_start`	end of the kernel code and data that is loaded initially.

Each device init typically takes `memory_start` and returns an updated value if it allocates space at `memory_start` (by simply grabbing it). `paging_init()` initializes the page tables in the `swapper_pg_dir` (starting at 0xc0000000) to cover all of the physical memory from `memory_start` to `memory_end`. Actually the first 4 MB is done in `startup_32` (head.S). `memory_start` is incremented if any new `page_tables` are added. The first page is zeroed to trap null pointer references in the kernel.

In `sched_init()` the `ldt` and `tss` descriptors for `task[0]` are set in the GDT, and loaded into the TR and LDTR (the only time it's done explicitly). A trap gate (0x80) is set up for `system_call()`. The nested task flag is turned off in preparation for entering user mode. The timer is turned on. The `task_struct` for `task[0]` appears in its entirety in `<linux/sched.h>`.

`mem_map` is then constructed by `mem_init()` to reflect the current usage of physical pages. This is the state reflected in the physical memory map of the previous section.

Then Linux moves into user mode with an `iret` after pushing the current `ss`, `esp`, etc. Of course the user segments for `task[0]` are mapped right over the kernel segments so execution continues exactly where it left off.

`task[0]`:

- `pg_dir = swapper_pg_dir` which means the the only addresses mapped are in the range 3 GB to 3 GB + `high_memory`.

- `LDT[1]` = user code, base=0xc0000000, size = 640K

- `LDT[2]` = user data, base=0xc0000000, size = 640K

The first `exec()` sets the LDT entries for `task[1]` to the user values of base = 0x0, limit = TASK_SIZE = 0xc0000000. Thereafter, no process sees the kernel segments while in user mode.

5.5.1 Processes and the Memory Manager

Memory-related work done by `fork()`:

- Memory allocation

  - 1 page for the `task_struct`.
  - 1 page for the kernel stack.
  - 1 for the `pg_dir` and some for `pg_tables` (copy_page_tables)

- Other changes

  - `ss0` set to kernel stack segment (0x10) to be sure?
  - `esp0` set to top of the newly allocated `kernel_stack_page`
  - `cr3` set by `copy_page_tables()` to point to newly allocated page directory.
  - `ldt = _LDT(task_nr)` creates new ldt descriptor.
  - descriptors set in gdt for new tss and `ldt[]`.
  - The remaining registers are inherited from parent.

The processes end up sharing their code and data segments (although they have separate local descriptor tables, the entries point to the same segments). The stack and data pages will be copied when the parent or child writes to them (copy-on-write).

Memory-related work done by `exec()`:

- memory allocation

  - 1 page for exec header entire file for omagic
  - 1 page or more for stack (MAX_ARG_PAGES)

- `clear_page_tables()` used to remove old pages.

- `change_ldt()` sets the descriptors in the new `LDT[]`

- `ldt[1]` = code base=0x00, limit=TASK_SIZE

- ldt[2] = data base=0x00, limit=TASK_SIZE
  These segments are DPL=3, P=1, S=1, G=1. type=a (code) or 2 (data)

- Up to MAX_ARG_PAGES dirty pages of argv and envp are allocated and stashed at the top of the data segment for the newly created user stack.

- Set the instruction pointer of the caller eip = ex.a_entry

- Set the stack pointer of the caller to the stack just created (esp = stack pointer) These will be popped off the stack when the caller resumes.

- update memory limits
  end_code = ex.a_text
  end_data = end_code + ex.a_data
  brk = end_data + ex.a_bss

Interrupts and traps are handled within the context of the current task. In particular, the page directory of the current process is used in address translation. The segments, however, are kernel segments so that all linear addresses point into kernel memory. For example, assume a user process invokes a system call and the kernel wants to access a variable at address 0x01. The linear address is 0xc0000001 (using kernel segments) and the physical address is 0x01. The later is because the process' page directory maps this range exactly as page_pg_dir.

The kernel space (0xc0000000 + high_memory) is mapped by the kernel page tables which are themselves part of the RESERVED memory. They are therefore shared by all processes. During a fork copy_page_tables() treats RESERVED page tables differently. It sets pointers in the process page directories to point to kernel page tables and does not actually allocate new page tables as it does normally. As an example the kernel_stack_page (which sits somewhere in the kernel space) does not need an associated page_table allocated in the process' pg_dir to map it.

The interrupt instruction sets the stack pointer and stack segment from the privilege 0 values saved in the tss of the current task. Note that the kernel stack is a really fragmented object — it's not a single object, but rather a bunch of stack frames each allocated when a process is created, and released when it exits. The kernel stack should never grow so rapidly within a process context that it extends below the current frame.

5.6   Acquiring and Freeing Memory: Paging Policy

When any kernel routine wants memory it ends up calling get_free_page(). This is at a lower level than kmalloc() (in fact kmalloc() uses get_free_page() when it needs more memory).

get_free_page() takes one parameter, a priority. Possible values are GFP_BUFFER, GFP_KERNEL, and GFP_ATOMIC. It takes a page off of the free_page_list, updates mem_map, zeroes the page and returns the physical address of the page (note that kmalloc() returns a physical address. The logic of the mm depends on the identity map between logical and physical addresses).

That itself is simple enough. The problem, of course, is that the free_page_list may be empty. If you did not request an atomic operation, at this stage, you enter into the realm of page stealing which we'll go into in a moment. As a last resort (and for atomic requests) a page is torn off from the secondary_page_list (as you may have guessed, when pages are freed, the secondary_page_list gets filled up first).

The actual manipulation of the page_lists and mem_map occurs in this mysterious macro called REMOVE_FROM_MEM_QUEUE() which you probably never want to look into. Suffice it to say that interrupts are disabled. [**I think that this should be explained here. It is not** *that* **hard. . .**]

Now back to the page stealing bit. `get_free_page()` calls `try_to_free_page()` which repeatedly calls `shrink_buffers()` and `swap_out()` in that order until it is successful in freeing a page. The priority is increased on each successive iteration so that these two routines run through their page stealing loops more often.

Here's one run through `swap_out()`:

- Run through the process table and get a swappable task say **Q**.

- Find a user page table (not RESERVED) in **Q**'s space.

- For each **page** in the table `try_to_swap_out(` **page** `)`.

- Quit when a page is freed.

Note that `swap_out()` (called by `try_to_free_page()`) maintains static variables so it may resume the search where it left off on the previous call.

`try_to_swap_out()` scans the page tables of all user processes and enforces the stealing policy:

1. Do not fiddle with RESERVED pages.

2. Age the page if it is marked accessed (1 bit).

3. Don't tamper with recently acquired pages (`last_free_pages[]`).

4. Leave dirty pages with `map_count`s > 1 alone.

5. Decrement the `map_count` of clean pages.

6. Free clean pages if they are unmapped.

7. Swap dirty pages with a `map_count` of 1.

Of these actions, 6 and 7 will stop the process as they result in the actual freeing of a physical page. Action 5 results in one of the processes losing an unshared clean page that was not accessed recently (decrement `Q->rss`) which is not all that bad, but the cumulative effects of a few iterations can slow down a process considerably. At present, there are 6 iterations, so a page shared by 6 processes can get stolen if it is clean.

Page table entries are updated and the TLB invalidated. **[Wonder about the latter. It seems unnecessary since accessed pages aren't offed and there is a walk through many page tables between iterations . . . may be in case an interrupt came along and wanted the most recently axed page?]**

The actual work of freeing the page is done by `free_page()`, the complement of `get_free_page()`. It ignores RESERVED pages, updates `mem_map`, then frees the page and updates the `page_lists` if it is unmapped. For swapping (in 6 above), `write_swap_page()` gets called and does nothing remarkable from the memory management perspective.

The details of `shrink_buffers()` would take us too far afield. Essentially it looks for free buffers, then writes out dirty buffers, then goes at busy buffers and calls `free_page()` when its able to free all the buffers on a page.

Note that page directories and page tables along with RESERVED pages do not get swapped, stolen or aged. They are mapped in the process page directory through reserved page tables. They are freed only on exit from the process.

5.7   The page fault handlers

When a process is created via fork, it starts out with a page directory and a page or so of the executable. So the page fault handler is the source of most of a processes' memory.

The page fault handler do_page_fault() retrieves the faulting address from the register cr2. The error code (retrieved in sys_call.S) differentiates user/supervisor access and the reason for the fault — write protection or a missing page. The former is handled by do_wp_page() and the latter by do_no_page().

If the faulting address is greater than TASK_SIZE the process receives a SIGKILL. **[Why this check? This can only happen in kernel mode because of segment level protection.]**

These routines have some subtleties as they can get called from an interrupt. You can't assume that it is the 'current' task that is executing.

do_no_page() handles three possible situations:

1. The page is swapped.

2. The page belongs to the executable or a shared library.

3. The page is missing — a data page that has not been allocated.

In all cases get_empty_pgtable() is called first to ensure the existence of a page table that covers the faulting address. In case 3 get_empty_page() is called to provide a page at the required address and in case of the swapped page, swap_in() is called.

In case 2, the handler calls share_page() to see if the page is shareable with some other process. If that fails it reads in the page from the executable or library (It repeats the call to share_page() in case another process did the same meanwhile). Any portion of the page beyond the brk value is zeroed.

A page read in from the disk is counted as a major fault (maj_flt). This happens with a swap_in() or when it is read from the executable or a library. Other cases are deemed minor faults (min_flt).

When a shareable page is found, it is write-protected. A process that writes to a shared page will then have to go through do_wp_page() which does the copy-on-write.

do_wp_page() does the following:

- send SIGSEGV if any user process is writing to current code_space.

- If the old page is not shared then just unprotect it.
  Else get_free_page() and copy_page(). The page acquires the dirty flag from the old page. Decrement the map count of the old page.

5.8   Paging

Paging is swapping on a page basis rather than by entire processes. We will use swapping here to refer to paging, since Linux only pages, and does not swap, and people are more used to the word "swap" than "page." Kernel pages are never swapped. Clean pages are also not written to swap. They are freed and reloaded when required. The swapper maintains a single bit of aging info in the PAGE_ACCESSED bit of the page table entries. **[What are the maintenance details? How is it used?]**

Linux supports multiple swap files or devices which may be turned on or off by the swapon and swapoff system calls. Each swap file or device is described by a struct swap_info_struct (swap.c).

```
static struct swap_info_struct {
    unsigned long flags;
    struct inode * swap_file;
    unsigned int swap_device;
    unsigned char * swap_map;
    char * swap_lockmap;
    int lowest_bit;
    int highest_bit;
} swap_info[MAX_SWAPFILES];
```

The flags field (SWP_USED or SWP_WRITEOK) is used to control access to the swap files. When SWP_WRITEOK is off space will not be allocated in that file. This is used by swapoff when it tries to unuse a file. When swapon adds a new swap file it sets SWP_USED. A static variable nr_swapfiles stores the number of currently active swap files. The fields lowest_bit and highest_bit bound the free region in the swap file and are used to speed up the search for free swap space.

The user program mkswap initializes a swap device or file. The first page contains a signature ('SWAP-SPACE') in the last 10 bytes, and holds a bitmap. Initially 0's in the bitmap signal bad pages. A '1' in the bitmap means the corresponding page is free. This page is never allocated so the initialization needs to be done just once.

The syscall swapon() is called by the user program swapon typically from /etc/rc. A couple of pages of memory are allocated for swap_map and swap_lockmap.

swap_map holds a byte for each page in the swap file. It is initialized from the bitmap to contain a 0 for available pages and 128 for unusable pages. It is used to maintain a count of swap requests on each page in the swap file. swap_lockmap holds a bit for each page that is used to ensure mutual exclusion when reading or writing swap files.

When a page of memory is to be swapped out an index to the swap location is obtained by a call to get_swap_page(). This index is then stored in bits 1–31 of the page table entry so the swapped page may be located by the page fault handler, do_no_page() when needed.

The upper 7 bits of the index give the swap file (or device) and the lower 24 bits give the page number on that device. That makes as many as 128 swap files, each with room for about 64 GB, but the space overhead due to the swap_map would be large. Instead the swap file size is limited to 16 MB, because the swap_map then takes 1 page.

The function swap_duplicate() is used by copy_page_tables() to let a child process inherit swapped pages during a fork. It just increments the count maintained in swap_map for that page. Each process will swap in a separate copy of the page when it accesses it.

swap_free() decrements the count maintained in swap_map. When the count drops to 0 the page can be reallocated by get_swap_page(). It is called each time a swapped page is read into memory (swap_in()) or when a page is to be discarded (free_one_table(), etc.).

5.9   80386 Memory Management

A logical address specified in an instruction is first translated to a linear address by the segmenting hardware. This linear address is then translated to a physical address by the paging unit.

5.9.1   Paging on the 386

There are two levels of indirection in address translation by the paging unit. A **page directory** contains pointers to 1024 page tables. Each **page table** contains pointers to 1024 pages. The register CR3 contains the physical base address of the page directory and is stored as part of the TSS in the `task_struct` and is therefore loaded on each task switch.

A 32-bit Linear address is divided as follows:

31 22	21 12	11 0
DIR	TABLE	OFFSET

Physical address is then computed (in hardware) as:

CR3 + DIR	points to the table_base.
table_base + TABLE	points to the page_base.
physical_address =	page_base + OFFSET

Page directories (page tables) are page aligned so the lower 12 bits are used to store useful information about the page table (page) pointed to by the entry.

Format for Page directory and Page table entries:

31 12	11 9	8	7	6	5	4	3	2	1	0
ADDRESS	OS	0	0	D	A	0	0	U/S	R/W	P

- D   1 means page is dirty (undefined for page directory entry).
- R/W   0 means read-only for user.
- U/S   1 means user page.
- P   1 means page is present in memory.
- A   1 means page has been accessed (set to 0 by aging).
- OS   bits can be used for LRU etc, and are defined by the OS.

The corresponding definitions for Linux are in `<linux/mm.h>`.

When a page is swapped, bits 1–31 of the page table entry are used to mark where a page is stored in swap (bit 0 must be 0).

Paging is enabled by setting the highest bit in CR0. **[in head.S?]** At each stage of the address translation access permissions are verified and pages not present in memory and protection violations result in page faults. The fault handler (in memory.c) then either brings in a new page or write-enables a page or does whatever needs to be done.

Page Fault handling Information

- The register CR2 contains the linear address that caused the last page fault.

- Page Fault Error Code (16 bits):

bit	cleared	set
0	page not present	page level protection
1	fault due to read	fault due to write
2	supervisor mode	user mode

The rest are undefined. These are extracted in sys_call.S.

The Translation Lookaside Buffer (TLB) is a hardware cache for physical addresses of the most recently used virtual addresses. When a virtual address is translated the 386 first looks in the TLB to see if the information it needs is available. If not, it has to make a couple of memory references to get at the page directory and then the page table before it can actually get at the page. Three physical memory references for address translation for every logical memory reference would kill the system, hence the TLB.

The TLB is flushed if CR3 loaded or by task switch that changes CR0. It is explicitly flushed in Linux by calling `invalidate()` which just reloads CR3.

5.9.2 Segments in the 80386

Segment registers are used in address translation to generate a linear address from a logical (virtual) address.

```
linear_address = segment_base + logical_address
```

The linear address is then translated into a physical address by the paging hardware.

Each segment in the system is described by a 8 byte segment descriptor which contains all pertinent information (base, limit, type, privilege).

The segments are:
Regular segments

- code and data segments

System segments

- (TSS) task state segments
- (LDT) local descriptor tables

Characteristics of system segments:

- System segments are task specific.

- There is a Task State Segment (TSS) associated with each task in the system. It contains the `tss_struct` (sched.h). The size of the segment is that of the `tss_struct` excluding the `i387_union` (232 bytes). It contains all the information necessary to restart the task.

- The LDT's contain regular segment descriptors that are private to a task. In Linux there is one LDT per task. There is room for 32 descriptors in the Linux `task_struct`. The normal LDT generated by Linux has a size of 24 bytes, hence room for only 3 entries as above. Its contents are:

    - LDT[0] Null (mandatory)
    - LDT[1] user code segment descriptor.
    - LDT[2] user data/stack segment descriptor.

- The user segments all have base=0x00 so that the linear address is the same as the logical address.

To keep track of all these segments, the 386 uses a global descriptor table (GDT) that is setup in memory by the system (located by the GDT register). The GDT contains a segment descriptors for each task state segment, each local descriptor tablet and also regular segments. The Linux GDT contains just two normal segment entries:

- GDT[0] is the null descriptor.

- GDT[1] is the kernel code segment descriptor.

- GDT[2] is the kernel data/stack segment descriptor.

The rest of the GDT is filled with TSS and LDT system descriptors:

- GDT[3] ???

- GDT[4] = TSS0, GDT[5] = LDT0,

- GDT[6] = TSS1, GDT[7] = LDT1

- ... etc ...

Note LDT[n] != LDTn

- LDT[n] = the nth descriptor in the LDT of the current task.

- LDTn = a descriptor in the GDT for the LDT of the nth task.

At present the GDT has a total of 256 entries or room for as many as 126 tasks. The kernel segments have base 0xc0000000 which is where the kernel lives in the linear view. Before a segment can be used, the contents of the descriptor for that segment must be loaded into the segment register. The 386 has a complex set of criteria regarding access to segments so you can't simply load a descriptor into a segment register. Also these segment registers have programmer invisible portions. The visible portion is what is usually called a segment register: cs, ds, es, fs, gs, and ss.

The programmer loads one of these registers with a 16-bit value called a selector. The selector uniquely identifies a segment descriptor in one of the tables. Access is validated and the corresponding descriptor loaded by the hardware.

Currently Linux largely ignores the (overly?) complex segment level protection afforded by the 386. It is biased towards the paging hardware and the associated page level protection. The segment level rules that apply to user processes are

1. A process cannot directly access the kernel data or code segments

2. There is always limit checking but given that every user segment goes from 0x00 to 0xc0000000 it is unlikely to apply. **[This has changed, and needs updating, please.]**

5.9.3   Selectors in the 80386

A segment selector is loaded into a segment register (cs, ds, etc.) to select one of the regular segments in the system as the one addressed via that segment register.

Segment selector Format:

15	3	2 1	0
index		TI	RPL

TI Table indicator:
        0 means selector indexes into GDT
        1 means selector indexes into LDT

RPL Privilege level. Linux uses only two privilege levels.
    0 means kernel
    3 means user

Examples:

Kernel code segment
    TI=0, index=1, RPL=0, therefore selector = 0x08 (GDT[1])

User data segment
    TI=1, index=2, RPL=3, therefore selector = 0x17 (LDT[2])

Selectors used in Linux:

TI	index	RPL	selector	segment	
0	1	0	0x08	kernel code	GDT[1]
0	2	0	0x10	kernel data/stack	GDT[2]
0	3	0	???	???	GDT[3]
1	1	3	0x0F	user code	LDT[1]
1	2	3	0x17	user data/stack	LDT[2]

Selectors for system segments are not to be loaded directly into segment registers. Instead one must load the TR or LDTR.

On entry into syscall:

- ds and es are set to the kernel data segment (0x10)

- fs is set to the user data segment (0x17) and is used to access data pointed to by arguments to the system call.

- The stack segment and pointer are automatically set to ss0 and esp0 by the interrupt and the old values restored when the syscall returns.

5.9.4 Segment descriptors

There is a segment descriptor used to describe each segment in the system. There are regular descriptors and system descriptors. Here's a descriptor in all its glory. The strange format is essentially to maintain compatibility with the 286. Note that it takes 8 bytes.

63–54	55	54	53	52	51–48	47	46	45	44–40	39–16	15–0
Base 31–24	G	D	R	U	Limit 19–16	P	DPL	S	TYPE	Segment Base 23–0	Segment Limit 15–0

Explanation:
- **R** reserved (0)
- **DPL** 0 means kernel, 3 means user
- **G** 1 means 4K granularity (Always set in Linux)
- **D** 1 means default operand size 32bits
- **U** programmer definable
- **P** 1 means present in physical memory
- **S** 0 means system segment, 1 means normal code or data segment.
- **Type** There are many possibilities. Interpreted differently for system and normal descriptors.

Linux system descriptors:
TSS: P=1, DPL=0, S=0, type=9, limit = 231 room for 1 `tss_struct`.
LDT: P=1, DPL=0, S=0, type=2, limit = 23 room for 3 segment descriptors.
The base is set during `fork()`. There is a TSS and LDT for each task.

Linux regular kernel descriptors: (head.S)
code: P=1, DPL=0, S=1, G=1, D=1, type=a, base=0xc0000000, limit=0x3ffff
data: P=1, DPL=0, S=1, G=1, D=1, type=2, base=0xc0000000, limit=0x3ffff

The LDT for task[0] contains: (sched.h)
code: P=1, DPL=3, S=1, G=1, D=1, type=a, base=0xc0000000, limit=0x9f
data: P=1, DPL=3, S=1, G=1, D=1, type=2, base=0xc0000000, limit=0x9f

The default LDT for the remaining tasks: (`exec()`)
code: P=1, DPL=3, S=1, G=1, D=1, type=a, base=0, limit= 0xbffff
data: P=1, DPL=3, S=1, G=1, D=1, type=2, base=0, limit= 0xbffff

The size of the kernel segments is 0x40000 pages (4KB pages since G=1 = 1 Gigabyte. The type implies that the permissions on the code segment is read-exec and on the data segment is read-write.

Registers associated with segmentation. Format of segment register: (Only the selector is programmer visible)

16-bit	32-bit	32-bit	
selector	physical base addr	segment limit	attributes

The invisible portion of the segment register is more conveniently viewed in terms of the format used in the descriptor table entries that the programmer sets up. The descriptor tables have registers associated with them that are used to locate them in memory. The GDTR (and IDTR) are initialized at startup once the tables are defined. The LDTR is loaded on each task switch.

Format of GDTR (and IDTR):

32-bits	16-bits
Linear base addr	table limit

The TR and LDTR are loaded from the GDT and so have the format of the other segment registers. The task register (TR) contains the descriptor for the currently executing task's TSS. The execution of a jump to a TSS selector causes the state to be saved in the old TSS, the TR is loaded with the new descriptor and the registers are restored from the new TSS. This is the process used by schedule to switch to various user tasks. Note that the field `tss_struct.ldt` contains a selector for the LDT of that task. It is used to load the LDTR. (sched.h)

5.9.5   Macros used in setting up descriptors

Some assembler macros are defined in sched.h and system.h to ease access and setting of descriptors. Each TSS entry and LDT entry takes 8 bytes.

Manipulating GDT system descriptors:

- _TSS(n),
  _LDT(n) These provide the index into the GDT for the n'th task.

- _LDT(n) is stored in the the ldt field of the tss_struct by fork.

- _set_tssldt_desc(n, addr, limit, type)
  ulong *n points to the GDT entry to set (see fork.c). The segment base (TSS or LDT) is set to 0xc0000000 + addr. Specific instances of the above are, where ltype refers to the byte containing P, DPL, S and type:

  set_ldt_desc(n, addr) ltype = 0x82
                       P=1, DPL=0, S=0, type=2 means LDT entry. limit = 23 => room for 3 segment descriptors.

  set_tss_desc(n, addr) ltype = 0x89
                       P=1, DPL=0, S=0, type = 9, means available 80386 TSS limit = 231 room for 1 tss_struct.

- load_TR(n),
  load_ldt(n) load descriptors for task number n into the task register and ldt register.

- ulong get_base (struct desc_struct ldt) gets the base from a descriptor.

- ulong get_limit (ulong segment) gets the limit (size) from a segment selector. Returns the size of the segment in bytes.

- set_base(struct desc_struct ldt, ulong base),
  set_limit(struct desc_struct ldt, ulong limit)
  Will set the base and limit for descriptors (4K granular segments). The limit here is actually the size in bytes of the segment.

- _set_seg_desc(gate_addr, type, dpl, base, limit)
  Default values 0x00408000 =) D=1, P=1, G=0
  Present, operation size is 32 bit and max size is 1M.
  gate_addr must be a (ulong *)

Appendix A

Bibliography

Two bibliographies for now...

A.1 Normal Bibliography

Bibliography

[ANS]   *Draft Proposed American National Standard for Information Systems: Small Computer System Interface –
2 (SCSI-2).* (X3T9.2/86-109, revision 10h, October 17, 1991).

[Int90]   Intel. *i486 Processor Programmer's Reference Manual.* Intel/McGraw-Hill, 1990.

[LXT91] *LXT SCSI Products: Specification and OEM Technical Manual*, 1991.

[Nor85] Peter Norton. *The Peter Norton Programmer's Guide to the IBM PC.* Bellevue, Washington: Microsoft
Press, 1985.

A.2   Annotated Bibliography

This annotated bibliography covers books on operating system theory as well as different kinds of programming in a UN⋆X environment. The price marked may or may not be an exact price, but should be close enough for government work. [**If you have a book that you think should go in the bibliography, please write a short review of it and send all the necessary information (title, author, publisher, ISBN, and approximate price) and the review to** johnsonm@sunsite.unc.edu]

This version is slowly going away, in favor of a real bibliography.

Title:	The Design of the UNIX Operating System
Author:	Maurice J. Bach
Publisher:	Prentice Hall, 1986
ISBN:	0-13-201799-7
Appr. Price:	$65.00

This is one of the books that Linus used to design Linux. It is a description of the data structures used in the System V kernel. Many of the names of the important functions in the Linux source come from this book, and are named after the algorithms presented here. For instance, if you can't quite figure out what exactly getblk(), brelse(), bread(), breada(), and bwrite() are, chapter 3 explains very well.

While most of the algorithms are similar or the same, a few differences are worth noting:

- The Linux buffer cache is dynamically resized, so the algorithm for dealing with getting new buffers is a bit different. Therefore the above referenced explanation of getblk() is a little different than the getblk() in Linux.

- Linux does not currently use streams, and if/when streams are implemented for Linux, they are likely to have somewhat different semantics.

- The semantics and calling structure for device drivers is different. The concept is similar, and the chapter on device drivers is still worth reading, but for details on the device driver structures, the *The Linux Kernel Hackers' Guide* is the proper reference.

- The memory management algorithms are somewhat different.

There are other small differences as well, but a good understanding of this text will help you understand the Linux source.

Title:	Advanced Programming in the UNIX Environment
Author:	W. Richard Stevens
Publisher:	Addison Wesley, 1992
ISBN:	0-201-56317-7
Appr. Price:	$50.00

This excellent tome covers the stuff you *really* have to know to write *real* UN*X programs. It includes a discussion of the various standards for UN*X implementations, including POSIX, X/Open XPG3, and FIPS, and concentrates on two implementations, SVR4 and pre-release 4.4 BSD, which it refers to as 4.3+BSD. The book concentrates heavily on application and fairly complete specification, and notes which features relate to which standards and releases.

The chapters include: Unix Standardization and Implementations, File I/O, Files and Directories, Standard I/O Library, System Data Files and Information, The Environment of a Unix Process, Process Control, Process Relationships, Signals, Terminal I/O, Advanced I/O (non-blocking, streams, async, memory-mapped, etc.), Daemon Processes, Interprocess Communication, Advanced Interprocess Communication, and some example applications, including chapters on A Database Library, Communicating with a PostScript Printer, A Modem Dialer, and then a seemingly misplaced final chapter on Pseudo Terminals.

I have found that this book makes it possible for me to write usable programs for UN*X. It will help you achieve POSIX compliance in ways that won't break SVR4 or BSD, as a general rule. This book will save you ten times its cost in frustration.

Title:	Advanced 80386 Programming Techniques
Author:	James L. Turley
Publisher:	Osborne McGraw-Hill, 1988
ISBN:	0-07-881342-5
Appr. Price:	$22.95

This book covers the 80386 quite well, without touching on any other hardware. Some code samples are included. All major features are covered, as are many of the concepts needed. The chapters of this book are: Basics, Memory Segmentation, Privilege Levels, Paging, Multitasking, Communicating Among Tasks, Handling Faults and Interrupts, 80286 Emulation, 8086 Emulation, Debugging, The 80387 Numeric Processor Extension, Programming for Performance, Reset and Real Mode, Hardware, and a few appendices, including tables of the memory management structures as a handy reference.

The author has a good writing style: If you are technically minded, you will find yourself caught up just reading this book. One strong feature of this book for Linux is that the author is very careful not to explain how to do things under DOS, nor how to deal with particular hardware. In fact, the only times he mentions DOS and PC-compatible hardware are in the introduction, where he promises never to mention them again.

Title:	The C Programming Language, second edition
Author:	Brian W. Kernighan and Dennis M. Ritchie
Publisher:	Prentice Hall, 1988
ISBN:	0-13-110362-8 (paper) 0-13-110370-9 (hard)
Appr. Price:	$35.00

The C programming bible. Includes a C tutorial, UN⋆X interface reference, C reference, and standard library reference.

You program in C, you buy this book. It's that simple.

Title:	Operating Systems: Design and Implementation
Author:	Andrew S. Tanenbaum
Publisher:	Prentice Hall, 1987
ISBN:	0-13-637406-9
Appr. Price:	$50.00

This book, while a little simplistic in spots, and missing some important ideas, is a fairly clear exposition of what it takes to write an operating system. Half the book is taken up with the source code to a UN⋆X clone called Minix, which is based on a microkernel, unlike Linux, which sports a monolithic design. It has been said that Minix shows that it is possible to to write a microkernel-based UN⋆X, but does not adequately explain *why* one would do so.

Linux was originally intended to be a free Minix replacement:[1] In fact, it was originally to be binary-compatible with Minix-386. Minix-386 was the development environment under which Linux was bootstrapped. No Minix code is in Linux, but vestiges of this heritage live on in such things as the minix filesystem in Linux. Early in Linux's existence, Andrew Tanenbaum started a flame war with Linus about OS design, which was interesting, if not enlightening. . .

However, this book might still prove worthwhile for those who want a basic explanation of OS concepts, as Tanenbaum's explanations of the basic concepts remain some of the clearer (and more entertaining, if you like to be entertained) available. Unfortunately, basic is the key work here, as many things such as virtual memory are not covered at all.

Title:	Modern Operating Systems
Author:	Andrew S. Tanenbaum
Publisher:	Prentice Hall, 1992
ISBN:	0-13-588187-0
Appr. Price:	$51.75

The first half of this book is a rewrite of Tanenbaum's earlier *Operating Systems*, but this book covers several things that the earlier book missed, including such things as virtual memory.

---

[1]Linus' Minix, Linus tells us.

Minix is not included, but overviews of MS-DOS and several distributed systems are. This book is probably more useful to someone who wants to do something with his or her knowledge than Tanenbaum's earlier *Operating Systems: Design and Implementation.* Some clue as to the reason may be found in the title... However, what DOS is doing in a book on *modern* operating systems, many have failed to discover.

Title:	Operating Systems
Author:	William Stallings
Publisher:	Macmillan, 1992 (800-548-9939)
ISBN:	0-02-415481- 4
Appr. Price:	$??.??

A very thorough text on operating systems, this book gives more in-depth coverage of the topics covered in Tannebaum's books, and covers more topics, in a much brisker style. This book covers all the major topics that you would need to know to build an operating system, and does so in a clear way. The author uses examples from three major systems, comparing and contrasting them: UN⋆X, OS/2, and MVS. With each topic covered, these example systems are used to clarify the points and provide an example of an implementation.

Topics covered in *Operating Systems* include threads, real-time systems, multiprocessor scheduling, distributed systems, process migration, and security, as well as the standard topics like memory management and scheduling. The section on distributed processing appears to be up-to-date, and I found it very helpful.

Title:	UNIX Network Programming
Author:	W. Richard Stevens
Publisher:	Prentice Hall, 1990
ISBN:	0-13-949876-1
Appr. Price:	$48.75

This book covers several kinds of networking under UN⋆X, and provides very thorough references to the forms of networking that it does not cover directly. It covers TCP/IP and XNS most heavily, and fairly exhaustively describes how all the calls work. It also has a description and sample code using System V's TLI, and pretty complete coverage of System V IPC. This book contains a lot of source code examples to get you started, and many useful procedures. One example is code to provide usable semaphores, based on the partially broken implementation that System V provides.

Title:	Programming in the UNIX environment
Author:	Brian W. Kernighan and Robert Pike
Publisher:	Prentice Hall, 1984
ISBN:	0-13-937699 (hardcover) 0-13-937681-X (paperback)
Appr. Price:	$??.??

no abstract

Title:	Writing UNIX Device Drivers
Author:	George Pajari
Publisher:	Addison Wesley, 1992
ISBN:	0-201-52374-4
Appr. Price:	$32.95

This book is written by the President and founder of Driver Design Labs, a company which specializes in the development of UN⋆X device drivers. This book is an excellent introduction to the sometimes wacky world of device driver design. The four basic types of drivers (character, block, tty, STREAMS) are first discussed briefly. Many full examples of device drivers of all types are given, starting with the simplest and progressing in complexity. All examples are of drivers which deal with UN⋆X on PC-compatible hardware. **Chapters include:** Character Drivers I: A Test Data Generator Character Drivers II: An A/D Converter Character Drivers III: A Line Printer Block Drivers I: A Test Data Generator Block Drivers II: A RAM Disk Driver Block Drivers III: A SCSI Disk Driver Character Drivers IV: The Raw Disk Driver Terminal Drivers I: The COM1 Port Character Drivers V: A Tape Drive STREAMS Drivers I: A Loop-Back Driver STREAMS Drivers II: The COM1 Port (Revisited) Driver Installation Zen and the Art of Device Driver Writing

Although many of the calls used in the book are not Linux-compatible, the general idea is there, and many of the ideas map directly into Linux.

Title:	title
Author:	author
Publisher:	pub,yr
ISBN:	isbn
Appr. Price:	$??.??

no abstract

Appendix B

Tour of the Linux kernel source

[This is an alpha release of a chapter written by Alessandro Rubini, rubini@ipvvis.unipv.it. **I'm including it here as it gets worked on for comments.]**

This chapter tries to explain the Linux source code in an orderly manner, trying to help the reader to achieve a good understanding of how the source code is laid out and how the most relevant unix features are implemented. The target is to help the experienced C programmer who is not accustomed to Linux in getting familiar with the overall Linux design. That's why the chosen entry point for the kernel tour is the kernel own entry point: system boot.

A good understanding of C language is required to understand this material, as well as some familiarity with both UN★X concepts and the PC architecture. However, no C code will appear in this chapter, but rather pointers to the actual code. The finest issues of kernel design are explained in other chapters of this guide, while this chapter tends to remain an informal overview.

Any pathname for files referenced in this chapter is referred to the main source-tree directory, usually /usr/src/linux.

> Most of the information reported here is taken from the source code of Linux release 1.0. Nonetheless, references to later versions are provided at times. Any paragraph within the tour shaped like this one is meant to underline changes the kernel has undergone after the 1.0 release. If no such paragraph is present, then no changes occurred up to release 1.0.9 – 1.1.76.

> Sometimes a paragraph like this occurs in the text. It is a pointer to the right sources to get more information on the subject just covered. Needless to say, *the source* is the primary source.

B.1 Booting the system

When the PC is powered up, the 80x86 processor finds itself in real mode and executes the code at address 0xFFFF0, which corresponds to a ROM-BIOS address. The PC BIOS performs some tests on the system and initializes the interrupt vector at physical address 0. After that it loads the first sector of a bootable device to 0x7C00, and jumps to it. The device is usually the floppy or the hard drive. The preceding description is quite a simplified one, but it's all that's needed to understand the kernel initial workings.

The very first part of the Linux kernel is written in 8086 assembly language (boot/bootsect.S). When run, it moves itself to absolute address 0x90000, loads the next 2 kBytes of code from the boot device to address 0x90200, and the rest of the kernel to address 0x10000. The message "Loading..." is displayed during system load. Control is then passed to the code in `boot/Setup.S`, another real-mode assembly source.

The setup portion identifies some features of the host system and the type of vga board. If requested to, it asks the user to choose the video mode for the console. It then moves the whole system from address 0x10000 to address 0x1000, enters protected mode and jumps to the rest of the system (at 0x1000).

The next step is kernel decompression. The code at 0x1000 comes from `zBoot/head.S` which initializes registers and invokes `decompress_kernel()`, which in turn is made up of `zBoot/inflate.c`, `zBoot/unzip.c` and `zBoot/misc.c`. The decompressed data goes to address 0x100000 (1 Meg), and this is the main reason why Linux can't run with less than 2 megs ram.

Encapsulation of the kernel in a gzip file is accomplished by `Makefile` and utilities in the `zBoot` directory. They are interesting files to look at.

Kernel release 1.1.75 moved the `boot` and `zBoot` directories down to `arch/i386/boot`. This change is meant to allow true kernel builds for different architectures. Nonetheless, I'll stick to i386-specific information.

Decompressed code is executed at address 0x1010000 [**Maybe I've lost track of physical addresses, here, as I don't know very well gas source code**], where all the 32-bit setup is accomplished: IDT, GDT and LDT are loaded, the processor and coprocessor are identified, and paging is setup; eventually, the routine `start_kernel` is invoked. The source for the above operations is in `boot/head.S`. It is probably the trickiest code in the whole kernel.

Note that if an error occurs during any of the preceding steps, the computer will lockup. The OS can't deal with errors when it isn't yet fully operative.

`start_kernel()` resides in `init/main.c`, and never returns. Anything from now on is coded in C language, left aside interrupt management and system call enter/leave (well, most of the macros embed assembly code, too).

B.2 Spinning the wheel

After dealing with all the tricky questions, `start_kernel()` initializes all the parts of the kernel, specifically:

- Sets the memory bounds and calls `paging_init()`.

- Initializes the traps, IRQ channels and scheduling.

- Parses the command line.

- If requested to, allocates a profiling buffer.

- Initializes all the device drivers and disk buffering, as well as other minor parts.

- Calibrates the delay loop (computes the "BogoMips" number).

- Checks if interrupt 16 works with the coprocessor.

Finally, the kernel is ready to `move_to_user_mode()`, in order to fork the `init` process, whose code is in the same source file. Process number 0 then, the so-called idle task, keeps running in an infinite idle loop.

The `init` process tries to execute `/etc/init`, or `/bin/init`, or `/sbin/init`.

If none of them succeeds, code is provided to execute "/bin/sh /etc/rc" and fork a root shell on the first terminal. This code dates back to Linux 0.01, when the OS was made by the kernel alone, and no login process was available.

After exec()ing the init program from one of the standard places (let's assume we have one of them), the kernel has no direct control on the program flow. Its role, from now on is to provide processes with system calls, as well as servicing asynchronous events (such as hardware interrupts). Multitasking has been setup, and it is now init who manages multiuser access by fork()ing system daemons and login processes.

Being the kernel in charge of providing services, the tour will proceed by looking at those services (the "system calls"), as well as by providing general ideas about the underlying data structures and code organization.

B.3   How the kernel sees a process

From the kernel point of view, a process is an entry in the process table. Nothing more.

The process table, then, is one of the most important data structures within the system, together with the memory- management tables and the buffer cache. The individual item in the process table is the task_struct structure, quite a huge one, defined in include/linux/sched.h. Within the task_struct both low-level and high-level information is kept— ranging from the copy of some hardware registers to the inode of the working directory for the process.

The process table is both an array and a double-linked list, as well as a tree. The physical implementation is a static array of pointers, whose length is NR_TASKS, a constant defined in include/linux/tasks.h, and each structure resides in a reserved memory page. The list structure is achieved through the pointers next_task and prev_task, while the tree structure is quite complex and will not be described here. You may wish to change NR_TASKS from the default value of 128, but be sure to have proper dependency files to force recompilation of all the source files involved.

After booting is over, the kernel is always working on behalf of one of the processes, and the global variable current, a pointer to a task_struct item, is used to record the running one. current is only changed by the scheduler, in kernel/sched.c. When, however, all processes must be looked at, the macro for_each_task is used. It is considerably faster than a sequential scan of the array, when the system is lightly loaded.

A process is always running in either "user mode" or "kernel mode". The main body of a user program is executed in user mode and system calls are executed in kernel mode. The stack used by the process in the two execution modes is different—a conventional stack segment is used for user mode, while a fixed-size stack (one page, owned by the process) is used in kernel mode. The kernel stack page is never swapped out, because it must be available whenever a system call is entered.

System calls, within the kernel, exist as C language functions, their 'official' name being prefixed by 'sys_'. A system call named, for example, *burnout* invokes the kernel function sys_*burnout*().

The system call mechanism is described in chapter 3 of this guide. Looking at for_each_task and SET_LINKS, in include/linux/sched.h can help understanding the list and tree structures in the process table.

B.4 Creating and destroying processes

A unix system creates a process though the `fork()` system call, and process termination is performed either by `exit()` or by receiving a signal. The Linux implementation for them resides in `kernel/fork.c` and `kernel/exit.c`.

Forking is easy, and `fork.c` is short and ready understandable. Its main task is filling the data structure for the new process. Relevant steps, apart from filling fields, are

- getting a free page to hold the `task_struct`

- finding an empty process slot (`find_empty_process()`)

- getting another free page for the `kernel_stack_page`

- copying the father's LDT to the child

- duplicating `mmap` information of the father

`sys_fork()` also manages file descriptors and inodes.

> The 1.0 kernel offers some vestigial support to threading, and the `fork()` system call shows some hints to that. Kernel threads is work-in-progress outside the mainstream kernel.

Exiting from a process is trickier, because the parent process must be notified about any child who exits. Moreover, a process can exit by being `kill()`ed by another process (these are UN★X features). The file `exit.c` is therefore the home of `sys_kill()` and the various flavors of `sys_wait()`, in addition to `sys_exit()`.

The code belonging to `exit.c` is not described here—it is not that interesting. It deals with a lot of details in order to leave the system in a consistent state. The POSIX standard, then, is quite demanding about signals, and it must be dealt with.

B.5 Executing programs

After `fork()`ing, two copies of the same program are running. One of them usually `exec()`s another program. The `exec()` system call must locate the binary image of the executable file, load and run it. The word 'load' doesn't necessarily mean "copy in memory the binary image", as Linux supports demand loading.

The Linux implementation of `exec()` supports different binary formats. This is accomplished through the `linux_binfmt` structure, which embeds two pointers to functions—one to load the executable and the other to load the library, each binary format representing both the executable and the library. Loading of shared libraries is implemented in the same source file as `exec()` is, but let's stick to `exec()` itself.

The UN★X systems provide the programmer with six flavors of the `exec()` function. All but one of them can be implemented as library functions, and the Linux kernel implements `sys_execve()` alone. It performs quite a simple task: loading the head of the executable, and trying to execute it. If the first two bytes are "`#!`", then the first line is parsed and an interpreter is invoked, otherwise the registered binary formats are sequentially tried.

The native Linux format is supported directly within `fs/exec.c`, and the relevant functions are `load_aout_binary` and `load_aout_library`. As for the binaries, the function loading an *a.out* executable ends up either in `mmap()`ing the disk file, or in calling `read_exec()`. The former way uses the

Linux demand loading mechanism to fault-in program pages when they're accessed, while the latter way is used when memory mapping is not supported by the host filesystem (for example the "msdos" filesystem).

> Late 1.1 kernels embed a revised msdos filesystem, which supports mmap(). Moreover, the struct linux_binfmt is a linked list rather than an array, to allow loading a new binary format as a kernel module. Finally, the structure itself has been extended to access format-related core-dump routines.

B.6   Accessing filesystems

It is well known that the filesystem is the most basic resource in a UN*X system, so basic and ubiquitous that it needs a more handy name — I'll stick to the standard practice of calling it simply "fs".

I'll assume the reader already knows the basic UN*X fs ideas — access permissions, inodes, the superblock, mounting and umounting. Those concepts are well explained by smarter authors than me within the standard UN*X literature, so I won't duplicate their efforts and I'll stick to Linux specific issues.

While the first Unices used to support a single fs type, whose structure was widespread in the whole kernel, today's practice is to use a standardized interface between the kernel and the fs, in order to ease data interchange across architectures. Linux itself provides a standardized layer to pass information between the kernel and each fs module. This interface layer is called VFS, for "virtual filesystem".

Filesystem code is therefore split into two layers: the upper layer is concerned with the management of kernel tables and data structures, while the lower layer is made up of the set of fs-dependent functions, and is invoked through the VFS data structures.

All the fs-independent material resides in the fs/*.c files. They address the following issues:

- Managing the buffer cache (buffer.c);

- Responding to the fcntl() and ioctl() system calls (fcntl.c and ioctl.c);

- Mapping pipes and FIFOs on inodes and buffers (fifo.c, pipe.c);

- Managing file- and inode-tables (file_table.c, inode.c);

- Locking and unlocking files and records (locks.c);

- Mapping names to inodes (namei.c, open.c);

- Implementing the tricky select() function (select.c);

- Providing information (stat.c);

- mounting and umounting filesystems (super.c);

- exec()ing executables and dumping cores (exec.c);

- Loading the various binary formats (bin_fmt*.c, as outlined above).

The VFS interface, then, consists of a set of relatively high-level operations which are invoked from the fs-independent code and are actually performed by each filesystem type. The most relevant structures are inode_operations and file_operations, though they're not alone: other structures exist as well. All of them are defined within include/linux/fs.h.

The kernel entry point to the actual file system is the structure file_system_type. An array of file_system_types is embodied within fs/filesystems.c and it is referenced whenever a mount is issued. The function `read_super` for the relevant fs type is then in charge of filling a `struct super_block` item, which in turn embeds a `struct super_operations` and a `struct *type*_sb_info`. The former provides pointers to generic fs operations for the current fs-type, the latter embeds specific information for the fs-type.

> The array of filesystem types has been turned in a linked list, to allow loading new fs types as kernel modules. The function (un-)`register_filesystem` is coded within `fs/super.c`.

B.7   Quick Anatomy of a Filesystem Type

The role of a filesystem type is to perform the low-level tasks used to map the relatively high level VFS operations on the physical media (disks, network or whatever). The VFS interface is flexible enough to allow support for both conventional UN*X filesystems and exotic situations such as the `msdos` and `umsdos` types.

Each fs-type is made up of the following items, in addition to its own directory:

- An entry in the `file_systems[]` array (`fs/filesystems.c`);

- The superblock include file (`include/linux/`*type*`_fs_sb.h`);

- The inode include file (`include/linux/`*type*`_fs_i.h`);

- The generic own include file (`include/linux/`*type*`_fs.h`);

- Two `#include` lines within `include/linux/fs.h`, as well as the entries in `struct super_block` and `struct inode`.

The own directory for the fs type contains all the real code, responsible of inode and data management.

> The chapter about `procfs` in this guide uncovers all the details about low-level code and VFS interface for that fs type. Source code in `fs/procfs` is quite understandable after reading the chapter.

We'll now look at the internal workings of the VFS mechanism, and the `Minix` filesystem source is used as a working example. I chose the `Minix` type because it is small but complete; moreover, any other fs type in Linux derives from the `Minix` one. The `ext2` type, the de-facto standard in recent Linux installations, is much more complex than that and its exploration is left as an exercise for the smart reader.

When a minix-fs is mounted, `minix_read_super` fills the `super_block` structure with data read from the mounted device. The `s_op` field of the structure will then hold a pointer to `minix_sops`, which is used by the generic filesystem code to dispatch superblock operations.

Chaining the newly mounted fs in the global system tree relies on the following data items (assuming sb is the `super_block` structure and `dir_i` points to the inode for the mount point):

- `sb->s_mounted` points to the root-dir inode of the mounted filesystem (`MINIX_ROOT_INO`);

- `dir_i->i_mount` holds `sb->s_mounted`;

- `sb->s_covered` holds `dir_i`

Unmounting will eventually be performed by `do_umount`, which in turn invokes `minix_put_super`.

Whenever a file is accessed, `minix_read_inode` comes into play; it fills the system-wide `inode` structure with fields coming form `minix_inode`. The `inode->i_op` field is filled according to `inode->i_mode` and it is responsible for any further operation on the file. The source for the Minix functions just described are to be found in `fs/minix/inode.c`.

The `inode_operations` structure is used to dispatch inode operations (you guessed it) to the fs-type specific kernel functions; the first entry in the structure is a pointer to a `file_operations` item, which is the data-management equivalent of `i_op`. The Minix fs-type allows three instances of inode-operation sets (for directories, for files and for symbolic links) and two instances of file-operation sets (symlinks don't need one).

Directory operations (`minix_readdir` alone) are to be found in `fs/minix/dir.c`; file operations (read and write) appear within `fs/minix/file.c` and symlink operations (reading and following the link) in `fs/minix/symlink.c`.

The rest of the minix directory implements the following tasks:

- `bitmap.c` manages allocation and freeing of inodes and blocks (the `ext2` fs, otherwise, has two different source files);

- `fsynk.c` is responsible for the `fsync()` system calls — it manages direct, indirect and double indirect blocks (I assume you know about them, it's common UN*X knowledge);

- `namei.c` embeds all the name-related inode operations, such as creating and destroying nodes, renaming and linking;

- `truncate.c` performs truncation of files.

B.8   The console driver

Being the main I/O device on most Linux boxes, the console driver deserves some attention. The source code related to the console, as well as the other character drivers, is to be found in `drivers/char`, and we'll use this very directory as our reference point when naming files.

Console initialization is performed by the function `tty_init()`, in `tty_io.c`. This function is only concerned in getting major device numbers and calling the init function for each device set. `con_init()`, then is the one related to the console, and resides in `console.c`.

> Initialization of the console has changed quite a lot during 1.1 evolution. `console_init()` has been detached from `tty_init()`, and is called directly by `../../main.c`. The virtual consoles are now dynamically allocated, and quite a good deal of code has changed. So, I'll skip the details of initialization, allocation and such.

B.8.1   How file operations are dispatched to the console

This paragraph is quite low-level, and can be happily skipped over.

Needless to say, a UN*X device is accessed though the filesystem. This paragraph details all steps from the device file to the actual console functions. Moreover, the following information is extracted from the 1.1.73 source code, and it may be slightly different from the 1.0 source.

When a device inode is opened, the function `chrdev_open()` (or `blkdev_open()`, but we'll stick to character devices) in `../../fs/devices.c` gets executed. This function is reached by means of the structure `def_chr_fops`, which in turn is referenced by `chrdev_inode_operations`, used by all the filesystem types (see the previous section about filesystems).

chrdev_open takes care of specifying the device operations by substituting the device specific file_operations table in the current filp and calls the specific open(). Device specific tables are kept in the array chrdevs[], indexed by the major device number, and filled by the same ../../fs/devices.c.

If the device is a tty one (aren't we aiming at the console?), we come to the tty drivers, whose functions are in tty_io.c, indexed by tty_fops. Thus, tty_open() calls init_dev(), which allocates any data structure needed by the device, based on the minor device number.

The minor number is also used to retrieve the actual driver for the device, which has been registered through tty_register_driver(). The driver, then, is still another structure used to dispatch computation, just like file_ops; it is concerned with writing and controlling the device. The last data structure used in managing a tty is the line discipline, described later. The line discipline for the console (and any other tty device) is set by initialize_tty_struct(), invoked by init_dev.

Everything we touched in this paragraph is device-independent. The only console-specific particular is that console.c, has registered its own driver during con_init(). The line discipline, on the contrary, in independent of the device.

> The tty_driver structure is fully explained within. <linux/tty_driver.h>
>
> The above information has been extracted from 1.1.73 source code. It isn't unlikely for your kernel to be somewhat different ("This information is subject to change without notice").

B.8.2   Writing to the console

When a console device is written to, the function con_write gets invoked. This function manages all the control characters and escape sequences used to provide applications with complete screen management. The escape sequences implemented are those of the vt102 terminal. This means that your environment should say TERM=vt102 when you are telnetting to a non-Linux host; the best choice for local activities, however, is TERM=console because the Linux console offers a superset of vt102 functionality.

con_write(), thus, is mostly made up of nested switch statements, used to handle a finite state automaton interpreting escape sequences one character at a time. When in normal mode, the character being printed is written directly to the video memory, using the current attr-ibute. Within console.c, all the fields of struct vc are made accessible through macros, so any reference to (for example) attr, does actually refer to the field in the structure vc_cons[currcons], as long as currcons is the number of the console being referred to.

> Actually, vc_cons in newer kernels is no longer an array of structures , it now is an array of pointers whose contents are kmalloc()ed. The use of macros greatly simplified changing the approach, because much of the code didn't need to be rewritten.

Actual mapping and unmapping of the console memory to screen is performed by the functions set_scrmem() (which copies data from the console buffer to video memory) and get_scrmem (which copies back data to the console buffer). The private buffer of the current console is physically mapped on the actual video RAM, in order to minimize the number of data transfers. This means that get- and set--scrmem() are static to console.c and are called only during a console switch.

B.8.3   Reading the console

Reading the console is accomplished through the line-discipline. The default (and unique) line discipline in Linux is called tty_ldisc_N_TTY. The line discipline is what "disciplines input through a line". It is another function table (we're used to the approach, aren't we?), which is concerned with reading the device. With the help of `termios` flags, the line discipline is what controls input from the tty: raw, cbreak and cooked mode; `select()`; `ioctl()` and so on.

The read function in the line discipline is called `read_chan()`, which reads the tty buffer independently of whence it came from. The reason is that character arrival through a tty is managed by asynchronous hardware interrupts.

> The line discipline `N_TTY` is to be found in the same `tty_io.c`, though
> later kernels use a different `n_tty.c` source file.

The lowest level of console input is part of keyboard management, and thus it is handled within `keyboard.c`, in the function `keyboard_interrupt()`.

B.8.4   Keyboard management

Keyboard management is quite a nightmare. It is confined to the file `keyboard.c`, which is full of hexadecimal numbers to represent the various key codes appearing in keyboards of different manufacturers.

> I won't dig in keyboard.c, because no relevant information is there to the kernel hacker.

> For those readers who are really interested in the Linux keyboard, the
> best approach to `keyboard.c` is from the last line upward. Lowest level
> details occur mainly in the first half of the file.

B.8.5   Switching the current console

The current console is switched through invocation of the function `change_console()`, which resides in `tty_io.c` and is invoked by both `keyboard.c` and `vt.c` (the former switches console in response to key presses, the latter when a program requests it by invoking an `ioctl()` call).

The actual switching process is performed in two steps, and the function `complete_change_console()` takes care of the second part of it. Splitting the switch is meant to complete the task after a possible handshake with the process controlling the tty we're leaving. If the console is not under process control, `change_console()` calls `complete_change_console()` by itself. Process intervention is needed to successfully switch from a graphic console to a text one and vice-versa, and the X server (for example) is the controlling process of its own graphic console.

B.8.6   The selection mechanism

"`selection`" is the cut and paste facility for the Linux text consoles. The mechanism is mainly handled by a user-level process, which can be instantiated by either `selection` or `gpm`. The user-level program uses `ioctl()` on the console to tell the kernel to highlight a region of the screen. The selected text, then, is copied to a selection buffer. The buffer is a static entity in `console.c`. Pasting text is accomplished by 'manually' pushing characters in the tty input queue. The whole selection mechanism is protected by `#ifdef` so users can disable it during kernel configuration to save a few kilobytes of RAM.

Selection is a very-low-level facility, and its workings are hidden from any other kernel activity. This means that most `#ifdef`'s simply deals with removing the highlight before the screen is modified in any way.

Newer kernels feature improved code for selection, and the mouse pointer can be highlighted independently of the selected text (1.1.32 and later). Moreover, from 1.1.73 onward a dynamic buffer is used for selected text rather than a static one, making the kernel 4kB smaller.

B.8.7 `ioctl()`ling the device

The `ioctl()` system call is the entry point for user processes to control the behavior of device files. Ioctl management is spawned by `../../fs/ioctl.c`, where the real `sys_ioctl()` resides. The standard `ioctl` requests are performed right there, other file-related requests are processed by `file_ioctl()` (same source file), while any other request is dispatches to the device-specific `ioctl()` function.

The `ioctl` material for console devices resides in `vt.c`, because the console driver dispatches ioctl requests to `vt_ioctl()`.

The information above refer to 1.1.7x. The 1.0 kernel doesn't have the "driver" table, and `vt_ioctl()` is pointed to directly by the `file_operations()` table.

Ioctl material is quite confused, indeed. Some requests are related to the device, and some are related to the line discipline. I'll try to summarize things for the 1.0 and the 1.1.7x kernels and anything that happened in between.

The 1.1.7x series features the following approach: `tty_ioctl.c` implements only line discipline requests (namely `n_tty_ioctl()`, which is the only n_tty function outside of `n_tty.c`), while the `file_operations` field points to `tty_ioctl()` in `tty_io.c`. If the request number is not resolved by `tty_ioctl()`, it is passed along to `tty->driver.ioctl` or, if it fails, to `tty->ldisc.ioctl`. Driver-related stuff for the console it to be found in `vt.c`, while line discipline material is in `tty_ioctl.c`.

In the 1.0 kernel, `tty_ioctl()` is in `tty_ioctl.c` and is pointed to by generic tty `file_operations`. Unresolved requests are passed along to the specific ioctl function or to the line-discipline code, in a way similar to 1.1.7x.

Note that in both cases, the `TIOCLINUX` request is in the device-independent code. This implies that the console selection can be set by `ioctl`ling any tty (`set_selection()` always operates on the foreground console), and this is a security hole. It is also a good reason to switch to a newer kernel, where the problem is fixed by only allowing the superuser to handle the selection.

A variety of requests can be issued to the console device, and the best way to know about them is to browse the source file `vt.c`.

Appendix C

The GNU General Public License

Printed below is the GNU General Public License (the *GPL* or *copyleft*), under which Linux is licensed. It is reproduced here to clear up some of the confusion about Linux's copyright status — Linux is *not* shareware, and it is *not* in the public domain. The bulk of the Linux kernel is copyright © 1993 by Linus Torvalds, and other software and parts of the kernel are copyrighted by their authors. Thus, Linux *is* copyrighted, however, you may redistribute it under the terms of the GPL printed below.

GNU GENERAL PUBLIC LICENSE
Version 2, June 1991

Copyright (C) 1989, 1991 Free Software Foundation, Inc. 675 Mass Ave, Cambridge, MA 02139, USA. Everyone is permitted to copy and distribute verbatim copies of this license document, but changing it is not allowed.

C.1 Preamble

The licenses for most software are designed to take away your freedom to share and change it. By contrast, the GNU General Public License is intended to guarantee your freedom to share and change free software– to make sure the software is free for all its users. This General Public License applies to most of the Free Software Foundation's software and to any other program whose authors commit to using it. (Some other Free Software Foundation software is covered by the GNU Library General Public License instead.) You can apply it to your programs, too.

When we speak of free software, we are referring to freedom, not price. Our General Public Licenses are designed to make sure that you have the freedom to distribute copies of free software (and charge for this service if you wish), that you receive source code or can get it if you want it, that you can change the software or use pieces of it in new free programs; and that you know you can do these things.

To protect your rights, we need to make restrictions that forbid anyone to deny you these rights or to ask you to surrender the rights. These restrictions translate to certain responsibilities for you if you distribute copies of the software, or if you modify it.

For example, if you distribute copies of such a program, whether gratis or for a fee, you must give the recipients all the rights that you have. You must make sure that they, too, receive or can get the source code. And you must show them these terms so they know their rights.

We protect your rights with two steps: (1) copyright the software, and (2) offer you this license which gives you legal permission to copy, distribute and/or modify the software.

Also, for each author's protection and ours, we want to make certain that everyone understands that there is no warranty for this free software. If the software is modified by someone else and passed on, we want its recipients to know that what they have is not the original, so that any problems introduced by others will not reflect on the original authors' reputations.

Finally, any free program is threatened constantly by software patents. We wish to avoid the danger that redistributors of a free program will individually obtain patent licenses, in effect making the program proprietary. To prevent this, we have made it clear that any patent must be licensed for everyone's free use or not licensed at all.

The precise terms and conditions for copying, distribution and modification follow.

C.2   Terms and Conditions for Copying, Distribution, and Modification

0. This License applies to any program or other work which contains a notice placed by the copyright holder saying it may be distributed under the terms of this General Public License. The "Program", below, refers to any such program or work, and a "work based on the Program" means either the Program or any derivative work under copyright law: that is to say, a work containing the Program or a portion of it, either verbatim or with modifications and/or translated into another language. (Hereinafter, translation is included without limitation in the term "modification".) Each licensee is addressed as "you".

   Activities other than copying, distribution and modification are not covered by this License; they are outside its scope. The act of running the Program is not restricted, and the output from the Program is covered only if its contents constitute a work based on the Program (independent of having been made by running the Program). Whether that is true depends on what the Program does.

1. You may copy and distribute verbatim copies of the Program's source code as you receive it, in any medium, provided that you conspicuously and appropriately publish on each copy an appropriate copyright notice and disclaimer of warranty; keep intact all the notices that refer to this License and to the absence of any warranty; and give any other recipients of the Program a copy of this License along with the Program.

   You may charge a fee for the physical act of transferring a copy, and you may at your option offer warranty protection in exchange for a fee.

2. You may modify your copy or copies of the Program or any portion of it, thus forming a work based on the Program, and copy and distribute such modifications or work under the terms of Section 1 above, provided that you also meet all of these conditions:

   a. You must cause the modified files to carry prominent notices stating that you changed the files and the date of any change.

   b. You must cause any work that you distribute or publish, that in whole or in part contains or is derived from the Program or any part thereof, to be licensed as a whole at no charge to all third parties under the terms of this License.

   c. If the modified program normally reads commands interactively when run, you must cause it, when started running for such interactive use in the most ordinary way, to print or display an announcement including an appropriate copyright notice and a notice that there is no warranty (or else, saying that you provide a warranty) and that users may redistribute the program under these conditions, and telling the user how to view a copy of this License. (Exception: if the Program itself is interactive but does not normally print such an announcement, your work based on the Program is not required to print an announcement.)

These requirements apply to the modified work as a whole. If identifiable sections of that work are not derived from the Program, and can be reasonably considered independent and separate works in themselves, then this License, and its terms, do not apply to those sections when you distribute them as separate works. But when you distribute the same sections as part of a whole which is a work based on the Program, the distribution of the whole must be on the terms of this License, whose permissions for other licensees extend to the entire whole, and thus to each and every part regardless of who wrote it.

Thus, it is not the intent of this section to claim rights or contest your rights to work written entirely by you; rather, the intent is to exercise the right to control the distribution of derivative or collective works based on the Program.

In addition, mere aggregation of another work not based on the Program with the Program (or with a work based on the Program) on a volume of a storage or distribution medium does not bring the other work under the scope of this License.

3. You may copy and distribute the Program (or a work based on it, under Section 2) in object code or executable form under the terms of Sections 1 and 2 above provided that you also do one of the following:

   a. Accompany it with the complete corresponding machine-readable source code, which must be distributed under the terms of Sections 1 and 2 above on a medium customarily used for software interchange; or,

   b. Accompany it with a written offer, valid for at least three years, to give any third party, for a charge no more than your cost of physically performing source distribution, a complete machine-readable copy of the corresponding source code, to be distributed under the terms of Sections 1 and 2 above on a medium customarily used for software interchange; or,

   c. Accompany it with the information you received as to the offer to distribute corresponding source code. (This alternative is allowed only for noncommercial distribution and only if you received the program in object code or executable form with such an offer, in accord with Subsection b above.)

The source code for a work means the preferred form of the work for making modifications to it. For an executable work, complete source code means all the source code for all modules it contains, plus any associated interface definition files, plus the scripts used to control compilation and installation of the executable. However, as a special exception, the source code distributed need not include anything that is normally distributed (in either source or binary form) with the major components (compiler, kernel, and so on) of the operating system on which the executable runs, unless that component itself accompanies the executable.

If distribution of executable or object code is made by offering access to copy from a designated place, then offering equivalent access to copy the source code from the same place counts as distribution of the source code, even though third parties are not compelled to copy the source along with the object code.

4. You may not copy, modify, sublicense, or distribute the Program except as expressly provided under this License. Any attempt otherwise to copy, modify, sublicense or distribute the Program is void, and will automatically terminate your rights under this License. However, parties who have received copies, or rights, from you under this License will not have their licenses terminated so long as such parties remain in full compliance.

5. You are not required to accept this License, since you have not signed it. However, nothing else grants you permission to modify or distribute the Program or its derivative works. These actions

are prohibited by law if you do not accept this License. Therefore, by modifying or distributing the Program (or any work based on the Program), you indicate your acceptance of this License to do so, and all its terms and conditions for copying, distributing or modifying the Program or works based on it.

6. Each time you redistribute the Program (or any work based on the Program), the recipient automatically receives a license from the original licensor to copy, distribute or modify the Program subject to these terms and conditions. You may not impose any further restrictions on the recipients' exercise of the rights granted herein. You are not responsible for enforcing compliance by third parties to this License.

7. If, as a consequence of a court judgment or allegation of patent infringement or for any other reason (not limited to patent issues), conditions are imposed on you (whether by court order, agreement or otherwise) that contradict the conditions of this License, they do not excuse you from the conditions of this License. If you cannot distribute so as to satisfy simultaneously your obligations under this License and any other pertinent obligations, then as a consequence you may not distribute the Program at all. For example, if a patent license would not permit royalty-free redistribution of the Program by all those who receive copies directly or indirectly through you, then the only way you could satisfy both it and this License would be to refrain entirely from distribution of the Program.

If any portion of this section is held invalid or unenforceable under any particular circumstance, the balance of the section is intended to apply and the section as a whole is intended to apply in other circumstances.

It is not the purpose of this section to induce you to infringe any patents or other property right claims or to contest validity of any such claims; this section has the sole purpose of protecting the integrity of the free software distribution system, which is implemented by public license practices. Many people have made generous contributions to the wide range of software distributed through that system in reliance on consistent application of that system; it is up to the author/donor to decide if he or she is willing to distribute software through any other system and a licensee cannot impose that choice.

This section is intended to make thoroughly clear what is believed to be a consequence of the rest of this License.

8. If the distribution and/or use of the Program is restricted in certain countries either by patents or by copyrighted interfaces, the original copyright holder who places the Program under this License may add an explicit geographical distribution limitation excluding those countries, so that distribution is permitted only in or among countries not thus excluded. In such case, this License incorporates the limitation as if written in the body of this License.

9. The Free Software Foundation may publish revised and/or new versions of the General Public License from time to time. Such new versions will be similar in spirit to the present version, but may differ in detail to address new problems or concerns.

Each version is given a distinguishing version number. If the Program specifies a version number of this License which applies to it and "any later version", you have the option of following the terms and conditions either of that version or of any later version published by the Free Software Foundation. If the Program does not specify a version number of this License, you may choose any version ever published by the Free Software Foundation.

10. If you wish to incorporate parts of the Program into other free programs whose distribution conditions are different, write to the author to ask for permission. For software which is copyrighted by the Free Software Foundation, write to the Free Software Foundation; we sometimes make exceptions for this. Our decision will be guided by the two goals of preserving the free status of all derivatives of our free software and of promoting the sharing and reuse of software generally.

NO WARRANTY

11. BECAUSE THE PROGRAM IS LICENSED FREE OF CHARGE, THERE IS NO WARRANTY FOR THE PROGRAM, TO THE EXTENT PERMITTED BY APPLICABLE LAW. EXCEPT WHEN OTHERWISE STATED IN WRITING THE COPYRIGHT HOLDERS AND/OR OTHER PARTIES PROVIDE THE PROGRAM "AS IS" WITHOUT WARRANTY OF ANY KIND, EITHER EXPRESSED OR IMPLIED, INCLUDING, BUT NOT LIMITED TO, THE IMPLIED WARRANTIES OF MERCHANTABILITY AND FITNESS FOR A PARTICULAR PURPOSE. THE ENTIRE RISK AS TO THE QUALITY AND PERFOR-MANCE OF THE PROGRAM IS WITH YOU. SHOULD THE PROGRAM PROVE DEFECTIVE, YOU ASSUME THE COST OF ALL NECESSARY SERVICING, REPAIR OR CORRECTION.

12. IN NO EVENT UNLESS REQUIRED BY APPLICABLE LAW OR AGREED TO IN WRITING WILL ANY COPYRIGHT HOLDER, OR ANY OTHER PARTY WHO MAY MODIFY AND/OR REDIS-TRIBUTE THE PROGRAM AS PERMITTED ABOVE, BE LIABLE TO YOU FOR DAMAGES, IN-CLUDING ANY GENERAL, SPECIAL, INCIDENTAL OR CONSEQUENTIAL DAMAGES ARISING OUT OF THE USE OR INABILITY TO USE THE PROGRAM (INCLUDING BUT NOT LIMITED TO LOSS OF DATA OR DATA BEING RENDERED INACCURATE OR LOSSES SUSTAINED BY YOU OR THIRD PARTIES OR A FAILURE OF THE PROGRAM TO OPERATE WITH ANY OTHER PRO-GRAMS), EVEN IF SUCH HOLDER OR OTHER PARTY HAS BEEN ADVISED OF THE POSSIBILITY OF SUCH DAMAGES.

END OF TERMS AND CONDITIONS

C.3   Appendix: How to Apply These Terms to Your New Programs

If you develop a new program, and you want it to be of the greatest possible use to the public, the best way to achieve this is to make it free software which everyone can redistribute and change under these terms.

To do so, attach the following notices to the program. It is safest to attach them to the start of each source file to most effectively convey the exclusion of warranty; and each file should have at least the "copyright" line and a pointer to where the full notice is found.

⟨one line to give the program's name and a brief idea of what it does.⟩ Copyright © 19yy ⟨name of author⟩

This program is free software; you can redistribute it and/or modify it under the terms of the GNU General Public License as published by the Free Software Foundation; either version 2 of the License, or (at your option) any later version.

This program is distributed in the hope that it will be useful, but WITHOUT ANY WARRANTY; without even the implied warranty of MERCHANTABILITY or FITNESS FOR A PARTICULAR PURPOSE. See the GNU General Public License for more details.

You should have received a copy of the GNU General Public License along with this program; if not, write to the Free Software Foundation, Inc., 675 Mass Ave, Cambridge, MA 02139, USA.

Also add information on how to contact you by electronic and paper mail.

If the program is interactive, make it output a short notice like this when it starts in an interactive mode:

```
Gnomovision version 69, Copyright (C) 19yy name of author Gnomovision comes
with ABSOLUTELY NO WARRANTY; for details type 'show w'.  This is free
software, and you are welcome to redistribute it under certain conditions;
type 'show c' for details.
```

The hypothetical commands 'show w' and 'show c' should show the appropriate parts of the General Public License. Of course, the commands you use may be called something other than 'show w' and 'show c'; they could even be mouse-clicks or menu items — whatever suits your program.

You should also get your employer (if you work as a programmer) or your school, if any, to sign a "copyright disclaimer" for the program, if necessary. Here is a sample; alter the names:

Yoyodyne, Inc., hereby disclaims all copyright interest in the program 'Gnomovision' (which makes passes at compilers) written by James Hacker.

⟨signature of Ty Coon⟩, 1 April 1989 Ty Coon, President of Vice

This General Public License does not permit incorporating your program into proprietary programs. If your program is a subroutine library, you may consider it more useful to permit linking proprietary applications with the library. If this is what you want to do, use the GNU Library General Public License instead of this License.

Part III

The Linux Network Administrators' Guide

For Britta

Contents

List of Figures

Preface

With the Internet much of a buzzword recently, and otherwise serious people joyriding along the "Informational Superhighway," computer networking seems to be moving toward the status of TV sets and microwave ovens. The Internet is recently getting an unusually high media coverage, and social science majors are descending on Usenet newsgroups to conduct researches on the "Internet Culture." Carrier companies are working to introduce new transmission techniques like ATM that offer many times the bandwidth the average network link of today has.

Of course, networking has been around for a long time. Connecting computers to form local area networks has been common practice even at small installations, and so have been long-haul links using public telephone lines. A rapidly growing conglomerate of world-wide networks has, however, made joining the global village a viable option even for small non-profit organizations of private computer users. Setting up an Internet host with mail and news capabilities offering dial-up access has become affordable, and the advent of ISDN will doubtlessly accelerate this trend.

Talking of computer networks quite frequently means talking about UNIX. Of course, UNIX is neither the only operating system with network capabilities, nor will it remain a front-runner forever, but it has been in the networking business for a long time, and will surely continue to do so for some time to come.

What makes it particularly interesting to private users is that there has been much activity to bring free UNIXoid operating systems to the PC, being 386BSD, FreeBSD — and Linux. However, Linux is *not* UNIX. That is a registered trademark of whoever currently holds the rights to it (Univel, while I'm typing this), while Linux is an operating system that strives to offer all functionality the POSIX standards require for UNIX-like operating systems, but is a complete reimplementation.

The Linux kernel was written largely by Linus Torvalds, who started it as a project to get to know the Intel i386, and to "make MINIX better." MINIX was then another popular PC operating system offering vital ingredients of UNIX functionality, and was written by Prof. Andrew S. Tanenbaum.

Linux is covered by the GNU General Public License (GPL), which allows free distribution of the code (please read the GPL in appendix C for a definition of what "free software" means). Outgrowing its child's diseases, and drawing from a large and ever-growing base of free application programs, it is quickly becoming the operating system of choice for many PC owners. The kernel and C library have become that good that most standard software may be compiled with no more effort than is required on any other mainstream UNIXish system, and a broad assortment of packaged Linux distributions allows you to almost drop it onto your hard disk and start playing.

Documentation on Linux

One of the complaints that are frequently levelled at Linux (and free software in general) is the sorry state or complete lack of documentation. In the early days it was not unusual for a package to come with a handful of *README*s and installation notes. They gave the moderately experienced UNIX wizard enough information to successfully install and run it, but left the average newbie out in the cold.

Back in late 1992, Lars Wirzenius and Michael K. Johnson suggested to form the Linux Documentation Project, or LDP, which aims at providing a coherent set of manuals. Stopping short of answering questions like "How?", or "Why?", or "What's the meaning of life, universe, and all the rest?", these manuals attempt to cover most aspects of running and using a Linux system users without requiring a prior degree in UNIX.

Among the achievements of the LDP are the *Installation and Getting Started Guide*, written by Matt Welsh, the *Kernel Hacker's Guide* by Michael K. Johnson, and the manpage project coordinated by Rik Faith, which so far supplied a set of roughly 450 manual pages for most system and C library calls. The *System Administrators' Guide*, written by Lars Wirzenius, is still at the Alpha stage. A User's Guide is being prepared.

This book, the *Linux Network Administrators' Guide*, is part of the LDP series, too. As such, it may be copied and distributed freely under the LDP copying license which is reproduced on the second page.

However, the LDP books are not the only source of information on Linux. At the moment, there are more than a dozen HOWTOs that are posted to **comp.os.linux.announce** regularly and archived at various FTP sites. HOWTOs are short documents of a few pages that give you a brief introduction into topics such as Ethernet support under Linux, or the configuration of Usenet news software, and answer frequently asked questions. They usually provide the most accurate and up-to-date information avaliable on the topic. A list of available HOWTOs is produced in the "Annotated Bibliography" toward the end of this book.

About This Book

When I joined the Linux Documentation Project in 1992, I wrote two small chapters on UUCP and *smail*, which I meant to contribute to the System Administrator's Guide. Development of TCP/IP networking was just beginning, and when those "small chapters" started to grow, I wondered aloud if it wouldn't be nice to have a Networking Guide. "Great", everyone said, "I'd say, go for it!" So I went for it, and wrote a first version of the Networking Guide, which I released in September 1993.

The new Networking Guide you are reading right now is a complete rewrite that features several new applications that have become available to Linux users since the first release.

The book is organized roughly in the sequence of steps you have to take to configure your system for networking. It starts by discussing basic concepts of networks, and TCP/IP-based networks in particular. We then slowly work our way up from configuring TCP/IP at the device level to the setup of common applications such as *rlogin* and friends, the Network File System, and the Network Information System. This is followed by a chapter on how to set up your machine as a UUCP node. The remainder of the book is dedicated to two major applications that run on top of both TCP/IP and UUCP: electronic mail and news.

The email part features an introduction of the more intimate parts of mail transport and routing, and the myriads of addressing schemes you may be confronted with. It describes the configuration and management of *smail*, a mail transport agent commonly used on smaller mail hubs, and *sendmail*, which is for people who have to do more complicated routing, or have to handle a large volume of mail. The *sendmail* chapter has been written and contributed by Vince Skahan.

The news part attempts to give you an overview of how Usenet news works, covers C news, the most widely used news transport software at the moment, and the use of NNTP to provide newsreading access to a local network. The book closes with a short chapter on the care and feeding of the most popular newsreaders on Linux.

The Official Printed Version

In autumn 1993, Andy Oram, who has been around the LDP mailing list from almost the very beginning, asked me about publishing my book at O'Reilly and Associates. I was excited about this; I had never imagined my book being that successful. We finally agreed that O'Reilly would produce an enhanced Official Printed Version of the Networking Guide with me, while I retained the original copyright so that the source of the book could be freely distributed.[1] This means that you can choose freely: you can get the LaTeX source distributed on the network (or the preformatted DVI or PostScript versions, for that matter), and print it out. Or you can purchase the official printed version from O'Reilly, which will be available some time later this year.

Then, why would you want to pay money for something you can get for free? Is Tim O'Reilly out of his

---

[1] The copyright notice is reproduced on the page immediately following the title page.

mind for publishing something everyone can print and even sell herself?[2] Or is there any difference between these versions?

The answers are "it depends," "no, definitely not," and "yes and no." O'Reilly and Associates do take a risk in publishing the Networking Guide, but I hope it will finally pay off for them. If it does, I believe this project can serve as an example how the free software world and companies can cooperate to produce something both benefit from. In my view, the great service O'Reilly is doing to the Linux community (apart from the book being readily available in your local bookstore) is that it may help Linux being recognized as something to be taken seriously: a viable and useful alternative to commercial PC UNIX operating systems.

So what about the differences between the printed version and the online one? Andy Oram has made great efforts at transforming my early ramblings into something actually worth printing. (He has also been reviewing the other books put out by the Linux Documentation Project, trying to contribute whatever professional skills he can to the Linux community.)

Since Andy started reviewing the Networking Guide and editing the copies I sent him, the book has improved vastly over what it was half a year ago. It would be nowhere close to where it is now without his contributions. All his edits have been fed back into online version, as will any changes that will be made to the Networking Guide during the copy-editing phase at O'Reilly. So there will be no difference in content. Still, the O'Reilly version *will* be different: On one hand, people at O'Reilly are putting a lot of work into the look and feel, producing a much more pleasant layout than you could ever get out of standard LaTeX. On the other hand, it will feature a couple of enhancements like an improved index, and better and more figures.

More Information

If you follow the instructions in this book, and something does not work nevertheless, please be patient. Some of your problems may be due to stupid mistakes on my part, but may also be caused by changes in the networking software. Therefore, you should probably ask on **comp.os.linux.help** first. There's a good chance that you are not alone with your problems, so that a fix or at least a proposed workaround is likely to be known. If you have the opportunity, you should also try to get the latest kernel and network release from one of the Linux FTP sites, or a BBS near you. Many problems are caused by software from different stages of development, which fail to work together properly. After all, Linux is "work in progress".

Another good place to inform yourself about current development is the Networking HOWTO. It is maintained by Terry Dawson[3]. It is posted to **comp.os.linux.announce** once a month, and contains the most up-to-date information. The current version can also be obtained (among others) from **tsx-11.mit.edu**, in */pub/linux/doc*. For problems you can't solve in any other way, you may also contact the author of this book at the address given in the preface. However, please, refrain from asking developers for help. They are already devoting a major part of their spare time to Linux anyway, and occasionally even have a life beyond the net :-)

On the Authors

Olaf has been a UNIX user and part-time administrator for a couple of years while he was studying mathematics. At the moment, he's working as a UNIX programmer and is writing a book. One of his favorite sports is doing things with *sed* that other people would reach for their *perl* interpreter for. He has about as much fun with this as with mountain hiking with a backpack and a tent.

Vince Skahan has been administering large numbers of UNIX systems since 1987 and currently runs sendmail+IDA on approximately 300 UNIX workstations for over 2000 users. He admits to losing considerable sleep from editing quite a few *sendmail.cf* files 'the hard way' before discovering sendmail+IDA in 1990. He also admits to anxiously awaiting the delivery of the first perl-based version of sendmail for even more obscure fun[4]...

Olaf can be reached at the following address:

> Olaf Kirch
> Kattreinstr. 38
> 64295 Darmstadt
> Germany

---

[2]Note that while you are allowed to print out the online version, you may *not* run the O'Reilly book through a photocopier, and much less sell any of those (hypothetical) copies.

[3]Terry Dawson can be reached at **terryd@extro.ucc.su.oz.au**.

[4]Don't you think we could do it with *sed*, Vince?

okir@monad.swb.de

Vince can be reached at:

Vince Skahan
vince@victrola.wa.com

We are open to your questions, comments, postcards, etc. However, we ask you *not* to telephone us unless it's really important.

Thanks

Olaf says: This book owes very much to the numerous people who took the time to proofread it and helped iron out many mistakes, both technical and grammatical (never knew that there's such a thing as a dangling participle). The most vigorous among them was Andy Oram at O'Reilly and Associates.

I am greatly indebted to Andres Sepúlveda, Wolfgang Michaelis, Michael K. Johnson, and all developers who spared the time to check the information provided in the Networking Guide. I also wish to thank all those who read the first version of the Networking Guide and sent me corrections and suggestions. You can find hopefully complete list of contributors in the file *Thanks* in the online distribution. Finally, this book would not have been possible without the support of Holger Grothe, who provided me with the critical Internet connectivity.

I would also like to thank the following groups and companies who printed the first edition of the Networking Guide and have donated money either to me, or to the Linux Documentation Project as a whole.

- Linux Support Team, Erlangen, Germany

- S.u.S.E. GmbH, Fuerth, Germany

- Linux System Labs, Inc., United States

Vince says: Thanks go to Neil Rickert and Paul Pomes for lots of help over the years regarding the care and feeding of sendmail+IDA and to Rich Braun for doing the initial port of sendmail+IDA to Linux. The biggest thanks by far go to my wife Susan for all the support on this and other projects.

Typographical Conventions

In writing this book, a number of typographical conventions were employed to mark shell commands, variable arguments, etc. They are explained below.

Bold Font   Used to mark hostnames and mail addresses, as well as new concepts and warnings.

Italics Font   Used to mark file names, UNIX commands, and keywords in configuration files. Also used for *emphasis* in text.

`Typewriter Font`
                    Used to represent screen interaction, such as user interaction when running a program.

                    Also used for code examples, whether it is a configuration file, a shell script, or something else.

Typewriter Slanted Font
                    Used to mark meta-variables in the text, especially in representations of the command line. For example,

```
$ ls -l foo
```

                    where *foo* would "stand for" a filename, such as */tmp*.

Key   Represents a key to press. You will often see it in this form:

                    Press return to continue.

◇   A diamond in the margin, like a black diamond on a ski hill, marks "danger" or "caution." Read paragraphs marked this way carefully.

$ and #   When preceding a shell command to be typed, these denote the shell prompt. The '$' symbol is used when the command may be executed as a normal user; '#' means that the command requires super user privileges.

The Linux Documentation Project

The Linux Documentation Project, or LDP, is a loose team of writers, proofreaders, and editors who are working together to provide complete documentation for the Linux operating system. The overall coordinator of the project is Matt Welsh, who is heavily aided by Lars Wirzenius and Michael K. Johnson.

This manual is one in a set of several being distributed by the LDP, including a Linux Users' Guide, System Administrators' Guide, Network Administrators' Guide, and Kernel Hackers' Guide. These manuals are all available in LaTeX source format, .dvi format, and postscript output by anonymous FTP from nic.funet.fi, in the directory /pub/OS/Linux/doc/doc-project, and from tsx-11.mit.edu, in the directory /pub/linux/docs/guides.

We encourage anyone with a penchant for writing or editing to join us in improving Linux documentation. If you have Internet e-mail access, you can join the DOC channel of the Linux-Activists mailing list by sending mail to

```
linux-activists-request@niksula.hut.fi
```

with the line

```
X-Mn-Admin:  join DOC
```

in the header or as the first line of the message body. An empty mail without the additional header line will make the mail-server return a help message. To leave the channel, send a message to the same address, including the line

```
X-Mn-Admin:  leave DOC
```

Filesystem Standards

Throughout the past, one of the problems that afflicted Linux distributions as well as separate packages was that there was no single accepted file system layout. This resulted in incompatibilities between different packages, and confronted users and administrators alike with the task to locate various files and programs.

To improve this situation, in August 1993, several people formed the Linux File System Standard Group, or FSSTND Group for short, coordinated by Daniel Quinlan. After six months of discussion, the group presented a draft that presents a coherent file sytem structure and defines the location of most essential programs and configuration files.

This standard is supposed to be implemented by most major Linux distributions and packages. Throughout this book, we will therefore assume that any files discussed reside in the location specified by the standard; only where there is a long tradition that conflicts with this specification will alternative locations be mentioned.

The Linux File System Standard can be obtained from all major Linux FTP sites and their mirrors; for instance, you can find it on **sunsite.unc.edu** below */pub/linux/docs*. Daniel Quinlan, the coordinator of the FSSTND group can be reached at **quinlan@netcom.com**.

Chapter 1

Introduction to Networking

1.1 History

The idea of networking is probably as old as telecommunications itself. Consider people living in the stone age, where drums may have been used to transmit messages between individuals. Suppose caveman A wants to invite caveman B for a game of hurling rocks at each other, but they live too far apart for B to hear A banging his drum. So what are A's options? He could 1) walk over to B's place, 2) get a bigger drum, or 3) ask C, who lives halfway between them, to forward the message. The last is called networking.

Of course, we have come a long way from the primitive pursuits and devices of our forebears. Nowadays, we have computers talk to each other over vast assemblages of wires, fiber optics, microwaves, and the like, to make an appointment for Saturday's soccer match.[1] In the following, we will deal with the means and ways by which this is accomplished, but leave out the wires, as well as the soccer part.

We will describe two types of networks in this guide: those based on UUCP, and those based on TCP/IP. These are protocol suites and software packages that supply means to transport data between two computers. In this chapter, we will look at both types of networks, and discuss their underlying principles.

We define a network as a collection of *hosts* that are able to communicate with each other, often by relying on the services of a number of dedicated hosts that relay data between the participants. Hosts are very often computers, but need not be; one can also think of X-terminals or intelligent printers as hosts. Small agglomerations of hosts are also called *sites*.

Communication is impossible without some sort of language or code. In computer networks, these languages are collectively referred to as *protocols*. However, you shouldn't think of written protocols here, but rather of the highly formalized code of behavior observed when heads of state meet, for instance. In a very similar fashion, the protocols used in computer networks are nothing but very strict rules for the exchange of messages between two or more hosts.

1.2 UUCP Networks

UUCP is an abbreviation for Unix-to-Unix Copy. It started out as a package of programs to transfer files over serial lines, schedule those transfers, and initiate execution of programs on remote sites. It has undergone major changes since its first implementation in the late seventies, but is still rather spartan in the services it offers. Its main application is still in wide-area networks based on dial-up telephone links.

UUCP was first developed by Bell Laboratories in 1977 for communication between their Unix-development sites. In mid-1978, this network already connected over 80 sites. It was running email as an application, as well as remote printing. However, the system's central use was in distributing new software and bugfixes.[2] Today, UUCP is not confined to the UNIX environment anymore. There are both free and commercial ports available for a variety of platforms, including AmigaOS, DOS, Atari's TOS, etc.

---

[1] The original spirit of which (see above) still shows on some occasions in Europe.
[2] Not that the times had changed that much...

One of the main disadvantages of UUCP networks is their low bandwidth. On one hand, telephone equipment places a tight limit on the maximum transfer rate. On the other hand, UUCP links are rarely permanent connections; instead, hosts rather dial up each other at regular intervals. Hence, most of the time it takes a mail message to travel a UUCP network it sits idly on some host's disk, awaiting the next time a connection is established.

Despite these limitations, there are still many UUCP networks operating all over the world, run mainly by hobbyists, which offer private users network access at reasonable prices. The main reason for the popularity of UUCP is that it is dirt cheap compared to having your computer connected to The Big Internet Cable. To make your computer a UUCP node, all you need is a modem, a working UUCP implementation, and another UUCP node that is willing to feed you mail and news.

1.2.1   How to Use UUCP

The idea behind UUCP is rather simple: as its name indicates, it basically copies files from one host to another, but it also allows certain actions to be performed on the remote host.

Suppose your machine is allowed to access a hypothetical host named **swim**, and have it execute the *lpr* print command for you. Then you could type the following on your command line to have this book printed on **swim**:[3]

```
$ uux -r swim!lpr !netguide.dvi
```

This makes *uux*, a command from the UUCP suite, schedule a *job* for **swim**. This job consists of the input file, *netguide.dvi*, and the request to feed this file to *lpr*. The -r flag tells *uux* not to call the remote system immediately, but to rather store the job away until a connection is established at a later occasion. This is called *spooling*.

Another property of UUCP is that it allows to forward jobs and files through several hosts, provided they cooperate. Assume that **swim** from the above examples has a UUCP link with **groucho**, which maintains a large archive of UNIX applications. To download the file *tripwire-1.0.tar.gz* to your site, you might issue

```
$ uucp -mr swim!groucho!~/security/tripwire-1.0.tar.gz trip.tgz
```

The job created will request **swim** to fetch the file from **groucho**, and send it to your site, where UUCP will store it in *trip.tgz* and notify you via mail of the file's arrival. This will be done in three steps. First, your site sends the job to **swim**. When **swim** establishes contact with **groucho** the next time, it downloads the file. The final step is the actual transfer from **swim** to your host.

The most important services provided by UUCP networks these days are electronic mail and news. We will come back to these later, so we will give only a brief introduction here.

Electronic mail – email for short – allows you to exchange messages with users on remote hosts without actually having to know how to access these hosts. The task of directing a message from your site to the destination site is performed entirely by the mail handling system. In a UUCP environment, mail is usually transported by executing the *rmail* command on a neighboring host, passing it the recipient address and the mail message. *rmail* will then forward the message to another host, and so on, until it reaches the destination host. We will look at this in detail in chapter 13.

News may best be described as sort of a distributed bulletin board system. Most often, this term refers to Usenet News, which is by far the most widely known news exchange network with an estimated number of 120,000 participating sites. The origins of Usenet date back to 1979, when, after the release of UUCP with the new Unix V7, three graduate students had the idea of a general information exchange within the Unix community. They put together some scripts, which became the first netnews system. In 1980, this network connected **duke**, **unc**, and **phs**, at two Universities in North Carolina. Out of this, Usenet eventually grew. Although it originated as a UUCP-based network, it is no longer confined to one single type of network.

---

[3]When using *bash*, the GNU Bourne Again Shell, you might have to escape the exclamation mark, because it uses it as its history character.

The basic unit of information is the article, which may be posted to a hierarchy of newsgroups dedicated to specific topics. Most sites receive only a selection of all newsgroups, which carry an average of 60MB worth of articles a day.

In the UUCP world, news is generally sent across a UUCP link by collecting all articles from the groups requested, and packing them up in a number of *batches*. These are sent to the receiving site, where they are fed to the *rnews* command for unpacking and further processing.

Finally, UUCP is also the medium of choice for many dial-up archive sites which offer public access. You can usually access them by dialing them up with UUCP, logging in as a guest user, and download files from a publicly accessible archive area. These guest accounts often have a login name and password of **uucp/nuucp** or something similar.

1.3   TCP/IP Networks

Although UUCP may be a reasonable choice for low-cost dial-up network links, there are many situations in which its store-and-forward technique proves too inflexible, for example in Local Area Networks (LANs). These are usually made up of a small number of machines located in the same building, or even on the same floor, that are interconnected to provide a homogeneous working environment. Typically, you would want to share files between these hosts, or run distributed applications on different machines.

These tasks require a completely different approach to networking. Instead of forwarding entire files along with a job description, all data is broken up in smaller chunks (packets), which are forwarded immediately to the destination host, where they are reassembled. This type of network is called a *packet-switched* network. Among other things, this allows to run interactive applications over the network. The cost of this is, of course, a greatly increased complexity in software.

The solution that UNIX system — and many non-UNIX sites — have adopted is known as TCP/IP. In this section, we will have a look at its underlying concepts.

1.3.1   Introduction to TCP/IP-Networks

TCP/IP traces its origins to a research project funded by the United States DARPA (Defense Advanced Research Projects Agency) in 1969. This was an experimental network, the ARPANET, which was converted into an operational one in 1975, after it had proven to be a success.

In 1983, the new protocol suite TCP/IP was adopted as a standard, and all hosts on the network were required to use it. When ARPANET finally grew into the Internet (with ARPANET itself passing out of existence in 1990), the use of TCP/IP had spread to networks beyond the Internet itself. Most notable are UNIX local area networks, but in the advent of fast digital telephone equipment, such as ISDN, it also has a promising future as a transport for dial-up networks.

For something concrete to look at as we discuss TCP/IP throughout the following sections, we will consider Groucho Marx University (GMU), situated somewhere in Fredland, as an example. Most departments run their own local area networks, while some share one, and others run several of them. They are all interconnected, and are hooked to the Internet through a single high-speed link.

Suppose your Linux box is connected to a LAN of UNIX hosts at the Mathematics Department, and its name is **erdos**. To access a host at the Physics Department, say **quark**, you enter the following command:

```
$ rlogin quark.physics
Welcome to the Physics Department at GMU
(ttyq2) login:
```

At the prompt, you enter your login name, say **andres**, and your password. You are then given a shell on **quark**, to which you can type as if you were sitting at the system's console. After you exit the shell, you are returned to your own machine's prompt. You have just used one of the instantaneous, interactive applications that TCP/IP provides: remote login.

While being logged into **quark**, you might also want to run an X11-based application, like a function plotting program, or a PostScript previewer. To tell this application that you want to have its windows displayed on your host's screen, you have to set the *DISPLAY* environment variable:

```
$ export DISPLAY=erdos.maths:0.0
```

If you now start your application, it will contact your X server instead of **quark**'s, and display all its windows on your screen. Of course, this requires that you have X11 runnning on **erdos**. The point here is that TCP/IP allows **quark** and **erdos** to send X11 packets back and forth to give you the illusion that you're on a single system. The network is almost transparent here.

Another very important application in TCP/IP networks is NFS, which stands for *Network File System*. It is another form of making the network transparent, because it basically allows you to mount directory hierarchies from other hosts, so that they appear like local file systems. For example, all users' home directories can be on a central server machine, from which all other hosts on the LAN mount the directory. The effect of this is that users can log into any machine, and find themselves in the same home directory. Similarly, it is possible to install applications that require large amounts of disk space (such as TEX) on only one machine, and export these directories to other machines. We will come back to NFS in chapter 11.

Of course, these are only examples of what you can do over TCP/IP networks. The possibilities are almost limitless.

We will now have a closer look at the way TCP/IP works. You will need this to understand how and why you have to configure your machine. We will start by examining the hardware, and slowly work our way up.

1.3.2   Ethernets

The type of hardware most widely used throughout LANs is what is commonly known as *Ethernet*. It consists of a single cable with hosts being attached to it through connectors, taps or transceivers. Simple Ethernets are quite inexpensive to install, which, together with a net transfer rate of 10 Megabits per second accounts for much of its popularity.

Ethernets come in three flavors, called *thick* and *thin*, respectively, and *twisted pair*. Thin and thick Ethernet each use a coaxial cable, differing in width and the way you may attach a host to this cable. Thin Ethernet uses a T-shaped "BNC" connector, which you insert into the cable, and twist onto a plug on the back of your computer. Thick Ethernet requires that you drill a small hole into the cable, and attach a transceiver using a "vampire tap". One or more hosts can then be connected to the transceiver. Thin and thick Ethernet cable may run for a maximum of 200 and 500 meters, respectively, and are therefore also called 10base-2 and 10base-5. Twisted pair uses a cable made of two copper wires which is also found in ordinary telephone installations, but usually requires additional hardware. It is also known as 10base-T.

Although adding a host to a thick Ethernet is a little hairy, it does not bring down the network. To add a host to a thinnet installation, you have to disrupt network service for at least a few minutes because you have to cut the cable to insert the connector.

Most people prefer thin Ethernet, because it is very cheap: PC cards come for as little as US$ 50, and cable is in the range of a few cent per meter. However, for large-scale installations, thick Ethernet is more appropriate. For example, the Ethernet at GMU's Mathematics Department uses thick Ethernet, so traffic will not be disrupted each time a host is added to the network.

One of the drawbacks of Ethernet technology is its limited cable length, which precludes any use of it other than for LANs. However, several Ethernet segments may be linked to each other using repeaters, bridges or routers. Repeaters simply copy the signals between two or more segments, so that all segments together will act as if it was one Ethernet. timing requirements, there may not be more than four repeaters any two hosts on the network. Bridges and Routers are more sophisticated. They analyze incoming data and forward it only when the recipient host is not on the local Ethernet.

Ethernet works like a bus system, where a host may send packets (or *frames*) of up to 1500 bytes to another host on the same Ethernet. A host is addressed by a six-byte address hardcoded into the firmware of its Ethernet board. These addresses are usually written as a sequence of two-digit hex numbers separated by colons, as in **aa:bb:cc:dd:ee:ff**.

A frame sent by one station is seen by all attached stations, but only the destination host actually picks it up and processes it. If two stations try to send at the same time, a *collision* occurs, which is resolved by the two stations aborting the send, and reattempting it a few moments later.

1.3.3 Other Types of Hardware

In larger installations, such as Groucho Marx University, Ethernet is usually not the only type of equipment used. At Groucho Marx University, each department's LAN is linked to the campus backbone, which is a fiber optics cable running FDDI (*Fiber Distributed Data Interface*). FDDI uses an entirely different approach to transmitting data, which basically involves sending around a number of *tokens*, with a station only being allowed to send a frame if it captures a token. The main advantage of FDDI is a speed of up to 100 Mbps, and a maximum cable length of up to 200 km.

For long-distance network links, a different type of equipment is frequently used, which is based on a standard named X.25. Many so-called Public Data Networks, like Tymnet in the U.S., or Datex-P in Germany, offer this service. X.25 requires special hardware, namely a Packet Assembler/Disassembler or *PAD*. X.25 defines a set of networking protocols of its own right, but is nevertheless frequently used to connect networks running TCP/IP and other protocols. Since IP packets cannot simply be mapped onto X.25 (and vice versa), they are simply encapsulated in X.25 packets and sent over the network.

Frequently, radio amateurs use their equipment to network their computers; this is called *packet radio* or *ham radio*. The protocol used by ham radios is called AX.25, which was derived from X.25.

Other techniques involve using slow but cheap serial lines for dial-up access. These require yet another protocol for transmission of packets, such as SLIP or PPP, which will be described below.

1.3.4 The Internet Protocol

Of course, you wouldn't want your networking to be limited to one Ethernet. Ideally, you would want to be able to use a network regardless of what hardware it runs on and how many subunits it is made up of. For example, in larger installations such as Groucho Marx University, you usually have a number of separate Ethernets that have to be connected in some way. At GMU, the maths department runs two Ethernets: one network of fast machines for professors and graduates, and another one with slow machines for students. Both are linked to the FDDI campus backbone.

This connection is handled by a dedicated host, a so-called *gateway*, which handles incoming and outgoing packets by copying them between the two Ethernets and the fiber optics cable. For example, if you are at the Maths Department, and want to access **quark** on the Physics Deparment's LAN from your Linux box, the networking software cannot send packets to **quark** directly, because it is not on the same Ethernet. Therefore, it has to rely on the gateway to act as a forwarder. The gateway (name it **sophus**) then forwards these packets to its peer gateway **niels** at the Physics Department, using the backbone, with **niels** delivering it to the destination machine. Data flow between **erdos** and **quark** is shown in figure 1.1 (With apologies to Guy L. Steele).

This scheme of directing data to a remote host is called *routing*, and packets are often referred to as *datagrams* in this context. To facilitate things, datagram exchange is governed by a single protocol that is independent of the hardware used: IP, or *Internet Protocol*. In chapter 2, we will cover IP and the issues of routing in greater detail.

The main benefit of IP is that it turns physically dissimilar networks into one apparently homogeneous network. This is called internetworking, and the resulting "meta-network" is called an *internet*. Note the subtle difference between *an* internet and *the* Internet here. The latter is the official name of one particular global internet.

Of course, IP also requires a hardware-independent addressing scheme. This is achieved by assigning each host a unique 32-bit number, called the *IP address*. An IP address is usually written as four decimal numbers, one for each 8-bit portion, separated by dots. For example, **quark** might have an IP address of **0x954C0C04**, which would be written as **149.76.12.4**. This format is also called *dotted quad* notation.

You will notice that we now have three different types of addresses: first there is the host's name, like **quark**, then there are IP addresses, and finally, there are hardware addresses, like the 6-byte Ethernet address.

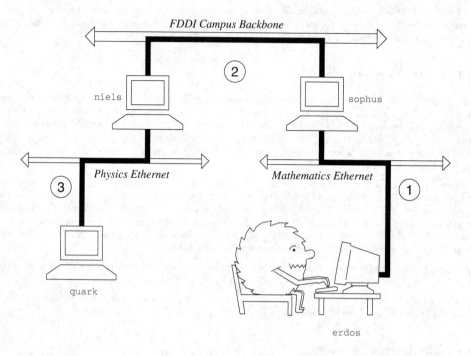

Figure 1.1: The three steps of sending a datagram from **erdos** to **quark**.

All these somehow have to match, so that when you type *rlogin quark*, the networking software can be given **quark**'s IP address; and when IP delivers any data to the Physics Department's Ethernet, it somehow has to find out what Ethernet address corresponds to the IP address. Which is rather confusing.

We will not go into this here, and deal with it in chapter 2 instead. For now, it's enough to remember that these steps of finding addresses are called *hostname resolution*, for mapping host names onto IP addresses, and *address resolution*, for mapping the latter to hardware addresses.

1.3.5 IP over Serial Lines

On serial lines, a "de facto" standard known as SLIP or *Serial Line IP* is frequently used. A modification of SLIP is known as CSLIP, or *compressed SLIP*, and performs compression of IP headers to make better use of the relatively low bandwidth provided by serial links.[4] A different serial protocol is PPP, or *Point-to-Point Protocol*. PPP has many more features than SLIP, including a link negotiation phase. Its main advantage over SLIP is, however, that it isn't limited to transporting IP datagrams, but that it was designed to allow for any type of datagrams to be transmitted.

1.3.6 The Transmission Control Protocol

Now, of course, sending datagrams from one host to another is not the whole story. If you log into **quark**, you want to have a reliable connection between your *rlogin* process on **erdos** and the shell process on **quark**. Thus, the information sent to and fro must be split up into packets by the sender, and reassembled into a character stream by the receiver. Trivial as it seems, this involves a number of hairy tasks.

A very important thing to know about IP is that, by intent, it is not reliable. Assume that ten people on your Ethernet started downloading the latest release of XFree86 from GMU's FTP server. The amount of

---

[4]SLIP is described in RFC 1055. The header compression CSLIP is based in is described in RFC 1144.

traffic generated by this might be too much for the gateway to handle, because it's too slow, and it's tight on memory. Now if you happen to send a packet to **quark**, **sophus** might just be out of buffer space for a moment and therefore unable to forward it. IP solves this problem by simply discarding it. The packet is irrevocably lost. It is therefore the responsibility of the communicating hosts to check the integrity and completeness of the data, and retransmit it in case of an error.

This is performed by yet another protocol, TCP, or *Transmission Control Protocol*, which builds a reliable service on top of IP. The essential property of TCP is that it uses IP to give you the illusion of a simple connection between the two processes on your host and the remote machine, so that you don't have to care about how and along which route your data actually travels. A TCP connection works essentially like a two-way pipe that both processes may write to and read from. Think of it as a telephone conversation.

TCP identifies the end points of such a connection by the IP addresses of the two hosts involved, and the number of a so-called *port* on each host. Ports may be viewed as attachment points for network connections. If we are to strain the telephone example a little more, one might compare IP addresses to area codes (numbers map to cities), and port numbers to local codes (numbers map to individual people's telephones).

In the *rlogin* example, the client application (*rlogin*) opens a port on **erdos**, and connects to port 513 on **quark**, which the *rlogind* server is known to listen to. This establishes a TCP connection. Using this connection, *rlogind* performs the authorization procedure, and then spawns the shell. The shell's standard input and output are redirected to the TCP connection, so that anything you type to *rlogin* on your machine will be passed through the TCP stream and be given to the shell as standard input.

1.3.7 The User Datagram Protocol

Of course, TCP isn't the only user protocol in TCP/IP networking. Although suitable for applications like *rlogin*, the overhead involved is prohibitive for applications like NFS. Instead, it uses a sibling protocol of TCP called UDP, or *User Datagram Protocol*. Just like TCP, UDP also allows an application to contact a service on a certain port on the remote machine, but it doesn't establish a connection for this. Instead, you may use it to send single packets to the destination service – hence its name.

Assume you have mounted the TeX directory hierarchy from the department's central NFS server, *galois*, and you want to view a document describing how to use LaTeX. You start your editor, who first reads in the entire file. However, it would take too long to establish a TCP connection with *galois*, send the file, and release it again. Instead, a request is made to *galois*, who sends the file in a couple of UDP packets, which is much faster. However, UDP was not made to deal with packet loss or corruption. It is up to the application – NFS in this case – to take care of this.

1.3.8 More on Ports

Ports may be viewed as attachment points for network connections. If an application wants to offer a certain service, it attaches itself to a port and waits for clients (this is also called *listening* on the port). A client that wants to use this service allocates a port on its local host, and connects to the server's port on the remote host.

An important property of ports is that once a connection has been established between the client and the server, another copy of the server may attach to the server port and listen for more clients. This permits, for instance, several concurrent remote logins to the same host, all using the same port 513. TCP is able to tell these connections from each other, because they all come from different ports or hosts. For example, if you twice log into **quark** from **erdos**, then the first *rlogin* client will use the local port 1023, and the second one will use port 1022. Both however, will connect to the same port 513 on **quark**.

This example shows the use of ports as rendezvous points, where a client contacts a specific port to obtain a specific service. In order for a client to know the proper port number, an agreement has to be reached between the administrators of both systems on the assignment of these numbers. For services that are widely used, such as *rlogin*, these numbers have to be administered centrally. This is done by the IETF (or *Internet Engineering Task Force*), which regularly releases an RFC titled *Assigned Numbers*. It describes, among other things, the port numbers assigned to *well-known services*. Linux uses a file mapping service names to numbers, called */etc/services*. It is described in section The *services* and *protocols* Files.

It is worth noting that although both TCP and UDP connections rely on ports, these numbers do not conflict. This means that TCP port 513, for example, is different from UDP port 513. In fact, these ports serve as access points for two different services, namely *rlogin* (TCP) and *rwho* (UDP).

1.3.9   The Socket Library

In UNIX operating systems, the software performing all the tasks and protocols described above is usually part of the kernel, and so it is in Linux. The programming interface most common in the UNIX world is the *Berkeley Socket Library*. Its name derives from a popular analogy that views ports as sockets, and connecting to a port as plugging in. It provides the (*bind(2)*) call to specifiy a remote host, a transport protocol, and a service which a program can connect or listen to (using *connect(2)*, *listen(2)*, and *accept(2)*). The socket library is however somewhat more general, in that it provides not only a class of TCP/IP-based sockets (the *AF_INET* sockets), but also a class that handles connections local to the machine (the *AF_UNIX* class). Some implementations can also handle other classes as well, like the XNS (*Xerox Networking System*) protocol, or X.25.

In Linux, the socket library is part of the standard *libc* C library. Currently, it only supports *AF_INET* and *AF_UNIX* sockets, but efforts are made to incorporate support for Novell's networking protocols, so that eventually one or more socket classes for these would be added.

1.4   Linux Networking

Being the result of a concerted effort of programmers around the world, Linux wouldn't have been possible without the global network. So it's not surprising that already in early stages of development, several people started to work on providing it with network capabilities. A UUCP implementation was running on Linux almost from the very beginning, and work on TCP/IP-based networking started around autumn 1992, when Ross Biro and others created what now has become known as Net-1.

After Ross quit active development in May 1993, Fred van Kempen began to work on a new implementation, rewriting major parts of the code. This ongoing effort is known as Net-2. A first public release, Net-2d, was made in Summer 1992 (as part of the 0.99.10 kernel), and has since been maintained and expanded by several people, most notably Alan Cox, as Net-2Debugged. After heavy debugging and numerous improvements to the code, he changed its name to Net-3 after Linux 1.0 was released. This is the version of the networking code currently included in the official kernel releases.

Net-3 offers device drivers for a wide variety of Ethernet boards, as well as SLIP (for sending network traffic over serial lines), and PLIP (for parallel lines). With Net-3, Linux has a TCP/IP implementation that behaves very well in a local area network environment, showing uptimes that beat some of the commercial PC Unices. Development currently moves toward the necessary stability to reliably run it on Internet hosts.

Beside these facilities, there are several projects going on that will enhance the versatility of Linux. A driver for PPP (the point-to-point protocol, another way to send network traffic over serial lines), is at Beta stage currently, and an AX.25 driver for ham radio is at Alpha stage. Alan Cox has also implemented a driver for Novell's IPX protocol, but the effort for a complete networking suite compatible with Novell's has been put on hold for the moment, because of Novell's unwillingness to provide the necessary documentation. Another very promising undertaking is *samba*, a free NetBIOS server for Unices, written by Andrew Tridgell.[5]

1.4.1   Different Streaks of Development

In the meanwhile, Fred continued development, going on to Net-2e, which features a much revised design of the networking layer. At the time of writing, Net-2e is still Beta software. Most notable about Net-2e is the incorporation of DDI, the *Device Driver Interface*. DDI offers a uniform access and configuration method to all networking devices and protocols.

Yet another implemtation of TCP/IP networking comes from Matthias Urlichs, who wrote an ISDN driver for Linux and FreeBSD. For this, he integrated some of the BSD networking code in the Linux kernel.

For the foreseeable future, however, Net-3 seems to be here to stay. Alan currently works on an implementation of the AX.25 protocol used by ham radio amateurs. Doubtlessly, the yet to be developed "module" code

---

[5]NetBIOS is the protocol on which applications like *lanmanager* and Windows for Workgroups are based.

for the kernel will also bring new impulses to the networking code. Modules allow you to add drivers to the kernel at run time.

Although these different network implementations all strive to provide the same service, there are major differences between them at the kernel and device level. Therefore, you will not be able to configure a system running a Net-2e kernel with utilities from Net-2d or Net-3, and vice versa. This only applies to commands that deal with kernel internals rather closely; applications and common networking commands such as *rlogin* or *telnet* run on either of them.

Nevertheless, all these different network version should not worry you. Unless you are participating in active development, you will not have to worry about which version of the TCP/IP code you run. The official kernel releases will always be accompanied by a set of networking tools that are compatible with the networking code present in the kernel.

1.4.2 Where to Get the Code

The latest version of the Linux network code can be obtained by anonymous FTP from various sites. The official FTP site for Net-3 is **sunacm.swan.ac.uk**, mirrored by **sunsite.unc.edu** below *system/Network/sunacm*. The latest Net-2e patch kit and binaries are available from **ftp.aris.com**. Matthias Urlichs' BSD-derived networking code can be gotten from **ftp.ira.uka.de** in */pub/system/linux/netbsd*.

The latest kernels can be found on **nic.funet.fi** in */pub/OS/Linux/PEOPLE/Linus*; **sunsite** and **tsx-11.mit.edu** mirror this directory.

1.5 Maintaining Your System

Throughout this book, we will mainly deal with installation and configuration issues. Administration is, however, much more than that — after setting up a service, you have to keep it running, too. For most of them, only little attendance will be necessary, while some, like mail and news, require that you perform routine tasks to keep your system up-to-date. We will discuss these tasks in later chapters.

The absolute minimum in maintenance is to check system and per-application log files regularly for error conditions and unusual events. Commonly, you will want to do this by writing a couple of administrative shell scripts and run them from *cron* periodically. The source distribution of some major applications, like *smail* or C News, contain such scripts. You only have to tailor them to suit your needs and preferences.

The output from any of your *cron* jobs should be mailed to an administrative account. By default, many applications will send error reports, usage statistics, or logfile summaries to the **root** account. This only makes sense if you log in as **root** frequently; a much better idea is to forward **root**'s mail to your personal account setting up a mail alias as described in chapter 14.

However carefully you have configured your site, Murphy's law guarantees that some problem *will* surface eventually. Therefore, maintaining a system also means being available for complaints. Usually, people expect that the system administrator can at least be reached via email as **root**, but there are also other addresses that are commonly used to reach the person responsible for a specific aspect of maintenance. For instance, complaints about a malfunctioning mail configuration will usually be addressed **postmaster**; and problems with the news system may be reported to **newsmaster** or **usenet**. Mail to **hostmaster** should be redirected to the person in charge of the host's basic network services, and the DNS name service if you run a name server.

1.5.1 System Security

Another very important aspect of system administration in a network environment is protecting your system and users from intruders. Carelessly managed systems offer malicious people many targets: attacks range from password guessing to Ethernet snooping, and the damage caused may range from faked mail messages to data loss or violation of your users' privacy. We will mention some particular problems when discussing the context they may occur in, and some common defenses against them.

This section will discuss a few examples and basic techniques in dealing with system security. Of course, the topics covered can not treat all security issues you may be faced with exhaustively; they merely serve to illustrate the problems that may arise. Therefore, reading a good book on security is an absolute must, especially in a networked system. Simon Garfinkel's "Practical UNIX Security" (see [Spaf93]) is highly recommendable.

System security starts with good system administration. This includes checking the ownership and permissions of all vital files and directories, monitoring use of privileged accounts, etc. The COPS program, for instance, will check your file system and common configuration files for unusual permissions or other anomalies. It is also wise to use a password suite that enforces certain rules on the users' passwords that make them hard to guess. The shadow password suite, for instance, requires a password to have at least five letters, and contain both upper and lower case numbers and digits.

When making a service accessible to the network, make sure to give it "least privilege," meaning that you don't permit it to do things that aren't required for it to work as designed. For example, you should make programs setuid to **root** or some other privileged account only when they really need this. Also, if you want to use a service for only a very limited application, don't hesitate to configure it as restrictively as your special application allows. For instance, if you want to allow diskless hosts to boot from your machine, you must provide the TFTP (trivial file transfer service) so that they can download basic configuration files from the */boot* directory. However, when used unrestricted, TFTP allows any user anywhere in the world to download any world-readable file from your system. If this is not what you want, why not restrict TFTP service to the */boot* directory?[6]

Along the same line of thought, you might want to restrict certain services to users from certain hosts, say from your local network. In chapter 9, we introduce *tcpd* which does this for a variety of network applications.

Another important point is to avoid "dangerous" software. Of course, any software you use can be dangerous, because software may have bugs that clever people might exploit to gain access to your system. Things like these happen, and there's no complete protection against this. This problem affects free software and commercial products alike.[7] However, programs that require special privilege are inherently more dangerous than others, because any loophole can have drastic consequences.[8] If you install a setuid program for network purposes be doubly careful that you don't miss anything from the documentation, so that you don't create a security breach by accident.

You can never rule out that your precautions might fail, regardless how careful you have been. You should therefore make sure you detect intruders early. Checking the system log files is a good starting point, but the intruder is probably as clever, and will delete any obvious traces he or she left. However, there are tools like *tripwire*[9] that allow you to check vital system files to see if their contents or permissions have been changed. *tripwire* computes various strong checksums over these files and stores them in a database. During subsequent runs, the checksums are re-computed and compared to the stored ones to detect any modifications.

1.6 Outlook on the Following Chapters

The next few chapters will deal with configuring Linux for TCP/IP networking, and with running some major applications. Before getting our hands dirty with file editing and the like, we will examine IP a little closer in chapter 2. If you already know about the way IP routing works, and how address resolution is performed, you might want to skip this chapter.

Chapter 3 deals with the very basic configuration issues, such as building a kernel and setting up your Ethernet board. The configuration of your serial ports is covered in a separate chapter, because the discussion does not apply to TCP/IP networking only, but is also relevant for UUCP.

Chapter 5 helps you to set up your machine for TCP/IP networking. It contains installation hints for standalone hosts with only loopback enabled, and hosts connected to an Ethernet. It will also introduce you to a few useful tools you can use to test and debug your setup. The next chapter discusses how to configure hostname resolution, and explains how to set up a name server.

---

[6]We will come back to this in chapter 9.

[7]There have been commercial Unices you have to pay lots of money for that came with a setuid-**root** shell script which allowed users to gain **root** privilege using a simple standard trick.

[8]In 1988, the RTM worm brought much of the Internet to a grinding halt, partly by exploiting a gaping hole in some *sendmail* programs. This hole has long been fixed since.

[9]Written by Gene Kim and Gene Spafford.

This is followed by two chapters featuring the configuration and use of SLIP and PPP, respectively. Chapter 7 explains how to establish SLIP connections, and gives a detailed reference of *dip*, a tool that allows you to automate most of the necessary steps. Chapter 8 covers PPP and *pppd*, the PPP daemon you need for this.

Chapter 9 gives a short introduction to setting up some of the most important network applications, such as *rlogin*, *rcp*, etc, in chapter 9. This also covers how services are managed by the *inetd* super, and how you may restrict certain security-relevant services to a set of trusted hosts.

The next two chapters discuss NIS, the Network Information System, and NFS, the Network File System. NIS is a useful tool to distribute administative information such as user passwords in a local area network. NFS allows you to share file systems between several hosts in your network.

Chapter 12 gives you an extensive introduction to the administration of Taylor UUCP, a free implementation of the UUCP suite.

The remainder of the book is taken up by a detailed tour of electronic mail and Usenet News. Chapter 13 introduces you to the central concepts of electronic mail, like what a mail address looks like, and how the mail handling system manages to get your message to the recipient.

Chapters 14 and 15 each cover the setup of *smail* and *sendmail*, two mail transport agents you can use for Linux. This book explains both of them, because *smail* is easier to install for the beginner, while *sendmail* is more flexible.

Chapters 16 and 17 explain the way news are managed in Usenet, and how you install and use C news, a popular software package for managing Usenet news. Chapter 18 briefly covers how to set up an NNTP daemon to provide news reading access for your local network. Chapter 19 finally shows you how to configure and maintain various newsreaders.

Chapter 2

Issues of TCP/IP Networking

We will now turn to the details you'll come in touch with when connecting your Linux machine to a TCP/IP network including dealing with IP addresses, host names, and sometimes routing issues. This chapter gives you the background you need in order to understand what your setup requires, while the next chapters will cover the tools to deal with these.

2.1   Networking Interfaces

To hide the diversity of equipment that may be used in a networking environment, TCP/IP defines an abstract *interface* through which the hardware is accessed. This interface offers a set of operations which is the same for all types of hardware and basically deals with sending and receiving packets.

For each peripheral device you want to use for networking, a corresponding interface has to be present in the kernel. For example, Ethernet interfaces in Linux are called *eth0* and *eth1*, and SLIP interfaces come as *sl0*, *sl1*, etc. These interface names are used for configuration purposes when you want to name a particular physical device to the kernel. They have no meaning beyond that.

To be useable for TCP/IP networking, an interface must be assigned an IP address which serves as its identifcation when communicating with the rest of the world. This address is different from the interface name mentioned above; if you compare an interface to door, then the address is like the name-plate pinned on it.

Of course, there are other device parameters that may be set; one of these is the maximum size of datagrams that can be processed by that particular piece of hardware, also called *Maximum Transfer Unit*, or MTU. Other attributes will be introduced later.

2.2   IP Addresses

As mentioned in the previous chapter, the addresses understood by the IP networking protocol are 32-bit numbers. Every machine must be assigned a number unique to the networking environment. If you are running a local network that does not have TCP/IP traffic with other networks, you may assign these numbers according to your personal preferences. However, for sites on the Internet, numbers are assigned by a central authority, the Network Information Center, or NIC.[1]

For easier reading, IP addresses are split up into four 8 bit numbers called *octets*. For example, **quark.physics.groucho.edu** has an IP address of **0x954C0C04**, which is written as **149.76.12.4**. This format is often referred to as the *dotted quad notation*.

Another reason for this notation is that IP addresses are split into a *network* number, which is contained in the leading octets, and a *host* number, which is the remainder. When applying to the NIC for IP addresses, you are not assigned an address for each single host you plan to use. Instead, you are given a network number,

---

[1]Frequently, IP addresses will be assigned to you by the provider you buy your IP connectivity from. However, you may also apply to NIC directly for an IP address for your network by sending a mail to **hostmaster@internic.net**.

and are allowed to assign all valid IP addresses within this range to hosts on your network according to your preferences.

Depending on the size of the network, the host part may need to be smaller or larger. To accomodate different needs, there are several classes of networks, defining different splits of IP addresses.

Class A   Class A comprises networks **1.0.0.0** through **127.0.0.0**. The network number is contained in the first octet. This provides for a 24 bit host part, allowing roughly 1.6 million hosts.

Class B   Class B contains networks **128.0.0.0** through **191.255.0.0**; the network number is in the first two octets. This allows for 16320 nets with 65024 hosts each.

Class C   Class C networks range from **192.0.0.0** through **223.255.255.0**, with the network number being contained in the first three octets. This allows for nearly 2 million networks with up to 254 hosts.

Classes D, E, and F
                   Addresses falling into the range of **224.0.0.0** through **254.0.0.0** are either experimental, or are reserved for future use and don't specify any network.

If we go back to the example in the previous chapter, we find that **149.76.12.4**, the address of **quark**, refers to host **12.4** on the class B network **149.76.0.0**.

You may have noticed that in the above list not all possible values were allowed for each octet in the host part. This is because host numbers with octets all **0** or all **255** are reserved for special purposes. An address where all host part bits are zero refers to the network, and one where all bits of the host part are 1 is called a broadcast address. This refers to all hosts on the specified network simultaneously. Thus, **149.76.255.255** is not a valid host address, but refers to all hosts on network **149.76.0.0**.

There are also two network addresses that are reserved, **0.0.0.0** and **127.0.0.0**. The first is called the *default route*, the latter the *loopback address*. The default route has something to do with the way IP routes datagrams, which will be dealt with below.

Network **127.0.0.0** is reserved for IP traffic local to your host. Usually, address **127.0.0.1** will be assigned to a special interface on your host, the so-called *loopback interface*, which acts like a closed circuit. Any IP packet handed to it from TCP or UDP will be returned to them as if it had just arrived from some network. This allows you to develop and test networking software without ever using a "real" network. Another useful application is when you want to use networking software on a standalone host. This may not be as uncommon as it sounds; for instance, many UUCP sites don't have IP connectivity at all, but still want to run the INN news system nevertheless. For proper operation on Linux, INN requires the loopback interface.

2.3   Address Resolution

Now that you've seen how IP addresses are made up, you may be wondering how they are used on an Ethernet to address different hosts. After all, the Ethernet protocol identifies hosts by a six-octet number that has absolutely nothing in common with an IP address, doesn't it?

Right. That's why a mechanism is needed to map IP addresses onto Ethernet addresses. This is the so-called *Address Resolution Protocol*, or ARP. In fact, ARP is not confined to Ethernets at all, but is used on other types networks such as ham radio as well. The idea underlying ARP is exactly what most people do when they have to find Mr. X. Ample in a throng of 150 people: they go round, calling out his name, confident that he will respond if he's there.

When ARP wants to find out the Ethernet address corresponding to a given IP address, it uses a feature of Ethernet known as "broadcasting," where a datagram is addressed to all stations on the network simultaneously. The broadcast datagram sent by ARP contains a query for the IP address. Each receiving host compares this to its own IP address, and if it matches, returns an ARP reply to the inquiring host. The inquiring host can now extract the sender's Ethernet address from the reply.

Of course you might wonder how a host may know on which of the zillions of Ethernets throughout the world it is to find the desired host, and why this should even be an Ethernet. These questions all involve what is called routing, namely finding out the physical location of a host in a network. This will be the topic of the following section.

For a moment, let's talk about ARP a little longer. Once a host has discovered an Ethernet address, it stores it in its ARP cache, so that it doesn't have to query for it the next time it wants to send a datagram to the host in question. However, it is unwise to keep this information forever; for instance, the remote host's Ethernet card may be replaced because of technical problems, so the ARP entry becomes invalid. To force another query for the IP address, entries in the ARP cache are therefore discarded after some time.

Sometimes, it is also necessary to find out the IP address associated with a given Ethernet address. This happens when a diskless machine wants to boot from a server on the network, which is quite a common situation on local area networks. A diskless client, however, has virtually no information about itself – except for its Ethernet address! So what it basically does is broadcast a message containing a plea for boot servers to tell it its IP address. There's another protocol for this, named *Reverse Address Resolution Protocol*, or RARP. Along with the BOOTP protocol, it serves to define a procedure for bootstrapping diskless clients over the network.

2.4   IP Routing

2.4.1   IP Networks

◇   When you write a letter to someone, you usually put a complete address on the envelope, specifying the country, state, zip code, etc. After you put it into the letter box, the postal service will deliver it to its destination: it will be sent to the country indicated, whose national service will dispatch it to the proper state and region, etc. The advantage of this hierarchical scheme is rather obvious: Wherever you post the letter, the local postmaster will know roughly the direction to forward the letter to, but doesn't have to care which way the letter will travel by within the destination country.

IP networks are structured in a similar way. The whole Internet consists of a number of proper networks, called *autonomous systems*. Each such system performs any routing between its member hosts internally, so that the task of delivering a datagram is reduced to finding a path to the destination host's network. This means, as soon as the datagram is handed to *any* host that is on that particular network, further processing is done exclusively by the network itself.

2.4.2   Subnetworks

This structure is reflected by splitting IP addresses into a host and network part, as explained above. By default, the destination network is derived from the network part of the IP address. Thus, hosts with identical IP network numbers should be found within the same network, and vice versa.[2]

It makes sense to offer a similar scheme *inside* the network, too, since it may consist of a collection of hundreds of smaller networks itself, with the smallest units being physical networks like Ethernets. Therefore, IP allows you to subdivide an IP network into several *subnets*.

A subnet takes over responsibility for delivering datagrams to a certain range of IP addresses from the IP network it is part of. As with classes A, B, or C, it is identified by the network part of the IP addresses. However, the network part is now extended to include some bits from the host part. The number of bits that are interpreted as the subnet number is given by the so-called *subnet mask*, or *netmask*. This is a 32 bit number, too, which specifies the bit mask for the network part of the IP address.

The campus network of Groucho Marx University is an example of such a network. It has a class B network number of **149.76.0.0**, and its netmask is therefore **255.255.0.0**.

Internally, GMU's campus network consists of several smaller networks, such as the LANs of various departments. So the range of IP addresses is broken up into 254 subnets, **149.76.1.0** through **149.76.254.0**. For example, the Department of Theoretical Physics has been assigned **149.76.12.0**. The campus backbone is a network by its own right, and is given **149.76.1.0**. These subnets share the same IP network number, while the third octet is used to distinguish between them. Thus they will use a subnet mask of **255.255.255.0**.

---

[2]Autonomous systems are slightly more general, however. They may comprise more than one IP network.

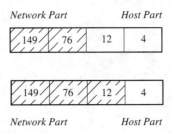

Figure 2.1: Subnetting a class B network

Figure 2.1 shows how **149.76.12.4**, the address of **quark**, is interpreted differently when the address is taken as an ordinary class B network, and when used with subnetting.

It is worth noting that subnetting (as the technique of generating subnets is called) is only an *internal division* of the network. Subnets are generated by the network owner (or the administrators). Frequently, subnets are created to reflect existing boundaries, be they physical (between two Ethernets), administrative (between two departments), or geographical, and authority over these subnets is delegated to some contact person. However, this structure affects only the network's internal behavior, and is completely invisible to the outside world.

2.4.3 Gateways

Subnetting is not only an organizational benefit, it is frequently a natural consequence of hardware boundaries. The viewpoint of a host on a given physical network, such as an Ethernet, is a very limited one: the only hosts it is able to talk to directly are those of the network it is on. All other hosts can be accessed only through so-called *gateways*. A gateway is a host that is connected to two or more physical networks simultaneously and is configured to switch packets between them.

For IP to be able to easily recognize if a host is on a local physical network, different physical networks have to belong to different IP networks. For example the network number **149.76.4.0** is reserved for hosts on the mathematics LAN. When sending a datagram to **quark**, the network software on **erdos** immediately sees from the IP address, **149.76.12.4**, that the destination host is on a different physical network, and therefore can be reached only through a gateway (**sophus** by default).

sophus itself is connected to two distinct subnets: the Mathematics Department, and the campus backbone. It accesses each through a different interface, *eth0* and *fddi0*, respectively. Now, what IP address do we assign it? Should we give it one on subnet **149.76.1.0**, or on **149.76.4.0**?

The answer is: both. When talking to a host on the Maths LAN, **sophus** should use an IP address of **149.76.4.1**, and when talking to a host on the backbone, it should use **149.76.1.4**.

Thus, a gateway is assigned one IP address per network it is on. These addresses — along with the corresponding netmask — are tied to the interface the subnet is accessed through. Thus, the mapping of interfaces and addresses for **sophus** would look like this:

iface	address	netmask
eth0	**149.76.4.1**	**255.255.255.0**
fddi0	**149.76.1.4**	**255.255.255.0**
lo	**127.0.0.1**	**255.0.0.0**

The last entry describes the loopback interface *lo*, which was introduced above.

Figure 2.2 shows a part of the network topology at Groucho Marx University (GMU). Hosts that are on two subnets at the same time are shown with both addresses.

Generally, you can ignore the subtle difference between attaching an address to a host or its interface. For hosts that are on one network only, like **erdos**, you would generally refer of the host as having this-and-that

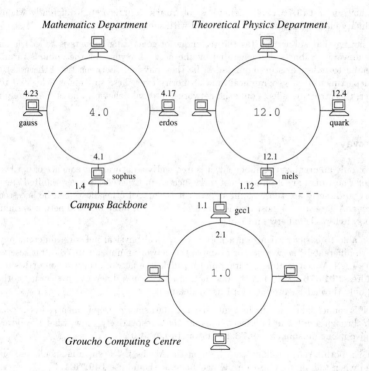

Figure 2.2: A part of the net topology at Groucho Marx Univ.

IP address although strictly speaking, it's the Ethernet interface that has this IP address. However, this distinction is only really important when you refer to a gateway.

2.4.4 The Routing Table

We are now focusing our attention on how IP chooses a gateway to use when delivering a datagram to a remote network.

We have seen before that **erdos**, when given a datagram for **quark**, checks the destination address and finds it is not on the local network. It therefore sends it to the default gateway, **sophus**, which is now basically faced with the same task. **sophus** recognizes that **quark** is not on any of the networks it is connected to directly, so it has to find yet another gateway to forward it through. The correct choice would be *niels*, the gateway to the Physics Department. **sophus** therefore needs some information to associate a destination network with a suitable gateway.

The routing information IP uses for this is basically a table linking networks to gateways that reach them. A catch-all entry (the *default route*) must generally be supplied, too; this is the gateway associated with network **0.0.0.0**. All packets to an unknown network are sent through the default route. On **sophus**, this table might look like this:

Network	Gateway	Interface
149.76.1.0	-	fddi0
149.76.2.0	**149.76.1.2**	fddi0
149.76.3.0	**149.76.1.3**	fddi0
149.76.4.0	-	eth0
149.76.5.0	**149.76.1.5**	fddi0
...	...	...
0.0.0.0	**149.76.1.2**	fddi0

Routes to a network that **sophus** is directly connected to don't require a gateway; therefore they show a gateway entry of "-".

Routing tables may be built by various means. For small LANs, it is usually most efficient to construct them by hand and feed them to IP using the *route* command at boot time (see chapter 5). For larger networks, they are built and adjusted at run-time by *routing daemons*; these run on central hosts of the network and exchange routing information to compute "optimal" routes between the member networks.

Depending on the size of the network, different routing protocols will be used. For routing inside autonomous systems (such as Groucho Marx campus), the *internal routing protocols* are used. The most prominent one is RIP, the Routing Information Protocol, which is implemented by the BSD *routed* daemon. For routing between autonomous systems, *external routing protocols* like EGP (External Gateway Protocol), or BGP (Border Gateway Protocol) have to be used; these (as well as RIP) have been implemented in the University of Cornell's *gated* daemon.[3]

2.4.5 Metric Values

Dynamic routing based on RIP chooses the best route to some destination host or network based on the number of "hops", that is, the gateways a datagram has to pass before reaching it. The shorter a route is, the better RIP rates it. Very long routes with 16 or more hops are regarded as unusable, and are discarded.

To use RIP to manage routing information internal to your local network, you have to run *gated* on all hosts. At boot time, *gated* checks for all active network interfaces. If there is more than one active interface (not counting the loopback interface), it assumes the host is switching packets between several networks, and will actively exchange and broadcast routing information. Otherwise, it will only passively receive any RIP updates and update the local routing table.

When broadcasting the information from the local routing table, *gated* computes the length of the route from the so-called *metric value* associated with the routing table entry. This metric value is set by the system

---

[3] *routed* is considered broken by many people. Since *gated* supports RIP as well, it is better to use that instead.

administrator when configuring the route and should reflect the actual cost of using this route. Therefore, the metric of a route to a subnet the host is directly connected to should always be zero, while a route going through two gateways should have a metric of two. However, note that you don't have to bother about metrics when you don't use *RIP* or *gated*.

2.5   The Internet Control Message Protocol

IP has a companion protocol that we haven't talked about yet. This is the *Internet Control Message Protocol* (ICMP) and is used by the kernel networking code to communicate error messages and the like to other hosts. For instance, assume that you are on **erdos** again and want to *telnet* to port 12345 on **quark**, but there's no process listening on that port. When the first TCP packet for this port arrives on **quark**, the networking layer will recognize this and immediately return an ICMP message to **erdos** stating "Port Unreachable".

There are quite a number of messages ICMP understands, many of which deal with error conditions. However, there is one very interesting message called the Redirect message. It is generated by the routing module when it detects that another host is using it as a gateway, although there is a much shorter route. For example, after booting the routing table of **sophus** may be incomplete, containing the routes to the Mathematics network, to the FDDI backbone, and the default route pointing at the Groucho Computing Center's gateway (**gcc1**). Therefore, any packets for **quark** would be sent to **gcc1** rather than to **niels**, the gateway to the Physics Department. When receiving such a datagram, **gcc1** will notice that this is a poor choice of route, and will forward the packet to **niels**, at the same time returning an ICMP Redirect message to **sophus** telling it of the superior route.

Now, this seems a very clever way to avoid having to set up any but the most basic routes manually. However be warned that relying on dynamic routing schemes, be it RIP or ICMP Redirect messages, is not always a good idea. ICMP Redirect and RIP offer you little or no choice in verifying that some routing information is indeed authentic. This allows malicious good-for-nothings to disrupt your entire network traffic, or do even worse things. For this reason, there are some versions of the Linux networking code that treat Redirect messages that affect network routes, as if they were only Redirects for host routes.

2.6   The Domain Name System

2.6.1   Hostname Resolution

◇   As described above, addressing in TCP/IP networking revolves around 32 bit numbers. However, you will have a hard time remembering more than a few of these. Therefore, hosts are generally known by "ordinary" names such as **gauss** or **strange**. It is then the application's duty to find the IP address corresponding to this name. This process is called *host name resolution*.

An application that wants to find the IP address of a given host name does not have to provide its own routines for looking up a hosts and IP addresses. Instead, it relies on number of library functions that do this transparently, called *gethostbyname(3)* and *gethostbyaddr(3)*. Traditionally, these and a number of related procedures were grouped in a separate library called the resolver library; on Linux, these are part of the standard *libc*. Colloquially, this collection of functions are therefore referred to as "the resolver".

Now, on a small network like an Ethernet, or even a cluster of them, it is not very difficult to maintain tables mapping host names to addresses. This information is usually kept in a file named */etc/hosts*. When adding or removing hosts, or reassigning addresses, all you have to do is update the *hosts* on all hosts. Quite obviously, this will become burdensome with networks than comprise more than a handful of machines.

One solution to this problem is NIS, the *Network Information System* developed by Sun Microsystems, colloquially called YP, or *Yellow Pages*. NIS stores the *hosts* file (and other information) in a database on a master host, from which clients may retrieve it as needed. Still, this approach is only suitable for medium-sized networks such as LANs, because it involves maintaining the entire *hosts* database centrally, and distributing it to all servers.

On the Internet, address information was initially stored in a single *HOSTS.TXT* database, too. This file was maintained at the Network Information Center, or NIC, and had to be downloaded and installed by all participating sites. When the network grew, several problems with this scheme arose. Beside the administrative overhead involved in installing *HOSTS.TXT* regularly, the load on the servers that distributed it became too high. Even more severe was the problem that all names had to be registered with the NIC, which had to make sure that no name was issued twice.

This is why, in 1984, a new name resolution scheme has been adopted, the *Domain Name System*. DNS was designed by Paul Mockapetris, and addresses both problems simultaneously.

2.6.2 Enter DNS

DNS organizes host names in a hierarchy of domains. A domain is a collection of sites that are related in some sense — be it because they form a proper network (e.g. all machines on a campus, or all hosts on BITNET), because they all belong to a certain organization (like the U.S. government), or because they're simply geographically close. For instance, universities are grouped in the **edu** domain, with each University or College using a separate *subdomain* below which their hosts are subsumed. Groucho Marx University might be given the **groucho.edu** domain, with the LAN of the Mathematics Department being assigned **maths.groucho.edu**. Hosts on the departmental network would have this domain name tacked onto their host name; so **erdos** would be known as **erdos.maths.groucho.edu**. This is called the *fully qualified domain name*, or FQDN, which uniquely identifies this host world-wide.

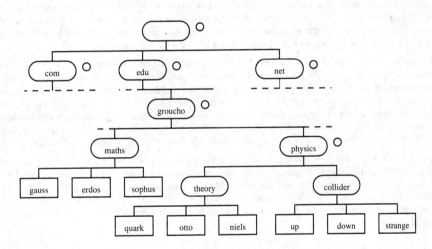

Figure 2.3: A part of the domain name space

Figure 2.3 shows a section of the name space. The entry at the root of this tree, which is denoted by a single dot, is quite appropriately called the *root domain*, and encompasses all other domains. To indicate that a host name is a fully qualified domain name, rather than a name relative to some (implicit) local domain, it is sometimes written with a trailing dot. This signifies that the name's last component is the root domain.

Depending on its location in the name hierarchy, a domain may be called top-level, second-level, or third-level. More levels of subdivision occur, but are rare. These are a couple of top-level domains you may see frequently:

edu   (Mostly US) educational institutions like universities, etc.

com   Commercial organizations, companies.

org   Non-commercial organizations. Often private UUCP networks are in this domain.

net   Gateways and other administrative host on a network.

mil   US military institutions.

gov   US government institutions.

uucp   Officially, all site names formerly used as UUCP names without domain, have been moved to
                   this domain.

Technically, the first four of these belong to the US part of the Internet, but you may also see non-US sites
in these domains. This is especially true of the **net** domain. However, **mil** and **gov** are used exclusively in the
US.

Outside the US, each country generally uses a top-level domain of its own named after the two-letter country
code defined in ISO-3166. Finland, for instance, uses the **fi** domain, **fr** is used by France, **de** by Germany,
or **au** by Australia etc. Below this top-level domain, each country's NIC is free to organize host names in
whatever way they want. Australia, for example, has second-level domain similar to the international top-level
domains, named **com.au**, **edu.au**, and so on. Others, like Germany, don't use this extra level, but rather have
slightly longish names that refer directly to the organizations running a particular domain. For example, it's
not uncommon to see host names like **ftp.informatik.uni-erlangen.de**. Chalk that up to German efficiency.

Of course, these national domains do not imply that a host below that domain is actually located in that
country; it only signals that the host has been registered with that country's NIC. A Swedish manufacturer
might have a branch in Australia, and still have all its hosts registered with the **se** top-level domain.

Now, organizing the name space in a hierarchy of domain names nicely solves the problem of name unique-
ness; with DNS, a host name has to be unique only within its domain to give it a name different from all other
hosts world-wide. Furthermore, fully qualified names are quite easy to remember. Taken by themselves, these
are already very good resaons to split up a large domain into several subdomains.

But DNS does even more for you than than this: it allows you to delegate authority over a subdomain to
its administrators. For example, the maintainers at the Groucho Computing Center might create a subdomain
for each department; we already encountered the **maths** and **physics** subdomains above. When they find
the network at the Physics Department too large and chaotic to manage from outside (after all, physicists are
known to be an unruly bunch of people), they may simply pass control over the **physics.groucho.edu** domain
to the administrators of this network. These are then free to use whatever host names they like, and assign
them IP addresses from their network in whatever fashion the like, without outside interference.

To this end, the name space is split up into *zones*, each rooted at a domain. Note the subtle difference
between a zone and a domain: the *domain* **groucho.edu** encompasses all hosts at the Groucho Marx University,
while the *zone* **groucho.edu** includes only the hosts that are managed by the Computing Center directly, for
example those at the Mathematics Department. The hosts at the Physics Department belong to a different
zone, namely **physics.groucho.edu**. In figure 2.3, the start of a zone is marked by a small circle to the right
of the domain name.

2.6.3   Name Lookups with DNS

At first glance, all this domain and zone fuss seems to make name resolution an awfully complicated business.
After all, if no central authority controls what names are assigned to which hosts, then how is a humble
application supposed to know?!

Now comes the really ingenuous part about DNS. If you want to find out the IP address of **erdos**, then,
DNS says, go ask the people that manage it, and they will tell you.

In fact, DNS is a giant distributed database. It is implemented by means of so-called name servers that
supply information on a given domain or set of domains. For each zone, there are at least two, at most a few,
name servers that hold all authoritative information on hosts in that zone. To obtain the IP address of **erdos**,
all you have to do is contact the name server for the **groucho.edu** zone, which will then return the desired
data.

Easier said than done, you might think. So how do I know how to reach the name server at Groucho Marx
University? In case your computer isn't equipped with an address-resolving oracle, DNS provides for this, too.
When your application wants to look up information on **erdos**, it contacts a local name server, which conducts
a so-called iterative query for it. It starts off by sending a query to a name server for the root domain, asking for
the address of **erdos.maths.groucho.edu**. The root name server recognizes that this name does not belong
to its zone of authority, but rather to one below the **edu** domain. Thus, it tells you to contact an **edu** zone

name server for more information, and encloses a list of all **edu** name servers along with their addresses. Your local name server will then go on and query one of those, for instance **a.isi.edu**. In a manner similar to the root name server, **a.isi.edu** knows that the **groucho.edu** people run a zone of their own, and point you to their servers. The local name server will then present its query for **erdos** to one of these, which will finally recognize the name as belonging to its zone, and return the corresponding IP address.

Now, this looks like a lot of traffic being generated for looking up a measly IP address, but it's really only miniscule compared to the amount of data that would have to be transferred if we were still stuck with *HOSTS.TXT*. But there's still room for improvement with this scheme.

To improve response time during future queries, the name server will store the information obtained in its local *cache*. So the next time anyone on your local network wants to look up the address of a host in the **groucho.edu** domain, your name server will not have to go through the whole process again, but will rather go to the **groucho.edu** name server directly.[4]

Of course, the name server will not keep this information forever, but rather discard it after some period. This expiry interval is called the *time to live*, or TTL. Each datum in the DNS database is assigned such a TTL by administrators of the responsible zone.

2.6.4 Domain Name Servers

Name servers that hold all information on hosts within a zone are called *authoritative* for this zone, and are sometimes referred to as *master name servers*. Any query for a host within this zone will finally wind down at one of these master name servers.

To provide a coherent picture of a zone, its master servers must be fairly well synchronized. This is achieved by making one of them the *primary* server, which loads its zone information from data files, and making the others *secondary* servers who transfer the zone data from the primary server at regular intervals.

One reason to have several name servers is to distribute work load, another is redundancy. When one name server machine fails in a benign way, like crashing or losing its network connection, all queries will fall back to the other servers. Of course, this scheme doesn't protect you from server malfunctions that produce wrong replies to all DNS requests, e.g. from software bugs in the server program itself.

Of course, you can also think of running a name server that is not authoritative for any domain.[5] This type of server is useful nevertheless, as it is still able to conduct DNS queries for the applications running on the local network, and cache the information. It is therefore called a *caching-only* server.

2.6.5 The DNS Database

We have seen above that DNS does not only deal with IP addresses of hosts, but also exchanges information on name servers. There are in fact a whole bunch of different types of entries the DNS database may have.

A single piece of information from the DNS database is called a *resource record*, or RR for short. Each record has a type associated with it, describing the sort of data it represents, and a class specifying the type of network it applies to. The latter accomodates the needs of different addressing schemes, like IP addresses (the IN class), or addresses of Hesiod networks (used at MIT), and a few more. The prototypical resource record type is the A record which associates a fully qualified domain name with an IP address.

Of course, a host may have more than one name. However, one of these names must be identified as the official, or *canonical host name*, while the others are simply aliases referring to the former. The difference is that the canocical host name is the one with an A record associated, while the others only have a record of type CNAME which points to the canonical host name.

We will not go through all record types here, but save them for a later chapter, but rather give you a brief example here. Figure 2.4 shows a part of the domain database that is loaded into the name servers for the **physics.groucho.edu** zone.

Apart from A and CNAME records, you can see a special record at the top of the file, stretching several lines. This is the SOA resource record, signalling the *Start of Authority*, which holds general information on

---

[4]If it didn't, then DNS would be about as bad as any other method, because each query would involve the root name servers.
[5]Well, almost. A name server at least has to provide name service for **localhost** and reverse lookups of **127.0.0.1**.

```
;
; Authoritative Information on physics.groucho.edu
@                      IN    SOA          {
                       niels.physics.groucho.edu.
                       hostmaster.niels.physics.groucho.edu.
                       1034              ; serial no
                       360000            ; refresh
                       3600              ; retry
                       3600000           ; expire
                       3600              ; default ttl
                }
;
; Name servers
                       IN    NS     niels
                       IN    NS     gauss.maths.groucho.edu.
gauss.maths.groucho.edu. IN  A     149.76.4.23
;
; Theoretical Physics (subnet 12)
niels                  IN    A      149.76.12.1
                       IN    A      149.76.1.12
nameserver             IN    CNAME  niels
otto                   IN    A      149.76.12.2
quark                  IN    A      149.76.12.4
down                   IN    A      149.76.12.5
strange                IN    A      149.76.12.6
...
; Collider Lab. (subnet 14)
boson                  IN    A      149.76.14.1
muon                   IN    A      149.76.14.7
bogon                  IN    A      149.76.14.12
...
```

Figure 2.4: An excerpt from the *named.hosts* file for the Physics Department.

the zone the server is authoritative for. This comprises, for instance, the default time-to-live for all records.

Note that all names in the sample file that do not end with a dot should be interpreted relative to the **groucho.edu** domain. The special name "@" used in the SOA record refers to the domain name by itself.

We have seen above that the name servers for the **groucho.edu** domain somehow have to know about the **physics** zone so that they can point queries to their name servers. This is usually achieved by a pair of records: the NS record that gives the server's FQDN, and an A record associating an address with that name. Since these records are what holds the name space together, they are frequently called the *glue records*. They are the only instances of records where a parent zone actually holds information on hosts in the subordinate zone. The glue records pointing to the name servers for **physics.groucho.edu** are shown in figure 2.5.

```
;
; Zone data for the groucho.edu zone.
@                       IN      SOA        {
                        vax12.gcc.groucho.edu.
                        hostmaster.vax12.gcc.groucho.edu.
                        233               ; serial no
                        360000            ; refresh
                        3600              ; retry
                        3600000           ; expire
                        3600              ; default ttl
                        }
....
;
; Glue records for the physics.groucho.edu zone
physics                 IN      NS         niels.physics.groucho.edu.
                        IN      NS         gauss.maths.groucho.edu.
niels.physics           IN      A          149.76.12.1
gauss.maths             IN      A          149.76.4.23
...
```

Figure 2.5: An excerpt from the *named.hosts* file for GMU.

2.6.6 Reverse Lookups

Beside looking up the IP address belonging to a host, it is sometimes desirable to find out the canonical host name corresponding to an address. This is called *reverse mapping* and is used by several network services to verify a client's identity. When using a single *hosts* file, reverse lookups simply involve searching the file for a host that owns the IP address in question. With DNS, an exhaustive search of the name space is out of the question, of course. Instead, a special domain, **in-addr.arpa**, has been created which contains the IP addresses of all hosts in a reverted dotted-quad notation. For instance, an IP address of **149.76.12.4** corresponds to the name **4.12.76.149.in-addr.arpa**. The resource record type linking these names to their canonical host names is PTR.

Creating a zone of authority usually means that its administrators are given full control over how they assign addresses to names. Since they usually have one or more IP networks or subnets at their hands, there's a one-to-many mapping between DNS zones and IP networks. The Physics Department, for instance, comprises the subnets **149.76.8.0**, **149.76.12.0**, and **149.76.14.0**.

As a consequence, new zones in the **in-addr.arpa** domain have to be created along with the **physics** zone and delegated to the network administrators at the department: **8.76.149.in-addr.arpa**, **12.76.149.in-addr.arpa**, and **14.76.149.in-addr.arpa**. Otherwise, installing a new host at the Collider Lab would require them to contact their parent domain to have the new address entered into their **in-addr.arpa** zone file.

The zone database for subnet 12 is shown in figure 2.6. The corresponding glue records in the database of their parent zone is shown in figure 2.7.

One important consequence of this is that zones can only be created as supersets of IP networks, and, even more severe, that these network's netmasks have to be on byte boundaries. All subnets at Groucho Marx University have a netmask of **255.255.255.0**, whence an **in-addr.arpa** zone could be created for each subnet.

```
;
; the 12.76.149.in-addr.arpa domain.
@               IN      SOA     {
                        niels.physics.groucho.edu.
                        hostmaster.niels.physics.groucho.edu.
                        233 360000 3600 3600000 3600
                    }
2               IN      PTR         otto.physics.groucho.edu.
4               IN      PTR         quark.physics.groucho.edu.
5               IN      PTR         down.physics.groucho.edu.
6               IN      PTR         strange.physics.groucho.edu.
```

Figure 2.6: An excerpt from the *named.rev* file for subnet 12.

```
;
; the 76.149.in-addr.arpa domain.
@                   IN      SOA         {
                        vax12.gcc.groucho.edu.
                        hostmaster.vax12.gcc.groucho.edu.
                        233 360000 3600 3600000 3600
                    }
...
; subnet 4: Mathematics Dept.
1.4                 IN      PTR         sophus.maths.groucho.edu.
17.4                IN      PTR         erdos.maths.groucho.edu.
23.4                IN      PTR         gauss.maths.groucho.edu.
...
; subnet 12: Physics Dept, separate zone
12                  IN      NS          niels.physics.groucho.edu.
                    IN      NS          gauss.maths.groucho.edu.
niels.physics.groucho.edu. IN  A 149.76.12.1
gauss.maths.groucho.edu. IN  A    149.76.4.23
...
```

Figure 2.7: An excerpt from the *named.rev* file for network **149.76**.

However, if the netmask was **255.255.255.128** instead, creating zones for the subnet **149.76.12.128** would be impossible, because there's no way to tell DNS that the **12.76.149.in-addr.arpa** domain has been split in two zones of authority, with host names ranging from **1** through **127**, and **128** through **255**, respectively.

Chapter 3

Configuring the Networking Hardware

3.1 Devices, Drivers, and all that

Up to now, we've been talking quite a bit about network interfaces and general TCP/IP issues, but didn't really cover exactly *what* happens when "the networking code" in the kernel accesses a piece of hardware. For this, we have to talk a little about the concept of interfaces and drivers.

First, of course, there's the hardware itself, for example an Ethernet board: this is a slice of Epoxy, cluttered with lots of tiny chips with silly numbers on them, sitting in a slot of your PC. This is what we generally call a device.

For you to be able to use the Ethernet board, special functions have to be present in your Linux kernel that understand the particular way this device is accessed. These are the so-called device drivers. For example, Linux has device drivers for several brands of Ethernet boards that are very similar in function. They are known as the "Becker Series Drivers", named after their author, Donald Becker. A different example is the D-Link driver that handles a D-Link pocket adaptor attached to a parallel port.

But, what do we mean when we say a driver "handles" a device? Let's go back to that Ethernet board we examined above. The driver has to be able to communicate with the peripheral's on-board logic somehow: it has to send commands and data to the board, while the board should deliver any data received to the driver.

In PCs, this communication takes place through an area of I/O memory that is mapped to on-board registers and the like. All commands and data the kernel sends to the board have to go through these registers. I/O memory is generally described by giving its starting or *base address*. Typical base addresses for Ethernet boards are 0x300, or 0x360.

Usually, you don't have to worry about any hardware issues such as the base address, because the kernel makes an attempt at boot time to detect a board's location. This is called autoprobing, which means that the kernel reads several memory locations and compares the data read with what it should see if a certain Ethernet board was installed. However, there may be Ethernet boards it cannot detect automatically; this is sometimes the case with cheap Ethernet cards that are not-quite clones of standard boards from other manufacturers. Also, the kernel will attempt to detect only one Ethernet device when booting. If you're using more than one board, you have to tell the kernel about this board explicitly.

Another such parameter that you might have to tell the kernel about is the interrupt request channel. Hardware components usually interrupt the kernel when they need care taken of them, e.g. when data has arrived, or a special condition occurs. In a PC, interrupts may occur on one of 15 interrupt channels numbered 0, 1, and 3 through 15. The interrupt number assigned to a hardware component is called its *interrupt request number*, or IRQ.[1]

As described in chapter 2, the kernel accesses a device through a so-called interface. Interfaces offer an abstract set of functions that is the same across all types of hardware, such as sending or receiving a datagram.

Interfaces are identified by means of names. These are names defined internally in the kernel, and are not device files in the */dev* directory. Typical names are *eth0*, *eth1*, etc, for Ethernet interfaces. The assignment

---

[1] IRQs 2 and 9 are the same because the PC has two cascaded interrupt processors with eight IRQs each; the secondary processor is connected to IRQ 2 of the primary one.

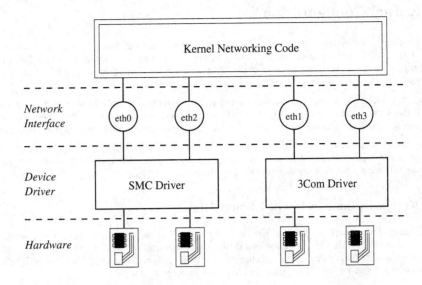

Figure 3.1: The relationship between drivers, interfaces, and the hardware.

of interfaces to devices usually depends on the order in which devices are configured; for instance the first Ethernet board installed will become *eth0*, the next will be *eth1*, and so on. One exception from this rule are SLIP interfaces, which are assigned dynamically; that is, whenever a SLIP connection is established, an interface is assigned to the serial port.

The picture given in figure 3.1 tries to show the relationship between the hardware, device drivers and interfaces.

When booting, the kernel displays what devices it detects, and what interfaces it installs. The following is an excerpt of a typical boot screen:

```
This processor honours the WP bit even when in supervisor mode. Good.
Floppy drive(s): fd0 is 1.44M
Swansea University Computer Society NET3.010
IP Protocols: ICMP, UDP, TCP
PPP: version 0.2.1 (4 channels) OPTIMIZE_FLAGS
TCP compression code copyright 1989 Regents of the University of California
PPP line discipline registered.
SLIP: version 0.7.5 (4 channels)
CSLIP: code copyright 1989 Regents of the University of California
dl0: D-Link DE-600 pocket adapter, Ethernet Address: 00:80:C8:71:76:95
Checking 386/387 coupling... Ok, fpu using exception 16 error reporting.
Linux version 1.1.11 (okir@monad) #3 Sat May 7 14:57:18 MET DST 1994
```

This shows that the kernel has been compiled with TCP/IP enabled, and drivers for SLIP, CSLIP, and PPP included. The third line from below says that a D-Link pocket adaptor was detected, and installed as interface *dl0*. If you have a different type of Ethernet card, the kernel will usually print a line starting with *eth0*, followed by the type of card detected. If you have an Ethernet card installed but don't see any such message, this means that the kernel is unable to detect your board properly. This is dealt with in a later section.

3.2 Kernel Configuration

Most Linux distributions come along with boot disks that work for all common types of PC hardware. This means that the kernel on those disks has all sorts of drivers configured in that you will never need, but which waste precious system memory because parts of the kernel cannot be swapped out. Therefore, you will generally roll your own kernel, including only those drivers you actually need or want.

When running a Linux system, you should be familiar with building a kernel. The basics of this are explained in Matt Welsh's "Installation and Getting Started" Guide, which is also part of the Linux Documentation Project's series. In this section, we will therefore discuss only those configuration options that affect networking.

When running `make config`, you will first be asked general configurations, for instance whether you want kernel math emulation or not, etc. One of these asks you whether you want TCP/IP networking support. You must answer this with y to get a kernel capable of networking.

3.2.1 Kernel Options in Linux 1.0 and Higher

After the general option part is complete, the configuration will go on to ask you for various features such as SCSI drivers, etc. The subsequent list questions deal with networking support. The exact set of configuration options is in constant flux because of the ongoing development. A typical list of options offered by most kernel versions around 1.0 and 1.1 looks like this (comments are given in italics):

```
*
* Network device support
*
Network device support? (CONFIG_ETHERCARDS) [y]
```

Despite the macro name displayed in brackets, you must answer this question with y if you want to use *any* type of networking devices, regardless of whether this is Ethernet, SLIP, or PPP. When answering this question with y, support for Ethernet-type devices is enabled automatically. Support for other types of network drivers must be enabled separately:

```
SLIP (serial line) support? (CONFIG_SLIP) [y]
 SLIP compressed headers (SL_COMPRESSED) [y]
PPP (point-to-point) support (CONFIG_PPP) [y]
PLIP (parallel port) support (CONFIG_PLIP) [n]
```

These questions concern the various link layer protocols supported by Linux. SLIP allows you to transport IP datagrams across serial lines. The compressed header option provides support for CSLIP, a technique that compresses TCP/IP headers to as little as three bytes. Note that this kernel option does not turn on CSLIP automatically, it merely provides the necessary kernel functions for it.

PPP is another protocol to send network traffic across serial lines. It is much more flexible than SLIP, and is not limited to IP, but will also support IPX once it is implemented. As PPP support has been completed only lately, this option may not be present in your kernel.

PLIP provides for a way to send IP datagrams across a parallel port connection. It is mostly used to communicate with PCs running DOS.

The following questions deal with Ethernet boards from various vendors. As more drivers are being developed, you are likely to see questions added to this section. If you want to build a kernel you can use on a number of different machines, you can enable more than one driver.

```
NE2000/NE1000 support (CONFIG_NE2000) [y]
WD80*3 support (CONFIG_WD80x3) [n]
SMC Ultra support (CONFIG_ULTRA) [n]
3c501 support (CONFIG_EL1) [n]
3c503 support (CONFIG_EL2) [n]
3c509/3c579 support (CONFIG_EL3) [n]
HP PCLAN support (CONFIG_HPLAN) [n]
```

```
     AT1500 and NE2100 (LANCE and PCnet-ISA) support (CONFIG_LANCE) [n]
     AT1700 support (CONFIG_AT1700) [n]
     DEPCA support (CONFIG_DEPCA) [n]
     D-Link DE600 pocket adaptor support (CONFIG_DE600) [y]
     AT-LAN-TEC/RealTek pocket adaptor support (CONFIG_ATP) [n]
     *
     * CD-ROM drivers
     *
     ...
```

Finally, in the filesystem section, the configuration script will ask you whether you want support for NFS, the networking filesystem. NFS lets you export filesystems to several hosts, which makes the files appear as if they were on an ordinary hard disk attached to the host.

```
     NFS filesystem support (CONFIG_NFS_FS) [y]
```

3.2.2 Kernel Options in Linux 1.1.14 and Higher

Starting with Linux 1.1.14, which added alpha support for IPX, the configuration procedure changed slightly. The general options section now asks whether you want networking support in general. It is immediately followed by a couple of question on miscellaneous networking options.

```
     *
     * Networking options
     *
     TCP/IP networking (CONFIG_INET) [y]
```

To use TCP/IP networking, you must answer this question with **y**. If you answer with **n**, however, you will still be able to compile the kernel with IPX support.

```
     IP forwarding/gatewaying (CONFIG_IP_FORWARD) [n]
```

You have to enable this option if your system acts as a gateway between two Ethernets, or between and Ethernet and a SLIP link, etc. Although it doesn't hurt to enable this by default, you may want to disable this to configure a host as a so-called firewall. Firewalls are hosts that are connected to two or more networks, but don't route traffic between them. They are commonly used to provide users from a company network with Internet access at a minimal risk to the internal network. Users will be allowed to log into the firewall and use Internet services, but the company's machines will be protected from outside attacks because any incoming connections can't cross the firewall.

```
     *
     * (it is safe to leave these untouched)
     *
     PC/TCP compatibility mode (CONFIG_INET_PCTCP) [n]
```

This option works around an incompatibility with some versions of PC/TCP, a commercial TCP/IP implementation for DOS-based PCs. If you enable this option, you will still be able to communicate with normal UNIX machines, but performance may be hurt over slow links.

```
     Reverse ARP (CONFIG_INET_RARP) [n]
```

This function enables RARP, the Reverse Address Resolution Protocol. RARP is used by diskless clients and X terminals to inquire their IP address when booting. You should enable RARP only when you plan to serve this sort of clients. The latest package of network utilities (*net-0.32d*) contains a small utility named *rarp* that allows you to add systems to the RARP cache.

```
     Assume subnets are local (CONFIG_INET_SNARL) [y]
```

When sending data over TCP, the kernel has to break up the stream into several packets before giving it to IP. For hosts that can be reached over a local network such as an Ethernet, larger packets will be used than for hosts where data has to go through long-distance links.[2] If you don't enable *SNARL*, the kernel will assume only those networks are local that it actually has an interface to. However, if you look at the class B network at Groucho Marx University, the whole class B network is local, but most hosts interface to only one or two subnets. If you enable *SNARL*, the kernel will assume *all* subnets are local and use large packets when talking to all hosts on campus.

If you do want to use smaller packet sizes for data sent to specific hosts (because, for instance, the data goes through a SLIP link), you can do so using the *mtu* option of *route*, which is briefly discussed at the end of this chapter.

```
Disable NAGLE algorithm (normally enabled) (CONFIG_TCP_NAGLE_OFF) [n]
```

Nagle's rule is a heuristic to avoid sending particularly small IP packets, also called tinygrams. Tinygrams are usually created by interactive networking tools that transmit single keystrokes, such as *telnet* or *rsh*. Tinygrams can become particularly wasteful on low-bandwidth links like SLIP. The Nagle algorithm attempts to avoid them by holding back transmission of TCP data briefly under some circumstances. You might only want to disable Nalge's algorithm if you have severe problems with packets getting dropped.

```
The IPX protocol (CONFIG_IPX) [n]
```

This enables support for IPX, the transport protocol used by Novell Networking. It is still under development, and isn't really useful yet. One benefit of this will be that you can exchange data with IPX-based DOS utilities one day, and route traffic between your Novell-based networks through a PPP link. Support for the high-level protocols of Novell networking is however not in sight, as the specifications for these are available only at horrendous cost and under a non-disclosure agreement.

Starting in the 1.1.16 kernel, Linux supports another driver type, the dummy driver. The following question appears toward the start of the device driver section.

```
Dummy net driver support (CONFIG_DUMMY) [y]
```

The dummy driver doesn't really do much, but is quite useful on standalone or SLIP hosts. It is basically a masqueraded loopback interface. The reason to have this sort of interface is that on hosts that do SLIP but have no Ethernet, you want to have an interface that bears your IP address all the time. This is discussed in a little more detail in section The Dummy Interface in chapter 5.

3.3   A Tour of Linux Network Devices

The Linux kernel supports a number of hardware drivers for various types of equipment. This section gives a short overview of the driver families available, and the interface names used for them.

There are a number of standard names for interfaces in Linux, which are listed below. Most drivers support more than one interface, in which case the interfaces are numbered, as in *eth0*, *eth1*, etc.

lo   The local loopback interface. It is used for testing purposes, as well as a couple of network applications. It works like a closed circuit in that any datagram written to it will be immediately returned to the host's networking layer. There's always one loopback device present in the kernel, and there's little sense in having fewer or more.

ethn   The *n*-th Ethernet card. This is the generic interface name for most Ethernet boards.

dln   These interfaces access a D-Link DE-600 pocket adapter, another Ethernet device. It is a little special in that the DE-600 is driven through a parallel port.

---

[2]This is to avoid fragmentation by links that have a very small maximum packet size.

sln   The *n*-th SLIP interface. SLIP interfaces are associated with serial lines in the order in which they are allocated for SLIP; i.e., the first serial line being configured for SLIP becomes *sl0*, etc. The kernel supports up to four SLIP interfaces.

pppn   The *n*-th PPP interface. Just like SLIP interfaces, a PPP interface is associated with a serial line once it is converted to PPP mode. At the moment, up to four interfaces are supported.

plipn   The *n*-th PLIP interface. PLIP transports IP datagrams over parallel lines. Up to three PLIP interfaces are supported. They are allocated by the PLIP driver at system boot time, and are mapped onto parallel ports.

For other interface drivers that may be added in the future, like ISDN, or AX.25, other names will be introduced. Drivers for IPX (Novell's networking protocol), and AX.25 (used by ham radio amateurs) are under development, but are at alpha stage still.

During the following sections, we will discuss the details of using the drivers described above.

3.4   Ethernet Installation

The current Linux network code supports various brands of Ethernet cards. Most drivers were written by Donald Becker (**becker@cesdis.gsfc.nasa.gov**), who authored a family of drivers for cards based on the National Semiconductor 8390 chip; these have become known as the Becker Series Drivers. There are also drivers for a couple of products from D-Link, among them the D-Link pocket adaptor that allows you to access an Ethernet through a parallel port. The driver for this was written by Bjørn Ekwall (**bj0rn@blox.se**). The DEPCA driver was written by David C. Davies (**davies@wanton.lkg.dec.com**).

3.4.1   Ethernet Cabling

If you're installing an Ethernet for the first time in your life, a few words about the cabling may be in order here. Ethernet is very picky about proper cabling. The cable must be terminated on both ends with a 50 Ohm resistor, and you must not have any branches (i.e. three cables connected in a star-shape). If you are using a thin coax cable with T-shaped BNC junctions, these junctions must be twisted on the board's connector directly; you should not insert a cable segment.

If you connect to a thicknet installation, you have to attach your host through a transceiver (sometimes called Ethernet Attachment Unit). You can plug the transceiver into the 15-pin AUI port on your board directly, but may also use a shielded cable.

3.4.2   Supported Boards

A complete list of supported boards is available in the Ethernet HOWTOs posted monthly to **comp.os.linux.announce** by Paul Gortmaker.[3]

Here's a list of the more widely-known boards supported by Linux. The actual list in the HOWTO is about three times longer. However, even if you find your board in this list, check the HOWTO first; there are sometimes important details about operating these cards. A case in point is the case of some DMA-based Ethernet boards that use the same DMA channel as the Adaptec 1542 SCSI controller by default. Unless you move either of them to a different DMA channel, you will wind up with the Ethernet board writing packet data to arbitrary locations on your hard disk.

3Com EtherLink
                Both 3c503 and 3c503/16 are supported, as are 3c507 and 3c509. The 3c501 is supported, too, but is too slow to be worth buying.

Novell Eagle   NE1000 and NE2000, and a variety of clones. NE1500 and NE2100 are supported, too.

---

[3]Paul can be reached at **gpg109@rsphysse.anu.edu.au**.

Western Digital/SMC

>WD8003 and WD8013 (same as SMC Elite and SMC Elite Plus) are supported, and also the newer SMC Elite 16 Ultra.

Hewlett Packard

>HP 27252, HP 27247B, and HP J2405A.

D-Link

>DE-600 pocket adaptor, DE-100, DE-200, and DE-220-T. There's also a patch kit for the DE-650-T, which is a PCMCIA card.[4]

DEC

>DE200 (32K/64K), DE202, DE100, and DEPCA rev E.

Allied Teliesis   AT1500 and AT1700.

To use one of these cards with Linux, you may use a precompiled kernel from one of the major Linux distributions. These generally have drivers for all of them built in. In the long term, however, it's better to roll your own kernel and compile in only those drivers you actually need.

3.4.3   Ethernet Autoprobing

At boot time, the Ethernet code will try to locate your board and determine its type. Cards are probed for at the following addresses and in the following order:

Board	Addresses probed for
WD/SMC	0x300, 0x280, 0x380, 0x240
SMC 16 Ultra	0x300, 0x280
3c501	0x280
3c503	0x300, 0x310, 0x330, 0x350, 0x250, 0x280, 0x2a0, 0x2e0
NEx000	0x300, 0x280, 0x320, 0x340, 0x360
HP	0x300, 0x320, 0x340, 0x280, 0x2C0, 0x200, 0x240
DEPCA	0x300, 0x320, 0x340, 0x360

There are two limitations to the autoprobing code. For one, it may not recognize all boards properly. This is especially true for some of the cheaper clones of common boards, but also for some WD80x3 boards. The second problem is that the kernel will not auto-probe for more than one board at the moment. This is a feature, because it is assumed you want to have control about which board is assigned which interface.

If you are using more than one board, or if the autoprobe should fail to detect your board, you have to tell the kernel explicitly about the card's base address and name.

In Net-3, you have can use two different schemes to accomplish this. One way is to change or add information in the *drivers/net/Space.c* file in the kernel source code that contains all information about drivers. This is recommended only if you are familiar with the networking code. A much better way is to provide the kernel with this information at boot time. If you use *lilo* to boot your system, you can pass parameters to the kernel by specifying them through the *append* option in *lilo.conf.* To inform the kernel about an Ethernet device, you can pass the following parameter:

>ether=*irq,base_addr,param1,param2,name*

The first four parameters are numerical, while the last is the device name. All numerical values are optional; if they are omitted or set to zero, the kernel will try to detect the value by probing for it, or use a default value.

The first parameter sets the IRQ assigned to the device. By default, the kernel will try to auto-detect the device's IRQ channel. The 3c503 driver has a special feature that selects a free IRQ from the list 5, 9, 3, 4, and configures the board to use this line.

---

[4]It can be gotten – along with other Laptop-related stuff – from **tsx-11.mit.edu** in *packages/laptops.*

The *base_addr* parameter gives the I/O base address of the board; a value of zero tells the kernel to probe the addresses listed above.

The remaining two parameters may be used differently by different drivers. For shared-memory boards such as the WD80x3, they specify start and end addresses of the shared memory area. Other cards commonly use *param1* to set the level of debugging information that is being displayed. Values of 1 through 7 denote increasing levels of verbosity, while 8 turns them off altogether; 0 denotes the default. The 3c503 driver uses *param2* to select the internal transceiver (default) or an external transceiver (a value of 1). The former uses the board's BNC connector; the latter uses its AUI port.

If you have two Ethernet boards, you can have Linux autodetect one board, and pass the second board's parameters with *lilo*. However, you must make sure the driver doesn't accidentally find the second board first, else the other one won't be registered at all. You do this by passing *lilo* a **reserve** option, which explicitly tells the kernel to avoid probing the I/O space taken up by the second board.

For instance, to make Linux install a second Ethernet board at 0x300 as *eth1*, you would pass the following parameters to the kernel:

```
reserve=0x300,32 ether=0,0x300,eth1
```

The *reserve* option makes sure no driver accesses the board's I/O space when probing for some device. You may also use the kernel parameters to override autoprobing for *eth0*:

```
reserve=0x340,32 ether=0,0x340,eth0
```

To turn off autoprobing altogether, you can specify a *base_addr* argument of -1:

```
ether=0,-1,eth0
```

3.5 The PLIP Driver

PLIP stands for *Parallel Line IP* and is a cheap way to network when you want to connect only two machines. It uses a parallel port and a special cable, achieving speeds of 10kBps to 20kBps.

PLIP was originally developed by Crynwr, Inc. Its design is rather ingenuous (or, if you prefer, hackish): for a long time, the parallel ports on PCs used to be only uni-directional printer ports; that is, the eight data lines could only be used to send from the PC to the peripheral device, but not the other way round. PLIP works around this by using the port's five status line for input, which limits it to transferring all data as nibbles (half bytes) only. This mode of operation is called mode zero PLIP. Today, these uni-directional ports don't seem to be used much anymore. Therefore, there is also a PLIP extension called mode 1 that uses the full 8 bit interface.

Currently, Linux only supports mode 0. Unlike earlier versions of the PLIP code, it now attempts to be compatible with the PLIP implementations from Crynwr, as well as the PLIP driver in NCSA *telnet*.[5] To connect two machines using PLIP, you need a special cable sold at some shops as "Null Printer" or "Turbo Laplink" cable. You can, however, make one yourself fairly easily. Appendix A shows you how.

The PLIP driver for Linux is the work of almost countless persons. It is currently maintained by Niibe Yutaka. If compiled into the kernel, it sets up a network interface for each of the possible printer ports, with *plip0* corresponding to parallel port *lp0*, *plip1* corresponding to *lp1*, etc. The mapping of interface to ports is currently this:

Interface	I/O Port	IRQ
plip0	0x3BC	7
plip1	0x378	7
plip2	0x278	5

---

[5]NCSA *telnet* is a popular program for DOS that runs TCP/IP over Ethernet or PLIP, and supports *telnet* and FTP.

If you have configured your printer port in a different way, you have to change these values in *drivers/net/Space.c* in the Linux kernel source, and build a new kernel.

This mapping does not mean, however, that you cannot use these parallel ports as usual. They are accessed by the PLIP driver only when the corresponding interface is configured *up*.

3.6   The SLIP and PPP Drivers

SLIP (Serial Line IP), and PPP (Point-to-Point Protocol) are a widely used protocol for sending IP packets over a serial link. A number of institutions offer dialup SLIP and PPP access to machines that are on the Internet, thus providing IP connectivity to private persons (something that's otherwise hardly affordable).

To run SLIP or PPP, no hardware modifications are necessary; you can use any serial port. Since serial port configuration is not specific to TCP/IP networking, a separate chapter has been devoted to this. Please refer to chapter 4 for more information.

Chapter 4

Setting up the Serial Hardware

There are rumors that there are some people out there in netland who only own one PC and don't have the money to spend on a T1 Internet link. To get their daily dose of news and mail nevertheless, they are said to rely on SLIP links, UUCP networks, and bulletin board systems (BBS's) that utilize public telephone networks.

This chapter is intended to help all those people who rely on modems to maintain their link. However, there are many details that this chapter cannot go into, for instance how to configure your modem for dialin. All these topics will be covered in the upcoming Serial HOWTO by Greg Hankins,[1] to be posted to **comp.os.linux.announce** on a regular basis.

4.1 Communication Software for Modem Links

There are a number of communication packages available for Linux. Many of them are *terminal programs* which allow a user to dial into another computer as if she was sitting in front of a simple terminal. The traditional terminal program for Unices is *kermit*. It is, however, somewhat Spartan. There are more comfortable programs available that support a dictionary of telephone numers, script languages for calling and logging into remote computer systems, etc. One of them is *minicom*, which is close to some terminal programs former DOS users might be accustomed to. There are also X-based communications packages, e.g. *seyon*.

Also, a number of Linux-based BBS packages are available for people that want to run a bulletin board system. Some of these packages can be found at **sunsite.unc.edu** in */pub/Linux/system/Network*.

Apart from terminal programs, there is also software that uses a serial link non-interactively to transport data to or from your computer. The advantage of this technique is that it takes much less time to download a few dozen kilobytes automatically, than it might take you to read your mail on-line in some mailbox and browse a bulletin board for interesting articles. On the other hand, this requires more disk storage because of the loads of useless information you usually get.

The epitome of this sort of communications software is UUCP. It is a program suite that copies files from one host to another, executes programs on a remote host, etc. It is frequently used to transport mail or news in private networks. Ian Taylor's UUCP package, which also runs under Linux, is described in the following chapter. Other non-interactive communication software is, for example, used throughout Fidonet. Ports of Fidonet applications like *ifmail* are also available.

SLIP, the serial line Internet protocol, is somewhat between, allowing both interactive and non-interactive use. Many people use SLIP to dial up their campus network or some other sort of public SLIP server to run FTP sessions, etc. SLIP may however also be used over permanent or semi-permanent connections for LAN-to-LAN coupling, although this is really only interesting with ISDN.

---

[1] To be reached at **gregh@cc.gatech.edu**.

4.2   Introduction to Serial Devices

The devices a UNIX kernel provides for accessing serial devices are typically called *ttys*. This is an abbreviation for *Teletype*™, which used to be one of the major manufacturers of terminals in the early days of Unix. The term is used nowadays for any character-based data terminal. Throughout this chapter, we will use the term exclusively to refer to kernel devices.

Linux distinguishes three classes of ttys: (virtual) consoles, pseudo-terminals (similar to a two-way pipe, used by application such as X11), and serial devices. The latter are also counted as ttys, because they permit interactive sessions over a serial connection; be it from a hard-wired terminal or a remote computer over a telephone line.

Ttys have a number of configurable parameters which can be set using the *ioctl(2)* system call. Many of them apply only to serial devices, since they need a great deal more flexibility to handle varying types of connections.

Among the most prominent line parameters are the line speed and parity. But there are also flags for the conversion between upper and lower case characters, of carriage return into line feed, etc. The tty driver may also support various *line disciplines* which make the device driver behave completely different. For example, the SLIP driver for Linux is implemented by means of a special line discipline.

There is a bit of ambiguity about how to measure a line's speed. The correct the term is *Bit rate*, which is related to the line's transfer speed measured in bits per second (or bps for short). Sometimes, you hear people refer to it as the *Baud rate*, which is not quite correct. These two terms are, however, not interchangeable. The Baud rate refers to a physical characteristic of some serial device, namely the clock rate at which pulses are transmitted. The bit rate rather denotes a current state of an existing serial connection between two points, namely the average number of bits transferred per second. It is important to know that these two values are usually different, as most devices encode more than one bit per electrical pulse.

4.3   Accessing Serial Devices

Like all devices in a UNIX system, serial ports are accessed through device special files, located in the */dev* directory. There are two varieties of device files related to serial drivers, and for each port, there is one device file from each of them. Depending on the file it is accessed by, the device will behave differently.

The first variety is used whenever the port is used for dialing in; it has a major number of 4, and the files are named *ttyS0*, *ttyS1*, etc. The second variety is used when dialing out through a port; the files are called *cua0*, etc, and have a major number of 5.

Minor numbers are identical for both types. If you have your modem on one of the ports *COM1* through *COM4*, its minor number will be the *COM* port number plus 63. If your setup is different from that, for example when using a board supporting multiple serial lines, please refer to the Serial Howto.

Assume your modem is on *COM2*. Thus its minor number will be 65, and its major number will be 5 for dialing out. There should be a device *cua1* which has these numbers. List the serial ttys in the */dev* directory. Columns 5 and 6 should show major and minor numbers, respectively:

```
$ ls -l /dev/cua*
crw-rw-rw-   1 root     root       5,   64 Nov 30 19:31 /dev/cua0
crw-rw-rw-   1 root     root       5,   65 Nov 30 22:08 /dev/cua1
crw-rw-rw-   1 root     root       5,   66 Oct 28 11:56 /dev/cua2
crw-rw-rw-   1 root     root       5,   67 Mar 19  1992 /dev/cua3
```

If there is no such device, you will have to create one: become super-user and type

```
# mknod -m 666 /dev/cua1 c 5 65
# chown root.root /dev/cua1
```

Some people suggest making */dev/modem* a symbolic link to your modem device, so that casual users don't have to remember the somewhat unintuitive *cua1*. However, you cannot use *modem* in one program, and the real device file name in another. This is because these programs use so-called *lock files* to signal that the device is used. By convention, the lock file name for *cua1*, for instance, is *LCK..cua1*. Using different device files for the same port means that programs will fail to recognize each other's lock files, and will both use the device at the same time. As a result, both applications will not work at all.

4.4   Serial Hardware

Linux currently supports a wide variety of serial boards which use the RS-232 standard. RS-232 is currently the most common standard for serial communcications in the PC world. It uses a number of circuits for transmitting single bits as well as for synchronization. Additional lines may be used for signaling the presence of a carrier (used by modems), and handshake.

Although hardware handshake is optional, it is very useful. It allows either of the two stations to signal whether it is ready to receive more data, or if the other station should pause until the receiver is done processing the incoming data. The lines used for this are called "Clear to Send" (CTS) and "Ready to Send" (RTS), respectively, which accounts for the colloquial name of hardware handshake, namely "RTS/CTS".

In PCs, the RS-232 interface is usually driven by a UART chip derived from the National Semiconductor 16450 chip, or a newer version thereof, the NSC 16550A[2]. Some brands (most notably internal modems equipped with the Rockwell chipset) also use completely different chips that have been programmed to behave as if they were 16550's.

The main difference between 16450's and 16550's that the latter have a FIFO buffer of 16 Bytes, while the former only have a 1-Byte buffer. This makes 16450's suitable for speeds up to 9600 Baud, while higher speeds require a 16550-compatible chip. Besides these chips, Linux also supports the 8250 chip, which was the original UART for the PC-AT.

In the default configuration, the kernel checks the four standard serial ports *COM1* through *COM4*. These will be assigned device minor numbers 64 through 67, as described above.

If you want to configure your serial ports properly, you should install Ted Tso's *setserial* command along with the *rc.serial* script. This script should be invoked from */etc/rc* at system boot time. It uses *setserial* to configure the kernel serial devices. A typical *rc.serial* script looks like this:

```
# /etc/rc.serial - serial line configuration script.
#
# Do wild interrupt detection
/sbin/setserial -W /dev/cua*

# Configure serial devices
/sbin/setserial /dev/cua0 auto_irq skip_test autoconfig
/sbin/setserial /dev/cua1 auto_irq skip_test autoconfig
/sbin/setserial /dev/cua2 auto_irq skip_test autoconfig
/sbin/setserial /dev/cua3 auto_irq skip_test autoconfig

# Display serial device configuration
/sbin/setserial -bg /dev/cua*
```

Please refer to the documentation that comes along with *setserial* for an explanation of the parameters.

If your serial card is not detected, or the *setserial -bg* command shows an incorrect setting, you will have to force the configuration by explicitly supplying the correct values. Users with internal modems equipped with the Rockwell chipset are reported to experience this problem. If, for example, the UART chip is reported to be a NSC 16450, while in fact it is NSC 16550-compatible, you have to change the configuration command for the offending port to

```
/sbin/setserial /dev/cua1 auto_irq skip_test autoconfig uart 16550
```

Similar options exist to force *COM* port, base address, and IRQ setting. Please refer to the *setserial(8)* manual page.

---

[2]There was also a NSC 16550, but it's FIFO never really worked.

If your modem supports hardware handshake, you should make sure to enable it. Surprising as it is, most communication programs do not attempt to enable this by default; you have to set it manually instead. This is best performed in the *rc.serial* script, using the *stty* command:

```
$ stty crtscts < /dev/cua1
```

To check if hardware handshake is in effect, use

```
$ stty -a < /dev/cua1
```

This gives you the status of all flags for that device; a flag shown with a preceding minus as in -crtscts means that the flag has been turned off.

Chapter 5

Configuring TCP/IP Networking

In this chapter, we will go through all the steps necessary to setting up TCP/IP networking on your machine. Starting with the assignment of IP addresses, we will slowly work our way through the configuration of TCP/IP network interfaces, and introduce a few tools that come quite handy when hunting down problems with your network installation.

Most of the tasks covered in this chapter you will generally have to do only once. Afterwards, you have to touch most configuration files only when adding a new system to your network, or when you reconfigure your system entirely. Some of the commands used to configure TCP/IP, however, have to be executed each time the system is booted. This is usually done by invoking them from the system /etc/rc scripts.

Commonly, the network-specific part of this procedure is contained in a script called *rc.net* or *rc.inet*. Sometimes, you will also see two scripts named *rc.inet1* and *rc.inet2*, where the former initializes the kernel part of networking, while the latter starts basic networking services and applications. Throughout the following, I will adhere to the latter concept.

Below, I will discuss the actions performed by *rc.inet1*, while applications will be covered in later chapters. After finishing this chapter, you should have established a sequence of commands that properly configure TCP/IP networking on your computer. You should then replace any sample commands in *rc.inet1* with your commands, make sure *rc.inet1* is executed at startup time, and reboot your machine. The networking *rc* scripts that come along with your favorite Linux distribution should give you a good example.

5.1 Setting up the *proc* Filesystem

Some of the configuration tools of the Net-2 release rely on the *proc* filesystem for communicating with the kernel. This is an interface that permits access to kernel run-time information through a filesystem-like mechanism. When mounted, you can list its files like any other filesystem, or display their contents. Typical items include the *loadavg* file that contains the system load average, or *meminfo*, which shows current core memory and swap usage.

To this, the networking code adds the *net* directory. It contains a number of files that show things like the kernel ARP tables, the state of TCP connections, and the routing tables. Most network administration tools get their information from these files.

The *proc* filesystem (or *procfs* as it is also known) is usually mounted on /proc at system boot time. The best method is to add the following line to /etc/fstab:

```
# procfs mont point:
none /proc proc defaults
```

and execute "mount /proc" from your /etc/rc script.

The *procfs* is nowadays configured into most kernels by default. If the *procfs* is not in your kernel, you will get a message like "mount: fs type procfs not supported by kernel". You will then have to recompile the kernel and answer "yes" when asked for *procfs* support.

5.2   Installing the Binaries

If you are using one of the pre-packaged Linux distributions, it will most probably contain the major networking applications and utilities along with a coherent set of sample files. The only case where you might have to obtain and install new utilities is when you install a new kernel release. As they occasionally involve changes in the kernel networking layer, you will need to update the basic configuration tools. This at least involves recompiling, but sometimes you may also be required to obtain the latest set of binaries. These are usually distributed along with the kernel, packaged in an archive called *net-XXX.tar.gz*, where *XXX* is the version number. The release matching Linux 1.0 is 0.32b, the latest kernel as of this writing (1.1.12 and later) require 0.32d.

If you want to compile and install the standard TCP/IP network applications yourself, you can obtain the sources from most Linux FTP servers. These are more or less heavily patched versions of programs from Net-BSD or other sources. Other applications, such as *Xmosaic*, *xarchie*, or Gopher and IRC clients must be obtained separately. Most of them compile out of the box if you follow the instructions.

The official FTP site for Net-3 is **sunacm.swan.ac.uk**, mirrored by **sunsite.unc.edu** below *system/Network/sunacm*. The latest Net-2e patch kit and binaries are available from **ftp.aris.com**. Matthias Urlichs' BSD-derived networking code can be gotten from **ftp.ira.uka.de** in */pub/system/linux/netbsd*.

5.3   Another Example

For the remainder of this book, let me introduce a new example that is less complex than Groucho Marx University, and may be closer to the tasks you will actually encounter. Consider the Virtual Brewery, a small company that brews, as the name indicates, virtual beer. To manage their business more efficiently, the virtual brewers want to network their computers, which all happen to be PCs running a bright and shiny Linux 1.0.

On the same floor, just across the hall, there's the Virtual Winery, who work closely with the brewery. They run an Ethernet of their own. Quite naturally, the two companies want to link their networks once they are operational. As a first step, they want to set up a gateway host that forwards datagrams between the two subnets. Later, they also want to have a UUCP link to the outside world, through which they exchange mail and news. In the long run, the also want to set up a SLIP connection to connect to the Internet occasionally.

5.4   Setting the Hostname

Most, if not all, network applications rely on the local host's name having been set to some reasonable value. This is usually done during the boot procedure by executing the *hostname* command. To set the hostname to *name*, it is invoked as

```
# hostname name
```

It is common practice to use the unqualified hostname without any domain name for this. For instance, hosts at the Virtual Brewery might be called **vale.vbrew.com**, **vlager.vbrew.com**, etc. These are their official, fully qualified domain names. Their local hostnames would be only the first component of the name, such as **vale**. However, as the local hostname is frequently used to look up the host's IP address, you have to make sure that the resolver library is able to look up the host's IP address. This usually means that you have to enter the name in */etc/hosts* (see below).

Some people suggest to use the *domainname* command to set the kernel's idea of a domain name to the remaining part of the FQDN. In this way you could combine the output from *hostname* and *domainname* to get the FQDN again. However, this is at best only half correct. *domainname* is generally used to set the host's NIS domain, which may be entirely different from the DNS domain your host belongs to. NIS is covered in chapter 10.

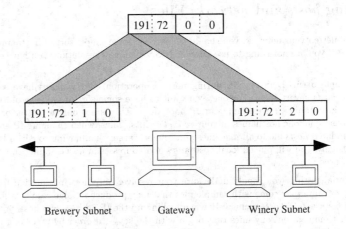

Figure 5.1: Virtual Brewery and Virtual Winery – the two subnets.

5.5   Assigning IP Addresses

If you configure the networking software on your host for standalone operation (for instance, to be able to run the INN netnews software), you can safely skip this section, because you will need an IP address just for the loopback interface, which is always **127.0.0.1**.

Things are a little more complicated with real networks like Ethernets. If you want to connect your host to an existing network, you have to ask its administrators to give you an IP address on this network. When setting up the network all by yourself, you have to assign IP addresses yourself as described below.

Hosts within a local network should usually share addresses from the same logical IP network. Hence you have to assign an IP network address. If you have several physical networks, you either have to assign them different network numbers, or use subnetting to split your IP address range into several subnetworks.

If your network is not connected to the Internet, you are free to choose any (legal) network address. You only have to make sure to choose one from classes A, B, or C, else things will most likely not work properly. However, if you intend to get on the Internet in the near future, you should obtain an official IP address *now*. The best way to proceed is to ask your network service provider to help you. If you want to obtain a network number just in case you might get on the Internet someday, request a Network Address Application Form from **hostmaster@internic.net**.

To operate several Ethernets (or other networks, once a driver is available), you have to split your network into subnets. Note that subnetting is required only if you have more than one *broadcast network*; point-to-point links don't count. For instance, if you have one Ethernet, and one or more SLIP links to the outside world, you don't need to subnet your network. The reason for this will be explained in chapter 7.

As an example, the brewery's network manager applies to the NIC for a class B network number, and is given **191.72.0.0**. To accomodate the two Ethernets, she decides to use eight bits of the host part as additional subnet bits. This leaves another eight bits for the host part, allowing for 254 hosts on each of the subnets. She then assigns subnet number 1 to the brewery, and gives the winery number 2. Their respective network addresses are thus **191.72.1.0** and **191.72.2.0**. The subnet mask is **255.255.255.0**.

vlager, which is the gateway between the two networks, is assigned a host number of 1 on both of them, which gives it the IP addresses **191.72.1.1** and **191.72.2.1**, respectively. Figure 5.1 shows the two subnets, and the gateway.

Note that in this example I am using a class B network to keep things simple; a class C network would be more realistic. With the new networking code, subnetting is not limited to byte boundaries, so even a class C network may be split into several subnets. For instance, you could use 2 bits of the host part for the netmask, giving you four possible subnets with 64 hosts on each.[1]

---

[1]The last number on each subnet is reserved as the broadcast address, so it's in fact 63 hosts per subnet.

5.6   Writing *hosts* and *networks* Files

After you have subnetted your network, you should prepare for some simple sort of hostname resolution using the */etc/hosts* file. If you are not going to use DNS or NIS for address resolution, you have to put all hosts in the *hosts* file.

Even if you want to run DNS or NIS during normal operation, you want to have some subset of all hostnames in */etc/hosts* nevertheless. For one, you want to have some sort of name resolution even when no network interfaces are running, for example during boot time. This is not only a matter of convenience, but also allows you to use symbolic hostnames in your *rc.inet* scripts. Thus, when changing IP addresses, you only have to copy an updated *hosts* file to all machines and reboot, rather than having to edit a large number of *rc* files separately. Usually, you will put all local hostnames and addresses in *hosts*, adding those of any gateways and NIS servers if used.[2]

Also, during intial testing, you should make sure your resolver only uses information from the *hosts* file. Your DNS or NIS software may come with sample files that may produce strange results when being used. To make all applications use */etc/hosts* exclusively when looking up the IP address of a host, you have to edit the */etc/host.conf* file. Comment out any lines that begin with the keyword *order* by preceding them with a hash sign, and insert the line

```
order hosts
```

The configuration of the resolver library will be covered in detail in chapter 6.

The *hosts* file contains one entry per line, consisting of an IP address, a hostname, and an optional list of aliases for the hostname. The fields are separated by spaces or tabs, and the address field must begin in column one. Anything following a hash sign (#) is regarded as a comment and is ignored.

Hostnames can be either fully qualified, or relative to the local domain. For **vale**, you would usually enter the the fully qualified name, **vale.vbrew.com**, and **vale** by itself in the *hosts* file, so that it is known by both its official name and the shorter local name.

This is an example how a *hosts* file at the Virtual Brewery might look. Two special names are included, **vlager-if1** and **vlager-if2** that give the addresses for both interfaces used on **vlager**.

```
#
# Hosts file for Virtual Brewery/Virtual Winery
#
# IP           local        fully qualified domain name
#
127.0.0.1      localhost
#
191.72.1.1     vlager       vlager.vbrew.com
191.72.1.1     vlager-if1
191.72.1.2     vstout       vstout.vbrew.com
191.72.1.3     vale         vale.vbrew.com
#
191.72.2.1     vlager-if2
191.72.2.2     vbeaujolais  vbeaujolais.vbrew.com
191.72.2.3     vbardolino   vbardolino.vbrew.com
191.72.2.4     vchianti     vchianti.vbrew.com
```

Just as with a host's IP address, you sometimes would like to use a symbolic name for network numbers, too. Therefore, the *hosts* file has a companion called */etc/networks* that maps network names to network numbers and vice versa. At the Virtual Brewery, we might install a *networks* file like this:[3]

```
# /etc/networks for the Virtual Brewery
brew-net      191.72.1.0
wine-net      191.72.2.0
```

---

[2]You will need the address of any NIS servers only if you use Peter Eriksson's NYS. Other NIS implementations locate their servers at run-time only by using *ypbind*.

[3]Note that names in *networks* must not collide with hostnames from the *hosts* file, else some programs may produce strange results.

5.7   Interface Configuration for IP

After setting up your hardware as explained in the previous chapter, you have to make these devices known to the kernel networking software. A couple of commands are used to configure the network interfaces, and initialize the routing table. These tasks are usually performed from the *rc.inet1* script each time the system is booted. The basic tools for this are called *ifconfig* (where "if" stands for interface), and *route*.

ifconfig is used to make an interface accessible to the kernel networking layer. This involves the assignment of an IP address and other parameters, and activating the interface, also known as "taking up." Being active here means that the kernel will send and receive IP datagrams through the interface. The simplest way to invoking it is

```
ifconfig interface ip-address
```

which assigns *ip-address* to *interface* and activates it. All other parameters are set to default values. For instance, the default subnet mask is derived from the network class of the IP address, such as **255.255.0.0** for a class B address. *ifconfig* is described in detail at the end of this chapter.

route allows you to add or remove routes from the kernel routing table. It can be invoked as

```
route [add|del] target
```

where the add and del arguments determine whether to add or delete the route to *target*.

5.7.1   The Loopback Interface

The very first interface to be activated is the loopback interface:

```
# ifconfig lo 127.0.0.1
```

Occasionally, you will also see the dummy hostname **localhost** being used instead of the IP address. *ifconfig* will look up the name in the *hosts* file where an entry should declare it as the hostname for **127.0.0.1**:

```
# Sample /etc/hosts entry for localhost
localhost      127.0.0.1
```

To view the configuration of an interface, you invoke *ifconfig* giving it the interface name as argument:

```
$ ifconfig lo
lo        Link encap Local Loopback
          inet addr 127.0.0.1  Bcast [NONE SET]  Mask 255.0.0.0
          UP BROADCAST LOOPBACK RUNNING  MTU 2000  Metric 1
          RX packets 0 errors 0 dropped 0 overrun 0
          TX packets 0 errors 0 dropped 0 overrun 0
```

As you can see, the loopback interface has been assigned a netmask of **255.0.0.0**, since **127.0.0.1** is a class A address. As you can see, the interface doesn't have a broadcast address set, which isn't normally very useful for the loopback anyway. However, if you run the *rwhod* daemon on your host, you may have to set the loopback device's broadcast address in order for *rwho* to function properly. Setting the broadcast is explained in section "All about *ifconfig*" below.

Now, you can almost start playing with your mini-"network." What is still missing is an entry in the routing table that tells IP that it may use this interface as route to destination **127.0.0.1**. This is accomplished by typing

```
# route add 127.0.0.1
```

Again, you can use **localhost** instead of the IP address.

Next, you should check that everything works fine, for example by using *ping*. *ping* is the networking equivalent of a sonar device[4] and is used to verify that a given address is actually reachable, and to measure the delay that occurs when sending a datagram to it and back again. The time required for this is often referred to as the round-trip time.

```
# ping localhost
PING localhost (127.0.0.1): 56 data bytes
64 bytes from 127.0.0.1: icmp_seq=0 ttl=32 time=1 ms
64 bytes from 127.0.0.1: icmp_seq=1 ttl=32 time=0 ms
64 bytes from 127.0.0.1: icmp_seq=2 ttl=32 time=0 ms
^C

--- localhost ping statistics ---
3 packets transmitted, 3 packets received, 0% packet loss
round-trip min/avg/max = 0/0/1 ms
```

When invoking *ping* as shown here, it will go on emitting packets forever unless interrupted by the user. The ^C above marks the place where we pressed Ctrl-C.

The above example shows that packets for **127.0.0.1** are properly delivered and a reply is returned to *ping* almost instantaneously. This shows you have succeeded in setting up your first network interface.

If the output you get from *ping* does not resemble that shown above, you are in trouble. Check any error if they indicate some file hasn't been installed properly. Check that the *ifconfig* and *route* binaries you use are compatible with the kernel release you run, and, above all, that the kernel has been compiled with networking enabled (you see this from the presence of the */proc/net* directory). If you get an error message saying "Network unreachable," then you probably have got the *route* command wrong. Make sure you use the same address as you gave to *ifconfig*.

The steps described above are enough to use networking applications on a standalone host. After adding the above lines to *rc.inet1* and making sure both *rc.inet* scripts are executed from */etc/rc*, you may reboot your machine and try out various applications. For instance, "*telnet localhost*" should establish a *telnet* connection to your host, giving you a login prompt.

However, the loopback interface is useful not only as an example in networking books, or as a testbed during development, but is actually used by some applications during normal operation.[5] Therefore, you always have to configure it, regardless of whether your machine is attached to a network or not.

5.7.2   Ethernet Interfaces

Configuring an Ethernet interface goes pretty much the same as with the loopback interface, it just requires a few more parameters when you are using subnetting.

At the Virtual Brewery, we have subnetted the IP network, which was originally a class B network, into class C subnetworks. To make the interface recognize this, the *ifconfig* incantation would look like this:

```
# ifconfig eth0 vstout netmask 255.255.255.0
```

This assigns the *eth0* interface the IP address of **vstout** (**191.72.1.2**). If we had omitted the netmask, *ifconfig* would have deduced the the netmask from the IP network class, which would have resulted in a netmask of **255.255.0.0**. Now a quick check shows:

```
# ifconfig eth0
eth0      Link encap 10Mps Ethernet HWaddr  00:00:C0:90:B3:42
          inet addr 191.72.1.2 Bcast 191.72.1.255 Mask 255.255.255.0
          UP BROADCAST RUNNING  MTU 1500  Metric 1
```

---

[4]Anyone remember Pink Floyd's "Echoes"?

[5]For instance, all applications based on RPC use the loopback interface to register themselves with the *portmapper* daemon at startup.

```
        RX packets 0 errors 0 dropped 0 overrun 0
        TX packets 0 errors 0 dropped 0 overrun 0
```

You can see that *ifconfig* automatically set the broadcast address (the `Bcast` field above) to the usual value, which is the hosts network number with the host bits all set. Also, the message transfer unit (the maximum size of Ethernet frames the kernel will generate for this interface) has been set to the maximum value of 1500 bytes. All these values can be overridden with special options that will be described later.

Quite similar to the loopback case, you now have to install a routing entry that informs the kernel about the network that can be reached through *eth0*. For the Virtual Brewery, you would invoke *route* as

```
# route add -net 191.72.1.0
```

At first, this looks a little like magic, because it's not really clear how *route* detects which interface to route through. However, the trick is rather simple: the kernel checks all interfaces that have been configured so far and compares the destination address (**191.72.1.0** in this case) to the network part of the interface address (that is, the bitwise and of the interface address and the netmask). The only interface that matches is *eth0*.

Now, what's that `-net` option for? This is used because *route* can handle both routes to networks and routes to single hosts (as you have seen above with **localhost**). When being given an address in dotted quad notation, it attempts to guess whether it is a network or a hostname by looking at the host part bits. If the address' host part is zero, *route* assumes it denotes a network, otherwise it takes it as a host address. Therefore, *route* would think that **191.72.1.0** is a host address rather than a network number, because it cannot know that we use subnetting. We therefore have to tell it explicitly that it denotes a network, giving it the `-net` flag.

Of course, the above *route* command is a little tedious to type, and it's prone to spelling mistakes. A more convenient approach is to use the network names we have defined in */etc/networks* above. This makes the command much more readable; even the `-net` flag can now be omitted, because *route* now knows that **191.72.1.0** denotes a network.

```
# route add brew-net
```

Now that you've finished the basic configuration steps, we want to make sure your Ethernet interface is indeed running happily. Choose a host from your Ethernet, for instance **vlager**, and type

```
# ping vlager
PING vlager: 64 byte packets
64 bytes from 191.72.1.1: icmp_seq=0. time=11. ms
64 bytes from 191.72.1.1: icmp_seq=1. time=7. ms
64 bytes from 191.72.1.1: icmp_seq=2. time=12. ms
64 bytes from 191.72.1.1: icmp_seq=3. time=3. ms
^C

----vstout.vbrew.com PING Statistics----
4 packets transmitted, 4 packets received, 0% packet loss
round-trip (ms)  min/avg/max = 3/8/12
```

If you don't see any output similar to this, then something is broken, obviously. If you encounter unusual packet loss rates, this hints at a hardware problem, like bad or missing terminators, etc. If you don't receive any packets at all, you should check the interface configuration with *netstat*. The packet statistics displayed by *ifconfig* should tell you whether any packets have been sent out on the interface at all. If you have access to the remote host, too, you should go over to that machine and check the interface statistics, too. In this way, you can determine exactly where the packets got dropped. In addition, you should display the routing information with *route* to see if both hosts have the correct routing entry. *route* prints out the complete kernel routing table when invoked without any arguments (the `-n` option only makes it print addresses as dotted quad instead of using the hostname):

```
# route -n
Kernel routing table
Destination     Gateway         Genmask          Flags Metric Ref Use    Iface
127.0.0.1       *               255.255.255.255  UH    1      0   112 lo
191.72.1.0      *               255.255.255.0    U     1      0    10 eth0
```

The detailed meaning of these fields is explained below in the section, Checking with *netstat*. The `Flag` column contains a list of flags set for each interface. `U` is always set for active interfaces, and `H` says the destination address denotes a host. If the `H` flag is set for a route that you meant to be a network route, then you have to specify the `-net` option with the *route* command. To check whether a route you have entered is used at all, check if the `Use` field in the second to last column increases between two invocations of *ping*.

5.7.3   Routing through a Gateway

In the previous section, I covered only the case of setting up a host on a single Ethernet. Quite frequently, however, one encounters networks connected to one another by gateways. These gateways may simply link two or more Ethernets, but may provide a link to the outside world, the Internet, as well. In order to use the service of a gateway, you have to provide additional routing information to the networking layer.

For instance, the Ethernets of the Virtual Brewery and the Virtual Winery are linked through such a gateway, namely the host **vlager**. Assuming that **vlager** has already been configured, we only have to add another entry to **vstout**'s routing table that tells the kernel it can reach all hosts on the Winery's network through **vlager**. The appropriate incantation of *route* is shown below; the `gw` keyword tells it that the next argument denotes a gateway.

```
# route add wine-net gw vlager
```

Of course, any host on the Winery network you wish to talk to must have a corresponding routing entry for the Brewery's network, otherwise you would only be able to send data from **vstout** to **vbardolino**, but any response returned by the latter would go into the great bit bucket.

This example describes only a gateway that switches packets between two isolated Ethernets. Now assume that **vlager** also has a connection to the Internet (say, through an additional SLIP link). Then we would want datagrams to *any* destination network other than the Brewery to be handed to **vlager**. This can be accomplished by making it the default gateway for **vstout**:

```
# route add default gw vlager
```

The network name **default** is a shorthand for **0.0.0.0**, which denotes the default route. You do not have to add this name to */etc/networks*, because it is built into *route*.

When you see high packet loss rates when *ping*ing a host behind one or more gateways, this may hint at a very congested network. Packet loss is not so much due to technical deficiencies as due to temporary excess loads on forwarding hosts, which makes them delay or even drop incoming datagrams.

5.7.4   Configuring a Gateway

Configuring a machine to switch packets between two Ethernets is pretty straightforward. Assume we're back at **vlager**, which is equipped with two Ethernet boards, each being connected to one of the two networks. All you have to do is configure both interfaces separately, giving them their respective IP address, and that's it.

It is quite useful to add information on the two interfaces to the *hosts* file in the way shown below, so we have handy names for them, too:

```
191.72.1.1      vlager        vlager.vbrew.com
191.72.1.1      vlager-if1
191.72.2.1      vlager-if2
```

The sequence of commands to set up the two interfaces is then:

```
# ifconfig eth0 vlager-if1
# ifconfig eth1 vlager-if2
# route add brew-net
# route add wine-net
```

5.7.5 The PLIP Interface

When using a PLIP link to connect two machines, things are a little different from what you have to do when using an Ethernet. The former are so-called *point-to-point* links, because they involve ony two hosts ("points"), as opposed to broadcast networks.

As an example, we consider the laptop computer of some employee at the Virtual Brewery that is connected to **vlager** via PLIP. The laptop itself is called **vlite**, and has only one parallel port. At boot time, this port will be registered as *plip1*. To activate the link, you have to configure the *plip1* interface using the following commands:[6]

```
# ifconfig plip1 vlite pointopoint vlager
# route add default gw vlager
```

The first command configures the interface, telling the kernel that this is a point-to-point link, with the remote side having the address of **vlager**. The second installs the default route, using **vlager** as gateway. On **vlager**, a similar *ifconfig* command is necessary to activate the link (a *route* invocation is not needed):

```
# ifconfig plip1 vlager pointopoint vlite
```

The interesting point is that the *plip1* interface on **vlager** does not have to have a separate IP address, but may also be given the address **191.72.1.1**.[7]

Now, we have configured routing from the laptop to the Brewery's network; what's still missing is a way to route from any of the Brewery's hosts to **vlite**. One particularly cumbersome way is to add a specific route to every host's routing table that names **vlager** as a gateway to **vlite**:

```
# route add vlite gw vlager
```

A much better option when faced with temporary routes is to use dynamic routing. One way to do so is to use *gated*, a routing daemon, which you would have to install on each host in the network in order to distribute routing information dynamically. The easiest way, however, is to use *proxy* ARP. With proxy ARP, **vlager** will respond to any ARP query for **vlite** by sending its own Ethernet address. The effect of this is that all packets for **vlite** will wind up at **vlager**, which then forwards them to the laptop. We will come back to proxy ARP in section Checking the ARP Tables below.

Future Net-3 releases will contain a tool called *plipconfig* which will allow you to set the IRQ of the printer port to use. Later, this may even be replaced by a more general *ifconfig* command.

5.7.6 The SLIP and PPP Interface

Although SLIP and PPP links are only simple point-to-point links like PLIP connections, there is much more to be said about them. Usually, establishing a SLIP connection involves dialing up a remote site through your modem, and setting the serial line to SLIP mode. PPP is used in a similar fashion. The tools required for setting up a SLIP or PPP link will be described in chapters 7 and 8.

5.7.7 The Dummy Interface

The dummy interface is really a little exotic, but rather useful nevertheless. Its main benefit is with standalone hosts, and machines whose only IP network connection is a dial-up link. In fact, the latter are standalone hosts most of the time, too.

The dilemma with standalone hosts is that they only have a single network device active, the loopback device, which is usually assigned the address **127.0.0.1**. On some occasions, however, you need to send data

---

[6]Note that `pointopoint` is not a typo. It's really spelt like this.

[7]Just as a matter of caution, you should however configure a PLIP or SLIP link only after you have completely set up the routing table entries for your Ethernets. With some older kernels, your network route might otherwise end up pointing at the point-to-point link.

to the 'official' IP address of the local host. For instance, consider the laptop **vlite**, that has been disconnected from any network for the duration of this example. An application on **vlite** may now want to send some data to another application on the same host. Looking up **vlite** in */etc/hosts* yields an IP address of **191.72.1.65**, so the application tries to send to this address. As the loopback interface is currently the only active interface on the machine, the kernel has no idea that this address actually refers to itself! As a consequence, the kernel discards the datagram, and returns an error to the application.

This is where the dummy device steps in. It solves the dilemma by simply serving as the alter ego of the loopback interface. In the case of **vlite**, you would simply give it the address **191.72.1.65** and add a host route pointing to it. Every datagram for **191.72.1.65** would then be delivered locally. The proper invocation is:

```
# ifconfig dummy vlite
# route add vlite
```

5.8   All About *ifconfig*

There are a lot more parameters to *ifconfig* than we have described above. Its normal invocation is this:

```
ifconfig interface [[-net|-host] address [parameters]]
```

interface is the interface name, and *address* is the IP address to be assigned to the interface. This may either be an IP address in dotted quad notation, or a name *ifconfig* will look up in */etc/hosts* and */etc/networks*. The -net and -host options force *ifconfig* to treat the address as network number or host address, respectively.

If *ifconfig* is invoked with only the interface name, it displays that interface's configuration. When invoked without any parameters, it displays all interfaces you configured so far; an option of -a forces it to show the inactive ones as well. A sample invocation for the Ethernet interface *eth0* may look like this:

```
# ifconfig eth0
eth0      Link encap 10Mbps Ethernet  HWaddr 00:00:C0:90:B3:42
          inet addr 191.72.1.2 Bcast 191.72.1.255 Mask 255.255.255.0
          UP BROADCAST RUNNING  MTU 1500  Metric 0
          RX packets 3136 errors 217 dropped 7 overrun 26
          TX packets 1752 errors 25 dropped 0 overrun 0
```

The MTU and Metric fields show the current MTU and metric value for that interface. The metric value is traditionally used by some operating systems to compute the cost of a route. Linux doesn't use this value yet, but defines it for compatibility nevertheless.

The RX and TX lines show how many packets have been received or transmitted error free, how many errors occurred, how many packets were dropped, probably because of low memory, and how many were lost because of an overrun. Receiver overruns usually happen when packets come in faster than the kernel can service the last interrupt. The flag values printed by *ifconfig* correspond more or less to the names of its command line options; they will be explained below.

The following is a list of parameters recognized by *ifconfig* with the corresponding flag names are given in brackets. Options that simply turn on a feature also allow it to be turned off again by preceding the option name by a dash (-).

up   This marks an interface "up", i.e. accessible to the IP layer. This option is implied when an
                address is given on the command line. It may also be used to re-eenable an interface that has
                been taken down temporarily using the down option.

                (This option corresponds to the flags UP RUNNING.)

down   This marks an interface "down", i.e. inaccessible to the IP layer. This effectively disables any
                IP traffic through the interface. Note that this does not delete all routing entries that use
                this interface automatically. If you take the interface down permanently, you should to delete
                these routing entries and supply alternative routes if possible.

netmask *mask* This assigns a subnet mask to be used by the interface. It may be given as either a 32-bit hexadecimal number preceded by 0x, or as a dotted quad of decimal numbers.

pointopoint *address*

This option is used for point-to-point IP links that involve only two hosts. This option is needed to configure, for example, SLIP or PLIP interfaces.

(If a point-to-point address has been set, *ifconfig* displays the `POINTOPOINT` flag.)

broadcast *address*

The broadcast address is usually made up from the network number by setting all bits of the host part. Some IP implementations use a different scheme; this option is there to adapt to these strange environments.

(If a broadcast address has been set, *ifconfig* displays the `BROADCAST` flag.)

metric *number*

This option may be used to assign a metric value to the routing table entry created for the interface. This metric is used by the Routing Information Protocol (RIP) to build routing tables for the network.[8] The default metric used by *ifconfig* is a value of zero. If you don't run a RIP daemon, you don't need this option at all; if you do, you will rarely need to change the metric value.

mtu *bytes* This sets the Maximum Transmission Unit, which is the maximum number of octets the interface is able to handle in one transaction. For Ethernets, the MTU defaults to 1500; for SLIP interfaces, this is 296.

arp This is an option specific to broadcast networks such as Ethernets or packet radio. It enables the use of ARP, the Address Resolution Protocol, to detect the physical addresses of hosts attached to the network. For broadcast networks, is on by default.

(If ARP is disabled, *ifconfig* displays the flag `NOARP`.)

-arp Disables the use of ARP on this interface.

promisc Puts the interface in promiscuous mode. On a broadcast network, this makes the interface receive all packets, regardless of whether they were destined for another host or not. This allows an analysis of network traffic using packet filters and such, also called *Ethernet snooping*. Usually, this is a good technique of hunting down network problems that are otherwise hard to come by.

On the other hand, this allows attackers to skim the traffic of your network for passwords and do other nasty things. One protection against this type of attack is not to let anyone just plug in their computers in your Ethernet. Another option is to use secure authentication protocols, such as Kerberos, or the SRA login suite.[9]

(This option corresponds to the flag `PROMISC`.)

-promisc Turns off promiscuous mode.

allmulti Multicast addresses are some sort of broadcast to a group of hosts who don't necessarily have to be on the same subnet. Multicast addresses are not yet supported by the kernel.

(This option corresponds to the flag `ALLMULTI`.)

-allmulti Turns off multicast addresses.

---

[8] RIP chooses the optimal route to a given host based on the "length" of the path. It is computed by summing up the individual metric values of each host-to-host link. By default, a hop has length 1, but this may be any positive integer less than 16. (A route length of 16 is equal to infinity. Such routes are considered unusable.) The `metric` parameter sets this hop cost, which is then broadcast by the routing daemon.

[9] SRA can be obtained from **ftp.tamu.edu** in */pub/sec/TAMU*.

5.9   Checking with *netstat*

Next, I will turn to a useful tool for checking your network configuration and activity. It is called *netstat* and is, in fact, rather a collection of several tools lumped together. We will discuss each of its functions in the following sections.

5.9.1   Displaying the Routing Table

When invoking *netstat* with the -r flag, it displays the kernel routing table in the way we've been doing this with *route* above. On **vstout**, it produces:

```
# netstat -nr
Kernel routing table
Destination    Gateway         Genmask         Flags Metric Ref Use   Iface
127.0.0.1      *               255.255.255.255 UH    1      0        50 lo
191.72.1.0     *               255.255.255.0   U     1      0       478 eth0
191.72.2.0     191.72.1.1      255.255.255.0   UGN   1      0       250 eth0
```

The -n option makes *netstat* print addresses as dotted quad IP numbers rather than the symbolic host and network names. This is especially useful when you want to avoid address lookups over the network (e.g. to a DNS or NIS server).

The second column of *netstat*'s output shows the gateway the routing entry points to. If no gateway is used, an asterisk is printed instead. Column three shows the "generality" of the route. When given an IP address to find a suitable route for, the kernel goes through all routing table entries, taking the bitwise AND of the address and the genmask before comparing it to the target of the route.

The fourth column displays various flags that describe the route:

G   The route uses a gateway.

U   The interface to be used is up.

H   Only a single host can be reached through the route. For example, this is the case for the loopback entry **127.0.0.1**.

D   This is set if the table entry has been generated by an ICMP redirect message (see section 2.5).

M   This is set if the table entry was modified by an ICMP redirect message.

The Ref column of *netstat*'s output shows the number of references to this route, that is, how many other routes (e.g. through gateways) rely on the presence of this route. The last two columns show the number of times the routing entry has been used, and the interface that datagrams are passed to for delivery.

5.9.2   Displaying Interface Statistics

When invoked with the -i flag, *netstat* will display statistics for the network interfaces currently configured. If, in addition, the -a option is given, it will print *all* interfaces present in the kernel, not only those that have been configured currently. On **vstaout**, the output from *netstat* will look like this:

```
$ netstat -i
Kernel Interface table
Iface   MTU Met   RX-OK RX-ERR RX-DRP RX-OVR  TX-OK TX-ERR TX-DRP TX-OVR Flags
lo        0   0    3185      0      0      0   3185      0      0      0 BLRU
eth0   1500   0  972633     17     20    120 628711    217      0      0 BRU
```

The MTU and Met fields show the current MTU and metric value for that interface. The RX and TX columns show how many packets have been received or transmitted error free (RX-OK/TX-OK), damaged

(RX-ERR/TX-ERR), how many were dropped (RX-DRP/TX-DRP), and how many were lost because of an overrun (RX-OVR/TX-OVR).

The last column shows the flags that have been set for this interface. These are one-character versions of the long flag names the are printed when you display the interface configuration with *ifconfig*.

B   A broadcast address has been set.

L   This interface is a loopback device.

M   All packets are received (promiscuous mode).

N   Trailers are avoided.

O   ARP is turned off for this interface.

P   This is a point-to-point connection.

R   Interface is running.

U   Interface is up.

5.9.3   Displaying Connections

netstat supports a set of options to display active or passive sockets. The options -t, -u, -w, and -x show active TCP, UDP, RAW, or UNIX socket connections. If you provide the -a flag in addition, sockets that are waiting for a connection (i.e. listening) are displayed as well. This will give you a list of all servers that are currently running on your system.

Invoking *netstat -ta* on **vlager** produces

```
$ netstat -ta
Active Internet connections
Proto Recv-Q Send-Q Local Address     Foreign Address    (State)
tcp       0      0 *:domain          *:*                LISTEN
tcp       0      0 *:time            *:*                LISTEN
tcp       0      0 *:smtp            *:*                LISTEN
tcp       0      0 vlager:smtp       vstout:1040        ESTABLISHED
tcp       0      0 *:telnet          *:*                LISTEN
tcp       0      0 localhost:1046    vbardolino:telnet  ESTABLISHED
tcp       0      0 *:chargen         *:*                LISTEN
tcp       0      0 *:daytime         *:*                LISTEN
tcp       0      0 *:discard         *:*                LISTEN
tcp       0      0 *:echo            *:*                LISTEN
tcp       0      0 *:shell           *:*                LISTEN
tcp       0      0 *:login           *:*                LISTEN
```

This shows most servers simply waiting for an incoming connection. However, the fourth line shows an incoming SMTP connection from **vstout**, and the sixth line tells you there is an outgoing *telnet* connection to **vbardolino**.[10]

Using the -a flag all by itself will display all sockets from all families.

5.10   Checking the ARP Tables

On some occasions, it is useful to view or even alter the contents of the kernel's ARP tables, for example when you suspect a duplicate Internet address is the cause for some intermittent network problem. The *arp* tool was made for things like these. Its command line options are

---

[10]You can tell whether a connection is outgoing or not from the port numbers involved. The port number shown for the *calling* host will always be a simple integer, while on the host being called, a well-known service port will be in use, for which *netstat* uses the symbolic name found in */etc/services*.

```
arp [-v] [-t hwtype] -a [hostname]
arp [-v] [-t hwtype] -s hostname hwaddr
arp [-v] -d hostname [hostname...]
```

All *hostname* arguments may be either symbolic host names or IP addresses in dotted quad notation.

The first invocation displays the ARP entry for the IP address or host specified, or all hosts known if no *hostname* is given. For example, invoking *arp* on **vlager** may yield

```
# arp -a
IP address      HW type          HW address
191.72.1.3      10Mbps Ethernet  00:00:C0:5A:42:C1
191.72.1.2      10Mbps Ethernet  00:00:C0:90:B3:42
191.72.2.4      10Mbps Ethernet  00:00:C0:04:69:AA
```

which shows the Ethernet addresses of **vlager**, **vstout** and **vale**.

Using the -t option you can limit the display to the hardware type specified. This may be *ether*, *ax25*, or *pronet*, standing for 10Mbps Ethernet, AMPR AX.25, and IEEE 802.5 token ring equipment, respectively.

The -s option is used to permanently add *hostname*'s Ethernet address to the ARP tables. The *hwaddr* argument specifies the hardware address, which is by default expected to be an Ethernet address, specified as six hexadecimal bytes separated by colons. You may also set the hardware address for other types of hardware, too, using the -t option.

One problem which may require you to manually add an IP address to the ARP table is when for some reasons ARP queries for the remote host fail, for instance when its ARP driver is buggy or there is another host in the network that erroneously identifies itself with that host's IP address. Hard-wiring IP addresses in the ARP table is also a (very drastic) measure to protect yourself from hosts on your Ethernet that pose as someone else.

Invoking *arp* using the -d switch deletes all ARP entries relating to the given host. This may be used to force the interface to re-attempt to obtain the Ethernet address for the IP address in question. This is useful when a misconfigured system has broadcast wrong ARP information (of course, you have to reconfigure the broken host before).

The -s option may also be used to implement *proxy* ARP. This is a special technique where a host, say **gate**, acts as a gateway to another host named **fnord**, by pretending that both addresses refer to the same host, namely **gate**. It does so by publishing an ARP entry for **fnord** that points to its own Ethernet interface. Now when a host sends out an ARP query for **fnord**, **gate** will return a reply containing its own Ethernet address. The querying host will then send all datagrams to **gate**, which dutifully forwards them to **fnord**.

These contortions may be necessary, for instance, when you want to access **fnord** from a DOS machine with a broken TCP implementation that doesn't understand routing too well. When you use proxy ARP, it will appear to the DOS machine as if **fnord** was on the local subnet, so it doesn't have to know about how to route through a gateway.

Another very useful application of proxy ARP is when one of your hosts acts as a gateway to some other host only temporarily, for instance through a dial-up link. In a previous example, we already encountered the laptop **vlite** which was connected to **vlager** through a PLIP link only from time to time. Of course, this will work only if the address of the host you want to provide proxy ARP for is on the same IP subnet as your gateway. For instance, **vstout** could proxy ARP for any host on the Brewery subnet (**191.72.1.0**), but never for a host on the Winery subnet (**191.72.2.0**).

The proper invocation to provide proxy ARP for **fnord** is given below; of course, the Ethernet address given must be that of **gate**.

```
# arp -s fnord 00:00:c0:a1:42:e0 pub
```

The proxy ARP entry may be removed again by invoking:

```
# arp -d fnord
```

5.11   The Future

Linux networking is still evolving. Major changes at the kernel layer will bring a very flexible configuration scheme that will allow you to configure the network devices at run time. For instance, the *ifconfig* command will take arguments that set the IRQ line and DMA channel.

Another change to come soon is the additional mtu flag to the *route* command which will set the Maximum Transmission Unit for a particular route. This route-specific MTU overrides the MTU specified for the interface. You will typically use this option for routes through a gateway, where the link between the gateway and the destination host requires a very low MTU. For instance, assume host **wanderer** is connected to **vlager** through a SLIP link. When sending data from **vstout** to **wanderer**, the networking layer on **wanderer** would would use packets of up to 1500 bytes, because packets are sent across the Ethernet. The SLIP link, on the other hand, is operated with an MTU of 296, so the network layer on **vlager** would have to break up the IP packets into smaller fragments that fit into 296 bytes. If instead, you would have configured the route on **vstout** to use a MTU of 296 right from the start, this relatively expensive fragmentation could be avoided:

```
# route add wanderer gw vlager mtu 296
```

Note that the mtu option also allows you to selectively undo the effects of the 'Subnets Are Local' Policy (SNARL). This policy is a kernel configuration option and is described in chapter 3.

Chapter 6

Name Service and Resolver Configuraton

As discussed in chapter 2, TCP/IP networking may rely on different schemes to convert names into addresses. The simplest way, which takes no advantage of the way the name space has been split up into zones is a host table stored in */etc/hosts*. This is useful only for small LANs that are run by one single administrator, and otherwise have no IP traffic with the outside world. The format of the *hosts* file has already been described in chapter 5.

Alternatively, you may use BIND – the Berkeley Internet Name Domain Service – for resolving host names to IP addresses. Configuring BIND may be a real chore, but once you've done it, changes in the network topology are easily made. On Linux, as on many other UNIXish systems, name service is provided through a program called *named*. At startup, it loads a set of master files into its cache, and waits for queries from remote or local user processes. There are different ways to set up BIND, and not all require you to run a name server on every host.

This chapter can do little more but give a rough sketch of how to operate a name server. If you plan to use BIND in an environment with more than just a small LAN and probably an Internet uplink, you should get a good book on BIND, for instance Cricket Liu's "DNS and BIND" (see [AlbitzLiu92]). For current information, you may also want to check the release notes contained in the BIND sources. There's also a newsgroup for DNS questions called **comp.protocols.tcp-ip.domains**.

6.1 The Resolver Library

When talking of "the resolver", we do not mean any special application, but rather refer to the *resolver library*, a collection of functions that can be found in the standard C library. The central routines are *gethostbyname(2)* and *gethostbyaddr(2)* which look up all IP addresses belonging to a host, and vice versa. They may be configured to simply look up the information in *hosts*, query a number of name servers, or use the *hosts* database of NIS (Network Information Service). Other applications, like *smail*, may include different drivers for any of these, and need special care.

6.1.1 The *host.conf* File

The central file that controls your resolver setup is *host.conf*. It resides in */etc* and tells the resolver which services to use, and in what order.

Options in *host.conf* must occur on separate lines. Fields may be separated by white space (spaces or tabs). A hash sign (#) introduces a comment that extends to the next newline.

The following options are available:

order   This determines the order in which the resolving services are tried. Valid options are *bind* for querying the name server, *hosts* for lookups in */etc/hosts*, and *nis* for NIS lookups. Any or all of them may be specified. The order in which they appear on the line detemines the order in which the respective services are tried.

multi Takes *on* or *off* as options. This detemines if a host in */etc/hosts* is allowed to have several IP addresses, which is usually referred to as being "multi-homed". This flag has no effect on DNS or NIS queries.

nospoof As explained in the previous chapter, DNS allows you to find the hostname belonging to an IP address by using the **in-addr.arpa** domain. Attempts by name servers to supply a false hostname are called "*spoofing*". To guard against this, the resolver may be configured to check if the original IP address is in fact associated with the hostname obtained. If not, the name is rejected and an error returned. This behavior is turned on by setting *nospoof on*.

alert This option takes *on* or *off* as arguments. If it is turned on, any spoof attempts (see above) will cause the resolver to log a message to the *syslog* facility.

trim This option takes a domain name as an argument, which will be removed from hostnames before lookup. This is useful for *hosts* entries, where you might only want to specify hostnames without local domain. A lookup of a host with the local domain name appended will have this removed, thus allowing the lookup in */etc/hosts* to succeed.

trim options accumulate, making it possible to consider your host as being local to several domains.

A sample file for **vlager** is shown below:

```
# /etc/host.conf
# We have named running, but no NIS (yet)
order    bind hosts
# Allow multiple addrs
multi    on
# Guard against spoof attempts
nospoof on
# Trim local domain (not really necessary).
trim     vbrew.com.
```

6.1.2 Resolver Environment Variables

The settings from *host.conf* may be overridden using a number of environment variables. These are:

RESOLV_HOST_CONF

This specifies a file to be read instead of */etc/host.conf*.

RESOLV_SERV_ORDER

Overrides the *order* option given in *host.conf*. Services are given as *hosts*, *bind*, and *nis*, separated by a space, comma, colon, or semicolon.

RESOLV_SPOOF_CHECK

Determines the measures taken against spoofing. It is completely disabled by *off*. The values *warn* and *warn off* enable spoof checking, but turn logging on and off, respectively. A value of * turns on spoof checks, but leaves the logging facility as defined in *host.conf*.

RESOLV_MULTI A value of *on* or *off* may be used to override the *multi* options from tt host.conf.

RESOLV_OVERRIDE_TRIM_DOMAINS

This environment specifies a list of trim domains which override those given in *host.conf*.

RESOLV_ADD_TRIM_DOMAINS

This environment specifies a list of trim domains which are added to those given in *host.conf*.

6.1.3   Configuring Name Server Lookups — *resolv.conf*

When configuring the resolver library to use the BIND name service for host lookups, you also have to tell it which name servers to use. There is a separate file for this, called *resolv.conf*. If this file does not exist or is empty, the resolver assumes the name server is on your local host.

If you run a name server on your local host, you have to set it up separately, as will be explained in the following section. If your are on a local network and have the opportunity to use an existing nameserver, this should always be preferred.

The most important option in *resolv.conf* is *nameserver*, which gives the IP address of a name server to use. If you specifiy several name servers by giving the *nameserver* option several times, they are tried in the order given. You should therefore put the most reliable server first. Currently, up to three name servers are supported.

If no *nameserver* option is given, the resolver attempts to connect to the name server on the local host.

Two other options, *domain* and *search* deal with default domains that are tacked onto a hostname if BIND fails to resolve it with the first query. The *search* option specifies a list of domain names to be tried. The list items are separated by spaces or tabs.

If no *search* option is given, a default search list is constructed from the local domain name by using the domain name itself, plus all parent domains up to the root. The local domain name may be given using the *domain* statement; if none is given, the resolver obtains it through the *getdomainname(2)* system call.

If this sounds confusing to you, consider this sample *resolv.conf* file for the Virtual Brewery:

```
# /etc/resolv.conf
# Our domain
domain          vbrew.com
#
# We use vlager as central nameserver:
nameserver      191.72.1.1
```

When resolving the name **vale**, the resolver would look up **vale**, and failing this, **vale.vbrew.com**, and **vale.com**.

6.1.4   Resolver Robustness

If you are running a LAN inside a larger network, you definitely should use central name servers if they are available. The advantage of this is that these will develop rich caches, since all queries are forwarded to them. This scheme, however has a drawback: when a fire recently destroyed the backbone cable at our university, no more work was possible on our department's LAN, because the resolver couldn't reach any of the name servers anymore. There was no logging in on X terminals anymore, no printing, etc.

Although it is not very common for campus backbones to go down in flames, one might want to take precautions against cases like these.

One option is to set up a local name server that resolves hostnames from your local domain, and forwards all queries for other hostnames to the main servers. Of course, this is applicable only if you are running your own domain.

Alternatively, you can maintain a backup host table for your domain or LAN in */etc/hosts*. In */etc/host.conf* you would then include "*order bind hosts*" to make the resolver fall back to the hosts file if the central name server is down.

6.2   Running *named*

The program that provides domain name service on most UNIX machines is usually called *named* (pronounced *name-dee*). This is a server program originally developed for BSD providing name service to clients, and possibly to other name servers. The version currently used on most Linux installations seems to be BIND-4.8.3. The new version, BIND-4.9.3, is being Beta-tested at the moment, and should be available on Linux soon.

This section requires some understanding of the way the Domain Name System works. If the following discussion is all Greek to you, you may want to re-read chapter 2, which has some more information on the basics of DNS.

named is usually started at system boot time, and runs until the machine goes down again. It takes its information from a configuration file called */etc/named.boot*, and various files that contain data mapping domain names to addresses and the like. The latter are called *zone files*. The formats and semantics of these files will be explained in the following section.

To run *named*, simply enter

```
# /usr/sbin/named
```

at the prompt. *named* will come up, read the *named.boot* file and any zone files specified therein. It writes its process id to */var/run/named.pid* in ASCII, downloads any zone files from primary servers, if necessary, and starts listening on port 53 for DNS queries.[1]

6.2.1 The *named.boot* File

The *named.boot* file is generally very small and contains little else but pointers to master files containing zone information, and pointers to other name servers. Comments in the boot file start with a semicolon and extend to the next newline. Before we discuss the format of *named.boot* in more detail, we will take a look at the sample file for **vlager** given in figure 6.1.[2]

```
;
; /etc/named.boot file for vlager.vbrew.com
;
directory       /var/named
;
;               domain                  file
;-------------------------------------------------------
cache           .                       named.ca
primary         vbrew.com               named.hosts
primary         0.0.127.in-addr.arpa    named.local
primary         72.191.in-addr.arpa     named.rev
```

Figure 6.1: The *named.boot* file for *vlager*.

The *cache* and *primary* commands shown in this example load information into *named*. This information is taken from the master files specified in the second argument. They contain textual representations of DNS resource records, which we will look at below.

In this example, we configured *named* as the primary name server for three domains, as indicated by the *primary* statements at the end of the file. The first of these lines, for instance, instructs *named* to act as a primary server for **vbrew.com**, taking the zone data from the file *named.hosts*. The *directory* keyword tells it that all zone files are located in */var/named*.

The *cache* entry is very special and should be present on virtually all machines running a name server. Its function is two-fold: it instructs *named* to enable its cache, and to load the *root name server hints* from the cache file specified (*named.ca* in our example). We will come back to the name server hints below.

Here's a list of the most important options you can use in *named.boot*:

---

[1]There are various *named* binaries floating around Linux FTP sites, each configured a little differently. Some have their pid file in */etc*, some store it in */tmp* or */var/tmp*.

[2]Note that the domain names in this example are given *without* trailing dot. Earlier versions of *named* seem to treat trailing dots in *named.boot* as an error, and silently discards the line. BIND-4.9.3 is said to fix this.

directory   This specifies a directory in which zone files reside. Names of files may be given relative to
                  this directory. Several directories may be specified by repeatedly using *directory*. According
                  to the Linux filesystem standard, this should be */var/named*.

primary   This takes a *domain name* and a *file name* as an argument, declaring the local server author-
                  itative for the named domain. As a primary server, *named* loads the zone information from
                  the given master file.

                  Generally, there will always be at least one *primary* entry in every boot file, namely for reverse
                  mapping of network **127.0.0.0**, which is the local loopback network.

secondary   This statement takes a *domain name*, an *address list*, and a *file name* as an argument. It
                  declares the local server a secondary master server for the domain specified.

                  A secondary server holds authoritative data on the domain, too, but it doesn't gather it from
                  files, but tries to download it from the primary server. The IP address of at least one primary
                  server must thus be given to *named* in the address list. The local server will contact each
                  of them in turn until it successfully transfers the zone database, which is then stored in the
                  backup file given as the third argument. If none of the primary servers responds, the zone
                  data is retrieved from the backup file instead.

                  named will then attempt to refresh the zone data at regular intervals. This is explained below
                  along in connection with the SOA resource record type.

cache   This takes a *domain* and a *file name* as arguments. This file contains the root server hints,
                  that is a list of records pointing to the root name servers. Only NS and A records will be
                  recognized. The *domain* argument is generally the root domain name ".".

                  This information is absolutely crucial to *named*: if the *cache* statement does not occur in the
                  boot file, *named* will not develop a local cache at all. This will severely degrade performance
                  and increase network load if the next server queried is not on the local net. Moreover, *named*
                  will not be able to reach any root name servers, and thus it won't resolve any addresses except
                  those it is authoritative for. An exception from this rule is when using forwarding servers (cf.
                  the *forwarders* option below).

forwarders   This statement takes an *address list* as an argument. The IP addresses in this list specify a
                  list of name servers that *named* may query if it fails to resolve a query from its local cache.
                  They are tried in order until one of them responds to the query.

slave   This statement makes the name server a *slave* server. That is, it will never perform recursive
                  queries itself, but only forwards them to servers specified with the *forwarders* statement.

There are two options which we will not describe here, being *sortlist* and *domain*. Additionally, there are
two directives that may be used inside the zone database files. These are *$INCLUDE* and *$ORIGIN*. Since
they are rarely needed, we will not describe them here, either.

6.2.2   The DNS Database Files

Master files included by *named*, like *named.hosts*, always have a domain associated with them, which is called
the *origin*. This is the domain name specified with the *cache* and *primary* commands. Within a master file,
you are allowed to specify domain and host names relative to this domain. A name given in a configuration
file is considered *absolute* if it ends in a single dot, otherwise it is considered relative to the origin. The origin
all by itself may be referred to using "@".

All data contained in a master file is split up in *resource records*, or RRs for short. They make up the
smallest unit of information available through DNS. Each resource record has a type. A records, for instance,
map a hostname to an IP address, and a CNAME record associates an alias for a host with its official hostname.
As an example, take a look at figure 6.3 on page 392, which shows the *named.hosts* master file for the virtual
brewery.

Resource record representations in master files share a common format, which is

     [*domain*] [*ttl*] [*class*] *type rdata*

Fields are separated by spaces or tabs. An entry may be continued across several lines if an opening brace occurs before the first newline, and the last field is followed by a closing brace. Anything between a semicolon and a newline is ignored.

domain   This is the domain name to which the entry applies. If no domain name is given, the RR is assumed to apply to the domain of the previous RR.

ttl   In order to force resolvers to discard information after a certain time, each RR is associated a *"time to live"*, or *ttl* for short. The *ttl* field specifies the time in seconds the information is valid after it has been retrieved from the server. It is a decimal number with at most eight digits.

If no *ttl* value is given, it defaults to the value of the *minimum* field of the preceding SOA record.

class   This is an address class, like IN for IP addresses, or HS for objects in the Hesiod class. For TCP/IP networking, you have to make this IN.

If no *class* field is given, the class of the preceding RR is assumed.

type   This describes the type of the RR. The most common types are A, SOA, PTR, and NS. The following sections describe the various types of RR's.

rdata   This holds the data associated with the RR. The format of this field depends on the type of the RR. Below, it will be described for each RR separately.

The following is an incomplete list of RRs to be used in DNS master files. There are a couple more of them, which we will not explain. They are experimental, and of little use generally.

SOA   This describes a zone of authority (SOA means "Start of Authority"). It signals that the records following the SOA RR contain authoritative information for the domain. Every master file included by a *primary* statement must contain an SOA record for this zone. The resource data contains the following fields:

    origin   This is the canonical hostname of the primary name server for this domain. It is usually given as an absolute name.

    contact   This is the email address of the person responsible for maintaining the domain, with the '@' character replaced by a dot. For instance, if the responsible person at the Virtual Brewery is **janet**, then this field would contain *janet.vbrew.com*.

    serial   This is the version number of the zone file, expressed as a single decimal number. Whenever data is changed in the zone file, this number should be incremented.

The serial number is used by secondary name servers to recognize when zone information has changed. To stay up to date, secondary servers request the primary server's SOA record at certain intervals, and compare the serial number to that of the cached SOA record. If the number has changed, the secondary servers transfers the whole zone database from the primary server.

    refresh   This specifies the interval in seconds that the secondary servers should wait between checking the SOA record of the primary server. Again, this is a decimal number with at most eight digits.

Generally, the network topology doesn't change too often, so that this number should specify an interval of roughly a day for larger networks, and even more for smaller ones.

    retry   This number determines the intervals at which a secondary server should retry contacting the primary server if a request or a zone refresh fails. It must not be too low, or else a temporary failure of the server or a network problem may cause the secondary server to waste network resources. One hour, or perhaps one half hour, might be a good choice.

expire   This specifies the time in seconds after which the server should finally discard all zone data if it hasn't been able to contact the primary server. It should normally be very large. Craig Hunt ([Hunt92]) recommends 42 days.

minimum   This is the default ttl value for resource records that do not explicitly specify one. This requires other name servers to discard the RR after a certain amount of time. It has however nothing to do with the time after which a secondary server tries to update the zone information.

minimum should be a large value, especially for LANs where the network topology almost never changes. A value of around a week or a month is probably a good choice. In the case that single RRs may change more frequently, you can still assign them different ttl's.

A   This associates an IP address with a hostname. The resource data field contains the address in dotted quad notation.

For each host, there must be only one A record. The hostname used in this A record is considered the official or *canonical* hostname. All other hostnames are aliases and must be mapped onto the canonical hostname using a CNAME record.

NS   This points to a master name server of a subordinate zone. For an explanation why one has to have NS records, see section 2.6. The resource data field contains the hostname of the name server. To resolve the hostname, an additional A record is needed, the so-called *glue record* which gives the name server's IP address.

CNAME   This associates an alias for a host with its *canonical hostname*. The canonical hostname is the one the master file provides an A record for; aliases are simply linked to that name by a CNAME record, but don't have any other records of their own.

PTR   This type of record is used to associate names in the **in-addr.arpa** domain with hostnames. This is used for reverse mapping of IP addresses to hostnames. The hostname given must be the canonical hostname.

MX   This RR announces a *mail exchanger* for a domain. The reasons to have mail exchangers are discussed in section Mail Routing on the Internet in chapter 13. The syntax of an MX record is

          [*domain*] [*ttl*] [*class*] `MX` *preference host*

host names the mail exchanger for *domain*. Every mail exchanger has an integer *preference* associated with it. A mail transport agent who desires to deliver mail to *domain* will try all hosts who have an MX record for this domain until it succeeds. The one with the lowest preference value is tried first, then the others in order of increasing preference value.

HINFO   This record provides information on the system's hardware and software. Its syntax is

          [*domain*] [*ttl*] [*class*] `HINFO` *hardware software*

The *hardware* field identifies the hardware used by this host. There are special conventions to specify this. A list of valid names is given in the "Assigned Numbers" (RFC 1340). If the field contains any blanks, it must be enclosed in double quotes. The *software* field names the operating system software used by the system. Again, a valid name from the "Assigned Numbers" RFC should be chosen.

6.2.3 Writing the Master Files

Figures 6.2, 6.3, 6.4, and 6.5 give sample files for a name server at the brewery, located on *vlager*. Owing to the nature of the network discussed (a single LAN), the example is pretty straightforward. If your requirements are more complex, and you can't get *named* going, get "DNS and BIND" by Cricket Liu and Paul Albitz ([AlbitzLiu92]).

The *named.ca* cache file shown in figure 6.2 shows sample hint records for a root name server. A typical cache file usually describes about a dozen name servers, or so. You can obtain the current list of name servers for the root domain using the *nslookup* tool described toward the end of this chapter.[3]

```
;
; /var/named/named.ca          Cache file for the brewery.
;                   We're not on the Internet, so we don't need
;                   any root servers. To activate these
;                   records, remove the semicolons.
;
; .                99999999  IN   NS  NS.NIC.DDN.MIL
; NS.NIC.DDN.MIL   99999999  IN   A   26.3.0.103
; .                99999999  IN   NS  NS.NASA.GOV
; NS.NASA.GOV      99999999  IN   A   128.102.16.10
```

Figure 6.2: The *named.ca* file.

6.2.4 Verifying the Name Server Setup

There's a fine tool for checking the operation of your name server setup. It is called *nslookup*, and may be used both interactively and from the command line. In the latter case, you simply invoke it as

```
nslookup hostname
```

and it will query the name server specified in *resolv.conf* for *hostname*. (If this file names more than one server, *nslookup* will choose one at random).

The interactive mode, however, is much more exciting. Besides looking up individual hosts, you may query for any type of DNS record, and transfer the entire zone information for a domain.

When invoked without argument, *nslookup* will display the name server it uses, and enter interactive mode. At the '>' prompt, you may type any domain name it should query for. By default, it asks for class A records, those containing the IP address relating to the domain name.

You may change this type by issuing "**set type=***type*", where *type* is one of the resource record names described above in section 6.2, or ANY.

For example, you might have the following dialogue with it:

```
$ nslookup
Default Name Server:  rs10.hrz.th-darmstadt.de
Address:  130.83.56.60

> sunsite.unc.edu
Name Server:  rs10.hrz.th-darmstadt.de
Address:  130.83.56.60

Non-authoritative answer:
Name:     sunsite.unc.edu
Address:  152.2.22.81
```

---

[3]Note that you can't query your name server for the root servers if you don't have any root server hints installed: Catch 22! To escape this dilemma, you can either make *nslookup* use a different name server, or you can use the sample file in figure 6.2 as a starting point, and then obtain the full list of valid servers.

```
;
; /var/named/named.hosts      Local hosts at the brewery
;                             Origin is vbrew.com
;
@               IN  SOA   vlager.vbrew.com. (
                          janet.vbrew.com.
                          16        ; serial
                          86400     ; refresh: once per day
                          3600      ; retry:   one hour
                          3600000   ; expire:  42 days
                          604800    ; minimum: 1 week
                          )
                IN  NS    vlager.vbrew.com.
;
; local mail is distributed on vlager
                IN  MX    10 vlager
;
; loopback address
localhost.      IN  A     127.0.0.1
; brewery Ethernet
vlager          IN  A     191.72.1.1
vlager-if1      IN  CNAME vlager
; vlager is also news server
news            IN  CNAME vlager
vstout          IN  A     191.72.1.2
vale            IN  A     191.72.1.3
; winery Ethernet
vlager-if2      IN  A     191.72.2.1
vbardolino      IN  A     191.72.2.2
vchianti        IN  A     191.72.2.3
vbeaujolais     IN  A     191.72.2.4
```

Figure 6.3: The *named.hosts* file.

```
;
; /var/named/named.local      Reverse mapping of 127.0.0
;                             Origin is 0.0.127.in-addr.arpa.
;
@               IN  SOA   vlager.vbrew.com. (
                          joe.vbrew.com.
                          1         ; serial
                          360000    ; refresh: 100 hrs
                          3600      ; retry:   one hour
                          3600000   ; expire:  42 days
                          360000    ; minimum: 100 hrs
                          )
                IN  NS    vlager.vbrew.com.
1               IN  PTR   localhost.
```

Figure 6.4: The *named.local* file.

```
;
; /var/named/named.rev          Reverse mapping of our IP addresses
;                               Origin is 72.191.in-addr.arpa.
;
@                   IN  SOA  vlager.vbrew.com. (
                             joe.vbrew.com.
                             16        ; serial
                             86400     ; refresh: once per day
                             3600      ; retry:   one hour
                             3600000   ; expire:  42 days
                             604800    ; minimum: 1 week
                             )
                    IN  NS   vlager.vbrew.com.
; brewery
1.1                 IN  PTR  vlager.vbrew.com.
2.1                 IN  PTR  vstout.vbrew.com.
3.1                 IN  PTR  vale.vbrew.com.
; winery
1.2                 IN  PTR  vlager-if1.vbrew.com.
2.2                 IN  PTR  vbardolino.vbrew.com.
3.2                 IN  PTR  vchianti.vbrew.com.
4.2                 IN  PTR  vbeaujolais.vbrew.com.
```

Figure 6.5: The *named.rev* file.

If you try to query for a name that has no IP address associated, but other records were found in the DNS database, *nslookup* will come back with an error message saying "`No type A records found`". However, you can make it query for records other than type A by issuing the "`set type`" command. For example, to get the SOA record of **unc.edu**, you would issue:

```
> unc.edu
*** No address (A) records available for unc.edu
Name Server: rs10.hrz.th-darmstadt.de
Address:  130.83.56.60

> set type=SOA
> unc.edu
Name Server: rs10.hrz.th-darmstadt.de
Address:  130.83.56.60

Non-authoritative answer:
unc.edu
        origin = ns.unc.edu
        mail addr = shava.ns.unc.edu
        serial = 930408
        refresh = 28800 (8 hours)
        retry   = 3600 (1 hour)
        expire  = 1209600 (14 days)
        minimum ttl = 86400 (1 day)

Authoritative answers can be found from:
UNC.EDU nameserver = SAMBA.ACS.UNC.EDU
SAMBA.ACS.UNC.EDU      internet address = 128.109.157.30
```

In a similar fashion you can query for MX records, etc. Using a type of ANY returns all resource records associated with a given name.

```
> set type=MX
> unc.edu
Non-authoritative answer:
```

```
unc.edu preference = 10, mail exchanger = lambada.oit.unc.edu
lambada.oit.unc.edu     internet address = 152.2.22.80

Authoritative answers can be found from:
UNC.EDU nameserver = SAMBA.ACS.UNC.EDU
SAMBA.ACS.UNC.EDU       internet address = 128.109.157.30
```

A practical application of *nslookup* beside debugging is to obtain the current list of root name servers for the *named.ca* file. You can do this by querying for all type NS records associated with the root domain:

```
> set typ=NS
> .
Name Server:  fb0430.mathematik.th-darmstadt.de
Address:  130.83.2.30

Non-authoritative answer:
(root)  nameserver = NS.INTERNIC.NET
(root)  nameserver = AOS.ARL.ARMY.MIL
(root)  nameserver = C.NYSER.NET
(root)  nameserver = TERP.UMD.EDU
(root)  nameserver = NS.NASA.GOV
(root)  nameserver = NIC.NORDU.NET
(root)  nameserver = NS.NIC.DDN.MIL

Authoritative answers can be found from:
(root)  nameserver = NS.INTERNIC.NET
(root)  nameserver = AOS.ARL.ARMY.MIL
(root)  nameserver = C.NYSER.NET
(root)  nameserver = TERP.UMD.EDU
(root)  nameserver = NS.NASA.GOV
(root)  nameserver = NIC.NORDU.NET
(root)  nameserver = NS.NIC.DDN.MIL
NS.INTERNIC.NET internet address = 198.41.0.4
AOS.ARL.ARMY.MIL        internet address = 128.63.4.82
AOS.ARL.ARMY.MIL        internet address = 192.5.25.82
AOS.ARL.ARMY.MIL        internet address = 26.3.0.29
C.NYSER.NET     internet address = 192.33.4.12
TERP.UMD.EDU    internet address = 128.8.10.90
NS.NASA.GOV     internet address = 128.102.16.10
NS.NASA.GOV     internet address = 192.52.195.10
NS.NASA.GOV     internet address = 45.13.10.121
NIC.NORDU.NET   internet address = 192.36.148.17
NS.NIC.DDN.MIL  internet address = 192.112.36.4
```

The complete set of commands available with *nslookup* may be obtained by the `help` command from within *nslookup*.

6.2.5   Other Useful Tools

There are a few tools that can help you with your tasks as a BIND administrator. I will briefly describe two of them here. Please refer to the documentation that comes with these tools for information on how to use them.

hostcvt is a tool that helps you with your initial BIND configuration by converting your */etc/hosts* file into master files for *named*. It generates both the forward (A) and reverse mapping (PTR) entries, and takes care of aliases and the like. Of course, it won't do the whole job for you, as you may still want to tune the timeout values in the SOA record, for instance, or add MX records and the like. Still, it may help you save a few aspirins. *hostcvt* is part of the BIND source, but can also be found as a standalone package on a few Linux FTP servers.

After setting up your name server, you may want to test your configuration. The ideal (and, to my knowledge) only tool for this is *dnswalk*, a *perl*-based package that walks your DNS database, looking for common mistakes and verifying that the information is consistent. *dnswalk* has been released on **comp.sources.misc** recently, and should be available on all FTP sites that archive this group (**ftp.uu.net** should be a safe bet if you don't know of any such site near you).

Chapter 7

Serial Line IP

The serial line protocols, SLIP and PPP, provide the Internet connectivity for the poor. Apart from a modem and a serial board equipped with a FIFO buffer, no hardware is needed. Using it is not much more complicated than a mailbox, and an increasing number of private organizations offer dial-up IP at an affordable cost to everyone.

There are both SLIP and PPP drivers available for Linux. SLIP has been there for quite a while, and works fairly reliable. A PPP driver has been developed recently by Michael Callahan and Al Longyear. It will be described in the next chapter.

7.1 General Requirements

To use SLIP or PPP, you have to configure some basic networking features as described in the previous chapters, of course. At the least, you have to set up the loopback interface, and provide for name resolution. When connecting to the Internet, you will of course want to use DNS. The simplest option is to put the address of some name server into your *resolv.conf* file; this server will be queried as soon as the SLIP link is activated. The closer this name server is to the point where you dial in, the better.

However, this solution is not optimal, because all name lookups will still go through your SLIP/PPP link. If you worry about the bandwidth this consumes, you can also set up a *caching-only* name server. It doesn't really serve a domain, but only acts as a relay for all DNS queries produced on your host. The advantage of this scheme is that it builds up a cache, so that most queries have to be sent over the serial line only once. A *named.boot* file for a caching-only server looks like this:

```
; named.boot file for caching-only server
directory                        /var/named

primary      0.0.127.in-addr.arpa    db.127.0.0 ; loopback net
cache        .                       db.cache   ; root servers
```

In addition to this *name.boot* file, you also have to set up the *db.cache* file with a valid list of root name servers. This is described toward the end of the Resolver Configuration chapter.

7.2 SLIP Operation

Dial-up IP servers frequently offer SLIP service through special user accounts. After logging into such an account, you are not dropped into the common shell; instead a program or shell script is executed that enables the server's SLIP driver for the serial line and configures the appropriate network interface. Then you have to do the same at your end of the link.

On some operating systems, the SLIP driver is a user-space program; under Linux, it is part of the kernel, which makes it a lot faster. This requires, however, that the serial line be converted to SLIP mode explicitly.

This is done by means of a special tty line discipline, SLIPDISC. While the tty is in normal line discipline (DISC0), it will exchange data only with user processes, using the normal *read(2)* and *write(2)* calls, and the SLIP driver is unable to write to or read from the tty. In SLIPDISC, the roles are reversed: now any user-space processes are blocked from writing to or reading from the tty, while all data coming in on the serial port will be passed directly to the SLIP driver.

The SLIP driver itself understands a number of variations on the SLIP protocol. Apart from ordinary SLIP, it also understands CSLIP, which performs the so-called Van Jacobson header compression on outgoing IP packets.[1] This improves throughput for interactive sessions noticeably. Additionally, there are six-bit versions for each of these protocols.

A simple way to convert a serial line to SLIP mode is by using the *slattach* tool. Assume you have your modem on */dev/cua3*, and have logged into the SLIP server successfully. You will then execute:

```
# slattach /dev/cua3 &
```

This will switch the line discipline of *cua3* to SLIPDISC, and attach it to one of the SLIP network interfaces. If this is your first active SLIP link, the line will be attached to *sl0*; the second would be attached to *sl1*, and so on. The current kernels support up to eight simultaneous SLIP links.

The default encapsulation chosen by *slattach* is CSLIP. You may choose any other mode using the -p switch. To use normal SLIP (no compression), you would use

```
# slattach -p slip /dev/cua3 &
```

Other modes are cslip, slip6, cslip6 (for the six-bit version of SLIP), and **adaptive** for adaptive SLIP. The latter leaves it to the kernel to find out which type of SLIP encapsulation the remote end uses.

Note that you must use the same encapsulation as your peer does. For example, if **cowslip** uses CSLIP, you have to do so, too. The symptoms of a mismatch will be that a *ping* to the remote host will not receive any packets back. If the other host *pings* you, you may also see messages like "Can't build ICMP header" on your console. One way to avoid these difficulties is to use adaptive SLIP.

In fact, *slattach* does not only allow you to enable SLIP, but other protocols that use the serial line as well, like PPP or KISS (another protocol used by ham radio people). For details, please refer to the *slattach(8)* manual page.

After turning over the line to the SLIP driver, you have to configure the network interface. Again, we do this using the standard *ifconfig* and *route* commands. Assume that from **vlager**, we have dialed up a server named **cowslip**. You would then execute

```
# ifconfig sl0 vlager pointopoint cowslip
# route add cowslip
# route add default gw cowslip
```

The first command configures the interface as a point-to-point link to **cowslip**, while the second and third add the route to **cowslip** and the default route using **cowslip** as a gateway.

When taking down the SLIP link, you first have to remove all routes through **cowslip** using *route* with the del option, take the interface down, and send *slattach* the hangup signal. Afterwards you have to hang up the modem using your terminal program again:

```
# route del default
# route del cowslip
# ifconfig sl0 down
# kill -HUP 516
```

---

[1]Van Jacobson header compression is described in RFC 1441.

7.3   Using *dip*

Now, that was rather simple. Nevertheless, you might want to automate the above steps so that you only have to invoke a simple command that performs all steps shown above. This is what *dip* is for.[2] The current release as of this writing is version 3.3.7. It has been patched very heavily by a number of people, so that you can't speak of *the dip* program anymore. These different strains of development will hopefully be merged in a future release.

dip provides an interpreter for a simple scripting language that can handle the modem for you, convert the line to SLIP mode, and configure the interfaces. This is rather primitive and restrictive, but sufficient for most cases. A new release of *dip* may feature a more versatile language one day.

To be able to configure the SLIP interface, *dip* requires root privilege. It would now be tempting to make *dip* setuid to **root**, so that all users can dial up some SLIP server without having to give them root access. This is very dangerous, because setting up bogus interfaces and default routes with *dip* may disrupt routing on your network badly. Even worse, this will give your users the power to connect to *any* SLIP server, and launch dangerous attacks on your network. So if you want to allow your users to fire up a SLIP connection, write small wrapper programs for each prospective SLIP server, and have these wrappers invoke *dip* with the specific script that establishes the connection. These programs can then safely be made setuid **root**.[3]

7.3.1   A Sample Script

A sample script is produced in figure 7.1. It can be used to connect to **cowslip** by invoking *dip* with the script name as argument:

```
# dip cowslip.dip
DIP: Dialup IP Protocol Driver version 3.3.7 (12/13/93)
Written by Fred N. van Kempen, MicroWalt Corporation.

connected to cowslip.moo.com with addr 193.174.7.129
#
```

After connecting to **cowslip** and enabling SLIP, *dip* will detach from the terminal and go to the background. You can then start using the normal networking services on the SLIP link. To terminate the connection, simply invoke **dip** with the -k option. This sends a hangup signal to *dip* process, using the process id *dip* records in */etc/dip.pid*:[4]

```
# kill -k
```

In *dip*'s scripting language, keywords prefixed with a dollar symbol denote variable names. *dip* has a predefined set of variables which will be listed below. *$remote* and *$local*, for instance, contain the hostnames of the local and remote host involved in the SLIP link.

The first two statements in the sample script are *get* commands, which is *dip*'s way to set a variable. Here, the local and remote hostname are set to **vlager** and **cowslip**, respectively.

The next five statements set up the terminal line and the modem. The *reset* sends a reset string to the modem; for Hayes-compatible modems, this is the *ATZ* command. The next statement flushes out the modem response, so that the login chat in the next few lines will work properly. This chat is pretty straight-forward: it simply dials 41988, the phone number of **cowslip**, and logs into the account *Svlager* using the password *hey-jude*. The *wait* command makes *dip* wait for the string given as its first argument; the number given as second argument make the wait time out after that many seconds if no such string is received. The *if* commands interspersed in the login procedure check that no error has occurred while executing the command.

The final commands executed after logging in are *default*, which makes the SLIP link the default route to all hosts, and *mode*, which enables SLIP mode on the line and configures the interface and routing table for you.

---

[2] *dip* means *Dialup IP*. It was written by Fred van Kempen.
[3] *diplogin* can (and must) be run setuid, too. See the section at the end of this chapter.
[4] See the newsgroup **alt.tla** for more palindromic fun with three-letter acronyms.

```
# Sample dip script for dialing up cowslip

# Set local and remote name and address
get $local vlager
get $remote cowslip

port cua3               # choose a serial port
speed 38400             # set speed to max
modem HAYES             # set modem type
reset                   # reset modem and tty
flush                   # flush out modem response

# Prepare for dialing.
send ATQOV1E1X1\r
wait OK 2
if $errlvl != 0 goto error
dial 41988
if $errlvl != 0 goto error
wait CONNECT 60
if $errlvl != 0 goto error

# Okay, we're connected now
sleep 3
send \r\n\r\n
wait ogin: 10
if $errlvl != 0 goto error
send Svlager\n
wait ssword: 5
if $errlvl != 0 goto error
send hey-jude\n
wait running 30
if $errlvl != 0 goto error

# We have logged in, and the remote side is firing up SLIP.
print Connected to $remote with address $rmtip
default                 # Make this link our default route
mode SLIP               # We go to SLIP mode, too
# fall through in case of error

error:
print SLIP to $remote failed.
```

Figure 7.1: A sample *dip* script

7.3.2   A *dip* Reference

Although widely used, *dip* hasn't been very well documented yet. In this section, we will therefore give a reference for most of *dip*'s commands. You can get an overview of all commands it provides by invoking *dip* in test mode, and entering the *help* command. To find out about the syntax of a command, you may enter it without any arguments; of course this does not work with commands that take no arguments.

```
$ dip -t
DIP: Dialup IP Protocol Driver version 3.3.7 (12/13/93)
Written by Fred N. van Kempen, MicroWalt Corporation.

DIP> help
DIP knows about the following commands:

databits default dial    echo    flush
get      goto    help    if      init
mode     modem   parity  print   port
reset    send    sleep   speed   stopbits
term     wait

DIP> echo
Usage: echo on|off
DIP> _
```

Throughout the following, examples that display the DIP> prompt show how to enter a command in test mode, and what output it produces. Examples lacking this prompt should be taken as script excerpts.

The Modem Commands

There is a number of commands *dip* provides to configure your serial line and modem. Some of these are obvious, such as *port*, which selects a serial port, and *speed*, *databits*, *stopbits*, and *parity*, which set the common line parameters.

The *modem* command selects a modem type. Currently, the only type supported is *HAYES* (capitalization required). You have to provide *dip* with a modem type, else it will refuse to execute the *dial* and *reset* commands. The *reset* command sends a reset string to the modem; the string used depends on the modem type selected. For Hayes-compatible modems, this is *ATZ*.

The *flush* code can be used to flush out all responses the modem has sent so far. Otherwise a chat script following the *reset* might be confused, because it reads the *OK* responses from earlier commands.

The *init* command selects an initialization string to be passed to the modem before dialling. The default for Hayes modems is "*ATE0 Q0 V1 X1*", which turns on echoing of commands and long result codes, and selects blind dialing (no checking of dial tone).

The *dial* command finally sends the initialization string to the modem and dials up the remote system. The default dial command for Hayes modems is *ATD*.

echo and *term*

The *echo* command serves as a debugging aid, in that using *echo on* makes *dip* echo to the console everything sends to the serial device. This can be turned off again by calling *echo off*.

dip also allows you to leave script mode temporarily and enter terminal mode. In this mode, you can use *dip* just like any ordinary terminal program, writing to the serial line and reading from it. To leave this mode, enter Ctrl-] .

The *get* Command

The *get* command is *dip*'s way of setting a variable. The simplest form is to set a variable to a constant, as used throughout the above example. You may, however, also prompt the user for input by specifying the keyword *ask* instead of a value:

```
DIP> get $local ask
Enter the value for $local: _
```

A third method is to try to obtain the value from the remote host. Bizarre as it seems first, this is very useful in some cases: Some SLIP servers will not allow you to use your own IP address on the SLIP link, but will rather assign you one from a pool of addresses whenever you dial in, printing some message that informs you about the address you have been assigned. If the message looks something like this "**Your address: 193.174.7.202**", then the following piece of *dip* code would let you pick up the address:

```
... login chat ....
wait address: 10
get $locip remote
```

The *print* Command

This is the command to echo text to the console *dip* was started from. Any of *dip*'s variables may be used in print commands, such as

```
DIP> print Using port $port at speed $speed
Using port cua3 at speed 38400
```

Variable Names

dip only understands a predefined set of variables. A variable name always begins with a dollar symbol and must be written in lower-case letters.

The *$local* and *$locip* variables contain the local host's name and IP address. Setting the hostname makes *dip* store the canonical hostname in *$local*, at the same time assigning *$locip* the corresponding IP address. The analogous thing happens when setting the *$locip*.

The *$remote* and *$rmtip* variables do the same for the remote host's name and address. *$mtu* contains the MTU value for the connection.

These five variables are the only ones that may be assigned values directly using the *get* command. A host of other variables can only be set through corresponding commands, but may be used *print* statements; these are *$modem*, *$port*, and *$speed*.

$errlvl is the variable through which you can access the result of the last command executed. An error level of 0 indicates success, while a non-zero value denotes an error.

The *if* and *goto* Commands

The *if* command is rather a conditional branch than what one usually calls an if. Its syntax is

```
if var op number goto label
```

where the expression must be a simple comparison between one of the variables *$errlvl*, *$locip*, and *$rmtip*. The second operand must be an integer number; the operator *op* may be one of ==, !=, <, >, <=, and >=.

The *goto* command makes the execution of the script continue at the line following that bearing the label. A label must occur as the very first token on the line, and must be followed immediately by a colon.

send, *wait* **and** *sleep*

These commands help implement simple chat scripts in *dip*. *send* outputs its arguments to the serial line. It does not support variables, but understands all C-style backslash character sequences such as \n and \b. The tilde character (˜) is used as an abbreviation for carriage return/newline.

wait takes a word as an argument, and scans all input on the serial line until it recognizes this word. The word itself may not contain any blanks. Optionally, you may give *wait* a timeout value as second argument; if the expected word is not received within that many seconds, the command will return with an *$errlvl* value of one.

The *sleep* statement may be used to wait for a certain amount of time, for instance to patiently wait for any login sequence to complete. Again, the interval is specified in seconds.

mode **and** *default*

These commands are used to flip the serial line to SLIP mode and configure the interface.

The *mode* command is the last command executed by *dip* before gong into daemon mode. Unless an error occurs, the command does not return.

mode takes a protocol name as argument. *dip* currently recognizes *SLIP* and *CSLIP* as valid names. The current version of *dip* does not understand adaptive SLIP, however.

After enabling SLIP mode on the serial line, *dip* executes *ifconfig* to configure the interface as a point-to-point link, and invokes *route* to set the route to the remote host.

If, in addition, the script executes the *default* command before *mode*, *dip* will also make the default route point to the SLIP link.

7.4   Running in Server Mode

Setting up your SLIP client was the hard part. Doing the opposite, namely configuring your host to act as a SLIP server, is much easier.

One way to do this is to to use *dip* in server mode, which can be achieved by invoking it as *diplogin*. Its main configuration file is */etc/diphosts*, which associates login names with the address this host is assigned. Alternatively, you can also use *sliplogin*, a BSD-derived tool that features a more flexible configuration scheme that lets you execute shell scripts whenever a host connects and disconnects. It is currently at Beta.

Both programs require that you set up one login account per SLIP client. For instance, assume you provide SLIP service to Arthur Dent at **dent.beta.com**, you might create an account named **dent** by adding the following line to your *passwd* file:

```
dent:*:501:60:Arthur Dent's SLIP account:/tmp:/usr/sbin/diplogin
```

Afterwards, you would set **dent**'s password using the *passwd* utility.

Now, when **dent** logs in, *dip* will start up as a server. To find out if he is indeed permitted to use SLIP, it will look up the user name in */etc/diphosts*. This file details the access rights and connection parameter for each SLIP user. A sample entry for **dent** could look like this:

```
dent::dent.beta.com:Arthur Dent:SLIP,296
```

The first of the colon-separated fields is the name the user must log in as. The second field may contain an additional password (see below). The third is the hostname or IP address of the calling host. Next comes an informational field without any special meaning (yet). The last field describes the connection parameters. This is a comma-separated list specifying the protocol (currently one of *SLIP* or *CSLIP*), followed by the MTU.

When **dent** logs in, *diplogin* extracts the information on him from the *diphosts* file, and, if the second field is not empty, prompts for an "external security password". The string entered by the user is compared to the (unencrypted) password from *diphosts*. If they do not match, the login attempt is rejected.

Otherwise, *diplogin* proceeds by flipping the serial line to CSLIP or SLIP mode, and sets up the interface and route. This connection remains established until the user disconnects and the modem drops the line. *diplogin* will then return the line to normal line discipline, and exit.

diplogin requires super-user privilege. If you don't have *dip* running setuid **root**, you should make *diplogin* a separate copy of *dip* instead of a simple link. *diplogin* can then safely be made setuid, without affecting the status of *dip* itself.

Chapter 8

The Point-to-Point Protocol

8.1 Untangling the P's

Just like SLIP, PPP is a protocol to send datagrams across a serial connection, but addresses a couple of deficiencies of the former. It lets the communicating sides negotiate options such as the IP address and the maximum datagram size at startup time, and provides for client authorization. For each of these capabilities, PPP has a separate protocol. Below, we will briefly cover these basic building blocks of PPP. This discussion is far from complete; if you want to know more about PPP, you are urged to read its specification in RFC 1548, as well as the dozen or so companion RFCs.[1]

At the very bottom of PPP is the *High-Level Data Link Control* Protocol, abbreviated HDLC,[2] which defines the boundaries around the individual PPP frames, and provides a 16 bit checksum. As opposed to the more primitive SLIP encapsulation, a PPP frame is capable of holding packets from other protocols than IP, such as Novell's IPX, or Appletalk. PPP achieves this by adding a protocol field to the basic HDLC frame that identifies the type of packet is carried by the frame.

LCP, the Link Control Protocol, is used on top of HDLC to negotiate options pertaining to the data link, such as the Maximum Receive Unit (MRU) that states the maximum datagram size one side of the link agrees to receive.

An important step at the configuration stage of a PPP link is client authorization. Although it is not mandatory, it is really a must for dial-up lines. Usually, the called host (the server) asks the client to authorize itself by proving it knows some secret key. If the caller fails to produce the correct secret, the connection is terminated. With PPP, authorization works both ways; that is, the caller may also ask the server to authenticate itself. These authentication procedures are totally independent of each other. There are two protocols for different types of authorization, which we will discuss further below. They are named Password Authentication Protocol, or PAP, and Challenge Handshake Authentication Protocol, or CHAP.

Each network protocol that is routed across the data link, like IP, AppleTalk, etc, is configured dynamically using a corresponding Network Control Protocol (NCP). For instance, to send IP datagrams across the link, both PPPs must first negotiate which IP address each of them uses. The control protocol used for this is IPCP, the Internet Protocol Control Protocol.

Beside sending standard IP datagrams across the link, PPP also supports Van Jacobson header compression of IP datagrams. This is a technique to shrink the headers of TCP packets to as little as three bytes. It is also used in CSLIP, and is more colloquially referred to as VJ header compression. The use of compression may be negotiated at startup time through IPCP as well.

---

[1] The relevant RFCs are listed in the Annotated Bibiliography at the end of this book.

[2] In fact, HDLC is a much more general protocol devised by the International Standards Organization (ISO).

8.2 PPP on Linux

On Linux, PPP functionality is split up in two parts, a low-level HDLC driver located in the kernel, and the user space *pppd* daemon that handles the various control protocols. The current release of PPP for Linux is *linux-ppp-1.0.0*, and contains the kernel PPP module, *pppd*, and a program named *chat* used to dial up the remote system.

The PPP kernel driver was written by Michael Callahan. *pppd* was derived from a free PPP implementation for Sun and 386BSD machines, which was written by Drew Perkins and others, and is maintained by Paul Mackerras. It was ported to Linux by Al Longyear.[3] *chat* was written by Karl Fox.[4]

Just like SLIP, PPP is implemented by means of a special line discipline. To use some serial line as a PPP link, you first establish the connection over your modem as usual, and subsequently convert the line to PPP mode. In this mode, all incoming data is passed to the PPP driver, which checks the incoming HDLC frames for validity (each HDLC frame carries a 16 bit checksum), and unwraps and dispatches them. Currently, it is able to handle IP datagrams, optionally using Van Jacobson header compression. As soon as Linux supports IPX, the PPP driver will be extended to handle IPX packets, too.

The kernel driver is aided by *pppd*, the PPP daemon, which performs the entire initialization and authentication phase that is necessary before actual network traffic can be sent across the link. *pppd*'s behavior may be fine-tuned using a number of options. As PPP is rather complex, it is impossible to explain all of them in a single chapter. This book therefore cannot cover all aspects of *pppd*, but only give you an introduction. For more information, refer to the manual pages and *README*s in the *pppd* source distribution, which should help you sort out most questions this chapter fails to discuss. If your problems persist even after reading all documentation, you should turn to the newsgroup **comp.protocols.ppp** for help, which is the place where you will reach most of the people involved in the development of *pppd*.

8.3 Running *pppd*

When you want to connect to the Internet through a PPP link, you have to set up basic networking capabilities such as the loopback device, and the resolver. Both have been covered in the previous chapters. There are some things to be said about using DNS over a serial link; please refer to the SLIP chapter for a discussion of this.

As an introductory example of how to establish a PPP connection with *pppd*, assume you are at **vlager** again. You have already dialed up the PPP server, **c3po**, and logged into the **ppp** account. **c3po** has already fired up its PPP driver. After exiting the communications program you used for dialing, you execute the following command:

```
# pppd /dev/cua3 38400 crtscts defaultroute
```

This will flip the serial line *cua3* to PPP mode and establish an IP link to **c3po**. The transfer speed used on the serial port will be 38400bps. The *crtscts* option turns on hardware handshake on the port, which is an absolute must at speeds above 9600 bps.

The first thing *pppd* does after starting up is to negotiate several link characteristics with the remote end, using LCP. Usually, the default set of options *pppd* tries to negotiate will work, so we won't go into this here. We will return to LCP in more detail in some later section.

For the time being, we also assume that **c3po** doesn't require any authentication from us, so that the configuration phase is completed successfully.

pppd will then negotiate the IP parameters with its peer using IPCP, the IP control protocol. Since we didn't specify any particular IP address to *pppd* above, it will try to use the address obtained by having the resolver look up the local hostname. Both will then announce their address to each other.

---

[3]Both authors have said they will be very busy for some time to come. If you have any questions on PPP in general, you'd best ask the people on the NET channel of the Linux activists mailing list.

[4]**karl@morningstar.com**.

Usually, there's nothing wrong with these defaults. Even if your machine is on an Ethernet, you can use the same IP address for both the Ethernet and the PPP interface. Nevertheless, *pppd* allows you to use a different address, or even to ask your peer to use some specific address. These options are discussed in a later section.

After going through the IPCP setup phase, *pppd* will prepare your host's networking layer to use the PPP link. It first configures the PPP network interface as a point-to-point link, using *ppp0* for the first PPP link that is active, *ppp1* for the second, and so on. Next, it will set up a routing table entry that points to the host at the other end of the link. In the example shown above, *pppd* will make the default network route point to **c3po**, because we gave it the *defaultroute* option.[5] This causes all datagrams to hosts not on your local network to be sent to **c3po**. There are a number of different routing schemes *pppd* supports, which we will cover in detail later in this chapter.

8.4   Using Options Files

Before *pppd* parses its command line arguments, it scans several files for default options. These files may contain any valid command line arguments, spread out across an arbitrary number of lines. comments are introduced by has signs.

The first options file is */etc/ppp/options*, which is always scanned when *pppd* starts up. Using it to set some global defaults is a good idea, because it allows you to keep your users from doing several things that may compromise security. For instance, to make *pppd* require some kind of authentication (either PAP or CHAP) from the peer, you would add the `auth` option to this file. This option cannot be overridden by the user, so that it becomes impossible to establish a PPP connection with any system that is not in our authentication databases.

The other option file, which is read after */etc/ppp/options*, is *.ppprc* in the user's home directory. It allows each user to specify her own set of default options.

A sample */etc/ppp/options* file might look like this:

```
# Global options for pppd running on vlager.vbrew.com
auth              # require authentication
usehostname       # use local hostname for CHAP
lock              # use UUCP-style device locking
domain vbrew.com  # our domain name
```

The first two of these options apply to authentication and will be explained below. The `lock` keyword makes *pppd* comply to the standard UUCP method of device locking. With this convention, each process that accesses a serial device, say */dev/cua3*, creates a lock file named *LCK..cua3* in the UUCP spool directory to signal that the device is in use. This is necessary to prevent any other programs such as *minicom* or *uucico* to open the serial device while used by PPP.

The reason to provide these options in the global configuration file is that options such as those shown above cannot be overridden, and so provide for a reasonable level of security. Note however, that some options can be overridden later; one such an example is the *connect* string.

8.5   Dialing out with *chat*

One of the things that may have struck you as inconvenient in the above example is that you had to establish the connection manually before you could fire up *pppd*. Unlike *dip*, *pppd* does not have its own scripting language for dialing the remote system and logging in, but rather relies on some external program or shell script to do this. The command to be executed can be given to *pppd* with the *connect* command line option. *pppd* will redirect the command's standard input and output to the serial line. One useful program for this is *expect*, written by Don Libes. It has a very powerful language based on Tcl, and was designed exactly for this sort of application.

The *pppd* package comes along with a similar program called *chat*, which lets you specify a UUCP-style chat script. Basically, a chat script consists of an alternating sequence of strings that we expect to receive from the

---
[5]The default network route is only installed if none is present yet.

remote system, and the answers we are to send. We will call the expect and send strings, respectively. This is a typical excerpt from a chat script;

```
ogin: b1ff ssword: s3kr3t
```

This tells *chat* to wait for the remote system to send the login prompt, and return the login name **b1ff**. We only wait for `ogin:` so that it doesn't matter if the login prompt starts with an uppercase or lowercase l, or if it arrives garbled. The following string is an expect-string again that makes *chat* wait for the password prompt, and send our password in response.

This is basically all that chat scripts are about. A complete script to dial up a PPP server would, of course, also have to include the appropriate modem commands. Assume your modem understands the Hayes command set, and the server's telephone number was 318714. The complete *chat* invocation to establish a connection with **c3po** would then be

```
$ chat -v '' ATZ OK ATDT318714 CONNECT '' ogin: ppp word: GaGariN
```

By definition, the first string must be an expect string, but as the modem won't say anything before we have kicked it, we make *chat* skip the first expect by specifying an empty string. We go on and send `ATZ`, the reset command for Hayes-compatible modems, and wait for its response (`OK`). The next string sends the dial command along with the phone number to *chat*, and expects the `CONNECT` message in response. This is followed by an empty string again, because we don't want to send anything now, but rather wait for the login prompt. The remainder of the chat script works exactly as described above.

The `-v` option makes *chat* log all activities to the *syslog* daemon's *local2* facility.[6]

Specifying the chat script on the command line bears a certain risk, because users can view a process' command line with the *ps* command. You can avoid this by putting the chat script in a file, say *dial-c3po*. You make *chat* read the script from the file instead of the command line by giving it the `-f` option, followed by the file name. The complete *pppd* incantation would now look like this:

```
# pppd connect "chat -f dial-c3po" /dev/cua3 38400 -detach \
     crtscts modem defaultroute
```

Beside the *connect* option that specifies the dial-up script, we have added two more options to the command line: *-detach*, which tells *pppd* not to detach from the console and become a background process. The *modem* keyword makes it perform some modem-specific actions on the serial device, like hanging up the line before and after the call. If you don't use this keyword, *pppd* will not monitor the port's DCD line, and will therefore not detect if the remote end hangs up unexpectedly.

The examples shown above were rather simple; *chat* allows for much more complex chat scripts. One very useful feature is the ability to specify strings on which to abort the chat with an error. Typical abort strings are messages like `BUSY`, or `NO CARRIER`, that your modem usually generates when the called number is busy, or doesn't pick up the phone. To make *chat* recognize these immediately, rather than timing out, you can specify them at the beginning of the script using the `ABORT` keyword:

```
$ chat -v ABORT BUSY ABORT 'NO CARRIER' '' ATZ OK ...
```

In a similar fashion, you may change the timeout value for parts of the chat scripts by inserting `TIMEOUT` options. For details, please check the *chat(8)* manual page.

Sometimes, you'd also want to have some sort of conditional execution of parts of the chat script. For instance, when you don't receive the remote end's login prompt, you might want to send a BREAK, or a carriage return. You can achieve this by appending a sub-script to an expect string. It consists of a sequence of send- and expect-strings, just like the overall script itself, which are separated by hyphens. The sub-script is executed whenever the expected string they are appended to is not received in time. In the example above, we would modify the chat script as follows:

---

[6]If you edit *syslog.conf* to redirect these log messages to a file, make sure this file isn't world readable, as *chat* also logs the entire chat script by default – including passwords and all.

```
ogin:-BREAK-ogin: ppp ssword: GaGariN
```

Now, when *chat* doesn't see the remote system send the login prompt, the sub-script is executed by first sending a BREAK, and then waiting for the login prompt again. If the prompt now appears, the script continues as usual, otherwise it will terminate with an error.

8.6   Debugging Your PPP Setup

By default, *pppd* will log any warnings and error messages to *syslog*'s *daemon* facility. You have to add an entry to *syslog.conf* that redirects this to a file, or even the console, otherwise *syslog* simply discards these messages. The following entry sends all messages to */var/log/ppp-log*:

```
daemon.*                /var/log/ppp-log
```

If your PPP setup doesn't work at once, looking into this log file should give you a first hint of what goes wrong. If this doesn't help, you can also turn on extra debugging output using the **debug** option. This makes *pppd* log the contents of all control packets sent or received to *syslog*. All messages will go to the *daemon* facility.

Finally, the most drastic feature is to enable kernel-level debugging by invoking *pppd* with the *kdebug* option. It is followed by a numeric argument that is the bitwise OR of the following values: 1 for general debug messages, 2 for printing the contents of all incoming HDLC frames, and 4 to make the driver print all outgoing HDLC frames. To capture kernel debugging messages, you must either run a *syslogd* daemon that reads the */proc/kmsg* file, or the *klogd* daemon. Either of them directs kernel debugging to *syslog*'s *kernel* facility.

8.7   IP Configuration Options

IPCP is used to negotiate a couple of IP parameters at link configuration time. Usually, each peer may send an IPCP Configuration Request packet, indicating which values it wants to change from the defaults, and to what value. Upon receipt, the remote end inspects each option in turn, and either acknowledges or rejects it.

pppd gives you a lot of control about which IPCP options it will try to negotiate. You can tune this through various command line options we will discuss below.

8.7.1   Choosing IP Addresses

In the example above, we had *pppd* dial up **c3po** and establish an IP link. No provisions were taken to choose a particular IP address on either end of the link. Instead, we picked **vlager**'s address as the local IP address, and let **c3po** provide its own. Sometimes, however, it is useful to have control over what address is used on one or the other end of the link. *pppd* supports several variations of this.

To ask for particular addresses, you generally provide *pppd* with the following option:

local_addr:*remote_addr*

where *local_addr* and *remote_addr* may be specified either in dotted quad notation, or as hostnames.[7] This makes *pppd* attempt to use the first address as its own IP address, and the second as the peer's. If the peer rejects either of them during IPCP negotiation, no IP link will be established.[8]

If you want to set only the local address, but accept any address the peer uses, you simply leave out the *remote_addr* part. For instance, to make **vlager** use the IP address **130.83.4.27** instead of its own, you would give it `130.83.4.27:` on the command line. Similarly, to set the remote address only, you would leave the *local_addr* field blank. By default, *pppd* will then use the address associated with your hostname.

---

[7]Using hostnames in this option has consequences on CHAP authentication. Please refer to the section on CHAP below.

[8]You can allow the peer PPP to override your ideas of IP addresses by giving *pppd* the `ipcp-accept-local` and `ipcp-accept-remote` options. Please refer to the manual page for details.

Some PPP servers that handle a lot of client sites assign addresses dynamically: addresses are assigned to systems only when calling in, and are claimed after they have logged off again. When dialing up such a server, you must make sure that *pppd* doesn't request any particular IP address from the server, but rather accept the address the server asks you to use. This means that you mustn't specify a *local_addr* argument. In addition, you have to use the `noipdefault` option, which makes *pppd* wait for the peer to provide the IP address instead of using the local host's address.

8.7.2   Routing Through a PPP Link

After setting up the network interface, *pppd* will usually set up a host route to its peer only. If the remote host is on a LAN, you certainly want to be able to connect to hosts "behind" your peer as well; that is, a network route must be set up.

We have already seen above that *pppd* can be asked to set the default route using the `defaultroute` option. This option is very useful if the PPP server you dialed up will act as your Internet gateway.

The reverse case, where your system acts as a gateway for a single host, is also relatively easy to accomplish. For example, take some employee at the Virtual Brewery whose home machine is called **loner**. When connecting to **vlager** through PPP, he uses an address on the Brewery's subnet. At **vlager**, we can now give *pppd* the `proxyarp` option, which will install a proxy ARP entry for **loner**. This will automatically make **loner** accessible from all hosts at the Brewery and the Winery.

However, things aren't always as easy as that, for instance when linking two local area networks. This usually requires adding a specific network route, because these networks may have their own default routes. Besides, having both peers use the PPP link as the default route would generate a loop, where packets to unknown destinations would ping-pong between the peers until their time-to-live expired.

As an example, suppose the Virtual Brewery opens a branch in some other city. The subsidiary runs an Ethernet of their own using the IP network number **191.72.3.0**, which is subnet 3 of the Brewery's class B network. They want to connect to the Brewery's main Ethernet via PPP to update customer databases, etc. Again, **vlager** acts as the gateway; its peer is called **sub-etha** and has an IP address of **191.72.3.1.**.

When **sub-etha** connects to **vlager**, it will make the default route point to **vlager** as usual. On **vlager**, however, we will have to install a network route for subnet 3 that goes through **sub-etha**. For this, we use a feature of *pppd* not discussed so far – the *ip-up* command. This is a shell script or program located in */etc/ppp* that is executed after the PPP interface has been configured. When present, it is invoked with the following parameters:

>   ip-up *iface device speed local_addr remote_addr*

where *iface* names the network interface used, *device* is the pathname of the serial device file used (*/dev/tty* if stdin/stdout are used), and *speed* is the device's speed. *local_addr* and *remote_addr* give the IP addresses used at both ends of the link in dotted quad notation. In our case, the *ip-up* script may contain the following code fragment:

```
#!/bin/sh
case $5 in
191.72.3.1)                 # this is sub-etha
        route add -net 191.72.3.0 gw 191.72.3.1;;
...
esac
exit 0
```

In a similar fashion, */etc/ppp/ip-down* is used to undo all actions of *ip-up* after the PPP link has been taken down again.

However, the routing scheme is not yet complete. We have set up routing table entries on both PPP hosts, but so far, all other hosts on both networks don't know anything about the PPP link. This is not a big problem if all hosts at the subsidiary have their default route pointing at **sub-etha**, and all Brewery hosts route to **vlager** by default. If this is not the case, your only option will usually be to use a routing daemon like *gated*. After creating the network route on **vlager**, the routing daemon would broadcast the new route to all hosts on the attached subnets.

8.8   Link Control Options

Above, we already encountered LCP, the Link Control Protocol, which is used to negotiate link characteristics, and to test the link.

The two most important options that may be negotiated by LCP are the maximum receive unit, and the Asynchronous Control Character Map. There are a number of other LCP configuration options, but they are far too specialized to discuss here. Please refer to RFC 1548 for a description of those.

The Asynchronous Control Character Map, colloquially called the async map, is used on asynchronous links such as telephone lines to identify control characters that must be escaped (replaced by a specific two-character sequence). For instance, you may want to avoid the XON and XOFF characters used for software handshake, because some misconfigured modem might choke upon receipt of an XOFF. Other candidates include Ctrl-] (the *telnet* escape character). PPP allows you to escape any of the characters with ASCII codes 0 through 31 by specifying them in the async map.

The async map is a bitmap 32 bits wide, with the least significant bit corresponding to the ASCII NUL character, and the most significant bit corrsponding to ASCII 31. If a bit is set, it signals that the corresponding character must be escaped before sending it across the link. Initially, the async map is set to *0xffffffff*, that is, all control characters will be escaped.

To tell your peer that it doesn't have to escape all control characters but only a few of them, you can specify a new asyncmap to *pppd* using the asyncmap option. For instance, if only ^S and ^Q (ASCII 17 and 19, commonly used for XON and XOFF) must be escaped, use the following option:

```
asyncmap 0x000A0000
```

The Maximum Receive Unit, or MRU, signals to the peer the maximum size of HDLC frames we want to receive. Although this may remind you of the MTU value (Maximum Transfer Unit), these two have little in common. The MTU is a parameter of the kernel networking device, and describes the maximum frame size the interface is able to handle. The MRU is more of an advice to the remote end not to generate any frames larger than the MRU; the interface must nevertheless be able to receive frames of up to 1500 bytes.

Choosing an MRU is therefore not so much a question of what the link is capable of transferring, but of what gives you the best throughput. If you intend to run interactive applications over the link, setting the MRU to values as low as 296 is a good idea, so that an occasional larger packet (say, from an FTP session) doesn't make your cursor "jump". To tell *pppd* to request an MRU of 296, you would give it the option mru 296. Small MRUs, however, only make sense if you don't have VJ header compression disabled (it is enabled by default).

pppd understands also a couple of LCP options that configure the overall behavior of the negotiation process, such as the maximum number of configuration requests that may be exchanged before the link is terminated. Unless you kow exactly what you are doing, you should leave these alone.

Finally, there are two options that apply to LCP echo messages. PPP defines two messages, Echo Request and Echo Response. *pppd* uses this feature to check if a link is still operating. You can enable this by using the lcp-echo-interval option together with a time in seconds. If no frames are received from the remote host within this interval, *pppd* generates an Echo Request, and expects the peer to return an Echo Response. If the peer does not produce a response, the link is terminated after a certain number of requests sent. This number can be set using the lcp-echo-failure option. By default, this feature is disabled altogether.

8.9   General Security Considerations

A misconfigured PPP daemon can be a devastating security breach. It can be as bad as letting anyone plug in their machine into your Ethernet (and that is very bad). In this section, we will discuss a few measures that should make your PPP configuration safe.

One problem with *pppd* is that to configure the network device and the routing table, it requires **root** privilege. You will usually solve this by running it setuid **root**. However, *pppd* allows users to set various security-relevant options. To protect against any attacks a user may launch by manipulating these options, it is suggested you set a couple of default values in the global */etc/ppp/options* file, like those shown in the sample file in section Using Options Files. Some of them, such as the authentication options, cannot be overridden by the user, and so provide a reasonable protection against manipulations.

Of course, you have to protect yourself from the systems you speak PPP with, too. To fend off hosts posing as someone else, you should always some sort of authentication from your peer. Additionally, you should not allow foreign hosts to use any IP address they choose, but restrict them to at least a few. The following section will deal with these topics.

8.10 Authentication with PPP

8.10.1 CHAP versus PAP

With PPP, each system may require its peer to authenticate itself using one of two authentication protocols. These are the Password Authentication Protocol (PAP), and the Challenge Handshake Authentication Protocol (CHAP). When a connection is established, each end can request the other to authenticate itself, regardless of whether it is the caller or the callee. Below I will loosely talk of 'client' and 'server' when I want to distinguish between the authenticating system and the authenticator. A PPP daemon can ask its peer for authentication by sending yet another LCP configuration request identifying the desired authentication protocol.

PAP works basically the same way as the normal login procedure. The client authenticates itself by sending a user name and an (optionally encrypted) password to the server, which the server compares to its secrets database. This technique is vulnerable to eavesdroppers who may try to obtain the password by listening in on the serial line, and to repeated trial and error attacks.

CHAP does not have these deficiencies. With CHAP, the authenticator (i.e. the server) sends a randomly generated "challenge" string to the client, along with its hostname. The client uses the hostname to look up the appropriate secret, combines it with the challenge, and encrypts the string using a one-way hashing function. The result is returned to the server along with the client's hostname. The server now performs the same computation, and acknowledges the client if it arrives at the same result.

Another feature of CHAP is that it doesn't only require the client to authenticate itself at startup time, but sends challenges at regular intervals to make sure the client hasn't been replaced by an intruder, for instance by just switching phone lines.

pppd keeps the secret keys for CHAP and PAP in two separate files, called */etc/ppp/chap-secrets* and *pap-secrets*, respectively. By entering a remote host in one or the other file, you have a fine control over whether CHAP or PAP is used to authenticate ourselves with our peer, and vice versa.

By default, *pppd* doesn't require authentication from the remote, but will agree to authenticate itself when requested by the remote. As CHAP is so much stronger than PAP, *pppd* tries to use the former whenever possible. If the peer does not support it, or if *pppd* can't find a CHAP secret for the remote system in its *chap-secrets* file, it reverts to PAP. If it doesn't have a PAP secret for its peer either, it will refuse to authenticate altogether. As a consequence, the connection is closed down.

This behavior can be modified in several ways. For instance, when given the auth keyword, *pppd* will require the peer to authenticate itself. *pppd* will agree to use either CHAP or PAP for this, as long as it has a secret for the peer in its CHAP or PAP database, respectively. There are other options to turn a particular authentication protocol on or off, but I won't describe them here. Please refer to the *pppd(8)* manual page for details.

If all systems you talk PPP with agree to authenticate themselves with you, you should put the auth option in the global */etc/ppp/options* file and define passwords for each system in the *chap-secrets* file. If a system doesn't support CHAP, add an entry for it to the *pap-secrets* file. In this way, you can make sure no unauthenticated system connects to your host.

The next two sections discuss the two PPP secrets files, *pap-secrets* and *chap-secrets*. They are located in */etc/ppp* and contain triples of clients, servers and passwords, optionally followed by a list of IP addresses. The interpretation of the client and server fields is different for CHAP and PAP, and also depends on whether we authenticate ourselves with the peer, or whether we require the server to authenticate itself with us.

8.10.2 The CHAP Secrets File

When it has to authenticate itself with some server using CHAP, *pppd* searches the *pap-secrets* file for an entry with the client field equal to the local hostname, and the server field equal to the remote hostname sent in the CHAP Challenge. When requiring the peer to authenticate itself, the roles are simply reversed: *pppd* will then look for an entry with the client field equal to the remote hostname (sent in the client's CHAP Response), and the server field equal to the local hostname.

The following is a sample *chap-secrets* file for **vlager**:[9]

```
# CHAP secrets for vlager.vbrew.com
#
# client            server            secret                addrs
#-----------------------------------------------------------------
vlager.vbrew.com   c3po.lucas.com    "Use The Source Luke" vlager.vbrew.com
c3po.lucas.com     vlager.vbrew.com  "riverrun, pasteve"   c3po.lucas.com
*                  vlager.vbrew.com  "VeryStupidPassword"  pub.vbrew.com
```

When establishing a PPP connection with **c3po**, **c3po** asks **vlager** to authenticate itself using CHAP by sending a CHAP challenge. *pppd* then scans *chap-secrets* for an entry with the client field equal to **vlager.vbrew.com** and the server field equal to **c3po.lucas.com**,[10] and finds the first line shown above. It then produces the CHAP Response from the challenge string and the secret (Use The Source Luke), and sends it off to **c3po**.

At the same time, *pppd* composes a CHAP challenge for **c3po**, containing a unique challenge string, and its fully qualified hostname **vlager.vbrew.com**. **c3po** constructs a CHAP Response in the manner we just discussed, and returns it to **vlager**. *pppd* now extracts the client hostname (**c3po.vbrew.com**) from the Response, and searches the *chap-secrets* file for a line matching **c3po** as a client, and **vlager** as the server. The second line does this, so *pppd* combines the CHAP challenge and the secret riverrun, pasteve, encrypts them, and compares the result to **c3po**'s CHAP respnose.

The optional fourth field lists the IP addresses that are acceptable for the clients named in the first field. The addresses may be given in dotted quad notation or as hostnames that are looked up with the resolver. For instance, if **c3po** requests to use an IP address during IPCP negotiation that is not in this list, the request will be rejected, and IPCP will be shut down. In the sample file shown above, **c3po** is therefore limited to using its own IP address. If the address field is empty, any addresses will be allowed; a value of - prevents the use of IP with that client altogether.

The third line of the sample *chap-secrets* file allows any host to establish a PPP link with **vlager** because a client or server field of * matches any hostname. The only requirement is that it knows the secret, and uses the address of **pub.vbrew.com**. Entries with wildcard hostnames may appear anywhere in the secrets file, since *pppd* will always use the most specific entry that applies to a server/client pair.

There are some words to be said about the way *pppd* arrives at the hostnames it looks up in the secrets file. As explained before, the remote hostname is always provided by the peer in the CHAP Challenge or Response packet. The local hostname will be derived by calling the *gethostname(2)* function by default. If you have set the system name to your unqualified hostname, such you have to provide *pppd* with the domain name in addition using the **domain** option:

```
# pppd ...domain vbrew.com
```

This will append the Brewery's domain name to **vlager** for all authentication-related activities. Other options that modify progpppd's idea of the local hostname are **usehostname** and **name**. When you give the local IP address on the command line using "*local*:varremote", and *local* is a name instead of a dotted quad, *pppd* will use this as the local hostname. For details, please refer to the *pppd(8)* manual page.

---

[9]The double quotes are not part of the password, they merely serve to protect the white space within the password.
[10]This hostname is taken from the CHAP challenge.

8.10.3   The PAP Secrets File

The PAP secrets file is very similar to that used by CHAP. The first two fields always contain a user name and a server name; the third holds the PAP secret. When the remote sends an authenticate request, *pppd* uses the entry that has a server field equal to the local hostname, and a user field equal to the user name sent in the request. When authenticating itself with the peer, *pppd* picks the secret to be sent from the line with the user field equal to the local user name, and the server field equal to the remote hostname.

A sample PAP secrets file might look like this:

```
# /etc/ppp/pap-secrets
#
# user          server        secret        addrs
vlager-pap      c3po          cresspahl     vlager.vbrew.com
c3po            vlager        DonaldGNUth   c3po.lucas.com
```

The first line is used to authenticate ourselves when talking to **c3po**. The second line describes how a user named **c3po** has to authenticate itself with us.

The name **vlager-pap** in column one is the user name we send to **c3po**. By default, *pppd* will pick the local hostname as the user name, but you can also specify a different name by giving the **user** option, followed by that name.

When picking an entry from the *pap-secrets* file for authentication with the peer, *pppd* has to know the remote host's name. As it has no way of finding that out, you have to specify it on the command line using the **remotename** keyword, followed by the peer's hostname. For instance, to use the above entry for authentication with **c3po**, we have to add the following option to *pppd*'s command line:

```
\#{} pppd ... remotename c3po user vlager-pap
```

In the fourth field (and all fields following), you may specify what IP addresses are allowed for that particular host, just as in the CHAP secrets file. The peer may then only request addresses from that list. In the sample file, we require **c3po** to use its real IP address.

Note that PAP is a rather weak authentication method, and it is suggested you use CHAP instead whenever possible. We will therefore not cover PAP in greater detail here; if you are interested in using PAP, you will find some more PAP features in the *pppd(8)* manual page.

8.11   Configuring a PPP Server

Running *pppd* as a server is just a matter of adding the appropriate options to the command line. Ideally, you would create a special account, say **ppp**, and give it a script or program as login shell that invokes *pppd* with these options. For instance, you would add the following line to */etc/passwd*:

```
ppp:*:500:200:Public PPP Account:/tmp:/etc/ppp/ppplogin
```

Of course, you may want to use different uids and gids than those shown above. You would also have to set the password for the above account using the *passwd* command.

The *ppplogin* script might then look like this:

```
#!/bin/sh
# ppplogin - script to fire up pppd on login
mesg n
stty -echo
exec pppd -detach silent modem crtscts
```

The *mesg* command disables other users to write to the tty using, for instance, the *write* command. The *stty* command turns off character echoing. The is necessary, because otherwise everything the peer sends would be echoed back to it. The most important *pppd* option given above is **-detach**, because it prevents *pppd* drom detaching from the controlling tty. If we didn't specify this option, it would go to the background, making the shell script exit. This would in turn would cause the serial line to be hung up and the connection to be dropped. The *silent* option causes *pppd* to wait until it receives a packet from the calling system before it starts sending. This prevents transmit timeouts to occur when the calling system is slow in firing up its PPP client. The **modem** makes *pppd* watch the DTR line to see if the peer has dropped the connection, and **crtscts** turns on hardware handshake.

Beside these options, you might want to force some sort of authentication, for example by specifying **auth** on *pppd*'s command line, or in the global options file. The manual page also discusses more specific options for turning individual authentication protocols on and off.

Chapter 9

Various Network Applications

After successfully setting up IP and the resolver, you have to turn to the services you want to provide over the network. This chapter covers the configuration of a few simple network applications, including the *inetd* server, and the programs from the *rlogin* family. The Remote Procedure Call interface that services like the Network File System (NFS) and the Network Information System (NIS) are based upon will be dealt with briefly, too. The configuration of NFS and NIS, however, takes up more room, will be described in separate chapters. This applies to electronic mail and netnews as well.

Of course, we can't cover all network applications in this book. If you want to install one that's not discussed here, like *talk*, *gopher*, or *Xmosaic* please refer to its manual pages for details.

9.1 The *inetd* Super-Server

Frequently, services are performed by so-called *daemons*. A daemon is a program that opens a certain port, and waits for incoming connections. If one occurs, it creates a child process which accepts the connection, while the parent continues to listen for further requests. This concept has the drawback that for every service offered, a daemon has to run that listens on the port for a connection to occur, which generally means a waste of system resources like swap space.

Thus, almost all UNIX installations run a "super-server" that creates sockets for a number of services, and listens on all of them simultaneously using the *select(2)* system call. When a remote host requests one of the services, the super-server notices this and spawns the server specified for this port.

The super-server commonly used is *inetd*, the Internet Daemon. It is started at system boot time, and takes the list of services it is to manage from a startup file named */etc/inetd.conf*. In addition to those servers invoked, there are a number of trivial services which are performed by *inetd* itself called *internal services*. They include *chargen* which simply generates a string of characters, and *daytime* which returns the system's idea of the time of day.

An entry in this file consists of a single line made up of the following fields:

> service type protocol wait user server cmdline

The meaning of each field is as follows:

service
: gives the service name. The service name has to be translated to a port number by looking it up in the */etc/services* file. This file will be described in section The *services* and *protocols* Files below.

type
: specifies a socket type, either *stream* (for connection-oriented protocols) or *dgram* (for datagram protocols). TCP-based services should therefore always use *stream*, while UDP-based services should always use *dgram*.

protocol
: names the transport protocol used by the service. This must be a valid protocol name found in the *protocols* file, also explained below.

wait   This option applies only to *dgram* sockets. It may be either *wait* or *nowait*. If *wait* is speci-
                 fied, *inetd* will only execute one server for the specified port at any time. Otherwise, it will
                 immediately continue to listen on the port after executing the server.

                 This is useful for "single-threaded" servers that read all incoming datagrams until no more
                 arrive, and then exit. Most RPC servers are of this type and should therefore specify *wait*.
                 The opposite type, "multi-threaded" servers, allow an unlimited number of instances to run
                 concurrently; this is only rarely used. These servers should specify *nowait*.

                 stream sockets should always use *nowait*.

user   This is the login id of the user the process is executed under. This will frequently be the
                 root user, but some services may use different accounts. It is a very good idea to apply
                 the principle of least privilege here, which states that you shouldn't run a command under a
                 privileged account if the program doesn't require this for proper functioning. For example, the
                 NNTP news server will run as **news**, while services that may pose a security risk (such as *tftp*
                 or *finger*) are often run as **nobody**.

server   gives the full path name of the server program to be executed. Internal services are marked
                 by the keyword *internal*.

cmdline   This is the command line to be passed to the server. This includes argument 0, that is the
                 command name. Usually, this will be the program name of the server, unless the program
                 behaves differently when invoked by a different name.

                 This field is empty for internal services.

```
#
# inetd services
ftp        stream tcp nowait root    /usr/sbin/ftpd    in.ftpd -l
telnet     stream tcp nowait root    /usr/sbin/telnetd in.telnetd -b/etc/issue
#finger    stream tcp nowait bin     /usr/sbin/fingerd in.fingerd
#tftp      dgram  udp wait   nobody /usr/sbin/tftpd   in.tftpd
#tftp      dgram  udp wait   nobody /usr/sbin/tftpd    in.tftpd /boot/diskless
login      stream tcp nowait root    /usr/sbin/rlogind in.rlogind
shell      stream tcp nowait root    /usr/sbin/rshd    in.rshd
exec       stream tcp nowait root    /usr/sbin/rexecd  in.rexecd
#
#      inetd internal services
#
daytime    stream tcp nowait root internal
daytime    dgram  udp nowait root internal
time       stream tcp nowait root internal
time       dgram  udp nowait root internal
echo       stream tcp nowait root internal
echo       dgram  udp nowait root internal
discard    stream tcp nowait root internal
discard    dgram  udp nowait root internal
chargen    stream tcp nowait root internal
chargen    dgram  udp nowait root internal
```

Figure 9.1: A sample */etc/inetd.conf* file.

A sample *inetd.conf* file is shown in figure 9.1. The *finger* service commented out, so that it is not available.
This is often done for security reasons, because may be used by attackers to obtain names of users on your
system.

The *tftp* is shown commented out as well. *tftp* implements the *Primitive File Transfer Protocol* that allows
to transfer any world-readable files from your system without password checking etc. This is especially harmful
with the */etc/passwd* file, even more so when you don't use shadow password.

TFTP is commonly used by diskless clients and X terminals to download their code from a boot server. If you need to run *tftpd* for this reason, make sure to limit its scope to those directories clients will retrieve files from by adding those directory names to *tftpd*'s command line. This is shown in the second *tftp* line in the example.

9.2   The *tcpd* access control facility

Since opening a computer to network access involves many security risks, applications are designed to guard against several types of attacks. Some of these, however, may be flawed (most drastically demonstrated by the RTM Internet worm), or do not distinguish between secure hosts from which requests for a particular service will be accepted, and insecure hosts whose requests should be rejected. We already briefly discussed the *finger* and *tftp* services above. Thus, one would want to limit access to these services to "trusted hosts" only, which is impossible with the usual setup, where *inetd* either provides this service to all clients, or not at all.

A useful tool for this is *tcpd*,[1] a so-called daemon wrapper. For TCP services you want to monitor or protect, it is invoked instead of the server program. *tcpd* logs the request to the *syslog* daemon, checks if the remote host is allowed to use that service, and only if this succeeds will it executes the real server program. Note that this does not work with UDP-based services.

For example, to wrap the *finger* daemon, you have to change the corresponding line in *inetd.conf* to

```
# wrap finger daemon
finger  stream  tcp     nowait  root    /usr/sbin/tcpd  in.fingerd
```

Without adding any access control, this will appear to the client just as a usual *finger* setup, except that any requests are logged to *syslog*'s *auth* facility.

Access control is implemented by means of two files called */etc/hosts.allow* and */etc/hosts.deny*. They contain entries allowing and denying access, respectively, to certain services and hosts. When *tcpd* handles a request for a service such as *finger* from a client host named **biff.foobar.com**, it scans *hosts.allow* and *hosts.deny* (in this order) for an entry matching both the service and client host. If a matching entry is found in *hosts.allow*, access is granted, regardless of any entry in *hosts.deny*. If a match is found in *hosts.deny*, the request is rejected by closing down the connection. If no match is found at all, the request is accepted.

Entries in the access files look like this:

> *servicelist*:   *hostlist* [:*shellcmd*]

servicelist is a list of service names from */etc/services*, or the keyword *ALL*. To match all services except *finger* and *tftp*, use "*ALL EXCEPT finger, tftp*".

hostlist is a list of host names or IP addresses, or the keywords *ALL*, *LOCAL*, or *UNKNOWN*. *ALL* matches any host, while *LOCAL* matches host names not containing a dot.[2] *UNKNOWN* matches any hosts whose name or address lookup failed. A name starting with a dot matches all hosts whose domain is equal to this name. For example, *.foobar.com* matches **biff.foobar.com**. There are also provisions for IP network addresses and subnet numbers. Please refer to the *hosts_access(5)* manual page for details.

To deny access to the *finger* and *tftp* services to all but the local hosts, put the following in */etc/hosts.deny*, and leave */etc/hosts.allow* empty:

```
in.tftpd, in.fingerd:  ALL EXCEPT LOCAL, .your.domain
```

The optional *shellcmd* field may contain a shell command to be invoked when the entry is matched. This is useful to set up traps that may expose potential attackers:

```
in.ftpd: ALL EXCEPT LOCAL, .vbrew.com : \
    echo "request from %d@%h" >> /var/log/finger.log; \
    if [ %h != "vlager.vbrew.com" ]; then \
        finger -l @%h >> /var/log/finger.log \
    fi
```

---

[1] Written by Wietse Venema, **wietse@wzv.win.tue.nl**.
[2] Usually only local host names obtained from lookups in */etc/hosts* contain no dots.

The *%h* and *%d* arguments are expanded by *tcpd* to the client host name and service name, respectively. Please refer to the *hosts_access(5)* manual page for details.

9.3   The *services* and *protocols* Files

The port numbers on which certain "standard" services are offered are defined in the "Assigned Numbers" RFC. To enable server and client programs to convert service names to these numbers, at least a part of the list is kept on each host; it is stored in a file called */etc/services*. An entry is made up like this:

> *service port/protocol [aliases]*

Here, *service* specifies the service name, *port* defines the port the service is offered on, and *protocol* defines which transport protocol is used. Commonly, this is either *udp* or *tcp*. It is possible for a service to be offered for more than one protocol, as well as offering different services on the same port, as long as the protocols are different. The *aliases* field allows to specify alternative names for the same service.

Usually, you don't have to change the services file that comes along with the network software on your Linux system. Nevertheless, we give a small excerpt from that file below.

```
# The services file:
#
# well-known services
echo            7/tcp                      # Echo
echo            7/udp                      #
discard         9/tcp    sink null         # Discard
discard         9/udp    sink null         #
daytime        13/tcp                      # Daytime
daytime        13/udp                      #
chargen        19/tcp    ttytst source     # Character Generator
chargen        19/udp    ttytst source     #
ftp-data       20/tcp                      # File Transfer Protocol (Data)
ftp            21/tcp                      # File Transfer Protocol (Control)
telnet         23/tcp                      # Virtual Terminal Protocol
smtp           25/tcp                      # Simple Mail Transfer Protocol
nntp          119/tcp    readnews          # Network News Transfer Protocol
#
# UNIX services
exec          512/tcp                      # BSD rexecd
biff          512/udp    comsat            # mail notification
login         513/tcp                      # remote login
who           513/udp    whod              # remote who and uptime
shell         514/tcp    cmd               # remote command, no passwd used
syslog        514/udp                      # remote system logging
printer       515/tcp    spooler           # remote print spooling
route         520/udp    router routed     # routing information protocol
```

Note that, for example, the *echo* service is offered on port 7 for both TCP and UDP, and that port 512 is used for two different services, namely the COMSAT daemon (which notifies users of newly arrived mail, see *xbiff(1x)*), over UDP, and for remote execution (*rexec(1)*), using TCP.

Similar to the services file, the networking library needs a way to translate protocol names — for example, those used in the services file — to protocol numbers understood by the IP layer on other hosts. This is done by looking up the name in the */etc/protocols* file. It contains one entry per line, each containing a protocol name, and the associated number. Having to touch this file is even more unlikely than having to meddle with */etc/services*. A sample file is given below:

```
#
# Internet (IP) protocols
#
```

```
ip      0       IP          # internet protocol, pseudo protocol number
icmp    1       ICMP        # internet control message protocol
igmp    2       IGMP        # internet group multicast protocol
tcp     6       TCP         # transmission control protocol
udp     17      UDP         # user datagram protocol
raw     255     RAW         # RAW IP interface
```

9.4 Remote Procedure Call

A very general mechanism for client-server applications is provided by RPC, the *Remote Procedure Call* package. RPC was developed by Sun Micrsystems, and is a collection of tools and library functions. Important applications built on top of RPC are NFS, the Network Filesystem, and NIS, the Network Information System, both of which will be introduced in later chapters.

An RPC server consists of a collection of procedures that client may call by sending an RPC request to the server, along with the procedure parameters. The server will invoke the indicated procedure on behalf of the client, handing back the return value, if there is any. In order to be machine-independent, all data exchanged between client and server is converted to a so-called *External Data Representation* format (XDR) by the sender, and converted back to the machine-local representation by the receiver.

Sometimes, improvements to an RPC application introduce incompatible changes in the procedure call interface. Of course, simply changing the server would crash all application that still expect the original behavior. Therefore, RPC programs have version numbers assigned to them, usually starting with 1, and with each new version of the RPC interface this counter will be bumped. Often, a server may offer several versions simultaneously; clients then indicate by the version number in their requests which implementation of the service they want to use.

The network communication between RPC servers and clients is somewhat peculiar. An RPC server offers one or more collections of procedures; each set is being called a *program*, and is uniquely identified by a *program number*. A list mapping service names to program numbers is usually kept in */etc/rpc*, an excerpt of which is reproduced below in figure 9.2.

```
#
# /etc/rpc - miscellaenous RPC-based services
#
portmapper      100000  portmap sunrpc
rstatd          100001  rstat rstat_svc rup perfmeter
rusersd         100002  rusers
nfs             100003  nfsprog
ypserv          100004  ypprog
mountd          100005  mount showmount
ypbind          100007
walld           100008  rwall shutdown
yppasswdd       100009  yppasswd
bootparam       100026
ypupdated       100028  ypupdate
```

Figure 9.2: A sample */etc/rpc* file.

In TCP/IP networks, the authors of RPC were faced with the problem of mapping program numbers to generic network services. They chose to have each server provide both a TCP and a UDP port for each program and each version. Generally, RPC applications will use UDP when sending data, and only fall back to TCP when the data to be transferred doesn't fit into a single UDP datagram.

Of course, client programs have to have a way to find out which port a program number maps to. Using a configuration file for this would be too unflexible; since RPC applications don't use reserved ports, there's no guarantee that a port originally meant to be used by our database application hasn't been taken by some other process. Therefore, RPC applications pick any port they can get, and register it with the so-called *portmapper daemon*. The latter acts as a service broker for all RPC servers running on its machine: a client that wishes to contact a service with a given program number will first query the portmapper on the server's host which returns the TCP and UDP port numbers the service can be reached at.

This method has the particular drawback that it introduces a single point of failure, much like the *inetd* daemon does for the standard Berkeley services. However, this case is even a little worse, because when the portmapper dies, all RPC port information is lost; this usually means you have to restart all RPC servers manually, or reboot the entire machine.

On Linux, the portmapper is called *rpc.portmap* and resides in */usr/sbin*. Other than making sure it is started form *rc.inet2*, the portmapper doesn't require any configuration work.

9.5   Configuring the *r* Commands

There are a number of commands for executing commands on remote hosts. These are *rlogin*, *rsh*, *rcp* and *rcmd*. They all spawn a shell on the remote host and allow the user to execute commands. Of course, the client needs to have an account on the host where the commmand is to be executed. Thus all these commands perform an authorization procedure. Usually, the client will tell the user's login name to the server, which in turn requests a password that is validated in the usual way.

Sometimes, however, it is desirable to relax authorization checks for certain users. For instance, if you frequently have to log into other machines on your LAN, you might want to be admitted without having to type your password every time.

Disabling authorization is advisable only on a small number of hosts whose password databases are synchronized, or for a small number of privileged users who need to access many machines for administrative reasons. Whenever you want to allow people to log into your host without having to specify a login id or password, make sure that you don't accidentally grant access to anybody else.

There are two ways to disable authorization checks for the *r* commands. One is for the super user to allow certain or all users on certain or all hosts (the latter definitely being a bad idea) to log in without being asked for a password. This access is controlled by a file called */etc/hosts.equiv*. It contains a list of host and user names that are considered equivalent to users on the local host. An alternative option is for a user to grant other users on certain hosts access to her account. These may be listed in the file *.rhosts* in the user's home directory. For security reasons, this file must be owned by the user or the super user, and must not be a symbolic link, otherwise it will be ignored.[3]

When a client requests an *r* service, her host and user name are searched in the */etc/hosts.equiv* file, and then in the *.rhosts* file of the user she wants to log in as. As am example, assume **janet** is working on **gauss** and tries to log into **joe**'s account on **euler**. Throughout the following, we will refer to Janet as the *client* user, and to Joe as the *local* user. Now, when Janet types

```
$ rlogin -l joe euler
```

on **gauss**, the server will first check *hosts.equiv*[4] if Janet should be granted free access, and if this fails, it will try to look her up in *.rhosts* in **joe**'s home directory.

The *hosts.equiv* file on **euler** looks like this:

```
gauss
euler
-public
quark.physics.groucho.edu        andres
```

An entry consists of a host name, optionally followed by a user name. If a host name appears all by itself, all users from that host will be admitted to their local accounts without any checks. In the above example, Janet would be allowed to log into her account **janet** when coming from **gauss**, and the same applies to any other user except **root**. However, if Janet wants to log in as **joe**, she will be prompted for a password as usual.

---

[3]In an NFS environment, you may need to give it a protection of 444, because the super user is often very restricted in accessing files on disks mounted via NFS.

[4]Note that the *hosts.equiv* file is *not* searched when someone attempts to log in as **root**.

If a host name is followed by a user name, as in the last line of the above sample file, this user is given password-free access to _all_ accounts except the **root** account.

The host name may also be preceded by a minus sign, as in the entry "**-public**". This requires authorization for all accounts on **public**, regardless of what rights individual users grant in their _.rhosts_ file.

The format of the _.rhosts_ file is identical to that of _hosts.equiv_, but its meaning is a little different. Consider Joe's _.rhosts_ file on **euler**:

```
chomp.cs.groucho.edu
gauss       janet
```

The first entry grants **joe** free access when logging in from **chomp.cs.groucho.edu**, but does not affect the rights of any other account on **euler** or **chomp**. The second entry is a slight variation of this, in that it grants **janet** free access to Joe's account when logging in from **gauss**.

Note that the client's host name is obtained by reverse mapping the caller's address to a name, so that this feature will fail with hosts unknown to the resolver. The client's host name is considered to match the name in the hosts files in one of the following cases:

- The client's canonical host name (not an alias) literally matches the host name in the file.

- If the client's host name is a fully qualified domain name (such as returned by the resolver when you have DNS running), and it doesn't literally match the host name in the hosts file, it is compared to that host name expanded with the local domain name.

Chapter 10

The Network Information System

When you are running a local area network, your overall goal is usually to provide an environment to your users that makes the network transparent. An important stepping stone to this end is to keep vital data such as user account information synchronized between all hosts. We have seen before that for host name resolution, a powerful and sophisticated service exists, being DNS. For others tasks, there is no such specialized service. Moreover, if you manage only a small LAN with no Internet connectivity, setting up DNS may not seem worth the trouble for many administrators.

This is why Sun developed NIS, the *Network Information System*. NIS provides generic database access facilities that can be used to distribute information such as that contained in the *passwd* and *groups* files to all hosts on your network. This makes the network appear just as a single system, with the same accounts on all hosts. In a similar fashion, you can use NIS to distribute the hostname information form */etc/hosts* to all machines on the network.

NIS is based on RPC, and comprises a server, a client-side library, and several administrative tools. Originally, NIS was called *Yellow Pages*, or YP, which is still widely used to informally refer this service. On the other hand, Yellow Pages is a trademark of British Telecom, which required Sun to drop that name. As things go, some names stick with people, and so YP lives on as a prefix to the names of most NIS-related commands such as *ypserv*, *ypbind*, etc.

Today, NIS is available for virtually all Unices, and there are even free implementations of it. One is from the BSD Net-2 release, and has been derived from a public domain reference implementation donated by Sun. The library client code from this release has been in the GNU *libc* for a long time, while the administrative programs have only recently been ported to Linux by Swen Thümmler.[1] An NIS server is missing from the reference implementation. Tobias Reber has written another NIS package including all tools and a server; it is called *yps*.[2]

Currently, a complete rewrite of the NIS code called NYS is being done by Peter Eriksson,[3] which supports both plain NIS and Sun's much revised NIS+. NYS not only provides a set of NIS tools and a server, but also adds a whole new set of library functions which will most probably make it into the standard *libc* eventually. This includes a new configuration scheme for hostname resolution that replaces the current scheme using *host.conf*. The features of these functions will be discussed below.

This chapter will focus on NYS rather than the other two packages, to which I will refer as the "traditional" NIS code. If you do want to run any of these packages, the instructions in this chapter may or may not be enough. To obtain additional information, please get a standard book on NIS, such as Hal Stern's *NFS and NIS* (see [Stern92]).

For the time being, NYS is still under development, and therefore standard Linux utilities such as the network programs or the *login* program are not yet aware of the NYS configuration scheme. Until NYS is merged into the mainstream *libc* you therefore have to recompile all these binaries if you want to make them use NYS. In any of these applications' *Makefiles*, specify *-lnsl* as the last option before *libc* to the linker. This links in the relevant functions from *libnsl*, the NYS library, instead of the standard C library.

---

[1] To be reached at **swen@uni-paderborn.de**. The NIS clients are available as yp-linux.tar.gz from **sunsite.unc.edu** in *system/Network*.

[2] The current version (as of this writing) is yps-0.21 and can be obtained from **ftp.lysator.liu.se** in the */pub/NYS* directory.

[3] To be reached at **pen@lysator.liu.se**.

10.1 Getting Acquainted with NIS

NIS keeps database information is in so-called *maps* containing key-value pairs. Maps are stored on a central host running the NIS server, from which clients may retrieve the information through various RPC calls. Quite frequently, maps are stored in DBM files.[4]

The maps themselves are usually generated from master text files such as */etc/hosts* or */etc/passwd*. For some files, several maps are created, one for each search key type. For instance, you may search the *hosts* file for a host name as well as for an IP address. Accordingly, two NIS maps are derived from it, called *hosts.byname* and *hosts.byaddr*, respectively. Table 10.1 lists common maps and the files they are generated form.

Master File	Map(s)	
/etc/hosts	*hosts.byname*	*hosts.byaddr*
/etc/networks	*networks.byname*	*networks.byaddr*
/etc/passwd	*passwd.byname*	*passwd.byuid*
/etc/group	*group.byname*	*group.bygid*
/etc/services	*services.byname*	*services.bynumber*
/etc/rpc	*rpc.byname*	*rpc.bynumber*
/etc/protocols	*protocols.byname*	*protocols.bynumber*
/usr/lib/aliases	*mail.aliases*	

Table 10.1: Some standard NIS maps and the corresponding files.

There are other files and maps you may find support for in some NIS package or other. These may contain information for applications not discussed in this book, such as the *bootparams* map that may used by some BOOTP servers, or which currently don't have any function in Linux (like the *ethers.byname* and *ethers.byaddr* maps).

For some maps, people commonly use *nicknames*, which are shorter and therefore easier to type. To obtain a full list of nicknames understood by your NIS tools, run the following command:

```
$ ypcat -x
NIS map nickname translation table:
        "passwd" -> "passwd.byname"
        "group" -> "group.byname"
        "networks" -> "networks.byaddr"
        "hosts" -> "hosts.byname"
        "protocols" -> "protocols.bynumber"
        "services" -> "services.byname"
        "aliases" -> "mail.aliases"
        "ethers" -> "ethers.byname"
        "rpc" -> "rpc.bynumber"
        "netmasks" -> "netmasks.byaddr"
        "publickey" -> "publickey.byname"
        "netid" -> "netid.byname"
        "passwd.adjunct" -> "passwd.adjunct.byname"
        "group.adjunct" -> "group.adjunct.byname"
        "timezone" -> "timezone.byname"
```

The NIS server is traditionally called *ypserv*. For an average network, a single server usually suffices; large networks may choose to run several of these on different machines and different segments of the network to relieve the load on the server machines and routers. These servers are synchronized by making one of them the *master server*, and the others *slave servers*. Maps will be created only on the master server's host. From there, they are distributed to all slaves.

You will have noticed that we have been talking about "networks" very vaguely all the time; of course there's a distinctive concept in NIS that refers to such a network, that is the collection of all hosts that share part of

---

[4]DBM is a simple database management library that uses hashing techniques to speed up search operations. There's a free DBM implementation from the GNU project called *gdbm*, which is part of most Linux distributions.

their system configuration data through NIS: the *NIS domain*. Unfortunately, NIS domains have absolutely nothing in common with the domains we encountered in DNS. To avoid any ambiguity throughout this chapter, I will therefore always specify which type of domain I mean.

NIS domains have a purely administrative function only. They are mostly invisible to users, except for the sharing of passwords between all machines in the domain. Therefore, the name given to a NIS domain is relevant only to the administrators. Usually, any name will do, as long as it is different from any other NIS domain name on your local network. For instance, the administrator at the Virtual Brewery may choose to create two NIS domains, one for the Brewery itself, and one for the Winery, which she names **brewery** and **winery**, respectively. Another quite common scheme is to simply use the DNS domain name for NIS as well. To set and display the NIS domain name of your host, you can use the *domainname* command. When invoked without any argument, it prints the current NIS domain name; to set the domain name, you must become super user and type:

```
# domainname brewery
```

NIS domains determine which NIS server an application will query. For instance, the *login* program on a host at the Winery should, of course, only query the Winery's NIS server (or one of them, if there were several) for a user's password information; while an application on a Brewery host should stick with the Brewery's server.

One mystery now remains to be solved, namely how a client finds out which server to connect to. The simplest approach would be to have a configuration file that names the host on which to find the server. However, this approach is rather inflexible, because it doesn't allow clients to use different servers (from the same domain, of course), depending on their availability. Therefore, traditional NIS implementations rely on a special daemon called *ypbind* to detect a suitable NIS server in their NIS domain. Before being able to perform any NIS queries, any application first finds out from *ypbind* which server to use.

ypbind probes for servers by broadcasting to the local IP network; the first to respond is assumed to be the potentially fastest one and will be used in all subsequent NIS queries. After a certain interval has elapsed, or if the server becomes unavailable, *ypbind* will probe for active servers again.

Now, the arguable point about dynamic binding is that you rarely need it, and that it introduces a security problem: *ypbind* blindly believes whoever answers, which could be a humble NIS server as well as a malicious intruder. Needless to say this becomes especially troublesome if you manage your password databases over NIS. To guard against this, NYS does *not* use *ypbind* by default, but rather picks up the server host name from a configuration file.

10.2   NIS versus NIS+

NIS and NIS+ share little more than their name and a common goal. NIS+ is structured in an entirely different way. Instead of a flat name space with disjoint NIS domains, it uses a hierarchical name space similar to that of DNS. Instead of maps, so called *tables* are used that are made up of rows and columns, where each row represents an object in the NIS+ database, while the columns cover those properties of the objects that NIS+ knows and cares about. Each table for a given NIS+ domain comprises those of its parent domains. In addition, an entry in a table may contain a link to another table. These features make it possible to structure information in many ways.

Traditional NIS has an RPC version number of 2, while NIS+ is version 3.

NIS+ does not seem to be very widely used yet, and I don't really know that much about it. (Well, almost nothing). For this reason, we will not deal with it here. If you are interested in learning more about it, please refer to Sun's NIS+ administration manual ([NISPlus]).

10.3   The Client Side of NIS

If you are familiar with writing or porting network applications, you will notice that most NIS maps listed above correspond to library functions in the C library. For instance, to obtain *passwd* information, you generally use the *getpwnam(3)* and *getpwuid(3)* functions which return the account information associated with the given user name or numerical user id, repsectively. Under normal circumstances, these functions will perform the requested lookup on the standard file, such as */etc/passwd*.

A NIS-aware implementation of these functions, however, will modify this behavior, and place an RPC call to have the NIS server look up the user name or id. This happens completely transparent to the application. The function may either "append" the NIS map to or "replace" the original file with it. Of course, this does not refer to a real modification of the file, it only means that it *appears* to the application as if the file had been replaced or appended to.

For traditional NIS implementations, there used to be certain conventions as to which maps replaced, and which were appended to the original information. Some, like the *passwd* maps, required kludgy modifications of the *passwd* file which, when done wrong, would open up security holes. To avoid these pitfalls, NYS uses a general configuration scheme that determines whether a particular set of client functions uses the original files, NIS, or NIS+, and in which order. It will be described in a later section of this chapter.

10.4   Running a NIS Server

After so much theoretical techno-babble, it's time to get our hands dirty with actual configuration work. In this section, we will cover the configuration of a NIS server. If there's already a NIS server running on your network, you won't have to set up your own server; in this case, you may safely skip this section.

◇ Note that if you are just going to experiment with the server, make sure you don't set it up for a NIS domain name that is already in use on your network. This may disrupt the entire network service and make a lot of people very unhappy, and very angry.

There are currently two NIS servers freely available for Linux, one contained in Tobias Reber's *yps* package, and the other in Peter Eriksson's *ypserv* package. It shouldn't matter which one you run, regardless of whether you use NYS or the standard NIS client code that is in *libc* currently. At the time of this writing, the code for the handling of NIS slave servers seems to be more complete in *yps*. So if you have to deal with slave servers, *yps* might be a better choice.

After installing the server program (*ypserv*) in */usr/sbin*, you should create the directory that is going to hold the map files your server is to distribute. When setting up a NIS domain for the **brewery** domain, the maps would go to */var/yp/brewery*. The server determines if it is serving a particular NIS domain by checking if the map directory is present. If you are disabling service for some NIS domain, make sure to remove the directory as well.

Maps are usually stored in DBM files to speed up lookups. They are created from the master files using a program called *makedbm* (for Tobias' server) or *dbmload* (for Peter's server). These may not be interchangeable. Transforming a master file into a form parseable by *dbmload* usually requires some *awk* or *sed* magic, which tend to be a little tedious to type and hard to remember. Therefore, Peter Eriksson's *ypserv* package contains a Makefile (called *ypMakefile*) that does all these jobs for you. You should install it as *Makefile* in your map directory, and edit it to reflect the maps you want to distribute. Towards the top of the file, you find the *all* target that lists the services *ypserv* is to offer. By default, the line looks something like this:

```
all: ethers hosts networks protocols rpc services passwd group netid
```

If you don't want to produce the *ethers.byname* and *ethers.byaddr* maps, for example, simply remove the *ethers* prerequisite from this rule. To test your setup, it may suffice to start with just one or two maps, like the *services.* * maps.

After editing the *Makefile*, while in the map directory, type "`make`". This will automatically generate and install the maps. You have to make sure to update the maps whenever you change the master files, otherwise the changes will remain invisible to the network.

The next section explains how to configure the NIS client code. If your setup doesn't work, you should try to find out whether any requests arrive at your server or not. If you specify the `-D` command line flag to the NYS server, it prints debugging messages to the console about all incoming NIS queries, and the results returned. These should give you a hint as to where the problem lies. Tobias' server has no such option.

10.5   Setting up a NIS Client with NYS

Throughout the remainder of this chapter, we will cover the configuration of a NIS client.

Your first step should be to tell NYS which server to use for NIS service, setting it in the */etc/yp.conf* configuration file. A very simple sample file for a host on the Winery's network may look like this:

```
# yp.conf - YP configuration for NYS library.
#
domainname winery
server vbardolino
```

The first statement tells all NIS clients that they belong to the **winery** NIS domain. If you omit this line, NYS will use the domain name you assigned your system through the *domainname* command. The *server* statement names the NIS server to use. Of course, the IP address corresponding to **vbardolino** must be set in the *hosts* file; alternatively, you may use the IP address itself with the *server* statement.

In the form shown above, the *server* command tells NYS to use the named server whatever the current NIS domain may be. If, however, you are moving your machine between different NIS domains frequently, you may want to keep information for several domains in the *yp.conf* file. You can have information on the servers for various NIS domains in *yp.conf* by adding the NIS domain name to the *server* statement. For instance, you might change the above sample file for a laptop to look like this:

```
# yp.conf - YP configuration for NYS library.
#
server vbardolino winery
server vstout     brewery
```

This allows you to bring up the laptop in any of the two domains by simply setting the desired NIS domain at boot time through the *domainname* command.

After creating this basic configuration file and making sure it is world-readable, you should run your first test to check if you can connect to your server. Make sure to choose any map your server distributes, like *hosts.byname*, and try to retrieve it by using the *ypcat* utility. *ypcat*, like all other administrative NIS tools, should live in */usr/sbin*.

```
# ypcat hosts.byname
191.72.2.2      vbeaujolais    vbeaujolais.linus.lxnet.org
191.72.2.3      vbardolino     vbardolino.linus.lxnet.org
191.72.1.1      vlager         vlager.linus.lxnet.org
191.72.2.1      vlager         vlager.linus.lxnet.org
191.72.1.2      vstout         vstout.linus.lxnet.org
191.72.1.3      vale           vale.linus.lxnet.org
191.72.2.4      vchianti       vchianti.linus.lxnet.org
```

The output you get should look somthing like that shown above. If you get an error message instead that says "Can't bind to server which serves domain" or something similar, then either the NIS domain name you've set doesn't have a matching server defined in *yp.conf*, or the server is unreachable for some reason. In the latter case, make sure that a *ping* to the host yields a positive result, and that it is indeed running a NIS server. You can verify the latter by using *rpcinfo*, which should produce the following output:

```
# rpcinfo -u serverhost ypserv
program 100004 version 2 ready and waiting
```

10.6   Choosing the Right Maps

Having made sure you can reach the NIS server, you have to decide which configuration files to replace or augment with NIS maps. Commonly, you will want use NIS maps for the host and password lookup functions.

The former is especially useful if you do not run BIND. The latter permits all users to log into their account from any system in the NIS domain; this usually requires sharing a central */home* directory between all hosts via NFS. It is explained detail in section 10.7 below. Other maps, like *services.byname*, aren't such a dramatic gain, but save you some editing work if you install any network applications that use a service name that's not in the standard *services* file.

Generally, you want to have some freedom of choice when a lookup function uses the local files, and when it queries the NIS server. NYS allows you to configure the order in which a function accesses these services. This is controlled through the */etc/nsswitch.conf* file, which stands for *Name Service Switch* but of course isn't limited to the name service. For any of the data lookup functions supported by NYS, it contains a line naming the services to use.

The right order of services depends on the type of data. It is unlikely that the *services.byname* map will contain entries differing from those in the local *services* file; it may only contain more. So a good choice may be to query the local files first, and check NIS only if the service name wasn't found. Hostname information, on the other hand, may change very frequently, so that DNS or the NIS server should always have the most accurate account, while the local *hosts* file is only kept as a backup if DNS and NIS should fail. In this case, you would want to check the local file last.

The example below shows how to configure *gethostbyname(2)*, *gethostbyaddr(2)*, and *getservbyname(2)* functions as described above. They will try the listed services in turn; if a lookup succeeds, the result is returned, otherwise the next service is tried.

```
# small sample /etc/nsswitch.conf
#
hosts:     nis dns files
services:  files nis
```

The complete list of services that may be used with an entry in the *nsswitch.conf* file is shown below. The actual maps, files, servers and objects being queried depend on the entry name.

nisplus or *nis+*
    Use the NIS+ server for this domain. The location of the server is obtained from the */etc/nis.conf* file.

nis
    Use the current NIS server of this domain. The location of the server queried is configured in the *yp.conf* file as shown in the previous section. For the *hosts* entry, the maps *hosts.byname* and *hosts.byaddr* are queried.

dns
    Use the DNS name server. This service type is only useful with the *hosts* entry. The name servers queried are still determined by the standard *resolv.conf* file.

files
    Use the local file, such as the */etc/hosts* file for the *hosts* entry.

dbm
    Look up the information from DBM files located in */var/dbm*. The name used for the file is that of the corresponding NIS map.

Currently, NYS supports the following *nsswitch.conf* entries: *hosts*, *networks*, *passwd*, *group*, *shadow*, *gshadow*, *services*, *protocols*, *rpc*, and *ethers*. More entries are likely to be added.

Figure 10.1 shows a more complete example which introduces another feature of *nsswitch.conf*: the *[NOT-FOUND=return]* keyword in the *hosts* entry tells NYS to return if the desired item couldn't be found in the NIS or DNS database. That is, NYS will continue and search the local files *only* if calls to the NIS and DNS servers failed for some other reason. The local files will then only be used at boot time and as a backup when the NIS server is down.

10.7 Using the *passwd* and *group* Maps

One of the major applications of NIS is in synchronizing user and account information on all hosts in a NIS domain. To this end, you usually keep only a small local */etc/passwd* file, to which the site-wide information

```
# /etc/nsswitch.conf
#
hosts:        nis dns [NOTFOUND=return] files
networks:     nis [NOTFOUND=return] files

services:     files nis
protocols:    files nis
rpc:          files nis
```

Figure 10.1: Sample *nsswitch.conf* file.

from the NIS maps is appended. However, simply enabling NIS lookups for this service in *nsswitch.conf* is not nearly enough.

When relying on the password information distributed by NIS, you first have to make sure that the numeric user id's of any users you have in your local *passwd* file match the NIS server's idea of user id's. You will want this for other purposes as well, like mounting NFS volumes from other hosts in your network.

If any of the numeric ids in */etc/passwd* or */etc/group* deviate from those in the maps, you have to adjust file ownerships for all files that belong to that user. First you should change all uids and gids in *passwd* and *group* to the new values; then find all files that belong to the users just changed, and finally change their ownership. Assume **news** used to have a user id of 9, and **okir** had a user id of 103, which were changed to some other value; you could then issue the following commands:

```
# find / -uid   9 -print >/tmp/uid.9
# find / -uid 103 -print >/tmp/uid.103
# cat /tmp/uid.9   | xargs chown news
# cat /tmp/uid.103 | xargs chown okir
```

It is important that you execute these commands with the *new passwd* file installed, and that you collect all file names before you change the ownership of any of them. To update the group ownerships of files, you will use a similar command.

Having done this, the numerical uid's and gid's on your system will agree with those on all other hosts in your NIS domain. The next step will be to add configuration lines to *nsswitch.conf* that enables NIS lookups for user and group information:

```
# /etc/nsswitch.conf - passwd and group treatment
passwd: nis files
group:  nis files
```

This makes the *login* command and all its friends first query the NIS maps when a user tries to log in, and if this lookup fails, fall back to the local files. Usually, you will remove almost all users from your local files, and only leave entries for **root** and generic accounts like **mail** in it. This is because some vital system tasks may require to map uids to user names or vice versa. For example, administrative *cron* jobs may execute the *su* command to temporarily become **news**, or the UUCP subsystem may mail a status report. If **news** and **uucp** don't have entries in the local *passwd* file, these jobs will fail miserably during a NIS brownout.

There are two big caveats in order here: on one hand, the setup as described up to here only works for login suites that don't use shadow password, like those included in the *util-linux* package. The intricacies of using shadow passwords with NIS will be covered below. On the other hand, the login commands are not the only ones that access the *passwd* file – look at the *ls* command which most people use almost constantly. Whenever doing a long listing, *ls* will display the symbolic names for user and group owners of a file; that is, for each uid and gid it encounters, it will have to query the NIS server once. This will slow things down rather badly if your local network is clogged, or, even worse, when the NIS server is not on the same physical network, so that datagrams have to pass through a router.

Still, this is not the whole story yet. Imagine what happens if a user wants to change her password. Usually, she will invoke *passwd*, which reads the new password and updates the local *passwd* file. This is impossible with NIS, since that file isn't available locally anymore, but having users log into the NIS server whenever they want to change their password is not an option either. Therefore, NIS provides a drop-in replacement for *passwd* called *yppasswd*, which does the analoguous thing in the presence of NIS. To change the password on the server host, it contacts the *yppasswdd* daemon on that host via RPC, and provides it with the updated password information. Usually, you install *yppasswd* over the normal program by doing something like this:

```
# cd /bin
# mv passwd passwd.old
# ln yppasswd passwd
```

At the same time you have to install *rpc.yppasswdd* on the server and start it from *rc.inet2*. This will effectively hide any of the contortions of NIS from your users.

10.8   Using NIS with Shadow Support

There is no NIS support yet for sites that use the shadow login suite. John F. Haugh, the author of the shadow suite, recently released a version of the shadow library functions covered by the GNU Library GPL to **comp.sources.misc**. It already has some support for NIS, but it isn't complete, and the files haven't been added to the standard C library yet. On the other hand, publishing the information from */etc/shadow* via NIS kind of defeats the purpose of the shadow suite.

Although the NYS password lookup functions don't use a *shadow.byname* map or anything likewise, NYS supports using a local */etc/shadow* file transparently. When the NYS implementation of *getpwnam* is called to look up information related to a given login name, the facilities specified by the *passwd* entry in *nsswitch.conf* are queried. The *nis* service will simply look up the name in the *passwd.byname* map on the NIS server. The *files* service, however, will check if */etc/shadow* is present, and if so, try to open it. If none is present, or if the user doesn't have **root** privilege, if reverts to the traditional behavior of looking up the user information in */etc/passwd* only. However, if the *shadow* file exists and can be opened, NYS will extract the user password from *shadow*. The *getpwuid* function is implemented accordingly. In this fashion, binaries compiled with NYS will deal with a local the shadow suite installation transparently.

10.9   Using the Traditional NIS Code

If you are using the client code that is in the standard *libc* currently, configuring a NIS client is a little different. On one hand, it uses a *ypbind* daemon to broadcast for active servers rather than gathering this information from a configuration file. You therefore have to make sure to start *ypbind* at boot time. It must be invoked after the NIS domain has been set and the RPC portmapper has been started. Invoking *ypcat* to test the server should then work as shown above.

Recently, there have been numerous bug reports that NIS fails with an error message saying "clntudp_create: RPC: portmapper failure - RPC: unable to receive". These are due to an incompatible change in the way *ypbind* communicates the binding information to the library functions. Obtaining the latest sources for the NIS utilities and recompiling them should cure this problem.[5]

Also, the way traditional NIS decides if and how to merge NIS information with that from the local files deviates from that used by NYS. For instance, to use the NIS password maps, you have to include the following line somewhere in your */etc/passwd* map:

```
+:*:0:0:::
```

This marks the place where the password lookup functions "insert" the NIS maps. Inserting a similar line (minus the last two colons) into */etc/group* does the same for the *group.** maps. To use the *hosts.** maps distributed by NIS, change the *order* line in the *host.conf* file. For instance, if you want to use NIS, DNS, and the */etc/hosts* file (in that order), you need to change the line to

```
order yp bind hosts
```

The traditional NIS implementation does not support any other maps at the moment.

---

[5]The source for *yp-linux* can be gotten from **ftp.uni-paderborn.de** in directory */pub/Linux/LOCAL*.

Chapter 11

The Network File System

NFS, the network filesystem, is probably the most prominent network services using RPC. It allows to access files on remote hosts in exactly the same way as a user would access any local files. This is made possible by a mixture of kernel functionality on the client side (that uses the remote file system) and an NFS server on the server side (that provides the file data). This file access is completely transparent to the client, and works across a variety of server and host architectures.

NFS offers a number of advantages:

- Data accessed by all users can be kept on a central host, with clients mounting this directory at boot time. For example, you can keep all user accounts on one host, and have all hosts on your network mount /home from that host. If installed alongside with NIS, users can then log into any system, and still work on one set of files.

- Data consuming large amounts of disk space may be kept on a single host. For example, all files and programs relating to LaTeX and METAFONT could be kept and maintained in one place.

- Administrative data may be kept on a single host. No need to use *rcp* anymore to install the same stupid file on 20 different machines.

Linux NFS is largely the work of Rick Sladkey,[1] who wrote the NFS kernel code and large parts of the NFS server. The latter is derived from the *unfsd* user-space NFS server originally written by Mark Shand, and the *hnfs* Harris NFS server written by Donald Becker.

Let's have a look now at how NFS works: A client may request to mount a directory from a remote host on a local directory just the same way it can mount a physical device. However, the syntax used to specify the remote directory is different. For example, to mount /home from host **vlager** to /users on **vale**, the administrator would issue the following command on **vale**:[2]

```
# mount -t nfs vlager:/home /users
```

mount will then try to connect to the *mountd* mount daemon on **vlager** via RPC. The server will check if **vale** is permitted to mount the directory in question, and if so, return it a file handle. This file handle will be used in all subsequent requests to files below /users.

When someone accesses a file over NFS, the kernel places an RPC call to *nfsd* (the NFS daemon) on the server machine. This call takes the file handle, the name of the file to be accessed, and the user's user and group id as parameters. These are used in determining access rights to the specified file. In order to prevent unauthorized users from reading or modifying files, user and group ids must be the same on both hosts.

On most UNIX implementations, the NFS functionality of both client and server are implemented as kernel-level daemons that are started from user space at system boot. These are the NFS daemon (*nfsd*) on the server

---

[1] Rick can be reached at **jrs@world.std.com**.
[2] Note that you can omit the **-t nfs** argument, because *mount* sees from the colon that this specifies an NFS volume.

host, and the *Block I/O Daemon* (*biod*) running on the client host. To improve throughput, *biod* performs asynchronous I/O using read-ahead and write-behind; also, several *nfsd* daemons are usually run concurrently.

The NFS implementation of Linux is a little different in that the client code is tightly integrated in the virtual file system (VFS) layer of the kernel and doesn't require additional control through *biod*. On the other hand, the server code runs entirely in user space, so that running several copies of the server at the same time is almost impossible because of the synchronization issues this would involve. Linux NFS currently also lacks read-ahead and write-behind, but Rick Sladkey plans to add this someday.[3]

The biggest problem with the Linux NFS code is that the Linux kernel as of version 1.0 is not able to allocate memory in chunks bigger than 4K; as a consequence, the networking code cannot handle datagrams bigger than roughly 3500 bytes after subtracting header sizes etc. This means that transfers to and from NFS daemons running on systems that use large UDP datagrams by default (e.g. 8K on SunOS) need to be downsized artificially. This hurts performance badly under some circumstances.[4] This limit is gone in late Linux-1.1 kernels, and the client code has been modified to take advantage of this.

11.1 Preparing NFS

Before you can use NFS, be it as server or client, you must make sure your kernel has NFS support compiled in. Newer kernels have a simple interface on the proc filesystem for this, the */proc/filesystems* file, which you can display using *cat*:

```
$ cat /proc/filesystems
minix
ext2
msdos
nodev proc
nodev nfs
```

If *nfs* is missing from this list, then you have to compile your own kernel with NFS enabled. Configuring the kernel network options is explained in section "Kernel Configuration" in chapter 3.

For older kernels prior to Linux 1.1, the easiest way to find out whether your kernel has NFS support enabled is to actually try to mount an NFS file system. For this, you could create a directory below */tmp*, and try to mount a local directory on it:

```
# mkdir /tmp/test
# mount localhost:/etc /tmp/test
```

If this mount attempt fails with an error message saying "`fs type nfs no supported by kernel`", you must make a new kernel with NFS enabled. Any other error messages are completely harmless, as you haven't configured the NFS daemons on your host yet.

11.2 Mounting an NFS Volume

NFS volumes[5] are mounted very much the way usual file systems are mounted. You invoke *mount* using the following syntax:

```
# mount -t nfs nfs_volume local_dir options
```

---

[3]The problem with write-behind is that the kernel buffer cache is indexed by device/inode pairs, and therefore can't be used for NFS-mounted file systems.

[4]As explained to me by Alan Cox: The NFS specification requires the server to flush each write to disk before it returns an acknowledgement. As BSD kernels are only capable of page-sized writes (4K), writing a 4 chunks of 1K each to a BSD-based NFS server results in 4 write operations of 4K each.

[5]One doesn't say file system, because these are not proper file systems.

nfs_volume is given as *remote_host:remote_dir*. Since this notation is unique to NFS file systems, you can leave out the -t nfs option.

There are a number of additional options that you may specify to *mount* upon mounting an NFS volume. These may either be given following the -o switch on the command line, or in the options field of the */etc/fstab* entry for the volume. In both cases, multiple options are separated from each other by commas. Options specified on the command line always override those given in the *fstab* file.

A sample entry in */etc/fstab* might be

```
# volume              mount point        type   options
news:/usr/spool/news  /usr/spool/news    nfs    timeo=14,intr
```

This volume may then be mounted using

```
# mount news:/usr/spool/news
```

In the absence of a *fstab* entry, NFS *mount* invocations look a lot uglier. For instance, suppose you mount your users' home directories from a machine named **moonshot**, which uses a default block size of 4K for read/write operations. You might decrease block size to 2K to suit Linux' datagram size limit by issuing

```
# mount moonshot:/home /home -o rsize=2048,wsize=2048
```

The list of all valid options is described in its entirety in the *nfs(5)* manual page that comes with Rick Sladkey's NFS-aware *mount* tool which can be found in Rik Faith's *util-linux* package). The following is an incomplete list of those you would probably want to use:

rsize=n and *wsize=n*

These specify the datagram size used by the NFS clients on read and write requests, respectively. They currently default to 1024 bytes, due to the limit on UDP datagram size described above.

timeo=n   This sets the time (in tenths of a second) the NFS client will wait for a request to complete. The default values is 0.7 seconds.

hard   Explicitly mark this volume as hard-mounted. This is on by default.

soft   Soft-mount the driver (as opposed to hard-mount).

intr   Allow signals to interrupt an NFS call. Useful for aborting when the server doesn't respond.

Except for *rsize* and *wsize*, all of these options apply to the client's behavior if the server should become inaccessible temporarily. They play together in the following way: whenever the client sends a request to the NFS server, it expects the operation to have finished after a given interval (specified in the *timeout* option). If no confirmation is received within this time, a so-called *minor timeout* occurs, and the operation is retried with the timeout interval doubled. After reaching a maximum timeout of 60 seconds, a *major timeout* occurs.

By default, a major timeout will cause the client to print a message to the console and start all over again, this time with an initial timeout interval twice that of the previous cascade. Potentially, this may go on forever. Volumes that stubbornly retry an operation until the server becomes available again are called *hard-mounted*. The opposite variety, *soft-mounted* volumes generenates an I/O error for the calling process whenever a major timeout occurs. Because of the write-behind introduced by the buffer cache, this error condition is not propagated to the process itself before it calls the *write(2)* function the next time, so a program can never be sure that a write operation to a soft-mounted volume has succeeded at all.

Whether you hard- or soft-mount a volume is not simply a question of taste, but also has to do with what sort of information you want to access from this volume. For example, if you mount your X programs by NFS, you certainly would not want your X session to go berserk just because someone brought the network to a grinding halt by firing up seven copies of *xv* at the same time, or by pulling the Ethernet plug for a moment. By hard-mounting these, you make sure that your computer will wait until it is able to re-establish contact with your NFS-server. On the other hand, non-critical data such as NFS-mounted news partititons or FTP archives may as well be soft-mounted, so it doesn't hang your session in case the remote machine should be temporarily unreachable, or down. If your network connection to the server is flakey or goes through a loaded router, you may either increase the initial timeout using the *timeo* option, or hard-mount the volumes, but allow for signals interrupting the NFS call so that you may still abort any hanging file access.

Usually, the *mountd* daemon will in some way or other keep track of which directories have been mounted by what hosts. This information can be displayed using the *showmount* program, which is also included in the NFS server package. The Linux *mountd*, however, does not do this yet.

11.3   The NFS Daemons

If you want to provide NFS service to other hosts, you have to run the *nfsd* and *mountd* daemons on your machine. As RPC-based programs, they are not managed by *inetd*, but are started up at boot time, and register themselves with the portmapper. Therefore, you have to make sure to start them only after *rpc.portmap* is running. Usually, you include the following two lines in your *rc.inet2* script:

```
if [ -x /usr/sbin/rpc.mountd ]; then
        /usr/sbin/rpc.mountd; echo -n " mountd"
fi
if [ -x /usr/sbin/rpc.nfsd ]; then
        /usr/sbin/rpc.nfsd; echo -n " nfsd"
fi
```

The ownership information of files a NFS daemon provides to its clients usually contains only numerical user and group id's. If both client and server associate the same user and group names with these numerical id's, they are said to share the same uid/gid space. For example, this is the case when you use NIS to distribute the *passwd* information to all hosts on your LAN.

On some occasions, however, they do not match. Rather updating the uid's and gid's of the client to match those of the server, you can use the *ugidd* mapping daemon to work around this. Using the *map_daemon* option explained below, you can tell *nfsd* to map the server's uid/gid space to the client's uid/gid space with the aid of the *ugidd* on the client.

ugidd is an RPC-based server, and is started from *rc.inet2* just like *nfsd* and *mountd*.

```
if [ -x /usr/sbin/rpc.ugidd ]; then
        /usr/sbin/rpc.ugidd; echo -n " ugidd"
fi
```

11.4   The *exports* File

While the above options applied to the client's NFS configuration, there is a different set of options on the server side that configure its per-client behavior. These options must be set in the */etc/exports* file.

By default, *mountd* will not allow anyone to mount directories from the local host, which is a rather sensible attitude. To permit one or more hosts to NFS-mount a directory, it must *exported*, that is, must be specified in the *exports* file. A sample file may look like this:

```
# exports file for vlager
/home           vale(rw) vstout(rw) vlight(rw)
/usr/X386       vale(ro) vstout(ro) vlight(ro)
/usr/TeX        vale(ro) vstout(ro) vlight(ro)
/               vale(rw,no_root_squash)
/home/ftp       (ro)
```

Each line defines a directory, and the hosts allowed to mount it. A host name is usually a fully qualified domain name, but may additionally contain the * and ? wildcard, which act the way they do with the Bourne shell. For instance, **lab*.foo.com** matches **lab01.foo.com** as well as **laber.foo.com**. If no host name is given, as with the */home/ftp* directory in the example above, any host is allowed to mount this directory.

When checking a client host against the *exports* file, *mountd* will look up the client's hostname using the *gethostbyaddr(2)* call. With DNS, this call returns the client's canonical hostname, so you must make sure not to use aliases in *exports*. Without using DNS, the returned name is the first hostname found in the *hosts* file that matches the client's address.

The host name is followed by an optional, comma-separated list of flags, enclosed in brackets. These flags may take the following values:

insecure   Permit non-authenticated access from this machine.

unix-rpc   Require UNIX-domain RPC authentication from this machine. This simply requires that requests originate from a reserved internet port (i.e. the port number has to be less than 1024). This option is on by default.

secure-rpc   Require secure RPC authentication from this machine. This has not been implemented yet. See Sun's documentation on Secure RPC.

kerberos   Require Kerberos authentication on accesses from this machine. This has not been implemented yet. See the MIT documentation on the Kerberos authentication system.

root_squash   This is a security feature that denies the super user on the specified hosts any special access rights by mapping requests from uid 0 on the client to uid 65534 (-2) on the server. This uid should be associated with the user **nobody**.

no_root_squash   Don't map requests from uid 0. This option is on by default.

ro   Mount file hierarchy read-only. This option is on by default.

rw   Mount file hierarchy read-write.

link_relative   Convert absolute symbolic links (where the link contents start with a slash) into relative links by prepending the necessary number of ../'s to get from the directory containing the link to the root on the server. This option only makes sense when a host's entire file system is mounted, else some of the links might point to nowhere, or even worse, files they were never meant to point to.

                    This option is on by default.

link_absolute   Leave all symbolic link as they are (the normal behavior for Sun-supplied NFS servers).

map_identity   The *map_identity* option tells the server to assume that the client uses the same uid's and gid's as the server. This option is on by default.

map_daemon   This option tells the NFS server to assume that client and server do not share the same uid/gid space. *nfsd* will then build a list mapping id's between client and server by querying the client's *ugidd* daemon.

An error parsing the *exports* file is reported to *syslogd*'s *daemon* facility at level *notice* whenever *nfsd* or *mountd* is started up.

Note that host names are obtained from the client's IP address by reverse mapping, so you have to have the resolver configured properly. If you use BIND and are very security-conscious, you should enable spoof checking in your *host.conf* file.

11.5   The Linux Automounter

Sometimes, it is wasteful to mount all NFS volumes users might possibly want to access; either because of the sheer number of volumes to be mounted, or because of the time this would take at startup. A viable alternative to this is a so-called *automounter*. This is a daemon that automatically and transparently mounts any NFS volume as needed, and unmounts them after they have not been used for some time. One of the clever things about an automounter is that it is able to mount a certain volume from alternative places. For instance, you may keep copies of your X programs and support files on two or three hosts, and have all other hosts mount them via NFS. Using an automounter, you may specify all three of them to be mounted on */usr/X386*; the automounter will then try to mount any of these until one of the mount attempts succeeds.

The automounter commonly used with Linux is called *amd*. It was originally written by Jan-Simon Pendry and has been ported to Linux by Rick Sladkey. The current version is *amd-5.3*.

Explaining *amd* is beyond the scope of this chapter; for a good manual please refer to the sources; they contain a texinfo file with very detailed information.

Chapter 12

Managing Taylor UUCP

12.1   History

UUCP was designed in the late seventies by Mike Lesk at AT&T Bell Laboratories to provide a simple dial-up network over public telephone lines. Since most people that want to have email and Usenet News on their home machine still communicate through modems, UUCP has remained very popular. Although there are many implementations running on a wide variety of hardware platforms and operating systems, they are compatible to a high degree.

However, as with most software that has somehow become "standard" over the years, there is no UUCP which one would call *the* UUCP. It has undergone a steady process of evolution since the first version which was implemented in 1976. Currently, there are two major species which differ mainly in their support of hardware and their configuration. Of these, various implementations exist, each varying slightly from its siblings.

One species is the so-called "Version 2 UUCP", which dates back to a 1977 implementation by Mike Lesk, David A. Novitz, and Greg Chesson. Although it is fairly old, it is still in frequent use. Recent implementations of Version 2 provide much of the comfort of the newer UUCP species.

The second species was developed in 1983, and is commonly referred to as BNU (Basic Networking Utilities), HoneyDanBer UUCP, or HDB for short. The name is derived from the authors' names, P. Honeyman, D. A. Novitz, and B. E. Redman. HDB was conceived to eliminate some of Version 2 UUCP's deficiencies. For example, new transfer protocols were added, and the spool directory was split so that now there is one directory for each site you have UUCP traffic with.

The implementation of UUCP currently distributed with Linux is Taylor UUCP 1.04,[1] which is the version this chapter is based upon. Taylor UUCP Version 1.04 was released in February 1993. Apart from traditional configuration files, Taylor UUCP may also be compiled to understand the new-style – a.k.a. "Taylor" – configuration files.

Version 1.05 has been released recently, and will soon make its way into most distributions. The differences between these versions mostly affect features you will never use, so you should be able to configure Taylor UUCP 1.05 using the information form this book.

As included in most Linux distributions, Taylor UUCP is usually compiled for BNU compatibility, or the Taylor configuration scheme, or both. As the latter is much more flexible, and probably easier to understand than the often rather obscure BNU configuration files, I will describe the Taylor scheme below.

The purpose of this chapter is not to give you an exhaustive description of what the command line options for the UUCP commands are and what they do, but to give you an introduction on how to set up a working UUCP node. The first section gives a hopefully gentle introduction about how UUCP implements remote execution and file transfers. If you are not entirely new to UUCP, you might want to skip this and move on to section UUCP Configuration Files, which explains the various files used to set up UUCP.

We will however assume that you are familiar with the user programs of the UUCP suite. These are *uucp* and *uux*. For a description, please refer to the on-line manual pages.

---

[1] Written and copyrighted by Ian Taylor, 1993.

Besides the publicly accessible programs, *uux* and *uucp*, the UUCP suite contains a number of commands used for administrative purposes only. They are used to monitor UUCP traffic across your node, remove old log files, or compile statistics. None of these will be described here, because they're peripheral to the main tasks of UUCP. Besides, they're well documented and fairly easy to understand. However, there is a third category, which comprises the actual UUCP "work horses". They are called *uucico* (where cico stands for copy-in copy-out), and *uuxqt*, which executes jobs sent from remote systems.

12.1.1   More Information on UUCP

Those who don't find everything they need in this chapter should read the documentation that comes along with the package. This is a set of texinfo files that describe the setup using the Taylor configuration scheme. Texinfo can be converted to DVI and to GNU info files using *tex* and *makeinfo*, respectively.

If you want to use BNU or even (shudder!) Version 2 configuration files, there is a very good book, "Managing UUCP and Usenet" ([OReilly89]). I find it very useful. Another good source for information about UUCP on Linux is Vince Skahan's UUCP-HOWTO, which is posted regularly to **comp.os.linux.announce**.

There's also a newsgroup for the discussion of UUCP, called **comp.mail.uucp**. If you have questions specific to Taylor UUCP, you may be better off asking them there, rather than on the **comp.os.linux** groups.

12.2   Introduction

12.2.1   Layout of UUCP Transfers and Remote Execution

Vital to the understanding of UUCP is the concept of *jobs*. Every transfer a user initiates with *uucp* or *uux* is called a job. It is made up of a *command* to be executed on a remote system, and a collection of *files* to be transferred between sites. One of these parts may be missing.

As an example, assume you issued the following command on your host, which makes UUCP copy the file *netguide.ps* to host **pablo**, and makes it execute the *lpr* command to print the file.

```
$ uux -r pablo!lpr !netguide.ps
```

UUCP does not generally call the remote system immediately to execute a job (else you could make do with *kermit*). Instead, it temporarily stores the job description away. This is called *spooling*. The directory tree under which jobs are stored is therefore called the *spool directory* and is generally located in */var/spool/uucp*. In our example, the job description would contain information about the remote command to be executed (*lpr*), the user who requested the execution, and a couple of other items. In addition to the job description, UUCP has to store the input file, *netguide.ps*.

The exact location and naming of spool files may vary, depending on some compile-time options. HDB-compatible UUCP's generally store spool files in a directory named */var/spool/uucp/site*, where *site* is the name of the remote site. When compiled for Taylor configuration, UUCP will create subdirectories below the site-specific spool directory for different types of spool files.

At regular intervals, UUCP dials up the remote system. When a connection to the remote machine is established, UUCP transfers the files describing the job, plus any input files. The incoming jobs will not be executed immediately, but only after the connection terminates. This is done by *uuxqt*, which also takes care of forwarding any jobs if they are designated for another site.

To distinguish between important and less important jobs, UUCP associates a *grade* with each job. This is a single letter, ranging from 0 through 9, A though Z, and a through z, in decreasing precedence. Mail is customarily spooled with grade B or C, while news is spooled with grade N. Jobs with higher grade are transferred earlier. Grades may be assigned using the -g flag when invoking *uucp* or *uux*.

You can also disallow the transfer of jobs below a given grade at certain times. This is also called the *maximum spool grade* allowed during a conversation and defaults to z. Note the terminological ambiguity here: a file is transferred only if it is *equal or above* the maximum spool grade.

12.2.2   The Inner Workings of *uucico*

◇   To understand why *uucico* needs to know certain things, a quick description of how it actually connects to a remote system might be in order here.

When you execute *uucico -s system* from the command line, it first has to connect physically. The actions taken depend on the type of connection to open – e.g. when using telephone line, it has to find a modem, and dial out. Over TCP, it has to call *gethostbyname(3)* to convert the name to a network address, find out which port to open, and bind the address to the corresponding socket.

After this connection has been established, an authorization procedure has to be passed. It generally consists of the remote system asking for a login name, and possibly a password. This is commonly called the *login chat*. The authorization procedure is performed either by the usual *getty/login* suite, or – on TCP sockets – by *uucico* itself. If authorization succeeds, the remote end fires up *uucico*. The local copy of *uucico* which initiated the connection is referred to as *master*, the remote copy as *slave*.

Next follows the *handshake phase*: the master now sends its hostname, plus several flags. The slave checks this hostname for permission to log in, send and receive files, etc. The flags describe (among other things) the maximum grade of spool files to transfer. If enabled, a conversation count, or *call sequence number* check takes place here. With this feature, both sites maintain a count of successful connections, which are compared. If they do not match, the handshake fails. This is useful to protect yourself against impostors.

Finally, the two *uucico*'s try to agree on a common *transfer protocol*. This protocol governs the way data is transferred, checked for consistency, and retransmitted in case of an error. There is a need for different protocols because of the differing types of connections supported. For example, telephone lines require a "safe" protocol which is pessimistic about errors, while TCP transmission is inherently reliable and can use a more efficient protocol that foregoes most extra error checking.

After the handshake is complete, the actual transmission phase begins. Both ends turn on the selected protocol driver. The drivers possibly perform a protocol-specific initialization sequence.

First, the master sends all files queued for the remote system whose spool grade is high enough. When it has finished, it informs the slave that it is done, and that the slave may now hang up. The slave now can either agree to hang up, or take over the conversation. This is a change of roles: now the remote system becomes master, and the local one becomes slave. The new master now sends its files. When done, both *uucico*'s exchange termination messages, and close the connection.

We will not go into this in greater detail: please refer to either the sources or any good book on UUCP for this. There is also a really antique article floating around the net, written by David A. Novitz, which gives a detailed description of the UUCP protocol. The Taylor UUCP FAQ also disucsses some details of the way UUCP is implemented. It is posted to **comp.mail.uucp** regularly.

12.2.3   *uucico* Command Line Options

This section describes the most important command line options for *uucico*. For a complete list, please refer to the *uucico(1)* manual page.

-s *system*   Call the named *system* unless prohibited by call time restrictions.

-S *system*   Call the named *system* unconditionally.

-r1   Start *uucico* in master mode. This is the default when -s or -S is given. All by itself, the -r1 option causes *uucico* to try to call all systems in *sys*, unless prohibited by call or retry time restrictions.

-r0   Start *uucico* in slave mode. This is the default when no -s or -S is given. In slave mode, either standard input/output are assumed to be connected to a serial port, or the TCP port specified by the -p option is used.

-x *type*, -X *type*
                 Turn on debugging of the specified type. Several types may be given as a comma-separated list. The following types are valid: *abnormal, chat, handshake, uucp-proto, proto, port, config,*

spooldir, execute, incoming, outgoing. Using *all* turns on all options. For compatibility with other UUCP implementations, a number may be specified instead, which turns on debugging for the first *n* items from the above list.

Debugging messages will be logged to the file *Debug* below */var/spool/uucp.*

12.3 UUCP Configuration Files

In contrast to simpler file transfer programs, UUCP was designed to be able to handle all transfers automatically. Once it is set up properly, interference by the administrator should not be necessary on a day-to-day basis. The information required for this is is kept in a couple of *configuration files* that reside in the directory */usr/lib/uucp.* Most of these files are used only when dialing out.

12.3.1 A Gentle Introduction to Taylor UUCP

To say that UUCP configuration is hard would be an understatement. It is really a hairy subject, and the sometimes terse format of the configuration files doesn't make things easier (although the Talyor format is almost easy reading compared to the older formats in HDB or Version 2).

To give you a feel how all these files interact, we will introduce you to the most important ones, and have a look at sample entries of these files. We won't explain everything in detail now; a more accurate account is given in separate sections below. If you want to set up your machine for UUCP, you had best start with some sample files, and adapt them gradually. You can pick either those shown below, or those included in your favorite Linux distribution.

All files described in this section are kept in */usr/lib/uucp* or a subdirectory thereof. Some Linux distributions contain UUCP binaries that have support for both HDB and Taylor configuration enabled, and use different subdirectories for each configuration file set. There will usually be a *README* file in */usr/lib/uucp.*

For UUCP to work properly, these files must be owned by the **uucp** user. Some of them contain passwords and telephone numbers, and therefore should have permissions of 600.[2]

The central UUCP configuration file is */usr/lib/uucp/config*, and is used to set general parameters. The most important of them (and for now, the only one), is your host's UUCP name. At the Virtual Brewery, they use **vstout** as their UUCP gateway:

```
# /usr/lib/uucp/config - UUCP main configuration file
hostname        vstout
```

The next important configuration file is the *sys* file. It contains all system-specific information of sites you are linked to. This includes the site's name, and information on the link itself, such as the telephone number when using a modem link. A typical entry for a modem-connected site called **pablo** would be

```
# /usr/lib/uucp/sys - name UUCP neighbors
# system: pablo
system          pablo
time            Any
phone           123-456
port            serial1
speed           38400
chat            ogin: vstout ssword: lorca
```

The *port* names a port to be used, and *time* specifies the times at which it may be called. *chat* describes the login chat scripts – the sequence of strings that must be exchanged between to allow *uucico* to log into **pablo**. We will get back to chat scripts later. The *port* command does not name a device special file such as

---

[2]Note that although most UUCP commands must be setuid to **uucp**, you must make sure the *uuchk* program is *not*. Otherwise, users will be able to display passwords even though they have mode 600.

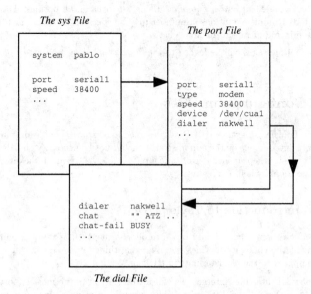

Figure 12.1: Interaction of Taylor UUCP Configuration Files.

/dev/cua1, but rather names an entry in the *port* file. You can assign these names as you like as long as they refer to a valid entry in *port*.

The *port* file holds information specific to the link itself. For modem links, it describes the device special file to be used, the range of speeds supported, and the type of dialing equipment connected to the port. The entry below describes */dev/cua1* (a.k.a. COM 2), to which a NakWell modem is connected that is capable of running at speeds up to 38400bps. The entry's name way chosen to match the port name given in the *sys* file.

```
# /usr/lib/uucp/port - UUCP ports
# /dev/cua1 (COM2)
port            serial1
type            modem
device          /dev/cua1
speed           38400
dialer          nakwell
```

The information pertaining to the dialers itself is kept in yet another file, called – you guessed it: *dial*. For each dialer type, it basically contains the sequence of commands to be issued to dial up a remote site, given the telephone number. Again, this is specified as a chat script. For example, the entry for the above NakWell might look like this:

```
# /usr/lib/uucp/dial - per-dialer information
# NakWell modems
dialer          nakwell
chat            "" ATZ OK ATDT\T CONNECT
```

The line starting with *chat* specifies the modem chat, which is the sequence of commands sent to and received from the modem to initialize it and make it dial the desired number. The "*T*" sequence will be replaced with the phone number by *uucico*.

To give you a rough idea how *uucico* deals with these configuration files, assume you issued the command

```
$ uucico -s pablo
```

on the command line. The first thing *uucico* does is look up **pablo** in the *sys* file. From the *sys* file entry for **pablo** it sees that it should use the *serial1* port to establish the connection. The *port* file tells it that this is a modem port, and that it has a NakWell modem attached.

uucico now searches *dial* for the entry describing the NakWell modem, and having found one, opens the serial port */dev/cua1* and executes the dialer chat. That is, it sends "ATZ", waits for the "OK" response, etc. When encountering the string "\T", it substitutes the phone number (123–456) extracted from the *sys* file.

After the modem returns CONNECT, the connection has been established, and the modem chat is complete. *uucico* now returns to the *sys* file and executes the login chat. In our example, it would wait for the "login:" prompt, then send its user name (**neruda**), wait for the "password:" prompt, and send its password, "lorca".

After completing authorization, the remote end is assumed to fire up its own *uucico*. The two will then enter the handshake phase described in the previous section.

The way the configuration files depend on each other is also shown in figure 12.1.

12.3.2 What UUCP Needs to Know

Before you start writing the UUCP configuration files, you have to gather some information it needs to know.

First, you will have to figure out what serial device your modem is attached to. Usually, the (DOS) ports COM1 through COM4 map to the device special files */dev/cua0* through */dev/cua3*. Most distributions, such as Slackware, create a link */dev/modem* as a link to the appropriate *cua** device file, and configure *kermit*, *seyon*, etc, to use this generic file. In this case, you should either use */dev/modem* in your UUCP configuration, too.

The reason for this is that all dial-out programs use so-called *lock files* to signal when a serial port is in use. The names of these lock files are a concatenation of the string *LCK..* and the device file name, for instance *LCK..cua1*. If programs use different names for the same device, they will fail to recognize each other's lock files. As a consequence, they will disrupt each other's session when started at the same time. This is not an unlikely event when you schedule your UUCP calls using a *crontab* entry.

For details of setting up your serial ports, please refer to chapter 4.

Next, you must find out at what speed your modem and Linux will communicate. You will have to set this to the maximum effective transfer rate you expect to get. The effective transfer rate may be much higher than the raw physical transfer rate your modem is capable of. For instance, many modems send and receive data at 2400bps (bits per second). Using compression protocols such as V.42bis, the actual transfer rate may climb up to 9600bps.

Of course, if UUCP is to do anything, you will need the phone number of a system to call. Also, you will need a valid login id and possibly a password for the remote machine.[3]

You will also have to know *exactly* how to log into the system. E.g., do you have to press the BREAK key before the login prompt appears? Does it display login: or user:? This is necessary for composing the *chat script*, which is a recipe telling *uucico* how to log in. If you don't know, or if the usual chat script fails, try to call the system with a terminal program like *kermit* or *minicom*, and write down exactly what you have to do.

12.3.3 Site Naming

As with TCP/IP-based networking, your host has to have a name for UUCP networking. As long as you simply want to use UUCP for file transfers to or from sites you dial up directly, or on a local network, this name does not have to meet any standards.[4]

However, if you use UUCP for a mail or news link, you should think about having the name registered with the UUCP Mapping project. The UUCP Mapping Project is described in chapter 13. Even if you participate in a domain, you might consider having an official UUCP name for your site.

---

[3]If you're just going to try out UUCP, get the number of an archive site near you. Write down the login and password – they're public to make anonymous downloads possible. In most cases, they're something like **uucp/uucp** or **nuucp/uucp**.

[4]The only limitation is that it shouldn't be longer than 7 characters, so as to not confuse hosts with filesystems that impose a narrow limit on file names.

Frequently, people choose their UUCP name to match the first component of their fully qualified domain name. Suppose your site's domain address is **swim.twobirds.com**, then your UUCP host name would be **swim**. Think of UUCP sites as knowing each other on a first-name basis. Of course, you can also use a UUCP name completely unrelated to your fully qualified domain name.

However, make sure not to use the unqualified site name in mail addresses unless you have registered it as your official UUCP name.[5] At the very best, mail to an unregistered UUCP host will vanish in some big black bit bucket. If you use a name already held by some other site, this mail will be routed to that site, and cause its postmaster no end of headaches.

By default, the UUCP suite uses the name set by *hostname* as the site's UUCP name. This name is commonly set in the */etc/rc.local* script. If your UUCP name is different from what you set your host name to, you have to use the *hostname* option in the *config* file to tell *uucico* about your UUCP name. This is described below.

12.3.4   Taylor Configuration Files

We now return to the configuration files. Taylor UUCP gets its information from the following files:

config   This is the main configuration file. You can define your site's UUCP name here.

sys   This file describes all sites known to you. For each site, it specifies its name, at what times to call it, which number to dial (if any), what type of device to use, and how to log on.

port   Contains entries describing each port available, together with the line speed supported and the dialer to be used.

dial   Describes dialers used to establish a telephone connection.

dialcode   Contains expansions for symbolic dialcodes.

call   Contains the login name and password to be used when calling a system. Rarely used.

passwd   Contains login names and passwords systems may use when logging in. This file is used only when *uucico* does its own password checking.

Taylor configuration files are generally made up of lines containing keyword-value pairs. A hash sign introduces a comment that extends to the end of the line. To use a hash sign by itself, you may escape it with a backslash.

There are quite a number of options you can tune with these configuration files. We can't go into all parameters here, but will only cover the most important ones. They you should be able to configure a modem-based UUCP link. Additional sections will describe the modifications necessary if you want to use UUCP over TCP/IP or over a direct serial line. A complete reference is given in the Texinfo documents that accompany the Taylor UUCP sources.

When you think you have configured your UUCP system completely, you can check your configuration using the *uuchk* tool (located in */usr/lib/uucp*). *uuchk* reads your configuration files, and prints out a detailed report of the configuration values used for each system.

12.3.5   General Configuration Options – the *config* File

You won't generally use this file to describe much beside your UUCP hostname. By default, UUCP will use the name you set with the *hostname* command, but it is generally a good idea to set the UUCP name explicitly. A sample file is shown below:

```
# /usr/lib/uucp/config - UUCP main configuration file
hostname          vstout
```

_____

[5]The UUCP Mapping Project registers all UUCP hostnames world-wide and makes sure they are unique. To register your UUCP name, ask the maintainers of the site that handles your mail; they will be able to help you with it.

Of course, there are a number of miscellaneous parameters that may be set here, too, such as the name of the spool directory, or access rights for anonymous UUCP. The latter will be described in a later section.

12.3.6 How to Tell UUCP about other Systems – the *sys* File

The *sys* file describes the systems your machine knows about. An entry is introduced by the *system* keyword; the subsequent lines up to the next *system* directive detail the parameters specific to that site. Commonly, a system entry will define parameters such as the telephone number and the login chat.

Parameters before the very first *system* line set default values used for all systems. Usually, you will set protocol paramters and the like in the defaults section.

Below, the most prominent fields are discussed in some detail.

System Name

The *system* command names the remote system. You must specify the correct name of the remote system, not an alias you invented, because *uucico* will check it against what the remote system says it is called when you log on.[6]

Each system name may appear more only once. If you want to use several sets of configurations for the same system (such as different telephone numbers *uucico* should try in turn), you can specify *alternates*. Alternates are described below.

Telephone Number

If the remote system is to be reached over a telephone line, the *phone* field specifies the number the modem should dial. It may contain several tokens interpreted by *uucico*'s dialing procedure. An equal sign means to wait for a secondary dial tone, and a dash generates a one-second pause. For instance, some telephone installations will choke when you don't pause between dialing the prefix code and telephone number.

[**Don't know the proper English term for this – you know, something like a company's private internal installation where you have to dial a 0 or 9 to get a line to the outside.**]

Any embedded alphabetic string may be used to hide site-dependent information like area codes. Any such string is translated to a dialcode using the *dialcode* file. Suppose you have the following *dialcode* file:

```
# /usr/lib/uucp/dialcode - dialcode translation
Bogoham         024881
Coxton          035119
```

With these translations, you can use a phone number such as *Bogoham7732* in the *sys* file, which makes things probably a little more legible.

Port and Speed

The *port* and *speed* options are used to select the device used for calling the remote system, and the maximum speed to which the device should be set.[7] A *system* entry may use either option alone, or both options in conjunction. When looking up a suitable device in the *port* file, only those ports are selected that have a matching port name and/or speed range.

Generally, using the *speed* option should suffice. If you have only one serial device defined in *port*, *uucico* will always pick the right one, anyway, so you only have to give it the desired speed. If you have several modems attached to your systems, you still often don't want to name a particular port, because if *uucico* finds that there are several matches, it tries each device in turn until it finds an unused one.

---

[6]Older Version 2 UUCP's don't broadcast their name when being called; however, newer implementations often do, and so does Taylor UUCP.

[7]The Baud rate of the tty must be at least as high as the maximum transfer speed.

The Login Chat

Above, we already encountered the login chat script, which tells *uucico* how to log into the remote system. It consists of a list of tokens, specifying strings expected and sent by the local *uucico* process. The intention is to make *uucico* wait until the remote machine sends a login prompt, then return the login name, wait for the remote system to send the password prompt, and send the password. Expect and send strings are given in alternation. *uucico* automatically appends a carriage return character (\r) to any send string. Thus, a simple chat script would look like

```
ogin:  vstout ssword:  catch22
```

You will notice that the expect fields don't contain the whole prompts. This is to make sure that the login succeeds even if the remote system broadcasts `Login:` instead of `login:`.

uucico also allows for some sort of conditional execution, for example in the case that the remote machine's *getty* needs to be reset before sending a prompt. For this, you can attach a sub-chat to an expect string, offset by a dash. The sub-chat is executed only if the main expect fails, i.e. a timeout occurs. One way to use this feature is to send a BREAK if the remote site doesn't display a login prompt. The following example gives an allround chat script that should also work in case you have to hit return before the login appears. `""` tells UUCP to not wait for anything and continue with the next send string immediately.

```
"" \n\r\d\r\n\c ogin:-BREAK-ogin: vstout ssword: catch22
```

There are a couple of special strings and escape characters which may occur in the chat script. The following is an incomplete list of characters legal in expect strings:

`""`   The empty string. It tells *uucico* not to wait for anything, but proceed with the next send string immediately.

`\t`   Tab character.

`\r`   Carriage return character.

`\s`   Space character. You need this to embed spaces in a chat string.

`\n`   Newline character.

`\\`   Backslash character.

On send strings, the following escape characters and strings are legal in addition to the above:

EOT   End of transmission character (^D).

BREAK   Break character.

`\c`   Suppress sending of carriage return at end of string.

`\d`   Delay sending for 1 second.

`\E`   Enable echo checking. This requires *uucico* to wait for the echo of everything it writes to be read back from the device before it can continue with the chat. It is primarily useful when used in modem chats (which we will encounter below). Echo checking is off by default.

`\e`   Disable echo checking.

`\K`   Same as *BREAK*.

`\p`   Pause for fraction of a second.

Alternates

Sometimes it is desirable to have multiple entries for a single system, for instance if the system can be reached on different modem lines. With Taylor UUCP, you can do this by defining a so-called *alternate*.

An alternate entry retains all settings from the main system entry, and and specifies only those values that should be overridden in the default system entry, or added to it. An alternate is offset from the system entry by a line containing the keyword *alternate*.

To use two phone numbers for **pablo**, you would modify its *sys* entry in the following way:

```
system          pablo
phone           123-456
... entries as above ...
alternate
phone           123-455
```

When calling **pablo**, *uucico* will now first dial 123-456, and if this fails, try the alternate. The alternate entry retains all settings from the main system entry, and overrides only the telephone number.

Restricting Call Times

Taylor UUCP provides a number of ways you may restrict the times when calls can be placed to a remote system. You might do this either because of limitations the remote host places on its services during business hours, or simply to avoid times with high call rates. Note that it is always possible to override call time restrictions by giving *uucico* the -S or -f option.

By default, Taylor UUCP will disallow connections at any time, so you *have* to use some sort of time specification in the *sys* file. If you don't care about call time restrictions, you can specify the *time* option with a value of *Any* in your *sys* file.

The simplest way to restrict call time is the *time* entry, which is followed by a string made up of a day and a time subfield. Day may be any of *Mo, Tu, We, Th, Fr, Sa, Su* combined, or *Any, Never*, or *Wk* for weekdays. The time consists of two 24-hour clock values, separated by a dash. They specify the range during which calls may be placed. The combination of these tokens is written without white space in between. Any number of day and time specifications may be grouped together with commas. For example,

```
time            MoWe0300-0730,Fr1805-2000
```

allows calls on Monday and Wednesdays from 3 a.m. to 7.30, and on Fridays between 18.05 and 20.00. When a time field spans midnight, say *Mo1830-0600*, it actually means Monday, between midnight and 6 a.m., and between 6.30 p.m. and midnight.

The special time strings *Any* and *Never* mean what they say: Calls may be placed at any or no time, respectively.

The *time* command takes an optional second argument that describes a retry time in minutes. When an attempt to establish a connection fails, *uucico* will not allow another attempt to dial up the remote host within a certain interval. By default, *uucico* uses an exponential backoff scheme, where the retry interval increases with each repeated failure. For instance, when you specify a retry time of 5 minutes, *uucico* will refuse to call the remote system within 5 minutes after the last failure.

The *timegrade* command allows you to attach a maximum spool grade to a schedule. For instance, assume you have the following *timegrade* commands in a *system* entry:

```
timegrade       N Wk1900-0700,SaSu
timegrade       C Any
```

This allows jobs with a spoolgrade of C or higher (usually, mail is queued with grade B or C) to be transferred whenever a call is established, while news (usually queued with grade N) will be transferred only during the night and at weekends.

Just like *time*, the *timegrade* command takes a retry interval in minutes as an optional third argument.

However, a caveat about spool grades is in order here: First, the *timegrade* option applies only to what *your* systems sends; the remote system may still transfer anything it likes. You can use the *call-timegrade* option to explicitly request it to send only jobs above some given spool grade; but there's no guarantee it will obey this request.[8]

Similarly, the *timegrade* field is not checked when a remote system calls in, so any jobs queued for the calling system will be sent. However, the remote system can explicitly request your *uucico* to restrict itself to a certain spool grade.

12.3.7   What Devices there are – the *port* File

The *port* file tells *uucico* about the available ports. These may be modem ports, but other types such as direct serial lines and TCP sockets are supported as well.

Like the *sys* file, *port* consists of separate entries starting with the keyword *port*, followed by the port name. This name may be used by in the *sys* file's *port* statement. The name need not be unique; if there are several ports with the same name, *uucico* will try each in turn until it finds one that is not currently being used.

The *port* command should be immediately followed by the *type* statement that describes what type of port is described. Valid types are *modem*, *direct* for direct connections, and *tcp* for TCP sockets. If the *port* command is missing, the port type defaults to modem.

In this section, we will cover only modem ports; TCP ports and direct lines are discussed in a later section.

For modem and direct ports, you have to specify the device for calling out using the *device* directive. Usually, this is the name of a device special file in the */dev* directory, like */dev/cua1*.[9]

In the case of a modem device, the port entry also determines what type of modem is connected to the port. Different types of modems have to be configured differently. Even modems that claim to be Hayes-compatible needn't be really compatible with each other. Therefore, you have to tell *uucico* how to initialize the modem and how to make it dial the desired number. Taylor UUCP keeps the descriptions of all dialers in a file named *dial*. To use any of these, you have to specify the dialer's name using the *dialer* command.

Sometimes, you will want to use a modem in different ways, depending on which system you call. For instance, some older modems don't understand when a high-speed modem attempts to connect at 14400bps; they simply drop the line instead of negotiating a connect at, say, 9600bps. When you know site **drop** uses such a dumb modem, you have to set up your modem differently when calling them. For this, you need an additional port entry in the *port* file that specifies a different dialer. Now you can give the new port a different name, such as *serial1-slow*, and use the *port* directive in **drop** system entry in *sys*.

A better way is to distinguish the ports by the speeds they support. For instance, the two port entries for the above situation may look like this:

```
# NakWell modem; connect at high speed
port            serial1         # port name
type            modem           # modem port
device          /dev/cua1       # this is COM2
speed           38400           # supported speed
dialer          nakwell         # normal dialer

# NakWell modem; connect at low speed
port            serial1         # port name
type            modem           # modem port
device          /dev/cua1       # this is COM2
speed           9600            # supported speed
dialer          nakwell-slow    # don't attempt fast connect
```

The system entry for site **drop** would now give *serial1* as port name, but request to use it at 9600bps only. *uucico* will then automatically use the second port entry. All remaining sites that have a speed of 38400bps in the system entry will be called using the first port entry.

---

[8]If the remote system runs Talyor UUCP, it will obey.

[9]Some people use the *ttyS** devices instead, which are intended for dial-in only.

12.3.8 How to Dial a Number – the *dial* File

The *dial* file describes the way various dialers are used. Traditionally, UUCP talks of dialers rather than modems, because in earlier times, it was usual practice to have one (expensive) automatic dialing device serve a whole bank of modems. Today, most modems have dialing support built in, so this distinction gets a little blurred.

Nevertheless, different dialers or modems may require a different configuration. You can describe each of them in the *dial* file. Entries in *dial* start with the *dialer* command that gives the dialer's name.

The most important entry beside this is the modem chat, specified by the *chat* command. Similar to the login chat, it consists of a sequence of strings *uucico* sends to the dialer and the responses it expects in return. It is commonly used to reset the modem to some known state, and dial the number. The following sample dialer entry shows a typical modem chat for a Hayes-compatible modem:

```
# NakWell modem; connect at high speed
dialer          nakwell        # dialer name
chat            "" ATZ OK\r ATH1EOQO OK\r ATDT\T CONNECT
chat-fail       BUSY
chat-fail       ERROR
chat-fail       NO\sCARRIER
dtr-toggle      true
```

The modem chat begins with "", the empty expect string. *uucico* will therefore send the first command (ATZ) right away. ATZ is the Hayes command to reset the modem. It then waits until the modem has sent OK, and sends the next command which turns off local echo, and the like. After the modem returns OK again, *uucico* sends the dialing command (ATDT). The escape sequence \T in this string is replaced with the phone number taken from the system entry *sys* file. *uucico* then waits for the modem to return the string CONNECT, which signals that a connection with the remote modem has been established successfully.

Often, the modem fails to connect to the remote system, for instance if the other system is talking to someone else and the line is busy. In this case, the modem will return some error message indicating the reason. Modem chats are not capable to detect such messages; *uucico* will continue to wait for the expected string until it times out. The UUCP log file will therefore only show a bland "timed out in chat script" instead of the true reason.

However, Taylor UUCP allows you to tell *uucico* about these error messages using the *chat-fail* command as shown above. When *uucico* detects a chat-fail string while executing the modem chat, it aborts the call, and logs the error message in the UUCP log file.

The last command in the example shown above tells UUCP to toggle the DTR line before starting the modem chat. Most modems can be configured to go on-hook when detecting a change on the DTR line, and enter command mode.[10]

12.3.9 UUCP Over TCP

Absurd as it may sound at the first moment, using UUCP to transfer data over TCP not that bad an idea, especially when transferring large amount of data such as Usenet news. On TCP-based links, news is generally exchanged using the NNTP protocol, where articles are requested and sent individually, without compression or any other optimization. Although adequate for large sites with several concurrent newsfeeds, this technique is very unfavorable for small sites that receive their news over a slow connection such as ISDN. These sites will usually want to combine the qualities of TCP with the advantages of sending news in large batches, which can be compressed and thus transferred with very low overhead. A standard way to transfer these batches is to use UUCP over TCP.

In *sys*, you would specify a system to be called via TCP in the following way:

```
system          gmu
address         news.groucho.edu
```

---

[10]You can also configure some modems to reset themselves when detecting a transition on DTR. Some of them, however, don't seem to like this, and occasionally get hung.

```
time                Any
port                tcp-conn
chat                ogin: vstout word: clouseau
```

The *address* command gives the IP address of the host, or its fully qualified domain name. The corresponding *port* entry would read:

```
port                tcp-conn
type                tcp
service             540
```

The entry states that a TCP connection should be used when a *sys* entry references *tcp-conn*, and that *uucico* should attempt to connect to the TCP network port 540 on the remote host. This is the default port number of the UUCP service. Instead of the port number, you may also give a symbolic port name to the *service* command. The port number corresponding to this name will be looked up in */etc/services*. The common name for the UUCP service is *uucpd*.

12.3.10   Using a Direct Connection

Assume you use a direct line connecting your system **vstout** to **tiny**. Very much like in the modem case, you have to write a system entry in the *sys* file. The *port* command identifies the serial port *tiny* is hooked up to.

```
system              tiny
time                Any
port                direct1
speed               38400
chat                ogin: cathcart word: catch22
```

In the *port* file, you have to describe the serial port for the direct connection. A *dialer* entry is not needed, because there's no need for dialing.

```
port                direct1
type                direct
speed               38400
```

12.4   The Do's and Dont's of UUCP – Tuning Permissions

12.4.1   Command Execution

UUCP's task is to copy files from one system to another, and to request execution of certain commands on remote hosts. Of course, you as an administrator would want to control what rights you grant other systems – allowing them to execute any command on your system is definitely not a good idea.

By default, the only commands Taylor UUCP allows other systems to execute on your machine are *rmail* and *rnews*, which are commonly used to to exchange email and Usent news over UUCP. The default search path used by *uuxqt* is a compile-time option, but should usually contain */bin*, */usr/bin*, and */usr/local/bin*. To change the set of commands for a particular system, you can use the *commands* keyword in the *sys* file. Similarly, the search path can be changed with the *command-path* statement. For instance, you may want to allow system **pablo** to execute the *rsmtp* command in addition to *rmail* and *rnews*:[11]

```
system              pablo
...
commands            rmail rnews rsmtp
```

---

[11] *rsmtp* is used to deliver mail with batched SMTP. This is described in the mail chapters.

12.4.2   File Transfers

Taylor UUCP also allows you to fine-tune file transfers in great detail. At one extreme, you can disable transfers to and from a particular system. Just set *request* to *no*, and the remote system will not be able either to retrieve files from your system or send it any files. Similarly, you can prohibit your users from transferring files to or from a system by setting *transfer* to *no*. By default, users on both the local and the remote system are allowed to up- and download files.

In addition, you can configure the directories to and from which files may be copied. Usually, you will want to restrict access from remote systems to a single directory hierarchy, but still allow your users to send files from their home directory. Commonly, remote users will be allowed to receive files only from the public UUCP directory, */var/spool/uucppublic*. This is the traditional place to make files publicly available; very much like FTP servers on the Internet. It is commonly referred to using the tilde character.

Therefore, Taylor UUCP provides four different commands to configure the directories for sending and receiving files. They are *local-send*, which specifies the list of directories a user may ask UUCP to send files from; *local-receive*, which gives the the list of directories a user may ask to receive files to; and *remote-send* and *remote-receive*, which do the analogous for requests from a foreign system. Consider the following example:

```
system          pablo
...
local-send      /home ~
local-receive   /home ~/receive
remote-send     ~ !~/incoming !~/receive
remote-receive  ~/incoming
```

The *local-send* command allows users on your host to send any files below */home* and from the public UUCP directory to **pablo**. The *local-receive* command allows them to receive files either to the world-writable *receive* directory in the *uucppublic*, or any world-writable directory below */home*. The *remote-send* directive allows **pablo** to request files from */var/spool/uucppublic*, except for files below the *incoming* and *receive* directories. This is signaled to *uucico* by preceding the directory names with exclamation marks. Finally, the last line allows **pablo** to upload any files to **incoming**.

One of the biggest problems with file transfers using UUCP is that will only receive files to directories that are world-writable. This may tempt some users to set up traps for other users, etc. However, there's no way escaping this problem except disabling UUCP file transfers altogether.

12.4.3   Forwarding

UUCP provides a mechanism to have other systems execute file transfers on your behalf. For instance, this allows you to make **seci** retrieve a file from **uchile** for you, and send it to your system. The following command would achieve this:

```
$ uucp -r seci!uchile!~/find-ls.gz ~/uchile.files.gz
```

This technique of passing a job through several systems is called *forwarding*. In the above example, the reason to use forwarding may be that **seci** has UUCP access to **uchile**, but your host doesn't. However, if you run a UUCP system, you would want to limit the forwarding service to a few hosts you trust not to run up a horrendous phone bill by making you download the latest X11R6 source release for them.

By default, Taylor UUCP disallows forwarding altogether. To enable forwarding for a particular system, you can use the *forward* command. This command specifies a list of sites the system may request you to forward jobs to and from. For instance, the UUCP administrator of **seci** would have to add the following lines to the *sys* file to allow **pablo** to request files from **uchile**:

```
###################
# pablo
system          pablo
...
forward         uchile
```

```
####################
# uchile
system          uchile
...
forward-to      pablo
```

The *forward-to* entry for **uchile** is necessary so that any files returned by it are actually passed on to **pablo**. Otherwise UUCP would drop them. This entry uses a variation of the *forward* command that permits **uchile** only to send files to **pablo** through **seci**; not the other way round.

To permit forwarding to any system, use the special keyword *ANY* (capital letters required).

12.5 Setting up your System for Dialing in

If you want to set up your site for dialing in, you have to permit logins on your serial port, and customize some system files to provide UUCP accounts. This will be the topic of the current section.

12.5.1 Setting up *getty*

If you want to use a serial line as a dialin port, you have to enable a *getty* process on this port. However, some *getty* implementations aren't really suitable for this, because you usually want to use a serial port for dialing in and out. You therefore have to make sure to use a *getty* that is able to share the line with other programs like *uucico*, or *minicom*. One program that does this is *uugetty* from the *getty_ps* package. Most Linux distributions have it; check for *uugetty* in your */sbin* directory. Another program I am aware of is Gert Doering's *mgetty*, which also supports reception of facsimiles. You can also obtain the latest versions of these from **sunsite.unc.edu** as either binary or source.

Explaining the differences in the way *uugetty* and *mgetty* handle logins is beyond the scope of this little section; for more information, please refer to the Serial HOWTO by Grag Hankins, as well as the documentation that comes along with *getty_ps* and *mgetty*.

12.5.2 Providing UUCP Accounts

Next, you have to set up user accounts that let remote sites log into your system and establish a UUCP connection. Generally, you will provide a separate login name to each system that polls you. When setting up an account for system **pablo**, you would probably give it **Upablo** as the user name.

For systems that dial in through the serial port, you usually have to add these accounts to the system password file, */etc/passwd*. A good practice is to put all UUCP logins in a special group such as **uuguest**. The account's home directory should be set to the public spool directory */var/spool/uucppublic*; its login shell must be *uucico*.

If you have the shadow password suite installed, you can do this with the *useradd* command:

```
# useradd -d /var/spool/uucppublic -G uuguest -s /usr/lib/uucp/uucico Upablo
```

If you don't use the shadow password suite, you probably have to edit */etc/passwd* by hand, adding a line like that shown below, where 5000 and 150 are the numerical uid and gid assigned to user **Upablo** and group **uuguest**, respectively.

```
Upablo:x:5000:150:UUCP Account:/var/spool/uucppublic:/usr/lib/uucp/uucico
```

After installing the account, you have to activate it by setting its password with the *passwd* command.

To serve UUCP systems that connect to your site over TCP, you have to set up *inetd* to handle incoming connections on the *uucp* port. You do this by adding the following line to */etc/inetd.conf*.[12]

---

[12]Note that usually, *tcpd* has mode 700, so that you must invoke it as user **root**, not **uucp** as you would usually do.

```
uucp    stream  tcp   nowait  root  /usr/sbin/tcpd /usr/lib/uucp/uucico -l
```

The -l option makes *uucico* perform its own login authorization. It will prompt for a login name and a password just like the standard *login* program, but will rely on its private password database instead of */etc/passwd*. This private password file is named */usr/lib/uucp/passwd* and contains pairs of login names and passwords:

```
Upablo  IslaNegra
Ulorca  co'rdoba
```

Of course, this file must be owned by **uucp** and have permissions of 600.

If this database sounds like such a good idea you would like to use on normal serial logins, too, you will be disappointed to hear that this isn't possible at the moment without major contortions. First off, you need Taylor UUCP 1.05 for this, because it allows *getty* to pass the login name of the calling user to *uucico* using the -u option.[13] Then, you have to trick the *getty* you are using into invoking *uucico* instead of the usual */bin/login*. With *getty_ps*, you can do this by setting the *LOGIN* option in the configuration file. However, this disables interactive logins altogether. *mgetty*, on the other hand, has a nice feature that allows you to invoke different login commands based on the name the user provided. For instance, you can tell *mgetty* to use *uucico* for all users that provide a login name beginning with a capital U, but let everyone else be handled by the standard *login* command.

To protect your UUCP users from callers giving a false system name and snarfing all their mail, you should add *called-login* commands to each system entry in the *sys* file. This is described in section Protecting Yourself Against Swindlers above.

12.5.3 Protecting Yourself Against Swindlers

One of the biggest problems about UUCP is that the calling system can lie about its name; it announces its name to the called system after logging in, but the server doesn't have a way to check this. Thus, an attacker could log into his or her own UUCP account, pretend to be someone else, and pick up that other site's mail. This is particularly troublesome if you offer login via anonymous UUCP, where the password is made public.

Unless you know you can trust all sites that call your system to be honest, you *must* guard against this sort of impostors. The cure against this disease is to require each system to use a particular login name by specifying a *called-login* in *sys*. A sample system entry may look like this:

```
system        pablo
... usual options ...
called-login  Upablo
```

The upshot of this is that whenever a system logs in and pretends it is **pablo**, *uucico* will check whether it has logged in as **Upablo**. If it hasn't, the calling system will be turned down, and the connection is dropped. You should make it a habit to add the *called-login* command to every system entry you add to your *sys* file. It is important that you do this for *all* sytems, regardless of whether they will ever call your site or not. For those sites that never call you, you should probably set *called-login* to some totally bogus user name, such as **neverlogsin**.

12.5.4 Be Paranoid – Call Sequence Checks

Another way to fend off and detect impostors is to use call sequence checks. Call sequence checks help you protect against intruders that somehow managed to find out the password you log into your UUCP system with.

When using call sequence checks, both machines keep track of the number of connections established so far. It is incremented with each connection. After logging in, the caller sends its call sequence number, and the

---

[13]The -u option is present in 1.04, too, but is only a no-op.

callee checks it against its own number. If they don't match, the connection attempt will be rejected. If the initial number is chosen at random, attackers will have a hard time guessing the correct call sequence number.

But call sequence checks do more for you than this: even if some very clever person should detect your call sequence number as well as your password, you will find this out. When the attacker call your UUCP feed and steals your mail, this will increase the feeds call sequence number by one. The next time *you* call your feed and try to log in, the remote *uucico* will refuse you, because the numbers don't match anymore!

If you have enabled call sequence checks, you should check your log files regularly for error messages that hint at possible attacks. If your system rejects the call sequence number the calling system offers it, *uucico* will put a message into the log file saying something like "Out of sequence call rejected". If your system is rejected by its feed because the sequence numbers are out of sync, it will put a message in the log file saying "Handshake failed (RBADSEQ)".

To enable call sequence checks, you have to add following command to the system entry:

```
# enable call sequence checks
sequence        true
```

Beside this, you have to create the file containing the sequence number itself. Taylor UUCP keeps the sequence number is in a file called *.Sequence* in the remote site's spool directory. It *must* be owned by **uucp**, and must be mode 600 (i.e. readable and writeable only by **uucp**). It is best to initialize this file with an arbitrary, agreed-upon start value. Otherwise, an attacker might manage to guess the number by trying out all values smaller than, say, 60.

```
# cd /var/spool/uucp/pablo
# echo 94316 > .Sequence
# chmod 600 .Sequence
# chown uucp.uucp .Sequence
```

Of course, the remote site has to enable call sequence checks as well, and start by using exactly the same sequence number as you.

12.5.5   Anonymous UUCP

If you want to provide anonymous UUCP access to your system, you first have to set up a special account for it as described above. A common practive is to give it a login name and a password of **uucp**.

In addition, you have to set a few of the security options for unknown systems. For instance, you may want to prohibit them from executing any commands on your system. However, you cannot set these parameters in a *sys* file entry, because the *system* command requires the system's name, which you don't have. Taylor UUCP solves this dilemma through the *unknown* command. *unknown* can be used in the *config* file to specify any command that can usually appear in a system entry:

```
unknown         remote-receive ~/incoming
unknown         remote-send ~/pub
unknown         max-remote-debug none
unknown         command-path /usr/lib/uucp/anon-bin
unknown         commands rmail
```

This will restrict unknown systems to downloading files from below the *pub* directory and uploading files to the *incoming* directory below */var/spool/uucppublic*. The next line will make *uucico* ignore any requests from the remote system to turn on debugging locally. The last two lines permit unknown systems to execute *rmail*; but the command path specified makes *uucico* look for the *rmail* command in a private directory named *anon-bin* only. This allows you to provide some special *rmail* that, for instance, forwards all mail to the super-user for examination. This allows anonymous users to reach the maintainer of the system, but prevents them at the same time from injecting any mail to other sites.

To enable anonymous UUCP, you must specify at least one *unknown* statement in *config*. Otherwise *uucico* will reject any unknown systems.

12.6 UUCP Low-Level Protocols

To negotiate session control and file transfers with the remote end, *uucico* uses a set of standardized messages. This is often referred to as the high-level protocol. During the initialization phase and the hangup phase these are simply sent across as strings. However, during the real transfer phase, an additional low-level protocol is employed which is mostly transparent to the higher levels. This is to make error checks possible when using unreliable lines, for instance.

12.6.1 Protocol Overview

As UUCP is used over different types of connections, such as serial lines or TCP, or even X.25, specific low-level protocols are needed. In addition, several implementations of UUCP have introduced different protocols that do roughly the same thing.

Protocols can be divided into two categories: streaming and packet-oriented protocols. Protocols of the latter variety transfer a file as a whole, possibly computing a checksum over it. This is nearly free of any overhead, but requires a reliable connection, because any error will cause the whole file to be retransmitted. These protocols are commonly used over TCP connections, but are not suitable for use over telephone lines. Although modern modems do quite a good job at error correction, they are not perfect, nor is there any error detection between your computer and the modem.

On the other hand, packet protocols split up the file into several chunks of equal size. Each packet is sent and received separately, a checksum is computed, and an acknowledgement is returned to the sender. To make this more efficient, sliding-window protocols were invented, which allow for a limited number (a window) of outstanding acknoledgements at any time. This greatly reduces the amount of time *uucico* has to wait during a transmission. Still, the relatively large overhead compared to a streaming protocol make packet protocls inefficient for use over TCP.

The width of the data path also makes a difference. Sometimes, sending eight-bit characters over a serial connection is impossible, for instance if the connection goes through a stupid terminal server. In this case, characters with the eighth bit set have to be quoted on transmission. When you transmit eight-bit characters over a seven-bit connection, they have to be Under worst-case assumptions, this doubles the amount of data to be transmitted, although compression done by the hardware may compensate for this. Lines that can transmit arbitrary eight-bit characters are usually called eight-bit clean. This is the case for all TCP connections, as well as for most modem connections.

The following protocols are available with Taylor UUCP 1.04:

g	This is the most common protocol and should be understood by virtually all *uucico*'s. It does thorough error checking and is therefore well-suited for noisy telephone links. *g* requires an eight-bit clean connection. It is a packet-oriented protocol which uses a sliding-window technique.
i	This is a bidirectional packet protocol which can send and receive files at the same time. It requires a full-duplex connection and an eight-bit clean data path. It is currently understood only by Taylor UUCP.
t	This is a protocol intended for use over a TCP connection, or other truly error-free networks. It uses packets of 1024 bytes and requires an eight-bit clean connection.
e	This should basically do the same as *t*. The main difference is that *e* is a streaming protocol.
f	This is intended for use with reliable X.25 connections. It is a streaming protocol and expects a seven-bit data path. Eight-bit characters are quoted, which can make it very inefficient.
G	This is the System V Release 4 version of the *g* protocol. It is also understood by some other versions of UUCP.
a	This protocol is similiar to ZMODEM. It requires an eight bit connection, but quotes certain control characters like XON and XOFF.

12.6.2   Tuning the Transmission Protocol

All protocols allow for some variation in packet sizes, timeouts, and the like. Usually, the defaults provided work well under standard circumstances, but may not be optimal for your situation. The *g* protocol, for instance, uses window sizes from 1 to 7, and packet sizes in powers of 2 ranging from 64 through 4096.[14] If your telephone line is usually so noisy that it drops more than 5 percent all packets, you should probably lower the packet size and shrink the window. On the other hand, on very good telephone lines the protocol overhead of sending ACKs for every 128 bytes may prove wasteful, so that you might increase the packet size to 512 or even 1024.

Taylor UUCP provides a meachanism to suit your needs by tuning these parameters with the *protocol-parameter* command in the *sys* file. For instance, to set the *g* protocol's packet size to 512 when talking to **pablo**, you have to add:

```
system          pablo
...
protocol-parameter g  packet-size  512
```

The tunable parameters and their names vary from protocol to protocol. For a complete list of them please refer to the documentation enclosed in the Taylor UUCP source.

12.6.3   Selecting Specific Protocols

Not every implementation of *uucico* speaks and understand each protocol, so during the initial handshake phase, both processes have to agree on a common protocol. The master *uucico* offers the slave a list of supported protocols by sending P*protlist*, from which the slave may pick one.

Based on the type of port used (modem, TCP, or direct), *uucico* will compose a default list of protocols. For modem and direct connections, this list usually comprises *i*, *a*, *g*, *G*, and *j*. For TCP connections, the list is *t*, *e*, *i*, *a*, *g*, *G*, *j*, and *f*. You can override this default list with the *protocols* command, which may be specified in a system entry as well as a port entry. For instance, you might edit the *port* file entry for your modem port like this:

```
port            serial1
...
protocols       igG
```

This will require any incoming or outgoing connection through this port to use *i*, *g*, or *G*. If the remote system does not support any of these, the conversation will fail.

12.7   Troubleshooting

This section describes what may go wrong with your UUCP connection, and makes suggestions where to look for the error. However, the questions were compiled off the top of my head. There's much more that can go wrong.

In any case, enable debugging with `-xall`, and take a look at the output in *Debug* in the spool directory. It should help you to quickly recognize where the problem lies. Also, I have always found it helpful to turn on my modem's speaker when it didn't connect. With Hayes-compatible modems, this is accomplished by adding "ATL1M1 OK" to the modem chat in the *dial* file.

The first check always should be whether all file permissions are set correctly. *uucico* should be setuid **uucp**, and all files in */usr/lib/uucp*, */var/spool/uucp* and */var/spool/uucppublic* should be owned by **uucp**. There are also some hidden files[15] in the spool directory which must be owned by **uucp** as well.

uucico **keeps saying "Wrong time to call":** This probably means that in the system entry in *sys*, you didn't specify a *time* command that details when the remote system may be called, or you gave one which

---

[14]Most binaries included in Linux distributions default to a window size of 7 and 128 byte packets.

[15]That is, files whose name begins with a dot. Such files aren't normally displayed by the *ls* command.

actually forbids calling at the current time. If no call schedule is given, *uucico* assumes that the system may never be called.

uucico **complains that the site is already locked**: This means that *uucico* detected a lock file for the remote system in */var/spool/uucp*. The lock file may be from an earlier call to the system that crashed, or was killed. However, it's also likely that there's another *uucico* process sitting around that is trying to dial the remote system and got stuck in a chat script, etc. If this *uucico* process doesn't succeed in connecting to the remote system, kill it with a hangup signal, and remove any lock files it left lying around.

I can connect to the remote site, but the chat script fails: Look at the text you receive from the remote site. If it's garbled, this might be a speed-related problem. Otherwise, confirm if it really agrees with what your chat script expects. Remember, the chat script starts with an expect string. If you receive the login prompt, then send your name, but never get the password prompt, insert some delays before sending it, or even in-between the letters. You might be too fast for your modem.

My modem does not dial: If your modem doesn't indicate that the DTR line has been raised when *uucico* calls out, you possibly haven't given the right device to *uucico*. If your modem recognizes DTR, check with a terminal program that you can write to it. If this works, turn on echoing with \E at the start of the modem chat. If it doesn't echo your commands during the modem chat, check if your line speed is too high or low for your modem. If you see the echo, check if you have disabled modem responses, or set them to number codes. Verify that the chat script itself is correct. Remember that you have to write two backslashes to send one to the modem.

My modem tries to dial, but doesn't get out: Insert a delay into the phone number. This is especially useful when dialing out from a company's internal telephone net. For people in Europe, who usually dial pulse-tone, try touch-tone. In some countries, postal services have been upgrading their nets recently. Touch-tone sometimes helps.

I log file says I have extremely high packet loss rates: This looks like a speed problem. Maybe the link between computer and modem is too slow (remember to adapt it to the highest effective rate possible)? Or is it your hardware that is too slow to service interrupts in time? With a NSC 16550A chipset on your serial port, 38kbps are said to work reasonably well; however, without FIFOs (like 16450 chips), 9600 bps is the limit. Also, you should make sure hardware handshake is enabled on the serial line.

Another likely cause is that hardware handshake isn't enabled on the port. Taylor UUCP 1.04 has no provisions for turning on RTS/CTS handshake. You have to enable this explicitly from *rc.serial* using the following command:

```
$ stty crtscts < /dev/cua3
```

I can log in, but handshake fails: Well, there can be a number of problems. The output in the log file should tell you a lot. Look at what protocols the remote site offers (It sends a string P*protlist* during the handshake). Maybe they don't have any in common (did you select any protocols in *sys* or *port*?).

If the remote system sends RLCK, there is a stale lockfile for you on the remote system. If it's not because you're already connected to the remote system on a different line, ask to have it removed.

If it sends RBADSEQ, the other site has conversation count checks enabled for you, but numbers didn't match. If it sends RLOGIN, you were not permitted to login under this id.

12.8   Log Files

When compiling the UUCP suite to use Taylor-style logging, you have only three global log files, all of which reside in the spool directory. The main log file is named *Log* and contains all information about connections established and files transferred. A typical excerpt looks like this (after a little reformatting to make it fit the page):

```
uucico pablo - (1994-05-28 17:15:01.66 539) Calling system pablo (port cua3)
uucico pablo - (1994-05-28 17:15:39.25 539) Login successful
uucico pablo - (1994-05-28 17:15:39.90 539) Handshake successful
                (protocol 'g' packet size 1024 window 7)
```

```
uucico pablo postmaster (1994-05-28 17:15:43.65 539) Receiving D.pabloB04aj
uucico pablo postmaster (1994-05-28 17:15:46.51 539) Receiving X.pabloX04ai
uucico pablo postmaster (1994-05-28 17:15:48.91 539) Receiving D.pabloB04at
uucico pablo postmaster (1994-05-28 17:15:51.52 539) Receiving X.pabloX04as
uucico pablo postmaster (1994-05-28 17:15:54.01 539) Receiving D.pabloB04c2
uucico pablo postmaster (1994-05-28 17:15:57.17 539) Receiving X.pabloX04c1
uucico pablo - (1994-05-28 17:15:59.05 539) Protocol 'g' packets: sent 15,
               resent 0, received 32
uucico pablo - (1994-05-28 17:16:02.50 539) Call complete (26 seconds)
uuxqt pablo postmaster (1994-05-28 17:16:11.41 546) Executing X.pabloX04ai
               (rmail okir)
uuxqt pablo postmaster (1994-05-28 17:16:13.30 546) Executing X.pabloX04as
               (rmail okir)
uuxqt pablo postmaster (1994-05-28 17:16:13.51 546) Executing X.pabloX04c1
               (rmail okir)
```

The next important log file is *Stats*, which lists file transfer statistics. The section of *Stats* corresponding to the above transfer looks like this:

```
postmaster pablo (1994-05-28 17:15:44.78)
                      received 1714 bytes in 1.802 seconds (951 bytes/sec)
postmaster pablo (1994-05-28 17:15:46.66)
                      received 57 bytes in 0.634 seconds (89 bytes/sec)
postmaster pablo (1994-05-28 17:15:49.91)
                      received 1898 bytes in 1.599 seconds (1186 bytes/sec)
postmaster pablo (1994-05-28 17:15:51.67)
                      received 65 bytes in 0.555 seconds (117 bytes/sec)
postmaster pablo (1994-05-28 17:15:55.71)
                      received 3217 bytes in 2.254 seconds (1427 bytes/sec)
postmaster pablo (1994-05-28 17:15:57.31)
                      received 65 bytes in 0.590 seconds (110 bytes/sec)
```

Again, the lines have been split to make it fit the page.

The third file if *Debug*. This is the place where debugging information is written. If you use debugging, you should make sure that this file has a protection mode of 600. Depending on the debug mode you selected, it may contain the login and password you use to connect to the remote system.

Some UUCP binaries included in Linux distributions have been compiled to use HDB-style logging. HDB UUCP uses a whole bunch of log files stored below */var/spool/uucp/.Log*. This directory contains three more directories, named *uucico*, *uuxqt*, and *uux*. They contain the logging output generated by each of the corresponding commands, sorted into different files for each site. Thus, output from *uucico* when calling site **pablo** will go into *.Log/uucico/pablo*, while the subsequent *uuxqt* run will write to *.Log/uuxqt/pablo*. The lines written to the various lofiles are however the same as with Taylor logging.

When you enable debugging output with HDB-style logging compiled in, it will go to the *.Admin* directory below */var/spool/uucp*. During outgoing calls, debugging information will be sent to *.Admin/audit.local*, while the output from *uucico* when someone calls in will go to *.Admin/audit*.

Chapter 13

Electronic Mail

One of the most prominent uses of networking since the first networks were devised, has been eletronic mail. It started as a simple service that copied a file from one machine to another, and appended it to the recipient's *mailbox* file. Basically, this is still what email is all about, although an ever growing net with its complex routing requirements and its ever increasing load of messages has made a more elaborate scheme necessary.

Various standards of mail exchange have been devised. Sites on the Internet adhere to one laid out in RFC 822, augmented by some RFCs that describe a machine-independent way of transferring special characters, and the like. Much thought has also been given recently to "multi-media mail", which deals with including pictures and sound in mail messages. Another standard, X.400, has been defined by CCITT.

Quite a number of mail transport programs have been implemented for UNIX systems. One of the best-known is the University of Berkeley's *sendmail*, which is used on a number of platforms. The original author was Eric Allman, who is now actively working on the *sendmail* team again. There are two Linux ports of *sendmail-5.56c* available, one of which will be described in chapter 15. The *sendmail* version currently being developed is 8.6.5.

The mail agent most commonly used with Linux is *smail-3.1.28*, written and copyrighted by Curt Landon Noll and Ronald S. Karr. This is the one included in most Linux distributions. In the following, we will refer to it simply as *smail*, although there are other versions of it which are entirely different, and which we don't describe here.

Compared to *sendmail*, *smail* is rather young. When handling mail for a small site without complicated routing requirements, their capabilities are pretty close. For large sites, however, *sendmail* always wins, because its configuration scheme is much more flexible.

Both *smail* and *sendmail* support a set of configuration files that have to be customized. Apart from the information that is required to make the mail subsystem run (such as the local hostname), there are many more parameters that may be tuned. *sendmail*'s main configuration file is very hard to understand at first. It looks as if your cat had taken a nap on your keyboard with the shift key pressed. *smail* configuration files are more structured and easier to understand than *sendmail*'s, but don't give the user as much power in tuning the mailer's behavior. However, for small UUCP or Internet sites the work required in setting up any of them is roughly the same.

In this chapter, we will deal with what email is and what issues you as an administrator will have to deal with. Chapters 14 and 15 will give instructions on setting up *smail* and *sendmail* for the first time. The information provided there should suffice to get smaller sites operational, but there are many more options, and you can spend many happy hours in front of your computer configuring the fanciest features.

Toward the end of the current chapter we will briefly cover setting up *elm*, a very common mail user agent on many UNIXish systems, including Linux.

For more information about issues specific to electronic mail on Linux, please refer to the Electronic Mail HOWTO by Vince Skahan, which is posted to **comp.os.linux.announce** regularly. The source distributions of *elm*, *smail* and *sendmail* also contain very extensive documentation that should answer most of your questions on setting them up. If you are looking for information on email in general, there's a number of RFCs that deal with this topic. They are listed in the bibliography at the end of the book.

13.1   What is a Mail Message?

A Mail message generally consists of a message body, which is the text the sender wrote, and special data specifying recipients, transport medium, etc., very much like what you see when you look at a letter's envelope.

This administrative data falls into two categories; in the first category is any data that is specific to the transport medium, like the address of sender and recipient. It is therefore called *the envelope*. It may be transformed by the transport software as the message is passed along.

The second variety is any data necessary for handling the mail message, which is not particular to any transport mechanism, such as the message's subject line, a list of all recipients, and the date the message was sent. In many networks, it has become standard to prepend this data to the mail message, forming the so-called *mail header*. It is offset from the *mail body* by an empty line.[1]

Most mail transport software in the UNIX world uses a header format outlined in a RFC 822. Its original purpose was to specify a standard for use on the ARPANET, but since it was designed to be independent from any environment, it has been easily adapted to other networks, including many UUCP-based networks.

RFC 822 however is only the greatest common denominator. More recent standards have been conceived to cope with growing needs as, for example, data encryption, international character set support, and multi-media mail extensions (MIME).

In all these standards, the header consists of several lines, separated by newline characters. A line is made up of a field name, beginning in column one, and the field itself, offset by a colon and white space. The format and semantics of each field vary depending on the field name. A header field may be continued across a newline, if the next line begins with a TAB. Fields can appear in any order.

A typical mail header may look like this:

```
From brewhq.swb.de!ora.com!andyo Wed Apr 13 00:17:03 1994
Return-Path: <brewhq.swb.de!ora.com!andyo>
Received: from brewhq.swb.de by monad.swb.de with uucp
        (Smail3.1.28.1 #6) id m0pqq1T-00023aB; Wed, 13 Apr 94 00:17 MET DST
Received: from ora.com (ruby.ora.com) by brewhq.swb.de with smtp
        (Smail3.1.28.1 #28.6) id <m0pqoQr-0008qhC>; Tue, 12 Apr 94 21:47 MEST
Received: by ruby.ora.com (8.6.8/8.6.4) id RAA26438; Tue, 12 Apr 94 15:56 -0400
Date: Tue, 12 Apr 1994 15:56:49 -0400
Message-Id: <199404121956.PAA07787@ruby>
From: andyo@ora.com (Andy Oram)
To: okir@monad.swb.de
Subject: Re: Your RPC section
```

Usually, all necessary header fields are generated by the mailer interface you use, like *elm*, *pine*, *mush*, or *mailx*. Some however are optional, and may be added by the user. *elm*, for example, allows you to edit part of the message header. Others are added by the mail transport software. A list of common header fields and their meaning are given below:

From: This contains the sender's email address, and possibly the "real name". A complete zoo of
                 formats is used here.

To: This is the recipient's email address.

Subject: Describes the content of the mail in a few words. At least that's what it *should* do.

Date: The date the mail was sent.

Reply-To: Specifies the address the sender wants the recipient's reply directed to. This may be useful if
                 you have several accounts, but want to receive the bulk of mail only on the one you use most
                 frequently. This field is optional.

Organization:
                 The organization that owns the machine from which the mail originates. If your machine is

---

[1] It is customary to append a *signature* or *.sig* to a mail message, usually containing information on the author, along with a joke or a motto. It is offset from the mail message by a line containing "-- ".

owned by you privately, either leave this out, or insert "private" or some complete nonsense. This field is optional.

Message-ID: A string generated by mail transport on the originating system. It is unique to this message.

Received: Every site that processes your mail (including the machines of sender and recipient) inserts such a field into the header, giving its site name, a message id, time and date it received the message, which site it is from, and which transport software was used. This is so that you can trace which route the message took, and can complain to the person responsible if something went wrong.

X-anything: No mail-related programs should complain about any header which starts with X-. It is used to implement additional features that have not yet made it into an RFC, or never will. This is used by the Linux Activists mailing list, for example, where the channel is selected by the X-Mn-Key: header field.

The one exception to this structure is the very first line. It starts with the keyword From which is followed by a blank instead of a colon. To distinguish it from the ordinary From: field, it is frequently referred to as From_. It contains the route the message has taken in UUCP bang-path style (explained below), time and date when it was received by the last machine having processed it, and an optional part specifying which host it was received from. Since this field is regenerated by every system that processes the message, it is sometimes subsumed under the envelope data.

The From_ field is there for backward compatibilty with some older mailers, but is not used very much anymore, except by mail user interfaces that rely on it to mark the beginning of a message in the user's mailbox. To avoid potential trouble with lines in the message body that begin with "From ", too, it has become standard procedure to escape any such occurence by preceding it with ">".

13.2   How is Mail Delivered?

Generally, you will compose mail using a mailer interface like *mail* or *mailx*, or more sophisticated ones like *elm*, *mush*, or *pine*. These programs are called *mail user agents*, or MUA's for short. If you send a mail message, the interface program will in most cases hand it to another program for delivery. This is called the *mail transport agent*, or MTA. On some systems, there are different mail transport agents for local and remote delivery; on others, there is only one. The command for remote delivery is usually called *rmail*, the other is called *lmail* (if it exists).

Local delivery of mail is, of course, more than just appending the incoming message to the recipient's mailxbox. Usually, the local MTA will understand aliasing (setting up local recipient addresses pointing to other addresses), and forwarding (redirecting a user's mail to some other destination). Also, messages that cannot be delivered must usually be *bounced*, that is, returned to the sender along with some error message.

For remote delivery, the transport software used depends on the nature of the link. If the mail must be delivered over a network using TCP/IP, SMTP is commonly used. SMTP stands for Simple Mail Transfer Protocol, and is defined in RFC 788 and RFC 821. SMTP usually connects to the recipient's machine directly, negotiating the message transfer with the remote side's SMTP daemon.

In UUCP networks, mail will usually not be delivered directly, but rather be forwarded to the destination host by a number of intermediate systems. To send a message over a UUCP link, the sending MTA will usually execute *rmail* on the forwarding system using *uux*, and feed it the message on standard input.

Since this is done for each message separately, it may produce a considerable work load on a major mail hub, as well as clutter the UUCP spool queues with hundreds of small files taking up an unproportional amount of disk space.[2] Some MTAs therefore allow you to collect several messages for a remote system in a single batch file. The batch file contains the SMTP commands that the local host would normally issue if a direct SMTP connection was used. This is called BSMTP, or *batched* SMTP. The batch is then fed to the *rsmtp* or *bsmtp* program on the remote system, which will process the input as if a normal SMTP connection had occurred.

---

[2]This is because disk space is usually allocated in blocks of 1024 Bytes. So even a message of at most 400 Bytes will eat a full KB.

13.3   Email Addresses

For electronic mail, an address is made up of at least the name of a machine handling the person's mail, and a user identification recognized by this system. This may be the recipient's login name, but may also be anything else. Other mail addressing schemes, like X.400, use a more general set of "attributes" which are used to look up the recipient's host in an X.500 directory server.

The way a machine name is interpreted, i.e. at which site your message will finally wind up, and how to combine this name with the recipient's user name greatly depends on the network you are on.

Internet sites adhere to the RFC 822 standard, which requires a notation of **user@host.domain**, where **host.domain** is the host's fully qualified domain name. The middle thing is called an "at" sign. Because this notation does not involve a route to the destination host but gives the (unique) hostname instead, this is called an *absolute* address.

In the original UUCP environment, the prevalent form was **path!host!user**, where **path** described a sequence of hosts the message had to travel before reaching the destination **host**. This construct is called the *bang path* notation, because an exclamation mark is loosely called a "bang". Today, many UUCP-based networks have adopted RFC 822, and will understand this type of address.

Now, these two types of addressing don't mix too well. Assume an address of **hostA!user@hostB**. It is not clear whether the '@' sign takes precedence over the path, or vice versa: do we have to send the message to **hostB**, which mails it to **hostA!user**, or should it be sent to **hostA**, which fowards it to **user@hostB**?

Addresses that mix different types of address operators are called *hybrid addresses*. Most notorious is the above example. It is usually resolved by giving the '@' sign precedence over the path. In the above example, this means sending the message to **hostB** first.

However, there is a way to specify routes in RFC 822-conformant ways: **<@hostA,@hostB:user@hostC>** denotes the address of **user** on **hostC**, where **hostC** is to be reached through **hostA** and **hostB** (in that order). This type of address is freqeuently called a *route-addr address*.

Then, there is the '%' address operator: **user%hostB@hostA** will first be sent to **hostA**, which expands the rightmost (in this case, only) percent sign to an '@' sign. The address is now **user@hostB**, and the mailer will happily forward your message to **hostB** which delivers it to **user**. This type of address is sometimes referred to as "Ye Olde ARPANET Kludge", and its use is discouraged. Nevertheless, many mail transport agents generate this type of address.

Other networks have still different means of addressing. DECnet-based networks, for example, use two colons as an address separator, yielding an address of *host::user*.[3] Lastly, the X.400 standard uses an entirely different scheme, by describing a recipient by a set of attribute-value pairs, like country and organization.

On FidoNet, each user is identified by a code like **2:320/204.9**, consisting of four numbers denoting zone (2 is for Europe), net (320 being Paris and Banlieue), node (the local hub), and point (the individual user's PC). Fidonet addresses can be mapped to RFC 822; the above would be written as **Thomas.Quinot@p9.f204.n320.z2.fidonet.org**. Now didn't I say domain names are easy to remember?

There are some implications to using these different types of addressing which will be described throughout the following sections. In a RFC 822 environment, however, you will rarely use anything else than absolute addresses like *user@host.domain*.

13.4   How does Mail Routing Work?

The process of directing a message to the recipient's host is called *routing*. Apart from finding a path from the sending site to the destination, it involves error checking as well as speed and cost optimization.

There is a big difference between the way a UUCP site handles routing, and the way an Internet site does. On the Internet, the main job of directing data to the recipient host (once it is known by it's IP address) is done by the IP networking layer, while in the UUCP zone, the route has to be supplied by the user, or generated by the mail transfer agent.

---

[3]When trying to reach a DECnet address from an RFC 822 environment, you may use "*host::user*"*@relay*, where *relay* is the name of a known Internet-DECnet relay.

13.4.1 Mail Routing on the Internet

On the Internet, it depends entirely on the destination host whether any specific mail routing is performed at all. The default is to deliver the message to the destination host directly by looking up its IP address, and leave the actual routing of the data to the IP transport layer.

Most sites will usually want to direct all inbound mail to a highly available mail server that is capable of handling all this traffic, and have it distribute this mail locally. To announce this service, the site publishes a so-called MX record for their local domain in the DNS database. MX stands for *Mail Exchanger* and basically states that the server host is willing to act as a mail forwarder for all machines in this domain. MX records may also be used to handle traffic for hosts that are not connected to the Internet themselves, like UUCP networks, or company networks with hosts carrying confidential information.

MX records also have a *preference* associated with them. This is a positive integer. If several mail exchangers exist for one host, the mail transport agent will try to transfer the message to the exchanger with the lowest preference value, and only if this fails will it try a host with a higher value. If the local host is itself a mail exchanger for the destination address, it must not forward messages to any MX hosts with a higher preference than its own; this is a safe way of avoiding mail loops.

Suppose that an organization, say Foobar Inc., want all their mail handled by their machine called **mailhub**. They will then have an MX record like this in the DNS database:

```
foobar.com       IN   MX    5    mailhub.foobar.com
```

This announces **mailhub.foobar.com** as a mail exchanger for **foobar.com** with a preference value of 5. A host that wishes to deliver a message to **joe@greenhouse.foobar.com** will check DNS for **foobar.com**, and finds the MX record pointing at **mailhub**. If there's no MX with a preference smaller than 5, the message will be delivered to **mailhub**, which then dispatches it to **greenhouse**.

The above is really only a sketch of how MX records work. For more information on the mail routing on the Internet, please refer to RFC 974.

13.4.2 Mail Routing in the UUCP World

Mail routing on UUCP networks is much more complicated than on the Internet, because the transport software does not perform any routing itself. In earlier times, all mail had to be addressed using bang paths. Bang paths specified a list of hosts through which to forward the message, separated by exclamation marks, and followed by the user's name. To address a letter to Janet User on a machine named **moria**, you would have used the path **eek!swim!moria!janet**. Whis would have sent the mail from your host to **eek**, from there on to **swim** and finally to **moria**.

The obvious drawback of this technique is that it requires you to remember much about the network topology, fast links, etc. Much worse than that, changes in the network topology — like links being deleted or hosts being removed — may cause messages to fail simply because you weren't aware of the change. And finally, in case you move to a different place, you will most likely have to update all these routes.

One thing, however, that made the use of source routing necessary was the presence of ambiguous hostnames: For instance, assume there are two sites named **moria**, one in the U.S., and one in France. Which site now does **moria!janet** refer to? This can be made clear by specifying what path to reach **moria** through.

The first step in disambiguating hostnames was the founding of *The UUCP Mapping Project*. It is located at Rutgers University, and registers all official UUCP hostnames, along with information on their UUCP neighbors and their geographic location, making sure no hostname is used twice. The information gathered by the Mapping Project is published as the *Usenet Maps*, which are distributed regularly through Usenet.[4] A typical system entry in a Map (after removing the comments) looks like this.

```
moria
        bert(DAILY/2),
        swim(WEEKLY)
```

---

[4]Maps for sites registered with The UUCP Mapping Project are distributed through the newsgroup **comp.mail.maps**; other organizations may publish separate maps for their network.

This entry says that **moria** has a link to **bert**, which it calls twice a day, and **swim**, which it calls weekly. We will come back to the Map file format in more detail below.

Using the connectivity information provided in the maps, you can automatically generate the full paths from your host to any destination site. This information is usually stored in the *paths* file, also called *pathalias database* sometimes. Assume the Maps state that you can reach **bert** through **ernie**, then a pathalias entry for **moria** generated from the Map snippet above may look like this:

```
     moria          ernie!bert!moria!%s
```

If you now give a destination address of **janet@moria.uucp**, your MTA will pick the route shown above, and send the message to **ernie** with an envelope address of **bert!moria!janet**.

Building a *paths* file from the full Usenet maps is however not a very good idea. The information provided in them is usually rather distorted, and occasionally out of date. Therefore, only a number of major hosts use the complete UUCP world maps to build their *paths* file. Most sites only maintain routing information for sites in their neighborhood, and send any mail to sites they don't find in their databases to a smarter host with more complete routing information. This scheme is called *smart-host routing*. Hosts that have only one UUCP mail link (so-called *leaf sites*) don't do any routing of their own; they rely entirely on their smart-host.

13.4.3   Mixing UUCP and RFC 822

The best cure against the problems of mail routing in UUCP networks so far is the adoption of the domain name system in UUCP networks. Of course, you can't query a name server over UUCP. Nevertheless, many UUCP sites have formed small domains that coordinate their routing internally. In the Maps, these domains announce one or two host as their mail gateways, so that there doesn't have to be a map entry for each host in the domain. The gateways handle all mail that flows into and out of the domain. The routing scheme inside the domain is completely invisible to the outside world.

This works very well with the smart-host routing scheme described above. Global routing information is maintained by the gateways only; minor hosts within a domain will get along with only a small hand-written *paths* file that lists the routes inside their domain, and the route to the mail hub. Even the mail gateways do not have to have routing information for every single UUCP host in the world anymore. Beside the complete routing information for the domain they serve, they only need to have routes to entire domains in their databases now. For instance, the pathalias entry shown below will route all mail for sites in the **sub.org** domain to **smurf**:

```
     .sub.org       swim!smurf!%s
```

Any mail addressed to **claire@jones.sub.org** will be sent to **swim** with an envelope address of **smurf!jones!claire**.

The hierarchical organization of the domain name space allows mail servers to mix more specific routes with less specific ones. For instance, a system in France may have specific routes for subdomains of **fr**, but route any mail for hosts in the **us** domain toward some system in the U.S. In this way, domain-based routing (as this technique is called) greatly reduces the size of routing databases as well as the administrative overhead needed.

The main benefit of using domain names in a UUCP environment, however, is that compliance with RFC 822 permits easy gatewaying between UUCP networks and the Internet. Many UUCP domains nowadays have a link with an Internet gateway that acts as their smart-host. Sending messages across the Internet is faster, and routing information is much more reliable because Internet hosts can use DNS instead of the Usenet Maps.

In order to be reachable from the Internet, UUCP-based domains usually have their Internet gateway announce an MX record for them (MX records were described above). For instance, assume that **moria** belongs to the **orcnet.org** domain. **gcc2.groucho.edu** acts as their Internet gateway. **moria** would therefore use **gcc2** as its smart-host, so that all mail for foreign domains is delivered across the Internet. On the other hand, **gcc2** would announce an MX record for **orcnet.org**, and deliver all incoming mail for **orcnet** sites to **moria**.

The only remaining problem is that the UUCP transport programs can't deal with fully qualified domain names. Most UUCP suites were designed to cope with site names of up to eight characters, some even less, and using non-alphanumeric characters such as dots is completely out of the question for most.

Therefore, some mapping between RFC 822 names and UUCP hostnames is needed. The way this mapping is done is completely implementation-dependent. One common way of mapping FQDNs to UUCP names is to use the pathalias file for this:

```
moria.orcnet.org  ernie!bert!moria!%s
```

This will produce a pure UUCP-style bang path from an address that specifies a fully qualified domain name. Some mailers provide a special files for this; *sendmail*, for instance, uses the *uucpxtable* for this.

The reverse transformation (colloquially called domainizing) is sometimes required when sending mail from a UUCP network to the Internet. As long as the mail sender uses the fully qualified domain name in the destination address, this problem can be avoided by not removing the domain name from the envelope address when forwarding the message to the smart-host. However, there are still some UUCP sites that are not part of any domain. They are usually domainized by appending the pseudo-domain **uucp**.

13.5 Pathalias and Map File Format

The pathalias database provides the main routing information in UUCP-based networks. A typical entry looks like this (site name and path are separated by TABs):

```
moria.orcnet.org  ernie!bert!moria!%s
moria             ernie!bert!moria!%s
```

This makes any message to **moria** be delivered via **ernie** and **bert**. Both **moria**'s fully qualified name and its UUCP name have to be given if the mailer does not have a separate way to map between these name spaces.

If you want to direct all messages to hosts inside some domain to its mail relay, you may also specify a path in the pathalias database, giving the domain name as target, preceded by a dot. For example, if all hosts in the **sub.org** may be reached through **swim!smurf**, the pathalias entry might look like this:

```
.sub.org       swim!smurf!%s
```

Writing a pathalias file is acceptable only when you are running a site that does not have to do much routing. If you have to do routing for a large number of hosts, a better way is to use the *pathalias* command to create the file from map files. Maps can be maintained much easier, because you may simply add or remove a system by editing the system's map entry, and re-create the map file. Although the maps published by the Usenet Mapping Project aren't used for routing very much anymore, smaller UUCP networks may provide routing information in their own set of maps.

A map file mainly consists of a list of sites, listing the sites each system polls or is polled by. The system name begins in column one, and is followed by a comma-separated list of links. The list may be continued across newlines if the next line begins with a tab. Each link consists of the name of the site, followed by a cost given in brackets. The cost is an arithmetic expression, made up of numbers and symbolic costs. Lines beginning with a hash sign are ignored.

As an example, consider **moria**, which polls **swim.twobirds.com** twice a day, and **bert.sesame.com** once per week. Moreover, the link to **bert** only uses a slow 2400bps modem. **moria**'s would publish the following maps entry:

```
moria.orcnet.org
        bert.sesame.com(DAILY/2),
        swim.twobirds.com(WEEKLY+LOW)

moria.orcnet.org = moria
```

The last line would make it known under its UUCP name, too. Note that it must be *DAILY/2*, because calling twice a day actually halves the cost for this link.

Using the information from such map files, *pathalias* is able to calculate optimal routes to any destination site listed in the paths file, and produce a pathalias database from this which can then be used for routing to these sites.

pathalias provides a couple of other features like site-hiding (i.e. making sites accessible only through a gateway) etc. See the manual page for *pathalias* for details, as well as a complete list of link costs.

Comments in the map file generally contain additional information on the sites described in it. There is a rigid format in which to specify this, so that it can be retrieved from the maps. For instance, a program called *uuwho* uses a database created from the map files to display this information in a nicely formatted way.

When you register your site with an organization that distributes map files to its members, you generally have to fill out such a map entry.

Below is a sample map entry (in fact, it's the one for my site):

```
#N      monad, monad.swb.de, monad.swb.sub.org
#S      AT 486DX50; Linux 0.99
#O      private
#C      Olaf Kirch
#E      okir@monad.swb.de
#P      Kattreinstr. 38, D-64295 Darmstadt, FRG
#L      49 52 03 N / 08 38 40 E
#U      brewhq
#W      okir@monad.swb.de (Olaf Kirch); Sun Jul 25 16:59:32 MET DST 1993
#
monad   brewhq(DAILY/2)
# Domains
monad = monad.swb.de
monad = monad.swb.sub.org
```

The white space after the first two characters is a TAB. The meaning of most of the fields is pretty obvious; you will receive a detailed description from whichever domain you register with. The *L* field is the most fun to find out: it gives your geographical position in latitude/longitude and is used to draw the postscript maps that show all sites for each country, as well as world-wide.[5]

13.6   Configuring *elm*

elm stands for "electronic mail" and is one of the more reasonably named UNIX tools. It provides a full-screen interface with a good help feature. We won't discuss here how to use *elm*, but only dwell on its configuration options.

Theoretically, you can run *elm* unconfigured, and everything works well — if you are lucky. But there are a few options that must be set, although only required on occasions.

When it starts, *elm* reads a set of configuration variables from the *elm.rc* file in */usr/lib/elm*. Then, it will attempt to read the file *.elm/elmrc* in your home directory. You don't usually write this file yourself. It is created when you choose "save options" from *elm*'s options menu.

The set of options for the private *elmrc* file is also available in the global *elm.rc* file. Most settings in your private *elmrc* file override those of the global file.

13.6.1   Global *elm* Options

In the global *elm.rc* file, you must set the options that pertain to your host's name. For example, at the Virtual Brewery, the file for **vlager** would contain the following:

```
#
# The local hostname
```

---
[5]They are posted regularly in **news.lists.ps-maps**. Beware. They're HUGE.

```
hostname = vlager
#
# Domain name
hostdomain = .vbrew.com
#
# Fully qualified domain name
hostfullname = vlager.vbrew.com
```

These options set *elm*'s idea of the local hostname. Although this information is rarely used, you should set these options nevertheless. Note that these options only take effect when giving them in the global configuration file; when found in your private *elmrc*, they will be ignored.

13.6.2 National Character Sets

Recently, there have been proposals to amend the RFC 822 standard to support various types of messages, such as plain text, binary data, Postscript files, etc. The set of standards and RFCs covering these aspects are commonly referred to as MIME, or Multipurpose Internet Mail Extensions. Among other things, this also lets the recipient know if a character set other than standard ASCII has been used when writing the message, for example using French accents, or German umlauts. This is supported by *elm* to some extent.

The character set used by Linux internally to represent characters is usually referred to as ISO-8859-1, which is the name of the standard it conforms to. It is also known as Latin-1. Any message using characters from this character set should have the following line in its header:

```
Content-Type:  text/plain; charset=iso-8859-1
```

The receiving system should recognize this field and take appropriate measures when displaying the message. The default for *text/plain* messages is a *charset* value of *us-ascii*.

To be able to display messages with character sets other than ASCII, *elm* must know how to print these characters. By default, when *elm* receives a message with a *charset* field other than *us-ascii* (or a content type other than *text/plain*, for that matter), it tries to display the message using a command called *metamail*. Messages that require *metamail* to be displayed are shown with an 'M' in the very first column in the overview screen.

Since Linux' native character set is ISO-8859-1, calling *metamail* is not necessary to display messages using this character set. If *elm* is told that the display understands ISO-8859-1, it will not use *metamail* but will display the message directly instead. This can be done by setting the following option in the global *elm.rc*:

```
displaycharset = iso-8859-1
```

Note that you should set this options even when you are never going to send or receive any messages that actually contain characters other than ASCII. This is because people who do send such messages usually configure their mailer to put the proper `Content-Type:` field into the mail header by default, whether or not they are sending ASCII-only messages.

However, setting this option in *elm.rc* is not enough. The problem is that when displaying the message with its builtin pager, *elm* calls a library function for each character to determine whether it is printable or not. By default, this function will only recognize ASCII characters as printable, and display all other characters as "`^?`". You may overcome this by setting the environment variable *LC_CTYPE* to *ISO-8859-1*, which tells the library to accept Latin-1 characters as printable. Support for this and other features is available since *libc-4.5.8*.

When sending messages that contain special characters from ISO-8859-1, you should make sure to set two more variables in the *elm.rc* file:

```
charset = iso-8859-1
textencoding = 8bit
```

This makes *elm* report the character set as ISO-8859-1 in the mail header, and send it as an 8 bit value (the default is to strip all characters to 7 bit).

Of course, any of these options can also be set in the private *elmrc* file instead of the global one.

Chapter 14

Getting smail Up and Running

This chapter will give you a quick introduction to setting up *smail*, and an overview of the functionality it provides. Although *smail* is largely compatible with *sendmail* in its behaviour, their configuration files are completely different.

The main configuration file is the */usr/lib/smail/config*. You always have to edit this file to reflect values specific to your site. If you are only a UUCP leaf site, you will have relatively little else to do, ever. Other files that configure routing and transport options may also be used; they will be dealt with briefly, too.

By default, *smail* processes and delivers all incoming mail immediately. If you have relatively high traffic, you may instead have *smail* collect all messages in the so-called *queue*, and process it at regular intervals only.

When handling mail within a TCP/IP network, *smail* is frequently run in daemon mode: at system boot time, it is invoked from *rc.inet2*, and puts itself in the background where it waits for incoming TCP connections on the SMTP port (usually port 25). This is very beneficial whenever you expect to have a significant amount of traffic, because *smail* isn't started up separately for every incoming connection. The alternative would be to have *inetd* manage the SMTP port, and have it spawn *smail* whenever there is a connection on this port.

smail has a lot a flags that control it behavior; describing them in detail here wouldn't make help you much. Fortunately, *smail* supports a number of standard modes of operation that are enabled when you invoke it by a special command name, like *rmail*, or *smtpd*. Usually, these aliases are symbolic links to the *smail* binary itself. We will encounter most of them when discussing the various features of *smail*.

There are two links to *smail* you should have under all circumstances; namely */usr/bin/rmail* and */usr/sbin/sendmail*.[1] When you compose and send a mail message with a user agent like *elm*, the message will be piped into *rmail* for delivery, with the recipient list given to it on the command line. The same happens with mail coming in via UUCP. Some versions of *elm*, however, invoke */usr/sbin/sendmail* instead of *rmail*, so you need both of them. For example, if you keep *smail* in */usr/local/bin*, type the following at the shell prompt:

```
# ln -s /usr/local/bin/smail /usr/bin/rmail
# ln -s /usr/local/bin/smail /usr/sbin/sendmail
```

If you want to dig further into the details of configuring *smail*, please refer to the manual pages *smail(1)* and *smail(5)*. If it isn't included in your favorite Linux distribution, you can get it from the source to *smail*.

14.1 UUCP Setup

To use *smail* in a UUCP-only environment, the basic installation is rather simple. First, you must make sure you have the two symbolic links to *rmail* and *sendmail* mentioned above. If you expect to receive SMTP batches from other sites, you also have to make *rsmtp* a link to *smail*.

---

[1]This is the new standard location of *sendmail* according to the Linux File System Standard. Another common location is */usr/lib*.

In Vince Skahan's *smail* distribution, you will find a sample configuration file. It is named *config.sample* and resides in */usr/lib/smail*. You have to copy it to *config* and edit it to reflect values specific to your site.

Assume your site is named *swim.twobirds.com*, and is registered in the UUCP maps as *swim*. Your smarthost is *ulysses*. Then your *config* file should look like this:

```
#
# Our domain names
visible_domain=two.birds:uucp
#
# Our name on outgoing mails
visible_name=swim.twobirds.com
#
# Use this as uucp-name as well
uucp_name=swim.twobirds.com
#
# Our smarthost
smart_host=ulysses
```

The first statement tells *smail* about the domains your site belongs to. Insert their names here, separated by colons. If your site name is registered in the UUCP maps, you should also add *uucp*. When being handed a mail message, *smail* determines your host's name using the *hostname(2)* system call, and checks the recipient's address against this hostname, tacking on all names from this list in turn. If the address matches any of these names, or the unqualified hostname, the recipient is considered local, and *smail* attempts to deliver the message to a user or alias on the local host. Otherwise, the recipient is considered remote, and delivery to the destination host is attempted.

visible_name should contain a single, fully qualified domain name of your site that you want to use on outgoing mails. This name is used when generating the sender's address on all outgoing mail. You must make sure to use a name that *smail* recognizes as referring to the local host (i.e. the hostname with one of the domains listed in the *visible_domain* attribute). Otherwise, replies to your mails will bounce off your site.

The last statement sets the path used for smart-host routing (described in section 13.4). With this sample setup, *smail* will forward any mail for remote addresses to the smart host. The path specified in the *smart_path* attribute will be used as a route to the smart host. Since messages will be delivered via UUCP, the attribute must specify a system known to your UUCP software. Please refer to chapter 12 on making a site known to UUCP.

There's one option used in the above file that we haven't explained yet; this is *uucp_name*. The reason to use the option is this: By default, *smail* uses the value returned by *hostname(2)* for UUCP-specific things such as the return path given in the *From_* header line. If your hostname is *not* registered with the UUCP mapping project, you should tell *smail* to use your fully qualified domain name instead.[2] This can be done by adding the *uucp_name* option to the *config* file.

There is another file in */usr/lib/smail*, called *paths.sample*. It is an example of what a *paths* file might look like. However, you will not need one unless you have mail links to more than one site. If you do, however, you will have to write one yourself, or generate one from the Usenet maps. The *paths* file will be described later in this chapter.

14.2   Setup for a LAN

If you are running a site with two or more hosts connected by a LAN, you will have to designate one host that handles your UUCP connection with the outside world. Between the hosts on your LAN, you will most probably want to exchange mail with SMTP over TCP/IP. Assume we're back at the Virtual Brewery again, and **vstout** is set up as the UUCP gateway.

In a networked environment, it is best to keep all user mailboxes on a single file system, which is NFS-mounted on all other hosts. This allows users to move from machine to machine, without having to move

---

[2]The reason is this: Assume your hostname is *monad*, but is not registered in the maps. However, there is a site in the maps called *monad*, so every mail to *monad!root*, even sent from a direct UUCP neighbor of yours, will wind up on the other *monad*. This is a nuisance for everybody.

their mail around (or even worse, check some three or four machines for newly-arrived mail each morning). Therefore, you also want to make sender addresses independent from the machine the mail was written on. It is common practice to use the domain name all by itself in the sender address, instead of a hostname. Janet User, for example, would specify **janet@vbrew.com** instead of **janet@vale.vbrew.com**. We will explain below how to make the server recognize the domain name as a valid name for your site.

A different way of keeping all mailboxes on a central host is to use POP or IMAP. POP stands for *Post Office Protocol* and lets users access their mailboxes over a simple TCP/IP conection. IMAP, the *Interactive Mail Access Protocol*, is similar to POP, but more general. Both clients and servers for IMAP and POP have been ported to Linux, and are available from **sunsite.unc.edu** below */pub/Linux/system/Network*.

14.2.1 Writing the Configuration Files

The configuration for the Brewery works as follows: all hosts except the mail server **vstout** itself route all outgoing mail to the server, using smart host routing. **vstout** itself sends all outgoing mail to the real smart host that routes all of the Brewery's mail; this host is called **moria**.

The standard *config* file for all hosts other than **vstout** looks like this:

```
#
# Our domain:
visible_domain=vbrew.com
#
# What we name ourselves
visible_name=vbrew.com
#
# Smart-host routing: via SMTP to vstout
smart_path=vstout
smart_transport=smtp
```

This is very similar to what we used for a UUCP-only site. The main difference is that the transport used to send mail to the smart host is, of course, SMTP. The *visible_domain* attribute makes *smail* use the domain name instead of the local hostname on all outgoing mail.

On the UUCP mail gateway **vstout**, the *config* file looks a little different:

```
#
# Our hostnames:
hostnames=vbrew.com:vstout.vbrew.com:vstout
#
# What we name ourselves
visible_name=vbrew.com
#
# in the uucp world, we're known as vbrew.com
uucp_name=vbrew.com
#
# Smart transport: via uucp to moria
smart_path=moria
smart_transport=uux
#
# we're authoritative for our domain
auth_domains=vbrew.com
```

This *config* file uses a different scheme to tell *smail* what the local host is called. Instead of giving it a list of domains and letting it find the hostname with a system call, it specifies a list explicitly. The above list contains both the fully qualified and the unqualified hostname, and the domain name all by itself. This makes *smail* recognize **janet@vbrew.com** as a local address, and deliver the message to **janet**.

The *auth_domains* variable names the domains for which **vstout** is considered to be authoritative. That is, if *smail* receives any mail addressed to *host.***vbrew.com** where *host* does not name an existing local machine, it rejects the message and returns it to the sender. If this entry isn't present, any such message will be sent to the smart-host, who will return it to **vstout**, and so on until it is discarded for exceeding the maximum hop count.

14.2.2 Running *smail*

First, you have to decide whether to run *smail* as a separate daemon, or whether to have *inetd* manage the SMTP port and invoke *smail* only whenever an SMTP connection is requested from some client. Usually, you will prefer daemon operation on the mail server, because this loads the machine far less than spawning *smail* over and over again for each single connection. As the mail server also delivers most incoming mail directly to the users, you will choose *inetd* operation on most other hosts.

Whatever mode of operation you choose for each individual host, you have to make sure you have the following entry in your */etc/services* file:

```
smtp            25/tcp              # Simple Mail Transfer Protocol
```

This defines the TCP port number that *smail* should use for SMTP conversations. 25 is the standard defined by the Assigned Numbers RFC.

When run in daemon mode, *smail* will put itself in the background, and wait for a connection to occur on the SMTP port. When a connection occurs, it forks and conducts an SMTP conversation with the peer process. The *smail* daemon is usually started by invoking it from the *rc.inet2* script using the following command:

```
/usr/local/bin/smail -bd -q15m
```

The -bd flag turns on daemon mode, and -q15m makes it process whatever messages have accumulated in the message queue every 15 minutes.

If you want to use *inetd* instead, your */etc/inetd.conf* file should contain a line like this:

```
smtp     stream  tcp nowait  root  /usr/sbin/smtpd smtpd
```

smtpd should be a symbolic link to the *smail* binary. Remember you have to make *inetd* re-read *inetd.conf* by sending it a *HUP* signal after making these changes.

Daemon mode and *inetd* mode are mutually exclusive. If you run *smail* in deamon mode, you should make sure to comment out any line in *inetd.conf* for the *smtp* service. Equivalently, when having *inetd* manage *smail*, make sure that *rc.inet2* does not start the *smail* daemon.

14.3 If You Don't Get Through...

If something goes wrong with your installation, there are a number of features that may help you to find what's at the root of the problem. The first place to check are *smail*'s log files. They are kept in */var/spool/smail/log*, and are named *logfile* and *paniclog*, respectively. The former lists all transactions, while the latter is only for error messages related to configuration errors and the like.

A typical entry in *logfile* looks like this:

```
04/24/94 07:12:04: [m0puwU8-00023UB] received
|               from: root
|            program: sendmail
|               size: 1468 bytes
04/24/94 07:12:04: [m0puwU8-00023UB] delivered
|                via: vstout.vbrew.com
|                 to: root@vstout.vbrew.com
|            orig-to: root@vstout.vbrew.com
|             router: smart_host
|          transport: smtp
```

This shows that a message from **root** to **root@vstout.vbrew.com** has been properly delivered to host **vstout** over SMTP.

Messages *smail* could not deliver generate a similar entry in the log file, but with an error message instead of the `delivered` part:

```
04/24/94 07:12:04: [m0puwU8-00023UB] received
|          from: root
|       program: sendmail
|          size: 1468 bytes
04/24/94 07:12:04: [m0puwU8-00023UB] root@vstout.vbrew.com ... deferred
 (ERR_148) transport smtp: connect: Connection refused
```

The above error is typical for a situation in which *smail* properly recognizes that the message should be delivered to **vstout** but was not able to connect to the SMTP service on **vstout**. If this happens, you either have a configuration problem, or TCP support is missing from your *smail* binaries.

This problem is not as uncommon as one might think. There have been precompiled *smail* binaries around, even in some Linux distributions, without support for TCP/IP networking. If this is the case for you, you have to compile *smail* yourself. Having installed *smail*, you can check if it has TCP networking support by telnetting to the SMTP port on your machine. A successful connect to the SMTP server is shown below (your input is marked *like this*):

```
$ telnet localhost smtp
Trying 127.0.0.1...
Connected to localhost.
Escape character is '^]'.
220 monad.swb.de Smail3.1.28.1 #6 ready at Sun, 23 Jan 94 19:26 MET
QUIT
221 monad.swb.de closing connection
```

If this test doesn't produce the SMTP banner (the line starting with the 220 code), first make sure that your configuration is *really* correct before you go through compiling *smail* yourself, which is described below.

If you encounter a problem with *smail* that you are unable to locate from the error message *smail* generates, you may want to turn on debugging messages. You can do this using the `-d` flag, optionally followed by a number specifying the level of verbosity (you may not have any space between the flag and the numerical argument). *smail* will then print a report of its operation to the screen, which may give you more hints about what is going wrong.

[**Don't know,... Maybe people don't find this funny:**] If nothing else helps, you may want to invoke *smail* in Rogue mode by giving the `-bR` option on the command line. The manpage says on this option: "Enter the hostile domain of giant mail messages, and RFC standard scrolls. Attempt to make it down to protocol level 26 and back." Although this option won't solve your problems, it may provide you some comfort and consolation.[3]

14.3.1 Compiling *smail*

If you know for sure that *smail* is lacking TCP network support, you have to get the source. It is probably included in your distribution, if you got it via CD-ROM, otherwise you may get it from the net via FTP.[4]

When compiling *smail*, you had best start with the set of configuration files from Vince Skahan's *newspak* distribution. To compile in the TCP networking driver, you have to set the *DRIVER_CONFIGURATION* macro in the *conf/EDITME* file to either *bsd-network* or *arpa-network*. The former is suitable for LAN installations, but the Internet requires *arpa-network*. The difference between these two is that the latter has a special driver for BIND service that is able to recognize MX records, which the former doesn't.

---

[3]Don't use this if you're in a really bad mood.

[4]If you bought this with a Linux distribution from a vendor, you are entitled to the source code "for a nominal shipping charge", according to *smail*'s copying conditions.

14.4   Mail Delivery Modes

As noted above, *smail* is able to deliver messages immediately, or queue them for later processing. If you choose to queue messages, *smail* will store away all mail in the *messages* directory below */var/spool/smail*. It will not process them until explicitly told so (this is also called "running the queue").

You can select one of three delivery modes by setting the *delivery_mode* attribute in the *config* file to either of *foreground*, *background*, or *queued*. These select delivery in the foreground (immediate processing of incoming messages), in the background, (message is delivered by a child of the receiving process, with the parent process exiting immediately after forking), and queued. Incoming mail will always be queued regardless of this option if the boolean variable *queue_only* is set in the *config* file.

If you turn on queuing, you have to make sure the queues are checked regularly; probably every 10 or 15 minutes. If you run *smail* in daemon mode, you have to add the option `-q10m` on the command line to process the queue every 10 minutes. Alternatively, you can invoke *runq* from *cron* at these intervals. *runq* should be a link to *smail*.

You can display the current mail queue by invoking *smail* with the `-bp` option. Equivalently, you can make *mailq* a link to *smail*, and invoke *mailq*:

```
$ mailq -v
m0pvB1r-00023UB From: root  (in /var/spool/smail/input)
                Date: Sun, 24 Apr 94 07:12 MET DST
                Args: -oem -oMP sendmail root@vstout.vbrew.com
 Log of transactions:
  Xdefer: <root@vstout.vbrew.com> reason: (ERR_148) transport smtp:
  connect: Connection refused
```

This shows a single message sitting in the message queue. The transaction log (which is only displayed if you give *mailq* the `-v` option) may give an additional reason why it is still waiting for delivery. If no attempt has been made yet to deliver the message, no transaction log will be displayed.

Even when you don't use queuing, *smail* will occasionally put messages into the queue when it finds immediate delivery fails for a transient reason. For SMTP connections, this may be an unreachable host; but messages may also be deferred when the file system is found to be full. You should therefore put in a queue run every hour or so (using *runq*), else any deferred message will stick around the queue forever.

14.5   Miscellaneous *config* Options

There are quite a number of options you may set in the *config* file, which, although useful, are not essential to running *smail*, and which we will not discuss here. Instead, we will only mention a few that you might find a reason to use:

error_copy_postmaster
 If this boolean variable is set, any error will generate a message to the postmaster. Usually, this is only done for errors that are due to a faulty configuration. The variable can be turned on by putting it in the *config* file, preceded by a plus (+).

max_hop_count   If the hop count for a message (i.e. the number of hosts already traversed) equals or exceeds this number, attempts at remote delivery will result in an error message being returned to the sender. This is used to prevent messages from looping forever. The hop count is generally computed from the number of *Received:* fields in the mail header, but may also be set manually using the `-h` option on the command line.

 This variable defaults to 20.

postmaster   The postmaster's address. If the address **Postmaster** cannot be resolved to a valid local address, then this is used as the last resort. The default is **root**.

14.6   Message Routing and Delivery

smail splits up mail delivery into three different tasks, the router, director, and transport module.

The router module resolves all remote addresses, determining to which host the message should be sent to next, and which transport must be used. Depending on the nature of the link, different transports such as UUCP or SMTP may be used.

Local addresses are given to the director task which resolves any forwarding or aliasing. For example, the address might be an alias or a mailing list, or the user might want to forward her mail to another address. If the resulting address is remote, it is handed to the router module for additional routing, otherwise it is assigned a transport for local delivery. By far the most common case will be delivery to a mailbox, but messages may also be piped into a command, or appended to some arbitrary file.

The transport module, finally, is responsible for whatever method of delivery has been chosen. It tries to deliver the message, and in case of failure either generates a bounce message, or defers it for a later retry.

With *smail*, you have much freedom in configuring these tasks. For each of them, a number of drivers are available, from which you can choose those you need. You describe them to *smail* in a couple of files, namely *routers*, *directors*, and *transports*, located in */usr/lib/smail*. If these files do not exist, reasonable defaults are assumed that should be suitable for many sites that either use SMTP or UUCP for transport. If you want to change *smail*'s routing policy, or modify a transport, you should get the sample files from the *smail* source distribution,[5] copy the sample files to */usr/lib/smail*, and modify them according to your needs. Sample configuration files are also given in Appendix B.

14.7   Routing Messages

When given a message, *smail* first checks if the destination is the local host, or a remote site. If the target host address is one of the local hostnames configured in *config*, the message is handed to the director module. Otherwise, *smail* hands the destination address to a number of router drivers to find out which host to forward a message to. They can be described in the *routers* file; if this file does not exist, a set of default routers are used.

The destination host is passed to all routers in turn, and the one finding the most specific route is selected. Consider a message addressed to **joe@foo.bar.com**. Then, one router might know a default route for all hosts in the **bar.com** domain, while another one has information for **foo.bar.com** itself. Since the latter is more specific, it is chosen over the former. If there are two routers that provide a "best match", the one coming first in the *routers* file is chosen.

This router now specifies the transport to be used, for instance UUCP, and generates a new destination address. The new address is passed to the transport along with the host to forward the message to. In the above example, *smail* might find out that **foo.bar.com** is to be reached via UUCP using the path **ernie!bert**. It will then generate a new target of **bert!foo.bar.com!user**, and have the UUCP transport use this as the envelope address to be passed to **ernie**.

When using the default setup, the following routers are available:

- If the destination host address can be resolved using the *gethostbyname(3)* or *gethostbyaddr(3)* library call, the message will be delivered via SMTP. The only exception is if the address is found to refer to the local host, it is handed to the director module, too.

  smail also recognizes IP addresses written as dotted quad as a legal hostname, as long as they can be resolved through a *gethostbyaddr(3)* call. For example, **scrooge@[149.76.12.4]** would be a valid although highly unusual mail address for **scrooge** on **quark.physics.groucho.edu**.

  If your machine is on the Internet, these routers are not what you are looking for, because they do not support MX records. See below for what to do in this case.

- If */usr/lib/smail/paths*, the pathalias database, exists, *smail* will try to look up the target host (minus any trailing **.uucp**) in this file. Mail to an address matched by this router will be delivered using UUCP, using the path found in the database.

---

[5]The default configuration files can be found in *samples/generic* below the source directory.

- The host address (minus any trailing **.uucp**) will be compared to the output of the *uuname* command to check if the target host is in fact a UUCP neighbor. If this is the case, the message will be delivered using the UUCP transport.

- If the address has not been matched by any of the above routers, it will be delivered to the smart host. The path to the smart host as well as the transport to be used are set in the *config* file.

These defaults work for many simple setups, but fail if routing requirements get a little more complicated. If you are faced with any of the problems discussed below, you will have to install your own *routers* file to override the defaults. A sample *routers* file you might start with is given in appendix B. Some Linux distributions also come with a set of configuration files that are tailored to work around these difficulties.

Probably the worst problems arise when your host lives in a dual universe with both dialup IP and UUCP links. You will then have hostnames in your *hosts* file that you only talk occasionally to through your SLIP link, so *smail* will attempt to deliver any mail for these hosts via SMTP. This is usually not what you want, because even if the SLIP link is activated regularly, SMTP is much slower than sending the mail over UUCP. With the default setup, there's no way escaping *smail*.

You can avoid this problem by having *smail* check the *paths* file before querying the resolver, and put all hosts you want to force UUCP delivery to into the *paths* file. If you don't want to send any messages over SMTP *ever*, you can also comment out the resolver-based routers altogether.

Another problem is that the default setup doesn't provide for true Internet mail routing, because the resolver-based router does not evaluate MX records. To enable full support for Internet mail routing, comment out this router, and uncomment the one that used BIND instead. There are, however, *smail* binaries included in some Linux distributions that don't have BIND support compiled in. If you enable BIND, but get a message in the *paniclog* file saying "`router inet_hosts:  driver bind not found`", then you have to get the sources and recompile *smail* (see section 14.2 above).

Finally, it is not generally a good idea to use the *uuname* driver. For one, it will generate a configuration error when you don't have UUCP installed, because no *uuname* command will be found. The second is when you have more sites listed in your UUCP *Systems* file than you actually have mail links with. These may be sites you only exchange news with, or sites you occasionally download files from via anonymous UUCP, but have no traffic with otherwise.

To work around the first problem, you can substitute a shell script for *uuname* which does a simple *exit 0*. The more general solution is, however, to edit the *routers* file and remove this driver altogether.

14.7.1   The *paths* database

smail expects to find the pathalias database in the *paths* file below */usr/lib/smail*. This file is optional, so if you don't want to perform any pathalias routing at all, simply remove any existing *paths* file.

paths must be a sorted ASCII file that contains entries which map destination site names to UUCP bang paths. The file has to be sorted because *smail* uses a binary search for looking up a site. Comments are not allowed in this file, and the site name must be separated from the path using a TAB. Pathalias databases are discussed in somewhat greater detail in chapter 13.

If you generate this file by hand, you should make sure to include all legal names for a site. For example, if a site is known by both a plain UUCP name and a fully qualified domain name, you have to add an entry for each of them. The file can be sorted by piping it through the *sort(1)* command.

If your site is only a leaf site, however, then no *paths* file should be necessary at all: just set up the smart host attributes in your *config* file, and leave all routing to your mail feed.

14.8   Delivering Messages to Local Addresses

Most commonly, a local address is just a user's login name, in which case the message is delivered to her mailbox, */var/spool/mail/user*. Other cases include aliases and mailing list names, and mail forwarding by the user. In these cases, the local address expands to a new list of addresses, which may be either local or remote.

Apart from these "normal" addresses, *smail* can handle other types of local message destinations, like file names, and pipe commands. These are not addresses in their own right, so you can't send mail to, say, **/etc/passwd@vbrew.com**; they are only valid if they have been taken from forwarding or alias files.

A *file name* is anything that begins with a slash (/) or a tilde (~). The latter refers to the user's home directory, and is possible only if the filename was taken from a *.forward* file or a forwarding entry in the mailbox (see below). When delivering to a file, *smail* appends the messages to the file, creating it if necessary.

A *pipe command* may be any UNIX command preceded by the pipe symbol (|). This causes *smail* to hand the command to the shell along with its arguments, but without the leading '|'. The message itself is fed to this command on standard input.

For example, to gate a mailing list into a local newsgroup, you might use a shell script named *gateit*, and set up a local alias which delivers all messages from this mailing list to the script using *"—gateit"*.

If the invocation contains white space, it has to be enclosed in double quotes. Due to the security issues involved, care is taken not to execute the command if the address has been obtained in a somewhat dubious way (for example, if the alias file from which the address was taken was writable by everyone).

14.8.1   Local Users

The most common case for a local address is to denote a user's mailbox. This mailbox is located in */var/spool/mail* and has the name of the user. It is owned by her, with a group of **mail**, and has mode 660. If it does not exist, it is created by *smail*.

Note that although */var/spool/mail* is currently the standard place to put the mailbox files, some mail software may have different paths compiled in, for example */usr/spool/mail*. If delivery to users on your machine fails consistently, you should try if it helps to make this a symbolic link to */var/spool/mail*.

There are two addresses *smail* requires to exist: **MAILER-DAEMON** and **Postmaster**. When generating a bounce message for an undeliverable mail, a carbon copy is sent to the **postmaster** account for examination (in case this might be due to a configuration problem). The **MAILER-DAEMON** is used as the sender's address on the bounce message.

If these addresses do not name valid accounts on your system, *smail* implicitly maps **MAILER-DAEMON** to **postmaser**, and **postmaster** to **root**, respectively. You should usually override this by aliasing the **postmaster** account to whoever is responsible for maintaining the mail software.

14.8.2   Forwarding

A user may redirect her mail by having it forwarded to an alternative address using one of two methods supported by *smail*. One option is to put

```
Forward to recipient,...
```

in the first line of her mailbox file. This will send all incoming mail to the specified list of recipients. Alternatively, she might create a *.forward* file in her home directory, which contains the comma-separated list of recipients. With this variety of forwarding, all lines of the file are read and interpreted.

Note that any type of address may be used. Thus, a practical example of a *.forward* file for vacations might be

```
janet, "|vacation"
```

The first address delivers the incoming message to **janet**'s mailbox nevertheless, while the *vacation* command returns a short notification to the sender.

14.8.3   Alias Files

smail is able to handle alias files compatible with those known by Berkeley's *sendmail*. Entries in the alias file may have the form

>   *alias: recipients*

recipients is a comma-separated list of addresses that will be substituted for the alias. The recipient list may be continued across newlines if the next line begins with a TAB.

There is a special feature that allows *smail* to handle mailing lists from the alias file: if you specify ":`include:`*filename*" as recipient, *smail* will read the file specified, and substitute its contents as a list of recipients.

The main aliases file is */usr/lib/aliases*. If you choose to make this file world-writable, *smail* will not deliver any messages to shell commands given in this file. A sample file is shown below:

```
# vbrew.com /usr/lib/aliases file
hostmaster: janet
postmaster: janet
usenet: phil
# The development mailing list.
development: joe, sue, mark, biff
        /var/mail/log/development
owner-development: joe
# Announcements of general interest are mailed to all
# of the staff
announce: :include: /usr/lib/smail/staff,
        /var/mail/log/announce
owner-announce: root
# gate the foobar mailing list to a local newsgroup
ppp-list: "|/usr/local/lib/gateit local.lists.ppp"
```

If an error occurs while delivering to an address generated from the *aliases* file, *smail* will attempt to send a copy of the error message to the "alias owner". For example, if delivery to **biff** fails when delivering a message to the **development** mailing list, a copy of the error message will be mailed to the sender, as well as to **postmaster** and **owner-development**. If the owner address does not exist, no additional error message will be generated.

When delivering to files or when invoking programs given in the *aliases* file, *smail* will become the **nobody** user to avoid any security hassles. Especially when delivering to files, this can be a real nuisance. In the file given above, for instance, the log files must be owned and writable by **nobody**, or delivery to them will fail.

14.8.4   Mailing Lists

Instead of using the *aliases* file, mailing lists may also be managed by means of files in the */usr/lib/smail/lists* directory. A mailing list named *nag-bugs* is described by the file *lists/nag-bugs*, which should contain the members' addresses, separated by commas. The list may be given on multiple lines, with comments being introduced by a hash sign.

For each mailing list, a user (or alias) named **owner-**_listname_ should exist; any errors occurring when resolving an address are reported to this user. This address is also used as the sender's address on all outgoing messages in the `Sender:` header field.

14.9   UUCP-based Transports

There are a number of transports compiled into *smail* that utilize the UUCP suite. In a UUCP environment, messages are usually passed on by invoking *rmail* on the next host, giving it the message on standard input and the envelope address on the command line. On your host, *rmail* should be a link to the *smail* command.

When handing a message to the UUCP transport, *smail* converts the target address to a UUCP bang path. For example, **user@host** will be transformed to **host!user**. Any occurrence of the '%' address operator is preserved, so **user%host@gateway** will become **gateway!user%host**. However, *smail* will never generate such addresses itself.

Alternatively, *smail* can send and receive BSMTP batches via UUCP. With BSMTP, one or more messages are wrapped up in a single batch that contains the commands the local mailer would issue if a real SMTP connection had be established. BSMTP is frequently used in store-and-forward (e.g. UUCP-based) networks to save disk space. The sample *transports* file in appendix B contains a transport dubbed *bsmtp* that generates partial BSMTP batches in a queue directory. They must be combined into the final batches later, using a shell script that adds the appropriate *HELO* and *QUIT* command.

To enable the *bsmtp* transport for specific UUCP links you have to use so-called *method* files (please refer to the *smail(5)* manual page for details). If you have only one UUCP link, and use the smart host router, you enable sending SMTP batches by setting the *smart_transport* configuration variable to *bsmtp* instead of *uux*.

To receive SMTP batches over UUCP, you must make sure that you have the unbatching command the remote site sends its batches to. If the remote site uses *smail*, too, you need to make *rsmtp* a link to *smail*. If the remote site runs *sendmail*, you should additionally install a shell script named */usr/bin/bsmtp* that does a simple "*exec rsmtp*" (a symbolic link won't work).

14.10 SMTP-based Transports

smail currently supports an SMTP driver to deliver mail over TCP connections.[6] It is capable of delivering a message to any number of addresses on one single host, with the hostname being specified as either a fully qualified domain name that can be resolved by the networking software, or in dotted quad notation enclosed in square brackets. Generally, addresses resolved by any of the BIND, *gethostbyname(3)*, or *gethostbyaddr(3)* router drivers will be delivered to the SMTP transport.

The SMTP driver will attempt to connect to the remote host immediately through the *smtp* port as listed in */etc/services*. If it cannot be reached, or the connection times out, delivery will be reattempted at a later time.

Delivery on the Internet requires that routes to the destination host be specified in the *route-addr* format described in chapter 13, rather than as a bang path.[7] *smail* will therefore transform **user%host@gateway**, where **gateway** is reached via **host1!host2!host3**, into the source-route address **¡@host2,@host3:user%host@gateway¿**, which will be sent as the message's envelope address to **host1**. To enable these transformation (along with the built-in BIND driver), you have to edit the entry for the *smtp* driver in the *transports* file. A sample *transports* file is given in Appendix B.

14.11 Hostname Qualification

Sometimes it is desirable to catch unqualified hostnames (i.e. those that don't have a domain name) specified in sender or recipient addresses, for example when gatewaying between two networks, where one requires fully qualified domain names. On an Internet-UUCP relay, unqualifed hostnames should be mapped to the **uucp** domain by default. Other address modifications than these are questionable.

The */usr/lib/smail/qualify* file tells *smail* which domain names to tack onto which hostnames. Entries in the *qualify* file consists of a hostname beginning in column one, followed by domain name. Lines containing a hash sign as its first non-white character are considered comments. Entries are searched in the order they appear in.

If no *qualify* file exists, no hostname qualification is performed at all.

A special hostname of * matches any hostnames, thus enabling you to map all hosts not mentioned before into a default domain. It should be used only as the last entry.

At the Virtual Brewery, all hosts have been set up to use fully qualified domain names in the sender's addresses. Unqualified recipient addresses are considered to be in the **uucp** domain, so only a single entry in the *qualify* file is needed.

```
# /usr/lib/smail/qualify, last changed Feb 12, 1994 by janet
```

---

[6]The authors call this support "simple". For a future version of *smail*, they advertise a complete backend which will handle this more efficiently.

[7]However, the use of routes in the Internet is discouraged altogether. Fully qualified domain names should be used instead.

```
#
*          uucp
```

Chapter 15

Sendmail+IDA

15.1 Introduction to Sendmail+IDA

It's been said that you aren't a *real* Unix system administrator until you've edited a *sendmail.cf* file. It's also been said that you're crazy if you've attempted to do so twice:-)

Sendmail is an incredibly powerful program. It's also incredibly difficult to learn and understand for most people. Any program whose definitive reference (*Sendmail*, published by O'Reilly and Associates) is 792 pages long quite justifiably scares most people off.

Sendmail+IDA is different. It removes the need to edit the always cryptic *sendmail.cf* file and allows the administrator to define the site-specific routing and addressing configuration through relatively easy to understand support files called *tables*. Switching to sendmail+IDA can save you many hours of work and stress.

Compared to the other major mail transport agents, there is probably nothing that can't be done faster and simpler with sendmail+IDA. Typical things that are needed to run a normal UUCP or Internet site become simple to accomplish. Configurations that normally are extremely difficult are simple to create and maintain.

At this writing, the current version of *sendmail5.67b+IDA1.5* is available via anonymous FTP from **vixen.cso.uiuc.edu**. It compiles without any patching required under Linux.

All the configuration files required to get sendmail+IDA sources to compile, install, and run under Linux are included in *newspak-2.2.tar.gz* which is available via anonymous FTP on **sunsite.unc.edu** in the directory */pub/Linux/system/Mail*.

15.2 Configuration Files — Overview

Traditional sendmail is set up through a system configuration file (typically */etc/sendmail.cf* or */usr/lib/sendmail.cf*), that is not anything close to any language you've seen before. Editing the *sendmail.cf* file to provide customized behavior can be a humbling experience.

Sendmail+IDA makes such pain essentially a thing of the past by having all configuration options table-driven with rather easy to understand syntax. These options are configured by running *m4* (a macro processor) or *dbm* (a database processor) on a number of data files via Makefiles supplied with the sources.

The *sendmail.cf* file defines only the default behavior of the system. Virtually all special customization is done through a number of optional tables rather than by directly editing the *sendmail.cf* file. A list of all *sendmail* tables is given in figure 15.1.

mailertable	defines special behavior for remote hosts or domains.
uucpxtable	forces UUCP delivery of mail to hosts that are in DNS format.
pathtable	defines UUCP bang-paths to remote hosts or domains.
uucprelays	short-circuits the pathalias path to well-known remote hosts.
genericfrom	converts internal addresses into generic ones visible to the outside world.
xaliases	converts generic addresses to/from valid internal ones.
decnetxtable	converts RFC-822 addresses to DECnet-style addresses.

Figure 15.1: *sendmail* Support Files.

15.3   The *sendmail.cf* File

The *sendmail.cf* file for sendmail+IDA is not edited directly, but is generated from an *m4* configuration file provided by the local system administrator. In the following, we will refer to it as *sendmail.m4*.

This file contains a few definitions and otherwise merely points to the tables where the real work gets done. In general, it is only necessary to specify:

- the pathnames and filenames used on the local system.
- the name(s) the site is known by for e-mail purposes.
- which default mailer (and perhaps smart relay host) is desired.

There are a large variety of parameters that can be defined to establish the behavior of the local site or to override compiled-in configuration items. These configuration options are identified in the file *ida/cf/OPTIONS* in the source directory.

A *sendmail.m4* file for a minimal configuration (UUCP or SMTP with all non-local mail being relayed to a directly connected smart-host) can be as short as 10 or 15 lines excluding comments.

15.3.1   An Example *sendmail.m4* File

A *sendmail.m4* file for **vstout** at the Virtual Brewery is shown below. **vstout** uses SMTP to talk to all hosts on the Brewery's LAN, and sends all mail for other destinations to **moria**, its Internet relay host, via UUCP.

15.3.2   Typically Used *sendmail.m4* Parameters

A few or the items in the *sendmail.m4* file are required all the time; others can be ignored if you can get away with defaults. The following sections describe each of the items in the example *sendmail.m4* file in more detail.

Items that Define Paths

```
dnl #define(LIBDIR,/usr/local/lib/mail)dnl   # where all support files go
```

LIBDIR defines the directory where sendmail+IDA expects to find configuration files, the various dbm tables, and special local definitions. In a typical binary distribution, this is compiled into the sendmail binary and does not need to be explicitly set in the sendmail.m4 file.

The above example has a leading *dnl* which means that this line is essentially a comment for information only.

To change the location of the support files to a different location, remove the leading *dnl* from the above line, set the path to the desired location, and rebuild and reinstall the *sendmail.cf* file.

```
dnl #----------------- SAMPLE SENDMAIL.M4 FILE -----------------
dnl # (the string 'dnl' is the m4 equivalent of commenting out a line)
dnl # you generally don't want to override LIBDIR from the compiled in paths
dnl #define(LIBDIR,/usr/local/lib/mail)dnl       # where all support files go
define(LOCAL_MAILER_DEF, mailers.linux)dnl       # mailer for local delivery
define(POSTMASTERBOUNCE)dnl                      # postmaster gets bounces
define(PSEUDODOMAINS, BITNET UUCP)dnl            # don't try DNS on these
dnl #----------------------------------------------------------
dnl #
define(PSEUDONYMS, vstout.vbrew.com  vstout.UUCP vbrew.com)
dnl                                              # names we're known by
define(DEFAULT_HOST, vstout.vbrew.com)dnl        # our primary 'name' for mail
define(UUCPNAME, vstout)dnl                      # our uucp name
dnl #
dnl #----------------------------------------------------------
dnl #
define(UUCPNODES, |uuname|sort|uniq)dnl          # our uucp neighbors
define(BANGIMPLIESUUCP)dnl                       # make certain that uucp
define(BANGONLYUUCP)dnl                          #  mail is treated correctly
define(RELAY_HOST, moria)dnl                     # our smart relay host
define(RELAY_MAILER, UUCP-A)dnl                  # we reach moria via uucp
dnl #
dnl #-----------------------------------------------------------
dnl #
dnl # the various dbm lookup tables
dnl #
define(ALIASES, LIBDIR/aliases)dnl               # system aliases
define(DOMAINTABLE, LIBDIR/domaintable)dnl       # domainize hosts
define(PATHTABLE, LIBDIR/pathtable)dnl           # paths database
define(GENERICFROM, LIBDIR/generics)dnl          # generic from addresses
define(MAILERTABLE, LIBDIR/mailertable)dnl       # mailers per host or domain
define(UUCPXTABLE, LIBDIR/uucpxtable)dnl         # paths to hosts we feed
define(UUCPRELAYS, LIBDIR/uucprelays)dnl         # short-circuit paths
dnl #
dnl #------------------------------------------------------------
dnl #
dnl # include the 'real' code that makes it all work
dnl # (provided with the source code)
dnl #
include(Sendmail.mc)dnl                          # REQUIRED ENTRY !!!
dnl #
dnl #----------- END OF SAMPLE SENDMAIL.M4 FILE -------
```

Figure 15.2: A sample *sendmail.m4* file for **vstout**.

Defining the Local Mailer

```
define(LOCAL_MAILER_DEF, mailers.linux)dnl   # mailer for local delivery
```

Most operating systems provide a program to handle local delivery of mail. Typical programs for many of the major variants of Unix are already built into the sendmail binary.

In Linux, it is necessary to explicitly define the appropriate local mailer since a local delivery program is not necessarily present in the distribution you've installed. This is done by specifying *LOCAL_MAILER_DEF* in the *sendmail.m4* file.

For example, to have the commonly used *deliver* program[1] provide this service, you would set *LOCAL_MAILER_DEF* to *mailers.linux*.

The following file should then be installed as *mailers.linux* in the directory pointed to by *LIBDIR*. It explicitly defines the *deliver* program in the internal *Mlocal* mailer with the proper parameters to result in *sendmail* correctly delivering mail targeted for the local system. Unless you are a sendmail expert, you probably do not want to alter the following example.

```
# -- /usr/local/lib/mail/mailers.linux --
#     (local mailers for use on Linux )
Mlocal, P=/usr/bin/deliver, F=SlsmFDMP, S=10, R=25/10, A=deliver $u
Mprog,  P=/bin/sh,          F=lsDFMeuP,  S=10, R=10,    A=sh -c $u
```

There is a also built-in default for *deliver* in the *Sendmail.mc* file that gets included into the *sendmail.cf* file. To specify it, you would not use the mailers.linux file and would instead define the following in your *sendmail.m4* file:

```
dnl --- (in sendmail.m4) ---
define(LOCAL_MAILER_DEF, DELIVER)dnl       # mailer for local delivery
```

Unfortunately, *Sendmail.mc* assumes deliver is installed in */bin*, which is not the case with Slackware1.1.1 (which installs it in */usr/bin*). In that case you'd need to either fake it with a link or rebuild deliver from sources so that it resides in */bin*.

Dealing with Bounced Mail

```
define(POSTMASTERBOUNCE)dnl                    # postmaster gets bounces
```

Many sites find that it is important to ensure that mail is sent and received with close to a 100% success rate. While examining *syslogd(8)* logs is helpful, the local mail administrator generally needs to see the headers on bounced mail in order to determine if the mail was undeliverable because of user error or a configuration error on one of the systems involved.

Defining *POSTMASTERBOUNCE* results in a copy of each bounced message being set to the person defined as **Postmaster** for the system.

Unfortunately, setting this parameter also results in the *text* of the message being sent to the Postmaster, which potentially has related privacy concerns for people using mail on the system.

Site postmasters should in general attempt to discipline themselves (or do so via technical means through shell scripts that delete the text of the bounce messages they receive) from reading mail not addressed to them.

Domain Name Service Related Items

```
define(PSEUDODOMAINS, BITNET UUCP)dnl       # don't try DNS on these
```

There are several well known networks that are commonly referenced in mail addresses for historical reasons but that are not valid for DNS purposes. Defining *PSEUDODOMAINS* prevents needless DNS lookup attempts that will always fail.

---

[1] *deliver* was written by Chip Salzenberg (**chip%tct@ateng.com**). It is part of several Linux distributions and can be found in the usual anonymous FTP archives such as **ftp.uu.net**.

Defining Names the Local System is Known by

```
define(PSEUDONYMS, vstout.vbrew.com  vstout.UUCP vbrew.com)
dnl                                    # names we're known by
define(DEFAULT_HOST, vstout.vbrew.com)dnl  # our primary 'name' for mail
```

Frequently, systems wish to hide their true identity, serve as mail gateways, or receive and process mail addressed to 'old' names by which they used to be known.

PSEUDONYMS specifies the list of all hostnames for which the local system will accept mail.

DEFAULT_HOST specifies the hostname that will appear in messages originating on the local host. It is important that this parameter be set to a valid value or all return mail will be undeliverable.

UUCP-Related Items

```
define(UUCPNAME, vstout)dnl              # our uucp name
define(UUCPNODES, |uuname|sort|uniq)dnl  # our uucp neighbors
define(BANGIMPLIESUUCP)dnl               # make certain that uucp
define(BANGONLYUUCP)dnl                  #  mail is treated correctly
```

Frequently, systems are known by one name for DNS purposes and another for UUCP purposes. *UUCP-NAME* permits you to define a different hostname that appears in the headers of outgoing UUCP mail.

UUCPNODES defines the commands that return a list of hostnames for the systems we are connected directly to via UUCP connections.

BANGIMPLIESUUCP and *BANGONLYUUCP* ensure that mail addressed with UUCP 'bang' syntax is treated according to UUCP behavior rather than the more current Domain Name Service behavior used today on Internet.

Relay Systems and Mailers

```
define(RELAY_HOST, moria)dnl     # our smart relay host
define(RELAY_MAILER, UUCP-A)dnl  # we reach moria via UUCP
```

Many system administrators do not want to be bothered with the work needed to ensure that their system is able to reach all the networks (and therefore systems) on all networks worldwide. Instead of doing so, they would rather relay all outgoing mail to another system that is known to be indeed "smart".

RELAY_HOST defines the UUCP hostname of such a smart neighboring system.

RELAY_MAILER defines the mailer used to relay the messages there.

It is important to note that setting these parameters results in your outgoing mail being forwarded to this remote system, which will affect the load of their system. Be certain to get explicit agreement from the remote Postmaster before you configure your system to use another system as a general purpose relay host.

The Various Configuration Tables

```
define(ALIASES, LIBDIR/aliases)dnl          # system aliases
define(DOMAINTABLE, LIBDIR/domaintable)dnl  # domainize hosts
define(PATHTABLE, LIBDIR/pathtable)dnl      # paths database
define(GENERICFROM, LIBDIR/generics)dnl     # generic from addresses
define(MAILERTABLE, LIBDIR/mailertable)dnl  # mailers per host or domain
define(UUCPXTABLE, LIBDIR/uucpxtable)dnl    # paths to hosts we feed
define(UUCPRELAYS, LIBDIR/uucprelays)dnl    # short-circuit paths
```

With these macros, you can change the location where sendmail+IDA looks for the various dbm tables that define the system's "real" behavior. It is generally wise to leave them in *LIBDIR*.

The Master *Sendmail.mc* **File**

```
include(Sendmail.mc)dnl                          # REQUIRED ENTRY !!!
```

The authors of sendmail+IDA provide the *Sendmail.mc* file which contains the true "guts" of what becomes the sendmail.cf file. Periodically, new versions are released to fix bugs or add functionality without requiring a full release and recompilation of sendmail from sources.

It is important *not* to edit this file.

So Which Entries are Really Required?

When not using any of the optional dbm tables, sendmail+IDA delivers mail via the *DEFAULT_MAILER* (and possibly *RELAY_HOST* and *RELAY_MAILER*) defined in the *sendmail.m4* file used to generate *sendmail.cf*. It is easily possible to override this behavior through entries in the *domaintable* or *uucpxtable*.

A generic site that is on Internet and speaks Domain Name Service, or one that is UUCP-only and forwards all mail via UUCP through a smart *RELAY_HOST*, probably does not need any specific table entries at all.

Virtually all systems should set the *DEFAULT_HOST* and *PSEUDONYMS* macros, which define the canonical site name and aliases it is known by, and *DEFAULT_MAILER*. If all you have is a relay host and relay mailer, you don't need to set these defaults since it works automagically.

UUCP hosts will probably also need to set *UUCPNAME* to their official UUCP name. They will also probably set *RELAY_MAILER*, and *RELAY_HOST* which enable smart-host routing through a mail relay. The mail transport to be used is defined in *RELAY_MAILER* and should usually be *UUCP-A* for UUCP sites.

If your site is SMTP-only and talks 'Domain Name Service', you would change the *DEFAULT_MAILER* to *TCP-A* and probably delete the *RELAY_MAILER* and *RELAY_HOST* lines.

15.4   A Tour of Sendmail+IDA Tables

Sendmail+IDA provides a number of tables that allow you to override the default behavior of sendmail (specified in the *sendmail.m4* file) and define special behavior for unique situations, remote systems, and networks. These tables are post-processed with *dbm* using the Makefile provided with the distribution.

Most sites will need few, if any, of these tables. If your site does not require these tables, the easiest thing is probably to make them zero length files (with the *touch* command) and use the default Makefile in *LIBDIR* rather than editing the Makefile itself.

15.4.1   *mailertable*

The *mailertable* defines special treatment for specific hosts or domains based on the remote host or network name. It is frequently used on Internet sites to select an intermediate mail relay host or gateway to reach a remote network through, and to specify a particular protocol (UUCP or SMTP) to be used. UUCP sites will generally not need to use this file.

Order is important. Sendmail reads the file top-down and processes the message according to the first rule it matches. So it is generally wise to place the most explicit rules at the top of the file and the more generic rules below.

Suppose you want to forward all mail for the Computer Science department at Groucho Marx University via UUCP to a relay host **ada**. To do so, you would have a *mailertable* entry that looked like the following:

```
# (in mailertable)
#
# forward all mail for the domain .cs.groucho.edu via UUCP to ada
UUCP-A,ada          .cs.groucho.edu
```

Suppose you want all mail to the larger **groucho.edu** domain to go to a different relayhost **bighub** for address resolution and delivery. The expanded mailertable entries would look quite similar.

```
# (in mailertable)
#
# forward all mail for the domain cs.groucho.edu via UUCP to ada
UUCP-A,ada        .cs.groucho.edu
#
# forward all mail for the domain groucho.edu via UUCP to bighub
UUCP-A,bighub     .groucho.edu
```

As mentioned above, order is important. Reversing the order of the two rules shown above will result in all mail to **.cs.groucho.edu** going through the more generic **bighub** path instead of the explicit **ada** path that is really desired.

```
# (in mailertable)
#
# forward all mail for the domain .groucho.edu via UUCP to bighub
UUCP-A,bighub     .groucho.edu
#
# (it is impossible to reach the next line because
#    the rule above will be matched first)
UUCP-A,ada        .cs.groucho.edu
#
```

In the mailertable examples above, the *UUCP-A* mailer makes *sendmail* use UUCP delivery with domainized headers.

The comma between the mailer and remote system tells it to forward the message to **ada** for address resolution and delivery.

Mailertable entries are of the format:

mailer delimiter relayhost   *host_or_domain*

There are a number of possible mailers. The differences are generally in how they treat addresses. Typical mailers are *TCP-A* (TCP/IP with Internet-style addresses), *TCP-U* (TCP/IP with UUCP-style addresses), and *UUCP-A* (UUCP with Internet-style addresses).

The character that separates the mailer from the host portion on the left-hand-side of a mailertable line defines how the address is modified by the mailertable. The important thing to realize is that this only rewrites the envelope (to get the mail into the remote system). Rewriting anything other than the envelope is generally frowned upon due to the high probability of breaking the mail configuration.

!   An exclamation point strips off the recipient hostname before forwarding to the mailer. This can be used when you want to wish to essentially force mail into a misconfigured remote site.

,   A comma does not change the address in any way. The message is merely forwarded via the specified mailer to the specified relay host.

:   A colon removes the recipient hostname only if there are intermediate hosts between you and the destination. Thus, **foo!bar!joe** will have **foo** removed, while **xyzzy!janet** will remain unchanged.

15.4.2 *uucpxtable*

Usually, mail to hosts with fully-qualified domain names is delivered via Internet style (SMTP) delivery using Domain Name Service (DNS), or via the relay host. The *uucpxtable* forces delivery via UUCP routing by converting the domainized name into a UUCP-style un-domainized remote hostname.

It is frequently used when you're a mail forwarder for a site or domain or when you wish to send mail via a direct and reliable UUCP link rather than potentially multiple hops through the default mailer and any intermediate systems and networks.

UUCP sites that talk to UUCP neighbors who use domainized mail headers would use this file to force delivery of the mail through the direct UUCP point-to-point link between the two systems rather than using the less direct route through the *RELAY_MAILER* and *RELAY_HOST* or through the *DEFAULT_MAILER*.

Internet sites who do not talk UUCP probably would not use the *uucpxtable*.

Suppose you provide mail forwarding service to a system called **sesame.com** in DNS and **sesame** in the UUCP maps. You would need the following *uucpxtable* entry to force mail for their host to go through your direct UUCP connection.

```
#============== /usr/local/lib/mail/uucpxtable ============
# Mail sent to joe@sesame.com is rewritten to sesame!joe and
# therefore delivered via UUCP
#
sesame      sesame.com
#
#-----------------------------------------------------------
```

15.4.3 *pathtable*

The *pathtable* is used to define explicit routing to remote hosts or networks. The *pathtable* file should be in pathalias-style syntax, sorted alphabetically. The two fields on each line must be separated by a real TAB, else *dbm* might complain.

Most systems will not need any *pathtable* entries.

```
#=============== /usr/local/lib/mail/pathtable ================
#
# this is a pathalias-style paths file to let you kick mail to
# UUCP neighbors to the direct UUCP path so you don't have to
# go the long way through your smart host that takes other traffic
#
# you want real tabs on each line or m4 might complain
#
# route mail through one or more intermediate sites to a remote
# system using UUCP-style addressing.
#
sesame!ernie!%s          ernie
#
# forwarding to a system that is a UUCP neighbor of a reachable
# internet site.
#
swim!%s@gcc.groucho.edu    swim
#
# The following sends all mail for two networks through different
# gateways (see the leading '.' ?).
# In this example, "uugate" and "byte" are specific systems that serve
# as mail gateways to the .UUCP and .BITNET pseudo-domains respectively
#
%s@uugate.groucho.edu        .UUCP
byte!%s@mail.shift.com       .BITNET
#
#=================== end of pathtable =====================
```

15.4.4 *domaintable*

The *domaintable* is generally used to force certain behavior after a DNS lookup has occurred. It permits the administrator to make shorthand names available for commonly referenced systems or domains by replacing the shorthand name with the proper one automatically. It can also be used to replace incorrect host or domain names with the "correct" information.

Most sites will not need any *domaintable* entries.

The following example shows how to replace an incorrect address people are attempting to mail to with the correct address:

```
#============= /usr/local/lib/mail/domaintable =================
#
#
brokenhost.correct.domain          brokenhost.wrong.domain
#
#
#================== end of domaintable ========================
```

15.4.5 *aliases*

Aliases permit a number of things to happen:

- They provide a shorthand or well-known name for mail to be addressed to in order to go to one or more persons.

- They invoke a program with the mail message as the input to the program.

- They send mail to a file.

All systems require aliases for **Postmaster** and **MAILER-DAEMON** to be RFC-compliant.

Always be extremely aware of security when defining aliases that invoke programs or write to programs since sendmail generally runs setuid-root.

Changes to the *aliases* file do not take effect until the command

```
# /usr/lib/sendmail -bi
```

is executed to build the required dbm tables. This can also be done by executing the *newaliases* command, usually from cron.

Details concerning mail aliases may be found in the *aliases(5)* manual page.

```
#-------------------- /usr/local/lib/mail/aliases ------------------
#
# demonstrate commonly seen types of aliases
#
usenet:        janet                   # alias for a person
admin:         joe,janet               # alias for several people
newspak-users: :include:/usr/lib/lists/newspak
                                       # read recipients from a file
changefeed:    | /usr/local/lib/gup    # alias that invokes a program
complaints:    /var/log/complaints     # alias that writes mail to a file
#
# The following two aliases must be present to be RFC-compliant.
# It is important to have them resolve to 'a person' who reads mail routinely.
#
postmaster:    root                    # required entry
MAILER-DAEMON: postmaster              # required entry
#
#----------------------------------------------------------------
```

15.4.6 Rarely Used Tables

The following tables are available, but rather infrequently used. Consult with the documentation that comes with the sendmail+IDA sources for details.

uucprelays   The *uucprelays* file is used to "short-circuit" the UUCP path to especially well known sites rather than using a multi-hop or unreliable path generated by processing the UUCP maps with *pathalias*.

genericfrom and *xaliases*

The *genericfrom* file hides local usernames and addresses from the outside world by automatically converting local usernames to generic sender addresses that do not match internal usernames.

The associated *xalparse* utility automates the generation of the genericfrom and aliases file so that both incoming and outgoing username translations occur from a master xaliases file.

decnetxtable   The *decnetxtable* rewrites domainized addresses into decnet-style addresses much like the domaintable can be used to rewrite undomainized addresses into domainized SMTP-style addresses.

15.5   Installing *sendmail*

In this section, we'll take a look at how to install a typical binary distribution of sendmail+IDA, and walk through what needs to be done to make it localized and functional.

The current binary distribution of sendmail+IDA for Linux can be gotten from **sunsite.unc.edu** in */pub/Linux/system/Mail*. Even if you have an earlier version of *sendmail* I strongly recommend you go to the *sendmail5.67b+IDA1.5* version since all required Linux-specific patches are now in the vanilla sources and several significant security holes have been plugged that were in versions prior to about December 1, 1993.

If you are building *sendmail* from the sources, you should follow the instructions in the *README*s included in the source distribution. The current sendmail+IDA source is available from **vixen.cso.uiuc.edu**. To build sendmail+IDA on Linux, you also need the Linux-specific configuration files from *newspak-2.2.tar.gz*, which is available on **sunsite.unc.edu** in the */pub/Linux/system/Mail* directory.

If you have previously installed *smail* or another mail delivery agent, you'll probably want to remove (or rename) all the files from smail to be safe.

15.5.1   Extracting the binary distribution

First, you have to unpack the archive file in some safe location:

```
$ gunzip -c sendmail5.65b+IDA1.5+mailx5.3b.tgz | tar xvf -
```

If you have a "modern" *tar*, for example from a recent Slackware Distribution, you can probably just do a `tar -zxvf` *filename*`.tgz` and get the same results.

Unpacking the archive creates a directory named *sendmail5.65b+IDA1.5+mailx5.3b*. In this directory, you find a complete installation of sendmail+IDA plus a binary of the *mailx* user agent. All file paths below this directory reflect the location where the files should be installed, so it's safe to work up a *tar* command to move 'em over:

```
# cd sendmail5.65b+IDA1.5+mailx5.3b
# tar cf - . | (cd /; tar xvvpoof -)
```

15.5.2   Building *sendmail.cf*

To build a *sendmail.cf* file customized for your site, you have to write a *sendmail.m4* file, and process it with m4. In */usr/local/lib/mail/CF*, you find a sample file called *sample.m4*. Copy it to *yourhostname.m4*, and edit it to reflect the situation of your site.

The sample file is set up for a UUCP-only site that has domainized headers and talks to a smart host. Sites like this only need to edit a few items.

In the current section, I will only give a short overview of the macros you have to change. For a complete description of what they do, please refer to the earlier discussion of the *sendmail.m4*.

LOCAL_MAILER_DEF
>Define define the file that defines the mailers for local mail delivery. See section "Defining the Local Mailer" above for what goes in here.

PSEUDONYMS
>Define all the names your local host is known by.

DEFAULT_HOST
>Put in your fully qualified domain name. This name will appear as your hostname in all outgoing mail.

UUCPNAME Put in your unqualified hostname.

RELAY_HOST and *RELAY_MAILER*
>If you talk UUCP to a smart-host, set *RELAY_HOST* to the UUCP name of your 'smart relay' uucp neighbor. Use the UUCP-A mailer if you want domainized headers.

DEFAULT_MAILER
>If you are on Internet and talk DNS, you should set this to *TCP-A*. This tells sendmail to use the *TCP-A* mailer, which delivers mail via SMTP using normal RFC style addressing for the envelope. Internet sites probably do not need to define *RELAY_HOST* or *RELAY_MAILER*.

To create the *sendmail.cf* file, execute the command

```
# make yourhostname.cf
```

This processes the *yourhostname.m4* file and creates *yourhostname.cf* from it.

Next, you should test whether the configuration file you've created does what you expect it to do. This is explained in the following two sections.

Once you're happy with its behavior, copy it into place with the command:

```
# cp yourhostname.cf /etc/sendmail.cf
```

At this point, your sendmail system is ready for action. Put the following line in the appropriate startup file (generally */etc/rc.inet2*). You can also execute it by hand to have the process start up now.

```
# /usr/lib/sendmail -bd -q1h
```

15.5.3 Testing the *sendmail.cf* file

To put sendmail into 'test' mode, you invoke it with the **-bt** flag. The default configuration file is the sendmail.cf file that is installed on the system. You can test an alternate file by using the **-C***filename* option.

In the following examples, we test *vstout.cf*, the configuration file generated from the *vstout.m4* file shown in figure 15.2.

```
# /usr/lib/sendmail -bt -Cvstout.cf
ADDRESS TEST MODE
Enter <ruleset> <address>
[Note: No initial ruleset 3 call]
>
```

The following tests ensure that *sendmail* is able to deliver all mail to users on your system. In all cases the result of the test should be the same and point to the local system name with the *LOCAL* mailer.

First test how a mail to a local user would be delivered.

```
# /usr/lib/sendmail -bt -Cvstout.cf
ADDRESS TEST MODE
Enter <ruleset> <address>
[Note: No initial ruleset 3 call]
> 3,0 me
rewrite: ruleset  3   input: me
rewrite: ruleset  7   input: me
rewrite: ruleset  9   input: me
rewrite: ruleset  9 returns: < me >
rewrite: ruleset  7 returns: < > , me
rewrite: ruleset  3 returns: < > , me
rewrite: ruleset  0   input: < > , me
rewrite: ruleset  8   input: < > , me
rewrite: ruleset 20   input: < > , me
rewrite: ruleset 20 returns: < > , @ vstout . vbrew . com , me
rewrite: ruleset  8 returns: < > , @ vstout . vbrew . com , me
rewrite: ruleset 26   input: < > , @ vstout . vbrew . com , me
rewrite: ruleset 26 returns: $# LOCAL $@ vstout . vbrew . com $: me
rewrite: ruleset  0 returns: $# LOCAL $@ vstout . vbrew . com $: me
```

The output shows how *sendmail* processes the address internally. It is handed to various rulesets which analyze it, invoke other rulesets in turn, and break it up into its components.

In our example, we passed the address **me** to rulesets 3 and 0 (this is the meaning of the 3,0 entered before the address). The last line shows the parsed address as returned by ruleset 0, containing the mailer the message would be delivered by, and the host and user name given to the mailer.

Next, test mail to a user on your system with UUCP syntax.

```
# /usr/lib/sendmail -bt -Cvstout.cf
ADDRESS TEST MODE
Enter <ruleset> <address>
[Note: No initial ruleset 3 call]
> 3,0 vstout!me
rewrite: ruleset  3   input: vstout ! me
[...]
rewrite: ruleset  0 returns: $# LOCAL $@ vstout . vbrew . com $: me
>
```

Next, test mail addressed to a user on your system with Internet syntax to your fully qualified hostname.

```
# /usr/lib/sendmail -bt -Cvstout.cf
ADDRESS TEST MODE
Enter <ruleset> <address>
[Note: No initial ruleset 3 call]
> 3,0 me@vstout.vbrew.com
rewrite: ruleset  3   input: me @ vstout . vbrew . com
[...]
rewrite: ruleset  0 returns: $# LOCAL $@ vstout . vbrew . com $: me
>
```

You should repeat the above two tests with each of the names you specified in the *PSEUDONYMS* and *DEFAULT_NAME* parameters in your *sendmail.m4* file.

Lastly, test that you can mail to your relay host.

```
# /usr/lib/sendmail -bt -Cvstout.cf
ADDRESS TEST MODE
Enter <ruleset> <address>
[Note: No initial ruleset 3 call]
> 3,0 fred@moria.com
rewrite: ruleset  3   input: fred @ moria . com
rewrite: ruleset  7   input: fred @ moria . com
rewrite: ruleset  9   input: fred @ moria . com
rewrite: ruleset  9 returns: < fred > @ moria . com
rewrite: ruleset  7 returns: < @ moria . com > , fred
rewrite: ruleset  3 returns: < @ moria . com > , fred
rewrite: ruleset  0   input: < @ moria . com > , fred
rewrite: ruleset  8   input: < @ moria . com > , fred
rewrite: ruleset  8 returns: < @ moria . com > , fred
rewrite: ruleset 29   input: < @ moria . com > , fred
rewrite: ruleset 29 returns: < @ moria . com > , fred
rewrite: ruleset 26   input: < @ moria . com > , fred
rewrite: ruleset 25   input: < @ moria . com > , fred
rewrite: ruleset 25 returns: < @ moria . com > , fred
rewrite: ruleset  4   input: < @ moria . com > , fred
rewrite: ruleset  4 returns: fred @ moria . com
rewrite: ruleset 26 returns: < @ moria . com > , fred
rewrite: ruleset  0 returns: $# UUCP-A $@ moria $: < @ moria . com > , fred
>
```

15.5.4 Putting it all together - Integration Testing *sendmail.cf* and the tables

At this point, you've verified that mail will have the desired default behavior and that you'll be able to both send and received validly addressed mail. To complete the installation, it may be necessary to create the appropriate dbm tables to get the desired final results.

After creating the table(s) that are required for your site, you must process them through *dbm* by typing *make* in the directory containing the tables.

If you are UUCP-only, you do *not* need to create any of the tables mentioned in the *README.linux* file. You'll just have to touch the files so that the Makefile works.

If you're UUCP-only and you talk to sites in addition to your smart-host, you'll need to add *uucpxtable* entries for each (or mail to them will also go through the smart host) and run *dbm* against the revised *uucpxtable*.

First, you need to make certain that mail through your *RELAY_HOST* is sent to them via the *RE-LAY_MAILER*.

```
# /usr/lib/sendmail -bt -Cvstout.cf
ADDRESS TEST MODE
Enter <ruleset> <address>
[Note: No initial ruleset 3 call]
> 3,0 fred@sesame.com
rewrite: ruleset  3   input: fred @ sesame . com
rewrite: ruleset  7   input: fred @ sesame . com
rewrite: ruleset  9   input: fred @ sesame . com
rewrite: ruleset  9 returns: < fred > @ sesame . com
rewrite: ruleset  7 returns: < @ sesame . com > , fred
rewrite: ruleset  3 returns: < @ sesame . com > , fred
rewrite: ruleset  0   input: < @ sesame . com > , fred
rewrite: ruleset  8   input: < @ sesame . com > , fred
rewrite: ruleset  8 returns: < @ sesame . com > , fred
rewrite: ruleset 29   input: < @ sesame . com > , fred
rewrite: ruleset 29 returns: < @ sesame . com > , fred
rewrite: ruleset 26   input: < @ sesame . com > , fred
rewrite: ruleset 25   input: < @ sesame . com > , fred
```

```
rewrite: ruleset 25 returns: < @ sesame . com > , fred
rewrite: ruleset 4   input: < @ sesame . com > , fred
rewrite: ruleset 4 returns: fred @ sesame . com
rewrite: ruleset 26 returns: < @ sesame . com > , fred
rewrite: ruleset 0 returns: $# UUCP-A $@ moria $: < @ sesame . com > , fred
>
```

If you have UUCP neighbors other than your *RELAY_HOST*, you need to ensure that mail to them has the proper behavior. Mail addressed with UUCP-style syntax to a host you talk UUCP with should go directly to them (unless you explicitly prevent it with a *domaintable* entry). Assume host **swim** is a direct UUCP neighbor of yours. Then feeding **swim!fred** to *sendmail* should produce the following result:

```
# /usr/lib/sendmail -bt -Cvstout.cf
ADDRESS TEST MODE
Enter <ruleset> <address>
[Note: No initial ruleset 3 call]
> 3,0 swim!fred
rewrite: ruleset 3   input: swim ! fred
[...lines omitted...]
rewrite: ruleset 0 returns: $# UUCP $@ swim $: < > , fred
>
```

If you have *uucpxtable* entries to force UUCP delivery to certain UUCP neighbors who send their mail with Internet style domainized headers, that also needs to be tested.

```
# /usr/lib/sendmail -bt -Cvstout.cf
ADDRESS TEST MODE
Enter <ruleset> <address>
[Note: No initial ruleset 3 call]
> 3,0 dude@swim.2birds.com
rewrite: ruleset 3   input: dude @ swim . 2birds . com
[...lines omitted...]
rewrite: ruleset 0 returns: $# UUCP $@ swim . 2birds $: < > , dude
>
```

15.6 Administrivia and Stupid Mail Tricks

Now that we've discussed the theory of configuring, installing, and testing a sendmail+IDA system, lets take a few moments to look into things that *do* happen routinely in the life of a mail administrator.

Remote systems sometimes break. Modems or phone lines fail, DNS definitions are set incorrectly due to human error. Networks go down unexpectedly. In such cases, mail administrators need to know how to react quickly, effectively, and *safely* to keep mail flowing through alternate routes until the remote systems or service providers can restore normal services.

The rest of this chapter is intended to provide you with the solutions to the most frequently encountered "electronic mail emergencies".

15.6.1 Forwarding Mail to a Relay Host

To forward mail for a particular host or domain to a designated relay system, you generally use the *mailertable*.

For example, to forward mail for **backwood.org** to their UUCP gateway system **backdoor**, you'd put the following entry into *mailertable*:

```
UUCP-A,backdoor   backwood.org
```

15.6.2 Forcing Mail into Misconfigured Remote Sites

Frequently, Internet hosts will have trouble getting mail into misconfigured remote sites. There are several variants of this problem, but the general symptom is that mail is bounced by the remote system or never gets there at all.

These problems can put the local system administrator in a bad position because your users generally don't care that you don't personally administer every system worldwide (or know how to get the remote administrator to fix the problem). They just know that their mail didn't get through to the desired recipient on the other end and that you're a likely person to complain to.

A remote site's configuration is their problem, not yours. In all cases, be certain to *not* break your site in order to communicate with a misconfigured remote site. If you can't get in touch with the Postmaster at the remote site to get them to fix their configuration in a timely manner, you have two options.

- It is generally possible to force mail into the remote system successfully, although since the remote system is misconfigured, replies on the remote end might not work... but then that's the remote administrator's problem.

  You can fix the bad headers in the envelope on your outgoing messages only by using a *domaintable* entry for their host/domain that results in the invalid information being corrected in mail originating from your site:

        braindead.correct.domain.com   braindead.wrong.domain.com

- Frequently, misconfigured sites 'bounce' mail back to the sending system and effectively say "that mail isn't for this site" because they do not have their *PSEUDONYMNS* or equivalent set properly in their configuration. It is possible to totally strip off all hostname and domain information from the envelope of messages going from your site to them.

  The *!* in the following *mailertable* delivers mail to their remote site making it appear to their *sendmail* as if it had originated locally on their system. Note that this changes only the envelope address, so the proper return address will still show up in the message.

        TCP!braindead.correct.domain.com   braindead.wrong.domain.com

Regardless, even if you get mail into their system, there is no guarantee that they can reply to your message (they're broken, remember...) but then their users are yelling at their administrators rather than your users yelling at you.

15.6.3 Forcing Mail to be Transferred via UUCP

In an ideal world (from the Internet perspective), all hosts have records in the Domain Name Service (DNS) and will send mail with fully qualified domain names.

If you happen to talk via UUCP to such a site, you can force mail to go through the point-to-point UUCP connection rather than through your default mailer by essentially "undomainizing" their hostname through the *uucpxtable*.

To force UUCP delivery to **sesame.com**, you would put the following in your *uucpxtable*:

        # un-domainize sesame.com to force UUCP delivery
        sesame   sesame.com

The result is that sendmail will then determine (via *UUCPNODES* in the *sendmail.m4* file) that you are directly connected to the remote system and will queue the mail for delivery with UUCP.

15.6.4   Preventing Mail from Being Delivered via UUCP

The opposite condition also occurs. Frequently, systems may have a number of direct UUCP connections that are used infrequently or that are not as reliable and always available as the default mailer or relay host.

For example, in the Seattle area there are a number of systems that exchange the various Linux distributions via anonymous UUCP when the distributions are released. These systems talk UUCP only when necessary, so it is generally faster and more reliable to send mail through multiple very reliable hops and common (and always available) relay hosts.

It is easily possible to prevent UUCP delivery of mail to a host that you are directly connected to. If the remote system has a fully-qualified domain name, you can add an entry like this to the *domaintable*:

```
# prevent mail delivery via UUCP to a neighbor
snorkel.com      snorkel
```

This will replace any occurence of the UUCP name with the FQDN, and thus prevent a match by the *UUCPNODES* line in the *sendmail.m4* file. The result is generally that mail will go via the *RELAY_MAILER* and *RELAY_HOST* (or *DEFAULT_MAILER*).

15.6.5   Running the Sendmail Queue on Demand

To process queued messages immediately, merely type '/usr/lib/runq'. This invokes sendmail with the appropriate options to cause sendmail to run through the queue of pending jobs immediately rather than waiting for the next scheduled run.

15.6.6   Reporting Mail Statistics

Many site administrators (and the persons they work for) are interested in the volume of mail passing to, from, and through the local site. There are a number of ways to quantify mail traffic.

- Sendmail comes with a utility called *mailstats* that reads a file called */usr/local/lib/mail/sendmail.st* and reports the number of messages and number of bytes transferred by each of the mailers used in the *sendmail.cf* file. This file must be created by the local administrator manually for sendmail logging to occur. The running totals are cleared by removing and recreating the *sendmail.st* file. One way is to do the following:

```
# cp /dev/null /usr/lib/local/mail/sendmail.st
```

- Probably the best way to do quality reporting regarding who uses mail and how much volume passes to, from, and through the local system is to turn on mail debugging with *syslogd(8)*. Generally, this means running the */etc/syslogd* daemon from your system startup file (which you should be doing anyway), and adding a line to */etc/syslog.conf(5)* that looks something like the following:

```
mail.debug                      /var/log/syslog.mail
```

If you use *mail.debug* and get any medium to high mail volume, the syslog output can get quite large. Output files from *syslogd* generally need to be rotated or purged on a routine basis from *crond(8)*.

There are a number of commonly available utilities that can summarize the output of mail logging from syslogd. One of the more well known utilities is *syslog-stat.pl*, a *perl* script that is distributed with the sendmail+IDA sources.

15.7   Mixing and Matching Binary Distributions

There is no true standard configuration of electronic mail transport and delivery agents and there is no "one true directory structure."

Accordingly, it is necessary to ensure that all the various pieces of the system (USENET news, mail, TCP/IP) agree on the location of the local mail delivery program (*lmail, deliver*, etc.), remote mail delivery program (*rmail*), and the mail transport program (*sendmail* or *smail*). Such assumptions are not generally documented, although use of the *strings* command can help determine what files and directories are expected. The following are some problems we've seen in the past with some of the commonly available Linux binary distributions and sources.

- Some versions of the NET-2 distribution of TCP/IP have services defined for a program called *umail* rather than *sendmail*.

- There are various ports of *elm* and *mailx* that look for a delivery agent of */usr/bin/smail* rather than sendmail.

- Sendmail+IDA has a built-in local mailer for *deliver*, but expects it to be located in */bin* rather than the more typical Linux location of */usr/bin*.

Rather than go through the trouble of building all the mail clients from sources, we generally fake it with the appropriate soft links. . .

15.8 Where to Get More Information

There are many places you can look for more information on *sendmail*. For a list, see the Linux MAIL Howto posted regularly to **comp.answers**. It is also available for anonymous FTP on **rtfm.mit.edu**. However, the definitive place is in the sendmail+IDA sources. Look in the directory *ida/cf* below the source directory for the files *DBM-GUIDE*, *OPTIONS*, and *Sendmail.mc*.

Chapter 16

Netnews

16.1 Usenet History

The idea of network news was born in 1979 when two graduate students, Tom Truscott and Jim Ellis, thought of using UUCP to connect machines for the purpose of information exchange among UNIX users. They set up a small network of three machines in North Carolina.

Initially, traffic was handled by a number of shell scripts (later rewritten in C), but they were never released to the public. They were quickly replaced by "A" news, the first public release of news software.

"A" news was not designed to handle more than a few articles per group and day. When the volume continued to grow, it was rewritten by Mark Horton and Matt Glickman, who called it the "B" release (a.k.a. Bnews). The first public release of Bnews was version 2.1 in 1982. It was expanded continuously, with several new features being added. Its current version is Bnews 2.11. It is slowly becoming obsolete, with its last official maintainer having switched to INN.

Another rewrite was done and released in 1987 by Geoff Collyer and Henry Spencer; this is release "C", or C News. In the time following there have been a number of patches to C News, the most prominent being the C News Performance Release. On sites that carry a large number of groups, the overhead involved in frequently invoking *relaynews*, which is responsible for dispatching incoming articles to other hosts, is significant. The Performance Release adds an option to *relaynews* that allows to run it in *daemon mode*, in which the program puts itself in the background.

The Performance Release is the C News version currently included in most Linux releases.

All news releases up to "C" are primarily targeted for UUCP networks, although they may be used in other environments as well. Efficient news transfer over networks like TCP/IP, DECNet, or related requires a new scheme. This was the reason why, in 1986, the "Network News Transfer Protocol", NNTP, was introduced. It is based on network connections, and specifies a number of commands to interactively transfer and retrieve articles.

There are a number of NNTP-based applications available from the Net. One of them is the *nntpd* package by Brian Barber and Phil Lapsley, which you can use, among other things, to provides newsreading service to a number of hosts inside a local network. *nntpd* was designed to complement news packages such as Bnews or C News to give them NNTP features.

A different NNTP package is INN, or Internet News. It is not merely a front end, but a news system by its own right. It comprises a sophisticated news relay daemon that is capable of maintaining several concurrent NNTP links efficiently, and is therefore the news server of choice for many Internet sites.

16.2 What *is* Usenet, Anyway?

One of the most astounding facts about Usenet is that it isn't part of any organization, or has any sort of centralized network management authority. In fact, it's part of Usenet lore that except for a technical description, you cannot define *what* it is, you can only say what it isn't. If you have Brendan Kehoe's excellent

496

"Zen and the Art of the Internet" (available online or through Prentice-Hall, see [Kehoe92]) at hand, you will find an amusing list of Usenet's non-properties.

At the risk of sounding stupid, one might define Usenet as a collaboration of separate sites who exchange Usenet news. To be a Usenet site, all you have to do is find another site Usenet site, and strike an agreement with its owners and maintainers to exchange news with you. Providing another site with news is also called *feeding* it, whence another common axiom of Usenet philosophy originates: "Get a feed and you're on it."

The basic unit of Usenet news is the article. This is a message a user writes and "posts" to the net. In order to enable news sytems to deal with it, it is prepended with administrative information, the so-called article header. It is very similar to the mail header format laid down in the Internet mail standard RFC 822, in that it consists of several lines of text, each beginning with a field name terminated by a colon, which is followed by the field's value.[1]

Articles are submitted to one or more *newsgroups*. One may consider a newsgroup a forum for articles relating to a common topic. All newsgroups are organized in a hierarchy, with each group's name indicating its place in the hierarchy. This often makes it easy to see what a group is all about. For example, anybody can see from the newsgroup name that **comp.os.linux.announce** is used for announcements concerning a computer operating system named Linux.

These articles are then exchanged between all Usenet sites that are willing to carry news from this group. When two sites agree to exchange news, they are free to exchange whatever newsgroups they like to, and may even add their own local news hierarchies. For example, **groucho.edu** might have a news link to **barnyard.edu**, which is a major news feed, and several links to minor sites which it feeds news. Now, Barnyard College might receive all Usenet groups, while GMU only wants to carry a few major hierarchies like **sci**, **comp**, **rec**, etc. Some of the downstream sites, say a UUCP site called **brewhq**, will want to carry even fewer groups, because they don't have the network or hardware resources. On the other hand, **brewhq** might want to receive newsgroups from the **fj** hierarchy, which GMU doesn't carry. It therefore maintains another link with **gargleblaster.com**, who carry all **fj** groups, and feed them to **brewhq**. The news flow is shown in figure 16.1.

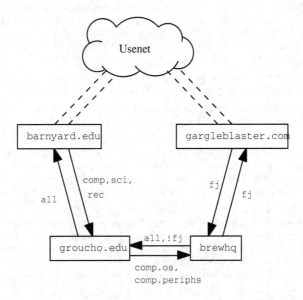

Figure 16.1: Usenet news flow through Groucho Marx University.

The labels on the arrows originating from **brewhq** may require some explanation, though. By default, it wants all locally generated news to be sent to **groucho.edu**. However, as **groucho.edu** does not carry the **fj**

---

[1]The format of Usenet news messages is specified in RFC 1036, "Standard for interchange of USENET messages".

groups, there's no pointing in sending it any messages from those groups. Therefore, the feed from **brewhq** to GMU is labelled **all,!fj**, meaning that all groups except those below **fj** are sent to it.

16.3   How Does Usenet Handle News?

Today, Usenet has grown to enormous proportions. Sites that carry the whole of netnews usually transfer something like a paltry sixty megabytes a day.[2] Of course this requires much more than pushing around files. So let's take a look at the way most UNIX systems handle Usenet news.

News is distributed through the net by various transports. The historical medium used to be UUCP, but today the main traffic is carried by Internet sites. The routing algorithm used is called *flooding*. Each site maintains a number of links (*news feeds*) to other sites. Any article generated or received by the local news system is forwarded to them, unless it has already been seen at that site, in which case it is discarded. A site may find out about all other sites the article has already traversed by looking at the **Path:** header field. This header contains a list of all systems the article has been forwarded by in bang path notation.

To distinguish articles and recognize duplicates, Usenet articles have to carry a message id (specified in the **Message-Id:** header field), which combines the posting site's name and a serial number into "<*serial@site*>". For each article processed, the news system logs this id into a *history* file against which all newly arrived articles are checked.

The flow between any two sites may be limited by two criteria: for one, an article is assigned a distribution (in the **Distribution:** header field) which may be used to confine it to a certain group of sites. On the other hand, the newsgroups exchanged may be limited by both the sending or receiving system. The set of newsgroups and distributions allowed for transmission to a site are usually kept in the *sys* file.

The sheer number of articles usually requires that improvements be made to the above scheme. On UUCP networks, the natural thing to do is to collect articles over a period of time, and combine them into a single file, which is compressed and sent to the remote site. This is called *batching*.[3]

An alternative technique is the *ihave/sendme* protocol that prevents duplicate articles from being transferred in the first place, thus saving net bandwidth. Instead of putting all articles in batch files and sending them along, only the message ids of articles are combined into a giant "ihave" message and sent to the remote site. It reads this message, compares it to its history file, and returns the list of articles it wants in a "sendme" message. Only these articles are then sent.

Of course, ihave/sendme only makes sense if it involves two big sites that receive news from several independent feeds each, and who poll each other often enough for an efficient flow of news.

Sites that are on the Internet generally rely on TCP/IP-based software that uses the Network News Transfer Protocol, NNTP.[4] It transfers news between feeds and provides Usenet access to single users on remote hosts.

NNTP knows three different ways to transfer news. One is a real-time version of ihave/sendme, also referred to as *pushing* news. The second technique is called *pulling* news, in which the client requests a list of articles in a given newsgroup or hierarchy that have arrived at the server's site after a specified date, and chooses those it cannot find in its history file. The third mode is for interactive newsreading, and allows you or your newsreader to retrieve articles from specified newgroups, as well as post articles with incomplete header information.

At each site, news are kept in a directory hierarchy below */var/spool/news*, each article in a separate file, and each newsgroup in a separate directory. The directory name is made up of the newsgroup name, with the components being the path components. Thus, **comp.os.linux.misc** articles are kept in */var/spool/news/comp/os/linux/misc*. The articles in a newsgroup are assigned numbers in the order they arrive. This number serves as the file's name. The range of numbers of articles currently online is kept in a file called *active*, which at the same time serves as a list of newsgroups known at your site.

Since disk space is a finite resource,[5] one has to start throwing away articles after some time. This is called *expiring*. Usually, articles from certain groups and hierarchies are expired at a fixed number of days after they arrive. This may be overridden by the poster by specifying a date of expiration in the **Expires:** field of the article header.

---

[2]Wait a moment: 60 Megs at 9600 bps, that's 60 million by 1200, that is... mutter, mutter,... Hey! That's 34 hours!
[3]The golden rule of netnews, according to Geoff Collyer: "Thou shalt batch thine articles."
[4]Described in RFC 977.
[5]Some people claim that Usenet is a conspiracy by modem and hard disk vendors.

Chapter 17

C News

One of the most popular software packages for Netnews is C News. It was designed for sites that carry news over UUCP links. This chapter will discuss the central concepts of C News, and the basic installation and maintenance tasks.

C News stores its configuration files in */usr/lib/news*, and most of its binaries in the */usr/lib/news/bin* directory. Articles are kept below */var/spool/news*. You should make sure virtually all files in these directories are owned by user **news**, group **news**. Most problems arise from files being inaccessible to C News. Make it a rule for you to become user **news** using *su* before you touch anything in there. The only exceptions is *setnewsids*, which is used to set the real user id of some news programs. It must be owned by **root** and must have the setuid bit set.

In the following, we describe all C News configuration files in detail, and show you what you have to do to keep your site running.

17.1 Delivering News

Articles may be fed to C News in several ways. When a local user posts an article, the newsreader usually hands it to the *inews* command, which completes the header information. News from remote sites, be it a single article or a whole batch, is given to the *rnews* command, which stores it in the */var/spool/newsin.coming* directory, from where it will be picked up at a later time by *newsrun*. With any of these two techniques, however, the article will eventually be handed to the *relaynews* command.

For each article, the *relaynews* command first checks if the article has already been seen at the local site by looking up the message id in the *history* file. Duplicate articles will be dropped. Then, *relaynews* looks at the **Newsgroups:** header line to find out if the local site requests articles from any of these groups. If it does, and the newsgroup is listed in the *active* file, *relaynews* tries to store the article in the corresponding directory in the news spool area. If this directory does not exist, it is created. The article's message id will then be logged to the *history* file. Otherwise, *relaynews* drops the article.

If *relaynews* fails to store an incoming article because a group it has been posted to is not listed in your *active* file, the article will be moved to the **junk** group.[1] *relaynews* will also check for stale or misdated articles and reject them. Incoming batches that fail for any other reason are moved to */var/spool/news/in.coming/bad*, and an error message is logged.

After this, the article will be relayed to all other sites that request news from these groups, using the transport specified for each particular site. To make sure it isn't sent to a site that already has seen it, each destination site is checked against the article's **Path:** header field, which contains the list of sites the article has traversed so far, written in bang path style. Only if the destination site's name does not appear in this list will the article be sent to it.

---

[1]There may be a difference between the groups that exist at your site, and those that your site is willing to receive. For example, the subscription list may specify **comp.all**, which means all newsgroups below the **comp** hierarchy, but at your site, only a number of **comp** groups are listed in *active*. articles posted to those groups will be moved to **junk**.

C News is commonly used to relay news between UUCP sites, altough it is also possible to use it in a NNTP environment. To deliver news to a remote UUCP site — either single articles or whole batches — *uux* is used to execute the *rnews* command on the remote site, and feed the article or batch to it on standard input.

When batching is enabled for a given site, C News does not send any incoming article immediately, but appends its path name to a file, usually *out.going/site/togo*. Periodically, a batcher program is executed from a crontab entry,[2] which puts the articles in one or more files, optionally compresses them, and sends them to *rnews* at the remote site.

Figure 17.1 shows the news flow through *relaynews*. Articles may be relayed to the local site (denoted by *ME*), to some site named **ponderosa** via email, and a site named **moria**, for which batching is enabled.

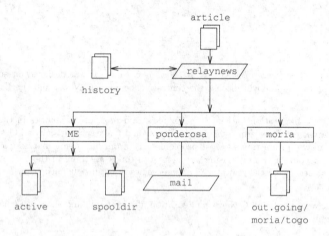

Figure 17.1: News flow through *relaynews*.

17.2 Installation

To install C News, untar the files into their proper places if you haven't done so yet, and edit the configuration files listed below. They are all located in */usr/lib/news*. Their formats will be described in the following sections.

sys   You probably have to modify the *ME* line that describes your system, although using *all/all* is always a safe bet. You also have to add a line for each site you feed news to.

                If you are a leaf site, you only need a line that sends all locally generated articles to your feed. Assume your feed is **moria**, then your *sys* file should look like this:

```
ME:all/all::
moria/moria.orcnet.org:all/all,!local:f:
```

organization   Your organization's name. For example, "Virtual Brewery, Inc.". On your home machine, enter "private site", or anything else you like. Most people will not call your site properly configured if you haven't customized this file.

newsgroups

mailname   Your site's mail name, e.g. **vbrew.com**.

whoami   Your site's name for news purposes. Quite often, the UUCP site name is used, for example **vbrew**.

---

[2]Note that this should be the crontab of **news**, in order not to mangle file permissions.

explist   You should probably edit this file to reflect your preferred expiry times for some special newsgroups. Disk space may play an important role in it.

To create an initial hierarchy of newsgroups, obtain an *active* and a *newsgroups* file from the site that feeds you, and install them in */usr/lib/news*, making sure they are owned by news and have a mode of 644. Remove all **to.*** groups from the active file, and add **to.***mysite* and **to.***feedsite*, as well as **junk** and **control**. The **to.*** groups are normally used for exchanging ihave/sendme messages, but you should create them regardless of whether you plan to use ihave/sendme or not. Next, replace all article numbers in the second and third field of *active* using the following command:

```
# cp active active.old
# sed 's/ [0-9]* [0-9]* / 0000000000 00001 /' active.old > active
# rm active.old
```

The second command is an invocation of *sed(1)*, one of my favorite UNIX commands. This invocation replaces two strings of digits with a string of zeroes and the string 000001, respectively.

Finally, create the news spool directory and the subdirectories used for incoming and outgoing news:

```
# cd /var/spool
# mkdir news news/in.coming news/out.going
# chown -R news.news news
# chmod -R 755 news
```

If you're using a later release of C News, you may also have to create the *out.master* directory in the news spool directory.

If you're using newsreaders from a different distribution than the C News you have running, you may find that some expect the news spool on */usr/spool/news* rather than in */var/spool/news*. If your newsreader doesn't seem to find any articles, create a symbolic from */usr/spool/news* to */var/spool/news*.

Now, you are ready to receive news. Note that you don't have to create any directories other than those shown above, because each time C News receives an article from a group for which there's no spool directory yet, it will create it.

In particular, this happens to *all* groups an article has been crossposted to. So, after a while, you will find your news spool cluttered with directories for newsgroups you have never subscribed to, like **alt.lang.teco**. You may prevent this by either removing all unwanted groups from *active*, or by regularly running a shell script which removes all empty directories below */var/spool/news* (except *out.going* and *in.coming*, of course).

C News needs a user to send error messages and status reports to. By default, this is **usenet**. If you use the default, you have to set up an alias for it which forwards all of its mail to one or more responsible persons. (Chapters 14 and 15 explain how to do so for *smail* and *sendmail*). You may also override this behavior by setting the environment variable *NEWSMASTER* to the appropriate name. You have to do so in **news**' crontab file, as well as every time you invoke an administrative tool manually, so installing an alias is probably easier.

While you're hacking */etc/passwd*, make sure that every user has her real name in the *pw_gecos* field of the password file (this is the fourth field). It is a question of Usenet netiquette that the sender's real name appears in the `From:` field of the article. Of course, you will want to do so anyway when you use mail.

17.3   The sys file

The *sys* file, located in */usr/lib/news*, controls which hierarchies you receive and forward to other sites. Although there are maintenance tools named *addfeed* and *delfeed*, I think it's better to maintain this file by hand.

The *sys* file contains entries for each site you forward news to, as well as a description of the groups you will accept. An entry looks like

    site[*/exclusions*] : *grouplist*[*/distlist*] [: *flags*[: *cmds*]]

Entries may be continued across newlines using a backslash (\). A hash sign (#) denotes a comment.

site   This is the name of the site the entry applies to. One usually chooses the site's UUCP name
                for this. There has to be an entry for your site in the *sys* file, too, else you will not receive any
                articles yourself.

                The special site name *ME* denotes your site. The *ME* entry defines all groups you are willing
                to store locally. Articles that aren't matched by the *ME* line will go to the **junk** group.

                Since C News checks *site* against the site names in the **Path:** header field, you have to make
                sure they really match. Some sites use their fully qualified domain name in this field, or an
                alias like **news.***site.domain*. To prevent any articles from being returned to these sites, you
                have to add these to the exclusion list, separated by commas.

                For the entry applying to site **moria**, for instance, the site field would contain **mo-
                ria/moria.orcnet.org**.

grouplist   This is a comma-separated subscription list of groups and hierarchies for that particular site.
                A hierarchy may be specified by giving the hierarchy's prefix (such as **comp.os** for all groups
                whose name starts with this prefix), optionally followed by the keyword **all** (e.g. **comp.os.all**).

                A hierarchy or group is excluded from forwarding by preceding it with an exclamation mark.
                If a newsgroup is checked against the list, the longest match applies. For example, if *grouplist*
                contains

                    !comp,comp.os.linux,comp.folklore.computers

                no groups from the **comp** hierarchy except **comp.folklore.computers** and all groups below
                comp.os.linux will be fed to that site.

                If the site requests to be forwarded all news you receive yourself, enter *all* as *grouplist*.

distlist   is offset from the *grouplist* by a slash, and contains a list of distributions to be forwarded.
                Again, you may exclude certain distributions by preceding them with an exclamation mark.
                All distributions are denoted by *all*. Omitting *distlist* implies a list of *all*.

                For example, you may use a distribution list of *all,!local* to prevent news for local use only
                from being sent to remote sites.

                There are usually at least two distributions: *world*, which is often the default distribution used
                when none is specified by the user, and *local*. There may be other distributions that apply to
                a certain region, state, country, etc. Finally, there are two distributions used by C News only;
                these are *sendme* and *ihave*, and are used for the sendme/ihave protocol.

                The use of distributions is a subject of debate. For one, some newsreaders create bogus
                distributions by simply using the top level hierarchy, for example **comp** when posting to
                comp.os.linux. Distributions that apply to regions are often questionable, too, because news
                may travel outside of your region when sent across the Internet.[3] Distributions applying to an
                organization, however, are very meaningful, for example to prevent confidential information
                from leaving the company network. This purpose, however, is generally served better by
                creating a separate newsgroup or hierarchy.

flags   This describes certain parameters for the feed. It may be empty, or a combination of the
                following:

                F   This flag enables batching.

                f   This is almost identical to the *F* flag, but allows C News to calculate the size
                                  of outgoing batches more precisely.

                I   This flag makes C News produce an article list suitable for use by
                                  ihave/sendme. Additional modifications to the *sys* and the *batchparms* file
                                  are required to enable ihave/sendme.

─────────────────
[3]It is not uncommon for an article posted in, say Hamburg, to go to Frankfurt via **reston.ans.net** in the Netherlands, or even
via some site in the U.S.

n   This creates batch files for active NNTP transfer clients like *nntpxmit* (see chapter 18). The batch files contain the article's filename along with its message id.

L   This tells C News to transmit only articles posted at your site. This flag may be followed by a decimal number *n*, which makes C News only transfer articles posted within *n* hops from your site. C News determines the number of hops from the `Path:` field.

u   This tells C News to batch only articles from unmoderated groups.

m   This tells C News to batch only articles from moderated groups.

You may use at most one of *F*, *f*, *I*, or *n*.

cmds   This field contains a command to be executed for each article, unless batching is enabled. The article will be fed to the command on standard input. This should only be used for very small feeds; otherwise the load on both systems will be too high.

The default command is

```
uux - -r -z system!rnews
```

which invokes *rnews* on the remote system, feeding it the article on standard input.

The   default   search   path   for   commands   given   in this field is */bin:/usr/bin:/usr/lib/news/bin/batch*. The latter directory contains a number of shell scripts whose name starts with *via*; they are briefly described later in this chapter.

If batching is enabled using either of the *F* or *f*, *I* or *n* flags, C News expects to find a file name in this field rather than a command. If the file name does not begin with a slash (*/*), it is assumed to be relative to */var/spool/news/out.going*. If the field is empty, it defaults to *system/togo*.

When setting up C News, you will most probably have to write your own *sys* file. To help you with it, we give a sample file for **vbrew.com** below, from which you might copy what you need.

```
# We take whatever they give us.
ME:all/all::

# We send everything we receive to moria, except for local and
# brewery-related articles. We use batching.
moria/moria.orcnet.org:all,!to,to.moria/all,!local,!brewery:f:

# We mail comp.risks to jack@ponderosa.uucp
ponderosa:comp.risks/all::rmail jack@ponderosa.uucp

# swim gets a minor feed
swim/swim.twobirds.com:comp.os.linux,rec.humor.oracle/all,!local:f:

# Log mail map articles for later processing
usenet-maps:comp.mail.maps/all:F:/var/spool/uumaps/work/batch
```

17.4 The *active* file

The *active* file is located in */usr/lib/news* and lists all groups known at your site, and the articles currently online. You will rarely have to touch it, but we explain it nevertheless for sake of completeness. Entries take the following form:

newsgroup high low perm

newsgroup is, of course, the group's name. *low* and *high* are the lowest and highest numbers of articles currently available. If none are available at the moment, *low* is equal to *high*+1.

At least, that's what the *low* field is meant to do. However, for efficiency reasons, C News doesn't update this field. This wouldn't be such a big loss if there weren't some newsreaders that depend on it. For instance, *trn* checks this field to see if it can purge any articles from its thread database. To update the *low* field, you therefore have to run the *updatemin* command regularly (or, in earlier version of C News, the *upact* script).

perm is a parameter detailing the access users are granted to the group. It takes one of the following values:

y   Users are allowed to post to this group.

n   Users are not allowed to post to this group. However, the group may still be read.

x   This group has been disabled locally. This happens sometimes when news admininistrators (or their superiors) take offense to articles posted to certain groups.

             Articles received for this group are not stored locally, although they are forwarded to the sites that request them.

m   This denotes a moderated group. When a user tries to post to this group, an intelligent newsreader will notify her of this, and send the article to the moderator instead. The moderator's address is taken from the *moderators* file in */usr/lib/news*.

=real-group This marks *newsgroup* as being a local alias for another group, namely *real-group*. All articles posted to *newsgroup* will be redirected to it.

In C News, you will generally not have to access this file directly. Groups may be added or deleted locally using *addgroup* and *delgroup* (see below in section Maintenance Tools and Tasks). When groups are added or deleted for the whole of Usenet, this is usually done by sending a *newgroup* or *rmgroup* control message, respectively. *Never send such a message yourself!* For instructions on how to create a newsgroup, read the monthly postings in **news.announce.newusers**.

A file closely related to *active* is *active.times*. Whenever a group is created, C News logs a message to this file, containing the name of the group created, the date of creation, whether it was done by a *newgroup* control message or locally, and who did it. This is for the convenience of newsreaders who may notify the user of any recently created groups. It is also used by the *NEWGROUPS* command of NNTP.

17.5 Article Batching

Newsbatches follow a particular format which is the same for Bnews, C News, and INN. Each article is preceded by a line like this:

```
#! rnews count
```

where *count* is the number of bytes in the article. When batch compression is used, the resulting file is compressed as a whole, and preceded by another line, indicated by the message to be used for unpacking. The standard compression tool is **compress**, which is marked by

```
#! cunbatch
```

Sometimes, when having to send batches via mail software that removes the eighth bit from all data, a compressed batch may be protected using what is called c7-encoding; these batches will be marked by *c7unbatch*.

When a batch is fed to *rnews* on the remote site, it checks for these markers and processes the batch appropriately. Some sites also use other compression tools, like *gzip*, and precede their gzipped files with *zunbatch* instead. C News does not recognize non-standard headers like these; you have to modify the source to support them.

In C News, article batching is performed by */usr/lib/news/bin/batch/sendbatches*, which takes a list of articles from the *site/togo* file, and puts them into several newsbatches. It should be executed once per hour or even more frequently, depending on the volume of traffic.

Its operation is controlled by the *batchparms* file in */usr/lib/news*. This file describes the maximum batch size allowed for each site, the batching and optional compression program to be used, and the transport for delivering it to the remote site. You may specify batching parameters on a per-site basis, as well as a set of default parameters for sites not explicitly mentioned.

To perform batching for a specific site, you invoke it as

```
# su news -c "/usr/lib/news/bin/batch/sendbatches site"
```

When invoked without arguments, *sendbatches* handles all batch queues. The interpretation of "all" depends on the presence of a default entry in *batchparms*. If one is found, all directories in */var/spool/news/out.going* are checked, otherwise, it cycles through all entries in *batchparms*. Note that *sendbatches*, when scanning the *out.going* directory, takes only those directories that contain no dot or at sign (@) as site names.

When installing C News, you will most likely find a *batchparms* file in your distribution which contains a reasonable default entry, so there's a good chance that you wouldn't have to touch the file. Just in case, we describe its format nevertheless. Each line consists of six fields, separated by spaces or tabs:

> *site size max batcher muncher transport*

The meaning of these fields is as follows:

site is the name of the site the entry applies to. The *togo* file for this site must reside in *out.going/togo* below the news spool. A site name of */default/* denotes the default entry.

size is the maximum size of article batches created (before compression). For single articles larger than this, C News makes an exception and puts them in a single batch by themselves.

max is the maximum number of batches created and scheduled for transfer before batching stalls for this particular site. This is useful in case the remote site should be down for a long time, because it prevents C News from cluttering your UUCP spool directories with zillions of newsbatches.

C News determines the number of queued batches using the *queuelen* script in */usr/lib/news/bin*. Vince Skahan's *newspak* release should contain a script for BNU-compatible UUCPs. If you use a different flavor of spool directories, for example, Taylor UUCP, you might have to write your own.[4]

The *batcher* field contains the command used for producing a batch from the list of articles in the *togo* file. For regular feeds, this is usually *batcher*. For other purposes, alternative batchers may be provided. For instance, the ihave/sendme protocol requires the article list to be turned into ihave or sendme control messages, which are posted to the newsgroup **to.***site*. This is performed by *batchih* and *batchsm*.

The *muncher* field specifies the command used for compression. Usually, this is **compcun**, a script that produces a compressed batch.[5] Alternatively, you might provide a muncher that uses *gzip*, say *gzipcun* (to be clear: you have to write it yourself). You have to make sure that *uncompress* on the remote site is patched to recognize files compressed with *gzip*.

If the remote site does not have an *uncompress* command, you may specify *nocomp* which does not do any compression.

The last field, *transport*, describes the transport to be used. A number of standard commands for different transports are available whose names begin with *via*. *sendbatches* passes them the destination site name on the command line. If the *batchparms* entry was not */default/*, it derives the site name from the *site* field by stripping of anything after and including the first dot or slash. If entry was */default/*, the directory names in *out.going* are used.

---

[4]If you don't care about the number of spool files (because you're the only person using your computer, and you don't write articles by the megabyte), you may replace the script's contents by a simple *exit 0* statement.

[5]As shipped with C News, **compcun** uses **compress** with the 12 bit option, since this is the least common denominator for most sites. You may produce a copy of it, say **compcun16**, where you use 16 bit compression. The improvement is not too impressive, though.

There are two commands that use *uux* to execute *rnews* on the remote system; *viauux* and *viauuxz*. The latter sets the -z flag for (older versions of) *uux* to keep it from returning success messages for each article delivered. Another command, *viamail*, sends article batches to the user **rnews** on the remote system via mail. Of course, this requires that the remote system somehow feeds all mail for **rnews** to their local news system. For a complete list of these transports, refer to the *newsbatch(8)* manual page.

All commands from the last three fields must be located in either of *out.going/site* or */usr/lib/news/bin/batch*. Most of them are scripts, so that you may easily tailor new tools for your personal needs. They are invoked as a pipe. The list of articles is fed to the batcher on standard input, which produces the batch on standard output. This is piped into the muncher, and so on.

A sample file is given below.

```
# batchparms file for the brewery
# site       | size   |max   |batcher  |muncher    |transport
#------------+--------+------+---------+-----------+-----------
/default/      100000 22      batcher   compcun     viauux
swim           10000  10      batcher   nocomp      viauux
```

17.6   Expiring News

In Bnews, expiring used to be performed by a program called *expire*, which took a list of newsgroups as arguments, along with a time specification after which articles had to be expired. To have different hierarchies expired at different times, you had to write a script that invoked *expire* for each of them separately. C News offers a more convenient solution to this: in a file called *explist*, you may specify newsgroups and expiration intervals. A command called *doexpire* is usually run once a day from *cron*, and processes all groups according to this list.

Occasionally, you may want to retain articles from certain groups even after they have been expired; for example, you might want to keep programs posted to **comp.sources.unix**. This is called *archiving*. *explist* permits you to mark groups for archiving.

An entry in *explist* looks like this:

> *grouplist perm times archive*

grouplist is a comma-separated list of newsgroups to which the entry applies. Hierarchies may be specified by giving the group name prefix, optionally appended with *all*. For example, for an entry applying to all groups below **comp.os**, you might either enter **comp.os** or **comp.os.all** in *grouplist*.

When expiring news from a group, the name is checked against all entries in *explist* in the order given. The first matching entry applies. For example, to throw away the majority of **comp** after four days, except for **comp.os.linux.announce** which you want to keep for a week, you simply have an entry for the latter, which specifies a seven-day expiration period, followed by that for **comp**, which specifies four days.

The *perm* field details if the entry applies to moderated, unmoderated, or any groups. It may take the values *m*, *u*, or *x*, which denote moderated, unmoderated, or any type.

The third field, *times*, usually contains only a single number. This is the number of days after which articles will be expired if they haven't been assigned an artificial expiration date in an `Expires:` field in the article header. Note that this is the number of days counting from its *arrival* at your site, not the date of posting.

The *times* field may, however, be more complex than that. It may be a combination of up to three numbers, separated from one another by a dash. The first denotes the number of days that have to pass before the article is considered a candidate for expiration. It is rarely useful to use a value other than zero. The second field is the above-mentioned default number of days after which it will be expired. The third is the number of days after which an article will be expired unconditionally, regardless of whether it has an `Expires:` field or not. If only the middle number is given, the other two take default values. These may be specified using the special entry */bounds/*, which is described below.

The fourth field, *archive*, denotes whether the newsgroup is to be archived, and where. If no archiving is intended, a dash should be used. Otherwise, you either use a full path name (pointing to a directory), or an at sign (@). The at sign denotes the default archive directory which must then be given to *doexpire* by using the -a flag on the command line. An archive directory should be owned by **news**. When *doexpire* archives an article from, say **comp.sources.unix**, it stores it in the directory **comp/sources/unix** below the archive directory, creating it if not existent. The archive directory itself, however, will not be created.

There are two special entries in your *explist* file that *doexpire* relies on. Instead of a list of newsgroups, they have the keywords */bounds/* and */expired/*. The */bounds/* entry contains the default values for the three values of the *times* field described above.

The */expired/* field determines how long C News will hold on to lines in the *history* file. This is needed because C News will not remove a line from the history file once the corresponding article(s) have been expired, but will hold on to it in case a duplicate should arrive after this date. If you are fed by only one site, you can keep this value small. Otherwise, a couple of weeks is advisable on UUCP networks, depending on the delays you experience with articles from these sites.

A sample *explist* file with rather tight expiry intervals is reproduced below:

```
# keep history lines for two weeks. Nobody gets more than three months
/expired/                       x       14      -
/bounds/                        x       0-1-90  -

# groups we want to keep longer than the rest
comp.os.linux.announce          m       10      -
comp.os.linux                   x       5       -
alt.folklore.computers          u       10      -
rec.humor.oracle                m       10      -
soc.feminism                    m       10      -

# Archive *.sources groups
comp.sources,alt.sources        x       5       @

# defaults for tech groups
comp,sci                        x       7       -

# enough for a long weekend
misc,talk                       x       4       -

# throw away junk quickly
junk                            x       1       -

# control messages are of scant interest, too
control                         x       1       -

# catch-all entry for the rest of it
all                             x       2       -
```

With expiring in C News, there are a number of potential troubles looming. One is that your newsreader might rely on the third field of the active file, which contains the number of the lowest article on-line. When expiring articles, C News does not update this field. If you need (or want) to have this field represent the real situation, you need to run a program called *updatemin* after each run of *doexpire*.[6]

Second, C News does not expire by scanning the newsgroup's directory, but simply checks the *history* file if the article is due for expiration.[7] If your history file somehow gets out of sync, articles may be around on your disk forever, because C News has literally forgotten them.[8] You can repair this using the *addmissing* script in */usr/lib/news/bin/maint*, which will add missing articles to the *history* file, or *mkhistory*, which re-builds the entire file from scratch. Don't forget to become **news** before invoking it, else you will wind up with a *history* file unreadable by C News.

---

[6] In older versions of C News, this was done by a script called *upact*.

[7] The article's date of arrival is kept in the middle field of the history line, given in seconds since January 1, 1970.

[8] I don't know *why* this happens, but for me, it does from time to time.

17.7   Miscellaneous Files

There are a number of files that control C News' behavior, but are not essential to its functioning. All of them reside in */usr/lib/news*. We will describe them briefly.

newsgroups   This is a companion file of *active* which contains a list of newsgroup names, along with a one-line description of its main topic. This file is automatically updated when C News receives a *checknews* control message (see section 17.8).

localgroups   If you have a number of local groups that you don't want C News to complain about every time you receive a *checknews* message, put their names and descriptions in this file, just like they would appear in *newsgroups*.

mailpaths   This file contains the moderator's address for each moderated group. Each line contains the group name, followed by the moderator's email address (offset by a tab).

Two special entries are provided as default. These are *backbone* and *internet*. Both provide — in bang-path notation — the path to the nearest backbone site, and the site that understands RFC 822-style addresses (**user@host**). The default entries are

```
internet     backbone
```

You will not have to change the *internet* entry if you have *smail* or *sendmail* installed, because they understand RFC 822-addressing.

The *backbone* entry is used whenever a user posts to a moderated group whose moderator is not listed explicitly. If the newsgroup's name is **alt.sewer**, and the *backbone* entry contains *path!%s*, C News will mail the article to *path!alt-sewer*, hoping that the backbone machine is able to forward the article. To find out which path to use, ask the news admins at the site that feeds you. As a last resort, you can also use **uunet.uu.net!%s**.

distributions   This file is not really a C News file, but it is used by some newsreaders, and *nntpd*. It contains the list of distributions recognized by your site, and a description of its (intended) effect. For example, Virtual Brewery has the following file:

```
world          everywhere in the world
local          Only local to this site
nl             Netherlands only
mugnet         MUGNET only
fr             France only
de             Germany only
brewery        Virtual Brewery only
```

log   This file contains a log of all C News activities. It is culled regularly by running *newsdaily*; copies of the old logfiles are kept in *log.o*, *log.oo*, etc.

errlog   This is a log of all error messages created by C News. These do not include articles junked due to wrong group, etc. This file is mailed to the newsmaster (**usenet** by default) automatically by *newsdaily* if it is found to be non-empty.

errlog is cleared by *newsdaily*. Old copies are kept in *errlog.o* and companions.

batchlog   This logs all runs of *sendbatches*. It is usually of scant interest only. It is also attended by *newsdaily*.

watchtime   This is an empty file created each time *newswatch* is run.

17.8   Control Messages

The Usenet news protocol knows a special category of articles which evoke certain responses or actions by the news system. These are called *control* messages. They are recognized by the presence of a `Control:` field in the article header, which contains the name of the control operation to be performed. There are several types of them, all of which are handled by shell scripts located in */usr/lib/news/ctl*.

Most of these will perform their action automatically at the time the article is processed by C News, without notifying the newsmaster. By default, only *checkgroups* messages will be handed to the newsmaster,[9] but you may change this by editing the scripts.

17.8.1 The *cancel* Message

The most widely known message is *cancel*, with which a user may cancel an article sent by her earlier. This effectively removes the article from the spool directories, if it exists. The *cancel* message is forwarded to all sites that receive news from the groups affected, regardless of whether the article has been seen already or not. This is to take into account the possibility that the original article has been delayed over the cancellation message. Some news systems allow users to cancel other person's messages; this is of course a definite no-no.

17.8.2 *newgroup* and *rmgroup*

Two messages dealing with creation or removal of newsgroups are the *newgroup* and *rmgroup* message. Newsgroups below the "usual" hierarchies may be created only after a discussion and voting has been held among Usenet readers. The rules applying to the **alt** hierarchy allow for something close to anarchy. For more information, see the regular postings in **news.announce.newusers** and **news.announce.newgroups**. Never send a *newgroup* or *rmgroup* message yourself unless you definitely know that you are allowed to.

17.8.3 The *checkgroups* Message

checkgroups messages are sent by news administrators to make all sites within a network synchronize their *active* files with the realities of Usenet. For example, commercial Internet service providers might send out such a message to their customers' sites. Once a month, the "official" *checkgroups* message for the major hierarchies is posted to **comp.announce.newgroups** by its moderator. However, it is posted as an ordinary article, not as a control message. To perform the *checkgroups* operation, save this article to a file, say */tmp/check*, remove everything up to the beginning of the control message itself, and feed it to the *checkgroups* script using the following command:

```
# su news -c "/usr/lib/news/bin/ctl/checkgroups" < /tmp/check
```

This will update your *newsgroups* file, adding the groups listed in *localgroups*. The old *newsgroups* file will be moved to *newsgroups.bac*. Note that posting the message locally will rarely work, because *inews* refuses to accept that large an article.

If C News finds mismatches between the *checkgroups* list and the *active* file, it will produce a list of commands that would bring your site up to date, and mail it to the news administrator. The output typically looks like this:

```
From news Sun Jan 30 16:18:11 1994
Date: Sun, 30 Jan 94 16:18 MET
From: news (News Subsystem)
To: usenet
Subject: Problems with your active file

The following newsgroups are not valid and should be removed.
        alt.ascii-art
        bionet.molbio.gene-org
        comp.windows.x.intrisics
        de.answers
```

---

[9]There's a funny typo in RFC 1036 (p.12): "Implementors and administrators may choose to allow control messages to be carried out automatically, or to queue them for annual processing."

You can do this by executing the commands:

```
        /usr/lib/news/bin/maint/delgroup alt.ascii-art
        /usr/lib/news/bin/maint/delgroup bionet.molbio.gene-org
        /usr/lib/news/bin/maint/delgroup comp.windows.x.intrisics
        /usr/lib/news/bin/maint/delgroup de.answers
```

The following newsgroups were missing.

```
        comp.binaries.cbm
        comp.databases.rdb
        comp.os.geos
        comp.os.qnx
        comp.unix.user-friendly
        misc.legal.moderated
        news.newsites
        soc.culture.scientists
        talk.politics.crypto
        talk.politics.tibet
```

When you receive a message like this from your news system, don't believe it blindly. Depending on who sent the *checkgroups* message, it may lack a few groups or even entire hierarchies; so you should be careful about removing any groups. If you find groups are listed as missing that you want to carry at your site, you have to add them using the *addgroup* script. Save the list of missing groups to a file and feed it to the following little script:

```
#!/bin/sh
cd /usr/lib/news

while read group; do
    if grep -si "^$group[[:space:]].*moderated" newsgroup; then
        mod=m
    else
        mod=y
    fi
    /usr/lib/news/bin/maint/addgroup $group $mod
done
```

17.8.4   *sendsys*, *version*, **and** *senduuname*

Finally, there are three messages that may be used to find out about the network's topology. These are *sendsys*, *version*, and *senduuname*. They cause C News to return to the sender the *sys* file, a software version string, and the output of *uuname(1)*, respectively. C News is very laconic about *version* messages; it returns a simple, unadorned "C".

Again, you should *never* issue such a message, unless you have made sure that it cannot leave a your (regional) network. Replies to *sendsys* messages can quickly bring down a UUCP network.[10]

17.9   C News in an NFS Environment

A simple way to distribute news within a local network is to keep all news on a central host, and export the relevant directories via NFS, so that newsreaders may scan the articles directly. The advantage of this method over NNTP is that the overhead involved in retrieving and threading articles is significantly lower. NNTP, on the other hand, wins in a heterogeneous network where equipment varies widely among hosts, or where users don't have equivalent accounts on the server machine.

When using NFS, articles posted on a local host have to be forwarded to the central machine, because accessing adminstrative files might otherwise expose the system to race-conditions that leave the files inconsis-

---

[10]I wouldn't try this on the Internet, either.

tent. Also, you might want to protect your news spool area by exporting it read-only, which requires forwarding to the central machine, too.

C News handles this transparently. When you post an article, your newsreader usually invokes *inews* to inject the article into the news system. This command runs a number of checks on the article, completes the header, and checks the file *server* in */usr/lib/news*. If this file exists and contains a hostname different from the local host's name, *inews* is invoked on that server host via *rsh*. Since the *inews* script uses a number of binary commands and support files from C News, you have to either have C News installed locally, or mount the news software from the server.

For the *rsh* invocation to work properly, each user must have an equivalent account on the server system, i.e. one to which she can log in without being asked for a password.

Make sure that the hostname given in *server* literally matches the output of the *hostname(1)* command on the server machine, else C News will loop forever when trying to deliver the article.

17.10   Maintenance Tools and Tasks

Despite the complexity of C News, a news administrator's life can be fairly easy, because C News provides you with a wide variety of maintenance tools. Some of these are intended to be run regularly from *cron*, like *newsdaily*. Using these scripts reduces daily care and feeding requirements of your C News installation greatly.

Unless stated otherwise, these commands are located in */usr/lib/news/bin/maint*. Note that you must become user **news** before invoking these commands. Running them as super-user may render these files inaccessible to C News.

newsdaily	The name already says it: runs this once a day. It is an important script that helps you keep log files small, retaining copies of each from the last three runs. It also tries to sense any anomalies, like stale batches in the incoming and outgoing directories, postings to unkown or moderated newsgroups, etc. Resulting error messages will be mailed to the newsmaster.
newswatch	This is a script that should be run regularly to look for anomalies in the news system, once an hour or so. It is intended to detect problems that will have immediate effect on the operability of your news system and mail a trouble report to the newsmaster. Things checked include stale lock files that don't get removed, unattended input batches, and disk space shortage.
addgroup	Adds a group to your site locally. The proper invocation is

    addgroup *groupname* y|n|m|=*realgroup*

The second argument has the same meaning as the flag in the *active* file, meaning that anyone may post to the group (*y*), that no-one may post (*n*), that it is moderated (*m*), or that it is an alias for another group (=*realgroup*).

You might also want to use *addgroup* when the first articles in a newly created group arrive earlier than the *newgroup* control message that is intended to create it.

delgroup	Allows you to delete a group locally. Invoke it as

    delgroup *groupname*

You still have to delete the articles that remain in the newsgroup's spool directory. Alternatively, you might leave it to the natural course of events (a.k.a. *expire*) to make them go away.

addmissing	Adds missing articles to the *history* file. Run this script when there are articles that seem to hang around forever.[11]
newsboot	This script should be run at system boot time. It removes any lock files left over when news processes were killed at shutdown, and closes and executes any batches left over from NNTP connections that were terminated when shutting down the system.

---

[11] Ever wondered how to get rid of that "Help! I can't get X11 to work with 0.97.2!!!" article?

newsrunning   This resides in */usr/lib/news/bin/input*, and may be used to disable unbatching of incoming news, for instance during work hours. You may turn off unbatching by invoking

>   */usr/lib/news/bin/*`input/newsrunning off`

It is turned on by using *on* instead of *off*.

Chapter 18

A Description of NNTP

18.1 Introduction

Due to the different network transport used, NNTP provides for a vastly different approach to news exchange from C news. NNTP stands for "Network News Transfer Protocol", and is not a particular software package, but an Internet Standard.[1] It is based on a stream-oriented connection – usually over TCP – between a client anywhere in the network, and a server on a host that keeps netnews on disk storage. The stream connection allows the client and server to interactively negotiate article transfer with nearly no turnaround delay, thus keeping the number of duplicate articles low. Together with the Internet's high transfer rates, this adds up to a news transport that surpasses the original UUCP networks by far. While some years ago it was not uncommon for an article to take two weeks or more before it arrived in the last corner of Usenet, this is now often less than two days; on the Internet itself, it is even within the range of minutes.

Various commands allow clients to retrieve, send and post articles. The difference between sending and posting is that the latter may involve articles with incomplete header information.[2] Article retrieval may be used by news transfer clients as well as newsreaders. This makes NNTP an excellent tool for providing news access to many clients on a local network without going through the contortions that are necessary when using NFS.

NNTP also provides for an active and a passive way of news transfer, colloquially called "pushing" and "pulling". Pushing is basically the same as the C news ihave/sendme protocol. The client offers an article to the server through the "*IHAVE <varmsgid>*" command, and the server returns a response code that indicates whether it already has the article, or if it wants it. If so, the client sends the article, terminated by a single dot on a separate line.

Pushing news has the single disadvantage that it places a heavy load on the server system, since it has to search its history database for every single article.

The opposite technique is pulling news, in which the client requests a list of all (available) articles from a group that have arrived after a specified date. This query is performed by the *NEWNEWS* command. From the returned list of message ids, the client selects those articles it does not yet have, using the *ARTICLE* command for each of them in turn.

The problem with pulling news is that it needs tight control by the server over which groups and distributions it allows a client to request. For example, it has to make sure that no confidential material from newsgroups local to the site are sent to unauthorized clients.

There are also a number of convenience commands for newsreaders that permit them to retrieve the article header and body separately, or even single header lines from a range of articles. This lets you keep all news on a central host, with all users on the (presumably local) network using NNTP-based client programs for reading and posting. This is an alternative to exporting the news directories via NFS which is described in chapter 17.

An overall problem of NNTP is that it allows the knowledgeable to insert articles into the news stream

---

[1] Formally specified in RFC 977.

[2] When posting an article over NNTP, the server always adds at least one header field, which is `Nntp-Posting-Host:`. It contains the client's host name.

with false sender specification. This is called *news faking*.[3] An extension to NNTP allows to require a user authentication for certain commands.

There are a number of NNTP packages available. One of the more widely known is the NNTP daemon, also known as the *reference implementation*. Originally, it was written by Stan Barber and Phil Lapsley to illustrate the details of RFC 977. Its most recent version is *nntpd-1.5.11*, which will be described below. You may either get the sources and compile it yourself, or use the *nntpd* from Fred van Kempen's *net-std* binary package. No ready-to-go binaries of *nntpd* are provided, because of various site-specific values that must be compiled in.

The *nntpd* package consists of a server and two clients for pulling and pushing news, respectively, as well as an *inews* replacement. They live in a B-news environment, but with a little tweaking, they will be happy with C-news, too. However if you plan to use NNTP for more than offering newsreaders access to your news server, the reference implementation is not really an option. We will therefore discuss only the NNTP daemon contained in the *nntpd* package, and leave out the client programs.

There is also a package called "InterNet News", or INN for short, that was written by Rich Salz. It provides both NNTP and UUCP-based news transport, and is more suitable for large news hubs. When it comes to news transport over NNTP, it is definitely better than *nntpd*. INN is currently at version *inn-1.4sec*. There is a kit for building INN on a Linux machine from Arjan de Vet; it is available from **sunsite.unc.edu** in the *system/Mail* directory. If you want to set up INN, please refer to the documentation that comes along with the source, as well as the INN FAQ posted regularly to **news.software.b**.

18.2   Installing the NNTP server

The NNTP server is called *nntpd*, and may be compiled in two ways, depending on the expected load on the news system. There are no compiled versions available, because of some site-specific defaults that are hard-coded into the executable. All configuration is done through macro definines in *common/conf.h*.

nntpd may be configured as either a standalone server that is started at system boot time from *rc.inet2*, or a daemon managed by *inetd*. In the latter case you have to have the following entry in */etc/inetd.conf*:

```
nntp     stream  tcp nowait      news    /usr/etc/in.nntpd    nntpd
```

If you configure *nntpd* as standalone, make sure that any such line in *inetd.conf* is commented out. In either case, you have to make sure there's the following line in */etc/services*:

```
nntp    119/tcp    readnews untp    # Network News Transfer Protocol
```

To temporarily store any incoming articles, etc, *nntpd* also needs a *.tmp* directory in your news spool. You should create it using

```
# mkdir /var/spool/news/.tmp
# chown news.news /var/spool/news/.tmp
```

18.3   Restricting NNTP Access

Access to NNTP resources is governed by the file *nntp_access* in */usr/lib/news*. Lines in the file describe the access rights granted to foreign hosts. Each line has the following format:

```
site read|xfer|both|no post|no [!exceptgroups]
```

If a client connects to the NNTP port, *nntpd* attempts to obtain the host's fully qualified domain name from its IP address by reverse lookup. The client's hostname and IP address are checked against the *site* field of each entry in the order in which they appear in the file. Matches may be either partial or exact. If an entry matches exactly, it applies; if the match is partial, it only applies if there is no other match following which is at least as good. *site* may be specified in one of the following ways:

---
[3]The same problem exists with SMTP, the Simple Mail Transfer Protocol.

hostname   This is a fully qualified domain name of a host. If this matches the client's canonical hostname literally, the entry applies, and all following entries are ignored.

IP address   This is an IP address in dotted quad notation. If the client's IP address matches this, the entry applies, and all following entries are ignored.

domain name   This is a domain name, specified as ***.*domain*. If the client's hostname matches the domain name, the entry matches.

network name   This is the name of a network as specified in */etc/networks*. If the network number of the client's IP address matches the network number associated with the network name, the entry matches.

default   The *default* matches any client.

Entries with a more general site specification should be specified earlier, because any matches by these will be overridden by later, more exact matches.

The second and third field describe the access rights granted to the client. The second details the permissions to retrieve news by pulling (*read*), and transmit news by pushing (*xfer*). A value of *both* enables both, *no* denies access altogether. The third field grants the client the right to post articles, that is, deliver articles with incomplete header information which is completed by the news software. If the second field contains *no*, the third field is ignored.

The fourth field is optional, and contains a comma-separated list of groups the client is denied access to.

A sample *nntp_access* file is shown below:

```
#
# by default, anyone may transfer news, but not read or post
default            xfer          no
#
# public.vbrew.com offers public access via modem, we allow
# them to read and post to any but the local.* groups
public.vbrew.com       read          post     !local
#
# all other hosts at the brewery may read and post
*.vbrew.com            read          post
```

18.4   NNTP Authorization

When capitalizing the access tokens like *xfer* or *read* in the *nntp_acces* file, *nntpd* requires the authorization from the client for the respective operations. For instance, when specifying a permission of *Xfer* or *XFER*, *nntpd* will not let the client transfer articles to your site unless it passes authorization.

The authorization procedure is implemented by means of a new NNTP command named *AUTHINFO*. Using this command, the client transmits a user name and a password to the NNTP server. *nntpd* will validate them by checking them against the */etc/passwd* database, and verify that the user belongs to the **nntp** group.

The current implementation of NNTP authorization is only experimental, and has therefore not been implemented very portably. The result of this is that it works only with plain-style password databases; shadow passwords will not be recognized.

18.5   *nntpd* Interaction with C News

When receiving an article, *nntpd* has to deliver it to the news subsystem. Depending on whether it was received as a result of an *IHAVE* or *POST* command, the article is handed to *rnews* or *inews*, respectively. Instead of invoking *rnews*, you may also configure it (at compile time) to batch the incoming articles and move the resulting batches to */var/spool/news/in.coming*, where they are left for *relaynews* to pick them up at the next queue run.

To be able to properly perform the ihave/sendme protocol, *nntpd* has to be able to access the *history* file. At compile time, you therefore have to make sure the path is set correctly. You should also make sure that C news and *nntpd* agree on the format of your history file. C news uses *dbm* hashing functions to access it; however, there are quite a number of different and slightly incompatible implementations of the *dbm* library. If C news has been linked with the a different *dbm* library than you have in your standard *libc*, you have to link *nntpd* with this library, too.

A typical symptom of *nntpd* and C news disagreeing on the database format are error messages in the system log that *nntpd* could not open it properly, or duplicate articles received via NNTP. A good test is to pick an article from your spool area, telnet to the *nntp* port, and offer it to *nntpd* as shown in the example below (your input is marked *like this*). Of course, you have to replace <*msg@id*> with the message-ID of the article you want to feed to *nntpd* again.

```
$ telnet localhost nntp
Trying 127.0.0.1...
Connected to loalhost
Escape characters is '^]'.
201 vstout NNTP[auth] server version 1.5.11t (16 November 1991) ready at Sun Feb 6 16:02:32
1194 (no posting)
IHAVE <msg@id>
435 Got it.
QUIT
```

This conversation shows the proper reaction of *nntpd*; the message "Got it" tells you that it already has this article. If you get a message of "335 Ok" instead, the lookup in the history file failed for some reason. Terminate the conversation by typing Ctrl-D. You can check what has gone wrong by checking the system log; *nntpd* logs all kinds of messages to the *daemon* facility of *syslog*. An incompatible *dbm* library usually manifests itself in a message complaining that *dbminit* failed.

Chapter 19

Newsreader Configuration

Newsreaders are intended to offer the user functionality that allows her to access the functions of the news system easily, like posting articles, or skimming the contents of a newsgroup in a comfortable way. The quality of this interface is subject of endless flame wars.

There are a couple of newsreaders available which have been ported to Linux. Below I will describe the basic setup for the three most popular ones, namely *tin*, *trn*, and *nn*.

One of the most effective newsreaders is

```
$ find /var/spool/news -name '[0-9]*' -exec cat {} \; | more
```

This is the way UNIX die-hards read their news.

The majority of newsreaders, however, are much more sophisticated. They usually offer a full-screen interface with separate levels for displaying all groups the user has subscribed to, for displaying an overview of all articles in one group. and for individual articles.

At the newsgroup level, most newsreaders display a list of articles, showing their subject line, and the author. In big groups, it is impossible for the user to keep track of articles relating to each other, although it is possible to identify responses to earlier articles.

A response usually repeats the original article's subject, prepending it with "`Re:` ". Additionally, the message id of the article it is a direct follow-up to may be given in the `References:` header line. Sorting articles by these two criteria generates small clusters (in fact, trees) of articles, which are called *threads*. One of the tasks in writing a newsreader is devising an efficient scheme of threading, because the time required for this is proportional to the square of the number of articles.

Here, we will not dig any further into how the user interfaces are built. All newsreaders currently available for Linux have a good help function, so you ought to get along.

In the following, we will only deal with administrative tasks. Most of these relate to the creation of threads databases and accounting.

19.1   *tin* Configuration

The most versatile newsreader with respect to threading is *tin*. It was written by Iain Lea and is loosely modeled on an older newsreader named *tass*.[1] It does its threading when the user enters the newsgroup, and it is pretty fast at this unless you're doing this via NNTP.

On an 486DX50, it takes roughly 30 seconds to thread 1000 articles when reading directly from disk. Over NNTP to a loaded news server, this would be somewhere above 5 minutes.[2] You may improve this by regularly updating your index file with the `-u` option, or by invoking *tin* with the `-U` option.

---

[1]Written by Rich Skrenta.
[2]Things improve drastically if the NNTP server does the threading itself, and lets the client retrieve the threads databases; INN-1.4 does this, for instance.

Usually, *tin* dumps its threading databases in the user's home directory below *.tin/index*. This may however be costly in terms of resources, so that you should want to keep a single copy of them in a central location. This may be achieved by making *tin* setuid to **news**, for example, or some entirely unprivileged account.[3] *tin* will then keep all thread databases below */var/spool/news/.index*. For any file access or shell escape, it will reset its effective uid to the real uid of the user who invoked it.[4]

A better solution is to install the *tind* indexing daemon that runs as a daemon and regularly updates the index files. This daemon is however not included in any release of Linux, so you would have to compile it yourself. If you are running a LAN with a central news server, you may even run *tind* on the server and have all clients retrieve the index files via NNTP. This, of course, requires an extension to NNTP. Patches for *nntpd* that implement this extension are included in the *tin* source.

The version of *tin* included in some Linux distributions has no NNTP support compiled in, but most do have it now. When invoked as *rtin* or with the -r option, *tin* tries to connect to the NNTP server specified in the file */etc/nntpserver* or in the **NNTPSERVER** environment variable. The *nntpserver* file simply contains the server's name on a single line.

19.2   *trn* Configuration

trn is the successor to an older newsreader, too, namely *rn* (which means *read news*). The "t" in its name stands for "threaded". It was written by Wayne Davidson.

Unlike *tin*, *trn* has no provision for generating its threading database at run-time. Instead, it uses those prepared by a program called *mthreads* that has to be invoked regularly from *cron* to update the index files.

Not running *mthreads*, however, doesn't mean you cannot access new articles, it only means you will have all those "Novell buys out Linix!!" articles scattered across your article selection menu, instead of a single thread you may easily skip.

To turn on threading for particular newsgroups, *mthreads* is invoked with the list of newsgroups on the command line. The list is made up in exactly the same fashion as the one in the *sys* file:

```
mthreads comp,rec,!rec.games.go
```

will enable threading for all of **comp** and **rec**, except for **rec.games.go** (people who play Go don't need fancy threads). After that, you simply invoke it without any option at all to make it thread any newly arrived articles. Threading of all groups found in your *active* file can be turned on by invoking *mthreads* with a group list of **all**.

If you're receiving news during the night, you will customarily run *mthreads* once in the morning, but you can also to do so more frequently if needed. Sites that have very heavy traffic may want to run *mthreads* in daemon mode. When it is started at boot time using the -d option, it puts itself in the background, and wakes up every 10 minutes to check if there are any newly-arrived articles, and threads them. To run *mthreads* in daemon mode, put the following line in your *rc.news* script:

```
/usr/local/bin/rn/mthreads -deav
```

The -a option makes *mthread* automatically turn on threading for new groups as they are created; -v enables verbose log messages to *mthreads*' log file, *mt.log* in the directory where you have *trn* installed.

Old articles no longer available must be removed from the index files regularly. By default, only articles whose number is below the low water mark will be removed.[5] Articles above this number who have been expired nevertheless (because the oldest article has been assigned an long expiry date by an `Expires:` header field) may be removed by giving *mthreads* the -e option to force an "enhanced" expiry run. When *mthreads* is running in daemon mode, the -e option makes it put in such an enhanced expiry run once a day, shortly after midnight.

19.3   *nn* Configuration

nn, written by Kim F. Storm, claims to be a newsreader whose ultimate goal is not to read news. It's name stands for "No News", and its motto is "No news is good news. *nn* is better."

---

[3]However, do *not* use **nobody** for this. As a rule, no files or commands whatsoever should be associated with this user.
[4]This is the reason why you will get ugly error messages when invoking it as super user. But then, you shouldn't work as **root**, anyway.
[5]Note that C news doesn't update this low water mark automatically; you have to run *updatemin* to do so. Please refer to chapter 17.

To achieve this ambitious goal, *nn* comes along with a large assortment of maintenance tools that not only allow generation of threads, but also extensive checks on the consistency of these databases, accounting, gathering of usage statistics, and access restrictions. There is also an administration program called *nnadmin*, which allows you to perform these tasks interactively. It is very intuitive, hence we will not dwell on these aspects, and only deal with the generation of the index files.

The *nn* threads database manager is called *nnmaster*. It is usually run as a daemon, started from the *rc.news* or *rc.inet2* script. It is invoked as

```
/usr/local/lib/nn/nnmaster -l -r -C
```

This enables threading for all newsgroups present in your *active* file.

Equivalently, you may invoke *nnmaster* periodically from *cron*, giving it a list of groups to act upon. This list is very similar to the subscription list in the *sys* file, except that it uses blanks instead of commas. Instead of the fake group name **all**, an empty argument of "" should be used to denote all groups. A sample invocation is

```
# /usr/local/lib/nn/nnmaster !rec.games.go rec comp
```

Note that the order is significant here: The leftmost group specification that matches always wins. Thus, if we had put *!rec.games.go* after *rec*, all articles from this group had been threaded nevertheless.

nn offers several methods to remove expired articles from its databases. The first is to update the database by scanning the news group directories and discarding the entries whose corresponding article is no longer available. This is the default operation obtained by invoking *nnmaster* with the -E option. It is reasonably fast unless you're doing this via NNTP.

Method 2 behaves exactly like a default expiry run of *mthreads*, in that it only removes those entries that refer to articles whose number is below the low water mark in the *active* file. It may be enabled using the -e option.

Finally, a third strategy is to discard the entire database and recollect all articles. This may be done by giving -E3 to *nnmaster*.

The list of groups to be expired is given by the -F option in the same fashion as above. However, if you have *nnmaster* running as daemon, you must kill it (using -k) before expiry can take place, and to re-start it with the original options afterwards. Thus the proper command to run expire on all groups using method 1 is:

```
# nnmaster -kF ""
# nnmaster -lrC
```

There are many more flags that may be used to fine-tune the behavior of *nn*. If you are concerned about removing bad articles or digestifying article digests, read the *nnmaster* manual page.

nnmaster relies on a file named *GROUPS*, which is located in */usr/local/lib/nn*. If it does not exist initially, it is created. For each newsgroup, it contains a line that begins with the group's name, optionally followed by a time stamp, and flags. You may edit these flags to enable certain behavior for the group in question, but you may not change the order in which the groups appear.[6] The flags allowed and their effects are detailed in the *nnmaster* manual page, too.

---

[6]This is because their order has to agree with that of the entries in the (binary) *MASTER* file.

Appendix A

A Null Printer Cable for PLIP

To make a Null Printer Cable for use with a PLIP connection, you need two 25-pin connectors (called DB-25) and some 11-conductor cable. The cable must be at most 15 meters long.

If you look at the connector, you should be able to read tiny numbers at the base of each pin, from 1 for the pin top left (if you hold the broader side up) to 25 for the pin bottom right. For the Null Printer cable, you have to connect the following pins of both connectors with each other:

D0	2—15	ERROR
D1	3—13	SLCT
D2	4—12	PAPOUT
D3	5—10	ACK
D4	6—11	BUSY
GROUND	25—25	GROUND
ERROR	15— 2	D0
SLCT	13— 3	D1
PAPOUT	12— 4	D2
ACK	10— 5	D3
BUSY	11— 6	D4

All remaining pins remain unconnected. If the cable is shielded, the shield should be connected to the DB-25's metallic shell on one end only.

Appendix B

Sample smail Configuration Files

This section shows sample configuration files for a UUCP leaf site on a local area network. They are based on the sample files included in the source distribution of *smail-3.1.28*. Although I make a feeble attempt to explain how these files work, you are advised to read the very fine *smail(8)* manual page, which discusses these files in great length. Once you've understood the basic idea behind *smail* configuration, it's worthwhile reading. It's easy!

The first file shown is the *routers* file, which describes a set of routers to *smail*. When *smail* has to deliver a message to a given address, it hands the address to all routers in turn, until one of them matches it. Matching here means that the router finds the destination host in its database, be it the *paths* file, */etc/hosts*, or whatever routing mechanism the router interfaces to.

Entries in *smail* configuration files always begin with a unique name identifying the router, transport, or director. They are followed by a list of attributes that define its behavior. This list consists of a set of global attributes, such as the *driver* used, and private attributes that are only understood by that particular driver. Attributes are separated by commas, while the sets of global and private attributes are separated from each other using a semicolon.

To make these fine distinctions clear, assume you want to maintain two separate pathalias files; one containing the routing information for your domain, and a second one containing global routing information, probably generated from the UUCP maps. With *smail*, you can now specify two routers in the *routers* file, both of which use the *pathalias* driver. This driver looks up hostnames in a pathalias database. It expects to be given the name of the file in a private attribute:

```
#
# pathalias database for intra-domain routing
domain_paths:
        driver=pathalias,           # look up host in a paths file
        transport=uux;              # if matched, deliver over UUCP

        file=paths/domain,          # file is /usr/lib/smail/paths/domain
        proto=lsearch,              # file is unsorted (linear search)
        optional,                   # ignore if the file does not exist
        required=vbrew.com,         # look up only *.vbrew.com hosts

#
# pathalias database for routing to hosts outside our domain
world_paths:
        driver=pathalias,           # look up host in a paths file
        transport=uux;              # if matched, deliver over UUCP

        file=paths/world,           # file is /usr/lib/smail/paths/world
        proto=bsearch,              # file is sorted with sort(1)
        optional,                   # ignore if the file does not exist
        -required,                  # no required domains
        domain=uucp,                # strip ending ".uucp" before searching
```

The second global attribute given in each of the two *routers* entries above defines the transport that should be used when the router matches the address. In our case, the message will be delivered using the *uux* transport. Transports are defined in the *transports* file, which is exlained below.

521

You can fine-tune by which transport a message will be delivered if you specify a method file instead of the *transports* attribute. Method files provide a mapping from target hostnames to transports. We won't deal with them here.

The following *routers* file defines routers for a local area network that query the resolver library. On an Internet host, however, you would want to use a router that handles MX records. You should therefore uncomment the alternative *inet_bind* router that uses *smail*'s builtin BIND driver.

In an environment that mixes UUCP and TCP/IP, you may encounter the problem that you have hosts in your */etc/hosts* file that you have only occasional SLIP or PPP contact with. Usually, you would still want to send any mail for them over UUCP. To prevent the *inet_hosts* driver from matching these hosts, you have to put them into the *paths/force* file. This is another pathalias-style database, and is consulted before *smail* queries the resolver.

```
# A sample /usr/lib/smail/routers file
#
# force - force UUCP delivery to certain hosts, even when
#         they are in our /etc/hosts
force:
        driver=pathalias,         # look up host in a paths file
        transport=uux;            # if matched, deliver over UUCP

        file=paths/force,         # file is /usr/lib/smail/paths/force
        optional,                 # ignore if the file does not exist
        proto=lsearch,            # file is unsorted (linear search)
        -required,                # no required domains
        domain=uucp,              # strip ending ".uucp" before searching


# inet_addrs - match domain literals containing literal
#       IP addresses, such as in janet@[191.72.2.1]
inet_addrs:
        driver=gethostbyaddr,     # driver to match IP domain literals
        transport=smtp;           # deliver using SMTP over TCP/IP

        fail_if_error,            # fail if address is malformed
        check_for_local,          # deliver directly if host is ourself

# inet_hosts - match hostnames with gethostbyname(3N)
#       Comment this out if you wish to use the BIND version instead.
inet_hosts:
        driver=gethostbyname,     # match hosts with the library function
        transport=smtp;           # use default SMTP

        -required,                # no required domains
        -domain,                  # no defined domain suffixes
        -only_local_domain,       # don't restrict to defined domains


# inet_hosts - alternate version using BIND to access the DNS
#inet_hosts:
#       driver=bind,              # use built-in BIND driver
#       transport=smtp;           # use TCP/IP SMTP for delivery
#
#       defnames,                 # use standard domain searching
#       defer_no_connect,         # try again if the nameserver is down
#       -local_mx_okay,           # fail (don't pass through) an MX
#                                 # to the local host


#
# pathalias database for intra-domain routing
domain_paths:
        driver=pathalias,         # look up host in a paths file
        transport=uux;            # if matched, deliver over UUCP

        file=paths/domain,        # file is /usr/lib/smail/paths/domain
        proto=lsearch,            # file is unsorted (linear search)
        optional,                 # ignore if the file does not exist
```

```
              required=vbrew.com,      # look up only *.vbrew.com hosts


#
# pathalias database for routing to hosts outside our domain
world_paths:
        driver=pathalias,        # look up host in a paths file
        transport=uux;           # if matched, deliver over UUCP


        file=paths/world,        # file is /usr/lib/smail/paths/world
        proto=bsearch,           # file is sorted with sort(1)
        optional,                # ignore if the file does not exist
        -required,               # no required domains
        domain=uucp,             # strip ending ".uucp" before searching



# smart_host - a partially specified smarthost director
#       If the smart_path attribute is not defined in
#       /usr/lib/smail/config, this router is ignored.
#       The transport attribute is overridden by the global
#       smart_transport variable
smart_host:
        driver=smarthost,        # special-case driver
        transport=uux;           # by default deliver over UUCP


        -path,                   # use smart_path config file variable
```

The handling of mail for local addresses is configured in the *directors* file. It is made up just like the *routers* file, with a list of entries that define a director each. Directors do *not* deliver a message, they merely perform all the redirection that is possible, for instance through aliases, mail forwarding, and the like.

When delivering mail to a local address, such as **janet**, *smail* passes the usr name to all directors in turn. If a director matches, it either specifies a transport the message should be delivered by (for instance, to the user's mailbox file), or generates a new address (for instance, after evaluating an alias).

Because of the security issues involved, directors usually do a lot of checking of whether the files they use may be compromised or not. Addresses obtained in a somewhat dubious way (for instance from a world-writable *aliases* file) are flagged as unsecure. Some transport drivers will turn down such addresses, for instance the transport that delivers a message to a file.

Apart from this, *smail* also *associates a user* with each address. Any write or read operations are performed as the user. For delivery to, say **janet**'s mailbox, the address is of course associated with **janet**. Other addresses, such as those obtained from the *aliases* file, have other users associated from them, for instance, the **nobody** user.

For details of these features, please refer to the *smail(8)* manpage.

```
# A sample /usr/lib/smail/directors file

# aliasinclude - expand ":include:filename" addresses produced
#       by alias files
aliasinclude:
        driver=aliasinclude,     # use this special-case driver
        nobody;                  # access file as nobody user if unsecure


        copysecure,              # get permissions from alias director
        copyowners,              # get owners from alias director

# forwardinclude - expand ":include:filename" addrs produced
#       by forward files
forwardinclude:
        driver=forwardinclude,   # use this special-case driver
        nobody;                  # access file as nobody user if unsecure


        checkpath,               # check path accessibility
        copysecure,              # get perms from forwarding director
        copyowners,              # get owners from forwarding director
```

```
# aliases - search for alias expansions stored in a database
aliases:
        driver=aliasfile,      # general-purpose aliasing director
        -nobody,               # all addresses are associated
                               # with nobody by default anyway
        sender_okay,           # don't remove sender from expansions
        owner=owner-$user;     # problems go to an owner address

        file=/usr/lib/aliases, # default: sendmail compatible
        modemask=002,          # should not be globally writable
        optional,              # ignore if file does not exist
        proto=lsearch,         # unsorted ASCII file

# dotforward - expand .forward files in user home directories
dotforward:
        driver=forwardfile,    # general-purpose forwarding director
        owner=real-$user,      # problems go to the user's mailbox
        nobody,                # use nobody user, if unsecure
        sender_okay;           # sender never removed from expansion

        file=~/.forward,       # .forward file in home directories
        checkowner,            # the user can own this file
        owners=root,           # or root can own the file
        modemask=002,          # it should not be globally writable
        caution=0-10:uucp:daemon, # don't run things as root or daemons
        # be extra careful of remotely accessible home directories
        unsecure="~ftp:~uucp:~nuucp:/tmp:/usr/tmp",

# forwardto - expand a "Forward to " line at the top of
#        the user's mailbox file
forwardto:
        driver=forwardfile,
        owner=Postmaster,      # errors go to Postmaster
        nobody,                # use nobody user, if unsecure
        sender_okay;           # don't remove sender from expansion

        file=/var/spool/mail/${lc:user}, # location of user's mailbox
        forwardto,             # enable "Forward to " check
        checkowner,            # the user can own this file
        owners=root,           # or root can own the file
        modemask=0002,         # under System V, group mail can write
        caution=0-10:uucp:daemon, # don't run things as root or daemons

# user - match users on the local host with delivery to their mailboxes
user:   driver=user;           # driver to match usernames

        transport=local,       # local transport goes to mailboxes

# real_user - match usernames when prefixed with the string "real-"
real_user:
        driver=user;           # driver to match usernames

        transport=local,       # local transport goes to mailboxes
        prefix="real-",        # for example, match real-root

# lists - expand mailing lists stored below /usr/lib/smail/lists
lists:  driver=forwardfile,
        caution,               # flag all addresses with caution
        nobody,                # and then associate the nobody user
        sender_okay,           # do NOT remove the sender
        owner=owner-$user;     # the list owner
```

```
                # map the name of the mailing list to lower case
                file=lists/${lc:user},
```

After successfully routing or directing a message, *smail* hands the message to the transport specified by the router or director that matched the address. These transports are defined in the *transports* file. Again, a transport is defined by a set of global and private options.

The most important option defined by each entry is driver that handles the transport, for instance the *pipe* driver, which invokes the command specified in the *cmd* attribute. Apart from this, there are a number of global attributes a transport may use, that perform various transformations on the message header, and possibly message body. The *return_path* attribute, for instance, makes the transport insert a *return_path* field in the message header The *unix_from_hack* attribute makes it precede every occurrence of the word From at the beginning of a line with a > sign.

```
# A sample /usr/lib/smail/transports file

# local - deliver mail to local users
local:  driver=appendfile,      # append message to a file
        return_path,            # include a Return-Path: field
        from,                   # supply a From_ envelope line
        unix_from_hack,         # insert > before From in body
        local;                  # use local forms for delivery

        file=/var/spool/mail/${lc:user}, # location of mailbox files
        group=mail,             # group to own file for System V
        mode=0660,              # group mail can access
        suffix="\n",            # append an extra newline

# pipe - deliver mail to shell commands
pipe:   driver=pipe,            # pipe message to another program
        return_path,            # include a Return-Path: field
        from,                   # supply a From_ envelope line
        unix_from_hack,         # insert > before From in body
        local;                  # use local forms for delivery

        cmd="/bin/sh -c $user", # send address to the Bourne Shell
        parent_env,             # environment info from parent addr
        pipe_as_user,           # use user-id associated with address
        ignore_status,          # ignore a non-zero exit status
        ignore_write_errors,    # ignore write errors, i.e., broken pipe
        umask=0022,             # umask for child process
        -log_output,            # do not log stdout/stderr

# file - deliver mail to files
file:   driver=appendfile,
        return_path,            # include a Return-Path: field
        from,                   # supply a From_ envelope line
        unix_from_hack,         # insert > before From in body
        local;                  # use local forms for delivery

        file=$user,             # file is taken from address
        append_as_user,         # use user-id associated with address
        expand_user,            # expand ~ and $ within address
        suffix="\n",            # append an extra newline
        mode=0600,              # set permissions to 600

# uux - deliver to the rmail program on a remote UUCP site
uux:    driver=pipe,
        uucp,                   # use UUCP-style addressing forms
        from,                   # supply a From_ envelope line
        max_addrs=5,            # at most 5 addresses per invocation
        max_chars=200;          # at most 200 chars of addresses

        cmd="/usr/bin/uux - -r -a$sender -g$grade $host!rmail $(($user)$)",
```

```
                pipe_as_sender,        # have uucp logs contain caller
                log_output,            # save error output for bounce messages
#               defer_child_errors,    # retry if uux returns an error

# demand - deliver to a remote rmail program, polling immediately
demand: driver=pipe,
                uucp,                  # use UUCP-style addressing forms
                from,                  # supply a From_ envelope line
                max_addrs=5,           # at most 5 addresses per invocation
                max_chars=200;         # at most 200 chars of addresses

                cmd="/usr/bin/uux - -a$sender -g$grade $host!rmail $(($user)$)",
                pipe_as_sender,        # have uucp logs contain caller
                log_output,            # save error output for bounce messages
#               defer_child_errors,    # retry if uux returns an error

# hbsmtp - half-baked BSMTP. The output files must
#          be processed regularly and sent out via UUCP.
hbsmtp: driver=appendfile,
                inet,                  # use RFC 822-addressing
                hbsmtp,                # batched SMTP w/o HELO and QUIT
                -max_addrs, -max_chars; # no limit on number of addresses

                file="/var/spool/smail/hbsmtp/$host",
                user=root,             # file is owned by root
                mode=0600,             # only read-/writable by root.

# smtp - deliver using SMTP over TCP/IP
smtp:   driver=tcpsmtp,
                inet,
                -max_addrs, -max_chars; # no limit on number of addresses

                short_timeout=5m,         # timeout for short operations
                long_timeout=2h,          # timeout for longer SMTP operations
                service=smtp,             # connect to this service port
# For internet use: uncomment the below 4 lines
#               use_bind,                 # resolve MX and multiple A records
#               defnames,                 # use standard domain searching
#               defer_no_connect,         # try again if the nameserver is down
#               -local_mx_okay,           # fail an MX to the local host
```

Appendix C

The GNU General Public License

Printed below is the GNU General Public License (the *GPL* or *copyleft*), under which Linux is licensed. It is reproduced here to clear up some of the confusion about Linux's copyright status—Linux is *not* shareware, and it is *not* in the public domain. The bulk of the Linux kernel is copyright ©1993 by Linus Torvalds, and other software and parts of the kernel are copyrighted by their authors. Thus, Linux *is* copyrighted, however, you may redistribute it under the terms of the GPL printed below.

GNU GENERAL PUBLIC LICENSE
Version 2, June 1991

Copyright (C) 1989, 1991 Free Software Foundation, Inc. 675 Mass Ave, Cambridge, MA 02139, USA Everyone is permitted to copy and distribute verbatim copies of this license document, but changing it is not allowed.

C.1 Preamble

The licenses for most software are designed to take away your freedom to share and change it. By contrast, the GNU General Public License is intended to guarantee your freedom to share and change free software–to make sure the software is free for all its users. This General Public License applies to most of the Free Software Foundation's software and to any other program whose authors commit to using it. (Some other Free Software Foundation software is covered by the GNU Library General Public License instead.) You can apply it to your programs, too.

When we speak of free software, we are referring to freedom, not price. Our General Public Licenses are designed to make sure that you have the freedom to distribute copies of free software (and charge for this service if you wish), that you receive source code or can get it if you want it, that you can change the software or use pieces of it in new free programs; and that you know you can do these things.

To protect your rights, we need to make restrictions that forbid anyone to deny you these rights or to ask you to surrender the rights. These restrictions translate to certain responsibilities for you if you distribute copies of the software, or if you modify it.

For example, if you distribute copies of such a program, whether gratis or for a fee, you must give the recipients all the rights that you have. You must make sure that they, too, receive or can get the source code. And you must show them these terms so they know their rights.

We protect your rights with two steps: (1) copyright the software, and (2) offer you this license which gives you legal permission to copy, distribute and/or modify the software.

Also, for each author's protection and ours, we want to make certain that everyone understands that there is no warranty for this free software. If the software is modified by someone else and passed on, we want its recipients to know that what they have is not the original, so that any problems introduced by others will not reflect on the original authors' reputations.

Finally, any free program is threatened constantly by software patents. We wish to avoid the danger that redistributors of a free program will individually obtain patent licenses, in effect making the program proprietary. To prevent this, we have made it clear that any patent must be licensed for everyone's free use or not licensed at all.

The precise terms and conditions for copying, distribution and modification follow.

C.2   Terms and Conditions for Copying, Distribution, and Modification

0. This License applies to any program or other work which contains a notice placed by the copyright holder saying it may be distributed under the terms of this General Public License. The "Program", below, refers to any such program or work, and a "work based on the Program" means either the Program or any derivative work under copyright law: that is to say, a work containing the Program or a portion of it, either verbatim or with modifications and/or translated into another language. (Hereinafter, translation is included without limitation in the term "modification".) Each licensee is addressed as "you".

   Activities other than copying, distribution and modification are not covered by this License; they are outside its scope. The act of running the Program is not restricted, and the output from the Program is covered only if its contents constitute a work based on the Program (independent of having been made by running the Program). Whether that is true depends on what the Program does.

1. You may copy and distribute verbatim copies of the Program's source code as you receive it, in any medium, provided that you conspicuously and appropriately publish on each copy an appropriate copyright notice and disclaimer of warranty; keep intact all the notices that refer to this License and to the absence of any warranty; and give any other recipients of the Program a copy of this License along with the Program.

   You may charge a fee for the physical act of transferring a copy, and you may at your option offer warranty protection in exchange for a fee.

2. You may modify your copy or copies of the Program or any portion of it, thus forming a work based on the Program, and copy and distribute such modifications or work under the terms of Section 1 above, provided that you also meet all of these conditions:

   a. You must cause the modified files to carry prominent notices stating that you changed the files and the date of any change.

   b. You must cause any work that you distribute or publish, that in whole or in part contains or is derived from the Program or any part thereof, to be licensed as a whole at no charge to all third parties under the terms of this License.

   c. If the modified program normally reads commands interactively when run, you must cause it, when started running for such interactive use in the most ordinary way, to print or display an announcement including an appropriate copyright notice and a notice that there is no warranty (or else, saying that you provide a warranty) and that users may redistribute the program under these conditions, and telling the user how to view a copy of this License. (Exception: if the Program itself is interactive but does not normally print such an announcement, your work based on the Program is not required to print an announcement.)

   These requirements apply to the modified work as a whole. If identifiable sections of that work are not derived from the Program, and can be reasonably considered independent and separate works in themselves, then this License, and its terms, do not apply to those sections when you distribute them as separate works. But when you distribute the same sections as part of a whole which is a work based on the Program, the distribution of the whole must be on the terms of this License, whose permissions for other licensees extend to the entire whole, and thus to each and every part regardless of who wrote it.

   Thus, it is not the intent of this section to claim rights or contest your rights to work written entirely by you; rather, the intent is to exercise the right to control the distribution of derivative or collective works based on the Program.

   In addition, mere aggregation of another work not based on the Program with the Program (or with a work based on the Program) on a volume of a storage or distribution medium does not bring the other work under the scope of this License.

3. You may copy and distribute the Program (or a work based on it, under Section 2) in object code or executable form under the terms of Sections 1 and 2 above provided that you also do one of the following:

   a. Accompany it with the complete corresponding machine-readable source code, which must be distributed under the terms of Sections 1 and 2 above on a medium customarily used for software interchange; or,

   b. Accompany it with a written offer, valid for at least three years, to give any third party, for a charge no more than your cost of physically performing source distribution, a complete machine-readable copy of the corresponding source code, to be distributed under the terms of Sections 1 and 2 above on a medium customarily used for software interchange; or,

   c. Accompany it with the information you received as to the offer to distribute corresponding source code. (This alternative is allowed only for noncommercial distribution and only if you received the program in object code or executable form with such an offer, in accord with Subsection b above.)

The source code for a work means the preferred form of the work for making modifications to it. For an executable work, complete source code means all the source code for all modules it contains, plus any associated interface definition files, plus the scripts used to control compilation and installation of the executable. However, as a special exception, the source code distributed need not include anything that is normally distributed (in either source or binary form) with the major components (compiler, kernel, and so on) of the operating system on which the executable runs, unless that component itself accompanies the executable.

If distribution of executable or object code is made by offering access to copy from a designated place, then offering equivalent access to copy the source code from the same place counts as distribution of the source code, even though third parties are not compelled to copy the source along with the object code.

4. You may not copy, modify, sublicense, or distribute the Program except as expressly provided under this License. Any attempt otherwise to copy, modify, sublicense or distribute the Program is void, and will automatically terminate your rights under this License. However, parties who have received copies, or rights, from you under this License will not have their licenses terminated so long as such parties remain in full compliance.

5. You are not required to accept this License, since you have not signed it. However, nothing else grants you permission to modify or distribute the Program or its derivative works. These actions are prohibited by law if you do not accept this License. Therefore, by modifying or distributing the Program (or any work based on the Program), you indicate your acceptance of this License to do so, and all its terms and conditions for copying, distributing or modifying the Program or works based on it.

6. Each time you redistribute the Program (or any work based on the Program), the recipient automatically receives a license from the original licensor to copy, distribute or modify the Program subject to these terms and conditions. You may not impose any further restrictions on the recipients' exercise of the rights granted herein. You are not responsible for enforcing compliance by third parties to this License.

7. If, as a consequence of a court judgment or allegation of patent infringement or for any other reason (not limited to patent issues), conditions are imposed on you (whether by court order, agreement or otherwise) that contradict the conditions of this License, they do not excuse you from the conditions of this License. If you cannot distribute so as to satisfy simultaneously your obligations under this License and any other pertinent obligations, then as a consequence you may not distribute the Program at all. For example, if a patent license would not permit royalty-free redistribution of the Program by all those who receive copies directly or indirectly through you, then the only way you could satisfy both it and this License would be to refrain entirely from distribution of the Program.

If any portion of this section is held invalid or unenforceable under any particular circumstance, the balance of the section is intended to apply and the section as a whole is intended to apply in other circumstances.

It is not the purpose of this section to induce you to infringe any patents or other property right claims or to contest validity of any such claims; this section has the sole purpose of protecting the integrity of the free software distribution system, which is implemented by public license practices. Many people have made generous contributions to the wide range of software distributed through that system in reliance on consistent application of that system; it is up to the author/donor to decide if he or she is willing to distribute software through any other system and a licensee cannot impose that choice.

This section is intended to make thoroughly clear what is believed to be a consequence of the rest of this License.

8. If the distribution and/or use of the Program is restricted in certain countries either by patents or by copyrighted interfaces, the original copyright holder who places the Program under this License may add an explicit geographical distribution limitation excluding those countries, so that distribution is permitted only in or among countries not thus excluded. In such case, this License incorporates the limitation as if written in the body of this License.

9. The Free Software Foundation may publish revised and/or new versions of the General Public License from time to time. Such new versions will be similar in spirit to the present version, but may differ in detail to address new problems or concerns.

Each version is given a distinguishing version number. If the Program specifies a version number of this License which applies to it and "any later version", you have the option of following the terms and conditions either of that version or of any later version published by the Free Software Foundation. If the Program does not specify a version number of this License, you may choose any version ever published by the Free Software Foundation.

10. If you wish to incorporate parts of the Program into other free programs whose distribution conditions are different, write to the author to ask for permission. For software which is copyrighted by the Free Software Foundation, write to the Free Software Foundation; we sometimes make exceptions for this. Our decision will be guided by the two goals of preserving the free status of all derivatives of our free software and of promoting the sharing and reuse of software generally.

NO WARRANTY

11. BECAUSE THE PROGRAM IS LICENSED FREE OF CHARGE, THERE IS NO WARRANTY FOR THE PROGRAM, TO THE EXTENT PERMITTED BY APPLICABLE LAW. EXCEPT WHEN OTHERWISE

STATED IN WRITING THE COPYRIGHT HOLDERS AND/OR OTHER PARTIES PROVIDE THE PRO-
GRAM "AS IS" WITHOUT WARRANTY OF ANY KIND, EITHER EXPRESSED OR IMPLIED, INCLUDING,
BUT NOT LIMITED TO, THE IMPLIED WARRANTIES OF MERCHANTABILITY AND FITNESS FOR A
PARTICULAR PURPOSE. THE ENTIRE RISK AS TO THE QUALITY AND PERFORMANCE OF THE
PROGRAM IS WITH YOU. SHOULD THE PROGRAM PROVE DEFECTIVE, YOU ASSUME THE COST
OF ALL NECESSARY SERVICING, REPAIR OR CORRECTION.

12. IN NO EVENT UNLESS REQUIRED BY APPLICABLE LAW OR AGREED TO IN WRITING WILL ANY
COPYRIGHT HOLDER, OR ANY OTHER PARTY WHO MAY MODIFY AND/OR REDISTRIBUTE THE
PROGRAM AS PERMITTED ABOVE, BE LIABLE TO YOU FOR DAMAGES, INCLUDING ANY GEN-
ERAL, SPECIAL, INCIDENTAL OR CONSEQUENTIAL DAMAGES ARISING OUT OF THE USE OR IN-
ABILITY TO USE THE PROGRAM (INCLUDING BUT NOT LIMITED TO LOSS OF DATA OR DATA
BEING RENDERED INACCURATE OR LOSSES SUSTAINED BY YOU OR THIRD PARTIES OR A FAIL-
URE OF THE PROGRAM TO OPERATE WITH ANY OTHER PROGRAMS), EVEN IF SUCH HOLDER
OR OTHER PARTY HAS BEEN ADVISED OF THE POSSIBILITY OF SUCH DAMAGES.

END OF TERMS AND CONDITIONS

C.3   Appendix: How to Apply These Terms to Your New Programs

If you develop a new program, and you want it to be of the greatest possible use to the public, the best way to achieve this is to make it free software which everyone can redistribute and change under these terms.

To do so, attach the following notices to the program. It is safest to attach them to the start of each source file to most effectively convey the exclusion of warranty; and each file should have at least the "copyright" line and a pointer to where the full notice is found.

⟨one line to give the program's name and a brief idea of what it does.⟩ Copyright ©19yy ⟨name of author⟩

This program is free software; you can redistribute it and/or modify it under the terms of the GNU General Public License as published by the Free Software Foundation; either version 2 of the License, or (at your option) any later version.

This program is distributed in the hope that it will be useful, but WITHOUT ANY WARRANTY; without even the implied warranty of MERCHANTABILITY or FITNESS FOR A PARTICULAR PURPOSE. See the GNU General Public License for more details.

You should have received a copy of the GNU General Public License along with this program; if not, write to the Free Software Foundation, Inc., 675 Mass Ave, Cambridge, MA 02139, USA.

Also add information on how to contact you by electronic and paper mail.

If the program is interactive, make it output a short notice like this when it starts in an interactive mode:

```
Gnomovision version 69, Copyright (C) 19yy name of author Gnomovision comes with ABSOLUTELY
NO WARRANTY; for details type 'show w'.  This is free software, and you are welcome to
redistribute it under certain conditions; type 'show c' for details.
```

The hypothetical commands 'show w' and 'show c' should show the appropriate parts of the General Public License. Of course, the commands you use may be called something other than 'show w' and 'show c'; they could even be mouse-clicks or menu items–whatever suits your program.

You should also get your employer (if you work as a programmer) or your school, if any, to sign a "copyright disclaimer" for the program, if necessary. Here is a sample; alter the names:

Yoyodyne, Inc., hereby disclaims all copyright interest in the program 'Gnomovision' (which makes passes at compilers) written by James Hacker.

⟨signature of Ty Coon⟩, 1 April 1989 Ty Coon, President of Vice

This General Public License does not permit incorporating your program into proprietary programs. If your program is a subroutine library, you may consider it more useful to permit linking proprietary applications with the library. If this is what you want to do, use the GNU Library General Public License instead of this License.

Glossary

An enormous difficulty in networking is to remember what all the abbreviations and terms one encounters really mean. Here's a list of those used frequently throughout the guide, along with a short explanation.

ACU   Automatic Call Unit. A modem.[1]

ARP   Address Resolution Protocol. Used to map IP addresses to Ethernet addresses.

ARPA   Advanced Research Project Agency, later DARPA. Founder of the Internet.

ARPANET   The ancestor of today's Internet; an experimental network funded by the U.S. Defense Advanced Research Project Agency (DARPA).

Assigned Numbers

         The title of an *RFC* published regularly that lists the publicly allocated numbers used for various things in TCP/IP networking. For example, it contains the list of all port numbers of well-known services like *rlogin*, *telnet*, etc. The most recent release of this document is RFC 1340.

bang path   In UUCP networks, a special notation for the path from one UUCP site to another. The name derives from the use of exclamation marks ('bangs') to separate the host names. Example: **foo!bar!ernie!bert** denotes a path to host **bert**, travelling (in this order) **foo**, **bar**, and **ernie**.

BBS   Bulletin Board System. A dial-up mailbox system.

BGP   Border Gateway Protocol. A protocol for exchanging routing information between autonomous systems.

BIND   The Berkeley Internet Name Domain server. An implementation of a DNS server.

BNU   Basic Networking Utilities. This is the most common UUCP variety at the moment. It is also known as HoneyDanBer UUCP. This name is derived from the authors' names: P. Honeyman, D.A. Novitz, and B.E. Redman.

broadcast network

         A network that allows one station to address a datagram to all other stations on the network simultaneously.

BSD   Berkeley Software Distribution. A UNIX flavor.

canonical hostname

         A host's primary name within the Domain Name System. This is the host's only name that has an A record associated with it, and which is returned when performing a reverse lookup.

CCITT   Comiteé Consultatif International de Télégraphique et Téléphonique. An International organization of telephone services, etc.

CSLIP   Compressed Serial Line IP. A protocol for exchanging IP packets over a serial line, using header compression of most TCP/IP datagrams.

DNS   Domain name system. This is a distributed database used on the Internet for mapping of host names to IP addresses.

EGP   External Gateway Protocol. A protocol for exchanging routing information between autonomous

---

[1] Alternatively: A teenager with a telephone.

systems.

Ethernet   In colloquial terms, the name of a sort of network equipment. Technically, Ethernet is part of a set of standards set forth by the IEEE. The Ethernet hardware uses a single piece of cable, frequently coax cable, to connect a number of hosts, and allows transfer rates of up to 10Mbps. The Ethernet protocol defines the manner in which hosts may communicate over this cable.[2]

FQDN   Fully Qualified Domain Name. A hostname with a domain name tacked onto it, so that it is a valid index into the Domain Name database.

FTP   File Transfer Protocol. The protocol one of the best-known file transfer service is based on and named after.

FYI   "For Your Information." Series of documents with informal information on Internet topics.

GMU   Groucho Marx University. Fictitious University used as an example throughout this book.

GNU   GNU's not Unix – this recursive acronym is the name of a project by the Free Software Association to provide a coherent set of UNIX-tools that may be used and copied free of charge. All GNU software is covered by a special Copyright notice, also called the GNU General Public License (GPL), or Copyleft. The GPL is reproduced in section C.

HoneyDanBer   The name of a UUCP variety. See also BNU.

host   Generally, a network node: something that is able to receive and transmit network messages. This will usually be a computer, but you can also think of X-Terminals, or smart printers.

ICMP   Internet Control Message Protocol. A networking protocol used by IP to return error information to the sending host, etc.

IEEE   Institute of Electrical and Eletronics Engineers. Another standards organization. From a UNIX user's point of view, their most important achievement are probably the POSIX standards which define aspects of a UNIX systems, ranging from system call interfaces and semantics to administration tools.

               Apart from this, the IEEE developed the specifications for Ethernet, Token Ring, and Token Bus networks. A widely-used standard for binary representation of real numbers is also due to the IEEE.

IETF   Internet Engineering Task Force.

internet   A computer network formed of a collection of individual smaller networks.

Internet   A particular world-wide internet.

IP   Internet Protocol. A networking protocol.

ISO   International Standards Organization.

ISDN   Integrated Services Digital Network. New telecommunications technology using digital instead of analogue circuitry.

LAN   Local Area Network. A small computer network.

MX   Mail Exchanger. A DNS resource record type used for marking a host as mail gateway for a domain.

network, packet-switched
               A variety of networks that provide instantaneous forwarding of data by all data up in small packets, which are tramsported to their destination individually. Packet-switched networks rely on permanent or semi-permanent connections.

network, store-and-forward
               They are pretty much the opposite of packet-switched networks. These networks transfer data as entire files, and don't use permanent connections. Instead, hosts conect to each other at certain intervals only, and transfer all data at once. This requires that data be stored intermediately until a connection is established.

NFS   Network File System. A standard networking protocol and software suite for accessing data on remote disks transparently.

---

[2]As an aside, the Ethernet *protocol* commonly used by TCP/IP is *not* exactly the same as IEEE 802.3. Ethernet frames have a type field where IEEE 802.3 frames have a length field.

NIS	Network Information System. An RPC-based application that allows to share configuration files such as the password file between several hosts. See also the entry under YP.
NNTP	Network News Transfer Protocol. Used to transfer news over TCP network connections.
octet	On the Internet, the technical term referring to a quantity of eight bits. It is used rather than *byte*, because there are machines on the Internet that have byte sizes other than eight bits.
OSI	Open Systems Interconnection. An ISO standard on network software.
path	Often used in UUCP networks as a synonym for *route*. Also see *bang path*.
PLIP	Parallel Line IP. A protocol for exchanging IP packets over a parallel line such as a printer port.
port, TCP or UDP	Ports are TCP's and UDP's abstraction of a service endpoint. Before a process can provide or access some networking service, it must claim (bind) a port. Together with the hosts' IP addresses, ports uniquely identify the two peers of a TCP connection.
portmapper	The portmapper is the mediator between the program numbers used by RPC as an identification of individual RPC servers, and the TCP and UDP port numbers those services are listening to.
PPP	The point-to-point protocol. PPP is a flexible and fast link-layer protocol to send various network protocols such as IP or IPX across a point-to-point connection. Apart from being used on serial (modem) links, PPP can also be employed as the link-level protocol on top of ISDN.
RARP	Reverse Address Resolution Protocol. It permits hosts to find out their IP address at boot time.
resolver	This is a library responsible for mapping hostnames to IP addresses and vice versa.
resource record	This is the basic unit of information in the DNS database, commonly abbreviated as RR. Each record has a certain type and class associated with it, for instance a record mapping a host name to an IP address has a type of A (for address), and a class of IN (for the Internet Protocol).
reverse lookup	The act of looking up a host's name based on a given IP address. Within DNS, this is done by looking up the host's IP address in the **in-addr.arpa** domain.
RFC	Request For Comments. Series of documents describing Internet standards.
RIP	Routing Information Protocol. This is a routing protocol used dynamically adjust routes inside a (small) network.
route	The sequence of hosts a piece of information has to travel from the originating host to the destination host. Finding an appropriate route is also called *routing*.
routing daemon	In larger networks, network topology changes are hard to adapt to manually, so facilities are used to distribute current routing information to the network's member hosts. This is called dynamic routing; the routing information is exchanged by *routing daemons* running on central hosts in the network. The protocols they employ are called *routing protocols*.
RPC	Remote Procedure Call. Protocol for executing procdures inside a process on a remote host.
RR	Short for *resource record*.
RS-232	This is a very common standard for serial interfaces.
RTS/CTS	A colloquial name for the hardware handshake performed by two devices communicating over RS-232. The name derives from the two cicuits involved, RTS ("Ready To Send"), and CTS ("Clear To Send").
RTM Internet Worm	A Virus-like program that used several flaws in VMS and BSD 4.3 Unix to spread through the Internet. Several "mistakes" in the program caused it to multiply without bound, and so effectively bringing down large parts of the Internet. RTM are the author's initials (Robert T. Morris), which he left in the program.
site	An agglomeration of hosts which, to the outside, behave almost like a single network node. For example, when speaking from an Internet point of view, one would call a Groucho Marx University a site, regardless of the complexity of its interior network.
SLIP	Serial Line IP. This is a protocol for exchanging IP packets over a serial line, see also CSLIP.

SMTP	Simple Mail Transfer Protocol. Used for mail transport over TCP connections, but also for mail batches transported over UUCP links (batched SMTP).
SOA	Start of Authority. A DNS resource record type.
System V	A UNIX flavor.
TCP	Transmission Control Protocol. A networking protocol.
TCP/IP	Sloppy description of the Internet protocol suite as a whole.
UDP	User Datagram Protocol. A networking protocol.
UUCP	Unix to Unix Copy. A suite of network transport commands for dial-up networks.

Version 2 UUCP
: An aging UUCP variety.

virtual beer
: Every Linuxer's favorite drink. The first mention of virtual beer I remember was in the release note of the Linux 0.98.X kernel, where Linus listed the "Oxford Beer Trolls" in his credits section for sending along some virtual beer.

well-known services
: This term is frequently used to refer to common networking services such as *telnet* and *rlogin*. In a more technical sense, it describes all services that have been assigned an official port number in the "Assigned Numbers" RFC.

YP
: Yellow Pages. An older name for NIS which is no longer used, because Yellow Pages is a trademark of British Telecom. Nevertheless, most NIS utilities have retained names with a prefix of *yp*.

Annotated Bibliography

Books

The following is a list of books you might want to read to if you want to know more about some of the topics covered in the Networking Guide. It is not very complete or systematic, I just happen to have read them and find them quite useful. Any additions to, and enhancement of this list are welcome.

General Books on the Internet

[Kehoe92]   Brendan P. Kehoe: *Zen and the Art of the Internet.* .

"Zen" was one of, if not *the* first Internet Guide, introducing the novice user to the various trades, services and the folklore of the Internet. Being a 100-page tome, it covered topics ranging from email to Usenet news to the Internet Worm. It is available via anonymous FTP from many FTP servers, and may be freely distributed and printed. A printed copy is also available from Prentice-Hall.

Administration Issues

[Hunt92]   Craig Hunt: *TCP/IP Network Administration.* O'Reilly and Associates, 1992. ISBN 0-937175-82-X.

If the Linux Network Administrators' Guide is not enough for you, get this book. It deals with everything from obtaining an IP address to troubleshooting your network to security issues.

Its focus is on setting up TCP/IP, that is, interface configuration, the setup of routing, and name resolution. It includes a detailed description of the facilities offered by the routing daemons `routed` and `gated`, which supply dynamic routing.

It also describes the configuration of application programs and network daemons, such as `inetd`, the `r` commands, NIS, and NFS.

The appendix has a detailed reference of `gated`, and `named`, and a description of Berkeley's `sendmail` configuration.

[Stern92]   Hal Stern: *Managing NIS and NFS.* O'Reilly and Associates, 1992. ISBN 0-937175-75-7.

This is a companion book to Craig Hunt's "TCP/IP Network Administration" book. It covers the use of NIS, the Network Information System, and NFS, the Network File System, in extenso, including the configuration of an automounter, and PC/NFS.

[OReilly89]   Tim O'Reilly and Grace Todino: *Managing UUCP and Usenet, 10th ed.* O'Reilly and Associates, 1992. ISBN 0-93717593-5.

This is the standard book on UUCP networking. It covers Version 2 UUCP as well as BNU. It helps you to set up your UUCP node from the start, giving practical tips and solutions for many problems, like testing the connection, or writing good chat scripts. It also deals with more exotic topics, like how to set up a travelling UUCP node, or the subtleties present in different flavors of UUCP.

The second part of the book deals with Usenet and netnews software. It explains the configuration of both Bnews (version 2.11) and C news, and introduces you to netnews maintenance tasks.

[Spaf93]   Gene Spafford and Simson Garfinkel: *Practical UNIX Security*. O'Reilly and Associates, 1992. ISBN 0-937175-72-2.

This is a must-have for everyone who manages a system with network access, and for others as well. The book discusses all issues relevant to computer security, ranging the basic security features UNIX offers physical security. Although you should strive to secure all parts of your system, the discussion of networks and security is the most interesting part of the book in our context. Apart from basic security policies that concern the Berkeley services (*telnet*, *rlogin*, etc), NFS and NIS, it also deals with enhanced security features like MIT's Kerberos, Sun's Secure RPC, and the use of firewalls to shield your network from attacks from the Internet.

[AlbitzLiu92]   Paul Albitz and Cricket Liu: *DNS and BIND*. O'Reilly and Associates, 1992. ISBN 1-56592-010-4.

This book is useful for all those that have to manage DNS name service. It explains all features of DNS in great detail and give examples that make even those BIND options plausible that appear outright weird at first sight. I found it fun to read, and really learned a lot from it.

[NISPlus]   Rick Ramsey: *All about Administering NIS+*. Prentice-Hall, 1993. ISBN 0-13-068800-2.

The Background

The following is a list of books that might be of interest to people who want to know more about *how* TCP/IP and its applications work, but don't want to read RFCs.

[Stevens90]   Richard W. Stevens: *UNIX Network Programming*. Prentice-Hall International, 1990. ISBN 0-13-949876-X.

This is probably *the* most widely used book on TCP/IP network programming, which, at the same time, tells you a lot about the nuts and bolts of the Internet Protocols.[3]

[Tanen89]   Andrew S. Tanenbaum: *Computer Networks*. Prentice-Hall International, 1989. ISBN 0-13-166836-6[4].

This book gives you a very good insight into general networking issues. Using the OSI Reference Model, it explains the design issues of each layer, and the algorithms that may be used to achieve these. At each layer, the implementations of several networks, among them the ARPAnet, are compared to each other.

The only drawback this book has is the abundance of abbreviations, which sometimes makes it hard to follow what the author says. But this is probably inherent to networking.

[Comer88]   Douglas R. Comer: *Internetworking with TCP/IP: Principles, Protocols, and Architecture*. Prentice-Hall International, 1988.

---

[3]Note that Stevens has just written a new TCP/IP, called *TCP/IP Illustrated, Volume 1, The Protocols*, published by Addison Wesley. I didn't have the time to look at it, though.

[4]The ISBN under which it is available in North America might be different.

HOWTOs

The following is an excerpt of the HOWTO-INDEX, version 2.0 (17 March 1994), written by Matt Welsh.

What are Linux HOWTOs?

Linux HOWTOs are short online documents which describe in detail a certain aspect of configuring or using the Linux system. For example, there is the Installation HOWTO, which gives instructions on installing Linux, and the Mail HOWTO, which describes how to set up and configure mail under Linux. Other examples include the NET-2-HOWTO (previously the NET-2-FAQ) and the Printing HOWTO.

Information in HOWTOs is generally more detailed and in-depth than what can be squeezed into the Linux FAQ. For this reason, the Linux FAQ is being rewritten. A large amount of the information contained therein will be relegated to various HOWTO documents. The FAQ will be a shorter list of frequently asked questions about Linux, covering small specific topics. Most of the "useful" information in the FAQ will now be covered in the HOWTOs.

HOWTOs are comprehensive documents—much like an FAQ but generally not in question-and-answer format. However, many HOWTOs contain an FAQ section at the end. For example, the NET-2-FAQ has been renamed to the NET-2-HOWTO, because it wasn't in question-and-answer format. However, you will see the NET-2-HOWTO named as the NET-2-FAQ in many places. The two docs are one and the same.

Where to get Linux HOWTOs

HOWTOs can be retrieved via anonymous FTP from the following sites:

- *sunsite.unc.edu:/pub/Linux/docs/HOWTO*
- *tsx-11.mit.edu:/pub/linux/docs/HOWTO*

as well as the many mirror sites, which are listed in the Linux META-FAQ (see below).

The Index, printed below, lists the currently available HOWTOs.

HOWTOs are also posted regularly to the newsgroups **comp.os.linux** and **comp.os.linux.announce**. In addition, a number of the HOWTOs will be crossposted to **news.answers**. Therefore, you can find the Linux HOWTOs on the **news.answers** archive site **rtfm.mit.edu**.

HOWTO Index

The following Linux HOWTOs are currently available.

- Linux Busmouse HOWTO, by **mike@starbug.apana.org.au** (Mike Battersby). Information on bus mouse compatibility with Linux.
- Linux CDROM HOWTO, by **tranter@software.mitel.com** (Jeff Tranter). Information on CD-ROM drive compatibility for Linux.
- Linux DOSEMU HOWTO, by **deisher@enws125.EAS.ASU.EDU** (Michael E. Deisher). HOWTO about the Linux MS-DOS Emulator, DOSEMU.
- Linux Distribution HOWTO, by **mdw@sunsite.unc.edu** (Matt Welsh). A list of mail order distributions and other commercial services.
- Linux Ethernet HOWTO, by Paul Gortmaker **gpg109@rsphysse.anu.edu.au**. Information on Ethernet hardware compatibility for Linux.
- Linux Ftape HOWTO, by **ftape@mic.dth.dk** (Linux ftape-HOWTO maintainer). Information on ftape drive compatibility with Linux.
- Linux HOWTO Index, by **mdw@sunsite.unc.edu** (Matt Welsh). Index of HOWTO documents about Linux.
- Linux Hardware Compatibility HOWTO, by **erc@apple.com** (Ed Carp). A near-extensive list of hardware known to work with Linux.
- Linux Installation HOWTO, by **mdw@sunsite.unc.edu** (Matt Welsh). How to obtain and install the Linux software.
- Linux JE-HOWTO, by Yasuhiro Yamazaki **hiro@rainbow.physics.utoronto.ca**. Information on JE, a set of Japanese language extensions for Linux.

- Linux Keystroke HOWTO, by Zenon Fortuna (**zenon@netcom.com**). HOWTO bind macro actions to keystrokes under Linux.

- Linux MGR HOWTO, by **broman@Np.nosc.mil** (Vincent Broman). Information on the MGR graphics interface for Linux.

- Linux Electronic Mail HOWTO, by **vince@victrola.wa.com** (Vince Skahan). Information on Linux-based mail servers and clients.

- Linux NET-2 HOWTO, by **terryd@extro.ucc.su.oz.au** (Terry Dawson). HOWTO configure TCP/IP networking, SLIP, PLIP, and PPP under Linux.

- Linux News HOWTO, by **vince@victrola.wa.com** (Vince Skahan). Information on USENET news server and client software for Linux.

- Linux PCI-HOWTO, by Michael Will **michaelw@desaster.student.uni-tuebingen.de**. Information on PCI-architecture compatibility with Linux.

- Linux Printing HOWTO, by **gtaylor@cs.tufts.edu** (Grant Taylor). HOWTO on printing software for Linux.

- Linux SCSI HOWTO, by Drew Eckhardt **drew@kinglear.cs.Colorado.EDU**. Information on SCSI driver compatibility with Linux.

- Linux Serial HOWTO, by **gregh@cc.gatech.edu** (Greg Hankins). Information on use of serial devices and communications software.

- Linux Sound HOWTO, by **tranter@software.mitel.com** (Jeff Tranter). Sound hardware and software for the Linux operating system.

- Linux Term HOWTO, by Bill Reynolds **bill@goshawk.lanl.gov**. HOWTO use the 'term' communications package on Linux systems.

- Linux Tips HOWTO, by Vince Reed **reedv@rpi.edu**. HOWTO on miscellaneous tips and tricks for Linux.

- Linux UUCP HOWTO, by **vince@victrola.wa.com** (Vince Skahan). Information on UUCP software for Linux.

- Linux XFree86 HOWTO, by **geyer@polyhymnia.iwr.uni-heidelberg.de** (Helmut Geyer). HOWTO on installation of XFree86 (X11R5) for Linux.

Miscellaneous and Legalese

If you have questions, please feel free to mail **mdw@sunsite.unc.edu**. The Linux FAQ rewrite is being coordinated by Ian Jackson, **ijackson@nyx.cs.du.edu**, with help from others.

Unless otherwise stated, Linux HOWTO documents are copyrighted by their respective authors. Linux HOWTO documents may be reproduced and distributed in whole or in part, in any medium physical or electronic, without permission of the author. Translations and derivative works are similarly permitted without express permission. Commercial redistribution is allowed and encouraged; however, the author would like to be notified of any such distributions.

In short, we wish to promote dissemination of this information through as many channels as possible. However, we do wish to retain copyright on the HOWTO documents, and would like to be notified of any plans to redistribute the HOW-TOs. If you have questions, please contact Matt Welsh, the Linux HOWTO coordinator, at **mdw@sunsite.unc.edu**.

RFCs

The following is a list of RFCs mentioned throughout this book. All RFCs are available via anonymous FTP from **nic.ddn.mil**, **ftp.uu.net**. To obtain an RFC via email, send a message to **service@nic.ddn.mil**, putting the request send RFC-*number*.TXT in the subject header line.

1340	Assigned Numbers, *Postel, J.*, and *Reynolds, J.* The Assigned Numbers RFC defines the meaning of numbers used in various protocols, such as the port numbers standard TCP and UDP servers are known to listen on, and the protocol numbers used in the IP datagram header.
1144	Compressing TCP/IP headers for low-speed serial links, *Jacobson, V.* This document describes the algorithm used to compress TCP/IP headers in CSLIP and PPP. Very worthwhile reading!
1033	Domain Administrators Operations Guide, *Lottor, M.* Together with its companion RFCs, RFC 1034 and RFC 1035, this is the definitive source on DNS, the Domain Name System.
1034	Domain Names - Concepts and Facilities, *Mockapetris, P.V.* A companion to RFC 1033.
1035	Domain names - Implementation and Specification, *Mockapetris, P.V.* A companion to RFC 1033.

974   Mail Routing and the Domain System, *Partridge, C.* This RFC describes mail routing on the Internet. Read this for the full story about MX records...

977   Network News Transfer Protocol, *Kantor, B.*, and *Lapsley, P.* The definition of NNTP, the common news transport used on the Internet.

1094   NFS: Network File System Protocol specification, *Nowicki, B.* The formal specification of the NFS and mount protocols (version 2).

1055   Nonstandard for Transmission of IP Datagrams over Serial Lines: SLIP, *Romkey, J.L.* Describes SLIP, the Serial Line Internet Protocol.

1057   RPC: Remote Procedure Call Protocol Specification: Version 2, *Sun Microsystems, Inc*

1058   Routing Information Protocol, *Hedrick, C.L.* Describes RIP, which is used to exchange dynamic routing information within LANs and MANs.

821   Simple Mail Transfer Protocol, *Postel, J.B.* Defines SMTP, the mail transport protocol over TCP/IP.

1036   Standard for the Interchange of USENET messages, *Adams, R.*, and *Horton, M.R.* This RFC describes the format of Usenet News messages, and how they are exchanged on the Internet as well as on UUCP networks. A revision of this RFC is expected to be released sometime soon.

822   Standard for the Format of ARPA Internet text messages, *Crocker, D.* This is the definitive source of wisdom regarding, well, RFC-conformant mail. Everyone knows it, few have really read it.

968   Twas the Night Before Start-up, *Cerf, V.* Who says the heroes of networking remain unsung?

Part I

LINUX **System Administrator's Guide 0.2**

This is a manual and tutorial for keeping a LINUX system up and running. This version is not finished, but the finished version is supposed to cover all the central topics except networking (for which see the Linux Network Administrators' Guide). This manual does not try to be a reference manual, or a manual to all the different programs that a system administrator might use. Separate documentation (such as man pages) exist for those.

Lars Wirzenius, Hernesaarenkatu 15 A 2, Fin-00150 Helsinki, Finland
lars.wirzenius@helsinki.fi

Contents

Chapter 1

Introduction to the ALPHA Versions

This is an ALPHA version of the LINUX System Administrator's Guide. That means that I don't even pretend it contains anything useful, or that anything contained within it is factually correct. In fact, if you believe anything that I say in this version, and you are hurt because of it, I will cruelly laugh at your face if you complain.

Well, almost. I won't laugh, but I also will not consider myself responsible for anything.

The purpose of an ALPHA version is to get the stuff out so that other people can look at it and comment on it. The latter part is the important one: Unless the author gets feedback, the ALPHA version isn't doing anything good. Therefore, if you read this 'book', please, *please*, **please** let me hear your opinion about it. I don't care whether you think it is good or bad, I want you to tell me about it.

If at all possible, you should mail your comments directly to me, otherwise there is a largish chance I will miss them. If you want to discuss things in public (one of the `comp.os.linux` newsgroups or the mailing list), that is ok by me, but please send a copy via mail directly to me as well.

I do not much care about the format in which you send your comments, but it is essential that you clearly indicate what part of my text you are commenting on.

I can be contacted at the following e-mail addresses:

```
lars.wirzenius@helsinki.fi
wirzeniu@cc.helsinki.fi
wirzeniu@cs.helsinki.fi
wirzeniu@kruuna.helsinki.fi
wirzeniu@hydra.helsinki.fi
```

(they're all actually the same account, but I give all these, just in case there is some weird problem).

This text contains a lot of notes that I have inserted as notes to myself. They are identified with "**META:** ". They indicate things that need to be worked on, that are missing, that are wrong, or something like that. They are mostly for my own benefit and for your amusement, they are not things that I am hoping someone else will write for me.

Parts of the chapters in this version are still unwritten. If someone wishes to fill things in, I'm glad to have it, but I will probably write it myself, anyway (mixing text from several people in one chapter usually makes for a less good manual). If you are serious about wanting to write a whole chapter or more, please contact me for ideas.

If you think that this version of the manual is missing a lot, you are right. I am including only those chapters that are at least half finished. New chapters will be released as they are written.

For reference: This is version 0.2, released 1995-02-04.

The LDP Rhyme[1]

A wondrous thing,
and beautiful,
'tis to write,
a book.

I'd like to sing,
of the sweat,
the blood and tear,
which it also took.

It started back in,
nineteen-ninety-two,
when users whined,
"we can nothing do!"

They wanted to know,
what their problem was,
and how to fix it
(by yesterday).

We put the answers in,
a Linux f-a-q,
hoped to get away,
from any more writin'.

"That's too long,
it's hard to search,
and we don't read it,
any-which-way!"

Then a few of us,
joined toghether
(virtually, you know),
to start the LDP.

We started to write,
or plan, at least,
several books,
one for every need.

The start was fun,
a lot of talk,
an outline,
then a slew.

Then silence came,
the work began,
some wrote less,
others more.

A blank screen,
oh its horrible,
it sits there,
laughs in the face.

We still await,
the final day,
when everything,
will be done.

Until then,
all we have,
is a draft,
for you to comment on.

---

[1] The author wishes to remain anonymous. It was posted to
the mailing list by Matt Welsh.

Chapter 2

Introduction

This manual, the LINUX System Administrator's Guide, describes the system administration aspects of using LINUX. It is intended for people who know next to nothing about system administration (as in "what is it?"), but who already master at least the basics of normal usage, which means roughly the material covered by the (as yet unpublished) LINUX User's Guide. This manual also doesn't tell you how to install LINUX, that is described in the Getting Started document. There is some overlap between all manuals, however, but they all look at things from slightly different angles. See below for more information about LINUX manuals.

What, then, is system administration? It is all the things that one has to do to keep a computer system in a useable shape. Things like backing up files (and restoring them if necessary), installing new programs, creating accounts for users (and deleting them when no longer needed), making certain that the filesystem is not corrupted, and so on. If a computer were a house, say, system administration would be called maintenance, and would include cleaning, fixing broken windows, and other such things. System administration is not called maintenance, because that would be too simple. [1]

The structure of this manual is such that many of the chapters should be usable independently, so that if you need information about, say, backups, you can read just that chapter. This hopefully makes the book easier to use as a reference manual, and makes it possible to read just a small part when needed, instead of having to read everything. We have tried to create a good index as well, to make it easier to find things. However, this manual is first and foremost a tutorial, and a reference manual only as a lucky coincidence.

This manual is not intended to be used completely by itself. Plenty of the rest of the LINUX documentation is also important for system administrators. After all, a system administrator is just a user with special privileges and duties. A very important resource is the man pages, which should always be consulted when a command is not familiar. however.)

While this manual is targeted at LINUX, a general principle has been that it should be useful with other UNIX based operating systems as well. Unfortunately, since there is so much variance between different versions of UNIX in general, and in system administration in particular, there is little hope for us to cover all variants. Even covering all possibilities for LINUX is difficult, due to the nature of its development. There is no one official LINUX distribution, so different people have different setups, many people have a setup they have built up themselves. When possible, we have tried to point out differences, and explain several alternatives. In order to cater to the hackers and DIY types that form the driving force behind LINUX development, we have tried to describe how things work, rather than just listing "five easy steps" for each task. This means that there is much information here that is not necessary for everyone, but those parts are marked as such and can be skipped if you use a preconfigured system. Reading everything will, naturally, increase your understanding of the system and should make using and administering it more pleasant.

Like all other LINUX related development, the work was done on a volunteer basis: we did it because

---

[1] There are some people who *do* call it that, but that's just because they have never read this manual, poor things.

we thought it might be fun and/or because we felt it should be done. However, like all volunteer work, there is a limit to how much effort we have been able to spend on this work, and also on how much knowledge and experience we have. This means that the manual is not necessarily as good as it would be if a wizard had been paid handsomely to write it and had spent a few years to perfect it. We think, of course, that it is pretty nice, but be warned. Also, on the general principle that *no* single source of information is enough, we have compiled a short bibliography of books, magazines, and papers related to UNIX system administration.

One particular point where we have cut corners and reduced our workload is that we have not covered very thoroughly many things that are already well documented in other freely available manuals. This applies especially to program specific documentation, such as all the details of using `mkfs(8)`; we only describe the purpose of the program, and as much of its usage as is necessary for the purposes of this manual. For further information, we refer the gentle reader to these other manuals. Usually, all of the referred to documentation is part of the full LINUX documentation set.

While we have tried to make this manual as good as possible, we would really like to hear from you if you have any ideas on how to make it better. Bad language, factual errors, ideas for new areas to cover, rewritten sections, information about how various UNIX versions do things, we are interested in all of it. The maintainer of the manual is Lars Wirzenius. You can contact him via electronic mail with the Internet domain address `lars.wirzenius@helsinki.fi`, or by traditional paper mail using the address

> Lars Wirzenius / Linux docs
> Hernesaarentie 15 A 2
> 00150 Helsinki
> Finland

META: acks

2.1 The LINUX Documentation Project

The LINUX Documentation Project, or LDP, is a loose team of writers, proofreaders, and editors who are working together to provide complete documentation for the LINUX operating system. The overall coordinator of the project is Matt Welsh, who is heavily aided by Lars Wirzenius and Michael K. Johnson.

This manual is one in a set of several being distributed by the LDP, including a Linux Users' Guide, System Administrators' Guide, Network Administrators' Guide, and Kernel Hackers' Guide. These manuals are all available in LATEX source format, .dvi format, and postscript output by anonymous FTP from `nic.funet.fi`, in the directory `/pub/OS/Linux/doc/doc-project`, and from `tsx-11.mit.edu`, in the directory `/pub/linux/docs/guides`.

We encourage anyone with a penchant for writing or editing to join us in improving Linux documentation. If you have Internet e-mail access, you can join the DOC channel of the Linux-Activists mailing list by sending mail to

```
linux-activists-request@niksula.hut.fi
```

with the line

```
X-Mn-Admin:  join DOC
```

in the header or as the first line of the message body.

2.2 Copyright, trademarks, other legalese

UNIX is a trademark of Unix System Labratories
Linux is not a trademark, and has no connection to UNIX™ or Unix System Labratories.

Linux System Administrator's Guide may be reproduced and distributed in whole or in part, subject to the following conditions:

0. The copyright notice above and this permission notice must be preserved complete on all complete or partial copies.

1. Any translation or derivative work of *Linux System Administrator's Guide* must be approved by the author in writing before distribution.

2. If you distribute *Linux System Administrator's Guide* in part, instructions for obtaining the complete version of this manual must be included, and a means for obtaining a complete version provided.

3. Small portions may be reproduced as illustrations for reviews or **quotes** in other works without this permission notice if proper citation is given.

Exceptions to these rules may be granted for academic purposes: Write to Lars Wirzenius, at the above address, or email lars.wirzenius@helsinki.fi, and ask. These restrictions are here to protect us as authors, not to restrict you as educators and learners.

Chapter 3

Directory Tree Overview

META: This chapter is waiting a major rewrite

    META: Give sample contents of important files, e.g. /etc/passwd, /etc/group (not here, in the chapter that discusses the relevant subject)

    META: Give a sample listing of sensible ownerships and permissions for all the important files, and *explain* why they are sensible. Explain what must be done in a specific way, and what can be altered to make the system more open or more secure.

    META: timezone files, /etc/skel.

    META: mention where files / programs come from, if not typically in the distribution

This chapter contains a quick overview of the most important files and directories on a UNIX system. It does not go into detail about the contents of files, only summarizes their purpose, possibly mentions connections to other files and programs, and points to the relevant document that describes things in more detail.

The set of directories and the division of files between directories is based on an assumption that some things are on a **root filesystem**, the first filesystem that is mounted when when LINUX boots, while others are on other filesystems, and that some files need to be accessable before those other filesystems are mounted. The 'other' filesystem is usually called /usr, and everything else in the root directory is assumed to be on the root filesystem. While this configuration is not true for all systems, especially LINUX systems, it was true when the directory tree was originally designed in the early history of UNIX. It is good to understand this, because many things do not otherwise make much sense (e.g. why both /bin and /usr/bin?).

3.1 The /etc and /usr/etc Directories

The /etc directory contains files that have to do with system administration, that are required during bootup or shutdown, that contain system-wide configuration data or are system-wide startup scripts.

The /usr/etc directory, on systems where it exists, is similar to /etc, but it typically contains only configuration files for programs in /usr/bin, not system-wide things. On some systems, however, /usr/etc is just a symlink to /etc, in which case both are the same thing.

    META: the items below should be sorted

/etc/rc This is a /bin/sh shell script that is automatically run when the system is booted. It should start the background processes that provide useful services to user programs (e.g. update, crond, inetd), mount filesystems, turn on swapping areas, and do other similar tasks. In some installations /etc/rc.local or /etc/rc.[0-9] are invoked by /etc/rc; the intention is that all changes that need to be made for a given site are done in those files so that /etc/rc can be automatically updated when a new version of the operating system is installed.

META: Describe /etc/rc.[0-9] better: which is what, and so on; sysvinit: rc.d

/etc/passwd This is a text file that contains information about users. See the passwd(5) man page for more information.

/etc/psdatabase This is used by some versions of the LINUX ps(1) command. It contains information about where in the kernel memory certain kernel data structures reside. ps(1) reads that data directly from /dev/kmem, and at least /etc/psdatabase needs to be updated when a new version of the kernel is used; sometimes ps itself needs recompilation and even changes. Other versions of ps use the /proc filesystem, and hence do not need any special attention when upgrading the kernel.

META: needed for procps too! wchan

/etc/disktab Contains the disk geometry for SCSI disks for those drivers that do not provide the information (for example the generic SCSI driver).

/etc/fdprm Floppy disk parameter table. This file describes what different floppy disk formats look like. The program setfdprm(1) looks in this file to see. See the man page fdprm(5) for more information.

/etc/fstab This file lists the filesystems and swap areas that are mounted by the mount -a command in /etc/rc. See the mount(8) man page for more information, and subsection 5.6.5.

META: root fs must be declared correctly, or else there will be problems with libc

/etc/getty This is the program that waits for somebody to log in via a terminal (or virtual console). It is started automatically by init, once per terminal line (or virtual console) via which it should be possible to log in. Some "terminal" lines (really, serial lines) might not be intended for logins, e.g. when a mouse is connected to that line, so getty is not invoked on all lines. getty waits until somebody enters a username and then runs login(1).

/etc/uugetty Another version of getty. See the section on logins for more information.

/etc/gettydefs **META:** On my system this is just a symlink to /etc/gettytab. sysv uses this name.

/etc/gettytab Describes how getty should use the terminal lines (speeds, parity settings, and so on).

META: I think this is something like it, gotta find a man page first. bsd uses this name.

META: mail from jwl (1993-07-22)

/etc/group This is a file similar to /etc/passwd, but it describes groups instead of users. See the group(5) man page for more information.

/etc/init This is the program that is started as process 1 by the kernel at boot time. After init is started, the kernel booting is done. init then runs /etc/rc, starts the gettys, and so on.

/etc/inittab This file lists the processes that init starts.

META: for some inits, much more info.

/etc/issue This file contains the text that getty outputs before the login prompt.

/etc/lilo This directory contains files for LILO, a program that allows LINUX to boot from a hard disk. See the LILO documentation for more information.

/etc/magic This is the configuration file for file(1). It contains the descriptions of various file formats based on which file guesses the type of the file.

/etc/motd This contains the **message of the day** that is automatically copied to the users terminal after his password is validated. It typically contains important messages from the sysadmin, such as warnings about downtime in the future. It is also common to have a short description of the type of the computer and the operating system.

META: .hushlogin?

/etc/mtab This file contains information about the currently mounted filesystems. It is removed by /etc/rc, set up by mount -a, and maintained automatically by the mount(8) and umount(8) commands, and used when a list of mounted filesystems is needed, for example by df(1).

/etc/mtools This is a configuration file for mtools, a package for using MS-DOS format disks with UNIX. mtools is typically unnecessary with LINUX, since LINUX itself understands the MS-DOS filesystem (although that driver can be configured out when compiling the kernel, in which case mtools is needed).

/etc/shadow This file contains the shadow passwords on systems where the shadow password software is installed. Shadow passwords mean that the password is not stored to the world-readable /etc/passwd file, but into /etc/shadow which only root can read. This way it is not possible to get the encrypted version of a password, and hence not possible to decipher it either.

/etc/login.defs This is a configuration file for the login(1) command.

/etc/printcap Like /etc/termcap, but intended for printers. Different syntax.

/etc/profile This file is sourced at login time by the Bourne shell /bin/sh (and /bin/bash; although they are the same on most LINUX systems), and the Korn shell /bin/ksh, before the user's own .profile file. This allows the sysadmin to introduce global settings easily.

/etc/securetty Identifies secure terminals. root can login only from the terminals listed in this file. Typically only the virtual consoles are listed, so that it becomes impossible (or at least harder) to gain superuser privileges by breaking into a system over a modem or a network.

/etc/shells Lists trusted shells. The chsh(1) command allows users to change their login shell only to shells listed in this file. ftpd, the server process that provides FTP services for a machine, will check that the user's shell is listed in /etc/shells and will not let people log in unles the shell is listed there.

/etc/startcons **META:** old sls? not used anymore? forget it?

/etc/termcap The terminal capability database. Describes by what "escape sequences" various terminals can be controlled. Programs are written so that instead of directly outputting an escape sequence that only works on a particular brand of terminal, they look up the correct sequence to do whatever it is they want to do in /etc/termcap. As a result most programs work with most kinds of terminals. /etc/termcap is a text file; see termcap(5) for more information.

/etc/ttytype Lists default terminal types for terminal lines. Used by login(1).

/etc/update This is one of the background programs that is started by /etc/rc or init(8) (depending on which init is installed). It syncs (forces all unwritten data in the buffer cache to be physically written) every 30 seconds. The idea is to make certain that if there is a power failure, a kernel panic, or some other horrible thing that completely ruins everything, you won't lose more than 30 seconds' worth of writes at the most.

/etc/utmp This is a binary file that records information about who, if anybody, is currently logged in on each terminal, and some other information about the login. Each terminal has its own record in the file. When a user logs in, login(1) updates the record for the terminal in question to show that somebody is logged in, and when he logs out, init(8) records that information.

/etc/wtmp This is like /etc/utmp, except that all the records written are appended instead of overwritten on the existing records. This means that /etc/wtmp grows indefinitely, although slowly. If and when it grows big enough, it will have to be trimmed.

`/etc/ftpusers`, `/etc/ftpaccess`, `/etc/rpc`, `/etc/rpcinit`, `/etc/exports` These have to do with networking. See the Linux Network Administrator's Guide for more information.

3.2 Devices, `/dev`

The `/dev` directory contains the special device files for all the devices. See the man pages for descriptions for which file stands for which device and what the device is.

META: include list of at least the most important devices

3.3 The Program Directories, `/bin`, `/usr/bin`, and Others

Programs in UNIX are usually scattered in many directories. The two most important ones are `/bin` and `/usr/bin`. Traditionally, all programs intended for the user (as opposed to the sysadmin) to run are in these directories. `/bin` contains the stuff that is needed on the root partition, that is everything which is needed before `/usr` is mounted (assuming it is on a different partition), and also tools useful for recovering from disasters. `/usr/bin` contains most other things.

Usually `/bin` and `/usr/bin` contain programs that are part of the operating system, i.e. they are provided by the OS vendor, not by the user or a third party. Most systems have a place where locally written software, and freeware snarfed from Usenet or other places is installed. This is typically called `/usr/local`, with subdirectories `bin`, `etc`, `lib`, and `man` (and others as necessary). This way those programs are not in the way when a new version of the operating system is installed, especially since the upgrade procedure might wipe out all of `/bin` and `/usr/bin`. (`/usr/local` would then preferably be either a mount point or a symbolic link so that it is not erased during the upgrade.)

In addition to these, many people prefer to install large packages in their own directories so that they can be easily uninstalled, and so that they don't have to worry about overwriting existing files from other packages when installing. It can also be nice to have all files that belong to a package in a central place. An example of this is that, on LINUX, X and X programs are usually installed to `/usr/X386`, which is a similar directory tree to `/usr/local`. TeX and GNU Emacs are also usually installed this way on LINUX.

On some systems[1] with shared libraries, the directory `/sbin` holds statically linked versions of some of the most important programs. The intent is that if the shared library images become corrupt or are accidentally removed, it is still possible to fix things without having to boot. Typical binaries would be `ln`, `cp`, `mount`, and `sync`.

META: check mail from geyer (1993-07-22) and SunOS

See section 3.5 for an example of how the shared libraries might become fouled up.

The drawback of `/sbin` is that statically linked binaries take a lot more disk space. When a binary of `ln` might be a couple of kilobytes when linked with shared libraries, it might be a couple of hundred kilobytes if linked statically. If you are willing to have to boot if you mess up your shared libraries—and have an emergency boot disk always available—it is never necessary to have `/sbin`. If you can't afford to boot, and you can afford the disk space, then `/sbin` is a very good idea. There is not, however, a single answer that is correct for everyone on this issue.

META: hlu's sln is 320 bytes!

3.4 The `/usr/lib` Directory

The `/usr/lib` directory contains code libraries, configuration and data files for individual programs, auxiliary programs that are only invoked by other programs, and other stuff like that. The contents

---

[1] SunOS, and some LINUX distributions at least

are pretty varied. Some programs want to have their support files directly in /usr/lib, some use a subdirectory below that.

/usr/lib is used only by programs in /usr/bin (programs in /bin shouldn't need /usr/lib, since /usr might not have been mounted). Programs in /usr/local/bin use /usr/local/lib, and programs that are installed in their own directory tree (like X in /usr/X386) use a place in that tree (/usr/X386/lib).

Of the files in /usr/lib, files named libsomething.a are usually libraries of subroutines in some programming language. The most important ones are libc.a, the standard C library (the one that contains printf, strcpy; everything except math stuff), libm.a (the math stuff), and libg.a (a debugging version of libc.a).

Note that on LINUX there are several versions of the C libraries, static, and two types of shared libraries. The libsomething.a files are the static versions, the shared images are in libsomething.so.version (usually installed in lib, see below) and the stub functions (needed for linking with the shared images) are in libsomething.sa.

3.5   Shared Library Images, /lib

The /lib directory contains the shared images of the shared libraries, that is the actual machine code that is run when a routine in a shared library is called. They are not in /usr/lib because /usr can be on a different partition and might not be mounted when the shared images are needed (e.g. by programs in /bin).

A shared library usually has a name such as /lib/libc.so.4.3.2, which in this case would indicate version 4.3.2 of the standard C library. The .so bit indicates that it is a shared library image ("shared object", if you prefer).

There can be several versions of a shared library installed at the same time. A typical reason for this is that when a shared library is upgraded, the old version is usually kept around until the new version has proved to be reliable. Also, some programs are linked so that they require a specific version of a shared library. Most programs, however, are linked to use a name like /lib/libc.so.4, i.e. using only the major version number. That name is then actually a symlink to whatever version of the shared library that is installed and intended to be used on the system. The contents of /lib might then look like

```
cpp -> /usr/lib/gcc-lib/i386-linux/2.3.3/cpp*
libc.so.4 -> libc.so.4.3.2*
libc.so.4.3.2*
libm.so.4 -> libm.so.4.3.2*
libm.so.4.0*
libm.so.4.3.2*
```

Note that there seems to be two versions of the C math library, libm.so.4.0 and libm.so.4.3.2. The symlink libm.so.4 points at the latter, so that's what gets used unless a program explicitly requires the other one. The reason why both versions are on the disk might be that some program that is used on the system does indeed require that version.[2]

A shared library image can be updated by shutting down the system, booting with a special boot floppy, or by some other means that doesn't mount the normal root filesystem, and then copying the new shared library image to the /lib directory and fixing up the symlink. The system can then be brought up in a normal manner. This procedure avoids the problems described below if something goes wrong during the update, since the shared library images on the partition that is being updated aren't ever used.

This is a bit of work, however, so the way it is actually done in practice is to do it while the system is up and running. There is no problem with this, except for a distinct possibility of making it impossible to run any program that uses a shared library, if you make a mistake. The correct way to do it is

---

[2] Yup, that's the reason all right. I should know, it's my system. . .

```
ln -sf /lib/libc.so.new /lib/libc.so.major
```

with appropriate values substituted for *new* and *major*. Note that it is imperative that the operation of replacing the old link with the new one is done atomically, in one operation, not as two separate commands. The following is an *incorrect* way of updating the link:

```
rm -f /lib/libc.so.major    DON'T DO THIS
ln -s /lib/libc.so.new /lib/libc.so.major
```

The problem with the above two commands is that what happens after the `rm`? When `ln` starts it tries to use the shared library `/lib/libc.so.4`, but that was just deleted! Not only can't you create the new link, you can't run any other program that uses the shared library either! If you reboot and use a different root partition (and therefore a different set of shared libraries) to do the update, or if you use some carefully selected statically linked binaries (`ln` comes to mind), you can reduce the probability of this problem, if you are afraid you are going to make the mistake.

META: fixing the missing link; getting rid of old images

3.6   C/C++ Programming, `/usr/include`, `/usr/g++include`

META: C++ should be typeset prettier.

The `/usr/include` directory contains the standard headers for the C programming language, or at least most of them (see GCC documentation for details); `/usr/g++include` contains similar headers for C++. (If this doesn't make any sense to you, don't worry, you can probably ignore it in that case.)

The symbolic links `/usr/include/asm` and `/usr/include/linux` point to the similarly named directories in the kernel source tree (see `/usr/src`) for whatever kernel version you are running. They are needed because some type declarations are kernel version dependent. (You may need to update these links when you upgrade the kernel, or the header files.)

3.7   Source Codes, `/usr/src`

The customary place to keep source code for the kernel and standard programs is `/usr/src`. In particular, `/usr/src/linux` is usually the directory with the source code for the running version of the kernel. Kernel source code, or at least the headers[3], is needed because the headers of the C library refer to headers in the kernel source for kernel version dependent information, such as some types. Because of this, `/usr/include/asm` and `/usr/include/linux` are typically symbolic links to `/usr/src/linux/include/asm` and `linux`, respectively.

3.8   Administrativia, `/usr/adm`

The `/usr/adm` directory contains administrative log files generated by various demons and system programs.

3.9   On-line Manuals, `/usr/man`

On-line man pages are stored below `/usr/man`, at least for programs in `/bin` and `/usr/bin`. Programs installed elsewhere (e.g. `/usr/local`) often get their man pages installed similarly elsewhere as well, but not always.

---

[3]If you're short of disk space, deleting everything but the headers can save a couple of megabytes.

UNIX man pages are divided into eight numbered chapters (after the chapters in the original UNIX manuals). Each chapter has a subdirectory below /usr/man, called man*0* where *0* stands for the number of the chapter, and a man page is installed into the appropriate subdirectory. (Man page directories in other places, e.g. /usr/local/man, usually have a similar organization.)

META: linux has chapter 9 as well? some man pages need -mandoc instead of -man

In addition to the troff(1) source code for the man page in /usr/man/man?, its formatted version (formatted for a simple printer or a text screen) is stored into /usr/man/cat*0*, where *0* again stands for the chapter. This way, if you need the source (in order to print it on a laser printer, for example), you can get it from /usr/man/man?, and if you are satisfied with the pre-formatted version, you can get it quickly from /usr/man/cat?. The man(1) command uses the correct one automatically: the formatted one if it exists, else it formats the unformatted one on the fly, saving the formatted version in the appropriate place.

Man pages can easily take up a lot of space, so they are sometimes stored in compressed format. On some systems, the man program understands compressed files and automatically uncompresses the man page while it is read.

Another way to save space is to not have both formatted and unformatted man pages installed. (Or to not have them installed at all, of course.)

3.10   More Manuals, /usr/info

Besides the traditional documentation form for UNIX, man pages, LINUX also uses the **Info** system develop by the GNU Project (based on the ITS info system). See Texinfo documentation for more information. The formatted info documents are put into /usr/info (or /usr/emacs/info, or /usr/lib/emacs/info, or /usr/local/emacs/info; the possibilities are almost endless, but /usr/info is usually either the place itself, or a symlink to the place). The file dir in the info directory is the toplevel, or directory, node and should be edited to contain a link to the new document when one is added to the directory.

META: info and texinfo 3 understand compressed man pages; emacs does not

3.11   /home, **Sweet** /home

Users' home directories are placed in different places on different systems. The oldest convention was to put them in /usr, but that is confusing since /usr contains a lot of other things as well. /home is one common place, and the place most LINUXers seem to prefer (although some prefer to call it /users, /usr/homes, or something else that isn't /usr.) The home directory of user liw would then be /home/liw.

3.12   **Temporary Files,** /tmp **and** /usr/tmp

META: /tmp on root can be a bad idea

Many programs need to create temporary files. In order not to fill the users' directories (and disks, on systems where home directories are on different disks) with such, sometimes large and plentiful, files, the directories /tmp and /usr/tmp exist. Most programs automatically place temporary files in one of these. Conventions differ from system to system, but generally it is considered better for programs to use /usr/tmp, because then the root filesystem (where /tmp resides) need not be as large. In fact, some systems even make /tmp a symbolic link to /usr/tmp (although this only works after /usr has been mounted) to force temporary files out of the root filesystem (this greatly reduces the size requirements for the root filesystem). Some large systems mount an especially fast disk on /tmp (or `/usr/tmp`); temporary files are usually used for a short time only, or as an extension to physical memory, so having `/tmp` be fast hopefully makes the system faster on the whole.

On many systems, `/tmp` is automatically cleaned (by an appropriate command in `/etc/rc` and/or `cron(8)`), so that the temporary files won't remain and take up space when they are no longer needed. `/usr/tmp` is usually not cleaned automatically (**META:** why?).

3.13   The `/mnt` and `/swap` Directories

The `/mnt` directory is the customary mounting point for temporarily mounted filesystems in LINUX. It is an empty directory, and the intent is that if you have to, for instance, mount a floppy, you can use `/mnt` as its mount point and don't have to create a new directory each time. It is just for convenience, no programs contain embedded information about `/mnt`. Some people call their `/mnt` something else, such as `/floppy`. Others prefer to have subdirectories below `/mnt`, so that they can have several mount points, e.g. `/mnt/a` for the first floppy drive, or `/mnt/dos` for the MS-DOS hard disk partition.

The `/swap` directory is similarly only a commonly used mount point. As the name implies, it is intended as the mount point for the swap partition. **META:** mount understands 'none' as the mount point, `/swap` is not needed anymore, but it might be a good place to keep swap files, if there are many

3.14   Process Information, `/proc`

The `/proc` directory is where the **proc filesystem** is usually mounted. The proc filesystem provides a way in which one can get information about the processes running without having to poke in kernel memory to find it. Poking in kernel memory is both a security hole and inconvenient, since the places and methods for poking vary from kernel version to kernel version, not to mention operating system to operating system. See the Linux Kernel Hackers' Guide for more information.

3.15   The `/install` Directory

The `/install` directory is specific to the SLS distribution of LINUX. It contains files needed for uninstallation of packages installed with the SLS installation tools.

Chapter 4

Boots And Shutdowns

This section explains what goes on when a LINUX system is turned on and off, and how it should be done properly.

META: don't power cycle too often

4.1 An Overview of Boots and Shutdowns

META: explain "bootstrapping"

META: boot: bios read boot sector; boot sector reads in kernel; kernel initializes itself and runs init; init runs /etc/rc and/or other scripts and starts gettys and other programs

META: shutdown: all processes are told to quit (sigterm); wait; then kill any that didn't quit (sigkill); sync; unmount all filesystems; halt the system; just cutting the power might cause something to go wrong

4.2 The Boot Process in Closer Look

META: see Linus' notes

You can boot LINUX either from a floppy or from the hard disk. The installation section in the Getting Started guide tells you how to install LINUX so you can boot it the way you want to.

When the computer is booted, the BIOS will do various tests to check that everything looks all-right[1], and will then start the actual booting. It will choose a disk drive (typically the first floppy drive, if there is a floppy inserted, otherwise the first hard disk, if one is installed in the computer) and read its very first sector. This is called the **boot sector**; for a hard disk, it is also called the **master boot record** (since a hard disk can contain several partitions, each with their own boot sectors).

The boot sector contains a small program (small enough to fit into one sector) whose responsibility it is to read the actual operating system from the disk and start it. When booting LINUX from a floppy disk, the boot sector contains code that just reads the first 512 kB (**META:** depends on kernel size) to a predetermined place in memory. (On a LINUX boot floppy, there is no filesystem, the kernel is just stored in consecutive sectors, since this simplifies the boot process.)

When booting from the hard disk, the code in the master boot record will examine the partition table, identify the active partition (the partition that is marked to be bootable), read the boot sector from that partition, and then start the code in that boot sector. The code in the partition's boot sector does what a floppy disk's boot sector does: it will read in the kernel from the partition and start it.

---

[1] These is called the **power on self test**, or **POST** for short.

The details vary, however, since it is generally not useful to have a separate partition for just the kernel image, so the code in the partition's boot sector can't just read the disk in sequential order, it has to find the sectors whereever the filesystem has put them. There are several ways around this problem, but the most common way is to use LILO. (The details about how to do this are irrelevant for this discussion, however; see the LILO documentation for more information.)

When booting with LILO, it will normally go right ahead and read in and boot the default kernel. It is also possible to configure LILO to be able to boot one of several kernels, or even other operating systems than LINUX, and it is possible for the user to choose which kernel or operating system is to be booted at boot time. LILO can be configured so that if one holds down the ⌈alt⌋, ⌈shift⌋, or ⌈ctrl⌋ key at boot time (i.e. when LILO is loaded), LILO will ask what is to be booted and not boot the default right away. Alternatively, LILO can be configured so that it will always ask, with an optional timeout that will cause the default kernel to be booted.

The are other boot loaders than LILO. However, since LILO has been written especially for LINUX, it has some features that are useful and that only it provides, for example the ability to pass arguments to the kernel at boot time, or overriding some configuration options built into the kernel. Hence, it is usually the best choice. Among the alternatives are bootlin and bootactv[2]

Booting from floppy and booting hard disk have both their advantages, but generally booting from the hard disk is easier, since it avoids the hassle of playing around with floppies. It is also faster. However, it can be more troublesome to install the system so it can boot from the hard disk, so many people will first boot from floppy, then, when the system is otherwise installed and working well, will install LILO and start booting from the hard disk.

After the LINUX kernel has been read into the memory, by whatever means, and is started for real, roughly the following things happen:

- If the kernel was installed compressed, it will first uncompress itself. (The beginning of the compressed kernel contains a small program that does this.)

- If you have a super-VGA card that LINUX thinks it recognizes and that has some special text modes (such as 100 columns by 40 rows[3]), LINUX asks you which mode you want to use. (During the kernel compilation, it is possible to preset a video mode, so that this is never asked. This can also be done with LILO.)

- After this the kernel checks what other hardware there is (hard disks, floppies, network adapters. . .), and configures some of its device drivers appropriately; while it does this, it outputs messages about its findings. For example, when I boot, I it looks like this:

```
LILO boot:
Loading linux.
Console: colour EGA+ 80x25, 8 virtual consoles
Serial driver version 3.94 with no serial options enabled
tty00 at 0x03f8 (irq = 4) is a 16450
tty01 at 0x02f8 (irq = 3) is a 16450
lp_init: lp1 exists (0), using polling driver
Memory: 7332k/8192k available (300k kernel code, 384k reserved, 176k data)
Floppy drive(s): fd0 is 1.44M, fd1 is 1.2M
Loopback device init
Warning WD8013 board not found at i/o = 280.
Math coprocessor using irq13 error reporting.
Partition check:
  hda: hda1 hda2 hda3
VFS: Mounted root (ext filesystem).
Linux version 0.99.p19-1 (root@haven) 05/01/93 14:12:20
```

(The exact texts are different on different systems, depending on the hardware, the version of LINUX being used, and how it has been configured.)

---

[2] I don't know much about any of the alternatives. If and when I learn, I will add more descriptions.
[3] Incidentally, this is the mode preferred by Linus himself.

- After all this configration business is complete, LINUX switches the processor into protected mode. The switch is not visible to the user, but is an important step for the kernel. A big leap for the kernel, a small step for the userkind.

- Then the kernel will try to mount the root filesystem. The place—which floppy or partition—is configurable at compilation time, with rdev (see man page), or with LILO (see LILO documentation). The filesystem type is detected automatically. If the mounting of the root filesystem fails, the kernel panics and halts the system (there isn't much one can do, anyway).

  META: read-only mounting of root fs, then re-mounting after fsck

- After this, the kernel starts the program /etc/init in the background (this will always become process number 1), which does various startup chores. The exact things it does depends on the version of init being used; see the section on init for more information.

  META: doshell

- The init program then starts a getty for virtual consoles and serial lines as configured in /etc/gettytabs. getty is the program which lets people log in via virtual consoles and serial terminals.

  META: check /etc/gettytabs filename (no s at end?)

- After this, the boot is complete, and the system is up and running normally.

META: explain doshell

4.3   More about Shutdowns

It is important to follow the correct procedures when you shut down a LINUX system. If you do not do so, your filesystems may become trashed and/or the files may become scrambled. This is because LINUX has a disk cache that won't write things to disk at once, but only at intervals. This greatly improves performance but also means that if you just turn off the power at a whim the cache may hold a lot of data and that what is on the disk may not be a fully working filesystem (because only some things have been written to the disk).

Another reason against just flipping the power switch is that in a multi-tasking system there can be lots of things going on in the background, and shutting the power can be quite disastrous. This is especially true for machines that several people use at the same time.

So, how does one shut down a LINUX system properly? The program for doing this is called /bin/shutdown or /etc/shutdown (the place varies between systems). There are two popular ways of using it.

If you are running a system where you are the only user, the usual way of using shutdown is to quit all running programs, log out on all virtual consoles, log in as root on one of them (or stay logged in as root if you already are, but you should change to the root directory, to avoid problems with unmounting), then give the command shutdown -q now (substitute now for a number in minutes if you want a delay, though you usually don't on a single user system).

Alternatively, if your system has many users, the usual way is to use the command shutdown 10, and give a short explanation of why the system is shutting down when prompted to do so. This will warn everybody that the system will shut down in ten minutes (although you can choose another time if you want, of course) and that they'd better get lost or loose data (perhaps not in these words). The warning is automatically repeated a few times before the boot, with shorter and shorter intervals as the time runs out.

META: /etc/shutdown.rc

Using either method, when the shutting down starts after any delays, all filesystems (except the root one) are unmounted, user processes (if anybody is still logged in) are killed, demons are shut down, and generally everything settles down. When that is done, shutdown prints out a message that you can power down the machine. Then, *and only then*, should you move your fingers towards the on/off button.

META: root fs is unmounted too?

There is another similar command, called reboot, which is identical to shutdown, but it boots the machine right away instead of asking you to power down the system. Use reboot instead of shutdown if that's what you want to do.

META: halt, fastboot, options to shutdown

Sometimes, although rarely on any good system, it is impossible to shut down properly. For instance, if the kernel panics and crashes and burns and generally misbehaves, it might be completely impossible to give any new commands, hence shutting down properly is somewhat difficult, and just about everything you can do is hope that nothing has been too severely damaged and turn off the power. If the troubles are a bit less severe (say, somebody merely hit your keyboard with an axe), and the kernel and the update program still run normally, it is probably a good idea to wait a couple of minutes to give update a chance to sync the disks, and only cut the power after that.

Some people like to shut down using the command sync three times, waiting for the disk I/O to stop, then turn off the power. If there are no running programs, this is about equivalent to using shutdown. However, it does not unmount any filesystems (this can lead to problems with the ext2fs "clean filesystem" flag). The triple-sync method is not recommended.

(In case you're wondering: the reason for *three* syncs is that in the early days of UNIX, when the commands were typed separately, that usually gave sufficient time for most disk I/O to be finished.)

Chapter 5

Using Disks and Other Storage Media

On a clear disk you can seek forever.

When you install or upgrade your system, you need to do a fair amount of work on your disks. You have to make filesystems on your disks so that files can be stored on them and reserve space for the different parts of your system.

This chapter explains all these initial activities. Usually, once you get your system set up, you won't have to go through the work again, except for using floppies. You'll need to come back to this chapter if you add a new disk or want to fine-tune your disk usage.

The basic tasks in administering disks are:

- Format your disk. This does various things to prepare it for use, such as checking for bad sectors. (Formatting is nowadays not necessary for most hard disks.)

- Partition a hard disk, if you want to use it for several activities that aren't supposed to interfere with one another. One reason for partitioning is to store different operating systems on the same disk. Another reason is to keep user files separate from system files, which simplifies back-ups and helps protect the system files from corruption.

- Make a filesystem (of a suitable type) on each disk or partition. The disk means nothing to LINUX until you make a filesystem; then files can be created and accessed on it.

- Mount different filesystems in a single tree structure, either automatically, or manually as needed. (Manually mounted filesystems usually need to be unmounted manually as well.)

Chapter 6 contains information about virtual memory and disk caching, of which you also need to be aware of when using disks.

This chapter explains what you need to know for hard disks and floppies. Unfortunately, because I lack the equipment, I cannot tell you much about using other types of media, such as tapes or CD-ROM's.

5.1 Two kinds of devices

UNIX, and therefore LINUX, recognizes two different kinds of devices: random-access block devices (such as disks), and serial character devices (such as tapes and serial lines). Each supported device is represented in the filesystem as a **device file**. When you read or write a device file, the data comes from or goes to the device it represents. This way no special programs (and no special application programming methodology, such as catching interrupts or polling a serial port) are necessary to access devices; for example, to send a file to the printer, one could just say

```
ttyp5 root ~ $ cat filename > /dev/lp1
ttyp5 root ~ $
```

and the contents of the file are printed (the file must, of course, be in a form that the printer understands). However, since it is not a good idea to have several people cat their files to the printer at the same time, one usually uses a special program to send the files to be printed (usually lpr(1)). This program makes sure that only one file is being printed at a time, and will automatically send files to the printer as soon as it finishes with the previous file. Something similar is needed for most devices. In fact, one seldom needs to worry about device files at all.

Since devices show up as files in the filesystem (in the /dev directory), it is easy to see just what device files exist, using ls(1) or another suitable command. In the output of ls -l, the first column contains the type of the file and its permissions. For example, inspecting a serial device gives on my system

```
ttyp5 root ~ $ ls -l /dev/cua0
crw-rw-rw-  1 root      uucp      5,  64 Nov 30  1993 /dev/cua0
ttyp5 root ~ $
```

The first character in the first column, i.e., 'c' in crw-rw-rw- above, tells an informed user the type of the file, in this case a character device. For ordinary files, the first character is '-', for directories it is 'd', and for block devices 'b'; see the ls(1) man page for further information.

Note that usually all device files exist even though the device itself might be not be installed. So just because you have a file /dev/sda, it doesn't mean that you really do have an SCSI hard disk. Having all the device files makes the installation programs simpler, and makes it easier to add new hardware (there is no need to find out the correct parameters for and create the device files for the new device).

5.2   Hard disks

This subsection introduces terminology related to hard disks. If you already know the terms and concepts, you can skip this subsection.

See figure 5.1 for a schematic picture of the important parts in a hard disk. A hard disk consists of one or more circular **platters**,[1] of which either or both **surfaces** are coated with a magnetic substance used for recording the data. For each surface, there is a **read-write head** that examines or alters the recorded data. The platters rotate on a common axis; a typical rotation speed is 3600 rotations per minute, although high-performance hard disks have higher speeds. The heads move along the radius of the platters; this movement combined with the rotation of the platters allows the head to access all parts of the surfaces.

The processor (CPU) and the actual disk communicate through a **disk controller**. This relieves the rest of the computer from knowing how to use the drive, since the controllers for different types of disks can be made to use the same interface towards the rest of the computer. Therefore, the computer can say just "hey disk, gimme what I want", instead of a long and complex series of electric signals to move the head to the proper location and waiting for the correct position to come under the head and doing all the other unpleasant stuff necessary. (In reality, the interface to the controller is still complex, but much less so than it would otherwise be.) The controller can also do some other stuff, such as caching, or automatic bad sector replacement.

The above is usually what one needs to understand about the hardware. There is also a bunch of other stuff, such as the motor that rotates the platters and moves the heads, and the electronics that control the operation of the mechanical parts, but that is mostly not relevant for understanding the working principle of a hard disk.

The surfaces are usually divided into concentric rings, called **tracks**, and these in turn are divided into **sectors**. This division is used to specify locations on the hard disk and to allocate disk space to files. To find a given place on the hard disk, one might say "surface 3, track 5, sector 7". Usually the

---

[1] The platters are made of a hard substance, e.g., aluminium, which gives the hard disk its name.

number of sectors is the same for all tracks, but some hard disks put more sectors in outer tracks (all sectors are of the same physical size, so more of them fit in the longer outer tracks). Typically, a sector will hold 512 bytes of data. The disk itself can't handle smaller amounts of data than one sector.

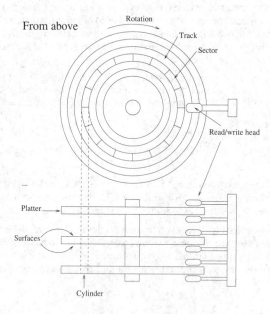

Figure 5.1: A schematic picture of a hard disk.

Each surface is divided into tracks (and sectors) in the same way. This means that when the head for one surface is on a track, the heads for the other surfaces are also on the corresponding tracks. All the corresponding tracks taken together are called a **cylinder**. It takes time to move the heads from one track (cylinder) to another, so by placing the data that is often accessed together (say, a file) so that it is within one cylinder, it is not necessary to move the heads to read all of it. This improves performance. It is not always possible to place files like this; files that are stored in several places on the disk are called **fragmented**.

The number of surfaces (or heads, which is the same thing), cylinders, and sectors vary a lot; the specification of the number of each is called the **geometry** of a hard disk. The geometry is usually stored in a special, battery-powered memory location called the **CMOS RAM**, from where the operating system can fetch it.

Unfortunately, the BIOS[2] has a design limitation, which makes it impossible to specify a track number that is larger than 1024 in the CMOS RAM, which is too little for a large hard disk. To overcome this, the hard disk controller lies about the geometry, and **translates the addresses** given by the computer into something that fits reality. For example, a hard disk might have 8 heads, 2048 tracks, and 35 sectors per track[3]. Its controller could lie to the computer and claim that it has 16 heads, 1024 tracks, and 35 sectors per track, thus not exceeding the limit on tracks, and translates the address that the computer gives it by halving the head number, and doubling the track number. The math can be more complicated in reality, because the numbers are not as nice as here (but again, the details are not relevant for understanding the principle). This translation distorts the operating system's view of how the disk is organized, thus making it impractical to use the all-data-on-one-cylinder trick to boost performance.

The translation is only a problem for IDE disks. SCSI disks use a sequential sector number (i.e., the

---

[2] The BIOS is some built-in software stored on ROM chips. It takes care, among other things, of the initial stages of booting.
[3] The numbers are completely imaginary.

controller translates a sequential sector number to head/cylinder/sector), and a completely different method for the CPU to talk with the controller, so they are insulated from the problem. Note, however, that the computer might not know the real geometry of an SCSI disk either.

Since LINUX often will not know the real geometry of a disk, it doesn't even try to keep files within a single cylinder. Instead, it tries to assign sequentially numbered sectors to files, which almost always gives similar performance. The issue is further complicated by on-controller caches, and automatic prefetches done by the controller.

Each hard disk is represented by a separate device file. There can (usually) be only two IDE hard disks. These are known as `/dev/hda` and `/dev/hdb`, respectively. SCSI hard disks are known as `/dev/sda`, `/dev/sdb`, and so on. Similar naming conventions exist for other hard disk types Note that the device files for the hard disks give access to the entire disk, with no regard to partitions (which will be discussed below), and it's easy to mess up the partitions or the data in them if you aren't careful. The disks' device files are usually used only to get access to the master boot record (which will also be discussed below).

5.3   Floppies

A floppy disk consists of a flexible membrane covered on one or both sides with similar magnetic substance as a hard disk. The floppy disk itself doesn't have a read-write head, that is included in the drive. A floppy corresponds to one platter in a hard disk, but is removable and one drive can be used to access different floppies, whereas the hard disk is one indivisible unit.

Like a hard disk, a floppy is divided into tracks and sectors (and the two corresponding tracks on either side of a floppy form a cylinder), but there are many fewer of them than on a hard disk.

A floppy drive can usually use several different types of disks; for example, a $3\frac{1}{2}$ inch drive can use both 720 kB and 1.44 MB disks. Since the drive has to operate a bit differently and the operating system must know how big the disk is, there are many device files for floppy drives, one per combination of drive and disk type. Therefore, `/dev/fd0H1440` is the first floppy drive (`fd0`), which must be a $3\frac{1}{2}$ inch drive, using a $3\frac{1}{2}$ inch, high density disk (`H`) of size 1440 kB (`1440`), i.e., a normal $3\frac{1}{2}$ inch HD floppy. For more information on the naming conventions for the floppy devices.

The names for floppy drives are complex, however, and LINUX therefore has a special floppy device type that automatically detects the type of the disk in the drive. It works by trying to read the first sector of a newly inserted floppy using different floppy types until it finds the correct one. This naturally requires that the floppy is formatted first. The automatic devices are called `/dev/fd0`, `/dev/fd1`, and so on.

The parameters the automatic device uses to access a disk can also be set using the program `setfdprm(8)`. This can be useful if you need to use disks that do not follow any usual floppy sizes, e.g., if they have an unusual number of sectors, or if the autodetecting for some reason fails and the proper device file is missing.

LINUX can handle many nonstandard floppy disk formats in addition to all the standard ones. Some of these require using special formatting programs. We'll skip these disk types for now.

5.4   Formatting

Formatting is the process of writing marks on the magnetic media that are used to mark tracks and sectors. Before a disk is formatted, its magnetic surface is a complete mess of magnetic signals. When it is formatted, some order is brought into the chaos by essentially drawing lines where the tracks go, and where they are divided into sectors. The actual details are not quite exactly like this, but that is irrelevant. What is important, is that a disk cannot be used unless it has been formatted.

The terminology is a bit confusing here: in MS-DOS, the word formatting is used to cover also the process of creating a filesystem (which will be discussed below). There, the two processes are often combined, especially for floppies. When the distinction needs to be made, the real formatting is called **low-level formatting**, while making the filesystem is called **high-level formatting**. In UNIX circles, the two are called formatting and making a filesystem, so that's what is used in this book as well.

For IDE and some SCSI disks the formatting is actually done at the factory and doesn't need to be repeated; hence most people rarely need to worry about it. In fact, formatting a hard disk can cause it to work less well, for example because a disk might need to be formatted in some very special way to allow automatic bad sector replacement to work.

Disks that need or can be formatted, often require a special program anyway, because the interface to the formatting logic inside the drive is different from drive to drive. The formatting program is often either on the controller BIOS, or is supplied as an MS-DOS program; neither of these can easily be used from within LINUX.

During formatting one might encounter bad spots on the disk, called **bad blocks** or **bad sectors**. These are sometimes handled by the drive itself, but even then, if more of them develop, something needs to be done to avoid using those parts of the disk. The logic to do this is built into the filesystem; how to add the information into the filesystem is described below. Alternatively, one might create a small partition that covers just the bad part of the disk; this approach might be a good idea if the bad spot is very large, since filesystems can sometimes have trouble with very large bad areas.

Floppies are formatted with fdformat(8). The floppy device file to use is given as the parameter. For example, the following command would format a high density, $3\frac{1}{2}$ inch floppy in the first floppy drive:

```
ttyp5 root ~ $ fdformat /dev/fd0H1440
Double-sided, 80 tracks, 18 sec/track. Total capacity 1440 kB.
Formatting ... done
Verifying ... done
ttyp5 root ~ $
```

Note that if you want to use an autodetecting device (e.g., /dev/fd0), you *must* set the parameters of the device with setfdprm(8) first. To achieve the same effect as above, one would have to do the following:

```
ttyp5 root ~ $ setfdprm /dev/fd0 1440/1440
ttyp5 root ~ $ fdformat /dev/fd0
Double-sided, 80 tracks, 18 sec/track. Total capacity 1440 kB.
Formatting ... done
Verifying ... done
ttyp5 root ~ $
```

It is usually more convenient to choose the correct device file that matches the type of the floppy. Note that it is unwise to format floppies to contain more information than what they are designed for.

fdformat will also validate the floppy, i.e., check it for bad blocks. It will try a bad block several times (you can usually hear this, the drive noise changes dramatically). If the floppy is only marginally bad (due to dirt on the read/write head, some errors are false signals), fdformat won't complain, but a real error will abort the validation process. The kernel will print log messages for each I/O error it finds; these will go to the console or, if syslog is being used, to the file /usr/adm/messages. fdformat itself won't tell where the error is (one usually doesn't care, floppies are cheap enough that a bad one is automatically thrown away).

```
ttyp5 root ~ $ fdformat /dev/fd0H1440
Double-sided, 80 tracks, 18 sec/track. Total capacity 1440 kB.
Formatting ... done
Verifying ... read: Unknown error
ttyp5 root ~ $
```

The badblocks(8) command can be used to search any disk or partition for bad blocks (including a floppy). It does not format the disk, so it can be used to check even existing filesystems. The example below checks a $3\frac{1}{2}$ inch floppy with two bad blocks.

```
ttyp5 root ~ $ badblocks /dev/fd0H1440 1440
718
719
ttyp5 root ~ $
```

`badblocks` outputs the block numbers of the bad blocks it finds. Most filesystems can avoid such bad blocks. They maintain a list of known bad blocks, which is initialized when the filesystem is made, and can be modified later. The initial search for bad blocks can be done by the `mkfs` command (which initializes the filesystem), but later checks should be done with `badblocks` and the new blocks should be added with `fsck`. We'll describe `mkfs` and `fsck` later.

5.5 Partitions

A hard disk can be divided into several **partitions**. Each partition functions as if it were a separate hard disk. The idea is that if you have one hard disk, and want to have, say, two operating systems on it, you can divide the disk into two partitions. Each operating system uses its partition as it wishes and doesn't touch the other one's. This way the two operating systems can co-exist peacefully on the same hard disk. Without partitions one would have to buy a hard disk for each operating system.

Floppies are not partitioned. There is no technical reason against this, but since they're so small, partitions would be useful only very rarely.

5.5.1 The MBR, boot sectors and partition table

The information about how a hard disk has been partitioned is stored in its first sector (that is, the first sector of the first track on the first disk surface). The first sector is the **master boot record** (MBR) of the disk; this is the sector that the BIOS reads in and starts when the machine is first booted. The master boot record contains a small program that reads the partition table, checks which partition is active (that is, marked bootable), and reads the first sector of that partition, the partition's **boot sector** (the MBR is also a boot sector, but it has a special status and therefore a special name). This boot sector contains another small program that reads the first part of the operating system stored on that partition (assuming it is bootable), and then starts it.

The partitioning scheme is not built into the hardware, or even into the BIOS. It is only a convention that many operating systems follow. Not all operating systems do follow it, but they are the exceptions. Some operating systems support partitions, but they occupy one partition on the hard disk, and use their internal partitioning method within that partition. The latter type exists peacefully with other operating systems (including LINUX), and does not require any special measures, but an operating system that doesn't support partitions cannot co-exist on the same disk with any other operating system.

As a safety precaution, it is a good idea to write down the partition table on a piece of paper, so that if it ever corrupts you don't have to lose all your files. (A bad partition table can be fixed with `fdisk`).

5.5.2 Extended and logical partitions

The original partitioning scheme for PC hard disks allowed only four partitions. This quickly turned out to be too little in real life, partly because some people want more than four operating systems (LINUX, MS-DOS, OS/2, Minix, FreeBSD, NetBSD, or Windows/NT, to name a few), but primarily because sometimes it is a good idea to have several partitions for one operating system. For example, swap space is usually best put in its own partition for LINUX instead of in the main LINUX partition for reasons of speed (see below).

To overcome this design problem, **extended partitions** were invented. This trick allows partitioning a **primary partition** into sub-partitions. The primary partition thus subdivided is the extended partition; the subpartitions are **logical partitions**. They behave like primary[4] partitions, but are created differently.

The partition structure of a hard disk might look like that in figure 5.2. The disk is divided into three primary partitions, the second of which is divided into two logical partitions. Part of the disk is not partitioned at all. The disk as a whole and each primary partition has a boot sector.

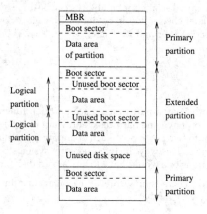

Figure 5.2: A sample hard disk partitioning.

5.5.3 Partition types

The partition tables (the one in the MBR, and the ones for extended partitions) contain one byte per partition that identifies the type of that partition. This attempts to identify the operating system that uses the partition, or what it uses it for. The purpose is to make it possible to avoid having two operating systems accidentally using the same partition. However, in reality, operating systems do not really care about the partition type byte; e.g., LINUX doesn't care at all what it is. Worse, some of them use it incorrectly; e.g., at least some versions of DR-DOS ignore the most significant bit of the byte, while others don't.

There is no standardization agency to specify what each byte value means, but some commonly accepted ones are included in the table in table 5.1. The same list is available in the LINUX `fdisk(8)` program.

Table 5.1: Partition types (from the LINUX `fdisk(8)` program).

0	Empty	40	Venix 80286	94	Amoeba BBT
1	DOS 12-bit FAT	51	Novell?	a5	BSD/386
2	XENIX root	52	Microport	b7	BSDI fs
3	XENIX usr	63	GNU HURD	b8	BSDI swap
4	DOS 16-bit <32M	64	Novell	c7	Syrinx
5	Extended	75	PC/IX	db	CP/M
6	DOS 16-bit ≥32M	80	Old MINIX	e1	DOS access
7	OS/2 HPFS	81	Linux/MINIX	e3	DOS R/O
8	AIX	82	Linux swap	f2	DOS secondary
9	AIX bootable	83	Linux native	ff	BBT
a	OS/2 Boot Manag	93	Amoeba		

---

[4] Illogical?

5.5.4 Partitioning a hard disk

There are many programs for creating and removing partitions. Most operating systems have their own, and it can be a good idea to use each operating system's own, just in case it does something unusual that the others can't. Many of the programs are called fdisk, including the LINUX one, or variations thereof. Details on using the LINUX fdisk are given on its man page. The cfdisk command is similar to fdisk, but has a nicer (full screen) user interface.

When using IDE disks, the boot partition (the partition with the bootable kernel image files) must be completely within the first 1024 cylinders. This is because the disk is used via the BIOS during boot (before the system goes into protected mode), and BIOS can't handle more than 1024 cylinders. It is sometimes possible to use a boot partition that is only partly within the first 1024 cylinders. This works as long as all the files that are read with the BIOS are within the first 1024 cylinders. Since this is difficult to arrange, it is *a very bad idea* to do it; you never know when a kernel update or disk defragmentation will result in an unbootable system. Therefore, make sure your boot partition is completely within the first 1024 cylinders.

Some newer versions of the BIOS and IDE disks can, in fact, handle disks with more than 1024 cylinders. If you have such a system, you can forget about the problem; if you aren't quite sure of it, put it within the first 1024 cylinders.

Each partition should have an even number of sectors, since the LINUX filesystems use a 1 kB block size, i.e., two sectors. An odd number of sectors will result in the last sector being unused. This won't result in any problems, but it is ugly, and some versions of fdisk will warn about it.

Changing a partition's size usually requires first backing up everything you want to save from that partition (preferably the whole disk, just in case), deleting the partition, creating new partition, then restoring everything to the new partition. There is a program for MS-DOS, called fips, which does this without requiring the backup and restore, but for other filesystems it is still necessary.

5.5.5 Device files and partitions

Each partition and extended partition has its own device file. The naming convention for these files is that a partition's number is appended after the name of the whole disk, with the convention that 1–4 are primary partitions (regardless of how many primary partitions there are) and 5–8 are logical partitions (regardless of within which primary partition they reside). For example, /dev/hda1 is the first primary partition on the first IDE hard disk, and /dev/sdb7 is the third extended partition on the second SCSI hard disk.

5.6 Filesystems

5.6.1 What are filesystems?

A **filesystem** is the methods and data structures that an operating uses to keep track of files on a disk or partition that is, the way the files are organized on the disk. The word is also used to refer to a partition or disk that is used to store the files or the type of the filesystem. Thus, one might say "I have two filesystems" meaning one has two partitions on which one stores files, or that one is using the "extended filesystem", meaning the type of the filesystem.

The difference between a disk or partition and the filesystem it contains is important. A few programs—including, reasonably enough, programs that create filesystems—operate directly on the raw sectors of a disk or partition; if there is an existing file system there it can be destroyed or seriously corrupted. Most programs operate on a filesystem, and therefore won't work on a partition that doesn't contain one (or that contains one of the wrong type).

Before a partition or disk can be used as a filesystem, it needs to be initialized, and the bookkeeping data structures need to be written to the disk. This process is called **making a filesystem**.

Most UNIX filesystem types have a similar general structure, although the exact details vary quite a bit. The central concepts are **superblock**, **inode**, **data block**, **directory block**, and **indirection block**. The superblock contains information about the filesystem as a whole, such as its size (the exact information here depends on the filesystem). An inode contains all information about a file, excepts its name. The name is stored in the directory, together with the number of the inode. A directory entry consists of a filename and the number of the inode which represents the file. The inode contains the numbers of several data blocks, which are used to store the data in the file. There is space only for a few data blocks in the inode, however, and if more are needed, more space for pointers to the data blocks is allocated dynamically. These dynamically allocated blocks are indirect blocks; the name indicates that in order to find the data block, one has to find its number in the indirect block first.

UNIX filesystems usually allow one to create a **hole** in a file (this is done with `lseek(2)`; check the manual page), which means that the filesystem just pretends that at a particular place in the file there is just zero bytes, but no actual disk sectors are reserved for that place in the file (this means that the file will use a bit less disk space). This happens especially often for small binaries, LINUX shared libraries, some databases, and a few other special cases. (Holes are implemented by storing a special value as the address of the data block in the indirect block or inode. This special address means that no data block is allocated for that part of the file, ergo, there is a hole in the file.)

Holes are moderately useful. On the author's system, a simple measurement showed a potential for about 4 MB of savings through holes of about 200 MB total used disk space. That system, however, contains relatively few programs and no database files. The measurement tool is described in appendix B.

5.6.2 Filesystems galore

LINUX supports several types of filesystems. As of this writing the most important ones are:

minix	The oldest, presumed to be the most reliable, but quite limited in features (some time stamps are missing, at most 30 character filenames) and restricted in capabilities (at most 64 MB per filesystem).
xia	A modified version of the minix filesystem that lifts the limits on the filenames and filesystem sizes, but does not otherwise introduce new features. It is not very popular, but is reported to work very well.
ext2	The most featureful of the native LINUX filesystems, currently also the most popular one. It is designed to be easily upwards compatible, so that new versions of the filesystem code do not require re-making the existing filesystems.
ext	An older version of `ext2` that wasn't upwards compatible. It is hardly ever used in new installations any more, and most people have converted to `ext2`.

In addition, support for several foreign filesystem exists, to make it easier to exchange files with other operating systems. These foreign filesystems work just like native ones, except that they may be lacking in some usual UNIX features, or have curious limitations, or other oddities.

msdos	Compatibility with MS-DOS (and OS/2 and Windows NT) FAT filesystems.
umsdos	Extends the `msdos` filesystem driver under LINUX so that LINUX can see long filenames, owners, permissions, links, and device files. This allows a normal `msdos` filesystem to be used as if it were a LINUX one, thus removing the need for a separate partition for LINUX.
iso9660	The standard CD-ROM filesystem; the popular Rock Ridge extensions to

the CD-ROM standard that allow longer file names are supported auto-matically.

nfs A networked filesystem that allows sharing a filesystem between many computers to allow easy access to the files from all of them.

hpfs The OS/2 filesystem.

sysv SystemV/386, Coherent, and Xenix filesystems.

The choice of filesystem to use depends on the situation. If compatibility or other reasons make one of the non-native filesystems necessary, then that one must be used. If one can choose freely, then it is probably wisest to use ext2, since it has all the features but does not suffer from lack of performance.

There is also the proc filesystem, usually accessible as the /proc directory, which is not really a filesystem at all, even though it looks like one. The proc filesystem makes it easy to access certain kernel data structures, such as the process list (hence the name). It makes these data structures look like a filesystem, and that filesystem can be manipulated with all the usual file tools. For example, to get a listing of all processes one might use the command

```
ttyp5 root ˜ $  ls -l /proc
total 0
dr-xr-xr-x  4 root    root          0 Jan 31 20:37 1
dr-xr-xr-x  4 liw     users         0 Jan 31 20:37 63
dr-xr-xr-x  4 liw     users         0 Jan 31 20:37 94
dr-xr-xr-x  4 liw     users         0 Jan 31 20:37 95
dr-xr-xr-x  4 root    users         0 Jan 31 20:37 98
dr-xr-xr-x  4 liw     users         0 Jan 31 20:37 99
-r--r--r--  1 root    root          0 Jan 31 20:37 devices
-r--r--r--  1 root    root          0 Jan 31 20:37 dma
-r--r--r--  1 root    root          0 Jan 31 20:37 filesystems
-r--r--r--  1 root    root          0 Jan 31 20:37 interrupts
-r--------  1 root    root    8654848 Jan 31 20:37 kcore
-r--r--r--  1 root    root          0 Jan 31 11:50 kmsg
-r--r--r--  1 root    root          0 Jan 31 20:37 ksyms
-r--r--r--  1 root    root          0 Jan 31 11:51 loadavg
-r--r--r--  1 root    root          0 Jan 31 20:37 meminfo
-r--r--r--  1 root    root          0 Jan 31 20:37 modules
dr-xr-xr-x  2 root    root          0 Jan 31 20:37 net
dr-xr-xr-x  4 root    root          0 Jan 31 20:37 self
-r--r--r--  1 root    root          0 Jan 31 20:37 stat
-r--r--r--  1 root    root          0 Jan 31 20:37 uptime
-r--r--r--  1 root    root          0 Jan 31 20:37 version
ttyp5 root ˜ $
```

(There will be a few extra files that don't correspond to processes, though. The above example has been shortened.)

Note that even though it is called a filesystem, no part of the proc filesystem touches any disk. It exists only in the kernel's imagination. Whenever anyone tries to look at any part of the proc filesystem, the kernel makes it look as if the part existed somewhere, even though it doesn't. So, even though there is a multi-megabyte /proc/kmem file, it doesn't take any disk space.

5.6.3 Which filesystem should be used?

There is usually little point in using many different filesystems. Currently, ext2fs is the most popular one, and it is probably the wisest choice. Depending on the overhead for bookkeeping structures, speed, (perceived) reliability, compatibility, and various other reasons, it may be advisable to use another file system. This needs to be decided on a case-by-case basis.

5.6.4 Creating a filesystem

Filesystems are created, i.e., initialized, with the mkfs(8) command. There is actually a separate program for each filesystem type. mkfs is just a front end that runs the appropriate program depending on the desired filesystem type. The type is selected with the -t fstype option.

The programs called by mkfs have slightly different command line interfaces. The common and most important options are summarized below; see the manual pages for more.

-t *fstype* Select the type of the filesystem.

-c Search bad bad blocks and initialize the bad block list accordingly.

-l *filename* Read the initial bad block list from the file *filename*.

To create an ext2 filesystem on a floppy, one would give the following commands:

```
ttyp6 root ~ $ fdformat -n /dev/fd0H1440
Double-sided, 80 tracks, 18 sec/track. Total capacity 1440 kB.
Formatting ... done
ttyp6 root ~ $ badblocks /dev/fd0H1440 1440 > bad-blocks
ttyp6 root ~ $ mkfs -t ext2 -l bad-blocks /dev/fd0H1440
mke2fs 0.5a, 5-Apr-94 for EXT2 FS 0.5, 94/03/10
360 inodes, 1440 blocks
72 blocks (5.00%) reserved for the super user
First data block=1
Block size=1024 (log=0)
Fragment size=1024 (log=0)
1 block group
8192 blocks per group, 8192 fragments per group
360 inodes per group

Writing inode tables: done
Writing superblocks and filesystem accounting information: done
ttyp6 root ~ $
```

First, the floppy was formatted (the -n option prevents validation, i.e., bad block checking). Then bad blocks were searched with badblocks, with the output redirected to a file, bad-blocks. Finally, the filesystem was created, with the bad block list initialized by whatever badblocks found.

The -c option could have been used with mkfs instead of badblocks and a separate file. The example below does that.

```
ttyp6 root ~ $ mkfs -t ext2 -c /dev/fd0H1440
mke2fs 0.5a, 5-Apr-94 for EXT2 FS 0.5, 94/03/10
360 inodes, 1440 blocks
72 blocks (5.00%) reserved for the super user
First data block=1
Block size=1024 (log=0)
Fragment size=1024 (log=0)
1 block group
8192 blocks per group, 8192 fragments per group
360 inodes per group

Checking for bad blocks (read-only test): done
Writing inode tables: done
Writing superblocks and filesystem accounting information: done
ttyp6 root ~ $
```

The -c is more convenient than a separate use of badblocks, but badblocks is necessary for checking after the filesystem has been created.

The process to prepare to filesystems on hard disks or partitions is the same as for floppies, except that the formatting isn't needed.

5.6.5 Mounting and unmounting

Before one can use a filesystem, it has to be **mounted**. The operating system then does various bookkeeping things to make sure that everything works. Since all files in UNIX are in a single directory tree, the mount operation will make it look like the contents of the new filesystem are the contents of an existing subdirectory in some already mounted filesystem.

For example, figure 5.3 shows three separate filesystems, each with their own root directory. When the last two filesystems are mounted below /home and /usr, respectively, on the first filesystem, we can get a single directory tree, as in figure 5.4.

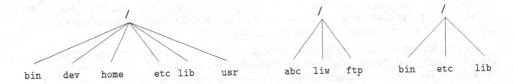

Figure 5.3: Three separate filesystems.

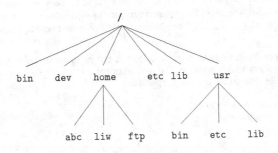

Figure 5.4: /home and /usr have been mounted.

The mounts could be done as in the following example:

```
ttyp6 root ~ $   mount /dev/hda2 /home
ttyp6 root ~ $   mount /dev/hda3 /usr
ttyp6 root ~ $
```

The mount(8) command takes two arguments. The first one is the device file corresponding to the disk or partition containing the filesystem. The second one is the directory below which it will be mounted. After these commands the contents of the two filesystems look just like the contents of the /home and /usr directories, respectively. One would then say that "/dev/hda2 **is mounted on** /home", and similarly for /usr. To look at either filesystem, one would look at the contents of the directory on which it has been mounted, just as it were any other directory. Note the difference between the device file, /dev/hda2, and the mounted-on directory, /home. The device file gives access to the raw contents of the disk, the mounted-on directory gives access to the files on the disk. The mounted-on directory is called the **mount point**.

The mounted-on directory need not be empty, although it must exist. Any files in it, however, will be inaccessible by name while the filesystem is mounted. (Any files that have already been opened will still be accessible. Files that have hard links from other directories can be accessed using those names.) There is no harm done with this, and it can even be useful. For instance, some people like to have /tmp and /usr/tmp synonymous, and make /tmp be a symbolic link to /usr/tmp. When the system is booted, before the /usr filesystem is mounted, a /usr/tmp directory residing on the root filesystem is used instead. When /usr is mounted, it will make the /usr/tmp directory on the root filesystem inaccessible. If /usr/tmp didn't exist on the root filesystem, it would be impossible to use temporary files before mounting /usr.

If you don't intend to write anything to the filesystem, use the -r switch for mount to do a **readonly mount**. This will make the kernel stop any attempts at writing to the filesystem, and will also stop the kernel from updating file access times in the inodes. Read-only mounts are necessary for unwritable media, e.g., CD-ROM's.

The alert reader has already noticed a slight logistical problem. How is the first filesystem (called the **root filesystem**, because it contains the root directory) mounted, since it obviously can't be mounted on another filesystem? Well, the answer is that it is done by magic.[5] The root filesystem is magically mounted at boot time, and one can rely on it to always be mounted—if the root filesystem can't be mounted, the system does not boot. The name of the filesystem that is magically mounted as root is either compiled into the kernel, or set using LILO or rdev.

The root filesystem is usually first mounted readonly. The startup scripts will then run fsck(8) to verify its validity, and if there are no problems, they will **re-mount** it so that writes will also be allowed. fsck should not be run on a mounted filesystem, since any changes to the filesystem while fsck is running *will* cause trouble. Since the root filesystem is mounted readonly while it is being checked, fsck can fix any problems without worry.

On many systems there are other filesystems that should also be mounted automatically at boot time. These are specified in the /etc/fstab file; see the fstab(5) man page for details on the format. The details of exactly when the extra filesystems are mounted depend on many factors, and can be configured by each administrator if need be. When the chapter on booting is finished, you may read all about it there.

When a filesystem no longer needs to be mounted, it can be unmounted with umount(8)[6]. umount takes one argument: either the device file or the mount point. For example, to unmount the directories of the previous example, one could use the commands

```
ttyp6 root ~ $   umount /dev/hda2
ttyp6 root ~ $   umount /usr
ttyp6 root ~ $
```

See the man page for further instructions on how to use the command. It is imperative that you always unmount a mounted floppy. *Don't just pop the floppy out of the drive!* Because of disk caching, the data is not necessarily written to the floppy until you unmount it, so removing the floppy from the drive too early might cause the contents to become garbled. If you just read from the floppy, this is not very likely, but if you write, even accidentally, the result may be catastrophic.

Mounting and unmounting requires super user priviledges, i.e., only root can do it. The reason for this is that if any user can mount a floppy on any directory, then it is rather easy to create a floppy with, say, a Trojan horse disguised as /bin/sh, or any other often used program. However, it is often necessary to allow users to use floppies, and there are several ways to do this:

- Give the users the root password. This is obviously bad security, but is the easiest solution. It works well if there is no need for security anyway, which is the case on many non-networked, personal systems.

- Use a program such as sudo(8) to allow users to use mount. This is still bad security, but doesn't directly give super user priviledges to everyone.[7]

- Make the users use mtools, a package for manipulating MS-DOS filesystems, without mounting them. This works well if MS-DOS floppies are the only thing that is needed, but is rather awkward otherwise.

---

[5] For more information, see the kernel source or the Kernel Hackers' Guide.

[6] It should of course be unmount(8), but the n mysteriously disappeared in the 70's, and hasn't been seen since. Please return it to Bell Labs, NJ, if you find it.

[7] It requires several seconds of hard thinking on the users' behalf.

- List the floppy devices and their allowable mount points together with the suitable options in /etc/fstab.

The last alternative can be implemented by adding a line like the following to /etc/fstab:

```
/dev/fd0 /floppy msdos user,noauto
```

The columns are: device file to mount, directory to mount on, filesystem type, and options. The noauto option stops this mount to be done automatically when the system is started (i.e., it stops mount -a from mounting it). The user option allows any user to mount the filesystem, and, because of security reasons, disallows execution of programs (normal or setuid) and interpretation of device files from the mounted filesystem. After this, any user can mount a floppy with an msdos filesystem with the following command:

```
ttyp6 root ~ $   mount /floppy
ttyp6 root ~ $
```

The floppy can (and needs to, of course) be unmounted with the corresponding umount command.

5.6.6   Keeping filesystems healthy

Filesystems are complex creatures, and as such, they tend to be somewhat error-prone. A filesystem's correctness and validity can be checked using the fsck(8) command. It can be instructed to repair any minor problems it finds, and to alert the user if there any unrepairable problems. Fortunately, the code to implement filesystems is debugged quite effectively, so there are seldom any problems at all, and they are usually caused by power failures, failing hardware, or operator errors; for example, by not shutting down the system properly.

Most systems are setup to run fsck automatically at boot time, so that any errors are detected (and hopefully corrected) before the system is used. Use of a corrupted filesystem tends to make things worse: if the data structures are messed up, using the filesystem will probably mess them up even more, resulting in more data loss. However, fsck can take a while to run on big filesystems, and since errors almost never occur if the system has been shut down properly, a couple of tricks are used to avoid doing the checks in such cases. The first is that if the file /etc/fastboot exists, no checks are made. The second is that the ext2 filesystem has a special marker in its superblock that tells whether the filesystem was unmounted properly after the previous mount. This allows e2fsck (the version of fsck for the ext2 filesystem) to avoid checking the filesystem if the flag indicates that the unmount was done (the assumption being that a proper unmount indicates no problems). Whether the /etc/fastboot trick works on your system depends on your startup scripts, but the ext2 trick works every time you use e2fsck—it has to be explicitly bypassed with an option to e2fsck to be avoided. (See the e2fsck(8) man page for details on how.)

The automatic checking only works for the filesystems that are mounted automatically at boot time. Use fsck manually to check other filesystems, e.g., floppies.

If fsck finds unrepairable problems, you need either in-depth knowlege of how filesystems work in general, and the type of the corrupt filesystem in particular, or good backups. The latter is easy (although sometimes tedious) to arrange, the former can sometimes be arranged via a friend, the LINUX newsgroups and mailing lists, or some other source of support, if you don't have the know-how yourself. I'd like to tell you more about it, but my lack of education and experience in this regard hinders me. The debugfs(8) program by Theodore T'so should be useful.

fsck must only be run on unmounted filesystems, never on mounted filesystems (with the exception of the read-only root during startup). This is because it accesses the raw disk, and can therefore modify the filesystem without the operating system realizing it. There *will* be trouble, if the operating system is confused.

It can be a good idea to periodically check for bad blocks. This is done with the badblocks command. It outputs a list of the numbers of all bad blocks it can find. This list can be fed to fsck to be recorded in the filesystem data structures so that the operating system won't try to use the bad blocks for storing data. The following example will show how this could be done.

```
ttyp6 root ~ $ badblocks /dev/fd0H1440 1440 > bad-blocks
ttyp6 root ~ $ fsck -t ext2 -l bad-blocks /dev/fd0H1440
Parallelizing fsck version 0.5a (5-Apr-94)
e2fsck 0.5a, 5-Apr-94 for EXT2 FS 0.5, 94/03/10
Pass 1: Checking inodes, blocks, and sizes
Pass 2: Checking directory structure
Pass 3: Checking directory connectivity
Pass 4: Check reference counts.
Pass 5: Checking group summary information.

/dev/fd0H1440: ***** FILE SYSTEM WAS MODIFIED *****
/dev/fd0H1440: 11/360 files, 63/1440 blocks
ttyp6 root ~ $
```

5.7   Disks without filesystems

Not all disks or partitions are used as filesystems. A swap partition, for example, will not have a filesystem on it. Many floppies are used in a tape-drive emulating fashion, so that a `tar` or other file is written directly on the raw disk, without a filesystem. This has the advantages of making more of the disk usable (a filesystem always has some bookkeeping overhead) and more easily compatible with other systems: the `tar` file format is the same on all systems, while filesystems are different on most systems. You will quickly get used to disks without filesystems if you need them. Bootable LINUX floppies also do not necessarily have a filesystem, although that is also possible.

One reason to use raw disks is to make image copies of them. For instance, if the disk contains a partially damaged filesystem, it is a good idea to make an exact copy of it before trying to fix it, since then you can start again if your fixing breaks thing even more. One way to do this is to use `dd(1)`:

```
ttyp2 root /usr/tmp $  dd if=/dev/fd0H1440 of=floppy-image
2880+0 records in
2880+0 records out
ttyp2 root /usr/tmp $  dd if=floppy-image of=/dev/fd0H1440
2880+0 records in
2880+0 records out
ttyp2 root /usr/tmp $
```

The first `dd` makes an exact image of the floppy to the file `floppy-image`, the second one writes the image to the floppy. (The user has presumably switched the floppy before the second command. Otherwise the command pair is of doubtful usefulness.)

5.8   Allocating disk space

5.8.1   Partitioning schemes

It is not easy to partition a disk in the best possible way. Worse, there is no universally correct way to do it; there are too many factors involved.

The traditional way is to have a (relatively) small root filesystem, which contains `/bin`, `/etc`, `/dev`, `/lib`, `/tmp`, and other stuff that is needed to get the system up and running. This way, the root filesystem (in its own partition or on its own disk) is all that is needed to bring up the system. The reasoning is that if the root filesystem is small and is not heavily used, it is less likely to become corrupt when the system crashes, and you will therefore find it easier to fix any problems caused by the crash. Then you create separate partitions or use separate disks for the directory tree below `/usr`, the users' home directories (often under `/home`), and the swap space. Separating the home directories (with the users' files) in their own partition makes backups easier, since it is usually not necessary to backup programs (which reside below `/usr`). In a networked environment it is also possible to share `/usr` among several machines (e.g., by using NFS), thereby reducing the total disk space required by several tens or hundreds of megabytes times the number of machines.

The problem with having many partitions is that it splits the total amount of free disk space into many small pieces. Nowadays, when disks and (hopefully) operating systems are more reliable, many people prefer to have just one partition that holds all their files. On the other hand, it can be less painful to back up (and restore) a small partition.

For a small hard disk (assuming you don't do kernel development), the best way to go is probably to have just one partition. For large hard disks, it is probably better to have a few large partitions, just in case something does go wrong. (Note that 'small' and 'large' are used in a relative sense here; your needs for disk space decide what the threshold is.)

If you have several disks, you might wish to have the root filesystem (including /usr) on one, and the users' home directories on another.

It is a good idea to be prepared to experiment a bit with different partitioning schemes (over time, not just while first installing the system). This is a bit of work, since it essentially requires you to install the system from scratch several times, but it is the only way to be sure you do it right.

5.8.2 Space requirements

The LINUX distribution you install will give some indication of how much disk space you need for various configurations. Programs installed separately may also do the same. This will help you plan your disk space usage, but you should prepare for the future and reserve some extra space for things you will notice later that you need.

The amount you need for user files depends on what your users wish to do. Most people seem to need as much space for their files as possible, but the amount they will live happily with varies a lot. Some people do only light text processing and will survive nicely with a few megabytes, others do heavy image processing and will need gigabytes.

By the way, when comparing file sizes given in kilobytes or megabytes and disk space given in megabytes, it can be important to know that the two units can be different. Some disk manufacturers like to pretend that a kilobyte is 1000 bytes and a megabyte is 1000 kilobytes, while all the rest of the computing world uses 1024 for both factors. Therefore, my 345 MB hard disk is really a 330 MB hard disk.[8]

Swap space allocation is discusses in section 6.5.

5.8.3 Examples of hard disk allocation

I used to have a 109 MB hard disk, and am now using a 330 MB hard disk. I'll explain how and why I partitioned these disks.

The 109 MB disk I partitioned in a lot of ways, when my needs and the operating systems I used changed; I'll explain two typical scenarios. First, I used to run MS-DOS together with LINUX. For that, I needed about 20 MB of hard disk, or just enough to have MS-DOS, a C compiler, an editor, a few other utilities, the program I was working on, and enough free disk space to not feel claustrophobic. For LINUX, I had a 10 MB swap partition, and the rest, or 79 MB, was a single partition with all the files I had under LINUX. I experimented with having separate root, /usr, and /home partitions, but there was never enough free disk space in one piece to do much interesting.

When I didn't need MS-DOS anymore, I repartitioned the disk so that I had a 12 MB swap partition, and again had the rest as a single filesystem.

The 330 MB disk is partitioned into several partitions, like this:

---

[8]Sic transit discus mundi.

5 MB	root filesystem
10 MB	swap partition
180 MB	/usr filesystem
120 MB	/home filesystem
15 MB	scratch partition

The scratch partition is for playing around with things that require their own partition, e.g., trying different LINUX distributions, or comparing speeds of filesystems. When not needed for anything else, it is used as swap space (I like to have a *lot* of open windows).

5.8.4 Adding more disk space for LINUX

Adding more disk space for LINUX is easy, at least after the hardware has been properly installed (the hardware installation is outside the scope of this book). You format it if necessary, then create the partitions and filesystem as described above, and add the proper lines to /etc/fstab so that it is mounted automatically.

5.8.5 Tips for saving disk space

The best tip for saving disk space is to avoid installing unnecessary programs. Most LINUX distributions have an option to install only part of the packages they contain, and by analyzing your needs you might notice that you don't need most of them. This will help save a lot of disk space, since many programs are quite large. Even if you do need a particular package or program, you might not need all of it. For example, some on-line documentation might be unnecessary, as might some of the Elisp files for GNU Emacs, some of the fonts for X11, or some of the libraries for programming.

If you cannot uninstall packages, you might look into compression. Compression programs such as gzip(1) or zip(1) will compress (and uncompress) individual files or groups of files. The gzexe system will compress and uncompress programs invisibly to the user (unused programs are compressed, then uncompressed as they are used). The experimental DouBle system will compress all files in a filesystem, invisibly to the programs that use them. (If you are familiar with products such as Stacker for MS-DOS, the principle is the same.)

Chapter 6

Memory Management

Minnet, jag har tappat mitt minne,
är jag svensk eller finne
kommer inte ihåg. . .

Inne, är jag ute eller inne
jag har luckor i minnet,
sådär små ALKO-HÅL
Men besinne,
man tätar med det brännvin man får,
fastän minnet och helan går.

(Bosse Österberg)

This section describes the LINUX memory management features, i.e., virtual memory and the disk buffer cache. The purpose and workings and the things the system administrator needs to take into consideration are described.

6.1 What is virtual memory?

LINUX supports **virtual memory**, that is, using a disk as an extension of RAM so that the effective size of usable memory grows correspondingly. The kernel will write the contents of a currently unused block of memory to the hard disk so that the memory can be used for another purpose. When the original contents are needed again, they are read back into memory. This is all made completely transparent to the user; programs running under LINUX only see the larger amount of memory available and don't notice that parts of them reside on the disk from time to time. Of course, reading and writing the hard disk is slower (on the order of a thousand times slower) than using real memory, so the programs don't run as fast. The part of the hard disk that is used as virtual memory is called the **swap space**.

LINUX can use either a normal file in the filesystem or a separate partition for swap space. A swap partition is faster, but it is easier to change the size of a swap file (there's no need to repartition the whole hard disk, and possibly install everything from scratch). When you know how much swap space you need, you should go for a swap partition, but if you are uncertain, you can use a swap file first, use the system for a while so that you can get a feel for how much swap you need, and then make a swap partition when you're confident about its size.

You should also know that LINUX allows one to use several swap partitions and/or swap files at the same time. This means that if you only occasionally need an unusual amount of swap space, you can set up an extra swap file at such times, instead of keeping the whole amount allocated all the time.

579

6.2   Creating a swap area

A swap file is an ordinary file; it is in no way special to the kernel. The only thing that matters to the kernel is that it has no holes, and that it is prepared for use with mkswap(8).

The bit about holes is important. The swap file reserves the disk space so that the kernel can quickly swap out a page without having to go through all the things that are necessary when allocating a disk sector to a file. The kernel merely uses any sectors that have already been allocated to the file. Because a hole in a file means that there are no disk sectors allocated (for that place in the file), it is not good for the kernel to try to use them.

One good way to create the swap file without holes is through the following command:

```
ttyp5 root ~ $ dd if=/dev/zero of=/extra-swap bs=1024 count=1024
1024+0 records in
1024+0 records out
ttyp5 root ~ $
```

where /extra-swap is the name of the swap file and the size of is given after the count=. It is best for the size to be a multiple of 4, because the kernel writes out **memory pages**, which are 4 kilobytes in size. If the size is not a multiple of 4, the last couple of kilobytes may be unused.

A swap partition is also not special in any way. You create it just like any other partition; the only difference is that it is used as a raw partition, that is, it will not contain any filesystem at all. It is a good idea to mark swap partitions as type 82 (LINUX swap); this will the make partition listings clearer, even though it is not strictly necessary to the kernel.

After you have created a swap file or a swap partition, you need to write a signature to its beginning; this contains some administrative information and is used by the kernel. The command to do this is mkswap(8), used like this:

```
ttyp5 root ~ $ mkswap /extra-swap 1024
Setting up swapspace, size = 1044480 bytes
ttyp5 root ~ $
```

Note that the swap space is still not in use yet: it exists, but the kernel does not use it to provide virtual memory.

The LINUX memory manager limits the size of each swap area to 127.5 MB. A larger swap space can be created, but only the first 127.5 MB are actually used. You can, however, use up to 16 swap spaces simultaneously, for a total of almost 2 GB.[1]

6.3   Using a swap area

An initialized swap area is taken into use with swapon(8). This command tells the kernel that the swap area can be used. The path to the swap area is given as the argument, so to start swapping on a temporary swap file one might use the following command.

```
swapon /usr/tmp/temporary-swap-file ttyp5 root ~ $ swapon /extra-swap
ttyp5 root ~ $
```

Swap areas can be used automatically by listing them in the /etc/fstab file.

```
/dev/hda8 swap swap defaults
```

The startup scripts will run the command swapon -a, which will start swapping on all the swap areas listed in /etc/fstab. Therefore, the swapon command is usually used only when extra swap is needed.

---

[1] A gigabyte here, a gigabyte there, pretty soon we start talking about real memory.

You can monitor the use of swap areas with `free(1)`. It will tell the total amount of swap space used. The same information is available via `top(1)`, or using the `proc` filesystem in file `/proc/meminfo`. It is currently difficult to get information on the use of a specific swap area.

A swap area can be removed from use with `swapoff(8)`. It is usually not necessary to do it, except for temporary swap areas. Any pages in use in the swap area are swapped in first; if there is not sufficient physical memory to hold them, they will then be swapped out (to some other swap area). If there is not enough virtual memory to hold all of the pages LINUX will start to trash; after a long while it should recover, but meanwhile the system is unusable. You should check (e.g., with `free`) that there is enough free memory before removing a swap space from use.

All the swap areas that are used automatically with `swapon -a` can be removed from use with `swapoff -a`; it looks at the file `/etc/fstab` to find what to remove. Any manually used swap areas will remain in use.

Sometimes a lot of swap space can be in use even though there is a lot of free physical memory. This can happen for instance if at one point there is need to swap, but later a big process that occupied much of the physical memory terminates and frees the memory. The swapped-out data is not automatically swapped in until it is needed, so the physical memory may remain free for a long time. There is no need to worry about this, but it can be comforting to know what is happening.

6.4   Sharing swap areas with other operating systems

Virtual memory is built into many operating systems. Since they each need it only when they are running, i.e., never at the same time, the swap areas of all but the currently running one are being wasted. It would be more efficient for them to share a single swap area. This is possible, but can require a bit of hacking. The Tips-HOWTO contains some advice on how to implement this.

6.5   Allocating swap space

Some people will tell you that you should allocate twice as much swap space as you have physical memory, but this is a bogus rule. Here's how to do it properly:

1. Estimate your total memory needs. This is the largest amount of memory you'll probably need at a time, that is the sum of the memory requirements of all the programs you want to run at the same time. This can be done by running at the same time all the programs you are likely to ever be running at the same time.

   For instance, if you want to run X, you should allocate about 8 MB for it, gcc wants several megabytes (some files need an unusually large amount, up to several tens of megabytes, but usually about four should do), and so on. The kernel will use about a megabyte by itself, and the usual shells and other small utilities perhaps a few hundred kilobytes (say a megabyte together). There is no need to try to be exact, rough estimates are fine, but you might want to be on the pessimistic side. Remember that if there are going to be several people using the system at the same time, they are all going to consume memory. (However, if two people run the same program at the same time, the total memory consumption is usually not double, since code pages and shared libraries exist only once.) The `free(8)` and `ps(1)` commands are useful for estimating the memory needs.

2. Add some security to the estimate in step 1. This is because estimates of program sizes will probably be wrong, because you'll probably forget some programs you want to run, and to make certain that you have some extra space just in case. A couple of megabytes should be fine. (It is better to allocate too much than too little swap space, but there's no need to over-do it and allocate the whole disk, since unused swap space is wasted space; see later about adding more swap.) Also, since it is nicer to deal with even numbers, you can round the value up to the next full megabyte.

3. Based on the computations in steps 1 and 2, you know how much memory you'll be needing in total. So, in order to allocate swap space, you just need to subtract the size of your physical memory from the total memory needed, and you know how much swap space you need. (On some versions of UNIX, you need to allocate space for an image of the physical memory as well, so the amount computed in step 2 is what you need and you shouldn't do the subtraction.)

6.6 The buffer cache

Reading from a disk[2] is very slow compared to accessing (real) memory. In addition, it is common to read the same part of a disk several times during relatively short periods of time. For example, one might first read an e-mail message, then read the letter into an editor when replying to it, then make the mail program read it again when copying it to a folder. Or, consider how often the command ls might be run on a system with many users. By reading the information from disk only once and then keeping it in memory until no longer needed, one can speed up all but the first read. This is called **disk buffering**, and the memory used for the purpose is called the **buffer cache**.

Since memory is, unfortunately, a finite, nay, scarce resource, the buffer cache usually cannot be big enough (it can't hold all the data one ever wants to use). When the cache fills up, the data that has been unused for the longest time is discarded and the memory thus freed is used for the new data.

Disk buffering works for writes as well. On the one hand, data that is written is often soon read again (e.g., a source code file is saved to a file, then read by the compiler), so putting data that is written in the cache is a good idea. On the other hand, by only putting the data into the cache, not writing it to disk at once, the program that writes runs quicker. The writes can then be done in the background, without slowing down the other programs.

Most operating systems have buffer caches (although they might be called something else), but not all of them work according to the above principles. Some are **write-through**: the data is written to disk at once (it is kept in the cache as well, of course). The cache is called **write-back** if the writes are done at a later time. Write-back is more efficient than write-through, but also a bit more prone to errors: if the machine crashes, or the power is cut at a bad moment, or the floppy is removed from the disk drive before the data in the cache waiting to be written gets written, the changes in the cache are usually lost. This might even mean that the filesystem (if there is one) is not in full working order, perhaps because the unwritten data held important changes to the bookkeeping information. Because of this, you should never turn off the power without using a proper shutdown procedure (see an as yet unwritten chapter), or remove a floppy from the disk drive until it has been unmounted (if it was mounted) or after whatever program is using it has signaled that it is finished and the floppy drive light doesn't shine anymore. The sync(8) command **flushes** the buffer, i.e., forces all unwritten data to be written to disk, and can be used when one wants to be sure that everything is safely written. In traditional UNIX systems, there is a program running in the background which does a sync every 30 seconds, so it is usually not necessary to use sync. LINUX has an additional daemon, bdflush(8), that does a more imperfect sync more frequently to avoid the sudden freeze due to heavy disk I/O that sync sometimes causes.

The cache does not actually buffer files, but blocks, which are the smallest units of disk I/O (under LINUX, they are usually 1 kB). This way, also directories, super blocks, other filesystem bookkeeping data, and non-filesystem disks are cached.

The effectiveness of a cache is primarily decided by its size. A small cache is next to useless: it will hold so little data that all all cached data is flushed from the cache before it is reused. The critical size depends on how much data is read and written, and how often the same data is accessed. The only way to know is to experiment.

If the cache is of a fixed size, it is not very good to have it too big, either, because that might make the free memory too small and cause swapping (which is also slow). To make the most efficient use of real memory, LINUX automatically uses all free RAM for buffer cache, but also automatically makes the cache smaller when programs need more memory.

---

[2] Except a RAM disk, for obvious reasons.

Under LINUX, you do not need to do anything to make use of the cache, it happens completely automatically. Except for following the proper procedures for shutdown and removing floppies, you do not need to worry about it.

Chapter 7

Backups

Hardware is indeterministically reliable.
Software is deterministically unreliable.
People are indeterministically unreliable.
Nature is deterministically reliable.

This chapter explains about why, how, and when to make backups, and how to restore things from backups.

META: backup strategies, horror stories, what media should be used, always verify, compressed vs uncompressed, discuss everything vs only the "important" stuff, automatic backups, off-site backups

7.1 Why backup?

Your data is valuable. It will cost you time and effort, and therefore money or at least personal grief and tears, to re-create it; sometimes it can't even be re-created, e.g., if it is the results of some measurements. Since it is an investment, you should protect it and take steps to avoid losing it.

There are basically four reasons why you might lose data: hardware failures, software bugs, human action, or natural disasters. Although modern hardware tends to be quite reliable, it can still break seemingly spontaneously. The most critical piece of hardware for storing data is the hard disk, which relies on tiny magnetic fields remaining intact in a world filled with electromagnetic noise. Modern software doesn't even tend to be reliable; a rock solid program is an exception, not a rule. Humans are quite deterministically unreliable, they will either make a mistake, or they will be malicious and destroy data on purpose. Nature might not be evil, but it can wreak havoc even when being good. All in all, it is a small miracle that anything works at all.

Backups are a way to protect the investment in data. By having several copies of the data, it does not matter as much if one is destroyed (the cost is only that of the restoration of the lost data from the backup).

7.2 Things to ponder

META: Considerations for backups: safety, speed, convenience, portability, rate of change, what to backup,

The purpose of backups is to enable you to rebuild the system if necessary. You must weigh all decisions about backups with this in mind. You should consider at least the following points (note that they influence each other to some degree):

- How paranoid to be?

  How much do you trust your system? Can you get the software (operating system, applications) from elsewhere quickly and reliably enough, or should you keep local copies? Can you get compatible versions? Will you be able to use the same hardware and software to restore? What disasters do expect? Do you care about unexpected disasters?

- What to backup?

  Can you get compatible copies of the software from elsewhere, whenever you need them, or should you keep local copies? Will it be easy to re-install, or should you backup your complete system?

  Important things to remember are non-files, such as the partition table, boot sectors, hardware setups, and well-hidden files, such as many configuration files.

- How often?

  How much and how often does your data change? The more often it changes, the more often you will need to back up.

- What media to use?

  A good backup media is reliable (it won't fail) and portable (it will work on other machines as well).

- What tools to use?

  A good tool is reliable (will detect and correct errors in the backup medium) and portable. It should also be convenient and efficient to use.

- How to verify?

  How much do you trust your backup medium? It's hardware, it too can fail. The backup tools might not work correctly, or you might be making a silly mistake using them, so you'll have to verify your backups, i.e., check that they work correctly.

- How to automate?

  Backing up can be quite tedious, and that makes them unpleasant to do. If you can automate the process as much as possible, it will be much more reliable and, most importantly, it will be done.

7.3 Backup levels

META: "backup volumes", rotation, backup levels, when to backup and how much each time, don't keep all backup media in one place

It is rarely possible to make a full copy of all your files every day. There is too much to copy, and it is too much work and takes too long.

7.4 Backup media

META: backup media: floppies, tapes, worm, mo disks, network disks, removable hard disks, other hard disks

7.5 Various tools

META: an overview of the tools: tar, cpio, afio, tbackup (+newer version), dump, GNU's shell scripts, other shell scripts

7.6 A sample plan for a small system

META: a sample plan for a very simple system

7.7 A more demanding backup plan

META: how I do my backups

Appendix A

Design and Implementation of the Second Extended Filesystem

This appendix is a paper by the designers and implementors of the ext2 filesystem. It was first published in the Proceedings to the First Dutch International Symposium on Linux, ISBN 90 367 0385 9.

Introduction

Linux is a Unix-like operating system, which runs on PC-386 computers. It was implemented first as extension to the Minix operating system [?] and its first versions included support for the Minix filesystem only. The Minix filesystem contains two serious limitations: block addresses are stored in 16 bit integers, thus the maximal filesystem size is restricted to 64 mega bytes, and directories contain fixed-size entries and the maximal file name is 14 characters.

We have designed and implemented two new filesystems that are included in the standard Linux kernel. These filesystems, called "Extended File System" (Ext fs) and "Second Extended File System" (Ext2 fs) raise the limitations and add new features.

In this paper, we describe the history of Linux filesystems. We briefly introduce the fundamental concepts implemented in Unix filesystems. We present the implementation of the Virtual File System layer in Linux and we detail the Second Extended File System kernel code and user mode tools. Last, we present performance measurements made on Linux and BSD filesystems and we conclude with the current status of Ext2fs and the future directions.

A.1 History of Linux filesystems

In its very early days, Linux was cross-developed under the Minix operating system. It was easier to share disks between the two systems than to design a new filesystem, so Linus Torvalds decided to implement support for the Minix filesystem in Linux. The Minix filesystem was an efficient and relatively bug-free piece of software.

However, the restrictions in the design of the Minix filesystem were too limiting, so people started thinking and working on the implementation of new filesystems in Linux.

In order to ease the addition of new filesystems into the Linux kernel, a Virtual File System (VFS) layer was developed. The VFS layer was initially written by Chris Provenzano, and later rewritten by Linus Torvalds before it was integrated into the Linux kernel. It will be described in section A.3 of this paper.

After the integration of the VFS in the kernel, a new filesystem, called the "Extended File System" was implemented in April 1992 and added to Linux 0.96c. This new filesystem removed the two big Minix limitations: its maximal size was 2 giga bytes and the maximal file name size was 255 characters. It was an improvement over the Minix filesystem but some problems were still present in it. There was no support for the separate access, inode modification, and data modification timestamps. The filesystem used linked lists to keep track of free blocks and inodes and this produced bad performances: as the filesystem was used, the lists became unsorted and the filesystem became fragmented.

As a response to these problems, two new filesytems were released in Alpha version in January 1993: the Xia filesystem and the Second Extended File System. The Xia filesystem was heavily based on the Minix filesystem kernel code and only added a few improvements over this filesystem. Basically, it provided long file names, support for bigger partitions and support for the three timestamps. On the other hand, Ext2fs was based on the Extfs code with many reorganizations and many improvements. It had been designed with evolution in mind and contained space for future improvements. It will be described with more details in section A.4.

When the two new filesystems were first released, they provided essentially the same features. Due to its minimal design, Xia fs was more stable than Ext2fs. As the filesystems were used more widely, bugs were fixed in Ext2fs and lots of improvements and new features were integrated. Ext2fs is now very stable and has become the de-facto standard Linux filesystem.

The table A.1 contains a summary of the features provided by the different filesystems.

Table A.1: Summary of the filesystem features

	Minix FS	Ext FS	Ext2 FS	Xia FS
Max FS size	64 MB	2 GB	4 TB	2 GB
Max file size	64 MB	2 GB	2 GB	64 MB
Max file name	16/30 c	255 c	255 c	248 c
3 times support	No	No	Yes	Yes
Extensible	No	No	Yes	No
Var. block size	No	No	Yes	No
Maintained	Yes	No	Yes	?

A.2 Basic File System Concepts

Every Linux filesystem implements a basic set of common concepts derivated from the Unix operating system [?]: files are represented by inodes, directories are simply files containing a list of entries and devices can be accessed by requesting I/O on special files.

A.2.1 Inodes

Each file is represented by a structure, called an inode. Each inode contains the description of the file: file type, access rights, owners, timestamps, size, pointers to data blocks. The addresses of data blocks allocated to a file are stored in its inode. When a user requests an I/O operation on the file, the kernel code converts the current offset to a block number, uses this number as an index in the block addresses table and reads or writes the physical block. Figure A.1 represents the structure of an inode.

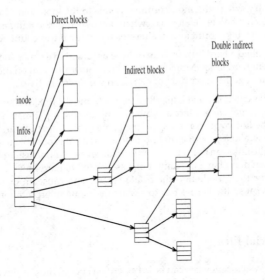

Figure A.1: Structure of an inode

A.2.2 Directories

Directories are structured in a hierarchical tree. Each directory can contain files and subdirectories.

Directories are implemented as a special type of files. Actually, a directory is a file containing a list of entries. Each entry contains an inode number and a file name. When a process uses a pathname, the kernel code searchs in the directories to find the corresponding inode number. After the name has been converted to an inode number, the inode is loaded into memory and is used by subsequent requests.

Figure A.2 represents a directory.

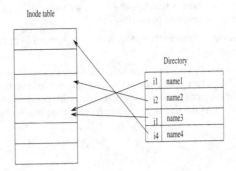

Figure A.2: Structure of a directory

A.2.3 Links

Unix filesystems implement the concept of link. Several names can be associated with a inode. The inode contains a field containing the number associated with the file. Adding a link simply consists in creating a directory entry, where the inode number points to the inode, and in incrementing the links count in the inode. When a link is deleted, i.e. when one uses the rm command to remove a filename, the kernel decrements the links count and deallocates the inode if this count becomes zero.

This type of link is called a hard link and can only be used within a single filesystem: it is impossible to create cross-filesystem hard links. Moreover, hard links can only point on files: a directory hard link cannot be created to prevent the apparition of a cycle in the directory tree.

Another kind of links exists in most Unix filesystems. Symbolic links are simply files which contain a filename. When the kernel encounters a symbolic link during a pathname to inode conversion, it replaces the name of the link by its contents, i.e. the name of the target file, and restarts the pathname interpretation. Since a symbolic link does not point to an inode, it is possible to create cross-filesystems symbolic links. Symbolic links can point to any type of file, even on nonexistent files. Symbolic links are very useful because they don't have the limitations associated to hard links. However, they use some disk space, allocated for their inode and their data blocks, and cause an overhead in the pathname to inode conversion because the kernel has to restart the name interpretation when it encounters a symbolic link.

A.2.4 Device special files

In Unix-like operating systems, devices can be accessed via special files. A device special file does not use any space on the filesystem. It is only an access point to the device driver.

Two types of special files exist: character and block special files. The former allows I/O operations in character mode while the later requires data to be written in block mode via the buffer cache functions. When an I/O request is made on a special file, it is forwarded to a (pseudo) device driver. A special file is referenced by a major number, which identifies the device type, and a minor number, which identifies the unit.

A.3 The Virtual File System

A.3.1 Principle

The Linux kernel contains a Virtual File System layer which is used during system calls acting on files. The VFS is an indirection layer which handles the file oriented system calls and calls the necessary functions in the physical filesystem code to do the I/O.

This indirection mechanism is frequently used in Unix-like operating systems to ease the integration and the use of several filesystem types [?, ?].

When a process issues a file oriented system call, the kernel calls a function contained in the VFS. This function handles the structure independent manipulations and redirects the call to a function contained in the physical filesystem code, which is responsible for handling the structure dependent operations. Filesystem code uses the buffer cache functions to request I/O on devices. This scheme is illustrated on figure A.3.

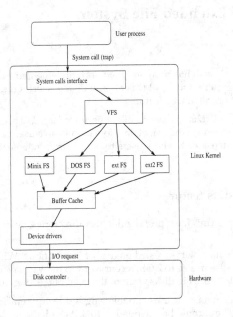

Figure A.3: The VFS Layer

A.3.2 The VFS structure

The VFS defines a set of functions that every filesystem has to implement. This interface is made up of a set of operations associated to three kinds of objects: filesystems, inodes, and open files.

The VFS knows about filesystem types supported in the kernel. It uses a table defined during the kernel configuration. Each entry in this table describes a filesystem type: it contains the name of the filesystem type and a pointer on a function called during the mount operation. When a filesystem is to be mounted, the appropriate mount function is called. This function is responsible for reading the superblock from the disk, initializing its internal variables, and returning a mounted filesystem descriptor to the VFS. After the filesystem is mounted, the VFS functions can use this descriptor to access the physical filesystem routines.

A mounted filesystem descriptor contains several kinds of data: informations that are common to every filesystem types, pointers to functions provided by the physical filesystem kernel code, and private data maintained by the physical filesystem code. The function pointers contained in the filesystem descriptors allow the VFS to access the filesystem internal routines.

Two other types of descriptors are used by the VFS: an inode descriptor and an open file descriptor. Each descriptor contains informations related to files in use and a set of operations provided by the physical filesystem code. While the inode descriptor contains pointers to functions that can be used to act on any file (e.g. `create`, `unlink`), the file descriptors contains pointer to functions which can only act on open files (e.g. `read`, `write`).

A.4   The Second Extended File System

A.4.1 Motivations

The Second Extended File System has been designed and implemented to fix some problems present in the first Extended File System. Our goal was to provide a powerful filesystem, which implements Unix file semantics and offers advanced features.

Of course, we wanted to Ext2fs to have excellent performance. We also wanted to provide a very robust filesystem in order to reduce the risk of data loss in intensive use. Last, but not least, Ext2fs had to include provision for extensions to allow users to benefit from new features without reformatting their filesystem.

A.4.2 "Standard" Ext2fs features

The Ext2fs supports standard Unix file types: regular files, directories, device special files and symbolic links.

Ext2fs is able to manage filesystems created on really big partitions. While the original kernel code restricted the maximal filesystem size to 2 GB, recent work in the VFS layer have raised this limit to 4 TB. Thus, it is now possible to use big disks without the need of creating many partitions.

Ext2fs provides long file names. It uses variable length directory entries. The maximal file name size is 255 characters. This limit could be extended to 1012 if needed.

Ext2fs reserves some blocks for the super user (`root`). Normally, 5% of the blocks are reserved. This allows the administrator to recover easily from situations where user processes fill up filesystems.

A.4.3 "Advanced" Ext2fs features

In addition to the standard Unix features, Ext2fs supports some extensions which are not usually present in Unix filesystems.

File attributes allow the users to modify the kernel behavior when acting on a set of files. One can set attributes on a file or on a directory. In the later case, new files created in the directory inherit these attributes.

BSD or System V Release 4 semantics can be selected at mount time. A mount option allows the administrator to choose the file creation semantics. On a filesystem mounted with BSD semantics, files are created with the same group id as their parent directory. System V semantics are a bit more complex: if a directory has the setgid bit set, new files inherit the group id of the directory and subdirectories inherit the group id and the setgid bit; in the other case, files and subdirectories are created with the primary group id of the calling process.

BSD-like synchronous updates can be used in Ext2fs. A mount option allows the administrator to request that metadata (inodes, bitmap blocks, indirect blocks and directory blocks) be written synchronously on the disk when they are modified. This can be useful to maintain a strict metadata consistency but this leads to poor performances. Actually, this feature is not normally used, since in addition to the performance loss associated with using synchronous updates of the metadata, it can cause corruption in the user data which will not be flagged by the filesystem checker.

Ext2fs allows the administrator to choose the logical block size when creating the filesystem. Block sizes can typically be 1024, 2048 and 4096 bytes. Using big block sizes can speed up I/O since fewer I/O requests, and thus fewer disk head seeks, need to be done to access a file. On the other hand, big blocks waste more disk space: on the average, the last block allocated to a file is only half full, so as blocks get bigger, more space is wasted in the last block of each file. In addition, most of the advantages of larger block sizes are obtained by Ext2 filesystem's preallocation techniques (see section A.4.5).

Ext2fs implements fast symbolic links. A fast symbolic link does not use any data block on the filesystem. The target name is not stored in a data block but in the inode itself. This policy can save some disk space (no data block needs to be allocated) and speeds up link operations (there is no need to read a data block when accessing such a link). Of course, the space available in the inode is limited so not every link can be implemented as a fast symbolic link. The maximal size of the target name in a fast symbolic link is 60 characters. We plan to extend this scheme to small files in a near future.

Ext2fs keeps track of the filesystem state. A special field in the superblock is used by the kernel code to indicate the status of the file system. When a filesystem is mounted in read/write mode, its state is set to "Not Clean". When it is unmounted or remounted in read-only mode, its state is reset to "Clean". At boot time, the filesystem checker uses this information to decide if a filesystem must be checked. The kernel code also records errors in this field. When an inconsistency is detected by the kernel code, the filesystem is marked as "Erroneous". The filesystem checker tests this to force the check of the filesystem regardless of its apparently clean state.

Always skipping filesystem checks may sometimes be dangerous so Ext2fs provides two ways to force checks at regular intervals. A mount counter is maintained in the superblock. Each time the filesystem is mounted in read/write mode, this counter is incremented. When it reaches a maximal value (also recorded in the superblock), the filesystem checker forces the check even if the filesystem is "Clean". A last check time and a maximal check interval are also maintained in the superblock. These two fields allow the administrator to request periodical checks. When the maximal check interval has been reached, the checker ignores the filesystem state and forces a filesystem check.

Ext2fs offers tools to tune the filesystem behavior. The `tune2fs` program can be used to modify:
- the error behavior. When an inconsistency is detected by the kernel code, the filesystem is marked as "Erroneous" and one of the three following actions can be done: continue normal execution, remount the filesystem in read-only mode to avoid corrupting the filesystem, make the kernel panic and reboot to run the filesystem checker.
- the maximal mount count.
- the maximal check interval.
- the number of logical blocks reserved for the super user.

Mount options can also be used to change the kernel error behavior.

An attribute allows the users to request secure deletion on files. When such a file is deleted, random data is written in the disk blocks previously allocated to the file. This prevents malicious people from gaining access to the previous content of the file by using a disk editor.

Last, new types of files inspired from the 4.4 BSD filesystem have recently been added to Ext2fs. Immutable files can only be read: nobody can write or delete them. This can be used to protect sensitive configuration files. Append-only files can be opened in write mode but data is always appended at the end of the file. Like immutable files, they cannot be deleted or renamed. This is especially useful for log files which can only grow.

A.4.4 Physical Structure

The physical structure of Ext2 filesystems has been strongly influenced by the layout of the BSD filesystem [?]. A filesystem is made up of block groups. Block groups are analogous to BSD FFS's cylinder groups. However, block groups are not tied to the physical layout of the blocks on the disk, since modern drives tend to be optimized for sequential access and hide their physical geometry to the operating system.

The physical structure of a filesystem is represented on figure A.4.

Boot Sector	Block Group 1	Block Group 2	... ...	Block Group N

Figure A.4: Physical structure of an Ext2 filesystem

Each block group contains a redundant copy of crucial filesystem control informations (superblock and the filesystem descriptors) and also contains a part of the filesystem (a block bitmap, an inode bitmap, a piece of the inode table, and data blocks). The structure of a block group is represented on figure A.5.

Super Block	FS descriptors	Block Bitmap	Inode Bitmap	Inode Table	Data Blocks

Figure A.5: Structure of a block group

Using block groups is a big win in terms of reliability: since the control structures are replicated in each block group, it is easy to recover from a filesystem where the superblock has been corrupted. This structure also helps to get good performances: by reducing the distance between the inode table and the data blocks, it is possible to reduce the disk head seeks during I/O on files.

In Ext2fs, directories are managed as linked lists of variable length entries. Each entry contains the inode number, the entry length, the file name and its length. By using variable length entries, it is possible to implement long file names without wasting disk space in directories. The structure of a directory entry is shown on figure A.6.

inode number	entry length	name length	filename

Figure A.6: Structure of a directory entry

As an example, figure A.7 represents the structure of a directory containing three files: `file1`, `long_file_name`, and `f2`.

i1	16	05	file1	i2	40	14	long_file_name	i3	12	02	f2

Figure A.7: Example of directory

A.4.5 Performance optimizations

The Ext2fs kernel code contains many performance optimizations, which tend to improve I/O speed when reading and writing files.

Ext2fs takes advantage of the buffer cache management by performing readaheads: when a block has to be read, the kernel code requests the I/O on several contiguous blocks. This way, it tries to ensure that the next block to read will already be loaded into the buffer cache. Readaheads are normally performed during sequential reads on files and Ext2fs extends them to directory reads, either explicit reads (`readdir(2)` calls) or implicit ones (namei kernel directory lookup).

Ext2fs also contains many allocation optimizations. Block groups are used to cluster together related inodes and data: the kernel code always tries to allocate data blocks for a file in the same group as its inode. This is intended to reduce the disk head seeks made when the kernel reads an inode and its data blocks.

When writing data to a file, Ext2fs preallocates up to 8 adjacent blocks when allocating a new block. Preallocation hit rates are around 75% even on very full filesystems. This preallocation achieves good write performances under heavy load. It also allows contiguous blocks to be allocated to files, thus it speeds up the future sequential reads.

These two allocation optimizations produce a very good locality of:

- related files through block groups
- related blocks through the 8 bits clustering of block allocations.

A.5   The Ext2fs library

To allow user mode programs to manipulate the control structures of an Ext2 filesystem, the libext2fs library was developed. This library provides routines which can be used to examine and modify the data of an Ext2 filesystem, by accessing the filesystem directly through the physical device.

The Ext2fs library was designed to allow maximal code reuse through the use of software abstraction techniques. For example, several different iterators are provided. A program can simply pass in a function to `ext2fs_block_interate()`, which will be called for each block in an inode. Another iterator function allows an user-provided function to be called for each file in a directory.

Many of the Ext2fs utilities (`mke2fs`, `e2fsck`, `tune2fs`, `dumpe2fs`, and `debugfs`) use the Ext2fs library. This greatly simplifies the maintainance of these utilities, since any changes to reflect new features in the Ext2 filesystem format need only be made in one place — in the Ext2fs library. This code reuse also results in smaller binaries, since the Ext2fs library can be built as a shared library image.

Because the interfaces of the Ext2fs library are so abstract and general, new programs which require direct access to the Ext2fs filesystem can very easily be written. For example, the Ext2fs library was used during the port of the 4.4BSD dump and restore backup utilities. Very few changes were needed to adapt these tools to Linux: only a few filesystem dependent functions had to be replaced by calls to the Ext2fs library.

The Ext2fs library provides access to several classes of operations. The first class are the filesystem-oriented operations. A program can open and close a filesystem, read and write the bitmaps, and create a new filesystem on the disk. Functions are also available to manipulate the filesystem's bad blocks list.

The second class of operations affect directories. A caller of the Ext2fs library can create and expand directories, as well as add and remove directory entries. Functions are also provided to both resolve a pathname to an inode number, and to determine a pathname of an inode given its inode number.

The final class of operations are oriented around inodes. It is possible to scan the inode table, read and write inodes, and scan through all of the blocks in an inode. Allocation and deallocation routines are also available and allow user mode programs to allocate and free blocks and inodes.

A.6   The Ext2fs tools

Powerful management tools have been developed for Ext2fs. These utilities are used to create, modify, and correct any inconsistencies in Ext2 filesystems. The `mke2fs` program is used to initialize a partition to contain an empty Ext2 filesystem.

The `tune2fs` program can be used to modify the filesystem parameters. As explained in section A.4.3, it can change the error behavior, the maximal mount count, the maximal check interval, and the number of logical blocks reserved for the super user.

The most interesting tool is probably the filesystem checker. E2fsck is intended to repair filesystem inconsistencies after an unclean shutdown of the system. The original version of `e2fsck` was based on Linus Torvald's fsck program for the Minix filesystem. However, the current version of `e2fsck` was rewritten from scratch, using the Ext2fs library, and is much faster and can correct more filesystem inconsistencies than the original version.

The `e2fsck` program is designed to run as quickly as possible. Since filesystem checkers tend to be disk bound, this was done by optimizing the algorithms used by `e2fsck` so that filesystem structures are not repeatedly accessed from the disk. In addition, the order in which inodes and directories are checked are sorted by block number to reduce the amount of time in disk seeks. Many of these ideas were originally explored by [?] although they have since been further refined by the authors.

In pass 1, `e2fsck` iterates over all of the inodes in the filesystem and performs checks over each inode as an unconnected object in the filesystem. That is, these checks do not require any cross-checks to other filesystem objects. Examples of such checks include making sure the file mode is legal, and that all of the blocks in the inode are valid block numbers. During pass 1, bitmaps indicating which blocks and inodes are in use are compiled.

If e2fsck notices data blocks which are claimed by more than one inode, it invokes passes 1B through 1D to resolve these conflicts, either by cloning the shared blocks so that each inode has its own copy of the shared block, or by deallocating one or more of the inodes.

Pass 1 takes the longest time to execute, since all of the inodes have to be read into memory and checked. To reduce the I/O time necessary in future passes, critical filesystem information is cached in memory. The most important example of this technique is the location on disk of all of the directory blocks on the filesystem. This obviates the need to re-read the directory inodes structures during pass 2 to obtain this information.

Pass 2 checks directories as unconnected objects. Since directory entries do not span disk blocks, each directory block can be checked individually without reference to other directory blocks. This allows e2fsck to sort all of the directory blocks by block number, and check directory blocks in ascending order, thus decreasing disk seek time. The directory blocks are checked to make sure that the directory entries are valid, and contain references to inode numbers which are in use (as determined by pass 1).

For the first directory block in each directory inode, the '.' and '..' entries are checked to make sure they exist, and that the inode number for the '.' entry matches the current directory. (The inode number for the '..' entry is not checked until pass 3.)

Pass 2 also caches information concerning the parent directory in which each directory is linked. (If a directory is referenced by more than one directory, the second reference of the directory is treated as an illegal hard link, and it is removed).

It is noteworthy to note that at the end of pass 2, nearly all of the disk I/O which e2fsck needs to perform is complete. Information required by passes 3, 4 and 5 are cached in memory; hence, the remaining passes of e2fsck are largely CPU bound, and take less than 5-10% of the total running time of e2fsck.

In pass 3, the directory connectivity is checked. E2fsck traces the path of each directory back to the root, using information that was cached during pass 2. At this time, the '..' entry for each directory is also checked to make sure it is valid. Any directories which can not be traced back to the root are linked to the /lost+found directory.

In pass 4, e2fsck checks the reference counts for all inodes, by iterating over all the inodes and comparing the link counts (which were cached in pass 1) against internal counters computed during passes 2 and 3. Any undeleted files with a zero link count is also linked to the /lost+found directory during this pass.

Finally, in pass 5, e2fsck checks the validity of the filesystem summary information. It compares the block and inode bitmaps which were constructed during the previous passes against the actual bitmaps on the filesystem, and corrects the on-disk copies if necessary.

The filesystem debugger is another useful tool. Debugfs is a powerful program which can be used to examine and change the state of a filesystem. Basically, it provides an interactive interface to the Ext2fs library: commands typed by the user are translated into calls to the library routines.

Debugfs can be used to examine the internal structures of a filesystem, manually repair a corrupted filesystem, or create test cases for e2fsck. Unfortunately, this program can be dangerous if it is used by people who do not know what they are doing; it is very easy to destroy a filesystem with this tool. For this reason, debugfs opens filesytems for read-only access by default. The user must explicitly specify the -w flag in order to use debugfs to open a filesystem for read/write access.

A.7   Performance Measurements

A.7.1   Description of the benchmarks

We have run benchmarks to measure filesystem performances. Benchmarks have been made on a middle-end PC, based on a i486DX2 processor, using 16 MB of memory and two 420 MB IDE disks. The tests were run on Ext2 fs and Xia fs (Linux 1.1.62) and on the BSD Fast filesystem in asynchronous and synchronous mode (FreeBSD 2.0 Alpha — based on the 4.4BSD Lite distribution).

We have run two different benchmarks. The Bonnie benchmark tests I/O speed on a big file — the file size was set to 60 MB during the tests. It writes data to the file using character based I/O, rewrites the contents of the whole file, writes data using block based I/O, reads the file using character I/O and block I/O, and seeks into the file. The Andrew Benchmark was developed at Carneggie Mellon University and has been used at the University of Berkeley to benchmark BSD FFS and LFS. It runs in five phases: it creates a directory hierarchy, makes a copy of the data, recursively examine the status of every file, examine every byte of every file, and compile several of the files.

A.7.2   Results of the Bonnie benchmark

The results of the Bonnie benchmark are presented in table A.2.

Table A.2: Results of the Bonnie benchmark

	Char Write (KB/s)	Block Write (KB/s)	Rewrite (KB/s)	Char Read (KB/s)	Block Read (KB/s)
BSD Async	710	684	401	721	888
BSD Sync	699	677	400	710	878
Ext2 fs	452	1237	536	397	1033
Xia fs	440	704	380	366	895

The results are very good in block oriented I/O: Ext2 fs outperforms other filesystems. This is clearly a benefit of the optimizations included in the allocation routines. Writes are fast because data is written in cluster mode. Reads are fast because contiguous blocks have been allocated to the file. Thus there is no head seek between two reads and the readahead optimizations can be fully used.

On the other hand, performance is better in the FreeBSD operating system in character oriented I/O. This is probably due to the fact that FreeBSD and Linux do not use the same stdio routines in their respective C libraries. It seems that FreeBSD has a more optimized character I/O library and its performance is better.

A.7.3   Results of the Andrew benchmark

The results of the Andrew benchmark are presented in table A.3.

Table A.3: Results of the Andrew benchmark

	P1 Create (ms)	P2 Copy (ms)	P3 Stat (ms)	P4 Grep (ms)	P5 Compile (ms)
BSD Async	2203	7391	6319	17466	75314
BSD Sync	2330	7732	6317	17499	75681
Ext2 fs	790	4791	7235	11685	63210
Xia fs	934	5402	8400	12912	66997

The results of the two first passes show that Linux benefits from its asynchronous metadata I/O. In passes 1 and 2, directories and files are created and BSD synchronously writes inodes and directory entries. There is an anomaly, though: even in asynchronous mode, the performance under BSD is poor. We suspect that the asynchronous support under FreeBSD is not fully implemented.

In pass 3, the Linux and BSD times are very similar. This is a big progress against the same benchmark run six months ago. While BSD used to outperform Linux by a factor of 3 in this test, the addition of a file name cache in the VFS has fixed this performance problem.

In passes 4 and 5, Linux is faster than FreeBSD mainly because it uses an unified buffer cache management. The buffer cache space can grow when needed and use more memory than the one in FreeBSD, which uses a fixed size buffer cache. Comparison of the Ext2fs and Xiafs results shows that the optimizations included in Ext2fs are really useful: the performance gain between Ext2fs and Xiafs is around 5–10 %.

A.8   Conclusion

The Second Extended File System is probably the most widely used filesystem in the Linux community. It provides standard Unix file semantics and advanced features. Moreover, thanks to the optimizations included in the kernel code, it is robust and offers excellent performance.

Since Ext2fs has been designed with evolution in mind, it contains hooks that can be used to add new features. Some people are working on extensions to the current filesystem: access control lists conforming to the Posix semantics [?], undelete, and on the fly file compression.

Ext2fs was first developed and integrated in the Linux kernel and is now actively being ported to other operating systems. An Ext2fs server running on top of the GNU Hurd has been implemented. People are also working on an Ext2fs port in the LITES server, running on top of the Mach microkernel [?], and in the VSTa operating system. Last, but not least, Ext2fs is an important part of the Masix operating system [?], currently under development by one of the authors.

Acknowledgments

The Ext2fs kernel code and tools have been written mostly by the authors of this paper. Some other people have also contributed to the development of Ext2fs either by suggesting new features or by sending patches. We want to thank these contributors for their help.

Appendix B

Measuring Holes

This appendix contains the interesting part of the program used to measure the potential for holes in a filesystem. The source distribution of the book contains the full source code.

```
int process(FILE *f, char *filename) {
        static char *buf = NULL;
        static long prev_block_size = -1;
        long zeroes;
        char *p;

        if (buf == NULL || prev_block_size != block_size) {
                free(buf);
                buf = xmalloc(block_size + 1);
                buf[block_size] = 1;
                prev_block_size = block_size;
        }
        zeroes = 0;
        while (fread(buf, block_size, 1, f) == 1) {
                for (p = buf; *p == '\0'; )
                        ++p;
                if (p == buf+block_size)
                        zeroes += block_size;
        }
        if (zeroes > 0)
                printf("%ld %s\n", zeroes, filename);
        if (ferror(f)) {
                errormsg(0, -1, "read failed for '%s'", filename);
                return -1;
        }
        return 0;
}
```

Appendix C

Bibliography

This chapter contains a bibliography of all the books referenced elsewhere in this manual, as well as a number of other books. Where possible, some comments on each book are given. Since the author of this book is unfortunately unable to afford all the books, the comments come from several sources (source is indicated, but withheld if so requested).

META: the c/unix book list should be a good source

META: HD-list

Title:	The New Hacker's Dictionary
Author:	Raymond, E. (ed)
Publisher:	MIT Press, 1991
ISBN:	0-262-18145-2 (hc), 0-262-68069-6 (pbk)
Appr. Price:	$10.95

From Lars Wirzenius: A dictionary of the slang and jargon used by hackers. A book version of the *Jargon File*, which contains all the text of the book (typically in a more up-to-date form), and which is in the public domain.

Title:	UNIX System Administration Handbook
Author:	Evi Nemeth, Garth Snyder and Scott Seebass
Publisher:	Prentice-Hall, 1989
ISBN:	0-13-933441-6
Appr. Price:	$?

From Anonymous: I haven't seen any others to compare this one to, so I don't know that I'd particularly recommend it. It does cover both BSD and SYSV, though, so it might be more useful to a Linux sysadmin than a single book that focussed on BSD or SYSV exclusively.

Title:	UNIX Power Tools
Author:	Jerry Peek, Tim O'Reilly, and Mike Loukide
Publisher:	Bantam, 1993
ISBN:	0-679-79073-X

Appr. Price: $price

From Anonymous: Not a comprehensive guide to much of anything, but it does include a LOT of hints and tips at the sysadmin level. This comes with a CD-ROM full of useful Unix programs, too.

Part V

The LINUX Users' Guide

All you need to know to start using LINUX, a free Unix clone. This manual covers the basic Unix commands, as well as the more specific LINUX ones. This manual is meant for the beginning Unix user, although it may be useful for more experienced users for reference purposes.

UNIX is a trademark of X/Open
MS-DOS and Microsoft Windows are trademarks of Microsoft Corporation
OS/2 and Operating System/2 are trademarks of IBM
LINUX is not a trademark, and has no connection to UNIX or to Unix System Labratories.
Please bring all unacknowledged trademarks to the attention of the author.

These are some of the typographical conventions used in this book.

Bold   Used to mark **new concepts**, **WARNINGS**, and **keywords** in a language.

italics   Used for *emphasis* in text. It is also used to indicate commands for the user to type when showing screen interaction (see below).

slanted   Used to mark **meta-variables** in the text, especially in representations of the command line. For example,

> ls -l *foo*

where *foo* would "stand for" a filename, such as /bin/cp.

Typewriter   Used to represent screen interaction.

Also used for code examples, whether it is "C" code, a shell script, or something else, and to display general files, such as configuration files. When necessary for clarity's sake, these examples or figures will be enclosed in thin boxes.

`Key`   Represents a key to press. You will often see it in this form:

> Press `return` to continue.

◇   A diamond in the margin, like a black diamond on a ski hill, marks "danger" or "caution." Read paragraphs marked this way carefully.

X   This X in the margin indicates special instructions for users of the X Window System.

Acknowledgements

The author would like to thank the following people for their invaluable help either with LINUX itself, or in writing *The* LINUX *Users' Guide*:

Linus Torvalds for providing something to write this manual about.

Karl Fogel has given me much help with writing my LINUX documentation and wrote Chapter 8 and Chapter 9. I cannot give him enough credit.

Maurizio Codogno wrote much of Chapter 11.

David Channon wrote the appendix on `vi`. (Appendix C)

The `fortune` program for supplying me with many of the wonderful quotes that start each chapter. They cheer me up, if no one else.

Contents

Chapter 1

Introduction

> How much does it cost to entice a dope-smoking Unix system guru to Dayton?
> Brian Boyle, *Unix World*'s First Annual Salary Survey

1.1 Who Should Read This Book

Are you someone who should read this book? Let's answer by asking some other questions: Have you just gotten LINUX from somewhere, installed it, and want to know what to do next? Or are you a non-Unix computer user who is considering LINUX but wants to find out what it can do for you?

If you have this book, the answer to these questions is probably "yes." Anyone who has LINUX, the free Unix clone written by Linus Torvalds, on their PC but doesn't know what to do next should read this book. In this book, we'll cover most of the basic Unix commands, as well as some of the more advanced ones. We'll also talk about GNU Emacs, a powerful editor, and several other large Unix applications.

1.1.1 What You Should Have Done Before Reading This Book

This book relies on a few things that the author can't control. First of all, this book assumes that you have access to a Unix system. (Unfortunately, it's a bit hard to learn without getting wet!) More importantly, this Unix system should be an Intel PC running LINUX. This requirement isn't necessary, but when versions of Unix differ, I'll be talking about how LINUX acts—nothing else.

LINUX is available in many forms, called distributions. It is hoped that you've found a complete distribution such as SoftLanding Linux Systems or the MCC-Interim release and have installed it. There are differences between the various distributions of LINUX, but for the most part they're small and unimportant. (Occasionally in this book you'll find places that seem a little off. If you do, it's probably because you're using a different distribution from mine. The author is interested in all such cases.)

If you're the superuser (the maintainer, the installer) of the system, you also should have created a normal user account for yourself. Please consult the installation manual(s) for this information. If you aren't the superuser, you should have obtained an account from the superuser.

You should have time and patience. Learning LINUX isn't easy—most people find learning the Macintosh Operating System is easier. However, many people feel that LINUX is more powerful.

In addition, this book assumes that you are moderately familiar with some computer terms. Although this requirement isn't necessary, it makes reading the book easier. You should know about computer terms such as 'program' and 'execution'. If you don't, you might want to get someone's help with learning Unix.

1.2   How to Avoid Reading This Book

The best way to learn about almost any computer program is at your computer. Most people find that reading a book without using the program isn't very beneficial. Thus, the best way to learn Unix and LINUX is by using them. Use LINUX for everything you can. Experiment. Don't be afraid—it's *possible* to mess things up, but you can always reinstall. Keep backups and have fun!

For better or for worse, though, Unix isn't as intuitively obvious as some other operating systems. Thus, you will probably end up reading at least the first couple of chapters in this book.

The number one way to avoid using this book is to use the on-line documentation that's available. Learn how to use the man command—it's described in Section 4.2.

1.3   How to Read This Book

The suggested way of learning Unix is to read a little, then to play a little. Keep playing until you're comfortable with the concepts, and then start skipping around in the book. You'll find a variety of topics are covered, some of which you might find interesting. After a while, you should feel confident enough to start using commands without knowing what they should do. This is a good thing.

What most people regard as Unix is the Unix shell, a special program that interprets commands. In practice, this is a fine way of looking at things, but you should be aware that Unix really consists of many more things, or much less. (Depending on how you look at it.) This book tells you about how to use the shell, programs that Unix usually comes with, and some programs Unix doesn't always come with.

The current chapter is a meta-chapter—it discusses this book and how to apply this book to getting work done. The other chapters contain:

Chapter 2 discusses where Unix and LINUX came from, and where they might be going. It also talks about the Free Software Foundation and the GNU Project.

Chapter 3 talks about how to start and stop using your computer, and what happens at these times. Much of it deals with topics not needed for using LINUX, but still quite useful and interesting.

Chapter 4 introduces the Unix shell. This is where people actually do work, and run programs. It talks about the basic programs and commands you must know to use Unix.

Chapter 5 covers the X Window System. X is the primary graphical front-end to Unix, and some distributions set it up by default.

Chapter 6 covers some of the more advanced parts of the Unix shell. Learning techniques described in this chapter will help make you more efficent.

Chapter 8 describes the Emacs text editor. Emacs is a very large program that integrates many of Unix's tools into one interface.

Chapter 7 has short descriptions of many different Unix commands. The more tools a user knows how to use, the quicker he will get his work done.

Chapter 11 describes some of the larger, harder to use commands.

Chapter 12 talks about easy ways to avoid errors in Unix and LINUX.

1.4   LINUX **Documentation**

This book, *The LINUX Users' Guide*, is intended for the Unix beginner. Luckily, the Linux Documentation Project is also writing books for the more experienced users.

1.4.1 Other LINUX **Books**

The other books include *Installation and Getting Started*, a guide on how to aquire and install LINUX, *The* LINUX *System Adminstrator's Guide*, how to organize and maintain a LINUX system, and *The* LINUX *Kernel Hackers' Guide*, a book about how to modify LINUX. *The* LINUX *Network Administration Guide* talks about how to install, configure, and use a network connection.

1.4.2 HOWTOs

In additon to the books, the Linux Documentation Project has made a series of short documents describing how to setup a particular aspect of LINUX. For instance, the SCSI-HOWTO describes some of the complications of using SCSI—a standard way of talking to devices—with LINUX.

These HOWTOs are available in several forms.

1.4.3 What's the Linux Documentation Project?

Like almost everything associated with LINUX, the Linux Documentation Project is a collection of people working across the globe. Originally organized by Lars Wirzenius, the Project is now coordinated by Matt Welsh with help from Michael K. Johnson.

It is hoped that the Linux Documentation Project will supply books that will meet all the needs of documenting LINUX at some point in time. Please tell us if we've succeeded or what we should improve on. You can contact the author at greenfie@gauss.rutgers.edu and Matt Welsh at mdw@cs.cornell.edu.

1.5 Operating Systems

An operating system's primary purpose is to support programs that actually do the work you're insterested in. For instance, you may be using an editor so you can create a document. This editor could not do its work without help from the operating system—it needs this help for interacting with your terminal, your files, and the rest of the computer.

If all the operating system does is support your applications, why do you need a whole book just to talk about the operating system? There are lots of routine maintenance activities (apart from your major programs) that you also need to do. In the case of LINUX, the operating system also contains a lot of "mini-applications" to help you do your work more efficently. Knowing the operating system can be helpful when you're not working in one huge application.

Operating systems (OS, for short) can be simple and minimalist, like DOS, or big and complex, like OS/2 or VMS.[1] Unix tries to be a middle ground. While it supplies more resources and does more than early operating systems, it doesn't try to do *everything* like some other operating systems.

The original design philosophy for Unix was to distribute functionality into small parts, the programs.[2] That way, you can relatively easily achieve new functionality and new features by combining the small parts (programs) in new ways. And if new utilities appear (and they do), you can integrate them into your old toolbox. Unfortunately, programs grow larger and more feature-packed on Unix as well these days, but some of the flexibility and interoperability is there to stay. When I write this document, for example, I'm using these programs actively; fvwm to manage my "windows", emacs to edit the text, LATEX to format it, xdvi to preview it, dvips to prepare it for printing and then lpr to print it. If I got a new, better dvi previewer tommorow, I could use it instead of xdvi without changing the rest of my setup.

---

[1] Apologies to DOS, OS/2, and VMS users. I've used all three, and each have their good points.
[2] This was actually determined by the hardware Unix original ran on. For some strange reason, the resulting operating system was very useful on other hardware.

When you're using an operating system, you want to minimize the amount of work you put into getting your job done. Unix supplies many tools that can help you, but only if you know what these tools do. Spending an hour trying to get something to work and then finally giving up isn't very productive. Hopefully, you already know how to use the correct tools—that way, you won't use the hammer to try and tighten a screw.

The key part of an operating system is called the "kernel." In many operating systems, like Unix, OS/2, or VMS, the kernel supplies functions for running programs to use, and schedules them to be run. It basically says program A can get so much time, program B can get this much time, etc. One school of thought says that kernels should be very small, and not supply a lot of resources, depending on programs to pick up the work. This allows the kernel to be small and fast, but may make programs bigger. Kernels designed like this are called micro-kernels. Another group of people believe that kernels that offer more services to applications are better and make more efficent operating systems. Most versions of Unix are designed like this, including LINUX. While it may seem at first that all micro-kernels should be smaller than all macro-kernels, the terms "micro" and "macro" really aren't referring to size of the kernel but a philosophy of operating system design.

Chapter 2

What's Unix, anyway?

Ken Thompson has an automobile which he helped design. Unlike most automobiles, it has neither speedometer, nor gas gage, nor any of the numerous idiot lights which plague the modern driver. Rather, if the driver makes any mistake, a giant "?" lights up in the center of the dashboard. "The experienced driver," he says, "will usually know what's wrong."

2.1 Unix History

In 1965, Bell Telephone Laboratories (Bell Labs, a division of AT&T) was working with General Electric and Project MAC of MIT to write an operating system called Multics. To make a long story slightly shorter, Bell Labs decided the project wasn't going anywhere and broke out of the group. This, however, left Bell Labs without a good operating system.

Ken Thompson and Dennis Ritchie decided to sketch out an operating system that would meet Bell Labs' needs. When Thompson needed a development environment (1970) to run on a PDP-7, he implemented their ideas. As a pun on Multics, Brian Kernighan gave the system the name UNIX.

Later, Dennis Ritchie invented the "C" programming language. In 1973, UNIX was rewritten in C, which would have a major impact later on. In 1977, UNIX was moved to a new machine, away from the PDP machines it had run on previously. This was aided by the fact UNIX was written in C.

Unix was slow to catch on outside of academic institutions but soon was popular with businesses as well. The Unix of today is different from the Unix of 1970. It has two major versions: System V, from Unix System Laboratories (USL), a subsiderary of Novell[1], and BSD, Berkeley Software Distribution. The USL version is now up to its forth release, or SVR4[2], while BSD's latest version is 4.4. However, there are many different versions of Unix besides these two. Most versions of Unix are developed by software companies and derive from one of the two groupings. Recently, the versions of Unix that are actually used incorporate features from both of them.

USL is a company that was 'spun off' from AT&T, and has taken over the maintenance of UNIX since it stopped being a research item. Unix now is much more commercial than it once was, and the licenses cost much more.

Please note the difference between Unix and UNIX. When I say "Unix" I am talking about Unix versions in generally, whether or not USL is involved in them. "UNIX" is the current version of Unix from USL. The distinction is because UNIX is a trademark of X/Open. (Officially, anybody can create a UNIX operating system, as long as it passes tests from X/Open. Since the tests haven't been created yet and are likely to cost money, LINUX is currently not a "real" UNIX.)

Current versions of UNIX for Intel PCs cost between $500 and $2000.

---

[1] It was recently sold to Novell. Previously, USL was owned by AT&T.
[2] System five, revision four.

2.2   LINUX **History**

LINUX was written by Linus Torvalds, and has been improved by countless numbers of people around the world. It is a clone, written entirely from scratch, of the Unix operating system. Neither USL, nor the University of California, Berkeley, was involved in writing LINUX. One of the more interesting facts about LINUX is that development simulataneously occurs around the world. People from Austrialia to Finland contributed to LINUX, and hopefully will continue to contribute.

LINUX began with a project to explore the 386 chip. One of Linus's earlier projects was a program that would switch between printing AAAA and BBBB. This later evolved to LINUX.

LINUX has been copyrighted under the terms of the GNU General Public License (GPL). This is a license written by the Free Software Foundation (FSF) that is designed to prevent people from restricting the distribution of software. In brief it says that although you can charge as much as you'd like for giving a copy away, you can't prevent the person you sold it to from giving it away for free. It also means that the source code[3] must also be available. This is useful for programmers. The license also says that anyone who modifies the program must also make his version freely redistributable.

LINUX supports most of the popular Unix software, including The X Window System. This is a rather large program from MIT allowing computers to create graphical windows, and is used on many different Unix platforms. LINUX is mostly System V, mostly BSD compatible and mostly POSIX-1 (a document trying to standardize operating systems) compliant. LINUX probably complies with much of POSIX-2, another document from the IEEE to standardize operating systems. It's a mix of all three standards: BSD, System V, and POSIX.

Many of the utilities included with LINUX distributions are from the Free Software Foundation and are part of GNU Project. The GNU Project is an effort to write a portable, advanced operating system that will look a lot like Unix. "Portable" means that it will run on a variety of machines, not just Intel PCs, Macintoshes, or whatever. LINUX is not easily ported (moved to another computer architechure) because it was written only with the 80386 in mind.

Of course, Torvalds isn't the only big name in LINUX's development. The following people also deserve to be recognized:

H. J. Lu has maintained gcc and the LINUX C Library, two items needed for programming.

Of course, I must have missed people in the above list. Sincere thanks and apologies go out to anyone not mentioned here—there must be dozens if not hundreds of you!

2.2.1   LINUX **Now**

LINUX development has split into two different branches. The first, signified with version numbers starting with "1.0" is supposed to be a more stable, dependable version of LINUX. The second, signified with versions numbered "1.1" is a more daring, quicker developing and therefore (unfortunately) more buggy version of LINUX.

The items changing the fastest in LINUX right now are TCP/IP support[4] and bug fixes. LINUX is a large system and unfortunately contains bugs which are found and then fixed. Although some people still experience bugs regularly, it is normally because of non-standard or faulty hardware; bugs that effect everyone are few and far between.

Of course, those are just the kernel bugs. Bugs can be present in almost every facet of the system, and inexperienced users have trouble seperating different programs from each other. For instance, a problem might arise that all the characters are some type of gibberish—is it a bug or a "feature"? Surprisingly, this is a feature—the gibberish is caused by certain control sequences that somehow appeared[5]. Hopefully, this book will help you to tell the different situations apart.

---

[3] The instructions that people write, as distinct from zeros and ones.

[4] That's a form of networking. More on that later.

[5] However, because you have all the source code, you can easily disable this particular escape sequence and recompile the

2.2.2 Trivial LINUX Matters

Before we embark on our long voyage, let's get the ultra-important out of the way.

Question: Just how do you pronounce LINUX?

Answer: According to Linus, it should be pronounced with a short *ih* sound, like prInt, mInImal, etc. LINUX should rhyme with Minix, another Unix clone. It should *not* be pronounced like (American pronounciation of) the "Peanuts" character, Linus, but rather *LIH-nucks*. And the *u* is sharp as in rule, not soft as in ducks.

2.2.3 Commercial Software in LINUX

For better or for worse, there is now commercial software available for LINUX. Although it isn't a fancy word processing application, Motif is a package that must be payed for, and the source isn't given out. Motif is a user interface for The X Window System that vaguely resembles Microsoft Windows.

For any readers interested in the legalities of LINUX, this is allowed by the LINUX license. While the GNU General Public License (reproduced in Appendix A) covers the LINUX kernel, the GNU Library General Public License (reproduced in Appendix B) covers most of the computer code applications depend on.

Please note that those two documents are copyright notices, and not licenses to use. They do *not* regulate how you may use the software, merely under what circumstances you can copy it and any derivative works. Also, copyright notices are enforced by lawsuits by the copyright holders, either the Free Software Foundation or Linus Torvalds. In general, this means you can't go wrong if you obey the spirit of what they're asking—they probably won't sue you and all will be well. (Unless the rights get sold.) It's also a good idea not to think up schemes to get around these two copyrights—it's almost definitely possible, but merely causes grief to all parties involved.

---

kernel.

Chapter 3

Getting Started

This login session: $13.99, but for you $11.88.

3.1 Starting to Use Your Computer

You may have previous experience with MS-DOS or other single user operating systems, such as OS/2 or the Macintosh. In these operating systems, you didn't have to identify yourself to the computer before using it; it was assumed that you were the only user of the system and could access everything. Well, Unix is a multi-user operating system—not only can more than one person use it at a time, different people are treated differently.[1]

To tell people apart, Unix needs a user to identify him or herself[2] by a process called **logging in**. You see, when you first turn on the computer, several things happen. Since this guide is geared towards LINUX, I'll tell you what happens during the LINUX boot-up sequence.

Please note that if you're using LINUX on some type of computer besides an Intel PC, some things in this chapter won't apply to you. Mostly, they'll be in Section 3.1.1 and Section 3.1.2. (Some parts of Section 3.1.2 will pertain.)

3.1.1 Power to the Computer

The first thing that happens when you turn an Intel PC on is that the BIOS executes. BIOS stands for **B**asic **I**nput/**O**utput **S**ystem. It's a program permenantly stored in the computer on read-only chips, normally. For our purposes, the BIOS can never be changed. It performs some minimal tests, and then looks for a floppy disk in the first disk drive. If it finds one, it looks for a "boot sector" on that disk, and starts executing code from it, if any. If there is a disk, but no boot sector, the BIOS will print a message like:

    Non-system disk or disk error

Removing the disk and pressing a key will cause the boot process to continue.

If there isn't a floppy disk in the drive, the BIOS looks for a master boot record (MBR) on the hard disk. It will start executing the code found there, which loads the operating system. On LINUX systems, LILO, the **LI**nux **LO**ader, can occupy the MBR position, and will load LINUX. For now, we'll assume that happens and that LINUX starts to load. (Your particular distribution may handle booting from the hard disk differently. Check with the documentation included in that distribution. Another good reference is the LILO documentation, [1].)

---

[1] Discrimination? Perhaps. You decide.

[2] From here on in this book, I shall be using the masculine pronouns to identify all people. This is the standard English convention, and people shouldn't take it as a statement that only men can use computers.

3.1.2   LINUX **Takes Over**

Before reading this section, you should know that nothing in it is needed to actually *use* LINUX. It is only here for your own enjoyment and interest, but if you find it boring or overly technical, skip over it!

After the BIOS passes control to LILO, LILO passes control to LINUX. (This is assuming you have configured LINUX to boot by default. It is also possible for LILO to call DOS or some other PC operating system.) The first thing that LINUX does once it starts executing is to change to protected mode. The 80386[3] CPU that controls your computer has two modes (for our purposes) called real mode and protected mode. DOS runs in real mode, as does the BIOS. However, for more advanced operating systems, it is necessary to run in protected mode. Therefore, when LINUX boots, it discards the BIOS.

LINUX then looks at the type of hardware it's running on. It wants to know what type of hard disks you have, whether or not you have a bus mouse, whether or not you're on a network, and other bits of trivia like that. LINUX can't remember things between boots, so it has to ask these questions each time it starts up. Luckily, it isn't asking *you* these questions—it is asking the hardware! During boot-up, the LINUX kernel will print variations on several messages. You can read about the messages in Section 3.3.

The kernel merely manages other programs, so once it is satisfied everything is okay, it must start another program to do anything useful. The program the kernel starts is called init . (Notice the difference in font. Things in that font are usually the names of programs, files, directories, or other computer related items.) After the kernel starts init, it never starts another program. The kernel becomes a manager and a provider, not an active program.

So to see what the computer is doing after the kernel boots up, we'll have to examine init. init goes through a complicated startup sequence that isn't the same for all computers. For LINUX there are many versions of init, and each does things its own way. It also matters whether your computer is on a network, or what distribution you used to install LINUX. Some things that might happen once init is started:

- The file systems might be checked. What is a file system, you might ask? A file system is the layout of files on the hard disk. It let's Unix know which parts of the disk are already used, and which aren't. Unfortunately, due to various factors such as power losses, what the file system information thinks is going on in the rest of the disk and the actually layout of the rest of the disk are in conflict. A special program, called fsck, can find these situations and hopefully correct them.

- Special routing programs for networks are run.

- Temporary files left by some programs may be deleted.

- The system clock can be correctly updated. This is trickier then one might think, since Unix, by default, wants the time in GMT and your CMOS clock, a battery powered clock in your computer, is probably set on local time.

After init is finished with its duties at boot-up, it goes on to its regularly scheduled activities. init can be called the parent of all processes on a Unix system. A process is simple a running program; since any one program can be running more than once, there can be two or more processes for any particular program. (Processes can also be sub-programs, but that isn't important right now.) There are as many processes operating as there are programs.

In Unix, a process, an instance of a program, is created by a system call, a service provided by the kernel, called fork. init forks a couple of processes, which in turn fork some of their own. On your LINUX system, what init runs are several instances of a program called getty. getty will be covered in. . .

---

[3]When I refer to the 80386, I am also talking about the 80486 unless I specifically say so. Also, I'll be abbreviating 80386 as 386.

3.1.3   The User Acts

This section actually contains information needed to know how to use LINUX.

The first thing you have to do to use a Unix machine is to identify yourself. This process, knowing as "logging in", is Unix's way of knowing that users are authorized to use the system. It asks for an account name and password. An account name is normally similar to your regular name; you should have already received one from your system administrator, or created your own if you are the system administrator. (Information on doing this should be available in *Installation and Getting Started* or *The* LINUX *System Adminstrator's Guide*.)

You should see, after all the boot-up procedures are done, something like the following:

```
Welcome to the mousehouse. Please, have some cheese.

mousehouse login:
```

However, it's possible that what the system presents you with does *not* look like this. Instead of a boring text mode screen, it is graphical. However, it will still ask you to login, and will function mostly the same way. If this is the case on your system, you are going to be using The X Window System. This means that you will be presented with a windowing system. Chapter 5 will discuss some of the differences that you'll be facing. However, logging in will be similar. If you are using X, look for a giant X is the margin.

This is, of course, your invitation to **login**. Throughout this manual, we'll be using the fictional (or not so fictional, depending on your machine) user `larry`. Whenever you see `larry`, you should be substituting your own account name. Account names are usually based on real names; bigger, more serious Unix systems will have accounts using the user's last name, or some combination of first and last name, or even some numbers. Possible accounts for Larry Greenfield might be: `larry`, `greenfie`, `lgreenfi`, `lg19`.

`mousehouse` is, by the way, the "name" of the machine I'm working on. It is possible that when you installed LINUX, you were prompted for some very witty name. It isn't very important, but whenever it comes up, I'll be using `mousehouse` or, rarely, `lionsden`.

After entering `larry`, I'm faced with the following:

```
mousehouse login: larry
Password:
```

What LINUX is asking for is your **password**. When you type in your password, you won't be able to see what you type. Type carefully: it is possible to delete, but you won't be able to see what you are editing. Don't type too slowly if people are watching—they'll be able to learn your password. If you mistype, you'll be presented with another chance to login.

If you've typed your login name and password correctly, a short message will appear, called the message of the day. This could say anything—the system adminstrator decides what it should be. After that, a **prompt** appears. A prompt is just that, something prompting you for the next command to give the system. It should look like this:

```
/home/larry#
```

If you've already determined you're using X Windows, you'll probably see a prompt like the one above in a "window" somewhere on the screen. (A "window" is simply a rectangular box.) To type into the prompt, move the mouse cursor (it probably looks like a big "x") using the mouse into the window.

3.2   Leaving the Computer

Do not just turn off the computer! You risk losing valuable data!

Unlike most versions of DOS, it's a bad thing to just hit the power switch when you're done using the computer. It is also bad to reboot the machine (with the reset button) without first taking proper precautions. LINUX, in order to improve performance, caches the disk. This means it temporarily stores part of the permanent storage in RAM. The idea of what LINUX thinks the disk should be and what the disk actually contains is syncronized every 30 seconds. In order to turn off or reboot the computer, you'll have to go through a procedure telling it to stop caching disk information.

If you're done with the computer, but are logged in (you've entered a username and password), first you must logout. To do so, enter the command logout. All commands are sent by pressing the key marked "Enter" or "Return". Until you hit enter, nothing will happen, and you can delete what you've done and start over.

```
/home/larry# logout

Welcome to the mousehouse. Please, have some cheese.

mousehouse login:
```

Now another user can login.

3.2.1 Turning the Computer Off

If this is a single user system, you might want to turn the computer off when you're done with it.[4] To do so, you'll have to log into a special account called root. The root account is the system adminstrator's account and can access any file on the system. If you're going to turn the computer off, get the password from the system adminstrator. (In a single user system, that's *you*! Make sure you know the default root password.) Login as root:

```
mousehouse login: root
Password:

Linux, version 0.99pl10.
/# shutdown now

************ GET THE SHUTDOWN MESSAGE CORRECT ***********
```

The command shutdown now prepares the system to be reset or turned off. Wait for a message saying it is safe to and then reset or turn off the system. You must go through this procedure, however. You risk losing your work if you don't.

A quick message to the lazy: an alternative to the logout/login approach is to use the command su. As a normal user, from your prompt, type su and ⎡return⎤. It should prompt you for the root password, and then give you root privileges. Now you can shutdown the system.

3.3 Kernel Messages

The messages printed by the kernel vary from machine to machine, and from kernel version to version. The version of LINUX that is discussed in *this* section is "0.99.10". (Please note that this is a big book, and LINUX develops quickly. Versions in other sections might be different. Usually, this distinction is unimportant.)

---

[4]To avoid possibly weakening some hardware components, only turn off the computer when you're done for the day.

3.3.1   Starting Messages

When LINUX first starts up, it writes many messages to the screen which you might not be able to see. LINUX maintains a special file, called `/proc/kmsg`, which stores all these messages for later viewing, and I've included a sample startup sequence here.

- The first thing LINUX does is decides what type of video card and screen you have, so it can pick a good font size. (The smaller the font, the more that can fit on the screen on any one time.) LINUX may ask you if you want a special font, or it might have had a choice compiled in.[5]

  ```
  Console: colour EGA+ 80x25, 8 virtual consoles Serial driver version
  ```

  In this example, the machine owner decided he wanted the standard, large font at compile time. Also, note the misspelling of the word "color." Linus evidently learned the wrong version of English.[6]

- LINUX has now switched to protected mode, and the serial driver has started to ask questions about the hardware. A driver is a part of the kernel that controls a device, usually a peripheral.

  ```
  Serial driver version 3.95 with no serial options enabled
  tty00 at 0x03f8 (irq = 4) is a 16450
  tty01 at 0x02f8 (irq = 3) is a 16450
  tty02 at 0x03e8 (irq = 4) is a 16450
  ```

  Here, it found 3 serial ports. A serial port is the equivalent of a DOS COM port, and is a device normally used with modems and mice.

  What it is trying to say is that serial port 0 (COM1) has an address of 0x03f8. When it interrupts the kernel, usually to say that it has data, it uses IRQ 4. An IRQ is another means of a peripheral talking to the software. Each serial port also has a controller chip. The usual one for a port to have is a 16450; other values possible are 8250 and 16550. The differences are beyond the scope of this book.

- Next comes the parallel port driver. A parallel port is normally connected to a printer, and the names for the parallel ports (in LINUX) start with `lp`. `lp` stands for **Line Printer**, although it could be a laser printer.

  ```
  lp_init: lp0 exists (0), using polling driver
  ```

  That message says it has found one parallel port, and is using the standard driver for it.

- The LINUX kernel also tells you a little about memory usage:

  ```
  Memory: 7296k/8192k available (384k kernel code, 384k reserved, 128k data)
  ```

  This said that the machine had 8 megabytes of memory. Some of this memory was reserved for the kernel—just the operating system. The rest of it could be used by programs.

  The other type of "memory" is general called a hard disk. It's like a large floppy disk permenantly in your computer—the contents stay around even when the power is off.

- The kernel now moves onto looking at your floppy drives. In this example, the machine has two drives. In DOS, drive "A" is a 5 1/4 inch drive, and drive "B" is a 3 1/2 inch drive. LINUX calls drive "A" `fd0`, and drive "B" `fd1`.

  ```
  Floppy drive(s): fd0 is 1.2M, fd1 is 1.44M
  floppy: FDC version 0x90
  ```

- Now LINUX moves onto less needed things, such as network cards. The following should be described in *The LINUX Networking Guide*, and is beyond the scope of this document.[7]

---

[5] "Compiled" is the process by which a computer program that a human writes gets translated into something the computer understands. A feature that has been "compiled in" has been included in the program.

[6] An editor has scolded me for my United States chauvinism, so you don't have to send me mean mail messages!

[7] This may change in latter 'versions' of this book.

```
SLIP: version 0.7.5 (4 channels): OK
plip.c:v0.04 Mar 19 1993 Donald Becker (becker@super.org)
plip0: using parallel port at 0x3bc, IRQ 5.
plip1: using parallel port at 0x378, IRQ 7.
plip2: using parallel port at 0x278, IRQ 2.
8390.c:v0.99-10 5/28/93 for 0.99.6+ Donald Becker (becker@super.org)
WD80x3 ethercard probe at 0x280: FF FF FF FF FF FF not found (0x7f8).
3c503 probe at 0x280:  not found.
8390 ethercard probe at 0x280 failed.
HP-LAN ethercard probe at 0x280: not found (nothing there).
No ethernet device found.
d10: D-Link pocket adapter: probe failed at 0x378.
```

- The next message you normally won't see as the machine boots up. LINUX supports a FPU, a floating point unit. This is a special chip (or part of a chip, in the case of a 80486DX CPU) that performs arithmetic dealing with non-whole numbers. Some of these chips are bad, and when LINUX tries to identify these chips, the machine "crashes". That is to say, the machine stops functioning. If this happens, you'll see:

```
You have a bad 386/387 coupling.
```

Otherwise, you'll see:

```
Math coprocessor using exception 16 error reporting.
```

if you're using a 486DX. If you are using a 386 with a 387, you'll see:

```
Math coprocessor using irq13 error reporting.
```

If you don't have any type of math coprocessor at all, you'll see:

```
What will they see?
```

- The kernel also scans for any hard disks you might have. If it finds any (and it should) it'll look at what partitions you have on them. A partition is a logical separation on a drive that is used to keep operating systems from interfering with each other. In this example, the computer had one hard disk (hda) with four partitions.

```
Partition check:
  hda: hda1 hda2 hda3 hda4
```

- Finally, LINUX **mounts** the root partition. The root partition is the disk partition where the LINUX operating system resides. When LINUX "mounts" this partition, it is making the partition available for use by the user.

```
VFS: Mounted root (ext filesystem).
```

3.3.2 Run-time Messages

The LINUX kernel occasionally sends messages to your screen. The following is a list of some of these messages and what they mean. Frequently, these messages indicate something is wrong. Some of these messages are **critical**, which means the operating system (and all your programs!) stops working. When these messages occur, you should write them down and what you where doing at the time, and send them to Linus. See Section 12.2.2.

Luckily, some of these messages are merely informational—hopefully, you'll see them more often!

-
```
   Adding Swap: 10556k swap-space
   lp0 on fire
   ******** OBVIOUSLY INCOMPLETE
```

Chapter 4

The Unix Shell

A UNIX saleslady, Lenore,
Enjoys work, but she likes the beach more.
　　　　She found a good way
　　　　To combine work and play:
She sells C shells by the seashore.

4.1　Unix Commands

When you first log into a Unix system, you are presented with something that looks like the following:

```
/home/larry#
```

This is called a **prompt**. As its name would suggest, it is prompting you to enter a command. Every Unix command is a sequence of letters, numbers, and characters. There are no spaces, however. Thus, valid Unix commands include `mail`, `cat`, and `CMU_is_Number-5`. Some characters aren't allowed—that's covered later. Unix is also **case-sensitive**. This means that `cat` and `Cat` are different commands.

Case sensitivity is a very personal thing. Some operating systems, such as OS/2 or Windows NT are case preserving, but not case sensitive. In practice, Unix rarely uses the different cases. It is unusual to have a situation where `cat` and `Cat` are different commands.

The prompt is displayed by a special program called the **shell**. The MS-DOS shell is called `COMMAND.COM`, and is very simple compared to most Unix shells. Shells accept commands, and run those commands. They can also be programmed in their own language, and programs written in that language are called "shell scripts".

There are two major types of shells in Unix, Bourne shells, and C shells. Bourne shells are named after their inventor, Steven Bourne. There are many implementations of this shell, and all those specific shell programs are called Bourne shells. Another class of shells, C shells (originally implemented by Bill Joy), are also common. Traditionally, Bourne shells have been used for compatibility, and C shells have been used for interactive use.

LINUX comes with a Bourne shell called `bash`, written by the Free Software Foundation. `bash` stands for **B**ourne **A**gain **Sh**ell, one of the many bad puns in Unix. It is an advanced Bourne shell, with many features commonly found in C shells, and is the default.

When you first login, the prompt is displayed by `bash`, and you are running your first Unix program, the `bash` shell.

4.1.1 A Typical Unix Command

The first command to know is `cat`. To use it, type `cat`, and then `return` :

```
/home/larry# cat
```

If you now have a cursor on a line by itself, you've done the correct thing. There are several variances you could have typed—some would work, some wouldn't.

- If you misspelled `cat`, you would have seen

```
/home/larry# ct
ct: command not found
/home/larry#
```

Thus, the shell informs you that it couldn't find a program named "ct" and gives you another prompt to work with. Remember, Unix is case sensitive: `CAT` is a misspelling.

- You could have also placed whitespace before the command, like this:[1]

```
/home/larry#␣␣␣␣␣cat
```

This produces the correct result and runs the `cat` program.

- You might also press return on a line by itself. Go right ahead—it does absolutely nothing.

I assume you are now in `cat`. Hopefully, you're wondering what it is doing. For all you hopefuls, no, it is not a game. `cat` is a useful utility that won't seem useful at first. Type anything, and hit return. What you should have seen is:

```
/home/larry# cat
Help! I'm stuck in a Linux program!
Help!  I'm stuck in a Linux program!
```

(The *slanted* text indicates what the user types.) What `cat` seems to do is echo the text right back at yourself. This is useful at times, but isn't right now. So let's get out of this program and move onto commands that have more obvious benefits.

To end many Unix commands, type `Ctrl-d` [2]. `Ctrl-d` is the end-of-file character, or EOF for short. Alternatively, it stands for end-of-text, depending on what book you read. I'll refer to it as an end-of-file. It is a control character that tells Unix programs that you (or another program) is done entering data. When `cat` sees you aren't typing anything else, it terminates.

For a similar idea, try the program `sort`. As its name indicates, it is a sorting program. If you type a couple of lines, then press `Ctrl-d` , it will output those lines in a sorted order. By the way, these types of programs are called **filters**, because they take in text, filter it, and output the text slightly differently. (Well, `cat` is a very basic filter and doesn't change the input.) We will talk more about filters later.

4.2 Helping Yourself

The `man` command displays reference pages for the command[3] you spesify. For example;

---

[1] The '␣' indicates that the user typed a space.
[2] Hold down the key labeled "Ctrl" and press "d", then let go.
[3] Or system call, subroutine, file format etc.

```
/home/larry# man cat

cat(1)                                               cat(1)

NAME
  cat - Concatenates or displays files

SYNOPSIS
  cat [-benstuvAET] [--number] [--number-nonblank] [--squeeze-blank]
  [--show-nonprinting] [--show-ends] [--show-tabs] [--show-all]
  [--help] [--version] [file...]


DESCRIPTION
  This manual page documents the GNU version of cat ...
```

There's about one full page of information about cat. Try it. Don't expect to understand it, though. It assumes quite some Unix knowledge. When you've read the page, there's probably a little black block at the bottom of your screen, reading --more--, Line 1 or something similar. This is the more-prompt, and you'll learn to love it.

Instead of just letting the text scroll away, man stops at the end of each page, waiting for you to decide what to do now. If you just want to go on, press ⎡Space⎤ and you'll advance a page. If you want to exit (quit) the manual page you are reading, just press ⎡q⎤. You'll be back at the shell prompt, and it'll be waiting for you to enter a new command.

There's also a keyword function in man. For example, say you're interested in any commands that deal with Postscript, the printer control language from Adobe. Type man -k ps or man -k Postscript, you'll get a listing of all commands, system calls, and other documented parts of Unix that have the word "ps" (or "Postscript") in their name or short description. This can be very useful when you're looking for a tool to do something, but you don't know it's name—or if it even exists!

4.3 Storing Information

Filters are very useful once you are an experienced user, but they have one small problem. How do you store the information? Surely you aren't expected to type everything in each time you are going to use the program! Of course not. Unix provides **files** and **directories**.

A directory is like a folder: it contains pieces of paper, or files. A large folder can even hold other folders—directories can be inside directories. In Unix, the collection of directories and files is called the file system. Initially, the file system consists of one directory, called the "root" directory. Inside this directory, there are more directories, and inside those directories are files and yet more directories.[4]

Each file and each directory has a name. It has both a short name, which can be the same as another file or directory somewhere else on the system, and a long name which is unique. A short name for a file could be joe, while it's "full name" would be /home/larry/joe. The full name is usually called the **path**. The path can be decode into a sequence of directories. For example, here is how /home/larry/joe is read:

/home/larry/joe
First, we are in the root directory.
  This signifies the directory called home. It is inside the root directory.
    This is the directory larry, which is inside home.
        joe is inside larry. A path could refer to either a directory or a filename,
        so joe could be either. All the items *before* the short name must be directories.

An easy way of visualizing this is a tree diagram. To see a diagram of a typical LINUX system, look at Figure 4.1. Please note that this diagram isn't complete—a full LINUX system has over 8000

---

[4]There may or may not be a limit to how "deep" the file system can go. You can easily have directories 10 levels down.

Figure 4.1: A typical (abridged) Unix directory tree.

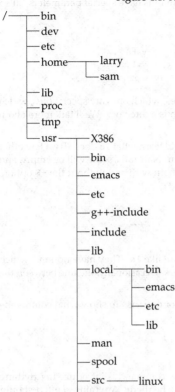

files!—and shows only some of the standard directories. Thus, there may be some directories in that diagram that aren't on your system, and your system almost certainly has directories not listed there.

4.3.1   Looking at Directories with `ls`

Now that you know that files and directories exist, there must be some way of manipulating them. Indeed there is. The command `ls` is one of the more important ones. It **lists** files. If you try `ls` as a command, you'll see:

```
/home/larry# ls
/home/larry#
```

That's right, you'll see nothing. Unix is intentionally terse: it gives you nothing, not even "no files" if there aren't any files. Thus, the lack of output was `ls`'s way of saying it didn't find any files.

But I just said there could be 8000 or more files lying around: where are they? You've run into the concept of a "current" directory. You can see in your prompt that your current directory is /home/larry, where you don't have any files. If you want a list of files of a more active directory, try the root directory:

```
/home/larry# ls /
bin      etc     install  mnt    root    user    var
dev      home    lib      proc   tmp     usr     vmlinux
/home/larry#
```

In the above command, "ls /", the directory is a **parameter**. The first word of the command is the command name, and anything after it is a parameter. Some commands have special parameters called **options** or **switches**. To see this, try:

```
/home/larry# ls -F /
bin/     etc/      install/  mnt/     root/    user/    var@
dev/     home/     lib/      proc/    tmp/     usr/     vmlinux
/home/larry#
```

The -F is an option that lets you see which ones are directories, which ones are special files, which are programs, and which are normal files. Anything with a slash is a directory. We'll talk more about ls's features later. It's a surprisingly complex program!

Now, there are two lessons to be learned here. First, you should learn what ls does. Try a few other directories that are shown in Figure 4.1, and see what they contain. Naturally, some will be empty, and some will have many, many files in them. I suggest you try ls both with and without the -F option. For example, ls /usr/local looks like:

```
/home/larry# ls /usr/local
archives  bin     emacs    etc     ka9q    lib     tcl
/home/larry#
```

The second lesson is more general. Many Unix commands are like ls. They have options, which are generally one character after a dash, and they have parameters. Occasionally, the line between the two isn't so clear.

Unlike ls, some commands require certain parameters and/or options. To show what commands generally look like, we'll use the following form:

```
ls [-arF] [directory]
```

That's a command template and you'll see it whenever a new command is introduced. Anything contained in brackets ("[" and "]") is optional: it doesn't have to be there. Anything *slanted* should usually be changed before trying the command. You'll rarely have a directory *named* directory.

4.3.2   The Current Directory and cd

Using directories would be cumbersome if you had to type the full path each time you wanted to access a directory. Instead, Unix shells have a feature called the "current" or "present" or "working" directory. Your setup most likely displays your directory in your prompt: /home/larry. If it doesn't, try the command pwd, for **p**resent **w**orking **d**irectory.

```
mousehouse>pwd
/home/larry
mousehouse>
```

As you can see, pwd tells you your current directory[5]—a very simple command. Most commands act, by default, on the current directory, such as ls. We can change our current directory using cd. For instance, try:

```
/home/larry# cd /home
/home# ls -F
larry/    sam/      shutdown/  steve/    user1/
/home#
```

A generic template looks like:

---

[5] You'll see all the terms in this book: present working directory, current directory, or working directory. I prefer "current directory", although at times the other forms will be used for stylistic purposes.

cd [*directory*]

If you omit the *directory*, you're returned to your home, or original, directory. Otherwise, cd will change you to the specified directory. For instance:

```
/home# cd
/home/larry# cd /
/# cd home
/home# cd /usr
/usr# cd local/bin
/usr/local/bin#
```

As you can see, cd allows you to give either absolute or relative pathnames. An "absolute" path starts with / and specifies all the directories before the one you wanted. A "relative" path is in relation to your current directory. In the above example, when I was in /usr, I made a relative move to local/bin—local is a directory under usr, and bin is a directory under local!

There are two directories used *only* for relative pathnames: "." and "..". . The directory "." refers to the current directory and ".." is the parent directory. These are "shortcut" directories. They exist in *every* directory, but don't really fit the "folder in a folder" concept. Even the root directory has a parent directory—it's its own parent!

The file ./chapter-1 would be the file called chapter-1 in the current directory. Occasionally, you need to put the "./" for some commands to work, although this is rare. In most cases, ./chapter-1 and chapter-1 will be identical.

The directory ".." is most useful in backing up:

```
/usr/local/bin# cd ..
/usr/local# ls -F
archives/   bin/      emacs@      etc/       ka9q/      lib/       tcl@
/usr/local# ls -F ../src
cweb/       linux/    xmris/
/usr/local#
```

In this example, I changed to the parent directory using cd .., and I listed the directory /usr/src from /usr/local using ../src. Note that if I was in /home/larry, typing ls -F ../src wouldn't do me any good!

One other shortcut for lazy users: the directory ~/ is your home directory:

```
/usr/local# ls -F ~/
/usr/local#
```

You can see at a glance that there isn't anything in your home directory! Actually, ~/ will become more useful as we learn more about how to manipulate files.

4.3.3 Using mkdir to Create Your Own Directories

Creating your own directories is extremely simple under Unix, and can be a useful organizational tool. To create a new directory, use the command mkdir. Of course, mkdir stands for **make dir**ectory.

mkdir *directory*

Let's do a small example to see how this works:

```
/home/larry# ls -F
/home/larry# mkdir report-1993
/home/larry# ls -F
report-1993/
/home/larry# cd report-1993
/home/larry/report-1993#
```

mkdir can actually take more than one parameter, and you can specify either the full pathname or a relative pathname; report-1993 in the above example is a relative pathname.

```
/home/larry/report-1993# mkdir /home/larry/report-1993/chap1 ~/report-1993/chap2
/home/larry/report-1993# ls -F
chap1/  chap2/
/home/larry/report-1993#
```

Finally, there is the opposite of mkdir, rmdir for **remove dir**ectory. rmdir works exactly as you think it should work:

rmdir *directory*

An example of rmdir is:

```
/home/larry/report-1993# rmdir chap1 chap3
rmdir: chap3: No such file or directory
/home/larry/report-1993# ls -F
chap2/
/home/larry/report-1993# cd ..
/home/larry# rmdir report-1993
rmdir: report-1993: Directory not empty
/home/larry#
```

As you can see, rmdir will refuse to remove a non-existent directory, as well as a directory that has anything in it. (Remember, report-1993 has a subdirectory, chap2, in it!) There is one more interesting thing to think about rmdir: what happens if you try to remove your current directory? Let's find out:

```
/home/larry# cd report-1993
/home/larry/report-1993# ls -F
chap2/
/home/larry/report-1993# rmdir chap2
/home/larry/report-1993# rmdir .
rmdir: .: Operation not permitted
/home/larry/report-1993#
```

Another situation you might want to consider is what happens if you try to remove the parent of your current directory. In fact, this isn't even a problem: the parent of your current directory isn't empty, so it can't be removed!

4.4   Moving Information

All of these fancy directories are very nice, but they really don't help unless you have some place to store you data. The Unix Gods saw this problem, and they fixed it by giving the users "files". We will learn more about creating and editing files in the next few chapters.

The primary commands for manipulating files under Unix are cp, mv, and rm. Respectively, they stand for copy, move, and remove.

4.4.1   cp **Like a Monk**

cp is a very useful utility under Unix, and extremely powerful. It enables one person to copy more information in a second than a fourteenth century monk could do in a year.

◇   Be careful with cp if you don't have a lot of disk space. No one wants to see Error saving--disk full. cp can also overwrite existing files—I'll talk more about that danger later.

The first parameter to cp is the file to copy—the last is where to copy it. You can copy to either a different filename, or a different directory. Let's try some examples:

```
/home/larry# ls -F /etc/rc
/etc/rc
/home/larry# cp /etc/rc .
/home/larry# ls -F
rc
/home/larry# cp rc frog
/home/larry# ls -F
frog  rc
/home/larry#
```

The first cp command I ran took the file /etc/rc, which contains commands that the Unix system runs on boot-up, and copied it to my home directory. cp doesn't delete the source file, so I didn't do anything that could harm the system. So two copies of /etc/rc exist on my system now, both named rc, but one is in the directory /etc and one is in /home/larry.

Then I created a *third* copy of /etc/rc when I typed cp rc frog—the three copies are now: /etc/rc, /home/larry/rc and /home/larry/frog. The contents of these three files are the same, even if the names aren't.

The above example illustrates two uses of the command cp. Are there any others? Let's take a look:

- cp can copy files between directories if the first parameter is a file and the second parameter is a directory.

- It can copy a file and change it's name if both parameters are file names. Here is one danger of cp. If I typed cp /etc/rc /etc/passwd, cp would normally create a new file with the contents identical to rc and name it passwd. However, if /etc/passwd already existed, cp would destroy the old file without giving you a chance to save it!

- Let's look at another example of cp:

```
/home/larry# ls -F
frog  rc
/home/larry# mkdir rc_version
/home/larry# cp frog rc rc_version
/home/larry# ls -F
frog          rc          rc_version/
/home/larry# ls -F rc_version
frog  rc
/home/larry#
```

How did I just use cp? Evidentally, cp can take *more* than two parameters. What the above command did is copied all the files listed (frog and rc) and placed them in the rc_version directory. In fact, cp can take any number of parameters, and interprets the first $n-1$ parameters to be files to copy, and the nth n<h6>th</h6> parameter as what directory to copy them too.

◇   You cannot rename files when you copy more than one at a time—they always keep their short name. This leads to an interesting question. What if I type cp frog rc toad, where frog and rc exist and toad isn't a directory? Try it and see.

One last thing in this section—how can you show the parameters that cp takes? After all, the parameters can mean two different things. When that happens, we'll have two different lines:

cp *source destination-name*
cp *file1 file2 . . . fileN destination-directory*

4.4.2 Pruning Back with rm

Now that we've learned how to create millions of files with cp (and believe me, you'll find new ways to create more files soon), it may be useful to learn how to delete them. Actually, it's very simple: the command you're looking for is rm, and it works just like you'd expect.

Any file that's a parameter to rm gets deleted:

rm *file1 file2 . . . fileN*

For example:

```
/home/larry# ls -F
frog        rc          rc_version/
/home/larry# rm frog toad rc
rm: toad: No such file or directory
/home/larry# ls -F
rc_version/
/home/larry#
```

As you can see, rm is extremely unfriendly. Not only does it not ask you for confirmation, but it will also delete things even if the whole command line wasn't correct. This could actually be dangerous. Consider the difference between these two commands:

```
/home/larry# ls -F
toad  frog/
/home/larry# ls -F frog
toad
/home/larry# rm frog/toad
/home/larry#
```

and this

```
/home/larry# rm frog toad
rm: frog is a directory
/home/larry# ls -F
frog/
/home/larry#
```

◇   As you can see, the difference of *one* character made a world of difference in the outcome of the command. It is vital that you check your command lines before hitting ⌗return⌗!

4.4.3 A Forklift Can Be Very Handy

Finally, the other file command you should be aware of is mv. mv looks a lot like cp, except that it deletes the original file after copying it. Thus, it's a lot like using cp and rm together. Let's take a look at what we can do:

```
/home/larry# cp /etc/rc .
/home/larry# ls -F
rc
/home/larry# mv rc frog
/home/larry# ls -F
frog
/home/larry# mkdir report
/home/larry# mv frog report
/home/larry# ls -F
report/
/home/larry# ls -F report
frog
/home/larry#
```

As you can see, `mv` will rename a file if the second parameter is a file. If the second parameter is a directory, `mv` will move the file to the new directory, keeping it's shortname the same:

> `mv` *old-name new-name*
> `mv` *file1 file2 . . . fileN new-directory*

◇   You should be very careful with `mv`—it doesn't check to see if the file already exists, and will remove any old file in its way. For instance, if I had a file named `frog` already in my directory `report`, the command `mv frog report` would delete the file `~/report/frog` and replace it with `~/frog`.

In fact, there is one way to make `rm`, `cp` and `mv` ask you before deleting files. The `-i` option. If you use an **alias**, you can make the shell do `rm -i` automatically when you type `rm`. You'll learn more about this later.

Chapter 5

The X Window System

Any good quotes about X11?

◇   This chapter only applies to those using the X Window System. If you encounter a screen with multiply windows, colors, or a cursor that is only movable with your mouse, you are using X11. (If you are interested in using X11, but are not by default, see Section 5.4.)

5.1   What is The X Window System?

The X Window System is a distributed, graphical method of working developed primarily at the Massachusetts Institute of Technology. It has since been passed to a consortium of vendors (aptly named "The X Consortium") and is being maintained by them.

The X Window System (hereafter abbreviated as "X"[1]) has new versions every few years, called releases. As of this writing, the latest revision is X11R6, or release six. The eleven in X11 is officially the version number.

There are two terms when dealing with X that you should be familiar. The **client** is a X program. For instance, xterm is the client that displays your shell when you log on. The **server** is a program that provides services to the client program. For instance, the server draws the window for xterm and communicates with the user.

Since the client and the server are two separate programs, it is possible to run the client and the server *on two physically separate machines*. This is the real beauty of X. In addition to supplying a standard method of doing graphics, you can run a program on a remote machine (across the country, if you like!) and have it display on the workstation right in front of you.

A third term you should be familiar with is the **window manager**. The window manager is a special client that tells the server where to position various windows and provides a way for the user to move these windows around. The server, by itself, does nothing for the user. It is merely there to provide a buffer between the user and the client.

5.2   What's This on my Screen?

When you first start X, several programs are started. First, the server is started. Then, several clients are usually started. Unfortunately, this is not standardized across various distributions. It is likely that among these clients are a window manager, either fvwm or twm, a prompt, xterm, and a clock, xclock.

---

[1] There are several acceptable ways to refer to The X Window System, although "X Windows" is *not* one of them.

5.2.1 XClock

I'll explain the simplest one first: `xclock` functions exactly as you'd expect it would. It ticks off the seconds, minutes and hours in a small window.

No amounts of clicking or typing in `xclock`'s window will affect it—that's *all* it does. Or is it? In fact, there are various different options you can give to the program to have it act in different ways. For instance, `xclock -digital` will create a digital clock. `xclock -update 1` will create a second hand that moves every second, while `-update 5` will create a second hand that moves every 5 seconds.

For more information on `xclock`'s options, consult its manpage—`man xclock`. If you're going to try running a few of your own `xclock`s, you should probably read Section 6.4.

5.2.2 XTerm

The window with a prompt in it (something that probably looks like: `/home/larry#` or some such, is being controlled by a program called `xterm`. `xterm` is a deceptively complicated program. At first glance, it doesn't seem to do much, but it actually has to do a lot of work. `xterm` emulates a terminal so that regular text-mode Unix applications work correctly.

For much of this book, we're going to be learning about the Unix command-line, and you'll find that inside your `xterm` window. In order to type into `xterm`, you *usually* have to move your mouse cursor (possibly shaped like an "X" or an arrow) into the `xterm` window. However, this behavior is dependant on the window manager.

5.3 Window Managers

On LINUX, there are two different window managers that are commonly used. One of them, called `twm` is short for "Tab Window Manager". It is larger than the other window manager usually used, `fvwm`. (`fvwm` stands for "F(?) Virtual Window Manager"—the author neglected to tie down exactly what the f stood for.) Both `twm` and `fvwm` are highly configurable, which means I can't tell you exactly what keys do what in your particular setup.

To learn about `twm`'s configuration, look at Section 9.2.1. `fvwm`'s configuration is covered in Section 9.2.2.

5.3.1 When New Windows are Created

There are three possible things a window manager will do when a new window is created. It is possible to configure a window manager so that an outline of the new window is shown, and you are allowed to position it on your screen. That is called "manual placement".

It is also possible that the window manager will place the new window somewhere on the screen by itself. This is known as "random placement".

Finally, sometimes an application will ask for a specific spot on the screen, or the window manager will be configured to display certain applications on the same place of the screen all the time. (For instance, I could specify that I want `xclock` to always appear in the upper right hand corner of the screen.)

5.3.2 Focus

The window manager controls some important things. The first thing you'll be interested in is "focus". The focus of the server is which window will get what you type into the keyboard. Usually in X the focus is determined by the position of the mouse cursor. If the mouse cursor is in one `xterm`'s window[2], that xterm will get your keypresses. Note that this is different from many other windowing systems, such as Microsoft Windows, OS/2, or the Macintosh where you must click the mouse in a window before that window gets focus. Also, usually under X, if your mouse cursor wanders from that window, focus will be lost and you'll no longer be able to type there.

Note, however, that it is possible to configure both twm and fvwm so that you must click on or in a window to gain focus, and click somewhere else to lose it. Either discover how your window manager is configured by trial and error, or consult local documentation.

5.3.3   Moving Windows

Another very configurable thing in X is how to move windows around. In my personal configuration of twm, there are three different ways of moving windows around. The most obvious method is to move the mouse cursor onto the **title bar** and drag the window around the screen. Unfortunately, this may be done with any of the left, right, or middle buttons[3]. (To drag, move the cursor above the title bar, and hold down on the buttons *while* moving the mouse.)

Another way of moving windows may be holding down a key while dragging the mouse. For instance, in *my* configuration, if I hold down the $\boxed{\text{Alt}}$ key, move the cursor above a window, I can drag the window around.

Again, you may be able to understand how the window manager is configured by trial and error, or by seeing local documentation. Additionally, if you want to try to interpret the window manager's configuration file, see Section 9.2.1 for twm or Section 9.2.2 for fvwm.

5.3.4   Depth

Since windows are allowed to overlap in X, there is a concept of **depth**. Even though the windows and the screen are both two dimensional, one window can be in front of another, partially or completely obscuring the rear window.

There are several operations that deal with depth:

- **Raising** the window, or bringing a window to the front. This is usually accomplished by clicking on a window's title bar with one of the buttons. Depending on how the window manager is configured, it could be any one of the buttons. (It is also possible that more then one button will do the job.)

- **Lowering** the window, or pushing the window to the back. This can generally be accomplished by a different click in the title bar. It is also possible to configure some window managers so that one click will bring the window foward if there is anything over it, while that same click will lower it when it is in the front.

- **Cycling** through windows is another operation many window managers allow. This brings each window to the front in an orderly cycle.

5.3.5   Iconization and Maximization

There are several other operations that can obscure windows or hide them completely. First is the idea of "iconization". Depending on the window manager, this can be done in many different ways. In twm, many people configure an **icon manager**. This is a special window that contains a list of all the other windows on the screen. If you click on a name (depending on the setup, it could be with any of the buttons!) the window disappears—it is iconified. The window is still active, but you can't see it. Another click in the icon manager restores the window to the screen.

---

[2]You can have more then one copy of xterm running at the same time!

[3]Many PCs have only two button mice. If this is the case for you, you should be able to emulate a middle button by using the left and right buttons simultaneously.

This is quite useful. For instance, you could have remote xterms to many different computers that you occansionally use. However, since you rarely use all of them at a given time, you can keep most of the xterm windows iconified while you work with a small subset. The only problem with this is it becomes easy to "lose" windows. It is also easy to create new windows that duplicate the functionality of iconified windows, since you forgot about the iconified windows.

Other window managers might create actual icons across the bottom of the screen, or might just leave icons littering across the root window.

Another operation most window managers support is maximization. In twm, for instance, you can maximize the height, the width, or both dimensions of a window. This is called "zooming" in twm's language although I prefer maximization since different applications respond differently to changes in their window size. (For instance, xterm won't make the font bigger, it will give you a larger workspace!)

Unfortunately, it is extremely non-standard on how to maximize windows.

5.3.6   Menus

Another purpose for window managers is for them to provide menus for the user to quickly accomplish tasks that are done over and over. For instance, I might make a menu choice that automatically launches Emacs, a powerful text editor, or an additional xterm for me. That way I don't need to type in an xterm—an especially good thing if there aren't any running xterms!

In general, different menus can be accessed by clicking on the root window, which is an immovable window behind all the other ones. By default, it is colored gray, but could look like anything. (There are programs that put fish in the background for you.) To try to see a menu, click and hold down a button on the desktop. A menu should pop up. To make a selection, move (without releasing the mouse button) the cursor over one of the items any then release the mouse button.

5.4   Starting and Stopping the X Window System

5.4.1   Starting X

Even if X doesn't start automatically when you login, it is possible to start it from the regular text-mode shell prompt. There are two possible commands that will start X, either startx or xinit. Try startx first. If the shell complains that no such command is found, try using xinit and see if X starts. If neither command works, you may not have X installed on your system—consult local documentation for your distribution.

5.4.2   Exiting X

One important menu entry should be "Exit Window Manager" or "Exit X" or some like entry. Try to find that entry (remember, there could be more than one menu—try different mouse buttons!) and choose it. If X was automatically started when you logged in, this should log you out. Simply login again to return. If you started X manually, this should return you to the text mode prompt.

5.5   X Programs

There are many programs that take advantage of X. Some programs, like emacs, can be run either as a text-mode program *or* as a program that creates its own X window. However, most X programs can only be run under X.

5.5.1 Geometry

There are a few things common to all programs running under X. In X, the concept of **geometry** is where and how large a window is.

5.5.2 Standard Options

Chapter 6

Working with Unix

```
better !pout !cry
better watchout
lpr why
santa claus <north pole >town

cat /etc/passwd >list
ncheck list
ncheck list
cat list | grep naughty >nogiftlist
cat list | grep nice >giftlist
santa claus <north pole > town

who | grep sleeping
who | grep awake
who | egrep 'bad|good'
for (goodness sake) {
        be good
}
```

Unix is a powerful system for those who know how to harness its power. In this chapter, I'll try to describe various ways to use Unix's shell, `bash`, more efficently.

6.1   Wildcards

In the previous chapter, you learned about the file maintence commands `cp`, `mv`, and `rm`. Occasionally, you want to deal with more than one file at once—in fact, you might want to deal with many files at once. For instance, you might want to copy all the files beginning with `data` into a directory called `~/backup`. You could do this by either running many `cp` commands, or you could list every file on one command line. Both of these methods would take a long time, however, and you have a large chance of making an error.

A better way of doing that task is to type:

```
/home/larry/report# ls -F
1993-1          1994-1          data1           data5
1993-2          data-new        data2
/home/larry/report# mkdir ~/backup
/home/larry/report# cp data* ~/backup
/home/larry/report# ls -F ~/backup
data-new        data1           data2           data5
/home/larry/report#
```

As you can see, the asterisk told cp to take all of the files beginning with data and copy them to ~/backup. Can you guess what cp d*w ~/backup would have done?

6.1.1 What *Really* Happens?

Good question. Actually, there are a couple of special characters intercepted by the shell, bash. The character "*", an asterisk, says "replace this word with all the files that will fit this specification". So, the command cp data* ~/backup, like the one above, gets changed to cp data-new data1 data2 data5 ~/backup before it gets run.

To illustrate this, let me introduce a new command, echo. echo is an extremely simple command; it echoes back, or prints out, any parameters. Thus:

```
/home/larry# echo Hello!
Hello!
/home/larry# echo How are you?
How are you?
/home/larry# cd report
/home/larry/report# ls -F
1993-1          1994-1          data1          data5
1993-2          data-new        data2
/home/larry/report# echo 199*
1993-1 1993-2 1994-1
/home/larry/report# echo *4*
1994-1
/home/larry/report# echo *2*
1993-2 data2
/home/larry/report#
```

As you can see, the shell expands the wildcard and passes all of the files to the program you tell it to run. This raises an interesting question: what happens if there are *no* files that meet the wildcard specification? Try echo /rc/fr*og and see what happens. . . bash will pass the wildcard specification verbatim to the program.

One word about that, though. Other shells, like tcsh, will, instead of just passing the wildcard verbatim, will reply No match.

```
mousehouse>echo /rc/fr*og
echo: No match.
mousehouse>
```

The last question you might want to know is what if I wanted to have data* echoed back at me, instead of the list of file names? Well, under both bash and tcsh, just include the string in quotes:

```
/home/larry/report# echo "data*"          mousehouse>echo "data*"
data*                             OR        data*
/home/larry/report#                         mousehouse>
```

6.1.2 The Question Mark

In addition to the asterisk, the shell also interprets a question mark as a special character. A question mark will match one, and only one character. For instance, ls /etc/?? will display all two letter files in the the /etc directory.

6.2 Time Saving with bash

6.2.1 Command-Line Editing

Occasionally, you've typed a long command to bash and, before you hit return, notice that there was a spelling mistake early in the line. You could just delete all the way back and retype everything you need to, but that takes much too much effort! Instead, you can use the arrow keys to move back there, delete the bad character or two, and type the correct information.

There are many special keys to help you edit your command line, most of them similar to the commands used in GNU Emacs. For instance, C-t flips two adjacent characters.[1] You'll be able to find most of the commands in the chapter on Emacs, Chapter 8.

6.2.2 Command and File Completion

Another feature of bash is automatic completion of your command lines. For instance, let's look at the following example of a typical cp command:

```
/home/larry# ls -F
this-is-a-long-file
/home/larry# cp this-is-a-long-file shorter
/home/larry# ls -F
shorter             this-is-a-long-file
/home/larry#
```

It's a big pain to have to type every letter of this-is-a-long-file whenever you try to access it. So, create this-is-a-long-file by copying /etc/rc to it[2]. Now, we're going to do the above cp command very quickly and with a smaller chance of mistyping.

Instead of typing the whole filename, type cp th and press and release the Tab. Like magic, the rest of the filename shows up on the command line, and you can type in shorter. Unfortunately, bash cannot read your thoughts, and you'll have to type all of shorter.

When you type Tab, bash looks at what you've typed and looks for a file that starts like that. For instance, if I type /usr/bin/ema and then hit Tab, bash will find /usr/bin/emacs since that's the only file that begins /usr/bin/ema on my system. However, if I type /usr/bin/ld and hit Tab, bash beeps at me. That's because three files, /usr/bin/ld, /usr/bin/ldd, and /usr/bin/ld86 start /usr/bin/ld on my system.

If you try a completion and bash beeps, you can immediately hit Tab again to get a list of all the files your start matches so far. That way, if you aren't sure of the exact spelling of your file, you can start it and scan a much smaller list of files.

6.3 The Standard Input and The Standard Output

Let's try to tackle a simple problem: getting a listing of the /usr/bin directory. If all we do is ls /usr/bin, some of the files scroll off the top of the screen. How can we see all of the files?

6.3.1 Unix Concepts

The Unix operating system makes it very easy for programs to use the terminal. When a program writes something to your screen, it is using something called **standard output**. Standard output, abbreviated

---

[1] C-t means hold down the key labeled "Ctrl", then press the "t" key. Then release the "Ctrl" key.
[2] cp /etc/rc this-is-a-long-file

as stdout, is how the program writes things to a user. The name for what you tell a program is **standard input** (stdin). It's possible for a program to communicate with the user without using standard input or output, but very rare—all of the commands we have covered so far use stdin and stdout.

For example, the `ls` command prints the list of the directories to standard output, which is normally "connected" to your terminal. An interactive command, such as your shell, `bash`, reads your commands from standard input.

It is also possible for a program to write to **standard error**, since it is very easy to make standard output point somewhere besides your terminal. Standard error, stderr, is almost always connected to a terminal so an actual human will read the message.

In this section, we're going to examine three ways of fiddling with the standard input and output: input redirection, output redirection, and pipes.

6.3.2 Output Redirection

A very important feature of Unix is the ability to **redirect** output. This allows you, instead of viewing the results of a command, to save it in a file or send it directly to a printer. For instance, to redirect the output of the command `ls /usr/bin`, we place a > sign at the end of the line, and say what file we want the output to be put in:

```
/home/larry# ls
/home/larry# ls -F /usr/bin > listing
/home/larry# ls
listing
/home/larry#
```

As you can see, instead of writing the names of all the files, the command created a totally new file in your home directory. Let's try to take a look at this file using the command `cat`. If you think back, you'll remember `cat` was a fairly useless command that copied what you typed (the standard input) to the terminal (the standard output). `cat` can also print a file to the standard output if you list the file as a parameter to `cat`:

```
/home/larry# cat listing
...
/home/larry#
```

The exact output of the command `ls /usr/bin` appeared in the contents of `listing`. All well and good, although it didn't solve the original problem.[3]

However, `cat` does do some interesting things when it's output is redirected. What does the command `cat listing > newfile` do? Normally, the > `newfile` says "take all the output of the command and put it in `newfile`." The output of the command `cat listing` is the file `listing`. So we've invented a new (and not so efficent) method of copying files.

How about the command `cat > fox`? `cat` by itself reads in each line typed at the terminal (standard input) and prints it right back out (standard output) until it reads Ctrl-d . In this case, standard output has been redirected into the file `fox`. Now `cat` is serving as a rudimentary editor:

```
/home/larry# cat > fox
The quick brown fox jumps over the lazy dog.
press Ctrl-d
```

We've now created the file `fox` that contains the sentence "The quick brown fox jumps over the lazy dog." One last use of the versitile `cat` command is to concatenate files together. `cat` will print out

---

[3]For impatient readers, the command you might want to try is `more`. However, there's still a bit more to talk about before we get there.

every file it was given as a parameter, one after another. So the command `cat listing fox` will print out the directory listing of `/usr/bin`, and then it will print out our silly sentence. Thus, the command `cat listing fox > listandfox` will create a new file containing the contents of both `listing` and `fox`.

6.3.3 Input Redirection

Like redirecting standard output, it is also possible to redirect standard input. Instead of a program reading from your keyboard, it will read from a file. Since input redirection is related to output redirection, it seems natural to make the special character for input redirection be `<`. It too, is used after the command you wish to run.

This is generally useful if you have a data file and a command that expects input from standard input. Most commands also let you specify a file to operate on, so `<` isn't used as much in day-to-day operations as other techniques.

6.3.4 Solution: The Pipe

Many Unix commands produce a large amount of information. For instance, it is not uncommon for a command like `ls /usr/bin` to produce more output than you can see on your screen. In order for you to be able to see all of the information that a command like `ls /usr/bin`, it's necessary to use another Unix command, called `more`.[4] `more` will pause once every screenful of information. For instance, `move < /etc/rc` will display the file `/etc/rc` just like `cat /etc/rc` would, except that `more` will let you read it.[5]

However, that doesn't help the problem that `ls /usr/bin` displays more information than you can see. `more < ls /usr/bin` won't work—input redirection only works with files, not commands! You *could* do this:

```
/home/larry# ls /usr/bin > temp-ls
/home/larry# more temp-ls
...
/home/larry# rm temp-ls
```

However, Unix supplies a much cleaner way of doing that. You can just use the command `ls /usr/bin | more`. The character "`|`" indicates a **pipe**. Like a water pipe, a Unix pipe controls flow. Instead of water, we're controlling the flow of information!

A useful tool with pipes are programs called **filters**. A filter is a program that reads the standard input, changes it in some way, and outputs to standard output. `more` is a filter—it reads the data that it gets from standard input and displays it to standard output one screen at a time, letting you read the file.

Other filters include the programs `cat`, `sort`, `head`, and `tail`. For instance, if you wanted to read only the first ten lines of the output from `ls`, you could use `ls /usr/bin | head`.

6.4 Multitasking

6.4.1 The Basics

Job control refers to the ability to put processes (another word for programs, essentially) in the background and bring them to the foreground again. That is to say, you want to be able to make

---

[4]`more` is named because that's the prompt it originally displayed: `--more--`. In many versions of LINUX the `more` command is identical to a more advanced command that does all that `more` can do and more. Its name? `less`, of course!

[5]`more` also allows the command `more /etc/rc`.

something run while you go and do other things, but have it be there again when you want to tell it something or stop it. In Unix, the main tool for job control is the shell—it will keep track of jobs for you, if you learn how to speak its language.

The two most important words in that language are fg, for "foreground", and bg, for "background". To find out how they work, use the command yes at a prompt.

```
/home/larry# yes
```

This will have the startling effect of running a long column of y's down the left hand side of your screen, faster than you can follow. (There are good reasons for this strange command to exist, but we won't go into them now). To get them to stop, you'd normally type ctrl-C to kill it, but instead you should type ctrl-Z this time. It appears to have stopped, but there will be a message before your prompt, looking more or less like this:

```
[1]+  Stopped                 yes
```

It means that the process yes has been *suspended* in the background. You can get it running again by typing fg at the prompt, which will put it into the foreground again. If you wish, you can do other things first, while it's suspended. Try a few ls's or something before you put it back in the foreground.

Once it's returned to the foreground, the y's will start coming again, as fast as before. You do not need to worry that while you had it suspended it was "storing up" more y's to send to the screen: when a program is suspended the whole program doesn't run until you bring it back to life. (And you can type ctrl-C to kill it for good, once you've seen enough).

Let's pick apart that message we got from the shell:

```
[1]+  Stopped                 yes
```

The number in brackets is the **job number** of this job, and will be used when we need to refer to it specifically. (Naturally, since job control is all about running multiple processes, we need some way to tell one from another). The + following it tells us that this is the "current job" — that is, the one most recently moved from the foreground to the background. If you were to type fg, you would put the job with the + in the foreground again. (More on that later, when we discuss running multiple jobs at once). The word Stopped means that the job is "stopped". The job isn't dead, but it isn't running right now. Linux has saved it in a special suspended state, ready to jump back into the action should anyone request it. Finally, the yes is the name that was typed on the command line to start the program.

Before we go on, let's kill this job and start it again in a different way. The command is named kill and can be used in the following way:

```
/home/larry# kill %1
[1]+  Stopped                 yes
```

That message about it being "stopped" again is misleading. To find out whether it's still alive (that is, either running or frozen in a suspended state), type jobs:

```
/home/larry# jobs
[1]+  Terminated              yes
```

There you have it—the job has been terminated! (It's possible that the jobs command showed nothing at all, which just means that there are no jobs running in the background. If you just killed a job, and typing jobs shows nothing, then you know the kill was successful. Usually it will tell you the job was "terminated".)

Now, start yes running again, like this:

```
/home/larry# yes > /dev/null
```

If you read the section about input and output redirection, you know that this is sending the output of yes into the special file /dev/null. /dev/null is a black hole that eats any output sent to it (you can imagine that stream of y's coming out the back of your computer and drilling a hole in the wall, if that makes you happy).

After typing this, you will not get your prompt back, but you will not see that column of y's either. Although output is being sent into /dev/null, the job is still running in the foreground. As usual, you can suspend it by hitting ctrl-Z. Do that now to get the prompt back.

```
/home/larry# yes > /dev/null
["yes" is running, and if we type ctrl-z right now, we'll suspend
 it and get the prompt back.  Imagine that I just did that...]
[1]+  Stopped                 yes >/dev/null

/home/larry#
```

Hmm...is there any way to get it to actually *run* in the background, while still leaving us the prompt for interactive work? Of course there is, otherwise I wouldn't have asked. The command to do that is **bg**:

```
/home/larry# bg
[1]+ yes >/dev/null &
/home/larry#
```

Now, you'll have to trust me on this one: after you typed bg, yes > /dev/null began to run again, but this time in the background. In fact, if you do things at the prompt, like ls and stuff, you might notice that your machine has been slowed down a little bit (piping a steady stream of single letters out the back of the machine does take some work, after all!) Other than that, however, there are no effects. You can do anything you want at the prompt, and yes will happily continue to sending its output into the black hole.

There are now two different ways you can kill it: with the kill command you just learned, or by putting the job in the foreground again and hitting it with an interrupt (ctrl-C). Let's try the second way, just to understand the relationship between fg and bg a little better;

```
/home/larry# fg
yes >/dev/null

[now it's in the foreground again.  Imagine that I hit ctrl-C
to terminate it]

/home/larry#
```

There, it's gone. Now, start up a few jobs running in simultaneously, like this:

```
/home/larry# yes  > /dev/null &
[1] 1024
/home/larry# yes | sort > /dev/null &
[2] 1026
/home/larry# yes | uniq > /dev/null
[and here, type ctrl-Z to suspend it, please]

[3]+  Stopped                 yes | uniq >/dev/null
```

The first thing you might notice about those commands is the trailing & at the end of the first two. Putting an & after a command tells the shell to start in running in the background right from the very beginning. (It's just a way to avoid having to start the program, type ctrl-Z, and then type bg.) So, we started those two commands running in the background. The third is suspended and inactive at the moment. You may notice that the machine has become slower now, as the two running ones require significant amounts of CPU time.

Each one told you it's job number. The first two also showed you their **Process IDentification numbers**, or PID's, immediately following the job number. The PID's are normally not something you need to know, but occasionally come in handy.

Let's kill the second one, since I think it's making your machine slow. You could just type `kill %2`, but that would be too easy. Instead, do this:

```
/home/larry # fg %2
[and then hit ctrl-C to kill it]
```

As this demonstrates, `fg` takes parameters beginning with % as well. In fact, you could just have typed this:

```
/home/larry # %2
[and then hit ctrl-C to kill it]
```

This works because the shell automatically interprets a job number as a request to put that job in the foreground. It can tell job numbers from other numbers by the preceding %. Now type `jobs` to see which jobs are left running:

```
/home/larry # jobs
[1]-  Running                yes >/dev/null  &
[3]+  Stopped                yes | uniq >/dev/null
```

That pretty much says it all. The - means that job number 1 is second in line to be put in the foreground, if you just type `fg` without giving it any parameters. However, you can get to it by naming it, if you wish:

```
/home/larry # fg %1
yes >/dev/null
[now type ctrl-Z to suspend it]

[1]+  Stopped                yes >/dev/null
```

Having changed to job number 1 and then suspending it has also changed the priorities of all your jobs. You can see this with the `jobs` command:

```
/home/larry # jobs
[1]+  Stopped                yes >/dev/null
[3]-  Stopped                yes | uniq >/dev/null
```

Now they are both stopped (because both were suspended with ctrl-Z), and number 1 is next in line to come to the foreground by default. This is because you put it in the foreground manually, and then suspended it. The + always refers to the most recent job that was suspended from the foreground. You can start it running again:

```
/home/larry # bg
[1]+ yes >/dev/null  &
/home/larry# jobs
[1]-  Running                yes >/dev/null
[3]+  Stopped                yes | uniq >/dev/null
```

Notice that now it is running, and the other job has moved back up in line and has the +.

Well, enough of that. Kill them all so you can get your machine back:

```
/home/larry# kill %1
/home/larry# kill %3
```

You should see various messages about termination of jobs – nothing dies quietly, it seems. To summarize what you should know about job control now:

ctrl-z | DOS equiv.: Hah! DOS doesn't have real job control. . .

This key combination usually causes a program to suspend, although a few programs ignore it. Once suspended, the job can be run in the background or killed.

Parameters: none — it's not really a command, just a signal.

fg | DOS equiv.: none whatsoever. Maybe someday. . .

This is a shell-builtin command that returns a job to the foreground. To find out which one this is by default, type `jobs` and look for the one with the +.

Parameters: job number (optional – defaults to the one with +).

& | When an `&` is added to the end of the command line, it tells the command to run in the background automatically. This job is then subject to all the usual methods of job control detailed here.

bg | This is a shell-builtin command that causes a suspended job to run in the background. To find out which one this is by default, type `jobs` and look for the one with the +. One way to think of bg is that it's really just `fg &`!

Parameters: job number (optional – defaults to the one with +).

kill | This is a shell-builtin command that causes a background job, either suspended or running, to terminate. You should always specify the job number or PID, and if you are using job numbers, remember to precede them with a %.

Parameters: job number (preceded by %) or PID (no % necessary).

jobs | This shell command just lists information about the jobs currently running or suspending. Sometimes it also tells you about ones that have just exited or been terminated.

ctrl-c | This is the generic interrupt character. Usually, if you type it while a program is running in the foreground, it will kill the program (sometimes it takes a few tries). However, not all programs will respond to this method of termination.

6.4.2 What Is Really Going On Here?

It is important to understand that job control is done by the shell. There is no program on the system called fg; rather, fg, bg, &, jobs, and kill are all shell-builtins (actually, sometimes kill is an independent program, but the bash shell used by Linux has it built in). This is a logical way to do it: since each user wants their own job control space, and each user already has their own shell, it is easiest to just have the shell keep track of the user's jobs. Therefore, each user's job numbers are meaningful only to that user: my job number [1] and your job number [1] are probably two totally different processes. In fact, if you are logged in more than once, each of your shells will have unique job control data, so you as a user might have two different jobs with the same number running in two different shells.

The way to tell for sure is to use the Process ID numbers (PID's). These are system-wide — each process has its own unique PID number. Two different users can refer to a process by its PID and know that they are talking about the same process (assuming that they are logged into the same machine!)

Let's take a look at one more command to understand what PIDs are. The ps command will list all running processes, including your shell. Try it out. It also has a few options, the most important of which (to many people) are a, u, and x. The a option will list processes belonging to any user, not just your own. The x switch will list processes that don't have a terminal associated with them.[6] Finally, the u switch will give additionally information about the process that is frequently useful.

To really get an idea of what your system is doing, put them all together: ps -aux. You can then see the process that uses the more memory by looking at the %MEM column, and the most CPU by looking at the %CPU column. (The TIME column lists the *total* amount of CPU time used.)

---

[6]This only makes sense for certain system programs that don't have to talk to users through a keyboard.

Another quick note about PIDs. `kill`, in addition to taking options of the form *%job#*, will take options of raw PIDs. So, put a `yes > /dev/null` in the background, run `ps`, and look for `yes`. Then type `kill PID`.[7]

If you start to program in C on your Linux system, you will soon learn that the shell's job control is just an interactive version of the function calls `fork` and `execl`. This is too complex to go into here, but may be helpful to remember later on when you are programming and want to run multiple processes from a single program.

6.5 Virtual Consoles: Being in Many Places at Once

Linux supports **virtual consoles**. These are a way of making your single machine seem like multiple terminals, all connected to one Linux kernel. Thankfully, using virtual consoles is one of the simplest things about Linux: there are "hot keys" for switching among the consoles quickly. To try it, log in to your Linux system, hold down the left `Alt` key, and press `F2` (that is, the function key number 2).[8]

You should find yourself at another login prompt. Don't panic: you are now on virtual console (VC) number 2! Log in here and do some things — a few `ls`'s or whatever — to confirm that this is a real login shell. Now you can return to VC number 1, by holding down the left `Alt` and pressing `F1`. Or you can move on to a *third* VC, in the obvious way (`Alt`-`F3`).

Linux systems generally come with four VC's enabled by default. You can increase this all the way to eight; this should be covered in *The* LINUX *System Adminstrator's Guide*. It involves editing a file in `/etc` or two. However, four should be enough for most people.

Once you get used to them, VC's will probably become an indispensable tool for getting many things done at once. For example, I typically run Emacs on VC 1 (and do most of my work there), while having a communications program up on VC 3 (so I can be downloading or uploading files by modem while I work, or running jobs on remote machines), and keep a shell up on VC 2 just in case I want to run something else without tying up VC 1.

---

[7] In general, it's easier to just kill the job number instead of using PIDs.

[8] Make sure you are doing this from text consoles: if you are running X windows or some other graphical application, it probably won't work, although rumor has it that X Windows will soon allow virtual console switching under Linux.

Chapter 7

Powerful Little Programs

7.1 The Power of Unix

The power of Unix is hidden in small commands that don't seem too useful when used alone, but when combined with other commands (either directly or indirectly) produce a system that's much more powerful and flexible than most other operating systems. The commands I'm going to talk about in this chapter include sort, grep, more, cat, wc, spell, diff, head, and tail. Unfortunately, it isn't totally intuitive what these names mean right now.

Let's cover what each of these utilities do separately and then I'll give some examples of how to use them together.[1]

7.2 Operating on Files

In addition to the commands like cd, mv, and rm you learned in Chapter 4, there are other commands that just operate on files but not the data in them. These include touch, chmod, du, and df. All of these files don't care what is *in* the file—the merely change some of the things Unix remembers about the file.

Some of the things these commands manipulate:

- The time stamp. Each file has three dates associated with it.[2] The three dates are the creation time (when the file was created), the last modification time (when the file was last changed), and the last access time (when the file was last read).

- The owner. Every file in Unix is owned by one user or the other.

- The group. Every file also has a group of users it is associated with. The most common group for user files is called users, which is usually shared by all the user account on the system.

- The permissions. Every file has permissions (sometimes called "privileges") associated with it which tell Unix who can access what file, or change it, or, in the case of programs, execute it. Each of these permissions can be toggled separately for the owner, the group, and all other users.

    touch *file1 file2 . . . fileN*

---

[1] Please note that the short summaries on commands in this chapter are not comprehensive. Please consult the command's manpage if you want to know every option.

[2] Older filesystems in LINUX only stored one date, since they were derived from Minix. If you have one of these filesystems, some of the information will merely be unavailable—operation will be mostly unchanged.

touch will update the time stamps of the files listed on the command line to the current time. If a file doesn't exist, touch will create it. It is also possible to specify the time that touch will set files to—consult the the manpage for touch.

chmod [-Rfv] *mode file1 file2 . . . fileN*

The command used to change the permissions on a file is called chmod, short for **change mod**e. Before I go into how to use the command, let's discuss what permissions are in Unix. Each file has a group of permissions associated with it. These permissions tell Unix whether or not the file can be read from, written to, or executed as a program. (In the next few paragraphs, I'll talk about users doing these things. Naturally, any programs a user runs are allowed to do the same things a user is. This can be a security problem if you don't know what a particular program does.)

However, Unix recognizes three different people: first, the owner of the file (and the person allowed to use chmod on that file). The group of most of your files might be "users", meaning the normal users of the system. (To find out the group of a particular file, use ls -l *file*.) Then, there's everybody else who isn't the owner and isn't a member of the group.

So, a file could have read and write permissions for the owner, read permissions for the group, and no permissions for all others. Or, for some reason, a file could have read/write permissions for the group and others, but *no* permissions for the owner!

Let's try using chmod to change a few permissions. First, create a new file using cat, emacs, or any other program. By default, you'll be able to read and write this file. (The permissions given other people will vary depending on how the system and your account is setup.) Make sure you can read the file using cat. Now, let's take away your read privilege by using chmod u-r *filename*. (The parameter u-r decodes to "user minus read".) Now if you try to read the file, you get a Permission denied error! Add read privileges back by using chmod u+r *filename*.

Directory permissions use the same three ideas: read, write, and execute, but act slightly differently. The read privilege allows the user (or group or others) to read the directory—list the names of the files. The write permission allows the user (or group or others) to add or remove files. The execute permission allows the user to access files in the directory or any subdirectories. (If a user doesn't have execute permissions for a directory, they can't even cd to it!)

To use chmod, replace the *mode* with what to operate on, either **u**ser, **g**roup, **o**ther, or **a**ll, and what to do with them. (That is, use a plus sign to indicate adding a privilege or a minus sign to indicate taking one away. Or, an equals sign will specify the exact permissions.) The possible permissions to add are **r**ead, **w**rite, and e**x**ecute.

chmod's R flag will change a directory's permissions, and all files in that directory, and all subdirecties, all the way down the line. (The 'R' stands for recursive.) The f flag forces chmod to attempt to change permissions, even if the user isn't the owner of the file. (If chmod is given the f flag, it won't print an error message when it fails to change a file's permissions.) The v flag makes chmod verbose—it will report on what it's done.

7.3 System Statistics

Commands in this section will display statistics about the operating system, or a part of the operating system.

du [-abs] [*path1 path2 . . . pathN*]

du stands for **d**isk **u**sage. It will count the amount of disk space a given directory *and all its subdirectories* take up on the disk. du by itself will return a list of how much space every subdirectory of the current directory consumes, and, at the very bottom, how much space the current directory (plus all the previously counted subdirectories) use. If you give it an option parameter or two, it will count the amount of space used by those files or directories instead of the current one.

The a flag will display a count for files, as well as directories. An option of b will display, instead of kilobytes (1024 characters), the total in bytes. One byte is the equivalent of one letter in a text document. And the s flag will just display the directories mentioned on the command-line and *not* their subdirectories.

df

df is short for something, although this author isn't quite sure what.[3] df summarizes the amount of disk space in use. For each filesystem (remember, different filesystems are either on different drives or partitions) it shows the total amount of disk space, the amount used, the amount available, and the total capacity of the filesystem that's used.

One odd thing you might encounter is that it's possible for the capacity to go over 100%, or the used plus the available not to equal the total. This is because Unix reserves some space on each filesystem only for root. That way, if a user accidentally fills the disk, the system will still have a little room to keep on operating.

For most people, df doesn't have any useful options.

uptime

The uptime program does exactly what one would suspect. It prints the amount of time the system has been "up"—the amount of time from the last Unix boot.

uptime also gives the current time and the load average. The load average is the average number of jobs waiting to run in a certain time period. uptime displays the load average for the last minute, five minutes, and ten minutes. A load average near zero indicates the system has been relatively idle. A load average near one indicates that the system has been almost fully utilized but nowhere near overtaxed. High load averages are the result of several programs being run simultaneously.

Amazingly, uptime is one of the few Unix programs that have *no* options!

who

who displays the current users of the system and when they logged in. If given the parameters am i (as in: who am i), it displays the current user.

w [-f] [*username*]

The w program displays the current users of the system and what they're doing. (It basically combines the functionality of uptime and who. The header of w is exactly the same as uptime, and each line shows a user, when the logged on (and how long they've been idle). JCPU is the total amount of CPU time used by that user, while PCPU the the total amount of CPU time used by their present task.

If w is given the option f, it shows the remote system they logged in from, if any. The optional parameter restricts w to showing only the named user.

7.4 What's in the File?

There are two major commands used in Unix for listing files, cat and more. I've talked about both of them in Chapter 6.

cat [-nA] [*file1 file2 ... fileN*]

---

[3]One cancelled US stamp to the first person who tells me what is does stand for!

`cat` is not a user friendly command—it doesn't wait for you to read the file, and is mostly used in conjuction with pipes. However, `cat` does have some useful command-line options. For instance, n will number all the lines in the file, and A will show control characters as normal characters instead of (possibly) doing strange things to your screen. (Remember, to see some of the stranger and perhaps "less useful" options, use the man command: man cat.) `cat` will accept input from stdin if no files are specified on the command-line.

`more` [-l] [+*linenumber*] [*file1 file2 . . . fileN*]

`more` is much more useful, and is the command that you'll want to use when browsing ASCII text files. The only interesting option is l, which will tell `more` that you aren't interested in treating the character Ctrl-L as a "new page" character. `more` will start on a specified linenumber.

Since `more` is an interactive command, I've summarized the major interactive commands below:

Spacebar — Moves to the next screen of text.

d — This will scroll the screen by 11 lines, or about half a normal, 25-line, screen.

/ — Searches for a regular expression. While a regular expression can be quite complicated, you can just type in a text string to search for. For example, /toad return would search for the next occurrence of "toad" in your current file. A slash followed by a return will search for the next occurrence of what you last searched for.

n — This will also search for the next occurrence of your regular expression.

: n — If you specified more than one file on the command line, this will move to the next file.

: p — This will move the the previous file.

q — Exits from `more`.

`head` [-*lines*] [*file1 file2 . . . fileN*]

`head` will display the first ten lines in the listed files, or the first ten lines of stdin if no files are specified on the command line. Any numeric option will be taken as the number of lines to print, so head -15 frog will print the first fifteen lines of the file `frog`.

`tail` [-*lines*] [*file1 file2 . . . fileN*]

Like `head`, `tail` will display only a fraction of the file. Naturally, `tail` will display the end of the file, or the last ten lines that come through stdin. `tail` also accepts an option specifying the number of lines.

`file` [*file1 file2 . . . fileN*]

The `file` command attempts to identify what format a particular file is written in. Since not all files have extentions or other easy to identify marks, the `file` command performs some rudimentary checks to try and figure out exactly what it contains.

Be careful, though, because it is quite possible for `file` to make a wrong identification.

7.5 Information Commands

This section discusses the commands that will alter a file, perform a certain operation on the file, or display statistics on the file.

grep [-nvwx] [-*number*] *expression* [*file1 file2 . . . fileN*]

One of the most useful commands in Unix is grep, the generalized regular expression parser. This is a fancy name for a utility which can only search a text file. The easiest way to use grep is like this:

```
/home/larry# cat animals
Animals are very interesting creatures. One of my favorite animals is
the tiger, a fearsome beast with large teeth.
I also like the lion---it's really neat!
/home/larry# grep iger animals
the tiger, a fearsome beast with large teeth.
/home/larry#
```

One disadvantage of this is, although it shows you all the lines containing your word, it doesn't tell you where to look in the file—no line number. Depending on what you're doing, this might be fine. For instance, if you're looking for errors from a programs output, you might try a.out | grep error, where a.out is your program's name.

If you're interested in where the match(es) are, use the n switch to grep to tell it to print line numbers. Use the v switch if you want to see all the lines that *don't* match the specified expression.

Another feature of grep is that it matches only parts of a word, like my example above where iger matched tiger. To tell grep to only match whole words, use the w, and the x switch will tell grep to only match whole lines.

Remember, if you don't specify any files, grep will examine stdin.

wc [-clw] [*file1 file2 . . . fileN*]

wc stands for **w**ord **c**ount. It simply counts the number of words, lines, and characters in the file(s). If there aren't any files specified on the command line, it operates on stdin.

The three parameters, clw, stand for **c**haracter, **l**ine, and **w**ord respectively, and tell wc which of the three to count. Thus, wc -cw will count the number of characters and words, but not the number of lines. wc defaults to counting everything—words, lines, and characters.

One nice use of wc is to find how many files are in the present directory: ls | wc -w. If you wanted to see how many files that ended with .c there were, try ls *.c | wc -w.

spell [*file1 file2 . . . fileN*]

spell is a very simple Unix spelling program, usually for American English.[4] spell is a filter, like most of the other programs we've talked about, which sucks in an ASCII text file and outputs all the words it considers misspellings. spell operates on the files listed in the command line, or, if there weren't any there, stdin.

A more sophisticated spelling program, ispell is probably also available on your machine. ispell will offer possible correct spellings and a fancy menu interface if a filename is specified on the command line or will run as a filter-like program if no files are specified.

While operation of ispell should be fairly obvious, consult the man page if you need more help.

---

[4]While there are versions of this for several other European languages, the copy on your LINUX machine is most likely for American English and only American English. Sorry.

cmp *file1* [*file2*]

cmp **comp**ares two files. The first must be listed on the command line, while the second is either listed as the second parameter or is read in from standard input. cmp is very simple, and merely tells you where the two files first differ.

diff *file1* *file2*

One of the most complicated standard Unix commands is called diff. The GNU version of diff has over twenty command line options! It is a much more powerful version of cmp and shows you what the differences are instead of merely telling you where the first one is.

Since talking about even a good portion of diff is beyond the scope of this book, I'll just talk about the basic operation of diff. In short, diff takes two parameters and displays the differences between them on a line-by-line basis. For instance:

```
/home/larry# cat frog
Animals are very interesting creatures. One of my favorite animals is
the tiger, a fearsome beast with large teeth.
I also like the lion---it's really neat!
/home/larry# cp frog toad
/home/larry# diff frog toad
/home/larry# cat dog
Animals are very nteresting creatures. One of my favorite animals is

the tiger, a fearsome beast with large teeth.
I also   like the lion---it's really neat!
/home/larry# diff frog dog
1c1,2
< Animals are very interesting creatures. One of my favorite animals is
---
> Animals are very nteresting creatures. One of my favorite animals is
>
3c4
< I also like the lion---it's really neat!
---
> I also   like the lion---it's really neat!
/home/larry#
```

As you can see, diff outputs nothing when the two files are identical. Then, when I compared two different files, it had a section header, 1c1,2 saying it was comparing line 1 of the left file, frog, to lines 1–2 of dog and what differences it noticed. Then it compared line 3 of frog to line 4 of dog. While it may seem strange at first to compare different line numbers, it is much more efficient then listing out every single line if there is an extra return early in one file.

Chapter 8

Editing files with Emacs

FUNNY SOMETHING OR OTHER

8.1 What's Emacs?

In order to get anything done on a computer, you need a way to put text into files, and a way to change text that's already in files. An **editor** is a program for doing this. Emacs is one of the most popular editors around—partly because it's very easy for a complete beginner to get actual work done with it. (The classic Unix editor, vi, is covered in Appendix C.)

To learn emacs, you need to find a file of plain text (letters, numbers, and the like), copy it to your home directory[1] (we don't want to modify the actual file, if it contains important information), and invoke Emacs on the file:

```
/home/larry# emacs README
```

(Of course, if you decided to copy /etc/rc, /etc/inittab, or any other file, substitute that file name for README. For instance, if you cp /etc/rc ~/rc, then emacs rc.)

 "Invoking" Emacs can have different effects depending on where where you do it. From a plain console displaying only text characters, Emacs will just take over the whole console. If you invoke it from X, Emacs will actually bring up its own window. I will assume that you are doing it from a text console, but everything carries over logically into the X Windows version—just substitute the word "window" in the places I've written "screen". Also, remember that you have to move the mouse pointer into Emacs's window to type in it!

Your screen (or window, if you're using X) should now resemble Figure 8.1. Most of the screen contains your text document, but the last two lines are especially interesting if you're trying to learn Emacs. The second-to-last line (the one with the long string of dashes) is called the **mode line**.

---

[1] For instance, cp /usr/src/linux/README ./README

```
          Linux kernel release 1.0

These are the release notes for linux version 1.0.  Read them carefully,
as they tell you what this is all about, explain how to install the
kernel, and what to do if something goes wrong.

WHAT IS LINUX?

   Linux is a Unix clone for 386/486-based PCs written from scratch by
   Linus Torvalds with assistance from a loosely-knit team of hackers
   across the Net.  It aims towards POSIX compliance.

   It has all the features you would expect in a modern fully-fledged
   Unix, including true multitasking, virtual memory, shared libraries,
   demand loading, shared copy-on-write executables, proper memory
   management and TCP/IP networking.

   It is distributed under the GNU General Public License - see the
   accompanying COPYING file for more details.

INSTALLING the kernel:
-----Emacs: README          (Fundamental)--Top-----------------------------
```

Figure 8.1: Emacs was just started with emacs README

In my mode line, you see "Top". It might be "All" instead, and there may be other minor differences. (Many people have the current time displayed in the mode line.) The line immediately below the mode line is called the **minibuffer**, or sometimes the **echo area**. Emacs uses the minibuffer to flash messages at you, and occasionally uses it to read input from you, when necessary. In fact, right now Emacs is telling you "For information about the GNU Project and its goals, type C-h C-p." Ignore it for now; we won't be making much use of the minibuffer for a while.

Before you actually change any of the text in the file, you need to learn how to move around. The cursor should be at the beginning of the file, in the upper-left corner of the screen. To move forward, type C-f (that is, hold down the Control key while you press "f", for "forward"). It will move you forward a character at a time, and if you hold both keys down, your system's automatic key-repeat should take effect in a half-second or so. Notice how when you get to the end of the line, the cursor automatically moves to the next line. C-b (for "backward") has the opposite behavior. And, while we're at it, C-n and C-p take you to the next and previous lines, respectively.[2]

Using the control keys is usually the quickest way of moving around when you're editing. The goal of Emacs is to keep your hands over the alpha-numeric keys of the keyboard, where most of your work gets done. However, if you want to, the arrow keys should also work.

X   In fact, when you're using X, you should be able to position the mouse pointer and click with the left button to move the cursor where you want. However, this is very slow—you have to move your hand all the way to your mouse! Most people who use Emacs primarily use the keyboard for getting around.

Use C-p and C-b to get all the way back to the upper-left corner. Now keep C-b held a little longer. You should hear an annoying bell sound, and see the message "Beginning of buffer" appear in the minibuffer. At this point you might wonder, "But what is a buffer?"

When Emacs works on a file, it doesn't actually work on the file itself. Instead, it copies the contents of the file into a special Emacs work area called a **buffer**, where you can modify it to your heart's content. When you are done working, you tell Emacs to save the buffer—in other words, to write the buffer's contents into the corresponding file. Until you do this, the file remains unchanged, and the buffer's contents exist only inside of Emacs.

With that in mind, prepare to insert your first character into the buffer. Until now, everything we have done has been "non-destructive", so this is a big moment. You can choose any character you

---

[2] In case you hadn't noticed yet, many of Emacs's movement commands consist of combining Control with a single mnemonic letter.

like, but if you want to do this in style, I suggest using a nice, solid, capital "X". As you type it, take a look at the beginning of the mode line at the bottom of the screen. When you change the buffer so that its contents are no longer the same as those of the file on disk, Emacs displays two asterisks at the beginning of the mode line, to let you know that the buffer has been modified:

```
--**-Emacs: some_file.txt          (Fundamental)--Top---------------------
```

These two asterisks are displayed as soon as you modify the buffer, and remain visible until you save the buffer. You can save the buffer multiple times during an editing session—the command to do so is just `C-x C-s` (hold down `Control` and hit "x" and "s" while it's down...okay, so you probably already figured that out!). It's deliberately easy to type, because saving your buffers is something best done early and often.

I'm going to list a few more commands now, along with the ones you've learned already, and you can practice them however you like. I'd suggest becoming familiar with them before going any further:

`C-f`	Move forward one character.
`C-b`	Move backward one character.
`C-n`	Go to next line.
`C-p`	Go to previous line.
`C-a`	Go to beginning of line.
`C-e`	Go to end of line.
`C-v`	Go to next page/screenful of text.
`C-l`	Redraw the screen, with current line in center.
`C-d`	Delete this character (practice this one).
`C-k`	Delete text from here to end of line.
`C-x C-s`	Save the buffer in its corresponding file.
`Backspace`	Delete preceding character (the one you just typed).

8.2   Getting Started Quickly in X

 If all you're interesting in is editing a few files quickly, an X user doesn't have to go much further beyond the menus at the top of the screen:

```
Buffers File Edit Help
```

These menus are not available in text mode.

When you first start Emacs, there will be four menus at the top of the screen: Buffers, File, Edit, and Help. To use a menu, simply move the mouse pointer over the name (like File, click and hold down on the left button. Then, move the pointer to the action you want and release the mouse button. If you change your mind, move the mouse pointer away from the menu and release the button.

The Buffers menu lists the different files you've been editing in this incarnation of Emacs.The File menu shows a bunch of commands for loading and saving files—many of them will be described later. The Edit menu displays some commands for editing one buffer, and the Help menu should hopefully give on-line documentation.

You'll notice keyboard equivalents are listed next to the choices in the menu. Since, in the long run, they'll be quicker, you might want to learn them. Also, for better or for worse, most of Emacs's functionality is *only* available through the keyboard—you might want to read the rest of this chapter.

8.3   Editing Many Files at Once

Emacs can work on more than one file at a time. In fact, the only limit on how many buffers your Emacs can contain is the actual amount of memory available on the machine. The command to bring a new file into an Emacs buffer is C-x C-f. When you type it, you will be prompted for a filename in the minibuffer:

```
Find file: ~/
```

The syntax here is the same one used to specify files from the shell prompt; slashes represent subdirectories, ~means your home directory. You also get **filename completion**, meaning that if you've typed enough of a filename at the prompt to identify the file uniquely, you can just hit Tab to complete it (or to show possible completions, if there are more than one). Space also has a role in filename completion in the minibuffer, similar to Tab , but I'll let you experiment to find out how the two differ. Once you have the full filename in the minibuffer, hit Return , and Emacs will bring up a buffer displaying that file. In Emacs, this process is known as **finding** a file. Go ahead and find some other unimportant text file now, and bring it into Emacs (do this from our original buffer some_file.txt). Now you have a new buffer; I'll pretend it's called another_file.txt, since I can't see your mode line.

Your original buffer seems to have disappeared—you're probably wondering where it went. It's still inside Emacs, and you can switch back to it with C-x b. When you type this, you will see that the minibuffer prompts you for a buffer to switch to, and it names a default. The default is the buffer you'd get if you just hit Return at the prompt, without typing a buffer name. The default buffer to switch to is always the one most recently left, so that when you are doing a lot of work between two buffers, C-x b always defaults to the "other" buffer (which saves you from having to type the buffer name). Even if the default buffer is the one you want, however, you should try typing in its name anyway.

Notice that you get the same sort of completion you got when finding a file: hitting Tab completes as much of a buffer name as it can, and so on. Whenever you are being prompted for something in the minibuffer, it's a good idea to see if Emacs is doing completion. Taking advantage of completion whenever it's offered will save you a lot of typing. Emacs usually does completion when you are choosing one item out of some predefined list.

Everything you learned about moving around and editing text in the first buffer applies to the new one. Go ahead and change some text in the new buffer, but don't save it (i.e. don't type C-x C-s). Let's assume that you want to discard your changes without saving them in the file. The command for that is C-x k, which "kills" the buffer. Type it now. First you will be asked which buffer to kill, but the default is the current buffer, and that's almost always the one you want to kill, so just hit Return . Then you will be asked if you *really* want to kill the buffer—Emacs always checks before killing a buffer that has unsaved changes in it. Just type "yes" and hit Return , if you want to kill it.

Go ahead and practice loading in files, modifying them, saving them, and killing their buffers. Make sure you don't modify any important system files in a way that will cause trouble[3], of course, but do try to have at least five buffers open at once, so you can get the hang of switching between them.

8.4   Ending an Editing Session

When you are done with your work in Emacs, make sure that all buffers are saved that should be saved, and exit Emacs with C-x C-c. Sometimes C-x C-c will ask you a question or two in the minibuffer before it lets you leave—don't be alarmed, just answer them in the obvious ways. If you think that you might be returning to Emacs later, don't use C-x C-c at all; use C-z, which will suspend Emacs. You

---

[3]If you are not the "root" user on the machine, you shouldn't be able to hurt the system anyway, but be careful just the same.

can return to it with the shell command "fg" later. This is more efficient than stopping and starting Emacs multiple times, especially if you have edit the same files again later.

X Under X, hitting C-z will merely iconize the window. See the section on iconization in Chapter 5. This gives you two ways of iconizing Emacs—the normal way your window manager offers, and C-z. Remember, when you iconize, a simply fg won't bring the window back—you'll have to use your window manager.

8.5 The Meta Key

You've already learned about one "modifier key" in Emacs, the [Control] key. There is a second one, called the **Meta** key, which is used almost as frequently. However, not all keyboards have their Meta key in the same place, and some don't have one at all. The first thing you need to do is find where your Meta key is located. Chances are, your keyboard's [Alt] keys are also Meta keys, if you are using an IBM PC or other another keyboard that has an [Alt] key.

The way to test this is to hold down a key that you think might be a Meta key and type "x". If you see a little prompt appear in the minibuffer (like this: M-x) then you've found it. To get rid of the prompt and go back to your Emacs buffer, type C-g.

If you didn't get a prompt, then there is still one solution. You can use the [Escape] key as a Meta key. But instead of holding it down while you type the next letter, you have to tap it and release it quickly, and *then* type the letter. This method will work whether or not you have a real Meta key, so it's the safest way to go. Try tapping [Escape] and then typing "x" now. You should get that tiny prompt again. Just use C-g to make it go away. C-g is the general way in Emacs to quit out of something you don't mean to be in. It usually beeps annoyingly at you to let you know that you have interrupted something, but that's fine, since that's what you intended to do if you typed C-g![4]

The notation M-x is analogous to C-x (substitute any character for "x"). If you have found a real Meta key, use that, otherwise just use the [Escape] key. I will simply write M-x and you'll have to use your own Meta key.

8.6 Cutting, Pasting, Killing and Yanking

Emacs, like any good editor, allows you to cut and paste blocks of text. In order to do this, you need a way to define the start and end of the block. In Emacs, you do this by setting two locations in the buffer, known as **mark** and **point**. To set the mark, go to the place you want your block to begin and type C-SPC ("SPC" means [Space], of course). You should see the message "Mark set" appear in the minibuffer.[5] The mark has now been set at that place. There will be no special highlighting indicating that fact, but you know where you put it, and that's all that matters.

What about **point**? Well, it turns out that you've been setting point every time you move the cursor, because "point" just refers to your current location in the buffer. In formal terms, point is the spot where text would be inserted if you were to type something. By setting the mark, and then moving to the end of the block of text, you have actually defined a block of text. This block is known as the **region**. The region always means the area between mark and point.

Merely defining the region does not make it available for pasting. You have to tell Emacs to copy it in order to be able to paste it. To copy the region, make sure that mark and point are set correctly, and type M-w. It has now been recorded by Emacs. In order to paste it somewhere else, just go there and type C-y. This is known as **yanking** the text into the buffer.

---

[4] Occasionally, even one C-g isn't enough to persuade Emacs that you really wanted to interrupt what you're doing. Just keep at it, and Emacs will usually return to a saner mode.
[5] On some terminals, C-SPC doesn't work. For these machines, you must use C-@.

If you want to actually move the text of the region to somewhere else, type C-w instead of M-w. This will **kill** the region—all the text inside it will disappear. In fact, it has been saved in the same way as if you had used M-w. You can yank it back out with C-y, as always. The place Emacs saves all this text is known as the **kill-ring**. Some editors call it the "clipboard" or the "paste buffer".

There's another way to do cutting and pasting: whenever you use C-k to kill to the end of a line, the killed text is saved in the kill-ring. If you kill more than one line in a row, they are all saved in the kill-ring together, so that the next yank will paste in all the lines at once. Because of this feature, it is often faster to use repeated C-k's to kill some text than it is to explicitly set mark and point and use C-w. However, either way will work. It's really a matter of personal preference how you do it.

8.7 Searching and Replacing

There are several ways to search for text in Emacs. Many of them are rather complex, and not worth going into here. The easiest and most entertaining way is to use **isearch**. "Isearch" stands for "incremental search". Suppose you want to search for the string "gadfly" in the following buffer:

```
I was growing afraid that we would run out of gasoline, when my passenger exclaimed
''Gadzooks!  There's a gadfly in here!''.
```

You would move to the beginning of the buffer, or at least to some point that you know is before the first occurrence of the goal word, "gadfly", and type C-s. That puts you in isearch mode. Now start typing the word you are searching for, "gadfly". But as soon as you type the "g", you see that Emacs has jumped you to the first occurrence of "g" in the buffer. If the above quote is the entire contents of the buffer, then that would be the first "g" of the word "growing". Now type the "a" of "gadfly", and Emacs leaps over to "gasoline", which contains the first occurrence of a "ga". The "d" gets you to gadzooks, and finally, "f" gets you to "gadfly", without your having had to type the entire word.

What you are doing in an isearch is defining a string to search for. Each time you add a character to the end of the string, the number of matches is reduced, until eventually you have entered enough to define the string uniquely. Once you have found the match you are looking for, you can exit the search with $\boxed{\text{Return}}$ or any of the normal movement commands. If you think the string you're looking for is behind you in the buffer, then you should use C-r, which does an isearch backwards.

If you encounter a match, but it's not the one you were looking for, then hit C-s again while still in the search. This will move you forward to the next complete match, each time you hit it. If there is no next match, it will say that the search failed, but if you press C-s again at that point, the search will wrap around from the beginning of the buffer. The reverse holds true for C-r — it wraps around the end of the buffer.

Try bringing up a buffer of plain English text and doing an isearch for the string "the". First you'd type in as much as you wanted, then use repeated C-s's to go to all instances of it. Notice that it will match words like "them" as well, since that also contains the substring "the". To search only for "the", you'd have to do add a space to the end of your search string. You can add new characters to the string at any point in the search, even after you've hit C-s repeatedly to find the next matches. You can also use $\boxed{\text{Backspace}}$ or $\boxed{\text{Delete}}$ to remove characters from the search string at any point in the search, and hitting $\boxed{\text{Return}}$ exits the search, leaving you at the last match.

Emacs also allows you to replace all instances of a string with some new string—this is known as **query-replace**. To invoke it, type query-replace and hit $\boxed{\text{Return}}$. Completion is done on the command name, so once you have typed "query-re", you can just hit $\boxed{\text{Tab}}$ to finish it. Say you wish to replace all instances of "gadfly" with "housefly". At the "Query replace: " prompt, type "gadfly", and hit $\boxed{\text{Return}}$. Then you will be prompted again, and you should enter "housefly". Emacs will then step through the buffer, stopping at every instance of the word "gadfly", and asking if you want to replace it. Just hit "y" or "n" at each instance, for "Yes" or "No", until it finishes. If this doesn't make sense as you read it, then try it out.

8.8 What's Really Going On Here?

Actually, all these **keybindings** you have been learning are shortcuts to Emacs functions. For example, C-p is a short way of telling Emacs to execute the internal function previous-line. However, all these internal functions can be called by name, using M-x. If you forgot that previous-line is bound to C-p, you could just type M-x previous-line Return , and it would move you up one line. Try this now, to understand how M-x previous-line and C-p are really the same thing.

The designer of Emacs started from the ground up, first defining a whole lot of internal functions, and then giving keybindings to the most commonly-used ones. Sometimes it's easier just to call a function explicitly with M-x than to remember what key it's bound to. The function query-replace, for example, is bound to M-% in some versions of Emacs. But who can remember such an odd keybinding? Unless you use query-replace extremely often, it's easier just to call it with M-x.

Most of the keys you type are letters, meant to be inserted into the text of the buffer. So each of those keys is **bound** to the function self-insert-command, which does nothing but insert that letter into the buffer. Combinations that use the Control key with a letter are generally bound to functions that do other things, like moving you around. For example, C-v is bound to a function called scroll-up, which scrolls the buffer up by one screenful (meaning that your position in the buffer moves *down*, of course).

If you ever actually wanted to insert a Control character into the buffer, then, how would you do it? After all, the Control characters are ASCII characters, although rarely used, and you might want them in a file. There is a way to prevent Control characters from being interpreted as commands by Emacs. The key C-q[6] is bound to a special function named quoted-insert. All quoted-insert does is read the next key and insert it literally into the buffer, without trying to interpret it as a command. This is how you can put Control characters into your files using Emacs. Naturally, the way to insert a C-q is to press C-q twice!

Emacs also has many functions that are not bound to any key. For example, if you're typing a long message, you don't want to have to hit return at the end of every line. You can have Emacs do it for you (you can have Emacs do anything for you)—the command to do so is called auto-fill-mode, but it's not bound to any keys by default. In order to invoke this command, you would type "M-x auto-fill-mode". "M-x" is the key used to call functions by name. You could even use it to call functions like next-line and previous-line, but that would be very inefficient, since they are already bound to C-n and C-p!

By the way, if you look at your mode line after invoking auto-fill-mode, you will notice that the word "Fill" has been added to the right side. As long as it's there, Emacs will fill (wrap) text automatically. You can turn it off by typing "M-x auto-fill-mode" again—it's a toggle command.

The inconvenience of typing long function names in the minibuffer is lessened because Emacs does completion on function names the same way it does on file names. Therefore, you should rarely find yourself typing in the whole function name, letter by letter. If you're not sure whether or not you can use completion, just hit Tab . It can't hurt: the worst thing that will happen is that you'll just get a tab character, and if you're lucky, it'll turn out that you can use completion.

8.9 Asking Emacs for Help

Emacs has extensive help facilities—so extensive, in fact, that we can only touch on them here. The most basic help features are accessed by typing C-h and then a single letter. For example, C-h k gets help on a key (it prompts you to type a key, then tells you what that key does). C-h t brings up a short Emacs tutorial. Most importantly, C-h C-h C-h gets you help on help, to tell you what's available once you have typed C-h the first time. If you know the name of an Emacs function (save-buffer, for example), but can't remember what key sequence invokes it, then use C-h w, for "where-is", and type

---

[6]We call C-q a "key", even though it is produced by holding down Control and pressing "q", because it is a single ASCII character.

in the name of the function. Or, if you want to know what a function does in detail, use C-h f, which prompts for a function name.

Remember, since Emacs does completion on function names, you don't really have to be sure what a function is called to ask for help on it. If you think you can guess the word it might start with, type that and hit `Tab` to see if it completes to anything. If not, back up and try something else. The same goes for file names: even if you can't remember quite what you named some file that you haven't accessed for three months, you can guess and use completion to find out if you're right. Get used to using completion as means of asking questions, not just as a way of saving keystrokes.

There are other characters you can type after C-h, and each one gets you help in a different way. The ones you will use most often are C-h k, C-h w, and C-h f. Once you are more familiar with Emacs, another one to try is C-h a, which prompts you for a string and then tells you about all the functions who have that string as part of their name (the "a" means for "apropos", or "about").

Another source of information is the **Info** documentation reader. Info is too complex a subject to go into here, but if you are interested in exploring it on your own, type C-h i and read the paragraph at the top of the screen. It will tell you how get more help.

8.10   Specializing Buffers: Modes

Emacs buffers have **modes** associated with them[7]. The reason for this is that your needs when writing a mail message are very different from your needs when, say, writing a program. Rather than try to come up with an editor that would meet every single need all the time (which would be impossible), the designer of Emacs[8] chose to have Emacs behave differently depending on what you are doing in each individual buffer. Thus, buffers have modes, each one designed for some specific activity. The main features that distinguish one mode from another are the keybindings, but there can be other differences as well.

The most basic mode is fundamental mode, which doesn't really have any special commands at all. In fact, here's what Emacs has to say about Fundamental Mode:

```
Fundamental Mode:

Major mode not specialized for anything in particular.
Other major modes are defined by comparison with this one.
```

I got that information like this: I typed C-x b, which is switch-to-buffer, and entered "foo" when it prompted me for a buffer name to switch to. Since there was previously no buffer named "foo", Emacs created one and switched me to it. It was in fundamental-mode by default, but it it hadn't been, I could have typed "M-x fundamental-mode" to make it so. All mode names have a command called <modename>-mode which puts the current buffer into that mode. Then, to find out more information about that major mode, I typed C-h m, which gets you help on the current major mode of the buffer you're in.

There's a slightly more useful mode called text-mode, which has the special commands M-S, for center-paragraph, and M-s, which invokes center-line. M-S, by the way, means exactly what you think it does: hold down both the `Meta` and the `Shift` key, and press "S".

Don't just take my word for this—go make a new buffer, put it into text-mode, and type C-h m. You may not understand everything Emacs tells you when you do that, but you should be able to get some useful information out of it.

Here is an introduction to some of the more commonly used modes. If you use them, make sure that you type C-h m sometime in each one, to find out more about each mode.

---

[7] To make matters worse, there are "Major Modes" and "Minor Modes", but you don't need to know about that right now.
[8] Richard Stallman, also sometimes referred to as "rms", because that's his login name.

8.11   Programming Modes

8.11.1   C Mode

If you use Emacs for programming in the C language, you can get it to do all the indentation for you automatically. Files whose names end in ".c" or ".h" are automatically brought up in c-mode. This means that certain special editing commands, useful for writing C-programs, are available. In C-mode, `Tab` is bound to c-indent-command. This means that hitting the `Tab` key does not actually insert a tab character. Instead, if you hit `Tab` anywhere on a line, Emacs automatically indents that line correctly for its location in the program. This implies that Emacs knows something about C syntax, which it does (although nothing about semantics—it cannot insure that your program has no errors!)

In order to do this, it assumes that the previous lines are indented correctly. That means that if the preceding line is missing a parenthesis, semicolon, curly brace, or whatever, Emacs will indent the current line in a funny way. When you see it do that, you will know to look for a punctuation mistake on the line above.

You can use this feature to check that you have punctuated your programs correctly—instead of reading through the entire program looking for problems, just start indenting lines from the top down with `Tab`, and when something indents oddly, check the lines just before it. In other words, let Emacs do the work for you!

8.11.2   Scheme Mode

This is a major mode that won't do you any good unless you have a compiler or an interpreter for the Scheme programming language on your system. Having one is not as normal as having, say, a C compiler, but it's becoming more and more common, so I'll cover it too. Much of what is true for Scheme mode is true for Lisp mode as well, if you prefer to write in Lisp.

Well, to make matters painful, Emacs comes with two different Scheme modes, because people couldn't decide how they wanted it to work. The one I'm describing is called cmuscheme, and later on, in the section on customizing Emacs, I'll talk about how there can be two different Scheme modes and what to do about it. For now, don't worry about it if things in your Emacs don't quite match up to what I say here. A customizable editor means an unpredictable editor, and there's no way around that!

You can run an interactive Scheme process in Emacs, with the command M-x run-scheme. This creates a buffer named "*scheme*", which has the usual Scheme prompt in it. You can type in Scheme expressions at the prompt, hit `Return`, and Scheme will evaluate them and display the answer. Thus, in order to interact with the Scheme process, you could just type all your function definitions and applications in at the prompt. Chances are you have previously-written Scheme source code in a file somewhere, and it would be easier to do your work in that file and send the definitions over to the Scheme process buffer as necessary.

If that source file ends in ".ss" or ".scm", it will automatically be brought up in **Scheme mode** when you find it with C-x C-f. If for some reason, it doesn't come up in Scheme mode, you can do it by hand with M-x scheme-mode. This scheme-mode is not the same thing as the buffer running the Scheme process; rather, the source code buffer's being in scheme-mode means that it has special commands for communicating with the process buffer.

If you put yourself inside a function definition in the Scheme source code buffer and type C-c C-e, then that definition will be "sent" to the process buffer — exactly as if you had typed it in yourself. C-c M-e sends the definition and then brings you to the process buffer to do some interactive work. C-c C-l loads a file of Scheme code (this one works from either the process buffer or the source code buffer). And like other programming language modes, hitting `Tab` anywhere on a line of code correctly indents that line.

If you're at the prompt in the process buffer, you can use M-p and M-n to move through your previous commands (also known as the **input history**). So if you are debugging the function 'rotate', and have already applied it to arguments in the process buffer, like so:

```
> (rotate '(a b c d e))
```

then you can get that command back by typing M-p at the prompt later on. There should be no need to retype long expressions at the Scheme prompt — get in the habit of using the input history and you'll save a lot of time.

Emacs knows about quite a few programming languages: C, C++, Lisp, and Scheme are just some. Generally, it knows how to indent them in intuitive ways.

8.11.3   Mail Mode

You can also edit and send mail in Emacs. To enter a mail buffer, type C-x m. You need to fill in the To: and Subject: fields, and then use C-n to get down below the separator line into the body of the message (which is empty when you first start out). Don't change or delete the separator line, or else Emacs will not be able to send your mail—it uses that line to distinguish the mail's headers, which tell it where to send the mail, from the actual contents of the message.

You can type whatever you want below the separator line. When you are ready to send the message, just type C-c C-c, and Emacs will send it and then make the mail buffer go away.

8.12   Being Even More Efficient

Experienced Emacs users are fanatical about efficiency. In fact, they will often end up wasting a lot of time searching for ways to be more efficient! While I don't want that to happen to you, there are some easy things you can do to become a better Emacs user. Sometimes experienced users make novices feel silly for not knowing all these tricks—for some reason, people become religious about using Emacs "correctly". I'd condemn that sort of elitism more if I weren't about to be guilty of it myself. Here we go:

When you're moving around, use the fastest means available. You know that C-f is forward-char—can you guess that M-f is forward-word? C-b is backward-char. Guess what M-b does? That's not all, though: you can move forward a sentence at a time with M-e, as long as you write your sentences so that there are always two spaces following the final period (otherwise Emacs can't tell where one sentence ends and the next one begins). M-a is backward-sentence.

If you find yourself using repeated C-f's to get to the end of the line, be ashamed, and make sure that you use C-e instead, and C-a to go to the beginning of the line. If you use many C-n's to move down screenfuls of text, be very ashamed, and use C-v forever after. If you are using repeated C-p's to move up screenfuls, be embarrassed to show your face, and use M-v instead.

If you are nearing the end of a line and you realize that there's a mispelling or a word left out somewhere earlier in the line, *don't* use Backspace or Delete to get back to that spot. That would require retyping whole portions of perfectly good text. Instead, use combinations of M-b, C-b, and C-f to move to the precise location of the error, fix it, and then use C-e to move to the end of the line again.

When you have to type in a filename, don't ever type in the whole name. Just type in enough of it to identify it uniquely, and let Emacs's completion finish the job by hitting Tab or Space . Why waste keystrokes when you can waste CPU cycles instead?

If you are typing some kind of plain text, and somehow your auto-filling (or auto-wrapping) has gotten screwed up, use M-q, which is fill-paragraph in common text modes. This will "adjust" the paragraph you're in as if it had been wrapped line by line, but without your having to go mess around with it by hand. M-q will work from inside the paragraph, or from its very beginning or end.

Sometimes it's helpful to use `C-x u`, (**undo**), which will try to "undo" the last change(s) you made. Emacs will guess at how much to undo; usually it guesses very intelligently. Calling it repeatedly will undo more and more, until Emacs can no longer remember what changes were made.

8.13   Customizing Emacs

Emacs is *so* big, and *so* complex, that it actually has its own programming language! I'm not kidding: to really customize Emacs to suit your needs, you have to write programs in this language. It's called Emacs Lisp, and it's a dialect of Lisp, so if you have previous experience in Lisp, it will seem quite friendly. If not, don't worry: I'm not going to go into a great deal of depth, because it's definitely best learned by doing. To really learn about programming Emacs, you should consult the Info pages on Emacs Lisp, and read a lot of Emacs Lisp source code.

Most of Emacs's functionality is defined in files of Emacs Lisp[9] code. Most of these files are distributed with Emacs and collectively are known as the "Emacs Lisp library". This library's location depends on how Emacs was installed on your system — common locations are `/usr/lib/emacs/lisp`, `/usr/lib/emacs/19.19/lisp/`, etc. The "19.19" is the version number of Emacs, and might be different on your system.

You don't need to poke around your filesystem looking for the lisp library, because Emacs has the information stored internally, in a variable called **load-path**. To find out the value of this variable, it is necessary to **evaluate** it; that is, to have Emacs's lisp interpreter get its value. There is a special mode for evaluating Lisp expressions in Emacs, called **lisp-interaction-mode**. Usually, there is a buffer called "*scratch*" that is already in this mode. If you can't find one, create a new buffer of any name, and type `M-x lisp-interaction-mode` inside it.

Now you have a workspace for interacting with the Emacs Lisp interpreter. Type this:

```
load-path
```

and then press `C-j` at the end of it. In lisp-interaction-mode, `C-j` is bound to `eval-print-last-sexp`. An "sexp" is an "**s-expression**", which means a balanced group of parentheses, including none. Well, that's simplifying it a little, but you'll get a feel for what they are as you work with Emacs Lisp. Anyway, evaluating `load-path` should get you something like this:

```
load-path C-j
("/usr/lib/emacs/site-lisp/vm-5.35" "/home/kfogel/elithp"
 "/usr/lib/emacs/site-lisp" "/usr/lib/emacs/19.19/lisp")
```

It won't look the same on every system, of course, since it is dependent on how Emacs was installed. The above example comes from my 386 PC running Linux. As the above indicates, `load-path` is a list of strings. Each string names a directory that might contain Emacs Lisp files. When Emacs needs to load a file of Lisp code, it goes looking for it in each of these directories, in order. If a directory is named but does not actually exist on the filesystem, Emacs just ignores it.

When Emacs starts up, it automatically tries to load the file `.emacs` in your home directory. Therefore, if you want to make personal customizations to Emacs, you should put them in `.emacs`. The most common customizations are keybindings, so here's how to do them:

```
(global-set-key "\C-cl" 'goto-line)
```

`global-set-key` is a function of two arguments: the key to be bound, and the function to bind it to. The word "`global`" means that this keybinding will be in effect in all major modes (there is another function, `local-set-key`, that binds a key in a single buffer). Above, I have bound `C-c l` to the function `goto-line`. The key is described using a string. The special syntax "`\C-<char>`" means

---

[9]Sometimes unofficially called "Elisp".

the ⟨Control⟩ key held down while the key <char> is pressed. Likewise, "\M-<char>" indicates the ⟨Meta⟩ key.

All very well, but how did I know that the function's name was "goto-line"? I may know that I want to bind C-c l to some function that prompts for a line number and then moves the cursor to that line, but how did I find out that function's name?

This is where Emacs's online help facilities come in. Once you have decided what kind of function you are looking for, you can use Emacs to track down its exact name. Here's one quick and dirty way to do it: since Emacs gives completion on function names, just type C-h f (which is describe-function, remember), and then hit ⟨Tab⟩ without typing anything. This asks Emacs to do completion on the empty string — in other words, the completion will match every single function! It may take a moment to build the completion list, since Emacs has so many internal functions, but it will display as much of it as fits on the screen when it's ready.

At that point, hit C-g to quit out of describe-function. There will be a buffer called "*Completions*", which contains the completion list you just generated. Switch to that buffer. Now you can use C-s, isearch, to search for likely functions. For example, it's a safe assumption that a function which prompts for a line number and then goes to that line will contain the string "line" in its name. Therefore, just start searching for the string "line", and you'll find what you're looking for eventually.

If you want another method, you can use C-h a, command-apropos, to show all functions whose names match the given string. The output of command-apropos is a little harder to sort through than just searching a completion list, in my opinion, but you may find that you feel differently. Try both methods and see what you think.

There is always the possibility that Emacs does not have any predefined function to do what you're looking for. In this situation, you have to write the function yourself. I'm not going to talk about how to do that — you should look at the Emacs Lisp library for examples of function definitions, and read the Info pages on Emacs Lisp. If you happen to know a local Emacs guru, ask her how to do it. Defining your own Emacs functions is not a big deal — to give you an idea, I have written 131 of them in the last year or so. It takes a little practice, but the learning curve is not steep at all.

Another thing people often do in their .emacs is set certain variables to preferred values. For example, put this in your .emacs and then start up a new Emacs:

```
(setq inhibit-startup-message t)
```

Emacs checks the value of the variable inhibit-startup-message to decide whether or not to display certain information about version and lack of warranty when it starts up. The Lisp expression above uses the command setq to set that variable to the value 't', which is a special Lisp value that means **true**. The opposite of 't' is 'nil', which is the designated **false** value in Emacs Lisp. Here are two things that are in my .emacs that you might find useful:

```
(setq case-fold-search nil) ; gives case-insensitivity in searching
;; make C programs indent the way I like them to:
(setq c-indent-level 2)
```

The first expression causes searches (including isearch) to be case-insensitive; that is, the search will match upper- or lower-case versions of a character even though the search string contains only the lower-case version. The second expression sets the default indentation for C language statements to be a little smaller than it is normally — this is just a personal preference; I find that it makes C code more readable.

The comment character in Lisp is ";". Emacs ignores anything following one, unless it appears inside a literal string, like so:

```
;; these two lines are ignored by the Lisp interpreter, but the
;; s-expression following them will be evaluated in full:
(setq some-literal-string "An awkward pause; for no purpose.")
```

It's a good idea to comment your changes to Lisp files, because six months later you will have no memory of what you were thinking when you modified them. If the comment appears on a line by itself, precede it with two semicolons. This aids Emacs in indenting Lisp files correctly.

You can find out about internal Emacs variables the same ways you find out about functions. Use C-h v, describe-variable to make a completion list, or use C-h C-a, apropos. Apropos differs from C-h a, command-apropos, in that it shows functions and variables instead of just functions.

The default extension for Emacs Lisp files is ".el", as in "c-mode.el". However, to make Lisp code run faster, Emacs allows it to be **byte-compiled**, and these files of compiled Lisp code end in ".elc" instead of ".el". The exception to this is your .emacs file, which does not need the .el extension because Emacs knows to search for it on startup.

To load a file of Lisp code interactively, use the command M-x load-file. It will prompt you for the name of the file. To load Lisp files from inside other Lisp files, do this:

```
(load "c-mode") ; force Emacs to load the stuff in c-mode.el or .elc
```

Emacs will first add the .elc extension to the filename and try to find it somewhere in the load-path. If it fails, it tries it with the .el extension; failing that, it uses the literal string as passed to load. You can byte-compile a file with the command M-x byte-compile-file, but if you modify the file often, it's probably not worth it. You should never byte-compile your .emacs, though, nor even give it a .el extension.

After your .emacs has been loaded, Emacs searches for a file named default.el to load. Usually it's located in a directory in load-path called site-lisp or local-elisp or something (see the example load-path I gave a while ago). People who maintain Emacs on multi-user systems use default.el to make changes that will affect everyone's Emacs, since everybody's Emacs loads it after their personal .emacs. Default.el should not be byte-compiled either, since it tends to be modified fairly often.

If a person's .emacs contains any errors, Emacs will not attempt to load default.el, but instead will just stop, flashing a message saying "Error in init file." or something. If you see this message, there's probably something wrong with your .emacs.

There is one more kind of expression that often goes in a .emacs. The Emacs Lisp library sometimes offers multiple packages for doing the same thing in different ways. This means that you have to specify which one you want to use (or you'll get the default package, which is not always the best one for all purposes). One area in which this happens is Emacs's Scheme interaction features. There are two different Scheme interfaces distributed with Emacs (in version 19 at least): xscheme and cmuscheme.

```
prompt> ls /usr/lib/emacs/19.19/lisp/*scheme*
/usr/lib/emacs/19.19/lisp/cmuscheme.el
/usr/lib/emacs/19.19/lisp/cmuscheme.elc
/usr/lib/emacs/19.19/lisp/scheme.el
/usr/lib/emacs/19.19/lisp/scheme.elc
/usr/lib/emacs/19.19/lisp/xscheme.el
/usr/lib/emacs/19.19/lisp/xscheme.elc
```

I happen to like the interface offered by cmuscheme much better than that offered by xscheme, but the one Emacs will use by default is xscheme. How can I cause Emacs to act in accordance with my preference? I put this in my .emacs:

```
;; notice how the expression can be broken across two lines.  Lisp
;; ignores whitespace, generally:
(autoload 'run-scheme "cmuscheme"
"Run an inferior Scheme, the way I like it." t)
```

The function autoload takes the name of a function (quoted with "'", for reasons having to do with how Lisp works) and tells Emacs that this function is defined in a certain file. The file is the second argument, a string (without the ".el" or ".elc" extension) indicating the name of the file to search for in the load-path.

The remaining arguments are optional, but necessary in this case: the third argument is a documentation string for the function, so that if you call `describe-function` on it, you get some useful information. The fourth argument tells Emacs that this autoloadable function can be called interactively (that is, by using `M-x`). This is very important in this case, because one should be able to type `M-x run-scheme` to start a scheme process running under Emacs.

Now that `run-scheme` has been defined as an autoloadable function, what happens when I type `M-x run-scheme`? Emacs looks at the function `run-scheme`, sees that it's set to be autoloaded, and loads the file named by the autoload (in this case, "cmuscheme"). The byte-compiled file `cmuscheme.elc` exists, so Emacs will load that. That file *must* define the function `run-scheme`, or there will be an autoload error. Luckily, it does define `run-scheme`, so everything goes smoothly, and I get my preferred Scheme interface[10].

An `autoload` is a like a promise to Emacs that, when the time comes, it can find the specified function in the file you tell it to look in. In return, you get some control over what gets loaded. Also, autoloads help cut down on Emacs's size in memory, by not loading certain features until they are asked for. Many commands are not really defined as functions when Emacs starts up. Rather, they are simply set to autoload from a certain file. If you never invoke the command, it never gets loaded. This space saving is actually vital to the functioning of Emacs: if it loaded every available file in the Lisp library, Emacs would take twenty minutes just to start up, and once it was done, it might occupy most of the available memory on your machine. Don't worry, you don't have to set all these autoloads in your `.emacs`; they were taken care of when Emacs was built.

8.14   Finding Out More

I have not told you everything there is to know about Emacs. In fact, I don't think I have even told you 1% of what there is to know about Emacs. While you know enough to get by, there are still lots of time-saving tricks and conveniences that you ought to find out about. The best way to do this is to wait until you find yourself needing something, and then look for a function that does it.

The importance of being comfortable with Emacs's online help facilities cannot be emphasized enough. For example, suppose you want to be able to insert the contents of some file into a buffer that is already working on a different file, so that the buffer contains both of them. Well, if you were to guess that there is a command called `insert-file`, you'd be right. To check your educated guess, type `C-h f`. At the prompt in the minibuffer, enter the name of a function that you want help on. Since you know that there is completion on function names, and you can guess that the command you are looking for begins with "insert", you type insert and hit `Tab`. This shows you all the function names that begin with "insert", and "insert-file" is one of them.

So you complete the function name and read about how it works, and then use `M-x insert-file`. If you're wondering whether it's also bound to a key, you type `C-h w insert-file Return`, and find out. The more you know about Emacs's help facilities, the more easily you can ask Emacs questions about itself. The ability to do so, combined with a spirit of exploration and a willingness to learn new ways of doing things, can end up saving you a lot of keystrokes.

To order a copy of the Emacs user's manual and/or the Emacs Lisp Programming manual, write to:

Free Software Foundation
675 Mass Ave
Cambridge, MA 02139
USA

Both of these manuals are distributed electronically with Emacs, in a form readable by using the Info documentation reader (`C-h i`), but you may find it easier to deal with treeware than with the

---

[10] By the way, `cmuscheme` was the interface I was talking about earlier, in the section on working with Scheme, so if you want to use any of the stuff from that tutorial, you need to make sure that you run `cmuscheme`.

online versions. Also, their prices are quite reasonable, and the money goes to a good cause — quality free software! At some point, you should type C-h C-c to read the copyright conditions for Emacs. It's more interesting than you might think, and will help clarify the concept of free software. If you think the term "free software" just means that the program doesn't cost anything, please do read that copyright as soon as you have time!

Chapter 9

I Gotta Be Me!

If God had known we'd need foresight, she would have given it to us.

9.1 bash Customization

One of the distinguishing things about the Unix philosophy is that the system's designers did not attempt to predict every need that users might have; instead, they tried to make it easy for each individual user to tailor the environment to their own particular needs. This is mainly done through **configuration files**. These are also known as "init files", "rc files" (for "run control"), or even "dot files", because the filenames often begin with ".". If you'll recall, filenames that start with "." aren't normally displayed by ls.

The most important configuration files are the ones used by the shell. Linux's default shell is bash, and that's the shell this chapter covers. Before we go into how to customize bash, we should know what files bash looks at.

9.1.1 Shell Startup

There are several different ways bash can run. It can run as a **login shell**, which is how it runs when you first login. The login shell should be the first shell you see.

Another way bash can run is as an **interactive shell**. This is any shell which presents a prompt to a human and waits for input. A login shell is also an interactive shell. A way you can get a non-login interactive shell is, say, a shell inside xterm. Any shell that was created by some other way besides logging in is a non-login shell.

Finally, there are **non-interactive shells**. These shells are used for executing a file of commands, much like MS-DOS's batch files—the files that end in .BAT. These **shell scripts** function like mini-programs. While they are usually much slower than a regular compiled program, it is often true that they're easier to write.

Depending on the type of shell, different files will be used at shell startup:

Type of Shell	Action
Interactive login	The file .bash_profile is read and executed
Interactive	The file .bashrc is read and executed
Non-interactive	The shell script is read and executed

```
alias ls="ls -F"           # give characters at the end of listing
alias ll="ls -l"           # special ls
alias la="ls -a"
alias ro="rm *~; rm .*~"   # this removes backup files created by Emacs
alias rd="rmdir"           # saves typing!
alias md="mkdir"
alias pu=pushd             # pushd, popd, and dirs weren't covered in this
alias po=popd              # manual---you might want to look them up
alias ds=dirs              # in the bash manpage
# these all are just keyboard shortcuts
alias to="telnet cs.oberlin.edu"
alias ta="telnet altair.mcs.anl.gov"
alias tg="telnet wombat.gnu.ai.mit.edu"
alias tko="tpalk kold@cs.oberlin.edu"
alias tjo="talk jimb@cs.oberlin.edu"
alias mroe="more"          # spelling correction!
alias moer="more"
alias email="emacs -f rmail" # my mail reader
alias ed2="emacs -d floss:0 -fg \"grey95\" -bg \"grey50\""
                           # one way of invoking emacs
```

Figure 9.1: Some sample aliases for bash.

9.1.2 Startup Files

Since most users want to have largely the same environment no matter what type of interactive shell they wind up with, whether or not it's a login shell, we'll start our configuration by putting a very simple command into our .bash_profile: "source ~/.bashrc". The source command tells the shell to interpret the argument as a shell script. What it means for us is that everytime .bash_profile is run, .bashrc is *also* run.

Now, we'll just add commands to our .bashrc. If you ever want a command to only be run when you login, add it to your .bash_profile.

9.1.3 Aliasing

What are some of the things you might want to customize? Here's something that I think about 90% of Bash users have put in their .bashrc:

```
alias ll="ls -l"
```

That command defined a shell **alias** called ll that "expands" to the normal shell command "ls -l" when invoked by the user. So, assuming that Bash has read that command in from your .bashrc, you can just type ll to get the effect of "ls -l" in only half the keystrokes. What happens is that when you type ll and hit [Return], Bash intercepts it, because it's watching for aliases, replaces it with "ls -l", and runs that instead. There is no actual program called ll on the system, but the shell automatically translated the alias into a valid program.

Some sample aliases are in Figure 9.1.3. You could put them in your own .bashrc. One especially interesting alias is the first one. With that alias, whenever someone types ls, they automatically have a -F flag tacked on. (The alias doesn't try to expand itself again.) This is a common way of adding options that you use every time you call a program.

Notice the comments with the # character in Figure 9.1.3. Whenever a # appears, the shell ignores the rest of the line.

You might have noticed a few odd things about them. First of all, I leave off the quotes in a few of the aliases—like pu. Strictly speaking, quotes aren't necessary when you only have one word on the right of the equal sign.

It never hurts to have quotes either, so don't let me get you into any bad habits. You should certainly use them if you're going to be aliasing a command with options and/or arguments:

```
alias rf="refrobnicate -verbose -prolix -wordy -o foo.out"
```

Also, the final alias has some funky quoting going on:

```
alias ed2="emacs -d floss:0 -fg \"grey95\" -bg \"grey50\""
```

As you might have guessed, I wanted to pass double-quotes in the options themselves, so I had to quote those with a backslash to prevent bash from thinking that they signaled the end of the alias.

Finally, I have actually aliased two common typing mistakes, "mroe" and "moer", to the command I meant to type, more. Aliases do not interfere with your passing arguments to a program. The following works just fine:

```
/home/larry# mroe hurd.txt
```

In fact, knowing how to make your own aliases is probably at least half of all the shell customization you'll ever do. Experiment a little, find out what long commands you find yourself typing frequently, and make aliases for them. You'll find that it makes working at a shell prompt a much more pleasant experience.

9.1.4 Environment Variables

Another major thing one does in a .bashrc is set **environment variables**. And what are environment variables? Let's go at it from the other direction: suppose you are reading the documentation for the program fruggle, and you run across these sentences:

> Fruggle normally looks for its configuration file, .frugglerc, in the user's home directory. However, if the environment variable FRUGGLEPATH is set to a different filename, it will look there instead.

Every program executes in an **environment**, and that environment is defined by the shell that called the program[1]. The environment could be said to exist "within" the shell. Programmers have a special routine for querying the environment, and the fruggle program makes use of this routine. It checks the value of the environment variable FRUGGLEPATH. If that variable turns out to be undefined, then it will just use the file .frugglerc in your home directory. If it is defined, however, fruggle will use the variable's value (which should be the name of a file that fruggle can use) instead of the default .frugglerc.

Here's how you can change your environment in bash:

```
/home/larry# export PGPPATH=/home/larry/secrets/pgp
```

You may think of the export command as meaning "Please export this variable out to the environment where I will be calling programs, so that its value is visible to them." There are actually reasons to call it export, as you'll see later.

This particular variable is used by Phil Zimmerman's infamous public-key encryption program, pgp. By default, pgp uses your home directory as a place to find certain files that it needs (containing encryption keys), and also as a place to store temporary files that it creates when it's running. By setting variable PGPPATH to this value, I have told it to use the directory /home/larry/secrets/pgp instead. I had to read the pgp manual to find out the exact name of the variable and what it does, but it is farily standard to use the name of the program in capital letters, prepended to the suffix "PATH".

It is also useful to be able to query the environment:

---

[1] Now you see why shells are so important. Imagine if you had to pass a whole environment by hand every time you called a program!

Variable name	Contains	Example
HOME	Your home directory	/home/larry
TERM	Your terminal type	xterm, vt100, or console
SHELL	The path to your shell	/bin/bash
USER	Your login name	larry
PATH	A list to search for programs	/bin:/usr/bin:/usr/local/bin:/usr/bin/X11

Figure 9.2: Some important environment variables.

```
/home/larry# echo $PGPPATH
/home/larry/.pgp
/home/larry#
```

Notice the "$"; you prefix an environment variable with a dollar sign in order to extract the variable's value. Had you typed it without the dollar sign, echo would have simply echoed its argument(s):

```
/home/larry# echo PGPPATH
PGPPATH
/home/larry#
```

The "$" is used to *evaluate* environment variables, but it only does so in the context of the shell—that is, when the shell is interpreting. When is the shell interpreting? Well, when you are typing commands at the prompt, or when bash is reading commands from a file like .bashrc, it can be said to be "interpreting" the commands.

There's another command that's very useful for querying the environment: env. env will merely list all the environment variables. It's possible, especially if you're using X, that the list will scroll off the screen. If that happens, just pipe env through more: env | more.

A few of these variables can be fairly useful, so I'll cover them. Look at Figure 9.1.4. Those four variables are defined automatically when you login: you don't set them in your .bashrc or .bash_login.

Let's take a closer look at the TERM variable. To understand that one, let's look back into the history of Unix: The operating system needs to know certain facts about your console, in order to perform basic functions like writing a character to the screen, moving the cursor to the next line, etc. In the early days of computing, manufacturers were constantly adding new features to their terminals: first reverse-video, then maybe European character sets, eventually even primitive drawing functions (remember, these were the days before windowing systems and mice). However, all of these new functions represented a problem to programmers: how could they know what a terminal supported and didn't support? And how could they support new features without making old terminals worthless?

In Unix, the answer to these questions was /etc/termcap. /etc/termcap is a list of all of the terminals that your system knows about, and how they control the cursor. If a system administrator got a new terminal, all they'd have to do is add an entry for that terminal into /etc/termcap instead of rebuilding all of Unix. Sometimes, it's even simpler. Along the way, Digital Equipment Corporation's vt100 terminal became a pseudo-standard, and many new terminals were built so that they could emulate it, or behave as if they were a vt100.

Under LINUX, TERM's value is sometimes console, which is a vt100-like terminal with some extra features.

Another variable, PATH, is also crucial to the proper functioning of the shell. Here's mine:

```
/home/larry# env | grep ^PATH
PATH=/home/larry/bin:/bin:/usr/bin:/usr/local/bin:/usr/bin/X11:/usr/TeX/bin
/home/larry#
```

Your PATH is a colon-separated list of the directories the shell should search for programs, when you type the name of a program to run. When I type ls and hit ⎢Return⎥, for example, the Bash first looks in /home/larry/bin, a directory I made for storing programs that I wrote. However, I didn't write ls (in fact, I think it might have been written before I was born!). Failing to find it in /home/larry/bin, Bash looks next in /bin—and there it has a hit! /bin/ls does exist and is executable, so Bash stops searching for a program named ls and runs it. There might well have been another ls sitting in the directory /usr/bin, but bash would never run it unless I asked for it by specifying an explicit pathname:

```
/home/larry# /usr/bin/ls
```

The PATH variable exists so that we don't have to type in complete pathnames for every command. When you type a command, Bash looks for it in the directories named in PATH, in order, and runs it if it finds it. If it doesn't find it, you get a rude error:

```
/home/larry# clubly
clubly: command not found
```

Notice that my PATH does not have the current directory, ".", in it. If it did, it might look like this:

```
/home/larry# echo $PATH
.:/home/larry/bin:/bin:/usr/bin:/usr/local/bin:/usr/bin/X11:/usr/TeX/bin
/home/larry#
```

This is a matter of some debate in Unix-circles (which you are now a member of, whether you like it or not). The problem is that having the current directory in your path can be a security hole. Suppose that you cd into a directory where somebody has left a "Trojan Horse" program called ls, and you do an ls, as would be natural on entering a new directory. Since the current directory, ".", came first in your PATH, the shell would have found this version of ls and executed it. Whatever mischief they might have put into that program, you have just gone ahead and executed (and that could be quite a lot of mischief indeed). The person did not need root privileges to do this; they only needed write permission on the directory where the "false" ls was located. It might even have been their home directory, if they knew that you would be poking around in there at some point.

On your own system, it's highly unlikely that people are leaving traps for each other. All the users are probably friends or colleagues of yours. However, on a large multi-user system (like many university computers), there could be plenty of unfriendly programmers whom you've never met. Whether or not you want to take your chances by having "." in your path depends on your situation; I'm not going to be dogmatic about it either way, I just want you to be aware of the risks involved[2]. Multi-user systems really are communities, where people can do things to one another in all sorts of unforseen ways.

The actual way that I set my PATH involves most of what you've learned so far about environment variables. Here is what is actually in my .bashrc:

```
export PATH=${PATH}:.:${HOME}/bin:/bin:/usr/bin:/usr/local/bin:/usr/bin/X11:/usr/TeX/bin
```

Here, I am taking advantage of the fact that the HOME variable is set before Bash reads my .bashrc, by using its value in setting my PATH. The curly braces ("{...}") are a further level of quoting; they delimit the extent of what the "$" is to evaluate, so that the shell doesn't get confused by the text immediately following it ("/bin" in this case). Here is another example of the effect they have:

```
/home/larry# echo ${HOME}foo
/home/larryfoo
/home/larry#
```

Without the curly braces, I would get nothing, since there is no environment variables named HOMEfoo.

---

[2] Remember that you can always execute programs in the current directory by being explicit about it, i.e.: "./foo".

```
/home/larry# echo $HOMEfoo

/home/larry#
```

Let me clear one other thing up in that path: the meaning of "$PATH". What that does is includes the value of any PATH variable *previously* set in my new PATH. Where would the old variable be set? The file /etc/profile serves as a kind of global .bash_profile that is common to all users. Having one centralized file like that makes it easier for the system administrator to add a new directory to everyone's PATH or something, without them all having to do it individually. If you include the old path in your new path, you won't lose any directories that the system already setup for you.

You can also control what your prompt looks like. This is done by setting the value of the environment variable **PS1**. Personally, I want a prompt that shows me the path to the current working directory—here's how I do it in my .bashrc:

```
export PS1='$PWD# '
```

As you can see, there are actually *two* variables being used here. The one being set is PS1, and it is being set to the value of PWD, which can be thought of as either "Print Working Directory" or "Path to Working Directory". But the evaluation of PWD takes place inside single quotes. The single quotes serve to evaluate the expression inside them, which itself evaluates the variable PWD. If you just did export PS1=$PWD, your prompt would constantly display the path to the current directory *at the time that* PS1 *was set*, instead of constantly updating it as you change directories. Well, that's sort of confusing, and not really all that important. Just keep in mind that you need the quotes if you want the current directory displayed in your prompt.

You might prefer export PS1='$PWD>', or even the name of your system: export PS1='`hostname`'>'. Let me dissect that last example a little further.

That last example used a *new* type of quoting, the back quotes. These don't protect something—in fact, you'll notice that "hostname" doesn't appear anywhere in the prompt when you run that. What actually happens is that the command inside the backquotes gets evaluated, and the output is put in place of the backquotes and the command name.

Try echo `ls` or wc `ls`. As you get more experienced using the shell, this technique gets more and more powerful.

There's a lot more to configuring your .bashrc, and not enough room to explain it here. You can read the bash man page for more, or ask questions of experienced Bash users. Here is a complete .bashrc for you to study; it's fairly standard, although the search path is a little long.

```
# some random stuff:
ulimit -c unlimited
export history_control=ignoredups
export PS1='$PWD>'
umask 022

# application-specific paths:
export MANPATH=/usr/local/man:/usr/man
export INFOPATH=/usr/local/info
export PGPPATH=${HOME}/.pgp

# make the main PATH:
homepath=${HOME}:~/bin
stdpath=/bin:/usr/bin:/usr/local/bin:/usr/ucb/:/etc:/usr/etc:/usr/games
pubpath=/usr/public/bin:/usr/gnusoft/bin:/usr/local/contribs/bin
softpath=/usr/bin/X11:/usr/local/bin/X11:/usr/TeX/bin
export PATH=.:${homepath}:${stdpath}:${pubpath}:${softpath}
# Technically, the curly braces were not necessary, because the colons
# were valid delimiters; nevertheless, the curly braces are a good
# habit to get into, and they can't hurt.
```

```
# aliases
alias ls="ls -CF"
alias fg1="fg %1"
alias fg2="fg %2"
alias tba="talk sussman@tern.mcs.anl.gov"
alias tko="talk kold@cs.oberlin.edu"
alias tji="talk jimb@totoro.bio.indiana.edu"
alias mroe="more"
alias moer="more"
alias email="emacs -f vm"
alias pu=pushd
alias po=popd
alias b="~/.b"
alias ds=dirs
alias ro="rm *~; rm .*~"
alias rd="rmdir"
alias ll="ls -l"
alias la="ls -a"
alias rr="rm -r"
alias md="mkdir"
alias ed2="emacs -d floss:0 -fg \"grey95\" -bg \"grey50\""

function gco
{
  gcc -o $1 $1.c -g
}
```

9.2   The X Window System Init Files

X Most people prefer to do their work inside a graphical environment, and for Unix machines, that usually means using X. If you're accustomed to the Macintosh or to Microsoft Windows, the X Window System may take a little getting used to, especially in how it is customized.

With the Macintosh or Microsoft Windows, you customize the environment from *within* the environment: if you want to change your background, for example, you do by clicking on the new color in some special graphical setup program. In X, system defaults are controlled by text files, which you edit directly—in other words, you'd type the actual color name into a file in order to set your background to that color.

There is no denying that this method just isn't as slick as some commercial windowing systems. I think this tendency to remain text-based, even in a graphical environment, has to do with the fact that X was created by a bunch of programmers who simply weren't trying to write software that their grandparents could use. This tendency may change in future versions of X (at least I hope it will), but for now, you just have to learn to deal with more text files. It does at least give you very flexible and precise control over your configuration.

Here are the most important files for configuring X:

```
.xinitrc    A script run by X when it starts up.
.twmrc      Read by an X window manager, twm.
.fvwmrc     Read by an X window manager, fvwm.
```

All of these files should be located in your home directory, if they exist at all.

The .xinitrc is a simple shell script that gets run when X is invoked. It can do anything any other shell script can do, but of course it makes the most sense to use it for starting up various X programs and setting window system parameters. The last command in the .xinitrc is usually the name of a window manager to run, for example /usr/bin/X11/twm.

What sort of thing might you want to put in a .xinitrc file? Perhaps some calls to the xsetroot program, to make your root (background) window and mouse cursor look the way you want them to look. Calls to `xmodmap`, which tells the server[3] how to interpret the signals from your keyboard. Any other programs you want started every time you run X (for example, `xclock`).

Here is some of my `.xinitrc`; yours will almost certainly look different, so this is meant only as an example:

```
#!/bin/sh
# The first line tells the operating system which shell to use in
# interpreting this script.  The script itself ought to be marked as
# executable; you can make it so with "chmod +x ~/.xinitrc".

# xmodmap is a program for telling the X server how to interpret your
# keyboard's signals.  It is *definitely* worth learning about. You
# can do "man xmodmap", "xmodmap -help", "xmodmap -grammar", and more.
# I don't guarantee that the expressions below will mean anything on
# your system (I don't even guarantee that they mean anything on
# mine):
xmodmap -e 'clear Lock'
xmodmap -e 'keycode 176 = Control_R'
xmodmap -e 'add control = Control_R'
xmodmap -e 'clear Mod2'
xmodmap -e 'add Mod1 = Alt_L Alt_R'

# xset is a program for setting some other parameters of the X server:
xset m 3 2 &         # mouse parameters
xset s 600 5 &       # screen saver prefs
xset s noblank &     # ditto
xset fp+ /home/larry/x/fonts # for cxterm
# To find out more, do "xset -help".

# Tell the X server to superimpose fish.cursor over fish.mask, and use
# the resulting pattern as my mouse cursor:
xsetroot -cursor /home/lab/larry/x/fish.cursor /home/lab/larry/x/fish.mask &

# a pleasing background pattern and color:
xsetroot -bitmap /home/lab/larry/x/pyramid.xbm -bg tan

# todo: xrdb here?  What about .Xdefaults file?

# You should do "man xsetroot", or "xsetroot -help" for more
# information on the program used above.

# A client program, the imposing circular color-clock by Jim Blandy:
/usr/local/bin/circles &

# Maybe you'd like to have a clock on your screen at all times?
/usr/bin/X11/xclock -digital &

# Allow client X programs running at occs.cs.oberlin.edu to display
# themselves here, do the same thing for juju.mcs.anl.gov:
xhost occs.cs.oberlin.edu
xhost juju.mcs.anl.gov

# You could simply tell the X server to allow clients running on any
# other host (a host being a remote machine) to display here, but this
# is a security hole -- those clients might be run by someone else,
# and watch your keystrokes as you type your password or something!
# However, if you wanted to do it anyway, you could use a "+" to stand
# for all possible hostnames, instead of a specific hostname, like
```

---

[3]The "server" just means the main X process on your machine, the one with which all other X programs must communicate in order to use the display. These other programs are known as "clients", and the whole deal is called a "client-server" system.

```
# this:
# xhost +

# And finally, run the window manager:
/usr/bin/X11/twm
# Some people prefer other window managers.  I use twm, but fvwm is
# often distributed with Linux too:
# /usr/bin/X11/fvwm
```

Notice that some commands are run in the background (i.e.: they are followed with a "&"), while others aren't. The distinction is that some programs will start when you start X and keep going until you exit—these get put in the background. Others execute once and then exit immediately. xsetroot is one such; it just sets the root window or cursor or whatever, and then exits.

Once the window manager has started, it will read its own init file, which controls things like how your menus are set up, which positions windows are brought up at, icon control, and other earth-shakingly important issues. If you use twm, then this file is .twmrc in your home directory. If you use fvwm, then it's .fvwmrc, etc. I'll deal with only those two, since they're the window managers you'll be most likely to encounter with Linux.

9.2.1   Twm Configuration

The .twmrc is not a shell script—it's actually written in a language specially made for twm, believe it or not![4] The main thing people like to play with in their .twmrc is window style (colors and such), and making cool menus, so here's an example .twmrc that does that:

```
# Set colors for the various parts of windows.  This has a great
# impact on the "feel" of your environment.
Color
{
        BorderColor "OrangeRed"
        BorderTileForeground "Black"
        BorderTileBackground "Black"
        TitleForeground "black"
        TitleBackground "gold"
        MenuForeground "black"
        MenuBackground "LightGrey"
        MenuTitleForeground "LightGrey"
        MenuTitleBackground "LightSlateGrey"
        MenuShadowColor "black"
        IconForeground "DimGray"
        IconBackground "Gold"
        IconBorderColor "OrangeRed"
        IconManagerForeground "black"
        IconManagerBackground "honeydew"
}

# I hope you don't have a monochrome system, but if you do...
Monochrome
{
        BorderColor "black"
        BorderTileForeground "black"
        BorderTileBackground "white"
        TitleForeground "black"
        TitleBackground "white"
```

---

[4]This is one of the harsh facts about init files: they generally each have their own idiosyncratic command language. This means that users get very good at learning command languages quickly. I suppose that it would have been nice if early Unix programmers had agreed on some standard init file format, so that we wouldn't have to learn new syntaxes all the time, but to be fair it's hard to predict what kinds of information programs will need.

```
}

# I created beifang.bmp with the program "bitmap".  Here I tell twm to
# use it as the default highlight pattern on windows' title bars:
Pixmaps
{
    TitleHighlight "/home/larry/x/beifang.bmp"
}


# Don't worry about this stuff, it's only for power users :-)
BorderWidth     2
TitleFont       "-adobe-new century schoolbook-bold-r-normal--14-140-75-75-p-87-iso8859-1"
MenuFont        "6x13"
IconFont        "lucidasans-italic-14"
ResizeFont      "fixed"
Zoom 50
RandomPlacement

# These programs will not get a window titlebar by default:
NoTitle
{
  "stamp"
  "xload"
  "xclock"
  "xlogo"
  "xbiff"
  "xeyes"
  "oclock"
  "xoid"
}


# "AutoRaise" means that a window is brought to the front whenever the
# mouse pointer enters it.  I find this annoying, so I have it turned
# off.  As you can see, I inherited my .twmrc from people who also did
# not like autoraise.
AutoRaise
{
  "nothing"     # I don't like auto-raise  # Me either  # nor I
}


# Here is where the mouse button functions are defined.  Notice the
# pattern: a mouse button pressed on the root window, with no modifier
# key being pressed, always brings up a menu.  Other locations usually
# result in window manipulation of some kind, and modifier keys are
# used in conjunction with the mouse buttons to get at the more
# sophisticated window manipulations.
#
# You don't have to follow this pattern in your own .twmrc -- it's
# entirely up to you how you arrange your environment.

# Button = KEYS : CONTEXT : FUNCTION
# ---------------------------------
Button1 =       : root    : f.menu "main"
Button1 =       : title   : f.raise
Button1 =       : frame   : f.raise
Button1 =       : icon    : f.iconify
Button1 = m     : window  : f.iconify

Button2 =       : root    : f.menu "stuff"
Button2 =       : icon    : f.move
Button2 = m     : window  : f.move
```

```
Button2 =       : title    : f.move
Button2 =       : frame    : f.move
Button2 = s     : frame    : f.zoom
Button2 = s     : window   : f.zoom

Button3 =       : root     : f.menu "x"
Button3 =       : title    : f.lower
Button3 =       : frame    : f.lower
Button3 =       : icon     : f.raiselower

# You can write your own functions; this one gets used in the menu
# "windowops" near the end of this file:
Function "raise-n-focus"
{
    f.raise
    f.focus
}


# Okay, below are the actual menus referred to in the mouse button
# section).  Note that many of these menu entries themselves call
# sub-menus.  You can have as many levels of menus as you want, but be
# aware that recursive menus don't work.  I've tried it.

menu "main"
{
"Vanilla"       f.title
"Emacs"         f.menu "emacs"
"Logins"        f.menu "logins"
"Xlock"         f.menu "xlock"
"Misc"          f.menu "misc"
}

# This allows me to invoke emacs on several different machines.  See
# the section on .rhosts files for more information about how this
# works:
menu "emacs"
{
"Emacs"         f.title
"here"          !"/usr/bin/emacs &"
""              f.nop
"phylo"         !"rsh phylo \"emacs -d floss:0\" &"
"geta"          !"rsh geta \"emacs -d floss:0\" &"
"darwin"        !"rsh darwin \"emacs -d floss:0\" &"
"ninja"         !"rsh ninja \"emacs -d floss:0\" &"
"indy"          !"rsh indy \"emacs -d floss:0\" &"
"oberlin"       !"rsh cs.oberlin.edu \"emacs -d floss.life.uiuc.edu:0\" &"
"gnu"           !"rsh gate-1.gnu.ai.mit.edu \"emacs -d floss.life.uiuc.edu:0\" &"
}


# This allows me to invoke xterms on several different machines.  See
# the section on .rhosts files for more information about how this
# works:
menu "logins"
{
"Logins"        f.title
"here"          !"/usr/bin/X11/xterm -ls -T `hostname` -n `hostname` &"
"phylo"         !"rsh phylo \"xterm -ls -display floss:0 -T phylo\" &"
"geta"          !"rsh geta \"xterm -ls -display floss:0 -T geta\" &"
"darwin"        !"rsh darwin \"xterm -ls -display floss:0 -T darwin\" &"
"ninja"         !"rsh ninja \"xterm -ls -display floss:0 -T ninja\" &"
"indy"          !"rsh indy \"xterm -ls -display floss:0 -T indy\" &"
```

```
}

# The xlock screensaver, called with various options (each of which
# gives a different pretty picture):
menu "xlock"
{
"Hop"    !"xlock -mode hop &"
"Qix"    !"xlock -mode qix &"
"Flame" !"xlock -mode flame &"
"Worm" !"xlock -mode worm &"
"Swarm" !"xlock -mode swarm &"
"Hop NL"   !"xlock -mode hop -nolock &"
"Qix NL"   !"xlock -mode qix -nolock &"
"Flame NL" !"xlock -mode flame -nolock &"
"Worm NL" !"xlock -mode worm -nolock &"
"Swarm NL" !"xlock -mode swarm -nolock &"
}

# Miscellaneous programs I run occasionally:
menu "misc"
{
"Xload"         !"/usr/bin/X11/xload &"
"XV"            !"/usr/bin/X11/xv &"
"Bitmap"        !"/usr/bin/X11/bitmap &"
"Tetris"        !"/usr/bin/X11/xtetris &"
"Hextris"       !"/usr/bin/X11/xhextris &"
"XRoach"        !"/usr/bin/X11/xroach &"
"Analog Clock" !"/usr/bin/X11/xclock -analog &"
"Digital Clock" !"/usr/bin/X11/xclock -digital &"
}

# This is the one I bound to the middle mouse button:
menu "stuff"
{
"Chores"     f.title
"Sync"       !"/bin/sync"
"Who"        !"who | xmessage -file - -columns 80 -lines 24 &"
"Xhost +"    !"/usr/bin/X11/xhost + &"
"Rootclear"  !"/home/larry/bin/rootclear &"
}

# X functions that are sometimes convenient:
menu "x"
{
"X Stuff"        f.title
"Xhost +"        !"xhost + &"
"Refresh"        f.refresh
"Source .twmrc"  f.twmrc
"(De)Iconify"    f.iconify
"Move Window"    f.move
"Resize Window"  f.resize
"Destroy Window" f.destroy
"Window Ops"     f.menu "windowops"
""               f.nop
"Kill twm"       f.quit
}

# This is a submenu from above:
menu "windowops"
{
"Window Ops"        f.title
```

```
"Show Icon Mgr"          f.showiconmgr
"Hide Icon Mgr"          f.hideiconmgr
"Refresh"                f.refresh
"Refresh Window"         f.winrefresh
"twm version"            f.version
"Focus on Root"          f.unfocus
"Source .twmrc"          f.twmrc
"Cut File"               f.cutfile
"(De)Iconify"            f.iconify
"DeIconify"              f.deiconify
"Move Window"            f.move
"ForceMove Window"       f.forcemove
"Resize Window"          f.resize
"Raise Window"           f.raise
"Lower Window"           f.lower
"Raise or Lower"         f.raiselower
"Focus on Window"        f.focus
"Raise-n-Focus"          f.function "raise-n-focus"
"Destroy Window"         f.destroy
"Kill twm"               f.quit
}
```

Whew! Believe me, that's not even the most involved .twmrc I've ever seen. It's quite probable that some decent example .twmrc files came with your X. Take a look in the directory /usr/lib/X11/twm/ or /usr/X11/lib/X11/twm and see what's there.

One bug to watch out for with .twmrc files is forgetting to put the & after a command on a menu. If you notice that X just freezes when you run certain commands, chances are that this is the cause. Break out of X with [Control]-[Alt]-[Backspace], edit your .twmrc, and try again.

9.2.2 Fvwm Configuration

If you are using fvwm, the directory /usr/lib/X11/fvwm/ (or /usr/X11/lib/X11/fvwm/) has some good example config files in it, as well.

[Folks: I don't know anything about fvwm, although I might be able to grok something from the example config files. Then again, so could the reader :-). Also, given the decent but small system.twmrc in the above-mentioned directory, I wonder if it's worth it for me to provide that lengthy example with my own .twmrc. It's in for now, but I don't know whether we want to leave it there or not. -Karl]

9.3   Other Init Files

Some other initialization files of note are:

- .emacs   Read by the Emacs text editor when it starts up.
- .netrc   Gives default login names and passwords for ftp.
- .rhosts   Makes your account remotely accessible.
- .forward   For automatic mail forwarding.

9.3.1   The Emacs Init File

If you use emacs as your primary editor, then the .emacs file is quite important. It is dealt with at length in Chapter 8.

9.3.2 FTP Defaults

Your .netrc file allows you to have certain ftp defaults set before you run ftp. Here is a small sample .netrc:

```
machine floss.life.uiuc.edu login larry password fishSticks
machine darwin.life.uiuc.edu login larry password fishSticks
machine geta.life.uiuc.edu login larry password fishSticks
machine phylo.life.uiuc.edu login larry password fishSticks
machine ninja.life.uiuc.edu login larry password fishSticks
machine indy.life.uiuc.edu login larry password fishSticks

machine clone.mcs.anl.gov login fogel password doorm@
machine osprey.mcs.anl.gov login fogel password doorm@
machine tern.mcs.anl.gov login fogel password doorm@
machine altair.mcs.anl.gov login fogel password doorm@
machine dalek.mcs.anl.gov login fogel password doorm@
machine juju.mcs.anl.gov login fogel password doorm@

machine sunsite.unc.edu login anonymous password larry@cs.oberlin.edu
```

Each line of your .netrc specifies a machine name, a login name to use by default for that machine, and a password. This is a great convenience if you do a lot of ftp-ing and are tired of constantly typing in your username and password at various sites. The ftp program will try to log you in automatically using the information found in your .netrc file, if you ftp to one of the machines listed in the file.

You can tell ftp to ignore your .netrc and not attempt auto-login by invoking it with the -n option: "ftp -n".

You must make sure that your .netrc file is readable *only* by you. Use the chmod program to set the file's read permissions. If other people can read it, that means they can find out your password at various other sites. This is about as big a security hole as one can have; to encourage you to be careful, ftp and other programs that look for the .netrc file will actually refuse to work if the read permissions on the file are bad.

There's more to the .netrc file than what I've said; when you get a chance, do "man .netrc" or "man ftp".

9.3.3 Allowing Easy Remote Access to Your Account

If you have an .rhosts file in your home directory, it will allow you to run programs on this machine remotely. That is, you might be logged in on the machine cs.oberlin.edu, but with a correctly configured .rhosts file on floss.life.uiuc.edu, you could run a program on floss.life.uiuc.edu and have the output go to cs.oberlin.edu, without ever having to log in or type a password.

A .rhosts file looks like this:

```
frobnozz.cs.knowledge.edu jsmith
aphrodite.classics.hahvaahd.edu wphilps
frobbo.hoola.com trixie
```

The format is fairly straightforward: a machine name, followed by username. Suppose that that example is in fact my .rhosts file on floss.life.uiuc.edu. That would mean that I could run programs on floss, with output going to any of the machines listed, as long as I were also logged in as the corresponding user given for that machine when I tried to do it.

The exact mechanism by which one runs a remote program is usually the rsh program. It stands for "remote shell", and what it does is start up a shell on a remote machine and execute a specified command. For example:

```
frobbo$ whoami
trixie
frobbo$ rsh floss.life.uiuc.edu "ls ~"
foo.txt    mbox   url.ps    snax.txt
frobbo$ rsh floss.life.uiuc.edu "more ~/snax.txt"
[snax.txt comes paging by here]
```

User trixie at floss.life.uiuc.edu, who had the example `.rhosts` shown previously, explicitly allows trixie at frobbo.hoola.com to run programs as trixie from floss.

You don't have to have the same username on all machines to make a `.rhosts` work right. Use the "`-l`" option to `rsh`, to tell the remote machine what username you'd like to use for logging in. If that username exists on the remote machine, and has a `.rhosts` file with your current (i.e.: local) machine and username in it, then your `rsh` will succeed.

```
frobbo$ whoami
trixie
frobbo$ rsh -l larry floss.life.uiuc.edu "ls ~"
[Insert a listing of my directory on floss here]
```

This will work if user `larry` on `floss.life.uiuc.edu` has a `.rhosts` file which allows `trixie` from `frobbo.hoopla.com` to run programs in his account. Whether or not they are the same person is irrelevant: the only important things are the usernames, the machine names, and the entry in larry's `.rhosts` file on floss. Note that trixie's `.rhosts` file on frobbo doesn't enter into it, only the one on the remote machine matters.

There are other combinations that can go in a `.rhosts` file—for example, you can leave off the username following a remote machine name, to allow any user from that machine to run programs as you on the local machine! This is, of course, a security risk: someone could remotely run a program that removes your files, just by virtue of having an account on a certain machine. If you're going to do things like leave off the username, then you ought to make sure that your `.rhosts` file is readable by you and no one else.

9.3.4   Mail Forwarding

You can also have a `.forward` file, which is not strictly speaking an "init file". If it contains an email address, then all mail to you will be forwarded to that address instead. This is useful when you have accounts on many different systems, but only want to read mail at one location.

There is a host of other possible initialization files. The exact number will vary from system to system, and is dependent on the software installed on that system. One way to learn more is to look at files in your home directory whose names begin with "`.`". These files are not all guaranteed to be init files, but it's a good bet that most of them are.

9.4   Seeing Some Examples

The ultimate example I can give you is a running Linux system. So, if you have Internet access, feel free to telnet to `floss.life.uiuc.edu`. Log in as "guest", password "explorer", and poke around. Most of the example files given here can be found in `/home/kfogel`, but there are other user directories as well. You are free to copy anything that you can read. Please be careful: floss is not a terribly secure box, and you can almost certainly gain root access if you try hard enough. I prefer to rely on trust, rather than constant vigilance, to maintain security.

Chapter 10

Talking to Others

"One basic notion underlying Usenet is that it is a cooperative."

Having been on Usenet for going on ten years, I disagree with this. The basic notion underlying Usenet is the flame.

Chuq Von Rospach

Unix networks extremely well. Two different Unix computers can exchange information is many, many different ways. This chapter is going to try to talk about how you can take advantage of strong network ability.

We'll try to cover electronic mail, Usenet news, and several basic Unix utilities used for communication.

10.1   Electronic Mail

One of the most popular standard features of Unix is electronic mail. With it, you are spared the usual hassle of finding an envelope, a piece of paper, a pen, a stamp, and the postal service.

10.1.1   Sending Mail

All you need to do is type `mail` *username* and type your message.

For instance, suppose I wanted to send mail to a user named `sam`:

```
/home/larry# mail sam
Subject: The user documentation
Just testing out the mail system.
EOT
/home/larry#
```

The `mail` program is very simple. Like `cat`, it accepts input from standard input, one line at a time, until it gets the end-of-text character on a line by itself: Ctrl-d. So, to send my message off I had to hit return and then Ctrl-d.

`mail` is the quickest way to send mail, and is quite useful when used with pipes and redirection. For instance, if I wanted to mail the file `report1` to "Sam", I could `mail sam < report1`, or I could have even run "`sort report1 | mail sam`".

However, the downside of using `mail` to send mail means a very crude editor. You can't change a line once you've hit return! So, I recommend you send mail (when not using a pipe or redirection) is with Emacs's mail mode. It's covered in Section 8.10.

10.1.2   Reading Mail

The mail program offers a clumsy way of reading mail. If you type mail without any parameter, you'll see the following:

```
/home/larry# mail
No mail for larry
/home/larry#
```

I'm going to send myself some mail so I can play around with the mailreader:

```
/home/larry# mail larry
Subject: Frogs!
and toads!
EOT
/home/larry# echo "snakes" | mail larry
/home/larry# mail
Mail version 5.5 6/1/90.  Type ? for help.
"/usr/spool/mail/larry": 2 messages 2 new
>N  1 larry              Tue Aug 30 18:11  10/211   "Frogs!"
 N  2 larry              Tue Aug 30 18:12   9/191
&
```

The prompt inside the mail program is an ampersand ("&"). It allows a couple of simple commands, and will give a short help screen if you type ? and then return .

The basic commands for mail are:

t *message-list*   Show (or type) the messages on the screen.

d *message-list*   Delete the messages.

s *message-list file*
                   Save the messages into *file*.

r *message-list*   Reply to the messages—that is, start composing a new message to whoever sent you the listed messages.

q   Quit and save any messages you didn't delete into a file called mbox in your home directory.

What's a *message-list*? It consists of a list of integers separated by spaces, or even a range, such as 2-4 (which is identical to "2 3 4"). You can also enter the username of the sender, so the command t sam would type all the mail from Sam. If a message list is omitted, it is assumed to be the last message displayed (or typed).

There are several problems with the mail program's reading facilities. First of all, if a message is longer than your screen, the mail program doesn't stop! You'll have to save it and use more on it later. Second of all, it doesn't have a very good interface for old mail—if you wanted to save mail and read it later.

Emacs also has a facility for reading mail, called rmail, but it is not covered in this book. Additionally, most Linux systems have several other mailreaders available, such as elm or pine.

10.2   More than Enough News

10.3   Searching for People

10.4   Using Systems by Remote

X If you're using X, let's create a new xterm for the other system we're travelling to. Use the command "xterm -title "lionsden" -e telnet lionsden &". This will create a new xterm window that's automatically running telnet. (If you do something like that often, you might want to create an alias or shell script for it.)

10.5   Exchanging Files on the Fly

Chapter 11

Funny Commands

Well, most people who had to do with the UNIX commands exposed in this chapter will not agree with this title. "What the heck! You have just shown me that the Linux interface is very standard, and now we have a bunch of commands, each one working in a completely different way. I will never remember all those options, and you are saying that they are *funny*?" Yes, you have just seen an example of hackers' humor. Besides, look at it from the bright side: there is no MS-DOS equivalent of these commands. If you need them, you have to purchase them, and you never know how their interface will be. Here they are a useful – and inexpensive – add-on, so enjoy!

The set of commands dwelled on in this chapter covers find, which lets the user search in the directory tree for specified groups of files; tar, useful to create some archive to be shipped or just saved; dd, the low-level copier; and sort, which ... yes, sorts files. A last proviso: these commands are by no means standardized, and while a core of common options could be found on all **IX systems, the (GNU) version which is explained below, and which you can find in your Linux system, has usually many more capabilities. So if you plan to use other UNIX-like operating systems, please don't forget to check their man page in the target system to learn the maybe not-so-little differences.

11.1 find, the file searcher

11.1.1 Generalities

Among the various commands seen so far, there were some which let the user recursively go down the directory tree in order to perform some action: the canonical examples are ls -R and rm -R. Good. find is *the* recursive command. Whenever you are thinking "Well, I have to do so-and-so on all those kind of files in my own partition", you have better think about using find. In a certain sense the fact that find finds files is just a side effect: its real occupation is to evaluate.

The basic structure of the command is as follows:

find *path* [. . .] *expression* [. . .]

This at least on the GNU version; other version do not allow to specify more than one path, and besides it is very uncommon the need to do such a thing. The rough explanation of the command syntax is rather simple: you say from where you want to start the search (the *path* part; with GNU find you can omit this and it will be taken as default the current directory .), and which kind of search you want to perform (the *expression* part).

The standard behavior of the command is a little tricky, so it's worth to note it. Let's suppose that in your home directory there is a directory called garbage, containing a file foobar. You happily type find . -name foobar (which as you can guess searches for files named foobar), and you obtain ... nothing else than the prompt again. The trouble lies in the fact that find is by default a silent command; it just returns 0 if the search was completed (with or without finding anything) or a non-zero value if there had been some problem. This does not happen with the version you can find on Linux, but it is useful to remember it anyway.

11.1.2   Expressions

The *expression* part can be divided itself in four different groups of keywords: *options, tests, actions,* and *operators*. Each of them can return a true/false value, together with a side effect. The difference among the groups is shown below.

options affect the overall operation of find, rather than the processing of a single file. An example is -follow, which instructs `find` to follow symbolic links instead of just stating the inode. They always return true.

tests are real tests (for example, -empty checks whether the file is empty), and can return true or false.

actions have also a side effect the name of the considered file. They can return true or false too.

operators do not really return a value (they can conventionally be considered as true), and are used to build compress expression. An example is -or, which takes the logical OR of the two subexpressions on its side. Notice that when juxtaposing expression, a -and is implied.

Note that `find` relies upon the shell to have the command line parsed; it means that all keyword must be embedded in white space and especially that a lot of nice characters have to be escaped, otherwise they would be mangled by the shell itself. Each escaping way (backslash, single and double quotes) is OK; in the examples the single character keywords will be usually quoted with backslash, because it is the simplest way (at least in my opinion. But it's me who is writing these notes!)

11.1.3   Options

Here there is the list of all options known by GNU version of `find`. Remember that they always return true.

- -daystart measures elapsed time not from 24 hours ago but from last midnight. A true hacker probably won't understand the utility of such an option, but a worker who programs from eight to five does appreciate it.

- -depth processes each directory's contents before the directory itself. To say the truth, I don't know many uses of this, apart for an emulation of rm -F command (of course you cannot delete a directory before all files in it are deleted too . . .

- -follow deferences (that is, follows) symbolic links. It implies option -noleaf; see below.

- -noleaf turns off an optimization which says "A directory contains two fewer subdirectories than their hard link count". If the world were perfect, all directories would be referenced by each of their subdirectories (because of the .. option), as . inside itself, and by it's "real" name from its parent directory.

  That means that every directory must be referenced at least twice (once by itself, once by its parent) and any additional references are by subdirectories. In practice however, symbolic links and distributed filesystems[1] can disrupt this. This option makes `find` run slightly slower, but may give expected results.

---

[1] Distributed filesystems allow files to appear like their local to a machine when they are actually located somewhere else.

- -maxdepth *levels*, -mindepth *levels*, where *levels* is a non-negative integer, respectively say that at most or at least *levels* levels of directories should be searched. A couple of examples is mandatory: -maxdepth 0 indicates that it the command should be performed just on the arguments in the command line, i.e., without recursively going down the directory tree; -mindepth 1 inhibits the processing of the command for the arguments in the command line, while all other files down are considered.

- -version just prints the current version of the program.

- -xdev, which is a misleading name, instructs find **not** to cross device, i.e. changing filesystem. It is very useful when you have to search for something in the root filesystem; in many machines it is a rather small partition, but a find / would otherwise search the whole structure!

11.1.4 Tests

The first two tests are very simple to understand: -false always return false, while -true always return true. Other tests which do not need the specification of a value are -empty, which returns true whether the file is empty, and the couple -nouser / -nogroup, which return true in the case that no entry in /etc/passwd or /etc/group match the user/group id of the file owner. This is a common thing which happens in a multiuser system; a user is deleted, but files owned by her remain in the strangest part of the filesystems, and due to Murphy's laws take a lot of space.

Of course, it is possible to search for a specific user or group. The tests are -uid *nn* and -gid *nn*. Unfortunately it is not possibile to give directly the user name, but it is necessary to use the numeric id, *nn*.

allowed to use the forms +*nn*, which means "a value strictly greater than *nn*", and −*nn*, which means "a value strictly less than *nn*". This is rather silly in the case of UIDs, but it will turn handy with other tests.

Another useful option is -type *c*, which returns true if the file is of type *c*. The mnemonics for the possible choices are the same found in ls; so we have **b** when the file is a block special; **c** when the file is character special; **d** for directories; **p** for named pipes; **l** for symbolic links, and **s** for sockets. Regular files are indicated with **f**. A related test is -xtype, which is similar to -type except in the case of symbolic links. If -follow has not been given, the file pointed at is checked, instead of the link itself. Completely unrelated is the test -fstype *type*. In this case, the filesystem type is checked. I think that the information is got from file /etc/mtab, the one stating the mounting filesystems; I am certain that types nfs, tmp, msdos and ext2 are recognized.

Tests -inum *nn* and -links *nn* check whether the file has inode number *nn*, or *nn* links, while -size *nn* is true if the file has *nn* 512-bytes blocks allocated. (well, not precisely: for sparse files unallocated blocks are counted too). As nowadays the result of ls -s is not always measured in 512-bytes chunks (Linux for example uses 1k as the unit), it is possible to append to *nn* the character *b*, which means to count in butes, or *k*, to count in kilobytes.

Permission bits are checked through the test -perm *mode*. If *mode* has no leading sign, then the permission bits of the file must exactly match them. A leading − means that all permission bits must be set, but makes no assumption for the other; a leading + is satisfied just if any of the bits are set. Oops! I forgot saying that the mode is written in octal or symbolically, like you use them in chmod.

Next group of tests is related to the time in which a file has been last used. This comes handy when a user has filled his space, as usually there are many files he did not use since ages, and whose meaning he has forgot. The trouble is to locate them, and find is the only hope in sight. -atime *nn* is true if the file was last accessed *nn* days ago, -ctime *nn* if the file status was last changed *nn* days ago – for example, with a chmod – and -mtime *nn* if the file was last modified *nn* days ago. Sometimes you need a more precise timestamp; the test -newer *file* is satisfied if the file considered has been modified later than *file*. So, you just have to use touch with the desired date, and you're done. GNU find add the tests -anewer and -cnewer which behave similarly; and the tests -amin, -cmin and -mmin which count time in minutes instead than 24-hours periods.

Last but not the least, the test I use more often. -name *pattern* is true if the file name exactly matches *pattern*, which is more or less the one you would use in a standard ls. Why 'more or less'? Because of course you have to remember that all the parameters are processed by the shell, and those lovely metacharacters are expanded. So, a test like −name foo* won't return what you want, and you should either write −name foo or −name "foo*". This is probably one of the most common mistakes made by careless users, so write it in BIG letters on your screen. Another problem is that, like with ls, leading dots are not recognized. To cope with this, you can use test -path *pattern* which does not worry about dot and slashes when comparing the path of the considered file with *pattern*.

11.1.5 Actions

I have said that actions are those which actually do something. Well, -prune rather does not do something, i.e. descending the directory tree (unless -depth is given). It is usally find together with -fstype, to choose among the various filesystems which should be checked.

The other actions can be divided into two broad categories;

- Actions which *print* something. The most obvious of these – and indeed, the default action of find – is -print which just print the name of the file(s) matching the other conditions in the command line, and returns true. A simple variants of -print is -fprint *file*, which uses *file* instead of standard output, -ls lists the current file in the same format as ls -dils; -printf *format* behaves more or less like C function printf(), so that you can specify how the output should be formatted, and -fprintf *file format* does the same, but writing on *file*. These action too return true.

- Actions which *execute* something. Their syntax is a little odd and they are used widely, so please look at them.

  -exec *command* \; the command is executed, and the action returns true if its final status is 0, that is regular execution of it. The reason for the \; is rather logical: find does not know where the command ends, and the trick to put the exec action at the end of the command is not applicable. Well, the best way to signal the end of the command is to use the character used to do this by the shell itself, that is ';', but of course a semicolon all alone on the command line would be eaten by the shell and never sent to find, so it has to be escaped. The second thing to remember is how to specify the name of the current file within *command*, as probably you did all the trouble to build the expression to do something, and not just to print date. This is done by means of the string {}. Some old versions of find require that it must be embedded in white space – not very handy if you needed for example the whole path and not just the file name – but with GNU find could be anywhere in the string composing *command*. And shouldn't it be escaped or quoted, you surely are asking? Amazingly, I never had to do this neither under tcsh nor under bash (sh does not consider { and } as special characters, so it is not much of a problem). My idea is that the shells "know" that {} is not an option making sense, so they do not try to expand them, luckily for find which can obtain it untouched.

  -ok *command* \; behaves like -exec, with the difference that for each selected file the user is asked to confirm the command; if the answer starts with y or Y, it is executed, otherwise not, and the action returns false.

11.1.6 Operators

There are a number of operators; here there is a list, in order of decreasing precedence.

\(*expr* \)
    forces the precedence order. The parentheses must of course be quoted, as they are meaningful for the shell too.

! *expr*
-not *expr*

change the truth value of expression, that is if *expr* is true, it becomes false. The exclamation mark
needn't be escaped, because it is followed by a white space.

expr1 expr2
expr1 -a *expr2*
expr1 -and *expr2*
all correspond to the logical AND operation, which in the first and most common case is implied.
expr2 is not evaluated, if *expr1* is false.

expr1 -o *expr2*
expr1 -or *expr2*
correspond to the logical OR operation. *expr2* is not evaluated, if *expr1* is true.

expr1 , *expr2*
is the list statement; both *expr1* and *expr2* are evaluated (together with all side effects, of course!), and
the final value of the expression is that of *expr2*.

11.1.7 Examples

Yes, I know that `find` has too many options. But there are a lot of instances which are worth remembering, because they are used often. Let's see some of them.

```
% find . -name foo\* -print
```

finds all file names starting with `foo`. If the string is embedded in the name, probably it is more
sensitive to write something like `"*foo*"`, rather than `foo`.

```
% find /usr/include -xtype f -exec grep foobar \
            /dev/null {} \;
```

is a grep executed recursively starting from directory /usr/include. In this case, we are interested both
in regular file and in symbolic links which point to regular files, hence the -xtype test. Many times
it is simpler to avoid specifing it, especially if we are rather sure no binary file contains the wanted
string. And why the /dev/null in the command? It's a trick to force grep to write the file name where
a match has been found. The command grep is applied to each file in a different invocation, and so it
doesn't think it is necessary to output the file name. But now there are *two* files, i.e. the current one and
/dev/null! Another possibility should be to pipe the command to `xargs` and let it perform the grep.
I just tried it, and completely smashed my filesystem (together with these notes which I am trying to
recover by hand :-( ).

```
% find /  -atime +1 -fstype ext2 -name core \
              -exec rm {} \;
```

is a classical job for crontab. It deletes all file named `core` in filesystems of type ext2 which have not
been accessed in the last 24 hours. It is possible that someone wants to use the core file to perform a
post mortem dump, but nobody could remember what he was doing after 24 hours. . .

```
% find /home -xdev -size +500k -ls > piggies
```

is useful to see who has those files who clog the filesystem. Note the use of -xdev; as we are interested
in just one filesystem, it is not necessary to descend other filesystems mounted under /home.

11.1.8   A last word

Keep in mind that find is a very time consuming command, as it has to access each and every inode of the system in order to perform its operation. It is therefore wise to combine how many operations you need in a unique invocation of find, especially in the 'housekeeping' jobs usually ran via a crontab job. A enlightening example is the following: let's suppose that we want to delete files ending in .BAK and change the protection of all directories to 771 and that of all files ending in .sh to 755. And maybe we are mounting NFS filesystems on a dial-up link, and we'd like not to check for files there. Why writing three different commands? The most effective way to accomplish the task is this:

```
% find . \( -fstype nfs -prune \) -o \
         \( -type d       -a -exec chmod 771 {} \; \) -o \
         \( -name "*.BAK" -a -exec /bin/rm {}  \; \) -o \
         \( -name "*.sh"  -a -exec chmod 755 {} \; \)
```

It seems ugly (and with much abuse of backslashes!), but looking closely at it reveals that the underlying logic is rather straightforward. Remember that what is really performed is a true/false evaluation; the embedded command is just a side effect. But this means that it is performed only if find must evaluate the exec part of the expression, that is only if the left side of the subexpression evaluates to true. So, if for example the file considered at the moment is a directory then the first exec is evaluated and the permission of the inode is changed to 771; otherwise it forgets everything and steps to the next subexpression. It's probably easier to see it in practice than in writing; but after a while, it will become a natural thing.

11.2   tar, the tape archiver

11.2.1   Introduction

11.2.2   Main options

11.2.3   Modifiers

11.2.4   Examples

11.3   dd, the data duplicator

Legend says that back in the mists of time, when the first UNIX was created, its developers needed a low level command to copy data between devices. As they were in a hurry, they decided to borrow the syntax used by IBM-360 machines, and to later develop an interface consistent with that of the other commands. As time passed, everyone used dd and it's odd syntax stuck. I don't know whether this is true, but it is a nice story to tell.

11.3.1   Options

To say the truth, dd it's not completely unlike the other Unix command: it is indeed a **filter**, that is it reads by default from the standard input and writes to the standard output. So if you just type dd at the terminal it remains quiet, waiting for input, and a ctrl-C is the only sensitive thing to type.

The syntax of the command is as follows:

```
dd [if=file] [of=file] [ibs=bytes] [obs=bytes]
   [bs=bytes] [cbs=bytes] [skip=blocks] [seek=blocks]
```

```
[count=blocks] [conv={ascii,ebcdic,ibm,block,
     unblock,lcase,ucase,swab,noerror,notrunc,sync}]
```

so all options are of the form *option=value*. No space is allowed either before or after the equal sign; this used to be annoying, because the shell did not expand a filename in this situation, but the version of bash present in Linux is rather smart, so you don't have to worry about that. It is important also to remember that all numbered values (`bytes` and `blocks` above) can be followed by a multiplier. The possible choices are **b** for block, which multiplies by 512, **k** for kilobytes (1024), **w** for word (2), and **xm** multiplies by **m**.

The meaning of options if explained below.

- if=*filein* and of=*fileout* instruct `dd` to respectively read from *filein* and write to *fileout*. In the latter case, the output file is truncated to the value given to `seek`, or if the keyword is not present, to 0 (that is deleted), before performing the operation. But look below at option `notrunc`.

- ibs=*nn* and obs=*nn* specify how much bytes should be read or write at a time. I think that the default is 1 block, i.e. 512 bytes, but I am not very sure about it: certainly it works that way with plain files. These parameters are very important when using special devices as input or output; for example, reading from the net should set `ibs` at 10k, while a high density 3.5" floppy has as its natural block size 18k. Failing to set these values could result not only in longer time to perform the command, but even in timeout errors, so be careful.

- bs=*nn* both reads and writes *nn* bytes at a time. It overrides `ibs` and `obs` keywords.

- cbs=*nn* sets the conversion buffers to *nn* bytes. This buffer is used when translating from ASCII to EBCDIC, or from an unblocked device to a blocked one. For example, files created under VMS have often a block size of 512, so you have to set `cbs` to 1b when reading a foreign VMS tape. Hope that you don't have to mess with these things!

- skip=*nbl* and seek=*nbl* tell the program to skip *nbl* blocks respectively at the beginning of input and at the beginning of output. Of course the latter case makes sense if conversion `notrunc` is given, see below. Each block's size is the value of `ibs` (`obs`). Beware: if you did not set `ibs` and write `skip=1b` you are actually skipping 512×*512 bytes, that is 256KB. It was not precisely what you wanted, wasn't it?

- count=*nbl* means to copy only *nbl* blocks from input, each of the size given by `ibs`. This option, together with the previous, turns useful if for example you have a corrupted file and you want to recover how much it is possible from it. You just skip the unreadable part and get what remains.

- conv=*conversion*,[*conversion*. . .] convert the file as specified by its argument. Possible conversions are `ascii`, which converts from EBCDIC to ASCII; `ebcdic` and `ibm`, which both perform an inverse conversion (yes, there is not a unique conversion from EBCDIC to ASCII! The first is the standard one, but the second works better when printing files on a IBM printer); `block`, which pads newline-terminated records to the size of `cbs`, replacing newline with trailing spaces; `unblock`, which performs the opposite (eliminates trailing spaces, and replaces them with newline); `lcase` and `ucase`, to convert test to lowercase and uppercase; `swab`, which swaps every pair of input bytes (for example, to use a file containing short integers written on a 680x0 machine in an Intel-based machine you need such a conversion); `noerror`, to continue processing after read errors; `sync`, which pads input block to the size of `ibs` with trailing NULs.

11.3.2   Examples

The canonical example is the one you have probably bumped at when you tried to create the first Linux diskette: how to write to a floppy without a MS-DOS filesystem. The solution is simple:

```
% dd if=disk.img of=/dev/fd0 obs=18k count=80
```

I decided not to use `ibs` because I don't know which is the better block size for a hard disk, but in this case no harm would have been if instead of `obs` I use `bs` – it could even be a trifle quicker. Notice the explicitation of the number of sectors to write (18KB is the occupation of a sector, so `count` is set to 80) and the use of the low-level name of the floppy device.

Another useful application of `dd` is related to the network backup. Let's suppose that we are on machine *alpha* and that on machine *beta* there is the tape unit `/dev/rst0` with a tar file we are interested in getting. We have the same rights on both machines, but there is no space on *beta* to dump the tar file. In this case, we could write

```
% rsh beta 'dd if=/dev/rst0 ibs=8k obs=20k' | tar xvBf -
```

to do in a single pass the whole operation. In this case, we have used the facilities of `rsh` to perform the reading from the tape. Input and output sizes are set to the default for these operations, that is 8KB for reading from a tape and 20KB for writing to ethernet; from the point of view of the other side of the tar, there is the same flow of bytes which could be got from the tape, except the fact that it arrives in a rather erratic way, and the option B is necessary.

I forgot: I don't think at all that `dd` is an acronym for "data duplicator", but at least this is a nice way to remember its meaning ...

11.4 `sort`, **the data sorter**

11.4.1 Introduction

11.4.2 Options

11.4.3 Examples

Chapter 12

Errors, Mistakes, Bugs, and Other Unpleasantries

> Unix was never designed to keep people from doing stupid things, because that policy
> would also keep them from doing clever things.
>
> Doug Gwyn

12.1 Avoiding Errors

Many users report frustration with the Unix operating system at one time or another, frequently because of their own doing. A feature of the Unix operating system that many users' love when they're working well and hate after a late-night session is how very few commands ask for confirmation. When a user is awake and functioning, they rarely think about this, and it is an asset since it let's them work smoother.

However, there are some disadvantages. rm and mv never ask for confirmation and this frequently leads to problems. Thus, let's go through a small list that might help you avoid total disaster:

- Keep backups! This applies especially to the one user system—all system adminstrators should make regular backups of their system! Once a week is good enough to salvage many files. See the *The* LINUX *System Adminstrator's Guide* for more information.

- Individual user's should keep there own backups, if possible. If you use more than one system regularly, try to keep updated copies of all your files on each of the systems. If you have access to a floppy drive, you might want to make backups onto floppies of your critical material. At worst, keep additional copies of your most important material lying around your account *in a separate directory*!

- Think about commands, especially "destructive" ones like mv, rm, and cp before you act. You also have to be careful with redirection (>)—it'll overwrite your files when you aren't paying attention. Even the most harmless of commands can become sinister:

      /home/larry/report# cp report-1992 report-1993 backups

  can easily become disaster:

      /home/larry/report# cp report-1992 report-1993

- The author also recommends, from his personal experience, not to do file maintenance late at night. Does you directory structure look a little messy at 1:32am? Let it stay—a little mess never hurt a computer.

- Keep track of your present directory. Sometimes, the prompt you're using doesn't display what directory you are working in, and danger strikes. It is a sad thing to read a post on `comp.unix.admin`[1] about a `root` user who was in / instead of /tmp! For example:

```
mousehouse> pwd
/etc
mousehouse> ls /tmp
passwd
mousehouse> rm passwd
```

The above series of commands would make the user very unhappy, seeing how they have just removed the password file for their system. Without it, people can't login!

12.2   Not Your Fault

Unfortunately for the programmers of the world, not all problems are caused by user-error. Unix and LINUX are complicated systems, and all known versions have bugs. Sometimes these bugs are hard to find and only appear under certain circumstances.

First of all, what is a bug? An example of a bug is if you ask the computer to compute "5+3" and it tells you "7". Although that's a trivial example of what can go wrong, most bugs in computer programs involve arithmetic in some extremely strange way.

12.2.1   When Is There a Bug

If the computer gives a wrong answer (verify that the answer is wrong!) or crashes, it is a bug. If any one program crashes or gives an operating system error message, it is a bug.

If a command never finishes running can be a bug, but you must make sure that you didn't tell it to take a long time doing whatever you wanted it to do. Ask for assistance if you didn't know what the command did.

Some messages will alert you of bugs. Some messages are not bugs. Check Section 3.3 and any other documentation to make sure they aren't normal informational messages. For instance, messages like "disk full" or "lp0 on fire" aren't software problems, but something wrong with your hardware—not enough disk space, or a bad printer.

If you can't find anything about a program, it is a bug in the documentation, and you should contact the author of that program and offer to write it yourself. If something is incorrect in existing documentation[2], it is a bug with that manual. If something appears incomplete or unclear in the manual, that is a bug.

If you can't beat `gnuchess` at chess, it is a flaw with your chess algorithm, but not necessarily a bug with your brain.

12.2.2   Reporting a bug

After you are sure you found a bug, it is important to make sure that your information gets to the right place. Try to find what program is causing the bug—if you can't find it, perhaps you could ask for help in `comp.os.linux.help` or `comp.unix.misc`. Once you find the program, try to read the manual page to see who wrote it.

The preferred method of sending bug reports in the LINUX world is via electronic mail. If you don't have access to electronic mail, you might want to contact whoever you got LINUX from—eventually, you're bound to encounter someone who either has electronic mail, or sells LINUX commercially and

---

[1] A discussion group in Usenet, which talks about administering Unix computers.
[2] Especially this one!

therefore wants to remove as many bugs as possible. Remember, though, that no one is under any obligation to fix any bugs unless you have a contract!

When you send a bug report in, include all the information you can think of. This includes:

- A description of what you think is incorrect. For instance, "I get 5 when I compute 2+2" or "It says `segmentation violation -- core dumped`." It is important to say exactly what is happening so the maintainer can fix *your* bug!

- Include any relevant environment variables.

- The version of your kernel (see the file `/proc/version`) and your system libraries (see the directory `/lib`—if you can't decipher it, send a listing of `/lib`).

- How you ran the program in question, or, if it was a kernel bug, what you were doing at the time.

- **All** peripheral information. For instance, the command w may not be displaying the current process for certain users. Don't just say, "w doesn't work when for a certain user". The bug could occur because the user's name is eight characters long, or when he is logging in over the network. Instead say, "w doesn't display the current process for use `greenfie` when he logs in over the network."

- And remember, be polite. Most people work on free software for the fun of it, and because they have big hearts. Don't ruin it for them—the LINUX community has already disillusioned too many developers, and it's still early in LINUX's life!

Appendix A

The GNU General Public License

GNU GENERAL PUBLIC LICENSE
Version 2, June 1991

Preamble

The licenses for most software are designed to take away your freedom to share and change it. By contrast, the GNU General Public License is intended to guarantee your freedom to share and change free software—to make sure the software is free for all its users. This General Public License applies to most of the Free Software Foundation's software and to any other program whose authors commit to using it. (Some other Free Software Foundation software is covered by the GNU Library General Public License instead.) You can apply it to your programs, too.

When we speak of free software, we are referring to freedom, not price. Our General Public Licenses are designed to make sure that you have the freedom to distribute copies of free software (and charge for this service if you wish), that you receive source code or can get it if you want it, that you can change the software or use pieces of it in new free programs; and that you know you can do these things.

To protect your rights, we need to make restrictions that forbid anyone to deny you these rights or to ask you to surrender the rights. These restrictions translate to certain responsibilities for you if you distribute copies of the software, or if you modify it.

For example, if you distribute copies of such a program, whether gratis or for a fee, you must give the recipients all the rights that you have. You must make sure that they, too, receive or can get the source code. And you must show them these terms so they know their rights.

We protect your rights with two steps: (1) copyright the software, and (2) offer you this license which gives you legal permission to copy, distribute and/or modify the software.

Also, for each author's protection and ours, we want to make certain that everyone understands that there is no warranty for this free software. If the software is modified by someone else and passed on, we want its recipients to know that what they have is not the original, so that any problems introduced by others will not reflect on the original authors' reputations.

Finally, any free program is threatened constantly by software patents. We wish to avoid the danger that redistributors of a free program will individually obtain patent licenses, in effect making the program proprietary. To prevent this, we have made it clear that any patent must be licensed for everyone's free use or not licensed at all.

The precise terms and conditions for copying, distribution and modification follow.

Terms and Conditions

0. This License applies to any program or other work which contains a notice placed by the copyright holder saying it may be distributed under the terms of this General Public License. The "Program", below, refers to any such program or work, and a "work based on the Program" means either the Program or any derivative work under copyright law: that is to say, a work containing the Program or a portion of it, either verbatim or with modifications and/or translated into another language. (Hereinafter, translation is included without limitation in the term "modification".) Each licensee is addressed as "you".

   Activities other than copying, distribution and modification are not covered by this License; they are outside its scope. The act of running the Program is not restricted, and the output from the Program is covered only if its contents constitute a work based on the Program (independent of having been made by running the Program). Whether that is true depends on what the Program does.

1. You may copy and distribute verbatim copies of the Program's source code as you receive it, in any medium, provided that you conspicuously and appropriately publish on each copy an appropriate copyright notice and disclaimer of warranty; keep intact all the notices that refer to this License and to the absence of any warranty; and give any other recipients of the Program a copy of this License along with the Program.

   You may charge a fee for the physical act of transferring a copy, and you may at your option offer warranty protection in exchange for a fee.

2. You may modify your copy or copies of the Program or any portion of it, thus forming a work based on the Program, and copy and distribute such modifications or work under the terms of Section 1 above, provided that you also meet all of these conditions:

   a. You must cause the modified files to carry prominent notices stating that you changed the files and the date of any change.

   b. You must cause any work that you distribute or publish, that in whole or in part contains or is derived from the Program or any part thereof, to be licensed as a whole at no charge to all third parties under the terms of this License.

   c. If the modified program normally reads commands interactively when run, you must cause it, when started running for such interactive use in the most ordinary way, to print or display an announcement including an appropriate copyright notice and a notice that there is no warranty (or else, saying that you provide a warranty) and that users may redistribute the program under these conditions, and telling the user how to view a copy of this License. (Exception: if the Program itself is interactive but does not normally print such an announcement, your work based on the Program is not required to print an announcement.)

   These requirements apply to the modified work as a whole. If identifiable sections of that work are not derived from the Program, and can be reasonably considered independent and separate works in themselves, then this License, and its terms, do not apply to those sections when you distribute them as separate works. But when you distribute the same sections as part of a whole which is a work based on the Program, the distribution of the whole must be on the terms of this License, whose permissions for other licensees extend to the entire whole, and thus to each and every part regardless of who wrote it.

   Thus, it is not the intent of this section to claim rights or contest your rights to work written entirely by you; rather, the intent is to exercise the right to control the distribution of derivative or collective works based on the Program.

   In addition, mere aggregation of another work not based on the Program with the Program (or with a work based on the Program) on a volume of a storage or distribution medium does not bring the other work under the scope of this License.

3. You may copy and distribute the Program (or a work based on it, under Section 2) in object code or executable form under the terms of Sections 1 and 2 above provided that you also do one of the following:

a. Accompany it with the complete corresponding machine-readable source code, which must be distributed under the terms of Sections 1 and 2 above on a medium customarily used for software interchange; or,

b. Accompany it with a written offer, valid for at least three years, to give any third party, for a charge no more than your cost of physically performing source distribution, a complete machine-readable copy of the corresponding source code, to be distributed under the terms of Sections 1 and 2 above on a medium customarily used for software interchange; or,

c. Accompany it with the information you received as to the offer to distribute corresponding source code. (This alternative is allowed only for noncommercial distribution and only if you received the program in object code or executable form with such an offer, in accord with Subsection b above.)

The source code for a work means the preferred form of the work for making modifications to it. For an executable work, complete source code means all the source code for all modules it contains, plus any associated interface definition files, plus the scripts used to control compilation and installation of the executable. However, as a special exception, the source code distributed need not include anything that is normally distributed (in either source or binary form) with the major components (compiler, kernel, and so on) of the operating system on which the executable runs, unless that component itself accompanies the executable.

If distribution of executable or object code is made by offering access to copy from a designated place, then offering equivalent access to copy the source code from the same place counts as distribution of the source code, even though third parties are not compelled to copy the source along with the object code.

4. You may not copy, modify, sublicense, or distribute the Program except as expressly provided under this License. Any attempt otherwise to copy, modify, sublicense or distribute the Program is void, and will automatically terminate your rights under this License. However, parties who have received copies, or rights, from you under this License will not have their licenses terminated so long as such parties remain in full compliance.

5. You are not required to accept this License, since you have not signed it. However, nothing else grants you permission to modify or distribute the Program or its derivative works. These actions are prohibited by law if you do not accept this License. Therefore, by modifying or distributing the Program (or any work based on the Program), you indicate your acceptance of this License to do so, and all its terms and conditions for copying, distributing or modifying the Program or works based on it.

6. Each time you redistribute the Program (or any work based on the Program), the recipient automatically receives a license from the original licensor to copy, distribute or modify the Program subject to these terms and conditions. You may not impose any further restrictions on the recipients' exercise of the rights granted herein. You are not responsible for enforcing compliance by third parties to this License.

7. If, as a consequence of a court judgment or allegation of patent infringement or for any other reason (not limited to patent issues), conditions are imposed on you (whether by court order, agreement or otherwise) that contradict the conditions of this License, they do not excuse you from the conditions of this License. If you cannot distribute so as to satisfy simultaneously your obligations under this License and any other pertinent obligations, then as a consequence you may not distribute the Program at all. For example, if a patent license would not permit royalty-free redistribution of the Program by all those who receive copies directly or indirectly through you, then the only way you could satisfy both it and this License would be to refrain entirely from distribution of the Program.

If any portion of this section is held invalid or unenforceable under any particular circumstance, the balance of the section is intended to apply and the section as a whole is intended to apply in other circumstances.

It is not the purpose of this section to induce you to infringe any patents or other property right claims or to contest validity of any such claims; this section has the sole purpose of protecting the integrity of the free software distribution system, which is implemented by public license practices. Many people have made generous contributions to the wide range of software distributed through that system in reliance on consistent application of that system; it is up to the author/donor to decide if he or she is willing to distribute software through any other system and a licensee cannot impose that choice.

This section is intended to make thoroughly clear what is believed to be a consequence of the rest of this License.

8. If the distribution and/or use of the Program is restricted in certain countries either by patents or by copyrighted interfaces, the original copyright holder who places the Program under this License may add an explicit geographical distribution limitation excluding those countries, so that distribution is permitted only in or among countries not thus excluded. In such case, this License incorporates the limitation as if written in the body of this License.

9. The Free Software Foundation may publish revised and/or new versions of the General Public License from time to time. Such new versions will be similar in spirit to the present version, but may differ in detail to address new problems or concerns.

Each version is given a distinguishing version number. If the Program specifies a version number of this License which applies to it and "any later version", you have the option of following the terms and conditions either of that version or of any later version published by the Free Software Foundation. If the Program does not specify a version number of this License, you may choose any version ever published by the Free Software Foundation.

10. If you wish to incorporate parts of the Program into other free programs whose distribution conditions are different, write to the author to ask for permission. For software which is copyrighted by the Free Software Foundation, write to the Free Software Foundation; we sometimes make exceptions for this. Our decision will be guided by the two goals of preserving the free status of all derivatives of our free software and of promoting the sharing and reuse of software generally.

NO WARRANTY

11. BECAUSE THE PROGRAM IS LICENSED FREE OF CHARGE, THERE IS NO WARRANTY FOR THE PROGRAM, TO THE EXTENT PERMITTED BY APPLICABLE LAW. EXCEPT WHEN OTHERWISE STATED IN WRITING THE COPYRIGHT HOLDERS AND/OR OTHER PARTIES PROVIDE THE PROGRAM "AS IS" WITHOUT WARRANTY OF ANY KIND, EITHER EXPRESSED OR IMPLIED, INCLUDING, BUT NOT LIMITED TO, THE IMPLIED WARRANTIES OF MERCHANTABILITY AND FITNESS FOR A PARTICULAR PURPOSE. THE ENTIRE RISK AS TO THE QUALITY AND PERFORMANCE OF THE PROGRAM IS WITH YOU. SHOULD THE PROGRAM PROVE DEFECTIVE, YOU ASSUME THE COST OF ALL NECESSARY SERVICING, REPAIR OR CORRECTION.

12. IN NO EVENT UNLESS REQUIRED BY APPLICABLE LAW OR AGREED TO IN WRITING WILL ANY COPYRIGHT HOLDER, OR ANY OTHER PARTY WHO MAY MODIFY AND/OR REDISTRIBUTE THE PROGRAM AS PERMITTED ABOVE, BE LIABLE TO YOU FOR DAMAGES, INCLUDING ANY GENERAL, SPECIAL, INCIDENTAL OR CONSEQUENTIAL DAMAGES ARISING OUT OF THE USE OR INABILITY TO USE THE PROGRAM (INCLUDING BUT NOT LIMITED TO LOSS OF DATA OR DATA BEING RENDERED INACCURATE OR LOSSES SUSTAINED BY YOU OR THIRD PARTIES OR A FAILURE OF THE PROGRAM TO OPERATE WITH ANY OTHER PROGRAMS), EVEN IF SUCH HOLDER OR OTHER PARTY HAS BEEN ADVISED OF THE POSSIBILITY OF SUCH DAMAGES.

How to Apply These Terms to Your New Programs

If you develop a new program, and you want it to be of the greatest possible use to the public, the best way to achieve this is to make it free software which everyone can redistribute and change under these terms.

To do so, attach the following notices to the program. It is safest to attach them to the start of each source file to most effectively convey the exclusion of warranty; and each file should have at least the "copyright" line and a pointer to where the full notice is found.

one line to give the program's name and an idea of what it does.
Copyright © 19*yy name of author*

This program is free software; you can redistribute it and/or modify it under the terms of the GNU General Public License as published by the Free Software Foundation; either version 2 of the License, or (at your option) any later version.

This program is distributed in the hope that it will be useful, but WITHOUT ANY WARRANTY; without even the implied warranty of MERCHANTABILITY or FITNESS FOR A PARTICULAR PURPOSE. See the GNU General Public License for more details.

You should have received a copy of the GNU General Public License along with this program; if not, write to the Free Software Foundation, Inc., 675 Mass Ave, Cambridge, MA 02139,

Also add information on how to contact you by electronic and paper mail.

If the program is interactive, make it output a short notice like this when it starts in an interactive mode:

Gnomovision version 69, Copyright © 19*yy name of author*
Gnomovision comes with ABSOLUTELY NO WARRANTY; for details type 'show w'. This is free software, and you are welcome to redistribute it under certain conditions; type 'show c' for details.

The hypothetical commands 'show w' and 'show c' should show the appropriate parts of the General Public License. Of course, the commands you use may be called something other than 'show w' and 'show c'; they could even be mouse-clicks or menu items—whatever suits your program.

You should also get your employer (if you work as a programmer) or your school, if any, to sign a "copyright disclaimer" for the program, if necessary. Here is a sample; alter the names:

Yoyodyne, Inc., hereby disclaims all copyright interest in the program 'Gnomovision' (which makes passes at compilers) written by James Hacker.

signature of Ty Coon, 1 April 1989
Ty Coon, President of Vice

This General Public License does not permit incorporating your program into proprietary programs. If your program is a subroutine library, you may consider it more useful to permit linking proprietary applications with the library. If this is what you want to do, use the GNU Library General Public License instead of this License.

Appendix B

The GNU Library General Public License

Preamble

The licenses for most software are designed to take away your freedom to share and change it. By contrast, the GNU General Public Licenses are intended to guarantee your freedom to share and change free software–to make sure the software is free for all its users.

This license, the Library General Public License, applies to some specially designated Free Software Foundation software, and to any other libraries whose authors decide to use it. You can use it for your libraries, too.

When we speak of free software, we are referring to freedom, not price. Our General Public Licenses are designed to make sure that you have the freedom to distribute copies of free software (and charge for this service if you wish), that you receive source code or can get it if you want it, that you can change the software or use pieces of it in new free programs; and that you know you can do these things.

To protect your rights, we need to make restrictions that forbid anyone to deny you these rights or to ask you to surrender the rights. These restrictions translate to certain responsibilities for you if you distribute copies of the library, or if you modify it.

For example, if you distribute copies of the library, whether gratis or for a fee, you must give the recipients all the rights that we gave you. You must make sure that they, too, receive or can get the source code. If you link a program with the library, you must provide complete object files to the recipients so that they can relink them with the library, after making changes to the library and recompiling it. And you must show them these terms so they know their rights.

Our method of protecting your rights has two steps: (1) copyright the library, and (2) offer you this license which gives you legal permission to copy, distribute and/or modify the library.

Also, for each distributor's protection, we want to make certain that everyone understands that there is no warranty for this free library. If the library is modified by someone else and passed on, we want its recipients to know that what they have is not the original version, so that any problems introduced by others will not reflect on the original authors' reputations.

Finally, any free program is threatened constantly by software patents. We wish to avoid the danger that companies distributing free software will individually obtain patent licenses, thus in effect transforming the program into proprietary software. To prevent this, we have made it clear that any patent must be licensed for everyone's free use or not licensed at all.

Most GNU software, including some libraries, is covered by the ordinary GNU General Public License, which was designed for utility programs. This license, the GNU Library General Public License, applies to certain designated libraries. This license is quite different from the ordinary one; be sure to read it in full, and don't assume that anything in it is the same as in the ordinary license.

The reason we have a separate public license for some libraries is that they blur the distinction we usually make between modifying or adding to a program and simply using it. Linking a program with a library, without changing the library, is in some sense simply using the library, and is analogous to running a utility program or application program. However, in a textual and legal sense, the linked executable is a combined work, a derivative of the original library, and the ordinary General Public License treats it as such.

Because of this blurred distinction, using the ordinary General Public License for libraries did not effectively promote software sharing, because most developers did not use the libraries. We concluded that weaker conditions might promote sharing better.

However, unrestricted linking of non-free programs would deprive the users of those programs of all benefit from the free status of the libraries themselves. This Library General Public License is intended to permit developers of non-free programs to use free libraries, while preserving your freedom as a user of such programs to change the free libraries that are incorporated in them. (We have not seen how to achieve this as regards changes in header files, but we have achieved it as regards changes in the actual functions of the Library.) The hope is that this will lead to faster development of free libraries.

The precise terms and conditions for copying, distribution and modification follow. Pay close attention to the difference between a "work based on the library" and a "work that uses the library". The former contains code derived from the library, while the latter only works together with the library.

Note that it is possible for a library to be covered by the ordinary General Public License rather than by this special one.

Terms and Conditions for Copying, Distribution and Modification

0. This License Agreement applies to any software library which contains a notice placed by the copyright holder or other authorized party saying it may be distributed under the terms of this Library General Public License (also called "this License"). Each licensee is addressed as "you".

   A "library" means a collection of software functions and/or data prepared so as to be conveniently linked with application programs (which use some of those functions and data) to form executables.

   The "Library", below, refers to any such software library or work which has been distributed under these terms. A "work based on the Library" means either the Library or any derivative work under copyright law: that is to say, a work containing the Library or a portion of it, either verbatim or with modifications and/or translated straightforwardly into another language. (Hereinafter, translation is included without limitation in the term "modification".)

   "Source code" for a work means the preferred form of the work for making modifications to it. For a library, complete source code means all the source code for all modules it contains, plus any associated interface definition files, plus the scripts used to control compilation and installation of the library.

   Activities other than copying, distribution and modification are not covered by this License; they are outside its scope. The act of running a program using the Library is not restricted, and output from such a program is covered only if its contents constitute a work based on the Library (independent of the use of the Library in a tool for writing it). Whether that is true depends on what the Library does and what the program that uses the Library does.

1. You may copy and distribute verbatim copies of the Library's complete source code as you receive it, in any medium, provided that you conspicuously and appropriately publish on each copy an appropriate copyright notice and disclaimer of warranty; keep intact all the notices that refer to this License and to the absence of any warranty; and distribute a copy of this License along with the Library.

   You may charge a fee for the physical act of transferring a copy, and you may at your option offer warranty protection in exchange for a fee.

2. You may modify your copy or copies of the Library or any portion of it, thus forming a work based on the Library, and copy and distribute such modifications or work under the terms of Section 1 above, provided that you also meet all of these conditions:

   a. The modified work must itself be a software library.

   b. You must cause the files modified to carry prominent notices stating that you changed the files and the date of any change.

   c. You must cause the whole of the work to be licensed at no charge to all third parties under the terms of this License.

   d. If a facility in the modified Library refers to a function or a table of data to be supplied by an application program that uses the facility, other than as an argument passed when the facility is invoked, then you must make a good faith effort to ensure that, in the event an application does not supply such function or table, the facility still operates, and performs whatever part of its purpose remains meaningful.

      (For example, a function in a library to compute square roots has a purpose that is entirely well-defined independent of the application. Therefore, Subsection 2d requires that any application-supplied function or table used by this function must be optional: if the application does not supply it, the square root function must still compute square roots.)

   These requirements apply to the modified work as a whole. If identifiable sections of that work are not derived from the Library, and can be reasonably considered independent and separate works in themselves, then this License, and its terms, do not apply to those sections when you distribute them as separate works. But when you distribute the same sections as part of a whole which is a work based on the Library, the distribution of the whole must be on the terms of this License, whose permissions for other licensees extend to the entire whole, and thus to each and every part regardless of who wrote it.

   Thus, it is not the intent of this section to claim rights or contest your rights to work written entirely by you; rather, the intent is to exercise the right to control the distribution of derivative or collective works based on the Library.

   In addition, mere aggregation of another work not based on the Library with the Library (or with a work based on the Library) on a volume of a storage or distribution medium does not bring the other work under the scope of this License.

3. You may opt to apply the terms of the ordinary GNU General Public License instead of this License to a given copy of the Library. To do this, you must alter all the notices that refer to this License, so that they refer to the ordinary GNU General Public License, version 2, instead of to this License. (If a newer version than version 2 of the ordinary GNU General Public License has appeared, then you can specify that version instead if you wish.) Do not make any other change in these notices.

   Once this change is made in a given copy, it is irreversible for that copy, so the ordinary GNU General Public License applies to all subsequent copies and derivative works made from that copy.

   This option is useful when you wish to copy part of the code of the Library into a program that is not a library.

4. You may copy and distribute the Library (or a portion or derivative of it, under Section 2) in object code or executable form under the terms of Sections 1 and 2 above provided that you accompany it with the complete corresponding machine-readable source code, which must be distributed under the terms of Sections 1 and 2 above on a medium customarily used for software interchange.

   If distribution of object code is made by offering access to copy from a designated place, then offering equivalent access to copy the source code from the same place satisfies the requirement to distribute the source code, even though third parties are not compelled to copy the source along with the object code.

5. A program that contains no derivative of any portion of the Library, but is designed to work with the Library by being compiled or linked with it, is called a "work that uses the Library". Such a work, in isolation, is not a derivative work of the Library, and therefore falls outside the scope of this License.

   However, linking a "work that uses the Library" with the Library creates an executable that is a derivative of the Library (because it contains portions of the Library), rather than a "work that uses the library". The executable is therefore covered by this License. Section 6 states terms for distribution of such executables.

   When a "work that uses the Library" uses material from a header file that is part of the Library, the object code for the work may be a derivative work of the Library even though the source code is not. Whether this is true is especially significant if the work can be linked without the Library, or if the work is itself a library. The threshold for this to be true is not precisely defined by law.

   If such an object file uses only numerical parameters, data structure layouts and accessors, and small macros and small inline functions (ten lines or less in length), then the use of the object file is unrestricted, regardless of whether it is legally a derivative work. (Executables containing this object code plus portions of the Library will still fall under Section 6.)

   Otherwise, if the work is a derivative of the Library, you may distribute the object code for the work under the terms of Section 6. Any executables containing that work also fall under Section 6, whether or not they are linked directly with the Library itself.

6. As an exception to the Sections above, you may also compile or link a "work that uses the Library" with the Library to produce a work containing portions of the Library, and distribute that work under terms of your choice, provided that the terms permit modification of the work for the customer's own use and reverse engineering for debugging such modifications.

   You must give prominent notice with each copy of the work that the Library is used in it and that the Library and its use are covered by this License. You must supply a copy of this License. If the work during execution displays copyright notices, you must include the copyright notice for the Library among them, as well as a reference directing the user to the copy of this License. Also, you must do one of these things:

   a. Accompany the work with the complete corresponding machine-readable source code for the Library including whatever changes were used in the work (which must be distributed under Sections 1 and 2 above); and, if the work is an executable linked with the Library, with the complete machine-readable "work that uses the Library", as object code and/or source code, so that the user can modify the Library and then relink to produce a modified executable containing the modified Library. (It is understood that the user who changes the contents of definitions files in the Library will not necessarily be able to recompile the application to use the modified definitions.)

   b. Accompany the work with a written offer, valid for at least three years, to give the same user the materials specified in Subsection 6a, above, for a charge no more than the cost of performing this distribution.

   c. If distribution of the work is made by offering access to copy from a designated place, offer equivalent access to copy the above specified materials from the same place.

   d. Verify that the user has already received a copy of these materials or that you have already sent this user a copy.

For an executable, the required form of the "work that uses the Library" must include any data and utility programs needed for reproducing the executable from it. However, as a special exception, the source code distributed need not include anything that is normally distributed (in either source or binary form) with the major components (compiler, kernel, and so on) of the operating system on which the executable runs, unless that component itself accompanies the executable.

It may happen that this requirement contradicts the license restrictions of other proprietary libraries that do not normally accompany the operating system. Such a contradiction means you cannot use both them and the Library together in an executable that you distribute.

7. You may place library facilities that are a work based on the Library side-by-side in a single library together with other library facilities not covered by this License, and distribute such a combined library, provided that the separate distribution of the work based on the Library and of the other library facilities is otherwise permitted, and provided that you do these two things:

   a. Accompany the combined library with a copy of the same work based on the Library, uncombined with any other library facilities. This must be distributed under the terms of the Sections above.

   b. Give prominent notice with the combined library of the fact that part of it is a work based on the Library, and explaining where to find the accompanying uncombined form of the same work.

8. You may not copy, modify, sublicense, link with, or distribute the Library except as expressly provided under this License. Any attempt otherwise to copy, modify, sublicense, link with, or distribute the Library is void, and will automatically terminate your rights under this License. However, parties who have received copies, or rights, from you under this License will not have their licenses terminated so long as such parties remain in full compliance.

9. You are not required to accept this License, since you have not signed it. However, nothing else grants you permission to modify or distribute the Library or its derivative works. These actions are prohibited by law if you do not accept this License. Therefore, by modifying or distributing the Library (or any work based on the Library), you indicate your acceptance of this License to do so, and all its terms and conditions for copying, distributing or modifying the Library or works based on it.

10. Each time you redistribute the Library (or any work based on the Library), the recipient automatically receives a license from the original licensor to copy, distribute, link with or modify the Library subject to these terms and conditions. You may not impose any further restrictions on the recipients' exercise of the rights granted herein. You are not responsible for enforcing compliance by third parties to this License.

11. If, as a consequence of a court judgment or allegation of patent infringement or for any other reason (not limited to patent issues), conditions are imposed on you (whether by court order, agreement or otherwise) that contradict the conditions of this License, they do not excuse you from the conditions of this License. If you cannot distribute so as to satisfy simultaneously your obligations under this License and any other pertinent obligations, then as a consequence you may not distribute the Library at all. For example, if a patent license would not permit royalty-free redistribution of the Library by all those who receive copies directly or indirectly through you, then the only way you could satisfy both it and this License would be to refrain entirely from distribution of the Library.

If any portion of this section is held invalid or unenforceable under any particular circumstance, the balance of the section is intended to apply, and the section as a whole is intended to apply in other circumstances.

It is not the purpose of this section to induce you to infringe any patents or other property right claims or to contest validity of any such claims; this section has the sole purpose of protecting the integrity of the free software distribution system which is implemented by public license practices. Many people have made generous contributions to the wide range of software distributed through that system in reliance on consistent application of that system; it is up to the author/donor to decide if he or she is willing to distribute software through any other system and a licensee cannot impose that choice.

This section is intended to make thoroughly clear what is believed to be a consequence of the rest of this License.

12. If the distribution and/or use of the Library is restricted in certain countries either by patents or by copyrighted interfaces, the original copyright holder who places the Library under this License may add an explicit geographical distribution limitation excluding those countries, so that distribution is permitted only in or among countries not thus excluded. In such case, this License incorporates the limitation as if written in the body of this License.

13. The Free Software Foundation may publish revised and/or new versions of the Library General Public License from time to time. Such new versions will be similar in spirit to the present version, but may differ in detail to address new problems or concerns.

Each version is given a distinguishing version number. If the Library specifies a version number of this License which applies to it and "any later version", you have the option of following the terms and conditions either of that version or of any later version published by the Free Software Foundation. If the Library does not specify a license version number, you may choose any version ever published by the Free Software Foundation.

14. If you wish to incorporate parts of the Library into other free programs whose distribution conditions are incompatible with these, write to the author to ask for permission. For software which is copyrighted by the Free Software Foundation, write to the Free Software Foundation; we sometimes make exceptions for this. Our decision will be guided by the two goals of preserving the free status of all derivatives of our free software and of promoting the sharing and reuse of software generally.

NO WARRANTY

11. BECAUSE THE LIBRARY IS LICENSED FREE OF CHARGE, THERE IS NO WARRANTY FOR THE LIBRARY, TO THE EXTENT PERMITTED BY APPLICABLE LAW. EXCEPT WHEN OTHERWISE STATED IN WRITING THE COPYRIGHT HOLDERS AND/OR OTHER PARTIES PROVIDE THE LIBRARY "AS IS" WITHOUT WARRANTY OF ANY KIND, EITHER EXPRESSED OR IMPLIED, INCLUDING, BUT NOT LIMITED TO, THE IMPLIED WARRANTIES OF MERCHANTABILITY AND FITNESS FOR A PARTICULAR PURPOSE. THE ENTIRE RISK AS TO THE QUALITY AND PERFORMANCE OF THE LIBRARY IS WITH YOU. SHOULD THE LIBRARY PROVE DEFECTIVE, YOU ASSUME THE COST OF ALL NECESSARY SERVICING, REPAIR OR CORRECTION.

12. IN NO EVENT UNLESS REQUIRED BY APPLICABLE LAW OR AGREED TO IN WRITING WILL ANY COPYRIGHT HOLDER, OR ANY OTHER PARTY WHO MAY MODIFY AND/OR REDISTRIBUTE THE LIBRARY AS PERMITTED ABOVE, BE LIABLE TO YOU FOR DAMAGES, INCLUDING ANY GENERAL, SPECIAL, INCIDENTAL OR CONSEQUENTIAL DAMAGES ARISING OUT OF THE USE OR INABILITY TO USE THE LIBRARY (INCLUDING BUT NOT LIMITED TO LOSS OF DATA OR DATA BEING RENDERED INACCURATE OR LOSSES SUSTAINED BY YOU OR THIRD PARTIES OR A FAILURE OF THE LIBRARY TO OPERATE WITH ANY OTHER SOFTWARE), EVEN IF SUCH HOLDER OR OTHER PARTY HAS BEEN ADVISED OF THE POSSIBILITY OF SUCH DAMAGES.

How to Apply These Terms to Your New Libraries

If you develop a new library, and you want it to be of the greatest possible use to the public, we recommend making it free software that everyone can redistribute and change. You can do so by permitting redistribution under these terms (or, alternatively, under the terms of the ordinary General Public License).

To apply these terms, attach the following notices to the library. It is safest to attach them to the start of each source file to most effectively convey the exclusion of warranty; and each file should have at least the "copyright" line and a pointer to where the full notice is found.

> *one line to give the library's name and a brief idea of what it does.*
> Copyright (C) *year name of author*

> This library is free software; you can redistribute it and/or modify it under the terms of the GNU Library General Public License as published by the Free Software Foundation; either version 2 of the License, or (at your option) any later version.

> This library is distributed in the hope that it will be useful, but WITHOUT ANY WARRANTY; without even the implied warranty of MERCHANTABILITY or FITNESS FOR A PARTICULAR PURPOSE. See the GNU Library General Public License for more details.

> You should have received a copy of the GNU Library General Public License along with this library; if not, write to the Free Software Foundation, Inc., 675 Mass Ave, Cambridge, MA 02139, USA.

Also add information on how to contact you by electronic and paper mail.

You should also get your employer (if you work as a programmer) or your school, if any, to sign a "copyright disclaimer" for the library, if necessary. Here is a sample; alter the names:

> Yoyodyne, Inc., hereby disclaims all copyright interest in the library 'Frob' (a library for tweaking knobs) written by James Random Hacker.

> *signature of Ty Coon*, 1 April 1990
> Ty Coon, President of Vice

That's all there is to it!

Appendix C

Introduction to Vi

vi (pronounced "vee eye") is really the only editor you can find at almost every Unix installation. It was originally written at the University of California at Berkeley and versions can be found it almost every vendor's edition of Unix, including LINUX. It is initially somewhat hard to get used to, but it has many powerful features. In general, we suggest that a new user learn Emacs, which is generally easier to use. However, people who will use more than one platform or find they dislike Emacs may want to try to learn vi.

A brief historical view of vi is necessary to understand how the key $\boxed{k}$ can mean move cursor up one line and why there are three different modes of use. If you are itchy to learn the editor, then the two tutorials will guide you from being a raw beginner, through to having enough knowledge of the command set you are ever likely to need. The chapter also incorporates a command guide, which makes a useful reference to keep by the terminal.

Even if vi does not become your regular text editor, the knowledge of its use is not wasted. It is almost certain that the Unix system you are using will have some variant of the vi editor. It may be necessary to use vi while installing another editor, such as Emacs. Many Unix tools, applications and games use a subset of the vi command set.

C.1   A Quick History of Vi

Early text editors were line oriented and typically were used from dumb printing terminals. A typical editor that operates in this mode is **ed**. The editor is powerful and efficient, using a very small amount of computer resources, and worked well with the display equipment of the time. vi offers the user a visual alternative with a significantly expanded command set compared with ed.

vi as we know it today started as the line editor **ex**. In fact ex is seen as a special editing mode of vi, although actually the converse is true. The visual component of ex can be initiated from the command line by using the vi command, or from within ex.

The ex/vi editor was developed at the University of California at Berkeley by William Joy. It was originally supplied as an unsupported utility until its official inclusion in the release of AT&T System V Unix. It has steadily become more popular, even with the challenges of more modern full screen editors.

Due to the popularity of vi there exists many clone variants and versions can be found for most operation systems. It is not the intention of this chapter to include all the commands available under vi or its variants. Many clones have expanded and changed the original behaviour of vi. Most clones do not support all the original commands of vi.

If you have a good working knowledge of ed then vi offers a smaller learning curve to master. Even if you have no intention of using vi as your regular editor, a basic knowledge of vi can only be an asset.

C.2   Quick ed Tutorial

The aim of this tutorial is to get you started using ed. ed is designed to be easy to use, and requires little training to get started. The best way to learn is to practice, so follow the instructions and try the editor before discounting its practical advantages.

C.2.1   Creating a file

ed is only capable of editing one file at a time. Follow the next example to create your first text file using ed.

```
/home/larry# ed
a
This is my first text file using ed.
This is really fun.
.
w firstone.txt
/home/larry# q
```

You can verify the file's contents using the Unix concatenate utility.

```
/home/larry# cat firstone.txt
```

The above example has illustrated a number of important points. When invoking ed as above you will have an empty file. The key $\boxed{a}$ is used to add text to the file. To end the text entering session, a period $\boxed{.}$ is used in the first column of the text. To save the text to a file, the key $\boxed{q}$ is used in combination with the file's name and finally, the key $\boxed{q}$ is used to exit the editor.

The most important observation is the two modes of operation. Initially the editor is in command mode. A command is defined by characters, so to ascertain what the user's intention is, ed uses a **text mode**, and a **command mode**.

C.2.2   editing a existing file

To add a line of text to an existing file follow the next example.

```
/home/larry# ed firstone.txt
a
This is a new line of text.
.
w
q
```

If you check the file with cat you'll see that a new line was inserted between the original first and second lines. How did ed know where to place the new line of text?

When ed reads in the file it keeps track of the current line. The command $\boxed{a}$ will add the text after the current line. ed can also place the text before the current line with the key command $\boxed{i}$. The effect will be the insertion of the text before the current line.

Now it is easy to see that ed operates on the text, line by line. All commands can be applied to a chosen line.

To add a line of text at the end of a file.

```
/home/larry# ed firstone.txt
        $a
        The last line of text.
        .
        w
        q
```

The command modifier $\boxed{\$}$ tells ed to add the line after the last line. To add the line after the first line the modifier would be $\boxed{1}$. The power is now available to select the line to either add a line of text after the line number, or insert a line before the line number.

How do we know what is on the current line? The command key $\boxed{p}$ will display the contents of the current line. If you want to change the current line to line 2 and see the contents of that line then do the following.

```
/home/larry# ed firstone.txt
        2p
        q
```

C.2.3   Line numbers in detail

You have seen how to display the contents of the current line, by the use of the $\boxed{p}$ command. We also know there are line number modifiers for the commands. To print the contents of the second line.

```
    2p
```

There are some special modifiers that refer to positions that can change, in the lifetime of the edit session. The $\boxed{\$}$ is the last line of the text. To print the last line.

```
    $p
```

The current line number uses the special modifier symbol $\boxed{.}$. To display the current line using a modifier.

```
    .p
```

This may appear to be unnecessary, although it is very useful in the context of line number ranges.

To display the contents of the text from line 1 to line 2 the range needs to be supplied to ed.

```
    1,2p
```

The first number refers to the starting line, and the second refers to the finishing line. The current line will subsequently be the second number of the command range.

If you want to display the contents of the file from the start to the current line.

```
    1,.p
```

To display the contents from the current line to the end of the file.

```
    .,$p
```

All that is left is to display the contents of the entire file which is left to you.

How can you delete the first 2 lines of the file.

```
    1,2d
```

The command key $\boxed{\text{d}}$ deletes the text line by line. If you wanted to delete the entire contents you would issue.

```
    1,$d
```

If you have made to many changes and do not want to save the contents of the file, then the best option is to quit the editor without writing the file beforehand.

Most users do not use ed as the main editor of choice. The more modern editors offer a full edit screen and more flexible command sets. Ed offers a good introduction to vi and helps explain where its command set originates.

C.3   Quick Vi Tutorial

The aim of this tutorial is to get you started using the vi editor. This tutorial assumes no vi experience, so you will be exposed to the ten most basic vi commands. These fundamental commands are enough to perform the bulk of your editing needs, and you can expand your vi vocabulary as needed. It is recommended you have a machine to practice with, as you proceed through the tutorial.

C.3.1   Invoking vi

To invoke vi, simply type the letters vi followed by the name of the file you wish to create. You will see a screen with a column of tildes (~) along the left side. vi is now in command mode. Anything you type will be understood as a command, not as text to be input. In order to input text, you must type a command. The two basic input commands are the following:

```
    i       insert text to the left of the cursor
    a       append text to the right of the cursor
```

Since you are at the beginning of an empty file, it doesn't matter which of these you type. Type one of them, and then type in the following text (a poem by Augustus DeMorgan found in *The Unix Programming Environment* by B.W. Kernighan and R. Pike):

```
    Great fleas have little fleas<Enter>
      upon their backs to bite 'em,<Enter>
    And little fleas have lesser fleas<Enter>
      and so ad infinitum.<Enter>
    And the great fleas themselves, in turn,<Enter>
      have greater fleas to go on;<Enter>
    While these again have greater still,<Enter>
      and greater still, and so on.<Enter>
    <Esc>
```

Note that you press the $\boxed{\text{Esc}}$ key to end insertion and return to command mode.

C.3.2   Cursor movement commands

```
    h       move the cursor one space to the left
    j       move the cursor one space down
    k       move the cursor one space up
    l       move the cursor one space to the right
```

These commands may be repeated by holding the key down. Try moving around in your text now. If you attempt an impossible movement, e.g., pressing the letter **k** when the cursor is on the top line, the screen will flash, or the terminal will beep. Don't worry, it won't bite, and your file will not be harmed.

C.3.3   Deleting text

```
x     delete the character at the cursor
dd    delete a line
```

Move the cursor to the second line and position it so that it is underneath the apostrophe in *'em*. Press the letter $\boxed{\text{x}}$, and the ' will disappear. Now press the letter $\boxed{\text{i}}$ to move into insert mode and type the letters **th**. Press $\boxed{\text{Esc}}$ when you are finished.

C.3.4   File saving

```
:w    save (write to disk)
:q    exit
```

Make sure you are in command mode by pressing the $\boxed{\text{Esc}}$ key. Now type **:w**. This will save your work by writing it to a disk file.

The command for quitting vi is $\boxed{\text{q}}$. If you wish to combine saving and quitting, just type **:wq**. There is also a convenient abbreviation for **:wq** — **ZZ**. Since much of your programming work will consist of running a program, encountering a problem, calling up the program in the editor to make a small change, and then exiting from the editor to run the program again, **ZZ** will be a command you use often. (Actually, **ZZ** is not an exact synonym for **:wq** — if you have not made any changes to the file you are editing since the last save, **ZZ** will just exit from the editor whereas **:wq** will (redundantly) save before exiting.)

If you have hopelessly messed things up and just want to start all over again, you can type **:q!** (remember to press the $\boxed{\text{Esc}}$ key first). If you omit the **!**, vi will not allow you to quit without saving.

C.3.5   What's next

The ten commands you have just learned should be enough for your work. However, you have just scratched the surface of the vi editor. There are commands to copy material from one place in a file to another, to move material from one place in a file to another, to move material from one file to another, to fine tune the editor to your personal tastes, etc. In all, there about 150 commands.

C.4   Advanced Vi Tutorial

The advantage and power of vi is the ability to use it successfully with only knowing a small subset of the commands. Most users of vi feel a bit awkward at the start, however after a small amount of time they find the need for more command knowledge.

The following tutorial is assuming the user has completed the quick tutorial (above) and hence feels comfortable with vi. It will expose some of the more powerful features of ex/vi from copying text to macro definitions. There is a section on ex and its settings which helps customize the editor. This tutorial describes the commands, rather then taking you set by set through each of them. It is recommended you spend the time trying the commands out on some example text, which you can afford to destroy.

This tutorial does not expose all the commands of vi though all of the commonly used commands and more are covered. Even if you choose to use an alternative text editor, it is hoped you will appreciate vi and what it offers those who do choose to use it.

C.4.1 Moving around

The most basic functionality of an editor, is to move the cursor around in the text. Here are more movement commands.

```
h          move the cursor one space to the left
j          move one line down
k          move one line up
l          move one line right
```

```
Some implementations also allow the arrows keys to move the cursor.
```

```
w          move to the start of the next word
e          move to the end of the next word
E          move to the end of the next word before a space
b          move to the start of the previous word
0          move to the start of the line
^          move to the first word of the current line
$          move to the end of the line
<CR>       move to the start of the next line
-          move to the start of the previous line
G          move to the end of the file
1G         move to the start of the file
nG         move to line number n
<Cntl> G   display the current line number
%          to the matching bracket
H          top line of the screen
M          middle line of the screen
L          bottom of the screen
n|         more cursor to column n
```

The screen will automatically scroll when the cursor reaches either the top or the bottom of the screen. There are alternative commands which can control scrolling the text.

```
<Cntl> f   scroll forward a screen
<Cntl> b   scroll backward a screen
<Cntl> d   scroll down half a screen
<Cntl> u   scroll down half a screen
```

The above commands control cursor movement. Some of the commands use a command modifier in the form of a number preciding the command. This feature will usually repeat the command that number of times.

To move the cursor a number of positions left.

```
nl         move the cursor n positions left
```

If you wanted to enter a number or spaces in front of the some text you could use the command modifier to the insert command. Enter the repeat number then $\boxed{\text{i}}$ followed by the space then press $\boxed{\text{ESC}}$.

```
ni         insert some text and repeat the text n times.
```

The commands that deal with lines use the modifier to refer to line numbers. The $\boxed{\text{G}}$ is a good example.

```
1G          Move the cursor to the first line.
```

vi has a large set of commands which can be used to move the cursor around the file. Single character movement through to direct line placement of the cursor. vi can also place the cursor at a selected line from the command line.

```
vi +10 myfile.tex
```

This command opens the file called *myfile.tex* and places the cursor 10 lines down from the start of the file.

Try out some of the commands in this section. Very few people can remember all of them in one session. Most users use only a subset of the above commands.

You can move around, so how do you change the text?

C.4.2 Modifing Text

The aim is to change the contents of the file and vi offers a very large set of commands to help in this process.

This section will focus on adding text, changing the existing text and deleting the text. At the end of this section you will have the knowledge to create any text file desired. The remaining sections focus on more desirable and convenient commands.

When entering text, multiple lines can be entered by using the $\boxed{\text{return}}$ key. If a typing mistake needs to be corrected and you are on the entering text on the line in question. You can use the $\boxed{\text{backspace}}$ key to move the cursor over the text. The different implementations of vi behave differently. Some just move the cursor back and the text can still be viewed and accepted. Others will remove the text as you backspace. Some clones even allow the arrow keys to be used to move the cursor when in input mode. This is not normal vi behaviour. If the text is visible and you use the $\boxed{\text{ESC}}$ key when on the line you have backspaced on the text after the cursor will be cleared. Use your editor to become accustomed to its' behaviour.

```
a          Append some text from the current cursor postion
A          Append at the end of the line
i          Insert text to the Left of the cursor
I          Inserts text to the Left of the first non-white character
               on current line
o          Open a new line and adds text Below current line
O          Open a new line and adds text Above the current line
```

We give it and we take it away. vi has a small set of delete commands which can be enhanced with the use of command modifiers.

```
x          Delete one character from under the cursor
dw         Delete from the current position to the end of the word
dd         Delete the current line.
D          Delete from the current position to the end of the line
```

The modifiers can be used to add greater power to the commands. The following examples are a subset of the posibilities.

```
nx            Delete n characters from under the cursor
ndd           Delete n lines
dnw           Deletes n words. (Same as ndw)
dG            Delete from the current position to the end of the file
d1G           Delete from the current postion to the start of the file
d$            Delete from current postion to the end of the line
              (This is the same as D)
dn$           Delete from current line the end of the nth line
```

The above command list shows the delete operating can be very powerful. This is evident when applied in combination with the cursor movement commands. One command to note is $\boxed{\text{D}}$ since it ignores the modifier directives.

On occasions you may need to undo the changes. The following commands restore the text after changes.

```
u             Undo the last command
U             Undo the current line from all changes on that line
:e!           Edit again. Restores to the state of the last save
```

vi not only allows you to undo changes, it can reverse the undo. Using the command $\boxed{\text{5dd}}$ delete 5 lines then restore the lines with $\boxed{\text{u}}$. The changes can be restored by the $\boxed{\text{u}}$ again.

vi offers commands which allow changes to the text to be made without first deleting then typing in the new version.

```
rc            Replace the character under the cursor with c
              (Moves cursor right if repeat modifier used eg 2rc)
R             Overwrites the text with the new text
cw            Changes the text of the current word
c$            Changes the text from current position to end of the line
cnw           Changes next n words.(same as ncw)
cn$           Changes to the end of the nth line
C             Changes to the end of the line (same as c$)
cc            Changes the current line
s             Substitutes text you type for the current character
ns            Substitutes text you type for the next n characters
```

The series of change commands which allow a string of characters to be entered are exited with the $\boxed{\text{ESC}}$ key.

The $\boxed{\text{cw}}$ command started from the current location in the word to the end of the word. When using a change command that specifies a distance the change will apply. vi will place a $ at the last character position. The new text can overflow or underflow the original text length.

C.4.3   Copying and Moving sections of text

Moving text involves a number of commands all combined to achieve the end result. This section will introduce named and unnamed buffers along with the commands which cut and paste the text.

Coping text involves three main steps.

1. **Yanking** (copying) the text to a buffer.

2. **Moving** the cursor to the destination location.

3. **Pasting** (putting) the text to the edit buffer.

To **Yank** text to the unnamed use $\boxed{y}$ command.

```
yy         Move a copy of the current line to the unnamed buffer.
Y          Move a copy of the current line to the unnamed buffer.
nyy        Move the next n lines to the unnamed buffer
nY         Move the next n lines to the unnamed buffer
yw         Move a word to the unnamed buffer.
ynw        Move n words to the unnamed buffer.
nyw        Move n words to the unnamed buffer.
y$         Move the current position to the end of the line.
```

The unnamed buffer is a tempory buffer that is easily corrupted by other common commands. On occasions the text may be needed for a long period of time. In this case the named buffers would be used. `vi` has 26 named buffers. The buffers use the letters of the alphabet as the identification name. To distinguish the difference between a command or a named buffer, `vi` uses the $\boxed{"}$ character. When using a named buffer by the lowercase letter the contents are over written while the uppercase version appends to the current contents.

```
"ayy       Move current line to named buffer a.
"aY        Move current line to named buffer a.
"byw       Move current word to named buffer b.
"Byw       Append the word the contents of the named buffer b.
"by3w      Move the next 3 words to named buffer b.
```

Use the $\boxed{p}$ command to paste the contents of the cut buffer to the edit buffer.

```
p          Paste from the unnamed buffer to the RIGHT of the cursor
P          Paste from the unnamed buffer to the LEFT of the cursor
nP         Paste n copies of the unnamed buffer to the LEFT of the cursor
"ap        Paste from the named buffer a RIGHT of the cursor.
"b3P       Paste 3 copies from the named buffer b LEFT of the cursor.
```

When using `vi` within an xterm you have one more option for copying text. Highlight the section of text you wish to copy by dragging the mouse cursor over text. Holding down the left mouse button and draging the mouse from the start to the finish will invert the text. This automatically places the text into a buffer reserved by the X server. To paste the text press the middle button. Remember the put `vi` into insert mode as the input could be interpreted as commands and the result will be unknown. Using the same techinque a single word can be copied by double clicking the left mouse button over the word. Just the single word will be copied. Pasting is the same as above. The buffer contents will only change when a new highlighted area is created.

Moving the text has three steps.

1. **Delete** text to a named or unnamed buffer.

2. **Moving** the cursor the to destination location.

3. **Pasting** the named or unnamed buffer.

The process is the same as copying with the change on step one to delete. When the command $\boxed{dd}$ is performed the line is deleted and placed into the unnamed buffer. You can then paste the contents just as you had when copying the text into the desired position.

```
"add       Delete the line and place it into named buffer a.
"a4dd      Delete 4 lines and place into named buffer a.
dw         Delete a word and place into unnamed buffer
```

See the section on modifying text for more examples of deleting text.

On the event of a system crash the named and unnamed buffer contents are lost but the edit buffers content can be recovered (See Useful commands).

C.4.4 Searching and replacing text

vi has a number of search command. You can search for individual characters through to regular expressions.

The main two character based search commands are $\boxed{\text{f}}$ and $\boxed{\text{t}}$.

```
fc          Find the next character c. Moves RIGHT to the next.
Fc          Find the next character c. Moves LEFT to the preceding.
tc          Move RIGHT to character before the next c.
Tc          Move LEFT to the character following the preceding c.
            (Some clones this is the same as Fc)
;           Repeats the last f,F,t,T command
,           Same as ; but reverses the direction to the orginal command.
```

If the character you were searching for was not found, vi will beep or give some other sort of signal.

vi allows you to search for a string in the edit buffer.

```
/str        Searches Right and Down for the next occurrence of str.
?str        Searches Left and UP for the next occurrence of str.
n           Repeat the last / or ? command
N           Repeats the last / or ? in the Reverse direction.
```

When using the $\boxed{\text{/}}$ or $\boxed{\text{?}}$ commands a line will be cleared along the bottom of the screen. You enter the search string followed by $\boxed{\text{RETURN}}$.

The string in the command $\boxed{\text{/}}$ or $\boxed{\text{?}}$ can be a regular expression. A regular expression is a description of a set of characters. The description is build using text intermixed with special characters. The special characters in regular expressions are . * [] ^$.

```
.           Matches any single character except newline.
\           Escapes any special characters.
*           Matches 0 or More occurrences of the preceding character.
[]          Matches exactly one of the enclosed characters.
^           Match of the next character must be at the begining of the line.
$           Matches characters preceding at the end of the line.
[^]         Matches anything not enclosed after the not character.
[-]         Matches a range of characters.
```

The only way to get used to the regular expression is to use them. Following is a series of examples.

```
c.pe        Matches cope, cape, caper etc
c\.pe       Matches c.pe, c.per etc
sto*p       Matches stp, stop, stoop etc
car.*n      Matches carton, cartoon, carmen etc
xyz.*       Matches xyz to the end of the line.
^The        Matches any line starting with The.
atime$      Matches any line ending with atime.
^Only$      Matches any line with Only as the only word in the line.
b[aou]rn    Matches barn, born, burn.
```

```
       Ver[D-F]    Matches VerD, VerE, VerF.
       Ver[^1-9]   Matches Ver followed by any non digit.
    the[ir][re]   Matches their,therr, there, theie.
[A-Za-z][A-Za-z]* Matches any word.
```

vi uses ex command mode to perform search and replace operations. All commands which start with a colon are requests in ex mode.

The search and replace command allows regular expression to be used over a range of lines and replace the matching string. The user can ask for confirmation before the substitution is performed. It may be well worth a review of line number representation in the ed tutorial.

```
:<start>,<finish>s/<find>/<replace>/g    General command

:1,$s/the/The/g      Search the entire file and replace the with The.
:%s/the/The/g        % means the complete file. (Same as above).
:.,5s/^.*//g         Delete the contents from the current to 5th line.
:%s/the/The/gc       Replace the with The but ask before substituting.
:%s/^....//g         Delete the first four characters on each line.
```

The search command is very powerful when combined with the regular expression search strings. If the $\boxed{g}$ directive is not included then the change is performed only on the first occurrence of a match on each line.

Sometimes you may want to use the original search string in the replacement result. You could retype the command on the line but vi allows the replacement string to contain some special characters.

```
:1,5s/help/&ing/g    Replaces help with helping on the first 5 lines.
:%s/ */&&/g          Double the number of spaces between the words.
```

Using the complete match string has its limits hence vi uses the escaped parentheses $\boxed{(}$ and $\boxed{)}$ to select the range of the substitution. Using an escaped digit $\boxed{1}$ which identifies the range in the order of the definition the replacement can be build.

```
:s/^\(.*\):.*/\1/g   Delete everything after and including the colon.
:s/\(.*\):\(.*\)/\2:\1/g   Swap the words either side of the colon.
```

You will most likely read the last series of gems again. vi offers powerful commands that many more modern editors do not or can not offer. The cost for this power is also the main argument against vi. The commands can be difficult to learn and read. Though most good things can be a little awkward at first. With a little practice and time, the vi command set will become second nature.

Bibliography

[1] Almesberger, Werner. *LILO: Generic Boot Loader for Linux*. Available electronically: `tsx-11.mit.edu`. July 3, 1993.

[2] Bach, Maurice J. *The Design of the UNIX Operating System*. Englewood Cliffs, New Jersey: Prentice-Hall, Inc. 1986.

[3] Lamport, Leslie. *LATEX: A Document Preparation System*. Reading, Massachusetts: Addison-Wesley Publishing Company. 1986.

[4] Stallman, Richard M. *GNU Emacs Manual*, eighth edition. Cambridge, Massachusetts: Free Software Foundation. 1993.

Part VI

LILO User's guide

Copyright Werner Almesberger werner.almesberger@lrc.di.epfl.ch
Version 0.16 February 26, 1995

Contents

LILO is a versatile boot loader for Linux. It does not depend on a specific file system, can boot Linux kernel images from floppy disks and from hard disks and can even boot other operating systems.[3]

One of up to sixteen different images can be selected at boot time. Various parameters, such as the root device, can be set independently for each kernel. LILO can even be used as the master boot record.

This document introduces the basics of disk organization and booting, continues with an overview of common boot techniques and finally describes installation and use of LILO in greater detail. The troubleshooting section at the end describes diagnostic messages and contains suggestions for most problems that have been observed in the past.

Please read the sections about installation and configuration if you're already using an older version of LILO. This distribution is accompanied by a file named INCOMPAT that describes further incompatibilities to older versions.

For the impatient: there is a quick-installation script to create a simple but quite usable installation. See section 4.1.2 for details.

But wait . . . here are a few easy rules that will help you avoiding most problems people experience with LILO:

- **Don't panic.** If something doesn't work, try to find out what is wrong, try to verify your assumption and only then attempt to fix it.

- Read the documentation. Especially if what the system does doesn't correspond to what you think it should do.

- Make sure you have an emergency boot disk, that you know how to use it, and that it is always kept up to date.

- Run /sbin/lilo **whenever** the kernel or any part of LILO, including its configuration file, has changed.

- If using LILO as the MBR, de-install it **before** performing a destructive upgrade and/or erasing your Linux partitions.

---

[3]PC/MS-DOS, DR DOS, OS/2, 386BSD, SCO UNIX, Unixware, . . .

- Don't trust setup scripts. Always verify the `/etc/lilo.conf` they create before booting.

- If using a big disk, be prepared for inconveniences: you may have to use the `linear` option.

Chapter 1

Introduction

1.1   Disk organization

When designing a boot concept, it is important to understand some of the subtleties of how PCs typically organize disks. The most simple case are floppy disks. They consist of a boot sector, some administrative data (FAT or super block, etc.) and the data area. Because that administrative data is irrelevant as far as booting is concerned, it is regarded as part of the data area for simplicity.

Boot sector
Data area

The entire disk appears as one device (e.g. `/dev/fd0`) on Linux.

The MS-DOS boot sector has the following structure:

0x000	Jump to the program code
0x003	Disk parameters
0x02C/0x03E	Program code
0x1FE	Magic number (0xAA55)

LILO uses a similar boot sector, but it does not contain the disk parameters part. This is no problem for Minix, Ext2 or similar file systems, because they don't look at the boot sector, but putting a LILO boot sector on an MS-DOS file system would make it inaccessible for MS-DOS.

Hard disks are organized in a more complex way than floppy disks. They contain several data areas called partitions. Up to four so-called primary partitions can exist on an MS-DOS hard disk. If more partitions are needed, one primary partition is used as an extended partition that contains several logical partitions.

The first sector of each hard disk contains a partition table, and an extended partition and **each** logical partition contains a partition table too.

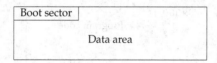

Partition table	/dev/hda
Partition 1	/dev/hda1
Partition 2	/dev/hda2

The entire disk can be accessed as `/dev/hda`, `/dev/hdb`, `/dev/sda`, etc. The primary partitions are `/dev/hda1` ... `/dev/hda4`.

Partition table	/dev/hda
Partition 1	/dev/hda1
Partition 2	/dev/hda2
Extended partition	/dev/hda3
Extended partition table	
Partition 3	/dev/hda5
Extended partition table	
Partition 4	/dev/hda6

This hard disk has two primary partitions and an extended partition that contains two logical partitions. They are accessed as `/dev/hda5` ...

Note that the partition tables of logical partitions are not accessible as the first blocks of some devices, while the main partition table, all boot sectors and the partition tables of extended partitions are.

Partition tables are stored in partition boot sectors. Normally, only the partition boot sector of the entire disk is used as a boot sector. It is also frequently called the master boot record (MBR).

0x000	Program code
0x1BE	Partition table
0x1FE	Magic number (0xAA55)

The LILO boot sector is designed to be usable as a partition boot sector. (I.e. there is room for the partition table.) Therefore, the LILO boot sector can be stored at the following locations:

- boot sector of a Linux floppy disk. (`/dev/fd0`, ...)
- MBR of the first hard disk. (`/dev/hda`, ...)
- boot sector of a primary Linux file system partition on the first hard disk. (`/dev/hda1`, ...)
- partition boot sector of an extended partition on the first hard disk. (`/dev/hda1`, ...)[1]

It **can't** be stored at any of the following locations:

- boot sector of a non-Linux floppy disk or primary partition.
- a Linux swap partition.
- boot sector of a logical partition in an extended partition.[2]
- on the second hard disk. (Unless for backup installations, if the current first disk will be removed or disabled, or if some other boot loader is used, that is capable of loading boot sectors from other drives.)

LILO typically doesn't detect attempts to put its boot sector at an invalid location.

[1]Most FDISK-type programs don't believe in booting from an extended partition and refuse to activate it. LILO is accompanied by a simple program (**activate**) that doesn't have this restriction. Linux fdisk also supports activating extended partitions.

[2]LILO can be forced to put the boot sector on such a partition by using the `-b` option or the `boot` variable. However, only few programs that operate as master boot records support booting from a logical partition.

1.2   Booting basics

When booting from a floppy disk, the first sector of the disk, the so-called boot sector, is loaded. That boot sector contains a small program that loads the respective operating system. MS-DOS boot sectors also contain a data area, where disk and file system parameters (cluster size, number of sectors, number of heads, etc.) are stored.

When booting from a hard disk, the very first sector of that disk, the so-called master boot record (MBR) is loaded. This sector contains a loader program and the partition table of the disk. The loader program usually loads the boot sector, as if the system was booting from a floppy.

Note that there is no functional difference between the MBR and the boot sector other than that the MBR contains the partition information but doesn't contain any file system-specific information (e.g. MS-DOS disk parameters).

The first 446 (0x1BE) bytes of the MBR are used by the loader program. They are followed by the partition table, with a length of 64 (0x40) bytes. The last two bytes contain a magic number that is sometimes used to verify that a given sector really is a boot sector.

There is a large number of possible boot configurations. The most common ones are described in the following sections.

1.2.1   MS-DOS alone

Master Boot Record	Boot sector	Operating system
DOS-MBR ⟶	MS-DOS ⟶	COMMAND.COM

This is what usually happens when MS-DOS boots from a hard disk: the DOS-MBR determines the active partition and loads the MS-DOS boot sector. This boot sector loads MS-DOS and finally passes control to COMMAND.COM. (This is greatly simplified.)

1.2.2   BOOTLIN[3]

Master Boot Record	Boot sector	Operating systems	
DOS-MBR ⟶	MS-DOS ⟶	COMMAND.COM	
	⟶	BOOTLIN ⟶	Linux

A typical BOOTLIN setup: everything happens like when booting MS-DOS, but in CONFIG.SYS or AUTOEXEC.BAT, BOOTLIN is invoked. Typically, a program like BOOT.SYS is used to choose among configuration sections in CONFIG.SYS and AUTOEXEC.BAT. This approach has the pleasant property that no boot sectors have to be altered.

Please refer to the documentation accompanying the package for installation instructions and further details.

1.2.3   LILO started by DOS-MBR

Master Boot Record	Boot sector	Operating system
DOS-MBR ⟶	LILO ⟶	Linux
	⟶ other OS	

This is a "safe" LILO setup: LILO is booted by the DOS-MBR. No other boot sectors have to be touched. If the other OS (or one of them, if there are several other operating systems being used) should be booted without using LILO, the other partition has to be marked "active" with fdisk or activate.

Installation:

- install LILO with its boot sector on the Linux partition.

---

[3]A more recent program called LOADLIN uses the same approach. Those who wish to use this method of booting are advised to use LOADLIN instead of BOOTLIN.

- use fdisk or activate to make that partition active.

- reboot.

Deinstallation:

- make a different partition active.

- install whatever should replace LILO or Linux.

1.2.4   Several alternate branches

Master Boot Record	Boot sector	Operating systems
DOS-MBR ⟶	MS-DOS ⟶	COMMAND.COM
	⟶	BOOTLIN ⟶ Linux
⟶	LILO ⟶	Linux
	⟶	MS-DOS — · · ·

An extended form of the above setup: the MBR is not changed and both branches can either boot Linux or MS-DOS. (LILO could also boot any other operating system.)

1.2.5   LILO started by BOOTACTV[4]

Master Boot Record	Boot sector	Operating system
BOOTACTV ⟶	LILO ⟶	Linux
⟶	other OS	

Here, the MBR is replaced by BOOTACTV (or any other interactive boot partition selector) and the choice between Linux and the other operating system(s) can be made at boot time. This approach should be used if LILO fails to boot the other operating system(s).[5]

Installation:

- boot Linux.

- make a backup copy of your MBR on a floppy disk, e.g.
  ```
  dd if=/dev/hda of=/fd/MBR bs=512 count=1
  ```

- install LILO with the boot sector on the Linux partition.

- install BOOTACTV as the MBR, e.g.
  ```
  dd if=bootactv.bin of=/dev/hda bs=446 count=1
  ```

- reboot.

Deinstallation:

- boot Linux.

- restore the old MBR, e.g.
  ```
  dd if=/MBR of=/dev/hda bs=446 count=1
  ```
  or FDISK /MBR under MS-DOS.

---

[4]Other, possibly better known boot switchers, e.g. OS/2 Bootmanager operate in a similar way. The installation procedures typically vary.

[5]And the author would like to be notified if booting the other operating system(s) doesn't work with LILO, but if it works with an other boot partition selector.

If replacing the MBR appears undesirable and if a second Linux partition exists (e.g. /usr, **not** a swap partition), **BOOTACTV** can be merged with the partition table and stored as the "boot sector" of that partition. Then, the partition can be marked active to be booted by the DOS-MBR.

Example:

```
# dd if=/dev/hda of=/dev/hda3 bs=512 count=1
# dd if=bootactv.bin of=/dev/hda3 bs=446 count=1
```

WARNING: Whenever the disk is re-partitioned, the merged boot sector on that "spare" Linux partition has to be updated too.

1.2.6 LILO alone

Master Boot Record	Operating system
LILO ————————→	**Linux**
——→	other OS

LILO can also take over the entire boot procedure. If installed as the MBR, LILO is responsible for either booting Linux or any other OS. This approach has the disadvantage, that the old MBR is overwritten and has to be restored (either from a backup copy, with FDISK /MBR on recent versions of MS-DOS or by overwriting it with something like **BOOTACTV**) if Linux should ever be removed from the system.

You should verify that LILO is able to boot your other operating system(s) before relying on this method.

Installation:

- boot Linux.

- make a backup copy of your MBR on a floppy disk, e.g.
  dd if=/dev/hda of=/fd/MBR bs=512 count=1

- install LILO with its boot sector as the MBR.

- reboot.

Deinstallation:

- boot Linux.

- restore the old MBR, e.g.
  dd if=/fd/MBR of=/dev/hda bs=446 count=1

If you've installed LILO as the master boot record, you have to explicitly specify the boot sector (configuration variable boot=...) when updating the map. Otherwise, it will try to use the boot sector of your current root partition, which may even work, but will probably leave your system unbootable.

1.2.7 Names

The following names have been used to describe boot sectors or parts of operating systems:

"DOS-MBR" is the original MS-DOS MBR. It scans the partition table for a partition that is marked "active" and loads the boot sector of that partition. Programs like MS-DOS' **FDISK**, Linux **fdisk** or **activate** (accompanies LILO) can change the active marker in the partition table.

"MS-DOS" denotes the MS-DOS boot sector that loads the other parts of the system (IO.SYS, etc.).

"COMMAND.COM" is the standard command interpreter of MS-DOS.

"BOOTLIN" and "LOADLIN" are programs that load a Linux kernel image from an MS-DOS partition into memory and execute it. They are usually invoked from `CONFIG.SYS` and used in combination with a `CONFIG.SYS` configuration switcher, like BOOT.SYS.[6]

"LILO" can either load a Linux kernel or the boot sector of any other operating system. It has a first stage boot sector that loads the remaining parts of LILO from various locations.[7]

"BOOTACTV" permits interactive selection of the partition from which the boot sector should be read. If no key is pressed within a given interval, the partition marked active is booted. BOOTACTV is included in the pfdisk package. There are also several similar programs, like PBOOT and OS-BS.[8]

1.3 Choosing the "right" boot concept

Although LILO can be installed in many different ways, the choice is usually limited by the present setup and therefore, typically only a small number of configurations which fit naturally into an existing system remains.

The configuration file `/etc/lilo.conf` for the examples could look like this:

```
boot = /dev/hda2
compact
image = /vmlinuz
image = /vmlinuz.old
other = /dev/hda1
  table = /dev/hda
  label = msdos
```

It installs a Linux kernel image (`/vmlinuz`), an alternate Linux kernel image (`/vmlinuz.old`) and a chain loader to boot MS-DOS from `/dev/hda1`. The option `compact` on the second line instructs the map installer to optimize loading.

In all examples, the names of the IDE-type hard disk devices (`/dev/hda...`) are used. Everything applies to other disk types (e.g. SCSI disks; `/dev/sda...`) too.

1.3.1 BIOS restrictions

Nowadays, an increasing number of systems is equipped with comparably large disks or even with multiple disks. At the time the disk interface of the standard PC BIOS has been designed (about 15 years ago), such configurations were apparently considered to be too unlikely to be worth supporting.

The most common BIOS restrictions that affect LILO are the limitation to two hard disks and the inability to access more than 1024 cylinders per disk. LILO can detect both conditions, but in order to solve the underlying problems, manual intervention is necessary.

[6]BOOTLIN is available for anonymous FTP from
`nic.funet.fi:/pub/OS/Linux/tools/bootlin.zip`
LOADLIN is available for anonymous FTP from
`sunsite.unc.edu:/pub/Linux/system/Linux-boot/lodlin15.tgz`
BOOT.SYS is available for anonymous FTP from
`sunsite.unc.edu:/pub/Linux/system/Linux-boot/boot142.zip` or
`nic.funet.fi:/pub/OS/Linux/tools/boot142.zip`
[7]LILO can be found in
`tsx-11.mit.edu:/pub/linux/packages/lilo/lilo.n.tar.gz`
`sunsite.unc.edu:/pub/Linux/system/Linux-boot/lilo/lilo.n.tar.gz`
`nic.funet.fi:/pub/OS/Linux/tools/lilo.n.tar.gz`
[8]pfdisk is available for anonymous FTP from
`sunsite.unc.edu:/pub/Linux/utils/disk-management/pfdisk.tar.Z` or
`nic.funet.fi:/pub/OS/Linux/tools/pfdisk.tar.Z`
PBOOT can be found in
`nic.funet.fi:/pub/OS/Linux/tools/pboot.zip`

The drive limit does not exist in every BIOS. Some modern motherboards and disk controllers are equipped with a BIOS that supports more (typically four) disk drives. When attempting to access the third, fourth, etc. drive, LILO prints a warning message but continues. Unless the BIOS really supports more than two drives, the system will **not** be able to boot in that case.[9]

The cylinder limit is a very common problem with IDE disks. There, the number of cylinders typically exceeds 1024 if the drive has a capacity of more than 504 MB. Many SCSI driver BIOSes present the disk geometry in a way that makes the limit occur near 1 GB. Modern disk controllers may even push the limit up to about 8 GB. All cylinders beyond the 1024th are inaccessible for the BIOS. LILO detects this problem and aborts the installation (unless the `linear` option is used, see section 3.2.2).

Note that large partitions that only partially extend into the "forbidden zone" are still in jeopardy even if they appear to work at first, because the file system does not know about the restrictions and may allocate disk space from the area beyond the 1024th cylinder when installing new kernels. LILO therefore prints a warning message but continues as long as no imminent danger exists.

There are four approaches of how such problems can be solved:

- use of a different partition which is on an accessible disk and which does not exceed the 1024 cylinder limit. If there is only a DOS partition which fulfills all the criteria, that partition can be used to store the relevant files. (See section 1.3.8.)

- rearranging partitions and disks. This is typically a destructive operation, so care should be taken to make good backups.

- if the system is running DOS, **LOADLIN** can be used instead of LILO.

- if all else fails, installation of a more capable BIOS, a different controller or a different disk configuration.

LILO depends on the BIOS to load the following items:

- `/boot/boot.b`

- `/boot/map` (created when running `/sbin/lilo`)

- all kernels

- the boot sectors of all other operating systems it boots

- the startup message, if one has been defined

Normally, this implies that the Linux root file system should be in the "safe" area. However, it is already sufficient to put all kernels into `/boot` and to either mount a "good" partition on `/boot` or to let `/boot` be a symbolic link pointing to or into such a partition.

See also `/usr/src/linux/drivers/block/README.ide` for a detailed description of problems with large disks.

1.3.2 One disk, Linux on a primary partition

If at least one primary partition of the first hard disk is used as a Linux file system (`/`, `/usr`, etc. but **not** as a swap partition), the LILO boot sector should be stored on that partition and it should be booted by the original master boot record or by a program like **BOOTACTV**.

MBR	/dev/hda
MS-DOS	/dev/hda1
→ Linux /	/dev/hda2

In this example, the `boot` variable could be omitted, because the boot sector is on the root partition.

---

[9]If only "unimportant" parts of the system are located on the "high" drives, some functionality may be available.

1.3.3 One disk, Linux on a logical partition

If no primary partition is available for Linux, but at least one logical partition of an extended partition on the first hard disk contains a Linux file system, the LILO boot sector should be stored in the partition sector of the extended partition and it should be booted by the original master boot record or by a program like BOOTACTV.

MBR	/dev/hda
MS-DOS	/dev/hda1
Extended	/dev/hda2
Linux	/dev/hda5
...	/dev/hda6

(→ pointing to the Extended row)

Because many disk partitioning programs refuse to make an extended partition (in our example /dev/hda2) active, you might have to use activate, which comes with the LILO distribution.

OS/2 BootManager should be able to boot LILO boot sectors from logical partitions. The installation on the extended partition itself is not necessary in this case.

1.3.4 Two disks, Linux (at least partially) on the first disk

This case is equivalent to the configurations where only one disk is in the system. The Linux boot sector resides on the first hard disk and the second disk is used later in the boot process.

Only the location of the boot sector matters – everything else (/boot/boot.b, /boot/map, the root file system, a swap partition, other Linux file systems, etc.) can be located anywhere on the second disk.

1.3.5 Two disks, Linux on second disk, first disk has an extended partition

If there is no Linux partition on the first disk, but there is an extended partition, the LILO boot sector can be stored in the partition sector of the extended partition and it should be booted by the original master boot record or by a program like BOOTACTV.

First disk

MBR	/dev/hda
MS-DOS	/dev/hda1
Extended	/dev/hda2
...	/dev/hda5
...	/dev/hda6

(→ pointing to the Extended row)

Second disk

MBR	/dev/hdb
Linux	/dev/hdb1
...	/dev/hdb2

The program activate, that accompanies LILO, may have to be used to set the active marker on an extended partition, because MS-DOS' FDISK and some older version of Linux fdisk refuse to do that. (Which is generally a good idea.)

1.3.6 Two disks, Linux on second disk, first disk has no extended partition

If there is neither a Linux partition nor an extended partition on the first disk, then there's only one place left, where a LILO boot sector could be stored: the master boot record.

In this configuration, LILO is responsible for booting all other operating systems too.

First disk

MBR	/dev/hda
MS-DOS	/dev/hda1
...	/dev/hda2

(→ pointing to the MBR row)

Second disk

MBR	/dev/hdb
Linux	/dev/hdb1
...	/dev/hdb2

You should back up your old MBR before installing LILO and verify that LILO is able to boot your other operating system(s) before relying on this approach.

The line `boot = /dev/hda2` in `/etc/lilo.conf` would have to be changed to `boot = /dev/hda` in this example.

1.3.7 More than two disks

On systems with more than two disks, typically only the first two can be accessed. The configuration choices are therefore the same as with two disks.

When attempting to access one of the extra disks, LILO displays a warning message (`Warning: BIOS drive 0xnumber may not be accessible`) but does not abort. This is done in order to allow the lucky few whose BIOS (or controller-BIOS) does support more than two drives to make use of this feature. By all others, this warning should be considered a fatal error.

Note that the two disks restriction is only imposed by the BIOS. Linux normally has no problems using all disks once it is booted.

1.3.8 `/boot` on a DOS partition

Recent kernels support all the functions LILO needs to map files also on MS-DOS (or UMSDOS) file systems. Since DOS partitions tend to occupy exactly the places where BIOS restrictions (see section 1.3.1) are invisible, they're an ideal location for `/boot` if the native Linux file systems can't be used because of BIOS problems.

In order to accomplish this, the DOS partition is mounted read-write, a directory (e.g. `/dos/linux`) is created, all files from `/boot` are moved to that directory, `/boot` is replaced by a symbolic link to it, the kernels are also moved to the new directory, their new location is recorded in `/etc/lilo.conf`, and finally `/sbin/lilo` is run.

From then on, new kernels must always be copied into that directory on the DOS partition before running `/sbin/lilo`, e.g. when recompiling a kernel, the standard procedure changes from

```
# make zlilo
```

to

```
# make zImage
# mv /dos/linux/vmlinuz /dos/linux/vmlinuz.old
# mv arch/i386/boot/zImage /dos/linux/vmlinuz
# /sbin/lilo
```

WARNING: De-fragmenting such a DOS partition is likely to make Linux or even the whole system unbootable. Therefore, the DOS partition should either not be de-fragmented, or a Linux boot disk should be prepared (and tested) to bring up Linux and to run `/sbin/lilo` after the de-fragmentation.[10]

---

[10]Setting the "system" attribute from DOS on the critical files (e.g. everything in `C:\LINUX`) may help to protect them from being rearranged. However, the boot floppy should still be ready, just in case.

Chapter 2

The boot prompt

Immediately after it's loaded, LILO checks whether one of the following is happening:

- any of the [Shift], [Control] or [Alt] keys is being pressed.

- [CapsLock] or [ScrollLock] is set.

If this is the case, LILO displays the `boot:` prompt and waits for the name of a boot image (i.e. Linux kernel or other operating system). Otherwise, it boots the default boot image[1] or – if a delay has been specified – waits for one of the listed activities until that amount of time has passed.

At the boot prompt, the name of the image to boot can be entered. Typing errors can be corrected with [BackSpace], [Delete], [Ctrl U] and [Ctrl X]. A list of known images can be obtained by pressing [?] (on the US keyboard) or [Tab].

If [Enter] is pressed and no file name has been entered, the default image is booted.

2.1 Boot command-line options

LILO is also able to pass command-line options to the kernel. Command-line options are words that follow the name of the boot image and that are separated by spaces.

Example:

```
boot: linux single root=200
```

2.1.1 Standard options

The 1.1.90 kernel recognizes the options `debug`, `no387`, `no-hlt`, `ramdisk=`*size*, `reserve=`*base*, *size*,..., `root=`*device*, `ro`, and `rw`, and all current init programs also recognize the option `single`. The options `lock` and `vga` are processed by the boot loader itself. Boot command-line options are always case-sensitive.

`single` boots the system in single-user mode. This bypasses most system initialization procedures and directly starts a root shell on the console. Multi-user mode can typically be entered by exiting the single-user shell or by rebooting.

---

[1]The default boot image is either the first boot image, the image specified with the `default` variable, or the image that has been selected at the boot prompt.

root=*device* changes the root device. This overrides settings that may have been made in the boot image and on the LILO command line. *device* is either the hexadecimal device number [2] or the full path name of the device, e.g. /dev/hda3.[3]

reserve=*base*,*size*,... reserves IO port regions. This can be used to prevent device drivers from auto-probing addresses where other devices are located, which get confused by the probing.

ro instructs the kernel to mount the root file system read-only. rw mounts it read-write. If neither ro nor rw is specified, the setting from the boot image is used.

no-hlt avoids executing a HLT instructions whenever the system is idle. HLT normally significantly reduces power consumption and therefore also heat dissipation of the CPU, but may not work properly with some clone CPUs. no387 disables using the hardware FPU even if one is present.

debug enables more verbose console logging.

vga=*mode* alters the VGA mode set at startup. The values normal, extended, ask or a decimal number are recognized. (See also page 747.)

Finally, lock stores the current command-line as the default command-line, so that LILO boots the same image with the same options (including lock) when invoked the next time.

2.1.2 Device-specific options

There is also a large number of options to specify certain characteristics (e.g. IO and memory addresses) of devices. The 1.1.90 kernel understands the following device options (if the corresponding devices are included): ether, max_scsi_luns, hd, hda, hdb,hdc, hdd, st, bmouse, st0x, tmc8xx, t128, pas16, ncr5380, aha152x, aha1542, aha274x, buslogic, xd, mcd, aztcd, sound, sbpcd, and cdu31a. The usage of these options is *option*=*number*,.... Please consult the corresponding FAQs and HOWTOs for details.

2.1.3 Other options

Options of the type *variable*=*value* which are neither standard options nor device-specific options, cause the respective variables to be set in the environment passed to init. The case of the variable name is preserved. (I.e. it's not automatically converted to upper case.)

Note that environment variables passed to init are typically available in system initialization scripts (e.g. /etc/rc.local), but they're not visible from ordinary login sessions, because the login program removes them from the user's environment.

2.1.4 Repeating options

The effect of repeating boot command-line options depends on the options.[4] There are three possible behaviours:

Options that only enable or disable a certain functionality can be repeated any number of times. debug, lock, no-hlt, and no387 fall into this category.

[2]This is a list of device numbers of some frequently used devices:

/dev/fd0	200	/dev/hda1	301	/dev/sda1	801
/dev/fd1	201	/dev/hda2	302	/dev/sda2	802
...		...		...	
		/dev/hdb1	341	/dev/sdb1	811
		/dev/hdb2	342	/dev/sdb2	812
		...		...	

[3]The device names are hard-coded in the kernel. Therefore, only the "standard" names are supported and some less common devices may not be recognized. In those cases, only numbers can be used.

[4]Options are frequently repeated when a string defined with append or literal is prepended to the parameters typed in by the user. Also, LILO implicitly prepends the options ramdisk, ro, root, or rw when ramdisk, read-only, read-write, or root, respectively, are set in the configuration file. (lock and vga are handled by a different internal mechanism.)

Other options change a global setting whenever they appear, so only the value or presence of the last option matters. The antagonists `ro` and `rw` are such options. Also, `ramdisk`, `root`, and `vga` work this way. Example: `ro rw` would mount the root file system read-write.

Finally, when `reserve` and many device-specific options are repeated, each occurrence has its own meaning, e.g. `hd=... hd=...` would configure two hard disks, and `reserve=0x300,8 reserve=0x5f0,16` would reserve the ranges 0x300 to 0x307 and 0x5f0 to 0x5ff (which is equivalent to writing `reserve=0x300,8,0x5f0,16`).

2.1.5   Implicit options

LILO always passes the string `BOOT_IMAGE=`*name* to the kernel, where *name* is the name by which the kernel is identified (e.g. the label). This variable can be used in `/etc/rc` to select a different behaviour, depending on the kernel.

When booting automatically, the word `auto` is also passed on the command line. This can be used by init to suppress interactive prompts in the boot phase.

2.2   Boot image selection

The details of selecting the boot image are somewhat complicated. The following tables illustrate them. First, if neither `prompt` is set nor a shift key is being pressed:

Externally provided cmd. line[5]	Command line in map file[6]	Automatic boot[7]	Booted image
No	No	Yes	Default image
Yes	—	Yes	Specified by external command line
No	Yes	Yes	Specified by command line in map file

If `prompt` is not set and a shift key is being pressed:

Input timeout	Empty cmd.l.	Extern. cmd.l.	Cmd.l. in map file	Automatic boot	Booted image
No	No	—	—	No	Specified by the user
No	Yes	—	—	No	Default image
Yes	n/a	—	—	Yes	Default image

Finally, if the configuration variable `prompt` is set:

Input timeout	Empty cmd.l.	Extern. cmd.l.	Cmd.l. in map file	Automatic boot	Booted image
No	No	No	No	No	Specified by the user
No	Yes	No	No	No	Default image
Yes	n/a	No	No	Yes	Default image
n/a	n/a	Yes	—	Yes	Specified by external command line
n/a	n/a	No	Yes	Yes	Specified by command line in map file

[5]Externally provided command lines could be used to add front-ends to LILO. They would pass the respective command string to LILO, which would then interpret it like keyboard input. This feature is currently not used.

[6]This command line is set by invoking the map installer with the `-R` option or by using the boot command-line option `lock`.

[7]I.e. the keyword `auto` is added.

Note that LILO pauses for the amount of time specified in `delay` when at the end of a default command line. The automatic boot can then be interrupted by pressing a shifting key.

The default image is the first image in the map file or the image specified with the `default` variable. However, after an unsuccessful boot attempt, the respective image becomes the default image.

Chapter 3

Map installer

The map installer program /sbin/lilo updates the boot sector and creates the map file. If the map installer detects an error, it terminates immediately and does not touch the boot sector and the map file.

Whenever the map installer updates a boot sector, the original boot sector is copied to /boot/boot.*number*, where *number* is the hexadecimal device number. If such a file already exists, no backup copy is made. Similarly, a file /boot/part.*number* is created if LILO modifies the partition table. (See page 744.)

3.1 Command-line options

The LILO map installer can be invoked in the following ways:

3.1.1 Show current installation

The currently mapped files are listed. With -v, also many parameters are shown.

/sbin/lilo [-C *config_file*] [-q] [-m *map_file*] [-v ...]

-C *config_file*
  Specifies the configuration file that is used by the map installer (see section 3.2). If -C is omitted, /etc/lilo.conf is used.

-m *map_file*
  Specifies an alternate map file. See also sections 3.1.7 and 3.2.2.

-q
  Lists the currently mapped files.

-v ...
  Increase verbosity. See also sections 3.1.7 and 3.2.2.

3.1.2 Create or update map

A new map is created for the images described in the configuration file /etc/lilo.conf and they are registered in the boot sector.

/sbin/lilo [-C *config_file*] [-b *boot_device*] [-c] [-l] [-i *boot_sector*] [-f *disk_tab*]

```
[ -m map_file ]
[ -d delay ]
[ -v ... ]
[ -t ]
[ -s save_file |
-S save_file ]
[ -P fix |
-P ignore ]
[ -r root_dir ]
```

-b *boot_device*
> Specifies the boot device. See also sections 3.1.7 and 3.2.2.

-c
> Enables map compaction. See also sections 3.1.7 and 3.2.2.

-C *config_file*
> Specifies an alternate configuration file. See also section 3.1.1.

-d *delay*
> Sets the delay before LILO boots the default image. Note that the delay is specified in **tenths** of a second. See also sections 3.1.7 and 3.2.2.

-f *disk_tab*
> Specifies a disk parameter table file. See also sections 3.1.7 and 3.2.2.

-i *boot_sector*
> Specifies an alternate boot file. See also sections 3.1.7 and 3.2.2.

-l
> Enables linear sector addresses. See also sections 3.1.7 and 3.2.2.

-m *map_file*
> Specifies an alternate map file. See also sections 3.1.7 and 3.2.2.

-P *mode*
> Specifies how invalid partition table entries should be handled. See also sections 3.1.7 and 3.2.2.

-r *root_directory*
> Chroots to the specified directory before doing anything else. This is useful when running the map installer while the normal root file system is mounted somewhere else, e.g. when recovering from an installation failure with a recovery disk. The -r option is implied if the environment variable ROOT is set.[1] The current directory is changed to the new root directory, so using relative paths may not work.

-s *save_file*
> Specifies an alternate boot sector save file. See also sections 3.1.7 and 3.2.2.

-S *save_file*
> Like -s, but overwrites old save file.

-t
> Test only. This performs the entire installation procedure except replacing the map file, writing the modified boot sector and fixing partition tables. This can be used in conjunction with the -v option to verify that LILO will use sane values.

-v ...
> Increase verbosity. See also sections 3.1.7 and 3.2.2.

---

[1]E.g. if your root partition is mounted on /mnt, you can update the map by simply running ROOT=/mnt /mnt/sbin/lilo

3.1.3   Change default command line

Changes LILO's default command line. See also section 2.2.

/sbin/lilo [-C *config_file*] [-m *map_file*] [-R [*word* ...]]

-C *config_file*
>   Specifies an alternate configuration file. See also section 3.1.1.

-m *map_file*
>   Specifies an alternate map file. See also sections 3.1.7 and 3.2.2.

-R *word* ...
>   Stores the specified words in the map file. The boot loader uses those words as the default command
>   line when booting the next time. That command line is removed from the map file by the boot loader
>   by overwriting the sector immediately after reading it. The first word has to be the name of a boot
>   image. If -R is not followed by any words, the current default command line in the map file is erased.[2]
>   An error message is issued and a non-zero exit code is returned if the command line is not accepted.

3.1.4   Kernel name translation

Determines the path of the kernel.

/sbin/lilo [-C *config_file*] -I *name* [*options*]

-C *config_file*
>   Specifies an alternate configuration file. See also section 3.1.1.

-I *name* [*options*]
>   Translates the specified label name to the path of the corresponding kernel image and prints that path
>   on standard output. This can be used to synchronize files that depend on the kernel (e.g. the ps
>   database). The image name can be obtained from the environment variable BOOT_IMAGE. An error
>   message is issued and a non-zero exit code is returned if no matching label name can be found. The
>   existence of the image file is verified if the option character v is added.

3.1.5   De-installation

Restores the boot sector that was used before the installation of LILO. Note that this option only works
properly if LILO's directories (e.g. /boot) have not been touched since the first installation. See also section
4.4.

/sbin/lilo [-C *config_file*] [-s *save_file*] -u | -U [*boot_device*]

-C *config_file*
>   Specifies an alternate configuration file. See also section 3.1.1.

-s *save_file*
>   Specifies an alternate boot sector save file. See also sections 3.1.7 and 3.2.2.

---

[2]-R is typically used in reboot scripts, e.g.
```
#!/bin/sh
cd /
if /sbin/lilo -R "$*"; then
    echo | shutdown -r now
fi
```

-u [*device_name*]
> Restores the backup copy of the specified boot sector. If no device is specified, the value of the `boot` variable is used. If this one is also unavailable, LILO uses the current root device. The name of the backup copy is derived from the device name. The `-s` option or the `backup` variable can be used to override this. LILO validates the backup copy by checking a time stamp.

-U [*device_name*]
> Like -u, but does not check the time stamp.

3.1.6 Print version number

```
/sbin/lilo -V
```

-V
> Print the version number and exit.

3.1.7 Options corresponding to configuration variables

There are also many command-line options that correspond to configuration variables. See section 3.2.2 for a description.

Command-line option	Configuration variable
-b *boot_device*	boot=*boot_device*
-c	compact
-d *tsecs*	delay=*tsecs*
-D *name*	default=*name*
-i *boot_sector*	install=*boot_sector*
-f *disktab_file*	disktab=*disktab_file*
-l	linear
-m *map_file*	map=*map_file*
-P fix	fix-table
-P ignore	ignore-table
-s *backup_file*	backup=*backup_file*
-S *backup_file*	force-backup=*backup_file*
-v ...	verbose=*level*

3.2 Configuration

The configuration information is stored in the file /etc/lilo.conf and consists of variable assignments.

3.2.1 Syntax

The following syntax rules apply:

- flag variables consist of a single word and are followed by whitespace or the end of the file.

- string variables consist of the variable name, optional whitespace, an equal sign, optional whitespace, the value and required whitespace, or the end of the file.

- a non-empty sequence of blanks, tabs, newlines and comments counts as whitespace.

- variable names are case-insensitive. Values are usually case-sensitive, but there are a few exceptions. (See below.)

- tabs and newlines are special characters and may not be part of a variable name or a value. The use of other control characters and non-ASCII characters is discouraged.

- blanks and equal signs may only be part of a variable name or a value if they are escaped by a backslash or if the value is embedded in double quotes. An equal sign may not be the only character in a name or value.

- an escaped tab is converted to an escaped blank. An escaped newline is removed from the input stream. An escaped backslash (i.e. two backslashes) is converted to a backslash. Inside quoted strings, only double quotes and backslashes can be escaped.

- comments begin with a number sign and end with the next newline. All characters (including backslashes) until the newline are ignored.

3.2.2   Global options

`/etc/lilo.conf` begins with a possibly empty global options section. Many global options can also be set from the command line, but storing permanent options in the configuration file is more convenient.

The following global options are recognized:

`backup=`*backup_file* Copy the original boot sector to *backup_file* (which may also be a device, e.g. `/dev/null`) instead of `/boot/boot.`*number*

`boot=`*boot_device* Sets the name of the device (e.g. a hard disk partition) that contains the boot sector. If `boot` is omitted, the boot sector is read from (and possibly written to) the device that is currently mounted as root.

`compact` Tries to merge read requests for adjacent sectors into a single read request. This drastically reduces load time and keeps the map smaller. Using `compact` is especially recommended when booting from a floppy disk.

`default=`*name* Uses the specified image as the default boot image. If `default` is omitted, the image appearing first in the configuration file is used.

`delay=`*tsecs* Specifies the number of tenths of a second LILO should wait before booting the first image. This is useful on systems that immediately boot from the hard disk after enabling the keyboard. LILO doesn't wait if `delay` is omitted or if `delay` is set to zero.

`disk=`*device_name* Defines non-standard parameters for the specified disk. See section 3.4 for details.

`disktab=`*disktab_file* Specifies the name of the disk parameter table (see section 3.4.3). The map installer looks for `/etc/disktab` if `disktab` is omitted. The use of disktabs is discouraged; see section 3.4 for a vastly superior approach.

`fix-table` allows LILO to adjust 3D addresses in partition tables. Each partition entry contains a 3D (sector/head/cylinder) and a linear address of the first and the last sector of the partition. If a partition is not track-aligned and if certain other operating systems (e.g. PC/MS-DOS or OS/2) are using the same disk, they may change the 3D address. LILO can store its boot sector only on partitions where both address types correspond. LILO re-adjusts incorrect 3D start addresses if `fix-table` is set.

WARNING: This does not guarantee that other operating systems may not attempt to reset the address later. It is also possible that this change has other, unexpected side-effects. The correct fix is to re-partition the drive with a program that does align partitions to tracks. Also, with some disks (e.g. some large EIDE disks with address translation enabled), under some circumstances, it may even be unavoidable to have conflicting partition table entries.

`force-backup=`*backup_file* Like `backup`, but overwrite an old backup copy if it exists. `backup=`*backup_file* is ignored if `force-backup` appears in the same configuration file.

`ignore-table` tells LILO to ignore corrupt partition tables.

`install=`*boot_sector* Install the specified file as the new boot sector. If `install` is omitted, `/boot/boot.b` is used as the default.

`linear` Generate linear sector addresses instead of sector/head/cylinder addresses. Linear addresses are translated at run time and do not depend on disk geometry. Note that boot disks may not be portable if `linear` is used, because the BIOS service to determine the disk geometry does not work reliably for floppy disks. When using `linear` with large disks, `/sbin/lilo` may generate references to inaccessible disk areas (see section 1.3.1), because 3D sector addresses are not known before boot time.

`lock` Enables automatic recording of boot command lines as the defaults for the following boots. This way, LILO "locks" on a choice until it is manually overridden.

`map=`*map_file* Specifies the location of the map file. If `map` is omitted, a file `/boot/map` is used.

`message=`*message_file* specifies a file containing a message that is displayed before the boot prompt. No message is displayed while waiting for a shifting key after printing "LILO ". In the message, the FF character ([Ctrl L]) clears the local screen. The size of the message file is limited to 65535 bytes. The map file has to be rebuilt if the message file is changed or moved.

`nowarn` Disables warnings about possible future dangers.

`optional` makes all images optional. (See below.)

`password=`*password* sets a password for all images. (See below.)

`prompt` forces entering the boot prompt without expecting any prior key-presses. Unattended reboots are impossible if `prompt` is set and `timeout` isn't.

`restricted` relaxes the password protection. (See below.)

`serial=`*parameters* enables control from a serial line. The specified serial port is initialized and LILO is accepting input from it and from the PC's keyboard. Sending a break on the serial line corresponds to pressing a shift key on the console in order to get LILO's attention. All boot images should be password-protected if the serial access is less secure than access to the console, e.g. if the line is connected to a modem. The parameter string has the following syntax:
port, *bps parity bits*
The components *bps*, *parity* and *bits* can be omitted. If a component is omitted, all following components have to be omitted too. Additionally, the comma has to be omitted if only the port number is specified.

> *port* the number of the serial port, zero-based. 0 corresponds to COM1 alias `/dev/ttyS0`, etc. All four ports can be used (if present).

> *bps* the baud rate of the serial port. The following baud rates are supported: 110, 150, 300, 600, 1200, 2400, 4800 and 9600 bps. Default is 2400 bps.

> *parity* the parity used on the serial line. LILO ignores input parity and strips the 8th bit. The following (upper or lower case) characters are used to describe the parity: n for no parity, e for even parity and o for odd parity.

> *bits* the number of bits in a character. Only 7 and 8 bits are supported. Default is 8 if parity is "none", 7 if parity is "even" or "odd".

> If `serial` is set, the value of `delay` is automatically raised to 20.

> Example: `serial=0,2400n8` initializes COM1 with the default parameters.

`timeout=`*tsecs* sets a timeout (in tenths of a second) for keyboard input. If no key is pressed for the specified time, the first image is automatically booted. Similarly, password input is aborted if the user is idle for too long. The default timeout is infinite.

`verbose=`*level* Turns on lots of progress reporting. Higher numbers give more verbose output. If `-v` is additionally specified on the command line, *level* is increased accordingly. The following verbosity levels exist:

<0 only warnings and errors are shown

0 prints one line for each added or skipped image

1 mentions names of important files and devices and why they are accessed. Also displays informational messages for exceptional but harmless conditions and prints the version number.

2 displays statistics and processing of temporary files and devices

3 displays disk geometry information

4 lists sector mappings as they are written into the map file (i.e. after compaction, in a format suitable to pass it to the BIOS)

5 lists the mapping of each sector (i.e. before compaction, raw)

When using the `-q` option, the levels have a slightly different meaning:

0 displays only image names

1 also displays all global and per-image settings

2 displays the address of the first map sector

Additionally, the kernel configuration parameters `append`, `ramdisk`, `read-only`, `read-write`, `root` and `vga` can be set in the global options section. They are used as defaults if they aren't specified in the configuration sections of the respective kernel images. See below for a description.

The plethora of options may be intimidating at first, but in "normal" configurations, hardly any options but `boot`, `compact`, `delay`, `root`, and `vga` are used.

3.2.3   General per-image options

LILO uses the main file name (without its path) of each image specification to identify that image. A different name can be used by setting the variable `label` (see the example above). A second name for the same entry can be used by specifying the `alias=`*name* option.

Images are protected by a password if the variable `password` is set. If the variable `restricted` is set in addition to `password`, a password is only required to boot the respective image if parameters are specified on the command line (e.g. `single`). `password` and `restricted` can also be set in the options section to be the default password and password protection mode for all images. Because the configuration file contains unencrypted passwords when using `password`, it should only be readable for the super-user.

If an image section contains the variable `optional` (or if that variable is set in the options section), the respective image is omitted if its main file is not available at map creation time. This is useful to specify test kernels that are not always present.

3.2.4   Per-image options for kernels

Each (kernel or non-kernel) image description begins with a special variable (see section 3.3) which is followed by optional variables. The following variables can be used for all image descriptions that describe a Linux kernel:

`append=`*string* Appends the options specified in *string* to the parameter line passed to the kernel. This is typically used to specify parameters of hardware that can't be entirely auto-detected, e.g.
`append = "hd=64,32,202"`

`literal=`*string* Like `append`, but removes all other options (e.g. setting of the root device). Because vital options can be removed unintentionally with `literal`, this option cannot be set in the global options section.

ramdisk=*size* specifies the size of the optional RAM disk. A value of zero indicates that no RAM disk should be created. If this variable is omitted, the RAM disk size configured into the boot image is used.

read-only specifies that the root file system should be mounted read-only. Typically, the system startup procedure re-mounts the root file system read-write later (e.g. after fsck'ing it).

read-write specifies that the root file system should be mounted read-write.

root=*root_device* specifies the device that should be mounted as root. If the special name current is used, the root device is set to the device on which the root file system is currently mounted. If the root has been changed with -r, the respective device is used. If the variable root is omitted, the root device setting contained in the kernel image is used. It can be changed with the rdev program.

vga=*mode* specifies the VGA text mode that should be selected when booting. The following values are recognized (case is ignored):

normal select normal 80x25 text mode.

extended select 80x50 text mode. The word extended can be abbreviated to ext.

ask stop and ask for user input (at boot time).

number use the corresponding text mode. A list of available modes can be obtained by booting with vga=ask and pressing [Enter].

If this variable is omitted, the VGA mode setting contained in the kernel image is used. rdev supports manipulation of the VGA text mode setting in the kernel image.

If one of ramdisk, read-only, read-write, root, or vga is omitted in the configuration file and the corresponding value in the kernel image is changed, LILO or the kernel will use the new value.

It is perfectly valid to use different settings for the same image, because LILO stores them in the image descriptors and not in the images themselves.

Example:

```
image = /vmlinuz
  label = lin-hd
  root = /dev/hda2
image = /vmlinuz
  label = lin-fd
  root = /dev/fd0
```

3.3   Boot image types

LILO can boot the following types of images:

- kernel images from a file.
- kernel images from a block device. (E.g. a floppy disk.)
- the boot sector of some other operating system.

The image type is determined by the name of the initial variable of the configuration section.

The image files can reside on any media that is accessible at boot time. There's no need to put them on the root device, although this certainly doesn't hurt.

In the configuration sections of all boot images, the following variables are recognized: alias, label, lock, optional, password and restricted.

In the configuration sections of all kernels (i.e. every boot image type except "other operating system"), the following variables are recognized: append, literal, ramdisk, read-only, read-write, root and vga.

3.3.1 Booting kernel images from a file

The image is specified as follows: `image=`*name*

Example:

```
image = /linux
```

3.3.2 Booting kernel images from a device

The range of sectors that should be mapped, has to be specified. Either a range (*start*-*end*) or a start and a distance (*start*+*number*) have to be specified. *start* and *end* are zero-based. If only the start is specified, only that sector is mapped.

The image is specified as follows: `image=`*device_name*   Additionally, the `range` variable must be set.

Example:

```
image = /dev/fd0
  range = 1+512
```

3.3.3 Booting a foreign operating system

LILO can even boot other operating systems, i.e. MS-DOS. To boot an other operating system, the name of a loader program, the device or file that contains the boot sector and the device that contains the partition table have to be specified.

The boot sector is merged with the partition table and stored in the map file.

Currently, the loaders `chain.b`, `os2_d.b`, `any_b.b` and `any_d.b` exist. `chain.b` simply starts the specified boot sector.[3] `os2_d.b` can boot OS/2 from the second hard disk. `any_b.b` and `any_d.b` install resident drivers that swap the first and the second floppy or hard disk drive. They can boot any operating system from the second hard disk, if it uses only the BIOS. This is known to work for PC/MS-DOS.

The image is specified as follows: `other=`*device_name* or `other=`*file_name*

The following additional variables are recognized: `loader`, `table` and `unsafe`.

`loader=`*chain_loader* specifies the chain loader that should be used. If it is omitted, `/boot/chain.b` is used. The chain loader must be specified if booting from a device other than the first hard or floppy disk.

`table=`*device* specifies the device that contains the partition table. LILO does not pass partition information to the booted operating system if this variable is omitted. (Some operating systems have other means to determine from which partition they have been booted. E.g. MS-DOS usually stores the geometry of the boot disk or partition in its boot sector.) Note that `/sbin/lilo` must be re-run if a partition table mapped referenced with `table` is modified.

`unsafe` do not access the boot sector at map creation time. This disables some sanity checks, including a partition table check. If the boot sector is on a fixed-format floppy disk device, using `unsafe` avoids the need to put a readable disk into the drive when running the map installer. `unsafe` and `table` are mutually incompatible.

Example:

```
other = /dev/hda2
  label = os2
  table = /dev/hda
```

---

[3]The boot sector is loaded by LILO's secondary boot loader before control is passed to the code of `chain.b`.

3.4 Disk geometry

For floppies and most hard disks, LILO can obtain the disk geometry information from the kernel. Unfortunately, there are some exotic disks or adapters which may either not supply this information or which may even return incorrect information.

If no geometry information is available, LILO reports either the error
`geo_query_dev HDIO_GETGEO (dev 0x`*number*`)`
or
`Device 0x`*number*`:  Got bad geometry` *sec*/*hd*/*cyl*

If incorrect information is returned, booting may fail in several ways, typically with a partial "LILO" banner message. In this document, that is called a "geometry mismatch".

The next step should be to attempt setting the `linear` configuration variable or the `-l` command-line option. If this doesn't help, the entire disk geometry has to be specified explicitly. Note that `linear` doesn't always work with floppy disks.

3.4.1 Obtaining the geometry

The disk geometry parameters can be obtained by booting MS-DOS and running the program `DPARAM.COM` with the hexadecimal BIOS code of the drive as its argument, e.g. `dparam 0x80` for the first hard disk. It displays the number of sectors per track, the number of heads per cylinder and the number of cylinders. All three numbers are one-based.

Alternatively, the geometry may also be determined by reading the information presented by the "setup" section of the ROM-BIOS or by using certain disk utilities under operating systems accessing the disk through the BIOS.

3.4.2 Specifying the geometry

Disk geometry parameters are specified in the options section of the configuration file. Each disk parameter sub-section begins with `disk=`*disk_device*, similar to the way how boot images are specified. It is suggested to group disk parameter sections together, preferably at the beginning or the end of the options section.

For each disk, the following variables can be specified:

`bios=`*bios_device_code* Is the number the BIOS uses to refer to that device. Normally, it's `0x80` for the first hard disk and `0x81` for the second hard disk. Note that hexadecimal numbers have to begin with "0x". If `bios` is omitted, LILO tries to "guess" that number.

`sectors=`*sectors* and

`heads=`*heads* specify the number of sectors per track and the number of heads, i.e. the number of tracks per cylinder. Both parameters have to be either specified together or they have to be entirely omitted. If omitted, LILO tries to obtain that geometry information from the kernel.

`cylinders=`*cylinders* Specifies the number of cylinders. This value is only used for sanity checks. If `cylinders` is omitted, LILO uses the information obtained from the kernel if geometry information had to be requested in order to determine some other parameter. Otherwise,[4] it just assumes the number of cylinders to be 1024, which is the cylinder limit imposed by the BIOS.

Additionally, partition sub-sub-sections can be added with `partition=`*partition_device*. Each partition section can contain only one variable:

`start=`*partition_offset* Specifies the zero-based number of the start sector of that partition. The whole disk always has a partition offset of zero. The partition offset is only necessary when using devices for which the kernel does not provide that information, e.g. CD-ROMs.

---

[4]I.e. if the BIOS device code, the number of sectors, the number of heads and the partition start are specified. Note that the number of cylinders may appear to vary if `cylinders` is absent and only some of the partition starts are specified.

Example:

```
disk = /dev/sda
  bios = 0x80
  sectors = 32
  heads = 64
  cylinders = 632
  partition = /dev/sda1
    start = 2048
  partition = /dev/sda2
    start = 204800
  partition = /dev/sda3
    start = 500000
  partition = /dev/sda4
    start = 900000
```

Because many SCSI controllers don't support more than 1 GB when using the BIOS interface, LILO can't access files that are located beyond the 1 GB limit of large SCSI disks on such controllers and reports errors in these cases.

3.4.3 Disk parameter table

The file `/etc/disktab` is the obsolete way to define the disk geometry. It is described here only for completeness. Its use with LILO 0.15 and newer is deprecated.

For each device (`/dev/hda` → 0x300, `/dev/sda` → 0x800, `/dev/sda1` → 0x801, etc.), the BIOS code and the disk geometry have to be specified, e.g.

```
# /etc/disktab  -  LILO disk parameter table
#
# This table contains disk parameters for non-standard disks.
# Parameters in disktab _always_ override auto-detected disk parameters.
# Note: this file is typically not needed for normal use of LILO.


# Dev.  BIOS    Secs/   Heads/  Cylin-  Part.
# num.  code    track   cylin.  ders    offset
#                                       (optional)

0x800   0x80    32      64      631     0           # /dev/sda
0x801   0x80    32      64      631     32          # /dev/sda1
0x802   0x80    32      64      631     204800      # /dev/sda2
```

Those parameters are just a random example from my system. However, many SCSI controllers re-map the drives to 32 sectors and 64 heads. The number of cylinders does not have to be exact, but it shouldn't be lower than the number of effectively available cylinders.

Note that the device number and the BIOS code have to be specified as hexadecimal numbers with the "0x" prefix. Also note that the complete information has to be repeated for each partition.

Chapter 4

Installation and updates

4.1 Installation

This section describes the installation of LILO. See section 4.4 for how to uninstall LILO.

4.1.1 Compatibility

The kernel header files have to be in `/usr/include/linux` and the kernel usually has to be configured by running `make config` before LILO can be compiled.

`/bin/sh` has to be a real Bourne shell. bash is sufficiently compatible, but some ksh clones may cause problems.

Using command-line options that are handled by init usually works with any current version of init. All currently available init packages typically support new features of LILO in the respective next release.

A file named `INCOMPAT` is included in the distribution. It describes incompatibilities to older versions of LILO and may also contain further compatibility notes.

4.1.2 Quick installation

If you want to install LILO on your hard disk and if you don't want to use all its features, you can use the quick installation script. Read `QuickInst` for details.

QuickInst can only be used for first-time installations or to entirely replace an existing installation, **not** to update or modify an existing installation of LILO. Be sure you've extracted LILO into a directory that doesn't contain any files of other LILO installations.

4.1.3 Files

Some of the files contained in `lilo.16.tar.gz`:

`lilo/README`
> This documentation in plain ASCII format. Some sections containing complex tables are only included in the LaTeX version in `doc/user.tex`

`lilo/INCOMPAT`
> List of incompatibilities to previous versions of LILO.

`lilo/CHANGES`
> Change history.

`lilo/QuickInst`
> Quick installation script.

`lilo/Makefile`
> Makefile to generate everything else.

`lilo/*.c, lilo/*.h`
> LILO map installer C source.

`lilo/*.S`
> LILO boot loader assembler source.

`lilo/activate.c`
> C source of a simple boot partition setter.

`lilo/dparam.s`
> Assembler source of a disk parameter dumper.

`lilo/disktab`
> Sample disk parameter table. (Obsolete.)

`lilo/mkdist`
> Shell script used to create the current LILO distribution.

`lilo/doc/README`
> Description of how the documentation is generated.

`lilo/doc/Makefile`
> Makefile used to convert the LaTeX source into either DVI output or the plain ASCII README file.

`lilo/doc/user.tex`
> LaTeX source of LILO's user's guide (this document).

`lilo/doc/tech.tex`
> LaTeX source of LILO's technical overview.

`lilo/doc/*.fig`
> Various **xfig** pictures used in the technical overview.

`lilo/doc/fullpage.sty`
> Style file to save a few square miles of forest.

`lilo/doc/rlatex`
> Shell script that invokes LaTeX repeatedly until all references have settled.

`lilo/doc/t2a.pl`
> **Perl** script to convert the LaTeX source of the user's guide to plain ASCII.

Files created after `make` in `lilo/` (among others):

`lilo/any_b.b`
> Chain loader that swaps the first two floppy drives (i.e. "A:" and "B:"). `make install` puts this file into `/boot`

`lilo/any_d.b`
> Chain loader that swaps the first two hard disk devices (i.e. "C:" and "D:"). `make install` puts this file into `/boot`

`lilo/boot.b`
> Combined boot sector. `make install` puts this file into `/boot`

`lilo/chain.b`
> Generic chain loader. `make install` puts this file into `/boot`

`lilo/os2_d.b`
> Chain loader to load **OS/2** from the second hard disk. `make install` puts this file into `/boot`

`lilo/lilo`
> LILO (map) installer. `make install` puts this file into `/sbin`

`lilo/activate`
> Simple boot partition setter.

`lilo/dparam.com`
> MS-DOS executable of the disk parameter dumper.

4.1.4 Normal first-time installation

First, you have to install the LILO files:

- extract all files from `lilo.`*version*`.tar.gz` in a new directory.[1]
- configure the `Makefile` (see section 4.2)
- run `make` to compile and assemble all parts.
- run `make install` to copy all LILO files to the directories where they're installed. `/sbin` should now contain the file `lilo`, `/etc` should contain `disktab`[2] and `/boot` should contain the following files: `any_b.b`, `any_d.b`, `boot.b`, `chain.b` and `os2_d.b`.

If you want to use LILO on a non-standard disk, you might have to determine the parameters of your disk(s) and specify them in the configuration file. See section 3.4 for details. If you're using such a non-standard system, the next step is to test LILO with the boot sector on a floppy disk:

- insert a blank (but low-level formatted) floppy disk into `/dev/fd0`.
- run `echo image=`*kernel_image* `|`
  `/sbin/lilo -C - -b /dev/fd0 -v -v -v`[3]
- reboot. LILO should now load its boot loaders from the floppy disk and then continue loading the kernel from the hard disk.

Now, you have to decide, which boot concept you want to use. Let's assume you have a Linux partition on `/dev/hda2` and you want to install your LILO boot sector there. The DOS-MBR loads the LILO boot sector.

- get a working boot disk, e.g. an install or recovery disk. Verify that you can boot with this setup and that you can mount your Linux partition(s) with it.
- if the boot sector you want to overwrite with LILO is of any value (e.g. it's the MBR or if it contains a boot loader you might want to use if you encounter problems with LILO), you should mount your boot disk and make a backup copy of your boot sector to a file on that floppy, e.g. `dd if=/dev/hda of=/fd/boot_sector bs=512 count=1`
- create the configuration file `/etc/lilo.conf`, e.g.
  global settings
     image specifications
     `...`
  Be sure to use absolute paths for all files. Relative paths may cause unexpected behaviour when using the `-r` option.

---

[1] E.g. `/usr/src/lilo`
[2] Actually, it shouldn't, because `disktab` is now obsolete.
[3] If you've already installed LILO on your system, you might not want to overwrite your old map file. Use the `-m` option to specify an alternate map file name.

- now, you can check what LILO would do if you were about to install it on your hard disk:
  `/sbin/lilo -v -v -v -t`
- if you need some additional boot utility (i.e. BOOTACTV), you should install that now
- run `/sbin/lilo` to install LILO on your hard disk
- if you have to change the active partition, use fdisk or activate to do that
- reboot

4.2   Build-time configuration

Certain build-time parameters can be configured. They can either be edited in the top-level `Makefile` or they can be stored in a file `/etc/lilo.defines`. Settings in the `Makefile` are ignored if that file exists.

The following items can be configured:

IGNORECASE   Makes image name matching case-insensitive, i.e. "linux" and "Linux" are identical. This option is enabled by default. Note that password matching is always case-sensitive.

NO1STDIAG   Do not generate diagnostics on read errors in the first stage boot loader. This avoids possibly irritating error codes if the disk controller has transient read problems. This option is disabled by default.

NOINSTDEF   If the option `install` is omitted, don't install a new boot sector, but try to modify the old boot sector instead. This option is disabled by default.

ONE_SHOT   Disables the command-line timeout (configuration variable `timeout`) if any key is pressed. This way, very short timeouts can be used if `prompt` is set. ONE_SHOT is disabled by default.

READONLY   Disallows overwriting the default command line sector of the map file. This way, command lines set with `-R` stay in effect until they are explicitly removed. This option is disabled by default.

VARSETUP   Enables the use of variable-size setup segments. This option is enabled by default and is only provided to fall back to fixed-size setup segments in the unlikely case of problems when using old kernels.

`/etc/lilo.defines` should be used if one wishes to make permanent configuration changes. The usual installation procedures don't touch that file. Example:

```
-DIGNORECASE -DONE_SHOT
```

4.3   Updates

LILO is affected by updates of kernels, the whole system and (trivially) of LILO itself. Typically, only `/sbin/lilo` has to be run after any of those updates and everything will be well again (at least as far as LILO is concerned).

4.3.1   LILO update

When updating to a new version of LILO, the initial steps are the same as for a first time installation: extract all files, configure the `Makefile`, run `make` to build the executables and run `make install` to install the files.

The old versions of `boot.b`, `chain.b`, etc. are automatically renamed to `boot.old`, `chain.old`, etc. This is done to ensure that you can boot even if the installation procedure does not finish. `boot.old`, `chain.old`, etc. can be deleted after the map file is rebuilt.

Because the locations of `boot.b`, `chain.b`, etc. have changed and because the map file format may be different too, you have to update the boot sector and the map file. Run `/sbin/lilo` to do this.

4.3.2 Kernel update

Whenever any of the kernel files that are accessed by LILO is moved or overwritten, the map has to be re-built.[4] Run `/sbin/lilo` to do this.

The kernel has a make target "zlilo" that copies the kernel to `/vmlinuz` and runs `/sbin/lilo`.

4.3.3 System upgrade

Normally, system upgrades (i.e. installation or removal of packages, possibly replacement of large a part of the installed binaries) do not affect LILO. Of course, if a new kernel is installed in the process, the normal kernel update procedure has to be followed (see section 4.3.2). Also, if kernels are removed or added, it may be necessary to update the configuration file.

If LILO is updated by this system upgrade, `/sbin/lilo` should be run before booting the upgraded system. It is generally a good idea not to rely on the upgrade procedure to perform this essential step automatically.

However, system upgrades which involve removal and re-creation of entire partitions (e.g. `/`, `/usr`, etc.) are different. First, they should be avoided, because they bear a high risk of losing other critical files, e.g. the `/etc/Xconfig` you've spent the last week fiddling with. If an upgrade really has to be performed in such a brute-force way, this is equal with total removal of LILO, followed by a new installation. Therefore, the procedures described in the sections 4.4 and 4.3.1 have to be performed. If you've forgotten to make a backup copy of `/etc/lilo.conf` (and possibly also of `/etc/disktab`) before the destructive upgrade, you might also have to go through section 4.1.4 again.

4.4 LILO de-installation

In order to stop LILO from being invoked when the system boots, its boot sector has to be either removed or disabled. All other files belonging to LILO can be deleted **after** removing the boot sector, if desired.[5]

Again, **when removing Linux, LILO must be de-installed before (!) its files (`/boot`, etc.) are deleted.** This is especially important if LILO is operating as the MBR.

LILO 0.14 (and newer) can be de-installed with `lilo -u`. If LILO 0.14 or newer is currently installed, but the first version of LILO installed was older than 0.14, `lilo -U` may work. When using `-U`, the warning at the end of this section applies.

If LILO's boot sector has been installed on a primary partition and is booted by the "standard" MBR or some partition switcher program, it can be disabled by making a different partition active. MS-DOS' FDISK, Linux fdisk or LILO's activate can do that.

If LILO's boot sector is the master boot record (MBR) of a disk, it has to be replaced with a different MBR, typically MS-DOS' "standard" MBR. When using MS-DOS 5.0 or above, the MS-DOS MBR can be restored with `FDISK /MBR`. This only alters the boot loader code, not the partition table.

LILO automatically makes backup copies when it overwrites boot sectors. They are named `/boot/boot.nnnn`, with *nnnn* corresponding to the device number, e.g. `0300` is `/dev/hda`, `0800` is `/dev/sda`, etc. Those backups can be used to restore the old MBR if no easier method is available. The commands are
`dd if=/boot/boot.0300 of=/dev/hda bs=446 count=1` or
`dd if=/boot/boot.0800 of=/dev/sda bs=446 count=1`
respectively.

---

[4]It is advisable to keep a second, stable, kernel image that can be booted if you forget to update the map after a change to your usual kernel image.

[5]Backup copies of old boot sectors may be needed when removing the boot sector. They are stored in `/boot`.

WARNING: Some Linux distributions install `boot.`*nnnn* files from the system where the distribution was created. Using those files may yield unpredictable results. Therefore, the file creation date should be carefully checked.

4.5 Installation of other operating systems

Some other operating systems (e.g. MS-DOS 6.0) appear to modify the MBR in their install procedures. It is therefore possible that LILO will stop to work after such an installation and Linux has to be booted from floppy disk. The original state can be restored by either re-running `/sbin/lilo` (if LILO is installed as the MBR) or by making LILO's partition active (if it's installed on a primary partition).

It is generally a good idea to install LILO after the other operating systems have been installed. E.g. OS/2 is said to cause trouble when attempting to add it to an existing Linux system. (However, booting from floppy and running `/sbin/lilo` should get around most interferences.)

Typically, the new operating system then has to be added to LILO's configuration (and `/sbin/lilo` has to be re-run) in order to boot it.

See also section 5.4 for a list of known problems with some other operating systems.

Chapter 5

Troubleshooting

All parts of LILO display some messages that can be used to diagnose problems.

5.1 Map installer warnings and errors

Most messages of the map installer (/sbin/lilo) should be self-explanatory. Some messages that indicate common errors are listed below. They are grouped into fatal errors and warnings (non-fatal errors).

5.1.1 Fatal errors

`Boot sector of` *device_name* `doesn't have a boot signature`

`Boot sector of` *device_name* `doesn't have a LILO signature`
: The sector from which LILO should be uninstalled doesn't appear to be a LILO boot sector.

`Can't put the boot sector on logical partition` *number*
: An attempt has been made to put LILO's boot sector on the current root file system partition which is on a logical partition. This usually doesn't have the desired effect, because common MBRs can only boot primary partitions. This check can be bypassed by explicitly specifying the boot partition with the -b option or by setting the configuration variable `boot`.

`Checksum error`
: The descriptor table of the map file has an invalid checksum. Refresh the map file **immediately** !

`Device 0x`*number*`:  Got bad geometry` *sec/hd/cyl*
: The device driver for your SCSI controller does not support geometry detection. You have to specify the geometry explicitly (see section 3.4).

`Device 0x`*number*`:  Invalid partition table, entry` *number*
: The 3D and linear addresses of the first sector of the specified partition don't correspond. This is typically caused by partitioning a disk with a program that doesn't align partitions to tracks and later using PC/MS-DOS or OS/2 on that disk. LILO can attempt to correct the problem, see page 744.

device_name `is not a valid partition device`
: The specified device is either not a device at all, a whole disk, or a partition on a different disk than the one in whose section its entry appears.

device_name `is not a whole disk device`
: Only the geometry of whole disks (e.g. /dev/hda, /dev/sdb, etc.) can be redefined when using disk sections.[1]

---

[1]When using a `disktab` file, you don't have this restriction. The additional flexibility offered by this is, however, useless and dangerous.

`DISKTAB and DISK are mutually exclusive`
> You cannot use a `disktab` file and disk geometry definitions in the configuration file at the same time. Maybe `/etc/disktab` was accidentally used, because that's the default for backward-compatibility. You should delete `/etc/disktab` after completing the transition to `disk` sections.

`Duplicate entry in partition table`
> A partition table entry appears twice. The partition table has to be fixed with fdisk.

`Duplicate geometry definition for *device_name*`
> A disk or partition geometry definition entry for the same device appears twice in the configuration file. Note that you mustn't write a partition section for the whole disk — its start sector is always the first sector of the disk.

`First sector of *device* doesn't have a valid boot signature`
> The first sector of the specified device does not appear to be a valid boot sector. You might have confused the device name.[2]

`geo_comp_addr:  Cylinder *number* beyond end of media (*number*)`
> A file block appears to be located beyond the last cylinder of the disk. This probably indicates an error in the disk geometry specification (see sections 3.4 and 3.4.3) or a file system corruption.

`geo_comp_addr:  Cylinder number is too big (*number* > 1023)`
> Blocks of a file are located beyond the 1024th cylinder of a hard disk. LILO can't access such files, because the BIOS limits cylinder numbers to the range $0\dots1023$. Try moving the file to a different place, preferably a partition that is entirely within the first 1024 cylinders of the disk.

`Hole found in map file (*location*)`
> The map installer is confused about the disk organization. Please report this error.

`*item* doesn't have a valid LILO signature`
> The specified item has been located, but is not part of LILO.

`*item* has an invalid stage code (*number*)`
> The specified item has probably been corrupted. Try re-building LILO.

`*item* is version *number*.  Expecting version*number*.`
> The specified entity is either too old or too new. Make sure all parts of LILO (map installer, boot loaders and chain loaders) are from the same distribution. [3]

`Kernel *name* is too big`
> The kernel image (without the setup code) is bigger than 512 kbytes. LILO would overwrite itself when trying to load such a kernel. Try removing some unused drivers and compiling the kernel again. With recent (compressed) kernels, the reason for this error is most likely that the kernel image is damaged or that it contains trailing "junk", e.g. as the result of copying an entire boot floppy to the hard disk.

`Map *path* is not a regular file.`
> This is probably the result of an attempt to omit writing a map file, e.g. with `-m /dev/null`. The `-t` option should be used to accomplish this.

`Must specify LOADER for BIOS device *number*`
> When booting an operating system from any device than the first hard or floppy disk, specifying the chain loader (option `loader` in the image section) is now mandatory.

`Must specify SECTORS and HEADS together`
> It is assumed that disks with a "strange" number of sectors will also have a "strange" number of heads. Therefore, it's all or nothing.

---

[2]Because different partition programs may display the partitions in a different order, it is possible that what you think is your first partition isn't `/dev/hda1`, etc. A good method to verify the content of a partition is to try to mount it.

[3]The expected version number may be different from the version number of the LILO package, because file version numbers are only increased when the file formats change.

`Partition entry not found`

> The partition from which an other operating system should be booted isn't listed in the specified partition table. This either means that an incorrect partition table has been specified or that you're trying to boot from a logical partition. The latter usually doesn't work. You can bypass this check by omitting the partition table specification (e.g. omitting the variable `table`).

`Sorry, don't know how to handle device` *number*

> LILO uses files that are located on a device for which there is no easy way to determine the disk geometry. Such devices have to be explicitly described, see section 3.4.

`Timestamp in boot sector of` *device* `differs from date of` *file*

> The backup copy of the boot sector does not appear to be an ancestor of the current boot sector. If you are absolutely sure that the boot sector is indeed correct, you can bypass this check by using `-U` instead of `-u`.

`Trying to map files from your RAM disk.  Please check -r option or ROOT environment variable.`

> Most likely, you or some installation script is trying to invoke LILO in a way that some of the files is has to access reside on the RAM disk. Normally, the `ROOT` environment variable should be set to the mount point of the effective root device if installing LILO with a different root directory. See also sections 3.1.2 and 4.1.4.

`write` *item*: *error_reason*

> The disk is probably full or mounted read-only.

5.1.2 Warnings

Warnings labeled with "Warning" can be turned off with the `nowarn` option.

`FIGETBSZ` *file_name*: *error_reason*

> The map installer is unable to determine the block size of a file system. It assumes a block size of two sectors (1kB).

`Ignoring entry` '*variable_name*'

> The command-line option corresponding to the specified variable is set. Therefore, the configuration file entry is ignored.

`Setting DELAY to 20 (2 seconds)`

> Because accidentally booting the wrong kernel or operating system may be very inconvenient on systems that are not run from a local display, the minimum delay is two seconds if the `serial` variable is set.

`(temp)` *item*: *error_reason*

> Deleting a temporary file has failed for the specified reason.

`Warning:  BIOS drive 0x`*number* `may not be accessible`

> Because most BIOS versions only support two floppies and two hard disks, files located on additional disks may be inaccessible. This warning indicates that some kernels or even the whole system may be unbootable.

`Warning:` *config_file* `should be owned by root`

> In order to prevent users from compromising system integrity, the configuration file should be owned by root and write access for all other users should be disabled.

`Warning:` *config_file* `should be readable only for root if using PASSWORD`

> Users should not be allowed to read the configuration file when using the `password` option, because then, it contains unencrypted passwords.

`Warning:` *config_file* `should be writable only for root`

> See "`Warning:` *config_file* `should be owned by root`".

`Warning: device 0x`*number* `exceeds 1024 cylinder limit`
> A disk or partition exceeds the 1024 cylinder limit imposed by the BIOS. This may result in a fatal error in the current installation run or in later installation runs. See "`geo_comp_addr:` `Cylinder number is too big (`*number* `> 1023)`" for details.

`Warning:` *device* `is not on the first disk`
> The specified partition is probably not on the first disk. LILO's boot sector can only be booted from the first disk unless some special boot manager is used.

`WARNING: The system is unbootable !`
> One of the last installation steps has failed. This warning is typically followed by a fatal error describing the problem.

5.2   LILO start message

When LILO loads itself, it displays the word "LILO". Each letter is printed before or after performing some specific action. If LILO fails at some point, the letters printed so far can be used to identify the problem. This is described in more detail in the technical overview.

Note that some hex digits may be inserted after the first "L" if a transient disk problem occurs. Unless LILO stops at that point, generating an endless stream of error codes, such hex digits do not indicate a severe problem.

(*nothing*) No part of LILO has been loaded. LILO either isn't installed or the partition on which its boot sector is located isn't active.

`L`*error*... The first stage boot loader has been loaded and started, but it can't load the second stage boot loader. The two-digit error codes indicate the type of problem. (See also section 5.3.) This condition usually indicates a media failure or a geometry mismatch (e.g. bad disk parameters, see section 3.4).

`LI` The first stage boot loader was able to load the second stage boot loader, but has failed to execute it. This can either be caused by a geometry mismatch or by moving `/boot/boot.b` without running the map installer.

`LIL` The second stage boot loader has been started, but it can't load the descriptor table from the map file. This is typically caused by a media failure or by a geometry mismatch.

`LIL?` The second stage boot loader has been loaded at an incorrect address. This is typically caused by a subtle geometry mismatch or by moving `/boot/boot.b` without running the map installer.

`LIL-` The descriptor table is corrupt. This can either be caused by a geometry mismatch or by moving `/boot/map` without running the map installer.

`LILO` All parts of LILO have been successfully loaded.

5.3   Disk error codes

If the BIOS signals an error when LILO is trying to load a boot image, the respective error code is displayed. The following BIOS error codes are known:

`0x00` "Internal error". This code is generated by the sector read routine of the LILO boot loader whenever an internal inconsistency is detected. This might be caused by corrupt files. Try re-building the map file.

`0x01` "Illegal command". This shouldn't happen, but if it does, it may indicate an attempt to access a disk which is not supported by the BIOS. See also "Warning: BIOS drive 0x*number* may not be accessible" in section 5.1.2.

0x02 "Address mark not found". This usually indicates a media problem. Try again several times.

0x03 "Write-protected disk". This shouldn't happen.

0x04 "Sector not found". This typically indicates a geometry mismatch. If you're booting a raw-written disk image, verify whether it was created for disks with the same geometry as the one you're using. If you're booting from a SCSI disk or a large IDE disk, you should check, whether LILO has obtained correct geometry data from the kernel or whether the geometry definition corresponds to the real disk geometry. (See section 3.4.) Removing compact may help too. So may adding linear.

0x06 "Change line active". This should be a transient error. Try booting a second time.

0x08 "DMA overrun". This shouldn't happen. Try booting again.

0x09 "DMA attempt across 64k boundary". This shouldn't happen. Try omitting the compact option and report this problem to the author.

0x0C "Invalid media". This shouldn't happen and might be caused by a media error. Try booting again.

0x10 "CRC error". A media error has been detected. Try booting several times, running the map installer a second time (to put the map file at some other physical location or to write "good data" over the bad spot), mapping out the bad sectors/tracks and, if all else fails, replacing the media.

0x20 "Controller error". This shouldn't happen.

0x40 "Seek failure". This might be a media problem. Try booting again.

0x80 "Disk timeout". The disk or the drive isn't ready. Either the media is bad or the disk isn't spinning. If you're booting from a floppy, you might not have closed the drive door. Otherwise, trying to boot again might help.

Generally, invalid geometry and attempts to use more than two disks without a very modern BIOS may yield misleading error codes. Please check carefully if /sbin/lilo doesn't emit any warnings. Then try using the linear option (see section 3.2.2).

5.4 Other problems

This section contains a collection of less common problems that have been observed. See also section 4.5 for general remarks on using LILO with other operating systems. Some of the problems are obscure and so are the work-arounds.

- If LILO doesn't go away even if you erase its files, format your Linux partition, etc., you've probably installed LILO as your MBR and you've forgotten to deinstall it before deleting its files. See section 4.4 for what you can do now.

- For yet unknown reasons, LILO may fail on some systems with AMI BIOS if the "Hard Disk Type 47 RAM area" is set to "0:300" instead of "DOS 1K".

- Some disk controller BIOSes perform disk geometry/address translations that are incompatible with the way the device's geometry is seen from Linux, i.e. without going through the BIOS. Particularly, large IDE disks and some recent PCI SCSI controllers appear to have this problem. In such cases, either the translated geometry has to be specified in a disk section or the sector address translation can be deferred by using the linear option. In a setup where floppies are not normally used for booting, the linear approach should be preferred, because this avoids the risk of specifying incorrect numbers.

- OS/2 is said to be bootable from a logical partition with LILO acting as the primary boot selector if LILO is installed on the MBR, the OS/2 BootManager is on an active primary partition and LILO boots BootManager. Putting LILO on an extended partition instead is said to crash the OS/2 FDISK in this scenario.

  Note that booting LILO from BootManager (so BootManager is the primary selector) or booting OS/2 directly from a primary partition (without BootManager) should generally work. See also section 4.5.

- Windows NT is reported to be bootable with LILO when LILO acts as the MBR and the Windows NT boot loader is on the DOS partition. However, NT's disk manager complains about LILO's MBR when trying to edit the partition table.

- Some PC UNIX systems (SCO and Unixware have been reported to exhibit this problem) depend on their partition being active. Such a setup can currently only be obtained by installing LILO as the MBR and making the respective partition active.[4]

- Future Domain TMC-1680 adapters with the BIOS versions 3.4 and 3.5 assign BIOS device numbers in the wrong order, e.g. on a two-disk system, /dev/sda becomes 0x81 and /dev/sdb becomes 0x80. This can be fixed with the following disk section:
  ```
  disk=/dev/sda bios=0x81 disk=/dev/sdb bios=0x80
  ```
  Note that this is only valid for a two-disk system. In three-disk systems, /dev/sdc would become 0x80, etc. Also, single-disk systems don't have this problem (and the "fix" would break them).

---

[4]Future versions of LILO may be able to change the active flag dynamically.

Part VII

LILO Technical Overview

Contents

This document describes internals of LILO and related parts of its environment (kernel, etc.). It is not necessary to read or understand this document in order to install or use LILO. A general introduction and installation instructions can be found in the user's guide.

Chapter 1

Load sequence

The boot sector is loaded by the ROM-BIOS at address 0x07C00. It moves itself to address 0x9A000, sets up the stack (growing downwards from 0x9B000 to 0x9A200), loads the secondary boot loader at address 0x9B000 and transfers control to it. It displays an "L" after moving itself and an "I" before starting the secondary boot loader. If a read error occurs when loading the secondary boot loader, a two-digit hex code is displayed after the "L". This results in an endless stream of error codes if the problem is permanent. Displaying these error codes is disabled if the build-time option NO1STDIAG is set.

The secondary boot loader loads the descriptor table at 0x9D200 and the sector containing the default command line at 0x9D600. If the default command line is enabled, its magic number is invalidated and the sector is written back to disk. This potentially dangerous operation can be disabled by defining LCF_READONLY when passing second.S through cpp. Next, the secondary boot loader checks for user input. If either the default is used or if the user has specified an alternate image, the options sector is loaded at 0x9D000 and the parameter line is constructed at 0x9D800. If the resulting line contains the option lock, the command line as entered by the user (it is saved before the final line is constructed) is written to the disk as the new default command line. Next, the floppy boot sector of that image is loaded at 0x90000[1], the setup part is loaded at 0x90200 and the kernel part is loaded at 0x10000. During the load operation, the sectors of the map file are loaded at 0x9D000.

If the loaded image is a kernel image, control is transferred to its setup code. If a different operating system is booted, things are a bit more difficult: the chain loader is loaded at 0x90200 and the boot sector of the other OS is loaded at 0x90400. The chain loader moves the partition table (loaded at 0x903BE as part of the chain loader) to 0x00600 and the boot sector to 0x07C00. After that, it passes control to the boot sector.

Chain loaders that allow booting from a second drive (either floppy or hard disk) also install a small function to intercept BIOS calls and to swap the drive numbers at the top of available memory.

The secondary boot loader displays an "L" after being started and an "O" after loading the descriptor table and the default command line. Before loading the descriptor table, it checks, whether it has been loaded at the correct location and displays a question mark if it hasn't. If the descriptor table has an incorrect checksum, a minus sign is displayed.

---

[1]The floppy boot sector is only used as a source of setup information.

0x00000		1982 bytes
0x007BE	Partition table	64 bytes
0x007FE		29 kB
0x07C00	Boot load area	512 bytes
0x07E00		32.5 kB
0x10000		448 kB
	Kernel	
0x90000	Floppy boot sector	512 bytes
0x90200	Setup (kernel)	39.5 kB (2 kB used)
0x9A000	Primary boot loader	512 bytes
0x9A200	Stack	3.5 kB
0x9B000	Secondary boot loader	8 kB (3.5 kB used)
0x9D000	Map load area	512 bytes
0x9D200	Descriptor table	1 kB
0x9D600	Default command line	512 bytes
0x9D800	Parameter line construction area	1 kB
0x9DC00		8 kB
	Drive swapper	1 kB
0xA0000		

The area 0x90020-0x90023 is overlaid by a command-line descriptor while the secondary boot loader is running.

Chapter 2

File references

This section describes the references among files involved in the boot procedures.

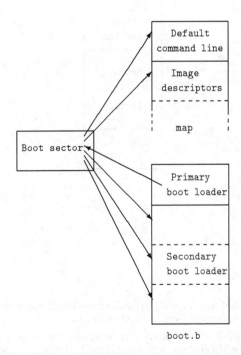

The boot sector contains the primary boot loader, the address of the default command line sector, the address of both descriptor table sectors and the addresses of the sectors of the secondary boot loader. The generic boot sector is copied from boot.b.

The primary boot loader can store up to eight sector addresses of the secondary boot loader.

```
+-----------------+
|    Default      |
|  command line   |
|                 |
+-----------------+
|                 |
|     Image       |
| - - - - - - - - |
|  descriptors    |
+-----------------+
|                 |
|  Zero sector    |
+-----------------+
|     First       |
|    section      |
+-----------------+
|    Second       |
| - -  ⟍ - - - - - |
|    section      |
+-----------------+
|     Third       |
|    section      |
+-----------------+
```

The map file consists of so-called sections and of special data sectors. Each section spans an integral number of disk sectors and contains addresses of sectors of other files.

There are three exceptions: 1. If a "hole" is being covered or if the floppy boot sector of an unstripped kernel has been omitted, the address of the zero sector is used. This sector is part of the map file. 2. When booting a different operating system, the first sector is the merged chain loader that has been written to the map file before that section. 3. Each map section describing an image is followed by a sector containing the options line of that image.

The last address slot of each map sector is either unused (if the map section ends in this sector) or contains the address of the next map sector in the section.

The four sectors at the beginning of the map file are special: the first sector contains the default command line, the next two sectors contain the boot image descriptor table and the fourth sector is filled with zero bytes. This sector is mapped whenever a file contains a "hole".

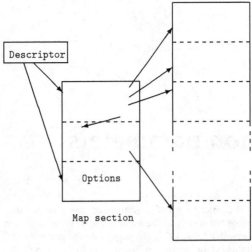

Map section

Kernel image

A kernel image consists simply of a sequence of sectors being loaded. The descriptor also contains a pointer to a sector with parameter line options. This sector is stored in the map file. Images that are loaded from a device are treated exactly the same way as images that are loaded from a file.

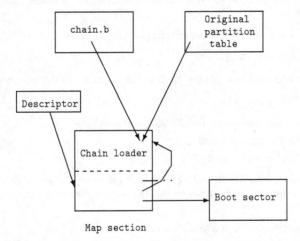

Map section

When booting another operating system, the chain loader (chain.b) is merged with the patched partition table[1] and written into the map file. The map section of this boot image starts after that sector and contains only the address of a dummy floppy boot sector (the zero sector, but its contents are irrelevant), the loader sector and the boot sector of the other operating system.

[1]If the partition table is omitted, that area is filled with zero bytes.

Chapter 3

Configuration parameters

The boot sector of each kernel contains a set of configuration parameters that have to be available at boot time before the kernel can access file systems. These parameters can be set when the kernel is compiled and later be changed with programs like rdev. LILO can supersede the parameters (in memory) at boot time by placing the corresponding items on the parameter line passed to the kernel.

The parameters are stored at the following (decimal) offsets:

497 the size of the setup code in sectors (512 bytes). Older kernels may put a zero at this place.

498-499 is a flag specifying whether the root file system should be mounted read-only (if non-zero) or read-write (if zero).

500-501 the size of the kernel, counted in paragraphs (16 bytes).

502-503 this parameter is currently unused.

504-505 the size of the RAM disk in kilobytes. No RAM disk is created if this parameter is set to zero.

506-507 the text mode the VGA is set to.

> **0xFFFD** the user is asked to specify the VGA mode at boot time.
>
> **0xFFFE** uses 80x50 ("extended") mode.
>
> **0xFFFF** uses 80x25 ("normal") mode.
>
> Any other value selects the corresponding mode as displayed in the interactive VGA mode selection menu. This is the only option that is set by LILO by patching the boot sector instead of passing it on the parameter line.

508 the minor number of the device that should be mounted as root.

509 the major number of the device that should be mounted as root.

Chapter 4

Parameter line interface

The kernel supports processing of parameters that are provided by the boot loader. The parameter string is a NUL-terminated ASCII string that contains space-separated words or *variable=value* pairs. A description of how they are interpreted can be found in the section of the user's guide labeled "The boot prompt".

The following descriptor has to be set up to pass a parameter string to the kernel:

0x90020 the magic number 0xA33F.

0x90022 the offset of the first byte of the parameter line relative to 0x90000.

The boot loader composes the parameter line from the command line, from the options sector and from some internally generated prefixes (typically `auto` and `BOOT_IMAGE=`), as follows:

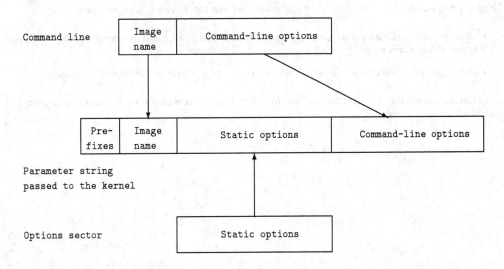

Example:
Command line: `vmlinuz root=802`
Options sector: `root=801 ro`

yields `BOOT_IMAGE=vmlinuz root=801 ro root=802`

Because parameter line options can typically be overridden, the first `root` option is ignored by the kernel.

Chapter 5

External interface

LILO is able to receive its command line from a program that is booted before it. This externally provided command line is only used if the user does not use the normal mechanism to invoke the boot prompt.

The following register contents are expected:

DL contains the value 0xFE.

ES:SI points to the string "LILO". The string must be in upper case and no terminating character is needed. The string must not cross segment boundaries, i.e. **SI** must be below 0xFFFD.

ES:BX points to a NUL-terminated string that is used as the command line. This string has a maximum length of 78 characters (not including the terminating NUL) and must not cross segment boundaries.

There are two values of the externally provided command line that have a special meaning:

- an empty string (**ES:BX** points to a NUL byte) is interpreted as a request to enter the boot prompt and to accept keyboard input.

- a string that consists only of blanks is interpreted as a request to boot the default boot image.

LILO can also obtain the default command line from the map file. It is only used if no externally provided command line is available.

Chapter 6

Default command line in map file

The first sector of the map file is reserved for a default command line. Unless the user invokes the boot prompt by pressing a shift key or unless an externally provided command line is present, the command line in the map file is interpreted as if it had been typed on the keyboard.

The first two bytes of the first sector of the map file have to contain the magic number DC_MAGIC (0xF4F2) in little-endian byte order. They are followed by a NUL-terminated string with a maximum length of 510 bytes, including the NUL. Note that the boot loader limits command lines to 78 characters after removing duplicate spaces.

The command line is disabled by either clobbering the magic number or by using an empty string (i.e. only a NUL byte) as the command line.

Part VIII

Linux HOWTO Index

Copyright by Greg Hankins, gregh@sunsite.unc.edu
v2.6.2, 20 May 1995
This is an index to the Linux HOWTO documents.

Contents

1   What are Linux HOWTOs?

Linux HOWTOs are short online documents which describe in detail a certain aspect of configuring or using the Linux system. For example, there is the *Installation HOWTO*, which gives instructions on installing Linux, and the *Mail HOWTO*, which describes how to set up and configure mail under Linux. Other examples include the *NET-2-HOWTO* (previously the *NET-2-FAQ*) and the *Printing HOWTO*.

Information in HOWTOs is generally more detailed and in-depth than what can be squeezed into the Linux FAQ. For this reason, the Linux FAQ is being rewritten. A large amount of the information contained therein will be relegated to various HOWTO documents. The FAQ will be a shorter list of frequently asked questions about Linux, covering small specific topics. Most of the "useful" information in the FAQ will now be covered in the HOWTOs.

HOWTOs are comprehensive docs—much like an FAQ but generally not in question-and-answer format. However, many HOWTOs contain an FAQ section at the end. For example, the *NET-2-FAQ* has been renamed to the *NET-2-HOWTO*, because it wasn't in question-and-answer format. However, you will see the *NET-2-HOWTO* named as the *NET-2-FAQ* in many places. The two docs are one and the same.

There are several HOWTO formats: plain text, PostScript, dvi, and html formats are all available. You can also browse *HOWTOs* (http://sunsite.unc.edu/mdw/HOWTO/) on the World Wide Web.

In addition to the HOWTOs, there are a multitude of "mini-HOWTOs". These are very short, specific HOWTOs, such as the *Colour-ls HOWTO*. They are only available in plain text format.

2   Where to get Linux HOWTOs

HOWTOs can be retrieved via anonymous FTP from the following sites:

- `sunsite.unc.edu:/pub/Linux/docs/HOWTO`

- `tsx-11.mit.edu:/pub/linux/docs/HOWTO`

as well as the many *mirror sites* (`ftp://sunsite.unc.edu/pub/Linux/MIRRORS.html`).

You can also browse *HOWTOs* (`http://sunsite.unc.edu/mdw/HOWTO/`) on the Web. Many *mirror sites* (`http://sunsite.unc.edu/mdw/hmirrors.html`) also mirror the HTML versions.

`sunsite` is heavily used, so please use a mirror site if possible.

HOWTOs are also posted regularly to the newsgroup `comp.os.linux.answers`, and other appropriate newsgroups.

3   HOWTO Index

The following Linux HOWTOs are currently available: (The German-HOWTO, JE-HOWTO, and Printing-HOWTO are only available in plain text format. This is because they have not been converted to the SGML source format. Conversion to SGML is in progress.)

- *Linux Bootdisk HOWTO* (`Bootdisk-HOWTO.html`),
  by Graham Chapman <grahamc@zeta.org.au>. How to create a boot/root maintenance disk for Linux. Updated 6 February 1995.

- *Linux Busmouse HOWTO* (`Busmouse-HOWTO.html`),
  by Mike Battersby <mike@starbug.apana.org.au>. Information on bus mouse compatibility with Linux. Updated 2 August 1994.

- *Linux CDROM HOWTO* (`CDROM-HOWTO.html`),
  by Jeff Tranter <tranter@software.mitel.com>. Information on CD-ROM drive compatibility for Linux. Updated 2 December 1994.

- *Linux Commercial HOWTO* (`Commercial-HOWTO.html`),
  by Harald Milz <hm@ix.de>. Listing of commercial software products for Linux. Updated May 1995.

- *Linux DOSEMU HOWTO* (`DOSEMU-HOWTO.html`),
  by Michael E. Deisher <deisher@enws125.EAS.ASU.EDU>. HOWTO about the Linux MS-DOS Emulator, DOSEMU. Updated 17 April 1995.

- *Linux Danish HOWTO* (`Danish-HOWTO.html`),
  by Thomas Petersen <petersen@risoe.dk>. How to configure Linux for use with the Danish characterset. Updated 9 March 1994.

- *Linux Distribution HOWTO* (`Distribution-HOWTO.html`),
  by Erik Troan <ewt@sunsite.unc.edu>. A list of mail order distributions and other commercial services. Updated 10 February 1995.

- *Linux ELF HOWTO* (`ELF-HOWTO.html`),
  by Riccardo Facchetti <riccardo@cdc8g5.cdc.polimi.it>. How to install the ELF binary file format. Updated 11 May 1995.

- *Linux Ethernet HOWTO* (`Ethernet-HOWTO.html`),
  by Paul Gortmaker <gpg109@rsphysse.anu.edu.au>. Information on Ethernet hardware compatibility for Linux. Updated 11 February 1995.

- *Linux Firewall HOWTO* (Firewall-HOWTO.html),
  by David Rudder <drig@execpc.com>. How to set up a firewall using Linux. Updated 23 April 1995.

- *Linux Ftape HOWTO* (Ftape-HOWTO.html),
  by Kai Harrekilde-Petersen <khp@pip.dknet.dk>. Information on ftape drive compatibility with Linux. Updated 13 May 1995 for ftape-2.03b.

- **Linux German HOWTO**,
  by Winfried Truemper <truemper@MI.Uni-Koeln.DE>. Information on using Linux with German-specific features.

- *Linux HAM HOWTO* (HAM-HOWTO.html),
  by Terry Dawson <terryd@extro.ucc.su.oz.au>. HOWTO configure amateur radio software for Linux. Updated 8 April 1995.

- *Linux HOWTO Index* (HOWTO-INDEX.html),
  by Greg Hankins <gregh@sunsite.unc.edu>. Index of HOWTO documents about Linux. Updated 14 May 1995.

- *Linux Hardware Compatibility HOWTO* (Hardware-HOWTO.html),
  by Tawei Wan <frac@ksc.au.ac.th>. A list of hardware known to work with Linux. Updated 2 May 1995.

- *Linux INFO-SHEET* (INFO-SHEET.html),
  by Michael K. Johnson <johnsonm@sunsite.unc.edu>. Generic introduction to the Linux operating system. Updated 31 March 1994.

- *Linux Installation HOWTO* (Installation-HOWTO.html),
  by Matt Welsh <mdw@sunsite.unc.edu>. How to obtain and install the Linux software. Updated 11 December 1994.

- **Linux JE HOWTO**,
  by Hiroo Yamagata <hiyori13@interramp.com>. Information on JE, a set of Japanese language extensions for Linux.

- *Linux Kernel HOWTO* (Kernel-HOWTO.html),
  by Brian Ward <ward@blah.tu-graz.ac.at>. Upgrading and compiling the Linux kernel. Updated 31 March 1995.

- *Linux META-FAQ* (META-FAQ.html),
  by Michael K. Johnson <johnsonm@sunsite.unc.edu>. A listing of Linux sources of information. Updated 12 November 1994.

- *Linux MGR HOWTO* (MGR-HOWTO.html),
  by Vincent Broman <broman@Np.nosc.mil>. Information on the MGR graphics interface for Linux. Updated 16 November 1994.

- *Linux Electronic Mail HOWTO* (Mail-HOWTO.html),
  by Vince Skahan <vince@halcyon.com>. Information on Linux-based mail servers and clients. Updated 31 March 1995.

- *Linux NET-2 HOWTO* (NET-2-HOWTO.html),
  by Terry Dawson <terryd@extro.ucc.su.oz.au>. HOWTO configure TCP/IP networking, SLIP, PLIP, and PPP under Linux. Updated 8 April 1995.

- *Linux NIS HOWTO* (NIS-HOWTO.html),
  by Erwin Embsen <erwin@nioz.nl>. Information on using NIS/YP on Linux systems. Updated 24 January 1995.

- *Linux News HOWTO* (News-HOWTO.html),
  by Vince Skahan <vince@halcyon.com>. Information on USENET news server and client software for Linux. Updated 31 March 1995.

- *Linux PCI-HOWTO* (PCI-HOWTO.html),
  by Michael Will <michaelw@desaster.student.uni-tuebingen.de>. Information on PCI-architecture compatibility with Linux. Updated March 1995.

- *Linux PCMCIA HOWTO* (PCMCIA-HOWTO.html),
  by Dave Hinds <dhinds@allegro.stanford.edu>. How to install and use PCMCIA Card Services. Updated 9 April 1995.

- *Linux PPP HOWTO* (PPP-HOWTO.html),
  by Al Longyear <longyear@netcom.com>. Information on using PPP networking with Linux. Updated 15 May 1995.

- **Linux Printing HOWTO**,
  by Grant Taylor <gtaylor@cs.tufts.edu>. HOWTO on printing software for Linux.

- *Linux SCSI HOWTO* (SCSI-HOWTO.html),
  by Drew Eckhardt <drew@kinglear.cs.Colorado.EDU>. Information on SCSI driver compatibility with Linux. Updated 20 March 1995.

- *Linux SCSI Programming HOWTO* (SCSI-Programming-HOWTO.html),
  by Heiko Eissfeldt <heiko@colossus.escape.de>. Information on programming the generic Linux SCSI interface. Updated 14 April 1995.

- *Linux Serial HOWTO* (Serial-HOWTO.html),
  by Greg Hankins <greg.hankins@cc.gatech.edu>. Information on use of serial devices and communications software. Updated 28 March 1995.

- *Linux Sound HOWTO* (Sound-HOWTO.html),
  by Jeff Tranter <tranter@software.mitel.com>. Sound hardware and software for the Linux operating system. Updated 3 December 1994.

- *Linux Term HOWTO* (Term-HOWTO.html),
  by Patrick Reijnen <patrickr@cs.kun.nl>. HOWTO use the 'term' communications package on Linux systems. Updated 12 May 1995.

- *Linux Tips HOWTO* (Tips-HOWTO.html),
  by Vince Reed <reedv@rpi.edu>. HOWTO on miscellaneous tips and tricks for Linux. Updated 30 August 1994.

- *Linux UPS HOWTO* (UPS-HOWTO.html),
  by Harvey J. Stein <hjstein@math.huji.ac.il>. Information on using a UPS power supply with Linux. Updated 16 April 1995.

- *Linux UUCP HOWTO* (UUCP-HOWTO.html),
  by Vince Skahan <vince@halcyon.com>. Information on UUCP software for Linux. Updated 31 March 1995.

- *Linux XFree86 HOWTO* (XFree86-HOWTO.html),
  by Matt Welsh <mdw@sunsite.unc.edu>. How to obtain, install, and configure XFree86 3.1.1 (X11R6). Updated 15 March 1995.

The following mini-HOWTOs are available:

- *Linux Anon FTP Setup mini-HOWTO* (mini/Anon-FTP-Setup),
  by Christopher Klaus <cklaus@shadow.net>. How to set up a secure anonymous FTP site. Updated 24 July 1994.

- *Linux Backup with MSDOS mini-HOWTO* (mini/Backup-With-MSDOS),
  by Christopher Neufeld <neufeld@physics.utoronto.ca>. How to backup MSDOS machines with Linux. Updated ???.

- *Linux Boca mini-HOWTO* (mini/Boca),
  by David H Dennis <david@amazing.cinenet.net>. How to install a Boca 16-port serial card (Boca 2016). Updated ???.

- *Linux BogoMips mini-HOWTO* (mini/BogoMips),
  by Wim C.A. van Dorst <baron@clifton.hobby.nl>. Information about BogoMips. Updated 1 May 1995.

- *Linux CD Writer mini-HOWTO* (mini/CD-Writer),
  by Matt Cutts <cutts@ms.uky.edu>. How to write CDs. Updated 17 December 1994.

- *Linux Caching named mini-HOWTO* (mini/Caching-named),
  by Nicolai Langfeldt <janl@ifi.uio.no>. How to set up a caching nameserver. Updated 20 March 1995.

- *Linux Colour ls mini-HOWTO* (mini/Colour-ls),
  by Thorbjoern Ravn Andersen <ravn@imada.ou.dk>. How to set up the colours with 'ls'. Updated 12 December 1994.

- *Linux Consoles mini-HOWTO* (mini/Consoles),
  by R. Mark Salathiel <RSalathi@nyx.cs.du.edu>. How to set up multiple virtual consoles. Updated 25 December 1994.

- *Linux getty-ps mini-HOWTO* (mini/Getty-ps),
  by Mark Horton <mah@ka4ybr.com>. How to set up 'getty_ps'. Updated ???.

- *Linux IO Port mini-HOWTO* (mini/IO-Port),
  by Riku Saikkonen <riku.saikkonen@compart.fi>. How to use I/O ports in C programs. Updated 18 October 1994.

- *Linux Key Setup mini-HOWTO* (mini/Key-Setup),
  by Stephen Lee <sl14@cornell.edu>. How to set up cursor control keys. Updated 13 May 1995.

- *Linux Keystroke mini-HOWTO* (mini/Keystroke),
  by Zenon Fortuna <zenon@netcom.com>. How to assign special action to keys. Updated 4 April 1995.

- *Linux Large IDE mini-HOWTO* (mini/Large-IDE),
  by Patrick LoPresti <patl@lcs.mit.edu>. How to use large IDE drives (kernel versions < 1.1.39). Updated ???.

- *Linux Man Page mini-HOWTO* (mini/Man-Page),
  by Jens Schweikhardt <jens@kssun3.rus.uni-stuttgart.de>. How to write man pages. Updated March 1995.

- *Linux Modeline mini-HOWTO* (mini/Modeline),
  by Rick Niles <niles@axp745.gsfc.nasa.gov>. How to use 'modeline'. Updated 11 February 1995.

- *Linux Multiple Ethernet mini-HOWTO* (mini/Multiple-Ethernet.html),
  by Don Becker <becker@cesdis.gsfc.nasa.gov>. How to use multiple ethernet cards (HTML format). Updated ???.

- *Linux Online Support mini-HOWTO* (mini/Online-Support),
  by lilo <TaRDiS@mail.utexas.edu>. Information about the Linux Internet Support Cooperative. Updated 2 January 1995.

- *Linux Proxy ARP mini-HOWTO* (mini/Proxy-ARP),
  by Al Longyear <longyear@netcom.com>. A small treatise on the use of Proxy ARP. Updated 5 December 1994.

- *Linux Reading List* (mini/Reading-List),
  by James H. Haynes <haynes@cats.ucsc.edu>. Interesting books pertaining to Linux subjects. Updated 16 February 1995.

- *Linux Stacker mini-HOWTO* (mini/Stacker),
  by Corey Sweeney <corey@bbs.xnet.com>. How to mount MSDOS Stacked filesystems. Updated ???.

- *Linux Swap Space mini-HOWTO* (mini/Swap-Space),
  by H. Peter Anvin <hpa@nwu.edu>. How to share swap space between Linux and Windows. Updated 13 November 1994.

- *Linux Term Firewall mini-HOWTO* (mini/Term-Firewall),

  by Barak Pearlmutter <bap@learning.scr.siemens.com>. How to use 'term' over a firewall. Updated March 2 1995.

- *Linux Visual Bell mini-HOWTO* (mini/Visual-Bell),
  by Alessandro Rubini <rubini@ipvvis.unipv.it>. How to disable audible bells, and enable visual bells. Updated May 1999.

- *Linux WordPerfect mini-HOWTO* (mini/WordPerfect),
  by Wade Hampton<tasi029@tmn.com>. How to set up SCO WordPerfect for Linux. Updated 17 May 1995.

4 Wanted HOWTOs

I would be very happy if someone would write the following HOWTO documents, and submit them to me (see the instructions in the next section below). Most of these are modifications of existing FAQ documents, and should be easy to put into HOWTO format. Keep in mind that HOWTOs generally aren't in FAQ format, but can contain an FAQ section at the end.

Some of these are under construction; however, if you're interested in working on one of them, please let me know.

- **GCC/LIBRARY HOWTO**. Discussing installation/upgrading of the GCC and shared libraries under Linux. How to build shared libraries. Most of the material would come from Mitchum DeSouza's GCC FAQ.

- If you have an idea for another HOWTO, please mail me!

5 Writing and submitting a HOWTO

If you would like to write a Linux HOWTO document, there are a few guidelines that you should follow.

- Format the document neatly. HOWTOs must be available in plain ASCII format, but you are free to use a formatting tool (texinfo, LameTeX, nroff) to format the document. Try to use meaningful structure and organization, and write clearly. Remember that many of the people reading HOWTOs do not speak English as their first language.

- You   may
  wish to use the Linuxdoc-SGML package, available from ftp.cs.cornell.edu:/pub/mdw/, to format the HOWTO. This package allows you to produce LaTeX, plain ASCII, and HTML from a single source document, and was designed specifically with the HOWTOs in mind. If you are writing a new HOWTO you should seriously consider this.

- Make sure that all of the information is correct. I can't stress this enough. When in doubt, speculate, but make it clear that you're only guessing.

- Make sure that you are covering the most recent version of the available software. Also, be sure to include full instructions on where software can be downloaded from (FTP site name, full pathname).

- Include an FAQ section at the end, if appropriate. Many HOWTO documents need an "FAQ" or "Common Problems" section to cover information which can't be covered in the regular text.

- Use other HOWTOs as a model.

After you have written the HOWTO, mail it to me (Greg Hankins) at gregh@sunsite.unc.edu. If you have use Linuxdoc-SGML, simply mail me the SGML source; I take care of formatting the documents. I'll also take care of archiving the HOWTO and posting it to the various newsgroups.

It is important that you go through me when submitting a HOWTO, as I maintain the archives and need to keep track of what HOWTOs are being written and who is doing what.

All you have to do is send me periodic updates (every month or so, as needed) and I will take care of posting the HOWTO regularly.

6   Miscellaneous and Legalese

If you have questions, please feel free to mail gregh@sunsite.unc.edu. The Linux FAQ rewrite is being coordinated by Ian Jackson, ijackson@nyx.cs.du.edu, with help from others.

Unless otherwise stated, Linux HOWTO documents are copyrighted by their respective authors. Linux HOWTO documents may be reproduced and distributed in whole or in part, in any medium physical or electronic, without permission of the author. Translations and derivative works are similarly permitted without express permission. Commercial redistribution is allowed and encouraged; however, the author would like to be notified of any such distributions.

In short, we wish to promote dissemination of this information through as many channels as possible. However, we do wish to retain copyright on the HOWTO documents, and would like to be notified of any plans to redistribute the HOWTOs. If you have questions, please contact Greg Hankins, the Linux HOWTO coordinator, at gregh@sunsite.unc.edu.

Part IX

The Linux Bootdisk HOWTO

Copyright Graham Chapman, grahamc@zeta.org.au
v1.01, 6 February 1995
This document describes how to create Linux boot, boot/root and utility maintenance disks. These disks could be used as rescue disks or to test new kernels.

Contents

1 Introduction

1.1 Why Build Boot Disks?

Linux boot disks are useful in a number of situations, such as:

- Testing a new kernel.

- Recovering from disk or system failure. Such a failure could be anything from a lost boot sector to a disk head crash.

There are several ways of producing boot disks:

- Use one from a distribution such as Slackware. This will at least allow you to boot.

- Use a rescue package to set up disks designed to be used as rescue disks.

- Learn what is required for each of the various types of disk to operate, then build your own.

I choose the last option - learn how it works so that you can do it yourself. That way, if something breaks, you can work out what to do to fix it. Plus you learn a lot about how Linux works along the way.

Experienced Linux users may find little of use in this document. However users new to Linux system administration who wish to protect against root disk loss and other mishaps may find it useful.

A note on versions - this document has been updated to support the following packages and versions:

- Linux 1.1.73

- LILO 0.15

Copyright (c) Graham Chapman 1995.

Permission is granted for this material to be freely used and distributed, provided the source is acknowledged. No warranty of any kind is provided. You use this material at your own risk.

1.2 Feedback and Credits

I welcome any feedback, good or bad, on the content of this document. Please let me know if you find any errors or omissions.

I thank the following people for correcting errors and providing useful suggestions for improvement:

```
Randolph Bentson
Bjxrn-Helge Mevik
Johannes Stille
```

1.3 Change History

v1.01, 6 February 1995

- Fix: DO NOT cp <kernel file> /dev/fd0 - this will overwrite any file system on the diskette.

- Fix: Put LILO boot.b and map files on target disk.

- Add: -dp flags to cp commands to avoid problems.

- Chg: restructure to try to improve readability.

- Add: can now use ext2 filesystem on root diskettes.

- Chg: can now separate boot and root diskettes.

- Add: credits section in Introduction.

- Add: FAQ.

v1.0, 2 January 1995

- Converted to conform to HOWTO documentation standards.

- Added new section - Change History.

- Various minor corrections.

v0.10, 1 November 1994 Original version, labelled "draft".

2 Disks

2.1 Summary of Disk Types

I classify boot-related disks into 4 types. The discussion here and throughout this document uses the term "disk" to refer to diskettes unless otherwise specified. Most of the discussion could be equally well applied to hard disks.

A summary of disk types and uses is:

boot

> A disk containing a kernel which can be booted. The disk can contain a filesystem and use a boot loader to boot, or it can simply contain the kernel only at the start of the disk. The disk can be used to boot the kernel using a root file system on another disk. This could be useful if you lost your boot loader due to, for example, an incorrect installation attempt.

root

> A disk with a file system containing everything required to run a Linux system. It does not necessarily contain either a kernel or a boot loader.

> This disk can be used to run the system independently of any other disks, once the kernel has been booted. A special kernel feature allows a separate root disk to be mounted after booting, with the root disk being automatically copied to a ramdisk.

> You could use this type of disk to check another disk for corruption without mounting it, or to restore another disk following disk failure or loss of files.

boot/root

> A disk which is the same as a root disk, but contains a kernel and a boot loader. It can be used to boot from, and to run the system. The advantage of this type of disk is that is it compact - everything required is on a single disk. However the gradually increasing size of everything means that it won't necessarily always be possbile to fit everything on a single diskette.

utility

> A disk which contains a file system, but is not intended to be mounted as a root file system. It is an additional data disk. You would use this type of disk to carry additional utilities where you have too much to fit on your root disk.

> The term "utility" only really applies to diskettes, where you would use a utility disk to store additional recovery utility software.

2.2 Boot

2.2.1 Overview

All PC systems start the boot process by executing code in ROM to load the sector from sector 0, cylinder 0 of the boot drive and try and execute it. On most bootable disks, sector 0, cylinder 0 contains either:

- code from a boot loader such as LILO, which locates the kernel, loads it and executes it to start the boot proper.

- the start of an operating system kernel, such as Linux.

If a Linux kernel has been written to a diskette as a raw device, then the first sector will be the first sector of the Linux kernel itself, and this sector will continue the boot process by loading the rest of the kernel and running Linux. For a more detailed description of the boot sector contents, see the documentation in lilo-01.5 or higher.

An alternative method of storing a kernel on a boot disk is to create a filesystem, not as a root filesystem, but simply as a means of installing LILO and thus allowing boot-time command line options to be specified. For example, the same kernel could then be used to boot using a hard disk root filesystem, or a diskette root filesystem. This could be useful if you were trying to rebuild the hard disk filesystem, and wanted to repeatedly test results.

2.2.2   Setting Pointer to Root

The kernel must somehow obtain a pointer to the drive and partititon to be mounted as the root drive. This can be provided in several ways:

- By setting `ROOT_DEV = <device>` in the Linux kernel makefile and rebuilding the kernel (for advice on how to rebuild the kernel, read the Linux FAQ and look in `/usr/src/linux`). Comments in the Linux makefile describe the valid values for `<device>`.

- By running the rdev utility:

```
rdev {$<$}filename{$>$} {$<$}device{$>$}
```

This will set the root device of the kernel contained in `<filename>` to be `<device>`. For example:

```
rdev Image /dev/sda1
```

This sets the root device in the kernel in Image to the first partition on the first SCSI drive.

There are some alternative ways of issuing the rdev command. Try:

```
rdev -?
```

and it will display command usage.

There is usually no need to configure the root device for boot diskette use, because the kernel currently used to boot from probably already points to the root drive device. The need can arise, howoever, if you obtain a kernel from another machine, for example, from a distribution, or if you want to use the kernel to boot a root diskette. It never hurts to check, though. To use rdev to check the current root device in a kernel file, enter the command:

```
rdev -r <filename>
```

It is possible to change the root device set in a kernel by means other than using rdev. For details, see the FAQ at the end of this document.

2.2.3   Copying Kernel to Boot Diskette

Once the kernel has been configured then it must be copied to the boot diskette.

If the disk is not intended to contain a file system, then the kernel must be copied using the dd command, as follows:

```
dd if={$<$}filename{$>$} of={$<$}device{$>$}

where   {$<$}filename{$>$} is the name of the kernel
and     {$<$}device{$>$} is the diskette raw device,
        usually /dev/fd0
```

The seek parameter to the dd command should NOT be used. The file must be copied to start at the boot sector (sector 0, cylinder 0), and omitting the seek parameter will do this.

The output device name varies. Many systems have /dev/fd0 as an alias of one sort or another for the "real" device name for the default diskette drive. For example, where the default drive (i.e. "drive A:" in DOS) is a high density 3 1/2 inch diskette drive, the device name will be /dev/fd0H1440, but usually /dev/fd0 points to the same device.

Where the kernel is to be copied to a boot disk containing a filesystem, then the disk is mounted at a suitable point in a currently-mounted filesystem, then the cp command is used. For example:

```
mount -t ext2 /dev/fd0 /mnt
cp Image /mnt
umount /mnt
```

2.3   Root

2.3.1   Overview

A root disk contains a complete working Linux system, but without necessarily including a kernel. In other words, the disk may not be bootable, but once the kernel is running, the root disk contains everything needed to support a full Linux system. To be able to do this, the disk must include the minimum requirements for a Linux system:

- File system.

- Minimum set of directories - dev, proc, bin, etc, lib, usr, tmp.

- Basic set of utilities - bash (to run a shell), ls, cp etc.

- Minimum set of config files - rc, inittab, fstab etc.

- Runtime library to provide basic functions used by utilities.

Of course, any system only becomes useful when you can run something on it, and a root diskette usually only becomes useful when you can do something like:

- Check a file system on another drive, for example to check your root file system on your hard drive, you need to be able to boot Linux from another drive, as you can with a root diskette system. Then you can run fsck on your original root drive while it is not mounted.

- Restore all or part of your original root drive from backup using archive/compression utilities including cpio, tar, gzip and ftape.

2.4   Boot/Root

This is essentially the same as the root disk, with the addition of a kernel and a boot loader such as LILO.

With this configuration, a kernel file is copied to the root file system, and LILO is then run to install a configuration which points to the kernel file on the target disk. At boot time, LILO will boot the kernel from the target disk.

Several files must be copied to the diskette for this method to work. Details of these files and the required LILO configuration, including a working sample, are given below in the section titled "LILO".

2.4.1   RAM Drives and Root Filesystems on Diskette

For a diskette root filesystem to be efficient, you need to be able to run it from a ramdrive, i.e. an emulated disk drive in main memory. This avoids having the system run at a snail's pace, which a diskette would impose.

There is an added benefit from using a ramdrive - the Linux kernel includes an automatic ramdisk root feature, whereby it will, under certain circumstances, automatically copy the contents of a root diskette to a RAM disk, and then switch the root drive to be the RAM disk instead of the diskette. This has two major benefits:

- The system runs a lot faster.

- The diskette drive is freed up to allow other diskettes to be used on a single-diskette drive system.

The requirements for this feature to be invoked are:

- The file system on the diskette drive must be either a minix or an ext2 file system. The ext2 file system is generally the preferred file system to use. Note that if you have a Linux kernel earlier than 1.1.73, then you should see the comments in the section below titled "File Systems" to see whether your kernel will support ext2. If your kernel is old then you may have to use minix. This will not cause any significant problems.

- A RAM disk must be configured into the kernel, and it must be at least as big as the diskette drive.

A RAM disk can be configured into the kernel in several ways:

- By uncommenting the RAMDISK macro in the Linux kernel makefile, so that it reads:

```
RAMDISK = -DRAMDISK=1440
```

to define a ramdisk of 1440 1K blocks, the size of a high-density diskette.

- By running the rdev utility, available on most Linux systems. This utility displays or sets values for several things in the kernel, including the desired size for a ramdisk. To configure a ramdisk of 1440 blocks into a kernel in a file named Image, enter:

```
rdev -r Image 1440
```

this might change in the future, of course. To see what your version of rdev does, enter the command:

```
rdev -?
```

and it should display its options.

- By using the boot loader package LILO to configure it into your kernel at boot time. This can be done using the LILO configuration parameter:

```
ramdisk = 1440
```

to request a RAM drive of 1440 1K blocks at boot time.

- By interrupting a LILO automatic boot and adding ramdisk=1440 to the command line. For example, such a command line might be:

```
vmlinux ramdisk=1440
```

See the section on LILO for more details.

- By editing the kernel file and altering the values near the start of the file which record the ramdisk size. This is definitely a last resort, but can be done. See the FAQ near the end of this document for more details.

The easiest of these methods is LILO configuration, because you need to set up a LILO configuration file anyway, so why not add the ramdisk size here?

LILO configuration is briefly described in a section titled "LILO" below, but it is advisable to obtain the latest stable version of LILO from your nearest Linux mirror site, and read the documentation that comes with it.

2.5 Utility

Often one disk is not sufficient to hold all the software you need to be able to perform rescue functions of analysing, repairing and restoring corrupted disk drives. By the time you include tar, gzip e2fsck, fdisk, Ftape and so on, there is enough for a whole new diskette, maybe even more if you want lots of tools.

This means that a rescue set often requires a utility diskette, with a file system containing any extra files required. This file system can then be mounted at a convenient point, such as /usr, on the boot/root system.

Creating a file system is fairly easy, and is described above in the section titled "File Systems" above.

3 Components

3.1 File Systems

The Linux kernel now supports two file system types for root disks to be automatically copied to ramdisk. These are minix and ext2, of which ext2 is the preferred file system. The ext2 support was added sometime between 1.1.17 and 1.1.57, I'm not sure exactly which. If you have a kernel within this range then edit /usr/src/linux/drivers/block/ramdisk.c and look for the word "ext2". If it is not found, then you will have to use a minix file system, and therefore the "mkfs" command to create it.

To create an ext2 file system on a diskette on my system, I issue the following command:

```
mke2fs /dev/fd0
```

The mke2fs command will automatically detect the space available and configure itself accordingly. It does not therefore require any parameters.

An easy way to test the result is to create a system using the above command or similar, and then attempt to mount the diskette. If it is an ext2 system, then the command:

```
mount -t ext2 /dev/fd0 /<mount point>
```

should work.

3.2 Kernel

3.2.1 Building a Custom Kernel

In most cases it would be possible to copy your current kernel and boot the diskette from that. However there may be cases where you wish to build a separate one.

One reason is size. The kernel is one of the largest files in a minimum system, so if you want to build a boot/root diskette, then you will have to reduce the size of the kernel as much as possible. The kernel now supports changing the diskette after booting and before mounting root, so it is not necessary any more to squeeze the kernel into the same disk as everything else, therefore these comments apply only if you choose to build a boot/root diskette.

There are two ways of reducing kernel size:

- Building it with the minumum set of facilities necessary to support the desired system. This means leaving out everything you don't need. Networking is a good thing to leave out, as well as support for any disk drives and other devices which you don't need when running your boot/root system.

- Compressing it, using the standard compressed-kernel option included in the makefile:

```
make zImage
```

Refer to the documentation included with the kernel source for up-to-date information on building compressed kernels. Note that the kernel source is usually in /usr/src/linux.

Having worked out a minimum set of facilities to include in a kernel, you then need to work out what to add back in. Probably the most common uses for a boot/root diskette system would be to examine and restore a corrupted root file system, and to do this you may need kernel support.

For example, if your backups are all held on tape using Ftape to access your tape drive, then, if you lose your current root drive and drives containing Ftape, then you will not be able to restore from your backup tapes. You will have to reinstall Linux, download and reinstall Ftape, and then try and read your backups.

It is probably desirable to maintain a copy of the same version of backup utilities used to write the backups, so that you don't waste time trying to install versions that cannot read your backup tapes.

The point here is that, whatever I/O support you have added to your kernel to support backups should also be added into your boot/root kernel. Note, though, that the Ftape module (or at least the one I have) is quite large and will not fit on your boot/root diskette. You will need to put it on a utility diskette - this is described below in the section titled "ADDING UTILITY DISKETTES".

The procedure for actually building the kernel is described in the documentation that comes with the kernel. It is quite easy to follow, so start by looking in /usr/src/linux. Note that if you have trouble building a kernel, then you should probably not attempt to build boot/root systems anyway.

3.3 Devices

A /dev directory containing a special file for all devices to be used by the system is mandatory for any Linux system. The directory itself is a normal directory, and can be created with the mkdir command in the normal way. The device special files, however, must be created in a special way, using the mknod command.

There is a shortcut, though - copy your existing /dev directory contents, and delete the ones you don't want. The only requirement is that you copy the device special files using the -R option. This will copy the directory without attempting to copy the contents of the files. Note that if you use lower caser, as in "-r", there will be a vast difference, because you will probably end up copying the entire contents of all of your hard disks - or at least as much of them as will fit on a diskette! Therefore, take care, and use the command:

```
cp -dpR /dev /mnt
```

assuming that the diskette is mounted at /mnt. The dp switches ensure that symbolic links are copied as links (rather than the target file being copied) and that the original file attributes are preserved, thus preserving ownership information.

If you want to do it the hard way, use ls -l to display the major and minor device numbers for the devices you want, and create them on the diskette using mknod.

Many distributions include a shell script called MAKEDEV in the /dev directory. This shell script could be used to create the devices, but it is probably easier to just copy your existing ones, especially for rescue disk purposes.

3.4 Directories

It might be possible to get away with just /dev, /proc and /etc to run a Linux system. I don't know - I've never tested it. However a reasonable minimum set of directories consists of the following:

/dev

Required to perform I/O with devices

/proc

Required by the ps command

/etc

    System configuration files

/bin

    Utility executables considered part of the system

/lib

    Shared libraries to provide run-time support

/mnt

    A mount point for maintenance on other disks

/usr

    Additional utilities and applications

Note that the directory tree presented here is for root diskette use only. Refer to the Linux File System Standard for much better information on how file systems should be structured in "standard" Linux systems.

Four of these directories can be created very easily:

- /dev is described above in the section titled DEVICES.

- /proc only needs to exist. Once the directory is created using mkdir, nothing more is required.

- Of the others, /mnt and /usr are included in this list only as mount points for use after the boot/root system is running. Hence again, these directories only need to be created.

The remaining 3 directories are described in the following sections.

3.4.1 /etc

This directory must contain a number of configuration files. On most systems, these can be divided into 3 groups:

- Required at all times, e.g. rc, fstab, passwd.

- May be required, but no-one is too sure.

- Junk that crept in.

Files which are not essential can be identified with the command:

```
ls -ltru
```

This lists files in reverse order of date last accessed, so if any files are not being accessed, then they can be omitted from a root diskette.

On my root diskettes, I have the number of config files down to 15. This reduces my work to dealing with three sets of files:

- The ones I must configure for a boot/root system:

```
rc       system startup script
fstab    list of file systems to be mounted
inittab  parameters for the init process - the
         first process started at boot time.
```

- the ones I should tidy up for a boot/root system:

```
passwd   list of logins
shadow   contains passwords
```

These should be pruned on secure systems to avoid copying user's passwords off the system, and so that when you boot from diskette, unwanted logins are rejected.

- The rest. They work at the moment, so I leave them alone.

Out of this, I only really have to configure two files, and what they should contain is suprisingly small.

- rc should contain:

```
#!/bin/sh
/etc/mount -av
/bin/hostname boot_root
```

and I don't really need to run hostname - it just looks nicer if I do. Even mount is actually only needed to mount /proc to support the ps command - Linux will run without it.

- fstab should contain:

```
/dev/fd0          /              ext2    defaults
/proc             /proc          proc    defaults
```

I don't think that the first entry is really needed, but I find that if I leave it out, mount won't mount /proc.

Inittab should be ok as is, unless you want to ensure that users on serial ports cannot login. To prevent this, comment out all the entries for /etc/getty which include a ttys or ttyS device at the end of the line. Leave in the tty ports so that you can login at the console.

For the rest, just copy all the text files in your /etc directory, plus all the executables in your /etc directory that you cannot be sure you do not need. As a guide, consult the sample ls listing in "Sample Boot/Root ls-lR Directory Listing" - this is what I have, so probably it will be sufficient for you if you copy only those files.

3.4.2 /bin

Here is a convenient point to place the extra utilities you need to perform basic operations, utilities such as ls, mv, cat, dd etc.

See the section titled "Sample Boot/Root ls-lR Directory Listing" for the list of files that I place in my boot/root /bin directory. You may notice that it does not include any of the utilities required to restore from backup, such as cpio, tar, gzip etc. That is because I place these on a separate utility diskette, to save space on the boot/root diskette. Once I have booted my boot/root diskette, it then copies itself to the ramdisk leaving the diskette drive free to mount another diskette, the utility diskette. I usually mount this as /usr.

Creation of a utility diskette is described below in the section titled "Adding Utility Diskettes".

3.4.3 /lib

Two libraries are required to run many facilities under Linux:

- ld.so

- libc.so.4

If they are not found in your /lib directory then the system will be unable to boot. If you're lucky you may see an error message telling you why.

These should be present in you existing /lib directory. Note that libc.so.4 may be a symlink to a libc library with version number in the filename. If you issue the command:

```
ls -l /lib
```

you will see something like:

```
libc.so.4 -> libc.so.4.5.21
```

In this case, the libc library you want is libc.so.4.5.21.

3.5 LILO

3.5.1 Overview

For the boot/root to be any use, it must be bootable. To achieve this, the easiest way (possibly the only way?) is to install a boot loader, which is a piece of executable code stored at sector 0, cylinder 0 of the diskette. See the section above titled "BOOT DISKETTE" for an overview of the boot process.

LILO is a tried and trusted boot loader available from any Linux mirror site. It allows you to configure the boot loader, including:

- Which device is to be mounted as the root drive.

- Whether to use a ramdisk.

3.5.2 Sample LILO Configuration

This provides a very convenient place to specify to the kernel how it should boot. My root/boot LILO configuration file, used with LILO 0.15, is:

```
boot = /dev/fd0
install = ./mnt/boot.b
map = ./mnt/lilo.map
delay = 50
message = ./mnt/lilo.msg
timeout = 150
compact
image = ./mnt/vmlinux
        ramdisk = 1440
        root = /dev/fd0
```

Note that boot.b, lilo.msg and the kernel must first have been copied to the diskette using a command similar to:

```
cp /boot/boot.b ./mnt
```

If this is not done, then LILO will not run correctly at boot time if the hard disk is not available, and there is little point setting up a rescue disk which requires a hard disk in order to boot.

I run lilo using the command:

```
/sbin/lilo -C <configfile>
```

I run it from the directory containing the mnt directory where I have mounted the diskette. This means that I am telling LILO to install a boot loader on the boot device (/dev/fd0 in this case), to boot a kernel in the root directory of the diskette.

I have also specified that I want the root device to be the diskette, and I want a RAM disk created of 1440 1K blocks, the same size as the diskette. Since I have created an ext2 file system on the diskette, this completes all the conditions required for Linux to automatically switch the root device to the ramdisk, and copy the diskette contents there as well.

The ramdisk features of Linux are described further in the section above titled "RAM DRIVES AND BOOT/ROOT SYSTEMS".

It is also worth considering using the "single" parameter to cause Linux to boot in single-user mode. This could be useful to prevent users logging in on serial ports.

I also use the "DELAY" "MESSAGE" and "TIMEOUT" statements so that when I boot the disk, LILO will give me the opportunity to enter command line options if I wish. I don't need them at present, but I never know when I might want to set a different root device or mount a filesystem read-only.

The message file I use contains the message:

```
Linux Boot/Root Diskette
========================

Enter a command line of the form:

      vmlinux [ command-line options]

If nothing is entered, linux will be loaded with
defaults after 15 seconds.
```

This is simply a reminder to myself what my choices are.

Readers are urged to read the LILO documentation carefully before atttempting to install anything. It is relatively easy to destroy partitions if you use the wrong "boot = " parameter. If you are inexperienced, do NOT run LILO until you are sure you understand it and you have triple-checked your parameters.

3.5.3   Removing LILO

One other thing I might as well add here while I'm on the LILO topic: if you mess up lilo on a drive containing DOS, you can always replace the boot sector with the DOS boot loader by issuing the DOS command:

```
FDISK /MBR
```

where MBR stands for "Master Boot Record". Note that some purists disagree with this, and they may have grounds, but it works.

3.5.4   Useful LILO Options

LILO has several useful options which are worth keeping in mind when building boot disks:

- Command line options - you can enter command line options to set the root device, ramdrive size, special device parameters, or other things. If you include the DELAY = nn statement in your LILO configuration file, then LILO will pause to allow you to select a kernel image to boot, and to enter, on the same line, any options. For example:

  ```
  vmlinux aha152x=0x340,11,3,1 ro
  ```

  will pass the aha152x parameters through to the aha152x SCSI disk driver (provided that driver has been included when the kernel was built) and will ask for the root filesystem to be mounted read-only.

- Command line "lock" option - this option asks LILO to store the command line entered as the default command line to be used for all future boots. This is particularly useful where you have a device which cannot be autoselected. By using "lock" you can avoid having to type in the device parameter string every time you boot. For example:

```
vmlinux aha152x=0x340,11,3,1 root=/dev/sda8 ro lock
```

- APPEND configuration statement - this allows device parameter strings to be stored in the configuration, as an alternative to using the "lock" command line option. Note that any keywords of the form word=value MUST be enclosed in quotes. For example:

```
APPEND = "aha152x=0x340,11,3,1"
```

- DELAY configuration statement - this pauses for DELAY tenths of seconds and allows the user to interrupt the automatic boot of the default command line, so that the user can enter an alternate command line.

4 Samples

4.1 Disk Directory Listings

This lists the contents of files and directories that I keep on my hard disk to use when building boot/root and utility diskettes. It shows which files I put in the /etc and /bin directories on my diskettes.

The sample shell scripts in the next section use these directories and files as a model to build the diskettes.

4.1.1 Boot/Root Disk ls-lR Directory Listing

The boot/root listing is of directory boot_disk:

```
total 226
drwxr-xr-x   2 root     root        1024 Oct  8 13:40 bin/
drwxr-xr-x   2 root     root        3072 Sep  8 16:37 dev/
drwxr-xr-x   2 root     root        1024 Oct  8 12:38 etc/
drwxr-xr-x   2 root     root        1024 Sep 10 14:58 lib/
-rw-r--r--   1 root     root      297956 Jan 25 21:55 vmlinux

boot_disk/bin:
total 366
-rwxr-xr-x   1 root     root        4376 Sep  9 21:34 cat*
-rwxr-xr-x   1 root     root        4112 Sep  9 21:34 chown*
-rwxr-xr-x   1 root     root       12148 Sep  9 21:34 cp*
-rwxr-xr-x   1 root     root        4376 Sep  9 21:34 cut*
-rwxr-xr-x   1 root     root        7660 Sep  9 21:34 dd*
-rwxr-xr-x   1 root     root        4696 Sep  9 21:34 df*
-rwx--x--x   1 root     root        1392 Sep 10 14:13 hostname*
-rwxr-xr-x   1 root     root        5252 Sep  9 21:34 ln*
-rwsr-xr-x   1 root     root        6636 Sep  9 21:34 login*
-rwxr-xr-x   1 root     root       13252 Sep  9 21:34 ls*
-rwxr-xr-x   1 root     root        4104 Sep  9 21:34 mkdir*
-rwxr-xr-x   1 root     root       21504 Sep 10 15:27 more*
-rwxr-xr-x   1 root     root        6744 Sep  9 21:34 mv*
-rwxr-xr-x   1 root     root        9780 Sep  9 21:34 ps*
-rwxr-xr-x   1 root     root        5076 Sep  9 21:34 rm*
-r-xr-xr-x   1 root     root       12604 Sep  9 21:34 sed*
-rwxr-xr-x   1 root     root      222208 Sep  9 21:34 sh*
-rws--x--x   1 root     root       16464 Sep  9 21:34 su*
-rwxr-xr-x   1 root     root        1216 Sep  9 21:34 sync*

boot_disk/dev:
total 73
-rwxr-xr-x   1 root     root        8331 Sep  8 16:31 MAKEDEV*
crw-r--r--   1 root     root      10,   3 Sep  8 16:31 bmouseatixl
```

```
crw-r--r--   1 root      root      10,    0 Sep   8 16:31 bmouselogitec
crw-r--r--   1 root      root      10,    2 Sep   8 16:31 bmousems
crw-r--r--   1 root      root      10,    1 Sep   8 16:31 bmouseps2
crw-------   1 root      root       0,    0 Sep   8 16:31 boot0
crw-r--r--   1 root      root       4,    0 Sep   8 16:31 console
crw-r--r--   1 root      root       5,   64 Sep   8 16:31 cua0
crw-r--r--   1 root      root       5,   65 Sep   8 16:31 cua1
crw-r--r--   1 root      root       5,   66 Sep   8 16:31 cua2
crw-r--r--   1 root      root       5,   67 Sep   8 16:31 cua3
brw-r--r--   1 root      root       2,    0 Sep   8 16:31 fd0
brw-r--r--   1 root      root       2,   12 Sep   8 16:31 fd0D360
brw-r--r--   1 root      root       2,   16 Sep   8 16:31 fd0D720
brw-r--r--   1 root      root       2,   28 Sep   8 16:31 fd0H1440
brw-r--r--   1 root      root       2,   12 Sep   8 16:31 fd0H360
brw-r--r--   1 root      root       2,   16 Sep   8 16:31 fd0H720
brw-r--r--   1 root      root       2,   16 Sep   8 16:31 fd0Q720
brw-r--r--   1 root      root       2,    4 Sep   8 16:31 fd0d360
brw-r--r--   1 root      root       2,    8 Sep   8 16:31 fd0h1200
brw-r--r--   1 root      root       2,   20 Sep   8 16:31 fd0h360
brw-r--r--   1 root      root       2,   24 Sep   8 16:31 fd0h720
brw-r--r--   1 root      root       2,   24 Sep   8 16:31 fd0q720
brw-r--r--   1 root      root       2,    1 Sep   8 16:31 fd1
brw-r--r--   1 root      root       2,   13 Sep   8 16:31 fd1D360
brw-r--r--   1 root      root       2,   17 Sep   8 16:31 fd1D720
brw-r--r--   1 root      root       2,   29 Sep   8 16:31 fd1H1440
brw-------   1 root      root       2,   31 Sep   8 16:31 fd1H1722
brw-r--r--   1 root      root       2,   13 Sep   8 16:31 fd1H360
brw-r--r--   1 root      root       2,   17 Sep   8 16:31 fd1H720
brw-r--r--   1 root      root       2,   17 Sep   8 16:31 fd1Q720
brw-r--r--   1 root      root       2,    5 Sep   8 16:31 fd1d360
brw-r--r--   1 root      root       2,    9 Sep   8 16:31 fd1h1200
brw-r--r--   1 root      root       2,   21 Sep   8 16:31 fd1h360
brw-r--r--   1 root      root       2,   25 Sep   8 16:31 fd1h720
brw-r--r--   1 root      root       2,   25 Sep   8 16:31 fd1q720
brw-r-----   1 root      root       3,    0 Sep   8 16:31 hda
brw-r-----   1 root      root       3,    1 Sep   8 16:31 hda1
brw-r-----   1 root      root       3,    2 Sep   8 16:31 hda2
brw-r-----   1 root      root       3,    3 Sep   8 16:31 hda3
brw-r-----   1 root      root       3,    4 Sep   8 16:31 hda4
brw-r-----   1 root      root       3,    5 Sep   8 16:31 hda5
brw-r-----   1 root      root       3,    6 Sep   8 16:31 hda6
brw-r-----   1 root      root       3,    7 Sep   8 16:31 hda7
brw-r-----   1 root      root       3,    8 Sep   8 16:31 hda8
brw-r-----   1 root      root       3,   64 Sep   8 16:31 hdb
brw-r-----   1 root      root       3,   65 Sep   8 16:31 hdb1
brw-r-----   1 root      root       3,   66 Sep   8 16:31 hdb2
brw-r-----   1 root      root       3,   67 Sep   8 16:31 hdb3
brw-r-----   1 root      root       3,   68 Sep   8 16:31 hdb4
brw-r-----   1 root      root       3,   69 Sep   8 16:31 hdb5
brw-r-----   1 root      root       3,   70 Sep   8 16:31 hdb6
brw-r-----   1 root      root       3,   71 Sep   8 16:31 hdb7
brw-r-----   1 root      root       3,   72 Sep   8 16:31 hdb8
crw-r-----   1 root      root       1,    2 Sep   8 16:31 kmem
brw-------   1 root      root      12,    0 Sep   8 16:31 loop0
brw-------   1 root      root      12,    1 Sep   8 16:31 loop1
crw-r--r--   1 root      root       6,    0 Sep   8 16:31 lp0
crw-r--r--   1 root      root       6,    1 Sep   8 16:31 lp1
crw-r--r--   1 root      root       6,    2 Sep   8 16:31 lp2
brw-r--r--   1 root      root      12,    0 Sep   8 16:31 mcd0
crw-r-----   1 root      root       1,    1 Sep   8 16:31 mem
crw-r--r--   1 root      root       5,   65 Sep   8 16:31 modem
```

```
crw-r--r--   1 root     root      5,  64 Sep  8 16:31 mouse
crw-r--r--   1 root     root     27,   4 Sep  8 16:31 nrft0
crw-r--r--   1 root     root     27,   5 Sep  8 16:31 nrft1
crw-r--r--   1 root     root     27,   6 Sep  8 16:31 nrft2
crw-r--r--   1 root     root     27,   7 Sep  8 16:31 nrft3
crw-------   1 root     root      9, 128 Sep  8 16:31 nrmt0
crw-r--r--   1 root     root      1,   3 Sep  8 16:31 null
crw-r-----   1 root     root      6,   0 Sep  8 16:31 par0
crw-r-----   1 root     root      6,   1 Sep  8 16:31 par1
crw-r-----   1 root     root      6,   2 Sep  8 16:31 par2
crw-r--r--   1 root     root      1,   4 Sep  8 16:31 port
crw-r--r--   1 root     root     10,   1 Sep  8 16:31 ps2aux
crw-r--r--   1 root     root      4, 128 Sep  8 16:31 ptyp0
crw-r--r--   1 root     root      4, 129 Sep  8 16:31 ptyp1
crw-r--r--   1 root     root      4, 130 Sep  8 16:31 ptyp2
crw-r--r--   1 root     root      4, 131 Sep  8 16:31 ptyp3
crw-r--r--   1 root     root      4, 132 Sep  8 16:31 ptyp4
crw-r--r--   1 root     root      4, 133 Sep  8 16:31 ptyp5
crw-r--r--   1 root     root      4, 134 Sep  8 16:31 ptyp6
crw-r--r--   1 root     root      4, 135 Sep  8 16:31 ptyp7
crw-r--r--   1 root     root      4, 136 Sep  8 16:31 ptyp8
crw-r--r--   1 root     root      4, 137 Sep  8 16:31 ptyp9
crw-r--r--   1 root     root      4, 138 Sep  8 16:31 ptypa
crw-r--r--   1 root     root      4, 139 Sep  8 16:31 ptypb
crw-r--r--   1 root     root      4, 140 Sep  8 16:31 ptypc
crw-r--r--   1 root     root      4, 141 Sep  8 16:31 ptypd
crw-r--r--   1 root     root      4, 142 Sep  8 16:31 ptype
crw-r--r--   1 root     root      4, 143 Sep  8 16:31 ptypf
brw-r-----   1 root     root      1,   0 Sep  8 16:31 ram
crw-r--r--   1 root     root     27,   0 Sep  8 16:31 rft0
crw-r--r--   1 root     root     27,   1 Sep  8 16:31 rft1
crw-r--r--   1 root     root     27,   2 Sep  8 16:31 rft2
crw-r--r--   1 root     root     27,   3 Sep  8 16:31 rft3
crw-------   1 root     root      9,   0 Sep  8 16:31 rmt0
brw-r-----   1 root     root      8,   0 Sep  8 16:31 sda
brw-r-----   1 root     root      8,   1 Sep  8 16:31 sda1
brw-r-----   1 root     root      8,   2 Sep  8 16:31 sda2
brw-r-----   1 root     root      8,   3 Sep  8 16:31 sda3
brw-r-----   1 root     root      8,   4 Sep  8 16:31 sda4
brw-r-----   1 root     root      8,   5 Sep  8 16:31 sda5
brw-r-----   1 root     root      8,   6 Sep  8 16:31 sda6
brw-r-----   1 root     root      8,   7 Sep  8 16:31 sda7
brw-r-----   1 root     root      8,   8 Sep  8 16:31 sda8
brw-r-----   1 root     root      8,  16 Sep  8 16:31 sdb
brw-r-----   1 root     root      8,  17 Sep  8 16:31 sdb1
brw-r-----   1 root     root      8,  18 Sep  8 16:31 sdb2
brw-r-----   1 root     root      8,  19 Sep  8 16:31 sdb3
brw-r-----   1 root     root      8,  20 Sep  8 16:31 sdb4
brw-r-----   1 root     root      8,  21 Sep  8 16:31 sdb5
brw-r-----   1 root     root      8,  22 Sep  8 16:31 sdb6
brw-r-----   1 root     root      8,  23 Sep  8 16:31 sdb7
brw-r-----   1 root     root      8,  24 Sep  8 16:31 sdb8
brw-------   1 root     root      8,  32 Sep  8 16:31 sdc
brw-------   1 root     root      8,  33 Sep  8 16:31 sdc1
brw-------   1 root     root      8,  34 Sep  8 16:31 sdc2
brw-------   1 root     root      8,  35 Sep  8 16:31 sdc3
brw-------   1 root     root      8,  36 Sep  8 16:31 sdc4
brw-------   1 root     root      8,  37 Sep  8 16:31 sdc5
brw-------   1 root     root      8,  38 Sep  8 16:31 sdc6
brw-------   1 root     root      8,  39 Sep  8 16:31 sdc7
brw-------   1 root     root      8,  40 Sep  8 16:31 sdc8
```

```
brw-------  1 root     root      8,   48 Sep  8 16:31 sdd
brw-------  1 root     root      8,   49 Sep  8 16:31 sdd1
brw-------  1 root     root      8,   50 Sep  8 16:31 sdd2
brw-------  1 root     root      8,   51 Sep  8 16:31 sdd3
brw-------  1 root     root      8,   52 Sep  8 16:31 sdd4
brw-------  1 root     root      8,   53 Sep  8 16:31 sdd5
brw-------  1 root     root      8,   54 Sep  8 16:31 sdd6
brw-------  1 root     root      8,   55 Sep  8 16:31 sdd7
brw-------  1 root     root      8,   56 Sep  8 16:31 sdd8
brw-------  1 root     root      8,   64 Sep  8 16:31 sde
brw-------  1 root     root      8,   65 Sep  8 16:31 sde1
brw-------  1 root     root      8,   66 Sep  8 16:31 sde2
brw-------  1 root     root      8,   67 Sep  8 16:31 sde3
brw-------  1 root     root      8,   68 Sep  8 16:31 sde4
brw-------  1 root     root      8,   69 Sep  8 16:31 sde5
brw-------  1 root     root      8,   70 Sep  8 16:31 sde6
brw-------  1 root     root      8,   71 Sep  8 16:31 sde7
brw-------  1 root     root      8,   72 Sep  8 16:31 sde8
brw-r--r--  1 root     root     11,    0 Sep  8 16:31 sr0
brw-r-----  1 root     root     11,    1 Sep  8 16:31 sr1
brw-r-----  1 root     root     11,    2 Sep  8 16:31 sr2
brw-r-----  1 root     root      3,    1 Sep  8 16:31 swap
crw-r--r--  1 root     root      5,    0 Sep  8 16:31 tty
crw-r--r--  1 root     root      4,    0 Sep  8 16:31 tty0
crw-------  1 root     root      4,    1 Sep  8 16:31 tty1
crw-r--r--  1 root     root      4,    2 Sep  8 16:31 tty2
-rw-r--r--  1 root     root          20 Sep  8 16:31 tty21
crw-r--r--  1 root     root      4,    3 Sep  8 16:31 tty3
crw-r--r--  1 root     root      4,    4 Sep  8 16:31 tty4
crw-r--r--  1 root     root      4,    5 Sep  8 16:31 tty5
crw-r--r--  1 root     root      4,    6 Sep  8 16:31 tty6
crw-------  1 root     root      4,    7 Sep  8 16:31 tty7
crw-------  1 root     root      4,    8 Sep  8 16:31 tty8
crw-r--r--  1 root     root      4,   64 Sep  8 16:31 ttyS0
crw-r--r--  1 root     root      4,   65 Sep  8 16:31 ttyS1
crw-r--r--  1 root     root      4,   66 Sep  8 16:31 ttyS2
crw-r--r--  1 root     root      4,  192 Sep  8 16:31 ttyp0
crw-r--r--  1 root     root      4,  193 Sep  8 16:31 ttyp1
crw-r--r--  1 root     root      4,  194 Sep  8 16:31 ttyp2
crw-r--r--  1 root     root      4,  195 Sep  8 16:31 ttyp3
crw-r--r--  1 root     root      4,  196 Sep  8 16:31 ttyp4
crw-r--r--  1 root     root      4,  197 Sep  8 16:31 ttyp5
crw-r--r--  1 root     root      4,  198 Sep  8 16:31 ttyp6
crw-r--r--  1 root     root      4,  199 Sep  8 16:31 ttyp7
crw-r--r--  1 root     root      4,  200 Sep  8 16:31 ttyp8
crw-r--r--  1 root     root      4,  201 Sep  8 16:31 ttyp9
crw-r--r--  1 root     root      4,  202 Sep  8 16:31 ttypa
crw-r--r--  1 root     root      4,  203 Sep  8 16:31 ttypb
crw-r--r--  1 root     root      4,  204 Sep  8 16:31 ttypc
crw-r--r--  1 root     root      4,  205 Sep  8 16:31 ttypd
crw-r--r--  1 root     root      4,  206 Sep  8 16:31 ttype
crw-r--r--  1 root     root      4,  207 Sep  8 16:31 ttypf
-rw-------  1 root     root       63488 Sep  8 16:31 ttys0
crw-r--r--  1 root     root      4,   67 Sep  8 16:31 ttys3
crw-r--r--  1 root     root      1,    5 Sep  8 16:31 zero

boot_disk/etc:
total 173
-rw-r--r--  1 root     root          53 Sep  8 18:48 boot.env
-rwxr-xr-x  1 root     root       27408 Sep  8 18:48 e2fsck*
-rwxr-xr-x  1 root     root       18540 Sep  8 18:48 fdisk*
```

```
-rw-r--r--  1 root      root            69 Oct   8 12:27 fstab
-r-x------  1 root      root         13312 Sep   8 18:48 getty*
-rw-r--r--  1 root      root           334 Sep   8 18:48 group
-rw-r--r--  1 root      root            12 Sep   8 18:48 host.conf
-rw-r--r--  1 root      root            62 Sep   8 18:48 hosts
-r-x------  1 root      root          6684 Sep   8 18:48 ifconfig*
-rwxr-xr-x  1 root      root         11492 Sep   8 18:48 init*
-rw-r--r--  1 root      root          1017 Sep   9 22:12 inittab
-rw-r--r--  1 root      root             0 Oct   8 12:19 issue
-rw-r-----  1 root      root          5137 Sep   8 18:48 login.defs
-rwxr-xr-x  1 root      root         14028 Sep   8 18:48 mke2fs*
-rwxr-x---  1 root      root          2436 Sep   8 18:48 mkswap*
-rwxr-xr-x  1 root      root         11288 Sep   8 18:48 mount*
-rw-r--r--  1 root      root           327 Sep   8 18:48 passwd
-rwxr-xr-x  1 root      root           383 Sep  10 16:02 profile*
-rw-r--r--  1 root      root            94 Sep   8 18:48 protocols
-rwxr-xr-x  1 root      root           334 Oct   8 12:27 rc*
-rwxr-xr-x  1 root      root          9220 Sep   8 18:48 reboot*
-r-x------  1 root      root          4092 Sep   8 18:48 route*
-rw-r--r--  1 root      root            20 Sep   8 18:48 securetty
-rw-r--r--  1 root      root          9749 Sep   8 18:48 services
-rw-r--r--  1 root      root            36 Sep   8 18:48 shells
-rwxr-xr-x  1 root      root         13316 Sep   8 18:48 shutdown*
-rwxr-xr-x  1 root      root          2496 Sep   8 18:48 swapoff*
-rwxr-xr-x  1 root      root          2496 Sep   8 18:48 swapon*
-rw-r--r--  1 root      root          5314 Sep   8 18:48 termcap
-rwxr-xr-x  1 root      root          5412 Sep   8 18:48 umount*
-rw-r--r--  1 root      root           224 Sep   8 18:48 utmp
-rw-r--r--  1 root      root           280 Sep   8 18:48 wtmp

boot_disk/lib:
total 629
-rwxr-xr-x  1 root      root         17412 Sep  10 14:58 ld.so*
-rwxr-xr-x  1 root      root        623620 Sep   8 18:33 libc.so.4*
```

<sect2>Utility Disk ls-1R Directory Listing
<p>
The utility listing is of directory util_disk:

```
total 1
drwxr-xr-x  2 root      root          1024 Sep  10 16:05 bin/

util_disk/bin:
total 897
-rwxr-xr-x  1 root      root         41984 Sep  10 14:11 cpio*
-rwxr-xr-x  1 root      root        504451 Sep   9 21:39 ftape.o*
-rwxr-xr-x  1 root      root         63874 Sep   9 21:40 gzip*
-rwxr-xr-x  1 root      root         13316 Sep   9 21:34 insmod*
-rwxr-xr-x  1 root      root            58 Sep   9 21:34 lsmod*
-rwxr-xr-x  1 root      root          3288 Sep   9 21:34 mknod*
-rwxr-xr-x  1 root      root          9220 Sep   9 21:34 rmmod*
-rwxr-xr-x  1 root      root        226308 Sep   9 22:13 tar*
```

4.2 Shell Scripts to Build Diskettes

There are two shell scripts:

- mkroot - builds a root or boot/root diskette.

- mkutil - builds a utility diskette.

Both are currently configured to run in the parent directory of boot_disk and util_disk, each of which contains everything to be copied to it's diskette. Note that these shell scripts will *NOT* automatically set up and copy all the files for you - you work out which files are needed, set up the directories and copy the files to those directories. The shell scripts are samples which will copy the contents of those directories. Note that they are primitive shell scripts and are not meant for the novice user.

The scripts both contain configuration variables at the start which allow them to be easily configured to run anywhere. First, set up the model directories and copy all the required files into them. Then check the configuration variables in the shell scripts and change them as required before running the scripts.

4.2.1   mkroot - Make Root or Boot/Root Diskette

```
# mkroot: make a boot/boot disk - creates a boot/root diskette
#       by building a file system on it, then mounting it and
#       copying required files from a model.
#       Note: the model to copy from must first be set up,
#       then change the configuration variables below to suit
#       your system.
#
# usage: mkroot [nokernel]
#       if the parameter is omitted, then the kernel and LILO
#       are copied.

# Copyright (c) Graham Chapman 1994. All rights reserved.
# Permission is granted for this material to be freely
# used and distributed, provided the source is acknowledged.
# No warranty of any kind is provided. You use this material
# at your own risk.

# Configuration variables...
BOOTDISKDIR=./boot_disk       # name of boot disk directory
MOUNTPOINT=./mnt              # temporary mount point for diskette
LILODIR=/sbin                 # directory containing lilo
LILOBOOT=/boot/boot.b         # lilo boot sector
LILOMSG=./lilo.msg            # lilo message to display at boot time
LILOCONFIG=./lilo.conf        # lilo parms for boot/root diskette
DISKETTEDEV=/dev/fd0          # device name of diskette drive

echo $0: create boot/root diskette
echo Warning: data on diskette will be overwritten!
echo Insert diskette in $DISKETTEDEV and and press any key...
read anything

mke2fs $DISKETTEDEV
if [ $? -ne 0 ]
then
        echo mke2fs failed
        exit
fi

mount -t ext2 $DISKETTEDEV $MOUNTPOINT
if [ $? -ne 0 ]
then
        echo mount failed
        exit
fi

# copy the directories containing files
for i in bin etc lib
do
        cp -dpr $BOOTDISKDIR/$i $MOUNTPOINT
```

```
    done

    # copy dev *without* trying to copy the files in it
    cp -dpR $BOOTDISKDIR/dev $MOUNTPOINT

    # create empty directories required
    mkdir $MOUNTPOINT/proc
    mkdir $MOUNTPOINT/tmp
    mkdir $MOUNTPOINT/mnt
    mkdir $MOUNTPOINT/usr

    # copy the kernel
    if [ "$1" != "nokernel" ]
    then
            echo "Copying kernel"
            cp $BOOTDISKDIR/vmlinux $MOUNTPOINT
            echo kernel copied

            # setup lilo
            cp $LILOBOOT $MOUNTPOINT
            cp $LILOMSG $MOUNTPOINT
            $LILODIR/lilo -C $LILOCONFIG
            echo LILO installed
    fi

    umount $MOUNTPOINT

    echo Root diskette complete
```

4.2.2   mkutil - Make Utility Diskette

```
    # mkutil: make a utility diskette - creates a utility diskette
    #         by building a file system on it, then mounting it and
    #         copying required files from a model.
    #         Note: the model to copy from from must first be set up,
    #         then change the configuration variables below to suit
    #         your system.

    # Copyright (c) Graham Chapman 1994. All rights reserved.
    # Permission is granted for this material to be freely
    # used and distributed, provided the source is acknowledged.
    # No warranty of any kind is provided. You use this material
    # at your own risk.

    # Configuration variables...
    UTILDISKDIR=./util_disk     # name of directory containing model
    MOUNTPOINT=./mnt            # temporary mount point for diskette
    DISKETTEDEV=/dev/fd0        # device name of diskette drive

    echo $0: create utility diskette
    echo Warning: data on diskette will be overwritten!
    echo Insert diskette in $DISKETTEDEV and and press any key...
    read anything

    mke2fs $DISKETTEDEV
    if [ $? -ne 0 ]
    then
            echo mke2fs failed
            exit
    fi
```

```
# Any file system type would do here
mount -t ext2 $DISKETTEDEV $MOUNTPOINT
if [ $? -ne 0 ]
then
        echo mount failed
        exit
fi

# copy the directories containing files
cp -dpr $UTILDISKDIR/bin $MOUNTPOINT

umount $MOUNTPOINT

echo Utility diskette complete
```

5 FAQ

5.1 Q. How can I make a boot disk with a XXX driver?

The easiest way is to obtain a Slackware kernel from your nearest Slackware mirror site. Slackware kernels are generic kernels which atttempt to include drivers for as many devices as possible, so if you have a SCSI or IDE controller, chances are that a driver for it is included in the Slackware kernel.

Go to the a1 directory and select either IDE or SCSI kernel depending on the type of controller you have. Check the xxxxkern.cfg file for the selected kernel to see the drivers which have been included in that kernel. If the device you want is in that list, then the corresponding kernel should boot your computer. Download the xxxxkern.tgz file and copy it to your boot diskette as described above in the section on making boot disks.

You must then check the root device in the kernel, using the rdev command:

```
rdev vmlinuz
```

Rdev will then display the current root device in the kernel. If this is not the same as the root device you want, then use rdev to change it. For example, the kernel I tried was set to /dev/sda2, but my root SCSI partition is /dev/sda8. To use a root diskette, you would have to use the command:

```
rdev vmlinuz /dev/fd0
```

If you want to know how to set up a Slackware root disk as well, that's outside the scope of this HOWTO, so I suggest you check the Linux Install Guide or get the Slackware distribution. See the section in this HOWTO titled "References".

5.2 Q. How do I update my boot floppy with a new kernel?

Just copy the kernel to your boot diskette using the dd command for a boot diskette without a filesystem, or the cp command for a boot/root disk. Refer to the section in this HOWTO titled "Boot" for details on creating a boot disk. The description applies equally to updating a kernel on a boot disk.

5.3 Q. How do I remove LILO so that I can use DOS to boot again?

This is not really a Bootdisk topic, but it is asked so often, so: the answer is, use the DOS command:

```
FDISK /MBR
```

MBR stands for Master Boot Record, and it replaces the boot sector with a clean DOS one, without affecting the partition table. Some purists disagree with this, but even the author of LILO, Werner Almesberger, suggests it. It is easy, and it works.

You can also use the dd command to copy the backup saved by LILO to the boot sector - refer to the LILO documentation if you wish to do this.

5.4 Q. How can I boot if I've lost my kernel AND my boot disk?

If you don't have a boot disk standing by, then probably the easiest method is to obtain a Slackware kernel for your disk controller type (IDE or SCSI) as described above for "How do I make a boot disk with a XXX driver?". You can then boot your computer using this kernel, then repair whatever damage there is.

The kernel you get may not have the root device set to the disk type and partition you want. For example, Slackware's generic SCSI kernel has the root device set to /dev/sda2, whereas my root Linux partition happens to be /dev/sda8. In this case the root device in the kernel will have to be changed.

You can still change the root device and ramdisk settings in the kernel even if all you have is a kernel, and some other operating system, such as DOS.

Rdev changes kernel settings by changing the values at fixed offsets in the kernel file, so you can do the same if you have a hex editor available on whatever systems you do still have running - for example, Norton Utilities Disk Editor under DOS. You then need to check and if necessary change the values in the kernel at the following offsets:

```
0x01F8   Low byte of RAMDISK size
0x01F9   High byte of RAMDISK size
0x01FC   Minor device number - see below
0X01FD   Major device number - see below
```

The ramdisk size is the number of blocks of ramdisk to create. If you want to boot from a root diskette then set this to decimal 1440, which is 0x05A0, thus set offset 0x01F8 to 0xA0 and offset 0x01F9 to 0x05. This will allocate enough space for a 1.4Mb diskette.

The major and minor device numbers must be set to the device you want to mount your root filesystem on. Some useful values to select from are:

```
device          major minor
/dev/fd0            2     0   1st floppy drive
/dev/hda1           3     1   partition 1 on 1st IDE drive
/dev/sda1           8     1   partition 1 on 1st SCSI drive
/dev/sda8           8     8   partition 8 on 1st SCSI drive
```

Once you have set these values then you can write the file to a diskette using either Norton Utilities Disk Editor, or a program called rawrite.exe. This program is included in several distributions, including the SLS and Slackware distributions. It is a DOS program which writes a file to the "raw" disk, starting at the boot sector, instead of writing it to the file system. If you use Norton Utilities, then you must write the file to a physical disk starting at the beginning of the disk.

5.5 Q. How can I make extra copies of boot/root diskettes?

It is never desirable to have just one set of rescue disks - 2 or 3 should be kept in case one is unreadable.

The easiest way of making copies of any diskettes, including bootable and utility diskettes, is to use the dd command to copy the contents of the original diskette to a file on your hard drive, and then use the same command to copy the file back to a new diskette. Note that you do not need to, and should not, mount the diskettes, because dd uses the raw device interface.

To copy the original, enter the command:

```
dd if={$<$}device{$>$} of={$<$}filename{$>$}
where   {$<$}device{$>$} = the device name of the diskette
        drive
and     {$<$}filename{$>$} = the name of the file where you
        want to copy to
```

For example, to copy from /dev/fd0 to a temporary file called /tmp/diskette.copy, I would enter the command:

```
dd if=/dev/fd0 of=/tmp/diskette.copy
```

Omitting the "count" parameter, as we have done here, means that the whole diskette of 2880 (for a high-density) blocks will be copied.

To copy the resulting file back to a new diskette, insert the new diskette and enter the reverse command:

```
dd if=<filename> of=<device>
```

Note that the above discussion assumes that you have only one diskette drive. If you have two of the same type, then you can copy diskettes using a command like:

```
dd if=/dev/fd0 of=/dev/fd1
```

5.6   Q. How can I boot without typing in "ahaxxxx=nn,nn,nn" every time?

Where a disk device cannot be autodetected it is necessary to supply the kernel with a command device parameter string, such as:

```
aha152x=0x340,11,3,1
```

This parameter string can be supplied in several ways using LILO:

- By entering it on the command line every time the system is booted via LILO. This is boring, though.
- By using the LILO "lock" keyword to make it store the command line as the default command line, so that LILO will use the same options every time it boots.
- By using the APPEND statement in the lilo config file. Note that the parameter string must be enclosed in quotes.

For example, a sample command line using the above parameter string would be:

```
vmlinux aha152x=0x340,11,3,1 root=/dev/sda1 lock
```

This would pass the device parameter string through, and also ask the kernel to set the root device to /dev/sda1 and save the whole command line and reuse it for all future boots.

A sample APPEND statement is:

```
APPEND = "aha152x=0x340,11,3,1"
```

Note that the parameter string must NOT be enclosed in quotes on the command line, but it MUST be enclosed in quotes in the APPEND statement.

Note also that for the parameter string to be acted on, the kernel must contain the driver for that disk type. If it does not, then there is nothing listening for the parameter string, and you will have to rebuild the kernel to include the required driver. For details on rebuilding the kernel, cd to /usr/src/linux and read the README, and read the Linux FAQ and Installation HOWTO. Alternatively you could obtain a generic kernel for the disk type and install that.

Readers are strongly urged to read the LILO documentation before experimenting with LILO installation. Incautious use of the "BOOT" statement can damage partitions.

6   References

In this section, vvv is used in package names in place of the version, to avoid referring here to specific versions. When retrieving a package, always get the latest version unless you have good reasons for not doing so.

6.1   LILO - Linux Loader

Written by Werner Almesberger. Excellent boot loader, and the documentation includes information on the boot sector contents and the early stages of the boot process.

Ftp from: `tsx-11.mit.edu:/pub/linux/packages/lilo/lilo.vvv.tar.gz` also on sunsite and mirror sites.

6.2   Linux FAQ and HOWTOs

These are available from many sources. Look at the usenet newsgroups `news.answers` and `comp.os.linux.announce`.

Ftp from: `sunsite.unc.edu:/pub/Linux/docs`

- FAQ is in `/pub/linux/docs/faqs/linux-faq`
- HOWTOs are in `/pub/Linux/docs/HOWTO`

For WWW, start at the Linux documentation home page:

> `http://sunsite.unc.edu/mdw/linux.html`

If desperate, send mail to:

> `mail-server@rtfm.mit.edu`

with the word "help" in the message, then follow the mailed instructions.

Note: if you haven't read the Linux FAQ and related documents such as the Linux Installation HOWTO and the Linux Install Guide, then you should not be trying to build boot diskettes.

6.3   Rescue Shell Scripts

Written by Thomas Heiling. This contains shell scripts to produce boot and boot/root diskettes. It has some dependencies on specific versions of other software such as LILO, and so might need some effort to convert to your system, but it might be useful as a starting point if you wanted more comprehensive shell scripts than are provided in this document.

Ftp from: `sunsite.unc.edu:/pub/Linux/system/Recovery/rescue.tgz`

6.4   SAR - Search and Rescue

Written by Karel Kubat. SAR produces a rescue diskette, using several techniques to minimize the space required on the diskette. The manual includes a description of the Linux boot/login process.

Ftp from: `ftp.icce.rug.nl:/pub/unix/SAR-vvv.tar.gz`

The manual is available via WWW from:

`http://www.icce.rug.nl/karel/programs/SAR.html`

6.5   Slackware Distribution

Apart from being one of the more popular Linux distributions around, it is also a good place to get a generic kernel. It is available from almost everywhere, so there is little point in putting addresses here.

Part X

The Linux Busmouse Howto

Copyright Mike Battersby, mike@starbug.apana.org.au
1.2, 1994/08/02

Contents

1   Introduction.

This document is a guide to getting your busmouse working with Linux. I've written this in the hope that the ten people a week who post "how do I get my busmouse to work" questions in the comp.os.linux.* newsgroups will read it first, though I won't be holding my breath.

Busmouse support has been in the kernel for as long as I can remember, and hasn't changed in a long time, so this document should be relevant to any version of Linux you're likely to have.

1.1   Disclaimer.

The information in this document is correct to the best of my knowledge, but there's a always a chance I've made some mistakes, so don't follow everything too blindly, especially if it seems wrong. Nothing here should have a detrimental effect on your computer, but just in case I take no responsibility for any damages incurred from the use of the information contained herein.

```
Microsoft(R) is a Trademark of Microsoft Corporation.
```

[trademark notices for other mice, anyone? — Mike]

1.2   Feedback.

If you find any mistakes in this document, have any comments about its contents or an update or addition, send them to me at the address listed at the top of this howto.

1.3   Acknowledgements.

This howto has been, in the spirit of Linux, a community effort. Many thanks go to Johan Myreen for the sections on the PS/2 mice, Robert T. Harris for help on the ATI-XL sections and Reuben Sumner for miscellaneous info and constructive criticism.

Thanks also to the multitudes of people who have sent me mouse information, fixes or words of encouragement.

2   Determining your mouse type.

There are two separate but important characteristics you will need to know about your mouse before you go on: what interface it uses and what protocol it uses. The interface is the hardware aspect of the mouse, taking into account things like which i/o ports it uses and how to check if it is installed. This is the part which the kernel is concerned with, so that it knows how to read data from the mouse. The protocol is the software aspect of the mouse. Applications need to know the protocol to interpret the raw mouse data they receive from the kernel.

2.1   Mouse interfaces.

The Linux kernel currently supports four different kinds of bus mouse interface : Inport (Microsoft), Logitech, PS/2 and ATI-XL. The majority of bus mice have Inport interfaces, although lately PS/2 interfaces are becoming more popular. There is no surefire way of determining your mouse interface — mouse developers generally do their own thing when it comes to standards. The following sections may help, otherwise you'll just have to make it up.

2.2   Inport mice.

This includes most of the old style Microsoft mice which are shaped like a bar of dove soap. U.S. users who have purchased Gateway computers should note that the mice that come with them are not Inport mice but PS/2 mice (see below). Inport mice generally connect to an interface card which plugs into the bus on your motherboard. If the plug which connects your mouse cord to the interface card is round, has 9 pins, and a notch in one side you likely have an Inport mouse.

As far as I can tell, apart from the ATI-XL, all ATI mice (such as those on the Graphics Ultra cards) are plain Inport mice.

2.3   Logitech mice.

Logitech mice in general appear almost exactly the same as Inport mice. They too connect to an interface card via a 9 pin mini-din connector. Hopefully, it will have come in a Logitech box or have "Logitech" printed on the connector card so that you can tell it actually is a Logitech mouse.

There are also some truly ancient Microsoft mice (ones with ball bearings on the bottom as well as the mouse ball and a DB9 connector) which also use the Logitech protocol.

2.4   PS/2 mice.

PS/2 mice aren't really bus mice at all. The PS/2 mouse interface is not on an expansion card, the mouse is connected to the PS/2 Auxiliary Device port on the keyboard controller. A PS/2 mouse port uses a 6-pin mini DIN connector, similar to the keyboard connector. Many laptops also use this kind of interface to their trackballs — except for the connector, of course.

2.5   ATI-XL mice.

ATI-XL mice are a variant of Inport mice, with some slight differences. They come on the ATI-XL combined video adaptor/mouse card. Unless you know you have an ATI-XL card (and thus an ATI-XL mouse), you probably don't have one of these. It is possible for ATI-XL mice to use either the ATI-XL or Inport kernel drivers, although the ATI-XL driver should give better results.

2.6   Mouse protocols.

The PC world is full of different and conflicting mouse protocols. Fortunately, the choice for bus mice is considerable smaller than that for serial mice. Most Inport, Logitech and ATI-XL mice use the "BusMouse" protocol, although there are some ancient Logitech mice which use the "MouseSystems" protocol, and some even older Microsoft mice which use the Logitech protocol. PS/2 mice use the "PS/2" protocol.

3   Getting your mouse working.

Once you have figured out your mouse interface and protocol types, you're ready to proceed.

3.1   Setting the mouse interrupt.

Now, you'll need to know which interrupt number your mouse is using, and make sure it doesn't conflict with any other peripherals you have installed.

You should make sure that your mouse is not trying to use the same interrupt as any of your other devices — it is not possible for the mouse to share an interrupt under Linux, even though it may work fine under other operating systems. Check the documentation for all your peripherals to see which interrupt they use. In most cases IRQ4 is used for the first serial port (/dev/ttyS0), IRQ3 for the second (/dev/ttyS1) (these are assuming you actually have such devices — if you don't you can happily use their IRQ's), and IRQ5 for some SCSI adaptors.

Note that for ATI-XL, Inport and Logitech mice the kernel default is to use IRQ5, so if you are stuck with a pre-compiled kernel (eg, CD-ROM users) you will have to use that.

3.2 Inport and Logitech mice.

If you open up your computer's case and look at the card which your mouse plugs into, you should notice a block of jumpers on the card (hopefully labeled "INTERRUPT") with positions for interrupt (otherwise known as IRQ) numbers 2,3,4 and 5. To change the interrupt simply move the jumper from its current position onto the correct pair of pins.

```
*****************************************************
***     MAKE SURE YOUR COMPUTER IS TURNED OFF    ***
***     BEFORE CHANGING THE JUMPERS AROUND.      ***
*****************************************************
```

3.3 ATI-XL mice.

ATI-XL busmice have a software selectable IRQ - you should have received with your mouse a MS-DOS program (VSETUP.EXE) to set the IRQ. In order to do so you must (temporarily) boot MS-DOS and run this program. Note that the VSETUP program takes an optional parameter "/70" to increase the vertical refresh rate (which results in less flicker). The VSETUP program also allows you to select either the primary or secondary mouse address - you should set this to the primary address or the kernel will not be able to detect your mouse.

Once VSETUP has been run you must perform a hard reset for the new configuration to take effect.

3.4 PS/2 mice.

The PS/2 mouse always uses IRQ12 – there is no way of changing this (except with a soldering gun.) In the rare case that some other device is using IRQ12, you'll have to rejumper that peripheral to use another IRQ number.

3.5 Compiling the kernel.

In order for your busmouse to operate correctly you will need to recompile your kernel with the busmouse support compiled in.

Change to your kernel directory (here assumed to be (/usr/src/linux) and do a

```
make config
```

If you are unsure as to your mouse type, the first time you recompile the kernel you may wish to enable all of the busmouse options in the hope that the kernel will autodetect your mouse properly. People have mixed sucess with this: it doesn't always work, but on the other hand it might save you any further compiles.

3.5.1 Inport, Logitech and ATI-XL mice.

Answer "y" to the question pertaining to your type of busmouse interface and "n" to all the other busmouse questions. For example, if you have an Inport mouse you should answer "y" to

```
Microsoft busmouse support
```

and "n" to all other busmouse questions. Answer the non-mouse related questions as you usually would.

If you have a Logitech or Inport mouse, edit the file `/usr/src/linux/include/linux/busmouse.h` and change the line which says

```
#define MOUSE_IRQ 5
```

to reflect the interrupt number for your mouse (see section 3.1 for details on finding your interrupt number).

If you have an ATI-XL mouse, edit the file `/usr/src/linux/drivers/char/atixlmouse.c` and change the line which says

```
#define ATIXL_MOUSE_IRQ 5
```

to reflect your mouse's interrupt number.

Due to the vagaries of the PC architecture, if you have set your mouse to use interrupt 2, you must set the #define to use interrupt 9.

Examples

For a mouse on interrupt 3, you should change the line to read

```
#define MOUSE_IRQ 3
```

For a mouse on interrupt 2, you should change the line to read

```
#define MOUSE_IRQ 9
```

Next, compile your kernel as per the instructions which come with it, and boot from the new kernel. You should now have the busmouse support correctly compiled in.

3.5.2 PS/2 mice.

To compile the kernel with PS/2 mouse support answer "y" to the question.

```
PS/2 mouse (aka "auxiliary device") support
```

The PS/2 mouse driver actually supports two kinds of devices: the standard PS/2 Auxiliary Device controller and a special PS/2 mouse interface chip from Chips & Technologies which is used in the Texas Instruments Travelmate and Gateway Nomad laptops. To compile in support for the trackballs on these computers, answer "y" to the

```
C&T 82C710 mouse port support (as on TI Travelmate)
```

question. Note that you will still have to answer "y" to the question about the standard PS/2 driver to even get a chance to answer this question, since the 82C710 driver is actually an add-on to the standard PS/2 mouse driver.

When configured both for a standard PS/2 mouse device and the 82C710 device, the driver first tries to locate a 82C710 chip at boot time. Failing this, the standard driver is used instead, so using a kernel configured for both types of interface on a machine with a standard PS/2 mouse port should work too. However, there has been one report of a falsely detected 82C710 chip, so to be on the safe side do not configure in support for the 82C710 if you don't need it.

Compile your new kernel and boot from it as you normally would.

3.5.3 Selection.

Regardless of your mouse type you should answer "y" to the

```
Selection (cut and paste for virtual consoles)
```

question if you wish to run the selection program (see section 4.1 for more details).

3.6   The mouse devices.

Mice under Linux are accessed via the devices in the /dev directory. The following table gives a list of interface types and which device you should use.

```
INTERFACE          DEVICE          MAJOR    MINOR
-------------------------------------------------
Logitech           /dev/logibm       10       0
PS/2               /dev/psaux        10       1
Inport             /dev/inportbm     10       2
ATI-XL             /dev/atibm        10       3

     Table 1.  Mouse devices.
```

Note:
> If you are using your ATI-XL mouse with the Inport driver, you should use the /dev/inportbm device, not the /dev/atibm device.

The major and minor entries are the device numbers for that particular device.

If you find that you do not have these devices, you should create them first. To do so, execute the following as root.

```
mknod /dev/logibm    c 10 0
mknod /dev/psaux     c 10 1
mknod /dev/inportbm  c 10 2
mknod /dev/atibm     c 10 3
```

Note:
> Some time in the (progressively less) recent history of Linux the names for the busmouse devices have changed. The following device names have been superceded by those above and should be removed: bmousems, bmouseps2, bmouseatixl, bmouselogitech.

Many people like to create a symbolic link from their mouse device to /dev/mouse so that they don't have to remember which device they need to be using. If you have one of the current Linux distributions you will almost certainly find that you have such a link. If you have such a link, or create one, you should make sure that it is pointing to the correct device for your mouse.

3.7   Testing your mouse.

Get the file selection-1.6.tar.gz from your local Linux ftp site and compile the program "test-mouse" within it, according to the instructions (all you should need to do is type "make test-mouse"). Run the program like this

```
test-mouse -t <mouse arg> -m <mouse dev>
```

where <mouse arg> is "bm" (without the quotes) if you use the BusMouse protocol, or "ps2" if you use the PS/2 protocol, and <mouse dev> is your mouse device name from table 1.

If your mouse is working correctly, you should be able to paint on the screen by holding down the right or left mouse button and dragging the mouse. Push the left and right mouse buttons simultaneously to exit the program.

4   Using your mouse.

4.1   Selection.

Selection is a program which allows you to do mouse based 'cut- and-paste' between virtual consoles under Linux. Selection can be found as the file `selection-1.6.tar.gz` at your friendly Linux FTP site (such as `sunsite.unc.edu`), and contains instructions for getting it compiled. Some Linux distributions, such as Slackware, come with a precompiled selection binary.

When invoking selection, use the -t switch to selection to indicate which protocol your mouse is using and the -m option to indicate which mouse device you are using. The default is to use the `/dev/mouse` device, so you can omit the -m option if you have the appropriate symbolic link. For example, if you use the BusMouse protocol, selection should be run like this:

```
selection -t bm
```

or if you use the PS/2 protocol:

```
selection -t ps2
```

You should then be able to cut and paste text between virtual consoles using the mouse buttons. Read the documentation with selection, or do a "man selection" for more information on how to operate it.

There have been a couple of reports of selection not working correctly with certain laptop trackballs (under the PS/2 interface). Replacing the line

```
{ 0xcc,    0x00,    0x00,    0x00,    3         }    /* PS/2 */
```

in selection's mouse.c file with the line

```
{ 0xcc,    0x08,    0x00,    0x00,    3         }    /* PS/2 */
```

may help if you are having problems and can't track it down to anything else.

4.2   XFree86.

To use your busmouse under XFree86, you will need to set your mouse protocol type in your Xconfig file. If you have a BusMouse protocol mouse, your Xconfig should contain (including the quotes)

```
Busmouse          "/dev/mouse"
```

For PS/2 mice it should have

```
ps/2          "/dev/mouse"
```

If you have a two button mouse, it should also contain the line

```
Emulate3Buttons
```

which will allow you to emulate the use of the middle mouse button by pressing both mouse buttons simultaneously. All other mouse related lines, such as "BaudRate" and "SampleRate" should be commented out, as these have no effect on bus mice.

4.3   XFree86 and selection.

Unlike serial mice, you cannot share busmice between processes. This means you will have to kill any copies of "selection" (see section 4.1) you have running before you start up Xfree86. If you try to run X with selection running, you will get errors like the following

```
Fatal server error:
Cannot open mouse (Device or resource busy)
```

Version 1.6 of selection allows you to terminate running copies of selection by executing

```
selection -k
```

This should be done before starting up X11. You may wish to add a line containing the above command to the top of your `startx` script so that the mouse is shut down automatically. If you have an older version of selection which does not support the `-k` switch you will have to kill selection by hand.

5   Still can't get your mouse going?

So you've read through this howto a dozen times, done everything exactly as you think you should have, and your mouse still doesn't work? The best advice I can give you is this: experiment. Sure, it's a pain in the posterior, but in the end the only way to find out what is going to work with your mouse is to try all of the alternatives until you have success.

As always, if there is something you don't understand, try reading the manual page first and see if that helps. If you have a specific question, or a problem you think I might be able to help with, feel free to contact me at the address listed at the top of this howto, and I'll see if I can help you out or point you to someone who can.

The `comp.os.linux.help` newsgroup is the appropriate forum for discussion and/or questions regarding mice — please don't post questions to other groups, and especially don't crosspost questions to two or more of the Linux groups, they are more than cluttered enough as it is! When posting, you will get a much better response (and much fewer flames) if you use appropriate Subject: and Keywords: lines. For example:

```
Subject: BUSMICE - Gateway 2000 mouse wont work.
Keywords: mouse busmouse gateway
```

Part XI

The Linux CD-ROM HOWTO

Copyright Jeff Tranter, Jeff_Tranter@Mitel.COM
v1.4, 2 December 1994
This document describes how to install, configure, and use CD-ROM drives under Linux. It lists the supported hardware and answers a number of frequently asked questions. The intent is to bring new users up to speed quickly and reduce the amount of traffic in the usenet news groups.

Contents

1   Introduction

This is the Linux CD-ROM HOWTO document. It is intended as a quick reference covering everything you need to know to install and configure CD-ROM hardware under Linux. Frequently asked questions related to CD-ROM are answered, and references are given to other sources of information related to CD-ROM applications and technology.

1.1   Acknowledgments

Much of this information came from the file `README.sbpcd` provided with the Linux kernel source code and written by Eberhard Moenkeberg (`eberhard_moenkeberg@rollo.central.de`), the internet alt.cd-rom FAQ, and input from Linux users.

Thanks to the Linuxdoc-SGML package, this HOWTO is available in several formats, all generated from a common source file.

1.2   Revision History

Version 1.0

> first version made publicly available

Version 1.1

> CDU33A is explicitly supported as of 1.1.20 kernel; notes on Reveal FX; info on reading audio tracks; info on some alpha drivers; added troubleshooting section; a few other minor additions

Version 1.2

> ISO9660 file systems must be mounted read-only starting with 1.1.33 kernel; clarified that SB16 SCSI is supported and newer Aztech drives are not supported; references to photocd and xpcd programs; note new on sbpcd autoeject feature

Version 1.3

> minor change to the way SBPCD eject feature is disabled starting with the 1.1.49 kernel; added info on XA discs and how to identify them

Version 1.4

> HOWTO now available in other languages; IBM and Longshine drives now supported by SBPCD; alpha driver for Aztech drives; CDU-33 driver no longer auto-probes, supports PhotoCD and audio; more than 2 SCSI drives are supported; new driver for IDE; reminder to check drive jumpers; can now set SBPCD auto-eject with IOCTL; list drivers with multisession support; question on flashing light on CDU-33

1.3   New Versions Of This Document

New versions of this document will be periodically posted to `comp.os.linux.announce`. They will also be uploaded to various anonymous ftp sites that archive such information including `sunsite.unc.edu:/pub/Linux/docs/HOWTO`.

Hypertext versions of this and other Linux HOWTOs are available on many World-Wide-Web sites. You can also buy printed copies from several vendors.

A French translation of this HOWTO, by Bruno Cornec (`cornec@stna7.stna.dgac.fr`) is available at `ftp.ibp.fr:/pub2/linux/french/docs/HOWTO`. A Japanese translation is also in progress.

1.4   Feedback

I rely on you, the users, to make this HOWTO useful. If you have any suggestions, corrections, or comments, please send them to the author and I will try to incorporate them in the next revision.

2   CD-ROM Technology

```
"CD-ROM is read-only memory, and audio compact disc system is
available as package-media of digital data for those purpose. For
playing audio CD, please insert Head-phone jack."
--- from a CD-ROM instruction manual
```

Don't Panic! The world of CD-ROM technology is not as confusing as your instruction manual.

CD-ROM stands for *Compact Disc Read-Only Memory*, a mass storage medium utilizing an optical laser to read microscopic pits on the aluminized layer of a polycarbonate disc. The same format is used for audio Compact Discs. Because of its high storage capacity, reliability, and low cost, CD-ROM has become an increasingly popular storage media.

The storage capacity of a CD-ROM disc is approximately 650 megabytes, equivalent to over 500 high density 3.5" floppy disks or roughly 250,000 typed pages.

First generation drives (known as *single speed*), provide a transfer rate of approximately 150 kilobytes per second. Double speed drives are commonly available, and triple and quad speed drives have recently been introduced.

Most CD-ROM drives use either the Small Computer Systems Interface (SCSI) or a vendor proprietary interface. They also typically support playing audio CDs via an external headphone jack or line level output.

CD-ROMs are usually formatted with an ISO-9660 (formerly called *High Sierra*) file system. This format restricts filenames to the MS-DOS style (8+3 characters). The *Rock Ridge Extensions* use undefined fields in the ISO-9660 standard to support longer filenames and additional Unix style information (e.g. file ownership, symbolic links, etc.).

PhotoCD is a standard developed by Kodak for storing photographic images as digital data on a CD-ROM. With appropriate software, you can view the images on a computer, manipulate them, or send them to a printer.

CD recorders (CD-R) have recently become available. They use a different media and specialized equipment for recording, but the resulting disc can be read by any CD-ROM drive.

3 Supported Hardware

This section lists the CD-ROM drivers and interfaces that are currently supported under Linux. The information here is based on the latest Linux kernel, which at time of writing was version 1.1.69.

3.1 SCSI CD-ROM Drives

SCSI (Small Computer Systems Interface) is a popular format for CD-ROM drives. Its chief advantages are a reasonably fast transfer rate, multi-device capability, and support on a variety of computer platforms.

Any SCSI CD-ROM drive with a block size of 512 or 2048 bytes should work under Linux; this includes the vast majority of CD-ROM drives on the market.

You will also need a supported SCSI controller card; see the SCSI HOWTO for more information on interface hardware.

Note that some CD-ROMs include a controller with a modified interface that is not fully SCSI compatible (e.g. it may not support adding other SCSI devices on the bus).

3.2 Proprietary CD-ROM Drives

Several CD-ROM drives using proprietary interfaces are available; the interface is often provided on a sound card. Simple interface cards equivalent to that provided on the sound card are also available. These drives generally tend to be lower in cost and smaller than SCSI drives.

The following proprietary CD-ROM drives are supported by the Linux kernel (drives listed together are compatible):

- Matsushita/Kotobuki/Panasonic/Creative Labs models CR-521, CR-522, CR-523, CR-562, CR-563, Longshine LCS-7260, IBM

- Mitsumi/Radio Shack

- Sony CDU31A and CDU33A

- Sony CDU535 and CDU531 (driver is available as a kernel patch)

- LMS/Philips CD205/225/202 (driver is available as a kernel patch)
- NEC CDR-260 (driver is available as a kernel patch)
- Aztech CD268A (driver is available as a kernel patch)

The following sound card interfaces are supported:

- SoundBlaster/Pro
- SoundBlaster/16 (both the proprietary interface and SCSI versions)
- Galaxy
- SoundFX
- Spea Media FX sound card (Sequoia S-1000)

The following interface cards are also supported:

- Panasonic CI-101P
- LaserMate
- Aztech (see below)
- WDH-7001C

IBM sells an external CD-ROM drive and interface card that is compatible with the Panasonic CR-562 driver.

Only the older Aztech drives compatible with the Matsushita/Panasonic driver. There is an ALPHA driver available separately for the CD268A drive. You can find it at ftp.gwdg.de in the directory pub/linux/cdrom/drivers/aztech.

Drivers for some additional devices are in development and may be available as kernel patches. They can most likely be found on sunsite.unc.edu in the directory /pub/Linux/kernel/patches/cdrom. Check the Linux Software Map for availability.

3.3   IDE CD-ROM Drives

CD-ROM drives based on a modified version the IDE hard disk (ATAPI) standard have recently been introduced. One such drive is the NEC CDR-260. An alpha release of a Linux kernel driver for IDE hard disks and CD-ROM drives is available on sunsite.unc.edu. It works with the NEC CDR-260 and possibly others.

Note that the proprietary interfaces are sometimes erroneously referred to as IDE interfaces, because like IDE, they use a simple interface based on the PC/AT bus.

4   Installation

Installation of CD-ROM under Linux consists of these steps:

1. Installing the hardware.
2. Configuring and building the Linux kernel.
3. Creating the necessary device files.
4. Mounting the media.

4.1 Installing Hardware

Follow the manufacturer's instructions for installing the hardware or have your dealer perform the installation. The details will vary depending on whether the drive is internal or external and on the type of interface used. There are no special installation requirements for Linux. You may need to set jumpers on the drive and/or interface card for correct operation.

4.2 Configuring and Building the Kernel

In order to use a CD-ROM you need the appropriate device drivers. To mount most CD-ROM discs you also need the ISO-9660 file system support in the kernel. Follow your usual procedure for building the kernel: do a "make config" and select the appropriate drivers when prompted.

For SCSI CD-ROMs you need to answer "yes" to "SCSI support?", and then enable "Scsi CDROM support" and the driver for the appropriate SCSI interface (e.g. "Adaptec AHA1542 support").

For the proprietary interface drives, select "Sony CDU31A/CDU33A CDROM driver support", "Mitsumi CDROM driver support", or "Matsushita/Panasonic CDROM driver support", according to your drive type. The Matsushita driver also supports up to 4 controllers.

For other drive types you must obtain the driver separately and apply it as a kernel patch.

If you are using the Matsushita/Panasonic drive, you have the choice of letting the kernel auto-probe for the drive, passing it on the kernel command line, or explicitly setting it in the file `/usr/src/linux/include/linux/sbpcd.h`. It is recommended that you initially set it to auto-probe. Later you can set the type and save some time during bootup.

As of the 1.1.64 kernel, autoprobing for the CDU-31A drives has been removed. You now need to either add your drive to the configuration table in the driver or use a LILO boot-line configuration. The format of the LILO command line is:

```
cdu31a=<I/O address>,<interrupt>[,PAS]
```

Setting the interrupt to 0 will disable the interrupts and use polled I/O. The PAS option is for ProAudioSpectum16 sound card users that are not using the sound driver. A typical card would have a configuration like one of the following:

```
cdu31a=0x340,0
cdu31a=0x340,5
```

The easiest way to set this up is to add a line such as the following to your LILO configuration file:

```
append="cdu31a=0x1f88,0,PAS"
```

Again, remember to compile in the ISO-9660 file system support. The Rock Ridge extensions are fully supported by the kernel driver.

If you have a sound card that is supported under Linux, you should enable and configure the kernel sound driver at this time as well.

After selecting the device drivers, compile the kernel and install it following your usual procedure.

4.3 Creating the Device Files

If you are running a standard Linux distribution you may have created the necessary device files during installation. Under Slackware Linux, for example, there is a menu-based `setup` tool that includes CD-ROM setup, and most systems have a `/dev/MAKEDEV` script. It is recommended that you at least verify the device files against the information in this section.

Create the device file by running the shell commands indicated for your drive type. This should be done as user `root`. Note that some Linux distributions may use slightly different CD-ROM device names from those listed here.

It is recommended that you also create a symbolic link to the CD-ROM device to make it easier to remember. For example, for a Panasonic CD-ROM drive, the link would be created using

```
% ln -s /dev/sbpcd /dev/cdrom
```

If you want to play audio CDs, you will need to set the protection on the device files to allow users to read and write, e.g.

```
% chmod 666 /dev/sbpcd
```

4.3.1 Matsushita/Kotobuki/Panasonic/Creative Labs/IBM

Up to four drives per controller are supported. Only the first device is needed if you have only one drive. If you have more than one controller, create devices with major numbers 26, 27, and 28, up to a maximum of 4 controllers (this is 16 CD-ROM drives in total; hopefully enough for most users :-).

```
% mknod /dev/sbpcd  b 25 0
% mknod /dev/sbpcd0 b 25 0
% mknod /dev/sbpcd1 b 25 1
% mknod /dev/sbpcd2 b 25 2
% mknod /dev/sbpcd3 b 25 3
```

4.3.2 Sony CDU31A/CDU33A

Only one drive is supported by this kernel driver. See the comments in the file `/usr/src/linux/drivers/block/cdu31a.c` for information on configuring the interface card. As of the 1.1.60 kernel, the driver supports playing audio CDs and PhotoCD (but not multisession yet).

```
% mknod /dev/cdu31a b 15 0
```

See the kernel source file cdu31a.c for information on configuring the drive interface card. Also see the notes given previously about specifying the configuration on the LILO command line.

4.3.3 Sony CDU535/CDU531

Note again that the driver is currently only available as a kernel patch.

```
% mknod /dev/cdu535 b 24 0
```

Some Linux distributions use `/dev/sonycd` for this device. Older versions of the driver used major device number 21; make sure your device file is correct.

4.3.4 Mitsumi

The kernel supports one Mitsumi drive. Recent kernels (1.1.25) incorporate changes to improve performance.

```
% mknod /dev/mcd b 23 0
```

4.3.5 LMS/Philips

Note again that this driver is currently only available as a kernel patch. See the README file included with the patches for more information.

```
% mknod /dev/lmscd b 24 0
```

4.3.6 SCSI

Multiple drives are supported (up to the limit of the number of devices on the SCSI bus). Create device files with major number 11 and minor numbers starting at zero:

```
% mknod /dev/scd0 b 11 0
% mknod /dev/scd1 b 11 1
```

4.3.7 IDE Drives

Information on creating the devices files are included with the kernel patch for these drives.

4.4   Mounting/Unmounting/Ejecting Devices

You can now reboot with the new kernel. Watch for a message such as the following indicating that the CD-ROM has been found by the device driver (the message will vary depending on the drive type):

```
SBPCD version 2.5 Eberhard Moenkeberg <emoenke@gwdg.de>
SBPCD: Looking for a SoundBlaster/Matsushita CD-ROM drive
SBPCD:
SBPCD: = = = = = = = = = = W A R N I N G = = = = = = = = = =
SBPCD: Auto-Probing can cause a hang (f.e. touching an ethernet card).
SBPCD: If that happens, you have to reboot and use the
SBPCD: LILO (kernel) command line feature like:
SBPCD:
SBPCD:    LILO boot: linux sbpcd=0x230,SoundBlaster
SBPCD: or like:
SBPCD:    LILO boot: linux sbpcd=0x300,LaserMate
SBPCD: or like:
SBPCD:    LILO boot: linux sbpcd=0x330,SPEA
SBPCD:
SBPCD: with your REAL address.
SBPCD: = = = = = = = = = = END of WARNING = = = = = = = = = =
SBPCD:
SBPCD: Trying to detect a SoundBlaster CD-ROM drive at 0x230.
SBPCD: - Drive 0: CR-562-x (0.76)
SBPCD: 1 SoundBlaster CD-ROM drive(s) at 0x0230.
SBPCD: init done.
```

(If the bootup messages scroll by too quickly to read, you should be able to retrieve them with the dmesg command)

To mount a CD-ROM, insert a disc in the drive, and run the mount command as root (this assumes you created a symbolic link to your device file as recommended above):

```
% mount -t iso9660 -r /dev/cdrom /mnt
```

The CD can now be accessed under the directory /mnt. Note that /mnt is commonly used as a temporary mount point; a more suitable name for a permanent installation might be something like /cdrom. There are other options to the mount command that you may wish to use; see the mount(8) man page for details.

You can add an entry to /etc/fstab to automatically mount a CD-ROM when Linux boots or to specify parameters to use when it is mounted; see the fstab(5) man page.

Note that to play audio CDs you should *not* try to mount them.

To unmount a CD-ROM, use the umount command as root:

```
% umount /mnt
```

The disc can only be unmounted if no processes are currently accessing the drive (including having their default directory set to the mounted drive). You can then eject the disc. Most drives have an eject button; there is also a standalone eject program that allows ejecting CD-ROMs under software control.

Note that you should not eject a disc while it is mounted (this may or may not be possible depending on the type of drive). The sbpcd driver will automatically eject a CD-ROM when it is unmounted and insert the CD tray when a disc is mounted (you can turn this feature off when compiling the kernel or by using a software command).

4.5 Troubleshooting

If you still encounter problems, here are some things to check.

If you recompiled the kernel yourself, verify that you are running the new kernel by looking at the timestamp:

```
% uname -a
Linux fizzbin 1.1.31 #1 Wed Jul 20 16:53:35 EDT 1994 i386
```

With recent 1.1.x kernels, you can see what drivers are compiled in by looking at /proc/devices:

```
% cat /proc/devices
Character devices:
 1 mem
 4 tty
 5 cua
 6 lp
14 sound
15 Joystick

Block devices:
 2 fd
 3 hd
25 sbpcd
```

If your drive has hardware jumpers for addressing, check that they are set correctly (e.g. drive 0 if you have only one drive).

Try reading from the CD-ROM drive. Typing the following command should cause the drive activity light come on and no errors should be reported. Use whatever device file is appropriate for your drive and make sure a CD-ROM is inserted; use Control-C to exit.

```
dd if=/dev/cdrom of=/dev/null bs=2048
^C
124+0 records in
124+0 records out
```

If you can read from the drive but cannot mount it, verify that you compiled in ISO9660 file system support. With the 1.1.x kernels this can be done as follows:

```
% cat /proc/filesystems
        ext2
        msdos
nodev   proc
        iso9660
```

Make sure you are mounting the drive with the "-t iso9660" and "-r" options and that a known good CD-ROM (not Audio CD) is inserted in the drive.

Make sure that the CD-ROM device files are correct, according to the information in the previous section.

If you are running the syslog daemon, there may be error messages from the kernel that you are not seeing. Try using the "dmesg" command:

```
% dmesg
SBPCD: sbpcd_open: no disk in drive
```

There may also be errors logged to files in /var/adm, depending on how you system is configured.

5   Applications

This section briefly lists some of the key applications related to CD-ROM that are available under Linux. Check the Linux Software Map for the latest versions and archive sites.

5.1   Audio CD players

Several programs are available for playing audio CDs, either through a headphone jack or an attached sound card.

Workman

a graphical player running under X11 and supporting a CD database and many other features

WorkBone

an interactive text-mode player

xcdplayer

a simple X11 based player

cdplayer

a very simple command line based player

Xmcd

an X11/Motif based player

xmitsumi

another X11 based player for Mitsumi drives

xplaycd

another X11 based player, bundled with sound mixer and VU meter programs

cdtool

command line tools for playing audio CDs

Some of these programs are coded to use a specific device file for the CD-ROM (e.g. /dev/cdrom). You may be able to pass the correct device name as a parameter, or you can create a symbolic link in the /dev directory. If sending the CD output to a sound card, you may wish to use a mixer program to set volume settings or select the CD-ROM input for recording.

5.2   Inheriting File System

The Inheriting File System (IFS) is a kernel driver that allows mounting multiple file systems at the same point. It is similar to the Translucent File System provided under SunOS. By mounting a hard disk directory over a CD-ROM file system, you can effectively obtain a writable CD-ROM file system.

The current version is experimental and was written for the 0.99pl11 and pl12 kernels; it may or may not work with more recent revisions. The author is Werner Almesberger (`almesber@bernina.ethz.ch`).

5.3   PhotoCD

PhotoCDs use an ISO-9660 file system containing image files in a proprietary format. Not all CD-ROM drives support reading PhotoCDs.

The `hpcdtoppm` program by Hadmut Danisch converts PhotoCD files to the portable pixmap format. It can be obtained from `ftp.gwdg.de:/pub/linux/hpcdtoppm` or as part of the PBM (portable bit map) utilities, available on many archive sites (look for "pbm" or "netpbm").

The `photocd` program by Gerd Knorr `kraxel@cs.tu-berlin.de` can convert PhotoCD images into targa or Windows and OS/2 bitmap files.

The same author has written the program xpcd, an X11-based program for handling PhotoCD images. You can select the images with a mouse, preview the image in a small window, and load the image with any of the five possible resolutions. You can also mark a part of the Image and load only the selected part. Look for these packages at `ftp.cs.tu-berlin.de:/pub/linux/Local/misc`.

(I've actually tried a PhotoCD! If anyone wants more detail on how to view files, etc... let me know and I can expand this section).

5.4   Mkisofs

Eric Youngdale's `mkisofs` package allows creating an ISO-9660 file system on a hard disk partition. This can then be used to assist in creating and testing CD-ROM file systems before mastering discs.

The tools for actually writing data to writable CD-ROM drives tend to be vendor specific. They also require writing the data with no interruptions, so a multitasking operating system like Linux is not particularly well suited.

5.5   9660_u

These are some utilities for verifying the format of ISO-9660 formatted discs; you may find them useful for testing suspect CDs. The package can be found on `ftp.cdrom.com` in the `/pub/ptf` directory. They were written by Bill Siegmund and Rich Morin.

6   Answers to Frequently Asked Questions

6.1   How can a non-root user mount and unmount discs?

Some mount commands support the *user* option. If you make an entry such as the following in `/etc/fstab`:

```
/dev/sbpcd   /cdrom    iso9660      user,noauto,ro
```

then an ordinary user will be allowed to mount and unmount the drive using these commands:

```
% mount /cdrom
% umount /cdrom
```

The disc will be mounted with some options that ensure security (e.g. programs cannot executed, device files are ignored); in some cases this may be too restrictive.

Another method is to get the `usermount` package which allows non-root users to mount and unmount removable devices such as floppies and CD-ROMs, but restricts access to other devices (such as hard disk partitions). It is available on major archive sites.

The archive site `ftp.cdrom.com` has the source file `mount.c` which allows mounting an unmounting of CD-ROMs (only) by normal users. It runs as a setuid executable.

6.2 Why do I get `device is busy` when unmounting a CD-ROM?

The disc cannot be unmounted if any processes are accessing the drive, including having their default directory set to the mounted filesystem. If you cannot identify the processes using the disc, you can use the `fuser` command, as shown in the following example.

```
% umount /cdrom
umount: /dev/sbpcd: device is busy
% fuser -v /cdrom
/cdrom:              USER      PID ACCESS COMMAND
                     tranter    50 ..c..  bash
```

6.3 How do I export a CD-ROM to other hosts over NFS?

You need to add an entry to the `/etc/exports` file; see the `exports(5)` man page for details.

6.4 Can I boot Linux from a CD-ROM?

The easiest way to boot from CD-ROM is to use a boot floppy. Several of the Linux CD-ROM distributions (e.g. Yggdrasil) include one, or you can use the boot disk(s) from one of the Linux distributions (e.g. Slackware) that includes the necessary CD-ROM drivers for your system.

In the future it may be possible to boot from IDE CD-ROM drives which have the appropriate ROM BIOS functions.

6.5 Why doesn't the kernel recognize my CD-ROM drive?

If you have a proprietary interface at a non-standard address, you may need to set the i/o port location in the appropriate kernel header file. Similarly, auto-probing by the kernel driver may conflict with another device (e.g. network card) and cause your system to hang.

For the Matsushita/Kotubuki/Panasonic/Creative Labs drives, you need to edit the file `sbpcd.h`. For the Mitsumi drives it is `mcd.h` and for Sony drives it is `cdu31a.h`. All of these files are normally installed in `/usr/include/linux`. Alternatively you can set the drive parameters on the LILO command line.

6.6 How can I read digital data from audio CDs?

Only a few CD-ROM drives support this. Heiko Eissfeldt (`heiko@colossus.escape.de`) and Olaf Kindel have written a utility that reads audio data and saves it as `.wav` format sound files. It only works with the Toshiba XM3401 and XM4101 SCSI drives. The package is called `cdda2wav.tar.gz` and can be found on `sunsite.unc.edu`.

The Panasonic SBPCD driver also has support for reading sound data beginning with the 2.0 driver included in the 1.1.22 kernel. A modified version of the cdda2wav program that works with this can be found at `ftp.gwdg.de` in `/pub/linux/misc/cdda2wav-sbpcd.2.tar.gz`.

Even though the standard cdda2wav program claims to support the Panasonic drives, it does not yet work properly, because of the need to handle "overlap" of the data.

The CDU-33 driver now supports reading audio data. It is said to work with the cdda2wav program.

For more information on this subject, see the alt.cd-rom FAQ listed in the references section.

6.7 How do I turn off the autoprobing messages on boot?

The SBPCD driver displays a lot of information during bootup. If you want to suppress this, set the variable `sbpcd_debug` in the file `sbpcd.c`. The comments in the file explain the various values that this can be set to.

6.8 Why doesn't the `find` command work properly?

On ISO-9660 formatted discs without the Rock Ridge Extensions, you need to add the `-noleaf` option to the `find` command.

The reason for this is that the number of links for each directory file is not easily obtainable, so it is set to 2. The default behavior for the `find` program is to look for (i_links - 2) subdirectories in each directory, and it then assumes that the rest are regular files. The `-noleaf` switch disables this optimization.

6.9 Is the Reveal Multimedia Effects kit CD-ROM supported?

(the following was provided by `Horne@leader.pfc.mit.edu`)

Here's what I discovered about the Reveal Multimedia kits that are available fairly cheap ($300 or so) from department stores. After some thrashing I discovered how to make the following CD work under linux.

This is a Reveal Multimedia FX kit, which includes a Sound FX SC400 sound card, which has interfaces for Sony CDU33A, Panasonic CR-563, and Mitsumi LU005s. My kit includes a Sony.

The tricks to making the Sony CD work are as follows:

- Decide which kernel to patch. I pulled the 1.0 kernel off the Trans-Ameritech CD-ROM via DOS (My system started out as SLS a long time ago)

- Add addresses 0x634, 0x654 to the table at the top of the cdu31a driver:

```
static unsigned short cdu31a_addresses[] =
{
    0x340,          /* Standard configuration Sony Interface */
    0x1f88,         /* Fusion CD-16 */
    0x230,          /* SoundBlaster 16 card */
    0x360,          /* Secondary standard Sony Interface */
    0x320,          /* Secondary standard Sony Interface */
    0x330,          /* Secondary standard Sony Interface */
    0x634,
    0x654,
    0
};
```

- Recompile your kernel, specifying Sony CDU31A and ISO9960 support

- Create the device file (use major number 15, not 21 as in the Transameritech doc)

```
% mknod /dev/cd b 15 0
```

- Mount the drive

```
% mount -t iso9660 -r /dev/cd /cdrom
```

I'm still working on the actual sound support (I don't really need it yet) but that should be much easier.

Thanks to Reveal tech support for the info that the CD interface is at 0x414 off of the soundcard base address, Roman at Trans-Ameritech (roman@btr.btr.com) who suggested patching the CDU31A driver, and Dale Elrod (dale@post.dungeon.com) who provided an existence proof (Dale, your zImage didn't recognize the drive - I expect you actually have slightly different hardware. I'd have returned this thing a week ago, though, if I hadn't thought you had it working.)

The original driver is due to minyard@wf-rch.cirr.com, and Linus made it all possible.

6.10 Does Linux support any recordable CD-ROM drives?

According to Adam J. Richter, adam@yggdrasil.com:

The Yggdrasil distribution can drive a Philips CD writer with an Adaptec 154x SCSI controller. I'm not sure which other SCSI controllers, if any, will work. You can use mkisofs to make an ISO-9660 filesystem and cdwrite to write it to the CD. If you want us to help you set this up, you can call us on our 900 technical support number: 1-900-446-6075 extension 835 (US$2.95/minute, U.S. only).

6.11 The eject function (e.g. from Workman) does not work!

The SBPCD driver had a problem where the drive could be locked and the eject ioctl() would fail. This appears to be corrected starting with the 1.1.29 kernel.

6.12 You say I need to configure and build a kernel - how do I do that?

This is not the kernel HOWTO (any volunteers?). Until one is written, try reading the file /usr/src/linux/README; it is reasonably complete.

If you really don't want to compile a kernel, you may be able to find a precompiled kernel that has the drivers you need as part of a Linux distribution (e.g. the Slackware "q" series of disks).

6.13 Why do I get mount: Read-only file system when mounting a CD-ROM?

With older kernels you could mount a CD-ROM for read/write; attempts to write data to the CD would not generate any errors. As of kernel version 1.1.33 this was corrected so that CD-ROMs must be mounted read only (e.g. using the -r option to mount).

6.14 Why does the disc tray open when I shut down the system?

As of the 1.1.38 kernel, the sbpcd driver ejects the CD when it is unmounted or closed. If you shut down the system, a mounted CD will be unmounted.

This feature is for convenience when changing discs. If the tray is open when you mount or read a CD, it will also automatically be closed.

I found that this caused problems with a few programs (e.g. cdplay and workbone). As of the 1.1.60 kernel you can control this feature under software control. A sample program is included in the README.sbpcd file (or use the "eject" program).

6.15   I have a "special" CD that can't be mounted

The "special" CD is likely an XA disc (like all Photo CDs or "one-offs" created using CD-R drives). Most of the Linux kernel CD-ROM drivers do not support XA discs, although you may be able to find a patch to add support on one of the archive sites.

The sbpcd driver *does* support XA. If you are using this driver you can determine if the disc is XA using the following procedure: go into the file sbpcd.c and enable the display of the "Table of Contents" (DBG_TOC). Build and install the new kernel and boot from it. During each mount the TOC info will be written (either to the console or to a log file). If the first displayed value in the TOC header line is "20", then it is an XA disc. That byte is "00" with normal disks. If the TOC display shows different tracks, that is also a sign that it is an XA disc.

(thanks to Eberhard Moenkeberg for the above information)

6.16   Which kernel drivers support multisession?

The SBPCD driver supports multisession.

The SCSI CD-ROM driver supports multisession with NEC and TOSHIBA drives.

The CDU-31A driver has some multi-session support written but it does not yet work.

Some drivers available as kernel patches may support multisession for other drives.

6.17   Why does the drive light flash on my CDU-33 drive?

This is normal and was added in a recent revision of the driver. It flashes the drive light when a CD is mounted (it's not a bug, it's a feature...).

7   References

Information on the Panasonic CD-ROM driver can be found in the file `/usr/src/linux/drivers/block/README.sbpcd`.

The following usenet FAQs are posted periodically to `news.answers` and archived at internet FTP sites such as `rtfm.mit.edu`:

- alt.cd-rom FAQ

- comp.periphs.scsi FAQ

Several other Linux HOWTOs have useful information relevant to CD-ROM:

- SCSI HOWTO

- Hardware Compatibility HOWTO

- Sound HOWTO

- Distribution HOWTO

At least 10 companies sell Linux distributions on CD-ROM; most of them are listed in the Distribution HOWTO.

The following Usenet news groups cover CD-ROM related topics:

- comp.publish.cdrom.hardware

- comp.publish.cdrom.multimedia

- comp.publish.cdrom.software

- comp.sys.ibm.pc.hardware.cd-rom

- alt.cd-rom

- alt.cd-rom.reviews

The internet site `ftp.cdrom.com` has a large archive of CD-ROM information and software; look in the directory `/pub/cdrom`.

The Linux Documentation Project has produced several books on Linux, including *Linux Installation and Getting Started*. These are freely available by anonymous FTP from major Linux archive sites or can be purchased in hardcopy format.

The *Linux Software Map* (LSM) is an invaluable reference for locating Linux software. The LSM can be found on various anonymous FTP sites, including `sunsite.unc.edu:/pub/Linux/docs/LSM.gz`.

Part XII

Linux Commercial-HOWTO

Contents

1   Introduction

Having a free Unix-like operating system like Linux is Really Nice (TM). All the corresponding source code is publicly available, wither via FTP, on CD-ROMs or in specialized BBSes.

"Free Software", however, does not necessarily mean that the software is available for free – it just implies what you are allowed to do with it once you have it. This is the interpretation of the term "Free Software" pushed by the *Free Software Foundation* (gnu@prep.ai.mit.edu), especially by *Richard Stallman* (rms@ai.mit.edu) (the founder of the GNU project and the developer of GNU Emacs). My opinion is in perfect sync with that. However when it comes to widespread commercial use of the free operating system we are talking about, this is virtually impossible without commercial applications running on it.

2   About this document

This is the Linux Commercial-HOWTO. It contains commercial application software which is available for Linux. The Commercial-HOWTO will not contain Linux distributions and related stuff – that's what the Distribution-HOWTO is for.

This HOWTO will contain tabular entries for each product (example follows). The entry format is similar to the new Linux Software Map (LSM) entry (field/stanza lengths are arbitrary). Please: KEEP SHORT. Otherwise I'll have to shorten your data, and I hate work (and you don't want to have important data omitted, right?) ;-)

Description:

> SHORT description of the package, just the basic functionality

Distribution Media:

> diskettes, CD-ROM, tapes or others

Licensing Policy:

> whatever applies. is there a free demo or shareware version available via FTP? Where?

OS Provisions:

> kernel version, XFree86 version, Motif version, RAM, harddisk usage, etc.

Documentation:

> printed documentation, page number, online help, language

Product Support:

> update service, maintenance, training and prices thereof

Linux Support:

> if you bundle a complete Linux system with your software, which kind of support do you offer for the operating system? prices?

Extra Features and Add-Ons:

> and their prices

Available Since:

> the date you started shipping the Linux version

Countries with Distribution:

> if you ship in too many countries to name them all, naming regional distribution channels is okay.

Price Range:

> whatever it costs

Installed Base:

> how many copies of the Linux version did you sell by now? (This piece of information will be kept secret if you wish. I'd just like to know what's going on... thank you.)

Vendor:

```
address
phone
fax
e-mail address
contact person
```

I'll post the list to several national and international newsgroups on a monthly basis. In addition, the Commercial-HOWTO is available via *FTP* (`ftp://ftp.ix.de/pub/ix/Linux/docs/HOWTO`) (the latest and greatest, ASCII, DVI, Postscript and HTML formats) and will be uploaded to *sunsite.unc.edu* (`ftp://sunsite.unc.edu/pub/Linux/docs/HOWTO`) if there were changes. WWW users can access the document at URL *http://www.ix.de/ix/linux/Commercial-HOWTO.html* (`http://www.ix.de/ix/linux/Commercial-HOWTO.html`)   (mirrored   at *http://fvkma.tu-graz.ac.at/howto/Commercial-HOWTO.html* (`http://fvkma.tu-graz.ac.at/howto/Commercial-HOWTO.html`)).

There   is   a   French   version   of   sections   1,   2   and   3   available via *WWW* (`ftp://ftp.ix.de/pub/ix/Linux/docs/HOWTO/Commercial-HOWTO.French.html`) (outdated).

The Commercial-HOWTO is not a forum for product announcements or marketing hypes and no ad space – it is a service to potential customers and the whole Linux community. Resellers will not be listed – the list is for companies who produce their software themselves. Two main goals are being aimed at:

1. It shall help companies who want to run Linux to find software solutions and applications. The international distribution of this list will enhance the contact opportunity.

2. It is meant to prove the commercial usability of Linux and thus to encourage other vendors to port their software as well.

Companies and developers who are offering their products for Linux and interested in joining the Commercial-HOWTO are invited to fill in the following form and contact me via e-mail (*hm@ix.de* (`mailto:hm@ix.de`), preferred) or fax (+49 (0)511/5352-361). If you happen to know a company which does, please drop me a note. If you send me an entry for your product(s), please don't forget to send me timely updates if appropriate.

Please do me a favor and see the section "Marketing aspects ..." for a questionnaire concerning marketing aspects ...

3   Disclaimer

This HOWTO is not actually a HOWTO in the sense of the *Linux Documentation Project* (`http://sunsite.unc.edu/pub/Linux/docs/HOWTO/INDEX.html`). Instead, it is an instrument to investigate the commercial Linux opportunity and to list applications which were already ported and marketed in a native Linux version. As a software vendor, you probably know that you can alternatively offer Linux users a statically linked SCO version of your application which would probably run under the iBCS2 emulator (albeit with a small performance penalty and higher memory requirements). Such applications will not be listed here (but see the *iBCS2 documentation* (`ftp://tsx-11.mit.edu/pub/linux/BETA/ibcs2/`)).

I will not select nor deselect any particular product. Instead, everyone who wants to have his/her product included will be serviced. However, I reserve the right to shorten individual entries to keep things in shape.

If you don't find a particular product or vendor in this list, this is probably due to one of the following reasons:

- I never heard of that product or vendor and thus didn't try to get in contact.

- I did get in contact, but the vendor didn't answer yet.

- I did get in contact, but the vendor stated positively that he doesn't sell his product for Linux (yet).

In any case, please kick me if you feel someone's missing, also if you discover any errors in the file. But don't forget: I'm not being paid for that job ;-) .

Sometimes two vendor's addresses are mentioned in the "Vendor:" field. In these cases I received the information from the German subsidiary / distributor. The original manufacturer's address is always mentioned first.

My comments in the text are enclosed in parentheses () and marked with my initials "hm".

4   Related Information

There's another html page which covers commercial Linux software. It is provided by *LINUX.ORG.UK* (`http://www.linux.org.uk/LxCommercial.html`) and maintained by *Alan Cox* (`mailto:Alan.Cox@linux.org`).

5   Marketing aspects of commercial Linux applications

This section was suggested by (*Orest Zborowski* (`mailto:orestz@eskimo.com`)) and is still under construction. It is meant to help potential commercial software developers to market their products. There are several caveats to watch when doing this, e.g. the *GNU General Public License* (`ftp://ftp.germany.eu.net/pub/packages/gnu/COPYING`) (GPL) and the *GNU Library General Public License* (`ftp://ftp.germany.eu.net/pub/packages/gnu/COPYING.LIB`) (LGPL). I'd appreciate anyone who wants to share his/her experience with Linux-specific marketing issues to send me some lines (see questionnaire which follows). Please make sure that people interested in more specific items can contact you via e-mail or fax.

5.1   Investigation

Here is a questionnaire which I ask you to fill in and send me. Answers will be handled anonymously, and I will only disclose facts, no names. The facts you tell me will be of great value to get an idea how the commercial Linux market looks like. If you do not market your application in a native Linux version, please tell my why. If not stated otherwise, *"application"* stands for *"native Linux version of your application"*.

- Why did you start marketing your *application*? Why didn't you do it earlier?

- How many copies of the application do you expect to sell

  - for Linux,
  - for all the other Unix variants,

  during the planned product life? (This information is kept confidential if you require)

- How many copies of your application did you already sell

  - for Linux?
  - for all the other Unix variants?

  (This information is kept confidential if you require)

- Which technical problems did you have porting your application to Linux? How did you solve/circumvent them?

- How many employees are working on

    – porting to Linux,

    – providing support to end users/distributors?

  (This information is kept confidential if you require)

- Does your company offer the support for the *application* or did you (attempt to) outsource the support? If you provide support yourself, would you like to outsource it?

- Which issues were important for the pricing? Is the *application*

    – more expensive,

    – equally priced,

    – cheaper,

    – shareware priced,

  compared to versions for other Unix variants?

- What types of end users you you address with the *application*?

- According to your experience, was it a good decision to start marketing the *application*? Will you port and market other *applications* too?

- Are there any copy protection issues you have/like to consider? If yes, how did you solve the problem?

- How do you think about the *iBCS2 emulator* (ftp://tsx-11.mit.edu/pub/linux/BETA/ibcs2/) and offering a statically linked SCO/ISC or other version runnable under the emulator? Why did you choose to offer a native Linux version instead?

- What is your warranty strategy (Do you restrict the usage to certain kernel/C-lib versions etc.)?

- Which country-specific (e.g. legal) issues did you have to take into consideration? How did you cope with them?

- Are there any other important issues which I possibly (probably) forgot to ask?

5.2 Some Aspects

Porting to Linux simply means recompiling in many, many cases. Sometimes some #include tweaking may be necessary. If you develop your apps using GNU C/C++ which is very useful sometimes, there should be virtually no further work to do.

One big **advantage with Linux** is that all the source code of the operating system is freely available. Experienced programmers can easily spot the locations where problems occur and contact the "responsible" developer for assistance. I never encountered any of those guys being impolite – just make sure you read the respective documentation first...

The persons responsible for the Linux port should know where to get vital information in case of problems. The
Linux Documentation Project (http://sunsite.unc.edu/pub/Linux/docs/HOWTO/INDEX.html) offers plenty information about all and everything and the kitchen sink. The *Linux INFO-SHEET* (http://sunsite.unc.edu/pub/Linux/docs/HOWTO/INFO-SHEET) is a good place to start with for beginners.

The key to success with your Linux port is **Internet access**, particularly **FTP access** to the big Linux FTP servers as *sunsite.unc.edu* (ftp://sunsite.unc.edu/pub/Linux) or *tsx-11.mit.edu* (ftp://tsx-11.mit.edu/pub/linux) and their legion mirrors.

It appears that one big problem is **after-sales support**. If you do market your software for Linux, you should consider to employ someone who knows whom and where to ask in case of problems with the OS itself. On the other hand, you may expect problems with Linux to be solved **much** faster than problems with commercial Unix variants. For example, the */bin/login* bug allowing people to log onto Unix hosts as root without entering a password (known publicly in September 1994) was solved in a fortnight under Linux, whereas IBM shipped AIX with the broken */bin/login* for another couple of months (and didn't tell customers although there was a fix available via FTP).

After-sales support for Linux, on the other hand, can be a good opportunity for small companies and startups. If you want to sell a Linux version of your product you might want to find such a company to outsource the after-sales support (see respective section). They might even help you with the porting.

Some companies selling big and expensive software packages **offer completely installed systems**, i.e. the hardware, the OS and their specific software. In the contract, you can restrict your warranty to specific kernel / library versions so that problems are unlikely to occur at a later time.

The *GNU General Public License* (ftp://ftp.germany.eu.net/pub/packages/gnu/COPYING) (GPL) and the *GNU Library General Public License* (ftp://ftp.germany.eu.net/pub/packages/gnu/COPYING.LIB) (LGPL) contain no restriction in terms of marketing products developed with GNU tools as the GNU C/C++ compiler. Anyway, the legal strength of the GPL was never checked at court – I doubt it can be *enforced* outside the U.S.A. If you violate the GPL, you may expect being sued by the FSF and being bashed publicly by the Linux community – the GPL has a strong *ethic* value. In case of doubts, you might want to contact the *Free Software Foundation* (mailto:gnu@prep.ai.mit.edu). A very comprehensive interpretation in German is printed in section 1.7 of Kai Petzke's book "Unix fuer jedermann – Einfuehrung in Linux", Bernd-Michael Paschke Verlag, Berlin 1995, ISBN 3-929711-07-9.

Pricing: Well, there are three major philosophies around. Some companies offer a full or limited version for a very low fee or even for free. Others consider the Linux version as valuable as those for other OS's and offer it at a reasonable discount. Third, the price is equal to that of, say, the Solaris or the HP/UX version. Finding a reasonable price for your product may be somewhat more difficult than for other Unixes because there are many Linux users expecting to get everything for free ;-). Others (seriously interested customers, i.e. business people and decision makers) know that nothing is for free. You'll have to decide for the target customer.

A word concerning **fast version shifts**. This is clearly a prejudice. From the view of a software vendor, this is clearly **not true**. Linux is no moving target. It *is* true that *Linus Torvalds* (mailto:torvalds@cs.helsinki.fi) sometimes releases two or more kernel patches per week (or even more) in the **hackers' corner** (odd minor kernel release numbers). However, if you found a kernel doing what it's designed to do (version 1.0.9 or 1.2.3 being good choices), there's no reason to upgrade. Leave everything as it is and limit your warranty to certain kernel releases. Selling complete systems helps here, too, because you can ensure the respective kernel and its device drivers work in perfect harmony with the computer, its peripherals and your application.

You might consider offering a **statically linked Linux version** too (as it is very popular for SCO due to some nasty bugs in several SCO runtime libraries) but please tell your customer about the additional memory requirement.

If you intend to offer a shrink-wrapped systems (i.e. a complete hardware/software installation) please **avoid IDE harddisks**. Those disks are a perfect **performance bottleneck** for a real-world multitasking OS.

Two killer applications are needed under Linux: a good **text processing system** and a good **spread sheet**. With Xess, a useful spread sheet is available, but a good text processor a la Word for Windows is still missing. Many users use the statically linked SCO version of Wordperfect V6 under the iBCS2 emulator (actually, Wordperfect Corp. has been selling more copies for use under Linux than under SCO) but at a bad memory penalty. A native Linux version is still missing. Why do Wordperfect, Star Division and the others hesitate ... ?

Copy protection is virtually impossible under Linux. Because the kernel and all the associated tools are available as source code, any experienced hacker can hook dongle or key card `ioctl()` calls. On a PC, you don't have a machine/CPU id available. You don't want to build a specialized kernel for a certain (and given) hardware configuration, not disclosing the corresponding source code; such a kernel would be a "derived work" according to the GPL, and doing so would clearly violate the GPL.

Last not least, don't forget that **university and college students** who are the majority of Linux users worldwide are the **decision makers of tomorrow**. If you offer them a reasonably priced product for their beloved operating system today (think of campus licenses), there's little question which application they will choose tomorrow.

6 Migrating to ELF format

On March 28, 1995, *H.J. Lu* (`mailto:hjl@nynexst.com`), the maintainer of the binary distributions of GCC, LIBC and the associated binary utilities (binutils), posted in `comp.os.linux.announce`:

```
Hi,

In the next few weeks, Linux will move to the ELF binary format. A
new set of the ELF-based development tools will be released for
testing during the week of March 27. All the new binaries generated
by the new development tools will be in ELF. We have compiled the
kernel, XFree86 3.1.1 and many packages in ELF. They are all working
fine. The next module utilities will also support ELF.

In the meantime, a new and last a.out DLL shared C library 4.7.x will
also be provided for bug fixing. All the old a.out binaries should
continue running fine. But all the new features will only be in the
Linux C library 5.x.x which will be in ELF only.

To help smoothly transfer to ELF, I hope the commercial software
vendors please get in touch with me. I will provide all the necessary
supports to migrate to ELF, which should be very easy. I'd like
to see the ELF versions of Motif, Netscape, Mac emulator, ...
to just name a few. I have some documentations and examples which
are useful for using ELF.

Thanks.

H.J
```

7 Linux vs. other free Unix flavors

Why port to Linux and not to one of the free BSD versions like 386BSD and its derivatives FreeBSD and NetBSD (short: *BSD)? Well, that depends on your application. If it was originally written for a SystemV-based system as AIX, HP/UX or Solaris 2, porting to Linux should be fairly easy. *BSD lacks certain SystemV features (such as the `termio` interface), and you'll have to carefully check the amount of work necessary. On the other hand, FreeBSD and NetBSD are maintained by a closed developers' team (as opposed to the open and sometimes chaotic and anarchic Linux developers' community), and e.g. for FreeBSD there is only one so-called distribution available per *FTP* (`freebsd.cdrom.com`). You might want to mail *info@FreeBSD.org* (`mailto:info@FreeBSD.org`) or look on *http://www.cdrom.com/titles/freebsd.html* (`http://www.cdrom.com/titles/freebsd.html`).

By   the   way,   the   *FAQ*   *for*   *comp.unix.bsd.netbsd.announce*
(ftp://ftp.uni-paderborn.de/pub/doc/FAQ/comp.unix.bsd.netbsd.announce/) concerning the *BSD flavors says (short excerpt):

```
5.  Where BSD and POSIX differ, 386BSD conforms by default to
BSD; Linux to POSIX.  Furthermore, while both run mostly GNU
utilities, Linux tends toward the SysV flavor (e.g. init)
where 386BSD sticks with the BSD style.  However, sources for
different flavors of utilities are available for both, and
both support compiler options which allow more BSD or more
POSIX semantics.
```

And later it says:

```
1) the 386BSD family started with BSD, and Linux started with
POSIX.  NetBSD/FreeBSD/386BSD have been adding POSIX and System
V compatibility, and Linux has been adding Berkeley and System
V compatibility.  So there's a good deal of overlap.  But ...BSD
is still a better choice if you want to program in a Berkeley
environment and Linux if you want a POSIX environment.
```

8 Product Groups

This list is divided into several product groups to make finding a specific product more easy. I'd really like
to present a better index here but the current linuxdoc-sgml version doesn't offer support for that (especially
not for the HTML output). I don't intend (and don't have the time) to develop some tools to implement
that ... sorry.

Once this section grows too big (yielding an overall document size of more than, say, 100 pages), I will strip
some less important items from the template and the existing entries.

8.1   Databases

Database products are well appreciated, even under Linux ;-)

8.1.1   AccountFlex

Description:

AccountFlex is a powerfull full featured accounting system that includes modules for Order Entry,
Inventory, Purchasing, A/R, A/P, G/L, Payroll, and Jobcost. Accountflex uses Infoflex, an SQL based
4GL lanquage that is compatible with Informix (see information in this HOWTO. hm).

Distribution Media:

Diskette, Tape

Licensing Policy:

Source, runtime and unlimited runtimes are available. Demos and source are available for Linux,
UNIX, DOS, or VMS.

OS Provisions:

Character Based Screen images.

Documentation:

Printed documentation.

Product Support:

Phone support charged by time usage. Onsite training and custom programming available.

Linux Support:

N/A

Extra Features and Add-Ons:

N/A

Available Since:

October 1994

Countries with Distribution:

USA

Price Range:

USD795 per module including source.

Installed Base:

11 (as of date of entry. hm)

Vendor:

```
Infoflex Inc.
840 Hinckley Road, Suite 107
Burlingame, CA 94010, USA
Phone: +1 (415) 697-6045
Fax: +1 (415) 697-7696
Contact: Gerard Menicucci
```

Entered:

May 10, 1995

8.1.2   CONZEPT 16

Description:

CONZEPT 16 is a complete software development system based on a relational database. It runs on different platforms and in heterogenous networks. A version with graphical user interface is available too. Client/Server technology optional. CONZEPT 16 is a high performance system, for which there are hardly limitations.

Distribution Media:

Diskettes

Licensing Policy:

Copy-protected

OS Provisions:

Kernel version 1.1.26; RAM: at least 2 MByte, recommended: 8 MByte, harddisk: about 3-4 MByte

Documentation:

German, English, training documentation and reference (700 pages each), Online help

Product Support:

   Available (prices on request)

Linux Support:

   N/A

Extra Features and Add-Ons:

   OEM-KIT, Recovery (prices on request)

Available Since:

   Sep 1, 1994

Countries with Distribution:

   worldwide

Price Range:

   upon request

Installed Base:

   N/A

Vendor:

```
vectorsoft Gesellschaft fuer Datentechnik mbH
Seligenstaedter Grund 2
D-63150 Heusenstamm, Germany
Phone:   +49 6104/6477
Fax:     +49 6104/65250
Mailbox: +49 6104/5022
```

Entered:

   April 6, 1995

8.1.3   D-ISAM

Description:

   Multikey B+ tree Isam File Handler. Follows the C-ISAM (Informix) file structure and function calls. Sold with Source.

Distribution Media:

   5.25" and 3.5" Floppy disk

Licensing Policy:

   Free distribution of the first 100 D-ISAM'd executables. Royalties apply after that.

OS Provisions:

   Independent

Documentation:

   Documentation in English. Unix Style manual.

Product Support:

   email, bbs, fax, telephone. First 90 days free. US$450/year for ongoing.

Linux Support:

   N/A

Extra Features and Add-Ons:

Transaction Processing functions: US$295.00

Available Since:

June 1994

Countries with Distribution:

UK, Germany, USA, Canada (manufacturer)

Price Range:

Single Programmer License with Source: US$595, Transaction Processing Add-on: US$295, Additional Programmers: US$100, Runtime Licenses per 100: US$695 (after the first 100), Unlimited Runtime: US$6950. A free D-ISAM for Linux library is available for development, but not for commercial use, via *ftp* (ftp://ftp.wimsey.com/pub/linux/d-isam)

Installed Base:

Vendor:

```
Byte Designs Ltd
20568 - 32 Avenue
Langley, BC V3A 4P5, Canada
Phone:  +1 (604) 534-0722
Fax:    +1 (604) 534-2601
Contact: Heinz Wittenbecher
E-mail: sales@byted.com
```

Entered:

Sep 08, 1994

8.1.4   ESQLFlex

Description:

ESQLFlex is a low cost clone of the Informix-ESQL/C and Informix standard Engine products. ESQLFlex will allow developers to completely replace Informix-ESQL and Informix standard engine without having to modify their existing application. ESQLFlex enables developers to build, modify, and/or query databases using standard SQL calls from within "C" programs.

Distribution Media:

Diskette, Tape

Licensing Policy:

Source, runtime and unlimited runtimes are available. Demos and source are available for Linux, UNIX, DOS, or VMS.

OS Provisions:

Character Based Screen images.

Documentation:

Printed documentation.

Product Support:

Phone support charged by time usage. Onsite training and custom programming available.

Linux Support:

N/A

Extra Features and Add-Ons:

N/A

Available Since:

October 1994

Countries with Distribution:

USA, Spain, France, Germany

Price Range:

USD495

Installed Base:

35 (as of date of entry. hm)

Vendor:

```
Infoflex Inc.
840 Hinckley Road, Suite 107
Burlingame, CA 94010, USA
Phone: +1 (415) 697-6045
Fax: +1 (415) 697-7696
Contact: Gerard Menicucci
```

Entered:

May 10, 1995

8.1.5   Flagship

Description:

CA-Clipper5, Fox, dBase & beyond for Unix. XBase 4GL applications development system & database. Superset of CA-Clipper. Can be used to port.

Distribution Media:

3 3.5" Diskettes, other media extra charge.

Licensing Policy:

No royalty or licensing for software you create and distribute. For more information available via *ftp* (ftp://ftp.wgs.com/pub2/wgs/Filelist)

OS Provisions:

Linux 0.99 and later, has been tested on many. Requires C compiler, libraries and linker. Make and other utilities useful. 4 MByte RAM & 5 MByte Hard disk needed to run. More is better.

Documentation:

1200 page printed manual extra charge, same manual online is shipped as part of the product.

Product Support:

Support via phone, email, fax (email preferred), unlimited for 30 days, chargeable thereafter. Maintenance agreements including discounts on upgrades are available. All of this is country dependent.

Linux Support:

Country Dependent

Extra Features and Add-Ons:

FS2 Toolbox, FoxKit, and others. Country dependent.

Available Since:

July 1994

Countries with Distribution:

We sell to all countries, and have regional distributors in most major areas, and on all continents.

Price Range:

Country dependent. North America: Single user US$199, Unlimited User US$499 until Nov 15, 1994. US$499 Single & US$999 Unlimited after that.

Installed Base:

Vendor:

```
multisoft Datentechnik GmbH
PO Box 312
D-82027 Gruenwald, Germany
Phone:   +49 (0)89/6417904
Fax:     +49 (0)89/6412974
E-Mail: 100031.267@compuserve.com
Contact:  Dorte Balek

North America:
WorkGroup Solutions, Inc
PO Box 460190
Aurora, CO 80046-0190, USA
Phone:  +1 (303) 699-7470
Fax:    +1 (303) 699-2793
E-Mail: info@wgs.com
Contact: Virginia Lane
```

Entered:

Sep 19, 1994

8.1.6   InfoFlex

Description:

InfoFlex is a complete 4GL that streamlines the design process with a consistent WYSIWYG approach to developing menus, screens and reports. Infoflex is compatable with the Informix database and is similar in syntax. Demos, source, and unlimited licenses are available for UNIX, DOS, or VMS.

Distribution Media:

Diskette, Tape

Licensing Policy:

Source, runtime and unlimited runtimes are available. Demos and source are available for Linux, UNIX, DOS, or VMS.

OS Provisions:

Character Based Screen images.

Documentation:

Printed documentation

Product Support:

Phone support charged by time usage. Onsite training and custom programming available.

Linux Support:

N/A

Extra Features and Add-Ons:

N/A

Available Since:

October 1994

Countries with Distribution:

USA, Spain, France, Germany

Price Range:

USD995

Installed Base:

18 (as of date of entry. hm)

Vendor:

```
Infoflex Inc.
840 Hinckley Road, Suite 107
Burlingame, CA 94010, USA
Phone: +1 (415) 697-6045
Fax: +1 (415) 697-7696
Contact: Gerard Menicucci
```

Entered:

May 10, 1995

8.1.7 Just Logic/SQL Database Manager

Description:

The Just Logic/SQL Database Manager is a relational database system made to be used from C and C++ applications. It includes a complete set of libraries, utilities and a database engine. It comes with three programming interfaces: a C API interface, a C++ Class definitions and a C Precompiler. The client-server version permits Windows and Unix applications to access a remote server on Unix across TCP/IP. WWW: *http://www.to.com/jlt* (http://www.to.com/jlt)

Distribution Media:

Diskettes.

Licensing Policy:

Unlimited runtime license of applications.

OS Provisions:

SLS 1.0, 400K RAM, plus 100K per user, and 1.2 Meg Hard Disk, plus 1 Meg for client-server.

Documentation:

User manual (175 pages)

Product Support:

phone, email, fax

Linux Support:

N/A

Extra Features and Add-Ons:

Fully compatibles versions on SCO, BSDI, UnixWare, FreeBSD, DOS, Windows and OS/2.

Available Since:

August 94

Countries with Distribution:

Sold to all countries. Distributors in US and Germany.

Price Range:

The Linux release is priced at USD149 (USD219 with client-server).

Installed Base:

250 (Linux release)

Vendor:

```
Just Logic Technologies Inc.
P.O. Box 63050
40 Commerce St.
Nun's Island, Quebec H3E 1V6, Canada
Phone:  +1 (800) 267-6887 (toll free USA and Canada)
        +1 (514) 761-6887
Fax:    +1 (514) 642-6480 (has voice-fax autodetection)
E-mail: 71563.3370@CompuServe.COM
```

Entered:

Sep 08, 1994 (update: May 10.1995)

8.1.8   POET 2.1

Description:

POET 2.1 ODBMS for C++. Database functionality for C++ objects. Full support of encapsulation, inheritance, polymorphism and objectidentity. Two versions available : Personal Edition (Single/User 1 Developer) Professional Edition (Client/Server up to 4 Developer)

Distribution Media:

Diskettes

Licensing Policy:

SDK license from US$ 99. Runtime Licenses for commercial Products and for Public Domain or Share Products available.

OS Provisions:

kernel version > 1.0; SDK needs 4 MBytes on harddisk

Documentation:

handbook and tutorial (450+ pages)

Product Support:

hotline support, training please contact vendor

Linux Support:

N/A

Extra Features and Add-Ons:

N/A

Available Since:

March 1994

Countries with Distribution:

many; please contact vendor.

Price Range:

Personal Edition US$ 99 / DM 170. Professional Edition US$ 1990 / DM 3.990 (includes 1 year hotline support)

Installed Base:

234 copies as of July 1994

Vendor:

```
POET Software GmbH
Fossredder 12
D-22359 Hamburg, Germany
Phone:   +49 (0)40/609 90 18
Fax:     +49 (0)40/603 98 51
E-Mail: info@poet.de
Contact: Detlef Meyer
```

Entered:

Sep 19, 1994

8.1.9   /rdb

Description:

/rdb is a RDBMS consisting of more than 125 shell level commands which read tables from the standard input and write tables to the standard output. Applications are typically written in shell scripts, mixing /rdb commands with ordinary system commands. A runtime library is also included.

Distribution Media:

3.5" diskettes

Licensing Policy:

/rdb is licensed by the CPU. Time stamped licenses are available to allow for hardware up-grades.   An example of a full-text search using /rdb can be found at the *Melody Shop* (http://www.branch.com/ rsw).

OS Provisions:

kernel version 0.99.12 or later; consumes about 3MB storage.

Documentation:

230 page manual, both printed and on line. Some on-line help. Informational and error message tables provided for translation.

Product Support:

free email support; maintenance costs 10% of license fee/year.

Linux Support:

N/A

Extra Features and Add-Ons:

N/A

Available Since:

October 1993

Countries with Distribution:

US, Canada, South America, Australia, Germany, France, Ireland, Great Britain

Price Range:

USD149 qty 1 / CPU.

Installed Base:

101+

Vendor:

```
Revolutionary Software
131 Rathburn Way
Santa Cruz, CA 95062-1035
Phone:  +1 (408) 429 6229
E-mail: rdb@rsw.com
Contact: Evan Schaffer
```

Entered:

April 7, 1995

8.1.10   Veritas

Description:

Veritas is a system for German drinks wholesalers ("Getränkegrosshändler"). It's based on Onyx which is my 4gl and database project, which of course stays under the *GNU Public License 2.0* (`ftp://ftp.ix.de/pub/Linux/COPYING-2.0`). Ftp to *wowbagger.pc-labor.uni-bremen.de* (`ftp://wowbagger.pc-labor.uni-bremen.de/pub/unix/databases`) if you like to take a look at Onyx.

The first version of Veritas was developed for PCOS Olivetti in 1992, later Xenix versions followed. The recent 3rd release features twelve years of experience with this kind of market, so you can expect to have nearly anything a drinks wholesaler needs, e.g. Pfand, Sektsteuer, Brauereiabrechnung, Bruchvergütung, etc.

Several servers can be linked via SLIP or UUCP and replicate transactions to share data. Clients are connected via ethernet to a local server and can run MS Windows or better Linux.

Distribution Media:

Directly installed on the customer's hardware. Plus a Tape containing (I hope) all of the GNU'ish sources including Onyx and a bunch of different databases.

Licensing Policy:

Veritas is licensed according to a *German translation of the GNU Public License 2.0* (`http://www.suse.de/gpl-ger.html`), restricted in a way that any changes made must be mailed to the author, and that any customer must know that I'm the author and give support.

Although the license is very much like the GPL, I really recommend to purchase a copy if you prefer to get support.

OS Provisions:

Linux 1.0.9 (MCC), XFree86 2.1. Servers: 8-16 MB RAM, 200-500 MB harddisk, tape, modem. Clients: 8 MB RAM, 40 MB harddisk.

Documentation:

About 41 pages printed for Veritas in German, and about 43 pages online documentation for Onyx in English.

Product Support:

Retail price includes one week of training, and one year first class support over modem lines and D2 phone directly from the author. If you are interested in Onyx support, contact the author directly.

Linux Support:

Support for the installed sites is included in the installation price for one year.

Extra Features and Add-Ons:

N/A

Available Since:

The 3rd version of veritas is now in BETA in Bremerhaven.

Countries with Distribution:

Only distributed in Germany because of the user interface language and a lot of German tax related features.

If sold outside the northern part of Germany we need a VAR able to handle Linux, and sell and install the right hardware for a share.

Price Range:

Between 10,000 and 20,000 DM without hardware which depends on the number of servers and additional tailoring.

Installed Base:

Vendor:

```
Michael Koehne
Loss Datensysteme
Bremerstr. 117
D-28816 Brinkum, Germany
Phone:   +49 (0)421/87 55 00
V32bis: +49 (0)421/87 05 32
Fax:     +49 (0)421/87 55 51
E-Mail: kraehe@nordwest.de (company)
        kraehe@bakunin.north.de (private)
```

Entered:

Sep 08, 1994

8.1.11   Yard SQL

Description:

The YARD company offers 5 SQL products as follows:

- YARD-SQL – Relational SQL database server with compliance to X/Open XPG4 and ANSI SQL 92
- YARD-ESQLC – Embedded SQL for C.
- YARD-ODBC – ODBC interface for MS Windows clients
- YARD-NET – Remote access to YARD databases via TCP/IP.
- YARD-X – Motif client for database access (No development tool)

Distribution Media:

Floppy disk and streamer tapes

Licensing Policy:

License number and activation key for each product and installation with user dependent licenses for the SQL-Server.

OS Provisions:

LINUX 1.0.9 and upwards compatible versions; Motif 1.2.3; RAM Usage: 1 MByte (minimum) for Shared Memory, 500 KByte per User; Disk Usage: YARD-SQL 7 MByte, YARD-ESQLC 1 MByte, YARD-ODBC 1,5 MByte, YARD-NET 1 MByte, YARD-X 5 MByte

Documentation:

Printed 600 pages reference and users guide in German. English documentation will be available early 1995.

Product Support:

Release Update, Price 25% Version Update, Price 50% Technical support according to a special maintenance agreement (20% of total pricing). Training on request

Linux Support:

Extra Features and Add-Ons:

All products also available for other widely distributed Unix systems (e.g. SCO UNIX, SPARC Solaris).

Available Since:

January 1994

Countries with Distribution:

Current distribution in Germany through Distributor Ordix Software (info@ordix.de), Paderborn, Germany. Europeean/international distribution scheduled for early 1995.

Price Range:

YARD-SQL 590,00 (1 user) - 8.490,00 DEM (unlimited user) YARD-ESQLC 390,00 DEM YARD-ODBC 490,00 DEM YARD-NET 490,00 DEM YARD-X 990,00 DEM

Installed Base:

Vendor:

```
YARD Software GmbH
Hansestr. 99
D-51149 Koeln, Germany
Phone:  +49 (0)22 03/45 71 30
Fax:    +49 (0)22 03/45 71 31
E-Mail: yard@yard.de
Contact: Thomas Schonhoven (thomass@yard.de)
```

Entered:

Sep 24, 1994

8.2 Data Visualisation, CAD

CAD tools, renderers, OCR software and such stuff.

8.2.1   Ghostscript 3.x

Description:

Aladdin Ghostscript 3.n is a full PostScript Level 2 language interpreter. It can display PostScript files on the screen with X Windows, convert them to various raster formats (TIFF/F, GIF, PCX, PPM), and print them on many non-PostScript printers, such as the H-P inkjet and laser printers.

Distribution Media:

PC diskettes only, normally compressed with *tar + gzip*. A shareware version is available via *ftp* (ftp://ftp.cs.wisc.edu/pub/ghost/aladdin) for non-commercial use only.

Licensing Policy:

Redistribution in non-commercial contexts (i.e., if no money changes hands in connection with the distribution) is allowed without license. Any commercial distribution of any kind requires a commercial license, with a negotiated license fee. If you are a commercial organization and intend to distribute Aladdin Ghostscript in a manner for which you believe you don't need a license, please check with us: "in connection with" is only a shorthand for the terms of the actual non-commercial license.

OS Provisions:

Will run on any Linux version. Will display on any X11R4 or R5 compatible window system.

Documentation:

English, probably about 30 pages. On-line only (no printed doc). No on-line help.

Product Support:

No training available. Maintenance (bug fixing) and updates are available with commercial licenses and unavailable otherwise.

Linux Support:

N/A

Extra Features and Add-Ons:

We offer commercial-quality sets of the 35 standard PostScript fonts at a price of $10 to end users and a much lower price to commercial licensees.

Available Since:

August 1994.

Countries with Distribution:

We distribute worldwide. Our only current overseas distributor is in Germany.

Price Range:

We will ship diskettes to end-users for a charge of $58 to cover service and materials costs. There is an additional charge for $50 for a custom configuration and of $20 (domestic) or $30 (international) for next-day mail. Commercial licensing prices are negotiated, and vary considerably.

Installed Base:

(L. Peter Deutsch estimates the number of users of the commercial version under Linux at about 12,000, as of Sep 23, 1994.)

Vendor:

```
Aladdin Enterprises
203 Santa Margarita Ave.
Menlo Park, CA 94025, USA
Phone:  +1 (415) 322-0103
Fax:    +1 (415) 322-1734
E-mail: ghost@aladdin.com
```

Entered:

Aug 26, 1994

8.2.2 MRJ Symbolic OCR

Description:

MRJ SOCR (Symbolic OCR) (TM) is an OCR program for Japanese text. SOCR reads TIFF files and recognizes Japanese text in scanned images. Output formats include PC, Mac, and Unix formats with Unicode, Shift-JIS, JIS, and EUC encodings. Also available for Sun OS.

Distribution Media:

3.5" Floppy Disks.

Licensing Policy:

One SOCR license per workstation.

OS Provisions:

Operating System: Linux 1.x, Window System: Motif run time library required, System RAM: 16 MB, Hard Disk: 6 MB.

Documentation:

Installation Guide and User Manual. All documentation is in English.

Product Support:

Technical support available via telephone, e-mail, and FAX.

Linux Support:

The Linux version of SOCR is fully supported. See Product Support.

Extra Features and Add-Ons:

Contact MRJ for information on OEM and software developer versions of SOCR.

Available Since:

August 1994

Countries with Distribution:

Distribution from U.S. Available for export.

Price Range:

Special Introductory Offer – $895 through 30 September 1994.

Installed Base:

Vendor:

```
MRJ, Inc.
10455 White Granite Drive
Oakton, VA 22124, USA
Phone:  +1 (703) 385-0700
Fax:    +1 (703) 385-4637
E-Mail: socr@mrj.com
```

Entered:

Sep 08,1994

8.2.3 SISCAD-P 1.3-3

Description:

SISCAD-P is a 2D-CAD system that gives engineers a production implementation of new design technologies - parametrics, variational geometry, inference sketching, a fully customizable user interface, constraint-based modeling and feature-based modeling. Today there is only a German version of SISCAD-P available. Unfortunately we can not yet provide a SISCAD-P version in any foreign language but we are already working on an English version. The release date for this version is not certain yet.

Distribution Media:

available   via   *ftp*
(sunsite.unc.edu://pub/Linux/X11/xapps/graphics/draw/siscadp1.3-3.tar.gz).
On diskette and CD-ROM available from several Linux distributors (i.e. CDs with sunsite mirrors. hm)

Licensing Policy:

SISCAD-P is running on several Unix workstations and is available as shareware for Linux. The shareware version is a FULL featured package which is restricted to at maximum 10 parts with each 2000 objects. It is provided at no charge to the user for evaluation. With this concept, the user can test all features of SISCAD-P and has a chance to try before buying it. After a reasonable trial period, the user must make a registration payment and will receive a license code which will disable all limitations.

OS Provisions:

X Windows running under Linux. 8 MByte of memory minimum, 16 MByte or more recommended. Slackware Linux 0.19pl14 or newer. Fvwm or Mwm window manager recommended.

Documentation:

Online help and several documents in PostScript, DVI and ASCII format.

Product Support:

Product support for registered users via e-mail, fax and BBS

Linux Support:

N/A

Extra Features and Add-Ons:

N/A

Available Since:

February 1994

Countries with Distribution:

Germany (worldwide via ftp).

Price Range:

DM 399 commercial users; DM 49 students version.

Installed Base:

20 registered users as per Sep 22, 1994.

Vendor:

```
Staedtler Mars GmbH & Co
Geschaeftsbereich Informationssysteme - SIS
Moosaeckerstrasse 3
D-90427 Nuernberg, Germany
Phone: +49 (0)911/3080-691
Fax:   +49 (0)911/3080-692
BBS:   +49 (0)911/3080-609, login: info, password: gast
E-Mail: support@SIS.Staedtler.DE
Contact: Helmrich Streitmatter
```

Entered:

Sep 19, 1994

8.2.4 TecPlot 6.0

Description:

Tecplot is a plotting program for visualizing and analyzing engineering and scientific data. The standard version includes XY, 2D and 3D-surface plotting. An optional extension (called 3DV) adds the capability to visualize 3D volumetric data. With Tecplot you don't have to write a program, just input your data and start visualizing immediately. (for more information consult vendor. hm)

Distribution Media:

3.5-inch floppies, 150MB-QIC, 4mm DAT, 8mm tape, (CD-ROM available November 1994)

Licensing Policy:

Single-computer license (node-locked) Evaluation copies are available.

OS Provisions:

4 MByte is minimum RAM, required hard disk space is 20 MByte.

Documentation:

Printed Users Manual 512 pages, partial online help info. English.

Product Support:

Update and technical support included with license for first three months and available for extra charge after that. Training classes are available; price is negotiable.

Linux Support:

N/A

Extra Features and Add-Ons:

3DV is an optional package of volumetric features available for an additional $300 USD.

Available Since:

August 1993

Countries with Distribution:

(many, please consult vendor. For Germany, see below. hm)

Price Range:

USD 995 to USD 1395 per Node-locked License

Installed Base:

Vendor:

```
Amtec Engineering, Inc
PO Box 3633
Bellevue, WA 98009-3633, USA
Phone:   +1 (206) 827-3304 (800-676-7568 in US/Canada)
Fax:     +1 (206) 827-3989
E-Mail: tecplot@amtec.com
Contact: Tom Chan

For Germany:
GENIAS Software GmbH
Erzgebirgstr. 2
D-93073 Neutraubling, Germany
Phone: +49 (0)94 01/92 00-11
Fax: +49 (0)94 01/92 00-92
Contact: Johannes Grawe
E-mail: jo@genias.de
```

Entered:

Sep 24, 1994 (updated May 15, 1995)

8.3 Development tools

Compilers, development environments and so on.

8.3.1 Basmark QuickBASIC

Description:

The Basmark QuickBASIC Compiler is a multi-user IBM-PC BASICA, MBASIC and Microsoft Quick-BASIC Compiler designed to provide performance and consistency across a variety of machines (e.g. i386 and i486, Pentium, SPARC, RS/6000, HP PA-Risc) under Unix, AIX, SunOS, Linux, HP-UX, Xenix.

Distribution Media:

3.5" diskette

Licensing Policy:

Per machine, no run-time restrictions.

OS Provisions:

GNU GAS and LD must be installed.

Documentation:

400+ page manual, release and installation notes.

Product Support:

Updates available for $39.00 less shipping. Maintenance contracts available.

Linux Support:

N/A

Extra Features and Add-Ons:

C-ISAM (Informix Inc.) Interface in C source code form. Cost $35.00.

Available Since:

December 1993

Countries with Distribution:

to purchase from manufacturer directly.

Price Range:

$195.00 (less shipping)

Installed Base:

Vendor:

```
Basmark Corporation
P.O. Box 40450
Cleveland, OH 44140, USA
Phone:  +1 (216) 871-8855
Fax:    +1 (216) 871-9011
E-Mail: jgo@ios.com  (for orders)
Contact: Joseph O'Toole (for orders)
```

Entered:

Sep 23, 1994

8.3.2   CODINE

Description:

CODINE Job Management System – A Job-Queueing System that allows optimal utilization of a heterogeneous workstation cluster. The system features static and dynamic loadbalancing, checkpointing, support for parallel programs etc. It is available for SUN, HP, IBM, SGI, CRAY, CONVEC, DEC and LINUX

Distribution Media:

QIC tape, DAT tape, ftp

Licensing Policy:

free   demo   available   at   *ftp://129.69.18.15/pub/info/producer/genias/codine* (ftp://129.69.18.15/pub/info/producer/genias/codine)

OS Provisions:

The GUI requires Motif, however the GUI is not necessary to use the system. A command line interface is available. RAM: 1,5 MB for the master daemon; HD: some Megs.

Documentation:

Manual in English available (also via ftp in PS format)

Product Support:

GENIAS offers training and support for the CODINE system. Please ask for prices.

Linux Support:

N/A

Extra Features and Add-Ons:

N/A

Available Since:

1994

Countries with Distribution:

Switzerland, Sweden, Taiwan, USA, Italy

Price Range:

N/A

Installed Base:

some 20. LINUX PC's are mostly only add-ons to a larger cluster.

Vendor:

```
GENIAS Software GmbH
Erzgebirgstr. 2
D-93073 Neutraubling, Germany
Tel.: 09401/9200-11, Fax: 09401/9200-92
Phone: +49 94 01/92 00-11
Fax: +49 94 01/92 00-92
Contact: Johannes Grawe
E-mail: jo@genias.de
```

Entered:

May 10, 1995

8.3.3   ICC11

Description:

ICC11 is a full featured C Compiler for the HC11 microcontrollers: including floating point support, interspersed C and assembly listing, and much more. It's available in native Linux version, as well as DOS and OS2 versions.

Distribution Media:

It's available on 3.5" diskette. Latest upgrades are available via FTP, usually for free or for a minimal charge.

Licensing Policy:

There   is   an
early version of the compiler available for free use in *ftp://ftp.netcom.com/pub/im/imagecft/icc11/free*
(ftp://ftp.netcom.com/pub/im/imagecft/icc11/free)

OS Provisions:

There is no special hardware or software requirement to run ICC11.

Documentation:

The product comes with a 100 page manual.

Product Support:

Preferred   technical   support   via   e-mail.   Send   mail   to   *imagecft@netcom.com*
(mailto:imagecft@netcom.com).

Linux Support:

N/A

Extra Features and Add-Ons:

N/A

Available Since:

Feb 95. Version 2 with floating point support available now.

Countries with Distribution:

N/A

Price Range:

USD45 plus USD5 S&H for U.S.A. and Canada, USD10 S&H for elsewhere.

Installed Base:

We have over 400 customers worldwide.

Vendor:

```
ImageCraft
P.O. Box 64226
Sunnyvale, CA 94088-4226, USA
Phone/Fax: +1 (408) 749-0702
Contact: Richard Man or Christina Willrich
E-mail: imagecft@netcom.com
```

Entered:

April 10, 1995

8.3.4   INSURE++

Description:

INSURE++ runtime debugger for C and C++ programms. INSURE detects memory leaks, problems in memory mismanagements during runtime.

Distribution Media:

DAT tape, QIC tape

Licensing Policy:

free   demo   at   *ftp://129.69.18.15/pub/info/producer/genias/insure*
(`ftp://129.69.18.15/pub/info/producer/genias/insure`).

OS Provisions:

N/A

Documentation:

N/A

Product Support:

N/A

Linux Support:

N/A

Extra Features and Add-Ons:

Available Since:

1994

Countries with Distribution:

USA, Sweden, Netherlands

Price Range:

DEM 895 (with 25% educational discount)

Installed Base:

few

Vendor:

```
GENIAS Software GmbH
Erzgebirgstr. 2
D-93073 Neutraubling, Germany
Tel.: 09401/9200-11, Fax: 09401/9200-92
Phone: +49 94 01/92 00-11
Fax: +49 94 01/92 00-92
Contact: Johannes Grawe
E-mail: jo@genias.de
```

Entered:

May 10, 1995

8.3.5   ISE Eiffel 3

Description:

ISE Eiffel 3 provides a powerful and user-friendly O-O programming environment designed for large, complex systems. It is an integrated GUI workbench consisting of a variety of Eiffel-based components: EiffelBench melting-ice workbench, EiffelBuild interface builder and application generator, EiffelVision graphics and GUI library, and EiffelBase basic libraries.

Distribution Media:

1/4 inch Tape, DAT.

Licensing Policy:

Each hardware platform type requires a different runtime. The standard delivery of the EiffelBench comes with the runtime for the given platform type; additional runtimes may be purchased for cross-development.

ISE charges run-time license fees, only for copyrighted commercial products built using ISE's technology. For further information contact vendor.

OS Provisions:

Motif required

Documentation:

Documentation including the Prentice Hall books "Eiffel: The Language, Reusable Software: The Base Object-Oriented Component Libraries" and "An Object-Oriented Environment: Principles & Practices".

Product Support:

The purchase prices include free technical support for three months. The price of technical support per year is 30% (payable in advance) of the standard software purchase and provides assistance with problems encountered in the use of the software. Support is provided by electronic mail, fax or telephone.

Linux Support:

N/A

Extra Features and Add-Ons:

A special license for students and individuals of ISE Eiffel on Linux includes the full graphical environment.

Available Since:

June 1994

Countries with Distribution:

(many individual distributors worldwide; too many to name them here. please consult vendor. hm)

Price Range:

US$295.00 plus shipping & handling. USA: $15.00 for UPS Ground, $20.00 for UPS 2nd Day Air; Canada: $35.00 for UPS 2nd Day Air; Other: $60.00 for UPS International Air

Installed Base:

Vendor:

```
Interactive Software Engineering, Inc.
270 Storke Road, Suite 7
Goleta, CA 93117, USA
Phone:  +1 (805) 685-1006
Fax:    +1 (805) 685-6869
E-mail: queries@eiffel.com
```

Entered:

Sep 09, 1994

8.3.6   Metacard

Description:

MetaCard is a hypermedia/Rapid Application Development environment for X11/Unix workstations that is compatible with Apple Corp.'s HyperCard. MetaCard can be used by programmers and sophisticated end users to build Motif applications and hypermedia documents using a powerful, direct manipulation editor and a simple scripting language. Stacks developed with MetaCard are portable among all supported platforms (14 for release 1.3) and can be distributed with the MetaCard engine without licensing fees or royalties.

Distribution Media:

Anonymous FTP and 3.5" diskettes.

Licensing Policy:

MetaCard can be licensed to a single, named individual, but can be used on any machine or combination of machines by that user. Multiple user packages are also available.

The save-disabled distribution is available via anonymous FTP from *ftp.metacard.com* (`ftp://ftp.metacard.com/MetaCard`) and *ftp.uu.net* (`ftp://ftp.uu.net/vendor/MetaCard`).

OS Provisions:

The 1.4 release was built on Linux 0.99pl14. 8 MByte RAM minimum, 16MByte recommended. 800x600 minimum display resolution. Requires about 5 MByte disk space.

Documentation:

Complete on-line documentation is supplied. Printed documentation is an extra-cost option.

Product Support:

Free email technical support. Free upgrades during the 1.X series of releases.

Linux Support:

N/A

Extra Features and Add-Ons:

A library version of MetaCard that can be linked directly to C programs (Embedded MetaCard) is available at extra cost.

Available Since:

February 1994

Countries with Distribution:

Direct sales world wide.

Price Range:

$247.50. $495 for a license that works on Linux and all Unix platforms.

Installed Base:

Vendor:

```
MetaCard Corporation
4710 Shoup pl.
Boulder, CO 80303, USA
Phone:  +1 (303) 447-3936
Fax:    +1 (303) 499-9855
E-Mail: info@metacard.com
Contact: Scott Raney
```

Entered:

Sep 20, 1994

8.3.7 tgdb

Description:

tgdb is a graphical user interface for gdb, the GNU debugger.

Distribution Media:

Anonymous   ftp,   available
as *source* (`ftp://sunsite.unc.edu:/pub/Linux/devel/debuggers/tgdb-1.0.src.tgz`)
package   or   *Linux*   *binary*
(`ftp://sunsite.unc.edu:/pub/Linux/devel/debuggers/tgdb-1.0.srcbin-linux.tgz`)
package.

Licensing Policy:

Shareware

OS Provisions:

Any Un*x-like OS (including Linux); requires X11R5.

Documentation:

Comprehensive online/hypertext help (English); can be converted into various formats for printing.

Product Support:

Updated when required; hotline and email support available.

Linux Support:

N/A

Extra Features and Add-Ons:

N/A

Available Since:

August 1994

Countries with Distribution:

worldwide (ftp)

Price Range:

US$30 or DM50.00 per user; site licenses available.

Installed Base:

Vendor:

```
HighTec EDV-Systeme GmbH
Neue Bahnhofstr. 37
D-66386 St. Ingbert, Germany
Phone: +49 (0)6894/87 00 41
Fax:   +49 (0)6894/87 00 44
Email: tgdb@hightec.saarlink.de
Contact: Michael Schumacher
```

Entered:

Sep 09, 1994

8.3.8 TowerEiffel

Description:

TowerEiffel is a complete software engineering tool for creating scalable systems in the object oriented programming language Eiffel. TowerEiffel for Linux includes a high performance Eiffel 3 compiler, open development environment, programming tools including debugger, browser and automatic documentation generation, and a base set of reusable software components. Key features include fast executable code, global system optimization, user controllable garbage collection, clear and precise error messages, exception handling, genericity, automatic system builds, automatic documentation generation and built in test support. A unique capability of TowerEiffel is Eiffel, C, and C++ interoperability.

Distribution Media:

4 Diskettes or QIC150 Tape

Licensing Policy:

TowerEiffel is licensed on a per user, right-to-use basis. There are no run-time fees. Two types of licenses are available:
1) Non-Commercial license for students and individuals developing software which will no be distributed for commercial use. Upon permission from Tower, software can be published as shareware.
2) Commercial license for commercial developers who will distribute or deploy developed software for commercial use.

OS Provisions:

no special requirements

Documentation:

500+ page user reference manual in English

Product Support:

60 days free technical support provided with purchase. Non-Commercial support is 30% per year of current retail price. Includes technical support via email or fax, and free upgrades (excluding shipping cost). Different support programs available for commercial developers.

Linux Support:

n/a

Extra Features and Add-Ons:

TowerEiffel supports interoperability with C and C++. Motif GUI Libraries, and Data Structure Library (Booch) sold as add-ons.

Available Since:

November 1994

Countries with Distribution:

TowerEiffel is available worldwide with authorized distributors in UK, Ireland, Germany, Switzerland, Japan, and China

Price Range:

USD249 for non-commercial license; USD1295 for commercial license

Installed Base:

N/A

Vendor:

```
Tower Technology Corporation
1501 West Koenig Lane
Austin, TX 78756, USA
Phone:   800 285 5124 or +1 512 452 9455
Fax:     +1 512 452 1721
E-mail: tower@twr.com
www: http://www.cm.cf.ac.uk/Tower/
```

Entered:

April 5, 1995

8.4   Financial Software

All about financial tools.

8.4.1   BB Tool

Description:

BB Tool is a powerful stock charting, technical analysis and portfolio management tool.

Distribution Media:

FTP download, or 3.5" diskettes

Licensing Policy:

Per machine license.   FREE demo version is available via FTP at *ftp://ftp.portal.com/pub/ctor* (ftp://ftp.portal.com/pub/ctor)

OS Provisions:

kernel version 1.1.52+, XFree86 3.1.1

Documentation:

PostScript formatted document is available via FTP download (file bb_doc.ps.gz). The document has 42 pages including tutorial and reference guide. Man pages are also provided. BB Tool has extensive context sensitive online help. Available in English only.

Product Support:

Free patch of current version available via Email or FTP.

Linux Support:

   N/A

Extra Features and Add-Ons:

   Historic stock data on US Stock Exchange (NYSE, AMEX, NASDAQ) are available at USD1.00 per
   stock. Daily stock quote is available FREE, distributed via Email.

Available Since:

   Sun SPARC version available since December 1993. Linux version available April 1995.

Countries with Distribution:

   USA

Price Range:

   Linux version: USD79; Sun SPARC version: USD89 Plus tax and shipping (if applicable)

Installed Base:

   N/A

Vendor:

```
Falkor Technologies
P.O.Box 14201
Fremont, CA 94539, U.S.A.
Phone: +1 (510) 505-0700
Contact: Henry Chen
Email: ctor@shell.portal.com
```

Entered:

   May 10, 1995

8.5   Network Management

Network management tools that are Linux based can save quite a bit on your budget ;-)

8.5.1   NetEye

Description:

   NetEye is a complete SNMP based Network Management System. NetEye's main features are:
   Standard X-Window System and OSF/Motif user interface
   Autodiscovery and automapping of all IP based objects
   MIB Browser to simplify the navigation of all MIB-2 and private.enterprise variables
   Trouble ticketing system capable of storing and forwarding tickets via email and fax
   Capture, filtering and storing of SNMP device traps
   Topological, logical and spatial network views using color codes
   User definable bitmaps to represent network objects on maps
   User definable alarm and warning thresholds and time plots of any number of MIB variables
   Builtin address book to store and retrieve all fax and email addresses of other network managers
   Online hyper help for unexperienced operators

Distribution Media:

   3.5" Floppy disk or ftp

Licensing Policy:

Licensed per CPU, also available for OEM and source licensing. Full product is available on request for one month free of charge evaluation.

OS Provisions:

X11R5 and a video card capable of handling 256 colors. An ethernet card or PPP dialup connection. Minimum hardware requirements are 16 MByte RAM and a 386/40 CPU for managing small networks. Best performances using a 486DX2/66 CPU. Disk requirements: 12 MByte for basic installation that will grow depending on use and size of database of managed objects.

Documentation:

Documentation in English. Booklet of about 100 pages detailing all operations.

Product Support:

email, fax, telephone. First 90 days free. USD450/year for ongoing support and updates.

Linux Support:

N/A

Extra Features and Add-Ons:

Comes with a compiled and ready to use copy of University Ingres 8.9

Available Since:

September 1993

Countries with Distribution:

UK, USA, Canada, Italy and worldwide (manufacturer)

Price Range:

Complete network management system with trouble ticketing service: USD5500 list price. Source and OEM contracts: contact manufacturer.

Vendor:

```
Soft*Star s.r.l.
Via Camburzano 9
10143 Torino, Italy
Phone:   +39 11 746092
Fax:     +39 11 746487
Contact: Enrico Badella
E-mail: softstar@pol88a.polito.it
        eb@relay1.iunet.it
```

Entered:

November 1, 1994

8.6 Text Processing

All kind of text processing, ASCII- and GUI-based

8.6.1 CRISP

Description:

CRISP is a graphical text editor on various Unix and Windows platforms which is 100% compatible with BRIEF. What makes Crisp different is that it tries to deliver its power in an intuitive point & click environment, without taking away the keyboard.

Distribution Media:

3.5" diskettes. Tapes available at extra charge.

Licensing Policy:

Both node locked and floating licenses are available. Demonstration copy is archived at *ftp.uu.net* (ftp://ftp.uu.net/vendor/vital).

OS Provisions:

RAM: 0.5 MByte, harddisk: 6 MByte (full), 2 MByte minimum. Openlook / Motif / Character versions are available on just about all commercial Unix platforms, Linux and Windows 3.1/NT.

Documentation:

printed, on-line manuals, on-line help, English

Product Support:

updates and maintenance can be purchased at $100.00 US per license per year. It provides free upgrades for one year.

Linux Support:

We are currently giving away Slackware Professional 2.0 away for users ordering Crisp. This promotion however is only valid till end of October.

Extra Features and Add-Ons:

N/A

Available Since:

March 1994

Countries with Distribution:

International Distributor: VITAL; Europe: Lasermoon

Price Range:

$99.99 without printed manuals. Printed user manual can be purchased at an additional $40.00

Installed Base:

Vendor:

```
VITAL SOLUTIONS INC
4109 Candlewyck Drive
Plano, TX 75024, USA
Phone:  +1 (214) 491-6907
Fax:    +1 (214) 491-6909
E-Mail: info@vital.com
Contact: Gigi Mehrotra
```

Entered:

Sep 20, 1994

8.6.2 ibgsXaed

Description:

ibgsXaed is an editor which is portable to every X Window System that offers OSF/Motif. The editor has normal edit functions and a lot of special features that support newcomers and professionals (f.e. function keys for system commands execution, variable fonts, undo, redo, online help, hotlist, iconbar, etc.).

Distribution Media:

3.5" diskette

Licensing Policy:

free demo version

OS Provisions:

X Window System X11R5, OSF/Motif 1.2, approx. 2 MByte harddisk

Documentation:

printed manual, online help, both in English or German

Product Support:

hotline, updates

Linux Support:

N/A

Extra Features and Add-Ons:

N/A

Available Since:

July 1994

Countries with Distribution:

Price Range:

DM 799,- for one license, sliding prices for more licenses

Installed Base:

Vendor:

```
ibgs GmbH
Promenade 7
D-52076 Aachen, Germany
Phone:  +49 (0)2408/9455-53
Fax:    +49 (0)2408/9455-15
Contact: Mr.Sohn
```

Entered:

Sep 28,1994

8.7 X Windows related stuff

Alternative X Windows servers, widget sets, window managers.

8.7.1 Metrolink Motif

Description:

Motif 1.2.4 - Graphical User Interface - Complete Runtime and Development package with Color Pixmap Support.

Distribution Media:

3.5" diskettes (3), or FTP: The customer places the order with a credit card, then we email him our license agreement, installation instructions, release notes, and the FTP instructions – including the current password.

Licensing Policy:

Licensing is per CPU. NFS mounting not allowed. Site licenses are available for 10 or more copies.

OS Provisions:

Linux 0.99pl15g or higher, 8-16 MByte RAM, 9 MByte HardDisk

Documentation:

OSF User's Manual (120 pages), man pages (electronic), English.

Product Support:

90 days free tech support, 30-day money back guarantee, Extended Tech Support Contract $100 US per year.

Linux Support:

N/A

Extra Features and Add-Ons:

N/A

Available Since:

Motif 1.2.4 for Linux since August 1994 (Motif 1.2.2 for Linux since June 1993).

Countries with Distribution:

USA, Germany, France.

Price Range:

$149.00 US through October 31, 1994; $199 US after that if the special offer isn't extended.

Installed Base:

2,600 copies as of Sep 23, 1994

Vendor:

```
Metro Link Incorporated
4711 N. Powerline Rd.
Fort Lauderdale, FL 33309, USA
Phone:  +1 (305) 938-0283
Fax:    +1 (305) 938-1982
E-Mail: sales@metrolink.com (general info)
Contact:  Holly Robinson (holly@metrolink.com, other questions \& orders)
```

Entered:

Sep 19, 1994

8.7.2   X Inside X Servers

Description:

Replacement X Server for the XFree86 and other Servers for Linux. Supports Actix, ColorGraphics, Compaq, ELSA, Matrox, Number 9, ATI, Boca, Diamond, Orchid, Reveal, STB, TechWorks. Chipsets include Matrox, Number 9 Imagine-128, ATI Mach64, S3 964. Supports Mouse Systems, Microsoft, Logitech mice.

Distribution Media:

single floppy diskette

Licensing Policy:

Per cpu license. Site licenses available.

OS Provisions:

Tested on versions of Linux between 1.0.8 and 1.1.18. No known problems with any Linux distribution. Requires around 3MB hard disk. Best used with a mouse...

Documentation:

Postscript formatted manual available via *ftp* (`ftp://ftp.xinside.com/accelx/1.0/Manual`). Hardcopy shipped with first copy of Server license.

Product Support:

Installation support included in price; available by email, Fax (and by phone if we have to).

Update service available, US$100 for four revisions a year, to track new chipsets and other performance improvements. US$50 to upgrade to specified revision (e.g. 1.1 to 1.2).

Product automatically sends email on failure. We may respond to a problem before you know you have it!

Linux Support:

N/A

Extra Features and Add-Ons:

Various extensions will be offered, starting with PEX.

Available Since:

May 94

Countries with Distribution:

Distribution currently in negotiation. Complete information available via *ftp* (`ftp://ftp.xinside.com/accelx/1.0/All/prodinfo.txt`). Europe: Delix Computers, Stuttgart

Price Range:

US$199.00. Student, academic and VAR discount programs. Student discount is 20% for Release 1.0 and 50% for Release 1.1. Post & Packing is between US$3 for US Mail to US$15 for Next Day delivery. Delix: Accelerated X DEM 159, Motif 2.0 DEM 259.

Installed Base:

Vendor:

```
X Inside Incorporated
P.O. Box 10774
Golden, CO 80401-0610, USA
Phone:   +1 (303) 384-9999
Fax:     +1 (303) 384-9778
```

```
E-mail: info@xinside.com

Europe:
Delix Computer GmbH
Hasenbergstr. 113
D-70176 Stuttgart, Germany
Phone:  +49 711/636 22 20
Fax:    +49-711/636 22 30
E-mail: info@delix.de
```

Entered:

April 7,1995

8.8   Other Software

Everything else that does not fit in one of the other sections by now.

8.8.1   Amadeus music software

Description:

Fully professional music notation and printing software. Supports MIDI-interface for realtime and step input. Printer drivers to some matrix-, Ink-jet and Laserprinters. Supports postscript translation for output on PS-printers or use in Ghostscript for printing on any printer supported by GS. Supports TIFF (import and export). The functionality is somewhat of a roff or TEX look alike. ASCII-files (one per system) containing source are processed into files, containing one page each, which can be converted into graphic files for viewing or editing on screen or printing, or into other formats as PS or TIFF. The software is highly automated in the actual note drawing. This makes it possible for blind musicians to print music for seeing if they use a blindsign-display to handle the computer.

Distribution Media:

Diskettes in tar-format (About 10)

Licensing Policy:

Strictly commercial. No demo at hand. Postscriptfile with detailed information and lots of music examples available. Post a message to *m8770@abc.se* (mailto:m8770@abc.se) and it will be sent to you.

OS Provisions:

Package contains kernel. XFree86 needed (not for blind users). 8Mb RAM, about 20 Mb HD.

Documentation:

Doc. in English and German.

Product Support:

Support via Tel. or Fax. Support free if the information not is available in the manuals. Updates about once a year, prices varies.

Linux Support:

Only if it is strictly related to the software

Extra Features and Add-Ons:

Are developed if requested. Price related to the work needed.

Available Since:

March 1994

Countries with Distribution:

Directly to the entire world from the developer except for Scandinavia. For Scandinavian customers: see Vendor

Price Range:

DEM 4000; Blind version DEM 6500; Upgrade from the Idris-version (Atari) DEM 2000

Installed Base:

N/A

Vendor:

```
Wolfgang Hamann
Amadeus Notenzats
Winterstr. 5
D-81543 Muenchen, Germany
Phone:   +49 89 669678
Fax:     +49 89 669579
Contact: Wolfgang Hamann

Scandinavian customers and e-mail:
Jerker Elsgard
MIDIBIT AB
Box 161
S-618 23 KOLMARDEN, Sweden
Phone/Fax: +46 11 391663
Contact: Jerker Elsgard
E-mail:  m8770@abc.se
```

Entered:

April 5, 1995

8.8.2   aqua_zis

Description:

(Time Series Information System). A system to store and maintain huge amounts of measurement data (mainly hydrological data). Time series with several 100,000's of values can be handled. You may retrieve, edit and insert data very fast. A lot of statistical and arithmetical operators are applicable. Time series may be visualized in a full scale GUI, includeing high performance zooming and scrolling. The user may define individual GUI's in an easy script language and with the time series programming language Azur. Reports on any paper size including full graphics are possible through Azur. Output is produced in Postscript and HPGL formats.

Distribution Media:

We install at your site. Demo disk available (*tar*)

Licensing Policy:

machine or site licenses available. Test licenses are limited in time.

OS Provisions:

Linux version 0.99pl6 or later. Motif required if you use the GUI features. When set up as a time series database server, no graphics is needed. RAM usage 8 – 16 MB. Disk space required: some 15 MB for executables and help files. For the data: several GB's.

Documentation:

printed manuals covering end user and admin tools (English version soon to appear). Program documentation and design available only in English.

Product Support:

12 months warranty, maintenance contract recommended. One day training at your site included.

Linux Support:

N/A

Extra Features and Add-Ons:

aqua_trop precipitation reconstruction tool using GIS methods. DigiTul digitizing of precipitation, water-level etc. paper registrations. aqua_log ground water data management.

Available Since:

Jan 1994

Countries with Distribution:

Germany, Austria, soon EC.

Price Range:

machine license: 39,000 DM, multiple machines: graduated discounts, site licenses on request, reasonable discout for universities.

Installed Base:

some 4 Linux-only systems are running.

Vendor:

```
aqua_plan
Ing.-Ges. fuer Problemloesungen
in Hydrologie und Umweltschutz mbH
Mozartstr. 16
D-52064 Aachen, Germany
Phone:   +49 (0)241/31430
Fax:     +49 (0)241/31499
```

Entered:

Aug 26, 1994

8.8.3 Maple V

Description:

Maple V Release 3 is a powerful general purpose computer algebra system. Maple V is a system for solving mathematical problems symbolically (instead of using paper and pencil and a lot of time) and numerically. Maple V's graphics (various types of 2D, 3D, animation) visualizes the solutions. Maple V also has a programming language (Pascal like) which allows you to extend the library of 2500+ functions.

Distribution Media:

3.5" disks

Licensing Policy:

License for unlimited use in time of the bought version, floating license with user based pricing

OS Provisions:

Linux kernel 1.0; XFree86 or Motif possible but not necessary; release number 2100: at least 8 MByte RAM suggested

Documentation:

3 books ("First Leaves: A Tutorial Introduction" 253 pgs., "Language Reference Manual", 267 pgs. and "The Maple Handbook" 497 pgs.), Installation Manual. Manual pages of all functions and commands, help browser, keyword search. Documentation and help in English, some books in various languages exist.

Product Support:

updates/maintenance depending on license, please call the distributor or WMSI.

Linux Support:

N/A

Extra Features and Add-Ons:

share library via email and *ftp* (`ftp://daisy.uwaterloo.ca/pub/maple`). Free mailing list available (`maple_group@daisy.waterloo.edu`).

Available Since:

September 94

Countries with Distribution:

US/Canada, Europe, Asia

Price Range:

German list price: DM 1785 (plus shipping and handling plus VAT). Please call the national distributor or WMSI.

Installed Base:

Vendor:

```
Waterloo Maple Software
450 Phillip Street, Waterloo, Ontario, Canada N2L 5J2
Phone: +1 (519) 747-2373
Fax:   +1 (519) 747-5284
email: info@maplesoft.on.ca

Germany, Switzerland and Austria:
Scientific Computers GmbH
Franzstr. 106
D-52064 Aachen, Germany
Phone: +49 (0)241/26041
Fax:   +49 (0)241/44983
E-Mail: info@scientific.de
Contact: Monika Germ
```

Entered:

Sep 19, 1994

8.8.4 PROCHEM-C

Description:

PROCHEM-C is an integrated Software System for users dealing with design, construction, maintenance, operation and control of plants in the fields of

- Pipeline Construction
- Chemical & Pharmaceutical Industry
- Power Plant Construction

- Petrochemical Industry
- Food Processing
- Environment Technology

Distribution Media:

DAT or QIC150

Licensing Policy:

per Workstation or Server-License

OS Provisions:

kernel version 1.0 , modified portmapper/mount XFree86 Version 2.1, Motif Version 1.2.3, RAM : 32 - 64 MByte (min. 16 MByte) DISK: 1 GByte (min. 500 MByte) Swap 120 MByte (min. 80 MByte)

Documentation:

ON-Line integrated in PROCHEM-C (printed optional) ca. 1700 Pages. German or English.

Product Support:

Update Service : All 3 Months or on User-request. Prices for Maintenance and Training on request.

Linux Support:

Only for Problems concerning LINUX <-> PROCHEM-C

Extra Features and Add-Ons:

N/A

Available Since:

1983, LINUX Version since 1993

Countries with Distribution:

N/A

Price Range:

DEM 2,000 to DEM 65,000 (i.a.w. amount of features. hm)

Installed Base:

N/A

Vendor:

```
COMPLANSOFT CAD GmbH
Sulzbacher Strasse 15 - 21
D-65812 Bad Soden, Germany
Phone:  +49 6196/56 06-0
Fax  :  +49 6196/56 06-66
Contact : Chris Chirila
```

Entered:

April 6, 1995

8.8.5 Reduce

Description:

REDUCE is a general purpose system for the symbolic manipulation of mathematical formulae (computer algebra) in science and engineering. More information via *WWW* (http://www.zib-berlin.de/Symbolik/reduce).

Distribution Media:

REDUCE for Linux is normally distributed on 3.5 inch diskettes. Tape cartridges of different formats are available on request.

Licensing Policy:

One time fee per installation. Discount for multiple licenses. Free demo version available via *ftp* (ftp://ftp.zib-berlin.de/pub/reduce/demo/linux).

OS Provisions:

Independent of LINUX kernel: the .c and .s sources for the LISP kernel are included and can be recompiled locally. X Windows not necessary but recommended. 8 Mbyte RAM recommended, better more.

Documentation:

A 230 page User's manual is available. A reference manual is accessible in hypertext style on line under X Windows. All documents in English. The manual and additional documentation on disk in LaTeX.

Product Support:

Free patches of the current version available via electronic mail or ftp.

Linux Support:

N/A

Extra Features and Add-Ons:

N/A

Available Since:

July 1993

Countries with Distribution:

All countries except Iraq and Yugoslavia. Local distributors in Russia, Japan, Czec Republic, China.

Price Range:

Personal REDUCE: approx. USD99; Professional REDUCE: approx. USD499. Plus freight and tax.

Installed Base:

several dozens

Vendor:

```
Konrad-Zuse-Zentrum Berlin
Heilbronner Str. 10
D-10711 Berlin-Wilmersdorf, Germany
Phone:   +49 (0)30/89604-195
Fax:     +49 (0)30/89604-125
E-Mail: melenk@zib-berlin.de
Contact: H.Melenk
```

Entered:

Sep 28, 1994

8.8.6 ROSIN NC

Description:

ROSIN-NC-Werkbank (*ger*: workbench) The ROSIN-NC-Werkbank is a comprehensive set of tools which accomplish a CAD system. These tools comprise the ROSIN-VDAFS-Processor to process digitized data, and data in the VDAFS format; the ROSIN-Post Processors to generate 2- to 5-axis milling programs for all major CNC process controls; the ROSIN-NC-Editor to analyze and edit existing NC programs; the ROSIN-NC-Visualiser to visualize the tool path and generate printed information about a NC program; the ROSIN-Engraver to mill logos or fonts of any kind.

Distribution Media:

Tapes (DAT, QuarterInch) or floppy disk

Licensing Policy:

All tools of the ROSIN-NC-Werkbank are independently licensed via the ROSIN License System, the customer gets a production license for each purchased tool. The combination of license types with different tools is possible. There are individual licenses for single users, 2-5 users etc. Please consult vendor for more information.

OS Provisions:

Kernel Version higher or equal to 0.99pl14; Motif; RAM 16 MByte, recommended 20 MByte; the necessary disk space for a complete installation with all tools is 25 MByte. It is recommended to ensure a free disk space of at least 1,5 times the size of the input file(s).

Documentation:

An Online Help Function is available with all tools. With the purchase of each tool a manual is supplied in the language chosen by the customer (languages available: German, English, French and Italian, other languages on request). Size of manuals: Depending on the tool from 60 to 170 pages each.

Product Support:

Maintenance contracts are offered for all tools and cost 1,3% per month of the license price. With a maintenance contract the customer gets regular product updates and manual updates. Migration to a different hardware platform is significantly cheaper (3% of the license price instead of 12% for customers without maintenance contract). The telephone hotline is free of charge. Our telephone hotline is available from 8.30 to 17.00 MET, languages are German and English. We offer special prices for product installation and training courses (75% of the normal service prices) for product customers. Prices for product updates can be provided on request.

Linux Support:

(there was no "official" statement by ROSIN, however, I was told on the phone that ROSIN ships complete systems with pre-installed software, and that they would offer limited Linux support as far as handling their software is concerned. hm)

Extra Features and Add-Ons:

N/A

Available Since:

1994

Countries with Distribution:

Germany, France and Mexico (please consult vendor for more information). We are looking for distributors in the UK, Spain and Italy.

Price Range:

The lower prices (in DM) are for Single User Licenses, the higher ones for Multi User Licenses, floating type. Prices for all other licenses are included in this price range.

ROSIN-VDAFS-Processor 7500 to 9750 ROSIN-3-axis Post Processor 4500 to 11050 ROSIN-5-axis Post Processor 13500 to 32500 ROSIN-NC-Editor 7500 to 9750 ROSIN-NC-Visualiser 3500 to 4550 ROSIN-Engraver 1500 to 1950

Installed Base:

Vendor:

```
ROSIN Gesellschaft fuer technische Datenverarbeitung mbH
Roniger Weg 13
D-53545 Linz am Rhein, Germany
Phone:   +49 (0)2644/97003-0
Fax:     +49 (0)2644/97003-32
Contact: Gisela Buechner (Marketing)
```

Entered:

Sep 19, 1994

8.8.7 Unix Cockpit

Description:

The Unix Cockpit (UC) is a nifty new file manager for Unix/X11 that smoothly integrates a directory tree, file browsers, custom menus and the classic Unix shells into one highly customizable productivity tool of a kind long missed on Unix systems.

Distribution Media:

anon. ftp from ftp.uu.net (192.48.96.9), directory /vendor/UniX11/linux.

Licensing Policy:

On Linux, USD25 shareware. For the people who wrote Linux, free.

OS Provisions:

Kernel 1.0.8 or higher. Small, single file executable (500k). No installation necessary.

Documentation:

Fully indexed, postscript version of tutorial is available via ftp. Tutorial is also available online from within UC. UC has full context sensitive online help. The language used is English.

Product Support:

Small updates and bug fixes are free and made available via ftp. Extra support is via email courtesy support hotline at support@UniX11.com. Special training/installation help on request.

Linux Support:

N/A

Extra Features and Add-Ons:

N/A

Available Since:

The Linux version is beta testing since 11/94. The SGI versions have been shipping since 9/94. SunOS, HP & DEC Alpha versions are in beta, too.

Countries with Distribution:

All distribution goes over the internet.

Price Range:

USD25 shareware.

Installed Base:

It is still a beta version, which is free, so no Linux copies have sold. Quite a few beta testers, though.

Vendor:

```
Henrik Klagges
UniX11 Software Development Corp
Moorbachweg 7
D-83209 Prien, Germany
E-mail: henrik@UniX11.com
```

Entered:

April 5, 1995

8.9   Free Software for Commercial Hardware

This section is somewhat "exotic". It covers free Linux software (drivers et cetera) for specialized hardware. This is no "commercial software", however, the software is unusable without the hardware.

8.9.1   Cyclades Cyclom-Y

Description:

Cyclom-Y is serial multiport card for ISA/EISA PC's. 8 and 16-port models are available. There are RJ-12 and DB-25 connector options. It is based on the Cirrus Logic CD1400 serial processor. This RISC-based processor supports on-board character processing and allows speeds up to 115.2 kbps. Drivers for Xenix, SCO, ISC and UnixWare are available from Cyclades. There is a driver for Linux available in the Internet. Board variants: Cyclom-8Ys: 8 ports, RJ-12 connectors (no RTS signal); Cyclom-8Yo: 8 ports, DB-25 connectors in a octopus cable (full-modem); Cyclom-8Yb: 8 ports, DB-25 connectors in a external box (full-modem); Cyclom-8Yb+: 8 ports, same as 8Yb with surge protection; Cyclom-16Y: 16 ports, DB-25 connectors in a external box (full-modem).

Distribution Media:

3.5" diskettes

Licensing Policy:

The Linux device driver software is free and is available via ftp at *sunsite.unc.edu* (`ftp://sunsite.unc.edu/pub/Linux/kernel/patches/misc`).

OS Provisions:

(the driver is available as a patch relative to Linux 1.1.8. A driver for newer kernels is under development. hm)

Documentation:

The user's manual contains all the reference information to configure and install the card. Specific information about the Linux driver can be found in readme files.

Product Support:

SW updates from Internet. Cyclades will provide technical support on the hardware, but the driver is a freeware and is provided "as is". Cyclades makes no warranties about the suitability of this software for any purposes. Some companies bundle the driver in their Linux distributions and can help in the installation and configuration of the card.

Linux Support:

N/A

Extra Features and Add-Ons:

N/A

Available Since:

July 1994

Countries with Distribution:

worldwide

Price Range:

```
List Price (end user):

CYCLOM 8YS \$459
CYCLOM-8YO \$549
CYCLOM-8YB \$599
CYCLOM-8YB+ \$699
CYCLOM-16Y/DB25 \$794

Promotion for resellers only (first-time buyer):
CYCLOM 8YS \$99
CYCLOM-8YO \$199
CYCLOM-16Y/DB25 \$399

NOTE:  All prices are F.O.B. Fremont, CA, USA
```

Installed Base:

Vendor:

```
Cyclades Corporation.
44140 Old Warm Springs Blvd
Fremont, CA 94538, USA
Phone:  +1 (510) 770-9727 or (800) 347-6601
Fax:    +1 (510) 770-0355
E-Mail: cyclades@netcom.com
Contact: Doris Li (Sales and Marketing).
```

Entered:

Sep 24, 1994

8.10   German corner

This section contains software which is only marketed in Germany and/or other German-speaking countries or which is otherwise specific for Germany or German-speaking countries. The companies listed here sent me entries in German ...

Dieser Abschnitt enthaelt Software, die nur in Deutschland und oder anderen deutschsprachigen Laendern vertrieben wird, oder die anderweitig spezifisch fuer den deutschen oder deutschsprachigen Raum ist. Die hier gelisteten Firmen schickten mir deutsche Eintraege...

8.10.1 Orgaplus

Description:

Orgaplus vertreibt eine ganze Auswahl branchenspezifischer Loesungen:

- J5 - Projektmanagement & Controlling fuer Agenturen und Projektierende Unternehmen (ab DM 6000,-)
- netConnect - Kabelmanagement & Endstellenverwaltung (ab DM 5500,-)
- R4 - Warenwirtschaft fuer den Reifenhandel (ab DM 6500,-)
- W5 - Warenwirtschaft (ab DM 6500,-)
- S2 - Technik / Wartung / Service (ab DM 3500,-)
- M3 - Menue- & Security-Management entspr. ISO 9000 Audit Vorschriften (ab DM 850,-)
- F4 - Finanzbuchhaltung (ab DM 1750,-)
- APAS - Lohn & Gehalt mit Voll-DUEVO. AOK-Systemgeprueft (ab DM 2800,-)
- A7 - Vertrieb- & Marketingmanagement (ab DM 1250,-)
- T5 - Textverarbeitung (integriert in die opus Software) (ab DM 300,-)
- G4 - Reportgenerator fuer den Sachbearbeiter (ab DM 1500,-)
- V2 - Versandpapierschreibung, Zollabwicklung (ab DM 4500,-)
- B2 - Anlagenbuchhaltung (ab DM 2500,-)
- K4 - Kostenrechnung (ab DM 4500,-)
- E2 - Elektronische Archivierung (ab DM 20000,-)
- Data Dictionary (ab DM 4500,-)
- Klassenbibliothek (ab DM 8500,-)
- Programmgenerator (ab DM 12500,-)
- Maskengenerator Text + GUI (ab DM 2500,-)

Distribution Media:

Disketten, DAT

Licensing Policy:

Demonstration erfolgt in unserem Haus oder nach Vereinbarung, Kurzpraesentation ueber WWW ik Construktion.

OS Provisions:

Kernel Version 1.2, XFree86 alle Versionen, Motif nicht noetig, mind. 8 MByte RAM, mind. 30 MByte freien Speicherplatz.

Documentation:

Deutsches Handbuch, Online-Hilfe

Product Support:

Update-Service, Schulung, persoenliche und telefonische Betreuung, Fernwartung, Fernschulung. Preise siehe beiliegendem Honorarverzeichnis.

Linux Support:

Installation von Linux, komplette Einrichtung von Linux. Preisgestaltung nach Aufwand, wegen unterschiedlichen Kundenanforderungen.

Extra Features and Add-Ons:

Available Since:

Maerz 1995

Countries with Distribution:

Deutschland, Oesterreich, Schweiz, Niederlande

Price Range:

User- und modulabhaengige Staffelung siehe Preisliste.

Installed Base:

Vendor:

```
orgaplus Software GmbH
Tel.: +49 71 31/59 75-0
Fax: +49 71 31/59 75-99
E-mail: info@orgaplus.de
Contact: Herr Michael Walz (Geschaeftsfuehrer), Herr Jaeger (Vertrieb)
```

Entered:

10. Mai 1995

9 Support

Who you're gonna call ...

This section contains some companies who provide for Linux support. The raw format is as follows:

```
Company name
Address
Phone
Fax
E-mail
Contact
Type of support (via phone, e-mail, inhouse, training etc.)
sample prices
```

9.1 Companies

The following list is virtually alphabetically sorted.

- ARIS Technology, Inc.
  Mississippi Research & Technology Park, Suite 204
  Starkville, MS 39759, USA
  Phone: +1 (615) 325-2319
  Fax: +1 (615)323-3726
  Email: *info@aris.com* (mailto:info@aris.com)
  Contact: Dr. Michael L. Stokes
  Type of support: Local Area networking support, Linux/UNIX/Windows compatibility software, Custom software, Web Authoring, Internet Access(Broadband 65kpbs and above)
  Sample prices: Technical support (USD25/hour). For Internet prices, see *http://www.aris.com* (http://www.aris.com)

- Bitbybit Information Systems
  Radex Complex, Kluyverweg 2A
  NL-2629 HT Delft, The Netherlands

Phone: ++31-15-682569
Fax: ++31-15-682530
E-mail: *bitbybit@runner.knoware.nl* (mailto:bitbybit@runner.knoware.nl)
Contact: Ir. N. Simon
Type of support: On-site, Network
Sample prices: Hfl 120,- per hour.
Specialities: Installation, Internet Connectivity. Consulting, Custom-Made Software, Timetabling Systems, Database Interoperability.

- ClearVu TWS
  95 Clearview Drive
  Christiansburg, VA 24073, USA
  Phone: +1 (703) 231-3938
  Email: *Thomas Dunbar* (mailto:tdunbar@gserver.grads.vt.edu)
  Sample prices: email/phone USD70/hr; inhouse USD70/hr + traveling expenses
  Speciality: custom typesetting systems

- Couvares Consulting
  146 Mill Lane
  Amherst, MA 01002, USA
  Phone: +1 (413) 253-2589
  Email: *couvares@family.hampshire.edu* (mailto:couvares@family.hampshire.edu)
  Contact: Peter F. Couvares
  Type of support: We offer phone/email support, installation, ongoing administration, training, and specialized consulting for free software and Linux (and other UNIX) systems.
  Sample prices: USD40/hour commercial, USA20/hour nonprofit, sliding scale for personal

- Gregg Weber
  1076 Carol Lane #3
  Lafayette, CA 94549, USA
  Phone: +1 (510) 283-6264
  E-mail: *gregg@netcom.com* (mailto:gregg@netcom.com)
  Contact: Gregg Weber
  Type of support: ?
  Sample prices: USD40/hour, or per job quote. Free initial discussion of job requirements.
  Specialities: Installation, problem solving, C and assembly language programming, Embedded controller microcoding, cumputer systems and peripheral electronic design and development. Systems integration. Dos, MS-Windoze, X-Windows, Novell, Lantastic, internet email

- Frontier Internet Services Limited
  Allied House
  45 Hatton Garden
  London EC1N 8EX, England
  phone +44 (0)171 242 3383
  fax +44 (0)171 242 3384
  Email: *info@ftech.net* (mailto:info@ftech.net)
  Contact: Gareth Bult, Piers Cawley
  Type of support: All.
  Sample prices: UKP250/day

Specialities: Internet Services Providers Systems/Network Integraters (Unix/Novell/Windows) General Consultancy

- LEMIS
  Schellnhausen 2
  D-36325 Feldatal, Germany
  Phone: +49 (0)66 37/91 91 23
  Fax: +49 (0)66 37/91 91 22
  E-mail: *lemis@lemis.de* (mailto:lemis@lemis.de)
  Contact: Greg Lehey
  Type of support: Phone, Email, inhouse
  Sample prices Hotline: DEM 3 per minute or part thereof; Contract: DEM 150/hour

- Michael Koehne
  Bremer Strasse 117
  D-28816 Brinkum, Germany
  Phone: +49 (0)421 / 87 55 00
  Fax: +49 (0)421 / 87 55 51
  E-mail: *kraehe@bakunin.north.de* (mailto:kraehe@bakunin.north.de) (private)
  Type of support: N/A
  Sample prices: to be negotiated
  Specialities: Linux installation for database or internetworking use. OS/2 and WfW conectivity. Applications for Getraenkegrosshaendler, Buchhandlungen, Wasserwirtschaftsaemter.

- Randysoft Software
  286 Cresta Vista Way
  San Jose, CA 95119, USA
  Phone: +1 (408) 229-0119
  E-mail: *randy@randysoft.com* (mailto:randy@randysoft.com)
  Contact: Randy Hootman
  Type of support: Via phone, e-mail, inhouse, training, software development. C/C++, Perl, Shell, networking, internet, installation.
  Sample prices: Prices vary according to type of work and length of contract.

- Signum Support AB
  Box 2044
  S-580 02 Linkoping, Sweden
  Phone: +46 (0)13 21 46 00
  Fax: +46 (0)13 21 47 00
  E-mail: *info@signum.se* (mailto:info@signum.se)
  Contact: *Magnus Redin* (mailto:redin@signum.se), *Inge Wallin* (mailto:ingwa@signum.se)
  Type of support: Phone, fax and email support
  Sample prices: Linux on CDROM with manual and installation support for one system, SEK 1,380; Internet server with WWW, Gopher, FTP, Sendmail, News/INN and DNS with administrationing tools that fits a pc system administrator and 40h support, SEK 30,000
  Specialities: Linux, GCC, CVS version management, Emacs, Tcl/Tk and Internet services: WWW, Gopher, FTP, Sendmail, News/INN

- The Silk Road Group, Ltd.
  13628 Bent Tree Circle #201
  Centreville, VA 22020, USA
  Phone: +1 (703)222-4243
  Fax: +1 (703)222-7320
  Email: *bass@silkroad.com* (mailto:bass@silkroad.com)
  Contact:Tim Bass
  Sample Prices: subject to project and availability
  Specialities: IP network management specialists using Linux platforms for Internet Information Services, including httpd servers, DNS and news servers, SMTP mail relay hosts, IP firewalls. Large scale system and network design and integration for large corporations and goverment agencies. Clients include the USAF and the National Science Foundation. More info on *http://www.silkroad.com/* (http://www.silkroad.com/)

- Systems Software
  22 Irvington Cres
  Willowdale, On, Canada M2N 2Z1
  Phone: +1 (416) 225-1592
  Email: *Drew Sullivan* (mailto:drew@ss.org)
  Sample prices: $90 Canadian/hour
  Specialities: Unix Systems & Internet Consulting

- Sytek s.r.l.
  Via Cernaia 14
  I-10122 Torino, Italy
  Phone: +39 11 9884111
  Fax: +39 11 9951487
  E-mail: *mario@sytek.it* (mailto:mario@sytek.it), *info@sytek.it* (mailto:info@sytek.it)
  Contact: Mariotti Mario
  Type of support: by e-mail, inhouse/outhouse, training
  Sample prices approx. USD60 per hour
  Specialities: General Unix Consultant, X11/Motif Experts, we own a GUI Builder for Motif (Xad), we have great experience in writing Unix Device Drivers (char & block).

- Wizvax Communications
  1508 Tibbits Ave
  Troy, NY 12180 USA
  Phone: +1 (518) 273-4325
  Fax: +1 (518) 271-6289
  Contacts: *Richard Shetron* (mailto:multics@wizvax.net) (owner/manager), *Stephanie Gilgut* (mailto:stephie@wizvax.net) (Linux/SunOS/Unix wizard)
  Support: We prefer to do as much support as possible via e-mail, phone, telnet.
  Sample prices: Prices vary depending on both level of service desired (24 hr/7 day, business hours, phone, email, etc.) and term of contract (one-shot, monthly, yearly, etc.). Typical prices range from USD45/hr for classes for beginners taught by JR level staff to USD120/hr for one-shot emergency calls to fix systems broken by incorrectly installed software/hardware by non-customers with no support contracts.
  Specialities: We primarily support the multiport serial boards and cables we sell. Support for products we sell is free for installation and initial setup. We can do Linux consulting, training, seminars, etc.

Part XIII

The Linux Danish/International HOWTO

Copyright Thomas Petersen, `petersen@risoe.dk`
v1.0, 9 March 1994
This document describes how to configure Linux and various Linux applications for use with the Danish characterset and keyboard. It is hoped that Linux users from other places in Western Europe will find this document of use too.

Contents

1   Introduction

All European users of almost any operating system have two problems: The first is to tell the OS that you have a non-American keyboard, and the second is to get the OS to display the special letters.

Under Linux you change the way your computer interprets the keyboard with the commands `xmodmap` and `loadkeys`. `loadkeys` will modify the keyboard for plain Linux while 'xmodmap' makes the modifications necessary when the handshaking between X and Linux is imperfect.

To display the characters you need to tell your applications that you use the ISO-8859-Latin-1 international set of glyphs. Mostly this is not necessary, but a number of key applications need special attention.

This Mini-Howto is intended to tell Danish users how to do this, but will hopefully be of help to many other people.

If you continue to have troubles after reading this you should try the German HOWTO, the Keystroke HOWTO for Linux or the ISO 8859-1 FAQ. They have tips for many applications. Many of the hints contained herein are cribbed from there. The HOWTOs are available from all respectable mirrors of `sunsite.unc.edu` while the ISO 8859-1 FAQ is available from `ftp.vlsivie.tuwien.ac.at` in `/pub/8bit/FAQ-ISO-8859-1`.

2   Keyboard setup

2.1   Loading a Danish keytable

Keyboard mappings are in `/usr/lib/kbd/keytables/`. Try typing either of these two commands to load one

```
/usr/bin/loadkeys /usr/lib/kbd/keytables/dk.map
/usr/bin/loadkeys /usr/lib/kbd/keytables/dk-lat1.map
```

The difference between the two lines is that `dk-lat1.map` uses 'dead' keys while `dk.map` doesn't. Dead keys are explained in section 2.3.

You can change the keymapping loaded at boot by editing the file `/etc/rc.d/rc.keymap`.

If this doesn't work you simply haven't installed support for international keyboards.

2.2   Getting the `AltGr` key to work under X

Edit the file `/etc/Xconfig` (under XFree86 2.0) or `/etc/X11/XF86Config` (underXFree86 3.x) and make sure the line

```
RightAlt    ModeShift
```

appears in the `Keyboard` section. Usually you can do this by uncommenting an appropriate line.

2.3   Dead keys and accented characters

Dead keys are those who don't type anything until you hit another key. Tildes and umlauts are like this by default under Microsoft Windows and if you use the `dk-lat1.map` keymap under Linux.

2.3.1   Removing dead key functionality

Under plain Linux type

```
loadkeys dk.map
```

2.3.2   Invoking dead key functionality

- Invoking dead key functionality under plain Linux
  Under plain Linux type

  ```
  loadkeys dk-lat1.map
  ```

- Invoking dead key functionality under X11R5 sessions
  Insert the following lines in a file `~/.Xmodmap` or `/etc/X11/Xmodmap`

```
    keycode 21 = acute       Dgrave_accent          bar
    keycode 35 = Ddiaeresis Dcircumflex_accent      Dtilde
```

You can now make the dead keys work by typing (e.g.) xmodmap .Xmodmap. Using the Slackware distribution this commando will be automatically executed next time you run X.

- Invoking dead key functionality under X11R6 sessions

Under X11R6 applications dead keys won't work unless they were compiled with support for unusual input methods. The only application reported to do so is kterm - an xterm substitute. Eventually the situation might improve, but as it is you can't do much but revert to X11R5 or hack every application you own. Do not attempt the method described for X11R5.

2.4 Making ⊘ (oslash) ⊘ (Ooblique) and the dollar sign work

2.4.1 ⊘ (oslash) and ⊘ (Ooblique)

Find out what keymap you load at boot-up. You should be able to find out by typing less /etc/rc.d/rc.keymap. On my computer it is called /usr/lib/kbd/keytables/dk-lat1.map. Find the line for keycode 40 in this file and change it from

```
    keycode  40 = cent             yen
```

to

```
    keycode  40 = oslash           Ooblique
```

and load the keytable as described in section 2.1.

Note: This bug appears to have been fixed in version 0.88 of the international keytable package.

2.4.2 Dollar sign

The dollar sign is accessed with Shift-4 instead of AltGr-4 by default. You can fix this by changing the line

```
    keycode   5 = four             dollar          dollar
```

in the keymap file to e.g.

```
    keycode   5 = four             asciicircum     dollar
```

It doesn't matter if you something else instead asciicircum if it is just a valid symbol name. See section 3.2 for a list of valid symbols.

3 Display and application setup

3.1 International character sets in specific applications

A number of applications demand special attention. This section descibes how to set up configuration files for them.

- bash v.1.13+ : Put the following in your .inputrc file

```
set meta-flag on
set convert-meta off
set output-meta on
```

- `tcsh`: Put the following in your `/etc/csh.login` or `.tcshrc` file

  ```
  setenv LC_CTYPE ISO-8859-1
  stty pass8
  ```

- `less`: Set the following environment variable

  ```
  LESSCHARSET=latin1
  ```

- `elm`: Set the following environment variables

  ```
  LANG=C
  LC_CTYPE=ISO-8859-1
  ```

- `emacs`: Put the following in your `.emacs` or the `/usr/lib/emacs/site-lisp/default.el` file:

  ```
  (standard-display-european t)

  (set-input-mode (car (current-input-mode))
          (nth 1 (current-input-mode))
          0)
  ```

- TeX / LaTeX: Cribbed from the ISO 8859-1 FAQ by Michael Gschwind `<mike@vlsivie.tuwien.ac.at>`:

  In LaTeX 2.09, use

  ```
  \documentstyle[isolatin]{article}
  ```

  to include support for ISO latin1 characters. In LaTeX2e, the commands

  ```
  \documentclass{article}
  \usepackage{isolatin}
  ```

  will do the job. `isolatin.sty` is available from all CTAN servers and from URL `ftp://ftp.vlsivie.tuwien.ac.at/pub/8bit`.

3.2   What characters you can display under Linux

Type `dumpkeys -l | less` at the prompt to find out what is readily available. You can map them to your keyboard via the keymap files mentioned in section 2.1.

X11R5 Note: The dead keys don't get the correct names under X11R5 with this scheme. Generally

```
dead_* (under plain Linux) => D* or D*_accent (under X11R5)
```

(i.e. the tilde may be `dead_tilde` in `dk-lat1.map` but X11R5 expects the dead tilde to be called `Dtilde`.) This does not apply to X11R6.

3.3   Loading the Latin-1 characer set on the console

Execute the following commands under the `bash` shell:

```
setfont /usr/lib/kbd/consolefonts/lat1-16.psf
mapscrn /usr/lib/kbd/consoletrans/trivial
echo -ne '\033(K'
```

Note: This only has effect under plain Linux. Do not try it under X.

4 Post-amble: Acknowledgements and Copyright

Thanks to Peter Dalgaard, Anders Majland, the authors of the German Howto and Michael Gschwind for help with several questions.

This Mini-Howto is copyrighted by Thomas Petersen and distributed as other Linux HOWTOs under the terms described below.

Part I
Linux Allocated Devices

Maintained by H. Peter Anvin <Peter.Anvin@linux.org>

This list is the successor to Rick Miller's Linux Device List, which he stopped maintaining when he lost network access in 1993. It is a registry of allocated major device numbers, as well as the recommended /dev directory nodes for these devices.

This list is available via FTP from ftp.yggdrasil.com in the directory /pub/device-list; filename is devices.*format* where *format* is txt (ASCII), tex (LaTeX), dvi (DVI) or ps (PostScript). In cases of discrepancy, the LaTeX version has priority.

This document is included by reference into the Linux Filesystem Standard (FSSTND). The FSSTND is available via FTP from tsx-11.mit.edu in the directory /pub/linux/docs/linux-standards/fsstnd.

To have a major number allocated, or a minor number in situations where that applies (e.g. busmice), please contact me. Also, if you have additional information regarding any of the devices listed below, I would like to know.

Allocations marked (68k) apply to Linux/68k only.

1 Major numbers

0		Unnamed devices (NFS mounts, loopback devices)
1	char	Memory devices
	block	RAM disk
2	char	Reserved for PTY's <tytso@athena.mit.edu>
	block	Floppy disks
3	char	Reserved for PTY's <tytso@athena.mit.edu>
	block	First MFM, RLL and IDE hard disk/CD-ROM interface
4	char	TTY devices
5	char	Alternate TTY devices
6	char	Parallel printer devices
7	char	Virtual console access devices
8	block	SCSI disk devices
9	char	SCSI tape devices
	block	Multiple disk devices
10	char	Non-serial mice, misc features
11	block	SCSI CD-ROM devices
12	char	QIC-02 tape
	block	MSCDEX CD-ROM callback support
13	char	Reserved for PC speaker
	block	8-bit MFM/RLL/IDE controller
14	char	Sound card
	block	BIOS harddrive callback support
15	char	Joystick
	block	Sony CDU-31A/CDU-33A CD-ROM
16	char	Reserved for scanners
	block	GoldStar CD-ROM
17	char	Chase serial card (Under development)
	block	Optics Storage CD-ROM (Under development)
18	char	Chase serial card – alternate devices
	block	Sanyo CD-ROM (Under development)
19	char	Cyclades serial card
	block	Double compressed disk
20	char	Cyclades serial card – alternate devices
	block	Hitachi CD-ROM (Under development)
21	char	Generic SCSI access
22	char	Digiboard serial card
	block	Second MFM, RLL and IDE hard disk/CD-ROM interface
23	char	Digiboard serial card – alternate devices

	block	Mitsumi proprietary CD-ROM
24	block	Sony CDU-535 CD-ROM
25	block	First Matsushita (Panasonic/SoundBlaster) CD-ROM
26	block	Second Matsushita (Panasonic/SoundBlaster) CD-ROM
27	char	QIC-117 tape
	block	Third Matsushita (Panasonic/SoundBlaster) CD-ROM
28	block	Fourth Matsushita (Panasonic/SoundBlaster) CD-ROM
	block	ACSI disk (68k)
29	char	Universal frame buffer
	block	Aztech/Orchid/Okano/Wearnes CD-ROM
30	char	iBCS-2
	block	Philips LMS-205 CD-ROM
31	block	ROM/flash memory card
32	block	Philips LMS-206 CD-ROM
33	block	Modular RAM disk
34–223		Unallocated
224–254		Local use
255		Reserved

2 Minor numbers

0		Unnamed devices (NFS mounts, loopback devices)	
		0	reserved as null device number

1	char	Memory devices	
		1 /dev/mem	Physical memory access
		2 /dev/kmem	Kernel virtual memory access
		3 /dev/null	Null device
		4 /dev/port	I/O port access
		5 /dev/zero	Null byte source
		6 /dev/core	OBSOLETE – should be a link to /proc/kcore
		7 /dev/full	Returns ENOSPC on write
	block	RAM disk	
		1 /dev/ramdisk	RAM disk

2	char	Reserved for PTY's <tytso@athena.mit.edu>	
	block	Floppy disks	
		0 /dev/fd0	First floppy disk autodetect
		1 /dev/fd1	Second floppy disk autodetect
		2 /dev/fd2	Third floppy disk autodetect
		3 /dev/fd3	Fourth floppy disk autodetect

To specify format, add to the autodetect device number

0	/dev/fd?	Autodetect format
4	/dev/fd?d360	5.25" 360K in a 360K drive
20	/dev/fd?h360	5.25" 360K in a 1200K drive
48	/dev/fd?h410	5.25" 410K in a 1200K drive
64	/dev/fd?h420	5.25" 420K in a 1200K drive
24	/dev/fd?h720	5.25" 720K in a 1200K drive
80	/dev/fd?h880	5.25" 880K in a 1200K drive

8	/dev/fd?h1200	5.25" 1200K in a 1200K drive
40	/dev/fd?h1440	5.25" 1440K in a 1200K drive
56	/dev/fd?h1476	5.25" 1476K in a 1200K drive
72	/dev/fd?h1494	5.25" 1494K in a 1200K drive
92	/dev/fd?h1600	5.25" 1600K in a 1200K drive
12	/dev/fd?u360	3.5" 360K Double Density
16	/dev/fd?u720	3.5" 720K Double Density
120	/dev/fd?u800	3.5" 800K Double Density
52	/dev/fd?u820	3.5" 820K Double Density
68	/dev/fd?u830	3.5" 830K Double Density
84	/dev/fd?u1040	3.5" 1040K Double Density
88	/dev/fd?u1120	3.5" 1120K Double Density
28	/dev/fd?u1440	3.5" 1440K High Density
124	/dev/fd?u1600	3.5" 1600K High Density
44	/dev/fd?u1680	3.5" 1680K High Density
60	/dev/fd?u1722	3.5" 1722K High Density
76	/dev/fd?u1743	3.5" 1743K High Density
96	/dev/fd?u1760	3.5" 1760K High Density
116	/dev/fd?u1840	3.5" 1840K High Density
100	/dev/fd?u1920	3.5" 1920K High Density
32	/dev/fd?u2880	3.5" 2880K Extra Density
104	/dev/fd?u3200	3.5" 3200K Extra Density
108	/dev/fd?u3520	3.5" 3520K Extra Density
112	/dev/fd?u3840	3.5" 3840K Extra Density
36	/dev/fd?CompaQ	Compaq 2880K drive; probably obsolete

NOTE: The letter in the device name (d, q, h or u) signifies the type of drive supported: 5.25" Double Density (d), 5.25" Quad Density (q), 5.25" High Density (h) or 3.5" (any type, u). The capital letters D, H, or E for the 3.5" models have been deprecated, since the drive type is insignificant for these devices.

| 3 | char | Reserved for PTY's <tytso@athena.mit.edu> |
| | block | First MFM, RLL and IDE hard disk/CD-ROM interface |

0	/dev/hda	Master: whole disk (or CD-ROM)
64	/dev/hdb	Slave: whole disk (or CD-ROM)

For partitions, add to the whole disk device number

0	/dev/hd?	Whole disk
1	/dev/hd?1	First primary partition
2	/dev/hd?2	Second primary partition
3	/dev/hd?3	Third primary partition
4	/dev/hd?4	Fourth primary partition
5	/dev/hd?5	First logical partition
6	/dev/hd?6	Second logical partition
7	/dev/hd?7	Third logical partition
	. . .	
63	/dev/hd?63	59th logical partition

| 4 | char | TTY devices |

0	/dev/console	Console device
1	/dev/tty1	First virtual console
	. . .	
63	/dev/tty63	63rd virtual console

		64 /dev/ttyS0	First serial port
		...	
		127 /dev/ttyS63	64th serial port
		128 /dev/ptyp0	First pseudo-tty master
		...	
		191 /dev/ptysf	64th pseudo-tty master
		192 /dev/ttyp0	First pseudo-tty slave
		...	
		255 /dev/ttysf	64th pseudo-tty slave

Pseudo-tty's are named as follows:

- Masters are pty, slaves are tty;

- the fourth letter is one of pqrs indicating the 1st, 2nd, 3rd, 4th series of 16 pseudo-ttys each, and

- the fifth letter is one of 0123456789abcdef indicating the position within the series.

5	char	Alternate TTY devices	
		0 /dev/tty	Current TTY device
		64 /dev/cua0	Callout device corresponding to ttyS0
		...	
		127 /dev/cua63	Callout device corresponding to ttyS63

6	char	Parallel printer devices	
		0 /dev/lp0	First parallel printer (0x3bc)
		1 /dev/lp1	Second parallel printer (0x378)
		2 /dev/lp2	Third parallel printer (0x278)

Not all computers have the 0x3bc parallel port, why the "first" printer may be either /dev/lp0 or /dev/lp1.

7	char	Virtual console access devices	
		0 /dev/vcs	Current vc text access
		1 /dev/vcs1	tty1 text access
		...	
		63 /dev/vcs63	tty63 text access
		128 /dev/vcsa	Current vc text/attribute access
		129 /dev/vcsa1	tty1 text/attribute access
		...	
		191 /dev/vcsa63	tty63 text/attribute access

NOTE: These devices permit both read and write access.

8	block	SCSI disk devices	
		0 /dev/sda	First SCSI disk whole disk
		16 /dev/sdb	Second SCSI disk whole disk
		32 /dev/sdc	Third SCSI disk whole disk
		...	
		240 /dev/sdp	Sixteenth SCSI disk whole disk

Partitions are handled in the same way as for IDE disks (see major number 3) except that the limit on logical partitions is 11 rather than 59 per disk.

9	char	SCSI tape devices		
		0 /dev/st0	First SCSI tape	
		1 /dev/st1	Second SCSI tape	
		. . .		
		128 /dev/nst0	First SCSI tape, no rewind-on-close	
		129 /dev/nst1	Second SCSI tape, no rewind-on-close	
		. . .		
	block	Multiple disk devices		
		0 /dev/md0	First device group	
		1 /dev/md1	Second device group	
		. . .		

The multiple device driver is used to span a filesystem across multiple physical disks.

10	char	Non-serial mice, misc features	
		0 /dev/logibm	Logitech bus mouse
		1 /dev/psaux	PS/2-style mouse port
		2 /dev/inportbm	Microsoft Inport bus mouse
		3 /dev/atibm	ATI XL bus mouse
		4 /dev/jbm	J-mouse
		4 /dev/amigamouse	Amiga Mouse (68k)
		5 /dev/atarimouse	Atari Mouse (68k)
		128 /dev/beep	Fancy beep device
		129 /dev/modreq	Kernel module load request

11	block	SCSI CD-ROM devices	
		0 /dev/sr0	First SCSI CD-ROM
		1 /dev/sr1	Second SCSI CD-ROM
		. . .	

The prefix /dev/scd instead of /dev/sr has been used as well, and might make more sense.

12	char	QIC-02 tape	
		2 /dev/ntpqic11	QIC-11, no rewind-on-close
		3 /dev/tpqic11	QIC-11, rewind-on-close
		4 /dev/ntpqic24	QIC-24, no rewind-on-close
		5 /dev/tpqic24	QIC-24, rewind-on-close
		6 /dev/ntpqic120	QIC-120, no rewind-on-close
		7 /dev/tpqic120	QIC-120, rewind-on-close
		8 /dev/ntpqic150	QIC-150, no rewind-on-close
		9 /dev/tpqic150	QIC-150, rewind-on-close

The device names specified are proposed – if there are "standard" names for these devices, please let me know.

	block	MSCDEX CD-ROM callback support	
		0 /dev/dos_cd0	First MSCDEX CD-ROM

```
                    1 /dev/dos_cd1        Second MSCDEX CD-ROM
                    ...
```

13   char   Reserved for PC speaker

        block   8-bit MFM/RLL/IDE controller
```
                    0 /dev/xda            First XT disk whole disk
                   64 /dev/xdb            Second XT disk whole disk
```

Partitions are handled in the same way as IDE disks (see major number 3).

14   char   Sound card
```
                    0 /dev/mixer          Mixer control
                    1 /dev/sequencer      Audio sequencer
                    2 /dev/midi00         First MIDI port
                    3 /dev/dsp            Digital audio
                    4 /dev/audio          Sun-compatible digital audio
                    6 /dev/sndstat        Sound card status information
                    8 /dev/sequencer2     Sequencer – alternate device
                   16 /dev/mixer1         Second soundcard mixer control
                   17 /dev/patmgr0        Sequencer patch manager
                   18 /dev/midi01         Second MIDI port
                   19 /dev/dsp1           Second soundcard digital audio
                   20 /dev/audio1         Second soundcard Sun digital audio
                   33 /dev/patmgr1        Sequencer patch manager
                   34 /dev/midi02         Third MIDI port
                   50 /dev/midi03         Fourth MIDI port
```

        block   BIOS harddrive callback support
```
                    0 /dev/dos_hda        First BIOS harddrive whole disk
                   64 /dev/dos_hdb        Second BIOS harddrive whole disk
                  128 /dev/dos_hdc        Third BIOS harddrive whole disk
                  192 /dev/dos_hdd        Fourth BIOS harddrive whole disk
```

Partitions are handled in the same way as IDE disks (see major number 3).

15   char   Joystick
```
                    0 /dev/js0            First joystick
                    1 /dev/js1            Second joystick
```

        block   Sony CDU-31A/CDU-33A CD-ROM
```
                    0 /dev/sonycd         Sony CDU-31A CD-ROM
```

16   char   Reserved for scanners
        block   GoldStar CD-ROM
```
                    0 /dev/gscd           GoldStar CD-ROM
```

17   char   Chase serial card (Under development)
```
                    0 /dev/ttyH0          First Chase port
                    1 /dev/ttyH1          Second Chase port
```

. . .

	block	Optics Storage CD-ROM (Under development)	
		0 /dev/optcd	Optics Storage CD-ROM

18	char	Chase serial card – alternate devices	
		0 /dev/cuh0	Callout device corresponding to `ttyH0`
		1 /dev/cuh1	Callout device corresponding to `ttyH1`
		. . .	

	block	Sanyo CD-ROM (Under development)	
		0 ?	Sanyo CD-ROM

19	char	Cyclades serial card	
		32 /dev/ttyC0	First Cyclades port
		. . .	
		63 /dev/ttyC31	32nd Cyclades port

It would make more sense for these to start at 0...

	block	"Double" compressed disk	
		0 /dev/double0	First compressed disk
		. . .	
		7 /dev/double7	Eighth compressed disk
		128 /dev/cdouble0	Mirror of first compressed disk
		. . .	
		135 /dev/cdouble7	Mirror of eighth compressed disk

See the Double documentation for an explanation of the "mirror" devices.

20	char	Cyclades serial card – alternate devices	
		32 /dev/cub0	Callout device corresponding to `ttyC0`
		. . .	
		63 /dev/cub31	Callout device corresponding to `ttyC31`

	block	Hitachi CD-ROM (Under development)	
		0 /dev/hitcd	Hitachi CD-ROM

21	char	Generic SCSI access	
		0 /dev/sg0	First generic SCSI device
		1 /dev/sg1	Second generic SCSI device
		. . .	

22	char	Digiboard serial card	
		0 /dev/ttyD0	First Digiboard port
		1 /dev/ttyD1	Second Digiboard port
		. . .	

	block	Second MFM, RLL and IDE hard disk/CD-ROM interface	
		0 /dev/hdc	Master: whole disk (or CD-ROM)
		64 /dev/hdd	Slave: whole disk (or CD-ROM)

Partitions are handled the same way as for the first interface (see major number 3).

23	char	Digiboard serial card – alternate devices	
		0 /dev/cud0	Callout device corresponding to `ttyD0`
		1 /dev/cud1	Callout device corresponding to `ttyD1`
		. . .	
	block	Mitsumi proprietary CD-ROM	
		0 /dev/mcd	Mitsumi CD-ROM
24	block	Sony CDU-535 CD-ROM	
		0 /dev/cdu535	Sony CDU-535 CD-ROM
25	block	First Matsushita (Panasonic/SoundBlaster) CD-ROM	
		0 /dev/sbpcd0	Panasonic CD-ROM controller 0 unit 0
		1 /dev/sbpcd1	Panasonic CD-ROM controller 0 unit 1
		2 /dev/sbpcd2	Panasonic CD-ROM controller 0 unit 2
		3 /dev/sbpcd3	Panasonic CD-ROM controller 0 unit 3
26	char	Frame grabbers	
		0 /dev/wvisfgrab	Quanta WinVision frame grabber
	block	Second Matsushita (Panasonic/SoundBlaster) CD-ROM	
		0 /dev/sbpcd4	Panasonic CD-ROM controller 1 unit 0
		1 /dev/sbpcd5	Panasonic CD-ROM controller 1 unit 1
		2 /dev/sbpcd6	Panasonic CD-ROM controller 1 unit 2
		3 /dev/sbpcd7	Panasonic CD-ROM controller 1 unit 3
27	char	QIC-117 tape	
		0 /dev/rft0	Unit 0, rewind-on-close
		1 /dev/rft1	Unit 1, rewind-on-close
		2 /dev/rft2	Unit 2, rewind-on-close
		3 /dev/rft3	Unit 3, rewind-on-close
		4 /dev/nrft0	Unit 0, no rewind-on-close
		5 /dev/nrft1	Unit 1, no rewind-on-close
		6 /dev/nrft2	Unit 2, no rewind-on-close
		7 /dev/nrft3	Unit 3, no rewind-on-close
	block	Third Matsushita (Panasonic/SoundBlaster) CD-ROM	
		0 /dev/sbpcd8	Panasonic CD-ROM controller 2 unit 0
		1 /dev/sbpcd9	Panasonic CD-ROM controller 2 unit 1
		2 /dev/sbpcd10	Panasonic CD-ROM controller 2 unit 2
		3 /dev/sbpcd11	Panasonic CD-ROM controller 2 unit 3
28	block	Fourth Matsushita (Panasonic/SoundBlaster) CD-ROM	
		0 /dev/sbpcd12	Panasonic CD-ROM controller 3 unit 0
		1 /dev/sbpcd13	Panasonic CD-ROM controller 3 unit 1
		2 /dev/sbpcd14	Panasonic CD-ROM controller 3 unit 2
		3 /dev/sbpcd15	Panasonic CD-ROM controller 3 unit 3
	block	ACSI disk (68k)	

		0 /dev/ada	First ACSI disk whole disk
		16 /dev/adb	Second ACSI disk whole disk
		32 /dev/adc	Third ACSI disk whole disk
		...	
		240 /dev/adp	Sixteenth ACSI disk whole disk

Partitions are handled in the same way as for IDE disks (see major number 3) except that the limit on logical partitions is 11 rather than 59 per disk.

29	char	Universal frame buffer	
		0 /dev/fb0current	First frame buffer
		1 /dev/fb0autodetect	
		...	
		16 /dev/fb1current	Second frame buffer
		17 /dev/fb1autodetect	
		...	

The universal frame buffer device is currently supported only on Linux/68k. The current device accesses the frame buffer at current resolution; the autodetect one at bootup (default) resolution. Minor numbers 2–15 within each frame buffer assignment are used for specific device-dependent resolutions. There appear to be no standard naming for these devices.

	block	Aztech/Orchid/Okano/Wearnes CD-ROM	
		0 /dev/aztcd	Aztech CD-ROM

30	char	iBCS-2 compatibility devices	
		0 /dev/socksys	Socket access
		1 /dev/spx	SVR3 local X interface
		2 /dev/inet/arp	Network access
		2 /dev/inet/icmp	Network access
		2 /dev/inet/ip	Network access
		2 /dev/inet/udp	Network access
		2 /dev/inet/tcp	Network access

iBCS-2 requires /dev/nfsd to be a link to /dev/socksys and /dev/X0R to be a link to /dev/null.

	block	Philips LMS CM-205 CD-ROM	
		0 /dev/cm205cd	Philips LMS CM-205 CD-ROM

/dev/lmscd is an older name for this drive. This driver does not work with the CM-205MS CD-ROM.

31	block	ROM/flash memory card	
		0 /dev/rom0	First ROM card (rw)
		...	
		7 /dev/rom7	Eighth ROM card (rw)
		8 /dev/rrom0	First ROM card (ro)
		...	
		15 /dev/rrom0	Eighth ROM card (ro)
		16 /dev/flash0	First flash memory card (rw)

. . .
23 /dev/flash7   Eighth flash memory card (rw)
24 /dev/rflash0   First flash memory card (ro)
. . .
31 /dev/rflash7   Eighth flash memory card (ro)

The read-write (rw) devices support back-caching written data in RAM, as well as writing to flash RAM devices. The read-only devices (ro) support reading only.

32	block	Philips LMS CM-206 CD-ROM	
		0 /dev/cm206cd	Philips LMS CM-206 CD-ROM

33	block	Modular RAM disk	
		0 /dev/ram0	First modular RAM disk
		1 /dev/ram1	Second modular RAM disk
		. . .	
		255 /dev/ram255	256th modular RAM disk

34–223   Unallocated

224–254   Local/experimental use

For devices not assigned official numbers, this range should be used, in order to avoid conflict with future assignments. Please note that MAX_CHRDEV and MAX_BLKDEV in linux/include/linux/major.h must be set to a value greater than the highest used major number. For a kernel using local/experimental devices, it is probably easiest to set both of these equal to 256. The memory cost above using the default value of 64 is 3K.

255   Reserved

3 Additional /dev directory entries

This section details additional entries that should or may exist in the /dev directory. It is preferred if symbolic links use the same form (absolute or relative) as is indicated here. Links are classified as *hard* or *symbolic* depending on the preferred type of link; if possible, the indicated type of link should be used.

3.1 Compulsory links

These links should exist on all systems:

/dev/fd	/proc/self/fd	symbolic	File descriptors
/dev/stdin	fd/0	symbolic	Standard input file descriptor
/dev/stdout	fd/1	symbolic	Standard output file descriptor
/dev/stderr	fd/2	symbolic	Standard error file descriptor

3.2 Recommended links

It is recommended that these links exist on all systems:

/dev/X0R	null	symbolic	Used by iBCS-2
/dev/nfsd	socksys	symbolic	Used by iBCS-2
/dev/core	/proc/kcore	symbolic	Backward compatibility
/dev/scd?	sr?	hard	Alternate name for CD-ROMs

3.3 Locally defined links

The following links may be established locally to conform to the configuration of the system. This is merely a tabulation of existing practice, and does not constitute a recommendation. However, if they exist, they should have the following uses.

/dev/mouse	*mouse port*	symbolic	Current mouse device
/dev/tape	*tape device*	symbolic	Current tape device
/dev/cdrom	*CD-ROM device*	symbolic	Current CD-ROM device
/dev/modem	*modem port*	symbolic	Current dialout device
/dev/root	*root device*	symbolic	Current root filesystem
/dev/swap	*swap device*	symbolic	Current swap device

/dev/modem should not be used for a modem which supports dialin as well as dialout, as it tends to cause lock file problems. If it exists, /dev/modem should point to the appropriate dialout (alternate) device.

3.4 Sockets and pipes

Non-transient sockets or named pipes may exist in /dev. Common entries are:

/dev/printer	socket	lpd local socket
/dev/log	socket	syslog local socket

Part XV

The dosemu HOWTO

Copyright edited by Mike Deisher, `deisher@dspsun.eas.asu.edu`
v0.52.8, 30 Mar 1995
This is the 'Frequently Asked Questions' (FAQ) / HOWTO document for dosemu. The most up-to-date
version of the dosemu-HOWTO may be found in `dspsun.eas.asu.edu:/pub/dosemu`.

Contents

1 The preliminaries

1.1 What is dosemu, anyway?

To quote the manual, "dosemu is a user-level program which uses certain special features of the Linux kernel and the 80386 processor to run MS-DOS in what we in the biz call a 'DOS box.' The DOS box, a combination of hardware and software trickery, has these capabilities:

o the ability to virtualize all input/output and processor control instructions

o the ability to support the word size and addressing modes of the iAPX86 processor family's "real mode," while still running within the full protected mode environment

o the ability to trap all DOS and BIOS system calls and emulate such calls as are necessary for proper operation and good performance

o the ability to simulate a hardware environment over which DOS programs are accustomed to having control.

o the ability to provide MS-DOS services through native Linux services; for example, dosemu can provide a virtual hard disk drive which is actually a Linux directory hierarchy."

1.2 What's the newest version of dosemu and where can I get it?

The newest version of dosemu is `dosemu0.52` and can be ftp'ed from the following sites:

```
dspsun.eas.asu.edu:/pub/dosemu/
tsx-11.mit.edu:/pub/linux/ALPHA/dosemu/
```

However, pre-release versions are also available for developers and ALPHA testers. They may be found in

```
dspsun.eas.asu.edu:/pub/dosemu/Development/
tsx-11.mit.edu:/pub/linux/ALPHA/dosemu/Development
```

and have names of the form `pre0.53_??`. The pre-release code has the distinct advantage that it is compatible with the most recent Linux kernels. Also, it includes new features (most notably X support). Remember that this is ALPHA code, however: there may be serious bugs and very little documentation for new features.

Release 0.60 is due out in late April 1995. It will have some nice new features (e.g., X-support, runs 32-bit games like DOOM II, and–rumor has it–the beginnings of support for running MS-Windows 3.1). There should be new documentation available with (or soon after) the release so stay tuned!

1.3 Where can I follow the development?

If you want to follow the development of dosemu, you should consider subscribing to the linux-msdos mailing list. To subscribe, send mail to `Majordomo@vger.rutgers.edu` with the following command in the body of your email message:

```
subscribe linux-msdos your_username@your.email.address
```

If you ever want to remove yourself from the mailing list, you can send mail to `Majordomo@vger.rutgers.edu` with the following command in the body of your email message:

```
unsubscribe linux-msdos your_username@your.email.address
```

1.4   What documentation is available for dosemu?

The dosemu manual (`dosemu.texinfo`) written by Robert Sanders has not been updated in some time but is still a good source of information. It is distributed with dosemu.

The "dosemu Novice's Altering Guide" or DANG is a road map to the inner workings of dosemu. It is designed for the adventurous, those who wish to modify the source code themselves. The DANG is maintained by Alistair MacDonald (`am20@unix.york.ac.uk`) and is posted once in a while to the MSDOS channel of Linux Activists.

The EMU success list (EMUsuccess.txt) is a list of all programs that have been reported to work with dosemu. It is posted once in a while to the MSDOS channel of Linux Activists. The most recent version can be found on dspsun.eas.asu.edu:/pub/dosemu.

And then, of course, there is the dosemu FAQ/HOWTO. But you already know about that, don't you. It is also posted once in a while to the MSDOS channel of Linux Activists. The most recent version can be found on `dspsun.eas.asu.edu:/pub/dosemu`.

1.5   How do I submit changes or additions to the HOWTO?

The preferred method is to edit the file, `dosemu-HOWTO-xx.x.sgml` to incorporate the changes, create a diff file by typing something like

```
diff original-file new-file
```

and send it to `deisher@dspsun.eas.asu.edu`. If you do not know SGML, that's ok. Changes or new information in any form will be accepted. Creating the diff file just makes it easier on the HOWTO maintainer. :-)

1.6   Message from Matt...

Unless otherwise stated, Linux HOWTO documents are copyrighted by their respective authors. Linux HOWTO documents may be reproduced and distributed in whole or in part, in any medium physical or electronic, as long as this copyright notice is retained on all copies. Commercial redistribution is allowed and encouraged; however, the author would like to be notified of any such distributions.

All translations, derivative works, or aggregate works incorporating any Linux HOWTO documents must be covered under this copyright notice. That is, you may not produce a derivative work from a HOWTO and impose additional restrictions on its distribution. Exceptions to these rules may be granted under certain conditions; please contact the Linux HOWTO coordinator at the address given below.

In short, we wish to promote dissemination of this information through as many channels as possible. However, we do wish to retain copyright on the HOWTO documents, and would like to be notified of any plans to redistribute the HOWTOs.

If you have questions, please contact Matt Welsh, the Linux HOWTO coordinator, at mdw@sunsite.unc.edu. You may finger this address for phone number and additional contact information.

2   Compiling and installing dosemu

2.1   Where are the installation instructions?

The installation instructions are in the file, "QuickStart", included in the distribution.

2.2   Why won't dosemu 0.52 compile?

(7/9/94)

There is a bug in the makefile of dosemu 0.52. The makefile expects the source to be located in `/usr/src/dosemu????`. Either install the source under `/usr/src` or try `make clean ; make config ; make dep ; make all`.

Of course, this is not the only possible reason (see below).

2.3   How can I be a bone-head when installing dosemu?

a.k.a. Top Ten Stupid Mistakes installing dosemu (7/9/94)

```
1. Don't read the QuickStart Guide.
2. Try to compile with a kernel older than 1.0.8.
3. Try to compile with an *unpatched* kernel >= 1.0.8.
4. Try to compile with a kernel older than 1.1.12.
5. Use dosemu with a kernel that does not have IPC compiled in.
6. Compile with gcc older than 2.5.8 or libc older than 4.5.21.
7. Forget to edit your /etc/dosemu.conf file.
8. Forget to run "FDISK /mbr" on your hdimage.
9. Forget to run "mkpartition" when using partition access.
10. Don't compile dosemu with sufficient privileges (i.e., root).
```

[Please send me your stupid mistakes for inclusion in this list. I promise you will remain anonymous. ;-)]

3   Hard disk setup

3.1   How do I use my hard disk with dosemu?

First, mount your dos hard disk partition as a Linux subdirectory. For example, you could create a directory in Linux such as /dos (mkdir -m 755 /dos) and add a line like

```
/dev/hda1        /dos      msdos    umask=022
```

to your /etc/fstab. (In this example, the hard disk is mounted read-only. You may want to mount it read/write by replacing "022" with "000" and using the -m 777 option with mkdir). Now `mount /dos`. Now you can add a line like

```
lredir d: linux\fs/dos
```

to the AUTOEXEC.BAT file in your hdimage (see the comments on LREDIR below). On a multi-user system you may want to use

```
lredir d: linux\fs\${home}
```

where "home" is the name of an environmental variable that contains the location of the dos directory (/dos in this example).

Tim Bird (Tim_R_Bird@Novell.COM) states that LREDIR users should

be careful when they use LREDIR in the autoexec, because COMMAND.COM will continue parsing the autoexec.bat from the redirected drive as the same file offset where it left off in the autoexec.bat on the physical drive. For this reason, it is safest to have the autoexec.bat on the redirected drive and the physical drive (diskimage) be the same.

Robert D. Warren (`rw11258@xx.acs.appstate.edu`) reported (4/28/94) that

I boot off a small hdimage file (less than 1 MB - and twice as large as needs be at that), and the next to last line in my config.sys file on the hdimage boot image is:

```
install=c:\lredir.exe LINUX\FS\home/dos
```

This will execute lredir just before the command interpreter runs. And I have successfully run it with both command.com and 4DOS. This eliminates the offset problem using lredir in autoexec.bat.

3.2   Can I use my stacked/double-spaced/super-stored disk?

At this time, compressed drives cannot be accessed via the redirector (lredir or emufs). However, many people have had success by simply uncommenting the

```
disk { wholedisk "/dev/hda" }          # 1st partition on 1st disk
```

line in their dosemu config file. Others have had success using

```
disk { partition "/dev/hda1" 1 }
```

and running the `mkpartition` utility (included in the dosemu distribution).

[WARNING: Make sure your dos partitions are not mounted and writeable from Linux while you are using dosemu with wholedisk or partition access. This is an easy way to destroy the data on your dos partition.]

If LILO is installed, the above will not work. However...

Thomas Mockridge (`thomas@aztec.co.za`) reported (8/5/94) that

To boot dosemu with LILO and Stacker 4.0 I did a little work around...

1. `dd` the MBR to a file. (or norton utility, etc., first 512 bytes)

2. Boot dos (from full boot not emu), do a fdisk /mbr, make your dos partition active with (dos) fdisk.

3. Copy the new MBR to a file.

4. Replace the original MBR

5. Copy the second MBR to /var/lib/dosemu/partition.hda? (Whichever is your dos partition)

6. Set dosemu.conf

```
disk {partition "/dev/hda? ?"}
```

7. Start dosemu and and voila! No LILO.

Holger Schemel (`q99492@pbhrzx.uni-paderborn.de`) reported (2/10/94) that

Works even fine under DOSEMU with MS-DOS 6.0. If you have problems, then you have to edit the file 'DBLSPACE.INI' manually and change the disk letter to the letter your drive gets under DOSEMU.

Darren J Moffat (`moffatd@dcs.gla.ac.uk`) also reported (3/27/94)

"...use 6.2 if you can get it!! Just make sure you have a lilo boot disk on hand since dos 6{.2} will change the MBR of the boot HD."

3.3 I get an error message about my config.sys file but it looks fine.

Corey Sweeney (corey@amiganet.xnet.com) reported (12/8/93) that

Sometimes when loading config.sys you will get a error message saying something like "error in line 6 of config.sys". The problem will go away if you add several carriage returns at the end of your config.sys.

3.4 Is it safe to use dosemu with DOUBLE?

Joep Mathijssen (joep@tm.tno.nl) reported (7/9/94) that

Last night I installed DOSEMU-0.52 on a DouBle'd disk (compressed file system for Linux). But when I tried to put a system on my hdimage, I got an "ERROR ON DRIVE C:" message. After putting the hdimage on a normal filesystem, it worked fine. Afterwards, I found the my compressed filesystem was ruined. Ah well, DouBle is an Alpha version, so problems like these can be expected.

4 Parallel ports, serial ports and mice

4.1 Where are the (microsoft compatible) mouse drivers?

Tom Kimball (tk@pssparc2.oc.com) reported (11/24/93) that

Several people said to use a different mouse driver and suggested some. I found a couple that seem to work fine.

```
oak.oakland.edu:/pub/msdos/mouse/mouse701.zip   (mscmouse)
oak.oakland.edu:/pub/msdos/mouse/gmous102.zip   (gmouse)
```

4.2 Why doesn't the mouse driver work?

Scott D. Heavner (sdh@fishmonger.nouucp) reported (11/27/93) that

If you start the mouse driver and it just hangs (it might actually take 30-60s), but if you are waiting longer than a minute for the mouse driver to start, remove any "timer" lines in your config file.

4.3 Why does dosemu clobber COM4?

Rob Janssen (rob@pe1chl.ampr.org) reported (3/24/94) that

According to jmorriso@bogomips.ee.ubc.ca, "dosemu still clobbers COM4 (0x2e8, IRQ 5). 0x2e8 isn't in ports{} in config. I have to run setserial /dev/cua3 irq 5 on it after dosemu exits."

This is caused by your VGA BIOS. I have found that by enabling the IO port trace and seeing where it was clobbered.

Disable the "allowvideoportaccess on" line in config and it will work fine. When you then have problems with the video, try to enable more selective ranges of IO addresses (e.g., 40-43).

4.4 How do I use dosemu over the serial ports?

Corey Sweeney (corey@amiganet.xnet.com) reported (12/8/93) that

If you plan to be using dosemu over a serial line, telnet session, or just don't want to use raw console mode, then you will probably want to get to know the termcap file. For those who don't know, the termcap file is usually located in the /etc directory. It contains the information on what sequences of characters to send to your terminal, and what sequences of characters from your terminal represent what keystrokes. If when you hit F5, and it does not work, it will usually be the fault of a incorrect termcap entry. (To learn more about termcaps look up the termcap man page.)

Now the information in the termcap relates to entries in the dosemu code. So after you put k5=\E[[E in your termcap, whenever your terminal sends \E[[E, dosemu translates that and says "he hit the k5 key!" Then it is up to dosemu to figure out what the proper scancode for the k5 key is, and push that into the buffer in some magical way. To determine the scancode, it looks up in a little table in termio.c. In termio.c under the line which (currently) says

```
#define FUNKEYS 20
```

There exist several lines following the form

```
{NULL, "termcap code", scancode} /* name of key */
```

so when it says

```
{NULL, "k5", 0x3f00} /* F5 */
```

it's saying that 0x3f00 is the scancode for F5, and that when the person activates the k5 sequence (defined in the termcap) to stuff the F5 scancode into the buffer.

Now that's all fine and dandy for analyzing how dosemu does this, but you probably want to be able to do something with this new information. Well you can add functionality for the F11 and F12 keys (and any other keys that you can find the scancode for).

All you have to do is add a line to the termio.c table that says:

```
{NULL, "ka", 0x8500} /* F11 */
```

Then to actually get it to read the line you just put in, add one to the FUNKEYS number.

```
#define FUNKEYS 21
```

Then add a "ka" entry to your termcap. After that, every time you hit the sequence stored in your termcap for ka, your dos program recognizes an "F11."

Warning: Make sure that ka is not in use in your termcap. If it is you are headed for trouble.

Note: The scancode for F12 is 0x8600.

4.5   How can I switch between dosemu and a shell over the serial line?

John Taylor (taylor@pollux.cs.uga.edu) reported (5/25/94) that

I am running Linux 1.1.13 and want to point out a great feature that should be protected and not taken out (IMHO). With the 52 version, I can run the program, "screen." From screen, i can invoke dos -D-a. What is really great (IMHO) is the screen commands (the CTRL-A cmds) still work. This means I can do a CTRL-A C and add another unix shell, and switch between the two (DOS / UNIX). This allows me to use dosemu over the serial line really well, because switching is made easy.

4.6   How can I get the parallel ports to work?

Dennis Flaherty (dennisf@flaherty.elk.miles.com) reported (3/2/95) that

The dosemu.conf has lines at the end to redirect printers to either lpr or a file. If you want direct access to the bare metal, comment out these emulation lines, and add the line

```
ports { 0x3b8 0x3b9 0x3ba 0x3bb 0x3bc 0x3bd 0x3be 0x3bf } # lpt0
```

for the "monitor card" printer port (corresponds to /dev/lp0), or

```
ports { 0x378 0x379 0x37a 0x37b 0x37c 0x37d 0x37e 0x37f } # lpt1
ports { 0x278 0x279 0x27a 0x27b 0x27c 0x27d 0x27e 0x27f } # lpt2
```

for LPT1 (/dev/lp1) and LPT2 (/dev/lp2) respectively.

5   Multiple users and Non-interactive sessions

5.1   Can I use dosemu on a multi-user system?

Corey Sweeney (corey@amiganet.xnet.com) reported (12/8/93) that

If you are running dosemu on a system in which more then one person may want to run dosemu, then you may want to change the directory of your hard drive image. Currently in the /etc/dosemu.conf file there exists the line saying that the hard drive image is "hdimage". If you change this to /var/lib/dosemu/hdimage then people do not have to worry about what directory they are in when they run dosemu, and hdimage does not have to be moved each time you upgrade to the next patch level.

If you do do this for multi-user dosemu, then you will want to make the hdimage in /var/lib/dosemu read-only for everyone but the dosemu administrator.

Note that you can use the new emufs.sys thing to mount a "public" directory and/or a "private" directory (a sub-directory in each person's home directory).

[Note: Users may also create a personal configuration file named ~/.dosrc (same format as /etc/dosemu.conf) to run their own copy of dos.]

5.2   How can I run dos commands non-interactively?

I have been meaning to write an article on this for quite some time but have not gotten around to it. Here are some hints from others:

Dan Newcombe (newcombe@aa.csc.peachnet.edu) reported (1/27/94) that

Here is an idea (untested) to be able to run a DOS command from the command line (or menu choice, etc...) without modifying the actual emulator. [Your dos partition is assumed to be mounted under Linux, already.]

Suppose you wanted to run wp60.exe with the parameter "wp60 d:\doc\paper.txt". You would do something like "dosrun wp60 d:\doc\paper.txt". "dosrun" would be a linux shell program that would a) edit/modify/recreate the dos autoexec.bat from your dos partition and b) simply run dosemu (e.g., "dos -C >/dev/null". Step a) would somehow keep all the stuff you'd normally want in autoexec.bat (e.g., mouse.com) and the last line would be "wp60 d:\doc\paper.txt".

On the dosemu side, beforehand, you would have to modify the config.sys file (located in hdimage) so that it 1) uses emufs to access the dos partition as D:, 2) sets "COMPSEC=D:\ (I think. I don't have a DOS manual around.), and 3) sets "shell=c:\command.com /p".

The idea is that for each time that you load the DOS emulator, you will recreate an autoexec.bat that is specific to that session. What makes it specific is that the last line will execute the program you want. The modifications on the hdimage are to tell the emulator/DOS that you want to use (and effectivly) boot off of D:, which will be the actual DOS partition.

If you do not use hdimage and access the DOS filesystem directly upon boot-up of DOSEMU, then this will work, and you don't have to go through the hdimage part of this all.

Daniel T. Schwager (danny@dragon.s.bawue.de) reported (7/2/94) that

You can use different dosemuf.conf files (and different hd-boot-images with different autoexec.bat's) and call dosemu like

```
$ dos -F my_quicken_q_exe_dosemu.conf
```

Dietmar Braun (braun@math20.mathematik.uni-bielefeld.de) reported (7/4/94) that

This is no problem at all when you use the redirector of dosemu. It is possible to redirect a drive letter to a linux path given by an environment variable.

So I have a shell script named "DOS" which does something like

```
mkdir /tmp/dos.\$\$
DOSTMP=/tmp/dos.\$\$; export DOSTMP
```

and then a little trick to get "echo $* > $DOSTMP/startup.bat" really working (actually a small C Program which turns '/' in '\' and terminates lines correctly for messy dos with cr/lf pairs and adds ^Z at the end of the file), creates startup files, links and so on in this directory, and then starts dosemu. Within "autoexec.bat" drive c: is redirected from hdimage to this tmp-directory, which has links for $HOME and $PWD.

So if I want to see my filenames shortened to 8.3 I can type "DOS dir" and I get my current directory listing. So I have full DOS multi user (I don't have any DOS partition and redirecting to Linux preserves user permissions) and multi tasking. (dosemu sessions are completely independent). I did this once to be able to use a dos driver for my printer. My printcap df is actually a DOS program. So you can even make DOS executables act as lpr filters.

6 dosemu and Netware

6.1 How do I get Netware access from dosemu?

James B. MacLean (jmaclean@fox.nstn.ns.ca) reported (11/28/94) that

Dosemu now supports pdipx (an IPX over pktdrvr) and pdether (uses Novell's MLID spec) to access Novell LAN's via the built in packet driver. The packet driver sits at interrupt 0x60, and abids by the normal packet driver rules. That said, beware of trying any DOS TCP/IP just yet. Single access can be made by:

```
1) cd ./net
2) cp libpacket.c.single libpacket.c
3) cp pktnew.c.single pktnew.c
4) recompile DOSEMU
5) run dosemu
6) load pdether as described by its docs (pdipx is another method)
7) load netx
8) enjoy netware access :-)
```

If you need special access to your NIC, read on. By default dosemu will not get interrupts from the kernel. That said, if you'd like to give your NIC to dosemu for it to control, maybe for access to Netware on the network through a NETX client, I do have a driver (Silly Interrupt Generator) to put in the kernel that any program, like dosemu can use to get at the interrupt for your NIC. I use it in DOSEMU to access a Novell Lite network in the past until the packet driver existed.

Any interested parties should E-mail me (jmaclean@fox.nstn.ns.ca) and I'll pass along some directions.

Want multiple DOSEMU's access to Novell?

```
1) compile current [pre-release] DOSEMU
2) follow directions in ./v-net/dosnet.README
3) carry on from 5) above.
```

6.2 The Netware-HOWTO

Lauri Tischler (ltischler@fipower.pp.fi) has authored this section of the HOWTO (Thanks Lauri!!!).
This is Rev. 0.1, 26 Nov 1994.

IMPORTANT NOTE: This information applies to the pre-release versions of dosemu (pre0.53_??) only!

This is my first attempt to write some kind of advice on how to connect to a Netware server from your
Linux box.

Due to the first attempt and the scope of this note, it is not a real HOWTO, not even a 'mini-HOWTO'. You
might call it a 'nano-HOWTO' if you like.

As in most sites the Netware is really just an extension to PC's running DOS and DOS applications (Windows
is JUST another DOS-application), the Netware providing fileserver and printing support, I will concentrate
on getting the connection via DOSEMU only.

It is possible to access Netware server via NFS from Linux directly, but that requires the Novell NFS nlm-
module for the server. Unless you have $x000 of extra dough around you better forget it. Besides all the
applications are DOS programs anyway, so you can't run them in Linux native mode. Also, if there is
filenamelength limitations in Novell NFS it is quite useless in *nix environment. (I really don't know NFS,
never seen the beast).

So, how to get the connection to the Netware server, that is the question.

We have a Netware network with 3 servers and appr. 110 PC's connected to it. It is TOTALLY Dos/Windows
environment, running 'Novell standard' Ethernet_802.3 frames, really very ordinary commercial REAL LIFE
setup.

I use in my PC (in addition to DOS) Linux 1.1.65 and Dosemu pre0.53_35 and it works in my machine with
my hardware and our network. The following may or may not work on Your pile of iron.

1) Linux kernel requirements (NONE). There is a config parameter 'IPX-SUPPORT'. It makes no difference
to use it or not to use it. It is provided for future hooks to kernel. There are no working hooks which use it,
not at least in dosemu, not in various configurations I have tested.

2) dosemu requirements (FEW) Here is a fragment of dosemu.conf file. Comment out ipxsupport on and
pktdriver novell_hack

```
#************************** NETWORKING SUPPORT ****************************
#
#     Turn the following option 'on' if you require IPX/SPX emulation.
#     Therefore, there is no need to load IPX.COM within the DOS session.
#     The following option does not emulate LSL.COM, IPXODI.COM, etc.
#     NOTE: MUST HAVE IPX PROTOCOL ENABLED IN KERNEL !!
#ipxsupport on
#
#     Enable Novell 8137->raw 802.3 translation hack in new packet driver.
#pktdriver novell_hack
```

The ipx support does not work yet in dosemu and the novell_hack has been disabled in the latest dosemu
(pl35). There is a gallant effort for better support, look at directory v-net for info, but we are not there yet.

In stock dosemu release (at least in pre0.53_35) in directory net the two files pktnew.c and libpacket.c are the
experimental multi-version. They do not work yet. You need to copy the single-versions over the original
multi-versions.

```
cp pktnew.c.single pktnew.c
```

```
cp libpacket.c.single libpacket.c
```

Remake your dosemu, normally 'make most' and we are almost there.

Test your newly made dosemu and when you are convinced that everything is on order, continue..

3) The shell.

To connect to Netware server you need the driver (ipx) and the shell (netx or vlm).

As a driver you can use either PDIPX, which is really an ipx-to-packet driver shim, or PDETHER which is also ipx-to-packet driver shim, but masquerading as an ODI compliant driver. Which one to use depends really on what frametypes is your Netware server using.

```
a) If the Netware runs on Ethernet_802.3  use PDIPX
b) If the Netware runs on Ethernet_II      use PDETHER
```

If you use PDIPX, you just load

```
PDIPX
NETX
```

and voila there You are, connected...

You can use PDIPX on Ethernet_II frame but then you need to run program called econfig against PDIPX, see Novell docs for info.

If you use PDETHER, because PDETHER is an ODI driver, you load..

```
LSL
PDETHER
IPXODI
NETX
```

and again You should be connected... Because PDETHER is an ODI driver, there must be corresponding section in Your net.cfg file. Read the PDETHER.DOC for info.

There is NO WAY to use PDETHER on Ethernet_802.3 frames. If your Netware runs on 802.3 and you MUST use ODI drivers then you need to run both frametypes on Netware server. You need to load the NIC-driver second time in your server. This time specifying Ethernet_II frame, like I do..

```
load SMCE32 port=6810 Name=Nv Frame=Ethernet_802.3   ; 'novell' frame
load SMCE32 port=6810 Name=Nl Frame=Ethernet_II      ; 'normal' frame
bind ipx to Nv Net=E1
bind ipx to Nl Net=E2
```

Both nets E1 and E2 are really the same net. If I use original PDIPX I connect to E1 with PDETHER I connect to E2.

Some people might want to use VLM drivers, because in DOS environment they are much faster. Don't bother, for reasons unknown, in DOSEMU the VLM drivers are dogs.

With above mentioned setup it IS POSSIBLE to connect to Netware server and even do some useful work, but slowly.

Here is some benchmarking I did using NETX and VLM shells, with and without packetburst. The testprogram was TESTNET.EXE, available somewhere in NetWire. It tests the network transfer speed. I can saturate my ethernet with two stations running at full tilt. Maximum aggregate speed is appr. 900 kilobytes/sec. I'm using SMC Elite 32 EISA board in Server and SMC Elite Ultra in workstation.

	NETX	VLM(0)	VLM(3)
Dos6.2	620	560	760
DosEmu	107	111	60

The figures denote transferspeed in kilobytes/second. VLM(0) means packetburst disabled, VLM(3) packetburst enabled. You can see that the connection with dosemu is not very fast, barely usable.

Few months ago I had a NE2000 clone in my box, with DOS6.2/NETX it would run to appr. 460 kbs. I could live with that. There is still work to be done.

I am well aware that I'm missing a lot of things in here, like

- multiuser dos-session, I don't think it works yet, anyway the speed would be comparable to dead snail.

- tcp-connections from dosemu, I havn't the faintest idea, the only *nix machine in our net is my Linuxbox.

Also I may have totally mixed the working and not working things. As the Dosemu as well as the Kernel are evolving, living things it is sometimes difficult to keep up with the beasts. I do apologize for any mistakes and will gratefully accept and include any corrections and additions to this note.

We all know that the DOSEMU is still ALPHA but it is not really far from BETA. There is some interesting work going on by Vinod G Kulkarni and others, read the relevant pieces in dosemu release (READMEs and such).

Regards, Lauri Tischler ltischler@fipower.pp.fi

7   dosemu and X-windows

7.1   Can I run dosemu in console mode while running X?

Ronald Schalk (R.Schalk@uci.kun.nl) reported (1/17/94) that

Yes, no problem. Just remember to use ctrl-alt-<Fn> to go to a Virtual Console (VC), and you can run any Linux application (dosemu is a linux-application). I've got almost always WP5.1 in a dos session.

[Note: Use ctrl-alt-F7 to switch back to X from dosemu.]

[Note: Some people have reported problems when dosemu is started before X]

7.2   Is it possible to run dosemu in an xterm?

Evmorfopoulos Dimitris (devmorfo@mtu.edu) reported (12/10/93) that

It is possible to run dosemu under an xterm, but without any graphics, and with no more than 128 characters.

H. Peter Anvin (hpa@hook.eecs.nwu.edu) adds (2/6/94)

no more than 128 characters... unless you use a special font. Someone has an IBM PC (CP 437) X font for use with ANSI-graphics on BBS's, as well as a patch for Xterm that *might* include character translation (for letters like \305, \304, \326 for example.

8   Video and sound

8.1   Exiting from dosemu gives me a screen full of garbage.

Keith A Grider (kgrider@magnus.acs.ohio-state.edu) reported (12/5/93) that

I have seen many postings concerning this with exit from X as well as exiting from a graphic dos screen. it seems to be prevalent among ATI graphic card users as well as a few others. The problem is that the font information for the vga text screen is not being saved. The only way I have been able to fix it is to download the vgalib-090.tar.gz file from sunsite.unc.edu. It is (I believe) in the pub/Linux/GCC directory. You get a lot of stuff that is not directly used to solve this problem, but in the fonts directory that is created when you untar the file, there are 2 files of interest, runx and restorefont. Read the README file in this directory. Copy runx and restorefont to a directory in your path. when runx is used, for example, it saves the font information in tmp/fontdata. I use a file called fix which consists of the line:

```
restorefont -r /tmp/fontdata
```

so that it is easy to 'fix' a vt when I go there from X (i.e. `ctrl-alt-f2`). This should also work for dosemu. I think the XFree86 people know about the problem and are working on a solution as this is a bit of a kludge.

8.2   How do I get dosemu to work with my Trident/Actix/other video card?

[The screen flickers violently, displays the video BIOS startup message, and hangs.]

Andrew Tridgell (`tridge@nimbus.anu.edu.au`) reported (1/29/94) that

I found with early versions it would work if I used:

```
ports { 0x42 }
```

but that sometimes my machine would crash when it was cycling the video bios in dosemu. This is because you're allowing the VGA bios to re-program your clock, which severely stuffs with Linux.

This prompted me to write the readonly and masking patches for dosemu, which I believe are still in the latest version. I now use:

```
ports { readonly 0x42 }
```

and it boots dosemu more slowly, but more reliably.

Tim Shnaider (`tims@kcbbs.gen.nz`) also reported (1/18/94) that

One way of fixing this is to use the GETROM program to dump your video bios to a file and edit the config file in the `/etc/dosemu` directory There will be a few video lines. Here is my video line

```
video { vga console graphics chipset trident memsize 1024 vbios_file
/etc/dosemu/vbios }
```

where vbios is the file generated by typing

```
getrom > vbios
```

Douglas Gleichman (`p86884@tcville.edsg.hac.com`) reported (9/1/94) that (with the ATI Graphics Ultra)

For DOSEMU 0.52 you need to add this line to your dosemu.conf file:

```
ports  { 0x1ce 0x1cf 0x238 0x23b 0x23c 0x23f 0x9ae8 0x9ae9 0x9aee 0x9aef }
```

The board self test will list a failure but graphics programs will run fine.

8.3   Why doesn't my soundcard software work with dosemu?

Hannu Savolainen (`hsavolai@cs.Helsinki.FI`) reported (3/21/94) that

The DOSEMU and any DOS program with it run under control of a protected mode operating system. This means that the memory is not mapped as the program expects. If it somehow manages to start DMA based recording with SB, the recorded sound doesn't find it's way to the application. It just destroys some data in the memory.

James B. MacLean (jmaclean@fox.nstn.ns.ca) reported (6/19/94) that

Sorry to disappoint, but at this time DOSEMU does not support directly the necessary interception of interrupts or DMA generally required for sound card access via DOSEMU :-(.

It's bound to happen at some future date though :-),

9 Other Hardware

9.1 How do I get my xxxxx device working under dosemu?

Corey Sweeney (corey@bbs.xnet.com) reported (5/30/94) that

Here is a log of my adventures trying to get devices working under dosemu. So far I've gotten my voice mail system working and my scanner half working. Here's how:

1. Look in your manual and find if your card uses any ports. If your manual gives you some, put them in your config file at the "ports" line. Remember that sometimes you need to have several ports in a row, and the first one might be the only one documented.

2. Try it out. If it doesn't work, or you don't have a manual (or your manual is as crappy as my AT&T manual:) then run dosemu with "dos -D+i 2> /tmp/io.debug". Run your device software, then exit dosemu. Look through /tmp/io.debug and find any port numbers it might give you. Try adding those to the port lines and try running dosemu again.

3. If you still fail then you may need interrupts. Find out what interrupt the card uses and get the SIG.tgz (silly interrupt generator) from somewhere on tsx-11.mit.edu. Install it as specified in the instructions.

and that's about it...

Question: What if my card uses DMA? Answer: You're screwed.

10 Problems and fixes

10.1 Why does dosemu 0.52 fail under kernels newer than 1.1.30?

(8/5/94)

Dosemu 0.52 is not compatible with kernels newer than 1.1.30. This problem will be fixed in dosemu 0.53.

10.2 I've enabled EMS memory in dosemu.conf but it does not help.

Rob Janssen (rob@pe1chl.ampr.org) reported (7/11/94)

Don't forget to load the provided ems.sys from the config.sys file.

10.3 How do I get rid of all those annoying "disk change" messages?

(8/11/94)

Grab and install klogd. Try

sunsite.unc.edu:/pub/Linux/system/Daemons/sysklogd1.2.tgz

10.4   Why is the cursor position wrong?

(7/9/94)

This is a known bug in dosemu 0.52. It will be fixed in dosemu 0.53.

10.5   Why does my busmouse act funny under dosemu 0.52?

James B. MacLean (jmaclean@fox.nstn.ns.ca) reported (7/8/94) that

Busmouse support is quite ALPHA at this time (as is DOSEMU :-)), and will be continually refined for a while :-). Look for better support in the upcoming releases.

10.6   Why won't dosemu run a second time after exiting in console mode?

Aldy Hernandez (aldy@sauron.cc.andrews.edu) reported (7/8/94) that

You should disable your video and/or bios caching.

10.7   Some dos applications still do not detect DPMI under dosemu0.52.

James B. MacLean (jmaclean@fox.nstn.ns.ca) reported (6/19/94) that

At this time (as of 0.52 release) DOSEMU is still growing with respect to DPMI. It will run certain DPMI programs, but has a ways to go yet. As suggested there needs to be more of the calls implemented, etc. Please be patient :-), as it's bound to come in time.

10.8   Why does dosemu give "divide overflow" errors after running for more than 24-hours?

(1/17/94)

This is a known bug. It will (hopefully) be fixed in an upcoming release. For now, you can simply exit dosemu and start it again.

10.9   Why will dosemu run in a term but not in the console?

JyiJiin Luo (jjluo@casbah.acns.nwu.edu) reported (4/19/94) that

I experienced exactly the same problem before. I figured out all the video shadow in my AMI BIOS must be disabled. Now dosemu runs fine on my system.

10.10   How can I speed up dosemu?

Mark Rejhon (mdrejhon@undergrad.math.uwaterloo.ca) reported (4/7/94) that

TIP: Speed up your DOS "dir" listings by about 25%-50% or so by typing break off at the DOS prompt or including it in autoexec.bat.

TIP: Use the nnansi.com ANSI driver to speed up the "dir" output even more at roughly 50%-100% more. It works properly in non-graphics mode, unlike turbo.com.

Joel M. Hoffman (joel@rac1.wam.umd.edu) reported (4/23/94) that

Ironically, I've found that it's sometimes faster to run dosemu in an Emacs terminal emulator rather than directly to the console. Emacs's output optimization is what makes the difference here.

Put the following in your .emacs:

```
(defun do-dos ()
  (interactive)
  (terminal-emulator "dos" "/usr/local/bin/dos" ()))
```

and then "emacs -f do-dos" will run the dosemu inside the buffer. Make sure you emacs window is 25x80, of course.

Pete Heist (`heistp@rpi.edu`) reported (5/13/94) that

If you compile it with the "`-funroll-all-loops`" option you will get MUCH faster screen output. Some other parts of the emulator will run much faster as well. Realize that the consequence of this is a larger executable which eats a little more memory, even though it's demand loaded.

Georg Wiegand (`gw@gwcomp.e.open.de`) reported (5/16/94) that

You also can use the keyword `HogThreshold` in `/etc/dosemu.conf`. The greater the following number the more calculating-time dosemu gets. For example, I use "`HogThreshold 60000`" on my 386/87-20 laptop.

10.11 My CDROM drive has problems reading some files under dosemu.

Vinod G Kulkarni (`vinod@cse.iitb.ernet.in`) reported (4/7/94) that

When a CDROM is mounted from linux and used from within DOSEMU (mapped drive), there could be some problems. The cdrom driver (iso9660) in the kernel tries to find out the type of the file (i.e. binary or text). If it can't find, it tries to guess the type of the file using a heuristic. This heuristic fails under some circumstances when a (almost) text file is to be treated as binary. (I do not know if it is a bug or feature.)

The result of this is that if you copy such a file from cdrom (from linux itself, and not necessarily dosemu), the resulting file will be usually bigger than original file. (Blanks get added before ^J,^M.) So a program running in dosemu gives an error or hangs, which may be mistaken as problem of dosemu.

Rob Janssen (`pe1chl@rabo.nl`) reported (8/10/94) that

The way to solve this is to turn off conversion altogether. Pass the option "`-o conv=binary`" to the mount command mounting the CDROM, or use the following in `/etc/fstab`:

```
/dev/cdrom      /cdrom          iso9660 conv=binary,ro
```

No patches to the kernel are necessary.

10.12 Where did the debugging output go?

As of dosemu0.49pl4, stderr is automatically redirected to /dev/null. Try "dos -D+a 2>debug" to turn on debugging information and redirect it to the file "debug".

10.13 Why does dosemu lock up after one keystroke?

(12/17/93)

You need to turn on the keyboard interrupt in the dosemu config file. Add a line to the config file:

```
keybint on
```

Shouldn't be a problem in dosemu0.52.

10.14   Why are my keystrokes echoed ttwwiiccee??

Nick Holloway (`alfie@dcs.warwick.ac.uk`) reported (2/22/94) that

After running dos after playing with some stty settings, I was getting doubled key presses. I can now reveal what the reason is!

It only happens when dos is run on the console with 'istrip' set. This is (I think) because the raw scancodes are mutilated by the 'istrip', so that key release events look like key press events.

So, the input processing needs to be turned off when using the scan codes on a console (it wouldn't be a good idea to do it for tty lines).

10.15   Why are characters < 128 highlighted and blinking?

Chris Kuehnke (`Christian.Kuehnke@Informatik.Uni-Oldenburg.DE`) reported (3/21/94) that

I think I've found a bug in dosemu0.50pl1; with a MDA card displayed characters > 128 automagically appeared as highlighted and blinking.

This patch fixed the problem for me [but on the other hand, maybe I'm totally wrong ;-)]:

```
--- video.c~     Sat Mar 19 00:50:25 1994
+++ video.c      Sat Mar 19 20:36:10 1994
@@ -721,7 +721,7 @@
    int x, y, i, tmp;
    unsigned int s;
    static int gfx_flag = 0;
-   char c;
+   u_char c;
    us *sm;

    if (d.video >= 3)
```

11   Contributing to the dosemu project

11.1   Who is responsible for dosemu?

(3/18/94)

Dosemu is built upon the work of Matthias Lautner and Robert Sanders.   James B. MacLean (`jmaclean@fox.nstn.ns.ca`) is responsible for organizing the latest releases of dosemu.

```
              History of dosemu

    Version    Date                Person
    -------------------------------------------------
    0.1        September 3, 1992    Matthias Lautner
    0.2        September 13, 1992   Matthias Lautner
    0.3        ???                  Matthias Lautner
    0.4        November 26, 1992    Matthias Lautner
    0.47       January 27, 1993     Robert Sanders
```

```
0.47.7      February 5, 1993      Robert  Sanders
0.48        February 16, 1993     Robert  Sanders
0.48p11     February 18, 1993     Robert  Sanders
0.49        May 20, 1993          Robert  Sanders
0.49p12     November 18, 1993     James  MacLean
0.49p13     November 30, 1993     James  MacLean
0.49p13.3   December 3, 1993      James  MacLean
0.50        March 4, 1994         James  MacLean
0.50p11     March 18, 1994        James  MacLean
0.52        June 16, 1994         James  MacLean
```

11.2   I want to help. Who should I contact?

The dosemu project is a team effort. If you wish to contribute, see the DPR (DOSEMU Project Registry). A current copy may be found in `dspsun.eas.asu.edu:/pub/dosemu`.

Part XVI

The Linux Distribution HOWTO

Copyright by Erik Troan, `ewt@sunsite.unc.edu`
v3.0, 10 February 1995
This document lists the various software distributions and services available for Linux via mail order, anonymous FTP, and other sources. It is based on previous versions by Matt Welsh, `mdw@sunsite.unc.edu`.

Contents

1   Introduction

There is no single distribution of the Linux software. Instead, there are many such distributions, available both via anonymous FTP and mail order on floppy, tape, or CD-ROM. This document is an attempt to present information on many of the available distributions of Linux. This document also contains information on many miscellaneous services and goods available for Linux, ranging from consulting and support to T-shirts and virtual beer.

The purpose of this document is to provide short summaries of the many Linux distributions and mail-order services, and to provide pointers for the reader to find more information. You shouldn't base your decision of which Linux distribution to use based solely on this document.

This is a PRELIMINARY version of the Distribution HOWTO. It is far from complete; there are many more Linux distributions and services than are listed here. Unfortunately, I have not received submissions from many of the organizations providing these services. Please see Section 4 at the end of this document for information on making a submission. It's easy and will take less then five minutes.

1.1   New versions of this document

New versions of this document will be posted periodically (about once a month) to the newsgroups `comp.os.linux.answers` and `comp.os.linux.misc`. The document is archived on a number of Linux FTP sites, including `sunsite.unc.edu` in `pub/Linux/docs/HOWTO`.

You can also view the latest version of this on the World Wide Web via the URL `http://sunsite.unc.edu/mdw/HOWTO/Distribution-HOWTO.html`.

1.2   And so on...

Please see section "New `comp.os.linux.announce` Policy" at the end of this document for information on how to make submissions to this document.

Disclaimer: I make absolutely *no* guarantee as to the correctness of the information, prices, and ordering details given in this document. Several of the entries in this HOWTO are a bit outdated; check the last modified field of each to get an idea. Furthermore, unless otherwise stated the Linux software comes with *ABSOLUTELY NO WARRANTY*.

I do not endorse or work for any of the distributors listed in this document. I merely include their information here as a service to the Linux community, as a "buyer's guide". Inclusion in this document does not mean that I recommend any of the products listed here.

The entries for each distributor are included as they sent them to me. I am not responsible for any spelling errors or mistakes in the content of this document; most of the entries here have only been edited to a limited extent by myself.

Feel free to mail any questions or comments about this HOWTO to Erik Troan, `ewt@sunsite.unc.edu`.

And now for the good stuff.

2 Linux Software Distributions

This section describes complete distributions of Linux software, available either via anonymous FTP or from mail order.

In each of the following entries, my own comments are followed by the information from the distributors themselves. You may safely disregard anything I say. :)

An oft-recurring question in the Linux world is, "What distribution should I choose?" This is not an easy question to answer: It depends greatly on your needs and available resources.

The current de facto standard distribution is the Slackware release. Slackware is easy to install and fairly complete. It's also more or less up-to-date with current versions of Linux software. The Linux Installation HOWTO documents installation of Slackware. I personally recommend Slackware for most new Linux users.

However, if you have a CD-ROM drive, you have more distributions to choose from. I haven't personally reviewed most of them, and you're more likely to get help from people on the Net for distributions such as Slackware (which is available freely on the Net, as well as on CD-ROM). On the other hand, some CD-ROM distributions come with documentation and support of their own. All I can say is that a good number of people have had success installing and using the Slackware distribution.

The Debian distribution is currently under development by a "semi-closed" group of developers (rather then an individual) and has been adopted as the Free Software Foundation's Linux distribution.

Other distributions such as Slackware Pro, Red Hat Linux, and Yggdrasil take advantage of the storage space available on CD-ROM to minimize the amount of hard disk space Linux takes.

The bottom line is that there's no easy way to pick a distribution out of the air. My own suggestion is to use Slackware. Other people will suggest MCC-Interim, TAMU, and others based on their own experience. By way of disclaimer, I don't use Slackware myself (in fact, I don't use any standard Linux distribution), but I have installed it for testing purposes.

2.1 Slackware Linux Distribution

Distributor:

> Patrick Volkerding, `volkerdi@mhd1.moorhead.msus.edu`.

Description:

> Slackware Linux is a full featured distribution of the Linux operating system designed for 386/486 computers with a 3.5" floppy. Slackware changes rapidly, but here's a current (partial) feature list:

> **A:**

>> Base Linux system

AP:

Various applications that do not need X

D:

Program Development (C, C++, Kernel source, Lisp, Perl, etc.)

E:

GNU Emacs (19.27, with and without X11 support. Your choice.)

F:

FAQ lists (last updated: Oct 1994)

I:

Info pages.

IV:

Interviews: libraries, include files, Doc and Idraw apps for X

N:

Networking (TCP/IP, UUCP, Mail)

OOP:

Object Oriented Programming (GNU Smalltalk 1.1.1) and X11 interface

Q:

All kinds of extra kernels (based on Linux 1.1.59)

T:

TeX

TCL:

Tcl/Tk/TclX, Tcl language, and Tk toolkit for developing X apps

X:

XFree-86 3.1 Base X Window System

XAP:

Applications for X

XD:

XFree-86 3.1 X server development, PEX extensions, and man pages

XV:

XView3.2p1-X11R6. (OpenLook *virtual* Window Manager, apps)

Y:

Games (that do not require X)

Availability:

The home site is `ftp.cdrom.com`, where the latest distribution can be found in `/pub/linux/slackware`.

Ordering:

FTP only, although various independent distributors provide it on disk, floppy, and CD.

Entry last modified:

14 Dec 1994

2.2   MCC Interim Linux

The current MCC-Interim release is based on Linux 1.0 with a few patches. . If you are one of those people who demands to be on top of the current release, this release isn't for you. However, if you're looking for a small and stable Linux system, this makes a good starting point.

Distributor:

Dr. A. V. Le Blanc, LeBlanc@mcc.ac.uk.

Description:

Base Linux installation. Complete sources and patches for all included software are available. Full details vary from release to release; see /pub/linux/mcc-interim/*/Acknowledgements at ftp.mcc.ac.uk. Roughly: this includes the kernel (with source), C, C++, groff, man pages, basic utilities, networking. The binaries fit on 6 or 7 floppies. It is also possible to have them on a DOS or Linux partition on a hard drive (plus one floppy) or on an NFS-mountable partition (plus two floppies). New versions appear at 2-3 month intervals, depending on various factors.

Availability:

By anonymous ftp from ftp.mcc.ac.uk; mirrored at tsx-11.mit.edu, nic.funet.fi, sunsite.unc.edu, and elsewhere. At ftp.mcc.ac.uk, in /pub/linux/mcc-interim.

Miscellaneous:

Suggestions and contributions are welcome.

Entry last modified:

14 Dec 1994

2.3   TAMU Linux Distribution

Distributor:

Dave Safford, Texas A&M University, dave.safford@net.tamu.edu.

Description:

TAMU.99p12+ is the latest release in the TAMU linux series. Unlike previous releases, this one includes both *integrated source* and binary sets, with the entire binary set created from a single top level source make. This ensures that all programs are compiled and linked with the same current tools and libraries, and guarantees availability of working source for every program in the binary set. In addition, the new boot diskette fully automates the installation process, including partitioning, lilo bootstrapping, and network configuration. Installation requires no rebooting, and requires the user to know only the host's name and IP address. At every step of installation, the program provides intelligent defaults, making it a snap for novices, while allowing experts full flexibility in setting installation parameters. Reliability has been improved over past TAMU installation by the use of labels on all disk images, so that the program can detect and recover from bad or misordered diskettes.

This release is a full featured package, including XFree86-1.3, emacs-19.18, net-2, bootutils, and sources for all installation programs (without any use restrictions :-).

Availability:

The latest TAMU release is available by anonymous ftp from net.tamu.edu:pub/linux.

Entry last modified:

31 Oct 1993.

2.4   The BOGUS Linux Release

Distributor:

The BOGUS Group, `linux-bogus@cs.unc.edu`

Description:

BOGUS is an unsupported, ftp-able distribution targeted at competent Linux hackers who want a stable development system. If you do not have experience developing, installing, and maintaining a Linux system, BOGUS is probably not for you.

BOGUS is a "bootstrapping" release: all of the patches needed to compile the complete system are provided, including explicit instructions on how we did the compilation. Indeed, the final build was totally automatic, and required the user to invoke a single command.

BOGUS has many other features, but the inclusion of pristine source, detailed patches, and a utility to support automatic patch application and compilation is the most important feature of BOGUS. For more information and a complete list of features, license restrictions, and other details, please see the Announce-BOGUS-* files at the ftp sites.

Availability:

The following sites are official mirror sites for the BOGUS release:

- ftp.cdrom.com:/pub/bogus
- ftp.gwdg.de:/pub/linux/bogus
- ftp.cps.cmich.edu:/pub/linux/packages/bogus
- ftp.nvg.unit.no:/pub/linux/bogus
- ftp.thepoint.com:/pub/linux/BOGUS
- ftp.ibp.fr:/pub/linux/distributions/bogus
- sunsite.unc.edu:/pub/Linux/distributions/bogus

Ordering:

BOGUS 1.0.1 is also available on the Trans-Ameritech Systems "Linux Plus BSD CD-ROM" (Fall Supplement 2, November 1994) for $19.95. Trans-Ameritech may be contacted at: 408.727.3883 (voice), 408.727.3882 (fax), or order@trans-am.com.

Miscellaneous:

To join the BOGUS mailing list, send mail to "majordomo@cs.unc.edu" with "subscribe linux-bogus" in the body of the message (i.e., *NOT* in the subject). When you do this, make sure that you have a valid return address – many people who set up a mailer for the first time have a return address which looks like joe@pizza instead of joe@pizza.cs.unc.edu. If you interact with the majordomo server successfully, you will receive mail. If you don't receive mail in about an hour, please don't continue to use the majordomo server as test bed.

Please note that the BOGUS release is COMPLETELY UNSUPPORTED: mail sent to the mailing list may not be answered, bugs may not be fixed, and it may be quite a while before there is another BOGUS release.

Entry last modified:

14 Dec 1994.

2.5   Linux Support Team Erlangen Distribution (LST)

Distributor:

The Linux Support Team Erlangen, a small group of students at the University of Erlangen-Nuernberg. Contact Stefan Probst (`snprobst@cip.informatik.uni-erlangen.de`) or Ralf Flaxa (`rfflaxa@informatik.uni-erlangen.de`). Probably, there will be a collective address soon.

Description:

The LST distribution's goal is to provide a solid, reliable, easy to install (even for beginners) and well-documented system. We are not hunting for the newest kernel or gcc versions. We do updates when they are necessary or provide really new functionality, are well tested, integrated in the system and working smoothly with the rest of the system. The distribution consists of a base system and additional packages. Currently the following packages are available: doku (doc), text, tex, develop, xdevelop, xbasis, xappl, xemacs, tinyx, network, grafik, src, misc.

The complete system is 50 HD disks and 1500 pages printed documentation including the LDP guides (IGS,KHG,NAG), HOWTOs, FAQs, the German Linuxhandbuch, install-guide and many other useful documents we collected over the time.

Our distribution is preconfigured for German users and comes with a 50 page step by step installation guide that leads you through the menu-driven installation scripts (both in German). We started this distribution to help newcomers with their first steps into Linux. Therefore our scripts are smart enough to handle all of the "dirty work" like setting up system configuraton (including LILO, modem, mouse, mounts, mtools, access to DOS, users, X11) and network configuration (TCP/IP, Routing, Mail, News, UUCP, SLIP).

Historically (and of course easier for us) most of the documentation for this distribution is written in German, sorry, but we are planning to translate those documents in English, but at the moment we don't have time for this. Any volunteers are welcome!

Our scripts also accept to install SLS and Slackware packages, but with no warranty if they work well together with the rest of the system.

Availability:

Via anonymous ftp: `ftp.uni-erlangen.de` under `pub/Linux/LST.Distribution`, or on 3.5" disks (also on one QIC-80 tape).

Ordering:

order at following address: Stefan Probst, In der Reuth 200, 91056 Erlangen, Germany.

- complete documentation (IGS, LHB, KHG, GDB, NAG, HOWTOs, FAQs, Installguide) together over 1500 pages for DM 139,– (plus shipping).

- complete documentation plus complete distribution on QIC-80 tape (about 65 MB) for DM 199,– (including shipping in Germany).

- complete documentation plus complete distribution on about 50 3.5" disks for DM 269,– (including shipping in Germany).

Entry last modified:

21 Dec 1993.

2.6   S.u.S.E. GmbH German Linux CD-ROM

Distributor:

```
S.u.S.E. GmbH
Gebhardtstr. 2
90762 Fuerth
Germany
```

Description:

This is a CD especially for German users. It contains a german version of the Slackware Distribution and two additional german distributions based on Slackware and SLS. It contains additional software, such as the Postgres system, the pbm-Tools and lots of other tools and utilities (ctwm window manager, GREAT environment, andrew toolkit, the POV-ray raytracer and so on). The source code of the complete system is included, too, as is a live system to enable using software without the need to install everything to the hard drive. The current version of the CD contains version 1.2.0 of the Slackware distribution containing version 1.0 of the linux kernel, version 2.5.8 of the GNU-Compiler and XFree86*tm* 2.1.

A german installation guide will help new users to successfully install the system.

The CD ist updated every three months, so the next one will be released in July 1994.

Ordering:

You can order by mail, by phone (49-911-74053-31), by Fax (49-911-7417755) or by sending email to `bestellung@suse.de`.

Price: The price for a single CD is 89,– DM for new customers. If you are already a S.u.S.E.-customer, you will get the CD for an update-price of 78,– DM. There is also the possibility to subscribe for one year; then you will receive 4 CDs for the price of 230,– DM.

Disks: Of course, you can get the German version of the Slackware Distribution on 3,5" disks. You can get either a basis version of the distribution (about 28 disks) for 89,– DM, the "standard" version (about 38 disks) for 119,– DM or the "full" version (about 59 disks) for 159,– DM. The update prices are 69,– DM, 94,– DM and 139,– DM respectively.

Documentation: S.u.S.E. is selling high-quality printed issues of the books from the Linux Documentation project (LDP) for people that would like to have a real book and not only printed loose papers. The prices are 24,– DM for Matt Welsh's *Linux Installation and Getting Started*, 39,– DM for Olaf Kirch's *Network Administrators' Guide* and 29,– DM for Michael K. Johnson's *Kernel Hackers' guide*. Additionally, S.u.S.E. offers the complete O'Reilly series which is the best documentation available for Unix in general. Of course you can order the well known german Linux books: *Deutsches Anwenderhandbuch* for 49,– DM and *Linux - vom PC zur Workstation* for 38,– DM.

Motif: Metrolink Motif for Linux is available for the price of 169,– DM for the runtime system only and for the price of 288,– DM you will get the runtime and development system.

Miscellaneous:

Service and support for our customers by Email, Fax, snail mail and phone (hotline Monday and Thursday from 13:00h-17:00h.)

Free info material and catalogues of CDROMs and books. (All Infomagic Unix CDs available).

Selling commercial software for Linux.

Development of individual software for Linux and other Unix systems.

Almost anything concerning Linux - just ask!

Entry last modified:

23 May 1994

2.7   Debian Linux Distribution

Distributor:

Ian A. Murdock, `imurdock@gnu.ai.mit.edu`.

Description:

For those of you who are not familiar with Debian, it is an effort to create a well thought-out, powerful, flexible yet complete Linux distribution. The motivations behind Debian are detailed in the Debian Manifesto, a copy of which can be acquired as described below.

For   up-to-date   information, please look at the files in the directory `/pub/Linux/distributions/debian/info` at `sunsite.unc.edu`. If you do not have access to the Internet or FTP, you may obtain printed copies by sending a self-addressed, stamped envelope to:

```
The Debian Linux Association
Station 11
P.O. Box 3121
West Lafayette, IN  47906
USA
```

This information includes how Debian can be obtained (via FTP or mail-order), why Debian is being constructed (the Manifesto) and other general information (including how to join the Debian mailing lists).

Availability:

Debian has not yet been "officially" released, but BETA releases are available to the general public at `sunsite.unc.edu` in the directory `/pub/Linux/distributions/debian`.

Entry last modified:

21 Feb 1994.

2.8 Yggdrasil Plug-and-Play Linux CD-ROM and the Linux Bible

Distributor:

```
Yggdrasil Computing, Incorporated
4880 Stevens Creek Blvd., Suite 205
San Jose, CA 95129-1034
toll free (800) 261-6630, (408) 261-6630, fax (408) 261-6631
info@yggdrasil.com
```

Description:

Yggdrasil Plug-and-Play Linux is a complete CD-ROM distribution of the Linux operating system. It includes a great deal of software—nearly every package that you would expect to find on a complete UNIX system is available. A complete file list is available via FTP from `yggdrasil.com`.

The Linux Bible is a compendium of Linux documentation, including 3 books from the Linux Documentation Project, The Yggdrasil installation manual, and the complete set of Linux HOWTO guides.

At the top of the sophistication hierarchy, programmers who want to explore or add the occasional feature know that Yggdrasil is the Linux distribution with a fully buildable source tree and with the ability to automatically trace installed files back to their sources.

Users who want maximum performance will appreciate that the major system components have been recompiled with -O6 optimization, and the SCSI clustering which reduces the build time on the source tree from 28 to 22 hours (over 20%) on 486DX2-66. Using IDE? Activate the multisector IDE code!

Everybody, especially new users, will appreciate the Plug-and-Play operation for which Yggdrasil's product is named. Put the media in a computer with supported hardware, turn the computer on, and it's running everything, straight from the CDROM.

The login screen lists a number of preconfigured user names, including "install", which installs the system, giving paragraphs of explanation about every question that it asks the user. The install script even searches for a modem, and, upon finding it, configures mail and UUCP so that mail sent to an internet address is transparently delivered through a bulletin board system at Yggdrasil.

X windows configuration is automated too, prompting the user for configuration information the first time `xinit` is run.

From X windows, a graphical control panel allows simple "fill in the blanks" configuration of networking, SLIP, outgoing UUCP, the printer, NNTP, and many other features that previously required the knowledge of a system administrator to configure.

For more information, send mail to `info@yggdrasil.com`, FTP to `yggdrasil.com`, or contact us by any convenient method.

Ordering:

Plug-and-Play Linux costs $39.95 is and available directly from Yggdrasil or from your local computer, software or technical book store. If Plug-and-Play Linux is not available from your favorite reseller, help promote Linux by making it your mission to change that. Give your reseller our phone number and demand that they carry Plug-and-Play Linux.

Yggdrasil offers a $10 discount for upgrades or crossgrades. Send us your old Yggdrasil release and a check for $29.95 + $5 shipping and handling to upgrade. Or do the same, but send us a competing distribution such any version of SCO, Esix, Minix, or one of the CD's with the slackware floppy images, and tell us where you got it, so that we can make sure that your favorite reseller carries our products too.

Miscellaneous:

Yggdrasil also sells OSF/Motif and The Linux Bible, a compilation of works from the Linux Documentation project. In addition to a copy of the Plug-and-Play Linux manual, The Linux Bible includes *Linux Installation and Getting Started*, *Network Administrator's Guide*, *Kernel Hacker's Guide*, and HOWTO guides on hardware compatibility, distributions, DOS emulation, ethernet, floppy tape, installation, mail, networking version 2, MGR (an alternative to X windows), X windows, usenet news, printing, SCSI, serial communications, sound, and UUCP. The Linux Bible costs $39.95 and is printed on recycled paper. $1 from every copy sold is donated to the Linux Documentation Project. OSF/Motif costs $149.95, $5 of which is donated to the development of a free Motif clone.

Entry last modified:

16 May 1994

2.9   Linux from Nascent CD-ROM

Distributor:

Nascent Technology

Description:

The Linux from Nascent CDROM is a new distribution of the Linux operating system which includes over 400 megabytes of source code, binaries, and documentation for Linux and applications. It features automated root, swap, package, network, and user account installation from CDROM. Linux can be can be run directly from the CDROM and floppy. The Nascent CDROM features Xwindows, Openlook, TeX, GNU compiler and utilities, Magic and Spice electronic design tools, and over 100 high resolution images translated from Kodak PhotoCD(TM). Each source archive is distributed with an associated notes file to allow you to browse and install applications using a consistent interface.

A listing of the contents of the Nascent CDROM as well as a current copy of the CDROM announcement and order form may be obtained via anonymous ftp at `netcom.com:/pub/nascent`.

Ordering:

The Linux from Nascent CDROM, Version 1.0, is only $39.95 plus shipping and handling. Nascent also offers the Linux from Nascent Plus package for only $89.95, which includes six months of email support and a 30
the CDROM with your CDROM purchase. Nascent accepts Mastercard, VISA, checks, and money orders as payment.

To order your Linux from Nascent CDROM, mail, email or fax a completed order form to:

```
Nascent Technology
Linux from Nascent CDROM
P.O. Box 60669
Sunnyvale CA 94088-0669 USA
Tel: (408) 737-9500
Fax: (408) 241-9390
Email: nascent@netcom.com
```

Entry last modified:

28 Nov 1993.

2.10   Red Hat Software Linux CD-ROM

Distributor:

Red Hat Software, info@redhat.com

Description:

RHS Linux contains over 650Mb of binaries and source code and comes with a manual that covers the installation process and the RHS Linux system administration tools. In addition the manual contains the entire Linux Installation and Getting Started book by Matt Welsh, and Ian Jackson's Linux FAQ. Included with the purchase of RHS Linux is 30 days of free installation support, and a card for a complimentary copy of the Linux Journal. More details are available from our FTP site.

Availibility:

Available directly from Red Hat Software and most distributors of Linux related products.

Ordering:

Please contact Red Hat Software for ordering details. (see contact info below). Suggested retail price is $49.95.

Miscellaneous:

```
Red Hat Software
PO Box 4325
Chapel Hill, NC 27515
(919) 309-9560
```

Entry last modified:

13 Dec 1994.

2.11   Unifix 1.02 CD-ROM

Distributor:

Unifix Software GmbH, Braunschweig, Germany

Description:

This is a Linux CD-ROM distribution with emphasis on easy and fast installation. Though it is possible to install everything on the hard disk, we do not recommend so, because it runs fast enough directly from CD. For example starting emacs the first time (in text mode) takes:

```
From single speed Mitsumi: 24 s
From double speed Mitsumi: 11 s
From Toshiba 3401:          7 s
```

The dynamic buffer cache of Linux takes care of the second and subsequent times a program is started, which needs less than one second.

Our system requires about 5 MB on the hard disk for configuration files and system management tools. Additionally we recommend a 16 MB swap partition. The distribution contains most of the standard programs in current versions, e.g. Linux 0.99.15e, XFree 2.0, emacs 19.22 and gcc 2.5.7. Full preconfigured source for everything is included.

Because Unifix is a European distribution it provides full support for iso8859-1 character sets. From the shells and emacs through ls, TeX and the print system everything supports 8-bit characters.

Printing is supported through System V compatible printer drivers which can be controlled through lp's -o options. Printer drivers are included for dumb text mode printers, for postscript- or ghostscript-compatible printers and for networked printing. These drivers know how to guess the type of the files so e.g. compressed man pages or DVI files can be printed directly.

Ordering:

Unifix is available only on CD. It comes in a Unifix/Linux binder with two boot floppies and about 70 pages of installation instructions in german. An english version will be available Apr 94. The price is 159 DM (about $100) and includes taxes and shipping; Eurocard/Mastercard/Visa are accepted.

```
Telephone        +49 (0)531 515161
Fax              +49 (0)531 515162
Mail             Unifix Software GmbH
                 Postfach 4918
                 D-38039 Braunschweig
                 Germany
```

Entry last modified:

18 Feb 1994.

3 Redistributors and Miscellany

This section lists re-sellers or re-distributors of the Linux distributions listed above. In other words, the people selling the below software more than likely do NOT maintain or support the software itself.

This section also lists distributors selling commercial software for Linux (such as Motif) and miscellany, such as documentation.

3.1 Clark Internet Services

Distributor:

Clark Internet Services, C/O Stephen Balbach

Description:

The latest version of Linux on disk and tape direct from the net at affordable prices. 120MB installed on 3.5" disks. 90MB installed on 5.25" disks.

Ordering:

Slackware on 32 3.5" disks: $50 (USPS 2nd day). SLS on 32 5.25" disks: $40 (USPS 2nd day).

Installation and Getting Started (c) Copyright Matt Welsh. 150+page laser printed, professional bound manual. Everything to get installed and running in one easy book. $15 if ordering set (at cost price!). $20 separate.

Availability:

For more complete information, including a multipage description of Linux, a hardware compatibility sheet, and more detailed package descriptions send mail to linux-all@clark.net for auto-reply info (30k of text).

Ordering:

Check, money-order

```
Stephen Balbach
5437 Enberend Terrace
Columbia, MD 21045
```

Credit Card orders call 410-740-1157 (Visa, MasterCard, AmXpres)

Entry last modified:

31 Oct 1993.

3.2   Extent Verlag, LDP Distribution

Distributor:

Extent Verlag Berlin, Germany

Description:

Extent has published the *Linux Installation and Getting Started* manual, Version 2.0 by Matt Welsh in order to make it available to Linux users within Germany and Europe. In spite of being non-commercial, the manual was printed with 2540 dpi and bound in soft cover. It's handy paperback format is 148 x 210 mm. Other LDP manuals are being prepared as soon as possible.

Extent also tries to make SLACKWARE available to everybody within Germany and Europe just for the ordinary diskette price. This means, you pay only the diskettes and get the newest SLACKWARE distribution for free, just in the sense of Free Software. The 3.5" diskettes are fully error-checked, of course.

Availability:

Extent Verlag Berlin, Postfach 12 66 48, D-10594 Berlin, Germany. phone +49 30 3244021, fax +49 30 3249685.

Ordering:

Linux Installation and Getting Started, 192 pages. ISBN 3-926671-12-2. Costs within Germany DM 15.80 (tax and shipping included), within Europe DM 16.50 (shipping included).

Full Slackware (latest version) on 50 diskettes. Within Germany, DM 100.00 plus DM 10.00 for shipping. Within Europe, DM 100.00 plus DM 20.00 for shipping.

Ordering by sending cheque to address above or money order (don't forget your address!) to Extent Verlag Berlin, Germany Postbank Berlin, BLZ 10010010, bank account 1769-104 or every book store.

Entry last modified:

25 March 1994.

3.3   Fintronic Linux Systems

Distributor:

Fintronic Linux Systems

Description:

We sell fully installed, custom configured Linux systems for about the price which you'd pay for the hardware alone. We offer desktop and notebook machines. We ship worldwide and accept payment by check and credit cards. If you have any questions or would like to be added to our mailing list, send mail to linux@fintronic.com.

Availability:

For   our   latest   pricelist,   finger   linux@fintronic.com   or Web to http://www.fintronic.com/linux/catalog.html. Prices change frequently as we are constantly looking for the best deals for our customers.

Ordering:

```
email:  linux@fintronic.com
  fax:  +1.415.325-4908
voice:  +1.415.325-4474
 Mail:  Fintronic USA, Inc.
        1360 Willow Rd., Suite 205
        Menlo Park, CA 94025
        USA
```

Entry last modified:

24 Mar 1994.

3.4   InfoMagic Developer's Resource CD-ROM kit

Distributor:

InfoMagic, Inc.

Description:

The InfoMagic Linux Developer's Resource is a complete snapshot of the sunsite.unc.edu and tsx-11.mit.edu archives. It also includes the complete GNU software collection (in source form). The following Linux "distributions" are included on the discs: Slackware, Bogus, Debian, SLS, TAMU, MCC, and JE (Japanese Extensions).

The Slackware distribution has been completely unpacked allowing many packages to be run directly from the disc. Sources for all the packages in Slackware are also included.

The Linux HOWTO documents have been formatted for use with the Microsoft Multimedia Viewer (which is included) to allow browsing and full-text search under Microsoft Windows.

InfoMagic also distributes the "Installation and Getting Started Guide", by Matt Welsh as well as Linux T-Shirts.

Availability:

```
InfoMagic, Inc.
PO Box 30370
Flagstaff, AZ 86003-0370

Tel: 800-800-6613 (within the US)/602-683-9565
Fax: 602-526-9573
email: Orders@InfoMagic.com
```

Ordering:

The 3-CD set is $25/copy. Shipping within the US is $5 (USPS Priority Mail), outside the US $10 (International Airmail), FedEx and UPS on request. Orders may be placed via phone, fax, or email (a PGP key is available: finger orders@InfoMagic.com). We accept Visa, Mastercard, and AMEX. 1-year subscriptions are available for $150 (within the US) and $175 (outside the US) including shipping. A 1yr subscription consists of 6 releases, one every two months.

Miscellaneous:

The contents of the CD's may be found at either: InfoMagic.com:/pub/Linux, ftp.uu.net:/vendor/InfoMagic/cd-roms/linux, or on http://www.infomagic.com.

This 3-CD set is updated every two months. Please call for latest info on contents, availability and pricing.

Entry last modified:

11 Jan 1995.

3.5   Lasermoon Ltd.

Distributor:

Lasermoon Ltd., info@lasermoon.co.uk, support@lasermoon.co.uk.

Description: We are specialists in UNIXLinux Freeware and stock products from : Infomagic, PrimeTime Freeware, Yggdrasil, Linux Journal, SSC, O'Reilly Associates, Addison Wedsley, SWiM (Motif) 1.2.3 & 1.2.4, Morse Telecommunications (Slackware Pro), VITAL (Crisp Editor), BASMARK (Language Products), Systek s.r.l (Application Builders), VERSASOFT (dBMAN), LINUX BIBLE and reference works. We are the sole UK/European/USA distributors for some of the above.

If you don't see what you want, please call us!

We provide free technical support for the above products which are competitively priced.

Dealers : Please contact us! We are looking for dealers in Europe and Aisa.

Availability:

CD-ROM, floppy disk and other media. ftp access for some products (ie SWiM)

Ordering:

We are pleased to accept : VISA, ACCESS, MASTERCARD, EuroCARD, Euro Cheque/Cheque/money order drawn on a UK bank in Pounds Sterling, Cash - (in desperation) Pounds Sterling (please send by recorded delivery).

```
Lasermoon Ltd
2a Beaconsfield Road
Fareham
Hants
England, PO16 0QB
```

Entry last modified:

14 Dec 1994.

3.6   Linux Journal

Publisher:

Linux Journal, P.O. Box 85867, Seattle, WA 98145-1867. Phone (206) 782-7753 (206-PUBS-REF), FAX 206-782-7191.

Description:

Linux Journal is a monthly publication covering the Linux Community. Most material in LJ is new (not reprinted from Usenet). Each issue includes columns and articles on Linux programming, Free Software Foundation issues, systems administration, Questions and Answers, interviews and more. LJ is a professional-quality magazine for the Linux community. Michael K. Johnson is the editor of Linux Journal.

Availability:

Subscriptions are $19/year (US), $24/year (Canada/Mexico), $29/year (elsewhere).

Ordering:

Payment can be made using VISA, MasterCard or American Express (make sure you include the credit card number, expiration date and signature). We can also accept checks in US $ on US banks. If you have a question concerning appropriate method of payment, phone or FAX our subscription numbers or send e-mail to subs@ssc.com For security reasons we discourage sending credit card numbers via e-mail.

Miscellaneous:

If you are interested in advertising in LJ, call, write or e-mail at linux@ssc.com. Article queries, new product announcements and other editorial material should be sent to our address above or e-mailed to `ljeditor@sunsite.unc.edu`. Generic questions can be sent to `linux@fylz.com`.

Entry last modified:

11 Jan 1995.

3.7   The Linux Quarterly CD-ROM

Distributor:

Morse Telecommunication, Inc.

Description:

The Linux Quarterly CDROM contains the complete contents of `tsx-11.mit.edu`, the one of the most popular Internet Linux sites which provides both source and binaries of major Linux distributions, utilities, source code and documentation. This includes Slackware, SLS, MCC and Debian releases of Linux. Additionally, beginning with the Spring 1994 edition, the complete contents of `prep.ai.mit.edu`, the repository of the FSF's GNU source archives, is included. For first-time users, this CDROM contains a Microsoft Windows(tm) front-end to assist the user in creating boot disks that can be used to install Linux directly from The Linux Quarterly CDROM. Support for the UMSDOS filesystem is now also included. This gives the user the ability to install Linux directly to an MSDOS system without having to repartition their hard drive. Ninety days of technical support is provided with each disc at no additional charge.

Availability:

```
Morse Telecommunication, Inc.
26 East Park Avenue, Suite 240
Long Beach, NY 11561
Orders:  (800) 60-MORSE
Tech Support:  (516) 889-8610
Fax:  (516) 889-8665
Email Orders:  Order@morse.net
Email info:  Linux@morse.net
Hours:  9AM - 5PM EST, Monday through Friday.  Fax available 24 hours.
```

Ordering:

Orders may be placed via phone, fax or email as listed above. The Linux Quarterly CDROM is priced at $29.95 plus $5 shipping and handling per order. Existing customers may upgrade for $22.95 plus S/H. All orders generally ship the same day if received by 4PM EST.

Miscellaneous:

The contents of the CDROM, the cover artwork in JPEG format, and the text of the USENET announcement can be found on the following FTP sites:

```
tsx-11.mit.edu:/pub/linux/advertisements/TLQ-Spring94.tar.z
sunsite.unc.edu:/pub/Linux/distributions/cdrom/TLQ-Spring94.tar.z
```

Entry last modified:

23 May 1994

3.8   Linux Systems Labs

Distributor:

Linux Systems Labs, info@lsl.com

Description:

Slackware (all 50 disks and I&GS) for $69.95 (updated weekly), resell the Yggdrasil CDROM and bundle the latest version of Slackware with Motif (version1.2.4) for $215.00 (Motif alone for $175.00). We currently print LDP documents duplex on a 600 DPI laser printer. We publish *Dr. Linux*, an impressive compendium (1170 pages) of the Linux Documentation Project for $49.95 and include a free CD with purchase. A free CD also comes with our other book, *Linux: Getting Started* (550 pages), which sells for $29.95.

Our newest product is Just Logic SQL Database Manager. It is an interactive multiuser SQL server+client for Linux. It also includes C++ class descriptions and API for interfacing with C and C++.

Availability:

Linux Systems Labs, 18300 Tara Drive, Clinton Twp MI 48036. Phone (313)954-2829, (800)432-0556, fax (313)954-2806.

Ordering:

See above for prices. We take MasterCard, Visa and American Express and will discount all products (except SQL) 20% for internet customers.

Entry last modified:

9 Feb 1995.

3.9   Sequoia International Motif Development Package

Distributor:

Sequoia International, Inc., 600 West Hillsboro Blvd, Suite 300, Deerfield Beach, FL 33441, Tel: (305) 480-6118, FAX: (305) 480-6198, info@seq.com

Description:

Sequoia International, Inc. has a complete Motif 1.2.3 Runtime and Development package called SWiM 1.2.3 available for $149.95. In addition to providing *shared* library versions of libXm and libMrm, the following is included in each package: The Window Manager (mwm), Shared Libraries (libXm, libMrm), Static Libraries (libXm, libMrm, libUil), UIL Compiler, Header and Include Files, Complete On-Line Manual Pages, Source Code to OSF/Motif Demo Programs, Complete OSF/Motif Users Guide.

Requirements:

Linux 0.99pl13 or higher, libc 4.4.4, XFree 2.0, 12M Free Disk, 8-12M RAM Suggested.

Ordering:

USA: Sequoia International, Inc. (305-480-6118), info@seq.com. Japan: Fortune Co., Ltd (03-5481-8974). England: Lasermoon Ltd. (+44-0-329-826444). Australia: Space Age Import-Export Proprietary (61-7-266-3418).

Entry last modified:

24 March 1994.

3.10 Discount Linux

Distributor:

Spheric Microsystems, Inc., info@spheric.com.

Description:

Spheric has the Linux distribution to fit your tastes, at discount prices. Here's just a sample, call for latest versions or a catalog:

Slackware Pro 2.0
retail $49.95, only $34.95. (Also available in floppy)

Yggdrasil Plug and Play Fall '94
retail $49.95, only $29.95

InfoMagic Archives
October 1994, kernel 1.1.50, Doom, retail $20.00, only $17.95

Linux Installation & Getting Started Guide
2.1, retail $14.95, only $9.95

Linux Bible - The GNU Testament
retail $49.95, only $39.95

Unix in a Nutshell, O'Reilly reference book
retail $9.95, only $8.95

Unix PowerTools, best tips and tricks
with CD, retail $59.95, only $44.95

The Whole Internet User's Guide
2nd Edition, retail $24.95, only $19.95

Source Code CDROM
many from source news groups, retail $39.95, only $24.95

C User's Group CD, volume 100-411
retail $49.95, only $29.95

Ordering:

```
Visa, MasterCard, American Express, check, money-orders accepted.
Call 1-800-869-8649, 9am-9pm Eastern.
NYS Residents add local sales tax.
$5 shipping per order.
```

Miscellaneous:

Spheric has been distributing Linux since 1992 (back when a few floppies made a great distribution :^). Commercial Linux software, general UNIX books, and CD-ROM subscription plans also available.

Entry last modified:

14 December 1994.

3.11 Spire Technologies Inc.

Distributor:

Spire Technologies, info@spiretech.com

Description:

Spire is a complete solution provider for Linux offering Networking, Custom systems, Consulting, Technical Support, and Distribution.

Our current services are consulting services, complete custom systems, networks and we offer the Linux Bible and the Info-Magic and Yggdrasil cdroms. We will soon have anonymous ftp available at ftp.spiretech.com (Feb 1995) and will be providing subscription internet access (Jan/Feb 1995).

Ordering:

You can reach Spire Technologies at info@spiretech.com or:

```
Spire Technologies
1439 SW Columbia
Portland, Or  97201
(503)222-3086
(503)222-5102 FAX
```

Entry last modified:

11 Jan 1994.

3.12   SSC Books and Linux Documentation Project Manuals

Distributor:

SSC, Inc., `sales@ssc.com`.

Availability:

SSC has printed the *Linux Installation and Getting Started* manual, Version 2.2.1 to make it available for those who do not have the capability to print it themself and to support our customers who buy Linux distributions from us. The book is perfect-bound with a 2-color cover. SSC has also published the Network Administrator's Guide from the LDP and will soon publish the Kernel Hacker's Guide. In addition, SSC has published The Linux Sampler, a book which includes new material plus articles from back issues of Linux Journal. Other products include Linux T-shirts, mouse pads and bumper stickers.

Ordering:

Linux Installation and Getting Started, Version 2.1 is available for $12.95 plus shipping ($3 in the U.S.). The Linux Network Administrator's Guide and The Linux Sampler are $18.95 each plus shipping. Finger bookshelf@ssc.com for information on these and other Linux books that we will make available. We can accept credit card orders (Visa, MasterCard or AmEx). Orders can be phoned in to 206-782-7191 (206-PUBS-REF) or faxed to 206-782-7191. Or mail orders to SSC, P.O. Box 55549, Seattle, WA 98155.

Miscellaneous:

SSC also publishes a series of reference cards on Unix and Unix-related programs such as Emacs, VI, Korn Shell, C language, etc. SSC also sells the InfoMagic, Yggdrasil and Trans Ameritech distributions, Free Software Foundation books and a complete Linux package consisting of *Linux Installation and Getting Started*, a Linux distribution on CD, 4 SSC Pocket References and a 1-year subscription to Linux Journal for $64.95. Call or e-mail `sales@ssc.com` for a free catalog.

Entry last modified:

11 Jan 1995.

3.13 Takelap Systems Ltd.

Distributor:

Takelap Systems Ltd., info@ddrive.demon.co.uk.

Description:

The SLS 1.04 distribution on diskettes. 25 3.5" or 30 5.25" diskettes including 0.99.13 kernel, X11R5, TeX, doc (WYSIWYG), GNU s/w development tools and more.

The SLS 1.04 Linux Distribution on CDROM: 0.99.13 kernel, X11R5, TeX, Andrew, GNU s/w development tools. May be installed and optionally run from CDROM mounted remotely. Many installation and operational options.

The Yggdrasil LGX Fall 93 Linux distribution on CDROM: 0.99.13 kernel, X11R5, TeX, Andrew 5.1, Postgres 4.1, GNU s/w development tools.

Availability:

Takelap Systems Ltd., The Reddings, Court Robin Lane, Llangwm, Usk, Gwent, United Kingdom NP5 1ET. tel: +44 (0)291 650357, fax: +44 (0)291 650500, email: info@ddrive.demon.co.uk.

Ordering:

SLS on Diskettes, price ukp42.00 +ukp1.50 p&p + VAT. SLS CD-ROM, ukp66.00 +ukp1.50 p&p + VAT. Yggdrasil LGX CD-ROM, ukp40.00 +ukp1.50 p&p + VAT. Visa and Mastercard accepted.

Miscellaneous:

Free catalogue of CDROMs and books (mostly UNIX related) on request.

Entry last modified:

31 Oct 93.

3.14 Trans-Ameritech Linux plus BSD CD-ROM

Distributor:

Trans-Ameritech corporation.

Description:

Trans-Ameritech has published 6 releases of Linux by the end of 94. CD-ROM based on the Slackware distribution of Linux with all the sources plus full uncompressed filesystem plus NetBSD source and binary distribution. The current full release is Release 4 and a Supplement 2 is also available with updates and additional software. The previous releases cover Linux from 0.99 p.9 (on the SLS release) to the current versions and have FreeBSD, NetBSD and the original 386BSD.

- The installation is highly automated by the Slackware scripts fine tuned to this CDROM but leaves a lot of room for customization. New Linux users will appreciate the DOS based menu driven program that helps to select and prepare the right boot floppy.

- To minimize the possibility of hardware conflicts many extra kernels are provided for different configurations. They are usable for installation and normal operation.

- Many on-line documents are provided for quick reference, including the Linux Documentation Project files in source, dvi and ps formats.
  - A lot of applications are included:
  - The C/C++ compiler GNU GCC ,
  - GNU and international versions of the ispell spell-checker.
  - The communications apps: term, minicom, Seyon (X-Windows based).
  - Editors: elvis (vi clone), joe, jove
  - PostScript clone ghostscript

- Network package with news and email:
- TCP/IP, UUCP, SLIP, CSLIP
- Object oriented GNU Smalltalk, and the Smalltalk Interface to X.
- TCL/Tk (Powerful scripting language with Motif-like X interface)
- Programs for electrical engineers and HAM enthusiasts
- Several window managers - openwin, twm, gwm, fvwm.
- Easy X-Windows configuration with many real-life examples.
- Many X applications
- Interviews libraries, include files, and the doc word processor and idraw drawing program.
- Typesetting: TeX, LaTeX, xdvi, dvips, Metafont, groff
- Andrew multimedia word processor with hyperlinks.
- Send and receive fax on either class 1 or class 2 fax modems.
- A lot more.

- To help the first time Linux users many documentation files are provided that are readable from DOS even before installing Linux.
- All the sources are available on the CDROM. The most often needed sources are uncompressed and can be used directly from CDROM.
- An uncompressed Linux filesystem is available for reference and disk space conservation. You can run programs directly from CDROM! There is a large info directory for on-line reference and many man pages.
- For hacker's reference uncompressed 386 BSD sources are provided.

The latest upgrades and patches are always available through Trans-Ameritech Linux BBS (408)980-9840. It's free for all Trans-Ameritech customers.

The Internet price for Linux Supplement CD 2 is $20

The price for our current (Release 4) Linux Plus CD is $30

The price for a package order: Linux Plus CD (Release 4) and Linux Supplement 2 CD (Trans-Ameritech Linux Package) in one shipment is - $40

Availability and Ordering:

You can order by e-mail, by phone (408)727-3883 or fax (408)727-3882.   (email: order@Trans-Ameritech.com)

If you prefer to send a cheque/money order, our address is:

```
Trans-Ameritech Enterprises, Inc.
2342A Walsh Ave
Santa Clara, CA 95051
USA
```

If you order with a credit card (VISA, MC, American Express) please indicate the card number, expiration date and your mailing address.

The order will be processed and the CD shipped the same day.

Shipping and handling in US is $5, Canada/Mexico $6, Overseas $8. COD is available in the US only for $4.50.

California residents please add sales tax.

Annual subscriptions (4 releases) are available for $80 plus S&H. (note: there are 4 shipments in a subscription) Example subscription in US is: $80 + $5 x 4 = $100 Subscription in EuropeJapan etc. is: $80 + $8 x 4 = $112

Miscellaneous:

If you have any further questions, please contact us at the above address, or (408) 727-3883, FAX (408) 727-3882, or info@trans-am.com

Entry last modified:

11 Jan 1995.

3.15 Universal CD-ROM

Distributor:

Universal CD-ROM, c/o Charles Liu

Description:

We are the publisher of Linux World Book '95 (Word Book '95 is a complete Linux reference book) and UCR Linux CD. In addition we also carry a complete line of Linux distribution such as: Slackware 2.1, Plug & Play, Walnut Creek CDs, InfoMagic Linux CDs, etc.

Availability:

You can get the latest price list from:

```
phone:     (408)992-0453
fax:       (408)992-0457
email:     ucr@bigmall.com
WWW:       http://www.bigmall.com
```

Ordering:

We accept: Visa, MasterCard, Money order and Checks. We ship worldwide from Silicon valley.

```
email:     sale@bigmall.com
fax:       (408)992-0457
voice:     (408)992-0453
mail:      520 Lawrence Expressway, #307
           Sunnyvale, CA 94086
           USA
```

Entry last modified:

16 Mar 1995

3.16 Unifix Custom Linux CD-ROM Mastering

Distributor:

Unifix Software GmbH, Braunschweig, Germany

Description:

We use our own (Linux based) premastering system to make custom CDs which include the customer's programs in addition to our Linux distribution. This enables our customers to sell their Unix based applications together with operating system tested and ready to run. Our CD recorder makes it possible to create prototypes and very small series at interesting prices.

Availability:

Ask us for more information or prices:

```
Telephone   +49 (0)531 515161
Fax         +49 (0)531 515162
Mail        Unifix Software GmbH
            Postfach 4918
            D-38039 Braunschweig
            Germany
```

3.17   UPython SLS and Slackware Diskette Labels

Distributor:

UPython Computer and Network Services

Description:

Labels for Softlanding and Slackware disks

Availability:

The labels that we print for you are available in several formats at `sunsite.unc.edu:/pub/linux/distributions/SLSlabels`.

Ordering:

For order information, send mail to `DGray@uh.edu`. Cost is $6.50 per set and domestic shipping in included. Overseas orders must send payment in US funds and add $1 for shipping. Texas residents add sales tax (6

Entry last modified:

11 Nov 1993.

3.18   Wizvax Communications

Distributor:

Richard Shetron (`multics@acm.rpi.edu`) Stephanie Gilgut (`stephie@acm.rpi.edu`) Sean Haus (`hans@wizvax.com`)

Description:

We sell modem and terminal cables for multi-port serial boards (mainly the Boca Research BB2016, BB1008, BB1004 and the IOAT66). We also sell multi-port serial boards. We can supply other products and services, please ask. We are also an internet provider with dialups and telnet accounts.

Availability:

```
email:  orders@wizvax.wizvax.com  (orders only, please)
        catalog@wizvax.wizvax.com  (automatic response robot)
        multics@wizvax.wizvax.com
        stephie@wizvax.wizvax.com
        hans@wizvax.com

phone:  (518) 271-6005 (US) 9am-7pm M-sa.
Fax:    (518) 271-6289
Snailmail:
        Wizvax Communications
        1508 Tibbits Ave.
        Troy, NY 12180 USA
```

Ordering:

Send for a catalog (see addresses above). Send orders to addresses listed above. Payment can be personal/company check, US Postal Money Order, Money Order, or Bank check. Orders will not be sent until payment clears. Inquire about PO's.

Miscellaneous:

Wizvax provides an anonymous posting and contact service. email acs@wizvax.com for help. Wizvax also provides space and resources for mucks, muds and such, for a fee. Email hans@wizvax.com regarding this.

4 Submissions to this document

Here's information on how to make submissions to this document, and on the policy that we are using for postings to `comp.os.linux.announce` regarding commercial and mail-order announcements.

4.1 `comp.os.linux.announce` policy

One of the purposes of this document is to present short summaries of the many Linux distributions in a compact form for new users to browse over. This document is not merely a concatenation of the various announcements of Linux distributions and the like.

Another purpose of this document is to remove some of the 'advertisement' traffic from the newsgroup `comp.os.linux.announce`. The moderators of `c.o.l.a` (as well as many of the readers) feel that those people who are re-distributors of Linux distributions which they do not maintain should not be allowed to post periodic advertisements in `c.o.l.a`.... after all, `c.o.l.a` is for announcements important to the Linux community; it is not a moderated sales board.

Therefore, if you are distributing Linux software which you do not maintain, the only way that you will be allowed to post information to `c.o.l.a` is through this HOWTO. Information on submitting entries to this HOWTO is given below. (To submit a posting for `c.o.l.a`, mail it to `linux-announce@tc.cornell.edu`. Exceptions are given below.

Here's an example. If you are, for example, reselling the SLS distribution of Linux on floppies via mail order, the first time that your mail-order service is available, you may post an announcement to `c.o.l.a`. Thereafter, you must submit an entry in this HOWTO, which will be periodically posted to the newsgroup. Only in the event that you do something dramatically new with your service will you be allowed to post to `c.o.l.a` about it. ('Dramatically new' does not include changing your prices or the versions of the software that you distribute. The moderators have the final say on just what consititutes 'dramatically new'. :)) The purpose of this is to reduce the number of periodic postings from people who are using `c.o.l.a` as an electronic billboard.

However, if you maintain and organize your own distribution of Linux (whether it be available for anonymous FTP, mail order, or both), then you will be allowed to post to `c.o.l.a` whenever you release a new version. You will not be allowed to make periodic postings about your distribution, in order to 'advertise' it every month; only when a new version is released will you be allowed to post to `c.o.l.a` about it. Of course, you should include information on your distribution in this HOWTO.

Hopefully this policy is not too confusing; the one basic rule is that we won't permit postings to `c.o.l.a` which are merely advertisements for your distribution or mail order service. The posting must include new information which is of interest to the Linux community at large. Remember that `c.o.l.a` postings are archived on `sunsite.unc.edu`; once your posting is out of the news spool it is not gone forever.

4.2 How to submit an entry for this HOWTO

I encourage anyone and everyone who maintains a Linux distribution or mail order service (or consulting service, and the like), to submit information on their service to this HOWTO. It's easy and fun, and it's free advertising. This document is posted to many places and is archived (see the next section).

4.2.1 Types of submissions

We are interested in submissions for:

- Complete distributions of Linux software, available either via anonymous FTP, UUCP, or mail order. By 'complete distribution' we mean any set of software which can be used to build a complete Linux system from scratch.

- Layered products or individual software packages available only via mail order. If your software package is available via anonymous FTP, chances are people can find it. Software products only available via mail-order include commercial things such as Motif, and any other commercial software ported to Linux.

- Any other LINUX-SPECIFIC goods available via mail order, such as Linux-specific books and documentation, T-shirts, and assorted paraphernalia.

- LINUX-SPECIFIC services such as telephone or e-mail consulting and technical support. This category also includes miscellany such as development contracts.

If the number of submissions for services and layered products is large, I'll create a separate HOWTO for these items.

4.2.2 How to submit

To submit an entry to this HOWTO, please send mail to mdw@sunsite.unc.edu with the following information. This 'format' is not machine-parsable; any of the fields may be any length that you wish, but I'd like to keep each entry down to, say, 50 lines.

Name:

Name of service or distribution

Distributor:

Name of company, person, etc. who distributes/maintains the service or distribution

Description:

Description of the distribution or service that you provide. If this is a software distribution, please include information such as what software is included, versions, general overview of installation, requirements, and so on.

Availability:

Where your service or distribution is available. This can be an FTP site (including directory pathname, please), a mailing address, phone number, e-mail address, etc.

Ordering:

How to order your distribution or service, if applicable. Include prices, shipping information, methods of payment, etc.

Miscellaneous:

Anything else that you find relevant.

Please keep your entry as short as possible. If you need to include extensive information, please make a reference to where one can FTP or mail to get more information on your distribution; these entries are only meant to be POINTERS to where one can find information on your service or distribution.

If you provide more than one service or distribution, please use SEPARATE ENTRIES for each.

Some things (such as books, t-shirts, etc.) won't fit exactly into this entry; just be sure to include all relevant information. In other words, this "entry form" is simply the bare minimum that you must include in your submission to the Distribution-HOWTO; feel free to change, add, or leave out "fields" as you see fit.

I will more than likely edit your entries to some degree if I find any irrelevant information, or if the entry is overly verbose. Otherwise the content should remain the same.

When making submissions to the Distribution-HOWTO, you grant implicit permission for me to use the entries in other materials, such as books from the LDP, and other online documents. For example, information from the Distribution-HOWTO may be included in a published Linux book. If you do not want me to include your entry in materials other than the Distribution-HOWTO, please say so.

4.3 Acknowledgements

Thanks to Bill Riemers, who produced the first version of the Distribution HOWTO and Matt Welsh who produced the second.. Also, thanks to all of the people who have contributed to this document. I hope that future releases of this HOWTO will be useful to the Linux community; unfortunately, gathering information on the many services out there is a difficult task. Your contributions make this task much easier.

Part XVII

The Linux ELF HOWTO

v1.1, 11 May 1995
This HOWTO describes the procedure to build your ELF development system guiding you, step by step, from the informations needed to get the source files to the last tests on the final binaries.

Contents

[In the last two weeks, I've faced the problem of jump-table -> ELF migration].

Some time after... here the new version, revised in the text and references, with a new FAQ section and formatted with SGML.

The Linux binary format is destined to migrate to ELF and sooner or later we will be forced to re-install all the binaries or re-compile them (unless we want to have systems in an half-way state with both ELF and jump-table libraries for long time).

I had started asking around where could I find gcc/gas/gld/libc binaries to produce ELF binary executables; unfortunately no one gave me useful information.

After this first try, I've decided to bootstrap an ELF development package on my own.

I have collected all the stages in this HOWTO, the ELF HOWTO.

1 Introduction

This is the Linux ELF HOWTO.

This document describes the way I have started the migration of my system to the ELF binary file format.

This HOWTO was written during the Real Thing; all the things written here have been tested by me directly.

- This file is provided 'as-is', see the disclaimer

- The Author is Riccardo Facchetti

- **Read CAREFULLY all the HOWTO if you want to do the things described!**

- Someone pointed out how outdated this document is now, stating something about how the chosen installation directory tree is old. I must advise you, the reader, that this document is **ONLY** a set of hints on how to **build an ELF development system over a jump-table one** and its final purpose is to have both development systems installed on your machine. This lets you migrate to ELF system by recompiling the old binaries instead of re-installing the whole system. **To have both development systems installed, we have to choose a directory tree, different from the standard one, in which install the ELF system.**

- This document was made step-by-step during the real work, using the libc version 4, so I can say nothing for sure about libc version 5. Someone has pointed out that it is best use the libc version 5 instead of libc version 4. I do not thave he time to check and re-compile the whole thing, so I can only suggest you to use the libc version 5 instead of version 4, but you are on your own.

- This document is **NOT** for those who have already an all-ELF system. There are now some distributions that are all-ELF, one of these is the Linux-FT. I do not recommend that someone with an all-ELF distribution installed read this document further.

- This document is **ONLY** for those who already have an installed jump-table system and that do not want to backup/reinstall/selective-restore their systems. It is for those who want to have **BOTH** ELF and jump-table compilers.

- Using a different directory tree for the new library/compilers will force you, when your system has been migrated to ELF, to re-compile the libraries/compilers, setting the compilation-time paths to the standard ones, or install the standard libc/compiler ELF distribution (that installs into the right installation paths). Of course then you will have all the ELF binaries that are searching for the /lib/elf/ld-linux.so.1, the ELF loader. Even if you have only a minimum of imagination, you alredy know that when you erase your jump-table /lib/*, replacing the files with the ELF library ones, you will have to do something like

```
mv <none or mount point>/lib/elf/* <none or mount point>/lib
rmdir <none or mount point>/lib/elf
ln -s <none or mount point>/lib <none or mount point>/lib/elf
```

```
I suggest you to do this operation after booting from a boot/root floppy
pair and mounting your Linux root partition, because moving around shared
libraries can lock your system, when the executables can't find the shared
libraries linked with them.
```

- GNU Make v. 3.72.1 seems to have a bug, I use GNU Make v. 3.70

- If you install g++, you may want to install libg++ too. The installation of libg++ is NOT discussed here because it is out of the scope of this HOWTO.

- For text-formatting reasons, in some example or code boxes you can find text that is splitted in more than one line. I have adopted the (?standard) continuation character to allow a best formatting without loss of meaning. Sometimes you will find boxes with lines, typically of code or examples, like this:

```
ld -shared -o libnam.so.ver -soname libnam.so.majver \
crtbeginS.o *.o crtendS.o
```

```
As you can see, the line is splitted in two parts, but the continuation
character, the \, means that these two lines are one line only, that was
splitted to avoid line wrapping.  It is not too much difficult, given the
context, know when a line is splitted.
```

- More information about ELF and linux status can be found at: (http://sable.ox.ac.uk/ jo95004/elf.html) and at (ftp://sunsite.unc.edu/pub/Linux/GCC/private/dontuse), but be careful because the private/dontuse/* files are for experienced Linuxers only. In the next weeks an official distribution for the ELF stuff (compilers and libraries) will probably be release. Keep your eyes open.

- I just want to point out a thing. ELF HOWTO will be completely out of date when all the installed Linux systems will be ELF systems. For those who want to try out the migration way, this document is enough. There will **NOT** be any revision about the informations contained in this document. There will eventually be only bugfix revisions. All the flames about **bad directory tree** or **bad idea** or **bad compilers or libc version** will be directed to **/dev/null**

- Since the subject of this HOWTO, the ELF stuff, is going to change very fast, I suggest you to look at the information sources described here before start to work on this thing. Check the state of the ELF stuff!

- On the 11th of July I will leave for my year of military duty, so all the bug reports and suggestions should be posted (via e-mail) before the 15th of June. I have planned a possible last update the 15th of June. After this date, no more updates will be made to this document. If someone want to replace me in mantaining this document, please let me know before the same date. Any e-mail posted after that date, will be answered, but at random time.

- I have to thank all the persons that have appreciated and will appreciate this work, reading it and reporting me bugs and successes.

1.1 Copyright

impose additional restrictions on its distribution. Exceptions to these rules may be granted under certain conditions; please contact the Linux HOWTO coordinator at the address given below.

In short, we wish to promote dissemination of this information through as many channels as possible. However, we do wish to retain copyright on the HOWTO documents, and would like to be notified of any plans to redistribute the HOWTOs.

If you have questions, please contact Matt Welsh, the Linux HOWTO coordinator, at mdw@sunsite.unc.edu. You may finger this address for phone number and additional contact information.

1.2   Feedback

Since this HOWTO will be maintained in a relaxed way, because of the little time I can spend on it, please send me suggestions, bugs and comments, but don't expect them to be included in a short-term update.

You can reach me via e-mail at:

`riccardo@cdc8g5.cdc.polimi.it`

or via snail-mail at:

```
Riccardo Facchetti
Via PAOLO VI, 29
22053 - Lecco (Lc)
ITALY
```

1.3   Disclaimer

This document is **not** bible. The Author is not responsible for any damages incurred due to actions taken based on the information included in this document.

2   FAQ

This is a little collection of FAQs I have answered in the last months.

2.1   What is ELF ?

ELF, Executable and Linkable Format, was originally developed by UNIX System Labs as part of the Application Binary Interface (ABI). The ELF format was selected by the Tool Interface Committee as a portable object file format that works on different operating systems running on the 32-bit Intel Architecture. This allow developers to have a binary interface definition that is the same in a wide variety of operating environments, reducing needs of recoding and recompiling the software. Linux users, for example, can run SYSV ELF executables by simply loading the iBCS (Intel Binary Compatibility Specification) kernel module.

2.2   Can I produce an ELF executable jammed with jump-table and ELF C libraries ?

ELF and jump-table libraries are not mixable in executables. Dynamically linked executables (you may see it as impure executables) need a final loader, or dynamic linker, that loads the shared libraries needed by the a.out and link them with the impure executable to produce a runnable image. This linking is done at run time. Since the jump-table and ELF technologies are not the same, their dynamic linkers are different, and can not handle a mixed set of libraries. The real reason is deeper. ELF and jump-table binaries have a different a.out layout. Get ELF technical informations to have an idea about this subject (see 2.4).

2.3 Why ELF is better than jump-table ?

- ELF binary file format it is portable (see 2.1).

- ELF shared libraries are easier to produce than jump-table ones (see 2.5).

2.4 Where can I find more informations about ELF ?

This document is a **migration howto**, not a technical review of ELF technology. You can find more information about ELF technology:

- (ftp://sunsite.unc.edu/pub/linux/GCC/elf.tar.gz) It is a postscript file that describes the internals of ELF technology.

- In the "UNIX SYSTEM V RELEASE 4 Programmers Guide: Ansi C and Programming Support Tools" book.

- Linux Journal in one of its issues, January or February 1995 I don't remember, discussed about ELF subject.

2.5 How can I produce ELF shared libraries ?

Producing ELF shared libraries is really an easy task. You have just to produce the ELF object files that will contribute to compose the library, then you have just to call the ELF linker with the following command-line syntax:

```
gcc-elf -fPIC -O2 -m486 -c *.c
ld -shared -o libnam.so.ver -soname libnam.so.majver \
crtbeginS.o *.o crtendS.o
```

or, as stated by gcc, and only if gcc (ELF version) support this:

```
gcc -fPIC -c xxxxxx *.[c|cc|C]
gcc -shared [-Wl,-soname -Wl,libfoo.so.y] -o libfoo.so.y.x.x *.o
```

3 What do I need to start up ?

To build ELF executables you need an ELF C compiler, an ELF assembler, an ELF linker, and ELF C libraries (static/dynamic/debug/profile).

These are the sources you need to build the ELF system: **if you change some source** (e.g. you would like to use gcc-2.6.3 instead of gcc-2.6.2) you are on your own. I think you should follow this document anyway because the things contained here are generalized enough. If you use a binutils package newer than binutils-2.5.2 you may not need to patch it with the patch 2.5.2 => 2.5.2.6 If you use a newer gcc you might be able to follow this HOWTO step by step. If you use a newer libc, you may not need to edit all the files I have edited.

Do not do anything without thinking (be sure of what you are doing)!!!

ELF C compiler:

gcc-2.6.2 as is

ELF assembler:

binutils-2.5.2 patched to 2.5.2.6

ELF linker:

binutils-2.5.2 patched to 2.5.2.6

ELF C libraries:

libc-4.6.27 as is

C libraries header files:

inc-4.6.27 as is

PATCH binutils-2.5.2 => binutils-2.5.2.6:

at the end of announce-4.6.27

3.1   Where can I find all these things ?

gcc-2.6.2:

(ftp://ftp.gnu.ai.mit.edu/pub/gnu/gcc-2.6.2.tar.gz)

binutils-2.5.2:

(ftp://ftp.gnu.ai.mit.edu/pub/gnu/binutile-2.5.2.tar.gz)

libc-4.6.27:

(ftp://sunsite.unc.edu/pub/linux/GCC/libc-4.6.27.tar.gz)

inc-4.6.27:

(ftp://sunsite.unc.edu/pub/linux/GCC/inc-4.6.27.tar.gz)

PATCH binutils-2.5.2 => binutils-2.5.2.6:

(ftp://sunsite.unc.edu/pub/linux/GCC/release.binutils-2.5.2.6)

3.2   Other requirements

- You need to have the libc-4.6.27 jump-table version and inc-4.6.27 installed on your system. You can find it in every major linux site (ftp://sunsite.unc.edu/pub/linux/GCC)

- You need to know how to edit/change/save a text file

- **You need at least 50 Mbytes of HD space**

- You need jump-table development system (gcc/gas/ld/make/includes/kernel/etc)

- You need to compile the BINFMT_ELF option into the kernel

- To build ELF development system you need the kernel 1.1.72 or above as stated by libc-4.6.27 announcement. excerpt from libc-4.6.27 announce

```
You need <linux/elf.h> in the kernel 1.1.72 or above if you want to
compile the ELF libraries yourself. Otherwise, please join the Linux
gcc list.

You need to recompile the libraries with the kernel 1.1.65 or above
to gain the support for 57600 and 115200 bps.
```

end of excerpt.

4   Theory of operation

The problem of building the development system for ELF binaries is that we need to bootstrap the ELF system from jump-table one. On the other hand, we NEED to keep the jump-table system separate from the ELF one because we may want to use both development systems. We also need to have a /lib for jump-table and one for ELF, a gcc/gas/ld for jump-table and one for ELF (this is our goal of course :) So we need to do the following operations:

```
1. Choose an alternate directory tree for ELF system.

2. Build jump-table binaries of binutils-2.5.2.6, to create the ELF
   assembler (gas) and linker (ld)

3. Install the things listed in 2

4. Build jump-table binaries of gcc-2.6.2 to create the ELF C compiler

5. Install the things listed in 4

6. Build ELF binaries of libc-4.6.27, to create ELF C libraries

7. Install the things listed in 6

8. 2-7 are the first stage:  they create the jump-table binaries of the ELF
   compilers.  To create gcc/gas/ld ELF binary files you must repeat the
   steps 2-7 (2nd stage) using the ELF compilers.
```

4.1   Choose an alternate directory tree

You must choose an alternate directory tree for your ELF system. You must do this only if you want to build an ELF system that will live with the jump-table one. I have chosen:

```
/lib/elf/ . . . . . . . . . . . . . . . . for ELF shared libraries
/usr/i486-linuxelf/ . . . . . . . . . . . for all the ELF related files
/usr/i486-linuxelf/bin/ . . . . . . . . . for ELF binaries
/usr/i486-linuxelf/lib/ . . . . . . . . . for libraries
/usr/i486-linuxelf/lib/gcc-lib/ . . . . . for gcc and its files
```

so the installation prefix will be /usr/i486-linuxelf .

5   Building binutils-2.5.2.6

5.1   Preparing binutils-2.5.2.6 for compilation

5.1.1   Unpacking the archive

```
cd /usr/src
tar xfvz binutils-2.5.2.tar.gz
cd binutils-2.5.2
```

5.1.2   Patching binutils-2.5.2 to binutils-2.5.2.6

```
patch -p0 < release.binutils-2.5.2.6
```

where release.binutils-2.5.2.6 is this patch file. The patch, made by H.J. Lu, fixes some binutils-2.5.2 bugs and allow the support for ELF.

5.1.3   Search for rejected patches

```
find . -name *.rej -print
```

should find nothing

5.1.4   Search and erase the original files

```
find . -name *.orig -print -exec rm -f {} \;
```

5.1.5   Edit bfd/elf32-i386.c

```
vi bfd/elf32-i386.c
```

at line 194 you should find:

```
#define ELF_DYNAMIC_INTERPRETER "/usr/lib/libc.so.1"
```

change it to:

```
#define ELF_DYNAMIC_INTERPRETER "/lib/elf/ld-linux.so.1"
```

The libc-4.6.27 will put the dynamic linker in /lib/elf and ld-linux.so.1 will be a symlink to the real linker -> /lib/elf/ld-linux.so.1.0.14 This is needed because the ELF executables will use this run-time linker to link the shared libraries.

5.1.6   Configure the binutils-2.5.2.6

If you have an i386:

```
configure i386-linuxelf
```

for a 486:

```
configure i486-linuxelf
```

have a little break during configuration, it may take few minutes.

5.1.7   Edit Makefile

```
vi Makefile
```

at line 36 you should find:

```
prefix = /usr/local
```

change it to:

```
prefix = /usr/i486-linuxelf
```

to reflect the installation directory tree we have chosen

at line 82 you should find:

```
CFLAGS = -g
```

change it to:

```
CFLAGS = -O2 -m486 -fomit-frame-pointer
```

(use the -m486 only if you have an i486; if you have a Pentium processor with the igcc, the Pentium gcc, you may want to try the -mpentium) for optimization.

5.1.8   Edit ld/Makefile to change the default emulation mode:

```
vi ld/Makefile
```

at line 189 you should find:

```
EMUL=i386linux
EMUL_EXTRA1=elf_i386
```

change it to:

```
EMUL_EXTRA1=i386linux
EMUL=elf_i386
```

to set the default emulation to elf_i386 (this will be the ELF linker, not the jump-table one).

5.2   Compiling binutils-2.5.2.6

do the

```
make
```

and have a long coffee break.

5.3   Installing binutils-2.5.2.6

do the

```
make install
```

and it is done.

Now if you are short of disk space you may want to

```
cd /usr/src
rm -rf binutils-2.5.2
```

6   Building gcc-2.6.2

Now we have in /usr/i486-linuxelf/bin the as (gas) and ld (gld), both compiled for ELF support. Now we will compile gcc-2.6.2 to generate ELF code. We need ELF assembler because in the final step, when make generates the libgcc using the xgcc, the xgcc is an ELF compiler so it needs the ELF assembler.

Note:

gcc-2.6.2 seems to have a bug in ELF generation code of the profiler section. When you build code to be profiled (-p or -pg), gcc-2.6.2 generates a call to mcount() function. Unfortunately, this code is generated in assembly stage and gcc fails to generate it.

In fact it generates:

```
call _mcount
```

instead of

```
call mcount
```

The ELF binary format does not prepend the '_' (underscore) when compiling C to asm functions, so you will end up with a lot of

undefined reference to '_mcount' messages.

I do not use the profiler. Anyway I think the best way to correct this bug is to modify libgcc because I do not have the stomach to put my hands on the gcc :) (see 7.1)

6.1 Preparing gcc-2.6.2 for compilation

6.1.1 Unpacking the archive

```
cd /usr/src
tar xfvz gcc-2.6.2.tar.gz
cd gcc-2.6.2
```

6.1.2 If you are short of disk space

Now you need 30 Mbytes to compile gcc. If you are running short of disk space, you may need to erase some unneeded documentation:

```
rm -f ChangeLog*
rm -f gcc.info*
rm -f cpp.info*
rm -f texinfo.tex gcc.ps
```

6.1.3 Configure the gcc-2.6.2

If you have an i386:

```
configure --with-elf i386-linux
```

for a 486:

```
configure --with-elf i486-linux
```

6.1.4 Edit Makefile

```
vi Makefile
```

at line 154 you should find:

```
prefix = /usr/local
```

change it to:

```
prefix = /usr/i486-linuxelf
```

at line 159 you should find:

```
local_prefix = /usr/local
```

change it to:

```
local_prefix = /usr/i486-linuxelf
```

to reflect the installation path we have chosen.

6.1.5 Configuring gcc package to use the ELF assembler/linker in libgcc2.a

compilation

```
ln -s /usr/i486-linuxelf/bin/as .
ln -s /usr/i486-linuxelf/bin/ld .
```

with these two links, we enable the xgcc (the gcc just compiled) to make use of the ELF assembler/linker.

and it is done.

Now if you are short of disk space you may want to

```
cd /usr/src
rm -rf gcc-2.6.2
```

6.4   Try it now!

Just to be sure everything is okay up to now:

check your gcc installation with 'gcc-elf -v', then try to compile something:

```
cd /tmp
```

edit a file called p.c

```
vi p.c

[start]
main()
{
printf("prova\n");
}
[end]
```

('prova' means 'test' in Italian :) then compile it to the object file (only to object because we still do not have the C library)

```
gcc-elf -v -c p.c
```

You should be able to see that gcc-elf invokes all the /usr/i486-linuxelf stuff.

Now to check the kind of file gcc-elf has built, do a:

```
file p.o
```

and it should say that p.o is an

```
ELF 32-bit LSB relocatable i386 (386 and up) Version 1
```

Of course you must have the ELF definition in /etc/magic file. If gcc-elf builds ELF objects, we are on the right path!

7   Building libc-4.6.27

Now we have the ELF compiler/assembler/linker. We need an ELF C library. This step will build the libc-4.6.27 in static/shared/debug/profile versions.

7.1   Preparing libc-4.6.27 for compilation

7.1.1   Unpacking the archive

```
cd /usr/src
tar xfvz libc-4.6.27.tar.gz
cd libc-linux
```

7.1.2 Configuring the libc-4.6.27

```
configure

Values correct (y/n) [y] ? n
Build 386, 486 or m68k library code (486 default) 4/3/m [4] ?
The target platform [i486-linux] ?
The target OS [linux] ?
Build targets (static/shared default) s/a [a] ?
Root path to i486-linux related files [/usr] ?
Bin path to gcc [/usr/bin] ?
The gcc version [2.6.2] ?
Fast build/save space (fast default) f/s [f] ?
GNU 'make' executable [make] ?
Root path to installation dirs [/] ?
Build a NYS libc from nys* (y default)  y/n [n] ?
Values correct (y/n) [y] ?
```

- all the above configuration parameters are defaults but you MUST do the ./configure to reset the config.in

7.1.3 Edit Makeconfig

```
vi Makeconfig
```

at line 368 you should find:

```
PIC_OPT_CFLAGS= -fPIC -O1 -funroll-loops -fomit-frame-pointer
```

change it to:

```
PIC_OPT_CFLAGS= -fPIC -D__PIC__ -O1 -funroll-loops -fomit-frame-pointer
```

we need to define __PIC__ because the syscall?() macros are different for PIC and non-PIC code.

at line 327 you should find:

```
REALCC  =gcc-elf -V $(GCCVERSION) -b $(TARGET_MACHINE) \
```

change it to:

```
REALCC  =gcc-elf \
```

we do not need the -V -b switches because gcc-elf should use the right binaries and -V -b confuses the compiler.

7.1.4 Edit elf/Makefile

```
vi elf/Makefile
```

at line 29 you can find:

```
if [ "1" = "1" ]; then \
```

change it to:

```
if [ "0" = "1" ]; then \
```

to make use of the linker directly and not through gcc-elf because, sadly, gcc-elf do not support the -shared switch.

7.1.5   Edit elf/d-link/libdl/Makefile

```
vi elf/d-link/libdl/Makefile
```

at line 29 you should find:

```
ELF_LDFLAGS=--shared -nostdlib # using GNU ld
```

change it to:

```
ELF_LDFLAGS=-Wl,-shared -nostdlib # using GNU ld
```

to pass the -shared switch directly to the linker, see above.

7.1.6   Edit elf/d-link/readelflib1.c

This is important because the ld-linux.so (ELF shlib loader) must know that the standard ELF shlib path is /lib/elf/ and not /lib/

At line 122 you should find:

```
pnt1 = "/lib/";
```

change it to:

```
pnt1 = "/lib/elf/";
```

7.1.7   Edit sysdeps/linux/i386/gmon/gmon.c

This change is needed if you want to use the profile option with gcc-2.6.2 (see the Note in section 6)

- if you upgrade the gcc (say to gcc-2.6.3) you have to check if this new gcc is able to handle ELF profiling code. You can do it this way:

```
vi p.c

[start]
main()
{
printf("Prova\n");
}
[end]
```

Now compile it this way:

```
gcc-elf -p -S p.c
```

gcc generate a file called p.s. It is the assembly output of the p.c C source. Edit p.s:

```
vi p.s
```

in the assembly listing, somewhere, you should find:

```
call _mcount
```

or

```
call mcount
```

in the first case your gcc is buggy so you should apply the next patch to gmon.c, in the second case, gcc is okay so don't apply the next patch.

at line 50 you should find:

```
extern void mcount(); /* asm ("mcount"); */
```

change it to:

```
extern void _mcount(); /* asm ("_mcount"); */
```

at line 221 you should find:

```
mcount()
```

change it to:

```
_mcount()
```

7.2   Compiling libc-4.6.27

Now it is time to compile the libc-4.6.27. My suggestion is to launch the compilation and then go to sleep or something like that because it takes a LOT of time, (If you have better things to do other than sleep, your time is not lost doing such nice things :)

do

```
nohup make ELF=true &
```

(for those who use the zsh now they should do a 'disown %1')

now you can logout/exit/ctrl-d

- the nohup is important because it logs all the compilation in a file called nohup.out . At the end of compilation, before going to the next step, you must check the nohup.out (1.5 Mbytes) for errors. Do:

```
grep Error nohup.out
```

  it should print out nothing. If any error is encountered, investigate and try to correct it.

7.3   Installing libc-4.6.27

To install the ELF libraries do:

```
make install.elf
```

and it is done!

Now you can delete the libc-linux:

```
cd /usr/src
rm -rf libc-linux
```

7.4   Try the Whole Thing!

```
cd /tmp
```

edit a file called p.c:

```
vi p.c

[start]
main()
{
printf("prova\n");
}
[end]
```

now try to compile the file to use the shared ELF library:

```
gcc-elf -O -v p.c -o p
```

and

```
file p
```

should say:

```
p: ELF 32-bit LSB executable i386 (386 and up) Version 1
```

run './p' and you should see the output 'prova'

repeat the above operations to check the static/debug/profile compilation with these command lines:

```
gcc-elf -static -O -v p.c -o p
gcc-elf -g -v p.c -o p
gcc-elf -p -v p.c -o p
gcc-elf -pg -v p.c -o p
```

launch the './p' for every compilation to check the output of p.

If you cannot see the output 'prova', you may have done something wrong. Make sure you have executed all the steps described in this HOWTO and if you find some error, please let me know.

If this last test is passed, you have succeeded installing the bootstrap ELF development system.

8   Recompiling the Whole Thing: Stage 2

Now you MUST go on recompiling the Whole Thing to be sure everything is okay. The recompilation is not only the way to have ELF binaries, it is a way to test the reliability of the binaries we have just compiled. Think of this as the Stage 2 (a la gcc Stage 2). I do not think a Stage 3 will be useful, but if you like you can do the Stage 3 too :) (e.g. Stage 3 compiled files should be the same as Stage 2, given the same compilation flags.)

You have to repeat the steps 5 6 7 with one small difference: in the Stage 2 you will use the gcc-elf!

8.1   Recompiling binutils-2.5.2.6

Follow section 5.1

Now you must change the gcc with gcc-elf in Makefile

8.1.1 Edit Makefile

```
vi Makefile
```

at line 72 you should find:

```
CC = cc
```

change it to:

```
CC = gcc-elf
```

Now follow the 5.2 and 5.3 sections.

You are done with binutils-2.5.2.6

8.2 Recompiling gcc-2.6.2

Follow section 6.1 for configuration.

Now compile the compiler stage1, do:

```
make LANGUAGES=c CC=gcc-elf CFLAGS="-O2 -m486 -fomit-frame-pointer -N"
```

Be warned: all things related to enquire.c and float.h are still valid!! We now have the ELF C lib but enquire will compile and link the right way only if we copy the installed gcc-elf specs file in gcc source directory (xgcc must know where to find crt and libc), so you have to wait until the gcc compilation is finished, then you will cp the correct specs:

```
cp /usr/i486-linuxelf/lib/gcc-lib/i486-linux/2.6.2/specs .
```

then remove enquire (an invalid file):

```
rm ./enquire
```

then re-compile with the same command line as the first compilation, and it will finish the compilation: do the above for all compilation stages, after every build.

Now make stage2 and stage3 of the compiler to build g++ and obj-c.

Here are the commands:

```
        *** First compilation (stage1) ***

ln -s /usr/i486-linuxelf/bin/as .
ln -s /usr/i486-linuxelf/bin/ld .
make LANGUAGES=c CC=gcc-elf CFLAGS="-O2 -m486 -fomit-frame-pointer -N"
cp /usr/i486-linuxelf/lib/gcc-lib/i486-linux/2.6.2/specs .
rm ./enquire
make LANGUAGES=c CC=gcc-elf CFLAGS="-O2 -m486 -fomit-frame-pointer -N"

        *** Second compilation (stage2) ***

make stage1
ln -s /usr/i486-linuxelf/bin/as stage1/as
ln -s /usr/i486-linuxelf/bin/ld stage1/ld
make LANGUAGES=c CC="stage1/xgcc -Bstage1/" \
CFLAGS="-O2 -m486 -fomit-frame-pointer -N"
```

```
cp /usr/i486-linuxelf/lib/gcc-lib/i486-linux/2.6.2/specs .
rm ./enquire
make LANGUAGES=c CC="stage1/xgcc -Bstage1/" \
CFLAGS="-O2 -m486 -fomit-frame-pointer -N"

            *** Third compilation (stage3) ***

make stage2
ln -s /usr/i486-linuxelf/bin/as stage2/as
ln -s /usr/i486-linuxelf/bin/ld stage2/ld
make CC="stage2/xgcc -Bstage2/" \
CFLAGS="-O2 -m486 -fomit-frame-pointer -N"
cp /usr/i486-linuxelf/lib/gcc-lib/i486-linux/2.6.2/specs .
rm ./enquire
make CC="stage2/xgcc -Bstage2/" \
CFLAGS="-O2 -m486 -fomit-frame-pointer -N"

    Now compare the objects of stage2 and stage3: they MUST be equal!!!!

for file in *.o
do
echo $file
cmp $file stage2/$file
done
```

Now for installation do

```
    make install
```

Make sure /usr/i486-linuxelf/lib/gcc-lib/i486-linux/2.6.2/specs is correct.

8.3   Recompiling libc-4.6.27

Follow sections 7.1, 7.2 and 7.3.

9   Patch binutils-2.5.2 ==> binutils-2.5.2.6

See 3.1 for the location of this patch.

Note:

You can apply this patch by simply

```
    cd /usr/src
    patch -p0 {$<$} release.binutils-2.5.2.6
```

This is an excerpt from the patch file:

```
    H.J. Lu
    hjl@nynexst.com
    12/16/94

    This patch contains some necessary bug fixes for binutils 2.5.2 to
    support ELF. It is called 2.5.2.6 by me. The fixes may not be the same
    as the ones in the next public release of binutils.
```

Part XVIII

Linux Ethernet-Howto

Copyright Paul Gortmaker, Editor.
v2.3, 11/02/95
This is the Ethernet-Howto, which is a compilation of information about which ethernet devices can be used for Linux, and how to set them up. It hopefully answers all the frequently asked questions about using ethernet cards with Linux. Note that this Howto is focused on the hardware and low level driver aspect of the ethernet cards, and does not cover the software end of things. See the NET2-Howto for that stuff.

Contents

1   Introduction

The Ethernet-Howto covers what cards you should and shouldn't buy; how to set them up, how to run more than one, and other common problems and questions. It contains detailed information on the current level of support for *all of the most common ethernet cards available*. It does *not* cover the software end of things, as that is covered in the NET-2 Howto. Also note that general non-Linux specific questions about Ethernet are not (or at least they should not be) answered here. For those types of questions, see the excellent amount of information in the *comp.dcom.lans.ethernet* FAQ. You can FTP it from `dorm.rutgers.edu` in the directory `/pub/novell/info_and_docs/`

This present revision covers kernels up to and including v1.1.91

The Ethernet-Howto is edited and maintained by:

Paul Gortmaker, `Paul.Gortmaker@anu.edu.au`

The primary source of the information for the Ethernet-Howto is from:

Donald J. Becker, becker@cesdis.gsfc.nasa.gov

who we have to thank for writing the vast majority of ethernet card drivers that are presently available for Linux. He also is the original author of the NFS server too. Thanks Donald! We owe ya one! :-)

Net-surfers may wish to check out the following URL:

Donald Becker (http://cesdis.gsfc.nasa.gov/pub/people/becker/whoiam.html)

1.1 Using the Ethernet-Howto

As this guide is getting bigger and bigger, you probably don't want to spend the rest of your afternoon reading the whole thing. And you don't *have* to read it all. If you haven't got an ethernet card, then you will want to start with 2 to see what you should buy, and what you should avoid. If you have already got an ethernet card, but are not sure if you can use it with Linux, then you will want to read 3 which contains specific information on each manufacturer, and their cards. If you are having trouble with your card, then you will want to read the specific information about your card mentioned above, and the troubleshooting information in 9. If you are interested in some of the technical aspects of the device drivers, then you can find that information in 7

1.2 Disclaimer and Copyright

This document is *not* gospel. However, it is probably the most up to date info that you will be able to find. Nobody is responsible for what happens to your hardware but yourself. If your ethercard or any other hardware goes up in smoke (...nearly impossible!) we take no responsibility. ie. THE AUTHORS ARE NOT RESPONSIBLE FOR ANY DAMAGES INCURRED DUE TO ACTIONS TAKEN BASED ON THE INFORMATION INCLUDED IN THIS DOCUMENT.

This document is Copyright (c) 1994 by Donald Becker and Paul Gortmaker. Permission is granted to make and distribute verbatim copies of this manual provided the copyright notice and this permission notice are preserved on all copies.

Permission is granted to copy and distribute modified versions of this document under the conditions for verbatim copying, provided that this copyright notice is included exactly as in the original, and that the entire resulting derived work is distributed under the terms of a permission notice identical to this one.

Permission is granted to copy and distribute translations of this document into another language, under the above conditions for modified versions.

If you are intending to incorporate this document into a published work, please contact me, and I will make an effort to ensure that you have the most up to date information available. In the past, out of date versions of the Linux howto documents have been published, which caused the developers undue grief from being plagued with questions that were already answered in the up to date versions.

1.3 Mailing Lists and the Linux Newsgroups

If you have questions about your ethernet card, please READ this document first. You may also want to join the NET channel of the Linux-activists mailing list by sending mail to

linux-activists-request@niksula.hut.fi

with the line

X-Mn-Admin: join NET

at the top of the message body (not the subject). If you want to learn how to use the mailing channels, then send an empty message to the above address, and you will get an instruction manual sent back to you in a few hours. However, it is worth noting that the NET channel is primarily used for discussion of the networking code, and you may not see much discussion about a particular driver.

Furthermore keep in mind that the NET channel is for development discussions only. General questions on how to configure your system should be directed to comp.os.linux.help unless you are actively involved in the development of part of the networking for Linux. We ask that you *please* respect this general guideline for content.

Recently, a similar group of mailing lists has started on the host `vger.rutgers.edu`, using the much more common `majordomo` mailing list server. Send mail to `majordomo@vger.rutgers.edu` to get help with what lists are available, and how to join them.

Also, the news groups *comp.sys.ibm.pc.hardware.networking* and *comp.dcom.lans.ethernet* should be used for questions that are not Linux specific.

1.4   Related Documentation

Much of this info came from saved postings from the comp.os.linux groups, which shows that it is a valuable resource of information. Other useful information came from a bunch of small files by Donald himself. Of course, if you are setting up an Ethernet card, then you will want to read the NET-2 Howto so that you can actually configure the software you will use. And last but not least, the contributions from the individuals and companies listed in 10.3 is greatly appreciated as well. Oh yeah, if you fancy yourself as a bit of a hacker, you can always scrounge some additional info from the driver source files as well. There is usually a paragraph in there describing any important points.

For those looking for information that is not specific in any way to Linux (i.e. what is 10BaseT, what is AUI, what does a hub do, etc.) I strongly recommend the **Ethernet-FAQ** from the newsgroup *comp.dcom.lans.ethernet*. Look on the FTP site `dorm.rutgers.edu` in the directory `/pub/novell/info_and_docs/` or grab it from the following URL:

Ethernet FAQ (`ftp://dorm.rutgers.edu/pub/novell/info_and_docs/Ethernet.FAQ`)

Don't let the fact that it was last revised in 1993 scare you, as not much has happened to Ethernet since then. (Discounting the upcoming 100Base-whatever, of course.)

1.5   New Versions of this Document

New versions of this document can be retrieved via anonymous FTP from sunsite.unc.edu, in `/pub/Linux/docs/HOWTO/*` and various Linux ftp mirror sites. Updates will be made as new information / drivers becomes available. If this copy that you are reading is more than 2 months old, it is either out of date, or it means that I have been lazy and haven't updated it. This document was produced by using the SGML system that was specifically set up for the Linux Howto project, and there are various output formats available, including, postscript, dvi, ascii, html, and soon TeXinfo.

I would recommend viewing it in the html (via Mosaic) or the Postscript/dvi format. Both of these contain cross-references that are lost in the ascii translation.

If you want to get the official copy off sunsite, here is URL.

Ethernet-HOWTO (`http://sunsite.unc.edu/mdw/HOWTO/Ethernet-HOWTO.html`)

If minor additions and changes have been made, you can view the latest working copy from this URL.

Working Copy (`http://rsphy1.anu.edu.au/ gpg109/Ethernet-HOWTO.html`)

2 What card should I buy for Linux?

For impatient users that just want a quick, cheap answer the summary is: get 16 bit thinnet 8013 cards. For those who want the absolute best performance, get an AMD PC-Net/Lance based card. For more detail as to the who what where and why, read on.

2.1 Eight bit vs 16 bit

Unless you are a light user, or are confined to using the smaller ISA slot, the use of the 8 bit cards like the wd8003, the 3c503 and the ne1000 is usually not worth the cost savings. Get the 8013 or the 3c503/16, or the ne2000 instead. (The 3c501 is not included in this discussion, as it shouldn't be used under any circumstances.)

However, so not to leave you with a bad taste in your mouth if you happen to already have one, you can still expect to get about 500kB/s ftp download speed to an 8 bit wd8003 card (on a 16MHz ISA bus) from a fast host. And if most of your net-traffic is going to remote sites, then the bottleneck in the path will be elsewhere, and the only speed difference you will notice is during net activity on your local subnet.

A note to NFS users: Some people have found that using 8 bit cards in NFS clients causes poorer than expected performance, when using 8kB (native Sun) NFS packet size.

The possible reason for this could be due to the difference in on board buffer size between the 8 bit and the 16 bit cards. The 8 bit cards have an 8kB buffer, and the 16 bit cards have a 16kB buffer. The Linux driver will reserve 3kB of that buffer (for Tx ping-pong buffers), leaving only 5kB for an 8 bit card. The maximum ethernet packet size is about 1500 bytes. Now that 8kB NFS packet will arrive as about 6 back to back maximum size ethernet packets. Both the 8 and 16 bit cards have no problem Rx'ing back to back packets. The problem arises when the machine doesn't remove the packets from the cards buffer in time, and the buffer overflows. The fact that 8 bit cards take an extra ISA bus cycle per transfer doesn't help either. What you *can* do if you have an 8 bit card is either set the NFS transfer size to 4kB, or try increasing the ISA bus speed in order to get the card's buffer cleared out faster.

2.2 Low price Ethernet cards

The lowest price seen so far was in the March '94 edition of LAN magazine. There was an ad for Addtron AE-200 cards (jumper settable NE2000 clones) for a measly $19 ea! Unfortunately this offer has since expired. However, you might want to check to see what their everyday price is.

You can also call AT-LAN-TEC at 301-948-7070. Ask for their technical support person. As with all purchases, you should indicate you are buying this for a Linux system. NB: Their current NE2000 clone is a model that 'traps' other drivers that probe into their address space. AT-LAN-TEC also carries a clone, non-EEPROM 8013 board for somewhat more, and a NE2100 clone. Either is a better choice if the very lowest price isn't essential.

And a recent addition is the VLB and PCI cards offered by Boca Research. These are selling for around the $70 mark, and these are supported with the latest kernel. These use the new 32 bit versions of the LANCE chip from AMD. See 3.10 for more info.

If you require an ISA card, you can use the the Allied Telesis AT1500 which uses the ISA version of the LANCE chip from AMD. It is offered at a good price by many vendors. Even Inmac, known for their premium markup, has this card for under $100. See 3.3.1 for more info.

2.3 Vendors and Brands to Avoid

These vendors have decided *not* to release programming information about their products, without signing a NDA (non-disclosure agreement). Hence it is strongly advised that you avoid buying products offered from these companies.

(1) Cabletron (see 3.11)

(2) Xircom (see 3.28)

These particular cards should be avoided, as they are obsolete. The reasons as to why they have been classified as such can be found in their respective sections. For your particular application, these reasons may not be a concern, so you should have a read of the reasons listed.

(1) 3c501 (see 3.1.1)

(2) Arcnet based cards (see 3.7)

(3) Any 8-bit cards (see 2.1)

2.4 Type of cable that your card should support

Unless you have to conform to an existing network, you will want to use thinnet or thin ethernet cable. This is the style with the standard BNC connectors. See 5 for other concerns with different types of ethernet cable.

Most ethercards also come in a 'Combo' version for only $10-$20 more. These have both twisted pair and thinnet transceiver built-in, allowing you to change your mind later.

The twisted pair cables, with the RJ-45 (giant phone jack) connectors is technically called 10BaseT. You may also hear it called UTP (Unsheilded Twisted Pair).

The thinnet, or thin ethernet cabling, (RG-58 coaxial cable) with the BNC (metal push and turn-to-lock) connectors is technically called 10Base2.

The older thick ethernet (10mm coaxial cable) which is only found in older installations is called 10Base5.

Large corporate installations will most likely use 10BaseT instead of 10Base2. 10Base2 does not offer an easy upgrade path to the new upcoming 100Base-whatever.

3 Vendor/Manufacturer/Model Specific Information

The only thing that one needs to use an ethernet card with Linux is the appropriate driver. For this, it is essential that the manufacturer will release the technical programming information to the general public without you (or anyone) having to sign your life away. A good guide for the likelihood of getting documentation (or, if you aren't writing code, the likelihood that someone else will write that driver you really, really need) is the availability of the Crynwr (nee Clarkson) packet driver. Russ Nelson runs this operation, and has been very helpful in supporting the development of drivers for Linux. *Net-surfers* can try this URL to look up Russ' software.

Russ Nelson's Packet Drivers (http://www.crynwr.com/crynwr/home.html)

Given the documentation, you can write a driver for your card and use it for Linux (at least in theory) and if you intend to write a driver, have a look at 7.2 as well. Keep in mind that some old hardware that was designed for XT type machines will not function very well in a multitasking environment such as Linux. Use of these will lead to major problems if your network sees a reasonable amount of traffic.

Most cards come with drivers for MS-DOS interfaces such as NDIS and ODI, but these are useless for Linux. Many people have suggested directly linking them in or automatic translation, but this is nearly impossible. The MS-DOS drivers expect to be in 16 bit mode and hook into 'software interrupts', both incompatible with the Linux kernel. This incompatibility is actually a feature, as some Linux drivers are considerably better than their MS-DOS counterparts. The '8390' series drivers, for instance, use ping-pong transmit buffers, which are only now being introduced in the MS-DOS world.

Keep in mind that PC ethercards have the widest variety of interfaces (shared memory, programmed I/O, bus-master, or slave DMA) of any computer hardware for anything, and supporting a new ethercard sometimes requires re-thinking most of the lower-level networking code. (If you are interested in learning more about these different forms of interfaces, see 7.5.)

Also, similar product numbers don't always indicate similar products. For instance, the 3c50* product line from 3Com varies wildly between different members.

Enough talk. Let's get down to the information you want.

3.1   3Com

If you are not sure what your card is, but you think it is a 3Com card, you can probably figure it out from the assembly number. 3Com has a document 'Identifying 3Com Adapters By Assembly Number' (ref 24500002) that would most likely clear things up. See 7.7 for info on how to get documents from 3Com.

Also note that 3Com has a FTP site with various goodies: `ftp.3Com.com` that you may want to check out.

3.1.1   3c501

Status – *Semi-Supported*

Too brain-damaged to use. Available surplus from many places. Avoid it like the plague. Again, do not purchase this card, even as a joke. It's performance is horrible, and it breaks in many ways.

Cameron L. Spitzer of 3Com said: "I'm speaking only for myself here, of course, but I believe 3Com advises against installing a 3C501 in a new system, mostly for the same reasons Donald has discussed. You probably won't be happy with the 3C501 in your Linux box. The data sheet is marked '(obsolete)' on 3Com's Developers' Order Form, and the board is not part of 3Com's program for sending free Technical Reference Manuals to people who need them. The decade-old things are nearly indestructible, but that's about all they've got going for them any more."

For those not yet convinced, the 3c501 can only do one thing at a time – while you are removing one packet from the single-packet buffer it cannot receive another packet, nor can it receive a packet while loading a transmit packet. This was fine for a network between two 8088-based computers where processing each packet and replying took 10's of msecs, but modern networks send back-to-back packets for almost every transaction.

Donald writes: 'The driver is now in the std. kernel, but under the following conditions: This is unsupported code. I know the usual copyright says all the code is unsupported, but this is _really_ unsupported. I DON'T want to see bug reports, and I'll accept bug fixes only if I'm in a good mood that day.

I don't want to be flamed later for putting out bad software. I don't know all all of the 3c501 bugs, and I know this driver only handles a few that I've been able to figure out. It has taken a long intense effort just to get the driver working this well.'

AutoIRQ works, DMA isn't used, the autoprobe only looks at `0x280` and `0x300`, and the debug level is set with the third boot-time argument.

Once again, the use of a 3c501 is *strongly discouraged*! Even more so with a IP multicast kernel, as you will grind to a halt while listening to *all* multicast packets. See the comments at the top of the source code for more details.

3.1.2   3c503, 3c503/16

Status – *Supported*

3Com shared-memory ethercards. They also have a programmed I/O mode that doesn't use the 8390 facilities (their engineers found too many bugs!) It should be about the same speed as the same bus width WD80x3, Unless you are a light user, spend the extra money and get the 16 bit model, as the price difference isn't significant. The 3c503 does not have "EEPROM setup", so the diagnostic/setup program isn't needed before running the card with Linux. The shared memory address of the 3c503 is set using jumpers that are shared with the boot PROM address. This is confusing to people familiar with other ISA cards, where you always leave the jumper set to "disable" unless you have a boot PROM.

The Linux 3c503 driver can also work with the 3c503 programmed-I/O mode, but this is slower and less reliable than shared memory mode. Also, programmed-I/O mode is not tested when updating the drivers, the deadman (deadcard?) check code may falsely timeout on some machines, and the probe for a 3c503 in programmed-I/O mode is turned off by default in some versions of the kernel. This was a panic reaction to the general device driver probe explosion; the 3c503 shared memory probe is a safe read from memory, rather than an extensive scan through I/O space. As of 0.99pl13, the kernel has an I/O port registrar that makes I/O space probes safer, and the programmed-I/O 3c503 probe has been re-enabled. You still shouldn't use the programmed-I/O mode though, unless you need it for MS-DOS compatibility.

The 3c503's IRQ line is set in software, with no hints from an EEPROM. Unlike the MS-DOS drivers, the Linux driver has capability to autoIRQ: it uses the first available IRQ line in {5,2/9,3,4}, selected each time the card is ifconfig'ed. (Older driver versions selected the IRQ at boot time.) The ioctl() call in 'ifconfig' will return EAGAIN if no IRQ line is available at that time.

Some common problems that people have with the 503 are discussed in 9.5.

3.1.3   3c505

Status – *Semi-Supported*

This is a driver that was written by Craig Southeren geoffw@extro.ucc.su.oz.au. These cards also use the i82586 chip. I don't think there are that many of these cards about. It is included in the standard kernel, but it is classed as an alpha driver. See 9.1 for important information on using alpha-test ethernet drivers with Linux.

There is also the file /usr/src/linux/drivers/net/README.3c505 that you should read if you are going to use one of these cards. It contains various options that you can enable/disable. Technical information is available in 7.6.

3.1.4   3c507

Status – *Semi-Supported*

This card uses one of the Intel chips, and the development of the driver is closely related to the development of the Intel Ether Express driver. The driver is included in the standard kernel release, but as an alpha driver.

See 9.1 for important information on using alpha-test ethernet drivers with Linux. Technical information is available in 7.6.

3.1.5   3c509 / 3c509B

Status – *Supported*

It's fairly inexpensive and has excellent performance for a non-bus-master design. The drawbacks are that the original 3c509 _requires_ very low interrupt latency. The 3c509B shouldn't suffer from the same problem, due to having a larger buffer. (See below.)

Note that the ISA card detection uses a different method than most cards. Basically, you ask the cards to respond by sending data to an ID_PORT (port 0x100). Note that if you have some other strange ISA card using an I/O range that includes the ID_PORT of the 3c509, it will probably not get detected. Note that you can change the ID_PORT to 0x110 or 0x120 or... in 3c509.c if you have a conflicting ISA card, and the 3c509 will still be happy. Also note that this detection method means that it is difficult to predict which card will get detected first in a multiple ISA 3c509 configuration. The card with the lowest hardware ethernet address will end up being eth0. This shouldn't matter to anyone, except for those people who want to assign a 6 byte hardware address to a particular interface.

A working 3c509 driver was first included as an alpha-test version in the 0.99pl13 kernel sources. It is now in the standard kernel.

The original 3c509 has a tiny Rx buffer (2kB), causing the driver to occasionally drop a packet if interrupts are masked for too long. To minimize this problem, you can try unmasking interrupts during IDE disk transfers (see `hdparm(8)`) and/or increasing your ISA bus speed so IDE transfers finish sooner. (Note that the driver could be completely rewritten to use predictive interrupts, but performance re-writes of working drivers are low priority unless there is some particular incentive or need.)

The newer model 3c509B has 8kB on board, and the driver can set 4, 5 or 6kB for an Rx buffer. This setting can also be stored on the EEPROM. This should alleviate the above problem with the original 3c509. At this point in time, the Linux driver is not aware of this, and treats the 3c509B as an older 3c509.

Apparently, 3c509B users may have to use the supplied DOS utility to disable the *plug and play* support, and to set the output media to what they require.

Cameron Spitzer writes: "Beware that if you put a '509 in EISA addressing mode by mistake and save that in the EEPROM, you'll have to use an EISA machine or the infamous Test Via to get it back to normal, and it will conflict at IO location 0 which may hang your ISA machine. I believe this problem is corrected in the 3C509B version of the board."

3.1.6 3c523

Status – *Not Supported*

This MCA bus card uses the i82586, and now that people are actually running Linux on MCA machines, someone may wish to try and recycle parts of the 3c507 driver into a driver for this card.

3.1.7 3c527

Status – *Not Supported*

Yes, another MCA card. No, not too much interest in it. Better chances with the 3c523 or the 3c529.

3.1.8 3c529

Status – *Not Supported*

This card actually uses the same chipset as the 3c509. Donald actually put hooks into the 3c509 driver to check for MCA cards after probing for EISA cards, and before probing for ISA cards. But it hasn't evolved much further than that. Donald writes:

"I don't have access to a MCA machine (nor do I fully understand the probing code) so I never wrote the `mca_adaptor_select_mode()` or `mca_adaptor_id()` routines. If you can find a way to get the adaptor I/O address that assigned at boot time, you can just hard-wire that in place of the commented-out probe. Be sure to keep the code that reads the IRQ, if_port, and ethernet address."

3.1.9 3c579

Status – *Supported*

The EISA version of the 509. The current EISA version uses the same 16 bit wide chip rather than a 32 bit interface, so the performance increase isn't stunning. The EISA probe code was added to 3c509.c for 0.99pl14. We would be interested in hearing progress reports from any 3c579 users. (Read the above 3c509 section for info on the driver.)

Cameron Spitzer writes: "The 3C579 (Etherlink III EISA) should be configured as an EISA card. The IO Base Address (window 0 register 6 bits 4:0) should be 1f, which selects EISA addressing mode. Logic outside the ASIC decodes the IO address s000, where s is the slot number. I don't think it was documented real well. Except for its IO Base Address, the '579 should behave EXACTLY like the'509 (EL3 ISA), and if it doesn't, I want to hear about it (at my work address)."

3.1.10   3c589 / 3c589B

Status – *Semi-Supported*

Many people have been using this PCMCIA card for quite some time now. Note that support for it is not (at present) included in the default kernel source tree. Note that you will need a supported PCMCIA controller chipset. There are drivers available on Donald's ftp site:

```
cesdis.gsfc.nasa.gov:/pub/linux/pcmcia/README.3c589
cesdis.gsfc.nasa.gov:/pub/linux/pcmcia/3c589.c
cesdis.gsfc.nasa.gov:/pub/linux/pcmcia/dbether.c
```

Or for those that are *net-surfing* you can try:

Don's PCMCIA Stuff (`http://cesdis.gsfc.nasa.gov/linux/pcmcia.html`)

You will still need a PCMCIA socket enabler as well.

See 8.3 for more info on PCMCIA chipsets, socket enablers, etc.

The "B" in the name means the same here as it does for the 3c509 case.

3.2   Accton

3.2.1   Accton MPX

Status – *Supported*

Don't let the name fool you. This is still supposed to be a NE2000 compatible card. The MPX is supposed to stand for MultiPacket Accelerator, which, according to Accton, increases throughput substantially. But if you are already sending back-to-back packets, how can you get any faster...

3.2.2   Accton EN2212 PCMCIA Card

Status – *Semi-Supported*

David Hinds has been working on a driver for this card, and you are best to check the latest release of his PCMCIA package to see what the present status is.

3.3   Allied Telesis

3.3.1   AT1500

Status –*Supported*

These are a series of low-cost ethercards using the 79C960 version of the AMD LANCE. These are bus-master cards, and thus probably the fastest ISA bus ethercards available (although the 3c509 has lower latency thanks to predictive interrupts).

DMA selection and chip numbering information can be found in 3.4.1.

More technical information on AMD LANCE based Ethernet cards can be found in 7.8.

3.3.2   AT1700

Status – *Supported*

The Allied Telesis AT1700 series ethercards are based on the Fujitsu MB86965. This chip uses a programmed I/O interface, and a pair of fixed-size transmit buffers. This allows small groups of packets to sent be sent back-to-back, with a short pause while switching buffers.

A unique feature is the ability to drive 150ohm STP (Shielded Twisted Pair) cable commonly installed for Token Ring, in addition to 10baseT 100ohm UTP (unshielded twisted pair).

The Fujitsu chip used on the AT1700 has a design flaw: it can only be fully reset by doing a power cycle of the machine. Pressing the reset button doesn't reset the bus interface. This wouldn't be so bad, except that it can only be reliably detected when it has been freshly reset. The solution/work-around is to power-cycle the machine if the kernel has a problem detecting the AT1700.

Some production runs of the AT1700 had another problem: they are permanently wired to DMA channel 5. This is undocumented, there are no jumpers to disable the "feature", and no driver dares use the DMA capability because of compatibility problems. No device driver will be written using DMA if installing a second card into the machine breaks both, and the only way to disable the DMA is with a knife.

The at1700 driver is included in the standard kernel source tree.

3.4   AMD / Advanced Micro Devices

3.4.1   AMD LANCE (7990, 79C960, PCnet-ISA)

Status – *Supported*

There really is no AMD ethernet card. You are probably reading this because the only markings you could find on your card said AMD and the above number. The 7990 is the original 'LANCE' chip, but most stuff (including this document) refer to all these similar chips as 'LANCE' chips. (...incorrectly, I might add.)

These above numbers refer to chips from AMD that are the heart of many ethernet cards. For example, the Allied Telesis AT1500 (see 3.3.1) the NE1500/2100 (see 3.22.2) and the Boca-VLB/PCI cards (see 3.10.1)

The 79C960 (a.k.a. PCnet-ISA) contains enhancements and bug fixes over the original 7990 LANCE design.

Chances are that the existing LANCE driver will work with all AMD LANCE based cards. (except perhaps the NI65XX - see 3.24.2 for more info on that one.) This driver should also work with NE1500 and NE2100 clones.

For the ISA bus master mode all structures used directly by the LANCE, the initialization block, Rx and Tx rings, and data buffers, must be accessible from the ISA bus, i.e. in the lower 16M of real memory. If more than 16MB of memory is installed, low-memory 'bounce-buffers' are used when needed.

The DMA channel can be set with the low bits of the otherwise-unused dev->mem_start value (a.k.a. PARAM_1). (see 10.1.1) If unset it is probed for by enabling each free DMA channel in turn and checking if initialization succeeds.

The HP-J2405A board is an exception: with this board it's easy to read the EEPROM-set values for the IRQ, and DMA.

See 7.8 for more info on these chips.

3.4.2   AMD 79C961 (PCnet-ISA+)

Status – *Supported*

This is the PCnet-ISA+ – an enhanced version of the 79C960. It has support for jumper-less configuration and Plug and Play. See the info in the above section.

3.4.3   AMD 79C965 (PCnet-32)

Status – *Supported*

This is the PCnet-32 – a 32 bit bus-master version of the original LANCE chip for VL-bus and local bus systems. Minor cleanups were added to the original lance driver around v1.1.50 to support these 32 bit versions of the LANCE chip. The main problem was that the current versions of the '965 and '970 chips have a minor bug. They clear the Rx buffer length field in the Rx ring when they are explicitly documented not to. Again, see the above info.

3.4.4   AMD 79C970 (PCnet-PCI)

Status – *Supported*

This is the PCnet-PCI – similar to the PCnet-32, but designed for PCI bus based systems. Again, see the above info. Donald has modified the LANCE driver to use the PCI BIOS structure that was introduced by Drew Eckhardt for the PCI-NCR SCSI driver. This means that you need to build a kernel with PCI BIOS support enabled.

3.4.5   AMD 79C974 (PCnet-SCSI)

Status – *Supported*

This is the PCnet-SCSI – which is basically treated like a '970 from an Ethernet point of view. A minor '974 specific fix was added to the 1.1.8x kernels, so get a 1.1.90 or newer kernel. Also see the above info. Don't ask if the SCSI half of the chip is supported – this is the *Ethernet-Howto*, not the SCSI-Howto.

3.5   Ansel Communications

3.5.1   AC3200 EISA

Status – *Semi-Supported*

This driver is included in the present kernel as an alpha test driver. Please see 9.1 in this document for important information regarding alpha drivers. If you use it, let Donald know how things work out, as not too many people have this card and feedback has been low.

3.6   Apricot

3.6.1   Apricot Xen-II On Board Ethernet

Status – *Supported*

This on board ethernet uses an i82596 bus-master chip. It can only be at i/o address 0x300. The author of this driver is Mark Evans. By looking at the driver source, it appears that the IRQ is hardwired to 10.

Earlier versions of the driver had a tendency to think that anything living at 0x300 was an apricot NIC. Since then the hardware address is checked to avoid these false detections.

3.7   Arcnet

Status – *Semi-Supported*

With the very low cost and better performance of ethernet, chances are that most places will be giving away their Arcnet hardware for free, resulting in a lot of home systems with Arcnet.

An advantage of Arcnet is that all of the cards have identical interfaces, so one driver will work for everyone.

Recent interest in getting Arcnet going has picked up again and Avery Pennarun's alpha driver has been put into the default kernel sources for 1.1.80 and above. The arcnet driver uses 'arc0' as its name instead of the usual 'eth0' for ethernet devices. Bug reports and success stories can be mailed to:

`apenwarr@tourism.807-city.on.ca`

3.8 AT&T

Note that AT&T's StarLAN is an orphaned technology, like SynOptics LattisNet, and can't be used in a standard 10Base-T environment.

3.8.1 AT&T T7231 (LanPACER+)

Status – *Not Supported*

These StarLAN cards use an interface similar to the i82586 chip. At one point, Matthijs Melchior (`matthijs.n.melchior@att.com`) was playing with the 3c507 driver, and almost had something usable working. Haven't heard much since that.

3.9 AT-Lan-Tec / RealTek

3.9.1 AT-Lan-Tec / RealTek Pocket adaptor

Status – *Supported*

This is a generic, low-cost OEM pocket adaptor being sold by AT-Lan-Tec, and (likely) a number of other suppliers. A driver for it is included in the standard kernel. Note that there is substantial information contained in the driver source file 'atp.c'. BTW, the adaptor (AEP-100L) has both 10baseT and BNC connections! You can reach AT-Lan-Tec at 1-301-948-7070. Ask for the model that works with Linux, or ask for tech support.

In the Netherlands a compatible adaptor is sold under the name SHI-TEC PE-NET/CT, and sells for about $125. The vendor was Megasellers. They state that they do not sell to private persons, but this doesn't appear to be strictly adhered to. They are: Megasellers, Vianen, The Netherlands. They always advertise in Dutch computer magazines. Note that the newer model EPP-NET/CT appears to be significantly different than the PE-NET/CT, and will not work with the present driver. Hopefully someone will come up with the programming information and this will be fixed up.

In Germany, a similar adaptor comes as a no-brand-name product. Prolan 890b, no brand on the casing, only a roman II. Resellers can get a price of about $130, including a small wall transformer for the power.

The adaptor is 'normal size' for the product class, about 57mm wide, 22mm high tapering to 15mm high at the DB25 connector, and 105mm long (120mm including the BNC socket). It's switchable between the RJ45 and BNC jacks with a small slide switch positioned between the two: a very intuitive design.

Donald performed some power draw measurements, and determined that the average current draw was only about 100mA @ 5V. This power draw is low enough that you could buy or build a cable to take the 5V directly from the keyboard/mouse port available on many laptops. (Bonus points here for using a standardized power connector instead of a proprietary one.)

Note that the device name that you pass to `ifconfig` is *not* `eth0` but `atp0` for this device.

3.10 Boca Research

Yes, they make more than just multi-port serial cards. :-)

3.10.1 Boca BEN (PCI, VLB)

Status – *Supported*

These cards are based on AMD's PCnet chips, used in the AT1500 and the like. You can pick up a combo (10BaseT and 10Base2) PCI card for under $70 at the moment.

Supposedly Boca PCI cards can have trouble with Pentium systems that are operating faster than 66MHz. You may want to check with Boca on this one. Note that this is not a driver problem, as it hits DOS/Win/NT users as well. Any additional info on this as it develops would be appreciated.

More information can be found in 3.4.1.

More technical information on AMD LANCE based Ethernet cards can be found in 7.8.

3.11   Cabletron

Donald writes: 'Yes, another one of these companies that won't release its programming information. They waited for months before actually confirming that all their information was proprietary, deliberately wasting my time. Avoid their cards like the plague if you can. Also note that some people have phoned Cabletron, and have been told things like 'a D. Becker is working on a driver for linux' – making it sound like I work for them. This is NOT the case.'

If you feel like asking them why they don't want to release their low level programming info so that people can use their cards, write to support@ctron.com. Tell them that you are using Linux, and are disappointed that they don't support open systems. And no, the usual driver development kit they supply is useless. It is just a DOS object file that you are supposed to link against. Which you aren't allowed to even reverse engineer.

3.11.1   E10**, E10**-x, E20**, E20**-x

Status – *Semi-Supported*

These are NEx000 almost-clones that are reported to work with the standard NEx000 drivers, thanks to a ctron-specific check during the probe. If there are any problems, they are unlikely to be fixed, as the programming information is unavailable.

3.11.2   E2100

Status – *Semi-Supported*

Again, there is not much one can do when the programming information is proprietary. The E2100 is a poor design. Whenever it maps its shared memory in during a packet transfer, it maps it into the *whole 128K region!* That means you **can't** safely use another interrupt-driven shared memory device in that region, including another E2100. It will work most of the time, but every once in a while it will bite you. (Yes, this problem can be avoided by turning off interrupts while transferring packets, but that will almost certainly lose clock ticks.) Also, if you mis-program the board, or halt the machine at just the wrong moment, even the reset button won't bring it back. You will *have* to turn it off and *leave* it off for about 30 seconds.

Media selection is automatic, but you can override this with the low bits of the dev->mem_end parameter. See 10.1.1

Also, don't confuse the E2100 for a NE2100 clone. The E2100 is a shared memory NatSemi DP8390 design, roughly similar to a brain-damaged WD8013, whereas the NE2100 (and NE1500) use a bus-mastering AMD LANCE design.

There is an E2100 driver included in the standard kernel. However, seeing as programming info isn't available, don't expect bug-fixes. Don't use one unless you are already stuck with the card.

3.12   D-Link

Some people have had difficulty in finding vendors that carry D-link stuff. This should help.

```
(714) 455-1688    in the US
(081) 203-9900    in the UK
6196-643011       in Germany
(416) 828-0260    in Canada
(02) 916-1600     in Taiwan
```

3.12.1 DE-100, DE-200, DE-220-T

Status – *Supported*

The manual says that it is 100 % compatible with the NE2000. This is not true. You should call them and tell them you are using their card with Linux, and they should correct their documentation. Some pre-0.99pl12 driver versions may have trouble recognizing the DE2** series as 16 bit cards, and these cards are the most widely reported as having the spurious transfer address mismatch errors. Note that there are cards from Digital (DEC) that are also named DE100 and DE200, but the similarity stops there.

3.12.2 DE-530

Status – *Semi-Supported*

This appears to be a generic DEC 21040 PCI chip implementation, and will most likely work with the generic 21040 driver. However, nobody has verified this yet, and until that has happened, it will remain listed as *Semi-Supported*.

See 3.14.4 for more information on these cards, and the present driver situation.

3.12.3 DE-600

Status – *Supported*

Laptop users and other folk who might want a quick way to put their computer onto the ethernet may want to use this. The driver is included with the default kernel source tree. Bjorn Ekwall `bj0rn@blox.se` wrote the driver. Expect about 80kb/s transfer speed from this via the parallel port. You should read the README.DLINK file in the kernel source tree.

Note that the device name that you pass to `ifconfig` is *now* eth0 and not the previously used dl0.

If your parallel port is *not* at the standard `0x378` then you will have to recompile. Bjorn writes: "Since the DE-620 driver tries to sqeeze the last microsecond from the loops, I made the irq and port address constants instead of variables. This makes for a usable speed, but it also means that you can't change these assignments from e.g. lilo; you _have_ to recompile..." Also note that some laptops implement the on-board parallel port at `0x3bc` which is where the parallel ports on monochrome cards were/are.

Supposedly, a no-name ethernet pocket adaptor marketed under the name 'PE-1200' is DE-600 compatible. It is available in Europe from:

```
SEMCON Handels Ges.m.b.h
Favoritenstrasse 20
A-1040 WIEN
Telephone: (+43) 222 50 41 708
Fax      : (+43) 222 50 41 706
```

3.12.4 DE-620

Status – *Supported*

Same as the DE-600, only with two output formats. Bjorn has written a driver for this model, for kernel versions 1.1 and above. See the above information on the DE-600.

3.12.5 DE-650

Status – *Semi-Supported*

Some people have been using this PCMCIA card for some time now with their notebooks. It is a basic 8390 design, much like a NE2000. The LinkSys PCMCIA card and the IC-Card Ethernet (available from Midwest Micro) are supposedly DE-650 clones as well. Note that at present, this driver is *not* part of the standard kernel, and so you will have to do some patching.

See 8.3 in this document, and if you can, have a look at:

Don's PCMCIA Stuff (http://cesdis.gsfc.nasa.gov/linux/pcmcia.html)

3.13 DFI

3.13.1 DFINET-300 and DFINET-400

Status – *Supported*

These cards are now detected (as of 0.99pl15) thanks to Eberhard Moenkeberg emoenke@gwdg.de who noted that they use 'DFI' in the first 3 bytes of the prom, instead of using 0x57 in bytes 14 and 15, which is what all the NE1000 and NE2000 cards use. (The 300 is an 8 bit pseudo NE1000 clone, and the 400 is a pseudo NE2000 clone.)

3.14 Digital / DEC

3.14.1 DEPCA, DE100, DE200/1/2, DE210, DE422

Status – *Supported*

As of linux v1.0, there is a driver included as standard for these cards. It was written by David C. Davies. There is documentation included in the source file 'depca.c', which includes info on how to use more than one of these cards in a machine. Note that the DE422 is an EISA card. These cards are all based on the AMD LANCE chip. See 3.4.1 for more info. A maximum of two of the ISA cards can be used, because they can only be set for 0x300 and 0x200 base I/O address. If you are intending to do this, please read the notes in the driver source file depca.c in the standard kernel source tree.

3.14.2 Digital EtherWorks 3 (DE203, DE204, DE205)

Status – *Supported*

Included into kernels v1.1.62 and above is this driver, also by David C. Davies of DEC. These cards use a proprietary chip from DEC, as opposed to the LANCE chip used in the earlier cards like the DE200. These cards support both shared memory or programmed I/O, although you take about a 50%performance hit if you use PIO mode. The shared memory size can be set to 2kB, 32kB or 64kB, but only 2 and 32 have been tested with this driver. David says that the performance is virtually identical between the 2kB and 32kB mode. There is more information (including using the driver as a loadable module) at the top of the driver file ewrk3.c and also in README.ewrk3. Both of these files come with the standard kernel distribution.

Other interesting notes are that it appears that David is/was working on this driver for the unreleased version of Linux for the DEC Alpha AXP. And the standard driver has a number of interesting ioctl() calls that can be used to get or clear packet statistics, read/write the EEPROM, change the hardware address, and the like. Hackers can see the source code for more info on that one.

David has also written a configuration utility for this card (along the lines of the DOS program NICSETUP.EXE) along with other tools. These can be found on sunsite.unc.edu in the directory /pub/Linux/system/Network/management – look for the file ewrk3tools-X.XX.tar.gz.

3.14.3 DE425 (EISA), DE434, DE435

Status – *Supported*

These cards are based on the 21040 chip mentioned below. Included into kernels v1.1.86 and above is this driver, also by David C. Davies of DEC. It sure is nice to have support from someone on the inside ;-) Have a read of the 21040 section for extra info.

Note that as of 1.1.91, David has added a compile time option that may allow non-DEC cards (such as the ZYNX cards) to work with this driver. Have a look at `README.de4x5` for details.

3.14.4 DEC 21040, 21140, Tulip

Status – *Supported*

The DEC 21040 is a bus-mastering single chip ethernet solution from Digital, similar to AMD's PCnet chip. The 21040 is specifically designed for the PCI bus architecture. SMC's new EtherPower PCI card uses this chip. The new 21140 recently announced is for supporting 100Base-? and is supposed to be able to work with drivers for the 21040 chip.

You have a choice of *two* drivers for cards based on this chip. There is the DE425 driver discussed above, and the generic 21040 driver that Donald has written.

To use David's `de4x5` driver with non-DEC cards, have a look at `README.de4x5` for details.

Donald is doing his generic 21040 driver development on a SMC EtherPower PCI card at the moment, and this driver is included in the standard kernel source as of 1.1.84. Note that this driver is still considered an *alpha* driver (see 9.1) at the moment, and should be treated as such. To use it, you will have to edit `arch/i386/config.in` and uncomment the line for `CONFIG_DEC_ELCP` support.

3.15 Farallon

Farallon sells EtherWave adaptors and transceivers. This device allows multiple 10baseT devices to be daisy-chained.

3.15.1 Farallon Etherwave

Status – *Supported*

This is reported to be a 3c509 clone that includes the EtherWave transceiver. People have used these successfully with Linux and the present 3c509 driver. They are too expensive for general use, but are a great option for special cases. Hublet prices start at $125, and Etherwave adds $75-$100 to the price of the board – worth it if you have pulled one wire too few, but not if you are two network drops short.

3.16 Hewlett Packard

The 272** cards use programmed I/O, similar to the NE*000 boards, but the data transfer port can be 'turned off' when you aren't accessing it, avoiding problems with autoprobing drivers.

Thanks to Glenn Talbott for helping clean up the confusion in this section regarding the version numbers of the HP hardware.

3.16.1 27245A

Status – *Supported*

8 Bit 8390 based 10BaseT, not recommended for all the 8 bit reasons. It was re-designed a couple years ago to be highly integrated which caused some changes in initialization timing which only affected testing

programs, not LAN drivers. (The new card is not 'ready' as soon after switching into and out of loopback mode.)

3.16.2   HP PC Lan+ (27247A, 27247B, 27252A)

Status – *Supported*

The HP PC Lan+ is different to the standard HP PC Lan card. This driver was added to the list of drivers in the standard kernel at about v1.1.3X. Note that even though the driver is included, the entry in 'config.in' seems to have been omitted. If you want to use it, and it doesn't come up in 'config.in' then add the following line to 'config.in' under the 'HP PCLAN support' line:

```
bool 'HP PCLAN Plus support' CONFIG_HPLAN_PLUS n
```

Then run `make config;make dep;make zlilo` or whatever.

The 47B is a 16 Bit 8390 based 10BaseT w/AUI, and the 52A is a 16 Bit 8390 based ThinLAN w/AUI. These cards are high performers (3c509 speed) without the interrupt latency problems (32K onboard RAM for TX or RX packet buffering). They both offer LAN connector autosense, data I/O in I/O space (simpler) or memory mapped (faster), and soft configuration.

The 47A is the older model that existed before the 'B'. Two versions 27247-60001 or 27247-60002 have part numbers marked on the card. Functionally the same to the LAN driver, except bits in ROM to identify boards differ. -60002 has a jumper to allow operation in non-standard ISA busses (chipsets that expect IOCHRDY early.)

3.16.3   HP-J2405A

Status – *Supported*

These are lower priced, and slightly faster than the 27247B/27252A, but are missing some features, such as AUI, ThinLAN connectivity, and boot PROM socket. This is a fairly generic LANCE design, but a minor design decision makes it incompatible with a generic 'NE2100' driver. Special support for it (including reading the DMA channel from the board) is included thanks to information provided by HP's Glenn Talbott.

More technical information on LANCE based cards can be found in 7.8

3.16.4   HP-Vectra On Board Ethernet

Status – *Supported*

The HP-Vectra has an AMD PCnet chip on the motherboard. Earlier kernel versions would detect it as the HP-J2405A but that would fail, as the Vectra doesn't report the IRQ and DMA channel like the J2405A. Get a kernel newer than v1.1.53 to avoid this problem.

DMA selection and chip numbering information can be found in 3.4.1.

More technical information on LANCE based cards can be found in 7.8

3.17   IBM / International Business Machines

3.17.1   IBM Thinkpad 300

Status – *Supported*

This is compatible with the Intel based Zenith Z-note. See 3.29.1 for more info.

Supposedly this site has a comprehensive database of useful stuff for newer versions of the Thinkpad. I haven't checked it out myself yet.

Thinkpad-info (`http://peipa.essex.ac.uk/html/linux-thinkpad.html`)

For those without a WWW browser handy, try `peipa.essex.ac.uk:/pub/tp750/`

3.17.2 IBM Credit Card Adaptor for Ethernet

Status – *Semi-Supported*

People have been using this PCMCIA card with Linux as well. Similar points apply, those being that you need a supported PCMCIA chipset on your notebook, and that you will have to patch the PCMCIA support into the standard kernel.

See 8.3 in this document, and if you can, have a look at:

Don's PCMCIA Stuff (`http://cesdis.gsfc.nasa.gov/linux/pcmcia.html`)

3.18 Intel Ethernet Cards

3.18.1 Ether Express

Status – *Semi-Supported*

This card uses the intel i82586. (Surprise, huh?) The driver is in the standard release of the kernel, as an alpha driver. See 9.1 for important information on using alpha-test ethernet drivers with Linux.

The reason is that the driver works well with slow machines, but the i82586 occasionally hangs from the packet buffer contention that a fast machine can cause. One reported hack/fix is to change all of the outw() calls to outw_p(). Also, the driver is missing promiscuous and multicast modes. (See 7.9)

There is also the standard way of using the chip (read slower) that is described in the chip manual, and used in other i82586 drivers, but this would require a re-write of the entire driver.

There is some technical information available on the i82586 in 7.6 and also in the source code for the driver 'eexpress.c'. Don't be afraid to read it. ;-)

3.18.2 Ether Express PRO

Status – *Not-Supported*

This card uses the Intel 82595. If it is as ugly to use as the i82586, then don't count on anybody writing a driver.

3.19 LinkSys

3.19.1 LinkSys PCMCIA Adaptor

Status – *Semi-Supported*

This is supposed to be a re-badged DE-650. See the information on the DE-650 in 3.12.5.

3.20 Microdyne

3.20.1 Microdyne Exos 205T

Status – *Not-Supported*

Another i82586 based card. At one point, dabn100@hermes.cam.ac.uk had written a driver that "almost worked" that was based on the 3c507 code. More details as they are received...

3.21   Mylex

3.21.1   Mylex LNP101, LNP104

Status – *Semi-Supported*

These are PCI cards that are based on DEC's 21040 chip. The LNP104 uses the 21050 chip to deliver *four* independent 10BaseT ports. The standard LNP101 is selectable between 10BaseT, 10Base2 and 10Base5 output. The LNP101 card *should* work with the generic 21040 driver, but nobody has verified this yet. As for the LNP 104, well...

See the section on the 21040 chip (3.14.4) for more information.

Mylex can be reached at the following numbers, in case anyone wants to ask them anything.

```
MYLEX CORPORATION, Fremont
Sales:  800-77-MYLEX, (510) 796-6100
FAX:    (510) 745-8016.
```

3.22   Novell Ethernet, NExxxx and associated clones.

The prefix 'NE' came from Novell Ethernet. Novell followed the cheapest NatSemi databook design and sold the manufacturing rights (spun off?) Eagle, just to get reasonably-priced ethercards into the market. (The now ubiquitous NE2000 card.)

3.22.1   NE1000, NE2000

Status – *Supported*

The now-generic name for a bare-bones design around the NatSemi 8390. They use programmed I/O rather than shared memory, leading to easier installation but slightly lower performance and a few problems. Again, the savings of using an 8 bit NE1000 over the NE2000 are only warranted if you expect light use. Some recently introduced NE2000 clones use the National Semiconductor 'AT/LANTic' 83905 chip, which offers a shared memory mode similar to the 8013 and EEPROM or software configuration. Some problems can arise with poor clones. See 9.3, and 4.1 In general it is not a good idea to put a NE2000 clone at I/O address 0x300 because nearly *every* device driver probes there at boot. Some poor NE2000 clones don't take kindly to being prodded in the wrong areas, and will respond by locking your machine.

Donald has written a NE2000 diagnostic program, but it is still presently in alpha test. (ne2k) See 6.2 for more information.

3.22.2   NE1500, NE2100

Status – *Supported*

These cards use the original 7990 LANCE chip from AMD and are supported using the Linux lance driver.

Some earlier versions of the lance driver had problems with getting the IRQ line via autoIRQ from the original Novell/Eagle 7990 cards. Hopefully this is now fixed. If not, then specify the IRQ via LILO, and let us know that it still has problems.

DMA selection and chip numbering information can be found in 3.4.1.

More technical information on LANCE based cards can be found in 7.8

3.22.3 NE3200

Status – *Not Supported*

This card uses a lowly 8MHz 80186, and hence you are better off using a cheap NE2000 clone. Even if a driver was available, the NE2000 card would most likely be faster.

3.23 Pure Data

3.23.1 PDUC8028, PDI8023

Status – *Supported*

The PureData PDUC8028 and PDI8023 series of cards are reported to work, thanks to special probe code contributed by Mike Jagdis `jaggy@purplet.demon.co.uk`. The support is integrated with the WD driver.

3.24 Racal-Interlan

3.24.1 NI52**

Status – *Semi-Supported*

Michael Hipp has written a driver for this card. It is included in the standard kernel as an 'alpha' driver. Michael would like to hear feedback from users that have this card. See 9.1 for important information on using alpha-test ethernet drivers with Linux.

Michael says that "the internal sysbus seems to be slow. So we often lose packets because of overruns while receiving from a fast remote host."

This card also uses one of the Intel chips. See 7.6 for more technical information.

3.24.2 NI65**

Status – *Semi-Supported*

There is also a driver for the LANCE based NI6510, and it is also written by Michael Hipp. Again, it is also an 'alpha' driver. For some reason, this card is not compatible with the generic LANCE driver. See 9.1 for important information on using alpha-test ethernet drivers with Linux.

3.25 Sager

3.25.1 Sager NP943

Status – *Semi-Supported*

This is just a 3c501 clone, with a different S.A. PROM prefix. I assume it is equally as brain dead as the original 3c501 as well. Kernels 1.1.53 and up check for the NP943 i.d. and then just treat it as a 3c501 after that. See 3.1.1 for all the reasons as to why you really don't want to use one of these cards.

3.26 Schneider & Koch

3.26.1 SK G16

Status – *Supported*

This driver was included into the v1.1 kernels, and it was written by PJD Weichmann and SWS Bern. It appears that the SK G16 is similar to the NI6510, in that it is based on the first edition LANCE chip (the 7990). Once again, I have no idea as to why this card won't work with the generic LANCE driver.

3.27 Western Digital / SMC (Standard Microsystems Corp.)

The ethernet part of Western Digital has been bought by SMC. One common mistake people make is that the relatively new SMC Elite Ultra is the same as the older SMC Elite16 models – this is **not** the case.

Here is how to contact SMC (not that you should need to.)

SMC / Standard Microsystems Corp., 80 Arkay Drive, Hauppage, New York, 11788, USA.

Technical Support via phone:

```
800-992-4762  (USA)
800-433-5345  (Canada)
516-435-6250  (Other Countries)
```

Literature requests:

```
800-SMC-4-YOU  (USA)
800-833-4-SMC  (Canada)
516-435-6255   (Other Countries)
```

Technical Support via E-mail:

```
techsupt@ccmail.west.smc.com
```

FTP Site:

```
ftp.smc.com
```

3.27.1 WD8003, SMC Elite

Status – *Supported*

These are the 8-bit versions of the card. The 8 bit 8003 is slightly less expensive, but only worth the savings for light use. Note that some of the non-EEPROM cards (clones with jumpers, or old *old* old wd8003 cards) have no way of reporting the IRQ line used. In this case, auto-irq is used, and if that fails, the driver silently assigns IRQ 5. Information regarding what the jumpers on old non-EEPROM wd8003 cards do can be found in conjunction with the SMC setup/driver disks stored on dorm.rutgers.edu in the directory /pub/novell/nic_drvs/. Note that some of the newer SMC 'SuperDisk' programs will fail to detect the old EEPROM-less cards. The file SMCDSK46.EXE seems to be a good all-round choice. Also the jumper settings for old cards are in an ascii text file in the aforementioned archive. The latest (greatest?) version can be obtained from ftp.smc.com.

As these are basically the same as their 16 bit counterparts (WD8013 / SMC Elite16), you should see the next section for more information.

3.27.2 WD8013, SMC Elite16

Status – *Supported*

Over the years the design has added more registers and an EEPROM. Clones usually go by the '8013' name, and usually use a non-EEPROM (jumpered) design. This part of WD has been sold to SMC, so you'll usually see something like SMC/WD8013 or SMC Elite16 Plus (WD8013). Late model SMC cards will have two main PLCC chips on board; the SMC 83c690 and the SMC 83c694. The shared memory design makes the cards 10-20 % faster, especially with larger packets. More importantly, from the driver's point of view, it avoids a few bugs in the programmed-I/O mode of the 8390, allows safe multi-threaded access to the packet buffer, and it doesn't have a programmed-I/O data register that hangs your machine during warm-boot probes.

Non-EEPROM cards that can't just read the selected IRQ will attempt auto-irq, and if that fails, they will silently assign IRQ 10. (8 bit versions will assign IRQ 5)

Also see 4.2 and 9.4.

3.27.3 SMC Elite Ultra

Status – *Supported*

This ethercard is based on a new chip from SMC, with a few new features. While it has a mode that is similar to the older SMC ethercards, it's not compatible with the old WD80*3 drivers. However, in this mode it shares most of its code with the other 8390 drivers, while operating somewhat faster than a WD8013 clone.

Since part of the Ultra *looks like* an 8013, the Ultra probe is supposed to find an Ultra before the wd8013 probe has a chance to mistakenly identify it.

Std. as of 0.99pl14, and made possible by documentation and ethercard loan from Duke Kamstra. If you plan on using an Ultra with Linux send him a note of thanks to let him know that there are Linux users out there!

Donald mentioned that it is possible to write a separate driver for the Ultra's 'Altego' mode which allows chaining transmits at the cost of inefficient use of receive buffers, but that will probably not happen right away. Performance re-writes of working drivers are low priority unless there is some particular incentive or need.

Bus-Master SCSI host adaptor users take note: In the manual that ships with Interactive UNIX, it mentions that a bug in the SMC Ultra will cause data corruption with SCSI disks being run from an aha-154X host adaptor. This will probably bite aha-154X compatible cards, such as the BusLogic boards, and the AMI-FastDisk SCSI host adaptors as well.

Supposedly SMC has acknowledged the problem occurs with Interactive, and older Windows NT drivers. It is supposed to be a hardware conflict that can be worked around in the driver design. More on this as it develops.

Some Linux users with an Ultra + aha-154X compatible cards have experienced data corruption, while others have not. Donald tried this combination himself, and wasn't able to reproduce the problem. You have been warned.

3.27.4 SMC 8416 (EtherEZ)

Status – *Supported*

This card uses SMC's 83c795 chip and supports the Plug 'n Play specification. It also has an *SMC Ultra* compatible mode, which allows it to be used with the Linux Ultra driver. In this compatibility mode, it uses shared memory instead of programmed i/o. Be sure to set your card for this compatibility mode.

Note that the EtherEZ specific checks were added to the SMC Ultra driver in 1.1.84, and hence earlier kernel versions will not handle these cards correctly.

3.27.5 SMC 8432 PCI (EtherPower)

Status – *Supported*

These cards appear to be a basic DEC 21040 implementation, i.e. one big chip and a couple of transceivers. Donald has used one of these cards for his development of the generic 21040 driver. Thanks to Duke Kamstra, once again, for supplying a card to do development on. See 3.14.4 for more details on using one of these cards, and the current status of the driver.

3.27.6　SMC 3008

Status – *Not Supported*

These 8 bit cards are based on the Fujitsu MB86950, which is an ancient version of the MB86965 used in the Linux at1700 driver. Russ says that you could probably hack up a driver by looking at the at1700.c code and his DOS packet driver for the Tiara card (tiara.asm)

3.27.7　SMC 3016

Status – *Not Supported*

These are 16bit i/o mapped 8390 cards, much similar to a generic NE2000 card. If you can get the specifications from SMC, then porting the NE2000 driver would probably be quite easy.

3.27.8　SMC 9000

Status – *Not Supported*

These cards are VLB cards based on the 91c92 chip. They are fairly expensive, and hence the demand for a driver is pretty low at the moment.

3.28　Xircom

Another group that won't release documentation. No cards supported. Don't look for any support in the future unless they release their programming information. And this is highly unlikely, as they *forbid* you from even reverse- engineering their drivers. If you are already stuck with one, see if you can trade it off on some DOS (l)user.

And if you just want to verify that this is the case, you can reach Xircom at 1-800-874-7875, 1-800-438-4526 or +1-818-878-7600. They used to advertise that their products "work with all network operating systems", but have since stopped. Wonder why...

3.28.1　PE1, PE2, PE3-10B*

Status – *Not Supported*

Not to get your hopes up, but if you have one of these parallel port adaptors, you may be able to use it in the DOS emulator with the Xircom-supplied DOS drivers. You will have to allow DOSEMU access to your parallel port, and will probably have to play with SIG (DOSEMU's Silly Interrupt Generator). I have no idea if this will work, but if you have any success with it, let me know, and I will include it here.

3.29　Zenith

3.29.1　Z-Note

Status – *Supported*

The built-in Z-Note network adaptor is based on the Intel i82593 using *two* DMA channels. There is an (alpha?) driver available in the present kernel version. As with all notebook and pocket adaptors, it is under the 'Pocket and portable adaptors' section when running make config. See 7.6 for more technical information. Also note that the IBM ThinkPad 300 is compatible with the Z-Note.

3.30 Zynx

3.30.1 Zynx (DEC 21040 based)

Status – *Supported*

You have a choice of *two* drivers for cards based on this chip. There is the DE425 driver written by David, and the generic 21040 driver that Donald has written.

Note that as of 1.1.91, David has added a compile time option that may allow non-DEC cards (such as the Zynx cards) to work with this driver. Have a look at README.de4x5 for details.

See 3.14.4 for more information on these cards, and the present driver situation.

4 Clones of popular Ethernet cards.

Due to the popular design of some cards, different companies will make 'clones' or replicas of the original card. However, one must be careful, as some of these clones are not 100 % compatible, and can be troublesome. Some common problems with 'not-quite-clones' are noted in 9.

This section used to have a listing of a whole bunch of clones that were reported to work, but seeing as nearly *all* clones will work, it makes more sense to list the ones that don't work 100 % .

4.1 Poor NE2000 Clones

Here is a list of some of the NE-2000 clones that are known to have various problems. Most of them aren't fatal. In the case of the ones listed as 'bad clones' – this usually indicates that the cards don't have the two NE2000 identifier bytes. NEx000-clones have a Station Address PROM (SAPROM) in the packet buffer memory space. NE2000 clones have 0x57, 0x57 in bytes 0x0e, 0x0f of the SAPROM, while other supposed NE2000 clones must be detected by their SA prefix.

Accton NE2000 – might not get detected at boot, see 9.3.

Aritsoft LANtastic AE-2 – OK, but has flawed error-reporting registers.

AT-LAN-TEC NE2000 – clone uses Winbond chip that traps SCSI drivers

ShineNet LCS-8634 – clone uses Winbond chip that traps SCSI drivers

Cabletron E10**, E20**, E10**-x, E20**-x – bad clones, but the driver checks for them. See 3.11.1.

D-Link Ethernet II – bad clones, but the driver checks for them. See 3.12.1.

DFI DFINET-300, DFINET-400 – bad clones, but the driver checks for them. See 3.13.1

4.2 Poor WD8013 Clones

I haven't heard of any bad clones of these cards, except perhaps for some chameleon-type cards that can be set to look like a ne2000 card or a wd8013 card. There is really no need to purchase one of these 'double-identity' cards anyway.

5   Cables, Coax, Twisted Pair

If you are starting a network from scratch, it's considerably less expensive to use thin ethernet, RG58 co-ax cable with BNC connectors, than old-fashioned thick ethernet, RG-5 cable with N connectors, or 10baseT, twisted pair telco-style cables with RJ-45 eight wire 'phone' connectors. See 2.4 for an introductory look at cables.

Also note that the FAQ from *comp.dcom.lans.ethernet* has a lot of useful information on cables and such. Look in `dorm.rutgers.edu` for the file `/pub/novell/info_and_docs/Ethernet.FAQ`

5.1   Thin Ethernet (thinnet)

Thin ethernet is the 'ether of choice'. The cable is inexpensive. If you are making your own cables solid-core RG58A is $0.27/m. and stranded RG58AU is $0.45/m. Twist-on BNC connectors are < $2 ea., and other misc. pieces are similarly inexpensive. It is essential that you properly terminate each end of the cable with 50 ohm terminators, so budget $2 ea. for a pair. It's also vital that your cable have no 'stubs' – the 'T' connectors must be attached directly to the ethercards. The only drawback is that if you have a big loop of machines connected together, and some bonehead breaks the loop by taking one cable off the side of his tee, the whole network goes down because it sees an infinite impedance (open circuit) instead of the required 50 ohm termination. Note that you can remove the tee piece from the card itself without killing the whole subnet, as long as you don't remove the cables from the tee itself. Of course this will disturb the machine that you pull the actual tee off of. 8-) And if you are doing a small network of two machines, you *still* need the tees and the 50 ohm terminators – you *can't* just cable them together!

5.2   Twisted Pair

Twisted pair networks require active hubs, which start around $200, and the raw cable cost can actually be higher than thinnet. They are usually sold using the claim that you can use your existing telephone wiring, but it's a rare installation where that turns out to be the case. The claim that you can upgrade to higher speeds is also suspect, as most proposed schemes use higher-grade (read $$) cable and more sophisticated termination ($$$) than you would likely install on speculation. New gizmos are floating around which allow you to daisy-chain machines together, and the like. For example, Farallon sells EtherWave adaptors and transceivers. This device allows multiple 10baseT devices to be daisy-chained. They also sell a 3c509 clone that includes the EtherWave transceiver. The drawback is that it's more expensive and less reliable than a cheap ($100-$150) mini-hub and another ethercard. You probably should either go for the hub approach or switch over to 10base2 thinnet.

On the other hand, hubs are rapidly dropping in price, all 100Mb/sec ethernet proposals use twisted pair, and most new business installations use twisted pair. (This is probably to avoid the problem with idiots messing with the BNC's as described above.)

Also, Russ Nelson adds that 'New installations should use Category 5 wiring. Anything else is a waste of your installer's time, as 100Base-whatever is going to require Cat 5.'

If you are only connecting two machines, it is possible to avoid using a hub, by swapping the Rx and Tx pairs (1-2 and 3-6).

If you hold the RJ-45 connector facing you (as if you were going to plug it into your mouth) with the lock tab on the top, then the pins are numbered 1 to 8 from left to right. The pin usage is as follows:

```
Pin Number           Assignment
----------           ----------
1                    Output Data (+)
2                    Output Data (-)
3                    Input Data (+)
4                    Reserved for Telephone use
5                    Reserved for Telephone use
```

```
        6               Input Data (-)
        7               Reserved for Telephone use
        8               Reserved for Telephone use
```

Some cards, like the wd8013 can sense reversed polarity, and will adjust accordingly. Also note that 3 and 6 **must** be a twisted pair. If you make 3-4 a twisted pair, and 5-6 the other twisted pair, your cable may work for lengths less than a metre, but will *fail miserably* for longer lengths.

Note that before 10BaseT was ratified as a standard, there existed other network formats using RJ-45 connectors, and the same wiring scheme as above. Examples are SynOptics's LattisNet, and AT&T's StarLAN. In some cases, (as with early 3C503 cards) you could set jumpers to get the card to talk to hubs of different types, but in most cases cards designed for these older types of networks will not work with standard 10BaseT networks/hubs. (Note that if the cards also have an AUI port, then there is no reason as to why you can't use that, combined with an AUI to 10BaseT transceiver.)

5.3   Thick Ethernet

Thick ethernet is mostly obsolete, and is usually used only to remain compatible with an existing implementation. You can stretch the rules and connect short spans of thick and thin ethernet together with a passive $3 N-to-BNC connector, and that's often the best solution to expanding an existing thicknet. A correct (but expensive) solution is to use a repeater in this case.

6   Software Configuration and Card Diagnostics

In most cases, if the configuration is done by software, and stored in an EEPROM, you will usually have to boot DOS, and use the supplied DOS program to set the cards IRQ, I/O, mem_addr and whatnot. Besides, hopefully it is something you will only be setting once. For those that don't have the DOS utility available, note that a fair number of NIC setup/driver disks (e.g. 3Com, SMC/WD and Allied Telesis NIC's) are available from `dorm.rutgers.edu` in the directory `/pub/novell/nic_drvs/` However, there are some cards for which Linux versions of the config utils exist, and they are listed here.

Also, Donald has written a few small card diagnostic programs that run under Linux. Most of these are a result of debugging tools that he has created while writing the various drivers. Don't expect fancy menu-driven interfaces. You will have to read the source code to use most of these. Even if your particular card doesn't have a corresponding diagnostic, you can still get lots of information just by typing `cat /proc/net/dev` – assuming that your card was at least detected at boot.

In either case, you will have to run most of these programs as root (to allow I/O to the ports) and you probably want to shut down the ethercard before doing so by typing `ifconfig eth0 down` (Note: replace `eth0` with `atp0` or whatever when appropriate.)

6.1   Configuration Programs for Ethernet Cards

For people with wd80x3 cards, there is the program `wdsetup` which can be found in `wdsetup-0.6a.tar.gz` on Linux ftp sites. I am not sure if it is being actively maintained or not, as it has not been updated for quite a while. If it works fine for you then great, if not, use the DOS version that you should have got with your card. If you don't have the DOS version, you will be glad to know that the SMC setup/driver disks are available at the `dorm.rutgers.edu` site mentioned above. Of course, you *have* to have an EEPROM card to use this utility. Old, *old* wd8003 cards, and some wd8013 clones use jumpers to set up the card instead.

The Digital EtherWorks 3 card can be configured in a similar fashion to the DOS program `NICSETUP.EXE`. David C. Davies wrote this and other tools for the EtherWorks 3 in conjunction with the driver. Look on `sunsite.unc.edu` in the directory `/pub/linux/system/Network/management` for the file that is named `ewrk3tools-X.XX.tar.gz`.

Some Nat Semi DP83905 implementations (such as the AT/LANTIC and the NE2000+) are software configurable. (Note that this card can also emulate a wd8013!) You can get the file `/pub/linux/setup/atlantic.c` from Donald's ftp server, `cesdis.gsfc.nasa.gov` to configure this card. Be careful when configuring NE2000+ cards, as you can give them bad setting values which will require you to open the case and switch a jumper to force it back to sane settings.

The 3Com Etherlink III family of cards (i.e. 3c5x9) can be configured by using another config utility from Donald. You can get the file `/pub/linux/setup/3c5x9setup.c` from Donald's ftp server, `cesdis.gsfc.nasa.gov` to configure these cards. (Note that the DOS 3c5x9B config utility may have more options pertaining to the new "B" series of the Etherlink III family.)

6.2 Diagnostic Programs for Ethernet Cards

Any of the diagnostic programs that Donald has written can be obtained from this URL.

Ethercard Diagnostics (`http://cesdis.gsfc.nasa.gov/pub/linux/diag/diagnostic.html`)

Allied Telesis AT1700 – look for the file `/pub/linux/diag/at1700.c` on `cesdis.gsfc.nasa.gov`.

Cabletron E21XX – look for the file `/pub/linux/diag/e21.c` on `cesdis.gsfc.nasa.gov`.

HP PCLAN+ – look for the file `/pub/linux/diag/hp+.c` on `cesdis.gsfc.nasa.gov`.

Intel EtherExpress – look for the file `/pub/linux/diag/eexpress.c` on `cesdis.gsfc.nasa.gov`.

NE2000 cards – look for the file `/pub/linux/diag/ne2k.c` on `cesdis.gsfc.nasa.gov`.

RealTek (ATP) Pocket adaptor – look for the file `/pub/linux/diag/atp-diag.c` on `cesdis.gsfc.nasa.gov`.

All Other Cards – try typing `cat /proc/net/dev` and see what useful info the kernel has on the card in question.

7 Technical Information

For those who want to play with the present drivers, or try to make up their own driver for a card that is presently unsupported, this information should be useful. If you do not fall into this category, then perhaps you will want to skip this section.

7.1 Probed Addresses

While trying to determine what ethernet card is there, the following addresses are autoprobed, assuming the type and specs of the card have not been set in the kernel. The file names below are in `/usr/src/linux/drivers/net/`

```
3c501.c       0x280, 0x300
3c503.c:      0x300, 0x310, 0x330, 0x350, 0x250, 0x280, 0x2a0, 0x2e0
3c505.c:      0x300, 0x280, 0x310
3c507.c:      0x300, 0x320, 0x340, 0x280
3c509.c:      Special ID Port probe
apricot.c     0x300
at1700.c:     0x300, 0x280, 0x380, 0x320, 0x340, 0x260, 0x2a0, 0x240
atp.c:        0x378, 0x278, 0x3bc
depca.c       0x300, 0x200
de600.c:      0x378
de620.c:      0x378
eexpress.c:   0x300, 0x270, 0x320, 0x340
hp.c:         0x300, 0x320, 0x340, 0x280, 0x2C0, 0x200, 0x240
```

```
hp-plus.c          0x200, 0x240, 0x280, 0x2C0, 0x300, 0x320, 0x340
lance.c:           0x300, 0x320, 0x340, 0x360
ne.c:              0x300, 0x280, 0x320, 0x340, 0x360
ni52.c             0x300, 0x280, 0x360, 0x320, 0x340
ni65.c             0x300, 0x320, 0x340, 0x360
smc-ultra.c:       0x200, 0x220, 0x240, 0x280, 0x300, 0x340, 0x380
wd.c:              0x300, 0x280, 0x380, 0x240
```

There are some NE2000 clone ethercards out there that are waiting black holes for autoprobe drivers. While many NE2000 clones are safe until they are enabled, some can't be reset to a safe mode. These dangerous ethercards will hang any I/O access to their 'dataports'. The typical dangerous locations are:

```
Ethercard jumpered base     Dangerous locations (base + 0x10 - 0x1f)
        0x300 *                     0x310-0x317
        0x320                       0x330-0x337
        0x340                       0x350-0x357
        0x360                       0x370-0x377
```

* The 0x300 location is the traditional place to put an ethercard, but it's also a popular place to put other devices (often SCSI controllers). The 0x320 location is often the next one chosen, but that's bad for for the AHA1542 driver probe. The 0x360 location is bad, because it conflicts with the parallel port at 0x378. If you have two IDE controllers, or two floppy controlers, then 0x360 is also a bad choice, as a NE2000 card will clobber them as well.

Note that kernels > 1.1.7X keep a log of who uses which i/o ports, and will not let a driver use i/o ports registered by an earlier driver. This may result in probes silently failing. You can view who is using what i/o ports by typing `cat /proc/ioports` if you have the proc filesystem enabled.

To avoid these lurking ethercards, here are the things you can do:

- Probe for the device's BIOS in memory space. This is easy and always safe, but it only works for cards that always have BIOSes, like primary SCSI controllers.

- Avoid probing any of the above locations until you think you've located your device. The NE2000 clones have a reset range from <base>+0x18 to <base>+0x1f that will read as 0xff, so probe there first if possible. It's also safe to probe in the 8390 space at <base>+0x00 - <base>+0x0f, but that area will return quasi-random values

- If you must probe in the dangerous range, for instance if your target device has only a few port locations, first check that there isn't an NE2000 there. You can see how to do this by looking at the probe code in /usr/src/linux/net/inet/ne.c

- Use the 'reserve' boot time argument to protect volatile areas from being probed. See the information on using boot time arguments with LILO in 10.1.2

7.2   Skeleton / prototype driver

OK. So you have decided that you want to write a driver for the Foobar Ethernet card, as you have the programming information, and it hasn't been done yet. (...these are the two main requirements ;-) You can use the skeleton network driver that is provided with the Linux kernel source tree. It can be found in the file /usr/src/linux/drivers/net/skeleton.c as of 0.99pl15, and later.

It's also very useful to look at the Crynwr (nee Clarkson) driver for your target ethercard, if it's available. Russ Nelson nelson@crynwr.com has been actively updating and writing these, and he has been very helpful with his code reviews of the current Linux drivers.

7.3   Driver interface to the kernel

Here are some notes that may help when trying to figure out what the code in the driver segments is doing, or perhaps what it is supposed to be doing.

```
int ethif_init(struct device *dev)
{
    ...
        dev->send_packet = &ei_send_packet;
        dev->open = &ei_open;
        dev->stop = &ei_close;
        dev->hard_start_xmit = &ei_start_xmit;
        ...
}

int ethif_init(struct device *dev)
```

This function is put into the device structure in Space.c. It is called only at boot time, and returns '0' iff the ethercard 'dev' exists.

```
static int ei_open(struct device *dev)
static int ei_close(struct device *dev)
```

This routine opens and initializes the board in response to an socket ioctl() usually called by 'ifconfig'. It is commonly stuffed into the 'struct device' by ethif_init().

The inverse routine is ei_close(), which should shut down the ethercard, free the IRQs and DMA channels if the hardware permits, and turn off anything that will save power (like the transceiver).

```
static int ei_start_xmit(struct sk_buff *skb, struct device *dev)
        dev->hard_start_xmit = &ei_start_xmit;
```

This routine puts packets to be transmitted into the hardware. It is usually stuffed into the 'struct device' by ethif_init().

When the hardware can't accept additional packets it should set the dev->tbusy flag. When additional room is available, usually during a transmit-complete interrupt, dev->tbusy should be cleared and the higher levels informed with mark_bh(INET_BH).

```
if (dev_rint(buffer, length, is_skb ? IN_SKBUFF : 0, dev))
        stats->rx_dropped++;
```

A received packet is passed to the higher levels using dev_rint(). If the unadorned packet data in a memory buffer, dev_rint will copy it into a 'skbuff' for you. Otherwise a new skbuff should be kmalloc()ed, filled, and passed to dev_rint() with the IN_SKBUFF flag.

```
int s=socket(AF_INET,SOCK_PACKET,htons(ETH_P_ALL));
```

Gives you a socket receiving every protocol type. Do recvfrom() calls to it and it will fill the sockaddr with device type in sa_family and the device name in the sa_data array. I don't know who originally invented SOCK_PACKET for Linux (its been in for ages) but its superb stuff. You can use it to send stuff raw too (both only as root).

7.4 Interrupts and Linux

There are two kinds of interrupt handlers in Linux: fast ones and slow ones. You decide what kind you are installing by the flags you pass to irqaction(). The fast ones, such as the serial interrupt handler, run with _all_ interrupts disabled. The normal interrupt handlers, such as the one for ethercard drivers, runs with other interrupts enabled.

There is a two-level interrupt structure. The 'fast' part handles the device register, removes the packets, and perhaps sets a flag. After it is done, and interrupts are re-enabled, the slow part is run if the flag is set.

The flag between the two parts is set by:

```
mark_bh(INET_BH);
```

Usually this flag is set within dev_rint() during a received-packet interrupt, and set directly by the device driver during a transmit-complete interrupt.

You might wonder why all interrupt handlers cannot run in 'normal mode' with other interrupts enabled. Ross Biro uses this scenario to illustrate the problem:

- You get a serial interrupt, and start processing it. The serial interrupt is now masked.

- You get a network interrupt, and you start transferring a maximum-sized 1500 byte packet from the card.

- Another character comes in, but this time the interrupts are masked!

The 'fast' interrupt structure solves this problem by allowing bounded-time interrupt handlers to run without the risk of leaving their interrupt lines masked by another interrupt request.

There is an additional distinction between fast and slow interrupt handlers – the arguments passed to the handler. A 'slow' handler is defined as

```
static void
handle_interrupt(int reg_ptr)
{
    int irq = -(((struct pt_regs *)reg_ptr)->orig_eax+2);
    struct device *dev = irq2dev_map[irq];
    ...
```

While a fast handler gets the interrupt number directly

```
static void
handle_fast_interrupt(int irq)
{
    ...
```

A final aspect of network performance is latency. The only board that really addresses this is the 3c509, which allows a predictive interrupt to be posted. It provides an interrupt response timer so that the driver can fine-tune how early an interrupt is generated.

Alan Cox has some advice for anyone wanting to write drivers that are to be used with 0.99pl14 kernels and newer. He says:

'Any driver intended for 0.99pl14 should use the new alloc_skb() and kfree_skbmem() functions rather than using kmalloc() to obtain a sk_buff. The new 0.99pl14 skeleton does this correctly. For drivers wishing to remain compatible with both sets the define 'HAVE_ALLOC_SKB' indicates these functions must be used.

In essence replace

```
skb=(struct sk_buff *)kmalloc(size)
```

with

```
skb=alloc_skb(size)
```

and

```
kfree_s(skb,size)
```

with

```
kfree_skbmem(skb,size) /* Only sk_buff memory though */
```

Any questions should I guess be directed to me (Alan Cox) since I made the change. This is a change to allow tracking of sk_buff's and sanity checks on buffers and stack behaviour. If a driver produces the message'File: ??? Line: ??? passed a non skb!' then it is probable the driver is not using the new sk_buff allocators.'

7.5   Programmed I/O vs. Shared Memory vs. DMA

Ethernet is 10Mbs. (Don't be pedantic, 3Mbs and 100Mbs don't count.) If you can already send and receive back-to-back packets, you just can't put more bits over the wire. Every modern ethercard can receive back-to-back packets. The Linux DP8390 drivers come pretty close to sending back-to-back packets (depending on the current interrupt latency) and the 3c509 and AT1500 hardware has no problem at all automatically sending back-to-back packets.

The ISA bus can do 5.3MB/sec (42Mb/sec), which sounds like more than enough. You can use that bandwidth in several ways:

7.5.1   Programmed I/O

Pro: Doesn't use any constrained system resources, just a few I/O registers, and has no 16M limit.

Con: Usually the slowest transfer rate, the CPU is waiting the whole time, and interleaved packet access is usually difficult to impossible.

7.5.2   Shared memory

Pro: Simple, faster than programmed I/O, and allows random access to packets.

Con: Uses up memory space (a big one for DOS users, only a minor issue under Linux), and it still ties up the CPU.

7.5.3   Slave (normal) Direct Memory Access

Pro: Frees up the CPU during the actual data transfer.

Con: Checking boundary conditions, allocating contiguous buffers, and programming the DMA registers makes it the slowest of all techniques. It also uses up a scarce DMA channel, and requires aligned low memory buffers.

7.5.4 Master Direct Memory Access (bus-master)

Pro: Frees up the CPU during the data transfer, can string together buffers, can require little or no CPU time lost on the ISA bus.

Con: Requires low-memory buffers and a DMA channel. Any bus-master will have problems with other bus-masters that are bus-hogs, such as some primitive SCSI adaptors. A few badly-designed motherboard chipsets have problems with bus-masters. And a reason for not using *any* type of DMA device is using a Cyrix 486 processor designed for plug-in replacement of a 386: these processors must flush their cache with each DMA cycle. (This includes the Cx486DLC, Ti486DLC, Cx486SLC, Ti486SLC, etc.)

7.6 Programming the Intel chips (i82586 and i82593)

These chips are used on a number of cards, namely the 3c507 ('86), the Intel EtherExpress 16 ('86), Microdyne's exos205t ('86), the Z-Note ('93), and the Racal-Interlan ni5210 ('86).

Russ Nelson writes: 'Most boards based on the 82586 can reuse quite a bit of their code. More, in fact, than the 8390-based adapters. There are only three differences between them:

- The code to get the Ethernet address,

- The code to trigger CA on the 82586, and

- The code to reset the 82586.

The Intel EtherExpress 16 is an exception, as it I/O maps the 82586. Yes, I/O maps it. Fairly clunky, but it works.

Garrett Wollman did an AT&T driver for BSD that uses the BSD copyright. The latest version I have (Sep '92) only uses a single transmit buffer. You can and should do better than this if you've got the memory. The AT&T and 3c507 adapters do; the ni5210 doesn't.

The people at Intel gave me a very big clue on how you queue up multiple transmit packets. You set up a list of NOP-> XMIT-> NOP-> XMIT-> NOP-> XMIT-> beginning) blocks, then you set the 'next' pointer of all the NOP blocks to themselves. Now you start the command unit on this chain. It continually processes the first NOP block. To transmit a packet, you stuff it into the next transmit block, then point the NOP to it. To transmit the next packet, you stuff the next transmit block and point the previous NOP to *it*. In this way, you don't have to wait for the previous transmit to finish, you can queue up multiple packets without any ambiguity as to whether it got accepted, and you can avoid the command unit start-up delay.'

7.7 Technical information from 3Com

```
From: Cameron Spitzer 764-6339 <camerons@nad.3com.com>
Subject: getting 3Com Adapter manuals
Date: Mon, 27 Sep 1993 21:17:07 +0200
```

Since this is becoming a FAQ, I'm going to tread the thin ice of No Commercial Use and answer it here.

3Com's Ethernet Adapters are documented for driver writers in our 'Technical References' (TRs). These manuals describe the programmer interfaces to the boards but they don't talk about the diagnostics, installation programs, etc that end users can see.

The Network Adapter Division marketing department has the TRs to give away. To keep this program efficient, we centralized it in a thing called 'CardFacts.' CardFacts is an automated phone system. You call it with a touch-tone phone and it faxes you stuff. To get a TR, call CardFacts at 408-727-7021. Ask it for Developer's Order Form, document number 9070. Have your fax number ready when you call. Fill out the order form and fax it to 408-764-5004. Manuals are shipped by Federal Express 2nd Day Service.

If you don't have a fax and nobody you know has a fax, really and truly, *then* send mail to Terry_Murphy@3Mail.3Com.com and tell her about your problem. PLEASE use the fax thing if you possibly can.

After you get a manual, if you still can't figure out how to program the board, try our 'CardBoard' BBS at 1-800-876-3266, and if you can't do that, write Andy_Chan@3Mail.3com.com and ask him for alternatives. If you have a real stumper that nobody has figured out yet, the fellow who needs to know about it is Steve_Lebus@3Mail.3com.com.

There are people here who think we are too free with the manuals, and they are looking for evidence that the system is too expensive, or takes too much time and effort. That's why it's important to try to use CardFacts *before* you start calling and mailing the people I named here.

There are even people who think we should be like Diamond and Xircom, requiring tight 'partnership' with driver writers to prevent poorly performing drivers from getting written. So far, 3Com customers have been really good about this, and there's no problem with the level of requests we've been getting. We need your continued cooperation and restraint to keep it that way.

Cameron Spitzer, 408-764-6339 3Com NAD Santa Clara work: camerons@nad.3com.com home: cls@truffula.sj.ca.us

7.8 Notes on AMD PCnet / LANCE Based cards

The AMD LANCE (Local Area Network Controller for Ethernet) was the original offering, and has since been replaced by the 'PCnet-ISA' chip, otherwise known as the 79C960. A relatively new chip from AMD, the 79C960, is the heart of many new cards being released at present. Note that the name 'LANCE' has stuck, and some people will refer to the new chip by the old name. Dave Roberts of the Network Products Division of AMD was kind enough to contribute the following information regarding this chip:

'As for the architecture itself, AMD developed it originally and reduced it to a single chip – the PCnet(tm)-ISA – over a year ago. It's been selling like hotcakes ever since.

Functionally, it is equivalent to a NE1500. The register set is identical to the old LANCE with the 1500/2100 architecture additions. Older 1500/2100 drivers will work on the PCnet-ISA. The NE1500 and NE2100 architecture is basically the same. Initially Novell called it the 2100, but then tried to distinguish between coax and 10BASE-T cards. Anything that was 10BASE-T only was to be numbered in the 1500 range. That's the only difference.

Many companies offer PCnet-ISA based products, including HP, Racal-Datacom, Allied Telesis, Boca Research, Kingston Technology, etc. The cards are basically the same except that some manufacturers have added 'jumperless' features that allow the card to be configured in software. Most have not. AMD offers a standard design package for a card that uses the PCnet-ISA and many manufacturers use our design without change. What this means is that anybody who wants to write drivers for most PCnet-ISA based cards can just get the data-sheet from AMD. Call our literature distribution center at (800)222-9323 and ask for the Am79C960, PCnet-ISA data sheet. It's free.

A quick way to understand whether the card is a 'stock' card is to just look at it. If it's stock, it should just have one large chip on it, a crystal, a small IEEE address PROM, possibly a socket for a boot ROM, and a connector (1, 2, or 3, depending on the media options offered). Note that if it's a coax card, it will have some transceiver stuff built onto it as well, but that should be near the connector and away from the PCnet-ISA.'

There is also some info regarding the LANCE chip in the file lance.c which is included in the standard kernel.

A note to would-be card hackers is that different LANCE implementations do 'restart' in different ways. Some pick up where they left off in the ring, and others start right from the beginning of the ring, as if just initialized. This is a concern when setting the multicast list.

7.9 Multicast and Promiscuous Mode

Another one of the things Donald has worked on is implementing multicast and promiscuous mode hooks. All of the *released* (i.e. **not** ALPHA) ISA drivers now support promiscuous mode. There was a minor problem with 8390 based cards with capturing multicast packets, in that the promiscuous mode setting in 8390.c around line 574 should be 0x18 and not 0x10. If you have an up to date kernel, this will already be fixed.

Donald writes: 'At first I was planning to do it while implementing either the /dev/* or DDI interface, but that's not really the correct way to do it. We should only enable multicast or promiscuous modes when something wants to look at the packets, and shut it down when that application is finished, neither of which is strongly related to when the hardware is opened or released.

I'll start by discussing promiscuous mode, which is conceptually easy to implement. For most hardware you only have to set a register bit, and from then on you get every packet on the wire. Well, it's almost that easy; for some hardware you have to shut the board (potentially dropping a few packet), reconfigure it, and then re-enable the ethercard. This is grungy and risky, but the alternative seems to be to have every application register before you open the ethercard at boot-time.

OK, so that's easy, so I'll move on something that's not quite so obvious: Multicast. It can be done two ways:

1. Use promiscuous mode, and a packet filter like the Berkeley packet filter (BPF). The BPF is a pattern matching stack language, where you write a program that picks out the addresses you are interested in. Its advantage is that it's very general and programmable. Its disadvantage is that there is no general way for the kernel to avoid turning on promiscuous mode and running every packet on the wire through every registered packet filter. See 7.10 for more info.

2. Using the built-in multicast filter that most etherchips have.

I guess I should list what a few ethercards/chips provide:

```
Chip/card     Promiscuous  Multicast filter
------------------------------------------------
Seeq8001/3c501    Yes      Binary filter (1)
3Com/3c509        Yes      Binary filter (1)
8390              Yes      Autodin II six bit hash (2) (3)
LANCE             Yes      Autodin II six bit hash (2) (3)
i82586            Yes      Hidden Autodin II six bit hash (2) (4)
```

1. These cards claim to have a filter, but it's a simple yes/no 'accept all multicast packets', or 'accept no multicast packets'.

2. AUTODIN II is the standard ethernet CRC (checksum) polynomial. In this scheme multicast addresses are hashed and looked up in a hash table. If the corresponding bit is enabled, this packet is accepted. Ethernet packets are laid out so that the hardware to do this is trivial – you just latch six (usually) bits from the CRC circuit (needed anyway for error checking) after the first six octets (the destination address), and use them as an index into the hash table (six bits – a 64-bit table).

3. These chips use the six bit hash, and must have the table computed and loaded by the host. This means the kernel must include the CRC code.

4. The 82586 uses the six bit hash internally, but it computes the hash table itself from a list of multicast addresses to accept.

Note that none of these chips do perfect filtering, and we still need a middle-level module to do the final filtering. Also note that in every case we must keep a complete list of accepted multicast addresses to recompute the hash table when it changes.

My first pass at device-level support is detailed in the new outline driver skeleton.c

It looks like the following:

```
#ifdef HAVE_MULTICAST
static void set_multicast_list(struct device *dev, int num_addrs,
                void *addrs);
#endif
.
.
.

ethercard_open() {
...
#ifdef HAVE_MULTICAST
        dev->set_multicast_list = &set_multicast_list;
#endif
...


#ifdef HAVE_MULTICAST
/* Set or clear the multicast filter for this adaptor.
    num_addrs -- -1      Promiscuous mode, receive all packets
    num_addrs -- 0       Normal mode, clear multicast list
    num_addrs > 0        Multicast mode, receive normal and
        MC packets, and do best-effort filtering.
 */
static void
set_multicast_list(struct device *dev, int num_addrs, void *addrs)
{
...
```

Any comments, criticism, etc. are welcome.'

7.10   The Berkeley Packet Filter (BPF)

The general idea of the developers is that the BPF functionality should not be provided by the kernel, but should be in a (hopefully little-used) compatibility library.

For those not in the know: BPF (the Berkeley Packet Filter) is an mechanism for specifying to the kernel networking layers what packets you are interested in. It's implemented as a specialized stack language interpreter built into a low level of the networking code. An application passes a program written in this language to the kernel, and the kernel runs the program on each incoming packet. If the kernel has multiple BPF applications, each program is run on each packet.

The problem is that it's difficult to deduce what kind of packets the application is really interested in from the packet filter program, so the general solution is to always run the filter. Imagine a program that registers a BPF program to pick up a low data-rate stream sent to a multicast address. Most ethernet cards have a hardware multicast address filter implemented as a 64 entry hash table that ignores most unwanted multicast packets, so the capability exists to make this a very inexpensive operation. But with the BFP the kernel must switch the interface to promiscuous mode, receive _all_ packets, and run them through this filter. This is work, BTW, that's very difficult to account back to the process requesting the packets.

8   Networking with a Laptop/Notebook Computer

There are currently only a few ways to put your laptop on a network. You can use the SLIP code (and run at serial line speeds); you can buy one of the few laptops that come with a NE2000-compatible ethercard; you can get a notebook with a supported PCMCIA slot built-in; you can get a laptop with a docking station and plug in an ISA ethercard; or you can use a parallel port Ethernet adapter such as the D-Link DE-600.

8.1   Using SLIP

This is the cheapest solution, but by far the most difficult. Also, you will not get very high transmission rates. Since SLIP is not really related to ethernet cards, it will not be discussed further here. See the NET-2 Howto.

8.2   Built in NE2000

This solution severely limits your laptop choices and is fairly expensive. Be sure to read the specifications carefully, as you may find that you will have to buy an additional non-standard transceiver to actually put the machine on a network. A good idea might be to boot the notebook with a kernel that has ne2000 support, and make sure it gets detected and works before you lay down your cash.

8.3   PCMCIA Support

As this area of Linux development is fairly young, I'd suggest that you join the LAPTOPS mailing channel. See 1.3 which describes how to join a mailing list channel.

Try and determine exactly what hardware you have (ie. card manufacturer, PCMCIA chip controller manufacturer) and then ask on the LAPTOPS channel. Regardless, don't expect things to be all that simple. Expect to have to fiddle around a bit, and patch kernels, etc. Maybe someday you will be able to type 'make config' 8-)

At present, the two PCMCIA chipsets that are supported are the Databook TCIC/2 and the intel i82365.

There is a number of programs on tsx-11.mit.edu in /pub/linux/packages/laptops/ that you may find useful. These range from PCMCIA Ethercard drivers to programs that communicate with the PCMCIA controller chip. Note that these drivers are usually tied to a specific PCMCIA chip (ie. the intel 82365 or the TCIC/2)

For NE2000 compatible cards, some people have had success with just configuring the card under DOS, and then booting linux from the DOS command prompt via `loadlin`.

For those that are *net-surfing* you can try:

Don's PCMCIA Stuff (`http://cesdis.gsfc.nasa.gov/linux/pcmcia.html`)

Anyway, the PCMCIA driver problem isn't specific to the Linux world. It's been a real disaster in the MS-DOS world. In that world people expect the hardware to work if they just follow the manual. They might not expect it to interoperate with any other hardware or software, or operate optimally, but they do expect that the software shipped with the product will function. Many PCMCIA adaptors don't even pass this test.

Things are looking up for Linux users that want PCMCIA support, as substantial progress is being made. Pioneering this effort is David Hinds. His latest PCMCIA support package can be obtained from `cb-iris.stanford.edu` in the directory `/pub/pcmcia/`. Look for a file like `pcmcia-cs-X.Y.Z.tgz` where X.Y.Z will be the latest version number. This is most likely uploaded to `tsx-11.mit.edu` as well.

Note that Donald's PCMCIA enabler works as a user-level process, and David Hinds' is a kernel-level solution. You may be best served by David's package as it is much more widely used.

8.4   ISA Ethercard in the Docking Station.

Docking stations for laptops typically cost about $250 and provide two full-size ISA slots, two serial and one parallel port. Most docking stations are powered off of the laptop's batteries, and a few allow adding extra batteries in the docking station if you use short ISA cards. You can add an inexpensive ethercard and enjoy full-speed ethernet performance.

8.5   Pocket / parallel port adaptors.

The 'pocket' ethernet adaptors may also fit your need. Until recently they actually costed more than a docking station and cheap ethercard, and most tie you down with a wall-brick power supply. At present, you can choose from the D-Link, or the RealTek adaptor. Most other companies, especially Xircom, (see 3.28) treat the programming information as a trade secret, so support will likely be slow in coming. (if ever!)

Note that the transfer speed will not be all that great (perhaps 100kB/s tops?) due to the limitations of the parallel port interface.

See 3.12.3 and 3.9.1 for supported pocket adaptors.

You can sometimes avoid the wall-brick with the adaptors by buying or making a cable that draws power from the laptop's keyboard port. (See 3.9.1)

9   Frequently Asked Questions

Here are some of the more frequently asked questions about using Linux with an Ethernet connection. Some of the more specific questions are sorted on a 'per manufacturer basis'. However, since this document is basically 'old' by the time you get it, any 'new' problems will not appear here instantly. For these, I suggest that you make efficient use of your newsreader. For example, nn users would type

```
nn -xX -s'3c'
```

to get all the news articles in your subscribed list that have '3c' in the subject. (ie. 3com, 3c509, 3c503, etc.) The moral: Read the man page for your newsreader.

9.1   Alpha Drivers – Getting and Using them

I heard that there is an alpha driver available for my card. Where can I get it?

The newest of the 'new' drivers can be found on Donald's new ftp site: `cesdis.gsfc.nasa.gov` in the `/pub/linux/` area. Things change here quite frequently, so just look around for it. There is still all the stuff on the old ftp site `ftp.super.org` in `/pub/linux`, but this is not being actively maintained, and hence will be of limited value to most people.

As of recent v1.1 kernels, the 'usable' alpha drivers have been included in the standard kernel source tree. When running `make config` you will be asked if you want to be offered ALPHA test drivers.

Now, if it really is an alpha, or pre-alpha driver, then please treat it as such. In other words, don't complain because you can't figure out what to do with it. If you can't figure out how to install it, then you probably shouldn't be testing it. Also, if it brings your machine down, don't complain. Instead, send us a well documented bug report, or even better, a patch!

People reading this while *net-surfing* may want to check out:

Don's Linux Home Page (http://cesdis.gsfc.nasa.gov/pub/linux/linux.html)

for the latest dirt on what is new and upcoming.

9.2 Using More than one Ethernet Card per Machine

What needs to be done so that Linux can run two ethernet cards?

The hooks for multiple ethercards are all there. However, note that only *one* ethercard is auto-probed for by default. This avoids a lot of possible boot time hangs caused by probing sensitive cards.

There are two ways that you can enable auto-probing for the second (and third, and...) card. The easiest method is to pass boot-time arguments to the kernel, which is usually done by LILO.Probing for the second card can be achieved by using a boot-time argument as simple as `ether=0,0,eth1`. In this case `eth0` and `eth1` will be assigned in the order that the cards are found at boot. Say if you want the card at `0x300` to be `eth0` and the card at `0x280` to be `eth1` then you could use

```
LILO: linux ether=5,0x300,eth0 ether=15,0x280,eth1
```

The `ether=` command accepts more than the IRQ + i/o + name shown above. Please have a look at 10.1 for the full syntax, card specific parameters, and LILO tips.

These boot time arguments can be made permanent so that you don't have to re-enter them every time. See the LILO configuration option 'append' in the LILO manual.

The second way (not recommended) is to edit the file `Space.c` and replace the `0xffe0` entry for the i/o address with a zero. The `0xffe0` entry tells it not to probe for that device – replacing it with a zero will enable autoprobing for that device. If you *really* need more than four ethernet cards in one machine, then you can clone the `eth3` entry and change `eth3` to `eth4`.

Note that if you are intending to use Linux as a gateway between two networks, you will have to re-compile a kernel with IP forwarding enabled. Usually using an old AT/286 with something like the 'kbridge' software is a better solution.

If you are viewing this while *net-surfing*, you may wish to look at a mini-howto Donald has on his WWW site. Check out *Multiple Ethercards* (`http://cesdis.gsfc.nasa.gov/linux/misc/multicard.html`).

9.3 Problems with NE1000 / NE2000 cards (and clones)

Problem: NE*000 ethercard at `0x360` doesn't get detected anymore.

Reason: Recent kernels (> 1.1.7X) have more sanity checks with respect to overlapping i/o regions. Your NE2000 card is `0x20` wide in i/o space, which makes it hit the parallel port at `0x378`. Other devices that could be there are the second floppy controller (if equipped) at `0x370` and the secondary IDE controller at `0x376--0x377`. If the port(s) are already registered by another driver, the kernel will not let the probe happen.

Solution: Either move your card to an address like `0x280`, `0x340`, `0x320` or compile without parallel printer support.

Problem: Network 'goes away' every time I print something (NE2000)

Reason: Same problem as above, but you have an older kernel that doesn't check for overlapping i/o regions. Use the same fix as above, and get a new kernel while you are at it.

Problem: NE*000 ethercard probe at 0xNNN: 00 00 C5 ... not found. (invalid signature yy zz)

Reason: First off, do you have a NE1000 or NE2000 card at the addr. 0xNNN? And if so, does the hardware address reported look like a valid one? If so, then you have a poor NE*000 clone. All NE*000 clones are supposed to have the value `0x57` in bytes 14 and 15 of the SA PROM on the card. Yours doesn't – it has 'yy zz' instead.

Solution: The driver (/usr/src/linux/drivers/net/ne.c) has a "Hall of Shame" list at about line 42. This list is used to detect poor clones. For example, the DFI cards use 'DFI' in the first 3 bytes of the prom, instead of using 0x57 in bytes 14 and 15, like they are supposed to.

You can determine what the first 3 bytes of your card PROM are by adding a line like:

```
printk("PROM prefix: %#2x %#2x %#2x\n",SA_prom[0],SA_prom[1],SA_prom[2]);
```

into the driver, right after the error message you got above, and just before the "return ENXIO" at line 227.

Reboot with this change in place, and after the detection fails, you will get the three bytes from the PROM like the DFI example above. Then you can add your card to the bad_clone_list[] at about line 43. Say the above line printed out:

```
PROM prefix:  0x3F 0x2D 0x1C
```

after you rebooted. And say that the 8 bit version of your card was called the "FOO-1k" and the 16 bit version the "FOO-2k". Then you would add the following line to the bad_clone_list[]:

```
{"FOO-1k", "FOO-2k", {0x3F, 0x2D, 0x1C,}},
```

Note that the 2 name strings you add can be anything – they are just printed at boot, and not matched against anything on the card. You can also take out the "printk()" that you added above, if you want. It shouldn't hit that line anymore anyway. Then recompile once more, and your card should be detected.

Problem: Errors like DMA address mismatch

Is the chip a real NatSemi 8390? (DP8390, DP83901, DP83902 or DP83905)? If not, some clone chips don't correctly implement the transfer verification register. MS-DOS drivers never do error checking, so it doesn't matter to them.

Are most of the messages off by a factor of 2? If so: Are you using the NE2000 in a 16 bit slot? Is it jumpered to use only 8 bit transfers?

The Linux driver expects a NE2000 to be in a 16 bit slot. A NE1000 can be in either size slot. This problem can also occur with some clones, notably D-Link 16 bit cards, that don't have the correct ID bytes in the station address PROM.

Are you running the bus faster than 8Mhz? If you can change the speed (faster or slower), see if that makes a difference. Most NE2000 clones will run at 16MHz, but some may not. Changing speed can also mask a noisy bus.

What other devices are on the bus? If moving the devices around changes the reliability, then you have a bus noise problem – just what that error message was designed to detect. Congratulations, you've probably found the source of other problems as well.

Problem: The machine hangs during boot right after the '8390...' or 'WD....' message. Removing the NE2000 fixes the problem.

Solution: Change your NE2000 base address to 0x340. Alternatively, you can use the device registrar implemented in 0.99pl13 and later kernels.

Reason: Your NE2000 clone isn't a good enough clone. An active NE2000 is a bottomless pit that will trap any driver autoprobing in its space. The other ethercard drivers take great pain to reset the NE2000 so that it's safe, but some clones cannot be reset. Clone chips to watch out for: Winbond 83C901. Changing the NE2000 to a less-popular address will move it out of the way of other autoprobes, allowing your machine to boot.

Problem: The machine hangs during the SCSI probe at boot.

Reason: It's the same problem as above, change the ethercard's address, or use the device registrar.

Problem: The machine hangs during the soundcard probe at boot.

Reason: No, that's really during the silent SCSI probe, and it's the same problem as above.

Problem: Errors like eth0: DMAing conflict in ne_block_input

This bug came from timer-based packet retransmissions. If you got a timer tick _during_ a ethercard RX interrupt, and timer tick tried to retransmit a timed-out packet, you could get a conflict. Because of the design of the NE2000 you would have the machine hang (exactly the same the NE2000-clone boot hangs).

Early versions of the driver disabled interrupts for a long time, and didn't have this problem. Later versions are fixed. (ie. kernels after 0.99p9 should be OK.)

Problem: NE2000 not detected at boot - no boot messages at all

Donald writes: 'A few people have reported a problem with detecting the Accton NE2000. This problem occurs only at boot-time, and the card is later detected at run-time by the identical code my (alpha-test) ne2k diagnostic program. Accton has been very responsive, but I still haven't tracked down what is going on. I've been unable to reproduce this problem with the Accton cards we purchased. If you are having this problem, please send me an immediate bug report. For that matter, if you have an Accton card send me a success report, including the type of the motherboard. I'm especially interested in finding out if this problem moves with the particular ethercard, or stays with the motherboard.'

Here are some things to try, as they have fixed it for some people:

- Change the bus speed, or just move the card to a different slot.

- Change the 'I/O recovery time' parameter in the BIOS chipset configuration.

9.4 Problems with WD80*3 cards

Problem: A WD80*3 is falsely detected. Removing the sound or MIDI card eliminates the 'detected' message.

Reason: Some MIDI ports happen to produce the same checksum as a WD ethercard.

Solution: Update your ethercard driver: new versions include an additional sanity check. If it is the midi chip at 0x388 that is getting detected as a WD living at 0x380, then you could also use:

```
LILO: linux reserve=0x380,8
```

Problem: You get messages such as the following with your 80*3:

```
eth0:  bogus packet size, status = ........  kmalloc called with impossibly
large argument (65400) eth0:  Couldn't allocate sk_buff of size 65400 eth0:
receiver overrun
```

Reason: There is a shared memory problem.

Solution: If the problem is sporadic, you have hardware problems. Typical problems that are easy to fix are board conflicts, having cache or 'shadow ROM' enabled for that region, or running your bus faster than 8Mhz. There are also a surprising number of memory failures on ethernet cards, so run a diagnostic program if you have one for your ethercard.

If the problem is continual, and you have have to reboot to fix the problem, record the boot-time probe message and mail it to becker@cesdis.gsfc.nasa.gov - Take particular note of the shared memory location.

Problem: WD80*3 will not get detected at boot.

Reason: Earlier versions of the Mitsumi CD-ROM (mcd) driver probe at 0x300 will succeed if just about *anything* is that I/O location. This is bad news and needs to be a bit more robust. Once another driver registers that it 'owns' an I/O location, other drivers (incl. the wd80x3) are 'locked out' and can not probe that addr for a card.

Solution: Recompile a new kernel without any excess drivers that you aren't using, including the above mcd driver. Or try moving your ethercard to a new I/O addr. Valid I/O addr. for all the cards are listed in 7.1 You can also point the mcd driver off in another direction by a boot-time parameter (via LILO) such as:

```
mcd=0x200,12
```

Problem: Old wd8003 and/or jumper-settable wd8013 always get the IRQ wrong.

Reason: The old wd8003 cards and jumper-settable wd8013 clones don't have the EEPROM that the driver can read the IRQ setting from. If the driver can't read the IRQ, then it tries to auto-IRQ to find out what it is. And if auto-IRQ returns zero, then the driver just assigns IRQ 5 for an 8 bit card or IRQ 10 for a 16 bit card.

Solution: Avoid the auto-IRQ code, and tell the kernel what the IRQ that you have jumpered the card to is via a boot time argument. For example, if you are using IRQ 9, using the following should work.

```
LILO: linux ether=9,0,eth0
```

9.5   Problems with 3Com cards

Problem: The 3c503 picks IRQ N, but this is needed for some other device which needs IRQ N. (eg. CD ROM driver, modem, etc.) Can this be fixed without compiling this into the kernel?

Solution: The 3c503 driver probes for a free IRQ line in the order {5, 9/2, 3, 4}, and it should pick a line which isn't being used. Very old drivers used to pick the IRQ line at boot-time, and the current driver (0.99pl12 and newer) chooses when the card is open()/ifconfig'ed.

Alternately, you can fix the IRQ at boot by passing parameters via LILO. The following selects IRQ9, base location 0x300, <ignored value>, and if_port #1 (the external transceiver).

```
LILO: linux ether=9,0x300,0,1,eth0
```

The following selects IRQ3, probes for the base location, <ignored value>, and the default if_port #0 (the internal transceiver)

```
LILO: linux ether=3,0,0,0,eth0
```

Problem: 3c503: Configured interrupt number XX is out of range.

Reason: Whoever built your kernel fixed the ethercard IRQ at XX. The above is truly evil, and worse than that, it is not necessary. The 3c503 will autoIRQ when it gets ifconfig'ed, and pick one of IRQ{5, 2/9, 3, 4}.

Solution: Use LILO as described above, or rebuild the kernel, enabling autoIRQ by not specifying the IRQ line.

Problem: The supplied 3c503 drivers don't use the AUI (thicknet) port. How does one choose it over the default thinnet port?

Solution: The 3c503 AUI port can be selected at boot-time with 0.99pl12 and later. The selection is overloaded onto the low bit of the currently-unused dev->rmem_start variable, so a boot-time parameter of:

```
LILO: linux ether=0,0,0,1,eth0
```

should work. A boot line to force IRQ 5, port base 0x300, and use an external transceiver is:

```
LILO: linux ether=5,0x300,0,1,eth0
```

Also note that kernel revisions 1.00 to 1.03 had an interesting 'feature'. They would switch to the AUI port when the internal transceiver failed. This is a problem, as it will *never* switch back if for example you momentarily disconnect the cable. Kernel versions 1.04 and newer only switch if the very first Tx attempt fails.

9.6 Problems with Hewlett Packard Cards

Problem: HP Vectra using built in AMD LANCE chip gets IRQ and DMA wrong.

Solution: The HP Vectra uses a different implementation to the standard HP-J2405A. The 'lance.c' driver used to *always* use the value in the setup register of an HP Lance implementation. In the Vectra case it's reading an invalid 0xff value. Kernel versions newer than about 1.1.50 now handle the Vectra in an appropriate fashion.

Problem: HP Card is not detected at boot, even though kernel was compiled with 'HP PCLAN support'.

Solution: You probably have a HP PCLAN+ – note the 'plus'. Support for the PCLAN+ was added to final versions of 1.1, but some of them didn't have the entry in 'config.in'. If you have the file hp-plus.c in /linux/drivers/net/ but no entry in config.in, then add the following line under the 'HP PCLAN support' line:

```
bool 'HP PCLAN Plus support' CONFIG_HPLAN_PLUS n
```

Kernels up tp 1.1.54 are missing the line in 'config.in' still. Do a 'make mrproper;make config;make dep;make zlilo' and you should be in business.

9.7 FAQs Not Specific to Any Card.

9.7.1 `ifconfig` reports the wrong i/o address for the card.

No it doesn't. You are just interpreting it incorrectly. This is *not* a bug, and the numbers reported are correct. It just happens that some 8390 based cards (wd80x3, smc-ultra, etc) have the actual 8390 chip living at an offset from the first assigned i/o port. Try `cd /usr/src/linux/drivers/net;grep NIC_OFFSET *.c|more` to see what is going on. This is the value stored in `dev->base_addr`, and is what `ifconfig` reports. If you want to see the full range of ports that your card uses, then try `cat /proc/ioports` which will give the numbers you expect.

9.7.2 Token Ring

Is there token ring support for Linux?

To support token ring requires more than only a writing a device driver, it also requires writing the source routing routines for token ring. It is the source routing that would be the most time comsuming to write.

Alan Cox adds: 'It will require (...) changes to the bottom socket layer to support 802.2 and 802.2 based TCP/IP. Don't expect anything soon.'

Peter De Schrijver has been spending some time on Token Ring lately, and has patches that are available for IBM ISA and MCA token ring cards. Don't expect miracles here, as he has just started on this as of 1.1.42. You can get the patch from:

`aix13ps2.cc.kuleuven.ac.be:/pub/Linux/TokenRing.patch-1.1.49.gz`

9.7.3 32 Bit / VLB / PCI Ethernet Cards

What is the selection for 32 bit ethernet cards?

There aren't many 32 bit ethercard device drivers because there aren't that many 32 bit ethercards.

There aren't many 32 bit ethercards out there because a 10Mbs network doesn't justify spending the 5x price increment for the 32 bit interface. See 7.5 as to why having an ethercard on an 8MHz ISA bus is really not a bottleneck.

This might change now that AMD has introduced the 32 bit PCnet-VLB and PCnet-PCI chips. The street price of the Boca PCnet-VLB board should be under $70 from a place like CMO (see Computer Shopper). See 3.10.1 for info on these cards.

See 3.4.3 for info on the 32 bit versions of the LANCE / PCnet-ISA chip.

The DEC 21040 PCI chip is another option (see 3.14.4) for power-users. The 21140 100Base-? chip could prove interesting as well, as it is supposedly driver compatible with the 21040. Should be good for uncovering any race-conditions, if nothing else...

9.7.4   FDDI

Is there FDDI support for Linux?

Donald writes: 'No, there is no Linux driver for any FDDI boards. I come from a place with supercomputers, so an external observer might think FDDI would be high on my list. But FDDI never delivered end-to-end throughput that would justify its cost, and it seems to be a nearly abandoned technology now that 100base{X,Anynet} seems imminent. (And yes, I know you can now get FDDI boards for <$1K. That seems to be a last-ditch effort to get some return on the development investment. Where is the next generation of FDDI going to come from?)'

9.7.5   Linking 10BaseT without a Hub

Can I link 10BaseT (RJ45) based systems together without a hub?

You can link 2 machines easily, but no more than that, without extra devices/gizmos. See 5.2 – it explains how to do it. And no, you can't hack together a hub just by crossing a few wires and stuff. It's pretty much impossible to do the collision signal right without duplicating a hub.

9.7.6   SIOCSFFLAGS: Try again

I get 'SIOCSFFLAGS: Try again' when I run 'ifconfig' – Huh?

Some other device has taken the IRQ that your ethercard is trying to use, and so the ethercard can't use the IRQ. You don't necessarily need to reboot to resolve this, as some devices only grab the IRQs when they need them and then release them when they are done. Examples are some sound cards, serial ports, floppy disk driver, etc. You can type `cat /proc/interrupts` to see which interrupts are presently *in use*. Most of the Linux ethercard drivers only grab the IRQ when they are opened for use via 'ifconfig'. If you can get the other device to 'let go' of the required IRQ line, then you should be able to 'Try again' with ifconfig.

9.7.7   Link UNSPEC and HW-addr of 00:00:00:00:00:00

When I run ifconfig with no arguments, it reports that LINK is UNSPEC (instead of 10Mbs Ethernet) and it also says that my hardware address is all zeros.

This is because people are running a newer version of the 'ifconfig' program than their kernel version. This new version of ifconfig is not able to report these properties when used in conjunction with an older kernel. You can either upgrade your kernel, 'downgrade' ifconfig, or simply ignore it. The kernel knows your hardware address, so it really doesn't matter if ifconfig can't read it.

9.7.8   Huge Number of RX and TX Errors

When I run ifconfig with no arguments, it reports that I have a huge error count in both rec'd and transmitted packets. It all seems to work ok – What is wrong?

Look again. It says `RX packets` *big number* **PAUSE** `errors` 0 **PAUSE** `dropped` 0 **PAUSE** `overrun` 0. And the same for the `TX` column. Hence the big numbers you are seeing are the total number of packets that your machine has rec'd and transmitted. If you still find it confusing, try typing `cat /proc/net/dev` instead.

9.7.9 Entries in /dev/ for Ethercards

I have /dev/eth0 as a link to /dev/xxx. Is this right?

Contrary to what you have heard, the files in /dev/* are not used. You can delete any /dev/wd0, /dev/ne0 and similar entries.

9.7.10 Linux and "trailers"

Should I disable trailers when I 'ifconfig' my ethercard?

You can't disable trailers, and you shouldn't want to. 'Trailers' are a hack to avoid data copying in the networking layers. The idea was to use a trivial fixed-size header of size 'H', put the variable-size header info at the end of the packet, and allocate all packets 'H' bytes before the start of a page. While it was a good idea, it turned out to not work well in practice. If someone suggests the use of '-trailers', note that it is the equivalent of sacrificial goats blood. It won't do anything to solve the problem, but if problem fixes itself then someone can claim deep magical knowledge.

9.7.11 Non-existent Apricot NIC is detected

I get `eth0: Apricot 82596 at 0x300, 00 00 00 00 00 00 IRQ 10` and `apricot.c:v.0.02 19/05/94` when I boot, but I don't have an "Apricot". And then the card I do have isn't detected.

A few kernel releases had a version of the Apricot driver which only used a simple checksum to detect if an Apricot is present. This would mistakenly think that almost everything was an Apricot NIC. It really should look at the vendor prefix instead. However there is now a check to see if the hardware address is all zeros, so this shouldn't happen. Your choices are to move your card off of `0x300` (the only place the Apricot driver probes), or better yet, get a new kernel.

10 Miscellaneous.

Any other associated stuff that didn't fit in anywhere else gets dumped here. It may not be relevant, and it may not be of general interest but it is here anyway.

10.1 Passing Ethernet Arguments to the Kernel

Here are two generic kernel commands that can be passed to the kernel at boot time. This can be done with LILO, loadlin, or any other booting utility that accepts optional arguments.

For exmaple, if the command was 'blah' and it expected 3 arguments (say 123, 456, and 789) then, with LILO, you would use:

`LILO: linux blah=123,456,789`

Note: PCI cards have their i/o and IRQ assigned by the BIOS at boot. This means that any boot time arguments for a PCI card's IRQ or i/o ports are ignored.

10.1.1 The ether command

In its most generic form, it looks something like this:

```
ether=IRQ,BASE_ADDR,PARAM_1,PARAM_2,NAME
```

All arguments are optional. The first non-numeric argument is taken as the NAME.

IRQ: Obvious. An IRQ value of '0' (usually the default) means to autoIRQ. It's a historical accident that the IRQ setting is first rather than the base_addr – this will be fixed whenever something else changes.

BASE_ADDR: Also obvious. A value of '0' (usually the default) means to probe a card-type-specific address list for an ethercard.

PARAM_1: It was orginally used as an override value for the memory start for a shared-memory ethercard, like the WD80*3. Some drivers use the low four bits of this value to set the debug message level. 0 – default, 1-7 – level 1..7, (7 is maximum verbosity) 8 – level 0 (no messages). Also, the LANCE driver uses the low four bits of this value to select the DMA channel. Otherwise it uses auto-DMA.

PARAM_2: The 3c503 driver uses this to select between the internal and external transceivers. 0 – default/internal, 1 – AUI external. The Cabletron E21XX card also uses the low 4 bits of PARAM_2 to select the output media. Otherwise it detects automatically.

NAME: Selects the network device the values refer to. The standard kernel uses the names 'eth0', 'eth1', 'eth2' and 'eth3' for bus-attached ethercards, and 'atp0' for the parallel port 'pocket' ethernet adaptor. The arcnet driver uses 'arc0' as its name. The default setting is for a single ethercard to be probed for as 'eth0'. Multiple cards can only be enabled by explicitly setting up their base address using these LILO parameters. The 1.0 kernel has LANCE-based ethercards as a special case. LILO arguments are ignored, and LANCE cards are always assigned 'eth<n>' names starting at 'eth0'. Additional non-LANCE ethercards must be explicitly assigned to 'eth<n+1>', and the usual 'eth0' probe disabled with something like 'ether=0,-1,eth0'. (Yes, this is bug.)

10.1.2   The `reserve` **command**

This next lilo command is used just like 'ether=' above, ie. it is appended to the name of the boot select specified in lilo.conf

```
reserve=IO-base,extent{,IO-base,extent...}
```

In some machines it may be necessary to prevent device drivers from checking for devices (auto-probing) in a specific region. This may be because of poorly designed hardware that causes the boot to *freeze* (such as some ethercards), hardware that is mistakenly identified, hardware whose state is changed by an earlier probe, or merely hardware you don't want the kernel to initialize.

The `reserve` boot-time argument addresses this problem by specifying an I/O port region that shouldn't be probed. That region is reserved in the kernel's port registration table as if a device has already been found in that region. Note that this mechanism shouldn't be necessary on most machines. Only when there is a problem or special case would it be necessary to use this.

The I/O ports in the specified region are protected against device probes. This was put in to be used when some driver was hanging on a NE2000, or misidentifying some other device as its own. A correct device driver shouldn't probe a reserved region, unless another boot argument explicitly specifies that it do so. This implies that `reserve` will most often be used with some other boot argument. Hence if you specify a `reserve` region to protect a specific device, you must generally specify an explicit probe for that device. Most drivers ignore the port registration table if they are given an explicit address.

For example, the boot line

```
LILO: linux reserve=0x300,32 ether=0,0x300,eth0
```

keeps all device drivers except the ethercard drivers from probing 0x300-0x31f.

As usual with boot-time specifiers there is an 11 parameter limit, thus you can only specify 5 reserved regions per `reserve` keyword. Multiple `reserve` specifiers will work if you have an unusually complicated request.

10.2 Using the Ethernet Drivers as Modules

At present, all the modules are put in the subdirectory `modules` in your Linux kernel source tree (usually in the form of symbolic links). To actually generate the modules, you have to type `make modules` after you have finished building the kernel proper. Earlier kernels built them automatically, which wasn't fair to those compiling on 4MB 386sx-16 machines.

If you have an 8390 based card, you will have to insert *two* modules, 8390.o and then the module for your card. You can find out if your card uses an 8390 chip by reading the above documentation for your card, or by just typing something like `grep 8390 my_card_name.c` in the `drivers/net/` directory. If `grep` finds anything, then your card has an 8390 (or compatible) chip.

Once you have figured this out, you can insert the module(s) by typing `insmod mod_name.o` as root. The command `lsmod` will show you what modules are loaded, and `rmmod` will remove them.

Once a module is inserted, then you can use it just like normal, and give `ifconfig` commands. If you set up your networking at boot, then make sure your `/etc/rc*` files run the `insmod` command(s) before getting to the `ifconfig` command.

Also note that a *busy* module can't be removed. That means that you will have to `ifconfig eth0 down` (shut down the ethernet card) before you can remove the modules. Also, if you use an 8390 based card, you will have to remove the card module before removing the 8390 module, as the 8390 module is used by the card module.

10.3 Contributors

Other people who have contributed (directly or indirectly) to the Ethernet-Howto are, in alphabetical order:

```
Ross Biro              <bir7@leland.stanford.edu>
Alan Cox               <iialan@www.linux.org.uk>
David C. Davies        <davies@wanton.enet.dec.com>
Bjorn Ekwall           <bj0rn@blox.se>
David Hinds            <dhinds@allegro.stanford.edu>
Michael Hipp           <mhipp@student.uni-tuebingen.de>
Mike Jagdis            <jaggy@purplet.demon.co.uk>
Duke Kamstra           <kamstra@ccmail.west.smc.com>
Russell Nelson         <nelson@crynwr.com>
Cameron Spitzer        <camerons@NAD.3Com.com>
Dave Roberts           <david.roberts@amd.com>
Glenn Talbott          <gt@hprnd.rose.hp.com>
```

Many thanks to the above people, and all the other unmentioned testers out there.

10.4 Closing

If you have found any glaring typos, or outdated info in this document, please let one of us know. It's getting big, and it is easy to overlook stuff.

Thanks,

Paul Gortmaker, `Paul.Gortmaker@anu.edu.au`

Donald J. Becker, `becker@cesdis.gsfc.nasa.gov`

Part XIX

Firewalling and Proxy Server HOWTO

This document is designed to teach the basics of setting up a firewall on a Linux based PC. Also covered is the installation and use of Proxy Servers to allow greater access to the Internet from behind a firewall.

Contents

1   Introduction

Firewalls have gained great fame recently as the ultimate in Internet Security. Like most things that gain fame, with that fame has come misunderstanding. This **HOWTO** will go over the basics of what a **firewall** is, how to set one up, what **proxy servers** are, how to set up proxy servers, and the applications of this technology outside of the security realm.

1.1   Feedback

Any feedback is very welcome. I am particularly looking for feedback from people who use Macintosh computers, as the information I have on them is scant. **PLEASE PLEASE PLEASE REPORT ANY INAC-CURACIES IN THIS PAPER!!!** I am human, and prone to making mistakes. If you find any, fixing them is of my highest interest. I will try to answer all e-mail, but I am busy, so don't get insulted if I don't.

My email address is drig@execpc.com.

1.2   Disclaimer

This document is meant as an introduction to how Firewalls and Proxy Servers work. I am not, nor do I pretend to be, a security expert. I am just some guy who has read too much and likes computers more than people. I AM NOT RESPONSIBLE FOR ANY DAMAGES INCURRED DUE TO ACTIONS TAKEN BASED ON THIS DOCUMENT. Please, I am writing this to help get people acquainted with this subject, and I am not ready to stake my life on the accuracy of what is in here.

1.3   Copyright

1.4   TODO

- Learn how to do this on a Macintosh

- Learn different Windows TCP/IP packages

- Find a good UDP proxy server that works with Linux

2 Understanding Firewalls

A **Firewall** is a term derived from a part of a car. In cars, Firewalls are physical objects that separate the engine block from the passenger compartment. They are meant to protect the passenger in case the car explodes.

A **Firewall** in computers is a logical device that protects a private network from the public part. How they work is:

1. You take a computer that has routing capabilities (such as a Linux box)

2. Put in 2 interfaces (ie Serial ports, Ethernet, Token Ring, etc)

3. Turn *off* IP forwarding

4. Connect the Internet to one interface

5. Connect the protected network to the other interface

Now, you have two distinct networks, which share a computer. The firewall computer, from now on named "firewall", can reach both the protected network and the Internet. The protected network can not reach the Internet, and the Internet can not reach the protected network.

For someone to reach the Internet from inside the protected network, one must telnet to firewall, and use the Internet from there. Accordingly, in order to get into the protected network, one must go through the firewall first.

This provides excellent security against attacks from the Internet. If someone wants to make a concerted attack against the protected network, they must go through the firewall first, making it a two-step, and thus much harder, attack. If someone wants to attack the protected network via a more common method, such as mail bombing, or the infamous "Internet Worm", they will not be able to reach the protected network. This makes for excellent protection.

2.1 Drawbacks with Firewalls

The biggest problem with firewalls is that they greatly inhibit the access to the Internet from the inside. Basically, they reduce the usage of the Internet to that which one would have via a dial-up shell account. Having to login to firewall and then do all Internet access is a severe restriction. Programs like *Netscape*, which require a direct Internet connection, will not work from behind a firewall. Being unable to ftp directly to your computer is another big problem, requiring a two step, Internet->firewall->protected computer setup. The answer to these problems is having a **Proxy Server**.

2.2 Proxy Servers

Proxy servers are constructs that allow direct Internet access from behind a firewall. How they work is they open a socket on the server, and allow communication via that socket to the Internet. For example, if my computer, drig is inside the protected network, and I want to browse the Web using *Netscape*, I would set up a proxy server on firewall. The proxy server would be configured to allow requests from my computer, trying for port 80, to connect to its port 1080, and it would then redirect all requests to the proper places.

Anyone that has used *TIA* or *TERM* has seen this concept before. Using these two programs, you can redirect a port. A friend had TIA setup to allow anyone using 192.251.139.21 port 4024 to connect to his Web

Server. The proxy server works like this, but backwards. To connect to anyone else's port 80, you must use port 1080 (or whichever port you set it for).

The great thing about proxy servers is that they are completely secure, when configured correctly. They *will not* allow someone in through them.

3 Setting This All Up

3.1 Hardware requirements

For our example, the computer is a 486-DX66, 8 megs of memory, 500 megs Linux partition, with a PPP connection to its Internet provider over a 14.4 modem. This setup is your basic Linux box. To make it a firewall, we add one NE2000 Ethernet card. It is then connected to 3 PC's running Windows 3.1 with Trumpet Winsock and 2 Suns running SunOS 4.1. This setup was chosen because it is a fairly common and they are both platforms that I am familiar with. I imagine much of the same stuff that I am talking about here is doable with Macs, but since I don't use Macs frequently enough, I don't really know.

3.2 Setting up the Software

So, you have one Linux box connected to the Net via a 14.4 PPP line. You then have a Ethernet network connected to the Linux box and all the other computers. First, you must recompile the Linux kernel with the appropriate options. At this point, I would look at the **Kernel HOWTO**, the **Ethernet HOWTO**, and the **NET-2 HOWTO**. Then, do a `"make config"`:

1. Turn on Networking Support

2. Turn on TCP/IP Networking

3. Turn off IP Forwarding (CONFIG_IP_FORWARD).

4. Turn on IP Firewalling

5. Probably turn on IP accounting. Seems prudent since we are setting up a security measure

6. Turn on Networking Device Support

7. We turn on PPP and Ethernet support, but that depends on your interfaces

Then, we recompile, reinstall the kernel and reboot. The interfaces should show up in the boot-up sequence, and we should be fine. If not, go over the other HOWTOs again until it is working.

3.3 Configuring the Network Addresses

This is the real interesting part. Since we do not want the Internet to have access, we do not need to use real addresses. One good C Class to use is 192.0.2.xxx, which was set aside as a dummy test domain. Thus, no one uses it, and it will not conflict with any requests for the outside. So, in this configuration, only one real IP address is needed. The others are free for the taking and will not affect the network at all.

Assign the real IP to the serial port used for the PPP. Assign 192.0.2.1 to the Ethernet card on `firewall`. Assign all the other machines in the protected network some number in that domain.

3.4   Testing it out

First, try to ping the Internet from `firewall`. I used to use `nic.ddn.mil` as my test point. It's still a good test, but has proven to be less reliable than I had hoped. If it doesn't work at first, try pinging a couple other places that are not connected to your LAN. If this doesn't work, then your PPP is incorrectly setup. Reread the **Net-2 HOWTO**, and try again.

Now, try pinging between hosts within the protected network. All the computers should be able to ping each other. If not, go over the **NET-2 HOWTO** again and work on the network some more.

Then, every machine in the protected network should be able to ping `firewall`. If not, go back again. Remember, they should be able to ping 192.0.2.1, not the PPP address.

Then, try to ping the PPP address of `firewall` from inside the protected network. If you can, then you have not turned off *IP Forwarding* and you will have to recompile the kernel. Having assigned the protected network the 192.0.2.1 domain means that no packets will be routed to this network anyway, but it is safer to have IP Forwarding turned off anyway. This leaves the control in your hands, not in the hands of your PPP provider.

Finally, ping each machine within the protected network from `firewall`. By this time, there should be no problems.

Now, you have your basic firewall setup.

3.5   Securing the Firewall

The firewall is no good if it is left wide open to attacks. First, look at /etc/inetd.conf. This file is what is called a "super server". It runs a bunch of the server daemons as they are requested. Examples are:

- Telnet

- Talk

- FTP

- Daytime

Turn off everything that is not needed. Definitely turn off netstat, systat, tftp, bootp, and finger. You might also want to turn off telnet, and only allow rlogin, or vica-versa. To turn a service off, merely put a # in front of it. Then, send a SIG-HUP to the process by typing kill -HUP <pid>, where pid is the process number of inetd. This will make inetd re-read its configuration file (inetd.conf) and restart. Test it out by telneting to port 15 on `firewall`, the netstat port. If you get an output of netstat, you have not restarted it correctly.

4   The Proxy Server

4.1   Setting up the Proxy Server

The proxy server requires additional software. You can get this software from

`(ftp://sunsite.unc.edu/pub/Linux/system/Network/misc/socks-linux-src.tgz)`

There is also an example config file in that directory called `"socks-conf"`. Uncompress and untar the files into a directory on your system, and follow the instructions on how to make it. I had a couple problems in making it. Make sure that the Makefiles are correct. Some are, some are not.

4.2   Configuring the Proxy Server

The socks program needs two separate configuration files. One to tell the access allowed, and one to route the requests to the appropriate proxy server. The access file should be housed on the server. The routing file should be housed on every Un*x machine. The DOS and, presumably, Macintosh computers will do their own routing.

4.2.1   The Access File

With socks4.2 Beta, the access file is called `"sockd.conf"`. It should contain 2 lines, a permit and a deny line. Each line will have three entries:

- The Identifier (permit/deny)
- The IP address
- The address modifier

The identifier is either permit or deny. You should have both a permit and a deny line.

The IP address holds a four byte address in typical IP dot notation. Ie 192.0.2.0.

The address modifier is also a typical IP address four byte number. It works like a netmask. Envision this number to be 32 bits (1s or 0s). If the bit is a 1, the corresponding bit of the address that it is checking must match the corresponding bit in the IP address field. For instance, if the line is:

```
permit 192.0.2.23 255.255.255.255
```

then, it will permit only the IP address that matches every bit in 192.0.2.23, eg, only 192.0.2.3. The line:

```
permit 192.0.2.0 255.255.255.0
```

will permit every number within group 192.0.2.0 through 192.0.2.255, the whole C Class domain. One should not have the line:

```
permit 192.0.2.0 0.0.0.0
```

as this will permit every address, regardless.

So, first permit every address you want to permit, and then deny the rest. To allow everyone in the domain 192.0.2.xxx, the lines:

```
permit 192.0.2.0 255.255.255.0
```

```
deny 0.0.0.0 0.0.0.0
```

will work nicely. Notice the first `"0.0.0.0"` in the deny line. With a modifier of 0.0.0.0, the IP address field does not matter. All 0's is the norm because it is easy to type.

More than one entry of each is allowed.

Specific users can also be granted or denied access. This is done via *ident* authentication. Not all systems support *ident*, including Trumpet Winsock, so I will not go into it here. The documentation with socks is quite adequate on this subject.

4.2.2   The Routing File

The routing file in socks is poorly named **"socks.conf"**. I say "poorly named" because it is so close to the name of the access file that it is easy to get the two confused.

The routing file is there to tell the socks clients when to use socks and when not to. For instance, in our network, 192.0.2.3 will not need to use socks to talk with 192.0.2.1, `firewall`. It has a direct connection in via Ethernet. It defines 127.0.0.1, the loopback, automatically. Of course you do not need socks to talk to yourself. There are three entries:

- deny

- direct

- sockd

Deny tells socks when to reject a request. This entry has the same three fields as in `sockd.conf`, identifier, address and modifier. Generally, since this is also handled by `sockd.conf`, the access file, the modifier field is set to 0.0.0.0. If you want to preclude yourself from calling any place, you can do it here.

The direct entry tells which addresses to *not* use socks for. These are all the addresses that can be reached without the proxy server. Again we have the three fields, identifier, address and modifier. Our example would have

direct 192.0.2.0 255.255.255.0

Thus going direct for any on our protected network.

The sockd entry tells the computer which host has the socks server daemon on it. The syntax is:

```
sockd @=<serverlist> <IP address> <modifier>
```

Notice the @= entry. This allows you to set the IP addresses of a list of proxy servers. In our example, we only use one proxy server. But, you can have many to allow a greater load and for redundancy in case of failure.

The IP address and modifier fields work just like in the other examples. You specify which addresses go where through these.

4.3 Working With a Proxy Server

4.3.1 Unix

To have your applications work with the proxy server, they need to be "sockified". You will need two different telnets, one for direct communication, one for communication via the proxy server. Socks comes with instructions on how to sockify a program, as well as a couple pre-sockified programs. If you use the sockified version to go somewhere direct, socks will automatically switch over to the direct version for you. Because of this, we want to rename all the programs on our protected network and replace them with the sockified programs. "Finger" becomes "finger.orig", "telnet" becomes "telnet.orig", etc. You must tell socks about each of these via the include/socks.h file.

Certain programs will handle routing and sockifying itself. *Netscape* is one of these. You can use a proxy server under *Netscape* by entering the server's address (192.0.2.1 in our case) in the **SOCKs** field under **Proxies**. Each application will need at least a little messing with, regardless of how it handles a proxy server.

4.3.2 MS Windows with Trumpet Winsock

Trumpet Winsock comes with built in proxy server capabilities. In the "setup" menu, enter the IP address of the server, and the addresses of all the computers reachable directly. Trumpet will then handle all outgoing packets.

4.4 Getting the Proxy Server to work with UDP Packets

The socks package works only with *TCP* packets, not *UDP*. This makes it quite a bit less useful. Many useful programs, such as talk and Archie, use UDP. There is a package designed to be used as a proxy server for UDP packets called UDPrelay, by Tom Fitzgerald <fitz@wang.com>. Unfortunately, at the time of this writing, it is not compatible with Linux.

4.5 Drawbacks with Proxy Servers

The proxy server is, above all, a *security device*. Using it to increase Internet access with limited IP addresses will have many drawbacks. A proxy server will allow greater access from inside the protected network to the outside, but will keep the inside completely unaccessible from the outside. This means no servers, talk or Archie connections, or direct mailing to the inside computers. These drawbacks might seem slight, but think of it this way:

- You have left a report you are doing on your computer inside a firewall protected network. You are at home, and decide that you would like to go over it. You can not. You can not reach your computer because it is behind the firewall. You try to log into `firewall` first, but since everyone has proxy server access, no one has set up an account for you on it.

- Your daughter goes to college. You want to email her. You have some private things to talk about, and would rather have your mail sent directly to your machine. You trust your systems administrator completely, but still, this is private mail.

- The inability to use UDP packets represents a big drawback with the proxy servers. I imagine UDP capabilities will be coming shortly.

And, proxy servers run slow. Because of the greater overhead, almost any other means of getting this access will be faster.

Basically, if you have the IP addresses, and you are not worried about security, do not use a firewall and/or proxy servers. If you do not have the IP addresses, but you are also not worried about security, you might also want to look into using an IP emulator, like Term, Slirp or TIA. Term is available from `ftp://sunsite.unc.edu`, Slirp is available from ftp://blitzen.canberra.edu.au/pub/slirp, and TIA is available from `marketplace.com`. These packages will run faster, allow better connections, and provide a greater level of access to the inside network from the Internet. Proxy servers are good for those networks which have a lot of hosts that will want to connect to the Internet on the fly, with one setup and little work after that.

5 Advanced Configurations

There is one configuration I would like to go over before wrapping this document up. The one I have just outlined will probably suffice for most people. However, I think the next outline will show a more advanced configuration that can clear up some questions. If you have questions beyond what I have just covered, or are just interested in the versatility of proxy servers and firewalls, read on.

5.1 A large network with emphasis on security

Say, for instance, you are the leader of the *Milwaukee 23rd Discordian Cabal*. You wish to network your site. You have 50 computers and a subnet of 32 (5 bits) IP numbers. You have various levels of access. You tell your disciples different things according to each level. Obviously, you would want to protect certain parts of the network from the disciples that are not in that level.

Disclaimer: I am not a member of the Discordians. I do not know their terminology, nor do I really care. I am using them as an example only. Please send all flames to

The levels are:

1. **The external level**. This is the level that gets shown to everybody. Basically, this is the ranting and raving about Eris, Goddess of Discord, and all the rest of the drivel.

2. **Sage.** This is the level of people who have gotten beyond the external level. Here is where you tell them that discord and structure are really one, and that Eris is also Jehovah.

3. **Adept.** Here is where the *real* plan is. In this level is stored all the information on how the Discordian Society is going to take over the world through a devious, yet humorous, plan involving Newt Gingrich, Wheaties Cereal, O.J. Simpson, and five hundred crystals, all erroneously marked "6.5 MHz".

5.1.1   The Network Setup

The IP numbers are arranged as:

- 23 of the 32 IP addresses are allocated to 23 machines that will be accessible to the Internet.

- 1 extra IP goes to a Linux box on that network

- 1 extra goes to a different Linux box on that network.

- 2 IP #'s go to the router

- 5 are left over, but given domain names paul, ringo, john, george and billy, just to confuse things a bit.

- The protected networks both have the addresses 192.0.2.xxx

Then, two separate networks are built, each in different rooms. They are routed via Infrared Ethernet so that they are completely invisible to the outside room. Luckily, infrared Ethernet works just like normal Ethernet (or so I think), so we can just think of them like normal.

These networks are each connected to one of the Linux boxes with an extra IP address.

There is a file server connecting the two protected networks. This is because the plans for taking over the world involves some of the higher sages. The file server holds the address `192.0.2.17` for the sage network and `192.0.2.23` for the adept network. It has to have different IP addresses because it has to have different Ethernet cards. IP Forwarding on it is **turned off**.

IP Forwarding on both Linux boxes is also turned off. The router will not forward packets destined for 192.0.2.xxx unless explicitly told to do so, so the Internet will not be able to get in. The reason for turning off IP Forwarding here is so that packets from the sage network will not be able to reach the adept network, and vice versa.

The NFS server can also be set to offer different files to the different networks. This can come in handy, and a little trickery with symbolic links can make it so that the common files can be shared with all. Using this setup and another Ethernet card can offer this one file server for all three networks.

5.1.2   The Proxy Setup

Now, since all three levels want to be able to monitor the network for their own devious purposes, all three need to have net access. The external network is connected directly into the Internet, so we don't have to mess with proxy servers here. The adept and sage networks are behind firewalls, so it is necessary to set up proxy servers here.

Both networks will be setup very similarly. They both have the same IP addresses assigned to them. I will throw in a couple of parameters, just to make things more interesting though.

1. No one can use the file server for Internet access. This exposes the file server to viruses and other nasty things, and it is rather important, so its off limits.

2. We will not allow Sage access to the World Wide Web. They are in training, and this kind of information retrieval power might prove to be damaging.

So, the sockd.conf file on the sage Linux box will have this line:

```
deny 192.0.2.17 255.255.255.255
```

and on the adept machine:

```
deny 192.0.2.23 255.255.255.255
```

And, the sage linux box will have this line

```
deny 0.0.0.0 0.0.0.0 eq 80
```

This says to deny access to all machines trying to access the port equal (*eq*) to 80, the http port. This will still allow all other services, just deny Web access.

Then, both files will have:

```
permit 192.0.2.0 255.255.255.0
```

to allow all the computers on the 192.0.2.xxx network to use this proxy server except for those that have already been denied (ie. the file server and Web access from the sage network).

The sage sockd.conf file will look like:

```
deny 192.0.2.17 255.255.255.255

deny 0.0.0.0 0.0.0.0 eq 80

permit 192.0.2.0 255.255.255.0
```

and the adept file will look like:

```
deny 192.0.2.23 255.255.255.255

permit 192.0.2.0 255.255.255.0
```

This should configure everything correctly. Each network is isolated accordingly, with the proper amount of interaction. Everyone should be happy. Now, *look out for your 6.5 MHz crystals*

Part XX

ftape-HOWTO

Copyright Kai Harrekilde-Petersen, <khp@pip.dknet.dk>
v1.51, 13 May 1995 for ftape-2.03b

This HOWTO discuss the essentials of the do's and dont's for the `ftape` driver under Linux. The `ftape` driver interfaces to QIC-40, QIC-80, QIC-3010 and QIC-3020 compatible drives only. The QIC-3010 and QIC-3020 standards are also known as 'QIC-WIDE'. These drives connects via the floppy disk controller (FDC). It **does not** cover SCSI or QIC-02 tape drives. DAT tape drives usually (always?) connect to a SCSI controller. This is but one of the Linux HOWTO documents. You can get an index over the HOWTOs from *the Linux HOWTO index* (http://sunsite.unc.edu/mdw/HOWTO), while the real HOWTO's can be fetched (using `ftp`) from sunsite.unc.edu:pub/Linux/doc/HOWTO (this is the "official" place) or via the World Wide Web from *the Linux Documentation Project home page* (http://sunsite.unc.edu/mdw/linux.hmtl).

Contents

1 Legalese

This is the 'Frequently Asked Questions' (FAQ) / HOWTO document for the `ftape` driver (ftape-HOWTO), Copyright (C) 1993, 1994, 1995 Kai Harrekilde-Petersen.

Copyright statement:

You may distribute this document freely **as a whole** in any form and free of charge. You may distribute parts of this document, provided this copyright message is included and you include a message stating that it is not the full HOWTO document and a pointer to where the full document can be obtained. Specifically, it may be included in commercial distributions, without my prior consent. However, I would like to be informed of such usage.

You may translate this HOWTO into any language, whatsoever, provided that you leave this copyright statement and the disclaimer intact, and that you append a notice stating who translated the document.

DISCLAIMER:

While I have tried to include the most correct and up-to-date information available to me, I cannot guarantee that usage of the information in this document does not result in loss of data. I provide NO WARRANTY about the information in the HOWTO and I cannot be made liable for any consequences for any damage resulting from using information in this HOWTO.

2 News flash

IMPORTANT: The `ftape` discussion forum has moved per May 11th, 1995 from the `niksula.hut.fi` server to the `linux-tape` list on `vger.rutgers.edu`. Please turn to the section 4.5 on how to leave the `niksula` channel and subscribe to the `vger` list.

version 1.51 (May 13, 1995)

- Included patch for timeouts on long tapes (QIC-WIDE)

version 1.5 (May 11, 1995)

- Updated to `ftape-2.03a`
- The `ftape` discussion list has moved to `vger`
- Conner TSM850R added to list of drives
- Colorado FC-20 controller works as of v2.03

version 1.41 (Apr 1, 1995)

- More bad English corrected, thanks to Daniel Barclay (I'm not a native speaker `:-)`

version 1.4 (Mar 17, 1995)

- Mostly typos corrected.

version 1.3 (Feb 5, 1995)

- Escom Powerstream v3.0 added to list of formatting software
- New section on how to create an emergency boot disk added (written by Claus Tøndering, `<ct@login.dknet.dk>`).

3 The preliminaries

Note that I (the howto-maintainer) no longer use `ftape` myself, so I cannot give much up-to-date advice on e.g. compiling `ftape`. If you have a problem, try posting on `comp.os.linux.help`, or to the tape discussion list on `vger.rutger.edu` (see 4.5 below). You should try to post a summary of your problems and its solution(s), after you've got it working, even if you only got it partially working. Please also send me (`<khp@pip.dknet.dk>`) a copy of your solution so that I can add it to the HOWTO.

I read my mail daily, I try to respond to everyone, but I cannot guarantee that I will respond immediately. Also, I seldomly read the newsgroups (`comp.os.linux.help` et al), as my Internet access is through a modem line and I have to read news On-line `8-(`.

If you recieve this as part of a printed distribution or on a CD-ROM, please check out *the Linux Documentation home page* (`http://sunsite.unc.edu/mdw/linux.hmtl`) or ftp to `sunsite.unc.edu:/pub/Linux/doc/HOWTO` to see if there exists a more recent version. This could potentially save you a lot troubles.

4   Getting and installing `ftape`

I will eventually include an installation guide in this section. You'll have to do without it, for the moment being.

4.1   What is `ftape`

`ftape` is a driver program that controls various low-cost tape drives that connect to the floppy controller.

`ftape` is not a backup program as such; it is a device driver, which allows you to use the tape drive (just like the SoundBlaster 16 driver let you use your sound card) through the device file `/dev/[n]rft[0-3]`.

`ftape` is written by Bas Laarhoven <bas@vimec.nl>, with "a little help from his friends" to sort out the ECC (Error Correcting Code) stuff. `ftape` is copyrighted by Bas under the GNU General Public License, which basically says: "go ahead and share this with the world, just don't disallow other people from copying it further".

`ftape` is currently beta testing, and has been that for some time now. It is reliable enough for critical backups (but always remember to check your backups, so you wont get a nasty surprise some day).

`ftape` supports drives that conform to the QIC-117 and one of the QIC-80, QIC-40, QIC-3010, and QIC-3020 standards. `ftape` does **not** support QIC-02 tape drives or drives that connect via a SCSI interface, e.g. DAT drives. SCSI drives are accessed as `/dev/[n]st[0-7]` and are supported by the kernel through the SCSI drivers. If you look for help on SCSI tape drives, you should read the `SCSI-howto`. See section 5.1 and 5.3 for a list of supported and unsupported drives.

4.2   How fast is `ftape`?

You can achieve quite respectable backup and restore speeds with `ftape`: I have a Colorado DJ-20 and an Adaptec 1542CF controller, and have measured a 4.25Mbyte/min sustained data transfer rate (no compression) across a 70Mbyte tar archive, while comparing the archive on the tape with data on my IDE disk. The speed of `ftape` is mostly dependent on the data transfer rate of your FDC: The AHA1542CF has a "post-1991 82077" FDC, and it will push 1Mbit/sec at the tape drive. If you have an FDC which can only deliver 500Kbit/sec data rates, you will see half the transfer rate (well, roughly).

4.3   What you need to install `ftape`

There are three source distributions that you must have to get `ftape` running:

- `ftape` v2.03 / v2.03a
- `modules` v1.1.87
- Linux kernel v1.2.<something>

4.3.1   Getting `ftape`

`ftape` can be fetched from the following site (and its mirrors):

> sunsite.unc.edu [152.2.22.81]: /pub/Linux/kernel/tapes/

You should get the files: `ftape-2.03.tar.gz`, `ftape-2.03a-patch.gz` and `ftape-1sm`. The `.tar.gz` and `patch.gz` files are the `ftape` driver proper, while the `1sm` file is a Linux Software Map (LSM) file for the LSM project.

The following patch, which corrects timeouts on long tapes, was sent out by Bas on the Linux Tape list on May 13th:

```
--- 1.29          1995/05/10 16:09:36
+++ ftape-read.c        1995/05/12 17:36:37
@@ -478,10 +478,10 @@
      case QIC_TAPE_QIC80:
        segments_per_1000_inch = 488;
        break;
-     case QIC_TAPE_QIC3020:
+     case QIC_TAPE_QIC3010:
        segments_per_1000_inch = 730;
        break;
-     case QIC_TAPE_QIC3010:
+     case QIC_TAPE_QIC3020:
        segments_per_1000_inch = 1430;
        break;
      }
```

4.3.2 modules

Newer kernels (from 1.1.85 and on), have improved support for loadable modules (by Bjørn Ekwall and Jacques Gelinas), which (if possible) allows you to insert modules compiled for an 'old' kernel into a 'new' kernel. To compile the kernel with this improved module support, you need the modules-1.1.87.tar.gz file and the patch included with ftape. The modules packages can be found on tsx-11.mit.edu and sunsite.unc.edu. You must compile and install it before you compile the kernel.

NOTE: You *must* follow the instructions in the ftape package on how to update the insmod program; The insmod that comes with the modules packages has a bug that causes the kernel to generate an Oops when you try to insert the ftape module. (Mail about Oops'es when ftape is inserted will quietly go to /dev/null).

4.3.3 The Linux kernel

Since Linux version 1.2 has been out for some time I assume that everyone has switched over to it. If you have not already switched over, I assume you have a very good reason for not doing so, and that you can cope with the differences in installation etc, that it will make for you.

The kernel can be fetched from a large number of sites all over the world, including these:

```
sunsite.unc.edu [152.2.22.81]:   /pub/Linux/kernel/tapes/
tsx-11.mit.edu  [18.172.1.2]:    /pub/linux/sources/system/
ftp.funet.fi    [218.214.248.6]: /pub/OS/Linux/PEOPLE/Linus/
```

You will find a number of subdirectories, including two named v1.1 and v1.2. These contain (you guessed it!) v1.1 and v1.2 of the kernel. I suggest that you get version 1.2.x.

4.4   If you have ftape-2.02, or earlier

Since ftape both has been improved and some more bugs have been thrown out, you should consider upgrading to 2.03 or 2.03a mandatory.

4.5   Following the development of the ftape driver

If you want to follow the development of the ftape driver, you should consider subscribing to the TAPE mailing list on vger. To subscribe to it, send a mail saying 'subscribe linux-tape' to majordomo@vger.rutgers.edu. When you subscribe, you will be sent a greeting mail, which will tell you how to submit real mails and how to get off the list again.

Note for old users:

On May 11th, Bas announced (together with the 2.03a patch) that the 'official' mailing list from now on will we the `linux-tape` list on `vger`. Hence, all that are on the Linux-activists list on Niksula should move to the other list.

Since I once in a while see mail of the type "Help! I can't get off niksula", I am going to be a bit elaborate on how to get off (and what to do before despairing).

To   get   off   the   TAPE channel on Niksula, you send a mail to <`linux-activists-request@niksula.hut.fi`> with the line 'X-Mn-Admin: leave TAPE'.

If Niksula refuses, try sending a mail with the line 'X-Mn-Info: user <*yourloginname*>'. This should return you a mail which tells you under what email address you are subscribed. The Niksula mailer is very adamant on the point that you *must* unsubscribe with the same email address that you used to subscribe originally.

If the machine that you originally subscribed with has changed its address, you can try to fake the mail by adding the line 'From: <*foo@bar.site.edu*>' right before or after the 'leave TAPE' line. This *should* fool niksula into unsubscribing you. As a very last resort, you could talk someone into logging into the SMTP port on niksula and creating a faked mail.

4.6   Compiling and installing the `ftape` driver

There is included an installation guide (the file `Install-guide`) in the `ftape` distribution; please read that.

4.7   Can I format my tapes under Linux?

No! Honestly, noone is working on it: If you want to work on it, drop Bas a line. Until then, you'll have to use MessyDOS (arghhh!) instead or buy preformatted tapes. However, some of the preformatted tapes are *not* checked for bad sectors!. If the `ftape` driver encounters a tape with no bad blocks, it will issue a warning. If `ftape` barfs at your preformatted tapes, try out your DOS software. If both the DOS software *and* `ftape` barfs on your tapes, a reformat will very probably cure the problem.

Note that to be able to use your newly formatted tapes under ftape, you must *erase* the tape first:

```
mt -f /dev/nftape erase
```

4.8   Which formatting programs can I use under DOS?

These are known to work:

- Colorado Memory System's software (`tape.exe`)
- Conner Backup Basics v1.1 and all Windows versions
- Norton Backup
- QICstream version 2
- Tallgrass FileSecure v1.52
- Escom Powerstream 3.0 (`qs3.exe` – QICstream v3?)

These programs are known to be more or less buggy:

- Conner Backup Basics 1.0

- Colorado Windows tape program

- CP Backup (wastes tape space, but is OK apart from that)

In fact, most software under DOS should work. The Conner Backup Basics v1.0 has a parameter off by one (someone could not read the QIC-80 specs right!), which is corrected in version 1.1. However, ftape detects this, and will work around it. Dennis T. Flaherty (<dennisf@denix.elk.miles.com>) report that Conner C250MQ owners can obtain the new v1.1, by calling Conner at 1-800-4Conner (in the US) and ask for an upgrade (for a nominal fee for the floppy). The Windows versions should work fine. Some versions of Colorado's tape program for windows, has an off-by-one error in the number of segments. ftape also detect and work around that bug.

Central Point Backup can be used, but it wastes precious tape space when it encounters a bad spot on the tape.

NOTE: If you are running a formatting software under DOS, which is not mentioned here, please mail the relevant info to me (<khp@pip.dknet.dk>), so I can update the HOWTO.

4.9 Mixing ftape and floppies

Since both the floppy driver and ftape needs the FDC (and IRQ6), they cannot run concurrently. Thus, if you have mounted a floppy and then try to access the tape drive, ftape will complain that it cannot grab IRQ6 and then die. This is especially a problem when designing a emergency disk for use with ftape. This solution is to either load the boot/root disk into a ramdisk and then unmount the floppy, or have two FDC's.

5 (Un)supported hardware

5.1 Supported tape drives

All drives that are both QIC-117 compatible *and* either QIC-40 or QIC-80 compatible should work. There are also experimental support of QIC-3010 and QIC-3020 drives (QIC-3010/302 can use 8mm tapes. This is sometimes refered to as 'QIC-WIDE'). Currently, the list of drives that are known to work with ftape is:

- Alloy Retriever 250

- Archive 5580i / XL9250i

- Colorado DJ-10 / DJ-20 (aka: Jumbo 120 / Jumbo 250)

- Conner C250MQ

- Conner TSM420R

- Conner TSM850R

- Escom / Archive (Hornet) 31250Q

- Insight 80Mb

- Iomega 250

- Mountain FS8000

- Summit SE 150 / SE 250

- Tallgrass FS300 (needs a tiny hack to work with AHA1542B)

- Memorex tape drive backup system

- Wangtek 3080F

You can always check out the newest list of drives that are recognised by `ftape`, by looking in the file `vendors.h` in the `ftape` distribution.

Although I do not want to endorse one drive type over another, I want to mention that the Colorado DJ-20 drive is rather noisy, when compared to, say, a Conner C250MQ drive ('tis said that the Colorado is 5-10 times as noisy as the Conner drive. I can't tell for sure, but I have a Colorado, and it *is* quite noisy).

If you have a Tallgrass FS300 and an AHA1542B, you need to increase the bus-on / bus-off time of the 1542B. Antti Virjo (`<klanvi@uta.fi>`), says that changing `CMD_BUSON_TIME` to 4 and `CMD_BUSOFF_CMD` to 12 in `linux/drivers/scsi/aha1542.c` will do the trick.

One user has reported that `ftape` works (partially) the with Conner TSM420R drive, which supports both QIC-80 (normal) and 'QIC-WIDE' tapes. As of right now, `ftape` provides only **experimental** support for QIC-WIDE tapes, and you should be aware of this. Hopefully, the TSM420R drive, and other QIC-WIDE drives, will be supported fully soon. If you have a drive that can use QIC-WIDE tapes, are interested in getting it to work with `ftape`, and not afraid of being ALPHA tester, drop Bas `<bas@vimec.nl>` a mail, stating which drive you have.

NOTE: If you have a drive that works fine, but it is not listed here, please send a mail to the HOWTO maintainer (`<khp@pip.dknet.dk>`).

5.2 Supported special controllers

These dedicated high-speed tape controllers are supported by `ftape`:

- Colorado FC-10

- Colorado FC-20

- Mountain MACH-2

- IOmega Tape Accelerator II

Support for the FC-10 controller has been merged into the `ftape` driver in version 1.12. See the `RELEASE-NOTES` and the `Makefile` files in the `ftape` distribution. Since of version 2.03 of `ftape`, the FC-20 controller will work (but do check the Release notes!).

The support for the MACH-2 controller was added in `ftape-1.14d`.

To use the IOmega Tape Accelerator II, use `-DMACH2`, and set the right settings for I/O base, IRQ and DMA. This works (by the empirical testing of Scott Bailey `<sbailey@xcc.mc.xerox.com>`), with at least `ftape-2.02`.

Anti-Colorado message:

As of lately, Colorado has proved themselves totally unwilling to help with FC-10 and FC-20 support. This is sad, and can only force me to say: Don't buy a Colorado high-speed controller, or even a Colorado tape drive. Why support a manufacturer who does not want to support his own product?

5.3 Un-supported tape drives

- All drives that connect to the parallel port (eg: Colorado Trakker)

- High-Speed controller's. (eg: Colorado TC-15 & FC-20)

- Irwin AX250L / Accutrak 250. (not a QIC-80 drive)

- IBM Internal Tape Backup Unit (identical to the Irwin AX250L drive)

- COREtape light

Generally, ALL drives that connect to the parallel port are NOT supported. This is because these drives uses (different) proprietary interfaces, that are very much different from the QIC-117 standard.

The Colorado TC-15 controller (and its like) are not supported directly by the `ftape` driver. The only 'special' controllers that can be used with `ftape` is the Colorado FC-10 and the Mountain MACH-2 (see above).

The Irwin AX250L (and the IBM Internal Tape Backup Unit) does not work the `ftape`. This is because they only support QIC-117, but not the QIC-80 standard (they use Irwin's proprietary servoe (Rhomat) format). I know nothing about the Rhomat format, nor where to get any info on it. Sorry.

The COREtape light, does not accept the initialization commands, we're feeding it. This pretty much leaves the drive unusable.

5.4   Using an external tape drive with `ftape`

If you have a floppy controller which has a female DB37 connector on the bracket (and some means of delivering power to the drive), you can use it with `ftape`. OK, that sentence was not very obvious. Let's try it this way: Some FDC's (the very ancient one's), have a DB37 connector on the bracket, for connecting to external floppy drives.

If you make a suitable cable (from a quick glance on an FDC that I've got lying around, it seems to be a straight 1-to-1 cable. However, your milage may vary) from the DB37 connector (on the FDC) and to your external tape drive, you can get `ftape` to control your tape drive.

This is because that from a program's view there is no difference between the internal and the external connectors. So, from `ftape`'s point of view, they are identical.

5.5   Getting PCI motherboards to work with `ftape`

Unfortunately, some PCI motherboards cause problems when running `ftape`. Some people have experienced that `ftape` would not run in a PCI based box, but ran flawlessly in a normal ISA based 386DX machine. To quote from the RELEASE-NOTES file in the `ftape` distribution:

```
More PCI news:
--------------

There have been more reports about PCI problems, some of them
were solved by upgrading the (flash) BIOS.
Other rumours are that it has to do with the FDC being on the
PCI bus, but that is not the case with the Intel Premiere boards.

Here is a list of systems and the BIOS versions known to work:

board:                         bios revision:

Intel Premiere PCI (Revenge)   1.00.09.AF2

Intel Premiere PCI II (Plato)  1.00.08.AX1 (disable GAT in BIOS!)
                               1.00.10.AX1

To see if you're having the GAT problem, try making a backup
under DOS. If it's very slow and often repositions you're
probably having this problem.

PCI news:
---------
```

There have been some problem reports from people using PCI-bus based
systems getting overrun errors.
I wasn't able to reproduce these until I ran ftape on a Intel Plato
(Premiere PCI II) motherboard with bios version 1.00.08AX1.
It turned out that if GAT (Guaranteed Access Timing) is enabled (?)
ftape gets a lot of overrun errors.
The problem disappears when disabling GAT in the bios.
Note that Intel removed this setting (permanently disabled) from the
1.00.10AX1 bios !

It looks like that if GAT is enabled there are often large periods
(greater than 120 us !??) on the ISA bus that the DMA controller cannot
service the floppy disk controller.
I cannot imagine this being acceptable in a decent PCI implementation.
Maybe this is a 'feature' of the chipset. I can only speculate why
Intel choose to remove the option from the latest Bios...

The lesson of this all is that there may be other motherboard
implementations having the same of similar problems.
If you experience a lot of overrun errors during a backup to tape,
see if there is some setting in the Bios that may influence the
bus timing.

6 Backing up and restoring data

This section describes some simple uses of tar and mt.

6.1 Writing an archive to a tape

You can use 'tar', 'dd', 'cpio', and 'afio'. You will need to use 'mt' to get the full potential of your tapes
and the ftape driver. For a start I'd recommend using 'tar', as it can archive lots of directories and let
you pick out seperate files from an archive. I have been told that cpio creates smaller archives and is
more flexible than tar, but I haven't tried it myself. 'afio' creates backups where each file is compressed
individually and then concatenated. This will allow you to access the files "after" the point of the error. If
you use gzipped tar files, all data after the point of the error is lost! (to me, this is a pretty good reason
for NOT using compression on backups).

To make a backup of your kernel source tree using tar, do this (assuming you have the sources in
/usr/src/linux):

```
cd /usr/src
tar cf /dev/ftape linux
```

This will not compress the files, but gives you a smoother tape run. If you want the compression (and
you've got tar 1.11.2), you just include the -z flag(*), eg: 'tar czf /dev/ftape linux'

For further instructions on how to use tar, dd and mt look at the man pages and the texinfo files that comes
with the respective distributions.

(*) tar assumes that the first argument is options, so the '-' is not necessary, i.e. these two commands are
the same: 'tar xzf /dev/ftape' and 'tar -xzf /dev/ftape'

6.2 Restoring an archive

OK, let us restore the backup of the kernel source you made in section 6.1 above. To do this you simply say

```
        tar xf /dev/ftape
```

If you used compression, you will have to say

```
        tar xzf /dev/ftape
```

When you use compression, `gzip` will complain about trailing garbage after the very end of the archive (and this will lead to a 'broken pipe' message). This can be safely ignored.

For the other utilities, please read the man page.

6.3   Testing the archive

tar has an option (`-d`) for detecting differences between two archives. To test your backup of the kernel source say

```
        tar df /dev/ftape
```

If you do not have the man page for `tar`, you are not lost (yet); tar has a builtin option list: try '`tar --help 2>&1 | more`'

6.4   Putting more than one `tar` file on a tape

To put more than one `tar` file on a tape you must have the `mt` utility. You will probably have it already, if you got one of the mainline distributions, e.g. Slackware or Debian.

`tar` generates a single Tape ARchive (that's why it is called '`tar`') and knows nothing about multiple files or positioning of a tape, it just reads or writes from/to a device. `mt` knows everything about moving the tape back and forth, but nothing about reading the data off the tape. As you might have guessed, `tar` and `mt` in conjunction, does the trick.

By using the `nrft[0-3]` (`nftape`) device, you can use '`mt`' to position the tape the correct place ('`mt -f /dev/nftape fsf 2`' means step over two "file marks", i.e. `tar` files) and then use `tar` to read or write the relevant data.

6.5   Appending files to an archive

"Is there a way to extend an archive – put a file on the tape, then later, add more to the tape?"

No. The `tar` documentation will tell you to use '`tar -Ar`', but it does not work. This is a limitation of the current `ftape` driver.

6.6   Mount/unmounting tapes

Since a tape does not have a "filesystem" on it, you do not mount / unmount the tape. To backup, you just insert the tape and run your '`tar`' command (or whatever you use to access the tape with).

7   Creating an emergency boot floppy for `ftape`

This section was written by Claus Tøndering <`ct@login.dknet.dk`>.

Once you are the happy owner of a tape drive and several tapes full of backups, you will probably ask yourself this question: "If everything goes wrong, and I completely lose my hard disk, how do I restore my files from tape?"

What you need is an emergency floppy disk that contains enough files to enable you to boot Linux and restore your hard disk from tape.

The first thing you should do is to read "The Linux Bootdisk HOWTO" written by Graham Chapman <grahamc@zeta.org.au>. That document tells you almost everything you need to know about making an emergency floppy boot kit. The paragraphs below contain a few extra pieces of information that will make your life a bit easier when you follow Graham Chapman's procedures:

- You don't really need /etc/init, /etc/inittab, /etc/getty, and /etc/rc.d/* on your floppy disk. If Linux doesn't find /etc/init, it will start /bin/sh on your console, which is fine for restoring your system. Deleting these files gives you extra space on your floppy, which you will probably need.

- Find a small version of /bin/sh. They are frequently available on the boot floppies that come with a Linux distribution. This again will give you extra space.

- The /etc/fstab you include on your floppy disk should look like this:

```
/dev/fd0          /              minix    defaults
none              /proc          proc     defaults
```

Once you have booted from your floppy, give the command:

```
mount -av
```

- Make sure your floppy drive is not mounted when you access the streamer tape! Otherwise you may get the following error message:

```
Unable to grab IRQ6 for ftape driver
```

This implies that you **MUST** load the floppy into a RAMDISK.

This has the unfortunate consequence that the programs needed to restore the files from the tape must not be located on a separate floppy disk. You have two options here:

1. You place tar (or cpio or afio or whatever other backup program you use) on your root floppy disk. (This is where you'll need all the extra space created in the steps above.)

2. Before you start restoring from tape, copy tar (or cpio or afio or whatever) to your hard disk and load it from there.

- Apart from your backup program, you will probably need mt on your root floppy as well.

- Make sure your ftape device (typically /dev/nrft0) is present on your boot floppy.

- Finally: **TRY IT!** Of course, I don't recommend that you destroy your hard disk contents to see if you are able to restore everything. What I do recommend, however, is that you try booting from your emergency disks and make sure that you can at least make a file listing of the contents of your backup tape.

8 Frequently Asked Questions

This is a collection of questions I get asked once in a while, which could fall into the category of FAQ's. If you feel that there is some question that ought to be added to the list, please feel free to mail me (but do include an answer, thanks!).

8.1   Can I exchange tapes with someone using DOS?

No. The DOS software conforms to the QIC-80 specs about the layout of the DOS filesystem, and it should(?) be a small problem to write a program that can read/write the DOS format. In fact, I'd bet that creating a nice user interface would be a bigger problem.

8.2   How do I '....' with `tar`?

These are really `tar` questions: Please read the man page and the `info` page. If you have not got it either, try 'tar --help 2>&1 | more'.

If your version of `tar` is v1.11.1 or earlier, consider upgrading to v1.11.2 - This version can call GNU `zip` directly (i.e.: it supports the `-z` option) and has an elaborate help included. Also, it compiles right out of the box on Linux.

8.3   `ftape` DMA transfers gives ECC errors

Sadly to say there are some SVGA cards and ethernet cards that do not decode their addresses correct. This typically happens when the `ftape` buffers are in the range `0x1a0000` to `0x1c0000`. Somehow, the DMA write cycles get clobbered and every other byte written gets a bad value (`0xff`). These problems are reported to happen with both SVGA and ethernet cards. We know of at least one (bad?) ATI 16bit VGA card that caused this.

The easiest solution is to put the card in an 8bit slot (it is often not enough to reconfigure the card to 8bit transfers). Moving the `ftape` buffer away from the VGA range is only a partial solution; All DMA buffers used in Linux can have this problem! Let us make this one clear: This has nothing to do with the `ftape` software.

8.4   `insmod` says the kernel version is wrong

The `insmod` program checks the kernel version against the version recorded in the `ftape` driver. This is a string in `kernel-version.h`, (e.g.: `#define KERNEL_VERSION "1.1.72";`) which is extracted from the kernel you are running when you run 'make dep'. If you got the error when you tried to insert the `ftape` driver, remove the file 'kernel-version.h', type 'make dep; make' again and the `kernel-version.h` file should be updated. Remember that you will have to do this every time you change to another kernel version.

8.5   `ftape` complains that "`This tape has no 'Linux raw format'`"

You get this complaint, if you haven't *erased* your freshly formatted tape. This is because `ftape` wants a "magic header" on the tape, to be able that it is allowed to interpret the header segment in it's own way (eg: file marks). To remove the problem, say 'mt -f /dev/nftape erase'

8.6   Where can I find the `tar`/`mt`/`cpio`/`dd` binaries/sources/manpages?

All of these tools have been developed by the GNU project, and the source (and man page) can be fetched from just-about any ftp site in the world (including `ftp.funet.fi`, `tsx-11.mit.edu`, and `sunsite.unc.edu`). In any case they can be fetched from the official GNU home site: `prep.ai.mit.edu` `[18.71.0.38]:/pub/gnu`. The latest versions (by 26. march 94) are:

```
cpio:   2.3 (cpio-2.3.tar.gz)
dd:     3.9 (fileutils-3.9.tar.gz)
mt:     2.3 (cpio-2.3.tar.gz)
```

```
tar:    1.11.2 (tar-1.11.2.tar.gz)
gzip:   1.2.4 (gzip-1.2.4.tar.gz)
```

They all compile out of the box on Linux `v1.0.4` / `libc` `v4.5.19` / `gcc` `v2.5.8` (The `rmt` program does not compile out of the box, but it is not needed as it is only used for accessing the tape drive remotely). There is a patch for `mt` included in the `ftape` distribution, which makes the `mt` `status` command spew out usable information for `ftape` drives.

8.7   Where can I obtain the QIC standards?

If you wish to help develop `ftape`, or add some utility (e.g. a tape formatting program), you will need the appropriate QIC standards. The standard(s) to get is: QIC-80 and perhaps QIC-117. QIC-117 describes how commands are sent to the tape drive (including timing etc), so you would probably never need it. QIC-80 describes the tape layout, ECC code, standard filesystem and all such "higher-level" stuff. You can get the QIC standards from the following address:

```
Quarter Inch Cartridge Drive Standars, Inc.
311 East Carrillo Street
Santa Barbara, California 93101
Phone: (805) 963-3852
Fax:   (805) 962-1541
```

8.8   What block-size to use with `tar`

When using compression, and in all general, it can be a benefit to specify to `tar`, that it should block the output into chunks. Since `ftape` cuts things into 29Kbyte blocks, saying '`-b58`' should be optimum.

"Why 29Kbyte?", I hear you cry. Well, the QIC-80 standard specifies that all data should be protected by an Error Correcting Code (ECC) code. The code specified in the QIC-80 standard is known as a Reed-Solomon (R-S) code. The R-S code takes 29 data bytes and generates 3 parity bytes. To increase the performance of the ECC code, the parity bytes are generated across 29 1Kbyte sectors. Thus, `ftape` takes 29Kbytes of data, adds 3Kbytes of ECC parity, and writes 32Kbytes to the tape at a time. For this reason, ftape will always read 32K byte blocks to be able to detect (and correct) data errors.

If you are curious, and wish to know more, look in the `ecc.c` and `ecc.h` files, they an explanation of the code and a reference to a textbook on Reed-Solomon codes.

9   Debugging the `ftape` driver

9.1   The kernel/`ftape` crashes on me when I do '...' - is that a bug?

No, that is a feature ;-)

Seriously, reliable software do not crash. Especially kernels do not or rather **should** not crash. If the kernel crashes upon you when you are running `ftape`, and you can show that it is `ftape` that is messing things up, regard it as a Bug That Should Be Fixed. Mail the details to Bas (`<bas@vimec.nl>`) and to the tape channel.

9.2   OK, it's a bug ...ehhh... feature - How do I submit a report?

First, make sure you can reproduce the problem. Spurious errors are a pain in the ass, since they are just about impossible to hunt down :-/ This is a quick check list:

- Kernel version, and patches applied

- ftape version

- tape drive model / manufacturer

- Expansion bus type (EISA, ISA, PCI, or VL-bus)

- What you did to expose the problem

- What went wrong on your system.

- Do not delete the kernel and the ftape.o file. We may want you run try some patches out or run a different test on your system.

Increase the tracing level to 7 (just below maximum tracing) and run the offending command again. Get the tracing data from the kernel log or /proc/kmsg, depending on where you harvest your error messages. Try to look at what ftape spews out at you. It may look in-comprehensible to you at first, but you can get valuable information from the logfile. Most messages have a function name prepended, to make it easier to locate the problem. Look through the source, don't just cry "WOLF!", without giving it a try. If your version of the kernel (or ftape for that matter), is "old", when compared to the newest version of the kernel, try to get a newer (or even the newest) kernel and see if the problem goes away under the new kernel. When you post your problem report, include the information about ftape version, kernel version, expansion bus type (ISA, VL-bus, PCI or EISA), bus speed, floppy controller, and tape drive. State exactly what you did, and what happened on your system. Some people have experienced that ftape would not run in a PCI based box, but ran flawlessly in a normal ISA based 386DX machine (see section 5.5 on PCI machines above)

Also, please think of the poor souls who actually *pay* for their Internet access (like me): avoid posting a (huge) log from the ftape run, without reason. Instead, you could describe the problem, and offer to send the log to the interested parties.

Send your bug report to <linux-tape@vger.rutgers.edu>. You might also want to mail the bug to <bas@vimec.nl>.

9.3   How do I change the trace-level?

You can do this two ways: either change the default trace-level (the var 'tracing' in file 'ftape-rw.c') and recompile or say

```
mt -f /dev/ftape fsr <tracing-level>
```

The use of the fsr command in mt is a *hack*, and will probably disappear or change with time.

9.4   ftape keep saying '... new tape', what do I do?

[You cannot do this anymore; I do not know a way of fixing it]

To get rid of this, do this (blindfold): login as root and say 'rmmod ftape'. ftape should choke a few times, give three segmentation violations (or so), and give up life.

Check the activity LED on your floppy drive (you do have one, don't you?). If it is constantly lit, you have turned the floppy cable upside down somewhere. Check your cable between controller, tape drive *and* floppy drive. Usually, one (or more) of the connectors have been turned upside down, such that pin 1 in one end connects to pin 34 in the other end. (All the even-numbered pins are grounded, so you wont be able to use your floppy either). Don't worry; this cannot damage your hardware.

9.5   When I use /dev/nftape, I get garbage ... why?

This was a problem in 'the old days', before version 0.9.10. Nowadays, the non-rewinding devices are working. If you have anything earlier, I strongly recommend you to update to the 2.03(a) version.

Part XXI

Linux HAM-HOWTO, Amateur Radio Software List

Copyright Terry Dawson, VK2KTJ, `terryd@extro.ucc.su.oz.au`
v1.6 08 Apr 1995
It is hoped that this list will assist Amateur Radio operators in finding and trying the various amateur radio software that has been written for, or ported to Linux. It is also hoped that as a consequence of this information being available that more amateur radio operators will choose Linux as the platform of choice for their experimentation, and that software developers will choose Linux as the platform for their software development, further expanding the role of operating systems like Linux in the Amateur Radio field.

Contents

1 Introduction.

This list was prompted by comments that had been expressed in the various Linux newsgroups about the number of amateur radio operators that were involved with Linux. It seemed to me that I was catching snippets of information here and there relating to development efforts taking place, but I never really knew where to locate either the person responsible for a particular piece of software, or the software itself. The list is growing as new packages are found.

This list is not limited to non-commercial software in any way. Taking a serious look at most amateur radio fields shows that most good developments are those that are designed by individuals and that commercial entities have taken up and disseminated to the mass market. I'd like to see the same happen for Linux support for Amateur Radio software too.

This list was originally called the RADIOLINUX list, but Matt Welsh suggested that there was no reason why it shouldn't be distributed with the Linux Documentation Project documents, so it has been renamed the HAM-HOWTO and will be made available with the rest of the Linux Documentation. I make no apologies for the name.

1.1 Changes from the previous version

```
Additions:
        Added clx - packet cluster software
```

```
        Bruce Perens LinuxForHams CDROM
        SuperiorMorse - thanks Brian and John
        svgafft - Spectrum analyser

Corrections:
        Updated SatTrack to version 3.1 - thanks Manfred.
        Updated IPIP daemon to Bdale recombined version.
```

2 Where to obtain new versions of this list.

This list will be periodically posted to the `comp.os.linux.announce` newsgroup, and to the HAMS list on `niksula.hut.fi`.

It is also available from the following World Wide Web sites:

The Linux Documentation Project runs a Web Server and this list appears there as

The HAM-HOWTO (`http://sunsite.unc.edu/mdw/HOWTO/HAM-HOWTO.html`).

Dennis Boylan N4ZMZ <`dennis@nanovx.atl.ga.us`> makes it available at the following three locations:

www.com (`http://www.com/linux/radio/index.html`),

www.hboc.com (`http://www.hboc.com/linux/index.html`)

and

www.lan.com (`http://www.lan.com/linux/index.html`).

John Gotts N8QDW <`jgotts@engin.umich.edu`> makes it available at:

www.engin.umich.edu (`http://www.engin.umich.edu/ jgotts/linuxhamsoft.html`).

Alan Hargreaves VK2KVF <`alan@dap.CSIRO.AU`> makes it available in Australia at:

www.dap.csiro.au (`http://www.dap.csiro.au/RadioLinux`).

Please let me know if you'd like to make it available somewhere too. I'd like to see it on some Web Servers that are accessible from radio.

3 Satellite Software.

The following software is for use in experimentation with Satellite communication.

3.1 MicroSat Ground Station Software

Author

John Melton, G0ORX/N6LYT, g0orx@amsat.org and Jonathan Naylor G4KLX, g4klx@amsat.org

Description

Microsat Ground Station software.

Status

BETA. Version 0.9-Xaw released.

System requirements

Alan Cox's kernel based AX.25 support ver 1.1.12 or better. X-Windows. The programs make use of the Athena Widgets and look much better with the 3D libraries.

Detail

This software allows you to use of a KISS tnc to directly communicate with the Microsat series of satellites. It provides an Athena Widgets based X-Windows interface, and allows you a comprehensive range of means of interacting with the satellite. The software should work with any window manager.

The software provides the following programs:

xpb:
broadcast monitor

xpg:
ftl0 file upload program, message upload program

xtlm:
telemetry display program

downloaded:
downloaded file list viewer

directory:
directory list viewer

message:
message preparation application

viewtext:
uncompressed ASCII text file viewer

viewlog:
display the contents of some log files

xweber:
special program for downloading webersat images

phs:
general purpose PACSAT header stripper

Where and How to obtain it.

John's software is available from:

`(ftp://ftp.ucsd.edu/hamradio/packet/tcpip/incoming/microsat-0.9-Xaw.tar.gz)`

or

`(ftp://ftp.funet.fi/pub/ham/satellite/microsat/microsat-0.9-Xaw.tar.gz)`.

Please check for new versions.

Licensing/Copyright

GNU Public License. Freely redistributable, No warranty.

Contributed by:

John Melton, G0ORX/N6LYT, Alan Cox, GW4PTS, Jonathon Naylor, G4KLX

3.2   SatTrack - Satellite tracking program

Name

SatTrack

Author

Manfred Bester, DL5KR, manfred@ssl.berkeley.edu, (510) 849-9922

Description

Satellite realtime tracking and orbit prediction program with X11 color graphics.

Status

Version 3.1 has been released.

System requirements

A vt100 terminal and or X11 server. A Maths Coprocessor is useful but not essential for good performance.

Detail

SatTrack is a satellite tracking program that has been written in 'C' language on a UNIX workstation. It provides two different live displays, for single or multiple satellites, and two different orbit prediction facilities. Cursor controls used in both live displays are compatible with the VT100 standard, which allows the program to be run basically from any terminal. An optional X Window graphics display shows the typical world map tracking chart. The orbit prediction can be run either interactively or in a batch mode. In the latter case all necessary parameters are specified on the command line. The program uses the NORAD/NASA two-line Keplerian element (TLE) sets directly.

The current version of SatTrack can track a single satellite and/or display multiple satellites for a single ground station. It also can control suitable ground station hardware, like antennas and radio equipment, and has an autotrack mode in which it switches automatically between a number of specified satellites. For calibration purposes tracking of the Sun and the Moon are also provided. Future releases will provide more options. SatTrack requires about 5 MB of disk space in the full distribution with eight different world maps (2 styles, with 4 different sizes each, to fit everyone's screen and taste) and less than 1.5 MB of memory at run time.

More information can be obtained from the *SatTrack WWW Home Page* (http://ssl.berkeley.edu/isi_www/sattrack.html)

Compiling the software under Linux is quite straightforward. Manfred has designed the Makefile to compile the software directly under your home directory, this is easy to change.

The steps I took were:

```
# cd /usr/src
# export HOME=/usr/src
# gzip -dc sattrack.V3.1.tar.gz | tar xvf -
# cd SatTrack/src
# vi Makefile
  {Comment SUN4 compile options}
  {Uncomment the linux options}
  {Select the options you want}
# make
```

Where and How to obtain it.

SatTrack can be found at: *ftp.amsat.org* (ftp://ftp.amsat.org/amsat/software/Linux/sattrack.V3.1.tar.gz) or *ftp.jvnc.net* (ftp://ftp.jvnc.net/priv/kupiec/sattrack/sattrack.V3.1.tar.Z) or the *SatTrack WWW Home Page* (http://ssl.berkeley.edu/isi_www/sattrack-3.1.tar.gz)

Licensing/Copyright

The software is Copyright of Manfred Bester. It can be used without special permission for non-profit, non-commercial use. For commercial applications a license from the author is required.

Contributed by:

Manfred Bester, DL5KR

4   Shack Automation Software.

Software for simplifying tasks in the shack. Examples might include software for controlling the newer breed of radios, logging programs, QSL database, or antenna rotation.

5   Packet Radio

Software for use in conjunction with, or for facilitating packet radio.

5.1   Kernel Based AX.25 networking.

Author

Alan Cox, GW4PTS, iialan@iifeak.swan.ac.uk

Description

Software that allows the Linux Kernel to perform AX.25 networking.

Status

ALPHA. Quite stable though.

System requirements

Linux kernel 1.0 or later.

Detail

Alan's software provides the programmer with a Berkeley socket based interface to the AX.25 protocol. AX.25 sockets can opened for either connected, or connectionless modes of operation. Support to allow TCP/IP over AX.25 is provided. The user applications has been Jonathon G4KLX. The software comes in two parts, a kernel patch, and the user programs. The user programs included are:

axadd

to manipulate the AX.25 ARP table.

axattach

to convert a serial device into a KISS device.

axl

an AX.25 listener designed to start a PMS when it receives an incoming connection. The PMS is still very new.

axsetcall

to change the callsign of a port.

beacon

generated beacon messages every 30 minutes.

call

A linemode AX.25 connection program. Call allows you to make connections to other AX.25 nodes. It provides file transmit and receive capabilities, and newer versions allow YAPP binary file transfers.

listen

a demonstration of how to use intercept AX.25 frames at the raw packet level. Useful as a building block for packet tracing for example.

Where and How to obtain it.

There are a number of different versions of the software. You must choose the one that suits your version of Linux kernel. The software is available from:

(ftp://sunacm.swan.ac.uk/pub/misc/Linux/Radio/)

More detail on where and how to obtain the software is provided in

(ftp://sunsite.unc.edu/pub/Linux/docs/howto/NET-2-HOWTO)

or if you have WWW access at:

(http://sunsite.unc.edu/mdw/HOWTO/NET-2-HOWTO.html).

Licensing/Copyright

Most of the software is covered by the GNU Public License, some of the software is Copyright by the Regents of University California Berkeley, and small portions of the user programs are Copyright Phil Karn KA9Q, whose copyright allows unrestricted use by Amateur Radio, Educational Institutions and Commercial KA9Q OEM license holders.

Contributed by:

Terry Dawson, VK2KTJ.

5.2 JNOS

Author

Brandon Allbery, KF8NH, bsa@kf8nh.wariat.org

Description

Brandon ported JNOS to Linux. His port is currently of the 1.09 (aka 1.08df) release of JNOS. Future versions will probably be based on Doug Crompton's evolution of 1.08df. Brandon suggests that JNOS for Linux is primarily of interest to people with existing DOS-based NOS configurations (especially server/switch configurations) who wish to switch to Linux or to escape the 640K barrier.

Status

The current version is ALPHA.4. Brandon is still tracking down bugs, as well as evolving new features.

System Requirements.

Any version of Linux along with *ncurses* 1.8.1 or 1.8.5 (the latter is preferred). Optionally you will require Linux networking (at least loopback) and *slattach* (kernels pre-1.1.13 or post-1.1.20 required for this).

Detail

If you include the Linux networking code in addition to JNOS, you can link the two by a slip link running over a pty, so that Linux can provide services to your radio users. In this way you can easily add servers without having to build them into JNOS itself. Brandon has supplied the following list of known bugs:

- some servers seem to be causing unexplained exits.
- PPP is reported not to work in ALPHA.4, although it worked in ALPHA.3.
- BBS forwarding when convers is compiled in but not configured causes core dumps.
- the finger server is getting bad filenames.
- the bbs W command is case-munging filenames.

Where and How to obtain it.

You can obtain JNOS for Linux ALPHA.4 at:

`(ftp://ftp.ucsd.edu/hamradio/packet/tcpip/linux/j1091xA4.tgz)`

ncurses is available on most Linux ftp sites.

Licensing/Copyright

Brandon's modifications to JNOS are public domain. Most of the pre-existing NOS code is copyrighted and restricted to non-commercial use by the various contributors from Phil Karn on.

Contributed by:

Brandon Allbery, KF8NH

5.3   N0ARY Packet BBS for UN*X

Author

Bob Arasmith, N0ARY, ported to Linux (and others) by Bob Proulx, KF0UW, rwp@fc.hp.com

Description

A packet bbs implemented under UN*X.

Status

ALPHA. Bob is running version ARY-0.9 on both Linux and HP-UX. The next version from N0ARY which is called 4.0 is in alpha test/development release. Bob has not been able to bring this online yet and is still running 0.9+kf0uw mods. Bob has about half of it working with Alan Cox's AX.25 kernel which would be the desirable combination.

System Requirements.

Linux installation, C Compiler, plus HAM radio TNC hardware.

Detail

This bbs has an excellent packet user interface. It has a compatible set of commands with the RLI bbs so users will be familiar with it immediately. It then extends the command set to be a very nice natural language style interface (e.g "list at allus about KPC-3"). Many csh style bang commands are supported. Also included is a mail interface to provide a packet to internet gateway.

Currently you need to customize the source code for your installation so you need some C programming proficiency.

Where and How to obtain it.

For a Linux version or for Linux information send mail to rwp@fc.hp.com. For a SunOS version contact bob@arasmith.com. This code is not packaged for distribution yet since it is not past the alpha stage of development.

Licensing/Copyright

Copyright by Bob Arasmith, N0ARY, but freely redistributable.

Contributed by:

Bob Proulx, kf0uw, rwp@fc.hp.com

5.4   MBL/RLI message to NNTP and email converter.

Author

SM0OHI, pme@it.kth.se

Description

Software that will convert incoming MBL/RLI messages into either NNTP or RFC-822 formatted mail messages.

Status

Development, not yet released.

System requirements

Unknown.

Detail

This software would be ideally suited to those who want to establish a mail and news gateway between conventional TCP/IP networks and the amateur radio mail network.

Where and How to obtain it.

Not yet available.

Licensing/Copyright

Unknown.

Contributed by:

SM0OHI

5.5   Packet Cluster Node software

Author

Franta Bendl, DJ0ZY, and Bernhard ("Ben") Buettner, DL6RAI, root@dl6rai.muc.de

Description

A PacketCluster like system running on Linux.

Status

Released in March 1995.

System Requirements

Linux Kernel version 1.1.50 or greater with Alan Cox's AX.25 version 025 driver, TCP/IP networking, SysV IPC. Also needs Perl and KISS TNC hardware on serial device.

Detail

PacketCluster nodes have been available for about six years. The original software was written by Dick Newell, AK1A, and is running under DOS. *clx* is a system which clones a PacketCluster node. To the outside user commands and features are mostly identical, remote PacketCluster nodes, which can be networked, don't see the difference between a generic PacketCluster node and *clx*. So it fits well into an established network of PacketCluster nodes.

clx is not a user application, it is network node software. As such it is not of much use for the individual amateur. SysOPs of PacketCluster nodes with some experience on both PacketCluster and Linux will find this application interesting.

Here are some of the features of CLX:

- It is fully compatible with the internal PCxx protocol and from a users' point of view. It allows multitasking and different priorities for different things.

- The software detects looping DX spots without generating endless messages. *clx* filters out such duplicate information. We have implemented a concept which allows us to connect the network at multiple points, which would formerly have been called a "Cluster Loop". *clx* knows of so-called "active" and "passive" links. The outcome is that more DX information is seen by clx.

- An interface to call your external programs (even dialog programs).

- *clx* uses modern programming concepts like shared memory for common data, lex & yacc to implement command language, shared libraries to keep binaries small (this is still on our wish list), remote procedure calls for inter process communication. It is strictly modularized with its own dedicated process for every major task.

- Comprises the following modules:

  con_ctl
  interfaces AX.25 kernel code and provides a socket for local users.
  rcv_ctl
  manages receive spooling.
  snd_ctl
  manages transmit spooling.

rm_disp

receive message dispatcher, forwards messages to other processes.

usr_req

user database requests, forks a process for every database task to make it run in the background. The background process later sends the results directly to send_ctl.

mb_ctl

mailbox control. The mailbox keeps messages in a file system, header information is stored in the database.

usr_ctl

user administration (logins, logouts, logbook).

usc_mng

manages external user commands and command extensions.

iu_com

inter user communication (talk, conference).

send_ctl

transmit spooling, handling priorities.

icl_com

inter node communication (processing and generating PCxx messages).

clx_ctl

system administration, installing shared memory pages.

int_com

manages internal program communications.

- The following is the only application program which can be run on the console:

loc_usr

allows console operator(s) to log in like a normal user.

Future enhance planned are:

- A console monitor to watch ongoing activities
- Speed optimization
- An internal clx protocol
- An additional command shell for experienced users

Where and How to obtain it:

You can obtain *clx* from

(ftp://ftp.uni-erlangen.de/pub/public/pc-freeware/hamradio/packet/packclus/clx)

Licensing/Copyright

clx is available for non-commercial use, but the authors want to keep track of who is using their product, so before you can actually use the software you have to ask for an encrypted callsign string to be placed in the configuration file. You must send mail to <clx_us@dl6rai.muc.de> to organise this.

Contributed by:

Bernhard ("Ben") Buettner, DL6RAI

5.6   Single floppy disk AX.25 router.

Author

Alan Cox, GW4PTS, iialan@iifeak.swan.ac.uk

Description

A single floppy disk version of linux with enough software to allow a PC to act as an AX.25/IP router.

Status

Development, not yet released.

System requirements.

As for any Linux system a 386SX class PC or better.

Detail

No detail yet.

Where and How to obtain it.

Not yet available.

Licensing/Copyright

Unknown/Undecided.

Contributed by:

Terry Dawson, VK2KTJ

5.7 TNT.

Author

Mark Wahl, DL4YBG, DL4YBG @ DB0BLO.#.DEU.EU, wahlm@zelator.de

Description

A Hostmode terminal program for TNC's that support the WA8DED hostmode protocol.

Status

Version 0.8 is reportedly stable.

System requirements

TNC supporting WA8DED hostmode protocol, serial line.

Detail

TNT is a full featured hostmode terminal program. Compiling it on Linux is as difficult as untarring the source and typing 'make'. It provides both a 'dumb' terminal and X11 version. It comes with some comprehensive documentation which describes its features in some detail. Its main features are:

Multiple sessions:

TNT supports multiple packet radio connections on virtual screens that you can switch between. Each session window provides split screen (separate transmit and receive text) operation with a status line. Commands can be entered in either a command session, or in any terminal session using a command key. Each of the virtual screens can be larger than the physical screen and can be scrolled around.

Data capture, file transfer and logging:

A number of options are available for logging received text to files. You can log transmit, receive or both to a log file. You can overwrite or append received data to existing files. You can use the 'autobin' protocol to transmit or receive binary files.

Remote Shell operation:

You can provide a shell to remote users so that they can access other programs on your computer. You can also run a program and direct its input/output to a channel so that users can use it.

Redirection of devices to a channel:

TNT allows you to redirect input/output from a channel to a device, a modem for example.

Umlaut conversion:

TNT provides umlaut conversion if necessary.

Remote mode:

Remote users can issue command themselves if allowed to do so.

Socket mode:

You can configure tnt so that it opens a socket for users to telnet to that allows them operation just as you have from the console. This is useful where your linux machine is on an ethernet and you want other terminal on the net to have use of your radio.

Where and How to obtain it.

The software is available by anonymous ftp from:

`(ftp://ftp.funet.fi/pub/ham/unix/packet/tntsrc08.tgz)`

This site is mirrored at a number of places so you will probably find it at other places as well.

Licensing/Copyright

GNU Public License. Freely redistributable, no warranty.

Contributed by:

Steffen Weinreich, DL5ZBG.

5.8   IPIP encapsulation daemon.

Name

Mike Westerhof's IPIP encapsulation daemon.

Author

Mike Westerhof KA9WSB (original code), then Bdale Garbee N3EUA (port to BSD), then Ron Atkinson N8FOW and John Paul Morrison (port to Linux), then Bdale rolled it all back together again.

Description

A daemon that will allow you to use your linux machine as an IPIP encapsulating gateway.

Status

Ron is running this code himself, and the other version have been run quite successfully.

System requirements

KISS TNC, any version of Linux supporting RAW sockets.

Detail

If you've ever used an internet gateway from your amateur packet radio you have probably been connected by an encapsulation gateway of some descpription. Most run KA9Q's NOS and DOS, but others run Unix and this daemon. It allows you to encapsulate IP within IP, so that you can 'tunnel' IP connections over the Internet. The software allows you to connect a KISS TNC to your linux machine and to have all datagrams received on it carried across the Internet to a similar gateway. Bdale has installation instructions in the package.

Where and How to obtain it.

This software is available from

`(ftp:///col.hp.com/hamradio/packet/etc/ipip/ipip.tar.gz)`

Licensing/Copyright etc.

Freely distributable, though Bdale asks that if you use the code and like it you might send him a QSL card or a postcard.

Contributed by:

Ron Atkinson, N8FOW, and Bdale Garbee, N3EUA

5.9 AXIP encapsulation daemon.

Name

Mike Westerhof's AXIP encapsulation daemon.

Author

Mike Westerhof KA9WSB, ported to Linux by Ron Atkinson N8FOW.

Description

A daemon that will allow you to use your linux machine as an AXIP encapsulating gateway.

Status

Not properly tested, but assumed to work OK.

System requirements

KISS TNC, any version of Linux supporting RAW sockets.

Detail

This daemon is the partner to the IPIP encapsulation daemon. It allows you to encapsulate AX.25 frames in IP to carry them across the Internet. This is useful for linking AX.25 networks in remote areas. Ron has supplied a `Makefile` for linux, and with it the software compiled without errors on my system running a recent version kernel. Ron has also written some `README` files which give you the detail necessary to compile the system and the original documentation describes how to configure it.

Where and How to obtain it.

This software is available from

`(ftp://sunsite.unc.edu/pub/Linux/apps/ham/ax25ip.tar.gz)`

Licensing/Copyright etc.

Freely distributable so long as the original copyright notice is not removed.

Contributed by:

Ron Atkinson, N8FOW

5.10 Ping-Pong Convers Server

Name

Fred Baumgartens Convers Server for Linux.

Author

Fred Baumgarten, DC6IQ, <dc6iq@insu1.etec.uni-karlsruhe.de>

Description

This is a version of the convers server that allows multiple users to simultaneously chat with each other in a round-table style conversation. It is compatible with the NOS convers servers, but provides extra facilities such as saving/restoring of Personal Text and Channel Topics.

Status

In use of a number of popular convers servers, appears very stable.

System requirements.

Linux, GNU make, C compiler.

Detail.

Complete installation instructions are included in the `INSTALL` file that is included in the distribution.

Where and How to obtain it.

A distribution of this software is available from:

(ftp://sunsite.unc.edu/pub/Linux/apps/ham/convers-941122.tar.gz)

The home of the software is

(ftp://insu1.etec.uni-karlsruhe.de/pub/hamradio/convers/convers)

Licensing/Copright etc.

Presumably copyright Fred Baumgarten (not specifically stated), but some portions appear to be free for non-commercial use and copying provided the copyright notices stay intact.

Contributed by:

Terry Dawson, VK2KTJ

5.11 Wampes

A port of Wampes to Linux. Could someone send me details of the latest wampes release please ?

6 Morse Code

Software for use in conjunction with, or for facilitating Morse communication.

6.1 GW4PTS Morse trainer.

Author

Alan Cox, GW4PTS, iialan@iifeak.swan.ac.uk

Description

A Morse Code trainer that uses the PC internal speaker

Status

stable, works quite well, unfinished.

System requirements

Linux, any version

Detail

Alan wrote this small program in only an hour. It is quite neat, and allows you to play morse at a range of speeds and frequencies through the PC internal speaker. You can specify the text to be played either from the command line, from a file, or the program is capable of generating random character groups. As it stands you must invoke the program from a Linux Virtual Console, as it relies on certain kernel calls to produce the sound, and these don't work as easily from an XTerm. As it sounds each character it lists the character in verbal form (Di, Dit, Dah etc.) to the screen. Alan is hoping that someone will take the code and enhance it with the features he has listed in the comments at the head of the source file.

Where and How to obtain it.

I've had a large number of responses from people seeking this code, so I've obtained Alan's permission to make it available. You can obtain it from:

(ftp://sunsite.unc.edu/pub/Linux/apps/ham/GW4PTS.morse.tar.gz).

Copyright/Licensing

GNU Public License 2, freely redistributable, no warranty.

Contributed by:

Terry Dawson, VK2KTJ, terryd@extro.ucc.su.oz.au

6.2   morse (aka superiormorse)

Author

Joe Dellinger, Hawaii Institute of Geophysics, University of Hawaii at Manoa, joe@sep.stanford.edu, jdellinger@trc.amoco.com, joe@soest.hawaii.edu

Description

A morse-code practice program for UNIX workstations.

Status

Quite stable

System Requirements

Currently supports X11, Sun4, HP, Indigo, and Linux

Detail

Lots of features and options. Includes a utility for generating random content QSOs, similar to those used in the FCC exams.

Where and How to obtain it:

morse can be obtained from:

```
(ftp://sepftp.stanford.edu/pub/UNIX_utils/morse/morse.tar.gz).
```

Licensing/Copyright

Freely Redistributable

Contributed by:

Brian Suggs, AC6GV, and John Gotts, jgotts@engin.umich.edu

7   AMTOR Software.

Software for use in conjunction with, or for facilitating AMTOR.

8   PACTOR Software.

Software for use in conjunction with, or for facilitating PACTOR.

9   Slow Scan Television Software.

Software for use in conjunction with, or for facilitating Slow Scan Television.

10   Facsimile Software.

Software for use in conjunction with, or for facilitating Facsimile.

11   Design and Construction Software.

Software to assist in the design and construction of amateur radio related things. Antenna, Circuit Board, Filter, and QSL card design packages are all good candidates for this section.

11.1   Software Oscilloscope

Author

Jeff Tranter, Jeff_Tranter@Mitel.COM

Description

Scope is a simple software emulation of an oscilloscope. It graphically displays voltage as a function of time.

Status

ALPHA. First release.

System requirements

Sound card with input capability supported by the kernel sound driver. SVGALIB is used to do the display work.

Detail

Scope uses the `/dev/dsp` device to take audio in from the soundcard and displays it on the screen in a manner similar to an oscilloscope. Jeff claims Scope was written more for amusement value than for any serious purpose.

Where and How to obtain it.

You can obtain source, makefile and man page for Scope from:

`(ftp://sunsite.unc.edu/pub/Linux/apps/circuits/scope-0.1.tar.gz)`

Licensing/Copyright

GNU Public License, Freely redistributable, No warranty.

Contributed by:

Terry Dawson, VK2KTJ

11.2   irsim

Author

Dmitry Teytelman, dim@leland.stanford.edu

Description

An event-driven logic-level simulator for MOS circuits

Status

Version 8.6, production.

System Requirements

X-Windows.

Detail

irsim is an X11 based simulator for MOS circuits. It has two simulation modes, either *switch* where each transistor is modeled as a voltage controlled switch, or *linear* where each transistor is modeled as a resistor in series with a voltage controlled switch, and each node has a capacitance.

Where and How to obtain it.

You can obtain irsim from:

`(ftp://sunsite.unc.edu/pub/Linux/apps/circuits/irsim.tar.z).`

Licensing/Copyright

Freely Redistributable

Contributed by:

Terry Dawson, VK2KTJ

11.3   Spice

Author

University of California, Berkeley, ported by eoahmad@ntuix.ntu.ac.sg

Description

Spice is an analog circuit emulator.

Status

Stable release. Last fortran version produced.

System requirements

Unknown.

Detail

Spice allows you to design and test circuits in a computer modeled environment to see how they will behave without having to touch a soldering iron, or solder.

Where and How to obtain it.

You can obtain version 2g6 of Spice from:

`(ftp://sunsite.unc.edu/pub/Linux/apps/circuits/spice2g6.tar.z)`

Licensing/Copyright

Copyright held by University California, Berkeley. Freely redistributable.

Contributed by:

Terry Dawson, VK2KTJ

11.4   svgafft - Spectrum analyser

Author

Andrew Veliath, drewvel@ayrton.eideti.com

Description

svgafft is a spectrum analyser for Linux.

Status

Alpha software, but usable.

System requirements

Linux supported sound card, svgalib, a 486DX33 or better.

Detail

svgafft uses the `/dev/dsp` device and currently supports 16-bit and 8-bit sample resolution on supported Linux soundcards. It's display is something akin to a high-end spectrum analyzer with falling peaks.

Where and How to obtain it:

Look for `svgafft-0.2.tar.gz` on `sunsite.unc.edu`

Licensing/Copyright

Unknown, check any `README` supplied.

Contributed by:

Terry Dawson, VK2KTJ.

12   Training/Educational Software.

Software to assist in education or training for amateur radio. Morse Code tutorials, technical examination database, Computer Based Training software, and the like are listed here.

13   Miscellaneous Software.

Software that didn't neatly fit into any other category.

13.1   Linux for HAMS CD-ROM

Author

Bruce Perens, bruce@pixar.com

Description

A complete linux distribution on CDROM specifically designed for Amateur Radio operators.

Status

Not yet available.

System requirements.

Linux compatible hardware, some software will obviously require specialized hardware to operate. No additional software should be required.

Detail

A complete Linux distribution specifically catering for Amateur Radio operators. It will include a fully featured Linux installation plus a range of amateur radio specific software such as those listed in this document. Bruce has detail and updated status report available at:

`(http://www.rahul.net/perens/LinuxForHams)`. s

Where and how to obtain it:

It isn't yet available, details will be made available when it is released.

Licensing/Copyright

Unknown.

Contributed by:

Bruce Perens, bruce@pixar.com

13.2 SunClock

Author

John Mackin, john@cs.su.oz.AU

Description

A clock that will show you instantly what parts of the globe are exposed by sunlight and what parts aren't.

Status

Released.

System requirements.

X-Windows.

Detail

sunclock is another of those desktop gadgets that most people think look nice but really don't have a lot of use for. I use sunclock to obtain an at-a-glance indication of the time anywhere in the world. In its iconic form it sits in a small Mercator projection. When maximized it produces the same image but obviously larger with slightly more detail. It also displays the date, local time and UTC. sunclock actually calculates mathematically what parts of globe are sunlit and which aren't, it seems quite accurate, so long as you assume the earth has no atmosphere.

Where and How to obtain it.

I haven't seen any precompiled sunclock binaries for Linux about, so check your nearest *archie* server. sunclock compiled straight out of the box for me.

Licensing/Copyright

Public Domain and may be freely copied as long as the notices at the top of sunclock.c remain intact.

Contributed by:

Terry Dawson, VK2KTJ

13.3 Xearth

Author

Kirk Lauritz Johnson, tuna@cag.lcs.mit.edu, modified by Dimitris Evmorfopoulos, devmorfo@cs.mtu.edu.

Description

A rotating earth for X-windows root window. It has real life shading, and options for geostatic view, and non geostatic view. A prettier and more modern version of *sunclock* but requires a bit more processing power.

Status

released, stable.

System requirements.

X-Windows.

Detail

xearth is much like *sunclock* except that it draws a view of the earth onto your root map in blue and green, as the earth would be viewed from space. You have a number of options in determining the behaviour of the view. You can either have it so that the same part of the earth is displayed, and the sun rotates, so you'll have varying light and shadow on the display, or you can have it shown as if you were travelling with the sun, so the whole of the globe is visible, and the earth rotates. You can specify the latitude/longtitude that will be the centre of the display. *xearth* is also capable of producing *gif* and *ppm* graphics output, so you can generate custom graphics of the globe. When run as your root map, you can adjust the interval of time between updates. On my 486sx25 you notice a small degradation in performance when it is recalculating, but it's not annoying.

Where and How to obtain it.

A precompiled *xearth* binary is available from: **sunsite.unc.edu**, or the source can be obtained from just about any X11/contrib directory. Try **export.lcs.mit.edu** if you can't find it elsewhere.

Licensing/Copyright

Copyright (C) 1989, 1990, 1993 by Kirk Lauritz Johnson. The copyright notice included states that *xearth* is freely redistributable so long as the copyright notice is left intact, and be included in documentation.

Contributed by:

Alan Cox, GW4PTS.

14   How to contribute or update an entry.

I'd like for this list to be as complete and up-to-date as possible. So I'm keen to hear about any developments or products that I don't already know about, or that the entry is obselete or outdated for.

What I'd like as a minimum set of requirement would be something like the following:

Name

The name of the software in question.

Author

Who wrote, or ported the software. An email address, or some other means of contacting them is also essential.

Description

A single line description of what the software does.

Status

An indication of the software's status. Is it still in testing? Is it a production release? Is it still in the design stage?

System requirements

What does the software require to run? Does it require X-Windows? Does it need a soundcard? Does it need a certain version of kernel? Does it need other software to support it?

Detail

I'm not keen on including a large amount of detail on each piece of software as this would consume a lot of time reading and trying to keep up to date. So instead what I'd like to list is what makes this software unique, anything special about it. Perhaps its most outstanding features, that sort of thing.

Where and How to obtain it.

If the software is freely distributable then ftp details would be great. If it is commercial software then the name of the company distributing the software, and an address or telephone number. If it is available only by some other means, say mail order, then details on where and how to obtain it.

Licensing/Copyright

Is the software Copyleft? Copyright? Shareware? Public Domain? Restricted in use in any way?

Don't worry if you don't know all of these details, just send me what you do know and I'll list what I can. I'd rather have an incomplete listing than no listing at all.

Please mail any contributions to:

`terryd@extro.ucc.su.oz.au` or `terry@orac.dn.itg.telecom.com.au`

I'd list a packet radio address too but I'm still not properly operational again yet after moving house.

15 Discussion relating to Amateur Radio and Linux.

There are various places that discussion relating to Amateur Radio and Linux take place. They take place in the `comp.os.linux.*` newsgroups, they also take place on the `HAMS` list on `niksula.hut.fi`. Other places where they are held include the `tcp-group` mailing list at `ucsd.edu` (the home of amateur radio TCP/IP discussions), and I believe there is an 'IRC' channel that sometimes is used to discuss them as well.

To join the Linux **HAMS** channel on the mail list server, send mail to:

```
linux-activists@niksula.hut.fi
```

with the line:

```
X-Mn-Admin: join HAMS
```

at the top of the message body (not the subject line).

To join the `tcp-group` send mail to:

```
listserver@ucsd.edu
```

with the line:

```
subscribe tcp-group
```

in the body of the text.

Note: Please remember that the `tcp-group` is primarily for discussion of the use of advanced protocols, of which TCP/IP is one, in Amateur Radio. *Linux specific questions should not ordinarily go there.*

Part XXII

Linux Hardware Compatibility HOWTO

Copyright FRiC (Boy of Destiny), frac@ksc.au.ac.th
v6969, 14 April 1995
This document lists most of the hardwares supported by Linux and helps you locate any necessary drivers.

Contents

1   Introduction

1.1   Welcome

Welcome to the Linux Hardware Compatibility HOWTO. This document lists most of the hardwares supported by Linux, now if only people would read this first before posting their questions on Usenet.

Subsections titled Others list hardwares with alpha or beta drivers in varying degrees of usability or other drivers that aren't included in standard kernels. Also note that some drivers only exist in alpha kernels, so if you see something listed as supported but isn't in your version of the Linux kernel, upgrade.

The latest version of this document can be found on the usual sites with LDP docs, and on the web at (http://homepage.eznet.net/ frac/hardware.html). Many thanks to Paul Erkkila and E-Znet for the account. No more wacky *.th links.

If you know of any Linux hardware (in)compatibilities not listed here please let me know. Just send mail or find me on IRC. Thanks.

1.2   System architechures

This document only deals with Linux for Intel platforms, for other platforms check the following:

- *Linux/68k* (http://www-users.informatik.rwth-aachen.de/ hn/linux68k.html)

- *Linux/MIPS* (http://www.waldorf-gmbh.de/linux-mips-faq.html)

- *Linux/PowerPC*
  (ftp://sunsite.unc.edu/pub/Linux/docs/ports/Linux-PowerPC-FAQ.gz)

- *Linux for Acorn* (http://www.ph.kcl.ac.uk/ amb/linux.html)

- *MacLinux* (http://www.ibg.uu.se/maclinux/)

2   Computers/Motherboards/BIOS

ISA, VLB, EISA, and PCI buses are all supported.

PS/2 and Microchannel (MCA) is not supported in the standard kernel. Alpha test PS/2 MCA kernels are available but not yet recommended for beginners or serious use.

- *PS/2 MCA kernel* (ftp://invaders.dcrl.nd.edu/pub/misc/)

3   Laptops

Some laptops have unusual video adapters or power management, it is not uncommon to be unable to use the power management features.

PCMCIA drivers currently support Databook TCIC/2, Intel i82365SL, Cirrus PD67xx, and Vadem VG-468 chipsets.

- *APM BIOS* (ftp://ftp.aaug.org.au/pub/unix/linux/apm_bios.0.5.tar.gz)
- *APM* (ftp://tsx-11.mit.edu/pub/linux/packages/laptops/apm)
- *PCMCIA* (ftp://cb-iris.stanford.edu/pub/pcmcia/)
- *non-blinking* *cursor* (ftp://sunsite.unc.edu/pub/Linux/kernel/patches/console/noblink-1.5.tar.gz)
- *power savings* (WD7600 *chipset*) (ftp://sunsite.unc.edu/pub/Linux/system/Misc/low-level/pwrm-1.0.tar.Z)

Running Linux on laptops

- *Compaq Contura Aero* (http://domen.uninett.no/ hta/linux/aero-faq.html)
- *IBM ThinkPad* (http://peipa.essex.ac.uk/html/linux-thinkpad.html)
- *IBM ThinkPad 755Cs* (http://www.cica.fr/ basturk/linux/index.html)
- *other general info* (ftp://tsx-11.mit.edu/pub/linux/packages/laptops/)

4   CPU/FPU

Intel/AMD/Cyrix 386SX/DX/SL/DXL/SLC, 486SX/DX/SL/SX2/DX2/DX4, Pentium. Basically all 386 or better processors will work. Linux has built-in FPU emulation if you don't have a math coprocessor.

A few very early AMD 486DX's may hang in some special situations. All current chips should be okay and getting a chip swap for old CPU's should not be a problem.

ULSI Math*Co series has a bug in the FSAVE and FRSTOR instructions that causes problems with all protected mode operating systems. Some older IIT and Cyrix chips may also have this problem.

There are problems with TLB flushing in UMC U5S chips. Fixed in newer kernels.

- *enable cache on Cyrix processors* (ftp://sunsite.unc.edu/pub/Linux/kernel/patches/CxPatch030.tar.z)
- *Cyrix software cache control* (ftp://sunsite.unc.edu/pub/Linux/kernel/patches/linux.cxpatch)

5   Video cards

Linux will work with all video cards in text mode, VGA cards not listed below probably will still work with mono VGA and/or standard VGA drivers.

If you're looking into buying a cheap video card to run X, keep in mind that accelerated cards (ATI Mach, ET4000/W32p, S3) are MUCH faster than unaccelerated or partially accelerated (Cirrus, WD) cards. S3 801 (ISA), S3 805 (VLB), ET4000/W32p, and ATI Graphics Wonder (Mach32) are good low-end accelerated cards.

32 bit color means 24 bit color aligned on 32 bit boundaries. Modes with 24 bit packed pixels are not supported, so cards that can display 24 bit color in other OS's may not able to do this in X. These cards include Mach32, Cirrus 542x, S3 801/805, ET4000, and others.

5.1   Diamond video cards

Early Diamond cards are not supported by XFree86, but there are ways of getting them to work. Most recent Diamond cards ARE supported by the current release of XFree86.

- *Diamond support for XFree86* (http://www.diamondmm.com/linux.html)
- *Diamond FAQ (for older cards)* (ftp://sunsite.unc.edu/pub/Linux/X11/Diamond.FAQ)

5.2   SVGALIB

- VGA
- EGA
- ATI Mach32
- Cirrus 542x
- OAK OTI-037/67/77/87
- Trident TVGA8900/9000
- Tseng ET3000/ET4000/W32

5.3   XFree86 3.1.1, Accelerated

8 bpp unless noted.

- ATI Mach8
- ATI Mach32 (16 bpp - does not work with all Mach32 cards)
- ATI Mach64 (16/32 bpp)
- Cirrus Logic 5420, 542x/5430 (16 bpp), 5434 (16/32 bpp), 62x5
- IBM 8514/A
- IBM XGA, XGA-II
- IIT AGX-010/014/015/016
- Oak OTI-087
- S3 911, 924, 801, 805, 928, 864, 964, Trio32, Trio64

- see Appendix A for long list of supported cards

- Tseng ET4000/W32/W32i/W32p

- Weitek P9000 (16/32 bpp)

  - Diamond Viper VLB/PCI

  - Orchid P9000

- Western Digital WD90C31/33

5.4   XFree86 3.1.1, Unaccelerated

- ATI VGA Wonder series

- Avance Logic AL2101/2228/2301/2302/2308/2401

- Chips & Technologies 65520/65530/65540/65545

- Cirrus Logic 6420/6440

- Compaq AVGA

- Genoa GVGA

- MCGA (320x200)

- MX MX68000/MX68010

- NCR 77C22, 77C22E, 77C22E+

- Oak OTI-067, OTI-077

- Trident TVGA8800, TVGA8900, TVGA9xxx (not very fast)

- Tseng ET3000, ET4000AX

- VGA (standard VGA, 4 bit, slow)

- Video 7 / Headland Technologies HT216-32

- Western Digital/Paradise PVGA1, WD90C00/10/11/24/30/31/33

5.5   Monochrome

- Hercules mono

- Hyundai HGC-1280

- Sigma LaserView PLUS

- VGA mono

5.6   Others

- *EGA* (ftp://ftp.funet.fi/pub/OS/Linux/BETA/Xega/)

5.7   Works in progress

- Compaq QVision

- Number Nine Imagine 128

No, I do not know when support for these cards will be finished, please don't ask me. If you want support for these cards now get Accelerated-X.

5.8   Commercial X servers

Commercial X servers provide support for cards not supported by XFree86, and might give better performances for cards that are supported by XFree86. Only cards not supported by XFree86 are listed here. Contact the vendors directly or check the Commercial HOWTO for more info.

5.8.1   Accelerated-X

- Compaq QVision 2000

- Matrox MGA-I, MGA-II

- Number Nine I-128

$199 from X Inside, Inc. <info@xinside.com>. Accel-X 1.1 is available right now for a promotional price of $99.50, with free upgrade to 1.2.

16 bit support for ATI Mach32, ATI Mach 64, Cirrus 542x/543x, IBM XGA, IIT AGX-014/015, Matrox MGA, #9 I-128, Oak OTI-077/087, S3 cards, ET4000, ET4000/W32 series, Weitek P9000, WD90C30/31.

32 bit support for ATI Mach64, Cirrus 5434, Matrox MGA, #9 I-128, S3-928/864/964, ET4000/W32p, Weitek P9000.

Accel-X 1.2 will support 24 bit packed pixel modes and have support for many more video cards.

5.8.2   Metro-X

$150 from Metro Link <sales@metrolink.com>. Metro-X 2.3 is now available for special introductory price of $99.00.

Metro-X has similar hardware support as Accel-X, however I don't have much more information as I can't seem to view the PostScript files they sent me. Mail them directly for more info.

6   Controllers (hard drive)

Linux will work with standard IDE, MFM and RLL controllers. When using MFM/RLL controllers it is important to use ext2fs and the bad block checking options when formatting the disk.

Enhanced IDE (EIDE) interfaces are supported. With up to two IDE interfaces and up to four hard drives and/or CD-ROM drives. (1.1.76)

ESDI controllers that emulate the ST-506 (that is MFM/RLL/IDE) interface will also work. The bad block checking comment also applies to these controllers.

Generic 8 bit XT controllers also work.

7 Controllers (SCSI)

It is important to pick a SCSI controller carefully. Many cheap ISA SCSI controllers are designed to drive CD-ROM's rather than anything else. Such low end SCSI controllers are no better than IDE. See the SCSI HOWTO and look at UNIX performance figures before buying a SCSI card.

7.1 Supported

- AMI Fast Disk VLB/EISA (works with BusLogic drivers)
- Adaptec AVA-1505/1515 (ISA) (use 152x drivers)
- Adaptec AHA-1510/152x (ISA)
- Adaptec AHA-154x (ISA) (all models)
- Adaptec AHA-174x (EISA) (in enhanced mode)
- Adaptec AHA-274x (EISA) / 284x (VLB) (AIC-7770)
- Always IN2000
- BusLogic (all models)
- DPT Smartcache (EATA) (ISA/EISA)
- DTC 329x (EISA) (Adaptec 154x compatible)
- Future Domain TMC-16x0, TMC-3260 (PCI)
- Future Domain TMC-8xx, TMC-950
- NCR 53c7x0, 53c8x0 (PCI)
- Pro Audio Spectrum 16 SCSI (ISA)
- Qlogic / Control Concepts SCSI/IDE (FAS408) - ISA/VLB/PCMCIA, does not work with PCI (different chipset). PCMCIA cards must boot DOS to init card
- Seagate ST-01/ST-02 (ISA)
- SoundBlaster 16 SCSI-2 (Adaptec 152x) (ISA)
- Trantor T128/T128F/T228 (ISA)
- UltraStor 14F (ISA), 24F (EISA), 34F (VLB)
- Western Digital WD7000 SCSI

7.2 Others

- *Adaptec ACB-40xx SCSI-MFM/RLL bridgeboard* (ftp://sunsite.unc.edu/pub/Linux/kernel/patches/scsi/adaptec-40XX.tar.gz)
- *Adaptec AHA-2940 (PCI) (AIC-7870)* (ftp://remus.nrl.navy.mil/pub/Linux/)
- *Acculogic ISApport / MV Premium 3D SCSI (NCR 53c406a)* (ftp://sunsite.unc.edu/pub/Linux/kernel/patches/scsi/ncr53c406-0.10.patch.gz)
- *Always AL-500* (ftp://sunsite.unc.edu/pub/Linux/kernel/patches/scsi/al500_0.1.tar.gz)

- *Iomega*   *PC2/2B*
  (`ftp://sunsite.unc.edu/pub/Linux/kernel/patches/scsi/iomega_pc2-1.1.x.tar.gz`)

- *New*   *Media*   *Bus*   *Toaster*   *PCMCIA*
  (`ftp://lamont.ldeo.columbia.edu/pub/linux/bus_toaster-1.5.tgz`)

- *Ricoh GSI-8* (`ftp://tsx-11.mit.edu/pub/linux/ALPHA/scsi/gsi8.tar.gz`)

- *Trantor*   *T130B*   *(NCR*   *53c400)*
  (`ftp://sunsite.unc.edu/pub/Linux/kernel/patches/scsi/53c400.tar.gz`)

7.3 Unsupported

- Parallel port SCSI adapters
- Non Adaptec compatible DTC boards (327x, 328x)

8 Controllers (I/O)

Any standard serial/parallel/joystick/IDE combo cards. Linux supports 8250, 16450, 16550, and 16550A UART's.

See National Semiconductor's "Application Note AN-493" by Martin S. Michael. Section 5.0 describes in detail the differences between the NS16550 and NS16550A. Briefly, the NS16550 had bugs in the FIFO circuits, but the NS16550A (and later) chips fixed those. However, there were very few NS16550's produced by National, long ago, so these should be very rare. And many of the "16550" parts in actual modern boards are from the many manufacturers of compatible parts, which may not use the National "A" suffix. Also, some multiport boards will use 16552 or 16554 or various other multiport or multifunction chips from National or other suppliers (generally in a dense package soldered to the board, not a 40 pin DIP). Mostly, don't worry about it unless you encounter a very old 40 pin DIP National "NS16550" (no A) chip loose or in an old board, in which case treat it as a 16450 (no FIFO) rather than a 16550A. - Zhahai Stewart <zstewart@hisys.com>

9 Controllers (multiport)

9.1 Supported

- AST FourPort and clones
- Accent Async-4
- Bell Technologies HUB6
- Boca BB-1004, 1008 (4, 8 port) - no DTR, DSR, and CD
- Boca BB-2016 (16 port)
- Boca IO/AT66 (6 port)
- Boca IO 2by4 (4S/2P) - works with modems, but uses 5 IRQ's
- Cyclades Cyclom-8Y/16Y (8, 16 port)
- PC-COMM 4-port
- STB 4-COM
- Twincom ACI/550
- Usenet Serial Board II

9.2 Others

- *Comtrol RocketPort (8/16/32 port)* (ftp://tsx-11.mit.edu/pub/linux/packages/comtrol/)

- DigiBoard COM/Xi - contact Simon Park <si@wimpol.demon.co.uk>

- *DigiBoard PC/Xe (ISA) and PC/Xi (EISA)* (ftp://ftp.skypoint.com/pub/linux/digiboard/)

- *Specialix   SIO/XIO   (modular,   4   to   32   ports)* (ftp://sunsite.unc.edu/pub/Linux/kernel/patches/serial/sidrv0_5.taz)

- *Stallion   Technologies   EasyIO   /   EasyConnection   8/32* (ftp://sunsite.unc.edu/pub/Linux/kernel/patches/serial/stallion-0.1.5.tar.gz)

10   Network adapters

Ethernet adapters vary greatly in performance. In general the newer the design the better. Some very old cards like the 3C501 are only useful because they can be found in junk heaps for $5 a time. Be careful with clones, not all are good clones and bad clones often cause erratic lockups under Linux.

10.1   Supported

10.1.1   ISA

- 3Com 3C501 - "avoid like the plague"

- 3Com 3C503, 3C505, 3C507, 3C509 (ISA) / 3C579 (EISA)

- AMD LANCE (79C960) / PCnet-ISA/PCI (AT1500, HP J2405A, NE1500/NE2100)

- AT&T GIS WaveLAN

- Allied Telesis AT1700

- Cabletron E21xx

- DEC DEPCA and EtherWORKS

- HP PCLAN (27245 and 27xxx series)

- HP PCLAN PLUS (27247B and 27252A)

- Intel EtherExpress

- NE2000/NE1000 (be careful with clones)

- Racal-Interlan NI5210 (i82586 Ethernet chip)

- Racal-Interlan NI6510 (am7990 lance chip) - doesn't work with more than 16 megs RAM

- PureData PDUC8028, PDI8023

- SMC Ultra

- Schneider & Koch G16

- Western Digital WD80x3

10.1.2 EISA and onboard controllers

- Ansel Communications AC3200 EISA

- Apricot Xen-II

- Zenith Z-Note / IBM ThinkPad 300 built-in adapter

10.1.3 Pocket and portable adapters

- AT-Lan-Tec/RealTek parallel port adapter

- D-Link DE600/DE620 parallel port adapter

10.1.4 Slotless

- SLIP/CSLIP/PPP (serial port)

- PLIP (parallel port, using "LapLink cable" or bi-directional cable)

10.1.5 ARCnet

- works with all ARCnet cards

10.2 Others

10.2.1 ISDN

- *Diehl   SCOM   card*
  (ftp://sunsite.unc.edu/pub/Linux/kernel/patches/network/isdndrv-0.1.1.tar.gz)

- Sonix PC Volante only in asynchronous mode, not useful for some applications

- Teles ISDN card

10.2.2 Amateur radio cards

- Ottawa PI2

- Most generic 8530 based HDLC boards

No support for the PMP/Baycom board

10.2.3 *PCMCIA cards* (ftp://cb-iris.stanford.edu/pub/pcmcia/)

- 3Com 3C589

- Accton EN2212 EtherCard

- D-Link DE650

- IBM Credit Card Adapter

- IC-Card

- Kingston KNE-PCM/M

- LANEED Ethernet
- Linksys EthernetCard
- Network General "Sniffer"
- Novell NE4100
- Thomas-Conrad Ethernet
- possibly more

10.2.4 *Token Ring* (`ftp://ftp.cs.kuleuven.ac.be/pub/unix/linux/`)

10.3 Unsupported

- Xircom adapters are not supported.

11 Sound cards

11.1 Supported

- 6850 UART MIDI
- ATI Stereo F/X (SB compatible)
- Adlib
- ECHO-PSS (Orchid SW32, Cardinal DSP16, etc)
- Ensoniq SoundScape (boot DOS to init card)
- Gravis Ultrasound
- Gravis Ultrasound 16-bit sampling daughterboard
- Gravis Ultrasound MAX
- Logitech SoundMan Games (SBPro, 44kHz stereo support)
- Logitech SoundMan Wave (SBPro/MPU-401) (OPL4)
- Logitech SoundMan 16 (PAS-16 compatible)
- Microsoft Sound System (AD1848)
- MPU-401 MIDI
- Media Vision Premium 3D (Jazz16) (SBPro compatible)
- Media Vision Pro Sonic 16 (Jazz)
- Media Vision Pro Audio Spectrum 16
- SoundBlaster
- SoundBlaster Pro
- SoundBlaster 16/ASP/MCD/SCSI-2
- Sound Galaxy NX Pro
- ThunderBoard (SB compatible)
- WaveBlaster (and other SB16 daughterboards)

11.2 Others

- *MPU-401   MIDI   (intelligent   mode)*
  (ftp://sunsite.unc.edu/pub/Linux/kernel/sound/mpu401.0.11a.tar.gz)

- *PC   speaker   /   Parallel   port   DAC*
  (ftp://ftp.informatik.hu-berlin.de/pub/os/linux/hu-sound/)

11.3 Unsupported

The ASP chip on SoundBlaster 16 series and AWE32 is not supported. AWE32's special features (MIDI, effects) are not supported. They will probably never be supported.

SoundBlaster 16 with DSP 4.11's have a hardware bug that causes hung/stuck notes when you use a WaveBlaster or other MIDI devices attached to it. There is no known fix.

12 Hard drives

All hard drives should work if the controller is supported.

(From the SCSI HOWTO) All direct access SCSI devices with a block size of 256, 512, or 1024 bytes should work. Other block sizes will not work (Note that this can often be fixed by changing the block and/or sector sizes using the MODE SELECT SCSI command).

Large IDE (EIDE) drives work fine with newer kernels. The boot partition must lie in the first 1024 cylinders due to PC BIOS limitations.

Some Conner CFP1060S drives may have problems with Linux and ext2fs. The symptoms are inode errors during e2fsck and corrupt file systems. Conner has released a bugfix for this problem, contact Conner at 1-800-4CONNER (US) or +44-1294-315333 (Europe). Have the microcode version (found on the drive label, 9WA1.6x) handy when you call.

Certain Micropolis drives have problems with Adaptec and BusLogic cards, contact the manufacturers for firmware upgrades if you suspect problems.

13 Tape drives

13.1 Supported

- SCSI tape drives

(From the SCSI HOWTO) Drives using both fixed and variable length blocks smaller than the driver buffer length (set to 32k in the distribution sources) are supported. Virtually all drives should work. (Send mail if you know of any incompatible drives.)

- QIC-02

- *QIC-117, QIC-40/80 drives (Ftape)* (ftp://sunsite.unc.edu/pub/Linux/kernel/tapes)

Most tape drives using the floppy controller should work. Check the Ftape HOWTO for details. Colorado FC-10 is also supported.

13.2 Unsupported

- Linux does not work with Emerald and Tecmar QIC-02 tape controller cards. - Chris Ulrich <insom@math.ucr.edu>

- Drives that connect to the parallel port (eg: Colorado Trakker)

- Some high speed tape controllers (Colorado TC-15 / FC-20)

- Irwin AX250L / Accutrak 250 (not QIC-80)

- IBM Internal Tape Backup Unit (not QIC-80)

- COREtape Light

14   CD-ROM drives

14.1 Supported

(From the CD-ROM HOWTO) Any SCSI CD-ROM drive with a block size of 512 or 2048 bytes should work under Linux; this includes the vast majority of CD-ROM drives on the market.

- Aztech CDA268, Orchid CDS-3110, Okano/Wearnes CDD-110

- EIDE (ATAPI) CD-ROM drives

- Matsushita/Panasonic, Kotobuki (SBPCD)

- Mitsumi

- Sony CDU31A/CDU33A

- Sony CDU-535/CDU-531

14.2 Others

- *GoldStar R420* (ftp://ftp.gwdg.de/pub/linux/cdrom/drivers/goldstar/)

- *LMS/Philips*   *CM*   *205/225/202*
  (ftp://sunsite.unc.edu/pub/Linux/kernel/patches/cdrom/lmscd0.3d.tar.gz)

- *LMS*   *Philips*   *CM*   *206*
  (ftp://sunsite.unc.edu/pub/Linux/kernel/patches/cdrom/cm206.0.22b.tar.gz)

- *Mitsumi* (ftp://ftp.gwdg.de/pub/linux/cdrom/drivers/mitsumi/)

- *NEC*   *CDR-35D*   *(old)*
  (ftp://sunsite.unc.edu/pub/Linux/kernel/patches/cdrom/linux-neccdr35d.patch)

14.3 Notes

PhotoCD (XA) is supported.

All CD-ROM drives should work similarly for reading data. There are various compatibility problems with audio CD playing utilities. (Especially with some NEC drives.) Some alpha drivers may not have audio support yet.

Early (single speed) NEC CD-ROM drives may have trouble with currently available SCSI controllers.

15   Removable drives

All SCSI drives should work if the controller is supported, including optical drives, WORM, CD-R, floptical, and others. Bernoulli and SyQuest drives work fine.

Linux supports both 512 and 1024 bytes/sector disks. There's a problem with msdos filesystems on 1024 bytes/sector disks on some recent kernels (fixed in 1.1.75).

16   Mice

16.1   Supported

- Microsoft serial mouse

- Mouse Systems serial mouse

- Logitech Mouseman serial mouse

- Logitech serial mouse

- ATI XL Inport busmouse

- C&T 82C710 (QuickPort) (Toshiba, TI Travelmate)

- Microsoft busmouse

- Logitech busmouse

- PS/2 (auxiliary device) mouse

16.2   Others

- *Sejin*   *J-mouse*
  (`ftp://sunsite.unc.edu/pub/Linux/kernel/patches/console/jmouse.1.1.70-jmouse.tar.gz`)
- *MultiMouse   -   use   multiple   mouse   devices   as   single   mouse*
  (`ftp://sunsite.unc.edu/pub/Linux/system/Misc/MultiMouse-1.0.tgz`)

16.3   Notes

Newer Logitech mice (except the Mouseman) use the Microsoft protocol and all three buttons do work. Eventhough Microsoft's mice have only two buttons, the protocol allows three buttons.

The mouse port on the ATI Graphics Ultra and Ultra Pro use the Logitech busmouse protocol. (See the Busmouse HOWTO for details.)

17   Modems

All internal modems or external modems connected to the serial port.

A small number of modems come with DOS software that downloads the control program at runtime. These can normally be used by loading the program under DOS and doing a warm boot. Such modems are probably best avoided as you won't be able to use them with non PC hardware in the future.

PCMCIA modems should work with the PCMCIA drivers.

Fax modems need appropriated software to operate.

- *Digicom   Connection   96+/14.4+   -   DSP   code   downloading   program* (`ftp://sunsite.unc.edu/pub/Linux/system/Serial/smdl-linux.1.02.tar.gz`)

- *ZyXEL   U-1496   series   -   ZyXEL   1.4,   modem/fax/voice   control   program* (`ftp://sunsite.unc.edu/pub/Linux/system/Serial/ZyXEL-1.4.tar.gz`)

18   Printers/Plotters

All printers and plotters connected to the parallel or serial port should work.

- *HP   LaserJet   4   series   -   free-lj4,   printing   modes   control   program* (`ftp://sunsite.unc.edu/pub/Linux/system/Printing/free-lj4-1.1p1.tar.gz`)

- *BiTronics   parallel   port   interface* (`ftp://sunsite.unc.edu/pub/Linux/kernel/misc/bt-ALPHA-0.0.1.tar.gz`)

18.1   Ghostscript

Many Linux programs output PostScript files. Non-PostScript printers can emulate PostScript Level 2 using Ghostscript.

- *Ghostscript* (`ftp://ftp.cs.wisc.edu/pub/ghost/aladdin/`)

18.1.1   Ghostscript supported printers

- Apple Imagewriter
- C. Itoh M8510
- Canon BubbleJet BJ10e, BJ200
- Canon LBP-8II, LIPS III
- DEC LA50/70/75/75plus
- DEC LN03, LJ250
- Epson 9 pin, 24 pin, LQ series, Stylus, AP3250
- HP 2563B
- HP DesignJet 650C
- HP DeskJet/Plus/500
- HP DeskJet 500C/520C/550C/1200C color
- HP LaserJet/Plus/II/III/4
- HP PaintJet/XL/XL300 color
- IBM Jetprinter color
- IBM Proprinter
- Imagen ImPress
- Mitsubishi CP50 color
- NEC P6/P6+/P60

- Okidata MicroLine 182

- Ricoh 4081

- SPARCprinter

- StarJet 48 inkjet printer

- Tektronix 4693d color 2/4/8 bit

- Tektronix 4695/4696 inkjet plotter

- Xerox XES printers (2700, 3700, 4045, etc.)

18.1.2   Others

- *Canon BJC600 and Epson ESC/P color printers* (`ftp://petole.imag.fr/pub/postscript/`)

19   Scanners

- *A4 Tech AC 4096* (`ftp://ftp.informatik.hu-berlin.de/pub/local/linux/ac4096.tgz`)

- Fujitsu SCSI-2 scanners, contact Dr. G.W. Wettstein <greg%wind.UUCP@plains.nodak.edu>

- *Genius*   *GS-B105G*
  (`ftp://tsx-11.mit.edu/pub/linux/ALPHA/scanner/gs105-0.0.1.tar.gz`)

- *Genius*   *GeniScan*   *GS4500*   *handheld*   *scanner*
  (`ftp://tsx-11.mit.edu/pub/linux/ALPHA/scanner/gs4500-1.3.tar.gz`)

- *HP ScanJet, ScanJet Plus* (`ftp://ftp.ctrl-c.liu.se/unix/linux/wingel/`)

- *HP*   *ScanJet*   *II*   *series*   *SCSI*
  (`ftp://sunsite.unc.edu/pub/Linux/apps/graphics/hpscanpbm.c.gz`)

- *Logitech*   *Scanman*   *32*   */*   *256*
  (`ftp://tsx-11.mit.edu/pub/linux/ALPHA/scanner/logiscan-0.0.2.tar.gz`)

- *Mustek*   *M105*   *handheld*   *scanner*   *with*   *GI1904*   *interface*
  (`ftp://tsx-11.mit.edu/pub/linux/ALPHA/scanner/scan-driver-0.1.8.tar.gz`)

20   Other hardwares

20.1   VESA Power Savings Protocol (DPMS) monitors

20.2   Joysticks

- *Joysticks*
  (`ftp://sunsite.unc.edu/pub/Linux/kernel/patches/console/joystick-0.7.tgz`)

20.3 Video capture boards

- *FAST   Screen   Machine   II*
  (ftp://sunsite.unc.edu/pub/Linux/apps/video/ScreenMachineII_1.1.tgz)

- *ProMovie Studio* (ftp://sunsite.unc.edu/pub/Linux/apps/video/PMS-grabber.tgz)

- *VideoBlaster,   Rombo   Media   Pro+*
  (ftp://sunsite.unc.edu/pub/Linux/apps/video/vid_src.gz)

- *WinVision   video   capture   card*
  (ftp://sunsite.unc.edu/pub/Linux/apps/video/fgrabber-1.0.tgz)

20.4 UPS

- various UPS's are supported, read the UPS HOWTO

20.5 Miscellaneous

- *Mattel Powerglove* (ftp://sunsite.unc.edu/pub/Linux/apps/linux-powerglove.tgz)

- *HP   IEEE-488   (HP-IB)   interface*
  (ftp://beaver.chemie.fu-berlin.de/pub/linux/IEEE488/)

21 Related sources of information

- *Cameron Spitzer's hardware FAQ archive* (ftp://rahul.net/pub/cameron/PC-info/)

- *Computer-related   WWW/FTP/Newsgroup   resources*
  (http://www-bprc.mps.ohio-state.edu/cgi-bin/hpp/list.html)

- *Computer   Hardware   and   Software   Vendor   Phone   Numbers*
  (http://mtmis1.mis.semi.harris.com/comp_ph1.html)

- *System Optimization Information* (http://www.dfw.net/ sdw/)

22 Acknowledgments

Thanks to all the authors and contributors of other HOWTO's, many things here are shamelessly stolen from their works; to Zane Healy and Ed Carp, the original authors of this list; and to everyone else who sent in updates and feedbacks. Special thanks to Eric Boerner and lilo (the person, not the program) for the sanity checks. And thanks to Dan Quinlan for the original SGML conversion.

23   Appendix A. S3 cards supported by XFree86 3.1.1.

CHIPSET	RAMDAC	CLOCKCHIP	BPP	CARD
801/805	AT&T	20C490	16	Actix GE 32
				Orchid Fahrenheit 1280+
801/805	AT&T	20C490	16	STB PowerGraph X.24
805	S3 GENDAC		16	Miro 10SD VLB/PCI
				SPEA Mirage VLB
805	SS2410	ICD2061A	8	Diamond Stealth 24 VLB
928	AT&T 20C490		16	Actix Ultra
928	Sierra SC15025	ICD2061A	32	ELSA Winner 1000 ISA/VLB/EISA
928	Bt485	ICD2061A	32	STB Pegasus VL
928	Bt485	SC11412	16	SPEA Mercury VLB
928	Bt485	ICD2061A	32	#9 GXE Level 10/11/12
928	Ti3020	ICD2061A	32	#9 GXE Level 14/16
864	AT&T 20C498	ICS2494	32	Miro 20SD (BIOS 1.x)
864	AT&T 20C498/	ICD2061A/	32	ELSA Winner 1000 PRO VLB/PCI
	STG1700	ICS9161		MIRO 20SD (BIOS 2.x)
864	STG1700	ICD2061A	32?	Actix GE 64 VLB
864	AT&T 20C498/	ICS2595	16	SPEA Mirage P64 DRAM (BIOS 3.x)
	AT&T 21C498			
864	S3 86C716 SDAC		32	ELSA Winner 1000 PRO
				Miro 20SD (BIOS 3.x)
				SPEA Mirage P64 DRAM (BIOS 4.x)
				Diamond Stealth 64 DRAM
864	ICS5342	ICS5342	32	Diamond Stealth 64 DRAM (some)
864	AT&T 20C490	ICD2061A	32	#9 GXE64
864	AT&T 20C498-13	ICD2061A	32	#9 GXE64 PCI
964	AT&T 20C505	ICD2061A	32	Miro Crystal 20SV PCI
964	Bt485	ICD2061A	32	Diamond Stealth 64
964	Bt9485	ICS9161A	32	SPEA Mercury 64
964	Ti3020	ICD2061A	8	ELSA Winner 2000 PRO PCI
964	Ti3025	Ti3025	32	#9 GXE64 Pro VLB/PCI
				Miro Crystal 40SV
764	(Trio64)		32	SPEA Mirage P64 (BIOS 5.x)
				Diamond Stealth 64 DRAM
				#9 GXE64 Trio64
				STB PowerGraph 64

Part XXIII

The Linux Installation HOWTO

Copyright by Matt Welsh, `mdw@sunsite.unc.edu`
v3.3, 11 December 1994
This document describes how to obtain and install the Linux software, focusing on the popular Slackware distribution (version 2.0.1). It is the first document which a new Linux user should read to get started.

Contents

1   Introduction

Linux is a freely-distributable implementation of UNIX for 80386 and 80486 machines. It supports a wide range of software, including X Windows, Emacs, TCP/IP networking (including SLIP), the works. This document assumes that you have heard of and know about Linux, and just want to sit down and install it.

1.1   Other sources of information

If you have never heard of Linux before, there are several sources of basic information about the system. One is the Linux Frequently Asked Questions list (FAQ), available from sunsite.unc.edu:/pub/Linux/docs/FAQ. This document contains many common questions (and answers!) about Linux—it is a "must read" for new users.

In the directory /pub/Linux/docs on sunsite.unc.edu you'll find a number of other documents about Linux, including the Linux INFO-SHEET and META-FAQ, both of which you should read. Also take a look at the USENET newsgroups comp.os.linux.help and comp.os.linux.announce.

Another source of online Linux documentation is the Linux HOWTO archive, on sunsite.unc.edu:/pub/Linux/docs/HOWTO. The file HOWTO-INDEX in that directory explains what Linux HOWTOs are available.

The Linux Documentation Project is writing a set of manuals and books about Linux, all of which are freely distributable on the net. The directory /pub/Linux/docs/LDP on sunsite.unc.edu contains the current set of LDP manuals.

The book "Linux Installation and Getting Started" is a complete guide to getting and installing Linux, as well as how to use the system once you've installed it. It contains a complete tutorial to using and running the system, and much more information than is contained here. This HOWTO is simply a condensation of some of the most important information in that book. You can get "Linux Installation and Getting Started" from sunsite.unc.edu in /pub/Linux/docs/LDP/install-guide. The README file there describes how you can order a printed copy of the book (about 180 pages).

1.2   New versions of this document

New versions of the Linux Installation HOWTO will be periodically posted to comp.os.linux.announce, comp.os.linux.help, and news.answers. They will also be uploaded to various Linux FTP sites, including sunsite.unc.edu:/pub/Linux/docs/HOWTO.

1.3   Feedback

If you have questions or comments about this document, please feel free to mail Matt Welsh, at mdw@sunsite.unc.edu. I welcome any suggestions, criticism, or postcards. If you find a mistake with this document, please let me know so I can correct it in the next version. Thanks.

2   Hardware Requirements

What kind of system is needed to run Linux? This is a good question; the actual hardware requirements for the system change periodically. The Linux Hardware-HOWTO gives a (more or less) complete listing of hardware supported by Linux. The Linux INFO-SHEET provides another list.

At the very least, a hardware configuration that looks like the following is required:

Any ISA, EISA or VESA Local Bus 80386, 80486, or Pentium system will do. Currently, the MicroChannel (MCA) architecture (found on IBM PS/2 machines) is not supported. Many PCI bus systems are supported (see the Linux PCI HOWTO for details). Any CPU from the 386SX to the Pentium will work. You do not need a math coprocessor, although it is nice to have one.

You need at least 4 megabytes of memory in your machine. Technically, Linux will run with only 2 megs, but most installations and software require 4. The more memory you have, the happier you'll be. I suggest 8 or 16 megabytes if you're planning to use X-Windows.

Of course, you'll need a hard drive and an AT-standard drive controller. All MFM, RLL, and IDE drives and controllers should work. Many SCSI drives and adaptors are supported as well; the Linux SCSI-HOWTO contains more information on SCSI.

Linux can actually run on a single 5.25″ HD floppy, but that's only useful for installation and maintenance.

Free space on your hard drive is needed as well. The amount of space needed depends on how much software you plan to install. Most installations require somewhere in the ballpark of 40 to 80 megs. This includes space for the software, swap space (used as virtual RAM on your machine), and free space for users, and so on.

It's conceivable that you could run a minimal Linux system in 10 megs or less, and it's conceivable that you could use well over 100 megs or more for all of your Linux software. The amount varies greatly depending on the amount of software you install and how much space you require. More about this later.

Linux will co-exist with other operating systems, such as MS-DOS, Microsoft Windows, or OS/2, on your hard drive. (In fact you can even access MS-DOS files and run some MS-DOS programs from Linux.) In other words, when partitioning your drive for Linux, MS-DOS or OS/2 live on their own partitions, and Linux exists on its own. We'll go into more detail later.

You do NOT need to be running MS-DOS, OS/2, or any other operating system to use Linux. Linux is a completely different, stand-alone operating system and does not rely on other OS's for installation and use.

You also need a Hercules, CGA, EGA, VGA, or Super VGA video card and monitor. In general, if your video card and monitor work under MS-DOS then it should work under Linux. However, if you wish to run X Windows, there are other restrictions on the supported video hardware. The Linux XFree86-HOWTO contains more information about running X and its requirements.

In all, the minimal setup for Linux is not much more than is required for most MS-DOS or MS Windows systems sold today. If you have a 386 or 486 with at least 4 megs of RAM, then you'll be happy running Linux. Linux does not require huge amounts of diskspace, memory, or processor speed. I (used to) run Linux on a 386/16 MHz (the slowest machine you can get) with 4 megs of RAM, and was quite happy. The more you want to do, the more memory (and faster processor) you'll need. In my experience a 486 with 16 megabytes of RAM running Linux outdoes several models of workstation.

3 Getting Linux

In this section we'll cover how to obtain the Linux software.

3.1 Linux Distributions

Before you can install Linux, you need to decide on one of the "distributions" of Linux which are available. There is no single, standard release of the Linux software—there are many such releases. Each release has its own documentation and installation instructions.

Linux distributions are available both via anonymous FTP and via mail order on diskette, tape, and CD-ROM. The Linux Distribution HOWTO (see sunsite.unc.edu in the file /pub/Linux/docs/HOWTO/Distribution-HOWTO) includes a list of many Linux distributions available via FTP and mail order.

The release of Linux covered in this HOWTO is the Slackware distribution, maintained by Patrick J. Volkerding (volkerdi@mhd1.moorhead.msus.edu). It is one of the most popular distributions available; it is very up-to-date and includes a good amount of software including X-Windows, TeX, and others. The

Slackware distribution consists of a number of "disk sets", each one containing a particular type of software (for example, the d disk set contains development tools such as the gcc compiler, and so forth). You can elect to install whatever disk sets you like, and can easily install new ones later.

Slackware is also easy to install; it is *very* self-explanatory. (So self-explanatory, in fact, that this HOWTO may not be necessary.)

The version of Slackware described here is 2.0.0, of 25 June 1994. Installation of later versions of Slackware should be very similar to the information given here.

Information on other releases can be found in the Linux Installation and Getting Started manual from the LDP. You can also find other releases of Linux on various FTP sites, including sunsite.unc.edu:/pub/Linux/distributions See the Distribution-HOWTO (mentioned above) for details.

The instructions here should be general enough to be applicable to releases other than Slackware. I hate to be biased towards a single release, but I don't have time to keep up with them all! And Slackware appears to have what most Linux users are looking for.

3.2 Slackware Space Requirements

Unfortunately, Slackware does not maintain a complete list of diskspace requirements for each disk set. You need at least 7 megabytes to install just the A series of disks; a very rough estimate of the required diskspace would be 2 or 2.5 megabytes per disk.

The following disk sets are available:

A

> The base system. Enough to get up and running and have elvis and comm programs available. Based around the 1.0.9 Linux kernel, and the new filesystem standard (FSSTND).
>
> These disks are known to fit on 1.2M disks, although the rest of Slackware won't. If you have only a 1.2M floppy, you can still install the base system, download other disks you want and install them from your hard drive.

AP

> Various applications and add ons, such as the manual pages, groff, ispell (GNU and international versions), term, joe, jove, ghostscript, sc, bc, and the quota patches.

D

> Program development. GCC/G++/Objective C 2.5.8, make (GNU and BSD), byacc and GNU bison, flex, the 4.5.26 C libraries, gdb, kernel source for 1.0.9, SVGAlib, ncurses, clisp, f2c, p2c, m4, perl, rcs.

E

> GNU Emacs 19.25.

F

> A collection of FAQs and other documentation.

I

> Info pages for GNU software. Documentation for various programs readable by info or Emacs.

N

> Networking. TCP/IP, UUCP, mailx, dip, deliver, elm, pine, smail, cnews, nn, tin, trn.

OOP

> Object Oriented Programming. GNU Smalltalk 1.1.1, and the Smalltalk Interface to X (STIX).

Q

Alpha kernel source and images (currently contains Linux 1.1.18).

TCL

Tcl, Tk, TclX, blt, itcl.

Y

Games. The BSD games collection, and Tetris for terminals.

X

The base XFree86 2.1.1 system, with `libXpm`, `fvwm` 1.20, and `xlock` added.

XAP

X applications: X11 `ghostscript`, `libgr13`, `seyon`, `workman`, `xfilemanager`, `xv` 3.01, GNU `chess` and `xboard`, `xfm` 1.2, `ghostview`, and various X games.

XD

X11 program development. X11 libraries, server linkkit, PEX support.

XV

XView 3.2 release 5. XView libraries, and the Open Look virtual and non-virtual window managers.

IV

Interviews libraries, include files, and the `doc` and `idraw` apps. These run unreasonably slow on my machine, but they might still be worth looking at.

OI

ParcPlace's Object Builder 2.0 and Object Interface Library 4.0, generously made available for Linux developers according to the terms in the "copying" notice found in these directories. Note that these only work with `libc`-4.4.4, but a new version may be released once `gcc` 2.5.9 is available.

T

The TeX and LaTeX2e text formatting systems.

You must get the "a" disk set; the rest are optional. I suggest at least installing the a, ap, and d sets, as well as the x set if you plan to run X Windows.

3.3 Getting Slackware via Mail Order

Slackware is available for free from the Internet, as well as via mail order (if you don't have Internet access, or don't want to take the time to download it yourself). The next section describes how to download Slackware from the Internet.

The various mail order distributors for Slackware (and other Linux distributions) are listed in the *Linux Distribution HOWTO*, from `sunsite.unc.edu` in the directory `/pub/Linux/docs/HOWTO`.

3.4 Getting Slackware from the Internet

The Slackware release of Linux may be found on any number of FTP sites worldwide. The Linux META-FAQ lists several of the Linux FTP sites; we suggest that you try to find the software on the FTP site nearest you, to reduce net traffic. However, two of the major Linux FTP sites are `sunsite.unc.edu` and `tsx-11.mit.edu`.

The Slackware release may be found on the following FTP sites:

- `sunsite.unc.edu:/pub/Linux/distributions/slackware`

- tsx-11.mit.edu:/pub/linux/packages/slackware

- ftp.cdrom.com:/pub/linux/slackware

ftp.cdrom.com is Slackware's home site.

3.4.1   Downloading the files

You need to download the following files from the FTP sites listed above. Make sure that you use binary mode when FTPing them!

- The various README files, as well as SLACKWARE_FAQ. Be sure to read these files before attempting to install the software, to get any updates or changes to this document.

- A bootdisk image. This is a file that you will write to a floppy to create the Slackware boot disk. If you have a 1.44 megabyte boot floppy (3.5"), look in the directory bootdsks.144. If you have a 1.2 megabyte boot floppy (5.25"), look in the directory bootdsks.12. The README files in these directories describes what the files are.

  You need one of the following files. (The file READ.ME in these directories contains an up-to-date list of boot disk images.)

    - bare.gz. This is a boot floppy that has only IDE hard drive drivers. (No SCSI, CD-ROM, or networking support.) Use this if you only have an IDE hard drive controller and aren't going to be installing over the network or from CD-ROM.

    - xt.gz. This is a boot floppy with IDE and XT hard drive support.

    - cd.gz. Contains IDE hard drive and non-SCSI CD-ROM drivers. Get this if you're going to be installing from a (non-SCSI) CD-ROM (only relevant if you bought a Slackware CD-ROM of some kind).

    - cdscsi.gz. Contains IDE and SCSI hard drive support, and non-SCSI CD-ROM drivers.

    - scsi.gz. Contains IDE and SCSI hard drive support, and SCSI CD-ROM drivers.

    - net.gz. Contains IDE hard drive and TCP/IP networking support. Get this if you are going to install over the network using NFS.

    - scsinet.gz. Contains IDE and SCSI hard drive support, SCSI CD-ROM drivers, and TCP/IP networking support. You might want to try this one first; use bare.gz or one of the other boot floppies if this doesn't work for you.

  You need only **one** of the above bootdisk images, depending on the type hardware that you have in your system.

  The issue here is that some hardware drivers conflict with each other in strange ways, and instead of attempting to debug hardware problems on your system it's easier to use a boot floppy image with only certain drivers enabled. Most users should try scsi.gz or bare.gz.

- A rootdisk image. This is a file that you will write to a floppy to create the Slackware installation disk. As with the bootdisk image, look in rootdsks.144 or rootdsks.12 depending on the type of boot floppy drive that you have.

  You need one of the following files:

    - color144.gz. The menu-based color installation disk for 1.44 meg drives. Most users should use this rootdisk.

    - umsds144.gz. A version of the color144 disk for installing with the UMSDOS filesystem, which allows you to install Linux onto a directory of an MS-DOS filesystem. This installation method is not discussed in detail here, but it will prevent you from having to repartition your drive. More on this later.

- `tty144.gz`. The terminal-based installation disk for 1.44 meg drives. You should use `color144.gz`, but a few people have reported problems with it on their system. If `color144.gz` doesn't work for you, try `tty144.gz` instead. It is a bit dated and the installation procedure isn't identical, but it should work if `color144.gz` doesn't.

- `colrlite.gz`. The menu-based color installation disk for 1.2 meg drives. Some things have been trimmed off of this disk to make it fit on a 1.2 meg floppy, but it should work if you only have a 1.2 meg drive.

- `umsds12.gz`. A version of the `colrlite` disk for installing with the UMSDOS filesystem. See the description of `umsds144.gz`, above.

- `tty12.gz`. The terminal-based installation disk for 1.2 meg drives. Use this rootdisk if you have a 1.2 meg boot floppy and `colrlite.gz` doesn't work for you.

Again, you need only **one** of the above rootdisk images, depending on the type of boot floppy drive that you have.

- `GZIP.EXE`. This is an MS-DOS executable of the `gzip` compression program used to compress the boot and rootdisk files (the `.gz` extension on the filenames indicates this). This can be found in the `install` directory.

- `RAWRITE.EXE`. This is an MS-DOS program that will write the contents of a file (such as the boot and rootdisk images) directly to a floppy, without regard to format. You will use `RAWRITE.EXE` to create the boot and root floppies. This can be found in the `install` directory as well.

   You only need `RAWRITE.EXE` and `GZIP.EXE` if you plan to create the boot and root floppies from an MS-DOS system. If you have access to a UNIX workstation with a floppy drive instead, you can create the floppies from there, using the `dd` command. See the man page for `dd` and ask your local UNIX gurus for assistance.

- The files in the directories `slakware/a1`, `slakware/a2`, `slakware/a3`, and `slakware/a4`. These files make up the "a" disk set of the Slackware distribution. They are required. Later, you will copy these files to MS-DOS floppies for installation (or, you can install from your hard drive). Therefore, when you download these files, keep them in separate directories; don't mix the `a1` files with the `a2` files, and so on.

   Be sure that you get the files without periods in the filenames as well. That is, within FTP, use the command "`mget *`" instead of "`mget *.*`".

- The files in the directories `ap1`, `ap2`, etc., depending on what disk sets you are installing. For example, if you are installing the "x" disk series, get the files in the directories `x1` through `x5`. As with the "a" disk set, above, be sure to keep the files in separate directories when you download them.

3.4.2   Installation methods

Slackware provides several different means of installing the software. The most popular is installing from an MS-DOS partition on your hard drive; the other is to install from a set of MS-DOS floppies created from the disk sets that you downloaded.

You can also install Slackware from an NFS-mounted filesystem over a TCP/IP network. This is somewhat involved, however, and a discussion of how to do this is out of the range of this document. If you need help, ask your local UNIX gurus how to set up your system to mount an NFS filesystem which you can install Slackware from. (For this, you'll need another system on the network which has Slackware available on an exported filesystem.)

First we'll describe how to create the boot and root floppies, and then we'll describe how to set things up for either a hard drive or floppy installation.

Creating the boot and root floppies You must create floppies from the bootdisk and rootdisk images that you downloaded, no matter what type of installation you will be doing. This is where the MS-DOS programs GZIP.EXE and RAWRITE.EXE come into play.

First you must uncompress the bootdisk and rootdisk images using GZIP.EXE (on an MS-DOS system, of course). For example, if you're using the bare.gz bootdisk image, issue the MS-DOS command:

```
C:\> GZIP -D BARE.GZ
```

which will uncompress bare.gz and leave you with the file bare. You must similarly uncompress the rootdisk image. For example, if you are using the rootdisk color144.gz, issue the command:

```
C:\> GZIP -D COLOR144.GZ
```

which will uncompress the file and leave you with color144.

Next, you must have two *high-density* MS-DOS formatted floppies. (They must be of the same type; that is, if your boot floppy drive is a 3.5" drive, both floppies must be high-density 3.5" disks.) You will use RAWRITE.EXE to write the boot and rootdisk images to the floppies.

For example, if you're using the bare.gz bootdisk, use the command:

```
C:\> RAWRITE
```

Answer the prompts for the name of the file to write (such as BAREBOOT) and the floppy to write it to (such as A:). RAWRITE will copy the file, block-by-block, directly to the floppy. Also use RAWRITE for the root disk image (such as COLOR144). When you're done, you'll have two floppies: one containing the boot disk, the other containing the root disk. Note that these two floppies will no longer be readable by MS-DOS (they are "Linux format" floppies, in some sense).

Be sure that you're using brand-new, error-free floppies. The floppies must have no bad blocks on them.

Note that you do not need to be running MS-DOS in order to install Slackware. However, running MS-DOS makes it easier to create the boot and root floppies, and it makes it easier to install the software (as you can install directly from an MS-DOS partition on your system). If you are not running MS-DOS on your system, you can use someone else's MS-DOS system just to create the floppies, and install from there.

It is not necessary to use GZIP.EXE and RAWRITE.EXE under MS-DOS to create the boot and root floppies, either. You can use the gzip and dd commands on a UNIX system to do the same job. (For this, you will need a UNIX workstation with a floppy drive, of course.) For example, on a Sun workstation with the floppy drive on device /dev/rfd0, you can use the commands:

```
$ gunzip bare.gz
$ dd if=bare of=/dev/rfd0 obs=18k
```

You must provide the appropriate block size argument (the obs argument) on some workstations (e.g., Suns) or this will fail. If you have problems the man page for dd will be instructive.

Preparing for installation from hard drive If you're planning on installing the Slackware software directly from the hard drive (which is much faster and more reliable than a floppy installation), you will need an MS-DOS partition on the system that you're installing Slackware to. (That is, you must already be running MS-DOS on the system.)

Note: If you plan to install Slackware from an MS-DOS partition, that partition must NOT be compressed with DoubleSpace, Stacker, or any other MS-DOS drive compression utility. Linux cannot currently read DoubleSpace/Stacker MS-DOS partitions directly. (You can access them via the MS-DOS Emulator, but that is not an option when installing the Linux software.)

To prepare for hard drive installation, simply create a directory on the hard drive to store the Slackware files. For example,

```
C:\> MKDIR SLACKWAR
```

will create the directory C:\SLACKWAR to hold the Slackware files. Under this directory, you should create the subdirectories A1, A2, and so on, for each disk set that you downloaded. All of the files from the A1 disk should go into the directory SLACKWAR\A1, and so forth.

Now you're ready to go on and install the software; skip to the section "Installing the Software".

Preparing for floppy installation   If you wish to install Slackware from floppies instead of the hard drive, you'll need to have one blank, MS-DOS formatted floppy for each Slackware disk that you downloaded. These disks must be high-density format.

The A disk set (disks A1 through A4) may be either 3.5" or 5.25" floppies. However, the rest of the disk sets must be 3.5" disks. Therefore, if you only have a 5.25" floppy drive, you'll need to borrow a 3.5" drive from someone in order to install disk sets other than A. (Or, you can install from the hard drive, as explained in the previous section.)

To make the disks, simply copy the files from each Slackware directory onto an MS-DOS formatted floppy, using the MS-DOS COPY command. As so:

```
C:\> COPY A1\*.* A:
```

will copy the contents of the A1 disk to the floppy in drive A:. You should repeat this for each disk that you downloaded.

You do *not* need to modify or uncompress the files on the disks in any way; you merely need to copy them to MS-DOS floppies. The Slackware installation procedure takes care of uncompressing the files for you.

4   Installing the Software

In this section we'll describe how to prepare your system for installing Slackware, and finally how to go about installing it.

4.1   Repartitioning

On most systems, the hard drive is already dedicated to partitions for MS-DOS, OS/2, and so on. You need to resize these partitions in order to make space for Linux.

NOTE: If you use one of the umsds root diskettes, you can install Slackware TO a directory on your MS-DOS partition. (This is different than installing FROM an MS-DOS partition.) Instead, you use the "UMSDOS filesystem", which allows you to treat a directory of your MS-DOS partition as a Linux filesystem. In this way, you don't have to repartition your drive.

I only suggest using this method if your drive has four partitions and repartitioning would be more trouble than it's worth. Or, if you want to try Slackware out before repartitioning, this is a good way to do so. But in most cases you should repartition, as described here. If you do plan to use UMSDOS, you are on your own—it is not documented in detail here. From now on, we assume that you are NOT using UMSDOS, and that you will be repartitioning.

A *partition* is just a section of the hard drive set aside for a particular operating system to use. If you only have MS-DOS installed, your hard drive probably has just one partition, entirely for MS-DOS. To use Linux, however, you'll need to repartition the drive, so that you have one partition for MS-DOS, and one (or more) for Linux.

Partitions come in three flavors: *primary*, *extended*, and *logical*. Briefly, primary partitions are one of the four main partitions on your drive. However, if you wish to have more than four partitions per drive, you need to create an extended partition, which can contain many logical partitions. You don't store data directly on an extended partition—it is used only as a container for logical partitions. Data is stored only on either primary or logical partitions.

To put this another way, most people use only primary partitions. However, if you need more than four partitions on a drive, you create an extended partition. Logical partitions are then created on top of the extended partition, and there you have it—more than four partitions per drive.

Note that you can easily install Linux on the second drive on your system (known as D: to MS-DOS). You simply specify the appropriate device name when creating Linux partitions. This is described in detail below.

Back to repartitioning your drive: The problem with resizing partitions is that there is no way to do it (easily) without deleting the data on those partitions. Therefore, you will need to make a full backup of your system before repartitioning. In order to resize a partition, we simply delete the partition(s), and re-create them with smaller sizes.

NOTE: There is a non-destructive disk repartitioner available for MS-DOS, called FIPS. Look on `sunsite.unc.edu` in the directory `/pub/Linux/system/Install`. With FIPS, a disk optimizer (such as Norton Speed Disk), and a little bit of luck, you should be able to resize MS-DOS partitions without destroying the data on them. It's still suggested that you make a full backup before attempting this.

If you're not using FIPS, however, the classic way to modify partitions is with the program FDISK. For example, let's say that you have an 80 meg hard drive, dedicated to MS-DOS. You'd like to split it in half—40 megs for MS-DOS and 40 megs for Linux. In order to do this, you run FDISK under MS-DOS, delete the 80 meg MS-DOS partition, and re-create a 40 meg MS-DOS partition in its place. You can then format the new partition and reinstall your MS-DOS software from backups. 40 megabytes of the drive is left empty. Later, you create Linux partitions on the unused portion of the drive.

In short, you should do the following to resize MS-DOS partitions with FDISK:

1. Make a full backup of your system.

2. Create an MS-DOS bootable floppy, using a command such as

   ```
   FORMAT /S A:
   ```

3. Copy the files `FDISK.EXE` and `FORMAT.COM` to this floppy, as well as any other utilities that you need. (For example, utilities to recover your system from backup.)

4. Boot the MS-DOS system floppy.

5. Run FDISK, possibly specifying the drive to modify (such as C: or D:).

6. Use the FDISK menu options to delete the partitions which you wish to resize. **This will destroy all data on the affected partitions.**

7. Use the FDISK menu options to re-create those partitions, with smaller sizes.

8. Exit FDISK and re-format the new partitions with the FORMAT command.

9. Restore the original files from backup.

Note that MS-DOS FDISK will give you an option to create a "logical DOS drive". A logical DOS drive is just a logical partition on your hard drive. You can install Linux on a logical partition, but you don't want to create that logical partition with MS-DOS fdisk. So, if you're currently using a logical DOS drive, and want to install Linux in its place, you should delete the logical drive with MS-DOS FDISK, and (later) create a logical partition for Linux in its place.

The mechanism used to repartition for OS/2 and other operating systems is similar. See the documentation for those operating systems for details.

4.2 Creating partitions for Linux

After repartitioning your drive, you need to create partitions for Linux. Before describing how to do that, we'll talk about partitions and filesystems under Linux.

4.2.1 Filesystems and swap space

Linux requires at least one partition, for the *root filesystem*, which will hold the Linux software itself.

You can think of a *filesystem* as a partition formatted for Linux. Filesystems are used to hold files. Every system must have a root filesystem, at least. However, many users prefer to use multiple filesystems—one for each major part of the directory tree. For example, you may wish to create a separate filesystem to hold all files under the /usr directory. (Note that on UNIX systems, forward slashes are used to delimit directories, not backslashes as with MS-DOS.) In this case you have both a root filesystem, and a /usr filesystem.

Each filesystem requires its own partition. Therefore, if you're using both root and /usr filesystems, you'll need to create two Linux partitions.

In addition, most users create a *swap partition*, which is used for virtual RAM. If you have, say, 4 megabytes of memory on your machine, and a 10-megabyte swap partition, as far as Linux is concerned you have 14 megabytes of virtual memory.

When using swap space, Linux moves unused pages of memory out to disk, allowing you to run more applications at once on your system. However, because swapping is often slow, it's no replacement for real physical RAM. But applications that require a great deal of memory (such as the X Window System) often rely on swap space if you don't have enough physical RAM.

Nearly all Linux users employ a swap partition. If you have 4 megabytes of RAM or less, a swap partition is required to install the software. It is strongly recommended that you have a swap partition anyway, unless you have a great amount of physical RAM.

The size of your swap partition depends on how much virtual memory you need. It's often suggested that you have at least 16 megabytes of virtual memory total. Therefore, if you have 8 megs of physical RAM, you might want to create an 8-megabyte swap partition. Note that swap partitions can be no larger than 128 megabytes in size. Therefore, if you need more than 128 megs of swap, you must create multiple swap partitions. You may have up to 16 swap partitions in all.

4.2.2 Booting the installation disk

Specifying hardware parameters The first step is to boot the Slackware bootdisk. After the system boots, you will see the message:

```
Welcome to the Slackware Linux 2.0.0 Bootkernel disk!
```

Here, you are given the opportunity to specify various hardware parameters, such as your SCSI controller IRQ and address, or drive geometry, before booting the Linux kernel. This is necessary in case Linux does not detect your SCSI controller or hard drive geometry, for example.

In particular, many BIOS-less SCSI controllers require you to specify the port address and IRQ at boot time. Likewise, IBM PS/1, ThinkPad, and ValuePoint machines do not store drive geometry in the CMOS, and you must specify it at boot time.

To try booting the kernel without any special parameters, just press enter at the boot prompt.

Watch the messages as the system boots. If you have a SCSI controller, you should see a listing of the SCSI hosts detected. If you see the message

```
SCSI: 0 hosts
```

Then your SCSI controller was not detected, and you will have to use the following procedure.

Also, the system will display information on the drive partitions and devices detected. If any of this information is incorrect or missing, you will have to force hardware detection.

On the other hand, if all goes well and you hardware seems to be detected, you can skip to the following section, "Loading the root disk."

To force hardware detection, you must enter the appropriate parameters at the boot prompt, using the following syntax:

```
ramdisk <parameters...>
```

There are a number of such parameters available; here are some of the most common.

- `hd=cylinders,heads,sectors` Specify the drive geometry. Required for systems such as the IBM PS/1, ValuePoint, and ThinkPad. For example, if your drive has 683 cylinders, 16 heads, and 32 sectors per track, enter

    ```
    ramdisk hd=683,16,32
    ```

- `tmc8xx=memaddr,irq` Specify address and IRQ for BIOS-less Future Domain TMC-8xx SCSI controller. For example,

    ```
    ramdisk tmc8xx=0xca000,5
    ```

    Note that the `0x` prefix must be used for all values given in hex. This is true for all of the following options.

- `st0x=memaddr,irq` Specify address and IRQ for BIOS-less Seagate ST02 controller.

- `t128=memaddr,irq` Specify address and IRQ for BIOS-less Trantor T128B controller.

- `ncr5380=port,irq,dma` Specify port, IRQ, and DMA channel for generic NCR5380 controller.

- `aha152x=port,irq,scsi_id,1` Specify port, IRQ, and SCSI ID for BIOS-less AIC-6260 controllers. This includes Adaptec 1510, 152x, and Soundblaster-SCSI controllers.

For each of these, you must enter 'ramdisk' followed by the parameter that you wish to use.

If you have questions about these boot-time options, please read the Linux *SCSI HOWTO*, which should be available on any Linux FTP archive site (or from wherever you obtained this document). The *SCSI HOWTO* explains Linux SCSI compatibility in much more detail.

Loading the rootdisk   After booting the kernel, you will be prompted to enter the Slackware root disk:

```
Please remove the boot kernel disk from your floppy drive,
insert a disk to be loaded into the ramdisk, and press
[enter] to continue.
```

At this point you should remove the bootdisk from the drive and insert the rootdisk. Then press enter to go on.

The rootdisk will be loaded into memory, and you should be presented with a login prompt. Login as "root".

```
slackware login: root
#
```

4.2.3 Using fdisk

To create Linux partitions, we'll use the Linux version of the fdisk program. After logging in as root, run the command

    fdisk ⟨*drive*⟩

where ⟨*drive*⟩ is the name of the drive that you wish to create Linux partitions on. Hard drive device names are:

- /dev/hda First IDE drive

- /dev/hdb Second IDE drive

- /dev/sda First SCSI drive

- /dev/sdb Second SCSI drive

For example, to create Linux partitions on the first SCSI drive in your system, use the command

    fdisk /dev/sda

If you use fdisk without an argument, it will assume /dev/hda.

To create Linux partitions on the second drive on your system, simply specify either /dev/hdb (for IDE drives) or /dev/sdb (for SCSI drives) when running fdisk.

Your Linux partitions don't all have to be on the same drive. You might want to create your root filesystem partition on /dev/hda and your swap partition on /dev/hdb, for example. In order to do so just run fdisk once for each drive.

Use of fdisk is simple. The command "p" displays your current partition table. "n" creates a new partition, and "d" deletes a partition.

To Linux, partitions are given a name based on the drive which they belong to. For example, the first partition on the drive /dev/hda is /dev/hda1, the second is /dev/hda2, and so on. If you have any logical partitions, they are numbered starting with /dev/hda5, /dev/hda6 and so on up.

NOTE: You should not create or delete partitions for operating systems other than Linux with Linux fdisk. That is, don't create or delete MS-DOS partitions with this version of fdisk; use MS-DOS's version of FDISK instead. If you try to create MS-DOS partitions with Linux fdisk, chances are MS-DOS will not recognize the partition and not boot correctly.

Here's an example of using fdisk. Here, we have a single MS-DOS partition using 61693 blocks on the drive, and the rest of the drive is free for Linux. (Under Linux, one block is 1024 bytes. Therefore, 61693 blocks is about 61 megabytes.) We will create two Linux partitions: one for swap, and one for the root filesystem.

First, we use the "p" command to display the current partition table. As you can see, /dev/hda1 (the first partition on /dev/hda) is a DOS partition of 61693 blocks.

```
Command (m for help):    p
Disk /dev/hda: 16 heads, 38 sectors, 683 cylinders
Units = cylinders of 608 * 512 bytes

     Device Boot  Begin    Start     End   Blocks   Id  System
    /dev/hda1    *        1        1     203   61693    6  DOS 16-bit >=32M

Command (m for help):
```

Next, we use the "n" command to create a new partition. The Linux root partition will be 80 megs in size.

```
Command (m for help):  n
Command action
   e    extended
   p    primary partition (1-4)
p
```

Here we're being asked if we want to create an extended or primary partition. In most cases you want to use primary partitions, unless you need more than four partitions on a drive. See the section "Repartitioning", above, for more information.

```
Partition number (1-4): 2
First cylinder (204-683):   204
Last cylinder or +size or +sizeM or +sizeK (204-683): +80M
```

The first cylinder should be the cylinder AFTER where the last partition left off. In this case, /dev/hda1 ended on cylinder 203, so we start the new partition at cylinder 204.

As you can see, if we use the notation "+80M", it specifies a partition of 80 megs in size. Likewise, the notation "+80K" would specify an 80 kilobyte partition, and "+80" would specify just an 80 byte partition.

```
Warning: Linux cannot currently use 33090 sectors of this partition
```

If you see this warning, you can ignore it. It is left over from an old restriction that Linux filesystems could only be 64 megs in size. However, with newer filesystem types, that is no longer the case... partitions can now be up to 4 terabytes in size.

Next, we create our 10 megabyte swap partition, /dev/hda3.

```
Command (m for help): n
Command action
   e    extended
   p    primary partition (1-4)
p

Partition number (1-4): 3
First cylinder (474-683):   474
Last cylinder or +size or +sizeM or +sizeK (474-683):  +10M
```

Again, we display the contents of the partition table. Be sure to write down the information here, especially the size of each partition in blocks. You need this information later.

```
Command (m for help): p
Disk /dev/hda: 16 heads, 38 sectors, 683 cylinders
Units = cylinders of 608 * 512 bytes

    Device Boot   Begin    Start     End   Blocks   Id  System
   /dev/hda1   *      1        1     203    61693    6  DOS 16-bit >=32M
   /dev/hda2        204      204     473    82080   83  Linux native
   /dev/hda3        474      474     507    10336   83  Linux native
```

Note that the Linux swap partition (here, /dev/hda3) has type "Linux native". We need to change the type of the swap partition to "Linux swap" so that the installation program will recognize it as such. In order to do this, use the fdisk "t" command:

```
Command (m for help): t
Partition number (1-4): 3
Hex code (type L to list codes): 82
```

If you use "L" to list the type codes, you'll find that 82 is the type corresponding to Linux swap.

To quit fdisk and save the changes to the partition table, use the "w" command. To quit fdisk WITHOUT saving changes, use the "q" command.

After quitting fdisk, the system may tell you to reboot to make sure that the changes took effect. In general there is no reason to reboot after using fdisk—the version of fdisk on the Slackware distribution is smart enough to update the partitions without rebooting.

4.3   Preparing the swap space

If you have 4 megabytes of RAM (or less) in your machine, you need to create a swap partition (using fdisk) and enable it for use before installing the software. Here, we describe how to format and enable your swap partition(s).

If you have more than 4 megs of RAM, you need only create your partition(s)—it's not necessary to format and enable them before installing the software. In this case you can skip down to the section "Installing the Software".

If you get any "out of memory" errors during the installation procedure you should create a swap partition and enable it as described here.

To prepare the swap space for use, we use the mkswap command. It takes the form:

> mkswap -c ⟨**partition**⟩ ⟨**size**⟩

where ⟨**partition**⟩ is the partition name, such as /dev/hda3, and ⟨**size**⟩ is the size of the partition in blocks.

For example, if you created the swap partition /dev/hda3 of size 10336 blocks, use the command

> mkswap -c /dev/hda3 10336

The -c option tells mkswap to check for bad blocks on the partition when preparing the swap space. If you see any "read_intr" error messages during the mkswap operation, this means that bad blocks were found (and flagged). So you can ignore these errors.

To enable swapping on the new device, use the command

> swapon ⟨**partition**⟩

For example, for our swap space on /dev/hda3, we use

> swapon /dev/hda3

We're now swapping with about 10 megabytes more virtual memory.

You should execute mkswap and swapon for each swap partition that you created.

4.4   Installing the software

Installing the Slackware release is very simple; it's almost automatic. You use the setup command, which guides you through a series of menus which allow you to specify the means of installation, the partitions to use, and so forth. Almost everything is automatic.

Here, we're not going to document many of the specifics of using setup, because it changes from time to time. setup is very self-explanatory; it contains its own documentation. Just to give you an idea of what it's like, however, we'll describe what most installations are like using setup.

Before you begin, be sure that you have a high-density MS-DOS formatted floppy on hand. You will use this floppy to create a Linux boot diskette.

After running fdisk (and, perhaps, mkswap and swapon as described above), issue the command

```
# setup
```

This will present you with a colourful menu with various options such as "Addswap" (to set up your swap space), "Source" (to specify the source of the software to install, such as floppy or hard drive), "Target" (to specify where to install the software), and so on.

In general, you should go through the menu commands in the following order:

1. **Addswap.** If you created a swap partition (using fdisk), use the addswap menu option to tell the system about it. This option will present you with a list of possible swap partitions; just type in the name of the swap partition(s) that you wish to use (such as /dev/hda3). The system will then ask you if you want to format the swap partition, which you should do *unless* you already ran mkswap and swapon on it. That is, you should format the swap partition unless you already formatted and enabled it by hand as described in the previous section.

2. **Source.** This menu option lets you specify the source for the software to install. You can select several means of installation, such as from floppy or from hard drive. If you are installing from floppies, the system will ask you which floppy drive to use. If you are installing from hard drive, the system will ask you what partition the files are stored on, and what directory they are in.

   For example, if you are installing from an MS-DOS partition on your hard drive, and the Slackware files are under the directory C:\SLACKWAR, you should enter the name of the MS-DOS partition (such as /dev/hda1) and the name of the directory (such as /slackwar). Note that you should use forward slashes (/), not backslashes (\), in the directory name.

   There are other means of installation, such as CD-ROM. These should be self-explanatory as well.

3. **Target.** This menu item lets you specify what partition(s) to install the software on. The system will display a list of possible partitions. First you will be asked to enter the name of the *root partition*, such as /dev/hda2. You will be asked if you want to format the partition; unless you are installing on a partition previously formatted for Linux you should do so. You should use the Second Extended Filesystem (ext2fs) type for the partition.

   You will also be given a chance to use additional partitions for different parts of the directory tree. For example, if you created a separate partition for the /usr filesystem, you should enter the name of that partition and the directory that it corresponds to (/usr) when asked.

4. **Disksets.** This option allows you to specify the disksets you wish to install. Use the arrow keys to scroll through the list; pressing the spacebar selects or deselects a set. Press return when you're done selecting disk sets.

   You may wish to only install a minimal system at this time. That's fine. Only the A diskset is required. After you have installed the software you may run setup to install other disksets.

5. **Install.** After setting up all of the parameters above, you're ready to install the software. First the system will ask you what type of prompting to use; you should use the "normal" prompting method (unless you're an expert and have modified the installation tagfiles in some way).

The system will simply go through each disk set and install the software. For each software package, a dialog box will be displayed describing the software. Software packages that are required will be installed automatically. For optional software packages you will be given the option of either installing or not installing the package. (If you don't wish to install a certain package now, you can always use `setup` on your system to install it later).

While the software is installing, watch out for error messages that may be displayed. The most common error that you're likely to run into is "`device full`", which means that you have run out of space on your Linux partitions. Unfortunately, the Slackware installation procedure is not quite smart enough to detect this, and will attempt to continue installing the software regardless. If you get any kind of error messages during the installation procedure, you may wish to break out of the installation program (using `Ctrl-C`) to record them. The only solution for the "`device full`" problem is to re-create your Linux partitions with different sizes, or attempt to reinstall the software without several of the optional software packages.

4.5 After installation

After installation is complete, and if all goes well, you will be given the option of creating a "standard boot disk", which you can use to boot your newly-installed Linux system. For this you will need a blank, high-density MS-DOS formatted diskette of the type that you boot with on your system. Simply insert the disk when prompted and a boot diskette will be created.

You will also be given the chance to install LILO on your hard drive. LILO (which stands for LInux LOader) is a program that will allow you to boot Linux (as well as other operating systems, such as MS-DOS) from your hard drive. If you wish to do this, just select the appropriate menu option and follow the prompts.

If you are using OS/2's Boot Manager, the menu will include an option for configuring LILO for use with the Boot Manager, so that you can boot Linux from it.

Note that this automated LILO installation procedure is not foolproof; there are situations in which this can fail. Be sure that you have a way to boot MS-DOS, Linux, and other operating systems from floppy before you attempt to install LILO. If the LILO installation fails you will be able to boot your system from floppy and correct the problem.

More information on configuring LILO is given below.

The postinstallation procedure will also take you through several menu items allowing you to configure your system. This includes specifying your modem and mouse device, as well as your time zone. Just follow the menu options.

4.6 Booting your new system

If everything went as planned, you should be able to boot your Linux boot floppy (not the Slackware installation floppy, but the floppy created after installing the software). Or, if you installed LILO, you should be able to boot from the hard drive. After booting, login as `root`. Congratulations! You have your very own Linux system.

If you are booting using LILO, try holding down `shift` or `control` during boot. This will present you with a boot prompt; press `tab` to see a list of options. In this way you can boot Linux, MS-DOS, or whatever directly from LILO.

After booting your system and logging in as root, one of the first things you should do is create an account for yourself. The `adduser` command may be used for this purpose. For example,

```
# adduser
Login to add (^C to quit): ebersol
Full Name: Norbert Ebersol
GID [100]: 100
UID [501]: 501
Home Directory [/home/ebersol]: /home/ebersol
```

```
Shell [/bin/bash]: /bin/bash
Password [ebersol]: new.password

Information for new user [ebersol]:
Home directory: [/home/ebersol]  Shell: [/bin/bash]
Password: [new.password]  UID: [502] GID:[100]
Is this correct? [y/n]: y
```

adduser will prompt you for various parameters, such as the username, full name, GID (group ID), UID (user ID), and so on. For the most part you can use the defaults. If you're unfamiliar with creating users on a UNIX system, I strongly suggest getting a book on UNIX systems administration. It will help you greatly in setting up and using your new system.

You can now login as the new user. You can use the keys Alt-F1 through Alt-F8 to switch between *virtual consoles*, which will allow you to login multiple times from the console. The passwd command can be used to set the passwords on your new accounts; you should set a password for root and any new users that you create.

Also, the hostname of your machine is set at boot time in the file /etc/rc.d/rc.M. You should edit this file (as root) to change the hostname of the machine. You should edit the lines in this file which run the commands hostname or hostname_notcp. (The default hostname is darkstar.) You may also wish to edit the domainname commands in this file, if you are on a TCP/IP network. (On most Slackware systems the hostname and domain name are set in the file /etc/HOSTNAME, so editing this file will probably suffice.)

Obviously, there are many more things to setup and configure. A good book on UNIX systems administration should help. (I suggest *Essential Systems Administration* from O'Reilly and Associates.) You will pick these things up as time goes by. You should read various other Linux HOWTOs, such as the *NET-2-HOWTO* and *Printing-HOWTO*, for information on other configuration tasks.

After that, the system is all yours... have fun!

5 Configuring LILO

LILO is a boot loader, which can be used to select either Linux, MS-DOS, or some other operating system at boot time. If you install LILO as the *primary* boot loader, it will handle the first-stage booting process for all operating systems on your drive. This works well if MS-DOS is the only other operating system that you have installed. However, you might be running OS/2, which has it's own Boot Manager. In this case, you want OS/2's Boot Manager to be the primary boot loader, and use LILO just to boot Linux (as the *secondary* boot loader).

The Slackware installation procedure allows you to install and configure LILO. However, this method doesn't seem to be smart enough to handle several peculiar situations. It might be easier in some cases to configure LILO by hand.

In order to set up LILO for your system, just edit the file /etc/lilo.conf. Below we present an example of a LILO configuration file, where the Linux root partition is on /dev/hda2, and MS-DOS is installed on /dev/hdb1 (on the second hard drive).

```
# Tell LILO to install itself as the primary boot loader on /dev/hda.
boot = /dev/hda
# The boot image to install; you probably shouldn't change this
install = /boot/boot.b
# Do some optimization. Doesn't work on all systems.
compact

# The stanza for booting Linux.
image = /vmlinuz        # The kernel is in /vmlinuz
  label = linux         # Give it the name "linux"
  root = /dev/hda2      # Use /dev/hda2 as the root filesystem
  vga = ask             # Prompt for VGA mode
```

```
      append = "aha152x=0x340,11,7,1"   # Add this to the boot options,
                                         # for detecting the SCSI controller

# The stanza for booting MS-DOS
other = /dev/hdb1         # This is the MS-DOS partition
  label = msdos           # Give it the name "msdos"
  table = /dev/hdb        # The partition table for the second drive
```

Once you have edited the /etc/lilo.conf file, run /sbin/lilo as root. This will install LILO on your drive. Note that you must rerun /sbin/lilo anytime that you recompile your kernel (something that you don't need to worry about just now, but keep it in mind).

Note how we use the append option in /etc/lilo.conf to specify boot parameters as we did when booting the Slackware bootdisk.

You can now reboot your system from the hard drive. By default LILO will boot the operating system listed first in the configuration file, which in this case is Linux. In order to bring up a boot menu, in order to select another operating system, hold down shift or ctrl while the system boots; you should see a prompt such as

```
   Boot:
```

Here, enter either the name of the operating system to boot (given by the label line in the configuration file; in this case, either linux or msdos), or press tab to get a list.

Now let's say that you want to use LILO as the secondary boot loader; if you want to boot Linux from OS/2's Boot Manager, for example. In order to boot a Linux partition from OS/2 Boot Manager, unfortunately, you must create the partition using OS/2's FDISK (not Linux's), and format the partition as FAT or HPFS, so that OS/2 knows about it. (That's IBM for you.)

In order to have LILO boot Linux from OS/2 Boot Manager, you only want to install LILO on your Linux root filesystem (in the above example, /dev/hda2). In this case, your LILO config file should look something like:

```
boot = /dev/hda2
install = /boot/boot.b
compact

image = /vmlinuz
  label = linux
  root = /dev/hda2
  vga = ask
```

Note the change in the boot line. After running /sbin/lilo you should be able to add the Linux partition to Boot Manager. This mechanism should work for boot loaders used by other operating systems as well.

6   Miscellaneous

I don't like to be biased towards the Slackware release, however, in order to document multiple releases of Linux, this file would be much, much longer. It is simpler and more coherent to cover the specific instructions for a single release of Linux. The book *Linux Installation and Getting Started* currently includes *general* installation instructions which should be applicable to "any" distribution of Linux. However, because the installation procedures are so varied, covering them all would be very confusing both to myself and to the reader.

The basic concepts in this document still hold, no matter what release of Linux you choose. For example, all releases require you to run fdisk, and all of them (to my knowledge) include some kind of installation menu similar to the setup program. If you choose to use a release of Linux other than Slackware, the

READMEs and installation instructions that come with that release should be easy to understand in the context of the material presented here.

If you would like a more complete discussion of Linux installation (instead of the "quick" examples given here), read the book *Linux Installation and Getting Started*, from `sunsite.unc.edu` in `/pub/Linux/docs/LDP`. This book includes a complete discussion of how to obtain and install Linux, as well as a basic UNIX and systems administration tutorial for new users.

Please mail me at `mdw@sunsite.unc.edu` if any part of this document is confusing or incorrect. I depend on feedback from readers in order to maintain this document! I also like to help answer questions about Linux installation, if you have any.

I'd like to thank Patrick Volkerding for his work on the Slackware distribution and assistance in preparing this document.

Best of luck with your new Linux system!

Cheers, mdw

Part XXIV

Linux Japanese Extensions Howto

Copyright Hirondu ABE and Yasu Hiro
v1.10 4/11/1994

Contents

1   Introduction

1.1   Concept

JE(Japanese Extensions for Linux) is a collection of free software for a standard distribution of the Linux system such as Slackware or SLS for the convenience of Japanese users. Each program is ported or developed mostly by members of the Japanese Linux Mailing List, and is available as both pre-compiled binary and source codes, though the basic distribution only contains the binary. Although the binary is tar+gzip'ed like those in Slackware or SLS and could be installed by a standard installer such as pkgtool or sysinstall, JE has its own installer called "ezinst" which even does some basic configuration after the installation.

1.2   Contents

JE consists of software to display, input, edit, format, and print Japanese documents, as well as small but fancy made-in-Japan software. For example, kon, kterm and pxvt display Japanese documents on console or in the X-window system. Wnn, Canna, and sj3 are what we call "Japanese input methods" (or JIM) which convert an input string from standard keyboards into Japanese characters, words, phrases or symbols. Editors included are a Japanese vi clone, NEmacs (Nihongo [=Japanese] Emacs), and Mule (Multilingual Emacs). Japanese TeX system typesets beautiful or exotic(?) documents. Oneko is a cute mouse-cursor chaser for the X-window system. In addition, there are several programs prepared to read/write electronic mail and news, to convert among character code sets, and to handle Japanese characters in command line under Linux. See section E for more details.

Binaries in JE are made to handle the EUC-J character code set for electronic Japanese whenever choice is necessary at the time of compilation. This code set is most popular for UNIX workstations. Some software requires re-compilation to support SJIS, while others are run-time configurable. SJIS or Shift-JIS is the code set used by MS-DOS and other personal computers. JIS code set, yet another encoding, is widely used on the net to exchange Japanese information among computer systems. This is the only popular 7-bit code set with escape sequences, and others assign a two-byte 8-bit code for each letter. It is supported by editors and network related software in JE. This diversity is due to historical reasons, and developers couldn't come up with a better solution to this issue. Note that "nkf" will detect and convert among these three popular code sets.

1.3   Requirements

JE is designed to be installed over a standard distribution of Linux such as Slackware or SLS. The current version, JE-0.9.3, requires the shared library of libc-4.5.8 (SHARED_VERSION hereafter) or newer and libX-3.1.0 (XF_SHARED_VERSION) or greater, both of which are prepared in the JE1 disk set.

Note that the current JE assumes you have a shadow password system, but this requirement is expected to be removed very soon.

2 How to get help

2.1 New version of JE-HOWTO

The latest version of JE-HOWTO should be available as a part of the latest JE distribution, and will also be posted on "fj.os.linux" and other newsgroups when it is updated.

2.2 Network News

For general questions and discussions about JE, the use of "fj.os.linux", a network newsgroup is recommended, if available. This newsgroup is rich in information on how to use JE effectively. Although almost all posts are in Japanese, those in other languages are quite welcome such as in English, Spanish, Germany, French, Korean and so on. There might be some detectives who **decipher** what you write. :) Chances of your getting replies would be greatest, however, if you post either in English or in Japanese.

2.3 Mailing List

There is no mailing list specialized for JE at the moment. However, the Japanese Linux Mailing List is very active for discussions on JE, and, actually, this ML is the mother of JE. In addition, you may get a beta version of JE by its occasional circulation in tapes or disk media. You can join Japanese Linux ML by sending e-mail as:

Mail linux@colias.tutics.tut.ac.jp X-Mn-Cmd: join

To obtain a brief guide about the ML, send e-mail to

linux@colias.tutics.tut.ac.jp

with only "# guide" (without quotations) in its body.

A Mailing List in English was just born. It is called jewel-ML, "The Mailing List of JE for the World in the English Language". The e-mail address is,

jewel@colias.tutics.tut.ac.jp

and we, JE developers and coordinators, are waiting for you with a cup of coffee at hand. Please relax and join us.

2.4 Installation Guide

JE comes with "The Guide", an installation guide written in Japanese. This explains the installation procedure step by step. Although the current version is somewhat outdated, it surely helps if you can read Japanese. There is no English edition, and your help in creating it is strongly desired by the whole world !

2.5 Feedback

Bug reports and suggestions should be posted on the newsgroup "fj.os.linux" to get the attention of people, if possible. Also, je@Roy.dsl.tutics.ac.jp is ready to accept those by e-mail. Jewel-ML, mentioned in B-2, is also available for those too shy to post an article to the public.

However, please don't send e-mail to the original developers of each program in JE when you find a problem, because your problem may be due to our composer's faults and we don't want to bother the authors.

2.6   Other sources of information

The following two documents are made public to explain Japanese Linux matters. Both are written in Japanese and, unfortunately, no English version is available.

They are in the jd disk set of JE, and periodically posted on fj.os.linux and some BBSs in Japan.

"Linux Jouhou memo" by Y. Hiro Yamazaki ⟨hiro@ice3.ori.u-tokyo.ac.jp⟩ "JMETA-FAQ" by Tetsu Ono ⟨ono@eiehost.gee.kyoto-u.ac.jp⟩

There is a book in English which will help you understand how the Japanese language is handled on computers, including the complicated issue of the character code sets.

Understanding Japanese Information Processing Ken Lunde O'Reilly & Associates Inc ISBN 1-56592-043-0

You may find it easily, because the title is printed in large Kanjis.

3   Getting JE

3.1   Anonymous ftp

JE is available at the following anonymous ftp sites in Japan as the binary distribution: (after JMETA-FAQ 1.28)

colias.tutics.tut.ac.jp	133.15.144.11	/pub/linux/JE
ftp.kuis.kyoto-u.ac.jp	130.54.20.1	/Linux/JE
ftp.cs.keio.ac.jp	131.113.35.20	/pub/os/linux/Japanese/JE
etlport.etl.go.jp	192.31.197.99	/pub/linux/JE
ftp.huie.hokudai.ac.jp	133.50.16.80	/pub/system/Jlinux/JE
ftp.is.titech.ac.jp	131.112.40.1	/pub/linux/JE
ftp.ipc.chiba-u.ac.jp	133.82.241.128	/ftp.kyoto-u.ac.jp/.u6/JE
ftp.pu-toyama.ac.jp	133.55.0.133	/pub/ftpmail/ftp.kuis.kyoto-u.ac.jp/Linux/JE
srawgw.sra.co.jp	133.137.4.3	/pub/os/linux/JE
theta.iis.u-tokyo.ac.jp	157.82.96.67	/pub2/Linux/Japanese/JE
wnoc-fuk.wide.ad.jp	133.4.14.3	/pub/Linux/JE
turbo.te.chiba-u.ac.jp	133.82.181.125	/pub/Linux/JE
ftp.astec.co.jp	133.147.2.254	/pub/Linux/JE
ftp.hitachi-sk.co.jp	133.107.1.2	/pub/pds/linux/JE
ftp.kddlabs.co.jp	192.26.91.15	/pub/os/linux/Japanese/JE

"colias" is the source of JE. However, use of other sites is strongly recommended since the line to it is rather thin.

The following sites outside Japan are known to mirror colias everyday:

| sunsite.unc.edu | 152.2.22.81 | /pub/Linux/distributions/je |
| ftp.cdrom.com | 192.153.46.2 | /pub/linux/je |

Source codes are also available at the following sites:

colias.tutics.tut.ac.jp	133.15.144.11	/pub/linux/je-sources
ftp.kuis.kyoto-u.ac.jp	130.54.20.1	/Linux/JE-sources
ftp.huie.hokudai.ac.jp	133.50.16.80	/pub/system/Jlinux/JE-sources
theta.iis.u-tokyo.ac.jp	157.82.96.67	/pub2/Linux/je-sources
ftp.iij.ad.jp	192.244.176.50	/pub/linux-j/JE-sources

Linux patch is separated from its original if there is any. For example,

oneko-1.1b.tar.Z Original codes oneko-1.1b+lx.diff.gz Linux patch

Apply the Linux patch with extension of "+lx" or "+je" after applying others if any.

3.2   CD-ROM

JE is also available in CD-ROM:

CD-ROM Shop Laser5

Big Office Plaza, Suite 203

2-652-8 Higashi Ikebukuro

Toshima-ku,

170 Tokyo Japan

Phone: +81-3-5952-4639

FAX: +81-3-5952-7486

This CD-ROM contains JE with its source codes as well as Slackware and SLS distributions. The organizers are active members of Japanese Linux ML and reflect the feedback from Japanese users quickly.

Also available is "The best Linux plus FreeBSD CDROM ever" CD-ROM by Trans-Ameritech.

Trans-Ameritech

2342A Walsh Avenue

Santa Clara, CA 95051

phone +1-408-727-3883

FAX +1-408-727-3882

e-mail: roman@trans-ameritech.com

4   Installation

4.1   Procedure

This section briefly explains the installation procedure of JE. Please refer to "The Guide" for more information.

The custom installer called "ezinst" is in the JE disk set of JE. Use "pkgtool" of Slackware or "sysinstall" of SLS in your system to install ezinst itself.

(1) Prepare floppy disks of JE. Each disk set of JE should fit in a High Density floppy disk, 5" or 3.5" 2HD. Note that this step is not necessary if you install JE from HDD or CD-ROM, or via NFS.

(2) Install JE1 using pkgtool of Slackware or sysinstall of SLS as:

    # pkgtool

    or,

    # sysinstall -doprompt -series JE

Read the manpage of the installer if you don't want to install JE1 from floppies.

The JE1 disk contains the following packages:

ezinst: Easy installer for JE konbin: KON to display Kanji on console konfnt: Fonts for kon (the same as those for Minix/V) libc: Linux standard shared libraries [Optional] libx: XFree86 shared libraries (English version) [Optional]

Software in JE is compiled to use the standard shared libraries of SHARED_VERSION and XF86 shared libraries of XF_SHARED_VERSION, both of which are defined in A-3. So, you need to install these, ONLY if you use older ones. "kon" is necessary if you don't have any software which display Japanese and is supported by the curses, because "ezinst" speaks Japanese. You might be able to use "-e" option to use it with English messages, though this option is in its beta stage.

(3) Run your Japanese terminal software, such as "kon" for console:

kon

You may use "kterm" if you already have one. Also, if your machine is J3100SX made by Toshiba Japan, you may use Kanji-term for J3100 as well as kon with j3100 option:

kon j3100sx

(4) Start "ezinst".

If you install JE from floppy disks:

ezinst -fd /dev/fd0

To install from HDD, say from "/dos/JE":

ezinst -hd /dos/JE

To install from "install/JE" directory of CD-ROM:

ezinst -cd install/JE

To install via NFS from /linux/JE directory of a server Roy:

ezinst -nfs Roy:/linux/JE

The installer uses "/mnt" as a temporary mount point of the floppy disks or CD-ROM. Thus, you need to "umount /mnt" if you already have something mounted on it, unless you install JE via NFS or from HDD.

(5) Follow the instructions by ezinst to go on. Note that the next version of ezinst will be modified significantly to simplify the installation procedure.

4.2 Tips

If you can't install JE successfully, try adding user "wnn" and invoke ezinst again. You are facing the known problem of the current JE which requires a shadow password package in you Linux system. In this case, don't use software in JE such as "xklock" which requests your password. This problem will be fixed in the next release, and all software will be re-compiled without the shadow password library.

5 Contents of each disk set

5.1 Outline

The current JE consists of 44 disks, and they are divided into 11 disk sets, as in the following list.

JE1: disk set to install JE easily 1disk j? : nkf, lha, Emacs related packages 8disks jd?: Japanese documents mostly by JF project 1disk jw?: Wnn Input Method users' packages 3disks jc?: Canna Input Method users' packages 4disks js?: sj3 Input Method users' packages 3disks jn?: Network software such as mailers, newsreaders 2disks jt?: Japanese TeX packages 2disks jf?: Font packages for TeX and XFree86 13disks jx?: XFree86 Japanese client packages 2disks jxsi?: XFree86j (X11R5 with Xsi extensions) 5disks

The choice of Japanese input method depends mostly on your taste, and JE provides four of them though all you need is only one: SKK, Wnn, Canna, or sj3. The large size of JE is due to this diversity as well as numerous complicated characters in Japanese; count how many emacs' variants JE has! You can't install jw, jc and js all at the same time. In addition, the choice of emacs is more difficult. You need one of X or non-X version of emacs with the built-in interface for one of the input methods. Mule (multi- lingual emacs) has more features than NEmacs(emacs for English and Japanese), but it takes more disk space. Here are some examples that might be helpful: Hiro, a desktop PC user, uses Canna-Mule on his X window system, while a notebook user prefers to use non-X NEmacs with SKK; they are both happy with their choices and have little reason to have more than one emacs. Anyway, once you make the major decisions, the installer will help you choose which packages to install, since it knows the dependency among packages to some extent.

5.2 JE disk set

The JE disk set, actually a JE1 disk, is compiled to help you install JE. See section C-1 for the installation procedure.

ezinst: Easy installer for JE konbin: Binary of KON to display Japanese on console konfnt: Fonts for kon (the same as those for Minix/V) libc: Linux standard shared libraries libx: XFree86 shared libraries (English version)

(1) ezinst is the installer for the rest of the JE distribution. It works on kon (Kanji on console) and other Japanese terminals.

(2) libc and libx are shared libraries required by JE. JE-0.9.3 has libc.4.5.8 and libx.3.1.0. Don't install them if they are older than what you have in your system.

(3) kon (kanji on console) in JE-0.9.3 is version 0.991b which displays Japanese characters on the console. The next version will be able to show other languages and will be able to work even on a vacant virtual console to save the number of login shells. Kon might be useful not only for the installation but also for your daily work.

5.3 j disk set

jbase: lha, nkf, ed, jhd, pwd, ish. pf and other basic tools jless: Japanese less (pager) pcurses: Pelican's curses (for Japanese) jman: Manpage system with Japanese nroff dic: To consult a dictionary on CD-ROM recjis: Tool to recover damaged Japanese document jelvis: Japanese elvis (vi clone) ng: Japanese Micro GNU Emacs nemsup: NEmacs(Nihongo[=Japanese] Emacs) supporting files nemuty: NEmacs utilities nemlisp: Lisp package for NEmacs mulelisp: Mule lisp package mulesup: Mule supporting files muleuty: Mule utilities muleskk: SKK related lisp files for Mule nemskk: SKK elisp for NEmacs skkbin: SKK server binaries skkdic: SKK dictionary skkman: SKK manual bash: Japanese bash (mostly sh compatible) tcsh: Japanese tcsh (csh compatible) zsh: enhanced shell vnem: NEmacs without input method support vmenx: NEmacs without input method support for X vmule: Mule without input method support vmulex: Mule without input method support for X jgsbin: Japanese Ghostscript (binary) jgslib: Japanese Ghostscript (library) jgsgnt1: Fonts for Japanese Ghostscript (part 1) jgsfnt2: Fonts for Japanese Ghostscript (part 2)

(1) "jbase" is a package of basic tools: "lha" is an archiver widely used under MS-DOS especially in Japan, "pf" is a print tool for Japanese line printers.

(2) "jless" is a Japanese pager, which automatically judges the character code set in the document and converts it to display depending on the environment variable of LESSCHARSET which most Linuxers set as "japanese-ujis" in Japan.

(3) "pcurses" is a curses with a Japanese handling feature.

(4) "jman" is a manpage system with Japanese nroff, which enables you to look up the Japanese man pages.

(5) "dic" looks up a dictionary in 8cm CD-ROM, widely available in Japan for "Data Discman" made by SONY or for its compatibles. Also included is an e-lisp code to call it from your emacs.

(6) "recjis" will recover damaged Japanese documents encoded in JIS, SJIS, or UJIS code set which might have lost some information through network transfers or by other accidents.

(7) "jelvis" is Japanese elvis(vi clone), while "ng" a subset of Japanese Emacs. Use them with "uum", "canuum" or "kinput2" to input Japanese characters.

(8) "nemsup", "nemuty", and "nemlisp" are necessary to use NEmacs, the Japanese Emacs. The current JE contains NEmacs-3.3.2 based on emacs-18.59.

(9) "mulelisp", "mulesup", and "muleuty" are necessary to use Mule, the Multi lingual Emacs. The JE-0.9.3 has Mule-1.0pl1 (KIRITSUBO version).

(10) "skkbin", "skkdic", and "skkman" are SKK, a Japanese input method, accessible by Mule with "muleskk" or NEmacs with "nemskk". JE-0.9.3 comes with SKK-6.32.

(11) "bash", "tcsh", and "zsh" are enhanced shells. "bash"(bash-1.13.5j) and "tcsh" will pass 8-bit Japanese characters.

(12) "vnem" and "vnemx" are naked NEmacs based on emacs-18.59 without support of any input method for the console and X respectively. You don't have to install these if you decide to use either Wnn, Canna or sj3.

(13) "vmule" and "vmulex" are naked Mule-1.0pl1(KIRITSUBO version) without support of any input method for the console and X respectively. You don't have to install these if you decide to use either Wnn, Canna or sj3.

(14) "jgsbin", "jgslib", "jgsgnt1", and "jgsfnt2" makes a Japanese Ghostscript system which is an interpreter of Japanese PostScript, based on Ghostscript-2.6.1. The only allocated devices in JE binary kit are X window and VGA console. Run "gslx" script to use it on the console. Note that older JE used to contain a version of gs which required libsvga.so. Install libsvga.so.1 in Slackware of obtain new JE, if you have this.

5.4 jd disk set

This is a collection of Japanese documents for Linux.

jmemo: Linux Jouhou Memo (INFO-SHEET with Japan specific issues) jmeta: JMETA FAQ (Japan Edition of META-FAQ, not translation)

(1) "Linux Jouhou Memo" is a document explaining Linux to Japanese beginners, which is based on "Linux INFO-SHEET" by Michael K. Johnson (johnsonm@stolaf.edu) translated into Japanese and modified by Yasu Hiro Yamazaki at the University of Toronto with additional information.

(2) "JMETA-FAQ" is written by Tetsu Ono at Kyoto University to help Japanese Linuxers to get Linux itself and related information.

These authors are active in the Japanese Linux society, especially making better documents as a part of JF(Japanese FAQ) project, a Japanese version of LDP (Linux Documentation Project). Tetsu is the head of this project. Although this disk set currently consists of very a limited number of documents, it is expected to grow rapidly because JF has already made many more documents such as its original FAQ and translations of most HOWTOs with lots of help from Mr. Nakagome and other members. Contact one of the two authors above if you are interested in this project. Any help is more than welcome !

5.5   jw disk set

This disk set is necessary only if you decide to go with Wnn, which is the most popular Japanese input method.

wnnbin: Wnn4.109(binary)
wnndic: Wnn4.109(dictionary)
wnnman: Wnn4.109(manual)

wnnprog: Wnn4.109(programmer's kit) ki2wnn: kinput2 for Wnn users wnem: NEmacs-3.3.2 with Wnn interface wnemx: NEmacs-3.3.2 with Wnn interface for X window system wmule: Mule-1.01 with Wnn interface wmulex: Mule-1.01 with Wnn interface for X window system

(1) "wnnbin", "wnndic", "wnnman", and "wnnprog" make Wnn-4.109, the most popular Japanese Input Method on Unices, which enables you to input Japanese words and phrases by regular keybaords such as English 101.

(2) "ki2wnn" is kinput2-fix6 for Wnn users, which enables input of Japanese characters into some Japanese applications.

(3) "wnem" and "wnemx" are Japanese Emacs(NEmacs-3.3.2) with built-in support of Wnn for non-X and X environment respectively.

(4) "wmule" and "wmulex" are Multilingual Emacs(Mule-1.01) with Wnn support of Wnn for non-X and X environment respectively.

5.6   jc disk set

This disk set is necessary only if you decided to go with Canna. Canna is famous for its features and speed among Japanese input methods.

canbin: Canna2.2pl4(binary)
canman: Canna2.2pl4(manual)
canprog: Canna2.2pl4(programmer's kit)
candic: Canna2.2pl4(dictionary)

ki2can: kinput2 for Canna users cnem: NEmacs-3.3.2 with Canna interface cnemx: NEmacs-3.3.2 with Canna interface for X cmule: Mule-1.01 with Canna interface cmulex: Mule-1.01 with Canna interface for the X window system

(1) "canbin", "candic", "canman", and "canprog" make a Canna-2.2pl4 system, an Input Method with good features and speed, which converts your input into Japanese.

(2) "ki2can" is kinput2-fix6 for Canna users, which communicates with a Canna server to input Japanese into your Japanese application.

(3) "cnem" and "cnemx" are NEmacs-3.3.2 with a built-in interface to a Canna server for non-X and X environment respectively.

(4) "cmule" and "cmulex" are Mule-1.01 with a Canna interface for non-X and X environment respectively.

5.7 js disk set

This disk set is necessary only for SKK users. This enables input of Japanese characters into some Japanese applications.

sj3bin: sj3(binary)

sj3prog: sj3(programmer's kit) ki2sj3: kinput2 for sj3 user snem: NEmacs-3.3.2 with sj3 interface snemx: NEmacs-3.3.2 with sj3 interface for X smule: Mule-1.02 with sj3 interface smulex: Mule-1.02 with sj3 interface for the X window system

(1) "sj3bin", and "sj3prog" make the sj3 input method system.

(2) "ki2sj3" is kinput2-fix6 for sj3 users.

(3) "snem", and "snemx" are NEmacs-3.3.2 with built-in interface to sj3 for non-X and X environment respectively.

(4) "smule", and "smulex" are Mule-1.01 with sj3 interface for non-X and X environment respectively.

5.8 jn disk set

This is the collection of network related software.

cf: CF-3.2W4 (produces sendmail.cf) sendmail: sendmail-8.6.5 for Japanese networks mailx: mailer (mail, Mail, rmail) mhlib: MH-6.8jp2c (library) mhbin: MH-6.8jp2c (binary) mhman: MH-6.8jp2c (manual) nntpclt: inews for NNTP cnn: cnn-1.4.2 (news checker) ktin: Japanese tin (newsreader)

(1) "cf" helps to configure sendmail by producing sendmail.cf.

(2) "sendmail" is the most popular mail transport in the Unix world. This binary has some extensions to use over the Japanese networks, such as WIDE or TISN.

(3) "mailx" is one of the most popular mailers among Linuxers.

(4) "mhbin", "mhlib", and "mhman" make MH, a mail handling system with Japanese support.

(5) "nntpclt" is Japanese inews, which enables the exchange of Japanese e-mail.

(6) "cnn" checks if there are new articles posted on you favourite newsgroups via an NNTP connection.

(7) "ktin" is a newsreader with Japanese support.

Next JE is expected to contain "mnews".

5.9 jt disk set

This set contains all the necessary files for the TeX system except for fonts in the jf disk set, and xdvi in jx.

bptexbin: PTeX (Japanese big TeX binary) bptexfmt: PTeX (Japanese big TeX format file) sptexbin: pTeX (Japanese TeX binary) sptexfmt: pTeX (Japanese TeX format file) ptexlib: common resources for PTeX and pTeX jbibtex: Japanese BibTeX dvi2tty: DVI previewer for character terminals dviout: DVI previewer for VGA consoles dviprt: DVI printer driver fntuty: TeX font utility

(1) "bptexbin"+"bptexfmt" and "sptexbin"+"sptexfmt" are Japanese (big) TeX systems developed by ASCII, a Japanese publisher of computer books, naturally based on the famous TeX system. You have to install the PTeX system only if you want to handle large documents, otherwise you should go with pTeX. These can handle both English and Japanese documents.

(2) "ptexlib" is a package of common files of PTeX and pTeX systems.

(3) "jbibtex" is Japanese BiBTeX.

(4) "dvi2tty" is a DVI file previewer for character terminals.

(5) "dviout" is a DVI previewer for VGA while "dviprt" is a printer driver; both are ported from their DOS versions, which work under non-X environments. They are based on version 2.39 of dviout/prt.

(6) "fntuty" is a utility software to exchange formats among bitmap, PK, and vector fonts.

Note that DVI previewer for X environment is in the jx disk set for X applications.

5.10   jf disk set

This disk set contains bitmap and vector fonts for Japanese TeX and the X window system. Note that Japanese PK fonts are NOT necessary if you decide to go with vector fonts.

cmf118: 118dpi-PK Computer Modern font for TeX cmf180: 180dpi-PK Computer Modern font for TeX j118w98: 118dpi-PK Watanabe's jfonts for TeX j118w142: 118dpi-PK Watanabe's jfonts for TeX j118w204: 118dpi-PK Watanabe's jfonts for TeX j118w108: 118dpi-PK Watanabe's jfonts for TeX j118w129: 118dpi-PK Watanabe's jfonts for TeX j118w170: 118dpi-PK Watanabe's jfonts for TeX j118w118: 118dpi-PK Watanabe's jfonts for TeX j118w245: 118dpi-PK Watanabe's jfonts for TeX j118w294: 118dpi-PK Watanabe's jfonts for TeX j118wlnk: DNP fonts -> Watanabe's jfonts linkage asiya24: Round Gothic PK font for dviout/prt hokuto24: Brush typeface PK font for dviout/prt kfonts: other PK fonts for dviout/prt vmincho1: Zeit vector font in Mincho (JIS level1 kanji) vmincho2: Zeit vector font in Mincho (JIS level2 kanji) vasiya1: Zeit vector font in Round Gothic (JIS L1 kanjis) vasiya2: Zeit vector font in Round Gothic (JIS L1 kanjis) vhokuto: Zeit vector font in Brush typeface xfnt13: 13 dot alphabet and Kana font for X xfnt16: 16 dot Japanese fonts for X xfnt18: 18 dot Japanese fonts for X xfnt24: 24 dot Japanese fonts for X xfnt26: 26 dot Japanese fonts for X xmarufnt: Round typeface Japanese font for X

(1) TeX requires Computer Modern fonts of "cmf118" or "cmf180" depending on the resolution of your printer. If other fonts with different resolutions are required, you have to find them in the net or make them by yourself using the Metafont system.

(2) Most Japanese TeX systems also require DNP fonts designed by a printing company called "Dai-Nippon Printing". Although you can buy DNP fonts for TeX from them, free alternatives are available in JE as Watanabe's jfonts, and Zeit compatible vector font sets. The authors recommend the use of vector fonts to save your disk space. In addition, if you have better CPU than 386 SX, the use of the vector fonts results in better speed, because it is faster to read smaller fonts from disks.

(3) "asiya24", "hokuto24", and "kfonts" are PK (bitmap) fonts for dviout/prt. These are not necessary if you decide to use the vector font set.

(4) "vmincho1/2", "vasiya1/2", and "vhokuto" are Zeit compatible vector fonts for TeX (dviout/prt, xdvi) and Japanese Ghostscript. You can buy the original Zeit font from Zeit, a Japanese software vender, or you can get free alternatives here in JE.

(5) "xfnt??" and "xmarufnt" are Japanese fonts for the X-window system. Make sure to execute mkfontdir in /usr/lib/X11/fonts/misc after you install any of them.

5.11   jx disk set

This is a collection of X applications.

fvwm: small and good looking window manager (1.18d) k14: the famous 14 dot Kanji fonts for X kterm: kterm-5.2.0, xterm with Kanji support pxvt: small terminal emulator for X, based on rxvt xldimg: image file viewer for X oneko: a cat chasing your mouse cursor libtk: Tcl7.3Tk3.6jp (library) tkbin: Tcl7.3Tk3.6jp (binary) tkdemo: Tcl7.3Tk3.6jp (demo) tkman: Tcl7.3Tk3.6jp (manual) xdvi: DVI previewer with PK font support xdviz: DVI previewer with Zeit vector font support gview: ghostview-1.5 (X interface for ghostscript) tgif: tgif-2.13.2.j (a draw tool with Japanese support) xfig: xfig-2.0.pl9.j (a draw tool with Japanese support) xklock: screen lock with Kanji support

(1) "fvwm" is a small and good looking window manager for X, and is getting popular. You can configure it into mwm-like mode.

(2) "k14" is a set of Japanese fonts contributed to the X-window system. You may find it even in your English-only workstations in your office, since it is in the core distribution of X.

(3) "kterm" is a Kanji terminal emulator for X. It will be found in the contrib directory of X.

(4) "pxvt" is a small terminal emulator for X, based on rxvt.

(5) "xldimg" is a viewer of image files such as those in GIF format.

(6) "oneko" makes it easy to find your mouse cursor; a neko (a Japanese word for cat) chases your mouse on your screen. You may make it a dog chasing a bone.

(7) "tkbin", "libtk", "tkdemo", and "tkman" make Japanese Tcl/Tk. This package helps to make software with a Graphical User Interface with Japanese messages.

(8) "xdvi" and "xdviz" are DVI previewers for X. "xdviz" is compiled to use Zeit compatible vector fonts. See E-9 to decide which one to use.

(9) "gview" is a user-friendly interface for Ghostscript.

(10) "tgif" in JE is a drawing tool tgif with kinput2 interface to input Japanese strings. It can handle EPS files as well as its proprietary files.

(11) "xfig" in JE is a drawing tool xfig with a Japanese patch.

(12) "xklock" is a screen lock with Kanji support. It is currently linked with shadow password libraries.

5.12   jxsi disk set

This disk set contains internationalized XFree86-2.0 using the Xsi extension WITHOUT fonts.

xfs3.tgz: S3 server xfsvga.tgz: SVGA server xfvga16.tgz: VGA16 server xf8514.tgz: 8514 server xf-mach32.tgz: Mach32 server xfmach8.tgz: Mach8 server xfmono.tgz: VGA Mono server xfprog.tgz: programming kit xfbin.tgz: basic clients xflib.tgz: shared libraries and others xfxawk.tgz: Xaw-i18n + Xawk2 + Xwchar

This disk set was made through the following steps.

- Applied the latest patches to XFree86 source codes - Set Xsi, X_LOCALE, X_WCHAR and XML, and did "make World" - Merged Xawk2 and Xwchar into Xaw-i18n (xfxawk.tgz)

Xawk2 was chosen in order to use kinput2. This allows us to input Japanese characters into internationalized clients such as xcal-i18n with Canna or sj3. Xaw will be replaced by the internationalized version when you install "xfxawk.tgz".

"XFree86-j" is upper-compatible with its original, and even non- internationalized clients will run without problem. Moreover, the binaries might improve your X system, because they have the latest patches applied. However, you need to install it over your X window system beause this package is NOT complete. Intensive testing has not yet been done, either.

A new version based on XFree86-2.1 is in its testing stage, and is expected to come with the next release of JE.

6   Future Plan

We plan to improve the following aspects of JE.

(1) More and better documentation: Works of JF members will be made available in the jd disk set. Most major HOWTOs, Japanese FAQs and others are ready to come.

(2) More varieties of Emacs: New emacs package with temacs is under development.

(3) XFree86 with Ximp extensions: Some people prefer Ximp to Xsi, another implementation of internationalized X.

(4) Reform of fonts: /usr/share/fonts is the new candidate to store Japanese fonts. PK fonts for TeX might be removed from JE.

(5) Evolution toward Multilingual Extensions: Give us your opinions ! JE developers are not specialists in all languages.

JE was originally compiled as an extension of the SLS distribution of Linux, but the developers are moving toward Slackware while keeping their eyes on the Debian package.

7   Legalese and miscellaneous

Any trademark in this document is owned by its owner. This document is freely distributable, though it is copyrighted by the authors. However, please distribute the latest version available, whenever you do, and the authors will appreciate it very much if you let them know about your distribution. There is no warranty on any information in this document.

The authors express special thanks to the following people for their dedicated help.
Takashi MANABE   ⟨manaba@Roy.dsl.tutics.tut.ac.jp⟩
Nozomi YTOW   ⟨nozomi@yacca.cc.tsukuba.ac.jp⟩
Kuniko MIKI   ⟨kuniko@ori.u-tokyo.ac.jp⟩

Comments, suggestions, cheers or just greetings to the authors are quite welcome. They will be reached at the following addresses:

Hironobu ABE ⟨hironobu@ap.isl.melco.co.jp⟩

Yasu Hiro YAMAZAKI ⟨hiro@ice3.ori.u-tokyo.ac.jp⟩ 2696 Bloor St. W., Apt B3, Toronto Ontario, Canada M8X 1A5

Part XXV

The Linux Kernel HOWTO

Copyright Brian Ward, `ward@blah.tu-graz.ac.at`
version 0.31, 31 March 1995
This is a detailed guide to kernel configuration, compilation, and upgrades.

Contents

1   Introduction

This is release 0.31 of the Kernel-HOWTO. Should you read this document? Well, see if you've got any of the following symptoms:

- "Arg! This wizzo-46.5.6 package says it needs kernel release 1.1.193 and I still only have release 1.0.9!"

- There's a device driver in one of the newer kernels that you just gotta have

- You really have no idea at all how to compile a kernel

- "Is this stuff in the README *really* the whole story?"

- You came, you tried, it didn't work

- You know how to compile and install a kernel, and people seem to know this. Therefore, they keep whining to you to help them install their kernels.

1.1   Read this first! (I mean it)

Some of the examples in this document assume that you have GNU `tar`, `find`, and `xargs`. These are quite standard; this should not cause problems. It is also assumed that you know your system's filesystem structure; if you don't, it is critical that you keep a written copy of the `mount` command's output during normal system operation (or a listing of `/etc/fstab`, if you can read it). This information is important, and does not change unless you repartition your disk, add a new one, reinstall your system, or something similar.

The latest kernel version at the time of this writing was 1.2.2, meaning that the references and examples correspond to that release. Even though I try to make this document as version-independent as possible, the kernel is constantly under development, so if you get a newer release, it will inevitably have some differences. Again, this should not cause major problems, but it may create some confusion.

1.2   A word on style

`Text that looks like this` is either something that appears on your screen, a filename, or something that can be directly typed in, such as a command, or options to a command (if you're looking at a plain-text file, it doesn't look any different). Commands and other input are frequently quoted (with ' '), which causes the following classic punctuation problem: if such an item appears at the end of a sentence in quotes, people often type a '.' along with the command, because the American quoting style says to put the period inside of the quotation marks. Even though common sense should tell one to strip off the punctuation first, many people simply do not remember, so I will place it outside the quotation marks in such cases. For example, I would write '`make config`', not '`make config.`'

2 Important questions and their answers

2.1 What does the kernel do, anyway?

The Unix kernel acts as a mediator for your programs. First, it does the memory management for all of the running programs (processes), and makes sure that they all get a fair (or unfair, if you please) share of the processor's cycles. In addition, it provides a nice, fairly portable interface for programs to talk to your hardware.

Obviously, there is more to the kernel's operation than this, but the basic functions above are the most important to know.

2.2 Why would I want to upgrade my kernel?

Newer kernels generally offer the ability to talk to more types of hardware (that is, they have more device drivers), they can have better process management, they can run faster than the older versions, they could be more stable than the older versions, and they fix silly bugs in the older versions. Most people upgrade kernels because they want the device drivers and the bug fixes.

2.3 What kind of hardware do the newer kernels support?

See the Hardware-HOWTO. Alternatively, you can look at the 'config.in' file in the linux source, or just find out when you try 'make config'. This shows you all hardware supported by the standard kernel distribution, but not everything that linux supports; many common device drivers (such as the PCMCIA drivers and some tape drivers) are loadable modules maintained and distributed separately.

2.4 What version of gcc and libc do I need?

Linus recommends a version of gcc in the README file included with the linux source. If you don't have this version, the documentation in the recommended version of gcc should tell you if you need to upgrade your libc. This is not a difficult procedure, but it is important to follow the instructions.

2.5 What's a loadable module?

These are pieces of kernel code which are not linked (included) directly in the kernel. One compiles them separately, and can insert and remove them into the running kernel at almost any time. Due to its flexibility, this is now the preferred way to code certain kernel features. Many popular device drivers, such as the PCMCIA drivers and the QIC-80/40 tape driver, are loadable modules.

2.6 How much disk space do I need?

It depends on your particular system configuration. First, the compressed linux source is 2.35 megabytes large at version 1.2.0. Most keep this even after unpacking. Uncompressed, it takes up 10 MB. But that's not the end – you need more to actually compile the thing. This depends on how much you configure into your kernel. For example, on my 386, I have networking, the 3Com 3C503 driver, and five filesystems configured, using 18 MB. Adding the compressed linux source, you need about 20 MB for this particular configuration. On another system, without network device support (but still with networking support), and sound card support, it consumes 14 MB. Also, a newer kernel is certain to have a larger source tree than an older one, so, in general, if you have a lot of hardware, make sure that you have a big enough hard disk in that mess.

2.7   How long does it take?

For most people, the answer is "fairly long." The speed of your system and the amount of memory you have ultimately determines the time, but there is a small bit to do with the amount of stuff you configure into the kernel. On a 486DX4/100 notebook with 16 MB of RAM, on a kernel with five filesystems, networking support, and sound card drivers, it takes under 20 minutes. On a 386DX/40 (8 MB RAM) with a similar configuration, compilation lasts nearly 1.5 hours. It is a generally good recommendation to make a little coffee, watch some TV, knit, or whatever you do for fun while your machine compiles the kernel.

3   How to actually configure the kernel

3.1   Getting the source

You can obtain the source via anonymous ftp from `ftp.funet.fi` in `/pub/OS/Linux/PEOPLE/Linus`, a mirror, or other sites. It is typically labelled `linux-x.y.z.tar.gz`, where `x.y.z` is the version number. Newer (better?) versions and the patches are typically in subdirectories such as 'v1.1' and 'v1.2' The highest number is the latest version, and is usually a "test release," meaning that if you feel uneasy about beta or alpha releases, you should stay with a major release.

I *strongly* suggest that you use a mirror ftp site instead of ftp.funet.fi. Here is a short list of mirrors and other sites:

```
USA:         tsx-11.mit.edu:/pub/linux/sources/system
USA:         sunsite.unc.edu:/pub/Linux/kernel
UK:          unix.hensa.ac.uk:/pub/linux/kernel
Austria:     fvkma.tu-graz.ac.at:/pub/linux/linus
Germany:     ftp.Germany.EU.net:/pub/os/Linux/Local.EUnet/Kernel/Linus
Germany:     ftp.dfv.rwth-aachen.de:/pub/linux/kernel
France:      ftp.ibp.fr:/pub/linux/sources/system/patches
Australia:   kirk.bond.edu.au:/pub/OS/Linux/kernel
```

If you do not have ftp access, a list of BBS systems which carry linux is posted periodically to comp.os.linux.announce; try to obtain this.

3.2   Unpacking the source

Log in as or su to 'root', and cd to `/usr/src`. If you installed kernel source when you first installed linux (as most do), there will already be a directory called 'linux' there, which contains the entire old source tree. If you have the disk space and you want to play it safe, preserve that directory. A good idea is to figure out what version your system runs now and rename the directory accordingly. The command 'uname -r' prints the current kernel version. Therefore, if 'uname -r' said '1.1.47', you would rename (with 'mv') 'linux' to 'linux-1.1.47'. If you feel mildly reckless, just wipe out the entire directory. In any case, make certain there is no 'linux' directory in `/usr/src` before unpacking the full source code.

Now, in `/usr/src`, unpack the source with 'tar zxvf linux-x.y.z.tar.gz' (if you've just got a .tar file with no .gz at the end, 'tar xvf linux-x.y.z.tar' works.). The contents of the source will fly by. When finished, there will be a new 'linux' directory in `/usr/src`. cd to linux and look over the README file. There will be a section with the label 'INSTALLING the kernel'. Carry out the instructions when appropriate – symbolic links that should be in place, removal of stale .o files, etc.

3.3   Configuring the kernel

Note: Some of this is reiteration/clarification of a similar section in Linus' README file.

The command 'make config' while in /usr/src/linux starts a configure script which asks you many questions. It requires bash, so verify that bash is /bin/bash, /bin/sh, or $BASH.

You are ready to answer the questions, usually with 'y' (yes) or 'n' (no). Some of the more obvious and non-critical options are not described here; see the section "Other configuration options" for short descriptions of a few others.

3.3.1   Kernel math emulation

If you don't have a math coprocessor (you have a bare 386 or 486SX), you must say 'y' to this. If you do have a coprocessor and you still say 'y', don't worry too much – the coprocessor is still used and the emulation ignored. The only consequence is that the kernel will be larger (costing RAM).

3.3.2   Normal (MFM/RLL) disk and IDE disk/cdrom support

You probably need to support this; it means that the kernel will support standard PC hard disks, which most people have. This driver does not include SCSI drives; they come later in the configuration.

You will then be asked about the "old disk-only" and "new IDE" drivers. You want to choose one of them; the main difference is that the old driver only supports two disks on a single interface, and the new one supports a secondary interface and IDE/ATAPI cdrom drives. The new driver is 4k larger than the old one and is also supposedly "improved," meaning that aside from containing a different number of bugs, it might improve your disk performance, especially if you have newer hardware.

3.3.3   Networking support

In principle, you would only say 'y' if your machine is on a network such as the internet, or you want to use SLIP, PPP, term, etc to dial up for internet access. However, as many packages (such as X windows) require networking support even if your machine does not live on a real network, you should say 'y'. Later on, you will be asked if you want to support TCP/IP networking; again, say 'y' here if you are not absolutely sure.

3.3.4   Limit memory to low 16MB

There exist buggy 386 DMA controllers which have problems with addressing anything more than 16 MB of RAM; you want to say 'y' in the (rare) case that you have one.

3.3.5   System V IPC

One of the best definitions of IPC (Interprocess Communication) is in the Perl book's glossary. Not surprisingly, Perl employs it to let processes talk to each other, as well as many other packages, so it is not a good idea to say n unless you know exactly what you are doing.

3.3.6   Use -m486 flag for 486-specific optimizations

This optimizes the kernel for use on a 486 processor. The new kernel will be slightly larger, but will work fine on a 386.

3.3.7   SCSI support

If you have a SCSI device, say 'y'. You will be prompted for further information, such as support for CD-ROM, disks, and what kind of SCSI adapter you have. See the SCSI-HOWTO for greater detail.

3.3.8   Network device support

If you have a network card, or you would like to use SLIP, PPP, or a parallel port adapter, say 'y'. The config script will prompt for which kind of card you have, and which protocol to use.

3.3.9   Filesystems

The configure script then asks if you wish to support the following filesystems:

Standard (Minix) - Newer distributions don't create Minix filesystems, and many people don't use it, but it may still be a good idea to configure this one. Some "rescue disk" programs use it, and still more floppies may have a Minix filesystem, since the Minix filesystem is fairly optimal for floppy disks.

Extended fs - This was the first version of the extended filesystem, which is no longer in widespread use. Chances are, you'll know it if you need it.

Second extended - This is widely used in new distributions. You probably have one of these, and need to say 'y'.

xiafs filesystem - At one time, this was not uncommon, but at the time of this writing, I did not know of anyone using it.

msdos - If you want to use your MS-DOS hard disk partitions, or mount MS-DOS formatted floppy disks, say 'y'.

umsdos - This filesystem expands an MS-DOS filesystem with usual Unix-like features such as long file-names. It is not useful for people (like me) who "don't do DOS."

/proc - Another one of the greatest things since powdered milk (idea shamelessly stolen from Bell Labs, I guess). One doesn't make a proc filesystem on a disk; this is a filesystem interface to the kernel and processes. Many process listers (such as 'ps') use it. Try 'cat /proc/meminfo' or 'cat /proc/devices' sometime. Some shells (rc, in particular) use /proc/self/fd (known as /dev/fd on other systems) for I/O. You should almost certainly say 'y' to this; many important Linux tools depend on it.

NFS - If your machine lives on a network and you want to share files with other systems using NFS, say 'y'.

ISO9660 - Found on most CD-ROMs.

OS/2 HPFS - At the time of this writing, a read-only fs for OS/2 HPFS.

System V and Coherent - for partitions of System V and Coherent systems (These are other PC Unix variants).

But I don't know which filesystems I need!   Ok, type 'mount'. The output will look something like this:

```
blah# mount
/dev/hda1 on / type ext2 (defaults)
/dev/hda3 on /usr type ext2 (defaults)
none on /proc type proc (defaults)
/dev/fd0 on /mnt type msdos (defaults)
```

Look at each line; the word next to 'type' is the filesystem type. In this example, my / and /usr filesystems are second extended, I'm using /proc, and there's a floppy disk mounted using the msdos (bleah) filesystem.

You can try 'cat /proc/filesystems' if you have /proc currently enabled; it will list your current kernel's filesystems.

The configuration of rarely-used, non-critical filesystems can cause kernel bloat; see the section on modules for a way to avoid this.

3.3.10 Character devices

Here, you enable the drivers for your printer, busmouse, PS/2 mouse (many notebooks use the PS/2 mouse protocol for their built-in trackballs), some tape drives, and other such "character" devices. Say 'y' when appropriate.

Note: Selection is a program which allows the use of the mouse outside of X Windows for cut and paste between virtual consoles. It's fairly nice if you have a serial mouse, because it coexists well with X Windows, but you need to do special tricks for others. Selection support was a configuration option at one time, but is now standard.

3.3.11 Sound card

If you feel a great desire to hear `biff` bark, say 'y', and later on, another config program will compile and ask you all about your sound board. (A note on sound card configuration: when it asks you if you want to install the full version of the driver, you can say 'n' and save some kernel memory by picking only the features which you deem necessary.)

3.3.12 Kernel hacking

>From Linus' README:

the "kernel hacking" configuration details usually result in a bigger or slower kernel (or both), and can even make the kernel less stable by configuring some routines to actively try to break bad code to find kernel problems (kmalloc()). Thus you should probably answer 'n' to the questions for a "production" kernel.

3.4 Now what? (The Makefile)

After you `make config`, a message tells you that your kernel has been configured, and to "check the top-level `Makefile` for additional configuration," etc.

So, look at the `Makefile`. You probably will not need to change it, but it never hurts to look. You can also change its options with the 'rdev' command once the new kernel is in place.

4 Compiling the kernel

4.1 Cleaning and depending

When the configure script ends, it also tells you to 'make dep' and 'clean'. So, do the 'make dep'. This insures that all of the dependencies, such the include files, are in place. It does not take long, unless your computer is fairly slow to begin with. When finished, do a 'make clean'. This removes all of the object files and some other things that an old version leaves behind. *Don't* forget this step.

4.2 Compile time

After depending and cleaning, you may now 'make zImage' or 'make zdisk' (This is the part that takes a long time.) 'make zImage' will compile the kernel, and leave a file in arch/i386/boot called 'zImage' (among other things). This is the new compressed kernel. 'make zdisk' does the same thing, but also places the new zImage on a floppy disk which you hopefully put in drive "A:". 'zdisk' is fairly handy for testing new kernels; if it bombs (or just doesn't work right), just remove the floppy and boot with your old kernel. It can also be a handy way to boot if you accidentally remove your kernel (or something equally as dreadful). You can also use it to install new systems when you just dump the contents of one disk onto the other ("all this and more! NOW how much would you pay?").

All reasonably recent kernels are compressed, hence the 'z' in front of the names. A compressed kernel automatically decompresses itself when executed.

4.3 Other "make"ables

'make mrproper' will do a more extensive 'clean'ing. It is sometimes necessary; you may wish to do it at every patch. See the section on modules for a description of 'make modules'.

4.4 Installing the kernel

After you have a new kernel that seems to work the way you want it to, it's time to install it. Most people use LILO (Linux Loader) for this. 'make zlilo' will install the kernel, run LILO on it, and get you all ready to boot, BUT ONLY if lilo is configured in the following way on your system: kernel is /vmlinuz, lilo is in /sbin, and your lilo config (/etc/lilo.conf) agrees with this.

Otherwise, you need to use LILO directly. It's a fairly easy package to install and work with, but it has a tendency to confuse people with the configuration file. Look at the config file (either /etc/lilo/config for older versions or /etc/lilo.conf for new versions), and see what the current setup is. The config file looks like this:

```
image = /vmlinuz
    label = Linux
    root = /dev/hda1
    ...
```

The 'image =' is set to the currently installed kernel. Most people use /vmlinuz. 'label' is used by lilo to determine which kernel or operating system to boot, and 'root' is the / of that particular operating system. Make a backup copy of your old kernel and copy the zImage which you just made into place (you would say 'cp zImage /vmlinuz' if you use '/vmlinuz'). Then, rerun lilo – on newer systems, you can just run 'lilo', but on older stuff, you might have to do an /etc/lilo/install or even an /etc/lilo/lilo -C /etc/lilo/config.

If you would like to know more about LILO's configuration, or you don't have LILO, get the newest version from your favorite ftp site and follow the instructions.

To boot one of your old kernels off the hard disk (another way to save yourself in case you screw up the new kernel), copy the lines below (and including) 'image = xxx' in the LILO config file to the bottom of the file, and change the 'image = xxx' to 'image = yyy', where 'yyy' is the full pathname of the file you saved your backup kernel to. Then, change the 'label = zzz' to 'label = linux-backup' and rerun lilo. You may need to put a line in the config file saying 'delay=x', where x is an amount in tenths of a second, which tells LILO to wait that much time before booting, so that you can interrupt it (with the shift key, for example), and type in the label of the backup boot image (in case unpleasant things happen).

5   Patching the kernel

5.1   Applying a patch

Incremental upgrades of the kernel are distributed as patches. For example, if you have version 1.1.45, and you notice that there's a 'patch46.gz' out there for it, it means you can upgrade to version 1.1.46 through application of the patch. You might want to make a backup of the source tree first ('make clean' and then 'cd /usr/src; tar zcvf old-tree.tar.gz linux' will make a compressed tar archive for you.).

So, continuing with the example above, let's suppose that you have 'patch46.gz' in /usr/src. cd to /usr/src and do a 'zcat patch46.gz | patch -p0' (or 'patch -p0 < patch46' if the patch isn't compressed). You'll see things whizz by (or flutter by, if your system is that slow) telling you that it is trying to apply hunks, and whether it succeeds or not. Usually, this action goes by too quickly for you to read, and you're not too sure whether it worked or not, so you might want to use the `-s` flag to `patch`, which tells `patch` to only report error messages (you don't get as much of the "hey, my computer is actually doing something for a change!" feeling, but you may prefer this..). To look for parts which might not have gone smoothly, cd to `/usr/src/linux` and look for files with a `.rej` extension. Some versions of `patch` (older versions which may have been compiled with on an inferior filesystem) leave the rejects with a # extension. You can use 'find' to look for you;

```
find . -name '*.rej' -print
```

prints all files who live in the current directory or any subdirectories with a `.rej` extension to the standard output.

If everything went right, do a 'make clean', 'config', and 'dep' as described in sections 3 and 4.

There are quite a few options to the `patch` command. As mentioned above, `patch -s` will suppress all messages except the errors. If you keep your kernel source in some other place than `/usr/src/linux`, `patch -p1` (in that directory) will patch things cleanly. Other `patch` options are well-documented in the manual page.

5.2 If something goes wrong

The most frequent problem that used to arise was when a patch modified a file called 'config.in' and it didn't look quite right, because you changed the options to suit your machine. This has been taken care of, but one still might encounter it with an older release. To fix it, look at the `config.in.rej` file, and see what remains of the original patch. The changes will typically be marked with '+' and '-' at the beginning of the line. Look at the lines surrounding it, and remember if they were set to 'y' or 'n'. Now, edit `config.in`, and change 'y' to 'n' and 'n' to 'y' when appropriate. Do a

```
patch -p0 < config.in.rej
```

and if it reports that it succeeded (no fails), then you can continue on with a configuration and compilation. The `config.in.rej` file will remain, but you can get delete it.

If you encounter further problems, you might have installed a patch out of order. If patch says 'previously applied patch detected: Assume -R?', you are probably trying to apply a patch which is below your current version number; if you answer 'y', it will attempt to degrade your source, and will most likely fail; thus, you will need to get a whole new source tree (which might not have been such a bad idea in the first place).

To back out (unapply) a patch, use 'patch -R' on the original patch.

The best thing to do when patches really turn out wrong is to start over again with a clean, out-of-the-box source tree (for example, from one of the `linux-x.y.z.tar.gz` files), and start again.

5.3 Getting rid of the .orig files

After just a few patches, the `.orig` files will start to pile up. For example, one 1.1.51 tree I had was once last cleaned out at 1.1.48. Removing the .orig files saved over a half a meg.

```
find . -name '*.orig' -exec rm -f {} ';'
```

will take care of it for you. Versions of `patch` which use # for rejects use a tilde instead of `.orig`.

There are better ways to get rid of the `.orig` files, which depend on GNU `xargs`:

```
find . -name '*.orig' | xargs rm
```

or the "quite secure but a little more verbose" method:

```
find . -name '*.orig' -print0 | xargs --null rm --
```

5.4 Other patches

There are other patches (I'll call them "nonstandard") than the ones Linus distributes. If you apply these, Linus' patches may not work correctly and you'll have to either back them out, fix the source or the patch, install a new source tree, or a combination of the above. This can become very frustrating, so if you do not want to modify the source (with the possibility of a very bad outcome), back out the nonstandard patches before applying Linus', or just install a new tree. Then, you can see if the nonstandard patches still work. If they don't, you are either stuck with an old kernel, playing with the patch or source to get it to work, or waiting (possibly begging) for a new version of the patch to come out.

How common are the patches not in the standard distribution? You will probably hear of them. I use the noblink patch for my virtual consoles because I hate blinking cursors (This patch is frequently updated for new kernel releases.).

6 Additional packages

Your linux kernel has many features which are not explained in the kernel source itself; these features are typically utilized through external packages. Some of the most common are listed here.

6.1 kbd

The linux console probably has more features than it deserves. Among these are the ability to switch fonts, remap your keyboard, switch video modes (in newer kernels), etc. The kbd package has programs which allow the user to do all of this, plus many fonts and keyboard maps for almost any keyboard, and is available from the same sites that carry the kernel source.

6.2 util-linux

Rik Faith (faith@cs.unc.edu) keeps a large collection of linux utilities which are, by odd coincidence, called util-linux. Available via anonymous ftp from sunsite.unc.edu in /pub/Linux/system/Misc, it contains programs such as setterm, rdev, and ctrlaltdel, which are relevant to the kernel. As Rik says, *do not install without thinking;* you do not need to install everything in the package, and it could very well cause serious problems if you do.

6.3 hdparm

As with many packages, this was once a kernel patch and support programs. The patches made it into the official kernel, and the programs to optimize and play with your hard disk are distributed separately.

7 Some pitfalls

7.1 make clean

If your new kernel does really weird things after a routine kernel upgrade, chances are you forgot to make clean before compiling the new kernel. Symptoms can be anything from your system outright crashing, strange I/O problems, to crummy performance. Make sure you do a make dep, too.

7.2   Huge or slow kernels

If your kernel is sucking up a lot of memory, is too large, or just takes forever to compile even when you've got your new 486DX6/440 working on it, you've probably got lots of unneeded stuff (device drivers, filesystems, etc) configured. If you don't use it, don't configure it, because it does take up memory. The most obvious symptom of kernel bloat is extreme swapping in and out of memory to disk; if your disk is making a lot of noise, look over your kernel configuration.

You can find out how much memory the kernel is using by taking the total amount of memory in your machine and subtracting it from the amount of "total mem" in `/proc/meminfo` or the output of the command 'free'. You can also find out by doing a 'dmesg' (or by looking at the kernel log file, wherever it is on your system). There will be a line which looks like this:

```
Memory:  15124k/16384k available (552k kernel code, 384k reserved, 324k data)
```

My 386 (which has slightly less junk configured) says this:

```
Memory:  7000k/8192k available (496k kernel code, 384k reserved, 312k data)
```

7.3   Kernel doesn't compile

If it does not compile, then it is likely that a patch failed, or your source is somehow corrupt. Your version of gcc also might not be correct, or could also be corrupt (for example, the include files might be in error). Make sure that the symbolic links which Linus describes in the README are set up correctly. In general, if a standard kernel does not compile, something is seriously wrong with the system, and reinstallation of certain tools is probably necessary.

7.4   New version of the kernel doesn't seem to boot

You did not run LILO, or it is not configured correctly. One thing that "got" me once was a problem in the config file; it said 'boot = /dev/hda1' instead of 'boot = /dev/hda' (This can be really annoying at first, but once you have a working config file, you shouldn't need to change it.).

7.5   You forgot to run LILO, or system doesn't boot at all

Ooops! The best thing you can do here is to boot off of a floppy disk and prepare another bootable floppy (such as 'make zdisk' would do). You need to know where your root (/) filesystem is and what type it is (e.g. second extended, Minix). In the example below, you also need to know what filesystem your `/usr/src/linux` source tree is on, its type, and where it is normally mounted.

In the following example, / is `/dev/hda1`, and the filesystem which holds `/usr/src/linux` is `/dev/hda3`, normally mounted at `/usr`. Both are second extended filesystems. The working kernel image in `/usr/src/linux/arch/i386/boot` is called zImage.

The idea is that if there is a functioning zImage, it is possible to use that for the new floppy. Another alternative, which may or may not work better (it depends on the particular method in which you messed up your system) is discussed after the example.

First, boot from a boot/root disk combo or rescue disk, and mount the filesystem which contains the working kernel image:

```
mkdir /mnt
mount -t ext2 /dev/hda3 /mnt
```

If mkdir tells you that the directory already exists, just ignore it. Now, cd to the place where the working kernel image was. Note that

```
/mnt + /usr/src/linux/arch/i386/boot - /usr = /mnt/src/linux/arch/i386/boot
```

Place a formatted disk in drive "A:" (not your boot or root disk!), dump the image to the disk, and configure it for your root filesystem:

```
cd /mnt/src/linux/arch/i386/boot
dd if=zImage of=/dev/fd0
rdev /dev/fd0 /dev/hda1
```

cd to / and unmount the normal /usr filesystem:

```
cd /
umount /mnt
```

You should now be able to reboot your system as normal from this floppy. Don't forget to run lilo (or whatever it was that you did wrong) after the reboot!

As mentioned above, there is another common alternative. If you happened to have a working kernel image in / (/vmlinuz for example), you can use that for a boot disk. Supposing all of the above conditions, and that my kernel image is /vmlinuz, just make these alterations to the example above: change /dev/hda3 to /dev/hda1 (the / filesystem), /mnt/src/linux to /mnt, and if=zImage to if=vmlinuz. The note explaining how to derive /mnt/src/linux may be ignored.

7.6   It says 'warning: bdflush not running'

This can be a severe problem. Starting with a kernel release after 1.0 (around 20 Apr 1994), a program called 'update' which periodically flushes out the filesystem buffers, was upgraded/replaced. Get the sources to 'bdflush' (you should find it where you got your kernel source), and install it (you probably want to run your system under the old kernel while doing this). It installs itself as 'update' and after a reboot, the new kernel should no longer complain.

7.7   It says weird things about obsolete routing requests

Get new versions of the route program and any other programs which do route manipulation. /usr/include/linux/route.h (which is actually a file in /usr/src/linux) has changed.

7.8   Firewalling not working in 1.2.0

Upgrade to at least version 1.2.1.

8   Modules

Loadable kernel modules can save memory and ease configuration. The scope of modules has grown to include filesystems, ethernet card drivers, tape drivers, printer drivers, and more.

8.1   Installing the module utilities

The module utilities are available from wherever you got your kernel source as modules-x.y.z.tar.gz; choose the highest patchlevel x.y.z that is equal to or below that of your current kernel. Unpack it with 'tar zxvf modules-x.y.z.tar.gz', cd to the directory it creates (modules-x.y.z), look over the README, and carry out its installation instructions (which is usually something simple, such as make install). You should now have the programs insmod, rmmod, ksyms, lsmod, genksyms, modprobe, and depmod in /sbin. If you wish, test out the utilities with the "hw" example driver in insmod; look over the INSTALL file in that subdirectory for details.

insmod inserts a module into the running kernel. Modules usually have a .o extension; the example driver mentioned above is called drv_hello.o, so to insert this, one would say 'insmod drv_hello.o'. To see the modules that the kernel is currently using, use lsmod. The output looks like this:

```
blah# lsmod
Module:         #pages:  Used by:
drv_hello          1
```

'drv_hello' is the name of the module, it uses one page (4k) of memory, and no other kernel modules depend on it at the moment. To remove this module, use 'rmmod drv_hello'. Note that rmmod wants a *module name*, not a filename; you get this from lsmod's listing. The other module utilities' purposes are documented in their manual pages.

8.2 Modules distributed with the kernel

As of version 1.2.2, many filesystems, a few SCSI drivers, several ethernet adapter drivers, and other odds and ends are loadable as modules. To use them, first make sure that you don't configure them into the regular kernel; that is, don't say y to it during 'make config'. Compile a new kernel and reboot with it. Then, cd to /usr/src/linux again, and do a 'make modules'. This compiles all of the modules which you did not specify in the kernel configuration, and places links to them in /usr/src/linux/modules. You can use them straight from that directory or execute 'make modules_install', which installs them in /lib/modules/x.y.z, where x.y.z is the kernel release.

This can be especially handy with filesystems. You may not use the Minix or msdos filesystems frequently. For example, if I encountered an msdos (shudder) floppy, I would insmod /usr/src/linux/modules/msdos.o, and then rmmod msdos when finished. This procedure saves about 50k of RAM in the kernel during normal operation. A small note is in order for the Minix filesystem: you should *always* configure it directly into the kernel for use in "rescue" disks.

9   Other configuration options

This section contains descriptions of selected kernel configuration options (in make config) which are not listed in the configuration section. Most device drivers are not listed here.

9.1   General setup

Normal floppy disk support - is exactly that. You may wish to read over the file drivers/block/README.fd; this is especially important for IBM Thinkpad users.

XT hard disk support - if you want to use that 8 bit XT controller collecting dust in the corner.

PCI bios support - if you have PCI, you may want to give this a shot; be careful, though, as some old PCI motherboards could crash with this option. More information about the PCI bus under linux is found in the PCI-HOWTO.

Kernel support for ELF binaries - ELF is an effort to allow binaries to span architectures and operating systems; linux seems to be headed in that direction.

Set version information on all symbols for modules - in the past, kernel modules were recompiled along with every new kernel. If you say y, it will be possible to use modules compiled under a different patchlevel. Read README.modules for more details.

9.2   Networking options

Networking options are described in the NET-2-HOWTO.

10   Tips and tricks

10.1   Redirecting output of the make or patch commands

If you would like logs of what those 'make' or 'patch' commands did, you can redirect output to a file. First, find out what shell you're running: 'grep root /etc/passwd' and look for something like '/bin/csh'.

If you use sh or bash,

```
(command) 2>&1 | tee (output file)
```

will place a copy of (command)'s output in the file '(output file)'.

For csh or tcsh, use

```
(command) |& tee (output file)
```

For rc (Note: you probably do not use rc) it's

```
(command) >[2=1] | tee (output file)
```

10.2   Conditional kernel install

Other than using floppy disks, there are several methods of testing out a new kernel without touching the old one. Unlike many other Unix flavors, LILO has the ability to boot a kernel from anywhere on the disk (if you have a large (500 MB or above) disk, please read over the LILO documentation on how this may cause problems). So, if you add something similar to

```
image = /usr/src/linux/arch/i386/zImage
    label = new_kernel
```

to the end of your LILO configuration file, you can choose to run a newly compiled kernel without touching your old /vmlinuz (after running lilo, of course). The easiest way to tell LILO to boot a new kernel is to press the shift key at bootup time (when it says LILO on the screen, and nothing else), which gives you a prompt. At this point, you can enter 'new_kernel' to boot the new kernel.

If you wish to keep several different kernel source trees on your system at the same time (this can take up a *lot* of disk space; be careful), the most common way is to name them /usr/src/linux-x.y.z, where x.y.z is the kernel version. You can then "select" a source tree with a symbolic link; for example, 'ln -sf linux-1.2.2 /usr/src/linux' would make the 1.2.2 tree current. Before creating a symbolic link like this, make certain that the last argument to ln is not a real directory (old symbolic links are fine); the result will not be what you expect.

10.3   Kernel updates

Russell Nelson (nelson@crynwr.com) summarizes the changes in new kernel releases. These are short, and you might like to look at them before an upgrade. They are available with anonymous ftp from ftp.emlist.com in pub/kchanges or through the URL

```
http://www.nvg.unit.no/linux-changes/index.html
```

11 Misc

11.1 Author

The author and maintainer of the Linux Kernel-HOWTO is Brian Ward (ward@blah.tu-graz.ac.at). Please send me any comments, additions, corrections, or computers. Corrections are, in particular, the most important to me. You can look at my 'home page' at one of these URLs:

```
http://www.math.psu.edu/ward/
http://blah.tu-graz.ac.at/~ward/
```

Even though I try to be attentive as possible with mail, please remember that I get a *lot* of mail per day, so it may take a little time to get back to you. Especially when emailing me with a question, please try extra hard to be clear and detailed in your message. I do not care if you ask simple questions; remember, if you don't ask, you may never get an answer! I'd like to thank everyone who has given me feedback.

Version -0.1 was written on October 3, 1994; this document is available in SGML, PostScript, TeX, roff, and plain-text formats.

11.2 To do

The "Tips and tricks" section is a little small. I hope to expand on it with suggestions from others.

So is "Additional packages."

More debugging/crash recovery info needed.

11.3 Contributions

A small part of Linus' README (kernel hacking options) is inclusive. (Thanks, Linus!)

uc@brian.lunetix.de (Ulrich Callmeier): patch -s and xargs.

quinlan@yggdrasil.com (Daniel Quinlan): corrections and additions in many sections.

nat@nataa.frmug.fr.net (Nat MAKAREVITCH): mrproper

boldt@math.ucsb.edu (Axel Boldt): collected descriptions of kernel configuration options on the net; then provided me with the list

lembark@wrkhors.psyber.com (Steve Lembark): multiple boot suggestion

kbriggs@earwax.pd.uwa.edu.au (Keith Briggs): some corrections and suggestions

Eric.Dumas@emi.u-bordeaux.fr (Eric Dumas): did a French translation

donahue@tiber.nist.gov (Michael J Donahue): typos, winner of the "sliced bread competition"

The people who have sent me mail with questions and problems have also been quite helpful.

11.4 Copyright notice and copying

Part XXVI

Linux Keystroke HOWTO

Copyright Zenon Fortuna, zenon@netcom.com
v2.0, 4 April 1995
This document is for users, who want to assign special action to some of keys of the keyboard. The suggested method is to use the loadkeys(1) or to modify the defkeymap.c file and relink the kernel. This text does NOT discuss remapping of keyboard keys, e.g. Backspace or Delete keys. For information about remapping of keys read the Backspace Mini-HOWTO written by Stephen Lee. The method described below was tested on Linux 1.2.1 release, packaged in the Slackware 2.2.0 distribution.

Contents

1   History of changes

- April 4th '95, version: 2.0 Adapted for the Linux 1.2.1:
    - simple changes in suggested modification of the my_keytable.map
    - modified key_macro example with /dev/vcs* screen dumping
- May 7th '94, version: 1.0 The initial version of the *Keystroke-HOWTO*, which worked for the Linux 1.0.

2   Short description

The Linux virtual terminal and keyboard drivers assume default keyboard mapping as defined in the drivers/char/defkeymap.c file of the kernel source. The 12 PC keyboard function keys may get strings assigned to their action. After pressing any of those function keys, perhaps modified with the Alt or Ctrl keys, the current virtual terminal adds the specific string to its input and output buffers, in effect emulating entry of this string as typed in from the keyboard.

Setting an appropriate string for chosen function key, we can simplify execution of selected command, for example calling a Shell-script /usr/local/bin/key_macro, which we can create and modify as desired.

3   Tools for keyboard driver modification

We may use loadkeys(1), dumpkeys(1) and showkey(1): The loadkeys(1) utility helps to load new strings into the keyboard buffers or prepares the new C-code to modify the kernel. The dumpkeys(1) should be used to get the current keyboard mapping table for inspection or modification. The showkey(1) may assist us to obtain the keycode of the selected function key.

If your Linux system does not have these utilities, you may get them via anonymous ftp as kbd-0.90.tar.gz package from

- (ftp://sunsite.unc.edu:/pub/Linux/system/Keyboards)
- (ftp://tsx-11.mit.edu:/pub/linux/sources/system)

You should use the GNU tar to extract the needed files.

4   Modifying keytable file

Linux kernel includes compiled defkeymap.c code, which is generated with the loadkeys(1) utility from a defkeymap.map file. Both files are included in the src/linux/drivers/char directory.

We need to modify the defkeymap.map file, so let's make a local copy of it either by

```
cp defkeymap.map my_keytable.map
```

or

```
dumpkeys > my_keytable.map
```

There is also a large collection of different keytable files in the /usr/lib/kbd/keytables directory, from which defkeymap.map may be used as src/linux/drivers/char/defkeymap.map file on your system.

The method which uses the dumpkeys(1) utility is recommended, because it may happen, that your kernel was already modified or generated for you with different defkeymap.map file than the one you can find.

Lets read the contents of the my_keytable.map file: there are more than 300 lines of code, and we can find 3 groups of declarations: The first group consists of lines with the word keycode, maybe prepended with additional words like alt, control, etc. The second group consists of lines with the word string. The third group consists of lines with the word compose.

More about the keytables(5) syntax can be read with

```
man keytables
```

4.1   Example of keytable file modification

As an example of assigning a macro-string to a function key stroke, let's make the Ctrl-F1 call our /usr/local/bin/key_macro Shell-script.

First of all we should find out what is the keycode for the F1 function key. We may use the showkey(1) utility to find the keycode with pressing F1.

Instead we can search for the "F1" string in the my_keytable.map file to find the following line:

```
keycode 59 = F1
```

This suggests, that the keycode for the F1 function key is 59. This line defines also, that after pressing the F1 key the keyboard driver would send out the string denoted by the string-code "F1". To see the contents of this string, one can search for the "string F1" pattern, to find

```
string F1 = "\033[[A"
```

This means, that after pressing the F1 key, the keyboard driver sends the "Esc [[A " (without blank spaces).

We shouldn't change this string, because some applications depend on this string as default action of the F1 function key.

However, we may define the new action for Ctrl–F1, provided it is not reserved by your kernel for other special actions. To see the mappings of the F1 key modified with the Ctrl–, Shift– or other modes, we may inspect the "my_keytable.map" file with

```
grep 59 my_keytable.map
```

In case when there is no line with "control keycode 59" we may use the Ctrl-F1 without problems. (when a line with the "shift control keycode 59" exists it is still OK)

Let us add a following line to the "my_keytable.map" file:

```
control keycode 59 = key_symbol
```

where the fkey_symbol would define the action of the Ctrl-F1 key. The Linux 1.2.* allows a dynamic allocation of strings, but a name of the key_symbol may be picked up only from a fixed set of names. Between other names the key-symbols F1-F246 are allowed. For my_keytable.map on my system the F21 was unused, but you should inspect your my_keytable.map and choose a proper key-symbol. So, we may end up with a line

```
control keycode 59 = F21
```

Now we have to define the contents of the F21, adding a line

```
string F21 = "/usr/local/bin/key_macro\n"
```

In the summary, we made two changes to the original my_keytable.map file: we declared the new string F21, and we have declared that the Ctrl-F1 key will be calling the F21 contents.

4.2   Temporary modification of the keyboard setup

Having properly modified my_keytable.map we can copy the changes to the kernel keyboard driver, using the loadkeys(1) utility:

```
loadkeys my_keytable.map
```

The permission to modify the kernel keyboard driver is granted to everybody who has the read access to the /dev/console device.

To verify that the intended changes were installed, we can use the dumpkeys(1) utility to check the F21 value, for example

```
dumpkeys | grep F21
```

We may see:

```
keycode 59 = F1          F11      Console_13      F21

string F21 = "/usr/local/bin/key_macro\012"
```

which is OK, because "12", or LF, is equivalent to "".

Now, pressing "Ctrl-F1" should call the "/usr/local/bin/key_macro" Shell-script, as intended.

4.3 Permanent modification

The changes to the kernel keyboard driver imposed by the loadkeys(1) last until the next reboot (or the next call to loadkeys).

We can modify the /etc/rc.d/rc.local to call the loadkeys with our my_keytable.map file as an argument. Instead, we can modify the src/linux/drivers/char/defkeymap.c and re-link the kernel with new defaults.

We should not modify the defkeymap.c manually, but rather generate it with the loadkeys(1) utility:

```
mv defkeymap.c defkeymap.c.ORIG
loadkeys --mktable my_keytable.map > defkeymap.c
```

Then we should generate the new kernel, essentially changing directory to the root of the Linux kernel source, and using the make(1).

Finally, we should use the lilo(1) to install and boot our new kernel.

4.4 Example of the key_macro script

A particularly useful script for simple-key-stroke operation may be a Shell-script preparing, or printing, a screen dump.

This example has changed since the version 1.0 of Linux, because of the changes in the Linux kernel, which does not provide the ioctl(0,TIOCLINUX) system call anymore.

To read the virtual console screen dumps one should prepare first some device files. As "root" user we may create the following files:

```
mknod /dev/vcs1  c 7 1
mknod /dev/vcs2  c 7 2
...
mknod /dev/vcs63 c 7 63
```

Of course, it is sufficient to have only the /dev/vcs* files specific for the virtual consoles you are using.

The code below should be regarded as an example of possible /usr/local/bin/key_macro file:

```
#!/bin/sh
#
# This is an example of useful key_macro script
#

VT_NUMBER='tty|cut -c9-'
FILE=/tmp/vt$VT_NUMBER.dump
cp /dev/vcs$VT_NUMBER $FILE
```

```
echo SCREEN DUMP saved in $FILE
#
# Uncomment the line below if you want to print the resulted dump-file
# lpr $FILE
```

4.5   Comments

There is no practical limit on the sum of the lengths of all strings which we would like to load to the keyboard driver. The previous fixed buffer of the length of FUNC_BUFSIZE (set to 512 bytes), has been replaced in the Linux 1.2.* by a strategy of dynamic buffer allocation ... in chunks of 512 bytes each.

The most recent copy of the Keystroke-HOWTO can be found in:

- (ftp://ftp.netcom.com/pub/ze/zenon/linux/howto)

4.6   Further ideas ?

In case you find anything worth adding to this document, please send your comments to zenon@netcom.com – thanks (zf)

Part XXVII

The MGR Window System HOWTO

Copyright Vincent Broman
Draft 16 Nov 1994

Contents

1   This HOWTO

1.1   Archiving

This HOWTO is temporarily archived in `ftp://bugs.nosc.mil/pub/Mgr/MGR-HOWTO`, and more permanently in `ftp://sunsite.unc.edu/pub/Linux/docs/HOWTO/MGR-HOWTO`. A copy will appear in `ftp://archimedes.nosc.mil/pub/Mgr/MGR-HOWTO` since bugs is disappearing in late 1994. In the same directories may appear alternate formats like `MGR-HOWTO.sgml` or `MGR-HOWTO.txt`.

1.2   Credit for the HOWTO

While Vincent Broman first put together this HOWTO, much of the information and text was obtained from FAQs, READMEs, etc. written by Stephen Uhler, Michael Haardt, and other public-spirited net-persons. Email corrections and suggested changes to `broman@nosc.mil`.

Uhler was the main architect of **MGR** – see the Credit section below.

2   What is the MGR window system?

2.1   Function

MGR (ManaGeR) is a graphical window system. The **MGR** server provides a builtin window manager and windowed graphics terminal emulation on color and monochrome bitmap displays. **MGR** is controlled by mousing pop-up menus, by keyboard interaction, and by escape sequences written on pseudo-terminals by client software.

MGR provides each client window with: termcap-style terminal control functions, graphics primitives such as line and circle drawing; facilities for manipulating bitmaps, fonts, icons, and pop-up menus; commands to reshape and position windows; and a message passing facility enabling client programs to rendezvous and exchange messages. Client programs may ask to be informed when a change in the window system occurs, such as a reshaped window, a pushed mouse button, or a message sent from another client program. These changes are called events. **MGR** notifies a client program of an event by sending it an ASCII character string in a format specified by the client program. Existing applications can be integrated into the windowing environment without modification by having **MGR** imitate keystrokes in response to user defined menu selections or other events.

2.2   Requirements

MGR currently runs on Linux, Sun 3/4 workstations with SunOS, and Coherent. Various older versions of **MGR** run on the Macintosh, Atari ST MiNT, Xenix, 386-Minix, DEC 3100, and the 3b1 Unix-pc. Many small, industrial, real-time systems under OS9 or Lynx in Europe use Mgr for their user interface. The programming interface is implemented in C and in ELisp, although supporting clients written in other languages is quite easy.

Running **MGR** requires much less in resources than X, or even gcc. It does not have the user-base, software repertory, or high-level libraries of X or MS-Windows, say, but it is quite elegant and approachable.

It has been said that **MGR** is to X as Unix was to Multics.

2.3   How do MGR, X11 and 8.5 compare?

MGR consists of a server with builtin window manager and terminal emulator, and clients which run in this terminal emulator and use it to communicate with the server. No resource multiplexing is done.

X11 consists of a server and clients, which usually connect to the server using a socket. All user visible things like terminal emulators, window managers etc are done using clients. No resource multiplexing is done.

8.5, the Plan 9 window system, is a resource multiplexer, as each process running in a window can access `/dev/bitblt`, `/dev/mouse` and `/dev/kbd` in its own namespace. These are multiplexed to the `/dev/bitblit`, `/dev/mouse` and `/dev/kbd` in the namespace of 8.5. This approach allows one to run

8.5 in an 8.5 window, a very clean design. 8.5 further has an integrated window manager and terminal emulator.

3 Installing MGR

The latest source distribution can be FTPed from the directories `ftp://bugs.nosc.mil/pub/Mgr/65` and `ftp://archimedes.nosc.mil/pub/Mgr/65`. One used to be able to find older **MGR** sources at `ftp://ftp.thp.uni-koeln.de/pub/linux/mgr`, or alternatively on `ftp://134.95.80.1/pub/thp/linux/mgr`, but these may be gone. Even older versions of this distribution from Haardt can be found on `tsx-11.mit.edu` and elsewhere. Pre-Linux versions of **MGR** from Uhler and others can be found at `ftp://bellcore.com/pub/mgr`, although no one seems to maintain things there. **MGR** has been through a lot of versions and releases, but the current *Linux* version number is 0.65. This version number ought to arrive at 1.0 when stable 256-color VGA code for Linux appears. RCS version numbers have increased from Bellcore's 4.3 up to our 4.12 now.

Required tools to build this distribution of **MGR** are m4 (GNU, or perhaps another supporting the -D option), make (GNU, or perhaps another supporting include) and *roff for the docs. Also sh, awk, and POSIX install. Binary distributions have not been assembled yet, so you need an ANSI C compiler environment, e.g. gcc.

A Linux installation requires Linux 0.99.10 or better, an HGC, EGA, VGA, or SVGA graphics card, and a mouse. Mouses supported are: serial Microsoft mouse, serial MouseSystems 3 and 5 byte mouse, serial MMSeries mouse, serial Logitech mouse, PS/2 mouse, or a bus mouse. The VGA 640x480 monochrome graphics mode is supported out of the box, as is 640x350 and 640x200. To run 800x600, or other modes that your BIOS can initialize and which do not require bank-switching, you need to run a small program (supplied as `src/vgamisc/regs.exe`) under DOS to read the VGA registers and write a header file which you place in the directory `src/libbitblit/linux`, so that it can be included by the `vga.c` file there. Some VGA cards can use 128k windows, and these can run higher monochrome resolutions.

The Linux-colorport code also runs in the standard 320x200x256 color VGA mode without difficulty, because no bank switching is required. Non-fast, but simple, bank-switching code has been added in version 0.65, and it works with a Tseng ET4000 card in 640x480x256 and 800x600x256 modes. The S3 code does not work in super VGA resolutions, yet. Supporting new super VGA cards requires writing one function to switch banks and making sure that the desired screen mode can be initialized from a register dump, possibly with hand-tweaking. The Linux color servers generally mangle the screen fonts, necessitating use of restorefont as in runx.

Suns with SunOS 4.1.2 and `bwtwo`, `cgthree`, or `cgsix` frame buffers are supported. Coherent installations should refer to the `README.Coh` file in the source distribution. Porting the latest-and-greatest **MGR** to another POSIX-like system which provides `select()` and pty's and direct access to a bitmapped framebuffer ought to be straightforward, just implementing the `libbitblit` library based on the `sunmono` or `colorport` code, say.

If you want to install everything, you need 5 MB disk space for binaries, fonts, manual pages etc. The sources are about 2 MB, plus object files during compilation.

Normally, `/usr/mgr` should be either the directory or a link to the directory where you install **MGR** stuff for runtime use. Typing

```
chdir /usr/mgr; gunzip < whereveryouputit/mgrusr.tgz | tar xvf -
```

and optionally

```
chdir /usr/mgr; gunzip < wherever/morefonts.tgz | tar xvf -
```

will unpack these. The source can be put anywhere, e.g. typing

```
chdir /usr/src/local/mgr; gunzip < wherever/mgrsrc.tgz | tar xvf -
```

to unpack the sources from `bugs.nosc.mil`.

The source tree can be compiled from one top-level Makefile which invokes lower-level Makefiles, all of which "include" a "Configfile" at the top level. The `Configfile` is created by an interactive sh script named `Configure`, which runs m4 on a `Configfile.m4`. So you do something like this:

```
chdir /usr/src/local/mgr
sh ./Configure
make first
make depend
make install
make clean
```

It might be wise, before running make, to eyeball the `Configfile` generated by the `Configure` script, checking that it looks reasonable. (At least one m4 poops out (Sun `/usr/bin/m4`), creating a very short `Configfile`. If this happens, try editing a copy of `Configfile.sun` or `Configfile.lx`) Several flags in MGRFLAGS can be added/omitted to change some optional features in the server, viz:

-DWHO

   muck utmp file so "who" works

-DVI

   code for clicking the mouse in vi moving the cursor

-DDEBUG

   enable debugging output selectable with -d options.

-DFASTMOUSE

   XOR the mouse track

-DBUCKEY

   for hot-key server commands without mousing

-DPRIORITY

   for priority window scheduling instead of round-robin; the active window gets higher priority

-DCUT

   for cut/paste between windows and a global snarf buffer

-DALIGN

   forces window alignment for fast scrolling (monochr)

-DKILL

   kills windows upon tty i/o errors

-DSHRINK

   use only some of the screen ($MGRSIZE in environment)

-DNOSTACK

   don't permit event stacking

-DBELL

   really ring the bell

-DKBD

   read `mgr` input from the sun kbd, instead of stdin. This permits redirection of console msgs to a window.

-DFRACCHAR

> fractional character movement for proportional fonts

-DXMENU

> extended menu stuff (experimental)

-DMOVIE

> movie making extension which logs all operations to a file for later replay – not quite working under Linux

-DEMUMIDMSBUT

> Emulate a missing middle mouse button by chording

Not all combinations of these options work on all systems.

The BITBLITFLAGS macro should contain `-DBANKED` if you're trying out the super VGA color.

If a make complains about the lack of a `default_font.h` or an `icon_server.h` in the directory `src/mgr`, it means that you forgot to do this

```
make depend
```

recently enough. C code for the static variables containing icons and fonts is generated by a translator from icon and font files.

Not all the clients are compiled and installed by the Makefiles. Clients found under `src/clients` having capitalized names or not compiled by the supplied Makefiles may have problems compiling and/or running, but they may be interesting to hack on. Most of the screen drivers found under the `libbitblit` directory are of mainly archeological interest. Grave robbing can be profitable.

At some point check that your `/etc/termcap` and/or `terminfo` file contain entries for **MGR** terminals such as found in the `misc` directory. If all your software checks $TERMCAP in the environment, this is not needed, as long as you run `set_termcap` in each window.

MGR works better if run setuid root, because it wants to chown ptys and write in the utmp file. This helps the ify iconifier client work better and the event passing mechanism be more secure. On Linux, root permissions are required in order to do in/out on the screen device. Otherwise, you decide whether to trust it.

In versions around 0.62 there are troubles on the Sun with using the csh as the default shell. Programs seem to run in a different process group than the foreground process group of the window's pty. There is no trouble with bash, sh, or rc. Ideas why?

4 Running MGR

The only file *required* in an **MGR** installation is the server itself. That would give you terminal emulator windows with shells running in them, but no nice clocks, extra fonts, fancy graphics, etc. Depending on options, a monochrome server needs about 200K of RAM plus dynamic space for windows, bitmaps, etc.

If `/usr/mgr/bin` is in your PATH, then just type `"mgr"` to start up. After enjoying the animated startup screen, press any key. When the hatched background and mouse pointer appear, hold down the left mouse button, highlight the `"new window"` menu item, and release the button. Then drag the mouse from corner to corner where you want a window to appear. The window will have your default shell running in it. Hold down the left mouse button over an existing window to see another menu for doing things to that window. The menu you saw that pops-up over the empty background includes the quit command. For people with a two button mouse: press both buttons together to emulate the missing middle button.

When trying to run **MGR**, if you get:

can't find the screen

make sure you have a /dev entry for your display device, e.g. on a Sun /dev/bwtwo0. If not, as root cd to /dev, and type "MAKEDEV bwtwo0". Otherwise, you might need the -S/dev/bwtwo0 or (on Linux) the -S640x480 command line option when starting mgr.

can't find the mouse

make sure /dev/mouse exists, usually as a symbolic link to the real device name for your mouse. If you haven't permission to write in /dev, then something like a -m/dev/cua0 option can be given when starting mgr. Also, make sure you've supplied the right mouse protocol choice when you configured mgr. The mouse may speak Microsoft, even if that is not the brand name.

can't get a pty

make sure all of /dev/[tp]ty[pq]? are owned by root, mode 666, and all programs referenced with the "shell" option in your .mgrc startup file (if any) exist and are executable.

none but the default font

make sure **MGR** is looking in the right place for its fonts. Check the Configfile in the source or see whether a -f/usr/mgr/font option to mgr fixes the problem.

completely hung (not even the mouse track moves)

login to your machine from another terminal (or rlogin) and kill the mgr process. A buckey-Q key can quit **MGR** if the keyboard still works.

4.1 Applications not aware of MGR

Any tty-oriented application can be run in an **MGR** window without further ado. Screen-oriented applications using termcap or curses can get the correct number of lines and columns by your using shape(1) to reshape the window or using set_termcap(1) to obtain the correct termcap.

4.2 MGR Applications (clients) distributed with the server

bdftomgr

converts some BDF fonts to MGR fonts

browse

an icon browser

bury

bury this window

c_menu

vi menus from C compiler errors

clock

digital display of time of day

clock2

analog display of time of day

close

close this window, iconify

color

set the foreground and background color for text in this window

colormap

    read or write in the color lookup table

cursor

    change appearance of the character cursor

cut

    cut text from this window into the cut buffer

cycle

    display a sequence of icons

dmgr

    crude ditroff previewer

fade

    fade a home movie script from one scene to another

font

    change to a new font in this window

hpmgr

    hp 2621 terminal emulator

ico

    animate an icosahedron or other polyhedron

iconmail

    notification of mail arrival

iconmsgs

    message arrival notification

ify

    iconify and deiconify windows

loadfont

    load a font from the file system

maze

    a maze game

mclock

    micky mouse clock

menu

    create or select a pop-up menu

mgr

    bellcore window system server and window manager

mgrbd

    boulder-dash game

mgrbiff

    watch mailbox for mail and notify

mgrload

    graph of system load average

mgrlock

    lock the console

mgrlogin

    graphical login controller

mgrmag

    magnify a part of the screen, optionally dump to file

mgrmail

    notification of mail arrival

mgrmode

    set or clear window modes

mgrmsgs

    message arrival notification

mgrplot

    Unix "plot" graphics filter

mgrsclock

    sandclock

mgrshowfont

    browse through mgr fonts

mgrsketch

    a sketching/drawing program

mgrview

    view mgr bitmap images

mless

    start up less/more in separate window, menu added for less

mphoon

    display the current phase of the moon

mvi

    start up vi in a separate window, mouse pointing

oclose

    (old) close a window

omgrmail

    (old) notification of mail arrival

pbmrawtomgr

    convert pbm raw bitmap to mgr bitmap format

pbmstream

    split out a stream of bitmaps

pbmtoprt

   printer output from PBM

pgs

   ghostscript patch and front end

pilot

   a bitmap browser

resetwin

   cleanup window state after client crashes messily

rotate

   rotate a bitmap 90 degrees.

screendump

   write graphics screen dump to a bitmap file

set_console

   redirect console messages to this window

set_termcap

   output an appropriate TERM and TERMCAP setting

setname

   name a window, for messages and iconifying

shape

   reshape this window

square

   square this window

squeeze

   compress mgr bitmap using run-length encoding

startup

   produce a skeleton startup file for current window layout

texmgr

   TeX dvi file previewer

text2font, font2text

   convert between mgr font format and text dump

unsqueeze

   uncompress mgr bitmap using run length encoding

window_print

   print an image of a window

zoom

   an icon editor

bounce, grav, grid, hilbert, mgreyes, stringart, walk

   graphics demos

4.3   MGR-aware clients distributed separately, see "SUPPORT" file

calctool

on-screen calculator

chess

frontend to `/usr/games/chess`

gnu emacs

editor with `lisp/term/mgr.el` mouse & menu support

gnuplot

universal scientific data plotting

metafont

font design and creation

origami

folding editor

pbmplus

portable bitmap format conversions, manipulations

plplot

slick scientific data plotting

?

a groff PBM driver using Hershey fonts

5   Programming for MGR

The **MGR** programmers manual, the C language applications interface, is found in the doc directory in troff/nroff form. It covers general concepts, the function/macro calls controlling the server, a sample application, with an index and glossary.

Porting client code used with older versions of **MGR** sometimes requires the substitution of

```
#include <mgr/mgr.h>
```

for

```
#include <term.h>
#include <dump.h>
```

and clients using old-style B_XOR, B_CLEAR, et al instead of BIT_XOR, BIT_CLR, et al can be accommodated by writing

```
#define OLDMGRBITOPS
#include <mgr/mgr.h>
```

Compiling client code generally requires compiler options like the following.

```
-I/usr/mgr/include   -L/usr/mgr/lib -lmgr
```

One can get some interactive feel for the **MGR** server functions by reading and experimenting with the `mgr.el` terminal driver for GNU Emacs which implements the **MGR** interface library in ELisp.

The usual method of inquiring state from the server has the potential of stumbling on a race condition if the client also expects a large volume of event notifications. The problem arises if an (asynchronous) event notification arrives when a (synchronous) inquiry response was expected. If this arises in practice (unusual) then the **MGR** state inquiry functions would have to be integrated with your event handling loop.

The only major drawing function missing from the **MGR** protocol, it seems, is an area fill for areas other than upright rectangles. There is new code for manipulating the global colormap, as well as (advisory) allocation and freeing of color indices owned by windows.

If you are thinking of hacking on the server, you can find the mouse driver in `mouse.*` and `mouse_get.*`, the grotty parts of the keyboard interface in `kbd.c`, and the interface to the display in the `src/libbitblit/*` directories. The main procedure, much initialization, and the top level input loop are in `mgr.c`, and the interpretation of escape sequences is in `put_window.c`.

6 More documentation

The programmer's manual is essential for concepts.

Nearly all the clients supplied come with a man page which is installed into `/usr/mgr/man/man1` or `man6`. Other useful man pages are `bitblit.3`, `font.5`, and `bitmap.5`. There is some ambiguity in the docs in distinguishing the internal bitmap format found in your frame-buffer and the external bitmap format found in files, e.g. icons.

The `mgr.1` man page covers command line options, commands in the `~/.mgrc` startup file, mouse and menu interaction with the server, and hot-key shortcuts available on systems with such hot-keys.

Many of the fonts in `/usr/mgr/font/*` are described to some extent in `/usr/mgr/font/*.txt`, e.g. `/usr/mgr/font/FONTDIR.txt` gives X-style font descriptions for the fonts obtained in .bdf format. Font names end in `WxH`, where `W` and `H` are the decimal width and height in pixels of each character box.

7 Credit for MGR

Stephen Uhler, with others working at Bellcore, was the original designer and implementer of **MGR**, so Bellcore has copyrighted much of the code and documentation for **MGR** under the following conditions.

```
* Permission is granted to copy or use this program, EXCEPT that it
* may not be sold for profit, the copyright notice must be reproduced
* on copies, and credit should be given to Bellcore where it is due.
```

One required showing of the copyright notice is the startup title screen.

Other credits to:

- Stephen Hawley for his wonderful icons.
- Tommy Frandsen for the VGA linux library.
- Tom Heller for his Gasblit library.
- Andrew Haylett for the Mouse driver code.
- Dan McCrackin for his gasblit->linux patches.
- Dave Gymer, dgp@cs.nott.ac.uk, for the Startrek effect fix.
- Alex Liu for first releasing a working Linux version of **MGR**.

- Lars Aronsson (aronsson@lysator.liu.se) for text2font and an ISO8859-1 8-bit font.

- Harry Pulley (hcpiv@grumpy.cis.uoguelph.ca, hcpiv@snowhite.cis.uoguelph.ca) for the Coherent port.

- Vance Petree & Grant Edwards & Udo Munk for their work on Hercules.

- Udo Munk for his work on serial mouse initialization & select.

- Norman Bartek & Hal Snyder at Mark Williams Co. for their help with some bugs & with Coherent device drivers.

- Extra thanks to Zeyd Ben Halim for lots of helpful patches, especially the adaptation of selection.

- Bradley Bosch, brad@lachman.com, for lots of patches from his 3b1 port, which fix bugs and implement new and desirable features.

- Andrew Morton, applix@runxtsa.runx.oz.au, who first wrote the cut-word code.

- Kapil Paranjape, kapil@motive.math.tifr.res.in, for the EGA support.

- Michael Haardt for MOVIE support fixes, bug fixes, separation of the libbitblit code into output drivers, expansion of the libmgr, and origami folding of the code.

- Yossi Gil for many fonts.

- Carsten Emde, carsten@thlmak.pr.net.ch, for mphoon.

- Vincent Broman for middle mouse-button emulation, linting, Sun cgsix support, VGA colormap acess, and integration of the sunport code into Haardt's layering scheme.

All bitmap fonts from any source are strictly public domain in the USA. The 575 fixed-width fonts supplied with **MGR** were obtained from Uhler, the X distribution, Yossi Gil, and elsewhere. The Hershey vector fonts and the code for rendering them are probably freely redistributable.

Part XXVIII

The Linux Electronic Mail HOWTO

Copyright Vince Skahan, <vince@halcyon.com>
v1.18, 31 Mar 1995
This document describes the setup and care+feeding of Electronic Mail (e-mail) under Linux. You need to read this if you plan to communicate locally or to remote sites via electronic mail. You probably do *not* need to read this document if don't exchange electronic mail with other users on your system or with other sites.

Contents

1   Introduction

The intent of this document is to answer some of the questions and comments that appear to meet the definition of 'frequently asked questions' about e-mail software under Linux.

This document and the corresponding UUCP and News 'HOWTO' documents collectively supersede the UUCP-NEWS-MAIL-FAQ that has previously been posted to comp.os.linux.announce.

1.1   New versions of this document

New versions of this document will be periodically posted to comp.os.linux.announce, comp.answers, and news.answers. They will also be added to the various anonymous ftp sites who archive such information including `sunsite.unc.edu:/pub/Linux/docs/HOWTO`.

In addition, you should be generally able to find this document on the Linux WorldWideWeb home page at `http://sunsite.unc.edu/mdw/linux.html`.

1.2   Feedback

I am interested in any feedback, positive or negative, regarding the content of this document via e-mail. Definitely contact me if you find errors or obvious omissions.

I read, but do not necessarily respond to, all e-mail I receive. Requests for enhancements will be considered and acted upon based on that day's combination of available time, merit of the request, and daily blood pressure :-)

Flames will quietly go to /dev/null so don't bother.

In particular, the Linux filesystem standard for pathnames is an evolving thing. What's in this document is there for illustration only based on the current standard at the time that part of the document was written and in the paths used in the distributions or 'kits' I've personally seen. Please consult your particular Linux distribution(s) for the paths they use.

Feedback concerning the actual format of the document should go to the HOWTO coordinator - Matt Welsh (`mdw@sunsite.unc.edu`).

1.3   Copyright Information

The Mail-HOWTO is copyrighted (c)1994 Vince Skahan.

A verbatim copy may be reproduced or distributed in any medium physical or electronic without permission of the author. Translations are similarly permitted without express permission if it includes a notice on who translated it.

Short quotes may be used without prior consent by the author. Derivative work and partial distributions of the Mail-HOWTO must be accompanied with either a verbatim copy of this file or a pointer to the verbatim copy.

Commercial redistribution is allowed and encouraged; however, the author would like to be notified of any such distributions.

In short, we wish to promote dissemination of this information through as many channels as possible. However, we do wish to retain copyright on the HOWTO documents, and would like to be notified of any plans to redistribute the HOWTOs.

We further want that ALL information provided in the HOWTOS is disseminated. If you have questions, please contact Matt Welsh, the Linux HOWTO coordinator, at `mdw@sunsite.unc.edu`.

1.4 Standard Disclaimer

Of course, I disavow any potential liability for the contents of this document. Use of the concepts, examples, and/or other content of this document is entirely at your own risk.

1.5 Other sources of information

1.5.1 LINUX HOWTO Documents:

There is plenty of exceptional material provided in the other Linux HOWTO documents and from the Linux DOC project. In particular, you might want to take a look at the following:

- the Serial Communications HOWTO

- the Ethernet HOWTO

- the Linux Networking Administrators' Guide

1.5.2 USENET:

```
comp.mail.elm            the ELM mail system.
comp.mail.mh             The Rand Message Handling system.
comp.mail.mime           Multipurpose Internet Mail Extensions.
comp.mail.misc           General discussions about computer mail.
comp.mail.multi-media    Multimedia Mail.
comp.mail.mush           The Mail User's Shell (MUSH).
comp.mail.sendmail       the BSD sendmail agent.
comp.mail.smail          the smail mail agent.
comp.mail.uucp           Mail in the uucp environment.
```

1.5.3 Books

The following is a non-inclusive set of books that will help...

- "Managing UUCP and USENET" from O'Reilly and Associates is in my opinion the best book out there for figuring out the programs and protocols involved in being a USENET site.

- "Unix Communications" from The Waite Group contains a nice description of all the pieces (and more) and how they fit together.

- "Sendmail" from O'Reilly and Associates looks to be the definitive reference on sendmail-v8 and sendmail+IDA. It's a "must have" for anybody hoping to make sense out of sendmail without bleeding in the process.

- "The Internet Complete Reference" from Osborne is a fine reference book that explains the various services available on Internet and is a great source for information on news, mail, and various other Internet resources.

- "The Linux Networking Administrators' Guide" from Olaf Kirch of the Linux DOC Project is available on the net and is also published by (at least) O'Reilly and SSC. It makes a fine *one-stop shopping* to learn about everything you ever imagined you'd need to know about Unix networking. *Shameless plug mode ON* - the sendmail+IDA descriptions below have been very much expanded and more fully explained in Chapter 15 of the Linux Networking Administrators' Guide. I *strongly* recommend you grab a copy and read it.

1.6   Where *NOT* to look for help

There is nothing "special" about configuring and running mail under Linux (any more). Accordingly, you almost certainly do *NOT* want to be posting generic mail-related questions to the comp.os.linux.* newsgroups.

Unless your posting is truly Linux-specific (ie, "please tell me what routers are already compiled into the SLS1.03 version of smail3.1.28") you should be asking your questions in one of the newsgroups or mailing lists referenced above.

Let me repeat that.

There is virtually no reason to post anything mail-related in the comp.os.linux hierarchy any more. There are existing newsgroups in the comp.mail.* hierarchy to handle *ALL* your questions.

IF YOU POST TO COMP.OS.LINUX. FOR NON-LINUX-SPECIFIC QUESTIONS, YOU ARE LOOKING IN THE WRONG PLACE FOR HELP. THE ELECTRONIC MAIL EXPERTS HANG OUT IN THE PLACES INDICATED ABOVE AND GENERALLY DO NOT RUN LINUX.*

POSTING TO THE LINUX HIERARCHY FOR NON-LINUX-SPECIFIC QUESTIONS WASTES YOUR TIME AND EVERYBODY ELSE'S...AND IT FREQUENTLY DELAYS YOU FROM GETTING THE ANSWER TO YOUR QUESTION.

2   Hardware Requirements

There are no specific hardware requirements for mail under Linux.

You'll need some sort of 'transport' software to connect to remote systems, which means either tcp-ip or uucp. This could mean that you need a modem or ethernet card (depending on your setup).

3   Getting the software

In general, I grab my sources from `ftp.uu.net` and the other fine archive sites on Internet. In addition, Linux-specific binary ports are found in the usual Linux distrbutions and on the usual Linux anonymous ftp sites (`sunsite.unc.edu` and `tsx-11.mit.edu` in particular).

The `newspak-2.4.tar.z` distribution contains config files and readme files related to building uucp, news, and mail software under Linux from the various freely-available sources. It can usually be found in `sunsite.unc.edu:/pub/Linux/system/Mail/news`. If you can't find it on sunsite, please send me mail and I'll make sure you get a copy of it.

4 Mail 'Transport Agents'

This section contains information related to 'transport agents', which means the underlying software that connects your local system to remote systems.

4.1 Smail v3.1

Smail3.1 seems to be a de-facto standard transport agent for uucp-only sites and for some smtp sites. It compiles without patching from the sources. In addition, smail is provided in binary form in the SLS distribution of Linux.

The newspak distribution contains config files for smail3.1.28 under Linux that you can use to start with.

If you're building smail from sources, you need to have the following in your os/linux file so that 'sed' gives you shell scripts that work properly.

```
CASE_NO_NEWLINES=true
```

For a uucp-only system that has a MX-record and that wants a domainized header (who goes through a smart-host for everything), these are the entire config files you'll need:

- replace 'subdomain.domain' with your domain name

- replace 'myhostname' with you un-domainized hostname

- replace 'my_uucp_neighbor' with the uucp name of your upstream site

```
#-------- /usr/local/lib/smail/config -----------------
#
# domains we belong to
visible_domain=subdomain.domain:uucp
#
# who we're known as (fully-qualified-site-name)
visible_name=myhostname.subdomain.domain
#
# who we go through
smart_path=my_uucp_neighbor
#
#---------- /usr/local/lib/smail/paths -------------
#
# we're a domainized site, make sure we accept mail to both names
myhostname          %s
myhostname.subdomain.domain        %s
#
#-------------------------------------------------------------------
```

To run smail as a smtp daemon, add the following to /etc/inetd.conf:

```
smtp stream tcp nowait  root  /usr/bin/smtpd smtpd
```

Outgoing mail gets sent automatically, when using elm. If your internet link is down when you send mail, then the mail sits in "/usr/spool/smail/input". When the link next comes up, "runq" is run which causes the mail to be sent.

4.2   Sendmail+IDA

I run a ppp and uucp site and generally use sendmail5.67b+IDA1.5 instead of smail3.1.28 due to the incredible   ease   of use. There is a binary distribution in `sunsite.unc.edu:pub/Linux/system/Mail/delivery`. To install it:

- you'll probably want to remove (or rename) all the files from smail (see the /install/installed directory if you are SLS) to be safe.

- cd to / then "gunzip -c sendmail5.67b+IDA1.5.tpz | tar xvf -" If you have a "modern" tar from a recent Slackware (for example) you can probably just do a "tar -zxvf filename.tgz" and get the same results.

- cd to /usr/local/lib/mail/CF and copy the sample.m4 local.m4 file to "yourhostname.m4". Edit out the distributed hostname, aliases, and smarthost and put in the correct one for your site. The default file is for a uucp-only site who has domainized headers and who talks to a smart host. Then "make yourhostname.cf" and move the resulting file to /etc/sendmail.cf

- if you are uucp-only, you do *NOT* need to create any of the tables mentioned in the README.linux file. You'll just have to touch the files so that the Makefile works. Just edit the .m4 file, make sendmail.cf, and start testing it.

- if you're uucp-only and you talk to sites in addition to your "smart-host", you'll need to add uucpxtable entries for each (or mail to them will also go through the smart host) and run dbm against the revised uucpxtable.

- if you use my sendmail5.67b+IDA1.5 distribution you should not use a "freeze file".

- If you run Rich Braun's original binary distribution of 5.67a, you'll need to freeze the configuration if you change your .cf file with "/usr/lib/sendmail -bz" to make the changes take effect. You should also update your version to at least 5.67b since there is a nasty security hole in 5.67a and earlier.

Another nice thing is that if you have mail.debug set and you run syslogd, your incoming and outgoing mail messages will get logged. See the /etc/syslog.conf file for details.

The sources for sendmail+IDA may be found at vixen.cso.uiuc.edu. They require no patching to run under Linux if you're running something like a kernel of 1.00.

If you're running a current kernel of around 1.1.50 or later, you get the fun of reversing most of the Linux-specific patches that are now in the vanilla sources. It's extremely obvious where this needs to be done. Just type *make* and when it blows up, go to that line in the sources and comment out the Linux-specific code that's in there.

Sometime after things settle down, I'll send the 'unpatches' to the sendmail+IDA authors and ask'em to remove the now unnecessary patches.

If you're going to run sendmail+IDA, I strongly recommend you go to the sendmail5.67b+IDA1.5 version since all required Linux-specific patches are now in the vanilla sources and several security holes have been plugged that WERE (!!!) in the older version you may have grabbed or built before about December 1st, 1993.

The May/June 1994 edition of `Linux Journal` has an extensive article on the care and feeding of sendmail+IDA. The new edition of the Linux DOC Project `Networking Administrator's Guide` has an even more detailed and complete version.

4.2.1   The sendmail.m4 file

Sendmail+IDA requires you to set up a `sendmail.m4` file rather than editing the `sendmail.cf` file directly. The nice thing about this is that it is simple to set up mail configurations that are extremely difficult (if not totally impossible for most people to set up correctly) in smail or traditional sendmail.

The sendmail.m4 file that corresponds to the above smail example looks like the following:

```
dnl #------------------ SAMPLE SENDMAIL.M4 FILE ------------------
dnl #
dnl # (the string 'dnl' is the m4 equivalent of commenting out a line)
dnl #
dnl # you generally don't want to override LIBDIR from the compiled in paths
dnl #define(LIBDIR, /usr/local/lib/mail)dnl     # where all support files go
define(LOCAL_MAILER_DEF, mailers.linux)dnl      # mailer for local delivery
define(POSTMASTERBOUNCE)dnl                     # postmaster gets bounces
define(PSEUDODOMAINS, BITNET UUCP)dnl           # don't try DNS on these
dnl #
dnl #-----------------------------------------------------------
dnl #
dnl # names we're known by
define(PSEUDONYMS, myhostname.subdomain.domain myhostname.UUCP)
dnl #
dnl # our primary name
define(HOSTNAME, myhostname.subdomain.domain)
dnl #
dnl # our uucp name
define(UUCPNAME, myhostname)dnl
dnl #
dnl #-----------------------------------------------------------
dnl #
define(UUCPNODES, |uuname|sort|uniq)dnl          # our uucp neighbors
define(BANGIMPLIESUUCP)dnl                       # make certain that uucp
define(BANGONLYUUCP)dnl                          #  mail is treated correctly
define(RELAY_HOST, my_uucp_neighbor)dnl          # our smart relay host
define(RELAY_MAILER, UUCP-A)dnl                  # we reach moria via uucp
dnl #
dnl #-----------------------------------------------------------------
dnl #
dnl # the various dbm lookup tables
dnl #
define(ALIASES, LIBDIR/aliases)dnl               # system aliases
define(DOMAINTABLE, LIBDIR/domaintable)dnl       # domainize hosts
define(PATHTABLE, LIBDIR/pathtable)dnl           # paths database
define(GENERICFROM, LIBDIR/generics)dnl          # generic from addresses
define(MAILERTABLE, LIBDIR/mailertable)dnl       # mailers per host or domain
define(UUCPXTABLE, LIBDIR/uucpxtable)dnl         # paths to hosts we feed
define(UUCPRELAYS, LIBDIR/uucprelays)dnl         # short-circuit paths
dnl #
dnl #-----------------------------------------------------------------
dnl #
dnl # include the 'real' code that makes it all work
dnl # (provided with the source code)
dnl #
include(Sendmail.mc)dnl                          # REQUIRED ENTRY !!!
dnl #
dnl #------------ END OF SAMPLE SENDMAIL.M4 FILE -------
```

4.2.2 Defining a local mailer

Unlike most Unix distributions, Linux does not come with a local mail delivery agent by default. I recommend using the commonly available deliver program, which is an optional package in a number of the usual Linux distributions. In order to do so, you need to define a LOCAL_MAILER_DEF in the `sendmail.m4` file that points to a file that looks like:

```
# -- /usr/local/lib/mail/mailers.linux --
#      (local mailers for use on Linux )
Mlocal, P=/usr/bin/deliver, F=SlsmFDMP, S=10, R=25/10, A=deliver $u
Mprog,  P=/bin/sh,          F=lsDFMeuP,  S=10, R=10, A=sh -c $u
```

There is a also built-in default for `deliver` in the `Sendmail.mc` file that gets included into the `sendmail.cf` file. To specify it, you would not use the `mailers.linux` file but would instead define the following in your sendmail.m4 file:

```
dnl --- (in sendmail.m4) ---
define(LOCAL_MAILER_DEF, DELIVER)dnl          # mailer for local delivery
```

Unfortunately, Sendmail.mc assumes deliver is installed in /bin, which is not the case with Slackware1.1.1 (which installs it in /usr/bin). In that case you'd need to either fake it with a link or rebuild deliver from sources so that it resides in /bin.

4.2.3   The Sendmail+IDA dbm Tables

Setting up special behavior for sites or domains is done through a number of optional dbm tables rather than editing the `sendmail.cf` file directly. Refer to the July-1994 issue of Linux Journal, to the docs in the sources, or to the sendmail chapter in the newest version of the Linux DOC Project Networking Administration Guide which will be available real-soon-now for more details.

- mailertable - defines special behavior for remote hosts or domains.

- uucpxtable - forces UUCP delivery of mail to hosts that are in DNS format.

- pathtable - defines UUCP bang-paths to remote hosts or domains.

- uucprelays - short-circuits the pathalias path to well-known remote hosts.

- genericfrom - converts internal addresses into generic ones visible to the outside world.

- xaliases - converts generic addresses to/from valid internal ones.

- decnetxtable - converts RFC-822 addresses to DECnet-style addresses.

4.2.4   So Which Entries are Really Required?

When not using any of the optional dbm tables, sendmail+IDA delivers mail via the DEFAULT_MAILER (and possibly RELAY_HOST and RELAY_MAILER) defined in the sendmail.m4 file used to generate sendmail.cf. It is easily possible to override this behavior through entries in the domaintable or uucpxtable.

A generic site that is on Internet and speaks Domain Name Service, or one that is UUCP-only and forwards all mail via UUCP through a smart RELAY_HOST, probably does not need any specific table entries at all.

Virtually all systems should set the DEFAULT_HOST and PSEUDONYMS macros, which define the canonical site name and aliases it is known by, and DEFAULT_MAILER. If all you have is a relay host and relay mailer, you don't need to set these defaults since it works automagically.

UUCP hosts will probably also need to set UUCPNAME to their official UUCP name. They will also probably set RELAY_MAILER, and RELAY_HOST which enable smart-host routing through a mail relay. The mail transport to be used is defined in RELAY_MAILER and should usually be UUCP-A for UUCP sites.

If your site is SMTP-only and talks 'Domain Name Service', you would change the DEFAULT_MAILER to TCP-A and probably delete the RELAY_MAILER and RELAY_HOST lines.

If you're a SLIP site, you might want to take the easy way out and just forward all outgoing mail to your service provider to do the right thing with. To do so, you'd want to define ISOLATED_DOMAINS and VALIDATION_DOMAINS to be your domain, you'd also want to define RELAY_HOST to be your service provider and RELAY_MAILER to be TCP. Of course, you want to ask permission before you set any system up as your general purpose relay.

4.3 Sendmail 8.6

Sendmail 8.6.x from Berkeley is the latest major revision after sendmail5. It has wonderful built-in support for building under Linux. Just "make linux" and you'll be all set. You'll probably be best served by grabbing one of the various binary distributions off of the usual Linux archive sites rather than fighting things like Berkeley dbm yourself.

There's a nice distribution of sendmail 8.6.12 from Jason Haar - *j.haar@lazerjem.demon.co.uk* in sunsite.unc.edu:/pub/Linux/system/Mail/delivery/sendmail-8.6.12-bin.tgz that has the source documentation and a very nice quickie description of how to run sendmail v8 for common configurations.

Bottom line with sendmail v8 is that you want to configure the bare minimum necessary to get the job done. The following is an example that should get you close at least.

4.3.1 A Sample 8.6.x mc file

Much like sendmail+IDA, sendmail v8 uses m4 to process a config file into a full sendmail.cf that sendmail uses. The following is my current mc file for my site (ppp to Internet for outgoing mail, uucp for incoming mail).

```
dnl divert(-1)
#-------------------------------------------------------------------
#
# this is the .mc file for a linux host that's set up as follows:
#
#        - connected to Internet for outbound mail (ppp here)
#        - connected via UUCP for incoming mail
#        - domainized headers
#        - no local mailer (use 'deliver' instead)
#        - no DNS running so don't canonicalize outgoing via DNS
#        - all non-local outbound mail goes to the RELAY_HOST over smtp
#            (we run ppp and let our service provider do the work)
#
#                                       vds 3/31/95
#
#-------------------------------------------------------------------
include('../m4/cf.m4')
VERSIONID('linux nodns relays to slip service provider smarthost')dnl
Cwmyhostname.myprimary.domain myhostname.UUCP localhost
OSTYPE(linux)
FEATURE(nodns)dnl
FEATURE(always_add_domain)dnl
FEATURE(redirect)
FEATURE(nocanonify)
dnl MAILER(local)dnl
MAILER(smtp)dnl
MAILER(uucp)dnl
define('RELAY_HOST',  smtp:my.relay.host.domain)
define('SMART_HOST',  smtp:my.relay.host.domain)
define('UUCP_RELAY',  smtp:my.relay.host.domain)
```

```
define('LOCAL_MAILER_PATH', '/bin/deliver')
define('LOCAL_MAILER_ARGS', 'deliver $u')
```

4.3.2 Sendmail v8 tidbits

There are a few differences I suppose to the 'IDA bigots' among us. So far, I've found the following.

- Instead of 'runq', you type 'sendmail -q' to run the queue

4.4   Other "transport agents"

The following also are known to run under Linux. Consult "archie" for details regarding how to find them...

- smail2.5 - very simple UUCP-based smail

4.5   Local Delivery Agents

Unlike most operating systems, Linux does not have mail "built-in". You'll need a program to deliver the local mail. One good program is Rich Braun's "lmail" program, but I've switched to using the more commonly available "deliver" program.

Documentation for how to use either for local delivery is in the sendmail5.67b+IDA1.5 binary release (on sunsite) mentioned above.

5   Mail "User Agents"

This section contains information related to "user agents", which means the software the user sees and uses. This software relies on the "transport agents" mentioned above.

5.1   Elm

Elm compiles, installs, and runs flawlessly under Linux up to and through Slackware 1.1.1 (gcc2.4.5, gcclib 4.4.4). For more information, see the elm sources and installation instructions.

The only thing to know is that Elm's Configure script incorrectly sets the "ranlib" variable in config.sh. The Elm Development Team has been informed of this little problem, so please don't bother them with it (again).

- (from *Chip Rosenthal - chip@chinacat.unicom.com*) The easiest way to deal with this is to create a file called `config.over` at the top of you Elm source tree and include the line:

      ```
      ranlib='ranlib'
      ```

- Alternatively, you can just remember to correctly edit the line in config.sh when Configure gives you the chance to do so.

- Elm and filter need to be mode 2755 (group mail) with /usr/spool/mail mode 775 and group mail.

If you use a binary distribution, you'll need to create a /usr/local/lib/elm/elm.rc file to override the compiled-in hostname and domain information:

- replace "subdomain.domain" with your domain name replace

- "myhostname" with you un-domainized hostname replace

```
#---------- /usr/local/lib/elm/elm.rc ------------------
#
# this is the unqualified hostname
hostname = myhostname
#
# this is the local domain
hostdomain = subdomain.domain
#
# this is the fully qualified hostname
hostfullname = myhostname.subdomain.domain
#
#-----------------------------------------------------------
```

One thing you want to be aware of is that if you have Elm compiled to be MIME-able, you need metamail installed and in your path or Elm will not be able to read MIME mail you've received. Metamail is available on `thumper.bellcore.com` and of course via "archie".

We have heard reports that gcc and gcclib newer than v2.4.5 and v4.4.4 respectively are rather strict and fail to compile Elm. Here's the scoop as reported by *ccnp@unitrix.utr.ac.za (Neil Parker)* who forwarded a posting by *longyear@netcom.com (Al Longyear)*.

- ELM is using internal fields in the FILE structure in an effort to bypass the standards. (The _flag, _IOERR, and _IOEOF are old fields for the pre-POSIX runtime package. While POSIX doesn't say that you can't define these fields, it does not say that you _must_. Linux does not. It does say that programs should not be written to use them, even if they are in the implementation.)

```
where it does        if (fp->_flag & _IOERR) ...
change it to         if (ferror(fp))  ....

where it does        if (fp->_flag & _IOEOF) ...
change it to         if (feof(fp)) ...

These are the ANSI/POSIX definitions for the same function.
```

- While this item is not Linux-specific, it's perceived (wrongly) to be a nagging Elm bug nevertheless. We've heard that Elm sometimes fails with a message that it's unable to malloc() some massive number of bytes. The identified workaround is to remove the post-processed global mail aliases (aliases.dir and aliases.pag). *THIS IS NOT A BUG IN ELM*. It's an error in configuration of Elm by whomever you got your binary distribution of Elm from. Elm has an enhanced, and non-compatible, format for aliases. You need to ensure that the path Elm uses for aliases is different from the path sendmail/smail uses. From the volume of reports of this problem, it's apparent that at least one major distribution 'on the street' has in the past been misconfigured. The current Slackware does it correctly.

- (from *scot@catzen.gun.de (Scot W. Stevenson)*)

The current metamail package requires csh for some of its scripts. Failure to have csh (or tcsh) will cause most interesting errors...

5.2 Mailx

Safe yourself the pain. Just go and grab the mailx kit from Slackware 2.1.0 or later, which has a nice implementation of mailx5.5. If you're into building from sources, mailx v5.5 compiles without patching under Linux if you have `"pmake"` installed.

If anybody is still using it, I strongly recommend removing the old "edmail" stuff from SLS1.00 and replacing it with mailx.

5.3   Other user agents

The following also are known to run under Linux. Consult "archie" for details regarding how to find them...

- Pine - from the Univ. of Washington
- Metamail - allows MIME support
- mh - yet another way to handle mail
- deliver - file/process mail based on rules
- procmail - file/process mail based on rules
- Majordomo - manages e-mail lists
- Mserv - provide files-by-mail

6   Acknowledgements

The following people have helped in the assembly of the information (and experience) that helped make this document possible:

Steve Robbins, Ian Kluft, Rich Braun, Ian Jackson, Syd Weinstein, Ralf Sauther, Martin White, Matt Welsh, Ralph Sims, Phil Hughes, Chip Rosenthal, Scot Stevenson, Neil Parker

If I forgot anybody, my apologies...

Part XXIX

Linux NET-2/NET-3 HOWTO

Copyright Terry Dawson, `terryd@extro.ucc.su.oz.au`
v3.0, 08 Apr 1995
This document aims to describe how to obtain, install and configure the Linux NET-2 and NET-3 networking software. Some answers to some of the more frequently asked questions are included in the appendix. This document is not designed to teach you about TCP/IP networking, though some information of this kind is included where possible. Pointers to other documentation which does teach TCP/IP networking principles is listed.

Contents

1   Introduction.

This is the Linux NET-2-HOWTO. This document is a complete rewrite of the earlier NET-FAQ, and of the subsequent NET-2-HOWTO versions 1.0+, for the new NET-2 and NET-3 TCP/IP networking code for Linux kernels 1.0 and above.

1.1   Changes from the previous release.

```
Additions:
        Added icmpinfo package to network diagnostic tools section.
        Added Matthias Urlich's ISDN support.
        Added brief description on how to install PI driver.
        Added QuickGuide for SLIP Server installation.

Corrections/Updates:
        Updated for kernel version 1.2.0 release.
        Updated newsgroup names to reflect current Linux heirarchy.
        Updated Florians package information.
        Updated the ARCNet information.
        Updated the Token Ring driver information.
```

```
Corrected a buglet in the sample dip script - thanks Matthew Elvey
Updated the AX25 code to version 028
Updated Eric Schenks diald package to 0.7
Updated Joerg Reuter's 8530 driver to 1.8
```

1.2 A brief development history of Linux Networking.

Ross Biro <biro@yggdrasil.com> wrote the original kernel based networking code for Linux. He used ethernet drivers written by Donald Becker <becker@cesdis1.gsfc.nasa.gov>, a *SLIP* driver written by Laurence Culhane <loz@holmes.demon.co.uk>, and a D-Link driver by Bj0rn Ekwall <bj0rn@blox.se>.

The further development of the Linux networking code was later taken up by Fred van Kempen <waltje@hacktic.nl>, who took Ross's code and produced the *NET-2* release of network code. NET-2 went through a number of revisions until release NET-2d, when Alan Cox <iialan@iifeak.swan.ac.uk> took Fred's NET-2d code and set about debugging the code with the aim of producing a stable and working release of code for incorporation into the standard kernel releases. This code was called *NET-2D(ebugged)*, and has been incorporated into the standard kernel releases since some time before Linux vers 1.0 was released.

PPP support was added by Michael Callahan, <callahan@maths.ox.ac.uk> and Al Longyear, <longyear@netcom.com>, originally as patches to the kernel, and in later releases as part of the standard kernel distribution.

With the release of Linux vers 1.0, Linus made a decision to continue supporting Alan's code as the *'standard'* network kernel code.

The latest revision of the code, NET-3, appears in kernel releases 1.1.5 and later, and is essentially the same code, but with many fixes, corrections and enhancements.

Alan has added such features as IPX and AX.25 modules. Florian La Roche, <flla@stud.uni-sb.de> has produced an updated distribution of network applications.

Many other people have made contributions by way of bug fixes, ports of applications and by writing device drivers.

2 Disclaimer.

The Linux networking code is a brand new implementation of kernel based TCP/IP networking. It has been developed from scratch, and is not a port of any existing kernel networking code.

Because it is a fresh implementation it may still have a number of bugs or problems with it, and there may be a number of fixes and patches released. If you are worried about problems then just stick to the version of network code released with the standard kernel releases and utility sets. The networking code has a small team of dedicated people working on it, with a cast of thousands testing the code, and collecting and reporting bugs and problems. Any problem you experience is likely to have already been reported, and be being worked on, and will possible be corrected soon, so be patient, or if you can help, offer your assistance.

We do not, and cannot, know everything there is to know about the Linux network software. Please accept and be warned that this document probably does contain errors. Please read any README files that are included with any of the various pieces of software described in this document for more detailed and accurate information. We will attempt to keep this document as error-free and up-to-date as possible. Versions of software are current as at time of writing.

NOTE: While its name may appear similar to the *Berkeley Software Distribution NET-2 release*, the Linux network code actually has nothing at all to do with it. Please don't confuse them.

3   Questions already ?

'The only stupid question is the unasked one.'

If you have general configuration questions, and you have been unable to find the answers after reading the other various HOWTO and FAQ files, then you would be best served to post them to *comp.os.linux.networking*, or, if you believe your question to be specifically related to the Linux Network code, then you could post it to the NET mailing list. **Please include as much relevant information as possible**, there is nothing more annoying than to have a bug or problem reported without sufficient information to even begin searching for it.

Version numbers and revisions of code, a detailed account of the problem, and the circumstances that caused it to occur, are essential. Trace and debug messages where available should also be considered mandatory.

If you have a question relating to the configuration of, or problems experienced with, **any** Linux distribution, regardless of who has provided it, please contact the people who created the distribution first, before attempting to report the problem to the network code developers. The reason for this is that some of the distributions use non-standard directory structures, and supply test/non-standard versions of code and utilities. The developers of the NET-2 code cannot be expected to offer support for the network code as distributed in any form, other than as described in this document, or as per distributed Alpha/Beta test instructions.

To join the Linux **NET** channel on the mail list server, send mail to:

```
linux-activists@niksula.hut.fi

with the line:

X-Mn-Admin: join NET

at the top of the message body (not the subject line).
```

Remember, keep in mind that the NET channel is for development discussions only.

Note also that a PPP list has been established. To join it, use the same procedure as for joining the NET channel, except specify PPP in place of NET in the X-Mn-Admin: field.

Note also that a HAMS list has been established. This list has been established for the discussion of programs related to Amateur Radio. To join it, follow the same procedure as for joining the NET or PPP channels, except specify HAMS in place of NET in the X-Mn-Admin: field.

4   Related Documentation. (Where to learn about TCP/IP)

If you are looking for information about TCP/IP networking that this HOWTO does not cover, then you might try the following sources, as they provide some very useful information.

Olaf Kirch has written a substantial document as part of the *Linux Documentation Project* entitled the *Linux Network Administration Guide*. This is an excellent document. It covers all aspects of setting up and using the TCP/IP networking under Linux, including NFS, UUCP, mail, News, nameserver etc.

Olaf's book supplements this HOWTO, taking up where this document leaves off. This document covers the installation and configuration of the NET code, i.e. 'How to put your machine on the net'. If you are new to Unix networking, then I strongly urge you to obtain a copy and read it first. It will answer a lot of questions for you that are not within the scope of this document.

The current release version is available in:

sunsite.unc.edu

```
/pub/Linux/docs/linux-doc-project/network-guide/*
```

There are various versions of the document in this directory. The most common formats are supported, being plain ascii, Postscript, DVI, Latex and groff.

The *Linux Network Administrators Guide* is Copyright (c) by Olaf Kirch.

You should also read the other HOWTO documents relevant to networking with Linux.

They are:

The *Ethernet-HOWTO* (`ftp://sunsite.unc.edu/pub/Linux/docs/HOWTO/Ethernet-HOWTO`) which you should read if you intend using an ethernet card with Linux. It includes much more detail on how to select, install and configure an ethernet card for Linux.

The *PPP-HOWTO* (`http://sunsite.unc.edu/mdw/HOWTO/PPP-HOWTO.html`) if you intend using PPP.

The *Serial-HOWTO* (`http://sunsite.unc.edu/mdw/HOWTO/Serial-HOWTO.html`) if you intend using SLIP or PPP in server mode.

The *Mail-HOWTO* (`http://sunsite.unc.edu/mdw/HOWTO/Mail-HOWTO.html`) and the *News-HOWTO* (`http://sunsite.unc.edu/mdw/HOWTO/News-HOWTO.html`) for some specific information on setting up Mail and News on your system.

The *UUCP-HOWTO* (`http://sunsite.unc.edu/mdw/HOWTO/UUCP-HOWTO.html`) if you will be connecting to the net via UUCP.

The *NIS-HOWTO* (`http://sunsite.unc.edu/mdw/HOWTO/NIS-HOWTO.html`) if you are interested in running a version of Sun's Network Information Service.

For more general information on Unix network configuration another good place to look for help on setting up your network is the *O'Reilly and Associates* book *TCP/IP Network Administration*, (the one with the Crab on the cover). Keep in mind that the Linux Network code is now a fairly standard implementation of TCP/IP networking, this means that the commands to configure and use it will work in much the same way as for those for other Unix operating systems. Keep in mind though that some of the arguments and options might differ slightly from those in the book.

If you are after some basic tutorial information on TCP/IP networking generally, then I recommend you take a look at the following documents:

TCP/IP introduction

text version (`ftp://athos.rutgers.edu/runet/tcp-ip-intro.doc`),

postscript version (`ftp://athos.rutgers.edu/runet/tcp-ip-intro.ps`).

TCP/IP administration

text version (`ftp://athos.rutgers.edu/runet/tcp-ip-admin.doc`),

postscript version (`ftp://athos.rutgers.edu/runet/tcp-ip-admin.ps`).

If you are after some more detailed information on TCP/IP networking then I highly recommend:

```
"Internetworking with TCP/IP"
by Douglas E. Comer

ISBN 0-13-474321-0
Prentice Hall publications.
```

If you are wanting to learn about how to write network applications in a Unix compatible environment then I also highly recommend:

```
"Unix Network Programming"
by W. Richard Stevens

ISBN 0-13-949876-1
Prentice Hall publications.
```

4.1   New versions of this document.

If your copy of this document is more than a two months old then I strongly recommend you obtain a newer version. Because the networking support for Linux is changing so rapidly this document also changes fairly frequently. The latest released version of this document can always be retrieved by anonymous ftp from:

sunsite.unc.edu

```
/pub/Linux/docs/HOWTO/NET-2-HOWTO

or:

/pub/Linux/docs/HOWTO/other-formats/NET-2-HOWTO{-html.tar,ps,dvi}.gz
```

or via the World Wide Web from *Linux Documentation Project Web Server* (`http://sunsite.unc.edu/mdw/linux.html`),

at page: *NET-2-HOWTO* (`http://sunsite.unc.edu/mdw/HOWTO/NET-2-HOWTO.html`)

or directly from me, `<terryd@extro.ucc.su.oz.au>`. It will also be posted to the newsgroups: `comp.os.linux.announce`, `comp.os.linux.help`, and `news.answers` from time to time.

You can find `news.answers` FAQ postings, including this one, archived on `rtfm.mit.edu:/pub/usenet`.

4.2 Feedback.

Please send any comments, updates, or suggestions to me, `<terryd@extro.ucc.su.oz.au>`. The sooner I get feedback, the sooner I can update and correct this document. If you find any problems with it, please mail me instead of posting to one of the newsgroups, as I may miss it.

5   Some terms used in this document.

You will often see the terms `client` and `server` used in this document. They are normally fairly specific terms but in this document I have generalized their definitions a little so that they mean the following:

client

> The machine or program that initiates an action or a connection for the purpose of gaining use of some service or data.

server

> The machine or program that accepts incoming connections from multiple remote machines and provides a service or data to those.

These definitions are not very reliable either, but they provide a means of distinguishing the ends of peer to peer systems such as *SLIP* or *ppp* which truly do not actually have clients and servers.

Other terms you will see are:

datagram

> A datagram is a discrete package of data and headers which contain addresses, which is the basic unit of transmission across an IP network. You might also hear this called a 'packet'.

MTU

> The Maximum Transmission Unit (*MTU*) is a parameter that determines the largest datagram than can be transmitted by an IP interface without it needing to be broken down into smaller units. The

MTU should be larger than the largest datagram you wish to transmit unfragmented. Note, this only prevents fragmentation locally, some other link in the path may have a smaller MTU and the datagram will be fragmented there. Typical values are 1500 bytes for an ethernet interface, or 576 bytes for a SLIP interface.

MSS

The Maximum Segment Size (*MSS*) is the largest quantity of data that can be transmitted at one time. If you want to prevent local fragmentation MSS would equal MTU-IP header.

window

The *window* is the largest amount of data that the receiving end can accept at a given point in time.

route

The *route* is the path that your datagrams take through the network to reach their destination.

6   NET-2/NET-3 Supported functionality.

The NET code is a complete kernel based implementation of TCP/IP for Linux. The recent NET-2 and NET-3 versions of code support:

Ethernet Cards

Most popular ethernet cards are supported.

SLIP (Serial Line IP) and PPP

for TCP/IP networking over serial lines such as the telephone via modem, or a local cable between two machines.

Van Jacobsen Header Compression

for compressing the TCP/IP headers to improve SLIP/PPP performance over low speed lines.

PLIP (Parallel Lines IP)

to allow local connections between two machines using your printer ports.

NFS (Networked File System)

to allow you to remotely mount another machines filesystems.

AX.25 (A protocol used by Amateur Radio Operators)

Alan Cox has some experimental code working.

PI Card (An 8530 SCC based card used by Amateur Radio Operators)

An experimental PI Card driver is available.

IPX/SPX (Novell)

to allow you to write custom SPX/IPX applications, or to use Linux as an IPX router.

Sun's Network Information System - NIS

An NIS implementation has been ported to Linux should you wish to use it.

ARCNet

An ARCNet driver has been written and is included in recent kernels.

IBM's Token Ring

An experimental Token Ring driver has been written.

The NET-2 and NET-3 network code does not yet currently support:

NCP (Novell Netware) support

to allow Linux to serve and mount Novell network devices. This is being worked on but due to the proprietry nature of the product it may take some time.

ISDN Support

You can of course use Linux with an appropriate terminal adapter that supports serial or ethernet connections, but there are currently no drivers for ISDN cards for Linux. There is some experimental code being developed.

FDDI

There is currently no support that I know of for FDDI cards for Linux.

6.1 Supported Ethernet cards.

The 1.2.0 Linux kernel release supports the following types of Ethernet cards:

- WD80*3 and close compatibles.
- SMC Ultra.
- AMD LANCE and PCnet (AT1500 and NE2100) and close compatibles.
- 3Com 3c501 (obsolete and very slow).
- 3Com 3c503.
- 3Com 3c505.
- 3Com 3c507.
- 3Com 3c509/3c579.
- Cabletron E21xx.
- DEPCA and close compatibles.
- EtherWorks 3.
- ARCNet.
- AT1700 (not clones).
- EtherExpress.
- NI5210 and close compatibles.
- NI6510.
- WaveLAN.
- HP PCLAN+ (27247B and 27252A).
- HP PCLAN (27245 and other 27xxx series).
- NE2000/NE1000 and close compatibles.
- SK_G16.
- Ansel Communications EISA 3200.
- Apricot Xen-II on board ethernet.
- DE425, DE434, DE435.

- Zenith Z-Note.

- AT-LAN-TEC/RealTek pocket adaptor.

- D-Link DE600 pocket adaptor and close compatibles.

- D-Link DE620 pocket adaptor and close compatibles.

Later versions of the Kernel software may support a wider variety of cards.

If you intend using and ethernet card with Linux you should read the *Ethernet-HOWTO* (`ftp://sunsite.unc.edu/pub/Linux/docs/HOWTO/Ethernet-HOWTO`) as it contains a lot of very useful information on the supported ethernet cards, including information on how to choose an ethernet card if you are intending to puchase some specifically for Linux.

As mentioned above, Linux supports other means of network connection if you don't have access to an ethernet card or connection. Many universities and businesses worldwide offer some form of dial-up network access. Generally these forms of access will offer an option of either SLIP or PPP access, so you will be well catered for. All you will need is a telephone modem, the one you already have may well be good enough, and to configure your Linux system appropriately. There are sections below that describe exactly what you need.

7 Getting the NET-2/NET-3 software.

Before you can configure the networking software you must obtain all of the bits and pieces that make it up. These include the current version of the kernel code (version 1.0 or later), the correct system libraries, the TCP/IP configuration programs and files (e.g. /sbin/ifconfig, /etc/hosts etc.), and finally a set of network application programs (such as telnet, ftp, rlogin etc.).

If you obtained Linux from a distribution you may already have all that you need. Check and make sure that you do. For example, some Linux distributions come with all of the network configuration files, binaries, libraries, and kernel installed, so there's no reason to get the following files.

NOTE: they may be in directories and files different to those specified in this HOWTO document

If you **DO** have the network software, skip to the 'Configuring the kernel' section. If you **DO NOT** have the network software follow the following directions.

7.1 The kernel source.

Version 1.2.0 of the Linux kernel is the *production* version. Any of the Linux kernels after that release are enhancements or bug fixes. If you feel at all concerned about the possibility of having to patch and modify the kernel source, then you should stick to this release, as it will do most of what you want it to. In the case of the networking code though, I strongly suggest you just take a deep breath and follow the newer releases of code, as there have been many changes in the newer version kernels that affect networking. I know you hear it from everyone and everywhere, but when trying out any new version of kernel software you should always ensure that you have sufficient backups of your system just in case something goes seriously wrong while you are testing.

The current kernel version is found in:

ftp.funet.fi

```
/pub/OS/Linux/PEOPLE/Linus/v1.2/linux-1.2.0.tar.gz
```

This is a gzipped file, so you will need *gzip* to uncompress it.

To install it, try:

```
# cd /usr/src
# mv linux linux.old
# gzip -dc linux-1.2.0.tar.gz | tar xvf -
```

You may also find some files called `patch-1.2.1.gz` ... in the same directory. These are patch files. If you have a Linux kernel that is version 1.2.1 then what this means is that you have Linux kernel version 1.2.0 with patch 1 applied. So you don't need to patch 1. If there are any patch files that are greater than the version of kernel you have, you should obtain **all** of those above, and apply them, **in sequence**, with something like the following commands:

```
# cd /usr/src
# for patchfile in .../patch*
> do
> gzip -dc $patchfile | patch -p0 2>>patch.errs
> done

    ...
```

Check the output file (patch.errs) and search for the strings `fail`. If you can't find it then all of the patch files were applied ok. If it is there, then at least one of the patch files didn't apply correctly. If this happens what you should do is start again from a clean kernel archive and apply the patches one by one until you find the patch file that failed. If you can't work out why it didn't work then report it as a problem.

7.2   The libraries.

You'll want at **least** version 4.4.2 of *libc*, as there were problems with earlier version that affected subnet masks.

The current libraries (libc-4.6.20) can be found in:

sunsite.unc.edu

```
/pub/Linux/GCC/
```

You will need at least the following files:

- image-4.6.27.tar.gz

- inc-4.6.27.tar.gz

- extra-4.6.27.tar.gz

- release.libc-4.6.27

You **MUST** read **release.libc-4.6.27** before you install the libraries. Please note that to use release 4.5.26 or later you will also need at least GCC version 2.6.2, and Linux kernel 1.1.52 or later.

7.3   The network configuration tool suite.

You will need the utility suite that provides tools to configure your network support.

The current NET-2 utility suite is available from:

sunacm.swan.ac.uk

```
/pub/misc/Linux/Networking/PROGRAMS/NetTools/net-tools-1.1.95.tar.gz
```

Because the kernel networking code is still changing some changes to the network tools have been necessary as new kernels are released, so you will need to choose the version that is appropiate for the kernel version you intend to use.

The filenames reflect the earliest version of kernel that the tools will work with. Please choose the filename whose version equals, or is less than the version of kernel source you intend to use.

To build and install the tools, you should try:

```
# cd /usr/src
# mkdir net-tools
# cd net-tools
# gzip -dc net-tools-1.1.95.tar.gz | tar xvf -
# make
```

This will automatically run the `Configure.sh` script. If everything makes ok, then:

```
# make install
```

If you use a kernel version 1.1.26 or earlier you should look in:

sunacm.swan.ac.uk

```
/pub/misc/Linux/Networking/PROGRAMS/Other/net032/
```

In this directory you will find three versions of the network tools. The following table lists net-032 package name with the relevant kernel versions:

```
net-0.32d-net3.tar.gz     1.1.12+
net-0.32b.tar.gz          1.1.4+
net-0.32.old.tar.gz       pre 1.1.4 kernels
```

These packages include the essential network configuration programs such as *ifconfig, route, netstat* etc. These will be discussed later.

7.4   The network applications.

You will want a number of network application programs. These are programs like *telnet, ftp, finger* and their daemons at least. `Florian La Roche, <flla@stud.uni-sb.de>` has put together a fairly complete distribution of network applications in both binary and source form. The TCP/IP application binaries and some sample config files are found in:

ftp.funet.fi

```
/pub/OS/Linux/PEOPLE/Linus/net-source/base/NetKit-A-0.08.bin.tar.gz
/pub/OS/Linux/PEOPLE/Linus/net-source/base/NetKit-B-0.06.tar.gz
```

If there are newer versions then use the newer versions. Please read the README file **first** just to make sure that you have the necessary prerequisites.

Florian used to have a binary distribution of the networking applications (the B file) available but it is no longer there, so you will have to build the files yourself. You can use the following procedure:

```
# cd /usr/src
# gzip -dc NetKit-B-0.06.tar.gz | tar xpvlf -
# cd NetKit-B-0.06
```

Then, read the README file. You will need to edit the Makefile and set the HAVE_SHADOW_PASSWORDS
define appropriately. I don't use shadow passwords, so I commented it out by placing a # at the start of the
line. The rest should not need modifying, so then all you should have to do is:

```
# make
# make install
```

IMPORTANT NOTE: Florian has built and prepackaged these tar files for your convenience. Florian has
attempted to make them as complete as possible and has included a distribution of the binaries found in the
net-tools-n.n.nn releases. Unfortunately Florian has chosen not to use the same directory structure as
Alan did when he prepared the installation script for the net-tools. This will mean that you should be very
careful when installing them. Florian will change this later so that this difference is not a problem, but until
then, I suggest you do the following instead of the above:

```
-  Unpack the binaries somewhere safe:
# cd /usr/src
# mkdir NetKit
# cd NetKit
# gzip -dc NetKit-A-0.07.bin.tar.gz | tar xpvlf -
# gzip -dc NetKit-B-0.06.bin.tar.gz | tar xpvlf -

-  Remove Florians copies of the network tools previously described:
# rm ./bin/hostname ./sbin/route ./sbin/ifconfig ./sbin/netstat
# rm ./usr/sbin/arp ./usr/sbin/rarp ./usr/sbin/slattach

-  Copy Florian's files into their new home:
# cp -vrpd . /
```

7.5   Additional drivers or packages.

If you want to add some developmental, or Alpha/Beta test code, such as AX.25 support, you will need
to obtain the appropriate support software for those packages. Please check the relevant sections for those
packages in this document for more detail.

8   Configuring the kernel.

Before you can use any of the network tools, or configure any network devices, you must ensure that your
kernel has the necessary network support built into it. The best way of doing this is to compile your own,
selecting which options you want and which you don't.

Assuming you have obtained and untarred the kernel source already, and applied any patches that you
might need to have applied to get any nonstandard or developmental software installed, all you have to do
is edit /usr/src/linux/drivers/net/CONFIG. This file has many comments to guide you in editing
it, and in general you will need to edit very little, as it has sensible defaults. In my case I don't need to edit
it at all. This file is really necesary if your ethernet card is an unusual one, or is one that isn't automatically
detected by the ethernet driver. It allows you to hard code some of the elements of your ethernet hardware.
For example, if your ethernet card is a close, but not exact clone of a WD-8013, then you might have to
configure the shared memory address to ensure the driver detects and drives the card properly. Please check
the The *Ethernet-HOWTO* (ftp://sunsite.unc.edu/pub/Linux/docs/HOWTO/Ethernet-HOWTO)
for more definitive information on this file and its effect on ethernet cards. This file also contains configurable
parameters for PLIP, though the defaults should again be ok unless you have a particularly slow machine.

When you are happy that the CONFIG file is suitable for your purposes, then you can proceed to build
the kernel. Your first step will be to edit the top level Makefile to ensure the kernel will be built with the
appropriate VGA settings, and then you must run the kernel configuration program:

```
# cd /usr/src/linux
# make config
```

You will be asked a series of questions. There are four sections relevant to the networking code. They are the General setup, Networking options, Network device support, and the Filesystems sections. The most difficult to configure is the Network device support section, as it is where you select what types of physical devices you want configured. On the whole you can just use the default values for the other sections fairly safely. The following will give you an idea of how to proceed:

```
*
* General setup
*
  ...
  ...
Networking support (CONFIG_NET) [y] y
  ...
  ...
```

In the General setup section you simply select whether you want network support or not. Naturally you must answer yes.

```
*
* Networking options
*
TCP/IP networking (CONFIG_INET) [y]
IP forwarding/gatewaying (CONFIG_IP_FORWARD) [n]
IP multicasting (CONFIG_IP_MULTICAST) [n]
IP firewalling (CONFIG_IP_FIREWALL) [n]
IP accounting (CONFIG_IP_ACCT) [n]
*
* (it is safe to leave these untouched)
*
PC/TCP compatibility mode (CONFIG_INET_PCTCP) [n]
Reverse ARP (CONFIG_INET_RARP) [n]
Assume subnets are local (CONFIG_INET_SNARL) [y]
Disable NAGLE algorithm (normally enabled) (CONFIG_TCP_NAGLE_OFF) [n]
The IPX protocol (CONFIG_IPX) [n]
*
```

The second half of the Networking options section allows you to enable or disable some funky features that you can safely accept the defaults on until you have some idea why you want to change them. They are described briefly later if you are interested.

```
*
*
* Network device support
*
Network device support? (CONFIG_NETDEVICES) [y]
Dummy net driver support (CONFIG_DUMMY) [n]
SLIP (serial line) support (CONFIG_SLIP) [y]
 CSLIP compressed headers (CONFIG_SLIP_COMPRESSED) [y]
 16 channels instead of 4 (SL_SLIP_LOTS) [n]
PPP (point-to-point) support (CONFIG_PPP) [y]
PLIP (parallel port) support (CONFIG_PLIP) [n]
Do you want to be offered ALPHA test drivers (CONFIG_NET_ALPHA) [n]
Western Digital/SMC cards (CONFIG_NET_VENDOR_SMC) [y]
WD80*3 support (CONFIG_WD80x3) [y]
SMC Ultra support (CONFIG_ULTRA) [n]
AMD LANCE and PCnet (AT1500 and NE2100) support (CONFIG_LANCE) [n]
```

```
3COM cards (CONFIG_NET_VENDOR_3COM) [n]
Other ISA cards (CONFIG_NET_ISA) [n]
EISA, VLB, PCI and on board controllers (CONFIG_NET_EISA) [n]
Pocket and portable adaptors (CONFIG_NET_POCKET) [n]
*
```

This section is the most important, and the most involved. It is where you select what hardware devices you want to support. You can see that I have selected SLIP support with header compression, PPP, the WD80*3 driver, and nothing else. Other options will appear depending on what you select. If you answered 'n' to the 'SLIP..' option you not be presented with the compressed SLIP or 16 channel options. Simply answer 'y' to whatever you want to play with, and 'n' to those that you don't.

```
*
* Filesystems
*
  ...
  ...
/proc filesystem support (CONFIG_PROC_FS) [y]
NFS filesystem support (CONFIG_NFS_FS) [y]
  ...
  ...
```

If you wish to run an NFS client then you will want to include the NFS filesystem type. You will need to include the /proc filesystem because a number of the network utilities use it.

After you have completed the configuration, all that remains is to actually compile the kernel:

```
# make dep
# make
```

Don't forget to make zlilo if the new kernel compiles and tests ok.

8.1   What do all those funky Networking options actually do?

Newer kernels have a number of options that you are asked about when you do a make config. Generally you will not need to change these, but some of the options might be useful to you in certain circumstances.

TCP/IP networking

This one is obvious, it selects whether you configure the TCP/IP suite of protocols into your kernel. Chances are if you are reading this then you will want to answer 'y' to this one.

Dummy networking device

This was added to allow SLIP and PPP users to configure an address on their Linux machine that would not be dependent on their serial link being established. It is an easy way to give your Linux machine two addresses.

IP forwarding/gatewaying

This determines what your kernel will do when it receives a datagram that has a destination address that is not one of its own devices. You **must** have this option selected if you want your kernel to act as an IP router. Most SLIP and PPP servers will want this option selected.

IP multicasting

This is alpha test code support for IP multicasting, examples of which include services such as 'Internet Talk Radio' and live video. You will need additional programs to make use of this facility, this is just the kernel support.

IP firewalling

This option allows you to provide flexible security options for your Linux machine. You can selectively enable/disable access to TCP/IP ports from any address ranges you choose. This also needs additional programs to support it.

IP accounting

This option is for those people that want to use their Linux machine to provide internet connectivity to others on a commercial basis. It allows you to count and record incoming and outgoing bytes on a per port and address basis. With the addition of suitable software this would allow you to produce separate usage charges for each person using your systems networking capabilities.

PC/TCP compatibility mode

This option provides a work-around for a bug that causes problems when using the PC/TCP networking programs to talk to your Linux machine. There is a PC/TCP bug which provokes a difficult to remedy Linux bug, and this option prevents the two clashing. Normally you would leave this disabled, but if you have users on your network who use PC/TCP then you may have to enable this option to prevent problems.

Reverse ARP

This option allows you to configure the RARP protocol into your kernel. This option was added to allow the booting of Sun 3 systems. This is not generally very useful otherwise.

Assume subnets are local

This option selects whether you assume that your whole subnet is directly connected to your Linux machine, or whether it might be bridged or otherwise subdivided at a lower layer. In practice it will make little difference if you leave it set at the default.

Disable NAGLE algorithm

This is a timing option that determines when a datagram should be transmitted. The default setting provides for the best throughput in most situations and you should leave this set as it is, as disabling it will degrade your throughput. This option can be selectively changed from within a program with a socket option, and you would normally be much better off leaving it set at the default and specifically writing your programs to disable the NAGLE algorithm if they require extremely fast interactivity.

The IPX protocol

This option selects whether you compile the IPX protocol support into your kernel. The IPX protocol is an internetworking protocol similar in function to the IP protocol. This protocol is one of those used by the Novell suite.

Amateur Radio AX.25 Level 2

This option selects whether you compile in the Amateur Radio AX.25 protocol suite. If you select this option then a new class of network sockets are available for programming. The AX.25 protocol is used primarily by Amateur Radio Operators for packet radio use.

9 Configuring the Network Devices.

If everything has gone ok so far, then you will have a Linux kernel which supports the network devices you intend to use, and you also have the network tools with which to configure them. *Now comes the fun part!* You'll need to configure each of the devices you intend to use. This configuration generally amounts to telling each device things like what its IP address will be, and what network it is connected to.

In past versions of this document I have presented near complete versions of the various configuration files and included comments to modify or delete lines from them as appropriate. From this version onwards I will take a slightly different approach which I hope will result in you having a complete set of uncluttered configuration files that you have built from scratch so you know exactly what is in them, and why. I'll describe each of these files, and their function, as we come to them.

9.1   Configuring the special device files in /dev

You do not need to configure any special device files in the /dev directory for Linux Networking. Linux does not need or use them as other operating systems might. The devices are built dynamically in memory by the kernel, and since they are only names there is no need for them to have an appearance directly to you. The kernel provides all of the programming hooks and interfaces that you need to utilize them effectively.

9.2   What information do I need before I begin ?

Before you can configure the networking software, you will need to know a number of pieces of information about your network connection. Your network provider or administrator will be able to provide you with most of them.

9.2.1   IP Address.

This is the unique machine address, in dotted decimal notation, that your machine will use. An example is 128.253.153.54. Your network administrator will provide you with this information.

If you will be using a SLIP or PLIP connection you may not need this information, so skip it until we get to the SLIP device.

If you're using the loopback device only, ie no ethernet, SLIP or PLIP support, then you won't need an ip address as the loopback port always uses the address 127.0.0.1.

9.2.2   Network Mask ('netmask').

For performance reasons it is desirable to limit the number of hosts on any particular segment of a network. For this reason it is common for network administrators to divide their network into a number of smaller networks, known as *subnets*, which each have a portion of the network addresses assigned to them. The *network mask* is a pattern of bits, which when overlayed onto an address on your network, will tell you which subnetwork it belongs to. This is very important for routing, and if you find for example, that you can happily talk to people outside your network, but not to some people on your own network, then it is quite likely that you have specified an incorrect subnet mask.

Your network adminstrators will have chosen the netmask when the network was designed, and therefore they should be able to supply you with the correct mask to use. Most networks are class-C subnetworks which use 255.255.255.0 as their netmask. Other larger networks use class-B netmasks (255.255.0.0). The NET-2/NET-3 code will automatically select a default mask when you assign an address to a device. The default assumes that your network has **not** been subnetted.

The NET-2/NET-3 code will choose the following masks by default:

```
For addresses with the first byte:
1-127           255.0.0.0           (Class A)
128-191         255.255.0.0         (Class B)
192+            255.255.255.0       (Class C)
```

if one of these doesn't work for you, try another. If this doesn't work ask your network administrator or local network guru (dime a dozen) for help.

You don't need to worry about a netmask for the loopback port, or if you are running SLIP/PLIP.

9.2.3   Network Address.

This is your IP address masked (bitwise AND) with your netmask. For example:

```
If your netmask is:            255.255.255.0
and your IP address is:        128.253.154.32    &&
                               ---------------
your Network address is:       128.253.154.0     =
```

9.2.4 Broadcast Address.

'A shout is a whisper that everyone hears whether they need to or not'

This is normally your network address logically ORed with your netmask inverted. This is simpler than it sounds. For a Class-C network, with network mask 255.255.255.0, your *Broadcast Address* will be your network address (calculated above), logically ORed with 0.0.0.255, the network mask inverted.

A worked example might look like:

```
If your netmask is:            255.255.255.0      !
the netmask inverted is:         0.  0.  0.255    =
If your Network address is:    128.253.154.0      ||
                               ---------------
Your broadcast address is:     128.253.154.255    =
```

Note that for historical reasons some networks use the network address as the broadcast address. If you have any doubts contact your network administrator.

If you have access to a *sniffer*, or some other device capable of providing you with a trace of your network traffic, then you might be able to determine both the network and broadcast addresses by watching other traffic on the lan. Keep an eye open for, (or filter everything except), ethernet frames destined for the ethernet broadcast address: ff:ff:ff:ff:ff:ff. If any of them has an IP source address of your local router, and the protocol ID is not ARP, then check the destination IP address, because this datagram may well be a RIP routing broadcast from your router, in which case the destination IP address will be your broadcast address.

Once again, if you're not sure, check with your network administrator, they'd rather help you, than have you connect your machine misconfigured.

9.2.5 Router ('Gateway') Address.

'There must be some way out of here.'

This is the address of the machine that connects your network to the rest of the Internet. It is your 'gateway' to the outside world. A couple of conventions exist for allocating addresses to routers which your network might follow, they are: The router is the lowest numbered address on the network, the router is the highest numbered host on the network. Probably the most common is the first, where the router will have an address that is mostly the same as your own, except with a .1 as the last byte. eg. if your address is 128.253.154.32, then your router might be 128.253.154.1. The router can in fact have any address valid on your network and function properly, the address doesn't matter at all. There may in fact even be more than one router on your network. You will probably need to talk to your network adminstrator to properly identify your router address.

If you're using only loopback then you don't need a router address. If you're using PPP then you also don't need your router address, because PPP will automatically determine the correct address for you. If you're using SLIP, then your router address will be your SLIP server address.

9.2.6 Nameserver Address.

Most machines on the net have access to a name server which translates human tolerable hostnames into machine tolerable addresses, and *vice versa*. Your network administrators will again tell you the address of your nearest nameserver. You can in fact run a nameserver on your own machine by running *named,* in which case your nameserver address will be `127.0.0.1`, the *loopback* port address. However it is not required that you run *named* at all; see section 'named' for more information.

If you're only using loopback then you don't need to know the nameserver address since you're only going to be talking to your own machine.

9.2.7   NOTE for SLIP/PLIP/PPP users.

You may or may not in fact need to know any of the above information. Whether you do or not will depend on exactly how your network connection is achieved, and the capabilities of the machine at the other end of the link. You'll find more detail in the section relevant to configuration of the SLIP/PLIP and PPP devices.

9.3   /etc/rc.d/rc.inet1,2 or /etc/rc.net

While the commands to configure your network devices can be typed manually each time, you will probably want to record them somewhere so that your network is configured automatically when you boot your machine.

The `'rc'` files are specifically designed for this purpose. For the non-Unix-wizard: `'rc'` file are run at bootup time by the *init* program and start up all of the basic system programs such as *syslog*, *update*, and *cron*. They are analagous to the MS-DOS *autoexec.bat* file, and *rc* might stand for *'runtime commands'*. By convention these files are kept under the */etc* directory. The Linux Filesystem Standard doesn't go so far as to describe exactly where your *rc* files should go, stating that it is ok for them to follow either the BSD (/etc/rc.*) or System-V (/etc/rc.d/rc*) conventions. Alan, Fred and I all use the System-V convention, so that is what you will see described here. This means that these files are found in */etc/rc.d* and are called *rc.inet1* and *rc.inet2*. The first *rc* file that gets called at bootup time is `/etc/rc`, and it in turn calls others, such as `rc.inet1`, which in turn might called `rc.inet2`. It doesn't really matter where they are kept, or what they are called, so long as *init* can find them.

In some distributions the *rc* file for the network is called *rc.net* and is in the */etc* subdirectory. The *rc.net* file on these systems is simply the *rc.inet1* and the *rc.inet2* files combined into one file that gets executed. **It doesn't matter where the commands appear, so long as you configure the interfaces before starting the network daemons and applications.**

I will refer to these files as *rc.inet1* and *rc.inet2*, and I keep them in the `/etc/rc.d`, so if you are using one of the distributions that uses *rc.net*, or you want to keep the files somewhere else, then you will have to make appropriate adjustments as you go.

We will be building these files from scratch as we go.

9.3.1   rc.inet1

The *rc.inet1* file configures the basic TCP/IP interaces for your machine using two programs: */sbin/ifconfig*, and */sbin/route*.

ifconfig   */sbin/ifconfig* is used for configuring your interfaces with the parameters that they require to function, such as their IP address, network mask, broadcast addresses and similar. You can use the *ifconfig* command with no parameters to display the configuration of all network devices. Please check the *ifconfig* man page for more detail on its use.

route   */sbin/route* is used to create, modify, and delete entries in a table (the routing table) that the networking code will look at when it has a datagram that it needs to transmit. The routing table lists destination address, and the interface that that address is reachable via. You can use the *route* command with no parameters to display the contents of the routing table. Please check the *route* man page for more detail on its use.

9.3.2 rc.inet2

The *rc.inet2* file starts any network daemons such as *inetd*, *portmapper* and so on. This will be covered in more detail in section 'rc.inet2', so for the moment we will concentrate on *rc.inet1*. I have mentioned this file here so that if you have some other configuration, such as a single *rc.net* file you will understand what the second half of it represents. it is important to remember that you must start your network applications and daemons **after** you have configured your network devices.

9.4 Configuring the Loopback device (mandatory).

The loopback device isn't really a hardware device. It is a software construct that looks like a physical interface. Its function is to happily allow you to connect to yourself, and to test network software without actually having to be connected to a network of any kind. This is great if you are developing network software and you have a SLIP connection. You can write and test the code locally, and then when you are ready to test it on a live network, eatablish your SLIP connection and test it out. You won't hurt others users if your program misbehaves.

By convention, the loopback device always has an IP address of 127.0.0.1 and so you will use this address when configuring it.

The loopback device for Linux is called *'lo'*. You will now make the first entry into your *rc.inet1* file. The following code fragment will work for you:

```
#!/bin/sh
#
# rc.inet1  --  configures network devices.
#
# Attach the loopback device.
/sbin/ifconfig lo 127.0.0.1
#
# Add a route to point to the loopback device.
/sbin/route add 127.0.0.1
# End loopback
#
```

You have used the *ifconfig* program to give the loopback interface its IP address, and *route* program to create an entry in the routing table that will ensure that all datagrams destined for 127.0.0.1 will be sent to the loopback port.

There are two important points to note here.

Firstly, the netmask and broadcast addresses have been allowed to take the default values for the loopback device described earlier in section 'Network Mask'. To see what they are, try the *ifconfig* program without any arguments.

```
# ifconfig
lo        Link encap Local Loopback
   inet addr 127.0.0.1  Bcast 127.255.255.255  Mask 255.0.0.0
   UP BROADCAST LOOPBACK RUNNING  MTU 2000  Metric 1
   RX packets 0 errors 0 dropped 0 overrun 0
   TX packets 30 errors 0 dropped 0 overrun 0
 #
```

Secondly, its not obvious how the *route* command chose the loopback device as the device for the route to 127.0.0.1. The *route* program is smart enough to know that 127.0.0.1 belongs to the network supported by the loopback device. It works this out by checking the IP address and the netmask. You can use the *route* command with no arguments to display the contents of the routing table:

```
# route
Kernel routing table
Destination     Gateway         Genmask         Flags Metric Ref    Use Iface
127.0.0.0       *               255.0.0.0       U     0      0       30 lo
#
```

Note: You might want to use the -n argument if your name resolver is not yet configured properly. The -n argument tells *route* to just display the numeric addresses, and to not bother looking up the name.

9.5   Configuring an ethernet device. (optional)

You'll only be interested in this section if you wish to configure an ethernet card, if not then skip on ahead to the next section.

To configure an ethernet card is only slightly more complicated than configuring the loopback device. This time you should probably specify explicitly the network mask and the broadcast address, unless you are sure that the defaults will work ok, and they probably will.

For this you will need the IP address that you have been assigned, the network mask in use on your network, and the broadcast address in use.

The first ethernet device for a *Linux* system is called *'eth0'*, the second *'eth1'* and so forth. You will now **add** a section to your *rc.inet1* file. The following code fragment will work for you if you change the addresses specified for real ones:

```
#
# Attach an ethernet device
#
#   configure the IP address, netmask and broadcast address.
/sbin/ifconfig eth0 IPA.IPA.IPA.IPA
/sbin/ifconfig eth0 netmask NMK.NMK.NMK.NMK
/sbin/ifconfig eth0 broadcast BCA.BCA.BCA.BCA
#
# add a network route to point to it:
/sbin/route add -net NWA.NWA.NWA.NWA device eth0
#
# End ethernet
#
```

Where:

IPA.IPA.IPA.IPA

> represents your IP Address.

NMK.NMK.NMK.NMK

> represents your netmask.

BCA.BCA.BCA.BCA

> represents your Broadcast address.

NWA.NWA.NWA.NWA

> represents your Network Address.

Note the use of the -net argument to the *route* command. This tells *route* that the route to be added is a route to a *network*, and not to a *host*. There is an alternative method of achieving this, you can leave off the -net if you have the network address listed in the */etc/networks* file. This is covered later in section '/etc/networks'.

9.6   Configuring a SLIP device (optional)

SLIP (Serial Line Internet Protocol) allows you to use TCP/IP over a serial line, be that a phone line with a dialup modem, or a leased line of some sort. Of course to use SLIP you need access to a *SLIP-server* in your area. Many universities and businesses provide SLIP access all over the world.

SLIP uses the serial ports on your machine to carry IP datagrams. To do this it must take control of the serial device. SLIP device names are named *sl0*, *sl1* etc. How do these correspond to your serial devices ? The networking code uses what is called an *ioctl* (i/o control) call to change the serial devices into SLIP devices. There are two programs supplied that can do this, they are called *dip* and *slattach*

9.6.1   dip

dip (Dialup IP) is a smart program that is able to set the speed of the serial device, command your modem to dial the remote end of the link, automatically log you into the remote server, search for messages sent to you by the server, and extract information for them such as your IP address, and perform the *ioctl* necessary to switch your serial port into SLIP mode. *dip* has a powerful scripting ability, and it is this that you can exploit to automate your logon procedure.

dip used to be supplied with the *net-tools*, but since development of *dip* is now separate, you have to source it separately. There have been a number of other versions of *dip* produced which offer a variety of new features. The `dip-uri` version seems to be the more popular, but I suggest you take a close look at each to determine which offers enhancements that you find useful. Since `dip-uri` is is so popular, the examples described in this document are based on current versions of it.

You can find it at:

sunsite.unc.edu

```
    /pub/Linux/system/Network/serial/dip337j-uri.tgz
```

To install it, try the following:

```
    #
    # cd /usr/src
    # gzip -dc dip337j-uri.tgz | tar xvf -
    # cd dip.3.3.7j

    <edit Makefile>

    # make install
    #
```

The `Makefile` assumes the existence of a group called *uucp*, but you might like to change this to either *dip* or *SLIP* depending on your configuration.

9.6.2   slattach

slattach as contrasted with *dip* is a very simple program, that is very easy to use, but does not have the sophistication of *dip*. It does not have the scripting ability, all it does is configure your serial device as a SLIP device. It assumes you have all the information you need and the serial line is established before you invoke it. *slattach* is ideal to use where you have a permanent connection to your server, such as a physical cable, or a leased line.

9.6.3   When do I use which ?

You would use *dip* when your link to the machine that is your SLIP server is a dialup modem, or some other temporary link. You would use *slattach* when you have a leased line, perhaps a cable, between your machine and the server, and there is no special action needed to get the link working. See section 'Permanent SLIP connection' for more information.

Configuring SLIP is much like configuring an Ethernet interface (read section 'Configuring an ethernet device' above). However there are a few key differences.

First of all, SLIP links are unlike ethernet networks in that there is only ever two hosts on the network, one at each end of the link. Unlike an ethernet that is available for use as soon are you are cabled, with SLIP, depending on the type of link you have, you may have to initialise your network connection in some special way.

If you are using *dip* then this would not normally be done at boot time, but at some time later, when you were ready to use the link. It is possible to automate this procedure. If you are using *slattach* then you will probably want to add a section to your *rc.inet1* file. This will be described soon.

There are two major types of SLIP servers: Dynamic IP address servers and static IP address servers. Almost every SLIP server will prompt you to login using a username and password when dialing in. *dip* can handle logging you in automatically.

9.6.4   Static SLIP server with a dialup line and DIP.

A static SLIP server in one in which you have been supplied an IP address that is exclusively yours. Each time you connect to the server, you will configure your SLIP port with that address. The static SLIP server will answer your modem call, possibly prompt you for a username and password, and then route any datagrams destined for your address to you via that connection. If you have a static server, then you may want to put entries for your hostname and IP address (since you know what it will be) into your /etc/hosts. You should also configure some other files such as: rc.inet2, host.conf, resolv.conf, /etc/HOSTNAME, and rc.local. Remember that when configuring rc.inet1, you don't need to add any special commands for your SLIP connection since it is *dip* that does all of the hard work for you in configuring your interface. You will need to give *dip* the appropriate information, and it will configure the interface for you after commanding the modem to establish the call, and logging you into your SLIP server.

If this is how your SLIP server works then you can move to section 'Using Dip' to learn how to configure *dip* appropriately.

9.6.5   Dynamic SLIP server with a dialup line and DIP.

A *dynamic* SLIP server is one which allocates you an IP address randomly, from a pool of addresses, each time you logon. This means that there is no guarantee that you will have any particular address each time, and that address may well be used by someone else after you have logged off. The network administrator who configured the SLIP server will have assigned a pool of address for the SLIP server to use, when the server receives a new incoming call, it finds the first unused address, guides the caller through the login process, and then prints a welcome message that contains the IP address it has allocated, and will proceed to use that IP address for the duration of that call.

Configuring for this type of server is similar to configuring for a static server, except that you must add a step where you obtain the IP address that the server has allocated for you and configure your SLIP device with that.

Again, *dip* does the hard work, and new versions are smart enough to not only log you in, but to also be able to automatically read the IP address printed in the welcome message, and store it so that you can have it configure your SLIP device with it.

If this is how your SLIP server works then you can move to section 'Using Dip' to learn how to configure *dip* appropriately.

9.6.6 Using DIP.

As explained earlier, *dip* is a powerful program that can simplify and automate the process of dialing into the SLIP server, logging you in, starting the connection, and configuring your SLIP devices with the appropriate *ifconfig* and *route* commands.

Essentially to use *dip* you'll write a 'dip script', which is basically a list of commands that *dip* understands that tell *dip* how to perform each of the actions you want it to perform. See `sample.dip` that comes supplied with *dip* to get an idea of how it works. *dip* is quite a powerful program, with many options. Instead of going into all of them here you should looks at the *man* page, README and sample files that will have come with your version of *dip*.

You may notice that the `sample.dip` script assumes that you're using a static SLIP server, so you know what your IP address is beforehand. For dynamic SLIP servers, the newer versions of *dip* include a command you can use to automatically read and configure your SLIP device with the IP address that the dynamic server allocates for you. The following sample is a modified verson of the `sample.dip` that came supplied with *dip337j-uri.tgz*, and is probably a good starting point for you. You might like to save it as `/etc/dipscript` and edit it to suit your configuration:

```
#
# sample.dip    Dialup IP connection support program.
#
#               This file (should show) shows how to use the DIP
#          This file should work for Annex type dynamic servers, if you
#          use a static address server then use the sample.dip file that
#          comes as part of the dip337-uri.tgz package.
#
#
# Version:      @(#)sample.dip  1.40    07/20/93
#
# Author:       Fred N. van Kempen, <waltje@uWalt.NL.Mugnet.ORG>
#

main:
# Next, set up the other side's name and address.
# My dialin machine is called 'xs4all.hacktic.nl' (== 193.78.33.42)
get $remote xs4all.hacktic.nl
# Set netmask on sl0 to 255.255.255.0
netmask 255.255.255.0
# Set the desired serial port and speed.
port cua02
speed 38400

# Reset the modem and terminal line.
# This seems to cause trouble for some people!
reset

# Note! "Standard" pre-defined "errlevel" values:
#   0 - OK
#   1 - CONNECT
#   2 - ERROR
#
# You can change those grep'ping for "addchat()" in *.c...

# Prepare for dialing.
send ATQ0V1E1X4\r
wait OK 2
if $errlvl != 0 goto modem_trouble
dial 555-1234567
if $errlvl != 1 goto modem_trouble
```

```
# We are connected.  Login to the system.
login:
sleep 2
wait ogin: 20
if $errlvl != 0 goto login_trouble
send MYLOGIN\n
wait ord: 20
if $errlvl != 0 goto password_error
send MYPASSWD\n
loggedin:

# We are now logged in.
wait SOMEPROMPT 30
if $errlvl != 0 goto prompt_error

# Command the server into SLIP mode
send SLIP\n
wait SLIP 30
if $errlvl != 0 goto prompt_error

# Get and Set your IP address from the server.
#   Here we assume that after commanding the SLIP server into SLIP
#   mode that it prints your IP address
get $locip remote 30
if $errlvl != 0 goto prompt_error

# Set up the SLIP operating parameters.
get $mtu 296
# Ensure "route add -net default xs4all.hacktic.nl" will be done
default

# Say hello and fire up!
done:
print CONNECTED $locip ---> $rmtip
mode CSLIP
goto exit

prompt_error:
print TIME-OUT waiting for SLIPlogin to fire up...
goto error

login_trouble:
print Trouble waiting for the Login: prompt...
goto error

password:error:
print Trouble waiting for the Password: prompt...
goto error

modem_trouble:
print Trouble ocurred with the modem...
error:
print CONNECT FAILED to $remote
quit

exit:
exit
```

The above example assumes you are calling a *dynamic* SLIP server, if you are calling a *static* SLIP server, then the `sample.dip` file that comes with *dip337j-uri.tgz* should work for you.

When *dip* is given the *get $local* command it searches the incoming text from the remote end for a string that looks like an IP address, ie strings numbers separated by '.' characters. This modification was put in place specifically for *dynamic* SLIP servers, so that the process of reading the IP address granted by the server could be automated.

The example above will automaticaly create a default route via your SLIP link, if this is not what you want, you might have an ethernet connection that should be your default route, then remove the *default* command from the script. After this script has finished running, if you do an *ifconfig* command, you will see that you have a device *sl0*. This is your SLIP device. Should you need to, you can modify its configuration manually, after the *dip* command has finished, using the *ifconfig* and *route* commands.

Please note that *dip* allows you to select a number of different protocols to use with the mode command, the most common example is *cSLIP* for SLIP with compression. Please note that both ends of the link must agree, so you should ensure that whatever you select agrees with what your server is set to.

The above example is fairly robust and should cope with most errors. Please refer to the *dip* man page for more information. Naturally you could, for example, code the script to do such things as redial the server if it doesn't get a connection within a prescribed period of time, or even try a series of servers if you have access to more than one.

9.6.7 Permament SLIP connection using a leased line and slattach.

If you have a cable between two machines, or are fortunate enough to have a leased line, or some other permanent serial connection between your machine and another, then you don't need to go to all the trouble of using *dip* to set up your serial link. *slattach* is a very simple to use utility that will allow you just enough functionality to configure your connection.

Since your connection will be a permanent one, you will want to add some commands to your rc.inet1 file. In essence all you need to do for a permanent connection is ensure that you configure the serial device to the correct speed and switch the serial device into SLIP mode. *slattach* allows you to do this with one command. **Add** the following to your rc.inet1 file:

```
#
# Attach a leased line static SLIP connection
#
#  configure /dev/cua0 for 19.2kbps and cSLIP
/sbin/slattach -p cSLIP -s 19200 /dev/cua0 &
/sbin/ifconfig sl0 IPA.IPA.IPA.IPA pointopoint IPR.IPR.IPR.IPR up
#
# End static SLIP.
```

Where:

IPA.IPA.IPA.IPA

represents your IP address.

IPR.IPR.IPR.IPR

represents the IP address of the remote end.

slattach allocated the first unallocated SLIP device to the serial device specified. *slattach* starts with *sl0*. Therefore the first *slattach* command attaches SLIP device *sl0* to the serial device specified, and *sl1* the next time, etc.

slattach allows you to configure a number of different protocols with the -p argument. In your case you will use either *SLIP* or *cSLIP* depending on whether you want to use compression or not. Note: both ends must agree on whether you want compression or not.

9.7 Configuring a PLIP device. (optional)

plip (Parallel Line IP), is like SLIP, in that it is used for providing a *point to point* network connection between two machines, except that it is designed to use the parallel printer ports on your machine instead of the serial ports. Because it is possible to transfer more than one bit at a time with a parallel port, it is possible to attain higher speeds with the *plip* interface than with a standard serial device. In addition, even the simplest of parallel ports, printer ports, can be used, in lieu of you having to purchase comparatively expensive 16550AFN UART's for your serial ports.

Please note that some laptops use chipsets that will not work with PLIP because they do not allow some combinations of signals that PLIP relies on, that printers don't use.

The Linux *plip* interface is compatible with the *Crywyr Packet Driver PLIP*, and this will mean that you can connect your Linux machine to a DOS machine running any other sort of TCP/IP software via *plip*.

When compiling the kernel, there is only one file that might need to be looked at to configure *plip*. That file is `/usr/src/linux/driver/net/CONFIG`, and it contains *plip* timers in mS. The defaults are probably ok in most cases. You will probably need to increase them if you have an especially slow computer, in which case the timers to increase are actually on the **other** computer.

To configure a *plip* interface, you will need to **add** the following lines to your `rc.inet1` file:

```
#
# Attach a PLIP interface
#
#  configure first parallel port as a plip device
/sbin/ifconfig plip0 IPA.IPA.IPA.IPA pointopoint IPR.IPR.IPR.IPR up
#
# End plip
```

Where:

IPA.IPA.IPA.IPA

   represents your IP address.

IPR.IPR.IPR.IPR

   represents the IP address of the remote machine.

The *pointopoint* parameter has the same meaning as for SLIP, in that it specifies the address of the machine at the other end of the link.

In almost all respects you can treat a *plip* interface as though it were a *SLIP* interface, except that neither *dip* nor *slattach* need be, nor can be, used.

9.7.1 PLIP cabling diagram.

plip has been designed to use cables with the same pinout as those commonly used by the better known of the MS-DOS based pc-pc file transfer programs.

The pinout diagram (taken from `/usr/src/linux/drivers/net/plip.c`) looks as follows:

```
Pin Name     Connect pin - pin
---------    ---------------------------------
GROUND       25 - 25
D0->ERROR    2 - 15
ERROR->D0    15 - 2
D1->SLCT     3 - 13
SLCT->D1     13 - 3
D2->PAPOUT   4 - 12
```

```
PAPOUT->D2    12 - 4
D3->ACK       5 - 10
ACK->D3       10 - 5
D4->BUSY      6 - 11
BUSY->D4      11 - 6
D5            7*
D6            8*
D7            9*
STROBE        1*
FEED          14*
INIT          16*
SLCTIN        17*
```

Notes: Do not connect the pins marked with an asterisk '*'. Extra grounds are 18,19,20,21,22,23, and 24.

If the cable you are using has a metallic shield, it should be connected to the metallic DB-25 shell at **one end only**.

Warning: A miswired PLIP cable can destroy your controller card. Be very careful, and double check every connection to ensure you don't cause yourself any unnecessary work or heartache.

While you may be able to run PLIP cables for long distances, you should avoid it if you can. The specifications for the cable allow for a cable length of about 1 metre or so. Please be very careful when running long plip cables as sources of strong electromagnetic fields such as lightning, power lines, and radio transmitters can interfere with and sometimes even damage your controller. If you really want to connect two of your computers over a large distance you really should be looking at obtaining a pair of thin-net ethernet cards and running some coaxial cable.

10   Routing. (mandatory)

After you have configured all of your network devices you need to think about how your machine is going to route IP datagrams. If you have only one network device configured then your choice is easy, as all datagrams for any machine other than yours must go via that interface. If you have more than one network interface then your choice is a little more complicated. You might have both an ethernet device and SLIP connection to your machine at home. In this situation you must direct all datagrams for your machine at home via your SLIP interface, and all else via the ethernet device. Routing is actually a very simple mechanism, but don't worry if you find it slightly difficult to understand at first; everybody does.

You can display the contents of your routing table by using the *route* command without any options.

There are four commonly used routing mechanisms for Unix network configurations. I'll briefly discuss each in turn.

10.1   Static/Manual Routes.

Static routing, as its name implies, is 'hard coded' routing, that is, it will not change if your network suffers some failure, or if an alternate route becomes available. Static routes are often used in cases where you have a very simple network with no alternate routes available to a destination host, that is, there is only one possible network path to a destination host, or where you want to route a particular way to a host regardless of network changes.

In Linux there is a special use for manual routes, and that is for adding a route to a SLIP or plip host where you have used the *ifconfig pointopoint* parameter. If you have a SLIP/plip link, and have the *pointopoint* parameter specifying the address of the remote host, then you should add a static route to that address so that the ip routing software knows how to route datagrams to that address. The *route* command you would use for the SLIP/plip link via leased line example presented earlier would be:

```
#/sbin/route add IPR.IPR.IPR.IPR
```

Where:

IPR.IPR.IPR.IPR

represents the IP address of the remote end.

10.2   Default Route.

The *default route* mechanism is probably the most common and most useful to most end-user workstations and hosts on most networks. The *default* route is a special static route that matches every destination address, so that if there is no more specific route for a datagram to be sent to, then the *default* route will be used.

If you have a configuration where you have only a single ethernet interface, or a single SLIP interface device defined then you should point your default route via it. In the case of an ethernet interface, the Linux kernel knows where to send datagrams for any host on your network. It works this out using the network address and the network mask as discussed earlier. This means that the only datagrams the kernel won't know how to properly route will be those for people not on your network. To make this work you would normally have your default route point to your *router* address, as it is your means of getting outside of your local network. If you are using a SLIP connection, then your *SLIP server* will be acting as your *router*, so your default route will be via your *SLIP server*.

To configure your default route, **add** the following to your `rc.inet1` **after** all of your network device configurations:

```
#
# Add a default route.
#
/sbin/route add default gw RGA.RGA.RGA.RGA
#
```

Where:

RGA.RGA.RGA.RGA

represents your Router/Gateway Address.

10.3   Proxy ARP.

This method is ugly, hazard prone and should be used with extreme care, some of you will want to use it anyway.

Those with the greatest need for *proxy arp* will be those of you who are configuring your Linux machine as a SLIP dial-in server. For those of you who will be using PPP, the PPP daemon simplifies and automates this task, making it a lot safer to use.

Normally when a TCP/IP host on your ethernet network wants to talk to you, it knows your IP address, but doesn't know what hardware (ethernet) address to send datagrams to. The ARP mechanism is there specifically to provide that mapping function between network address and hardware address. The ethernet protocol provides a special address that is recognised by all ethernet cards, this is called the broadcast address. ARP works by sending a specially formatted datagram containing the IP address of the host it wishes to discover the hardware address of, and transmits it to the ethernet broadcast address. Every host will receive this datagram and the host that is configured with the matching IP address will reply with its hardware address. The host that performed the arp will then know what hardware address to use for the desired IP address.

If you want to use your machine as a server for other machines, you must get your machine to answer ARP requests for their IP addresses on their behalf, as they will not be physically connected to the ethernet network. Lets say that you have been assigned a number of IP addresses on your local network that you will be offering to dial-in SLIP users. Lets say those addresses are: `128.253.154.120-124`, and that you have an ethernet card with a hardware address of `00:00:C0:AD:37:1C`. (You can find the hardware address of your ethernet card by using the *ifconfig* command with no options). To instruct your Linux server to answer arp requests by proxy for these addresses you would need to **add** the following commands to the end of your `rc.inet1` file:

```
#
# Proxy ARP for those dialin users who will be using this
#          machine as a server:
#
/sbin/arp -s 128.263.154.120 00:00:C0:AD:37:1C pub
/sbin/arp -s 128.263.154.121 00:00:C0:AD:37:1C pub
/sbin/arp -s 128.263.154.122 00:00:C0:AD:37:1C pub
/sbin/arp -s 128.263.154.123 00:00:C0:AD:37:1C pub
/sbin/arp -s 128.263.154.124 00:00:C0:AD:37:1C pub
#
# End proxy arps.
```

The `pub` argument stands for *'publish'*. It is this argument that instructs your machine to answer requests for these addresses, even though they are not for your machine. When it answers it will supply the hardware address specified, which is of course its own hardware address.

Naturally you will need to ensure that you have routes configured in your Linux server that point these addresses to the SLIP device on which they will be connecting.

If you are using PPP, you don't need to worry about manually messing with the arp table, as the *pppd* will manage those entries for you if you use the *proxyarp* parameter, and as long as the IP addresses of the remote machine and the server machine are in the same network. You will need to supply the netmask of the network on the server's *pppd* command line.

10.4 gated - the routing daemon.

gated could be used in place of *proxy arp* in some cases, and would certainly be much cleaner, but its primary use is if you want your Linux machine to act as an intelligent *ip router* for your network. *gated* provides support for a number of routing protocols. Among these are RIP, BGP, EGP, HELLO, and OSPF. The most commonly used in small networks being *rip*. *rip* stands for *'Routing Information Protocol'*. If you run *gated*, configured for *rip*, your Linux machine will periodically broadcast a copy of its *routing table* to your network in a special format. In this way, all of the other machines on your network will know what addresses are accessible via your machine.

gated can be used to replace *proxy arp* when all hosts on your network run either *gated* or *routed*. If you have a network where you use a mixture of manual and dynamic routes, you should mark any manual routes as `passive` to ensure that they aren't destroyed by *gated* because it hasn't received an update for them. The best way to add static routes if you are using *gated* is to add a `static` stanza to your `/etc/gated.conf` file. This is described below.

gated would normally be started from your `rc.inet2` which is covered in the next section. You might already see a daemon called *routed* running. *gated* is superior to *routed* in that it is more flexible and more functional. So you should use *gated* and not *routed*.

10.4.1 Obtaining *gated*

Gated is available from:

sunsite.unc.edu

```
/pub/Linux/system/Network/daemons/gated.linux.bin.tgz
                                  /gated.linux.man.tgz
                                  /gated.linux.tgz
```

`gated.linux.tgz` is the source, so you probably won't need it unless you wish to recompile the binaries for some reason.

10.4.2 Installing *gated*

The *gated* binary distribution comprises three programs and two sample configuration files.

The programs are:

gated

> the actual *gated* daemon.

gdc

> the operational user interface for *gated*. *gdc* is for controlling the *gated* daemon, stopping and starting it, obtaining its status and the like.

ripquery

> a diagnostic tool to query the known routes of a gateway using either a 'rip query' or a 'rip poll'.

The configuration files are:

gated.conf

> this is the actual configuration file for the *gated* daemon. It allows you to specify how *gated* will behave when it is running. You can enable and disable any of the routing protocols, and control the behaviour of those routing protocols running.

gated.version

> a text file that describes the version number of the *gated* daemon

The *gated* binary distribution will not install the *gated* files in the correct place for you. Fortunately there aren't very many, so its fairly simple to do.

To install the binaries try the following:

```
# cd /tmp
# gzip -dc .../gated.linux.bin.tgz | tar xvf -
# install -m 500 bin/gated /usr/sbin
# install -m 444 bin/gated.conf bin/gated.version /etc
# install -m 555 bin/ripquery bin/gdc /sbin
# rm -rf /tmp/bin
```

I keep the networking daemons in `/usr/sbin`, if yours are somewhere else then naturally you'll have to change the target directory. The sample *gated* configuration file included configures *gated* to emulate the old *routed* daemon. It will probably work for you in most circumstances, and it looks like this:

```
#
#  This configuration emulates routed.  It runs RIP and only sends
#  updates if there are more than one interfaces up and IP forwarding is
#  enabled in the kernel.
#
#       NOTE that RIP *will not* run if UDP checksums are disabled in
#       the kernel.
#
rip yes ;
traceoptions all;
#
```

If you have any static routes you wish to add, you can add them in a `static` stanza appended to your `/etc/gated.conf` as follows:

```
#
static {
37.0.0.0 mask 255.0.0.0 gateway 44.136.8.97 ;
host 44.136.8.100 gateway 44.136.8.97 ;
} ;
#
```

The above example would create a static route to the Class A network `37.0.0.0` via gateway `44.136.8.97`, and a static route to a host with address `44.136.8.100` via gateway `44.136.8.97`. If you do this you do not need to add the routes using the *route* command, *gated* will add and manage the routes for you.

To install the *man* files, try the following:

```
# cd /tmp
# gzip -dc .../gated.linux.man.tgz | tar xvf -
# install -m 444 man/*.8 /usr/man/man8
# install -m 444 man/*.5 /usr/man/man5
# rm -rf /tmp/man
```

The *man* files contain concise and detailed information on the configuration and use of *gated*. For information on configuring *gated*, refer to the `gated-config` *man* page.

11   Configuring the network daemons.

As mentioned earlier, there are other files that you will need to complete your network installation. These files concern higher level configurations of the network software. Each of the important ones are covered in the following sub-sections, but you will find there are others that you will have to configure as you become more familiar with the network suite.

11.1   /etc/rc.d/rc.inet2 (the second half of rc.net)

If you have been following this document you should at this stage have built an *rc* file to configure each of your network devices with the correct addresses, and set up whatever routing you will need for your particular network configuration. You will now need to actually start some of the higher level network software.

Now would be a really good time to read Olaf's *Network Administrators Guide*, as it really should be considered the definitive document for this stage of the configuration process. It will help you decide what to include in this file, and more importantly perhaps, what **not** to include in this file. For the security conscious it is a fair statement to say that the more network services you have running, the more likely the chance of your system having a security hole: Run only what you need.

There are some very important *daemons* (system processes that run in the background) that you will need to know a little about. The *man* pages will tell you more, but they are:

11.1.1   inetd.

inetd is a program that sits in the background and manages internet connection requests and the like. It is smart enough that you don't need to leave a whole bunch of servers running when there is nothing connected to them. When it sees an incoming request for a particular service, eg *telnet*, or *ftp*, it will check the `/etc/services` file, find what server program needs to be run to manage the request, start it, and hand the connection over to it. Imagine it as a master server for your internet servers. It also has a few simple standard services inbuilt. These are *echo, discard* and *generate* services used for various types of network testing. *inetd* doesn't manage **all** servers and services that you might run, but it manages most of the usual ones. Normally services such as udp based services, or services that manage their own connection multiplexing such as World Wide Web servers or muds would be run independently of *inetd*. Generally the documentation accompanying such servers will tell you whether to use *inetd* or not.

11.1.2   syslogd.

syslogd is a daemon that handles all system logging. It accepts messages generated for it and will distribute them according to a set of rules contained in /etc/syslogd.conf. For example, certain types of messages you will want to send to the console, and also to a log file, where others you will want only to log to a file. *syslogd* allows you to specify what messages should go where.

11.2   A sample rc.inet2 file.

The following is a sample rc.inet2 file that Fred built. It starts a large number of servers, so you might want to trim it down to just those services that you actually want to run. To trim it down, simply delete or comment out the stanzas (*if* to *fi*) that you don't need. All each stanza does is test that the relevant module is a file, that it exists, echoes a comment that you can see when you boot your machine, and then executes the commands with the arguments supplied to ensure that it runs happily in the background. For more detailed information on each of the deamons, check either the *Network Administrators Guide* or the relevant *man* pages.

```
#! /bin/sh
#
# rc.inet2     This shell script boots up the entire INET system.
#              Note, that when this script is used to also fire
#              up any important remote NFS disks (like the /usr
#              distribution), care must be taken to actually
#              have all the needed binaries online _now_ ...
#
# Version:     @(#)/etc/rc.d/rc.inet2  2.18    05/27/93
#
# Author:      Fred N. van Kempen, <waltje@uwalt.nl.mugnet.org>
#

# Constants.
NET="/usr/sbin"
IN_SERV="lpd"
LPSPOOL="/var/spool/lpd"

# At this point, we are ready to talk to The World...
echo -e "\nMounting remote file systems ..."
/bin/mount -t nfs -v                # This may be our /usr runtime!!!

echo -e "\nStarting Network daemons ..."
# Start the SYSLOG daemon.  This has to be the first server.
# This is a MUST HAVE, so leave it in.
echo -n "INET: "
if [ -f ${NET}/syslogd ]
then
echo -n "syslogd "
${NET}/syslogd
fi

# Start the SUN RPC Portmapper.
if [ -f ${NET}/rpc.portmap ]
```

```
then
echo -n "portmap "
${NET}/rpc.portmap
fi

# Start the INET SuperServer
# This is a MUST HAVE, so leave it in.
if [ -f ${NET}/inetd ]
then
echo -n "inetd "
${NET}/inetd
else
echo "no INETD found.  INET cancelled!"
exit 1
fi

# Start the NAMED/BIND name server.
# NOTE: you probably don't need to run named.
#if [ ! -f ${NET}/named ]
#then
#          echo -n "named "
#              ${NET}/named
#fi

# Start the ROUTEd server.
# NOTE: routed is now obsolete. You should now use gated.
#if [ -f ${NET}/routed ]
#then
#          echo -n "routed "
#              ${NET}/routed -q #-g -s
#fi

# Start the GATEd server.
if [ -f ${NET}/gated ]
then
echo -n "gated "
${NET}/gated
fi

# Start the RWHO server.
if [ -f ${NET}/rwhod ]
then
echo -n "rwhod "
${NET}/rwhod -t -s
fi

# Start the U-MAIL SMTP server.
if [ -f XXX/usr/lib/umail/umail ]
then
echo -n "umail "
/usr/lib/umail/umail -d7 -bd </dev/null >/dev/null 2>&1 &
fi

# Start the various INET servers.
for server in ${IN_SERV}
do
if [ -f ${NET}/${server} ]
then
                echo -n "${server} "
                    ${NET}/${server}
    fi
```

```
done

# Start the various SUN RPC servers.
if [ -f ${NET}/rpc.portmap ]
then
if [ -f ${NET}/rpc.ugidd ]
then
                echo -n "ugidd "
                ${NET}/rpc.ugidd -d
fi
if [ -f ${NET}/rpc.mountd ]
then
                echo -n "mountd "
                ${NET}/rpc.mountd
fi
if [ -f ${NET}/rpc.nfsd ]
then
                echo -n "nfsd "
                ${NET}/rpc.nfsd
fi

# Fire up the PC-NFS daemon(s).
if [ -f ${NET}/rpc.pcnfsd ]
then
                echo -n "pcnfsd "
                ${NET}/rpc.pcnfsd ${LPSPOOL}
fi
if [ -f ${NET}/rpc.bwnfsd ]
then
                echo -n "bwnfsd "
                ${NET}/rpc.bwnfsd ${LPSPOOL}
fi

fi
echo network daemons started.
# Done!
```

11.3   Other necessary network configuration files.

There are other network configuraiton files that you will need to configure if you want to have people connect to and use your machine as a host. If you have installed your Linux from a distribution then you will probably already have copies of these files so just check them to make sure they look ok, and if not you can use the following samples.

11.3.1   A sample /etc/inetd.conf file.

Your /etc/rc.d/rc.inet2 file will have started *inetd*, *syslogd* and the various *rpc* servers for you. You will now need to configure the network daemons that will be managed by *inetd*. *inetd* uses a configuration file called /etc/inetd.conf.

The following is an example of how a simple configuration might look:

```
#
# The internal services.
#
# Authors:       Original taken from BSD UNIX 4.3/TAHOE.
#                Fred N. van Kempen, <waltje@uwalt.nl.mugnet.org>
#
echo     stream tcp nowait root  internal
```

```
echo    dgram  udp wait    root   internal
discard stream tcp nowait  root   internal
discard dgram  udp wait    root   internal
daytime stream tcp nowait  root   internal
daytime dgram  udp wait    root   internal
chargen stream tcp nowait  root   internal
chargen dgram  udp wait    root   internal
#
# Standard services.
#
ftp     stream tcp nowait root  /usr/sbin/tcpd in.ftpd ftpd
telnet  stream tcp nowait root  /usr/sbin/tcpd in.telnetd
#
# Shell, login, exec and talk are BSD protocols.
#
shell   stream tcp nowait root  /usr/sbin/tcpd in.rshd
login   stream tcp nowait root  /usr/sbin/tcpd in.rlogind
exec    stream tcp nowait root  /usr/sbin/tcpd in.rexecd
talk    dgram  udp wait   root  /usr/sbin/tcpd in.talkd
ntalk   dgram  udp wait   root  /usr/sbin/tcpd in.talkd
#
# Status and Information services.
#
finger  stream tcp nowait root  /usr/sbin/tcpd in.fingerd
systat  stream tcp nowait guest /usr/sbin/tcpd /usr/bin/ps -auwwx
netstat stream tcp nowait guest /usr/sbin/tcpd /bin/netstat
#
# End of inetd.conf.
```

The *inetd* man page describes what each of the fields are, but put simply, each entry describes what program should be executed when an incoming connection is received on the socket listed as the first entry. Those entries which have incoming where the program name and arguments would be are those services that are provided internally by the *inetd* program.

The conversion between the service name in the first column, and the actual socket number it refers to is performed by the /etc/services file.

11.3.2   A sample /etc/services file.

The /etc/services file is a simple table of Internet service names and the socket number and protocol is uses. This table is used by a number of programs including *inetd*, *telnet* and *tcpdump*. It makes life a little easier by allowing us to refer to services by name rather than by number.

The following is a sample of what a simple /etc/services file might look like:

```
#
# /etc/services - database of service name, socket number
#                 and protocol.
#
# Original Author:
#      Fred N. van Kempen, <waltje@uwalt.nl.mugnet.org>
#
tcpmux     1/tcp
echo       7/tcp
echo       7/udp
discard    9/tcp    sink null
discard    9/udp    sink null
systat     11/tcp   users
daytime    13/tcp
daytime    13/udp
```

```
netstat      15/tcp
chargen      19/tcp  ttytst source
chargen      19/udp  ttytst source
ftp-data     20/tcp
ftp          21/tcp
telnet       23/tcp
smtp         25/tcp  mail
time         37/tcp  timserver
time         37/udp  timserver
name         42/udp  nameserver
whois        43/tcp  nicname      # usually to sri-nic
domain       53/tcp
domain       53/udp
finger       79/tcp
link         87/tcp  ttylink
hostnames    101/tcp hostname    # usually to sri-nic
sunrpc       111/tcp
sunrpc       111/tcp portmapper # RPC 4.0 portmapper TCP
sunrpc       111/udp
sunrpc       111/udp portmapper # RPC 4.0 portmapper UDP
auth         113/tcp authentication
nntp         119/tcp usenet     # Network News Transfer
ntp          123/tcp            # Network Time Protocol
ntp          123/udp            # Network Time Protocol
snmp         161/udp
snmp-trap    162/udp
exec         512/tcp            # BSD rexecd(8)
biff         512/udp comsat
login        513/tcp            # BSD rlogind(8)
who          513/udp whod       # BSD rwhod(8)
shell        514/tcp cmd        # BSD rshd(8)
syslog       514/udp            # BSD syslogd(8)
printer      515/tcp spooler    # BSD lpd(8)
talk         517/udp            # BSD talkd(8)
ntalk        518/udp            # SunOS talkd(8)
route        520/udp routed     # 521/udp too
timed        525/udp timeserver
mount        635/udp            # NFS Mount Service
pcnfs        640/udp            # PC-NFS DOS Authentication
bwnfs        650/udp            # BW-NFS DOS Authentication
listen       1025/tcp listener  # RFS remote_file_sharing
ingreslock   1524/tcp           # ingres lock server
nfs          2049/udp           # NFS File Service
irc          6667/tcp           # Internet Relay Chat
# End of services.
```

The *telnet* entry tells us that the *telnet* service uses socket number 23 and the *tcp* protocol. The *domain* entry tells us that the Domain Name Service uses socket number 52 and both *tcp* and *udp* protocols. You should have an appropriate /etc/services entry for each /etc/inetd.conf entry.

11.3.3   A sample /etc/protocols file.

The /etc/protocols file is a table of protocol name with its corresponding protocol number. Since the number of protocols in use is small this file is quite trivial.

```
#
# /etc/protocols - database of protocols.
#
# Original Author:
```

```
#    Fred N. van Kempen, <waltje@uwalt.nl.mugnet.org>
#
ip   0    IP   # internet protocol
icmp 1    ICMP # internet control message protocol
igmp 2    IGMP # internet group multicast protocol
ggp  3    GGP  # gateway-gateway protocol
tcp  6    TCP  # transmission control protocol
pup  12   PUP  # PARC universal packet protocol
udp  17   UDP  # user datagram protocol
idp  22   IDP
raw  255  RAW
#
# End of protocols.
```

11.4   Name Resolution.

Name Resolution is the process of converting a hostname in the familiar dotted notation (e.g. tsx-11.mit.edu) into an IP address which the network software understands. There are two principal means of achieving this in a typical installation, one simple, and one more complex.

11.4.1   /etc/hosts

/etc/hosts contains a list of ip addresses and the hostnames they map to. In this way, you can refer to other machines on the network by name, as well as their ip address. Using a nameserver (see section 'named') allows you to do the same name->ip address translation automatically. (Running *named* allows you to run your own nameserver on your Linux machine). This file needs to contain at least an entry for 127.0.0.1 with the name localhost. If you're not only using loopback, you need to add an entry for your ip address, with your full hostname (such as loomer.vpizza.com). You may also wish to include entries for your gateways and network addresses.

For example, if loomer.vpizza.com has the ip address 128.253.154.32, the /etc/hosts file would contain:

```
# /etc/hosts
# List of hostnames and their ip addresses
127.0.0.1            localhost
128.253.154.32       loomer.vpizza.com loomer
# end of hosts
```

Once again you will need to edit this file to suit your own needs. If you're only using loopback, the only line in /etc/hosts should be for 127.0.0.1, with both localhost and your hostname after it.

Note that in the second line, above, there are two names for 128.253.154.32: loomer.vpizza.com and just loomer. The first name is the full hostname of the system, called the "Fully Qualified Domain Name", and the second is an alias for it. The second allows you to type only *rlogin loomer* instead of having to type the entire hostname. You should ensure that you put the Fully Qualified Domain Name in the line before the alias name.

11.4.2   named - do I need thee ?

'I dub thee ..'

named is the nameserver daemon for many Unix-like operating systems. It allows your machine to serve the name lookup requests, not only for itself, but also for other machines on the network, that is, if another machine wants to find the address for 'goober.norelco.com', and you have this machines address in your *named* database, then you can service the request and tell other machines what 'goobers' address is.

Under older implementations of Linux TCP/IP, to create aliases for machine names, (even for your own machine), you had to run *named* on your Linux machine to do the hostname to IP address conversion. One problem with this is that *named* is comparatively difficult to set up properly, and maintain. To solve this problem, a program called hostcvt.build was made available on Linux systems to translate your /etc/hosts file into the many files that make up *named* database files. However even with this problem overcome, *named* still uses CPU overhead and causes network traffic.

The bottom line is this: **You do not need to run named** on your Linux system. The SLS instructions will probably tell you to run hostcvt.build to setup *named*. This is simply unnecessary unless you want to make your Linux system function as a nameserver for other machines, in which case you probably should learn some more about *named* anyway. When looking up hostnames, your Linux machine will first check the /etc/hosts file, and then ask the nameserver out on the net.

The only reason you may want to run *named* would be if:

- You're setting up a network of machines, and need a nameserver for one of them, and don't have a nameserver out on the net somewhere.

- Your network administrators want you to run your Linux system as a nameserver for some reason.

- You have a slow SLIP connection, and want to run a small cache-only nameserver on your Linux machine so that you don't have to go out on the serial line for every name lookup that occurs. If you're only going to be connecting to a small number of hosts on the net, and you know what their addresses are, then you can put them in your hosts file and not need to query a nameserver at all. Generally namelookup isn't that slow and should work fine over a SLIP link anyway.

- You want to run a nameserver for fun and excitement.

In general, **you do NOT need to run named**: this means that you can comment it out from your rc.inet2 file, and you don't have to run hostcvt.build. If you want to alias machine names, for example, if you want to refer to loomer.vpizza.com as just loomer, then you can add as alias in /etc/hosts instead. There is no reason to run *named* unless you have a specific requirement to do so. If you have access to a nameserver, (and your network administrators will tell you its address), and most networks do, then don't bother running *named*.

If you're only using loopback, you can run *named* and set your nameserver address to 127.0.0.1, but since you are the only machine you can talk to, this would be quite bizarre, as you'd never need to call it.

11.4.3 /etc/networks

The /etc/networks file lists the names and addresses of your own, and other, networks. It is used by the *route* command, and allows you to specify a network by name, should you so desire.

Every network you wish to add a route to using the *route* command should have an entry in the /etc/networks file, unless you also specify the -net argument in the *route* command line.

Its format is similar to that of /etc/hosts file above, and an example file might look like:

```
#
# /etc/networks: list all networks that you wish to add route commands
#                for in here
#
default         0.0.0.0         # default route     - recommended
loopnet         127.0.0.0       # loopback network - recommended
mynet           128.253.154.0   # Example network CHANGE to YOURS
#
# end of networks
```

11.4.4 /etc/host.conf

The system has some library functions called the resolver library. This file specifies how your system will lookup host names. It should contain at least the following two lines:

```
order hosts,bind
multi on
```

These two lines tell the *resolve* libraries to first check the /etc/hosts file, and then to ask the nameserver (if one is present). The *multi* entry allows you to have multiple IP addresses for a given machine name in /etc/hosts.

This file comes from the implementation of the *resolv+* bind library for Linux. You can find further documentation in the *resolv+(8)* man page if you have it. If you don't, it can be obtained from:

sunsite.doc.ic.ac.uk

```
/computing/comms/tcpip/nameserver/resolv+/resolv+2.1.1.tar.Z
```

This file contains the *resolv+.8* man page for the resolver library.

11.4.5 /etc/resolv.conf

This file actually configures the system name resolver, and contains two types of entries: The addresses of your nameservers (if any), and the name of your domain, if you have one. If you're running your own nameserver (i.e running *named* on your Linux machine), then the address of your nameserver is 127.0.0.1, the loopback address.

Your domain name is your fully qualified hostname (if you're a registered machine on the Internet, for example), with the hostname component removed. That is, if your full hostname is loomer.vpizza.com, then your domain name is vpizza.com, without the hostname loomer.

For example, if you machine is goober.norelco.com, and has a nameserver at the address 128.253.154.5, then your /etc/resolv.conf file would look like:

```
domain norelco.com
nameserver 127.253.154.5
```

You can specify more than one nameserver. Each one must have a *nameserver* entry in the resolv.conf file.

Remember, if you're running on loopback, you don't need a nameserver.

11.4.6 Configuring your Hostname - /etc/HOSTNAME

After you have configured everything else, there is one small task that remains, you need to configure your own machine with a name. This is so that application programs like *sendmail* can know who you are to accept mail, and so that your machine can identify itself to other machines that it might be connected to.

There are two programs that are used to configure this sort of information, and they are commonly misused. They are *hostname* and *domainname*.

If you are using a release of net-tools earlier than 1.1.38 then you can include a command in your /etc/rc file that looks like this:

```
/bin/hostname -S
```

and this will cause the *hostname* command to read a file called /etc/HOSTNAME which it expects will contain a "Fully Qualified Domain Name", that is, your machines hostname **including** the domainname. It will split the F.Q.D.N. into its DNS hostname and domainname components and set them appropriately for you.

For example, the machine above would have the file /etc/HOSTNAME:

```
goober.norelco.com
```

If you are using the *hostname* that came with net-tools-1.1.38 or later, then you would add a command at the end of your /etc/rc.d/rc.inet1 file like:

```
/bin/hostname goober.norelco.com
```

or if you have upgraded from a previous release, you could add:

```
/bin/hostname -F /etc/HOSTNAME
```

and it would behave in the same way as for the earlier version.

The /bin/domainname command is for setting the **N.I.S.** domain name **NOT** the D.N.S. domain name. You do not need to set this unless you are running *NIS*, which is briefly described later.

11.5   Other files.

There are of course many other files in the /etc directory which you may need to dabble with later on. Instead of going into them here, I'm going to provide the bare minimum to get you on the net. More information is available in Olaf's *Network Administration Guide*. It picks up where this *HOWTO* ends, and some more information will be provided in later versions of this document.

Once you have all of the files set up, and everthing in the right place, you should be able to reboot you new kernel, and net away to your hearts content. However I strongly suggest that you keep a bootable copy of your old kernel and possibly even a 'recovery disk', in case something goes wrong, so that you can get back in and fix it. You might try HJLu's 'single disk boot disk', or 'disk1' from an SLS distribution.

12   Advanced Configurations.

The configurations above have described how a typical Linux workstation might be configured for normal end-user operation. Some of you will have other requirements which will require slightly more advanced configurations. What follows are examples of some the more common of these.

12.1   PPP - Point to Point Protocol.

The *Point to Point Protocol* is a modern and efficient protocol for conveying multiple protocols, TCP/IP for one, across serial links, that a lot of people use in place of SLIP. It offers enhanced functionality, error detection and security options. It corrects a number of deficiencies that are found in SLIP, and is suitable for both asynchronous links and synchronous links alike.

An important feature of PPP operation is dynamic address allocation, and this feature will almost certainly be exploited by your PPP server. This feature allows a PPP client, with a specially formatted frame, to request its address from the server. In this way configuration is somewhat less messy than with SLIP, since this ability to retrieve your address must occur outside of the protocol.

The authors of the Linux port are Michael Callahan, <callahan@maths.ox.ac.uk> and Al Longyear, <longyear@netcom.com>. Most of this information has come from the documentation that accompanies the PPP software. The documentation is quite complete, and will tell you much more than I present here.

The Linux PPP code has come out of Alpha testing and is now available as a public release. The 1.0.0 Linux PPP code is based on Paul Mackerras's free PPP for BSD-derivative operating systems. The 1.0.0 release is based on version 2.1.1 of the free PPP code.

The PPP code comes in two parts. The first is a kernel module which handles the assembly and disassembly of the frames, and the second is a set of protocols called LCP, IPCP, UPAP and CHAP, for negotiating link options, bringing the link into a functioning state and for authentication.

12.1.1   Why would I use PPP in place of SLIP ?

You would use PPP in place of SLIP for a few reasons. The most common are:

Your Internet Provider supports only PPP

> The most obvious reason you would use PPP in favour of SLIP is when your Internet Provider supports PPP and not SLIP. Ok, I said it was obvious.

You have a normally noisy serial line

> PPP provides a frame check sequence for each and every frame transmitted, SLIP does not. If you have a noisy serial line, and you are using SLIP, your error correction will be performed end to end, that is between your machine and the destination machine, whereas with PPP the error detection occurs locally, between your machine and the PPP server. This makes for faster recovery from errors.

You need to make use of some other feature PPP offers.

> PPP provides a number of features that SLIP does not. You might for example want to carry not only IP, but also DECNET, or AppleTalk frames over your serial link. PPP will allow you to do this.

12.1.2   Where to obtain the PPP software.

The ppp software is available from:

sunsite.unc.edu

```
/pub/Linux/system/Networking/serial/ppp-2.1.2b.tar.gz
```

This file contains the kernel source, and the *pppd* source and binary. Version 1.0.0 is meant for use with kernels 1.0.x and 1.1.x.

12.1.3   Installing the PPP software.

Installation of the PPP software is fairly straightforward.

The kernel driver.   Some support for *ppp* has been built into the kernel for some time. Configuring the kernel is fairly easy, the following should work ok:

```
# cd /usr/src
# gzip -dc ppp-2.1.2b.tar.gz | tar xvf -
```

and if you are running a kernel prior to 1.1.14:

```
# cp /usr/src/ppp-2.1.2b/linux/ppp.c /usr/src/linux/drivers/net
# cp /usr/src/ppp-2.1.2b/pppd/ppp.h /usr/src/linux/include/linux
```

other wise do **NOT** copy these files as they will overwrite the ones in the kernel source.

If you are running a kernel version earlier than 1.1.13, or 1.0.x, then you will then need to uncomment the `CONFIG_PPP` line in `/usr/src/linux/config.in`.

If you are running a version of the kernel that is 1.1.3 or lower, then you will also need to uncomment out the macro definition of `NET02D` in the file `/usr/src/linux/drivers/net/ppp.c` by removing the `/*` characters.

You can then do:

```
# make config    (remembering to answer yes to PPP support)
# make dep
# make
```

When you reboot with the new kernel you should see messages at boot time that look something like these:

```
PPP: version 0.2.7 (4 channels) NEW_TTY_DRIVERS OPTIMIZE_FLAGS
TCP compression code copyright 1989 Regents of the University of California
PPP line discipline registered.
```

These indicate that the PPP support has in fact been compiled into your kernel.

Now, try looking at the contents of `/proc/net/dev`. It should look something like this:

```
Inter-|   Receive                    |  Transmit
face  |packets errs drop fifo frame|packets errs drop fifo colls carrier
lo:        0    0    0    0    0        0    0    0    0    0    0
ppp0:      0    0    0    0    0        0    0    0    0    0    0
ppp1:      0    0    0    0    0        0    0    0    0    0    0
ppp2:      0    0    0    0    0        0    0    0    0    0    0
ppp3:      0    0    0    0    0        0    0    0    0    0    0
```

This indicates that the kernel driver is installed correctly.

pppd   If you want to recompile *pppd*, type *make* in the `pppd` subdirectory of the installation. There will be some warnings when compiling `lcp.c`, `upap.c` and `chap.c` but these are OK.

If you want to recompile *chat*, consult `README.linux` in the `chat` directory.

To install, type *make install* in the `chat` and `pppd` directories. This will put *chat* and *pppd* binaries in `/usr/sbin` and the `pppd.8` manual page in `/usr/man/man8`.

`pppd` needs to be run as *root*. You can either make it suid root or just use it when you are root. *make install* will try to install it suid root, so if you are root when you try to install it, it should work ok.

12.1.4 Configuring and using the PPP software.

Like SLIP, you can configure the PPP software as either a client or a server. The *chat* program performs a similar function to the *dip* program in that it is used to automate the dialing and login procedure to the remote machine, unlike *dip* though, it does not perform the *ioctl* to convert the serial line into a PPP line. This is performed by the *pppd* program. *pppd* can act as either the client or the server. When used as a client, it normally invokes the *chat* program to perform the connection and login, and then it takes over by performing the *ioctl* to change the line discipline to *ppp*, performs a number of steps in configuring your machine to talk to the remote machine and then steps out of the way to let you operate.

Please refer to the *pppd* and *chat* man pages for more information. Please also refer to the README file that comes with the ppp software, as its description of the operation of these utilities is much more complete than I have described here.

Configuring a PPP client by dial-up modem. This is perhaps what most of you will want to do, so it appears first. You would use this configuration when you have a network provider who supports ppp by dialup modem. When you want to establish your connection you simply have to invoke the *pppd* program with appropriate arguments.

The following example might look a little confusing at first, but it is easier to understand if you can see that all it is doing is taking a command line for the *chat* program as its first argument and then others for itself later.

```
pppd connect 'chat -v "" ATDT5551212 CONNECT "" ogin: ppp word: password'\
/dev/cua1 38400 debug crtscts modem defaultroute 192.1.1.17:
```

What this says is:

- Invoke the *chat* program with the command line:

  ```
  chat -v "" ATDT5551212 CONNECT "" ogin: ppp word: password
  ```

  Which says: Dial 5551212, wait for the 'CONNECT' string, transmit a carriage return, wait for the string 'ogin:', transmit the string 'ppp', wait for the string 'word:', transmit the string 'password', and quit.

- Use serial device /dev/cua1

- Set its speed to 38400 bps.

- *debug* means log status messages to *syslog*

- *crtscts* means use hardware handshaking to the modem - recommended.

- *modem* means that *pppd* will attempt to hang up the call before and after making the call.

- *defaultroute* instructs *pppd* to add a routing entry that makes this the default route. In most cases this will be what you want.

- *192.1.1.17:* says to set the ppp interfaces address to 192.1.1.17. This argument normally looks like x.x.x.x:y.y.y.y, where x.x.x.x is your ip address, and y.y.y.y is the ip address of the server. If you leave off the server's address, *pppd* will ask for it, and x.x.x.x will be set to your machines ip address.

Please refer to the *pppd* and *chat* man pages for more information. Please also refer to the README file that comes with the ppp software, as its description of the above is much more complete than I have described here.

Configuring a PPP client via a leased line. Configuring a PPP client via a leased line is very simple. You will still use the *pppd* program, but since you won't need to establish the modem link the arguments to the chat program can be much simpler.

The example I'm presenting here assumes that the ppp server doesn't require any special login procedure. I do this because every login procedure will be different, and if you are simply running a local connection then it is possible that you might have it set up this way.

```
pppd defaultroute noipdefault debug \
kdebug 2 /dev/cua0 9600
```

This will open the serial device, generate the *ioctl* to change it into a *ppp*device, set your default route via the *ppp* interface. The *noipdefault* argument instructs the *pppd* program to request the address to use for this device from the server. Debug messages will go to *syslog*. The *kdebug 2* argument causes the debug messages to be set to level 2, this will give you slightly more information on what is going on. It will use /dev/cua0 at 9600 bps.

If your ppp server does require some sort of login procedure, you can easily use the *chat* program as in the example for the dialup server to perform that function for you.

Please refer to the *pppd* and *chat* man pages for more information. Please also refer to the README file that comes with the ppp software, as its description of the above is much more complete than I have described here.

Configuring a PPP server.   Configuring a PPP server is similar to establishing a SLIP server. You can create a special 'ppp' account, which uses an executable script as its login shell. The `/etc/passwd` entry might look like:

```
ppp:EncPasswd:102:50:PPP client login:/tmp:/etc/ppp/ppplogin
```

and the `/etc/ppp/ppplogin` script might look like:

```
#!/bin/sh
exec /usr/sbin/pppd passive :192.1.2.23
```

The address that you provide will be the address that the **calling** machine will be assigned.

Naturally, if you want multiple users to have simultaneous access you would have to create a number of startup scripts and individual accounts for each to use, as you can only put one ip address in each script.

12.1.5   Where to obtain more information on PPP, or report bugs.

Most discussion on PPP for Linux takes place on the PPP mailing list.

To join the Linux **PPP** channel on the mail list server, send mail to:

```
linux-activists@niksula.hut.fi

with the line:

X-Mn-Admin: join PPP

at the top of the message body (not the subject line).
```

Please remember that when you are reporting bugs or problems you should include as much information relevant to the problem as you can to assist those that will help you understand your problem.

You might also like to check out:

RFCS 1548, 1331, 1332, 1333, and 1334. These are the definitive documents for PPP.

W. Richard Stevens also describes PPP in his book 'TCP/IP Illustrated Volume 1', (Addison-Wessley, 1994, ISBN 0-201-63346-9).

12.2   Configuring Linux as a SLIP Server.

If you have a machine that is perhaps network connected, that you'd like other people be able to dial into, and provide network services, then you will need to configure your machine as a server. If you want to use SLIP as the serial line protocol, then currently you have three options as to how to configure your Linux machine as a SLIP server. My preference would be to use the first presented, *SLIPlogin*, as it seems the easiest to configure and understand, but I will present a summary of each, so you make your mind.

12.2.1   SLIP Server using *SLIPlogin*.

SLIPlogin is a program that you can use in place of the normal login shell for SLIP users that converts the terminal line into a SLIP line. It allows you to configure your Linux machine as either a *static address server*, users get the same address everytime they call in, or a *dynamic address server*, where users get an address allocated for them which will not necessarily be the same as the last time they called.

The caller will login as per the standard login process, entering their username and password, but instead of being presented with a shell after their login, *SLIPlogin* is executed which searches its configuration file (/etc/SLIP.hosts) for an entry with a login name that matches that of the caller. If it locates one, it configures the line as an 8bit clean line, and uses an *ioctl* call to convert the line discipline to SLIP. When this process is complete, the last stage of configuration takes place, where *SLIPlogin* invokes a shell script which configures the SLIP interface with the relevant ip address, netmask and sets appropriate routing in place. This script is usually called /etc/SLIP.login, but in a similar manner to *getty*, if you have certain callers that require special initialization, then you can create configuration scripts called /etc/SLIP.login.loginname that will be run instead of the default specifically for them.

There are either three or four files that you need to configure to get *SLIPlogin* working for you. I will detail how and where to get the software, and how each is configured in detail. The files are:

- /etc/passwd, for the dialin user accounts.
- /etc/SLIP.hosts, to contain the information unique to each dial-in user.
- /etc/SLIP.login, which manages the configuration of the routing that needs to be performed for the user.
- /etc/SLIP.tty, which is required only if you are configuring your server for *dynamic address allocation* and contains a table of addresses to allocate
- /etc/SLIP.logout, which contains commands to clean up after the user has hung up or logged out.

Where to get *SLIPlogin*   *SLIPlogin* can be obtained from:

sunsite.unc.edu

        /pub/Linux/system/Network/serial/SLIPlogin-1.3.tar.gz

The tar file contains both source, precompiled binaries and a *man* page.

To ensure that only authorized users will be able to run *SLIPlogin* program, you should add an entry to your /etc/group file similar to the following:

```
  ..
SLIP::13:radio,fred
  ..
```

When you install the *SLIPlogin* package, the Makefile will change the group ownership of the *SLIPlogin* program to SLIP, and this will mean that only users who belong to that group will be able to execute it. The example above will allow only users radio and fred to execute *SLIPlogin*.

To install the binaries into your /sbin directory, and the *man* page into section 8, do the following:

```
# cd /usr/src
# gzip -dc .../SLIPlogin-1.3.tar.gz | tar xvf -
# cd src
# make install
```

If you want to recompile the binaries before installation, add a make clean before the make install. If you want to install the binaries somewhere else, you will need to edit the Makefile *install* rule.

Please read the README files that come with the package for more information.

Configuring `/etc/passwd` **for SLIP hosts.**   Normally you would create some special logins for SLIP callers in your `/etc/passwd` file. A convention commonly followed is to use the *hostname* of the calling host with a capital 'S' prefixing it. So, for example, if the calling host is called `radio` then you could create a `/etc/passwd` entry that looked like:

```
Sradio:FvKurok73:1427:1:radio SLIP login:/tmp:/sbin/SLIPlogin
```

It doesn't really matter what the account is called, so long as it is meaningful to you.

Note: the caller doesn't need any special home directory, as they will not be presented with a shell from this machine, so `/tmp` is a good choice. Also note that *SLIPlogin* is used in place of the normal login shell.

Configuring `/etc/SLIP.hosts`   The `/etc/SLIP.hosts` file is the file that *SLIPlogin* searches for entries matching the login name to obtain configuration details for this caller. It is this file where you specify the ip address and netmask that will be assigned to the caller, and configured for their use. Sample entries for two hosts, one a static configuration for host `radio`, and another, a dynamic configuration for user host `albert` might look like:

```
#
Sradio    44.136.8.99    44.136.8.100    0xffffff00    normal
Salbert   44.136.8.99    DYNAMIC         0xffffff00    compressed
#
```

The `/etc/SLIP.hosts` file entries are:

1. the login name of the caller.

2. ip address of the server machine, ie this machine.

3. ip address that the caller will be assigned. If this field is coded `DYNAMIC` then an ip address will be allocated based on the information contained in your `/etc/SLIP.tty` file discussed later. **Note:** you must be using at least version 1.3 of SLIPlogin for this to work.

4. the netmask assigned to the calling machine in hexadecimal notation eg 0xffffff00 for a Class C network mask.

5. optional parameters to enable/disable compression and other features.

Note: You can use either hostnames or IP addresses in dotted decimal notation for fields 2 and 3. If you use hostnames then those hosts must be resolvable, that is, your machine must be able to locate an ip address for those hostnames, otherwise the script will fail when it is called. You can test this by trying trying to telnet to the hostname, if you get the *Trying nnn.nnn.nnn...* message then your machine has been able to find an ip address for that name. If you get the message *Unknown host*, then it has not. If not, either use ip addresses in dotted decimal notation, or fix up your name resolver configuration (See section `Name Resolution`).

The most commonly used optional paramaters for the `opt1` and `opt2` fields are:

normal

to enable normal uncompressed SLIP.

compressed

to enable van Jacobsen header compression (cSLIP)

Naturally these are mutually exclusive, you can use one or the other. For more information on the other options available, refer to the *man* pages.

Configuring the /etc/SLIP.login **file.** After *SLIPlogin* has searched the /etc/SLIP.hosts and found a matching entry, it will attempt to execute the /etc/SLIP.login file to actually configure the SLIP interface with its ip address and netmask.

The sample /etc/SLIP.login file supplied with the *SLIPlogin* package looks like this:

```
#!/bin/sh -
#
#       @(#)SLIP.login  5.1 (Berkeley) 7/1/90
#
# generic login file for a SLIP line.  SLIPlogin invokes this with
# the parameters:
#     $1      $2        $3        $4         $5        $6     $7-n
#   SLIPunit ttyspeed loginname local-addr remote-addr mask opt-args
#
/sbin/ifconfig $1 $4 pointopoint $5 mtu 1500 -trailers up
/sbin/route add $5
arp -s $5 <hw_addr> pub
exit 0
#
```

You will note that this script simply uses the *ifconfig* and *route* commands to configure the SLIP device with its ipaddress, remote ip address and netmask, and creates a route for the remote address via the SLIP device. Just the same as you would if you were using the *slattach* command.

Note also the use of *Proxy ARP* to ensure that other hosts on the same ethernet as the server machine will know how to reach the dial-in host. The <hw_addr> field should be the hardware address of the ethernet card in the machine. If your server machine isn't on an ethernet network then you can leave this line out completely.

Configuring the /etc/SLIP.logout **file.** When the call drops out, you want to ensure that the serial device is restored to its normal state so that future callers will be able to login correctly. This is achieved with the use of the /etc/SLIP.logout file. It is quite simple in format.

```
#!/bin/sh -
#
#                 SLIP.logout
#
/sbin/ifconfig $1 down
/sbin/route del $5
arp -d $5
exit 0
#
```

All it does is 'down' the interface and delete the manual route previously created. It also uses the *arp* command to delete any proxy arp put in place, again, you don't need the *arp* command in the script if your server machine does not have an ethernet port.

Configuring the /etc/SLIP.tty **file.** If you are using dynamic ip address allocation (have any hosts configured with the DYNAMIC keyword in the /etc/SLIP.hosts file, then you must configure the /etc/SLIP.tty file to list what addresses are assigned to what port. You only need this file if you wish your server to dynamically allocate addresses to users.

The file is a table that lists the *tty* devices that will support dial-in SLIP connections and the ip address that should be assigned to users who call in on that port.

Its format is as follows:

```
# SLIP.tty    tty -> IP address mappings for dynamic SLIP
# format: /dev/tty?? xxx.xxx.xxx.xxx
#
/dev/ttyS0      192.168.0.100
/dev/ttyS1      192.168.0.101
#
```

What this table says is that callers that dial in on port `/dev/ttyS0` who have their remote address field in the `/etc/SLIP.hosts` file set to `DYNAMIC` will be assigned an address of `192.168.0.100`.

In this way you need only allocate one address per port for all users who do not require an dedicated address for themselves. This helps you keep the number of addresses you need down to a minimum to avoid wastage.

12.2.2   SLIP Server using *dip*.

Let me start by saying that some of the information below came from the *dip* man pages, where how to run Linux as a SLIP server is briefly documented. Please also beware that the following has been based on the *dip337j-uri.tgz* package and probably will not apply to other versions of *dip*.

dip has an input mode of operation, where it automatically locates an entry for the user who invoked it and configures the serial line as a SLIP link according to information it finds in the `/etc/diphosts` file. This input mode of operation is activated by invoking *dip* as *diplogin*. This therefore is how you use *dip* as a SLIP server, by creating special accounts where *diplogin* is used as the login shell.

The first thing you will need to do is to make a symbolic link as follows:

```
# ln -sf /usr/sbin/dip /usr/sbin/diplogin
```

You then need to add entries to both your `/etc/passwd` and your `/etc/diphosts` files. The entries you need to make are formatted as follows:

To configure Linux as a SLIP server with *dip*, you need to create some special SLIP accounts for users, where *dip* (in input mode) is used as the login shell. A suggested convention is that of having all SLIP accounts begin with a capital 'S', eg 'Sfredm'.

A sample `/etc/passwd` entry for a SLIP user looks like:

```
Sfredm:ij/SMxiTlGVCo:1004:10:Fred:/tmp:/usr/sbin/diplogin
^^      ^^            ^^   ^^  ^^   ^^   ^^
 |       |            |    |   |    |     \__ diplogin as login shell
 |       |            |    |   |     _____ Home directory
 |       |            |    |    _____ User Full Name
 |       |            |     _____ User Group ID
 |       |             _____ User ID
 |        _____ Encrypted User Password
  _____ SLIP User Login Name
```

After the user logs in, the *login(1)* program, if it finds and verifies the user ok, will execute the *diplogin* command. *dip*, when invoked as *diplogin* knows that it should automatically assume that it is being used a login shell. When it is started as *diplogin* the first thing it does is use the *getuid()* function call to get the userid of whoever has invoked it. It then searches the `/etc/diphosts` file for the first entry that matches either the userid or the name of the *tty* device that the call has come in on, and configures itself appropriately. By judicious decision as to whether to give a user an entry in the `diphosts` file, or whether to let the user be given the default configuration you can build your server in such a way that you can have a mix of static and dynamically assigned address users.

dip will automatically add a 'Proxy-ARP' entry if invoked in input mode, so you do not need to worry about manually adding such entries.

Configuring /etc/diphosts   /etc/diphosts is used by *dip* to lookup preset configurations for remote hosts. These remote hosts might be users dialing into your Linux machine, or they might be for machines that you dial into with your Linux machine.

The general format for /etc/diphosts is as follows:

```
  ..
  Suwalt::145.71.34.1:145.71.34.2:255.255.255.0:SLIP uwalt:CSLIP,1006
  ttyS1::145.71.34.3:145.71.34.2:255.255.255.0:Dynamic ttyS1:CSLIP,296
  ..
```

The fields are:

1. login name: as returned by getpwuid(getuid()) or tty name.

2. unused: compat. with passwd

3. Remote Address: IP address of the calling host, either numeric or by name

4. Local Address: IP address of this machine, again numeric or by name

5. Netmask: in dotted decimal notation

6. Comment field: put whatever you want here.

7. protocol: SLIP, CSLIP etc.

8. MTU: decimal number

An example /etc/net/diphosts entry for a remote SLIP user might be:

```
  Sfredm::145.71.34.1:145.71.34.2:255.255.255.0:SLIP uwalt:SLIP,296
```

which specifies a SLIP link with remote address of 145.71.34.1, and MTU of 296, or:

```
  Sfredm::145.71.34.1:145.71.34.2:255.255.255.0:SLIP uwalt:CSLIP,1006
```

which specifies a cSLIP-capable link with remote address 145.71.34.1, and MTU of 1006.

Therefore, all users who you wish to be allowed a statically allocated dial-up IP access should have an entry in the /etc/diphosts and if you want users who call a particular port to have their details dynamically allocated you must have an entry for the tty device and do not configure a user based entry. You should remember to configure at least one entry for each tty device that your dialup users use to ensure that a suitable configuration is available for them regardless of which modem they call in on.

When a user logs in, they will receive a normal login and password prompt, at which they should enter their SLIP-login userid and password. If they check out ok, then the user will see no special messages, they should just change into SLIP mode at their end, and then they should be able to connect ok, and be configured with the parameters from the diphosts file.

12.2.3   SLIP server using the *dSLIP* package.

Matt Dillon <dillon@apollo.west.oic.com> has written a package that does not only dial-in but also dial-out SLIP. Matt's package is a combination of small programs and scripts that manage your connections for you. You will need to have *tcsh* installed as at least one of the scripts requires it. Matt supplies a binary copy of the *expect* utility as it too is needed by one of the scripts. You will most likely need some experience with *expect* to get this package working to your liking, but don't let that put you off.

Matt has written a good set of installation instructions in the README file, so I won't bother repeating them.

You can get the *dSLIP* package from its home site at:

apollo.west.oic.com

```
/pub/linux/dillon_src/dSLIP203.tgz
```

or from:

sunsite.unc.edu

```
/pub/Linux/system/Network/serial/dSLIP203.tgz
```

Read the README file, and create the /etc/passwd and /etc/group entries **before** doing a make install.

12.3   Using the Automounter Daemon - AMD.

This section has been supplied by Mitch DSouza, and I've included it with minimal editing, as he supplied it. Thanks Mitch.

12.3.1   What is an automounter, and why would I use one ?

An *automounter* provides a convenient means of mounting filesystems on demand, i.e. when required. This will reduce both the server and the client load, and provides a great deal of flexibility even with non-NFS mounts. It also offers a redundancy mechanism whereby a mount point will automatically switch to a secondary server should a primary one be unavailable. A rather useful mount called the *union* mount gives the *automounter* the ability to *merge* the contents of multiple directories into a single directory. The documentation msut be read thoroughly to make full use of its extensive capabilities.

A few important points must be remembered - (in no particular order):

- *amd* maps are **not** compatible with Sun maps, which in turn are **not** compatible with HP maps *ad infinitum*. The point here however is that *amd* is freely available and compatible with all the systems mentioned above and more, thus giving you the ability to share maps if *amd* is installed throughout your network. Mitch uses it with a mixture of Linux/Dec/NeXt/Sun machines.

- *Sun* automount maps can be converted to *amd* style maps by using the *perl* script in the contrib directory - automount2amd.pl.

- You **must** have the *portmapper* running **before** starting *amd*.

- UFS mounts **do not** timeout.

- UFS mounts, in the case of Linux **only**, have been extended to deal with **all** varieties of native filesystems (i.e. Minix, ext, ext2, xiafs ...) with the default being Minix. This undocumented feature is accessed in the *opts* option like:

```
..., opts:=type=msdos,conv=auto
```

- Do not mount over existing directories unless you use a *direct* automount option, otherwise it is like mounting your disk on /home when some user directory is /home/fred.

- **Always** turn on full logging with the '-x all' option to *amd* if you have any troubles. Check also what the command:

```
% amq -ms
```

reports, as it will indicate problems as they occur.

- GNU *getopt()* is too clever for its own good sometimes. You should always use '–' before the non-options e.g.

```
# /etc/amd -x all -l syslog -a /amd -- /net /etc/amd.net
```

12.3.2   Where to get AMD, the automounter daemon.

amd can be obtained from:

sunsite.unc.edu

```
/pub/Linux/system/Misc/mount/amd920824upl67.tar.gz
```

This contains ready-to-run binaries, full sources and documentation in texinfo format.

12.3.3   An example AMD configuration.

You do not configure the *automounter* from the /etc/fstab file, which you will already be using to contain information about your fileystems, instead it is command line driven.

To mount two *nfs* filesystems using your /etc/fstab file you would use two entries that looked like:

```
server-1:/export/disk  /nfs/server-1  nfs  defaults
server-2:/export/disk  /nfs/server-2  nfs  defaults
```

i.e. you were *nfs* mounting server-1 and server-2 on your Linux disk on the /nfs/server-1 and /nfs/server-2 directories.

After commenting out, or deleting the above lines from your /etc/fstab file, you could *amd* to perform the same task with the following syntax:

```
/etc/amd -x all -l syslog -a /amd -- /nfs /etc/amd.server
   |      |  |    | |       | |     | | |  |  |
   |      |  |    | |       | |     | | |  |  |
   '------' '----' '--------' '-----' -' '--' '--------------'
   |        |      |          |       |  |    |
   |        |      |          |       |  |    |
   (1)      (2)    (3)        (4)    (5)(6)  (7)
```

Where:

1. The full *amd* binary path (obviously optional) depending on your $PATH setting, so just '*amd*' may be specified here.

2. '-x all' means turn full logging on. Read the documentation for the other logging levels

3. '-l syslog' means log the message via the *syslog* daemon. This could mean put it to a file, dump it, or pass it, to an unused tty console. This (*syslog*) can be changed to the name of a file, i.e. '-l foo' will record to a file called *foo*.

4. '-a /amd' means use the /amd directory as a temporary place for automount points. This directory is created automatically by *amd* and should be removed before starting *amd* in your /etc/rc scripts.

5. '–' means tell *getopt()* to stop attempting to parse the rest of the command line for options. This is especially useful when specifying the 'type:=' options on the command line, otherwise *getopt()* tries to decode it incorrectly.

6. '/nfs' is the **real** nfs mount point. Again this is automatically created and should **not** generally contain subdirectories unless the 'type:=direct' option is used.

7. The *amd* map (i.e. a file) named 'amd.server' contains the lines:

```
# /etc/amd.server
/defaults    opts:=rw;type:=nfs
server-1     rhost:=server-1;rfs:=/export/disk
server-2     rhost:=server-2;rfs:=/export/disk
```

Once started and successfully running, you can query the status of the mounts with the command:

```
% amq -ms
```

Now if you say:

```
% ls /nfs
```

you should see no files. However the command:

```
% ls /nfs/server-1
```

will mount the host 'server-1' automatically. *voila!* *amd* is running. After the default timeout has expired, this will automatically be unmounted. Your /etc/password file could contain entries like:

```
...
linus:EncPass:10:0:God:/nfs/server-1/home/linus:/bin/sh
mitch:EncPass:20:10:Mitch DSouza:/nfs/server-1/home/mitch:/bin/tcsh
matt:EncPass:20:10:Matt Welsh:/nfs/server-1/home/matt:/bin/csh
```

which would mean that when Linus, Matt, or Mitch are logged in, their home directory will be remotely mounted from the appropriate server, and umounted when they log out.

12.4   Using Linux as a router

Linux will function just fine as a router. You should run a routing daemon such as *gated*, or if you have simple routing requirements use hard coded routes. If you are using a late version kernel (1.1.*) then you should ensure that you have answered 'y' to:

```
IP forwarding/gatewaying (CONFIG_IP_FORWARD) [y] y
```

when building your kernel.

Olaf Kirch's Network Administrators Guide discusses network design and routing issues, and you should read it for more information. A reference to it is in the "Related Documentation" section of this document.

12.5   NIS - Sun Network Information System.

There is now an *NIS-HOWTO* (http://sunsite.unc.edu/mdw/HOWTO/NIS-HOWTO.html) which you should read if you are interested in using NIS. It details how to obtain, install and configure the NIS system for Linux.

13   Experimental and Developmental modules.

There are a number of people developing new features and modules for the Linux networking code. Some of these are in quite an advanced state (read *working*), and it is these that I intend to include in this section until they are standard release code, when they will be moved forward.

13.1 AX.25 - A protocol used by Amateur Radio Operators.

The *AX.25* protocol is used by Amateur Radio Operators worldwide. It offers both connected and connectionless modes of operation, and is used either by itself for point-point links, or to carry other protocols such as TCP/IP and netrom.

It is similar to X.25 level 2 in structure, with some extensions to make it more useful in the amateur radio environment.

Alan Cox has developed some kernel based AX.25 software support for Linux and these are available in ALPHA form for you to try. Alan's code supports both KISS based TNC's (Terminal Node Controllers), and the Z8530 SCC driver.

The User programs contain a P.M.S. (Personal Message System), a beacon facility, a line mode connect program, and 'listen' an example of how to capture all AX.25 frames at RAW interface level.

Be sure to read `/usr/local/ax25/README` as it contains more complete information regarding this software.

13.1.1 Where to obtain the AX.25 software.

The AX.25 software is available from:

sunacm.swan.ac.uk

```
/pub/misc/Linux/Radio/*
```

You will find a number of directories, each containing different versions of the code. Since it is closely linked with the kernel code, you will need to ensure that you choose the version appropriate for the kernel version you are running. The following table shows the mapping between the two:

```
AX25007          Prehistoric
AX25010          Obsolete
AX25012          for release 1.0.* kernels and higher
AX25016          for release 1.1.5 kernels
AX25017          for release 1.1.6 kernels
AX25018
AX25021
AX25022          for release 1.1.28 kernels
AX25023
AX25024
AX25026
AX25027
AX25028                              for release 1.1.88 kernels and later.
```

In each directory you will find at least two files, one called something like `krnl028.tgz`, and the other called something like `util028.tgz`. These are the kernel software, and the user programs respectively.

13.1.2 Installing the AX.25 software.

The software comes in two parts, the kernel drivers, and the user programs.

The kernel drivers. To install the kernel drivers, do the following:

```
# cd /usr/src
# gzip -dc krnl028.tgz | tar xvf -
```

you   will   need   to   uncomment
(remove the # symbol from) the line in the `/usr/src/linux/arch/i386/config.in` file that looks
like this:

```
bool 'Amateur Radio AX.25 Level 2' CONFIG_AX25 n
```

If you want your kernel to support the H.A.P.N. PI2 driver then you will have to edit the
`/usr/src/linux/arch/i386/config.in` file and add some text in the appropriate place.

Change:

```
bool 'PPP (point-to-point) support' CONFIG_PPP n
bool 'PLIP (parallel port) support' CONFIG_PLIP n
bool 'Do you want to be offered ALPHA test drivers' CONFIG_NET_ALPHA n
```

to:

```
bool 'PPP (point-to-point) support' CONFIG_PPP n
bool 'PLIP (parallel port) support' CONFIG_PLIP n
bool 'HAPN PI2 Card support' CONFIG_PI n
bool 'Do you want to be offered ALPHA test drivers' CONFIG_NET_ALPHA n
```

This will ensure the driver for the PI card is provided as an option when building the kernel. The driver
will automatically probe for the cards settings.

You should then:

```
# cd /usr/src/linux
# make config
# make dep;make
```

Be sure to answer 'yes' when you are asked if you should include the AX.25 support in the *make config* step.
You will also need to answer 'yes' to including SLIP if you want the AX.25 code to support a KISS TNC.

The user programs.   To install the user programs you should try:

```
# cd /usr/local
# gzip -dc util028.tgz | tar xvvof -
# cd ax25
```

You should then read the README file and follow its instructions. When you are happy you are ready to
compile, then do:

```
# cd /usr/local/ax25/src
# make clean
# make install
```

13.1.3   Configuring and using the AX.25 software.

Configuring an AX.25 port is very similar to configuring a SLIP device. The AX.25 software has been
designed to work with a TNC in *kiss* mode or a H.A.P.N. PI2 card. You will need to have the TNC
preconfigured and connected. You can use a comms program like *minicom* or *seyon* to configure the TNC
into kiss mode if you wish.

You use the *axattach* program in much the same way as you would use the *slattach* program. For example:

```
# /usr/local/ax25/bin/axattach -s 4800 /dev/cua1 VK2KTJ &
```

would configure your /dev/cua1 serial device to be a *kiss* interface at 4800 bps, with the hardware address VK2KTJ.

You would then use the *ifconfig* program to configure the ip address and netmask as for an ethernet device:

```
# /sbin/ifconfig sl0 44.136.8.5
# /sbin/ifconfig sl0 netmask 255.255.255.0
# /sbin/ifconfig sl0 broadcast 44.136.8.255
# /sbin/ifconfig sl0 arp mtu 257 up
```

To test it out, try the following:

```
/usr/local/ax25/bin/call VK2DAY via VK2RVT
```

The *call* program is a linemode terminal program for making ax.25 calls. It recognizes lines that start with ' ' as command lines. The '.' command will close the connection.

You also need to configure some items such as the window to use. This necessitates editing only one file. Edit the /usr/local/ax25/etc/ports file. This is an ascii file containing one line for each AX.25 port. You must have the entries in this file in the same order as you configure your AX.25 interfaces.

The format is as follows:

```
callsign baudrate window frequency
```

At this stage not much of this information is used, it will be picked up and used in later developments.

I haven't had a chance to try this code out yet. Please refer to the man pages in /usr/local/ax25/man and the README file in /usr/local/ax25 for more information.

13.2 Z8530 SCC driver.

The Zilog Z8530 SCC provides Synchronous/Asynchronous, HDLC, NRZI encoding and other capabilities. There are a number of peripheral cards that use the Z850 as the basis of their design. A driver has been written by Joerg Reuter, <DL1BKE@melaten.ihf.rwth-aachen.de>, that is generic enough to be pushed into service for just about any sort of 8530 card and is available on:

ftp.ucsd.edu

```
/hamradio/packet/tcpip/incoming/z8530drv-1.8.dl1bke.tar.gz
```

Please read the README file that accompanies the driver for more details.

13.3 Ottawa PI/PI2 card driver.

The Ottawa PI card is a Z8530 SCC based card for IBM PC type machines that is in common usage by Amateur Radio operators worldwide. While it is most commonly used by Amateur Radio Operators, it could be pressed into service in other fields where it is desirable to have the features of a Z8530. It supports a high speed half duplex (single DMA channel) port, and a low speed (<19.2kbps interrupt driven) full duplex port. The PI2 is a new version of the card that supports an on board radio modem, and improved hardware design.

A driver for this card has been written by David Perry, <dp@hydra.carleton.edu>, and is available from:

hydra.carleton.ca

```
/pub/hamradio/packet/tcpip/linux/pi2-0.5ALPHA.tgz
```

Please read the README file that accompanies the driver for more details.

13.4   snmp agent.

There is an experimental snmp agent for Linux, ported from the cmu-snmp source by Erik
Schoenfelder, <schoenfr@ibr.cs.tu-bs.de>.

It is available from:

ftp.ibr.cs.tu-bs.de

```
/pub/local/cmu-snmp2.1.213-src.tar.gz
```

Please **read** the file called cmu-snmp2.1.213.README, as it contains information that you will need to
know about the package.

This package provides a nearly complete MIB-II variable set. and parts of the host MIB. Setting of system
group variables is provided. The private community string is setable in the config file.

nstat.tar.gz contains a formatter of the output from /proc/net/snmp called *nstat*.

You will need Linux v1.1.60 and libc v4.6.27 or higher to compile and run the agent.

13.5   Experimental Token Ring driver

An   experimental   Token   Ring   driver   is
being developed by Peter De Schrijver <stud11@cc4.kuleuven.ac.be>. His latest version, at
the time of writing was available at:

linux3.cc.kuleuven.ac.be

```
/pub/Linux/TokenRing/TokenRing.patch-1.2.0.gz
```

ftp.cs.kuleuven.ac.be

```
/pub/unix/linux/TokenRing.patch-1.1.64.gz
```

There are a number of patch files against various kernel versions. Just pick the one that suits your kernel.

Note also that there are versions of the network tools to suit Token Ring in the same directory at
linux3.cc.kuleven.ac.be.

Most boards based on IBM's TROPIC chipset should work now. The following boards are known to be
working with the driver :

- IBM Token Ring Adapter II
- IBM Token Ring 16/4 Adapter
- IBM Token Ring Adapter/A
- IBM Token Ring 16/4 Adapter/A
- HyperRing Classic 16/4

Boards which use the TI chipset or busmastering DMA won't work with the current driver. However
someone is working on a driver for the IBM busmaster adapters.

13.6   V.35 interface board

V.35 is a C.C.I.T.T. standard interface that provides a high speed balanced serial interface suitable for speeds up to about 2 Mbps. The use of differential pair balanced transmission allows the V.35 interface to support longer cables than can the more familiar V.24/RS232C type interface and higher data rates.

`Pete Kruckenberg <kruckenb@sal.cs.utah.edu>` located a company that supplies V.35 interface hardware for ISA bus machines. The company is also developing a Linux driver for this card that is nearing Beta testing stage. This would allow you to directly connect your Linux machine to a 48/56kbps synchronous leased line. The card supports multiple protocols and allows for interface speeds of up to 12 Mbps.

More information is available from:

ftp.std.com

```
pub/sdl/n2
```

or you can email `Dale Dhillon <sdl@world.std.com>`

13.7   IPX bridge program

Vinod G Kulkarni `<vinod@cse.iitb.ernet.in>` has cowritten some software for Linux that will allow it to act as an IPX bridge.

The software is available from:

sunsite.unc.edu

```
/pub/Linux/Systems/Network/router/ipxbridge.tar.gz
```

13.8   IPX RIP and SAP support.

Alex Liu `<labrat@unitrx.com` has written support for the Novell RIP and SAP protocols to allow your Linux machine to act as a Novell router.

This software is **alpha** and includes a kernel patch. Be warned that you should take the usual precautions when testing this software.

You can obtain the software from:

sunsite.unc.edu

```
/pub/Linux/Incoming/ipxripd-002.tar.gz (until it is moved)
/pub/Linux//system/Network/router/ipxripd-002.tar.gz
```

A `README` file is included, and you should read this for installation and configuration details.

13.9   Demand Dial SLIP/PPP package

Eric Schenk `<schenk@cs.toronto.edu>` has written a demand dial daemon that will work with either SLIP or PPP. It relies on you having a SLIP device configured which the daemon connects to via a pty. When your SLIP connection is not active all datagrams for non local hosts will be routed to this device, and the daemon will detect them, when it receives a datagram it executes a script to activate your network link, and then reroutes datagrams to that link.

The software is available at:

sunsite.unc.edu

```
/pub/Linux/system/Network/serial/diald-0.7.tar.gz
```

Note: You must configure your kernel so that it includes the SLIP driver, even if you only want to run PPP. The included documentation describes how to install and configure the software.

13.10   ISDN support

Matthias Urlichs `<urlichs@smurf.noris.de>` has developed some experimental ISDN support for Linux. The most recent version was for kernel version 1.1.88 and is reported to work.

It is available at:

ftp.uni-stuttgart.de

```
/pub/systems/linux/isdn/kernel/1.1.83-88/*
```

Be warned, the documentation is in German, and the code is designed to support the European ISDN network.

14   Diagnostic tools - How do I find out what is wrong?

In this section I'll briefly describe some of the commonly used diagnostic tools that are available for your Linux network, and how you might use them to identify the cause of your network problems, or to teach yourself a bit more about how TCP/IP networking works. I'll gloss over some of the detail of how the tools work because this document is not an appropriate forum for describing that sort of detail, but I hope I'll have presented enough information that you'll have an understanding of how to use the tool, and to better understand the relevant *man* page or other documentation.

14.1   ping - are you there?

The *ping* tool is located in the NetKit-B distribution as detailed above in the 'Network Applications' section. *ping*, as the name implies, allows you to transmit a datagram at another host that it will reflect back at you if it is alive and working OK and the network in between is also OK. In its simplest form you would simply say:

```
# ping gw
PING gw.vk2ktj.ampr.org (44.136.8.97): 56 data bytes
64 bytes from 44.136.8.97: icmp_seq=0 ttl=254 time=35.9 ms
64 bytes from 44.136.8.97: icmp_seq=1 ttl=254 time=22.1 ms
64 bytes from 44.136.8.97: icmp_seq=2 ttl=254 time=26.0 ms
^C

--- gw.vk2ktj.ampr.org ping statistics ---
3 packets transmitted, 3 packets received, 0% packet loss
round-trip min/avg/max = 22.1/28.0/35.9 ms
#
```

What *ping* has done is resolved the hostname to an address, and using the *icmp* protocol has transmitted an *icmp echo request* datagram to the remote host periodically. For each *echo request* that the remote host receives it will formulate an *icmp echo reply* datagram which it will transmit back to you. Each line beginning with '64 bytes from ...' represents an *echo reply* received in response to an *echo request*. Each line tells you the address of the host that sent you the reply, the sequence number to which the reply was for, the *time to live* field and the total *round trip time* that was taken. The *round trip time* is the time between when the *echo request* datagram is transmitted, and the corresponding *echo reply* is received. This can be used as a measure of how fast or slow the network connection between the two machines is.

The last two lines tell you how many datagrams were transmitted, how many valid responses were received and what percentage of the datagrams were lost. The percentage lost figure is a measure of how good or error free the network connection is. High percentage lost figures indicate such problems as a high error rate on a link somewhere between the hosts, exhausted capacity on a router or link somewhere, or high collision rate on an ethernet lan. You can use *ping* to identify where this problem might be by running *ping* sessions to each of the routed points that make up the network path. When you find that you can ping somewhere without any datagram loss, but pinging anywhere past there causes you packet loss, you can deduce that the problem lies somewhere between those two points.

14.2   traceroute - How do I get there?

The *traceroute* tool is found in the NetKit-A distribution detailed earlier. *traceroute* is primarily used for testing and displaying the path that your network connection would take to a destination host. *traceroute* also uses the *icmp* protocol, but it uses a clever trick to get each point along the path to send it back a reply as it creeps its way along. Its trick is to manually manipulate the *time to live* field of the datagrams it transmits. The *time to live* field is a mechanism that ensures that rogue datagrams do not get caught in a routing loop. Each time a datagram passes through a router it decrements the *time to live* field by one. If the *time to live* reaches zero then that router or host sends an *icmp time to live expired* message back to the host who transmitted the datagram to let it know the datagram has expired. *traceroute* uses this mechanism by sending a series of *udp* datagrams with the *time to live* beginning set at one, and incrementing each step it takes. By recording the addresses from the *icmp time to live expired* replies it receives in response to the datagrams dying it can determine the path taken to get to the destination. An example of its use would look something like:

```
# traceroute minnie.vk1xwt.ampr.org
traceroute to minnie.vk1xwt (44.136.7.129), 30 hops max, 40 byte packets
 1  gw (44.136.8.97)  51.618 ms  30.431 ms  34.396 ms
 2  gw.uts (44.136.8.68) 2017.322 ms  2060.121 ms 1997.793 ms
 3  minnie.vk1xwt (44.136.7.129) 2205.335 ms  2319.728 ms  2279.643 ms
#
```

The first column tells us how many hops away (what the *ttl* value was), the second column is the hostname and address that responded if it could be resolved or just its address if it could not. The third, fourth and fifth columns are the round trip time for three consecutive datagrams to that point. This tells us that the first hop in the network route is via gw.vk2ktj, and the three figures following are the round trip times to that router. The next hop was via gw.uts.ampr.org, and minnie.vk1xwt.ampr.org is one hop further away. You can deduce information about the network route by looking at the difference in times between each step in the route. You can see that the round trip times to gw are fairly fast, it is an ethernet connected host. gw.uts is substantially slower to get to than gw, it is across a low speed radio link, so you have the ethernet time plus the radio link time added together. minnie.vk1xwt is only slightly slower than gw.uts, they are connected via a high speed network.

If you perform a traceroute and you see the string !N appear after the time figure, this indicates that your traceroute program received a *network unreachable* response. This message tells you that the host or router who sent you the message did not know how to route to the destination address. This normally indicates that there is a network link down somewhere. The last address listed is as far as you get before you find the faulty link.

Similarly if you see the string !H this indicates that a *host unreachable* message has been received. This might suggest that you got as far as the ethernet that the remote host is connected to, but the host itself is not responding or is faulty.

14.3   tcpdump - capturing and displaying network activity.

Adam Caldwell <acaldwel@103mort2.cs.ohiou.edu> has ported the *tcpdump* utlility to Linux. *tcpdump* allows you to take traces of network activity by intercepting the datagrams on their way in and out of your machine. This is useful for diagnosing difficult to identify network problems.

Both binary and sources are available, and version 3.0 has been tested on kernel versions 0.99.15, 1.0.8 and 1.1.28.

You can find the source and binaries at: *103mor2.cs.ohiou.edu* (ftp://103mort2.cs.ohiou.edu/linux/tcpdump-3.0-linux-src.tar.gz) or from: *sunsite.unc.edu* (ftp://sunsite.unc.edu/pub/Linux/system/Network/tcpdump-3.0-linux-src.tar.gz)

tcpdump decodes each of the datagrams that it intercepts and displays them in a slightly cryptic looking format in text. You would use *tcpdump* if you were trying to diagnose a problem like protocol errors, or strange disconnections, as it allows you to actually see what has happened on the network. To properly use *tcpdump* you would need some understanding of the protocols and how they work, but it is useful for simpler duties such as ensuring that datagrams are actually leaving your machine on the correct port if you are trying to diagnose routing problems and for seeing if you are receiving datagrams from remote destinations.

A sample of tcpdump output looks like this:

```
# tcpdump -i eth0
tcpdump: listening on eth0
13:51:36.168219 arp who-has gw.vk2ktj.ampr.org tell albert.vk2ktj.ampr.org
13:51:36.193830 arp reply gw.vk2ktj.ampr.org is-at 2:60:8c:9c:ec:d4
13:51:37.373561 albert.vk2ktj.ampr.org > gw.vk2ktj.ampr.org: icmp: echo request
13:51:37.388036 gw.vk2ktj.ampr.org > albert.vk2ktj.ampr.org: icmp: echo reply
13:51:38.383578 albert.vk2ktj.ampr.org > gw.vk2ktj.ampr.org: icmp: echo request
13:51:38.400592 gw.vk2ktj.ampr.org > albert.vk2ktj.ampr.org: icmp: echo reply
13:51:49.303196 albert.vk2ktj.ampr.org.1104 > gw.vk2ktj.ampr.org.telnet: \
     S 700506986:700506986(0) win 512 <mss 1436>
13:51:49.363933 albert.vk2ktj.ampr.org.1104 > gw.vk2ktj.ampr.org.telnet: \
     . ack 1103372289 win 14261
13:51:49.367328 gw.vk2ktj.ampr.org.telnet > albert.vk2ktj.ampr.org.1104: \
     S 1103372288:1103372288(0) ack 700506987 win 2048 <mss 432>
13:51:49.391800 albert.vk2ktj.ampr.org.1104 > gw.vk2ktj.ampr.org.telnet: \
     . ack 134 win 14198
13:51:49.394524 gw.vk2ktj.ampr.org.telnet > albert.vk2ktj.ampr.org.1104: \
     P 1:134(133) ack 1 win 2048
13:51:49.524930 albert.vk2ktj.ampr.org.1104 > gw.vk2ktj.ampr.org.telnet: \
     P 1:28(27) ack 134 win 14335


  . .
#
```

When you start *tcpdump* without arguments it grabs the first (lowest numbered) network device that is not the loopback device. You can specify which device to monitor with a command line argument as shown above. *tcpdump* then decodes each datagram transmitted or received and displays them, one line each, in a textual form. The first column is obviously the time the datagram was transmitted or received. The remainder of the line is then dependent on the type of datagram. The first two lines in the sample are what an arp request from albert.vk2ktj for gw.vk2ktj look like. The next four lines are two pings from albert.vk2ktj to gw.vk2ktj, note that *tcpdump* actually tells you the name of the *icmp* datagram transmitted or received. The greater-than (>) symbol tells you which way the datagram was transmitted, that is, from who, to who. It points from the sender, to the receiver. The remainder of the sample trace are the establishment of a telnet connection from albert.vk2ktj to gw.vk2ktj.

The number or name at the end of each hostname tells you what socket number is being used. *tcpdump* looks in your /etc/services file to do this translation.

tcpdump explodes each of the fields, and so you can see the values of the window and mss parameters in some of the datagrams.

The *man* page documents all of the options available to you.

Note for PPP users: The version of *tcpdump* that is currently available does not support the PPP suite of protocols. Al Longyear has produced a set of patches to correct this, but these have not been built into a *tcpdump* distribution yet.

14.4 icmpinfo - logs icmp messages received.

ICMP then Internet Control Message Protocol conveys useful information about the health of your IP network. Often ICMP messages are received and acted on silently with you never knowing of their presence. *icmpinfo* is a tool that will allow you to view ICMP messages much like tcpdump does. Laurent Demailly <dl@hplyot.obspm.fr> took the bsd ping source and modified it heavily.

Version 1.10 is available from:

hplyot.obspm.fr

```
/net/icmpinfo-1.10.tar.gz
```

Compilation is as simple as:

```
# cd /usr/src
# cd icmpinfo-1.10
# gzip -dc icmpinfo-1.10.tar.gz | tar xvf -
# make
```

You must be SuperUser to run *icmpinfo*. *icmpinfo* can either decode to the tty it was called from or send its output to the *syslog* utility.

To test out how it works, try running *icmpinfo* and starting a *traceroute* to a remote host. You will see the icmp messages that *traceroute* uses listed on the output.

15 Some Frequently Asked Questions, with Brief Answers.

Following are some questions and answers that are commonly asked.

15.1 General questions:

I have only a dialin terminal access to a machine on the net, can I use this as a network connection ?

Yes you can, take a look at TERM. TERM allows you you to run network connections over a normal terminal session. It requires some modifications to the network applications to work with it, but binaries and sources are available for the most common ones already. take a look at the *TERM-HOWTO* (http://sunsite.unc.edu/mdw/HOWTO/Term-HOWTO.html) for lots more information.

Why, when I telnet/ftp/rlogin to my machine does it take so long to answer?

You do not have your name resolver configured properly. Reread the section on /etc/resolv.conf.

I want to build my own standalone network, what addresses do I use ?

RFC1597 has specifically reserved some IP addresses for private networks. You should use these as they prevent anything nasty happening if you accidentally get connected to the Internet. The addresses reserved are:

```
    10.0.0.0        -    10.255.255.255
    172.16.0.0      -    172.31.255.255
    192.168.0.0     -    192.168.255.255
```

Note, reserved network addresses are of classes A, B and C, so you are not restricted in your network design or size. Since you won't be connecting to the Internet it doesn't matter if you use the same address as some other group or network, just so long as the addresses you use are unique within your network.

If sunacm.swan.ac.uk is down, how do I get the files specified ?

'sunacm' is mirrored on:

ftp.Uni-Mainz.DE

```
    /pub/Linux/packages/Net2Debugged
```

and/or:

ftp.infomagic.com

```
    /pub/mirrors/linux/sunacm
```

How do I know what version of kernel/net code I am running ?

The network code and kernel now have synchronized version numbers, so try:

```
uname -a
```

or:

```
cat /proc/version
```

How do I change the message that telnet users are given at connect?

The `/etc/issue` is the message that is given to normal getty users when they login. Some *telnetd* programs use a different file `/etc/issue.net` instead. So if you find that changing your `issue` file doesn't work, try changing the other.

15.2   Error messages:

I keep getting the error 'eth0: transmit timed out'. What does this mean?

This usually means that your Ethernet cable is unplugged, or that the setup parameters for your card (I/O address, IRQ, etc.) are not set correctly. Check the messages at boot time and make sure that your card is recognized with the correct Ethernet address. If it is, check that there is no conflict with any other hardware in your machine, eg you might have a soundblaster sharing the same IRQ or i/o control port.

I get errors 'check Ethernet cable' when using the network.

You probably have your Ethernet card configured incorrectly. Double check the settings in /usr/src/linux/drivers/net/CONFIG. If this checks out ok, you may in fact have a cabling problem, check the cables are plugged in securely.

15.3   Routing questions:

Why do I get the message 'obsolete route request' when I use the route command ?

You are using a version of route that is older than your kernel. You should upgrade to a newer version of route. Refer to the "The network configuration tool suite" section of this document for information on where to obtain the tool set.

Why do I get a 'network unreachable' message when I try and network?

This message means that yours, or some other, machine doesn't know how to route to the host that you are attempting to ping or connect to. If it occurs for all hosts that you try, then it is probable that you don't have your default route set up properly, reread the 'routing' section.

I can ping my server/gateway, but can't ping or connect to anyone remote.

This is probably due to a routing problem. Reread the 'routing' section in this document. If this looks ok, then make sure that the host you are attempting to connect to has a route to you. If you are a dialin user then this is a common cause of problems, ensure that your server is either running a routing program like *gated* or *routed*, or that it is *'prox arping'* for you, otherwise you will be able to get datagrams to the remote host, but it won't know how to return datagrams to you.

15.4 Using Linux with fileservers/NFS:

How do I use my existing Novell fileserver with my Linux machine ?

If you have the Novell NFS Daemon code then it is easy, just NFS mount the Novell volume that you wish to use. If you don't, and you are really desperate to be able to do this, and you have a spare pc machine laying about, you are in luck. You can run a program called Stan's Own Server on the spare PC. First, configure the pc as a novell workstation with maps to the directories you want to nfs mount, then run SOS, and export those drive maps. SOS is available from spdcc.com:pub/sos/sossexe.zoo

Files get corrupted when running NFS over a network.

Certain vendors (Sun primarily) shipped many machines running NFS without UDP checksums. Great on ethernet, suicide otherwise. UDP checksums can be enabled on most file servers. Linux has it enabled by default from pl13 onwards - but both ends need to have it enabled...

Why are my NFS files all read only ?

The Linux NFS server defaults to read only. RTFM the 'exports' and nfsd manual pages. With non Linux servers you may also need to alter /etc/exports

15.5 SLIP questions:

What do I do if I don't know my SLIP servers address ?

dip doesn't really need to know the address of your SLIP server for SLIP to function. The *remote* option was added as a convenience so that *dip* could automate the *ifconfig* and *route* commands for you. If you don't know, and cannot find out the address of your SLIP server then Peter D. Junger Junger@samsara.law.cwru.edu has suggested that he simply used his own address wherever a dip script called for a remote address. This is a small kludge but it works ok, as the server's address never actually appears in the SLIP headers anyway.

'dip' only works for root. How do I make it work for others?

dip needs to be setuid root to do some of the things it needs to do, such as modifying the routing table. Uri Blumenthal recommends the following:

- Create a new group called *dip* in your /etc/group file, and place each person who you want to allow dial out operation in it.

- Then when logged in as root, do the following:

```
# chown root.dip /usr/bin/dip
# chmod u=rx,g=x,o= /usr/bin/dip
# chmod u+s /usr/bin/dip
```

Dial-In users will be restricted in what they can do by what is contained in the /etc/diphosts file.

I get 'DIP: tty: set_disc(1): Invalid argument', **why?**

This usually suggests that your kernel has not been compiled with *SLIP* support in it. Check that /proc/net/dev contains devices called sl0, sl1 etc. It could also mean that your version of dip is very old. You should upgrade to a newer version.

When I ping a host I get 'wrong data byte #17...', **why?**

This generally means that you have your modem configured for XON/XOFF flow control. SLIP **must** have an eight bit clean line, so you cannot use XON/XOFF flow control. Hardware handshaking works better anyway, use it.

With SLIP I can ping my server, and other hosts, but telnet or ftp don't work.

This is most likely caused by a disagreement on the use of header compression between your server and your machine. Double check that both ends either are, or are not, using compression. They must match.

How can I hang up the phone line when I'm done using SLIP?

If you use dip to dial out on the SLIP line, just 'dip -k' should do the trick. If not, try to kill the dip process that is running. When dip dies it should hang up the call. To give it the best chance to clean up after itself, try killing the process in the following sequence: 'kill <pid>', 'kill -hup <pid>', and finally, if the dip process still refuses to die, try 'kill -9 <pid>'. The same philosophy should be applied to all Unix processes that you are attempting to kill.

I see a lot of overrun errors on my SLIP port, why ?

The older network tools incorrectly report number of packets compressed as the number of packets overrun. This has been corrected, and shouldn't occur if you are running the new version kernel and tools. If it still is it probably indicates that your machine isn't keeping up with the rate of data incoming. If you are not using 16550AFN UARTs then you should upgrade to them. 16450, or 8250 generate an interrupt for every character they receive and are therefore very reliant on the processor to be able to find time to stop what it is doing an collect the character from them to ensure none get lost. The 16550AFN has a 16 character FIFO, and they only generate interrupts when the FIFO is nearly full, or when they have had character waiting, this means that less interrupts get generated for the same amount of data, and that less time is spent servicing your serial port. If you want to use multiple serial ports you should mandatorily upgrade to 16550AFN UARTs anyway.

Can I use two SLIP interfaces ?

Yes. If you have, for example, three machines which you would like to interconnect, then you most certainly could use two SLIP interfaces on one machine and connect each of the other machines to it. Simply configure the second interface as you did the first. NOTE that the second interface will require a different IP address to the first. You may need to play with the routing a bit to get it to do what you want, but it should work.

I have a multiport i/o card, how do I use more than 4 SLIP ports ?

The kernel SLIP comes with a default of a maximum of 4 SLIP devices configured, this is set in the /usr/src/linux/drivers/net/SLIP.h file. To increase it, say to 16, change the #define SL_NRUNIT to 16, in place of the 4 that will be there. You also need to edit /usr/src/linux/drivers/net/Space.c and add sections for sl4, sl5 etc. You can copy the existing driver definition as a template to make it easier. You will need to recompile the kernel for the change to take effect.

15.6   PPP questions.

You should refer to the *PPP-HOWTO* (http://sunsite.unc.edu/mdw/HOWTO/PPP-HOWTO.html) for a list of PPP questions and answers compiled by Al Longyear.

16   Quick Guide - SLIP Server

Configuring your Linux machine as a SLIP server is a deceptively simple thing to do. The actual process is simple, but there are a number of different aspects to the configuration and understanding how each of the stages interact with each other is what will help you diagnose any problems you experience. Here are the steps that you must follow to configure your Linux machine as a SLIP server:

1. Assemble your hardware. Avoid IRQ and shared memory conflicts. Test each of the serial ports by connecting a dumb terminal to each of the ports and use a null modem cable and a comms program like *minicom* or *seyon* to talk to each. Make sure you can send and receive characters. If you intend running a number of serial ports then try to use a smart serial board or use `16550AFN` UARTs. This will help ease some of the work of handling interrupts generated by the serial ports.

2. Build your kernel, make sure it has networking configured, `IP Forwarding` enabled, and `SLIP` configured. Make sure you configure `CSLIP` if you wish to use it. Double check you have `IP Forwarding` enabled.

3. Install your kernel. Test the kernel. Check the `/proc/net/dev` file and make sure that you have `sl0` and other SLIP devices listed. If not then you have probably made some error in configuring your kernel, or you are not actually running your new kernel.

4. Configure a *getty* on the serial port(s) that you wish to use for your incoming calls. You should refer to the *Serial-HOWTO* (`http://sunsite.unc.edu/mdw/HOWTO/Serial-HOWTO.html`) for a description of how to do this. Remember to configure your modem so that the `DCD` pin tracks received carrier, this is how your *getty* will detect an incoming call.

5. Test the *getty* to make sure it works. It is important that you do this before you start worrying about the actual SLIP configuration. Try dialing into your system, you should get a `login:` prompt and be able to login normally.

6. Decide how you want your server to allocate addresses. If you want your users to get the same address each time they call then you want a `static` server, if you want to minimise the number of addresses you use and don't care what address your users are allocated then you want a `dynamic` server.

7. Decide how you are going to build the SLIP server, whether you are going to use *SLIPlogin*, *dip* or *dSLIP*. If you wish to use the *SLIPlogin* package then refer to the 12.2.1 section. If you are going to use *dip* then refer to section 12.2.2. If you want to build your SLIP server using the *dSLIP* package then refer to section 12.2.3. Ensure you have the appropriate software, it is a recent version and compile the software if necessary.

8. If the addresses you are allocating to you SLIP users are part of your ethernet network, then make sure you read the 10.3 section and configure a proxy arp for each address. You may do this in the `/etc/SLIPlogin` and `/etc/SLIPlogout` files if you are using the *SLIPlogin* package. If the addresses you are allocating are from a network separate to your ethernet network then you can use either proxy arp or *gated*. If you use *gated* then refer to the 10.4 section.

9. Test your SLIP server.

17   Known Bugs.

The Linux networking code is still an evolving thing. It still has bugs though they are becoming less frequently reported now. The *Linux Networking News* (`http://iifeak.swan.ac.uk/NetNews.html`) is a World Wide Web page maintained by Alan Cox which contains information on the status of the NET-3 networking code. You can obtain information on what is known and what isn't, by reading the `/usr/src/linux/net/inet/README` file that accompanies the kernel source, or by joining the NET channel.

18   Copyright Message.

The NET-2-HOWTO is copyright by Terry Dawson and Matt Welsh. A verbatim copy of this document may be reproduced and distributed in any medium, physical or electronic without permission of the authors. Translations are similarly permitted without express permission if such translations include a notice stating who performed the translation, and that it is a translation. Commercial redistribution is allowed and encouraged, however, the authors would like to be notified of any such distributions.

Short quotes may be used without prior consent by the authors. Derivative works and partial distributions of the NET-2-HOWTO must include either a verbatim copy of this file, or make a verbatim copy of this file available. If the latter is the case, a pointer to the verbatim copy must be stated at a clearly visible place.

In short, we wish to promote dissemination of this information through as many channels as possible. However, we wish to retain copyright on this HOWTO document, and would like to be notified of any plans to redistribute it. Further we desire that ALL information provided in this HOWTO be disseminated.

If you have any questions relating to the conditions of this copyright, please contact Matt Welsh, the Linux HOWTO coordinator, at: `mdw@sunsite.unc.edu`

19 Miscellaneous, and Acknowledgements.

There are so many people who have contributed comments and suggestions for this update that I have forgotten who you are. **Thanks**.

Please, if you have any comments or suggestions then mail them to me. I'm fairly busy these days, so I might not get back to you straight away, but I will certainly consider any suggestion you have.

The Linux networking code has come a long way, and it hasn't been an easy trip, but the developers, all of them, have done an excellent job in getting together something that is functional, versatile, flexible, and free for us to use. We all owe them a great debt of thanks. Linus, Ross, Fred, Alan, the Alpha/Beta testers, the tools developers, and those offering moral support have all contributed to the code as it is today.

For those that have an itch they want to scratch, happy hacking, here it is.

regards `Terry Dawson, vk2ktj`.

`<terryd@extro.ucc.su.oz.au>, or <terry@orac.dn.telecom.com.au>`

Part XXX

The Linux NIS(YP)/NIS+/NYS HOWTO

Copyright Andrea Dell'Amico, Mitchum DSouza, Erwin Embsen, Peter Eriksson
Version 0.5, Last Modified on January 24, 1995

Contents

1   Glossary of Terms

In this document a lot of acronyms are used. Here are the most important acronyms and a brief explanation:

DBM

DataBase Management, a library of functions which maintain key-content pairs in a data base.

DLL

Dynamically Linked Library, a library linked to an executable program at run-time.

domainname

A name "key" that is used by NIS clients to be able to locate a suitable NIS server that serves that domainname key. Please note that this does not necessarily have anything at all to do with the DNS "domain" (machine name) of the machine(s).

FTP

File Transfer Protocol, a protocol used to transfer files between two computers.

libnsl

Name services library, a library of name service calls (getpwnam, getservbyname, etc...) on SVR4 Unixes.

libsocket

Socket services library, a library for the socket service calls (socket, bind, listen, etc...) on SVR4 Unixes.

NIS

Network Information Service, a service that provides information, that has to be known throughout the network, to all machines on the network. There is support for NIS in Linux's standard libc library, which in the following text is referred to as "traditional NIS".

NIS+

Network Information Service (Plus :-), essentially NIS on steroids. NIS+ is designed by Sun Microsystems Inc. as a replacement for NIS with better security and better handling of _large_ installations.

NYS

This is the name of a project and stands for NIS+, YP and Switch and is managed by Peter Eriksson <pen@lysator.liu.se>. It contains among other things a complete reimplementation of the NIS (=YP) code that uses the Name Services Switch functionality of the NYS library.

RPC

Remote Procedure Call. RPC routines allow C programs to make procedure calls on other machines across the network. When people talk about RPC they most often mean the SunRPC variant.

YP

Yellow Pages(tm), a registered trademark in the UK of British Telecom plc.

TCP-IP

Transmission Control Protocol/Internet Protocol. It's a data communication protocol often used on Unix machines.

1.1 Some General Information

The next three lines are quoted from the Sun(tm) System & Network Administration Manual:

```
"NIS was formerly known as Sun Yellow Pages (YP) but
the name Yellow Pages(tm) is a registered trademark
in the United Kingdom of British Telecom plc and may
not be used without permission."
```

NIS stands for Network Information Service. It's purpose is to provide information, that has to be known throughout the network, to all machines on the network. Information likely to be distributed by NIS is:

- login names/passwords/home directories (/etc/passwd)

- group information (/etc/group)

So, for example, if your password entry is recorded in the NIS passwd database, you will be able to login on all machines on the net which have the NIS client programs running.

Sun is a trademark of Sun Microsystems, Inc. licensed to SunSoft, Inc.

2 Introduction

More and more, Linux machines are installed as part of a network of computers. To simplify network administration, most networks (mostly Sun-based networks) run the Network Information Service. Linux machines can take full advantage of existing NIS service or provide NIS service themselves. It can also (with the NYS library) act as a limited NIS+ client.

This document tries to answer questions about setting up NIS(YP) on your Linux machine. It does not talk about how to set up NIS+. Don't forget to read section 5.1, The RPC Portmapper.

2.1 New versions of this document

New versions of this document will be posted periodically (about every month) to the newsgroups comp.os.linux.announce and comp.os.linux.misc. The document is archived on a number of Linux FTP sites, including `sunsite.unc.edu` in `/pub/Linux/docs/HOWTO`.

2.2 Disclaimer

Although this document has been put together to the best of our knowledge it may, and probably does contain errors. Please read any README files that are bundled with any of the various pieces of software described in this document for more detailed and accurate information. We will attempt to keep this document as error free as possible.

2.3 Feedback

If you have any comments, questions or suggestions please email them to Erwin Embsen `<erwin@nioz.nl>`. Definitely contact him if you find errors or obvious omissions.

2.4 Acknowledgements

We would like to thank all the people who have contributed (directly or indirectly) to this document. In alphabetical order:

```
Andrea Dell'Amico {$<$}adellam@di.unipi.it>
Mitchum DSouza    {$<$}Mitch.Dsouza@Dubai.Sun.COM>
Erwin Embsen      {$<$}erwin@nioz.nl>
Byron A Jeff      {$<$}byron@cc.gatech.edu>
Peter Eriksson    {$<$}pen@lysator.liu.se>
```

Theo de Raadt <deraadt@fsa.ca> is responsible for the original yp-clients code. Swen Thuemmler <swen@uni-paderborn.de> ported the yp-clients code to Linux and also ported the yp-routines in libc (again based on Theo's work).

3 NIS or NIS+ ?

The choice between NIS and NIS+ is easy - use NIS if you don't have to use NIS+ or have severe security needs. NIS+ is _much_ more problematic to administer (it's pretty easy to handle on the client side, but the server side is horrible). Another problem is that the support for NIS+ under Linux is still under development - one major thing it still lacks is support for data encryption/authentication which is _the_ major thing why anyone would want to use NIS+...

3.1 Traditional NIS or the NYS library ?

The choice between Traditional NIS or the NIS code in the NYS library is a choice between laziness and maturity vs. flexibility and love of adventure.

The "traditional NIS" code is in the standard C library and has been around longer and sometimes suffers from it's age and slight inflexibility.

The NIS code in the NYS library, on the other hand requires you either to recompile and relink all your programs to the libnsl library, or recompile the libc library to include the libnsl code into the libc library (or maybe you can go get a precompiled version of libc from someone who has already done it).

Another difference is that the traditional NIS code has some support for NIS Netgroups, which the NYS code doesn't (yet). On the other hand the NYS code allows you to handle Shadow Passwords in a transparent way.

4 How it works

Within a network there must be at least one machine acting as a NIS server. You can have multiple NIS servers, each serving different NIS "domains" - or you can have cooperating NIS servers, where one is said to be the master NIS server, and all the other are so-called slave NIS servers (for a certain NIS "domain", that is!) - or you can have a mix of them...

Slave servers only have copies of the NIS databases and receive these copies from the master NIS server whenever changes are made to the master's databases. Depending on the number of machines in your network and the reliability of your network, you might decide to install one or more slave servers. Whenever a NIS server goes down or is too slow in responding to requests, a NIS client connected to that server will try to find one that is up or quicker.

NIS databases are in so-called DBM format, derived from ASCII databases. For example, the files /etc/passwd and /etc/group can be directly converted to DBM format using ASCII-to-DBM translation software ("dbload", it's included with the server software). The master NIS server should have both, the ASCII databases and the DBM databases.

Slave servers will be notified of any change to the NIS maps, (via the "yppush" program), and automatically retrieve the necessary changes in order to synchronize their databases. NIS clients does not need to do this since they always talks to the NIS server to read the information stored in it's DBM databases.

The author of the YP clients for linux has informed us that the newest ypbind (from yp-clients.tar.gz) is able to get the server from a configuration file - thus no need to broadcast (which is insecure - due to the fact that anyone may install a NIS server and answer the broadcast queries...)

5   What do you need to set up NIS?

5.1   The RPC Portmapper

To run any of the software mentioned below you will need to run the program /usr/sbin/rpc.portmap. Some Linux distributions already have the code in /etc/rc.d/rc.inet2 to start up this daemon. All you have to do is comment it out and reboot your Linux machine to activate it.

The RPC portmapper (portmap(8c)) is a server that converts RPC program numbers into TCP/IP (or UDP/IP) protocol port numbers. It must be running in order to make RPC calls (which is what the NIS client software does) to RPC servers (like a NIS server) on that machine. When an RPC server is started, it will tell portmap what port number it is listening to, and what RPC program numbers it is prepared to serve. When a client wishes to make an RPC call to a given program number, it will first contact portmap on the server machine to determine the port number where RPC packets should be sent.

Normally, standard RPC servers are started by inetd(8C), so portmap must be started before inetd is invoked.

5.2   Determine whether you are a Server, Slave or Client.

To answer this question you have to consider two cases:

1. Your machine is going to be part of a network with existing NIS servers

2. You do not have any NIS servers in the network yet

In the first case, you only need the client programs (ypbind, ypwhich, ypcat, yppoll, ypmatch). The most important program is ypbind. This program must be running at all times, that is, it should always appear in the list of processes. It's a so-called daemon process and needs to be started from the system's startup file (eg. /etc/rc.local). As soon as ypbind is running, your system has become a NIS client.

In the second case, if you don't have NIS servers, then you will also need a NIS server program (usually called ypserv). Section 6 describes how to set up a NIS server on your Linux machine using the "ypserv" implementation by Peter Eriksson (<pen@lysator.liu.se>). Note that this implementation does NOT support the master-slave concept talked about in section 3. Using this software, all your NIS servers will be master servers. There is also another free NIS server available, called "yps", written by Tobias Reber in Germany which does support the master-slave concept, but has other limitations.

5.3   The Software

The system library "/usr/lib/libc.a" (version 4.4.2 and better) or the shared library "/usr/lib/libc.sa" and its related DLL contain all necessary system calls to succesfully compile the NIS client and server software.

Some people reported that NIS only works with "/usr/lib/libc.a" version 4.5.21 and better so if you want to play it safe don't user older libc's. The NIS client software can be obtained from:

Site	Directory	File Name
ftp.uni-paderborn.de	/pcsoft2/linux/local/yp	yp-clients.tar.gz

```
ftp.funet.fi          /pub/OS/Linux/BETA/NYS/clients   yp-clients.tar.gz
ftp.lysator.liu.se    /pub/NYS/clients                 yp-clients.tar.gz
sunsite.unc.edu       /pub/Linux/system/Network/admin  yp-clients.tar.gz
```

Once you obtained the software, please follow the instructions which come with the software.

5.4   Setting up a NIS Client using Traditional NIS

Assuming you have succesfully compiled the software you are now ready to install the software. A suitable place for the ypbind daemon is the directory /usr/sbin.

You'll need to do this as root of course. The other binaries (ypwhich, ypcat, yppoll, ypmatch) should go in a directory accessible by all users, for example /usr/etc or /usr/local/bin. It might be a good idea to test ypbind before incorporating it in /etc/rc.d/rc.inet2.

To test ypbind do the following:

- Make sure you have your domain name set. If it is not set then issue the command:

```
/bin/domainname-yp nis.domain
```

  where nis.domain should be some string, _NOT_ normally associated with the domain name of your machine! The reason for this is that it makes it a little harder for external crackers to retreive the password database from your NIS servers. If you don't know what the NIS domain name is on your network, ask your system/network administrator.

- Start up "/usr/sbin/rpc.portmap" if it is not already running.

- Create the directory "/var/yp" if it does not exist.

- Start up "/usr/sbin/ypbind"

- Use the command "rpcinfo -p localhost" to check if ypbind was able to register its service with the portmapper. The rpcinfo should produce something like:

```
program vers proto   port
 100000   2    tcp    111  portmapper
 100000   2    udp    111  portmapper
 100007   2    udp    637  ypbind
 100007   2    tcp    639  ypbind
 300019   1    udp    660
```

- You may also run "rpcinfo -u localhost ypbind". This command should produce something like:

```
program 100007 version 2 ready and waiting
```

Finally, do not forget that for host lookups you must set (or add) "nis" to the lookup order line in your /etc/host.conf file. Please read the manpage "resolv+.8" for more details.

At this point you should be able to use NIS client programs like ypcat, etc... For example, "ypcat passwd" will give you the entire NIS password database.

IMPORTANT: If you skipped the test procedure then make sure you have set the domain name, and created the directory:

```
/var/yp
```

This directory MUST exist for ypbind to start up succesfully.

If the test worked you may now want to change the files /etc/rc.d/rc.M and /etc/rc.d/rc.inet2 on your system so that ypbind will be started up at boot time and your system will act as a NIS client. Edit the file /etc/rc.d/rc.M and look for the commands which set the domain name. Change the domain name into the name of your domain. Also, edit the file /etc/rc.d/rc.inet2, comment out the lines which start up the rpc.portmap daemon, and add the following lines just after the place where rpc.portmap is started:

```
#
# Start the ypbind daemon
#
if [ -f ${NET}/ypbind -a -d /var/yp ]; then
    echo -n " ypbind"
    ${NET}/ypbind
fi
```

Unlike Sun's implementation of NIS you do not need to edit /etc/passwd and /etc/group to take advantage of NIS. Sun's implementation needs a line "+:*:0:0:::" in /etc/passwd and a line "+:*:0:" in /etc/group to tell NIS to search the NIS password and group databases.

IMPORTANT: Note that the command finger will report "no such user" messages if you do not add the line "+:*:0:0:::" to /etc/passwd. Putting the line "+:*:0:0:::" back in /etc/passwd fixes finger.

Well, that's it. Reboot the machine and watch the boot messages to see if ypbind is actually started.

IMPORTANT: Note that the netgroup feature is implemented starting from libc 4.5.26. Netgroups allow access control for every machine and every user in the NIS domain, and they require an entry like:

```
+@this_machine_users
```

in /etc/passwd. But if you have a version of libc erlier than 4.5.26, every user in the NIS password database can access your linux machine if you run "ypbind".

6   What you need to set up NYS?

6.1   Determine whether you are a Server, Slave or Client.

To answer this question you have to consider two cases:

- Your machine is going to be part of a network with existing NIS servers
- You do not have any NIS servers in the network yet

In the first case you have two choices:

- Either you relink all client and daemon programs with the NYS library libnsl.so (or statically link them with libnsl.a). This means adding the line:

```
LIBS=-lnsl
```

to your Makefile signifying you want to link the Network Services Library. Basically all network daemons and the "login" program need to be recompiled.

- Or you can recompile the standard C library libc to include the NYS client library functions into the normal libc library, and then relink all statically linked programs (the dynamically linked programs automatically get the new version of libc). See section 6.5 below for more information about this option.

Similarly like in the case of traditional NIS, if you don't have NIS servers, then you will also need a NIS server program (usually called ypserv) and you have to designate one of the machines in your network as a master NIS server. Again, you might want to set up at least one slave server as well.

6.2   The Software

You need to retrieve and compile the NYS services library libnsl.so. If you don't have the DLL tools installed you may retrieve a precompiled shared, static and stub library from the same site mentioned below. Note, however, that the precompiled version may be (and probably is) older than the latest source code release.

The NYS library (source and precompiled version) can be obtained from:

Site	Directory	File Name
ftp.lysator.liu.se	/pub/NYS/libs	nys-0.27.4.tar.gz
ftp.lysator.liu.se	/pub/NYS/binaries/lib	libnsl.so.1.0.a26
ftp.funet.fi	/pub/OS/Linux/BETA/NYS/libs	nys-0.27.4.tar.gz
ftp.funet.fi	/pub/OS/Linux/BETA/NYS/lib	libnsl.so.1.0.a26

Precompiled "login" and "su" programs may also be fetched from

Site	Directory	File Name
ftp.lysator.liu.se	/pub/NYS/binaries/bin	login
ftp.lysator.liu.se	/pub/NYS/binaries/bin	su
ftp.funet.fi	/pub/OS/Linux/BETA/NYS/bin	login
ftp.funet.fi	/pub/OS/Linux/BETA/NYS/bin	su

Similarly, example configuration files may be retrieved from

Site	Directory	File Name
ftp.lysator.liu.se	/pub/NYS/binaries/etc	*conf
ftp.funet.fi	/pub/OS/Linux/BETA/NYS/etc	*conf

For compilation of the nsl library, please follow the instructions which come with the software. If you wish to compile the shared DLL library you must have the DLL tools installed in the standard place (/usr/dll). The DLL tools (the package tools-2.11.tar.gz or later) can be obtained from many sites.

6.3   Setting up a NYS Client using NYS

Unlike traditional NIS, there is no setting up required for a NIS client. All that is required is that the NIS configuration file (/etc/yp.conf) points to the correct server(s) for its information. Also, the Name Services Switch configuration file (/etc/nsswitch.conf) must be correctly set up.

Please refer to the examples provided with the source code.

6.4   The nsswitch.conf File

The Network Services switch file /etc/nsswitch.conf determines the order of lookups performed when a certain piece of information is requested, just like the /etc/host.conf file which determines the way host lookups are performed. Again, look at at the example file provided in the source distribution. For example, the line

```
        hosts: files nis dns
```

specifies that host lookup functions should first look in the local /etc/hosts file, followed by a NIS lookup and finally thru the domain name service (/etc/resolv.conf and named), at which point if no match is found an error is returned.

6.5   Making your binaries NYS aware

Instead of relinking each binary with the NYS library (libnsl.so), a cleaner solution has been achieved by providing the user with the ability to build a NYS aware libc. This means all you need to do is recompile a new libc and replace your existing /lib/libc.so.x.y.z for all (non-static compiled) programs to be NYS aware.

This merge also gives you the advantage over the traditional NIS implementation in the linux libc in that it allows transparent shadow passwords support (via the /etc/nisswitch.conf file).

Follow the simple steps below to rebuild a NYS aware libc.

- Make sure you have the latest DLL tools installed. Refer to the the GCC-FAQ for more info on where to get this.

- Get the latest libc sources. (again see GCC-FAQ)

- Get the latest nys sources from

```
        ftp.lysator.liu.se:/pub/NYS/libs
```

and extract it under this libc-linux source directory. The current NYS distribution is "nys-0.27.4.tar.gz".

- Do the ./configure as before and first answer "n" to the question

```
        Values correct (y/n) [y] ?
```

Then go thru all the other questions and the last question will now be

```
        Build a NYS libc from nys-0.27 (y default) ?
```

answer "y" to this.

- Then issue the command

```
        % make
```

The library generated after compilation is named something like

```
    libc.so.4.5.26
```

and placed under the directory jump/libc-nys. To install this library our advise would be copying it to /lib with a name lexiographically greater than the version number it currently has. Just appending the letter "a" should do the trick. For example:

```
    % cp jump/libc-nys/libc.so.4.5.26 /lib/libc.so.4.5.26a
```

Alternatively, append "nys" to it so you can quickly identify it. Now run the command

```
    % ldconfig
```

which will reset your cache to use the new library. The dynamic linker strategy may be examined with the command "ldconfig -p".

That's basically it. All your programs should now be NYS aware. Please note that usually the program "login" is compiled static and thus cannot access the new NYS functions from the NYS aware libc. You must either recompile "login" without the -static flag, or else statically link it to the libnsl.a library.

7   Setting up a NIS Server

7.1   The Server Program ypserv

This document only describes how to set up the "ypserv" NIS server. The "yps" server setup is similar, but not exactly the same so beware if you try to apply these instructions to "yps"!

The NIS server software can be found on:

```
Site                    Directory                              File Name

ftp.lysator.liu.se      /pub/NYS/servers                       ypserv-0.11.tar.gz
ftp.funet.fi            /pub/OS/Linux/BETA/NYS/servers          ypserv-0.11.tar.gz
mcsun.eu.net            /os/linux/BETA/NYS/servers             ypserv-0.11.tar.gz
ftp.univie.ac.at        /unix/system/linux/funet/BETA/NYS/servers
                                                               ypserv-0.11.tar.gz
```

The server setup is the same for both traditional NIS and NYS.

Compile the software to generate the "ypserv", "dbcat" and "dbload" programs. Firstly, determine what files you require to be available via NIS and then add or remove the appropriate entries to the ypMakefile. Install the file ypMakefile into /var/yp as the file Makefile.

Now build the DBM files by typing:

```
% cd /var/yp; make
```

Make sure the portmapper (rpc.portmap) is running, and start the server "ypserv". The command

```
% rpcinfo -u localhost ypserv
```

should output something like

```
program 100004 version 2 ready and waiting
```

That's it, your server is up and running.

7.2   The Program yppasswdd

Whenever users change their passwords, the NIS password database and probably other NIS databases, which depend on the NIS password database, should be updated. The program "yppasswdd" is a server that handles password changes and makes sure that the NIS information will be updated accordingly. The software for "yppasswdd" can be found on:

```
Site                    Directory                         File Name

ftp.lysator.liu.se      /pub/NYS                          yppasswdd-0.5.tar.gz
ftp.funet.fi            /pub/OS/Linux/BETA/NYS/servers    yppasswdd-0.5.tar.gz
```

Once you obtained the software, please follow the instructions which come with the software.

8   Verifying the NIS/NYS Installation

If everything is fine (as it should be), you should be able to verify your installation with a few simple commands. Assuming, for example, your passwd file is being supplied by NIS, the command

```
% ypcat passwd
```

should give you the contents of your NIS passwd file. The command

```
% ypmatch userid passwd
```

(where userid is the login name of an arbitrary user) should give you the user's entry in the NIS passwd file. The "ypcat" and "ypmatch" programs should be included with your distribution of traditional NIS or NYS.

9   Common Problems and Troubleshooting NIS

Here are some common problems reported by various users:

1. The libraries for 4.5.19 are broken. NIS won't work with it.

2. If you upgrade the libraries from 4.5.19 to 4.5.24 then the su command breaks. You need to get the su command from the slackware 1.2.0 distribution. Incidentally that's where you can get the updated libraries.

3. You could run into trouble with NIS and DNS on the same machine. My DNS server occasionally will not bring up NIS. Haven't yet tracked down why.

4. When a NIS server goes down and comes up again ypbind starts complaining with messages like:

```
yp_match: clnt_call:
                RPC: Unable to receive; errno = Connection refused
```

and logins are refused for those who are registered in the NIS database. Try to login as root and if you succeed, then kill ypbind and start it up again.

10   Frequently Asked Questions

Most of your questions should be answered by now. If there are still questions unanswered you might want to post a message to

```
comp.os.linux.help
```

or contact one of the authors of this HOWTO.

Part XXXI

The Linux News HOWTO

Copyright Vince Skahan, <vince@halcyon.com>
v1.15, 31 Mar 1995
This document describes the setup and care+feeding of USENET News under Linux. You need to read this if you plan to post or read USENET news either locally on your site or between your site and other sites. You probably do *not* need to read this document if don't plan to provide USENET news as a feature of your system.

Contents

1   Introduction

The intent of this document is to answer some of the questions and comments that appear to meet the definition of "frequently asked questions" about USENET News software under Linux in general, and the version in the Linux Slackware distribution in particular.

This document and the corresponding Mail and UUCP "HOWTO" documents collectively supersede the UUCP-NEWS-MAIL-FAQ that has previously been posted to comp.os.linux.announce.

1.1   New versions of this document

New versions of this document will be periodically posted to comp.os.linux.announce, comp.answers, and news.answers. They will also be added to the various anonymous ftp sites who archive such information including `sunsite.unc.edu:/pub/Linux/docs/HOWTO`.

In addition, you should be generally able to find this document on the Linux WorldWideWeb home page at `http://sunsite.unc.edu/mdw/linux.html`.

1.2   Feedback

I am interested in any feedback, positive or negative, regarding the content of this document via e-mail. Definitely contact me if you find errors or obvious omissions.

I read, but do not necessarily respond to, all e-mail I receive. Requests for enhancements will be considered and acted upon based on that day's combination of available time, merit of the request, and daily blood pressure :-)

Flames will quietly go to /dev/null so don't bother.

In particular, the Linux filesystem standard for pathnames is an evolving thing. What's in this document is there for illustration only based on the current standard at the time that part of the document was written and in the paths used in the distributions or 'kits' I've personally seen. Please consult your particular Linux distribution(s) for the paths they use.

Feedback concerning the actual format of the document should go to the HOWTO coordinator - Matt Welsh (`mdw@sunsite.unc.edu`).

1.3 Copyright Information

The News-HOWTO is copyrighted (c)1994 Vince Skahan.

A verbatim copy may be reproduced or distributed in any medium physical or electronic without permission of the author. Translations are similarly permitted without express permission if it includes a notice on who translated it.

Short quotes may be used without prior consent by the author. Derivative work and partial distributions of the News-HOWTO must be accompanied with either a verbatim copy of this file or a pointer to the verbatim copy.

Commercial redistribution is allowed and encouraged; however, the author would like to be notified of any such distributions.

In short, we wish to promote dissemination of this information through as many channels as possible. However, we do wish to retain copyright on the HOWTO documents, and would like to be notified of any plans to redistribute the HOWTOs.

We further want that ALL information provided in the HOWTOS is disseminated. If you have questions, please contact Matt Welsh, the Linux HOWTO coordinator, at `mdw@sunsite.unc.edu`.

1.4 Standard Disclaimer

Of course, I disavow any potential liability for the contents of this document. Use of the concepts, examples, and/or other content of this document is entirely at your own risk.

1.5 Other sources of information

1.5.1 USENET

```
news.admin.misc          General topics of network news administration.
news.admin.policy        Policy issues of USENET.
news.admin.technical     Maintaining network news. (Moderated)
news.software.b          Discussion about B-news-compatible software.
news.software.nn         Discussion about the "nn" news reader package.
news.software.nntp       The Network News Transfer Protocol.
news.software.readers    Software used to read network news.
news.sysadmin            Comments directed to system administrators.
news.announce.newusers   Explanatory postings for new users. (Moderated)
news.newusers.questions  Q & A for users new to the Usenet.
```

1.5.2 Books

The following is a non-inclusive set of books that will help

- "Managing UUCP and USENET" published by O'Reilly+Associates is in my opinion the best book out there for figuring out the programs and protocols involved in being a USENET site.

- "Unix Communications" published by The Waite Group contains a nice description of all the pieces (and more) and how they fit together.

- "Practical Unix Security" published by O'Reilly+Associates has a nice discussion of how to secure UUCP in general.

- "The Internet Complete Reference" from Osborne is a fine reference book that explains the various services available on Internet and is a great source for information on news, mail, and various other Internet resources.

- "The Linux Networking Administrators' Guide" from Olaf Kirch of the Linux DOC Project is available on the net and is also published by (at least) O'Reilly and SSC. It makes a fine *one-stop shopping* to learn about everything you ever imagined you'd need to know about Unix networking.

1.6   Where NOT to look for help

There is nothing "special" about configuring and running USENET news under Linux (any more). Accordingly, you almost certainly do *NOT* want to be posting generic news-related questions to the comp.os.linux.* newsgroups.

Unless your posting is truly Linux-specific (ie, "please tell me what patches are needed to run INN with the bash1.12 in SLS v1.03") you should be asking your questions in the newsgroups mentioned above.

Let me repeat that.

There is virtually no reason to post anything news-related in the comp.os.linux hierarchy any more. There are existing newsgroups in the news.* hierarchy to handle *ALL* your questions.

IF YOU POST TO COMP.OS.LINUX. FOR NON-LINUX-SPECIFIC QUESTIONS, YOU ARE LOOKING IN THE WRONG PLACE FOR HELP. THE USENET NEWS EXPERTS HANG OUT IN THE PLACES INDICATED ABOVE AND GENERALLY DO NOT RUN LINUX.*

POSTING TO THE LINUX HIERARCHY FOR NON-LINUX-SPECIFIC QUESTIONS WASTES YOUR TIME AND EVERYONE ELSE'S AND IT FREQUENTLY DELAYS YOU FROM GETTING THE ANSWER TO YOUR QUESTION.

2   Hardware Requirements

There are no specific hardware requirements for USENET News under Linux. The only requirement of any type is sufficient disk space to hold the software itself, the threads database(s), and the amount of news you wish to keep on the system. Figure on a minimum of 10 MB of disk space for starters.

3   Getting USENET News software

All the software referenced in this "HOWTO" is available on the usual Internet anonymous ftp sites.

Looking in /networking/news on `ftp.uu.net` is usually a good way to start.

The newspak-2.4.tar.z distribution contains config files and readme files related to building uucp, news, and mail software under Linux from the various freely-available sources. It can usually be found in `sunsite.unc.edu:/pub/Linux/system/Mail/news`. If you can't find it on sunsite, please send me mail and I'll make sure you get a copy of it.

4   News Transport Software

There are two main sets of news "transport" software for *nix these days, Cnews and INN. The old "Bnews" has been declared officially dead and unsupported by its authors.

News "transport" is defined here to be the software that works behind the scenes to post and propagate the news articles as well as making the articles available for the newsreaders to access.

You can set your paths to anything you like, as long as UUCP has the absolute path to rnews in the Permissions file and as long as you have your newsreaders configured so that they can find "inews" and "mail".

Important - you're asking for trouble if you try to intermix Cnews and INN. Pick one or the other. It's ok to add the NNTP "Reference Release" into Cnews since they're intended to play well together.

4.1   Cnews Cleanup Release

The current de-facto standard news software is Cnews. It has been around for a number of years, I first saw it sometime around 1988. The current version is called "Cnews Cleanup Release, with patch CR.E".

Cnews's main benefit is its maturity. It runs on about every *nix you can find and there are literally thousands of systems running it worldwide.

Its main disadvantage is that it seems to have been intended for uucp-over-modem connections between sites and as such requires the addition of NNTP software to handle realtime Internet feeds and reading.

Regardless, the beginning USENET admin should probably run Cnews first since it's so stable, well documented, and has many thousands of experienced administrators who can answer questions.

The 'Cleanup Release' claims that "Overview support has been fully integrated and is faster than it used to be." The result is that you can do things like use Cnews NOV support rather than running external threading packages for newsreaders such as nn, tin, and trn.

I haven't quite figured how to implement this part yet, since I switched to INN at home long ago. If anybody wants to clue me in to update this document, please drop me a line via e-mail.

The newspak distribution on sunsite contains working config files for the Cnews Cleanup Release under Linux as well as a couple line patch you'll need to make to `doexplode` to get around some problems with bash1.12.

Basically you run the new 'quiz' script and take the defaults. You'll have to refer to your /usr/include tree to answer a number of the questions, but that's rather straightforward.

4.1.1   Installing Cnews

Installing the Cleanup Release of Cnews is absolutely a "rtfm" project. Just grab the sources, extract them, and follow the instructions.

The `quiz.def` in newspak was generated by running "quiz" the first time and simply looking up the answers by checking out the /usr/include files to get the right answers.

Steve Robbins also has determined that the recent 'cleanup release' of Cnews has found a bug in GNU 'join' from shellutils-1.9. There are a few patches needed to the sources for join to deal with the problem. Steve's put them on sunsite as I recall.

4.1.2   Configuring Cnews

At the very least, you need to edit or at least take a look at the following files that all should be in /usr/local/lib/news:

```
active                - the active file
batchparms            - batch parameters
explist               - article expiration setup
mailname              - name in headers for mailed replies
mailpaths             - path to mail moderated postings to
organization          - your "org"
sys                   - control what you take and feed
whoami                - your hostname for the Path: line
```

4.1.3 Maintaining a Cnews Site

First, a significant rule of thumb is to not mess with files by hand that have utilities that configure them. In particular don't set up newsfeeds manually (run "addfeed" instead) and don't mess with your active file (run "addgroup"). When in doubt, read and re-read the docs in the source distribution.

Everything else can be done via cron. My crontab for "news" looks like the following:

```
# take the compressed batches that came in from other systems
# also, post (locally) articles that originated here
20 *        * * * /usenet/sw/news/bin/input/newsrun

# batch 'em up to go out
0 *         * * * /usenet/sw/news/bin/batch/sendbatches myfeedsite

# expire C-news
59 0        * * * /usenet/sw/news/bin/expire/doexpire

# monitor stuff and report if needed
10 5        * * * /usenet/sw/news/bin/newsdaily
00 5        * * * /usenet/sw/new/bin/newswatch

# turn processing of incoming news batches off 6:30AM - 4:00 PM
30 6        * * * /usenet/sw/news/bin/input/newsrunning off
00 16       * * * /usenet/sw/news/bin/input/newsrunning on
```

4.2 InterNetNews (INN)

INN is the newcomer on the scene, but it's gaining popularity as it matures. Its main benefit is speed and the fact that it contains an integrated nntp package. Its main drawback is that it's new and that it doesn't necessarily install and run flawlessly on the many "standard *nixes" yet. In addition, it operates by having a daemon (the innd) always running plus potentially a overchan daemon to do threading. The tradeoff seems to be memory vs. speed.

I've run up to a 5 MB/night newsfeed incoming over UUCP with INN on a 8 MB 386-33 (no Xwindows running normally) over a 14.4 KB modem with no problems at all.

New USENET admins should probably not try INN until they have experience with either B-news or Cnews. While it's fast and reliable under Linux, it's virtually undocumented for the beginning news administrator (though in practice it's rather simple to run once you figure it out).

INN is very particular about its permissions. Don't mess with them.

INN is also very particular about having a "quality" TCP/IP to work with. Linux is not necessarily all the way there at this time, so it is recommended that you grab a Linux-specific INN distribution from one of the usual Linux archive sites.

4.2.1 Installing INN

(from Arjan de Vet - devet@info.win.tue.nl)

I've made a patch + config kit for INN 1.4 to get it to run on Linux. It can be found at:

ftp.win.tue.nl:/pub/linux/ports/inn-1.4-linux.tar.gz

INN depends heavily on a good /bin/sh substitute. I use a beta version of bash 1.13 that is now available for Linux on the normal archive sites. bash 1.12 gives some small problems with newgroups not being handled correctly (maybe some other problems too, I don't remember).

4.2.2   Configuring INN

Basically follow Arjan's instructions and you'll be all set. Here's the summary of what to do:

- In config.data, make sure you have "HAVE_UNIX_DOMAIN DONT"

- Add the hostname of the system running innd to hosts.nntp For a uucp-only site, that's your sitename.

- Make sure you do not have a line for nntp in /etc/inetd.conf

- Make sure that you have innshellvars say "HAVE_UUSTAT DO" rather than the "DONT" in his example config.data if you have uustat from the Taylor UUCP package installed. If you have this defined wrong, it'll result in no outgoing news getting batched.

- If you run INN, definitely define the recommended syslogd stuff because it is very, very helpful.

There is a spectacular (!!!!)   FAQ for INN that comes out monthly.   Look on rtfm.mit.edu:/pub/usenet-by-hierarchy/news for it. You'll be glad you did.

4.2.3   Maintaining a INN Site

I've found that there's essentially zero care-and-feeding of a Linux INN site other than having a working cron. Basically you want a crontab that looks something like the following:

```
# daily maint, also expire the .overview database and articles
1 0 * * * /usenet/sw/inn/bin/news.daily expireover delayrm < /dev/null

# send 'em out
5 * * * * /usenet/sw/inn/lib/send-uucp
```

(if you switch to bash1.13, the "< /dev/null" above is not needed)

4.3   Other News Transport Agents

The following is a non-inclusive list of other news transport software known to work under Linux:

- dynafeed
- nntp1.5.11
- slurp1.05

5   News Readers

There is no "one true newsreader". As a result, there are many well-known newsreaders that port easily to Linux in particular. At this writing, "tin", "trn", and "nn" are in most of the commonly available distributions of Linux and in newspak.

When picking a newsreader, you basically want to find something that is easy to use, very configurable by the user, with threading and kill files (to select interesting articles or make the non-interesting ones not appear at all).

You can set your paths to anything you like as long as all the newsreaders can find "inews" from your Cnews or INN installation and a "mail" program to send mail replies to posts.

This section will talk briefly about several of the most popular ones. Before you ask, I use "nn" for lots of reasons :-)

5.1 Tin

Tin is a threaded newsreader generally intended to be easy for new users. It supports kill files and NOV threading. If you're running INN, it will read NOV .overview files by default and not write index files.

To compile Tin under linux, basically just edit the makefile to set the locations of the software (especially the location of inews) and type "make linux". There are no patches required for tin under Linux.

For threading, you can basically just say "tin -u" to update the index files.

To enable the ability to read via NNTP, compile with "NNTP_ABLE" defined. This will result in a file called "tin" for local and one called "rtin" for NNTP reading. "tin -r" will also get the same behavior as "rtin".

Iain Lea recommends the following crontab entry and says that you need to do a "make daemon" to make tind.

```
# thread the database
35 * * * * /usenet/bin/tind -u
```

I've run tin over a SLIP link as a NNTP-based newsreader. If you're connecting to a system that has a full newsfeed, you will grow extremely old waiting for it to load up the "active" file.

5.2 Trn/Mthreads

trn is a threaded derivative of the "rn" newsreader. trn3.2 and newer has the nice ability to select either the "mthreads" (trn's threading package) or NOV (threader from INN) threading.

To compile it, just run Configure and take the calculated defaults. You might need to have lib4.4.1 and bash-1.13 (there is a beta now available on the various Linux archive sites) to successfully run Configure. You'll probably need both bash1.13 and libs4.4.1 to get the new Configure to run properly.

The newspak distribution on sunsite contains working config files for trn under Linux.

It's probably unwise to try to edit a trn config.sh by hand unless you're doing something *VERY* simple like changing the paths to fit your tastes. If you do so, you'll need to run "Configure -S" before you "make depend", "make", and "make install".

Although "Configure" fails generally under Linux with bash1.12, "Configure -S" work fine so if you take the newspak config.sh as a starting point, you'll be very close.

Compiling for NNTP reading is as simple as answering "yes" when Configure asks you if you want to do so (assuming Configure runs ok on your system). A future release of newspak will include a config.sh for NNTP reading as well as the existing one for local reading for those of us who are still "bash-impaired" :-)

I've run trn over a SLIP link as a NNTP-based newsreader. If you're connecting to a system that has a full newsfeed, you will grow extremely old waiting for it to load up the "active" file and to thread the articles.

There are dozens of command line switches for trn to get all kinds of behavior. Read the "trn" man page for details. I use a nice feature to set all the switches easily:

- make a file with all the settings in a file called /.trnrc
- export TRNINIT=" /.trnrc"

The current newspak has a copy of my .trnrc file as an example.

trn3.2 and above has support for NOV or mthreads threading that's user-selectable. Accordingly, I recommend building the software to allow both threading mechanisms (it's a question in Configure). To pick one at runtime, try "trn -Zo" for NOV and "trn -Zt" for mthreads. I do it my aliasing trn to the right thing.

To build the mthreads database, do something like the following in the "news" crontab:

```
# thread the trn database
35 * * * * /usenet/bin/mthreads all
```

5.3 NN

The newspak distribution on sunsite contains working config files for nn6.4.18 that you can drop into place and type "make" under Linux. They also work with the 6.5b3 beta of the coming nn6.5 update.

When you're done compiling, you need to do the following:

- - run the "inst" program to install things. (install everything)
- - initialize the database
- - fire up nnmaster

See the nn docs for details. Compiling, configuring, and running nn under Linux is no different than running nn on any other *nix with the exception that you may want to run nnmaster as a cron entry rather than as a daemon. If you run it as a daemon under linux, it may not tend to wake up properly (the net effect of running it from cron is the same anyway).

Support of "nn" is as simple as the following crontab entries:

```
# run nnmaster to collect "nn" stuff
# (not needed if you use NOV from INN in nn-6.5beta3)
25 * * * * /usenet/sw/nn/lib/nnmaster

# expire the nn database
# (not needed if you use NOV from INN in nn-6.5beta3)
0   4       * * * /usenet/sw/nn/bin/nnadmin =EYW

# stash a copy of the active file for "nngoback" and keep last 7
0 3 * * * /usenet/sw/nn/lib/back_act 7
```

I've experimented a little with running nn as a NNTP-based newsreader over a SLIP connection. In this case, you'll want to edit the config.h file slightly. See the comments in the file for details. When running as a NNTP-based reader, nn runs a local copy of nnmaster to keep the threads database on the local system so that article selection is very fast (although you of course wait for the arcticle text a little if you're running SLIP over a modem).

The new version (6.5.x) of nn has support for INN's NOV database which makes it unnecessary for you to run nnmaster at all. This configuration is *highly* recommended, since as a result you won't have to spend the cpu time to run nnmaster at all and you won't get its database and the actual news articles available out of synch.

5.4 Other newsreaders

The following is a non-inclusive list of newsreaders said to install and run under Linux:

- tass
- xrn
- gnus

6 Acknowledgements

The following people have helped in the assembly of the information (and experience) that helped make this document possible:

Ed Carp, Steve Robbins, Ian Taylor, Greg Naber, Matt Welsh, Iain Lea, Arjan de Vet

If I forgot anybody, my apologies.

7 Frequently Asked Questions about USENET (in c.o.l.* anyway)

7.1 Why can't I post to moderated groups ?

Probably because the newsreader is trying to call /bin/mail to send the mail and it doesn't like it. Replace the /bin/mail in old versions of SLS with the port of mailx-5.5.tar.z from a modern Slackware and use Slackware's `pkgtool` to install the kit and you'll be all set.

Another possibility is that you have a moderated newsgroup set up on your local system as not-moderated and somebody upstream is quietly deleting the article (some system's software, not a person). Make sure you run a "checkgroups" every now and then when the checkgroups article rolls by in news.admin every few weeks.

7.2 Why do I have problems that appear to be permission-related ?

Because they are :-)

Check to see that your permissions are right and that you have a "news" username and group in /etc/passwd and /etc/group that matches the binary distribution you grabbed. It seems that there is not yet a Linux-standard for commonly available accounts.

All the stuff in /usr/local/lib/news should be news.news except /usr/local/lib/news/setnewsids which should be setuid root.

You can use whatever UID and GID you want for "news".

7.3 Why can I post articles locally, but they don't show up or get fed downstream ?

Probably because you didn't call newsrun from cron. Maybe because you edited your sys file and messed it up. Maybe because you don't have a /usr/spool/news/out.going tree or something. Maybe because you grabbed a distribution that has the 'Performance' or 'Cleanup' releases of Cnews, which batch things up and need 'newsrun' running from cron to process them to feed the other sites and to have them visible locally.

Do not create newsgroups or feeds by editing the active or sys files. Use the utilities in /usr/local/lib/news/bin/maint to do it.

7.4 Why doesn't my binary distribution have nntp ?

Because it's supposed to be plug-n-play under Linux and because I didn't want to make SLS's news stuff doubly big by having to maintain both nntp and non-nntp versions of the newsreaders and news transport programs. Also because it compiles in localized information that is not overridable at runtime via a config file.

7.5 Why does doexpire (or relaynews or) say "severe space shortage" when there's lots of room ?

Because it can't read /etc/mtab. Make it mode 644. This happens when you unmount a mounted filesystem by root with a umask that doesn't permit world-read of files owned by root.

7.6 Why does everything look normal, but posting doesn't happen ?

Older versions of Linux had a "broken" sed that Cnews was prone to blow up. In particular, if you've installed over an old SLS, be sure to check /bin and /usr/bin to be certain you have only one copy of sed and that it's a modern one.

Because as of the 'Performance Release' in about February 1993, you have to have 'newsrun' run from cron periodically to process things. That's a feature that apparently suprises some people.

7.7 Can I hook the new news overview (NOV) stuff into trn/tin/nn to replace the various independent thread databases ?

Yes. trn, tin, and the beta of nn support it now.

You can hook it into the Performance and Cleanup Releases of Cnews and various other readers as well.

The beta copy of nn6.5 I have here has NOV support and it works just dandy under Linux. I run it here and have nn running without having to run nnmaster (!). Look on uniwa.uwa.edu.au for a copy of it.

7.8 Why can't we have a binary distribution of NNTP ?

Because significant local-only information is compiled-in and cannot be determined auto-magically at runtime. If you're that into things, please grab INN rather than rolling your own with Cnews plus NNTP.

7.9 How do I set up NNTP to allow read/post across the network while *not* storing any news articles or databases locally.

(mdw@sunsite.unc.edu (Matt Welsh))

- 1) Grab the "reference implementation" of nntp and a copy or rn from your local archive site. If you connect to ftp.uu.net you'd grab:

  nntp.1.5.11.tar.Z from ftp.uu.net:/networking/news/nntp

- 2) compile nntp as follows: copy common/conf.h.dist to common/conf.h.

  Edit common/conf.h to set certain options: The only ones I set were:

  DOMAIN: undefine it (i.e. change the line to #undef DOMAIN).

  REALDOMAIN: Define this. It looks up the domain using the libraries.

  SERVER_FILE: Set this to the name of the file which will contain the hostname of the news server (i.e. the machine you'll read and post news through). I use "/usr/local/lib/news/server".

  PASSFILE: If your news server requires authorization (i.e. some kind of username/password) to post, set this to the name of the file which contains the username and password (described below). I use "/usr/local/lib/news/nntppass".

  I decided to keep all of the other news stuff in /usr/local/lib/news. So I set all of the rest of the pathnames in the file (i.e. ACTIVE_FILE, NEWSGROUPS_FILE, etc.) to use /usr/local/lib/news. Many of these files are only used by the NNTP server, not the client, but to be safe I changed them all to point to the right directory. You can of course use the default pathnames; just make sure you create the directory accordingly.

  3) Create the user "usenet" if you haven't already. The inews program runs as this user. All you need is a userid; you don't need a home directory or shell or anything for the user. Just plop the following line into your /etc/passwd:

  ```
  usenet:*:13:1::/:
  ```

  Make sure you set the userid ("13", above) to something unique. The group can be anything; I use "daemon" (gid 1).

- 4) Create the SERVER_FILE, above. For example, my news server is "wonton.tc.cornell.edu", so I created the file /usr/local/lib/news/server which contained one line:

```
wonton.tc.cornell.edu
```

- 5) Create the PASSFILE. This file contains lines of the form

```
<server name> <username> <password>
```

Let's say that your news server (the one in SERVER_FILE, above) is "shoop.vpizza.com", and to post on that machine you need to be authorized as the user "news" with a password of "floof". Thus, in the PASSFILE (I use /usr/local/lib/news/nntppass), you need the line

```
shoop.vpizza.com news floof
```

- 6) Make this file secure! The inews program runs as the user "usenet", so make this news directory owned by that user and the nntppass file as well.

```
chown usenet /usr/local/lib/news
chmod 755 /usr/local/lib/news
chown usenet /usr/local/lib/news/nntppass
chmod 600 /usr/local/lib/news/nntppass
```

So nobody else can read this file. No, the passwords in it are not encrypted.

- 7) Go back to the nntp.1.5.11 source directory; issue "make client". At this point you'll build the NNTP version of inews, which is the only software used by the NNTP client.

When I built inews, there was a bug in the library which caused the function uname() in uname.c to call itself eternally. This should be gone now; however, if inews seems to hang and your system starts slowing down *a lot* you should rename the function "uname()" in uname.c to something like "my_uname()", and change the calls to it (in inews.c) to call my_uname() instead. Mail me if you run into this problem.

```
(VDS note - this means mail to Matt-not me :-) )
```

- 8) Issue "make install_client". This will install the inews stuff. Also link /usr/local/lib/news/inews to /usr/local/bin/inews

Now you should be able to happily post (by hand). Try something like the following:

```
$ inews -h << EOF
Newsgroups: misc.test
From: me@foo.bar.com
Subject: Testing
Reply-To: my-real-address@wherever.edu

This is a test.
EOF
```

If this works, inews should post the article. You'll know because test-responders on misc.test will reply to the address on the Reply-To line, above. Please don't do test postings on real groups, like c.o.l. :)

Part XXXII

Linux PCI-HOWTO

Copyright by Michael Will, michaelw@desaster.student.uni-tuebingen.de
version 0.5c / 1995 March
Information on what works with Linux and PCI-boards and what does not.

Contents

1 Introduction

Many people, including me, would like to run Linux on a PCI-based machine. Since it is not obvious which PCI motherboards and PCI cards will work with Linux and which do not, I conducted a survey and spent some hours to compile the information contained herein.

If you have information to add, please mail me. If you have questions, feel free to ask.

Help with my style/grammar/language is welcome as well. I am not a native- speaker of English and expect to make occasional mistakes.

Note: "on-board chip" refers to a SCSI chip integrated onto the motherboard rather than on a PCI expansion card.

Also, "quotes" herein may have slight context editing.

2 Why PCI?

2.1 General overview

The PC-architecture has several BUS-Systems to choose from:

ISA

    cheap, slow (usually 8Mhz), standard, many cards available>

EISA

    expensive, fast, some cards available>

MCA

    ex-IBM-proprietary, fast but not very wide-spread>

VESA-Local-Bus

    based on ISA, cheap, fast, some cards available>

PCI-Local-Bus

    expensive, fast, some cards available, the upcoming standard>

ISA/VESA-Local-Bus had some problems with high bus-speeds, and was not very reliable, but mainly due to its low price and better-than-ISA performance, sold very well. Most VESA boards should be stable by now.

EISA was reliable, but rather expensive, and intended more for power-users and servers, than for the average user. It has fewer cards available than other busses.

PCI now has the advantage. Like EISA it is not proprietary. It is as fast as EISA (or even faster), and 64bits wide. This will be important with the i586 (That Intel would prefer we call the Pentium...).

PCI is not like ISA/Local-Bus processor-dependent. This means you can use the winner-1000-PCI in an Alpha-driven-PCI-board as well as in a i486/i586-driven PCI-Board, except for the BIOS, but the hardware should be about the same.)

PCI allows cheaper production of onboard components, and needs no glue-logic chips.

2.2 Performance

taken from Craig Sutphin's Pro-PCI-Propaganda

    Unlike some local buses, which are aimed at speeding up graphics alone, the PCI Local Bus is a total system solution, providing increased performance for networks, disk drives, full-motion video, graphics and the full range of high-speed peripherals. At 33 MHz, the synchronous PCI Local Bus transfers 32 bits of data at up to 132 Mbytes/sec. A transparent 64-bit extension of the 32-bit data and address buses can double the bus bandwidth (264 Mbytes/sec) and offer forward and backwards compatibility for 32 and 64-bit PCI Local Bus peripherals. Because it is processor-independent, the PCI Local Bus is optimized for I/O functions, enabling the local bus to operate concurrent with the processor/memory subsystem. For users of high-end desktop PC's, PCI makes high reliability, high performance and ease of use more affordable than ever before; no trivial task at 33 MHz bus-clock rates. Variable length linear or toggle mode bursting for both reads and writes improves write dependent graphics performance. By comprehending the loading and frequency requirements of the local bus at the component level, buffers and glue logic are eliminated.

2.3 The onboard-SCSI-II-chip NCR53c810

One very nice feature of some PCI mother boards is the NCR onboard-SCSI-II-chip, which is said to be as fast as the EISA-Adaptec-1742, but much cheaper. Drivers for DOS/OS2 are available. Drew Eckard has released version 3 of his NCR53c810-driver. I run kernel 1.1.78 at the moment (9JAN94).

This works so well I sold my adaptec-1542B-ISA months ago. :-)

The NCR53c810-chip is onboard on some PCI-motherboards. There are add-on-boards available too, for about US$ 70.00.

The NCR-patches and bootimages are available on tsx-11.mit.edu:/pub/linux/ALPHA/scsi/ncr (approximately). Newer releases of Slackware 2.0 have support for the ncr too. Newer versions of the test-kernels (1.1.41 for example) do not require any patches; they have the driver already included. Since Kernel 1.2 it is in the standard kernel.

There is only one thing I noticed does not work with the current NCR-drivers yet. Disconnect/Reconnect does not work, so using a SCSI-tape can be a pain especially when using "mt erase" or the like blocks the whole SCSI-bus until it has finished. This is very unsatisfying.

Drew said, he had most (all?) of the code done for half a year, but it is not debugged, and he does not see working on it any time in the near future. Rumors say, there is someone in germany working on it, but he does not want to be put under pressure so he does not release the name yet.

FreeBSD does support the NCR53c810 for quite a long time already, including Tagged Command Queues, FAST, WIDE and Disconnect for NCR 53c810, 815, 825. Drew said, it would be possible to adapt the FreeBSD driver to Linux. Any volunteers?

I personaly have the impression there are some important wheels invented more than once because of the differently evolving of FreeBSD and Linux. Some more cooperation could do both systems very well...

I use the NCR-driver at the moment, but I am inclined to shell out some money on the new DPT-boards mentioned in this article. (Michael Will, 09JAN94.)

2.4 Drew Eckhardt on PCI-SCSI:

Drew said on end of March about the SCSI on PCI: (slightly edited for clarity in context)

The Adaptec 2940, Buslogic BT946, BT946W, DPT PCI boards, Future Domain 3260, NCR53c810, NCR53c815, NCR53c820, and NCR53c825 all work for some definition of the word works.

- The Adaptec 2940 suffers from the same cabling sensitivity that plagues all recent boards, but otherwise works fine.

- The Future Domain boards are not busmasters, and the driver doesn't support multiple simultaenous commands. If you don't (currently) need multiple simultaneous commands, get a NCR board, which will be cheaper and is busmastering. If you need multiple simultaneous commands, get a Buslogic.

- The Buslogic BT956W will do WIDE SCSI with the Linux drivers (although you can't use targets 8-15), the Adaptec 2940W (with one line patch to the 2940 driver) won't, nor will the NCR53c820 and NCR53c825.

- The NCR boards are dirt cheap (< $70 US), are generally quite fast, but the driver currently doesn't support multiple simultaenous commands, and I don't know when this will change.

- Emulux, Forex, and other unmentioned PCI SCSI controllers will not work.

2.5 The EATA-DMA driver and the PCI SCSI controllers from DPT

The EATA-DMA SCSI driver has undergone extensive changes and now also supports PCI SCSI controllers, multiple controllers and all SCSI channels on the multichannel SmartCache/Raid boards.

The driver supports all EATA-DMA Protocol (CAM document CAM/89-004 rev. 2.0c) compliant SCSI controllers and has been tested with many of those controllers in mixed combinations.

```
Those are:              (ISA)   (EISA) (PCI)
      DPT Smartcache: PM2011  PM2012A
                              PM2012B
      Smartcache III: PM2021  PM2022  PM2024
                              PM2122  PM2124
                              PM2322
      SmartRAID     : PM3021  PM3122  PM3224
                              PM3222
      and some controllers from NEC and ATT.
```

On a "base" DPT card (no caching or RAID module), a MC680x0 controls the bus-mastering DMA chip(s) and the SCSI controller chip. The DPT SCSI card almost works like a SCSI coprocessor.

The DPT card also will emulate an IDE controller/drive (ST506 interface), which enables you to use it with all operating systems even if they don't have an EATA driver.

On a card with the caching module, the 680x0 maintains and manages the on-board caching. The DPT card supports up to 64 MB RAM for disk-caching.

On a card with the RAID module, the 680x0 also performs the management of the RAID, doing the mirroring on RAID-1, doing the striping and ECC info generation on RAID-5, etc.

The entry level boards utilize a Motorola 68000, the high-end, more raid specific DPT cards use a 68020, 68030 or 68040/40MHz processor.

Official list prices range from 245to1995 (December 1, 1994)

Since I've been asked numerous times where you can buy those boards in Europe, I asked DPT to send me a list of their official European distributors. Here is a small excerpt:

```
Austria: Macrotron GmbH          Tel:+43 1 408 15430   Fax:+43 1 408 1545
Denmark: Tallgrass Technologies A/S Tel:+45 86 14 7000   Fax:+45 86 14 7333
Finland: Computer 2000 Finnland OY Tel:+35 80 887 331    Fax:+35 80 887 333 43
France : Chip Technologies        Tel:+33 1 49 60 1011   Fax:+33 1 49 599350
Germany: Akro Datensysteme GmbH    Tel:+49 (0)89 3178701 Fax:+49 (0)89 31787299
Russia : Soft-tronik              Tel:+7 812 315 92 76   Fax:+7 812 311 01 08
U.K.   : Ambar Systems Ltd.       Tel:+44 296 435 511    Fax:+44 296 479 461
```

"IMHO, the DPT cards are the best-designed SCSI cards available for a PC. And I've written code for just about every type of SCSI card for the PC. (Although, in retrospect, I don't know why!) ;-)" Jon R. Taylor (jtaylor@magicnet.net) President, Visionix, Inc.

The latest version of the EATA-DMA driver and a Slackware bootdisk is available on: ftp.uni-mainz.de:/pub/Linux/Drivers/SCSI/EATA

Since patchlevel 1.1.81 the driver is included in the standard kernel distribution.

The author can be reached under these addresses: neuffer@goofy.zdv.uni-mainz.de or linux@uni-koblenz.de

2.6 Future Domain TMC-3260 PCI SCSI

Rik Faith (faith@cs.unc.edu) informed me on Wed, 1 Feb 1995 about the Future Domain TMC-3260 PCI SCSI card being supported by the Future Domain 16x0 SCSI driver. Newer information might be contained in the SCSI-HOWTO.

- Detection is not done well, and does not use standard PCI BIOS detection methods (someone who has a PCI board needs to send me patches to fix this problem). So, you might have to fiddle with the detection routine in the kernel to get it detected.

- The driver still does not support multiple outstanding commands, so your system will hang while your tape rewinds.

- The driver does not support the enhanced pseudo-32bit transfer mode supported by recent Future Domain chips, so you will not get transfer rates as high as under DOS.

- The driver only supports the SCSI-I protocol, so your really fast hard disks will not get used at the highest possible throughput. (Again, fixes for all these problems are solicited – no one is working on them at this time.)

2.7 other thoughts on SCSI

James Soutter (J.K.Soutter1@lut.ac.uk) asked me to add the following information on Fast-Wide-SCSI-2:

Fast Wide SCSI-2 is sometimes incorrectly called SCSI-3. It differs from the normal Fast SCSI-2 (like the Adapted 1542B?) because it uses a 16 bit data bus rather than the more usual 8 bit bus. This improves the maximum transfer rate from 10 MB/s to 20 MB/s but requires the use of special Fast Wide SCSI-2 drives. The added performance of Fast Wide SCSI-2 will not necessarily improve the speed of your system. Most hard disk drives have a maximum internal transfer rate of less than 10 MB/s and so one drive alone can not flood a FAST SCSI-2 bus.

In Seagate's Oct 1993 product overview, only one Fast Wide SCSI-2 drive has an internal transfer rate of more than 10 MB/s (the ST12450W). Most of the drives have a maximum internal transfer rate of 6 MB/s or less, although the ST12450W is not the only exception to the rule. In conclusion, Fast Wide SCSI is designed for the file server market and will not necessarily benefit a single user workstation style system.

Rather than buying a PCI system with a SCSI interface on the motherboard, or rather than waiting for the NCR driver, you could purchase a separate PCI based SCSI card. According to Drew, the only PCI SCSI option that stands a chance of working is the Buslogic 946. It purports to be Adaptec 1540 compatible, like the EISA/VESA/ISA boards in the series.

Drew commented that other PCI based SCSI controllers are unlikely to be supported under Linux or the BSD's because the NCR based controllers are cheaper and more prevalent.

I personally would tend to try the NCR-Driver.

According to broom@ocean.fit.qut.edu.au (Bradley Broom):

The Buslogic BT-946C PCI SCSI works if you disable the option "enable Disconnection" with the AUTOSCSI-program under DOS which comes with the card.

Ernst Kloecker (ernst@cs.tu-berlin.de) wrote: (edited)

Talus Corporation has finished a NS/FIP driver for PCI boards with NCR SCSI. It will be shipping very soon, might even be free because a third party might pay for the work and donate the driver to NeXT.

Not every PCI-Board has got the chip. ASUS does, and one of the J-Bond boards does, too. Some vendors provide an alternative as you can read in Drew's text...

The NCR-Chip is clever enough to work with drives formatted by other controllers, and should be no problem.

3 ASUS-Boards

3.1 Various types of ASUS Boards

3.1.1 ASUS SP3 with saturn chipset I (rev. 2) for 486,

- 2 x rs232 with 16550

- NCR53c810 onboard,

- slightly broken saturn-chipset I (rev. 2)

3.1.2 ASUS SP3G with saturn chipset II (rev. 4) for 486,

like SP3, but less buggy saturn chipset

3.1.3 ASUS SP3-SiS chipset, for 486

like SP3G, but SiS chipset, green functions, and no NCR53c810 onboard anymore.

3.1.4 ASUS AP4, for 486, with PCI/ISA/VesaLocalbus

green functions, 1VL, 3 ISA, 4 PCI slots, only EIDE onboard, no fd-controller, no rs232/centronics. Very small size.

does recognice AMD486DX2/66 as DX4/100 only. This can be corrected with soldering one pin (which?) to ground, but I would not recommend a board like this anyway.

The one I tested was broken for OS2 and Linux, but people are said to use it for both.

The VesaLocalbus-Slot is expected to be slower than the normal vesa-localbus boards because of the PCI2VL bridge, but without penalty to the PCI section.

3.1.5 ASUS SP4-SiS, for Pentium90, PCI/ISA

like SP3-SiS, but for Pentium90.

3.2 Detailed information on the old ASUS PCI-I-SP3 with saturn chipset from heinrich@zsv.gmd.de:

- 3 PCI, 4 ISA Slots (3x16, 1x8 Bit)

- ZIF Socket for the CPU

- room for 4 72pin-SIMMs (max. 128M)

- Award BIOS in Flash-Eprom

- Onboard: NCR-SCSI, 1par, 2ser (with FIFO), AT-Bus, Floppy

The board does like most in that price class – write-through cache, no write-back. This should not be significant, maybe 3% of performance.

The BIOS supports SCSI-drives under DOS/Windows without additional drivers, but with the board come additional drivers which are said to give better performance, for DOS/Windows(ASPI), OS2, Windows-NT, SCO-Unix, Netware (3.11 and 4, if interpreted correctly)

Gert Doering (gert@greenie.muc.de) was saying the SCO-Unix-driver for the onboard-SCSI-Chip was not working properly. After two or three times doing: "time dd if=/dev/rhd20 of=/dev/null bs=100k count=500" it kernel-panicked...

The trouble some people experienced with this board might be due to them using an outboard Adaptec-SCSI-Controller with "sync negotiation" turned on. (This predates the NCR driver release; hence the use of the Adaptec.) Please check that in the BIOS-Setup of the Adaptec-1542C if you use one and have problems with occasional hangups!

There is a new version of the ASUS-Board which should have definitely less problems. It is called ASUS-PCI-I/SP3G, the G is important. It has the new Saturn-chipset rev. 4 and the bugs should be gone. They use the Saturn-ZX-variant and the new SP3G has fully PCI conforming level-triggered (thus shareable), BIOS-configurable interrupts. It has an on-board PS/2-mouseport, EPA-power-saving-modes and DX4-support, too. It performs excellently. If you can get the German computer magazine C't from July (?), you will find a test report where the ASUS-Board is the best around.

Latest information about ASUS-SP3-G: You might experience crashes when using PCI-to-Memory-Posting. If you disable this, all works perfect. jw@peanuts.informatik.uni-tuebingen.de said he believed it to be a problem of the current Linux-kernel rather than the hardware, because part of the system still works when crashing, looking like a deadlock in the swapper, and OS2/DOS/WINDOZE don't crash at all.

4   Pat Dowler (dowler@pt1B1106.FSH.UVic.CA) with ASUS SP3G

- ASUS SP3G board (it is rev.4 == saturn II)

- AMD DX4-100 CPU (need to set jumper 36 to 1&2 rather than 2&3, otherwise it's set the same as other 486DXn chips)

- 256K cache (comes with 15ns cache :-)

- 16meg RAM (2x8meg)

- ET4000 ISA video card

- quantum IDE hard drive

- SMC Elitel16 combo ethernet card

Unlike some other reports, I find the mouse pointer moves very smoothy under X (just like the ol' 386) - it is jumpy under some, but not all, DOS games though...

Performance is great!! I ran some large floating point tests and found the performance in 3x33 (100MHz) mode to be almost 1.5x that in 2x (66MHz) mode (large being 500x500 doubles - 4meg or so)... I was a little dubious about clock-tripling but I seem to be getting full benefit :-)

The heavily configurable energy star stuff doesn't work with the current AMD DX4 chips - you need an SL chip

I really need a SCSI disk and a PCI video card :-)

5   confusion about saturn chipsets

Pat Duffy (duffy@theory.chem.ubc.ca) said:

```
Saturn I:  these are revisions 1 and 2 of the Saturn chipsets.
Saturn II: This is also called rev. 4 of the Saturn chipsets.

As far as I know, rev. 3 never actually shipped, and (from a few people who
```

have it) the SP3G now has rev. 4 (or Saturn II) in it.

Confused? Well, the only real definitive answer is to get ahold of the board and run the debug script in the PCI chipset list on it. As far as I know, though, the SP3G board is indeed shipping with rev. 4 (Saturn II).

6 Video-Cards

Linux people have successfully used # 9 XGE Level 12, ELSA Winner 1000, and S3-928 video cards. The XFree86(tm)-3.1.1 does support boards with the tseng et4000/w32 in accelerated mode, as well as S3 Vision 864 and 964 chipsets including boards like the ELSA Winner 1000Pro and 2000Pro, Number Nine GXE64 and GXE64Pro, Miro Crystal 20SV). Support in the S3 Server for the Chrontel 8391 clock chip has been added.

Trio32 and Trio64 S3 Boards like the SPEA V7 Mirage P64 PCI and MIRO Crystal 40SV, are also supported, the Mach32 and Mach64 are supported in accelerated mode, too.

The SVGA Driver

16bpp mode (65K colors instead of the usual 256) support for Mach32 boards as well as 32bpp for some S3 boards and the P9000 boards has been added.

tldraben@teleport.com reported:

- Diamond Stealth W32 (et4000/W32) – Text mode works, X11 suffered from "pixel dust", unbearable never got it to work and returned it.

- # 9GXE L12 – Works, virtual consoles corrupted when switched, fixed this with disabling the "fast dram mode" feature in his BIOS. Does not get a dot clock above 85, though.

Genoa Phantom 8900PCI card seems to work well. Genoa Phantom/W32 2MB does not work in an ASUS-Board. Tseng 3000/W32i chipset seems to work well. Spea-v7 mercury-lite works perfectly since XFree86(tm)-2.1.

Spea V7 Mirage P64 PCI 2M with Trio64 works nice since XFree86(tm)-3.1.1

ATI Graphics Ultra Pro for PCI with 2MB VRAM and an ATI68875C DAC run well as dem@skyline.dayton.oh.us tells us: "It's humming right along at 1280x1024 w/256 colors @74Hz non-interlaced. Looks great."

Paradise WD90C33 PCI did lock up on screensaver/X - this has been solved in the newer versions of the kernel. jbauer@badlands.NoDak.edu (John Edward Bauer)

miroChrystal 8S/PCI (1MB) S3 - no problem.

7 Ethernet Cards

Of course the ISA-ethernet-cards still work, but people are asking for PCI-based ones. The author of many (if not most) ethernet- drivers said the following:

From: Donald Becker (becker@cesdis.gsfc.nasa.gov) Subject: PCI ethernet cards supported? The LANCE code has been extended to handle the PCI version. I hope to get the PCI probe code (about a dozen extra lines in the LANCE driver) into the next kernel version. I'm working on the 32 bit mode code. I haven't yet started the 21040 code.

I'll write drivers for the PCnet32 mode and the DEC 21040. That will cover most of the PCI ethercard market.

file://cesdis.gsfc.nasa.gov/pub/people/becker/whoiam.html

In the new testkernels of 1.1.50 and above, the AMD-singlechip ethernetadapters are supported. With a pentium, they ought to then see 900K/second ftps +(assuming an NCR PCI SCSI controller) at about 20% cpu load. (AMD Lance).

Anything based on the AMD PCnet/PCI chip should work at the time being. In the US the Boca board costs under US$ 70

8 Motherboards

The people who answered were using the following boards:

8.1 ASUS

- Ruediger.Funck@Physik.TU-Muenchen.DE - successful.
- strauss@dagoba.escape.de - half-successful, works, but...
- Ulrich Teichert, Stormweg 24, D-24539 Neumuenster, Germany - successful.
- heinrich@zsv.gmd.de - successful
- CARSTEN@AWORLD.aworld.de - successful
- egooch@mc.com - successful - but trouble with the serial port
- archie@CS.Berkeley.EDU and his friend - successful after solving IDE-puzzle
- Lars Heinemann (lars@uni-paderborn.de) successful
- Michael Will (michaelw@desaster.student.uni-tuebingen.de) - successful.

8.2 Micronics P54i-90

root@intellibase.gte.com succesful bill.foster@mccaw.com successful karpens@ncssm-server.ncssm.edu successful

8.3 SA486P AIO-II

ah@doc.ic.ac.uk successful

8.4 Sirius SPACE

hi86@rz.uni-karlsruhe.de - successful

8.5 Gateway-2000

kenf@clark.net - no problems except the soundcard he tries to swap dmarples@comms.eee.strathclyde.ac.uk - successful, but... robert logan (rl@de-montfort.ac.uk) - flawless. James D. Levine (jdl@netcom.com) - flawless.

8.6 Intel-Premiere

grif@cs.ucr.edu - successful jeromem@amiserv.xnet.com - successful demarest@rerf.or.jp - successful (Premier-II)

8.7 DELL Poweredge SP4100 gbelow@pmail.sams.ch - successful

8.8 Comtrade Best Buy PCI / PCI48X MB Rev 1.0

tldraben@Teleport.Com - "Works, I believe it has buggy Saturn chipset. I would also like to add: I strongly recommend not buying from Contrade. Their service is horrible. "

8.9 IDeal PCI / PCI48X MB Rev 1.0

tldraben@Teleport.Com - "Did not work with PCI48X motherboard"

8.10 CMD Tech. PCI IDE / CSA-6400C

tldraben@TelePort.com - "Works"

8.11 GA-486iS (Gigabyte)

Stefan.Dalibor@informatik.uni-erlangen.de - success with problems.

8.12 GA-586-ID (Gigabyte) 90 Mhz Pentium PCI/EISA Board

kkeyte@esoc.bitnet - succesful

8.13 ESCOM 486dx2/66 - which board?

Works perfect except the ftape-streamer (archive)

8.14 J-Bond with i486dx2/66

Drew Eckhardt (drew@kinglear.cs.Colorado.EDU) - The NCR53c810 doesn't work too hot (yet), but I'm working on fixing that.

9 reports on success

9.1 Micronics P54i-90 (root@intellibase.gte.com)

Pentium with 90Mhz, 32M RAM and 512K L2-cache. Works extremely well (a kernel recompile takes 10 minutes :-).

The board includes:

- UART - two 16550A high speed UARTS

- ECP - one enhanced parallel port

- Onboard IDE controller

- Onboard floppy controller

Pros: Currently, I'm using it with an Adaptec 1542CF and a 1G Seagate drive, No problems. Graphics is ATI Graphics Pro Turbo (PCI). Very fast. The serial ports can keep up with a TeleBit T3000 modem (38400) without overruns. Caching above 16M does occur. There are 3 banks of SIMM slots (2 SIMM's per bank), with each bank capable of 64M each (2 32M 72-pin SIMM's). Each bank must be filled completely to be used (I'm only using bank 0 with 2 16Mx72-pin SIMM's). The CPU socket is a ZIF type socket. The BIOS is Phoenix, FLASH type.

Drawbacks: RAM is expandable to 192M, but the L2 cache is maxed at 512K. While the graphics are very fast, there is currently no XF86 server for the Mach64 (well, actually there is, but it doesn't use any of the accelerator features; it's just an SVGA server). I don't know if the onboard IDE hard drive controller works; I'm prejudiced against a standard that won't allow my peripherals to operate across platforms, so I didn't buy an IDE disk; instead, I got a Seagate 31200N and a NEC 3Xi.

Mitch

9.2 Angelo Haritsis (ah@doc.ic.ac.uk) about SA486P AIO-II:

The motherboard I eventually bought (in the UK) is one supporting 486 SX/DX/DX2/DX4 chips. It is called SA486P AIO-II. Features include:

- Intel Saturn v2 chipset

- Phoenix BIOS (flash eprom option)

- NCR SCSI BIOS v 3.04.00

- 256K 15ns cache (max 512) write back and write through

- 4 72-pin SIMM slots in 2 banks

- 3 PCI slots, 4 ISA

- On-board NCR 53c810 SCSI controller

- On-board IDE / floppy / 2 x 16550A uarts / enhanced parallel

I bought it from a company (UK) called ICS, (note I have no connections whatsoever with the company, just a happy customer). I use a 486/DX2-66 CPU.

Before I had a VLB 486 m/board with a buslogic BT-445S controller that I was borrowing. I have 2 SCSI devices: 1 barracuda 2.1GB ST12550N disk and a Wangtek 5525ES tape drive. I was expecting a lot of adventures by switching to the new motherboard, esp after hearing all these non-success stories on the net. To my surprise everything worked flawlessly on the 1st boot! (1.1.50). And it has been doing so for about a month now. I did not even have to repartition the disk: apparently the disk geometry bios translation of the 2 controllers is the same. Linux has had no problems at all. SCSI is visibly much faster as well (sorry, I have no actual performance measurements).

The only problems (related to Drew's linux ncr53c7,810 SCSI driver - thanks for the good work Drew!) are:

- no synchronous transfers are yet supported => performance hit

- disconnect/reconnect is disabled => disk SCSI ops "hold" during certain slow SCSI device opeartions (eg tape rewind)

- tagged queuing is not there (?) => performance hit

There has been no progress on the ncr driver since Sept 94. (current writing: 19 Jan 95).

If you get Windows complaiing about 32-bit disk driver problems, just disable 32-bit disk access via Control Panel. This should not hurt performance. (What I did is remove the WDCTRL driver from my SYSTEM.INI).

All else is fine. I tried the serial ports with some dos/windows s/w and worked ok. The IDE/floppy work ok as well. I have not tried the parallel yet. The motherboard is quite fast and so far I am very pleased with the upgrade. I have not yet tried a PCI graphics board. I will later on. I am using an old ISA S3 which is fine at the moment.

9.3 bill.foster@mccaw.com about his Micronics M5Pi

Micronics M5Pi motherboard with 60 MHz Pentium, PCI bus having the following components:

```
16Mb RAM/512k cache
onboard IDE, parallel, 16550A UARTS
2 X 340MB Maxtor IDE Hard Drives
Soundblaster 16 SCSI-II
Toshiba 3401B SCSI CD-ROM
Archive Viper 525MB SCSI Tape Drive
Viewsonic 17 monitor
Cardex Challenger PCI video card (ET4000/W32P)
A4-Tech Serial Mouse
```

Everything works great, Slackware installation was very easy, I can run Quicken 7 for DOS under DOSEMU. I run X at 1152x900 resolution at 67Hz.

9.4 Simon Karpen (karpens@ncssm-server.ncssm.edu) with Micronics M54pi

I have had no problems with the above board, the on-board PCI IDE (hopefully soon will also have SCSI), and an ATI Mach32 (GUP) with 2MB of VRAM.

9.5 Goerg von Below (gbelow@pmail.sams.ch) about DELL Poweredge

```
- Intel 486DX4/100
- 16 MB RAM
- DELL SCSI array (DSA) with Firmware A07, DSA-Manager 1.7
- 1 GB SCSI HD DIGITAL
- NEC SCSI CD-ROM
- 2 GB internal SCSI streamer
- 3-Com C579 EISA Ethernet card
- ATI 6800AX PCI VGA subsystem, 1024 MB RAM

CAVE! DELL SCSI Array controller (DSA) runs only with firmware Rev. A07 !
A06 is buggy, impossible to reboot !
To get it: ftp dell.com , file is /dellbbs/dsa/dsaman17.zip
```

Apart from this firmware-problem there where no problems for the last 2 months, running with linux 1.1.42 as primary nameserver, newsserver and www-server on internet.

9.6 zenon@resonex.com about Gateway2000 P-66

Gateway2000's P5-66 system with Intel's PCI motherboard, with 5 ISA slots and 3 PCI slots. The only PCI card I am using is the # 9 GXe level 12 PCI card (2 MB VRAM and 1 MB DRAM). This card was bought from Dell. Under Linux I am using the graphics in the 80x25 mode only (I am waiting for some XFree86 refinements before using it in 1280x1024 resolution), but under DOS/Windows I have used the card in 1280x1024x256 mode without problems. Etherlink 3C509 Ethernet card, Mitsumi bus-interface card,

Adaptec 1542C SCSI interface card and additional serial/parallel ports card (which makes the total of serial ports 3).

I have total of 32 MB RAM (recognized and used by both Linux and DOS). There is also a bus mouse (Microsoft in the PS2 mode).

No problems so far.

9.7 James D. Levine (jdl@netcom.com) with Gateway2000

Gateway 2000 P5-60 with an Intel Mercury motherboard, AMI-Flash-BIOS, (1.00.03.AF1, (c)'92) 16M RAM, on-board IDE controller and an ATI AX0 (Mach32 Ultra XLR) PCI display adapter. He had absolutely no problems with the hardware so far but has not tried anything fancy, such as accelerated IDE drivers or SCSI support.

9.8 hi86@rz.uni-karlsruhe.de with SPACE

SPACE-board, 8MB RAM, S3 805 1MB DRAM PCI 260MB Seagate IDE-hard disk because of lack of NCR53c810-Driver, 0.99pl15d, does seem to work well.

9.9 grif@cs.ucr.edu with INTEL

17 machines running a 60Mhz-i586 on Intel-Premier-PCI-Board

9.10 Jermoe Meyers (jeromem@amiserv.xnet.com) with Intel Premiere

Motherboard - Intel Premiere Plato-babyAT 90mhz with Buslogic bt946c w/4.86 mcode w/4.22 autoSCSI firmware, (note, mine came with 4.80 mcode and 4.17 autoSCSI firmware. (interrupt pins A,B,C conform to respective PCI slots!) ATI Xpression (Mach64) - using driver from sunsite, (running AcerView 56L monitor).

The motherboard has 4 IDE drives, Linux (Slackware 2.0) sees the first two and everything on the Buslogic as it emulates an adaptec 1542. Uh, yes, Dos sees them all. Buslogic is VERY accomodating in regards to shipping upgraded chips (you will have to know how to change PLCC (plastic leaded chip carrier) chips, 3 of them. Though, don't let that scare you :-) it's not that tough. Get a low end PLCC removal tool, and your in business. You also might want to "flash upgrade your system bios from Intel's IPAN BBS, a trivial process. Whats even more interesting is I also have a Sound Blaster SCSI-2 running a SCSI CDROM drive off it's adaptech 1522 onboard controller. So thats 4 IDE drives (2 under Linux) and 2 SCSI-2 controllers.

I hope this helps others who are struggling with PCI technology use Linux! Jerry (jeromem@xnet.com)

9.11 Timothy Demarest (demarest@rerf.or.jp) Intel Plato Premiere II

My system is configured as follows: 16Mb 60ns RAM, 3Com Etherlink-III 53C809 ethernet card (using 10base2), ATI Mach 64 2Mb VRAM, Toshiba 2x SCSI CDROM, NCR 53c810 PCI SCSI, Syquest 3270 270Mb Cartridge Drive, Viewsonic 17 monitor, Pentium-90 (FDIV Bug Free). Running Slackware 2.1.0, Kernel 1.2.0, with other misc patches/upgrades.

Everything is functioning flawlessly. I dont recommend the Syquest drives. I have used the 3105 and the 3270 and both a very, very fragile. Also, the cartridges are easily damaged and I have had frequent problems with them. I am in the process of looking for alternative removable storage (MO, Zip, Minidisc, etc).

Some information you might need:

9.11.1 Flash Bios upgrades

Flash Bios updates can be ftp'd from wuarchive.wustl.edu:/pub/MSDOS_UPLOADS/plato. The current version is 1.00.12.AX1. The BIOS upgrades *must* be done in order. 1.00.03.AZ1 to 1.00.06.AX1 to 1.00.08.AX1 to 1.00.10.AX1 to 1.00.12.AX1. The Flash BIOS updates can also be downloaded from the Intel BBS. I do not have that number right now.

9.11.2 NCR 53c810 BIOSless PCI SCSI

If you are using an NCR 53c810 BIOSless PCI SCSI card in the Plato, you may have trouble getting the card to be recognized. I had to change one of the jumpers on the NCR card: the jumper that controls whether there is 1 or 2 NCR SCSI cards in your system must be set to "2". I dont know why, but this is how I got it to work. The other jumper controls the INT setting (A,B,C,D). I left mine at A (the default).

9.11.3 apart from that - plug and play!

There are no settings in the motherboard BIOS for setting the NCR 53c810. Dont worry - once the card is jumpered correctly, it will be recognized! So much for PCI Plug-n-Play!

9.12 heinrich@zsv.gmd.de with ASUS

ASUS-PCI-Board (SP3) having:

- – Asus PCI-Board with AMD 486/dx2-66 and 16M RAM
- – Fujitsu 2196ESA 1G SCSI-II
- – Future Domain 850MEX Controller (cheap-SCSI-Controller, almost a clone to Seagate's ST01... want's to use ncr53c810 as soon as the driver comes out
- – ATI Graphics Ultra (the older one with Mach-8 Chip, ISA-Bus)
- – Slackware 1.1.1

He just exchanged the boards, plugged his cards in, connected the cables, and it worked perfect. He does not use any PCI-Cards yet, though.

9.13 CARSTEN@AWORLD.aworld.de with ASUS

ASUS-PCI-Board with 486DX66/2, miro-crystal 8s PCI driven by the S3-drivers of XFree86-2.0, using the onboard SCSI-Chip. No problems with compatibility at all.

9.14 Lars Heinemann (lars@uni-paderborn.de) with ASUS

ASUS PCI/I-486SP3 Motherboard w/ 486DX2/66 and 16M RAM (2x8), miroChrystal 8S/PCI (1MB) S3, Soundblaster PRO, Adaptec 1542b (3.20 ROM) SCSI host adapter with two hard disks (Fujitsu M2694ESA u. Quantum LPS52) and a QIC-150 Streamer attached. No problems at all!

9.15 Ruediger.Funck@Physik.TU-Muenchen.DE with ASUS

ASUS PCI/I-486SP3 / i486DX2-66 / 8 MB PS/2 70 ns BIOS: Award v 4.50 CPU TO DRAM write buffer: enabled CPU TO PCI write buffer: enabled PCI TO DRAM write buffer: disabled, unchangeable CPU TO PCI burst write: enabled Miro Crystal 8s PCI - S3 P86C805 - 1MB DRAM

Quantum LPS 540S SCSI-Harddisk on NCR53c810-controller.

9.16   robert logan (rl@de-montfort.ac.uk with GW/2000)

Gateway 2000 4DX2-66P 16 Megs RAM, PCI ATI AX0 2MB DRAM (ATI GUP). WD 2540 Hard Disk (528 Megs) CrystalScan 1776LE 17inch. (Runs up to 1280x1024) Slackware 1.1.2 (0.99pl15f)

It is giving no problems. He uses SLIP for networking and an Orchid-Soundwave-32 for niceties, awaiting the NCR-Driver. The only problem he has is that the IDE-Drive could be much faster on the PCI-IDE. It is one of the new Western Digital fast drives and in DOS/WfW it absolutely screams - on Linux it is just as slow as a good IDE-Drive.

9.17   archie@CS.Berkeley.EDU and his friend use ASUS

Archie and his friend have rather similar configurations:

- ASUS PCI-SP3 board (4 ISA, 3 PCI)

- Intel 486DX2/66

- Genoa Phantom 8900PCI card (friend: Tseng 3000/W32i chipset)

- Maxtor 345 MB IDE hard drive

- Supra 14.4 internal modem

- ViewSonic 6e monitor (Archie)

- NEC Multisync 4fge (friend)

- Slackware 1.2.0

The onboard-SCSI is disabled. First there were problems with the IDE-drive: "on the board there's a jumper which selects whether IRQ14 comes from the ISA bus or the PCI bus. The manual has an example where they show connecting it to PCI INT-A. Well, we did that just like the example... but then later our IDE drive would not work (the IDE controller is on board). Had to take it back. The guys at NCA were puzzled, then traced it back to this jumper. I guess the IDE controller uses IRQ14 or something? That's not documented anywhere in the manual. Other than that, seems to be kicking ass nicely now. Running X, modeming, etc. (for the Supra you have to explicitly tell the kernel that the COM port has a 16550A using setserial (in Slackware /etc/rc.d/rc.serial))".

9.18   Michael Will with ASUS-SP3 486 (the old one)

used the following:

- ASUS PCI-SP3-Board with 486dx2/66 and 16M RAM

- NCR53c810-SCSI-II chip driving a 1GB-Seagate-SCSI-II disk and a Wangtec-tape

- ATI-GUP PCI Mach32 Graphics card with 2M VRAM running perfectly with XFree86(tm)-3.1 8bpp and 16bpp

- Linux kernel 1.1.69

It runs perfectly and I am content with the speed, the ATI-GUP-PCI (Mach32) does not give as good benchmarks as expected, though. Since I got the money by now, I got me an ASUS-SP4 with P90 which gives me better throughput on Mach32-PCI... If I had even more money I'd get me another 16M of RAM and a Mach64-PCI with 4M RAM, though... I still keep on dreaming :-)

9.19   Karl Keyte (kkeyte@esoc.bitnet) Gigabyte GA586 Pentium

- PCI/EISA Board Gigabyte GA586-ID 90MHz Pentium (dual processor, one fitted)

- 32M RAM

- SCSI - no SCSI-NCR-chip on-board, using Adaptec 1542C,

- PCI ATI GUP 2M VRAM

- Adaptec 1742 EISA SCSI controller

- Soundblaster 16

- usual I/O

Everything under DOS AND Linux works perfectly. No problem whatsoever. A VERY fast machine! BYTE Unix benchmarks place it about the same as a Sun SuperSPARC-20 running Solaris 2.3. The PC is faster for integer arithmetic and process stuff (including context switching). The SPARC is faster for floating point and one of the disk benchmarks.

9.20   kenf@clark.net with G/W 2000

He uses a Gateway 2000 with no problems, except the soundcard (which one?). He is trading it in for a genuine soundblaster in hopes that will help.

9.21   Joerg Wedeck (jw@peanuts.informatik.uni-tuebingen.de) / ESCOM

originally bought a 486 DX2/66 from ESCOM (which board?) with onboard IDE and without (!) onboard NCR-SCSI-chip. ISA-adaptec 1542cf SCSI-controller instead spea v7 mercury lite (s3, PCI, 1MB), ISA-Soundblaster-16, mitsumi-cdrom (the slower one). Everything except the archive-streamer works with no problems. The spea-v7 works perfectly since XFree86-2.1

He abandoned the Intel-board in favour of an ASUS-SP3-g and has some problems with PCI-to-Memory burstmode which is crashing only on Linux, "looking like a deadlock in the swapper". If you have any information on this, please eMail the maintainer of the PCI-HOWTO.

After turning off the PCI-to-Memory posting feature it just works perfect.

Rather than sending him mail please read his http-homepage at "http://wsiserv.informatik.uni-tuebingen.de/ jw" where he keeps information about his PCI-system, too.

9.22   Ulrich Teichert / ASUS

ASUS-PCI board with AMD486dx40 (but actually running at 33Mhz?!) His ISA-ET3000 Optima 1024A ISA works nice. No problems with Quantum540S SCSI Harddisk attached to the onboard NCR53c810.

10   Reports of problems

10.1   hschmal@informatik.uni-rostock.de and SCSI-PCI-SC200

He reports that after plugging that card into his Pentium-board, Linux no longer boots. My first guess is that it is not supported.

10.2 dmarples@comms.eee.strathclyde.ac.uk G/W 2000

Gateway 2000 G/W 2000 4DX2/66 PCI ATI-Graphics-Ultra-Pro IDE of indeterminate make

It works well - only the IDE-Card runs in ISA-compatibility-mode, and works a lot faster when switched into PCI-Mode by a DOS-program... thus it's not that fast in Linux, and a patch would be nice.

10.3 cip574@wpax01.physik.uni-wuerzburg.de (Frank Hofmann) / ASUS

He uses the ASUS-board with 16MB-RAM, ISA-based S3/928, and the onboard-IDE-controller with a Seagate ST4550A hard disk. He's had no trouble with the newer Linux-kernels.

His problem:

```
using X, my mouse is not responding the way I was used to before.  It's
sometimes behind movement and makes jumps if moved quickly.  I think this was
discussed In a Linux newsgroup before (I don't know which one) and is due to
the use of 16550 serial chips for the onboard serial interfaces.  After two
weeks, I got used to it :-)
```

Reducing the threshold of the 16550 should help. There should be a patch to setserial available somewhere, but I do not know where.

10.4 axel@avalanche.cs.tu-berlin.de (Axel Mahler) / ASUS

ASUS PCI/I-486SP3 Motherboard (Award BIOS 4.50), 16 MB RAM the on-Board NCR Chip is disabled, he had the Genoa Phantom/W32 2MB for PCI and a Adaptec AHA-1542CF (BIOS v2.01) connected to:

- an IBM 1.05 GB Harddisk

- a Toshiba CD-ROM (XM4101-B)

- a HP DAT-Streamer (2GB)

when creating the filesystems, 'mke2fs' (0.4, v. 1.11.93) hung and installation was impossible. After replacing the Genoa Phantom/W32 2MB PCI with an ELSA Winner 1000 2MB PCI it worked perfectly. He tested it with an old Eizo VGA-ISA and it worked as well, so the problem was in the Genoa-PCI-card.

10.5 Frank Strauss (strauss@dagoba.escape.de) / ASUS

ASUS SP3 Board i486DX2/66 NCR53c810 disabled Adaptec 1542B in ISA Slot with 2 hard drives (200MB Maxtor, 420MB Fijutsu), SyQuest 88MB and Tandberg Streamer ELSA Winner 1000 PCI, 1MB-VRAM Sound-blaster Pro in ISA Slot at IRQ 5 Onboard IDE disabled Onboard serial, parallel, FD enabled

After a reset, the machine sometimes 'hangs' (soft and hard-reset the same) - this is probably not related to the Adaptec and the Soundcard, because even without these the system sometimes fails to come up. But if it runs, (and the ELSA-WINNER-1000-PCI-message appears) it runs ok.

The two serial ports are detected as 16550 as they should, but at some mailbox-sessions there was heavy data-loss at V42bis... The problem seems to be in the hardware...

CPU>-PCI-Burst seems to work well with DOS/MS-Windows

CPU->PCI-Burst does not work properly with linux0.99p15, Messing up when switching the virtual-consoles, crashing completely when calling big apps like ghostview, or xdvi, leaving the SCSI-LED on (!).

(I suspect these apps would be using a lot of CPU->PCI-burst because of the big heap of data to transmit to the PCI-Winner-1000)

After disabling CPU->PCI-Burst, it works well, the Winner-1000 at 1152x846 (not much font cache with 1MB) does 93k xstones. OpaqueMove with twm is more than just endureable :-)

He has got a SATURN.EXE which he loads under DOS before starting Linux, helping to turn on burst without hangs...

Someone stated that these problems might go away when turning off "sync negotiation" on the Adaptec - I do not know if this is possible with the adaptec1542B too? But I guess so.

With CPU->PCI-Burst it yielded 95k xstones, so he considers it as not too grave to do without. His only problem is that he would like to run his Winner-1000 at 1152x900 which fails because it seems to take any x-resolution higher than 1024pixels as a 1280pixel-resolution, thus wasting a lot end resulting in a y-resolution of 816pixels... but this is probably no PCI-related problem. It should have gone away with XFree86-2.1

10.6   egooch@mc.com / ASUS

- BOARD ASUS PCI/I-486 SP3 RAM: 16MB (4x4M-SIMM)
- CPU 486DX33 CPU
- BIOS Ver. 4.50 (12/30/93)
- Floppy Two floppy drives (1.2 and 1.44), using ASUS on-board floppy controller
- SCSI tried both WD7000 SCSI controller and Adaptec 1542CF and worked.
- Two SCSI 320M hard drives
- SCSI NEC84 CDROM drive
- SCSI QIC150 Archive tape drive
- Video - Tseng ET4000 ISA graphics card
- Sound PAS16 sound card
- Printer attached to on-board ASUS parallel port

He has nothing in the PCI-Slots yet, but wants to buy a PCI-Video-Card, currently uses WD7000 SCSI controller but will switch to the NCR-Chip onboard as soon as the driver is out.

Everything works perfectly - the first serial port which has a 14.4K-Modem attached does hang occasionally when reconnecting with the modem after having used it previously. He says that would not be unique to ASUS but rather a bug in the SMC-LSI device with its 16550UART. The logitech-serial-mouse on the second port works fine. Setting down the threshold of the 16550 for the mouseport would definitely help, one does seem to need a special patched setserial for that? I have not got the information yet, please contact me if you know more!

10.7   Stefan.Dalibor@informatik.uni-erlangen.de / GigaByte

- Board - GA-486iS from Gigabyte w/ 256Kb 2L-Cache, i486-DX2
- Bios - AMI, 93/8
- SCSI - no SCSI-NCR-chip on-board, using Adaptec 1542C,
- Video - ELSA Winner 1000
- Linux 0.99pl14 + SCSI-Clustering-Patches / Slackware 1.1.1

All seems to go well, but he has not tried neither networking, printing or a streamer yet. Before applying the clustering- patches he had some problems with hangs triggered by "find", but this no longer is the case - perhaps it was an older kernel-bug.

The ELSA-Winner-1000 sometimes hangs, with very strange patterns on the screen resolved only by rebooting... The dealer has told him it was a bug in the ELSA-Card, but the manufacturer claims it had solved the problem. The bug is not reproducible so he does not plan to take any action at the moment.

All in all the machine seems to work very well under heavy text processing (emacs, LaTeX, xfig, ghostview) usage. Interaction is surprisingly responsive, little difference between it and the 3-4X as expensive Sun he works on...

CPU->PCI-Burst is still disabled because the bios does not support the PCI-things well?

A problem with his new modem (v32 terbo) arose: it looses characters. Especially when using SLIP it complains a lot about RX and TX errors. As soon as he runs X it gets unusable. He said he activated FIFO and RTS/CTS with stty, but to no avail...

10.8   Tom Drabenstott (tldraben@Teleport.Com) with Comtrade / PCI48IX

PCI48IX Motherboard Rev. 1.0. Made by ??? documentation copyrighted by "exrc". The BIOS says not very much about PCI.

His E-315E Super IDE UMC (863+865) ISA-Controller-card does have problems. (It is a multifunction controller-card). It seems to work well under DOS/OS2 but not under Linux.

11   General tips for PCI-Motherboard + Linux NCR PCI SCSI

This was compiled by Angelo Haritsis (ah@doc.ic.ac.uk) from various people's postings:

11.1   DON'Ts:

Do *NOT* go for combination VLB/PCI motherboards. They usually have a lot of problems. Get a plain PCI version (with ISA slots as well of course). A lot of bad things have been heard about OPTI chipset PCI motherboards. Someone hints: "Avoid the OPTi (82C596/82C597/82C822) chipset based motherboards like the TMC PCI54PV".

(I know of at least one person having no problems with his TMC PCI54PV motherboard. He just had to put the NCR53c810 addonboard into slot-A which is the only slot capable of busmastering as it seems.)

Rumours say that Intel chipset PCI motherboards will have problems with more than one bus-mastering PCI board. I have not tried this one yet on mine and have nothing to suggest. I also heard that the Saturn II chipset is problematic, but this is the one I use and it is perfectly ok! Advice: Try to negotiate a 1-2 week money back agreement with your supplier, in case the motherboard you get has problems with the use you plan for it.

11.2   SIMM slots

Go for 72-pin only SIMMs for speed: Some (all?) of the mainboards which take 30 pin SIMMs use a 32 bit main memory interface, and will be significantly slower than the Intel based boards which all use a 64 bit or permanently interleaved memory interface. You might want to keep that in mind.

11.3   Praised PCI Pentium motherboard

The P90 Intel motherboard with the Intel Premiere II chipset (aka Plato). Get the latest BIOS which has concatenated NCR SCSI BIOS 3.04.00. Otherwise DOS won't see your SCSI disk(s) if you use a BIOS-less 53c810 based controller. NCR SCSI BIOS exists in the AMI BIOS of the plato after version 1.00.08 (or maybe verion 1.00.06). This BIOS is FLASH upgradeable so you should be able to get the upgrade on a floppy from your supplier. The current version is 1.00.10 and has all early problems fixed.

(Bios files should be available at ftp.demon.co.uk:/pub/ibmpc/intel, but I did not check that myself. the Author.)

11.4   irq-lines

The value in the interrupt line PCI configuration register is usually set manually (for compatability with legacy ISA boards) in the extended CMOS setup screens on a per-slot or per-device basis. Older PCI mainboards also force you to set jumpers for each PCI slot/device which select how PCI INTA and perhaps INTB, INTC, and INTD are mapped to an 8259 IRQ line, Obviously, if these jumpers exist on your board, they must match the settings in the extended CMOS setup. Also note that some boards (notably Viglens) have silkscreens and instruction manuals which disagree with the wiring, and some experimentation may be in order.

11.5   Info about the different NCR 8xx family SCSI chips:

All NCR 8XX Chips are direct connect PCI bus mastering devices, that have no performance difference whether on motherboard or add in option card. All devices comply with PCI 2.0 Specification, and can burst 32 bit data at the full 33 MHz (133Mbytes/Sec)

11.5.1   53C810

53C810 = 8 bit Fast SCSI-2 (10 MB/Sec) Single ended only Requires Integrated Mother board BIOS 100 pin Quad Flat Pack (PQFP) Worlds first PCI SCSI Chip, Volumes make it the most inexpensive.

11.5.2   53C815

53C815 = 8 bit Fast SCSI-2 (10 MB/Sec) Single Ended only Support ROM BIOS interface, which makes it ideal for add-in card Designs. 128 Pin QFP

11.5.3   53C825

53C825 = 8 bit Fast SCSI-2, Single ended or Differential 16 bit Fast SCSI-2 (20 MB/Sec), Single ended or Differetial Also has support for external Rom, making it a good candidate for add in cards. 160 pin QFP Not supported by linux yet. (See section below on news about the 825). Must have devices with wide or differential SCSI to use these features.

11.6   future of 53c8xx

There are 4 new devices planned for announcement late this year and into early next year. Footprint compatible with 810 and 825 with some new features.

All the Chips require a BIOS in DOS/Intel applications. The 810 is the only chip that needs it resident on the motherboard. Latest NCR SCSI BIOS version: 3.04.00 The bios supports disks >1GB for DOS.

11.7   Performance of the 53c810

C't magazine's DOS benchmarks showed that it was significantly faster than the Buslogic BT-946, one user noted a 10-15% performance increase versus an Adaptec 2940, and with a very fast disk it may be 2.5X as fast as an Adaptec 1540.

12   news about NCR53c825 support

Drew Eckhardt stated this would indeed work with the driver included into the newer Linux Kernels, but there would be two trivial changes necessary:

```
Yes, although you have to remove the 3 from inside the brackets
for the pci_chip_ids[] array, and add an 825: to an obvious case
statement.
```

12.1   Frederic POTTER (Frederic.Potter@masi.ibp.fr) about Pentium+NCR+Strap_bug

On some Intel Plato board, the NCR bios doesn't recognize the board, because it needs to see the board as a "secondary SCSI controller", and because on most SCSI board the jumper to select between primary/secondary has been ironed to primary (to spare 1 cent, presumably).

Solution:

```
near the NCR chip, they are 3 via ( kind of holes ) with a strap like
that
              O--O  O

      this mean primary is selected as default setting. For the Plato Intel
      Mainboard, it should be like that

         O  O--O

      The best solution is to get rid of the strap and to put a 2 position
      jumper instead.
```

12.2   PCIprobe in the latest Linux Kernels by Frederic Potter

Frederic Potter has added a PCI-Probe into the latest kernels. If you do a "cat /proc/pci" it should list all your cards. If you own cards which are not properly recogniced, please contact him via mail as "Frederic.Potter@masi.ibp.fr".

See arch/i386/kernel/bios32.c and include/linux/pci.h in the kernel source for more information on PCI-Probe-Stuff.

13   Conclusion

If you have some moneny to put into your machine, you'd be well off with a Pentium90, ASUS-SP4, which is what I use at the moment. If you can afford 32M RAM that would be much better than 16M RAM.

Real soon now the upcoming standard will be the Triton Chipset with support for special SIMMS called EDODRAM, which has cache on the SIMM and does not require any external cache anymore. At the time of writing (29th of March 95) this is fairly new and will evolve a lot, but you could expect more than a 30 percent increase in performance. The PCI Mach64 ATI-GUP-Turbo (not the cheaper GUP-Turbo-Windows) would be a good choice, with 4M RAM you can have truecolor in higher resolutions. It is well supported in the XFree86(tm)-3.1.1, and there are commercial X-Servers available of which I'd recommend Accelerated/X by Roell, which supports the Mach64 very well and fast. For SCSI I'd take the DPT rather than the (much cheaper and very fast) NCR53c810 in case you plan to use SCSI-Tapes a lot. The NCR53c810 driver on Linux does lack disconnect/reconnect support, thus blocking the SCSIbus on operations like "mt rewind", "mt fsf" etc. It bears a performance penalty on tar-operations

If you do not want to spend that much money on computer equipment (e.g.: you are having a life) you might go for an ASUS-SP3-SiS with AMD-DX2/66 or DX4/100. The SPEA V7 Mirage P64 PCI with 2M VRAM would be a good choice, since it uses the Trio64 S3 Chip, which is well supported by XFree86(tm)-3.1.1, quite cheap to buy and fast, too.

Intel Premiere-II (aka Plato) motherboard, and the number-nine GXE64Pro. Since I don't have that much money I'd opt for a 486 on the new ASUS-486-PCI-SP3-G Board with the saturn-chipset rev. 4. and the PCI-ATI-GUP Mach32 with 2M VRAM. I can use x-window in 16bpp or 8bpp (64K colors or 256 colors) in accelerated mode that way. Since the mach64 is not supported yet I would not recommend buying it for the time being. The current linux-kernels seem to have some problems with this ASUS-486-PCI-SP3-g board with PCI-to-Memory-posting enabled, but the system is still very fast when disabling that feature. If you come across a 486-board which works with all PCI-features enabled, please let me know.

Another fine card since XFree86(tm)-3.1 is the fast and cheap et4000/w32-PCI-card.

So whatever mainboard you buy, you should get one with the NCR53c810-SCSI-chip on board. It is unbeatable in its price/speed.

14 Thanks

I want to thank the following people for supporting this document:

- David Lesher (wb8foz@netcom.com) for extensive help with the english language

- Nathanael MAKAREVITCH (nat@nataa.frmug.fr.net) for translating into french

- Jun Morimoto (morimoto@lab.imagica.co.jp) for translating into japanese

- Donald Becker (becker@cesdis.gsfc.nasa.gov) for ethernet-informations

- Drew Eckhardt (drew@kinglear.cs.Colorado.EDU) for SCSI-informations

and many more people adding information mostly by mail and by posts, some of them will be named here:

```
CARSTEN@AWORLD.aworld.de,
dmarples@comms.eee.strathclyde.ac.uk,
drew@kinglear.cs.Colorado.EDU (Working at the PCI-NCR53c810-Driver),
duncan@spd.eee.strathclyde.ac.uk,
fm3@irz.inf.tu-dresden.de,
grif@ucrengr.ucr.edu,
heinrich@zsv.gmd.de,
hm@ix.de (iX-Magazine),
hm@seneca.ix.de,
kebsch.pad@sni.de,
kenf@clark.net,
matthias@penthouse.boerde.de,
ortloff@omega.informatik.uni-dortmund.de,
preberle@cip.informatik.uni-erlangen.de,
rob@me62.lbl.gov,
rsi@netcom.com,
sk001sp@unidui.uni-duisburg.de,
```

```
strauss@dagoba.escape.de,
strauss@dagoba.priconet.de,
hi86@rz.uni-karlsruhe.de,
Ulrich Teichert, Stormweg 24, D-24539 Neumuenster, Germany
Stefan.Dalibor@informatik.uni-erlangen.de,
tldraben@teleport.com
mundkur@eagle.ece.uci.edu,
ooch@jericho.mc.com,
Gert Doering (gert@greenie.muc.de),
James D. Levine (jdl@netcom.com),
Georg von Below (gbelow@pmail.sams.ch),
Jerome Meyers (jeromem@quake.xnet.com),
Angelo Haritsis (ah@doc.ic.ac.uk),
archie@CS.Berkeley.EDU and his friend kenf@clark.net.
```

15   copyright/legalese

(c)opyright 1993,94 by Michael Will - the GPL (Gnu Public License) applies. If you cannot obtain a copy of the GPL I will be happy to send you one.

If you sell this HOWTO on a CD or in a book I would really like to have a copy for reference.

(michaelw@desaster.student.uni-tuebingen.de)

Contact me, either via eMail or call +49-7071-67551.

Trademarks are owned by their owners. There is no warranty on the information in this document.

For german users I am offering tested, pre-installed / preconfigured and supported Linux-PCI-machines. Call me at 07071-67551.

Part XXXIII

Linux PCMCIA HOWTO

Copyright David Hinds, dhinds@allegro.stanford.edu
v1.33, 1995/04/03 05:43:42
This document describes how to install and use PCMCIA Card Services for Linux, and answers some frequently asked questions. The latest version of this document can always be found at cb-iris.stanford.edu in /pub/pcmcia/doc.

Contents

1   General information and hardware requirements

1.1   Introduction

Card Services for Linux is a complete PCMCIA support package. It includes a set of loadable kernel modules that implement a version of the PCMCIA Card Services applications program interface, a set of client drivers for specific cards, and a card manager daemon that can respond to card insertion and removal events, loading and unloading drivers on demand. It supports "hot swapping" of PCMCIA cards, so cards can be inserted and ejected at any time.

This is beta software. It probably contains bugs, and should be used with caution. I'll do my best to fix problems that are reported to me, but if you don't tell me, I may never know. If you use this code, I hope you will send me your experiences, good or bad!

If you have any suggestions for how this document could be improved, please let me know (dhinds@allegro.stanford.edu).

1.2   Copyright notice and disclaimer

Copyright (c) 1995 David A. Hinds

This document may be reproduced or distributed in any form without my prior permission. Parts of this document may be distributed, provided that this copyright message and a pointer to the complete document are included. Specifically, it may be included in commercial distributions without my prior consent. However, I would like to be informed of such usage.

This document may be translated into any language, provided this copyright statement is left intact.

This document is provided "as is", with no explicit or implied warranties. Use the information in this document at your own risk.

1.3   What is the latest version, and where can I get it?

The current release of Card Services is version 2.5.1.

The latest version is always available from cb-iris.stanford.edu in the /pub/pcmcia directory. There will sometimes be several versions here. In that case, the oldest version should be more stable, and newer versions generally contain more experimental code. It is up to you to decide which version is more appropriate, but the CHANGES file will summarize the most important differences.

`cb-iris.stanford.edu` is mirrored at `sunsite.unc.edu` in `/pub/Linux/kernel/pcmcia`. I'll also try to upload major releases to `tsx-11.mit.edu` under `/pub/linux/laptops/pcmcia/drivers` now and then.

1.4   What systems are supported?

This code should run on almost any Linux-capable laptop. All common PCMCIA controllers are supported, including Intel, Cirrus, Vadem, VLSI, and Databook chips. Custom controllers used in IBM and Toshiba laptops are also supported. Several people use the package on desktop systems with PCMCIA card adapters.

The Motorola 6AHC05GA controller used in some Hyundai laptops is not supported.

1.5   What PCMCIA cards are supported?

The current release includes drivers for a variety of ethernet cards, a driver for modem and serial port cards, several SCSI adapter drivers, and a simple memory card driver that should support most SRAM cards and read-only access to Flash cards. The SUPPORTED.CARDS file included with each release of Card Services lists all cards that are known to work in at least one actual system.

The likelihood that a card not on the supported list will work depends on the type of card. Essentially all modems should work with the supplied driver. Some network cards may work if they are OEM versions of supported cards. Other types of IO cards (hard drives, sound cards, etc) will not work until someone writes the appropriate drivers.

1.6   When will card X be supported?

Unfortunately, they don't pay me to write device drivers, so if you'd like to have a driver for your favorite card, you're probably going to have to do some of the work on your own. The SUPPORTED.CARDS file mentions some cards for which driver work is currently in progress. I will try to help where I can.

1.7   Mailing list

I maintain a database and mailing list of Linux PCMCIA users. This is used to announce new releases of the PCMCIA package. If you would like to be included, send me the following:

- Your name and email address
- What kind of laptop are you using?
- What PCMCIA controller is reported by the `probe` command?
- What PCMCIA cards are you using?
- Any special settings you use: compilation options, irq and port settings, `/etc/pcmcia/config` entries, `insmod` options, etc.

2   Compilation, installation, and configuration

2.1   Prerequisites and kernel setup

For the latest version, you will need to have kernel version 1.1.93 or higher, or kernel 1.2.0 or higher. There are no kernel patches specifically for PCMCIA support. You'll also need to have a relatively recent set of module utilities. If your man page for `insmod` describes the `[symbol=value ...]` syntax, your utilities are current enough.

You need to have a complete linux source tree for your kernel, not just an up-to-date kernel image, when you compile the PCMCIA package. The PCMCIA modules contain some references to kernel source files.

Current kernel sources and patches are available from sunsite.unc.edu in /pub/Linux/kernel/v1.1, or from tsx-11.mit.edu in /pub/linux/sources/system/v1.1. Current module utilities can be found in the same places, in the file modules-1.1.87.tgz.

When configuring your kernel, if you plan on using a PCMCIA ethernet card, you should turn on networking support but turn off the normal Linux network card drivers, including the "pocket and portable adapters". The PCMCIA network card drivers are all implemented as loadable modules. All of the PCMCIA net drivers except the 3Com 3c589 driver depend on the 8390.o driver module which is part of the Linux kernel.

If you want to use SLIP, PPP, or PLIP, you do need to either configure your kernel with these enabled, or use the loadable module versions of these drivers. There is an unfortunate deficiency in the kernel config process, in that it is not possible to set configuration options (like SLIP compression) for a loadable module, so it is probably better to just link SLIP into the kernel if you need it.

If you will be using a PCMCIA SCSI adapter, you should enable CONFIG_SCSI when configuring your kernel. Also, enable any top level drivers (SCSI disk, tape, cdrom, generic) that you expect to use. All low-level drivers for particular host adapters should be disabled. There is currently a bad interaction between the SCSI modules and CONFIG_MODVERSIONS, so you will need to disable this option if you plan to use one of these cards.

For recent kernels, you must explicitly do "make modules" followed by "make modules_install" in /usr/src/linux to build the loadable driver modules. They will be installed under /lib/modules.

2.2 Installation

Starting with release 2.4.8, this package includes an X-based card status utility called cardinfo. This utility is based on a public domain user interface toolkit called the Forms Library, which you will need to install before building cardinfo. A binary distribution is on cb-iris.stanford.edu in /pub/pcmcia/extras/bxform-0.61.tgz. There is a small bug in the Makefile: the line that starts with "ln -s" should have "; fi" added to the end.

Unpack the pcmcia-cs-2.5.1.tgz package in a convenient location, like /usr/src.

Make sure the definitions in make.options are consistent with your site setup. Running "make prereq" will check your system configuration to verify that it satisfies all prerequisites for installing PCMCIA support.

Running "make all" followed by "make install" will build and then install the kernel modules and utility programs. Kernel modules are installed under /lib/modules/<version>/pcmcia. The cardmgr and cardctl programs are installed in /sbin. If cardinfo is built, it is installed in /usr/bin/X11.

Configuration files are kept in the /etc/pcmcia directory: do "make install-etc" to set up this directory. If you are installing over an older version, the new config files will be installed with a ".N" suffix – you should replace or update your existing files by hand. Finally, "make install-man" will install man pages for all the loadable modules and programs.

If you don't know what kind of PCMCIA controller chip you have, you can use the probe utility in the cardmgr/ subdirectory to determine this. There are two major types: the Databook TCIC-2 type and the Intel i82365SL-compatible type.

A user-level daemon processes card insertion and removal events. This is called cardmgr. It is similar in function to Barry Jaspan's pcmciad in earlier PCMCIA releases. Cardmgr reads a configuration file describing known PCMCIA cards from /etc/pcmcia/config. This file also specifies what resources can be allocated for use by PCMCIA devices, and may need to be customized for your system. See the pcmcia man page for more information about this file.

The script rc.pcmcia, installed in /etc/rc.d, controls starting up and shutting down the PCMCIA system. "make install-etc" will use the probe command to determine your controller type and modify `rc.pcmcia` appropriately. You should add a line to your system startup file `/etc/rc.d/rc.M` to invoke this:

```
/etc/rc.d/rc.pcmcia start
```

If you are using a PCMCIA ethernet card, you should not try to configure it in `/etc/rc.d/rc.inet1`, since the card may not be present when this script is executed. Comment out everything except the loopback stuff in `rc.inet1` and instead edit the `/etc/pcmcia/network` script to match your local network setup. This script will be executed only when your ethernet card is actually present.

2.3 Site-specific configuration options

Card Services should automatically avoid allocating IO ports and interrupts already in use by other standard devices. This should work for any devices that have Linux drivers, like serial and parallel ports, IDE drives, and some sound cards. If a device is unsupported by Linux, you may need to explicitly exclude the resources it uses in `/etc/pcmcia/config`.

Some PCMCIA controllers have optional features that may or may not be implemented in a particular system. It is generally impossible for a socket driver to detect if these features are implemented. Check the man page for your driver to see what optional features may be enabled.

The low level socket drivers, `tcic` and `i82365`, have numerous bus timing parameters that may need to be adjusted for systems with particularly fast processors. Symptoms of timing problems include lock-ups under heavy loads, high error rates, or poor device performance. Check the corresponding man pages for more details, but here is a brief summary:

- Cirrus controllers have numerous configurable timing parameters. The most important is the `freq_bypass` flag which changes the multiplier for the PCMCIA bus clock to slow down all operations.

- The Cirrus CL6729 PCI controller has the `fast_pci` flag, which should be set if the PCI bus speed is greater than 25 MHz.

- For Vadem VG-468 controllers and Databook TCIC-2 controllers, the `async_clock` flag changes the relative clocking of PCMCIA bus and host bus cycles. Setting this flag adds extra wait states to some operations.

All these options should be configured by modifying the top of `/etc/rc.d/rc.pcmcia`. For example:

```
# Should be either i82365 or tcic
PCIC=i82365
# Put socket driver timing parameters here
OPTS="async_clock=1"
```

On some systems using Cirrus controllers, including the NEC Versa M, the BIOS puts the controller in a special suspended state at system startup time. On these systems, the `probe` command will fail to find any known PCMCIA controller. In this case, edit `/etc/rc.pcmcia` by hand as follows:

```
# Should be either i82365 or tcic
PCIC=i82365
# Put socket driver timing parameters here
OPTS="wakeup=1"
```

2.4   Can I install Linux via NFS with a PCMCIA network card?

I've created a set of 1.44MB boot and root disks with PCMCIA support for the Slackware 2.1 distribution. The files are pcboot14.gz and pcroot14.gz on cb-iris.stanford.edu and sunsite.unc.edu (see section 1.3). The root disk includes cardmgr, the core PCMCIA modules, and all the network drivers. As for how to use these, you should familiarize yourself with the Slackware installation instructions, available from the usual FTP sites. The PCMCIA drivers will be loaded automatically, and installation will be the same as for a non-PCMCIA net card. Note that Slackware root disks do not include any normal user-level network utilities (ftp, telnet, etc). They only include enough network support to establish an NFS mount.

After installation is complete, you'll have a non-PCMCIA setup on your root disk. It is possible to copy things from the boot and root disks to get a working network setup, but it is tricky to put everything in the right places by hand. First, with the boot disk mounted on /mnt, do:

```
cp /mnt/vmlinuz /linuz
rootflags /vmlinuz 1
lilo
```

Then, with the root disk mounted on /mnt, do:

```
cp /mnt/sbin/cardmgr /sbin
(cd /mnt ; tar cf - etc/pcmcia lib/modules) | (cd / ; tar xf -)
```

Edit /etc/pcmcia/config and un-comment the "start" and "stop" commands for the net cards, and edit /etc/pcmcia/network to conform to your network setup.

Alternatively, if your install server has a current set of source files, you can copy current kernel sources, pcmcia sources, and module utilities to your hard disk while it is NFS mounted. Then, after rebooting, build a new kernel and install the PCMCIA software as normal.

2.5   Why doesn't my system respond to card insertions?

In most cases, the socket driver (i82365 or tcic) will automatically probe and select an appropriate interrupt to signal card status changes. The automatic interrupt probe doesn't work on some Intel-compatible controllers, including Cirrus chips and the chips used in some IBM ThinkPads. In these cases, the i82365 driver may pick an interrupt that is used by another device.

With the i82365 driver, the irq_mask option can be used to limit the interrupts that will be tested. This mask limits the set of interrupts that can be used by PCMCIA cards as well as for monitoring card status changes. For the tcic driver, the cs_irq option can be used to explicitly set the interrupt to be used for monitoring card status changes.

If you can't find an interrupt number that works, there is also a polled status mode: both i82365 and tcic will accept a poll_interval=100 option, to poll once per second.

3   Usage and features

3.1   How do I tell if it is working?

The cardmgr daemon normally beeps when a card is inserted, and the tone of the beeps indicates the status of the newly inserted card. Two high beeps indicate the card was identified and configured successfully. A high beep followed by a lower beep indicates that the card was identified, but could not be configured for some reason. One low beep indicates that the card could not be identified.

If you are running X, the new cardinfo utility produces a slick graphical display showing the current status of all PCMCIA sockets.

If the modules are all loaded correctly, the output of the `lsmod` command should look like the following, with no cards inserted:

```
Module:          #pages:  Used by:
ds                  2
i82365              2
pcmcia_core         4      [ds i82365]
```

All the PCMCIA modules and the `cardmgr` daemon send status messages to the system log. This will usually be `/usr/adm/messages`. This file should be the first place you look when tracking down a problem. When submitting a bug report, you should always include the contents of this file. `Cardmgr` also records some current device information for each socket in `/etc/stab`.

3.2 How do I tell `cardmgr` how to identify a new card?

Assuming that your card is supported by an existing driver, all that needs to be done is to add an entry to `/etc/pcmcia/config` to tell `cardmgr` how to identify the card, and which driver(s) need to be linked up to this card. Check the man page for `pcmcia` for more information about the config file format. If you insert an unknown card, `cardmgr` will normally record some identification information in `/usr/adm/messages` that can be used to construct the config entry.

Here is an example of how cardmgr will report an unsupported card in `/usr/adm/messages`.

```
cardmgr[460]: unsupported card in socket 1
cardmgr[460]: version info: "MEGAHERTZ", "XJ2288", "V.34 PCMCIA MODEM"
```

The corresponding entry in `/etc/pcmcia/config` would be:

```
card "Megahertz XJ2288 V.34 Fax Modem"
  version "MEGAHERTZ", "XJ2288", "V.34 PCMCIA MODEM"
  bind "serial_cs"
```

You can use "*" to match strings that don't need to match exactly, like version numbers. When making new config entries, be careful to copy the strings exactly, preserving case and blank spaces. Also be sure that the config entry has the same number of strings as are reported in the log file.

After editing `/etc/pcmcia/config`, you can signal `cardmgr` to reload the file with:

```
kill -HUP `cat /var/run/cardmgr.pid`
```

If you do set up an entry for a new card, please send me a copy so that I can include it in `sample.config`.

3.3 How do I control which interrupts and ports are used by a device?

In theory, it should not really matter which interrupt is allocated to which device, as long as two devices are not configured to use the same interrupt. At the top of `/etc/pcmcia/config` you'll find a place for excluding interrupts that are used by non-PCMCIA devices.

The `ibmcc_cs`, `de650_cs`, `3c589_cs`, and `serial_cs` drivers each have a parameter called `irq_mask` for specifying which interrupts they may try to allocate. Each bit of irq_mask corresponds to one irq line: bit 0 is irq 0, bit 1 is irq 1, and so on. So, a mask of 0x1100 would correspond to irq 8 and irq 12. To limit a driver to use only one specific interrupt, its irq_mask should have only one bit set. These driver options should be set in your `/etc/pcmcia/config` file. For example:

```
device "serial_cs"
  module "serial_cs" opts "irq_mask=0x1100"
    ...
```

would specify that the serial driver should only use irq 8 or irq 12. Note that Card Services will never allocate an interrupt that is already in use by another device, or an interrupt that is excluded in the config file.

There is no way to directly specify the I/O addresses for a PCMCIA card to use. The `/etc/pcmcia/config` file allows you to specify ranges of ports available for use by all PCMCIA devices.

After modifying `/etc/pcmcia/config`, you can restart `cardmgr` with "`kill -HUP`".

3.4　When is it safe to insert or eject a PCMCIA card?

In theory, you can insert and remove PCMCIA cards at any time. However, it is a good idea not to eject a card that is currently being used by an application program. Kernels older than 1.1.77 would often lock up when serial/modem cards were ejected, but this should be fixed now.

3.5　How do I unload PCMCIA drivers?

To unload the entire PCMCIA package, invoke `rc.pcmcia` with:

```
/etc/rc.d/rc.pcmcia stop
```

This script will take several seconds to run, to give all client drivers time to shut down gracefully. If a PCMCIA device is currently in use, the shutdown will fail.

3.6　How does Card Services deal with suspend/resume?

Card Services can be compiled with support for APM (Advanced Power Management) if you've installed this package on your system. The current release of Stephen Rothwell's APM support package is version 0.5. Unlike the 0.4 release, 0.5 does not require a special patch to work with PCMCIA. The PCMCIA modules will automatically be configured for APM if a compatible version is detected on your system.

Without resorting to APM, you can do "`cardctl suspend`" before suspending your laptop, and "`cardctl resume`" after resuming, to properly shut down and restart your PCMCIA cards. This will not work with a PCMCIA modem that is in use, because the serial driver isn't able to save and restore the modem operating parameters.

APM seems to be unstable on some systems. If you experience trouble with APM and PCMCIA on your system, try to narrow down the problem to one package or the other before reporting a bug.

3.7　How do I turn off a PCMCIA card without ejecting it?

Use either the `cardctl` or `cardinfo` command. "`cardctl suspend #`" will suspend one socket, and turn off its power. The corresponding `resume` command will wake up the card in its previous state.

4　Problems with specific cards

4.1　Why doesn't my modem work?

That's a broad question, but here's a quick troubleshooting guide.

- Is your card recognized as a modem? Check `/usr/adm/messages` and make sure that `cardmgr` identifies the card correctly and starts up the `serial_cs` driver. If it doesn't, you may need to add a new entry to your `/etc/pcmcia/config` file so that it will be identified properly. See section 3.2 for details.

- Is the modem configured successfully by serial_cs? Again, check `/usr/adm/messages` and look for messages from the serial_cs driver. If you see "register_serial() failed", you may have an I/O port conflict with another device. Another tip-off of a conflict is if the device is reported to be an 8250; most modern PCMCIA modems should be identified as 16550A UART's. If you think you're seeing a port conflict, edit `/etc/pcmcia/config` and exclude the port range that was allocated for the modem.

- Is there an interrupt conflict? If `/usr/adm/messages` looks good, but the modem just doesn't seem to work, try using `setserial` to change the irq to 0, and see if the modem works. This causes the serial driver to use a slower polled mode instead of using interrupts. If this seems to fix the problem, it is likely that some other device in your system is using the interrupt selected by serial_cs. You should add a line to `/etc/pcmcia/config` to exclude this interrupt.

- Make sure your problem is really a PCMCIA one. It may help to see if the card works under DOS with the vendor's drivers. Also, don't test the card with something complex like SLIP until you are sure you can make simple connections. If simple things work but SLIP does not, your problem is with SLIP, not with PCMCIA.

4.2 Why does my Megahertz modem sometimes fail to work?

Earlier versions of the PCMCIA drivers often failed to properly initialize some Megahertz modems, specifically the 2144 model. This problem should be fixed in current releases.

I've also received one report from someone with a newer Megahertz modem that has a 16550-type UART. He says that he wasn't able to get this modem to work under Linux with cu until he configured the modem with:

```
echo 'ATS=QV1X4\&C1\&D2S95=2W1\&K3S36=7S95=255' > /dev/modem
```

This initialization string was supplied by Megahertz tech support.

4.3 Why doesn't my ethernet card work?

Here's another quick troubleshooting guide.

- Is your card recognized as an ethernet card? Check `/usr/adm/messages` and make sure that cardmgr identifies the card correctly and starts up one of the network drivers. If it doesn't, your card might still be usable if it is compatible with a supported card. This will be most easily done if the card claims to be "NE2000 compatible".

- Is the card configured properly? If you are using a supported card, and it was recognized by cardmgr, but still doesn't work, there might be an interrupt or port conflict with another device. Find out what resources the card is using (from `/usr/adm/messages`), and try excluding these in `/etc/pcmcia/config` to force the card to use something different.

- With Socket EA and 3Com 3c589 cards, you need to pick the transceiver type (10base2, 10baseT, AUI) when the driver module is loaded. Make sure that the transceiver type reported in `/usr/adm/messages` matches your connection.

- The Farallon EtherWave is actually based on the 3Com 3c589, with a special transceiver. Though the EtherWave uses 10baseT-style connections, its transceiver requires that the 3c589 be configured in 10base2 mode.

- Make sure your problem is really a PCMCIA one. It may help to see see if the card works under DOS with the vendor's drivers. Double check your modifications to the `/etc/pcmcia/network` script. Make sure your drop cable, "T" jack, terminator, etc are working.

- If your card seems to be configured properly, but sometimes locks up, particularly under high load, you may need to try changing your socket driver timing parameters. See section 2.3 for more information.

4.4   How do I select the transceiver type for my 3c589 card?

It would be nice if the driver could autodetect the difference between a 10baseT and a 10base2 connection, but I don't know how to do that. For now, you need to edit /etc/pcmcia/config and add an `if_ports=#` option to the `3c589_cs` module definition. Check the `tc589_cs` man page for more details, but to select 10base2 (also known as BNC, or thin net, or coax), change:

```
module "3c589_cs"
```

to:

```
module "3c589_cs" opts "if_port=3"
```

4.5   My network performance stinks. What can I do?

If you have an NE4100 or IBM CCAE adapter, increase the memory access time with the `mem_speed=#` option to the `ibmcc_cs` module definition. Try speeds of up to 1000 (in nanoseconds).

For other cards, you may need to try changing your socket driver timing parameters. Check the man page for your socket driver (`i82365` or `tcic`) to see what parameters are available.

4.6   How do I add support for an NE2000-compatible ethernet card?

First, see if the card is already recognized by `cardmgr`. Some cards not listed in SUPPORTED.CARDS are actually OEM versions of cards that are supported. If you find a card like this, let me know so I can add it to the list.

If it is not recognized, `cardmgr` will normally bind the "memory card" driver to the card. Check your system log to verify this, because you'll need to use this driver. You will also need to know your card's hardware ethernet address. This address is a series of six two-digit hex numbers, often printed on the card itself. If it is not printed on the card, you may be able to use a DOS driver to display the address. In any case, once you know it, run:

```
dd if=/dev/pcmem0a count=20 | od -Ax -t x1
```

and search the output for your address. Record the hex offset of the first byte of the address. Now, edit `modules/de650_cs.c` and find the `hw_info` structure. You'll need to create a new entry for your card. The first field is the offset multiplied by two. The next three fields are the first three bytes of the hardware address. The final field is just a descriptive name.

After editing `de650_cs`, install the new module. Edit /etc/pcmcia/config and create an entry for your card. See section 3.2 for details. And please send me copies of your new `hw_info` and config entries.

4.7   How do I use my PCMCIA floppy interface?

The PCMCIA floppy interface used in the Compaq Aero and a few other laptops is not yet supported by this package. If your laptop can initialize this card before Linux boots, you should be able to use it by telling Card Services to ignore that socket. Note that you will not be able to hot swap this card.

To configure Card Services to ignore a socket, use the `ignore=#` parameter when you load the `i82365` or `tcic` driver. See the man pages for more details.

4.8 What's up with support for Xircom cards?

Xircom does not share technical information about its cards without a non-disclosure agreement. This means that it is not really possible to develop freely distributable drivers for Xircom cards without doing legally dubious things like reverse engineering DOS drivers. Unless their policy changes, it is doubtful that Linux drivers for Xircom products will ever become available.

4.9 What's up with support for SCSI adapters?

The Qlogic FastSCSI and New Media Bus Toaster cards now work under Card Services. As of 1.1.81, the Linux kernel supports loadable SCSI driver modules, but you should try to use the latest available kernel. The PCMCIA driver modules for these cards are built by linking some PCMCIA-specific code (in `qlogic_cs.c` and `toaster_cs.c`) with a normal Linux SCSI driver. The Qlogic PCMCIA driver links with the normal QLogic driver; the Bus Toaster driver links with the Adaptec 152x driver. Pre-1.2.2 kernels require a patch for the Adaptec driver to make it PCMCIA-ready: the patch should be available from all the FTP sites mirroring `cb-iris.stanford.edu`.

The Adaptec SlimSCSI adapter is not currently supported. This card was originally sold under the Trantor name, and is not compatible with any of the existing Adaptec drivers for Linux. I'm not sure how hard it would be to write a driver; I don't think anyone has obtained the technical information from Adaptec.

Be very careful about ejecting a SCSI adapter. Be sure that all associated SCSI devices are unmounted and closed before ejecting the card. For now, all SCSI devices should be powered up before plugging in a SCSI adapter, and should stay connected until after you unplug the adapter and/or power down your laptop.

Roger Pao (`rpao@paonet.org`) adds:

Make sure there is a device capable of supplying termination power both to the terminating target device and to the PCMCIA SCSI card. This is vitally important as most PCMCIA SCSI cards do not supply termination power to its own terminators nor to the SCSI bus. This is usually to save laptop battery power and to isolate the laptop from the SCSI bus.

For a recommendation, the APS SCSI Sentry 2 ($100) is an external Centronics active terminator block (male on one end, female on the other) which uses an external power supply (115/230VAC) to supply termination power (5VDC 2.0A) to its own active terminator and to the PCMCIA SCSI card's terminators (be it active or passive). For more details, APS Technical Support can be reached at 800-334-7550.

5 Debugging tips and programming information

5.1 How can I submit a helpful bug report?

Here are some things that should be included in all bug reports:

- Your system type, and the output of the `probe` command

- What PCMCIA cards you are using

- Your Linux kernel version, and PCMCIA version

- Any changes you've made to the startup files in `/etc/pcmcia`

- Contents of `/usr/adm/messages`, even if you don't see anything that looks interesting.

The `make.options` file includes a few choices for building the kernel modules with various kinds of debugging code turned on. This may or may not be useful, depending on your problem. It is probably better to only turn on the really verbose debugging if I ask you to.

If your problem involves a kernel fault, the register dump from the fault is only useful if you can track down the fault address, EIP. If it is in the main kernel, look up the address in zSystem.map to identify the function at fault. If the fault is in a loadable module, it is a bit harder to trace. With the current module tools, "ksyms -m" will report the base address of each loadable module. Pick the module that contains the EIP address, and subtract its base address from EIP to get an offset inside that module. Then, run gdb on that module, and look up the offset with the list command. This will only work if you've compiled that module with -g to include debugging information.

Send bug reports to dhinds@allegro.stanford.edu. I prefer to handle bug reports by email – please avoid calling me at home or at work.

5.2   Low level PCMCIA debugging aids

The PCMCIA modules contain a lot of conditionally-compiled debugging code. The make.options file shows how to enable this code. A module compiled with PCMCIA_DEBUG set will have a parameter, pc_debug, that controls the verbosity of debugging output. This can be adjusted when the module is loaded, so output can be controlled on a per-module basis without recompiling.

There are a few debugging tools in the debug_tools/ subdirectory of the PCMCIA distribution. The dump_tcic and dump_i365 utilities generate complete register dumps of the PCMCIA controllers, and decode a lot of the register information. They are most useful if you have access to a datasheet for the corresponding controller chip. The dump_tuples utility lists a card's CIS (Card Information Structure), and decodes some of the important bits. And the dump_cisreg utility displays a card's local configuration registers.

The pcmem_cs memory card driver is also sometimes useful for debugging. It can be bound to any PCMCIA card, and does not interfere with other drivers. It can be used to directly access any card's attribute memory or common memory.

5.3   How do I write a Card Services driver for card X?

The Linux PCMCIA Programmer's Guide is the best documentation for the Linux PCMCIA interface. The latest version is always available from cb-iris.stanford.edu in /pub/pcmcia/doc.

For devices that are close relatives of normal ISA devices, you'll probably be able to use parts of existing Linux drivers. In some cases, the biggest stumbling block will be modifying an existing driver so that it can handle adding and removing devices after boot time. Of the current drivers, the memory card driver is the only "self-contained" driver that does not depend on other parts of the Linux kernel to do most of the dirty work.

I've written a skeleton driver with lots of comments that explains a lot of how a driver communicates with Card Services; you'll find this in the PCMCIA source distribution in modules/skeleton.c.

Part XXXIV

Linux PPP HOWTO

Copyright Al Longyear, longyear@netcom.com
v1.10, 15 May 1995
This document contains a list the most Frequently Asked Questions (FAQ) about PPP for Linux (and their answers). It is really *not* a HOWTO, but is in 'classical' Question / Answer form.

1 Preface

Please send any corrections to longyear@netcom.com.

This is but one of the Linux HOWTO/FAQ documents. You can get the HOWTO's from sunsite.unc.edu:/pub/Linux/docs/HOWTO (this is the 'official' place) or via WWW from *the Linux Documentation home page* (http://sunsite.unc.edu/mdw/linux.hmtl). You cannot rely on the HOWTO's being posted to comp.os.linux.answers, as some news feeds have complained about their size.

Throughout this document, I have used the word 'remote' to mean 'the system at the other end of the modem link'. It is also called 'peer' in the PPP documentation. Another name for this is called the 'gateway' when the term is use for routing. Its IP address will show as the 'P-t-P' address if you use ifconfig.

Microsoft is a registered trademark of Microsoft Corporation. Morning Star is a registered trademark of Morning Star Technologies Incorporated. All other products mentioned are trademarks of their respective companies.

2 General information

2.1 What is PPP?

PPP, or Point-to-Point Protocol, is a recognized 'official' internet protocol. It is a protocol used to exchange IP frames (and others) over a serial link. The current RFC for PPP is 1661. There are many related ones.

Contrary to what some people think, it does not mean "Peer to Peer Processing"; although you may do peer-peer communications using TCP/IP over a PPP link.

2.2 My university (company) does not support PPP. Can I use PPP?

In general, no. A 'classical' PPP implementation requires that you make changes to the routes and network devices supported by the operating system. This may mean that you will have to rebuild the kernel for the remote computer.

This is not a job for a general user. If you can convince your administration people that PPP is a 'good thing' then you stand a chance of getting it implemented. If you can't, then you probably can't use PPP.

However, if you are using a system which is supported by the people who are marketing the "TIA" (The Internet Adapter) package, then there is hope. I do not have much information on this package, however, from what I have found, they plan to support PPP in "the next version". (My information may be old. Contact them directly. Information on TIA is available at ftp.marketplace.com in the /pub/tia directory.)

If your system is not supported by TIA and you can't convince the admin group to support PPP then you should use the 'term' package. Some service providers will object to you running 'term'. They have many different reasons, however the most common is 'security concerns'.

There is a version of TIA for Linux.

2.3   Where is PPP?

It is in two parts. The first part is in the kernel. In the kernels from 1.1.13, the driver is part of the network system drivers.

Do not replace the driver in the kernel with a version from the pppd **package!!!**

The second part is the 'daemon' process, pppd. This is a **required** process. The source to it is in the file ppp-2.1.2c.tar.gz located on sunsite.unc.edu in the /pub/Linux/system/Network/serial directory.

For kernels before 1.1.13, the necessary driver is included in the daemon code.

2.4   I just obtained PPP. What do I do with it?

Read The Fine Material available.

Start by reading the README file and then the README.linux file. The documentation sources are listed below.

2.5   Where are additional sources of information for PPP? (Where's the documentation? Is there a HOWTO?, etc.)

There are several sources of information for the PPP protocol as implemented under Linux.

- The README file in the source package.
- The README.linux file in the source package.
- The Net-2-HOWTO document.
- The Network Administration Guide.
- The pppd man page.
- The ppp FAQ document. (This is not it, by the way.)

The HOWTO file is stored in the usual place for the Linux HOWTOs. That is currently on sunsite.unc.edu in the directory /pub/Linux/docs/HOWTO.

The Network Administration Guide is available in the docs/linux-doc-project/nag directory on sunsite. It is published by O'Rielly and Associates. So, if you want a really professional document, then buy a copy from your local bookstore.

The 'man' pages are included in the source package. You will probably have to move them to the normal man directory, /usr/man/man8 before the man command may find them. Alternately, you may use nroff and more to view them directly.

The PPP faq document describes the PPP protocol itself and the various implementations. You will find the FAQ for the usenet news group, comp.protocols.ppp, archived on rtfm.mit.edu in the /usenet directory. It is in eight parts at the present time.

2.6   Where should I post questions about PPP?

The primary usenet group for the PPP implementations is comp.protocols.ppp. Use this group for general questions such as "How do I use pppd?" or "Why doesn't this work?".

Questions such as "Why won't pppd compile?" are generally linux related and belong on the comp.os.linux.networking group.

Please don't use comp.os.linux.help.

2.7 The PPP software doesn't work. HELP!!!

This is one of the most sickening questions. I realize that this is a plea for help. However, it is practically useless to post this message **with no other information**. I, and most others, will only ignore it.

Please see the question regarding errors which normally occur at the modem's disconnection. They are not the cause of a problem, only a symptom. Posting a message with only those errors is also meaningless.

What is needed is the output of the system log (syslog) when you run the pppd program with the option 'debug'. In addition, if you are using chat then please use the '-v' option to run the sequence with verbose output.

Please include the output from the kernel's startup. This shows the various kernel hardware information such as your UART type, PPP version, etc.

Please include all information that you can relating to the problem. However your system configuration, disk drive configuration, terminal type, mouse location and button status, etc. are irrelevant. What is important is the system to which your are trying to contact, the ppp (or terminal server) that they are using, the modem types and speed that you are using, etc.

Take care and go through the output. Remove the references to the telephone number, your account name, and the password. They are not important to analyzing the problem and would pose a security risk to you if you published them to usenet. Also discard the lines which neither come from the kernel nor pppd.

Do **NOT** run the pppd program with the option 'kdebug 7' and post that!

If the problem warrants examining the data stream, then you will be contacted by email and asked to mail the trace. Usenet already costs too much for too many people.

Information is written to various levels. The debug information is written to the debug level. The informational messages are written to the info level. The errors are written to the error level. Please include all levels the the 'local2' group which come from the pppd process.

In addition, please do not delete the time stamp information. It is important.

2.8 How do I use PPP with a system which uses dynamic IP assignments? It assigns a different IP address to me with each call.

The assignment of the local IP address is a function of the options given to pppd and the IPCP protocol. You should use the 'magic' IP address of 0.0.0.0 if you must specify the local IP address. Most people simply leave the local IP address out of the option list.

The other option which is closely tied to this is called 'noipdefault'. The noipdefault option instructs the pppd process to not attempt to guess the local IP address from your hostname and the IP addresses in the /etc/hosts file. Most people use this option when the IP address is dynamically assigned. However, this option does not mean 'use dynamic IP addresses'. The use of dynamic IP addresses is automatic when the local IP address is not given.

2.9 How do I know what IP address was given to me when it is dynamically assigned?

Use the /etc/ppp/ip-up hook. The local IP address is the fourth parameter. This will be executed when pppd knows the IP address for the local system. The fifth parameter is the remote IP address if you should wish to know this value as well.

2.10 Can I use the same local IP address for each line of a PPP server?

Yes. The local address is not significant to the local system. You must have a unique remote IP address. The routing is performed based upon the remote IP address and not the local IP address.

3   Other implementations

3.1   Do you know of a implementation for PPP other than Linux? I would like one for HP-UX, or AIX, or ... (you fill in the blank) ?

Check the PPP FAQ document mentioned above.

AIX is due to be supported in the 2.2 version of the pppd process. HP-UX is, to my knowledge, only supported by the Morning Star commercial package.

If you don't find one listed then post to the `comp.protocols.ppp` group and not the Linux group.

(Please don't mail me asking for "Do you know of a PPP package for ..."? These requests will now be 'appropriately' filed. ;-))

3.2   Did you know that there is a program called 'dp'?

Yes, we know. The dp package was considered very early in the development stage quite a few months back. It is nice. It supports 'demand dial'. It also only works with systems which support streams. This is primarily the SunOS (Solaris) operating systems.

Linux, at the present time, does not supports streams.

There are several other packages for PPP available on the 'net'. The 'portable ppp' package is very much like the TIA code. There is another package called simply 'ppp'. There is code for PPP in the KA9Q package.

Of all of the packages available, the pppd package was the closest to the requirements and functions of Linux to warrant the port.

(If you want more information about these other packages, ask in the `comp.protocols.ppp` group!)

3.3   What RFCs describe the PPP protocol?

The current implementation of PPP is a mixture of several. The major portion of the PPP code is written against the RFCs 1331 and 1332. These RFCs were later obsoleted. 1331 was replaced by 1548 and that, in turn, was obsoleted by 1661 six months later.

Most implementations of PPP will be happy to talk to the Linux PPP code.

A complete list is in the PPP faq.

[to quote the FAQ document]:

> All of 1134, 1171, and 1172 (and 1055, for that matter :-) have been obsoleted. They're interesting only if you want to debug a connection with an ancient PPP implementation, and you're wondering why (e.g.) it asked you for IPCP option 2 with a length of only 4, and Compression-Type 0x0037. (There's a lot of that still running around - be careful out there.)

Linux PPP will not support this.

4   Compatibility

4.1   Can PPP talk to a SLIP interface?

No. SLIP works with SLIP. PPP works with PPP.

Some vendors may offer products which work both as SLIP and PPP. However, they must be configured to run in one mode or the other. There is no present method to determine, based upon the protocol passed at the time of a connection, which combination of SLIP protocols or PPP is being requested.

4.2   Which is better? PPP or SLIP?

IT DEPENDS UPON MANY FACTORS. The people who post this type of question have usually not read the `Net-2-HOWTO` document.

A good technical discussion is available at Morning Star's www server, `www.morningstar.com`.

4.3   Is CHAP or PAP better for authentication?

If you have the choice, use CHAP. Failing that, PAP is better than nothing.

5   Authentication files

5.1   What goes into the `/etc/ppp/pap-secrets` file? Do you have a sample?

The PAP protocol is most often implemented as your user name and password. You need to include the name of the remote system, your account name, and the password. If the user on abbot wishes to call costello, the entry would be similar to the following.

```
#remote     account     password     IP address list
*           abbot       firstbase
```

5.2   What goes into the `/etc/ppp/chap-secrets` file? Do you have a sample?

The most common problem is that people don't recognize that CHAP deals with a pair of secrets. Both computers involved in the link must have both secrets to work.

For example, if abbot wants to talk to costello, then abbot's file would have:

```
#local      remote      secret       IP address list
abbot       costello    firstbase
costello    abbot       who
```

And costello's file would have:

```
#local      remote      secret       IP address list
abbot       costello    firstbase
costello    abbot       who
```

6   Construction problems

6.1   I get compile errors when I try to compile the kernel

With the release of the 1.2 kernel for Linux, the ppp driver is a standard part of the network devices. Each kernel should include the software necessary to make the PPP support within the kernel. Please do not edit the ppp driver. It has been pre-configured for the kernel.

If you are attempting to run ppp on kernels prior to the 1.2, then please consider upgrading the kernel. The 1.0 kernels require patching to support the ppp driver. The 1.2 kernels supported ppp to some degree, but also required changes depending upon the specific patch level.

7 Problems running pppd

7.1 PPPD won't run unless you are root

The pppd process needs to make changes to the networking system and this can only be done if you are the root user. If you wish to run pppd from other than the root user then the pppd program needs to be secured 'suid to root'.

```
chown root pppd
chmod 4755 pppd
```

If you wish to control the pppd access to a select group of people, then make the pppd process owned by the group and do not permit all others to run the program.

7.2 The ppp-2.1.2c package says it needs the 4.6 libraries

Sorry, I goofed. You will have to forego the binaries and re-compile the code yourself. It is easy. Go to the pppd directory, delete the bad binary, and issue the command 'make'. Go to the chat directory and do the same if you want a corrected chat program.

You must have the C language compiler and GNU make installed to rebuild the PPP software.

It turns out that when I compiled the ppp-2.1.2c package, while I used the proper definitions, I used the 4.6 libraries. One of these days, Al may finally get his act together . . . .

Or, you can get binaries from the Slackware 2.0.2 (or later) package. They are in the **ppp.tgz** file in the 'n' series of disks.

Please use the source in the ppp-2.1.2c to compile the code. The source has been corrected over the 'a' package.

7.3 unable to create pid file: no such file or directory

You need to create the directory /var/run. On earlier Slackware distributions, this was a symbolic link to the /etc directory.

This is a warning. The ppp software will work normally in spite of this message. However, the ppp-off script depends upon this file. It is a good idea to create the directory or make the link to the appropriate location.

The posix header, paths.h, defines the location for the pid file under the name "_VAR_RUN". If you wish to use a different directory for PPP and others, change the value for this define and rebuild the software.

7.4 /etc/ppp/options: no such file or directory

You need to create the directory /etc/ppp and have a file called 'options' in that directory. It needs to be readable by the pppd process (root).

The file may be empty. To make an empty file use the 'touch' command.

See the pppd man page, pppd.8, for a description of this file.

7.5 Could not determine local IP address

This happens with many configurations of the Telebit Netblazer. The problem is not the terminal server, but the site which has not configured the terminal server with a set of IP addresses.

The Netblazer does not have your IP address. You do not have your IP address. The link will not work unless both IP addresses are known.

You must have been given a piece of paper with both IP addresses written upon it. You must tell the Netblazer the IP addresses to be used. Use the local IP address and the remote IP address as a parameter to the pppd process.

Use the pppd option format of:

local_ip:remote_ip

(That is the local IP address, a colon, and the remote IP address.)

7.6 Could not determine remote IP address

See the previous answer.

7.7 I keep getting the message to the effect that the magic number is always NAKed. The system will not connect.

There is a one in over four billion chance that the two systems have chosen the same magic number. If you get a continual failure about the magic number, the chances that this is a fluke will geometrically reduce.

The two most common reasons for this failure are:

- The remote ppp software is not running when you think it is. Is the remote system configured to run PPP? Is the ppp process in the expected location? Is the privileges suitable so that you may run it? This would indicate that the shell is doing the local echo of the data. This is the more common reason.

- The modem has disconnected immediately upon making the connection and logging you on to the remote. Most modems are configured to echo the data sent to them and you are seeing the local echo from the modem.

In either case, the Linux system is sending data to the remote which is being fed immediately back into the serial receiver. This is not an acceptable condition. You have what is called a "loop".

7.8 protocol reject for protocol fffb

This usually occurs when you are trying to connect to a Xyplex terminal server. Version 5.1 of the Xyplex terminal server software, according to Xyplex, has numerous problems with PPP. It is strongly recommended that you update the Xyplex software to at least version 5.3.

If you must use version 5.1, then use the pppd option "vj-max-slots 3" to limit the number of slots to three. The problem on the Xyplex server is that it will accept the request for the default 16 slots, but fail to operate beyond the third slot. It should have return a NAK frame with the limit, but it does not.

Alternately, you can disable the Van Jacobson header compression with the option "-vj".

7.9 The PPP software connects, sends quite a few frames, but still does not seem to connect. Why is that?

Examine the system log when you use the "debug" option. (You will need the system log data anyway if you are going to ask for help.) If the trace shows that it is sending the LCP-request frame over and over again and the id number is not incrementing then you are not exchanging frames with the remote PPP software.

Three common reasons for this are:

- You don't have the ppp software running on the other end. You are sending the PPP frames to some other program which is probably saying "What is this #$%ˆ ?" Please make sure that you have the ppp software started on the other end before you enter the ppp protocol sequence. Try to use a normal modem program and go through the logon sequence that you would normally do. Do you see the ppp frames being sent to you?

  The ppp frames are fairly distinctive. They will be about 16 characters in length and contain several { characters. They should not have a carriage return character after them and are sent out in a burst with a pause between the bursts.

- The line is not "eight bit clean". This means that you need to have eight data bits, no parity, and one stop bit. The PPP link absolutely requires eight data bits. The pppd software will automatically put the line into eight data bits, no parity, and one stop bit. The remote must match this configuration or framing and parity errors may occur.

  PPP will escape characters. It is not possible for it to escape bits as kermit does. PPP will *not* work with a seven bit communications link.

  There is a compile option in the ppp.c driver (part of the kernel) called **CHECK_CHARACTERS** which will include additional code in the driver to provide additional checking on the input characters. It will be able to tell you if the parity was enabled or if the remote system always sent the characters as seven bits.

- The remote is configured to require authentication such as PAP or CHAP. You have not configured the local system to use this feature. Therefore, the remote is discarding all of your frames until it sees a valid authentication frame from you. Since you are not configured to generate the frames, the IPCP frames which you send are being ignored. In this case, either configure the remote to not expect authentication or configure the local system to do authentication and supply the proper secrets.

  Examine the receipt of the LCP configure frame. If it shows an 'auth' type, then the remote is configured for authentication.

7.10   I can't connect to the merit network.

Some users of the merit network have indicated that it needs UPAP. Did you try UPAP authentication?

8   DIP

8.1   DIP does not have support for PPP's mode

The current version of dip-uri supports PPP in that it will execute the pppd process when you execute 'mode ppp'. However, there are many options which are needed for the proper operation of pppd. Since dip does not pass these to the program, they must be stored in the /etc/ppp/options file.

The dip program controls the establishment of the SLIP link. It controls the SLIP link with the aid of slattach, ifconfig, and route. These programs may be used to establish a SLIP link. They are not useful for the establishment of a PPP link.

The dip program may be used to dial the telephone and start the ppp software on the remote system. It is best used in this mode as the parameter to the 'connect' option. However, you have the option to use dip to control the link. It is not important how pppd be executed to run the ppp link. It is only important that it be executed as it is a mandatory program for the PPP protocol.

9   Process termination

9.1   Is there a 'dip -k' for PPP?

No. There is no 'dip -k'.

In the chat directory, there is a 'ppp-off' script. This will stop the ppp link in the same manner as the 'dip -k'.

I have included it below. (Cut it out. Store it in its own file. Make the file executable with chmod.)

```
#!/bin/sh
DEVICE=ppp0
#
# If the ppp0 pid file is present then the program is running. Stop it.
if [ -r /var/run/$DEVICE.pid ]; then
        kill -INT 'cat /var/run/$DEVICE.pid'
#
# If the kill did not work then there is no process running for this
# pid. It may also mean that the lock file will be left. You may wish
# to delete the lock file at the same time.
        if [ ! "$?" = "0" ]; then
                rm -f /var/run/$DEVICE.pid
                echo "ERROR: Removed stale pid file"
                exit 1
        fi
#
# Success. Let pppd clean up its own junk.
        echo "PPP link to $DEVICE terminated."
        exit 0
fi
#
# The ppp process is not running for ppp0
echo "ERROR: PPP link is not active on $DEVICE"
exit 1
```

9.2   PPP does not hangup the modem when it terminates

There are several reasons for this.

- Did you use the pppd 'modem' parameter? This parameter controls whether or not the pppd process is to control and honor the signals reflecting the modem status. This parameter is explained in the man page for pppd.

- Do you have the modem presenting the DCD signal and honoring DTR? The Hayes sequence for this is usually "&C1". If you reset the modem during the connection sequence with "ATZ" then ensure that your modem is configured correctly. The DTR signal is generated by the computer and instructs the modem to disconnect. Hayes sequence for this is usually "&D1" or "&D2" with "&D2" being the preferred setting for PPP. Many manufacturers will ignore the DTR condition in their 'factory defaults' setting.

- Did you use a cheap cable which does not pass the DCD signal? Macintosh 'classic' cables are notorious for this problem. That Macintosh does not use this signal.

- For dial-in connections, did you exec the pppd process properly?

The pppd process should be 'exec'ed from the script rather than simply executed. If you attempt to simply run the pppd process then it will be the shell which will receive the SIGHUP hangup signal and not the pppd process. The 'shell' script should have a format similar to the following:

```
#!/bin/sh
exec pppd -detach modem ...
```

10   Data Transfer related issues

10.1   The ftp transfers seems to die when I do a 'put' operation. They will work correctly if I 'get' a file. Why?

Do you have the flow control enabled? Flow control is set by the pppd option `crtscts` for RTS/CTS and `xonxoff` for XON/XOFF. If you don't enable the flow control then you will probably overrun the modem's buffers and this will prove to be disastrous with vj header compression.

10.2   How do I use XON/XOFF for flow control?

The better flow control is CTS/RTS. However, if you can not do the hardware flow control with the signals CTS and RTS, then use XON/XOFF. The following three steps need to be performed.

- You need to specify the pppd option `xonxoff`. This tells the pppd process to configure the serial device for XON/XOFF flow control and to load the two characters into the tty driver.

- You need to specify the XON and XOFF characters in the pppd parameter `asyncmap`. This tells the remote system that is should quote the XON and XOFF characters when it wishes to send them to you. It is normally specified as the pppd parameter '`asyncmap` **a0000**'.

- Of course, don't forget to tell the modem to use XON/XOFF flow control. My `ZyXEL` modem uses a sequence '&R1&H4' to do this.

10.3   The modem seems to always connect at a strange rate. When I use minicom, the modem will always use 14400. However, PPP is using 9600 or 7200 or even 2400. How do I fix this?

Put the desired rate as an option to the pppd process. If you don't put the rate, then pppd process will use whatever rate is set currently at the time. Not all programs will restore all of the parameters to the previous settings properly upon exit. This may lead to strange rates configured for the serial device.

10.4   The ftp transfers seems to be very slow when I do a 'get' operation. The 'put' operation is much faster. Why?

Did you specify the option:

asyncmap 0

when you ran pppd? If you forgot the option, the peer must quote (double) all of the control characters in the range from 00 to 1F (hex). This will result in a statistical loss of about 12.5% in speed for all of the data which you receive.

Did you configure the remote system? If so, did you forget flow control on its modem?

10.5 The proxyarp function fails to find the hardware address.

Use the `ppp-2.1.2c.tar.gz` package. The `pppd` process was erroneously compiled with the 1.1.8 kernel and it used `Net-3` rather than `Net-2` definitions.

Additionally, you should refer to the proxy-ARP mini-HOWTO about the requirements for using proxy-ARP.

11   Routing and other problems

11.1   My route to the remote keeps disappearing! It last for about 3 minutes and then the route just goes away. Help!

This is not a question for PPP.

Hint: **DON'T RUN** `routed`!

11.2   I can reach the remote server, but I can not get anywhere else.

Did you forget the '`defaultroute`' parameter to pppd? This parameter adds a default route into your routing system so that frames to all other IP addresses will be sent to the PPP device.

The PPP software will not replace the default route if you have one already set when you run pppd. This is done to prevent people from destroying their default route to the ethernet routers by accident. A warning message is written to the system log if the defaultroute parameter is not performed for this reason.

11.3   I have a default route and I still can't get anywhere else! Now what?

The problem then is not with the local Linux system. It most likely is routing problem on the remote end.

The remote system is not configured for '`IP forwarding`'. It is an RFC requirement that this option **NOT** be enabled by default. You must enable the option. For Linux systems, you will need to build the kernel and specify that you want IP forwarding/gatewaying.

The remote computers need a route back to you just as you need a route to them. This may be accomplished by one of four methods. Each has advantages and limitations. You need to do one and only one of these.

- Use a host route. At each host on the remote system, add a host route to your Linux IP address with the gateway being the terminal server that you use for your local access. This will work if you have a small number of host systems and a simple network without bridges, routers, gateways, etc.

- Use a network route. Subdivide the remote IP addresses so that your local Linux IP address and the remote terminal server address and the remote terminal server's ethernet address is on the same IP domain. This will work if you have the IP addresses to spare. It will work very well if you have a Class-B IP domain and can afford to put the all of the remote addresses on the same IP domain. Then add a network route on each of the gateways and routers so that any address of the remote network is sent to the terminal server. Most configurations have many hosts but few routers. (At `sii.com`, we have over 300 active host systems with only 3 routers.)

- Use `gated` on all of the gateways and on the terminal server. This will cause the terminal server to broadcast to the gateways that it can accept the frames for your IP address. Since the hosts will have a default route to one of the gateways, the gateways will generate the ICMP re-direct frame and the specific host will automatically add its host route.

- Use proxy ARP on the terminal server. This will only work if your remote IP address is in the same IP domain as one of the domains for the network cards.

There is no clear solution. You must choose one of these.

If your remote router requires to receive RIP frames in order to update the route to your system then you should use the bcastd program on sunsite.unc.edu. This will generate the RIP frames without actually running gated.

11.4   I can not ping my local IP address

You are not able to do this because you wont normally have a route to the address. This is the normal operating environment.

If you wish to ping your own system then use the loopback address of 127.0.0.1.

You may be able to ping the remote address. However, some terminal servers may not allow this as the address may be 'phony' to them. It depends upon their environment.

In general, don't try to ping either address. Choose a third address which is well known to be available on the remote network such as the name server IP address.

While the PPP software will not perform this task, you may add the route table entry yourself once the link has been established. The syntax for the route statement is:

```
route add -host 192.187.163.32 lo
```

where the local IP address is represented as 192.187.163.32 in this example. This will tell the network software to route all frames destined to your local IP address to the loopback adapter. Once you add the appropriate route to the local IP address then you may use this address as the target to IP frames.

You will be responsible for deleting the route when the link goes down.

12   Interactions with other PPP implementations

12.1   I am using a Trumpet (for MSDOS) and the connection simply terminates. Why is this happening?

Trumpet does not like any VJ header compression. Use the pppd option "-vj" to turn it off.

12.2   I am using dp-3.1.2 (with SunOS) and the system will not allow me to use anything but ping, or nslookup. Why is this happening?

There is a bug in the 3.1.2 version of dp. Please get the 3.1.2a or later file from the dp ftp home site harbor.ecn.purdue.ecu. Until you can put the patch into dp, disable the vj header compression.

12.3   I can not connect to/with my Windows NT code (a.k.a. 'Daytona')

Microsoft has chosen to support a non-standard authentication protocol with Windows NT. That is their right to do so provided that they have registered the protocol number with the IANA. (They have.) If the 'accept only Microsoft encrypted authentication' check box is set in the phone book entry, the connection will not complete. This setting mandates that the Daytona system only exchange PPP authentication with another Microsoft PPP implementation.

Linux does not support this authentication protocol.

If you have the option of changing the settings on the Daytona system then go to the Daytona Phone Book settings, advanced, security settings and ensure that the 'Accept any authentication including clear text' box is **checked** and the 'accept only Microsoft encrypted authentication' is **not checked**. The other checkboxes may be checked or not as you see fit.

Then use UPAP on the Linux side. Put your Daytona account name and password into the /etc/ppp/pap-secrets file.

The Microsoft authentication sequence is a UPAP style authentication with their DES encryption algorithm for the passwords. Normal UPAP sends the passwords in clear text. This would violate their C2 security goals.

Versions of the Linux ppp code earlier than 2.1.2c have a flaw in their decoding of the authentication request. They will not work with a Daytona system as they will not negotiate the proper authentication. Please used 2.1.2c or later if you wish to connect to Daytona.

13   Other messages written to the system log

13.1   `Alarm`

This is not a problem. It means that a timer has expired. Timers are a necessary part of the protocol establishment phase.

13.2   `SIGHUP`

The pppd process has received a HUP signal. The HUP signal is generated by the tty software when the remote system has disconnected the modem link. It means that the modem has put the 'telephone receiver back on the hook', or, 'Hung UP' the connection.

The kill program may also be used to send this signal to the pppd process.

The pppd process will terminate the link in an orderly fashion when it receives this signal.

13.3   `SIGINT`

The pppd process has received an INT signal. The INT signal is generated by the console software when you press the Ctrl-C key combination and pppd is the foreground process.

The kill program may also be used to send this signal to the pppd process. In fact, the recommended method to terminate the pppd link is to send the process an INT. See the question relating to "dip -k" for a script which will perform this task.

The pppd process will terminate the link in an orderly fashion when it receives this signal.

13.4   `Unknown protocol (c025) received!.`

The remote wishes to exchange Link Quality Reporting protocol with the Linux system. This protocol is presently not supported. This is not an error. It is merely saying that it has received the request and will tell the remote that "I can't do this now. Don't bother me with this!"

The Morning Star PPP package will always try to do LQR protocol. This is normal.

13.5   **The connection fails with an** `ioctl(TIOCSCTTY)` **error.**

Use the `ppp-2.1.2c.tar.gz` package. This was a bug which was not caught before the 'a' package was released.

13.6 The connection fails with errors "`ioctl(TIOCGETD): I/O error`" or "`ioctl(PPPIOCSINPSIG): I/O error`". What now?

Look at the boot messages when you boot the kernel. If it says "`PPP version 0.1.2`" then you have an old version of the `ppp.c` driver.

If it says "`PPP version 0.2.7`" then you have the current driver, however, it was not built with the same set of defines for the ioctl numbers. Ensure that you have only one file called "`ppp.h`". It should be located in the kernel's `include/linux` directory. Once you have done this, rebuild the kernel and the pppd process.

13.7 Sometimes   the messages "`ioctl(PPPIOCGDEBUG): I/O error`", "`ioctl(TIOCSETD): I/O error`" and "`ioctl(TIOCNXCL): I/O error`" occur. Why?

The remote system has disconnected the telephone. The tty drivers will re-establish the proper tty discipline and these errors are the result of the pppd process trying to do the same thing. These are to be expected.

13.8 My `ifconfig` has strange output for PPP.

Usually the ifconfig program reports information similar to the following:

```
ppp0        Link encap UNSPEC  HWaddr 00-00-00-00-00-00-00 ...
            inet addr 192.76.32.2  P-t-P 129.67.1.65  Mask 255.255.255.0
            UP POINTOPOINT RUNNING  MTU 1500  Metric 1
```

The information is for display purposes only. If you are using a recent 1.2 kernel then update the nettools package with the current one on `sunacm.swan.ac.uk` in the directory `/pub/Linux/networking/nettools`.

13.9 The file `/proc/net/dev` seems to be empty

Did you just issue the command "`ls -l /proc/net`" and are wondering why the size is zero? If so, this is normal. Instead, issue the command:

cat /proc/net/dev

You should not find the file empty. The size is always shown as zero, but that is the 'proc' file system. Don't believe the size. Do the command.

The 'more', 'less', and 'most' programs may not be used to view the file directly. If you wish to use these programs, use it as follows:

cat /proc/net/dev | less

14 Network routing issues (using PPP as a 'cheap' bridge)

14.1 `Slattach` and `ifconfig` don't work like SLIP

Do not use `slattach` and `ifconfig` with PPP. These are used for SLIP. The pppd process does these functions at the appropriate time. These must occur after the LCP and IPCP protocols have been exchanged.

You can not replace pppd with `slattach` and `ifconfig`. Most of the protocol support for PPP is in the pppd process. Only the IP (and IPX when it is completed) processing is in the kernel.

The host route to the remote system will be automatically added by pppd. There is no option to NOT add the route. The pppd process will terminate if the route could not be added.

The default route may or may not be added. This is controlled by the option 'defaultroute'. If you have a default route, it will not be changed.

If you must do routing for an entire network, then put the route command into the /etc/ppp/ip-up script. The parameters to the script are:

```
$0 - name of the script (/etc/ppp/ip-up or /etc/ppp/ip-down)
$1 - name of the network device (such as ppp0)
$2 - name of the tty device (such as /dev/cua0)
$3 - speed of the tty device in Bits Per Second (such as 38400)
$4 - the local IP address in dotted decimal notation
$5 - the remote IP address in dotted decimal notation
```

14.2 I want the route to the network and not the route to the host.

On sunsite there is a package called devinfo.tar.gz. It contains some useful little programs which will extract the data from the device and to do various things with the dotted IP addresses.

The documentation is in the man pages in the file.

For example, if you want to route the entire IP domain to the remote, the following may be used in /etc/ppp/ip-up.

Of course, if the values are not variable, then simply use the appropriate entry in the route command.

```
# Obtain the netmask for the ppp0 (or whatever) device
NETMASK = 'devinfo -d $1 -t mask'

# Obtain the IP domain (without the host address by removing the extra bits)
DOMAIN = 'netmath -a $5 $NETMASK'

# Do the network route now that the IP domain is known
route -net add $DOMAIN gw $5
```

15 Other features and protocols

15.1 What about support for 'demand dial'

Use the **diald** package. This is on sunsite in the same directory as the ppp source, /pub/Linux/system/Network/serial.

15.2 What about 'filtering'

There are no plans to put filtering into the PPP code. Run the ipfirewall code. It is on sunsite. Help the author debug that code. It will do the filtering that you want in a general solution.

The latest development kernels will include the patches to support filtering. (You will still need the ipfirewall code as the kernel only contains the patches which were in the ipfirewall code for the kernel.) Again, filtering is a network issue and not one specifically for PPP.

15.3 How about IPX?

The addition of support for IPX is fairly straight forward. Work is underway to include the IPX protocol.

15.4　How about NETBIOS?

There is a netbios PPP protocol. However, your better solution would be to use TCP/IP and the 'samba' code.

Microsoft and others have used Netbios PPP protocol.

The nbfcp protocol is a public document and available from several sources. The Netbios protocol is not a valid address family at the present time for Linux. Until Linux supports the protocol, there is little need to support Netbios over PPP for Linux.

15.5　I need ISDN support. Is there any?

ISDN support revolves around having a working ISDN driver. The present design of the ppp driver does not lend itself well to the concept of a block of data being received. This is being changed. A driver for the Sonix interface is being developed.

15.6　How about just standard synchronous PPP?

There are small changes needed to support a serial interface which uses synchronous communications. The redesign of the ppp driver will help with this function as well. Kate Marika Alhola has expressed an intrest in writing such a synchronous driver for her hardware. You should contact her at kate@digiw.fi for further information.

16　Miscellaneous

16.1　Do you have a PPP compatible mail reader?

Huh? You have the wrong group if you want MSDOS. PPP has nothing to do with the mail user agent. All of the mail agents are compatible with PPP.

16.2　How about a news reader?

Refer to the previous answer.

Part XXXIV Linux Printing HOWTO guide

Grant Taylor <gtaylor@cs.tufts.edu>
Brian McCauley <B.A.McCauley@bham.ac.uk>

Table of Contents

1 Intro

This is the Printing HOWTO for Linux. This is a member of the second generation of Linux FAQs. The original Linux FAQ gradually became a monolithic beast, and has now been re-written in a new syle, refering to HOWTOs for details. This HOWTO details how to properly set up most types of printers, how to configure software to make them print well, what types of fax software are available, and how to preview many types of printable output. It was originally written by Grant Taylor <gtaylor@cs.tufts.edu> and later incorporated the lpd-FAQ by Brian McCauley <B.A.McCauley@bham.ac.uk>. Other HOWTOs detail networking, kernel hacking, etc. All HOWTOs are found in several places, the official location being:
sunsite.unc.edu:/pub/Linux/docs/HOWTO

Like just about any usenet FAQs they can also be found on rtfm.mit.edu.

Please send comments, bug reports, etc, to <printing@god.ext.tufts.edu>. This address goes to both Brian and Grant.

If you know anything or can point us towards any useful programs not in this document that should be, please let us know!

Grant has a mail server set up on his machine. It stores documents and other things related to printing and previewing with Linux, including the latest and greatest version of this document. At some point in the future this will probably be superceded by our own directory on one of the major ftp servers. Mail to <listserv@god.ext.tufts.edu> with a body of 'info' will have you sent a list of available files. A body of 'get file1 [file2 file3...]' will send you specific files.

Summary of changes

Now in texinfo! Available from sunsite in texinfo, dvi and text forms. The info form may be read in emacs but less you are a real emacsphile or don't have X then you'd probably be better off using tkinfo.

tkinfo is available by anonymous ftp from: ptolemy.eecs.berkeley.edu:pub/misc
harbor.ecn.purdue.edu:pub/tcl/code

The ptolemy site will always have the latest version.

New mailserver info.

Much dead-wood removed.

Attributions on individual sections do not appear in the final version although they do in the texinfo source.

Assorted little changes

Incorporated Karl Auer's <Karl.Auer@anu.edu.au> document. This is still not seamless so you'll likely find some duplication and missing cross references - please let us know.

2 Printing software

These sections describe printing software known to be available for Linux. Note that most Un*x printing software can be easily compiled under Linux.

2.1 text

Under Linux, or under most any Un*x operating system, the easiest thing to print with most printers is plain ASCII. Any way you can arrange to send the text to the printer is perfectly valid. If you have a serial printer, then try devices /dev/ttyS?, /dev/ttys?, /dev/cua?, etc, and if you have a regular parallel hookup, use /dev/lp?. Typing 'cat *file* >/dev/????' should do it. You may need root privileges, or you may wish to chmod your printer device if this is all you ever print. (Note the security hole there if you've more than one user) Some printers (ie, HP DeskJet) want dos-style end of lines: newline+carriage return. These printers will show the 'staircase effect'. See Section 3.11 [The staircase effect], page 1334.

2.2 pr

Most plain ascii files in the un*x world have a tendency to be just that - plain, unformatted ascii with no page breaks or anything else to make a printed copy look nice and not have lines printed over perforations. The answer to this problem is to run your text through a formatter such as pr. Pr is a standard un*x utility designed to format plain text for printing on a line printer. The usual appearance of the resulting formatted text has a header and/or footer, page numbers, the date, possibly margins, double spacing, etc. As is common with un*x utils, pr has a bazillion options. They are detailed in the man page.

2.3 PostScript

Printing almost anything other than plain text under Un*x usually involves the ability to print PostScript. If you have a PostScript printer, you're all set. But for most, this is not so easy.

The established way to interpret PostScript under Linux is to use ghostscript, which, like nearly everything else, comes from the GNU project. Ghostscript is a PostScript interpreter which accepts PostScript input and generates output appropriate for X displays, most printers, some specialized display hardware, and fax software.

The following devices are available as of ghostscript 2.6.1pl4:

```
          linux    PC vga using linux svgalib
    #     x11      X Windows version 11, release >=4    [Unix and VMS only]
    # Printers:
    # *     appledmp  Apple Dot Matrix Printer (Imagewriter)
```

```
#        bj10e    Canon BubbleJet BJ10e
# *      bj200    Canon BubbleJet BJ200
# *      cdeskjet  H-P DeskJet 500C with 1 bit/pixel color
# *      cdjcolor  H-P DeskJet 500C with 24 bit/pixel color and
#                  high-quality color (Floyd-Steinberg) dithering
# *      cdjmono  H-P DeskJet 500C printing black only
# *      cdj500   H-P DeskJet 500C (same as cdjcolor)
# *      cdj550   H-P DeskJet 550C
# *      declj250  alternate DEC LJ250 driver
# +      deskjet  H-P DeskJet and DeskJet Plus
# *      dfaxhigh  DigiBoard, Inc.'s DigiFAX software format
# *      dfaxlow  DigiFAX low (normal) resolution
#        djet500  H-P DeskJet 500
# *      djet500c  H-P DeskJet 500C
#        epson    Epson-compatible dot matrix printers (9- or 24-pin)
# +      eps9high  Epson-compatible 9-pin, interleaved lines
#                  (triple resolution)
# *      epsonc   Epson LQ-2550 and Fujitsu 3400/2400/1200 color printers
# *      escp2    Epson ESC/P 2 language printers, including Stylus 800
# +      ibmpro   IBM 9-pin Proprinter
# *      jetp3852  IBM Jetprinter ink-jet color printer (Model #3852)
# +      laserjet  H-P LaserJet
# *      la50     DEC LA50 printer
# *      la75     DEC LA75 printer
# *      lbp8     Canon LBP-8II laser printer
# *      ln03     DEC LN03 printer
# *      lj250    DEC LJ250 Companion color printer
# +      ljet2p   H-P LaserJet IId/IIp/III* with TIFF compression
# +      ljet3    H-P LaserJet III* with Delta Row compression
# +      ljet4    H-P LaserJet 4 (defaults to 600 dpi)
# +      ljetplus  H-P LaserJet Plus
# *      m8510    C.Itoh M8510 printer
# *      necp6    NEC P6/P6+/P60 printers at 360 x 360 DPI resolution
# *      nwp533   Sony Microsystems NWP533 laser printer   [Sony only]
# *      oki182   Okidata MicroLine 182
#        paintjet  H-P PaintJet color printer
# *      pj       alternate PaintJet XL driver
# *      pjxl     H-P PaintJet XL color printer
# *      pjxl300  H-P PaintJet XL300 color printer
# *      r4081    Ricoh 4081 laser printer
# *      sparc    SPARCprinter
# *      t4693d2  Tektronix 4693d color printer, 2 bits per R/G/B component
# *      t4693d4  Tektronix 4693d color printer, 4 bits per R/G/B component
# *      t4693d8  Tektronix 4693d color printer, 8 bits per R/G/B component
# *      tek4696  Tektronix 4695/4696 inkjet plotter
#%*      trufax   TruFax facsimile driver   [Unix only]
# File formats and others:
#        bit      A plain "bit bucket" device
#        bmpmono  Monochrome MS Windows .BMP file format
#        bmp16    4-bit (EGA/VGA) .BMP file format
#        bmp256   8-bit (256-color) .BMP file format
#        bmp16m   24-bit .BMP file format
#        gifmono  Monochrome GIF file format
#        gif8     8-bit color GIF file format
#        pcxmono  Monochrome PCX file format
#        pcxgray  8-bit gray scale PCX file format
#        pcx16    Older color PCX file format (EGA/VGA, 16-color)
```

```
#        pcx256   Newer color PCX file format (256-color)
#        pbm      Portable Bitmap (plain format)
#        pbmraw   Portable Bitmap (raw format)
#        pgm      Portable Graymap (plain format)
#        pgmraw   Portable Graymap (raw format)
#        ppm      Portable Pixmap (plain format)
#        ppmraw   Portable Pixmap (raw format)
# *      tiffg3   TIFF/F (G3 fax)
```

Lines beginning with a '#' are drivers included with the gs261 source distribution.

Drivers marked with '%' require commercial software to work

Installations of ghostscript are available from several places:

A full, and presumably correct, installation comes with most distributions. Note that this binary installation may require libX.so.???, as it includes the X11 display driver.

The "official" installation is to obtain the sources and build it yourself:

```
prep.ai.mit.edu:/pub/gnu/ghostscript-xxxx.tar.gz
prep.ai.mit.edu:/pub/gnu/ghostscript-fonts-xxxx.tar.gz
```

This is probably best, as you can get the latest version (currently 2.6.1pl4 (the four patches are separate, they are available from my mail-server as gs261-patches)).

A patch which uses the Linux svgalib, and hence does not require X for previewing is available. See Section 4.6 [non-X previewing], page 1350.

A minimal binary installation of ghostscript and several other packages needed for printing the Linux documentation is available as:
sunsite.unc.edu:/pub/Linux/apps/tex/texmin/texmin-0.1.tar.z.

Note that this does not contain any PostScript fonts. (Nor do you need them to print dvi (aka [La]TEX).)

The main Ghostscript documentation is contained in the file use.doc, either in the source directory, or lib/ghostscript/doc/use.doc if you haven't the sources.

To print ps, first determine your driver name with 'gs -help' which lists installed drivers. If the device you need is not listed, you must compile gs yourself from the source distribution (do not panic. Do follow the instructions in make.doc. You will need 5 or 6 megs of space to build it in.) Then type 'gs -dNOPAUSE -sDEVICE=?????? -sOutputFile=/dev/???? file.ps' and your output should (hopefully) appear at your printer. Those of you with non-US paper sizes may wish to build gs yourself with the right default, or you may use the '-sPAPERSIZE=a4' option.

Ghostscript may be used to print at most of the resolutions your printer supports; '-r300', '-r150', '-r360x180' are examples of the option used to control this. Dot matrix printers in particular need to choose an appropriate resolution, since they do not typically run at the more standard 300dpi. Note that versions 2.6 and greater of ghostscript have more drivers.

2.4 fonts

(This section contains font information not specific to any ghostscript driver, nor even specific to ghostscript). Font information pertaining to the X11 gs drivers (and thus to ghostview) is included in the ghostview section under previewing)

All versions of ghostscript come with assorted public-domain fonts, most of which were generated from bitmaps, and are therefore of relatively poor quality. However, ghostscript can use any PostScript Type 1 or 3 fonts you may have handy. For example, the Adobe Type Manager (for any platform other than mac) comes with fonts you can use. Place the fonts (typically *.pc?) in lib/ghostscript/fonts/ and add to lib/ghostscript/Fontmap lines such as:

```
/Courier    (com_____.pfb) ;
```

A full fontmap file for the ususal set of fonts included with the Adobe Type Manager is available as 'fontmap.atm' from the printing mailserver.

TimesNewRomanPS and ArialMT fonts are interchangable with Times Roman and Helvetica, so you can alias them this way if this is what you have.

Adobe Type 1 fonts may be found on the net in several places:

```
ftp.cica.indiana.edu:/pub/pc/win3/fonts
archive.umich.edu:/msdos/mswindows/fonts
```

I have not looked in these places, but this information is lifted straight from the comp.fonts FAQ (which you should read if fonts are a thing for you. You can get a copy of this from rtfm.mit.edu).

Conversion between various font types is tricky. Ghostscript comes with the tools needed to take a bitmap (hopefully large) and make a scalable ps font. Groff comes with the tools to allow use of tfm/mf (TeX) and pfb (Type 1) fonts in *roff documents. X11R5 includes several font utilities and Type 1 rendering code contributed by IBM. I have used none of the above, but they all come with manpages, so read them. Other font conversion utilities are listed in the comp.fonts FAQ. Also look into the package fontutils on prep.ai.mit.edu:/pub/gnu/.

2.5 faxing

If you have a fax modem, you can arrage to fax things out (and in), including PostScript, dvi, ascii, etc... Arranging for e-mail to fax itself somewhere is also straightforward.

Fax modems support one of of two cammand sets: Class 1 or 2. Class one modems are have less of what goes on in a fax supported in firmware (thus the software has to do more. Supporting such timing-critical things under a preemptive multitasking environment like Linux is tricky at best). The class 1 standard is EIA 578. Class 2 modems tend to be more expensive and comply with the standard EIA 592. Mention of your fax modem's level of support should be in its manuals. Do not confuse class and group. You will, of course, want a group III fax modem.

Fax software which runs under Linux must convert input in whatever format into a Group III compatible image format for transmission. As usual, Ghostscript does the job. The device tiffg3 generates standard g3/tiff encoded fax messages. You must compile this device in if it is not there already; this is yet another reason to get the source. Some fax sofware on commercial platforms can use the display PostScript renderer to render the fax image; this is not yet an option under Linux.

The GNU program netfax supports Class 2 fax modems only. It builds nearly out of the box under linux. I have patches for version 3.2.1; you can get them from the printing mail server as 'netfaxpatch'. It runs a server and accepts jobs into a queue from the local machine and the net. Netfax is in use at MIT. It accepts PostScript, dvi, and ascii, and can be configured to work as an email gate. Documentation in the package is limited to compile notes and man pages for the individual programs; actual installation tips are few and far between.
```
prep.ai.mit.edu:/pub/gnu/fax-3.2.1.tar.gz
```

FlexFax is available from:
```
sgi.com(192.48.153.1):/sgi/fax/?????.src.tar.Z
```

It is written in C++, and thus requires g++ to build. FlexFax supports class 1 and 2 modems, uses ghostview (or a display PostScript server) for rendering, and generally is more complete, or at least general than the somewhat MIT-specific netfax. It also can run in place of getty and either receive a fax or spawn a login as appropriate for the type of call. It includes precise instructions on configuring smail3, sendmail, and other mail agents to send mail for so-and-so@12345678.fax to the fax at 12345678. This is the package I recommend if you have real faxing needs, as it is properly documented and full-featured. Version 2.x of FlexFax is in real release now and fully supports Linux - just type './configure' and 'make'.

mgetty+sendfax is a Linux and SCO-specific getty for faxmodems and a simple sendfax program. This package is available as sunsite.unc.edu:/pub/Linux/system/Serial/mgetty+sendfax-0.16.tar.gz. This is a good package for those who need to send a fax every now and then.

Finally, efax deserves mention. Class 2 only. no net, no mail, just send a tiff. Efax is available as:
```
sunsite.unc.edu:/pub/Linux/apps/comm/efax05.tar.gz
```

2.6 *roff, man pages

Man pages can sometimes be printed straight from the cat pages (in lieu of the normal nroff source pages) as though they were a normal text file (which they mostly are). However, many printers do not like the control characters for highlighting and what not that is imbedded in these. A filter for this purpose comes with the net-2 lpd package.

If you have the nroff source to the page (the finding of which I highly recommend) you can say 'man -t foobar | lpr' and your man program will (hopefully) format the man page using groff into PostScript, which will then be sent to your lpd and on to the printer. This form of man page output looks MUCH better than the plain ASCII version. Unfortunately, this depends very much on which man program and what supporting software you have installed. If your man doesn't do this, you might try the perl version of man, available near:
sunsite.unc.edu:/pub/Linux/system/Manual-pagers/

It is written entirely in perl, and is thus easily customizable (perl being an interpreted language reminiscent of C and sh).

You can also find the nroff source file in the man directories (most versions of man have an option to just spit out the filename) and do it yourself, into any format supported by groff.

```
groff -mandoc -Ttype foobar.1 | lpr
```

Where **type** is one of ascii, dvi, ps, X100, X75, latin8.

2.7 Printing text via PostScript

There are a number of utilities to allow text to be printed to a PostScript device.

2.7.1 mpage

The package mpage converts plain text into PostScript and/or prints more than one page onto each peice of paper given PostScript or text. It is available at (or at least near):
wuarchive.wustl.edu:/pub/mirrors/unix-c/PostScript/mpage.tar-z

Note that wuarchive uses the '-z' suffix to mean '.Z', ie, compress, not gzip or freeze. 'man -t foobar | mpage' will send a 2-up (depending on the environment variable MPAGE) version of the man page to lpr and its PostScript interpreter. This saves paper and speeds up printing.

2.7.2 a2ps

A2ps will take ASCII and turn it into a nice PostScript document with headers and footers and page numbers, printed two pages on one (or otherwise, if you say so). A2ps does a very nice job at this. It is available at the same place mpage is. Not that if you have a deskjet, many n-up programs will run into trouble by trying to print in that last half-inch.

2.7.3 enscript

Enscript is a program which does basically the same thing as a2ps. I do not know where to get it. It comes with most commercial Un*ces.

A clone version of enscript is called nenscript, available on sunsite.unc.edu as:
/pub/Linux/system/Printing/nenscript-1.13++.bin.tar.z
/pub/Linux/system/Printing/nenscript-1.13++.tar.z

2.7.4 gslp

Gslp is one of the uilities which comes with ghostscript 2.6.x and purports to do the same ascii ⇒ ps conversion as enscript and a2ps. I have not used it, but the docs say that

```
gs -q -sDEVICE=????? -dNOPAUSE -- gslp.ps text.file [options]
```

should do the trick. (gslp.ps is the actual program, which is written in PostScript. Here it is run with the argument *text.file*. PostScript is in many respects a programming language more than a mere printer command language.) Further documentation is in the file 'gslp.ps'. There is a script file which does the above for you.

2.8 PostScript utilities

Those of you who deal with large amounts of PostScript may wish for more utility programs. There are probably millions of little programs which do things to your PostScript. A representative package of them may be found in:
achilles.doc.ic.ac.uk:/tex/inter/psutils/
ftp.cs.psu.edu:/pub/src/psutil.tar.gz

These handle page selection, double-sided printing, booklet creation, etc. Most large ftp sites (eg, wuarchive.wustl.edu, ftp.uu.uunet) will have many such packages to choose from.

2.9 TEX/dvi

[La]TEX is the text formatting package used by many in the academic world and elsewhere. TEX works much like any other compiler – source code is run through the program `tex` to become a `.dvi` file (analogous to an .o object file in C) which can be further manipulated to produce printed output (a "binary"). This manipulation of a dvi (DeVice Independant) file usually takes a little bit of doing. It is well worth it; TEX's output is of professional quality.

If all you are given is a file with a `.tex` ending, try either '`tex file.tex`' or '`latex file.tex`'. One of these is bound to work. Then you have a dvi. (You may have to run it twice for indexing)

For those in the real world who cannot afford a dvi understanding printer, it is usually necessary to convert the dvi something the printer understands. These programs may be run manualy but are often built into lpd filters. See Section 3.24 [Writing lpd filters], page 1341.

2.9.1 `dvips`

`dvips` converts dvi into PostScript that you can pipe into ghostscript or send to a PostScript printer. Most installations come with functioning installations of both TEX and `dvips`. Typing '`dvips -f1 file.dvi | lpr`' will do it. `dvips` responds to either command line arguments or a file `/usr/TeX/lib/tex/ps/config.ps` (in the usual TEX layout, at least) in which you can arrange to have dvips automatically send its output to `lpr`. Thus '`dvips file.dvi`' will do everything that needs to be done.

Note that some `.dvi`'s may include PostScript graphics in the `dvips` stage rather than the TEX stage of the game; if they are not found, you will get a hole instead of a picture. This follows naturally from the object file analogy above. Usually, pre-made documentation in this form has a makefile or script to do everything for you. The LILO documentation is an example of this.

`dvips` has several interesting options; for example, '`dvips -r1 file.dvi`' will print it out backwards. We deskjet users love this one.

2.9.2 `eps`

Eps is a program which converts dvi files directly into the standard Epson printer language; thus it is a dvi driver for epsons. I beleive it supports MakeTeXPK, the automatic font rendering system used by many dvi drivers, and is available as:
```
sunsite.unc.edu:/pub/Linux/apps/tex/eps-061.tar.gz
ftp.ctd.comsat.com:/pub/
```

Note that it is still coming out with new versions fairly often, so there may be a newer version than 061.

2.9.3 `dvilj`

For LaserJet owners, there is a separate program that will take dvi and convert it directly into your printer's language (PCL). It is called dvilj2p or dvilj, and if not on tsx or sunsite, is certainly available on ftp.uu.net.

(Description by Nils Rennebarth)

Its a nice driver, but a little out of fashion in the sense that configuration (especially of font-paths) font-paths is not very flexible and that it doesn't support virtual fonts (at least the version 0.51 not). The biggest advantage over the dvips/ghostscript combo is that it uses downloadable fonts which:

reduces data transmission to the printer drastically, which makes the printer usable even on a serial line.

reduces printer-memory-requirements drastically. A standard Laserjet with 512k memory is able to print almost every TeX-document.

It has support for double side printing and most options you expect a driver to have. It compiles cleanly and worked flawlessly on our diverse hardware here.

2.10 texinfo

This is the native documentation format of the GNU project. Emacs can be coerced into producing an info file from TeXinfo, and TeX can produce nice printed documentation from the same file. It is a bit of a stretch for both systems, but it works. It is really just TeX source which expects the macro file `texinfo.tex` to be installed on your system. Just do '`tex` *filename*' twice (for index generation purposes), and you end up with a plain dvi file, to print or preview at your leisure.

In Emacs, you can also do `M-x texinfo-format-buffer` to convert the texinfo file into an info file viewable with Emacs `M-x info` or an info viewer of your choice.

There are also separate programs which read and format info from a texinfo file. These are available in: `prep.ai.mit.edu:/pub/gnu/`

2.11 Printing though a terminal

Many terminals and terminal emulators support the connection of a printer. The computer the terminal is conected to may then use a standard set of escape sequences to operate this printer. DEC VT's and most other ANSI terminals should offer this capability.

A simple shell script will enable you to print a text file using the printer connected to your terminal:

```
#!/bin/csh -f
# Transparent printing on a vt100-compatible terminal.
echo -n \[5i ; cat $* ; echo -n \[4i
```

If this script is called `vtprint`, then 'vtprint [*filename* [*filename*]]' will print file(s) (or stdin if no file were specified) on your printer.

2.12 hardware and drivers

There are two ways the kernel driver may be used to run the parallel ports. One, the original, is the polling driver. The other is the interrupt driver. In principle, the interrupt driver only deals with the port when it gets an interrupt and should therefore be more efficient. In practice, people have found that it depends on the machine. It probably doesn't make too much difference in most situations.

For the polling driver, you may adjust its polling frequency with the program tunelp without kernel twiddling. The actual driver is in the kernel source file `lp.c`.

To choose the interrupt driver rather than the polled, use the program tunelp to set it. (tunelp is available on sunsite, or from the printing mail server.) Just put the appropriate line in `/etc/rc.local`

Seven is the usual "LPT1:" IRQ, 5 is usual for "LPT2:" for an AT class machine. Note that if your printer is on lp0, the interrupt driver will probably not work. The first parameter should already contain the correct i/o base address. Many bios boot screens have this information if you need it.

DOS uses a polling driver so if you find that your printer works in DOS but not in Linux then you should try the polling driver.

`tunelp` is available from the printing mail server or:
`sunsite.unc.edu:/pub/Linux/system/Printing/tunelp-1.0.tar.z`

2.13 Printer device names

On an XT bus system LPT1: becomes /dev/lp0 (major=6, minor=0), on an AT LPT1: becomes /dev/lp1 (major=6, minor=1). To be more precise:

```
Name Major Minor I/O address
 lp0    6     0      0x3bc
 lp1    6     1      0x378
 lp2    6     2      0x278
```

For a serial printer use the /dev/ttyS? (or /devttys?, if you follow that scheme) device, not the /dev/cua? device. The /dev/ttyS? devices have major 4; the /dev/cua? devices have major 5.

3 LPR

This chapter used to the the `lpd-FAQ` then it became part of the `Linux-FAQ` and now it is part of the Printing-HOWTO. Who knows where it will go next?

3.1 Setting up print services

This section was originally writen Karl Auer <Karl.Auer@anu.oedu.au> 1/11/93 and has now been included here because it was felt that the Printing-HOWTO, being written in the style of a reference manual, was not doing its job properly, since it did not describe in a straightforward way what you need to do to set up print services on your Linux machine.

So far it has been included with little modification and may replicate or even contradict information elsewhere in the HOWTO. The overview it gives should nevertheless be very useful to those new to bsd print spooling.

3.1.1 Remote Printing Vs. Local Printing

Remote printing is allowing people to send print jobs to your computer from another computer. This will be needed if, for example, you are running as a server in a network, or if a printer attached to your machine is to be accessible from other Unix hosts.

Local printing is allowing users on your machine to send print jobs to a printer attached to your machine.

There is a third combination too - your own use of remote printing on other Unix machines. That is, where you wish to print on a printer that is not attached to your own computer.

3.1.2 What You Need

This document assumes you know how to edit a text file under Linux, and that you have a basic understanding of file ownership and permissions.

It also assumes that you have your Linux system set up and running correctly. In particular, if you are going to use remote printing your networking subsystems must be installed and operating correctly.

Check out the man pages on the commands `chmod` and `chown` for more information.

3.1.3 How Printing Works Under Linux

The simplest way to print under Unix (and thus under Linux) is to send the print data directly to the printer device. This command will send a directory listing to the first parallel printer (LPT1: in DOS terms):

```
ls > /dev/lp0
```

This method does not take advantage of the multitasking capabilities of Linux, because the time taken for this command to finish will be however long it takes the printer to actually physically print the data. On a slow printer, or a printer which is deselected or disconnected, this could be a long time.

A better method is to spool the data. That is, to collect the print data into a file, then start up a background process to send the data to the printer.

This is essentially how Linux works. For each printer, a spool area is defined. Data for the printer is collected in the spool area, one file per print job. A background process (called the printer daemon) constantly scans the spool areas for new files to print. When one appears, the data is sent to the appropriate printer or **despooled**. When more than one file is waiting to be printed, they will be printed in the order they were completed - first in, first out. Thus the spool area is effectively a queue, and the waiting jobs are often referred to as being "in the print queue", or "queued".

In the case of remote printing, the data is first spooled locally as for any other print job, but the background process is told to send the data to a particular printer on a particular remote machine.

The necessary information that the printer daemon needs to do its job - the physical device to use, the spool area to look in, the remote machine and printer for remote printing and so on - is all stored in a file called /etc/printcap. The details of this file are discussed below.

In the discussions that follow, the term "printer" will be used to mean a printer as specified in /etc/printcap. The term "physical printer" will be used to mean the thing that actually puts characters on paper. It is possible to have multiple entries in /etc/printcap which all describe one physical printer, but do so in different ways. If this is not clear to you, read the section on /etc/printcap.

3.1.4 The important programs

There are five programs which comprise the Unix print system. They should be in the locations shown, should all be owned by root and belong to the group daemon and have the permissions shown here:

```
-rwsr-sr-x /usr/bin/lpr
-rwsr-sr-x /usr/bin/lpq
-rwsr-sr-x /usr/bin/lpc
-rwsr-sr-x /usr/bin/lprm
-rwxr-s--- /etc/lpd
```

The first four are used to submit, cancel and inspect print jobs. `/etc/lpd` is the printer daemon.

(The locations, ownerships and permissions given here are a simplification and may be wrong for your system see Section 3.4 [lpd files and permissions], page 1329)

There are man pages for all these commands, which you should consult for more information. The important points are that by default `lpr`, `lprm`, `lpc` and `lpq` will operate on a printer called 'lp'. If you define an environment variable called PRINTER, the name thus defined will be used instead. Both these may be overridden by specifying the printer name to use on the command line thus:

    lpc -P*myprinter*

3.1.5 The `lpr` Command

The `lpr` command submits a job to the printer, or "queues a print job". What actually happens is that the file you specify is copied to the spool directory (see above), where it will be found by `lpd`, which then takes care of moving the data to the physical printer. If you don't specify a file, `lpr` uses standard input.

3.1.6 The `lpq` Command

The `lpq` command shows you the contents of the spool directory for a given printer. One important piece of information displayed by `lpq` is the job id, which identifies a particular job. This number must be specified if you wish to cancel a pending job.

`lpq` also shows a rank for each job in the queue - "active" means the file is actually printing (or at least that `lpd` is trying to print it). Otherwise a number shows you where in the queue the job is.

3.1.7 The `lprm` Command

The `lprm` command removes a job from the queue - that is, it removes unprinted files from the spool directory. You can either specify a job id (obtained by using the `lpq` command) or specify '-' as the job id, in which case all jobs belonging to you will be cancelled. If you do this as root, all jobs for the printer will be cancelled. If you are root and want to remove all the jobs belonging to a specific user, specify the user's name.

3.1.8 The `lpc` Command

The `lpc` command lets you check the status of printers and control some aspects of their use. In particular it lets you start and stop despooling on printers, lets you enable or disable printers and lets you rearrange the order of jobs in a print queue. The following commands disable printing on myprinter, enable the spool queue on yourprinter and move job number 37 to the top of the queue:

```
lpc down myprinter
lpc enable yourprinter
lpc topq 37
```

If invoked without any command arguments, lpc will be interactive, prompting you for actions to take. Read the man page for complete instructions. Bear in mind that some `lpc` functions are restricted to root.

3.1.9 The Important Directories

There is really only one important directory - the spool area where data to be printed is accumulated before `/etc/lpd` prints it. However, typically a system will be set up with multiple spool directories, one for each printer. This makes printer management easier. My system is set up to use `/usr/spool/lpd` as the main spool area, with each separate printer having a directory under that with the same name as the printer. Thus I have a printer called 'ps_nff' which has `/usr/spool/lpd/ps_nff` as its spool directory and so on.

The spool directories should belong to the daemon group and be user and group read/writable, and world -readable. That is, after creating the directory make sure it has permissions "-rwxrwxr-x" (0775). For the directory myprinter, the appropriate command would be:

```
chmod ug=rwx,o=rx myprinter
chgrp daemon myprinter
```

(The locations, ownerships and permissions given here are a simplification and may be wrong for your system see Section 3.4 [lpd files and permissions], page 1329)

3.1.10 The Important Files

Apart from the programs discussed above, each spool directory should contain four files - `.seq`, `errs`. `lock` and `status`. These files should have the permissions "-rw-rw-r–". The `.seq` file contains the job number counter for `lpr` to assign a and the `status` file contains the message to be reported by 'lpc stat'. The `lock` file is used by `lpd` to prevent itself trying to print two jobs to the same printer at once, and the `errs` file is a log of printer failures.

The file `errs` is not required and can actually be called whatever you like - the name is specified in `/etc/printcap`, but the file must exist for `lpd` to be able to log to it, so it is usually created manually when setting up the spool area. More on this later.

One very important file is the file `/etc/printcap`, which is described in detail in the following sections.

3.1.11 More About /etc/printcap

The file /etc/printcap is a text file, which may be edited with your favourite editor. It should be owned by root and have the permissions "-rw-r–r–".

The contents of /etc/printcap are typically very cryptic-looking, but once you know how it works they are much easier to understand. The problem is compounded by the fact that in some braindead distributions there is no man page for printcap, and the fact that most printcaps are created either by programs or by people with no thought for readability. For your own sanity, I recommend making the layout of your printcap file as logical and readable as possible, with lots of comments. And get the a man page from the lpd sources, if you don't already have it.

One printcap entry describes one printer. Essentially a printcap entry provides a logical name for a physical device, then describes how data to be sent to that device is to be handled. For example, a printcap entry will define what physical device is to be used, what spool directory data for that device should be stored in, what preprocessing should be performed on the data, where errors on the physical device should be logged and so forth. You can limit the amount of data which may be sent in a single job, or limit access to a printer to certain classes of user.

It is perfectly OK to have multiple printcap entries defining several different ways to handle data destined for the same physical printer. For example, a physical printer may support both PostScript and HP Laserjet data formats, depending on some setup sequence being sent to the physical printer before each job. It would make sense to define two printers, one of which preprocesses the data by prepending the HP LaserJet sequence while the other prepends the PostScript sequence. Programs which generate HP data would send it to the HP printer, while programs generating PostScript would print to the PostScript printer.

Programs which change the data before it is sent to the physical printer are called "filters". It is possible for a filter to send no data at all to a physical printer.

See Section 3.8 [The Syntax of /etc/printcap], page 1332

```
# Sample printcap entry with two aliases
myprinter|laserwriter:\
# lp is the device to print to - here the first parallel printer.
:lp=/dev/lp0: \
# sd means 'spool directory' - where print data is collected
:sd=/usr/spool/lpd/myprinter:
```

3.1.12 Fields in /etc/printcap

There are too many fields to describe here in full, so I'll just describe the most important ones. All fields in /etc/printcap (except for the names of the printer) are enclosed between a pair of colons and are denoted by a two-letter code. The two-letter code is followed by a value that depends on the type of field. There are three types of field - string, boolean and numeric See Section 3.8 [The Syntax of /etc/printcap], page 1332.

The following fields are the most common and most important ones:

```
lp      string          specify the device to print to, eg /dev/lp0
sd      string          specify the name of the spool directory for
                        this printer
lf      string          specify the file to which errors on this
                        printer are to be logged
if      string          specify the input filter name
rm      string          specify the name of a remote printing host
rp      string          specify the name of a remote printer
sh      boolean         specify this to suppress headers (banner pages)
sf      boolean         specify this to suppress end-of-job form feeds
mx      numeric         specify the maximum allowable print job size
                        (in blocks)
```

3.1.13 More on The 'lp' Field

If you specify /dev/null as the print device, all other processing will be performed correctly, but the final data will go to the bit bucket. This is rarely useful except for test printer configurations or with weird printers See Section 3.16 [Printers not in /dev], page 1338. When you are setting up a remote printer (that is, you have specified 'rm' and 'rp' fields), you should specify ':lp=:'.

Don't leave the field empty unless you are using a remote printer. The printer daemon will complain if you don't specify a print device.

3.1.14 More On The lf Field

Whatever file you specify should already exist, or logging will not occur.

3.1.15 More On The if Field

Input filters are programs which take print data on their standard input and generate output on their standard output. A typical use of an input filter is to detect plain text and convert it into PostScript. That is, raw text is its input, PostScript is its output. See Section 3.24 [Writing lpd filters], page 1341.

When you specify an input filter, the printer daemon does **not** send the spooled print data to the specified device. Instead, it runs the input filter with the spooled data as standard input and the print device as standard output. (For another use for input filters see Section 3.1.19 [A test printcap entry], page 1324).

3.1.16 More On The `rm` and `rp` Fields

Sending your print data to a printer attached to another machine is as simple as specifying the remote machine 'rm' and the remote printer 'rp', and making sure that the print device field 'lp' is empty. Note that data will still be spooled locally before being transferred to the remote machine, and any input filters you specify will be run also.

3.1.17 More On The `sh` and `sf` Fields

Unless you have a lot of different people using your printer, you will most likely not be interested in banner pages.

Suppressing form feeds is most useful if your printer is typically used for output from wordprocessing packages. Most WP packages create complete pages of data, so if the printer daemon is adding a form feed to the end of each job, you will get a blank page after each job. If the printer is usually used for program or directory listings, however, having that form feed ensures that the final page is completely ejected, so each listing starts at the top of a new page.

3.1.18 More On The `mx` Field

This field allows you to limit the size of the print data to be spooled. The number you specify is in BUFSIZE blocks (1K under Linux). If you specify zero, the limit is removed, allowing print jobs to be limited only by available disk space. Note that the limit is on the size of the spooled data, **not** the amount of data sent to the physical printer. If a user tries to exceed this limit the file is tuncated. The user will see a message saying "lpr: <filename>: copy file is too large".

For text physical printers, this is useful if you have users or programs that may deliberately or accidentally create excessively large output, but in most cases is not really very applicable.

For PostScript physical printers, the limit is not useful at all, because a very small amount of spooled PostScript data can generate a large number of output pages.

3.1.19 A Test Printcap Entry

The following shell script is a very simple input filter - it simply concatenates its input onto the end of a file in /tmp after an appropriate banner. We specify this filter in our printcap entry and specify /dev/null as the print device. The print device will never actually be used, but we have to set it to something because otherwise the printer daemon will complain.

```
#!/bin/sh
# This file should be placed in the printer's spool directory and
```

```
# named input_filter. It should be owned by root, group daemon, and be
# world executable (-rwxr-xr-x).
echo -------------------------------------------------- >> /tmp/testlp.out
date                                                     >> /tmp/testlp.out
echo -------------------------------------------------- >> /tmp/testlp.out
cat                                                      >> /tmp/testlp.out
```

Here's the printcap entry. Notice the (reasonably) readable format and the use of continuation characters on all but the last line:

```
myprinter|myprinter: \
:lp=/dev/null: \
:sd=/usr/spool/lpd/myprinter: \
:lf=/usr/spool/lpd/myprinter/errs: \
:if=/usr/spool/lpd/myprinter/input_filter: \
:mx#0: \
:sh: \
:sf:
```

3.1.20 Putting It All Together

Putting all the above bits together, here is a step by step guide to setting up a single printer on /dev/lp0. You can then extend this to other printers. You have to be root do do all this, by the way.

1. Check the permissions and locations of lpr, lprm, lpc, lpq and lpd See Section 3.1.4 [The important programs], page 1319.

2. Create the spool directory for your printer, which we will call 'myprinter' for now. Make sure both are owned by root, group daemon, and are user and group writeable, readonly for others (-rwxrwxr-x).
   ```
   mkdir /usr/spool/lpd /usr/spool/lpd/myprinter
   chown root.daemon /usr/spool/lpd /usr/spool/lpd/myprinter
   chmod ug=rwx,o=rx /usr/spool/lpd /usr/spool/lpd/myprinter
   ```

3. In the directory /usr/spool/lpd/myprinter, create the necessary files and give them the correct permissions and owner:
   ```
   cd /usr/spool/lpd/myprinter
   touch .seq errs status lock
   chown root.daemon .seq errs status lock
   chmod ug=rw,o=r .seq errs status lock
   ```

4. Create the shell script input_filter in the directory /usr/spool/lpd/myprinter. Use the input filter given above. Make sure that the file is owned by root, group daemon, and is executable by anyone.
   ```
   cd /usr/spool/lpd/myprinter
   chmod ug=rwx,o=rx input_filter
   ```

5. Create the file /etc/printcap if it doesn't already exist. Remove all entries in it and add the test printcap entry given above. Make sure the file is owned by root, and readonly to everyone else (-rw-r--r--).

6. Edit the file rc.local. Add the line '/etc/lpd' to the end. This will run the printer daemon each time the system boots. It is not necessary to boot now though - just run it by hand:
   ```
   lpd
   ```

7. Do a test print:

   ```
   ls -l | lpr -Pmyprinter
   ```

8. Look in `/tmp` for a file called `testlp.out` - it should contain your directory listing.

9. Edit `/etc/printcap`. Copy the myprinter entry, so you have two identical entries.

   > in the **first** entry, change both occurrences of '`myprinter`' to '`testlp`' in the first line only

   > in the **second** entry, change `/dev/null` to your real print device, eg., `/dev/lp0`

   > in the **second** entry, remove the '`if`' line completely

10. Either reboot the system or kill the printer daemon and restart it. This is because the printer daemon only looks at the `/etc/printcap` file when it first starts up.

11. Do a test print again - this one should come out on your physical printer!

    ```
    ls -l | lpr -Pmyprinter
    ```

3.1.21 More On Remote Printing

In order for any other machines to print using your printers, their names will have to be registered in either the file `/etc/hosts.equiv` or `/etc/hosts.lpd`. These are simple text files, one host name per line.

For preference, add hosts to `/etc/hosts.lpd`. `/etc/hosts.equiv` is used to give far wider access rights, and should be avoided wherever possible.

You can restrict remote users either by group name (specify the groups permitted using one or more rg fields in `/etc/printcap` - '`:rg=admin:`' will restrict access to a printer to those users belonging to the group admin. You can also restrict access to those users with accounts on your system, by specifying the boolean flag '`:rs:`' in your `/etc/printcap`.

3.1.22 The Fiddly Bits

If all the above worked, you will now have two printers defined in `/etc/printcap` - one called testlp, which appends output to `/tmp/testlp.out`, and one called myprinter which sends unmodified output to the physical printer attached to `/dev/lp0`. Both share the same spool directory. As an exercise, you might like to set up a separate spool directory for the testlp printer.

If your printer is a PostScript printer, it may not be able to handle plain text. If this is the case, you'll need to set up a filter to convert plain text to PostScript. An excellent freeware program called nenscript is available which does just this. See Section 2.3 [PostScript], page 1308. If you don't set up such a filter, you will have to make sure by other means that the printer is sent only PostScript.

You may like to add a line to your login script - or even to the default user login script - which sets up a `PRINTER` environment variable. Under bash, a suitable line would be '`export PRINTER=myprinter`'. This will prevent people having to specify '`-Pmyprinter`' every time they submit a print job.

To add more printers, just repeat the above process with different printer names. Remember you can have multiple printcap entries all using the same physical device. This lets you treat the same device differently, depending on what you call it when you submit a print job to it.

It is possible to "reuse" a printcap entry. If you specify your own machine as the remote host and another printer in your printcap file as the remote printer, you can effectively redirect print data from one printer to another. Remember if you use this technique that all the data will be processed by all input filters in the chain and spooled for each printer it goes through.

Although you can specify as many aliases for a printer as you like, it seems that for maximum usefulness the first two should be the same and should be the "real" printer name. Many programs will only ever use one of these two aliases. The lpc command will only report on the first alias, though lpc, lpr, lprm and lpq all understand any alias.

Rather than specify a maximum spool file size, you may want instead to prevent spool files expanding to fill your disk, even temporarily. To do so, put a file called minfree in each spool directory, specifying the amount of disk space that must remain for spooling data to be accepted. This file is a simple text file, containing the number of blocks to be left free. Usually this file is a link to a file in the main spool directory, as it is rare for different printers to have different minimums.

3.1.23 Troubleshooting

Problem: You get a message saying "lpd: connect: No such file or directory"

Answer: The printer daemon /etc/lpd is not running. You may have forgotten to add it to your /etc/rc.local file. Alternatively you did add it, but haven't booted since. Add it and reboot, OR just run /etc/lpd. Remember you have to be root to do this. See Section 3.5 [lpd not working], page 1331.

Problem: You get a message saying "Job queued, but cannot start daemon".

Answer: This often appears right after the "lpd: connect" message. Same problem.

Problem: You get a message saying "lpd: cannot create <spooldir>/.seq".

Answer: You have not created the spool directory specified in the printcap entry or have misnamed it. An alternative (though much less likely) answer is that you have too little disk space left.

Problem: You get a message saying "lpr: Printer queue is disabled".

Answer: As root, use 'lpc enable <*printername*>' to enable the printer. Note that as root, you can submit jobs even to a disabled printer.

Problem: You submit a print job, there are no error messages, but nothing comes out on the physical printer.

Answer: There could be many reasons. Make sure the physical printer is switched on, selected, and physically connected to the device specified in the /etc/printcap file. Use the lpq command to see whether the entry is in the queue. If it is, then the device may be busy, the printer may be down, or there may be an error on the printer. Check the error log specified in the printcap entry for clues. You can use the 'lpc status' command to check whether the printer is down and 'lpc up <*printername*>' to bring it back up if it is (you need to be root to do this).

If after checking as suggested your print jobs still do not come out, double check that any input filter you have specified is present in the correct directory and has the correct permissions. If you are running syslogd, you can look in your logs for messages from lpd. If you see log entries saying "cannot execv <name of input filter>", then this is almost certainly the problem.

Another possibility is that your printer is a PostScript printer and you are not sending PostScript to it. Most PostScript printers will ignore non-PostScript data. You may need to install an appropriate text-to-PostScript input filter.

Lastly (and you'll feel really silly if this is the cause!) check that your input filter actually generates output and that the output device is not /dev/null.

Problem: When remote printing, your jobs go into the remote queue but never get physically printed.

Answer: If you can, look at the entry for the remote printer in the /etc/printcap file on the remote machine. It may be restricting your access. The 'rg' field restricts access to members of a specific group which you may not be in, and the 'rs' field prevents access from users without accounts on the remote machine, which you may not have. Alternatively the printer on the remote machine may have been downed by the system administrator. See Section 3.23 [lpr over a network], page 1340.

3.2 What lpr and lpd do

Most Un*x systems use lpd (or the System V variant lp), the line printer daemon, and friends to spool print jobs and run them through all needed filters. While line printers are certainly on their way out, spooling print jobs and running them through filters is definitely a convenient thing. Thus lpr. (subliminal note: **PLEASE** find and read the lpr, lpd, printcap, lpc, lpq, and lprm man pages. They are in the source dist of the net-2, if you haven't got them.)

3.3 Getting hold of lpd

Lpd and family are available in several places. The new Linux net-2 package contains a working BSD-style lpd (although it has a couple of bugs and Makefile installs the binaries with the wrong permissions). I now use this one with my stock 0.99pl14 kernel after following the directions in Matt Welsh's Net-2 HOWTO to get my NET-2 going (you only need loopback). Most people (and this document) consider this to be **the** Linux lpd package. A slightly debugged version incorporating patches from earlier releases of this HOWTO is also available in:

```
tsx-11.mit.edu:/pub/linux/packages/net/new-net-2/lpd-590p?.tar.gz
```

Some of the prepackaged Linux distributions have a very poor record with respect to having a working lpd packages so don't be shy of getting a new one if you seem to be having trouble.

Fans of the SysV lp package should consider getting plp (however this HOWTO contains no information on that package)

An lpd binary package which can be coaxed into working with the old net things (pre 0.99pl10 kernel) may still be around but you'll probably find it a bit shakey and you really should update your kernel. Note a subtle difference between the two versions: the old one placed lock files and such in /var/spool, while the net-2 version requires the directory /var/spool/lpd to exist for its lock file.

You will need to edit /etc/printcap to configure lpd to use your printer. Setting up lpd to accept PostScript and print it is not very difficult; simply make a shell script filter. See Section 3.24 [Writing lpd filters], page 1341

Setting up lpd correctly is definitely worth the trouble if you are going to do any printing at all. Of course, if all you ever print is the occasional man page or instruction book, then you can probably get by without it (but even then it's nice).

Ghostscript 2.6.x also comes with a complicated script and utilities to generate printcap entries and manage multiple types of queues for a printer. I have not tested these, but I assume they can be made to work. If you are in a large-scale environment with varied printing needs, these may be worth a look.

3.4 Where Do The Files Go And What Should Their Permissions Be?

There is quite a bit of variation between the various releases but I'll try where possible to offer solutions that are universally applicable. Start lpd in your /etc/rc or /etc/rc.local (usually in /etc/rc.local after you start syslogd (if you use syslogd)).

Set the group fields of the file permissons/ownership as follows:

```
-rwxr-sr--   1 root      lp           37892 Nov 19 23:32 /etc/lpd
-rwxr-sr-x   1 root      lp           21508 Nov 19 23:32 /usr/bin/lpc
```

```
-rwsr-sr-x   1 root     lp          17412 Nov 19 23:32 /usr/bin/lpq
-rwxr-sr-x   1 root     lp          17412 Nov 19 23:32 /usr/bin/lpr
-rwxr-sr-x   1 root     lp          17412 Nov 19 23:32 /usr/bin/lprm
-rwxr-xr-x   1 root     lp           2816 May 10 13:37 /usr/bin/lptest

...and for each of the spool directories listed in the sd fields of
/etc/printcap...

/var/spool/lpd:
total 5
drwxrwxr-x   2 root     lp           1024 May 18 23:00 .
drwxr-xr-x  11 root     root         1024 Feb 19 20:56 ..
-rw-rw-r--   1 root     lp              4 May 18 23:00 .seq
-rw-rw-r--   1 root     lp             18 May 18 23:00 lock
-rw-rw-r--   1 root     lp             25 May 18 23:00 status
```

Note these 3 files are created by lpr and lpd so if you've never run these they will be absent. With some versions of the lpd package you had to touch them into being or they would be created with the wrong permissions but this bug seems to have been fixed.

In older versions the group id was 'daemon' not 'lp'. There's also a named socket but lpd creates/deletes it as needed. Also you may find the uid is sometimes set to 'daemon' or 'lp' rather than 'root' but this is of no consequence except on setuid binaries.

These permissions are the most pedantic so don't be surprised if your system works with different permissions. On the other hand if lpd is not working for you and you have different permissions please try these before mailing us or posting to usenet. (This may sound obvious but you'd be amazed how much mail I've had from people with the permissions set wrong).

People tell me that lpr must be setuid(root) but I've not seen evidence that this is really the case as long as the file permissions on the spool queues are right. Still as far as I know lpr is designed to be secure when installed setuid(root). This allows an alternative (sloppy) approach: just make lpr and lprm setuid(root) then you can almost forget the file permissions on the spool queues!

You're free to choose different directories for the executables on your system (notably lpc is usually in /etc (or /usr/sbin) even though it has commands that are useful to non-root). Of course since you are free to do this it implies the person who made up your distribution was also free to do so, so be careful to make sure you delete old components when you install new ones.

The master lpd lock file is fixed at compile time to be /var/spool/lpd/lpd.lock so you must have a /var/spool/lpd directory even if you choose not to keep your spool queue there. In the older binaries the lock file was /usr/spool/lpd.lock so this was not an issue.

My advice is to keep your primary spool queue in /usr/spool/lpd and make /var a symlink to usr or keep it in /var/spool/lpd and make /usr/spool a symlink to ../var/spool. This gives the greatest compatibility with the pathnames that are compiled into the various distributed binaries. Note that having a separate /var filesystem avoids the problem of your /usr filesystem filling up as a result of stuff in spool queues.

The main configuration file is /etc/printcap. Network printing also uses /etc/hosts.allow and /etc/hosts.lpd.

By now everyone should have libraries and binaries that look for config files in /etc. If you chose to keep your configs somewhere else (/conf or /usr/etc for example) then /etc must contain a symlink to the real file. If you still have a system which looks for files in /usr/etc or /etc/inet your system is way out of date and you should upgrade.

3.5 lpd not working

If 'ps ax' does not reveal a lpd then you daemon has died (or was never started) - usually a sign that it couldn't create its lockfile, or was unable to find /etc/services. (This will happen if you tried to start it before all your filesystems were mounted).

If lpr works only for root then you've probably got a permission problem.

If you can't even cat files to the printer then you may be using the wrong device name for the printer in /etc/printcap See Section 2.13 [Printer device names], page 1317 or you may need to fiddle with tunelp. See Section 2.12 [hardware and drivers], page 1317.

If you get "jobs queued, but cannot start daemon" or "lpc: connect: No such file or directory" while lpd **is** running then you are having trouble with the socket connection to lpd. "start" in the context of this error really means "wake". This problem has come and gone thoughout the history of Linux - I don't really understand this but it stems from an erroneous interaction between the networking stuff and "Unix domain" (non-network) sockets. Usually it has only shown up when the network is incorrectly configured. If you're not really on a network it is usually adequate just to have the following somewhere in your startup.

```
ifconfig lo localhost
route add localhost
```

You'll also need to have the /etc/hosts file. There's no need to run any daemons.

There is second and much more understandable way to produce this error - use a mixture of components from different releases of lpd that use different names for the Unix domain socket (new stuff uses /tmp/.printer, obsolete stuff /dev/printer). (For some time SLS was released this way).

At the time of writing I am quite unable to reproduce this error - I am using my debugged version of the net-2 lpd compiled with gcc-2.4.5 and libc-4.4.4 on kernel 0.99.14.

3.6 Where Do I Get A Printcap For Printer Model xxxxx?

This question is essentially meaningless so please don't ask it on usenet See Section 3.7 [The Semantics of /etc/printcap], page 1332.

3.7 The Semantics of `/etc/printcap`

Given the similarity in appearance and name between `/etc/termcap` and `/etc/printcap` one could be forgiven for assuming that they contain analogous information. This is not the case. Whereas `/etc/termcap` contains informations about terminal **types** - (mostly escape sequences) printcap contains information about **specific** printers (like the directory that holds the spool queue, the device name of the printer and what room it's in). The information about a printer model's escape sequences and so on are held in the various **filters** which are programs called by `lpd` to drive the printer. `/etc/printcap` simply gives the locations of these filters. For details RTFM(printcap). [Alternatively the net-HOWTO has a summary of some of the more important fields.]

One last point - you should always specify 'suppress header' `':sh:'` unless you have a **text** (not PostScript) printer and want banners. On a text printer they are usually a waste of time and paper. On a PostScript printer they usually stop your printer working. See Section 3.17 [Burst/banner pages], page 1338.

3.8 The Syntax of `/etc/printcap`

Ideally RTFM(termcap) (yes, I said **termcap**) but since most people don't have TFM(termcap) here are the essentials.

Lines starting with '#' are comments (as you might have guessed).

For each printer usable from the `lpr` command on your system there is one logical line in the file. For the sake of readability each logical line may be spread over several physical lines by making the last character on all but the last physical line a backslash.

Each logical line has the following format:

name1 | *name2* | *name3* : *string_capability*=*string* : \
          : *numeric_capability*#*number* : *boolean_capability* :

The leading spaces and colon on the second line are for readability only.

A printer can have as many names as you like but conventionally the final name is used as a longhand description of the printer. (Still people are free to say `'lpr -P "grotty teletype in room 213 "'` if that's the description you've given.) One of the names of your default printer must be `'lp'`.

The list of capabilities can be as long as needed and the order is not significant. Each **capability** is denoted by a two character code. (The name "capability" comes form the file format's termcap heritage - parameter or attribute would be a more sensible terms.) [Note from Ross Biro: capabilities with 3 character names don't work properly which is why the serial port stuff in the old binaries failed.] Capabilities having string value and have a = delimiter between the capability name and the value while those having a numeric value use a # (actually they can use either a # or an =). Boolean "capabilities" are true if they appear in the list and false if they do not.

Special characters in a string value can be expressed using backslash-escaped sequences as in C; in addition, '\E' stands for ESC. '^' is also a kind of escape character; '^' followed by **CHAR** stands for the control-equivalent of **CHAR**. Thus, '^a' stands for the character control-a, just like '\001'. '\' and '^' themselves can be represented as '\\' and '\^' respectively. '\:' for ':' seems to work but the source code contains a warning that it can confuse the parser and '\072' is a better idea.

Example:

```
lp|bam|Epson FX-80:lp=/dev/lp1:sd=/usr/spool/lp1:sh:mx#0:\
        :df=/usr/local/lib/magic-filter/lp.df:\
        :if=/usr/local/lib/magic-filter/lp.if:
```

The printer's name is lp (this is the printer that lpr uses by default). It's also known as bam or "Epson FX-80".

The printer is on /dev/lp1 (aka AT-bus LPT1:). I don't want a burst page. I don't want a file length limit. Files queued by 'lpr -d' are passed through /usr/local/lib/magic-filter/lp.df and those queued by lpr through /usr/local/lib/magic-filter/lp.1f.

See also the next section.

3.9 An /etc/printcap **gotcha**

Two /etc/printcap files can look identical and yet one works and the other doesn't.

See if 'lpc stat' reports a printer called ' :'. The last character on a continued line must be a backslash. If there are whitespace characters after the backslash then it doesn't register the next line as a continuation.

3.10 The Minimum /etc/printcap

This is a silly question but it is frequently asked. The answer is 'lp:sh' (that's 6 bytes including the required linefeed character on the end). To use this /etc/printcap you must make /dev/lp a symlink to your printer and create your spool queue directory as /usr/spool/lpd. (You might think that if you wanted banner pages you could loose the ':sh' but the termcap syntax requires at least one capability per entry).

3.11 How to prevent the 'Staircase Effect'

Un*x terminates each line of a file with a linefeed but not a carriage return so taken literally a Un*x text file printed on an ASCII device will start each line below the end of the previous line. Some printers can be set to treat "linefeed" as "carriage return, linefeed", others can't. If yours can then do simply do that. If the printer cannot be fixed create a shell script filter that reads:

```
#!/bin/sh
if [ "$1" = -c ]; then
   cat
else
   sed -e s/$/^M/
fi
# the ''echo -ne'' assumes that /bin/sh is really bash
echo -ne \\f
```

Where ^M is a carriage return character not a ^ followed by a M. To type ^M in Emacs use the sequence C-q C-m and in vi use C-v C-m. Conventionally this script is called /usr/lib/lpf. If you have more than one such script a better idea is to keep them in a subdirectory, say /usr/lib/lpd/. The test of $1 allows the insertion of carriage returns to be switched off by 'lpr -l'.

Install this filter as the 'if' filter by putting ':if=/usr/lib/lpf:' (or whatever) in your /etc/printcap entry for the printer.

Alternatively your printer may have an escape sequence that will set the way it handles linefeed characters. A simple filter that uses an 'echo -ne' command to send this sequence may be appropriate.

```
#!/bin/sh
# Filter for HP printers to treat LF as CRLF
# the ''echo -ne'' assumes that /bin/sh is really bash
echo -ne \\033\&k2G
cat
echo -ne \\f
```

3.12 Resetting the printer between each file printed

Either make your filters do it or define the 'tr' "capability" in /etc/printcap to be your printer's font reset command. For details of the format of this string see the question on the format of printcap. This may not work if a printout crashes in the middle of an escape sequence - putting a lot of ^@ on the front may help but this probably won't be enough it you were printing raster graphics when the filter died.

3.13 Preventing formfeed after each file printed

If you don't have an 'if' specified in /etc/printcap then lpd will automatically put a formfeed at the end of each file. If you're using a filter then it's up to the filter to decide if it wants to put a formfeed. To disable formfeed completely if you don't have an 'if' put ':ff=:' in your /etc/printcap. But please note this suppresses the formfeed that would usually be printed if a filter dies. If you want formfeeds after text printouts but not on printouts printed with 'lpr -l' then create the following 'if' filter:

```
#!/bin/sh
# the ''echo -ne'' assumes that /bin/sh is really bash
cat
if [ "$1" != -c ]; then
  echo -ne \\f
fi
```

If you want a formfeed after 'lpr -l' to be optional you can misuse the '-i' switch to suppress the formfeed with the following trick (after all 'lpr -i -l' would usually not be implemented).

```
#!/bin/sh
cat
# use lpr -i -l to print raw without trailing formfeed
if [ "$1" != -c -o "$4" = -i0 ]; then
  # the ''echo -ne'' assumes that /bin/sh is really bash
  echo -ne \\f
fi
```

3.14 Printing with lpd to a serial port

The first if lpd complains about "ioctl(TIOCEXCL)" being unimplemented you need a version of lpd that doesn't care (eg. lpd-590p2)

There are two sets of flags which you will need to set, plus the baud rate (Note: the 'fc' flag setting seems to override the 'br#' capability, so be sure to set that correctly as well as the 'br#'!).

Each of the flags can have bits set and cleared. Clearing is done first, so specify the clear flags ('fc#' and 'xc#') before the set flags ('fs' and 'xs').

Setting the 'br#' capability is self-explanatory. Example: 'br#9600'

It is very easy to translate from stty settings to printcap flag settings. If you need to, see the man page for stty now.

Use stty to set up the printer port so that you can cat a file to it and have it print correctly. Here's what 'stty -a' looks like for my printer port:

```
dina:/usr/users/andy/work/lpd/lpd# stty -a < /dev/ttyS2
speed 9600 baud; rows 0; columns 0; line = 0;
intr = ^C; quit = ^\; erase = ^?; kill = ^U; eof = ^D; eol = <undef>;
eol2 = <undef>; start = ^Q; stop = ^S; susp = ^Z; rprnt = ^R; werase = ^W;
lnext = ^V; min = 1; time = 0;
-parenb -parodd cs8 hupcl -cstopb cread -clocal -crtscts
-ignbrk -brkint -ignpar -parmrk -inpck -istrip -inlcr
-igncr -icrnl ixon -ixoff -iuclc -ixany -imaxbel
-opost -olcuc -ocrnl -onlcr -onocr -onlret -ofill -ofdel nl0 cr0 tab0
bs0 vt0 ff0
-isig -icanon -iexten -echo -echoe -echok -echonl -noflsh -xcase -tostop
-echoprt -echoctl -echoke
```

The only changes between this and the way the port is initialized at bootup are -clocal, -crtscts, and ixon. Your port may well be different depending on how your printer does flow control.

Once you have your stty settings right, so that 'cat file > /dev/ttyS2' (in my case) sends the file to the printer, look at the file /usr/src/linux/include/linux/termios.h. This contains a lot of #defines and a few structs (You may wish to cat this file to the printer (you do have that working, right?) and use it as scratch paper – I (Andrew Tefft <teffta@engr.dnet.ge.com> did!). Go to the section that starts out

```
/* c_cflag bit meaning */
#define CBAUD    0000017
```

This section lists the meaning of the 'fc#' and 'fs#' bits. You will notice that the names there (after the baud rates) match up with one of the lines of stty output. Didn't I say this was going to be easy?

Note which of those settings are preceded with a - in your stty output. Sum up all those numbers (they are octal). This represents the bits you want to **clear**, so the result is your 'fc#' capability. Of course, remember that you will be setting bits directly after you clear, so you can just use 'fc#0177777' (I do).

Now do the same for those settings (listed in this section) which do not have a - before them in your stty output. In my example the important ones are CS8 (0000060), HUPCL (0002000), and CREAD (0000200). Also note the flags for your baud rate – mine is 0000015. Add those all up, and in my example you get 0002275. This goes in your 'fs#' capability ('fs#02275' works fine in my example).

Do the same with set and clear for the next section of the include file, "c_lflag bits". In my case I didn't have to set anything, so I just use 'xc#0157777' and 'xs#0'.

Once your printcap is set up, try it out. If things don't work, see the next section.

3.15 cat works to the serial port, but not lpd (1)

Generally getting lpd up and running is explained elsewhere, but if you are having trouble with serial port settings you can prevent lpd from trying to configure your port by treating you printer as one that does not present a normal device interface. See Section 3.16 [Printers not in /dev], page 1338.

1. Set your printer (in your printcap) to /dev/null1. ('mknod /dev/null1 c 1 3' because you don't want /dev/null to be opened exclusively).

    remove the baud rate and flags settings from your printcap.

2. Create a script such as this:

    ```
    #!/bin/sh
    echo if: $* >> /var/spool/lpd/results
    # /dev/lp is linked to /dev/ttyS2 which has the printer
    exec your-old-input-filter $* > /dev/lp
    ```

    ...or if you didn't have an old 'if' installed...

    ```
    #!/bin/sh
    echo if: $* >> /var/spool/lpd/results
    cat > /dev/lp
    # the ''echo -ne'' assumes that /bin/sh is realy bash
    echo -en \\f > /dev/lp
    ```

    Make sure it's world-executable and world-readable. Try out your script ('/usr/lib/lpd/if < *some-file*') and see if it prints.

3. Set the 'if' capability in your printcap to call this script, e.g. 'if=/usr/lib/lpd/if'

4. Use stty to correctly set your port settings. Try to print now. You should be able to tell if things are being spooled, and things **should** be printed, if your manual testing of the 'if' script works. But this is a kludge, so the idea is not to use the 'if' script.

Assuming the above method using the 'if' filter works and that you believe that you have specified what you think are the correct flags and baud rate in printcap; check 'stty -a < /dev/ttyS2' (or whatever your printer port is). If the settings are not correct, check your flags against your printout from termios.h. If the settings are **way** not correct, you may need a fixed lpd. The patch follows, and you can probably see why it's needed :-) Note: this patch is reversed and has already been applied (uh... unapplied :-)) to lpd-590p2 so don't apply it if you already have that version or later.

(the patch is coming in just a sec)

When I was setting mine up, I followed a sequence like this:

```
lprm whatever # (make sure queue is empty and lpd is running)
stty correct settings < /dev/ttyS2
lpr something small
stty -a < /dev/ttyS2  # (often had to ctrl-c out of this one)
```

twiddle with flags

```
lprm whatever # make sure queue is empty again...
```

Here's the patch (I it's reversed so apply it with '-R' - or, in practice, by hand!):

```
-----------------------------Cut Here------------------------------------
*** lpd-590/lpd/printjob.c   Thu Jul  8 20:56:59 1993
--- lpd-590/lpd/printjob.c~  Sat Feb 27 09:07:01 1993
***************
*** 1271,1277 ****
        }
  #ifdef LINUX
        ttybuf.c_cflag &= ~FC;          /* not quite right! */
!       ttybuf.c_cflag |= FS;           /* not quite right! */
  #else
        ttybuf.sg_flags &= ~FC;
        ttybuf.sg_flags |= FS;
--- 1271,1277 ----
        }
  #ifdef LINUX
        ttybuf.c_cflag &= ~FC;          /* not quite right! */
!       ttybuf.c_cflag |= ~FS;          /* not quite right! */
  #else
        ttybuf.sg_flags &= ~FC;
        ttybuf.sg_flags |= FS;
-----------------------------Cut Here------------------------------------
```

3.16 Printers that are not simple devices

[Firstly I'll explain the subject.] The most common example is a printer that is connected via a network in some strange way. For example consider a printer connected to a host with which you can only communicate via E-mail.

To use such a printer through lpr the 'lp' capability of the print queue should be directed to a /dev/null type device (e.g. 'mknod /dev/null1 c 1 3') but not /dev/null itself as lpd opens the device exclusively. Each filter must must explicitly uuencode and mail its output.

In more complex cases if you already have an 'if' or 'of' filter for a strangely connected printer then other filters can pass their output to/through this filter to avoid duplication of effort. In this case the 'if' filter should usually be called with the '-c' switch to minimize the further manipulations if performs.

I've heard someone has had some success trying something like this with Novell NetWare and the free mail transfer agent "Charon".

3.17 Generating burst or banner pages

For a simple text printer (in particular not PostScript) and a simple text banner simply take ':sh:' out of the printcap record. If you want to prevent the banner coming out in whatever font was last used on the printer then define the 'tr' "capability" to be your printer's font reset command.

If you want a fancy customized banner (or have a PostScript printer) leave ':sh:' in the printcap and make each of your filters print the banner. All the information to put on the banner is included in the filter's positional parameters. RTFM(printcap) for details. [If you're using <B.A.McCauley@bham.ac.uk>'s magic-filter package then call the code to print the banners from the config script.]

3.18 Spooling text to a PostScript printer

You need a filter based on a program that converts ascii to PostScript. The most well known of these is enscript but it's also the hardest to find (being non-free). Others include a2ps, nenscript, and mpage. See Section 2.7 [Printing text via PostScript], page 1313.

3.19 Why graphics files are sometines truncated

This is usually because you've got a limit set on the maximum size file that can sit in the spool queue. Put 'mx#0' in your printcap.

3.20 Why 'lpr -i' doesn't work

To get 'lpr -i' to work you need a filter installed as 'if' that implements it. The '-i' switch is simply passed on by lpd to the filter. The filter called lpf that comes with lpd supports this feature but can only be used to print text. If you want to use this program but still want your filter to do some printer specific initialization then write the script thus:

```
#!/bin/sh
# My initialisation stuff goes here
exec /usr/lib/lpf $*
```

More reasonably you could have your filter script send the printer left margin sequence.

```
#!/usr/bin/perl
# This example is in perl for a change because converting numbers
# to characters is tricky in shell script

for ($i=0; !($_ = $ARGV[$i]) || !/^-i([0-9])+/; $i++) {}

print pack("cAc",27,"l",$1);

while (<STDIN>) { print; }
```

3.21 Why 'lpr -p' doesn't work?

Because it's broken. lpd always thinks that the printer is 0 characters wide regardless of what /etc/printcap or the lpr arguments say. The lpd-FAQ contained a patch but it has now been applied to lpd-590p1 and later. (Apologies to anyone who wanted this patch after the lpd-FAQ merged with printing-how.to. It was dropped in the mistaken belief that a new release of lpd-590 was imminent).

One other thing: lpd calls pr by full pathname so if you keep pr somewhere different from /usr/bin/pr you will need a symlink. (Where lpd expects to find pr may vary from version to version).

3.22 lpc and lpq warning of missing daemons

One lpd process runs all the time and it spawns children to handle each printer as needed. The health of the master daemon is not explicity reported by lpc but the absence of errors indicates that it is healthy. See Section 3.5 [lpd not working], page 1331. The 'lpc stat' command will display the message "no daemon present" for each queue that is not actually printing at the time - this is completely normal. If printing has been disabled or the queue is empty then this is not an error condition. lpq is even more alarmist and will say "Warning: no daemon present". If the daemon is absent when the queue has entries and has not been explicitly stopped then this warning probably indicates an error in a filter. Fix the filter then use 'lpd up *queue-name*' to restart it.

Sometimes when shutting down a printer lpc will get confused and try to kill a non existant daemon. This leads to irritating but harmless error messages. In lpd-590p2 these are much rarer.

3.23 Using lpr over a network

To print on the printer listed as foo in the printcap on machine bar.baz.net from the machine mine.baz.net you put an entry like this in your /etc/printcap (on mine.baz.net):

```
foo:lp=:rm=bar.baz.net:rp=foo:sd=/usr/lpd/spool/foo:
```

and, of course, create the spool directory /usr/lpd/spool/foo.

There's no point specifying filters and the like in mine.baz.net:/etc/printcap as it's the ones in bar.baz.net:/etc/printcap that will get used.

On the machine bar.baz.foo, you need to put mine.baz.net on a line by itself in either /etc/hosts.equiv or /etc/hosts.lpd; note that putting it in /etc/hosts.equiv will allow for unauthenticated logins as well as printing. /etc/hosts.lpd is for printing only.

The machines listed in `/etc/hosts.*` should be described canonical names or numbers as lpd starts with the IP address and performs a reverse DNS lookup to get the name. If you are not sure of cannonical name you can just list all the names you know for a machine. (If you have `dig` then the command '`dig -x` **a.b.c.d**' can be used to get the canonical name of IP address **a.b.c.d**.)

If the printer server is not running a BSD style spooler then it should still be possible to get it to work but the authority files may have different names or formats. For example Chris Nystrom <chrisn@medianet.com> found that he had to create a file on the remote machine called `/usr/spool/lp/admins/lp/Systems` that listed his Linux box's name. We do not know if this is a SYSV thing or something exclusive to dynix/ptx 2.0.3 that he is using on his Sequent.

If you can't get remote printing to work through lpd you may be able to simply use remote command execution like this:

```
rsh bar.baz.net "lp -dlp" < file
```

This example would be for a remote system using a SYSV type printing system on host `bar.baz.net`.

3.24 Writing lpd filters

In normal Un*x terminology, filters are just programs (so they must have execute permission) that read a stream from their standard input and write to their standard output.

lpd filters are filters in the sense that thay read STDIN and write to STDOUT, but are unusual in that they may assume that their standard input is a random access file and may perform lseek() operations on it.

All lpd filters have a common command line syntax (or more often simply ignore command line parameters). For details of the command line parameters RTFM(printcap).

If you want to write a shell script filter it must have a #!/bin/sh (or perl or csh) header. Here is the generic form of a filter to accept PostScript.

```
#!/bin/sh
/path.../gs -q -dSAFER -dNOPAUSE -r??? -sDevice=?????? -sOutputFile=- -
```

Place the full pathname of the script as one of the filters (but not 'of'!) parameter in the printcap for your printer. I suggest putting such scripts in `/usr/lib/lpd/`. It is also usual to keep filters in the spool directories but this goes against normal practice of keeping programs and data neatly apart. ('-dSAFER' attempts to protect against PostScript interpreter security holes, '-q' and '-dNOPAUSE' make it run nonstop, and Device is the appropriate special file for your printer).

Here is an Epson FX-80 dvi filter using ghostscript:

```
#!/bin/sh
/usr/TeX/bin/dvips -f | \
            /usr/bin/gs -q -dSAFER -sDEVICE=eps9high -r120x216 \
            -dNOPAUSE -sOutputFile=- -
```

More tools useful for making filters are described elsewhere in this document.

3.25 Debugging lpd filters

It's easier to debug filters if you test them in an immediate shell before you install them. (If your filter makes use of its command line arguments you'll have to specify them too). 'my-new-filter <*file* >/dev/lp1'

A trick most people find useful when testing filters that make use of their command line arguments is to include 'echo $* >>/tmp/filter-log' near the top of the script.

If the filter works when you test it but still doesn't work when called by lpd then you may have forgotten the '#!/bin/sh' header. You may also need to set PATH within the script since the daemon's PATH may not have everything you need. Note also that the filter is run with uid=daemon so any programs it calls should be world executable.

3.26 Output ('of') filters

Never use these. (Well strictly speaking there are circumstances but you're unlikely to meet them). Recently (early '94) there has been a spate of people on c.o.l.help advocating the use of output filters. Using 'of' filters means that if a printout is queued while another is already printing the 2 will be run together with a form-feed between. Any printer initialization or file type detection will therefore not be performed for the second file and it will probably be printed incorrectly. There are other more subtle ways in which output filters can do unexpected things. IMHO: If using an output filter is the answer, it was probably a silly question.

3.27 Getting filters for given printers

From: B.A.McCauley@bham.ac.uk (Brian McCauley)

Because writing a filter usually takes about 10 minutes once you've found the right program (gs, dvilj etc.) there's little call for ftp archives of printer filters but we are thinking of creating an extensive example file to go with this document.

If you already have a program to print, say DVI, on your printer by some mechanism, then making it into a filter is usually a matter of writing trivial shell script See Section 3.24 [Writing lpd filters], page 1341.

If the program you are using insists on reading a names file as input see the next question. Text mode filters are trivial too (see this HOWTO) unless you want lpr to have a choice of fonts in which case they are slightly harder than trivial. You will probably want to insert and 'echo -ne' command at the beginning and end of your filter to set up the font etc to your liking.

3.28 Filters from programs that won't read STDIN

Some of the programs that are used in writing `lpd` filters are not capable of taking their input from their standard input. For example `dvilj2p` insists on a named file as its input (and what's more expects one with a `.dvi` suffix) so do this:

```
#!/bin/sh
ln -s /proc/self/fd/0 /tmp/$$.dvi
dvilj2p /tmp/$$
rm /tmp/$$.dvi
```

Note: If it wasn't for the fact that `dvilj2p` adds a `.dvi` suffix you wouldn't need the temporary symlink and could just specify `/proc/self/fd/0` directly. People who use this trick often usually permanently 'ln -s /proc/self/fd/0 /dev/stdin'. If you're highly security conscious and don't allow access to `/proc` you'll need to create a temporary file.

3.29 Having many filters

Historically the `lpr` command was created to support a finite set of possible file types. You can, in fact, use any of the filters for any reason. If you're never going to use Benson Varian raster files you could use the '-v' switch for GIF files. You could even use '-d' for low res and -v for high res. Remember that if you create a filter for a file format that takes a long time to process then your printer may sit idle between print jobs even when there are things in the queue.

If you are on a network remember that the filter setups go on the print server. One way to avoid running out of filter options is to define several logical printers in `/etc/printcap` that all point to the same physical one and put each filter in the 'if' field of a different printcap entry. This has the advantage that you can set the `PRINTER` environment variable to choose your filter rather than having to specify it on the command line each time. One small problem with this is that you have no control over the order in which files from separate queues are printed.

Another (and these days more common) way to avoid running out of possible types is to use magic filters.

3.30 Magic Filters

Magic filters deduce their input files' types from 'magic numbers' (distinctive byte patterns at particular offsets). Magic filters are usually perl scripts, shell scripts or C programs that simply identify the file type then call the appropriate non-magic filter. Blatent plug :-) Brian has a generic magic filter bash script that selects the right filter to use based on the output of the `file` command. With a suitable magic filter (and 3 associated non-magic filters) you can do things like:

```
lpr -d file1.dvi file2.div.Z file3.ps file4.texinfo.gz
```

(BTW confguring `lpr` to handle texinfo files is getting a bit silly).

This is now on the mailserver or at: `tsx-11.mit.edu:pub/linux/sources/usr.bin/magic-filter-0.4.tar.gz` (Although the release number will possibly change in future).

`'apsfilter'` is a rather easy to use shell script that requires no additional filters and which is pre-configured for HP compatible laser printers. This is also available on the mailserver.

An example written in C, which may be easily adapted to most installations is available from the printing mail server as `'lpr_if.c'`.

Magic filters should never be specified as `'of'` as the output filter only gets called once if a number of files are printed without a gap. There are other more subtle problems too using `'of'`.

IMHO (Brian) magic filters as `'if'` are inelegant as they may prevent you from listing a PostScript or nroff file. (Most people disagree with me on this point.)

3.31 Magic Filter Examples

The following is an example of a magic shell script which should take either PostScript or text and deal with it:

```
#!/bin/sh
# This is based on a script I received from Scott Doty and which was
# written by Keith Walker.  Keith's script made use of the fact that
# lpd passes options to if:
#
#   <if> -w<width> -l<length> -i<indent> -n <user> -h <host> <accountingfile>
#
# to print text out well at any size.  This one does not.  These options
# are also handy if you want to do your own snazzy header page, much
# like NeWSPrint from Sun does (although running PostScript through
# the display server to get it interpreted is a bit much :)
#
#
```

```
# gs will reset the printer anyway, so the this text setup doesn't matter.
# setup should include the escape code for \n conversion, if applicable.
#
printf "<printer setup for text printing (escape codes, etc)>"

read first_line
first_two_chars='expr $first_line : '\(..\)''

if [ "$first_two_chars" = "%!" ]; then # it's PostScript

        /usr/bin/gs -dSAFER -dNOPAUSE -q -sDEVICE=??????? -sOutputFile=- -

else # it's plain text

        echo -n $first_line
        cat
        printf "\014"

fi
```

Note that for the paranoid, shell scripts run as someone other than the user are sometimes a security hole, but this is not the case with lpd filters as the script's environment is not under the control of the potential cracker.

4 Previewing

These sections describe various ways to preview things under Linux - that is, how to view them in a way approximating their final form without printing them out.

4.1 ghostview

Ghostview, a companion program for gs, previews PostScript on an X display. It also lets you select individual or ranges of pages from a PostScript document to print using lpr. The new version, 1.5, has fixed a few glitches which never bothered me but may make a difference to you. It also calls gs with the '-dSAFER' option and has a few more resource and command-line options relative to 1.4.1. The real installation is from: prep.ai.mit.edu:/pub/gnu/ghostview-*xxx*.tar.gz

It builds out of the box. Ghostview requires gs to work. The new version of gs, 2.6.x, will use X display fonts in an effort to improve legibility at the low resolutions of a video monitor (a previous failing of this pair relative to commercial display-PostScript based systems). This works very well for me at least, at the expense of exact character positioning (X fonts have different widths). In fact, I thought that Ghostview looks better than Sun's pageview the other day when I looked at the same page in oth programs side-by-side. Ghostview/Ghostscript also has much more intelligent color handling than pageview. You might wish to let gs render some Type 1 fonts you install instead of using platform fonts (or the awful fonts gs comes with. To do this while in Ghostview (or in any situation involving the X11 driver), place 'ghostscript.useExternalFonts: false' in your .Xdefaults file, and the platform fonts will not be used.

This is part of a message posted to gnu.ghostscript.bug by Tim Theisen <ghostview@cs.wisc.edu>:

> (note that the usual Linux X-server, XFree, is simply an enhanced version of MIT's effort at an i386 X-server (X386), and does contain the X11R5 Type 1 rasterizer which I beleive was contributed by IBM.)

> Ghostscript now uses the X Toolkit to pick up X Resources. Now ghostscript uses the standard X rules that allow more specific resources to override less specific ones giving users the full power of X resources to control the X11 driver. It also allows system administrators to establish an application defaults file with resources specific to their ghostscript installation.

> The customization choices mentioned in make.doc have been moved into X resources and are now configured at run time rather than compile time. Sorry, this section of make.doc did not get revised for the 2.6.1 release.

> If useBackingPixmap is set, ghostscript will attempt to allocate a backing pixmap. If one cannot be allocated, ghostscript will issue a warning and ask for backing store instead. (Since there were insufficient resources for a backing pixmap, the X server may not provide backing store either.)

> Color Handling was totally revamped for gs 2.6.

Ghostscript first checks for a suitable standard colormap. If you have static colormap in your X server, it would be best to store a standard colormap property on the root window describing the color layout. Ghostscript will then be able to take full advantage of the device. If you have a standard colormap installed, ghostscript will start slightly faster since it does not have to allocate colors for a cube or ramp.

If no standard colormap is available, ghostscript will allocate an RGB cube or gray ramp. Ghostscript tries for a 5x5x5 cube on a color device, and a 128 gray ramp on grayscale devices. It will never ask for more than 1/2 of the colors for a RGB cube or gray ramp. It also takes into account the number of significant bits per pixel. (i.e. It won't ask for 128 gray levels if you only have 16 available.)

Ghostscript will attempt to allocate colors that are off the color cube/ramp as the picture is being rendered. Ghostscript will keep track of 256 dynamic colors. After all these are allocated, ghostscript asks the X server directly.

The foreground and background color can be set explicitly. This is important for the visually impaired and when using the ghostview widget.

Color Resources:

1. `palette`(Palette): Default value: 'Color'. Other allowable settings: 'Grayscale', 'Monochrome'. The palette resource is used to restrict the palette used for display. One can set palette to 'Grayscale' or 'Monochrome' to see how a file would be rendered in grayscale or monochrome on a color display. I use it to avoid dithering of gray- scale figures on a color display with 4-bit DACs.

2. `maxGrayRamp`(MaxGrayRamp): Default value: 128. Maximum number of gray levels that ghostscript will attempt to allocate. (It won't try for more than this on an 8-bit pseudo color display even if you set it higher.) Set this lower if you want a smaller ramp and would prefer ghostscript to use dynamic colors.

3. `maxRGBCube`(MaxRGBCube): Default value: 5. Maximum number of colors levels that ghostscript will attempt to allocate. (It won't try for more than this on an 8-bit pseudo color display even if you set it higher.) Set this lower if you want a smaller ramp and would prefer ghostscript to use dynamic colors.

I believe these values to be a good compromise between dynamic allocation and fall back onto a fairly good color cube for dithering.

You can use the foreground and background colors to accomplish "reverse video". However, if you have a grayscale device, it may be better to reverse the gray ramp using the following PostScript code fragment:

```
[{1 exch sub} /exec load currenttransfer /exec load] cvx settransfer
```

The X11 driver now supports native X11 fonts. If you have installed the HP XLFD font extensions into your font or X server. Ghostscript will also be able to use platform fonts at rotations of 90 degrees, with mirroring, and anamorphic scaling.

The X11 driver does most if its work silently. You can get it to report when it is using an X11 font by setting the logExternalFonts boolean in your X resources.

The X11 driver is setup to use the standard fonts distributed with X11R5. We purchased the Adobe Type Manager and the Adobe Plus Pack. These font packages give all the fonts normally found in the Apple LaserWriter Plus. The X11 driver is setup to handle these fonts as well. (They are a superset of the bitmap fonts distributed with X11.)

You may set the regularFonts, symbolFonts, or dinbatFonts resources if you have different fonts available. Each font name must have 7 dashes or it will be ignored. Minimize the use of wildcards to promote faster matching. (I once encountered an X server that took many seconds to do a font lookup when wildcards were carelessly used.)

There is a different list of fonts for each common encoding. Regular fonts may be accessed in standard or ISO Latin 1 encoding. The bdf files that are distributed with X11 are in the ISO Latin 1 encoding. This leaves out the ligatures. Luckily, the ligatures are present in the bdf files, but are not given an encoding, essentially commenting them out. You can use the `fixfont` program from the xproof distribution (`Ftp.Cs.Wisc.Edu:/Pub/X/Xproof.Tar.Z`, or `Ftp.X.Org:/Contrib/Xproof.Tar.Z`) to reencode the bdf files and build X11 fonts that contain the ligatures (i.e standard encoding).

If you have the Type1 fonts mentioned above, and you installed the Type1 rasterizer into you font or X server, you can use the appended fonts.scale to name your fonts so that ghostscript can find them.

Font resources:

1. `useExternalFonts`(`UseExternalFonts`): Default value: true. This resource controls whether X11 fonts will be used.

2. `useScalableFonts`(`UseScalableFonts`): Default value: true. This resource controls whether scalable fonts will be used. If you have an outline scaler in your X server, you should have this on. If you have an X terminal, you may get slightly better performance with this on. If you have to use the X11 bitmap scaler, turn this off. Fonts scaled by the bitmap scaler look worse than the default ghostscript fonts.

3. `logExternalFonts`(`LogExternalFonts`): Default value: false. Controls whether to report when X11 fonts are being used.

The following fonts.scale makes all of the fonts of the Adobe Type Manager and Adobe Plus pack available in standard and ISO Latin 1 encoding. (We were able to purchase the above two packages at an educational discount price of $150.)

70
agw......pfb -Adobe-ITC Avant Garde Gothic-Book-r-normal–0-0-0-0-p-0-iso8859-1
agwo......pfb -Adobe-ITC Avant Garde Gothic-Book-o-normal–0-0-0-0-p-0-iso8859-1
agd......pfb -Adobe-ITC Avant Garde Gothic-Demi-r-normal–0-0-0-0-p-0-iso8859-1
agdo......pfb -Adobe-ITC Avant Garde Gothic-Demi-o-normal–0-0-0-0-p-0-iso8859-1
bkl......pfb -Adobe-ITC Bookman-Light-r-normal–0-0-0-0-p-0-iso8859-1
bkli......pfb -Adobe-ITC Bookman-Light-i-normal–0-0-0-0-p-0-iso8859-1
bkd......pfb -Adobe-ITC Bookman-Demi-r-normal–0-0-0-0-p-0-iso8859-1
bkdi......pfb -Adobe-ITC Bookman-Demi-i-normal–0-0-0-0-p-0-iso8859-1
com......pfb -Adobe-Courier-Medium-r-normal–0-0-0-0-m-0-iso8859-1
coo......pfb -Adobe-Courier-Medium-o-normal–0-0-0-0-m-0-iso8859-1
cob......pfb -Adobe-Courier-Bold-r-normal–0-0-0-0-m-0-iso8859-1
cobo......pfb -Adobe-Courier-Bold-o-normal–0-0-0-0-m-0-iso8859-1
hv......pfb -Adobe-Helvetica-Medium-r-normal–0-0-0-0-p-0-iso8859-1
hvo......pfb -Adobe-Helvetica-Medium-o-normal–0-0-0-0-p-0-iso8859-1

```
hvb_____.pfb -Adobe-Helvetica-Bold-r-normal--0-0-0-0-p-0-iso8859-1
hvbo_____.pfb -Adobe-Helvetica-Bold-o-normal--0-0-0-0-p-0-iso8859-1
hvn_____.pfb -Adobe-Helvetica-Medium-r-Narrow--0-0-0-0-p-0-iso8859-1
hvno_____.pfb -Adobe-Helvetica-Medium-o-Narrow--0-0-0-0-p-0-iso8859-1
hvnb_____.pfb -Adobe-Helvetica-Bold-r-Narrow--0-0-0-0-p-0-iso8859-1
hvnbo_____.pfb -Adobe-Helvetica-Bold-o-Narrow--0-0-0-0-p-0-iso8859-1
ncr_____.pfb -Adobe-New Century Schoolbook-Medium-r-normal--0-0-0-0-p-0-iso8859-1
nci_____.pfb -Adobe-New Century Schoolbook-Medium-i-normal--0-0-0-0-p-0-iso8859-1
ncb_____.pfb -Adobe-New Century Schoolbook-Bold-r-normal--0-0-0-0-p-0-iso8859-1
ncbi_____.pfb -Adobe-New Century Schoolbook-Bold-i-normal--0-0-0-0-p-0-iso8859-1
por_____.pfb -Adobe-Palatino-Medium-r-normal--0-0-0-0-p-0-iso8859-1
poi_____.pfb -Adobe-Palatino-Medium-i-normal--0-0-0-0-p-0-iso8859-1
pob_____.pfb -Adobe-Palatino-Bold-r-normal--0-0-0-0-p-0-iso8859-1
pobi_____.pfb -Adobe-Palatino-Bold-i-normal--0-0-0-0-p-0-iso8859-1
sy_____.pfb -Adobe-Symbol-Medium-r-normal--0-0-0-0-p-0-iso8859-1
tir_____.pfb -Adobe-Times-Medium-r-normal--0-0-0-0-p-0-iso8859-1
tii_____.pfb -Adobe-Times-Medium-i-normal--0-0-0-0-p-0-iso8859-1
tib_____.pfb -Adobe-Times-Bold-r-normal--0-0-0-0-p-0-iso8859-1
tibi_____.pfb -Adobe-Times-Bold-i-normal--0-0-0-0-p-0-iso8859-1
zcmi_____.pfb -Adobe-ITC Zapf Chancery-Medium-i-normal--0-0-0-0-p-0-iso8859-1
zd_____.pfb -Adobe-ITC Zapf Dingbats-Medium-r-normal--0-0-0-0-p-0-iso8859-1
agw_____.pfb -Adobe-ITC Avant Garde Gothic-Book-r-normal--0-0-0-0-p-0-adobe-fontspecific
agwo_____.pfb -Adobe-ITC Avant Garde Gothic-Book-o-normal--0-0-0-0-p-0-adobe-fontspecific
agd_____.pfb -Adobe-ITC Avant Garde Gothic-Demi-r-normal--0-0-0-0-p-0-adobe-fontspecific
agdo_____.pfb -Adobe-ITC Avant Garde Gothic-Demi-o-normal--0-0-0-0-p-0-adobe-fontspecific
bkl_____.pfb -Adobe-ITC Bookman-Light-r-normal--0-0-0-0-p-0-adobe-fontspecific
bkli_____.pfb -Adobe-ITC Bookman-Light-i-normal--0-0-0-0-p-0-adobe-fontspecific
bkd_____.pfb -Adobe-ITC Bookman-Demi-r-normal--0-0-0-0-p-0-adobe-fontspecific
bkdi_____.pfb -Adobe-ITC Bookman-Demi-i-normal--0-0-0-0-p-0-adobe-fontspecific
com_____.pfb -Adobe-Courier-Medium-r-normal--0-0-0-0-m-0-adobe-fontspecific
coo_____.pfb -Adobe-Courier-Medium-o-normal--0-0-0-0-m-0-adobe-fontspecific
cob_____.pfb -Adobe-Courier-Bold-r-normal--0-0-0-0-m-0-adobe-fontspecific
cobo_____.pfb -Adobe-Courier-Bold-o-normal--0-0-0-0-m-0-adobe-fontspecific
hv_____.pfb -Adobe-Helvetica-Medium-r-normal--0-0-0-0-p-0-adobe-fontspecific
hvo_____.pfb -Adobe-Helvetica-Medium-o-normal--0-0-0-0-p-0-adobe-fontspecific
hvb_____.pfb -Adobe-Helvetica-Bold-r-normal--0-0-0-0-p-0-adobe-fontspecific
hvbo_____.pfb -Adobe-Helvetica-Bold-o-normal--0-0-0-0-p-0-adobe-fontspecific
hvn_____.pfb -Adobe-Helvetica-Medium-r-Narrow--0-0-0-0-p-0-adobe-fontspecific
hvno_____.pfb -Adobe-Helvetica-Medium-o-Narrow--0-0-0-0-p-0-adobe-fontspecific
hvnb_____.pfb -Adobe-Helvetica-Bold-r-Narrow--0-0-0-0-p-0-adobe-fontspecific
hvnbo_____.pfb -Adobe-Helvetica-Bold-o-Narrow--0-0-0-0-p-0-adobe-fontspecific
ncr_____.pfb -Adobe-New Century Schoolbook-Medium-r-normal--0-0-0-0-p-0-adobe-fontspecific
nci_____.pfb -Adobe-New Century Schoolbook-Medium-i-normal--0-0-0-0-p-0-adobe-fontspecific
ncb_____.pfb -Adobe-New Century Schoolbook-Bold-r-normal--0-0-0-0-p-0-adobe-fontspecific
ncbi_____.pfb -Adobe-New Century Schoolbook-Bold-i-normal--0-0-0-0-p-0-adobe-fontspecific
por_____.pfb -Adobe-Palatino-Medium-r-normal--0-0-0-0-p-0-adobe-fontspecific
poi_____.pfb -Adobe-Palatino-Medium-i-normal--0-0-0-0-p-0-adobe-fontspecific
pob_____.pfb -Adobe-Palatino-Bold-r-normal--0-0-0-0-p-0-adobe-fontspecific
pobi_____.pfb -Adobe-Palatino-Bold-i-normal--0-0-0-0-p-0-adobe-fontspecific
sy_____.pfb -Adobe-Symbol-Medium-r-normal--0-0-0-0-p-0-adobe-fontspecific
tir_____.pfb -Adobe-Times-Medium-r-normal--0-0-0-0-p-0-adobe-fontspecific
tii_____.pfb -Adobe-Times-Medium-i-normal--0-0-0-0-p-0-adobe-fontspecific
tib_____.pfb -Adobe-Times-Bold-r-normal--0-0-0-0-p-0-adobe-fontspecific
tibi_____.pfb -Adobe-Times-Bold-i-normal--0-0-0-0-p-0-adobe-fontspecific
zcmi_____.pfb -Adobe-ITC Zapf Chancery-Medium-i-normal--0-0-0-0-p-0-adobe-fontspecific
zd_____.pfb -Adobe-ITC Zapf Dingbats-Medium-r-normal--0-0-0-0-p-0-adobe-fontspecific
```

4.2 gspreview

This is another front-end for Ghostscript. I have gotten and built it, and actually preferred the user interface, but it had a few bugs. It didn't seem as full-featured as ghostview, though. (Not that there are all **that** many features in ghostview, but it does its job well). `ftp.x.org:/contrib/gspreview...`

4.3 xdvi

A beautifully legible previewing program for dvi with a handy zoom+pan feature. Will not interpret PostScript specials, which are understood only by `dvips` (back to the compiler, object file, and now linker analogy :-) To view a file, do `'xdvi file.dvi'`. This comes with either TEX or X in most distributions. Either way, you've probably got one. If not, look in `ftp.x.org:/contrib/`.

4.4 xtex

Xtex is similar in purpose to xdvi. I have tried to build it under Linux and failed. It is available as: `ftp.x.org:/contrib/xtex-2.18.5.tar.z`

4.5 gxditview

Ditview produces a preview version of `troff` source using X fonts. `'groff -TX100 -mandoc man page'` will run gxditview to show you a typeset version of the man page. `'-TX75'` is the same thing, but tiny. Most distributions don't have a working one at all. A good one comes with the source to `groff`, which you might want to get anyway for the additional drivers (some distributions are missing some, including PostScript).
`prep.ai.mit.edu:/pub/gnu/groff-xxxx.tar.z`

4.6 non-X previewing

Ghostscript comes with pc video hardware drivers, but under un*x these are not a good thing. However, there are `gs` binaries around which will use the Linux VGA library (`svgalib`). The Ghostscript device for this is called linux, thus `'gs -sDEVICE=linux file.ps'` will show you an image of the PostScript. The environment variable `GSVGAMODE` is important for this. Set it to the nuber of the video mode you want, taken from the vga.h which comes with vgalib.

If you need this driver, a patch to put in Linux svgalib is available from the printing mail server or as:

```
ws105.zfn.uni-bremen.de:/pub/gs261-linuxdriver.sh
ws105.zfn.uni-bremen.de:/pub/gs261-svgalib.tar.gz
```

Another possibly different svgalib patch is found in:

`ftp.cdrom.com:/pub/linux/misc`

The plain vgalib driver is available on Sunsite.

Texmgr is a program which will preview dvi under MGR. I don't beleive that it currently works under Linux MGR, but if it does, MGR uses sufficiently less memory and disk that this might be an attractive option for some.

dvgt is a program which will preview dvi with Linux svgalib, or on one of several types of graphics terminals including vt, tek, or a PC with MS-Kermit. It is available on sunsite.

5 Ascii Translation

These sections describe various programs which can generate plain ascii from some file formats.

5.1 from TeX

Lametex will generate ascii from TeX source. It is available as:
`sunsite.unc.edu:/pub/Linux/apps/tex/lametex.tar.z`

LaTeX is used by the Linux Doc Projext to generate text versions of their manuals. I don't know where to find it.

5.2 from dvi

`dvi2tty` is a program which will process dvi into text. Apparently, it will also make an effort at reproducing graphics as well. I do not know where to find it.

5.3 from PostScript

Ghostscript 2.6.1 comes with a script file which will use `gs` to extract just the text from a ps file, called `ps2ascii`. (see Section 2.3 [PostScript], page 1308, for information above for where it can be found). Further documentation is in the Ghostscript 2.6.1 distribution files `gs_2asc.ps` and `use.doc`

5.4 from troff

`groff -Tascii` or `-Tlatin1` ...

5.5 from ascii/latin1

The GNU program `recode` handles conversion between various forms of straight text encoding, ie from Latin-1 to ASCII. This is available on prep.ai.mit.edu.

Part XXXVI

Linux SCSI HOWTO

Copyright Drew Eckhardt, drew@cs.colorado.edu
v2.15, 20 March 1995
This HOWTO covers the Linux SCSI subsystem, as implemented in Linux kernel revision 1.1.74 and newer alpha code. Earlier revisions of the SCSI code are *unsupported*, and may differ significantly in terms of the drivers implemented, performance, and options available.

Contents

1   Introduction

1.1   License

Noncommercial redistributions of a verbatim copy in any medium physical or electronic are permitted without express permission of the author. Translations are similarly permitted without express permission if they includes a notice on who translated it.

Commercial redistribution is allowed and encouraged, provided that the author is notified of any such distributions and given opportunity to to provide a more up-to-date version.

Short quotes may be used without prior consent by the author. Derivative work and partial distributions of the SCSI-HOWTO must include either a verbatim copy of this file or make a verbatim copy of this file available. If the latter is the case, a pointer to the verbatim copy must be stated at a clearly visible place.

In short, we wish to promote dissemination of this information through as many channels as possible. However, we do wish to retain copyright on the HOWTO documents, to be notified of any plans to redistribute the HOWTOs to insure that outdated versions don't spread too far, and for ALL the information provided in the HOWTOS to be disseminated. If you have questions on the Linux documentation project, please contact Matt Welsh, the Linux HOWTO coordinator, at mdw@sunsite.unc.edu. Questions regarding this document itself should be addressed to Drew Eckhardt, drew@Colorado.EDU.

1.2   Important Note

IMPORTANT:

BUG REPORTS WHICH FAIL TO FOLLOW THE PROCEDURE OUTLINED IN SECTION 2 WILL BE IGNORED.

For additional information, you may wish to join the SCSI channel of the Linux activists list - mail to linux-activists-request@joker.cs.hut.fi. with the line

```
X-Mn-Admin: join SCSI
```

in the header, as well as the Linux SCSI list by mailing majordomo@vger.rutgers.edu with the line

```
subscribe linux-scsi
```

in the text.

I'm aware that this document isn't the most user-friendly, and that there may be inaccuracies and oversights. If you have constructive comments on how to rectify the situation you're free to mail me about it.

2   Common Problems

This section lists some of the common problems that people have. If there is not anything here that answers your questions, you should also consult the sections for your host adapter and the devices in that are giving you problems.

2.1   General Flakiness

If you experience random errors, the most likely causes are cabling and termination problems.

Some products, such as those built around the newer NCR chips, feature digital filtering and active signal negation, and aren't very sensitive to cabling problems.

Others, such as the Adaptec 154xC, 154xCF, and 274x, are *extremely* sensitive and may fail with cables that work with other systems.

I reiterate: some host adapters are **extremely** sensitive to cabling and termination problems and therefore, cabling and termination should be the first things checked when there are problems.

To minimize your problems, you should use cables which

1. Claim SCSI-II compliance

2. Have a characteristic impedance of 132 ohms

3. All come from the same source to avoid impedance mismatches

4. Come from a reputable vendor such as Amphenol

Termination power should be provided by *all* devices on the SCSI bus, through a diode to prevent current backflow, so that sufficient power is available at the ends of the cable where it is needed. To prevent damage if the bus is shorted, TERMPWR should be driven through a fuse or other current limiting device.

If multiple devices, external cables, or FAST SCSI 2 are used, active or forced perfect termination should be used on both ends of the SCSI bus.

See the `comp.periphs.scsi` FAQ (`ftp://tsx-11.mit.edu/pub/linux/ALPHA/scsi`) for more information about active termination.

2.2 The kernel command line

Other parts of the documentation refer to a "kernel command line".

The kernel command line is a set of options you may specify from either the LILO: prompt after an image name, or in the append field in your LILO configuration file (LILO .14 and newer use /etc/lilo.conf, older versions use /etc/lilo/config).

Boot your system with LILO, and hit one of the alt, control, or shift keys when it first comes up to get a prompt. LILO should respond with

```
boot:
```

At this prompt, you can select a kernel image to boot, or list them with "?". Ie

```
boot: ?

ramdisk floppy harddisk
```

To boot that kernel with the command line options you have selected, simply enter the name followed by a white space delimited list of options, terminating with a return.

Options take the form of

```
variable=valuelist
```

Where valuelist may be a single value or comma delimited list of values with no whitespace. With the exception of root device, individual values are numbers, and may be specified in either decimal or hexadecimal.

Ie, to boot Linux with an Adaptec 1520 clone not recognized at bootup, you might type

```
boot: floppy aha152x=0x340,11,7,1
```

If you don't care to type all of this at boot time, it is also possible to use the LILO configuration file "append" option with LILO .13 and newer.

Ie,

```
append="aha152x=0x340,11,7,1"
```

2.3   A SCSI device shows up at all possible IDs

If this is the case, you have strapped the device at the same address as the controller (typically 7, although some boards use other addresses, with 6 being used by some Future Domain boards).

Please change the jumper settings.

2.4   A SCSI device shows up at all possible LUNs

The device has buggy firmware.

As an interim solution, you should try using the kernel command line option

```
max_scsi_luns=1
```

If that works, there is a list of buggy devices in the kernel sources in drivers/scsi/scsi.c in the variable blacklist. Add your device to this list and mail the patch to Linus.

2.5   You get sense errors when you know the devices are error free

Sometimes this is caused by bad cables or improper termination.

See 2.1: General Flakiness

2.6   A kernel configured with networking does not work.

The auto-probe routines for many of the network drivers are not passive, and will interfere with operation with some of the SCSI drivers.

2.7   Device detected, but unable to access.

A SCSI device is detected by the kernel, but you are unable to access it - i.e. mkfs /dev/sdc, tar xvf /dev/rst2, etc fails.

You don't have a special file in /dev for the device.

Unix devices are identified as either block or character (block devices go through the buffer cache, character devices do not) devices, a major number (i.e. which driver is used - block major 8 corresponds to SCSI disks) and a minor number (i.e. which unit is being accessed through a given driver - i.e. character major 4, minor 0 is the first virtual console, minor 1 the next, etc). However, accessing devices through this separate namespace would break the Unix/Linux metaphor of "everything is a file," so character and block device special files are created under /dev. This lets you access the raw third SCSI disk device as /dev/sdc, the first serial port as /dev/ttyS0, etc.

The preferred method for creating a file is using the MAKEDEV script:

```
cd /dev
```

and run MAKEDEV (as root) for the devices you want to create - i.e.

```
./MAKEDEV sdc
```

wildcards "should" work - i.e.

```
./MAKEDEV sd\*
```

"should" create entries for all SCSI disk devices (doing this should create /dev/sda through /dev/sdp, with fifteen partition entries for each)

```
./MAKEDEV sdc\*
```

"should" create entries for /dev/sdc and all fifteen permissible partitions on /dev/sdc, etc.

I say "should" because this is the standard Unix behavior - the MAKEDEV script in your installation may not conform to this behavior, or may have restricted the number of devices it will create.

If MAKEDEV won't do the right magic for you, you'll have to create the device entries by hand with the mknod command.

The block/character type, major, and minor numbers are specified for the various SCSI devices in Subsection 3: Device Files in the appropriate section.

Take those numbers, and use (as root)

```
mknod /dev/device b|c major minor
```

i.e. -

```
mknod /dev/sdc b 8 32
mknod /dev/rst0 c 9 0
```

2.8   SCSI System Lockups

This could be one of a number of things. Also see the section for your specific host adapter for possible further solutions.

There are cases where the lockups seem to occur when multiple devices are in use at the same time. In this case, you can try contacting the manufacturer of the devices and see if firmware upgrades are available which would correct the problem. If possible, try a different SCSI cable, or try on another system. This can also be caused by bad blocks on disks, or by bad handling of DMA by the motherboard (for host adapters that do DMA). There are probably many other possible conditions that could lead to this type of event.

Sometimes these problems occur when there are multiple devices in use on the bus at the same time. In this case, if your host adapter driver supports more than one outstanding command on the bus at one time, try reducing this to 1 and see if this helps. If you have tape drives or slow CD-ROM drives on the bus, this might not be a practical solution.

2.9   Configuring and building the kernel

Unused SCSI drivers eat up valuable memory, aggravating memory shortage problems on small systems because kernel memory is unpagable.

So, you will want to build a kernel tuned for your system, with only the drivers you need installed.

cd to /usr/src/linux

If you are using a root device other than the current one, or something other than 80x25 VGA, and you are writing a boot floppy, you should edit the makefile, and make sure the

```
ROOT_DEV =
```

and

```
SVGA_MODE =
```

lines are the way you want them.

If you've installed any patches, you may wish to guarantee that all files are rebuilt. If this is the case, you should type

```
make mrproper
```

Regardless of whether you ran make mrproper, type

```
make config
```

and answer the configuration questions. Then run

```
make depend
```

and finally

```
make
```

Once the build completes, you may wish to update the lilo configuration, or write a boot floppy. A boot floppy may be made by running

```
make zdisk
```

2.10   LUNS other than 0 don't work

This is often a problem with SCSI-> MFM, RLL, ESDI, SMD, and similar bridge boards.

At some point, we came to the conclusion that many SCSI-I devices were extremely broken, and added the following code

```
/* Some scsi-1 peripherals do not handle lun != 0.
   I am assuming that scsi-2 peripherals do better */
if((scsi_result[2] & 0x07) == 1 &&
   (scsi_result[3] & 0x0f) == 0) break;
```

to scan_scsis() in drivers/scsi/scsi.c. If you delete this code, your old devices should be detected correctly if you have not used the max_scsi_luns kernel command line option, or the NO_MULTI_LUN compile time define.

3   Reporting Bugs

The Linux SCSI developers don't necessarily maintain old revisions of the code due to space constraints. So, if you are not running the latest publically released Linux kernel (note that many of the Linux distributions, such as MCC, SLS, Yggdrasil, etc. often lag one or even twenty patches behind this) chances are we will be unable to solve your problem. So, before reporting a bug, please check to see if it exists with the latest publically available kernel.

If after upgrading, and reading this document thoroughly, you still believe that you have a bug, please mail a bug report to the SCSI channel of the mailing list where it will be seen by many of the people who've contributed to the Linux SCSI drivers.

In your bug report, please provide as much information as possible regarding your hardware configuration, the exact text of all of the messages that Linux prints when it boots, when the error condition occurs, and where in the source code the error is. Use the procedures outlined in Section 2.1 : Capturing messages and Section 2.2 : Locating the source of a panic().

Failure to provide the maximum possible amount of information may result in misdiagnosis of your problem, or developers deciding that there are other more interesting problems to fix.

The bottom line is that if we can't reproduce your bug, and you can't point at us what's broken, it won't get fixed.

3.1   Capturing messages

If you are not running a kernel message logging system :

Insure that the /proc filesystem is mounted.

```
grep proc /etc/mtab
```

If the /proc filesystem is not mounted, mount it

```
mkdir /proc
chmod 755 /proc
mount -t proc /proc /proc
```

Copy the kernel revision and messages into a log file

```
cat /proc/version >/tmp/log
cat /proc/kmsg >>/tmp/log
```

Type Ctrl-C after a second or two.

If you are running some logger, you'll have to poke through the appropriate log files (/etc/syslog.conf should be of some use in locating them), or use dmesg.

If Linux is not yet bootstrapped, format a floppy diskette under DOS. Note that if you have a distribution which mounts the root diskette off of floppy rather than RAM drive, you'll have to format a diskette readable in the drive not being used to mount root or use their ramdisk boot option.

Boot Linux off your distribution boot floppy, preferably in single user mode using a RAM disk as root.

```
mkdir /tmp/dos
```

Insert the diskette in a drive not being used to mount root, and mount it. I.E.

```
mount -t msdos /dev/fd0 /tmp/dos
```

or

```
mount -t msdos /dev/fd1 /tmp/dos
```

Copy your log to it

```
cp /tmp/log /tmp/dos/log
```

Unmount the DOS floppy

```
umount /tmp/dos
```

And shutdown Linux

```
shutdown
```

Reboot into DOS, and using your favorite communications software include the log file in your trouble mail.

3.2   Locating the source of a panic()

Like other Unices, when a fatal error is encountered, Linux calls the kernel panic() function. Unlike other Unices, Linux doesn't dump core to the swap or dump device and reboot automatically. Instead, a useful summary of state information is printed for the user to manually copy down. I.E. :

```
Unable to handle kernel NULL pointer dereference at virtual address c0000004
current->tss,cr3 = 00101000, \%cr3 = 00101000
*pde = 00102027
*pte = 00000027
Oops: 0000
EIP:     0010:0019c905
EFLAGS: 00010002
eax: 0000000a   ebx: 001cd0e8   ecx: 00000006   edx: 000003d5
esi: 001cd0a8   edi: 00000000   ebp: 00000000   esp: 001a18c0
ds: 0018   es: 0018   fs: 002b   gs: 002b   ss: 0018
Process swapper (pid: 0, process nr: 0, stackpage=001a09c8)
Stack: 0019c5c6 00000000 0019c5b2 00000000 0019c5a5 001cd0a8 00000002 00000000
001cd0e8 001cd0a8 00000000 001cdb38 001cdb00 00000000 001ce284 0019d001
001cd004 0000e800 fbfff000 0019d051 001cd0a8 00000000 001a29f4 00800000
Call Trace: 0019c5c6 0019c5b2 0018c5a5 0019d001 0019d051 00111508 00111502
0011e800 0011154d 00110f63 0010e2b3 0010ef55 0010ddb7
Code: 8b 57 04 52 68 d2 c5 19 00 e8 cd a0 f7 ff 83 c4 20 8b 4f 04
Aiee, killing interrupt handler
kfree of non-kmalloced memory: 001a29c0, next= 00000000, order=0
task[0] (swapper) killed: unable to recover
Kernel panic: Trying to free up swapper memory space
In swapper task - not syncing
```

Take the hexidecimal number on the EIP: line, in this case 19c905, and search through /usr/src/linux/zSystem.map for the highest number not larger than that address. I.E.,

```
0019a000 T _fix_pointers
0019c700 t _intr_scsi
0019d000 t _NCR53c7x0_intr
```

That tells you what function its in. Recompile the source file which defines that function file with debugging enabled, or the whole kernel if you prefer by editing /usr/src/linux/Makefile and adding a "-g" to the CFLAGS definition.

```
##standard CFLAGS
#
```

I.E.,

```
CFLAGS = -Wall -Wstrict-prototypes -O2 -fomit-frame-pointer -pipe
```

becomes

```
CFLAGS = -g -Wall -Wstrict-prototypes -O2 -fomit-frame-pointer -pipe
```

Rebuild the kernel, incrementally or by doing a

```
make clean
make
```

Make the kernel bootable by creating an entry in your /etc/lilo.conf for it

```
image = /usr/src/linux/zImage
label = experimental
```

and re-running LILO as root, or by creating a boot floppy

```
make zImage
```

Reboot and record the new EIP for the error.

If you have script installed, you may want to start it, as it will log your debugging session to the typescript file.

Now, run

```
gdb /usr/src/linux/tools/zSystem
```

and enter

```
info line *<your EIP>
```

I.E.,

```
info line *0x19c905
```

To which GDB will respond something like

```
(gdb) info line *0x19c905
Line 2855 of ''53c7,8xx.c'' starts at address 0x19c905 <intr_scsi+641>and ends
at 0x19c913 <intr_scsi+655>.
```

Record this information. Then, enter list < line number>

I.E.,

```
(gdb) list 2855
2850    /*        printk("scsi%d : target %d lun %d unexpected disconnect\n",
2851                   host->host_no, cmd->cmd->target, cmd->cmd->lun); */
2852              printk("host : 0x%x\n", (unsigned) host);
2853              printk("host->host_no : %d\n", host->host_no);
2854              printk("cmd : 0x%x\n", (unsigned) cmd);
2855              printk("cmd->cmd : 0x%x\n", (unsigned) cmd->cmd);
2856              printk("cmd->cmd->target : %d\n", cmd->cmd->target);
2857              if (cmd) {
2858                   abnormal_finished(cmd, DID_ERROR << 16);
2859              }
2860              hostdata->dsp = hostdata->script + hostdata->E_schedule /
2861                   sizeof(long);
2862              hostdata->dsp_changed = 1;
2863    /* SCSI PARITY error */
2864              }
2865
2866         if (sstat0_sist0 & SSTAT0_PAR) {
2867              fatal = 1;
2868              if (cmd && cmd->cmd) {
2869                   printk("scsi%d : target %d lun %d parity error.\n",
```

Obviously, quit will take you out of GDB.

Record this information too, as it will provide a context incase the developers' kernels differ from yours.

4   Hosts

This section gives specific information about the various host adapters that are supported in some way or another under Linux.

4.1   Supported and Unsupported Hardware

Drivers in the distribution kernel :

Adaptec 152x, Adaptec 154x (including clones from Bustek and DTC 329x boards), Adaptec 174x, Adaptec 274x/284x/2940, EATA-DMA protocol compilant boards (all DPT PMXXXXX/XX and SKXXXXX/XX except the PM2001, some boards from NEC and ATT), Future Domain 850, 885, 950, and other boards in that series (but not the 840, 841, 880, and 881 boards unless you make the appropriate patch), Future Domain 16x0 with TMC-1800, TMC-18C30, or TMC-18C50 chips, NCR53c8xx,PAS16 SCSI ports, Seagate ST0x, Trantor T128/T130/T228 boards, Ultrastor 14F, 24F, and 34F, and Western Digital 7000.

Alpha drivers: Richoh GSI-8

Many of the ALPHA drivers are available via anonymous FTP from (ftp://tsx-11.mit.edu:/pub/linux/ALPHA/scsi)

Drivers that are being developed, but aren't publically available yet, and modifications needed to make existing drivers compatable with other boards: DPT PM2001

Announcements WILL be made when drivers are available for public alpha testing. Until then, please don't use up the developers' valuable time with mail asking for release dates, etc.

- NCR53c8x0/7x0

  - A NCR53c8xx driver has been developed, and with modifications ranging from minor to severe should support these chips

- NCR53c720 - detection changes, initializaion changes, modification of the assembler to use the 720's register mapping
- NCR53c710 - detection changes, initialization changes, modification of assembler, modification of the NCR code to use fatal interrupts or GPIO generated non fatal interrupts for command completion.
- NCR53c700, NCR53c700-66 - detection changes, initialization changes, modification of NCR code to not use DSA, modification of Linux code to handle context switches.

- NCR53c9x family

- Qlogic

SCSI hosts that will not work :

- All parallel-> SCSI adapters

- Rancho SCSI boards

- and Grass Roots SCSI boards.

SCSI hosts that will NEVER work:

- Non Adaptec compatable DTC boards (including the 3270 and 3280).

  Aquiring programming information requires a non-disclosure agreement with DTC. This means that it would be impossible to distribute a Linux driver if one were written, since complying with the NDA would mean distributing no source, in violation of the GPL, and complying with the GPL would mean distributing source, in violation of the NDA.

If you want to run Linux on an unsupported piece of hardware, your options are to either write a driver yourself (Eric Youngdale and I are usually willing to answer technical questions concerning the Linux SCSI drivers) or to commision a driver.

4.1.1 Multiple host adapters

With some host adapters (see 9: Buyers' Guide : Feature Comparison), you can use multiple host adapters of the same type in the same system. With multiple adapters of the same type in the same system, generally the one at the lowest address will be scsi0, the one at the next address scsi1, etc.

In all cases, it is possible to use multiple host adapters of different types, provided that none of their addresses conflict. SCSI controllers are scanned in the order specified in the builtin_scsi_hosts[ ]array in drivers/scsi/hosts.c, with the order currently being

1. Ultrastor

2. Adaptec 151x/152x

3. Buslogic

4. Adaptec 154x

5. Adaptec 174x

6. Future Domain 16x0

7. Always IN2000

8. Generic NCR5380

9. PAS16

10. Seagate

11. Trantor T128/T130

12. NCR53c8xx

13. EATA-DMA

14. WD7000

15. debugging driver.

In most cases (i.e., you aren't trying to use both Buslogic and Adaptec drivers), this can be changed to suit your needs (i.e., keeping the same devices when new SCSI devices are added to the system on a new controller) by moving the individual entries.

4.2   Common Problems

4.2.1   SCSI timeouts

Make sure interrupts are enabled correctly, and there are no IRQ, DMA, or address conflicts with other boards.

4.2.2   Failure of autoprobe routines on boards that rely on

BIOS for autoprobe.

If your SCSI adapter is one of the following :

- Adaptec 152x
- Adaptec 151x
- Adaptec AIC-6260
- Adaptec AIC-6360
- Future Domain 1680
- Future Domain TMC-950
- Future Domain TMC-8xx
- Trantor T128
- Trantor T128F
- Trantor T228F
- Seagate ST01
- Seagate ST02
- Western Digital 7000

and it is not detected on bootup, i.e. you get a

```
scsi : 0 hosts
```

message or a

```
scsi\%d : type
```

message is not printed for each supported SCSI adapter installed in the system, you may have a problem with the autoprobe routine not knowing about your board.

Autodetection will fail for drivers using the BIOS for autodetection if the BIOS is disabled. Double check that your BIOS is enabled, and not conflicting with any other peripherial BIOSes.

Autodetection will also fail if the board's "signature" and/or BIOS address don't match known ones.

If the BIOS is installed, please use DOS and DEBUG to find a signature that will detect your board -

I.E., if your board lives at 0xc8000, under DOS do

```
debug
d c800:0
q
```

and send a message to the SCSI channel of the mailing list with the ASCII message, with the length and offset from the base address (i.e., 0xc8000). Note that the **exact** text is required, and you should provide both the hex and ASCII portions of the text.

If no BIOS is installed, and you are using an Adaptec 152x, Trantor T128, or Seagate driver, you can use command line or compile time overrides to force detection.

Please consult the appropriate subsection for your SCSI board as well as 2.1.

4.2.3 Failure of boards using memory mapped I/O

(This include the Trantor T128 and Seagate boards, but not the Adaptec, Generic NCR5380, PAS16, and Ultrastor drivers)

This is often caused when the memory mapped I/O ports are incorrectly cached. You should have the board's address space marked as uncachable in the XCMOS settings.

If this is not possible, you will have to disable cache entirely.

If you have manually specified the address of the board, remember that Linux needs the actual address of the board, and not the 16 byte segment the documentation may refer to. I.E., 0xc8000 would be correct, 0xc800 would not work and could cause memory corruption.

4.2.4 "kernel panic : cannot mount root device" when booting

an ALPHA driver boot floppy

You'll need to edit the binary image of the kernel (before or after writing it out to disk), and modify a few two byte fields (little endian) to gurantee that it will work on your system.

1. default swap device at offset 502, this should be set to 0x00 0x00

2. ram disk size at offset 504, this should be set to the size of the boot floppy in K - i.e., 5.25" = 1200, 3.5" = 1440.

   This means the bytes are

   ```
   3.5"  : 0xA0 0x05
   5.25" : 0xB0  0x04
   ```

3. root device offset at 508, this should be 0x00 0x00, i.e. the boot device.

dd or rawrite the file to a disk. Insert the disk in the first floppy drive, wait until it prompts you to insert the root disk, and insert the root floppy from your distribution.

4.2.5   Installing a device driver not included with the distribution kernel

You need to start with the version of the kernel used by the driver author. This revision may be alluded to in the documentation included with the driver.

Various   recent   kernel   revisions   can   be   found   at (ftp://nic.funet.fi/pub/OS/Linux/PEOPLE/Linus)

as linux-version.tar.gz

They are also mirrored at tsx-11.mit.edu and various other sites.

cd to /usr/src.

Remove your old Linux sources, if you want to keep a backup copy of them

```
mv linux linux-old
```

Untar the archive

```
gunzip <linux-0.99.12.tar.gz | tar xvfp -
```

Apply the patches. The patches will be relative to some directory in the filesystem. By examining the output file lines in the patch file (grep for ^—), you can tell where this is - i.e. patches with these lines

```
--- ./kernel/blk_drv/scsi/Makefile
```

```
--- ./config.in Wed Sep  1 16:19:33 1993
```

would have the files relative to /usr/src/linux.

Untar the driver sources at an appropriate place - you can type

```
tar tfv patches.tar
```

to get a listing, and move files as necessary (The SCSI driver files should live in /usr/src/linux/kernel/drivers/scsi).

Either cd to the directory they are relative to and type

```
patch -p0 <patch_file
```

or tell patch to strip off leading path components. I.E., if the files started with

```
--- linux-new/kernel/blk_drv/scsi/Makefile
```

and you wanted to apply them while in /usr/src/linux, you could cd to /usr/src/linux and type

```
patch -p1 < patches
```

to strip off the "linux-new" component.

After you have applied the patches, look for any patch rejects, which will be the name of the rejected file with a # suffix appended.

```
find /usr/src/linux/ -name ''*#'' -print
```

If any of these exist, look at them. In some cases, the differences will be in RCS identifiers and will be harmless, in other cases, you'll have to manually apply important parts. Documentation on diffs files and patch is beyond the scope of this document.

See also ??: Configuring and building the kernel

4.2.6   Installing a driver that has no patches

In some cases, a driver author may not offer patches with the .c and .h files which comprise his driver, or the patches may be against an older revision of the kernel and not go in cleanly.

1. Copy the .c and .h files into /usr/src/linux/drivers/scsi

2. Add the configuration option
   Edit /usr/src/linux/config.in, and add a line in the

   ```
       * SCSI low-level drivers
   ```

   section, add a boolean configuration variable for your driver. I.E.,

   ```
       bool 'Always IN2000 SCSI support' CONFIG_SCSI_IN2000 y
   ```

3. Add the makefile entries
   Edit /usr/src/linux/drivers/scsi/Makefile, and add an entry like

   ```
   ifdef CONFIG_SCSI_IN2000
   SCSI_OBS  := $(SCSI_OBJS) in2000.o
   SCSI_SRCS := $(SCSI_SRCS) in2000.c
   endif
   ```

   before the

   ```
   scsi.a: $(SCSI_OBJS)
   ```

   line in the makefile, where the .c file is the .c file you copied in, and the .o file is the basename of the .c file with a .o suffixed.

4. Add the entry points
   Edit /usr/src/linux/drivers/scsi/hosts.c, and add a #include for the header file, conditional on the CONFIG_SCSI preprocessor define you added to the configuration file. I.E., after

   ```
   #ifdef CONFIG_SCSI_GENERIC_NCR5380
   #include ''g_NCR5380.h''
   #endif
   ```

   you might add

   ```
   #ifdef CONFIG_SCSI_IN2000
   #include ''in2000.h''
   #endif
   ```

   You will also need to add the Scsi_Host_Template entry into the scsi_hosts[ ] array. Take a look into the .h file, and you should find a # define that looks something like this :

   ```
   #define IN2000 {''Always IN2000'', in2000_detect, \
   in2000_info, in2000_command,       \
   in2000_queuecommand,               \
   in2000_abort,                      \
   in2000_reset,                      \
   NULL,                              \
   in2000_biosparam,                  \
   1, 7, IN2000_SG, 1, 0, 0}
   ```

the name of the preprocessor define, and add it into the scsi_hosts[ ] array, conditional on definition of the preprocessor symbol you used in the configuration file.

I.E., after

```
#ifdef CONFIG_SCSI_GENERIC_NCR5380
GENERIC_NCR5380,
#endif
```

you might add

```
#ifdef CONFIG_SCSI_IN2000
IN2000,
#endif
```

See also **??**: Configuring and building the kernel

4.3 Adaptec 152x, 151x, Sound Blaster 16 SCSI, SCSI Pro, Gigabyte, and other AIC 6260/6360 based products (Standard)

4.3.1 Supported Configurations :

BIOS addresses:

0xd8000, 0xdc000, 0xd0000, 0xd4000, 0xc8000, 0xcc000, 0xe0 000, 0xe4000.

Ports:

0x140, 0x340

IRQs:

9, 10, 11, 12

DMA:

is not used.

IO:

port mapped

Autoprobe:

Works with many boards with an installed BIOS. All other board s, including the Adaptec 1510, and Sound Blaster16 SCSI must use a kernel comma nd line or compile time override.

Autoprobe Override:

None

Compile time:

Define PORTBASE, IRQ, SCSI_ID, RECONNECT as appropriate, see Defines

kernel command line

aha152x=< PORTBASE> ,< IRQ> ,< SCSI-ID> , < RECONNECT> Usually, SCSI-ID will be 7 and RE-CONNECT non-zero. To force d etection at 0x340, IRQ 11, at SCSI-ID 7, allowing disconnect/reconnect, you wou ld use the following command line option :

```
aha152x=0x340,11,7,1
```

Antiquity Problems, fix by upgrading:

The driver fails with VLB boards. There was a timing problem in kernels older than revision 1.0.5.

Defines:

AUTOCONF:
use configuration the controller reports (only 152x)
IRQ:
override interrupt channel (9,10,11 or 12) (default 11)
SCSI_ID:
override SCSI id of AIC-6260 (0-7) (default 7)
RECONNECT:
override target dis-/reconnection/multiple
outstanding command:
set to non-zero to enable, zero to disable.
DONT_SNARF:
Don't register ports (pl12 and below)
SKIP_BIOSTEST:
Don't test for BIOS signature (AHA-1510 or disabled BIOS)
PORTBASE:
Force port base. Don't try to probe

4.4 Adaptec 154x, AMI FastDisk VLB, Buslogic, DTC 329x (Standard)

Supported Configurations:

Ports:
0x330 and 0x334
IRQs:
9, 10, 11, 12, 14, 15
DMA channels:
5, 6, 7
IO:
port mapped, bus master

Autoprobe:

works with all supported configurations, does not require an installed BIOS.

Autoprobe override:

Note:

No suffix boards, and early 'A' suffix boards do not support scatter/gather, and thus don't work. However, they can be made to work for some definition of the word works if AHA1542_SCATTER is changed to 0 in drivers/scsi/aha1542.h.

Note:

Buslogic makes a series of boards that are software compatible with the Adaptec 1542, and these come in ISA, VLB and EISA flavors.

Antiquity Problems, fix by upgrading:

1. Linux kernel revisions prior to .99.10 don't support the 'C' revision.
2. Linux kernel revisions prior to .99.14k don't support the 'C' revision options for

- BIOS support for the extended mapping for disks > 1G
- BIOS support for > 2 drives
- BIOS support for autoscanning the SCSI bus

3. Linux kernel revisions prior to .99.15e don't support the 'C' with the BIOS support for > 2 drives turned on and the BIOS support for the extended mapping for disks > 1G turned off.

4. Linux kernel revisions prior to .99.14u don't support the 'CF' revisions of the board.

5. Linux kernel revisions prior to 1.0.5 have a race condition when multiple devices are accessed at the same time.

Common problems:

1. There are unexpected errors with a 154xC or 154xCF board,

    Early examples of the 154xC boards have a high slew rate on one of the SCSI signals, which results in signal reflections when cables with the wrong impedance are used.

    Newer boards aren't much better, and also suffer from extreme cabling and termination sensitivity.

    See also Common Problems # 2 and # 3 and Section 2: Common Problems, and Section 2.1: General Flakiness

2. There are unexpected errors with a 154xC or 154x with both internal and external devices connected.

    This is probably a termination problem. In order to use the software option to disable host adapter termination, you must turn switch 1 off.

    See also Common Problems # 2 and # 3 and Section 2: Common Problems, and Section 2.1: General Flakiness

3. The SCSI subsystem locks up completely.

    There are cases where the lockups seem to occur when multiple devices are in use at the same time. In this case, you can try contacting the manufacturer of the devices and see if firmware upgrades are available which would correct the problem. As a last resort, you can go into aha1542.h and change AHA1542_MAILBOX to 1. This will effectively limit you to one outstanding command on the SCSI bus at one time, and may help the situation. If you have tape drives or slow CD-ROM drives on the bus, this might not be a practical solution.

    See also Common Problems # 2 and # 3 and Section 2: Common Problems, Section 2.1: General Flakiness and Section 2.8:SCSI Lockups.

4. An "Interrupt received, but no mail" message is printed on bootup and your SCSI devices are not detected.

    Disable the BIOS options to support the extended mapping for disks > 1G, support for > 2 drives, and for autoscanning the bus. Or, upgrade to Linux .99.14k or newer.

4.5   Adaptec 174x

Supported Configurations:

Slots:

   1-8

Ports:

   EISA board, not applicable

IRQs:

   9, 10, 11, 12, 14, 15

DMA Channels:

   EISA board, not applicable

IO:

   port mapped, bus master

Autoprobe:

works with all supported configurations

Autoprobe override:

Note:

This board has been discontinued by Adaptec.

Common Problems:

1. If the Adaptec 1740 driver prints the message "aha1740: Board detected, but EBCNTRL = % x, so disabled it." your board was disabled because it was not running in enhanced mode. Boards running in standard 1542 mode are not supported.

4.6   Adaptec 274x, 284x, 294x (Standard)

Newer   revisions   may   be   available
at (ftp://ftp.cpsc.ucalgary.ca/pub/systems/linux/aha274x/aha274x-pre-alpha.tar
.gz)

Supported Configurations:

274x:

EISA Slots:

1-12

IRQs:

ALL

IO:

port mapped, bus master

284x:

Ports:

All

IRQs:

All

DMA Channels:

All

294x

PCI

Note:

BIOS MUST be enabled

Note:

The B channel on 2742AT boards is ignored.

4.7 Always IN2000 (ALPHA)

ALPHA driver available at `(ftp://tsx-11.mit.edu/pub/linux/ALPHA/SCSI/in2000)`. The
driver is in2000.tar.z, bootable kernel zImage

Port:

0x100, 0x110, 0x200, 0x220

IRQs:

10, 11, 14, 15

DMA:

not used

IO:

port mapped

Autoprobe:

BIOS not required

Autoprobe override:

Common Problems:

1. There are known problems in systems with IDE drives and with swapping.

4.8 EATA: DPT Smartcache, Smartcache Plus, Smartcache III (Standard)

Supported boards:

all, that support the EATA-DMA protocol (no PM2001).

DPT Smartcache:

PM2011 PM2012A PM2012B

Smartcache III:

PM2021 PM2022 PM2024 PM2122 PM2124 PM2322

SmartRAID:

PM3021 PM3222 PM3224 many of those boards are also available as SKXXXX versions, which
are supported as well.

Supported Configurations:

Slots:

ALL

Ports:

ALL

IRQs:

ALL level & edge triggered

DMA Channels:

ISA ALL, EISA/PCI not applicable

IO:

port mapped, bus master

SCSI Channels:

ALL

Autoprobe:

works with all supported configurations

Compile time:

diskgeometry in eata_dma.h for unusual disk geometries which came from the usage of the old DPTFMT utility. The latest version of the EATA-DMA driver and a Slackware bootdisk should be available on: (`ftp://ftp.uni-mainz.de/pub/Linux/arch/i386/system/EATA/`)

Common Problems:

1. The IDE driver detects the ST-506 interface of the EATA board.

   (a) This will look like similar to one of the following 2 examples:

   ```
   hd.c: ST-506 interface disk with more than 16 heads detected,
   probably due to non-standard sector translation. Giving up.
   (disk \% d: cyl=\% d, sect=63, head=64)
   ```

   ```
   hdc: probing with STATUS instead of ALTSTATUS
   hdc: MP0242 A, 0MB w/128KB Cache, CHS=0/0/0
   hdc: cannot handle disk with 0 physical heads
   hdd: probing with STATUS instead of ALTSTATUS
   hdd: MP0242 A, 0MB w/128KB Cache, CHS=0/0/0
   hdd: cannot handle disk with 0 physical heads
   ```

   If the IDE driver gets into trouble because of this, i.e.. you can't access your (real) IDE hardware, change the IO Port and/or the IRQ of the EATA board.

   (b) If the IDE driver finds hardware it can handle i.e.. harddisks with a capacity $< =504MB$, it will allocate the IO Port and IRQ, so that the eata driver can't utilize them. In this case also change IO Port and IRQ ($!= 14,15$).

2. Some old SK2011 boards have a broken firmware. Please contact DPT's customer support for an update.

4.9 Future Domain 16x0 with TMC-1800, TMC-18C30, TMC-18C50, or TMC-36C70 chip

Supported Configurations:

BIOSes:

2.0, 3.0, 3.2, 3.4, 3.5

BIOS Addresses:

0xc8000, 0xca000, 0xce000, 0xde000

Ports:

0x140, 0x150, 0x160, 0x170

IRQs:

3, 5, 10, 11, 12, 14, 15

DMA:

not used

IO:

port mapped

Autoprobe:

works with all supported configurations, requires installed BIOS

Autoprobe Override:

Antiquity Problems, fix by upgrading:

1. Old versions do not support the TMC-18C50 chip, and will fail with newer boards.
2. Old versions will not have the most current BIOS signatures for autodetection.
3. Versions prior to the one included in Linux 1.0.9 and 1.1.6 don't support the new SCSI chip or 3.4 BIOS.

4.10   Generic NCR5380 / T130B

Supported and Unsupported Configurations:

Ports:
> all

IRQs:
> all

DMA:
> not used

IO:
> port mapped

Autoprobe:

Autoprobe Override:

Compile time:
> Define GENERIC_NCR5380_OVERRIDE to be an array of tupples with port, irq, dma, board type
> - i.e.

```
#define GENERIC_NCR5380_OVERRIDE {{0x330, 5, DMA_NONE, BOARD_NCR5380}}
```

> for a NCR5380 board at port 330, IRQ 5.

```
#define GENERIC_NCR5380_OVERRIDE {{0x350, 5, DMA_NONE, BOARD_NCR53C400}}
```

> for a T130B at port 0x350.
> Older versions of the code eliminate the BOARD_* entry.
> The symbolic IRQs IRQ_NONE and IRQ_AUTO may be used.

kernel command line:
- ncr5380=port,irq
- ncr5380=port,irq,dma
- ncr53c400=port,irq

255 may be used for no irq, 254 for irq autoprobe.

Common Problems:

1. Using the T130B board with the old (pre public release 6) generic NCR5380 driver which doesn't support the ncr53c400 command line option.
   The NCR5380 compatible registers are offset eight from the base address. So, if your address is 0x350, use

   ```
   ncr53480=0x358,254
   ```

   on the kernel command line.

Antiquity problems, fix by upgrading :

> 1. The kernel locks up during disk access with T130B or other NCR53c400 boards
> Pre-public release 6 versions of the Generic NCR5380 driver didn't support interrupts on these boards. Upgrade.

Notes:

> the generic driver doesn't support DMA yet, and pseudo-DMA isn't supported in the generic driver.

4.11 NCR53c8xx (Standard)

Supported and Unsupported Configurations:

> **Base addresses:**
> > ALL
>
> **IRQs:**
> > ALL
>
> **DMA channels:**
> > PCI, not applicable
>
> **IO:**
> > port mapped, busmastering

Autoprobe:

> requires PCI BIOS, uses PCI BIOS routines to search for devices and read configuration space.
>
> The driver uses the pre-programmed values in some registers for initialization, so a BIOS must be installed.

Antiquity Problems, fix by upgrading:

> 1. Older versions of Linux had a problem with swapping
> See Section 5.2.7:System Hangs When Swapping
> 2. Older versions of Linux didn't recognize '815 and '825 boards.

Common Problems:

> 1. Many people have encountered problems where the chip worked fine under DOS, but failed under Linux with a timeout on test 1 due to a lost interrupt.
> This is often due to a mismatch between the IRQ hardware jumper for a slot or mainboard device and the value set in the CMOS setup.
> It may also be due to PCI INTB, INTC, or INTD being selected on a PCI board in a system which only supports PCI INTA.
> Finally, PCI should be using level-sensitive rather than edge triggered interrupts. Check that your board is jumpered for level-sensitive, and if that fails try edge-triggered because your system may be broken.
> This problem is especially common with Viglen some Viglen motherboards, where the mainboard IRQ jumper settings are NOT as documented in the manual. I've been told that what claims to be IRQ5 is really IRQ9, your mileage will vary.
> 2. Lockups occur when using an S3928P, X11, and the NCR chip at the same time.
> There are hardware bugs in at least some S3928P chip. Don't do this.
> 3. You get a message on boot up indicating that the I/O mapping was disabled because base address 0 bits 0..1 indicated a non I/O mapping
> This is due to a BIOS bug in some machines which results in dword reads of configuration regsisters returning the high and low 16 bit words swapped.

4. Some systems have problems if PCI write posting, or CPU->PCI buffering are enabled. If you have problems, disable these options.

5. Some systems with the NCR SDMS software in an onboard BIOS ROM and in the system BIOS are unable to boot DOS. Disabling the image in one place should rectify this problem.

6. Some systems have hideous, broken, BIOS chips. Don't make any bug reports until you've made sure you have the newest ROM from your vendor.

   - Intel P90 boards require revision 1.00.04.AX1

4.12 Seagate ST0x/Future Domain TMC-8xx/TMC-9xx

Supported and Unsupported Configurations :

Base addresses:

0xc8000, 0xca000, 0xcc000, 0xce000, 0xdc000, 0xde000

IRQs:

3, 5

DMA:

not used

IO:

memory mapped

Autoprobe:

probes for address only, IRQ is assumed to be 5, requires installed BIOS.

Autoprobe Override:

Compile time:

Define OVERRIDE to be the base address, CONTROLLER to FD or SEAGATE as appropriate, and IRQ to the IRQ.

kernel command line:

st0x=address,irq or tmc8xx=address,irq (only works for .99.13b and newer)

Antiquity Problems, fix by upgrading:

1. . Versions prior to the one in the Linux .99.12 kernel had a problem handshaking with some slow devices, where

   This is what happens when you write data out to the bus

   (a) Write byte to data register, data register is asserted to bus
   (b) time_remaining = 12us
   (c) wait while time_remaining > 0 and REQ is not asserted
   (d) if time_remaining > 0, assert ACK
   (e) wait while time remaining > 0 and REQ is asserted
   (f) deassert ACK

   The problem was encountered in slow devices that do the command processing as they read the command, where the REQ/ACK handshake takes over 12us - REQ didn't go false when the driver expected it to, so the driver ended up sending multiple bytes of data for each REQ pulse.

2. With Linux .99.12, a bug was introduced when I fixed the arbitration code, resulting in failed selections on some systems. This was fixed in .99.13.

4.12.1 Common Problems

Command Timeouts There are command timeouts when Linux attempts to read the partition table or do other disk access.

The board ships with the defaults set up for MSDOS, i.e. interrupts are disabled. To jumper the board for interrupts, on the Seagate use jumper W3 (ST01) or JP3 (ST02) and short pins F-G to select IRQ 5.

Some Devices Don't Work The driver can't handle some devices, particularly cheap SCSI tapes and CDROMs.

The Seagate ties the SCSI bus REQ/ACK handshaking into the PC bus IO CHANNEL READY and (optionally) 0WS signals. Unfortunately, it doesn't tell you when the watchdog timer runs out, and you have no way of knowing for certain that REQ went low, and may end up seeing one REQ pulse as multiple REQ pulses.

Dealing with this means using a tight loop to look for REQ to go low, with a timeout incase you don't catch the transition due to an interrupt, etc. This results in a performance decrease, so it would be undesireable to apply this to all SCSI devices. Instead, it is selected on a per-device basis with the "borken" field for the given SCSI device in the SCSI_devices array. If you run into problems, you should try adding your device to the list of devices for which borken is not reset to zero (currently, only the TENEX CDROM drives).

Future Domain does not work A Future Domain board (specific examples include the 840, 841, 880, and 881) doesn't work.

A few of the Future Domain boards use the Seagate register mapping, and have the MSG and CD bits of the status register flipped.

You should edit seagate.h, swapping the definitions for STAT_MSG and STAT_CD, and recompile the kernel with CONTROLLER defined to SEAGATE and an appropriate IRQ and OVERRIDE specified.

HDIO_REQ or HDIO_GETGEO failed When attempting to fdisk your drive, you get error messages indicating that the HDIO_REQ or HDIO_GETGEO ioctl failed, or

You must set heads sectors and cylinders. You can do this from the extra functions menu.

See Section **??**: Partitioning

Fdisk fails After manually specifying the drive geometry, subsequent attempts to read the partition table result in partition boundary not on a cylinder boundary, physical and logical boundaries don't match, etc. error messages.

See Section **??**: Partitioning

Used to work but now it doesn't Some systems which worked prior to .99.13 fail with newer versions of Linux. Older versions of Linux assigned the CONTROL and DATA registers in an order different than that outlined in the Seagate documentation, which broke on some systems. Newer versions make the assignment in the correct way, but this breaks other systems.

The code in seagate.c looks like this now :

```
cli();
DATA = (unsigned char) ((1 <<target) | (controller_type == SEAGATE ? 0x80 : 0x4
0));
CONTROL = BASE_CMD | CMD_DRVR_ENABLE | CMD_SEL |
(reselect ? CMD_ATTN : 0);
sti();
```

Changing this to

```
cli();
CONTROL = BASE_CMD | CMD_DRVR_ENABLE | CMD_SEL |
(reselect ? CMD_ATTN : 0);
DATA = (unsigned char) ((1 <<target) | (controller_type == SEAGATE ? 0x80 : 0x4
0));
sti()
```

may fix your problem.

4.12.2   Defines

FAST or FAST32 will use blind transfers where possible

ARBITRATE will cause the host adapter to arbitrate for the bus for better SCSI-II compatibility, rather than just waiting for BUS FREE and then doing its thing. Should let us do one command per LUN when I integrate my reorganization changes into the distribution sources.

SLOW_HANDSHAKE will allow compatibility with broken devices that don't handshake fast enough (i.e., some CD-ROM's) for the Seagate code.

SLOW_RATE=x, x some number will let you specify a default transfer rate if handshaking isn't working correctly.

4.13   PAS16 SCSI

Supported and Unsupported Configurations:

   Ports:

   0x388, 0x384, 0x38x, 0x288

   IRQs:

   10, 12, 14, 15

   IMPORTANT:

   IRQ MUST be different from the IRQ used for the sound portion of the board.

   DMA:

   not used for the SCSI portion of the board

   IO:

   port mapped

Autoprobe:

does not require BIOS

Autoprobe Override:

   Compile time:

   Define PAS16_OVERRIDE to be an array of port, irq tupples. I.E.

```
#define PAS16_OVERRIDE {{0x388, 10}}
```

for a board at port 0x388, IRQ 10.

kernel command line:

pas16=port,irq

Defines:

- AUTOSENSE - if defined, REQUEST SENSE will be performed automatically for commands that return with a CHECK CONDITION status.
- PSEUDO_DMA - enables PSEUDO-DMA hardware, should give a 3-4X performance increase compared to polled I/O.
- PARITY - enable parity checking. Not supported
- SCSI2 - enable support for SCSI-II tagged queueing. Untested
- UNSAFE - leave interrupts enabled during pseudo-DMA transfers. You only really want to use this if you're having a problem with dropped characters during high speed communications, and even then, you're going to be better off twiddling with transfersize.
- USLEEP - enable support for devices that don't disconnect. Untested.

Common problems:

1. Command timeouts, aborts, etc.

You should install the NCR5380 patches that I posted to the net some time ago, which should be integrated into some future alpha release. These patches fix a race condition in earlier NCR5380 driver cores, as well as fixing support for multiple devices on NCR5380 based boards.

If that fails, you should disable the PSEUDO_DMA option by changing the # define PSEUDO_DMA line in drivers/scsi/pas16.c to # undef PSEUDO_DMA.

Note that the later should be considered a last resort, because there will be a severe performance degradation.

4.14   Trantor T128/T128F/T228

Supported and Unsupported Configurations:

Base addresses:

0xcc000, 00xc8000, 0xdc000, 0xd8000

IRQs:

- none, 3, 5, 7 (all boards)
- 10, 12, 14, 15 (T128F only)

DMA:

not used.

IO:

memory mapped

Autoprobe:

works for all supported configurations, requires installed BIOS.

Autoprobe Override:

Compile time:

Define T128_OVERRIDE to be an array of address, irq tupples. I.E.

```
#define T128_OVERRIDE {{0xcc000, 5}}
```

for a board at address 0xcc000, IRQ 5.

The symbolic IRQs IRQ_NONE and IRQ_AUTO may be used.

kernel command line:

t128=address,irq

-1 may be used for no irq, -2 for irq autoprobe.

Defines:

AUTOSENSE

if defined, REQUEST SENSE will be performed automatically for commands that return with a CHECK CONDITION status.

PSEUDO_DMA

enables PSEUDO-DMA hardware, should give a 3-4X performance increase compared to polled I/O.

PARITY

enable parity checking. Not supported

SCSI2

enable support for SCSI-II tagged queueing. Untested

UNSAFE

leave interrupts enabled during pseudo-DMA transfers. You only really want to use this if you're having a problem with dropped characters during high speed communications, and even then, you're going to be better off twiddling with transfersize.

USLEEP

enable support for devices that don't disconnect. Untested.

Common Problems:

1. Command timeouts, aborts, etc.

You should install the NCR5380 patches that I posted to the net some time ago, which should be integrated into some future alpha release. These patches fix a race condition in earlier NCR5380 driver cores, as well as fixing support for multiple devices on NCR5380 based boards.

If that fails, you should disable the PSEUDO_DMA option by changing the # define PSEUDO_DMA line in drivers/scsi/pas16.c to # undef PSEUDO_DMA.

Note that the later should be considered a last resort, because there will be a severe performance degradation.

4.15   Ultrastor 14f (ISA), 24f (EISA), 34f (VLB)

Supported Configurations:

Ports:

0x130, 0x140, 0x210, 0x230, 0x240, 0x310, 0x330, 0x340

IRQs:

10, 11, 14, 15

DMA channels:

5, 6, 7

IO:

port mapped, bus master

Autoprobe:

does not work for boards at port 0x310, BIOS not required.

Autoprobe override:

compile time only, define PORT_OVERRIDE

Common Problems :

1. The address 0x310 is not supported by the autoprobe code, and may cause conflicts if networking is enabled.

   Please use a different address.

2. Using an Ultrastor at address 0x330 may cause the system to hang when the sound drivers are autoprobing.

   Please use a different address.

3. Various other drivers do unsafe probes at various addresses, if you are having problems with detection or the system is hanging at boot time, please try a different address.

   0x340 is recommended as an address that is known to work.

4. Linux detects no SCSI devices, but detects your SCSI hard disk on an Ultrastor SCSI board as a normal hard disk, and the hard disk driver refuses to support it. Note that when this occurs, you will probably also get a message

   hd.c: ST-506 interface disk with more than 16 heads detected, probably due to non-standard sector translation. Giving up. (disk % d: cyl=% d, sect=63, head=64)

   If this is the case, you are running the Ultrastor board in WD1003 emulation mode. You have to

   (a) Switch the ultrastor into native mode. This is the recommended action, since the SCSI driver can be significantly faster than the IDE driver, especially with the clustered read/write patches installed. Some users have sustained in excess of 2M/sec through the file system using these patches.

   Note that this will be necessary if you wish to use any non- hard disk, or more than two hard disk devices on the Ultrastor.

   (b) Use the kernel command line switch

   ```
   hd=cylinders,heads,sectors
   ```

   to override the default setting to bootstrap yourself, keeping number of cylinders < = 2048, number of heads < = 16, and number of sectors < = 255 such that cylinders * heads * sectors is the same for both mappings.

   You'll also have to manually specify the disk geometry when running fdisk under Linux. Failure to do so will result in incorrect partition entries being written, which will work correctly with Linux but fail under MSDOS which looks at the cylinder/head/sector entries in the table.

   Once Linux is up, you can avoid the inconvience of having to boot by hand by recompiling the kernel with an appropriately defined HD_TYPE macro in include/linux/config.h.

4.16   Western Digital 7000

Supported Configurations :

BIOS Addresses:

0xce000

Ports:

0x350

IRQs:

15

DMA Channels:

6

IO:

port mapped, bus master

Autoprobe:

requires installed BIOS

Common Problems :

1. There are several revisisions of the chip and firmware. Supposedly, revision 3 boards do not work, revision 5 boards do, chips with no suffix do not work, chips with an 'A' suffix do.

2. The board supports a few BIOS addresses which aren't on the list of supported addresses. If you run into this situation, please use one of the supported addresses and submit a bug report as outlined in Section 2, "Bug Reports"

5 Disks

This section gives information that is specific to disk drives.

5.1 Supported and Unsupported Hardware

All direct access SCSI devices with a block size of 256, 512, or 1024 bytes should work. Other block sizes will not work (Note that this can often be fixed by changing the block and/or sector sizes using the MODE SELECT SCSI command)

Sector size refers to the number of data bytes allocated per sector on a device, i.e. CDROMs use a 2048 byte sector size.

Block size refers to the size of the logical blocks used to interface with the device. Although this is usually identical to sector size, some devices map multiple smaller physical sectors (i.e., 256 bytes in the case of 55M Syquest drives) to larger logical blocks or vice versa (i.e., 512 byte blocks on SUN compatible CD-ROM drives).

Removeable media devices, including Bernoulis, flopticals, and MO drives work.

In theory, drives up to a terrabyte in size should work. There is definately no problem with tiny 9G drives.

5.2 Common Problems

5.2.1 Cylinder > 1024 message.

When partitioning, you get a warning message about "cylinder > 1024" or you are unable to boot from a partition including a logical cylinder past logical cylinder 1024.

This is a BIOS limitation.

See Section ??: Disk Geometry and Partitioning for a n explanation.

5.2.2 You are unable to partition "/dev/hd*"

/dev/hd* aren't SCSI devices, /dev/sd* are.

See Section 5.3: Device files, and Section ??, Disk Geometry and Partitioning for the correct device names and partitioning procedure.

5.2.3 Unable to eject media from a removeable media drive.

Linux attempts to lock the drive door when a piece of media is mounted to prevent filesystem corruption due to an inadvertant media change.

Please unmount your disks before ejecting them.

5.2.4 Unable to boot using LILO from a SCSI disk

In some cases, the SCSI driver and BIOS will disagree over the correct BIOS mapping to use, and will result in LILO hanging after 'LI' at boot time and/or other problems.

To workarround this, you'll have to determine your BIOS geometry mapping used under DOS, and make an entry for your disk in /etc/lilo/disktab.

Alternatively, you may be able to use the "linear" configuration file option.

5.2.5 Fdisk responds with

```
You must set heads sectors and cylinders.
You can do this from the extra functions menu.
and disk geometry is not 'remembered' when fdisk is rerun.
```

See Section **??**: Partitioning

5.2.6 Only one drive is detected on a bridge board with multiple drives connected.

Linux won't search LUNs past zero on SCSI devices which predate ANSI SCSI revision 1. If you wish devices on alternate LUNs to be recognized, you will have to modify drivers/scsi/scsi.c:scan_scsis().

5.2.7 System Hangs When Swapping

We think this has been fixed, try upgrading to 1.1.38.

5.2.8 Connor CFP1060S disks get corrupted

This is due to a microcode bug in the read-ahead and caching code.

>From Soenke Behrens of Conner tech. support:

```
During the past few weeks, we got several calls from customers stating
that they had severe problems with Conner CFP1060x 1GB SCSI drives
using the Linux operating system. Symptoms were corrupt filesystems
(damaged inodes) reported by e2fsck on each system boot and similar
errors.

There is now a fix available for customers with a CFP1060x (microcode
revisions 9WA1.62/1.66/1.68) and Linux. To apply the upgrade, you
will need a DOS boot disk and ASPI drivers that can access the hard
drive. The upgrade downloads new queuing and lookahead code into the
non-volatile SCSI RAM of the drive.

If you are experiencing problems with a disk that has microcode
revision 9WA1.60, you will have to contact your nearest Conner service
centre to get the disk upgraded. The microcode revision can be found
on the label of the drive and on the underside of the drive on a label
on one of the ICs.

If you are confident that you can perform the upgrade yourself, please
contact Conner Technical Support and have your microcode revision
ready. Conner Technical Support Europe can be reached on +44-1294-315333,
Conner Technical Support in the USA can be reached on 1-800-4CONNER.

Regards
```

Device	Target	Lun	SCSI disk
84M Seagate	0	0	/dev/sda
SCSI-> SMD bridge disk 0	3	0	/dev/sdb
SCSI-> SMD bridge disk 1	3	1	/dev/sdc
Wangtek tape	4	0	none
213M Maxtor	6	0	/dev/sdd
etc.			

Device	type	major	minor
/dev/sda	block	8	0
/dev/sda1	block	8	1
/dev/sda2	block	8	2
/dev/sda3	block	8	3
etc.			

```
Soenke Behrens
European Technical Support
```

5.3   Device Files

SCSI disks use block device major 8, and there are no "raw" devices ala BSD.

16 minor numbers are allocated to each SCSI disk, with minor % 16 == 0 being the whole disk, minors $1 < =$ (minor % 16) $< = 4$ the four primary partitions, minors $5 < =$ (minor % 16) $< = 15$ any extended partitions.

Due to constraints imposed by Linux's use of a sixteen bit dev_t with only eight bits allocated to the minor number, the SCSI disk minor numbers are assigned dynamically starting with the lowest SCSI HOST/ID/LUN.

I.E., a configuration may work out like this (with one host adapter)

The standard naming convention is

/dev/sd{letter} for the entire disk device ((minor % 16) == 0) /dev/sd{letter}{partition} for the partitions on that device ($1 < =$ (minor % 16) $< = 15$)

I.E.

5.4   Partitioning

You can partition your SCSI disks using the partitioning program of your choice, under DOS, OS/2, Linux or any other operating system supporting the standard partitioning scheme.

The correct way to run the Linux fdisk program is by specifying the device on the command line. I.E., to partition the first SCSI disk,

```
fdisk /dev/sda
```

If you don't explicitly specify the device, the partitioning program may default to /dev/hda, which isn't a SCSI disk.

In some cases, fdisk will respond with

```
You must set heads sectors and cylinders.
You can do this from the extra functions menu.
```

$$1 <= \text{heads} <= 256$$
$$1 <= \text{cylinders} <= 1024$$
$$1 <= \text{sectors} <= 63$$

```
Command (m for help):
```

and/or give a message to the effect that the HDIO_REQ or HDIO_GETGEO ioctl failed. In these cases, you must manually specify the disk geometry as outlined in Subsection ??: Disk Geometry when running fdisk, and also in /etc/disktab if you wish to boot kernels off that disk with LILO.

If you have manually specified the disk geometry, subsequent attempts to run fdisk will give the same error message. This is normal, since PCs don't store the disk geometry information in the partition table. In and of itself, will cause _NO PROBLEMS_, and you will have no problems accessing partitions you created on the drive with Linux. Some vendors' poor installation code will choke on this, in which case you should contact your vendor and insist that they fix the code.

In some cases, you will get a warning message about a partition ending past cylinder 1024. If you create one of these partitions, you will be unable to boot Linux kernels off of that partition using LILO. Note, however, that this restriction does not preclude the creation of a root partition partially or entirely above the 1024 cylinder mark, since it is possible to create a small /boot partition below the 1024 cylinder mark or to boot kernels off existing partitions.

5.5   Disk Geometry

Under Linux, each disk is viewed as the SCSI host adapter sees it : N blocks, numbered from 0 to N-1, all error free, where as DOS/BIOS predate intelligent disks and apply an arbitrary head / cylinder / sector mapping to this linear addressing.

This can pose a problem when you partition the drives under Linux, since there is no portable way to get DOS/BIOS's idea of the mapped geometry. In most cases, a HDIO_GETGEO ioctl() can be implemented to return this mapping. Unfortunately, when the vendor (i.e. Seagate) has chosen a perverse, non-standard, and undocumented mapping, this is not possible and geometry must be manually specified

If manual specification of the is required, you have one of several options :

1. If you don't care about using DOS, or booting kernels from the drive with LILO, create a translation such that heads * cylinders * sectors * 512 < size of your drive in bytes (a megabyte is defined as 2^20 bytes).

2. Use the BIOS mapping. In some cases, this will mean reconfiguring the disk so that it is at SCSI ID 0, and disabling the second IDE drive (if you have one).

   You can either use a program like NU, or you can use the following program:

```
begin 664 dparam.com
MBAZ''##_B+^!'+N!'(H'0SP@=/D\,'5:@#]X='6'/UAU4(!_'3AU2H!_'P!U
M1(I7'H#J,(#Z'7<Y@,*'M'C-$PCD=3-14HC()#\PY.@R'.@J'%J(\/[',.3H
M)0#H'0!8AL2Q!M+L0.@7'+K"'(0)S2'#NIP!ZR"ZQ0'K&[K5'>L6N]T!=+Y
M"@#W\8#",SN(%P'=^^')VK0)S2'#=7-A9V4Z(&1P87))A;2'P>#P#0H@("!O
L<B'@9'!A<F%M(#!X..#$-"B!).G,;;; G9A;%ED("&1R:79E#0H(""'D''''''D''!O
'
end
```

When run it prints the sectors, heads, and cylinders of the drive whose BIOS address was specified on the command line (0x80 is the first disk, 0x81 the second).

I.E.,

```
dparam 0x80
60 17 1007
```

Would mean that C: had 60 sectors, 17 heads, and 1007 cylinders.

6   CD-ROMs

This section gives information that is specific to CD-ROM drives.

6.1   Supported and Unsupported Hardware

SCSI CDs with a block size of 512 or 2048 bytes should work. Other block sizes will not work.

6.2   Common Problems

6.2.1   Unable to mount CD-ROM.

The correct syntax to mount an ISO-9660 CD-ROM is

```
mount -t iso9660 /dev/sr0 /mount_point -o ro
```

Note that for this to work, you must have the kernel configured with support for SCSI, your host adapter, the SCSI CD-ROM driver, and the iso9660 filesystem.

Note that as of Linux 1.1.32, read-only devices such as CD-ROMs *cannot* be mounted with the default read/write options.

6.2.2   Unable to eject CD-ROM.

Linux attempts to lock the drive door when a piece of media is mounted to prevent filesystem corruption due to an inadvertant media change.

6.2.3   Unable to play audio.

The programs Workman or xcdplayer will do this for you.

6.2.4   Workman or Xcdplayer do not work.

The functions to control audio functions are part of the SCSI-II command set, so any drive that is not SCSI-II will probably not work here. Also, many SCSI-I and some SCSI-II CD-ROM drives use a proprietary command set for accessing audio functions instead of the SCSI-II command set. For NEC drives, there is a version of xcdplayer specially adapted to use this command set floating around - try looking on (ftp://tsx-11.mit.edu/pub/linux/BETA/cdrom)

These programs may work with some of the non-SCSI CD-ROM drives if the driver implements the same ioctls as the SCSI drivers.

6.3   Device Files

SCSI CD-ROMs use major 11.

Minors are allocated dynamically (See Section 4: Disks, Subsection 4.3: Device Files for an example) with the first CD-ROM found being minor 0, the second minor 1, etc.

The standard naming convention is

/dev/sr{digit} i.e.

/dev/sr0 /dev/sr1

etc.

7   Tapes

This setion gives information that is specific to SCSI tape drives.

7.1   Supported and Unsupported Hardware

Drives using both fixed and variable length blocks smaller than the the driver buffer length (set to 32K in the distribution sources) are supported.

Parameters (block size, buffering, density) are set with ioctls (usually with the mt program), and remain in effect after the device is closed and reopened.

Virtually all drives should work, including :

- Archive Viper QIC drives, including the 150M and 525M models

- Exabyte 8mm drives

- Wangtek 5150S drives

- Wangdat DAT drives

7.2   Common Problems

7.2.1   Tape drive not recognized at boot time.

Try booting with a tape in the drive.

7.2.2   Tapes with multiple files cannot be read properly.

When reading a tape with multiple files, the first tar is successful, a second tar fails silently, and retrying the second tar is successful.

User level programs, such as tar, don't understand file marks. The first tar reads up until the end of the file. The second tar attempts to read at the file mark, gets nothing, but the tape spaces over the file mark. The third tar is successful since the tape is at the start of the next file.

Use mt on the no-rewind device to space forward to the next file.

7.2.3 Decompression fails.

Decompressing programs cannot handle the zeros padding the last block of the file.

To prevent warnings and errors, wrap your compressed files in a .tar file - i.e., rather than doing

```
tar cfvz /dev/nrst0 file.1 file.2 ...
```

do

```
tar cfvz tmp.tar.z file.1 file.2 ...

tar cf /dev/nrst0 tmp.tar.z
```

7.2.4 Problems taking tapes to/from other systems.

You can't read a tape made with another operating system or another operating system can't read a tape written in Linux.

Different systems often use different block sizes. On a tape device using a fixed blocksize, you will get errors when reading blocks written using a different block size.

To read these tapes, you must set the blocksize of the tape driver to match the blocksize used when the tape was written, or to variable.

Note: this is the hardware block size, not the blocking factor used with tar, dump, etc.

You can do this with the mt command -

```
mt setblk <size>
```

or

```
mt setblk 0
```

to get variable block length support.

Note that these mt flags are NOT supported under the GNU version of mt which is included with some Linux distributions. Instead, you must use the BSD derrived Linux SCSI mt command. Source should be available from

```
(ftp://tsx-11.mit.edu/pub/linux/ALPHA/scsi)
```

7.2.5 "No such device" error message.

All attempts to access the tape result in a

"No such device"

or similar error message. Check the type of your tape device - it **must** be a character device with major and minor numbers matching those specified in subsection C, Device Files.

7.2.6 Tape reads at a given density work, writes fail

Many tape drives support reading at lower densities for compatibility with older harware, but will not write at those same densities.

This is especially the case with QIC drives, which will read old 60M tapes but only write new 120, 150, 250, and 525M formats.

7.3 Device Files

SCSI tapes use character device major 9.

Due to constraints imposed by Linux's use of a sixteen bit dev_t with only eight bits allocated to the minor number, the SCSI tape minor numbers are assigned dynamically starting with the lowest SCSI HOST/ID/LUN.

Rewinding devices are numbered from 0 - with the first SCSI tape, /dev/rst0 being c 9 0, the second /dev/rst1 c 9 1, etc. Non-rewinding devices have the high bit set in the minor number, i.e. /dev/nrst0 is c 9 128.

The standard naming convention is */dev/nrst{digit}* for non-rewinding devices */dev/rst{digit} for rewinding devices*

8 Generic

This information gives information that is specific to the generic SCSI driver.

8.1 Supported Hardware

The Generic SCSI device driver provides an interface for sending SCSI commands to all SCSI devices - disks, tapes, CD-ROMs, media changer robots, etc.

Everything electrically compatible with your SCSI board should work.

8.2 Common Problems

None :-).

8.3 Device Files

SCSI generic devices use character major 21. Due to constraints imposed by Linux's use of a 16 bit dev_t, minor numbers are dynamically assigned from 0, one per device, with

/dev/sg0

corresponding to the lowest numerical target/lun on the first SCSI board.

9 Buyers' Guide

A frequent question is:

"Linux supports quite a number of different boards, so which SCSI host adapter should I get."

The answer depends upon how much performance you expect or need, motherboard, and the SCSI peripherals that you plan on attaching to your machine.

9.1 Transfer types

The biggest factor affecting performance (in terms of throughput and interactive response time during SCSI I/O) is going to be the transfer type used.

9.1.1 Pure Polled handshaking.

A pure polled I/O board will use the CPU to handle all of the SCSI processing, including the REQ/ACK

Even a fast CPU will be slower handling the REQ/ACK handshake sequence than a simple finite state machine, resulting in peak transfer rates of about 150K/sec on a fast machine, perhaps 60K/sec on a slow machine (through the filesystem).

The driver also must sit in a tight loop as long as the SCSI bus is busy, resulting in near 100% CPU utilitization and extremely poor responsiveness during SCSI/IO. Slow CD-ROMs which don't disconnect/reconnect will kill interactive performance with these boards.

Not recommended.

9.1.2 Interlocked Polled handshaking

Boards using interlocked polled I/O are essentially the same as pure polled I/O boards, only the SCSI REQ/ACK signals the PC bus handshaking signals. All SCSI processing beyond the handshaking is handled by the CPU.

Peak transfer rates of 500-600K/sec through the filesystem re possible on these boards.

As with pure polled I/O boards, the driver must sit in a tight loop as long as the SCSI bus is busy, resulting in CPU utilization dependant on the transfer rates of the devices, and when they disconnect/reconnect. CPU utilization may vary between 25% for single speed CDs which handle disconnect/reconnect properly to 100% for faster drives or broken CD-ROMs which fail to disconnect/reconnect.

On my 486-66, with a T128, I use 90% of my CPU time to sustain a throughput of 547K/sec on a drive with a headrate of 1080K/sec with a T128 board.

Sometimes acceptable for slow tapes and CD-ROMs when low cost is essential.

9.1.3 FIFO Polled

Boards using FIFO polled I/O put a small (typically 8K) buffer between the CPU and the SCSI bus, and often implement some amount of intelligence. The net effect is that the CPU is only tied up when it is transfering data at top speed to the FIFO and when it's handling the rest of the interrupt processing for FIFO empty conditions, disconnect/reconnect, etc.

Peak transfer rates should be sufficient to handle most SCSI devices, and have been measured at up to 4M/sec using raw SCSI commands to read 64K blocks on a fast Seagate Barcuda with an Adaptec 1520.

CPU utilization is dependant on the transfer rates of the devices, with faster devices generating more interrupts per unit time which require more CPU processing time. Although CPU usage may be high (perhaps 75%) with fast devices, the system usually remains usable. These boards will provide excellent interactive performance with broken devices which don't disconnect/reconnect (typically cheap CD-ROM drives)

Recommended for persons on a budget.

9.1.4 Slave DMA

Drivers for boards using slave DMA program the PC's DMA controller for a channel when they do a data transfer, and return control to the CPU.

Peak transfer rates are usually handicapped by the poor DMA controller used on PCs, with one such 8-bit board having problems going faster than 140-150K/sec with one mainboard.

CPU utilization is very reasonable, slightly less than what is seen with FIFO polled I/O boards. These boards are very tollerant of broken devices which don't disconnect/reconnect (typically cheap CSG limit DROM drives).

Acceptable for slow CD-ROM drives, tapes, etc.

9.1.5   Busmastering DMA

These boards are intelligent. Drivers for these boards throw a SCSI command, the destination target and lun, and where the data should end up in a structure, and tell the board "Hey, I have a command for you." The driver returns control to various running programs, and eventually the SCSI board gets back and says that it's done.

Since the intelligence is in the host adapter firmware and not the driver, drivers for these boards typically support more features - synchronous transfers, tagged queing, etc.

With the clustered read/write patches, peak transfer rates through the file system approach 100% of head rate writing, 75% reading.

CPU utilization is minimal, irregardless of I/O load, with a measured 5% CPU usage while accessing a double speed CD-ROM on an Adaptec 1540 and 20% while sustaining a 1.2M/sec transfer rate on a SCSI disk.

Recommended in all cases where money is not extremely tight, the main board is not broken (some broken main boards do not work with bus masters), and applications where time to data is more important than throughput are not being run (bus master overhead may hit 3-4ms per command).

9.2   Scatter/gather

The second most important driver/hardware feature with respect to performance is support for scatter/gather I/O. The overhead of executing a SCSI command is significant - on the order of milliseconds. Intelligent bus masters like the Adaptec 1540 may take 3-4ms to process a SCSI command before the target even sees it. On unbuffered devices, this overhead is allways enough to slip a revolution, resulting in a transfer rate of about 60K/sec (assuming a 3600RPM drive) per block transfered at a time. So, to maximize performance, it is necessary to minimize the number of SCSI commands needed to transfer a given amount of data by transfering more data per command. Due to the design of the Linux buffer cache, contiguous disk blocks are not contiguous in memory. With the clustered read/write patches, 4K worth of buffers are contiguous. So, the maximum amount of data which can be transfered per SCSI command is going to be 1K * # of scatter/gather regions without the clustered read/write patches, 4K * # of regions with. Experimentally, we've determined that 64K is a reasonable amount to transfer with a single SCSI command - meaning 64 scatter/gather buffers with clustered read/write patches, 16 without. With the change from 16K to 64K transfers, we saw an improvement from 50% of headrate, through the filesystem, reading and writing, to 75% and 100% respectively using an Adaptec 1540 series board.

9.3   Mailbox vs. non-mailbox

A number of intelligent host adapters, such as the Ultrastor, WD7000, Adaptec 1540, 1740, and Buslogic boards have used a mailbox-metaphor interface, where SCSI commands are executed by putting a SCSI command structure in a fixed memory location (mailbox), signaling the board (i.e., raising the outgoing mail flag), and waiting for a return (incoming mail). With this high level programming interface, users can often upgrade to a newer board revision to take advantage of new features, such as FAST + WIDE SCSI, without software changes. Drivers tend to be simpler to implement, may implement a larger feature set, and may be more stable.

Other intelligent host adapters, such as the NCR53c7/8xx family, and Adaptec AIC-7770/7870 chips (including the 274x, 284x, and 2940 boards) use a lower level programming interface. This may prove faster since processing can be shifted between the board's processor and faster host CPU, allow better flexibility in implementing certain features (i.e., target mode for arbitrary devices), and these boards can be built for less money (In some cases, this is passed on to the consumer (i.e., most NCR boards)). On the down side, drivers tend to be more complex, and must be modified to take advantage of the features present on newer chips.

9.4   Bus types

Bus type is the next thing to consider, with choices including ISA, EISA, VESA, and PCI. Marketing types often spout of absurd bandwidth numbers based on burst transfer rates and fiction, which isn't very useful. Instead, I've chosen to state "real-world" numbers based on measured performance with various peripherials.

9.4.1   ISA

Bandwidth is slightly better than 5M/sec for busmastering devices. With an ISA bus, arbitration for busmasters is performed by the venerable 8237 third party DMA controller, resulting in relatively high bus aquisition times. Interrupt drivers are tri-state and edge triggered, meaning interrupts cannot be shared. Generally, ISA is unbuffered, meaning the host/memory bus is tied up whenever a transfer is occuring. No mechanism is provided to prevent bus-hogging.

9.4.2   VESA

Bandwidth is about 30M/sec. Some VESA systems run the bus out of spec, rendering them incompatible with some boards, so this should be taken into consideration before purchasing hardware without a return guarantee. Generally, VESA is unbuffered, meaning meaning the host/memory bus is tied up whenever a transfer is occuring.

9.4.3   EISA

Bandwidth is about 30M/sec, with busmastering operations generally being faster than VESA. Some EISA systems buffer the bus, allowing burst transfers to the faster host/memory bus and minimizing impact on CPU performance. EISA interrupt drivers may be either tri-state edge-triggered or open collector level-active, allowing interrupt sharing with drivers that support it. Since EISA allocates a separate address space for each board, it is usually less prone to resource conflicts than ISA or VESA.

9.4.4   PCI

Bandwidth is about 60M/sec. Most PCI systems implement write posting buffers on the host bridge, allowing speed mismatches on either side to have a minimum impact on bus/CPU performance. PCI interrupt drivers are open collector level-active, allowing interrupt sharing with drivers that support it. Mechanisms are provided to prevent bus hogging, and for both master and slave to suspend a bus-mastering operation.

Since PCI provides a plug-n-play mechanism with writeable configuration registers on every board, in a separate address space, a propperly implemented PCI system is plug-and play.

PCI is extremely strict as to trace length, loading, mechanical specifications, etc. and ultimately should be more reliable than VESA or ISA.

In summary, PCI is the best PC bus, although it does have its dark side. PCI is still in its infancy, and although most manufacturers have ironed out the problems, there is still stock of older, buggy PCI hardware and broken main BIOSes. For this reason, I _strongly_ recommend a return guarantee on the hardware. While the latest PCI mainboards are truly plug-and-play, older PCI boards may require the user to set options with both jumpers and in software (i.e., interrupt assignments). Although many users have resolved their PCI problems, it has taken time and for this reason I cannot recommend a PCI purchase if having the system operational is extremely time critical.

For many slower SCSI devices, such as disks with head rates around 2M/sec or less, CD-ROMs, and tapes, there will be little difference in throughputs with the different PC bus interfaces. For faster contemporary SCSI drives (Typical high end multi-gigabyte drives have a head rate of 4-5M/sec, and at least one company is currently ALPHA testing a parallel head unit with a 14M/sec head rate), throughput will often be significantly better with controllers on faster busses, with one user noting a 2.5 fold performance improvement when going from an Adaptec 1542 ISA board to a NCR53c810 PCI board.

With the exception of situations where PCI write-posting or a similar write-buffering mechanism is being used, when one of the busses in your system is busy, all of the busses will be unaccessable. So, although bus saturation may not be interfering with SCSI performance, it may have a negative effect on interactive performance. I.E., if you have a 4M/sec SCSI disk under ISA, you'll have lost 80% of your bandwidth, and in an ISA/VESA system would only be able to bitblt at 6M/sec. In most cases, a similar impact on processing jobs in the background would also be felt.

Note that having over 16M of memory does not preclude using an ISA busmastering SCSI board. Unlike various broken operating systems, Linux will double buffer when using a DMA with an ISA controller and a transfer is ultimately destined for an area above 16M. Performance on these transfers only suffers by about 1.5%, i.e. not noticably.

Finally, the price difference between bus masters offered with the different bus interfaces is often minimal.

With all that in mind, based on your priorities you will have certain bus preferences.

Stability, time critical installations and poor return policies

EISA ISA VESA PCI

Performance, and typical hobbiest installations

PCI EISA VESA ISA

As I pointed out earlier, bus mastering versus other transfer modes is going to have a bigger impact on total system performance, and should be considered more important than bus type when purchasing a SCSI controller.

9.5 Multiple devices

If will you have multiple devices on your SCSI bus, you may want to see whether the host adapter/driver that you are considering supports more than one outstanding command at one time. This is very important if you are mixing devices of different speeds, like a tape drive and a disk drive. If the Linux driver only supports one outstanding command, you may be locked out of your disk drive while a tape in the tape drive is rewinding, for example. With two disk drives, the problem will not be as noticeable, allthough throughput would approach the average of the two transfer rates rather than the sum of the two transfer rates.

9.6 SCSI-I, SCSI-II, SCSI-III FAST and WIDE options, etc.

Over the years, SCSI has evolved, with new revisions of the standard introducing higher transfer rates, methods to increase throughput, standardized commands for new devices, and new commands for previously supported devices.

In and of themselves, the revision levels don't really mean anything. Excepting minor things like SCSI-II not allowing the single initiator option of SCSI-I, SCSI is backwards compatible, with new features being introduced as options and not mandatory. So, the descision to call a SCSI adapter SCSI, SCSI-II, or SCSI-III is almost entirely a marketing one.

9.7 Driver feature comparison

Driver feature comparison (supported chips are listed in parenthesis)

Driver	Transfer mode	Simultaneous Commands total/LUN	SG Limit	>1
aha152x (AIC6260, AIC6360)	FIFO(8k) Polled	1s/1s	255s	
aha1542	Busmastering DMA	8s/1s	16	Y
aha1740	Busmastering DMA	32s	16	
aha274x	Busmastering DMA	4s/1s	255s	Y
buslogic	Busmastering DMA	Y	64s, 8196h	
eata dma	Busmastering DMA	64s/16s	64s	Y
fdomain TMC1800 except TMC18c30 TMC18c30, with 2k FIFO TMC18c50, TMC36c70	FIFO(8k) Polled	1s	64s	
in2000*	FIFO(2k) Polled	1s	255s	
g NCR5380 (NCR5380, NCR53c80, NCR5381, NCR53c400)	Pure Polled	16s/2s	255s	Y
gsi8* (NCR5380)	Slave DMA	16s/2s	255s	
PAS16 (NCR5380) (fails on some systems!)	Pure Polled or Interlocked Polled	16s/2s	255s	Y
seagate	Interlocked Polled	1s	255s	N
wd7000	Busmastering DMA	8s	1	
t128 (NCR5380)	Interlocked Polled	16s	255s	Y
ultrastor	Busmastering DMA	Y		
53c7,8xx (NCR53c810)	Busmastering DMA	1s/1s	255s	Y

Notes :

1. drivers flagged with an '*' are not included with the distribution kernel, and binary boot images may be unavailable.

2. numbers suffixed with an 's' are arbitrary limits set in software which may be changed with a compile time define.

3. hardware limits are indicated by an 'h' suffix, and may differ from the software limits currently imposed by the Linux drivers.

4. unsuffixed numbers may indicate either hard or soft limits.

9.8 Board comparison

Board	Driver	Bus	Price	Notes
Adaptec AIC-6260	aha152x	ISA		chip, not board
Adaptec AIC-6360	aha152x	VLB		chip, not board (Used in most VESA/ISA multi-IO boards with SCSI, Zenon mainboards)
Adaptec 1520	aha152x	ISA		
Adaptec 1522	aha152x	ISA	$80	1520 w/FDC
Adaptec 1510	aha152x	ISA		1520 w/out boot ROM, won't autoprobe.
Adaptec 1540C	aha1542	ISA		
Adaptec 1542C	aha1542	ISA		1540C w/FDC
Adaptec 1540CF	aha1542	ISA		FAST SCSI-II
Adaptec 1542CF	aha1542	ISA	$200	1540CF w/FDC
Adaptec 1740	aha1740	EISA		discontinued
Adaptec 1742	aha1740	EISA		discontinued, 1740 w/FDC
Adaptec 2740	aha274x	EISA		
Adaptec 2742	aha274x	EISA		w/FDC
Adaptec 2840	aha274x	VLB		
Adaptec 2842	aha274x	VLB		w/FDC
Always IN2000	in2000	ISA		
Buslogic 445S	aha1542, buslogic	VLB	$250	FAST SCSI-II, active termination, w/FDC
Buslogic 747S	aha1542 buslogic	EISA		FAST SCSI-II, active termination, w/FDC
Buslogic 946S	buslogic	PCI		FAST SCSI-II, active termination.
DPT PM2011	eata dma	ISA		FAST SCSI-II
DPT PM2012A	eata dma	EISA		FAST SCSI-II
DPT PM2012B	eata dma	EISA		FAST SCSI-II
DPT PM2021	eata dma	ISA	$245	FAST SCSI-II
DPT PM2022	eata dma	EISA	$449	FAST SCSI-II active termination
DPT PM2024	eata dma	PCI	$395	FAST SCSI-II active termination
DPT PM2122	eata dma	EISA	$595	FAST SCSI-II active termination
DPT PM2124	eata dma	PCI	$595	FAST SCSI-II active termination
DPT PM2322	eata dma	EISA		FAST SCSI-II active termination
DPT PM3021	eata dma	ISA	$1595	FAST SCSI-II multichannel raid/simm sockets active termination
DPT PM3122	eata dma	EISA	$1795	FAST SCSI-II multichannel/raid active termination

DPT PM3222	eata dma	EISA	$1795	FAST SCSI-II multichannel raid/simm sockets active termination
DPT PM3224	eata dma	PCI	$1995	FAST SCSI-II multichannel raid/simm sockets active termination
DPT DTC 3	aha1542	EISA		Although it should work, due to documentation release polices, DTC hardware is unsupported
DTC 3292	aha1542	EISA		3290 w/FDC
DTC 3292	aha1542	EISA		3290 w/FDC
Future Domain 1680	fdomain	ISA		FDC
Future Domain 3260	fdomain	PCI		
NCR53c810 (boards sold by FIC, Chaintech, Nextor, Gigabyte, etc. Mainboards with chip by AMI, ASUS, J-Bond, etc. Common in DEC PCI systems)	53c7,8xx	PCI	$70	+chip, not board. Boards (board) don't include BIOS, although most non-NCR equipped main boards have the SDMS BIOS
NCR53c815 (Intel PCISCSIKIT, NCR8150S, etc)	53c7,8xx	PCI	$115	NCR53c810 plus bios
NCR53c825	53c7,8xx	PCI		Wide variant of NCR53c815. Note that the current Linux driver does not negotiate for wide transfers.
Pro Audio Spectrum 16	pas16	ISA		Sound board w/SCSI
Seagate ST01	seagate	ISA	$20	IOS only works with some drives
Seagate ST02	seagate	ISA	$40	ST01 w/FDC
Sound Blaster 16 SCSI	aha152x	ISA		Sound board w/SCSI
Western Digital 7000	wd7000	ISA		w/FDC
Trantor T128	t128	ISA		
Trantor T128F	t128	ISA		T128 w/FDC and support for high IRQs
Trantor T130B	g NCR5380	ISA		
Ultrastor 14F	ultrastor	ISA		w/FDC
Ultrastor 24F	ultrastor	EISA		w/FDC
Ultrastor 34F	ultrastor	VLB		

Notes:

1. Trantor was recently purchased by Adaptec, and some products are being sold under the Adaptec name.

2. Ultrastor recently filed for Chapter 11 Bankruptcy, so technical support is non-existant at this time.

3. Various Buslogic boards other than the 545S, 445S, 747S, and 946S _should_ work, although to my knowledge have not been tried.

4. The $70 price for the busmastering NCR53c810 boards is not a typo, includes the standard ASPI/CAM driver package for DOS, OS/2 and Windows (32 bit access), and other drivers are available for free

download.

If you can't find one at that price, try Technoland at 1-800-292-4500 or 1-408-992-0888 if you live in California, InteliSys at (703)385-0347, Superpower 1 (800) 736-0007, SW (swt@netcom.com) 214-907-0871 fax 214-907-9339

Insight Electronics at 1-609-985-5556 stocks NCR8150S '815 boards for $115 if you don't have a NCR SDMS BIOS in your main ROM.

5. Adaptec's recent SCSI chips show an unusual sensitivity to cabling and termination problems. For this reason, I cannot recommend the Adaptec 154x C and CF revisions or the 2xxx series.

   Note that the reliability problems do not apply to the older 154x B revision boards, 174x A revision boards, or to my knowledge AIC-6360/AIC-6260 based boards.

   Also, the quality of their technical support has slipped markedly, with long delays becoming more common, and their employees being ignorant (suggesting there were non-disclosure policies affecting certain literature when there were none), and hostile (i.e., refusing to pass questions on to some one else when they couldn't answer them).

   If users desire handholding, or wish to make a political statement, they should take this point into consideration. Otherwise, the Adaptec 152x/1510 are nicer than the other ISA boards in the same price range, and there are some excellent deals on used and surplus 154x B revision boards and 1742 boards which IMHO outweigh the support problems.

6. All given prices for the DPT controllers are official list prices. Street prices should be considerably lower. All boards can be upgraded with chache and raid modules, most of the boards are also available in Wide and/or Differential versions.

9.9 Summary

Most ISA, EISA, and VESA users will probably be served best by a Buslogic board, due to its performance, features such as active termination, and Adaptec 1540 compatibility. There are a number of models available with EISA, ISA, PCI, and VESA local bus interfaces, in single ended and differential, and 8/16 bit SCSI bus widths.

People with PCI systems should consider NCR53c810 based boards. These are bus mastering SCSI controllers, available in Q1 for about $70 (i.e., cheaper than the Adaptec 1520) with larger quantities being cheaper (I've seen $62 in Q20). In addition to being the cheapest PCI SCSI boards, the NCR boards were also benchmarked as faster than the Adaptec 2940 and Buslogic BT-946, and demonstrate excellent performance under Linux (up to 4M/sec through the file system) inspite of the performance optimizations being disabled in the current driver. The disadvantages of these boards versus the Buslogics are that they aren't Adaptec 1540 compatible, don't come with active termination, and to my knowledge are only supported under DOS+Windows, OS/2, Windows NT, SCO, NeXTstep, and Free BSD. Currently, the Linux driver appears quite stable on most systems (We've moved several gigabytes of data to NCR based devices with no problems), surprisingly fast (I've seen 4M/sec through the filesystem) and will eventually become more featureful. On the downside, the current Linux driver implementation doesn't support disconnect/reconnect, so you will be unable to access your SCSI disks if rewinding, retensioning,etc. SCSI tapes at the same time.

People wanting non-PCI SCSI on a limited budget will probably be happiest finding a surplus or used Adaptec 154x B revision or 174x A revision, or an Adaptec 1520 clone of some sort (about $80) if they want new hardware. These boards offer reasonable throughput and interactive performance at a modest price.

Part XXXVII

The Linux SCSI programming HOWTO

Copyright Heiko Eißfeldt `heiko@colossus.escape.de`
v1.3, 14 April 1995
This document deals with programming the Linux generic SCSI interface.

Contents

1 Introduction

This document is a guide to the installation and programming of the Linux generic SCSI interface.

It covers kernel prerequisites, device mappings, and basic interaction with devices. Some simple C programming examples are included. General knowledge of the SCSI command set is required; for more information on the SCSI standard and related information, see the appendix to this document.

2 What Is The Generic SCSI Interface?

The generic SCSI interface has been implemented to provide general SCSI access to (possibly exotic) pieces of SCSI hardware. It was developed by Lawrence Foard (`entropy@world.std.com`) and sponsored by Killy Corporation (see the comments in `drivers/scsi/sg.h`).

The interface makes special device handling possible from user level applications (i.e. outside the kernel). Thus, kernel driver development, which is more risky and difficult to debug, is not necessary.

However, if you don't program the driver properly it is possible to hang the SCSI bus, the driver, or the kernel. Therefore, it is important to properly program the generic driver and to first back up all files to avoid losing data. Another useful thing to do before running your programs is to issue a `sync` command to ensure that any buffers are flushed to disk, minimizing data loss if the system hangs.

Another advantage of the generic driver is that as long as the interface itself does not change, all applications are independent of new kernel development. In comparison, other low-level kernel drivers have to be synchronized with other internal kernel changes.

Typically, the generic driver is used to communicate with new SCSI hardware devices that require special user applications to be written to take advantage of their features (e.g. scanners, printers, CD-ROM jukeboxes). The generic interface allows these to be written quickly.

3   What Are The Requirements To Use It?

3.1   Kernel Configuration

You must have a supported SCSI controller, obviously. Furthermore, your kernel must have controller support as well as generic support compiled in. Configuring the Linux kernel (via `make config` under /usr/src/linux) typically looks like the following:

```
    . . .
  *
  * SCSI support
  *
  SCSI support? (CONFIG_SCSI) [n] y
  *
  * SCSI support type (disk, tape, CDrom)
  *
    . . .
  SCSI generic support (CONFIG_CHR_DEV_SG) [n] y
  *
  * SCSI low-level drivers
  *
    . . .
```

If available, modules can of course be built instead.

3.2   Device Files

The generic SCSI driver uses its own device files, separate from those used by the other SCSI device drivers. They can be generated using the `MAKEDEV` script, typically found in the /dev directory. Running `MAKEDEV` `sg` produces these files:

```
crw-------  1 root    system    21,   0 Aug 20 20:09 /dev/sga
crw-------  1 root    system    21,   1 Aug 20 20:09 /dev/sgb
crw-------  1 root    system    21,   2 Aug 20 20:09 /dev/sgc
crw-------  1 root    system    21,   3 Aug 20 20:09 /dev/sgd
crw-------  1 root    system    21,   4 Aug 20 20:09 /dev/sge
crw-------  1 root    system    21,   5 Aug 20 20:09 /dev/sgf
crw-------  1 root    system    21,   6 Aug 20 20:09 /dev/sgg
crw-------  1 root    system    21,   7 Aug 20 20:09 /dev/sgh
                                 |     |
                           major,   minor device numbers
```

Note that these are character devices for raw access. On some systems these devices may be called /dev/{sg0,sg1,...}, depending on your installation, so adjust the following examples accordingly.

3.3   Device Mapping

These device files are dynamically mapped to SCSI id/LUNs on your SCSI bus (LUN = logical unit). The mapping allocates devices consecutively for each LUN of each device on each SCSI bus found at time of the SCSI scan, beginning at the lower LUNs/ids/busses. It starts with the first SCSI controller and continues without interruption with all following controllers. This is currently done in the initialisation of the SCSI driver.

For example, assuming you had three SCSI devices hooked up with ids 1, 3, and 5 on the first SCSI bus (each having one LUN), then the following mapping would be in effect:

```
/dev/sga -> SCSI id 1
/dev/sgb -> SCSI id 3
/dev/sgc -> SCSI id 5
```

If you now add a new device with id 4, then the mapping (after the next rescan) will be:

```
/dev/sga -> SCSI id 1
/dev/sgb -> SCSI id 3
/dev/sgc -> SCSI id 4
/dev/sgd -> SCSI id 5
```

Notice the change for id 5 – the corresponding device is no longer mapped to /dev/sgc but is now /dev/sgd.

3.3.1 Rescanning the devices

To force a rescan, a modularized driver could be deleted and reinserted. At initialisation time it will rescan the busses. But in order to be able to delete the driver, none of its devices may be used at that time. When adding more devices to the SCSI busses keep in mind there are limited spare entries for new devices. The memory had been allocated at boot time and has room for 2 more disks, 2 more CDROMs, 2 more tapes and 2 more generic devices.

Scanning the SCSI busses on your own is not recommended. There are too many (buggy) devices that may hang the SCSI bus, when being addressed with a LUN value that is not 0. The kernel manages a private table with known flawed devices, where it scans with LUN 0 only.

4   Programmers Guide

The following sections are for programmers who want to use the generic SCSI interface in their own applications. An example will be given showing how to access a SCSI device with the INQUIRY and the TESTUNITREADY commands.

When using these code examples, note the following:

- the generic SCSI interface was extended in kernel version 1.1.68; the examples require at least this version. But please avoid kernel version 1.1.77 up to 1.1.89 since they had a broken generic SCSI interface.

- the constant DEVICE in the header section describing the accessed device should be set according to your available devices (see section 7.

5   Overview Of Device Programming

The header file drivers/scsi/sg.h under the Linux source tree contains a description of the interface (this is based on kernel version 1.1.68):

```
struct sg_header
  {
    int pack_len;
                    /* length of incoming packet <4096 (including header) */
    int reply_len;  /* maximum length <4096 of expected reply */
    int pack_id;    /* id number of packet */
    int result;     /* 0==ok, otherwise refer to errno codes */
    unsigned int twelve_byte:1;
```

```
                   /* Force 12 byte command length for group 6 & 7 commands */
    unsigned int other_flags:31;                    /* for future use */
    unsigned char sense_buffer[16]; /* used only by reads */
    /* command follows then data for command */
    };
```

This structure describes how a SCSI command is to be processed and has room to hold the results of the execution of the command. The individual structure components will be discussed later in section 7.

The general way of exchanging data with the generic driver is as follows: to send a command to an opened generic device, write() a block containing these three parts to it:

```
                    struct sg_header
                      SCSI command
                       output data
```

To obtain the result of a command, read() a block with this similar block structure:

```
                    struct sg_header
                       input data
```

NOTE: Up to recent kernel versions, it is necessary to block the SIGINT signal between the write() and the corresponding read() call (i.e. via sigprocmask()). A return after the write() part without any read() to fetch the results will block on subsequent accesses. This signal blocking has not yet been included in the example code.

This is a general overview of the process. The following sections describe each of the steps in more detail.

6   Opening The Device

A generic device has to be opened for read and write access:

```
        int fd = open (device_name, O_RDWR);
```

(This is the case even for a read-only hardware device such as a cdrom drive).

We have to perform a write to send the command and a read to get back any results. In the case of an error the return code is negative (see section B for a complete list).

7   The Header Structure

The header structure struct sg_header serves as a controlling layer between the application and the kernel driver. We now discuss its components in detail.

int pack_len

> defines the size of the block written to the driver. This is defined from the application side.

int reply_len

> defines the size of the block to be accepted at reply. This is defined from the application side.

int pack_id

> This field helps to assign replies to requests. The application can supply a unique id for each request. Suppose you have written several commands (say 4) to one device. They may work in parallel, one being the fastest. When getting replies via 4 reads, the replies do not have to have the order of the requests. To identify the correct reply for a given request one can use the pack_id field. Typically its value is incremented after each request (and wraps eventually).

int result

the result code of a `read` or `write` call. This is defined from the generic driver (kernel) side. These codes are defined in `errno.h` (0 meaning no error).

unsigned int twelve_byte:1

This field is necessary only when using non-standard vendor specific commands (in the range 0xc0 - 0xff). When these commands have a command length of 12 bytes instead of 10, this field has to be set to one before the write call. Other command lengths are not supported. This is defined from the application side.

unsigned char sense_buffer16

This buffer is set after a command is completed (after a `read()` call) and contains the SCSI sense code. Some command results have to be read from here (e.g. for TESTUNITREADY). Usually it contains just zero bytes. The value in this field is set by the generic driver (kernel) side.

The following example function interfaces directly with the generic kernel driver. It defines the header structure, sends the command via `write`, gets the result via `read` and does some (limited) error checking. The sense buffer data is available in the output buffer (unless a NULL pointer has been given, in which case it's in the input buffer). We will use it in the examples which follow.

Note: Set the value of `DEVICE` to your device descriptor.

```
/* Example program to demonstrate the generic SCSI interface */
#include <stdio.h>
#include <unistd.h>
#include <string.h>
#include <fcntl.h>
#include <errno.h>
#include <linux/../../drivers/scsi/sg.h>

#define DEVICE "/dev/sgc"

#define SCSI_OFF sizeof(struct sg_header)
static unsigned char cmd[SCSI_OFF + 18];       /* SCSI command buffer */
int fd;                                  /* SCSI device/file descriptor */

/* process a complete SCSI cmd. Use the generic SCSI interface. */
static int handle_SCSI_cmd(unsigned cmd_len,       /* command length */
                           unsigned in_size,       /* input data size */
                           unsigned char *i_buff,  /* input buffer */
                           unsigned out_size,      /* output data size */
                           unsigned char *o_buff   /* output buffer */
                           )
{
    int status = 0;
    struct sg_header *sg_hd;

    /* safety checks */
    if (!cmd_len) return -1;               /* need a cmd_len != 0 */
    if (!i_buff) return -1;                /* need an input buffer != NULL */
#ifdef SG_BIG_BUFF
    if (SCSI_OFF + cmd_len + in_size > SG_BIG_BUFF) return -1;
    if (SCSI_OFF + out_size > SG_BIG_BUFF) return -1;
#else
    if (SCSI_OFF + cmd_len + in_size > 4096) return -1;
    if (SCSI_OFF + out_size > 4096) return -1;
#endif

    if (!o_buff) out_size = 0;        /* no output buffer, no output size */
```

```
        /* generic SCSI device header construction */
        sg_hd = (struct sg_header *) i_buff;
        sg_hd->pack_len    = SCSI_OFF + cmd_len + in_size;
        sg_hd->reply_len   = SCSI_OFF + out_size;
        sg_hd->twelve_byte = cmd_len == 12;
#if    0
        sg_hd->pack_id;      /* not used */
        sg_hd->other_flags; /* not used */
#endif

        /* send command */
        status = write( fd, i_buff, SCSI_OFF + cmd_len + in_size );
        if ( status < 0 || status != SCSI_OFF + cmd_len + in_size ||
                        sg_hd->result ) {
            /* some error happened */
            fprintf( stderr, "write(generic) result = 0x%x cmd = 0x%x\n",
                        sg_hd->result, i_buff[SCSI_OFF] );
            perror("");
            return status;
        }

        if (!o_buff) o_buff = i_buff;       /* buffer pointer check */

        /* retrieve result */
        status = read( fd, o_buff, SCSI_OFF + out_size);
        if ( status < 0 || status != SCSI_OFF + out_size || sg_hd->result ) {
            /* some error happened */
            fprintf( stderr, "read(generic) status = 0x%x, result = 0x%x, "
                        "cmd = 0x%x\n",
                        status, sg_hd->result, o_buff[SCSI_OFF] );
            fprintf( stderr, "read(generic) sense "
                "%x %x %x %x %x %x %x %x %x %x %x %x %x %x %x %x\n",
                sg_hd->sense_buffer[0],          sg_hd->sense_buffer[1],
                sg_hd->sense_buffer[2],          sg_hd->sense_buffer[3],
                sg_hd->sense_buffer[4],          sg_hd->sense_buffer[5],
                sg_hd->sense_buffer[6],          sg_hd->sense_buffer[7],
                sg_hd->sense_buffer[8],          sg_hd->sense_buffer[9],
                sg_hd->sense_buffer[10],         sg_hd->sense_buffer[11],
                sg_hd->sense_buffer[12],         sg_hd->sense_buffer[13],
                sg_hd->sense_buffer[14],         sg_hd->sense_buffer[15]);
        }
        /* Look if we got what we expected to get */
        if (status == SCSI_OFF + out_size) status = 0; /* got them all */

        return status;  /* 0 means no error */
}
```

While this may look somewhat complex at first appearance, most of the code is for error checking and reporting (which is useful even after the code is working).

Handle_SCSI_cmd has a generalized form for all SCSI commands types, falling into each of these categories:

```
        Data Mode            | Example Command
==================================================
neither input nor output data | test unit ready
 no input data, output data   | inquiry, read
 input data, no output data   | mode select, write
   input data, output data    | mode sense
```

8 Inquiry Command Example

One of the most basic SCSI commands is the INQUIRY command, used to identify the type and make of the device. Here is the definition from the SCSI-2 specification (for details refer to the SCSI-2 standard).

```
                    Table 44: INQUIRY Command
+=====-========-========-========-========-========-========-========+
| Bit|   7    |   6    |   5    |   4    |   3    |   2    |   1    |   0    |
|Byte|        |        |        |        |        |        |        |        |
|=====+========================================================================|
| 0  |                    Operation Code (12h)                                |
|-----+-------------------------------------------------------------------|
| 1  | Logical Unit Number      |          Reserved          | EVPD |
|-----+-------------------------------------------------------------------|
| 2  |                        Page Code                                 |
|-----+-------------------------------------------------------------------|
| 3  |                        Reserved                                  |
|-----+-------------------------------------------------------------------|
| 4  |                     Allocation Length                            |
|-----+-------------------------------------------------------------------|
| 5  |                        Control                                   |
+=====================================================================+
```

The output data are as follows:

```
                 Table 45: Standard INQUIRY Data Format
+=====-========-========-========-========-========-========-========+
| Bit|   7    |   6    |   5    |   4    |   3    |   2    |   1    |   0    |
|Byte|        |        |        |        |        |        |        |        |
|=====+========================+=========================================|
| 0  | Peripheral Qualifier    |       Peripheral Device Type            |
|-----+-------------------------------------------------------------------|
| 1  | RMB  |           Device-Type Modifier                            |
|-----+-------------------------------------------------------------------|
| 2  | ISO Version  |   ECMA Version    |  ANSI-Approved Version         |
|-----+-------------------------------------------------------------------|
| 3  | AENC | TrmIOP | Reserved  |      Response Data Format              |
|-----+-------------------------------------------------------------------|
| 4  |                    Additional Length (n-4)                        |
|-----+-------------------------------------------------------------------|
| 5  |                        Reserved                                  |
|-----+-------------------------------------------------------------------|
| 6  |                        Reserved                                  |
|-----+-------------------------------------------------------------------|
| 7  | RelAdr | WBus32 | WBus16 | Sync | Linked |Reserved| CmdQue | SftRe |
|-----+-------------------------------------------------------------------|
| 8  | (MSB)                                                            |
|- - -+---               Vendor Identification               ---|
| 15 |                                                         (LSB) |
|-----+-------------------------------------------------------------------|
| 16 | (MSB)                                                            |
|- - -+---               Product Identification              ---|
| 31 |                                                         (LSB) |
|-----+-------------------------------------------------------------------|
| 32 | (MSB)                                                            |
|- - -+---               Product Revision Level             ---|
| 35 |                                                         (LSB) |
|-----+-------------------------------------------------------------------|
| 36 |                                                                  |
|- - -+---                  Vendor Specific                  ---|
```

```
| 55  |
|-----+------------------------------------------------------------------|
| 56  |
|- - -+---                      Reserved                              ---|
| 95  |
|=====+==================================================================|
|     |               Vendor-Specific Parameters                         |
|=====+==================================================================|
| 96  |
|- - -+---                    Vendor Specific                         ---|
| n   |
+=======================================================================+
```

The next example uses the low-level function handle_SCSI_cmd to perform the Inquiry SCSI command.

We first append the command block to the generic header, then call handle_SCSI_cmd. Note that the output buffer size argument for the handle_SCSI_cmd call excludes the generic header size. After command completion the output buffer contains the requested data, unless an error occurred.

```
#define INQUIRY_CMD      0x12
#define INQUIRY_CMDLEN   6
#define INQUIRY_REPLY_LEN 96
#define INQUIRY_VENDOR   8          /* Offset in reply data to vendor name */

/* request vendor brand and model */
static unsigned char *Inquiry ( void )
{
  unsigned char Inqbuffer[ SCSI_OFF + INQUIRY_REPLY_LEN ];
  unsigned char cmdblk [ INQUIRY_CMDLEN ] =
      { INQUIRY_CMD, /* command */
               0,  /* lun/reserved */
               0,  /* page code */
               0,  /* reserved */
INQUIRY_REPLY_LEN,  /* allocation length */
               0 };/* reserved/flag/link */

  memcpy( cmd + SCSI_OFF, cmdblk, sizeof(cmdblk) );

  if (handle_SCSI_cmd(sizeof(cmdblk), 0, cmd,
                    sizeof(Inqbuffer) - SCSI_OFF, Inqbuffer )) {
      fprintf( stderr, "Inquiry failed\n" );
      exit(2);
  }
  return (Inqbuffer + SCSI_OFF);
}
```

The example above follows this structure. The Inquiry function copies its command block behind the generic header (given by SCSI_OFF). Input data is not present for this command. Handle_SCSI_cmd will define the header structure. We can now implement the function main to complete this working example program.

```
void main( void )
{
  fd = open(DEVICE, O_RDWR);
  if (fd < 0) {
    fprintf( stderr, "Need read/write permissions for "DEVICE".\n" );
    exit(1);
  }

  /* print the result of Inquiry */
```

```
    printf( "%s\n", Inquiry() + INQUIRY_VENDOR );
}
```

We first open the device, check for errors, and then call the higher level subroutine. Then we print the results in human readable format including the vendor, product, and revision.

9   The Sense Buffer

Commands with no output data can give status information via the sense buffer (which is part of the header structure). Sense data is available when the previous command has terminated with a CHECK CONDITION status. In this case the kernel automatically retrieves the sense data via a REQUEST SENSE command. Its structure is:

```
+=====-========-========-========-========-========-========-========+
| Bit|   7    |   6    |   5    |   4    |   3    |   2    |   1    |   0    |
|Byte |        |        |        |        |        |        |        |        |
|=====+========+========================================================|
| 0   | Valid  |                 Error Code (70h or 71h)                |
|-----+----------------------------------------------------------------|
| 1   |                        Segment Number                          |
|-----+----------------------------------------------------------------|
| 2   |Filemark|  EOM  | ILI  |Reserved|          Sense Key            |
|-----+----------------------------------------------------------------|
| 3   | (MSB)                                                          |
|- - -+---                     Information                         ---|
| 6   |                                                        (LSB) |
|-----+----------------------------------------------------------------|
| 7   |                  Additional Sense Length (n-7)                |
|-----+----------------------------------------------------------------|
| 8   | (MSB)                                                          |
|- - -+---              Command-Specific Information              ---|
| 11  |                                                        (LSB) |
|-----+----------------------------------------------------------------|
| 12  |                    Additional Sense Code                      |
|-----+----------------------------------------------------------------|
| 13  |               Additional Sense Code Qualifier                 |
|-----+----------------------------------------------------------------|
| 14  |                  Field Replaceable Unit Code                  |
|-----+----------------------------------------------------------------|
| 15  | SKSV  |                                                        |
|- - -+------------           Sense-Key Specific             ---|
| 17  |                                                                |
|-----+----------------------------------------------------------------|
| 18  |                                                                |
|- - -+---                  Additional Sense Bytes             ---|
| n   |                                                                |
+=================================================================+
```

Note: The most useful fields are Sense Key (see section B.3), Additional Sense Code and Additional Sense Code Qualifier (see section C). The latter two are combined.

10   Example Using Sense Buffer

Here we will use the TEST UNIT READY command to check whether media is loaded into our device. The header declarations and function `handle_SCSI_cmd` from the inquiry example will be needed as well.

```
                    Table 73: TEST UNIT READY Command
+=====-========-========-========-========-========-========-========-========+
| Bit|   7    |   6    |   5    |   4    |   3    |   2    |   1    |   0    |
|Byte |        |        |        |        |        |        |        |        |
|=====+========================================================================|
| 0   |                       Operation Code (00h)                            |
|-----+------------------------------------------------------------------------|
| 1   | Logical Unit Number     |              Reserved                       |
|-----+------------------------------------------------------------------------|
| 2   |                           Reserved                                    |
|-----+------------------------------------------------------------------------|
| 3   |                           Reserved                                    |
|-----+------------------------------------------------------------------------|
| 4   |                           Reserved                                    |
|-----+------------------------------------------------------------------------|
| 5   |                           Control                                     |
+============================================================================+
```

Here is the function which implements it:

```
#define TESTUNITREADY_CMD 0
#define TESTUNITREADY_CMDLEN 6

#define ADD_SENSECODE 12
#define ADD_SC_QUALIFIER 13
#define NO_MEDIA_SC 0x3a
#define NO_MEDIA_SCQ 0x00

int TestForMedium ( void )
{
  /* request READY status */
  static unsigned char cmdblk [TESTUNITREADY_CMDLEN] = {
      TESTUNITREADY_CMD, /* command */
                     0, /* reserved */
                     0, /* reserved */
                     0, /* reserved */
                     0, /* reserved */
                     0};/* control */

  memcpy( cmd + SCSI_OFF, cmdblk, sizeof(cmdblk) );

  if (handle_SCSI_cmd(sizeof(cmdblk), 0, cmd,
                        0, NULL)) {
      fprintf (stderr, "Test unit ready failed\n");
      exit(2);
  }

  return
    *(((struct sg_header*)cmd)->sense_buffer +ADD_SENSECODE) !=
                                        NO_MEDIA_SC ||
    *(((struct sg_header*)cmd)->sense_buffer +ADD_SC_QUALIFIER) !=
                                        NO_MEDIA_SCQ;
}
```

Combined with this main function we can do the check.

```
void main( void )
{
  fd = open(DEVICE, O_RDWR);
  if (fd < 0) {
```

```
        fprintf( stderr, "Need read/write permissions for "DEVICE".\n" );
        exit(1);
    }

    /* look if medium is loaded */

    if (!TestForMedium()) {
        printf("device is unloaded\n");
    } else {
        printf("device is loaded\n");
    }
}
```

The file `generic_demo.c` from the appendix contains both examples.

11   Ioctl Functions

There are two ioctl functions available:

- `ioctl(fd, SG_SET_TIMEOUT, &Timeout);` sets the timeout value to `Timeout` * 10 milliseconds. `Timeout` has to be declared as int.

- `ioctl(fd, SG_GET_TIMEOUT, &Timeout);` gets the current timeout value. `Timeout` has to be declared as int.

12   Driver Defaults

12.1   Transfer Lengths

Currently (at least up to kernel version 1.1.68) input and output sizes have to be less than or equal than 4096 bytes unless the kernel has been compiled with `SG_BIG_BUFF` defined, if which case it is limited to `SG_BIG_BUFF` (e.g. 32768) bytes. These sizes include the generic header as well as the command block on input.

12.2   Timeout And Retry Values

The default timeout value is set to one minute (`Timeout` = 6000). It can be changed through an ioctl call (see section 11). The default number of retries is one.

13   Obtaining The SCSI Specifications

There are standards entitled SCSI-1 and SCSI-2 (and possibly soon SCSI-3). The standards are mostly upward compatible.

The SCSI-1 standard is (in the author's opinion) mostly obsolete, and SCSI-2 is the most widely used. SCSI-3 is very new and very expensive. These standardized command sets specify mandatory and optional commands for SCSI manufacturers and should be preferred over the vendor specific command extensions which are not standardized and for which programming information is seldom available. Of course sometimes there is no alternative to these extensions.

Electronic copies are available via anonymous ftp from:

- ftp.cs.tulane.edu:pub/scsi

- ncrinfo.ncr.com:/pub/standards

- ftp.cs.uni-sb.de:/pub/misc/doc/scsi

(I got my SCSI specification from the Yggdrasil Linux CD-ROM in the directory /usr/doc/scsi-2 and /usr/doc/scsi-1).

The SCSI FAQ also lists the following sources of printed information:

The SCSI specification: Available from:

```
        Global Engineering Documents
        15 Inverness Way East
        Englewood Co  80112-5704
        (800) 854-7179
          SCSI-1: X3.131-1986
          SCSI-2: X3.131-199x
          SCSI-3 X3T9.2/91-010R4 Working Draft

(Global Engineering Documentation in Irvine, CA (714)261-1455??)

SCSI-1: Doc \# X3.131-1986 from ANSI, 1430 Broadway, NY, NY 10018

IN-DEPTH EXPLORATION OF SCSI can be obtained from
Solution Technology, Attn: SCSI Publications, POB 104, Boulder Creek,
CA 95006, (408)338-4285, FAX (408)338-4374

THE SCSI ENCYLOPEDIA and the SCSI BENCH REFERENCE can be obtained from
ENDL Publishing, 14426 Black Walnut Ct., Saratoga, CA 95090,
(408)867-6642, FAX (408)867-2115

SCSI: UNDERSTANDING THE SMALL COMPUTER SYSTEM INTERFACE was published
by Prentice-Hall, ISBN 0-13-796855-8
```

14 Related Information Sources

The Linux **SCSI-HOWTO** by Drew Eckhardt covers all supported SCSI controllers as well as device specific questions. A lot of troubleshooting hints are given. It is available from sunsite.unc.edu in /pub/Linux/docs/LDP and its mirror sites.

General questions about SCSI are answered in the **SCSI-FAQ** from the newsgroup Comp.Periphs.Scsi (available on tsx-11 in pub/linux/ALPHA/scsi and mirror sites).

There is a **mailing list** for bug reports and questions regarding SCSI development under Linux. To join, send email to majordomo@vger.rutgers.edu with the line subscribe linux-scsi in the body of the message. Messages should be posted to linux-scsi@vger.rutgers.edu. Help text can be requested by sending the message line "help" to majordomo@vger.rutgers.edu. There is another mailing list server at niksula.hut.fi, but it has been very busy (read too busy) lately.

15 Other SCSI Access Interfaces

There are some other similar interfaces in use in the un*x world, but not available for Linux:

1. CAM (Common Access Method) developed by Future Domain and other SCSI vendors. This was a response to the ASPI interface. Linux has some support for a SCSI CAM system (mainly for booting from hard disk). CAM even supports target mode, so one could disguise ones computer as a peripheral hardware device (e.g. for a small SCSI net).

2. ASPI (Advanced SCSI Programming Interface) developed by Adaptec. This is the de facto standard for MS-DOS machines.

There are other application interfaces from SCO(TM), NeXT(TM), Silicon Graphics(TM) and SUN(TM) as well.

16   Final Comments

The generic SCSI interface bridges the gap between user applications and specific devices. But rather than bloating a lot of programs with similar sets of low-level functions, it would be more desirable to have a shared library with a generalized set of low-level functions for a particular purpose. The main goal should be to have independent layers of interfaces. A good design would separate an application into low-level and hardware independent routines. The low-level routines could be put into a shared library and made available for all applications. Here, standardized interfaces should be followed as much as possible before making new ones.

By now you should know more than I do about the Linux generic SCSI interface. So you can start developing powerful applications for the benefit of the global Linux community now...

17   Acknowledgments

Special thanks go to Jeff Tranter for proofreading and enhancing the text considerably as well as to Carlos Puchol for useful comments. Drew Eckhardt's and Eric Youngdale's help on my first (dumb) questions about the use of this interface has been appreciated.

A   Appendix

B   Error handling

The functions `open`, `ioctl`, `write` and `read` can report errors. In this case their return value is -1 and the global variable errno is set to the error number (negative). The errno values are defined in `/usr/include/errno.h`. Possible negative values are:

```
Function | Error         | Description
=========|===============|================================================
open     | -ENXIO        | not a valid device
         | -EACCES       | access mode is not read/write (O_RDWR)
         | -EBUSY        | device was requested for nonblocking access,
         |               | but is busy now.
         | -ERESTARTSYS  | this indicates an internal error. Try to
         |               | make it reproducible and inform the SCSI
         |               | channel (for details on bug reporting
         |               | see Drew Eckhardts SCSI-HOWTO).
ioctl    | -ENXIO        | not a valid device
read     | -EWOULDBLOCK  | the device would block. Try again later.
write    | -EIO          | the length is too small (smaller than the
         |               | generic header struct). Caution: Currently
         |               | there is no overlength checking.
         | -EWOULDBLOCK  | the device would block. Try again later.
         | -ERESTARTSYS  | this indicates an internal error. Try to
         |               | make it reproducible and inform the SCSI
         |               | channel (for details on bug reporting
         |               | see Drew Eckhardts SCSI-HOWTO).
```

```
|  -ENOMEM            |  memory required for this request could not be
|                     |  allocated. Try later again unless you
|                     |  exceeded the maximum transfer size (see above)
```

For read/write positive return values indicate as usual the amount of bytes that have been successfully transferred. This should equal the amount you requested.

B.1 Error status decoding

Furthermore a detailed reporting is done via the kernels hd_status and the devices reports in the sense_buffer (see section 9) from the header structure.

The meaning of hd_status can be found in drivers/scsi/scsi.h: This unsigned int is composed out of different parts:

```
    lsb  |    ...    |    ...    |  msb
    =======|===========|===========|============
    status | sense key | host code | driver byte
```

These macros from drivers/scsi/scsi.h can be used to separate the fields:

```
        Macro            | Description
    ==================== |============================================
    status_byte(result)  |  The SCSI device status. See above
    msg_byte(result)     |  The devices sense key. See above
    host_byte(result)    |  The host code from the kernel driver. See above
    driver_byte(result)  |  The first byte from the device
```

B.2 Status codes

The following status codes from the SCSI device (defined in drivers/scsi/scsi.h) should be used with the macro status_byte (see section B.1):

```
    Value | Symbol
    ======|====================
    0x00  |  GOOD
    0x01  |  CHECK_CONDITION
    0x02  |  CONDITION_GOOD
    0x04  |  BUSY
    0x08  |  INTERMEDIATE_GOOD
    0x0a  |  INTERMEDIATE_C_GOOD
    0x0c  |  RESERVATION_CONFLICT
```

Note that these symbol values have been **shifted right once**. From the SCSI-2 specification:

Table 27: Status Byte Code

7	6	5	4	3	2	1	0	Status
R	R	0	0	0	0	0	R	GOOD
R	R	0	0	0	0	1	R	CHECK CONDITION
R	R	0	0	0	1	0	R	CONDITION MET
R	R	0	0	1	0	0	R	BUSY
R	R	0	1	0	0	0	R	INTERMEDIATE

Bits of Status Byte

```
| R   R   0   1   0   1   0   R  | INTERMEDIATE-CONDITION MET  |
| R   R   0   1   1   0   0   R  | RESERVATION CONFLICT       |
| R   R   1   0   0   0   1   R  | COMMAND TERMINATED         |
| R   R   1   0   1   0   0   R  | QUEUE FULL                 |
|                                |                            |
|      All Other Codes           | Reserved                   |
|--------------------------------------------------------------|
| Key: R = Reserved bit                                        |
+==============================================================+
```

A definition of the status byte codes is given below.

GOOD. This status indicates that the target has successfully completed the command.

CHECK CONDITION. This status indicates that a contingent allegiance condition has occurred (see 6.6).

CONDITION MET. This status or INTERMEDIATE-CONDITION MET is returned whenever the requested operation is satisfied (see the SEARCH DATA and PRE-FETCH commands).

BUSY. This status indicates that the target is busy. This status shall be returned whenever a target is unable to accept a command from an otherwise acceptable initiator (i.e., no reservation conflicts). The recommended initiator recovery action is to issue the command again at a later time.

INTERMEDIATE. This status or INTERMEDIATE-CONDITION MET shall be returned for every successfully completed command in a series of linked commands (except the last command), unless the command is terminated with CHECK CONDITION, RESERVATION CONFLICT, or COMMAND TERMINATED status. If INTERMEDIATE or INTERMEDIATE-CONDITION MET status is not returned, the series of linked commands is terminated and the I/O process is ended.

INTERMEDIATE-CONDITION MET. This status is the combination of the CONDITION MET and INTERMEDIATE statuses.

RESERVATION CONFLICT. This status shall be returned whenever an initiator attempts to access a logical unit or an extent within a logical unit that is reserved with a conflicting reservation type for another SCSI device (see the RESERVE and RESERVE UNIT commands). The recommended initiator recovery action is to issue the command again at a later time.

COMMAND TERMINATED. This status shall be returned whenever the target terminates the current I/O process after receiving a TERMINATE I/O PROCESS message (see 5.6.22). This status also indicates that a contingent allegiance condition has occurred (see 6.6).

QUEUE FULL. This status shall be implemented if tagged queuing is implemented. This status is returned when a SIMPLE QUEUE TAG, ORDERED QUEUE TAG, or HEAD OF QUEUE TAG message is received and the command queue is full. The I/O process is not placed in the command queue.

B.3   SCSI Sense Keys

The sense key from the result should be retrieved with the macro msg_byte (see section B.1). These kernel symbols (from drivers/scsi/scsi.h) are predefined:

```
Value | Symbol
======|=================
```

```
0x00 | NO_SENSE
0x01 | RECOVERED_ERROR
0x02 | NOT_READY
0x03 | MEDIUM_ERROR
0x04 | HARDWARE_ERROR
0x05 | ILLEGAL_REQUEST
0x06 | UNIT_ATTENTION
0x07 | DATA_PROTECT
0x08 | BLANK_CHECK
0x0a | COPY_ABORTED
0x0b | ABORTED_COMMAND
0x0d | VOLUME_OVERFLOW
0x0e | MISCOMPARE
```

A verbatim list from the SCSI-2 doc follows (from section 7.2.14.3):

```
              Table 69: Sense Key (0h-7h) Descriptions
+=========-====================================================================+
| Sense  |  Description                                                        |
|  Key   |                                                                    |
|--------+-----------------------------------------------------------------------|
|  0h    |  NO SENSE.  Indicates that there is no specific sense key           |
|        |  information to be reported for the designated logical unit.  This |
|        |  would be the case for a successful command or a command that      |
|        |  received CHECK CONDITION or COMMAND TERMINATED status because one  |
|        |  of the filemark, EOM, or ILI bits is set to one.                  |
|--------+-----------------------------------------------------------------------|
|  1h    |  RECOVERED ERROR.  Indicates that the last command completed        |
|        |  successfully with some recovery action performed by the target.   |
|        |  Details may be determinable by examining the additional sense     |
|        |  bytes and the information field.  When multiple recovered errors  |
|        |  occur during one command, the choice of which error to report     |
|        |  (first, last, most severe, etc.) is device specific.              |
|--------+-----------------------------------------------------------------------|
|  2h    |  NOT READY.  Indicates that the logical unit addressed cannot be    |
|        |  accessed.  Operator intervention may be required to correct this  |
|        |  condition.                                                        |
|--------+-----------------------------------------------------------------------|
|  3h    |  MEDIUM ERROR.  Indicates that the command terminated with a non-   |
|        |  recovered error condition that was probably caused by a flaw in   |
|        |  the medium or an error in the recorded data.  This sense key may  |
|        |  also be returned if the target is unable to distinguish between a |
|        |  flaw in the medium and a specific hardware failure (sense key 4h).|
|--------+-----------------------------------------------------------------------|
|  4h    |  HARDWARE ERROR.  Indicates that the target detected a non-         |
|        |  recoverable hardware failure (for example, controller failure,    |
|        |  device failure, parity error, etc.) while performing the command  |
|        |  or during a self test.                                            |
|--------+-----------------------------------------------------------------------|
|  5h    |  ILLEGAL REQUEST.  Indicates that there was an illegal parameter in |
|        |  the command descriptor block or in the additional parameters      |
|        |  supplied as data for some commands (FORMAT UNIT, SEARCH DATA,      |
|        |  etc.).  If the target detects an invalid parameter in the command |
|        |  descriptor block, then it shall terminate the command without     |
|        |  altering the medium.  If the target detects an invalid parameter  |
|        |  in the additional parameters supplied as data, then the target may|
|        |  have already altered the medium.  This sense key may also indicate|
|        |  that an invalid IDENTIFY message was received (5.6.7).            |
|--------+-----------------------------------------------------------------------|
|  6h    |  UNIT ATTENTION.  Indicates that the removable medium may have been|
|        |  changed or the target has been reset.  See 6.9 for more detailed  |
```

```
|        |   information about the unit attention condition.                  |
|--------+----------------------------------------------------------------------|
|   7h   |   DATA PROTECT.  Indicates that a command that reads or writes the    |
|        |   medium was attempted on a block that is protected from this        |
|        |   operation.  The read or write operation is not performed.          |
+==============================================================================+
```

Table 70: Sense Key (8h-Fh) Descriptions

```
+==============================================================================+
| Sense  |  Description                                                         |
|  Key   |                                                                      |
|--------+----------------------------------------------------------------------|
|   8h   |  BLANK CHECK.  Indicates that a write-once device or a sequential-    |
|        |  access device encountered blank medium or format-defined end-of-    |
|        |  data indication while reading or a write-once device encountered a  |
|        |  non-blank medium while writing.                                     |
|--------+----------------------------------------------------------------------|
|   9h   |  Vendor Specific.  This sense key is available for reporting vendor   |
|        |  specific conditions.                                                |
|--------+----------------------------------------------------------------------|
|   Ah   |  COPY ABORTED.  Indicates a COPY, COMPARE, or COPY AND VERIFY         |
|        |  command was aborted due to an error condition on the source         |
|        |  device, the destination device, or both.  (See 7.2.3.2 for         |
|        |  additional information about this sense key.)                       |
|--------+----------------------------------------------------------------------|
|   Bh   |  ABORTED COMMAND.  Indicates that the target aborted the command.    |
|        |  The initiator may be able to recover by trying the command again.   |
|--------+----------------------------------------------------------------------|
|   Ch   |  EQUAL.  Indicates a SEARCH DATA command has satisfied an equal      |
|        |  comparison.                                                         |
|--------+----------------------------------------------------------------------|
|   Dh   |  VOLUME OVERFLOW.  Indicates that a buffered peripheral device has   |
|        |  reached the end-of-partition and data may remain in the buffer      |
|        |  that has not been written to the medium.  A RECOVER BUFFERED DATA   |
|        |  command(s) may be issued to read the unwritten data from the        |
|        |  buffer.                                                             |
|--------+----------------------------------------------------------------------|
|   Eh   |  MISCOMPARE.  Indicates that the source data did not match the data  |
|        |  read from the medium.                                               |
|--------+----------------------------------------------------------------------|
|   Fh   |  RESERVED.                                                           |
+==============================================================================+
```

B.4 Hostcodes

The following host codes are defined in `drivers/scsi/scsi.h`. They are set by the kernel driver and should be used with the macro `host_byte` (see section B.1):

```
Value | Symbol          | Description
======|=================|=======================================
0x00  | DID_OK          | No error
0x01  | DID_NO_CONNECT  | Couldn't connect before timeout period
0x02  | DID_BUS_BUSY    | BUS stayed busy through time out period
0x03  | DID_TIME_OUT    | TIMED OUT for other reason
0x04  | DID_BAD_TARGET  | BAD target
0x05  | DID_ABORT       | Told to abort for some other reason
0x06  | DID_PARITY      | Parity error
0x07  | DID_ERROR       | internal error
0x08  | DID_RESET       | Reset by somebody
0x09  | DID_BAD_INTR    | Got an interrupt we weren't expecting
```

C Additional sense codes and additional sense code qualifiers

From the SCSI-2 specification I include two tables. The first is in lexical, the second in numerical order.

C.1 ASC and ASCQ in lexical order

The following table list gives a list of descriptions and device types they apply to.

```
+=============================================================================+
|                 D - DIRECT ACCESS DEVICE                                    |
|                .T - SEQUENTIAL ACCESS DEVICE                                |
|                . L - PRINTER DEVICE                                         |
|                . P - PROCESSOR DEVICE                                       |
|                . .W - WRITE ONCE READ MULTIPLE DEVICE                       |
|                . . R - READ ONLY (CD-ROM) DEVICE                            |
|                . . S - SCANNER DEVICE                                       |
|                . . .O - OPTICAL MEMORY DEVICE                               |
|                . . . M - MEDIA CHANGER DEVICE                               |
|                . . . C - COMMUNICATION DEVICE                               |
|                . . . . .                                                    |
| ASC ASCQ  DTLPWRSOMC  DESCRIPTION                                           |
| --- ----             ------------------------------------------------------|
| 13h  00h  D  W O     ADDRESS MARK NOT FOUND FOR DATA FIELD                  |
| 12h  00h  D  W O     ADDRESS MARK NOT FOUND FOR ID FIELD                    |
| 00h  11h     R       AUDIO PLAY OPERATION IN PROGRESS                       |
| 00h  12h     R       AUDIO PLAY OPERATION PAUSED                            |
| 00h  14h     R       AUDIO PLAY OPERATION STOPPED DUE TO ERROR              |
| 00h  13h     R       AUDIO PLAY OPERATION SUCCESSFULLY COMPLETED            |
| 00h  04h  T    S     BEGINNING-OF-PARTITION/MEDIUM DETECTED                 |
| 14h  04h  T          BLOCK SEQUENCE ERROR                                   |
| 30h  02h  DT WR O    CANNOT READ MEDIUM - INCOMPATIBLE FORMAT               |
| 30h  01h  DT WR O    CANNOT READ MEDIUM - UNKNOWN FORMAT                    |
| 52h  00h  T          CARTRIDGE FAULT                                        |
| 3Fh  02h  DTLPWRSOMC CHANGED OPERATING DEFINITION                          |
| 11h  06h     WR O    CIRC UNRECOVERED ERROR                                 |
| 30h  03h  DT         CLEANING CARTRIDGE INSTALLED                           |
| 4Ah  00h  DTLPWRSOMC COMMAND PHASE ERROR                                    |
| 2Ch  00h  DTLPWRSOMC COMMAND SEQUENCE ERROR                                 |
| 2Fh  00h  DTLPWRSOMC COMMANDS CLEARED BY ANOTHER INITIATOR                  |
| 2Bh  00h  DTLPWRSO C COPY CANNOT EXECUTE SINCE HOST CANNOT DISCONNECT       |
| 41h  00h  D          DATA PATH FAILURE (SHOULD USE 40 NN)                   |
| 4Bh  00h  DTLPWRSOMC DATA PHASE ERROR                                       |
| 11h  07h     W O     DATA RESYCHRONIZATION ERROR                            |
| 16h  00h  D  W O     DATA SYNCHRONIZATION MARK ERROR                        |
| 19h  00h  D    O     DEFECT LIST ERROR                                      |
| 19h  03h  D    O     DEFECT LIST ERROR IN GROWN LIST                        |
| 19h  02h  D    O     DEFECT LIST ERROR IN PRIMARY LIST                      |
| 19h  01h  D    O     DEFECT LIST NOT AVAILABLE                              |
| 1Ch  00h  D    O     DEFECT LIST NOT FOUND                                  |
| 32h  01h  D  W O     DEFECT LIST UPDATE FAILURE                             |
| 40h  NNh  DTLPWRSOMC DIAGNOSTIC FAILURE ON COMPONENT NN (80H-FFH)           |
| 63h  00h     R       END OF USER AREA ENCOUNTERED ON THIS TRACK             |
| 00h  05h  T    S     END-OF-DATA DETECTED                                   |
| 14h  03h  T          END-OF-DATA NOT FOUND                                  |
| 00h  02h  T    S     END-OF-PARTITION/MEDIUM DETECTED                       |
| 51h  00h  T    O     ERASE FAILURE                                          |
| 0Ah  00h  DTLPWRSOMC ERROR LOG OVERFLOW                                     |
| 11h  02h  DT W SO    ERROR TOO LONG TO CORRECT                              |
| 03h  02h  T          EXCESSIVE WRITE ERRORS                                 |
```

```
| 3Bh  07h    L          FAILED TO SENSE BOTTOM-OF-FORM                             |
| 3Bh  06h    L          FAILED TO SENSE TOP-OF-FORM                                |
| 00h  01h    T          FILEMARK DETECTED                                          |
| 14h  02h    T          FILEMARK OR SETMARK NOT FOUND                              |
| 09h  02h      WR O     FOCUS SERVO FAILURE                                        |
| 31h  01h  D L    O     FORMAT COMMAND FAILED                                      |
| 58h  00h         O     GENERATION DOES NOT EXIST                                  |
+===================================================================================+
```

Table 71: (continued)

```
+===================================================================================+
| ASC ASCQ DTLPWRSOMC  DESCRIPTION                                                  |
| --- ----             -----------------------------------------------------------  |
| 1Ch  02h  D      O   GROWN DEFECT LIST NOT FOUND                                  |
| 00h  06h  DTLPWRSOMC  I/O PROCESS TERMINATED                                      |
| 10h  00h  D   W  O   ID CRC OR ECC ERROR                                          |
| 22h  00h  D          ILLEGAL FUNCTION (SHOULD USE 20 00, 24 00, OR 26 00) |
| 64h  00h       R     ILLEGAL MODE FOR THIS TRACK                                  |
| 28h  01h         M   IMPORT OR EXPORT ELEMENT ACCESSED                            |
| 30h  00h  DT  WR OM  INCOMPATIBLE MEDIUM INSTALLED                                |
| 11h  08h    T        INCOMPLETE BLOCK READ                                        |
| 48h  00h  DTLPWRSOMC  INITIATOR DETECTED ERROR MESSAGE RECEIVED                   |
| 3Fh  03h  DTLPWRSOMC  INQUIRY DATA HAS CHANGED                                    |
| 44h  00h  DTLPWRSOMC  INTERNAL TARGET FAILURE                                     |
| 3Dh  00h  DTLPWRSOMC  INVALID BITS IN IDENTIFY MESSAGE                            |
| 2Ch  02h         S   INVALID COMBINATION OF WINDOWS SPECIFIED                     |
| 20h  00h  DTLPWRSOMC  INVALID COMMAND OPERATION CODE                              |
| 21h  01h         M   INVALID ELEMENT ADDRESS                                      |
| 24h  00h  DTLPWRSOMC  INVALID FIELD IN CDB                                        |
| 26h  00h  DTLPWRSOMC  INVALID FIELD IN PARAMETER LIST                            |
| 49h  00h  DTLPWRSOMC  INVALID MESSAGE ERROR                                       |
| 11h  05h      WR O   L-EC UNCORRECTABLE ERROR                                     |
| 60h  00h         S   LAMP FAILURE                                                 |
| 5Bh  02h  DTLPWRSOM   LOG COUNTER AT MAXIMUM                                       |
| 5Bh  00h  DTLPWRSOM   LOG EXCEPTION                                               |
| 5Bh  03h  DTLPWRSOM   LOG LIST CODES EXHAUSTED                                    |
| 2Ah  02h  DTL WRSOMC  LOG PARAMETERS CHANGED                                      |
| 21h  00h  DT  WR OM  LOGICAL BLOCK ADDRESS OUT OF RANGE                           |
| 08h  00h  DTL WRSOMC  LOGICAL UNIT COMMUNICATION FAILURE                          |
| 08h  02h  DTL WRSOMC  LOGICAL UNIT COMMUNICATION PARITY ERROR                     |
| 08h  01h  DTL WRSOMC  LOGICAL UNIT COMMUNICATION TIME-OUT                         |
| 4Ch  00h  DTLPWRSOMC  LOGICAL UNIT FAILED SELF-CONFIGURATION                      |
| 3Eh  00h  DTLPWRSOMC  LOGICAL UNIT HAS NOT SELF-CONFIGURED YET                    |
| 04h  01h  DTLPWRSOMC  LOGICAL UNIT IS IN PROCESS OF BECOMING READY                |
| 04h  00h  DTLPWRSOMC  LOGICAL UNIT NOT READY, CAUSE NOT REPORTABLE                |
| 04h  04h  DTL    O   LOGICAL UNIT NOT READY, FORMAT IN PROGRESS                   |
| 04h  02h  DTLPWRSOMC  LOGICAL UNIT NOT READY, INITIALIZING COMMAND REQUIRED |
| 04h  03h  DTLPWRSOMC  LOGICAL UNIT NOT READY, MANUAL INTERVENTION REQUIRED |
| 25h  00h  DTLPWRSOMC  LOGICAL UNIT NOT SUPPORTED                                  |
| 15h  01h  DTL WRSOM   MECHANICAL POSITIONING ERROR                                |
| 53h  00h  DTL WRSOM   MEDIA LOAD OR EJECT FAILED                                  |
| 3Bh  0Dh         M   MEDIUM DESTINATION ELEMENT FULL                              |
| 31h  00h  DT  W  O   MEDIUM FORMAT CORRUPTED                                      |
| 3Ah  00h  DTL WRSOM   MEDIUM NOT PRESENT                                          |
| 53h  02h  DT  WR OM  MEDIUM REMOVAL PREVENTED                                     |
| 3Bh  0Eh         M   MEDIUM SOURCE ELEMENT EMPTY                                  |
| 43h  00h  DTLPWRSOMC  MESSAGE ERROR                                               |
| 3Fh  01h  DTLPWRSOMC  MICROCODE HAS BEEN CHANGED                                  |
| 1Dh  00h  D   W  O   MISCOMPARE DURING VERIFY OPERATION                           |
| 11h  0Ah  DT     O   MISCORRECTED ERROR                                           |
| 2Ah  01h  DTL WRSOMC  MODE PARAMETERS CHANGED                                     |
```

```
| 07h  00h  DTL WRSOM   MULTIPLE PERIPHERAL DEVICES SELECTED                    |
| 11h  03h  DT  W SO    MULTIPLE READ ERRORS                                    |
| 00h  00h  DTLPWRSOMC  NO ADDITIONAL SENSE INFORMATION                         |
| 00h  15h        R     NO CURRENT AUDIO STATUS TO RETURN                       |
| 32h  00h  D   W  O    NO DEFECT SPARE LOCATION AVAILABLE                      |
| 11h  09h  T           NO GAP FOUND                                           |
| 01h  00h  D   W  O    NO INDEX/SECTOR SIGNAL                                  |
| 06h  00h  D   WR OM   NO REFERENCE POSITION FOUND                            |
+===============================================================================+
```

Table 71: (continued)

```
+===============================================================================+
| ASC ASCQ  DTLPWRSOMC  DESCRIPTION                                             |
| --- ----             -------------------------------------------------------- |
| 02h  00h  D   WR OM   NO SEEK COMPLETE                                        |
| 03h  01h  T           NO WRITE CURRENT                                        |
| 28h  00h  DTLPWRSOMC  NOT READY TO READY TRANSITION, MEDIUM MAY HAVE CHANGED |
| 5Ah  01h  DT  WR OM   OPERATOR MEDIUM REMOVAL REQUEST                        |
| 5Ah  00h  DTLPWRSOM   OPERATOR REQUEST OR STATE CHANGE INPUT (UNSPECIFIED)   |
| 5Ah  03h  DT  W  O    OPERATOR SELECTED WRITE PERMIT                         |
| 5Ah  02h  DT  W  O    OPERATOR SELECTED WRITE PROTECT                        |
| 61h  02h        S     OUT OF FOCUS                                           |
| 4Eh  00h  DTLPWRSOMC  OVERLAPPED COMMANDS ATTEMPTED                          |
| 2Dh  00h  T           OVERWRITE ERROR ON UPDATE IN PLACE                     |
| 3Bh  05h      L       PAPER JAM                                              |
| 1Ah  00h  DTLPWRSOMC  PARAMETER LIST LENGTH ERROR                            |
| 26h  01h  DTLPWRSOMC  PARAMETER NOT SUPPORTED                                |
| 26h  02h  DTLPWRSOMC  PARAMETER VALUE INVALID                                |
| 2Ah  00h  DTL WRSOMC  PARAMETERS CHANGED                                     |
| 03h  00h  DTL W SO    PERIPHERAL DEVICE WRITE FAULT                          |
| 50h  02h  T           POSITION ERROR RELATED TO TIMING                       |
| 3Bh  0Ch        S     POSITION PAST BEGINNING OF MEDIUM                      |
| 3Bh  0Bh        S     POSITION PAST END OF MEDIUM                            |
| 15h  02h  DT  WR O    POSITIONING ERROR DETECTED BY READ OF MEDIUM           |
| 29h  00h  DTLPWRSOMC  POWER ON, RESET, OR BUS DEVICE RESET OCCURRED          |
| 42h  00h  D           POWER-ON OR SELF-TEST FAILURE (SHOULD USE 40 NN)       |
| 1Ch  01h  D      O    PRIMARY DEFECT LIST NOT FOUND                          |
| 40h  00h  D           RAM FAILURE (SHOULD USE 40 NN)                         |
| 15h  00h  DTL WRSOM   RANDOM POSITIONING ERROR                               |
| 3Bh  0Ah        S     READ PAST BEGINNING OF MEDIUM                          |
| 3Bh  09h        S     READ PAST END OF MEDIUM                                |
| 11h  01h  DT  W SO    READ RETRIES EXHAUSTED                                 |
| 14h  01h  DT  WR O    RECORD NOT FOUND                                       |
| 14h  00h  DTL WRSO    RECORDED ENTITY NOT FOUND                              |
| 18h  02h  D   WR O    RECOVERED DATA - DATA AUTO-REALLOCATED                 |
| 18h  05h  D   WR O    RECOVERED DATA - RECOMMEND REASSIGNMENT                |
| 18h  06h  D   WR O    RECOVERED DATA - RECOMMEND REWRITE                     |
| 17h  05h  D   WR O    RECOVERED DATA USING PREVIOUS SECTOR ID                |
| 18h  03h        R     RECOVERED DATA WITH CIRC                               |
| 18h  01h  D   WR O    RECOVERED DATA WITH ERROR CORRECTION & RETRIES APPLIED |
| 18h  00h  DT  WR O    RECOVERED DATA WITH ERROR CORRECTION APPLIED           |
| 18h  04h        R     RECOVERED DATA WITH L-EC                               |
| 17h  03h  DT  WR O    RECOVERED DATA WITH NEGATIVE HEAD OFFSET               |
| 17h  00h  DT  WRSO    RECOVERED DATA WITH NO ERROR CORRECTION APPLIED        |
| 17h  02h  DT  WR O    RECOVERED DATA WITH POSITIVE HEAD OFFSET               |
| 17h  01h  DT  WRSO    RECOVERED DATA WITH RETRIES                            |
| 17h  04h      WR O    RECOVERED DATA WITH RETRIES AND/OR CIRC APPLIED        |
| 17h  06h  D   W  O    RECOVERED DATA WITHOUT ECC - DATA AUTO-REALLOCATED     |
| 17h  07h  D   W  O    RECOVERED DATA WITHOUT ECC - RECOMMEND REASSIGNMENT    |
| 17h  08h  D   W  O    RECOVERED DATA WITHOUT ECC - RECOMMEND REWRITE         |
| 1Eh  00h  D   W  O    RECOVERED ID WITH ECC CORRECTION                       |
```

```
| 3Bh  08h   T             REPOSITION ERROR                                             |
| 36h  00h       L         RIBBON, INK, OR TONER FAILURE                                |
| 37h  00h   DTL WRSOMC    ROUNDED PARAMETER                                            |
| 5Ch  00h   D      O      RPL STATUS CHANGE                                            |
| 39h  00h   DTL WRSOMC    SAVING PARAMETERS NOT SUPPORTED                              |
| 62h  00h          S      SCAN HEAD POSITIONING ERROR                                  |
| 47h  00h   DTLPWRSOMC    SCSI PARITY ERROR                                            |
| 54h  00h        P        SCSI TO HOST SYSTEM INTERFACE FAILURE                        |
| 45h  00h   DTLPWRSOMC    SELECT OR RESELECT FAILURE                                   |
+===========================================================================+
```

Table 71: (concluded)

```
+=================================================================================+
| ASC ASCQ   DTLPWRSOMC    DESCRIPTION                                             |
| --- ----                 ------------------------------------------------------ |
| 3Bh  00h   TL            SEQUENTIAL POSITIONING ERROR                            |
| 00h  03h   T             SETMARK DETECTED                                        |
| 3Bh  04h       L         SLEW FAILURE                                            |
| 09h  03h          WR O   SPINDLE SERVO FAILURE                                   |
| 5Ch  02h   D      O      SPINDLES NOT SYNCHRONIZED                               |
| 5Ch  01h   D      O      SPINDLES SYNCHRONIZED                                   |
| 1Bh  00h   DTLPWRSOMC    SYNCHRONOUS DATA TRANSFER ERROR                         |
| 55h  00h        P        SYSTEM RESOURCE FAILURE                                 |
| 33h  00h   T             TAPE LENGTH ERROR                                       |
| 3Bh  03h       L         TAPE OR ELECTRONIC VERTICAL FORMS UNIT NOT READY        |
| 3Bh  01h   T             TAPE POSITION ERROR AT BEGINNING-OF-MEDIUM              |
| 3Bh  02h   T             TAPE POSITION ERROR AT END-OF-MEDIUM                    |
| 3Fh  00h   DTLPWRSOMC    TARGET OPERATING CONDITIONS HAVE CHANGED                |
| 5Bh  01h   DTLPWRSOM     THRESHOLD CONDITION MET                                 |
| 26h  03h   DTLPWRSOMC    THRESHOLD PARAMETERS NOT SUPPORTED                      |
| 2Ch  01h          S      TOO MANY WINDOWS SPECIFIED                              |
| 09h  00h   DT     WR O   TRACK FOLLOWING ERROR                                   |
| 09h  01h          WR O   TRACKING SERVO FAILURE                                  |
| 61h  01h          S      UNABLE TO ACQUIRE VIDEO                                 |
| 57h  00h            R     UNABLE TO RECOVER TABLE-OF-CONTENTS                    |
| 53h  01h   T             UNLOAD TAPE FAILURE                                     |
| 11h  00h   DT  WRSO      UNRECOVERED READ ERROR                                  |
| 11h  04h   D   W  O      UNRECOVERED READ ERROR - AUTO REALLOCATE FAILED         |
| 11h  0Bh   D   W  O      UNRECOVERED READ ERROR - RECOMMEND REASSIGNMENT         |
| 11h  0Ch   D   W  O      UNRECOVERED READ ERROR - RECOMMEND REWRITE THE DATA     |
| 46h  00h   DTLPWRSOMC    UNSUCCESSFUL SOFT RESET                                 |
| 59h  00h          O      UPDATED BLOCK READ                                      |
| 61h  00h          S      VIDEO ACQUISITION ERROR                                 |
| 50h  00h   T             WRITE APPEND ERROR                                       |
| 50h  01h   T             WRITE APPEND POSITION ERROR                             |
| 0Ch  00h   T    S        WRITE ERROR                                             |
| 0Ch  02h   D   W  O      WRITE ERROR - AUTO REALLOCATION FAILED                  |
| 0Ch  01h   D   W  O      WRITE ERROR RECOVERED WITH AUTO REALLOCATION            |
| 27h  00h   DT  W  O      WRITE PROTECTED                                         |
|                                                                                 |
| 80h  XXh       \                                                                |
| THROUGH        >         VENDOR SPECIFIC.                                        |
| FFh  XX        /                                                                |
|                                                                                 |
| XXh  80h       \                                                                |
| THROUGH        >         VENDOR SPECIFIC QUALIFICATION OF STANDARD ASC.          |
| XXh  FFh       /                                                                |
|                          ALL CODES NOT SHOWN ARE RESERVED.                       |
|-------------------------------------------------------------------------------- |
```

C.2   ASC and ASCQ in numerical order

Table 364: ASC and ASCQ Assignments

```
+==============================================================================+
|             D - DIRECT ACCESS DEVICE                                         |
|             .T - SEQUENTIAL ACCESS DEVICE                                    |
|             . L - PRINTER DEVICE                                             |
|             .  P - PROCESSOR DEVICE                                          |
|             .  .W - WRITE ONCE READ MULTIPLE DEVICE                          |
|             .  . R - READ ONLY (CD-ROM) DEVICE                               |
|             .  .  S - SCANNER DEVICE                                         |
|             .  .  .O - OPTICAL MEMORY DEVICE                                 |
|             .  .  . M - MEDIA CHANGER DEVICE                                 |
|             .  .  .  C - COMMUNICATION DEVICE                                |
|             .  .  .  .                                                       |
| ASC ASCQ  DTLPWRSOMC  DESCRIPTION                                            |
| --- ----                ---------------------------------------------------- |
|  00  00   DTLPWRSOMC  NO ADDITIONAL SENSE INFORMATION                        |
|  00  01    T          FILEMARK DETECTED                                      |
|  00  02    T     S    END-OF-PARTITION/MEDIUM DETECTED                       |
|  00  03    T          SETMARK DETECTED                                       |
|  00  04    T     S    BEGINNING-OF-PARTITION/MEDIUM DETECTED                 |
|  00  05    T     S    END-OF-DATA DETECTED                                   |
|  00  06   DTLPWRSOMC  I/O PROCESS TERMINATED                                 |
|  00  11         R     AUDIO PLAY OPERATION IN PROGRESS                       |
|  00  12         R     AUDIO PLAY OPERATION PAUSED                            |
|  00  13         R     AUDIO PLAY OPERATION SUCCESSFULLY COMPLETED            |
|  00  14         R     AUDIO PLAY OPERATION STOPPED DUE TO ERROR              |
|  00  15         R     NO CURRENT AUDIO STATUS TO RETURN                      |
|  01  00      DW   O   NO INDEX/SECTOR SIGNAL                                 |
|  02  00      DWR OM   NO SEEK COMPLETE                                       |
|  03  00   DTL W SO    PERIPHERAL DEVICE WRITE FAULT                          |
|  03  01    T          NO WRITE CURRENT                                       |
|  03  02    T          EXCESSIVE WRITE ERRORS                                 |
|  04  00   DTLPWRSOMC  LOGICAL UNIT NOT READY, CAUSE NOT REPORTABLE           |
|  04  01   DTLPWRSOMC  LOGICAL UNIT IS IN PROCESS OF BECOMING READY           |
|  04  02   DTLPWRSOMC  LOGICAL UNIT NOT READY, INITIALIZING COMMAND REQUIRED  |
|  04  03   DTLPWRSOMC  LOGICAL UNIT NOT READY, MANUAL INTERVENTION REQUIRED   |
|  04  04   DTL    O    LOGICAL UNIT NOT READY, FORMAT IN PROGRESS             |
|  05  00   DTL WRSOMC  LOGICAL UNIT DOES NOT RESPOND TO SELECTION             |
|  06  00      DWR OM NO REFERENCE POSITION FOUND                             |
|  07  00   DTL WRSOM   MULTIPLE PERIPHERAL DEVICES SELECTED                   |
|  08  00   DTL WRSOMC  LOGICAL UNIT COMMUNICATION FAILURE                     |
|  08  01   DTL WRSOMC  LOGICAL UNIT COMMUNICATION TIME-OUT                    |
|  08  02   DTL WRSOMC  LOGICAL UNIT COMMUNICATION PARITY ERROR                |
|  09  00   DT WR O     TRACK FOLLOWING ERROR                                  |
|  09  01      WR O     TRA CKING SERVO FAILURE                                |
|  09  02      WR O     FOC US SERVO FAILURE                                   |
|  09  03      WR O     SPI NDLE SERVO FAILURE                                 |
+==============================================================================+
```

Table 364: (continued)

```
+==============================================================================+
|             D - DIRECT ACCESS DEVICE                                         |
|             .T - SEQUENTIAL ACCESS DEVICE                                    |
|             . L - PRINTER DEVICE                                             |
|             .  P - PROCESSOR DEVICE                                          |
|             .  .W - WRITE ONCE READ MULTIPLE DEVICE                          |
|             .  . R - READ ONLY (CD-ROM) DEVICE                               |
|             .  . S - SCANNER DEVICE                                          |
```

```
|             .  .  .O - OPTICAL MEMORY DEVICE                             |
|             .  .  . M - MEDIA CHANGER DEVICE                             |
|             .  .  . C - COMMUNICATION DEVICE                            |
|             .  .  .  .                                                   |
| ASC ASCQ  DTLPWRSOMC  DESCRIPTION                                        |
| --- ----  ----------  ------------------------------------------------- |
| 0A  00    DTLPWRSOMC  ERROR LOG OVERFLOW                                 |
| 0B  00                                                                   |
| 0C  00    T      S    WRITE ERROR                                        |
| 0C  01    D    W   O  WRITE ERROR RECOVERED WITH AUTO REALLOCATION       |
| 0C  02    D    W   O  WRITE ERROR - AUTO REALLOCATION FAILED             |
| 0D  00                                                                   |
| 0E  00                                                                   |
| 0F  00                                                                   |
| 10  00    D    W   O  ID CRC OR ECC ERROR                                |
| 11  00    DT   WRSO   UNRECOVERED READ ERROR                             |
| 11  01    DT   W SO   READ RETRIES EXHAUSTED                             |
| 11  02    DT   W SO   ERROR TOO LONG TO CORRECT                          |
| 11  03    DT   W SO   MULTIPLE READ ERRORS                               |
| 11  04    D    W   O  UNRECOVERED READ ERROR - AUTO REALLOCATE FAILED    |
| 11  05         WR  O  L-EC UNCORRECTABLE ERROR                           |
| 11  06         WR  O  CIRC UNRECOVERED ERROR                             |
| 11  07         W   O  DATA RESYNCHRONIZATION ERROR                       |
| 11  08    T           INCOMPLETE BLOCK READ                              |
| 11  09    T           NO GAP FOUND                                       |
| 11  0A    DT      O   MISCORRECTED ERROR                                 |
| 11  0B    D    W   O  UNRECOVERED READ ERROR - RECOMMEND REASSIGNMENT    |
| 11  0C    D    W   O  UNRECOVERED READ ERROR - RECOMMEND REWRITE THE DATA|
| 12  00    D    W   O  ADDRESS MARK NOT FOUND FOR ID FIELD                |
| 13  00    D    W   O  ADDRESS MARK NOT FOUND FOR DATA FIELD              |
| 14  00    DTL  WRSO   RECORDED ENTITY NOT FOUND                          |
| 14  01    DT   WR  O  RECORD NOT FOUND                                   |
| 14  02    T           FILEMARK OR SETMARK NOT FOUND                      |
| 14  03    T           END-OF-DATA NOT FOUND                              |
| 14  04    T           BLOCK SEQUENCE ERROR                               |
| 15  00    DTL  WRSOM  RANDOM POSITIONING ERROR                           |
| 15  01    DTL  WRSOM  MECHANICAL POSITIONING ERROR                       |
| 15  02    DT   WR  O  POSITIONING ERROR DETECTED BY READ OF MEDIUM       |
| 16  00    DW      O   DATA SYNCHRONIZATION MARK ERROR                    |
| 17  00    DT   WRSO   RECOVERED DATA WITH NO ERROR CORRECTION APPLIED    |
| 17  01    DT   WRSO   RECOVERED DATA WITH RETRIES                        |
| 17  02    DT   WR  O  RECOVERED DATA WITH POSITIVE HEAD OFFSET           |
| 17  03    DT   WR  O  RECOVERED DATA WITH NEGATIVE HEAD OFFSET           |
| 17  04         WR  O  RECOVERED DATA WITH RETRIES AND/OR CIRC APPLIED    |
| 17  05    D           RECOVERED DATA USING PREVIOUS SECTOR ID            |
| 17  06    D    W   O  RECOVERED DATA WITHOUT ECC - DATA AUTO-REALLOCATED |
| 17  07    D    W   O  RECOVERED DATA WITHOUT ECC - RECOMMEND REASSIGNMENT|
| 17  08    D    W   O  RECOVERED DATA WITHOUT ECC - RECOMMEND REWRITE     |
| 18  00    DT   WR  O  RECOVERED DATA WITH ERROR CORRECTION APPLIED       |
| 18  01    D    WR  O  RECOVERED DATA WITH ERROR CORRECTION & RETRIES APPLIED|
| 18  02    D    WR  O  RECOVERED DATA - DATA AUTO-REALLOCATED             |
| 18  03         R      RECOVERED DATA WITH CIRC                           |
| 18  04         R      RECOVERED DATA WITH LEC                            |
| 18  05    D    WR  O  RECOVERED DATA - RECOMMEND REASSIGNMENT            |
| 18  06    D    WR  O  RECOVERED DATA - RECOMMEND REWRITE                 |
+=========================================================================+
```

Table 364: (continued)

```
+=========================================================================+
|          D - DIRECT ACCESS DEVICE                                       |
|          .T - SEQUENTIAL ACCESS DEVICE                                  |
```

```
|                 . L - PRINTER DEVICE                                        |
|                 .  P - PROCESSOR DEVICE                                     |
|                 .  .W - WRITE ONCE READ MULTIPLE DEVICE                     |
|                 .  . R - READ ONLY (CD-ROM) DEVICE                          |
|                 .  . S - SCANNER DEVICE                                     |
|                 .  . .O - OPTICAL MEMORY DEVICE                             |
|                 .  . . M - MEDIA CHANGER DEVICE                             |
|                 .  . . C - COMMUNICATION DEVICE                             |
|                 .  . . .                                                    |
| ASC ASCQ  DTLPWRSOMC  DESCRIPTION                                           |
| --- ----  ----------  ----------------------------------------------------- |
| 19  00    D      O    DEFECT LIST ERROR                                     |
| 19  01    D      O    DEFECT LIST NOT AVAILABLE                             |
| 19  02    D      O    DEFECT LIST ERROR IN PRIMARY LIST                     |
| 19  03    D      O    DEFECT LIST ERROR IN GROWN LIST                       |
| 1A  00    DTLPWRSOMC  PARAMETER LIST LENGTH ERROR                           |
| 1B  00    DTLPWRSOMC  SYNCHRONOUS DATA TRANSFER ERROR                       |
| 1C  00    D      O    DEFECT LIST NOT FOUND                                 |
| 1C  01    D      O    PRIMARY DEFECT LIST NOT FOUND                         |
| 1C  02    D      O    GROWN DEFECT LIST NOT FOUND                           |
| 1D  00    D   W  O    MISCOMPARE DURING VERIFY OPERATION                    |
| 1E  00    D   W  O    RECOVERED ID WITH ECC                                 |
| 1F  00                                                                      |
| 20  00    DTLPWRSOMC  INVALID COMMAND OPERATION CODE                        |
| 21  00    DT  WR OM   LOGICAL BLOCK ADDRESS OUT OF RANGE                    |
| 21  01           M    INVALID ELEMENT ADDRESS                               |
| 22  00    D           ILLEGAL FUNCTION (SHOULD USE 20 00, 24 00, OR 26 00)  |
| 23  00                                                                      |
| 24  00    DTLPWRSOMC  INVALID FIELD IN CDB                                  |
| 25  00    DTLPWRSOMC  LOGICAL UNIT NOT SUPPORTED                            |
| 26  00    DTLPWRSOMC  INVALID FIELD IN PARAMETER LIST                       |
| 26  01    DTLPWRSOMC  PARAMETER NOT SUPPORTED                               |
| 26  02    DTLPWRSOMC  PARAMETER VALUE INVALID                               |
| 26  03    DTLPWRSOMC  THRESHOLD PARAMETERS NOT SUPPORTED                    |
| 27  00    DT  W  O    WRITE PROTECTED                                       |
| 28  00    DTLPWRSOMC  NOT READY TO READY TRANSITION(MEDIUM MAY HAVE CHANGED)|
| 28  01           M    IMPORT OR EXPORT ELEMENT ACCESSED                     |
| 29  00    DTLPWRSOMC  POWER ON, RESET, OR BUS DEVICE RESET OCCURRED         |
| 2A  00    DTL WRSOMC  PARAMETERS CHANGED                                    |
| 2A  01    DTL WRSOMC  MODE PARAMETERS CHANGED                               |
| 2A  02    DTL WRSOMC  LOG PARAMETERS CHANGED                                |
| 2B  00    DTLPWRSO C  COPY CANNOT EXECUTE SINCE HOST CANNOT DISCONNECT      |
| 2C  00    DTLPWRSOMC  COMMAND SEQUENCE ERROR                                |
| 2C  01           S    TOO MANY WINDOWS SPECIFIED                            |
| 2C  02           S    INVALID COMBINATION OF WINDOWS SPECIFIED              |
| 2D  00    T           OVERWRITE ERROR ON UPDATE IN PLACE                    |
| 2E  00                                                                      |
| 2F  00    DTLPWRSOMC  COMMANDS CLEARED BY ANOTHER INITIATOR                 |
| 30  00    DT  WR OM   INCOMPATIBLE MEDIUM INSTALLED                         |
| 30  01    DT  WR O    CANNOT READ MEDIUM - UNKNOWN FORMAT                   |
| 30  02    DT  WR O    CANNOT READ MEDIUM - INCOMPATIBLE FORMAT              |
| 30  03    DT          CLEANING CARTRIDGE INSTALLED                          |
| 31  00    DT  W  O    MEDIUM FORMAT CORRUPTED                               |
| 31  01    D L    O    FORMAT COMMAND FAILED                                 |
| 32  00    D   W  O    NO DEFECT SPARE LOCATION AVAILABLE                    |
| 32  01    D   W  O    DEFECT LIST UPDATE FAILURE                            |
| 33  00    T           TAPE LENGTH ERROR                                     |
| 34  00                                                                      |
| 35  00                                                                      |
| 36  00    L           RIBBON, INK, OR TONER FAILURE                         |
+============================================================================+
```

```
Table 364: (continued)
+==============================================================================+
|               D - DIRECT ACCESS DEVICE                                       |
|               .T - SEQUENTIAL ACCESS DEVICE                                  |
|               . L - PRINTER DEVICE                                           |
|               .  P - PROCESSOR DEVICE                                        |
|               .  .W - WRITE ONCE READ MULTIPLE DEVICE                        |
|               .  . R - READ ONLY (CD-ROM) DEVICE                             |
|               .  . S - SCANNER DEVICE                                        |
|               .  . .O - OPTICAL MEMORY DEVICE                                |
|               .  . . M - MEDIA CHANGER DEVICE                                |
|               .  . . C - COMMUNICATION DEVICE                                |
|               .  . . .                                                       |
| ASC ASCQ  DTLPWRSOMC  DESCRIPTION                                            |
| --- ----  ----------  ----------------------------------------------------- |
|  37  00   DTL WRSOMC  ROUNDED PARAMETER                                      |
|  38  00                                                                      |
|  39  00   DTL WRSOMC  SAVING PARAMETERS NOT SUPPORTED                        |
|  3A  00   DTL WRSOM   MEDIUM NOT PRESENT                                     |
|  3B  00       TL      SEQUENTIAL POSITIONING ERROR                           |
|  3B  01       T       TAPE POSITION ERROR AT BEGINNING-OF-MEDIUM             |
|  3B  02       T       TAPE POSITION ERROR AT END-OF-MEDIUM                   |
|  3B  03        L      TAPE OR ELECTRONIC VERTICAL FORMS UNIT NOT READY       |
|  3B  04        L      SLEW FAILURE                                           |
|  3B  05        L      PAPER JAM                                              |
|  3B  06        L      FAILED TO SENSE TOP-OF-FORM                            |
|  3B  07        L      FAILED TO SENSE BOTTOM-OF-FORM                         |
|  3B  08       T       REPOSITION ERROR                                       |
|  3B  09            S  READ PAST END OF MEDIUM                                |
|  3B  0A            S  READ PAST BEGINNING OF MEDIUM                          |
|  3B  0B            S  POSITION PAST END OF MEDIUM                            |
|  3B  0C            S  POSITION PAST BEGINNING OF MEDIUM                      |
|  3B  0D              M  MEDIUM DESTINATION ELEMENT FULL                      |
|  3B  0E              M  MEDIUM SOURCE ELEMENT EMPTY                          |
|  3C  00                                                                      |
|  3D  00   DTLPWRSOMC  INVALID BITS IN IDENTIFY MESSAGE                       |
|  3E  00   DTLPWRSOMC  LOGICAL UNIT HAS NOT SELF-CONFIGURED YET               |
|  3F  00   DTLPWRSOMC  TARGET OPERATING CONDITIONS HAVE CHANGED               |
|  3F  01   DTLPWRSOMC  MICROCODE HAS BEEN CHANGED                             |
|  3F  02   DTLPWRSOMC  CHANGED OPERATING DEFINITION                           |
|  3F  03   DTLPWRSOMC  INQUIRY DATA HAS CHANGED                               |
|  40  00   D          RAM FAILURE (SHOULD USE 40 NN)                          |
|  40  NN   DTLPWRSOMC  DIAGNOSTIC FAILURE ON COMPONENT NN (80H-FFH)           |
|  41  00   D          DATA PATH FAILURE (SHOULD USE 40 NN)                    |
|  42  00   D          POWER-ON OR SELF-TEST FAILURE (SHOULD USE 40 NN)        |
|  43  00   DTLPWRSOMC  MESSAGE ERROR                                          |
|  44  00   DTLPWRSOMC  INTERNAL TARGET FAILURE                                |
|  45  00   DTLPWRSOMC  SELECT OR RESELECT FAILURE                             |
|  46  00   DTLPWRSOMC  UNSUCCESSFUL SOFT RESET                                |
|  47  00   DTLPWRSOMC  SCSI PARITY ERROR                                      |
|  48  00   DTLPWRSOMC  INITIATOR DETECTED ERROR MESSAGE RECEIVED              |
|  49  00   DTLPWRSOMC  INVALID MESSAGE ERROR                                  |
|  4A  00   DTLPWRSOMC  COMMAND PHASE ERROR                                    |
|  4B  00   DTLPWRSOMC  DATA PHASE ERROR                                       |
|  4C  00   DTLPWRSOMC  LOGICAL UNIT FAILED SELF-CONFIGURATION                 |
|  4D  00                                                                      |
|  4E  00   DTLPWRSOMC  OVERLAPPED COMMANDS ATTEMPTED                          |
|  4F  00                                                                      |
|  50  00       T       WRITE APPEND ERROR                                     |
|  50  01       T       WRITE APPEND POSITION ERROR                            |
|  50  02       T       POSITION ERROR RELATED TO TIMING                       |
```

```
| 51  00    T     O     ERASE FAILURE                                        |
| 52  00    T           CARTRIDGE FAULT                                      |
+==========================================================================+


Table 364: (continued)
+==========================================================================+
|            D - DIRECT ACCESS DEVICE                                       |
|            .T - SEQUENTIAL ACCESS DEVICE                                  |
|            . L - PRINTER DEVICE                                           |
|            .  P - PROCESSOR DEVICE                                        |
|            .  .W - WRITE ONCE READ MULTIPLE DEVICE                        |
|            .  . R - READ ONLY (CD-ROM) DEVICE                             |
|            .  . S - SCANNER DEVICE                                        |
|            .  . .O - OPTICAL MEMORY DEVICE                                |
|            .  . . M - MEDIA CHANGER DEVICE                                |
|            .  . . C - COMMUNICATION DEVICE                                |
|            .  . . .                                                       |
| ASC ASCQ  DTLPWRSOMC  DESCRIPTION                                         |
| --- ----             -------------------------------------------------   |
| 53  00    DTL WRSOM   MEDIA LOAD OR EJECT FAILED                          |
| 53  01    T           UNLOAD TAPE FAILURE                                 |
| 53  02    DT  WR OM   MEDIUM REMOVAL PREVENTED                            |
| 54  00       P        SCSI TO HOST SYSTEM INTERFACE FAILURE               |
| 55  00       P        SYSTEM RESOURCE FAILURE                             |
| 56  00                                                                    |
| 57  00            R   UNABLE TO RECOVER TABLE-OF-CONTENTS                 |
| 58  00    O           GENERATION DOES NOT EXIST                           |
| 59  00    O           UPDATED BLOCK READ                                  |
| 5A  00    DTLPWRSOM   OPERATOR REQUEST OR STATE CHANGE INPUT (UNSPECIFIED)|
| 5A  01    DT  WR OM   OPERATOR MEDIUM REMOVAL REQUEST                     |
| 5A  02    DT  W  O    OPERATOR SELECTED WRITE PROTECT                     |
| 5A  03    DT  W  O    OPERATOR SELECTED WRITE PERMIT                      |
| 5B  00    DTLPWRSOM   LOG EXCEPTION                                       |
| 5B  01    DTLPWRSOM   THRESHOLD CONDITION MET                             |
| 5B  02    DTLPWRSOM   LOG COUNTER AT MAXIMUM                              |
| 5B  03    DTLPWRSOM   LOG LIST CODES EXHAUSTED                            |
| 5C  00    D  O        RPL STATUS CHANGE                                   |
| 5C  01    D  O        SPINDLES SYNCHRONIZED                               |
| 5C  02    D  O        SPINDLES NOT SYNCHRONIZED                           |
| 5D  00                                                                    |
| 5E  00                                                                    |
| 5F  00                                                                    |
| 60  00            S   LAMP FAILURE                                        |
| 61  00            S   VIDEO ACQUISITION ERROR                            |
| 61  01            S   UNABLE TO ACQUIRE VIDEO                             |
| 61  02            S   OUT OF FOCUS                                        |
| 62  00            S   SCAN HEAD POSITIONING ERROR                        |
| 63  00            R   END OF USER AREA ENCOUNTERED ON THIS TRACK         |
| 64  00            R   ILLEGAL MODE FOR THIS TRACK                        |
| 65  00                                                                    |
| 66  00                                                                    |
| 67  00                                                                    |
| 68  00                                                                    |
| 69  00                                                                    |
| 6A  00                                                                    |
| 6B  00                                                                    |
| 6C  00                                                                    |
| 6D  00                                                                    |
| 6E  00                                                                    |
| 6F  00                                                                    |
+==========================================================================+
```

```
Table 364: (concluded)
+================================================================================+
|              D - DIRECT ACCESS DEVICE                                          |
|              .T - SEQUENTIAL ACCESS DEVICE                                     |
|              . L - PRINTER DEVICE                                              |
|              . P - PROCESSOR DEVICE                                            |
|              . .W - WRITE ONCE READ MULTIPLE DEVICE                            |
|              . . R - READ ONLY (CD-ROM) DEVICE                                 |
|              . . S - SCANNER DEVICE                                            |
|              . . .O - OPTICAL MEMORY DEVICE                                    |
|              . . . M - MEDIA CHANGER DEVICE                                    |
|              . . . C - COMMUNICATION DEVICE                                    |
|              . . . . .                                                         |
| ASC ASCQ  DTLPWRSOMC  DESCRIPTION                                              |
| --- ----             ------------------------------------------------------- |
| 70  00                                                                         |
| 71  00                                                                         |
| 72  00                                                                         |
| 73  00                                                                         |
| 74  00                                                                         |
| 75  00                                                                         |
| 76  00                                                                         |
| 77  00                                                                         |
| 78  00                                                                         |
| 79  00                                                                         |
| 7A  00                                                                         |
| 7B  00                                                                         |
| 7C  00                                                                         |
| 7D  00                                                                         |
| 7E  00                                                                         |
| 7F  00                                                                         |
|                                                                                |
| 80  xxh \                                                                      |
|   THROUGH >  VENDOR SPECIFIC.                                                   |
| FF  xxh /                                                                      |
|                                                                                |
| xxh 80 \                                                                       |
| THROUGH >  VENDOR SPECIFIC QUALIFICATION OF STANDARD ASC.                       |
| xxh FF /                                                                       |
|              ALL CODES NOT SHOWN OR BLANK ARE RESERVED.                         |
+================================================================================+
```

D   A SCSI command code quick reference

```
Table 365 is a numerical order listing of the command operation codes.

                    Table 365: SCSI-2 Operation Codes

+=================================================================================+
|              D - DIRECT ACCESS DEVICE              Device Column Key |
|              .T - SEQUENTIAL ACCESS DEVICE         M = Mandatory     |
|              . L - PRINTER DEVICE                  O = Optional      |
|              . P - PROCESSOR DEVICE                V = Vendor Specific|
|              . .W - WRITE ONCE READ MULTIPLE DEVICE R = Reserved      |
|              . . R - READ ONLY (CD-ROM) DEVICE                       |
|              . . S - SCANNER DEVICE                                 |
|              . . .O - OPTICAL MEMORY DEVICE                         |
|              . . . M - MEDIA CHANGER DEVICE                         |
|              . . . C - COMMUNICATION DEVICE                         |
```

```
|                . . . .                                                        |
|           OP DTLPWRSOMC Description                                           |
|----------+----------+-----------------------------------------------------------|
|           00 MMMMMMMMM TEST UNIT READY                                        |
|           01 M         REWIND                                                 |
|           01 O V OO OO REZERO UNIT                                            |
|           02 VVVVVV V                                                         |
|           03 MMMMMMMMM REQUEST SENSE                                          |
|           04   O        FORMAT                                                |
|           04 M      O   FORMAT UNIT                                           |
|           05 VMVVVV V   READ BLOCK LIMITS                                     |
|           06 VVVVVV V                                                         |
|           07         O  INITIALIZE ELEMENT STATUS                             |
|           07 OVV O  OV  REASSIGN BLOCKS                                       |
|           08        M GET MESSAGE(06)                                         |
|           08 OMV OO OV  READ(06)                                              |
|           08   O        RECEIVE                                               |
|           09 VVVVVV V                                                         |
|           0A  M         PRINT                                                 |
|           0A         M SEND MESSAGE(06)                                       |
|           0A  M         SEND(06)                                              |
|           0A OM  O  OV  WRITE(06)                                             |
|           0B O   OO OV  SEEK(06)                                              |
|           0B  O         SLEW AND PRINT                                        |
|           0C VVVVVV V                                                         |
|           0D VVVVVV V                                                         |
|           0E VVVVVV V                                                         |
|           0F VOVVVV V   READ REVERSE                                          |
|           10  O O       SYNCHRONIZE BUFFER                                    |
|           10 VM VVV     WRITE FILEMARKS                                       |
|           11 VMVVVV     SPACE                                                 |
|           12 MMMMMMMMM INQUIRY                                                |
|           13 VOVVVV     VERIFY(06)                                            |
|           14 VOOVVV     RECOVER BUFFERED DATA                                 |
|           15 OMO OOOOOO MODE SELECT(06)                                       |
|           16 M   MM MO  RESERVE                                               |
|           16 MM   M     RESERVE UNIT                                          |
|           17 M   MM MO  RELEASE                                              |
|           17  MM  M     RELEASE UNIT                                          |
|           18 OOOOOOOO   COPY                                                  |
|           19 VMVVVV     ERASE                                                 |
|           1A OMO OOOOOO MODE SENSE(06)                                        |
|           1B  O         LOAD UNLOAD                                           |
|           1B      O     SCAN                                                  |
|           1B  O         STOP PRINT                                            |
|           1B O  OO O    STOP START UNIT                                       |
+==============================================================================+
```

Table 365: (continued)

```
+==============================================================================+
|          D - DIRECT ACCESS DEVICE                    Device Column Key |
|          .T - SEQUENTIAL ACCESS DEVICE               M = Mandatory     |
|          . L - PRINTER DEVICE                        O = Optional       |
|          .  P - PROCESSOR DEVICE                     V = Vendor Specific|
|          . .W - WRITE ONCE READ MULTIPLE DEVICE      R = Reserved       |
|          . . R - READ ONLY (CD-ROM) DEVICE                              |
|          . .  S - SCANNER DEVICE                                        |
|          . .  .O - OPTICAL MEMORY DEVICE                                |
|          . .  . M - MEDIA CHANGER DEVICE                                |
|          . .  . C - COMMUNICATION DEVICE                                |
|          . . . . .                                                      |
```

```
|         OP DTLPWRSOMC Description                                             |
|----------+----------+--------------------------------------------------------|
|         1C OOOOOOOOOO RECEIVE DIAGNOSTIC RESULTS                              |
|         1D MMMMMMMMMM SEND DIAGNOSTIC                                         |
|         1E OO   OO OO  PREVENT ALLOW MEDIUM REMOVAL                           |
|         1F                                                                    |
|         20 V    VV V                                                          |
|         21 V    VV V                                                          |
|         22 V    VV V                                                          |
|         23 V    VV V                                                          |
|         24 V    VVM    SET WINDOW                                             |
|         25      O      GET WINDOW                                             |
|         25 M    M M    READ CAPACITY                                          |
|         25      M      READ CD-ROM CAPACITY                                   |
|         26 V    VV                                                            |
|         27 V    VV                                                           |
|         28          O GET MESSAGE(10)                                         |
|         28 M    MMMM  READ(10)                                               |
|         29 V    VV O   READ GENERATION                                        |
|         2A          O SEND MESSAGE(10)                                        |
|         2A      O     SEND(10)                                               |
|         2A M    M M    WRITE(10)                                              |
|         2B O          LOCATE                                                  |
|         2B         O  POSITION TO ELEMENT                                     |
|         2B O    OO O   SEEK(10)                                               |
|         2C V    O      ERASE(10)                                              |
|         2D V    O  O   READ UPDATED BLOCK                                     |
|         2E O    O  O   WRITE AND VERIFY(10)                                   |
|         2F O    OO O   VERIFY(10)                                             |
|         30 O    OO O   SEARCH DATA HIGH(10)                                   |
|         31      O      OBJECT POSITION                                        |
|         31 O    OO O   SEARCH DATA EQUAL(10)                                  |
|         32 O    OO O   SEARCH DATA LOW(10)                                    |
|         33 O    OO O   SET LIMITS(10)                                         |
|         34      O      GET DATA BUFFER STATUS                                 |
|         34 O    OO O   PRE-FETCH                                              |
|         34 O          READ POSITION                                          |
|         35 O    OO O   SYNCHRONIZE CACHE                                      |
|         36 O    OO O   LOCK UNLOCK CACHE                                      |
|         37 O    O      READ DEFECT DATA(10)                                   |
|         38      O O    MEDIUM SCAN                                            |
|         39 OOOOOOOO   COMPARE                                                 |
|         3A OOOOOOOO   COPY AND VERIFY                                         |
|         3B OOOOOOOOOO WRITE BUFFER                                            |
|         3C OOOOOOOOOO READ BUFFER                                             |
|         3D      O  O   UPDATE BLOCK                                           |
|         3E O    OO O   READ LONG                                             |
|         3F O    O  O   WRITE LONG                                            |
+==============================================================================+
```

Table 365: (continued)

```
+==============================================================================+
|         D - DIRECT ACCESS DEVICE                    Device Column Key |
|         .T - SEQUENTIAL ACCESS DEVICE               M = Mandatory     |
|         . L - PRINTER DEVICE                        O = Optional      |
|         .  P - PROCESSOR DEVICE                     V = Vendor Specific|
|         .  .W - WRITE ONCE READ MULTIPLE DEVICE     R = Reserved      |
|         .  . R - READ ONLY (CD-ROM) DEVICE                            |
|         .  .  S - SCANNER DEVICE                                      |
|         .  .  .O - OPTICAL MEMORY DEVICE                              |
|         .  .  . M - MEDIA CHANGER DEVICE                              |
```

```
|               .  .  . C - COMMUNICATION DEVICE                        |
|               .  .  .  .                                              |
|          OP DTLPWRSOMC Description                                    |
|----------+----------+-------------------------------------------------|
|          40 OOOOOOOOOO CHANGE DEFINITION                              |
|          41 O          WRITE SAME                                     |
|          42       O    READ SUB-CHANNEL                               |
|          43       O    READ TOC                                       |
|          44       O    READ HEADER                                    |
|          45       O    PLAY AUDIO(10)                                 |
|          46                                                           |
|          47       O    PLAY AUDIO MSF                                 |
|          48       O    PLAY AUDIO TRACK INDEX                         |
|          49       O    PLAY TRACK RELATIVE(10)                        |
|          4A                                                           |
|          4B       O    PAUSE RESUME                                   |
|          4C OOOOOOOOOO LOG SELECT                                     |
|          4D OOOOOOOOOO LOG SENSE                                      |
|          4E                                                           |
|          4F                                                           |
|          50                                                           |
|          51                                                           |
|          52                                                           |
|          53                                                           |
|          54                                                           |
|          55 OOO OOOOOO MODE SELECT(10)                                |
|          56                                                           |
|          57                                                           |
|          58                                                           |
|          59                                                           |
|          5A OOO OOOOOO MODE SENSE(10)                                 |
|          5B                                                           |
|          5C                                                           |
|          5D                                                           |
|          5E                                                           |
|          5F                                                           |
+======================================================================+
```

Table 365: (concluded)

```
+======================================================================+
|          D - DIRECT ACCESS DEVICE              Device Column Key      |
|          .T - SEQUENTIAL ACCESS DEVICE         M = Mandatory          |
|          . L - PRINTER DEVICE                  O = Optional           |
|          . P - PROCESSOR DEVICE                V = Vendor Specific     |
|          . .W - WRITE ONCE READ MULTIPLE DEVICE R = Reserved          |
|          . . R - READ ONLY (CD-ROM) DEVICE                            |
|          . . S - SCANNER DEVICE                                       |
|          . . .O - OPTICAL MEMORY DEVICE                               |
|          . . . M - MEDIA CHANGER DEVICE                               |
|          . . . C - COMMUNICATION DEVICE                               |
|          . . . .                                                      |
|          OP DTLPWRSOMC Description                                    |
|----------+----------+-------------------------------------------------|
|          A0                                                           |
|          A1                                                           |
|          A2                                                           |
|          A3                                                           |
|          A4                                                           |
|          A5       M    MOVE MEDIUM                                    |
|          A5       O    PLAY AUDIO(12)                                 |
|          A6         O  EXCHANGE MEDIUM                                |
```

```
|         A7                                                                    |
|         A8          O  GET MESSAGE(12)                                        |
|         A8      OO O   READ(12)                                               |
|         A9       O     PLAY TRACK RELATIVE(12)                                |
|         AA          O  SEND MESSAGE(12)                                       |
|         AA      O  O   WRITE(12)                                              |
|         AB                                                                    |
|         AC       O     ERASE(12)                                             |
|         AD                                                                    |
|         AE      O  O   WRITE AND VERIFY(12)                                   |
|         AF      OO O   VERIFY(12)                                             |
|         B0      OO O   SEARCH DATA HIGH(12)                                   |
|         B1      OO O   SEARCH DATA EQUAL(12)                                  |
|         B2      OO O   SEARCH DATA LOW(12)                                    |
|         B3      OO O   SET LIMITS(12)                                         |
|         B4                                                                    |
|         B5                                                                    |
|         B5          O  REQUEST VOLUME ELEMENT ADDRESS                         |
|         B6                                                                    |
|         B6          O  SEND VOLUME TAG                                        |
|         B7          O  READ DEFECT DATA(12)                                   |
|         B8                                                                    |
|         B8          O  READ ELEMENT STATUS                                    |
|         B9                                                                    |
|         BA                                                                    |
|         BB                                                                    |
|         BC                                                                    |
|         BD                                                                    |
|         BE                                                                    |
|         BF                                                                    |
+==============================================================================+
```

E   Example programs

Here is the C example program, which requests manufacturer/model and reports if a medium is loaded in the device.

```c
/* Example program to demonstrate the generic SCSI interface */
#include <stdio.h>
#include <unistd.h>
#include <string.h>
#include <fcntl.h>
#include <errno.h>
#include <linux/../../drivers/scsi/sg.h>

#define DEVICE "/dev/sgc"

#define SCSI_OFF sizeof(struct sg_header)
static unsigned char cmd[SCSI_OFF + 18];      /* SCSI command buffer */
int fd;                              /* SCSI device/file descriptor */

/* process a complete SCSI cmd. Use the generic SCSI interface. */
static int handle_scsi_cmd(unsigned cmd_len,        /* command length */
                    unsigned in_size,        /* input data size */
                    unsigned char *i_buff,   /* input buffer */
                    unsigned out_size,       /* output data size */
                    unsigned char *o_buff    /* output buffer */
                    )
{
```

```c
    int status = 0;
    struct sg_header *sg_hd;

    /* safety checks */
    if (!cmd_len) return -1;            /* need a cmd_len != 0 */
    if (!i_buff) return -1;             /* need an input buffer != NULL */
#ifdef SG_BIG_BUFF
    if (SCSI_OFF + cmd_len + in_size > SG_BIG_BUFF) return -1;
    if (SCSI_OFF + out_size > SG_BIG_BUFF) return -1;
#else
    if (SCSI_OFF + cmd_len + in_size > 4096) return -1;
    if (SCSI_OFF + out_size > 4096) return -1;
#endif

    if (!o_buff) out_size = 0;

    /* generic SCSI device header construction */
    sg_hd = (struct sg_header *) i_buff;
    sg_hd->pack_len    = SCSI_OFF + cmd_len + in_size;
    sg_hd->reply_len   = SCSI_OFF + out_size;
    sg_hd->twelve_byte = cmd_len == 12;
#if     0
    sg_hd->pack_id;     /* not used */
    sg_hd->other_flags; /* not used */
#endif

    /* send command */
    status = write( fd, i_buff, SCSI_OFF + cmd_len + in_size );
    if ( status < 0 || status != SCSI_OFF + cmd_len + in_size ||
                      sg_hd->result ) {
        /* some error happened */
        fprintf( stderr, "write(generic) result = 0x%x cmd = 0x%x\n",
                sg_hd->result, i_buff[SCSI_OFF] );
        perror("");
        return status;
    }

    if (!o_buff) o_buff = i_buff;       /* buffer pointer check */

    /* retrieve result */
    status = read( fd, o_buff, SCSI_OFF + out_size);
    if ( status < 0 || status != SCSI_OFF + out_size || sg_hd->result ) {
        /* some error happened */
        fprintf( stderr, "read(generic) result = 0x%x cmd = 0x%x\n",
                sg_hd->result, o_buff[SCSI_OFF] );
        fprintf( stderr, "read(generic) sense "
                "%x %x %x %x %x %x %x %x %x %x %x %x %x %x %x %x\n",
                sg_hd->sense_buffer[0],         sg_hd->sense_buffer[1],
                sg_hd->sense_buffer[2],         sg_hd->sense_buffer[3],
                sg_hd->sense_buffer[4],         sg_hd->sense_buffer[5],
                sg_hd->sense_buffer[6],         sg_hd->sense_buffer[7],
                sg_hd->sense_buffer[8],         sg_hd->sense_buffer[9],
                sg_hd->sense_buffer[10],        sg_hd->sense_buffer[11],
                sg_hd->sense_buffer[12],        sg_hd->sense_buffer[13],
                sg_hd->sense_buffer[14],        sg_hd->sense_buffer[15]);
        perror("");
    }
    /* Look if we got what we expected to get */
    if (status == SCSI_OFF + out_size) status = 0; /* got them all */

    return status;  /* 0 means no error */
```

```
}

#define INQUIRY_CMD     0x12
#define INQUIRY_CMDLEN  6
#define INQUIRY_REPLY_LEN 96
#define INQUIRY_VENDOR  8        /* Offset in reply data to vendor name */

/* request vendor brand and model */
static unsigned char *Inquiry ( void )
{
  unsigned char Inqbuffer[ SCSI_OFF + INQUIRY_REPLY_LEN ];
  unsigned char cmdblk [ INQUIRY_CMDLEN ] =
      { INQUIRY_CMD,  /* command */
                 0,  /* lun/reserved */
                 0,  /* page code */
                 0,  /* reserved */
  INQUIRY_REPLY_LEN,  /* allocation length */
                 0 };/* reserved/flag/link */

  memcpy( cmd + SCSI_OFF, cmdblk, sizeof(cmdblk) );

  if (handle_scsi_cmd(sizeof(cmdblk), 0, cmd,
                   sizeof(Inqbuffer) - SCSI_OFF, Inqbuffer )) {
      fprintf( stderr, "Inquiry failed\n" );
      exit(2);
  }
  return (Inqbuffer + SCSI_OFF);
}

#define TESTUNITREADY_CMD 0
#define TESTUNITREADY_CMDLEN 6

#define ADD_SENSECODE 12
#define ADD_SC_QUALIFIER 13
#define NO_MEDIA_SC 0x3a
#define NO_MEDIA_SCQ 0x00
int TestForMedium ( void )
{
  /* request READY status */
  static unsigned char cmdblk [TESTUNITREADY_CMDLEN] = {
      TESTUNITREADY_CMD, /* command */
                 0, /* reserved */
                 0, /* reserved */
                 0, /* reserved */
                 0, /* reserved */
                0};/* reserved */

  memcpy( cmd + SCSI_OFF, cmdblk, sizeof(cmdblk) );

  if (handle_scsi_cmd(sizeof(cmdblk), 0, cmd,
                      0, NULL)) {
      fprintf (stderr, "Test unit ready failed\n");
      exit(2);
  }

  return
   *(((struct sg_header*)cmd)->sense_buffer +ADD_SENSECODE) !=
                                        NO_MEDIA_SC ||
   *(((struct sg_header*)cmd)->sense_buffer +ADD_SC_QUALIFIER) !=
                                        NO_MEDIA_SCQ;
}
```

```
void main( void )
{
  fd = open(DEVICE, O_RDWR);
  if (fd < 0) {
    fprintf( stderr, "Need read/write permissions for "DEVICE".\n" );
    exit(1);
  }

  /* print the result of Inquiry */
  printf( "%s\n", Inquiry() + INQUIRY_VENDOR );

  /* look if medium is loaded */
  if (!TestForMedium()) {
    printf("device is unloaded\n");
  } else {
    printf("device is loaded\n");
  }
}
```

Part XXXVIII

The Linux Serial HOWTO

Copyright by Greg Hankins, `greg.hankins@cc.gatech.edu`
v1.8, 28 March 1995
This document describes how to set up serial communications devices on a Linux box.

Contents

1 Introduction

This is the Linux Serial HOWTO. All about how to set up modems and terminals under Linux, some serial tips, and troubleshooting.

1.1 Copyright

The Linux Serial HOWTO is copyright (C) 1993 - 1995 by Greg Hankins. Linux HOWTO documents may be reproduced and distributed in whole or in part, in any medium physical or electronic, as long as this copyright notice is retained on all copies. Commercial redistribution is allowed and encouraged; however, the author would *like* to be notified of any such distributions.

All translations, derivative works, or aggregate works incorporating any Linux HOWTO documents must be covered under this copyright notice. That is, you may not produce a derivative work from a HOWTO and impose additional restrictions on its distribution. Exceptions to these rules may be granted under certain conditions; please contact the Linux HOWTO coordinator at the address given below.

In short, we wish to promote dissemination of this information through as many channels as possible. However, we do wish to retain copyright on the HOWTO documents, and would *like* to be notified of any plans to redistribute the HOWTOs.

If you have questions, please contact Greg Hankins, the Linux HOWTO coordinator, at `gregh@sunsite.unc.edu` via email, or at +1 404 853 9989.

1.2 Other sources of information

- man pages for: `agetty(8)`, `getty(1m)`, `gettydefs(5)`, `init(1)`, `login(1)`, `mgetty(8)`, `setserial(8)`

- Your modem manual

- UUCP HOWTO: for information on setting up UUCP

- Printing HOWTO: for setting up a serial printer

- NET-2 HOWTO: all about networking, including SLIP, CSLIP, PLIP and PPP

- BUPS HOWTO: setting up UPS boxen connected to your serial port

- Term HOWTO: everything you wanted to know about the `term` program

- USENET newsgroups:

  comp.os.linux.advocacy
  Benefits of Linux compared to other operating systems.

comp.os.linux.announce

Announcements important to the Linux community.

comp.os.linux.answers

FAQs, How-To's, READMEs, etc. about Linux.

comp.os.linux.development.apps

Writing Linux applications, porting to Linux.

comp.os.linux.development.system

Linux kernels, device drivers, modules.

comp.os.linux.hardware

Hardware compatibility with the Linux operating system.

comp.os.linux.misc

Linux-specific topics not covered by other groups.

comp.os.linux.networking

Networking and communications under Linux.

comp.os.linux.setup

Linux installation and system administration.

comp.os.linux.x

Linux X Window System servers, clients, libs and fonts.

- the Linux serial mailing list. To join, send email to majordomo@vger.rutgers.edu, with "subscribe linux-serial" in the message body. If you send "help" in the message body, you get a help message.

1.3   New versions of this document

New versions of the Serial-HOWTO will be placed on
sunsite.unc.edu (ftp://sunsite.unc.edu:/pub/Linux/docs/HOWTO/Serial-HOWTO) and mirror sites. There are other formats, such as a PostScript and dvi version in the other-formats directory. The *Serial HOWTO* (http://sunsite.unc.edu/mdw/HOWTO/Serial-HOWTO.html) is also available for WWW clients such as mosaic. It will also be posted regularly to comp.os.linux.answers.

If you don't have FTP access, you can get Linux help files via email. Bill Riemers runs a mail handler on his account. Send mail to bcr@physics.purdue.edu with a subject of "help" for more infomation, and to get an index file.

1.4   Feedback

Please send me any questions, comments, suggestions, or additional material. I'm always eager to hear about what you think about the HOWTO. I'm also always on the lookout for improvements! Tell me exactly what you don't understand, or what could be clearer. You can reach me at greg.hankins@cc.gatech.edu via email. I can also be reached at:
Greg Hankins
College of Computing
801 Atlantic Drive
Atlanta, GA 30332-0280
via snail mail, and at *my home page* (http://www.cc.gatech.edu/staff/h/Greg.Hankins/) via the WWW.

Please include the version number of the Serial HOWTO when writing, this is version 1.8.

1.5   Disclaimer

Your mileage may vary. The answers given may not work for all systems and all setup combinations.

2   Supported serial hardware

Linux is known to work with the following serial hardware.

2.1   Standard PC hardware (COM1 - COM4)

- standard PC 2S/1P/1G serial boards (COM1 - COM4), to which external serial devices (modems, serial mice, etc...) can be connected

- standard PC internal modems (COM1 - COM4)

- Quickpath Systems Port-Folio 550e (allows IRQs of 3, 4, 5, 9, 10, 11, 12, and 15)

2.2   Multiport serial boards (with 16450/16550A UARTs)

- AST FourPort and clones (4 port)

- Accent Async-4 (4 port)

- Arnet Multiport-8 (8 port)

- Bell Technologies HUB6 (6 port)

- Boca BB-1004 (4 port), BB-1008 (8 port), BB-2016 (16 port)

- Boca IO/AT66 (6 port)

- Boca 2by4 (4S/2P)

- Computone ValuePort V4-ISA (AST FourPort compatible)

- PC-COMM (4 port)

- STB-4COM (4 port)

- Twincom ACI/550

- Usenet Serial Board II (4 port)

In general, Linux will support any serial board which uses a 8250, 16450, 16550, 16550A (or compatible) UART, or an internal modem which emulates one of the above UARTs.

Special note on the BB-1004 and BB-1008, they do not support DCD and RI lines, and thus are not usable for dialin modems. They will work fine for all other purposes.

2.3   Intelligent multiport serial boards

- Computone IntelliPort II (16Mhz 80186 - 4, 8, or 16 port) Computone IntelliPort II EXpandable (20Mhz 80186 - modular 16 - 64 port) (pre-ALPHA driver, contact Michael H. Warfield, mhw@wittsend.atl.ga.us)

- Cyclades Cyclom 8Y (8 port), and 16Y (16 port) (Cirrus Logic CD-1400 RISC UARTs) (contact cyclades@netcom.com)

- DigiBoard PC/Xe (12.5MHz 80186 processor - 2, 4, 8, or 16 port), and PC/Xi (12.5MHz 80186 processor - 8, or 16 port) (contact Troy De Jongh, troyd@digibd.com.   Driver location: ftp.digibd.com:/digiline/drivers/linux)

- Digiboard COM/Xi (10MHz 80188 processor - 4 or 8 port)
  (pre-ALPHA driver contact Simon Park, si@wimpol.demon.co.uk)

- Hayes ESP8 (8 port)
  (pre-ALPHA driver, contact Dennis Boylan, `dennis@lan.com`)

- Omega COMM-8 (8 port)
  (contact Vance Petree, `vpetree@infi.net`)

- Specialix SIO - (modular, 4 - 32 port)
  (ALPHA driver, contact Simon Allen, `simonallen@cix.compulink.co.uk`)

- Stallion EasyIO-4 (4 port), EasyIO-8 (8 port), and Stallion EasyConnection (modular, 8 - 32 port) (Cirrus Logic CD-1400 RISC UARTs) (contact Greg Ungerer, `gerg@stallion.oz.au`)

Drivers for the Cyclades, DigiBoard, Stallion and Specialix boards can be found on `sunsite.unc.edu:/pub/Linux/kernel/patches/serial` and mirror sites.

3   What are the names of the serial ports?

There are the 4 serial devices corresponding to COM1 - COM4:

```
/dev/cua0, /dev/ttyS0 (COM1) address 0x3f8 IRQ 4
/dev/cua1, /dev/ttyS1 (COM2) address 0x2f8 IRQ 3
/dev/cua2, /dev/ttyS2 (COM3) address 0x3e8 IRQ 4
/dev/cua3, /dev/ttyS3 (COM4) address 0x2e8 IRQ 3
```

The `/dev/ttyS`N devices are for incoming connections and `/dev/cua`N devices for outgoing connections. N is the serial port number. In this document, I refer to COM1 as `ttyS0`, COM2 as `ttyS1`, COM3 as `ttyS2`, and COM4 as `ttyS3`. If I am referring to a specific device in `/dev`, I will always prepend `/dev` to avoid confusing you.

On some installations, two extra devices will be created, `/dev/modem` for your modem and `/dev/mouse` for your mouse. Both of these are symbolic links to the appropriate `/dev/cua`N device which you specified during the installation (unless you have a bus mouse, then `/dev/mouse` will point to the bus mouse device).

There has been some discussion on the merits of `/dev/mouse` and `/dev/modem`. I *strongly* discourage the use of these links. In particular, if you are planning on using your modem for dialin you will run into problems because the lock files will not work correctly if you use `/dev/modem`. Use them if you like, but *be sure they point to the right device.*

3.1   Major and minor device numbers of serial devices in `/dev`

```
/dev/ttyS0 major 4, minor 64    /dev/cua0 major 5, minor 64
/dev/ttyS1 major 4, minor 65    /dev/cua1 major 5, minor 65
/dev/ttyS2 major 4, minor 66    /dev/cua2 major 5, minor 66
/dev/ttyS3 major 4, minor 67    /dev/cua3 major 5, minor 67
```

Note that all distributions should come with these devices already made correctly.

3.1.1   Creating devices in `/dev`

If you don't have a device, you will have to create it with the `mknod` command.

Example, suppose you needed to create devices for `ttyS0`:

```
linux# mknod -m 666 /dev/cua0 c 5 64
linux# mknod -m 666 /dev/ttyS0 c 4 64
```

You can also get the MAKEDEV script, available on the usual FTP sites. This simplifies the making of devices. For example, if you needed to make the devices for ttyS0 you would type:

```
linux# cd /dev
linux# MAKEDEV ttyS0
```

This handles the devices creation for the incoming and outgoing devices.

3.1.2 Notes for multiport boards

The devices your multiport board uses depends on what kind of board you have. These are listed in detail in the rc.serial which comes with the setserial program. You will probably need to create these devices. Either use the mknod command, or get the MAKEDEV script. Devices for mulitport boards are made by adding "64 + the port number". So, if you wanted to create devices for ttyS17, you would type:

```
linux# mknod -m 666 /dev/cua17 c 5 81
linux# mknod -m 666 /dev/ttyS17 c 4 81
```

Note that "64 + 17 = 81". Using the MAKEDEV script, you would type:

```
linux# cd /dev
linux# MAKEDEV ttyS17
```

4 What is getty?

getty is a program that handles the login process when you log onto a Unix box. There are 3 versions that are commonly used with Linux: agetty, getty_ps and mgetty.

4.1 About getty_ps

This version of getty was written by Paul Sutcliffe Jr., paul@devon.lns.pa.us. Kris Gleason, gleasokr@boulder.colorado.edu currently maintains it. 2.0.7e is the latest version, and supercedes any older versions. Most distributions come with the getty_ps package installed as /sbin/getty.

The getty_ps package contains two getties. getty is used for console, and terminal devices - and uugetty which is used for modems. I use this version of getty, so I will focus on the getty_ps package in this HOWTO.

4.2 About mgetty

mgetty is a version of getty written by Gert Doering, gert@greenie.muc.de. In addition to allowing logins, mgetty also provides class 2 FAX support through sendfax, which accompanies mgetty. mgetty+sendfax 0.22 is the latest version of this package. The mgetty documentation is quite good, and does not need supplementing. Please refer to it for installation instructions.

4.3 About agetty

agetty is the third variation of getty. It was original written by W.Z. Venema, wietse@wzv.win.tue.nl. It's a simple implementation of getty.

5 What is `setserial`?

`setserial` is a program which allows you to look at and change various attributes of a serial device, including its port address, its interrupt, and other serial port options. It was initially written Rick Sladkey, and was heavily modified by Ted T'so, `tytso@mit.edu`, who also maintains it. The newest version is 2.10, and can be found on the Linux FTP sites. You can find out what version you have by running `setserial` with no arguments.

When your Linux system boots, only `ttyS{0-3}` are configured, using the default IRQs of 4 and 3. So, if you have any other serial ports provided by other boards or if `ttyS{0-3}` have a non-standard IRQ, you *must* use this program in order to configure those serial ports. For the full listing of options, consult the man page.

6 How do I dial out with my modem?

6.1 Hardware requirements

First, make sure you have the right cable. Your modem requires a straight through cable, with no pins crossed. Any computer store should have these. Make sure you get the correct gender. If you are using the DB25 serial port, it will always be the male DB25. Do not confuse it with the parallel port, which is the female DB25. Hook up your modem to one of your serial ports. Consult your modem manual on how to do this if you need help.

6.1.1 Notes on internal modems

For an internal modem, you will not need a cable. An internal modem does not need a serial port, it has one built in. All you need to do is configure it to use an interrupt that is not being used, and configure the port I/O address. Consult your modem manual if you get stuck. Also, see section 9 if you need help on choosing interrupts or addresses.

Due to a bit of stupidity on IBM's part, you may encounter problems if you want your internal modem to be on `ttyS3`. If Linux does not detect your internal modem on `ttyS3`, you can use `setserial` and the modem will work fine. Internal modems on `ttyS{0-2}` should not have any problems being detected.

6.2 Talking to your modem

Use `kermit` or some other simple comm program to test the setup, before you go jumping into complex comm programs. (For legel reasons, `kermit` is not distributed with commercial distributions. You can find the lastest version of `kermit` on `sunsite.unc.edu:/pub/Linux/apps/comm` and mirror sites.) For example, say your modem was on `ttyS3`, and it could handle 38400 bps. You would do the following:

```
linux# kermit
C-Kermit 5A(188), 23 Nov 92, POSIX
Type ? or HELP for help
C-Kermit>set line /dev/cua3
C-Kermit>set speed 38400
/dev/cua3, 38400 bps
C-Kermit>c
Connecting to /dev/cua3, speed 38400.
The escape character is Ctrl-\ (ASCII 28, FS)
Type the escape character followed by C to get back,
or followed by ? to see other options.
AT
OK
<ctrl>-\-C
```

```
(Back at linux)
C-Kermit>quit
linux#
```

If your modem responds to AT commands, you can assume your modem is working correctly on the Linux side. Try calling another modem. If you don't like `kermit`, try one of the more advanced comm programs. Check out section 11 about comm programs if you need some pointers.

When you dial out with your modem, set the speed to the highest bps rate that your modem supports. Since there is no speed named 57600 or 115200 bps, you must use the `setserial` program to set your serial port to a higher speed. See section 10 for how to do this. Then, set the speed to 38400 bps in your comm program.

6.3 Dial out modem configuration

For dial out use only, you can configure your modem however you want. If you intend to use your modem for dialin, you *must* configure your modem at the same speed that you intend to run `getty` at. So, if you want to run `getty` at 38400 bps, set your speed to 38400 bps when you configure your modem. This is done to prevent speed mismatches between your computer and modem.

I like to see result codes, so I set Q0 - result codes are reported. To set this on my modem, I would have to preceed the register name with an AT command. Using `kermit` or some comm program, connect to your modem and type the following: ATQ0. If your modem says OK back to you, then the register is set. Do this for each register you want to set.

I also like to see what I'm typing, so I set E1 - command echo on. If your modem has data compression capabilities, you probably want to enable them. Consult your modem manual for more help, and a full listing of options. If your modem supports a stored profile, be sure to write the configuration to the modem (often done with AT&W, but varies between modem manufacturers) if not you will have to set the registers everytime you turn on, or reset your modem.

6.4 Hardware flow control

If your modem supports hardware flow control (RTS/CTS), I highly recommend you use it. This is particularly important for modems that support data compression. First, you have to enable RTS/CTS flow control on the serial port itself. This is best done on startup, like in `/etc/rc.d/rc.local` or `/etc/rc.d/rc.serial`. Make sure that these files are being run from the main etc/rc.d/rc.M/ file! You need to do the following for each serial port you want to enable hardware flow control on:

```
stty crtscts < /dev/cuaN
```

You must also enable RTS/CTS flow control on your modem. Consult your modem manual on how to do this, as it varies between modem manufacturers. Be sure to save your modem configuration if your modem supports stored profiles.

7 How do I dial in and out with my modem using `getty_ps`?

Get your modem to dial out correctly. If you haven't read section 6 go *read it now*! It contains *very* important setup information.

7.1 Dial in and out modem configuration

For dialin and dialout use, you *have* to set up your modem a certain way (again, using AT commands on your modem):

```
E1          command echo ON
Q0          result codes are reported
V1          verbose ON
S0=0        never answer (uugetty handles this with the WAITFOR option)
```

If you don't set these correctly, your `INIT` string in your config file may fail, hosing the whole process. But, more on config files below...

```
&C1         DCD is on after connect only
&S0         DSR is always on
            DTR on/off resets modem (depends on manufacturer - RTFM)
```

These affect what your modem does when calls start and end.

If your modem does not support a stored profile, you can set these through the `INIT` string in your config file. See below. Some modems come with DIP switches that affect register settings. Be sure these are set correctly, too.

I have started a collection of modem setups for different types of modems. So far, I only have a few of them, if you would like to send me your working configuration, please do so! If you would like me to send you one of the configurations, just mail me and ask. I'm not listing them here due to space concerns. I have setups for Supra, Telebit T1600, USR Courier and Sportster, and Zoom 14.4/28.8 modems.

7.2 Installing `getty_ps`

By default, `getty_ps` will be configured to be Linux FSSTND (**FileSystem STaNDard**) compliant, which means that the binaries will be in `/sbin`, and the config files will be named `/etc/conf.{uu}getty.ttySN`. This is not apparant from the documentation! It will also expect lock files to go in `/var/lock`. Make sure you have the `/var/lock` directory.

If you don't want FSSTND compliance, binaries will go in `/etc`, config files will go in `/etc/default/{uu}getty.ttySN`, and lock file will go in `/usr/spool/uucp`. I recommend doing things this way if you are using UUCP, because Taylor UUCP will have problems if you move the lock files to where it isn't looking for them.

`getty_ps` also uses `syslogd` to log messages. See the man pages for `syslogd(1)` and `syslog.conf(5)` for setting up `syslogd`, if you don't have it running already. Messages are logged with priority LOG_AUTH, errors use LOG_ERR, and debugging uses LOG_DEBUG. If you don't want to use `syslogd` you can edit `tune.h` in the `getty_ps` source files to use a log file for messages instead, namely `/var/adm/getty.log` by default.

When you have decided if you want FSSTND, and `syslog`, edit `tune.h` and the `Makefile` in the `getty_ps` source directory to reflect you decisions. Now, install according to the instructions.

From this point on, all references to `getty` will refer to `getty_ps`. References to `uugetty` will refer to the `uugetty` that comes with the `getty_ps` package.

7.3 Setting up `uugetty`

For dialing into, and out from your modem, we want to use `uugetty`. `uugetty` does important lock file checking. Update `/etc/gettydefs` to include entries for modems (note that the entries point to each other, these are not for fixed speed):

```
# Modem entries
38400# B38400 CS8 # B38400 SANE -ISTRIP HUPCL #@S @L @B login: #19200
19200# B19200 CS8 # B19200 SANE -ISTRIP HUPCL #@S @L @B login: #9600
9600# B9600 CS8 # B9600 SANE -ISTRIP HUPCL #@S @L @B login: #2400
2400# B2400 CS8 # B2400 SANE -ISTRIP HUPCL #@S @L @B login: #1200
1200# B1200 CS8 # B1200 SANE -ISTRIP HUPCL #@S @L @B login: #300
300# B300 CS8 # B300 SANE -ISTRIP HUPCL #@S @L @B login: #38400
```

If you have a 9600 bps or faster modem, with data compression, you can lock your serial port speed and let the modem handle the transitions to other bps rates. Then, instead of the step down series of lines listed above, `/etc/gettydefs` only needs to contain one line for the modem:

```
# 38400 fixed speed
F38400# B38400 CS8 # B38400 SANE - ISTRIP HUPCL #@S @L @B login: #F38400
# 19200 fixed speed
F19200# B19200 CS8 # B19200 SANE -ISTRIP HUPCL #@S @L @B login: #F19200
# 9600 fixed speed
F9600# B9600 CS8 # B9600 SANE - ISTRIP HUPCL #@S @L @B login: #F9600
```

If you have your modem set up to do RTS/CTS hardware flow control, you can add CRTSCTS to the entries:

```
# 38400 fixed speed with hardware flow control
F38400# B38400 CS8 CRTSCTS # B38400 SANE -ISTRIP HUPCL CRTSCTS
  #@S @L @B login: #F38400
# 19200 fixed speed with hardware flow control
F19200# B19200 CS8 CRTSCTS # B19200 SANE - ISTRIP HUPCL CRTSCTS
  #@S @L @B login: #F19200
# 9600 fixed speed with hardware flow control
F9600# B9600 CS8 CRTSCTS # B9600 SANE -ISTRIP HUPCL CRTSCTS
  #@S @L @B login: #F9600
```

If you want, you can make `uugetty` print interesting things in the login banner. In my examples, I have the system name, the serial line, and the current bps rate. You can add other things:

```
@B    The current (evaluated at the time the @B is seen) bps rate.
@D    The current date, in MM/DD/YY.
@L    The serial line to which getty is attached.
@S    The system name.
@T    The current time, in HH:MM:SS (24-hour).
@U    The number of currently signed-on users.  This is a
      count of the number of entries in the /etc/utmp file
      that have a non-null ut_name field.
@V    The value of VERSION, as given in the defaults file.
To display a single '@' character, use either '\@' or '@@'.
```

Next, make sure that you have an outgoing and incoming device for the serial port your modem is on. If you have your modem on `ttyS3` you will need the `/dev/cua3`, and `/dev/ttyS3` devices. If you don't have the correct devices, see section 3.1.1 on how to create devices, and create the devices.

7.4 Customizing `uugetty`

There are lots of parameters you can tweak for each port you have. These are implemented in separate config files for each port. The file `/etc/conf.uugetty` will be used by *all* instances of `uugetty`, and `/etc/conf.uugetty.ttySN` will only be used by that one port. Sample default config files can be found with the `getty_ps` source files, which come with most Linux distributions. Due to space concerns, they are not listed here. Note that if you are using older versions of `getty` (older than 2.0.7e), or aren't using FSSTND, then the default file will be `/etc/default/uugetty.ttySN`. My `/etc/conf.uugetty.ttyS3` looks like this:

```
# sample uugetty configuration file for a Hayes compatible modem to allow
# incoming modem connections
#
# alternate lock file to check... if this lock file exists, then uugetty is
# restarted so that the modem is re-initialized
ALTLOCK=cua3
ALTLINE=cua3
# line to initialize
INITLINE=cua3
```

```
# timeout to disconnect if idle...
TIMEOUT=60
# modem initialization string...
# format: <expect> <send> ... (chat sequence)
INIT="" AT\r OK\r\n
WAITFOR=RING
CONNECT="" ATA\r CONNECT\s\A
# this line sets the time to delay before sending the login banner
DELAY=1
#DEBUG=010
```

Add the following line to your /etc/inittab, so that uugetty is run on your serial port (substituting in the correct information for your environment - port, speed, and default terminal type):

```
S3:456:respawn:/sbin/uugetty ttyS3 F38400 vt100
```

Restart init:

```
linux# init q
```

For the speed parameter in your inittab, you want to use the highest bps rate that your modem supports. Since there is no speed named 57600 or 115200, you must use the setserial program to set your serial port to a higher speed. See section 10 for doing this. Then, use 38400 bps in your inittab.

Now Linux will be watching your serial port for connections. Dial in from another site and login to you Linux system. Rejoice.

uugetty has a lot more options, see the man page for getty(1m) for a full description. Among other things there is a scheduling feature, and a ringback feature. RTFM :-).

7.5 US Robotics Notes

To get my USR Courier modem to reset correctly when DTR drops, I had to set &D2 and S13=1.

7.6 Supra Notes

Supra modems treat DCD differently than other modems. If you are using a Supra, you must set &C0 and *not* &C1. You must also set &D2 to handle DTR correctly.

8 How do I set up a terminal connected to my PC?

8.1 Hardware requirements

Make sure you have the right kind of cable. A null modem cable bought at a computer store will do it. But it must be a *null modem* cable! Make sure you are using your serial port, the male DB25 or the DB9, and not your parallel port.

At a minimum, you should have (for a DB25 connector):

```
TxD    Transmit Data      2 - 3      RxD    Receive Data
RxD    Receive Data       3 - 2      TxD    Transmit Data
SG     Signal Ground      7 - 7      SGD    Signal Ground
```

If you want to have hardware handshaking signals, you must have a full null modem cable:

```
FG    Frame Ground           1  -  1     FG    Frame Ground
TxD   Transmit Data          2  -  3     RxD   Receive Data
RxD   Receive Data           3  -  2     TxD   Transmit Data
RTS   Request To Send        4  -  5     CTS   Clear To Send
CTS   Clear To Send          5  -  4     RTS   Request To Send
DSR   Data Set Ready         6  - 20     DTR   Data Terminal Ready
SG    Signal Ground          7  -  7     SG    Signal Ground
DCD   Carrier Detect         8  - 20     DTR   Data Terminal Ready
DTR   Data Terminal Ready   20  -  6     DSR   Data Set Ready
DTR   Data Terminal Ready   20  -  8     DCD   Carrier Detect
```

If you have a DB9 connector on your serial port, try the following:

```
                            DB9    DB25
RxD   Receive Data           2  -  2     TxD   Transmit Data
TxD   Transmit Data          3  -  3     RxD   Receive Data
SG    Signal Ground          5  -  7     SG    Signal Ground
```

Alternatively, a full DB9-DB25 null modem cable:

```
                            DB9    DB25
DCD   Carrier Detect         1  - 20     DTR   Data Terminal Ready
RxD   Receive Data           2  -  2     TxD   Transmit Data
TxD   Transmit Data          3  -  3     RxD   Receive Data
DTR   Data Terminal Ready    4  -  6     DSR   Data Set Ready
DTR   Data Terminal Ready    4  -  8     DCD   Carrier Detect
SG    Signal Ground          5  -  7     SG    Signal Ground
DSR   Data Set Ready         6  - 20     DTR   Data Terminal Ready
RTS   Request To Send        7  -  5     CTS   Clear To Send
CTS   Clear To Send          8  -  4     RTS   Request To Send
(RI   Ring Indicator         9  - 22     RI    Ring Indicator)
```

If you are not using a full null modem cable, you might have to do the following trick: on each side of the connector, connect RTS and CTS together, and also connect DSR, DCD and DTR together. This way, when the computer or terminal wants a certain handshaking signal, it will get it (from itself).

Now that you have the right kind of cable, connect your terminal to your computer. If you can, tell you terminal to ignore modem control signals. Try using 9600 bps, 8 data bits, 1 stop bit, no parity bits for the terminal's setup.

8.2 Setting up getty

Install getty_ps as described in REFERENCE. Add an entry for getty to use for your terminal in /etc/gettydefs:

```
# 38400 bps Dumb Terminal entry
DT38400# B38400 CS8 CLOCAL # B38400 SANE -ISTRIP CLOCAL #@S @L login: #DT38400
# 19200 bps Dumb Terminal entry
DT19200# B19200 CS8 CLOCAL # B19200 SANE -ISTRIP CLOCAL #@S @L login: #DT19200
# 9600 bps Dumb Terminal entry
DT9600# B9600 CS8 CLOCAL # B9600 SANE -ISTRIP CLOCAL #@S @L login: #DT9600
```

If you want, you can make getty print interesting things in the login banner. In my examples, I have the system name and the serial line printed. You can add other things:

```
@B    The current (evaluated at the time the @B is seen) bps rate.
@D    The current date, in MM/DD/YY.
@L    The serial line to which getty is attached.
@S    The system name.
@T    The current time, in HH:MM:SS (24-hour).
@U    The number of currently signed-on users.  This is  a
      count of the number of entries in the /etc/utmp file
      that have a non-null ut_name field.
@V    The value of VERSION, as given in the defaults file.
To display a single '@' character, use either '\@' or '@@'.
```

Edit your /etc/inittab file to run getty on the serial port (substituting in the correct information for your environment - port, speed, and default terminal type):

```
S1:456:respawn:/sbin/getty ttyS1 DT9600 vt100
```

Restart init:

```
linux# init q
```

At this point, you should see a login prompt on your terminal. You may have to hit return to get the terminal's attention. Rejoice.

8.3   Notes on setting up a PC as a terminal

Many people set up other PCs as terminals connected to Linux boxen. For example, old 8088 or 286 PCs are perfect for this purpose. All you need is a DOS boot disk containing a version of DOS suitable for your terminal-PC, and a communications program for your terminal-PC to run. kermit works very well for this purpose. You can find precompiled versions of kermit for nearly every OS in existence at watsun.cc.columbia.edu:/pub/ftp/kermit. Other popular DOS comm programs such as telix and procomm will work equally well. Be sure to input correct serial port information into your terminal-PC's communications setup.

9   Can I use more than 2 serial devices?

You don't need to read this section, unless you want to use 3 or more serial devices... (assuming you don't have a multiport board).

Providing you have another spare serial port, yes, you can.

The number of serial ports you can use is limited by the number of interrupts (IRQ) and port I/O addresses we have to use. This is not a Linux limitation, but a limitation of the PC bus. Each serial devices must be assigned it's own interrupt and address. A serial device can be a serial port, an internal modem, or a multiport serial board.

Multiport serial boards are specially designed to have multiple serial ports that share the same IRQ for all serial ports on the board. Linux gets data from them by using a different I/O address for each port on the card.

9.1   Choosing serial device interrupts

Your PC will normally come with ttyS0 and ttyS2 at IRQ 4, and ttyS1 and ttyS3 at IRQ 3. To use more than 2 serial devices, you will have to give up an interrupt to use. A good choice is to reassign an interrupt from your parallel port. Your PC normally comes with IRQ 5 and IRQ 7 set up as interrupts for your parallel ports, but few people use 2 parallel ports. You can reassign one of the interrupts to a serial device, and still happily use a parallel port. You will need the `setserial` program to do this. In addition, you have to play with the jumpers on your boards, check the docs for your board. Set the jumpers to the IRQ you want for each port.

You will need to set things up so that there is one, and only one interrupt for each serial device. Here is how I set mine up in `/etc/rc.d/rc.local` - you should do it upon startup somewhere:

```
/etc/setserial /dev/cua0 irq 3      # my serial mouse
/etc/setserial /dev/cua1 irq 4      # my Wyse dumb terminal
/etc/setserial /dev/cua2 irq 5      # my Zoom modem
/etc/setserial /dev/cua3 irq 9      # my USR modem
```

Standard IRQ assignments:

```
IRQ  0    Timer channel 0
IRQ  1    Keyboard
IRQ  2    Cascade for controller 2
IRQ  3    Serial port 2
IRQ  4    Serial port 1
IRQ  5    Parallel port 2
IRQ  6    Floppy diskette
IRQ  7    Parallel port 1
IRQ  8    Real-time clock
IRQ  9    Redirected to IRQ2
IRQ 10    not assigned
IRQ 11    not assigned
IRQ 12    not assigned
IRQ 13    Math coprocessor
IRQ 14    Hard disk controller
IRQ 15    not assigned
```

There is really no Right Thing to do when choosing interrupts. Just make sure it isn't being used by the motherboard, or your other cards. 2, 3, 4, 5, or 7 is a good choice. "not assigned" means that currently nothing standard uses these IRQs. Also note that IRQ 2 is the same as IRQ 9. You can call it either 2 or 9, the serial driver is very understanding.

If you have a serial card with a 16-bit bus connector, you can also use IRQ 10, 11, 12 or 15.

Just make sure you don't use IRQ 0, 1, 6, 8, 13 or 14! These are used by your mother board. You will make her very unhappy by taking her IRQs.

9.2   Setting serial device addresses

Next, you must set the port address. Check the manual on your board for the jumper settings. Like interrupts, there can only be one serial device at each address. Your ports will usually come configured as follows:

```
ttyS0 address 0x3f8
ttyS1 address 0x2f8
ttyS2 address 0x3e8
ttyS3 address 0x2e8
```

Choose which address you want each serial device to have and set the jumpers accordingly. I have my modem on `ttyS3`, my mouse on `ttyS0`, and my terminal on `ttyS2`.

When you reboot, Linux should see your serial ports at the address you set them. The IRQ Linux sees may not correspond to the IRQ you set with the jumpers. Don't worry about this. Linux does not do any IRQ detection when it boots, because IRQ detection is dicey and can be fooled. Use `setserial` to tell Linux what IRQ the port is using.

10 How do I set up my serial ports for higher speeds? What speed should I use with my modem?

This section should help you figure out what speed to use when using your modem with a communications program, or with a `getty` program.

- If you have something slower than a 9600 bps (V.32) modem, set your speed to the highest speed your modem supports. For example 300, 1200, or 2400 bps.

- If you have a 9600 bps (V.32) modem, with V.42bis data compression. use 38400 as your speed. V.42bis compression has a *theoretical* rate of 4:1, thus "4 * 9600 = 38400".

- If you have a 14400 bps (V.32bis) modem, with V.42bis data compression, use `setserial`, with the `spd_hi` flag to configure your serial port to use 57600 bps (4 * 14400 = 57600). Use the `spd_vhi` flag if you have a 28800 (V.FC or V.34) modem (4 * 28800 = 115200).

  Then, use 38400 as the speed in your comm program, or `inittab`. This is now the high speed you have set. There is no speed named 57600 or 115200 (although support was added in 1.1.65 and will be used soon). Make sure you have 16550A UARTs :-).

Put your modifications into `/etc/rc.d/rc.serial` or `/etc/rc.d/rc.local` so that they are done at startup. In my `/etc/rc.d/rc.local`, I set `ttyS3` to 115200 bps by doing:

```
/sbin/setserial /dev/cua3 spd_vhi
```

11 Communications programs and utilities

Once you get everything working, you may want to check out these more advanced programs, all are available on the usual FTP sites, if they didn't come with your distribution.

- `ecu` - a communications program

- `minicom` - `telix`-like comm program

- `procomm` - procommish comm program with zmodem

- `seyon` - X based comm program

- `xc` - xcomm communications package

These programs offer more features than just `kermit` alone, including telephone directories, auto-dialing and so on.

- Another useful program is `term`. `term` multiplexes many connections over one serial line. It is somewhat similar to SLIP, and offers some SLIP functionality. These include `rlogin`, `telnet`, `ftp`, `finger`, `rdate`, `xmosaic` and `tredir`. `tredir` is a special program which lets you redirect remote TCP/IP ports to your local machine. This allows for remote NNTP, and SMTP access. The good thing about `term` is that is runs entirely in user space, meaning it requires no kernel support, or sysadmin support (like SLIP does).

- `screen` is another multi-session program. This one behaves like the virtual consoles.

- `callback` is a program that will have your modem call you back immediately from where you just called.

- `mgetty+fax` handles FAX stuff, and provides an alternate `getty`

- ZyXEL is a control program for ZyXEL U-1496 modems. It handles dialin, dialout, dial back security, FAXing, and voice mailbox functions.

- Other things can be found on `sunsite.unc.edu:/pub/Linux/system/Serial` and `sunsite.unc.edu:/pub/Linux/apps/comm` or one of the many mirrors. These are the directories where all the serial type things are kept.

12 Serial Tips

Here are some serial tips you might find helpful...

12.1 `kermit` and zmodem

To use zmodem with `kermit`, add the following to your `.kermrc`:

```
define rz !rz < /dev/cua3 > /dev/cua3
define sz !sz \%0 > /dev/cua3 < /dev/cua3
```

Be sure to put in the correct port your modem is on. Then, to use it, just type `rz` or `sz  <filename>` at the `kermit` prompt.

12.2 Setting terminal types automagically

To set your terminal type automagically when you log in, add the terminal type to the entry in `/etc/inittab`. If I have a vt100 terminal on `ttyS1`, I would add "vt100" to the `getty` command:

```
S1:456:respawn:/sbin/getty ttyS1 DT9600 vt100
```

You can also get `tset` from `sunsite.unc.edu:/pub/Linux/system/Terminal-management` or a mirror site. See the docs that come with `tset` to learn how to use it. `tset` can establish terminal characteristics when you log in, and doesn't depend on any defaults.

12.3 Color `ls` on serial connections

If `ls` is screwing up your terminal emulation with the color feature, turn it off. `ls --color`, and `ls --colour` all use the color feature. Some installations have `ls` set to use color by default. Check `/etc/profile` and `/etc/csh.cshrc` for `ls` aliases. You can also alias `ls` to `ls --no-color`, if you don't want to change the system defaults.

12.4 Printing to a printer connected to a terminal

There is a program called `vtprint` that will do this, written by Garrett D'Amore `garrett@sdsu.edu`. It   is   available   from `ftp.sdsu.edu:/pub/vtprint`, and also from `http://www.sdsu.edu/~garrett/`. The following is from the `README` file that comes with the program:

vtprint is a program that allows users to print from a remote UNIX host to a printer attached to their local terminal or emulator, which makes it great for printing files at home, etc. (It only does text files, though.)

12.5   Can Linux configure the serial devices automagically?

Yes. To get Linux to detect and set up the serial devices automatically on startup, add the line:

```
/sbin/setserial /dev/cuaN auto_irq skip_test autoconfig
```

to your `/etc/rc.d/rc.local` or `/etc/rc.d/rc.serial` file. Do this for every serial port you want to auto configure. Be sure to give a device name that really does exist on your machine.

12.5.1   Notes for multiport boards

For board addresses, and IRQs, look at the `rc.serial` that comes with the `setserial` program. It has a lot of detail on multiport boards, including I/O addresses and device names.

13   Linux FTP sites

```
sunsite.unc.edu [152.2.22.81]:/pub/Linux        (NC, USA)
tsx-11.mit.edu [18.172.1.2]:/pub/linux          (MA, USA)
nic.funet.fi [128.214.6.100]:/pub/OS/Linux      (Finland, Europe)
```

`sunsite.unc.edu` is the official Linux FTP site, and has many mirrors. Please use a mirror site if at all possible to save `sunsite` some traffic.

`sunsite` mirrors (`sunsite.unc.edu:/pub/Linux/MIRRORS`):

```
* CONTINENT
- COUNTRY
   CITY... FTP Site    Directory
--------------------------------------------------------------------
* Africa
- None so far
* Asia
- Thailand
   Bangkok... ftp.nectec.or.th /pub/mirrors/linux/
- Hong Kong
   ... ftp.cs.cuhk.hk /pub/Linux/
- Republic of Singapore
   Singapore... ftp.nus.sg /pub/unix/Linux/
- Japan
   Unknown... ftp.spin.ad.jp /pub/linux/sunsite.unc.edu/
* Australia
   Adelaide... smug.student.adelaide.edu.au /pub/sunsite.linux/
   Brisbane... ftp.dstc.edu.au /pub/linux/
* Europe
- Austria
   Graz... ftp.tu-graz.ac.at /pub/Linux/
- Czech Republic
   Brno... ftp.fi.muni.cz /pub/UNIX/linux/
   Prague... pub.vse.cz /pub/386-unix/linux/
- France
   Angers... ftp.univ-angers.fr /pub/linux/
   Nancy... ftp.loria.fr /pub/linux/sunsite/
- Germany (Deutschland)
   Aachen... ftp.dfv.rwth-aachen.de /pub/linux/sunsite/
   Dortmund... ftp.germany.eu.net /pub/os/Linux/Mirror.SunSITE/
   Dresden... ftp.tu-dresden.de /pub/Linux/sunsite/
   Erlangen... ftp.uni-erlangen.de /pub/Linux/MIRROR.sunsite/
```

```
          Mannheim... ftp.ba-mannheim.de /pub/linux/mirror.sunsite/
          Paderborn... ftp.uni-paderborn.de /pub/Mirrors/sunsite.unc.edu/
          Rostock... ftp.uni-rostock.de /Linux/sunsite/
          Stuttgart... ftp.rus.uni-stuttgart.de /pub/unix/systems/linux/MIRROR.sunsite/
          Tuebingen... ftp.uni-tuebingen.de /pub/linux/Mirror.sunsite/
          Ulm... ftp.rz.uni-ulm.de /pub/mirrors/linux/sunsite/
          Unknown... ftp.gwdg.de /pub/linux/mirrors/sunsite/
      - Hungary
          Budapest... ftp.kfki.hu /pub/linux/
      - Italy
          Pisa... cnuce-arch.cnr.it /pub/Linux/
      - Switzerland
          Zurich... ftp.switch.ch /mirror/linux/
      - Turkey (Turkiye)
          Ankara... ftp.metu.edu.tr /pub/linux/sunsite/
      - United Kingdom
          Coventry... ftp.maths.warwick.ac.uk /mirrors/linux/sunsite.unc-mirror/
          London... src.doc.ic.ac.uk /packages/linux/sunsite.unc-mirror/
          Mildenhall... ftp.dungeon.com /pub/linux/sunsite-mirror/
    * North America
      - United States
          Atlanta, GA... ftp.cc.gatech.edu /pub/linux/
          Chapel Hill, NC... sunsite.unc.edu /pub/Linux/
          Fayetteville, AR... ftp.engr.uark.edu /pub/linux/sunsite/
          Flagstaff, AZ... ftp.infomagic.com /pub/mirrors/linux/sunsite/
          Midwest... ftp.wit.com /systems/unix/linux/
          Mt. Pleasant, MI... ftp.cps.cmich.edu /pub/linux/sunsite/
          Rochester, NY... ftp.rge.com /pub/linux/sunsite/
          Salt Lake City, UT... ftp.pht.com /mirrors/linux/sunsite/
          Urbana, IL... mrcnext.cso.uiuc.edu /pub/linux/
          Unknown... ftp.linux.org /pub/mirrors/sunsite/
          Unknown... ftp.orst.edu /pub/mirrors/sunsite.unc.edu/linux/
          Unknown... ftp.iquest.com /pub/linux/sunsite/
          Unknown... ftp.yggdrasil.com mirrors/sunsite/
    * South America
      - Chile
          ftp.inf.utfsm.cl                  /pub/Linux
    * Unknown
      - If you know where these sites are, please mail ewt@sunsite.unc.edu.
          ... ftp.linux.org /pub/mirrors/sunsite/
          ... ftp.gwdg.de /pub/linux/mirrors/sunsite/
          ... ftp.orst.edu /pub/mirrors/sunsite.unc.edu/linux/
          ... ftp.iquest.com /pub/linux/sunsite/
          ... ftp.spin.ad.jp /pub/linux/sunsite.unc.edu/
          ... ftp.yggdrasil.com mirrors/sunsite/
```

These FTP sites support anonymous FTP, which means login as `ftp`, and password as your email address (ie `logname@yourhost.yourdomain`).

14 One step further...

This section is not required reading, but may give you some further insight into Unix, and the world of telecommunications.

14.1 What are lock files?

Lock file are simply a file saying that a particular device is in use. They are kept in `/usr/spool/uucp`, or `/var/lock`. Linux lock files are named `LCK..`*name*, where *name* is either a device name, or a UUCP site name. Certain processes create these locks so that they can have exclusive access to devices, for instance if you dial out on your modem, a lock will appear telling other processes that someone is using the modem already. Locks mainly contain the PID of the process that has locked the device. Most programs look at the lock, and try to determine if that lock is still valid by checking the process table for the process that has locked the device. If the lock is found to be valid, the program (should) exit. If not, some programs remove the stale lock, and use the device, creating their own lock in the process. Other programs just exit and tell you that the device is in use.

14.2 "baud" vs. "bps"

"baud" and "bps" are prehaps one of the most misused terms in the computing/telecom field. Many people use these terms interchangeably, when in fact they are not!

baud

> The baud rate is a measure of how many times per second the signal sent by a modem (**mo**dulator-**dem**odulator) changes. For example, a baud rate of 1200 implies one signal change every 833 microseconds. Common baud rates are 50, 75, 110, 300, 600, 1200, and 2400. Most high speed modems run at 2400 baud. Because of the bandwidth limitations on voice-grade phone lines, baud rates greater than 2400 are harder to achieve, and only work under very pristine phone line quality. "baud" is named after Emile Baudot, the inventor of the asynchronous telegraph printer.

bps

> The bps rate is a measure of how many bits per second are transmitted. Common bps rates are 50, 75, 110, 300, 1200, 2400, 9600, ... 115200. With modems using V.42bis compression (4:1 compression), *theoretical* bps rates are possible up to 115200. This is what most people mean when they misuse the word "baud".

So, if high speed modems are running at 2400 baud, how can they send 14400 bps? The modems achive a bps greater than their baud rate by encoding a number of bits per baud. Thus, when 2 or more bits are encoded per baud, the bps rate exceeds the baud rate. If your modem connects at 14400 bps, it's going to be sending 6 bits per baud.

How did this confusion start? Well, back when today's low speed modems were yesterday's high speed modems, the bps rate actually did equal the baud rate. One bit would be encoded per baud. People would use bps and baud interchangeably, because they were the same number. For example, a 300 bps modem also had a baud rate of 300. This all changed when faster modems came around, and the bit rate exceeded the baud rate.

14.3   What are UARTs? How do they affect performance?

UARTs (Universal Asyncronous Receiver Transmitter) are chips on your PC serial card. Their purpose is to convert data to bits, send the bits down the serial line, and then rebuild the data again on the other end. UARTs deal with data in byte sized pieces, which is conveniently also the size of ASCII characters.

Say you have a terminal hooked up to your PC. When you type a character, the terminal gives that character to it's transmitter (also a UART of some sort). The transmitter sends that byte out onto the serial line, one bit at a time, at a specific rate. On the PC end, the receiving UART takes all the bits and rebuilds the byte and puts it in a buffer.

There are two different types of UARTs. You have probably heard of dumb UARTs - the 8250 and 16450, and FIFO UARTs - the 16550A. To understand their differences, first let's examine what happens when a UART has sent or received a byte.

The UART itself can't do anything with the data, it just sends and receives it. The CPU gets an interrupt from the serial device every time a byte has been sent or received. The CPU then moves the received byte out of the UART's buffer and into memory somewhere, or gives the UART another byte to send. The 8250 and 16450 UARTs only have a 1 byte buffer. That means, that every time 1 byte is sent or received, the CPU is interrupted. At low rates, this is OK. But, at high transfer rates, the CPU gets so busy dealing with the UART, that is doesn't have time to tend to other tasks. In some cases, the CPU does not get around to servicing the interrupt in time, and the byte is overwritten, because they are coming in so fast.

That's where the 16550A UARTs are useful. These chips come with 16 byte FIFOs. This means that it can receive or transmit up to 16 bytes before it has to interrupt the CPU. Not only can it wait, but the CPU then can transfer all 16 bytes at a time. Although the interrupt threshold is seldom set at 16, this is still a significant advantage over the other UARTs, which only have the 1 byte buffer. The CPU receives less interrupts, and is free to do other things. Data is not lost, and everyone is happy. (There is also a 16550 UART, but it is treated as a 16450)

In general, the 8250 and 16450 UARTs should be fine for speeds up to 38400 bps. At speeds greater than 38400 bps, you might start seeing data loss, and a reduction in interactive response time. Other PC operating systems (definition used loosely here), like DOS aren't multitasking, so they might be able to cope better with 8250 or 16450s. That's why some people don't see data loss, until they switch to Linux.

Non-UART, and intelligent multiport boards use DSP chips to do additional buffering and control, thus relieving the CPU even more. For example, the Cyclades Cyclom, and Stallion EasyIO boards use a Cirrus Logic CD-1400 RISC chip.

Keep in mind that these dumb UART types are not bad, they just aren't good for high speeds. You should have no problem connecting a terminal, or a mouse to these UARTs. But, for a high speed modem, the 16550A is definately a must.

You can buy serial cards with the 16550A UARTs for a little more money, just ask your dealer what type of UART is on the card. Or if you want to upgrade your existing card, you can simply purchase 16550A chips and replace your existing 16450 UARTs. They are pin-to-pin compatible. Some cards come with socketed UARTs for this purpose, if not you can solder. Note, that you'll probably save yourself a lot of trouble by just getting a new card, if you've got the money, they are under US$ 50.

14.4   What's the real difference between the `/dev/cuaN` and `/dev/ttySN` devices?

The only difference is the way that the devices are opened. The dialin devices `/dev/ttySN` are opened in blocking mode, until CD is asserted (ie someone connects). So, when someone wants to use a `/dev/cuaN` device, there is no conflict with a program watching the `/dev/ttySN` device.

The distinction is made to allow dialin and dialout use of the same serial port.

15   Troubleshooting

15.1   I keep getting "line *NNN* of inittab invalid".

Make sure you are using the correct syntax for your version of `init`. The different `init`'s that are out there use different syntax in the `/etc/inittab` file. Make sure you are using the correct syntax for your version of `getty`.

15.2   When I try to dial out, it says "/dev/cua*N*: Device or resource busy".

This problem can arise when DCD or DTR are not set correctly. DCD should only be set when there is an actual connection (ie someone is dialed in), not when `getty` is watching the port. Check to make sure that your modem is configured to only set DCD when there is a connection. DTR should be set whenever something is using, or watching the line, like `getty`, `kermit`, or some other comm program.

Another common cause of "device busy" errors, is that you set up your serial port with an interrupt already taken by something else. As each device initializes, it asks Linux for permission to use its hardware interrupt. Linux keeps track of which interrupt is assigned to whom, and if your interrupt is already taken, your device won't be able to initialize properly. The device really doesn't have much of any way to tell you that this happened, except that when you try to use it, it will return a "device-busy" error. Check the interrupts on all of your cards (serial, ethernet, SCSI, etc.). Look for IRQ conflicts.

15.3 I keep getting "Id SN respawning too fast: disabled for 5 minutes".

Make sure your modem is configured correctly. Look at registers E and Q. This can occur when your modem is chatting with `getty`.

Make sure you are calling `getty` correctly from your `/etc/inittab`. Using the wrong syntax or device names will cause serious problems.

This can also happen when the `uugetty` initialization is failing. Go to the "`getty` or `uugetty` still doesn't work" question.

15.4 Serial devices are slow or serial devices can only send in one direction.

You probably have an IRQ conflict. Make sure there are no IRQs being shared. Check all your cards (serial, ethernet, SCSI, etc...). Make sure the jumper settings, and the `setserial` parameters are correct for all your serial devices.

15.5 My modem is hosed after someone hangs up, or `uugetty` doesn't respawn.

This can happen when your modem doesn't reset when DTR is dropped. I saw my RD and SD LEDs go nuts when this happened to me. You need to have your modem reset. Most Hayes compatible modems do this with `&D3`, but on my USR Courier, I had to set `&D2` and `S13=1`. Check your modem manual.

15.6 I have my terminal connected to my PC, but after I type in a login name, it just locks up.

You probably don't have CLOCAL in your `/etc/gettydefs` entry for the terminal, and you're probably not using a full null modem cable. You need CLOCAL, which tells Linux to ignore modem control signals. Here is what it should look like:

```
# 38400 bps Dumb Terminal entry
DT38400# B38400 CS8 CLOCAL # B38400 SANE -ISTRIP CLOCAL #@S @L login: #D38400
# 19200 bps Dumb Terminal entry
DT19200# B19200 CS8 CLOCAL # B19200 SANE -ISTRIP CLOCAL #@S @L login: #DT19200
# 9600 bps Dumb Terminal entry
DT9600# B9600 CS8 CLOCAL # B9600 SANE -ISTRIP CLOCAL #@S @L login: #DT9600
```

Next, `kill` the `getty` process so a new one will be spawned with the new entry.

15.7 At high speeds, my modem loses data.

If you are trying to run your modem at > 19200 bps, and you don't have 16550A UARTs, you should upgrade them. See section 14.3 about UARTs.

15.8 On startup, Linux doesn't report the serial devices the way I have them configured.

This is true. Linux does not do any IRQ detection on startup, it only does serial device detection. Thus, disregard what it says about the IRQ, because it's just assuming the standard IRQs. This is done, because IRQ detection is unreliable, and can be fooled.

So, even though I have my `ttyS2` set at IRQ 5, I still see

```
Jan 23 22:25:28 misfits vmunix: tty02 at 0x03e8 (irq = 4) is a 16550A
```

You have to use `setserial` to tell Linux the IRQ you are using.

15.9 `rz` and/or `sz` don't work when I call my Linux box on my modem.

If Linux looks for `/dev/modem` when you try to transfer files, look at `/etc/profile`, and `/etc/csh.cshrc`. There are a bunch of aliases defined there on some distributions, most notably Slack-ware. These aliases mess up the zmodem programs. Take them out, or correct them.

15.10 My screen is printing funny looking characters.

This happens on virtual consoles when you send binary data to your screen, or sometimes on serial connections. The way to fix this is to type `echo ^v^[c`. For the control-character-impaired, thats `echo <ctrl>v<esc>c`.

15.11 `getty` or `uugetty` still doesn't work.

There is a DEBUG option that comes with `getty_ps`. Edit your config file `/etc/conf.{uu}getty.ttySN` and add DEBUG=*NNN*. Where *NNN* is one of the following combination of numbers according to what you are trying to debug:

```
D_OPT    001        option settings
D_DEF    002        defaults file processing
D_UTMP   004        utmp/wtmp processing
D_INIT   010        line initialization (INIT)
D_GTAB   020        gettytab file processing
D_RUN    040        other runtime diagnostics
D_RB     100        ringback debugging
D_LOCK   200        uugetty lockfile processing
D_SCH    400        schedule processing
D_ALL    777        everything
```

Setting `DEBUG=010` is a good place to start.

If you are running `syslogd`, debugging info will appear in your log files. If you aren't running `syslogd` info will appear in `/tmp/getty:ttySN` for debugging `getty` and `/tmp/uugetty:ttySN` for uugetty, and in `/var/adm/getty.log`. Look at the debugging info and see what is going on. Most likely, you will need to tune some of the parameters in your config file, and reconfigure your modem.

You could also try `mgetty`. Some people have better luck with it.

16 Contributions

There was no possible way to write this HOWTO alone. Although a lot of the HOWTO is my writing, I have rewritten many contributions to maintain continuity in the writing style and flow. Thanks to everyone who has contributed or commented, the list of people has gotten too long to list (somewhere over fifty). Special thanks to Ted T'so for answering questions about the serial drivers, Kris Gleason who maintains `getty_ps`, and Gert Doering who maintains `mgetty`.

END OF Serial-HOWTO

Part XXXIX

The Linux Sound HOWTO

This document describes sound support for Linux. It lists the supported sound hardware, describes how to configure the kernel drivers, and answers frequently asked questions. The intent is to bring new users up to speed more quickly and reduce the amount of traffic in the usenet news groups.

Contents

1 Introduction

This is the Linux Sound HOWTO document. It is intended as a quick reference covering everything you need to know to install and configure sound support under Linux. Frequently asked questions about sound under Linux are answered, and references are given to some other sources of information on a variety of topics related to computer generated sound and music.

The scope is limited to the aspects of sound cards pertaining to Linux. See the other documents listed in the *Other Sources of Information* section for more general information on sound cards and computer sound and music generation.

1.1 Acknowledgments

Much of this information came from the `Readme` files provided with the sound driver source code, by Hannu Savolainen (`hannu@voxware.pp.fi`). Thanks go to Hannu and the many other people who developed the Linux kernel sound drivers and utilities.

Thanks to the Linuxdoc-SGML package, this HOWTO is now available in several formats, including HTML hypertext (Mosaic), PostScript, and plain ASCII, all generated from a common source file.

1.2   Revision History

Version 1.1

first version; posted to SOUND channel of Linux activists mailing list only

Version 1.2

minor updates; first version available on archive sites

Version 1.3

converted to SGML; now available in several formats using Matt Welsh's Linuxdoc-SGML tools; appearance changed due to new format, only minor changes to content

Version 1.4

minor tweaking of SGML; added answer on PAS16 and Adaptec1542A SCSI adaptor incompatibilities

Version 1.5

2.5a sound driver is now in 1.1 kernel distribution; note on GUS-MAX support; other minor updates

Version 1.6

added info on "no space on device" error; added note that Hacker's Guide is in a "hidden" directory; added question on bidirectional mode; info on "device busy" errors; other minor changes

Version 1.7

added info on ASP and AWE32; VoxWare 2.9 is available; answer to question on using IRQ2; references to Sound and SCSI HOWTOs

Version 1.8

added question on errors under DOS; many minor things updated to match the version 2.90 sound driver; info on DOOM; answer on reducing noise

Version 1.9

questions on recording and clone cards

Version 1.10

mentioned that HOWTO is available on WWW, as printed copies, and translations; info on DMA conflict with QIC tape driver; info on Sound Galaxy NX Pro and Logitech BusMouse

1.3   New versions of this document

New versions of this document will be periodically posted to `comp.os.linux.announce`. They will also be uploaded to various anonymous ftp sites that archive such information including `sunsite.unc.edu:/pub/Linux/docs/HOWTO`.

Hypertext versions of this and other Linux HOWTOs are available on many World-Wide-Web sites. You can also buy printed copies from several vendors.

If your native language is not English, you may be able to obtain a translation of this document (French and Japanese translations are in progress).

1.4   Feedback

If you have any suggestions, corrections, or comments on the HOWTO, please send them to the author and I will try to incorporate them in the next release.

If you have sound related problems that are not answered in this HOWTO, feel free to send me a mail message and I will try to help.

1.5   Other Sources of Information

The Linux Sound User's Guide covers all of the user visible aspects of using sound under Linux in much more detail (approximately 40 pages). If you are interested in sound under Linux you should definitely get this document. The current version is ALPHA 0.1, and is available on `tsx-11.mit.edu` in the directory `/pub/linux/ALPHA/LDP`. I will continue to maintain the Sound-HOWTO as a concise guide for users who want to get sound up and running, or just find out what is required, without having to read the full user's guide.

If you have a sound card that supports a CD-ROM or SCSI interface, the Linux SCSI HOWTO and the Linux CD-ROM HOWTO have additional information that may be useful to you.

Hannu Savolainen has written a draft version of the *Hacker's Guide to VoxWare*. The latest version is draft 2, and can be found on `nic.funet.fi` in `/pub/OS/linux/ALPHA/sound`.

The following FAQs are regularly posted to the usenet newsgroup `news.announce` as well as being archived at the site `rtfm.mit.edu` in the directory `/pub/usenet/news.answers`:

```
PCsoundcards/generic-faq (Generic PC Soundcard FAQ)
PCsoundcards/soundcard-faq (comp.sys.ibm.pc.soundcard FAQ)
PCsoundcards/gravis-ultrasound/faq (Gravis UltraSound FAQ)
audio-fmts/part1 (Audio file format descriptions)
audio-fmts/part2 (Audio file format descriptions)
```

The FAQs also list several product specific mailing lists and archive sites. The following Usenet news groups discuss sound and/or music related issues:

```
alt.binaries.sounds.* (various groups for posting sound files)
alt.binaries.multimedia (for posting Multimedia files)
alt.sb.programmer (Soundblaster programming topics)
comp.multimedia (Multimedia topics)
comp.music (Computer music theory and research)
comp.sys.ibm.pc.soundcard.* (various IBM PC soundcard groups)
```

The Linux Activists mailing list has a SOUND channel. To find out how to join the mailing list, send mail to `linux-activists-request@joker.cs.hut.fi`.

The files `Readme`, `Readme.linux`, and `CHANGELOG` included with the kernel sound driver source code contain useful information about the sound card drivers. These can typically be found in the directory `/usr/src/linux/drivers/sound`.

The *Linux Software Map* (LSM) is an invaluable reference for locating Linux software. Searching the LSM for keywords such as *sound* is a good way to identify applications related to sound hardware. The LSM can be found on various anonymous FTP sites, including `sunsite.unc.edu:/pub/Linux/docs/LSM.gz`.

1.6   Version Information

At time of writing the latest Linux sound driver was version 2.90-2 and was included in the Linux kernel version 1.1.50 (and should be the same in Linux 1.2.0). This is a pre-release version of the upcoming version 3.0 driver which has a number of new features not in previous versions, some of which are disabled. While version 2.90 appears to be quite reliable, if you want a more stable driver you may prefer to use the version 2.5a sound driver provided in kernel revisions 1.1.10 through 1.1.30.

The author of the sound driver, Hannu Savolainen, typically also makes available newer BETA releases of the sound driver as kernel patches before they are included as part of the standard Linux kernel distribution.

2   Supported Sound Hardware

2.1   Sound Cards

The following sound cards are supported by the Linux kernel:

- Roland MPU-401 MIDI interface

- AdLib

- SoundBlaster (version 1 and 2) and compatibles, including ThunderBoard and ATI Stereo F/X

- SoundBlaster Pro (version 1 and 2)

- Sound Galaxy NX Pro (in its compatibility mode with SoundBlaster Pro 2.0 and support for its special mixer)

- SoundBlaster 16

- ProAudioSpectrum 16 (and the compatible Logitech SoundMan 16)

- Advanced Gravis UltraSound (GUS)

- GUS MAX (2.9 driver and later)

- Microsoft Sound System (2.9 driver and later)

- Personal Sound System (2.9 driver and later)

Other sound cards that are claimed to be compatible with one of the supported sound cards *may* work if they are hardware (i.e. register level) compatible. Some cards described as "100% SoundBlaster compatible" are *not* register compatible.

The Sound Galaxy NX Pro is supported as a SoundBlaster compatible. Answer "yes" to the question "Do you want support for the mixer of SG NX Pro" when the sound driver is configured (in versions prior to 2.9 you must manually add #define __SGNXPRO__ to the sound driver local.h file).

Note that if you have a Sound Galaxy NX Pro *and* a Logitech Busmouse, you *must* configure the card (using the SGPFIG utility on the driver diskettes) to use base address 0x240 in order to operate your mouse. The SGNXPRO has a Covox Speech Thing compatibility mode which has its control register at the base+0x01C which is the Logitech Busmouse control register address when the SGNXPRO base address is set to 0x220 (thanks to Matti Aarnio (mea@utu.fi) for this information).

The Linux kernel supports the SCSI port provided on some sound cards (e.g. ProAudioSpectrum 16). There is also support for CD-ROM drives attached to the Soundblaster Pro and SoundBlaster 16 CD-ROM port (see the file /usr/src/linux/drivers/block/README.sbpcd).

A loadable kernel module to support joystick ports, including those provided on some sound cards, is also available.

Note that the kernel SCSI, CD-ROM, and sound drivers are completely independent of each other.

2.2   PC Speaker

An alternate sound driver is available that requires no additional sound hardware; it uses the internal PC speaker. It is mostly software compatible with the sound card driver, but, as might be expected, provides much lower quality output and has much more CPU overhead. The results seem to vary, being dependent on the characteristics of the individual loudspeaker. For more information, see the documentation provided with the release.

The current version is 0.7, and can be found at site sunsite.unc.edu in the file /pub/Linux/kernel/patches/console/pcsndrv-0.7.tar.gz.

2.3   Parallel Port

Another option is to build a digital to analog converter using a parallel printer port. This provides better sound quality but still has a lot of CPU overhead. The PC sound driver package mentioned above supports this, and includes instructions for building the necessary hardware.

3   Configuring Linux for Sound Support

Configuring Linux to support sound involves the following steps:

1. Installing the sound card.

2. Configuring and building the kernel for sound support.

3. Creating the device files.

4. Testing the installation.

3.1   Installing the Sound Card

To install the card, follow the instructions provided by the manufacturer. Be sure to note down the jumper settings for IRQ, DMA channel, etc. If you are unsure, use the factory defaults. Try to avoid conflicts with other devices (e.g. ethernet cards, SCSI host adaptors, serial and parallel ports) if possible.

3.2   Configuring the Kernel

If you are using a recent kernel (0.99pl14 or later), the sound drivers are included with the kernel release. Follow the usual procedure for building the kernel. When you run `make config`, a configuration program will ask you what sound card options you want. Carefully read the information displayed by this program.

If you are upgrading from an older sound driver, make sure that the files `/usr/include/sys/soundcard.h` and `/usr/include/sys/ultrasound.h` are symbolic links to the corresponding files in `/usr/include/linux`, or that they simply contain the lines `#include <linux/soundcard.h>` and `#include <linux/ultrasound.h>`, respectively.

It's good idea to read the `Readme` files in the kernel `drivers/sound` directory since there could be some last minute information. The file `CHANGELOG` contains a list of enhancements and new features since the previous version.

Particularly with the 2.90 sound driver, read this documentation to be aware of potential incompatibilities with the older versions of sound drivers.

3.3   Creating the Device Files

The first time the kernel sound driver is configured, you need to create the sound device files. The easiest way to do this is to cut the short shell script from the end of the file `Readme.linux` (or possibly `Readme`) in the directory `/usr/src/linux/drivers/sound`, and run it as root.

If your device entries already exist, you might want to ensure they are correct, e.g. `/dev/audio` should have major and minor device numbers 14 and 4. If they are not, or if you are in doubt, run the above script and it will replace any existing entries with correct ones.

Some older Linux distributions provided install scripts which created incorrect sound device files. You may also have a `/dev/MAKEDEV` script for creating device files. Using the script included with the kernel sound driver is preferred since it should always be up to date with the latest supported sound devices.

3.4   Testing the Installation

You can now follow these steps to verify the sound hardware and software:

1. Reboot with the new kernel.

Follow your usual procedure for installing and rebooting the new kernel (keep the old kernel around in case of problems, of course).

2. Verify that the sound card is recognized during kernel initialization.

Check for a message such as the following on powerup (if they scroll by too quickly to read, you may be able to retrieve them with the "dmesg" command):

```
snd2 <SoundBlaster Pro 3.2> at 0x220 irq 5 drq 1
snd1 <Yamaha OPL-3 FM> at 0x388 irq 0 drq 0
```

This should match your sound card type and jumper settings.

The driver may also display some error messages and warnings during boot. Watch for these when booting the first time after configuring the sound driver.

If no sound card is detected when booting, here are some possible reasons:

- the configuration of the driver is incorrect and the driver was not able to detect your card in the given I/O address

- the sound driver was configured to be inactive or you booted with an old kernel (a common error).

3. Check the device file /dev/sndstat.

Reading the sound driver status device file should provide additional information on whether the sound card driver initialized properly. Sample output should look something like this:

```
% cat /dev/sndstat

Sound Driver:2.90-2 (Fri Aug 26 20:08:45 EDT 1994 root@fizzbin.ca)
Config options: 31402

Installed drivers:
Type 1: OPL-2/OPL-3 FM
Type 2: SoundBlaster

Card config:
SoundBlaster at 0x220 irq 5 drq 1
OPL-2/OPL-3 FM at 0x388 irq 0 drq 0

PCM devices:
0: SoundBlaster Pro 3.2

Synth devices:
0: Yamaha OPL-3

Midi devices:

MIDI Timers:
0: System Timer

1 mixer(s) installed
```

If the cat command displays "No such device", the sound driver is not active in the kernel. Make sure that you booted with the newly compiled kernel.

If the output contains no devices (PCM, Synth or MIDI), your soundcard was not detected. Verify that the "HW config" section contains correct information.

4. Play a simple sound file.

Get hold of a sample sound file, and send it to the sound device as a basic check of sound output, e.g.

```
% cat endoftheworld >/dev/dsp
% cat crash.au >/dev/audio
```

(Make sure you don't omit the ">" in the commands above).

Some sample sound files can be obtained from the file snd-data-0.1.tar.Z.

5. Verify sound recording.

If you have sound input capability, you can do a quick test of this using commands such as the following:

```
# record 4 seconds of audio from microphone
% dd bs=8k count=4 </dev/audio >sample.au
# play back sound
% cat sample.au >/dev/audio
```

If these tests pass, you can be reasonably confident that the sound hardware and software are working. If you experience problems, read the FAQ section of this document.

4   Applications Supporting Sound

Because *The Linux Sound User's Guide* describes the available Linux applications in detail, I will only give here a sample of the types of applications that you likely want if you have a sound card under Linux.

As a minimum, you will likely want to obtain the following sound applications:

- audio file format conversion utility (e.g. Sox)

- mixer utility (e.g. aumix or xmix)

- digitized file player/recorder (e.g. play or wavplay)

- MOD file player (e.g. tracker)

- MIDI file player (e.g. mp)

There are text-based as well as GUI-based versions of most of these tools. There are also some more esoteric applications (e.g. speech synthesis) that you may wish to try.

5   Answers To Frequently Asked Questions

This section answers some of the questions that have been commonly asked on the Usenet news groups and mailing lists.

5.1   What are the various sound device files?

These are the most "standard" device file names, some Linux distributions may use slightly different names.

/dev/audio

  Sun workstation compatible audio device (only a partial implementation, does not support Sun ioctl interface, just u-law encoding)

/dev/dsp

  digital sampling device

/dev/mixer

  sound mixer

/dev/mixer1

  second sound mixer

/dev/patmgr0

  Patch Manager (not implemented)

/dev/patmgr1

  Patch Manager (not implemented)

/dev/sequencer

  low level MIDI, FM, and GUS access

/dev/sequencer2

  high level sequencer interface (partially implemented)

/dev/midi00

  1st raw MIDI port

/dev/midi01

  2nd raw MIDI port

/dev/midi02

  3rd raw MIDI port

/dev/midi03

  4th raw MIDI port

/dev/sndstat

  displays sound driver status when read

/dev/audio1

  for second sound card

/dev/dsp1

  for second sound card

The PC speaker driver provides the following devices:

/dev/pcaudio

  equivalent to /dev/audio

/dev/pcsp

  equivalent to /dev/dsp

/dev/pcmixer

  equivalent to /dev/mixer

5.2   How can I play a sound sample?

Sun workstation (.au) sound files can be played by sending them to the `/dev/audio` device. Raw samples can be sent to `/dev/dsp`. Using a program such as `play` is preferable, as it will recognize most file types and set the sound card to the correct sampling rate, etc.

5.3   How can I record a sample?

Reading `/dev/audio` or `/dev/dsp` will return sampled data that can be redirected to a file. A program such as `vrec` makes it easier to control the sampling rate, duration, etc. You may also need a mixer program to select the appropriate input device.

5.4   Can I have more than one sound card?

Up to two sound cards is supported. It's possible to install a Gravis UltraSound or MPU-401 with a SoundBlaster, SoundBlaster Pro, SoundBlaster16 or ProAudioSpectrum16. It's *not* possible to have a ProAudioSpectrum16 and SoundBlaster at the same time (the PAS16 has an SB emulator in it). It's also not possible to have more than one card of the same type at the same time – for example, a GUS + GUS combination is not possible.

You can change the sound card configuration parameters at boot time using command line options from a boot loader such as LILO. See the kernel sound driver file `Readme.linux` for details.

5.5   Error: `No such file or directory` for sound devices

You need to create the sound driver device files. See the section on creating device files. If you do have the device files, ensure that they have the correct major and minor device numbers (some older CD-ROM distributions of Linux may not create the correct device files during installation).

5.6   Error: `No such device` for sound devices

You have not booted with a kernel containing the sound driver or the I/O address configuration doesn't match your hardware. Check that you are running the newly compiled kernel and verify that the settings entered when configuring the sound driver match your hardware setup.

5.7   Error: `No space left on device` for sound devices

This can happen if you tried to record data to /dev/audio or /dev/dsp without creating the necessary device file. The sound device is now a regular file, and has filled up your disk partition. You need to run the script described in the *Creating the Device Files* section of this document.

5.8   Error: `device busy` for sound devices

Only one process can open a given sound device at one time. Most likely some other process is using the device in question. One way to determine this is to use the fuser command:

```
% fuser -v /dev/dsp
/dev/dsp:                USER      PID ACCESS COMMAND
                         tranter   265 f....  tracker
```

In the above example, the fuser command showed that process 265 had the device open. Waiting for the process to complete or killing it will allow the sound device to be accessed once again.

5.9   I still get `device busy` errors!

According to Brian Gough, for the SoundBlaster cards which use DMA channel 1 there is a potential conflict with the QIC-02 tape driver, which also uses DMA 1, causing "device busy" errors. If you are using FTAPE, you may have this driver enabled. According to the FTAPE-HOWTO the QIC-02 driver is not essential for the use of FTAPE; only the QIC-117 driver is required. Reconfiguring the kernel to use QIC-117 but not QIC-02 allows FTAPE and the sound-driver to coexist.

(the following explanation was supplied by Harald Albrecht `albrecht@igpm.rwth-aachen.de`)

Some soundcards support using DMA channel 0. The sound driver configuration program allows this, and the kernel compiles properly, but accessing the sound device results in a "device busy" error message.

The reason is that the Linux kernel reserves DMA channel 0 for DRAM refresh. This is no longer true for modern 386/486 boards which use their own refresh logic. You can correct it by changing this line in the file /usr/src/linux/kernel/dma.c:

```
static volatile unsigned int dma_chan_busy[MAX_DMA_CHANNELS] = {
                1, 0, 0, 0, 1, 0, 0, 0
};
```

Replace the first 1 with a 0; this enables DMA channel 0. Don't do the same with DMA channel 4 as this is cascade and won't work! The code should now look like this:

```
static volatile unsigned int dma_chan_busy[MAX_DMA_CHANNELS] = {
                0, 0, 0, 0, 1, 0, 0, 0
};
```

Recompile and reboot with the new kernel.

5.10   Partial playback of digitized sound file

The symptom is usually that a sound sample plays for about a second and then stops completely or reports an error message about "missing IRQ" or "DMA timeout". Most likely you have incorrect IRQ or DMA channel settings. Verify that the kernel configuration matches the sound card jumper settings and that they do not conflict with some other card.

Another symptom is sound samples that "loop". This is usually caused by an IRQ conflict.

5.11   There are pauses when playing MOD files

Playing MOD files requires considerable CPU power. You may have too many processes running or your computer may be too slow to play in real time. Your options are to:

- try playing with a lower sampling rate or in mono mode

- eliminate other processes

- buy a faster computer

- buy a more powerful sound card (e.g. Gravis UltraSound)

If you have a Gravis UltraSound card, you should use one of the mod file players written specifically for the GUS (e.g. gmod).

5.12   Compile errors when compiling sound applications

The version 1.0c and earlier sound driver used a different and incompatible `ioctl()` scheme. Obtain newer source code or make the necessary changes to adapt it to the new sound driver. See the sound driver `Readme` file for details.

Also ensure that you have used the latest version of `soundcard.h` and `ultrasound.h` when compiling the application. See the installation instructions at beginning of this text.

5.13   SEGV when running sound binaries that worked previously

This is probably the same problem described in the previous question.

5.14   What known bugs or limitations are there in the sound driver?

See the `Readme` and `CHANGELOG` files included with the sound driver kernel source.

5.15   What version of the sound driver I should use?

If you are using version 1.0c or earlier, you definitely need to upgrade. Version 1.0c is not compatible with the applications written for version 2.0 or later.

There have been no significant changes after version 2.0, so if you don't have problems and that particular version fulfills your requirements, there are no compelling reasons to move to a more recent version (this should be true at least until September 1994).

The latest official version is in the latest Linux kernel distribution. There may also be some test and prototype versions lying around. If the version number is smaller than 2.9, the version should be quite safe. Any driver release having a version number of the form 2.99.XX is an incompletely implemented and experimental test release.

If you run DOOM under Linux, see the related question later in this document.

If you are interested in development of the sound driver, join the linux activists SOUND channel.

5.16   What do all the sound driver configuration options mean?

During configuration of the sound driver, a `configure` program is compiled and executed. This program asks you some questions and then generates the header file `local.h` that defines the sound card configuration.

The configuration file defines (or undefines) the following symbols:

```
Symbol                     Meaning
======                     =======
KERNEL_SOUNDCARD           enable/disable sound driver
EXCLUDE_PAS                ProAudioSpectrum support
EXCLUDE_SB                 SoundBlaster support
EXCLUDE_ADLIB              AdLib support
EXCLUDE_GUS                Gravis UltraSound support
EXCLUDE_MPU401             MPU-401 MIDI interface support
EXCLUDE_UART6850           6850 MIDI UART support
EXCLUDE_PSS                Professional Sound System support
EXCLUDE_GUS16              Gravis UltraSound support
EXCLUDE_GUSMAX             Gravis UltraSound Max support
EXCLUDE_MSS                Microsoft Sound System support
```

```
EXCLUDE_SBPRO              SoundBlaster Pro support
EXCLUDE_SB16              SoundBlaster 16 support
EXCLUDE_AUDIO             Digitized voice support
EXCLUDE_MIDI              MIDI interface support
EXCLUDE_YM3812            FM synthesizer (YM3812/OPL-3) support
EXCLUDE_SEQUENCER         MIDI sequencer support
EXCLUDE_PRO_MIDI          SoundBlaster Pro MIDI support
EXCLUDE_CHIP_MIDI         MIDI on CHIP support
SBC_BASE 0x220            SoundBlaster I/O base address
SBC_IRQ                  SoundBlaster IRQ number
SBC_DMA                  SoundBlaster DMA channel
SB16_DMA                 SoundBlaster 16 DMA channel
SB16_MIDI_BASE           base address of SoundBlaster 16 MIDI port
PAS_IRQ                  ProAudioSpectrum IRQ number
PAS_DMA                  ProAudioSpectrum DMA channel
GUS_IRQ                  Gravis UltraSound IRQ number
GUS_DMA                  Gravis UltraSound DMA channel
GUS_BASE                 base address of Gravis UltraSound
MPU_IRQ                  MPU-401 IRQ number
MPU_BASE                 base address of MPU-401 port
DSP_BUFFSIZE             DMA buffer size
```

Several other defines are also created, setting such things as the sound driver revision level and the time and date when configure was run.

There are other parameters that are not set by the configure program. If you need to change these, edit the file sound_config.h.

To disable the sound driver, run make config and answer "no" to the "Sound card support?" question.

5.17   What future enhancements are planned for the sound driver?

The sound driver is not just for Linux, it also supports several other Intel-based Unix operating systems. The package is now called "VoxWare". Some of the enhancements being considered are:

- implementing full MIDI support

- patch manager support

- document sound card driver (Hacker's Guide)

- support for new sound cards

- miscellaneous bug fixes

5.18   Where are the sound driver ioctls() etc. documented?

These are documented in the *Hacker's Guide to VoxWare*, currently available in draft form. The latest version is draft 2, and can be found on nic.funet.fi in /pub/OS/linux/ALPHA/sound. Note that this directory is "hidden" and will not appear in directory listings. If you "cd" to the directory and use the FTP "dir" command, the files *are* there.

5.19   What CPU resources are needed to play or record without pauses?

There is no easy answer to this question, as it depends on:

- whether using PCM sampling or FM synthesis

- sampling rate and sample size

- which application is used to play or record

- Sound Card hardware

- disk I/O rate, CPU clock speed, cache size, etc.

In general, any 386 machine should be able to play samples or FM synthesized music on an 8 bit soundcard with ease.

Playing MOD files, however, requires considerable CPU resources. Some experimental measurements have shown that playing at 44kHz requires more than 40% of the speed of a 486/50 and a 386/25 can hardly play faster than 22 kHz (these are with an 8 bit card sound such as a SoundBlaster). A card such as the Gravis UltraSound card performs more functions in hardware, and will require less CPU resources.

These statements assume the computer is not performing any other CPU intensive tasks.

Converting sound files or adding effects using a utility such as Sox is also much faster if you have a math coprocessor. The kernel driver itself does not do any floating point calculations, though.

5.20 Problems with a PAS16 and an Adaptec 1542 SCSI host adaptor

(the following explanation was supplied by `seeker@indirect.com`)

Linux only recognizes the 1542 at address 330 (default) or 333, and the PAS only allows the MPU-401 emulation at 330. Even when you disable the MPU-401 under software, something still wants to conflict with the 1542 if it's at its preferred default address. Moving the 1542 to 333 makes everyone happy.

Additionally, both the 1542 and the PAS-16 do 16-bit DMA, so if you sample at 16-bit 44KHz stereo and save the file to a SCSI drive hung on the 1542, you're about to have trouble. The DMAs overlap and there isn't enough time for RAM refresh, so you get the dread "PARITY ERROR - SYSTEM HALTED" message, with no clue to what caused it. It's made worse because a few second-party vendors with QIC-117 tape drives recommend setting the bus on/off times such that the 1542 is on even longer than normal. Get the SCSISEL.EXE program from Adaptec's BBS or several places on the internet, and reduce the BUS ON time or increase the BUS OFF time until the problem goes away, then move it one notch or more further. SCSISEL changes the EEPROM settings, so it's more permanent than a patch to the DOS driver line in CONFIG.SYS, and will work if you boot right into Linux (unlike the DOS patch). Next problem solved.

Last problem - the older Symphony chipsets drastically reduced the timing of the I/O cycles to speed up bus accesses. None of various boards I've played with had *any* problem with the reduced timing except for the PAS-16. Media Vision's BBS has SYMPFIX.EXE that's supposed to cure the problem by twiddling a diagnostic bit in Symphony's bus controller, but it's not a hard guarantee. You may need to:

- get the motherboard distributor to replace the older version bus chip,

- replace the motherboard, or

- buy a different brand of sound card.

Young Microsystems will upgrade the boards they import for around $30 (US); other vendors may be similar if you can figure out who made or imported the motherboard (good luck). The problem is in ProAudio's bus interface chip as far as I'm concerned; *nobody* buys a $120 sound card and sticks it in a 6MHz AT. Most of them wind up in 25-40MHz 386/486 boxes, and should be able to handle *at least* 12MHz bus rates if the chips are designed right. Exit soapbox (stage left).

The first problem depends on the chipset used on your motherboard, what bus speed and other BIOS settings, and the phase of the moon. The second problem depends on your refresh option setting (hidden or synchronous), the 1542 DMA rate and (possibly) the bus I/O rate. The third can be determined by calling Media Vision and asking which flavor of Symphony chip is incompatible with their slow design. Be warned, though - 3 of 4 techs I talked to were brain damaged. I would be very leery of trusting *anything* they said about someone else's hardware, since they didn't even know their own very well.

5.21 Problems with the FM synthesizer on a SoundBlaster Pro 1

The newer SB Pro has an OPL-3 FM chip, but the older version 1 used the OPL-2. The sound driver assumed the presence of an OPL-3. Version 2.5 of the sound driver corrects this problem.

5.22 Is the GUS-MAX supported?

With the 2.5a sound driver the GUS-MAX is not explicitly supported but it will work partially. The driver does not know about the additions such as the mixer or 16 bit sampling. Booting your system and initializing the card under MS-DOS and then booting Linux (using ctrl-alt-del) should allow it to work.

There is support for the GUS-MAX starting with the 2.9 sound driver.

5.23 What if my sound card is not supported?

First, make sure you really have an unsupported sound card. A few cards are compatible with supported cards (e.g. Logitech SoundMan 16 is compatible with ProAudioSpectrum 16). Post your question to the net or the Linux activists SOUND channel.

If your card truly is not supported, here are some options:

- replace it with a supported sound card
- write the driver yourself
- ask Hannu Savolainen to add support to the sound driver

The *Hacker's Guide to Voxware* has some comments on which sound cards may be supported in future.

5.24 Is it possible to read and write samples simultaneously?

Due to hardware limitations, this is not possible with most sound cards. The only supported card that can do this is the ProAudioSpectrum16. See the section on "bidirectional mode" in the *Hacker's Guide to Voxware* for more information.

5.25 My SB16 is set to IRQ 2, but configure does not allow this value.

On '286 and later machines, the IRQ 2 interrupt is cascaded to the second interrupt controller. It is equivalent to IRQ 9.

5.26 Are the SoundBlaster AWE32 or SoundBlaster16 ASP supported?

Creative Labs is not willing to release programming information for the ASP and Emu chips used in these cards. Unless they change their policy, there will be no support for this under Linux.

The Gravis UltraSound card has capabilities similar to the AWE32, and is supported under Linux. Cards based on other DSPs such as the Analog Devices ADSP-21xx may be supported in the future.

5.27   If I run Linux, then boot DOS, I get errors and/or sound applications do not work properly.

This happens after a soft reboot to DOS. Sometimes the error message misleadingly refers to a bad CONFIG.SYS file.

Most of the current sound cards have software programmable IRQ and DMA settings. If you use different settings between Linux and MS-DOS/Windows, this may cause problems. Some sound cards don't accept new parameters without a complete reset (i.e. cycle the power or use the hardware reset button).

The quick solution to this problem it to perform a full reboot using the reset button or power cycle rather than a soft reboot (e.g. Ctrl-Alt-Del).

The correct solution is to ensure that you use the same IRQ and DMA settings with MS-DOS and Linux (or not to use DOS :-).

5.28   You say I need to configure and build a kernel - how do I do that?

This is not the kernel HOWTO (any volunteers?).   Until one is written, try reading the file /usr/src/linux/README; it is reasonably complete.

If you really don't want to compile a kernel, you may be able to find a precompiled kernel that has the drivers you need as part of a Linux distribution (e.g. the Slackware "q" series of disks).

5.29   Problems running DOOM under Linux

Users of the recently released port of ID software's game DOOM for Linux may be interested in these notes.

For correct sound output you need version 2.90 or later of the sound driver; it has support for the new the real-time "DOOM mode".

The sound samples are 16-bit. If you have an 8-bit sound card there is a program called sndcvt available that converts the data from 16 to 8 bits on the fly. You also have to patch the DOOM sound server; the details are explained in the README file.

If performance of DOOM is poor on your system, disabling sound (by renaming the file sndserver) may improve it.

At least at time of writing, DOOM for Linux does not have any background music.

5.30   How can I reduce noise picked up by my soundcard?

Using good quality shielded cables and trying the sound card in different slots may help reduce noise. If the sound card has a volume control, you can try different settings (maximum is probably best).

Using a mixer program you can make sure that undesired inputs (e.g. microphone) are set to zero gain.

Some sound cards are simply not designed with good shielding and grounding and are prone to noise pickup.

Finally, on my system I found that the kernel command line option no-hlt reduces the noise level. This tells the kernel not to use the halt instruction when running the idle process loop. You can try this manually when booting, or set it up using the command append = "no-hlt" in your LILO configuration file.

5.31   I can play sounds, but not record.

If you can play sound but not record, try these steps:

- use a mixer program to select the appropriate device (e.g. microphone)

- use the mixer to set the input gains to maximum

- If you can, try to test sound card recording under MS-DOS to determine if there is a hardware problem

5.32   My "compatible" sound card only works if I first initialize under MS-DOS.

Some sound card clones are not 100% register compatible with the real thing; they sometimes contain extra circuitry such as mixers. You *may* be able to use these under Linux if you first initialize under MS-DOS, then soft boot Linux (i.e. Ctrl-Alt-Delete).

One user also reported that he had better results if he used LOADLIN rather than LILO to boot Linux after initializing his sound card under MS-DOS (this was with a Diamond sound card).,

They may or may not function reliably. The real solution is to find out from the manufacturer what the differences are and have the support added to the sound driver. This has been done, for example, for the Sound Galaxy NX Pro.

Part XL

TERM **HOWTO**

Copyright Patrick Reijnen `patrickr@cs.kun.nl`
v1.1, 12 May 1995

Contents

1   Legal Information

1.1   Copyright statement

This document may be distributed freely as a whole in any form and free of charge. Parts of this document may be distributed, provided that this copyright message is included and the reader is informed that this is not the full HOWTO document. Furthermore, there is to be a pointer as to where the full document can be obtained. Specifically, it may be included in commercial distributions, without prior consent. However, I would like to be informed of such usage.

This HOWTO may be translated into any language, whatsoever, provided that you leave this copyright statement and the disclaimer intact, and that a notice is appended stating who translated the document.

1.2   DISCLAIMER

While I have tried to include the most correct and up-to-date information available, I cannot guarantee that usage of the information in this document does not result in loss of data. I provide NO WARRANTY about the information in this HOWTO and I cannot be made liable for any consequences for any damage resulting from using information in this HOWTO.

2   Introduction

2.1   This Document

This HOWTO attempts to clear up some of the confusion of using TERM, Michael O'Reilly's remarkable program that allows you to multiplex your serial line and set up a network connection. By and large, the documents that come with TERM are quite good, and this HOWTO is not intended to replace them. The intention of this document is to give some background on how TERM works and detail the steps in getting some of the more common networking services working under TERM. It should be emphasized that this document does not cover everything there is to know about TERM. After reading it, the TERM manual pages should be read, since they include information not contained here.

2.2   What is TERM?

TERM is a program, written by Michael O'Reilly (michael@iinet.com.au) and maintained by Bill Riemers (bcr@physics.purdue.edu), that is run over a serial line to allow multiple connections to operate concurrently - *i.e.* you may be down-load a file via your modem while working on a (different) remote system via the same modem connection. TERM can also be used to open up X client windows over a serial connection. Through the `tredir` utility and the `tudpredir` utility TERM can provide almost all of the "traditional" TCP/IP and UDP network services: mail, news, ftp, telnet, xarchie, etc. In a sense, TERM is very much like other serial protocols such as SLIP or PPP. TERM's advantage is that it can be run entirely from user space, requiring no support from system or network administrators.

Unlike SLIP or PPP, your machine does not have its own IP address. All incoming traffic must be addressed to your remote host, and it will be redirected to your local computer by TERM.

3   How TERM works

Before experimenting with TERM it is strongly advised to first read this complete chapter and the INSTAL-LATION file provided with the package. Also take a look at the manual pages `linecheck`, `(term)test` and TERM. This will help you to work easier and faster.

3.1   Nomenclature

I assume you are dialing a system through some sort of terminal server. I use the terms *local* and *remote* to refer to the home and network connected systems respectively (unless I use them to mean something else :-).

TERM provides the local machine, which has no network connection, but is connected, via a serial line, to a remote machine which is in turn connected to a network with network services. Let us look at how a machine with a 'traditional' network connection provides these services. First the user invokes a program, like ftp or telnet, that requests a network service. What these programs do is make a system call requesting network services. The operating system then obtains these services via its network interface (*e.g.* it sends and receives packets over the ethernet). SLIP and PPP do exactly this, by converting your modem line into a network interface, which is in principle no different from an ethernet. The downside of this is that these protocols make the modem-connected machine part of the network, just like any other machine. This implies all the administrative burdens associated with being a network node (more actually, since the modem link must also be administered).

In the absence of a network connection like SLIP or PPP, what does one typically do? Well, you dial your network connected machine, read your mail, your news etc; if you need a file, you first transfer it to the remote machine and then download it to your local machine using kermit or some other communication program. This is a bit of a pain, especially since you can only really do one thing at a time that uses your modem link. The idea behind TERM is basically to automate and multiplex this process. TERM is invoked on both the local and remote machines, and the two processes communicate with one another over the modem line. When you need a network service, you make a request to the local TERM daemon, which forwards the request to the TERM daemon on the remote, network-connected, machine. The result is then returned over the modem line.

To be more concrete, say you want to retrieve a file by ftp. First you need a version of ftp that can speak to TERM. You invoke this termftp as you do a regular ftp, say termftp nethost.gov, but this special version makes its network request to the local TERM daemon instead of the kernel. The local TERM forwards this request, over the modem line, to the remote TERM, which opens an ftp connection to nethost.gov, and transmits the data back over the modem link. TERM is smart enough to have many different things going on at once; so you can have several different network sessions using the same modem link, *e.g.* you can be logged into another distant host via termtelnet while the termftp transfer is going on.

If this is too abstract (or unclear) do not worry; the important piece of information to get out of this section is that there are *two* copies of TERM running, one on each end of the modem link.

4   Setting Things Up

4.1   What has to be available

Before you start building and using TERM you have to make sure that you have built TCP/IP support into the kernel. Furthermore, make sure that the TCP/IP loopback interface is activated. When this is the case you can go on with the rest of this section.

4.2   Explanation of concepts

In newer TERM version two new concepts have entered TERM. These two concepts will be explained in the next two subsections.

4.2.1   Sharing

Starting with version 1.16 the concept of sharing the TERM connection with other users has entered TERM. This means that when you enable shared features, other people can use the same TERM connection you are using, i.e. when you are working on your remote machine via your TERM connection (say, from your local machine you used trsh to get in) another person on your local machine can use the same TERM connection at the same time to ftp a file to his login on your local machine from an ftp site somewhere in the world.

When you disable shared features (i.e. you execute TERM in private mode) you and only you (we do not count root :-) can use the TERM connection.

Of course, you only need to install shared TERM at the end at which you want to allow people to use the same TERM connection you are using. So, if other people have a login on your local machine and they want to use it from somewhere on your remote network you enable shared features on the remote end of your TERM connection. In this way all these people can login on your machine at the same time sharing the same TERM connection with each other and with you. (NOTE: the first example needed shared features to be enabled at the local end of the TERM connection).

NOTE for installation as root: When you install TERM as root you have to create a 'term' group first (before compilation) with no member by adding the following line in '/etc/group':

```
term::16:root
```

or any other unused GID than 16 when 16 is already in use.

After compilation and installation make TERM and its clients SGID 'term':

```
chgrp term <term_client>
chmod g+s <term_client>
```

Also any other program that you make TERM-aware must be made SGID 'term'.

4.2.2   Full TERM networking

Starting with TERM version 2.0.0 the statement full TERM networking is used. When your only connection with the outside world is a TERM connection, you have a full TERM network and you should build TERM with full TERM networking. In this case in the shared directory a file called termnet is placed. This tells TERM that your only connection to the outside world is via TERM.

When you also have some other type of network connection beside your TERM connection TERM-aware programs first try to fulfill their job using this network connection. When this fails TERM is invoked and it is tried to fulfill the job via the TERM connection. To make this more clear now an example is given in which TERM-aware telnet is used. This telnet should work both with and without TERM.

```
telnet localhost
```

does not use TERM to connect, but

```
telnet zeus.cs.kun.nl
```

will use TERM only if you do not have some other type of network connection.

Full TERM networking also means to lie about the host name, and say it is the remote host instead. Furthermore, it causes bind(0) to always act on the remote host. In essence it makes many programs unusable when they are not going through TERM, while TERM is running. Unfortunately, most UDP programs and daemons will not work with TERM without these nasty tricks.

4.3 Build TERM

When you are lucky, this should just involve a make. Most probably however, you need to do more. Due to new features in newer versions of TERM it is now a bit more complicated to create your TERM binary. A couple of ways can be followed to obtain your binary.

To cover all these ways TERM can be built this section will be split into three parts:

1. Build TERM, versions 2.0.0 and higher

2. Build TERM, versions 1.16 up to 1.19

3. Build TERM up to version 1.15

4.3.1 Build TERM, versions 2.0.0 and higher

First, make sure you have read the section about 'full TERM networking' above.

For TERM versions 2.0.0 and higher there are many ways to build the TERM binary and the clients. All of these can be done both by root and by ordinary user:

1. Build TERM in private mode without full TERM networking

2. Build TERM in private mode with full TERM networking

3. Build TERM in shared mode without full TERM networking

4. Build TERM in shared mode with full TERM networking

In these versions of TERM a new way for compilation has entered TERM using the script configure. When configure is run it checks on what operating system you are trying to install TERM, whether the source directory is available or not, and if any runtime options are set. According to the things found configure then creates a Makefile using Makefile.in which is provided in the TERM package.

Two of the more important options to configure are --root and --user which state whether TERM will be installed by root or an ordinary user. Other options can be used to install TERM the way you want (non-standard paths for example).

1. Build TERM in private mode without full TERM networking.

   To build TERM in this way you need to execute the following commands (both for root and ordinary user):

   ```
   ./configure --root  OR --user
   make install installman
   ```

   This builds the binaries and installs these binaries and the manual pages.

2. Build TERM in private mode with full TERM networking.

   To build TERM in this way you need to execute the following commands (both for root and ordinary user):

   ```
   ./configure --root  OR --user
   make installnet installman
   ```

   This builds the binaries and installs these binaries and the manual pages.

3. Build TERM in shared mode without full TERM networking.

   To build TERM in this way you need to execute the following commands (both for root and ordinary user):

```
./configure --root  OR --user
make share installman
```

This builds the binaries and installs these binaries and the manual pages.

4. Build TERM in shared mode with full TERM networking.

To build TERM in this way you need to execute the following commands (both for root and ordinary user):

```
./configure --root  OR --user
make share installnet installman
```

This builds the binaries and installs these binaries and the manual pages.

4.3.2   Build TERM, versions 1.16 up to 1.19

To build these versions of TERM you can now choose one of the following ways:

1. As an ordinary user, build TERM in private mode

2. As an ordinary user, build TERM in shared mode

3. As root, build TERM in private mode

4. As root, build TERM in shared mode

Below, it will be explained how to enable/disable shared features during the compilation of TERM.

1. You are an ordinary user (no root access) and you do NOT want to SHARE the TERM connection with other users.

   As a user who does not want to share the TERM connection with other users you should do the following to build TERM:

```
make DO=install OS-type
make installman
```

   After this TERM, its clients and the manual pages are built and installed.

   Furthermore, you need to create a directory '$HOME/.term'. This is the directory in which TERM will look for its 'termrc' file.

2. You are an ordinary user (no root access) and you want to SHARE the TERM connection with other users.

   As a user who wants to share the TERM connection you should do the following:

```
make DO=installshare USERSHARE=$HOME/term OS-type
make installman
```

   After this TERM, its clients and the manual pages are built and installed.

   Furthermore, you will have a directory '$HOME/term' (default) with permissions 'drwxrwxr-x'. In this directory you will find at least the socket used by TERM for its connection ('/tmp/private/socket=').

3. You are root and you do NOT want to SHARE the TERM connection with other users.

   As root who does not want the TERM connection to be shareable you should do the following to build TERM:

```
make DO=install OS-type
make installman
```

After this TERM, its clients and the manual pages are built and installed.

Furthermore, you now have a directory called '/usr/local/lib/term' (default) with permissions 'drwxr-xr-x'. In this directory you will at least find the socket used by TERM for its connection ('/tmp/private/socket=').

4. You are root and want to SHARE the TERM connection.

First, make sure you have read the section about 'sharing' above.

As root who wants to share the TERM connection you should do the following:

```
make DO=installshare OS-type
make installman
```

After this TERM, its clients and the manual pages are built and installed.

Furthermore, you now have a directory called '/usr/local/lib/term' (default) owned by group TERM and with permissions 'drwxrwxr-x'. In this directory you will at least find the socket used by TERM for its connection ('/tmp/private/socket=').

4.3.3   Build TERM up to version 1.15

For these versions of TERM building should invoke no more than the commands

```
make DO=install OS-type
make installman
```

You will find TERM, its clients and the manual pages nicely built and installed and ready for use after this.

Furthermore, you need to create a directory '$HOME/term'. This directory TERM will use to look for its termrc file.

The only thing you may want to do is change some of the paths in the `Makefile` or change some of the compiler flags.

4.4   client.a, libtermnet.a, libtermnet.sa, libtermnet.so

With TERM a library with functions for TERM clients is provided.

Up to version 1.16 this library was called `client.a`. During compilation of TERM this library was built and then used during the compilation of the TERM clients. It was not installed in another directory.

Starting with version 1.16 the name of the library is changed to `libtermnet.a`. Up to version 1.19 this library is created in the TERM directory and then used during compilation of the TERM clients. It is not installed in another directory.

Starting with version 2.0.0, beside libtermnet.a also `libtermnet.so` and `libtermnet.sa` (shared library and exported initialized library data) are created during compilation of the TERM package. During the installation of all the parts of the package also these three library files are installed in the directory '/usr/local/lib' (default). Then a link is made from libtermnet.so.2 to libtermnet.so.2.x.x. Finally, `ldconfig` is run to create the necessary links and cache (for use by the run-time linker, ld.so) to the most recent shared libraries found in the directories specified on the command line, in the file '/etc/ld.so.conf', and in the trusted directories ('/usr/lib' and '/lib'). If the installation is done correctly the three library files can now be used by TERM clients which are built with dynamic instead of static libraries. Also, these libraries can now be used to port your own software to make it TERM aware (see below).

4.5   Setting environment variables

TERM knows a couple of environment variables which can be set by users. The first three of those that I will explain are

- TERMDIR
- TERMSHARE
- TERMMODE

By setting these variables you can control the way TERM is run.

For TERM versions up to 1.15 only the variable TERMDIR is important (these versions do not know the shared mode). For these versions TERMDIR should be set as follows:

```
setenv TERMDIR $HOME        (csh or tcsh)
export TERMDIR=$HOME        (bash)
```

Starting with version 1.16 TERM also knows the variables TERMSHARE and TERMMODE. With these variables TERM can be told to run in private mode or in shared mode. I will explain how to set the variables for private mode and shared mode.

TERMMODE knows the following three values;

- 0 = private
- 1 = system shared
- 2 = user shared

1. Running TERM in private mode can be done setting the variables TERMDIR and TERMMODE in the following way:

   For csh or tcsh

   ```
   setenv TERMDIR $HOME
   setenv TERMMODE 0
   ```

   For bash

   ```
   export TERMDIR=$HOME
   export TERMMODE=0
   ```

2. When you want to use TERM in shared mode there are two ways of setting the variables:

   (a) When TERM is installed as a SUID program only TERMMODE has to be set.

   ```
   setenv TERMMODE 2      (csh or tcsh)
   export TERMMODE=2      (bash)
   ```

   (b) When TERM is installed as a SGID program the variables have to be set in the following way:

   For csh or tcsh

   ```
   setenv TERMMODE 1
   setenv TERMDIR /usr/local/lib/term
   setenv TERMSHARE $TERMDIR
   ```

   For bash

```
export TERMMODE=1
export TERMDIR=/usr/local/lib/term
export TERMSHARE=$TERMDIR
```

Setting the variables in this way makes it possible to start old clients (clients linked to an older version of client.a) in shared mode.

Starting with version 2.0.0 TERM also knows the variable TERMSERVER. You need to set this variable when you have multiple modems and you have more than one connection at a time. To specify which connection to use, you must start TERM with a server name:

```
nohup term -v /dev/modem1 Connection1 &
nohup term -v /dev/modem2 Connection2 &
```

Users should then set the variable TERMSERVER to the connection name they want to use:

```
setenv TERMSERVER Connection1      (csh or tcsh)
export TERMSERVER=Connection2      (bash)
```

4.6   Test TERM

Do a make test (or make termtest for newer versions of TERM) to build TERM's test daemon. (term)test works by running two copies of TERM on your system, a 'local' and a 'remote" copy. Both of these will read your 'termrc'; so you can adjust their behaviour. Now execute (term)test. You should now be able to do a trsh and a tupload (try

```
tupload ./term /usr/tmp
```

- you should get a copy of the TERM binary in '/usr/tmp'). The local TERM's output should show up in 'local.log', the remote's one in 'remote.log'. You can start TERM up with a -d255 flag to enable debugging output to be written to these files, or enable debugging in your 'termrc' file.

NOTE: Run test as ./test   so as to avoid your system's test.

4.7   TERM and communication programs

Before you can use TERM you must have established a connection via the modem using a communication program like kermit or seyon. In the documentation of your communication program you can find what you need to do to establish the conection with the remote machine.

When you have established the connection with the remote machine and you want to run TERM you need to suspend or quit your communication program without closing the connection with the remote machine. This needs to be done as otherwise the communication program will steal characters from linecheck or TERM.

Below for some communication programs I will explain how you can make sure that the connection will stay alive and the communication programs will not steal characters from linecheck or TERM.

4.7.1   Kermit

Starting TERM when you use kermit is easy. At the local kermit prompt you type *suspend*. Now you see back your Linux prompt. From this prompt you can establish your TERM connection.

4.7.2 Seyon

An easy way to start linecheck or TERM when you are using seyon is to put linecheck and TERM in the Transfer Menu (controlled by the file '$HOME/.seyon/protocols').

In the file '$HOME/.seyon/protocols' add:

```
"Line check" "$cd /tmp; linecheck"
"Term" "$term -c off -w 10 -t 150 -s 38400 -l $HOME/tlog"
```

Then, when you want to execute linecheck or TERM on the local machine, you can select the Transfer Menu, either the "Line check" or the "Term" item, and Go.

Of course, you can also use the shell command button, and type 'linecheck' or 'term' in the pop-up dialog box. This also does automatic redirection of input and output.

4.8 Make a Transparent Link

Presumably, you can establish a modem connection between your local and remote hosts. Typically, you are dialing into some kind of terminal server and connecting to your remote host from there. You are also using some kind of terminal software, such as kermit or seyon to talk to your modem (the examples in this document will use kermit, since that is what its author uses). If you are having trouble with your modem, or your terminal software, take a look at the Serial-HOWTO; that should help you out.

Having established your link, you want to make it as transparent as possible. Check the commands on the terminal server (help or ? will usually get you started). Go for the 8 bit options whenever possible. This may mean changing the way you log in to a system, *e.g.* if the server uses rlogin, you may have to use it and give it the -8 flag to make it transparent. Especially watch out for xon/xoff flow control. You do not want that. Try to enable rts/cts (hardware) flow control. You may need to check your modem documentation to learn how to configure it to do 8-bit rts/cts communications.

4.9 Run linecheck

WARNING: In some of the documents the command line options for linecheck are mentioned in an incorrect order. I have checked this and found the order of options mentioned below to be the correct ones.

NOTE: Starting with TERM version 2.3.0 linecheck no longer needs to have the name of a log-file on its command line. It will write its output to the file 'linecheck.log' in the directory you start linecheck in.

Linecheck is a program that is supplied with TERM. It checks the transparency of a link, providing configuration information that TERM needs to run correctly. linecheck will send each of the 256 possible eight bit characters over the link and verify that each was transmitted successfully. TERM needs to be configured to deal with characters that cannot be transmitted over the link, and linecheck determines what characters these are. You use linecheck after you have established as transparent a modem link as possible. To run linecheck, do the following

1. On the remote system run

   ```
   linecheck linecheck.log
   ```

2. Escape back to your local system and suspend your communication program (see above)

3. On the local system run

   ```
   linecheck linecheck.log > /dev/modem < /dev/modem
   ```

When linecheck is done, you will find a set of numbers at the bottom of the 'linecheck.log' files. These should be escaped in the termrc at the other end of the link. For example, in my system my local 'linecheck.log' said nothing and my remote 'linecheck.log' said to escape 29 and 157. Therefore, my local 'termrc' escapes these characters and my remote 'termrc' escapes nothing. If I *escape* a character at one end, I have to also *ignore* it at the other; so, in this example, I shall have to ignore 29 and 157 in my remote system.

If linecheck hangs, try using

```
linecheck linecheck.log 17 19
```

on the remote system and

```
linecheck linecheck.log 17 19 > /dev/modem < /dev/modem
```

on the local system. This will escape your xon/xoff (flow control) characters, which will hang your line if you have got software flow control. If this solves the hanging problems, you will want to *escape / ignore* 17/19 in both 'termrc's'. If your terminal server has other characters that will shut it down, try running linecheck with those characters escaped, as above. You can spot these characters if linecheck hangs. If this is the case, kill it, then look in the log-files. The last characters transmitted are likely to be the culprits. Try it again with these characters escaped.

In summary, my local termrc has the lines

```
escape 29
escape 157
```

and my remote termrc has the lines

```
ignore 29
ignore 157
```

since my *remote* 'linecheck.log' said to escape 29 and 157.

4.10   **Try Running** TERM

Log into the remote system, making the link as transparent as possible (if you have not already done so). Fire up TERM at the remote end. I use the following:

```
exec term -r -l $HOME/tlog -s 38400 -c off -w 10 -t 150.
```

Let us run down each option one by one (note that I could just as easily have put these options in my termrc. I did it this way because it saves editing a file while getting TERM set up).

exec means to destroy your current shell, running the given program in its place. I exec things because I do not intend to use my login shell again; so it is just wasting memory. If you are debugging the link and can reliably kill the remote TERM, you might not want to do an exec.

The -r option is needed at exactly one end. TERM will then see this end as the remote end of the connection (Note that TERM's remote end can thus be your local machine). If you do not use this option at one end TERM clients will spontaneously crash.

-l $HOME/tlog. This logs errors to the file tlog in my home directory. Very useful for debugging. No reason not to do this.

-s 38400 : I have got a 14400 baud modem, with compression. For optimal compression ratios, I want to be able to push bits down the pipe as fast as possible. For a slower modem, you should use something lower. Note that if you have a slower machine with 16450 uart on your serial port, high baud rates can cause data loss by overloading the chip on your serial port. TERM will recover from this, but if you see a lot of error messages in your log file, (or get overrun warnings from linux kernel versions 0.99pl15 and up) you again might want to lower this number.

`-c off`: This turns data compression off. I have got a compressing modem, and I do not want to compress things twice.

`-w 10 -t 150`: Again, these are options to optimize my fast modem link. I have set my window to 10 and my timeout to 150. This is according to the recommendation in the `term_setup` man page.

Escape back to your local machine and suspend your communication program (see above). You do not want it running while TERM is running, because it will fight with TERM over the serial port. If you can convince your modem to not hang up when you exit your communication program (when it toggles DTR), you could just exit the program at this point.

Now run TERM locally. I use:

```
term -c off -l $HOME/tlog -s 38400 -w 10 -t 150 {$<$} /dev/modem > /dev/modem \&
```

I need to tell TERM where the modem is; so I point both standard input and output at '/dev/modem' (that is what the < and > do). I also run it in the background; so I can use this screen for something else if I want to.

TERM should work now :-). Try a `trsh`, and see what happens. If you hang, or your link seems slow, take a look at your 'tlog' at each end. Are you getting timeouts or error messages? If so, then you have configured something incorrectly. Try again (after you have finished reading this :-). Note that the connection will not seem blazingly fast, especially if you are using compression - it will be a little jumpy. The real speed comes in during file transfer and the like.

4.11   Terminate your TERM connection

Most certainly, after you have done a lot of work using TERM, you want to finish your work and bring your TERM connection down. For this to be realized there are four ways:

1. Kill the TERM programs at both sides of the connection. This is the least recommended way of terminating your connection.

2. A better way is to execute the following command locally:

   ```
   echo '00000' > /dev/modem
   ```

   This will nicely terminate your TERM connection. It will work for all version of TERM. Make sure that the sequence of zeros contains at least *five* zeros.

3. In the termrc of TERM versions 2.0.0 and higher you can now enter a statement called `terminate` '`<some string>`'. This sets a string that will cause TERM to exit ('00000' by default). It must be at least *five* characters long, to avoid accidental terminations.

4. Starting with version 1.14 there is the program `tshutdown` (actually for version 1.14 it is available as a patch, for newer versions it is in the package). Executing tshutdown nicely terminates your TERM connection.

4.12   Removing TERM from your partition

Ok, you asked for this. As some of you want to get rid of TERM I here present you the steps to be done in removing TERM. In the process of removing TERM you have to fulfill the following steps:

- Removing directories with their contents. Depending on how you installed TERM, one or more of the following directories will exist on your machine:

```
$HOME/.term/termrc
$HOME/.term/termrc.<server>
$HOME/term/termrc
$HOME/term/termrc.<server>
/usr/local/lib/term/termrc
/usr/local/lib/term/termrc.<server>
/etc/termrc
/etc/termrc.<server>
```

These directories can be removed together with their contents. Use '/bin/rm -rf' to get this done.

- The group 'term'. For some of the ways of installation you had to create a group 'term'. Check the file '/etc/group' for the 'term' entry. When it exists you can remove the entry.

- The TERM-package and TERM-aware executables. This is probably the hardest part in removing TERM. For the executables coming with the TERM-package you have to look in the directory '/usr/local/bin' or the directory '$HOME/bin'.

  With executables you made TERM-aware yourself I cannot help you. You need to know what executables you made TERM-aware in order to know what executables you have to remove. Do not forget configuration, default and other files coming with some of these executables.

- Library files. To remove these you best can execute the following commands:

```
cd /
find . -name libtermnet* -exec /bin/rm {}
```

This will find and remove the library files.

- Include file. Also for this one the easiest way is to execute the following two commands:

```
cd /
find . -name termnet.h -exec /bin/rm {}
```

This will remove the include file.

- Manual pages. When you have installed the TERM manual pages you can now find them back in one of the following directories:

```
/usr/local/man/man1
/usr/local/man/cat1
$HOME/man/man1
$HOME/man/cat1
```

At least you have to check for the following manual pages: term, term_clients, term_setup, tdownload, linecheck, trdate, trdated, termrc, termtest, tmon, tredir, trsh, tshutdown, tudpredir, tupload, txconnand finally tiptest.

- Temporary user directory. This is the directory '/usr/tmp/private' and its contents.

After this exercise you can be quite sure that you have removed everything related to TERM.

4.13 Optimizing your connection

Once you have got TERM running, you might want to try to get things optimized. A good way to measure the speed of your link is to run tmon in one window while up/downloading a file in another. Try both (big) text files and compressed files; the plain text should go a factor of two-ish faster than the compressed files. The parameters you want to fiddle with are baud rate (-s), compression (-c), windows (-w), timeout (-t) and retrain (-A).

Watch out with the retrain parameter. With TERM version 1.19 I got a performance decrease of 80% to 90% compared to running TERM without the retrain parameter. It is not clear if this is a bug in TERM version 1.19 and if this problem exists only with TERM version 1.19.

Baudrate: the maximum number of bits per second TERM will try to send over the serial link. TERM will avoid sending characters at a higher data rate than this. The default is to use the speed of your computer's serial port, but be warned that this may be too high if your modem runs at a lower rate over the phone line. The baud rate option is intended for systems that buffer output to the modem. During setup and tuning it is better to use a small baud rate rather than one which is too large. For high speed links (> 38400), making it unlimited is probably advantageous. This is achieved by using the value 'off'. TERM will then rely solely on your kernel to do flow control.

Compression: you want this on if you do not have a compressing modem. If you do have such a modem, turn compression off, otherwise you will be compressing things twice, which typically *increases* the amount of data transmitted. Compressing modems are those that use the MNP-5 or V42.bis protocols. Check your modem documentation and the message when your modem connects.

Windows: this is the number of chunks of data, or packets, that TERM will let go over the line before it gets an acknowledgment (or ack) from the remote TERM. For fast modems, increasing this can be a win; for slower links this can overwhelm the remote end.

Timeout: the time TERM will wait for an ack. If you have increased windows, and you are getting timeouts in your log-file, try increasing this.

For 14400/V42.bis, I use -c off -w 10 -t 150. I get around 1700 cps on compressed files and 3500 cps on ASCII files using tupload.

4.14 Troubleshooting

In this section some thoughts are given about what to check when you have problems executing TERM or one of its clients.

- Did you clean up the TERM directory structure? With newer versions of TERM the structure of the directory tree under '/usr/local/lib/term' has changed a couple of times. If you are not aware of this, it can cause all kinds of error messages. The best thing to do is to delete the directory tree under '/usr/local/lib/term' (save your 'termrc') and then install your new TERM version. This way, you avoid the struggle with a messed up directory tree.

- Did you remove old sockets? When you update your TERM version remove all the sockets (called 'socket=') created by TERM. No doing this can cause strange problems. To find out what socket TERM is listening to you can use the "netstat" program.

- TERM does not compile correct on SunOS 4.1.3? You have configured TERM with './configure –user'. During compilation you are getting a assembler error on a unknown '-k' flag. The reason of this error is unknown. The solution to this error is to configure TERM with static libraries. So, you have to do './configure –user –static' and then continue with the compilation process the way you normally do. Now TERM should compile correct.

- termtest is presenting you the error: 'Term: failed to connect to term socket '/root/.term/sockettest"? When termtest runs it expects the executable 'term' to be in the same directory as termtest. When you do a 'make install' prior to running termtest, the TERM binary is moved to '/usr/local/bin' (or some other bin directory).

The workaround for this is to link the binary to the source directory:

```
ln -s /usr/local/bin/term /usr/src/term-<version_number>/term
```

- Are you running the right binary? TERM has been updated quite a lot, and many systems have different versions of the programs floating around. Make sure you are using the right version. Note that this applies to linecheck too. You can use bash's type -a or the whereis command to find which program is being run. TERM versions after 1.11 should print out their version number when they start up. (Although version 1.14 claims to be 1.12. Sigh.)

- Do you have the right 'termrc' in the right place? Depending on the version of TERM you are running and the way you installed TERM (being root or user) this file has to be in one of the following directories:

```
$HOME/.term/termrc
$HOME/.term/termrc.<server>
$HOME/term/termrc
$HOME/term/termrc.<server>
/usr/local/lib/term/termrc
/usr/local/lib/term/termrc.<server>
/etc/termrc
/etc/termrc.<server>
```

Some systems have pre-installed 'termrc' files; make sure they are gone before you set things up. If you are running things as root, lookout for '/.term'. TERM creates files (sockets actually) while it is running; so it has its own directory, '$HOME/.term', where the file 'termrc' goes (note, there is *no* leading dot in 'termrc'!).

- Does TERM find its 'termrc' file? when you start up TERM at both sides, you should see messages like the one below:

```
Term version: 2.2.9
Reading file:  /usr/local/lib/term/termrc
Using shared mode.
```

When the second line is missing TERM cannot find its 'termrc' file and you know that something is gone wrong during the installation (unless you are not using a 'termrc' file and enter all the options to the command line :-). Check the place and the permissions of the 'termrc' file on the site TERM cannot find its 'termrc' file.

- Is you 'term' or '.term' directory mounted with NFS? If your 'term' or '.term' directory is mounted with NFS you need to set the flag -DTERM_NFS_DIR in the CFLAGS line of the Makefile. Alas, for the author this flag causes a compile error when TERM 1.19 is compiled on a machine running SunOS 4.*.

- Are all files and directories owned by the correct user and group and do they have the correct permissions? This should be no problems as these permissions are set during the installation phase. However, when you port your own programs to TERM you must be aware of this. Also when you change the mode TERM is working in (i.e. from private mode to shared mode) file and directory ownerships and permissions have to be adapted.

- You are getting the error *gethostbyname: <hostname>: Non-authoritative 'host not found', or, server failed* To solve this you have to check the following things:

  1. Is the file '/etc/hosts' configured correctly? <hostname> is not the name of your host (old SLS releases and some old and new Slackware releases are shipped with hostname 'darkstar' for example). Change this in this file. It must at least contain a line like below (the format is described above it):

```
# Local Hosts Format:
#  IP_NUMBER              HOSTNAME          ALIASES
#
# Here is the name of your host, first, followed by any aliases
127.0.0.1       localhost       linuxpc.domain  linuxpc
```

2. Are your '/etc/rc*' and '/etc/resolv.conf' files world readable (chmod ugo+r)?

3. Last, make sure that you have installed the TCP/IP loopback-interface on your machine.

- You are getting all kinds of 'timed out' messages in your TERM log files? This means that your TERM connection is not optimized. A small number of these messages every now and then is not a problem. These are most certainly due to temporal factors influencing the physical connection between your local and remote hosts.

  When you get a lot of these messages all the time your connection will slow down considerably. You have to fiddle with the parameters mentioned in the section 'Optimizing your connection' above. Alas, this part of the installation is a process of trial and error. No hard rules can be given about the numbers to be presented to the various parameters as many factors have an influence on the connection. These factors differ between the connections and even in time.

- Normal FTP with redirected ports does not work for you? Alas, it is a known problem that redirection of the ports needed by FTP (20 and 21) does not give you a working FTP. The only solution is to get a TERM-aware ftp or ncftp version. Alas, also some TERM-aware ftp versions seem not to work.

5 TERM clients

TERM provides several default clients. They include trsh, tmon, tupload, tredir, txconn and in newer versions trdate, trdated. Furthermore, starting with version 2.0.0 tudpredir is available and from version 2.1.0 tdownload is available. This section will deal with trsh, tmon, tupload, tdownload, trdate and trdated. The others each have their own section. No TERM client will work until you have established a TERM link.

tmon is a simple utility to monitor the statistics of your link. It prints a time histogram of characters transmitted and received. It is invoked simply as tmon. Since around version 1.11, tmon has had a bug that causes some information to be garbled (??).

trsh is similar to rsh. Without arguments, it spawns an interactive shell on the remote system (*i.e.* it logs you in). trsh is one of the primary means of accessing the remote end of the link via TERM. If given an argument, trsh executes that argument as a command on the remote system. For example

```
trsh ls
```

would give you a listing of the files in your home directory on the remote system.

tupload will transfer a file, given as its first argument, from local to remote. By default, the files will be put in the same directory that you invoked TERM from at the other side. To put files in another directory, give their names as a second argument to tupload. For example, if I want to put a copy of the file 'term114.tar.gz' in '/usr/tmp' on the remote system, I would type

```
tupload term114.tar.gz /usr/tmp
```

When you use tupload you can use wild cards like in 'tupload a.*'. The shell expands the wild card and tupload is called as 'tupload a.1 a.2 ......'.

tdownload will transfer a file, given as its first argument, from remote to local. By default, the files will be put in the same directory that you invoked TERM from at the local side. To put files in another directory, give their names as a second argument to tdownload. For example, if I want to put a copy of the file 'term114.tar.gz' in '/usr/tmp' on the local system, I would type

```
tdownload term114.tar.gz /usr/tmp
```

When you use tdownload you *cannot* use wild cards like in 'tdownload a.*'. Reason for this is that the remote directory is not available to your local shell when you use tdownload; so your local shell cannot expand the wild cards.

trdate is a time setting utility. It reads the time on the remote machine and sets the local clock to the remote time. It must be run as root.

trdated is the daemon version of trdate. When it is started in 'rc.local' it is run as daemon in which case it updates the time every 5 minutes (default). Even when there is no TERM connection, this daemon will start up when set in the rc.local. Once a TERM connection is created it starts updating the time.

6   X and TERM

TERM allows users to open up X windows on the local machine from clients that are running on a machine on the network. This is done by using the txconn client. txconn is executed on the remote, network-connected machine; it is invoked simply as txconn. It goes into the background and returns a number on the standard output; this number is the display number that clients should use to access the X server on the local machine. An example should make this clear. I am logged in, via trsh, to my remote TERM host, named foo. On foo, I do the following

```
foo$ txconn
Xconn bound to screen 10
:10
foo$
```

Now, on any host that I wish to run an X client on, that is to display on my local machine's X server, I do

```
setenv DISPLAY foo:10
```

(for bash you should use export DISPLAY=foo:10). In some cases it can furthermore be necessary to do a

```
xhost + foo
```

or even a

```
xhost +
```

on your local machine. Now when I start the client, it will try to connect to screen 10 on machine foo, but txconn is listening to this screen, and will forward all X protocol packets via TERM to the X server on the local host - *i.e.* the window will open up on your local machine.

It is possible to go the other way - run a client on your local machine and have it open up a window on a remote machine on the network; however we will defer explaining this until after we have discussed tredir.

The X protocol is not very efficient; it wastes some bandwidth. This is usually not a problem over an ethernet, but can be murder over a modem. X11R6 is supposed to introduce a low bandwidth version of the X protocol, LBX. If however you are using X11R5 you can use a utility named sxpc which compresses the X protocol, improving response over serial lines. Sxpc includes a write-up on how to get it working with TERM, and is recommended. The sxpc package also explains how to use xauth; so it is doubly recommended.

7 tredir

`tredir` is one of TERM's most powerful utilities, allowing most important network services to be performed over a TERM link. Before we explain how to use tredir, it is necessary to give some background on network services. We have talked about network services before, but we have not said exactly what they are. Services are just that - services that are provided by the network. Examples of services include `telnet`, which provides logins between machines, the File Transfer Protocol, `ftp`, which transfers files between machines, and smtp, the Simple Mail Transfer Protocol, which is used whenever you send electronic mail. Each network service has a *port number* associated with it. The mapping of port numbers to services is given in the file '/etc/services'. This file should be the same on all internet-connected machines.

How are these services invoked? Each networked machine runs a daemon called `inetd`, which listens for attempts to connect to the network ports. These requests can come from either the network or the local machine. A network service is obtained by connecting to a particular inetd port. When a network request is made, inetd knows exactly which service is involved by the port number the request is made on. If inetd is configured to do so, it provides the relevant service to the requesting connection. inetd's configuration is given by the file '/etc/inetd.conf', which has a list of the services that inetd provides. For more information, see the man pages for inetd and inetd.conf.

You can communicate directly with network services by using `telnet` (*n.b.* not `termtelnet`). For example, to talk to the `sendmail`, (or smtp) daemon on machine `machine_name`, you can do a `telnet machine_name smtp`, or `telnet machine_name 25`, (since 25 is the number assigned to smtp in '/etc/services'). You should get a polite greeting from the daemon on the remote machine. This is a very useful trick for debugging network problems and checking ports redirected with tredir (see below).

Tredir works very much like inetd. It runs in the background as a daemon, listening to the network ports, waiting for a request. When a request for a service is made, instead of providing that service, as inetd does, tredir forwards the request over the TERM link to the remote TERM, which makes the request over the network, returning the result back over the link to the local client. Tredir can forward the request to any machine on the network, but by default sends it to the machine at the other end of the TERM link. Tredir *redirects* TCP (Transmission Control Protocol) network services over the TERM link.

The common command format of tredir is:

```
tredir [this_computer:]port [that_computer:]port
```

An example should make this clear. Let us redirect a local port to the telnet port on the remote machine. To do this we would do

```
tredir 2023 23
```

Now, anyone who connects to port 2023 on the local machine will be redirected to port 23 (telnet) on the remote machine. Here is an example session; the local machine is `mymachine.modem.home` and the remote machine is `netsun`.

```
$ tredir 2023 23
Redirecting 2023 to 23
$ telnet localhost 2023
Trying 127.0.0.1...
Connected to mymachine.modem.home
Escape character is '^]'.


SunOS UNIX (netsun)
login:
```

This example is actually quite useful. If I were instead to do the tredir on `netsun`. I could then telnet in to `mymachine` from the network simply by connecting to the redirected port on the networked machine (using telnet) - *i.e.* `telnet netsun 2023`.

The general principle in using tredir is to redirect the desired service to a machine on the network. Our next example will allow us to read news on the local machine over our TERM link from a news server on the network. News is provided by the nntp service, port number 119. All decent news readers allow you to specify what port number they will use, either via a configuration file or an environment variable. Let us specify this local port to be 2119. Now, let us say that our news server is `news.domain.org`. We will redirect port 2119 to port 119 on `news.domain.org`; we will then tell our news reading software that the nntp server is located at port 2119 on the local host. Since this will depend on the news reader that you use, I will just test the link with `telnet` instead of firing up a news reader:

```
$ tredir 2119 news.domain.org:119
Redirecting 2119 to news.domain.org:119
$ telnet localhost 2119
Trying 127.0.0.1...
Connected to mymachine.modem.home.
Escape character is '^]'.
200 news.domain.org InterNetNews NNRP server INN 1.4 07-Dec-41 ready
(posting ok).
```

If you can get this far, all you have to do is configure your news reader to be able to read news via TERM. (*n.b.*, if you read news like this, be sure that in all your posts you set a Reply-To: header to an network email address that you can be reached at, otherwise people who want to get in touch with you will be sending mail to whatever (wrong) data your news reader puts in the From: header).

7.1 `tredir` can bite!

The astute reader, after reading the last example will be wondering why port 2119 was redirected to port 119 - since news readers default to port 119, why could I not do a `tredir 119 news.domain.org:119` and skip the news reader configuration? The answer is that all ports numbered less than 1024 are "reserved ports", and only the superuser can listen to them. If one is willing to take a security risk and make tredir an SUID program, or run tredir as root, then one can redirect reserved ports and avoid the hassle of renaming services.

Another problem with using reserved ports is that inetd is often already listening to these ports, and only one program at a time can listen to a port. In order to use such a port, you must change 'inetd.conf' so that inetd no longer listens to the port you want to redirect. This is most easily done by commenting out the line with the offending service by putting a # character at the beginning of the line. The superuser must then send inetd a HUP signal (kill -1 inetd-pid) to get it to reread its configuration.

7.2 Stupid `tredir` tricks

In this section we will describe some of the more common uses for tredir. We have already described how to redirect nntp and telnet services; here we will give some more complicated examples.

7.2.1 X windows

In a previous section, we described how to get an X client running on the network to open a window on your home machine using `txconn`. The same technique could be used on your home machine to display a client on the machine at the remote end of your TERM link. But how does one display an X client on a network machine that is not the remote end? The answer lies in knowing that X uses a particular network service just like the other programs we have been discussing. An X server listens for a network request on a port whose number is given by the formula $port = 6000 + displaynumber$, *e.g.* an X server managing screen 0 on a machine would listen to port 6000, if it were managing screen 2, it would listen to port 6002. When you set your DISPLAY environment variable to `xmachine:n`, your X clients will try to connect to port $6000 + n$ on `xmachine`.

We can use this to trick X clients on your local machine to open up windows on remote displays. Let us say I want to open up an `xterm`, running on my local machine, on display 0 of machine `xmachine`, which is running some place on the network. I first pick a local display number, say 2 (do not use 0, since that is what your local X server will be using). I will map this display to display 0 on `xmachine`. In terms of ports, this means I want to redirect the local port 6002 to the remote port 6000. I do the following

```
$ tredir 6002 xmachine:6000
$ setenv DISPLAY localhost:2
$ xterm
```

This should open up an `xterm` on machine `xmachine`. Note that I set the DISPLAY to `localhost:2`. This is because X clients will sometimes use unix domain sockets instead of internet domain sockets, at their own option, when connecting to a local display, if DISPLAY is set to `:2`. `localhost:2` says to use a TCP connection.

Note that as far as `xmachine` is concerned, the X request is coming from the machine on the remote end of your TERM link (`remotemachine`) - so if you need to authorize the connection, you should either do an `xhost + remotemachine` on `xmachine` or use xauth to update the '.Xauthority' file on your local machine for display number 2, using the key from `xmachine`.

Again, to speed up X connections, you can use the program sxpc, which includes an explanation of how to use tredir to establish the link and authorize it using xauth.

7.2.2   Mail with TERM

Well, you asked for it. Electronic mail has the justifiable reputation of being one of the most difficult things to get working right on a UNIX system. To really get TERM working correctly with mail means that you have to understand how mail works, which is beyond the scope of this document. To learn more about mail, you should consult a book on UNIX system administration and/or the comp.mail.misc FAQ, available for anonymous ftp on rtfm.mit.edu:pub/usenet/comp.mail.misc. There are also currently two packages available for anonymous ftp on sunsite.unc.edu that will help you get mail running under TERM - they are `term.mailerd+smail` by Byron A. Jeff and the `BCRMailHandlerXXX` by Bill C. Riemers.

That being said, we will give a thumbnail description of how mail works. There are two parts to getting mail running, sending messages and receiving messages. We will begin with sending messages from your local box to the network.

There are two classes of mail programs. The first is the mail user agent (MUA). MUA's help you read, compose and send messages. Examples of MUA's are `elm`, `pine`, `Mail` and `vm`. MUA's do not really do any networking; they just put the messages together - the real work of sending mail is done by the second class of mail programs, the mail transfer agents (MTA's). These are invoked by the MUA's. They take the message, decide where to send it by looking at the address, and then actually deliver it over the network.

The two most common MTA's on Linux systems are `sendmail` and `smail`. The basic idea is to get your MTA to connect to another MTA running on a machine on the net that will know what to do with your message. This is done by redirecting a local port to the smtp port on the net machine. You then have to tell you MTA to take any message it does not know what to do with, and send it out over the redirected port on your local machine to the MTA on the remote machine, which will then route your message to its correct destination.

How do we do this using smail? We first redirect a port to the smtp port on the network mail machine (`mailhost`):

`tredir XXXX mailhost:25`

here XXXX is the port number that the `smail` on the localhost will connect to (note that I have to give this port a name in my '/etc/services' to get smail to recognize it). Smail has several configuration files that usually live in '/usr/local/lib/smail'. The ones we care about are 'config', 'routers' and 'transports'. Note that I am assuming you have already got smail configured correctly for local mail - delivery to files and pipes and such things. Again, consult the documentation if you have not.

In the file 'config', we put the following definition:

```
smart_path=localhost
```

localhost is the machine that smail connects to when it does not know what to do with a message.

In 'routers' we put

```
smart_host:
driver=smarthost,
transport=termsmtp;
path = localhost
```

In 'transports' we put

```
termsmtp:           driver=tcpsmtp,
     inet,
     return_path,
     remove_header="From",
     append_header="From: YOUR_NET_ADDRESS",
     -received,
     -max_addrs, -max_chars;
     service=YOUR_SMTP_SERVICE,
```

In the above, the header lines change the `From` header in all your outgoing mail to the address, YOUR_NET_ADDRESS, which is the network address you want mail sent to. If more than one user is going to be using your TERM link, you will have to do something more fancy, like keep a database of local user's network addresses and insert these in the `From:` headers.

The service line is the name of the local port number that you have redirected to the smtp port on the network connected machine. In my version of smail, I cannot just set this to a number, I have to set it to a name, like "foo", and then define "foo" in my '/etc/services' to be the number of my redirected port. If you use a SUID tredir and just redirect the smtp port (25), you do not need to define this.

This should be enough to get you going. If you decide to use `sendmail`, the principles are the same but the details differ. Ronald Florence (ron@mlfarm.com) told me that the stock Sun sendmail will not send multiple queued messages over a redirected port; BSD sendmail 8.6.9 works fine. He made the following changes to '/etc/sendmail.cf' to get it working with TERM. In his case, the default sendmail port (25) is used for SMTP traffic over a local ethernet so Internet mail is forwarded to a redirected TCP port.

```
#
#Create the termsmtp mailer, which sends mail via a re-directed TCP port
#
Mtermsmtp,P=[TCP], F=mDFMuCXe, S=22, R=22, A=TCP $h PORTNUMBER
```

Here, PORTNUMBER is the number of the redirected port on the local machine. This should be an unused port over 2000. We next tell sendmail which machine to connect to, and set termsmtp as the default mailer.

```
#
# major relay mailer
#
```

```
DMtermsmtp
#
# major relay host: use the $M mailer to send mail to other domains
#
DR HOSTNAME
CR HOSTNAME
```

Here `HOSTNAME` is the name of your local host (does `localhost` work?). The last entry goes under Rule 0 to forward Internet mail.

```
# Pass other valid names up the ladder to our forwarder
R$*<@$*.$+>$*          $#$M    $@$R $:$1<@$2.$3>$4        user@any.domain
```

When the `TERM` connection is established to the Internet host, run the following commands on the local machine.

```
tredir PORTNUMBER internet.host:25
/usr/lib/sendmail -q
```

We now turn to receiving electronic mail using `TERM`. We will assume that mail is sent to your account on the network machine `mailhost`. The simplest solution is to just use trsh or termtelnet to log on to `mailhost` and read your mail on there. However, it is also possible to have your mail automatically downloaded to your local machine. One way to do this is to use the Post Office Protocol, (POP). POP was designed for exactly this purpose: to deliver mail to machines that have intermittent network connections. To use POP, you must have a POP server installed on `mailhost`. Assuming that you do, you can then use a POP client to download your mail every few minutes. This is done, as you might expect, using tredir. The POP service is 110 (**note** that there is an older protocol, POP-2, which uses port 109; in this document we describe POP-3, which is the latest version of POP). There are several POP clients available. One, written in the script language `perl` is pop-perl-1.X, written by William Perry and maintained by myself - it can be found on sunsite.unc.edu:/pub/Linux/system/Mail.

To use POP, you redirect a local port to port 110 on `mailhost` and configure your client to retrieve your mail from localhost using the local port. As an example, we will assume that there is a POP server running on `mailhost`. We will redirect the local port 2110, and fire up the pop-perl client:

```
$ tredir 2110 mailhost:110
Redirecting 2110 to mailhost:110
$ pop
Username: bill
Password: <enter your password for mailhost>
Pop Host: name of local
Pop Port: 2110
Starting popmail daemon for bill
```

If you do not have a POP server available, the BCRMailHandler package has a program to download your mail over a `TERM` link to your local machine. I have not used it, but anyone who has is welcome to comment. You can also use the term.mailerd+smail package for this purpose. Alas, both BCRMailHandler and the term.mailerd.smail package do not work anymore with `TERM` versions 2.0.0 and higher.

8 `tudpredir`

`tudpredir` is similar to tredir when you look at what these programs do and how they are executed. The big difference between the two programs is that tredir is used to redirect TCP network services while `tudpredir` redirects UDP (User Datagram Protocol) network services over the `TERM` link. One more important difference between the two programs is that tredir becomes a background daemon once it has successfully established the local port, while tudpredir commands must be placed in the background manually.

The common command format of tudpredir is:

```
tudpredir [this_computer:]port [that_computer:]port
```

9 Automating Things

Now that you know how to get all your network services over TERM, it would be nice to set things up in such a way that your link is set up and configured automatically. There are basically an infinite number of ways of doing so, depending on what communication program you use and how you log in to your remote system.

One program that I have not used, but I have heard is quite nice, is fet: a front end for TERM. It is designed to log you into a remote system and fire up TERM and all your tredir's. Any comments on fet would be most welcome.

I shall now give an example of a set of commands that use kermit to log into the remote system and then performs all of the TERM initializations. Obviously, if you use these examples, you will have to modify them for your own login procedures.

The command which is actually invoked is the shell script 'knet', given by:

```
#!/bin/sh
/usr/bin/kermit -y $HOME/.kerm_term > $HOME/klog < /dev/null 2>& 1
exec $HOME/bin/tstart >> $HOME/klog 2>& 1
```

The script '.kerm_term' is given by:

```
pause 2
# The number you want to dial
output atdtXXXXXXX \13
# Login to the terminal server
input 145 {name: }
output MYNAME \13
input 3 {word: }
output MYPASSWORD \13
input 5 {xyplex>}
# Make the line transparent
output term telnet-t \13
output term stopb 1 \13
# Connect to the remote host
output telnet remotehost.somedomain.org \13
input 10 {ogin: }
output MYOTHERNAME \13
input 3 word:
output MYOTHERPASSWORD \13
pause 5
# Fire up term on the remote host
output exec term -s 38400 -l $HOME/tlog -w 10 -t 150  \13
! /usr/bin/term -r -l $HOME/tlog -s 38400 -c off -w 10 -t 150 < /dev/modem  > /dev/modem &
# Open other clients here
suspend
!killall -KILL term
```

and finally, the script 'tstart' which fires up the TERM clients is given by

```
#!/bin/sh
#
# This lets mail get out, can read news here, can pick up my mail here
#
/usr/local/bin/tredir 2025 25 2119 newshost:119 2110 pophost:110
#
# So I can open up Xwindows here
#
/usr/local/bin/trsh -s txconn
#
# So I will receive mail....
#
/usr/local/bin/pop
#
# Clean out the queue, in case of boo-boos
#
/usr/bin/runq
#
# Done now
#
echo ^G^G > /dev/console
```

When finally you want to close the connection, you resume and terminate kermit. The last line of the script kills the local TERM and returns the system in its initial state.

(Note of the author: instead of doing '!killall -KILL term', I think it should be possible just to do '!tshutdown'. This should also work?)

As I said, there are zillions of ways to do so; these are just meant as examples to get you started. Other examples can be found in the packages autoterm and JoelTermStuff.

10 Porting software for use with TERM

In principle, all programs that can be used over a network can also be used in combination with TERM. Some of them you can get as binaries with TERM support already built in. These include telnet, (nc)ftp, Mosaic and many others. Most of these programs are compiled for TERM 1.17 or earlier. They should, however, still work with the newer versions of TERM.

Another way to make programs TERM aware is to port them yourself. This process will be described in the next subsection.

The last way to make your programs TERM-aware is to termify them.

10.1 Port and compile the sources

Porting software to TERM can be done using a fairly simple porting procedure:

If installed in '/usr/local' by root:

1. Add to the compile flags -include /usr/local/include/termnet.h

2. and add to the library list -ltermnet

If installed in your home directory:

1. Add to the compile flags `-include $HOME/term/termnet.h`

2. and add to the library list `-L$HOME/term -ltermnet`

Now compile the software as described in the INSTALL or README document that came with the software. That should do!

At this point the commands should work both with and without TERM.

```
telnet localhost
```

does not use TERM to connect, but

```
telnet bohr.physics.purdue.edu
```

will use TERM only if you do not have some other type of network connection.

Some commands like `rlogin` can only be executed by root and the owner of the TERM connection (privileged persons).

Some TERM commands will be TERM transparent and only use TERM when there is not another option. Some common examples are telnet and ftp.

Others require an external flag to tell them it is all right to use TERM. These programs include xarchie, fsp and ytalk.

You can either flag these programs to use TERM by setting the environmental variable TERMMODE as specified in README.security, or running `make installnet`. Eventually, the 'termnet' file created will contain special networking instructions, but for now only its existence is checked.

If you add an `ethernet connection`, you can then simply remove the 'termnet' file and continue to use the same binaries!

NOTE: Programs that were ported back in the days of `client.a`, can still be recompiled for use with newer versions of TERM simply by changing the `client.a` reference to `libtermnet.a`.

10.2   Termify

This package will convert dynamically linked binaries for TERM use.

Before you can use `termify` you have to make sure that you have TERM version 2.2i (is this version 2.2.8?) or later and libc.so.4.5.26 or later. Then you have to create the file 'libt.so.4' in the directory '/lib' (see the README file in the package).

Problem at this moment is that you have to remake the file 'libt.so.4' every time you upgrade TERM versions.

After you have created the library you can let termify 'crunch' the program you want to make TERM-aware, by using the command:

```
termify <command name>
```

When you do not like the result you can 'un'termify the program you have just termified using the command:

```
termify -u <command name>
```

Last, the package also contains a script for completely termifying 'smail'; so no special transport definitions are necessary. The only thing you possibly want to change is the 'From: ' address.

11   Term clients

11.1   Term clients available on ftp sites.

Below a list of application running with TERM is given. I am not stating that this list is complete; so any completion is welcome. As far as possible I will present the site and directory where the application can be found (all to my knowledge). When I state sunsite.unc.edu as the place to find the application I mean that you can find it in one of the following two directories:

1. /pub/Linux/apps/comm/term/apps

2. /pub/Linux/apps/comm/term/extra

Here we go :-)

TERM **package:**

```
tupload
tdownload           (versions 2.1.0 and higher)
trsh
tmon
tredir
tudpredir           (versions 2.0.0 and higher)
txconn
trdate(d)
tshutdown
libtermnet
```

File transfer:

```
ftpd            sunsite.unc.edu
termncftp       sunsite.unc.edu
ncftp185        sunsite.unc.edu:/pub/Linux/system/Network/file-transfer
fsp             sunsite.unc.edu:/pub/Linux/system/Network/file-transfer
```

Information systems:

```
lynx
Mosaic          sunsite.unc.edu:/pub/Linux/system/Network/info-systems/Mosaic
chimera
netscape        sunsite.unc.edu:/pub/Linux/system/Network/info-systems
httpd
xgopher
gopher          sunsite.unc.edu
```

Remote login:

```
termtelnet      sunsite.unc.edu
rlogin          physics.purdue.edu:/pub/bcr/term/extra
rsh             physics.purdue.edu:/pub/bcr/term/extra
```

Netnews:

```
tin 1.3         sunsite.unc.edu:/pub/Linux/system/Mail/news
news2           sunsite.unc.edu
```

Mail:

```
slurp                 sunsite.unc.edu
smail                 sunsite.unc.edu
term.mailerd+smail    sunsite.unc.edu
BCRMailHandlerXXX     physics.purdue.edu:/pub/bcr/term
```

Automating scripts:

```
JoelTermStuff         sunsite.unc.edu
autoterm              sunsite.unc.edu
fet                   sunsite.unc.edu
```

Other programs:

```
inetd                 sunsite.unc.edu
rdate                 sunsite.unc.edu
xgospel               sunsite.unc.edu:/pub/Linux/games/x11/networked
termify               physics.purdue.edu:/pub/bcr/term/extra
xboard                sunsite.unc.edu
ircII                 sunsite.unc.edu:/pub/Linux/system/Network/chat
whois
xwebster              sunsite.unc.edu
sxpc                  ftp.x.org:/R5contrib
xztalk                sunsite.unc.edu:/pub/Linux/apps/sound/talk
```

11.2   The termnet package

The package `termnet-2.0.4-Linux-bin.tar.gz` (sunsite.unc.edu:/pub/Linux/apps/comm/term) contains a couple of pre-compiled TERM clients and a couple of scripts, manual pages and libtermnet.so.2.00.04. The clients are compiled using this version of libtermnet.so. The package contains the following clients:

```
fet        perl         sperl4.036   tmon       tshutdown   xgopher
finger     perl4.036    suidperl     trdate     tudpredir   ytalk
ftp        rcp          taintperl    trdated    tupload
fwhois     rlogin       telnet       tredir     txconn
ncftp      rsh          term         trsh       xarchie
```

WARNING: The package also contains the complete set of compiled clients of TERM 2.0.4 including TERM itself. Do not install this package before you are sure about what you want. You will destroy other versions of TERM and its clients when you start moving executables around.

11.3   Asked for but not yet supported

1. DOOM: The problem with this game seems to be the fact that it uses port 5029 both as client and as server.

2. NFS: The NFS server is only supposed to accept requests if the socket requesting the connection is bound to a port below 1024. This seems to be troublesome. However, some NFS servers have an 'insecure' option. In this case NFS might work eventually, if RPC support is added to Term.

12   Term and Security

In this section I will point to some security aspects of TERM. The problems will be explained and a way to improve security will be given.

12.1   trsh

Trsh is insecure when it is used to access the local Linux box from the remote system. The problem with TERM and its clients is that beside the owner of the TERM connection also 'root' can execute TERM-aware programs over the connection.

This also means that 'root' on the remote system can execute trsh and thus can enter the login which owns the TERM connection quite easy. If this owner on the local box is 'root' then you will be in hell.

The solution to this problem is easy: you just have to put the following line in the termrc· file on the local box:

```
denyrsh on
```

With this set in the 'termrc' file, nobody can use trsh on the remote site anymore to access your machine. When you and others want to access your local Linux box over the TERM connection this can still be done using telnet and redirected ports.

12.2   txconn and xauth

Txconn is not terribly secure; anyone can connect to your local server via TERM and perform all sorts of mischief. I you are worried about this sort of thing, it might be a good idea to consider using xauth to authorize your connections. See the next section for an example of using xauth for securing your connections.

12.3   sxpc, xhost and xauth

Sxpc in combination with 'xhost +' is very dangerous when you are not using xauth.

Using xauth is very important to maintaining security when using sxpc. If you do not use xauth when using sxpc all the dangers of running with 'xhost +' apply. These dangers include but are not limited to:

- Someone watching what is displayed on your screen

- Someone watching what you type

- Someone typing in one of your windows (for example: a command to delete all your files :-(

Xauth is available in X releases R4 and later. Here I will describe how to set up basic usage of xauth. This configuration is vulnerable to network snooping, but if you can live with that it should be fine.

NOTE: when using xauth your $DISPLAY variable must NOT be set to localhost (or localhost:whatever). If your $DISPLAY variable does use localhost the clients will be unable to find the appropriate authorization information. The workaround is to use the real hostname of the machine. If you follow the compilation instructions in the README, and compile without -DNOGETHOSTNAME then everything should work.

The machine where you will be running clients will be called C, the machine where you wish to display them will be called D.

First choose a 'key', up to 16 pairs of hexadecimal digits (so an even number of characters from the ranges 0-9 and a-f). You will need to supply this key in place of <key> in the example below.

On C:

```
% xauth
xauth:  creating new authority file $HOME/.Xauthority
Using authority file $HOME/.Xauthority
xauth> add Chostname:8 MIT-MAGIC-COOKIE-1 <key>
xauth> exit
```

On D:

```
% xauth
xauth:  creating new authority file $HOME/.Xauthority
Using authority file $HOME/.Xauthority
xauth> add Dhostname/unix:0 MIT-MAGIC-COOKIE-1 <key>
xauth> add Dhostname:0 MIT-MAGIC-COOKIE-1 <key>
xauth> exit
```

When starting the X server on D you should give the flag *-auth* $*HOME/.Xauthority*. You may need to edit or create a '$HOME/.xserverrc' to control how the X server is started. For example:

```
#!/bin/sh
exec X  -auth $HOME/.Xauthority $*
```

Make sure that your '.Xauthority' file is readable only by you on both C and D.

13   Things to remember

In this section I try to present you with a list of useful ftp addresses, URL's etc. where you can find software and information about TERM.

ftp:

```
sunsite.unc.edu:/pub/Linux/apps/comm/term/<whole-directory-tree>
sunsite.unc.edu:/pub/Linux/docs/HOWTO
physics.purdue.edu:/pub/bcr/term/<whole-directory-tree>
```

URL:

```
http://sunsite.unc.edu/mdw/HOWTO/Term-HOWTO.html
http://zeus.cs.kun.nl:4080/term-howto/Term-HOWTO.html
http://physics.purdue.edu/~bcr/homepage.html
```

netnews:

```
comp.os.linux.announce        announce of new TERM versions and Term-HOWTO
comp.os.linux.help            ask your questions about TERM here
comp.os.linux.misc            or here
comp.protocols.misc           answers to TERM questions are also posted here.
```

When you start asking questions on netnews please make sure that you give people in the groups as much information as they need to solve your problem (TERM version number, way you set up your connection etc.). At this moment many TERM versions are in use and all have their specific and common problems. Therefore, when you want a useful answer, at least state the version of TERM you are using. Otherwise, in some cases only wild guesses are possible to help you solve your problems.

14   Reliability of TERM versions

Many versions of TERM are around now. The maintainer of TERM, Bill Riemers, has made a list of TERM versions stating what versions are reliable and what versions you had better avoid. This list is the following:

```
         term110              --> cannot really say
         term111              --> cannot really say
         term112              --> cannot really say
         term113              --> cannot really say
         term114              --> fairly stable BETA version
         term115              --> unstable BETA version
         term116              --> unstable BETA version
         term117              --> unstable BETA version
         term118              --> semi-stable BETA version
         term119              --> stable GAMMA version
         term-2.0.X           --> semi-stable BETA versions
         term-2.1.X           --> more stable BETA versions
         term-2.2.X           --> new BETA versions
         term-2.3.X           -->
```

15   Term speed table

Thanks to Bill McCarthy we now have a table with TERM speed information for different modems, TERM versions and connection conditions. Its purpose is to give new and experienced users some idea what other people are using and the results they are getting.

```
                        LINUX TERM CHART 8/14/94


  |___modem speed/make___|___line speed__|__avg cps__|__high__|__term ver_|
  | 1)  USR SP 14.4       |  9600         |  950      |  963   | 1.17       |
  | 2)  USR SP 14.4       |  14400        |  1376     |  n/a   | 1.18p06    |
  | 3)  Zoom 2400         |  2400         |  220      |  230   | 1.19       |
  | 4)  Boca V.32bis 14   |  57600        |  1400     |  n/a   | 1.01/09?   |
  | 5)  Viva 14.4         |  14400        |  1300     |  n/a   | 1.16       |
  | 6)  USR SP 14.4       |  14400+       |  1550     |  1680  | 1.19       |
  | 7)  Intel 14.4 Fax    |  14400        |  1400     |  1650  | 2.0.4      |
  | 8)  cable tv hookup   |  57600        |  1500     |  1800  | 1.18p06    |
  | 9)  Twincom 144/DFi   |  57600        |  1500     |  4000? | 2.0.4      |
  | 10) USR SP 14.4       |  14400        |  1200     |  1500  | 1.08       |
  | 11) cable tv hookup   |  19200        |  1300     |  1800  | 1.19       |
  |-------------------------------------------------------------------------|
```

+Command flags/termrc settings:

```
1) default escapes    2) window 5        3) baudrate 2400     4) n/a
   baudrate 9600         timeout 200         window 3
   window 10                                 noise on
   timeout 150

5) compress off       6) baudrate 19200  7) ignore 19+17      8) compress off
   window 10             compress on         window 4             escape 0, 13,
   timeout 150                               timeout 90           16-19, 255
   baudrate 38400                                                 baudrate 0
                                                                  shift 224
                                                                  flowcrtl 500
                                                                  window 10
                                                                  timeout 70
                                                                  retrain on
                                                                  breakout 24

9) compress off      10) compress off    11) baudrate 19200
   baudrate 57600        baudrate 38400       compress on
   window 10             escape 17, 19        shift 224
   timeout 200           remote               escape 0, 13 16-17
```

```
    noise on                                     19, 255
    share on                                     window 10
    remote                                       timeout 40
```

```
Escaping characters at one end also implies ignoring them on the other end.
```

16   Hints and Tricks found on the net

In the Linux related newsgroups many questions about TERM are coming back every couple of weeks, together with the answers to these questions. To reduce traffic to the newsgroup, in this section I shall try to make a composition of these questions and the answers to them. Some of the answers have been checked by me as I also had related problems. Others, I have just taken from the newsgroups without testing them.

- Many people, especially those who are using Ultrix, seem to have trouble with vi presenting less than 24 lines on a window with 24 lines. There are three ways to get rid of this problem:

  1. Log in into the remote system using:

     ```
     trsh -s telnet {$<$}hostname>
     ```

  2. Put 'resize; clear' in your '.login' file

  3. The best solutions seems to be to enter the following remote:

     ```
     stty 38400
     ```

- Many people seem to have problems with crashing TERM connections, whatever may be the reason of the crashes. So before starting applications people want to know whether their TERM connection is still alive or not. This can be checked using the following small shell script examples:

  When you are using tcsh:

  ```
  if ( { trsh -s true } ) then
    ...
  endif
  ```

  When you are using bash:

  ```
  if trsh -s true; then
    ...
  fi
  ```

- The new WWW browser called Netscape is causing people problems to get it to work with TERM. The good news is that it will work under TERM. Here is how:

  ```
     1. Termify netscape
     2. Fire up termnetscape
           under Options | Preferences | Mail/Proxys
           leave _all_ of the proxy boxes blank
           set the SOCKS box to 'remotehost' & 80
     3. Ignore the error you get when you exit the Options menu.
     4. If termnetscape fails to work right:
           under Options | Preferences | Mail/Proxys
           leave _all_ of the proxy boxes blank
           set the SOCKS box to 'none' & 80
     5. Ignore the error you get when you exit the Options menu.
  ```

17   Other Things

Some things that might be included:

- Extension of troubleshooting
- Extension of security issues
- Termwrap
- Suggestions

Anyway, if you have suggestions, criticism, suggestions, or anything else to say about this document, please fire away. At the moment I, Patrick Reijnen, have taken over the authorship of the TERM-HOWTO. I can (currently) be reached at `patrickr@cs.kun.nl` or `patrickr@sci.kun.nl`.

18   Acknowledgements

A lot of people have to be thanked. First and foremost Michael O'Reilly and all the developers of TERM, who have provided us with such a great tool. I would also like to thank everyone who gave feedback and contributed to this HOWTO. They include Bill Reynolds, the former author of this HOWTO, Ronald Florence, Tom Payerle, Bill C. Riemers, Hugh Secker-Walker, Matt Welsh, Bill McCarthy, Sergio, Weyman Martin and everybody I forgot to mention.

Part XLI

The Linux Tips HOWTO

Copyright Vince Reed, reedv@rpi.edu
v0.1, 30 August 1994
This document describes time-saving ideas and procedures intended to make linux easier to configure and use. Items found here are too general to be included in one of the other howtos.

Contents

1   Introduction

Welcome to the **Linux Tips HOWTO**, a place to find swift answers to questions not covered in the more specific linux howtos. In the tips howto, you'll also find neat little tricks that make managing and using Linux systems easier. However, as this is only the second release of the tips howto, the number of tips mentioned is still rather small. The next issue needn't be this way though... Please send me your ideas to be included in future howtos. Thanks in advance!

Vince Reed *Maintainer–Linux TIPS HOWTO*

reedv@rpi.edu

2 Short Tips

2.1 Moving directories between filesystems. *Alan Cox,* `A.Cox@swansea.ac.uk`

Quick way to move an entire tree of files from one disk to another

```
(cd /source/directory; tar cf - . ) | (cd /dest/directory; tar xvfp -)
```

2.2 Pointer to patch for GNU Make 3.70 to change VPATH behavior. *Ted Stern,* `stern@amath.washington.edu`

I don't know if many people have this problem, but there is a "feature" of GNU make version 3.70 that I don't like. It is that VPATH acts funny if you give it an absolute pathname. There is an extremely solid patch that fixes this, which you can get from Paul D. Smith <psmith@wellfleet.com>. He also posts the documentation and patch after every revision of GNU make on the newsgroup 'gnu.utils.bug'. Generally, I apply this patch and recompile gmake on every system I have access to.

2.3 How do I stop my system from fscking on each reboot? *Dale Lutz,* `dal@wimsey.com`

Q: How do I stop e2fsck from checking my disk every time I boot up.

A: When you rebuild the kernel, the filesystem is marked as 'dirty' and so your disk will be checked with each boot. The fix is to run:

rdev -R /zImage 1

This fixes the kernel so that it is no longer convinced that the filesystem is dirty.

Note: If using lilo, then add `read-only` *to your linux setup in your lilo config file (Usually /etc/lilo.conf)*

2.4 How to avoid fscks caused by "device busy" at reboot time. *Jon Tombs,* `jon@gtex02.us.es`

If you often get device busy errors on shutdown that leave the filesystem in need of an fsck upon reboot, here is a simple fix:

To `/etc/brc` or `/sbin/brc`, add the line

```
mount -o remount,ro /mount.dir
```

for all your mounted filesystems except /, before the call to umount -a. This means if, for some reason, shutdown fails to kill all processes and umount the disks they will still be clean on reboot. Saves a lot of time at reboot for me

2.5 How to print pages with a margin for hole punching. *Mike Dickey,* `mdickey@thorplus.lib.purdue.edu`

```
#!/bin/sh
# /usr/local/bin/print
# a simple formatted printout, to enable someone to
# 3-hole punch the output and put it in a binder

cat $1 | pr -t -o 5 -w 85 | lpr
```

2.6 A way to search through trees of files for a particular regular expression. *Raul Deluth Miller,* `rockwell@nova.umd.edu`

I call this script 'forall'. Use it like this:

```
forall /usr/include grep -i ioctl
forall /usr/man grep ioctl
```

Here's forall:

```
#!/bin/sh
if [ 1 = 'expr 2 \> $#' ]
then
        echo Usage: $0 dir cmd [optargs]
        exit 1
fi
dir=$1
shift
find $dir -type f -print | xargs "$@"
```

2.7 A script for cleaning up after programs that creat autosave and backup files. *Barry Tolnas,* `tolnas@nestor.engr.utk.edu`

Here is a simple two-liner which recursively descends a directory hierarchy removing emacs auto-save ( ) and backup (#) files, .o files, and TeX .log files. It also compresses .tex files and README files. I call it 'squeeze' on my system.

```
#!/bin/sh
#SQUEEZE removes unnecessary files and compresses .tex and README files
#By Barry tolnas, tolnas@sun1.engr.utk.edu
#
echo squeezing $PWD
find  $PWD \( -name \*~ -or -name \*.o -or -name \*.log -or -name \*\#\) -exec
rm -f {} \;
find $PWD \( -name \*.tex -or -name \*README\* -or -name \*readme\* \) -exec gzip -9 {} \;
```

3 Detailed Tips

3.1 Sharing swap partitions between Linux and Windows. *Tony Acero,* `ace3@midway.uchicago.edu`

1. Format the partition as a dos partition, and create the Windows swap file on it, but don't run windows yet. (You want to keep the swap file completely empty for now, so that it compresses well).

2. Boot linux and save the partition into a file. For example if the partition was /dev/hda8:

   ```
   dd if=/dev/hda8 of=/etc/dosswap
   ```

3. Compress the dosswap file; since it is virtually all 0's it will compress very well

   ```
   gzip -9 /etc/dosswap
   ```

4. Add the following to the /etc/rc file to prepare and install the swap space under Linux:

   XXXXX is the number of blocks in the swap partition

   ```
   mkswap /dev/hda8 XXXXX
   swapon -av
   ```

Make sure you add an entry for the swap partition in your /etc/fstab file

5. If your init/reboot package supports /etc/brc or /sbin/brc add the following to /etc/brc, else do this by hand when you want to boot to dos | os/2 and you want to convert the swap partition back to the dos/windows version:

```
swapoff -av
zcat /etc/dosswap.gz | dd of=/dev/hda8 bs=1k count=100
```

Note that this only writes the first 100 blocks back to the partition. I've found empirically that this is sufficient

>> What are the pros and cons of doing this?

Pros: you save a substantial amount of disk space.

Cons: if step 5 is not automatic, you have to remember to do it by hand, and it slows the reboot process by a nanosecond :-)

3.2 How to configure xdm's chooser for host selection. *Arrigo Triulzi,* a.triulzi@ic.ac.uk

1. Edit the file that launches xdm most likely /etc/rc/rc.6 or /etc/rc.local) so that it contains the following lines in the xdm startup section.

```
/usr/bin/X11/xdm
exec /usr/bin/X11/X -indirect hostname
```

2. Edit /usr/lib/X11/xdm/Xservers and comment out the line which starts the server on the local machine *i.e.starting0* :

3. Reboot the machine and you're home and away.

I add this because when I was, desperately, trying to set it up for my own subnet over here it took me about a week to suss out all the problems.

Caveat: with old SLS (1.1.1) for some reason you can leave a -nodaemon after the xdm line – this does **NOT** work for later releases.

Part XLII

The UPS Howto

Contents

1   Introduction

This HOWTO covers connecting a UPS to a PC running Linux. The idea is to connect the two in such a way that Linux can shutdown cleanly when the power goes out. To a large extent this document is reduntant, because all the basic info is contained in the powerd man page that comes with the SysVinit package. None-the-less, there seems to periodically be alot of discussion on the net regarding connecting Linux PCs to UPSs (and the versions of Linux that I installed didn't come with a powerd man page). I figured having a HOWTO would be a good idea because:

- A second source of information might help to understand how to connect Linux to a UPS, even if it's just the same information written differently.

- The HOWTO can serve as a repository for UPS specific data.

- The HOWTO contains additional details that aren't in the powerd man page.

None the less, this does not replace the powerd man page. Hopefully, after reading both, people will be able to deal with UPSs.

1.1   Contributors

I am forever indebted to those from whom I've received help, suggestions, and UPS specific data. The list includes, in order of appearance in this document:

- Miquel van Smoorenburg (miquels@cistron.nl.mugnet.org)

- Danny ter Haar (danny@caution.cistron.nl.mugnet.org)

- Hennus Bergman (hennus@sky.nl.mugnet.org)

- Tom Webster (webster@kaiwan.com)

- Marek Michalkiewicz (ind43@sun1000.ci.pwr.wroc.pl)

- Christian G. Holtje (docwhat@uiuc.edu)

- Ben Galliart (bgallia@orion.it.luc.edu)

- Lam Dang (angit@netcom.com)

1.2   Important disclaimer

I really can't guarantee that any of this will work for you. Connecting a UPS to a computer can be a tricky business. One or the other or both might burn out, blow up, catch fire, or start World War Three. Furthermore, I only have direct experience with the Advice 1200 A UPS, and I didn't have to make a cable. So, BE CAREFUL. GATHER ALL INFORMATION YOU CAN ON YOUR UPS. THINK FIRST. DON'T IMPLICITLY TRUST ANYTHING YOU READ HERE.

On the other hand, I managed to get everything working with my UPSes, without much information from the manufacturer, and without burning out anything, so it is possible.

1.3   Other documents

This document does not cover the general features and capabilities of UPSs. For this type of information, you might turn to the UPS.faq, which is available via anonymous FTP from navigator.jpl.nasa.gov (128.149.23.82) in `pub/doc/faq/UPS.faq`, and can probably be found somewhere on rtfm.mit.edu. It is maintained by Nick Christenson (npc@minotaur.jpl.nasa.gov). In email to him, he'd like that you put UPS or UPS FAQ or something along these lines in the Subject line of the message.

2   What you need to do (summary)

- Plug the PC into the UPS.

- Connect the PC's serial port to the UPS with a special cable.

- Run powerd on the PC.

- Setup your initd to do something reasonable on powerfail and powerok events (like start a shutdown and kill any currently running shutdowns, respectively, for example).

3   How it's supposed to work

UPS's job

When the power goes out, the UPS continues to power the PC and signals that the power went out by throwing a relay or turning on an opticoupler on it's control port.

Cable's job

The cable is designed so that when the UPS throws said relay, this causes a particular serial port control line (typically DCD) to go high.

Powerd's job

Powerd monitors the serial port. Keeps raised/lowered whatever serial port control lines the UPS needs to have raised/lowered (typically, DTR must be kept high and whatever line shuts off the UPS must be kept low). When powerd sees the UPS control line go high, it writes FAIL to `/etc/powerfail` and sends the initd process a SIGPWR signal. When the control line goes low again, it writes OK to `/etc/powerfail` and sends initd a SIGPWR signal.

Initd's job (aside from everything else it does)

When it receives a SIGPWR, it looks at `/etc/powerfail`. If it contains FAIL it runs the `powerfail` entry from `/etc/inittab`. If it contains OK it runs the `powerokwait` entry from `inittab`.

4   Where to get the appropriate software

When I last looked, the package to pick up was `/pub/Linux/system/Daemons/SysVinit-2.50.tgz` from sunsite.unc.edu or a mirror. It includes a copy of powerd.c, shutdown.c, an initd that understands what to do with SIGPWR and can handle powerfail and powerokwait entries in the inittab file.

Of course, by now, I'm sure much newer versions are available. Whatever you get might differ from the description here, but will probably adhere to the overall philosophy.

5   How to set things up

The following presupposes that you have a cable that works properly with powerd.c. If you're not sure that your cable works (or how it works), see section 8 for information on dealing with poorly described cables and reconfiguring `powerd.c`. Sections 9 and 10 will also be useful.

If you need to make a cable, see section 7 for the overall details, and the subsection of section 11 that refers to your UPS. The latter might also include information on manufacturer supplied cables. You'll probably want to read all of section 11 because each section has a few additional generally helpful details.

- Edit `/etc/inittab`. Put in something like this:

```
# What to do when power fails (Halt system & drain battery :):
pf::powerfail:/etc/powerfailscript +5

# If power is back before shutdown, cancel the running shutdown.
pg:0123456:powerokwait:/etc/powerokscript
```

- Write scripts `/etc/powerfailscript` and `/etc/powerokscript` to shutdown in 5 minutes (or whatever's appropriate) and kill any existing shutdown, respectively. Depending on the version of shutdown that you're using, this will be either so trivial that you'll dispense with the scripts, or be a 1 line bash script, something along the lines of:

```
kill 'ps -aux | grep "shutdown" | grep -v grep | awk '{print $2}''
```

  and you'll keep the scripts. (In case it doesn't come out right, the first single quote on the above line is a backquote, the second and third are single quotes, and the last is also a backquote.)

- Tell initd to re-process the inittab file with the command:

```
telinit q
```

- Edit rc.local so that powerd gets run upon startup. The syntax is:

```
powerd <line>
```

  Replace `<line>` with the serial port that the modem is connected, such as `/dev/cua1`.

- Connect PC's serial port to UPS's serial port. DO NOT PLUG PC INTO UPS YET.

- Plug a light into the UPS.

- Turn on the UPS and the light.

- Run powerd.

- Test the setup:

  - Yank the UPS's plug.
    * Check that the light stays on.
    * Check that `/etc/powerfailscript` runs.

  * Check that shutdown is running.
- Plug the UPS back in.
  * Check that the light stays on.
  * Check that `/etc/powerokscript` runs.
  * Check that `/etc/powerfailscript` is not running.
  * Check that shutdown is no longer running.
- Yank the UPS's plug again. Leave it out and make sure that the PC shuts down properly in the proper amount of time.
- **The Dangerous Part.** After everything seems to be proper, powerdown the PC and plug it into the UPS. Run a script that sync's the hard disk every second or so. Simultaneously run a second script that keeps doing a find over your entire hard disk. The first is to make this a little safer and the second is to help draw lots of power. Now, pull the plug on the UPS, check again that shutdown is running and wait. Make sure that the PC shuts down cleanly before the battery on the UPS gives out. This is dangerous because if the power goes out before the PC shuts down, you can end up with a corrupt file system, and maybe even lose all your files. You'll probably want to do a full backup before this test, and set the shutdown time extremely short to begin with.

Congratulations! You now have a Linux PC that's protected by a UPS and will shutdown cleanly when the power goes out!

6 User Enhancements

- Hack `powerd.c` to monitor the line indicating that the batteries are low. When the batteries get low, do an **immediate** shutdown.

- Modify shutdown procedure so that if it's shutting down in a powerfail situation, then it turns off the UPS after doing everything necessary.

7 How to make a cable

This section is just from messages I've seen on the net. I haven't done it so I can't write from experience. If anyone has, please write this section for me :). See also the message about the GPS1000 contained in section 11.3

```
>From miquels@caution.cistron.nl.mugnet.org Wed Jul 21 14:26:33 1993
Newsgroups: comp.os.linux
Subject: Re: UPS interface for Linux?
From: miquels@caution.cistron.nl.mugnet.org (Miquel van Smoorenburg)
Date: Sat, 17 Jul 93 18:03:37
Distribution: world
Organization: Cistron Electronics.

In article <1993Jul15.184450.5193@excaliber.uucp>
joel@rac1.wam.umd.edu (Joel M. Hoffman) writes:
>I'm in the process of buying a UPS (Uninterruptable Power Supply), and
>notice that some of them have interfaces for LAN's to signal the LAN
>when the power fails.
>
>Is there such an interface for Linux?
>
```

>Thanks.
>
>-Joel
>(joel@wam.umd.edu)
>

When I worked on the last versioon of SysVinit (Now version 2.4),
I temporarily had a UPS on my computer, so I added support for it.
You might have seen that in the latest <signal.h> header files there
is a #define SIGPWR 30 now :-). Anyway, I did not have such a special
interface but the output of most UPS's is just a relais that makes or breaks
on power interrupt. I thought up a simple way to connect this to the
DCD line of the serial port. In the SysVinit package there is a daemon
called 'powerd' that keeps an eye on that serial line and sends SIGPWR
to init when the status changes, so that init can do something (such as
bringing the system down within 5 minutes). How to connect the UPS to
the serial line is described in the source "powerd.c", but I will
draw it here for explanation:

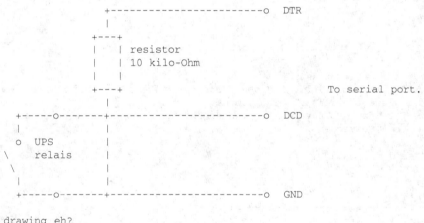

```
                          +-----------------------o  DTR
                          |
                      +---+
                      |   | resistor
                      |   | 10 kilo-Ohm
                      |   |
                      +---+                                 To serial port.
                        |
        +-----o-------+-----------------------o  DCD
        |            |
        o  UPS       |
         \    relais |
          \          |
          |          |
        +-----o-------+-----------------------o  GND
```

Nice drawing eh?

Hope this helps.
SysVinit can be found on sunsite (and tsx-11 probably) as
SysVinit2.4.tar.z

Mike.

--

Miquel van Smoorenburg, <miquels@cistron.nl.mugnet.org>
Ibmio.com: cannot open CONFIG.SYS: file handle broke off.

>From danny@caution.cistron.nl.mugnet.org Wed Jul 21 14:27:04 1993
Newsgroups: comp.os.linux
Subject: Re: UPS interface for Linux?
From: danny@caution.cistron.nl.mugnet.org (Danny ter Haar)
Date: Mon, 19 Jul 93 11:02:14
Distribution: world
Organization: Cistron Electronics.

```
In article <9307174330@caution.cistron.nl.mugnet.org>
miquels@caution.cistron.nl.mugnet.org (Miquel van Smoorenburg) writes:
>How to connect the UPS to the serial line is described in the source
>"powerd.c", but I will draw it here for explanation:

The drawing wasn't really clear, please use this one in stead !
>
>                       +------------------------o  DTR
>                       |
>                     +---+
>                     |   |  resistor
>                     |   |  10 kilo-Ohm
>                     |   |
>                     +---+                                 To serial port.
>                       |
>         +-----o-------+------------------------o  DCD
>         |
>         o   UPS
>         \     relais
>          \
>          |
>         +-----o-----------------------------------o  GND
>
```

```
The DTR is kept high, when the UPS's power input is gone it
will close the relais . The computer is monitoring
the DCD input port to go LOW . When this happens it will start a
shutdown sequence...
```

```
Danny
```

```
--
<=====================================================================>
Danny ter Haar  <dannyth@hacktic.nl> or <danny@cistron.nl.mugnet.org>
Robins law #103: 'a couple of lightyears can't part good friends'
```

8   Reverse-engineering cables and hacking powerd.c

Try to get documentation for the cables that your UPS seller supplies. In particular find out:

- What lines need to be kept high.
- What line(s) turn off the UPS.
- What lines the UPS toggles to indicate that:
  - Power is out.
  - Battery is low.

You then need to hack powerd.c appropriately.

If you have trouble getting the above information, or just want to check it (a *good* idea) the following program might help. It's a hacked version of powerd.c. It allows you to set the necessary port flags from the command line and then monitors the port, displaying the control lines every second. I used it as "upscheck

/dev/cua1 2" (for example) to set the 2nd bit (DTR) and to clear the other bits. The number base 2 indicates which bits to set, so for example to set bits 1, 2 and 3, (and clear the others) use 7. See the code for details.

Here's the (untested) upscheck.c program. It's untested because I edited the version I originally used to make it clearer, and can't test the new version at the moment.

```
/*
 * upscheck      Check how UPS & computer communicate.
 *
 * Usage:       upscheck <device> <bits to set>
 *              For example, upscheck /dev/cua4 4 to set bit 3 &
 *              monitor /dev/cua4.
 *
 * Author:      Harvey J. Stein <hjstein@math.huji.ac.il>
 *              (but really just a minor modification of Miquel van
 *              Smoorenburg's <miquels@drinkel.nl.mugnet.org> powerd.c
 *
 * Version:     1.0 19940802
 *
 */
#include <sys/types.h>
#include <sys/ioctl.h>
#include <fcntl.h>
#include <errno.h>
#include <stdlib.h>
#include <unistd.h>
#include <stdio.h>
#include <signal.h>

/* Main program. */
int main(int argc, char **argv)
{
  int fd;

/*  These TIOCM_* parameters are defined in <linux/termios.h>, which  */
/*  is indirectly included here.                                      */
  int dtr_bit = TIOCM_DTR;
  int rts_bit = TIOCM_RTS;
  int set_bits;
  int flags;
  int status, oldstat = -1;
  int count = 0;
  int pc;

  if (argc < 2) {
      fprintf(stderr, "Usage: upscheck <device> <bits-to-set>\n");
      exit(1);
  }

  /* Open monitor device. */
  if ((fd = open(argv[1], O_RDWR | O_NDELAY)) < 0) {
    fprintf(stderr, "upscheck: %s: %s\n", argv[1], sys_errlist[errno]);
    exit(1);}

  /* Get the bits to set from the command line. */
  sscanf(argv[2], "%d", &set_bits);

  while (1) {
    /* Set the command line specified bits (& only the command line */
    /* specified bits).                                             */
    ioctl(fd, TIOCMSET, &set_bits);
    fprintf(stderr, "Setting %o.\n", set_bits);
```

```
        sleep(1);

        /* Get the current line bits */
        ioctl(fd, TIOCMGET, &flags);
        fprintf(stderr, "Flags are %o.\n", flags);

/*  Fiddle here by changing TIOCM_CTS to some other TIOCM until    */
/*  this program detects that the power goes out when you yank     */
/*  the plug on the UPS.  Then you'll know how to modify powerd.c. */
        if (flags & TIOCM_CTS)
          {
            pc = 0 ;
            fprintf(stderr, "power is up.\n");
          }
        else
          {
            pc = pc + 1 ;
            fprintf(stderr, "power is down.\n");
          }
        }

    close(fd);
}
```

9   Serial port pin assignments

The previous section presupposes knowledge of the correspondence between terminal signals and serial port pins. Here's a reference for that correspondence, taken from David Tal's <GSRGAAO@TECHNION.BITNET> "Frequently Used Cables and Connectors" document. I'm including a diagram illustrating the connectors, and a table listing the correspondence between pin numbers and terminal line signals.

```
       1                          13        1         5
       ------------------------------       -----------------
       \  . . . . . . . . . . . . /         \  . . . . . /        RS232-connectors
        \  . . . . . . . . . . . /           \  . . . . /         seen from outside
         --------------------------           -----------         of computer.
       14                         25         6         9

DTE : Data Terminal Equipment (i.e. computer)
DCE : Data Communications Equipment (i.e. modem)
RxD : Data received; 1 is transmitted "low", 0 as "high"
TxD : Data sent; 1 is transmitted "low", 0 as "high"
DTR : DTE announces that it is powered up and ready to communicate
DSR : DCE announces that it is ready to communicate; low=modem hangup
RTS : DTE asks DCE for permission to send data
CTS : DCE agrees on RTS
RI  : DCE signals the DTE that an establishment of a connection is attempted
DCD : DCE announces that a connection is established
```

10   Ioctl to RS232 correspondence

Since you also might need to modify powerd.c to raise and lower the correct lines, you might also need the numeric values of different terminal signals. The can be found in /usr/include/linux/termios.h,

DB-25 Pin #	DB-9 Pin #	Name	EIA	CCITT	DTE-DCE	Description
1		FG	AA	101	—	Frame Ground/Chassis GND
2	3	TD	BA	103	—>	Transmitted Data, TxD
3	2	RD	BB	104	<—	Received Data, RxD
4	7	RTS	CA	105	—>	Request To Send
5	8	CTS	CB	106	<—	Clear To Send
6	6	DSR	CC	107	<—	Data Set Ready
7	5	SG	AB	102	—	Signal Ground, GND
8	1	DCD	CF	109	<—	Data Carrier Detect
9		–	–	-	-	Positive DC test voltage
10		–	–	-	-	Negative DC test voltage
11		QM	–	-	<—	Equalizer mode
12		SDCD	SCF	122	<—	Secondary Data Carrier Detect
13		SCTS	SCB	121	<—	Secondary Clear To Send
14		STD	SBA	118	—>	Secondary Transmitted Data
15		TC	DB	114	<—	Transmitter (signal) Clock
16		SRD	SBB	119	<—	Secondary Receiver Clock
17		RC	DD	115	—>	Receiver (signal) Clock
18		DCR	–	-	<—	Divided Clock Receiver
19		SRTS	SCA	120	—>	Secondary Request To Send
20	4	DTR	CD	108.2	—>	Data Terminal Ready
21		SQ	CG	110	<—	Signal Quality Detect
22	9	RI	CE	125	<—	Ring Indicator
23		–	CH	111	—>	Data rate selector
24		–	CI	112	<—	Data rate selector
25		TC	DA	113	<—	Transmitted Clock

Table 1: Pin Assignment for the Serial Port (RS-232C), 25-pin and 9-pin

but are reproduced here for reference. Since they could change, you're best off confirming these values against said file.

```
/* modem lines */
#define TIOCM_LE       0x001
#define TIOCM_DTR      0x002
#define TIOCM_RTS      0x004
#define TIOCM_ST       0x008
#define TIOCM_SR       0x010
#define TIOCM_CTS      0x020
#define TIOCM_CAR      0x040
#define TIOCM_RNG      0x080
#define TIOCM_DSR      0x100
#define TIOCM_CD       TIOCM_CAR
#define TIOCM_RI       TIOCM_RNG
```

Note that the 3rd column is in Hex.

11   Info on selected UPSs

This section contains UPS specific information. What I'd like is to have the UPS control port information (what each pin does and needs to have done), information on the manufacturer supplied cable (what it connects where), and a hacked version of powerd.c which works with the UPS. What I currently have is fairly complete descriptions of setting up each UPS. I'd try to distill out the relevant information, but since I can't test each UPS, it's hard to decide exactly what's relevant. Furthermore, each UPS seems to have some additional quirks that are nicely described by the authors of each section. So for now I'm leaving everything in. Makes for a hefty Howto.

Please send me your experiences for inclusion here.

11.1   General Experiences.

I've been saving peoples comments, but haven't gotten permission yet to include them here. Here's a general summary of what I've heard from people.

APC: Won't release info on their "smart" mode without your signature on a non-disclosure agreement. Thus, people are forced to run their "smart" UPSes in the "dumb" mode as outlined above.

Tripp Lite: One person reported that Tripp lite won't release info either.

Upsonic: One person reported that Upsonic has discussed technical details over the phone, answered questions via fax and are generally helpful.

11.2   Advice 1200 A

UPS from Advice Electronics, Tel Aviv Israel (they stick their own name on the things).

UPS Control Port's pin specifications.

- 2 - Power Fail.

- 5 - Battery Low.

- 6 - Shut Down UPS.

- 4 - Common ground for pin 2, 5, 6.

They also gave me the following picture which didn't help me, but may help you if you want to build a cable yourself:

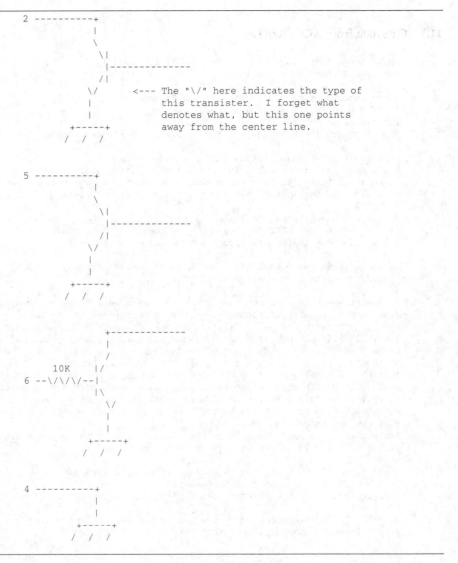

```
    2 ----------+
               |
               \
               \ |
               |--------------
              / |
              \ /         <--- The "\/" here indicates the type of
               |               this transister.  I forget what
               |               denotes what, but this one points
           +-----+           away from the center line.
           /  /  /


    5 ----------+
               |
               \
               \ |
               |--------------
              / |
              \ /
               |
               |
           +-----+
           /  /  /


              +--------------
               |
               /
    10K      |/
 6 --\/\/\/--|
             | \
              \ /
               |
               |
           +-----+
           /  /  /


    4 ----------+
               |
               |
           +-----+
           /  /  /
```

Cable supplied

They first gave me a cable that was part of a DOS UPS control package called RUPS. I used this for testing. When I was satisfied, they gave me a cable they use for Netware servers connected to UPSs. It functioned identically. Here are the details:

- DTR - Powers cable (make powerd.c keep it high).

- CTS - Power out (stays high and goes low when power goes out).

- DSR - Battery low (stays high. Goes low when battery does).

- RTS - Turns off UPS (keep it low. Set it high to turn off UPS).

(The powerd.c that comes with SysVinit set or left RTS high, causing the UPS to shut off immediately when powerd was started up!)

11.3 GPS1000 from ACCODATA

```
>From hennus@sky.nl.mugnet.org Thu Mar 10 15:10:22 1994
Newsgroups: comp.os.linux.help
Subject: Re: auto-shutdown with UPS
From: hennus@sky.nl.mugnet.org (Hennus Bergman)
Date: Tue, 1 Mar 1994 22:17:45 GMT
Distribution: world
Organization: The Organization For Removal Of On-Screen Logos

In article <CRAFFERT.94Feb28125452@nostril.lehman.com>,
Colin Owen Rafferty <craffert@nostril.lehman.com> wrote:
>I am about to buy an Uninterruptable Power Supply for my machine, and
>I would like to get one that has the "auto-shutdown" feature.
>
I just got one of those real cheap :-)
It's a GPS1000 by ACCODATA. Anybody know how good the output
signal of these things is? [Don't have a scope myself :-(]

>I assume that these each have some kind of serial connection that
>tells the system information about it.
>
I took it apart to find out how it worked. There were three optocouplers
(two output, one input) connected to a 9 pin connector at the back.
One turns on when the power fails, and goes off again when the power
returns. While the power is off, you can use the 'input' to shut the
battery off. [It releases the power-relay.] The third one is some kind
of feedback to tell that it did accept the 'shut-down command'.
I think the interface for my UPS was designed to be connected to TTL-level
signals, but with some resistors it could be connected to serial port.
It's wired in such a way that using a RS-232 port you cannot use both
output optocouplers; but the shutdown feedback is not necessary anyway,
just use the important one. ;-)
[Note that it is possible to blow the transistor part in optocouplers
with RS-232 levels if you wire it the wrong way round ;-)]

I was hoping I would be able to connect it to my unused game port,
but that doesn't have an output, does it?
I'll probably end up getting an extra printer port for this.

Not all UPS' use optocouplers, some use simple relays, which are
less critical to connect, but of course not as 'nice'.

>Has anyone written a package that watches the UPS and does a shutdown
>(or something) when the power is off?
SysVinit-2.4 (and probably 2.5 as well) has a 'powerd' daemon that
continually watches a serial port for presence of the CD (Carrier
Detect) line and signals init when it drops. Init then activates
shutdown with a time delay. If the power returns within a few minutes
the shutdown is cancelled. Very Nice.
The only problem I had with it is that it doesn't actually tell the
UPS to turn off when the shutdown is complete. It just sits there with
a root prompt. I'll probably write a small program to shut it down
>from /etc/brc. RSN.

>     Colin Rafferty, Lehman Brothers <craffert@lehman.com>
```

Hennus Bergman

11.4   TrippLite BC750LAN (Standby UPS)

```
From: Tom Webster <webster@kaiwan.com>
To: hjstein@MATH.HUJI.AC.IL (Harvey J. Stein)
Subject: Re: Help - Powerd & UPS - Help
Date: Mon, 8 Aug 1994 12:26:09 -0700 (PDT)
```

Harvey,

First off, let me say that I enjoyed reading your HOWTO. It is about
what I'd hoped my document might grow into. I wrote my pseudo-HOWTO
late on night because I kept seeing the "Can I hook a UPS up to
Linux...." message, about once a month on c.o.l.*. Mine deals
specifically with hooking one vendor's model of UPS (Tripplite's
BCxxx/LAN series) to a Linux box and making powerd work with it.

It is in need of some upkeep, things have been a little hectic. Now
that I have posted it three or four time in response to questions, I'm
finally getting some feedback (which catches these errors). The
problems that I know it has so far are:

The proper version of SysVinit is 2.4, not 2.04.

There is some argument about whether one or more resistors are needed
in my cable. The only place I really see that it might be needed is
in the inverter shutoff, to make sure that I don't send too much
voltage to the UPS. For the sensor circuit I don't see why a DTE
device can't stand to have its signal looped back to it. All that I'm
doing is connecting a line that is held high to the Carrier Detect
line.

I should be a little clearer about how the UPS acts when it goes into
powerfail mode. The Tripplites provide both an open and a closed
circuit on powerfail, two different pins and a common negative pin.
Thus all I have to do is wire a pin that it held high to the carrier
detect line and route this through the UPS's open on powerfail
circuit, to cause the carrier detect to drop. I think that this
confuses some people who read Miquel van Smoorenburg's description of
a UPS that only provides only a closed circuit on powerfail, and
requires a much more complex cable.

Well that is all I can think of for now. I'm planning on seeing if my
cable will still operate if I insert resistors into all of the
circuits. If it does then I'll make the changes to my document,
should find out this weekend.

Tom

Of Linux and Uninterruptible Power Supplies
[or How to connect a TrippLite BCXXXLAN UPS]

by Tom Webster <webster@kaiwan.com>
   05/20/94 (Version 1.0)

1.0 Introduction

I struggled through connecting a TrippLite BC750LAN (Standby UPS) to
my Linux box about six months ago. Since then I've seen several
requests for information on this subject, so I'm putting it in a
relatively stable format so I can just send this out when the question
reappears.

1.1 The Results
When the power fails in my apartment, several things happen:

1. The UPS switches its inverter on and the computer starts
    drawing off of the UPS. The warning beeper also starts going
    off. If the power comes back on, the UPS shuts the inverter
    down and switches back to line power. Nothing else happens,
    other than the beeper turns off.

2. If the power is off for ~15-30 seconds, the system will send
    a message to the users (via wall) and initiate a shutdown
    (to halt) in five minutes. If the power comes back on, the
    shutdown is canceled and a message stating this is sent
    to the users (via wall) stating that the shutdown has been
    canceled.

3. While the system is shutting itself down, its dying act is to
    shut off the inverter on the UPS, killing power to the system.
    This is done after the disks are unmounted, and is done to
    prevent the halted system from draining power from the UPS.

4. When the line power comes back on, the system restarts normally.

The BC750 has enough juice to keep my system going for quite some
time, so why do I only run it off of the UPS for five minutes? The
answer rests in a couple of 'rules-of-thumb' (your mileage may vary):

a. If the power browns out or blacks out, 90% of the time it will
    be out for 0-2 minutes.

b. If it is out for longer, it will be out for .5-3+ hours.

c. If it is out for a while (see b), the power will yo-yo at least
    once while the power company is working on it. (The power
    will come up for 5-45 seconds, and then fail again.)

So, I set my system up to cover the majority of the power outages I
get, without trying to cover the really long ones. I also keep plenty
of reserve in the UPS to handle yo-yo situations.

1.2 Disclaimer
I make no warranties or guarantees as to the suitability or sanity of
following my advice. This is how my system is setup, and as far as I
can tell it works fine for me. Your setup may need to be different to
fit your needs, especially if you are using different UPS hardware.

2.0 Hardware
In the case of my UPS, I thought that the RS-232 interface was
something of a misnomer. I was expecting the UPS to send and receive
data, like talking to your modem with Hayes "AT" commands. This was
not the case. It seems that it is called an RS-232 interface because
it stays within the voltage and signal limits of the RS-232 spec. To
communicate with the UPS, you need to be able to sense changes in
state on certain lines and change the state of other lines. The fact
that these lines may have nothing in common to the lines your system

might expect to use, if it were talking to say a modem or printer, is
probably why the UPS needs special cables to allow software (including
the manufacturer's) to communicate with the UPS.

Through trial and error with a RS-232 patch panel, I was able to come
up with this cable diagram for the cable between the UPS and the
computer. Please note that I did this without looking at the official
TrippLite cable and it may be different.

```
          UPS                 System
          DB-25               DB-25
            1 <--------------> 1          Ground

            2 <--------------> 4          Power Fail
            8 <--------------> 8          Sensing Circuit

            3 <--------------> 2          Inverter Shutdown
           20 <--------------> 22         Circuit
```

Once you have the cable patched together, just hook the UPS side to
the UPS and the System side to a free serial port on your Linux box.
You will probably have to mess around with 9->25 and 25->9 adapters
to get your cable to fit, but you and a good computer store should
be able to handle this.

3.0 Software
The software that I use is all available to Linux users and comes
with most distributions (SLS and Slackware at least). This setup
has worked for me through Kernels .99.9, .99.14, and 1.00.

3.1 System V Init
This package is needed to make the whole thing work. If you are
still using the "Simple Init" package, perhaps it is time you looked
at upgrading. The version I am using is 2.04, and I believe that
Miquel van Smoorenburg is the author of the package.

3.2 powerd
powerd is the power daemon, by default is sits and watches for a
change in state on the DCD line and reports these changes to the
system via the signal mechanism. The source for powerd is provided
in the System V Init package. Compile it, move it to a binary
directory (I put it in /sbin on my system), and alter your rc.local
script to start the daemon. The relevant part of my rc.local looks
like this:

```
    ----- snip -----
    # Add support for the UPS
    echo "Starting powerd daemon..."
    if [ -x /sbin/powerd ]; then
       /sbin/powerd /dev/cua4
    fi
    ----- snip -----
```

3.3 inittab
Your inittab needs to be modified to properly handle the signals
that powerd will send if there is a power failure. The relevant
lines of my inittab look like this:

```
    ----- snip -----
    # What to do when power fails (shutdown to single user).
    pf::powerfail:/sbin/shutdown -f +5 "THE POWER IS FAILING"
```

```
    # If power is back before shutdown, cancel the running shutdown.
    pg:0123456:powerokwait:/sbin/shutdown -c "THE POWER IS BACK"

    # If power comes back in single user mode, return to multi user mode.
    ps:S:powerokwait:/sbin/init 2
    ----- snip -----
```

3.4 rc.0 (brc)
Depending on how your system is setup either rc.0 or the brc script
is executed immediately prior to shutdown. These scripts take care
of things like unmounting disks and any other last minute clean-up.

The inverter shutdown circuit, is designed to signal an inverter
shutdown when data is sent out over the DTR line. In my case,
I just cat a short file to the serial port (/etc/passwd - since I
know it will always be there). My rc.0 is as follows, please note
that it is overly conservative, the sync can be removed and the
sleep times can probably be tightened, but it works so I haven't
messed with it.

```
    ----- snip -----
    #! /bin/sh
    #
    # brc      This file is executed by init(8) when the system is being
    #          shutdown (i.e. set to run at level 0).  It usually takes
    #          care of un-mounting all unneeded file systems.
    #
    # Version: @(#)/etc/brc            2.01    02/17/93
    #
    # Authors: Miquel van Smoorenburg, <miquels@drinkel.nl.mugnet.org>
    #          Fred N. van Kempen, <waltje@uwalt.nl.mugnet.org>
    #
    # Modified: 01/15/94 - Inverter shutdown support added.
    #           Tom Webster <webster@kaiwan.com>

    PATH=/sbin:/bin:/usr/sbin:/usr/bin
    echo Unmounting file systems.....
    sync
    umount -a
    sleep 2
    cat /etc/passwd > /dev/cua4
    sleep 5
    echo Done.
    ----- snip -----
```

(On my UPS the inverter is only running when the line power is off,
so there is no harm in sending the shutdown signal at every shutdown.)

4.0 Conclusion
Well that's how I hooked my TrippLite UPS up to my Linux box.
Feel free to drop me a line with the results of you attempts,
especially if you have any improvements. :->

From: Tom Webster <webster@kaiwan.com>
To: hjstein@MATH.HUJI.AC.IL (Harvey J. Stein)
Subject: Re: Help - Powerd & UPS - Help
Date: Thu, 11 Aug 1994 12:20:50 -0700 (PDT)

Harvey,

> Like I tried to say, powerd can just run shutdown directly in the
> event of a low battery, so that init doesn't need to deal with it &
> doesn't need to be hacked - no new signal necessary. Although this
> violates the nice separation of labor between powerd & init, it's
> easier than adding another signal. Or do you just mean another
> command? Something like having powerok/powerfail/powerfailnow as
> commands in inittab which execute when SIGPWR is received &
> /etc/powerfail contains OK/FAIL/LOWBATT (respectively). This would be
> cleanest, but having powerd execute shutdown -r now is trivial to do
> now, and might as well be done - the logic will be the same regardless
> of the action that powerd takes when it senses a low battery. For now
> it can just run shutdown, & when init gets hacked it can write LOWBATT
> to /etc/powerfail (or whatever the hell the file is called) & give
> init a SIGPWR.

I'd like to add the LOWBATT command, it would be the cleaner way to do
it. I just need to take a look at the code and see how hard it would
be to add it. Also need to look at my wiring, guess this may mean I've
got to run the system all the way down for a final test (once I think I
have it working.

Tom

From: Tom Webster <webster@kaiwan.com>
To: hjstein@MATH.HUJI.AC.IL (Harvey J. Stein)
Subject: Re: Help - Powerd & UPS - Help
Date: Mon, 15 Aug 1994 09:46:06 -0700 (PDT)

Harvey,

Well, I messed about all weekend taking readings with my multi-
tester and comparing it to the scant documentation that I have for
the UPS. The only conclusions I came to were:

1. My system has been working for about 8-9 months now. If I was
going to fry anything, it should have happened by now.

2. If my success is based on my serial hardware doing odd things
(I'm using an STB 4COM board), there is no way I'm going to be
able to find out on my system. I'll have to leave that to other
poor souls on the net.

3. As far as I can tell the only reason the 10kohm resistor was
in Miquel's diagram, was to keep the line higher than DCD, even
after the circuit had been shunted to ground.

4. The only circuit that is expected to do anything other that be
switched by the UPS (the inverter shutdown circuit) has a 40kohm
resistor built into it (inside the UPS). That should take care of
any worries there.

5. Miquel's circuit will work for power fail sensing, and might
be extrapolated to include the low battery circuit. If my circuit
proves unviable for others, it would just require more soldering
than I'd care to deal with in a cable.

In other related news, I broke down this morning and ordered a
cable from Tripplite. I ordered the LanTastic/LAN Manager/Win NT
cable, it's just a cable (9M-9F, no software). This will set me

back about $40 (the PC UNIX cable (w/ software) is about $140).
The motivation for doing this was three part.

(1) Within a year I'll probably be running Win 4.0, or WinNT 3.5
(I beta'ed 3.1) and both should support UPS monitoring (I know NT
does and saw the power management icon on a Win4.0 desktop in one
of the computer mags).

(2) My current cable isn't going to be compatible with any other
monitoring software for other OS's (except by random chance),
working to a known (and presumably soon to be common?) cable via a
hacked powerd, should widen the audience.

(3) I can always reverse engineer the cable to see if Tripplite
is indeed building any safety into their cables.

It should be here in a week or so. In the mean time, I'll start
looking into hacking powerd for LOWBATT.

Tom

11.5   APC Backup-UPS

There seems to be some controversy as to the accuracy of the information here on APC Back-UPSes. So,
please be careful. I'm prefacing this section with one message of caution I received. It might not make alot
of sense before the rest of this section is read, but this way, at least you're more likely to see it. And again,
since I don't have any APC UPS units, I can't verify the accuracy of either of these messages.

11.5.1   A message of caution

    From ind43@sun1000.ci.pwr.wroc.pl Sun Oct 9 11:00:42 1994
    Newsgroups: comp.os.linux.admin
    Subject: BUPS-HOWTO warning
    From: ind43@sun1000.ci.pwr.wroc.pl (Marek Michalkiewicz)
    Date: 6 Oct 1994 18:38:15 GMT
    Organization: Technical Univeristy of Wroclaw
    NNTP-Posting-Host: ci3ux.ci.pwr.wroc.pl
    X-Newsreader: TIN [version 1.2 PL2]

    If you want to connect the APC Back-UPS to your Linux box, this might
    be of interest to you.

    There is a good BUPS-HOWTO which describes how to do this. But it has
    one "bug".

    The RTS serial port signal is used to shut down the UPS. The UPS will
    shut down only if it operates from its battery. The manual says that
    the shutdown signal must be high for at least 0.5s. But few milliseconds
    is enough, at least for my APC Back-UPS 600.

    Using RTS to shut down the UPS can be dangerous, because the RTS goes
    high when the serial device is opened. The backupsd program then turns
    RTS off, but it is on (high) for a moment. This kills the power when
    backupsd is first started and there is a power failure at this time.
    This can happen for example when the UPS is shut down, unattended,
    and the power comes back for a while.

    Either start backupsd before mounting any filesystems for read-write,

```
or (better) use TX (pin 3) instead of RTS (pin 7) to shut down the
UPS (pin numbers are for 9-pin plug). Use ioctl(fd, TCSBRKP, 10);
to make TX high for one second, for example. Using TX should be safe.
Maybe I will post the diffs if time permits...

-- Marek Michalkiewicz
ind43@ci3ux.ci.pwr.wroc.pl
```

11.5.2   BUPS-HOWTO

Luminated Software Group Presents

HOWTO use Back-UPS (by APC) (to keep your linux box from frying)

Version: 1.01 BETA

Document by: Christian G. Holtje <docwhat@uiuc.edu> Cabling info and help: Ben Galliart <bgallia@orion.it.luc.edu>

This document, under one condition, is placed in Public Domain. The one condition is that credit is given where credit is due. Modify this as much as you want, just give some credit to us who worked.

** Warning! I, nor any of us who have written or helped with this document, make and guarantees or claims for this text/source/hints. If anything is damaged, we take NO RESPONSIBILITY! This works to the BEST OF OUR KNOWLEDGE, but we may have made mistakes. So be careful! **

Al right, you just bought (or are going to buy) a Back-UPS from APC. (Other brands might be able to use this info, with little or no modification, but we don't know) You've looked at the price of the Power-Chute software/cabling, and just are not sure it's worth the price. Well, I made my own cable, and my own software and am using it to automatically shut off the power to my linux box when a power failure hits. Guess what? You can too!

*** The Cable ***

This was the hardest part to figure out (I know little about hardware, so Ben did the most work for this). To build one, you need to buy from your local radio shack (or other part supplier) this stuff:

```
1 9-Position Male D-Subminature Connector (solder-type)
        [Radio Shack cat. no. 276-1537c]
1 9-Position Female D-Subminature Connector (solder-type)
        [Radio Shack cat. no. 276-1538c]
2 casings for the above plugs (usually sold separately)
Some stranded wire (wire made of strands, not solid wire)
```

You also need, but may be able to borrow:

```
1 soldering iron
solder
```

Okay...this is how you connect it up!

These diagrams are looking into the REVERSE SIDE (the side where you solder the wire onto the plugs) The letters G, R, and B represent the colors of the wires I used, and help to distinguish one line from the next. (NOTE: I'm use standard rs-232 (as near as we can tell) numbering. The APC book uses different numbers. Ignore them! Use ours...I already changed the numbers for you!)

```
     ---------------------    Male Side! (This goes into the UPS)
      \ B   R  *   *   * /
       \  *   *   *  G  /
        ---------------
```

```
    --------------------        Female Side! (This goes into your COM port)
    \  R  *  *  *  G /
     \  *  B  *  *  /
      ------------
```

For those who like the numbers better:

```
        Male            Female
--------------------------------------
         1               7              Black
         2               1              Red
         9               5              Green
```

————Aside: What the rs-232 pins are for!———— Since we had to dig this info up anyway:

\>From the REAR (the soldering side) the pins are numbered so:

```
    --------------------
    \  1  2  3  4  5 /
     \  6  7  8  9  /
      ------------
```

The pins mean:

```
    Number   Name                    Abbr.  (Sometimes written with D prefix)
    1        Carrier Detect          CD
    2        Receive Data            RD
    3        Transmit Data           TD(?)
    4        Data Terminal Ready     DTR
    5        Signal Ground           Gnd
    6        Data Set Ready          DSR
    7        Request to Send         RTS(?)
    8        Clear to Send           CS
    9        Ring Indicator          RI
```

What we did is connect the UPS's RS-232 Line Fail Output to the CD, the UPS's chassis to Gnd, and the UPS's RS-232 Shut Down Input to RTS. Easy now that we told you, no?

I have no idea if the software below will work, if you purchase the cable from APC. It might, and it might not.

*** The Software ***

Okay, I use the SysVInit package by Miquel van Smoorenburg for Linux. (see end for file locations, credits, email addresses, etc.) I don't know what would have to be changed to use someone elses init, but I know this code (following) will work with Miquel's stuff. Just so I give credit where credit's due. I looked at Miquel's code to figure out how ioctl()'s worked. If I didn't have that example, I'd have been in trouble. I also used the powerfail() routine (verbatim, I think), since it must interact with his init, I thought that he should know best. The .c file is at the end of this document, and just needs to be clipped off. To clip the file, edit away and extra '.sigs' and junk. This document should end on the line /* End of File */.....cut the rest.

This program can either be run as a daemon to check the status of the UPS and report it to init, or it can be run to send the kill-power command to the UPS. The power will only be killed if there is a power problem, and the UPS is running off the battery. Once the power is restored, it turns back on.

To run as a daemon, just type: backupsd /dev/backups

/dev/backups is a link to /dev/cua0 at the moment (COM 1, for you DOSers). The niceness of the link is that I can just re-link the device if I change to com 2 or 3.

Then, if the power dies init will run the commands for the powerwait. An example (This is from my /etc/inittab):

```
#Here are the actions for powerfailure.
pf::powerwait:/etc/rc.d/rc.power start
po::powerokwait:/etc/rc.d/rc.power stop
```

The powerwait will run, if the power goes down, and powerokwait will run if the power comes back up.

Here is my entire rc.power:

```
#! /bin/sh
#
# rc.power       This file is executed by init when there is a powerfailure.
#
# Version:       @(#)/etc/rc.d/rc.power   1.50    1994-08-10
#
# Author:        Christian Holtje, <docwhat@uiuc.edu>
#

        # Set the path.
        PATH=/sbin:/etc:/bin:/usr/bin:/sbin/dangerous

        # Find out how we were called.
        case "$1" in
            start)
                        echo "Warning there is Power problems."  | wall
                        # Save current Run Level
                        ps | gawk '{ if (($5 == "init") && ($1 == "1")) print $6 }' \
                                | cut -f2 -d[ | cut -f1 -d] \
                                > /tmp/run.level.power
                        /sbin/shutdown -h +1m
                        ;;
            stop)
                        echo "Power is back up.  Attempting to halt shutdown." | wall
                        shutdown -c
                        ;;
            *)
                        echo "Usage:  $0 [start|stop]"
                        exit 1
                        ;;
        esac
```

Pretty nifty, no? Actually, there is a problem here...I haven't had time to figure it out...If there is a 'sh' wizard out there....

There is one little detail left, that is having the UPS turn off the power if it was halted with the power out. This is accomplished by adding this line into the end of your halt script:

```
/sbin/backupsd /dev/backups killpower
```

This will only kill the power if there is no power being supplied to your UPS.

*** Testing the stuff ***

This is just a short section saying this:

BE CAREFUL!

I recommend backing up your linux partitions, syncing several times before testing and just being careful in general. Of course, I'm just recommending this. I wasn't careful at all, and had to clean my partition several times testing my config. But it works. :)

*** Where to Get It ***

Miquel van Smoorenburg's SysVInit can be gotten at:

`sunsite.unc.edu:/pub/Linux/system/Daemons/SysVinit-2.50.tgz`

and a fix for some bash shells is right next-door as:

`sunsite.unc.edu:/pub/Linux/system/Daemons/SysVinit-2.50.patch1`

As to getting this HOWTO, you can email me. docwhat@uiuc.edu with the subject saying 'request' and the keyword 'backups' in body of the letter. (I may automate this, and other stuff)

*** Credit Where Credit's Due Dept. ***

Thanks to Miquel van Smoorenburg <miquels@drinkel.nl.mugnet.org> for his wonderful SysVInit package and his powerd.c which helped me very much.

Christian Holtje <docwhat@uiuc.edu> Documentation backupsd.c (what wasn't Miquel's) rc.power

Ben Galliart <bgallia@orion.it.luc.edu> The cable Information for the RS-232 standard Lousy Jokes (none quoted here)

```
/*  backupsd.c -- Simple Daemon to catch power failure signals from a
 *              Back-UPS (from APC).
 *
 *  Parts of the code are from Miquel van Smoorenburg's powerd.c
 *  Other parts are original from Christian Holtje <docwhat@uiuc.edu>
 *  I believe that it is okay to say that this is Public Domain, just
 *  give credit, where credit is due.
 *
 *  Disclaimer:  We make NO claims to this software, and take no
 *              responsibility for it's use/misuse.
 */

#include <sys/types.h>
#include <sys/ioctl.h>
#include <fcntl.h>
#include <errno.h>
#include <stdlib.h>
#include <unistd.h>
#include <stdio.h>
#include <signal.h>

/* This is the file needed by SysVInit */
#define PWRSTAT         "/etc/powerstatus"

void powerfail(int fail);

/* Main program. */
int main(int argc, char **argv)
{
    int fd;
    int killpwr_bit = TIOCM_RTS;
    int flags;
    int status, oldstat = -1;
    int count = 0;

    if (argc < 2) {
        fprintf(stderr, "Usage: %s <device> [killpower]\n", argv[0]);
        exit(1);
    }

    /* Open the the device */
    if ((fd = open(argv[1], O_RDWR | O_NDELAY)) < 0) {
```

```
            fprintf(stderr, "%s: %s: %s\n", argv[0], argv[1], sys_errlist[errno]);
            exit(1);
    }

    if ( argc >= 3  && (strcmp(argv[2], "killpower")==0) )
        {
            /* Let's kill the power! */
            fprintf(stderr, "%s: Attempting to kill the power!\n",argv[0] );
            ioctl(fd, TIOCMBIS, &killpwr_bit);
            /* Hmmm..... If you have a power outtage, you won't make it! */
            exit(0);
        }
    else
        /* Since we don't want to kill the power, clear the RTS. (killpwr_bit) */
        ioctl(fd, TIOCMBIC, &killpwr_bit);

/* Become a daemon. */
  switch(fork()) {
  case 0: /* I am the child. */
                setsid();
                break;
  case -1: /* Failed to become daemon. */
                fprintf(stderr, "%s: can't fork.\n", argv[0]);
                exit(1);
  default: /* I am the parent. */
                exit(0);
  }


  /* Now sample the DCD line. */
  while(1) {
      ioctl(fd, TIOCMGET, &flags);
      status = (flags & TIOCM_CD);
      /* Did DCD jumps to high? Then the power has failed. */
      if (oldstat == 0 && status != 0) {
          count++;
          if (count > 3) powerfail(0);
          else { sleep(1); continue; }
      }
      /* Did DCD go down again? Then the power is back. */
      if (oldstat > 0 && status == 0) {
          count++;
          if (count > 3) powerfail(1);
          else { sleep(1); continue; }
      }
      /* Reset count, remember status and sleep 2 seconds. */
      count = 0;
      oldstat = status;
      sleep(2);
  }
  /* Error! (shouldn't happen) */
  return(1);
}


/* Tell init the power has either gone or is back. */
void powerfail(ok)
int ok;
{
  int fd;
```

```
        /* Create an info file needed by init to shutdown/cancel shutdown */
        unlink(PWRSTAT);
        if ((fd = open(PWRSTAT, O_CREAT|O_WRONLY, 0644)) >= 0) {
            if (ok)
                    write(fd, "OK\n", 3);
            else
                    write(fd, "FAIL\n", 5);
            close(fd);
        }
        kill(1, SIGPWR);
}


/* End of File */
```

11.6   APC Smart-UPS, Model 600

Many people have APC Smart UPSes. To the best of my knowledge, no one can run them in "smart"
mode under Linux. This is because APC refuses to release the protocol for the "smart" mode without a
non-disclosure agreement. Not very smart of them, I'd say :).

The general consensus is to buy from a brand which does release the information. I hear that Best is one
such brand.

If you are stuck with an APC Smart-UPS, you can still use it, but only in a dumb mode like all the other
UPSes and as outlined above.

Here's some info on how to make a cable for doing such. You'll probably have to hack powerd.c as outlined
in section 8

```
From dangit@netcom.com Mon Aug 22 10:16:23 1994
Newsgroups: comp.os.linux.misc
Subject: UPS Monitoring Cable For APC
From: dangit@netcom.com (Lam Dang)
Date: Fri, 19 Aug 1994 11:56:28 GMT
Organization: NETCOM On-line Communication Services (408 261-4700 guest)
X-Newsreader: TIN [version 1.2 PL1]

[Didn't make it the first time.]

A few netters have asked about UPS monitoring cables. This is what I
found when I made one for my APC Smart-UPS, Model 600. A disclaimer is in
order. This is just an experimenter's report; use it at your own risks.
Please read the User's Manual first, especially Section 6.4, Computer
Interface Port.

The cable is to run between a 9-pin female connector on the UPS and a
25-pin male connector on the PC. Since I cut off one end of a 9-pin
cable and replaced it with a 25-pin connector, I had to be VERY
CAREFUL ABOUT PIN NUMBERS. The 25-pin hood is big enough to contain a
voltage regulator and two resistors. I got all the materials (listed
below) from Radio Shack for less than 10 bucks. As required by Windows NT
Advanced Server 3.5 (Beta 2), the "interface" between the UPS connector
and the PC connector is as follows:

        UPS (9-pin)             PC (25-pin)

        1 (Shutdown)            20 (DTR)
        3 (Line Fail)            5 (CTS)
        4 (Common)               7 (GND)
        5 (Low Battery)          8 (DCD)
        9 (Chassis Ground)       1 (Chassis Ground)
```

This is pretty straightforward. You can use UPS pin 6 instead of 3 (they're the inverse of each other). The complication is in pulling up UPS open collector pins 3 (or 6) and 5.

This APC model provides an unregulated output of 24 Vdc at UPS pin 8. The output voltage is available all the time (at least until some time after Low Battery has been signalled). The supply is limited to 40 mA. To pull up, UPS pin 8 is input to a +5 Vdc voltage regulator. The output of the regulator goes into two 4.7K resistors. The other end of one resistor connects both UPS pin 3 (Line Fail) and PC pin 5 (CTS). That of the other resistor connects both UPS pin 5 (Low Battery) and PC pin 8 (DCD). The two resistors draw about 2 mA when closed.

Test your cable without connecting it to the PC. When the UPS is on line, pins 5 (CTS) and 8 (DCD) at the PC end of the cable should be very close to 5 Vdc, and applying a high to pin 20 (DTR) for 5 seconds should have no effect. Now pull the power plug to put the UPS on battery. Pin 5 (CTS) should go down to zero Vdc, pin 8 (DCD) should stay the same at 5 Vdc, and applying a high to pin 20 (DTR), e.g., by shorting pins 8 and 20, should shut down the UPS after about 15 seconds.

Keep the UPS on battery until Low Battery is lighted on its front panel. Now pin 8 (DCD) should go down to zero Vdc too. Wait until the UPS battery is recharged. Then connect your cable to the PC, disable the UPS option switches by turning all of them ON, and run your favorite UPS monitoring software.

For those who want to run it with Windows NT Advanced Server, the UPS interface voltages are NEGATIVE for both power failure (using UPS pin 3) and low battery conditions, and POSITIVE for remote shutdown. Serial line parameters such as baud rate don't matter.

I haven't tested my cable with Linux powerd. When you do, please let us know. I run NT as often as Linux on the same PC. I must conform to NT's UPS scheme. Perhaps somebody can modify powerd to work with it and post the source code here.

List of materials:

        1 shielded D-sub connector hood (Radio Shack 276-1510)
        1 25-pin female D-sub crimp-type connector (276-1430)
        1 7805 +5Vdc voltage regulator (276-1770)
        2 4.7K resistors
        1 component perfboard (276-148)
        1 cable with at least one 9-pin male connector.

You'll need a multimeter, a soldering iron, and a couple of hours.

Hope this helps.

Regards,

--
Lam Dang
dangit@netcom.com

12 How to shutdown other machines on the same UPS

Some people (myself included) have several Linux PCs connected to one UPS. One PC monitors the UPS and needs to get the other PCs to shut down when the power goes out. There are a number of ways to do this, all are do-it-yourself currently, and most are just hypothetical.

We assume the PCs can communicate over a network. Call the PC that monitors the UPS the master & the other PCs the slaves.

12.1 UPS status port method

Set up a port on the master which, when connected to, either sends "OK", "FAIL", or "BATLOW", the first when the power is ok, the second when the power has failed, and the third when the battery is low. Model this on port 13 (the time port) which one can telnet to & receive the local time.

Have the slaves run versions of powerd that look at this port instead of checking a serial line.

I think this is probably the best method, and intend to eventually upgrade my systems to use it.

12.2 Broadcast method

Same as section 12.1 except send an ethernet broadcast message that the power has just gone down.

This might have security implications, since it could be spoofed.

12.3 Dummy login method

Set up dummy logins on the slaves with login names powerok and powerfail, both with the same UID. Make /etc/powerokscript the shell of the powerok user, and make /etc/powerfailscript the shell of the powerfail user. On the master, have the /etc/powerokscript rlogin to each slave as user powerok and have the /etc/powerfailscript rlogin to each slave as user powerfail. Put a .rhosts file on each slave in the home directory of powerok and powerfail to allow root from the master to login as user powerok and powerfail to each slave.

This is the system I'm currently using. Unfortunately, there are some difficulties in getting the remote logins to execute and return without hanging. One probably wants the /etc/powerfailscript on the master to rsh to the slaves in background so that the /etc/powerfailscript doesn't hang. However, I never managed to get logging in in background to work right. I even tried arcane combinations such as having /etc/powerfailscript run foo in background and having foo log into the slave. Whatever I did gave problems with the thing being stopped for tty input (or output, I can't remember).

Also, this might create security holes.

Part XLIII

The Linux UUCP HOWTO

Copyright Vince Skahan, <vince@halcyon.com>
v1.12, 31 Mar 1995
This document describes the setup and care+feeding of UUCP under Linux. You need to read this if you plan to connect to remote sites via UUCP via a modem, via a direct-connection, or via Internet. You probably do *not* need to read this document if don't talk UUCP.

Contents

1   Introduction

The intent of this document is to answer some of the questions and comments that appear to meet the definition of "frequently asked questions" about UUCP software under Linux in general, and the version in the Linux SLS and Slackware distributions in particular.

This document and the corresponding Mail and News "HOWTO" documents collectively supersede the UUCP-NEWS-MAIL-FAQ that has previously been posted to *comp.os.linux.announce*.

1.1   New versions of this document

New versions of this document will be periodically posted to comp.os.linux.announce, comp.answers, and news.answers. They will also be added to the various anonymous ftp sites who archive such information including `sunsite.unc.edu:/pub/Linux/docs/HOWTO`.

In addition, you should be generally able to find this document on the Linux WorldWideWeb home page at `http://sunsite.unc.edu/mdw/linux.html`.

1.2   Feedback

I am interested in any feedback, positive or negative, regarding the content of this document via e-mail. Definitely contact me if you find errors or obvious omissions.

I read, but do not necessarily respond to, all e-mail I receive. Requests for enhancements will be considered and acted upon based on that day's combination of available time, merit of the request, and daily blood pressure :-)

Flames will quietly go to /dev/null so don't bother.

In particular, the Linux filesystem standard for pathnames is an evolving thing. What's in this document is there for illustration only based on the current standard at the time that part of the document was written and in the paths used in the distributions or 'kits' I've personally seen. Please consult your particular Linux distribution(s) for the paths they use.

Feedback concerning the actual format of the document should go to the HOWTO coordinator - Matt Welsh (`mdw@sunsite.unc.edu`).

1.3   Copyright Information

The UUCP-HOWTO is copyrighted (c)1994 Vince Skahan.

A verbatim copy may be reproduced or distributed in any medium physical or electronic without permission of the author. Translations are similarly permitted without express permission if it includes a notice on who translated it.

Short quotes may be used without prior consent by the author. Derivative work and partial distributions of the UUCP-HOWTO must be accompanied with either a verbatim copy of this file or a pointer to the verbatim copy.

Commercial redistribution is allowed and encouraged; however, the author would like to be notified of any such distributions.

In short, we wish to promote dissemination of this information through as many channels as possible. However, we do wish to retain copyright the HOWTO documents, and would like to be notified of any plans to redistribute the HOWTOs.

We further want that ALL information provided in the HOWTOS is disseminated. If you have questions, please contact Matt Welsh, the Linux HOWTO coordinator, at mdw@sunsite.unc.edu, or +1 607 256 7372.

1.4 Standard Disclaimer

Of course, I disavow any potential liability for the contents of this document. Use of the concepts, examples, and/or other content of this document is entirely at your own risk.

1.5 Other sources of information

1.5.1 Linux HOWTO Documents

There is plenty of exceptional material provided in the other Linux HOWTO documents and from the Linux DOC project. In particular, you might want to take a look at the following:

- the Serial Communications HOWTO

- the Ethernet HOWTO

- the Linux Networking Administrators' Guide

1.5.2 USENET

comp.mail.uucp can answer most of your UUCP questions

1.5.3 Mailing Lists

There is a Taylor UUCP mailing list.

To join (or get off) the list, send mail to

```
taylor-uucp-request@gnu.ai.mit.edu
```

This request goes to a person, not to a program, so please make sure that you include the address at which you want to receive mail in the text of the message.

To send a message to the list, send it to

```
taylor-uucp@gnu.ai.mit.edu
```

1.5.4 Books

HDB and V2 versions of UUCP are documented in about every vendor's documentation as well as in almost all *nix communications books.

Taylor config files are currently only documented in the info files provided with the sources (and in the SLS distribution hopefully). To read them, you can grab the nice "infosrc" program from the SLS "s" disks and compile it.

The following is a non-inclusive set of books that will help.

- `"Managing UUCP and USENET"` from O'Reilly and Associates is in my opinion the best book out there for figuring out the programs and protocols involved in being a USENET site.

- `"Unix Communications"` from The Waite Group contains a nice description of all the pieces (and more) and how they fit together.

- `"Practical Unix Security"` from O'Reilly and Associates has a nice discussion of how to secure UUCP in general.

- `"The Internet Complete Reference"` from Osborne is a fine reference book that explains the various services available on Internet and is a great source for information on news, mail, and various other Internet resources.

- `"The Linux Networking Administrators' Guide"` from Olaf Kirch of the Linux DOC Project is available on the net and is also published by (at least) O'Reilly and SSC. It makes a fine *one-stop shopping* to learn about everything you ever imagined you'd need to know about Unix networking.

1.6   Where *NOT* to look for help

There is nothing "special" about configuring and running UUCP under Linux (any more). Accordingly, you almost certainly do *NOT* want to be posting generic UUCP-related questions to the comp.os.linux.* newsgroups.

Unless your posting is truly Linux-specific (ie, "please tell me what config file support is built into the binaries for Taylor uucp v1.04 in SLS v1.02"), you should be asking your questions in comp.mail.uucp or on the Taylor UUCP mailing list as indicated above.

Let me repeat that.

There is virtually no reason to post anything uucp-related in the comp.os.linux hierarchy any more. There are existing newsgroups in the comp.mail.* hierarchy to handle *ALL* your questions.

IF YOU POST TO COMP.OS.LINUX. FOR NON-LINUX-SPECIFIC QUESTIONS, YOU ARE LOOKING IN THE WRONG PLACE FOR HELP. THE UUCP EXPERTS HANG OUT IN THE PLACES INDICATED ABOVE AND GENERALLY DO NOT RUN LINUX.*

POSTING TO THE LINUX HIERARCHY FOR NON-LINUX-SPECIFIC QUESTIONS WASTES YOUR TIME AND EVERYONE ELSE'S AND IT FREQUENTLY DELAYS YOU FROM GETTING THE ANSWER TO YOUR QUESTION.

2   Hardware Requirements

There are no specific hardware requirements for UUCP under Linux. Basically any Hayes-compatible modem works painlessly with UUCP.

In most cases, you'll want the fastest modem you can afford. In general, you want to have a 16550 UART on your serial board or built into your modem to handle speeds of above 9600 baud.

If you don't know what that last sentence means, please consult the *comp.dcom.modems* group or the various fine modem and serial communications FAQs and periodic postings on USENET.

3   Getting UUCP

Taylor UUCP (current version 1.05) is available on `prep.ai.mit.edu` in source form and in various Linux distributions in binary form.

The `newspak-2.4.tar.z` distribution contains config files and readme files related to building uucp, news, and mail software under Linux from the various freely-available sources. It can usually be found on `sunsite.unc.edu` in the directory `/pub/Linux/system/Mail/news`. If you can't find it on sunsite, please send me mail and I'll make sure you get a copy of it.

4   Installing the Software

(Much of this section is taken verbatim from the README file in the Taylor UUCP v1.05 sources - it's provided here so I can help you "rtfm" instead of just telling you to do so)

Detailed compilation instructions are in uucp.texi in the sources.

You can grab "known good" `conf.h` and `policy.h` files for Linux from the newspak distribution referred to in the "other sources of information" section above. In that case, you can probably go right to typing "make".

4.1   Extracting the compressed sources

To extract a gzip'd tar archive, I do the following:

```
gunzip -c filename.tar.z | tar xvf -
```

A "modern" tar can just do a:

```
tar -zxvf filename.tgz
```

4.2   Edit Makefile.in to set installation directories.

Here, I set `"prefix"` to "/usr" rather than the default of "/usr/local"

4.3   Run "configure"

Type `"sh configure"`.

The configure script will compile a number of test programs to see what is available on your system and will calculate many things.

The configure script will create `conf.h` from conf.h.in and `Makefile` from Makefile.in. It will also create config.status, which is a shell script which actually creates the files.

- Rather than editing the Makefile.in file in the sources as indicated above, you can get the same effect by:

```
"configure --prefix=/usr/lib"
```

4.4   Configure the future setup of the software

4.4.1   Examine conf.h and Makefile to make sure they're right.

I took the defaults

4.4.2 Edit `policy.h` for your local system.

- - set the type of lockfiles you want (HAVE_HDB_LOCKFILES)

- - set the type of config files you want built in (HAVE_TAYLOR_CONFIG, HAVE_V2_CONFIG, HAVE_HDB_CONFIG)

- - set the type of spool directory structure you want (SPOOLDIR_HDB)

- - set the type of logging you want (HAVE_HDB_LOGGING)

- - set the default search path for commands (I added /usr/local/bin to mine)

4.5 Compile and install the software

- Type `"make"`.

- Use `"uuchk | more"` to check configuration files. You can use `"uuconv"` to convert between configuration file formats.

- Type `"make install"` to install.

4.6 Set up the config files

I'd recommend you start by taking the attached known-good config files for HDB mode and installing them.

- Make sure that the `Permissions` file indicates exactly where rmail and rnews are to be found if you put them anywhere other than in the path you specified in policy.h

- Make sure that your `Devices` files matches the actual location of your modem (cua1=COM2 in the examples)

- Edit the `Systems` file to set up the system(s) you talk to with their speed, phone number, username, and password.

  `*PROTECT THIS FILE AGAINST WORLD READ*`

- Set up the `Permissions` file and add a set of lines for each site you talk to. For security reasons, it's recommended to make sure they each have a separate account (if you allow dialin) and home directory so you can track things.

4.7 Give it a try

        /usr/lib/uucp/uucico -r 1 -x 9 -s remote_system_name

The   `-x 9`   will
have maximum debugging information written to the `/usr/spool/uucp/.Admin/audit.local` file
for help in initial setup.

I normally run `-x 4` here since that level logs details that help me with login problems. Obviously, this contains cleartext information from your Systems file (account/password) so protect it against world-read.

- from *Pierre.Beyssac@emeraude.syseca.fr*

  Taylor has more logging levels. Use -x all to get the highest level possible.

  Also, do a `"tail -f /usr/spool/uucp/.Admin/audit.local"` while debugging to watch things happen on the fly.

4.8   It doesn't work - now what ?

In general, you can refer to the documentation mentioned above if things don't work. You can also refer to your more experienced UUCP neighbors for help. Usually, it's something like a typo anyway.

5   Frequently Asked Questions about Linux UUCP

5.1   Why is my binary of uucp configured in HDB rather than "Taylor" mode?

(religious mode on - I know some people are just as religious about "ease of use" as I am about "being standard". That's why they make source code you can build your own from :-))

Because IMHO it's the de-facto standard UUCP implementation at this time. There are thousands of sites with experienced admins and there are many places you can get incredibly good information concerning the HDB setup.

The uucp-1.04 that's in SLS 1.02 and later has all three modes of config files built in. While I can't test it, I did "rtfm" and Ian Taylor tells me that it should work.

The search order for config files is Taylor then V2 (L.sys) then HDB. Use the uuconv utility in /usr/lib/uucp to convert config files from one mode to another.

If you can't wait, grab the sources for uucp and specify HAVE_BNU_CONFIG, HAVE_V2_CONFIG *and* HAVE_TAYLOR_CONFIG in the policy.h file and type "make".

The following workaround is ugly, but it does work, if you want to run Taylor configs from binaries that don't have it built in.

- *From mbravo@tctube.spb.su (Michael E. Bravo)*

  - add `"-I /usr/local/lib/uucp/config"` to _every_ invocation of whatever program in uucp package

Also, the current Slackware has a nice setup where they separated the config files for the various configurations into separate directories. For example, the HDB config files would go into `/usr/lib/uucp/hdb_config`. While I used to 'roll my own' here, I've been running the out-of-the-box Slackware UUCP in HDB mode here with no problems for quite a while.

5.2   Why do I get "timeout" on connections when I upgraded to uucp-1.04 ?

- from *Ed Carp - erc@apple.com*

  If you use a "Direct" device in the Devices file, there's now a 10 second timeout compiled in. Make the name of the Device anything other than "Direct". If you tweak the example /usr/lib/uucp files provided with SLS, you won't have problems with this one.

- from *Greg Naber - greg@squally.halcyon.com*

  If you get chat script timeouts, you can tweak the sources by editing at line 323 in uuconf/syssub.c and changing the default timeouts from 10 seconds to something larger.

- from *Ed Rodda - ed@orca.wimsey.bc.ca*

  If you get chat script timeouts, typically connecting to other Taylor sites, a pause after login can fix this.

  `feed Any ACU,ag 38400 5551212 ogin: \c\d "" yourname word: passwd`

- from *Dr. Eberhard W. Lisse - el@lisse.NA*

  Some kernels experience modems hanging up after a couple of seconds. The following patch sent by Ian Taylor might help.

```
*** conn.c.orig Mon Feb 22 20:25:24 1993
--- conn.c      Mon Feb 22 20:33:10 1993
***************
*** 204,209 ****
--- 204,212 ----

      /* Make sure any signal reporting has been done before we set
         fLog_sighup back to TRUE.  */
+     /* SMR: it seems to me if we don't care about SIGHUPS, we should clear
+        the flag before we return  */
+     afSignal[INDEXSIG_SIGHUP] = FALSE;
      ulog (LOG_ERROR, (const char *) NULL);
      fLog_sighup = TRUE;
```

5.3   Why doesn't HDB anonymous uucp seem to work ?

The SLS anonymous uucp only works in Taylor mode because it's compiled with HAVE_TAYLOR_CONFIG.
If you want to do anon uucp in HDB mode, you'll have to recompile the sources with just HDB defined. Ian
Taylor is considering which way to deal with this "feature".

Also, Taylor in HDB mode seems to be sensitive to white space and blank lines. To be safe, make sure that
there are no blank lines or trailing spaces in the Permissions file.

Lastly, make sure that you have a file called remote.unknown in /usr/lib/uucp and that it's *NOT*
executable. See the O'Reilly+Assoc book "Managing UUCP and USENET" for details regarding this file.

5.4   What does "no matching ports found" mean ?

In all probability, you are attempting to use a device (/usr/lib/uucp/Devices) that doesn't exist, or the
device you've specified in the /usr/lib/uucp/Systems file doesn't match up with any valid devices in
the Devices file.

Following this are *sanitized* versions of my working Taylor 1.05 HDB config files that you can plug in and
use.

note the "ACU" in the Systems ? That tells which "port" to use in Devices

see the "scout" word in Systems ? That tells which dialer to use in Dialers.

If you had a ACU port, but none that matched the specified dialer on the same line in Systems, you'll get
that message.

5.5   What are known good config files for HDB mode ?

The following are "known-good" config files for Taylor 1.05 under Linux in HoneyDanBer mode. They work
on kernels of 0.99-8 or later. All files should be in /usr/lib/uucp unless you've tweaked the sources to put
the uucp library elsewhere.

If you *HAVE* put things in non-standard places, be aware that things like sendmail might get very
confused. You need to ensure that all communications-related programs agree on your idea of "standard"
paths.

If you're running a kernel of 0.99-7 or earlier, change "cua1" to "ttyS1".

```
#------------- Devices -------------
# make sure the device (cua1 here) matches your system
# cua1 = COM2
#
```

```
# here "scout" is the Digicom Scout Plus 19.2 modem I use
# tbfast etc. is for a Telebit Trailblazer Plus modem's various speeds
#
ACU cua1 - 19200 scout
ACU cua1 - 9600 tbfast
ACU cua1 - 1200 tbslow
ACU cua1 - 2400 tbmed

#------------- dialers --------------
# note the setting of the Trailblazer registers "on the fly"
# "scout" is a Digicom Scout Plus (Hayes-like) modem I use here
#
scout   =W-,     "" ATM0DT\T CONNECT
tbfast  =W-,     "" A\pA\pA\pT OK ATS50=255DT\T CONNECT\sFAST
tbslow  =W-,     "" A\pA\pA\pT OK ATS50=2DT\T CONNECT\s1200
tbmed   =W-,     "" A\pA\pA\pT OK ATS50=3DT\T CONNECT\s2400

#-------------- Systems -------------
# this is a very generic entry that will work for most systems
#
# the Any;1 means that you can call once per minute with using -f (force)
# the ACU,g means force "g" protocol rather than Taylor's default "i"
#
fredsys Any;1 ACU,g 19200 scout5555555 "" \r ogin:--ogin: uanon word: uanon

#----------------------------- Permissions -----------------------

# Taylor UUCP in HDB mode appears to be sensitive to blank lines.
# Make sure all Permissions lines are real or commented out.
#
# this is a anonymous uucp entry
#
LOGNAME=nuucp MACHINE=OTHER \
READ=/usr/spool/uucp/nuucp \
WRITE=/usr/spool/uucp/nuucp \
SENDFILES=yes REQUEST=yes \
COMMANDS=/bin/rmail
#
# this is a normal setup for a remote system that talks to us
# note the absolute path to rnews since this site puts things
# in locations that aren't "standard"
#
LOGNAME=fredsys MACHINE=fredsys \
READ=/usr/spool/uucp/fredsys:/usr/spool/uucp/uucppublic:/files \
WRITE=/usr/spool/uucp/fredsys:/usr/spool/uucppublic \
SENDFILES=yes REQUEST=yes \
COMMANDS=/bin/rmail:/usr/local/lib/news/bin/rnews
#-----------------------------------------------------------------
```

5.6 Getting uucico to call alternate numbers

The new v1.05 has an added '-z' switch to uucico that will try alternate numbers for a remote system.

6 Acknowledgements

The following people have helped in the assembly of the information (and experience) that helped make this document possible:

Ed Carp, Steve Robbins, Ian Taylor, Greg Naber, Matt Welsh, Pierre Beyssac

If I forgot anybody, my apologies.

Part XLIV

Wine Frequently Asked Questions & Answers

Copyright P. David Gardner pdg@primenet.com
2.9.1 April 1995
This is the mid-month posting of the FAQ (Frequently Asked Questions) for the Wine development project mad only to comp.emulaturs.ms-windows.wine. It contains both general and technical information about Wine: project status, how to obtain and configure and run it, and more. Please read this FAQ carefully before you post questions about Wine to Usenet to see if your question is already answered here first.

Contents

1 Introduction

NOTE: If you are reading this FAQ and it is April 30, 1995 or later, this document is out of date. Please get a new one from sources outlined below.

ALSO NOTE: As of this version of the FAQ, the World Wide Web version, located at (`http://www.primenet.com/ pdg/wine-faq.html`), has full hypertext links to all sites mentioned here, for obtaining Wine binaries via ftp, to obtaining the plaintext version of the FAQ via ftp, to linking to other sites that carry Wine related pages. I've also dressed things up a bit with some graphics to make the WWW version of the FAQ more interesting. The following answers have changed since the last issue of this FAQ:

- Sites to ftp the plaintext version of this FAQ

- 3.1 – Programs that run under Wine

- 3.6 – Compiling programs in MS Windows compilers running under Wine

- 5.1 – Places to get Wine

- 6.3 – WWW pages related to Wine

- 8.1 – Folks who contribute to Wine

Please note that since Wine is still alpha code, it may or may not work to varying degrees on your system. Neither the Wine developers nor the Wine FAQ author/maintainer can be held responsible for any damage that may be caused to your computer hardware or software by your obtaining, installing, configuring, operating and/or removing Wine. This FAQ will be posted monthly to these newsgroups:

- comp.answers

- comp.emulators.announce

- comp.emulators.ms-windows.wine

- comp.unix.bsd.freebsd.announce

- comp.unix.bsd.netbsd.announce

- comp.os.linux.answers

- comp.windows.x.i386unix

- news.answers

and is reposted mid-month to only:

- comp.emulators.ms-windows.wine

The plaintext version of this FAQ is also available by anonymous ftp from the following systems. These are hypertext links, so you can ftp the file by clicking on the desired site.

- (`ftp://ftp.primenet.com/pub/users/p/pdg/Wine.FAQ`)

- (`ftp://tsx-11.mit.edu/pub/linux/ALPHA/Wine/Wine.FAQ`)

-
  (ftp://rtfm.mit.edu/pub/usenet-by-newsgroup/comp.emulators.ms-windows.wine/WINE_
  (WINdows_ Emulator)_ Frequently_ Asked_ Questions)

- (ftp://sunsite.unc.edu/pub/Linux/ALPHA/wine/Wine.FAQ)

and quite likely most of the other sites around the globe that mirror the Wine distribution from the Wine project's main distribution site, tsx-11.mit.edu.

This FAQ is also available on the World Wide Web (WWW), reachable with any web browser such as Mosaic or Netscape, or the ASCII browser lynx, at the following URL:

- (http://www.primenet.com/ pdg/wine-faq.html)

If you have any technical questions about Wine, please post these have any suggestions for corrections, changes, expansion or further clarification of this FAQ, please send them to the Wine FAQ author and maintainer listed in question 8.2.

2   Overview

2.1   What is Wine, and what is it supposed to do?

Wine is both a program loader and an emulation library that will allow Unix users to run MS Windows applications on an x86 hardware platform running under some Unixes. The program loader will load and execute an MS Windows application binary, while the emulation library will take calls to MS Windows functions and translate these into calls to Unix/X, so that equivalent functionality is achieved.

MS Windows binaries will run directly; there will be no need for machine level emulation of program instructions. Sun has reported better performance with their version of WABI than is actually achieved under MS Windows, so theoretically the same result is possible under Wine.

2.2   What does the word Wine stand for?

The word Wine stands for one of two things: WINdows Emulator, or Wine Is Not an Emulator. Both are right. Use whichever one you like best.

2.3   What is the current version of Wine?

A new version of Wine will be distributed almost every week, usually on a Saturday or Sunday. You will be able to keep up on all the latest releases by reading the newsgroup comp.emulators.ms-windows.wine.

When downloading Wine from your ftp site of choice (see question 5.1 for some of these choices), you can make sure you are getting the latest version by watching the version numbers in the distribution filename. For instance, the distribution released on June 20, 1994 was called Wine-940620.tar.gz.

Weekly patches are also available. If you are current to the previous version, you can download and apply just the current patch file rather than the entire new distribution. The patch filenames follow the same conventions as the weekly distribution, so watch those version numbers!

2.4   When will Wine be ready for general distribution?

Because Wine is being developed solely by volunteers, it is difficult to predict when it will be ready for general distribution. Between 90-98% of the functions used by MS Windows applets, and 80-90% of the functions used by major programs, have been at least partially implemented at this time. However, the remaining 10% will likely take another 90% of the time, not including debugging.

3   Program Compatibility

3.1   Which MS Windows programs does wine currently run?

Since Wine is still under development, programs may break and then run again from release to release, so it is difficult to publish a complete and accurate list. However, I'll list some of the more stable successes here from now on.

Most of the aplets distributed with MS Windows now run to varying degrees of success. For instance, Solitaire (SOL.EXE) runs just fine now, including menu selections, as long as you don't try to access the help menu. Windows colors can vary from system to system, depending on your video card and monitor, but it's been reported that colors are generally darker under X and Wine than under native DOS/MS Windows.

A number of public domain and shareware games programs found on the ftp site ftp.cica.indiana.edu can run under Wine, with varying degrees of success.

To date, there have been no reports of successful runs of major MS Windows programs such as Word, WordPerfect, Paradox, and the like. Quicken has been reported to work from time to time under Wine.

Keep an eye on the newsgroup comp.emulators.ms-windows.wine for up-to-date reports of successes.

3.2   Which MS Windows programs do you expect Wine never to be able to run at all, and for what reason(s)?

Any MS Windows program that requires a special enhanced mode device driver (VxD) that cannot be rewritten specifically for Wine, will not run under Wine.

3.3   Will MS Windows programs typically run faster or slower under Unix and Wine than they do under MS-DOS and MS Windows? Will certain kinds of programs run slower or faster? Programs should typically run at about the same speed under Wine as they do under MS Windows.

3.4   Are there any advantages or disadvantages to running MS Windows applications under wine that I should be aware of?

As with OS/2, you will be running 16-bit MS Windows applications in a 32-bit operating system using emulation techniques, so you will have similar advantages and disadvantages.

There will be crash protection. That is, each MS Windows application running under Wine will be running in its own X window and its own portion of reserved memory, so that if one MS Windows application crashes, it will not crash the other MS Windows or Unix applications that you may have running at the same time.

Also, MS Windows programs should run at about the same speed under Wine as they do under MS Windows. When Wine is finished, you will be able to run your favorite MS Windows applications in a Unix environment.

However, be aware that any application written for a 16-bit operating system will run much less efficiently than its 32-bit cousin, so if you find a 32-bit application that fits your needs, you will be much better off switching.

3.5   Will   Wine   support   MS   Windows   networked   applications   that   use WINSOCK.DLL?

Yes, Wine will support such applications. You will be able to run MS Windows applications such as Netscape and Mosaic (though there are 32-bit native Unix versions of these available now).

3.6   I'm a software developer who wants to use Unix to develop programs rather than MS-DOS, but I need to write MS-DOS and MS Windows programs as well. Will I be able to run my favorite MS-DOS and/or MS Windows compilers under Wine?

Linux users report that DOSEMU, the MS-DOS emulator for Linux, is starting to support DPMI (DOS Protected Mode Interface). This means that folks can run MS Windows in standard mode under DOSEMU, and can also run (with varied degrees of success) Microsoft and Borland C++ compilers.

However, at last report, Wine cannot run these compilers, nor is it able to run any MS Windows debuggers, and may not be able to for some time.

Keep in mind that Wine is being designed to run existing MS Windows applications. Be aware too that a custom MS Windows program specifically written to be compatible with Wine may not work the same as when it is run under MS-DOS and MS Windows.

4   Hardware/Software Considerations

4.1   Under what hardware platform(s) and operating system(s) will Wine run?

Wine is being developed specifically to run on the Intel x86 class of CPUs under certain Unixes that run on the x86 platform. Unixes currently being tested for Wine compatibility include Linux, NetBSD and FreeBSD. The Wine development team hopes to attract the interest of commercial Unix and Unix clone vendors as well.

4.2   What minimum CPU must I have in my computer to be able to run Wine and MS Windows applications smoothly?

Wine is currently being developed specifically for use on Intel x86 CPUs, and needs a minimum 80386 CPU. It is known to also work in the 80486 and Pentium CPUs. Beyond that, the basic test is, if you can run X11 now, you should be able to run Wine and MS Windows applications. As always, the faster your CPU, the better. Having a math coprocessor is unimportant. However, having a graphics accelerated video card supported by X will help greatly.

4.3   How much disk space will the Wine source code and binaries take on my hard drive?

It is anticipated that when Wine is completed, you will need approximately 6-8 megabytes of hard drive space to store and compile the source code.

4.4   How much RAM do I need to have on my Unix system to be able to run Wine and MS Windows applications smoothly?

If you can run X smoothly on your Unix system now, you should be able to run Wine and MS Windows applications just fine too. A Wine workstation should realistically have at least 8 megabytes of RAM and a 12 megabyte swap partition. More is better, of course.

4.5   I have a Doublespaced or Stackered MS-DOS partition. Can Wine run MS Windows binaries located in such a partition?

Only if the operating system supports mounting those types of drives. Currently, NetBSD and FreeBSD do not. However, there is a patch for the Linux kernel that allows read-only access to a Doublespaced DOS partition, and it's available on sunsite.unc.edu as:

```
(ftp://sunsite.unc.edu/pub/Linux/system/Filesystems/thsfs.tgz)
```

4.6 Do I need to have a MS-DOS partition on my system to use Wine? Does MS Windows need to be loaded into that partition in order to run MS Windows programs under Wine?

You do not need DOS or MS Windows to install, configure and run Wine. However, Wine has to be able to 'see' an MS Windows binary if it is to run it. So, currently, you do need to have a DOS partition with MS Windows installed on your hard drive to use Wine in a practical manner. Your Unix OS must be able to 'see' this partition (check your /etc/fstab file or mount the partition manually) in order for Wine to run MS Windows binaries in your DOS partition.

However, when it is finished, Wine will not require that you have a MS-DOS partition on your system at all, meaning that you will not need to have MS Windows installed either. Wine programmers will provide an application setup program to allow you to install your MS Windows programs straight from your distribution diskettes into your Unix filesystem, or from within your Unix filesystem if you ftp an MS Windows program over the Internet.

4.7 If Wine completely replaces MS Windows, will it duplicate all of the functions of MS Windows?

Most of them, yes. However, some applications and aplets that come with MS Windows, such as File Manager and Calculator, can be considered by some to be redundant, since 32-bit Unix programs that duplicate these functions already exist.

4.8 Will I be able to install MS Windows applications in any Unix filesystem?

Wine is written to be filesystem independent, so MS Windows applications will install and run under any filesystem supported by your brand of Unix.

4.9 Will Wine run only under X, or can it run in character mode?

Being a GUI (graphical user interface), MS Windows does not have a character mode, so there will be no character mode for Wine. So yes, you must run Wine under X.

4.10 Will Wine run under any X window manager?

Wine is window manager independent, so the X window manager you choose to run has absolutely no bearing on your ability to run MS Windows programs under Wine. Wine uses standard X libraries, so no additional ones are needed.

4.11 What happens when Windows '95 is released? Will 32-bit Windows applications run under Wine?

Wine developers do eventually plan on supporting Win32s, but such support is not in the current version of Wine.

5   How to Find, Install, Configure and Run Wine

5.1   Where can I get Wine?

Wine can now be found on quite a few systems throughout the Internet. Here is an incomplete list of some of the systems where you will find Wine:

- (ftp://sunsite.unc.edu/pub/Linux/ALPHA/wine/Wine-950403.tar.gz)

- (ftp://tsx-11.mit.edu/pub/linux/ALPHA/Wine/development/Wine-950403.tar.gz)

-
    (ftp://ftp.infomagic.com/pub/mirrors/linux/wine/development/Wine-950403.tar.gz)

- (ftp://ftp.funet.fi:/pub/OS/Linux/ALPHA/Wine/Wine-950403.tar.gz)

It should also be available from any site that mirrors tsx-11 or sunsite.

Some of these ftp sites may archive previous versions of Wine as well as the current one. To determine which is the latest one, look at the distribution filename, which will take the form:

                    Wine-[yymmdd].tar.gz

Simply replace *yymmdd* in the distribution filename with the numbers for year, month and date respectively. The latest one is the one to get.

Note that weekly diff patches are now available, so you don't have to download, install and configure the entire distribution each week if you are current to the previous release. Diff releases follow the same numbering conventions as do the general releases, and take the form:

                    Wine-[yymmdd].diff.gz

Note that any mirror of tsx-11 will likely carry the Wine distribution as well, and may not be listed here in this FAQ. If you are mirroring the Wine distribution from the tsx-11 site and wish to be listed here in this FAQ, please send email to the FAQ author/maintainer listed in question 8.2

5.2   If I do not have an Internet account, how can I get Wine?

Some CD-ROM archives of Internet sites, notably those from Walnut Creek that archive ftp.cdrom.com and sunsite.unc.edu, do include Wine as part of the archive. However, the age of these distributions is always in question, as the "snapshot" of the site may have been taken anywhere from 1-4 months (or more) prior to purchase.

Your best bet to get the very latest distribution of Wine, if you do not have your own Internet account, is to find a friend who does have an Internet account and have him/her ftp the necessary files for you. If you have an email account on a BBS that can reach the Internet through a gateway, you may be able to use email to get the Wine release sent to you; check with your BBS system operator for details.

If you are running a BBS that is not connected to the Internet but does offer the Wine distribution for download, and would like to be listed in this FAQ, please forward such information to the FAQ author/maintainer as listed in question 8.2

5.3   How do I install Wine on my hard drive?

Just un-gzip and un-tar the file, and follow the instructions contained in the README file that will be located in the base Wine directory.

5.4   How do I compile the Wine distribution source code?

5.5   How do I configure Wine to run on my system?

All of the directions to perform these two steps are located in the README file that will be located in the base Wine directory after you untar the distribution file.

5.6   How do I run an MS Windows program under Wine?

Assuming you are running X already, call up a term window. Then, at the shell prompt, type:

```
wine [/path/progname]
```

Another X window will pop up on top of the shell window and the binary should begin to execute.

Let's assume that you want to run MS Windows Solitaire. Under MS-DOS, you had installed MS Windows on your C: drive under the subdirectory /WINDOWS. Under Unix, you have mounted the C: drive under /dos/c. To run MS Windows Solitaire, you would type:

```
wine /dos/c/windows/sol.exe
```

5.7   I have installed and configured Wine, but Wine cannot find MS Windows on my drive. Where did I go wrong?

First, make sure you have mounted your MS-DOS partition into your Unix filesystem, either by putting the entry into /etc/fstab, or by manually mounting it. Remember, it must not be located on a Doublespaced or Stackered partition, as neither Linux, FreeBSD, NetBSD or Wine cannot currently 'see' files located in such compressed DOS partitions.

Next, check your path statements in the 'wine.conf' file. No capital letters may be used in paths, as they are automatically converted to lowercase.

5.8   I think I've found a bug. How do I report this bug to the Wine programming team?

Bug reports should be posted to the newsgroup:

```
comp.emulators.ms-windows.wine
```

5.9   I was able to get various MS Windows programs to run, but their menus do not work. What is wrong?

Wine is not complete at this time, so the menus may not work. They will in time as more of the MS Windows API calls are included in Wine.

5.10   I have run various MS Windows programs but since the program menus do not work, how can I exit these programs?

Kill the shell window that you called up to run your MS Windows program, and the X window that appeared with the program will be killed too.

5.11   How do I remove Wine from my computer?

All you have to do is to type:

```
rm -fR [/path/]Wine*
```

Make sure you specify the exact path when using the powerful 'rm -fR' command. If you are afraid you might delete something important, or might otherwise delete other files within your filesystem, change into each Wine subdirectory singly and delete the files found there manually, one file or directory at a time. Neither the Wine programmers nor the Wine FAQ author/maintainer can be held responsible for your deleting any files in your filesystem.

6   How To Get Help

6.1   Is there a Usenet newsgroup for Wine?

Yes. It's called comp.emulators.ms-windows.wine, and the newsgroup's charter states that it will consist of announcements and discussion about Wine. The newsgroup serves as a place for developers to discuss Wine, and for minor announcements for the general public. Major announcements will be crossposted to other appropriate groups, such as the newsgroups comp.os.linux.announce, comp.windows.x.announce and comp.emulators.announce.

If your Usenet site does not carry this new newsgroup, please urge your sysadmin and/or uplink to add it.

6.2   Is there a gopher site set up for Wine?

To the best of my knowledge at the time of this writing, no. If you are installing or maintain a Gopher site pertaining to Wine, please contact the FAQ author/maintainer as noted in question 8.2for inclusion in the next edition of the Wine FAQ.

6.3   Is there a WWW site set up for Wine information?

Here are the URLs for a few sites reachable with your favorite web browser:

- (http://www.primenet.com/ pdg/wine-faq.html)
- (http://www.thepoint.com/unix/emulate/wine/index.html)
- (http://daedalus.dra.hmg.gb/gale/wine/wine.html)
- (http://www.ifi.uio.no/ dash/wine/index.html)

If you are installing or maintain a WWW page pertaining to Wine, please inform the FAQ author/maintainer as detailed in 8.2 for inclusion in the next edition of the Wine FAQ.

6.4   Is there a mailing list for Wine?

There is a seldom-used developers-only mailing list, whose contents are planned to be ported into comp.emulators.ms-windows.wine. If you are a Wine developer, or want to become one, you are welcome to join the list. Please leave a message on the newsgroup comp.emulators.ms-windows.wine expressing your interest.

Those with a general interest in Wine should participate in the newsgroup.

7 How You Can Help

7.1 How can I help contribute to the Wine project, and in what way(s)?

You can contribute programming skills, or monetary or equipment donations, to aid the Wine developers in reaching their goal. To find out who, what, where, when and why, please post your desire to contribute to the newsgroup comp.emulators.ms-windows.wine.

7.2 I want to help beta test Wine. How can I do this?

Beta testers are currently not needed, as Wine is still Alpha code at this time. However, anyone is welcome to download the latest version and try it out at any time.

7.3 I have written some code that I would like to submit to the Wine project. How do I go about doing this?

Send your weekly code contributions to the mail alias 'wine-new@amscons.com'. You should still verify that your code was included in the subsequent release of Wine, as project managers cannot guarantee that the mail server will not suffer some computer failure that will cause loss of your message and code after it is received.

8 Who is Responsible for Wine

8.1 Who is responsible for writing and maintaining the Wine source code?

Wine is available thanks to the work of Bob Amstadt, Dag Asheim, Martin Ayotte, Erik Bos, John Brezak, Andrew Bulhak, John Burton, Paul Falstad, Peter Galbavy, Jeffrey Hsu, Miguel de Icaza, Alexandre Julliard, Jon Konrath, Scott A. Laird, Martin von Loewis, Kenneth MacDonald, Peter MacDonald, David Metcalfe, Michael Patra, John Richardson, Johannes Ruscheinski, Yngvi Sigurjonsson, Rick Sladkey, William Smith, Jon Tombs, Linus Torvalds, Carl Williams, Karl Guenter Wuensch, and Eric Youngdale.

8.2 Who is responsible for writing and maintaining the Wine FAQ?

The FAQ is being maintained by Dave Gardner < pdg@primenet.com > , who is not connected with the Wine project in any way but as the FAQ author/maintainer. Please do not send technical questions about the Wine project to the FAQ maintainer, but rather post them to the newsgroup.

8.3 Who are the folks and organizations who have contributed money or equipment to the Wine project?

People and organizations who have given generous contributions of money and equipment include David L. Harper, Bob Hepple, Mark A. Horton, Kevin P. Lawton, the Syntropy Institute, and James Woulfe.

Part XLV

The Linux XFree86 HOWTO

Copyright by Matt Welsh, mdw@sunsite.unc.edu
v3.0, 15 March 1995
This document describes how to obtain, install, and configure version 3.1.1 of the XFree86 version of the X Window System (X11R6) for Linux systems. It is a step-by-step guide to configuring XFree86 on your system.

Contents

1 Introduction

The X Window System is a large and powerful (and somewhat complex) graphics environment for UNIX systems. The original X Window System code was developed at MIT; commercial vendors have since made X the industry standard for UNIX platforms. Virtually every UNIX workstation in the world runs some variant of the X Window system.

A free port of the MIT X Window System version 11, release 6 (X11R6) for 80386/80486/Pentium UNIX systems has been developed by a team of programmers originally headed by David Wexelblat (dwex@XFree86.org). The release, known as XFree86, is available for System V/386, 386BSD, and other x86 UNIX implementations, including Linux. It includes all of the required binaries, support files, libraries, and tools.

In this document, we'll give a step-by-step description of how to install and configure XFree86 for Linux, but you will have to fill in some of the details yourself by reading the documentation released with XFree86 itself. (This documentation is discussed below.) However, using and customizing the X Window System is far beyond the scope of this document—for this purpose you should obtain one of the many good books on using the X Window System.

2 Hardware requirements

As of XFree86 version 3.1.1, released in February 1995, the following video chipsets are supported. The documentation included with your video adaptor should specify the chipset used. If you are in the market for a new video card, or are buying a new machine that comes with a video card, have the vendor find out exactly what the make, model, and chipset of the video card is. This may require the vendor to call technical support on your behalf; in general vendors will be happy to do this. Many PC hardware vendors will state that the video card is a "standard SVGA card" which "should work" on your system. Explain that your software (mention Linux and XFree86!) does not support all video chipsets and that you must have detailed information.

You can also determine your videocard chipset by running the `SuperProbe` program included with the XFree86 distribution. This is covered in more detail below.

The following standard SVGA chipsets are supported:

- Tseng ET3000, ET4000AX, ET4000/W32

- Western Digital/Paradise PVGA1

- Western Digital WD90C00, WD90C10, WD90C11, WD90C24, WD90C30, WD90C31, WD90C33

- Genoa GVGA

- Trident TVGA8800CS, TVGA8900B, TVGA8900C, TVGA8900CL, TVGA9000, TVGA9000i, TVGA9100B, TVGA9200CX, TVGA9320, TVGA9400CX, TVGA9420

- ATI 18800, 18800-1, 28800-2, 28800-4, 28800-5, 28800-6, 68800-3, 68800-6, 68800AX, 68800LX, 88800

- NCR 77C22, 77C22E, 77C22E+

- Cirrus Logic CLGD5420, CLGD5422, CLGD5424, CLGD5426, CLGD5428, CLGD5429, CLGD5430, CLGD5434, CLGD6205, CLGD6215, CLGD6225, CLGD6235, CLGD6420

- Compaq AVGA

- OAK OTI067, OTI077

- Avance Logic AL2101

- MX MX68000, MX680010

- Video 7/Headland Technologies HT216-32

The following SVGA chipsets with accelerated features are also supported:

- 8514/A (and true clones)

- ATI Mach8, Mach32

- Cirrus CLGD5420, CLGD5422, CLGD5424, CLGD5426, CLGD5428, CLGD5429, CLGD5430, CLGD5434, CLGD6205, CLGD6215, CLGD6225, CLGD6235

- S3 86C911, 86C924, 86C801, 86C805, 86C805i, 86C928, 86C864, 86C964

- Western Digital WD90C31, WD90C33

- Weitek P9000

- IIT AGX-014, AGX-015, AGX-016

- Tseng ET4000/W32, ET4000/W32i, ET4000/W32p

Video cards using these chipsets are supported on all bus types, including VLB and PCI.

All of the above are supported in both 256 color and monochrome modes, with the exception of the Avance Logic, MX and Video 7 chipsets, which are only supported in 256 color mode. If your video card has enough DRAM installed, many of the above chipsets are supported in 16 and 32 bits-per-pixel mode (specifically, some Mach32, P9000, S3 and Cirrus boards). The usual configuration is 8 bits per pixel (that is, 256 colors).

The monochrome server also supports generic VGA cards, the Hercules monochrome card, the Hyundai HGC1280, Sigma LaserView, and Apollo monochrome cards. On the Compaq AVGA, only 64k of video memory is supported for the monochrome server, and the GVGA has not been tested with more than 64k.

This list will undoubtedly expand as time passes. The release notes for the current version of XFree86 should contain the complete list of supported video chipsets.

One problem faced by the XFree86 developers is that some video card manufacturers use non-standard mechanisms for determining clock frequencies used to drive the card. Some of these manufacturers either don't release specifications describing how to program the card, or they require developers to sign a non-disclosure statement to obtain the information. This would obviously restrict the free distribution of the XFree86 software, something that the XFree86 development team is not willing to do. For a long time, this has been a problem with certain video cards manufactured by Diamond, but as of release 3.1 of XFree86, Diamond has started to work with the development team to release free drivers for these cards.

The suggested setup for XFree86 under Linux is a 486 machine with at least 8 megabytes of RAM, and a video card with a chipset listed above. For optimal performance, we suggest using an accelerated card, such as an S3-chipset card. You should check the documentation for XFree86 and verify that your particular card is supported before taking the plunge and purchasing expensive hardware. Benchmark ratings comparisons for various video cards under XFree86 are posted routinely to the USENET newsgroups `comp.windows.x.i386unix` and `comp.os.linux.x`.

As a side note, my personal Linux system is a 486DX2-66, 20 megabytes of RAM, and is equipped with a VLB S3-864 chipset card with 2 megabytes of DRAM. I have run X benchmarks on this machine as well as on Sun Sparc IPX workstations. The Linux system is roughly 7 times faster than the Sparc IPX (for the curious, XFree86-3.1 under Linux, with this video card, runs at around 171,000 xstones; the Sparc IPX at around 24,000). In general, XFree86 on a Linux system with an accelerated SVGA card will give you much greater performance than that found on commercial UNIX workstations (which usually employ simple framebuffers for graphics).

Your machine will need at least 4 megabytes of physical RAM, and 16 megabytes of virtual RAM (for example, 8 megs physical and 8 megs swap). Remember that the more physical RAM that you have, the less that the system will swap to and from disk when memory is low. Because swapping is inherently slow (disks are very slow compared to memory), having 8 megabytes of RAM or more is necessary to run XFree86 comfortably. A system with 4 megabytes of physical RAM could run *much* (up to 10 times) more slowly than one with 8 megs or more.

3 Installing XFree86

The Linux binary distribution of XFree86 can be found on a number of FTP sites. On `sunsite.unc.edu`, it is found in the directory `/pub/Linux/X11`. (As of the time of this writing, the current version is 3.1.1; newer versions are released periodically).

It's quite likely that you obtained XFree86 as part of a Linux distribution, in which case downloading the software separately is not necessary.

If you are downloading XFree86 directly, this table lists the files in the XFree86-3.1 distribution.

One of the following servers is required:

XF86-3.1.1-8514.tar.gz

    Server for 8514-based boards.

XF86-3.1.1-AGX.tar.gz

Server for AGX-based boards.

XF86-3.1.1-Mach32.tar.gz

Server for Mach32-based boards.

XF86-3.1.1-Mach8.tar.gz

Server for Mach8-based boards.

XF86-3.1.1-Mono.tar.gz

Server for monochrome video modes.

XF86-3.1.1-P9000.tar.gz

Server for P9000-based boards.

XF86-3.1.1-S3.tar.gz

Server for S3-based boards.

XF86-3.1.1-SVGA.tar.gz

Server for Super VGA-based boards.

XF86-3.1.1-VGA16.tar.gz

Server for VGA/EGA-based boards.

XF86-3.1.1-W32.tar.gz

Server for ET4000/W32-based boards.

All of the following files are required:

XF86-3.1.1-bin.tar.gz

The rest of the X11R6 binaries.

XF86-3.1.1-cfg.tar.gz

Config files for `xdm`, `xinit` and `fs`.

XF86-3.1.1-doc.tar.gz

Documentation and man pages.

XF86-3.1.1-inc.tar.gz

Include files.

XF86-3.1.1-lib.tar.gz

Shared X libraries and support files.

XF86-3.1-fnt.tar.gz

Basic fonts.

The following files are optional:

XF86-3.1-ctrb.tar.gz

Selected contrib programs.

XF86-3.1-extra.tar.gz

Extra XFree86 servers and binaries.

XF86-3.1-lkit.tar.gz

Server linkkit for customization.

XF86-3.1-fnt75.tar.gz

75-dpi screen fonts.

XF86-3.1-fnt100.tar.gz

100-dpi screen fonts.

XF86-3.1-fntbig.tar.gz

Large Kanji and other fonts.

XF86-3.1-fntscl.tar.gz

Scaled fonts (Speedo, Type1).

XF86-3.1-man.tar.gz

Manual pages.

XF86-3.1-pex.tar.gz

PEX binaries, includes and libraries.

XF86-3.1-slib.tar.gz

Static X libraries and support files.

XF86-3.1-usrbin.tar.gz

Daemons which reside in /usr/bin.

XF86-3.1-xdmshdw.tar.gz

Shadow password version of xdm.

The XFree86 directory should contain README files and installation notes for the current version.

All that is required to install XFree86 is to obtain the above files, create the directory /usr/X11R6 (as root), and unpack the files from /usr/X11R6 with a command such as:

```
gzip -dc XF86-3.1.1-bin.tar.gz | tar xfB -
```

Remember that these tar files are packed relative to /usr/X11R6. so it's important to unpack the files there.

After unpacking the files, you first need to link the file /usr/X11R6/bin/X to the server that you're using. For example, if you wish to use the SVGA color server, /usr/bin/X11/X should be linked to /usr/X11R6/bin/XF86_SVGA. If you wish to use the monochrome server instead, relink this file to XF86_MONO with the command

```
ln -sf /usr/X11R6/bin/XF86_MONO /usr/X11R6/bin/X
```

The same holds true if you are using one of the other servers.

If you aren't sure which server to use, or don't know your video card chipset, you can run the SuperProbe program found in /usr/X11R6/bin (included in the XF86-3.1-bin listed above). This program will attempt to determine your video chipset type and other information; write down its output for later reference.

You need to make sure that /usr/X11R6/bin is on your path. This can be done by editing your system default /etc/profile or /etc/csh.login (based on the shell that you, or other users on your system, use). Or you can simply add the directory to your personal path by modifying /etc/.bashrc or /etc/.cshrc, based on your shell.

You also need to make sure that /usr/X11R6/lib can be located by ld.so, the runtime linker. To do this, add the line

```
/usr/X11R6/lib
```

to the file `/etc/ld.so.conf`, and run `/sbin/ldconfig`, as root.

4   Configuring XFree86

Setting up XFree86 is not difficult in most cases. However, if you happen to be using hardware for which drivers ar under development, or wish to obtain the best performance or resolution from an accelerated graphics card, configuring XFree86 can be somewhat time-consuming.

In this section we will describe how to create and edit the `XF86Config` file, which configures the XFree86 server. In many cases it is best to start out with a "basic" XFree86 configuration, one which uses a low resolution, such as 640x480, which should be supported on all video cards and monitor types. Once you have XFree86 working at a lower, standard resolution, you can tweak the configuration to exploit the capabilities of your video hardware. The idea is that you want to know that XFree86 works at all on your system, and that something isn't wrong with your installation, before attempting the sometimes difficult task of setting up XFree86 for real use.

In addition to the information listed here, you should read the following documentation:

- The   XFree86   documentation in `/usr/X11R6/lib/X11/doc` (contained within the `XFree86-3.1-doc` package). You should especially see the file `README.Config`, which is an XFree86 configuration tutorial.

- Several video chipsets have separate `README` files in the above directory (such as `README.Cirrus` and `README.S3`). Read one of these if applicable.

- The man page for `XFree86`.

- The man page for `XF86Config`.

- The man page for the particular server that you are using (such as `XF86_SVGA` or `XF86_S3`).

The main XFree86 configuration file is `/usr/X11R6/lib/X11/XF86Config`. This file contains information on your mouse, video card parameters, and so on. The file `XF86Config.eg` is provided with the XFree86 distribution as an example. Copy this file to `XF86Config` and edit it as a starting point.

The `XF86Config` man page explains the format of this file in detail. Read this man page now, if you have not done so already.

We are going to present a sample `XF86Config` file, piece by piece. This file may not look exactly like the sample file included in the XFree86 distribution, but the structure is the same.

Note that the `XF86Config` file format may change with each version of XFree86; this information is only valid for XFree86 version 3.1.

Also, you should not simply copy the configuration file listed here to your own system and attempt to use it. Attempting to use a configuration file which doesn't correspond to your hardware could drive the monitor at a frequency which is too high for it; there have been reports of monitors (especially fixed-frequency monitors) being damaged or destroyed by using an incorrectly configured `XF86Config` file. The bottom line is this: Make absolutely sure that your `XF86Config` file corresponds to your hardware before you attempt to use it.

Each section of the `XF86Config` file is surrounded by the pair of lines

```
Section "section-name"
  ...
EndSection
```

The first part of the `XF86Config` file is `Files`, which looks like this:

```
Section "Files"
    RgbPath      "/usr/X11R6/lib/X11/rgb"
    FontPath     "/usr/X11R6/lib/X11/fonts/misc/"
    FontPath     "/usr/X11R6/lib/X11/fonts/75dpi/"
EndSection
```

The RgbPath line sets the path to the X11R6 RGB color database, and each FontPath line sets the path to a directory containing X11 fonts. In general you shouldn't have to modify these lines; just be sure that there is a FontPath entry for each font type that you have installed (that is, for each directory in /usr/X11R6/lib/X11/fonts).

The next section is ServerFlags, which specifies several global flags for the server. In general this section is empty.

```
Section "ServerFlags"
# Uncomment this to cause a core dump at the spot where a signal is
# received.  This may leave the console in an unusable state, but may
# provide a better stack trace in the core dump to aid in debugging
#    NoTrapSignals

# Uncomment this to disable the <Crtl><Alt><BS> server abort sequence
#    DontZap
EndSection
```

Here, we have all lines within the section commented out.

The next section is Keyboard. This should be fairly intuitive.

```
Section "Keyboard"
    Protocol    "Standard"
    AutoRepeat  500 5
    ServerNumLock
EndSection
```

Other options are available as well—see the XF86Config file if you wish to modify the keyboard configuration. The above should work for most systems.

The next section is Pointer which specifies parameters for the mouse device.

```
Section "Pointer"

    Protocol    "MouseSystems"
    Device      "/dev/mouse"

# Baudrate and SampleRate are only for some Logitech mice
#    BaudRate   9600
#    SampleRate 150

# Emulate3Buttons is an option for 2-button Microsoft mice
#    Emulate3Buttons

# ChordMiddle is an option for some 3-button Logitech mice
#    ChordMiddle

EndSection
```

The only options that you should concern yourself with now are Protocol and Device. Protocol specifies the mouse *protocol* that your mouse uses (not the make or brand of mouse). Valid types for Protocol (under Linux—there are other options available for other operating systems) are:

- BusMouse

- Logitech

- Microsoft

- MMSeries

- Mouseman

- MouseSystems

- PS/2

- MMHitTab

BusMouse should be used for the Logitech busmouse. Note that older Logitech mice should use Logitech, but newer Logitech mice use either Microsoft or Mouseman protocols. This is a case in which the protocol doesn't necessarily have anything to do with the make of the mouse.

Device specifies the device file where the mouse can be accessed. On most Linux systems, this is /dev/mouse. /dev/mouse is usually a link to the appropriate serial port (such as /dev/cua0) for serial mice, or to the appropriate busmouse device for busmice. At any rate, be sure that the device file listed in Device exists.

The next section is Monitor, which specifies the characteristics of your monitor. As with other sections in the XF86Config file, there may be more than one Monitor section. This is useful if you have multiple monitors connected to a system, or use the same XF86Config file under multiple hardware configurations. In general, though, you will need a single Monitor section.

```
Section "Monitor"

    Identifier  "CTX 5468 NI"

    # These values are for a CTX 5468NI only! Don't attempt to use
    # them with your monitor (unless you have this model)

    Bandwidth    60
    HorizSync    30-38,47-50
    VertRefresh  50-90

    # Modes: Name      dotclock  horiz                vert

    ModeLine "640x480"   25      640 664 760 800      480 491 493 525
    ModeLine "800x600"   36      800 824 896 1024     600 601 603 625
    ModeLine "1024x768"  65      1024 1088 1200 1328  768 783 789 818

EndSection
```

The Identifier line is used to give an arbitrary name to the Monitor entry. This can be any string; you will use it to refer to the Monitor entry later in the XF86Config file.

they are listed below.

HorizSync specifies the valid horizontal sync frequencies for your monitor, in kHz. If you have a multisync monitor, this can be a range of values (or several comma-separated ranges), as seen above. If you have a fixed-frequency monitor, this will be a list of discrete values, such as:

```
    HorizSync    31.5, 35.2, 37.9, 35.5, 48.95
```

Your monitor manual should list these values in the technical specifications section. If you do not have this information available, you should either contact the manufacturer or vendor of your monitor to obtain it. There are other sources of information, as well;

VertRefresh specifies the valid vertical refresh rates (or vertical synchronization frequencies) for your monitor, in Hz. Like HorizSync this can be a range or a list of discrete values; your monitor manual should list them.

HorizSync and VertRefresh are used only to double-check that the monitor resolutions that you specify are in valid ranges. This is to reduce the chance that you will damage your monitor by attempting to drive it at a frequency for which it was not designed.

The ModeLine directive is used to specify a single resolution mode for your monitor. The format of ModeLine is

```
ModeLine name clock horiz-values vert-values
```

name is an arbitrary string, which you will use to refer to the resolution mode later in the file. dot-clock is the driving clock frequency, or "dot clock" associated with the resolution mode. A dot clock is usually specified in MHz, and is the rate at which the video card must send pixels to the monitor at this resolution. horiz-values and vert-values are four numbers each which specify when the electron gun of the monitor should fire, and when the horizontal and vertical sync pulses fire during a sweep.

How can you determine the ModeLine values for your monitor? The file VideoModes.doc, included with the XFree86 distribution, describes in detail how to determine these values for each resolution mode that your monitor supports. First of all, clock must correspond to one of the dot clock values that your video card can produce. Later in the XF86Config file you will specify these clocks; you can only use video modes which have a clock value supported by your video card.

There are two files included in the XFree86 distribution which may include ModeLine data for your monitor. These files are modeDB.txt and Monitors, both of which are found in /usr/X11R6/lib/X11/doc.

You should start with ModeLine values for the VESA standard monitor timings, which most monitors support. modeDB.txt includes timing values for VESA standard resolutions. In that file, you will see entries such as

```
# 640x480@60Hz Non-Interlaced mode
# Horizontal Sync = 31.5kHz
# Timing: H=(0.95us, 3.81us, 1.59us), V=(0.35ms, 0.064ms, 1.02ms)
#
# name       clock   horizontal timing      vertical timing      flags
  "640x480"  25.175  640  664  760  800     480  491  493  525
```

This is a VESA standard timing for a 640x480 video mode. It uses a dot clock of 25.175, which your video card must support to use this mode (more on this later). To include this entry in the XF86Config file, you'd use the line

```
ModeLine "640x480" 25.175 640 664 760 800 480 491 493 525
```

Note that the name argument to ModeLine (in this case "640x480") is an arbitrary string—the convention is to name the mode after the resolution, but name can technically be anything descriptive which describes the mode to you.

For each ModeLine used the server will check that the specifications for the mode fall within the range of values specified with Bandwidth, HorizSync and VertRefresh. If they do not, the server will complain when you attempt to start up X (more on this later). For one thing, the dot clock used by the mode should not be greater than the value used for Bandwidth. (However, in many cases it is safe to use modes with a slightly higher bandwidth than your monitor can support.)

If the VESA standard timings do not work for you (you'll know after trying to use them later) then the files modeDB.txt and Monitors include specific mode values for many monitor types. You can create ModeLine entries from the values found in those two files as well. Be sure to only use values for the specific model of monitor that you have. Note that many 14 and 15-inch monitors cannot support higher resolution modes, and often resolutions of 1024x768 at low dot clocks. This means that if you can't find high resolution modes for your monitor in these files, then your monitor probably does not support those resolution modes.

If you are completely at a loss, and can't find working `ModeLine` values for your monitor, you can follow the instructions in the `VideoModes.doc` file included in the XFree86 distribution to generate `ModeLine` values from the specifications listed in your monitor's manual. While your mileage will certainly vary when attempting to generate `ModeLine` values by hand, this is a good place to look if you can't find the values that you need. `VideoModes.doc` also describes the format of the `ModeLine` directive and other aspects of the XFree86 server in gory detail.

Lastly, if you do obtain `ModeLine` values which are almost, but not quite, right, then it may be possible to simply modify the values slightly to obtain the desired result. For example, if while running XFree86 the image on the monitor is shifted slightly, or seems to "roll", you can follow the instructions in the `VideoModes.doc` file to try to fix these values. Also, be sure to check the knobs and controls on the monitor itself! In many cases it is necessary to change the horizontal or vertical size of the display after starting up XFree86 in order for the image to be centered and be of the appropriate size. Having these controls on the front of the monitor can certainly make life easier.

You shouldn't use monitor timing values or `ModeLine` values for monitors other than the model that you own. If you attempt to drive the monitor at a frequency for which it was not designed, you can damage or even destroy it.

The next section of the `XF86Config` file is `Device`, which specifies parameters for your video card. Here is an example.

```
Section "Device"
        Identifier "#9 GXE 64"

        # Nothing yet; we fill in these values later.

    EndSection
```

This section defines properties for a particular video card. `Identifier` is an arbitrary string describing the card; you will use this string to refer to the card later.

Initially, you don't need to include anything in the `Device` section, except for `Identifier`. This is because we will be using the X server itself to probe for the properties of the video card, and entering them into the `Device` section later. The XFree86 server is capable of probing for the video chipset, clocks, RAMDAC, and amount of video RAM on the board.

Before we do this, however, we need to finish writing the `XF86Config` file. The next section is `Screen`, which specifies the monitor/video card combination to use for a particular server.

```
Section "Screen"
        Driver      "Accel"
        Device      "#9 GXE 64"
        Monitor     "CTX 5468 NI"
        Subsection "Display"
            Depth       16
            Modes       "1024x768" "800x600" "640x480"
            ViewPort    0 0
            Virtual     1024 768
        EndSubsection
    EndSection
```

The `Driver` line specifies the X server that you will be using. The value values for `Driver` are:

- `Accel`: For the `XF86_S3`, `XF86_Mach32`, `XF86_Mach8`, `XF86_8514`, `XF86_P9000`, `XF86_AGX`, and `XF86_W32` servers;

- `SVGA`: For the `XF86_SVGA` server;

- `VGA16`: For the `XF86_VGA16` server;

- VGA2: For the XF86_Mono server;

- Mono: For the non-VGA monochrome drivers in the XF86_Mono and XF86_VGA16 servers.

You should be sure that /usr/X11R6/bin/X is a symbolic link to the server that you are using.

The Device line specifies the Identifier of the Device section corresponding to the video card to use for this server. Above, we created a Device section with the line

```
Identifier "#9 GXE 64"
```

Therefore, we use "#9 GXE 64" on the Device line here.

Similarly, the Monitor line specifies the name of the Monitor section to be used with this server. Here, "CTX 5468 NI" is the Identifier used in the Monitor section described above.

Subsection "Display" defines several properties of the XFree86 server corresponding to your monitor/video card combination. The XF86Config file describes all of these options in detail; most of them are icing on the cake and not necessary to get the system working.

The options that you should know about are:

- Depth. Defines the number of color planes—the number of bits per pixel. Usually, Depth is set to 8. For the VGA16 server, you would use a depth of 4, and for the monochrome server a depth of 1. If you are using an accelerated video card with enough memory to support more bits per pixel, you can set Depth to 16, 24, or 32. If you have problems with depths higher than 8, set it back to 8 and attempt to debug the problem later.

- Modes. This is the list of video mode names which have been defined using the ModeLine directive in the Monitor section. In the above section, we used ModeLines named "1024x768", "800x600", and "640x480". Therefore, we use a Modes line of

```
Modes    "1024x768" "800x600" "640x480"
```

The first mode listed on this line will be the default when XFree86 starts up. After XFree86 is running, you can switch between the modes listed here using the keys ctrl-alt-numeric + and ctrl-alt-numeric -.

It might be best, when initially configuring XFree86, to use lower resolution video modes, such as 640x480, which tend to work on most systems. Once you have the basic configuration working you can modify XF86Config to support higher resolutions.

- Virtual. Sets the virtual desktop size. XFree86 has the ability to use any additional memory on your video card to extend the size of your desktop. When you move the mouse pointer to the edge of the display, the desktop will scroll, bringing the additional space into view. Therefore, even if you are running at a lower video resolution such as 800x600, you can set Virtual to the total resolution which your video card can support (a 1-megabyte video card can support 1024x768 at a depth of 8 bits per pixel; a 2-megabyte card 1280x1024 at depth 8, or 1024x768 at depth 16). Of course, the entire area will not be visible at once, but it can still be used.

The Virtual feature is a nice way to utilize the memory of your video card, but it is rather limited. If you want to use a true virtual desktop, we suggest using fvwm, or a similar window manager, instead. fvwm allows you to have rather large virtual desktops (implemented by hiding windows, and so forth, instead of actually storing the entire desktop in video memory at once). See the man pages for fvwm for more details about this; most Linux systems use fvwm by default.

- ViewPort. If you are using the Virtual option described above, ViewPort sets the coordinates of the upper-left-hand corner of the virtual desktop when XFree86 starts up. Virtual 0 0 is often used; if this is unspecified then the desktop is centered on the virtual desktop display (which may be undesirable to you).

Many other options for this section exist; see the XF86Config man page for a complete description. In practice these other options are not necessary to get XFree86 initially working.

5   Filling in video card information

Your `XF86Config` file is now ready to go, with the exception of complete information on the video card. What we're going to do is use the X server to probe for the rest of this information, and fill it into `XF86Config`.

Instead of probing for this information with the X server, the `XF86Config` values for many cards are listed in the files `modeDB.txt`, `AccelCards`, and `Devices`. These files are all found in `/usr/X11R6/lib/X11/doc`. In addition, there are various `README` files for certain chipsets. You should look in these files for information on your video card, and use that information (the clock values, chipset type, and any options) in the `XF86Config` file. If any information is missing, you can probe for it as described here.

In these examples we will demonstrate configuration for a #9 GXE 64 video card, which uses the `XF86_S3` chipset. This card happens to be the one which the author uses, but the discussion here applies to any video card.

The first thing to do is to determine the video chipset used on the card. Running `SuperProbe` (found in `/usr/X11R6/bin`) will tell you this information, but you need to know the chipset name as it is known to the X server.

To do this, run the command

```
X -showconfig
```

This will give the chipset names known to your X server. (The man pages for each X server list these as well.) For example, with the accelerated `XF86_S3` server, we obtain:

```
XFree86 Version 3.1 / X Window System
(protocol Version 11, revision 0, vendor release 6000)
Operating System: Linux
Configured drivers:
  S3: accelerated server for S3 graphics adaptors (Patchlevel 0)
      mmio_928, s3_generic
```

The valid chipset names for this server are `mmio_928` and `s3_generic`. The `XF86_S3` man page describes these chipsets and which videocards use them. In the case of the #9 GXE 64 video card, `mmio_928` is appropriate.

If you don't know which chipset to use, the X server can probe it for you. To do this, run the command

```
X -probeonly > /tmp/x.out 2>&1
```

if you use `bash` as your shell. If you use `csh`, try:

```
X -probeonly &> /tmp/x.out
```

You should run this command while the system is unloaded, that is, while no other activity is occurring on the system. This command will also probe for your video card dot clocks (as seen below), and system load can throw off this calculation.

The output from the above (in `/tmp/x.out` should contain lines such as the following:

```
XFree86 Version 3.1 / X Window System
(protocol Version 11, revision 0, vendor release 6000)
Operating System: Linux
Configured drivers:
  S3: accelerated server for S3 graphics adaptors (Patchlevel 0)
      mmio_928, s3_generic
  ...
```

```
(--) S3: card type: 386/486 localbus
(--) S3: chipset:   864 rev. 0
(--) S3: chipset driver: mmio_928
```

Here, we see that the two valid chipsets for this server (in this case, XF86_S3) are mmio_928 and s3_generic. The server probed for and found a video card using the mmio_928 chipset.

In the Device section of the XF86Config file, add a Chipset line, containing the name of the chipset as determined above. For example,

```
Section "Device"
        # We already had Identifier here...
        Identifier "#9 GXE 64"
        # Add this line:
        Chipset "mmio_928"
EndSection
```

Now we need to determine the driving clock frequencies used by the video card. A driving clock frequency, or dot clock, is simply a rate at which the video card can send pixels to the monitor. As we have seen, each monitor resolution has a dot clock associated with it. Now we need to determine which dot clocks are made available by the video card.

First you should look into the files (modeDB.txt, and so forth) mentioned above and see if your card's clocks are listed there. The dot clocks will usually be a list of 8 or 16 values, all of which are in MHz. For example, when looking at modeDB.txt we see an entry for the Cardinal ET4000 video board, which looks like this:

```
# chip    ram   virtual   clocks                       default-mode flags
  ET4000  1024  1024 768    25  28  38  36  40  45  32   0  "1024x768"
```

As we can see, the dot clocks for this card are 25, 28, 38, 36, 40, 45, 32, and 0 MHz.

In the Devices section of the XF86Config file, you should add a Clocks line containing the list of dot clocks for your card. For example, for the clocks above, we would add the line

```
        Clocks 25 28 38 36 40 45 32 0
```

to the Devices section of the file, after Chipset. Note that the order of the clocks is important! Don't resort the list of clocks or remove duplicates.

If you cannot find the dot clocks associated with your card, the X server can probe for these as well. Using the X -probeonly command described above, the output should contain lines which look like the following:

```
(--) S3: clocks:  25.18  28.32  38.02  36.15  40.33  45.32  32.00  00.00
```

We could then add a Clocks line containing all of these values, as printed. You can use more than one Clocks line in XF86Config should all of the values (sometimes there are more than 8 clock values printed) not fit onto one line. Again, be sure to keep the list of clocks in order as they are printed.

Be sure that there is no Clocks line (or that it is commented out) in the Devices section of the file when using X -probeonly to probe for the clocks. If there is a Clocks line present, the server will *not* probe for the clocks—it will use the values given in XF86Config.

Note that some accelerated video boards use a programmable clock chip. (See the XF86_Accel man page for details; this generally applies to S3, AGX, and XGA-2 boards.) This chip essentially allows the X server to tell the card which dot clocks to use. If this is the case, then you may not find a list of dot clocks for the card in any of the above files. Or, the list of dot clocks printed when using X -probeonly will only contain one or two discrete clock values, with the rest being duplicates or zero.

For boards which use a programmable clock chip, you would use a ClockChip line, instead of a Clocks line, in your XF86Config file. ClockChip gives the name of the clock chip as used by the video card; the man pages for each server describe what these are. For example, in the file README.S3, we see that several S3-864 video cards use an "ICD2061A" clock chip, and that we should use the line

```
ClockChip "icd2061a"
```

instead of `Clocks` in the `XF86Config` file. As with `Clocks`, this line should go in the `Devices` section, after `Chipset`.

Similarly, some accelerated cards require you to specify the RAMDAC chip type in the `XF86Config` file, using a `Ramdac` line. The `XF86_Accel` man page describes this option. Usually, the X server will correctly probe for the RAMDAC.

Some video card types require you to specify several options in the `Devices` section of `XF86Config`. These options will be described in the man page for your server, as well as in the various files (such as `README.cirrus` or `README.S3`. These options are enabled using the `Option` line. For example, the #9 GXE 64 card requires two options:

```
Option "number_nine"
Option "dac_8_bit"
```

Usually, the X server will work without these options, but they are necessary to obtain the best performance. There are too many such options to list here, and they each depend on the particular video card being used. If you must use one of these options, fear not—the X server man pages and various files in `/usr/X11R6/lib/X11/doc` will tell you what they are.

So, when you're finished, you should end up with a `Devices` section which looks something like this:

```
Section "Device"
        # Device section for the #9 GXE 64 only!
        Identifier "#9 GXE 64"
        Chipset "mmio_928"
        ClockChip "icd2061a"
        Option "number_nine"
        Option "dac_8_bit"
EndSection
```

Most video cards will require a `Clocks` line, instead of `ClockChip`, as described above. The above `Device` entry is only valid for a particular video card, the #9 GXE 64. It is given here only as an example.

There are other options that you can include in the `Devices` entry. Check the X server man pages for the gritty details, but the above should suffice for most systems.

6 Running XFree86

With your `XF86Config` file configured, you're ready to fire up the X server and give it a spin. First, be sure that `/usr/X11R6/bin` is on your path.

The command to start up XFree86 is

```
startx
```

This is a front-end to `xinit` (in case you're used to using `xinit` on other UNIX systems).

This command will start the X server and run the commands found in the file `.xinitrc` in your home directory. `.xinitrc` is just a shell script containing X clients to run. If this file does not exist, the system default `/usr/X11R6/lib/X11/xinit/xinitrc` will be used.

A standard `.xinitrc` file looks like this:

```
#!/bin/sh

xterm -fn 7x13bold -geometry 80x32+10+50 &
```

```
xterm -fn 9x15bold -geometry 80x34+30-10 &
oclock -geometry 70x70-7+7 &
xsetroot -solid midnightblue &

exec twm
```

This script will start up two `xterm` clients, an `oclock`, and set the root window (background) color to `midnightblue`. It will then start up `twm`, the window manager. Note that `twm` is executed with the shell's `exec` statement; this causes the `xinit` process to be replaced with `twm`. Once the `twm` process exits, the X server will shut down. You can cause `twm` to exit by using the root menus: depress mouse button 1 on the desktop background—this will display a pop up menu which will allow you to `Exit Twm`.

Be sure that the last command in `.xinitrc` is started with `exec`, and that it is not placed into the background (no ampersand on the end of the line). Otherwise the X server will shut down as soon as it has started the clients in the `.xinitrc` file.

Alternately, you can exit X by pressing `ctrl-alt-backspace` in combination. This will kill the X server directly, exiting the window system.

The above is a very, very simple desktop configuration. Many wonderful programs and configurations are available with a bit of work on your `.xinitrc` file. For example, the `fvwm` window manager will provide a virtual desktop, and you can customize colors, fonts, window sizes and positions, and so forth to your heart's content. Although the X Window System might appear to be simplistic at first, it is extremely powerful once you customize it for yourself.

If you are new to the X Window System environment, we strongly suggest picking up a book such as *The X Window System: A User's Guide*. Using and configuring X is far too in-depth to cover here. See the man pages for `xterm`, `oclock`, and `twm` for clues on getting started.

7 Running Into Trouble

Often, something will not be quite right when you initially fire up the X server. This is almost always caused by a problem in your `XF86Config` file. Usually, the monitor timing values are off, or the video card dot clocks set incorrectly. If your display seems to roll, or the edges are fuzzy, this is a clear indication that the monitor timing values or dot clocks are wrong. Also be sure that you are correctly specifying your video card chipset, as well as other options for the `Device` section of `XF86Config`. Be absolutely certain that you are using the right X server and that `/usr/X11R6/bin/X` is a symbolic link to this server.

If all else fails, try to start X "bare"; that is, use a command such as:

```
X > /tmp/x.out 2>&1
```

You can then kill the X server (using the `ctrl-alt-backspace` key combination) and examine the contents of `/tmp/x.out`. The X server will report any warnings or errors—for example, if your video card doesn't have a dot clock corresponding to a mode supported by your monitor.

The file `VideoModes.doc` included in the XFree86 distribution contains many hints for tweaking the values in your `XF86Config` file.

Remember that you can use `ctrl-alt-numeric +` and `ctrl-alt-numeric -` to switch between the video modes listed on the `Modes` line of the `Screen` section of `XF86Config`. If the highest resolution mode doesn't look right, try switching to lower resolutions. This will let you know, at least, that those parts of your X configuration are working correctly.

Also, check the vertical and horizontal size/hold knobs on your monitor. In many cases it is necessary to adjust these when starting up X. For example, if the display seems to be shifted slightly to one side, you can usually correct this using the monitor controls.

The USENET newsgroup `comp.windows.x.i386unix` is devoted to discussions about XFree86, as is `comp.os.linux.x`. It might be a good idea to watch that newsgroup for postings relating to your video configuration—you might run across someone with the same problems as your own.

8 Copyright

Index